The Editors

GERALD HAMMOND is Emeritus Professor of English at the University of Manchester. A Fellow of the British Academy, his many publications include *The Making of the English Bible; Fleeting Things: English Poets and Poems, 1616–1660; Sir Walter Raleigh's Selected Writings;* and *John Skelton's Selected Poems.* He contributed the essay on English Bible translation to *The Literary Guide to the Bible.*

AUSTIN BUSCH is Assistant Professor of Early World Literatures in the Department of English at the State University of New York College at Brockport. His articles have appeared in the *Journal of Biblical Literature, Biblical Interpretation,* and *The Classical Journal.* He is a contributing author of *Seneca and the Self* (Cambridge University Press).

The 1611 KJV contained a separate title page for the New Testament. Its elaborate wood-cut border, apparently recycled from previous editions of the Bishops' Bible, displays at the center top the tetragrammaton, the four-letter name of God (YHWH) in Hebrew. Underneath it stands a victorious lamb, an image of the risen Christ, and underneath that is a dove symbolizing the Holy Spirit. Beneath the title page's text is an altar with a bound lamb awaiting sacrifice that figures Jesus' death. At the corners of the bordered text sit the four evangelists with their associated symbols: Matthew accompanied by an angel, Mark by a lion, Luke by an ox, and John by an eagle. Toward the right are images of the twelve apostles (cf. Acts 1:13, 26); toward the left, tents of the twelve sons of Judah (roughly corresponding to Israel's twelve tribes).

A NORTON CRITICAL EDITION

THE ENGLISH BIBLE
KING JAMES VERSION

Volume Two
The New Testament and the Apocrypha

EDITED BY

GERALD HAMMOND

UNIVERSITY OF MANCHESTER

AND

AUSTIN BUSCH

STATE UNIVERSITY OF NEW YORK
COLLEGE AT BROCKPORT

W·W·NORTON & COMPANY · *New York* · *London*

W. W. Norton & Company has been independent since its founding in 1923, when William Warder Norton and Mary D. Herter Norton first published lectures delivered at the People's Institute, the adult education division of New York City's Cooper Union. The Nortons soon expanded their program beyond the Institute, publishing books by celebrated academics from America and abroad. By mid-century, the two major pillars of Norton's publishing program—trade books and college texts— were firmly established. In the 1950s, the Norton family transferred control of the company to its employees, and today—with a staff of four hundred and a comparable number of trade, college, and professional titles published each year—W. W. Norton & Company stands as the largest and oldest publishing house owned wholly by its employees.

The text of this book is composed in Fairfield Medium
with the display set in Bernhard Modern.
Design by Jo Anne Metsch.
Composition by Westchester Book Group.
Maps by Mapping Specialists.
Manufacturing by R. R. Donnelley.
Production manager: Eric Pier-Hocking.

Library of Congress Cataloging-in-Publication Data

Bible. English. Authorized. 2012.
    The English Bible : King James Version. — 1st ed.
        p. cm.
    "A Norton critical edition."
    Includes bibliographical references.
    ISBN 978-0-393-92745-0 (pbk., v. 1) — **ISBN 978-0-393-97507-9 (pbk., v. 2)**
1. Bible—Criticism, interpretation, etc.   I. Marks, Herbert.   II. Hammond, Gerald.
III. Busch, Austin.   IV. Title.
    BS1852012 .N49 2012
    220.5'2034—dc23

                                                                2011052997

W. W. Norton & Company, Inc., 500 Fifth Avenue, New York, NY 10110-0017
www.norton.com

W. W. Norton & Company Ltd., Castle House, 75/76 Wells Street, London W1T 3QT

1 2 3 4 5 6 7 8 9 0

Contents

CONTEXT, RECEPTION, CRITICISM

Part I. Historical Contexts   /   975

Part II. Exegesis / 1068

Part III. Poetic Reimaginings / 1275

Part V. Translation / 1494

MAPS

MAPS

Preface: An Introduction to the New Testament and the Apocrypha

In 2 Corinthians 3:6, Paul writes that God "hath made us able ministers of the new testament; not of the letter, but of the spirit: for the letter killeth, but the spirit giveth life." Readers sometimes assume that Paul contrasts the Christian gospel inscribed in the section of the Bible known today as the New Testament with the supposedly legalistic Judaism of the Old Testament. Some even take this verse as a hermeneutically programmatic passage that encourages readers to privilege the Bible's spiritual truth (whatever that might mean) over its literal significance, inferring that the New Testament offers a clearer view of this truth than does the Old, where it is putatively mired in obsolete legal codes and barbaric tales of a vengeful and violent God. Such a reading of 2 Corinthians 3:6 is erroneous on many levels.

The Greek word *diathēkē*, which the King James Version renders "testament," refers to a covenant, promise, or pact—often, in the New Testament, one that God makes with his people. The Bible narrates God's establishment of many such covenants and sometimes records their specific terms. When he uses the phrase "old testament" in 2 Corinthians, Paul refers to the covenant God made with Israel at Mount Sinai. The meaning of "new testament" is less clear, but in any case the eponymous divisions of the Christian biblical canon are not being invoked, for these did not exist as such until well after Paul wrote, and they received their traditional titles only from an anachronistic appropriation of this verse (probably beginning in the second century C.E.).

However we understand it, we probably ought not to call the "new testament" Christian. Paul never used the word "Christian" in his writings and our earliest evidence suggests that outsiders originally applied it to Jesus-believers; it was not something they called themselves (Acts 11:26; 26:28; 1 Pet 4:16). Paul understood himself to be a member of a Jewish religious movement that emphasized faithfulness to Jesus, the Messiah and Lord; the first historian of this movement, the author of the Acts of the Apostles, simply calls it the Way. That some of the Way's leaders were interested in reaching out to Gentiles, and that at least a few of them believed that non-Jews faithful to Jesus ought not to become circumcised, no more obviates the Way's essential Jewishness than does the frequent presence of Gentiles at synagogues throughout the Mediterranean world (at least according to Acts) obviate the Jewishness of these hellenistic Jewish congregations. In light of this observation, it should come as no surprise that Paul lifts the phrase "new testament" directly from the Hebrew Scriptures. He alludes in verse 6 and elsewhere in 2 Corinthians 3 to Jeremiah 31:31–34, which anticipates Israel's internalization of and spontaneous obedience to God's law—a new and better covenant than the one God made with Israel at Sinai (though no more or less legal than it), and one in which Paul is convinced that Gentiles as well as Jews may participate. It is thus not of Christianity that Paul claims to be a minister. He rather presents a particular understanding of the Jewish God's covenants with his people. In particular, he associates himself with Jeremiah's promise of a new covenant that will fulfill the unrealized potential of the one that God made with Israel at Sinai.

2 Corinthians 3:6, then, neither opposes the Christian to the Jewish nor refers to the divisions of the Bible later known as the New and Old Testament. It may be possible to infer from it a program for biblical interpretation, though the distinction between spiritual and literal meaning it is often invoked to justify seems so vague and subject to idiosyncratic application as to offer little reliable guidance. In light of the verse's often realized potential for misinterpretation, perhaps the soundest advice it offers is this: read closely and with careful attention to echoes of other relevant literature, contextualize appropriately, and beware of anachronistic presumptions. The introductions and annotations to the biblical books that follow provide information aimed at facilitating such reading, as does the balance of this preface, which, before introducing the Apocrypha, explores four important New Testament matrices, understood at the same time as generative sources from which New Testament writers draw language and ideas and as conceptual systems with which they assume their readers' familiarity.

The Biblical Matrix

The only Scripture that the New Testament writers knew was a version of what is today usually called the Hebrew Bible or the Old Testament, although in this context neither title fits. "Old Testament" assumes a New Testament, which, as noted above, did not come into existence until after the texts it would include were composed. "Hebrew Bible" also misleads because New Testament writers normally quote from the Septuagint, a Greek translation of the Hebrew Scriptures probably initiated in Alexandria and produced piecemeal during the third to the first centuries B.C.E. Its conventional title and standard abbreviation (LXX) round off the number seventy-two, which figures prominently in a popular legend preserved in the *Letter to Aristeas*. According to this text, a Hellenistic Egyptian king sponsored seventy-two learned Jews (six elders from each tribe) who worked for seventy-two days to translate the Hebrew Scriptures into Greek. The lost Hebrew texts on which the Septuagint presumably relies were often though not always quite close to the Masoretic Text, the recension of the Hebrew Bible that the King James Version translates. It is to the King James Old Testament that this volume's introductions and annotations refer, although they occasionally call attention to significant Septuagintal deviations.

The Old Testament represents the New Testament's most vital conceptual background. Episodes from the New Testament narratives often look like imaginative revisions of Old Testament stories. Even if these have a historical basis—as many do—the evangelists or the sources on which they drew freely assimilated events from Jesus' ministry or from the early history of the church to one or another Old Testament account. For example, the Gospels' miraculous feedings (Mark 6:30–44 and parallels) seem to be versions of the story of Elisha's feeding of one hundred men from twenty loaves of bread and some wheat (2 Kgs 4:42–44), and they incorporate elements from God's miraculous provision of manna in the wilderness as well (see Exod 16). The Pentecost story from Acts 2 is another example: it recalls and subverts the linguistic confusion of the story of Babel from Genesis 11:1–9. Sometimes the intertextual relationships are more fleeting and allusive than these examples might suggest. For instance, Jesus' birth and perilous infancy in Matthew 1:18–2:23 repeatedly echo the story of Moses' origins in Exodus 1–2, leading up to Jesus' first major discourse, the Sermon on the Mount (Matt 5–7), which explicitly quotes, interprets, and expands the law God promulgated through Moses at Mount Sinai. Jesus' engagement with Mosaic law in Matthew 5 is direct, but the parallels between Jesus' early life and Moses' in the book's opening chapters are rather subtle, and an inattentive or uninformed reader might miss them.

The New Testament rarely invokes the Old gratuitously, and thus each reference obliges readers to question what work the quoted or echoed passage performs in its new context. The allusions to Exodus in the opening chapters of Matthew, for instance, seem to present Jesus as a new Moses—an observation that initiates rather than ends interpretive investigation. What is this new Moses' relationship to the old one? Does his legislation in the Sermon on the Mount overturn Mosaic law or merely expose its latent implications? Does Jesus' sermon inaugurate a new covenant, or does it reinvigorate the covenant God made at Sinai through Moses?

An Old Testament echo or structural parallel sometimes lays bare interpretive possibilities that would remain latent without its recognition. Returning to Acts 2's allusion to Genesis 11:1–9 mentioned above, we might begin by noting that the linguistic confusion thematized by the Babel story reflects the chaos into which the world descends as Genesis's Primeval History progresses, and that this chaos culminates in God abandoning engagement with humanity at large in favor of a covenant with the descendants of Abraham in particular (Gen 12:1–9). From a related angle, God's election of Israel over other nations in Genesis 12 presupposes the fragmentation of humanity into diverse linguistic and ethnic groups that Genesis 10:1–11:9 recounts. In either case, Acts reverses the situation that obtains at the end of the Primeval History: the risen Christ prophesies that his followers will bear him witness at the center of Israel (Jerusalem), in Judea and Samaria, and finally in the world at large (1:8) just before Acts' author transforms the story of linguistic fragmentation at Babel into one of linguistic unification (chap. 2). The Old Testament episode's subversion gestures at a divine volte-face: no longer focused primarily on his covenant with Abraham's descendants, God extends himself in Acts to humanity at large. This outreach presupposes the human community's fundamental unity—precisely what the Pentecost miracle symbolically effects by undoing the linguistic confusion initiated at Babel.

Paul's engagement with the Old Testament may be the most probing in the entire New Testament. For Paul especially the Old Testament is not merely a reservoir of theological or literary types and motifs, of quotations, turns of phrase, and the like, but a conceptual and linguistic ocean in which to sail. Continuing our focus on the New Testament's allusions to the Primeval History, we might consider Paul's treatment of the story of the primeval transgression (i.e., "the Fall") in Romans 7:7–25. Romans 7 contains only one clear allusion to Genesis 3 (at v. 11; compare Eve's words in Gen 3:13), but the analogies between the situation Paul explores and the Old Testament episode his exploration echoes are so numerous and provocative that many interpreters see the passage from Romans as a rewriting of the Genesis story. In both, for instance, a proffered commandment serves to instigate rather than to prevent its own transgression; in both this subversion of the commandment's intent is labeled deception; in both the transgression is associated with death; and so on. Romans 7:7–25 amounts to an introspective and demythologized revision of Genesis 3. Having imagined the first human transgression of God's will from the perspective of the primeval transgressor Eve, Paul seizes the opportunity presented by this vantage to probe the psychological dynamics of a life lived in opposition to God's law.

Observation of the relationship between Romans 7 and Genesis 3 raises a number of important interpretive questions. What are the implications of Paul's adoption of a feminine persona (Eve, whose words Paul quotes in v. 11) and why have commentators so rarely acknowledged it, even when exploring Paul's engagement with Genesis 3? How does the self's alienation from itself in Romans 7:15–25 relate to the repercussions of Adam and Eve's transgression as spelled out in Genesis 3:14–21? More broadly (and more provocatively), does God, in giving human beings rules to follow, necessarily assume that they will transgress his will, or at least desire to transgress his will, even as he demands that they do not? And if so, might this imply that the promulgation of God's law itself marks humans' alienation from God, so that transgression is in some sense beside the point?

In order to facilitate readers' investigations of Old Testament echoes, allusions, and quotations, this edition's annotations cite parallels generously (though by no means exhaustively). Often, the original context of an Old Testament text shapes the role it plays in the New, and careful consideration of an allusion thus requires more than simply tracing the cross-reference. One must read enough of the original context to acquire a basic understanding of the passage in which the echoed or quoted text was originally embedded. No responsible reader of the New Testament can afford to ignore its Old Testament matrix; put positively, careful consideration of the New Testament's relationship with the Old lays the foundation for informed interpretations of its highly allusive writings.

The Jewish Matrix

Scholars today sometimes speak of ancient Judaisms rather than of ancient Judaism. Their choice of phrase recognizes the diversity that characterized Jewish religious culture during the latter part of the Second Temple period, which lasted from the late sixth century B.C.E. until 70 C.E., when the Romans sacked Jerusalem and destroyed the Herodian temple. In the New Testament alone we encounter multiple Jewish sects. The Pharisees figure prominently in the Gospels and Acts, as do the Sadducees. Acts also implies that the movement initiated by John the Baptist reached well beyond Judea (18:24–26; 19:1–3) and we read there of other prophetic movements with a political edge (5:37; 21:38). From different sources we learn of another Jewish sect, the Essenes, whose writings seem to have survived in the Dead Sea Scrolls. Though they do not really constitute sects or religious movements, we must not omit the temple functionaries in Jerusalem and the Greek-speaking Jewish communities scattered throughout the Mediterranean world. (At the time the New Testament writings were composed, more Jews lived outside Judea than within it.) It is in this rich diversity, whose contours we have only begun to trace, that the Jewish religious movement Jesus inaugurated and his disciples perpetuated must be situated.

Jesus was an itinerant preacher and miracle worker (neither was uncommon in the ancient Mediterranean world) and he seems to have presented himself as a Jewish prophet. None of these designations seems entirely sufficient, but scholars debate whether the historical Jesus went so far as to declare himself Messiah or whether it was his followers who identified him as such after his death. To be sure, Jesus' ministry and teaching were stirring; his parables especially seem to have left a powerful impression. But what many of his disciples found most important was what they understood to be his continued appearances to them after he had been publicly executed. At this point, the Jewish religious movement that Jesus initiated became focused on faithfulness to the risen Jesus himself, understood as God's Messiah and son.

According to Acts, the post-resurrection Jesus movement (the Way) began in Jerusalem and its members participated actively in the temple cult. Escalating disputes with the temple leadership and local synagogues prompted some adherents of the Way to leave Jerusalem, leading to the establishment of congregations of Jesus-believers throughout the Mediterranean world. Acts and other sources suggest that Gentiles sometimes found Jews' unique monotheistic religious traditions attractive and it seems that non-Jews found the Way particularly compelling, for it was largely Gentiles who made up many communities of Jesus-believers outside of Judea (above all those established by Paul). The extent of Gentiles' participation in the Way's growing network of congregations was controversial in the movement's early years and church leaders debated whether Gentiles faithful to Christ ought to be circumcised. Acts reports an official proclamation that answered this question in the negative, but Paul composed Galatians after it was supposedly issued and the debate was far from settled when he wrote.

The Way, then, originally constituted one Jewish sect among others, though significantly one especially attractive and open to Gentile members (even if Gentile inclusion proved controversial among many Jesus-believers). The conflicts that the New Testament records between the movement initiated by Jesus and other Jewish sects (e.g., the Pharisees) and influential constituencies (e.g., the temple leadership in Jerusalem) constituted one factor that would lead to the emergence of Christianity as a religion distinct from Judaism; the traumatic destruction of the

Herodian temple in 70 C.E. was another, for it prompted a Jewish theological and ideological consolidation ill-suited to the sectarian diversity that had characterized the religion in the Second Temple period. Though early Christians who defined their faith against emergent rabbinic Judaism had some basis for claiming as their own many of the writings that the New Testament came to include, we must not confuse continuity for equivalence. Strange as it may seem to say, careful readers of the New Testament must be wary of unduly Christianizing it.

That the New Testament is not straightforwardly Christian is often obvious. For example, the rigorous adherence to Mosaic law that Jesus demands of his followers in Matthew 5:17–20 is not easily compatible with most understandings of Christianity, ancient or modern; nor is Paul's unapologetic subordination of Christ to God in 1 Corinthians 15:28. More broadly, the New Testament's portrayal of and discourse about Jesus' resurrection—arguably the theological foundation of Christianity itself—makes the best sense within a Second Temple Jewish context.

Many Jews more or less contemporary with the New Testament writers adopted a religious perspective that scholars today call apocalyptic eschatology (from Greek words meaning "unveil" [*apokalyptō*] and "discourse" [*logos*] about the "end time" [*eschaton*]). Apocalyptic eschatology assumes, among other things, that the world has fallen under the control of evil spiritual forces who harm human beings directly (e.g., by possessing them) and who induce wicked temporal leaders to oppress the vulnerable righteous. It also assumes that God will intervene shortly and decisively to set the world aright, destroying these evil forces, rewarding righteous human beings, and punishing the wicked. And it assumes that through dreams, visions, and the like, God reveals hidden knowledge about all this to those he has chosen. In addition, in the Jewish context God's dramatic intervention was expected to entail the resurrection and judgment of the dead, an idea first attested in Daniel 12:1–4.

Jesus, his followers, and early adherents of the Way shared a Jewish apocalyptic-eschatological outlook. Dreams and visions are commonplace and the devil's control over the world is assumed (e.g., Luke 4:6). Moreover, the New Testament anticipates God's defeat of Satan's spiritual forces and can juxtapose this defeat to the resurrection of all who have died, of which Christ's resurrection is but an exemplar (see 1 Cor 15:20–26). Indeed, according to Matthew, others actually rose from the dead at the same time as Jesus (27:52–53).

Apocalyptic eschatology was controversial among Jews during the Second Temple period. For example, the Pharisees embraced it while Sadducees rejected it wholesale. The resurrection of the dead accordingly unites Jesus-believers and Pharisees against the Sadducees in Acts 23:6–9, where the Apostle Paul straightforwardly claims his identity as "a Pharisee, son of a Pharisee" long after having come to faith in Jesus (cf. Acts 15:5). Acts presents this and other conflicts in which Jesus-believers find themselves embroiled as Jewish sectarian debates, and followers of the Way sometimes found their agreement with members of competing Jewish sects on issues such as the eschatological resurrection of the dead no less significant than their disagreement regarding the status of Jesus, whom they believed already to have risen. The New Testament (especially the Gospel of John, but also Acts itself, on occasion) sometimes anticipates a move away from central tenets shared by most Jewish communities, but nonetheless it is generally appropriate to speak not merely of the New Testament's Jewish matrix but even of New Testament Judaism.

The Greco-Roman Matrix

Alexander the Great (356–323 B.C.E.) conquered the Mediterranean world for Macedonia, marching as far east as Afghanistan and Pakistan. This extensive territory proved unwieldy to control and when he died without naming a successor, his officers partitioned his conquests. Boundaries became stable only after several decades of conflict, which resulted in a basically tripartite division: Greece, Macedonia, and eventually Asia Minor went to Antigonous I Monophthalmos; Egypt (and Judea) to Ptolemy Lagus; and Mesopotamia and the regions eastward to Seleucus I Nicator.

The cultural impact of Alexander's conquests was at least as profound as the political. Alexander founded more than twenty cities he named "Alexandria," some of which continue to thrive today, including Egyptian Alexandria and Kandahar in Afghanistan. He established centers of Greek education (*gymnasia*) throughout the territories he conquered and disseminated Greek culture in other ways as well. His officers perpetuated this program of hellenization after his death and as a result Koine (literally, "common" or "standard") Greek became the Mediterranean basin's lingua franca. Within a few generations virtually all educated people in the areas Alexander had conquered possessed more than a passing knowledge of Greek literature and culture.

These developments affected Jews no less than other inhabitants of the Mediterranean world. A few decades after it took Judea from Ptolemiac Egypt in 198 B.C.E., the Seleucid Empire began an intense program of hellenization there. The apocryphal books of Maccabees indicate that different Judean factions responded to this program in different ways, but those who favored active resistance ultimately took the lead: Judea fought a series of battles against the Seleucids that culminated in independence—a short-lived period of autonomy lasting from the 130s B.C.E. until Rome's imperial expansion brought it to Judea in 63 B.C.E. By the time of Jesus' birth, Rome controlled almost the entire Mediterranean world, for the most part adopting the Greek language and cultural institutions that Alexander and his successors had imposed on the territories now under this Italian city's domain.

Despite resistance to hellenization by many Jews in Judea and elsewhere, Greek language and culture were crucially important to Jewish life in the centuries before, during, and after the period covered by the New Testament writings. A large corpus of ancient Jewish Greek literature survives, including Philo of Alexandria's philosophical and exegetical treatises, Josephus's histories, and a tragedy on the exodus by Ezekiel (not the prophet), as well as some books in the biblical Apocrypha and in a collection of literature sometimes called the Old Testament Pseudepigrapha. We find fragments of Greek writing even among the Dead Sea Scrolls, which are associated with a Jewish sectarian community located in Judea and frequently concerned with parochial issues such as the Levitical priesthood's purity. The most significant work of Hellenistic Jewish literature is surely the Septuagint, the influential translation of the Hebrew Bible into Greek discussed above. The writings that came to constitute the New Testament should also be located in this flurry of Hellenistic Jewish literary activity.

The writings of the New Testament are Hellenistic not only in that they were written in Greek during a period of Greek cultural ascendency; they also actively engage with classical Greek literature. Acts, for instance, contains structural parallels to Euripides' *Bacchae*, a classical tragedy tracing the disaster that ensues when Pentheus resists worship of the new god Dionysus—an obvious mythical archetype for Acts' story of resistance to the gospel's dissemination throughout Judea and the rest of the Mediterranean. Paul actually quotes the play to Agrippa at Acts 26:14. In another vein, Paul engages with Greco-Roman popular philosophical writing throughout his letters, adopting and sometimes ingeniously adapting its maxims, commonplaces, and rhetorical forms. The influence of Greek literature on the New Testament is not as pervasive as that of the Septuagint, to be sure, but it is quite important (the examples listed above are by no means exhaustive) and this volume's annotations signal a variety of resonant parallels.

Despite their productive engagement with Greek literature, the New Testament writers often seem ill at ease with the Hellenistic culture surrounding them. Most people in the ancient Mediterranean world adhered to a polytheistic religious tradition that scholars today call Greco-Roman paganism. Monotheistic Jews, who often found Greco-Roman paganism ridiculous and perverse, polemically labeled those devoted to pagan gods idolaters, sometimes insisting that they unwittingly worshipped devils. Ancient Jews might also prejudicially assume that pagans were morally corrupt. Even the Apostle Paul, whose primary ministry was to Greco-Roman pagan converts to the Way, can in passing contrast "sinners of the Gentiles" to "Jews by nature" (Gal 2:15) or say about a particularly heinous sexual transgression that "it is not so much as named [even] among the Gentiles" (1 Cor 5:1).

New Testament writers sometimes found elements of Greco-Roman paganism valuable, or at least not totally corrupt. Revelation adapts the myth of Python and Apollo (11:19–12:17) and Paul in Acts 17 claims that an altar to an unknown God at Athens actually honors YHWH. He goes on to quote a line of poetry from Aratus that may suggest his willingness to identify YHWH with Zeus, the chief god of the Greek pantheon. Analogously, Paul's advice in 1 Corinthians 8–10 about whether Gentile Jesus-believers may eat meat from animals that have been sacrificed to pagan gods addresses in a realistic and sensitive way the religiously diverse background and social environment of his ex-pagan Greek readers. These are arguably exceptions rather than the rule, however; the attitude toward Greco-Roman paganism that New Testament writers usually adopt is one of hostility and disparagement.

New Testament writers' stances toward Roman political rule are somewhat more complicated than their stances toward Greco-Roman paganism. There is no single New Testament perspective on the Roman Empire; indeed, a fair reading of this anthology of writings will conclude that the views of Rome it offers are sometimes diametrically opposed. While Revelation views Rome as satanic, Roman authorities save Paul from Jewish assassins in Acts (23:12–35) and in other ways as well facilitate the gospel's advancement in that book. Sometimes a single author expresses apparently contradictory views of Rome: Paul, for instance, can assume that Roman political authority is divinely ordained, fundamentally just, and worthy of obedience (Rom 13:1–7) but will also mock Roman political propaganda (1 Thess 5:3; see note). We also find political issues addressed with studied ambivalence. In the Synoptic Gospels (Matthew, Mark, and Luke), Jesus avoids answering a question his opponents pose about whether Jews should pay Roman taxes. Instead of taking a firm position one way or the other, he frames the issue in such a way as to clarify for his auditors what is at stake and to require them to come to their own conclusions (see Mark 12:13–17 and notes; Rom 13:1–7 addresses the issue more straightforwardly).

As this brief survey makes clear, Jews in the ancient Mediterranean world, including those faithful to Jesus, were concerned to maintain autonomy from the dominant Hellenistic culture—especially from Greco-Roman paganism—but at the same time they could write in standard Greek, were familiar with Hellenic literary traditions, and may even, on occasion, have been willing to countenance religious syncretism. Analogously, while they were sometimes suspicious of or even hostile to Roman hegemony, at other times they seem to embrace Rome's propagandistic claims to have brought the world justice and peace. For readers interested in how subjects negotiate the problems and potentialities of political and cultural identity in an imperial context, the New Testament offers exceptionally rich interpretive ground.

The Christian Matrix

Although calling individual New Testament writings "Christian" raises a number of problems, the New Testament as a collection was originally assembled, preserved, translated, and interpreted within the context of ancient Christianity and its students should have a fundamental understanding of the conditions under which these developments took place.

The emergence of the New Testament canon (from the Greek word *kanōn*, originally a "straight rod," whence "ruler" or "level," whence "standard of measure or evaluation," whence "rule" or "norm," whence "authoritative list" of scriptural books) is not very well understood, and scholars are divided as to its primary impetus.[1] Some see the New Testament canon as a proto-orthodox reaction to the proliferation of writings treated as scriptural by various sectarian Christian groups, such as the classic (Sethian) gnostics, the Valentinians, and the Marcionites. It is significant, these scholars note, that in the late second century C.E. Irenaeus, the first writer to quote and name the four New Testament gospels, does so in the context of a vigorous and tendentious argument that only these four are legitimate (*Against Heresies* 3.11.8–9). He is familiar with many more used by Christians whose theology and praxis he opposes, and he wants his proto-orthodox readers to know

---

1. See Bruce M. Metzger, *The Canon of the New Testament: Its Origin, Development, and Significance* (Oxford: Oxford University Press, 1987), 289–93.

which they may profitably study. Similarly, the New Testament collection of Paul's letters would have emerged in response to a Pauline collection that the sectarian teacher Marcion assembled and circulated. Marcion's collection is no longer extant, but it seems to have been heavily edited—in particular, he expurgated references to the God of Israel, refusing to identify YHWH with the Lord proclaimed by Jesus—and to have lacked the Pastoral Epistles (1 and 2 Timothy and Titus). Proto-orthodox churchmen assembled the Pauline collection that the New Testament came to include as the "official" corpus of Paul's writings, and it was supposed to expose as counterfeit the collection that Marcion and his followers privileged.

Other scholars believe that the New Testament canon's development was less reactionary than organic. Justin Martyr informs us in ca. 150 C.E. that "memoirs of the apostles" (his designation for at least the Synoptic Gospels of the New Testament) were read by the proto-orthodox alongside the Septuagint during Sunday worship (*First Apology* 67). This practice would have led to these works' acquisition of the scriptural status that proto-orthodox Christians granted the Septuagint. When church leaders began to assemble the collection of writings that would come to be known as the New Testament, they naturally would have gravitated toward texts that had been read publicly in such a context. Analogously, the letters of Paul themselves give evidence of having been publicly read (e.g., 1 Thess 5:27), widely circulated (e.g., Col 4:16), and carefully edited. 2 Corinthians in particular looks to be stitched together from a number of separate epistles, but since none of the original letters are extant, they must have been incorporated into this text at a very early stage. Finally, admirers of Paul within a generation or two of his death seem to have composed works in his name (probably the Pastoral Epistles; possibly Ephesians, Colossians, and 2 Thessalonians as well), which likewise suggests a broad and deep familiarity with his writings from early on. In other words, the New Testament Pauline collection indicates that Paul's letters were from virtually the moment of their delivery read publicly, disseminated widely, studied intently, subjected to careful editorial activity, and even imitated. It is arguably a short step from this to affording them the status of scripture and 2 Peter 3:15-16 takes that step, probably no later than the mid-second century C.E. By this account, Marcion's idiosyncratic Pauline collection would be a tendentious edition of an emerging proto-orthodox scriptural corpus of Paul's letters, not the impetus for the latter's development.

Whatever precisely impelled the New Testament canon's formation, we can begin to trace its development by looking at early lists of "Christian" books that were read publicly alongside the Hebrew Scriptures. The so-called Muratorian fragment, probably composed in Rome in the waning years of the second century C.E., mentions Luke, John, and Acts. The opening sentences are lost, but the first preserved line seems to refer to Mark and Matthew must have been mentioned in the missing section. The list goes on to include Paul's epistles to communities (two to the Corinthians, Ephesians, Philippians, Colossians, Galatians, two to the Thessalonians, and Romans) and to individuals (Philemon, Titus, and two to Timothy). After dismissing as spurious two letters attributed to Paul (Laodiceans and Alexandrians), it authorizes an epistle of Jude, two of John (it is unclear which of the three New Testament Johannine letters are meant), the Wisdom of Solomon, and the Apocalypses of John and Peter, though acknowledging debate about the latter two. The fragment makes special mention of the Shepherd of Hermas, a contemporary book that its writer admired but would not authorize for public reading in church. The incomplete Muratorian fragment goes on to name a number of sectarians whose writings it rejects. Missing from the list entirely are Hebrews, James, the two epistles of Peter, and one of John.

Eusebius's list (preserved in *Ecclesiastical History* 3.15) dates from the early fourth century C.E. and is more systematic. It divides books into those widely regarded as authoritative, those that are disputed, and those that are spurious. In the first category Eusebius places the four gospels (so well known by the time he is writing that he does not even name them), Acts, and the Pauline epistles (again without names; presumably he would include Hebrews here). Eusebius also includes 1 John, 1 Peter, and Revelation, though the last only provisionally. To the second category he assigns James, Jude, 2 Peter, and 2 and 3 John. Among spurious books he mentions a number not included in the New Testament today (including the Muratorian fragment's Apocalypse of Peter), as well as Revelation, whose authority, he admits, is far from secure.

The first list that contains all and only those books found in the King James New Testament and contemporary bibles is Athanasius' thirty-ninth *Festal Letter* of 367 C.E. While Athanasius's canon agrees with that of most Christians today, controversy by no means ceased with his letter and later ancient lists continued to diverge from the one he made. Indeed, it is exceedingly difficult to pinpoint a specific moment in history at which we can declare the New Testament canon closed. Many Latin Bibles throughout the Middle Ages incorporated Paul's Epistle to the Laodiceans, which John Wycliffe therefore included in the first English translation of the entire Bible (late fourteenth-century). In the sixteenth century, Martin Luther questioned the canonicity of Hebrews, James, Jude, and Revelation, on theological grounds (especially with regard to James) and on the basis of ancient Christians' misgivings about these texts.

This brief survey suggests that at a fairly early period, proto-orthodox and subsequently orthodox Christians (those whom the first Christian emperor Constantine supported and whose faith was encapsulated in the important Nicene Creed of 325 C.E.) came to agree on a canonical core consisting of the four gospels, Acts, and the Pauline Epistles; they disputed Hebrews, several of the Catholic Epistles, and above all Revelation, as well as a number of writings that the King James New Testament does not include. But we should hesitate before making this suggestion carry too much weight. For instance, the New Testament canon varied significantly by region. Ancient orthodox Christians in Syria used as their primary gospel the Diatessaron, a harmonized version of the New Testament gospels that perhaps relied on other sources as well, and they considered 3 Corinthians canonical too. Revelation was usually rejected by Greek-speaking Christians in the east and, as mentioned above, the pseudepigraphical Pauline Epistle to the Laodiceans was frequently included in Latin New Testaments in the west.

Despite significant agreement across the board, absolute consensus about an orthodox New Testament canon remained surprisingly elusive throughout most of Christian history.

Even such a properly qualified assessment as this is not adequate, however. Ancient Christians not only failed to agree on the shape of the New Testament canon; they also disagreed about the New Testament canon's nature or function.[2] Athanasius published his important list of canonical books as Alexandria's bishop, in which capacity he was concerned with issues of worship, liturgy, admission to the cult, ecclesiastical governance, pastoral care, and the like. He wrote in implicit opposition to an academic Christian constituency in his city—namely, study circles led by learned and charismatic teachers interested in theological inquiry and the discovery of God's truth in a wide variety of literature, including pagan philosophy and writings sometimes deemed heretical. Such theologians might have basically agreed with Athanasius about which books were and were not scriptural, but in practice they were far less concerned with limiting what might be read than with teaching students to read in such a way as to uncover hidden divine truth in whatever they studied. By advocating a closed collection of Scriptures that uniquely communicated God's truth as opposed to a more open canon to be explored by learned communities of faithful and imaginative scholars, Athanasius attempted to circumscribe the legitimate activity and influence of authoritative teachers like these, whose theological speculation some found dangerous, if not heretical. In this context it is significant that Athanasius's thirty-ninth *Festal Letter* insists that "though the Lord has appointed teachers [1 Cor 12:28] . . . rightly [Christ] alone is the Teacher" (Coptic version quoted). Athanasius thereby suggests that Christ teaches uniquely through those approved books that he lists.

Understanding the New Testament canon turns out to be a difficult task indeed. Its original impulse is uncertain, its emerging contours were frequently controversial, and there was not necessarily consensus about the function of the canon itself, even among Christians who might have agreed on its framework. Nor can we relegate such controversies to hoary antiquity, as such notable figures as Wycliffe and Luther remind us. The New Testament canon has often been a moving target rather than a fixed entity: many orthodox Christians throughout history would not accept as scriptural several of the texts readers today find in the New Testament, and conversely would embrace others that contemporary bibles omit.

The New Testament writings were not only defined but also preserved in the early church. The printing press was not invented until the mid-fifteenth century; before that, literature survived by being hand-copied—a laborious and expensive process. The prohibitive expense of copying, the relative lack of literacy in antiquity and the Middle Ages, and the tendency of written artifacts to deteriorate over time has resulted in a dearth of manuscript evidence for most ancient literary works. For instance, only books 1–6 and 11–16 of Tacitus's *Annals of Imperial*

---

2. For this paragraph, see David Brakke, "Canon Formation and Social Conflict in Fourth-Century Egypt: Athanasius of Alexandria's Thirty-Ninth *Festal Letter,*" *Harvard Theological Review* 87 (1994): 295–419.

Rome survive. All modern editions are based on just two medieval manuscripts: a ninth-century copy of the first surviving section and an eleventh-century copy of the second. As paltry a tradition as this is, it is robust compared to what survives for most ancient books, which is nothing. Usually, all we know of one or another ancient literary work is its title and maybe a handful of lines quoted in another work—itself perhaps fragmentary—that has managed to survive.

Scholars of the New Testament encounter precisely the opposite problem. Since this collection of writings has been so highly valued by so many people and for such a long time, the number of manuscripts preserving its text is overwhelmingly large (several thousand, depending on how they are counted). Witnesses consist primarily of the following: entire Greek New Testament books or fragments written on papyri, some of which may be dated to as early as the second or third centuries C.E.; parchment manuscripts, far more common, displaying a style of Greek handwriting that dates them to the fourth through the tenth centuries; and later parchment copies that are more numerous still. We should also count manuscript copies of ancient and medieval lectionaries and of other literature that quotes the New Testament, as well as handwritten copies of early translations of the New Testament into languages other than Greek, especially Latin, Syriac, Coptic, Armenian, Georgian, Ethiopic, Gothic, Arabic, Persian, and Old Church Slavonic.

Sorting through this mass of evidence in order to determine the best reading of any particular New Testament passage is a difficult endeavor, especially because scribes (frequently educated monks) not only made unintentional errors but also felt liberty to amend texts they assumed to be infected by errors a previous copyist had introduced. For instance, a scribe encountering Mark's reference to "the prophet Isaiah" in 1:2 and observing that this gospel actually quotes both Isaiah and Malachi in verses 2–3 apparently inferred that Mark wrote "the prophets" and that an earlier copyist mistakenly turned this vague but acceptable reference into an erroneous citation of Isaiah alone (perhaps because he recognized the words of Isaiah but not those of Malachi). The later scribe emended the text in order to rectify the assumed error, thereby introducing disagreement into the manuscript tradition. Since there are no surviving autographs of New Testament writings, scholars today can determine which reading is more likely to be original in a case like this only by applying their critical acumen to the textual evidence that emerges from a collation of the wealth of manuscripts.

Of course, textual critics grant special privilege to those copies of any particular New Testament text that are evidently early, that seem not to copy other extant copies, and that represent the work of competent scribes. They also apply analytical rules of thumb, such as the following: when the manuscript tradition attests competing readings of the same text, the more difficult one is most likely original. In the example from Mark 1:2 discussed above, it is easy to imagine a scribe "correcting" an originally inaccurate citation of Isaiah to introduce a quote combining Isaiah and Malachi. We have in fact explained how this might come about. It is somewhat more difficult (though not impossible; textual criticism cannot make absolute claims) to imagine a scribe changing an entirely appropriate (if vague) reference to "the prophets" into an erroneous reference to Isaiah alone.

Thus, the inaccuracy is likely original. Although the amount of manuscript evidence they must work through is daunting, most modern New Testament textual critics are confident that the analytical techniques they apply enable them to reconstruct something very similar to what the authors originally wrote, even if absolute certainty is unobtainable and, for a number of difficult passages, relative certainty too remains elusive.

The King James Version is not based on a Greek New Testament edited by modern textual critics.[3] The translators instead used a version (or versions) of the edition published by Desiderius Erasmus early in the sixteenth century. Erasmus's work seems to have taken less than a year and he himself later admitted that it was rushed. He did not have access to a manuscript of the entire New Testament. For all but Revelation he used two relatively late (twelfth-century) manuscripts of poor quality, one for the Gospels and another for Acts and the Epistles (both of which he emended with reference to a few other manuscripts at his disposal), and occasionally the Latin Vulgate as well. For Revelation the situation was worse. Erasmus could find only one manuscript, and it was missing the book's final verses, which he decided to translate from the Vulgate back into Greek for his edition. Erasmus's Greek New Testament improved as it saw successive editions, but even at its best it remains an inferior work of scholarship, by modern standards especially.

Nonetheless, it rapidly became the definitive version of the Greek New Testament in Europe, and most subsequent editions until Johann Griesbach's groundbreaking work in the late eighteenth century followed it closely. Within little more than a century of its original publication, the text-type Erasmus produced came to be called the *textus receptus* (received text), a title reflecting the authority it had somewhat arbitrarily been assigned. Of particular importance are the editions of the printer Robert Estienne (better known as Stephanus, his name in Latin), whose fourth edition, published in 1551, introduced the verse numbers that have since become conventional. In the second half of the sixteenth century, Théodore de Bèze (Beza) also prepared several editions. His copious annotations offer a large number of variant readings, but the text he prints basically amounts to that of Stephanus's fourth edition, which is itself closely related to Erasmus's. It is on the later editions of Beza's text (1589 and 1598) that the 1611 King James Version usually relies. The King James translators also used Erasmus's text, the Complutensian Polyglot (1514–17), and Stephanus's 1550 edition, and there are a few places where they seem to follow the Vulgate.

The King James New Testament, then, translates a Greek text that is frequently corrupt. Those corruptions are often so minor as not to affect the translation. For instance, the text on which the King James New Testament relies might alter the highly flexible Greek word order displayed in a given sentence without altering the sentence's sense in a way that translation into English, with its relatively fixed word order, could easily capture. However, the poor quality of the Greek text that the King James New Testament translates occasionally does

---

3.   For this paragraph and the next, see Bruce M. Metzger and Bart D. Ehrman, *The Text of the New Testament: Its Transmission, Corruption, and Restoration*, 4th ed. (New York: Oxford University Press, 2005), 137–64.

affect its English rendering, and sometimes drastically. The most famous example would be the final twelve verses of Mark, which the best reading of the manuscript tradition would omit. (Mark 16:9–20 is missing from important early witnesses, and some manuscripts that have the passage mark it as textually suspect.) Mark 1:41 offers a narrower example. There, according to the King James Version, Jesus was "moved with pity" to heal a man afflicted with leprosy. A better construal of the manuscript tradition has Jesus "moved with anger." ("Anger" represents the more difficult reading: it is more likely that a pious scribe eliminated Jesus' unmotivated anger at a recipient of his mercy than that such a scribe introduced it.) As a rule, we have noted in the annotations every place where the King James Bible translates a Greek reading that does not accord with the best construal of the manuscript tradition, provided its divergence could affect a close reading of the English translation. In deciding on the best reading of the manuscript tradition, the editors of this volume have generally followed the twenty-seventh edition of the Nestle-Aland *Novum Testamentum Graece*, edited by Barbara and Kurt Aland et al. (Stuttgart: Deutsche Bibelgesellschaft, 1993) and have also consulted the second edition of Bruce Metzger's *Textual Commentary on the Greek New Testament* (Stuttgart: Deutsche Bibelgesellschaft, 1994).

The system of chapters and verses that the Bible uses was introduced after the biblical books were originally written and for the New Testament should be assigned no interpretive authority. Indeed, the earliest New Testament manuscripts have no paragraphs or even punctuation and do not distinguish between capital and lowercase letters either. Division of the text into paragraphs therefore represents an editorial decision (ours, as the King James Bible's paragraphing is sporadic and incomplete), as does division into sentences, whenever the Greek syntax allows for competing interpretations. Other than paragraphing, the only meaningful changes we have made to the standard Cambridge University Press edition (itself a lightly corrected version of Benjamin Blayney's 1769 Oxford edition) are occasional alterations of its erratic punctuation in those places where the original punctuation stands in irresolvable tension with our understanding of how best to divide the text into meaningful paragraphs. Every one of the small handful of such changes is flagged in the annotations.

The King James Bible was conceived as a revision of the Bishops' Bible (first edition, 1568; second, 1572) and as an answer to the ever-popular Geneva Bible (1560; NT, 1557), privileged by the Puritans. It was supposed to rectify the obvious deficiencies of the former (the Anglican bishops responsible for it were neither strong philologists nor great prose stylists) while at the same time eschewing the kind of tendentious interpretive annotations in which the latter was thought occasionally to have indulged (a few of which apparently offended King James himself). It happily exceeded these rather modest expectations to become one of the most important works of English literature ever produced.

Approximately fifty scholars working in six companies began the project in 1604. Although King James commissioned this translation, neither he nor any other monarch ever "authorized" it (e.g., for public reading) and it was not until the nineteenth century that it was commonly referred to as the Authorized Version, a practice we accordingly eschew in this edition. The King James Bible owes a great deal to the monumental work of the translator and reformer William Tyndale, who first published his New Testament in 1526 and his Pentateuch in 1530. (He was arrested and executed by Catholic authorities in Antwerp before his translation of most of the rest of the Bible could be finalized and published.) Like Tyndale's, the King James Bible is a fairly literal translation; indeed, it often does a better job of capturing the strangeness of the New Testament's Greek than do modern versions. Jude 7 provides a representative example, with its puzzling reference to the inhabitants of Sodom and Gomorrah *apelthousai opisō sarkos heteras,* "going after other flesh." Modern translations usually paraphrase: "indulged in sexual immorality" (NRSV), "gave themselves up to sexual immorality" (NIV), "pursued unnatural lusts" (NJB), and so on. The King James translators render the phrase literally ("going after strange flesh"), thereby allowing the careful reader to discover that Jude imagines Sodom and Gomorrah's transgression to have been not a violent desire for homosexual sex, nor even a hubristic violation of ancient Near Eastern conventions of hospitality (another common interpretation of the passage), but rather an attempt to rape angels (angelic flesh being "other" than human, that is, foreign or "strange"), in particular those God had sent to visit them (see Gen 19:1–26; Jude 6–7 and notes). This is certainly not an interpretation of the story that most modern readers would intuitively leap to, and contemporary translators' decision to paraphrase rather than to reproduce the strangeness of Jude's Greek hopelessly obscures this book's surprising construal of the Old Testament episode. Their choice becomes particular disturbing when we recognize that Jude may be onto something: the story of Sodom's destruction clearly echoes the story of the flood from Genesis 6–9 (see Gen 19:1–38 and notes) and human-angelic miscegenation seems to have initiated that episode of divine judgment as well (Gen 6:1–4).

The King James Version sometimes violates its general tendency toward literal translation, however. For instance, it privileges English's predilection for variation of diction over a tendency displayed in the Old and New Testament to repeat key words and roots in rhetorically or thematically significant ways. It is also a Christian version and at times its translators' theological presuppositions lead to tendentious renderings. Yet for the most part, the King James Bible is a useful translation—careful, stately, and readable. That its translators were sophisticated philologists is revealed by the marginal notes they prepared along with their translation, as well as by the notes John Bois took while revising the translation of Romans through Revelation as a member of the final committee of review (as excerpted on pp. 1506–08 of this volume).

In the annotations to New Testament books, we sometimes propose a "better" translation, but that assessment is rarely meant as a critique of the King James Bible. A proposed rendering might be "better" merely because the words that the King James translators chose in the early seventeenth century have since acquired misleading connotations, or even different meanings, and an alternative translation more closely reflects contemporary English usage. It might also be "better" because it preserves thematically significant repetition in the original, though that does not imply that the King James translators made an error in deciding to avoid awkwardly redundant English. An alternative translation of a given word or phrase might also be "better" because it coheres with a more compelling interpretation of the book or episode in which it is embedded, even though the King James rendering might be grammatically feasible and exegetically defensible. Only on occasion is the King James New Testament's translation genuinely flawed (for example, Rom 6:17 and note; 11:11 and note), in which case the alternative translation that the notes propose is straightforwardly superior to what the King James Bible offers. Context makes such cases clear.

While the New Testament writings are not Christian per se, the New Testament itself has been assembled, preserved, translated, and interpreted in a Christian context, and the introductions and annotations that follow address all of these developments to one degree or another. The critical appendix, however, focuses especially on the last mentioned. It contains some contextual materials, but most of it is devoted to examples of biblical interpretation. Of course, the body of literature that interprets or otherwise responds to the New Testament is wildly expansive; it is probably no exaggeration to claim that more has been written about the New Testament than about any other comparable collection of literature ever. The appendix samples the history of New Testament interpretation and translation, frequently offering competing perspectives on the same interpretive issue or biblical passage. It gives the reader a sense of how Christians especially (but not exclusively) have read and responded to this collection of writings for the past two thousand years and may therefore be viewed as a continuation of this discussion of the New Testament's Christian matrix.

The Apocrypha

The Apocrypha contains a number of Jewish writings, for the most part composed in the Hellenistic period, that are not included in the Hebrew Bible. Some of these supplement Old Testament books: the Daniel and Esther additions; the Prayer of Manasses (cf. 2 Chr 33:11–13); 1 Esdras, which is closely related to Ezra-Nehemiah; and Baruch, with the Letter of Jeremiah attached (compare Jeremiah). Others offer later examples of genres that the Old Testament includes: the Wisdom of Solomon and Sirach (Ecclesiasticus) exemplify Wisdom literature (compare Proverbs); 1 and 2 Maccabees are histories (compare the books of Samuel); Tobit and Judith are romances (comparable to Ruth and Esther); 2 Esdras is an apocalypse (compare Daniel). The Greek word *apocrypha* means "hidden things," but it is far from clear why it came to be applied to these texts. Was it because their origins were unknown, since in many cases they survived only in Greek or Latin translation of a Hebrew or Aramaic original? Was it to suggest that they were not suitable for public reading? Or was there perhaps another reason? Certainly Catholics, who accept many of the Apocrypha's writings as canonical, are often uncomfortable with the appellation, especially since the word can imply falsity. They tend to refer to these books (minus 1 and 2 Esdras and the Prayer of Manasses) as "deuterocanonical"—that is, "of the second canon" as opposed to the first, the writings of the Hebrew Bible

It is difficult to assess these books' status among ancient Jews. They certainly did not enjoy the same widespread authority as the Hebrew Bible, which omits them. It may also be significant that the Jewish writings included in the New Testament quote from none of them (although allusions are not uncommon).

Presumably most of the works constituting the Apocrypha were viewed as authoritative in Alexandria, for it seems likely that the Septuagint (which included the
majority of them) originated there. Moreover, fragments from Tobit, Sirach, and
the Letter of Jeremiah were found among the Dead Sea Scrolls in Judea, and the
rabbis quote from Sirach. 1 and 2 Maccabees, too, have often been popular
among Jews. Nonetheless, with few exceptions no copies of these works survive
in their original Semitic languages, because it was Christians rather than Jews
who were responsible for preserving these texts in the copies of the Greek Septuagint they produced and used. This pattern of survival suggests that the texts
were not valued highly in the context of the ideological and theological consolidation of Judaism that took place under the rabbis after the Herodian temple's
destruction.

Jerome knew of no Hebrew copies of these texts (his translations rely on the
Septuagint's Greek) and he draws attention to their secondary status in his prefaces, where he also indicates his reluctance to include them at all in the Vulgate.
Most ancient and later medieval Christians accepted the books as canonical—a
consensus leading to Jerome's inclusion of them, despite reservations—but some
(John Wycliffe among them) continued to register questions, culminating in Protestants' final rejection of their canonicity. Yet many Protestant Bibles retained
the Apocrypha, merely segregating these from the rest of the biblical books in an
appendix; rejection of its canonical authority did not necessarily amount to rejection outright. The Church of England, for instance, declared it appropriate to draw
on the Apocrypha for instructing believers, but not for deciding doctrine. The
Counter-Reformation Catholic Church, of course, went much further: the Council of Trent in 1546 explicitly declared Tobit, Judith, Wisdom, Sirach, Baruch, and
1 and 2 Maccabees canonical, as well as alluding to the canonical status of the
Esther and Daniel additions and of the Letter of Jeremiah. It denied such status to 1 and 2 Esdras and the Prayer of Manasses, which had always been more
marginal. The Sixtine Vulgate, whose publication in 1590 Pope Sixtus V oversaw
in order to make available a version of the Scriptures adhering to the council's
directives, omitted these books; Pope Clement VIII's more influential revision
published two years later (the Clementine Vulgate) restored them, although relegating them to an appendix, much as Protestant Bibles treat the entire Apocrypha.
Eastern Orthodox Bibles contain slightly different collections of deuterocanonical
books and deal with them in different ways.

Readers may be surprised to find the Apocrypha in the King James Bible at all,
for from the nineteenth century on, especially in the United States, it became
increasingly popular to omit the Apocrypha from printings of the translation.
Accordingly, King James Bibles without the Apocrypha are more common today
than those that include it. The King James translators based their version on
numerous textual authorities, especially the Complutensian Polyglot. Yet that
edition of the Bible did not contain 1 and 2 Esdras or the Prayer of Manasses.
For the second and possibly third of these books, the translators relied primarily
on the Vulgate; for the first, they used the Aldus Greek Bible (1518) and also the
Roman Septuagint (1586). Except in the case of a few books (especially Sirach
and 2 Esdras, as explained in their introductions), the present edition's annotations do not trace the divergences of the Apocrypha from the best Greek or Latin

authorities with anything like the attention devoted to the New Testament's manuscript tradition, nor do they comment extensively on the originals of the translation, although information about the sometimes complicated textual traditions of each apocryphal book may be found in the introductions.

Acknowledgments

I have benefited more than I can say from the expertise and camaraderie of my colleagues in the English Department at the College at Brockport. I must single out Brooke Conti especially, who read various portions of this book in manuscript form and whose critiques and encouraging words I have come to value immensely. I am also grateful to department chair Roger Kurtz, who facilitated a crucial adjustment to my teaching schedule that enabled me to complete the manuscript on time. Nick Gresens, from the Department of Religion and Classics at the University of Rochester, generously lent me his philological expertise during my translation of Juvencus; his assistance saved me from more than one error.

Herb Marks, editor of the OT volume, has been the most valuable of partners and the NT volume frequently benefits from his deep learnedness and his keen sense of language. Working with him has been one of this project's great pleasures.

I am grateful to the editors at Norton, especially Carol Bemis and Rivka Genesen, for ably shepherding this project to completion. Alice Falk, perhaps the best copyeditor in the business, did a remarkable job of facilitating the transformation of my long and unwieldy manuscript into a book.

I want also to acknowledge my wife, Joy, and my son, Noah, who have suffered through and generously helped me negotiate the demands this prolonged project has made on my time and on our life together. My mother, Jane Busch, deserves special recognition, not only for encouraging me but also for reading the introductions and annotations and offering her astute comments as an intelligent layperson about where and how they might be made more helpful for a general reader.

I dedicate this book to my late grandmother, Fredella Levey, whose love for the biblical word first inspired my own.

AB

Abbreviations

With occasional exceptions, capitalization and abbreviations follow the guide-lines set out in *The SBL Handbook of Style: For Ancient Near Eastern, Biblical, and Early Christian Studies*, ed. Patrick H. Alexander et al. (Peabody, MA: Hendrickson, 1999). The following abbreviations are common:

B.C.E.	before the Common Era (B.C.)
ca.	circa
C.E.	Common Era (A.D.)
cf.	compare
chap(s).	chapter(s)
Gk.	Greek
Heb.	Hebrew
KJV	King James Version
Lat.	Latin
lit.	literally
LXX	Septuagint
MS(s)	manuscript(s)
MT	Masoretic Text (or Majority Text)
NJB	New Jerusalem Bible
NRSV	New Revised Standard Version
NT	New Testament
OT	Old Testament
RSV	Revised Standard Version
v(v).	verse(s)

The books of the Bible are abbreviated as follows:

Old Testament: Gen, Exod, Lev, Num, Deut, Josh, Judg, Ruth, 1–2 Sam, 1–2 Kgs, 1–2 Chr, Ezra, Neh, Esth, Job, Ps(s), Prov, Eccl, Song, Isa, Jer, Lam, Ezek, Dan, Hos, Joel, Amos, Obad, Jonah, Mic, Nah, Hab, Zeph, Hag, Zech, Mal;

New Testament: Matt, Mark, Luke, John, Acts, Rom, 1–2 Cor, Gal, Eph, Phil, Col, 1–2 Thess, 1–2 Tim, Titus, Phlm, Heb, Jas, 1–2 Pet, 1–3 John, Jude, Rev;

Apocrypha: 1–2 Esd, Tob, Jdt, Add Est, Wis, Sir, Bar, Ep Jer, Sg Three, Sus, Bel, Pr Man, 1–2 Macc.

THE
NEW TESTAMENT

Narratives

THE first five books of the New Testament are narratives: four accounts of Jesus' career, which have come to be known as "gospels," and the Acts of the Apostles (or simply Acts), a history of the early church. Acts is actually Luke's companion volume, the second book of a history of Christian origins that contemporary scholars call Luke-Acts. Separated from its partner, it serves as a transition from the stories of Jesus to the epistles of Paul and of other leaders in the early church, whose ministries it recounts.

The bulk of New Testament narrative focuses on Jesus. The four gospels each offer a distinct version of his story, much as 1–2 Samuel and 1–2 Chronicles provide competing accounts of David's reign. As the Chronicler relied on the Deuteronomistic History, so, scholars believe, literary dependence explains the relationship between at least the first three gospels. Matthew, Mark, and Luke display similarities so extensive and precise that they have earned the label "synoptic," from a Greek word meaning "seen together": the reader studying them side by side can profitably compare them—episode by episode, saying by saying.

Because the Synoptics' similarities involve extended verbatim repetition, we cannot simply posit that they are independent reports of the same events. Three witnesses of the same incident might produce compatible narratives, but not virtually identical descriptions, such as those often found in Matthew, Mark, and Luke.

Some speculate that independent reliance on common oral traditions might explain these similarities. Oral tradition certainly played a crucial role in transmitting and preserving information about Jesus before the Synoptics were composed, but it cannot account for the texts we have. First of all, oral transmission does not normally involve word-for-word memorization. It is possible, of course, that early oral preservation of traditions about Jesus was exceptional: eyewitnesses of Jesus' ministry (particularly the twelve apostles) could have exercised more or less formal control over the process of transmission, overseeing verbatim memorization of the stories and sayings of Jesus and ensuring their accurate recitation. Matthew, Mark, and Luke might then independently have drawn on the same body of carefully preserved oral traditions about Jesus to compose accounts of his career.

Under this scenario, however, the Synoptics should demonstrate rather more agreement than they in fact display. Along with word-for-word correspondences we find divergences as well—frequently substantive ones. If oral traditions about Jesus were preserved and transmitted with sufficient precision to ensure frequent verbatim agreement among the Synoptics, then lack of agreement must indicate that one or more of the evangelists has treated this traditional material very freely

1

and thus quite contrary to the practice of careful preservation on which the evangelists are supposed to have relied. In the end, special pleading is required of those using common reliance on oral tradition to explain the Synoptics' combination of verbatim similarity and consequential difference. They must posit an exceptionally controlled process of oral transmission to ensure meticulous preservation of Jesus' stories and sayings, while at the same time accepting the evangelists' willingness to make radical departures from that tradition. On balance it is easier to imagine an original author working with stories and sayings of Jesus that had never been meticulously memorized and recited but rather told and retold, with greater and lesser modifications to meet the needs of particular communities in particular circumstances. This evangelist incorporated that traditional material into a written narrative of Jesus' career, editing and arranging it according to his own literary and theological vision. Later authors then incorporated that document into their own compositions, sometimes revising, excising, and supplementing it significantly, and sometimes following it verbatim.

The Synoptic Problem

Charting the precise literary relationship among the Synoptics (i.e., solving the "Synoptic Problem") requires detailed consideration, but it makes available a powerful interpretive methodology. By carefully comparing the Synoptics and viewing their differences as the product of editorial alteration, readers can draw inferences about the effects and even possible motivations of a later evangelist's revision of an earlier gospel, thereby better grasping the later composition's stylistic, thematic, and theological concerns, as well as gaining insight into how the earlier work was originally interpreted. Such analysis, known as "redaction criticism," is a staple of New Testament studies, although it requires no special training. This volume's annotations facilitate its practice by noting parallel passages for every relevant episode in each Synoptic Gospel. In order to attempt it profitably, however, readers must first come to a tentative conclusion about which gospels are redacting and which are redacted: that is, they must determine in what literary relationship the Synoptics stand.

The conventional view holds that Mark was the first gospel written and that Matthew and Luke independently used Mark as their source. The force of the arguments supporting this position is more cumulative than individual. Among the most important are the arguments from omissions, from order, and from redaction.

Matthew and Luke together contain almost all of Mark's material. According to B. F. Streeter, Matthew alone includes about 90 percent of it, and Luke about 50 percent (*The Four Gospels* [2nd edn; London: Macmillan, 1930], 159–60). Mark, in contrast, lacks the majority of Matthew's and Luke's contents, including most of Jesus' ethical teaching (e.g., Matthew's Sermon on the Mount) and his parables (e.g., the parables of the Good Samaritan and Prodigal Son from Luke). Moreover, Matthew and Luke each contain considerable unique material. To explain all these omissions we can posit that Matthew and Luke independently used Mark as their primary source, supplementing it with additional material, some of which they both had access to, some of which only one or the other knew, but none of which was known by Mark. Otherwise, we have to imagine

Mark using Matthew, Luke, or both but expurgating in a way difficult to account for, and Matthew or Luke adopting the same procedure one toward the other.

The structure of the gospels also suggests that Mark has priority. As a rule, whenever the order of episodes included by Matthew and Luke agrees (which is often), that order also agrees with Mark—and even when the two disagree, one or the other continues to follow Mark's order. The similarities and differences in sequence that Matthew, Mark, and Luke display can be explained by positing that Matthew and Luke independently follow Mark, with occasional and usually separate deviations.

Finally, it is easy to interpret many differences that Mark, Matthew, and Luke display as the latters' independent revisions of the former; it is hard to explain them as Markan editorial alterations to Matthew or Luke.

Mark's Greek is sometimes awkward, and deviations in Luke or Matthew at the level of diction, grammar, and syntax often look like attempts to improve his writing. In addition, Mark is sometimes redundant: for example, "And at even, when the sun did set" (1:32). Only a single temporal marker is necessary, and therefore Matthew and Luke each eliminate one when they incorporate Mark into their gospels: Matthew has "When the even was come" (8:16); Luke writes "Now when the sun was setting" (4:40).

Mark also includes material that many early Jesus-believers presumably would have found troubling. His statement that Jesus *could there do no mighty work*, save that he laid his hands on a few sick folk, and healed them. And he marvelled because of their unbelief" (6:5–6; emphasis added) implies that Jesus' power depends on the faith of the people among whom he ministers. The parallel passage in Matthew eliminates that scandalous notion: "And *he did not many mighty works there* because of their unbelief" (13:58; emphasis added). It seems more plausible that Matthew revised what he saw to be an imprudent limitation of Jesus' power in Mark than that Mark imported into Matthew's statement a potentially disturbing idea.

Of particular relevance is the Synoptics' treatment of Jesus' disciples. Mark consistently depicts them as dim-witted and presumptuous, while Matthew's and Luke's somewhat more favorable portrayals look like attempts to salvage their reputation. Consider just one of the numerous examples. In Mark, James and John audaciously ask to sit at Jesus' right and left hand in eschatological glory (10:35–45). Luke replaces their appeal with a passing reference to a dispute among the disciples about which was greatest (22:24–27) and has Jesus promise them the eschatological authority that Mark's Jesus will not or cannot grant (22:28–30; cf. Mark 10:40). Matthew's change is even more revealing: he introduces the character of James and John's mother, to whom he attributes the brash request (20:20–28). Most scholars believe it more plausible that Matthew introduced a face-saving revision than that Mark transformed a mother's immoderate advocacy for her sons into two disciples' own gross presumption.

Such arguments, combined with others, convince most New Testament scholars that Matthew and Luke independently used Mark as a literary source. But this hypothesis must deal with a number of complications—most obviously, that Matthew and Luke share a great deal of material absent from Mark. Both alone have the Beatitudes (Matt 5:3–12; Luke 6:20–23), as well as the story of Satan's triple temptation of Jesus (Matt 4:1–11; Luke 4:1–13) and much else besides. Moreover, the non-Markan material that Matthew and Luke share demonstrates the same tendency toward verbatim agreement they display when drawing on Mark. Scholars therefore hypothesize that they used another literary source, which is conventionally designated Q (probably from the German *Quelle,* "source").

Matthew and Luke presumably exercised much more liberty with Q's order than they did with Mark's, for when they include identical material that Mark omits, it rarely appears at the same point in their narratives. For example, Matthew and Luke both have the non-Markan parable of the Lost Sheep, but Matthew locates it in Jesus' extended discourse on community discipline (18:10–14) while Luke's Jesus utters it in response to the scribes' and Pharisees' rejection of sinners (15:1–7). Moreover, when they do insert Q material at the same point in their narratives, the agreement usually points to common reliance on Mark's sequential order. For example, both expand Mark's account of John the Baptist's ministry with the same supplementary sayings of John (Matt 3:1–12; Luke 3:1–18; cf. Mark 1:2–6), and both locate their extended temptation stories immediately after Jesus' baptism, precisely where Mark reports Jesus was tempted (Matt 4:1–11; Luke 4:1–13; cf. Mark 1:12–13). Indeed, Q apparently lacked a coherent framework of its own: the non-Markan traditions that Matthew and Luke share consist primarily of sayings of Jesus, with a few attributed to John the Baptist as well. There are also a handful of stories (e.g., Jesus' healing of the centurion's son; Matt 8:5–13; Luke 7:1–10), most of which emphasize the authority of Jesus' sayings. Several ancient Christian collections of loosely connected sayings attributed to Jesus survive (e.g., the *Gospel of Thomas* [see Appendix, pp. 1034–45] and the *Gospel of Philip*); Q, presumably, was one that did not.

Perhaps the strongest argument against the Q hypothesis is that it is purely conjectural: the document is not extant. All that points to its existence is extensive verbatim agreement between non-Markan material in Matthew and Luke, which is more efficiently explained by positing that one of those gospels borrowed from the other. Q's plausibility, then, depends on the strength of the arguments for Matthew's and Luke's independent use of Mark as a source. If these arguments are persuasive, then we must hypothesize that a Q document once existed. Moreover, its disappearance is easy to understand: once Matthew's and Luke's coherent narratives incorporated the material that Q had preserved in disjointed form, no one in antiquity would have needed or wanted to read Q. The document would have ceased to circulate and to be copied and would have dropped out of existence.

Nineteenth-century German biblical scholars combined Markan priority and the Q hypothesis, and the resulting Two-Source Hypothesis is accepted by most New Testament scholars today as the best description of the literary relationship among the Synoptics. Yet despite the arguments in its favor and the widespread support it enjoys, this hypothesis is not without problems, and they too require careful attention. These difficulties can be found in each of the arguments for Markan priority outlined above.

The argument from omission relies on an assumption that demands examination: no evangelist would omit important information about Jesus that he knew.

Two-Source Hypothesis

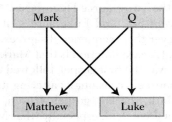

On its face this assumption seems sound. The gospels, after all, preserve traditional knowledge about Jesus for later generations, a purpose announced in the preface to Luke (1:1–4). This purpose would seem to imply reluctance to omit important material about Jesus, but there are reasons to question this implication.

Markan priority explains why Mark lacks much of what Matthew and Luke contain by positing that its writer had no knowledge of Matthew and Luke, or of the traditions they preserve. Yet that explanation cannot address its most vital omission: namely, the risen Christ's appearances to his disciples (see note to 16:9–20). The risen Jesus fails to appear in Mark, which in fact closes with a suggestion that the disciples never saw him after his resurrection (16:6–7 and notes). Matthew, Luke, John, and Acts, in contrast, each narrate distinct versions of Jesus' appearances to the Twelve and others. Their diverse accounts cannot be traced to a common source, and therefore indicate that such stories were widely disseminated in the early church. Confirmation is provided by Paul's discussion of the risen Christ in 1 Corinthians, universally believed to have been written before the gospels. Paul introduces and concludes a list of references to the resurrected Christ's appearances by noting that he merely passes on what he has learned from others and what all apostles attest (1 Cor 15:3–11). It is implausible that Mark had not heard of these traditions: thus, he chose to omit them. If this evangelist deems accounts of Jesus' resurrection appearances inessential, then how can we assume he would not also omit Matthew's Sermon on the Mount, or Luke's parable of the Prodigal Son, or indeed any and every other tradition that Matthew and Luke share but Mark lacks?

Some scholars avoid this problem by claiming that Mark did not originally end at 16:8 (see note) but included an account, now lost, of the risen Jesus' appearances to the disciples in Galilee (supposedly foreshadowed at 14:28; 16:7). No evidence supports this assertion. The best reading of Mark's MS tradition points to an ending at 16:8, and Matthew and Luke cease to agree with one another at this point; thus, even those who accept the hypothesis of Markan priority must conclude that the later evangelists used copies of Mark that ended there. A lost original ending would have to have vanished very early in Mark's history. Increasingly, contemporary scholars accept 16:8 as Mark's authentic close, even if it strikes them as a curiously unsatisfying ending. That acceptance significantly undercuts the argument from omission, though few have explored this implication.

A reasonable challenge to the argument from order likewise puts in question Markan priority and thus the Two-Source Hypothesis. As noted above, whenever the order of episodes in Matthew and Luke agrees, it also agrees with Mark's episodic sequence. Whenever their sequence disagrees, one or the other continues following Mark's order. One explanation is that Mark was written first; another possibility is that Matthew was the first gospel, followed by Luke. On this account, Luke used Matthew as a source, occasionally altering its order (as well as adding and omitting material). Mark, the last gospel written, used both Matthew and Luke as sources (omitting a great deal, especially what Matthew and Luke did not share). Augustine of Hippo proposed a version of this theory in 400 C.E. (*Harmony of the Gospels* 1.4; Appendix, pp. 1077–78), but it was first put forth in precisely this form in the late eighteenth century by Johann Jakob Griesbach. Bearing his name, it has become the chief competitor of the Two-Source Hypothesis, although today scholars who hold to it find themselves in the minority.

Griesbach Hypothesis

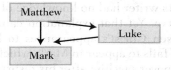

The Griesbach Hypothesis posits that when the order of Matthew and Luke agreed, Mark followed it; when their order disagreed, the evangelist chose to follow one or the other. It also explains the similarities between Matthew and Luke more efficiently than does the Two-Source Hypothesis, eliminating the need for the hypothetical Q.

The most compelling arguments in favor of Markan priority and, by extension, of the Two-Source Hypothesis are those from redaction, but they are not impervious to criticism. Against the case made above for Matthew and Luke resolving grammatical and stylistic infelicities in Mark, we might imagine Mark introducing them into accounts derived from Matthew or Luke—a credible procedure if we assume that Greek was not Mark's primary language. This charitable assumption, however, fails to explain Mark's redundancies—such as the example already given, "at even, when the sun did set" (Mark 1:32; cf. Matt 8:16; Luke 4:40), or his subsequent combination of Matthew's "all that were sick" (8:16) and Luke's "any infirm [KJV 'sick'] with divers diseases" (4:40) to produce "many that were sick of divers diseases" (1:34). The Griesbach Hypothesis posits a simple mechanism for such conflation, but its explanatory power depends on special pleading: one has to accept that Mark knew of and eliminated large swaths of material in Matthew and Luke, while at the same time faithfully preserving apparently random synonymous phrases from them.

That Mark may have introduced theological problems into Matthew or Luke is somewhat easier to accept. Regardless of its priority, Mark's failure to confirm Jesus' resurrection with traditional accounts of the risen Christ's appearances is a major theological complication. Though some have argued that Mark confirms the resurrection by means of the empty tomb, this evidence is ambiguous at best, and Matthew admits as much (28:11–15). Mark's willingness to complicate such a fundamental issue should make one pause before presuming he would not introduce other kinds of theological difficulties (e.g., at 6:5–6, as discussed above) into relatively straightforward stories from Matthew or Luke.

The least compelling evidence for Mark's editorial alteration of Matthew or Luke is his treatment of the disciples. The early Jesus-believing movement was far from unified; even idealized leaders of the church were not above sharp conflict. Galatians, for instance, records Paul's public denunciation of Peter (2:11–21), a disciple who comes off poorly in Mark's gospel as well. Whether or not Mark was the first gospel written, it criticizes Peter and the other disciples severely. Given the disputes among the early church's leaders and constituencies, we can as easily imagine a later evangelist inserting a reproof of Jesus' disciples as one expurgating such criticism to leave a more favorable depiction of them.

Another potential problem for the Two-Source Hypothesis arises from areas of agreement between Matthew and Luke against Mark. Since the Two-Source Hypothesis posits that Matthew and Luke used Mark independently, identical alterations of Mark must be coincidental, and thus should be infrequent. They are, but they still occur somewhat more often than one would expect. Matthew's and Luke's revision of Mark's story of the paralytic's restoration provides a case study (Mark 2:1–12; cf. Matt 9:1–8; Luke 5:17–26). Mark uses what appears to be a vernacular Greek word for the object on which the paralytic lies: *krabbatos*, a "mattress" or "pallet" (KJV "bed"). The apparent awkwardness of Mark's diction can explain why Matthew and Luke both remove the word from their versions— but not why their tactics of deletion are often the same.

Matthew and Luke both introduce the same alternative Greek word (*klinēs*, "bed") at the same point in their version of Mark's story (Matt 9:2; Luke 5:18). More surprisingly, they do so a sentence earlier than Mark's first reference to the paralytic's *krabbatos*. It is also unexpected that when Matthew and Luke delete *krabbatos* from Mark's narrative, half the time they eliminate it in the same way. They both excise it at the second of the four times it appears in Mark (2:9; cf. Matt 9:5; Luke 5:23) and they both change it to a form of *klinēs* at its third appearance (2:11; cf. Matt 9:6; Luke 5:24 [KJV "couch"]). The first and fourth time it appears in Mark they deal with it differently: Matthew deletes it from his equivalent of Mark 2:4 and 12 (see Matt 9:2, 7), while Luke changes it to a form of *klinēs* at 2:4 (Luke 5:19, "couch") and uses the periphrasis "that whereon he lay" in his version of Mark 2:12 (Luke 5:25). The Two-Source Hypothesis asks us to accept that when faced with an awkward term, Matthew and Luke independently alter Mark's text in the same way three times out of five. An exhaustive survey of such minor agreements between Matthew and Luke against Mark lends further support to what this case suggests: they occur slightly more often than might be expected were Matthew and Luke independent compositions.

In a few cases, the agreements against Mark are more substantial. Matthew, Mark, and Luke all include the accusation that Jesus uses demonic power to exorcise demons (Mark 3:22–30; cf. Matt 12:22–32; Luke 11:14–23; 12:10), but

Matthew and Luke share a version of the episode different from Mark's. The same is true of the parable of the Mustard Seed (Mark 4:30–32; cf. Matt 13:31–32; Luke 13:18–19), which not only appears in slightly different form in Matthew and Luke, but also in both immediately precedes the parable of the Leaven (Matt 13:33; Luke 13:20–21). Since Mark does not have the parable of the Leaven, the Two-Source Hypothesis explains their rare agreement in order against Mark by positing that the two parables stood side by side in Q. Matthew and Luke also have different versions of the sending out of the Twelve (Mark 6:7–13; cf. Matt 10:1, 9–14; Luke 9:1–6), of the teaching about divorce (Mark 10:11–12; cf. Matt 5:31–32; Luke 16:18), of the sayings from Mark 4:21–22 (for v. 21, cf. Matt 5:15; Luke 11:33; for v. 22, cf. Matt 10:26; Luke 12:2), and of other material as well. In addition, as noted above, Matthew and Luke have the same expanded version of Jesus' temptation, which differs from Mark's brief report (Matt 4:1–11; Luke 4:1–13; cf. Mark 1:12–13), and they have similar expanded versions of John the Baptist's preaching (Matt 3:7–12; Luke 3:7–18; cf. Mark 1:7–8).

Scholars usually explain these major agreements between Matthew and Luke against Mark as cases of Mark-Q overlap: Q contained some material very similar to what one finds in Mark, and Matthew and Luke independently chose to include Q's version rather than, or sometimes in addition to, what they found in Mark. This premise also addresses the occasional doubling of Markan material in Matthew and Luke. Matthew, for instance, twice includes Jesus' teaching about divorce, once in a context and form resembling Mark's (Matt 19:9; cf. Mark 10:11–12) and once in a form different from Mark's but similar to Luke's (Matt 5:31–32; Luke 16:18). According to the explanation just offered, Matthew has included both Mark's and Q's version of the teaching.

From one perspective, the idea of Mark-Q overlap is hardly objectionable. We would expect early Christian writings about Jesus by different authors to contain different versions of some of the same stories, which they could have learned independently from flexible oral traditions. From another perspective, however, the notion of Mark-Q overlap is disconcerting, for it violates the principle of explanatory economy (Occam's razor): it is far easier to explain that Matthew and Luke sometimes share material that Mark lacks and at other times share different versions of episodes Mark includes by positing that Luke used Matthew and that Mark used both, precisely as the Griesbach Hypothesis does. What the Two-Source Hypothesis attributes to the hypothetical document Q is more simply explained as evidence of Luke having used Matthew; what it then calls Mark's overlap with Q is again more easily explained as evidence of Mark's use of material shared by Matthew and Luke, with more or less significant alterations and eliminations.

This violation of the law of parsimony is especially troubling in light of how the idea of Mark-Q overlap alters our conception of Q. The document must have contained not only material that Matthew and Luke alone share, but also much that Matthew and Luke include along with Mark, albeit in somewhat different forms. Thus the hypothetical Q comes to approximate the real documents Matthew and Luke, which share material Mark lacks as well as material Mark includes. The Two-Source Hypothesis, then, requires us to explain Matthew's and Luke's major agreements against Mark by positing a lost document (for which there is no direct evidence) that would have resembled two extant documents. Would it not be more reasonable to turn to the Griesbach Hypothesis, an explanation that relies solely on actual documents?

Most scholars answer no, because they find the cumulative arguments for Markan priority and the related Two-Source Hypothesis convincing, and this volume tentatively accepts the consensus view. The annotations to the Synoptic Gospels therefore occasionally address how Matthew and Luke edit Mark; Mark receives more extensive annotation than either Matthew or Luke, whose notes often refer the reader to Mark for fuller background information and interpretive guidance, as well as for consideration of editorial alteration. But readers should be aware that the Two-Source Hypothesis is just that—a hypothesis. It remains open to challenge, and the Griesbach Hypothesis in particular can more efficiently and persuasively explain some aspects of the Synoptic Problem. Indeed, readers may find it useful to analyze parallel synoptic episodes from both theoretical perspectives, then compare the results and gauge which are more compelling.

The Gospel of John

The Gospel of John differs more from the Synoptics than do Matthew, Mark, or Luke from one another. On occasion the similarities between John and the Synoptics are close (compare John 6:1–21 with Matt 14:13–33 and Mark 6:30–52; cf. Luke 9:10–17); often they are looser (compare John 12:27–30 and Matt 26:36–46; Mark 14:32–42; Luke 22:39–46), and frequently there are none. Scholars therefore debate whether John employs Mark as a source (if so, it is in a very different way from Matthew and Luke), or relies on literary sources Mark or the other gospels might also have used, or simply draws on the same body of oral traditions about Jesus that directly or indirectly informed the Synoptics. Whatever the origin of the Fourth Gospel's information about Jesus, John seems to have supplemented that source by attributing to Jesus in the flesh words that originated as oracles spoken by early Christian prophets in the name of the risen Christ. The notes that follow observe John's parallels with the Synoptics, and on occasion the Fourth Gospel may be compared with them profitably; but John often raises interpretive problems very different from those in the Synoptics, and thus is generally treated independently.

The Gospels' Composition

Conclusions drawn about the Synoptics' literary relationship have implications for hypotheses about their authorship and dates of composition. If the authors of Matthew and Luke used Mark as a source, it is unlikely that either witnessed the events they recount. They presumably would not have relied so heavily on a literary source for information about events experienced firsthand. In fact, none of the Synoptics claims to present eyewitness accounts, although the third evangelist apparently consulted them (Luke 1:2–3). However, the Fourth Gospel authorizes itself as the eyewitness testimony of the anonymous "disciple whom Jesus loved" (John 21:20–25), and while it contains elements anachronistic for Jesus' time (e.g., see 9:22 and note), it may preserve older traditions as well.

If we take the gospels' titles as authentic attributions of authorship (and there is good reason not to do so), only Matthew's titular epigraph unambiguously claims composition by an original follower of Jesus. The purported evangelist Matthew appears in this gospel as a tax collector whom Jesus calls to follow him (9:9) and later appoints as one of the Twelve (10:3). The other Synoptics curiously identify the tax collector as Levi, not as the apostle Matthew, and it is unlikely that the same figure went by both names. Especially when interpreted from the perspective of the Two-Source Hypothesis, this peculiarity suggests that the First Gospel was not written by the apostle Matthew. If it were, why would the apostolic evangelist claim for himself an already-existing story of Levi's call instead of narrating his own experience of encountering Jesus? The title of the Fourth Gospel is usually thought to attribute composition to Zebedee's son, but the identity of "John" (a name common in antiquity, as today) is ambiguous, and some ancient Christians apparently believed the author to be a figure called John the Elder, who was not one of the Twelve but perhaps one of Jesus' other disciples. The titles of the Second and Third Gospels attribute authorship to Paul's fellow missionaries, neither of whom was among Jesus' followers: Mark (see Acts 12:25; 15:37–39; Phlm 24) and Luke (see Phlm 24), with Mark traditionally linked to Peter as well (cf. 1 Pet 5:13).

The authenticity of all these attributions is questionable. The earliest writing that quotes and names the four New Testament gospels is *Against Heresies* by Irenaeus of Lyons, written about a century after their composition (ca. 180 C.E.). Earlier Christian writings are more flexible in their quotations and citations: while they sometimes quote the gospels in forms recognizable from the New Testament, they never actually name them. Justin Martyr, writing a few decades before Irenaeus, calls the sources of his quotations *apomnēmoneumata tōn apostolōn*, "memoirs of (or 'about') the apostles," either because he understands them to contain traditions that the apostles taught or because he takes the apostles to be their central characters. He once identifies them collectively as "gospels" (*First Apology* 66), but never calls them by the names Irenaeus and later Christians employ or in fact by any specific titles, which suggests that the gospels lacked ascriptions when they came into Justin's hands. Perhaps they were originally anonymous, written for discrete local communities of Christians who would have had no need of labels to distinguish their "gospel" from others. For the community that used it, each of the gospels simply would have been "the gospel," the good news about Jesus.

Evidence from other second-century literature supports such an inference. Writers quote and allude to the gospels frequently, but never name them. Sometimes they refer to a text as "the Lord's gospel" (*Didache* 8.1–3, quoting Matthew's version of the Lord's Prayer) or even as "scripture" (*2 Clement* 2.4, quoting Mark 2:17 or Matt 9:13). Sometimes they discuss a tradition about Jesus in a form uniquely corresponding to a single New Testament gospel, but without citation (e.g., Ignatius, *Epistle to the Smyrnaeans* 1.1, alluding to Matthew's version of Jesus' baptism). Sometimes they quote a distinctive dominical saying, but again attribute it only to "the Lord" or even to "God," without naming the gospel in which it appears (e.g., *2 Clement* 13.4; cf. Luke 6:32, 36; or *Didache* 9.5; cf. Matt 7:6). Frequently quotations follow none of the New Testament gospels precisely, which may indicate quotation from memory, but perhaps more likely reliance on oral tradition or on written collections of material about Jesus no longer extant (e.g., *1 Clement* 13.2; 46.8).

Before Irenaeus only a single writer provides information about the gospels' authorial attributions. A fragment from *Expositions of the Sayings of the Lord*, written by Papias (bishop of Hierapolis, in Asia Minor) and probably published about 130 C.E., relates information about Matthew and Mark that the author attributes to John the Elder, a figure of the previous generation (Appendix, pp. 1017–19).

The meaning of Papias's single sentence on Matthew has sparked considerable debate. It should probably be translated as "Matthew, then, arranged the sayings in the Hebrew language, and each translated them as he was able"—a strange description of the First Gospel. Matthew as it appears in the New Testament offers no evidence of having been translated from a Semitic language and contains both narratives and sayings. Some scholars hold that differences between ancient and modern conceptions of translation explain how Papias might have mistaken the New Testament Matthew for a translation of sorts. Moreover, it has been argued that the Greek word rendered "sayings" in the quotation from Papias might actually refer to accounts of what Jesus said and did. Though the incongruities of Papias's description of Matthew (including others not mentioned above) can all be resolved, so many surface in the brief sentence that it is reasonable to suspect it might in fact not refer to the text known to readers today as Matthew's gospel.

Papias's statement about Mark has fewer problems: "Mark, having become Peter's translator, wrote accurately as much as he remembered—not, however, in order—about the things said and done by Christ." Justin Martyr may even confirm this claim, for at one point he attributes a quote from Mark to the "memoirs of Peter" (*Dialogue with Trypho* 106.3). However, the Greek phrase may instead mean "memoirs about Peter" and thus refer only to Peter's central role in Mark's gospel, not to Mark's reliance on Petrine testimony in composing it.

Papias's comments are intriguing, and Irenaeus seems to have taken them seriously, for his own statements about the gospels' authorship betray their influence (see *Against Heresies* 3.1). Nonetheless, it is odd that before Irenaeus, no one mentions the traditions Papias claims to preserve. Christian writers throughout the late first and early second centuries quote the gospels and frequently refer to Jesus' words and deeds, but no one except Papias ever calls them by the names they go by today, or indeed by any name at all. If Papias recounts an authentic tradition, then why is he the only one to preserve it?

Regardless of his intent, Papias may be reporting as traditional knowledge early Christian speculation about the gospels' authorship. Ancient readers ignorant of, say, the Second Gospel's author, may have inferred from its contents a reliance on Peter's testimony. They were confident, however, that if Peter himself had written it his authorship could hardly have remained concealed, and so they turned to other authoritative writings in search of an appropriate companion of his to whom they might attribute this gospel. They landed, reasonably enough, on

Mark, with whose family Peter apparently had a connection (see Acts 12:12) and about whom 1 Peter speaks affectionately (5:13). Likewise eager to name the First Gospel's author, early Christians might have seized on its unique identification of the apostle Matthew with the tax collector elsewhere named Levi, attributing this amendment to inside information most likely known by Matthew himself. Moreover, the claim that it is a translation from Hebrew may merely reflect its interest in Jewish law. Analogous explanations can be proposed for the attribution of the Third Gospel to Luke and of the Fourth to John, son of Zebedee, if that is indeed the "John" who is meant. All things considered, it is safest to view the gospels' titular attributions as later additions to originally anonymous writings about Jesus. The labels may preserve traditional knowledge, but they are just as likely to represent early Christians' educated guesses. In this volume, references to "Matthew," "Mark," "Luke," and "John" are conventional; they do not presume the validity of the gospels' authorial ascriptions.

Although the gospels are first quoted in the late first and early second centuries C.E., most scholars believe they were written earlier than that. The evidence for their dates primarily consists of allusive references to Rome's destruction of Jerusalem in the Jewish War of 66–70 C.E.—for example, the saying of Jesus about the temple at Mark 13:2 (cf. Matt 24:2; Luke 21:6): "Seest thou these great buildings? there shall not be left one stone upon another, that shall not be thrown down." Some interpret this as an historical allusion to the temple's destruction couched in ostensible prophecy; others, impressed by the lack of correspondence between the dominical saying and the event it purportedly prophesied, believe it to be an oracle spoken before the temple's fall. (Its destruction was not as complete as the saying suggests; to this day, stones lie upon stones on the Temple Mount.) Individual passages from Matthew and Luke more convincingly betray knowledge of Rome's destruction of Jerusalem (see Matt 22:7; Luke 21:20 and notes).

We must also consider Mark 9:1 and parallels (Matt 16:28; Luke 9:27), where Jesus tells his disciples, "Verily I say unto you, That there be some of them that stand here, which shall not taste of death, till they have seen the kingdom of God come with power." This unfulfilled prophecy's inclusion in the Synoptics indicates that they were composed while the first generation of Jesus' followers still lived. Were they written later, the prophecy presumably would have been altered or omitted. In fact, Luke does tone it down slightly. By removing Mark's "come with power," he invites readers to interpret the kingdom of God symbolically, in a way amenable to Jesus' teaching at 17:21: "Neither shall they say, Lo here! or, lo there! for, behold, the kingdom of God is within you." Luke's subtle revision of Mark may reflect his skepticism that Jesus' prediction would come to pass in a literal way, because most of Jesus' original followers had already died by the time he was writing.

None of this evidence is totally compelling, but its cumulative weight leads most scholars to suppose that Mark was written around the time of Jerusalem's destruction in 70 C.E., give or take a few years. Since Matthew and Luke likely used Mark as a source, we can infer that they were written later, and in fact their internal evidence points more strongly than Mark's to dates of composition after Jerusalem's destruction. Luke in particular seems to have been written near the end of the first generation of Jesus' followers. Many scholars date it to 85–95 C.E. and Matthew a bit earlier, to 80–90. Internal evidence in John also suggests a late date (see 9:22 and note). Though this gospel may include earlier material, a final date of composition in the waning years of the first century C.E. or even the opening decade of the second is a good guess.

The gospels, then, were likely written as Jesus' original followers were dying out, or soon after all had died. They seem to have preserved information about Jesus that originally circulated orally under the informal scrutiny of Jesus' original disciples, who could have rectified glaring errors and corrected or forestalled misunderstandings of their accounts by answering questions, providing interpretive commentary, and so on. As authoritative witnesses to Jesus' ministry disappeared, preserving their knowledge in written form would have become vital; but as Plato notes in the *Phaedrus*, creating such a record always has a cost:

> And when once it is written, every discourse wanders everywhere, in the same way in the presence both of those who know about the subject and of those who have nothing to do with it at all; and it does not know how to address those it should address and not those it should not. When it is wronged and unjustly abused, it always needs its father to help it, for it is incapable of defending or helping itself. (275e; trans. C. J. Rowe [altered])

The Gospels' original anonymity may suggest that the evangelists and some of their early readers in effect accepted the lack of authorial control over their discourse's dissemination and were not especially concerned to protect it from unauthorized interpretation. Not all Christians agreed, and some assigned the gospels titular epigraphs attributing their authorship to the apostles or to figures linked with them. Such labels already constrain interpretation significantly. For example, a reader of "the Gospel according to Mark" who is aware of Peter's affectionate relationship with the purported evangelist (cf. 1 Pet 5:13) might be blinded to the Second Gospel's devastating portrayal of Peter. Later Christians would introduce less subtle interpretive restrictions—for example, by adding accounts of the risen Christ's appearances to the end of Mark (16:9–20; see notes) in order to remove ambiguity about Jesus' resurrection and about the future status of Peter, who is no longer a disciple at the gospel's authentic close (16:7), or by closing all the gospels and Acts with "Amen." More explicit still are interpretive principles such as the rule of love articulated by Augustine in *On Christian Doctrine*, where he argues that any scriptural passage that does not promote love of God, or godly love of self and neighbor, must be interpreted as figurative (3.14–16).

Such developments are understandable: no one can ever encounter any text without presuppositions and interpretive conventions that restrict the range of meanings discovered in it. Traditions of apostolic authorization, textual alterations, and articulated hermeneutical principles do not simply impose restrictions on how the Gospels might be read. They also reflect the limited ways in which the gospels commonly were read: as records of the apostles' teaching, as heroic stories of Jesus and his but mildly flawed followers, as exhortations to charitable behavior, as dogmatic assertions requiring assent, and so forth. But the evangelists themselves, and some of their very first readers as well, were apparently comfortable enough without overtly coercive interpretive frames. Readers of the New Testament as literature are invited to welcome what the evangelists seem to have accepted, although Plato bemoans it: the absence of a living voice capable of restricting a written discourse's dissemination and of guiding its comprehension. By implication, they are invited to resist reducing the New Testament to a series of ideologically amenable assertions and to embrace the evangelists' own tolerance for complexity. This is an invitation not to undertake capricious interpretation, but on the contrary to approach New Testament narrative faithfully indeed: to read it closely and carefully as a series of interrelated stories about Jesus and the early church whose meaning is not predetermined by the sort of dogmatic hermeneutical constraints that the evangelists themselves, in their anonymity, seem to have shunned.

The Gospel According to St. Matthew

AN early Christian tradition holds that Matthew was composed in Hebrew (i.e., Aramaic) and translated into Greek, the language of its earliest extant copies. But the First Gospel's Greek shows no evidence of being a translation. Ancient Christians likely extrapolated a literary history from the gospel's thematic contents, especially its insistence on Jesus' fulfillment of Old Testament oracles and its sustained engagement with biblical law.

Fulfillment citations come with particular frequency in the opening stories of Jesus' birth and infancy, which may in fact be based on the Old Testament prophecies that Matthew claims these stories realize. The first evangelist, convinced that Old Testament oracles were fulfilled by the Messiah's birth, turned to such oracles in order to reconstruct the events that must have fulfilled them. This circular procedure points to the First Gospel's intricate balance between literary innovation and Old Testament dependence, which the dominical saying of 13:52 makes explicit: "every scribe which is instructed unto the kingdom of heaven is like unto a man that is an householder, which bringeth forth out of his treasure things new and old." Ancient Christians therefore strategically chose Matthew as the New Testament's first book: it opens with a genealogy tracing the Messiah's lineage back through David to Abraham, followed by birth and infancy narratives incorporating various Old Testament prophecies into a story patterned on Moses' birth. The First Gospel, and the entire New Testament which it introduces, thereby insists on continuity between God's "old covenant" with Israel and the new work that Jesus inaugurates.

Matthew's gospel engages carefully with the Hebrew Bible throughout, its very structure recalling the Torah's division into five books. The first of its five extended discourses, the Sermon on the Mount (chaps. 5–7), concentrates on biblical law. Although some of the sermon's directives are innovative with respect to the Hebrew Bible (e.g., its prohibition against divorce; 5:31–32), Jesus insists that his teaching fulfills rather than overturns biblical legislation (5:17–20). Interpreters often presume he radicalizes the Old Testament injunctions he cites (esp. at 5:21, 27, 33, 38, 43), with the new commandments that he distinguishes from the old somehow revealing the latter's authentic, inner meaning. At the heart of the Hebrew Bible's prohibition of murder, by this account, lies Jesus' more fundamental prohibition of anger (5:21–22): the former implies the latter, and Jesus makes the implicit explicit.

Jesus' strategy could just as easily be described as supplementing biblical commandments with additional regulations designed to prevent careless transgression. On this reading, the prohibitions against anger and cursing, as well as the requirement to reconcile with whomever one might have offended (5:21–26), augment rather than radicalize the sixth commandment. Jesus' proscriptions of lust and divorce play the same role with regard to the seventh, which forbids adultery (5:27–32). One who vigilantly guards against anger and resentment forecloses murder's motives and will never kill. By a similar logic, one who avoids lust will not wish to commit adultery.

This construal of Jesus' hermeneutic recalls the rabbinic tradition of "building a fence around the Torah"—that is, generating supplemental injunctions, based on oral tradition, to safeguard God's law from transgression (m. Avot 1:1). The resemblance is not coincidental, for rabbinic and Matthean biblical interpretation emerge from a common cultural and historical context. Scholars hypothesize that the First Gospel was written in Syria or even Palestine after the fall of the temple in 70 C.E. Before 70, Jewish sects proliferated; after the temple's destruction, rabbinic Judaism gradually emerged as dominant. This Jewish movement, from which virtually all later forms of Judaism derive, had its origins in Pharisaic Judaism, which placed a high value on interpreting the Torah. It relied on oral traditions to formulate readings of biblical legislation that expanded the original commandments and thereby revealed how the Bible's already archaic rules and obscure cultic regulations were relevant to the workaday lives of people in the Pharisees' and later the rabbis' own time. The community of Jesus-believing Jews for which Matthew was written would have felt an affinity for the Pharisaic and emergent rabbinic movement's approach to the Law, although its veneration of Jesus and its willingness to embrace Gentiles would have set this Jewish sect at odds with the increasingly influential rabbis.

Analysis of any number of Matthean passages from the perspective of the Two-Source Hypothesis suggests that the first evangelist assumes his readers carefully observed the Torah. For example, Matthew's revision of Mark's saying about defilement eliminates the Second Gospel's parenthetical claim that Jesus declared all foods clean (15:17–18; cf. Mark 7:18–19 and note at v. 19), presumably because Matthew did not believe Jesus to have overturned the Pentateuch's dietary legislation. Analogously, Matthew supplements Mark 13:18 ("pray ye that your flight be not in the winter") by adding "neither on the sabbath day" (24:20), probably because he expected his readers to keep the Sabbath faithfully. When Matthew argues for a loosening of Sabbath regulations at 12:1–8, his revision of Mark 2:23–28 is especially instructive: he strengthens and clarifies Mark's biblical support for exceptional breaking of the Sabbath, corrects a mistake that Mark makes regarding the story of David and the showbread, and eliminates Mark's sweeping relativization of Sabbath legislation to human needs. The attitude toward the Law that Matthew's Jesus evinces is always careful and searching, respectful of the Torah's integrity and authority.

Matthew's Jesus tacitly admits that the approach he takes toward the Law is amenable to the Pharisees': "The scribes and the Pharisees sit in Moses' seat: all therefore whatsoever they bid you observe, that observe and do" (23:2–3). The first evangelist apparently thought Pharisaic interpretation of the Torah to be generally sound, even if he believed the Pharisees themselves to be hypocrites who for all their professions of legal punctiliousness were not above privileging their own traditions when those opposed the Bible (see 15:1–9), and who did not themselves observe the law with consistent care: "Woe unto you, scribes and Pharisees, hypocrites! for ye pay tithe of mint and anise and cummin, and have omitted the weightier matters of the law, judgment, mercy, and faith: these ought ye to have done, and not to leave the other undone" (23:23). Matthew's vituperative polemic addresses not only—perhaps not even primarily—the Pharisees of Jesus' day but also leaders of the proto-rabbinic Jewish movement that was emerging when Matthew wrote. Jesus' prohibition against leaders being greeted as "Rabbi" (23:7–8) seems to anticipate the widespread use of this Hebrew honorific by members of the post–Second Temple Jewish movement that would take its name from the practice.

In light of the First Gospel's origins in tension between the nascent Jesus-believing and proto-rabbinic Jewish movements, the common charge that it is anti-Semitic is anachronistic to say the least. Consideration of how later Christian readers misinterpreted Matthew's intra-Jewish polemic as anti-Jewish slander is revealing, however. The fourth-century church father John Chrysostom construes Matt 27:25 ("His blood be on us, and on our children") as an authoritative assertion that Jews are universally and perpetually responsible for Jesus' death (*Discourses against Judaizing Christians* 1.5.1; 6.1.7), and he is not the only Christian to do so. This interpretation is perverse on a number of levels, most fundamentally in its reliance on a basic error of contextualization: in this passage, the evangelist does not refer to "the Jews" as an alien ethnic or religious group; indeed, he does not refer to "the Jews" at all. As a presumably Jewish believer in Jesus, the evangelist attempts to comprehend two traumatic events in his recent history: Jerusalem's rejection of Jesus, which led to Jesus' execution there, and the city's destruction by Rome a generation later. Matthew understands the latter ordeal in relation to the former, construing Jerusalem's downfall as its delayed punishment for Jesus' unjust death. After Jerusalem welcomes Jesus as "the prophet of Nazareth" (Matt 21:11), Jesus utters a prophetic oracle declaring the city's judgment for killing the prophets: "O Jerusalem, Jerusalem, thou that killest the prophets, and stonest them which are sent unto thee. . . . Behold, your house is left unto you desolate" (23:37–38). In light of these passages, the section of Matthew on which Chrysostom comments (27:22–25) portrays the inhabitants of Jerusalem who clamored for the prophet Jesus' death as accepting responsibility for killing him. Since Rome's capture of Jerusalem and destruction of the temple (alluded to in 23:38) occurred thirty to forty years after Jesus died, the reference to "our children" does not hold "the Jews" eternally responsible for Jesus' execution, but rather holds a single generation of Jerusalemites accountable for their parents' crimes. It invites an interpretation of Jerusalem's destruction in 70 as God's delayed punishment of the city for its role in crucifying Jesus a generation earlier.

The same logic of generationally deferred punishment surfaces in 2 Kings' description of Babylon's destruction of the first temple in Jerusalem, where the city's capture is presented as God's retribution for crimes King Manasseh committed a generation or two before the Babylonian conquest (2 Kgs 21:10–15; 23:26; 24:3). The Old Testament book evinces particular concern about the "innocent blood" King Manasseh shed (2 Kgs 21:16; 24:4), which was thought to include that of the prophet Isaiah (see 2 Kgs 21:16 note). Significantly, the phrase "innocent blood" surfaces in Matthew as well, with reference to the prophet Jesus' death at the hands of the chief priests (27:4; cf. v. 24). The first evangelist searched Scripture not only to reconstruct Jesus' birth and infancy out of prophetic oracles and structural parallels with the story of Moses, but also to explain traumatic events subsequent to Jesus' demise: like the destruction of Jerusalem's first temple, so must the devastation of its second represent God's deferred judgment for an earlier generation's shedding of innocent blood.

Matthew, then, far from being an anti-Jewish polemic, is a thoroughly Jewish book. It presents Jesus as an authoritative Jewish teacher of the Jewish law, which its presumably Jewish readers faithfully followed, and it interprets that law in a way that resembles rabbinic hermeneutical practices. Moreover, like 2 Kings, it is concerned to explain why God allowed Jerusalem and its temple to be destroyed. Matthew criticizes proto-rabbinic Judaism in the guise of the Pharisees, and the first evangelist apparently believed that God held Jerusalemites of his own day responsible for the city's shedding of Jesus' blood a generation earlier, but the First Gospel never slanders "Judaism" nor attacks "the Jews" from a position outside that ethnic and religious community (with one possible exception; see Matt 28:15).

We may therefore be tempted to dismiss Chrysostom's and analogous ancient Christian approaches to Matthew as perverse interpretations by craven bigots. Such dismissal would be unproductive. Chrysostom's invocations of Matt 27:25 occur in a series of sermons urging Christians not to observe Jewish religious rituals, and this context suggests that the anti-Semitic discourse he imposes on the First Gospel reflects his own anxiety about maintaining the distinctiveness of his upstart Christian religion against the rich and venerable traditions of ancient Judaism, to which "Christians" as late as the fourth century apparently continued to find themselves attached. As Chrysostom's comments reveal, the intra-Jewish disputes that Matthew reflects would ultimately culminate in "Christianity's" messy and protracted divorce from Judaism, but that divorce had not quite been finalized even in Chrysostom's time. In this church father's interpretation of the First Gospel we hear what may be described as the bitter recriminations of a resentful (ex-)spouse. In Matthew itself we encounter something more complex: a record of discourse from a time when the parties were fighting, but still cohabiting. From such a context the First Gospel emerged, a self-consciously Jewish narrative of Jesus' career that emulates the Torah and demands rigorous adherence to it, but that also effectively opens the anthology of writings known as the New Testament.

For further information about Matthew, consult W. D. Davies and D. C. Allison's authoritative three-volume commentary in the International Critical Commentary series, which informs this volume's annotations of Matthew and of the other Synoptic Gospels throughout: A *Critical and Exegetical Commentary on the Gospel According to Matthew* (London: T&T Clark, 1988–97).

THE GOSPEL ACCORDING TO
ST. MATTHEW

1 The book of the generation of Jesus Christ, the son of David, the son of Abraham.

²Abraham begat Isaac; and Isaac begat Jacob; and Jacob begat Judas and his brethren; ³and Judas begat Phares and Zara of Thamar; and Phares begat Esrom; and Esrom begat Aram; ⁴and Aram begat Aminadab; and Aminadab begat Naasson; and Naasson begat Salmon; ⁵and Salmon begat Booz of Rachab; and Booz begat Obed of Ruth; and Obed begat Jesse; ⁶and Jesse begat David the king; and David the king begat Solomon of her that had been the wife of Urias; ⁷and Solomon begat Roboam; and Roboam begat Abia: and Abia begat Asa; ⁸and Asa begat Josaphat; and Josaphat begat Joram; and Joram begat Ozias; ⁹and Ozias begat Joatham; and Joatham begat Achaz; and Achaz begat Ezekias; ¹⁰and Ezekias begat Manasses; and Manasses begat Amon; and Amon begat Josias; ¹¹and Josias begat Jechonias and his brethren, about the time they were carried away to Babylon: ¹²and after they were brought to Babylon, Jechonias begat Salathiel; and Salathiel begat Zorobabel; ¹³and Zorobabel begat Abiud; and Abiud begat Eliakim; and Eliakim begat Azor; ¹⁴and Azor begat Sadoc; and Sadoc begat Achim; and Achim begat Eliud; ¹⁵and Eliud begat Eleazar; and Eleazar begat Matthan; and Matthan begat Jacob; ¹⁶and Jacob begat Joseph the husband of Mary, of whom was born Jesus, who is called Christ.

1:1–17 Genealogy. Luke's genealogy (3:23–38) differs. Matthew's, based through v. 12 on 1 Chr 2–3, conventionally traces Jesus' descent through the male line, but mentions four sexually compromised Gentile women. **1:1** *The book . . . generation*: announcing the genealogy that follows (cf. Gen 5:1). *Jesus Christ*: see Mark 1:1 note. *Son of David*: see Mark 10:47 note. Matthew uses this title ten times, in contrast to Mark and Luke, who use it only three times each. **1:2** *Judas and his brethren*: the eponymous ancestors of Israel's tribes. Israel's kings came from the tribe of Judah. (*Judas* is the name's Greek form. KJV transliterates the Greek forms of the genealogy's names; modern versions prefer the Hebrew originals.) **1:3** *Thamar*: Tamar, Judah's daughter-in-law who seduced him after her husband died and he refused to comply with the levirate law and marry her to his son (Gen 38). **1:5** *Rachab*: Rahab, a Canaanite prostitute who sheltered Israelite spies (Josh 2). No known tradition before Matthew makes her Boaz's mother. *Ruth*: a Moabite refugee in Israel; she seduced Boaz, who married her (see Ruth). **1:6** *Of her . . . Urias*: a circumlocution for Bathsheba, reminding the reader that David impregnated the Hittite Uriah's wife and then killed him as part of an elaborate cover-up. She later bore Solomon (2 Sam 11–12). **1:7** *Asa*: better "Asaph" (MS tradition; also in v. 8). **1:10** *Amon*: better "Amos" (MS tradition). **1:11** *About the time . . . Babylon*: at which point the Davidic dynasty ceased (586 B.C.E.). **1:12** *Salathiel begat Zorobabel*: following LXX 1 Chr 3:19, which contradicts MT (but cf. Ezra 3:2). Matthew ceases following 1 Chr 2–3 after this point, presumably using a source no

¹⁷So all the generations from Abraham to David are fourteen generations; and from David until the carrying away into Babylon are fourteen generations; and from the carrying away into Babylon unto Christ are fourteen generations.

¹⁸Now the birth of Jesus Christ was on this wise: When as his mother Mary was espoused to Joseph, before they came together, she was found with child of the Holy Ghost. ¹⁹Then Joseph her husband, being a just man, and not willing to make her a publick example, was minded to put her away privily. ²⁰But while he thought on these things, behold, the angel of the Lord appeared unto him in a dream, saying, Joseph, thou son of David, fear not to take unto thee Mary thy wife: for that which is conceived in her is of the Holy Ghost. ²¹And she shall bring forth a son, and thou shalt call his name Jesus: for he shall save his people from their sins. ²²Now all this was done, that it might be fulfilled which was spoken of the Lord by the prophet, saying, ²³Behold, a virgin shall be with child, and shall bring forth a son, and they shall call his name Emmanuel, which being interpreted is, God with us. ²⁴Then Joseph being raised from sleep did as the angel of the Lord had bidden him, and took unto him his wife: ²⁵and knew her not till she had brought forth her firstborn son: and he called his name Jesus.

2 Now when Jesus was born in Bethlehem of Judæa in the days of Herod the king, behold, there came wise men from the east to Jerusalem, ²saying, Where is he that is born King of the Jews? for we have seen his star in the east, and are come to worship him. ³When Herod the king had heard these things, he

---

longer extant.   **1:17** *From David until the carrying away into Babylon*: from David until Josias, with the next division of fourteen generations beginning with Jechonias.

    1:18–2:23 Birth and infancy. Compare Luke 2:1–20, but the two accounts have little overlap. Matthew develops parallels between Jesus and Moses, whose birth and perilous infancy Exod 1–2 recounts.   **1:18–25** Jesus' birth.   **1:18** *Birth*: Gk. *genesis* (cf. v. 1 [KJV "generation"]). *Espoused*: betrothed; a state that had the legal force of marriage, without consummation. *Holy Ghost*: God's spirit, signaling his generative power (cf. Gen 1:2).   **1:19** *Put her away privily*: secretly divorce her, a procedure in line with OT law; cf. Deut 24:1.   **1:20** *Angel of the Lord*: the angel who frequently appears in the OT to communicate God's will, especially in regard to the destiny of offspring (cf. Gen 16:7–14; 22:11–18; Judg 13). *In a dream*: like his OT namesake, Joseph is a dreamer; see also 2:13, 19, 22.   **1:21** *Jesus: for he shall save*: a Greek form of Heb. *Joshua*, which a widely held etymology linked to the Hebrew word for "salvation."   **1:22–23** *Be fulfilled . . . us*: signifying one of Matthew's central conceits, that Jesus "fulfills" OT prophecies—in this case LXX Isa 7:14, where Gk. *parthenos*, "virgin," translates Heb. *'almah*, "young woman." This is the first of several OT fulfillment citations, each of which is similarly introduced (cf. 2:5–6, 15, 17–18, 23; 3:3; 4:14–16; 8:17; 12:17–21; 13:14–15, 35; 21:4–5; 26:54–56; 27:9–10).   **1:25** *Knew her not*: i.e., sexually. *Firstborn*: better omitted (MS tradition).   **2:1–12** The wise men's visit.   **2:1** *Bethlehem*: David's hometown, just south of Jerusalem. *Judæa*: see Mark 1:5 note. *Herod the king*: not of the Davidic lineage, the Herods were an Idumean family with close ties to Rome, whose Senate installed Herod (the Great) as king of Judea in 40 B.C.E. Jesus would have been born within a few years of Herod's death in 4 B.C.E. *Wise men*: Gk. *magoi*, which initially referred to Persian priests and later became a name for eastern sages. As the first Gentiles to pay Jesus homage, they foreshadow the risen Christ's final command that his disciples evangelize "all nations" (28:19). Partly on the basis of Ps 72:10–11 and Isa 60:3, 6, a later tradition identified them as three kings (Melchior, Balthasar, and Caspar), even though Matthew lists three gifts (v. 11), not three givers.   **2:2** *In the east*: rather "at its rising." *Worship*: Gk. *proskyneō* (so throughout, with the exception of 15:9), lit. "to prostrate oneself before," sometimes (depending on context) with the connotation of "worship."

was troubled, and all Jerusalem with him. ⁴And when he had gathered all the chief priests and scribes of the people together, he demanded of them where Christ should be born. ⁵And they said unto him, In Bethlehem of Judæa: for thus it is written by the prophet, ⁶And thou Bethlehem, in the land of Juda, art not the least among the princes of Juda: for out of thee shall come a Governor, that shall rule my people Israel.

⁷Then Herod, when he had privily called the wise men, inquired of them diligently what time the star appeared. ⁸And he sent them to Bethlehem, and said, Go and search diligently for the young child; and when ye have found him, bring me word again, that I may come and worship him also. ⁹When they had heard the king, they departed; and, lo, the star, which they saw in the east, went before them, till it came and stood over where the young child was. ¹⁰When they saw the star, they rejoiced with exceeding great joy. ¹¹And when they were come into the house, they saw the young child with Mary his mother, and fell down, and worshipped him: and when they had opened their treasures, they presented unto him gifts; gold, and frankincense, and myrrh. ¹²And being warned of God in a dream that they should not return to Herod, they departed into their own country another way.

¹³And when they were departed, behold, the angel of the Lord appeareth to Joseph in a dream, saying, Arise, and take the young child and his mother, and flee into Egypt, and be thou there until I bring thee word: for Herod will seek the young child to destroy him. ¹⁴When he arose, he took the young child and his mother by night, and departed into Egypt: ¹⁵and was there until the death of Herod: that it might be fulfilled which was spoken of the Lord by the prophet, saying, Out of Egypt have I called my son.

¹⁶Then Herod, when he saw that he was mocked of the wise men, was exceeding wroth, and sent forth, and slew all the children that were in Bethlehem, and in all the coasts thereof, from two years old and under, according to the time which he had diligently inquired of the wise men. ¹⁷Then was fulfilled that which was spoken by Jeremy the prophet, saying, ¹⁸In Rama was there a voice heard, lamentation, and weeping, and great mourning, Rachel weeping for her children, and would not be comforted, because they are not.

¹⁹But when Herod was dead, behold, an angel of the Lord appeareth in a dream to Joseph in Egypt, ²⁰saying, Arise, and take the young child and his mother, and go into the land of Israel: for they are dead which sought the young child's life.

2:4 *He had . . . together*: a similar group will later "gather" to judge Jesus (26:57 [KJV "were assembled"]). *Chief priests* directed the temple and its worship; *scribes* were trained interpreters of Jewish law.   2:6 *And thou . . . Israel*: cf. Mic 5:2.   2:11 *Frankincense, and myrrh*: used as incense in religious rituals.   2:13–23 Flight to Egypt and massacre of infants. This story has no known historical basis and may have been constructed on the foundation of the OT citations and parallels (especially with Moses) it features.   2:14 *Departed into Egypt*: Jesus, like Moses, grows up among Egyptians (cf. Exod 2:10).   2:15 *Out of . . . son*: Hos 11:1, identifying the son as Israel in exodus. 2:16 *Slew all . . . under*: like Moses, the baby Jesus escapes a slaughter of infants (cf. Exod 1:15–2:10). *Coasts*: territories.   2:18 *In Rama . . . are not*: Jer 31:15, a lament for Israel's exile in Babylon. 2:20–21 *Arise, and . . . Israel*: cf. Exod 4:19–20, where God tells Moses to return to Egypt

²¹And he arose, and took the young child and his mother, and came into the land of Israel. ²²But when he heard that Archelaus did reign in Judæa in the room of his father Herod, he was afraid to go thither: notwithstanding, being warned of God in a dream, he turned aside into the parts of Galilee: ²³and he came and dwelt in a city called Nazareth: that it might be fulfilled which was spoken by the prophets, He shall be called a Nazarene.

3 In those days came John the Baptist, preaching in the wilderness of Judæa, ²and saying, Repent ye: for the kingdom of heaven is at hand. ³For this is he that was spoken of by the prophet Esaias, saying, The voice of one crying in the wilderness, Prepare ye the way of the Lord, make his paths straight. ⁴And the same John had his raiment of camel's hair, and a leathern girdle about his loins; and his meat was locusts and wild honey. ⁵Then went out to him Jerusalem, and all Judæa, and all the region round about Jordan, ⁶and were baptized of him in Jordan, confessing their sins.

⁷But when he saw many of the Pharisees and Sadducees come to his baptism, he said unto them, O generation of vipers, who hath warned you to flee from the wrath to come? ⁸Bring forth therefore fruits meet for repentance: ⁹and think not to say within yourselves, We have Abraham to our father: for I say unto you, that God is able of these stones to raise up children unto Abraham. ¹⁰And now also the axe is laid unto the root of the trees: therefore every tree which bringeth not forth good fruit is hewn down, and cast into the fire. ¹¹I indeed baptize you with water unto repentance: but he that cometh after me is mightier than I, whose shoes I am not worthy to bear: he shall baptize you with the Holy Ghost, and with fire: ¹²whose fan is in his hand, and he will throughly purge his floor, and gather his wheat into the garner; but he will burn up the chaff with unquenchable fire.

¹³Then cometh Jesus from Galilee to Jordan unto John, to be baptized of him. ¹⁴But John forbad him, saying, I have need to be baptized of thee, and comest thou to me? ¹⁵And Jesus answering said unto him, Suffer it to be so now: for thus

with his family because Pharaoh has died.   **2:22** *Archelaus* reigned from 4 B.C.E. until 6 C.E., when the Romans exiled him because of his brutality. *In the room of*: in place of. *Galilee*: see Mark 1:9 note.   **2:23** *That it . . . Nazarene*: no particular OT text is quoted, which explains the plural *prophets* and the absence of "saying," variations from Matthew's standard introduction of fulfillment citations. Jesus' birthplace somehow fulfills a general prophetic message, perhaps by gesturing at a link between Jesus the Nazarene (Gk. *nazōraios*) and the Nazarites (Gk. *naziraioi*), dedicated to God by vows (cf. Num 6:1–21), sometimes even from birth (cf. Judg 13:2–7; 1 Sam 1:11).

3:1–4:25 Baptism, temptation, and initial ministry. 3:1–12 John the Baptist. Compare Mark 1:2–8 and notes; Luke 3:1–20; John 1:29–34.   **3:1** *Wilderness of Judæa*: the mountainous region west of the Dead Sea, extending north into the Jordan Valley.   **3:2** *Kingdom of heaven*: Matthew's substitution for the other gospels' "kingdom of God"; cf. Mark 1:15 and note.   **3:3** *The voice . . . straight*: Isa 40:3.   **3:4** *His raiment . . . loins*: clothed like Elijah (2 Kgs 1:8 and note). *Meat*: food (so throughout).   **3:7** For *Pharisees*, see Mark 2:16 note; for *Sadducees*, see Mark 12:18 note. *Generation*: or "brood." *Wrath to come*: God's eschatological judgment.   **3:8** *Meet*: fitting (so throughout).   **3:11** *The Holy . . . fire*: Davies and Allison suggest that since "ghost" translates Gk. *pneuma*, which also means "breath," the phrase may refer to God's blazing breath, an image of eschatological judgment at 2 Esd 13:8–11; cf. Isa 30:27–28.   **3:12** *Fan*: a basket or shovel used to separate wheat from chaff by throwing it into the air (*OED*). Threshing and winnowing can figure eschatological judgment in the OT; cf. Isa 41:15–16; Jer 15:7.   **3:13–17** Baptism. Compare Mark 1:9–11 and notes; Luke

it becometh us to fulfil all righteousness. Then he suffered him. [16]And Jesus, when he was baptized, went up straightway out of the water: and, lo, the heavens were opened unto him, and he saw the Spirit of God descending like a dove, and lighting upon him: [17]and lo a voice from heaven, saying, This is my beloved Son, in whom I am well pleased.

4 Then was Jesus led up of the Spirit into the wilderness to be tempted of the devil. [2]And when he had fasted forty days and forty nights, he was afterward an hungred. [3]And when the tempter came to him, he said, If thou be the Son of God, command that these stones be made bread. [4]But he answered and said, It is written, Man shall not live by bread alone, but by every word that proceedeth out of the mouth of God. [5]Then the devil taketh him up into the holy city, and setteth him on a pinnacle of the temple, [6]and saith unto him, If thou be the Son of God, cast thyself down: for it is written, He shall give his angels charge concerning thee: and in their hands they shall bear thee up, lest at any time thou dash thy foot against a stone. [7]Jesus said unto him, It is written again, Thou shalt not tempt the Lord thy God. [8]Again, the devil taketh him up into an exceeding high mountain, and sheweth him all the kingdoms of the world, and the glory of them; [9]and saith unto him, All these things will I give thee, if thou wilt fall down and worship me. [10]Then saith Jesus unto him, Get thee hence, Satan: for it is written, Thou shalt worship the Lord thy God, and him only shalt thou serve. [11]Then the devil leaveth him, and, behold, angels came and ministered unto him.

[12]Now when Jesus had heard that John was cast into prison, he departed into Galilee; [13]and leaving Nazareth, he came and dwelt in Capernaum, which is upon the sea coast, in the borders of Zabulon and Nephthalim: [14]that it might be

3:21–22; John 1:29–34.   **3:16** *The heavens . . . unto him*: a conventional introduction to descriptions of visions (note *he saw*); cf. Ezek 1:1; Acts 7:56; Rev 19:11.   **3:17** *This is . . . pleased*: in Matthew, the divine voice speaks about Jesus rather than to him, as in Mark 1:11.   **4:1–11** Temptation. Compare Mark 1:12–13 and notes; Luke 4:1–13. In this artfully composed narrative, upward movement (from *wilderness* to *pinnacle of the temple* to *an exceeding high mountain*) tracks escalating temptation. The episode recalls Israel's wilderness wanderings after the exodus, especially as the passage through the Red Sea was sometimes thought to foreshadow baptism (cf. 1 Cor 10:1–5), which Jesus has just undergone.   **4:1** *Wilderness*: Gk. *erēmos*, which also means "desert" (so throughout). *Tempted*: or "tested" (so throughout).   **4:2** *Forty days . . . nights*: the same length of time that Moses went without food on Mount Sinai when he received the law (Exod 34:28) and that Elijah spent in the wilderness, where he was fed by angels (1 Kgs 19:4–9; cf. Matt 4:11). The number may also echo Israel's forty years of wilderness wandering. *An hungred*: hungry (so throughout).   **4:3** *If thou . . . bread*: inviting Jesus to emulate God's miraculous provision of manna in the wilderness (Exod 16).   **4:4** *Man shall . . . God*: Deut 8:3, also with reference to manna.   **4:5** *The holy city*: Jerusalem.   **4:6** *He shall give . . . stone*: Ps 91:11–12.   **4:7** *Thou shalt not . . . God*: Deut 6:16, referring to Israel's murmuring at Massah (Exod 17:1–7; Num 20:2–13), which prompted Moses to prove God's faithfulness by producing water from a rock.   **4:8–9** *The devil . . . me*: presuming the devil's authority over the world, a commonplace in Jewish apocalyptic thought. Luke 4:6 makes the assumption explicit.   **4:8** *Into an . . . mountain*: perversely recalling God's display of the promised land to Moses from Mount Nebo (Deut 34:1; cf. Gen 13:14–15).   **4:10** *Thou shalt worship . . . serve*: Deut 6:13; 10:20.   **4:12–17** Return to Galilee. Compare Mark 1:14–15; Luke 4:14–15.   **4:12** *John was . . . prison*: 14:3–5 narrates John's arrest.   **4:13** *Capernaum*: see Mark 1:21 note. *Zabulon and Nephthalim*: tribes that had been assigned regions

fulfilled which was spoken by Esaias the prophet, saying, [15]The land of Zabulon, and the land of Nephthalim, by the way of the sea, beyond Jordan, Galilee of the Gentiles; [16]the people which sat in darkness saw great light; and to them which sat in the region and shadow of death light is sprung up. [17]From that time Jesus began to preach, and to say, Repent: for the kingdom of heaven is at hand.

[18]And Jesus, walking by the sea of Galilee, saw two brethren, Simon called Peter, and Andrew his brother, casting a net into the sea: for they were fishers. [19]And he saith unto them, Follow me, and I will make you fishers of men. [20]And they straightway left their nets, and followed him. [21]And going on from thence, he saw other two brethren, James the son of Zebedee, and John his brother, in a ship with Zebedee their father, mending their nets; and he called them. [22]And they immediately left the ship and their father, and followed him.

[23]And Jesus went about all Galilee, teaching in their synagogues, and preaching the gospel of the kingdom, and healing all manner of sickness and all manner of disease among the people. [24]And his fame went throughout all Syria: and they brought unto him all sick people that were taken with divers diseases and torments, and those which were possessed with devils, and those which were lunatick, and those that had the palsy; and he healed them. [25]And there followed him great multitudes of people from Galilee, and from Decapolis, and from Jerusalem, and from Judæa, and from beyond Jordan.

5 And seeing the multitudes, he went up into a mountain: and when he was set, his disciples came unto him: [2]and he opened his mouth, and taught them, saying, [3]Blessed are the poor in spirit: for theirs is the kingdom of heaven. [4]Blessed are they that mourn: for they shall be comforted. [5]Blessed are the meek: for they

---

partly corresponding to Galilee. **4:15–16** *The land . . . up*: Isa 9:1–2, originally referring to Assyria's occupation of Galilee (see notes). The quotation here foreshadows Jesus' encounters with Gentiles during the Galilean ministry; cf. 8:5–13, 28–34. **4:17** *Repent: for . . . hand*: echoing John's message (3:2). **4:18–22** Calling the first disciples. Compare Mark 1:16–20 and notes; Luke 5:1–11; and John 1:35–51 for a very different account. **4:23–25** Early ministry. Adapting Mark 1:39; 3:7–10; cf. Luke 4:44; 6:17–19. In Matthew, report of Jesus' ministry in Galilee spreads more widely and quickly than in Mark or Luke. **4:23** *Synagogues*: see Mark 1:21 note. *Gospel of the kingdom*: see Mark 1:1 note. **4:24** *Syria*: possibly confined to the area north and northeast of Galilee; or, in its wider sense, the entire Roman province, which included Palestine. *Lunatick*: this Latinate word and the Greek term it translates have similar etymologies. Both mean "moonstruck" and refer to epileptics. **4:25** *Decapolis*: a Gentile region; see Mark 5:20 note.

5:1–7:29 Sermon on the Mount. The first of Jesus' five extended discourses functions as a kind of constitution for the community he has begun to form. Although often understood as the apex of Christian ethical teaching, Jesus' sermon actually incorporates a great deal of traditional Jewish and Greco-Roman wisdom; the notes that follow signal some parallels. **5:1–2** Introduction. **5:1** *Multitudes . . . his disciples*: Jesus teaches his disciples in the presence of the multitudes (cf. 7:28–29). *Into a mountain*: recalling Moses' ascension to Mount Sinai before receiving and promulgating God's law (cf. Exod 24:12–13). Jesus will interpret this law (see esp. 5:17–48). *Set*: sitting down, as was customary for teaching rabbis. **5:3–12** Beatitudes. Compare Luke 6:20–23. Parallels between this section and Isa 61, which roughly contemporary Jewish writers often interpreted eschatologically, suggest that Jesus' sayings refer to the eschatological consummation (with the exception of vv. 3 and 10–12; see notes). **5:3** *Theirs is . . . heaven*: present tense, in contrast with the future promises of vv. 4–9. Jesus' ministry, which ushers in the kingdom of heaven (cf. 3:2–3; 4:17), brings this blessing to present fruition. **5:4** *Blessed are . . . mourn*: cf. Isa 61:1–7, where Israel mourns because foreign powers have conquered it. **5:5** *Blessed are . . . earth*: cf. Ps 37:11; LXX Isa 61:7, both with reference to the promised

shall inherit the earth. [6]Blessed are they which do hunger and thirst after righteousness: for they shall be filled. [7]Blessed are the merciful: for they shall obtain mercy. [8]Blessed are the pure in heart: for they shall see God. [9]Blessed are the peacemakers: for they shall be called the children of God. [10]Blessed are they which are persecuted for righteousness' sake: for theirs is the kingdom of heaven. [11]Blessed are ye, when men shall revile you, and persecute you, and shall say all manner of evil against you falsely, for my sake. [12]Rejoice, and be exceeding glad: for great is your reward in heaven: for so persecuted they the prophets which were before you.

[13]Ye are the salt of the earth: but if the salt have lost his savour, wherewith shall it be salted? it is thenceforth good for nothing, but to be cast out, and to be trodden under foot of men. [14]Ye are the light of the world. A city that is set on an hill cannot be hid. [15]Neither do men light a candle, and put it under a bushel, but on a candlestick; and it giveth light unto all that are in the house. [16]Let your light so shine before men, that they may see your good works, and glorify your Father which is in heaven.

[17]Think not that I am come to destroy the law, or the prophets: I am not come to destroy, but to fulfil. [18]For verily I say unto you, Till heaven and earth pass, one jot or one tittle shall in no wise pass from the law, till all be fulfilled. [19]Whosoever therefore shall break one of these least commandments, and shall teach men so, he shall be called the least in the kingdom of heaven: but whosoever shall do and teach them, the same shall be called great in the kingdom of heaven. [20]For I say unto you, That except your righteousness shall exceed the righteousness of the scribes and Pharisees, ye shall in no case enter into the kingdom of heaven.

---

land.   **5:8** *Pure in heart*: cf. Ps 24:3–4.   **5:9** *Children of God*: lit. "sons of God"; cf. John 1:12; Rom 8:14–15; Gal 3:26; etc.   **5:10** *Theirs is . . . heaven*: forming an inclusive frame with v. 3 and formally demarcating the first eight blessings from the ninth (vv. 11–12), which is longer and in the second-person plural. The present tense here and in v. 12 may suggest that martyrs need not await eschatological resurrection to experience a blessed afterlife. (Compare Phil 1:23, where Paul suggests that his death in prison would bring him directly to Christ, and Rev 20:4–6, which promises martyrs an earlier resurrection than others.)   **5:11** *Falsely*: better omitted (MS tradition) as a scribal emendation emphasizing persecuted believers' innocence.   **5:13–16** Salt and light. Compare Mark 9:50; Luke 14:34–35; 11:33.   **5:13** *Ye are the salt of the earth*: Jesus may refer to salt's use as a preservative, as a seasoning, as an ingredient in sacrifices (cf. Lev 2:13), as a symbol of wisdom (in rabbinic writings; cf. *m. Soṭah* 9:15), or in any number of other ways. *Lost his savour*: lit. "becomes foolish," which may hint at the saying's meaning, given salt's potential connection with wisdom.   **5:14** *A city . . . hill*: eschatological Jerusalem; cf. Isa 2:2–4; chap. 60; Mic 4:1–3. *Light of the world* picks up on Jerusalem's welcoming of Gentiles in these OT passages.   **5:15** *Bushel*: a vessel for measuring grain.   **5:17–20** The Law. Compare Luke 16:16–17. Matthew introduces one of his major themes, the primacy of biblical law as reinterpreted by Jesus. Jesus' hermeneutical approach involves generating additional directives that protect the original biblical commandments from violation. It reflects the same impulse as the rabbinic strategy of "building a fence around the Torah" (see introduction), which probably originated with the Pharisees.   **5:17** *The law . . . prophets*: Scripture, i.e., the OT.   **5:18** *Till heaven . . . law*: cf. Isa 40:8; 51:6. *Jot*: Gk. *iōta*, the smallest Greek letter. *Tittle*: apparently referring to part of a letter, or to a tiny accent or breathing mark associated with a letter. *In no wise*: in no way (so throughout). *Till all be fulfilled*: a different Greek word is used in v. 17. The phrase is better translated "until all is accomplished" (NRSV), with reference to the end time.

²¹Ye have heard that it was said by them of old time, Thou shalt not kill; and whosoever shall kill shall be in danger of the judgment: ²²but I say unto you, That whosoever is angry with his brother without a cause shall be in danger of the judgment: and whosoever shall say to his brother, Raca, shall be in danger of the council: but whosoever shall say, Thou fool, shall be in danger of hell fire. ²³Therefore if thou bring thy gift to the altar, and there rememberest that thy brother hath ought against thee; ²⁴leave there thy gift before the altar, and go thy way; first be reconciled to thy brother, and then come and offer thy gift. ²⁵Agree with thine adversary quickly, whiles thou art in the way with him; lest at any time the adversary deliver thee to the judge, and the judge deliver thee to the officer, and thou be cast into prison. ²⁶Verily I say unto thee, Thou shalt by no means come out thence, till thou hast paid the uttermost farthing.

²⁷Ye have heard that it was said by them of old time, Thou shalt not commit adultery: ²⁸but I say unto you, That whosoever looketh on a woman to lust after her hath committed adultery with her already in his heart. ²⁹And if thy right eye offend thee, pluck it out, and cast it from thee: for it is profitable for thee that one of thy members should perish, and not that thy whole body should be cast into hell. ³⁰And if thy right hand offend thee, cut it off, and cast it from thee: for it is profitable for thee that one of thy members should perish, and not that thy whole body should be cast into hell. ³¹It hath been said, Whosoever shall put away his wife, let him give her a writing of divorcement: ³²but I say unto you, That whosoever shall put away his wife, saving for the cause of fornication, causeth her to commit adultery: and whosoever shall marry her that is divorced committeth adultery.

³³Again, ye have heard that it hath been said by them of old time, Thou shalt not forswear thyself, but shalt perform unto the Lord thine oaths: ³⁴but I say unto you, Swear not at all; neither by heaven; for it is God's throne: ³⁵nor by the earth; for it is his footstool: neither by Jerusalem; for it is the city of the great King.

5:21–26 Anger. Compare Luke 12:57–59.   **5:21** *Thou shalt not kill*: Exod 20:13; Deut 5:17.   **5:22** *But*: Gk. *de* (also vv. 28, 34, 39, 44), a conjunction that is not necessarily adversative (and even when it is, its adversative force is relatively weak). Both context and grammar indicate that Jesus sees his words as complementing rather than superseding the law. *Without a cause*: better omitted (MS tradition) as a scribe's attempt to moderate Jesus' commandment. *Raca*: an Aramaic insult meaning "imbecile." *But whosoever*: better "and whosoever," as in the previous clause. *The council*: probably a local court. *Hell*: Gk. *gehenna*; see Mark 9:43 note.   **5:23–24** *Therefore if . . . offer thy gift*: cf. Mark 11:25.   **5:25–26** *Agree with . . . farthing*: presuming the conflict relates to payment of a debt.   **5:26** *Farthing*: Gk. *kodrantēs*, transliterating Lat. *quadrans*, one-quarter of an *assarius* (see 10:29 note).   **5:27–32** Adultery and divorce. Compare Luke 16:18.   **5:27** *By them . . . time*: better omitted (MS tradition). *Thou shalt not commit adultery*: Exod 20:14; Deut 5:18.   **5:29** *Offend*: see Mark 4:17 note.   **5:31** *Put away*: divorce (cf. Deut 24:1).   **5:32** *Whosoever shall marry . . . committeth adultery*: the prohibition against divorce (see 19:6; Mark 10:9; 1 Cor 7:10) and related prohibition of remarriage after divorce (see also 19:9; Mark 10:11–12; Luke 16:18) constitute the dominical teaching most often quoted in the NT. The doctrine opposes Deut 24:1–4 (a problem Jesus addresses in 19:3–9), but is anticipated by Mal 2:13–16. *Saving for the cause of fornication*: only Matthew includes this exception. *Causeth her to commit adultery*: this phrase assumes her social and economic vulnerability as a woman would force her to remarry.   **5:33–37** Oaths. Jesus reiterates this prohibition at 23:16–22. Jas 5:12 echoes the saying.   **5:33** *Thou shalt not forswear thyself*: not a precise reference to anything in the OT, but Lev 19:12 contains an injunction against profaning God's name by using it while swear-

³⁶Neither shalt thou swear by thy head, because thou canst not make one hair white or black. ³⁷But let your communication be, Yea, yea; Nay, nay: for whatsoever is more than these cometh of evil.

³⁸Ye have heard that it hath been said, An eye for an eye, and a tooth for a tooth: ³⁹but I say unto you, That ye resist not evil: but whosoever shall smite thee on thy right cheek, turn to him the other also. ⁴⁰And if any man will sue thee at the law, and take away thy coat, let him have thy cloke also. ⁴¹And whosoever shall compel thee to go a mile, go with him twain. ⁴²Give to him that asketh thee, and from him that would borrow of thee turn not thou away.

⁴³Ye have heard that it hath been said, Thou shalt love thy neighbour, and hate thine enemy. ⁴⁴But I say unto you, Love your enemies, bless them that curse you, do good to them that hate you, and pray for them which despitefully use you, and persecute you; ⁴⁵that ye may be the children of your Father which is in heaven: for he maketh his sun to rise on the evil and on the good, and sendeth rain on the just and on the unjust. ⁴⁶For if ye love them which love you, what reward have ye? do not even the publicans the same? ⁴⁷And if ye salute your brethren only, what do ye more than others? do not even the publicans so? ⁴⁸Be ye therefore perfect, even as your Father which is in heaven is perfect.

6 Take heed that ye do not your alms before men, to be seen of them: otherwise ye have no reward of your Father which is in heaven.

²Therefore when thou doest thine alms, do not sound a trumpet before thee, as the hypocrites do in the synagogues and in the streets, that they may have glory of men. Verily I say unto you, They have their reward. ³But when thou doest alms, let not thy left hand know what thy right hand doeth: ⁴that thine alms may be in secret: and thy Father which seeth in secret himself shall reward thee openly.

⁵And when thou prayest, thou shalt not be as the hypocrites are: for they love to pray standing in the synagogues and in the corners of the streets, that they may be

---

ing false oaths.   **5:37** *Evil* may be rendered "the evil one" (i.e., Satan; also in 6:13).   **5:38–42** Retaliation. Compare Luke 6:29–30.   **5:38** *An eye . . . for a tooth*: the *lex talionis*; see Exod 21:24; Lev 24:20; Deut 19:21.   **5:39** *Evil*: or "the evil one" (see v. 37 note), but here referring to an evil person. *Whosoever shall . . . also*: cf. Lam 3:27–30.   **5:40** *Thy coat . . . cloke*: inner and outer garments.   **5:41** *Compel*: the Greek word refers to military requisition (cf. 27:32).   **5:43–48** Enemies. Compare Luke 6:27–28, 32–36.   **5:43** *Thou shalt . . . neighbour*: Lev 19:18, which does not mention hating one's enemy. Jesus transforms an injunction aimed at communal harmony into a demand for universal peace.   **5:44** *Bless them . . . persecute you*: better "and pray for them which persecute you" (MS tradition).   **5:45** *For he . . . unjust*: cf. Seneca, *On Benefits* 4.25–26, esp. 26.1: "If you will imitate . . . the gods, then give benefits also to the ungrateful: for the sun rises even on criminals, and the sea lies open to pirates."   **5:46** *Publicans*: see Mark 2:15 note.   **5:47** *Salute*: lit. "greet," but that seems too weak here. Since the greeting would have taken the form of a wish for peace (see 10:12–13), perhaps the word connotes a sincere desire for the other's well-being. *Publicans*: better "Gentiles" (MS tradition), a common term of disparagement in the NT, connoting pagan sinner (6:7 [KJV "heathen"], 32; cf. Gal 2:15).   **6:1–4** Charity. Giving alms was a central tenet of Judaism; cf. Deut 15:11; Tob 12:9.   **6:1** *Do not your alms*: better "do not your righteousness" (MS tradition), with the sense "do not practice piety." Verse 1 therefore introduces all of 6:1–18.   **6:2** *When thou . . . reward*: a saying with numerous parallels in rabbinic Jewish texts. *Hypocrites*: Gk. *hypokritai*, "dissemblers" (originally a term for theater actors). *May have glory*: elsewhere Matthew uses this Greek word only of God.   **6:4** *Openly*: better omitted (MS tradition); also in vv. 6, 18.   **6:5–8** Prayer.

seen of men. Verily I say unto you, They have their reward. [6]But thou, when thou prayest, enter into thy closet, and when thou hast shut thy door, pray to thy Father which is in secret; and thy Father which seeth in secret shall reward thee openly. [7]But when ye pray, use not vain repetitions, as the heathen do: for they think that they shall be heard for their much speaking. [8]Be not ye therefore like unto them: for your Father knoweth what things ye have need of, before ye ask him.

[9]After this manner therefore pray ye: Our Father which art in heaven, Hallowed be thy name. [10]Thy kingdom come. Thy will be done in earth, as it is in heaven. [11]Give us this day our daily bread. [12]And forgive us our debts, as we forgive our debtors. [13]And lead us not into temptation, but deliver us from evil: For thine is the kingdom, and the power, and the glory, for ever. Amen. [14]For if ye forgive men their trespasses, your heavenly Father will also forgive you: [15]but if ye forgive not men their trespasses, neither will your Father forgive your trespasses.

[16]Moreover when ye fast, be not, as the hypocrites, of a sad countenance: for they disfigure their faces, that they may appear unto men to fast. Verily I say unto you, They have their reward. [17]But thou, when thou fastest, anoint thine head, and wash thy face; [18]that thou appear not unto men to fast, but unto thy Father which is in secret: and thy Father, which seeth in secret, shall reward thee openly.

[19]Lay not up for yourselves treasures upon earth, where moth and rust doth corrupt, and where thieves break through and steal: [20]but lay up for yourselves treasures in heaven, where neither moth nor rust doth corrupt, and where thieves do not break through nor steal: [21]for where your treasure is, there will your heart be also.

[22]The light of the body is the eye: if therefore thine eye be single, thy whole body shall be full of light. [23]But if thine eye be evil, thy whole body shall be full of darkness. If therefore the light that is in thee be darkness, how great is that darkness!

[24]No man can serve two masters: for either he will hate the one, and love the other; or else he will hold to the one, and despise the other. Ye cannot serve God and mammon.

6:7 *Use . . . vain repetitions*: probably "babble" (Gk. obscure).   **6:9–15** The Lord's Prayer. Compare Mark 11:25–26; Luke 11:1–4. This prayer resembles other Jewish prayers more or less contemporary with it, especially the Kaddish and the Eighteen Benedictions.   **6:11** *Daily*: Gk. obscure; alternatively "necessary" or "for tomorrow" (perhaps recalling God's extra provision of manna for the Sabbath; Exod 16:22–30).   **6:12** *Debts*: Luke 11:4 has "sins." *Forgive*: better "have forgiven" (MS tradition). **6:13** *Lead us not into temptation*: alternatively "do not bring us to the time of trial" (NRSV). *Evil*: see 5:37 note. *For thine . . . Amen*: this doxology, based on 1 Chr 29:11–13, is better omitted (MS tradition). It likely reflects the prayer's use in later Christian liturgy.   **6:14–15** *For if . . . your trespasses*: the saying has numerous parallels in ancient Jewish literature (e.g., Sir 28:2–5).   **6:16–18** Fasting. **6:16** *Sad countenance . . . faces*: the faster might adopt a posture of mourning; cf. Isa 58:3–5; Jonah 3:5–8.   **6:19–21** Treasures in heaven. Compare Luke 12:33–34. Jas 5:2–3 echoes this saying, the first in the sermon's series of maxims on wealth (vv. 19–34).   **6:19** *Rust*: lit. "eating"; hence, perhaps, "corrosion" or "rust." *Corrupt*: cf. v. 16 (KJV "disfigure").   **6:22–23** A sound eye. Compare Luke 11:34–36.   **6:22** *Light*: lamp. The ancients conventionally explained vision as a light emanating from the eye. *Single*: Gk. *haplous*, which connotes generosity, as in Rom 12:8 (KJV "simplicity"); 2 Cor 8:2 ("liberality"); 9:11 ("bountifulness"); etc.   **6:23** *Eye be evil*: the evil eye was commonly linked with stinginess and covetousness (see 20:15; Deut 15:9; Prov 28:22; etc).   **6:24** Serving two masters. Compare Luke 16:13. *Mammon*: probably "wealth" or "property." This Semitic word transliterated into Greek in

^{25}Therefore I say unto you, Take no thought for your life, what ye shall eat, or what ye shall drink; nor yet for your body, what ye shall put on. Is not the life more than meat, and the body than raiment? ^{26}Behold the fowls of the air: for they sow not, neither do they reap, nor gather into barns; yet your heavenly Father feedeth them. Are ye not much better than they? ^{27}Which of you by taking thought can add one cubit unto his stature? ^{28}And why take ye thought for raiment? Consider the lilies of the field, how they grow; they toil not, neither do they spin: ^{29}and yet I say unto you, That even Solomon in all his glory was not arrayed like one of these. ^{30}Wherefore, if God so clothe the grass of the field, which to day is, and to morrow is cast into the oven, shall he not much more clothe you, O ye of little faith? ^{31}Therefore take no thought, saying, What shall we eat? or, What shall we drink? or, Wherewithal shall we be clothed? ^{32}(For after all these things do the Gentiles seek:) for your heavenly Father knoweth that ye have need of all these things. ^{33}But seek ye first the kingdom of God, and his righteousness; and all these things shall be added unto you. ^{34}Take therefore no thought for the morrow: for the morrow shall take thought for the things of itself. Sufficient unto the day is the evil thereof.

7 Judge not, that ye be not judged. ^{2}For with what judgment ye judge, ye shall be judged: and with what measure ye mete, it shall be measured to you again. ^{3}And why beholdest thou the mote that is in thy brother's eye, but considerest not the beam that is in thine own eye? ^{4}Or how wilt thou say to thy brother, Let me pull out the mote out of thine eye; and, behold, a beam is in thine own eye? ^{5}Thou hypocrite, first cast out the beam out of thine own eye; and then shalt thou see clearly to cast out the mote out of thy brother's eye.

^{6}Give not that which is holy unto the dogs, neither cast ye your pearls before swine, lest they trample them under their feet, and turn again and rend you.

---

effect personifies wealth as an alien god, leading to the later use of *Mammon* as the name for a demon (most famously in Milton, *Paradise Lost* 1.678ff.). **6:25–34** Trusting providence. Compare Luke 12:22–31. **6:25** *Take no thought*: lit. "be not anxious" (so throughout). **6:26** *Your heavenly . . . them*: God's provision for animals is conventional; cf. Pss 104:10–28; 147:9; etc. **6:27** *Stature*: the Greek word primarily means "length of life." Since *cubit*, literally a measure of about eighteen inches, could also be used with reference to time, the sense is of extending one's life. **6:28** *Lilies*: it is not clear to what blossom the Greek word refers; it may be a generic designation for flowers. **6:29** *Solomon in all his glory*: see 1 Kgs 10:14–29. **6:30** *Which to day . . . oven*: grass and flowers conventionally figure human life's transitoriness (cf. Job 14:1–2; Ps 90:3–6; Isa 40:6–7), but Jesus distinguishes humans from these fragile flora, thereby gesturing at a possibility of eternal life (explored in 7:13–27). **6:33** *Seek ye . . . you*: recalling the combination of God's kingdom and daily provisions in the Lord's Prayer (vv. 10–11). **6:34** *Sufficient unto the day is the evil thereof*: elsewhere in the sermon, *evil* is Gk. *ponera*; here it is *kakia*, better "trouble" or "misfortune." Seneca's comparison of humans and nature is similar to Jesus': the human "mind hangs in suspense . . . worried by expectation of what's to come," while "beasts flee dangers when they see them and once they escape are free from anxiety" (*Epistle* 5.8–9). **7:1–5** Judging others. Compare Mark 4:24; Luke 6:37–38, 41–42. **7:3–5** *And why . . . brother's eye*: a commonplace in Greco-Roman literature; cf. Rom 2:1–24 and notes. For a closer parallel, see Horace, *Satire* 1.3.25–27: "When you survey your own evil with inflamed, ointment-smeared eyes, why do you discern the faults of your friend as keenly as an eagle . . . ?" **7:3** *Mote*: "speck" (of dust); lit. "splinter," in parallel with the *beam*. **7:6** Profaning the holy. The saying resembles conventional wisdom such as that found

⁷Ask, and it shall be given you; seek, and ye shall find; knock, and it shall be opened unto, you: ⁸for every one that asketh receiveth; and he that seeketh findeth; and to him that knocketh it shall be opened. ⁹Or what man is there of you, whom if his son ask bread, will he give him a stone? ¹⁰Or if he ask a fish, will he give him a serpent? ¹¹If ye then, being evil, know how to give good gifts unto your children, how much more shall your Father which is in heaven give good things to them that ask him? ¹²Therefore all things whatsoever ye would that men should do to you, do ye even so to them: for this is the law and the prophets.

¹³Enter ye in at the strait gate: for wide is the gate, and broad is the way, that leadeth to destruction, and many there be which go in thereat: ¹⁴because strait is the gate, and narrow is the way, which leadeth unto life, and few there be that find it.

¹⁵Beware of false prophets, which come to you in sheep's clothing, but inwardly they are ravening wolves. ¹⁶Ye shall know them by their fruits. Do men gather grapes of thorns, or figs of thistles? ¹⁷Even so every good tree bringeth forth good fruit; but a corrupt tree bringeth forth evil fruit. ¹⁸A good tree cannot bring forth evil fruit, neither can a corrupt tree bring forth good fruit. ¹⁹Every tree that bringeth not forth good fruit is hewn down, and cast into the fire. ²⁰Wherefore by their fruits ye shall know them. ²¹Not every one that saith unto me, Lord, Lord, shall enter into the kingdom of heaven; but he that doeth the will of my Father which is in heaven. ²²Many will say to me in that day, Lord, Lord, have we not prophesied in thy name? and in thy name have cast out devils? and in thy name done many wonderful works? ²³And then will I profess unto them, I never knew you: depart from me, ye that work iniquity.

²⁴Therefore whosoever heareth these sayings of mine, and doeth them, I will liken him unto a wise man, which built his house upon a rock: ²⁵and the rain descended, and the floods came, and the winds blew, and beat upon that house; and it fell not: for it was founded upon a rock. ²⁶And every one that heareth these sayings of mine, and doeth them not, shall be likened unto a foolish man, which built his house upon the sand: ²⁷and the rain descended, and the floods came,

---

at Prov 23:9.   **7:7–12** Asking God. Compare Luke 11:9–13; 6:31.   **7:12** *Therefore all . . . them:* parallels to the "golden rule" are found throughout ancient Jewish and Greco-Roman literature (e.g., Lev 19:18; Herodotus 3.142), and in other traditions as well (e.g., Confucius, *Analects* 15.23). *For this . . . prophets:* Paul likewise insists that this rule fulfills God's law; cf. Rom 13:8–9; Gal 5:14.   **7:13–14** Two paths and gates. Compare Luke 13:23–24. The motif of two paths was conventional in the OT and ancient Jewish literature; cf. Ps 1:6; Jer 21:8.   **7:14** *Strait is . . . narrow:* the colloquial "straight and narrow" apparently originated as a misreading of this verse that mistook *strait* ("constricted") for "straight." *Few there be that find it:* cf. 22:14, but contrast 8:11 and 20:28.   **7:15–23** False prophets. Compare Luke 6:43–46; 13:25–27. The widespread concern in NT writings about *false prophets,* charismatic itinerants who preached gospels potentially different from those endorsed by local church leaders (e.g., 24:23–28; 2 Cor 11:4–23; 2 Pet 2; 1 John 4:1–3), reveals how diverse and prone to disagreement the early Christian movement was.   **7:15** *Sheep's clothing . . . wolves:* Aesop's fable may lie in the background. The OT often figures God's people as vulnerable sheep (e.g., Ezek 34).   **7:19** *Every tree . . . fire:* cf. 3:10.   **7:21** *Lord:* see Mark 7:28 note. Christological confession is in view here and at v. 22; cf. Rom 10:9; 1 Cor 12:3.   **7:22** *In that day:* the day of judgment.   **7:23** *Depart from . . . iniquity:* quoting Ps 6:8.   **7:24–27** Hearing and doing. Compare Luke 6:47–49.   **7:25** *The rain . . . blew:* in 24:37–39, Jesus invokes the great deluge to figure God's eschatological judgment; the storm

and the winds blew, and beat upon that house; and it fell: and great was the fall of it.

²⁸And it came to pass, when Jesus had ended these sayings, the people were astonished at his doctrine: ²⁹for he taught them as one having authority, and not as the scribes.

8 When he was come down from the mountain, great multitudes followed him. ²And, behold, there came a leper and worshipped him, saying, Lord, if thou wilt, thou canst make me clean. ³And Jesus put forth his hand, and touched him, saying, I will; be thou clean. And immediately his leprosy was cleansed. ⁴And Jesus saith unto him, See thou tell no man; but go thy way, shew thyself to the priest, and offer the gift that Moses commanded, for a testimony unto them.

⁵And when Jesus was entered into Capernaum, there came unto him a centurion, beseeching him, ⁶and saying, Lord, my servant lieth at home sick of the palsy, grievously tormented. ⁷And Jesus saith unto him, I will come and heal him. ⁸The centurion answered and said, Lord, I am not worthy that thou shouldest come under my roof: but speak the word only, and my servant shall be healed. ⁹For I am a man under authority, having soldiers under me: and I say to this man, Go, and he goeth; and to another, Come, and he cometh; and to my servant, Do this, and he doeth it. ¹⁰When Jesus heard it, he marvelled, and said to them that followed, Verily I say unto you, I have not found so great faith, no, not in Israel. ¹¹And I say unto you, That many shall come from the east and west, and shall sit down with Abraham, and Isaac, and Jacob, in the kingdom of heaven. ¹²But the children of the kingdom shall be cast out into outer darkness: there shall be weeping and gnashing of teeth. ¹³And Jesus said unto the centurion, Go thy way; and as thou hast believed, so be it done unto thee. And his servant was healed in the selfsame hour.

---

represented here likewise symbolizes God's final judgment.   **7:28–29** Conclusion.   **7:28** *And it . . . pass*: Matthew's closing formula for each of Jesus' five main discourses; see 11:1; 13:53; 19:1; 26:1. *Doctrine*: teaching (so throughout).   **7:29** *Them*: apparently the disciples, not "the people" (v. 28; cf. 5:1–2), unless Matthew is being inconsistent.

8:1–9:34 Miracles. A series of nine miracle stories, told in groups of three (8:1–18; 8:23–9:8; 9:18–34), with more mundane interludes (8:19–22; 9:9–17). These stories contain a total of ten miracles (9:18–26 interlinks a pair of healings), perhaps corresponding to the ten that Moses performed (Exod 7–12).   **8:1–4** Healing a leprous man. Compare Mark 1:40–45 and notes; Luke 5:12–16.   **8:2** *Leper*: someone ritually unclean, and thus presumably not allowed into the crowd listening to the sermon.   **8:4** *Tell no man*: Matthew retains several such vestiges of Mark's messianic secret motif (see introduction to Mark), but does not thoroughly develop the theme. *That Moses commanded*: see Lev 13–14.   **8:5–13** Healing a centurion's servant. Compare Luke 7:1–10; 13:28–29; John 4:46–54. This episode recalls Elisha's healing of Naaman, a commander in the Syrian army (2 Kgs 5:1–19).   **8:5** *Centurion*: officer commanding a company of Roman soldiers. **8:6** *Servant*: Gk. *pais*, which can mean either "slave" or "child," reflecting the low view of children in the ancient Mediterranean world.   **8:8** *I am . . . roof*: the Gentile centurion is sensitive to the possibility that Jesus might be defiled by entering his home; cf. Acts 10:28; 11:2–3.   **8:9** *Servant*: Gk. *doulos*, unambiguously "slave."   **8:10** *Faith*: see Mark 2:5 note.   **8:11** *Many shall come . . . west*: recalling Ps 107:3, which actually refers to Israel's return to Palestine; but cf. Mal 1:11. *Sit down*: lit. "recline" at table (the customary posture for dining), alluding to an eschatological banquet—in particular, a wedding banquet (see Mark 2:19 note).   **8:12** *Children of the kingdom*: Jews. *Cast*

¹⁴And when Jesus was come into Peter's house, he saw his wife's mother laid, and sick of a fever. ¹⁵And he touched her hand, and the fever left her: and she arose, and ministered unto them. ¹⁶When the even was come, they brought unto him many that were possessed with devils: and he cast out the spirits with his word, and healed all that were sick: ¹⁷that it might be fulfilled which was spoken by Esaias the prophet, saying, Himself took our infirmities, and bare our sicknesses.

¹⁸Now when Jesus saw great multitudes about him, he gave commandment to depart unto the other side. ¹⁹And a certain scribe came, and said unto him, Master, I will follow thee whithersoever thou goest. ²⁰And Jesus saith unto him, The foxes have holes, and the birds of the air have nests; but the Son of man hath not where to lay his head. ²¹And another of his disciples said unto him, Lord, suffer me first to go and bury my father. ²²But Jesus said unto him, Follow me; and let the dead bury their dead.

²³And when he was entered into a ship, his disciples followed him. ²⁴And, behold, there arose a great tempest in the sea, insomuch that the ship was covered with the waves: but he was asleep. ²⁵And his disciples came to him, and awoke him, saying, Lord, save us: we perish. ²⁶And he saith unto them, Why are ye fearful, O ye of little faith? Then he arose, and rebuked the winds and the sea; and there was a great calm. ²⁷But the men marvelled, saying, What manner of man is this, that even the winds and the sea obey him!

²⁸And when he was come to the other side into the country of the Gergesenes, there met him two possessed with devils, coming out of the tombs, exceeding fierce, so that no man might pass by that way. ²⁹And, behold, they cried out, saying, What have we to do with thee, Jesus, thou Son of God? art thou come hither to torment us before the time? ³⁰And there was a good way off from them an herd of many swine feeding. ³¹So the devils besought him, saying, If thou cast us out,

---

out . . . teeth: Matthew's formula for Hell (see 13:42, 50; 22:13; etc.).   **8:14-17** Healing Peter's mother-in-law. Compare Mark 1:29-34 and note to v. 31; Luke 4:38-41.   **8:14** *Laid*: lying in bed. **8:15** *Unto them*: better "unto him" (MS tradition.)   **8:17** *Himself took . . . sicknesses*: Isa 53:4 (see 53:3 note), from one of Isaiah's Servant Songs.   **8:18-22** Following Jesus. Compare Luke 9:57-62. **8:18** *The other side*: of the Sea of Galilee, on whose shore Capernaum was located.   **8:19** *Master*: see Mark 4:38 note.   **8:20** *Son of man*: see Mark 2:10 note.   **8:21** *Suffer me . . . father*: cf. 1 Kgs 19:19-21, Elijah's calling of Elisha. This brutal call to discipleship stands in tension with vv. 14-15, where Jesus implicitly affirms Peter's concern for his family by healing his mother-in-law, though he had stopped supporting them to follow Jesus (4:20).   **8:23-27** Calming the storm. Compare Mark 4:35-41 and notes; Luke 8:22-25. Parallels between this episode and Jonah 1:1-16 suggest a revision of the Jonah story's first act. Jonah sleeps through a great storm (1:4-5) before mariners wake him and demand that he call on God to calm the sea (1:6-9), but the sea is calmed only after Jonah is cast into it (1:10-16). Jesus, on the contrary, calms the storm by word alone (8:26) and will later outdo Jonah in other ways as well (cf. 12:39-41).   **8:24** *Tempest*: Gk. *seismos*, lit. "earthquake" (cf. 24:7).   **8:25** *Lord, save . . . perish*: transforming the disciples' accusatory question in Mark (4:38) into a prayer (cf. Jonah 1:14).   **8:26** *O ye of little faith*: moderating Jesus' brutal rebuke of the disciples as utterly faithless in Mark (see 4:40 note). **8:28-34** Gergesene demoniacs. Compare Mark 5:1-20 and notes, where there is only one demoniac but multiple demons; Luke 8:26-39. Matthew occasionally doubles characters or props from Mark's narrative: e.g., 20:29-34 (two blind men; cf. Mark 10:46-52) and 21:1-11 (two asses; cf. Mark 11:1-10).   **8:28** *Gergesenes*: better "Gaderenes" (MS tradition); Gadara was a city in Gentile territory (the Decapolis) east of the Sea of Galilee. Mark and Luke read "Gerasenes."   **8:29** *The time*: the Last

suffer us to go away into the herd of swine. [32]And he said unto them, Go. And when they were come out, they went into the herd of swine: and, behold, the whole herd of swine ran violently down a steep place into the sea, and perished in the waters. [33]And they that kept them fled, and went their ways into the city, and told every thing, and what was befallen to the possessed of the devils. [34]And, behold, the whole city came out to meet Jesus: and when they saw him, they besought him that he would depart out of their coasts.

9 And he entered into a ship, and passed over, and came into his own city. [2]And, behold, they brought to him a man sick of the palsy, lying on a bed: and Jesus seeing their faith said unto the sick of the palsy; Son, be of good cheer; thy sins be forgiven thee. [3]And, behold, certain of the scribes said within themselves, This man blasphemeth. [4]And Jesus knowing their thoughts said, Wherefore think ye evil in your hearts? [5]For whether is easier, to say, Thy sins be forgiven thee; or to say, Arise, and walk? [6]But that ye may know that the Son of man hath power on earth to forgive sins, (then saith he to the sick of the palsy,) Arise, take up thy bed, and go unto thine house. [7]And he arose, and departed to his house. [8]But when the multitudes saw it, they marvelled, and glorified God, which had given such power unto men.

[9]And as Jesus passed forth from thence, he saw a man, named Matthew, sitting at the receipt of custom: and he saith unto him, Follow me. And he arose, and followed him. [10]And it came to pass, as Jesus sat at meat in the house, behold, many publicans and sinners came and sat down with him and his disciples. [11]And when the Pharisees saw it, they said unto his disciples, Why eateth your Master with publicans and sinners? [12]But when Jesus heard that, he said unto them, They that be whole need not a physician, but they that are sick. [13]But go ye and learn what that meaneth, I will have mercy, and not sacrifice: for I am not come to call the righteous, but sinners to repentance.

[14]Then came to him the disciples of John, saying, Why do we and the Pharisees fast oft, but thy disciples fast not? [15]And Jesus said unto them, Can the children of the bridechamber mourn, as long as the bridegroom is with them? but the days will come, when the bridegroom shall be taken from them, and then shall they fast. [16]No man putteth a piece of new cloth unto an old garment, for that which is put in to fill it up taketh from the garment, and the rent is made worse. [17]Neither do men put new wine into old bottles: else the bottles break, and the wine runneth out, and the bottles perish: but they put new wine into new bottles, and both are preserved.

Judgment.   **9:1–8** Healing a paralytic. Compare Mark 2:1–12 and notes; Luke 5:17–26. John 5:1–18 has a very different account.   **9:1** *His own city*: Capernaum.   **9:3** *Blasphemeth*: presumably because forgiving sins was the privilege of God alone, as Mark 2:7 specifies.   **9:8** *Marvelled*: better "became afraid" (MS tradition).   **9:9–17** Calling Matthew and the subsequent symposium. Compare Mark 2:13–22 and notes; Luke 5:27–39. In Mark and Luke, the man called is Levi. It is not clear why this gospel changes his name to that of one of the Twelve (cf. 10:3), but early readers may have seen in the episode a clue to its authorship, whence the traditional title "according to Matthew." **9:13** *I will . . . sacrifice*: Hos 6:6; cf. Matt 12:7. *To repentance*: better omitted (MS tradition). **9:15** *Children of the bridechamber*: wedding guests; cf. 8:11 and note.   **9:17** *Bottles*: lit. "wineskins."

¹⁸While he spake these things unto them, behold, there came a certain ruler, and worshipped him, saying, My daughter is even now dead: but come and lay thy hand upon her, and she shall live. ¹⁹And Jesus arose, and followed him, and so did his disciples.

²⁰And, behold, a woman, which was diseased with an issue of blood twelve years, came behind him, and touched the hem of his garment: ²¹for she said within herself, If I may but touch his garment, I shall be whole. ²²But Jesus turned him about, and when he saw her, he said, Daughter, be of good comfort; thy faith hath made thee whole. And the woman was made whole from that hour.

²³And when Jesus came into the ruler's house, and saw the minstrels and the people making a noise, ²⁴he said unto them, Give place: for the maid is not dead, but sleepeth. And they laughed him to scorn. ²⁵But when the people were put forth, he went in, and took her by the hand, and the maid arose. ²⁶And the fame hereof went abroad into all that land.

²⁷And when Jesus departed thence, two blind men followed him, crying, and saying, Thou Son of David, have mercy on us. ²⁸And when he was come into the house, the blind men came to him: and Jesus saith unto them, Believe ye that I am able to do this? They said unto him, Yea, Lord. ²⁹Then touched he their eyes, saying, According to your faith be it unto you. ³⁰And their eyes were opened; and Jesus straitly charged them, saying, See that no man know it. ³¹But they, when they were departed, spread abroad his fame in all that country.

³²As they went out, behold, they brought to him a dumb man possessed with a devil. ³³And when the devil was cast out, the dumb spake: and the multitudes marvelled, saying, It was never so seen in Israel. ³⁴But the Pharisees said, He casteth out devils through the prince of the devils.

³⁵And Jesus went about all the cities and villages, teaching in their synagogues, and preaching the gospel of the kingdom, and healing every sickness and every disease among the people. ³⁶But when he saw the multitudes, he was moved with compassion on them, because they fainted, and were scattered abroad, as sheep having no shepherd. ³⁷Then saith he unto his disciples, The harvest truly is plen-

9:18–26 Healing a girl and woman. Compare Mark 5:21–43 and notes; Luke 8:40–56.   9:20 *Issue of blood*: vaginal bleeding, which would have made her ritually unclean (cf. Lev 15:19–30).   9:21 *Whole*: "healthy" (also in v. 22); the Greek word (not the same as in v. 12) also means "saved."   9:23 *Minstrels*: flautists, who commonly played at funerals.   9:27–31 Healing blind men. Compare Mark 10:46–52 and notes; Luke 18:35–43. Matthew has apparently composed two stories (see also 20:29–34) on the model of Mark 10:46–52, perhaps in order to fill out a third triad of miracles or to establish that the prophecies Jesus quotes in 11:5 have been completely fulfilled.   9:30 *Straitly*: sternly.   9:32–34 Healing a dumb demoniac. Matthew has apparently composed two stories on the model of Q's version of the Beelzebub controversy (see also 12:22–24; cf. Luke 11:14–16), probably for the reasons mentioned in 9:27–31 note.   9:32 *Dumb*: the Greek word can mean "deaf" or "mute."

  9:35–11:1 **Discipleship.** This section features Jesus' second extended discourse, on mission (10:5–42).   9:35–10:4 Commissioning the Twelve. Compare Mark 6:34, 6b–7; 3:13–19 (see notes); Luke 10:1–2; 9:1; 6:13–16; Acts 1:13. This passage marks the beginning of God's eschatological gathering of Israel. Its culmination will coincide with the end time's consummation (cf. 24:31 and note).   9:36 *Fainted*: better "were distressed" (MS tradition). *Scattered abroad*: lit. "cast down" or "dejected." *As sheep . . . shepherd*: the OT commonly compares Israel to a flock without shepherd; e.g., Num 27:17; Ezek 34:5–6; Zech 10:2.   9:37 *The harvest . . . labourers*: cf. Mark 4:29 note; John

teous, but the labourers are few; [38]pray ye therefore the Lord of the harvest, that he will send forth labourers into his harvest.

10 And when he had called unto him his twelve disciples, he gave them power against unclean spirits, to cast them out, and to heal all manner of sickness and all manner of disease. [2]Now the names of the twelve apostles are these; the first, Simon, who is called Peter, and Andrew his brother; James the son of Zebedee, and John his brother; [3]Philip, and Bartholomew; Thomas, and Matthew the publican; James the son of Alphæus, and Lebbæus, whose surname was Thaddæus; [4]Simon the Canaanite, and Judas Iscariot, who also betrayed him.

[5]These twelve Jesus sent forth, and commanded them, saying, Go not into the way of the Gentiles, and into any city of the Samaritans enter ye not: [6]but go rather to the lost sheep of the house of Israel. [7]And as ye go, preach, saying, The kingdom of heaven is at hand. [8]Heal the sick, cleanse the lepers, raise the dead, cast out devils: freely ye have received, freely give. [9]Provide neither gold, nor silver, nor brass in your purses, [10]nor scrip for your journey, neither two coats, neither shoes, nor yet staves: for the workman is worthy of his meat. [11]And into whatsoever city or town ye shall enter, inquire who in it is worthy; and there abide till ye go thence. [12]And when ye come into an house, salute it. [13]And if the house be worthy, let your peace come upon it: but if it be not worthy, let your peace return to you. [14]And whosoever shall not receive you, nor hear your words, when ye depart out of that house or city, shake off the dust of your feet. [15]Verily I say unto you, It shall be more tolerable for the land of Sodom and Gomorrha in the day of judgment, than for that city. [16]Behold, I send you forth as sheep in the midst of wolves: be ye therefore wise as serpents, and harmless as doves.

4:35. Jesus' use of the metaphor here suggests that the end time is already present.   **9:38** *Send forth*: Gk. *ekbalē*, the same word used of casting out demons; perhaps "thrust" or "force out" would be better.   **10:1** *Twelve disciples*: mirroring Israel's twelve tribes (cf. 19:28). *Unclean spirits*: demons; cf. Zech 13:2.   **10:2** *Apostles*: lit. "those who are sent out." In time *apostles* became a technical term applied to a particular group in the early church (cf. 1 Cor 15:7), but the qualifications and precise responsibilities of an apostle are not clear.   **10:3** *Matthew the publican*: this gospel alone specifies Matthew's profession, thereby equating him with the Matthew of 9:9–13. *Lebbæus, whose . . . was*: better omitted (MS tradition).   **10:5–16** Instructions to the Twelve. Compare Mark 6:8–11 and notes; Luke 9:2–5; 10:3–12.   **10:5** *Go not . . . Gentiles*: Jesus progressively circumscribes this restriction as the First Gospel progresses. He himself ministers in Gentile territory in 15:21–39; he looks to a future time when his followers will preach to Gentiles at 24:14 (cf. Mark 13:10 and note); and after he rises from the dead, he commands them to initiate a Gentile ministry (28:19). *Samaritans*: Samaria lay between Judea to the south and Galilee to the north. Its residents shared an ethnic and religious heritage with Jews but differed from them on important doctrinal points, especially on the centrality of Jerusalem to YHWH's cult. Their ancestry is traditionally traced to those Israelites who remained in the Northern Kingdom after Assyria conquered it and deported much of the population, and to heathen foreigners who subsequently settled there. See 2 Kgs 17 for a polemical account of their origins.   **10:10** *Scrip*: a small satchel. *Staves*: better singular (MS tradition), i.e., "a staff." Jesus actually permits the Twelve to carry "a staff only" in Mark 6:8, and the scribal emendation may represent a lame attempt to avoid contradiction (the forbidden element understood as the plurality).   **10:11** *Inquire who . . . worthy*: this addition to Mark may urge missionaries to lodge solely with fellow believers.   **10:12** *Salute*: give a formal greeting—i.e., of "peace" (see v. 13).   **10:15** *Sodom and Gomorrha*: proverbial cities of evil, destroyed by God for gross inhospitality (see Gen 19:12–29).   **10:16** *Wise as serpents*: the

¹⁷But beware of men: for they will deliver you up to the councils, and they will scourge you in their synagogues; ¹⁸and ye shall be brought before governors and kings for my sake, for a testimony against them and the Gentiles. ¹⁹But when they deliver you up, take no thought how or what ye shall speak: for it shall be given you in that same hour what ye shall speak. ²⁰For it is not ye that speak, but the Spirit of your Father which speaketh in you. ²¹And the brother shall deliver up the brother to death, and the father the child: and the children shall rise up against their parents, and cause them to be put to death. ²²And ye shall be hated of all men for my name's sake: but he that endureth to the end shall be saved. ²³But when they persecute you in this city, flee ye into another: for verily I say unto you, Ye shall not have gone over the cities of Israel, till the Son of man be come. ²⁴The disciple is not above his master, nor the servant above his lord. ²⁵It is enough for the disciple that he be as his master, and the servant as his lord. If they have called the master of the house Beelzebub, how much more shall they call them of his household?

²⁶Fear them not therefore: for there is nothing covered, that shall not be revealed; and hid, that shall not be known. ²⁷What I tell you in darkness, that speak ye in light: and what ye hear in the ear, that preach ye upon the housetops. ²⁸And fear not them which kill the body, but are not able to kill the soul: but rather fear him which is able to destroy both soul and body in hell. ²⁹Are not two sparrows sold for a farthing? and one of them shall not fall on the ground without your Father. ³⁰But the very hairs of your head are all numbered. ³¹Fear ye not therefore, ye are of more value than many sparrows. ³²Whosoever therefore shall confess me before men, him will I confess also before my Father which is in heaven. ³³But whosoever shall deny me before men, him will I also deny before my Father which is in heaven.

³⁴Think not that I am come to send peace on earth: I came not to send peace, but a sword. ³⁵For I am come to set a man at variance against his father, and the daughter against her mother, and the daughter in law against her mother in law. ³⁶And a man's foes shall be they of his own household. ³⁷He that loveth father or

---

saying is proverbial, but Jesus may be invoking Gen 3:1.   **10:17–25** Predictions of persecution. Mark (13:9–13; see notes) and Luke (21:12–19; cf. 6:40; 12:11–12) assign this material to Jesus' apocalyptic discourse. Matthew duplicates some of it in his version of that sermon as well (cf. 24:9, 13). Also see John 14:26.   **10:17** *Councils*: local courts. *Scourge*: flog.   **10:18** *A testimony against*: or "a witness to."   **10:22** *Be hated . . . sake*: cf. 5:11.   **10:23** *But when . . . another*: the church later debated whether this phrase authorized Christians to flee in the face of imperial persecution; see, e.g., Tertullian, *Flight in Time of Persecution* (Appendix, pp. 1091–98).   **10:24** *Nor the . . . lord*: cf. John 13:16; 15:20. *Servant*: i.e., "slave" (so frequently).   **10:25** *Beelzebub*: see Mark 3:22 note; cf. Matt 9:34.   **10:26–33** Exhortation to bravery. Compare Luke 12:2–9.   **10:27** *In the ear*: whispered. **10:28** *Fear not . . . hell*: on *hell*, see Mark 9:43 note. Matthew suggests that the martyr's soul survives apart from the body after its death, later rejoining the resurrected body for eschatological vindication (cf. 5:10 note). See Rev 20 for a complicated development of this scenario.   **10:29** *Farthing*: Gk. *assarion* (a different word is used in 5:26), transliterating Lat. *assarius*, a Roman coin of notoriously little value.   **10:34–11:1** Realigning loyalties. Compare Luke 12:51–53; 14:26–27; 17:33; 10:16. **10:35–36** *For I . . . household*: adapting Mic 7:6, which some ancient Jewish writers treat as a

mother more than me is not worthy of me: and he that loveth son or daughter more than me is not worthy of me. [38]And he that taketh not his cross, and followeth after me, is not worthy of me. [39]He that findeth his life shall lose it: and he that loseth his life for my sake shall find it.

[40]He that receiveth you receiveth me, and he that receiveth me receiveth him that sent me. [41]He that receiveth a prophet in the name of a prophet shall receive a prophet's reward; and he that receiveth a righteous man in the name of a righteous man shall receive a righteous man's reward. [42]And whosoever shall give to drink unto one of these little ones a cup of cold water only in the name of a disciple, verily I say unto you, he shall in no wise lose his reward.

11 And it came to pass, when Jesus had made an end of commanding his twelve disciples, he departed thence to teach and to preach in their cities. [2]Now when John had heard in the prison the works of Christ, he sent two of his disciples, [3]and said unto him, Art thou he that should come, or do we look for another? [4]Jesus answered and said unto them, Go and shew John again those things which ye do hear and see: [5]the blind receive their sight, and the lame walk, the lepers are cleansed, and the deaf hear, the dead are raised up, and the poor have the gospel preached to them. [6]And blessed is he, whosoever shall not be offended in me.

[7]And as they departed, Jesus began to say unto the multitudes concerning John, What went ye out into the wilderness to see? A reed shaken with the wind? [8]But what went ye out for to see? A man clothed in soft raiment? behold, they that wear soft clothing are in kings' houses. [9]But what went ye out for to see? A prophet? yea, I say unto you, and more than a prophet. [10]For this is he, of whom it is written, Behold, I send my messenger before thy face, which shall prepare thy way before thee. [11]Verily I say unto you, Among them that are born of women there hath not risen a greater than John the Baptist: notwithstanding he that is least in the kingdom of heaven is greater than he. [12]And from the days of John the Baptist until

---

prophecy of eschatological strife.   **10:38** *Taketh . . . his cross*: in the ancient Mediterranean world the renunciation of family urged by Jesus would have amounted to self-denial so radical that he plausibly compares it to public execution, though persecution and martyrdom are also implied (cf. vv. 17–20).   **10:40** *He that receiveth you receiveth me*: in light of the risen Jesus' promised presence with his followers in their missionary activity (28:18–20), this statement may not be merely metaphorical. Compare Paul's equation of the community of believers with the risen Christ's body in 1 Cor 6:12–20; 12:12–31; etc. The verse has a parallel at John 13:20.   **10:42** *Little ones*: the disciples, who are little in the sense of having no obvious importance.

11:2–12:50 Opposition intensifies. As Jesus openly aligns himself with John the Baptist (11:2–19), adopting and expanding the prophet's urgent demands for repentance (11:20–30; cf. 3:7–12), the Pharisees' opposition to Jesus' ministry intensifies (see esp. 12:14) and his warnings to them in turn become more dire (12:1–45). The section ends with a disturbingly severe Jesus refusing even to acknowledge his family, instead insisting that shared obedience to God constitutes the only legitimate basis for loyalty (12:46–50).   **11:2–19** Jesus and John. Compare Luke 7:18–35; 16:16.   **11:2** *Sent two of*: better "sent word by" (MS tradition; NRSV).   **11:5** *The blind . . . them*: recapitulating the miracles and preaching described in chaps. 8–9 and evoking Isaianic oracles such as Isa 26:19; 29:18–19; 35:5–6; 61:1.   **11:10** *Behold, I . . . thee*: Mal 3:1.

now the kingdom of heaven suffereth violence, and the violent take it by force. [13]For all the prophets and the law prophesied until John. [14]And if ye will receive it, this is Elias, which was for to come. [15]He that hath ears to hear, let him hear.

[16]But whereunto shall I liken this generation? It is like unto children sitting in the markets, and calling unto their fellows, [17]and saying, We have piped unto you, and ye have not danced; we have mourned unto you, and ye have not lamented. [18]For John came neither eating nor drinking, and they say, He hath a devil. [19]The Son of man came eating and drinking, and they say, Behold a man gluttonous, and a winebibber, a friend of publicans and sinners. But wisdom is justified of her children.

[20]Then began he to upbraid the cities wherein most of his mighty works were done, because they repented not: [21]Woe unto thee, Chorazin! woe unto thee, Bethsaida! for if the mighty works, which were done in you, had been done in Tyre and Sidon, they would have repented long ago in sackcloth and ashes. [22]But I say unto you, It shall be more tolerable for Tyre and Sidon at the day of judgment, than for you. [23]And thou, Capernaum, which art exalted unto heaven, shalt be brought down to hell: for if the mighty works, which have been done in thee, had been done in Sodom, it would have remained until this day. [24]But I say unto you, That it shall be more tolerable for the land of Sodom in the day of judgment, than for thee.

[25]At that time Jesus answered and said, I thank thee, O Father, Lord of heaven and earth, because thou hast hid these things from the wise and prudent, and hast revealed them unto babes. [26]Even so, Father: for so it seemed good in thy sight. [27]All things are delivered unto me of my Father: and no man knoweth the Son, but the Father; neither knoweth any man the Father, save the Son, and he to whomsoever the Son will reveal him.

11:12 *The kingdom . . . force*: sometimes taken to mean that the kingdom is stormed by those zealous to enter it, but the negative interpretation is better: those identified with God's kingdom suffer persecution and other eschatological violence (cf. 10:16–36).   **11:14** *This is Elias*: identifying John as a second Elijah, whom Mal 4:5–6 links with the messenger and eschatological forerunner of Mal 3:1 (quoted in v. 10).   **11:16** *Like unto children*: possibly comparing John's and Jesus' ministries to a game of make-believe, with the people sulking like children refusing to join in. Alternatively, the simile may imply that the people behave like children by capriciously demanding the opposite of what John and Jesus offer: when John is somber, they condemn him for refusing celebration; when Jesus celebrates, they condemn him for refusing austerity.   **11:19** *Wisdom is . . . children*: the Bible commonly figures wisdom as a female (e.g., Prov 1:20–23), but a better reading of the MS tradition resists maternalizing her here, substituting "actions" for "children."   **11:20–24** Complaint against unrepentant cities. Compare Luke 10:12–15.   **11:21** *Woe unto thee . . . ashes*: *Chorazin* and *Bethsaida*, two Jewish cities in or near Galilee, are set against *Tyre* and *Sidon*, Gentile cities in Phoenicia that were often assailed by OT prophets (e.g., Isa 23; Ezek 28). *Sackcloth and ashes* signal mourning and repentance.   **11:23** *And thou . . . hell*: a better reading of the MS tradition preserves a more vivid rebuke: "And you, Capernaum, will you be exalted to heaven? You shall descend to hell!" (cf. Isa 14:12–15). *Hell* (also at 16:18) is Gk. *hadēs* (Hades), originally the name of the Greek god of the underworld, and often used in LXX to translate Heb. *She'ol*.   **11:25–30** Thanksgiving and invitation. Compare Luke 10:21–22.   **11:25** *Babes*: see 10:42 note.   **11:27** *No man . . . him*: compare the scriptural tradition that God and wisdom share exclusive knowledge of one another (e.g., Job 28:12–27; Wis 9:9–18). The mutual knowledge of God and Moses may also be relevant (cf. Exod 33:12–13).

²⁸Come unto me, all ye that labour and are heavy laden, and I will give you rest. ²⁹Take my yoke upon you, and learn of me; for I am meek and lowly in heart: and ye shall find rest unto your souls. ³⁰For my yoke is easy, and my burden is light.

12 At that time Jesus went on the sabbath day through the corn; and his disciples were an hungred, and began to pluck the ears of corn, and to eat. ²But when the Pharisees saw it, they said unto him, Behold, thy disciples do that which is not lawful to do upon the sabbath day. ³But he said unto them, Have ye not read what David did, when he was an hungred, and they that were with him; ⁴how he entered into the house of God, and did eat the shewbread, which was not lawful for him to eat, neither for them which were with him, but only for the priests? ⁵Or have ye not read in the law, how that on the sabbath days the priests in the temple profane the sabbath, and are blameless? ⁶But I say unto you, That in this place is one greater than the temple. ⁷But if ye had known what this meaneth, I will have mercy, and not sacrifice, ye would not have condemned the guiltless. ⁸For the Son of man is Lord even of the sabbath day.

⁹And when he was departed thence, he went into their synagogue: ¹⁰and, behold, there was a man which had his hand withered. And they asked him, saying, Is it lawful to heal on the sabbath days? that they might accuse him. ¹¹And he said unto them, What man shall there be among you, that shall have one sheep, and if it fall into a pit on the sabbath day, will he not lay hold on it, and lift it out? ¹²How much then is a man better than a sheep? Wherefore it is lawful to do well on the sabbath days. ¹³Then saith he to the man, Stretch forth thine hand. And he stretched it forth; and it was restored whole, like as the other. ¹⁴Then the Pharisees went out, and held a council against him, how they might destroy him.

¹⁵But when Jesus knew it, he withdrew himself from thence: and great multitudes followed him, and he healed them all; ¹⁶and charged them that they should not make him known: ¹⁷that it might be fulfilled which was spoken by Esaias the prophet, saying, ¹⁸Behold my servant, whom I have chosen; my beloved, in whom my soul is well pleased: I will put my spirit upon him, and he shall shew judgment to the Gentiles. ¹⁹He shall not strive, nor cry; neither shall any man hear his voice in the streets. ²⁰A bruised reed shall he not break, and smoking flax shall he not quench, till he send forth judgment unto victory. ²¹And in his name shall the Gentiles trust.

11:28–30 *Come unto . . . light:* cf. Sir 6:23–31; 51:18–30, where the yoke of wisdom is attractive, easy, and restful. **11:29** *Ye shall . . . souls:* quoting Jer 6:16. **11:30** *My burden is light:* perhaps in implicit contrast to the scribes and Pharisees' burdens (cf. 23:4). **12:1–14** Sabbath disputes. Compare Mark 2:23–3:6 and notes; Luke 6:1–11; 14:5. Matthew's omission of Mark 2:27, combined with his insistence that the disciples are innocent of breaking Sabbath regulations (v. 7), suggests that his community still kept the Sabbath. (See also 24:20 note.) **12:1** *Corn:* wheat. **12:2** *Not lawful . . . day:* cf. Exod 20:8–11. **12:3–4** *What David . . . shewbread:* see 1 Sam 21:1–6. **12:4** *Not lawful . . . priests:* cf. Lev 24:5–9. **12:5** *How that . . . blameless:* in Num 28:9–10, priests in effect work on the Sabbath. **12:7** *I will . . . sacrifice:* Hos 6:6; cf. Matt 9:13. **12:15–21** Healing multitudes. Compare Mark 3:7–12; Luke 6:17–19. In 8:16–17 Matthew also appends a quote from an Isaianic Servant Song to a summary of Jesus' healings. **12:18–21** *Behold my . . . trust:*

²²Then was brought unto him one possessed with a devil, blind, and dumb: and he healed him, insomuch that the blind and dumb both spake and saw. ²³And all the people were amazed, and said, Is not this the son of David? ²⁴But when the Pharisees heard it, they said, This fellow doth not cast out devils, but by Beelzebub the prince of the devils.

²⁵And Jesus knew their thoughts, and said unto them, Every kingdom divided against itself is brought to desolation; and every city or house divided against itself shall not stand: ²⁶and if Satan cast out Satan, he is divided against himself; how shall then his kingdom stand? ²⁷And if I by Beelzebub cast out devils, by whom do your children cast them out? therefore they shall be your judges. ²⁸But if I cast out devils by the Spirit of God, then the kingdom of God is come unto you. ²⁹Or else how can one enter into a strong man's house, and spoil his goods, except he first bind the strong man? and then he will spoil his house. ³⁰He that is not with me is against me; and he that gathereth not with me scattereth abroad.

³¹Wherefore I say unto you, All manner of sin and blasphemy shall be forgiven unto me: but the blasphemy against the Holy Ghost shall not be forgiven unto men. ³²And whosoever speaketh a word against the Son of man, it shall be forgiven him: but whosoever speaketh against the Holy Ghost, it shall not be forgiven him, neither in this world, neither in the world to come. ³³Either make the tree good, and his fruit good; or else make the tree corrupt, and his fruit corrupt: for the tree is known by his fruit. ³⁴O generation of vipers, how can ye, being evil, speak good things? for out of the abundance of the heart the mouth speaketh. ³⁵A good man out of the good treasure of the heart bringeth forth good things: and an evil man out of the evil treasure bringeth forth evil things. ³⁶But I say unto you, That every idle word that men shall speak, they shall give account thereof in the day of judgment. ³⁷For by thy words thou shalt be justified, and by thy words thou shalt be condemned.

³⁸Then certain of the scribes and of the Pharisees answered, saying, Master, we would see a sign from thee. ³⁹But he answered and said unto them, An evil and adulterous generation seeketh after a sign; and there shall no sign be given to it, but the sign of the prophet Jonas: ⁴⁰for as Jonas was three days and three nights in the whale's belly; so shall the Son of man be three days and three nights in the heart of the earth. ⁴¹The men of Nineveh shall rise in judgment with this genera-

---

LXX Isa 42:1–4, with the prophecy's focus on Gentiles anticipating 28:19–20. **12:22–37** The Beelzebub controversy. Compare Mark 3:19b–30 (with no exorcism reported) and notes; Luke 11:14–23; 12:10; 6:43–45. **12:24** *Beelzebub*: see Mark 3:22 note. **12:27** *Your children*: Pharisees and their supporters. **12:29** *Spoil*: plunder. **12:30** *He that . . . against me*: contrast Mark 9:40 (cf. Luke 9:50). **12:31** *Ghost*: Gk. *pneuma* (also vv. 28 [KJV "Spirit"] and 32), suggesting that the Pharisees are guilty of such blasphemy in attributing the Holy Spirit's activity to Beelzebul. **12:32** *World*: better "age" (Gk. *aiōn*), with the eschatological consummation in view (so frequently). **12:33** *The tree . . . by his fruit*: cf. 7:17; Sir 27:6. This and v. 34 recall John the Baptist's condemnation of the Pharisees and Sadducees at 3:7–8. **12:34** *Generation of vipers*: see 3:7 note. **12:35** *Of the heart*: better omitted (MS tradition). **12:38–42** Seeking signs. Mark 8:11–12 totally rejects the seeking of signs (see notes); Luke's Jesus (11:29–32) agrees with Matthew's in presenting the sign of Jonah. **12:39** *An evil and adulterous generation*: Jesus associates the scribes and Pharisees with the generation of Israelites that wandered in the wilderness (cf. Num 32:13; Deut 1:35). *Adulterous*: unfaithful to God; a dominant image in the OT prophets (e.g., Hos 2). **12:40** *Three days . . . belly*: see Jonah 1:17. **12:41** *Nineveh*: the Assyrian city to which Jonah was sent (Jonah 1:1–2).

tion, and shall condemn it: because they repented at the preaching of Jonas; and, behold, a greater than Jonas is here. [42]The queen of the south shall rise up in the judgment with this generation, and shall condemn it: for she came from the uttermost parts of the earth to hear the wisdom of Solomon; and, behold, a greater than Solomon is here.

[43]When the unclean spirit is gone out of a man, he walketh through dry places, seeking rest, and findeth none. [44]Then he saith, I will return into my house from whence I came out; and when he is come, he findeth it empty, swept, and garnished. [45]Then goeth he, and taketh with himself seven other spirits more wicked than himself, and they enter in and dwell there: and the last state of that man is worse than the first. Even so shall it be also unto this wicked generation.

[46]While he yet talked to the people, behold, his mother and his brethren stood without, desiring to speak with him. [47]Then one said unto him, Behold, thy mother and thy brethren stand without, desiring to speak with thee. [48]But he answered and said unto him that told him, Who is my mother? and who are my brethren? [49]And he stretched forth his hand toward his disciples, and said, Behold my mother and my brethren! [50]For whosoever shall do the will of my Father which is in heaven, the same is my brother, and sister, and mother.

13 The same day went Jesus out of the house, and sat by the sea side. [2]And great multitudes were gathered together unto him, so that he went into a ship, and sat; and the whole multitude stood on the shore. [3]And he spake many things unto them in parables, saying, Behold, a sower went forth to sow; [4]and when he sowed, some seeds fell by the way side, and the fowls came and devoured them up: [5]some fell upon stony places, where they had not much earth: and forthwith they sprung up, because they had no deepness of earth: [6]and when the sun was up, they were scorched; and because they had no root, they withered away. [7]And some fell among thorns; and the thorns sprung up, and choked them: [8]but other fell into good ground, and brought forth fruit, some an hundredfold, some sixtyfold, some thirtyfold. [9]Who hath ears to hear, let him hear.

They repented: Jonah 3:5; see Matt 11:21 for references to other Gentile cities that repent. **12:42** *Queen of the south*: the Queen of Sheba, who traveled from Arabia to question Solomon (1 Kgs 10:1–13). **12:43–45** The unclean spirit's return. Compare Luke 11:24–26. **12:43** *Dry places*: presuming an aversion to water, which would explain demons' residence in the desert wilderness (cf. 4:1) and perhaps Jesus' drowning of them in 8:32. **12:44** *Garnished*: put in order or decorated. **12:45** *Last state . . . first*: cf. 2 Pet 2:20. *This wicked generation*: see v. 39 and note. **12:46–50** Jesus' true relatives. Compare Mark 3:31–35; Luke 8:19–21. Jesus himself demonstrates the rejection of mundane loyalties he demands from his followers: his contempt for his family recalls his earlier claim to initiate familial strife (10:34–37), his refusal to allow a would-be disciple to bury his father (8:21–22), and James and John's abandonment of their father in order to follow Jesus (4:21–22). **13:1–13:53 Parables.** This section constitutes Jesus' third extended discourse, a collection of parables divided into three triads: vv. 1–23, 24–43, 44–52. A parable and its interpretation bracket the first two: the parable of the Sower (vv. 1–9) and its interpretation (vv. 18–23); the parable of the Weeds (vv. 24–30) and its interpretation (vv. 36–43). The third triad is also bracketed, beginning with the parable of the Treasure (v. 44) and ending with a discussion that explicitly likens Jesus' parabolic teaching to treasure (v. 52). **13:1–9** Parable of the Sower. Compare Mark 4:1–9 and notes; Luke 8:4-8. **13:1** *Went Jesus . . . house*: 12:46 assumes Jesus is indoors. *Sat*: see 5:1 note. **13:3** *Went forth*: Gk. *exēlthen*, as in v. 1 ("went Jesus out"), implicitly equating the sower with Jesus and his

[10]And the disciples came, and said unto him, Why speakest thou unto them in parables? [11]He answered and said unto them, Because it is given unto you to know the mysteries of the kingdom of heaven, but to them it is not given. [12]For whosoever hath, to him shall be given, and he shall have more abundance: but whosoever hath not, from him shall be taken away even that he hath. [13]Therefore speak I to them in parables: because they seeing see not; and hearing they hear not, neither do they understand. [14]And in them is fulfilled the prophecy of Esaias, which saith, By hearing ye shall hear, and shall not understand; and seeing ye shall see, and shall not perceive: [15]for this people's heart is waxed gross, and their ears are dull of hearing, and their eyes they have closed; lest at any time they should see with their eyes, and hear with their ears, and should understand with their heart, and should be converted, and I should heal them. [16]But blessed are your eyes, for they see: and your ears, for they hear. [17]For verily I say unto you, That many prophets and righteous men have desired to see those things which ye see, and have not seen them; and to hear those things which ye hear, and have not heard them.

[18]Hear ye therefore the parable of the sower. [19]When any one heareth the word of the kingdom, and understandeth it not, then cometh the wicked one, and catcheth away that which was sown in his heart. This is he which received seed by the way side. [20]But he that received the seed into stony places, the same is he that heareth the word, and anon with joy receiveth it; [21]yet hath he not root in himself, but dureth for a while: for when tribulation or persecution ariseth because of the word, by and by he is offended. [22]He also that received seed among the thorns is he that heareth the word; and the care of this world, and the deceitfulness of riches, choke the word, and he becometh unfruitful. [23]But he that received seed into the good ground is he that heareth the word, and understandeth it; which also beareth fruit, and bringeth forth, some an hundredfold, some sixty, some thirty.

[24]Another parable put he forth unto them, saying, The kingdom of heaven is likened unto a man which sowed good seed in his field: [25]but while men slept, his enemy came and sowed tares among the wheat, and went his way. [26]But when the blade was sprung up, and brought forth fruit, then appeared the tares also. [27]So the servants of the householder came and said unto him, Sir, didst not thou sow

---

sowing with Jesus' teaching. **13:10-17** Reason for parables. Compare Mark 4:10-12, 25 and notes; Luke 8:9-10, 18; 10:23-24; John 12:39-41. **13:13** *Because*: Gk. *hoti*, in contrast to Mark's *hina*, "in order that" (KJV "that," 4:12). Mark's Jesus tells parables as obscure mysteries that confuse his listeners and prevent them from repenting; Matthew construes Jesus' parables as a response to his listeners' obstinacy—perhaps to keep from them the truth they seem prone to reject (cf. 7:6) but more likely, in light of vv. 34-35, as a final attempt to deliver his message in a way they might recognize. **13:14-15** *By hearing . . . them*: Isa 6:9-10. **13:15** *Waxed gross*: grown fat, connoting obtuseness. *Be converted*: lit. "turn back" or "turn around." **13:17** *Many prophets . . . heard them*: a commonplace in ancient Jewish and Christian literature (cf. Eph 3:4-5; Heb 11:13; 1 Pet 1:10). **13:18-23** Interpretation of the parable of the Sower. Compare Mark 4:13-20 and notes; Luke 8:11-15. **13:19** *The word of the kingdom*: preaching about the kingdom of God. *The wicked one*: Satan. *This is he which received seed*: lit. "this is the one sown," referring to the seed rather than to the ground on which it falls (also in vv. 20, 22, 23). KJV's mistranslation clarifies the inconsistent allegory: while the earlier part of v. 19 assumes the seed's equation with the one hearing the word, the latter part assimilates it to the word itself. (The grammar of the Greek prevents "this" from referring to the sown seed.) **13:20** *Anon*: at once. **13:21** *Dureth*: endures. **13:24-30** Parable of the Weeds.

good seed in thy field? from whence then hath it tares? ²⁸He said unto them, An enemy hath done this. The servants said unto him, Wilt thou then that we go and gather them up? ²⁹But he said, Nay; lest while ye gather up the tares, ye root up also the wheat with them. ³⁰Let both grow together until the harvest: and in the time of harvest I will say to the reapers, Gather ye together first the tares, and bind them in bundles to burn them: but gather the wheat into my barn.

³¹Another parable put he forth unto them, saying, The kingdom of heaven is like to a grain of mustard seed, which a man took, and sowed in his field: ³²which indeed is the least of all seeds: but when it is grown, it is the greatest among herbs, and becometh a tree, so that the birds of the air come and lodge in the branches thereof.

³³Another parable spake he unto them; The kingdom of heaven is like unto leaven, which a woman took, and hid in three measures of meal, till the whole was leavened.

³⁴All these things spake Jesus unto the multitude in parables; and without a parable spake he not unto them: ³⁵that it might be fulfilled which was spoken by the prophet, saying, I will open my mouth in parables; I will utter things which have been kept secret from the foundation of the world.

³⁶Then Jesus sent the multitude away, and went into the house: and his disciples came unto him, saying, Declare unto us the parable of the tares of the field. ³⁷He answered and said unto them, He that soweth the good seed is the Son of man; ³⁸the field is the world; the good seed are the children of the kingdom; but the tares are the children of the wicked one; ³⁹the enemy that sowed them is the devil; the harvest is the end of the world; and the reapers are the angels. ⁴⁰As therefore the tares are gathered and burned in the fire; so shall it be in the end of this world. ⁴¹The Son of man shall send forth his angels, and they shall gather out of his kingdom all things that offend, and them which do iniquity; ⁴²and shall cast them into a furnace of fire: there shall be wailing and gnashing of teeth. ⁴³Then shall the righteous shine forth as the sun in the kingdom of their Father. Who hath ears to hear, let him hear.

13:31–33 Parables of Mustard Seed and Yeast. Compare Mark 4:30–32 (without the second parable) and notes; Luke 13:18–21. Both parables liken the kingdom of heaven to inexorable growth.   13:33 *Like unto leaven*: since leaven has negative associations (see Mark 8:15 note), this parable, like the previous one, makes a scandalous comparison (see Mark 4:32 note). *Three measures of meal*: flour enough for an enormous amount of bread (perhaps alluding to the eschatological banquet; see 8:11 note).   13:34–35 Jesus' use of parables. Compare Mark 4:33–34.   13:35 *I will open . . . world*: Ps 78:2, whose inscription attributes it to Asaph (a prophet, according to 2 Chr 29:30).   13:36–43 Interpretation of the parable of the Weeds. This passage was important for early Christian debates about ecclesiology, with some theologians (such as Augustine) seeing in it an image of the church as a combination of both good people and bad. God (rather than ecclesiastical authorities) would sort them out at the final judgment.   13:36 *Declare*: explain.   13:39 *World*: "age" (also v. 49; see 12:32 note); a different Greek word is used in v. 38. In 9:37 Jesus calls his disciples harvesters, perhaps suggesting that he understands the final judgment already to have begun.   13:41 *His kingdom*: the Son of Man claims the world (v. 38) for his eschatological kingdom; cf. Rev 11:15.   13:42 *Cast them . . . fire*: quoting Dan 3:6 (also in v. 50), where Israelites refusing to worship the idolatrous image are threatened with the same punishment.   13:43 *Then shall . . . sun*: an allusion to the eschatological resurrection; cf. Dan 12:2–3.   13:44–50 Parables of the Treasure, Pearl, and Net.

⁴⁴Again, the kingdom of heaven is like unto treasure hid in a field; the which when a man hath found, he hideth, and for joy thereof goeth and selleth all that he hath, and buyeth that field.

⁴⁵Again, the kingdom of heaven is like unto a merchant man, seeking goodly pearls: ⁴⁶who, when he had found one pearl of great price, went and sold all that he had, and bought it.

⁴⁷Again, the kingdom of heaven is like unto a net, that was cast into the sea, and gathered of every kind: ⁴⁸which, when it was full, they drew to shore, and sat down, and gathered the good into vessels, but cast the bad away. ⁴⁹So shall it be at the end of the world: the angels shall come forth, and sever the wicked from among the just, ⁵⁰and shall cast them into the furnace of fire: there shall be wailing and gnashing of teeth.

⁵¹Jesus saith unto them, Have ye understood all these things? They say unto him, Yea, Lord. ⁵²Then said he unto them, Therefore every scribe which is instructed unto the kingdom of heaven is like unto a man that is an householder, which bringeth forth out of his treasure things new and old.

⁵³And it came to pass, that when Jesus had finished these parables, he departed thence.

⁵⁴And when he was come into his own country, he taught them in their synagogue, insomuch that they were astonished, and said, Whence hath this man this wisdom, and these mighty works? ⁵⁵Is not this the carpenter's son? is not his mother called Mary? and his brethren, James, and Joses, and Simon, and Judas? ⁵⁶And his sisters, are they not all with us? Whence then hath this man all these things? ⁵⁷And they were offended in him. But Jesus said unto them, A prophet is not without honour, save in his own country, and in his own house. ⁵⁸And he did not many mighty works there because of their unbelief.

14 At that time Herod the tetrarch heard of the fame of Jesus, ²and said unto his servants, This is John the Baptist; he is risen from the dead; and there-

---

13:44 *Treasure*: observing that the word reappears in v. 52, the ancient Christian scholar Origen cannily read this verse's parable in light of the later passage, connecting the *field* with Scripture and the *treasure* with its hidden meaning (*Commentary on Matthew* 10.5–6, cf. 14–15).   **13:47** *Gathered of every kind*: cf. Ezek 47:9–10.   **13:48** *Gathered . . . away*: perhaps presuming a distinction between clean and unclean fish (cf. Lev 11:9–12).   **13:51–53** Treasures new and old. Some see in this image a self-portrait of this gospel's author.   **13:51** *Lord*: better omitted (MS tradition).   **13:52** *Is instructed unto*: better "has become a disciple to" (MS tradition). *Bringeth forth . . . old*: in *Jubilees* 45.15 Isaac gives his father's books to Levi so that he may "preserve them and renew them." Rabbinic texts also present scribes as at once hermeneutically innovative and conservative.

13:54–17:27 Ominous escalations. Jesus' rejection in his hometown (13:54–58), juxtaposed to the execution of his ally John the Baptist (14:1–12), signals a crucial shift. While he can still command great crowds, opposition to his ministry in Galilee becomes more hostile. Consequently we find Jesus venturing out of Judea and into Gentile territory (15:21–39), speaking openly of his expectation that he and his followers will die (16:21, 24–26; 17:22–23), and addressing the issue of his community's relationship to political authorities (17:24–27).   **13:54–58** Rejection in Nazareth. Compare Mark 6:1–6 and notes; Luke 4:16–30; John 7:3–5, 15; 6:42; 4:44. This episode both serves as an introduction to the section and recalls Jesus' rejection of his family in 12:46–50. Jesus' parable discourse (13:1–53) therefore finds itself bracketed between complementary notices of rejection.   **13:55** *Joses*: better "Joseph" (MS tradition); contrast Mark 6:3.   **13:58** *And he . . . there*: Matthew alters Mark 6:5 to remove any hint that Jesus' power is limited.   **14:1–12** Death of John the Baptist. Compare Mark 6:14–29 and notes; Luke 9:7–9; 3:19–20.   **14:1** *Herod the tetrarch*: see Mark 6:14 note.

fore mighty works do shew forth themselves in him. [3]For Herod had laid hold on John, and bound him, and put him in prison for Herodias' sake, his brother Philip's wife. [4]For John said unto him, It is not lawful for thee to have her. [5]And when he would have put him to death, he feared the multitude, because they counted him as a prophet. [6]But when Herod's birthday was kept, the daughter of Herodias danced before them, and pleased Herod. [7]Whereupon he promised with an oath to give her whatsoever she would ask. [8]And she, being before instructed of her mother, said, Give me here John Baptist's head in a charger. [9]And the king was sorry: nevertheless for the oath's sake, and them which sat with him at meat, he commanded it to be given her. [10]And he sent, and beheaded John in the prison. [11]And his head was brought in a charger, and given to the damsel: and she brought it to her mother. [12]And his disciples came, and took up the body, and buried it, and went and told Jesus.

[13]When Jesus heard of it, he departed thence by ship into a desert place apart: and when the people had heard thereof, they followed him on foot out of the cities. [14]And Jesus went forth, and saw a great multitude, and was moved with compassion toward them, and he healed their sick. [15]And when it was evening, his disciples came to him, saying, This is a desert place, and the time is now past; send the multitude away, that they may go into the villages, and buy themselves victuals. [16]But Jesus said unto them, They need not depart; give ye them to eat. [17]And they say unto him, We have here but five loaves, and two fishes. [18]He said, Bring them hither to me. [19]And he commanded the multitude to sit down on the grass, and took the five loaves, and the two fishes, and looking up to heaven, he blessed, and brake, and gave the loaves to his disciples, and the disciples to the multitude. [20]And they did all eat, and were filled: and they took up of the fragments that remained twelve baskets full. [21]And they that had eaten were about five thousand men, beside women and children.

[22]And straightway Jesus constrained his disciples to get into a ship, and to go before him unto the other side, while he sent the multitudes away. [23]And when he had sent the multitudes away, he went up into a mountain apart to pray: and when the evening was come, he was there alone. [24]But the ship was now in the midst of the sea, tossed with waves: for the wind was contrary. [25]And in the fourth watch of the night Jesus went unto them, walking on the sea. [26]And when the disciples saw him walking on the sea, they were troubled, saying, It is a spirit; and they cried out for fear. [27]But straightway Jesus spake unto them, saying, Be of good cheer; it is I; be not afraid. [28]And Peter answered him and said, Lord, if it be thou,

---

14:8 *Charger:* platter.　**14:12** *Body:* better "corpse" (MS tradition).　**14:13–21** Feeding five thousand. Compare Mark 6:30–44 and notes; Luke 9:10–17; John 6:1–13.　**14:22–33** Walking on water. Compare Mark 6:45–52 and notes; John 6:15–21. Matthew revises Mark radically, eliminating Mark's mysterious insistence that Jesus meant to pass the disciples by (6:48) and supplementing his presentation of their fearful and stubborn ignorance (6:49–52). In Matthew, Peter takes steps of faith that culminate in the disciples' worship of Jesus as God's son.　**14:22** *Jesus constrained:* better "he constrained" (MS tradition). Because Jesus is not specified as the subject until v. 27 at the earliest (see note), the reader is drawn into the disciples' confusion.　**14:25** *Jesus went unto them:* better "he went to them" (MS tradition).　**14:27** *Jesus spake:* some MSS do not specify Jesus as the subject of this verb, prolonging the story's disorientation.　**14:28–31** *Peter answered . . . doubt:* while stories of miraculous strolls over water are ubiquitous in antiquity, a Pāli Buddhist text (*Jātaka* 190)

bid me come unto thee on the water. [29]And he said, Come. And when Peter was come down out of the ship, he walked on the water, to go to Jesus. [30]But when he saw the wind boisterous, he was afraid; and beginning to sink, he cried, saying, Lord, save me. [31]And immediately Jesus stretched forth his hand, and caught him, and said unto him, O thou of little faith, wherefore didst thou doubt? [32]And when they were come into the ship, the wind ceased. [33]Then they that were in the ship came and worshipped him, saying, Of a truth thou art the Son of God.

[34]And when they were gone over, they came into the land of Gennesaret. [35]And when the men of that place had knowledge of him, they sent out into all that country round about, and brought unto him all that were diseased; [36]and besought him that they might only touch the hem of his garment: and as many as touched were made perfectly whole.

15 Then came to Jesus scribes and Pharisees, which were of Jerusalem, saying, [2]Why do thy disciples transgress the tradition of the elders? for they wash not their hands when they eat bread. [3]But he answered and said unto them, Why do ye also transgress the commandment of God by your tradition? [4]For God commanded, saying, Honour thy father and mother: and, He that curseth father or mother, let him die the death. [5]But ye say, Whosoever shall say to his father or his mother, It is a gift, by whatsoever thou mightest be profited by me; [6]and honour not his father or his mother, he shall be free. Thus have ye made the commandment of God of none effect by your tradition. [7]Ye hypocrites, well did Esaias prophesy of you, saying, [8]This people draweth nigh unto me with their mouth, and honoureth me with their lips; but their heart is far from me. [9]But in vain they do worship me, teaching for doctrines the commandments of men.

---

offers an exceptionally close parallel: a disciple meditating ecstatically on the Buddha walks over a river; halfway across he notices the waves and begins to sink, but then recovers his concentration and continues the trek.   **14:30–31** *Lord, save . . . faith*: cf. 8:25–26; some see an allusion to Ps 18:15–16.   **14:34–36** Healings at Gennesaret. Compare Mark 6:53–56.   **14:34** *Gennesaret*: a plain northwest of the Sea of Galilee.   **14:36** *Only touch . . . garment*: see Mark 5:27 and note. *Were made perfectly whole*: Gk. *diesōthēsan*, containing the same root as "save me" (*sōson*) in v. 30. **15:1–20** Defilement. Compare Mark 7:1–23 and notes. This episode likely reflects Matthew's concerns in writing for a Jewish community believing in Jesus and engaged in debates with proto-rabbinic Jews about the need to maintain ritual purity (cf. chap. 23, esp. vv. 1–8 and notes): Matthew eliminates Mark's description of Jewish customs (7:1–4), probably because his audience was familiar with them, as well as Mark's claim that Jesus declared all foods clean (see 7:19 note), presumably because he did not believe that Jesus overturned biblical dietary regulations.   **15:2** *Traditions of the elders*: oral teachings circulated by the Pharisees. Their authority was in dispute until sometime after the temple's destruction in 70 C.E., when rabbinic Judaism (an evolutionary descendent of the Pharisaic sect) became dominant and collected them in the Mishnah. The Pharisaic tradition apparently expanded to all of Israel biblical legislation directed specifically at priests (cf. Exod 30:17–21), the implication being that every Jew stands in the place of a priest and every home is a temple. Such expansive interpretation of OT law resembles Jesus' hermeneutic in 5:17–48 and may have influenced it.   **15:3** *Why do . . . tradition*: Jesus insists that the Pharisees' interpretation of biblical law actually leads to its violation.   **15:4** *Honour thy father . . . death*: cf. Exod 20:12; 21:17; Deut 5:16.   **15:5** *Gift*: referring to the practice of setting apart one's property for an offering to God. **15:6** *Or his mother*: better omitted (MS tradition). *He shall be free*: absent in the Greek; vv. 5–6 might be better rendered "But as you have it, whoever tells his father or his mother 'What you would have profited from me is devoted to God' shall never honor his father."   **15:8–9** *This people . . . men*: Isa 29:13. *Draweth nigh . . . and* is better omitted (MS tradition) as a scribal assimilation

¹⁰And he called the multitude, and said unto them, Hear, and understand: ¹¹Not that which goeth into the mouth defileth a man; but that which cometh out of the mouth, this defileth a man. ¹²Then came his disciples, and said unto him, Knowest thou that the Pharisees were offended, after they heard this saying? ¹³But he answered and said, Every plant, which my heavenly Father hath not planted, shall be rooted up. ¹⁴Let them alone: they be blind leaders of the blind. And if the blind lead the blind, both shall fall into the ditch. ¹⁵Then answered Peter and said unto him, Declare unto us this parable. ¹⁶And Jesus said, Are ye also yet without understanding? ¹⁷Do not ye yet understand, that whatsoever entereth in at the mouth goeth into the belly, and is cast out into the draught? ¹⁸But those things which proceed out of the mouth come forth from the heart; and they defile the man. ¹⁹For out of the heart proceed evil thoughts, murders, adulteries, fornications, thefts, false witness, blasphemies: ²⁰these are the things which defile a man: but to eat with unwashen hands defileth not a man.

²¹Then Jesus went thence, and departed into the coasts of Tyre and Sidon. ²²And, behold, a woman of Canaan came out of the same coasts, and cried unto him, saying, Have mercy on me, O Lord, thou Son of David; my daughter is grievously vexed with a devil. ²³But he answered her not a word. And his disciples came and besought him, saying, Send her away; for she crieth after us. ²⁴But he answered and said, I am not sent but unto the lost sheep of the house of Israel. ²⁵Then came she and worshipped him, saying, Lord, help me. ²⁶But he answered and said, It is not meet to take the children's bread, and to cast it to dogs. ²⁷And she said, Truth, Lord: yet the dogs eat of the crumbs which fall from their masters' table. ²⁸Then Jesus answered and said unto her, O woman, great is thy faith: be it unto thee even as thou wilt. And her daughter was made whole from that very hour.

²⁹And Jesus departed from thence, and came nigh unto the sea of Galilee; and went up into a mountain, and sat down there. ³⁰And great multitudes came unto him, having with them those that were lame, blind, dumb, maimed, and many others, and cast them down at Jesus' feet; and he healed them: ³¹insomuch that

---

of Jesus' words to the passage he quotes.   **15:11** *Not that . . . this defileth a man*: this sentiment seems to have been fairly widespread in the Greco-Roman world, even among some Jews; cf. Philo, *On the Special Laws* 3.209: "for the man who is unjust and impious is unclean in the proper sense."   **15:13** *Every plant . . . up*: recalling 13:29–30.   **15:15** *Declare*: explain.   **15:17** *Yet*: better omitted (MS tradition). *Draught*: latrine.   **15:21–28** Healing a Canaanite woman's daughter. Compare Mark 7:24–30 and notes.   **15:22** *Woman of Canaan*: Canaanites were the traditional enemies of Israel.   **15:23** *Send her away*: cf. 2 Kgs 4:27, Gehazi's rebuke of the Shunammite woman who wants Elisha to restore her ailing son.   **15:24** *I am . . . Israel*: cf. 10:5–6.   **15:26** *Cast it to dogs*: recalling 7:6. **15:29–31** Healing multitudes. Compare Mark 7:31–37, which focuses on the healing of a deaf-mute. *God of Israel* (v. 31) would be redundant, coming from Israelites; Jesus must still be in Gentile territory, with the reference to the Sea of Galilee (v. 29) specifying his location as the region of the Decapolis, on the sea's southeastern shore—precisely where Mark places Jesus during the parallel healing and second miraculous feeding. This admittedly does not make sense geographically, as Tyre and Sidon (cf. v. 21) were nowhere near the Decapolis. The confusion probably results from Mark's error about where the Decapolis was located (see Mark 7:31 note; Matthew's failure to identify the region as the Decapolis may constitute an attempt to smooth over Mark's geographical mistake). In any case, Jesus' encounter with the faithful Canaanite woman (vv. 21–28) has apparently prompted him to reconsider his previous ban on a Gentile mission (10:5–6; cf. 15:24).

the multitude wondered, when they saw the dumb to speak, the maimed to be whole, the lame to walk, and the blind to see: and they glorified the God of Israel.

³²Then Jesus called his disciples unto him, and said, I have compassion on the multitude, because they continue with me now three days, and have nothing to eat: and I will not send them away fasting, lest they faint in the way. ³³And his disciples say unto him, Whence should we have so much bread in the wilderness, as to fill so great a multitude? ³⁴And Jesus saith unto them, How many loaves have ye? And they said, Seven, and a few little fishes. ³⁵And he commanded the multitude to sit down on the ground. ³⁶And he took the seven loaves and the fishes, and gave thanks, and brake them, and gave to his disciples, and the disciples to the multitude. ³⁷And they did all eat, and were filled: and they took up of the broken meat that was left seven baskets full. ³⁸And they that did eat were four thousand men, beside women and children. ³⁹And he sent away the multitude, and took ship, and came into the coasts of Magdala.

16 The Pharisees also with the Sadducees came, and tempting desired him that he would shew them a sign from heaven. ²He answered and said unto them, When it is evening, ye say, It will be fair weather: for the sky is red. ³And in the morning, It will be foul weather to day: for the sky is red and lowring. O ye hypocrites, ye can discern the face of the sky; but can ye not discern the signs of the times? ⁴A wicked and adulterous generation seeketh after a sign; and there shall no sign be given unto it, but the sign of the prophet Jonas. And he left them, and departed.

⁵And when his disciples were come to the other side, they had forgotten to take bread. ⁶Then Jesus said unto them, Take heed and beware of the leaven of the Pharisees and of the Sadducees. ⁷And they reasoned among themselves, saying, It is because we have taken no bread. ⁸Which when Jesus perceived, he said unto them, O ye of little faith, why reason ye among yourselves, because ye have brought no bread? ⁹Do ye not yet understand, neither remember the five loaves of the five thousand, and how many baskets ye took up? ¹⁰Neither the seven loaves of the four thousand, and how many baskets ye took up? ¹¹How is it that ye do not understand that I spake it not to you concerning bread, that ye should beware of the leaven of the Pharisees and of the Sadducees? ¹²Then understood they how that he bade them not beware of the leaven of bread, but of the doctrine of the Pharisees and of the Sadducees.

15:31 *The dumb . . . see*: cf. Isa 35:5–6; this summary of Jesus' healing ministry recalls that of 11:5. **15:32–39** Feeding four thousand. Compare Mark 8:1–10 and notes. Like Mark, Matthew understands Jesus' second miraculous feeding to occur in Gentile territory. **15:39** *Magdala*: better "Magadan" (MS tradition). The place name is unknown, but like Dalmanutha in Mark 8:10 (also unknown), it signals Jesus' return to Jewish territory, for the Pharisees resurface. **16:1–4** Seeking signs. Compare Mark 8:11–13 and notes; Luke 11:16; 12:54–56; John 6:30. Matthew discussed the sign of Jonah earlier (12:38–42 and notes), where it seemed to figure his death and resurrection. In light of Jesus' recent ministry in Gentile territory, it should perhaps here be construed as a reference to the prophet's preaching in Nineveh (Jonah 3). **16:2–3** *When it . . . times*: probably better omitted (MS tradition). **16:5–12** Yeast of Pharisees and Sadducees. Compare Mark 8:14–21 and notes; Luke 12:1.

[13]When Jesus came into the coasts of Caesarea Philippi, he asked his disciples, saying, Whom do men say that I the Son of man am? [14]And they said, Some say that thou art John the Baptist: some, Elias; and others, Jeremias, or one of the prophets. [15]He saith unto them, But whom say ye that I am? [16]And Simon Peter answered and said, Thou art the Christ, the Son of the living God. [17]And Jesus answered and said unto him, Blessed art thou, Simon Bar-jona: for flesh and blood hath not revealed it unto thee, but my Father which is in heaven. [18]And I say also unto thee, That thou art Peter, and upon this rock I will build my church; and the gates of hell shall not prevail against it. [19]And I will give unto thee the keys of the kingdom of heaven: and whatsoever thou shalt bind on earth shall be bound in heaven: and whatsoever thou shalt loose on earth shall be loosed in heaven. [20]Then charged he his disciples that they should tell no man that he was Jesus the Christ.

[21]From that time forth began Jesus to shew unto his disciples, how that he must go unto Jerusalem, and suffer many things of the elders and chief priests and scribes, and be killed, and be raised again the third day. [22]Then Peter took him, and began to rebuke him, saying, Be it far from thee, Lord: this shall not be unto thee. [23]But he turned, and said unto Peter, Get thee behind me, Satan: thou art an offence unto me: for thou savourest not the things that be of God, but those that be of men.

[24]Then said Jesus unto his disciples, If any man will come after me, let him deny himself, and take up his cross, and follow me. [25]For whosoever will save his life shall lose it: and whosoever will lose his life for my sake shall find it. [26]For what is a man profited, if he shall gain the whole world, and lose his own soul? or what shall a man give in exchange for his soul? [27]For the Son of man shall come in the glory of his Father with his angels; and then he shall reward every man according to his works. [28]Verily I say unto you, There be some standing here, which shall not taste of death, till they see the Son of man coming in his kingdom.

16:13–23 Peter's confession and the first prediction of Jesus' death and resurrection. Compare Mark 8:27–33 and notes; Luke 9:18–22; John 6:67–71. This is an important passage in Roman Catholic theology, which sees in it Jesus' institution of the papacy.   16:13 *Caesarea Philippi*: a city about twenty-five miles north of the Sea of Galilee. *I the Son of man am*: better "the Son of man is" (MS tradition).   16:14 *Elias*: Elijah; cf. 11:14 and note.   16:17 *Bar-jona*: Gk. transliteration of the Aramaic for "Son of Jonah." *Flesh and . . . heaven*: by specifying that Peter's knowledge was divinely revealed, Matthew forecloses the possibility that his insight is demonic (cf. 8:29), a possibility Mark leaves open (see introduction to Mark).   16:18 *Thou art . . . church*: cf. Gen 17:1–8, where God renames Abram Abraham, "father of many nations," and where a new name likewise designates the founder of a new community. *Rock*: a wordplay on the Greek name Petros ("Rock"). *Church*: Gk. *ekklēsia*, lit. "assembly"; often used in LXX of the "congregation" or "assembly of Israel." Its sense in the NT is usually of a local (but sometimes global) community worshipping the risen Christ. Matthew is the only gospel to use the word (also at 18:17); the anachronism may suggest that vv. 18–19 originated as a prophetic oracle spoken by the risen Christ and attributed by the evangelist to the pre-risen Jesus.   16:19 *The keys . . . of heaven*: cf. Isa 22:22, where God uses similar language to vest Eliakim with authority over the royal household.   16:21 *The elders . . . scribes*: the Sanhedrin (see Mark 8:31 note).   16:23 *Get thee . . . Satan*: recalling the words Jesus speaks to the devil in 4:10. *Offence*: see Mark 4:17 note. *Savourest not*: do not consider.   16:24–28 Taking up the cross. Compare Mark 8:34–9:1 and notes; Luke 9:23–27. This is the second time that Matthew's Jesus speaks of carrying the cross in the context of following him (cf. 10:38–39).   16:26 *Soul*: rather "life" (Gk. *psychē*, as in v. 25).   16:27 *The Son . . . works*: cf. Dan 7:13.

17 And after six days Jesus taketh Peter, James, and John his brother, and bringeth them up into an high mountain apart, [2]and was transfigured before them: and his face did shine as the sun, and his raiment was white as the light. [3]And, behold, there appeared unto them Moses and Elias talking with him. [4]Then answered Peter, and said unto Jesus, Lord, it is good for us to be here: if thou wilt, let us make here three tabernacles; one for thee, and one for Moses, and one for Elias. [5]While he yet spake, behold, a bright cloud overshadowed them: and behold a voice out of the cloud, which said, This is my beloved Son, in whom I am well pleased; hear ye him. [6]And when the disciples heard it, they fell on their face, and were sore afraid. [7]And Jesus came and touched them, and said, Arise, and be not afraid. [8]And when they had lifted up their eyes, they saw no man, save Jesus only. [9]And as they came down from the mountain, Jesus charged them, saying, Tell the vision to no man, until the Son of man be risen again from the dead.

[10]And his disciples asked him, saying, Why then say the scribes that Elias must first come? [11]And Jesus answered and said unto them, Elias truly shall first come, and restore all things. [12]But I say unto you, That Elias is come already, and they knew him not, but have done unto him whatsoever they listed. Likewise shall also the Son of man suffer of them. [13]Then the disciples understood that he spake unto them of John the Baptist.

[14]And when they were come to the multitude, there came to him a certain man, kneeling down to him, and saying, [15]Lord, have mercy on my son: for he is lunatick, and sore vexed: for ofttimes he falleth into the fire, and oft into the water. [16]And I brought him to thy disciples, and they could not cure him. [17]Then Jesus answered and said, O faithless and perverse generation, how long shall I be with you? how long shall I suffer you? bring him hither to me. [18]And Jesus rebuked the devil; and he departed out of him: and the child was cured from that very hour. [19]Then came the disciples to Jesus apart, and said, Why could not we cast him out? [20]And Jesus said unto them, Because of your unbelief: for verily I say unto you, If ye have faith as a grain of mustard seed, ye shall say unto this mountain, Remove hence to yonder place; and it shall remove; and nothing shall be impossible unto you. [21]Howbeit this kind goeth not out but by prayer and fasting.

[22]And while they abode in Galilee, Jesus said unto them, The Son of man shall be betrayed into the hands of men: [23]and they shall kill him, and the third day he shall be raised again. And they were exceeding sorry.

17:1–9 Transfiguration. Compare Mark 9:2–10 and notes; Luke 9:28–36.   **17:2** *Face did shine*: clarifying Mark's latent parallel with Moses (Exod 34:29–35).   **17:4** *Let us make*: better "I will make" (MS tradition).   **17:5** *Hear ye him*: cf. Deut 18:15.   **17:10–13** Elijah's coming. Compare Mark 9:9–13 and notes.   **17:10–12** *Elias must . . . already*: cf. 11:14 and note.   **17:12** *Listed*: pleased   **17:14–21** Healing an epileptic boy. Compare Mark 9:14–29 and notes; Luke 9:37–43a; 17:6.   **17:15** *Lord, have mercy*: Gk. *kyrie, eleēson*, an ancient Christian liturgical phrase that became the first words of the mass; see also 20:30, 31. *Lunatick*: see 4:24 note.   **17:20** *Unbelief*: lit. "lack of faith," but "little faith" is better (MS tradition). *A grain . . . seed*: a figure of minuteness with potential for growth, as in 13:31. *Remove hence . . . remove*: moving mountains was a familiar idiom for accomplishing the impossible (see, e.g., Isa 54:10).   **17:21** *Howbeit this . . . fasting*: better omitted (MS tradition).   **17:22–23** Second prediction of Jesus' death and resurrection. Compare Mark 9:30–32; Luke 9:43b–45.   **17:22** *Abode*: better

²⁴And when they were come to Capernaum, they that received tribute money came to Peter, and said, Doth not your master pay tribute? ²⁵He saith, Yes. And when he was come into the house, Jesus prevented him, saying, What thinkest thou, Simon? of whom do the kings of the earth take custom or tribute? of their own children, or of strangers? ²⁶Peter saith unto him, Of strangers. Jesus saith unto him, Then are the children free. ²⁷Notwithstanding, lest we should offend them, go thou to the sea, and cast an hook, and take up the fish that first cometh up; and when thou hast opened his mouth, thou shalt find a piece of money: that take, and give unto them for me and thee.

18 At the same time came the disciples unto Jesus, saying, Who is the greatest in the kingdom of heaven? ²And Jesus called a little child unto him, and set him in the midst of them, ³and said, Verily I say unto you, Except ye be converted, and become as little children, ye shall not enter into the kingdom of heaven. ⁴Whosoever therefore shall humble himself as this little child, the same is greatest in the kingdom of heaven. ⁵And whoso shall receive one such little child in my name receiveth me. ⁶But whoso shall offend one of these little ones which believe in me, it were better for him that a millstone were hanged about his neck, and that he were drowned in the depth of the sea.

⁷Woe unto the world because of offences! for it must needs be that offences come; but woe to that man by whom the offence cometh! ⁸Wherefore if thy hand or thy foot offend thee, cut them off, and cast them from thee: it is better for thee to enter into life halt or maimed, rather than having two hands or two feet to be cast into everlasting fire. ⁹And if thine eye offend thee, pluck it out, and cast it from thee: it is better for thee to enter into life with one eye, rather than having two eyes to be cast into hell fire. ¹⁰Take heed that ye despise not one of these little ones; for I say unto you, That in heaven their angels do always behold the face of my Father which is in heaven.

¹¹For the Son of man is come to save that which was lost. ¹²How think ye? if a

---

"were gathering" (MS tradition).   **17:24–27** Paying the temple tax.   **17:24** *Tribute money*: Gk. *didrachmon*, a coin no longer used during Jesus' time; the word conventionally referred to the tax that Jews paid annually to support the temple; see Exod 30:11–16.   **17:25** *Prevented*: anticipated. *Custom or tribute*: Gk. *telos* and *kēnsos*, words referring to Roman taxes. *Strangers*: foreigners.   **17:27** *Piece of money*: Gk. *statēr*, a coin worth two *didrachma* (one for Peter and one for Jesus; see v. 24 note).

18:1–35 Community discipline. In his fourth extended discourse, Jesus ceases to instruct by replying to challenges his increasingly hostile opponents issue (cf. 15:1–20; 16:1–12; 17:24–27) and more positively defines the values and behaviors he expects of his community of disciples. As in the Sermon on the Mount, his expectations are high.   **18:1–10** Greatness in the kingdom of heaven. Compare Mark 9:33–37; 10:15; 9:42–48 and notes; Luke 9:46–48; 18:17; 17:1–2.   **18:3** *Be converted*: see 13:15 note.   **18:4** *Humble himself . . . child*: see 8:6 note.   **18:5** *Shall receive . . . me*: the echo of 10:40–42 (see notes) suggests that Jesus speaks metaphorically of his followers, as v. 6 ("which believe in me") confirms.   **18:7** *It must . . . come*: with eschatological *offences* in mind (see Mark 4:17 note); cf. 24:10–11.   **18:8–9** *If thy hand . . . fire*: repeating 5:29–30, but context suggests that here the imagery symbolizes the community and its members; see Mark 9:43 note.   **18:8** *Halt*: lame.   **18:10** *Their angels . . . heaven*: this and other ancient Jewish texts seem to assume something akin to the notion of guardian angels; cf. Ps 34:7; *Jubilees* 35.17; etc.   **18:11–14** Parable of the Lost Sheep. Compare Luke 15:3–7.   **18:11** *For the . . . lost*: better omitted (MS tradition). Sandwiched between the previous section's concern for "little ones" (v. 6) and the following section's communal advice,

man have an hundred sheep, and one of them be gone astray, doth he not leave the ninety and nine, and goeth into the mountains, and seeketh that which is gone astray? ¹³And if so be that he find it, verily I say unto you, he rejoiceth more of that sheep, than of the ninety and nine which went not astray. ¹⁴Even so it is not the will of your Father which is in heaven, that one of these little ones should perish.

¹⁵Moreover if thy brother shall trespass against thee, go and tell him his fault between thee and him alone: if he shall hear thee, thou hast gained thy brother. ¹⁶But if he will not hear thee, then take with thee one or two more, that in the mouth of two or three witnesses every word may be established. ¹⁷And if he shall neglect to hear them, tell it unto the church: but if he neglect to hear the church, let him be unto thee as an heathen man and a publican. ¹⁸Verily I say unto you, Whatsoever ye shall bind on earth shall be bound in heaven: and whatsoever ye shall loose on earth shall be loosed in heaven. ¹⁹Again I say unto you, That if two of you shall agree on earth as touching any thing that they shall ask, it shall be done for them of my Father which is in heaven. ²⁰For where two or three are gathered together in my name, there am I in the midst of them.

²¹Then came Peter to him, and said, Lord, how oft shall my brother sin against me, and I forgive him? till seven times? ²²Jesus saith unto him, I say not unto thee, Until seven times: but, Until seventy times seven.

²³Therefore is the kingdom of heaven likened unto a certain king, which would take account of his servants. ²⁴And when he had begun to reckon, one was brought unto him, which owed him ten thousand talents. ²⁵But forasmuch as he had not to pay, his lord commanded him to be sold, and his wife, and children, and all that he had, and payment to be made. ²⁶The servant therefore fell down, and worshipped him, saying, Lord, have patience with me, and I will pay thee all. ²⁷Then the lord of that servant was moved with compassion, and loosed him, and forgave him the debt. ²⁸But the same servant went out, and found one of his fellowser-

---

this parable demands that church leaders aggressively pursue those who wander from the community of faith. The shepherd stands for such leaders, who are to emulate the Son of Man. **18:12** *Doth he . . . astray*: "Does he not leave the ninety-nine on the mountains and go in search of the one that went astray?" (MS tradition; RSV). The reading KJV translates eliminates the shepherd's reckless abandonment of the remaining sheep on the mountains, but the parables of Jesus often trade on scandalous extravagance, by proposing outrageous comparisons or presenting exaggerated conduct; cf. Mark 4:30–32 and notes; Luke 16:1–9; etc. **18:15–20** Confronting a fellow believer. Compare Luke 17:3. **18:15** *Brother*: jargon for fellow believer in the NT. *Against thee*: better omitted (MS tradition). **18:16** *In the mouth . . . established*: quoting Deut 19:15. **18:17** *Church*: see 16:18 note. *An heathen . . . publican*: i.e., an outsider (cf. 5:46–47 and notes). **18:18** *Whatsoever ye shall bind . . . loosed in heaven*: repeating 16:19, though here with reference to the community rather than to its leader. John 20:23 seems to preserve an alternate version of this dominical saying. **18:20** *Where two . . . them*: this saying—like much of this section, which is patently anachronistic on Jesus' lips—probably originated as an early Christian prophetic oracle spoken by the risen Christ to confirm his presence in the community of believers. **18:21–35** Forgiveness. Jesus' demand for unlimited forgiveness (vv. 21–22) partly parallels Luke 17:3–4. The subsequent parable of the Unmerciful Servant (vv. 23–35) dramatizes this demand. **18:22** *Seven times . . . seven*: recalling and subverting the ratio of revenge in Gen 4:24. The Greek for *seventy times seven* may also be translated as "seventy-seven." **18:23** *Take account of*: settle his accounts with. **18:24** *Ten thousand talents*: an incredible sum, equivalent to millions of dollars in today's economy.

vants, which owed him an hundred pence: and he laid hands on him, and took him by the throat, saying, Pay me that thou owest. ²⁹And his fellowservant fell down at his feet, and besought him, saying, Have patience with me, and I will pay thee all. ³⁰And he would not: but went and cast him into prison, till he should pay the debt. ³¹So when his fellowservants saw what was done, they were very sorry, and came and told unto their lord all that was done. ³²Then his lord, after that he had called him, said unto him, O thou wicked servant, I forgave thee all that debt, because thou desiredst me: ³³shouldest not thou also have had compassion on thy fellowservant, even as I had pity on thee? ³⁴And his lord was wroth, and delivered him to the tormentors, till he should pay all that was due unto him. ³⁵So likewise shall my heavenly Father do also unto you, if ye from your hearts forgive not every one his brother their trespasses.

19 And it came to pass, that when Jesus had finished these sayings, he departed from Galilee, and came into the coasts of Judæa beyond Jordan; ²and great multitudes followed him; and he healed them there.

³The Pharisees also came unto him, tempting him, and saying unto him, Is it lawful for a man to put away his wife for every cause? ⁴And he answered and said unto them, Have ye not read, that he which made them at the beginning made them male and female, ⁵and said, For this cause shall a man leave father and mother, and shall cleave to his wife: and they twain shall be one flesh? ⁶Wherefore they are no more twain, but one flesh. What therefore God hath joined together, let not man put asunder. ⁷They say unto him, Why did Moses then command to give a writing of divorcement, and to put her away? ⁸He saith unto them, Moses because of the hardness of your hearts suffered you to put away your wives: but from the beginning it was not so. ⁹And I say unto you, Whosoever shall put away his wife, except it be for fornication, and shall marry another, committeth adultery: and whoso marrieth her which is put away doth commit adultery.

¹⁰His disciples say unto him, If the case of the man be so with his wife, it is not good to marry. ¹¹But he said unto them, All men cannot receive this saying, save they to whom it is given. ¹²For there are some eunuchs, which were so born from their mother's womb: and there are some eunuchs, which were made eunuchs of men: and there be eunuchs, which have made themselves eunuchs for the kingdom of heaven's sake. He that is able to receive it, let him receive it.

¹³Then were there brought unto him little children, that he should put his

---

18:28 *An hundred pence*: about one hundred days' wages for a manual laborer; see Mark 14:5 note. 18:34 *Delivered him . . . tormentors*: perhaps to prompt disclosure of hidden funds; alternatively, to induce his family to pay his debt.   18:35 *Their trespasses*: better omitted (MS tradition).

19:1–21:11 **Journey to Jerusalem.** This section's geographical notices gradually move Jesus from Galilee to Jerusalem (19:1; 20:17, 29; 21:1, 10).   19:1–12 Marriage, divorce, and eunuchs. Compare Mark 10:1–12 and notes.   19:1 *Came into . . . Jordan*: Jesus' route, east of the Jordon River, would avoid Samaria (cf. 10:5, in tension with the mission to Gentile territory of 15:21–39).   19:4 *Made them . . . female*: Gen 1:27.   19:5 *For this cause . . . flesh*: Gen 2:24.   19:7 *Moses then . . . away*: cf. Deut 24:1.   19:9 *Except it . . . fornication*: see 5:32 and note. *And whoso . . . adultery*: better omitted (MS tradition) as a scribal assimilation to 5:32.   19:12 *Eunuchs, which were so . . . men*: distinguishing between birth defect and castration. *Eunuchs for . . . sake*: probably those celibate for religious purposes, but possibly a reference to castration.   19:13–15 Blessing children. Compare Mark 10:13–16

hands on them, and pray: and the disciples rebuked them. [14]But Jesus said, Suffer little children, and forbid them not, to come unto me: for of such is the kingdom of heaven. [15]And he laid his hands on them, and departed thence.

[16]And, behold, one came and said unto him, Good Master, what good thing shall I do, that I may have eternal life? [17]And he said unto him, Why callest thou me good? there is none good but one, that is, God: but if thou wilt enter into life, keep the commandments. [18]He saith unto him, Which? Jesus said, Thou shalt do no murder, Thou shalt not commit adultery, Thou shalt not steal, Thou shalt not bear false witness, [19]Honour thy father and thy mother: and, Thou shalt love thy neighbour as thyself. [20]The young man saith unto him, All these things have I kept from my youth up: what lack I yet? [21]Jesus said unto him, If thou wilt be perfect, go and sell that thou hast, and give to the poor, and thou shalt have treasure in heaven: and come and follow me. [22]But when the young man heard that saying, he went away sorrowful: for he had great possessions.

[23]Then said Jesus unto his disciples, Verily I say unto you, That a rich man shall hardly enter into the kingdom of heaven. [24]And again I say unto you, It is easier for a camel to go through the eye of a needle, than for a rich man to enter into the kingdom of God. [25]When his disciples heard it, they were exceedingly amazed, saying, Who then can be saved? [26]But Jesus beheld them, and said unto them, With men this is impossible; but with God all things are possible. [27]Then answered Peter and said unto him, Behold, we have forsaken all, and followed thee; what shall we have therefore? [28]And Jesus said unto them, Verily I say unto you, That ye which have followed me, in the regeneration when the Son of man shall sit in the throne of his glory, ye also shall sit upon twelve thrones, judging the twelve tribes of Israel. [29]And every one that hath forsaken houses, or brethren, or sisters, or father, or mother, or wife, or children, or lands, for my name's sake, shall receive an hundredfold, and shall inherit everlasting life. [30]But many that are first shall be last; and the last shall be first.

---

and notes; Luke 18:15–17. **19:14** *Of such . . . heaven*: cf. 5:3, 10; 18:1–5. **19:16–30** Obtaining eternal life. Compare Mark 10:17–31 and notes; Luke 18:18–30; 22:28–30; 13:30. **19:16** *Good*: better omitted (MS tradition). **19:17** *Why callest . . . good*: better "why do you ask me about what is good?" (MS tradition). Matthew excises the Markan Jesus' reluctance (10:18) to be called "good," but retains Jesus' subsequent insistence that "there is none good but one, that is, God." Later scribes apparently saw in Matthew insufficient motivation for this insistence, and therefore had the man invoke Jesus as "good master" (v. 16; see note), in addition to restoring the Markan version of Jesus' question. **19:18–19** *Thou shalt . . . mother*: quoting commandments five through nine of the Decalogue (Exod 20:12–16; Deut 5:16–20). **19:19** *Love thy . . . thyself*: Lev 19:18; cf. Matt 5:43. **19:20** *From my youth up*: better omitted (MS tradition). **19:21** *If thou . . . me*: developing the tenth commandment, which prohibits covetousness (Exod 20:17; Deut 5:21), along the lines of Jesus' interpretation of the OT law in 5:21–48 (see notes). Like the present passage, that one ends with an exhortation to perfection (5:48). **19:23** *Hardly*: with difficulty. **19:28** *Regeneration*: Gk. *palingenesia*, originally a Stoic term and referring to the universe's renewal, the culmination/commencement of an infinitely recurring cycle of cosmic entropy and rebirth. Here it signifies the eschatological establishment of God's rule. *The Son . . . glory*: cf. Dan 7:13–14. **19:29** *Or wife*: better omitted (MS tradi-

20 For the kingdom of heaven is like unto a man that is an householder, which went out early in the morning to hire labourers into his vineyard. [2]And when he had agreed with the labourers for a penny a day, he sent them into his vineyard. [3]And he went out about the third hour, and saw others standing idle in the marketplace, [4]and said unto them; Go ye also into the vineyard, and whatsoever is right I will give you. And they went their way. [5]Again he went out about the sixth and ninth hour, and did likewise. [6]And about the eleventh hour he went out, and found others standing idle, and saith unto them, Why stand ye here all the day idle? [7]They say unto him, Because no man hath hired us. He saith unto them, Go ye also into the vineyard; and whatsoever is right, that shall ye receive. [8]So when even was come, the lord of the vineyard saith unto his steward, Call the labourers, and give them their hire, beginning from the last unto the first. [9]And when they came that were hired about the eleventh hour, they received every man a penny. [10]But when the first came, they supposed that they should have received more; and they likewise received every man a penny. [11]And when they had received it, they murmured against the goodman of the house, [12]saying, These last have wrought but one hour, and thou hast made them equal unto us, which have borne the burden and heat of the day. [13]But he answered one of them, and said, Friend, I do thee no wrong: didst not thou agree with me for a penny? [14]Take that thine is, and go thy way: I will give unto this last, even as unto thee. [15]Is it not lawful for me to do what I will with mine own? Is thine eye evil, because I am good? [16]So the last shall be first, and the first last: for many be called, but few chosen.

[17]And Jesus going up to Jerusalem took the twelve disciples apart in the way, and said unto them, [18]Behold, we go up to Jerusalem; and the Son of man shall be betrayed unto the chief priests and unto the scribes, and they shall condemn him to death, [19]and shall deliver him to the Gentiles to mock, and to scourge, and to crucify him: and the third day he shall rise again.

[20]Then came to him the mother of Zebedee's children with her sons, worshipping him, and desiring a certain thing of him. [21]And he said unto her, What wilt thou? She saith unto him, Grant that these my two sons may sit, the one on thy right hand, and the other on the left, in thy kingdom. [22]But Jesus answered and

---

tion).   **20:1–16** Parable of the Workers in the Vineyard. Following and illustrating the aphorism of 19:30 (cf. 20:8, 16), this parable is often taken as a warning against presuming eschatological rewards, but one should not allegorize too quickly. Its portrayal of a landowner willing to forgo fairness (equal wages for equal work) in favor of generosity is not unrelated to Jesus' command to the rich man in 19:21.   **20:2** *A penny*: see Mark 14:5 note.   **20:3** *Third hour*: 9 A.M.   **20:5** *Sixth and ninth hour*: noon and 3 P.M.   **20:6** *Eleventh hour*: 5 P.M.   **20:7** *And whatsoever . . . receive*: better omitted (MS tradition).   **20:8** *Even*: when hired servants were to be paid; see Deut 24:14–15.   **20:11** *They murmured*: perhaps recalling the Israelites' murmurs against God for want of sustenance (Exod 16). *Goodman of the house*: Gk. *oikodespotēs* (cf. v. 1 [KJV "householder"]).   **20:15** *Is thine eye evil*: see 6:23 note.   **20:16** *For many . . . chosen*: better omitted (MS tradition).   **20:17–19** Third prediction of Jesus' death and resurrection. Compare Mark 10:32–34 and notes; Luke 18:31–34.   **20:20–28** Request for the sons of Zebedee. Compare Mark 10:35–45 and notes; Luke 22:24–27.   **20:20** *The mother . . . sons*: altering Mark's version in order to blame the mother, rather than James and John, for the impudent request of v. 21.

said, Ye know not what ye ask. Are ye able to drink of the cup that I shall drink of, and to be baptized with the baptism that I am baptized with? They say unto him, We are able. ²³And he saith unto them, Ye shall drink indeed of my cup, and be baptized with the baptism that I am baptized with: but to sit on my right hand, and on my left, is not mine to give, but it shall be given to them for whom it is prepared of my Father. ²⁴And when the ten heard it, they were moved with indignation against the two brethren. ²⁵But Jesus called them unto him, and said, Ye know that the princes of the Gentiles exercise dominion over them, and they that are great exercise authority upon them. ²⁶But it shall not be so among you: but whosoever will be great among you, let him be your minister; ²⁷and whosoever will be chief among you, let him be your servant: ²⁸even as the Son of man came not to be ministered unto, but to minister, and to give his life a ransom for many.

²⁹And as they departed from Jericho, a great multitude followed him. ³⁰And, behold, two blind men sitting by the way side, when they heard that Jesus passed by, cried out, saying, Have mercy on us, O Lord, thou Son of David. ³¹And the multitude rebuked them, because they should hold their peace: but they cried the more, saying, Have mercy on us, O Lord, thou Son of David. ³²And Jesus stood still, and called them, and said, What will ye that I shall do unto you? ³³They say unto him, Lord, that our eyes may be opened. ³⁴So Jesus had compassion on them, and touched their eyes: and immediately their eyes received sight, and they followed him.

21 And when they drew nigh unto Jerusalem, and were come to Bethphage, unto the mount of Olives, then sent Jesus two disciples, ²saying unto them, Go into the village over against you, and straightway ye shall find an ass tied, and a colt with her: loose them, and bring them unto me. ³And if any man say ought unto you, ye shall say, The Lord hath need of them; and straightway he will send them. ⁴All this was done, that it might be fulfilled which was spoken by the prophet, saying, ⁵Tell ye the daughter of Sion, Behold, thy King cometh unto thee, meek, and sitting upon an ass, and a colt the foal of an ass. ⁶And the disciples went, and did as Jesus commanded them, ⁷and brought the ass, and the

---

20:22 *And to . . . am baptized with*: this and the reference to baptism in v. 23 are better omitted (MS tradition) as scribal emendations assimilating Matthew's version of the story to Mark's. **20:26** *Minister*: Gk. *diakonos*, helper, attendant, or servant. Its verbal form appears in v. 28. **20:27** *Chief*: Gk. *prōtos*; KJV "first" in 19:30; 20:8, 10, 16. **20:29–34** Healing blind men. Compare 9:27–31; Mark 10:46–52 and notes; Luke 18:35–43. **20:29** *Jericho*: a city about fifteen miles northwest of Jerusalem. **20:34** *And they followed him*: in contrast to 9:31. **21:1–11** Entering Jerusalem. Compare Mark 11:1–10; Luke 19:28–38; John 12:12–19. Although presenting Jesus' royal entry (esp. vv. 7–10; see notes), this episode culminates in his proclamation as "the prophet of Nazareth" (v. 11) rather than as the anticipated king (cf. "Son of David," 20:30). Moreover, Jesus' behavior in vv. 2–3 recalls the prophet Samuel's when he first encounters the future King Saul (cf. 1 Sam 9:1–10:16). That story culminates in the king's unexpected prophetic frenzy (10:9–13); like it, this episode shows the boundary between king and prophet to be remarkably fluid. **21:1** *Bethphage*: a village apparently on the slope of the Mount of Olives, just east of Jerusalem; its precise location is now unknown. **21:2** *An ass . . . her*: it is not clear why Matthew doubles the livestock from Mark's account; perhaps he has misread the poetic parallelism of Zech 9:9 (cf. v. 5). **21:5** *Tell ye . . . of an ass*: a composite of Isa 62:11 and Zech 9:9. **21:7–10** *And brought . . . moved*: recalling the story of Solomon's coronation in 1 Kgs 1:32–40, which involved the prince riding to his anointing on a mule (vv. 33, 38) and the earth shaking with the people's joyful noise (v. 40).

colt, and put on them their clothes, and they set him thereon. [8]And a very great multitude spread their garments in the way; others cut down branches from the trees, and strawed them in the way. [9]And the multitudes that went before, and that followed, cried, saying, Hosanna to the Son of David: Blessed is he that cometh in the name of the Lord; Hosanna in the highest. [10]And when he was come into Jerusalem, all the city was moved, saying, Who is this? [11]And the multitude said, This is Jesus the prophet of Nazareth of Galilee.

[12]And Jesus went into the temple of God, and cast out all them that sold and bought in the temple, and overthrew the tables of the moneychangers, and the seats of them that sold doves, [13]and said unto them, It is written, My house shall be called the house of prayer; but ye have made it a den of thieves. [14]And the blind and the lame came to him in the temple; and he healed them. [15]And when the chief priests and scribes saw the wonderful things that he did, and the children crying in the temple, and saying, Hosanna to the Son of David; they were sore displeased, [16]and said unto him, Hearest thou what these say? And Jesus saith unto them, Yea; have ye never read, Out of the mouth of babes and sucklings thou hast perfected praise? [17]And he left them, and went out of the city into Bethany; and he lodged there.

[18]Now in the morning as he returned into the city, he hungered. [19]And when he saw a fig tree in the way, he came to it, and found nothing thereon, but leaves only, and said unto it, Let no fruit grow on thee henceforward for ever. And presently the fig tree withered away. [20]And when the disciples saw it, they marvelled, saying, How soon is the fig tree withered away! [21]Jesus answered and said unto them, Verily I say unto you, If ye have faith, and doubt not, ye shall not only do this which is done to the fig tree, but also if ye shall say unto this mountain, Be thou removed, and be thou cast into the sea; it shall be done. [22]And all things, whatsoever ye shall ask in prayer, believing, ye shall receive.

[23]And when he was come into the temple, the chief priests and the elders of the people came unto him as he was teaching, and said, By what authority doest thou these things? and who gave thee this authority? [24]And Jesus answered and said

---

21:7 *They set him thereon*: lit. "he sat on them"—i.e., on both donkeys. KJV obscures the strangeness of the Greek.   **21:8** *Spread their garments in the way*: cf. 2 Kgs 9:13. *Cut down branches*: cf. 1 Macc 13:51.   **21:9** *Hosanna*: a transliterated Hebrew phrase meaning "save now" (also in v. 15). The multitudes quote from Ps 118 (vv. 25–26).

21:12–22:46 Conflict in the temple. 21:12–17 Cleansing the temple. Compare Mark 11:11, 15–19 and notes; Luke 19:45–48; and its earlier placement in John 2:13–22. Jesus' major opponents, the chief priests, make their first appearance since 2:4.   **21:12** *The moneychangers* exchanged idolatrous Roman coinage for acceptable currency. *Sold doves*: sold animals for sacrifice; cf. Lev 5:6–7; 12:6–8; etc.   **21:13** *My house . . . prayer*: Isa 56:7; but like Luke (19:46), Matthew omits "for all people," which Mark retains (11:17). *But ye . . . thieves*: Jer 7:11.   **21:14** *The blind . . . them*: Lev 21:18 prohibits those with such a deformity ("blemish") from approaching the sanctuary.   **21:16** *Out of . . . praise*: Ps 8:2.   **21:17** *Bethany*: the companion village to Bethphage.   **21:18–22** Cursing the fig tree. In Matthew the curse and the lesson to be drawn from it constitute an uninterrupted sequence, but Mark interlaces this episode (see 11:12–14, 20–26 and notes) with the previous one; Luke omits it altogether.   **21:19** *The fig . . . away*: a not uncommon figure for God's judgment; cf. Isa 34:4; Jer 8:13.   **21:21** *This mountain*: moving mountains was proverbially associated with faith (cf. 17:20; 1 Cor 13:2), but context and diction ("<u>this</u> mountain") suggest Jesus has in mind the Temple Mount's devastation.   **21:23–27** Jesus' authority. Compare Mark 11:27–33; Luke 20:1–8.

unto them, I also will ask you one thing, which if ye tell me, I in like wise will tell you by what authority I do these things. [25]The baptism of John, whence was it? from heaven, or of men? And they reasoned with themselves, saying, If we shall say, From heaven; he will say unto us, Why did ye not then believe him? [26]But if we shall say, Of men; we fear the people; for all hold John as a prophet. [27]And they answered Jesus, and said, We cannot tell. And he said unto them, Neither tell I you by what authority I do these things.

[28]But what think ye? A certain man had two sons; and he came to the first, and said, Son, go work to day in my vineyard. [29]He answered and said, I will not: but afterward he repented, and went. [30]And he came to the second, and said likewise. And he answered and said, I go, sir: and went not. [31]Whether of them twain did the will of his father? They say unto him, The first. Jesus saith unto them, Verily I say unto you, That the publicans and the harlots go into the kingdom of God before you. [32]For John came unto you in the way of righteousness, and ye believed him not: but the publicans and the harlots believed him: and ye, when ye had seen it, repented not afterward, that ye might believe him.

[33]Hear another parable: There was a certain householder, which planted a vineyard, and hedged it round about, and digged a winepress in it, and built a tower, and let it out to husbandmen, and went into a far country: [34]and when the time of the fruit drew near, he sent his servants to the husbandmen, that they might receive the fruits of it. [35]And the husbandmen took his servants, and beat one, and killed another, and stoned another. [36]Again, he sent other servants more than the first: and they did unto them likewise. [37]But last of all he sent unto them his son, saying, They will reverence my son. [38]But when the husbandmen saw the son, they said among themselves, This is the heir; come, let us kill him, and let us seize on his inheritance. [39]And they caught him, and cast him out of the vineyard, and slew him. [40]When the lord therefore of the vineyard cometh, what will he do unto those husbandmen? [41]They say unto him, He will miserably destroy those wicked men, and will let out his vineyard unto other husbandmen, which shall render him the fruits in their seasons. [42]Jesus saith unto them, Did ye never read in the scriptures, The stone which the builders rejected, the same is become the head of the corner: this is the Lord's doing, and it is marvellous in our eyes? [43]Therefore say I unto you, The kingdom of God shall be taken from you, and given to a nation bringing forth the fruits thereof. [44]And whosoever shall fall on this stone shall be broken: but on whomsoever it shall fall, it will grind him to powder. [45]And when the chief priests and Pharisees had heard his parables, they

21:28–32 Parable of the Two Sons. This parable introduces a set of three, all related to the failure of the chief priests and elders to embrace John's ministry and Jesus'. **21:33–46** Parable of the Wicked Tenants. Compare Mark 12:1–12 and notes; Luke 20:9–19. Jesus' parable develops the allegory of God's vineyard from Isa 5:1–7. **21:41** *Render him . . . seasons*: cf. Ps 1:3. **21:42** *The stone . . . eyes*: Ps 118:22–23. *Head of the corner*: either a building's cornerstone or a copestone. **21:43** *A nation*: perhaps suggesting that the church, which contained both Jews and Gentiles, constitutes a "nation" different from Israel. *Bringing forth the fruits*: lit. "producing the fruits," although the parable is concerned not with infertility but with refusal to hand fruit over. But compare the Isaianic allegory with which Jesus began (Isa 5:1–7, esp. v. 4). **21:44** *And whosoever . . . powder*: better omitted (MS tradi-

perceived that he spake of them. ⁴⁶But when they sought to lay hands on him, they feared the multitude, because they took him for a prophet.

22 And Jesus answered and spake unto them again by parables, and said, ²The kingdom of heaven is like unto a certain king, which made a marriage for his son, ³and sent forth his servants to call them that were bidden to the wedding: and they would not come. ⁴Again, he sent forth other servants, saying, Tell them which are bidden, Behold, I have prepared my dinner: my oxen and my fatlings are killed, and all things are ready: come unto the marriage. ⁵But they made light of it, and went their ways, one to his farm, another to his merchandise: ⁶and the remnant took his servants, and entreated them spitefully, and slew them. ⁷But when the king heard thereof, he was wroth: and he sent forth his armies, and destroyed those murderers, and burned up their city. ⁸Then saith he to his servants, The wedding is ready, but they which were bidden were not worthy. ⁹Go ye therefore into the highways, and as many as ye shall find, bid to the marriage. ¹⁰So those servants went out into the highways, and gathered together all as many as they found, both bad and good: and the wedding was furnished with guests. ¹¹And when the king came in to see the guests, he saw there a man which had not on a wedding garment: ¹²and he saith unto him, Friend, how camest thou in hither not having a wedding garment? And he was speechless. ¹³Then said the king to the servants, Bind him hand and foot, and take him away, and cast him into outer darkness; there shall be weeping and gnashing of teeth. ¹⁴For many are called, but few are chosen.

¹⁵Then went the Pharisees, and took counsel how they might entangle him in his talk. ¹⁶And they sent out unto him their disciples with the Herodians, saying, Master, we know that thou art true, and teachest the way of God in truth, neither carest thou for any man: for thou regardest not the person of men. ¹⁷Tell us therefore, What thinkest thou? Is it lawful to give tribute unto Cæsar, or not? ¹⁸But Jesus perceived their wickedness, and said, Why tempt ye me, ye hypocrites? ¹⁹Shew me the tribute money. And they brought unto him a penny. ²⁰And he saith unto them, Whose is this image and superscription? ²¹They say unto him, Cæsar's. Then saith he unto them, Render therefore unto Cæsar the things

---

tion) as a scribal importation from the Lukan parallel.   **22:1–14** Parable of the Wedding Banquet. Compare Luke 14:16–24.   **22:2** *Marriage*: Gk. *gamos* ("marriage" and "wedding" throughout this episode); it refers to a wedding celebration, with the eschatological banquet in mind (see Mark 2:19 note). **22:6** *Entreated them spitefully*: abused them.   **22:7** *And burned . . . city*: this sentence is not in Luke; Matthew may have added it to Q as an allusion to Rome's destruction of Jerusalem in 70 C.E.   **22:11** *Had not . . . garment*: commentators throughout history have cited Rev 19:7–8, which identifies the fine linen of the lamb's bride as "the righteousness of saints," to interpret this garment as good works. However, the donning of new clothing often symbolizes the new life of eschatological resurrection (cf. 1 Cor 15:53; 2 Cor 5:2; etc.); inappropriate attire may thus figure, rather than explain, eschatological condemnation.   **22:13** *Servants*: Gk. *diakonoi* (KJV "minister" at 20:26; see note); the different Greek word used earlier in this episode (vv. 3, 4, 6, 8) referred to slaves. The change in diction may suggest an allegorical reference to God's angels (cf. 13:49–50).   **22:14** *Many are . . . chosen*: a common formula in the Greco-Roman world, with variations in numerous ancient texts. Compare Plato: "as they say about initiation into the mysteries, 'Many carry the thyrsus, but few are Bacchantes'" (*Phaedo* 69c–d).   **22:15–22** Paying tribute to Caesar. Compare Mark 12:13–17 and notes; Luke 20:20–26.   **22:16** *Herodians*: see

which are Cæsar's; and unto God the things that are God's. [22]When they had heard these words, they marvelled, and left him, and went their way.

[23]The same day came to him the Sadducees, which say that there is no resurrection, and asked him, [24]saying, Master, Moses said, If a man die, having no children, his brother shall marry his wife, and raise up seed unto his brother. [25]Now there were with us seven brethren: and the first, when he had married a wife, deceased, and, having no issue, left his wife unto his brother: [26]likewise the second also, and the third, unto the seventh. [27]And last of all the woman died also. [28]Therefore in the resurrection whose wife shall she be of the seven? for they all had her. [29]Jesus answered and said unto them, Ye do err, not knowing the scriptures, nor the power of God. [30]For in the resurrection they neither marry, nor are given in marriage, but are as the angels of God in heaven. [31]But as touching the resurrection of the dead, have ye not read that which was spoken unto you by God, saying, [32]I am the God of Abraham, and the God of Isaac, and the God of Jacob? God is not the God of the dead, but of the living. [33]And when the multitude heard this, they were astonished at his doctrine.

[34]But when the Pharisees had heard that he had put the Sadducees to silence, they were gathered together. [35]Then one of them, which was a lawyer, asked him a question, tempting him, and saying, [36]Master, which is the great commandment in the law? [37]Jesus said unto him, Thou shalt love the Lord thy God with all thy heart, and with all thy soul, and with all thy mind. [38]This is the first and great commandment. [39]And the second is like unto it, Thou shalt love thy neighbour as thyself. [40]On these two commandments hang all the law and the prophets.

[41]While the Pharisees were gathered together, Jesus asked them, [42]saying, What think ye of Christ? whose son is he? They say unto him, The Son of David. [43]He saith unto them, How then doth David in spirit call him Lord, saying, [44]The LORD said unto my Lord, Sit thou on my right hand, till I make thine enemies thy footstool? [45]If David then call him Lord, how is he his son? [46]And no man was able to answer him a word, neither durst any man from that day forth ask him any more questions.

Mark 3:6 note. **22:23–33** Resurrection. Compare Mark 12:18–27 and notes; Luke 20:27–40. **22:23** *Sadducees*: this conservative Jewish sect's adherents rejected religious ideas and traditions not authorized by the Pentateuch, such as resurrection. **22:24** *If a man . . . unto his brother*: conflating Deut 25:5 and Gen 38:8, both dealing with levirate marriage. **22:25–27** *Now there . . . also*: extending to absurd lengths the story of Tamar from Gen 38 (quoted in v. 24). **22:32** *I am . . . living*: cf. Exod 3:6, 15–16; *4 Maccabees* 7.19. **22:34–40** The great commandment. Compare Mark 12:28–34; Luke 10:25–28, where it introduces the parable of the Good Samaritan. **22:35** *Lawyer*: legal expert. **22:37** *Thou shalt . . . mind*: Deut 6:5 (neither MT nor LXX is quoted precisely). **22:39** *Thou shalt love . . . thyself*: Lev 19:18, this verse's third appearance in Matthew (cf. 5:43; 19:19). **22:40** *The law . . . prophets*: cf. 5:17 and note. **22:41–46** David's son. Compare Mark 12:35–37 and notes; Luke 20:41–44. This episode reveals the limitations of a conception of the Christ as David's descendent, which surfaces repeatedly earlier (1:1; 9:27; 12:23; 15:22; 20:30; 21:9, 15), but after this never again. **22:43** *In spirit*: by inspiration. **22:44** *The Lord . . . footstool*: Ps 110:1; but a better reading of the MS tradition substitutes "put your enemies underneath your feet" (from Ps 8:6) for *make thine enemies thy footstool*.

23 Then spake Jesus to the multitude, and to his disciples, ²saying, The scribes and the Pharisees sit in Moses' seat: ³all therefore whatsoever they bid you observe, that observe and do; but do not ye after their works: for they say, and do not. ⁴For they bind heavy burdens and grievous to be borne, and lay them on men's shoulders; but they themselves will not move them with one of their fingers. ⁵But all their works they do for to be seen of men: they make broad their phylacteries, and enlarge the borders of their garments, ⁶and love the uppermost rooms at feasts, and the chief seats in the synagogues, ⁷and greetings in the markets, and to be called of men, Rabbi, Rabbi. ⁸But be not ye called Rabbi: for one is your Master, even Christ; and all ye are brethren. ⁹And call no man your father upon the earth: for one is your Father, which is in heaven. ¹⁰Neither be ye called masters: for one is your Master, even Christ. ¹¹But he that is greatest among you shall be your servant. ¹²And whosoever shall exalt himself shall be abased; and he that shall humble himself shall be exalted.

¹³But woe unto you, scribes and Pharisees, hypocrites! for ye shut up the kingdom of heaven against men: for ye neither go in yourselves, neither suffer ye them that are entering to go in. ¹⁴Woe unto you, scribes and Pharisees, hypocrites! for ye devour widows' houses, and for a pretence make long prayer: therefore ye shall receive the greater damnation. ¹⁵Woe unto you, scribes and Pharisees, hypocrites! for ye compass sea and land to make one proselyte, and when he is made, ye make him twofold more the child of hell than yourselves.

23:1–25:46 Religious hypocrisy and the end time. Jesus' fifth and final extended discourse is set in two locales. In the temple Jesus delivers to the multitudes a polemic against the scribes and the Pharisees, who stand in for leaders of the proto-rabbinic Jewish movement (cf. 23:7–8) that developed out of Pharisaism and came into prominence after the temple's destruction in 70 C.E (23:1–36). On the Mount of Olives he delivers an eschatological discourse to his disciples, culminating in a series of parables (24:3–25:46). Jesus' lament for Jerusalem and prediction of the temple's destruction (23:37–24:2) links the two parts. **23:1–36** Denunciation of scribes and Pharisees. Compare Mark 12:38–40; Luke 20:45–47; 11:39–52. **23:2** *Sit in Moses' seat*: figuratively, have authority to interpret and teach the Torah. **23:3** *Whatsoever they . . . and do*: see 5:17–20 note on Jesus' understanding of God's law in relation to the Pharisees'. By introducing Jesus' harangue with a call to respect the Pharisees' authority, Matthew in effect presents the vitriolic polemic that follows as part of an internal Jewish debate between differing sects. **23:4** *They bind heavy burdens*: cf. 11:30. *And grievous . . . borne*: better omitted (MS tradition). **23:5** *Phylacteries*: small leather boxes holding scriptural texts (bound to the head and arm in accordance with Exod 13:9, 16; Deut 6:6–8). *Borders*: tassels worn on the corners of garments in order to remind the wearer to follow God's law (see Num 15:38–39). In descriptions of Jesus' garment (9:20; 14:36), "hem" translates the same Greek word as *borders* here, suggesting that he wore these tassels. **23:6** *Uppermost, chief*: both share the Greek root *prōto-* (see 20:27 and note). **23:7** *Rabbi, Rabbi*: one is better omitted (MS tradition). *Rabbi* transliterates a Hebrew honorific commonly used of teachers (see v. 8 and note). Usually in the NT it is deferential; Jesus' prohibition of its employment in v. 8 may imply a critique of the proto-rabbinic movement. **23:8** *Master*: lit. "teacher" (a different Greek word is used in v. 10). *Even Christ*: better omitted (MS tradition). *Brethren*: cf. 18:15 and note. **23:9–10** *Call no . . . Christ*: perhaps amounting to a general prohibition of honorifics in Matthew's community. **23:13** *Woe unto you*: introducing a set of seven (or six; see v. 14 note) "woes," the opposite of "blessings" (cf. 5:3–12). *Shut up . . . to go in*: cf. 16:19. **23:14** *Woe unto you . . . damnation*: better omitted (MS tradition).

¹⁶Woe unto you, ye blind guides, which say, Whosoever shall swear by the temple, it is nothing; but whosoever shall swear by the gold of the temple, he is a debtor! ¹⁷Ye fools and blind: for whether is greater, the gold, or the temple that sanctifieth the gold? ¹⁸And, Whosoever shall swear by the altar, it is nothing; but whosoever sweareth by the gift that is upon it, he is guilty. ¹⁹Ye fools and blind: for whether is greater, the gift, or the altar that sanctifieth the gift? ²⁰Whoso therefore shall swear by the altar, sweareth by it, and by all things thereon. ²¹And whoso shall swear by the temple, sweareth by it, and by him that dwelleth therein. ²²And he that shall swear by heaven, sweareth by the throne of God, and by him that sitteth thereon.

²³Woe unto you, scribes and Pharisees, hypocrites! for ye pay tithe of mint and anise and cummin, and have omitted the weightier matters of the law, judgment, mercy, and faith: these ought ye to have done, and not to leave the other undone. ²⁴Ye blind guides, which strain at a gnat, and swallow a camel.

²⁵Woe unto you, scribes and Pharisees, hypocrites! for ye make clean the outside of the cup and of the platter, but within they are full of extortion and excess. ²⁶Thou blind Pharisee, cleanse first that which is within the cup and platter, that the outside of them may be clean also.

²⁷Woe unto you, scribes and Pharisees, hypocrites! for ye are like unto whited sepulchres, which indeed appear beautiful outward, but are within full of dead men's bones, and of all uncleanness. ²⁸Even so ye also outwardly appear righteous unto men, but within ye are full of hypocrisy and iniquity.

²⁹Woe unto you, scribes and Pharisees, hypocrites! because ye build the tombs of the prophets, and garnish the sepulchres of the righteous, ³⁰and say, If we had been in the days of our fathers, we would not have been partakers with them in the blood of the prophets. ³¹Wherefore ye be witnesses unto yourselves, that ye are the children of them which killed the prophets. ³²Fill ye up then the measure of your fathers. ³³Ye serpents, ye generation of vipers, how can ye escape the damnation of hell? ³⁴Wherefore, behold, I send unto you prophets, and wise men, and scribes: and some of them ye shall kill and crucify; and some of them shall ye scourge in your synagogues, and persecute them from city to city: ³⁵that upon you may come all the righteous blood shed upon the earth, from the blood of righteous Abel unto the blood of Zacharias son of Barachias, whom ye slew

---

23:16–22 *Woe unto you . . . thereon*: criticizing the practice of swearing by things regarded as not quite entirely holy in order to avoid being held accountable for the oath. Jesus insists that any oath gesturing toward God is binding. Compare his resistance to oaths in 5:33–37. **23:16** *A debtor*: lit. "bound"; Gk. *opheilei* (cf. v. 18 [KJV "guilty"]). **23:19** *Fools and*: better omitted (MS tradition). **23:23** *And not . . . undone*: Jesus encourages the impulse to tithe meticulously from one's "increase" (cf. Deut 14:22), even from herbs. **23:24** *Strain at*: filter (e.g., wine). Both gnats (Lev 11:20 and note) and camels (Lev 11:4) were considered unclean and might not be consumed. **23:25** *Make clean . . . platter*: a ritual practice (cf. Mark 7:4). **23:26** *And platter*: better omitted (MS tradition). *Of them*: better "of it" (MS tradition). **23:27** *Whited sepulchres*: tombs whitewashed to caution passersby against touching them and incurring ritual contamination (cf. Num 19:11–13). **23:30–31** *And say . . . prophets*: in distinguishing themselves from their murderous forefathers, the scribes and Pharisees admit their wicked ancestry. For the motif of the slain prophets, see, e.g., Neh 9:26; Jer 2:30. **23:33** *Generation of vipers*: see 3:7 note. **23:34** *I send . . . city*: Luke's Jesus attributes parallel words to "the wisdom of God" (11:49); cf. Jer 7:24. **23:35** *From the blood of righteous Abel*: cf. Gen 4:1–15; later traditions insist on Abel's righteousness (cf. Heb 11:4; 1 John 3:12). *Zacharias son of Barachias*: author of the OT book of Zechariah (Zech 1:1), who lived after the temple's destruction and apparently was not murdered. A tradition erroneously con-

between the temple and the altar. [36]Verily I say unto you, All these things shall come upon this generation.

[37]O Jerusalem, Jerusalem, thou that killest the prophets, and stonest them which are sent unto thee, how often would I have gathered thy children together, even as a hen gathereth her chickens under her wings, and ye would not! [38]Behold, your house is left unto you desolate. [39]For I say unto you, Ye shall not see me henceforth, till ye shall say, Blessed is he that cometh in the name of the Lord.

24 And Jesus went out, and departed from the temple: and his disciples came to him for to shew him the buildings of the temple. [2]And Jesus said unto them, See ye not all these things? verily I say unto you, There shall not be left here one stone upon another, that shall not be thrown down.

[3]And as he sat upon the mount of Olives, the disciples came unto him privately, saying, Tell us, when shall these things be? and what shall be the sign of thy coming, and of the end of the world? [4]And Jesus answered and said unto them, Take heed that no man deceive you. [5]For many shall come in my name, saying, I am Christ; and shall deceive many. [6]And ye shall hear of wars and rumours of wars: see that ye be not troubled: for all these things must come to pass, but the end is not yet. [7]For nation shall rise against nation, and kingdom against kingdom: and there shall be famines, and pestilences, and earthquakes, in divers places. [8]All these are the beginning of sorrows. [9]Then shall they deliver you up to be afflicted, and shall kill you: and ye shall be hated of all nations for my name's sake. [10]And then shall many be offended, and shall betray one another, and shall hate one another. [11]And many false prophets shall rise, and shall deceive many. [12]And because iniquity shall abound, the love of many shall wax cold. [13]But he that shall endure unto the end, the same shall be saved. [14]And this gospel of the kingdom shall be preached in all the world for a witness unto all nations; and then shall the end come.

---

flated him with Zechariah son of Jehoiada, who was stoned in the temple court (2 Chr 24:20–22). Matthew therefore refers to the first and last murders in the Hebrew Bible, which closes with 2 Chronicles. (In Christian bibles, the Prophets introduce the New Testament.) **23:37–24:2** Lament for Jerusalem and prediction of the temple's destruction. Compare Mark 13:1–2; Luke 13:34–35; 21:5–6. **23:37** *Killest the prophets . . . thee*: Jesus' words are ominous in light of Jerusalem's previous embrace of him as a prophet (21:11). *Would I . . . wings*: a conventional OT image describing God's protection of his people; cf. Deut 32:11–12; Ruth 2:12; Ps 17:8; etc. **23:38** *Your house . . . desolate*: echoing a number of OT texts (e.g., Jer 22:5; Hag 1:9). The phrasing here refers to the temple's impending destruction (cf. 24:1–2, 15), which, Matthew suggests, will be Jerusalem's punishment for killing the prophet Jesus. **23:39** *Blessed is . . . Lord*: again quoting Ps 118:26 (cf. Matt 21:9, 15), here with reference to the Son of Man's eschatological advent. Since Ps 118:26b locates the blessing in the temple, Jesus may be hinting at its eschatological reconstruction (cf. Tob 14:5; *1 Enoch* 90.28–29; contrast Rev 21:22). **24:3–14** Signs of the end. Compare Mark 13:3–13 and notes; Luke 21:7–19. Jesus' discourse throughout chap. 24 draws on eschatological imagery from OT and other Jewish literature. See Mark 13 notes for references. **24:3** *Coming*: Gk. *parousia* ("presence" or "arrival"), often used of a royal advent. It becomes a technical term in early Christianity for the (second) coming of Christ. **24:7** *And pestilences*: better omitted (MS tradition). **24:9–14** *Then shall . . . nations*: recalling Jesus' words to his disciples at 10:17–23, but here the mission is to *the nations* (i.e., Gentiles), not to Israel. **24:10** *Shall many be offended*: cf. 18:6–7. **24:14** *Preached in . . . come*: cf. 10:5 and note.

¹⁵When ye therefore shall see the abomination of desolation, spoken of by Daniel the prophet, stand in the holy place, (whoso readeth, let him understand:) ¹⁶then let them which be in Judæa flee into the mountains: ¹⁷let him which is on the housetop not come down to take any thing out of his house: ¹⁸neither let him which is in the field return back to take his clothes. ¹⁹And woe unto them that are with child, and to them that give suck in those days! ²⁰But pray ye that your flight be not in the winter, neither on the sabbath day: ²¹for then shall be great tribulation, such as was not since the beginning of the world to this time, no, nor ever shall be. ²²And except those days should be shortened, there should no flesh be saved: but for the elect's sake those days shall be shortened.

²³Then if any man shall say unto you, Lo, here is Christ, or there; believe it not. ²⁴For there shall arise false Christs, and false prophets, and shall shew great signs and wonders; insomuch that, if it were possible, they shall deceive the very elect. ²⁵Behold, I have told you before. ²⁶Wherefore if they shall say unto you, Behold, he is in the desert; go not forth: behold, he is in the secret chambers; believe it not. ²⁷For as the lightning cometh out of the east, and shineth even unto the west; so shall also the coming of the Son of man be. ²⁸For wheresoever the carcase is, there will the eagles be gathered together.

²⁹Immediately after the tribulation of those days shall the sun be darkened, and the moon shall not give her light, and the stars shall fall from heaven, and the powers of the heavens shall be shaken: ³⁰and then shall appear the sign of the Son of man in heaven: and then shall all the tribes of the earth mourn, and they shall see the Son of man coming in the clouds of heaven with power and great glory. ³¹And he shall send his angels with a great sound of a trumpet, and they shall gather together his elect from the four winds, from one end of heaven to the other.

³²Now learn a parable of the fig tree; When his branch is yet tender, and putteth forth leaves, ye know that summer is nigh: ³³so likewise ye, when ye shall see all these things, know that it is near, even at the doors. ³⁴Verily I say unto you, This generation shall not pass, till all these things be fulfilled. ³⁵Heaven and earth shall pass away, but my words shall not pass away. ³⁶But of that day and hour knoweth no man, no, not the angels of heaven, but my Father only.

24:15–22 Abomination of desolation. Compare Mark 13:14–20 and notes; Luke 21:20–24. **24:15** *Abomination of desolation*: a phrase from Daniel (9:27; 11:31; cf. 8:11–14), which here alludes to Rome's destruction of the temple in 70 C.E. (cf. 23:38 and note)—recent history to the evangelist. **24:20** *Neither on . . . day*: Matthew's addition to Mark (13:18) suggests that his community of believers kept the Sabbath; see 12:1–14 note. **24:21** *Then shall . . . be*: cf. Dan 12:1. **24:23–31** False messiahs and the Son of Man's coming. Compare Mark 13:21–27 and notes; Luke 17:21–24, 37; 21:25–28. **24:24** *False prophets*: cf. 7:15–23 and note. **24:27** *As the lightening*: compare the lightning at Sinai, in addition to the cloud and trumpet (Exod 19:16–20; cf. Matt 24:30–31). **24:28** *Wheresoever the carcase . . . together*: Pliny (cf. *Natural History* 10.3) and Aristotle categorize the vulture as a type of eagle; this phrase is thus probably proverbial, equivalent to "where there's smoke, there's fire"; cf. Job 39:30. **24:30** *They shall . . . glory*: Dan 7:13; cf. Matt 16:27; 19:28. **24:31** *A great sound of a trumpet*: a common eschatological motif; cf. Isa 27:13; 1 Cor 15:52; 1 Thess 4:16. *They shall gather . . . other*: cf. 9:35–10:4 and note. **24:32–36** Parable of the Fig Tree. Compare Mark 13:28–32 and notes; Luke 21:29–33. **24:34** *This generation . . . fulfilled*: cf. 16:28. **24:35** *Heaven and . . . not pass away*: cf. 5:18. **24:36** *Heaven*: better to add "nor the son" (MS tradition).

³⁷But as the days of Noe were, so shall also the coming of the Son of man be. ³⁸For as in the days that were before the flood they were eating and drinking, marrying and giving in marriage, until the day that Noe entered into the ark, ³⁹and knew not until the flood came, and took them all away; so shall also the coming of the Son of man be. ⁴⁰Then shall two be in the field; the one shall be taken, and the other left. ⁴¹Two women shall be grinding at the mill; the one shall be taken, and the other left. ⁴²Watch therefore: for ye know not what hour your Lord doth come.

⁴³But know this, that if the goodman of the house had known in what watch the thief would come, he would have watched, and would not have suffered his house to be broken up. ⁴⁴Therefore be ye also ready: for in such an hour as ye think not the Son of man cometh.

⁴⁵Who then is a faithful and wise servant, whom his lord hath made ruler over his household, to give them meat in due season? ⁴⁶Blessed is that servant, whom his lord when he cometh shall find so doing. ⁴⁷Verily I say unto you, That he shall make him ruler over all his goods. ⁴⁸But and if that evil servant shall say in his heart, My lord delayeth his coming; ⁴⁹and shall begin to smite his fellowservants, and to eat and drink with the drunken; ⁵⁰the lord of that servant shall come in a day when he looketh not for him, and in an hour that he is not aware of, ⁵¹and shall cut him asunder, and appoint him his portion with the hypocrites: there shall be weeping and gnashing of teeth.

25 Then shall the kingdom of heaven be likened unto ten virgins, which took their lamps, and went forth to meet the bridegroom. ²And five of them were wise, and five were foolish. ³They that were foolish took their lamps, and took no oil with them: ⁴but the wise took oil in their vessels with their lamps. ⁵While the bridegroom tarried, they all slumbered and slept. ⁶And at midnight there was a cry made, Behold, the bridegroom cometh; go ye out to meet him. ⁷Then all those vir-

---

24:37–42 The day and hour. Compare Luke 17:26–36 and notes. **24:38** *Marrying and . . . marriage*: perhaps referring to Gen 6:4, thought to narrate angelic couplings with human women, which preceded (and prompted?) God's destruction of the world. **24:39** *The flood*: 2 Pet 3:4–7 and other ancient texts compare the great deluge (Gen 6–8) to God's eschatological judgment. **24:40–41** *Then shall . . . left*: in light of v. 39 ("the flood . . . took"), this is an analogous reference to angels taking the wicked for judgment and leaving the righteous—precisely the scenario envisioned in 13:41–43, 49–50. (Some wrongly interpret this passage in light of 1 Thess 4:17: "we which . . . remain shall be caught up . . . in the clouds, to meet the Lord in the air.") **24:43–51** Parables of the Watchful Householder and the Faithful and Wise Servant. Compare Mark 13:33–37; Luke 12:39–46. This passage begins a series of parables about the eschatological consummation and its delay (24:43–25:46), which brings to an end Jesus' discourse. **24:43** *Goodman*: householder. *The thief*: early Christian literature regularly likens the Day of the Lord to a thief (cf. 1 Thess 5:2, 4; 2 Pet 3:10; Rev 3:3; 16:15), perhaps on the basis of this dominical saying. *Broken up*: broken into. **24:49** *Eat and drink*: cf. v. 38. **24:51** *Cut him asunder*: i.e., "dismember him," a grisly threat softened in some modern translations: RSV has "punish" and NJB has "cut off" (i.e., ostracized). **25:1–13** Parable of the Wise and Foolish Virgins. Compare Luke 12:35–36. **25:1** *Virgins*: bridesmaids who will escort the couple from the bride's parents' to the groom's house, where the wedding is held (cf. 22:2). It is odd that the parable makes no reference to the bride, and in fact an array of MSS add "and the bride" to the end of this verse. Perhaps reference to a bride was deleted in order to assimilate the parable to conventional Christian allegorical symbolism, with the bridesmaids awaiting the groom's (Christ's eschatological) arrival to claim his bride (the church), rather than his emergence with her from her parents' house. *Lamps*: rather "torches," a regular feature of ancient Mediterranean wedding processionals (cf. Euripides, *Trojan Women* 308–14; Virgil, *Aeneid*

gins arose, and trimmed their lamps. [8]And the foolish said unto the wise, Give us of your oil; for our lamps are gone out. [9]But the wise answered, saying, Not so; lest there be not enough for us and you: but go ye rather to them that sell, and buy for yourselves. [10]And while they went to buy, the bridegroom came; and they that were ready went in with him to the marriage: and the door was shut. [11]Afterward came also the other virgins, saying, Lord, Lord, open to us. [12]But he answered and said, Verily I say unto you, I know you not. [13]Watch therefore, for ye know neither the day nor the hour wherein the Son of man cometh.

[14]For the kingdom of heaven is as a man travelling into a far country, who called his own servants, and delivered unto them his goods. [15]And unto one he gave five talents, to another two, and to another one; to every man according to his several ability; and straightway took his journey. [16]Then he that had received the five talents went and traded with the same, and made them other five talents. [17]And likewise he that had received two, he also gained other two. [18]But he that had received one went and digged in the earth, and hid his lord's money. [19]After a long time the lord of those servants cometh, and reckoneth with them. [20]And so he that had received five talents came and brought other five talents, saying, Lord, thou deliveredst unto me five talents: behold, I have gained beside them five talents more. [21]His lord said unto him, Well done, thou good and faithful servant: thou hast been faithful over a few things, I will make thee ruler over many things: enter thou into the joy of thy lord. [22]He also that had received two talents came and said, Lord, thou deliveredst unto me two talents: behold, I have gained two other talents beside them. [23]His lord said unto him, Well done, good and faithful servant; thou hast been faithful over a few things, I will make thee ruler over many things: enter thou into the joy of thy lord. [24]Then he which had received the one talent came and said, Lord, I knew thee that thou art an hard man, reaping where thou hast not sown, and gathering where thou hast not strawed: [25]and I was afraid, and went and hid thy talent in the earth: lo, there thou hast that is thine. [26]His lord answered and said unto him, Thou wicked and slothful servant, thou knewest that I reap where I sowed not, and gather where I have not strawed: [27]thou oughtest therefore to have put my money to the exchangers, and then at my coming I should have received mine own with usury. [28]Take therefore the talent from him, and give it unto him which hath ten talents. [29]For unto every one that hath shall be given, and he shall have abundance: but from him that hath not shall be taken away even that which he hath. [30]And cast ye the unprofitable servant into outer darkness: there shall be weeping and gnashing of teeth.

4.338–39). **25:10** *Went in with him . . . shut*: cf. 22:11–14. *Marriage*: wedding celebration; see 22:2 note.   **25:13** *Wherein the . . . cometh*: better omitted (MS tradition).   **25:14–30** Parable of the Talents. Compare Luke 19:11–27.   **25:14** *The kingdom of heaven*: added by KJV; the Greek reads "it."   **25:15** *Talents*: transliterating Gk. *talanta*. A talent was a large sum of money (perhaps fifteen to twenty years' wages for a manual laborer). The common (and probably erroneous) interpretation of this parable as calling for responsible cultivation of one's natural endowments led to the current meaning of "talent." *Several*: individual.   **25:24–25** *Reaping where . . . earth*: in accusing his master of ruthless and irrational agriculture, the slave admits to his own foolish farming: money does not grow like seed, as the master observes (vv. 26–27). Whereas the previous parables address the need to be prepared for the Lord's return, this one focuses on the correct way to prepare. **25:27** *Exchangers*: money changers or bankers.   **25:29** *For unto . . . he hath*: echoing 13:12.

³¹When the Son of man shall come in his glory, and all the holy angels with him, then shall he sit upon the throne of his glory: ³²and before him shall be gathered all nations: and he shall separate them one from another, as a shepherd divideth his sheep from the goats: ³³and he shall set the sheep on his right hand, but the goats on the left. ³⁴Then shall the King say unto them on his right hand, Come, ye blessed of my Father, inherit the kingdom prepared for you from the foundation of the world: ³⁵for I was an hungred, and ye gave me meat: I was thirsty, and ye gave me drink: I was a stranger, and ye took me in: ³⁶naked, and ye clothed me: I was sick, and ye visited me: I was in prison, and ye came unto me. ³⁷Then shall the righteous answer him, saying, Lord, when saw we thee an hungred, and fed thee? or thirsty, and gave thee drink? ³⁸When saw we thee a stranger, and took thee in? or naked, and clothed thee? ³⁹Or when saw we thee sick, or in prison, and came unto thee? ⁴⁰And the King shall answer and say unto them, Verily I say unto you, Inasmuch as ye have done it unto one of the least of these my brethren, ye have done it unto me. ⁴¹Then shall he say also unto them on the left hand, Depart from me, ye cursed, into everlasting fire, prepared for the devil and his angels: ⁴²for I was an hungred, and ye gave me no meat: I was thirsty, and ye gave me no drink: ⁴³I was a stranger, and ye took me not in: naked, and ye clothed me not: sick, and in prison, and ye visited me not. ⁴⁴Then shall they also answer him, saying, Lord, when saw we thee an hungred, or athirst, or a stranger, or naked, or sick, or in prison, and did not minister unto thee? ⁴⁵Then shall he answer them, saying, Verily I say unto you, Inasmuch as ye did it not to one of the least of these, ye did it not to me. ⁴⁶And these shall go away into everlasting punishment: but the righteous into life eternal.

26 And it came to pass, when Jesus had finished all these sayings, he said unto his disciples, ²Ye know that after two days is the feast of the passover, and the Son of man is betrayed to be crucified. ³Then assembled together the chief priests, and the scribes, and the elders of the people, unto the palace of

25:31–46 The sheep and the goats. Although featuring a famous simile (v. 32), this passage is less a parable than a straightforward description of the final judgment, for which the previous parables have urged preparation. **25:31** *When the son . . . glory*: see 24:30 and note. **25:32** *All nations*: God's final gathering and judgment of the nations was a common eschatological expectation; cf. Isa 66:18; Joel 3:11–12; Zeph 3:8. *Nations* translates Gk. *ethnē*, a word Matthew elsewhere uses for Gentiles, often with the connotation of heathen sinners (cf. 5:47 note). This episode might describe the eschatological judgment of nonbelieving Gentiles, as opposed to Jews or Jesus-believing Gentiles, who would presumably be evaluated on the standard of faithfulness to the covenant law (cf. 5:17–20). Complicating such a reading is the fact that Israel can be accounted one of the nations (Deut 32:8; Isa 40:15–17; Acts 10:22), as might the church (see 21:43 and note). *A shepherd . . . goats*: cf. Ezek 34:17. **25:40** *The least . . . brethren*: perhaps referring to needy believers (cf. 18:5–10) or to Jesus-believing missionaries (cf. 10:40–42), but perhaps also to the destitute in general (cf. Prov 19:17 and note the absence of "my brethren" in v. 45). A reference to believers would imply an allusion to the risen Christ's presence in the church (see 10:40 and note; 18:20 and note; 28:20.) **25:44** *Minister*: see 20:26 and note.

26:1–27:66 Jesus' arrest, crucifixion, and burial. 26:1–16 Plot against Jesus and his anointing at Bethany. Compare Mark 14:1–11 and notes; Luke 22:1–6; 7:36–50; John 12:1–8. **26:2** *After two days*: the Passion Narrative's later echoes of Gen 22:2–5 (see 26:36 and note) suggest an allusion here to Gen 22:4, where Isaac is (almost) sacrificed "on the third day." *Son of . . . crucified*: an about-face from the triumphant atmosphere of chaps. 21–25. **26:3** *And the scribes*: better omitted (MS

the high priest, who was called Caiaphas, ⁴and consulted that they might take Jesus by subtilty, and kill him. ⁵But they said, Not on the feast day, lest there be an uproar among the people.

⁶Now when Jesus was in Bethany, in the house of Simon the leper, ⁷there came unto him a woman having an alabaster box of very precious ointment, and poured it on his head, as he sat at meat. ⁸But when his disciples saw it, they had indignation, saying, To what purpose is this waste? ⁹For this ointment might have been sold for much, and given to the poor. ¹⁰When Jesus understood it, he said unto them, Why trouble ye the woman? for she hath wrought a good work upon me. ¹¹For ye have the poor always with you; but me ye have not always. ¹²For in that she hath poured this ointment on my body, she did it for my burial. ¹³Verily I say unto you, Wheresoever this gospel shall be preached in the whole world, there shall also this, that this woman hath done, be told for a memorial of her.

¹⁴Then one of the twelve, called Judas Iscariot, went unto the chief priests, ¹⁵and said unto them, What will ye give me, and I will deliver him unto you? And they covenanted with him for thirty pieces of silver. ¹⁶And from that time he sought opportunity to betray him.

¹⁷Now the first day of the feast of unleavened bread the disciples came to Jesus, saying unto him, Where wilt thou that we prepare for thee to eat the passover? ¹⁸And he said, Go into the city to such a man, and say unto him, The Master saith, My time is at hand; I will keep the passover at thy house with my disciples. ¹⁹And the disciples did as Jesus had appointed them; and they made ready the passover.

²⁰Now when the even was come, he sat down with the twelve. ²¹And as they did eat, he said, Verily I say unto you, that one of you shall betray me. ²²And they were exceeding sorrowful, and began every one of them to say unto him, Lord, is it I? ²³And he answered and said, He that dippeth his hand with me in the dish, the same shall betray me. ²⁴The Son of man goeth as it is written of him: but woe unto that man by whom the Son of man is betrayed! it had been good for that man if he had not been born. ²⁵Then Judas, which betrayed him, answered and said, Master, is it I? He said unto him, Thou hast said.

²⁶And as they were eating, Jesus took bread, and blessed it, and brake it, and

---

tradition). *Caiaphas*: high priest, ca. 18–36 C.E. **26:4** *Subtilty*: trickery. **26:5** *On the feast day*: rather "during the festival." **26:11** *Ye have . . . you*: cf. Deut 15:11. **26:15** *Covenanted with him for*: rather "weighed out for him" (as on a scale), thereby vividly fulfilling Zech 11:12, whose LXX translation uses the same verb. *Thirty pieces of silver*: the amount assessed from a party responsible for accidentally injuring another's slave (Exod 21:32)—not a very large amount (see the sarcasm in Zech 11:12–13). **26:17–35** Celebrating Passover. Compare Mark 14:12–31 and notes; Luke 22:7–23, 39, 31–34; John 13:21–30, 36–38. **26:17** *The first . . . bread*: see Mark 14:1 note. **26:22** *Is it I*: rather "Surely, not I?" (NRSV). **26:24** *The Son . . . born*: cf. 18:6–7. *As it . . . him*: cf. vv. 54, 56. The early church believed that various OT texts predicted Jesus' fate. **26:25** *Master*: Gk. *Rabbi*. Judas is the only one of Jesus' disciples to address him, here and at v. 49 (when betraying him). Matthew thereby links Judas with Jesus' opponents; cf. 23:7 and note. *Is it I*: see v. 22 note. Judas's reiterated exclamation of innocence reveals his guilty conscience, as Jesus points out: "Thou hast said." **26:26–29** *Jesus took . . . kingdom*: Paul (1 Cor 11:23–25) joins the Synoptic Gospels in narrating this meal. **26:26** *Jesus took . . . disciples*: cf. 14:19 and 15:36 (the miraculous feedings).

gave it to the disciples, and said, Take, eat; this is my body. [27]And he took the cup, and gave thanks, and gave it to them, saying, Drink ye all of it; [28]for this is my blood of the new testament, which is shed for many for the remission of sins. [29]But I say unto you, I will not drink henceforth of this fruit of the vine, until that day when I drink it new with you in my Father's kingdom. [30]And when they had sung an hymn, they went out into the mount of Olives.

[31]Then saith Jesus unto them, All ye shall be offended because of me this night: for it is written, I will smite the shepherd, and the sheep of the flock shall be scattered abroad. [32]But after I am risen again, I will go before you into Galilee. [33]Peter answered and said unto him, Though all men shall be offended because of thee, yet will I never be offended. [34]Jesus said unto him, Verily I say unto thee, That this night, before the cock crow, thou shalt deny me thrice. [35]Peter said unto him, Though I should die with thee, yet will I not deny thee. Likewise also said all the disciples.

[36]Then cometh Jesus with them unto a place called Gethsemane, and saith unto the disciples, Sit ye here, while I go and pray yonder. [37]And he took with him Peter and the two sons of Zebedee, and began to be sorrowful and very heavy. [38]Then saith he unto them, My soul is exceeding sorrowful, even unto death: tarry ye here, and watch with me. [39]And he went a little further, and fell on his face, and prayed, saying, O my Father, if it be possible, let this cup pass from me: nevertheless not as I will, but as thou wilt. [40]And he cometh unto the disciples, and findeth them asleep, and saith unto Peter, What, could ye not watch with me one hour? [41]Watch and pray, that ye enter not into temptation: the spirit indeed is willing, but the flesh is weak. [42]He went away again the second time, and prayed, saying, O my Father, if this cup may not pass away from me, except I drink it, thy will be done. [43]And he came and found them asleep again: for their eyes were heavy. [44]And he left them, and went away again, and prayed the third time, saying the same words. [45]Then cometh he to his disciples, and saith unto them, Sleep on now, and take your rest: behold, the hour is at hand, and the Son of man is betrayed into the hands of sinners. [46]Rise, let us be going: behold, he is at hand that doth betray me.

[47]And while he yet spake, lo, Judas, one of the twelve, came, and with him a great multitude with swords and staves, from the chief priests and elders of the

---

26:27 *He took . . . of it*: cf. 20:22–23. **26:28** *New*: better omitted (MS tradition). *Testament*: covenant. *Remission*: Gk. *aphesis*, which refers to releasing; for a similar understanding of Jesus' death, see 20:28, where the Son of Man gives his life as "a ransom for many." **26:31** *I will smite . . . abroad*: Zech 13:7. **26:36–46** In Gethsemane. Compare Mark 14:32–42 and notes; Luke 22:39–46; John 18:1; 12:27–28. **26:36** *Gethsemane*: Greek transliteration of a Hebrew or Aramaic phrase meaning "oil press," perhaps evoking an orchard of olive trees on the Mount of Olives. *Sit ye . . . yonder*: recalling Abraham's words to his servants when he leaves them purportedly to worship with Isaac, but really to sacrifice him (Gen 22:5). **26:38** *Watch*: recalling Jesus' numerous commands to watch in the apocalyptic discourse (24:42, 43; 25:13); also in vv. 40–41. **26:39** *This cup*: cf. v. 27; 20:22–23. **26:40** *Could ye . . . hour*: recalling references in Jesus' apocalyptic sermon to the "hour" for which the disciples were to "watch" (24:36, 42, 44, 50; 25:13); also in v. 45. **26:41** *Pray, that . . . temptation*: cf. 6:13. **26:42** *If this . . . me*: better "if this cannot pass" (MS tradition). **26:45** *The hour . . . hand*: initiating the fulfillment of Jesus' passion predictions (16:21; 17:22–23; 20:18–19). **26:47–56** Arrest. Compare Mark 14:43–52 and notes; Luke 22:47–53; John 18:2–11.

people. ⁴⁸Now he that betrayed him gave them a sign, saying, Whomsoever I shall kiss, that same is he: hold him fast. ⁴⁹And forthwith he came to Jesus, and said, Hail, master; and kissed him. ⁵⁰And Jesus said unto him, Friend, wherefore art thou come? Then came they, and laid hands on Jesus, and took him. ⁵¹And, behold, one of them which were with Jesus stretched out his hand, and drew his sword, and struck a servant of the high priest's, and smote off his ear. ⁵²Then said Jesus unto him, Put up again thy sword into his place: for all they that take the sword shall perish with the sword. ⁵³Thinkest thou that I cannot now pray to my Father, and he shall presently give me more than twelve legions of angels? ⁵⁴But how then shall the scriptures be fulfilled, that thus it must be? ⁵⁵In that same hour said Jesus to the multitudes, Are ye come out as against a thief with swords and staves for to take me? I sat daily with you teaching in the temple, and ye laid no hold on me. ⁵⁶But all this was done, that the scriptures of the prophets might be fulfilled. Then all the disciples forsook him, and fled.

⁵⁷And they that had laid hold on Jesus led him away to Caiaphas the high priest, where the scribes and the elders were assembled. ⁵⁸But Peter followed him afar off unto the high priest's palace, and went in, and sat with the servants, to see the end. ⁵⁹Now the chief priests, and elders, and all the council, sought false witness against Jesus, to put him to death; ⁶⁰but found none: yea, though many false witnesses came, yet found they none. At the last came two false witnesses, ⁶¹and said, This fellow said, I am able to destroy the temple of God, and to build it in three days. ⁶²And the high priest arose, and said unto him, Answerest thou nothing? what is it which these witness against thee? ⁶³But Jesus held his peace. And the high priest answered and said unto him, I adjure thee by the living God, that thou tell us whether thou be the Christ, the Son of God. ⁶⁴Jesus saith unto him, Thou hast said: nevertheless I say unto you, Hereafter shall ye see the Son of man sitting on the right hand of power, and coming in the clouds of heaven.

⁶⁵Then the high priest rent his clothes, saying, He hath spoken blasphemy; what further need have we of witnesses? behold, now ye have heard his blasphemy. ⁶⁶What think ye? They answered and said, He is guilty of death. ⁶⁷Then did they

---

26:49 *And kissed him*: cf. 2 Sam 20:9–10. **26:50** *Wherefore art thou come*: perhaps to be construed as a question (so KJV), or even as a command missing the imperative verb ("do what you are here to do"; NRSV), but the Greek phrase may also be incomplete, as if interrupted by Jesus' arrest. **26:51–52** *One of them . . . place*: exemplifying the teaching from the Sermon on the Mount (5:38–48). **26:52** *For all . . . with the sword*: compare God's prohibition of murder in the covenant with Noah (Gen 9:6) and the decree against resisting persecution in Rev 13:10. **26:53** *More than . . . angels*: for *legions*, see Mark 5:9 note. The mention of *twelve legions* emphasizes that Jesus has no need for any of the twelve disciples to save him. **26:57–75** Jesus before the council and Peter's denial. Compare Mark 14:53–72 and notes; Luke 22:54–71; John 18:12–27. **26:59** *And elders*: better omitted (MS tradition). *Council*: Gk. *synedrion* (Sanhedrin); see Mark 8:31 note. **26:60** *But found . . . they none*: better "and they did not find many false witnesses" (MS tradition). *Two false witnesses*: see Deut 19:15; cf. 17:6–7. **26:61** *I am . . . days*: in the Synoptics Jesus never says this, but cf. John 2:19–22. **26:63** *Jesus held his peace*: cf. Isa 53:7. **26:64** *Thou hast said*: cf. 26:25. *Son of man . . . heaven*: conflating Ps 110:1 (cf. Matt 22:44) and Dan 7:13 (cf. Matt 16:27; 19:28; 24:30). **26:66** *Is guilty of*: deserves. **26:67** *Then did . . . hands*: cf. Isa 50:6.

spit in his face, and buffeted him; and others smote him with the palms of their hands, [68]saying, Prophesy unto us, thou Christ, Who is he that smote thee?

[69]Now Peter sat without in the palace: and a damsel came unto him, saying, Thou also wast with Jesus of Galilee. [70]But he denied before them all, saying, I know not what thou sayest. [71]And when he was gone out into the porch, another maid saw him, and said unto them that were there, This fellow was also with Jesus of Nazareth. [72]And again he denied with an oath, I do not know the man. [73]And after a while came unto him they that stood by, and said to Peter, Surely thou also art one of them; for thy speech bewrayeth thee. [74]Then began he to curse and to swear, saying, I know not the man. And immediately the cock crew. [75]And Peter remembered the word of Jesus, which said unto him, Before the cock crow, thou shalt deny me thrice. And he went out, and wept bitterly.

27 When the morning was come, all the chief priests and elders of the people took counsel against Jesus to put him to death: [2]and when they had bound him, they led him away, and delivered him to Pontius Pilate the governor.

[3]Then Judas, which had betrayed him, when he saw that he was condemned, repented himself, and brought again the thirty pieces of silver to the chief priests and elders, [4]saying, I have sinned in that I have betrayed the innocent blood. And they said, What is that to us? see thou to that. [5]And he cast down the pieces of silver in the temple, and departed, and went and hanged himself. [6]And the chief priests took the silver pieces, and said, It is not lawful for to put them into the treasury, because it is the price of blood. [7]And they took counsel, and bought with them the potter's field, to bury strangers in. [8]Wherefore that field was

26:68 *Who is . . . thee*: though universally attested in the MS tradition, these words make no sense in Matthew, which neglects to mention that Jesus was blindfolded, and are absent from Mark, though they appear in Luke—unexpectedly, if Matthew and Luke independently used Mark as their source. These problems together may suggest that at a very early stage Matthew's text here was assimilated to Luke's by scribes, or they may tell against the Two-Source Hypothesis. **26:69** *Without in the palace*: in the palace courtyard. *Damsel*: female slave. **26:72** *With an oath*: cf. 5:33–37, where Jesus forbids his disciples from using oaths. Gk. *horkos* ("oath") shares a root with "adjure" (*exorkizō*, v. 63), thereby linking Peter's denial of Jesus with Caiaphas's accusation of him. **26:73** *Bewrayeth*: betrays; Peter's Galilean accent discloses his identity, as does the Ephraimites' in Judg 12:5–6. **27:1–2** Jesus handed over to Pilate. Compare Mark 15:1 and note; Luke 23:1; John 18:28–32. **27:1** *Took counsel*: better "arrived at a decision," since deliberations had already occurred. **27:2** *Pontius Pilate*: prefect of the Roman province of Judea, ca. 26–37 C.E. **27:3–10** Judas's death. Only Matthew intercuts the trial with this episode. Acts 1:18–19 presents a different version of Judas's demise. Matthew presumably uses Scripture as the foundation for his imaginative expansion of an oral tradition about Judas's death. **27:3** *He was condemned*: i.e., Jesus. By juxtaposing Judas's suicide with Jesus' trial and sentencing, Matthew underscores thematic connections between Judas's remorse and Pilate's ambivalence, and between the chief priests' and Pilate's hypocrisy. **27:4** *Betrayed the innocent blood*: echoing LXX Deut 27:25: "cursed is he who takes a bribe to strike down the life of innocent blood." This may also recall Manasseh's crimes (see 2 Kgs 21:6). **27:5** *Cast down . . . temple*: cf. Zech 11:13, also echoed at 26:15. *Hanged himself*: as did Ahithophel, who betrayed King David (2 Sam 17:23). **27:6** *It is not . . . blood*: the priests piously avoid contaminating the temple treasury with money polluted (cf. Deut 23:18) by their own payment of it in exchange for Judas's promise to betray Jesus (cf. 26:15). **27:7** *The potter's field*: the name is perhaps taken from the reference to the potter in Zech 11:13 (cf. Matt 27:5, 9–10 and notes). In any case, Matthew expects his readers to know it not as *the potter's field* but as "the field of blood" (v. 8). *Strangers*: perhaps Gentiles, or pilgrims who died

called, The field of blood, unto this day. ⁹Then was fulfilled that which was spoken by Jeremy the prophet, saying, And they took the thirty pieces of silver, the price of him that was valued, whom they of the children of Israel did value; ¹⁰and gave them for the potter's field, as the Lord appointed me.

¹¹And Jesus stood before the governor: and the governor asked him, saying, Art thou the King of the Jews? And Jesus said unto him, Thou sayest. ¹²And when he was accused of the chief priests and elders, he answered nothing. ¹³Then said Pilate unto him, Hearest thou not how many things they witness against thee? ¹⁴And he answered him to never a word; insomuch that the governor marvelled greatly.

¹⁵Now at that feast the governor was wont to release unto the people a prisoner, whom they would. ¹⁶And they had then a notable prisoner, called Barabbas. ¹⁷Therefore when they were gathered together, Pilate said unto them, Whom will ye that I release unto you? Barabbas, or Jesus which is called Christ? ¹⁸For he knew that for envy they had delivered him.

¹⁹When he was set down on the judgment seat, his wife sent unto him, saying, Have thou nothing to do with that just man: for I have suffered many things this day in a dream because of him. ²⁰But the chief priests and elders persuaded the multitude that they should ask Barabbas, and destroy Jesus. ²¹The governor answered and said unto them, Whether of the twain will ye that I release unto you? They said, Barabbas. ²²Pilate saith unto them, What shall I do then with Jesus which is called Christ? They all say unto him, Let him be crucified. ²³And the governor said, Why, what evil hath he done? But they cried out the more, saying, Let him be crucified. ²⁴When Pilate saw that he could prevail nothing, but that rather a tumult was made, he took water, and washed his hands before the multitude, saying, I am innocent of the blood of this just person: see ye to it. ²⁵Then answered all the people, and said, His blood be on us, and on our children.

---

while visiting Jerusalem.   **27:9** *Jeremy the prophet*: some suggest allusions to Jer 18–19, where a number of shared motifs appear, but the citation is in fact of Zechariah.   **27:9–10** *And they . . . me*: cf. Zech 11:12–13.   **27:11–26** Jesus before Pilate. Compare Mark 15:2–15 and notes; Luke 23:2–5, 17–25; John 18:33–40; 19:4–16.   **27:11** *King of the Jews*: Pilate expresses concern not with blasphemy but with sedition. *Thou sayest*: cf. 26:25, 64.   **27:12** *He answered nothing*: for this and v. 14, see 26:63 and note.   **27:14** *The governor marvelled greatly*: compare Antiochus's amazement at the Jewish martyrs in *4 Maccabees* 17.17–24.   **27:16** *Barabbas*: better "Jesus Barabbas" (MS tradition; so throughout), probably changed by early scribes out of piety.   **27:19** *Set down . . . seat*: i.e., "sat on the bench." *His wife . . . of him*: recalling the Magi, Gentile dreamers who tried to foil Herod's scheme to put the young child Jesus to death (2:7–12), and also calling attention to Pilate's wickedness in allowing a *just man* to be executed in order to appease the masses.   **27:21** *Whether of the twain*: which of the two. **27:23** *But they . . . crucified*: cf. 21:9, where the multitudes joyfully bless Jesus as he enters Jerusalem. **27:24** *Washed his hands*: a conventional sign of innocence in the Hebrew Bible; cf. Ps 26:6; 73:13; Deut 21:1–9 (esp. vv. 6–7). *I am . . . it*: echoing the chief priests' statement to Judas ("see thou to that," v. 4) after his confession to having "betrayed the innocent blood." *The blood . . . person*: better "this blood" (MS tradition).   **27:25** *His blood . . . children*: this verse leads some readers to suppose that Matthew holds Jews universally accountable for Jesus' death, but its scope is limited: it portrays the people of Jerusalem as accepting responsibility for killing Jesus, with *on our children* alluding to Rome's destruction of Jerusalem and its temple in 70 C.E. (see 24:15 and note). Since the Jerusalemites recognized Jesus as a prophet when he entered the city (21:11), they are now liable to his promise

²⁶Then released he Barabbas unto them: and when he had scourged Jesus, he delivered him to be crucified.

²⁷Then the soldiers of the governor took Jesus into the common hall, and gathered unto him the whole band of soldiers. ²⁸And they stripped him, and put on him a scarlet robe. ²⁹And when they had platted a crown of thorns, they put it upon his head, and a reed in his right hand: and they bowed the knee before him, and mocked him, saying, Hail, King of the Jews! ³⁰And they spit upon him, and took the reed, and smote him on the head. ³¹And after that they had mocked him, they took the robe off from him, and put his own raiment on him, and led him away to crucify him.

³²And as they came out, they found a man of Cyrene, Simon by name: him they compelled to bear his cross. ³³And when they were come unto a place called Golgotha, that is to say, a place of a skull, ³⁴they gave him vinegar to drink mingled with gall: and when he had tasted thereof, he would not drink. ³⁵And they crucified him, and parted his garments, casting lots: that it might be fulfilled which was spoken by the prophet, They parted my garments among them, and upon my vesture did they cast lots. ³⁶And sitting down they watched him there; ³⁷and set up over his head his accusation written, This is Jesus the King of the Jews.

³⁸Then were there two thieves crucified with him, one on the right hand, and another on the left. ³⁹And they that passed by reviled him, wagging their heads, ⁴⁰and saying, Thou that destroyest the temple, and buildest it in three days, save thyself. If thou be the Son of God, come down from the cross. ⁴¹Likewise also the chief priests mocking him, with the scribes and elders, said, ⁴²He saved others; himself he cannot save. If he be the King of Israel, let him now come down from the cross, and we will believe him. ⁴³He trusted in God; let him deliver him now, if he will have him: for he said, I am the Son of God. ⁴⁴The thieves also, which were crucified with him, cast the same in his teeth.

---

of judgment for those who kill the prophets (23:29–38). That promise is fulfilled a generation later in the temple's destruction. **27:26** *Scourged Jesus*: cf. Isa 53:5. **27:27–31** Soldiers mock Jesus. Compare Mark 15:16–20 and notes; Luke 23:11; John 19:1–3. **27:27** *The common hall*: Gk. *praetō-rion*, transliterating Lat. *praetorium* (a governor's official residence). *Band*: cohort, consisting of several hundred soldiers. **27:28** *Scarlet*: like Mark's "purple," an ironic sign of royalty; but scarlet, the color of Roman soldiers' cloaks, is more appropriate. **27:29** *They bowed . . . Jews*: compare the Magi, Gentiles who bow to Jesus and hail him king of the Jews in sincerity (2:2, 11). **27:30** *They spit . . . head*: cf. 26:67; Isa 50:6. **27:32–56** Crucifixion. Compare Mark 15:21–41 and notes; Luke 23:26–49; John 19:17–37. OT echoes and allusions are now even more frequent than earlier in the Passion Narrative (cf. 26:24, 54, 56), explaining exactly how Jesus' death fulfills Scripture. **27:32** *Cyrene*: a city in North Africa. *Bear his cross*: cf. 10:38; 16:24. **27:33** *Golgotha*: "skull" (Aramaic). **27:34** *Vinegar to drink . . . gall*: cf. Ps 69:21 (but a better reading of the MS tradition substitutes "wine" for "vinegar," muting the allusion). The Bible commonly associates gall with anguish and resentment (e.g., Job 16:13; Acts 8:23). **27:35** *That it . . . lots*: better omitted (MS tradition) as a scribal assimilation to John 19:24. *Parted his garments, casting lots*: cf. Ps 22:18. **27:38** *Two thieves . . . left*: ironically recalling 20:23. **27:39** *They that . . . heads*: cf. Ps 22:7; Lam 2:15. **27:40** *Thou that . . . days*: cf. 26:61. *Save thyself*: cf. 16:25; 21:9 (see note), 15. *If thou . . . God*: Satan's formula of temptation (4:3, 6). Matthew presents the mockery as a final temptation, presumably for Jesus to call on angels to help him escape (cf. 4:5–7; 26:53; 27:43). **27:42** *If he . . . Israel*: better "he is the king of Israel" (MS tradition), ironically referring to the written accusation (v. 37). **27:43** *He trusted . . . now*: the Sanhedrin (unintentionally?) quotes Ps 22:8; cf. Wis 2:18. **27:44** *Cast the same in his teeth*:

⁴⁵Now from the sixth hour there was darkness over all the land unto the ninth hour. ⁴⁶And about the ninth hour Jesus cried with a loud voice, saying, Eli, Eli, lama sabachthani? that is to say, My God, my God, why hast thou forsaken me? ⁴⁷Some of them that stood there, when they heard that, said, This man calleth for Elias. ⁴⁸And straightway one of them ran, and took a spunge, and filled it with vinegar, and put it on a reed, and gave him to drink. ⁴⁹The rest said, Let be, let us see whether Elias will come to save him.

⁵⁰Jesus, when he had cried again with a loud voice, yielded up the ghost. ⁵¹And, behold, the veil of the temple was rent in twain from the top to the bottom; and the earth did quake, and the rocks rent; ⁵²and the graves were opened; and many bodies of the saints which slept arose, ⁵³and came out of the graves after his resurrection, and went into the holy city, and appeared unto many. ⁵⁴Now when the centurion, and they that were with him, watching Jesus, saw the earthquake, and those things that were done, they feared greatly, saying, Truly this was the Son of God. ⁵⁵And many women were there beholding afar off, which followed Jesus from Galilee, ministering unto him: ⁵⁶among which was Mary Magdalene, and Mary the mother of James and Joses, and the mother of Zebedee's children.

⁵⁷When the even was come, there came a rich man of Arimathæa, named Joseph, who also himself was Jesus' disciple: ⁵⁸he went to Pilate, and begged the body of Jesus. Then Pilate commanded the body to be delivered. ⁵⁹And when Joseph had taken the body, he wrapped it in a clean linen cloth, ⁶⁰and laid it in his own new tomb, which he had hewn out in the rock: and he rolled a great stone to the door of the sepulchre, and departed. ⁶¹And there was Mary Magdalene, and the other Mary, sitting over against the sepulchre.

⁶²Now the next day, that followed the day of the preparation, the chief priests and Pharisees came together unto Pilate, ⁶³saying, Sir, we remember that that deceiver said, while he was yet alive, After three days I will rise again. ⁶⁴Command

---

reproached him.   **27:45** *The sixth hour*: noon; for darkness at noon, see Amos 8:9–10. *The ninth hour*: 3 P.M.   **27:46** *Eli, Eli, lama sabachthani*: quoting Ps 22:1 (Aramaic, perhaps mixed with Hebrew).   **27:47** *This man . . . Elias*: they presumably mistake "Eli" for Elijah.   **27:48** *Filled it . . . drink*: another allusion to Ps 69:21 (cf. v. 34).   **27:51** *The veil . . . bottom*: an ambiguous sign; see Mark 15:38 note. *The earth did quake*: cf. 24:7. Behind this verse and v. 52 lies Zech 14:4–5. **27:52–53** *The graves . . . many*: for this general resurrection of the dead, see 1 Cor 15:20–26. (Paul does not believe anyone except Jesus has yet risen.)   **27:54** *The centurion . . . God*: perhaps implying conversion (contrast vv. 27–31), or simply signaling their awe at the portents accompanying Jesus' death.   **27:56** *Mary Magdalene*: see Luke 8:2 note. *Mary the mother . . . Joses*: Jesus' mother; cf. 13:55. *Joses*: better Joseph (MS tradition, differing from Mark). *Mother of Zebedee's children*: also differing from Mark, unless Matthew identifies James and John's mother (cf. 20:20) as Salome.   **27:57–66** Burial. Compare Mark 15:42–47 and notes; Luke 23:50–56; John 19:38–42.   **27:57** *Arimathæa*: perhaps Ramathaim (see 1 Sam 1:1). *Jesus' disciple*: in Mark, Joseph is a member of the Sanhedrin; by turning him into a disciple, Matthew suggests that Jesus was not totally abandoned by his male followers.   **27:58** *And begged the body*: in accordance with Deut 21:23.   **26:62** *The next day . . . preparation*: the Sabbath (see Mark 15:42 note).   **27:63** *That deceiver . . . again*: see 16:21; 17:23; 20:19.

therefore that the sepulchre be made sure until the third day, lest his disciples come by night, and steal him away, and say unto the people, He is risen from the dead: so the last error shall be worse than the first. [65]Pilate said unto them, Ye have a watch: go your way, make it as sure as ye can. [66]So they went, and made the sepulchre sure, sealing the stone, and setting a watch.

28 In the end of the sabbath, as it began to dawn toward the first day of the week, came Mary Magdalene and the other Mary to see the sepulchre. [2]And, behold, there was a great earthquake: for the angel of the Lord descended from heaven, and came and rolled back the stone from the door, and sat upon it. [3]His countenance was like lightning, and his raiment white as snow: [4]and for fear of him the keepers did shake, and became as dead men. [5]And the angel answered and said unto the women, Fear not ye: for I know that ye seek Jesus, which was crucified. [6]He is not here: for he is risen, as he said. Come, see the place where the Lord lay. [7]And go quickly, and tell his disciples that he is risen from the dead; and, behold, he goeth before you into Galilee; there shall ye see him: lo, I have told you. [8]And they departed quickly from the sepulchre with fear and great joy; and did run to bring his disciples word. [9]And as they went to tell his disciples, behold, Jesus met them, saying, All hail. And they came and held him by the feet, and worshipped him. [10]Then said Jesus unto them, Be not afraid: go tell my brethren that they go into Galilee, and there shall they see me.

[11]Now when they were going, behold, some of the watch came into the city, and shewed unto the chief priests all the things that were done. [12]And when they were assembled with the elders, and had taken counsel, they gave large money unto the soldiers, [13]saying, Say ye, His disciples came by night, and stole him away while we slept. [14]And if this come to the governor's ears, we will persuade him, and secure you. [15]So they took the money, and did as they were taught: and this saying is commonly reported among the Jews until this day.

[16]Then the eleven disciples went away into Galilee, into a mountain where Jesus had appointed them. [17]And when they saw him, they worshipped him: but

---

27:64 *Sure*: secure. *By night*: better omitted (MS tradition). *Error*: lit. "deception."
   28:1–20 Resurrection. 28:1–10 Empty tomb. Compare Mark 16:1–8 and notes; Luke 24:1–12; John 20:1–10.   **28:2** *There was . . . earthquake*: cf. 24:7; 27:51–53.   **28:3** *His countenance . . . snow*: cf. 17:2 and note; Dan 7:9; 10:6.   **28:4** *Keepers*: the "watch" of 27:66.   **28:6** *The Lord*: better "he" (MS tradition).   **28:7** *He goeth . . . Galilee*: cf. 26:32.   **28:9** *As they . . . disciples*: better omitted (MS tradition). *Held him . . . feet*: a posture of humble prayer as well as evidence of the risen Christ's tangibility.   **28:10** *My brethren*: the disciples.   **28:11–15** Bribing the soldiers. In combination with 27:62–66, this episode serves to refute an explanation for the ambiguous empty tomb that circulated when Matthew wrote (v. 15).   **28:12–15** *When they . . . taught*: the elaborate ruse, ironically perpetrated in order to prevent deception (27:63–64), draws final attention to the chief priests' hypocrisy. **28:14** *Secure*: protect.   **28:16–20** Jesus commissions his disciples. Compare Luke 24:36–39. This episode, the so-called Great Commission, recalls the commissioning of Joshua (Deut 31:23; Josh 1:1–9). **28:16** *Into a . . . them*: Jesus had not told them to go to a mountain, but Gk. *etaxato* (*appointed*) can also mean "give orders" or "command" (as in LXX Exod 29:43). Thus another translation might be "to the mountain where Jesus gave them commandments," i.e., the location of his first sermon (see 5:1). Matthew's tendency to liken Jesus to Moses also suggests an allusion to Moses' final ascent of Mount

some doubted. [18]And Jesus came and spake unto them, saying, All power is given unto me in heaven and in earth. [19]Go ye therefore, and teach all nations, baptizing them in the name of the Father, and of the Son, and of the Holy Ghost: [20]teaching them to observe all things whatsoever I have commanded you: and, lo, I am with you alway, even unto the end of the world. Amen.

Nebo in Deut 34.   **28:18** *All power . . . earth*: for the Son of Man's authority, cf. Dan 7:13–14. **28:19** *Go ye . . . nations*: broadening 10:5–7. *Baptizing them . . . Ghost*: perhaps differentiating baptism associated with Jesus from that of John (cf. 3:11), whose movement continued after his death and competed with the early church for adherents (see Acts 19:1–7 and note). The doctrine of the Trinity, that God is a union of Father, Son, and Holy Spirit, is postbiblical, but apparently based on such formulae as this and the one found in 2 Cor 13:14.   **28:20** *Lo, I . . . world*: unlike John (esp. 20:17) and Luke-Acts (Luke 24:51; Acts 1:6–11), Matthew does not refer to, let alone narrate, Jesus' ascension to heaven. He instead emphasizes the risen Christ's abiding presence with the church (cf. 10:40; 18:20; 25:40, 45 and notes), a role John and Luke both assign to the Holy Spirit. *Amen*: better omitted (MS tradition).

The Gospel According to St. Mark

WHETHER or not Mark knew the traditions about Jesus' birth that Matthew and Luke include, he does not mention them in his gospel, whose opening in comparison appears shockingly abrupt: as one of a throng of pilgrims coming for baptism by John, Jesus experiences a vision informing him he is God's "beloved Son" (1:11). After a period of testing, his ministry begins; but he immediately encounters fierce opposition, not only from demons but also from Jewish religious authorities, as well as from his own family, his hometown, and, most troubling of all, his chosen disciples. They defy and ultimately betray, desert, and deny him.

For the reader approaching Mark without misplaced presuppositions regarding Jesus' omniscience, the impact of the disciples' perfidy is profound. According to Mark, Jesus knows early on that he will die and even knows something about the manner of his death, but it is not until the night of his arrest that he realizes his followers will abandon him. Earlier, he expected his disciples to die with him (see 8:34–35; 10:38–39 and notes). They will not; Jesus is crucified alongside convicted criminals. His disciples will not even watch his execution, with the exception of some female followers who observe it from afar. Jesus dies alone, abandoned by everyone who had accompanied him during his brief ministry, including the God who had embraced him as "beloved Son" at the gospel's opening. Jesus' final words in Mark are "My God, my God, why hast thou forsaken me?" (15:34).

Mark offers no triumphant resurrection narrative to brighten this story of rejection and abandonment. The risen Jesus never even appears (see note to 16:9–20): instead of being represented his resurrection is announced, and not by angels (as in the other gospels) but merely by a young man who sits in Jesus' empty tomb and commands the women who would anoint Jesus' body to tell "his disciples and Peter" that Jesus will meet them in Galilee (16:5–7). This reunion never takes place, however, and Mark's gospel ends as abruptly as it begins, with the troubling notice that these women "fled from the sepulchre; for they trembled and were amazed: neither said they anything to any man; for they were afraid" (16:8). Of all his followers, these women alone had maintained a modicum of loyalty, but by the gospel's close they too have fled in fearful disobedience. Jesus' resurrection in Mark does not facilitate his faithless followers' redemption, as it does to one degree or another in the other New Testament gospels; it confirms their disloyalty.

Mark's story is not entirely hopeless, but the hope it offers takes a peculiar form. While Mark presents no rapprochement between the risen Jesus and the disciples who abandon him at his darkest hour, it does hint at the redemption of those responsible for Jesus' death. In chapter 15, a member of the council that plotted Jesus' murder requests his corpse in order to honor him with an elaborate burial. Pilate, the Roman governor who made the final decision to execute Jesus, not only proves more reluctant than anyone else to see him die but also allows Jesus' corpse to be removed from the cross for interment. Perhaps most significantly, the centurion who oversees Jesus' execution calls him "Son of God" at the moment of his demise (15:39).

These characters' surprisingly positive attitudes toward the crucified Jesus suggest a paradox that pervades Mark: those whom one expects to recognize and honor Jesus as God's special representative consistently fail to do so, while those opposed to Jesus often manage the feat. This can be adequately (though by no means exhaustively) demonstrated by considering who confesses Jesus' divine heritage, which God's voice announces at 1:11 and confirms at 9:7. Not only does the Roman centurion overseeing Jesus' execution call him God's son, but in the early chapters so do the demons. Jesus' followers, on the contrary, never grasp this aspect of his identity, with only one apparent exception to the pattern: in 8:29–33 Peter first responds to Jesus' query "whom do ye say that I am" by calling him "the Christ." But once Jesus explains the implications of that confession, Peter immediately rebukes him, prompting Jesus to rebuke him in turn. Peter's confession is usually treated separately from his and Jesus' mutual rebukes, with most modern bibles introducing a section break between verses 30 and 31. Jesus' words in verse 33 ("Get thee behind me, Satan") reveal the inserted break to be tendentious in the extreme. Peter's demonic possession explains both his confession that Jesus is the Christ and his hostility to his master, for demons in Mark regularly address Jesus as God's special representative and Jesus often responds by commanding their silence and issuing exorcistic rebukes. Precisely this pattern obtains here: Peter calls Jesus "Christ" (8:29), Jesus commands silence (v. 30), and, after Peter's hostility to Jesus (vv. 31–32), Jesus rebukes the demon inspiring him (v. 33). Jesus' followers, then, *never* grasp his true identity and honor him as God's son or special representative; that understanding is reserved for those most hostile to Jesus, particularly the unclean spirits that constantly oppose him and the Gentiles overseeing his execution.

Yet the responsibility for this troubling state of affairs lies squarely at the feet of Jesus, who actively endeavors to keep his identity as God's representative hidden. This tendency is known as Mark's messianic secrecy motif, and it pervades the gospel. Mark's Jesus constantly tries to avoid crowds, to suppress rumors of miracles that would draw attention to himself, and to conceal his divine identity. He teaches in deliberately obscure ways that baffle his closest followers, who therefore persistently misconstrue his doctrine and fail to trust him. Briefly summarized, the classic explanation of Mark's secrecy motif (originally formulated by Wilhelm Rede in 1901; see Appendix pp. 1129–49) proposes that the historical Jesus did not present himself as the Messiah, a proposition for which the synoptic tradition offers evidence: Jesus speaks about the messianic Son of Man, a figure whom his own preserved sayings (e.g., Mark 8:38; cf. Luke 12:8) suggest Jesus understood to be someone other than himself. The early church, in contrast, identified the two (an identification most of the synoptic Son of Man passages seem to reflect), but only after its encounter with the risen Christ, as the New Testament itself testifies in its early christological confessions stating that Jesus was designated Messiah at his resurrection (e.g., Acts 2:36; Rom 1:4). Early Christians, then, were left to explain the discrepancy between the historical Jesus' preaching and the church's proclamation about Christ, and Mark does so by presenting Jesus as consciously the Messiah, but endeavoring to keep his identity under wraps. The result is that until he died and rose again, even his disciples were not sure what to make of him (e.g., 4:41; 9:31–32). It is for this reason that when his most intimate followers catch a glimpse of his divinity at the Mount of Transfiguration (though they do not understand what they have seen; cf. 9:5–6 and notes), they are explicitly forbidden to say a word about it—precisely "till the Son of man were risen from the dead" (9:9).

This historicizing explanation must be broadened in order to take into account two additional aspects of Mark's narrative. First, Mark, unlike the other canonical gospels, never suggests that Jesus' resurrection actually altered his disciples' attitude toward him. Second, despite the disciples' ignorance, Jesus is somehow recognized and even honored by several other characters in the gospel, including unclean spirits and Gentiles. A historical explanation of the messianic secret that takes these elements into account will give due weight to the unexpected expansion of faith in Jesus among Gentiles in the early church, as well as the resistance that this expansion encountered among some Jewish believers. Jesus and his original followers were Jewish, and Jesus' teaching was deeply rooted in Jewish prophetic and apocalyptic traditions. Mark's portrayals of those whom one would expect to understand Jesus as rejecting him, and of those who should misconstrue Jesus as surprisingly open-minded and insightful about his identity, may thus reflect the traumatic experience of an originally Jewish community of Jesus-believers suddenly finding itself predominantly Gentile. Such an explanation is especially attractive in light of Paul's own struggles with this vexing issue (see Rom 9–11), and his conflicts with Peter and others regarding how Gentiles should be integrated into the nascent church (see Gal 2:11–17). If Mark is the product of an author familiar with Paul's writings or thought, as many scholars now believe, then his harsh portrayal of Peter and the other disciples might constitute a polemic against the ecclesiastical leadership provided by Jesus' original followers, who, Mark suggests, never really understood their master.

But perhaps no historical explanation of the messianic secret will suffice, for the motif ultimately reflects a Markan *theological* tension: Jesus is the Son of God—God's special representative and, in some attenuated sense, himself divine—and yet it is Jesus' destiny to die an ugly and solitary death, abandoned not only by his followers but also by God himself. Mark meditates on this paradox at various points in his gospel, most explicitly at 10:44–45: "Whosoever among you will be the chiefest, shall be servant of all. For even the Son of man came not to be ministered unto, but to minister, and to give his life a ransom for many." Though Mark's Jesus is often referred to as Son of God as well as by other triumphant titles, Jesus refers to himself by a more mundane name, Son of Man (see 2:10 note). And sometimes he does so in explicit response to more ostentatious forms of address, for Mark is careful to orchestrate a dialogue between these two crucial aspects of Jesus' identity, letting neither obtain the upper hand. This dialogue is evident at the end of chapter 8, discussed above, and the beginning of 9. Peter's confession that Jesus is "the Christ" (8:29; on the title's meaning, see 1:1 note) leads Jesus to insist that "the Son of man" must suffer, but satanic Peter finds this declaration distasteful and rebukes Jesus (8:31–32). Jesus' rebuke in return introduces a sustained discussion of the necessity of suffering, both for himself and for those who will follow him (8:33–38). But this emphasis does not overshadow Jesus' glory, which is immediately prophesied (9:1) and then demonstrated in the transfiguration that follows (9:2–9).

Mark's representation of Jesus and his ministry maintains a careful balance between suffering and glory, humiliation and exaltation, humanity and divinity. (Indeed, reading Mark alongside the other Synoptics and the Fourth Gospel reveals the extent to which Luke, John, and to a lesser degree Matthew are all willing to emphasize the latter element in each pair at the expense of the former.) Mark's story of Jesus is tragic, to be sure, but it is hopeful as well, even if the hope it offers is never quite realized. Jesus' resurrection is announced, but the risen Christ never appears to confirm the claim. Mark's closing image, Jesus' empty tomb, emblematizes this tension between devastating tragedy and hopeful anticipation. The Greek word used for "tomb" (*mnēmeion*; KJV "sepulchre") literarily means "memorial," and Jesus' elaborate rock-hewn grave certainly memorializes this dead hero—but the tomb is uncannily empty. Moreover, as soon as Jesus' followers, intent on anointing his corpse, are shown it, they are directed to leave in order to meet the risen Christ in Galilee: "Behold the place where they laid him. But go your way . . . into Galilee: there shall ye see him" (16:6–7). They apparently refuse to follow these orders (16:8); but Mark, who like all biblical authors expects more from his readers than literary appreciation and analysis, probably hopes to provoke a more complex response to his demoralizing narrative of perfidy and abandonment, which nonetheless insists on the possibility that the story does not end with Jesus' torturous and solitary death. Such a response will require an embrace of hope, but also a refusal to relinquish despair, which is an authentic response—it is Jesus' response!—to tragedies such as the one Mark's narrative presents. It demands resistance to seeing death as the ultimate reality, and at the same time a refusal to treat it as merely a "passing away" to a "better place." It entails an honest assessment of our most shameful failures and forbids that they be forgotten (it is remarkable that early Christian literature contains such a devastating portrait of Peter and the Twelve), but also refuses to let those failures define us. Such are the psychological, theological, and moral corollaries to the literary paradoxes that Mark relishes.

There are now a number of excellent English language commentaries on Mark. The best is Joel Marcus's two-volume Anchor Bible commentary, *Mark* (New York: Doubleday, 2000; New Haven: Yale University Press, 2009). Also useful are the Word Biblical Commentary, *Mark*, vol. 1 by Robert A. Guelich and vol. 2 by Craig A. Evans (Waco, TX: Thomas Nelson, 1989–2001), and Adela Yarbro Collins's Hermeneia commentary, *Mark* (Minneapolis: Fortress, 2007). The influence of all of these may be detected in the notes that follow.

THE GOSPEL ACCORDING TO

ST. MARK

1 The beginning of the gospel of Jesus Christ, the Son of God: [2]as it is written in the prophets, Behold, I send my messenger before thy face, which shall prepare thy way before thee. [3]The voice of one crying in the wilderness, Prepare ye the way of the Lord, make his paths straight. [4]John did baptize in the wilderness, and preach the baptism of repentance for the remission of sins. [5]And there went out unto him all the land of Judæa, and they of Jerusalem, and were all baptized of him in the river of Jordan, confessing their sins. [6]And John was clothed with camel's hair, and with a girdle of a skin about his loins; and he did eat locusts and wild honey; [7]and preached, saying, There cometh one mightier than I after me, the latchet of whose shoes I am not worthy to stoop down and unloose. [8]I indeed have baptized you with water: but he shall baptize you with the Holy Ghost.

1:1–15 Introduction. In contrast to the other Synoptic Gospels, Mark lacks any reference to Jesus' birth or infancy. Instead, after what may have been the original titular epigraph (v. 1), it launches into John's ministry (vv. 2–8; cf. Matt 3:1–12; Luke 3:1–20; John 1:19–28) and then briefly recounts Jesus' baptism (vv. 9–11; cf. Matt 3:13–17; Luke 3:21–22; John 1:29–34), temptation (vv. 12–13; cf. Matt 4:1–11; Luke 4:1–13), and initial preaching in Galilee (vv. 14–15; cf. Matt 4:12–17; Luke 4:14–15). **1:1** *Beginning*: echoing Gen 1:1. *Gospel*: Gk. *euangelion*, "good news," often used in the Greco-Roman world of an announcement of military victory. The word does not appear in Luke (but see Acts 15:7; 20:24) or John, and in Matthew it is always qualified (e.g., "the gospel of the kingdom" or "this gospel"); of the four gospels, only Mark uses the noun without qualification (see 1:15; 8:35; 10:29; etc.). Thus it here has virtually the technical sense it carries in Paul's letters, denoting proclamation about Jesus, but written instead of preached (see Rom 15:19–20; 16:25; 1 Cor 15:1; etc.). Mark's decision to inscribe the early church's proclamation as a story about Jesus was apparently innovative, but rapidly caught on (hence Matthew, Luke, John, and numerous noncanonical gospels) and led to the familiar use of "gospel" to refer to a genre of writing focused on Jesus. *Jesus Christ*: a name and a title, Jesus the messiah. *Christ* (Gk. *christos*) and "messiah" (Heb. *mashiah*) both mean "anointed," a mark of kingship. *The Son of God*: better omitted (MS tradition). **1:2–8** John the Baptist. **1:2** *Prophets*: better "prophet Isaiah" (MS tradition), altered by scribes because the quotation conflates Exod 23:20, Mal 3:1 (referring to Elijah; cf. Mal 4:5–6), and Isa 40:3. **1:4** *Baptize*: Gk. *baptizō*, "plunge" or "dip"; in the NT it is used exclusively of ritual cleansing. *Remission*: Gk. *aphesis* (cf. 3:29 [KJV "forgiveness"]); the same root is elsewhere translated "forgive." **1:5** *Judæa*: all of Palestine, or (as here) the region around and containing Jerusalem. **1:6** *Camel's hair . . . loins*: a camel-hair coat and a leather belt; compare Elijah in 2 Kgs 1:8 (see note). **1:8** *Holy Ghost*: the creative and inspiring power of God, which sometimes metonymically represents God himself (cf. "Spirit of God," Gen 1:2).

⁹And it came to pass in those days, that Jesus came from Nazareth of Galilee, and was baptized of John in Jordan. ¹⁰And straightway coming up out of the water, he saw the heavens opened, and the Spirit like a dove descending upon him: ¹¹and there came a voice from heaven, saying, Thou art my beloved Son, in whom I am well pleased.

¹²And immediately the Spirit driveth him into the wilderness. ¹³And he was there in the wilderness forty days, tempted of Satan; and was with the wild beasts; and the angels ministered unto him.

¹⁴Now after that John was put in prison, Jesus came into Galilee, preaching the gospel of the kingdom of God, ¹⁵and saying, The time is fulfilled, and the kingdom of God is at hand: repent ye, and believe the gospel.

¹⁶Now as he walked by the sea of Galilee, he saw Simon and Andrew his brother casting a net into the sea: for they were fishers. ¹⁷And Jesus said unto them, Come ye after me, and I will make you to become fishers of men. ¹⁸And straightway they forsook their nets, and followed him. ¹⁹And when he had gone a little further thence, he saw James the son of Zebedee, and John his brother, who also were in the ship mending their nets. ²⁰And straightway he called them: and they left their father Zebedee in the ship with the hired servants, and went after him.

1:9–11 Baptism. Jesus' baptism troubled the other evangelists because it suggested John's superiority. (See Acts 19:1–7 and note at v. 1.) In Matt 3:13–17 John resists baptizing him; Luke 3:19–22 suggests that John was arrested before Jesus was baptized; John 1:29–34 has no reference to his baptism. Matthew and Luke also objectify the episode's portentous events (Matt 3:16–17; Luke 3:21–22; cf. John 1:32), which Mark presents as Jesus' vision. **1:9** *Nazareth*: a village in *Galilee*, a small Palestinian region north of Judea beyond Samaria, and west of the Jordan River. **1:10** *Straightway*: Gk. *euthys*; the adverb appears approximately forty times in Mark, also rendered "immediately," "forthwith," etc. *Opened*: Gk. *schizomenous*, lit. "rent apart." Matthew (3:16) and Luke (3:21) both change Mark's word to the blander *anoigō*, "open." **1:11** *Thou art . . . pleased*: echoing Ps 2:7. *Beloved*: Gk. *agapētos*, which when applied to a son can have the sense "only." LXX uses it of Isaac when God commands Abraham to kill him (Gen 22:2, 12). *In whom*: better "in you" (MS tradition). **1:12–13** Temptation. Matthew (4:1–11) and Luke (4:1–13) contain longer versions, presumably drawing on another literary source (Q). **1:12** *Driveth*: Gk. *ekballei*, an aggressive word made more forceful by the historical present tense. Mark uses the same verb in his reports of exorcisms (1:34, 39; etc. [KJV "cast out"]). Matt 4:1 and Luke 4:1 substitute forms of the milder *agō* ("lead"). **1:13** *Forty days*: compare Elijah's forty days and nights in the wilderness, where he was fed by angels (1 Kgs 19:4–8); see Matt 4:2 note for other parallels. *Tempted*: or "tested" (so throughout). *Satan*: in the OT (where the name is often better translated "the adversary"; see Job 1:6 note), a divine courtier who brings accusations before YHWH (cf. Job 1–2; Ps 109:6–7; Zech 3:1–2). Probably under the influence of Persian dualism, Satan later appears as the chief demon, totally opposed to God, but here God's Spirit cooperates with Satan in testing Jesus (cf. Job 1–2; 2 Cor 12:7–9). **1:14** *Put in prison*: lit. "handed over"; cf. 10:33 (KJV "delivered unto") and 14:10–11 (KJV "betray"), of Jesus' betrayal. *Of the kingdom*: better omitted (MS tradition). **1:15** *Kingdom of God*: God's eschatological reign over the world.

1:16–2:12 Healings in Capernaum. After narrating Jesus' call of the four (1:16–20; cf. Matt 4:18–22 and Luke 5:1–11; John 1:35–51 has a very different account), Mark includes a series of healing stories, focusing on a demoniac (1:21–28; cf. Matt 7:28–29, omitting the healing; Luke 4:31–37), Peter's mother-in-law and many others at Peter's door (1:29–39; cf. Matt 8:14–17; Luke 4:38–43), a man with leprosy (1:40–45; cf. Matt 8:1–4; Luke 5:12–16), and a paralytic (2:1–12; cf. Matt 9:1–8 and Luke 5:17–26; John 5:1–18 has a very different account). **1:16–20** Calling the four. Mark's account recalls Elijah's similarly abrupt call of Elisha (1 Kgs 19:19–21), which likewise follows the protagonist's forty-day sojourn in the wilderness (1 Kgs 19:4–8; cf. Mark 1:13 and note). **1:16** *Simon*: Peter (see 3:16). **1:17** *Fishers of men*: a persuasive teacher could be likened to an angler (e.g., Plato, *Sophist*

²¹And they went into Capernaum; and straightway on the sabbath day he entered into the synagogue, and taught. ²²And they were astonished at his doctrine: for he taught them as one that had authority, and not as the scribes. ²³And there was in their synagogue a man with an unclean spirit; and he cried out, ²⁴saying, Let us alone; what have we to do with thee, thou Jesus of Nazareth? art thou come to destroy us? I know thee who thou art, the Holy One of God. ²⁵And Jesus rebuked him, saying, Hold thy peace, and come out of him. ²⁶And when the unclean spirit had torn him, and cried with a loud voice, he came out of him. ²⁷And they were all amazed, insomuch that they questioned among themselves, saying, What thing is this? what new doctrine is this? for with authority commandeth he even the unclean spirits, and they do obey him. ²⁸And immediately his fame spread abroad throughout all the region round about Galilee.

²⁹And forthwith, when they were come out of the synagogue, they entered into the house of Simon and Andrew, with James and John. ³⁰But Simon's wife's mother lay sick of a fever, and anon they tell him of her. ³¹And he came and took her by the hand, and lifted her up; and immediately the fever left her, and she ministered unto them.

³²And at even, when the sun did set, they brought unto him all that were diseased, and them that were possessed with devils. ³³And all the city was gathered together at the door. ³⁴And he healed many that were sick of divers diseases, and cast out many devils; and suffered not the devils to speak, because they knew him.

³⁵And in the morning, rising up a great while before day, he went out, and departed into a solitary place, and there prayed. ³⁶And Simon and they that were with him followed after him. ³⁷And when they had found him, they said unto him, All men seek for thee. ³⁸And he said unto them, Let us go into the next towns, that I may preach there also: for therefore came I forth. ³⁹And he preached in their synagogues throughout all Galilee, and cast out devils.

⁴⁰And there came a leper to him, beseeching him, and kneeling down to him, and saying unto him, If thou wilt, thou canst make me clean. ⁴¹And Jesus, moved

218d–222d). **1:21** *Capernaum*: a town on the northwest shore of the Sea of Galilee that served as the center of Jesus' ministry. *Synagogue*: Gk. *synagōgē*, here meaning "place of assembly"—a Jewish gathering place for worship, teaching, prayer, and other religious and social activities. **1:22** *Doctrine*: teaching (so throughout). *Scribes*: expert interpreters of the Jewish law, but not a particular sect like the Pharisees. **1:23** *With an unclean spirit*: possessed by a demon (perhaps echoing Zech 13:2). **1:24** *Let us alone*: better omitted (MS tradition). *What have . . . thee*: an ambiguous OT expression, which may imply that the two parties are totally separate and distinct (cf. 2 Kgs 3:13) or that they have no grounds for mutual hostility (cf. Judg 11:12). The first-person plural suggests that Jesus' exorcism represents an assault on all demonic forces, not just this demon. *Thou Jesus . . . God*: following the logic of Greco-Roman magic, the unclean spirit attempts to exercise authority over Jesus by employing his name. Like other demons in Mark (cf. 1:34; 3:11–12), this one recognizes Jesus as a divine representative. **1:25** *Hold thy peace*: a rebuke both consonant with Greco-Roman magic and part of a larger pattern in Mark's gospel: the messianic secret motif (see introduction). **1:26** *Torn*: a literal translation of a Greek word that probably refers to convulsion (so throughout). *Anon*: immediately. **1:31** *Ministered unto them*: as the angels ministered to Jesus (v. 13). **1:35** *Solitary place*: lit. "wilderness" (cf. 1:3, 12, 45 [KJV "desert places"]). **1:36** *Followed after*: better "hunted for" (NRSV). **1:40–45** Healing a man with leprosy. The parallel with Elisha's healing of leprous Namaan (2 Kgs 5:1–19) is part of an extended analogy between Jesus and Elisha; see also 6:30–44 note. **1:40** *Leper*: in the Bible "leprosy" describes a range of skin disorders (see note to Lev 13–14).

with compassion, put forth his hand, and touched him, and saith unto him, I will; be thou clean. ⁴²And as soon as he had spoken, immediately the leprosy departed from him, and he was cleansed. ⁴³And he straitly charged him, and forthwith sent him away; ⁴⁴and saith unto him, See thou say nothing to any man: but go thy way, shew thyself to the priest, and offer for thy cleansing those things which Moses commanded, for a testimony unto them. ⁴⁵But he went out, and began to publish it much, and to blaze abroad the matter, insomuch that Jesus could no more openly enter into the city, but was without in desert places: and they came to him from every quarter.

2 And again he entered into Capernaum, after some days; and it was noised that he was in the house. ²And straightway many were gathered together, insomuch that there was no room to receive them, no, not so much as about the door: and he preached the word unto them.

³And they come unto him, bringing one sick of the palsy, which was borne of four. ⁴And when they could not come nigh unto him for the press, they uncovered the roof where he was: and when they had broken it up, they let down the bed wherein the sick of the palsy lay. ⁵When Jesus saw their faith, he said unto the sick of the palsy, Son, thy sins be forgiven thee. ⁶But there were certain of the scribes sitting there, and reasoning in their hearts, ⁷Why doth this man thus speak blasphemies? who can forgive sins but God only? ⁸And immediately when Jesus perceived in his spirit that they so reasoned within themselves, he said unto them, Why reason ye these things in your hearts? ⁹Whether is it easier to say to the sick of the palsy, Thy sins be forgiven thee; or to say, Arise, and take up thy bed, and walk? ¹⁰But that ye may know that the Son of man hath power on earth to forgive sins, (he saith to the sick of the palsy,) ¹¹I say unto thee, Arise, and take up thy bed, and go thy way into thine house. ¹²And immediately he arose, took up the bed, and went forth before them all; insomuch that they were all amazed, and glorified God, saying, We never saw it on this fashion.

1:41 *Compassion*: better "anger" (MS tradition), altered by scribes so that Jesus not appear angry without clear cause. Matthew and Luke probably excise the phrase for the same reason. *Put forth . . . touched him*: Jesus' physical contact itself challenges the man's uncleanness.   **1:43** *Straitly charged*: scolded. *Sent him away*: Gk. *exebalen* (see v. 12 note).   **1:44** *Which Moses commanded*: Lev 13–14.   **1:45** *Desert places*: see v. 35 note.   **2:1–12** Healing a paralytic.   **2:1** *In the house*: presumably Peter's (cf. 1:29).   **2:2** *Preached the word*: God's word, but not necessarily Scripture.   **2:4** *Broken it up*: lit. "dug out" the thatched roof.   **2:5** *Faith*: Gk. *pistis*, a common element of Jesus' healing; cf. 5:34; 6:5–6; 10:52; etc. KJV translates the Greek word's verbal form as "believe" (cf. 1:15), but *pistis* involves active trust and commitment, not just intellectual assent. *Thy sins . . . thee*: the OT traces illness to sin (e.g., Lev 26:14–16; Deut 28:15–22, 27–29; 2 Chr 21:12–15, 18–19), a link Jesus assumes. Only in this episode (cf. Matt 9:2; Luke 5:20) and in Luke 7:48 does the synoptic tradition show him forgiving sins. **2:9** *Whether*: which.   **2:10** *Son of man*: the OT idiom meaning "human being" (e.g., Num 23:19; Ps 144:3) ultimately acquired eschatological connotations, probably as a result of Dan 7:13–14. The phrase is used in the gospels exclusively by Jesus, almost always with apparent reference to himself (but cf. v. 28; 8:38 and notes) and often with a view to the eschatological consummation.

   2:13–3:12 Initial conflicts. After narrating Jesus' call of Levi (2:13–14; cf. Matt 9:9, where Levi is named Matthew; Luke 5:27–28), Mark includes a series of conflict narratives, in which Jesus disputes with scribes, Pharisees, and others about his tendency to fraternize with sinners (2:15–17; cf. Matt 9:10–13; Luke 5:29–32), about fasting (2:18–22; cf. Matt 9:14–17; Luke 5:33–39), and about Sabbath observance (2:23–3:6; cf. Matt 12:1–14; Luke 6:1–11). The section begins (2:13) and ends (3:7–12; cf. Matt 12:15–21; Luke 6:17–19) with Jesus withdrawing to the sea.

¹³And he went forth again by the sea side; and all the multitude resorted unto him, and he taught them. ¹⁴And as he passed by, he saw Levi the son of Alphæus sitting at the receipt of custom, and said unto him, Follow me. And he arose and followed him.

¹⁵And it came to pass, that, as Jesus sat at meat in his house, many publicans and sinners sat also together with Jesus and his disciples: for there were many, and they followed him. ¹⁶And when the scribes and Pharisees saw him eat with publicans and sinners, they said unto his disciples, How is it that he eateth and drinketh with publicans and sinners? ¹⁷When Jesus heard it, he saith unto them, They that are whole have no need of the physician, but they that are sick: I came not to call the righteous, but sinners to repentance.

¹⁸And the disciples of John and of the Pharisees used to fast: and they come and say unto him, Why do the disciples of John and of the Pharisees fast, but thy disciples fast not? ¹⁹And Jesus said unto them, Can the children of the bridechamber fast, while the bridegroom is with them? as long as they have the bridegroom with them, they cannot fast. ²⁰But the days will come, when the bridegroom shall be taken away from them, and then shall they fast in those days. ²¹No man also seweth a piece of new cloth on an old garment: else the new piece that filled it up taketh away from the old, and the rent is made worse. ²²And no man putteth new wine into old bottles: else the new wine doth burst the bottles, and the wine is spilled, and the bottles will be marred: but new wine must be put into new bottles.

²³And it came to pass, that he went through the corn fields on the sabbath day; and his disciples began, as they went, to pluck the ears of corn. ²⁴And the Pharisees said unto him, Behold, why do they on the sabbath day that which is not lawful? ²⁵And he said unto them, Have ye never read what David did, when he had need, and was an hungred, he, and they that were with him? ²⁶How he went into

---

2:13 *The sea*: of Galilee (so throughout). **2:14** *Receipt of custom*: tax office. **2:15** *Sat* [lit. "reclined"] *at meat*: reclining was the customary posture for dining. (*Meat*, here and throughout, is food.) Banquets (Gk. *symposia*) are conventional settings for learned discourse in Greco-Roman literature, most famously in Plato's *Symposium*. *His house*: either Jesus' (presuming he was staying with Peter; cf. 1:29–34) or Levi's. *Many publicans and sinners*: apparently Levi's friends. KJV *publicans* (Gk. *telōnai*) are not technically Lat. *publicani* ("official tax collectors") but their local agents (Lat. *portitores*), subcontracted to extract taxes in their native regions. They were reviled as collaborationists who extorted more than was due and pocketed the profits (see Luke 3:12–13). **2:16** *And Pharisees*: better "of the Pharisees" (MS tradition), i.e., scribes belonging to the Pharisaic movement. *Pharisees* (from Heb. *perushim*, "set apart") were an influential Jewish sect that highly valued oral traditions as well as the written law, which it wanted to apply faithfully to every aspect of life. **2:17** *They that . . . sick*: a common adage in Greco-Roman literature. Jesus again links sin with illness (cf. v. 5 and note). *To repentance*: better omitted (MS tradition). **2:19** *Children of the bridechamber*: wedding guests. The nuptial imagery develops a common OT motif of Israel as the bride of God, to whom God remains faithful even when she goes "a whoring" after idols (cf. Exod 34:15–16; Isa 54:5–6; Hos 2). In the NT Christ is the bridegroom (cf. John 3:28–29; Eph 5:23–33), with the eschatological age often figured as his wedding banquet (see Matt 22:1–14; 25:1–13; Rev 19:7–9), on the basis of OT passages such as Isa 25:6–8; 62:4–5. **2:21–22** *No man . . . new bottles*: Jesus may stress the newness of his teaching, or he may deny it altogether. Luke suggests the latter by adding that no one prefers new wine to old (5:39). **2:22** *Bottles*: lit. "wineskins." *Is spilled . . . marred*: better "is destroyed along with the wineskins" (MS tradition). **2:23** *Corn*: grain. **2:24** *Not lawful*: see Exod 34:21. **2:25** *An hungred*: hungry. **2:26** *How he . . . him*: see 1 Sam 21:1–6.

the house of God in the days of Abiathar the high priest, and did eat the shew-bread, which is not lawful to eat but for the priests, and gave also to them which were with him? ²⁷And he said unto them, The sabbath was made for man, and not man for the sabbath: ²⁸therefore the Son of man is Lord also of the sabbath.

3 And he entered again into the synagogue; and there was a man there which had a withered hand. ²And they watched him, whether he would heal him on the sabbath day; that they might accuse him. ³And he saith unto the man which had the withered hand, Stand forth. ⁴And he saith unto them, Is it lawful to do good on the sabbath days, or to do evil? to save life, or to kill? But they held their peace. ⁵And when he had looked round about on them with anger, being grieved for the hardness of their hearts, he saith unto the man, Stretch forth thine hand. And he stretched it out: and his hand was restored whole as the other. ⁶And the Pharisees went forth, and straightway took counsel with the Herodians against him, how they might destroy him.

⁷But Jesus withdrew himself with his disciples to the sea: and a great multi-tude from Galilee followed him, and from Judæa, ⁸and from Jerusalem, and from Idumæa, and from beyond Jordan; and they about Tyre and Sidon, a great multitude, when they had heard what great things he did, came unto him. ⁹And he spake to his disciples, that a small ship should wait on him because of the multitude, lest they should throng him. ¹⁰For he had healed many; insomuch that they pressed upon him for to touch him, as many as had plagues. ¹¹And unclean spirits, when they saw him, fell down before him, and cried, saying, Thou art the Son of God. ¹²And he straitly charged them that they should not make him known.

The days . . . priest: Ahimelech was high priest at the time; Abiathar was his son (1 Sam 22:20–23) and became high priest only later (2 Sam 20:25). Matthew and Luke omit Mark's erroneous refer-ence. *The shewbread . . . priests*: see Lev 24:5–9.   **2:27** *The sabbath . . . sabbath*: a sweeping claim, which transforms into a general principle the exceptional subordination of the law to human needs in 1 Sam 21. The saying has parallels in later rabbinic literature (e.g., *Mekilta* on Exod 31:14), but both Matthew and Luke omit it (perhaps as too radical).   **2:28** *Son of man*: perhaps Jesus' eschato-logical alter ego, or perhaps any human being (see v. 10 and note).   **3:1** *Withered hand*: compare the healing of Jeroboam's hand (1 Kgs 13:1–10).   **3:2** *They*: apparently the Pharisees mentioned in the previous episode.   **3:5** *Hardness of their hearts*: a biblical commonplace for sinful stubbornness. **3:6** *The Pharisees . . . destroy him*: the Pharisees and *Herodians* work with the Sanhedrin against Jesus later in Mark (12:13). *Herodians*: supporters of Herod (precise identity unknown).   **3:8** *Idumæa*: Edom, a region south of Judea whose population, coerced into conversion under John Hyrancus in the late second century B.C.E., was considered only marginally Jewish. *Beyond Jordan*: the region east of the Jordan River, whose population was a mixture of Jews and Gentiles. *Tyre and Sidon*: Gentile cities in Phoenicia, northwest of Judea.   **3:10** *Plagues*: torments or sufferings, often used figuratively of disease.   **3:12** *Straitly charged*: rebuked (cf. 1:43).

   3:13–4:34 Parables. After narrating Jesus' call of the Twelve (3:13–19a; cf. Matt 10:1–4; Luke 6:12–16; Acts 1:13), Mark focuses on Jesus' parables, beginning with his parabolic response to the scribes' accusations (3:19b–35, esp. 23–27; cf. Matt 12:22–32, 46–50; Luke 11:14–23; 12:10; 8:19–21) and progressing to the parable of the Sower (4:1–9; cf. Matt 13:1–9; Luke 8:4–8) and its interpretation (4:13–20; cf. Matt 13:18–23; Luke 8:11–15), the parable of the Seed Growing Secretly (4:26–29), and the parable of the Mustard Seed (4:30–32; cf. Matt 13:31–32; Luke 13:18–19). Interspersed are state-ments addressing Jesus' tendency to speak obscurely: 4:10–12 (cf. Matt 13:10–15; Luke 8:9–10; John 12:39–41), 4:21–25 (cf. Matt 5:15; 10:26; 7:2; 13:12; Luke 8:16–18; 11:33; 12:2; 6:38b; 19:26), and

¹³And he goeth up into a mountain, and calleth unto him whom he would: and they came unto him. ¹⁴And he ordained twelve, that they should be with him, and that he might send them forth to preach, ¹⁵and to have power to heal sicknesses, and to cast out devils: ¹⁶and Simon he surnamed Peter; ¹⁷and James the son of Zebedee, and John the brother of James; and he surnamed them Boanerges, which is, The sons of thunder: ¹⁸and Andrew, and Philip, and Bartholomew, and Matthew, and Thomas, and James the son of Alphæus and Thaddæus, and Simon the Canaanite, ¹⁹and Judas Iscariot, which also betrayed him.

And they went into an house. ²⁰And the multitude cometh together again, so that they could not so much as eat bread. ²¹And when his friends heard of it, they went out to lay hold on him: for they said, He is beside himself.

²²And the scribes which came down from Jerusalem said, He hath Beelzebub, and by the prince of the devils casteth he out devils. ²³And he called them unto him, and said unto them in parables, How can Satan cast out Satan? ²⁴And if a kingdom be divided against itself, that kingdom cannot stand. ²⁵And if a house be divided against itself, that house cannot stand. ²⁶And if Satan rise up against himself, and be divided, he cannot stand, but hath an end. ²⁷No man can enter into a strong man's house, and spoil his goods, except he will first bind the strong man; and then he will spoil his house. ²⁸Verily I say unto you, All sins shall be forgiven

4:33–34 (cf. Matt 13:34–35). **3:13** *Goeth up . . . mountain*: compare Moses' ascent of Sinai with Israel's elders (Exod 24:1–4). **3:14** *Ordained*: better "appointed" (NRSV). *Twelve*: cf. Exod 24:4; Matt 10:1 note. *Send them forth*: Gk. *apostellō*, whence "apostle"; cf. 6:30; Matt 10:2 note. **3:15** *To heal . . . and*: better omitted (MS tradition). **3:16–18** *And Simon . . . Andrew*: cf. 1:16–20. **3:16** *Peter*: Gk. *Petros*, "Rock"; cf. Matt 16:18. **3:18** *Philip*: in all four apostolic lists (here; Matt 10:1–4; Luke 6:13–16; Acts 1:13); he figures prominently in John (1:43–51; 14:8–9). *Bartholomew*: in all four lists. *Matthew*: in all four lists, although Matthew's gospel conflates him with Levi (see Matt 10:3 note; 9:9; cf. Mark 2:13–14). *Thomas*: in all four lists, but he figures most prominently in John, where his faith is questioned (20:24–29). *James the son of Alphæus*: in all four lists; Mark apparently believes he is Levi's brother (cf. 2:14). *Thaddæus*: appearing only here and in Matthew's list (10:3). Luke 6:16 and Acts 1:13 substitute "Judas, the brother [or 'son'; see Luke 6:16 note] of James." *Simon the Canaanite*: in all four lists, but he is called "Zelotes" (i.e., "the Zealot") in Luke 6:15 and Acts 1:13, perhaps because the Greek word translated "Canaanite" derives from an Aramaic word meaning "zealot." **3:19** *Iscariot*: perhaps meaning "man from Karioth" (a town in Judea); or "the assassin" (from Gk. *sikarios*, "dagger"); or "from the tribe of Issachar." Other interpretations are possible. *Betrayed him*: in the erratic paragraphing of KJV, the second half of this verse, printed without an initial capital, is separated from the first by a colon. **3:19b–35** The Beelzebub controversy. The first appearance of Mark's so-called interpolation technique: interrupting one story (in this case, a conflict between Jesus and his family, vv. 19b–21; see 21 note) with another (a conflict between Jesus and the scribes, vv. 22–30) before returning to the original (vv. 31–35), and thereby inviting the reader to ponder the relationship between the two. Matthew (12:46–50) and Luke (8:19–21) separate Jesus' response to his family's call from the accusation of satanic collusion, and seem to privilege a version of the latter from Q (Matt 12:22–32; Luke 11:14–23). **3:19** *Into an house*: or simply "home." **3:21** *Friends*: better "family." *Beside himself*: out of his mind. **3:22** *Beelzebub*: apparently following the Vulgate, KJV replaces Gk. *Beelzeboul* with *Beelzebub*, a disdainful distortion (Heb. *ba'al zebub*, "Lord of Flies") of an honorific for the Canaanite god Baal (cf. 2 Kgs 1:2). "Beelzebul" seems to suggest a different distortion, "Lord of Dung," although other interpretations are possible. In any case, Mark equates the despised pagan god with Satan, *the prince of the devils* (vv. 22–23). **3:23** *Parables*: see 4:2 note. **3:24–27** *If a kingdom . . . his house*: Jesus' argument is inconsistent. On the assumption that Satan's kingdom and house stand, vv. 24–26 reason that Jesus' exorcistic power is not satanic; for if it were, Satan would be divided and could not stand. But v. 27 suggests the opposite, that Satan's kingdom or house has fallen before Jesus' power (see note). **3:27** *No man . . . his house*: Jesus (the thief) enters Satan's (the strong man's) realm of authority (house), restrains him, and

unto the sons of men, and blasphemies wherewith soever they shall blaspheme: [29]but he that shall blaspheme against the Holy Ghost hath never forgiveness, but is in danger of eternal damnation: [30]because they said, He hath an unclean spirit.

[31]There came then his brethren and his mother, and, standing without, sent unto him, calling him. [32]And the multitude sat about him, and they said unto him, Behold, thy mother and thy brethren without seek for thee. [33]And he answered them, saying, Who is my mother, or my brethren? [34]And he looked round about on them which sat about him, and said, Behold my mother and my brethren! [35]For whosoever shall do the will of God, the same is my brother, and my sister, and mother.

4 And he began again to teach by the sea side: and there was gathered unto him a great multitude, so that he entered into a ship, and sat in the sea; and the whole multitude was by the sea on the land. [2]And he taught them many things by parables, and said unto them in his doctrine, [3]Hearken; Behold, there went out a sower to sow: [4]and it came to pass, as he sowed, some fell by the way side, and the fowls of the air came and devoured it up. [5]And some fell on stony ground, where it had not much earth; and immediately it sprang up, because it had no depth of earth: [6]but when the sun was up, it was scorched; and because it had no root, it withered away. [7]And some fell among thorns, and the thorns grew up, and choked it, and it yielded no fruit. [8]And other fell on good ground, and did yield fruit that sprang up and increased; and brought forth, some thirty, and some sixty, and some an hundred. [9]And he said unto them, He that hath ears to hear, let him hear.

[10]And when he was alone, they that were about him with the twelve asked of him the parable. [11]And he said unto them, Unto you it is given to know the mystery of the kingdom of God: but unto them that are without, all these things are done in parables: [12]that seeing they may see, and not perceive: and hearing they may hear, and not understand; lest at any time they should be converted, and their sins should be forgiven them.

[13]And he said unto them, Know ye not this parable? and how then will ye know all parables? [14]The sower soweth the word. [15]And these are they by the way side, where the word is sown; but when they have heard, Satan cometh immediately,

---

liberates those he and his minions have possessed (plunders his goods). Mark has repeatedly portrayed Jesus doing precisely this (see 1:23–26, 34; 3:11–12), and diction supports the interpretation: the Greek word rendered *goods* (lit. "vessels") can refer to bodies or even to people (cf. 1 Thess 4:4 and note), *strong man* (Gk. *ischyros*) can designate a demon; and Mark identified Jesus himself as the "mightier one" in 1:7 (Gk. *ischyroteros*).   **3:29** *Blaspheme against . . . Ghost*: the vagueness of this grave sin seized hold of the later Christian imagination, perhaps most famously John Bunyan's (see *Grace Abounding to the Chief of Sinners*). *In danger*: lit. "guilty." *Damnation*: better "sin" (MS tradition).   **3:31** *Standing without*: outside the house; cf. v. 19b; 21 and note.   **3:32** *Brethren*: better to add "and sisters" (MS tradition).   **4:2** *Parables*: Gk. *parabolē*, "comparison"; this rhetorical term can denote many forms of concise, figurative discourse, including proverb, fable, and metaphor.   **4:8** *Some thirty . . . hundred*: three hyperbolic yields to counter the three instances of fruitless sowing.   **4:10** *Parable*: better "parables" (MS tradition).   **4:11** *To know*: better omitted (MS tradition).   **4:12** *That*: Gk. *hina*, "in order that." Mark presents Jesus' parables as obscure mysteries that confound his listeners and prevent them from obtaining forgiveness. *Seeing they . . . them*: cf. Isa 6:9–10. *Converted*: Gk. *epistrephō*, "turn back" or "turn around."   **4:14–20** Parable of the Sower interpreted. This may be an early Christian interpretation of Jesus' parable, anachronistically attributed by the Synoptics to Jesus himself. A possibly more primitive form of the parable circulated without the interpretation attached (see *Gospel of Thomas* 9; Appendix, pp. 1034–35).

and taketh away the word that was sown in their hearts. ¹⁶And these are they likewise which are sown on stony ground; who, when they have heard the word, immediately receive it with gladness; ¹⁷and have no root in themselves, and so endure but for a time: afterward, when affliction or persecution ariseth for the word's sake, immediately they are offended. ¹⁸And these are they which are sown among thorns; such as hear the word, ¹⁹and the cares of this world, and the deceitfulness of riches, and the lusts of other things entering in, choke the word, and it becometh unfruitful. ²⁰And these are they which are sown on good ground; such as hear the word, and receive it, and bring forth fruit, some thirtyfold, some sixty, and some an hundred.

²¹And he said unto them, Is a candle brought to be put under a bushel, or under a bed? and not to be set on a candlestick? ²²For there is nothing hid, which shall not be manifested; neither was any thing kept secret, but that it should come abroad. ²³If any man have ears to hear, let him hear. ²⁴And he said unto them, Take heed what ye hear: with what measure ye mete, it shall be measured to you: and unto you that hear shall more be given. ²⁵For he that hath, to him shall be given: and he that hath not, from him shall be taken even that which he hath.

²⁶And he said, So is the kingdom of God, as if a man should cast seed into the ground; ²⁷and should sleep, and rise night and day, and the seed should spring and grow up, he knoweth not how. ²⁸For the earth bringeth forth fruit of herself; first the blade, then the ear, after that the full corn in the ear. ²⁹But when the fruit is brought forth, immediately he putteth in the sickle, because the harvest is come.

³⁰And he said, Whereunto shall we liken the kingdom of God? or with what comparison shall we compare it? ³¹It is like a grain of mustard seed, which, when it is sown in the earth, is less than all the seeds that be in the earth: ³²but when it is sown, it groweth up, and becometh greater than all herbs, and shooteth out great branches; so that the fowls of the air may lodge under the shadow of it.

³³And with many such parables spake he the word unto them, as they were able to hear it. ³⁴But without a parable spake he not unto them: and when they were alone, he expounded all things to his disciples.

4:15 *In their hearts*: better "in them" (MS tradition).   **4:16** *These are . . . word*: here, as in v. 18, the interpretation loses syntactical consistency. The word is no longer sown (cf. v. 14); rather, its hearers are themselves the sown seed. The symbolic slippage invites readers to ponder how much responsibility Jesus the sower bears for his teaching's fruitlessness, a pressing question given Jesus' claim that his teaching obfuscates (v. 12).   **4:17** *Affliction or persecution*: the context is eschatological; cf. 13:11–13, 19. *Offended*: Gk. *skandalizō*, lit. "trap" or "snare"; in the NT the verb seems to mean "cause to stumble" or "cause to sin."   **4:19** *World*: lit. "age," as often in Mark. "This age" refers to the present (as opposed to the end time).   **4:21** *Bushel*: vessel for measuring grain.   **4:24** *Take heed . . . hear*: lit. "see what you hear" (cf. vv. 3, 12). *That hear*: better omitted (MS tradition).   **4:25** *For he . . . he hath*: the eschatological revelation of hidden truth (vv. 21–22) will exaggerate the division between insiders and outsiders established by Jesus' teaching (vv. 11–12).   **4:28** *Corn*: grain.   **4:29** *The harvest*: a conventional symbol of God's eschatological judgment (cf. Joel 3:13), with God and his angels often serving as harvesters (cf. Matt 13:30, 39; Rev 14:14–20).   **4:30** *With what . . . it*: better "in what parable shall we present it" (MS tradition; our translation).   **4:32** *It groweth . . . it*: recalling Ezek 17:22–23 (cf. Dan 4:10–12, 20–21), but replacing Ezekiel's sprig of a lofty cedar with a seed that grows not into a proud tree but into a sizable herb. While a cedar *shooteth out great branches*, the phrase is somewhat out of place when applied to mustard, and so the parable may ironically challenge expectations about the grandeur of God's kingdom.

³⁵And the same day, when the even was come, he saith unto them, Let us pass over unto the other side. ³⁶And when they had sent away the multitude, they took him even as he was in the ship. And there were also with him other little ships. ³⁷And there arose a great storm of wind, and the waves beat into the ship, so that it was now full. ³⁸And he was in the hinder part of the ship, asleep on a pillow: and they awake him, and say unto him, Master, carest thou not that we perish? ³⁹And he arose, and rebuked the wind, and said unto the sea, Peace, be still. And the wind ceased, and there was a great calm. ⁴⁰And he said unto them, Why are ye so fearful? how is it that ye have no faith? ⁴¹And they feared exceedingly, and said one to another, What manner of man is this, that even the wind and the sea obey him?

5 And they came over unto the other side of the sea, into the country of the Gadarenes. ²And when he was come out of the ship, immediately there met him out of the tombs a man with an unclean spirit, ³who had his dwelling among the tombs; and no man could bind him, no, not with chains: ⁴because that he had been often bound with fetters and chains, and the chains had been plucked asunder by him, and the fetters broken in pieces: neither could any man tame him. ⁵And always, night and day, he was in the mountains, and in the tombs, crying, and cutting himself with stones. ⁶But when he saw Jesus afar off, he ran and worshipped him, ⁷and cried with a loud voice, and said, What have I to do with thee, Jesus, thou Son of the most high God? I adjure thee by God, that thou torment me

4:35–5:43 Calming the storm and more healings. After narrating Jesus' calming of the storm (4:35–41; cf. Matt 8:18, 23–27; Luke 8:22–25), Mark records three more miraculous healings: Legion's exorcism (5:1–20; cf. Matt 8:28–34; Luke 8:26–39) and the restoration of Jairus's daughter, an episode interrupted by the hemorrhaging woman's healing (5:21–43; cf. Matt 9:18–26; Luke 8:40–56). **4:35** *The other side*: of the Sea of Galilee; see 5:1 note. **4:38** *Asleep*: as in Jonah; see Matt 8:23–27 note for this episode's numerous parallels with that OT book. *Master*: a title commonly applied to Jesus in the KJV Synoptic Gospels, often as the translation of a Greek (or sometimes Aramaic) word for teacher. **4:39** *And rebuked . . . still*: Jesus rebukes the storm, just as he does demons; cf. 1:25 (with the same Greek word [KJV "hold thy peace"]); 9:25; etc. Mark may allude to the OT tradition of God defeating sea monsters (e.g., Ps 74:12–15; Isa 51:9–10; cf. Mark 6:48 and note). **4:40** *How is . . . faith*: better "Do you still have no faith?" (MS tradition). Following on the heels of Mark's representation of the disciples as privileged recipients of Jesus' secret teachings (4:10–12, 33–34), this portrayal of them as faithless comes as a surprise, suggesting that the boundary between insider and outsider (cf. 4:11) is not stable. Matthew (8:26) and Luke (8:25) each soften Jesus' rebuke. **4:41** *What manner of man*: Gk. *tis*, "who"; KJV apparently assimilates Mark (and Luke 8:25) to Matt 8:27. **5:1** *Gadarenes*: better "Gerasenes" (MS tradition), but confusion among MSS and disagreement among the Synoptics (see Matt 8:28 note) point to early and widespread bewilderment about where this exorcism was supposed to have occurred. A number of locations in the Gentile territory (note the swine herding in vv. 11–14) of the Decapolis (cf. v. 20), east of the Sea of Galilee, have names that could have been corrupted into the variations recorded. **5:2** *Out of the tombs*: assimilating the demoniac to OT caricatures of unclean Gentile behavior (e.g., Isa 65:4, referring ironically to Israel). The man's dwelling among tombs also suggests that he is socially dead. **5:3** *Could bind him*: better to add "anymore" (MS tradition). **5:6** *Worshipped*: lit. "fell prostrate before." The Greek word implies veneration, but not necessarily that due to a god. **5:7** *What have . . . thee*: see 1:24 and note. *Son of the most high God*: on the function of names in Greco-Roman exorcisms, see 1:24 note. *Most high God*: an OT divine appellation commonly used by Gentiles (e.g., Gen 14:18–22; Num 24:15–16), or by Israelites when asserting YHWH's dominion over

not. ⁸For he said unto him, Come out of the man, thou unclean spirit. ⁹And he asked him, What is thy name? And he answered, saying, My name is Legion: for we are many. ¹⁰And he besought him much that he would not send them away out of the country.

¹¹Now there was there nigh unto the mountains a great herd of swine feeding. ¹²And all the devils besought him, saying, Send us into the swine, that we may enter into them. ¹³And forthwith Jesus gave them leave. And the unclean spirits went out, and entered into the swine: and the herd ran violently down a steep place into the sea, (they were about two thousand;) and were choked in the sea. ¹⁴And they that fed the swine fled, and told it in the city, and in the country. And they went out to see what it was that was done. ¹⁵And they come to Jesus, and see him that was possessed with the devil, and had the legion, sitting, and clothed, and in his right mind: and they were afraid. ¹⁶And they that saw it told them how it befell to him that was possessed with the devil, and also concerning the swine. ¹⁷And they began to pray him to depart out of their coasts. ¹⁸And when he was come into the ship, he that had been possessed with the devil prayed him that he might be with him. ¹⁹Howbeit Jesus suffered him not, but saith unto him, Go home to thy friends, and tell them how great things the Lord hath done for thee, and hath had compassion on thee. ²⁰And he departed, and began to publish in Decapolis how great things Jesus had done for him: and all men did marvel.

²¹And when Jesus was passed over again by ship unto the other side, much people gathered unto him: and he was nigh unto the sea. ²²And, behold, there cometh one of the rulers of the synagogue, Jairus by name; and when he saw him, he fell at his feet, ²³and besought him greatly, saying, My little daughter lieth at the point of death: I pray thee, come and lay thy hands on her, that she may be healed; and she shall live.

²⁴And Jesus went with him; and much people followed him, and thronged him. ²⁵And a certain woman, which had an issue of blood twelve years, ²⁶and had suffered many things of many physicians, and had spent all that she had, and was nothing bettered, but rather grew worse, ²⁷when she had heard of Jesus,

---

the world, especially over the nations (e.g., Deut 32:8; cf. Dan 4:17).   **5:9** *My name . . . many*: the alteration between singular and plural pronouns dramatizes the drowning of the man's identity into the demonic horde. *Legion*: Lat. *legio*, transliterated into Greek: a division of the Roman army consisting of several thousand soldiers. Mark's use of the term invites an allegorical reading of the parable as a critique of Rome's domination of the Levant. (Note that Legion begs Jesus not to expel them from the region, v. 10.)   **5:12** *All the devils*: better "they" (MS tradition). *Send us . . . them*: the unclean spirits have an affinity for unclean animals.   **5:17** *Coasts*: territory (so throughout).   **5:19** *Tell them . . . thee*: while Matthew's Jesus forbids preaching to the Gentiles (10:5; 15:24–26), at least until his resurrection (28:19–20), in Mark Jesus authorizes open discourse about his miracles among the Decapolis's Gentile populace as an exception to his normal policy of secrecy.   **5:20** *Decapolis*: a coalition of Hellenistic cities east of Galilee, with a primarily Gentile population.   **5:21** *Passed over . . . side*: Jesus returns to Jewish territory (cf. "synagogue," v. 22).   **5:23** *Healed*: Gk. *sōzō*, also "saved" (cf. vv. 28, 34 [KJV "be/made whole"]).   **5:25** *Issue of blood*: vaginal bleeding; this woman and anything she touched would have been ritually unclean (Lev 15:19–30).

came in the press behind, and touched his garment. [28]For she said, If I may touch but his clothes, I shall be whole. [29]And straightway the fountain of her blood was dried up; and she felt in her body that she was healed of that plague. [30]And Jesus, immediately knowing in himself that virtue had gone out of him, turned him about in the press, and said, Who touched my clothes? [31]And his disciples said unto him, Thou seest the multitude thronging thee, and sayest thou, Who touched me? [32]And he looked round about to see her that had done this thing. [33]But the woman fearing and trembling, knowing what was done in her, came and fell down before him, and told him all the truth. [34]And he said unto her, Daughter, thy faith hath made thee whole; go in peace, and be whole of thy plague.

[35]While he yet spake, there came from the ruler of the synagogue's house certain which said, Thy daughter is dead: why troublest thou the Master any further? [36]As soon as Jesus heard the word that was spoken, he saith unto the ruler of the synagogue, Be not afraid, only believe. [37]And he suffered no man to follow him, save Peter, and James, and John the brother of James. [38]And he cometh to the house of the ruler of the synagogue, and seeth the tumult, and them that wept and wailed greatly. [39]And when he was come in, he saith unto them, Why make ye this ado, and weep? the damsel is not dead, but sleepeth. [40]And they laughed him to scorn. But when he had put them all out, he taketh the father and the mother of the damsel, and them that were with him, and entereth in where the damsel was lying. [41]And he took the damsel by the hand, and said unto her, Talitha cumi; which is, being interpreted, Damsel, I say unto thee, arise. [42]And straightway the damsel arose, and walked; for she was of the age of twelve years. And they were astonished with a great astonishment. [43]And he charged them straitly that no man should know it; and commanded that something should be given her to eat.

6 And he went out from thence, and came into his own country; and his disciples follow him. [2]And when the sabbath day was come, he began to teach

---

5:27 *Touched his garment*: cf. 6:56; Acts 19:11–12.   **5:29** *Plague*: see 3:10 note (also at v. 34).   **5:30** *Virtue*: Gk. *dynamis*, also rendered "mighty works" (e.g., 6:2), "power" (9:1), or "miracle" (9:39).   **5:36** *As soon . . . heard*: better "overhearing" or "ignoring" (MS tradition), different meanings of the same Greek word. The latter would imply Jesus' refusal to acknowledge death's power.   **5:37** *Save Peter . . . John*: the same will accompany Jesus when he anguishes about his impending death (14:32–42) and witness his transfiguration (9:2–8), which foreshadows the resurrection.   **5:39** *The damsel . . . sleepeth*: Jesus denies in anticipation that he resurrects the girl. Unlike Luke (see 8:55) and Matthew (compare 9:18 and Mark 5:23), Mark never clarifies whether she rises from the dead or awakens from a coma. *Damsel*: lit. "child."   **5:40** *When he . . . out*: the privacy suits Jesus' tendency toward secrecy, but is also common in ancient stories of miraculous restoration (e.g., 2 Kgs 4:32–37; Mark 7:33; Ovid, *Metamorphoses* 7.255–93).   **5:41** *Talitha cumi*: a transliteration of the Aramaic, the alien utterance underscoring the numinous nature of the scene (cf. 7:33–34).   **5:42** *Twelve years*: the same length of time as the woman had been bleeding (v. 25), one of several points of contact between the episode's intercalated stories.

6:1–8:21 Commissioning the Twelve and the revelation of Gentile inclusion. As in chap. 3 (vv. 13–21, 31–35), Mark juxtaposes Jesus' rejection by his own (6:1–6a; cf. Matt 13:53–58; Luke 4:16–30; John 7:3–5; 4:44) to his turning to the Twelve. After the narrative of their mission and return (6:6b–13, 30–32; cf. Matt 9:35–10:1, 5–15; Luke 9:1–6; 10:1–12), which frames John's demise (6:14–29; Matt

in the synagogue: and many hearing him were astonished, saying, From whence hath this man these things? and what wisdom is this which is given unto him, that even such mighty works are wrought by his hands? ³Is not this the carpenter, the son of Mary, the brother of James, and Joses, and of Juda, and Simon? and are not his sisters here with us? And they were offended at him. ⁴But Jesus said unto them, A prophet is not without honour, but in his own country, and among his own kin, and in his own house. ⁵And he could there do no mighty work, save that he laid his hands upon a few sick folk, and healed them. ⁶And he marvelled because of their unbelief.

And he went round about the villages, teaching. ⁷And he called unto him the twelve, and began to send them forth by two and two; and gave them power over unclean spirits; ⁸and commanded them that they should take nothing for their journey, save a staff only; no scrip, no bread, no money in their purse: ⁹but be shod with sandals; and not put on two coats. ¹⁰And he said unto them, In what place soever ye enter into an house, there abide till ye depart from that place. ¹¹And whosoever shall not receive you, nor hear you, when ye depart thence, shake off the dust under your feet for a testimony against them. Verily I say unto you, It shall be more tolerable for Sodom and Gomorrha in the day of judgment, than for that city. ¹²And they went out, and preached that men should repent. ¹³And they cast out many devils, and anointed with oil many that were sick, and healed them.

¹⁴And king Herod heard of him; (for his name was spread abroad:) and he said, That John the Baptist was risen from the dead, and therefore mighty works do

---

14:1–12; Luke 9:7–9; 3:19–20), Mark includes a variety of material arranged in a way that explains and underscores the inclusion of Gentiles in Jesus' mission (already foreshadowed in 5:1–20; see esp. v. 19 and note), and suggests that the Twelve failed to grasp this aspect of his ministry: the miraculous feeding of five thousand Jews (6:30–44; cf. Matt 14:13–21; Luke 9:10–17; John 6:1–13), the disciples' failure to recognize Jesus walking on water (6:45–52; cf. Matt 14:22–33; John 6:15–21), healings at Gennesaret (6:53–56; cf. Matt 14:34–36), a dispute about defilement (7:1–23; cf. Matt 15:1–20), the healing of a Syrophoenician woman's daughter (7:24–30; cf. Matt 15:21–28), the healing of a (Gentile) deaf-mute (7:31–37; cf. Matt 15:29–31), the feeding of four thousand Gentiles (8:1–9; cf. Matt 15:32–38), and the Pharisees' rejected request for a sign (8:10–13; cf. Matt 12:38–39; Luke 11:16, 29), which leads to Jesus' rebuke of the disciples for failing to understand the miraculous feedings (8:14–21; cf. Matt 16:5–12; Luke 12:1).   **6:1** *His own country*: presumably the area around Nazareth.   **6:3** *Son of Mary*: identification of a son with reference to the mother is unusual. The phrase intimates that Jesus is illegitimate, which partly explains why Matthew (13:55) and Luke (4:22) alter it. The story of Jesus' miraculous conception, versions of which appear in Matthew and Luke, answers such charges. **6:4** *A prophet . . . house*: a common sentiment; parallels abound in ancient Mediterranean literature. **6:8** *Scrip*: Gk. *pēran*, a small satchel; customarily carried, with *a staff*, by itinerant Hellenistic philosophers such as the Cynics, from whom Jesus may be urging his disciples to differentiate themselves. Epictetus, for instance, speaks of Cynics' characteristic "little satchel [Gk. *pēridion*, diminutive of *pēran*], staff, and gigantic jaws" (*Discourses* 3.22.50).   **6:10** *In what . . . that place*: perhaps intended to limit garrulous visitations associated with false teachers in early Christianity (cf. 2 Tim 3:6), or to prohibit a missionary from leaving humble accommodations in order to enjoy more lavish hospitality in a wealthier home. Compare the concerns about freeloading itinerant prophets in *Didache* 11–12. **6:11** *Shake off . . . feet*: comprehensive rejection, extending even to the associated ground. *Verily I . . . city*: better omitted (MS tradition) as a scribal assimilation to Matthew (10:15) and Luke (10:12). **6:13** *Anointed with oil*: a common treatment for the infirm; cf. Isa 1:6; Luke 10:34; Jas 5:14.   **6:14** *King Herod*: Herod Antipas was actually tetrarch of Galilee and Perea, 4 B.C.E.–39 C.E.; cf. Matt 14:1; Luke 9:7. A tetrarch technically governed a quarter of a province, but by Herod's time the term was used of

shew forth themselves in him. ¹⁵Others said, That it is Elias. And others said, That it is a prophet, or as one of the prophets. ¹⁶But when Herod heard thereof, he said, It is John, whom I beheaded: he is risen from the dead. ¹⁷For Herod himself had sent forth and laid hold upon John, and bound him in prison for Herodias' sake, his brother Philip's wife: for he had married her. ¹⁸For John had said unto Herod, It is not lawful for thee to have thy brother's wife. ¹⁹Therefore Herodias had a quarrel against him, and would have killed him; but she could not: ²⁰for Herod feared John, knowing that he was a just man and an holy, and observed him; and when he heard him, he did many things, and heard him gladly. ²¹And when a convenient day was come, that Herod on his birthday made a supper to his lords, high captains, and chief estates of Galilee; ²²and when the daughter of the said Herodias came in, and danced, and pleased Herod and them that sat with him, the king said unto the damsel, Ask of me whatsoever thou wilt, and I will give it thee. ²³And he sware unto her, Whatsoever thou shalt ask of me, I will give it thee, unto the half of my kingdom. ²⁴And she went forth, and said unto her mother, What shall I ask? And she said, The head of John the Baptist. ²⁵And she came in straightway with haste unto the king, and asked, saying, I will that thou give me by and by in a charger the head of John the Baptist. ²⁶And the king was exceeding sorry; yet for his oath's sake, and for their sakes which sat with him, he would not reject her. ²⁷And immediately the king sent an executioner, and commanded his head to be brought: and he went and beheaded him in the prison, ²⁸and brought his head in a charger, and gave it to the damsel: and the damsel gave it to her mother. ²⁹And when his disciples heard of it, they came and took up his corpse, and laid it in a tomb.

³⁰And the apostles gathered themselves together unto Jesus, and told him all

---

local kings in regions dominated by Rome. **6:15** *Elias*: cf. 1:2, 6 (see notes); 9:11−13. *Or*: better omitted (MS tradition). The reference is to scriptural prophets. **6:17** *His brother Philip's wife*: according to Josephus (*Jewish Antiquities* 18.136−37), Herodias had been the wife not of Philip but of another brother (also named Herod). Luke (see 3:19 and note) and some MSS of Matt 14:3 correct Mark, reading only "his brother's wife." **6:18** *Not lawful*: Herod had apparently married Herodias while his brother was still alive, contrary to Lev 18:16. Josephus finds the union objectionable (see *Jewish Antiquities* 18.136), but blames John's arrest on Herod's fear of his influence over the potentially rebellious masses (*Jewish Antiquities* 18.116−19). **6:20** *Observed*: watched over or kept safe. *Did many things*: better "was very perplexed" (MS tradition). **6:21** *High captains*: military leaders. *Chief estates*: people of high status. **6:22** *The daughter . . . Herodias*: better "his daughter Herodias" (MS tradition), which injects an element of incest into this story of the (erotically) dancing girl. According to Josephus, Herodias's daughter was not named after her mother but was instead called Salome (*Jewish Antiquities* 18.136) and was begotten by Herod's brother Herod (see v. 17 note). The text KJV translates may reflect a later scribe's attempt to rectify Mark's confusion by assimilating the verse to Matt 14:6. **6:23** *Whatsoever thou . . . kingdom*: quoting the Persian king Ahasuerus's offers to the beautiful Esther (Esth 5:3, 6; 7:2). Whereas Esther uses her erotic influence to save the Jews and to kill their enemies (Esth 7:1−9:5), Herodias's daughter uses hers to kill a prophet. **6:25** *By and by*: at once. *Charger*: platter. **6:27** *Executioner*: rather "guard"; Gk. *spekoulatōr*, usually "spy" but also "military bodyguard." **6:29** *Laid it . . . tomb*: the end of John's story, in contrast to Jesus', which continues after his death and burial. **6:30−44** Feeding five thousand. This meal, which looks forward to the Last Supper (cf. 6:41; 14:22) and thence to the Eucharist (cf. 1 Cor 11:23−26), as well as to the eschatological banquet (e.g., Isa 25:6−9; see Mark 2:19 note), provides a sanctified antidote to the previous episode's unholy cannibalism (v. 25). It recalls and trumps Elisha's feeding of one hundred men from twenty loaves of bread and some wheat (2 Kgs 4:42−44), but of greater symbolic significance are parallels with God's miracu-

things, both what they had done, and what they had taught. ³¹And he said unto them, Come ye yourselves apart into a desert place, and rest a while: for there were many coming and going, and they had no leisure so much as to eat. ³²And they departed into a desert place by ship privately. ³³And the people saw them departing, and many knew him, and ran afoot thither out of all cities, and outwent them, and came together unto him. ³⁴And Jesus, when he came out, saw much people, and was moved with compassion toward them, because they were as sheep not having a shepherd: and he began to teach them many things. ³⁵And when the day was now far spent, his disciples came unto him, and said, This is a desert place, and now the time is far passed: ³⁶send them away, that they may go into the country round about, and into the villages, and buy themselves bread: for they have nothing to eat. ³⁷He answered and said unto them, Give ye them to eat. And they say unto him, Shall we go and buy two hundred pennyworth of bread, and give them to eat? ³⁸He saith unto them, How many loaves have ye? go and see. And when they knew, they say, Five, and two fishes. ³⁹And he commanded them to make all sit down by companies upon the green grass. ⁴⁰And they sat down in ranks, by hundreds, and by fifties. ⁴¹And when he had taken the five loaves and the two fishes, he looked up to heaven, and blessed, and brake the loaves, and gave them to his disciples to set before them; and the two fishes divided he among them all. ⁴²And they did all eat, and were filled. ⁴³And they took up twelve baskets full of the fragments, and of the fishes. ⁴⁴And they that did eat of the loaves were about five thousand men.

⁴⁵And straightway he constrained his disciples to get into the ship, and to go to the other side before unto Bethsaida, while he sent away the people. ⁴⁶And when he had sent them away, he departed into a mountain to pray. ⁴⁷And when even was come, the ship was in the midst of the sea, and he alone on the land. ⁴⁸And he saw them toiling in rowing; for the wind was contrary unto them: and about the fourth watch of the night he cometh unto them, walking upon the sea, and would have passed by them. ⁴⁹But when they saw him walking upon the sea, they supposed it had been a spirit, and cried out: ⁵⁰for they all saw him, and were troubled. And

---

lous provision of manna in the wilderness (Exod 16). **6:31** *Desert*: "uninhabited," but also "wilderness"; see 1:35 note. **6:34** *As sheep . . . shepherd*: the OT commonly compares Israel to a shepherdless flock (e.g., Num 27:17; Ezek 34:5–6; Zech 10:2), but this verse may specifically refer to John's death. **6:36** *Bread: for . . . eat*: better "something to eat" (MS tradition). **6:37** *Give ye them to eat*: Jesus earlier encouraged his disciples to rely on others' hospitality (vv. 8–10); now he instructs them to act as hosts. *Two hundred pennyworth*: about two hundred days' wages for a manual laborer (see 14:5 note). The question from the tired and hungry (cf. v. 31) apostles can only be interpreted as sarcastic, especially since Jesus had just forbidden them to carry money (v. 8). Matthew and Luke omit it. **6:39** *Companies*: Gk. *symposia*, "drinking parties" or "banquets." **6:40** *Ranks*: the Greek word normally refers to garden plots; the groups of people look like gardens against the green grass (v. 39). **6:43** *Twelve baskets full*: one for each disciple; complementarily, one for each of Israel's twelve tribes. **6:45** *Bethsaida*: a city on the northeast shore of the Sea of Galilee. **6:48** *About the fourth watch*: between 3 and 6 A.M. *Walking upon the sea*: in the OT, raging waters can symbolize the chaos YHWH conquers/orders when he creates the world; cf. Pss 74:12–17; 89:9–12; Gen 1:1–2 (a demythologized version of the same events; see notes). In this context, God is sometimes represented as treading on the furious sea (e.g., Job 9:8–9). *Would have . . . them*: perhaps recalling the theophanies of Exod 33:17–34:8 and 1 Kgs 19:11–13, where God "passes by" Moses and Elijah on Mount Horeb/Sinai. **6:49** *Spirit*: Gk. *phantasma*, "apparition"; the disciples' shocking misidentification frustrates the theophany.

immediately he talked with them, and saith unto them, Be of good cheer: it is I; be not afraid. ⁵¹And he went up unto them into the ship; and the wind ceased: and they were sore amazed in themselves beyond measure, and wondered. ⁵²For they considered not the miracle of the loaves: for their heart was hardened.

⁵³And when they had passed over, they came into the land of Gennesaret, and drew to the shore. ⁵⁴And when they were come out of the ship, straightway they knew him, ⁵⁵and ran through that whole region round about, and began to carry about in beds those that were sick, where they heard he was. ⁵⁶And whithersoever he entered, into villages, or cities, or country, they laid the sick in the streets, and besought him that they might touch if it were but the border of his garment: and as many as touched him were made whole.

7 Then came together unto him the Pharisees, and certain of the scribes, which came from Jerusalem. ²And when they saw some of his disciples eat bread with defiled, that is to say, with unwashen, hands, they found fault. ³For the Pharisees, and all the Jews, except they wash their hands oft, eat not, holding the tradition of the elders. ⁴And when they come from the market, except they wash, they eat not. And many other things there be, which they have received to hold, as the washing of cups, and pots, brasen vessels, and of tables. ⁵Then the Pharisees and scribes asked him, Why walk not thy disciples according to the tradition of the elders, but eat bread with unwashen hands? ⁶He answered and said unto them, Well hath Esaias prophesied of you hypocrites, as it is written, This people honoureth me with their lips, but their heart is far from me. ⁷Howbeit in vain do they worship me, teaching for doctrines the commandments of men. ⁸For laying aside the commandment of God, ye hold the tradition of men, as the washing of pots and cups: and many other such like things ye do. ⁹And he said unto them, Full well ye reject the commandment of God, that ye may keep your own tradition. ¹⁰For Moses said, Honour thy father and thy mother; and, Whoso curseth father or mother, let him die the death: ¹¹but ye say, If a man shall say to his father or mother, It is Corban, that is to say, a gift, by whatsoever thou mightest be profited by me; he shall be free. ¹²And ye suffer him no more to do ought for his father or his mother; ¹³making the word of God of none effect through your tradition, which ye have delivered: and many such like things do ye.

6:50 *It is I*: Gk. *egō eimi*, "I am," echoing YHWH's revelation of his name (Exod 3:14).   **6:52** *Considered not*: had failed to understand. *Miracle of the loaves*: lit. "the loaves." *Their heart was hardened*: cf. 3:5 (of the Pharisees).   **6:53** *Gennesaret*: a plain northwest of the Sea of Galilee. Apparently they had been blown off their course to Bethsaida.   **6:56** *Made whole*: see 5:23 note.   **7:2** *They found fault*: better omitted (MS tradition), leaving an incomplete sentence.   **7:3** *Tradition of the elders*: apparently expanding to all Israel OT legislation specifically directed at priests (Exod 30:17–21); see Matt 15:2 note. *Oft*: better "with a fist" (MS tradition); Gk. obscure (proposed explanations include "to the top of the hand" and "with cupped hand").   **7:4** *They have received to hold*: are traditions they maintain. *Washing of cups . . . tables*: certain vessels must be washed if touched by a man with an abnormal genital discharge (Lev 15:12), who also makes impure his bed (a better translation than KJV *tables*; Lev 15:5). *Washing*: a form of Gk. *baptizō* (see 1:4 note).   **7:6–7** *This people . . . men*: Isa 29:13.   **7:8** *As the washing . . . do*: better omitted (MS tradition).   **7:10** *Honour thy father . . . death*: cf. Exod 20:12; 21:17; Deut 5:16.   **7:11** *Corban*: a transliterated Hebrew word meaning "offering," used of property designated solely for a donation to God. *He shall be free*: added by KJV; alternatively (vv. 11–12) "But as you have it, if a man says to his father or mother, 'What you would have profited from me is *corban*' (that is, devoted to God), you no longer allow him to do anything for his father or his mother."

¹⁴And when he had called all the people unto him, he said unto them, Hearken unto me every one of you, and understand: ¹⁵there is nothing from without a man, that entering into him can defile him: but the things which come out of him, those are they that defile the man. ¹⁶If any man have ears to hear, let him hear. ¹⁷And when he was entered into the house from the people, his disciples asked him concerning the parable. ¹⁸And he saith unto them, Are ye so without understanding also? Do ye not perceive, that whatsoever thing from without entereth into the man, it cannot defile him; ¹⁹because it entereth not into his heart, but into the belly, and goeth out into the draught, purging all meats? ²⁰And he said, That which cometh out of the man, that defileth the man. ²¹For from within, out of the heart of men, proceed evil thoughts, adulteries, fornications, murders, ²²thefts, covetousness, wickedness, deceit, lasciviousness, an evil eye, blasphemy, pride, foolishness: ²³all these evil things come from within, and defile the man.

²⁴And from thence he arose, and went into the borders of Tyre and Sidon, and entered into an house, and would have no man know it: but he could not be hid. ²⁵For a certain woman, whose young daughter had an unclean spirit, heard of him, and came and fell at his feet: ²⁶the woman was a Greek, a Syrophenician by nation; and she besought him that he would cast forth the devil out of her daughter. ²⁷But Jesus said unto her, Let the children first be filled: for it is not meet to take the children's bread, and to cast it unto the dogs. ²⁸And she answered and said unto him, Yes, Lord: yet the dogs under the table eat of the children's crumbs. ²⁹And he said unto her, For this saying go thy way; the devil is gone out of thy daughter. ³⁰And when she was come to her house, she found the devil gone out, and her daughter laid upon the bed.

³¹And again, departing from the coasts of Tyre and Sidon, he came unto the sea of Galilee, through the midst of the coasts of Decapolis. ³²And they bring

---

7:16: *If any man . . . him hear*: better omitted (MS tradition).   **7:17** *The house*: better "a house" (it is unclear to which Mark refers).   **7:17–18** *His disciples . . . perceive*: recalling 4:10–13.   **7:19** *Draught*: latrine. *Purging all meats*: KJV's Greek text has this participial phrase modify *draught*, but it should agree with "Jesus" in v. 18 (MS tradition). NRSV therefore consigns this clause to a concluding parenthesis, "(Thus he declared all foods clean.)"; cf. Rom 14:20.   **7:21–22** *Evil thoughts . . . thefts*: the order of the first five sins varies in the MS tradition.   **7:22** *An evil eye*: stinginess (see Matt 6:23 note). *Blasphemy*: Gk. *blasphēmia*, here meaning "slander."   **7:24–30** Exorcising a Syrophoenician woman's daughter. In the second episode demonstrating his ministry to a Gentile (cf. 5:1–20), Jesus puts into practice, though perhaps with reluctance (v. 27), his teaching about what is and is not "unclean." **7:24** *And Sidon*: better omitted (MS tradition). *Tyre* and *Sidon* are Phoenician coastal cities.   **7:26** *Greek*: meaning "Gentile"; cf. Rom 1:16; 1 Cor 1:22–24.   **7:27** *Let the . . . dogs*: Jesus' response is at once rude and parabolic. *Dogs* may have been a pejorative term for Gentiles; *children* refers to the children of Israel.   **7:28** *Lord*: Gk. *kyrios* has a range of connotations, from sir to God's name YHWH (KJV "LORD"). *The dogs . . . crumbs*: a commonplace in ancient Mediterranean literature (cf. Philostratus, *Life of Apollonius* 1.19; *Gospel of Philip* 82.21–23). The response shows that this woman grasps Jesus' insulting parable. She accepts her designation as a Gentile dog whose feeding takes second place to that of God's children, the Jews, but challenges the latent assumption that God's resources are scarce. Her reference to *crumbs* recalls the prodigious leftovers from the miraculous feeding of the five thousand (6:30–44).   **7:31–37** Healing a deaf Gentile. Perhaps embarrassed by its implications of magic (see vv. 33–34 and note), Matthew (15:29–31) transforms this story into a straightforward description of Jesus healing people suffering from all kinds of ailments.   **7:31** *And Sidon, he came*: better "he came through Sidon" (MS tradition), the geography seems confused, as Sidon is north of Tyre while the Sea of Galilee is to its southeast. Moreover, the Decapolis setting

unto him one that was deaf, and had an impediment in his speech; and they beseech him to put his hand upon him. ³³And he took him aside from the multitude, and put his fingers into his ears, and he spit, and touched his tongue; ³⁴and looking up to heaven, he sighed, and saith unto him, Ephphatha, that is, Be opened. ³⁵And straightway his ears were opened, and the string of his tongue was loosed, and he spake plain. ³⁶And he charged them that they should tell no man: but the more he charged them, so much the more a great deal they published it; ³⁷and were beyond measure astonished, saying, He hath done all things well: he maketh both the deaf to hear, and the dumb to speak.

8 In those days the multitude being very great, and having nothing to eat, Jesus called his disciples unto him, and saith unto them, ²I have compassion on the multitude, because they have now been with me three days, and have nothing to eat: ³and if I send them away fasting to their own houses, they will faint by the way: for divers of them came from far. ⁴And his disciples answered him, From whence can a man satisfy these men with bread here in the wilderness? ⁵And he asked them, How many loaves have ye? And they said, Seven. ⁶And he commanded the people to sit down on the ground: and he took the seven loaves, and gave thanks, and brake, and gave to his disciples to set before them; and they did set them before the people. ⁷And they had a few small fishes: and he blessed, and commanded to set them also before them. ⁸So they did eat, and were filled: and they took up of the broken meat that was left seven baskets. ⁹And they that had eaten were about four thousand: and he sent them away.

¹⁰And straightway he entered into a ship with his disciples, and came into the parts of Dalmanutha. ¹¹And the Pharisees came forth, and began to question with him, seeking of him a sign from heaven, tempting him. ¹²And he sighed deeply in his spirit, and saith, Why doth this generation seek after a sign? verily I say unto you, There shall no sign be given unto this generation. ¹³And he left them, and entering into the ship again departed to the other side.

---

locates Jesus on the Sea of Galilee's eastern shore, even though in vv. 24–30 he was west of it, on the Mediterranean coast. Mark may have been mistaken as to where the Decapolis was located, but his thematic point is clear: Jesus travels through Gentile territory.   **7:33** *From the multitude*: the Greek adds "by himself."   **7:33–34** *He spit . . . Ephphatha*: spitting, sighing, and the utterance of foreign words are common components of Greco-Roman magic spells. Jesus' Aramaic words may have been preserved out of belief in their preternatural power (cf. "Talitha cumi," 5:41).   **7:35** *String*: bond or fetter.   **7:36** *The more . . . it*: Jesus' miraculous powers are again proclaimed openly in Gentile territory (though this time against his will; cf. 5:19–20).   **7:37** *He maketh . . . speak*: alluding to the eschatological vision of Isa 35:5–6.   **8:1–9** Feeding the four thousand. Jesus completes a second miraculous feeding—this one in Gentile territory (see 7:31 note)—corresponding to the first, which occurred in Jewish regions (6:30–44).   **8:4** *Bread here . . . wilderness*: the unconscious allusion to the manna given the Israelites during their wilderness wanderings (Exod 16) reveals the disciples' lack of faith in God's provision.   **8:8** *Seven*: symbolizing completion; compare the symbolic associations of twelve in the previous feeding (cf. 6:43 and note). *Baskets*: a different Greek word is used in 6:43; this one may suggest larger baskets.   **8:10** *Dalmanutha*: unidentified but presumably in Jewish territory, since the Pharisees reappear.   **8:11** *Seeking of him . . . heaven*: compare Aaron's signs for the Israelites (Exod 4:29–31). *Tempting*: cf. 1:13 and note; see also the Israelites' tempting of God during the wilderness wanderings (Exod 17:1–7), which likewise follows a miraculous wilderness feeding (Exod 16).   **8:12** *There shall . . . given*: lit. "if a sign shall be given," with the main clause (a self-curse) understood (cf. 2 Kgs 6:31). In Matthew and Luke, Jesus promises the "sign of the prophet Jonah"

¹⁴Now the disciples had forgotten to take bread, neither had they in the ship with them more than one loaf. ¹⁵And he charged them, saying, Take heed, beware of the leaven of the Pharisees, and of the leaven of Herod. ¹⁶And they reasoned among themselves, saying, It is because we have no bread. ¹⁷And when Jesus knew it, he saith unto them, Why reason ye, because ye have no bread? perceive ye not yet, neither understand? have ye your heart yet hardened? ¹⁸Having eyes, see ye not? and having ears, hear ye not? and do ye not remember? ¹⁹When I brake the five loaves among five thousand, how many baskets full of fragments took ye up? They say unto him, Twelve. ²⁰And when the seven among four thousand, how many baskets full of fragments took ye up? And they said, Seven. ²¹And he said unto them, How is it that ye do not understand?

²²And he cometh to Bethsaida; and they bring a blind man unto him, and besought him to touch him. ²³And he took the blind man by the hand, and led him out of the town; and when he had spit on his eyes, and put his hands upon him, he asked him if he saw ought. ²⁴And he looked up, and said, I see men as

---

(Matt 12:39; 16:4; Luke 11:29). **8:15** *Leaven*: a contagion (cf. Exod 12:15–20; Lev 2:11; 1 Cor 5:6). **8:16** *It is . . . bread*: they presumably think Jesus warns them against buying bread contaminated by the Pharisees or Herod. **8:17–18** *Perceive ye . . . hear ye not*: echoing 4:12 and 6:52, and definitively marking Jesus' disciples as outsiders. **8:17** *Yet hardened*: better simply "hardened" (MS tradition). **8:19–20** *When I . . . Seven*: the review invites the disciples and the readers to ponder the feedings' symbolic significance. Perhaps most fundamentally, Jesus develops his exchange with the Syrophoenician woman (7:24–30): he fed the Jews first (7:27; cf. 6:30–44), but, as the abundant leftovers (6:43) and the Syrophoenician woman (7:28) suggest, he has resources enough to nourish Gentiles too, and he ultimately provides them with their own plentiful meal (8:1–9, esp. v. 8). The specific numbers recall David's taking of the showbread (cf. 2:23–28). According to 1 Sam 21:1–6 (esp. v. 3), David took five of its twelve loaves (cf. Lev 24:5–9), leaving seven behind. In the first feeding five loaves are multiplied (6:38), producing twelve baskets of fragments; in the second, seven (8:5), producing seven. **8:20** *Baskets*: translating a Greek word different from that in v. 19 (see v. 8 note). **8:21** *How is . . . understand*: better "Do you not yet understand" (MS tradition), recalling Jesus' earlier question to the disciples, "Do you still have no faith?" (4:40; see note).

8:22–10:52 The journey to Jerusalem. Framed by similar accounts of blind men's healings (8:22–26 and 10:46–52; cf. Matt 9:27–31; 20:29–34; Luke 18:35–43; John 9:1–7), the material constituting Jesus' Jerusalem journey emphasizes the disciples' total misunderstanding of Jesus' mission, and at times open hostility to it: Peter's confession followed by Jesus' first passion prediction and their mutual rebukes (8:27–9:1; cf. Matt 16:13–28; Luke 9:18–27; John 6:66–71); Jesus' transfiguration and Peter, James, and John's confusion (9:2–13; cf. Matt 17:1–13; Luke 9:28–36); the disciples' failed exorcism (9:14–29; cf. Matt 17:14–21; Luke 9:37–43a); Jesus' second passion prediction, followed by the disciples' dispute about greatness (9:30–37; cf. Matt 17:22–23; 18:1–5; Luke 9:43b–48; John 12:44–45; 13:20); the disciples' misguided attempt to hinder an exorcist (9:38–50; cf. Matt 18:6–9; 5:13; Luke 9:49–50; 17:1–2; 14:34–35); Jesus' dispute with the Pharisees about divorce (10:1–12; cf. Matt 19:1–12); Jesus' rebuke of the disciples for keeping children away (10:13–16; cf. Matt 19:13–15; Luke 18:15–17); the story of the rich young man seeking eternal life (10:17–31; cf. Matt 19:16–30; Luke 18:18–30); and Jesus' third passion prediction, followed by James and John's request for glory (10:32–45; cf. Matt 20:17–28; Luke 18:31–34; 22:24–27). **8:22–26** The blind man of Bethsaida. The other Synoptics omit this episode, probably because Jesus' miraculous powers are not immediately effective in it. But in Mark the progressive restoration of sight, which involves the man looking twice and closely (see v. 25 and note) in order to see clearly, has symbolic resonance: the gradually healed blind man figures the disciples (cf. v. 17) and, by proxy, Mark's readers, who must read and reread in order to fathom the mystery of the bread (from the previous episode) and Jesus' disturbing predictions of and calls to martyrdom in the material that follows. **8:22** *Bethsaida*: see 6:45 note. **8:23** *Spit*: see 7:33 note.

trees, walking. ²⁵After that he put his hands again upon his eyes, and made him look up: and he was restored, and saw every man clearly. ²⁶And he sent him away to his house, saying, Neither go into the town, nor tell it to any in the town.

²⁷And Jesus went out, and his disciples, into the towns of Cæsarea Philippi: and by the way he asked his disciples, saying unto them, Whom do men say that I am? ²⁸And they answered, John the Baptist: but some say, Elias; and others, One of the prophets. ²⁹And he saith unto them, But whom say ye that I am? And Peter answereth and saith unto him, Thou art the Christ. ³⁰And he charged them that they should tell no man of him. ³¹And he began to teach them, that the Son of man must suffer many things, and be rejected of the elders, and of the chief priests, and scribes, and be killed, and after three days rise again. ³²And he spake that saying openly. And Peter took him, and began to rebuke him. ³³But when he had turned about and looked on his disciples, he rebuked Peter, saying, Get thee behind me, Satan: for thou savourest not the things that be of God, but the things that be of men.

³⁴And when he had called the people unto him with his disciples also, he said unto them, Whosoever will come after me, let him deny himself, and take up his cross, and follow me. ³⁵For whosoever will save his life shall lose it; but whosoever shall lose his life for my sake and the gospel's, the same shall save it. ³⁶For what shall it profit a man, if he shall gain the whole world, and lose his own soul? ³⁷Or what shall a man give in exchange for his soul? ³⁸Whosoever therefore shall be ashamed of me and of my words in this adulterous and sinful generation; of him also shall the Son of man be ashamed, when he cometh in the glory of his Father with the holy angels.

9 ¹And he said unto them, Verily I say unto you, That there be some of them that stand here, which shall not taste of death, till they have seen the kingdom of God come with power.

8:25 *Made him look up*: better "he looked intently" (MS tradition).   8:26 *Nor tell . . . town*: better omitted (MS tradition).   8:27 *Cæsarea Philippi*: a city about twenty-five miles north of the Sea of Galilee. Mark's subsequent geographical references bring Jesus south from this city to Jerusalem.   8:28 *John the Baptist . . . prophets*: compare Herod's musings (6:14–16).   8:30 *Charged*: Gk. epitimaō; cf. vv. 32–33 (KJV "rebuke"). Mark has used the word before of Jesus calming the raging sea (4:39) and silencing demons (1:25; 3:12).   8:31 *The Son . . . again*: the first prediction of Jesus' death and resurrection. *The elders . . . scribes*: members of the Jerusalem Sanhedrin (from the Hebrew transliteration of Gk. *synedrion*), the highest Jewish "council" (so KJV; cf. 14:55; 15:1) and court, which maintained public order and advised the Roman authorities: *elders* were lay leaders; *chief priests* directed the temple cult; on *scribes*, see 1:22 note.   8:32 *Spake that saying openly*: contrast v. 30.   8:33 *Savourest not*: do not consider.   8:34 *Take up his cross*: a vivid image of public execution. Here it refers primarily to persecution and martyrdom, although it may also figure radical self-denial more broadly understood.   8:36–37 *Soul*: Gk. psychē; better "life," as in v. 35.   8:38 *This adulterous . . . generation*: see Matt 12:39 note. *The Son . . . angels*: God's eschatological reign (cf. Dan 7:13–14). Jesus here seems to distinguish himself from the Son of Man (contrast Matt 10:33; 16:27); see 2:10 note.   9:1 *Shall not . . . death*: an allusion to the early church's imminent expectation of the end time, and also a transition to the subsequent episode.   9:2–13 Transfiguration. This story may recount an appearance of the risen Christ, interjected into the narrative of the earthly Jesus' ministry. Other ancient Christian texts have similar descriptions of Peter meeting the resurrected Christ on a mountain (e.g., *The Letter of Peter to Philip* 133.9–18; the Valentinion *Treatise on the Resurrection* 48.3–11); 2 Pet 1:16–18 may refer to the present

²And after six days Jesus taketh with him Peter, and James, and John, and leadeth them up into an high mountain apart by themselves: and he was transfigured
before them. ³And his raiment became shining, exceeding white as snow; so as no
fuller on earth can white them. ⁴And there appeared unto them Elias with Moses:
and they were talking with Jesus. ⁵And Peter answered and said to Jesus, Master, it
is good for us to be here: and let us make three tabernacles; one for thee, and one
for Moses, and one for Elias. ⁶For he wist not what to say; for they were sore afraid.
⁷And there was a cloud that overshadowed them: and a voice came out of the cloud,
saying, This is my beloved Son: hear him. ⁸And suddenly, when they had looked
round about, they saw no man any more, save Jesus only with themselves.

⁹And as they came down from the mountain, he charged them that they should
tell no man what things they had seen, till the Son of man were risen from the
dead. ¹⁰And they kept that saying with themselves, questioning one with another
what the rising from the dead should mean. ¹¹And they asked him, saying, Why
say the scribes that Elias must first come? ¹²And he answered and told them,
Elias verily cometh first, and restoreth all things; and how it is written of the Son
of man, that he must suffer many things, and be set at nought. ¹³But I say unto
you, That Elias is indeed come, and they have done unto him whatsoever they
listed, as it is written of him.

---

story as such an encounter (see notes). **9:2** *After six days*: cf. Exod 24:16 (God's glory abides on Sinai
for six days; on the seventh, God calls Moses up to reveal to him the law). *Peter, James, and John*: "Aaron,
Nadab, and Abihu" (along with seventy unnamed elders) accompany Moses to Sinai (Exod 24:1). *Transfigured*: Gk. *metemorphōthē*; cf. 2 Cor 3:18 (KJV "changed"), referring to Moses' glorious transformation
on his descent from Sinai with the law (Exod 34:29–35). **9:3** *Raiment became shining*: luminous bodies
and clothing conventionally characterize divine and resurrected existence (e.g., Dan 7:9; 12:2–3; Rev
3:4–5; 7:9). The shining of Moses' face (Exod 34:29–35) led Matthew (17:2) and Luke (9:29) to clarify
the parallel by mentioning Jesus' face as well as clothing. *As snow*: better omitted (MS tradition). *Fuller*:
launderer. **9:4** *Elias with Moses*: both experienced theophanies on Mount Horeb/Sinai (cf. 1 Kgs 19;
Exod 33). Also, both were thought to have avoided death by heavenly translation, in Elijah's case explicitly
(2 Kgs 2:9–12); Moses' hidden tomb (Deut 34:5–6) spurred later speculation that he too was taken up to
heaven before dying (cf. Josephus, *Jewish Antiquities* 4.323–26). See also Mal 4:4–6, which links Moses
with Elijah, the eschatological forerunner (cf. Mark 9:11–13). **9:5–6** *Let us . . . say*: Peter may want to
extend the experience by building a tent to house God's glory, as Moses did at the foot of Sinai (Exod
33:7–11); alternatively, since "tent" was a Hellenistic commonplace for the transitory mortal body (cf. 2
Cor 5:1–8), the offer may hint at Peter's blindness to the glimpse of future glory offered by Jesus' transfiguration. Whatever Peter meant, Mark suggests it was foolish. **9:6** *Wist*: knew. *Were sore afraid*: as
were those who saw Moses' shining face (Exod 34:30). **9:7** *Cloud*: a sign of God's glorious presence (see
Exod 33:8–10; etc.) or a shuttle between heaven and earth (Dan 7:13; Acts 1:9; Rev 11:12). *This is . . . Son*:
echoing the divine voice at Jesus' baptism (1:11 and note). *Hear him*: cf. Deut 18:15 (of Moses, as the
eschatological prophet); here the reference is to Jesus' predictions of his death and resurrection (8:31;
9:9), which Peter and the other disciples fail to understand (8:32–33; 9:10). **9:9** *He charged . . . dead*:
perhaps anticipating objections to this chronological transposition of a story widely known as
an account of the risen Jesus' appearance to Peter. Mark subtly suggests that the secrecy required
until Jesus' resurrection led the transfiguration to be misinterpreted as a resurrection appearance.
9:12 *Elias verily . . . things*: Elijah is the eschatological forerunner who "will restore the heart of the father
to the son, and the heart of a man to his neighbor" (LXX Mal 4:5–6). *How it . . . nought*: better a question ("how is it . . . ?") than a continuation of Jesus' assertion. See Isa 53:3; Ps 22:6–7; etc. **9:13** *Elias
is indeed come*: as John the Baptist (cf. 1:2, 6 and notes). *As it . . . him*: Elijah's persecution at the hands
of Ahab and Jezebel (1 Kgs 19:1–3) foreshadows John's persecution at the hands of Herod and his wife

¹⁴And when he came to his disciples, he saw a great multitude about them, and the scribes questioning with them. ¹⁵And straightway all the people, when they beheld him, were greatly amazed, and running to him saluted him. ¹⁶And he asked the scribes, What question ye with them? ¹⁷And one of the multitude answered and said, Master, I have brought unto thee my son, which hath a dumb spirit; ¹⁸and wheresoever he taketh him, he teareth him: and he foameth, and gnasheth with his teeth, and pineth away: and I spake to thy disciples that they should cast him out; and they could not. ¹⁹He answereth him, and saith, O faithless generation, how long shall I be with you? how long shall I suffer you? bring him unto me. ²⁰And they brought him unto him: and when he saw him, straightway the spirit tare him; and he fell on the ground, and wallowed foaming. ²¹And he asked his father, How long is it ago since this came unto him? And he said, Of a child. ²²And ofttimes it hath cast him into the fire, and into the waters, to destroy him: but if thou canst do any thing, have compassion on us, and help us. ²³Jesus said unto him, If thou canst believe, all things are possible to him that believeth. ²⁴And straightway the father of the child cried out, and said with tears, Lord, I believe; help thou mine unbelief. ²⁵When Jesus saw that the people came running together, he rebuked the foul spirit, saying unto him, Thou dumb and deaf spirit, I charge thee, come out of him, and enter no more into him. ²⁶And the spirit cried, and rent him sore, and came out of him: and he was as one dead; insomuch that many said, He is dead. ²⁷But Jesus took him by the hand, and lifted him up; and he arose. ²⁸And when he was come into the house, his disciples asked him privately, Why could not we cast him out? ²⁹And he said unto them, This kind can come forth by nothing, but by prayer and fasting.

³⁰And they departed thence, and passed through Galilee; and he would not that any man should know it. ³¹For he taught his disciples, and said unto them, The Son of man is delivered into the hands of men, and they shall kill him; and after that he is killed, he shall rise the third day. ³²But they understood not that saying, and were afraid to ask him.

³³And he came to Capernaum: and being in the house he asked them, What was it that ye disputed among yourselves by the way? ³⁴But they held their peace: for by the way they had disputed among themselves, who should be the greatest. ³⁵And he sat down, and called the twelve, and saith unto them, If any man desire

---

(6:14–29).   **9:15** *Were greatly amazed*: the Greek verb implies alarm. Perhaps the appearance of Jesus, still luminous like Moses (Exod 34:29–35), terrified the crowd even as it attracted them.   **9:17** *Dumb spirit*: the spirit prevents the boy from speaking.   **9:18** *Teareth*: throws down (cf. 9:20, 26 [KJV "rent"]). *Pineth away*: lit. "becomes dry"; cf. 3:1 (KJV "withered"). Perhaps the boy's body becomes stiff. **9:19** *Answereth him*: better "answers them" (MS tradition)—i.e., the disciples. *O faithless generation . . . suffer you?*: cf. 8:38; Deut 32:5. Though they were recently granted "power over unclean spirits" (6:7), the disciples' faithlessness results in a failed exorcism. (In contrast, faith often leads to healing; 2:5; 5:34; 10:52.)   **9:23** *If thou canst believe*: better "If thou canst!" (MS tradition), with Jesus sarcastically quoting the man's words back at him.   **9:24** *With tears, Lord*: better omitted (MS tradition).   **9:25** *Foul*: unclean.   **9:28** *The house*: see 7:17 note.   **9:29** *And fasting*: better omitted (MS tradition).   **9:31** *The Son . . . day*: the second prediction of Jesus' death and resurrection. *The third day*: better "after three days" (MS tradition).   **9:33** *In the house*: likely Peter's house.

to be first, the same shall be last of all, and servant of all. [36]And he took a child, and set him in the midst of them: and when he had taken him in his arms, he said unto them, [37]Whosoever shall receive one of such children in my name, receiveth me: and whosoever shall receive me, receiveth not me, but him that sent me.

[38]And John answered him, saying, Master, we saw one casting out devils in thy name, and he followeth not us: and we forbad him, because he followeth not us. [39]But Jesus said, Forbid him not: for there is no man which shall do a miracle in my name, that can lightly speak evil of me. [40]For he that is not against us is on our part. [41]For whosoever shall give you a cup of water to drink in my name, because ye belong to Christ, verily I say unto you, he shall not lose his reward. [42]And whosoever shall offend one of these little ones that believe in me, it is better for him that a millstone were hanged about his neck, and he were cast into the sea.

[43]And if thy hand offend thee, cut it off: it is better for thee to enter into life maimed, than having two hands to go into hell, into the fire that never shall be quenched: [44]where their worm dieth not, and the fire is not quenched. [45]And if thy foot offend thee, cut it off: it is better for thee to enter halt into life, than having two feet to be cast into hell, into the fire that never shall be quenched: [46]where their worm dieth not, and the fire is not quenched. [47]And if thine eye offend thee, pluck it out: it is better for thee to enter into the kingdom of God with one eye, than having two eyes to be cast into hell fire: [48]where their worm dieth not, and the fire is not quenched.

9:35 *Servant*: slave (as often).   **9:36** *Child*: Gk. *paidion*, also "young slave"—an indication of children's low social status in the ancient Mediterranean world.   **9:37** *Whosoever shall receive . . . sent me*: befitting his paradox (v. 35), Jesus associates himself at once with a lowly child and with God.   **9:38** *Answered him*: better "said to him" (MS tradition), marking a new episode.   **9:38–40** *Master, we . . . part*: having just been rebuked for their own failed exorcism (v. 19), the disciples now confess to having forbidden another from exorcising demons. Moreover, they take issue with an outsider's acting in Jesus' name, despite Jesus' instruction that they welcome others in his name (v. 37). Perhaps jealousy motivates their outrageous behavior (see vv. 33–34; cf. Num 11:27–29).   **9:39** *Lightly*: rather "soon after."   **9:40** *Part*: side. Q has a dominical saying to the opposite effect: "He that is not with me is against me" (Matt 12:30; Luke 11:23).   **9:41** *In my name . . . Christ*: better "on the basis of your belonging to Christ" (MS tradition).   **9:42** *Little ones*: i.e., having no obvious importance, like children; see v. 36 and note. *In me*: better omitted (MS tradition). *Millstone*: better "a millstone worked by a donkey" (MS tradition); i.e., a large stone. The threat was apparently conventional (cf. *Alexander Romance* β 2.41).   **9:43** *If thy hand . . . hell*: this saying and its sequels (vv. 45, 47) appear to draw an analogy from the communal (v. 42) to the individual. However, Greco-Roman writings regularly figure communities as bodies (e.g., 1 Cor 12), and thus Jesus may be calling for the excommunication of those who cause others to sin. *Hell*: Gk. *geenna*, as often in the Synoptic Gospels: a transliteration of Heb. *gehenna*, originally *ge hinnom* ("the valley of the children of Hinnom"), where children were sacrificed to Molech and other pagan gods (see 2 Kgs 23:10; Jer 19:2–9; 32:35; etc.). Gehenna later became the name of the place where flames were supposed to torture the evil dead. *The fire . . . quenched*: cf. Isa 66:24 (also at v. 48).   **9:44** *Where their worm . . . quenched*: better omitted (MS tradition; also at v. 46), as a scribe's anticipatory duplication of v. 48.   **9:45** *Into the fire . . . quenched*: better omitted (MS tradition) as a scribal duplication of

⁴⁹For every one shall be salted with fire, and every sacrifice shall be salted with salt. ⁵⁰Salt is good: but if the salt have lost his saltness, wherewith will ye season it? Have salt in yourselves, and have peace one with another.

10 And he arose from thence, and cometh into the coasts of Judæa by the farther side of Jordan: and the people resort unto him again; and, as he was wont, he taught them again.

²And the Pharisees came to him, and asked him, Is it lawful for a man to put away his wife? tempting him. ³And he answered and said unto them, What did Moses command you? ⁴And they said, Moses suffered to write a bill of divorcement, and to put her away. ⁵And Jesus answered and said unto them, For the hardness of your heart he wrote you this precept. ⁶But from the beginning of the creation God made them male and female. ⁷For this cause shall a man leave his father and mother, and cleave to his wife; ⁸and they twain shall be one flesh: so then they are no more twain, but one flesh. ⁹What therefore God hath joined together, let not man put asunder. ¹⁰And in the house his disciples asked him again of the same matter. ¹¹And he saith unto them, Whosoever shall put away his wife, and marry another, committeth adultery against her. ¹²And if a woman shall put away her husband, and be married to another, she committeth adultery.

¹³And they brought young children to him, that he should touch them: and his disciples rebuked those that brought them. ¹⁴But when Jesus saw it, he was much displeased, and said unto them, Suffer the little children to come unto me, and forbid them not: for of such is the kingdom of God. ¹⁵Verily I say unto you, Whosoever shall not receive the kingdom of God as a little child, he shall not enter therein. ¹⁶And he took them up in his arms, put his hands upon them, and blessed them.

¹⁷And when he was gone forth into the way, there came one running, and kneeled to him, and asked him, Good Master, what shall I do that I may inherit eternal life? ¹⁸And Jesus said unto him, Why callest thou me good? there is none

---

the end of v. 43. **9:49** *Salted with fire*: salt was used to season and to preserve. Fire's association with self-preservation here balances its use in vv. 43–48 as a figure of divine judgment. *And every . . . salt*: better omitted (MS tradition). This quotation of Lev 2:13 may have been written in the text's margin by a scribe trying to explain Jesus' mysterious words, and then later transferred by copyists into the text's body. The practice of including "the salt of the covenant" with burnt offerings, as Lev 2:13 requires, may indeed lie behind this saying. **10:1** *Coasts of Judæa . . . Jordan*: better "the region of Judea on the other side of the Jordan" or "the region of Judea and the other side of the Jordan" (MS tradition). All that can be certain is that Jesus headed south to Judea but also spent time east of the Jordan River, in Perea. **10:2** *Put away*: divorce; on Jesus' teaching about it, see Matt 5:32 note. *Tempting*: cf. 8:11 and note. **10:4** *Moses suffered . . . away*: see Deut 24:1. **10:5** *Hardness of your heart*: Jesus claims that Moses conceded to the Israelites' sinful stubbornness in allowing divorce. **10:6** *God made . . . female*: Gen 1:27; a Qumran text similarly draws on the same passage to condemn those remarrying after divorce or polygamists (it is unclear which): "[they] shall be caught in fornication twice by taking a second wife while the first is alive, whereas the principle of creation is 'Male and female created he them'" (*Damascus Document* IV 19–21; trans. Vermes). **10:7–8** *For this cause . . . be one flesh*: Gen 2:24. **10:10** *In the house*: it is unclear to which house Mark refers. **10:13** *His disciples . . . them*: patently rejecting Jesus' teaching in 9:35–37. **10:15** *As a little child*: i.e., humbly, as a gift from a superior; cf. 9:36 and note. **10:16** *And blessed them*: better omitted (MS tradition). **10:17** *Inherit*: the man's desire to receive eternal life as a birthright suggests elevated social status; contrast the lowly

good but one, that is, God. ¹⁹Thou knowest the commandments, Do not commit adultery, Do not kill, Do not steal, Do not bear false witness, Defraud not, Honour thy father and mother. ²⁰And he answered and said unto him, Master, all these have I observed from my youth. ²¹Then Jesus beholding him loved him, and said unto him, One thing thou lackest: go thy way, sell whatsoever thou hast, and give to the poor, and thou shalt have treasure in heaven: and come, take up the cross, and follow me. ²²And he was sad at that saying, and went away grieved: for he had great possessions.

²³And Jesus looked round about, and saith unto his disciples, How hardly shall they that have riches enter into the kingdom of God! ²⁴And the disciples were astonished at his words. But Jesus answereth again, and saith unto them, Children, how hard is it for them that trust in riches to enter into the kingdom of God! ²⁵It is easier for a camel to go through the eye of a needle, than for a rich man to enter into the kingdom of God. ²⁶And they were astonished out of measure, saying among themselves, Who then can be saved? ²⁷And Jesus looking upon them saith, With men it is impossible, but not with God: for with God all things are possible. ²⁸Then Peter began to say unto him, Lo, we have left all, and have followed thee. ²⁹And Jesus answered and said, Verily I say unto you, There is no man that hath left house, or brethren, or sisters, or father, or mother, or wife, or children, or lands, for my sake, and the gospel's, ³⁰but he shall receive an hundredfold now in this time, houses, and brethren, and sisters, and mothers,

---

children of 9:36 and 10:15 (see notes).   **10:19** *Do not commit . . . mother*: quoting the commandments of the Decalogue that regulate social relationships (five through nine; cf. Exod 20:12–16; Deut 5:16–20), with the exception of the prohibition against covetousness (commandment ten; see v. 21 note). The order of the first two is better reversed (MS tradition). *Defraud not*: expanding the prohibition against bearing false witness, which it follows, but not actually one of the commandments. Matthew (19:18–19) and Luke (18:20) therefore omit it.   **10:20** *From my youth*: he distances himself from childhood (contrast v. 15).   **10:21** *One thing thou lackest*: paradoxically identifying the man's possessions as a deficiency. *Sell whatsoever . . . me*: dramatically personalizing the tenth commandment (prohibiting covetousness; Exod 20:17; Deut 5:21), which is notably missing from the earlier catalogue. *Take up the cross*: better omitted (MS tradition).   **10:22** *For he . . . possessions*: only now does Mark reveal the man's wealth, apparently expecting this revelation and Jesus' subsequent teaching to shock (vv. 23–24). **10:23** *Hardly*: with difficulty.   **10:24** *For them . . . riches*: better omitted (MS tradition) as a scribal attempt to soften Jesus' saying. The interpolation misleadingly suggests that Jesus refers to those who trust in wealth, rather than to those who have it.   **10:25** *It is . . . needle*: a proverbial image of impossibility, which commentators have long erroneously tried to dilute—e.g., by emending the Greek word for "camel" to one meaning "rope" or by insisting (without historical evidence) that "the eye of a needle" named a low gateway in Jerusalem's wall. So Shakespeare paraphrased this verse in *Richard II*: "It is as hard to come as for a camel / To thread the postern of a small needle's eye" (5.5.16–17).   **10:26** *Who then can be saved?*: the disciples' question presumes that the wealthy are more likely than others to find eschatological salvation—precisely the opposite of what Jesus has been teaching.   **10:27** *With men . . . possible*: Jesus' answer echoes God's promise to give the elderly Sarah a son (Gen 18:14), thereby suggesting it will take a special miracle to save a rich man.   **10:28–31** *Lo, we . . . last first*: Jesus validates the disciples for following him—a short-lived respite from the tension between him and them that characterizes so much of Mark, especially during the Jerusalem journey.   **10:29** *Or wife*: better omitted (MS tradition). The order of "father" and "mother" should also be reversed.   **10:30** *Shall receive . . . persecutions*: the list of what will be received differs from the list of what has been

and children, and lands, with persecutions; and in the world to come eternal life. ³¹But many that are first shall be last; and the last first.

³²And they were in the way going up to Jerusalem; and Jesus went before them: and they were amazed; and as they followed, they were afraid. And he took again the twelve, and began to tell them what things should happen unto him, ³³saying, Behold, we go up to Jerusalem; and the Son of man shall be delivered unto the chief priests, and unto the scribes; and they shall condemn him to death, and shall deliver him to the Gentiles: ³⁴and they shall mock him, and shall scourge him, and shall spit upon him, and shall kill him: and the third day he shall rise again.

³⁵And James and John, the sons of Zebedee, come unto him, saying, Master, we would that thou shouldest do for us whatsoever we shall desire. ³⁶And he said unto them, What would ye that I should do for you? ³⁷They said unto him, Grant unto us that we may sit, one on thy right hand, and the other on thy left hand, in thy glory. ³⁸But Jesus said unto them, Ye know not what ye ask: can ye drink of the cup that I drink of? and be baptized with the baptism that I am baptized with? ³⁹And they said unto him, We can. And Jesus said unto them, Ye shall indeed drink of the cup that I drink of; and with the baptism that I am baptized withal shall ye be baptized: ⁴⁰but to sit on my right hand and on my left hand is not mine to give; but it shall be given to them for whom it is prepared.

⁴¹And when the ten heard it, they began to be much displeased with James and John. ⁴²But Jesus called them to him, and saith unto them, Ye know that they which are accounted to rule over the Gentiles exercise lordship over them; and their great ones exercise authority upon them. ⁴³But so shall it not be among you: but whosoever will be great among you, shall be your minister: ⁴⁴and whosoever of

---

abandoned (v. 29): no fathers will be received, perhaps in recognition that God is the ultimate father, and persecutions are to be expected.   **10:33–34** *Behold, we . . . again*: the third prediction of Jesus' death and resurrection is the most precise (cf. 8:31; 9:31–32). The events that will bring Jesus' life to an end come into clearer focus as he approaches Jerusalem.   **10:33** *The Gentiles*: i.e., the Roman authorities.   **10:34** *The third day*: see 9:31 note.   **10:35–45** The request of the sons of Zebedee. Their outrageous demand embarrassed Matthew and Luke: the former assigns it to their mother (20:20–28); the latter mentions no disciples by name, referring only to a "strife" about who "should be accounted the greatest" (22:24–27).   **10:37** *In thy glory*: see 8:38 and note.   **10:38** *Cup*: a common biblical image for one's allotment in life. Usually it is associated with suffering, in particular at God's hands (e.g., Ps 11:6; Isa 51:17, 22). The cup here foreshadows that of the Last Supper, symbolizing Jesus' impending demise (14:23; cf. 14:36), which in turn forecasts the eucharistic cup (cf. 1 Cor 11:25). *Be baptized . . . with*: ancient Christian liturgy apparently referred to baptism in Christ (Rom 6:3a; Gal 3:27; cf. 1 Cor 12:13), which Paul interprets as baptism into his death (cf. Rom 6:3b–4), an interpretation Mark presumably shared.   **10:40** *To sit . . . prepared*: this obscure saying is clarified at 15:27, which underscores how misguided is James and John's request for eschatological glory.   **10:42** *They which . . . upon them*: Roman imperial authorities.   **10:43–45** *But whosoever . . . minister*: an idea perhaps rarely applied but not uncommon in the Greco-Roman world. A good ruler was expected to serve his subjects beneficently; see esp. Seneca's *Of Clemency*, which links the emperor's power with both divine authority and servitude, perhaps even equating high rank with crucifixion: "This is slavery of the highest magnitude, to be unable to become less. But you [emperor Nero] have that obligation in common with the gods; for heaven holds them too in fetters, and it is no more permissible for them to descend than it is safe for you. You have been nailed to your high rank" (8.1.3).   **10:43** *Minister*: servant.

you will be the chiefest, shall be servant of all. ⁴⁵For even the Son of man came not to be ministered unto, but to minister, and to give his life a ransom for many.

⁴⁶And they came to Jericho: and as he went out of Jericho with his disciples and a great number of people, blind Bartimæus, the son of Timæus, sat by the highway side begging. ⁴⁷And when he heard that it was Jesus of Nazareth, he began to cry out, and say, Jesus, thou Son of David, have mercy on me. ⁴⁸And many charged him that he should hold his peace: but he cried the more a great deal, Thou Son of David, have mercy on me. ⁴⁹And Jesus stood still, and commanded him to be called. And they call the blind man, saying unto him, Be of good comfort, rise; he calleth thee. ⁵⁰And he, casting away his garment, rose, and came to Jesus. ⁵¹And Jesus answered and said unto him, What wilt thou that I should do unto thee? The blind man said unto him, Lord, that I might receive my sight. ⁵²And Jesus said unto him, Go thy way; thy faith hath made thee whole. And immediately he received his sight, and followed Jesus in the way.

11 And when they came nigh to Jerusalem, unto Bethphage and Bethany, at the mount of Olives, he sendeth forth two of his disciples, ²and saith unto them, Go your way into the village over against you: and as soon as ye be entered into it, ye shall find a colt tied, whereon never man sat; loose him, and bring him. ³And if any man say unto you, Why do ye this? say ye that the Lord hath need of him; and straightway he will send him hither. ⁴And they went their way, and found the colt tied by the door without in a place where two ways met; and they loose him. ⁵And certain of them that stood there said unto them, What do ye, loosing the colt? ⁶And they said unto them even as Jesus had commanded: and they let them go. ⁷And they brought the colt to Jesus, and cast their garments on him; and he sat

10:44 *Chiefest*: Gk. *prōtos*; cf. 9:35; 10:31 (KJV "first"). *Servant*: slave.   **10:45** *Ransom*: Gk. *lytron* (paid in exchange for slaves' or captives' freedom; cf. Lev 25:51–52). This metaphor for Jesus' death recalls YHWH's liberation of Israel from Egypt: "I am the Lord and I will lead you out from the Egyptians' tyranny and I will rescue you from slavery and I will ransom [Gk. *lytrōsomai*] you with my raised right arm and with great judgment" (LXX Exod 6:6).   **10:46–52** Healing Bartimaeus. Recalling the healing of the blind man in 8:22–26, which immediately precedes Jesus' journey to Jerusalem, this encounter initiates the journey's close.   **10:46** *Jericho*: a city about fifteen miles northeast of Jerusalem. *The son of Timæus*: glossing *Bartimæus*, who refers to Jesus by an analogous patronymic in the subsequent verses.   **10:47** *Son of David*: a messianic title alluding to God's promise that a Davidic heir would always rule (see 2 Sam 7:12–16; Ps 89:3–4). God had failed to keep that promise, but some expected him to fulfill it in the eschatological messiah.   **10:48** *Charged him . . . peace*: cf. 1:25 (KJV "rebuked him"). There Jesus, during his first exorcism, silenced the demon who confessed his true identity; now the crowd utters the same verbs while Jesus allows the confessor to speak.   **10:50** *Rose*: better "sprang up" (MS tradition).   **10:51** *What wilt . . . thee*: echoing vv. 35–36.

11:1–26 The Jerusalem entry and the temple's cleansing. Jesus' entry into Jerusalem (11:1–11; cf. Matt 21:1–11; Luke 19:28–38; John 12:12–17) resembles a royal processional, appropriately for the "Son of David" (10:47–48). His cleansing of the temple (vv. 15–19; cf. Matt 21:12–15; Luke 19:45–48; and its earlier placement in John 2:13–17) is interpolated within the story of the fig tree's curse (vv. 12–14; cf. Matt 21:18–19) and the curse's realization (vv. 20–26; cf. Matt 21:20–22).   **11:1** *Bethphage and Bethany*: villages east of Jerusalem.   **11:2** *A colt . . . sat*: for the image of the king approaching Jerusalem on a colt, see Zech 9:9.   **11:4** *A place . . . met*: better "the street."   **11:7–9** *They brought . . .*

upon him. ⁸And many spread their garments in the way: and others cut down branches off the trees, and strawed them in the way. ⁹And they that went before, and they that followed, cried, saying, Hosanna; Blessed is he that cometh in the name of the Lord: ¹⁰Blessed be the kingdom of our father David, that cometh in the name of the Lord: Hosanna in the highest. ¹¹And Jesus entered into Jerusalem, and into the temple: and when he had looked round about upon all things, and now the eventide was come, he went out unto Bethany with the twelve.

¹²And on the morrow, when they were come from Bethany, he was hungry: ¹³and seeing a fig tree afar off having leaves, he came, if haply he might find any thing thereon: and when he came to it, he found nothing but leaves; for the time of figs was not yet. ¹⁴And Jesus answered and said unto it, No man eat fruit of thee hereafter for ever. And his disciples heard it.

¹⁵And they come to Jerusalem: and Jesus went into the temple, and began to cast out them that sold and bought in the temple, and overthrew the tables of the moneychangers, and the seats of them that sold doves; ¹⁶and would not suffer that any man should carry any vessel through the temple. ¹⁷And he taught, saying unto them, Is it not written, My house shall be called of all nations the house of prayer? but ye have made it a den of thieves. ¹⁸And the scribes and chief priests heard it, and sought how they might destroy him: for they feared him, because all the people was astonished at his doctrine. ¹⁹And when even was come, he went out of the city.

²⁰And in the morning, as they passed by, they saw the fig tree dried up from the roots. ²¹And Peter calling to remembrance saith unto him, Master, behold, the fig tree which thou cursedst is withered away. ²²And Jesus answering saith unto them, Have faith in God. ²³For verily I say unto you, That whosoever shall say unto this mountain, Be thou removed, and be thou cast into the sea; and shall not doubt in his heart, but shall believe that those things which he saith shall come to pass; he shall have whatsoever he saith. ²⁴Therefore I say unto you, What things soever ye desire, when ye pray, believe that ye receive them, and ye shall have

---

Lord: recalling the coronation of Solomon (1 Kgs 1:32–40), as well as that of Jehu (2 Kgs 9:13), when military officers spread their cloaks at the feet of the newly anointed king. For cut branches, compare Simon Maccabeus's victorious entrance into the Jerusalem citadel (1 Macc 13:51; 2 Macc 10:7).

11:8 *Trees*: better "fields" (MS tradition). **11:9** *Hosanna*: a transliterated Hebrew phrase meaning "save now." The people quote from Ps 118 (vv. 25–26a), which culminates in an entrance into the temple's sanctuary (vv. 26b–27). **11:10** *In the . . . Lord*: better omitted (MS tradition). **11:15** *Moneychangers,* for a fee, exchanged Roman coinage, which displayed idolatrous words and images (see 12:13–17 and notes), for coins acceptable for the temple tax. The *doves* sold were pigeons, relatively affordable animals that the poor were instructed to sacrifice (see Lev 5:6–7; 12:6–8; etc.). **11:17** *My house . . . prayer*: Isa 56:7; the reference may suggest concern that the outer court of the temple complex (the so-called Court of the Gentiles, beyond which non-Jews desiring to worship YHWH might not pass) had been so overrun by commerce as to disrupt pious Gentiles' devotion. *But ye . . . thieves*: echoing Jer 7:11 (subsequent verses describe YHWH's destruction of the shrine at Shiloh, whose centrality to YHWH's cult preceded that of the Jerusalem temple). **11:20** *Fig tree . . . roots*: "every man under his vine and under his fig tree" is an OT slogan of communal prosperity (1 Kgs 4:25; Mic 4:4); accordingly, bad figs and shriveled trees sometimes figure divine wrath (cf. Isa 34:4; Jer 8:13). **11:23** *This mountain*: moving mountains was a familiar image for accomplishing the impossible, and was proverbially associated with faith (cf. Matt 17:20; 1 Cor 13:2). But since Jesus is approaching the temple (cf. vv. 20, 27), *this mountain* presumably refers to the Temple Mount, with Jesus counseling his disciples to pray for its destruction. **11:24** *That ye receive*: better

them. ²⁵And when ye stand praying, forgive, if ye have ought against any: that your Father also which is in heaven may forgive you your trespasses. ²⁶But if ye do not forgive, neither will your Father which is in heaven forgive your trespasses.

²⁷And they come again to Jerusalem: and as he was walking in the temple, there come to him the chief priests, and the scribes, and the elders, ²⁸and say unto him, By what authority doest thou these things? and who gave thee this authority to do these things? ²⁹And Jesus answered and said unto them, I will also ask of you one question, and answer me, and I will tell you by what authority I do these things. ³⁰The baptism of John, was it from heaven, or of men? answer me. ³¹And they reasoned with themselves, saying, If we shall say, From heaven; he will say, Why then did ye not believe him? ³²But if we shall say, Of men; they feared the people: for all men counted John, that he was a prophet indeed. ³³And they answered and said unto Jesus, We cannot tell. And Jesus answering saith unto them, Neither do I tell you by what authority I do these things.

12 And he began to speak unto them by parables. A certain man planted a vineyard, and set an hedge about it, and digged a place for the winefat, and built a tower, and let it out to husbandmen, and went into a far country. ²And at the season he sent to the husbandmen a servant, that he might receive from the husbandmen of the fruit of the vineyard. ³And they caught him, and beat him, and sent him away empty. ⁴And again he sent unto them another servant; and at him they cast stones, and wounded him in the head, and sent him away shamefully handled. ⁵And again he sent another; and him they killed, and many others; beating some, and killing some. ⁶Having yet therefore one son, his wellbeloved, he sent him also last unto them, saying, They will reverence my son. ⁷But those husbandmen said among themselves, This is the heir; come, let us kill him, and the inheritance shall be ours. ⁸And they took him, and killed him, and cast him out of the vineyard. ⁹What shall therefore the lord of the vineyard do? he will come and

---

"that ye have received" (MS tradition). **11:25** *And when . . . trespasses*: paralleled in the Sermon on the Mount (Matt 5:23–24; 6:14), but here it qualifies the previous prayer's disturbing violence by excluding personal resentment and arrogant condescension as legitimate motives. **11:26** *But if . . . trespasses*: better omitted (MS tradition).

11:27–13:2 Disputes in the temple. Jesus continues the temple's cleansing by rhetorically vanquishing the range of his opponents in it: priests, scribes, elders, Pharisees, Herodians, and Sadducees. **11:27–33** Jesus' authority. Compare Matt 21:23–27; Luke 20:1–8. **12:1–12** Parable of the Wicked Tenants. Compare Matt 21:33–46; Luke 20:9–19. **12:1** *A certain . . . tower*: see Isa 5:1–2. Jesus' parable develops Isaiah's allegory of God's vineyard inventively, but it still demands to be read in the context of Isa 5:1–7. Since Jesus' audience includes the chief priests (see 11:27), it may be significant that Jewish literature roughly contemporary with Mark links Isaiah's vineyard with the temple. *Winefat*: vat for pressing wine. *Let it . . . country*: the householder becomes an absentee landlord, a figure widely despised. **12:2** *Servant*: lit. "slave"; the OT frequently refers to prophets as servants or slaves whom God sends to his people (e.g., Jer 7:25; 25:4). For the motif of the killing of prophets, see, e.g., Neh 9:26. **12:4** *And at . . . stones*: better omitted (MS tradition). *Wounded him in the head*: perhaps alluding to John the Baptist's beheading (cf. 6:24–29). **12:6** *Having yet . . . my son*: the husbandmen's persistent brutalization of the servants makes the murderous plot of vv. 7–8 entirely predictable, drawing attention to the recklessness of this decision to send the son. *Wellbeloved*: Gk. *agapētos*; cf. 1:11 (see note); 9:7 (both KJV "beloved," of Jesus). It echoes God's command that Abraham kill Isaac in Gen 22:2. **12:7** *Come, let us . . . ours*: recalling the words of Joseph's brothers planning his murder (Gen 37:20).

destroy the husbandmen, and will give the vineyard unto others. ¹⁰And have ye not read this scripture; The stone which the builders rejected is become the head of the corner: ¹¹this was the Lord's doing, and it is marvellous in our eyes? ¹²And they sought to lay hold on him, but feared the people: for they knew that he had spoken the parable against them: and they left him, and went their way.

¹³And they send unto him certain of the Pharisees and of the Herodians, to catch him in his words. ¹⁴And when they were come, they say unto him, Master, we know that thou art true, and carest for no man: for thou regardest not the person of men, but teachest the way of God in truth: Is it lawful to give tribute to Cæsar, or not? ¹⁵Shall we give, or shall we not give? But he, knowing their hypocrisy, said unto them, Why tempt ye me? bring me a penny, that I may see it. ¹⁶And they brought it. And he saith unto them, Whose is this image and superscription? And they said unto him, Cæsar's. ¹⁷And Jesus answering said unto them, Render to Cæsar the things that are Cæsar's, and to God the things that are God's. And they marvelled at him.

¹⁸Then come unto him the Sadducees, which say there is no resurrection; and they asked him, saying, ¹⁹Master, Moses wrote unto us, If a man's brother die, and leave his wife behind him, and leave no children, that his brother should take his wife, and raise up seed unto his brother. ²⁰Now there were seven brethren: and the first took a wife, and dying left no seed. ²¹And the second took her, and died, neither left he any seed: and the third likewise. ²²And the seven had her, and left no seed: last of all the woman died also. ²³In the resurrection therefore, when they shall rise, whose wife shall she be of them? for the seven had her to wife. ²⁴And Jesus answering said unto them, Do ye not therefore err, because

12:10–11 *The stone . . . eyes*: Ps 118:22–23.   12:10 *Head of the corner*: either a cornerstone or a copestone.   12:12 *Lay hold on*: arrest.   12:13–17 Tribute to Caesar. Compare Matt 22:15–22; Luke 20:20–26.   12:14 *Thou regardest . . . men*: you do not show favoritism (a Semitic idiom). *Tribute*: Gk. *kēnson*, the Roman tax levied on the basis of the imperial census. The question touches on the second commandment (Exod 20:4–6; Deut 4:15–20), for the coin in which the tax was paid displayed Caesar's image and a legend proclaiming his divinity. More narrowly, the question invites Jesus to declare himself in support of or in opposition to Roman rule in Palestine. Either position could land him in trouble, with the presumably anti-Roman crowds or with the Roman authorities, respectively.   12:15 *Tempt*: or "test"; Mark may imply that the question tempts Jesus to violate the second commandment by expressing tolerance for pagan rulers and their idolatry.   12:17 *Render to Cæsar . . . God's*: cf. Rom 13:6–7. Unlike Paul, Mark's Jesus refuses to specify what is Caesar's and what is God's: the coin for the tax may be understood as Caesar's, for it contains his image and inscription; but since that inscription proclaims Caesar's divinity (most likely, "Tiberius Caesar Augustus, son of divine Augustus," found on contemporary Roman coinage), it is also possible that paying the tax entailed giving to Caesar what belongs to God alone.   12:18–27 Resurrection. Compare Matt 22:23–33; Luke 20:27–40.   12:18 *Sadducees*: a conservative sect associated with the temple whose adherents rejected religious ideas and traditions not authorized by the Pentateuch, such as resurrection.   12:19 *If a . . . unto his brother*: summarizing the law governing levirate marriage (cf. Deut 25:5–10) by conflating Deut 25:5 and Gen 38:8. *Raise up*: the verbal form of Gk. *anastasis*, "resurrection" (vv. 18, 23, 25). The semantic link draws attention to the Sadducees' and Jesus' conflicting understandings of afterlife: the pentateuchal idea of living on in one's offspring (see Gen 30:1; Exod 6:8; etc.) vs. living on in resurrected bodies.   12:20–22 *Now there . . . also*: extending to absurdity the story of Tamar (see Gen 38:6–11, quoted in v. 19), and thereby underscoring both a conflict between the Pentateuch and the later doctrine of eschatological resurrection and the levirate law's failure to "raise up" offspring even in the Pentateuch's own terms

ye know not the scriptures, neither the power of God? [25]For when they shall rise from the dead, they neither marry, nor are given in marriage; but are as the angels which are in heaven. [26]And as touching the dead, that they rise: have ye not read in the book of Moses, how in the bush God spake unto him, saying, I am the God of Abraham, and the God of Isaac, and the God of Jacob? [27]He is not the God of the dead, but the God of the living: ye therefore do greatly err.

[28]And one of the scribes came, and having heard them reasoning together, and perceiving that he had answered them well, asked him, Which is the first commandment of all? [29]And Jesus answered him, The first of all the commandments is, Hear, O Israel; The Lord our God is one Lord: [30]and thou shalt love the Lord thy God with all thy heart, and with all thy soul, and with all thy mind, and with all thy strength: this is the first commandment. [31]And the second is like, namely this, Thou shalt love thy neighbour as thyself. There is none other commandment greater than these. [32]And the scribe said unto him, Well, Master, thou hast said the truth: for there is one God; and there is none other but he: [33]and to love him with all the heart, and with all the understanding, and with all the soul, and with all the strength, and to love his neighbour as himself, is more than all whole burnt offerings and sacrifices. [34]And when Jesus saw that he answered discreetly, he said unto him, Thou art not far from the kingdom of God. And no man after that durst ask him any question.

[35]And Jesus answered and said, while he taught in the temple, How say the scribes that Christ is the Son of David? [36]For David himself said by the Holy

---

(i.e., biological reproduction).   **12:25** *When they . . . marriage*: cf. 1 Cor 7:25–31, where Paul cites the impending eschatological transformation in arguing against marrying. *As the angels*: like Paul, Jesus insists that resurrection entails radical transformation (cf. 1 Cor 15:35–54); but angels were usually viewed not as asexual but rather as sexually threatening (cf. Gen 6:1–4 and notes; perhaps 1 Cor 11:10). **12:26** *In the bush*: "in the story about the bush" (NRSV).   **12:26–27** *I am . . . living*: Exod 3:6, 15–16. *4 Maccabees* 7.19 (cf. 16.25) is also relevant, as it alludes to the same OT passage and likewise asserts that the three patriarchs continue to live with God. Jesus' claim that the patriarchs are "living" is puzzling, for his insistence on eschatological resurrection (in contrast to *4 Maccabees'* doctrine of an immortal soul) presupposes that they are currently dead and will live again only in the future. In any case, in response to the Sadducees' invocation of a story in which divine intervention causes (Gen 38:7) and then compounds (vv. 10–11) a generative crisis, Jesus' allusion draws attention to the patriarchs' miraculous success in fathering offspring in which each lived on after death (Gen 21:5–7; 25:21; 30:22). For Mark's Jesus (as for Paul; cf. Rom 4:16–25) this guarantees that God will raise the dead.   **12:28–34** The great commandment. Compare Matt 22:34–40; Luke 10:25–28.   **12:28** *One of the scribes*: the first of several characters in Mark's closing chapters who might be expected to oppose Jesus but show surprising sympathy to him or his teaching; cf. 15:1–15 (Pontius Pilate), 39 (the centurion), 43 (Joseph of Arimathea). Such characters serve as a foil to Jesus' disciples, who persistently misunderstand or reject Jesus' teaching, mission, and identity, and who ultimately betray, deny, and abandon him. More generally, they call attention to instability in the line between insider and outsider; cf. 4:10–12 and notes, 33–34.   **12:29–30** *Hear, O . . . strength*: the opening sentences of the Shema, the major Jewish declaration of belief (Deut 6:4–5; neither Jesus nor the scribes quote the passage in a form that LXX or MT preserves).   **12:30** *This is the first commandment*: better omitted (MS tradition).   **12:31** *Like, namely*: better omitted (MS tradition). *Thou shalt love . . . thyself*: Lev 19:18.   **12:32** *There is one God*: better "he is one" (MS tradition).   **12:33** *And with all . . . soul*: better omitted (MS tradition). *Is more . . . sacrifices*: a commonplace of the OT prophets (Hos 6:6; Mic 6:6–8; etc.).   **12:34** *Discreetly*: thoughtfully.   **12:35–37** The Son of David. Compare Matt 22:41–46; Luke 20:41–44. This episode challenges a conventional understanding

Ghost, The LORD said to my Lord, Sit thou on my right hand, till I make thine enemies thy footstool. [37]David therefore himself calleth him Lord; and whence is he then his son? And the common people heard him gladly.

[38]And he said unto them in his doctrine, Beware of the scribes, which love to go in long clothing, and love salutations in the marketplaces, [39]and the chief seats in the synagogues, and the uppermost rooms at feasts: [40]which devour widows' houses, and for a pretence make long prayers: these shall receive greater damnation.

[41]And Jesus sat over against the treasury, and beheld how the people cast money into the treasury: and many that were rich cast in much. [42]And there came a certain poor widow, and she threw in two mites, which make a farthing. [43]And he called unto him his disciples, and saith unto them, Verily I say unto you, That this poor widow hath cast more in, than all they which have cast into the treasury: [44]for all they did cast in of their abundance; but she of her want did cast in all that she had, even all her living.

13 And as he went out of the temple, one of his disciples saith unto him, Master, see what manner of stones and what buildings are here! [2]And Jesus answering said unto him, Seest thou these great buildings? there shall not be left one stone upon another, that shall not be thrown down.

[3]And as he sat upon the mount of Olives over against the temple, Peter and James and John and Andrew asked him privately, [4]Tell us, when shall these things

---

of the Christ as *Son of David* (cf. 10:47–48). **12:36** *The* LORD . . . *footstool*: Ps 110:1, the OT verse most often quoted in the NT. Jesus assumes that David, the psalm's purported author, records YHWH's dialogue with the Christ. In LXX Ps 110:1, which Mark quotes, each character is called Gk. *kyrios,* "Lord." KJV's LORD reflects the Hebrew, in which "YHWH" speaks to the Psalmist's "lord" (see 14:62 note). *Make thine enemies thy footstool*: better "put your enemies underneath your feet," a phrase from Ps 8:6 (MS tradition). **12:37** *David therefore . . . son*: Jesus' point is that if the *Lord* (i.e., the Christ) were merely David's descendent (*son*), then David (the psalmist) would not show such deference as to call him *my Lord.* Therefore, the Lord (Christ) rules at the LORD's (YHWH's) right hand not as a descendent of David, but as the resurrected son of God (cf. Rom 1:3–4; 1 Cor 15:20–28). *Common people*: better "large crowd." **12:38–40** Denunciation of scribes. Compare Luke 20:45–47 and the expanded versions of Jesus' denunciation of religious leaders in Matt 23:1–36; Luke 11:37–54. **12:39** *Uppermost rooms*: places of honor; cf. Luke 14:7–11. **12:40** *Long prayers*: showy prayer (more elaborately critiqued at Matt 6:5–8). *Damnation*: condemnation. **12:41–44** The widow's mites. Compare Luke 21:1–4. This episode is linked to the preceding denunciation through its focus on a widow (cf. v. 40), contrasting her humility with the scribes' and Pharisees' pretension. **12:42** *Mites*: Gk. *lepta,* copper coins of the smallest denomination. *Farthing*: see Matt 5:26 note. **12:44** *Living*: Gk. *bion,* "livelihood" or "life." **13:1–2** The temple's destruction prophesied. Compare Matt 24:1–2; Luke 21:5–6. **13:1** *See what . . . here*: in the late first century B.C.E. Herod the Great began the process of renovating the second temple. While the Herodian temple maintained the original's dimensions, the surrounding complex was larger and more opulent—by all accounts one of the most impressive monuments in the Roman Empire. **13:2** *There shall not be left . . . down*: prophesying Rome's destruction of this temple in 70 C.E., at the end of the Jewish War, which would have been an imminent expectation or recent memory of the evangelist. **13:3–37 The coming end.** This section consists of an apocalyptic discourse sometimes called the Synoptic Apocalypse, or the Little Apocalypse, or the Olivet Discourse, versions of which appear in Matt 24 and Luke 21. Prompted by the first four disciples' question about the temple (vv. 3–4; cf. Matt 24:3; Luke 21:7), Jesus' final sermon draws heavily on eschatological ideas and imagery from OT and other Jewish literature, some cited in the notes that follow. **13:4** *These things*: presumably referring to Jesus' previous statement about the temple (v. 2), but his response concerns the Son of

be? and what shall be the sign when all these things shall be fulfilled? [5]And Jesus answering them began to say, Take heed lest any man deceive you: [6]for many shall come in my name, saying, I am Christ; and shall deceive many. [7]And when ye shall hear of wars and rumours of wars, be ye not troubled: for such things must needs be; but the end shall not be yet. [8]For nation shall rise against nation, and kingdom against kingdom: and there shall be earthquakes in divers places, and there shall be famines and troubles: these are the beginnings of sorrows.

[9]But take heed to yourselves: for they shall deliver you up to councils; and in the synagogues ye shall be beaten: and ye shall be brought before rulers and kings for my sake, for a testimony against them. [10]And the gospel must first be published among all nations. [11]But when they shall lead you, and deliver you up, take no thought beforehand what ye shall speak, neither do ye premeditate: but whatsoever shall be given you in that hour, that speak ye: for it is not ye that speak, but the Holy Ghost. [12]Now the brother shall betray the brother to death, and the father the son; and children shall rise up against their parents, and shall cause them to be put to death. [13]And ye shall be hated of all men for my name's sake: but he that shall endure unto the end, the same shall be saved.

[14]But when ye shall see the abomination of desolation, spoken of by Daniel the prophet, standing where it ought not, (let him that readeth understand,) then let them that be in Judæa flee to the mountains: [15]and let him that is on the housetop not go down into the house, neither enter therein, to take any thing out of his house: [16]and let him that is in the field not turn back again for to take up his garment. [17]But woe to them that are with child, and to them that give suck in

---

Man's eschatological advent rather than the temple's destruction. Whereas Matthew resolves the inconsistency by having the disciples change subjects (24:3), here Jesus' non sequitur directs the disciples' attention even further away from the transient building. **13:5–8** Signs of the coming end. Compare Matt 24:4–8; Luke 21:8–11. **13:5** *Take heed*: lit. "see" (so throughout). Jesus' sermon repeatedly refers to seeing and watching: vv. 2, 5, 9, 14, 23, 33, 34, 35, 37. *Deceive*: deception was a conventional eschatological expectation; cf. 2 Thess 2:3. **13:6** *I am Christ*: Gk. *egō eimi*, "it is I" or "I am" (KJV adds "Christ"); see 6:50 note. **13:7–8** *Ye shall hear . . . against kingdom*: cf. 2 Chr 15:6; Isa 19:2; Jer 51:46. **13:8** *Earthquakes*: cf. Isa 29:6; Joel 2:10; etc. *And troubles*: better omitted (MS tradition). *Sorrows*: lit. "birth pangs," another common eschatological motif; cf. Isa 66:8–11; Jer 30:5–9; 1 Thess 5:3; etc. **13:9–13** Betrayal and persecution. Compare Matt 10:17–21; 24:9–14; Luke 21:12–19. **13:9** *Councils*: local courts. *A testimony against*: alternatively "a witness to." **13:10** *The gospel . . . nations*: many OT texts look forward to Gentiles worshiping YHWH in the eschatological future (e.g., Isa 2:2–4; Zech 8:23). Paul also understands Gentiles' evangelization as part of a complex eschatological timetable; see Rom 11:11–26a. *Published*: proclaimed. **13:11** *Lead you . . . up*: i.e., to trial or judgment. *Neither do ye premeditate*: better omitted (MS tradition). **13:12** *The brother . . . parents*: cf. Mic 7:6. This prophecy reverses the communal and familial restoration supposedly accomplished by John the Baptist (see 9:12 and note). **13:14–27** Cataclysm. Compare Matt 24:15–31; Luke 21:20–28; Luke 17:20–21 also draws on material from this passage, but develops it differently. **13:14** *Abomination of desolation*: the phrase used by Daniel (9:27; 11:31; cf. 8:11–14 and notes) to describe the pagan statue or altar that Antiochus erected in the temple in 167 B.C.E (cf. 1 Macc 1:54). Mark may be making a veiled reference to Rome's destruction of the temple (cf. Matt 23:38; 24:15; Luke 21:20). However, the neuter noun *abomination* (Gk. *to bdelygma*) is modified by the masculine participle *standing* (*estēkota*), which may imply a person—the enigmatic "man of sin" discussed at 2 Thess 2:3–12 or some other shadowy figure. *Spoken of . . . prophet*: better omitted (MS tradition) as a scribal gloss. **13:15–16** *On the housetop . . . field*: the *housetop* seems to have been a place of relaxation (cf. 2 Sam 11:2; Acts 10:9; etc.), in contrast to *the field*, a place of labor. **13:16** *Not turn back*: cf. Gen 19:17.

those days! [18]And pray ye that your flight be not in the winter. [19]For in those days shall be affliction, such as was not from the beginning of the creation which God created unto this time, neither shall be. [20]And except that the Lord had shortened those days, no flesh should be saved: but for the elect's sake, whom he hath chosen, he hath shortened the days. [21]And then if any man shall say to you, Lo, here is Christ; or, lo, he is there; believe him not: [22]for false Christs and false prophets shall rise, and shall shew signs and wonders, to seduce, if it were possible, even the elect. [23]But take ye heed: behold, I have foretold you all things.

[24]But in those days, after that tribulation, the sun shall be darkened, and the moon shall not give her light, [25]and the stars of heaven shall fall, and the powers that are in heaven shall be shaken. [26]And then shall they see the Son of man coming in the clouds with great power and glory. [27]And then shall he send his angels, and shall gather together his elect from the four winds, from the uttermost part of the earth to the uttermost part of heaven.

[28]Now learn a parable of the fig tree; When her branch is yet tender, and putteth forth leaves, ye know that summer is near: [29]so ye in like manner, when ye shall see these things come to pass, know that it is nigh, even at the doors. [30]Verily I say unto you, that this generation shall not pass, till all these things be done. [31]Heaven and earth shall pass away: but my words shall not pass away. [32]But of that day and that hour knoweth no man, no, not the angels which are in heaven, neither the Son, but the Father.

[33]Take ye heed, watch and pray: for ye know not when the time is. [34]For the Son of man is as a man taking a far journey, who left his house, and gave authority to his servants, and to every man his work, and commanded the porter to watch. [35]Watch ye therefore: for ye know not when the master of the house cometh, at even, or at midnight, or at the cockcrowing, or in the morning: [36]lest coming suddenly he find you sleeping. [37]And what I say unto you I say unto all, Watch.

13:18 *Your flight*: better "it" (MS tradition).   **13:19** *In those . . . neither shall be*: recalling and surpassing Dan 12:1.   **13:20** *Except that . . . the days*: a conventional hope; cf. Sir 36:1–12 (esp. v. 8); 2 Esd 2:13; etc.   **13:22** *False Christs . . . elect*: compare the warning about prophets and dreamers in Deut 13:1–5 and about the "man of sin" in 2 Thess 2:3–12. *False prophets*: see Matt 7:15–23 note. **13:24–25** *The sun . . . shaken*: drawing on the imagery of such prophetic passages as Isa 13:10; 34:4; Joel 2:10. These events may signal an end to God's original creation (cf. vv. 19, 31)—which began with light and the heavens (Gen 1:1–8)—in advance of the new created order that the Son of Man's advent initiates. Even so, the darkness is troubling given Jesus' numerous commands to "see" and "watch" (see v. 5 note).   **13:25** *The powers . . . heaven*: i.e., heavenly bodies, the spiritual beings thought to rule them (cf. Eph 6:12), or both.   **13:26** *Son of . . . glory*: Dan 7:13; cf. Mark 8:38. **13:27** *Gather together . . . heaven*: a conventional eschatological expectation; see Deut 30:4; Isa 43:6; LXX Zech 2:6; cf. 1 Thess 4:17.   **13:28–32** Parable of the Fig Tree. Compare Matt 24:32–36; Luke 21:29–33.   **13:30** *This generation . . . done*: cf. 9:1 and note.   **13:31** *Heaven and . . . not pass away*: see Isa 40:8; 51:6.   **13:32** *But of . . . Son*: contrast Dan 11–12 (esp. 12:11–13), which attempts to establish the day with some precision. The Son's authority over what happens at the end time is similarly limited at 10:40.   **13:33–37** Parable of the Returning Master.   **13:33** *And pray*: better omitted (MS tradition).   **13:34** *For the Son of man*: added by KJV; the Greek sentence's subject is "it" ("the time" of v. 33).   **13:35** *At even . . . morning*: the Roman imperial world conventionally divided night into four watches.   **13:36** *He find you sleeping*: cf. 1 Thess 5:6–7.

14 After two days was the feast of the passover, and of unleavened bread: and the chief priests and the scribes sought how they might take him by craft, and put him to death. ²But they said, Not on the feast day, lest there be an uproar of the people.

³And being in Bethany in the house of Simon the leper, as he sat at meat, there came a woman having an alabaster box of ointment of spikenard very precious; and she brake the box, and poured it on his head. ⁴And there were some that had indignation within themselves, and said, Why was this waste of the ointment made? ⁵For it might have been sold for more than three hundred pence, and have been given to the poor. And they murmured against her. ⁶And Jesus said, Let her alone; why trouble ye her? she hath wrought a good work on me. ⁷For ye have the poor with you always, and whensoever ye will ye may do them good: but me ye have not always. ⁸She hath done what she could: she is come aforehand to anoint my body to the burying. ⁹Verily I say unto you, Wheresoever this gospel shall be preached throughout the whole world, this also that she hath done shall be spoken of for a memorial of her.

¹⁰And Judas Iscariot, one of the twelve, went unto the chief priests, to betray him unto them. ¹¹And when they heard it, they were glad, and promised to give him money. And he sought how he might conveniently betray him.

¹²And the first day of unleavened bread, when they killed the passover, his disciples said unto him, Where wilt thou that we go and prepare that thou mayest eat the passover? ¹³And he sendeth forth two of his disciples, and saith unto them, Go ye into the city, and there shall meet you a man bearing a pitcher of water: follow him. ¹⁴And wheresoever he shall go in, say ye to the goodman of the house, The Master saith, Where is the guestchamber, where I shall eat the passover with my disciples? ¹⁵And he will shew you a large upper room furnished and

14:1–15:47 Jesus' arrest, crucifixion, and burial. 14:1–11 Plot against Jesus and anointing at Bethany. Compare Matt 26:1–16; Luke 22:1–6; Luke 7:36–50, locating the anointing earlier in Jesus' career; John 11:47–12:8, identifying Mary, sister of Martha and Lazarus, as the woman who anoints Jesus.   **14:1** *Passover*: the seven-day commemoration of Israel's deliverance from Egyptian slavery that features the feast of unleavened bread (cf. Exod 12:1–13:10).   **14:2** *On the feast day*: rather "during the festival." Jesus will be arrested on the feast day (vv. 43–52).   **14:3** *Simon the leper*: Mark's identification of the host calls attention to Jesus' penchant for dining with social outcasts; cf. 2:15–17. *Spikenard*: an aromatic Indian plant.   **14:4** *Some that . . . themselves*: other gospels variously identify the complainants as the disciples (Matt 26:8), a Pharisee named Simon (Luke 7:39–40), and Judas, motivated by greed (John 12:4–6).   **14:5** *Pence*: Gk. *dēnarios*, from Lat. *denarius*—apparently a manual laborer's standard daily wage (cf. Matt 20:2).   **14:7** *Ye have . . . you always*: see Deut 15:11.   **14:8** *To anoint . . . burying*: because anointing is a sign of kingship, Jesus' insistence on interpreting the woman's actions in a funereal context marks a transition from his regal arrival at Jerusalem (10:47–48; 11:1–11; etc.) to more somber tones, for which passages such as 10:43–45 have prepared the reader.   **14:9** *Memorial of her*: a somewhat ironic memorial, since she remains anonymous.   **14:10** *Betrayed*: Gk. *paradidōmi*; cf. 9:31; 10:33 ("delivered").   **14:11** *Promised to give him money*: unlike Matthew (26:15; cf. Luke 22:3–6), Mark does not offer greed as Judas' explicit motive for betrayal, but his willingness to accept money contrasts with the lavish generosity of the woman in the previous episode. An alternative interpretation would have Judas understand Jesus' reference to his impending burial as a signal to initiate the fulfillment of Jesus' repeated prophecies of death and resurrection (8:31; 9:31; 10:32–34), to which Judas was privy and which he follows to the letter (esp. 10:33; see 14:10 note).   **14:12–31** Celebrating the Passover. Compare Matt 26:17–35; Luke 22:7–23, 31–34; John 13:21–30, 36–38.   **14:12** *The passover*: i.e., the lamb sacrificed for the Passover festival.   **14:14** *Goodman*: master. *The guestchamber*:

prepared: there make ready for us. ¹⁶And his disciples went forth, and came into the city, and found as he had said unto them: and they made ready the passover.

¹⁷And in the evening he cometh with the twelve. ¹⁸And as they sat and did eat, Jesus said, Verily I say unto you, One of you which eateth with me shall betray me. ¹⁹And they began to be sorrowful, and to say unto him one by one, Is it I? and another said, Is it I? ²⁰And he answered and said unto them, It is one of the twelve, that dippeth with me in the dish. ²¹The Son of man indeed goeth, as it is written of him: but woe to that man by whom the Son of man is betrayed! good were it for that man if he had never been born.

²²And as they did eat, Jesus took bread, and blessed, and brake it, and gave to them, and said, Take, eat: this is my body. ²³And he took the cup, and when he had given thanks, he gave it to them: and they all drank of it. ²⁴And he said unto them, This is my blood of the new testament, which is shed for many. ²⁵Verily I say unto you, I will drink no more of the fruit of the vine, until that day that I drink it new in the kingdom of God.

²⁶And when they had sung an hymn, they went out into the mount of Olives. ²⁷And Jesus saith unto them, All ye shall be offended because of me this night: for it is written, I will smite the shepherd, and the sheep shall be scattered. ²⁸But after that I am risen, I will go before you into Galilee. ²⁹But Peter said unto him, Although all shall be offended, yet will not I. ³⁰And Jesus saith unto him, Verily I say unto thee, That this day, even in this night, before the cock crow twice, thou shalt deny me thrice. ³¹But he spake the more vehemently, If I should die with thee, I will not deny thee in any wise. Likewise also said they all.

³²And they came to a place which was named Gethsemane: and he saith to his disciples, Sit ye here, while I shall pray. ³³And he taketh with him Peter and James and John, and began to be sore amazed, and to be very heavy; ³⁴and saith unto

---

better "my guestchamber" (MS tradition).   **14:18** *One of you . . . me*: see Ps 41:9.   **14:19** *Is it I*: better "Surely, not I?" (NRSV). *And another . . . I*: better omitted (MS tradition).   **14:21** *As it is written*: the early church believed that various OT texts predicted Jesus' fate, and Mark's Passion Narrative alludes to many of them.   **14:22–25** *And as . . . God*: in addition to the Synoptic Gospels, Paul too narrates this meal (1 Cor 11:23–25).   **14:22** *Jesus took . . . them*: cf. 6:41; 8:6 (the miraculous feedings). *Eat*: better omitted (MS tradition). *This is my body*: Jesus' body will be broken on the cross, just as the bread was broken.   **14:23** *They all . . . it*: cf. 10:39.   **14:24** *Blood of the new testament*: better simply "blood of the testament" (MS tradition). KJV alternates between "testament" and "covenant" when rendering Gk. *diathēkē*, which in LXX consistently translates the Hebrew word for covenant. The phrase's allusions (esp. Exod 24:5–8; also Zech 9:11) indicate that Mark's Jesus believes his blood will reaffirm the Mosaic covenant (contrast Luke 22:20; 1 Cor 11:25).   **14:25** *Until that . . . God*: i.e., at the eschatological banquet (see 2:19 note), unless Mark is ironically referring to Jesus' execution as "king of the Jews" (15:26, 32).   **14:27** *Offended*: see 4:17 note. *Because of . . . night*: better omitted (MS tradition). *I will . . . scattered*: Zech 13:7; cf. Mark 6:34.   **14:31** *Wise*: manner.   **14:32–42** Jesus' agonizing prayer. Compare Matt 26:36–46; Luke 22:39–46; John 12:27–30.   **14:32** *Gethsemane*: Greek transliteration of a Hebrew or Aramaic phrase meaning "oil press," perhaps evoking an orchard of olive trees on the Mount of Olives.   **14:33** *Peter and James and John*: these three also accompanied Jesus at the healing of Jairus's daughter (5:37–43) and at the transfiguration (9:2–8). Along with Andrew, they alone heard Jesus' apocalyptic sermon (13:3–37). *Sore amazed*: in Mark's gospel, the crowds or the disciples are normally amazed by Jesus (e.g., 1:27; 9:15; 10:32; etc.); here Jesus is himself amazed, apparently at what he is about to do. *Heavy*: anxious or distressed.

them, My soul is exceeding sorrowful unto death: tarry ye here, and watch. [35]And he went forward a little, and fell on the ground, and prayed that, if it were possible, the hour might pass from him. [36]And he said, Abba, Father, all things are possible unto thee; take away this cup from me: nevertheless not what I will, but what thou wilt. [37]And he cometh, and findeth them sleeping, and saith unto Peter, Simon, sleepest thou? couldest not thou watch one hour? [38]Watch ye and pray, lest ye enter into temptation. The spirit truly is ready, but the flesh is weak. [39]And again he went away, and prayed, and spake the same words. [40]And when he returned, he found them asleep again, (for their eyes were heavy,) neither wist they what to answer him. [41]And he cometh the third time, and saith unto them, Sleep on now, and take your rest: it is enough, the hour is come; behold, the Son of man is betrayed into the hands of sinners. [42]Rise up, let us go; lo, he that betrayeth me is at hand.

[43]And immediately, while he yet spake, cometh Judas, one of the twelve, and with him a great multitude with swords and staves, from the chief priests and the scribes and the elders. [44]And he that betrayed him had given them a token, saying, Whomsoever I shall kiss, that same is he; take him, and lead him away safely. [45]And as soon as he was come, he goeth straightway to him, and saith, Master, master; and kissed him. [46]And they laid their hands on him, and took him. [47]And one of them that stood by drew a sword, and smote a servant of the high priest, and cut off his ear. [48]And Jesus answered and said unto them, Are ye come out, as against a thief, with swords and with staves to take me? [49]I was daily with you

---

14:34 *My soul . . . death*: echoing numerous cries of sorrow from the OT (e.g., Ps 42:5). *Watch*: Jesus twice asks the three to "watch" in this episode (cf. v. 38), recalling his repeated calls to "watch" and "take heed" in chap. 13 (esp. the concluding parable, 13:32–37; see 13:5 note). Numerous points of contact between chap. 13's apocalyptic discourse and Mark's Passion Narrative collapse the Son of Man's eschatological advent into Jesus' anguish, arrest, and execution, thereby undercutting any triumphalism possibly engendered by the earlier sermon's prediction of the Son of Man's glorious coming (see esp. 13:26–27). **14:35** *Hour*: cf. vv. 37, 41; 13:32. **14:36** *Abba, Father*: *Abba* means "father" (Aramaic). Its employment suggests that Mark's Greek-speaking readers were familiar with its use in combination with Gk. *ho patēr* ("the father"), and the same combination in fact appears in Paul's letters (Rom 8:15; Gal 4:6). The Pauline expression may have emulated Jesus' prayer, but Mark may be assimilating this prayer to an early Christian liturgical formula. Contextual analysis of "Abba, Father" in Paul's letters suggests that the phrase played a role in a baptismal liturgy, to which Mark may be alluding (cf. 10:38–39 and note to v. 38). *This cup*: see 10:38–39 and note to v. 38; 14:23. **14:37–38** *Sleepest thou . . . Watch ye*: cf. 13:33–37. **14:38** *The spirit . . . weak*: invoking a distinction that Greco-Roman philosophical thought commonly made between the ignoble flesh or body, weak and vulnerable to its basest appetites, and the superior spirit (or mind, or soul). Paul draws on the same distinction (e.g., Rom 8:1–17). **14:40** *Neither wist . . . him*: cf. 9:6. **14:41** *Sleep on . . . rest*: often translated as a question (e.g., NRSV: "Are you still sleeping and taking your rest?"), but KJV's command is also possible, inviting a reading of Jesus' words as bitterly ironic. His disciples have slept through his time of agonizing prayer; they might as well sleep through his arrest too. *It is enough*: Gk. *apechei* (interpretation obscure); since the word often means "to receive [a sum] in full," it may also be understood with reference to Judas: "he receives payment" (cf. vv. 10–11). *The hour . . . sinners*: initiating the fulfillment of Jesus' passion predictions, which this verse echoes; cf. 8:31; 9:31; 10:33–34. **14:43–15:15** Arrest, trial, and sentencing. Compare Matt 26:47–27:26; Luke 22:47–23:25; John 18:1–40; 19:4–16. **14:43** *Chief priests . . . elders*: members of the Sanhedrin; see 8:31 note. **14:44** *Safely*: "securely"—i.e., "under guard" (NRSV). **14:45** *Master, Master*: better to omit one (MS tradition). *And kissed him*: compare Joab's kiss of Amasa (2 Sam 20:9–10). **14:48** *Thief*: Gk. *lēstēs*, which can also refer to an insurrectionist (cf. 15:27).

in the temple teaching, and ye took me not: but the scriptures must be fulfilled. ⁵⁰And they all forsook him, and fled. ⁵¹And there followed him a certain young man, having a linen cloth cast about his naked body; and the young men laid hold on him: ⁵²and he left the linen cloth, and fled from them naked.

⁵³And they led Jesus away to the high priest: and with him were assembled all the chief priests and the elders and the scribes. ⁵⁴And Peter followed him afar off, even into the palace of the high priest: and he sat with the servants, and warmed himself at the fire. ⁵⁵And the chief priests and all the council sought for witness against Jesus to put him to death; and found none. ⁵⁶For many bare false witness against him, but their witness agreed not together. ⁵⁷And there arose certain, and bare false witness against him, saying, ⁵⁸We heard him say, I will destroy this temple that is made with hands, and within three days I will build another made without hands. ⁵⁹But neither so did their witness agree together. ⁶⁰And the high priest stood up in the midst, and asked Jesus, saying, Answerest thou nothing? what is it which these witness against thee? ⁶¹But he held his peace, and answered nothing. Again the high priest asked him, and said unto him, Art thou the Christ, the Son of the Blessed? ⁶²And Jesus said, I am: and ye shall see the Son of man sitting on the right hand of power, and coming in the clouds of heaven. ⁶³Then the high priest rent his clothes, and saith, What need we any further witnesses? ⁶⁴Ye have heard the blasphemy: what think ye? And they all condemned him to

---

14:49 *But the scriptures must be fulfilled*: see 14:21 note. The Greek phrase literally reads "but in order that the Scriptures may be fulfilled." **14:51–52** *There followed . . . naked*: this mysterious follower, so desperate to escape the scene of Jesus' arrest that he abandons his clothing, emblematizes the disciples' shameful abandonment of their master to die alone (cf. v. 50). His reappearance dressed in new garb to announce Jesus' resurrection at 16:5 may therefore gesture at hope for their rehabilitation. **14:51** *The young men*: better "they" (MS tradition). **14:52** *Linen cloth*: Gk. *sindōn*; cf. 15:46 (KJV "fine linen"). **14:54** *Palace*: better "courtyard" (cf. v. 66). **14:55** *Council*: Gk. *synedrion* (Sanhedrin); cf. 15:1. **14:56** *Bare false witness*: transgressing the ninth commandment (Exod 20:16; Deut 5:20). *Their witness . . . together*: multiple witnesses are required to sustain an accusation, especially of a capital offense (Deut 19:15; cf. 17:6–7). **14:58** *I will destroy . . . without hands*: Jesus never makes this claim in the Synoptic Gospels (although elements of it are to be found in 8:31; 9:31; 10:33–34; 13:2), and thus it is not surprising that the witnesses cannot agree (v. 59). John attributes the saying to Jesus, interpreting it as a prophecy of his death and resurrection (2:19–22). **14:60–61** *The high priest . . . Blessed*: the connection between rebuilding the temple and Jesus' messianic claims lies in God's promise in 2 Sam 7:12–14 that David's heir will both build God's house (i.e., temple) and be God's son. That passage refers to Solomon—"son of God" conventionally designates the Israelite king (cf. Ps 2 and notes)—but it was often interpreted as a reference to the eschatological messiah (see 10:47 note). **14:61** *He held . . . nothing*: perhaps alluding to the servant's silence in Isaiah's fourth Servant Song (53:7). *The Blessed*: a reverent circumlocution for YHWH. **14:62** *I am*: Jesus' only open acknowledgment in Mark of his messianic status. (On the implications of the phrase, see 6:50 note.) In light of the witnesses' lack of agreement, it appears to be this confession alone that does Jesus in. *The Son . . . heaven*: the phrase conflates Ps 110:1 (cf. Mark 12:35–37) and Dan 7:13 (cf. Mark 8:38; 13:26). On the basis of Ps 110:1, the NT often imagines the risen Christ as stationed at God's right hand (Acts 2:25, 33, 34; Rom 8:34; etc.). **14:63–64** *The high priest . . . death*: tearing one's clothes is an act that conventionally indicates emotional distress (cf. Gen 37:34; Job 1:20; Acts 14:14) but is forbidden to the high priest (Lev 21:10). His transgression of the prohibition is especially ironic since the Sanhedrin relies on Levitical statute and precedent in sentencing Jesus to death for blasphemy (Lev 24:10–16, 23). Perhaps v. 62 is blasphemous as an oblique claim of divinity (see note; cf. 2:5–7; John 10:33–36), though Jesus will actually be executed for sedition rather than blasphemy (see 15:2

be guilty of death. ⁶⁵And some began to spit on him, and to cover his face, and to buffet him, and to say unto him, Prophesy: and the servants did strike him with the palms of their hands.

⁶⁶And as Peter was beneath in the palace, there cometh one of the maids of the high priest: ⁶⁷and when she saw Peter warming himself, she looked upon him, and said, And thou also wast with Jesus of Nazareth. ⁶⁸But he denied, saying, I know not, neither understand I what thou sayest. And he went out into the porch; and the cock crew. ⁶⁹And a maid saw him again, and began to say to them that stood by, This is one of them. ⁷⁰And he denied it again. And a little after, they that stood by said again to Peter, Surely thou art one of them: for thou art a Galilæan, and thy speech agreeth thereto. ⁷¹But he began to curse and to swear, saying, I know not this man of whom ye speak. ⁷²And the second time the cock crew. And Peter called to mind the word that Jesus said unto him, Before the cock crow twice, thou shalt deny me thrice. And when he thought thereon, he wept.

15 And straightway in the morning the chief priests held a consultation with the elders and scribes and the whole council, and bound Jesus, and carried him away, and delivered him to Pilate. ²And Pilate asked him, Art thou the King of the Jews? And he answering said unto him, Thou sayest it. ³And the chief priests accused him of many things: but he answered nothing. ⁴And Pilate asked him again, saying, Answerest thou nothing? behold how many things they witness against thee. ⁵But Jesus yet answered nothing; so that Pilate marvelled.

⁶Now at that feast he released unto them one prisoner, whomsoever they desired. ⁷And there was one named Barabbas, which lay bound with them that had made insurrection with him, who had committed murder in the insurrection. ⁸And the multitude crying aloud began to desire him to do as he had ever done unto them.

---

and note, 26). **14:64** *Guilty of*: deserves. **14:65** *Some began . . . hands*: compare Isaiah's third Servant Song (50:6). **14:68** *He denied*: Mark artfully juxtaposes Peter's denial to Jesus' confession (cf. v. 62). *The cock crew*: recalling (with v. 72) both Jesus' prediction of Peter's denial (v. 30) and the times when the householder of chap. 13 may return: "at even, or at midnight, or at the cockcrowing, or in the morning" (13:35). Particular events in the Passion Narrative explicitly occur at three of these times: the Passover meal "in the evening" (14:17), Jesus' trial at the cockcrow (14:68, 72), and his delivery to Pilate for crucifixion "in the morning" (15:1; cf. 15:25 and note). The Gethsemane scene clearly occurs in the middle of the night (thus the disciples are unable to stay awake). The echoes of temporal markers from chap. 13's closing parable draw attention to the disciples' failure to discern the eschatological import of the events leading up to Jesus' death, despite Jesus' reiterated commands that they "watch" (see 13:5 note). **14:70** *And thy . . . thereto*: better omitted (MS tradition) as a scribal gloss (from Matt 26:73; see note). **14:72** *The second time the cock crew*: better introduced with "immediately" (MS tradition). *When he . . . wept*: Gk. obscure; other suggestions include "he broke down and wept," "he beat himself and wept," "he threw himself out and wept," and "he proceeded to weep." **15:1** *Delivered him to Pilate*: Pontius Pilate, the prefect of the Roman province of Judea, ca. 26–37 C.E. The Sanhedrin may hand Jesus over to him (in fulfillment of 10:33) because it was not authorized to carry out executions (cf. John 18:31 and note). **15:2** *Art thou . . . Jews*: i.e., a politically troublesome messianic poser. *King of the Jews* becomes a refrain leading up to the crucifixion (see vv. 9, 12, 18, 26, 32). **15:3** *But he answered nothing*: better omitted (MS tradition). **15:5** *Answered nothing*: see 14:61 and note. *Pilate marveled*: compare Antiochus's amazement at the Jewish martyrs (4 Maccabees 17.17–24). **15:6** *He released*: better "used to release." The custom of pardoning a criminal at Passover (cf. v. 8) is not otherwise recorded, but it is easy to imagine a Roman magistrate releasing a prominent prisoner to mollify the masses. **15:7** *Barabbas*: a patronymic, "Son of the father" (see 10:46; 14:36 notes). The crowd ironically chooses Barabbas over Jesus, the true "Son of the Father" (cf. 1:11; 9:7). *Who had . . . insurrection*:

⁹But Pilate answered them, saying, Will ye that I release unto you the King of the Jews? ¹⁰For he knew that the chief priests had delivered him for envy. ¹¹But the chief priests moved the people, that he should rather release Barabbas unto them. ¹²And Pilate answered and said again unto them, What will ye then that I shall do unto him whom ye call the King of the Jews? ¹³And they cried out again, Crucify him. ¹⁴Then Pilate said unto them, Why, what evil hath he done? And they cried out the more exceedingly, Crucify him. ¹⁵And so Pilate, willing to content the people, released Barabbas unto them, and delivered Jesus, when he had scourged him, to be crucified.

¹⁶And the soldiers led him away into the hall, called Prætorium; and they call together the whole band. ¹⁷And they clothed him with purple, and platted a crown of thorns, and put it about his head, ¹⁸and began to salute him, Hail, King of the Jews! ¹⁹And they smote him on the head with a reed, and did spit upon him, and bowing their knees worshipped him. ²⁰And when they had mocked him, they took off the purple from him, and put his own clothes on him, and led him out to crucify him.

²¹And they compel one Simon a Cyrenian, who passed by, coming out of the country, the father of Alexander and Rufus, to bear his cross. ²²And they bring him unto the place Golgotha, which is, being interpreted, The place of a skull. ²³And they gave him to drink wine mingled with myrrh: but he received it not. ²⁴And when they had crucified him, they parted his garments, casting lots upon them, what every man should take.

²⁵And it was the third hour, and they crucified him. ²⁶And the superscription of his accusation was written over, The King of the Jews. ²⁷And with him they crucify two thieves; the one on his right hand, and the other on his left. ²⁸And the scripture was fulfilled, which saith, And he was numbered with the transgressors.

---

the phrase refers to Barabbas's co-insurrectionists. (Many insurrections are recorded in other sources; e.g., Acts 5:36–37.)   **15:11** *The chief . . . people*: earlier the chief priests feared the people (11:32; 12:12) and Jesus' influence over them (11:18), but now they manipulate the masses to put Jesus to death.   **15:13** *Cried out*: cf. v. 14; 11:9, where many "cried" blessings to Jesus.   **15:15** *Scourged him*: cf. Isa 53:5 (the fourth Servant Song).   **15:16–47** Jesus' execution and burial. Compare Matt 27:27–61; Luke 23:26–56; John 19:1–3, 16–42.   **15:16** *Hall*: cf. 14:54 (KJV "palace") and note. *Prætorium*: the Greek transliterates Lat. *praetorium*, a governor's official residence. *Band*: cohort, consisting of several hundred soldiers.   **15:17** *Purple*: a color associated with royal apparel and thus—like the crown (v. 17), salute (v. 18), and obeisance (v. 19)—a mockery of Jesus' kingly pretensions.   **15:19** *They smote . . . upon him*: see 14:65 and note.   **15:21** *One Simon . . . Rufus*: as a Cyrenian, Simon is a North African from what is now Libya. Mark's readers may have recognized his two sons' names, and it is tempting to link the latter with the Rufus whom Paul greets in Rom 16:13. *Bear his cross*: weakened by his previous beatings (14:65; 15:19), Jesus is aided by this stranger; notably absent are his disciples (including another Simon, namely Peter), whom he had instructed to take up the cross and follow him (8:34).   **15:22** *Golgotha*: "Skull" (Aramaic), perhaps so named because it was a common location for executions.   **15:23** *Wine mingled with myrrh*: a delicacy, according to Pliny (*Natural History* 14.92–93)—perhaps offered to ridicule Jesus' regal pretensions, or to soothe his suffering (cf. Prov 31:6–7). Jesus' refusal to drink recalls 14:25.   **15:24** *They parted . . . take*: cf. Ps 22:18.   **15:25** *The third hour*: 9 A.M.   **15:26** *Written over . . . Jews*: Mark's portrayal of the soldiers having yet another laugh at Jesus' expense (cf. vv. 17, 19) may represent an authentic historical detail, but such sarcasm is not attested elsewhere in summaries of charges displayed with executed criminals, and John seems to recognize the tradition's oddity (19:19–22).   **15:27** *With him . . . left*: cf. 10:40 and note. Jesus' parodic coronation (cf. vv. 16–20) is completed by this perverse enthronement: he is elevated on the cross (v. 25) with the two criminals in places of honor beside him.   **15:28** *And the scripture . . . transgressors*:

²⁹And they that passed by railed on him, wagging their heads, and saying, Ah, thou that destroyest the temple, and buildest it in three days, ³⁰save thyself, and come down from the cross. ³¹Likewise also the chief priests mocking said among themselves with the scribes, He saved others; himself he cannot save. ³²Let Christ the King of Israel descend now from the cross, that we may see and believe. And they that were crucified with him reviled him.

³³And when the sixth hour was come, there was darkness over the whole land until the ninth hour. ³⁴And at the ninth hour Jesus cried with a loud voice, saying, Eloi, Eloi, lama sabachthani? which is, being interpreted, My God, my God, why hast thou forsaken me? ³⁵And some of them that stood by, when they heard it, said, Behold, he calleth Elias. ³⁶And one ran and filled a spunge full of vinegar, and put it on a reed, and gave him to drink, saying, Let alone; let us see whether Elias will come to take him down. ³⁷And Jesus cried with a loud voice, and gave up the ghost. ³⁸And the veil of the temple was rent in twain from the top to the bottom. ³⁹And when the centurion, which stood over against him, saw that he so cried out, and gave up the ghost, he said, Truly this man was the Son of God. ⁴⁰There were also women looking on afar off: among whom was Mary Magdalene, and Mary the mother of James the less and of Joses, and Salome; ⁴¹(who also, when he was in Galilee, followed him, and ministered unto him;) and many other women which came up with him unto Jerusalem.

Isa 53:12; better omitted (MS tradition).   **15:29** *They that . . . heads*: cf. Ps 22:7; Lam 2:15. *Railed on him*: Gk. *eblasphēmoun*; the same root is used in 14:64 ("blasphemy"). *Thou that . . . days*: cf. 14:58. **15:30** *Save thyself*: recalling the crowd's cries of "hosanna" (lit. "save now"), which welcomed Jesus as he entered Jerusalem (cf. 11:9–10). **15:33** *Sixth hour . . . ninth hour*: noon and 3 P.M.; for darkness at noon, see Amos 8:9; cf. Mark 13:24. **15:34** *Cried with a loud voice*: cf. v. 37; Mark has earlier used this same phrase of exorcised demons (1:26; 5:7). The echo may underscore Jesus' alienation from God, as does the rest of the verse. *Eloi, Eloi lama sabachthani*: quoting Ps 22:1 in Aramaic, perhaps mixed with Hebrew. Jesus experiences his death as total abandonment, first by his disciples (14:26–31, 50–52, 66–72) and finally by his father, God himself, but commentators sometimes argue that his words express confidence in God, because of the psalm's closure on a positive assurance of God's support. **15:35** *He calleth Elias*: they presumably mistake "Eloi" for a call on Elijah to deliver him to heaven (cf. v. 36; 2 Kgs 2:11). **15:36** *Vinegar*: spoiled wine; cf. Ps 69:21. *Let alone*: leave him be. **15:37** *Gave up the ghost*: lit. "expired" (cf. v. 39). **15:38** *The veil . . . bottom*: it is unclear which veil Mark means. Reference to the curtain hiding the inner sanctum (cf. Exod 26:31–35), where YHWH was thought to appear (Lev 16:2) and where once a year the priest would enter to make atonement for Israel's sin (Lev 16:16), might imply universal access to God's presence and mercy. Reference to the outer curtain (cf. Exod 26:36–37) might symbolically reiterate Jesus' prophecy of the temple's destruction (13:1–2). In either case, the rending (Gk. *schizō*) of the temple curtain at Jesus' death recalls the rending of the heavens at his baptism (1:10 and note). **15:39** *The centurion . . . God*: a remarkable change from the Roman soldiers' earlier brutality. The words might be a christological confession; an admission, made on the basis of the awesome portents accompanying Jesus' death (vv. 33, 38), that a holy hero has been unjustly executed ("truly this was a son of God"); or a sarcastic remark. It may also be significant that the centurion's words echo similar demonic declarations of Jesus' identity (e.g., 3:11; 5:7). *Cried out, and*: better omitted (MS tradition). **15:40** *Women looking . . . off*: Jesus' female disciples are somewhat more faithful than his male ones. References to them (vv. 40–41, 47) frame the story of his burial. *Mary Magdalene*: a prominent follower of Jesus named alongside the Twelve in Luke 8:2 (see note). *Mary the mother . . . Joses*: presumably Jesus' mother (cf. 6:3). By calling her the mother of Jesus' brothers rather than of Jesus, Mark recalls 3:31–35 and emphasizes that Jesus is dead (so that, strictly speaking, she is no longer his mother). *James the less*: the younger or the smaller James, presumably to distinguish him from James son of Zebedee. *Salome*: otherwise unknown; Matthew replaces her with

⁴²And now when the even was come, because it was the preparation, that is, the day before the sabbath, ⁴³Joseph of Arimathæa, an honourable counseller, which also waited for the kingdom of God, came, and went in boldly unto Pilate, and craved the body of Jesus. ⁴⁴And Pilate marvelled if he were already dead: and calling unto him the centurion, he asked him whether he had been any while dead. ⁴⁵And when he knew it of the centurion, he gave the body to Joseph. ⁴⁶And he bought fine linen, and took him down, and wrapped him in the linen, and laid him in a sepulchre which was hewn out of a rock, and rolled a stone unto the door of the sepulchre. ⁴⁷And Mary Magdalene and Mary the mother of Joses beheld where he was laid.

16 And when the sabbath was past, Mary Magdalene, and Mary the mother of James, and Salome, had bought sweet spices, that they might come and anoint him. ²And very early in the morning the first day of the week, they came unto the sepulchre at the rising of the sun. ³And they said among themselves, Who shall roll us away the stone from the door of the sepulchre? ⁴And when they looked, they saw that the stone was rolled away: for it was very great. ⁵And entering into the sepulchre, they saw a young man sitting on the right side, clothed in a long white garment; and they were affrighted. ⁶And he saith unto them, Be not affrighted: Ye seek Jesus of Nazareth, which was crucified: he is risen; he is not here: behold the place where they laid him. ⁷But go your way, tell his disciples and Peter that

---

or identifies her as the mother of James and John (27:56).   **15:42** *The preparation . . . sabbath*: when tasks not permitted on the Sabbath were to be accomplished. Since the Sabbath proper begins at Friday's sunset, the events narrated here take place late in the afternoon or early in the evening.   **15:43** *Arimathæa*: perhaps to be identified with Ramathaim (1 Sam 1:1), i.e., Ramah. *An honourable counseller*: Joseph appears to have been an influential member of the Sanhedrin. *Went in . . . Jesus*: Joseph's request is bold (and Pilate's assent generous) because it was Roman practice to leave the corpse exposed on the cross for some time after death. Joseph presumably obeys the injunction of Deut 21:22–23.   **15:44** *Pilate marvelled . . . already dead*: it usually took several days for the crucified to die.   **15:45** *Body*: better "corpse" (MS tradition).   **15:46** *Fine linen*: cf. 14:52 and note. *Sepulchre which . . . rock*: an extravagant tomb, by ancient standards.

16:1–8 The empty tomb. Compare Matt 28:1–10; Luke 24:1–12; John 20:1–18.   **16:1** *Sweet spices . . . him*: normally, interment followed the corpse's washing and anointing, but Jesus' was rushed to avoid violating the Sabbath (see 15:42 note); moreover, his body had already been anointed for burial (14:8).   **16:2** *First day*: i.e., Sunday; by inclusive counting, this is the third day after Jesus' death on Friday the Passover (cf. 8:31; 9:31; 10:34).   **16:5** *Young man*: Gk. *neaniskos.* (cf. 14:51). Use of the same Greek word suggests that this youth and the one who earlier fled naked are the same. Matthew presents the figure as an angel (28:2), as do Luke (24:4, 23) and John (20:12), who both insist two angels were present, but there is no compelling reason to assimilate Mark to the other evangelists. *Right side . . . garment*: since the risen Christ is regularly presented as sitting at God's "right hand" (see 14:62 and note), and since luminous white raiment often characterizes divine and resurrected figures (see 9:3 and note), some speculate that this young man stands in for or symbolizes the risen Jesus, who never actually appears in Mark (but see 9:2–10 and note).   **16:6–7** *Ye seek . . . you*: the young man straightforwardly describes the empty tomb and repeats Jesus' prophecy of 14:28—words he may have been present to hear (see 16:5 note). If so, he has presumably connected them with the empty tomb to infer Jesus' resurrection.   **16:7** *His disciples and Peter*: usually interpreted as giving prominence to Peter, who elsewhere is singled out for a special visitation by the risen Christ (Luke 24:34; 1 Cor 15:5), and whom in John the risen Christ rehabilitates (21:1–19), Mark's words actually make a negative distinction: having thrice denied knowing him (as Jesus had predicted, 14:29–31), Peter is no longer num-

he goeth before you into Galilee: there shall ye see him, as he said unto you. ⁸And they went out quickly, and fled from the sepulchre; for they trembled and were amazed: neither said they any thing to any man; for they were afraid.

⁹Now when Jesus was risen early the first day of the week, he appeared first to Mary Magdalene, out of whom he had cast seven devils. ¹⁰And she went and told them that had been with him, as they mourned and wept. ¹¹And they, when they had heard that he was alive, and had been seen of her, believed not.

¹²After that he appeared in another form unto two of them, as they walked, and went into the country. ¹³And they went and told it unto the residue: neither believed they them.

¹⁴Afterward he appeared unto the eleven as they sat at meat, and upbraided them with their unbelief and hardness of heart, because they believed not them which had seen him after he was risen. ¹⁵And he said unto them, Go ye into all the world, and preach the gospel to every creature. ¹⁶He that believeth and is baptized shall be saved; but he that believeth not shall be damned. ¹⁷And these signs shall follow them that believe; In my name shall they cast out devils; they shall speak with new tongues; ¹⁸they shall take up serpents; and if they drink any deadly thing, it shall not hurt them; they shall lay hands on the sick, and they shall recover.

¹⁹So then after the Lord had spoken unto them, he was received up into heaven, and sat on the right hand of God. ²⁰And they went forth, and preached every where, the Lord working with them, and confirming the word with signs following. Amen.

bered among Jesus' followers. *He goeth . . . Galilee*: where Jesus' ministry began; cf. 1:14. **16:8** *Quickly*: better omitted (MS tradition). *Neither said . . . afraid*: the best reading of the MS tradition ends Mark's gospel at this verse's close (see note to 16:9–20). Some scholars argue that Mark's authentic ending was lost at an early stage of its transmission, because they find the conclusion here too abrupt and suppose that 14:28 and 16:7 promise appearances of the risen Christ which Mark fails to deliver. In fact, however, 16:7 ("he goeth before you into Galilee") itself fulfills the promise of 14:28 ("after that I am risen, I will go before you into Galilee"), and the reader must interpret, rather than explain away, Mark's gloomy, sudden, and open-ended close, which omits any appearances of the risen Christ.
    16:9–20 The spurious "longer ending." Although vv. 9–20 are present in most MSS, this section is marked as textually suspect in some and is missing in important early witnesses. Some MSS contain the so-called shorter ending of Mark, either replacing or immediately preceding vv. 9–20: "And all that had been commanded them they told briefly to those around Peter. And afterward Jesus himself sent out through them, from east to west, the sacred and imperishable proclamation of eternal salvation" (NRSV). Other witnesses add after v. 14 a lengthy exchange between the risen Christ and the disciples, which blames Satan for their lack of faith in the resurrection. The numerous and substantial variations in the MS tradition (not to mention in the other Synoptics) suggest that Mark originally ended with the phrase *for they were afraid*. Early scribes, uncomfortable with this abrupt and troubling conclusion, appended numerous variations. The verses in KJV were likely composed by a second-century scribe on the basis of the other canonical gospels and Acts, echoes of which abound. **16:9** *He appeared . . . Magdalene*: cf. Matt 28:9–10; John 20:11–18. *Out of whom . . . devils*: cf. Luke 8:2. **16:10–11** *She went . . . not*: cf. Luke 24:9–11. **16:12–13** *He appeared . . . them*: summarizing Luke 24:13–35. **16:14** *He appeared . . . risen*: summarizing Luke 24:36–49. **16:15–16** *Go ye . . . damned*: recalling Matt 28:19, with an added threat of condemnation to unbelievers. **16:17–18** *Signs*: the first two and fifth *signs* were conventional in the early church; the third refers to Acts 28:3–6 (cf. Luke 10:19); and the fourth appears occasionally in nonbiblical early Christian literature. **16:19** *Received up into heaven*: cf. Luke 24:51; Acts 1:9–11. *Sat on . . . God*: see 14:62 note.

The Gospel According to St. Luke

FOLLOWING his own statement of intent in the opening sentence, readers often call the author of Luke's gospel a historian, committed to writing down in proper order the sequence of events that make up the life, death, and resurrection of Jesus. He traces their origins further back than the other synoptic evangelists, describing Jesus' conception and that of John the Baptist too, and he includes a genealogy tracing his hero's lineage all the way back to Adam. He also writes more about the risen Christ and supplements his gospel with Acts, a volume focusing on the history of the early church. Luke-Acts demands to be read as a unified literary work. Artificially isolated treatment of either part may mislead, and so here the two are introduced together.

Historians in Greco-Roman antiquity were as much narrative artists as chroniclers of the past, and as befits a rhetorically trained Greco-Roman historian, Luke writes with a keen literary awareness. He begins his gospel with a periodic sentence in the classical mode, before shifting in his introductory chapters to a more straightforward prose style which, as the annotations make clear, emulates scriptural narrative and poetry as it was known from the Septuagint translation of the Hebrew Bible. Scripture alone did not inspire Luke's writing. In Acts especially we find quotes from and allusions to Homer, Plato, Euripides, and Aratus, and the Gospel of Luke likewise displays the influence of Greco-Roman culture: Mary's divine conception, to cite only the most obvious example, resembles any number of pagan stories about gods impregnating human women to beget demigods with extraordinary power. (Heracles, born of Alcmene and Zeus, is perhaps the most famous of these semidivine heroes.) Luke may have adapted this well-known mythological pattern in order to explain the "Son of God" to Gentile readers, much as Luke's Paul will later identify YHWH with the "unknown god" to whom a pagan altar at Athens was dedicated, in an attempt to communicate his monotheistic gospel to a polytheistic audience (Acts 17:23).

Dennis R. MacDonald and a handful of other scholars have begun to explore Luke's use of pagan Greek literature, and the annotations that follow benefit from their work. But as important as this relationship with Hellenistic literature may be, Scripture's influence on Luke-Acts remains paramount, operating at the level of style, structure, and thought. Luke's sustained engagement with the Elijah and Elisha cycles exemplifies the Old Testament's centrality to his literary project: Jesus' resurrection of the widow's son at Nain (7:11–17) recalls Elijah's resurrection of the widow's son at Zarephath (1 Kgs 17:17–24); Luke's notice of the Samaritan village rejecting Jesus (9:51–56) likewise recalls Elijah's confrontation of King Ahaziah in Samaria (2 Kgs 1); soon thereafter, Jesus' call of an anonymous man

(9:59–62) recasts Elijah's calling of Elisha (1 Kgs 19:19–21), and the same Old Testament scene lies behind Jesus' summoning of the first disciples as well (5:1–11). These and other allusions to 1 and 2 Kings analogize Jesus to Elijah and his disciples to Elisha—a surprising typological configuration, since the other gospels display a competing tendency to present John the Baptist as the eschatological Elijah (an idea Luke puts forth only once; see Luke 1:17) and Jesus as the Elisha figure, who like that prophet obtains a "double portion" of the spirit empowering his master (see 2 Kgs 2:8–15, esp. v. 9; cf. Mark 1:4–11 and parallels).

Luke's distinctive assimilation of Jesus to Elijah and of the disciples to Elisha functions at the level not only of discrete episode but also of overarching plot. As just noted, immediately before Elijah ascends to heaven in the whirlwind, Elisha is promised a "double portion" of his spirit on the condition that he observe his master's heavenly ascent. Elisha does so and immediately thereafter performs a miracle paralleling an earlier one of Elijah's, thereby confirming his spiritual inheritance (2 Kgs 2:1–14). Luke follows this pattern carefully: at Luke 24:49 and Acts 1:8, just before he ascends to heaven, Jesus promises the Holy Spirit to the disciples. That promise is fulfilled at Pentecost (Acts 2) and confirmed immediately thereafter, when Peter performs a miracle resembling one that Jesus accomplished early in his ministry (Acts 3:1–10; cf. Luke 5:17–26). A number of meaningful parallels between the apostles and Elisha follow: Elisha's provision of oil for the widow (2 Kgs 4:1–7) finds a corollary in the church's institutionalized provision for widows (cf. Acts 6:1); Elisha's healing of the Gentile military commander Naaman (2 Kgs 5:1–19) corresponds to the story of Peter's conversion of the Roman centurion Cornelius (Acts 10:1–11:18); and so on. Luke, then, depicts the apostolic church "taking up the mantle" of Jesus, just as Elisha did Elijah's (cf. 2 Kgs 2:13–14). Not only does he draw on these Old Testament stories as models for individual episodes, but he finds in the Elijah and Elisha cycles, and especially in the transition between them, a structural model for the relationship his own narrative proposes between two discrete and potentially disjointed historical moments: the ministries of Jesus and of the church.

Scripture's influence on Luke is conceptual, as well as stylistic and structural, and its theological impact on Luke's gospel comes into special relief in the episode that serves as the gospel's thesis. In 4:16–30 Jesus articulates his understanding of the ministry on which he is embarking. He quotes Isa 61:1–2, which offers an eschatological interpretation of the Priestly Jubilee—the one year of every fifty during which Israel's land was to lie fallow, acquired property was to return to its ancestral owners, and indentured servants were to be set free (see Lev 25:8–55 and notes). In the Septuagint's Leviticus, the Jubilee year is called the year of "release" or "liberty" (Gk. *aphesis*; cf. Lev 25:10), and this key word appears in LXX Isa 61:1, where God promises "liberty to the captives." Luke quotes this phrase at 4:18 (KJV "deliverance to the captives") and supplements it with another reference to release from Isaiah: "to set at liberty [Gk. *aphesei*] them that are bruised" (LXX 58:6). Luke's Jesus goes on to insist that his ministry fulfills the eschatological Jubilee promised by the prophet, declaring, "This day is this scripture fulfilled in your ears" (4:21). The gospel validates this provocative claim by depicting Jesus delivering the liberty he promised in various ways. The Greek word *aphesis* and its cognates turn up throughout Luke to describe a range of freedoms Jesus offers: freedom from sin (e.g., 7:47–49, in KJV various forms of "forgiveness") and from disease (e.g., 4:39 [KJV "left"]); independence from constraining possessions (5:11 [KJV "forsook"]); and so on.

Jesus' opening claim about his ministry implies what Luke's gospel later articulates: "The kingdom of God cometh not with observation: neither shall they say, Lo here! or, lo there! for, behold, the kingdom of God is among [KJV 'within'] you" (17:20–21). Unlike the other Synoptics, which consistently portray Jesus anticipating the future establishment of God's kingdom on Earth, Luke's Jesus says that his ongoing ministry and the people it encompasses themselves constitute the kingdom of God. Lukan eschatology is complex, and it would be inaccurate to claim that Luke simply does away with expectation of cosmic cataclysm and future judgment. Immediately upon claiming that "the kingdom of God is among you," Jesus in fact promises the Son of Man's future eschatological arrival: "For as the lightning, that lighteneth out of the one part under heaven, shineth unto the other part under heaven; so shall also the Son of man be in his day" (17:24). But the evangelist qualifies the eschatological consummation he describes: by analogizing the day of the Son of Man to previous moments of divine judgment (the great deluge and the destruction of Sodom), he suggests that while the Son of Man's advent will be of great consequence, it will not be unprecedented. Cosmic upheaval and divine judgment are bound to come in the future, as they have come in the past, but their arrival may not herald the world's transformation into a just realm blessed by God's reign, as other New Testament texts expect. For Luke, Jesus' liberating ministry and its continuation in the church after his ascension embody eschatological transformation differently understood, accessible in the present rather than anticipated for the future.

Lukan parables provocatively imagine this present transformation by introducing outlandish behavior into mundane situations and then holding up that behavior as normal, even normative. In the parable of the Lost Sheep, for example, Jesus invites his audience to imagine themselves as shepherds—common enough in ancient Palestine—whose behavior is by any account bizarre: "What man of you, having an hundred sheep, if he lose one of them, doth not leave the ninety and nine in the wilderness, and go after that which is lost, until he find it?" (15:4). Only an incompetent shepherd would abandon his entire flock to search for a single wandering sheep, but Jesus' rhetorical question implies that to do this would be the most natural thing in the world. The parable's eccentricity expands as Jesus describes the shepherd's incongruously extravagant celebration: "And when he hath found it, he layeth it on his shoulders, rejoicing. And when he cometh home, he calleth together his friends and neighbours, saying unto them, Rejoice with me; for I have found my sheep which was lost" (15:5–6). Of course, the parable is not really about lost sheep and imprudent shepherds. It figures the restoration of those whose lives are characterized by persistent transgression of God's law, for Jesus directs it at Pharisees and scribes who have questioned his policy of embracing "sinners." These, they believe, should be avoided as polluted and polluting (15:1–2), but the parable invites religious leaders to adopt a different conception of their responsibilities: instead of giving up wayward sinners for lost, they should make desperate attempts to restore the recalcitrant, perhaps even at the expense of attention to the faithful. This is not a conventional approach to ministry; the shepherding analogy underscores its peculiarity. But Jesus claims that it reflects the view of heaven (15:7), and among those who embrace it may be found the kingdom of God.

Most of Jesus' parables function like that of the Lost Sheep, depicting extravagant or outrageous behavior as normative for those who embrace God's kingdom. The excessively liberal forgiveness of the prodigal son's father (15:22–23), for instance, or the extreme generosity of the good Samaritan (10:33–35), or the audacious deceit of the dishonest manager (16:1–8)—all are presented in one way or another as models to follow. By portraying normal characters behaving in eccentric ways, and then encouraging the auditors to go and do likewise, Jesus' parables invite them (and Luke's readers as well) to participate in the eschatological transformation of the world.

The kind of social transformation the parables envision and encourage finds a reflection in the economic policy that Luke's Jesus advocates, and that the early church puts into practice in Acts. Jesus' introduction of his ministry in Luke evinces a concern for "the poor" (see 4:18 note) that stands out from the other gospels and is sustained through much of Luke-Acts. The Lukan version of the Beatitudes, for instance, associates the kingdom of God with the "poor" (6:20); Matthew, in contrast, promises it to the "poor in spirit" (5:3). Soon thereafter Luke's Jesus guarantees blessed satiety to those "that hunger now" (6:21), again in contrast to Matthew's promise of abundance to those "who hunger and thirst after righteousness" (5:6). Analogously, Luke alone of the gospels depicts Jesus resurrecting an anonymous widow's only son (7:11–17), thereby relieving her from the economic disaster her loss and subsequent social isolation would entail. Such examples from the Third Gospel could be multiplied, but exploration of Luke's development of the same theme in the second half of his history is more revealing.

As soon as the church is established, its members sell all their possessions and share everything in common, enabling the apostles to distribute resources according to need (Acts 4:32–37). The distribution focuses on widows, as the church institutionalizes the concern demonstrated by Jesus himself for this especially vulnerable class. However, when confronted with the increasingly messy problem of how to fairly distribute stipends to the culturally diverse widows whom the congregation supported, the twelve apostles balk, insisting, "It is not pleasing that we should leave the word of God, and serve tables [Gk. *diakonein trapezais*]" (6:2). They order that administrators be appointed to relieve them, so that they can devote themselves "continually to prayer, and to the service [Gk. *diakonia* (KJV 'ministry')] of the word" (6:4). Of these seven supervisors, two (Stephen and Philip) manage the feat that the Twelve found impracticable, combining administrative responsibilities with ministries of prayer and preaching: Stephen embarks on a tour de force of biblical interpretation in his self-defense before the Sanhedrin, becoming the church's first martyr and praying for his murderers with his dying breath; Philip evangelizes the Samaritans and offers a christological interpretation of Isaiah to the Ethiopian eunuch, becoming the first Jesus-believer to spread the gospel outside of Jerusalem and to non-Jews.

This crucial moment of Luke's narrative initiates a gradual shift in focus from familiar characters (Peter and James) to new ones (Stephen, Philip, and Paul—all three of whom Luke contrives to introduce in chaps. 6–7). We ought not to assume that the transference of attention is neutral, especially in light of Jesus' teaching in the first volume of Luke's history: "he that is greatest among you, let him be as the younger; and he that is chief, as he that doth serve [Gk. *ho diakonōn*]. For whether is greater, he that sitteth at meat, or he that serveth [*ho diakonōn*]? is not he that sitteth at meat? But I am among you as he that serveth [*ho diakonōn*]" (Luke 22:26–27). By dismissing "service at tables" (Gk. *diakonein trapezais*)—in particular the feeding of poor widows—as a dispensable feature of their ministry (Acts 6:1–3), the apostles reveal a fundamental misunderstanding of their master's mission, for Jesus himself had defined that mission as service, especially of food to the poor. It therefore comes as no surprise that when they abandon this mission, the Twelve begin to relinquish their position as "chiefs" of Jesus' church and heroes of Luke's narrative. Jesus' brother James, not one of the Twelve, emerges to lead the Jerusalem congregation (see Acts 12:17; 15:13–21; 21:17–18). More significantly, the Twelve themselves begin to recede in importance and Stephen, Philip, and ultimately Paul come to dominate Luke's history, which begins to focus on the gospel's proliferation among non-Jews. While Peter is not totally excluded from this development, Luke circumscribes his significance: he is responsible for the conversion of just one Gentile household (Cornelius's, in 10:1–11:18) and, unlike Philip and Paul, he at first resists God's plan to reach out to Gentiles.

Paul, the self-styled apostle to the Gentiles (e.g., Rom 15:16), becomes the undisputed hero of Acts' second half, which depicts his dramatic conversion (narrated three separate times), his stirring missionary journeys, and ultimately his arrest by Roman authorities and perilous journey to the empire's capital. One moment of Paul's exciting story is often overlooked, however, and it demands careful attention in light of Luke-Acts' concern for the poor. Paul's ministry to Gentiles begins when he and Barnabas jointly lead the ethnically diverse congregation at Antioch. Luke offers only a single detail about this early period. When the Antioch church receives a prophetic oracle about an impending famine, it responds by taking up a collection for believers suffering in Judea (11:27–30), which Paul delivers personally. Paul's ministry among Gentiles thus begins with his administration of a charitable collection for the poor in Jerusalem—precisely the task that the Twelve had renounced.

As Jesus' ministry of liberation fulfilled eschatological prophecy, so does Paul's preaching of Jesus among the Gentiles. Indeed, Isaiah's promise of "a light to the Gentiles" (49:6) is thrice reiterated during the course of Luke's narrative, once in the same section in which Jesus introduces his ministry of liberation for the poor (Luke 2:32) and twice during the account of Paul's ministry (Acts 13:47; 26:17–18). Acts is sometimes thought to narrate a grand shift in God's covenant, as if Israel relinquished its privileged relationship with God because of its persistent rejection of Jesus and his evangelists. What we actually find in Luke-Acts is much more complex: Jews both resist Jesus and his gospel and are open to them. Even in the concluding scene, which does seem to depict divine precedence shifting from Jews to Gentiles (Acts 28:25–28), Luke points out that some Jews believed the gospel (v. 24), and notes that even those who didn't were willing to talk about it (v. 29).

It is easy to ignore such nuances in light of Luke-Acts' ideological thrust. By Luke's own admission, Roman imperial authorities executed Jesus and arrested Paul, whom they subjected to prolonged imprisonment, but at every juncture the third evangelist contrives to displace Roman hostility toward Jesus and the movement founded in his name onto the Jewish authorities and people. Pilate, therefore, did not really want to execute Jesus but was driven to do so by the Sanhedrin. The Roman cohort stationed at Jerusalem arrests Paul not because it perceives him doing anything wrong but in order to quell a Jewish riot at the temple. Felix draws out Paul's imprisonment unjustly, but he does so "to shew the Jews a pleasure" (24:27). At the end of Luke and throughout Acts' second half, the author again and again affirms that the Roman authorities saw nothing amiss in Jesus or his followers. Pilate repeatedly declares of Jesus that he has "found no fault in this man" (Luke 23:14; cf. vv. 15, 22), even as he orders his execution. Roman rulers twice insist that Paul has "nothing laid to his charge worthy of death or of bonds" (Acts 23:29; cf. 26:31), even as they hold him prisoner. It does not take an especially skeptical reader to detect historical revisionism. Anxious about Rome's increasing willingness to persecute Jesus-believers (exemplified in the brief Neronian persecution of 64 c.e.; cf. Tacitus, *Annals* 15.44; Appendix, pp. 983–84), Luke puts the best face possible on the numerous conflicts between Roman authorities and the religious movement whose early years he recounted, blaming "the Jews" for Jesus' and his later followers' trouble with the empire. This strategy's effectiveness depends on the Jesus-believing movement being seen as a religion different from Judaism, and not coincidentally the second volume of Luke's history emphasizes precisely this transformation (esp. 11:19–26; 28:26–28).

This political impulse helps account for Luke-Acts' final scene, which notes that Paul remained under house arrest in Rome for two years as he awaited his trial before Caesar. The author does not say what happened at the conclusion of that period, which is at first surprising—after all, his narrative is replete with ominous forebodings of Paul's death (e.g., Acts 20:22–24, 36–38; 21:8–14). Moreover, a reliable early Christian tradition confirms that Paul was in fact executed following his arrival at Rome. Luke's presumed suppression of this detail coheres with his tendency to downplay conflict between church and empire, but this observation does not exhaust the significance of his narrative's conclusion: "Paul dwelt two whole years in his own hired house, and received all that came in unto him, preaching the kingdom of God, and teaching those things which concern the Lord Jesus Christ, with all confidence, no man forbidding him" (Acts 28:30–31). Luke-Acts closes by portraying Paul doing exactly what Luke-Acts itself sets out to accomplish: "preaching the kingdom of God, and teaching those things which concern the Lord Jesus Christ" (see Luke 1:1–4; Acts 1:1–3). It thereby presents itself as an extension of Paul's ministry, a strategy that may also lie behind Acts' famous "we-sections," in which the narrative voice suddenly shifts to the first-person plural, implicitly identifying itself with one of Paul's fellow missionaries.

In the end, then, Luke-Acts is more than a history of Jesus' career and of the early church's ministry. It does not merely recount the ministry and message of Jesus, nor simply report the nascent church's struggle to proclaim the gospel. Rather, it presents itself as that gospel's authoritative proclamation. In this light,

Luke-Acts' failure to document Paul's death is an act not so much of suppression as of transcendence (a transcendence analogous to but more subtle than Jesus' resurrection): inasmuch as Luke-Acts itself continues "preaching the kingdom of God, and teaching those things which concern the Lord Jesus Christ," the mission of Paul—itself an extension of Jesus' (Acts 9:15)—goes on, even if Paul himself died at Rome.

For further information about Luke-Acts, see Joseph A. Fitzmyer's Anchor Bible commentaries: *The Gospel According to Luke: Introduction, Translation, and Notes,* 2 vols. (Garden City, NY: Doubleday, 1981–85) and *The Acts of the Apostles* (New York: Doubleday, 1998). C. K. Barrett's two-volume commentary on Acts in the International Critical Commentary series, *A Critical and Exegetical Commentary on the Acts of the Apostles* (Edinburgh: T&T Clark, 1994–98), is also strong, as is Joel B. Green's commentary on Luke in the New International Commentary series, *The Gospel of Luke* (Grand Rapids, MI: Eerdmans, 1997). Though Green's commentary is less exhaustive than the others, it presents a coherent and persuasive reading of Luke's gospel with careful attention to its literary and sociological dimensions. The influence of all of these may be detected throughout the notes that follow.

THE GOSPEL ACCORDING TO

ST. LUKE

1 Forasmuch as many have taken in hand to set forth in order a declaration of those things which are most surely believed among us, [2]even as they delivered them unto us, which from the beginning were eyewitnesses, and ministers of the word; [3]it seemed good to me also, having had perfect understanding of all things from the very first, to write unto thee in order, most excellent Theophilus, [4]that thou mightest know the certainty of those things, wherein thou hast been instructed.

[5]There was in the days of Herod, the king of Judæa, a certain priest named Zacharias, of the course of Abia: and his wife was of the daughters of Aaron, and her name was Elisabeth. [6]And they were both righteous before God, walking in all the commandments and ordinances of the Lord blameless. [7]And they had no child, because that Elisabeth was barren, and they both were now well stricken in years.

[8]And it came to pass, that while he executed the priest's office before God in the order of his course, [9]according to the custom of the priest's office, his lot was to burn incense when he went into the temple of the Lord. [10]And the whole multitude of the people were praying without at the time of incense. [11]And there appeared

1:1–4 Prologue. Adhering to the conventions of Greco-Roman historiography, Luke prefaces his narrative with an explanation of why he undertakes the work that follows. This elaborate sentence has two artfully coordinated segments (vv. 1–2 and 3–4): compare "many" (v. 1) and "me also" (v. 3); "set forth in order a declaration" (v. 1) and "write unto thee in order" (v. 3); etc. **1:1** *Declaration*: lit. "narrative." *Which are . . . believed*: lit. "that have been fulfilled." **1:2** *Eyewitnesses*: Gk. *autoptai*. Greek historians from Thucydides (1.22) on emphasize firsthand testimony. **1:3** *Had perfect understanding*: or carefully investigated. *Theophilus*: Luke's dedicatee and perhaps patron.
   1:5–2:52 Jesus' birth and childhood. Luke's infancy narrative includes material absent from or conflicting with Matthew, the other gospel narrating Jesus' nativity. In both substance and form, Luke's account depends on LXX (whose influence is traced to some extent in the following notes). But unlike Matthew, which primarily seeks to demonstrate that Jesus' birth fulfills discrete OT prophecies and patterns, this section consists of numerous divine promises, fulfillments, and responsive songs of praise, all intertwined to form a complex narrative structure through which Luke stresses broad continuity between God's redemptive work in Jesus and the ancient stories of YHWH's relationship with Israel. **1:5–25** The promise of John the Baptist's birth. The gospels all present John's ministry as preparing the way for Jesus', but Luke traces this temporal priority back to conception. The primary OT parallel is Abraham and Sarah, another aged couple whom God promised a son. **1:5** *In the days . . . Judæa*: recalling the beginnings of numerous OT books (Isa 1:1; Jer 1:2–3; etc.). *Herod*: see Matt 2:1 note. *Judæa*: here referring to Palestine in general (see Mark 1:5 note). *Course*: priestly division; Abia was eighth of twenty-four (see 1 Chr 24:1–31 and note). *Aaron*: Israel's original priest. **1:9** *According to . . . incense*: see Exod 30:7–8.

unto him an angel of the Lord standing on the right side of the altar of incense. [12]And when Zacharias saw him, he was troubled, and fear fell upon him. [13]But the angel said unto him, Fear not, Zacharias: for thy prayer is heard; and thy wife Elisabeth shall bear thee a son, and thou shalt call his name John. [14]And thou shalt have joy and gladness; and many shall rejoice at his birth. [15]For he shall be great in the sight of the Lord, and shall drink neither wine nor strong drink; and he shall be filled with the Holy Ghost, even from his mother's womb. [16]And many of the children of Israel shall he turn to the Lord their God. [17]And he shall go before him in the spirit and power of Elias, to turn the hearts of the fathers to the children, and the disobedient to the wisdom of the just; to make ready a people prepared for the Lord. [18]And Zacharias said unto the angel, Whereby shall I know this? for I am an old man, and my wife well stricken in years. [19]And the angel answering said unto him, I am Gabriel, that stand in the presence of God; and am sent to speak unto thee, and to shew thee these glad tidings. [20]And, behold, thou shalt be dumb, and not able to speak, until the day that these things shall be performed, because thou believest not my words, which shall be fulfilled in their season.

[21]And the people waited for Zacharias, and marvelled that he tarried so long in the temple. [22]And when he came out, he could not speak unto them: and they perceived that he had seen a vision in the temple: for he beckoned unto them, and remained speechless. [23]And it came to pass, that, as soon as the days of his ministration were accomplished, he departed to his own house.

[24]And after those days his wife Elisabeth conceived, and hid herself five months, saying, [25]Thus hath the Lord dealt with me in the days wherein he looked on me, to take away my reproach among men.

[26]And in the sixth month the angel Gabriel was sent from God unto a city of Galilee, named Nazareth, [27]to a virgin espoused to a man whose name was Joseph,

---

1:11 *Angel of the Lord*: see Matt 1:20 note. **1:13** *Thy prayer is heard*: Luke reports only the prayer of the people gathered outside the sanctuary (v. 10), not Zacharias's within, so the angel's declaration conflates his personal desire for a son with Israel's collective longing (cf. v. 14). **1:15** *Shall drink . . . drink*: the angel destines John for a Nazarite's life (cf. Num 6:2–4), just as the angel destined Samson in Judg 13:3–5. *Holy Ghost*: see Mark 1:8 note. **1:17** *Go before . . . children*: cf. Mal 3:1; 4:5–6 (on Elijah's eschatological advent). **1:18** *Whereby shall . . . years*: recalling the skepticism of the aged Abraham (Gen 15:8; 17:17) and Sarah (Gen 18:12) when God promised them offspring. **1:19** *Gabriel*: cf. Dan 8:16–19; 9:21–23. **1:20** *Thou shalt . . . performed*: though a punishment for disbelief, Zacharias's muteness recalls Daniel's inability to speak upon hearing the angel's message (Dan 10:15), as well as the angel's commands that Daniel keep silent "till the time of the end" (12:4, 9). **1:24** *Hid herself five months*: her seclusion seems to be motivated by shameful childlessness (v. 25; cf. Gen 30:23): Elizabeth will reappear in public only when her pregnancy shows. At the same time, her seclusion furthers the secrecy enjoined on Zacharias. **1:26–38** Jesus' promised birth (the Annunciation). In Matthew, the angel appears to Joseph (1:19–21). Though this episode and the previous are parallel in both form and diction, there are significant points of contrast. For example, John's birth is foretold in God's temple; Jesus' is announced in Galilee, a region traditionally disparaged as impure ("Galilee of the nations," Isa 9:1; cf. 1 Macc 5:15). John's confused question to Gabriel prompts a rebuke; Mary's is merely answered. Elizabeth will conceive despite her age; Mary becomes pregnant though a virgin. John will be "filled with the Holy Ghost, even from his mother's womb" (v. 15); the Holy Ghost itself bears responsibility for Jesus' conception. **1:26** *In the sixth month*: of Elizabeth's pregnancy. *A city . . . Nazareth*: see Mark 1:9 note. **1:27** *Espoused*: see

of the house of David; and the virgin's name was Mary. [28]And the angel came in unto her, and said, Hail, thou that art highly favoured, the Lord is with thee: blessed art thou among women. [29]And when she saw him, she was troubled at his saying, and cast in her mind what manner of salutation this should be. [30]And the angel said unto her, Fear not, Mary: for thou hast found favour with God. [31]And, behold, thou shalt conceive in thy womb, and bring forth a son, and shalt call his name Jesus. [32]He shall be great, and shall be called the Son of the Highest: and the Lord God shall give unto him the throne of his father David: [33]and he shall reign over the house of Jacob for ever; and of his kingdom there shall be no end.

[34]Then said Mary unto the angel, How shall this be, seeing I know not a man? [35]And the angel answered and said unto her, The Holy Ghost shall come upon thee, and the power of the Highest shall overshadow thee: therefore also that holy thing which shall be born of thee shall be called the Son of God. [36]And, behold, thy cousin Elisabeth, she hath also conceived a son in her old age: and this is the sixth month with her, who was called barren. [37]For with God nothing shall be impossible. [38]And Mary said, Behold the handmaid of the Lord; be it unto me according to thy word. And the angel departed from her.

[39]And Mary arose in those days, and went into the hill country with haste, into a city of Juda; [40]and entered into the house of Zacharias, and saluted Elisabeth. [41]And it came to pass, that, when Elisabeth heard the salutation of Mary, the babe leaped in her womb; and Elisabeth was filled with the Holy Ghost: [42]and she spake out with a loud voice, and said, Blessed art thou among women, and blessed is the fruit of thy womb. [43]And whence is this to me, that the mother of my Lord should come to me? [44]For, lo, as soon as the voice of thy salutation sounded in mine ears, the babe leaped in my womb for joy. [45]And blessed is she that believed: for there shall be a performance of those things which were told her from the Lord.

[46]And Mary said,

> My soul doth magnify the Lord,
> [47]And my spirit hath rejoiced in God my Saviour.

Matt 1:18 note.   **1:28** *Blessed art . . . women*: better omitted (MS tradition).   **1:31** *Behold, thou . . . son*: recalling the predictions of portentous births in Gen 16:11 and Isa 7:14. *Jesus*: see Matt 1:21 note.   **1:32** *The Highest*: a common divine title in Luke (vv. 35, 76; 6:35; etc.); cf. Mark 5:7 note. **1:32–33** *The Lord . . . end*: presenting Jesus as the eternally ruling descendent that God promised David (2 Sam 7:12–16), to whom he is supposedly related through Joseph (v. 27).   **1:34** *Know not a man*: i.e., have not had sex.   **1:35** *Son of God*: a traditional designation for the Davidic king (cf. v. 32; 2 Sam 7:14), but here linked with Jesus' divine conception.   **1:37** *With God . . . impossible*: cf. Gen 18:14 (God's words to Sarah).   **1:38** *Handmaid*: lit. "slave" (cf. v. 48).   **1:39–45** Mary visits Elisabeth. **1:41** *The babe . . . Ghost*: cf. v. 15.   **1:42** *Blessed*: Gk. *eulogēmenē*, "praised" (cf. v. 68; 2:28); a different word is used in v. 45.   **1:45** *Performance*: fulfillment.   **1:46–56** Mary's song of praise (Magnificat). Mary's psalm, whose traditional name derives from the opening word of its Vulgate translation, adopts the diction and themes of ancient Hebrew poetry (esp. the Song of Hannah, 1 Sam 2:1–10), as well as its parallelistic form. The song's conflation of praise for God's blessing of Mary (vv. 46–49) and of Israel (vv. 50–55) recalls Luke's earlier conflation of the crowd's prayer with Zacharias's (see v. 13 note), while its revolutionary imagery sets the stage for what will emerge as a dominant theme in Luke's gospel: status reversal. The scriptural references provided below are not exhaustive.   **1:46–47** *My soul . . . my spirit*: *soul* and *spirit*, poetic designations of the self, are also conjoined in Ps 77:2–3 (cf. Job 12:10;

⁴⁸For he hath regarded the low estate of his handmaiden; for,
        behold, from henceforth all generations shall call me blessed.
⁴⁹For he that is mighty hath done to me great things; and holy is
        his name.
⁵⁰And his mercy is on them that fear him from generation to
        generation.
⁵¹He hath shewed strength with his arm; he hath scattered the
        proud in the imagination of their hearts.
⁵²He hath put down the mighty from their seats and exalted them
        of low degree.
⁵³He hath filled the hungry with good things; and the rich he hath
        sent empty away.
⁵⁴He hath holpen his servant Israel, in remembrance of his mercy;
⁵⁵As he spake to our fathers, to Abraham, and to his seed for ever.
⁵⁶And Mary abode with her about three months, and returned to her own house.

⁵⁷Now Elisabeth's full time came that she should be delivered; and she brought
forth a son. ⁵⁸And her neighbours and her cousins heard how the Lord had shewed
great mercy upon her; and they rejoiced with her. ⁵⁹And it came to pass, that on
the eighth day they came to circumcise the child; and they called him Zacharias,
after the name of his father. ⁶⁰And his mother answered and said, Not so; but he
shall be called John. ⁶¹And they said unto her, There is none of thy kindred that
is called by this name. ⁶²And they made signs to his father, how he would have
him called. ⁶³And he asked for a writing table, and wrote, saying, His name is
John. And they marvelled all. ⁶⁴And his mouth was opened immediately, and his
tongue loosed, and he spake, and praised God. ⁶⁵And fear came on all that dwelt
round about them: and all these sayings were noised abroad throughout all the hill
country of Judæa. ⁶⁶And all they that heard them laid them up in their hearts, saying,
What manner of child shall this be! And the hand of the Lord was with him.

⁶⁷And his father Zacharias was filled with the Holy Ghost, and prophesied,
saying,
        ⁶⁸Blessed be the Lord God of Israel; for he hath visited and
                redeemed his people,

---

2 Esd 6:37).   **1:48** *Regarded the . . . handmaiden*: compare Hannah's vow (1 Sam 1:11).   **1:49** *Done to
me great things*: echoing Deut 10:21.   **1:50** *His mercy . . . to generation*: adapting Ps 103:17.   **1:51**
Strength with his arm: a common anthropomorphism used of YHWH in the OT (e.g., Ps 89:10; Isa 51:9).
Scattered the . . . hearts: perhaps recalling Ps 33:10.   **1:52** *Put down . . . degree*: cf. 1 Sam 2:7–8. *Seats*:
thrones.   **1:53** *Filled the hungry . . . away*: adapting Ps 34:10 (cf. 1 Sam 2:5).   **1:54** *Holpen*: helped. *In
remembrance . . . mercy*: cf. Ps 98:3.   **1:55** *He spake . . . ever*: recalling God's covenant with Abraham.
Luke, like Paul, understands Christ to fulfill it (cf. Rom 4:2–25; Gal 3:16–18).   **1:57–80** John the Baptist's birth. The song of vv. 68–79 is known as the Benedictus, after the first word of its Vulgate translation. Like the Magnificat, it resembles classical Hebrew poetry in diction, theme, and form. The
scriptural references provided below are not exhaustive.   **1:59** *On the eighth day*: cf. Gen 17:12; Lev 12:3.
Called: or were going to call.   **1:62** *They made signs*: the narrative assumes that Zacharias was deaf as
well as mute (two conditions commonly linked in the ancient world).   **1:63** *Table*: tablet; compare the
naming of Isaiah's son (Isa 8:1–4). *They marvelled all*: because Zacharias chose the same name as his wife
without having heard her speak it.   **1:66** *Laid them . . . hearts*: in the Bible, the heart is the seat not only of
emotion but also of volition (cf. 12:34; Ezek 11:19–20) and intellect (cf. Deut 8:5; Isa 6:10). This phrase
denotes "pondering" or "contemplation" (cf. 2:19, 51).   **1:68** *Blessed be . . . Israel*: cf. Pss 41:13; 72:18; 106:48.

⁶⁹And hath raised up an horn of salvation for us in the house of
     his servant David;

⁷⁰As he spake by the mouth of his holy prophets, which have been
     since the world began:

⁷¹That we should be saved from our enemies, and from the hand
     of all that hate us;

⁷²To perform the mercy promised to our fathers, and to remember
     his holy covenant;

⁷³The oath which he sware to our father Abraham,

⁷⁴That he would grant unto us, that we being delivered out of the
     hand of our enemies might serve him without fear,

⁷⁵In holiness and righteousness before him, all the days of our life.

⁷⁶And thou, child, shalt be called the prophet of the Highest: for
     thou shalt go before the face of the Lord to prepare his ways;

⁷⁷To give knowledge of salvation unto his people by the remission
     of their sins,

⁷⁸Through the tender mercy of our God; whereby the dayspring
     from on high hath visited us,

⁷⁹To give light to them that sit in darkness and in the shadow of
     death, to guide our feet into the way of peace.

⁸⁰And the child grew, and waxed strong in spirit, and was in the deserts till the
day of his shewing unto Israel.

2 And it came to pass in those days, that there went out a decree from Cæsar
Augustus, that all the world should be taxed. ²(And this taxing was first made

---

Redeemed: lit. "made ransom for"; cf. Mark 10:45 note.   **1:69** *Horn of salvation*: see Ps 18:2 (= 2 Sam
22:3); cf. 1 Sam 2:10; Ps 132:17.   **1:70** *Since the world began*: more literally "of old."   **1:71** *Saved
from our enemies . . . us*: echoing Ps 18:17 (= 2 Sam 22:18); cf. Ps 106:10.   **1:72** *To remember . . .
covenant*: echoing Ps 105:8.   **1:73** *The oath . . . Abraham*: cf. Gen 26:3; see 1:55 note. The reference to
this oath is apt, since John's circumcision occasions Zacharias's song.   **1:74–75** *That we . . . life*: recalling God's liberation of Israel from Egypt, "that they may serve me" (Exod 7:16; 8:1; etc.).   **1:76** *Go
before . . . ways*: cf. Isa 40:3; Mal 3:1.   **1:78** *Dayspring*: see LXX Jer 23:5; Zech 3:8; 6:12, three messianic prophecies in which the Hebrew word for "branch" is rendered Gk. *anatolē*, "dawn" or "dayspring";
see also Mal 4:2. *Hath visited*: better "will visit" (MS tradition).   **1:79** *Give light . . . death*: cf. Ps 107:10;
Isa 9:2. *To guide . . . peace*: cf. Isa 59:8.   **2:1–20** Jesus' birth. Matt 2 provides a very different account.
2:1 *Cæsar Augustus*: Roman emperor, 27 B.C.E.–14 C.E. Greco-Roman historians conventionally mention
simultaneous rulers (see "Cyrenius," v. 2) in order to fix an event chronologically. *Taxed*: enrolled, as in a
census. An assessment took place in Judea when Cyrenius (Quirinius) became legate of Syria, the
Roman province to which Judea was subordinated (see Acts 5:37 and note). Luke apparently invokes it
here to reconcile the tradition of Jesus' Bethlehem birth (probably based on a messianic reading of Mic
5:2; cf. Matt 2:6) with his knowledge of the Nazarene origins of Jesus' family, inferring that the census
required Joseph and Mary to travel from Nazareth to Bethlehem at the time of Jesus' birth. (Matt 2
reconciles these conflicting traditions differently.) However, Cyrenius became legate of Syria only in 6
C.E., which conflicts with the earlier claim that the events Luke narrates occurred during "the days of
Herod," who died in 4 B.C.E. (1:5; cf. Matt 2:1 note). Moreover, there is no other evidence that the census
required its subjects to travel to their ancestral homeland or that it involved the entire empire (contrast
vv. 1, 3). Indeed, an empirewide census carried out on this principle would have caused massive social
upheaval, and would certainly have left a larger historical footprint than this single reference in Luke.
Thematically, Luke's association of Jesus' birth with an empirewide census attributes to it a universal
relevance complementing the national significance that chap. 1 emphasizes.   **2:2** *And this . . . made*:

when Cyrenius was governor of Syria.) ³And all went to be taxed, every one into his own city. ⁴And Joseph also went up from Galilee, out of the city of Nazareth, into Judæa, unto the city of David, which is called Bethlehem; (because he was of the house and lineage of David:) ⁵to be taxed with Mary his espoused wife, being great with child. ⁶And so it was, that, while they were there, the days were accomplished that she should be delivered. ⁷And she brought forth her firstborn son, and wrapped him in swaddling clothes, and laid him in a manger; because there was no room for them in the inn.

⁸And there were in the same country shepherds abiding in the field, keeping watch over their flock by night. ⁹And, lo, the angel of the Lord came upon them, and the glory of the Lord shone round about them: and they were sore afraid. ¹⁰And the angel said unto them, Fear not: for, behold, I bring you good tidings of great joy, which shall be to all people. ¹¹For unto you is born this day in the city of David a Saviour, which is Christ the Lord. ¹²And this shall be a sign unto you; Ye shall find the babe wrapped in swaddling clothes, lying in a manger. ¹³And suddenly there was with the angel a multitude of the heavenly host praising God, and saying, ¹⁴Glory to God in the highest, and on earth peace, good will toward men.

¹⁵And it came to pass, as the angels were gone away from them into heaven, the shepherds said one to another, Let us now go even unto Bethlehem, and see this thing which is come to pass, which the Lord hath made known unto us. ¹⁶And they came with haste, and found Mary, and Joseph, and the babe lying in a manger. ¹⁷And when they had seen it, they made known abroad the saying which was told them concerning this child. ¹⁸And all they that heard it wondered at those things which were told them by the shepherds. ¹⁹But Mary kept all these things, and pondered them in her heart. ²⁰And the shepherds returned, glorifying and praising God for all the things that they had heard and seen, as it was told unto them.

²¹And when eight days were accomplished for the circumcising of the child, his name was called Jesus, which was so named of the angel before he was con-

---

better "this was the first registration." **2:4** *Bethlehem*: just south of Jerusalem. **2:7** *Firstborn son*: in light of the stress placed by Luke on Jesus' Davidic lineage (1:27, 32; 2:4; etc.), this phrase establishes his right to inherit David's throne. *Manger*: feeding trough. **2:8** *Country*: region. *Shepherds*: contrast Matt 2, where Jesus' birth attracts the attention of the elite. **2:9** *The glory . . . Lord*: the divine presence traditionally associated with the tabernacle or temple (see Exod 40:34–35; 1 Kgs 8:11). **2:10** *I bring . . . joy*: cf. 1:19. The announcement recalls Isaiah's praise of "the prince of peace" (9:6–7). **2:11** *Is born . . . Lord*: since the Roman emperor Augustus (see v. 1) was commonly honored as *Lord* and *Saviour*, and since both *Christ* (see Mark 1:1 note) and *city of David* have royal connotations, Luke presents Jesus as ruler of a topsy-turvy social and political order (the "kingdom of God"; cf. 6:20; 7:28; etc.): its throne is a manger (vv. 7, 12); its temple, a field grazed by sheep (v. 8); its king, an infant honored by lowly shepherds (vv. 15–18). **2:13** *Heavenly host*: army of heaven. **2:14** *On earth peace*: in the Greco-Roman world, this phrase (now a holiday commonplace) would have recalled Rome's conventional presentation of its rule over the Mediterranean world as the *pax Romana* ("Roman peace"). *Good will toward men*: better "among men of [God's] good pleasure" (MS tradition). **2:21–40** Circumcision and presentation at the temple. This section and the next are marked by a strong emphasis on piety, seen in Mary and Joseph's Torah observance, Simeon's faithful expectation of a messiah, and Anna's unceasing prayer at the temple. **2:21–24** *When eight . . . pigeons*: for laws regarding circumcision and purification after childbirth, see Lev 12. (The precise sacrifice Mary makes marks her as poor; cf. Lev 12:6, 8.) For the dedication and redemption of firstborn sons, see Exod 13:2, 13–15; Num 3:46–48; 18:15–16. (Luke does not mention the payment that

ceived in the womb. ²²And when the days of her purification according to the law of Moses were accomplished, they brought him to Jerusalem, to present him to the Lord; ²³(as it is written in the law of the Lord, Every male that openeth the womb shall be called holy to the Lord;) ²⁴and to offer a sacrifice according to that which is said in the law of the Lord, A pair of turtledoves, or two young pigeons.

²⁵And, behold, there was a man in Jerusalem, whose name was Simeon; and the same man was just and devout, waiting for the consolation of Israel: and the Holy Ghost was upon him. ²⁶And it was revealed unto him by the Holy Ghost, that he should not see death, before he had seen the Lord's Christ. ²⁷And he came by the Spirit into the temple: and when the parents brought in the child Jesus, to do for him after the custom of the law, ²⁸then took he him up in his arms, and blessed God, and said,

²⁹Lord, now lettest thou thy servant depart in peace, according to
　　thy word:
　　³⁰For mine eyes have seen thy salvation,
　　³¹Which thou hast prepared before the face of all people;
　　³²A light to lighten the Gentiles, and the glory of thy people Israel.

³³And Joseph and his mother marvelled at those things which were spoken of him. ³⁴And Simeon blessed them, and said unto Mary his mother, Behold, this child is set for the fall and rising again of many in Israel; and for a sign which shall be spoken against; ³⁵(yea, a sword shall pierce through thy own soul also,) that the thoughts of many hearts may be revealed.

³⁶And there was one Anna, a prophetess, the daughter of Phanuel, of the tribe of Aser: she was of a great age, and had lived with an husband seven years from her virginity; ³⁷and she was a widow of about fourscore and four years, which departed not from the temple, but served God with fastings and prayers night and day. ³⁸And she coming in that instant gave thanks likewise unto the Lord, and spake of him to all them that looked for redemption in Jerusalem. ³⁹And when they had performed all things according to the law of the Lord, they returned into Galilee, to their own city Nazareth. ⁴⁰And the child grew, and waxed strong in spirit, filled with wisdom: and the grace of God was upon him.

Numbers requires.)　**2:22** *Her purification*: better "their purification" (MS tradition), even though childbirth polluted only the mother.　**2:29–32** *Lord, now . . . Israel*: a brief hymn of praise known as the Nunc Dimittis after its opening words in the Vulgate. Given Simeon's patient expectation (v. 25), "now," the hymn's first word in Greek, carries strong eschatological significance. The song links Jesus' advent with the anticipation (realized in Acts) that YHWH would reach out to Gentiles at the end time (cf. Isa 49:6; Zech 8:23; etc.).　**2:29** *Lord*: Gk. *despota* ("lord" is usually *kyrios*); perhaps better "master." *Servant*: slave (as usual in Luke).　**2:32** *A light . . . Gentiles*: Isa 49:6.　**2:33** *Joseph*: better "his father" (MS tradition), which scribes altered in light of Jesus' divine conception. Analogous changes were apparently made at v. 41 (not affecting KJV) and at 43 (see note).　**2:34** *This child . . . Israel*: recalling 1:52–53, but perhaps also alluding to the idea that God made Jesus a "stumblingstone" over which many Jews would trip while Gentiles would embrace him; cf. Rom 9:32–33; 11:11–12.　**2:35** *A sword . . . also*: probably referring to Jesus' devaluing of natural family ties (8:21; 11:27–28; 12:51–53; 14:26–27), foreshadowed in the next episode (vv. 40–52).　**2:37** *Fourscore and four years*: her age is symbolic, 84 being 12 × 7.　**2:38** *In Jerusalem*: better "of Jerusalem" (MS tradition), which reveals a layer of irony. Jesus, himself Jerusalem's redemption, has been brought to Jerusalem for his redemption as firstborn son (v. 23).　**2:40** *In spirit*: better omitted (MS tradition).

⁴¹Now his parents went to Jerusalem every year at the feast of the passover. ⁴²And when he was twelve years old, they went up to Jerusalem after the custom of the feast. ⁴³And when they had fulfilled the days, as they returned, the child Jesus tarried behind in Jerusalem; and Joseph and his mother knew not of it. ⁴⁴But they, supposing him to have been in the company, went a day's journey; and they sought him among their kinsfolk and acquaintance. ⁴⁵And when they found him not, they turned back again to Jerusalem, seeking him.

⁴⁶And it came to pass, that after three days they found him in the temple, sitting in the midst of the doctors, both hearing them, and asking them questions. ⁴⁷And all that heard him were astonished at his understanding and answers. ⁴⁸And when they saw him, they were amazed: and his mother said unto him, Son, why hast thou thus dealt with us? behold, thy father and I have sought thee sorrowing. ⁴⁹And he said unto them, How is it that ye sought me? wist ye not that I must be about my Father's business? ⁵⁰And they understood not the saying which he spake unto them. ⁵¹And he went down with them, and came to Nazareth, and was subject unto them: but his mother kept all these sayings in her heart. ⁵²And Jesus increased in wisdom and stature, and in favour with God and man.

3 Now in the fifteenth year of the reign of Tiberius Cæsar, Pontius Pilate being governor of Judæa, and Herod being tetrarch of Galilee, and his brother Philip tetrarch of Ituræa and of the region of Trachonitis, and Lysanias the tetrarch of Abilene, ²Annas and Caiaphas being the high priests, the word of God came unto John the son of Zacharias in the wilderness. ³And he came into all the country about Jordan, preaching the baptism of repentance for the remission of sins; ⁴as it is written in the book of the words of Esaias the prophet, saying, The voice of one crying in the wilderness, Prepare ye the way of the Lord, make his paths straight. ⁵Every valley shall be filled, and every mountain and hill shall be brought low; and the crooked shall be made straight, and the rough ways shall be made smooth; ⁶and all flesh shall see the salvation of God.

2:41–52 Return to the temple. This episode from Jesus' youth is framed by summary statements of his maturation (vv. 40, 52). **2:41** *The feast of the passover*: Deut 16:1–8 (esp. vv. 5–7) mandates Passover pilgrimage to Jerusalem. **2:43** *Joseph and his mother*: better "his parents" (MS tradition); see 2:33 note. **2:44** *Company*: caravan. **2:46** *Doctors*: teachers of the law, also called "scribes" (cf. 5:17 and note, 21). **2:48** *Sought thee sorrowing*: cf. v. 35. **2:49** *Wist*: Knew. *My Father's business*: a discreet but harsh rebuke of Mary (cf. v. 48): Jesus reminds her where his true familial loyalty lies.

3:1–4:13 Preparing for Jesus' ministry. 3:1–20 John the Baptist. Compare Matt 3:1–12 and notes; Mark 1:2–8 and notes. **3:1** *Now in . . . Abilene*: on multiple references to rulers, see 2:1 note. *Tiberius* was emperor, 14–37 C.E., making the fifteenth year of his reign 28/29. *Pontius Pilate* was prefect of Judea, ca. 26–37 C.E., Herod the Great's son *Herod* Antipas ruled Galilee and Perea, 4 B.C.E.–39 C.E.; his son *Philip* ruled an area northeast of the Sea of Galilee containing *Ituræa* and *Trachonitis* from 4 B.C.E. to 34 C.E. (On *tetrarch*, see Mark 6:14 note.) Josephus discusses a *Lysanias* who died in the first century B.C.E., but may also refer to a later figure by that name (see *Jewish War* 2.247), and an inscription found near Abila (a town in Abilene about twenty miles northwest of Damascus) mentions a tetrarch named Lysanias who perhaps corresponds to this later figure. There is not enough information to date his reign. **3:2** *Annas and . . . priests*: there was only one high priest at a time: *Annas* served from 6 to 15 C.E.; his son-in-law *Caiaphas*, 18–36. Luke and John refer to both as high priests simultaneously (cf. John 18:13 and note), perhaps reflecting Annas's continued influence after he left office. *The word . . . came*: assimilating John to OT prophets; cf. 1 Kgs 12:22; Isa 38:4; Jer 1:1–2; etc. *Wilderness*: cf. 1:80 (KJV "deserts"). **3:4–6** *The voice . . . God*: Isa 40:3–5. **3:6** *All flesh . . . God*:

⁷Then said he to the multitude that came forth to be baptized of him, O generation of vipers, who hath warned you to flee from the wrath to come? ⁸Bring forth therefore fruits worthy of repentance, and begin not to say within yourselves, We have Abraham to our father: for I say unto you, That God is able of these stones to raise up children unto Abraham. ⁹And now also the axe is laid unto the root of the trees: every tree therefore which bringeth not forth good fruit is hewn down, and cast into the fire.

¹⁰And the people asked him, saying, What shall we do then? ¹¹He answereth and saith unto them, He that hath two coats, let him impart to him that hath none; and he that hath meat, let him do likewise. ¹²Then came also publicans to be baptized, and said unto him, Master, what shall we do? ¹³And he said unto them, Exact no more than that which is appointed you. ¹⁴And the soldiers likewise demanded of him, saying, And what shall we do? And he said unto them, Do violence to no man, neither accuse any falsely; and be content with your wages.

¹⁵And as the people were in expectation, and all men mused in their hearts of John, whether he were the Christ, or not; ¹⁶John answered, saying unto them all, I indeed baptize you with water; but one mightier than I cometh, the latchet of whose shoes I am not worthy to unloose: he shall baptize you with the Holy Ghost and with fire: ¹⁷whose fan is in his hand, and he will throughly purge his floor, and will gather the wheat into his garner; but the chaff he will burn with fire unquenchable. ¹⁸And many other things in his exhortation preached he unto the people. ¹⁹But Herod the tetrarch, being reproved by him for Herodias his brother Philip's wife, and for all the evils which Herod had done, ²⁰added yet this above all, that he shut up John in prison.

²¹Now when all the people were baptized, it came to pass, that Jesus also being baptized, and praying, the heaven was opened, ²²and the Holy Ghost descended in a bodily shape like a dove upon him, and a voice came from heaven, which said, Thou art my beloved Son; in thee I am well pleased.

---

this verse from Isaiah (not included in Matthew and Mark) recalls Simeon's universalizing hymn (2:29–32). **3:10–14** *The people . . . wages*: Luke alone of the Synoptics includes John's ethical advice. **3:11** *Meat*: food (so throughout). **3:12** *Publicans*: see Mark 2:15 note. **3:14** *Soldiers*: their association with tax collectors suggests they are Roman soldiers, who show up periodically in Luke-Acts (e.g., Luke 7:1–10; Acts 10). *Do violence . . . accuse any falsely*: both Greek verbs refer to extortion, as John's third command to soldiers suggests (NRSV: "Do not extort money from anyone by threats or false accusation"). **3:19–20** *But Herod . . . prison*: Luke displaces and abbreviates Mark's elaborate narrative of John's arrest (6:14–29; see notes), reporting it before Jesus' baptism and later mentioning John's execution only incidentally (9:9). Luke thereby subordinates John's ministry to Jesus'. His curtailment of John's ministry perhaps reflects his concern about a movement that did not recognize Jesus but still valued John's baptism, whose influence early Christian missionaries will encounter throughout the Mediterranean world (Acts 18:24–19:4; cf. 13:24–25). **3:19** *Brother Philip's*: better simply "brother's" (MS tradition); see Mark 6:17 note. **3:21–22** Baptism. Compare Matt 3:13–17; Mark 1:9–11 and notes. **3:21** *Now when . . . opened*: a more literal translation reveals that the Spirit descends not during Jesus' baptism but rather while he afterward prays: "It came about, when all the people were baptized, and Jesus also, having been baptized, was praying, that the heaven was opened." Luke frequently portrays Jesus in prayer, especially at key moments in his ministry: at its commencement (here), before he chooses the Twelve (6:12), before the first passion prediction (9:18), just before

²³And Jesus himself began to be about thirty years of age, being (as was supposed) the son of Joseph, which was the son of Heli, ²⁴which was the son of Matthat, which was the son of Levi, which was the son of Melchi, which was the son of Janna, which was the son of Joseph, ²⁵which was the son of Mattathias, which was the son of Amos, which was the son of Naum, which was the son of Esli, which was the son of Nagge, ²⁶which was the son of Maath, which was the son of Mattathias, which was the son of Semei, which was the son of Joseph, which was the son of Juda, ²⁷which was the son of Joanna, which was the son of Rhesa, which was the son of Zorobabel, which was the son of Salathiel, which was the son of Neri, ²⁸which was the son of Melchi, which was the son of Addi, which was the son of Cosam, which was the son of Elmodam, which was the son of Er, ²⁹which was the son of Jose, which was the son of Eliezer, which was the son of Jorim, which was the son of Matthat, which was the son of Levi, ³⁰which was the son of Simeon, which was the son of Juda, which was the son of Joseph, which was the son of Jonan, which was the son of Eliakim, ³¹which was the son of Melea, which was the son of Menan, which was the son of Mattatha, which was the son of Nathan, which was the son of David, ³²which was the son of Jesse, which was the son of Obed, which was the son of Booz, which was the son of Salmon, which was the son of Naasson, ³³which was the son of Aminadab, which was the son of Aram, which was the son of Esrom, which was the son of Phares, which was the son of Juda, ³⁴which was the son of Jacob, which was the son of Isaac, which was the son of Abraham, which was the son of Thara, which was the son of Nachor, ³⁵which was the son of Saruch, which was the son of Ragau, which was the son of Phalec, which was the son of Heber, which was the son of Sala, ³⁶which was the son of Cainan, which was the son of Arphaxad, which was the son of Sem, which was the son of Noe, which was the son of Lamech, ³⁷which was the son of

---

his arrest (22:41–44), etc.   **3:23–38** Genealogy. Matt 1:1–17 provides a different genealogy. Luke's, motivated by the divine pronouncement in v. 22, traces Jesus' ancestry backward for seventy-seven generations, through Joseph all the way to Adam, and thence to God. The best reading of the MS tradition (which adds a generation in v. 33; see note) reveals that Luke's genealogy is elaborately patterned, consisting of 21 (3 × 7) generations from Adam (v. 38) to Abraham (v. 34); 14 (2 × 7) generations from Isaac (v. 34) to David (v. 31); 21 (3 × 7) generations from David's son Nathan (v. 31) until the end of the Babylonian exile (Salathiel, v. 27); and 21 (3 × 7) generations from the return (Zorobabel, v. 27; cf. Ezra 2:2; 3:2) until Jesus (v. 23). Luke draws on three OT genealogies: many of the names in the series beginning with Zorobabel and ending with Abraham are found in 1 Chr 1–3; all the names from Thara (v. 34) to Sem (v. 36) come from LXX Gen 11; and all those from Sem to Adam come from Gen 5. But several names are completely unknown: all in the series beginning with Heli (v. 23) and ending with Rhesa (v. 27), and from Neri (v. 27) to Mattatha (v. 31), as well as Admin and Arni (v. 33; see note). Not surprisingly, the MS tradition preserves a staggering number of variations in spelling. Modern critical editions and the Greek text used by KJV often disagree on these matters, leading to a host of trivial differences among translations. In addition, KJV transliterates Luke's Greek versions of Hebrew names, while most modern translations substitute English forms of the Hebrew originals (e.g., Shem for Sem, and Noah for Noe; v. 36). Such variations receive no comment in the notes that follow.   **3:23** *Began to . . . age*: better "was about thirty years of age when he began [his ministry]."   **3:32** *Salmon*: better "Sala" (MS tradition), changed by later scribes to assimilate Luke to Matt 1:4–5; cf. LXX 1 Chr 2:11. **3:33** *Aminadab, which . . . Aram*: better "Aminadab, son of Admin, son of Arni" (MS tradition). Later scribes sacrificed Luke's numerical patterning to further assimilate his text to Matthew (1:3–4); cf. LXX

Mathusala, which was the son of Enoch, which was the son of Jared, which was the son of Maleleel, which was the son of Cainan, ³⁸which was the son of Enos, which was the son of Seth, which was the son of Adam, which was the son of God.

4 And Jesus being full of the Holy Ghost returned from Jordan, and was led by the Spirit into the wilderness, ²being forty days tempted of the devil. And in those days he did eat nothing: and when they were ended, he afterward hungered. ³And the devil said unto him, If thou be the Son of God, command this stone that it be made bread. ⁴And Jesus answered him, saying, It is written, That man shall not live by bread alone, but by every word of God. ⁵And the devil, taking him up into an high mountain, shewed unto him all the kingdoms of the world in a moment of time. ⁶And the devil said unto him, All this power will I give thee, and the glory of them: for that is delivered unto me; and to whomsoever I will I give it. ⁷If thou therefore wilt worship me, all shall be thine. ⁸And Jesus answered and said unto him, Get thee behind me, Satan: for it is written, Thou shalt worship the Lord thy God, and him only shalt thou serve. ⁹And he brought him to Jerusalem, and set him on a pinnacle of the temple, and said unto him, If thou be the Son of God, cast thyself down from hence: ¹⁰for it is written, He shall give his angels charge over thee, to keep thee: ¹¹and in their hands they shall bear thee up, lest at any time thou dash thy foot against a stone. ¹²And Jesus answering said unto him, It is said, Thou shalt not tempt the Lord thy God. ¹³And when the devil had ended all the temptation, he departed from him for a season.

¹⁴And Jesus returned in the power of the Spirit into Galilee: and there went out a fame of him through all the region round about. ¹⁵And he taught in their synagogues, being glorified of all.

¹⁶And he came to Nazareth, where he had been brought up: and, as his custom was, he went into the synagogue on the sabbath day, and stood up for to read.

---

1 Chr 2:9–10.   **4:1–13** Temptation. Compare Matt 4:1–11 and notes; Mark 1:12–13 and notes. Luke reverses the order of Matthew's final two temptations.   **4:2** *Tempted:* Gk. *peirazō*, also "tested" (so throughout).   **4:3** *If thou . . . God:* whereas the previous section confirms the heavenly voice's proclamation (3:22) by tracing Jesus' human ancestry to God (v. 38), the devil tempts Jesus to prove his divine pedigree by exercising superhuman powers.   **4:4** *Man shall not live . . . God:* Deut 8:3. *But by . . . God:* better omitted (MS tradition).   **4:5** *The devil . . . mountain:* better "taking him up, he . . ." (MS tradition).   **4:6** *For that . . . it:* in Jewish apocalyptic literature, the devil was understood to exercise authority over the sublunary world. Compare God's granting of authority to Satan ("the adversary") in Job 1:12; 2:6 (see 1:6 note).   **4:8** *Get thee . . . Satan:* better omitted (MS tradition). *Thou shalt worship . . . serve:* Deut 6:13.   **4:10–11** *He shall give . . . stone:* Ps 91:11–12.   **4:12** *Thou shalt not tempt . . . God:* Deut 6:16.   **4:13** *The devil . . . temptation:* the previous verse showed Jesus identifying with humanity by refusing to presume God's protection, but the devil's immediate departure suggests an equation between Jesus and v. 12's "the Lord thy God." *For a season:* more literally "until an appointed time," foreshadowing Satan's return to instigate Jesus' betrayal (22:3).

4:14–9:50 Galilean ministry. 4:14–15 Initial preaching. Compare Matt 4:12–17; Mark 1:14–15. This section forms an inclusive frame with vv. 31–32; Jesus' rejection at Nazareth (vv. 16–32) is presented as a brief digression from his ministry's enthusiastic reception elsewhere.   **4:16–32** Rejection in Nazareth. Compare the briefer and differently placed versions in Matt 13:54–58; 7:28–29 and Mark 6:1–6; 1:21–22; cf. John 7:3–5, 15; 6:42; 4:44. Luke presents Jesus' rejection as the first scene of his ministry, using it to announce his work's central themes, including continuity with Hebrew Scriptures, status reversal, Jesus' acceptance of Gentiles, and his own people's rejection of him.   **4:16** *Synagogue:* see Mark 1:21 note. *Stood up . . . read:* as a participant in a Jewish worship service,

¹⁷And there was delivered unto him the book of the prophet Esaias. And when he had opened the book, he found the place where it was written, ¹⁸The Spirit of the Lord is upon me, because he hath anointed me to preach the gospel to the poor; he hath sent me to heal the brokenhearted, to preach deliverance to the captives, and recovering of sight to the blind, to set at liberty them that are bruised, ¹⁹to preach the acceptable year of the Lord. ²⁰And he closed the book, and he gave it again to the minister, and sat down. And the eyes of all them that were in the synagogue were fastened on him.

²¹And he began to say unto them, This day is this scripture fulfilled in your ears. ²²And all bare him witness, and wondered at the gracious words which proceeded out of his mouth. And they said, Is not this Joseph's son? ²³And he said unto them, Ye will surely say unto me this proverb, Physician, heal thyself: whatsoever we have heard done in Capernaum, do also here in thy country. ²⁴And he said, Verily I say unto you, No prophet is accepted in his own country. ²⁵But I tell you of a truth, many widows were in Israel in the days of Elias, when the heaven was shut up three years and six months, when great famine was throughout all the land; ²⁶but unto none of them was Elias sent, save unto Sarepta, a city of Sidon, unto a woman that was a widow. ²⁷And many lepers were in Israel in the time of Eliseus the prophet; and none of them was cleansed, saving Naaman the Syrian. ²⁸And all they in the synagogue, when they heard these things, were filled with wrath, ²⁹and rose up, and thrust him out of the city, and led him unto the brow of

---

Jesus could be called upon to read Scripture and, perhaps, preach from it; cf. Acts 13:15.   **4:17** *Opened*: better "unrolled" (MS tradition); the *book* is a scroll.   **4:18–19** *The Spirit . . . Lord*: LXX Isa 61:1–2, with a phrase from 58:6.   **4:18** *To preach the gospel*: Gk. *euangelisasthai*, "to bring glad tidings" (1:19; 2:10; cf. 3:18). *The poor*: five of Luke's ten references to *the poor* occupy the primary or ultimate position in catalogues of detestable afflictions, such as leprosy, bodily mutilation, and lameness (see also 6:20; 7:22; 14:13, 21; cf. 16:20). The word in Luke implies not only penury but more broadly social ignominy. *To heal the brokenhearted*: better omitted (MS tradition) as a scribal assimilation of Luke's text to Isa 61:1. *Deliverance*: Gk. *aphesis*, "release"; KJV "liberty" later in this verse. To proclaim deliverance or liberty invokes the Priestly Jubilee (Lev 25:10), to which the Isaianic passage read here gives eschatological interpretation (see Isa 61:1 note). The Jubilee year is a key paradigm for Jesus' ministry in Luke, which emphasizes his liberation of people from the constricting power of destitution (e.g., 7:11–17 and notes), illness (e.g., 4:39 and note), sin (e.g., 5:20 and note; cf. 1:77; 3:3 [KJV "remission"], about John's ministry), demons (e.g., 13:11–12 and note), etc. *Recovering of sight . . . blind*: both literally (18:35–43) and figuratively (1:78–79; 2:29–32). *Bruised*: downtrodden or oppressed.   **4:20** *Minister*: attendant. *Sat down*: in order to teach, as was customary.   **4:21** *This day . . . ears*: in comparison with the other Synoptics, Luke tends to de-emphasize a future eschatological consummation; he presents Jesus' advent and ministry, and later the ministry of the church (e.g., Acts 2:17–21 and note), as themselves fulfilling eschatological expectations (cf. Luke 17:20–21). Luke's many pregnant references to "now," "this day," "to day," and the like (e.g., 2:29, 11; 5:26) underscore the point.   **4:23–27** *Ye will . . . Syrian*: the congregation's positive response to Jesus' message (v. 22) makes this a strangely belligerent reply. His tendentious invocation of these biblical stories as examples of God privileging Gentiles seems intentionally provocative.   **4:23** *Capernaum*: see Mark 1:21 note.   **4:24** *No prophet . . . country*: Luke eliminates Mark's reference to family (6:4), a change that complements his positive portrayal of Mary.   **4:25–26** *Many widows . . . widow*: Elijah miraculously aided the Gentile widow of Zarephath (1 Kgs 17:8–24).   **4:27** *Many lepers . . . Syrian*: Elisha's healing of the Gentile military commander Namaan (2 Kgs 5:1–19) foreshadows not only Jesus' healing of the Roman centurion's servant (7:1–10) but also the early church's ministry to Gentiles, in particular Peter's conversion of the centurion Cornelius (Acts 10:1–11:30).   **4:29** *Led him . . .*

the hill whereon their city was built, that they might cast him down headlong. [30]But he passing through the midst of them went his way, [31]and came down to Capernaum, a city of Galilee, and taught them on the sabbath days. [32]And they were astonished at his doctrine: for his word was with power.

[33]And in the synagogue there was a man, which had a spirit of an unclean devil, and cried out with a loud voice, [34]saying, Let us alone; what have we to do with thee, thou Jesus of Nazareth? art thou come to destroy us? I know thee who thou art; the Holy One of God. [35]And Jesus rebuked him, saying, Hold thy peace, and come out of him. And when the devil had thrown him in the midst, he came out of him, and hurt him not. [36]And they were all amazed, and spake among themselves, saying, What a word is this! for with authority and power he commandeth the unclean spirits, and they come out. [37]And the fame of him went out into every place of the country round about.

[38]And he arose out of the synagogue, and entered into Simon's house. And Simon's wife's mother was taken with a great fever; and they besought him for her. [39]And he stood over her, and rebuked the fever; and it left her: and immediately she arose and ministered unto them.

[40]Now when the sun was setting, all they that had any sick with divers diseases brought them unto him; and he laid his hands on every one of them, and healed them. [41]And devils also came out of many, crying out, and saying, Thou art Christ the Son of God. And he rebuking them suffered them not to speak: for they knew that he was Christ. [42]And when it was day, he departed and went into a desert place: and the people sought him, and came unto him, and stayed him, that he should not depart from them. [43]And he said unto them, I must preach the kingdom of God to other cities also: for therefore am I sent. [44]And he preached in the synagogues of Galilee.

5 And it came to pass, that, as the people pressed upon him to hear the word of God, he stood by the lake of Gennesaret, [2]and saw two ships standing by the lake: but the fishermen were gone out of them, and were washing their nets. [3]And he entered into one of the ships, which was Simon's, and prayed him that he would thrust out a little from the land. And he sat down, and taught the people out of the ship. [4]Now when he had left speaking, he said unto Simon, Launch out into the deep, and let down your nets for a draught. [5]And Simon answering

---

headlong: recalling the devil's third temptation (vv. 9–12).   **4:31–32** *And came . . . power*: cf. vv. 14–15 and note.   **4:32** *Doctrine*: teaching.   **4:33–44** Ministry in Capernaum. Compare Matt 8:14–17; 4:23; Mark 1:23–39 and notes. This material is chiastically structured: teaching (vv. 31–32), exorcism (vv. 33–37), and healing (vv. 38–39) are mirrored by healing (v. 40), exorcism (v. 41), and preaching (vv. 42–44).   **4:33** *Devil*: i.e., demon (as often in Luke).   **4:38–39** *He arose . . . them*: in Luke, before calling Simon as a disciple (5:1–11) Jesus heals Simon's mother-in-law, thereby motivating his willingness to follow.   **4:39** *It left her*: or "it released her" (translating the verbal form of Gk. *aphesis*; see v. 18 note).   **4:40** *When the sun was setting*: i.e., after the Sabbath had ended (cf. vv. 31, 33).   **4:41** *Thou art . . . God*: better "you are the Son of God" (MS tradition).   **4:44** *Galilee*: better "Judea" (MS tradition), referring to all Palestine.   **5:1–11** Calling the first disciples. Compare Matt 4:18–22; Mark 1:16–20 and notes, both of which lack the miraculous catch of fish. John has a different account of Jesus calling the first disciples (1:35–51) and attributes the miraculous catch to the risen Christ, associating it with Peter's rehabilitation rather than his recruitment (21:1–14).   **5:1** *Lake of Gennesaret*: Sea of Galilee.   **5:4** *Draught*: a catch with a dragnet.

said unto him, Master, we have toiled all the night, and have taken nothing: nevertheless at thy word I will let down the net. [6]And when they had this done, they inclosed a great multitude of fishes: and their net brake. [7]And they beckoned unto their partners, which were in the other ship, that they should come and help them. And they came, and filled both the ships, so that they began to sink. [8]When Simon Peter saw it, he fell down at Jesus' knees, saying, Depart from me; for I am a sinful man, O Lord. [9]For he was astonished, and all that were with him, at the draught of the fishes which they had taken: [10]and so was also James, and John, the sons of Zebedee, which were partners with Simon. And Jesus said unto Simon, Fear not; from henceforth thou shalt catch men. [11]And when they had brought their ships to land, they forsook all, and followed him.

[12]And it came to pass, when he was in a certain city, behold a man full of leprosy: who seeing Jesus fell on his face, and besought him, saying, Lord, if thou wilt, thou canst make me clean. [13]And he put forth his hand, and touched him, saying, I will: be thou clean. And immediately the leprosy departed from him. [14]And he charged him to tell no man: but go, and shew thyself to the priest, and offer for thy cleansing, according as Moses commanded, for a testimony unto them. [15]But so much the more went there a fame abroad of him: and great multitudes came together to hear, and to be healed by him of their infirmities. [16]And he withdrew himself into the wilderness, and prayed.

[17]And it came to pass on a certain day, as he was teaching, that there were Pharisees and doctors of the law sitting by, which were come out of every town of Galilee, and Judæa, and Jerusalem: and the power of the Lord was present to heal them. [18]And, behold, men brought in a bed a man which was taken with a palsy: and they sought means to bring him in, and to lay him before him. [19]And when they could not find by what way they might bring him in because of the multitude, they went upon the housetop, and let him down through the tiling with his couch into the midst before Jesus. [20]And when he saw their faith, he said unto him, Man, thy sins are forgiven thee. [21]And the scribes and the Pharisees began to reason, saying, Who is this which speaketh blasphemies? Who can forgive sins, but God alone? [22]But when Jesus perceived their thoughts, he answering said unto them, What reason ye in your hearts? [23]Whether is easier, to say, Thy sins be for-

---

5:5 *Master*: Gk. *epistatēs*; in the other Synoptics "master" is usually *didaskalos*, lit. "teacher." In Luke, Jesus' followers use the former word and others the latter.   **5:8** *Lord*: see Mark 7:28 note.   **5:10** *Catch*: Gk. *zōgreō*, "to capture alive" or even "to spare life" (see 2 Tim 2:26 note). Peter will catch people in order to save them.   **5:11** *Forsook*: Gk. *aphentes*, a verbal form of *aphesis* (see 4:18 note).   **5:12–16** Healing a man with leprosy. Compare Matt 8:1–4; Mark 1:40–45 and notes. Also compare Elisha's healing of Namaan (2 Kgs 5:1–19; cf. Luke 4:27 and note).   **5:14** *As Moses commanded*: see Lev 13–14.   **5:17–26** Healing a paralytic. Compare Matt 9:1–8; Mark 2:1–12 and notes. John 5:1–18 has a very different account.   **5:17** *Pharisees*: see Mark 2:16 note. Luke's decision to include them in his version of Mark's story (cf. Mark 2:6) is significant in light of the universal acclamation of Jesus with which it ends (see v. 26 and note). *Doctors of the law*: the "scribes" of v. 21 (see Mark 1:22 note). Their response to Jesus here differs drastically from that of 2:46–47.   **5:20** *Forgiven*: from Gk. *aphiēmi* (throughout this episode and often in Luke), the verbal form of *aphesis* (see 4:18 note).   **5:23** *Whether*: which.

given thee; or to say, Rise up and walk? [24]But that ye may know that the Son of man hath power upon earth to forgive sins, (he said unto the sick of the palsy,) I say unto thee, Arise, and take up thy couch, and go into thine house. [25]And immediately he rose up before them, and took up that whereon he lay, and departed to his own house, glorifying God. [26]And they were all amazed, and they glorified God, and were filled with fear, saying, We have seen strange things to day.

[27]And after these things he went forth, and saw a publican, named Levi, sitting at the receipt of custom: and he said unto him, Follow me. [28]And he left all, rose up, and followed him. [29]And Levi made him a great feast in his own house: and there was a great company of publicans and of others that sat down with them. [30]But their scribes and Pharisees murmured against his disciples, saying, Why do ye eat and drink with publicans and sinners? [31]And Jesus answering said unto them, They that are whole need not a physician; but they that are sick. [32]I came not to call the righteous, but sinners to repentance.

[33]And they said unto him, Why do the disciples of John fast often, and make prayers, and likewise the disciples of the Pharisees; but thine eat and drink? [34]And he said unto them, Can ye make the children of the bridechamber fast, while the bridegroom is with them? [35]But the days will come, when the bridegroom shall be taken away from them, and then shall they fast in those days. [36]And he spake also a parable unto them; No man putteth a piece of a new garment upon an old; if otherwise, then both the new maketh a rent, and the piece that was taken out of the new agreeth not with the old. [37]And no man putteth new wine into old bottles; else the new wine will burst the bottles, and be spilled, and the bottles shall perish. [38]But new wine must be put into new bottles; and both are preserved. [39]No man also having drunk old wine straightway desireth new: for he saith, The old is better.

5:24 *Son of man*: see Mark 2:10 note.   **5:26** *All*: including the Pharisees and scribes (v. 17). Luke's portrayal of the Pharisees is more multifaceted than the other gospels'. Their opposition to Jesus is not predetermined, but gradually emerges and intensifies throughout 5:17–6:11. Despite their hostility, some Pharisees evince concern for Jesus' safety (13:31); in Acts, moreover, Pharisees advocate for the apostles (5:34–39; 23:9) and are even counted among the church's members (15:5). Most prominently, Paul himself claims to be a Pharisee—well after his "conversion" (23:6).   **5:27–39** Symposium at Levi's house. Compare Matt 9:9–17; Mark 2:13–22 and notes.   **5:30** *Their scribes and Pharisees*: better "the Pharisees and their scribes" (MS tradition).   **5:33** *Why do*: better omitted (MS tradition), leaving a statement rather than a question.   **5:34** *Children of the bridechamber*: wedding guests.   **5:37** *Bottles*: lit. "wineskins."   **5:38** *And both are preserved*: better omitted (MS tradition).   **5:39** *No man . . . better*: attempts to deny Jesus' assimilation of his ministry to the privileged *old* abound in the history of this verse's interpretation, including capricious excision of it from Luke's gospel and tendentious claims that it merely implies that those whose hearts are stubbornly set in their traditional (i.e., "Jewish") ways will have difficulty embracing Jesus' radically new (i.e., "Christian") teaching. Such attempts should be abandoned, for Luke persistently incorporates OT language and themes into his story of Jesus and explicitly presents Jesus' ministry as the fulfillment of biblical prophecy (4:18–19). Luke's Jesus is not so much rejecting traditional forms of piety (v. 35) as fulfilling God's ancient purposes. *Straightway*: better omitted (MS tradition) as a scribal emendation, perhaps designed to bring Jesus' words in line with a tendentious interpretation of the verse. *Better*: better "good" (MS tradition), which later scribes altered to clarify the implicit

6 And it came to pass on the second sabbath after the first, that he went through the corn fields; and his disciples plucked the ears of corn, and did eat, rubbing them in their hands. ²And certain of the Pharisees said unto them, Why do ye that which is not lawful to do on the sabbath days? ³And Jesus answering them said, Have ye not read so much as this, what David did, when himself was an hungred, and they which were with him; ⁴how he went into the house of God, and did take and eat the shewbread, and gave also to them that were with him; which it is not lawful to eat but for the priests alone? ⁵And he said unto them, That the Son of man is Lord also of the sabbath.

⁶And it came to pass also on another sabbath, that he entered into the synagogue and taught: and there was a man whose right hand was withered. ⁷And the scribes and Pharisees watched him, whether he would heal on the sabbath day; that they might find an accusation against him. ⁸But he knew their thoughts, and said to the man which had the withered hand, Rise up, and stand forth in the midst. And he arose and stood forth. ⁹Then said Jesus unto them, I will ask you one thing; Is it lawful on the sabbath days to do good, or to do evil? to save life, or to destroy it? ¹⁰And looking round about upon them all, he said unto the man, Stretch forth thy hand. And he did so: and his hand was restored whole as the other. ¹¹And they were filled with madness; and communed one with another what they might do to Jesus.

¹²And it came to pass in those days, that he went out into a mountain to pray, and continued all night in prayer to God. ¹³And when it was day, he called unto him his disciples: and of them he chose twelve, whom also he named apostles; ¹⁴Simon, (whom he also named Peter,) and Andrew his brother, James and John, Philip and Bartholomew, ¹⁵Matthew and Thomas, James the son of Alphæus, and Simon called Zelotes, ¹⁶and Judas the brother of James, and Judas Iscariot, which also was the traitor.

¹⁷And he came down with them, and stood in the plain, and the company of his disciples, and a great multitude of people out of all Judæa and Jerusalem, and from the sea coast of Tyre and Sidon, which came to hear him, and to be healed of their diseases; ¹⁸and they that were vexed with unclean spirits: and they were healed. ¹⁹And the whole multitude sought to touch him: for there went virtue out of him, and healed them all.

---

comparison.   **6:1–11** The Sabbath. Compare Matt 12:1–14; Mark 2:23–3:6 and notes.   **6:1** *The second . . . first*: better simply "the Sabbath" (MS tradition). *Corn*: wheat.   **6:2** *Not lawful . . . days*: cf. Exod 34:21.   **6:3–4** *What David . . . him*: see 1 Sam 21:1–6.   **6:3** *An hungred*: hungry.   **6:4** *Not lawful . . . alone*: see Lev 24:5–9.   **6:5** *Also*: better omitted (MS tradition).   **6:9** *One thing*: better omitted (MS tradition).   **6:10** *Whole as the other*: better omitted (MS tradition).   **6:11** *Madness*: or foolishness.   **6:12–16** Choosing the apostles. Compare Matt 10:1–4; Mark 3:13–19 notes. **6:13** *Apostles*: see Matt 10:2 note.   **6:15** *Zelotes*: the Zealot.   **6:16** *Judas the brother of James*: the same Greek construction is employed in v. 15 ("James the son of Alphaeus"). It likely means that Judas (also called Jude, so as not to confuse him with Judas Iscariot) had a father named James. KJV makes him James's brother, thereby linking him with the author of the book of Jude (cf. Jude 1). *Was the traitor*: alternatively "became the traitor."   **6:17–19** Healing the multitudes. Matthew introduces the Sermon on the Mount with a related summary statement about Jesus' ministry (4:23–25); in Mark (3:7–12), similar material immediately precedes the apostles' calling.   **6:17** *Tyre and Sidon*: see Mark 3:8 note.   **6:19** *Virtue*:

²⁰And he lifted up his eyes on his disciples, and said, Blessed be ye poor: for yours is the kingdom of God. ²¹Blessed are ye that hunger now: for ye shall be filled. Blessed are ye that weep now: for ye shall laugh. ²²Blessed are ye, when men shall hate you, and when they shall separate you from their company, and shall reproach you, and cast out your name as evil, for the Son of man's sake. ²³Rejoice ye in that day, and leap for joy: for, behold, your reward is great in heaven: for in the like manner did their fathers unto the prophets. ²⁴But woe unto you that are rich! for ye have received your consolation. ²⁵Woe unto you that are full! for ye shall hunger. Woe unto you that laugh now! for ye shall mourn and weep. ²⁶Woe unto you, when all men shall speak well of you! for so did their fathers to the false prophets.

²⁷But I say unto you which hear, Love your enemies, do good to them which hate you, ²⁸bless them that curse you, and pray for them which despitefully use you. ²⁹And unto him that smiteth thee on the one cheek offer also the other; and him that taketh away thy cloke forbid not to take thy coat also. ³⁰Give to every man that asketh of thee; and of him that taketh away thy goods ask them not again. ³¹And as ye would that men should do to you, do ye also to them likewise. ³²For if ye love them which love you, what thank have ye? for sinners also love those that love them. ³³And if ye do good to them which do good to you, what thank have ye? for sinners also do even the same. ³⁴And if ye lend to them of whom ye hope to receive, what thank have ye? for sinners also lend to sinners, to receive as much again. ³⁵But love ye your enemies, and do good, and lend, hoping for nothing again; and your reward shall be great, and ye shall be the children of the Highest: for he is kind unto the unthankful and to the evil. ³⁶Be ye therefore merciful, as your Father also is merciful.

³⁷Judge not, and ye shall not be judged: condemn not, and ye shall not be condemned: forgive, and ye shall be forgiven: ³⁸give, and it shall be given unto you; good measure, pressed down, and shaken together, and running over, shall men

power.   **6:20-49** Sermon on the Plain. Luke's version of Matthew's much longer Sermon on the Mount (chaps. 5-7). Like that sermon, this is directed at the disciples in the presence of the crowds (vv. 19-20; cf. Matt 5:1-2) and serves as a charter for the community Jesus has begun to form (5:1-11; 6:12-16).   **6:20-26** Beatitudes and woes. Verses 20-23 parallel Matt 5:3-12 (see notes); the woes of vv. 24-26 are unique to Luke.   **6:20** *Ye poor*: contrast Matthew's "poor in spirit" (5:3).   **6:21** *Hunger now*: contrast Matthew's "hunger . . . after righteousness" (5:6).   **6:25** *That are full*: better to add "now" (MS tradition), assimilating the phrase to v. 21a.   **6:26** *So did . . . prophets*: well-liked prophets were often said to be deceptive; cf. Isa 30:9-10; Jer 5:31; 6:14; etc.   **6:27-42** Reciprocal behavior and judgment. Compare Matt 5:39-42, 44-48; 7:1-5, 12; 10:24-25; 15:14 and notes. Verses 27-31 consist of eight commands (followed by a summarizing coda—the golden rule, v. 31) that urge the disciples to behave in accordance not with how they are treated but rather with what treatment they desire, outlawing positive as well as negative reciprocal behavior (vv. 32-34). A second series of eight commands restores the principle of reciprocation, but in different form: the disciples are to seek divine reward by behaving toward others in such a way as to emulate God, the perfect benefactor (vv. 35-38). The prohibition against judging others (v. 37) is necessarily qualified (vv. 39-42) because such ethical standards presuppose and require mutual judgment so that members of the community they govern can hold one another accountable to them; cf. Acts 4:32-5:11.   **6:34** *Lend*: Gk. *daneizō* (also v. 35), which refers to loaning money; cf. Exod 22:25; Lev 25:36-37; Deut 23:19-20.   **6:38** *Good measure . . . over*: the image seems to be of a scandalously generous merchant trying to get as much grain as possible into a measuring vessel, continuously adding more by alternately

give into your bosom. For with the same measure that ye mete withal it shall be measured to you again. ³⁹And he spake a parable unto them, Can the blind lead the blind? shall they not both fall into the ditch? ⁴⁰The disciple is not above his master: but every one that is perfect shall be as his master. ⁴¹And why beholdest thou the mote that is in thy brother's eye, but perceivest not the beam that is in thine own eye? ⁴²Either how canst thou say to thy brother, Brother, let me pull out the mote that is in thine eye, when thou thyself beholdest not the beam that is in thine own eye? Thou hypocrite, cast out first the beam out of thine own eye, and then shalt thou see clearly to pull out the mote that is in thy brother's eye.

⁴³For a good tree bringeth not forth corrupt fruit; neither doth a corrupt tree bring forth good fruit. ⁴⁴For every tree is known by his own fruit. For of thorns men do not gather figs, nor of a bramble bush gather they grapes. ⁴⁵A good man out of the good treasure of his heart bringeth forth that which is good; and an evil man out of the evil treasure of his heart bringeth forth that which is evil: for of the abundance of the heart his mouth speaketh.

⁴⁶And why call ye me, Lord, Lord, and do not the things which I say? ⁴⁷Whosoever cometh to me, and heareth my sayings, and doeth them, I will shew you to whom he is like: ⁴⁸he is like a man which built an house, and digged deep, and laid the foundation on a rock: and when the flood arose, the stream beat vehemently upon that house, and could not shake it: for it was founded upon a rock. ⁴⁹But he that heareth, and doeth not, is like a man that without a foundation built an house upon the earth; against which the stream did beat vehemently, and immediately it fell; and the ruin of that house was great.

7 Now when he had ended all his sayings in the audience of the people, he entered into Capernaum. ²And a certain centurion's servant, who was dear unto him, was sick, and ready to die. ³And when he heard of Jesus, he sent unto him the elders of the Jews, beseeching him that he would come and heal his servant. ⁴And when they came to Jesus, they besought him instantly, saying, That he was worthy for whom he should do this: ⁵for he loveth our nation, and he hath built us a synagogue. ⁶Then Jesus went with them. And when he was now not far from the house, the centurion sent friends to him, saying unto him, Lord, trouble not thyself: for I am not worthy that thou shouldest enter under my roof: ⁷wherefore neither thought I myself worthy to come unto thee: but say in a word, and my servant shall be healed. ⁸For I also am a man set under authority, having under me

---

compacting the contents and shaking it so the grain will distribute evenly throughout, and finally just letting the vessel overflow. **6:39** *Parable*: see Mark 4:2 note. **6:42** *Either*: better omitted (MS tradition). **6:43–49** Speaking and doing good. Compare Matt 12:33–35; 7:16–21, 24–27 and notes. Verses 43–45 link a good heart (see 1:66 note) to a good confession; vv. 46–49 link a good confession to good deeds. **6:43** *Good*: Gk. *kalon*, here "free from defect"; a different word (*agathos*) is used in v. 45. **6:48** *For it . . . rock*: better "for it was well built" (MS tradition). **7:1–10** Healing a centurion's servant. Compare Matt 8:5–13 and notes. Luke expands the parallels with Elisha's healing of the Gentile soldier Namaan (2 Kgs 5:1–19; cf. Luke 4:27; 5:12–16 and notes) by introducing Jewish intercessors between the centurion and Jesus (vv. 3–5; cf. 2 Kgs 5:2–8). The episode here exemplifies the ethical paradigm that Jesus presented (6:27–38, esp. vv. 27, 35), by showing the Jewish elders and Jesus reaching across ethnic lines to assist a commander of Rome's occupying military force, and by presenting his slave's healing as a divine reward for the commander's beneficence to the

soldiers, and I say unto one, Go, and he goeth; and to another, Come, and he cometh; and to my servant, Do this, and he doeth it. [9]When Jesus heard these things, he marvelled at him, and turned him about, and said unto the people that followed him, I say unto you, I have not found so great faith, no, not in Israel. [10]And they that were sent, returning to the house, found the servant whole that had been sick.

[11]And it came to pass the day after, that he went into a city called Nain; and many of his disciples went with him, and much people. [12]Now when he came nigh to the gate of the city, behold, there was a dead man carried out, the only son of his mother, and she was a widow: and much people of the city was with her. [13]And when the Lord saw her, he had compassion on her, and said unto her, Weep not. [14]And he came and touched the bier: and they that bare him stood still. And he said, Young man, I say unto thee, Arise. [15]And he that was dead sat up, and began to speak. And he delivered him to his mother. [16]And there came a fear on all: and they glorified God, saying, That a great prophet is risen up among us; and, That God hath visited his people. [17]And this rumour of him went forth throughout all Judæa, and throughout all the region round about.

[18]And the disciples of John shewed him of all these things. [19]And John calling unto him two of his disciples sent them to Jesus, saying, Art thou he that should come? or look we for another? [20]When the men were come unto him, they said, John Baptist hath sent us unto thee, saying, Art thou he that should come? or look we for another? [21]And in that same hour he cured many of their infirmities and plagues, and of evil spirits; and unto many that were blind he gave sight. [22]Then Jesus answering said unto them, Go your way, and tell John what things ye have seen and heard; how that the blind see, the lame walk, the lepers are cleansed, the deaf hear, the dead are raised, to the poor the gospel is preached. [23]And blessed is he, whosoever shall not be offended in me.

[24]And when the messengers of John were departed, he began to speak unto the people concerning John, What went ye out into the wilderness for to see? A reed shaken with the wind? [25]But what went ye out for to see? A man clothed in soft raiment? Behold, they which are gorgeously apparelled, and live delicately, are in kings' courts. [26]But what went ye out for to see? A prophet? Yea, I say unto you, and much more than a prophet. [27]This is he, of whom it is written, Behold, I send my messenger before thy face, which shall prepare thy way before thee. [28]For I say unto you, Among those that are born of women there is not a greater prophet than John the Baptist: but he that is least in the kingdom of God is greater than

---

Jewish nation.   **7:11–17** Raising a widow's son. This episode recalls Elijah's resurrection of a widow's son (1 Kgs 17:17–24; cf. Luke 4:25–26).   **7:11** *Nain*: in southern Galilee.   **7:12** *Widow*: as a sonless widow, she would have been socially and economically marginalized.   **7:13** *Weep not*: cf. 6:21. **7:16** *A great . . . us*: underscoring the parallels with Elijah, but also echoing Deut 18:15–18, about the prophet like Moses. *God hath . . . people*: cf. 1:68, 78.   **7:18–35** Jesus and John. Compare Matt 11:2–19 and notes.   **7:19** *Jesus*: better "the Lord" (MS tradition).   **7:21** *Plagues*: see Mark 3:10 note. **7:22** *How that . . . preached*: alluding to a number of oracles from Isaiah (e.g., 26:19; 29:18–19; 35:5–6; 61:1–2, quoted at Luke 4:18–19).   **7:23** *Offended*: see Mark 4:17 note.   **7:27** *Behold, I . . . thee*: Exod 23:20; Mal 3:1.   **7:28** *There is . . . Baptist*: better "there is none greater than John" (MS tradition).

he. ²⁹And all the people that heard him, and the publicans, justified God, being baptized with the baptism of John. ³⁰But the Pharisees and lawyers rejected the counsel of God against themselves, being not baptized of him.

³¹And the Lord said, Whereunto then shall I liken the men of this generation? and to what are they like? ³²They are like unto children sitting in the marketplace, and calling one to another, and saying, We have piped unto you, and ye have not danced; we have mourned to you, and ye have not wept. ³³For John the Baptist came neither eating bread nor drinking wine; and ye say, He hath a devil. ³⁴The Son of man is come eating and drinking; and ye say, Behold a gluttonous man, and a winebibber, a friend of publicans and sinners! ³⁵But wisdom is justified of all her children.

³⁶And one of the Pharisees desired him that he would eat with him. And he went into the Pharisee's house, and sat down to meat. ³⁷And, behold, a woman in the city, which was a sinner, when she knew that Jesus sat at meat in the Pharisee's house, brought an alabaster box of ointment, ³⁸and stood at his feet behind him weeping, and began to wash his feet with tears, and did wipe them with the hairs of her head, and kissed his feet, and anointed them with the ointment. ³⁹Now when the Pharisee which had bidden him saw it, he spake within himself, saying, This man, if he were a prophet, would have known who and what manner of woman this is that toucheth him: for she is a sinner. ⁴⁰And Jesus answering said unto him, Simon, I have somewhat to say unto thee. And he saith, Master, say on. ⁴¹There was a certain creditor which had two debtors: the one owed five hundred pence, and the other fifty. ⁴²And when they had nothing to pay, he frankly forgave them both. Tell me therefore, which of them will love him most? ⁴³Simon answered and said, I suppose that he, to whom he forgave most. And he said unto him, Thou hast rightly judged. ⁴⁴And he turned to the woman, and said unto Simon, Seest thou this woman? I entered into thine house, thou gavest me no water for my feet: but she hath washed my feet with tears, and wiped them with the hairs of her head. ⁴⁵Thou gavest me no kiss: but this woman since the time I came in hath not ceased to kiss my feet. ⁴⁶My head with oil thou didst not

---

7:30 *Lawyers*: i.e., legal authorities (probably those elsewhere called "scribes"). *Counsel*: purpose or plan. **7:31** *And the Lord said*: better omitted (MS tradition). **7:35** *But*: the Greek reads "and." *Wisdom is . . . children*: the Bible commonly figures wisdom (a grammatically feminine noun in Hebrew and Greek) as a woman; cf. Prov 1:20–21. Here she is a mother whose justice is shown by the quality of her "offspring" (Gk. *teknoi*; a different word is used in v. 32). *Justified*: cf. v. 29, where God is justified by those who are baptized. **7:36–50** A woman anoints Jesus. Compare Matt 26:6–13; Mark 14:3–9 and notes; John 12:1–8. In Luke, the episode exemplifies the kind of dismissive rejection that Jesus has just condemned (vv. 31–35). **7:36** *Sat down*: lit. "reclined" (at table), the customary posture for formal eating. **7:37** *A woman . . . sinner*: probably a prostitute. *The city*: Nain (cf. v. 11). *Ointment*: the costly container hints at its value. Unlike in the other gospels, hostility arises not because a valuable commodity is being wasted, but because the woman sensuously offering it is contaminated. **7:38** *Weeping*: like the widow (v. 13; cf. 6:21). **7:39** *If he were a prophet*: as the crowd acclaimed (v. 16). Since the Pharisee *spake within himself*, Jesus' subsequent "answer" demonstrates that he is indeed a prophet. **7:40** *Simon*: Jesus suddenly calls this previously anonymous Pharisee by name. As Joel Green observes, unlike his host (who has just called the woman "a sinner," v. 39) and others of "this generation" (v. 31; cf. 33–34), Jesus will not traffic in flippant epithets. **7:41** *Pence*: see Mark 14:5 note. **7:42** *Frankly*: better omitted (MS tradition). **7:44–46** *He turned . . . ointment*: Simon's neglect of culturally appropriate courtesies is outrageous; the woman, far from

anoint: but this woman hath anointed my feet with ointment. [47]Wherefore I say unto thee, Her sins, which are many, are forgiven; for she loved much: but to whom little is forgiven, the same loveth little. [48]And he said unto her, Thy sins are forgiven. [49]And they that sat at meat with him began to say within themselves, Who is this that forgiveth sins also? [50]And he said to the woman, Thy faith hath saved thee; go in peace.

8 And it came to pass afterward, that he went throughout every city and village, preaching and shewing the glad tidings of the kingdom of God: and the twelve were with him, [2]and certain women, which had been healed of evil spirits and infirmities, Mary called Magdalene, out of whom went seven devils, [3]and Joanna the wife of Chuza Herod's steward, and Susanna, and many others, which ministered unto him of their substance.

[4]And when much people were gathered together, and were come to him out of every city, he spake by a parable: [5]A sower went out to sow his seed: and as he sowed, some fell by the way side; and it was trodden down, and the fowls of the air devoured it. [6]And some fell upon a rock; and as soon as it was sprung up, it withered away, because it lacked moisture. [7]And some fell among thorns; and the thorns sprang up with it, and choked it. [8]And other fell on good ground, and sprang up, and bare fruit an hundredfold. And when he had said these things, he cried, He that hath ears to hear, let him hear.

[9]And his disciples asked him, saying, What might this parable be? [10]And he said, Unto you it is given to know the mysteries of the kingdom of God: but to others in parables; that seeing they might not see, and hearing they might not understand.

[11]Now the parable is this: The seed is the word of God. [12]Those by the way side are they that hear; then cometh the devil, and taketh away the word out of their hearts, lest they should believe and be saved. [13]They on the rock are they, which, when they hear, receive the word with joy; and these have no root, which for a while believe, and in time of temptation fall away. [14]And that which fell among thorns are they, which, when they have heard, go forth, and are choked with cares and riches and pleasures of this life, and bring no fruit to perfection. [15]But

---

deserving Simon's scorn as "a sinner," supplants him in the privileged position of host. **7:47** *Forgiven*: see 5:20 and note. **7:48** *Thy sins are forgiven*: see Mark 2:5 note. **8:1–3** Ministering women. **8:2** *Mary called Magdalene*: her name's derivation from the town of Magdala (on the Sea of Galilee's northwest shore) suggests she has no husband, children, or (living) father. There is no reason to identify this prominent follower of Jesus with the woman who just anointed him (Mary of Bethany, according to John 11:1–2) or the adulterous woman of John 8:1–11, though later interpretive traditions conflated all three. **8:3** *Steward*: household manager; an elevated position, though one often held by slaves (cf. 12:42–43). *Unto him*: better "unto them" (MS tradition). *Substance*: property. **8:4–21** Responding to God's word. **8:4–8** Parable of the Sower. Compare Matt 13:1–9; Mark 4:1–9 and notes. **8:9–10** The reason for parables. Compare Matt 13:10–15; Mark 4:10–12 and notes. Because Luke eliminates Mark's change of scene as well as the reference to "them that are without" (Mark 4:11), the crowd (v. 4) has access to the following discourse (vv. 9–18; cf. Mark 4:10–25), which Mark's Jesus spoke in secret to the disciples (4:10). While recognizing that Jesus' teaching alienates some, Luke portrays him as leaving the doors to conversion always open and thus cuts short Mark's quote from Isa 6:9–10, omitting "lest at any time they should be converted, and their sins should be forgiven them" (Mark 4:12). For Luke, such obstruction is satanic (cf. v. 12). **8:11–15** Interpreting the parable of the Sower. Compare Matt 13:18–23; Mark 4:13–20 and notes.

that on the good ground are they, which in an honest and good heart, having heard the word, keep it, and bring forth fruit with patience.

¹⁶No man, when he hath lighted a candle, covereth it with a vessel, or putteth it under a bed; but setteth it on a candlestick, that they which enter in may see the light. ¹⁷For nothing is secret, that shall not be made manifest; neither any thing hid, that shall not be known and come abroad. ¹⁸Take heed therefore how ye hear: for whosoever hath, to him shall be given; and whosoever hath not, from him shall be taken even that which he seemeth to have.

¹⁹Then came to him his mother and his brethren, and could not come at him for the press. ²⁰And it was told him by certain which said, Thy mother and thy brethren stand without, desiring to see thee. ²¹And he answered and said unto them, My mother and my brethren are these which hear the word of God, and do it.

²²Now it came to pass on a certain day, that he went into a ship with his disciples: and he said unto them, Let us go over unto the other side of the lake. And they launched forth. ²³But as they sailed he fell asleep: and there came down a storm of wind on the lake; and they were filled with water, and were in jeopardy. ²⁴And they came to him, and awoke him, saying, Master, master, we perish. Then he arose, and rebuked the wind and the raging of the water: and they ceased, and there was a calm. ²⁵And he said unto them, Where is your faith? And they being afraid wondered, saying one to another, What manner of man is this! for he commandeth even the winds and water, and they obey him.

²⁶And they arrived at the country of the Gadarenes, which is over against Galilee. ²⁷And when he went forth to land, there met him out of the city a certain man,

8:15 *In an honest and good heart*: see 6:43–49, where a good heart gives rise to a good confession (v. 45) and to consonant good deeds (vv. 46–49). *Good* and *honest* are Gk. *agathos* and *kalos*; cf. 6:43 and note, 45.   **8:16–18** Disclosing what is hidden. Compare Matt 13:12; Mark 4:21–25 and notes. The crowd's presence (vv. 4, 19; see 9–10 note) alters the implications of the Markan dominical sayings. Like Mark, Luke promises that the eschatological revelation of what is now obscure will magnify the distinction between those who do and do not embrace God's word, but unlike Mark he insists that everyone has equal opportunity to respond in obedience.   **8:17** *Come abroad*: come to light.   **8:18** *How ye hear*: altering Mark's "what ye hear" (4:24) in order to connect this episode with the interpretation of the parable of the Sower (vv. 11–15) and to invite the audience to choose the type of soil it will be. **8:19–21** Jesus' true relatives. Compare Matt 12:46–50; Mark 3:31–35. By concluding Jesus' discourse on the proper response to God's word (vv. 4–18) with the story of his cavalier treatment of his family (differently contextualized in Mark and Matthew), Luke clarifies the previous episode's implications (see vv. 16–18 note): whoever in the crowd responds obediently to God's word shares Mary's privileged position in relation to Jesus.   **8:22–25** Jesus calms the storm. Compare Matt 8:23–27 and note for parallels with Jonah; Mark 4:35–41 and notes. Parallels with Jesus' call of the first disciples (which also involved a voyage on Lake Gennesaret; cf. 5:1–11) invite the reader to ponder why their faith has not grown more, though the implied critique is softer than in Mark's version of the story.   **8:24** *Master, master, we perish*: Luke transforms the disciples' accusatory question in Mark (4:38) into a frightened cry. **8:25** *Where is your faith*: Luke moderates Jesus' brutal rebuke of the disciples as utterly faithless in Mark 4:40 (see note). *What manner of man is this*: lit. "Who is this?" See Mark 4:41 note.   **8:26–39** The Gerasene demoniac. Compare Matt 8:28–34; Mark 5:1–20 and notes. Luke's references to the demoniac's lack of clothing and house (v. 27), combined with his statement that the demon drives the man into the wilderness (v. 29), develop Mark's suggestion that the possession constitutes a social death (see Mark 5:2 note), by emphasizing the demoniac's rejection of even the most basic social conventions. Luke's replacement of Legion's fear of ejection "out of the country" with fear of being sent "into the deep" (v. 31; cf. Mark 5:10) softens Mark's intimation that Legion's possession symbolizes Rome's control of Palestine (see Mark 5:9 note).   **8:26** *Gadarenes*: better "Gerasenes" (MS tradition; also in v. 37). Gerasa

which had devils long time, and ware no clothes, neither abode in any house, but in the tombs. [28]When he saw Jesus, he cried out, and fell down before him, and with a loud voice said, What have I to do with thee, Jesus, thou Son of God most high? I beseech thee, torment me not. [29](For he had commanded the unclean spirit to come out of the man. For oftentimes it had caught him: and he was kept bound with chains and in fetters; and he brake the bands, and was driven of the devil into the wilderness.) [30]And Jesus asked him, saying, What is thy name? And he said, Legion: because many devils were entered into him. [31]And they besought him that he would not command them to go out into the deep.

[32]And there was there an herd of many swine feeding on the mountain: and they besought him that he would suffer them to enter into them. And he suffered them. [33]Then went the devils out of the man, and entered into the swine: and the herd ran violently down a steep place into the lake, and were choked. [34]When they that fed them saw what was done, they fled, and went and told it in the city and in the country. [35]Then they went out to see what was done; and came to Jesus, and found the man, out of whom the devils were departed, sitting at the feet of Jesus, clothed, and in his right mind: and they were afraid. [36]They also which saw it told them by what means he that was possessed of the devils was healed. [37]Then the whole multitude of the country of the Gadarenes round about besought him to depart from them; for they were taken with great fear: and he went up into the ship, and returned back again. [38]Now the man out of whom the devils were departed besought him that he might be with him: but Jesus sent him away, saying, [39]Return to thine own house, and shew how great things God hath done unto thee. And he went his way, and published throughout the whole city how great things Jesus had done unto him.

[40]And it came to pass, that, when Jesus was returned, the people gladly received him: for they were all waiting for him. [41]And, behold, there came a man named Jairus, and he was a ruler of the synagogue: and he fell down at Jesus' feet, and besought him that he would come into his house: [42]for he had one only daughter, about twelve years of age, and she lay a dying.

But as he went the people thronged him. [43]And a woman having an issue of blood twelve years, which had spent all her living upon physicians, neither could be healed of any, [44]came behind him, and touched the border of his garment: and immediately her issue of blood stanched. [45]And Jesus said, Who touched me? When all denied, Peter and they that were with him said, Master, the multitude throng thee and press thee, and sayest thou, Who touched me? [46]And Jesus said, Somebody hath touched me: for I perceive that virtue is gone out of me. [47]And

---

belonged to the Decapolis, a confederacy of Hellenistic cities east of Galilee, with a primarily Gentile population. In Luke, this is Jesus' only expedition to Gentile territory. **8:31** *Deep*: Gk. *abyssos*, referring to the place of demonic confinement; cf. Rev 9:1–3; 20:1–3 (KJV "bottomless pit"). **8:35** *Sitting at the feet of Jesus*: suggesting he had become Jesus' disciple; cf. 10:39; Acts 22:3. **8:40–56** Healing Jairus' daughter and the hemorrhaging woman. Compare Matt 9:18–26; Mark 5:21–43 and notes. **8:42** *Thronged*: lit. "choked" (cf. v. 33). **8:43** *Issue of blood*: vaginal bleeding, which would have made her a source of ritual contamination (cf. Lev 15:19–30). *Had spent . . . any*: perhaps better "could not be healed by physicians" (MS tradition). **8:45** *And they . . . him*: better omitted (MS tradition). *And sayest . . . me*: better omitted (MS tradition). **8:46** *Virtue*: power.

when the woman saw that she was not hid, she came trembling, and falling down before him, she declared unto him before all the people for what cause she had touched him, and how she was healed immediately. ⁴⁸And he said unto her, Daughter, be of good comfort: thy faith hath made thee whole; go in peace.

⁴⁹While he yet spake, there cometh one from the ruler of the synagogue's house, saying to him, Thy daughter is dead; trouble not the Master. ⁵⁰But when Jesus heard it, he answered him, saying, Fear not: believe only, and she shall be made whole. ⁵¹And when he came into the house, he suffered no man to go in, save Peter, and James, and John, and the father and the mother of the maiden. ⁵²And all wept, and bewailed her: but he said, Weep not; she is not dead, but sleepeth. ⁵³And they laughed him to scorn, knowing that she was dead. ⁵⁴And he put them all out, and took her by the hand, and called, saying, Maid, arise. ⁵⁵And her spirit came again, and she arose straightway: and he commanded to give her meat. ⁵⁶And her parents were astonished: but he charged them that they should tell no man what was done.

9 Then he called his twelve disciples together, and gave them power and author- ity over all devils, and to cure diseases. ²And he sent them to preach the king- dom of God, and to heal the sick. ³And he said unto them, Take nothing for your journey, neither staves, nor scrip, neither bread, neither money; neither have two coats apiece. ⁴And whatsoever house ye enter into, there abide, and thence depart. ⁵And whosoever will not receive you, when ye go out of that city, shake off the very dust from your feet for a testimony against them. ⁶And they departed, and went through the towns, preaching the gospel, and healing every where.

⁷Now Herod the tetrarch heard of all that was done by him: and he was per- plexed, because that it was said of some, that John was risen from the dead; ⁸and of some, that Elias had appeared; and of others, that one of the old prophets was risen again. ⁹And Herod said, John have I beheaded: but who is this, of whom I hear such things? And he desired to see him.

¹⁰And the apostles, when they were returned, told him all that they had done. And he took them, and went aside privately into a desert place belonging to the

---

8:48 *Be of good comfort*: better omitted (MS tradition).   **8:52** *Weep not*: cf. 7:13. The answering deri- sive laughter (v. 53) perverts the eschatological mirth promised to those who weep (6:21).   **8:54** *Put them all out, and*: better omitted (MS tradition).   **8:55** *Her spirit came again*: along with "knowing that she was dead" (v. 53), this phrase eliminates the ambiguity introduced by Jesus at v. 52; see Mark 5:39 note.   **9:1–50** Mission and Christology. This section juxtaposes material laying out the ministry (vv. 1–6, 10–17, 23–27, 37–42) and proper attitude (vv. 46–50) of Jesus' disciples to recur- ring attempts to grasp Jesus' identity (vv. 7–9, 18–22, 28–36, 43–45). It emphasizes the intercon- nectedness of confession that Jesus is Lord and obedience to his directives (cf. 6:46). The section culminates in a series of brief narratives detailing the disciples' failure to understand Jesus' mes- sage and respond appropriately to it.   **9:1–6** Sending out the Twelve. Compare Matt 10:1, 5–15; Mark 6:6b–13 and notes.   **9:3** *Staves*: better "a staff" (MS tradition), which Mark's Jesus permits (6:8). *Scrip*: a small satchel.   **9:7–9** Herod's perplexity. Compare Matt 14:1–2; Mark 6:14–16 and notes.   **9:7** *By him*: better omitted (MS tradition), thereby suggesting that the disciples' mission has brought Jesus to Herod's attention.   **9:8** *Was risen again*: "has been raised up"; cf. LXX Deut 18:15–18; Luke 7:16 and note.   **9:10–17** Feeding five thousand. Compare Matt 14:13–21; Mark 6:30–44 and notes. Luke's single feeding story—the other Synoptics have two—fulfills the promise of 6:21; cf. 1:53.   **9:10** *A desert . . . Bethsaida*: better "a city called Bethsaida" (MS tradition); the

city called Bethsaida. ¹¹And the people, when they knew it, followed him: and he received them, and spake unto them of the kingdom of God, and healed them that had need of healing. ¹²And when the day began to wear away, then came the twelve, and said unto him, Send the multitude away, that they may go into the towns and country round about, and lodge, and get victuals: for we are here in a desert place. ¹³But he said unto them, Give ye them to eat. And they said, We have no more but five loaves and two fishes; except we should go and buy meat for all this people. ¹⁴For they were about five thousand men. And he said to his disciples, Make them sit down by fifties in a company. ¹⁵And they did so, and made them all sit down. ¹⁶Then he took the five loaves and the two fishes, and looking up to heaven, he blessed them, and brake, and gave to the disciples to set before the multitude. ¹⁷And they did eat, and were all filled: and there was taken up of fragments that remained to them twelve baskets.

¹⁸And it came to pass, as he was alone praying, his disciples were with him: and he asked them, saying, Whom say the people that I am? ¹⁹They answering said, John the Baptist; but some say, Elias; and others say, that one of the old prophets is risen again. ²⁰He said unto them, But whom say ye that I am? Peter answering said, The Christ of God. ²¹And he straitly charged them, and commanded them to tell no man that thing; ²²saying, The Son of man must suffer many things, and be rejected of the elders and chief priests and scribes, and be slain, and be raised the third day.

²³And he said to them all, If any man will come after me, let him deny himself, and take up his cross daily, and follow me. ²⁴For whosoever will save his life shall lose it: but whosoever will lose his life for my sake, the same shall save it. ²⁵For what is a man advantaged, if he gain the whole world, and lose himself, or be cast away? ²⁶For whosoever shall be ashamed of me and of my words, of him shall the Son of man be ashamed, when he shall come in his own glory, and in his Father's, and of the holy angels. ²⁷But I tell you of a truth, there be some standing here, which shall not taste of death, till they see the kingdom of God.

²⁸And it came to pass about an eight days after these sayings, he took Peter and John and James, and went up into a mountain to pray. ²⁹And as he prayed, the fashion of his countenance was altered, and his raiment was white and glistering. ³⁰And, behold, there talked with him two men, which were Moses and Elias: ³¹who appeared in glory, and spake of his decease which he should accomplish at

---

additional material was added by scribes to harmonize vv. 10 and 12. *Bethsaida* is just northeast of the Sea of Galilee. **9:18–22** Peter's confession and the first prediction of Jesus' death and resurrection. Compare Matt 16:13–23; Mark 8:27–33 and notes. Luke eliminates Peter's and Jesus' mutual rebukes (Mark 8:32–33). **9:19** *John the Baptist . . . again*: cf. vv. 7–9 and notes. **9:23–27** Conditions of discipleship. Compare Matt 16:24–28; 10:38–39; Mark 8:34–9:1 and notes. **9:23** *Daily*: this addition to the Markan dominical saying makes Jesus' speech figurative, pushing actual martyrdom from view. **9:26** *Son of man . . . angels*: cf. Dan 7:13–14. **9:28–36** Transfiguration. Compare Matt 17:1–8; Mark 9:2–8 and notes. **9:28** *Eight days after*: recalling the temporal framework for the Feast of Tabernacles (Lev 23:36); cf. v. 33. **9:29** *The fashion . . . altered*: clarifying Mark's latent parallel between Jesus and Moses (Exod 34:29–35). **9:31** *Decease*: Gk. *exodos*, lit. "departure." It can refer to a departure from life (cf. 2 Pet 1:15), but it is also a key LXX term for Israel's escape from Egypt. Luke suggests that Jesus' impending journey to Jerusalem (cf. v. 51) and death there is an act

Jerusalem. [32]But Peter and they that were with him were heavy with sleep: and when they were awake, they saw his glory, and the two men that stood with him. [33]And it came to pass, as they departed from him, Peter said unto Jesus, Master, it is good for us to be here: and let us make three tabernacles; one for thee, and one for Moses, and one for Elias: not knowing what he said. [34]While he thus spake, there came a cloud, and overshadowed them: and they feared as they entered into the cloud. [35]And there came a voice out of the cloud, saying, This is my beloved Son: hear him. [36]And when the voice was past, Jesus was found alone. And they kept it close, and told no man in those days any of those things which they had seen.

[37]And it came to pass, that on the next day, when they were come down from the hill, much people met him. [38]And, behold, a man of the company cried out, saying, Master, I beseech thee, look upon my son: for he is mine only child. [39]And, lo, a spirit taketh him, and he suddenly crieth out; and it teareth him that he foameth again, and bruising him hardly departeth from him. [40]And I besought thy disciples to cast him out; and they could not. [41]And Jesus answering said, O faithless and perverse generation, how long shall I be with you, and suffer you? Bring thy son hither. [42]And as he was yet a coming, the devil threw him down, and tare him. And Jesus rebuked the unclean spirit, and healed the child, and delivered him again to his father. [43]And they were all amazed at the mighty power of God.

But while they wondered every one at all things which Jesus did, he said unto his disciples, [44]Let these sayings sink down into your ears: for the Son of man shall be delivered into the hands of men. [45]But they understood not this saying, and it was hid from them, that they perceived it not: and they feared to ask him of that saying.

[46]Then there arose a reasoning among them, which of them should be greatest. [47]And Jesus, perceiving the thought of their heart, took a child, and set him by him, [48]and said unto them, Whosoever shall receive this child in my name receiveth me: and whosoever shall receive me receiveth him that sent me: for he that is least among you all, the same shall be great. [49]And John answered and said, Master, we saw one casting out devils in thy name; and we forbad him, because he followeth

---

of liberation akin to God's deliverance of Israel from Egypt.   **9:33** *As they . . . him*: this addition to Mark's version hints that Peter hopes to lengthen the visitation. Complementarily, the use of Gk. *exodos* (v. 31) and the echo of Lev 23:26 (v. 28) suggest that he proposes to celebrate Israel's exodus from Egypt according to the mandate of Lev 23:42–43 (see Mark 9:5–6 note).   **9:35** *Beloved Son*: cf. 3:22; but "chosen son" is better (MS tradition). *Hear him*: cf. Deut 18:15.   **9:37–50** The disciples' failure. Compare Matt 17:14–23; 18:1–5; Mark 9:14–41 and notes.   **9:39** *Teareth*: throws down (cf. v. 42).   **9:41** *O faithless . . . generation*: Jesus' address, which echoes Deut 32:5, is probably directed at the disciples (cf. 8:25) for their failure to exercise the "authority" over devils just granted them (v. 1).   **9:43–44** *And they . . . men*: while the others wonder at Jesus' power, Jesus insists on his impending suffering. Luke's omission of any reference to resurrection in this second passion prediction underscores that insistence (cf. Matt 17:23; Mark 9:31).   **9:45** *It was . . . not*: perhaps suggesting Satan has snatched "the word" from the disciples (cf. 8:12).   **9:46** *Reasoning*: argument.   **9:47** *Child*: children held low social status in the ancient Mediterranean world.   **9:48** *Shall be great*: better "is great" (MS tradition).   **9:49** *Master, we . . . us*: ironic, given the disciples' own recent exorcistic failure

not with us. [50]And Jesus said unto him, Forbid him not: for he that is not against us is for us.

[51]And it came to pass, when the time was come that he should be received up, he stedfastly set his face to go to Jerusalem, [52]and sent messengers before his face: and they went, and entered into a village of the Samaritans, to make ready for him. [53]And they did not receive him, because his face was as though he would go to Jerusalem. [54]And when his disciples James and John saw this, they said, Lord, wilt thou that we command fire to come down from heaven, and consume them, even as Elias did? [55]But he turned, and rebuked them, and said, Ye know not what manner of spirit ye are of. [56]For the Son of man is not come to destroy men's lives, but to save them. And they went to another village.

[57]And it came to pass, that, as they went in the way, a certain man said unto him, Lord, I will follow thee whithersoever thou goest. [58]And Jesus said unto him, Foxes have holes, and birds of the air have nests; but the Son of man hath not where to lay his head. [59]And he said unto another, Follow me. But he said, Lord, suffer me first to go and bury my father. [60]Jesus said unto him, Let the dead bury their dead: but go thou and preach the kingdom of God. [61]And another also said, Lord, I will follow thee; but let me first go bid them farewell, which are at home at my house. [62]And Jesus said unto him, No man, having put his hand to the plough, and looking back, is fit for the kingdom of God.

10 After these things the Lord appointed other seventy also, and sent them two and two before his face into every city and place, whither he himself would come. [2]Therefore said he unto them, The harvest truly is great, but the labourers are few: pray ye therefore the Lord of the harvest, that he would send forth labourers into his harvest. [3]Go your ways: behold, I send you forth as lambs

---

(v. 40) and Jesus' demand that they welcome others in his name (v. 48).   **9:50** *He that . . . for us*: a better reading of the MS tradition replaces "us" with "you." Jesus reverses this saying when confronting those who slander his own ministry of exorcism (11:23).
     9:51–19:44 Journey to Jerusalem. This long section traces Jesus' trek toward Jerusalem (alluded to in 9:31), culminating in his approach and his prophecy of the city's destruction. The circuitous journey gives him opportunity to continue instructing his obtuse disciples about God's kingdom.   **9:51–56** A Samaritan village rejects Jesus.   **9:51** *Received up*: alluding to Jesus' ascension (see 24:51; Acts 1:6–11) and perhaps—given this chapter's copious references to and parallels with the Elijah cycle (vv. 8, 19, 30, 33, 54, 59–62 and notes)—to Elijah's ascension at 2 Kgs 2:1–12. **9:52** *Samaritans*: see Matt 10:5 note. Their refusal to recognize the Jerusalem temple explains the refusal to host Jesus on his journey there.   **9:54** *Wilt thou . . . them*: contradicting Jesus' directive of v. 5. *As Elias did*: better omitted (MS tradition), leaving implicit the allusion to Elijah's confrontation of King Ahaziah in Samaria (2 Kgs 1).   **9:55–56** *And said . . . them*: better omitted (MS tradition). **9:57–62** How to follow Jesus. Compare Matt 8:19–22 and notes.   **9:57** *Lord*: better omitted (MS tradition).   **9:59–62** *Suffer me . . . God*: parallels with Elijah's call of Elisha (cf. 1 Kgs 19:19–21) are more extensive here than in Matthew's version.   **10:1–16** The ministry of the seventy(-two). This section incorporates material from elsewhere in the synoptic tradition, especially from the accounts of the sending out of the Twelve; cf. Matt 9:37–38; 10:8–16, 40; 11:21–23; Mark 6:7–12; Luke 9:1–6. **10:1** *Seventy*: better "seventy-two," also at v. 17 (MS tradition). Since seventy-two is the total number in the Table of Nations from LXX Gen 10 (MT has seventy), their mission foreshadows the early church's mission to Gentiles (note the privileging of Gentile cities in vv. 13–15). Analogously, the Twelve's earlier mission symbolizes outreach to (the twelve tribes of) Israel.   **10:2** *Harvest*: see

among wolves. ⁴Carry neither purse, nor scrip, nor shoes: and salute no man by the way. ⁵And into whatsoever house ye enter, first say, Peace be to this house. ⁶And if the son of peace be there, your peace shall rest upon it: if not, it shall turn to you again. ⁷And in the same house remain, eating and drinking such things as they give: for the labourer is worthy of his hire. Go not from house to house. ⁸And into whatsoever city ye enter, and they receive you, eat such things as are set before you: ⁹and heal the sick that are therein, and say unto them, The kingdom of God is come nigh unto you. ¹⁰But into whatsoever city ye enter, and they receive you not, go your ways out into the streets of the same, and say, ¹¹Even the very dust of your city, which cleaveth on us, we do wipe off against you: notwithstanding be ye sure of this, that the kingdom of God is come nigh unto you. ¹²But I say unto you, that it shall be more tolerable in that day for Sodom, than for that city.

¹³Woe unto thee, Chorazin! woe unto thee, Bethsaida! for if the mighty works had been done in Tyre and Sidon, which have been done in you, they had a great while ago repented, sitting in sackcloth and ashes. ¹⁴But it shall be more tolerable for Tyre and Sidon at the judgment, than for you. ¹⁵And thou, Capernaum, which art exalted to heaven, shalt be thrust down to hell. ¹⁶He that heareth you heareth me; and he that despiseth you despiseth me; and he that despiseth me despiseth him that sent me.

¹⁷And the seventy returned again with joy, saying, Lord, even the devils are subject unto us through thy name. ¹⁸And he said unto them, I beheld Satan as lightning fall from heaven. ¹⁹Behold, I give unto you power to tread on serpents and scorpions, and over all the power of the enemy: and nothing shall by any means hurt you. ²⁰Notwithstanding in this rejoice not, that the spirits are subject unto you; but rather rejoice, because your names are written in heaven.

²¹In that hour Jesus rejoiced in spirit, and said, I thank thee, O Father, Lord of heaven and earth, that thou hast hid these things from the wise and prudent, and hast revealed them unto babes: even so, Father; for so it seemed good in thy sight. ²²All things are delivered to me of my Father: and no man knoweth who the Son is, but the Father; and who the Father is, but the Son, and he to whom the Son will

---

Mark 4:29 note.   **10:4** *Scrip*: a small satchel. *Salute no man by the way*: compare Elisha's instruction to Gehazi (2 Kgs 4:29).   **10:7** *Go not from house to house*: see Mark 6:10 note.   **10:11** *Even the very dust . . . against you*: see Mark 6:11 note.   **10:12** *Sodom*: see Matt 10:15 note.   **10:13** *Woe unto thee . . . ashes*: *Chorazin* and *Bethsaida*, like Capernaum (v. 15), are Galilean cities; *Tyre* and *Sidon* are Gentile cities in Phoenicia whose inhabitants had visited Galilee to see Jesus (6:17). While the disciples crave the destruction of Samaritan villages that do not welcome Jesus (9:54), Jesus foretells woe for Galilean cities like Capernaum, which embraced him (cf. 4:23, 31–44; 7:1–10) but apparently did not repent.   **10:15** *And thou . . . hell*: see Matt 11:23 note; cf. Isa 14:12–15.   **10:17–24** The return of the seventy(-two). Verses 21–22 parallel Matt 11:25–27 (see notes); vv. 23–24 parallel Matt 13:16–17 (see v. 17 note).   **10:18** *I beheld . . . heaven*: echoing Isa 14:12: "How art thou fallen from heaven, O Lucifer, son of the morning!" The tradition equating Lucifer with Satan and taking the OT passage as a reference to Satan's primeval rebellion and expulsion from heaven probably postdates Luke and may even be influenced by (a misreading of) this verse. Here Jesus' echo of Isaiah draws out the cosmic implications of the seventy-two's subjugation of devils, which augurs Satan's defeat. It further links that defeat with the downfall of unrepentant cities such as Capernaum, whose future ruin Jesus has just prophesied with an echo of the same Isaianic passage (see v. 15 and note).   **10:19** *Give*: better "have given" (MS tradition).   **10:20** *Your names . . . heaven*: for the OT image of a

reveal him. ²³And he turned him unto his disciples, and said privately, Blessed are the eyes which see the things that ye see: ²⁴for I tell you, that many prophets and kings have desired to see those things which ye see, and have not seen them; and to hear those things which ye hear, and have not heard them.

²⁵And, behold, a certain lawyer stood up, and tempted him, saying, Master, what shall I do to inherit eternal life? ²⁶He said unto him, What is written in the law? how readest thou? ²⁷And he answering said, Thou shalt love the Lord thy God with all thy heart, and with all thy soul, and with all thy strength, and with all thy mind; and thy neighbour as thyself. ²⁸And he said unto him, Thou hast answered right: this do, and thou shalt live. ²⁹But he, willing to justify himself, said unto Jesus, And who is my neighbour? ³⁰And Jesus answering said, A certain man went down from Jerusalem to Jericho, and fell among thieves, which stripped him of his raiment, and wounded him, and departed, leaving him half dead. ³¹And by chance there came down a certain priest that way: and when he saw him, he passed by on the other side. ³²And likewise a Levite, when he was at the place, came and looked on him, and passed by on the other side. ³³But a certain Samaritan, as he journeyed, came where he was: and when he saw him, he had compassion on him, ³⁴and went to him, and bound up his wounds, pouring in oil and wine, and set him on his own beast, and brought him to an inn, and took care of him. ³⁵And on the morrow when he departed, he took out two pence, and gave them to the host, and said unto him, Take care of him; and whatsoever thou spendest more, when I come again, I will repay thee. ³⁶Which now of these three, thinkest thou, was neighbour unto him that fell among the thieves? ³⁷And he said, He that shewed mercy on him. Then said Jesus unto him, Go, and do thou likewise.

³⁸Now it came to pass, as they went, that he entered into a certain village: and a certain woman named Martha received him into her house. ³⁹And she had a sister called Mary, which also sat at Jesus' feet, and heard his word. ⁴⁰But Martha was cumbered about much serving, and came to him, and said, Lord, dost thou not care that my sister hath left me to serve alone? bid her therefore that she help me. ⁴¹And Jesus answered and said unto her, Martha, Martha, thou art careful and troubled about many things: ⁴²but one thing is needful: and Mary hath chosen that good part, which shall not be taken away from her.

---

divine roll of the living or righteous, see Exod 32:32–33; Ps 69:28; Dan 12:1.   **10:24** *Desired to see . . . heard them*: cf. 8:10.   **10:25–37** Parable of the Good Samaritan. The parable is unique to Luke, but in Matt 22:34–40 and Mark 12:28–31 (see notes) a scribe or lawyer asks a different question that prompts a similar response.   **10:25** *And, behold*: suggesting an interruption. *Tempted*: tested.   **10:27** *Thou shalt love . . . thyself*: combining Deut 6:4–5 (the opening sentences of the Shema—the major Jewish declaration of belief) and Lev 19:18.   **10:31** *Passed . . . other side*: here and in v. 32, presumably to avoid contamination from what appeared to be a corpse ("half dead," v. 30); cf. Num 19:11–13.   **10:32** *Levite*: one belonging to the tribe of Levi, but not a priestly descendent of Aaron. Levites commonly fulfilled lesser temple functions.   **10:33** *Samaritan*: cf. 9:51–56; see Matt 10:5 note.   **10:35** *Pence*: see Mark 14:5 note.   **10:38–42** Mary and Martha. They are identified as Lazarus's sisters in John 11.   **10:39** *Sat at Jesus' feet . . . word*: i.e., learned as a disciple; cf. Acts 22:3. *Jesus'*: better "the Lord's" (MS tradition).   **10:40** *Cumbered about*: distracted or burdened by.   **10:41** *Jesus*: better "the Lord" (MS tradition). *Careful*: anxious.

11 And it came to pass, that, as he was praying in a certain place, when he ceased, one of his disciples said unto him, Lord, teach us to pray, as John also taught his disciples. ²And he said unto them, When ye pray, say, Our Father which art in heaven, Hallowed be thy name. Thy kingdom come. Thy will be done, as in heaven, so in earth. ³Give us day by day our daily bread. ⁴And forgive us our sins; for we also forgive every one that is indebted to us. And lead us not into temptation; but deliver us from evil.

⁵And he said unto them, Which of you shall have a friend, and shall go unto him at midnight, and say unto him, Friend, lend me three loaves; ⁶for a friend of mine in his journey is come to me, and I have nothing to set before him? ⁷And he from within shall answer and say, Trouble me not: the door is now shut, and my children are with me in bed; I cannot rise and give thee. ⁸I say unto you, Though he will not rise and give him, because he is his friend, yet because of his importunity he will rise and give him as many as he needeth. ⁹And I say unto you, Ask, and it shall be given you; seek, and ye shall find; knock, and it shall be opened unto you. ¹⁰For every one that asketh receiveth; and he that seeketh findeth; and to him that knocketh it shall be opened. ¹¹If a son shall ask bread of any of you that is a father, will he give him a stone? or if he ask a fish, will he for a fish give him a serpent? ¹²Or if he shall ask an egg, will he offer him a scorpion? ¹³If ye then, being evil, know how to give good gifts unto your children: how much more shall your heavenly Father give the Holy Spirit to them that ask him?

¹⁴And he was casting out a devil, and it was dumb. And it came to pass, when the devil was gone out, the dumb spake; and the people wondered. ¹⁵But some of them said, He casteth out devils through Beelzebub the chief of the devils. ¹⁶And others, tempting him, sought of him a sign from heaven. ¹⁷But he, knowing their thoughts, said unto them, Every kingdom divided against itself is brought to desolation; and a house divided against a house falleth. ¹⁸If Satan also be divided against himself, how shall his kingdom stand? because ye say that I cast out devils through Beelzebub. ¹⁹And if I by Beelzebub cast out devils, by whom do your sons cast them out? therefore shall they be your judges. ²⁰But if I with the finger of God cast out devils, no doubt the kingdom of God is come upon you. ²¹When a strong man armed keepeth his palace, his goods are in peace: ²²but when a stronger than he shall come upon him, and overcome him, he taketh from him all his armour wherein he trusted, and divideth his spoils. ²³He that is not with me is against me: and he that gathereth not with me scattereth.

11:1–13 Prayer. Verses 1–4, the Lord's Prayer, parallel Matt 6:9–13 (see notes); vv. 9–13 parallel Matt 7:7–11.   **11:2** *Our Father . . . earth*: better "Father, hallowed be thy name. Thy kingdom come" (MS tradition), which later scribes assimilated to Matthew.   **11:4** *But deliver . . . evil*: better omitted (MS tradition) as another scribal assimilation.   **11:8** *Importunity*: lit. "shamelessness," referring either to the petitioner's begging for bread late at night (so KJV) or to the shamelessness the petitioned neighbor would demonstrate were he to refuse the request. The parable's placement next to Jesus' prayer, which linked God's reputation (v. 2) with his provision of bread (v. 3), favors the latter.   **11:11** *If a son . . . serpent*: according to a better reading of the MS tradition, the request for bread is omitted and Jesus begins with the request for a fish.   **11:13** *Give the Holy Spirit*: anticipating Acts 2:1–4; cf. Luke 24:49; Acts 1:8.   **11:14–26** The Beelzebub controversy. Compare Matt 12:22–30, 43–45 and notes; Mark 3:22–30 and notes.   **11:20** *The finger of God*: cf. Exod 8:19.   **11:23** *He that . . . against*

²⁴When the unclean spirit is gone out of a man, he walketh through dry places, seeking rest; and finding none, he saith, I will return unto my house whence I came out. ²⁵And when he cometh, he findeth it swept and garnished. ²⁶Then goeth he, and taketh to him seven other spirits more wicked than himself; and they enter in, and dwell there: and the last state of that man is worse than the first.

²⁷And it came to pass, as he spake these things, a certain woman of the company lifted up her voice, and said unto him, Blessed is the womb that bare thee, and the paps which thou hast sucked. ²⁸But he said, Yea rather, blessed are they that hear the word of God, and keep it.

²⁹And when the people were gathered thick together, he began to say, This is an evil generation: they seek a sign; and there shall no sign be given it, but the sign of Jonas the prophet. ³⁰For as Jonas was a sign unto the Ninevites, so shall also the Son of man be to this generation. ³¹The queen of the south shall rise up in the judgment with the men of this generation, and condemn them: for she came from the utmost parts of the earth to hear the wisdom of Solomon; and, behold, a greater than Solomon is here. ³²The men of Nineve shall rise up in the judgment with this generation, and shall condemn it: for they repented at the preaching of Jonas; and, behold, a greater than Jonas is here.

³³No man, when he hath lighted a candle, putteth it in a secret place, neither under a bushel, but on a candlestick, that they which come in may see the light. ³⁴The light of the body is the eye: therefore when thine eye is single, thy whole body also is full of light; but when thine eye is evil, thy body also is full of darkness. ³⁵Take heed therefore that the light which is in thee be not darkness. ³⁶If thy whole body therefore be full of light, having no part dark, the whole shall be full of light, as when the bright shining of a candle doth give thee light.

³⁷And as he spake, a certain Pharisee besought him to dine with him: and he went in, and sat down to meat. ³⁸And when the Pharisee saw it, he marvelled that he had not first washed before dinner. ³⁹And the Lord said unto him, Now do ye Pharisees make clean the outside of the cup and the platter; but your inward part is full of ravening and wickedness. ⁴⁰Ye fools, did not he that made that which is without make that which is within also? ⁴¹But rather give alms of such things as

---

me: cf. 9:50.   **11:24–26** *When the unclean spirit . . . first*: balancing the triumphalism of 10:17–20. **11:25** *Garnished*: put in order or decorated.   **11:27–28** Blessed keepers of God's word. Unique to Luke, but the Beelzebub episode in Mark closes with a similar slight of Jesus' mother (3:31–35). **11:27** *Blessed is . . . sucked*: cf. 1:42.   **11:28** *Keep*: Gk. *phylassō*, "guard," the word used in Jesus' metaphorical discussion of exorcism (v. 21).   **11:29–36** Seeking signs. Compare Matt 12:38–42; 16:1, 4; 5:15; 6:22–23 and notes; Mark 8:11–12.   **11:29** *Seek a sign*: cf. v. 16.   **11:30** *Ninevites*: the Gentiles to whom Jonah preached; see Jonah 3.   **11:31** *Queen of the south*: the Queen of Sheba; see 1 Kgs 10:1–13.   **11:33** *No man . . . light*: cf. 8:16. *Secret place*: or "cellar" (MS tradition). *Bushel*: a vessel for measuring grain.   **11:34** *Eye is evil . . . darkness*: recalling "evil generation" (v. 29). The association of the *single* and *evil eye* with generosity and greed, respectively (see Matt 6:22–23 notes), motivates Luke's inclusion of the Pharisee's dinner invitation (v. 37) and anticipates Jesus' condemnation of this Pharisee and his colleagues for rapaciousness (vv. 39, 41).   **11:37–54** Jesus attacks Pharisees and lawyers. Compare Matt 23:1–36 and notes.   **11:39** *Ye Pharisees . . . platter*: referring to ritual ablutions (see Mark 7:4 note), as in v. 38. *Wickedness*: cf. v. 34 (KJV "evil").   **11:41** *Such things . . . have*: lit.

ye have; and, behold, all things are clean unto you. ⁴²But woe unto you, Pharisees! for ye tithe mint and rue and all manner of herbs, and pass over judgment and the love of God: these ought ye to have done, and not to leave the other undone. ⁴³Woe unto you, Pharisees! for ye love the uppermost seats in the synagogues, and greetings in the markets. ⁴⁴Woe unto you, scribes and Pharisees, hypocrites! for ye are as graves which appear not, and the men that walk over them are not aware of them.

⁴⁵Then answered one of the lawyers, and said unto him, Master, thus saying thou reproachest us also. ⁴⁶And he said, Woe unto you also, ye lawyers! for ye lade men with burdens grievous to be borne, and ye yourselves touch not the burdens with one of your fingers. ⁴⁷Woe unto you! for ye build the sepulchres of the prophets, and your fathers killed them. ⁴⁸Truly ye bear witness that ye allow the deeds of your fathers: for they indeed killed them, and ye build their sepulchres. ⁴⁹Therefore also said the wisdom of God, I will send them prophets and apostles, and some of them they shall slay and persecute: ⁵⁰that the blood of all the prophets, which was shed from the foundation of the world, may be required of this generation; ⁵¹from the blood of Abel unto the blood of Zacharias, which perished between the altar and the temple: verily I say unto you, It shall be required of this generation. ⁵²Woe unto you, lawyers! for ye have taken away the key of knowledge: ye entered not in yourselves, and them that were entering in ye hindered. ⁵³And as he said these things unto them, the scribes and the Pharisees began to urge him vehemently, and to provoke him to speak of many things: ⁵⁴laying wait for him, and seeking to catch something out of his mouth, that they might accuse him.

12 In the mean time, when there were gathered together an innumerable multitude of people, insomuch that they trode one upon another, he began to say unto his disciples first of all, Beware ye of the leaven of the Pharisees, which is hypocrisy. ²For there is nothing covered, that shall not be revealed; neither hid, that shall not be known. ³Therefore whatsoever ye have spoken in darkness shall be heard in the light; and that which ye have spoken in the ear in closets shall be proclaimed upon the housetops.

⁴And I say unto you my friends, Be not afraid of them that kill the body, and after that have no more that they can do. ⁵But I will forewarn you whom ye shall fear: Fear him, which after he hath killed hath power to cast into hell; yea, I say

---

"the things within." **11:42** *Tithe mint . . . herbs*: see Deut 14:22. **11:44** *Scribes and . . . hypocrites*: better omitted (MS tradition). *As graves*: i.e., contaminating (cf. Num 19:11–13). **11:46** *Lade*: load down. **11:47** *Sepulchres*: cf. v. 44 (KJV "graves"). **11:49** *Also said . . . send*: in Matt 23:34 Jesus sends the prophets, but the early church sometimes equated him with God's wisdom; cf. John 1:1–18 and notes. *Some of them . . . persecute*: the persecution and slaying of prophets is a common biblical motif (e.g., Neh 9:26; Jer 2:30). **11:51** *Blood of Abel*: see Gen 4:8–10. *Blood of Zacharias*: see 2 Chr 24:20–22. Jesus refers to the first and last murders of the Hebrew Bible (see Matt 23:35 note). **11:53** *And as . . . them*: better "and when he went outside" (MS tradition), forming an inclusive frame with v. 37. *Urge*: lit. "be hostile toward." **11:54** *That they might accuse him*: better omitted (MS tradition). **12:1–12** Integrity amid persecution. The introductory statement about yeast finds a parallel in Matt 16:6, 12; Mark 8:15. For the other material, cf. Matt 10:26–33, 19–20; 12:32 and notes. **12:2** *There is . . . known*: cf. 8:17. **12:3** *In the ear*: in whispers. **12:5** *Hell*: see Mark 9:43

unto you, Fear him. ⁶Are not five sparrows sold for two farthings, and not one of them is forgotten before God? ⁷But even the very hairs of your head are all numbered. Fear not therefore: ye are of more value than many sparrows.

⁸Also I say unto you, Whosoever shall confess me before men, him shall the Son of man also confess before the angels of God: ⁹but he that denieth me before men shall be denied before the angels of God. ¹⁰And whosoever shall speak a word against the Son of man, it shall be forgiven him: but unto him that blasphemeth against the Holy Ghost it shall not be forgiven. ¹¹And when they bring you unto the synagogues, and unto magistrates, and powers, take ye no thought how or what thing ye shall answer, or what ye shall say: ¹²for the Holy Ghost shall teach you in the same hour what ye ought to say.

¹³And one of the company said unto him, Master, speak to my brother, that he divide the inheritance with me. ¹⁴And he said unto him, Man, who made me a judge or a divider over you? ¹⁵And he said unto them, Take heed, and beware of covetousness: for a man's life consisteth not in the abundance of the things which he possesseth. ¹⁶And he spake a parable unto them, saying, The ground of a certain rich man brought forth plentifully: ¹⁷and he thought within himself, saying, What shall I do, because I have no room where to bestow my fruits? ¹⁸And he said, This will I do: I will pull down my barns, and build greater; and there will I bestow all my fruits and my goods. ¹⁹And I will say to my soul, Soul, thou hast much goods laid up for many years; take thine ease, eat, drink, and be merry. ²⁰But God said unto him, Thou fool, this night thy soul shall be required of thee: then whose shall those things be, which thou hast provided? ²¹So is he that layeth up treasure for himself, and is not rich toward God.

²²And he said unto his disciples, Therefore I say unto you, Take no thought for your life, what ye shall eat; neither for the body, what ye shall put on. ²³The life is more than meat, and the body is more than raiment. ²⁴Consider the ravens: for they neither sow nor reap; which neither have storehouse nor barn; and God feedeth them: how much more are ye better than the fowls? ²⁵And which of you with taking thought can add to his stature one cubit? ²⁶If ye then be not able to do that thing which is least, why take ye thought for the rest? ²⁷Consider the lilies how they grow: they toil not, they spin not; and yet I say unto you, that Solomon in all his glory was not arrayed like one of these. ²⁸If then God so clothe the

note. **12:6** *Farthings*: see Matt 10:29 note. **12:9** *He that . . . God*: cf. 9:26. **12:10** *Whosoever . . . not be forgiven*: by specifying that speech against the Son of Man (including, presumably, denial of him; v. 9) is forgivable, Luke lays the groundwork for the rehabilitation of Peter, who "denies" Jesus (cf. 22:31–34, 54–62), and of Saul/Paul, who "breath[es] out threatenings and slaughter" against Jesus' disciples and therefore, according to the risen Lord, against Jesus himself (Acts 9:1; cf. vv. 4–5). **12:11** *Powers*: authorities. *Take ye no thought*: lit. "be not anxious" (so throughout). *Ye shall answer*: Gk. *apologēsēsthe*, a term used of a formal defense. **12:13–34** Possessions. Verses 22–34 parallel Matt 6:25–33, 19–21 (see notes). **12:14** *Who made . . . you*: cf. Exod 2:14. **12:17–18** *What shall . . . goods*: he plans to store them rather than to sell them for what would presumably be a price reduced by the year's rich harvest. Joseph does the same on Pharaoh's behalf (Gen 41:34–36), with ultimately nefarious aims (47:13–21). **12:19** *My soul, Soul*: Gk. *psychē* (twice; cf. vv. 22–23 [KJV "life"]), here a pretentious metonymic reference to one's self or entire existence. *Eat, drink, and be merry*: cf. Eccl 10:19. **12:25** *Can add . . . cubit*: see Matt 6:27 note. **12:27** *Solomon*

grass, which is to day in the field, and to morrow is cast into the oven; how much more will he clothe you, O ye of little faith? [29]And seek not ye what ye shall eat, or what ye shall drink, neither be ye of doubtful mind. [30]For all these things do the nations of the world seek after: and your Father knoweth that ye have need of these things. [31]But rather seek ye the kingdom of God; and all these things shall be added unto you. [32]Fear not, little flock; for it is your Father's good pleasure to give you the kingdom. [33]Sell that ye have, and give alms; provide yourselves bags which wax not old, a treasure in the heavens that faileth not, where no thief approacheth, neither moth corrupteth. [34]For where your treasure is, there will your heart be also.

[35]Let your loins be girded about, and your lights burning; [36]and ye yourselves like unto men that wait for their lord, when he will return from the wedding; that when he cometh and knocketh, they may open unto him immediately. [37]Blessed are those servants, whom the lord when he cometh shall find watching: verily I say unto you, that he shall gird himself, and make them to sit down to meat, and will come forth and serve them. [38]And if he shall come in the second watch, or come in the third watch, and find them so, blessed are those servants. [39]And this know, that if the goodman of the house had known what hour the thief would come, he would have watched, and not have suffered his house to be broken through. [40]Be ye therefore ready also: for the Son of man cometh at an hour when ye think not.

[41]Then Peter said unto him, Lord, speakest thou this parable unto us, or even to all? [42]And the Lord said, Who then is that faithful and wise steward, whom his lord shall make ruler over his household, to give them their portion of meat in due season? [43]Blessed is that servant, whom his lord when he cometh shall find so doing. [44]Of a truth I say unto you, that he will make him ruler over all that he hath. [45]But and if that servant say in his heart, My lord delayeth his coming; and shall begin to beat the menservants and maidens, and to eat and drink, and to be drunken; [46]the lord of that servant will come in a day when he looketh not for him, and at an hour when he is not aware, and will cut him in sunder, and will appoint him his portion with the unbelievers. [47]And that servant, which knew his lord's will, and prepared not himself, neither did according to his will, shall be beaten with many stripes. [48]But he that knew not, and did commit things worthy of stripes, shall be beaten with few stripes. For unto whomsoever much is given, of him shall be much required: and to whom men have committed much, of him they will ask the more.

---

in . . . glory: see 1 Kgs 10:14–29.   **12:29** *Seek not . . . mind*: corresponding to "eat, drink, and be merry" (v. 19).   **12:33** *Sell that . . . corrupteth*: Jesus' logic is mercantile: one should give alms because that is the safest capital investment. Luke will develop this idea in chap. 16.   **12:35–59** Eschatological division and expectation. Verses 35–38 recall the parable of the Wise and Foolish Virgins, Matt 25:1–13; vv. 39–46 parallel Matt 24:43–51; vv. 49–56 parallel Matt 10:34–36 and 16:2–3; vv. 57–59 parallel Matt 5:25–26 (for all, see notes).   **12:37** *Gird himself . . . serve them*: i.e., wait on them like a slave, with the eschatological banquet in mind (see Mark 2:19 note).   **12:39** *Goodman*: master. *Broken through*: broken into.   **12:41** *Lord*: shrewdly identifying Jesus with the "lord" of vv. 36–37.   **12:43** *Blessed is . . . doing*: cf. v. 37.   **12:46** *Cut him in sunder*: dismember him. *The unbelievers*: or

⁴⁹I am come to send fire on the earth; and what will I, if it be already kindled? ⁵⁰But I have a baptism to be baptized with; and how am I straitened till it be accomplished! ⁵¹Suppose ye that I am come to give peace on earth? I tell you, Nay; but rather division: ⁵²for from henceforth there shall be five in one house divided, three against two, and two against three. ⁵³The father shall be divided against the son, and the son against the father; the mother against the daughter, and the daughter against the mother; the mother in law against her daughter in law, and the daughter in law against her mother in law.

⁵⁴And he said also to the people, When ye see a cloud rise out of the west, straightway ye say, There cometh a shower; and so it is. ⁵⁵And when ye see the south wind blow, ye say, There will be heat; and it cometh to pass. ⁵⁶Ye hypocrites, ye can discern the face of the sky and of the earth; but how is it that ye do not discern this time? ⁵⁷Yea, and why even of yourselves judge ye not what is right? ⁵⁸When thou goest with thine adversary to the magistrate, as thou art in the way, give diligence that thou mayest be delivered from him; lest he hale thee to the judge, and the judge deliver thee to the officer, and the officer cast thee into prison. ⁵⁹I tell thee, thou shalt not depart thence, till thou hast paid the very last mite.

13 There were present at that season some that told him of the Galilæans, whose blood Pilate had mingled with their sacrifices. ²And Jesus answering said unto them, Suppose ye that these Galilæans were sinners above all the Galilæans, because they suffered such things? ³I tell you, Nay: but, except ye repent, ye shall all likewise perish. ⁴Or those eighteen, upon whom the tower in Siloam fell, and slew them, think ye that they were sinners above all men that dwelt in Jerusalem? ⁵I tell you, Nay: but, except ye repent, ye shall all likewise perish.

⁶He spake also this parable; A certain man had a fig tree planted in his vineyard; and he came and sought fruit thereon, and found none. ⁷Then said he unto the dresser of his vineyard, Behold, these three years I come seeking fruit on this fig tree, and find none: cut it down; why cumbereth it the ground? ⁸And he answering said unto him, Lord, let it alone this year also, till I shall dig about it, and dung it: ⁹and if it bear fruit, well: and if not, then after that thou shalt cut it down.

---

the unfaithful.   **12:49** *What will . . . kindled*: i.e., "what do I want, if it be already kindled?" Alternatively "how I wish it were already kindled!" (NRSV).   **12:50** *I have . . . with*: in Mark 10:38 the same phrase refers to Jesus' impending death (see note). Here (with v. 49) it recalls John the Baptist's prophecy of "one mightier" who "shall baptize . . . with fire" (3:16). *Straitened*: constricted or hemmed in; the Greek word may also mean "distressed."   **12:51** *Suppose ye . . . earth*: reversing the angelic host's announcement at his birth of "on earth peace" (2:14).   **12:53** *The father . . . mother in law*: cf. Mic 7:6. This prophecy of division reverses Gabriel's description of John's ministry (1:17).   **12:57** *Why even . . . right*: i.e., why do you not judge from mundane experience (cf. vv. 58–59) how to act in view of God's imminent judgment?   **12:59** *Mite*: see Mark 12:42 note.   **13:1–9** A warning to repent.   **13:1** *The Galilæans* would have been pilgrims visiting the temple. Those informing Jesus of this otherwise unattested event apparently thought it represented the divine judgment he had just mentioned (12:58–59). Jesus' rejection of this interpretation underscores that their report actually foreshadows his own death at Pilate's hands, as another Galilean pilgrim to Jerusalem.   **13:4** *Those eighteen . . . them*: another Jerusalem calamity not elsewhere attested.   **13:6–9** *A certain man . . . down*: Jesus' parable echoes John's call for repentance (3:8–9), although here the emphasis is on the number of opportunities to repent.   **13:6** *Fig tree . . . vineyard*: perhaps recalling the OT slogan of communal prosperity,

¹⁰And he was teaching in one of the synagogues on the sabbath. ¹¹And, behold, there was a woman which had a spirit of infirmity eighteen years, and was bowed together, and could in no wise lift up herself. ¹²And when Jesus saw her, he called her to him, and said unto her, Woman, thou art loosed from thine infirmity. ¹³And he laid his hands on her: and immediately she was made straight, and glorified God. ¹⁴And the ruler of the synagogue answered with indignation, because that Jesus had healed on the sabbath day, and said unto the people, There are six days in which men ought to work: in them therefore come and be healed, and not on the sabbath day. ¹⁵The Lord then answered him, and said, Thou hypocrite, doth not each one of you on the sabbath loose his ox or his ass from the stall, and lead him away to watering? ¹⁶And ought not this woman, being a daughter of Abraham, whom Satan hath bound, lo, these eighteen years, be loosed from this bond on the sabbath day? ¹⁷And when he had said these things, all his adversaries were ashamed: and all the people rejoiced for all the glorious things that were done by him.

¹⁸Then said he, Unto what is the kingdom of God like? and whereunto shall I resemble it? ¹⁹It is like a grain of mustard seed, which a man took, and cast into his garden; and it grew, and waxed a great tree; and the fowls of the air lodged in the branches of it. ²⁰And again he said, Whereunto shall I liken the kingdom of God? ²¹It is like leaven, which a woman took and hid in three measures of meal, till the whole was leavened.

²²And he went through the cities and villages, teaching, and journeying toward Jerusalem. ²³Then said one unto him, Lord, are there few that be saved? And he said unto them, ²⁴Strive to enter in at the strait gate: for many, I say unto you, will seek to enter in, and shall not be able. ²⁵When once the master of the house is risen up, and hath shut to the door, and ye begin to stand without, and to knock at the door, saying, Lord, Lord, open unto us; and he shall answer and say unto you, I know you not whence ye are: ²⁶then shall ye begin to say, We have eaten and drunk in thy presence, and thou hast taught in our streets. ²⁷But he shall say, I tell you, I know you not whence ye are; depart from me, all ye workers of iniquity. ²⁸There shall be weeping and gnashing of teeth, when ye shall see Abraham, and Isaac, and Jacob, and all the prophets, in the kingdom of God, and you yourselves thrust out. ²⁹And they shall come from the east, and from the west, and from the north, and from the south, and shall sit down in the kingdom of God. ³⁰And, behold, there are last which shall be first, and there are first which shall be last.

"every man under his vine and under his fig tree" (1 Kgs 4:25; Mic 4:4).   **13:10–21** Healing a crippled woman and the parables of Mustard Seed and Yeast. Verses 18–21 parallel Mark 4:30–32 (without the second parable) and Matt 13:31–33 (see notes to both).   **13:11** *Eighteen years*: the same number as those killed by the collapsing tower (v. 4).   **13:12** *Thou art loosed*: the emphasis on freedom from bondage (cf. v. 16) recalls 4:18–19 (see notes).   **13:14** *Six days . . . work*: cf. Exod 20:9–10; Deut 5:13–14.   **13:15** *Thou hypocrite*: better "you hypocrites" (MS tradition).   **13:18** *Then*: better "therefore" (MS tradition), more closely linking this paragraph with the preceding.   **13:19** *Great*: better omitted (MS tradition).   **13:22–30** Who will be saved? Compare Matt 7:13–14; 25:10b–12; 7:22–23; 8:11–12; 20:16 and notes.   **13:24** *Gate*: better "door" (MS tradition), which some scribes assimilated to Matt 7:13.   **13:27** *Depart from me . . . iniquity*: cf. Ps 6:8.   **13:29** *They shall come . . . God*: the image of a narrow door (v. 24) locked shut (vv. 25–28) yields to a vision of universal hospitality. *Sit down*: lit.

³¹The same day there came certain of the Pharisees, saying unto him, Get thee out, and depart hence: for Herod will kill thee. ³²And he said unto them, Go ye, and tell that fox, Behold, I cast out devils, and I do cures to day and to morrow, and the third day I shall be perfected. ³³Nevertheless I must walk to day, and to morrow, and the day following: for it cannot be that a prophet perish out of Jerusalem. ³⁴O Jerusalem, Jerusalem, which killest the prophets, and stonest them that are sent unto thee; how often would I have gathered thy children together, as a hen doth gather her brood under her wings, and ye would not! ³⁵Behold, your house is left unto you desolate: and verily I say unto you, Ye shall not see me, until the time come when ye shall say, Blessed is he that cometh in the name of the Lord.

14 And it came to pass, as he went into the house of one of the chief Pharisees to eat bread on the sabbath day, that they watched him. ²And, behold, there was a certain man before him which had the dropsy. ³And Jesus answering spake unto the lawyers and Pharisees, saying, Is it lawful to heal on the sabbath day? ⁴And they held their peace. And he took him, and healed him, and let him go; ⁵and answered them, saying, Which of you shall have an ass or an ox fallen into a pit, and will not straightway pull him out on the sabbath day? ⁶And they could not answer him again to these things.

⁷And he put forth a parable to those which were bidden, when he marked how they chose out the chief rooms; saying unto them, ⁸When thou art bidden of any man to a wedding, sit not down in the highest room; lest a more honourable man than thou be bidden of him; ⁹and he that bade thee and him come and say to thee, Give this man place; and thou begin with shame to take the lowest room. ¹⁰But when thou art bidden, go and sit down in the lowest room; that when he that bade thee cometh, he may say unto thee, Friend, go up higher: then shalt thou have worship in the presence of them that sit at meat with thee. ¹¹For whosoever exalteth himself shall be abased; and he that humbleth himself shall be exalted.

¹²Then said he also to him that bade him, When thou makest a dinner or a supper, call not thy friends, nor thy brethren, neither thy kinsmen, nor thy rich neighbours; lest they also bid thee again, and a recompence be made thee. ¹³But when thou makest a feast, call the poor, the maimed, the lame, the blind: ¹⁴and

---

"recline" (at table; see 7:36 note), with the eschatological banquet in view.   **13:31–35** Lament for Jerusalem. Verses 34–35 parallel Matt 23:37–39 (see notes).   **13:32** *Be perfected*: Gk. *teleioō*, which refers to reaching a goal.   **13:34** *Killest the prophets*: see 11:47–50 and notes.   **13:35** *Your house*: the Jerusalem temple. *Desolate*: better omitted (MS tradition), but the sense is that the house has been forsaken; cf. Jer 12:7. *Blessed is . . . Lord*: Ps 118:26.   **14:1–24** Symposium at a chief Pharisee's house. This section's first episode (vv. 1–6) closely parallels the healing of 13:10–17. The following parable (vv. 7–11) draws on Prov 25:6–7 to advise how to act when invited to a dinner, while vv. 12–14 recall 6:32–34 and give advice for issuing such invitations. Verses 15–24 parallel Matt 22:1–14.   **14:2** *The dropsy*: edema (a disease marked by an accumulation of fluids that causes swelling).   **14:4** *Let him go*: cf. 13:12 and note (KJV "loosed").   **14:5** *An ass*: better "a son" (MS tradition).   **14:7** *Bidden*: invited (so throughout). *Chief rooms*: honorable places to recline. *Chief* is Gk. *prōto-*; cf. v. 8 (KJV "highest"); 13:30 (KJV "first").   **14:9** *Lowest*: Gk. *eschaton* (cf. 13:30 [KJV "last"]).   **14:11** *Abased, humbleth*: the same

thou shalt be blessed; for they cannot recompense thee: for thou shalt be recompensed at the resurrection of the just.

[15]And when one of them that sat at meat with him heard these things, he said unto him, Blessed is he that shall eat bread in the kingdom of God. [16]Then said he unto him, A certain man made a great supper, and bade many: [17]and sent his servant at supper time to say to them that were bidden, Come; for all things are now ready. [18]And they all with one consent began to make excuse. The first said unto him, I have bought a piece of ground, and I must needs go and see it: I pray thee have me excused. [19]And another said, I have bought five yoke of oxen, and I go to prove them: I pray thee have me excused. [20]And another said, I have married a wife, and therefore I cannot come. [21]So that servant came, and shewed his lord these things. Then the master of the house being angry said to his servant, Go out quickly into the streets and lanes of the city, and bring in hither the poor, and the maimed, and the halt, and the blind. [22]And the servant said, Lord, it is done as thou hast commanded, and yet there is room. [23]And the lord said unto the servant, Go out into the highways and hedges, and compel them to come in, that my house may be filled. [24]For I say unto you, That none of those men which were bidden shall taste of my supper.

[25]And there went great multitudes with him: and he turned, and said unto them, [26]If any man come to me, and hate not his father, and mother, and wife, and children, and brethren, and sisters, yea, and his own life also, he cannot be my disciple. [27]And whosoever doth not bear his cross, and come after me, cannot be my disciple. [28]For which of you, intending to build a tower, sitteth not down first, and counteth the cost, whether he have sufficient to finish it? [29]Lest haply, after he hath laid the foundation, and is not able to finish it, all that behold it begin to mock him, [30]saying, This man began to build, and was not able to finish. [31]Or what king, going to make war against another king, sitteth not down first, and consulteth whether he be able with ten thousand to meet him that cometh against him with twenty

---

Greek verb.   **14:14** *Resurrection of the just*: this seems to imply that only the righteous will be raised at the end time. Other texts promise resurrection to both just and unjust, the latter to be condemned (e.g., Dan 12:2–3; Acts 24:15; cf. Luke 13:27).   **14:15** *Blessed is . . . God*: perhaps the blessing suggests that Jesus' advice is relevant to God's eschatological kingdom, not the real world. The ensuing story challenges the suggestion by portraying a mundane, if exaggerated application of the etiquette Jesus recommends. (Compare the similarly disruptive benediction of 11:27, which Jesus also challenges.) Alternatively, Jesus may accept the benediction, and then tell the story to explain that those who will feast in God's kingdom correspond to those whom Jesus urged the guests to invite to their own dinners (cf. vv. 13, 21 and note).   **14:18–20** *The first . . . come*: these excuses show a preoccupation with possessions and family that Luke consistently rejects (cf. 2:48–49; 12:13–34; 14:26; etc.), but they also recall legitimate reasons for avoiding military service (Deut 20:5–7; 24:5). By implicitly comparing the man's banquet to life-threatening battle, the invitees suggest that his generous invitation is a burdensome obligation.   **14:19** *Prove them*: i.e., determine their value by testing. Oddly, he does this only after the purchase.   **14:21** *Halt*: lame (as the same Greek word is translated in v. 13).   **14:23** *Highways and hedges*: areas outside the city, where the perpetually impure dwelled (cf. Lev 13:46); contrast "the streets and lanes of the city" (v. 21).   **14:25–35** Counting discipleship's cost. Verses 25–27 parallel Matt 10:37–38 (see v. 38 note); cf. Matt 16:24; Mark 8:34; Luke 9:23. Verses 34–35 parallel Matt 5:13; cf. Mark 9:50.   **14:26** *If any man . . . disciple*: Luke's version of this saying is harsher and more comprehensive than Matthew's (10:37).   **14:27** *Come after me*: the phrase should be understood both metaphorically (cf. 9:23 and note) and literally, applying to Jesus' current journey to Jerusalem (cf. 9:51; 13:22, 31–33).   **14:29** *Haply*: by chance.

thousand? [32]Or else, while the other is yet a great way off, he sendeth an ambassage, and desireth conditions of peace. [33]So likewise, whosoever he be of you that forsaketh not all that he hath, he cannot be my disciple.

[34]Salt is good: but if the salt have lost his savour, wherewith shall it be seasoned? [35]It is neither fit for the land, nor yet for the dunghill; but men cast it out. He that hath ears to hear, let him hear.

15 Then drew near unto him all the publicans and sinners for to hear him. [2]And the Pharisees and scribes murmured, saying, This man receiveth sinners, and eateth with them.

[3]And he spake this parable unto them, saying, [4]What man of you, having an hundred sheep, if he lose one of them, doth not leave the ninety and nine in the wilderness, and go after that which is lost, until he find it? [5]And when he hath found it, he layeth it on his shoulders, rejoicing. [6]And when he cometh home, he calleth together his friends and neighbours, saying unto them, Rejoice with me; for I have found my sheep which was lost. [7]I say unto you, that likewise joy shall be in heaven over one sinner that repenteth, more than over ninety and nine just persons, which need no repentance.

[8]Either what woman having ten pieces of silver, if she lose one piece, doth not light a candle, and sweep the house, and seek diligently till she find it? [9]And when she hath found it, she calleth her friends and her neighbours together, saying, Rejoice with me; for I have found the piece which I had lost. [10]Likewise, I say unto you, there is joy in the presence of the angels of God over one sinner that repenteth.

[11]And he said, A certain man had two sons: [12]and the younger of them said to his father, Father, give me the portion of goods that falleth to me. And he divided unto them his living. [13]And not many days after the younger son gathered all together, and took his journey into a far country, and there wasted his substance with riotous living. [14]And when he had spent all, there arose a mighty famine in that land; and he began to be in want. [15]And he went and joined himself to a citizen of that country; and he sent him into his fields to feed swine. [16]And he would fain have filled his belly with the husks that the swine did eat: and no man gave unto him. [17]And when he came to himself, he said, How many hired servants of my father's have bread enough and to spare, and I perish with hunger! [18]I will arise

---

14:33 *Forsaketh*: lit. "bid farewell to" (cf. 9:61; 2 Cor 2:13), alluding to the call to follow (v. 27). **14:34** *Salt is good*: better "salt therefore is good" (MS tradition), more closely linking the saying about preservative salt with the metaphors of vv. 28–32, which demonstrate the need for perseverance on the difficult journey of discipleship (vv. 27, 33). **14:35** *Nor yet for the dunghill*: i.e., not useful even as fertilizer. **15:1–32** Parables of the lost found. The parable of the Lost Sheep (vv. 3–7) parallels Matt 18:12–14 (see v. 12 note), while those of the Lost Coin and Prodigal Son are unique to Luke. The three parables constitute an elaborate response to the Pharisees' and scribes' murmuring about Jesus' association with sinners (vv. 1–2) and evince a pattern of gradual intensification: lost and then found are one sheep out of one hundred (vv. 3–7), one silver coin out of ten (vv. 8–10), and finally one son out of two (vv. 11–32). **15:6** *Calleth together*: Gk. root *-kaleō*, "invite"; cf. v. 9; 14:7–10; etc. (KJV "bid"). The shepherd's out-of-place celebration complements his reckless abandonment of the ninety-nine sheep in order to save one (v. 4). **15:8** *Either*: Or. *Pieces of silver*: Gk. *drachma*, a silver coin of roughly the same value as a denarius (see Mark 14:5 note). **15:12** *Give me . . . me*: the premature request for inheritance is presumptuous and cruel, amounting to a wish that the father were dead. **15:13** *Far country*: Gentile territory, as the swine herding (v. 15) suggests. **15:16** *Fain*: gladly **15:18** *Arise*: Gk. *anistēmi* (cf. v. 20); the verb used of Jesus' resurrection

and go to my father, and will say unto him, Father, I have sinned against heaven, and before thee, ¹⁹and am no more worthy to be called thy son: make me as one of thy hired servants. ²⁰And he arose, and came to his father. But when he was yet a great way off, his father saw him, and had compassion, and ran, and fell on his neck, and kissed him. ²¹And the son said unto him, Father, I have sinned against heaven, and in thy sight, and am no more worthy to be called thy son. ²²But the father said to his servants, Bring forth the best robe, and put it on him; and put a ring on his hand, and shoes on his feet: ²³and bring hither the fatted calf, and kill it; and let us eat, and be merry: ²⁴for this my son was dead, and is alive again; he was lost, and is found. And they began to be merry.

²⁵Now his elder son was in the field: and as he came and drew nigh to the house, he heard musick and dancing. ²⁶And he called one of the servants, and asked what these things meant. ²⁷And he said unto him, Thy brother is come; and thy father hath killed the fatted calf, because he hath received him safe and sound. ²⁸And he was angry, and would not go in: therefore came his father out, and intreated him. ²⁹And he answering said to his father, Lo, these many years do I serve thee, neither transgressed I at any time thy commandment: and yet thou never gavest me a kid, that I might make merry with my friends: ³⁰but as soon as this thy son was come, which hath devoured thy living with harlots, thou hast killed for him the fatted calf. ³¹And he said unto him, Son, thou art ever with me, and all that I have is thine. ³²It was meet that we should make merry, and be glad: for this thy brother was dead, and is alive again; and was lost, and is found.

16 And he said also unto his disciples, There was a certain rich man, which had a steward; and the same was accused unto him that he had wasted his goods. ²And he called him, and said unto him, How is it that I hear this of thee? give an account of thy stewardship; for thou mayest be no longer steward. ³Then the steward said within himself, What shall I do? for my lord taketh away from me the stewardship: I cannot dig; to beg I am ashamed. ⁴I am resolved what to do, that, when I am put out of the stewardship, they may receive me into their houses. ⁵So he called every one of his lord's debtors unto him, and said unto the first, How much owest thou unto my lord? ⁶And he said, An hundred measures of oil. And he said unto him, Take thy bill, and sit down quickly, and write fifty. ⁷Then said he to another, And how much owest thou? And he said, An hundred measures of wheat. And he said unto him, Take thy bill, and write fourscore. ⁸And the lord commended the unjust steward, because he had done wisely: for the children of this world are in their generation wiser than the children of light.

(18:33; 24:7, 46), a connection suggested in vv. 24, 32.   **15:20** *His father saw . . . him*: cf. Gen 33:4.   **15:21** *Thy son*: many early and important MSS add "make me as one of your hired servants," though this may have been imported by scribes from v. 19.   **15:22** *Bring forth . . . feet*: cf. Gen 41:42.   **15:29** *Do I serve thee*: lit. "have I been your slave"; compare the younger son's desire to become his father's servant (v. 19; cf. 21 note). In both cases, the father rejects this framing of their relationship (vv. 22–24, 31).   **15:32** *Meet*: appropriate.   **16:1–13** Parable of the Unjust Steward.   **16:1** *Steward*: see 8:3 note. *Wasted his goods*: cf. 15:13, "wasted his substance."   **16:6–7** *An hundred . . . wheat*: both amounts are large; the first debtor, apparently an olive farmer, owed about 900 gallons of oil.   **16:8** *Wisely*: see 12:42 for another wise steward. *World*: lit. "age," as often in Luke. *Children of light*: an apocalyptic self-designation in the Qumran texts, used occasionally in the NT as well (John 12:36; Eph 5:8;

⁹And I say unto you, Make to yourselves friends of the mammon of unrighteousness; that, when ye fail, they may receive you into everlasting habitations. ¹⁰He that is faithful in that which is least is faithful also in much: and he that is unjust in the least is unjust also in much. ¹¹If therefore ye have not been faithful in the unrighteous mammon, who will commit to your trust the true riches? ¹²And if ye have not been faithful in that which is another man's, who shall give you that which is your own? ¹³No servant can serve two masters: for either he will hate the one, and love the other; or else he will hold to the one, and despise the other. Ye cannot serve God and mammon.

¹⁴And the Pharisees also, who were covetous, heard all these things: and they derided him. ¹⁵And he said unto them, Ye are they which justify yourselves before men; but God knoweth your hearts: for that which is highly esteemed among men is abomination in the sight of God. ¹⁶The law and the prophets were until John: since that time the kingdom of God is preached, and every man presseth into it. ¹⁷And it is easier for heaven and earth to pass, than one tittle of the law to fail. ¹⁸Whosoever putteth away his wife, and marrieth another, committeth adultery: and whosoever marrieth her that is put away from her husband committeth adultery.

¹⁹There was a certain rich man, which was clothed in purple and fine linen, and fared sumptuously every day: ²⁰and there was a certain beggar named Lazarus, which was laid at his gate, full of sores, ²¹and desiring to be fed with the crumbs which fell from the rich man's table: moreover the dogs came and licked his sores. ²²And it came to pass, that the beggar died, and was carried by the angels into Abraham's bosom: the rich man also died, and was buried; ²³and in hell he lift up his eyes, being in torments, and seeth Abraham afar off, and Lazarus in his bosom. ²⁴And he cried and said, Father Abraham, have mercy on me, and send Lazarus, that he may dip the tip of his finger in water, and cool my tongue; for I am tormented in this flame. ²⁵But Abraham said, Son, remember that thou in thy lifetime receivedst thy good things, and likewise Lazarus evil things: but now he

1 Thess 5:5). **16:9** *Of the mammon*: by means of *the mammon* (see Matt 6:24 note). *Ye fail*: better "it fail" (MS tradition). *Everlasting habitations*: lit. "eternal tents," possibly referring to eschatologically resurrected bodies (see 2 Cor 5:1–8 and notes); cf. 12:33. **16:14–18** The Pharisees and the law. Verse 16 parallels Matt 11:12–13; v. 17 parallels Matt 5:18; v. 18 parallels Matt 5:32 (for all, see notes). **16:14** *Covetous*: lit. "friends of money," subverting Jesus' directive (v. 9). **16:15** *Ye are . . . hearts*: cf. Prov 21:2. *Abomination*: used frequently in the Pentateuch; e.g., of animals not to be eaten (Lev 11:20, 23; etc.), of sexual transgressions (Lev 18:22), and of dishonest financial dealings (Deut 25:13–16). **16:16** *Every man . . . it*: alternatively "every man is pressed into it." **16:19–31** Parable of the Rich Man and Lazarus. This parable combines the two preceding sections' main themes: the primacy of the law and the relationship between worldly wealth and "eternal dwellings." Though it has given rise to extensive speculation about the afterlife, the details of its portrait of the hereafter merely reflect the story's internal logic: the unbridgeable gulf in v. 26 corresponds to and amplifies the gate in v. 20, which the rich man could have opened to Lazarus but never did; the emphasis on Abraham that so many commentators find confusing underscores the parable's final point about the law and the prophets (vv. 29, 31; see notes). **16:19** *Rich man*: traditionally known as Dives (Lat. "Rich"), from the Vulgate. *Fared*: feasted. **16:20** *Lazarus*: the only character in Jesus' parables to be named (perhaps a gesture toward his final advantage in status over the anonymous rich man). **16:24** *Dip the tip . . . water*: vividly dramatizing their reversal: in life dogs licked Lazarus' sores as he sat at the

is comforted, and thou art tormented. ²⁶And beside all this, between us and you there is a great gulf fixed: so that they which would pass from hence to you cannot; neither can they pass to us, that would come from thence. ²⁷Then he said, I pray thee therefore, father, that thou wouldest send him to my father's house: ²⁸for I have five brethren; that he may testify unto them, lest they also come into this place of torment. ²⁹Abraham saith unto him, They have Moses and the prophets; let them hear them. ³⁰And he said, Nay, father Abraham: but if one went unto them from the dead, they will repent. ³¹And he said unto him, If they hear not Moses and the prophets, neither will they be persuaded, though one rose from the dead.

17 Then said he unto the disciples, It is impossible but that offences will come: but woe unto him, through whom they come! ²It were better for him that a millstone were hanged about his neck, and he cast into the sea, than that he should offend one of these little ones.

³Take heed to yourselves: If thy brother trespass against thee, rebuke him; and if he repent, forgive him. ⁴And if he trespass against thee seven times in a day, and seven times in a day turn again to thee, saying, I repent; thou shalt forgive him.

⁵And the apostles said unto the Lord, Increase our faith. ⁶And the Lord said, If ye had faith as a grain of mustard seed, ye might say unto this sycamine tree, Be thou plucked up by the root, and be thou planted in the sea; and it should obey you.

⁷But which of you, having a servant plowing or feeding cattle, will say unto him by and by, when he is come from the field, Go and sit down to meat? ⁸And will not rather say unto him, Make ready wherewith I may sup, and gird thyself, and serve me, till I have eaten and drunken; and afterward thou shalt eat and drink? ⁹Doth he thank that servant because he did the things that were commanded him? I trow not. ¹⁰So likewise ye, when ye shall have done all those things which are commanded you, say, We are unprofitable servants: we have done that which was our duty to do.

¹¹And it came to pass, as he went to Jerusalem, that he passed through the midst of Samaria and Galilee. ¹²And as he entered into a certain village, there met him ten men that were lepers, which stood afar off: ¹³and they lifted up their voices, and said, Jesus, Master, have mercy on us. ¹⁴And when he saw them, he said unto them, Go shew yourselves unto the priests. And it came to pass, that, as they

---

rich man's gate (vv. 20–21).   **16:29** *They have . . . them*: words all the more compelling from Abraham, who obeyed God without benefit of law or prophets.   **16:31** *If they . . . dead*: though this parable ends with a pointed refusal to raise Lazarus from the dead, in John 11 Jesus in fact resurrects a man named Lazarus.   **17:1–10** Faithful service. Verses 1–2 parallel Matt 18:6–7 and Mark 9:42 (see notes); vv. 3–4 parallel Matt 18:15, 21–22; vv. 5–6 parallel Matt 17:20; cf. Mark 11:22–23; Matt 21:21. **17:2** *These little ones*: i.e., those with no obvious significance (such as the destitute like Lazarus). **17:3** *Brother*: throughout the NT, a fellow believer; here it also recalls the fraternal strife in the parable of the Prodigal Son (15:11–32). *Against thee*: better omitted (MS tradition).   **17:4** *Saying, I repent*: in Matthew's version, Jesus' requirement to forgive is not contingent on repentance.   **17:5** *Increase our faith*: the apostles ask for Jesus' help in following the directives he has laid out. His response suggests that they need no extraordinary assistance (v. 6) and that they should not look for gratitude either (vv. 7–10).   **17:6** *Sycamine*: mulberry.   **17:9** *I trow not*: better omitted (MS tradition). **17:10** *Unprofitable servants*: lit. "useless slaves" (NRSV).   **17:11–19** Ten healed of leprosy. This episode recalls 5:12–16.   **17:11** *The midst of*: i.e., "the region between" (in fact, Samaria was adjacent to Galilee).   **17:13** *Master*: Gk. *epistatēs*, the disciples' usual title for Jesus.   **17:14** *Go shew . . .*

went, they were cleansed. ¹⁵And one of them, when he saw that he was healed, turned back, and with a loud voice glorified God, ¹⁶and fell down on his face at his feet, giving him thanks: and he was a Samaritan. ¹⁷And Jesus answering said, Were there not ten cleansed? but where are the nine? ¹⁸There are not found that returned to give glory to God, save this stranger. ¹⁹And he said unto him, Arise, go thy way: thy faith hath made thee whole.

²⁰And when he was demanded of the Pharisees, when the kingdom of God should come, he answered them and said, The kingdom of God cometh not with observation: ²¹neither shall they say, Lo here! or, lo there! for, behold, the kingdom of God is within you.

²²And he said unto the disciples, The days will come, when ye shall desire to see one of the days of the Son of man, and ye shall not see it. ²³And they shall say to you, See here; or, see there: go not after them, nor follow them. ²⁴For as the lightning, that lighteneth out of the one part under heaven, shineth unto the other part under heaven; so shall also the Son of man be in his day. ²⁵But first must he suffer many things, and be rejected of this generation. ²⁶And as it was in the days of Noe, so shall it be also in the days of the Son of man. ²⁷They did eat, they drank, they married wives, they were given in marriage, until the day that Noe entered into the ark, and the flood came, and destroyed them all. ²⁸Likewise also as it was in the days of Lot; they did eat, they drank, they bought, they sold, they planted, they builded; ²⁹but the same day that Lot went out of Sodom it rained fire and brimstone from heaven, and destroyed them all. ³⁰Even thus shall it be in the day when the Son of man is revealed. ³¹In that day, he which shall be upon the housetop, and his stuff in the house, let him not come down to take it away: and he that is in the field, let him likewise not return back. ³²Remember Lot's wife. ³³Whosoever shall seek to save his life shall lose it; and whosoever shall lose his life shall preserve it. ³⁴I tell you, in that night there shall be two men in one bed; the one shall be taken, and the other shall be left. ³⁵Two women shall be grinding together; the one shall be taken, and the other left. ³⁶Two men shall be in the field; the one shall be taken, and the other left. ³⁷And they answered and said unto him, Where, Lord? And he said unto them, Wheresoever the body is, thither will the eagles be gathered together.

---

priests: cf. Lev 13–14.   **17:16** *He was a Samaritan*: cf. 10:25–37.   **17:18** *Stranger*: foreigner. **17:20–37** The kingdom of God and the days of the Son of Man. Verses 23–27 parallel Matt 24:26– 27, 37–39 (see notes); v. 33 parallels Matt 10:39; vv. 34–37 parallel Matt 24:40–41, 28 (see notes). This section challenges eschatological preoccupation in a number of ways: by insisting that already "the kingdom of God is within you" (v. 21b; see note), by stating that the kingdom will come without signs (vv. 20–21a, but cf. 37), by suggesting that its eschatological consummation represents merely one moment of divine judgment among others (vv. 26–30), and by hinting throughout that it should perhaps not even be conceived of as a discrete moment of time ("days of the Son of man," vv. 22, 26).   **17:21** *Within you*: better "among you" (*you* is plural).   **17:24** *In his day*: better omitted (MS tradition).   **17:26** *In the days of Noe*: for the story of Noah, see Gen 6–9.   **17:28** *In the days of Lot*: see Gen 19.   **17:32** *Lot's wife*: see Gen 19:26.   **17:33** *Whosoever shall seek . . . preserve it*: cf. 9:24. *Save*: better "preserve" (MS tradition), a different Greek word from that in 9:24. *And whosoever shall lose his life shall preserve it*: lit. "and whosoever shall lose it shall keep it alive."   **17:36** *Two men . . . left*: better omitted (MS tradition).   **17:37** *Eagles*: or vultures.

18 And he spake a parable unto them to this end, that men ought always to pray, and not to faint; [2]saying, There was in a city a judge, which feared not God, neither regarded man: [3]and there was a widow in that city; and she came unto him, saying, Avenge me of mine adversary. [4]And he would not for a while: but afterward he said within himself, Though I fear not God, nor regard man; [5]yet because this widow troubleth me, I will avenge her, lest by her continual coming she weary me. [6]And the Lord said, Hear what the unjust judge saith. [7]And shall not God avenge his own elect, which cry day and night unto him, though he bear long with them? [8]I tell you that he will avenge them speedily. Nevertheless when the Son of man cometh, shall he find faith on the earth?

[9]And he spake this parable unto certain which trusted in themselves that they were righteous, and despised others: [10]Two men went up into the temple to pray; the one a Pharisee, and the other a publican. [11]The Pharisee stood and prayed thus with himself, God, I thank thee, that I am not as other men are, extortioners, unjust, adulterers, or even as this publican. [12]I fast twice in the week, I give tithes of all that I possess. [13]And the publican, standing afar off, would not lift up so much as his eyes unto heaven, but smote upon his breast, saying, God be merciful to me a sinner. [14]I tell you, this man went down to his house justified rather than the other: for every one that exalteth himself shall be abased; and he that humbleth himself shall be exalted.

[15]And they brought unto him also infants, that he would touch them: but when his disciples saw it, they rebuked them. [16]But Jesus called them unto him, and said, Suffer little children to come unto me, and forbid them not: for of such is the kingdom of God. [17]Verily I say unto you, Whosoever shall not receive the kingdom of God as a little child shall in no wise enter therein.

[18]And a certain ruler asked him, saying, Good Master, what shall I do to inherit eternal life? [19]And Jesus said unto him, Why callest thou me good? none is good, save one, that is, God. [20]Thou knowest the commandments, Do not commit adultery, Do not kill, Do not steal, Do not bear false witness, Honour thy father and thy mother. [21]And he said, All these have I kept from my youth up. [22]Now when Jesus heard these things, he said unto him, Yet lackest thou one thing: sell all that

---

18:1–8 Parable of the Widow and Unjust Judge. Having forbidden sign-seeking eschatological preoccupation, Jesus now demonstrates the prayerful posture that he wants his followers to assume as they await the day of the Son of Man. The parable develops themes from Sir 35:13–17.   **18:1** *Men*: better "they" (MS tradition)—i.e., the disciples (cf. 17:22). *Faint*: "lose heart" (NRSV).   **18:3** *Avenge me of*: Gk. root *-dikē*, "justice"; throughout the parable, justice rather than revenge is at issue.   **18:7** *Bear long*: the Greek word probably means "delay"; a better reading of the MS tradition makes this clause independent, suggesting "and will he delay long in helping them?" (NRSV).   **18:8** *When the Son . . . earth*: the phrase forms an inclusive frame with 17:20.   **18:9–19:10** Who is in the kingdom? This unit's material often answers that question in surprising ways.   **18:9–14** Parable of the Pharisee and Tax Collector.   **18:11** *With himself*: lit. "to himself."   **18:14** *Justified*: Gk. root *dikaio-*, "just"; cf. v. 9 (KJV "righteous"). *For every one . . . exalted*: see 14:11 and note.   **18:15–17** Blessing children. Compare Matt 19:13–15; Mark 10:13–16 and notes.   **18:15** *Also infants*: or "even infants," emphasizing how shocking is Jesus' interest in these lowliest members of society.   **18:18–30** A rich ruler. Compare Matt 19:16–30; Mark 10:17–31 and notes.   **18:18** *Ruler*: magistrate, as in 12:58.   **18:20** *Do not . . . mother*: commandments five through nine of the Decalogue, though not in the original order (cf. Exod

thou hast, and distribute unto the poor, and thou shalt have treasure in heaven: and come, follow me. ²³And when he heard this, he was very sorrowful: for he was very rich. ²⁴And when Jesus saw that he was very sorrowful, he said, How hardly shall they that have riches enter into the kingdom of God! ²⁵For it is easier for a camel to go through a needle's eye, than for a rich man to enter into the kingdom of God. ²⁶And they that heard it said, Who then can be saved? ²⁷And he said, The things which are impossible with men are possible with God. ²⁸Then Peter said, Lo, we have left all, and followed thee. ²⁹And he said unto them, Verily I say unto you, There is no man that hath left house, or parents, or brethren, or wife, or children, for the kingdom of God's sake, ³⁰who shall not receive manifold more in this present time, and in the world to come life everlasting.

³¹Then he took unto him the twelve, and said unto them, Behold, we go up to Jerusalem, and all things that are written by the prophets concerning the Son of man shall be accomplished. ³²For he shall be delivered unto the Gentiles, and shall be mocked, and spitefully entreated, and spitted on: ³³and they shall scourge him, and put him to death: and the third day he shall rise again. ³⁴And they understood none of these things: and this saying was hid from them, neither knew they the things which were spoken.

³⁵And it came to pass, that as he was come nigh unto Jericho, a certain blind man sat by the way side begging: ³⁶and hearing the multitude pass by, he asked what it meant. ³⁷And they told him, that Jesus of Nazareth passeth by. ³⁸And he cried, saying, Jesus, thou Son of David, have mercy on me. ³⁹And they which went before rebuked him, that he should hold his peace: but he cried so much the more, Thou Son of David, have mercy on me. ⁴⁰And Jesus stood, and commanded him to be brought unto him: and when he was come near, he asked him, ⁴¹saying, What wilt thou that I shall do unto thee? And he said, Lord, that I may receive my sight. ⁴²And Jesus said unto him, Receive thy sight: thy faith hath saved thee. ⁴³And immediately he received his sight, and followed him, glorifying God: and all the people, when they saw it, gave praise unto God.

19 And Jesus entered and passed through Jericho. ²And, behold, there was a man named Zacchæus, which was the chief among the publicans, and he was rich. ³And he sought to see Jesus who he was; and could not for the press, because he was little of stature. ⁴And he ran before, and climbed up into a sycomore

---

20:12–17; Deut 5:16–20). **18:24** *That he . . . sorrowful*: better simply "him" (MS tradition). *Hardly*: with difficulty.   **18:29** *House, or . . . children*: Luke's list of people abandoned, which includes wives and parents, is more expansive than Mark's and Matthew's.   **18:31–34** Third prediction of Jesus' death and resurrection. Compare Matt 20:17–19; Mark 10:32–34 and notes.   **18:32–33** *Be mocked . . . death*: echoing Isa 50:6 (as mention of "the prophets" [v. 31] underscores).   **18:34** *They understood . . . spoken*: see 9:45. The close repetition indicates how little progress the disciples have made during their journey to Jerusalem, now drawing to an end.   **18:35–43** Healing a blind man. Compare Matt 20:29–34; Mark 10:46–52.   **18:35** *Jericho*: a city several miles northeast of Jerusalem. **18:38** *Son of David*: cf. 1:32–35 and notes. The blind man's insight contrasts with the disciples' obtuseness (v. 34 and note).   **18:39** *They which went before*: presumably the disciples.   **19:1–10** Zacchaeus. This episode parallels and in some ways reverses the story of the rich ruler (18:18–23).   **19:2** *Chief*: Gk. root *arch-*, "leader"; cf. 18:18 (KJV "ruler").   **19:3** Zacchaeus's tremendous effort *to see Jesus who he was* underscores the disciples' inability to comprehend the implications of Jesus' identity, which are "hid

tree to see him: for he was to pass that way. ⁵And when Jesus came to the place, he looked up, and saw him, and said unto him, Zacchæus, make haste, and come down; for to day I must abide at thy house. ⁶And he made haste, and came down, and received him joyfully. ⁷And when they saw it, they all murmured, saying, That he was gone to be guest with a man that is a sinner. ⁸And Zacchæus stood, and said unto the Lord; Behold, Lord, the half of my goods I give to the poor; and if I have taken any thing from any man by false accusation, I restore him fourfold. ⁹And Jesus said unto him, This day is salvation come to this house, forsomuch as he also is a son of Abraham. ¹⁰For the Son of man is come to seek and to save that which was lost.

¹¹And as they heard these things, he added and spake a parable, because he was nigh to Jerusalem, and because they thought that the kingdom of God should immediately appear. ¹²He said therefore, A certain nobleman went into a far country to receive for himself a kingdom, and to return. ¹³And he called his ten servants, and delivered them ten pounds, and said unto them, Occupy till I come. ¹⁴But his citizens hated him, and sent a message after him, saying, We will not have this man to reign over us. ¹⁵And it came to pass, that when he was returned, having received the kingdom, then he commanded these servants to be called unto him, to whom he had given the money, that he might know how much every man had gained by trading. ¹⁶Then came the first, saying, Lord, thy pound hath gained ten pounds. ¹⁷And he said unto him, Well, thou good servant: because thou hast been faithful in a very little, have thou authority over ten cities. ¹⁸And the second came, saying, Lord, thy pound hath gained five pounds. ¹⁹And he said likewise to him, Be thou also over five cities. ²⁰And another came, saying, Lord, behold, here is thy pound, which I have kept laid up in a napkin: ²¹for I feared thee, because thou art an austere man: thou takest up that thou layedst not down, and reapest that thou didst not sow. ²²And he saith unto him, Out of thine own mouth will I judge thee, thou wicked servant. Thou knewest that I was an austere man, taking up that I laid not down, and reaping that I did not sow: ²³wherefore then gavest not thou my money into the bank, that at my coming I might have required mine own with usury? ²⁴And he said unto them that stood by, Take from him the pound, and give it to him that hath ten pounds. ²⁵(And they said unto him, Lord, he hath ten pounds.) ²⁶For I say unto you, That unto every one which hath shall be given; and from him that hath not, even that he hath shall be taken away from him. ²⁷But those mine enemies, which would not that I should reign over them, bring hither, and slay them before me.

---

from them" (18:34).   **19:8–9** *The half . . . Abraham*: recalling John the Baptist's directives in 3:8–14. **19:11–27** Parable of the Pounds. Compare Matt 25:14–30 and notes. As in 17:20–18:8, Luke shifts attention from preoccupation with God's coming kingdom and toward faithfulness while awaiting it. The scenario this parable envisions—a provincial conflict resolved when a central government confirms a regional ruler's authority—was a familiar one in Rome's eastern provinces, especially in Judea.   **19:13** *Pounds*: a pound (Gk. *mna*) was the equivalent of perhaps 100 drachmai; see 15:8 note. *Occupy*: do business.   **19:14** *Message*: delegation.   **19:22–23** *Thou knewest . . . usury*: this accusation may suggest an alternative motive for the slave's refusal to trade with his master's money: reluctance to be identified with the unpopular nobleman's interests (cf. v. 14).   **19:26** *Unto every . . . taken away from him*: cf. 8:18.

²⁸And when he had thus spoken, he went before, ascending up to Jerusalem. ²⁹And it came to pass, when he was come nigh to Bethphage and Bethany, at the mount called the mount of Olives, he sent two of his disciples, ³⁰saying, Go ye into the village over against you; in the which at your entering ye shall find a colt tied, whereon yet never man sat: loose him, and bring him hither. ³¹And if any man ask you, Why do ye loose him? thus shall ye say unto him, Because the Lord hath need of him. ³²And they that were sent went their way, and found even as he had said unto them. ³³And as they were loosing the colt, the owners thereof said unto them, Why loose ye the colt? ³⁴And they said, The Lord hath need of him. ³⁵And they brought him to Jesus: and they cast their garments upon the colt, and they set Jesus thereon. ³⁶And as he went, they spread their clothes in the way.

³⁷And when he was come nigh, even now at the descent of the mount of Olives, the whole multitude of the disciples began to rejoice and praise God with a loud voice for all the mighty works that they had seen; ³⁸saying, Blessed be the King that cometh in the name of the Lord: peace in heaven, and glory in the highest. ³⁹And some of the Pharisees from among the multitude said unto him, Master, rebuke thy disciples. ⁴⁰And he answered and said unto them, I tell you that, if these should hold their peace, the stones would immediately cry out.

⁴¹And when he was come near, he beheld the city, and wept over it, ⁴²saying, If thou hadst known, even thou, at least in this thy day, the things which belong unto thy peace! but now they are hid from thine eyes. ⁴³For the days shall come upon thee, that thine enemies shall cast a trench about thee, and compass thee round, and keep thee in on every side, ⁴⁴and shall lay thee even with the ground, and thy children within thee; and they shall not leave in thee one stone upon another; because thou knewest not the time of thy visitation.

⁴⁵And he went into the temple, and began to cast out them that sold therein, and them that bought; ⁴⁶saying unto them, It is written, My house is the house of

---

19:28–40 Arrival at Jerusalem. Compare Matt 21:1–11; Mark 11:1–10 and notes.   **19:29** *Bethphage and Bethany*: see Mark 11:1.   **19:30** *A colt . . . sat*: see LXX Zech 9:9.   **19:33** *Owners*: lit. "lords." **19:35–36** *They set . . . way*: recalling the coronation of Solomon (1 Kgs 1:32–40) and Jehu's proclamation as king (2 Kgs 9:13).   **19:37** *At the descent . . . Olives*: perhaps echoing Zechariah's eschatological vision (14:4).   **19:38** *Blessed be . . . LORD*: quoting Ps 118:26, a song of royal procession; *king* is inserted to emphasize its regal overtones. *Peace in heaven . . . highest*: cf. 2:14.   **19:40** *The stones . . . out*: recalling John's preaching in 3:8, and perhaps echoing Hab 2:11.   **19:41–44** Predicting Jerusalem's destruction. The prophecy echoes Jer 6:13–15 and other OT oracles.   **19:42** *If thou . . . peace*: better "if you had recognized on this day, even you, the things that make for peace" (MS tradition; cf. NRSV).   **19:43–44** *The days . . . another*: referring to Rome's siege and destruction of Jerusalem in 70 C.E., likely a decade or two before Luke wrote.

19:45–21:38 In the temple. The final stage of Jesus' ministry in Luke takes place entirely in the Jerusalem temple: unlike Matthew's and Mark's Jesus, Luke's is not reported to exit it until the section's close (21:37–38). This extended unit is introduced by the temple's cleansing (19:45–48) and contains a series of debates with and prophetic denunciations of the religious establishment at Jerusalem (20:1–21:4), followed by an extended eschatological discourse (21:5–36).   **19:45–48** Cleansing the temple. Compare Matt 21:12–17; Mark 11:15–19 and notes. See also its earlier placement in John (2:13–22).   **19:45** *Them that sold*: sellers of animals for sacrifice. *Therein, and . . . bought*: better omitted (MS tradition).   **19:46** *My house . . . thieves*: Isa 56:7; Jer 7:11. *My house is*:

prayer: but ye have made it a den of thieves. [47]And he taught daily in the temple. But the chief priests and the scribes and the chief of the people sought to destroy him, [48]and could not find what they might do: for all the people were very attentive to hear him.

[20] And it came to pass, that on one of those days, as he taught the people in the temple, and preached the gospel, the chief priests and the scribes came upon him with the elders, [2]and spake unto him, saying, Tell us, by what authority doest thou these things? or who is he that gave thee this authority? [3]And he answered and said unto them, I will also ask you one thing; and answer me: [4]The baptism of John, was it from heaven, or of men? [5]And they reasoned with themselves, saying, If we shall say, From heaven; he will say, Why then believed ye him not? [6]But and if we say, Of men; all the people will stone us: for they be persuaded that John was a prophet. [7]And they answered, that they could not tell whence it was. [8]And Jesus said unto them, Neither tell I you by what authority I do these things.

[9]Then began he to speak to the people this parable; A certain man planted a vineyard, and let it forth to husbandmen, and went into a far country for a long time. [10]And at the season he sent a servant to the husbandmen, that they should give him of the fruit of the vineyard: but the husbandmen beat him, and sent him away empty. [11]And again he sent another servant: and they beat him also, and entreated him shamefully, and sent him away empty. [12]And again he sent a third: and they wounded him also, and cast him out. [13]Then said the lord of the vineyard, What shall I do? I will send my beloved son: it may be they will reverence him when they see him. [14]But when the husbandmen saw him, they reasoned among themselves, saying, This is the heir: come, let us kill him, that the inheritance may be ours. [15]So they cast him out of the vineyard, and killed him. What therefore shall the lord of the vineyard do unto them? [16]He shall come and destroy these husbandmen, and shall give the vineyard to others. And when they heard it, they said, God forbid. [17]And he beheld them, and said, What is this then that is written, The stone which the builders rejected, the same is become the head of the corner? [18]Whosoever shall fall upon that stone shall be broken; but on whomsoever it shall fall, it will grind him to powder. [19]And the chief priests and the scribes the same hour sought to lay hands on him; and they feared the people: for they perceived that he had spoken this parable against them.

[20]And they watched him, and sent forth spies, which should feign themselves just men, that they might take hold of his words, that so they might deliver him

---

better "my house will be" (MS tradition).   **19:47** *Chief priests . . . people*: probably the Jerusalem Sanhedrin. *The chief of the people* are the "elders" (20:1); see Mark 8:31 note.   **19:48** *Very attentive . . . him*: lit. "hung on him, listening."   **20:1–8** Whence Jesus' authority? Compare Matt 21:23–27; Mark 11:27–33.   **20:7** *Could not tell*: lit. "did not know."   **20:9–19** Parable of the Wicked Tenants. Compare Matt 21:33–46; Mark 12:1–12 and notes.   **20:9** *A certain . . . vineyard*: Luke obscures the allusion to Isa 5:1–7 evident in Mark's version.   **20:11** *Entreated*: treated.   **20:13** *Beloved son*: cf. 3:22; 9:35 (but see note).   **20:14** *Come, let us kill him*: echoing Gen 37:20; cf. 19:47. **20:17** *The stone . . . corner*: Ps 118:22. *The head of the corner*: either the cornerstone or a copestone.   **20:20–26** Paying tribute to Caesar. Compare Matt 22:15–22; Mark 12:13–17 and notes.

unto the power and authority of the governor. ²¹And they asked him, saying, Master, we know that thou sayest and teachest rightly, neither acceptest thou the person of any, but teachest the way of God truly: ²²is it lawful for us to give tribute unto Cæsar, or no? ²³But he perceived their craftiness, and said unto them, Why tempt ye me? ²⁴Shew me a penny. Whose image and superscription hath it? They answered and said, Cæsar's. ²⁵And he said unto them, Render therefore unto Cæsar the things which be Cæsar's, and unto God the things which be God's. ²⁶And they could not take hold of his words before the people: and they marvelled at his answer, and held their peace.

²⁷Then came to him certain of the Sadducees, which deny that there is any resurrection; and they asked him, ²⁸saying, Master, Moses wrote unto us, If any man's brother die, having a wife, and he die without children, that his brother should take his wife, and raise up seed unto his brother. ²⁹There were therefore seven brethren: and the first took a wife, and died without children. ³⁰And the second took her to wife, and he died childless. ³¹And the third took her; and in like manner the seven also: and they left no children, and died. ³²Last of all the woman died also. ³³Therefore in the resurrection whose wife of them is she? for seven had her to wife. ³⁴And Jesus answering said unto them, The children of this world marry, and are given in marriage: ³⁵but they which shall be accounted worthy to obtain that world, and the resurrection from the dead, neither marry, nor are given in marriage: ³⁶neither can they die any more: for they are equal unto the angels; and are the children of God, being the children of the resurrection. ³⁷Now that the dead are raised, even Moses shewed at the bush, when he calleth the Lord the God of Abraham, and the God of Isaac, and the God of Jacob. ³⁸For he is not a God of the dead, but of the living: for all live unto him. ³⁹Then certain of the scribes answering said, Master, thou hast well said. ⁴⁰And after that they durst not ask him any question at all.

⁴¹And he said unto them, How say they that Christ is David's son? ⁴²And David himself saith in the book of Psalms, The LORD said unto my Lord, Sit thou on my right hand, ⁴³till I make thine enemies thy footstool. ⁴⁴David therefore calleth him Lord, how is he then his son?

⁴⁵Then in the audience of all the people he said unto his disciples, ⁴⁶Beware of the scribes, which desire to walk in long robes, and love greetings in the markets, and the highest seats in the synagogues, and the chief rooms at feasts; ⁴⁷which devour widows' houses, and for a shew make long prayers: the same shall receive greater damnation.

20:20 *Governor*: Roman provincial ruler.   **20:23** *Why tempt ye me*: better omitted (MS tradition).   **20:24** *Penny*: see Mark 14:5 note.   **20:27–40** *Resurrection*. Compare Matt 22:23–33; Mark 12:18–27 and notes.   **20:28** *If any . . . unto his brother*: see Deut 25:5–10, on levirate marriage; cf. Gen 38:8.   **20:29–32** *There were . . . also*: cf. Gen 38:6–11.   **20:37** *At the bush*: i.e., in the place where he writes about the (burning) bush.   **20:37–38** *The Lord . . . living*: cf. Exod 3:6, 15–16; 4 *Maccabees* 7.19.   **20:41–44** Son of David. Compare Matt 22:41–46; Mark 12:35–37a and notes.   **20:42–43** *The LORD . . . footstool*: Ps 110:1.   **20:45–47** Denouncing the scribes. Compare Mark 12:37b–40 and notes. This passage recalls the denunciation of 11:37–54.   **20:46** *Chief rooms at feasts*: see 14:7–11 and notes.   **20:47** *Damnation*: condemnation.

21 And he looked up, and saw the rich men casting their gifts into the treasury. ²And he saw also a certain poor widow casting in thither two mites. ³And he said, Of a truth I say unto you, that this poor widow hath cast in more than they all: ⁴for all these have of their abundance cast in unto the offerings of God: but she of her penury hath cast in all the living that she had.

⁵And as some spake of the temple, how it was adorned with goodly stones and gifts, he said, ⁶As for these things which ye behold, the days will come, in the which there shall not be left one stone upon another, that shall not be thrown down. ⁷And they asked him, saying, Master, but when shall these things be? and what sign will there be when these things shall come to pass?

⁸And he said, Take heed that ye be not deceived: for many shall come in my name, saying, I am Christ; and the time draweth near: go ye not therefore after them. ⁹But when ye shall hear of wars and commotions, be not terrified: for these things must first come to pass; but the end is not by and by. ¹⁰Then said he unto them, Nation shall rise against nation, and kingdom against kingdom: ¹¹and great earthquakes shall be in divers places, and famines, and pestilences; and fearful sights and great signs shall there be from heaven.

¹²But before all these, they shall lay their hands on you, and persecute you, delivering you up to the synagogues, and into prisons, being brought before kings and rulers for my name's sake. ¹³And it shall turn to you for a testimony. ¹⁴Settle it therefore in your hearts, not to meditate before what ye shall answer: ¹⁵for I will give you a mouth and wisdom, which all your adversaries shall not be able to gainsay nor resist. ¹⁶And ye shall be betrayed both by parents, and brethren, and kinsfolks, and friends; and some of you shall they cause to be put to death. ¹⁷And ye shall be hated of all men for my name's sake. ¹⁸But there shall not an hair of your head perish. ¹⁹In your patience possess ye your souls.

²⁰And when ye shall see Jerusalem compassed with armies, then know that the

21:1–4 The widow's mites. Compare Mark 12:41–44 and notes. 21:2 *Mites*: coins of the smallest denomination. 21:5–38 The coming end. See Mark 13:2–27 notes. The structure of Luke's version of Jesus' apocalyptic discourse is tighter than Mark's or Matthew's. After a prophecy about the temple's destruction (vv. 5–7) that ushers in an overview of the eschatological consummation (vv. 8–11), Jesus progresses chronologically; he moves from a time of persecution and testimony (vv. 12–19), which would correspond to the period narrated in Acts, to Jerusalem's destruction (vv. 20–24), an event that was probably fresh in the author's memory, to a series of cosmic cataclysms ending in the Son of Man's advent (vv. 25–28). The discourse closes (vv. 29–36) with an exhortation to watch and wait patiently for the eschatological consummation, but the reiterated commands for watchfulness stand in some tension with 17:20–37 (see note). 21:5–7 The temple's destruction. Compare Matt 24:1–3; Mark 13:1–4 and notes. 21:8–11 Signs of the coming end. Compare Matt 24:4–8; Mark 13:5–8 and notes. 21:8 *Take heed*: lit. "see" (so throughout). *I am Christ*: Gk. *egō eimi*, "it is I," echoing Exod 3:14. 21:9–10 *But when . . . against kingdom*: cf. 2 Chr 15:6; Isa 19:2; Jer 51:46; 2 Esd 13:31; etc. 21:9 *Commotions*: the Greek word can refer to political unrest. *By and by*: immediate. 21:11 *Great earthquakes . . . heaven*: cf. Joel 2:10, 30–31. 21:12–19 Impending persecution. Compare Matt 10:17–21; 24:9–14; Mark 13:9–13 and notes. 21:13 *It shall turn to you*: it shall give you opportunity. 21:14–15 *Settle it . . . resist*: cf. 12:11–12. 21:16 *Ye shall be betrayed . . . death*: echoing Mic 7:6, also alluded to in 12:53. 21:18 *There shall not . . . perish*: cf. 1 Sam 14:45; 2 Sam 14:11. 21:19 *In your patience . . . souls*: better "by your endurance, gain your lives" (MS tradition; our translation). 21:20–24 Jerusalem's desolation. Compare Matt 24:15–22; Mark 13:14–20 and notes. This section recalls Jesus' earlier oracle against Jerusalem (19:41–44). 21:20 *When*

desolation thereof is nigh. [21]Then let them which are in Judæa flee to the mountains; and let them which are in the midst of it depart out; and let not them that
are in the countries enter thereinto. [22]For these be the days of vengeance, that all
things which are written may be fulfilled. [23]But woe unto them that are with child,
and to them that give suck, in those days! for there shall be great distress in the
land, and wrath upon this people. [24]And they shall fall by the edge of the sword,
and shall be led away captive into all nations: and Jerusalem shall be trodden down
of the Gentiles, until the times of the Gentiles be fulfilled.

[25]And there shall be signs in the sun, and in the moon, and in the stars; and
upon the earth distress of nations, with perplexity; the sea and the waves roaring;
[26]men's hearts failing them for fear, and for looking after those things which are
coming on the earth: for the powers of heaven shall be shaken. [27]And then shall
they see the Son of man coming in a cloud with power and great glory. [28]And
when these things begin to come to pass, then look up, and lift up your heads; for
your redemption draweth nigh.

[29]And he spake to them a parable; Behold the fig tree, and all the trees; [30]when
they now shoot forth, ye see and know of your own selves that summer is now
nigh at hand. [31]So likewise ye, when ye see these things come to pass, know ye
that the kingdom of God is nigh at hand. [32]Verily I say unto you, This generation
shall not pass away, till all be fulfilled. [33]Heaven and earth shall pass away: but
my words shall not pass away.

[34]And take heed to yourselves, lest at any time your hearts be overcharged with
surfeiting, and drunkenness, and cares of this life, and so that day come upon you
unawares. [35]For as a snare shall it come on all them that dwell on the face of the
whole earth. [36]Watch ye therefore, and pray always, that ye may be accounted worthy to escape all these things that shall come to pass, and to stand before the Son
of man.

[37]And in the day time he was teaching in the temple; and at night he went out,
and abode in the mount that is called the mount of Olives. [38]And all the people
came early in the morning to him in the temple, for to hear him.

---

ye . . . nigh: Luke replaces Mark's obscure reference to the "abomination of desolation" (13:14) with
a clear reference to Rome's siege and destruction of Jerusalem in the Jewish War of 66–70 C.E.
21:21 *Countries*: countryside. **21:22** *Days of vengeance*: cf. LXX Hos 9:7. **21:24** *Be led . . .
nations*: cf. Deut 28:64; Jer 21:7; Ezek 32:9. The prophetic echoes assimilate Jerusalem's eschatological woes to those of the Southern Kingdom during the Babylonian captivity. *And Jerusalem shall
be trodden down of the Gentiles*: cf. LXX Zech 12:3. *Times of the Gentiles*: a reference to God's use
of Rome to destroy Jerusalem, and probably also to the Gentiles' evangelization, which Acts narrates. **21:25–28** The Son of Man's coming. Compare Matt 24:29–31; Mark 13:24–27 and notes.
21:25 *There shall be . . . stars*: cf. Isa 13:10; 34:4; Joel 2:10, 30–31; etc. **21:26** *Powers of heaven*: see
Mark 13:25 note. **21:27** *Son of man . . . glory*: see Dan 7:13–14; cf. Luke 9:26. **21:28** *Your redemption draweth nigh*: see 1:68 and note. **21:29–33** Parable of the Fig Tree. Compare Matt 24:32–36;
Mark 13:28–32 and notes. **21:32** *This generation . . . fulfilled*: cf. 9:27. **21:33** *Heaven . . . not pass
away*: recalling Isa 40:8; 51:6; cf. Luke 16:17. **21:34–36** Need for watchfulness. **21:34** *Overcharged*: burdened. **21:35** *As a snare . . . earth*: cf. Isa 24:17. **21:36** *Accounted worthy*: better "able"
(MS tradition). **21:37–38** *And in . . . hear him*: these verses form an inclusive frame with Jesus' entry
into the temple (19:45–20:1) and mark the end of his teaching there.

22 Now the feast of unleavened bread drew nigh, which is called the Pass-over. ²And the chief priests and scribes sought how they might kill him; for they feared the people.

³Then entered Satan into Judas surnamed Iscariot, being of the number of the twelve. ⁴And he went his way, and communed with the chief priests and captains, how he might betray him unto them. ⁵And they were glad, and covenanted to give him money. ⁶And he promised, and sought opportunity to betray him unto them in the absence of the multitude.

⁷Then came the day of unleavened bread, when the passover must be killed. ⁸And he sent Peter and John, saying, Go and prepare us the passover, that we may eat. ⁹And they said unto him, Where wilt thou that we prepare? ¹⁰And he said unto them, Behold, when ye are entered into the city, there shall a man meet you, bearing a pitcher of water; follow him into the house where he entereth in. ¹¹And ye shall say unto the goodman of the house, The Master saith unto thee, Where is the guestchamber, where I shall eat the passover with my disciples? ¹²And he shall shew you a large upper room furnished: there make ready. ¹³And they went, and found as he had said unto them: and they made ready the passover.

¹⁴And when the hour was come, he sat down, and the twelve apostles with him. ¹⁵And he said unto them, With desire I have desired to eat this passover with you before I suffer: ¹⁶for I say unto you, I will not any more eat thereof, until it be ful-filled in the kingdom of God. ¹⁷And he took the cup, and gave thanks, and said, Take this, and divide it among yourselves: ¹⁸for I say unto you, I will not drink of the fruit of the vine, until the kingdom of God shall come. ¹⁹And he took bread, and gave thanks, and brake it, and gave unto them, saying, This is my body which is given for you: this do in remembrance of me. ²⁰Likewise also the cup after supper, saying, This cup is the new testament in my blood, which is shed for you. ²¹But, behold, the hand of him that betrayeth me is with me on the table. ²²And truly the Son of man goeth, as it was determined: but woe unto that man by whom he is betrayed! ²³And they began to inquire among themselves, which of them it was that should do this thing.

²⁴And there was also a strife among them, which of them should be accounted the greatest. ²⁵And he said unto them, The kings of the Gentiles exercise lord-ship over them; and they that exercise authority upon them are called benefactors.

22:1–23:56 Jesus' arrest, crucifixion, and burial. **22:1–6** Conspiracy. Compare Matt 26:1–5, 14–16; Mark 14:1–2, 10–11 and notes. **22:1** *Passover*: see Exod 12:1–13:10. **22:3** *Then entered . . . Iscariot*: Luke alone of the Synoptics attributes Judas' betrayal to satanic influence (but see John 13:2, 27), thereby marking Satan's return to the narrative (see 4:13 note). **22:4** *Captains*: of the temple guard. **22:7–13** Passover preparations. Compare Matt 26:17–19; Mark 14:12–16 and notes. **22:7** *The passover*: i.e., the Passover lamb. **22:14–23** The Lord's Supper. Compare Matt 26:20–29; Mark 14:17–25 and notes; John 13:21–30. **22:14** *Twelve*: better omitted (MS tradition). **22:15** *With desire I have desired*: i.e., "I have strongly desired" (imitating a conventional LXX construction). **22:17–20** *He took . . . you*: in addition to the Synoptic Gospels, 1 Cor 11:23–25 narrates this meal. Jesus' serving of the wine (v. 17) and especially of bread (v. 19) recalls the earlier miraculous feeding (9:16). **22:20** *Testament*: better "covenant." For the "new covenant," see Jer 31:31–34 (cf. 2 Cor 3:6); for the covenant's association with blood, see Exod 24:8; Zech 9:11. **22:22** *The Son . . . betrayed*: cf. 17:1. **22:24–30** Priority in God's kingdom. Compare Matt 20:25–28; 19:28; Mark 10:42–45 and notes. Discussion about who would betray Jesus

²⁶But ye shall not be so: but he that is greatest among you, let him be as the younger; and he that is chief, as he that doth serve. ²⁷For whether is greater, he that sitteth at meat, or he that serveth? is not he that sitteth at meat? but I am among you as he that serveth. ²⁸Ye are they which have continued with me in my temptations. ²⁹And I appoint unto you a kingdom, as my Father hath appointed unto me; ³⁰that ye may eat and drink at my table in my kingdom, and sit on thrones judging the twelve tribes of Israel.

³¹And the Lord said, Simon, Simon, behold, Satan hath desired to have you, that he may sift you as wheat: ³²but I have prayed for thee, that thy faith fail not: and when thou art converted, strengthen thy brethren. ³³And he said unto him, Lord, I am ready to go with thee, both into prison, and to death. ³⁴And he said, I tell thee, Peter, the cock shall not crow this day, before that thou shalt thrice deny that thou knowest me.

³⁵And he said unto them, When I sent you without purse, and scrip, and shoes, lacked ye any thing? And they said, Nothing. ³⁶Then said he unto them, But now, he that hath a purse, let him take it, and likewise his scrip: and he that hath no sword, let him sell his garment, and buy one. ³⁷For I say unto you, that this that is written must yet be accomplished in me, And he was reckoned among the transgressors: for the things concerning me have an end. ³⁸And they said, Lord, behold, here are two swords. And he said unto them, It is enough.

³⁹And he came out, and went, as he was wont, to the mount of Olives; and his disciples also followed him. ⁴⁰And when he was at the place, he said unto them, Pray that ye enter not into temptation. ⁴¹And he was withdrawn from them about a stone's cast, and kneeled down, and prayed, ⁴²saying, Father, if thou be willing, remove this cup from me: nevertheless not my will, but thine, be done. ⁴³And there appeared an angel unto him from heaven, strengthening him. ⁴⁴And being in an agony he prayed more earnestly: and his sweat was as it were great drops of blood falling down to the ground. ⁴⁵And when he rose up from prayer, and was

---

gives way to a dispute about who is best. The apostles' wrangling over position amounts to a rejection of Jesus' previous teaching (cf. 9:46–48) and assimilates them to those Jesus rebuked at the chief Pharisee's dinner (14:7–11). **22:26** *As the younger:* cf. 9:46–47. **22:27** *Whether:* which. **22:28** *Continued with me in my temptations:* perhaps another hint at Satan's return to the narrative (cf. 4:13). **22:31–34** Peter's denial predicted. Compare Matt 26:31–35; Mark 14:27–31 and notes; John 13:36–38. **22:31** *And the Lord said:* better omitted (MS tradition). *Satan hath desired to have you:* lit. "Satan has requested you all." Luke imagines an exchange between Satan and God like that in Job 1–2. The similarity between Satan's desire to "sift" the apostles "as wheat" and John the Baptist's image of divine judgment (3:17) confirms God's collusion with Satan in the testing/temptation (vv. 40, 46). **22:32** *For thee:* only at this point in the Greek do the second-person pronouns shift to the singular, referring to Peter alone. *When thou art converted:* when you turn back. **22:35–38** Purse, bag, and sword. Jesus alters his earlier directives (cf. 9:3; 10:4). In light of his own impending treatment as a criminal (v. 37), he no longer assumes his disciples will be able to rely on others' good will. **22:37** *He was reckoned among the transgressors:* Isa 53:12. **22:38** *It is enough:* implying that two swords are sufficient or expressing exasperation at the apostles' eagerness for violence (cf. vv. 49–51). **22:39–46** Jesus' agonizing prayer. Compare Matt 26:36–46; Mark 14:32–42 and notes; John 12:27–30. **22:40** *Pray that . . . temptation:* repeated in v. 46; cf. 8:13; 11:4; 22:31–32. **22:42** *Cup:* see Mark 10:38 note. **22:43–44** *And there . . . ground:* better omitted (MS tradition), but this likely interpolation is very ancient. (Justin Martyr refers to it in the mid-second century.)

come to his disciples, he found them sleeping for sorrow, **⁴⁶**and said unto them, Why sleep ye? rise and pray, lest ye enter into temptation.

⁴⁷And while he yet spake, behold a multitude, and he that was called Judas, one of the twelve, went before them, and drew near unto Jesus to kiss him. **⁴⁸**But Jesus said unto him, Judas, betrayest thou the Son of man with a kiss? **⁴⁹**When they which were about him saw what would follow, they said unto him, Lord, shall we smite with the sword? **⁵⁰**And one of them smote the servant of the high priest, and cut off his right ear. **⁵¹**And Jesus answered and said, Suffer ye thus far. And he touched his ear, and healed him. **⁵²**Then Jesus said unto the chief priests, and captains of the temple, and the elders, which were come to him, Be ye come out, as against a thief, with swords and staves? **⁵³**When I was daily with you in the temple, ye stretched forth no hands against me: but this is your hour, and the power of darkness.

⁵⁴Then took they him, and led him, and brought him into the high priest's house. And Peter followed afar off. **⁵⁵**And when they had kindled a fire in the midst of the hall, and were set down together, Peter sat down among them. **⁵⁶**But a certain maid beheld him as he sat by the fire, and earnestly looked upon him, and said, This man was also with him. **⁵⁷**And he denied him, saying, Woman, I know him not. **⁵⁸**And after a little while another saw him, and said, Thou art also of them. And Peter said, Man, I am not. **⁵⁹**And about the space of one hour after another confidently affirmed, saying, Of a truth this fellow also was with him: for he is a Galilæan. **⁶⁰**And Peter said, Man, I know not what thou sayest. And immediately, while he yet spake, the cock crew. **⁶¹**And the Lord turned, and looked upon Peter. And Peter remembered the word of the Lord, how he had said unto him, Before the cock crow, thou shalt deny me thrice. **⁶²**And Peter went out, and wept bitterly.

⁶³And the men that held Jesus mocked him, and smote him. **⁶⁴**And when they had blindfolded him, they struck him on the face, and asked him, saying, Prophesy, who is it that smote thee? **⁶⁵**And many other things blasphemously spake they against him.

⁶⁶And as soon as it was day, the elders of the people and the chief priests and the scribes came together, and led him into their council, saying, **⁶⁷**Art thou the Christ? tell us. And he said unto them, If I tell you, ye will not believe: **⁶⁸**and if I also ask you, ye will not answer me, nor let me go. **⁶⁹**Hereafter shall the Son of man sit on the right hand of the power of God. **⁷⁰**Then said they all, Art thou then

---

22:45 *Sleeping for sorrow*: cf. 9:32. Mark's portrayal of the sleeping disciples is far less forgiving (14:37–41). **22:47–53** Jesus' arrest. Compare Matt 26:47–56; Mark 14:43–52 and notes; John 18:2–11. **22:47** *To kiss him*: cf. 2 Sam 20:9–10. **22:51** *Suffer ye thus far*: i.e., "allow even this." *He touched . . . him*: the slave's healing, which Luke alone records, represents Jesus' total repudiation of the violence his disciple adopted and exemplifies his teaching about love of enemies (6:27–36). Jesus' actions may amount to a prohibition against using the swords he had just urged his disciples to buy, suggesting that earlier he was speaking figuratively (see v. 38 and note). **22:54–71** Peter's denial and the council's judgment. Compare Matt 26:57–75; Mark 14:53–72 and notes; John 18:12–27. **22:55** *Hall*: better "courtyard." **22:63–65** *The men . . . him*: Luke's juxtaposition of this episode to Peter's denial, which Jesus prophesied, underscores the dramatic irony of their mockery. **22:64** *Struck him . . . and*: better omitted (MS tradition). **22:66** *Council*: Sanhedrin (see Mark 8:31 note). **22:68** *Me, nor . . . go*: better omitted (MS tradition). **22:69** *Sit on . . . God*: cf. Ps 110:1; Luke 20:42.

the Son of God? And he said unto them, Ye say that I am. ⁷¹And they said, What need we any further witness? for we ourselves have heard of his own mouth.

23 And the whole multitude of them arose, and led him unto Pilate. ²And they began to accuse him, saying, We found this fellow perverting the nation, and forbidding to give tribute to Cæsar, saying that he himself is Christ a King. ³And Pilate asked him, saying, Art thou the King of the Jews? And he answered him and said, Thou sayest it. ⁴Then said Pilate to the chief priests and to the people, I find no fault in this man. ⁵And they were the more fierce, saying, He stirreth up the people, teaching throughout all Jewry, beginning from Galilee to this place. ⁶When Pilate heard of Galilee, he asked whether the man were a Galilæan. ⁷And as soon as he knew that he belonged unto Herod's jurisdiction, he sent him to Herod, who himself also was at Jerusalem at that time.

⁸And when Herod saw Jesus, he was exceeding glad: for he was desirous to see him of a long season, because he had heard many things of him; and he hoped to have seen some miracle done by him. ⁹Then he questioned with him in many words; but he answered him nothing. ¹⁰And the chief priests and scribes stood and vehemently accused him. ¹¹And Herod with his men of war set him at nought, and mocked him, and arrayed him in a gorgeous robe, and sent him again to Pilate. ¹²And the same day Pilate and Herod were made friends together: for before they were at enmity between themselves.

¹³And Pilate, when he had called together the chief priests and the rulers and the people, ¹⁴said unto them, Ye have brought this man unto me, as one that perverteth the people: and, behold, I, having examined him before you, have found no fault in this man touching those things whereof ye accuse him: ¹⁵no, nor yet Herod: for I sent you to him; and, lo, nothing worthy of death is done unto him. ¹⁶I will therefore chastise him, and release him. ¹⁷(For of necessity he must release one unto them at the feast.) ¹⁸And they cried out all at once, saying, Away with this man, and release unto us Barabbas: ¹⁹(who for a certain sedition made in the city, and for murder, was cast into prison.) ²⁰Pilate therefore, willing to release Jesus, spake again to them. ²¹But they cried, saying, Crucify him, crucify him. ²²And he said unto them the third time, Why, what evil hath he done? I have found no cause

---

22:70 *I am*: Gk. *egō eimi*; cf. 21:8 and note.   **23:1–7** Before Pilate. Compare Matt 27:1–14; Mark 15:1–5; John 18:28–38.   **23:2** *Forbidding to give tribute to Cæsar*: cf. 20:20–26. *Christ a king*: better "an anointed king" (see Mark 1:1 note).   **23:4** *People*: Gk. *ochloi*, lit. "crowds" or "multitude"; in 22:47 the Greek word refers to the Sanhedrin and its attendants (cf. 22:52), as it must here—"the people" (Gk. *laos*) are named as another group in the very next verse.   **23:5** *Fierce*: or insistent. *Jewry*: lit. "Judea."   **23:8–12** Before Herod.   **23:8** *He was desirous . . . by him*: cf. 9:7–9; earlier he wished to kill Jesus (13:31).   **23:9** *He questioned . . . nothing*: cf. Isa 53:7.   **23:11** *Men of war*: soldiers.   **23:12** *Pilate and Herod . . . together*: cf. Ps 2:1–2, which Acts 4:25–28 cites as a prophecy of their relationship.   **23:13–25** Sentencing. Compare Matt 27:15–26; Mark 15:6–15 and notes; John 18:38b–19:16.   **23:14** *People*: Gk. *laos* (see v. 4 note). Here Luke refers to the Jerusalem populace, which had supported Jesus (e.g., 19:38) and which the Sanhedrin had feared (20:19; 22:2). Matthew and Mark explain the people's altered disposition toward Jesus (Matt 27:20; Mark 15:11), while John seems to avoid the problem (see 18:31 note). Luke offers no explanation of their change in heart, but implies that not all were of like mind (see vv. 27, 48 and notes).   **23:15** *I sent you to him*: better "he sent him [back] to us" (MS tradition). *Unto*: better "by."   **23:17** *For of necessity . . . feast*: better omitted (MS tradition) as a gloss, based on Matt 27:15 and Mark 15:6, to explain Pilate's actions.

of death in him: I will therefore chastise him, and let him go. ²³And they were instant with loud voices, requiring that he might be crucified. And the voices of them and of the chief priests prevailed. ²⁴And Pilate gave sentence that it should be as they required. ²⁵And he released unto them him that for sedition and murder was cast into prison, whom they had desired; but he delivered Jesus to their will.

²⁶And as they led him away, they laid hold upon one Simon, a Cyrenian, coming out of the country, and on him they laid the cross, that he might bear it after Jesus. ²⁷And there followed him a great company of people, and of women, which also bewailed and lamented him. ²⁸But Jesus turning unto them said, Daughters of Jerusalem, weep not for me, but weep for yourselves, and for your children. ²⁹For, behold, the days are coming, in the which they shall say, Blessed are the barren, and the wombs that never bare, and the paps which never gave suck. ³⁰Then shall they begin to say to the mountains, Fall on us; and to the hills, Cover us. ³¹For if they do these things in a green tree, what shall be done in the dry?

³²And there were also two other, malefactors, led with him to be put to death. ³³And when they were come to the place, which is called Calvary, there they crucified him, and the malefactors, one on the right hand, and the other on the left. ³⁴Then said Jesus, Father, forgive them; for they know not what they do. And they parted his raiment, and cast lots. ³⁵And the people stood beholding. And the rulers also with them derided him, saying, He saved others; let him save himself, if he be Christ, the chosen of God. ³⁶And the soldiers also mocked him, coming to him, and offering him vinegar, ³⁷and saying, If thou be the king of the Jews, save thyself. ³⁸And a superscription also was written over him in letters of Greek, and Latin, and Hebrew, This is the King of the Jews.

23:23 *Instant*: urgent. *And of the chief priests*: better omitted (MS tradition). **23:25** *Desired*: Gk. *aiteō*, "demand, require"; cf. vv. 23–24. *Their will*: as opposed to Pilate's (v. 20). **23:26–49** Crucifixion. Compare Matt 27:32–56; Mark 15:21–41 and notes; John 19:17–37. **23:26** *Cyrenian*: Cyrene was a city in North Africa. *Coming out . . . country*: i.e., he was not among those who demanded Jesus' death. *On him . . . Jesus*: cf. 9:23; 14:27. **23:27** *There followed . . . lamented him*: Luke refuses to paint the Jerusalemites with broad strokes, introducing citizens who apparently did not join the call for Jesus' death. Later, he displays Jerusalemites regretting Jesus' execution (see v. 48 and note) and in Acts' opening chapters, a good many of them will come to faith in Jesus. **23:28** *Weep not for me*: cf. 7:13–14; 8:52. **23:29** *Behold, the days are coming*: compare Luke's other oracles against Jerusalem: 13:34–35; 19:41–44; 21:20–24. *Blessed are . . . suck*: echoing Isa 54:1, but reversing its significance. **23:30** *To the mountains . . . cover us*: cf. Hos 10:8. **23:31** *For if . . . dry*: perhaps adapting a proverb. Jesus would be the green wood, difficult to set alight, while the Jerusalemites are dry wood, easily burned. **23:32** *Malefactors*: criminals (cf. vv. 33, 39). **23:33** *Calvary*: Gk. *kranion*, "skull"; the other gospels use the name "Golgotha," transliterating an Aramaic word for skull. "Calvary" derives from the Latin word for skull used in the Vulgate, *Calvaria*; it has no basis in the Greek text, but had long been a common English name for the site of Jesus' execution (appearing even in the Anglo-Saxon version of the verse: "þa stowe þe is genemned caluarie þæt is heafodpannan stow"). **23:34** *Then said . . . do*: better omitted (MS tradition) as a scribal addition that attributes to the dying Jesus the final sentiment of Stephen (Acts 7:60) and thereby supplements Luke's own assimilation of the two martyrdoms. *They parted . . . lots*: cf. Ps 22:18. **23:35** *Derided him . . . himself*: echoing Ps 22:7–8. Jesus' refusal to heed the repeated call to save himself (here, vv. 37, 39) should be understood in light of 9:24 and 17:33; cf. 4:9–12. *The chosen of God*: alluding to Isa 42:1 ("mine elect"); cf. 9:35 note. **23:36** *Vinegar*: cf. Ps 69:21. **23:38** *In letters . . . Hebrew*: better omitted (MS tradition) as

39And one of the malefactors which were hanged railed on him, saying, If thou be Christ, save thyself and us. 40But the other answering rebuked him, saying, Dost not thou fear God, seeing thou art in the same condemnation? 41And we indeed justly; for we receive the due reward of our deeds: but this man hath done nothing amiss. 42And he said unto Jesus, Lord, remember me when thou comest into thy kingdom. 43And Jesus said unto him, Verily I say unto thee, To day shalt thou be with me in paradise.

44And it was about the sixth hour, and there was a darkness over all the earth until the ninth hour. 45And the sun was darkened, and the veil of the temple was rent in the midst. 46And when Jesus had cried with a loud voice, he said, Father, into thy hands I commend my spirit: and having said thus, he gave up the ghost. 47Now when the centurion saw what was done, he glorified God, saying, Certainly this was a righteous man. 48And all the people that came together to that sight, beholding the things which were done, smote their breasts, and returned. 49And all his acquaintance, and the women that followed him from Galilee, stood afar off, beholding these things.

50And, behold, there was a man named Joseph, a counseller; and he was a good man, and a just: 51(the same had not consented to the counsel and deed of them;) he was of Arimathæa, a city of the Jews: who also himself waited for the kingdom of God. 52This man went unto Pilate, and begged the body of Jesus. 53And he took it down, and wrapped it in linen, and laid it in a sepulchre that was hewn in stone, wherein never man before was laid. 54And that day was the preparation, and the sabbath drew on. 55And the women also, which came with him from Galilee, followed after, and beheld the sepulchre, and how his body was laid. 56And they returned, and prepared spices and ointments; and rested the sabbath day according to the commandment.

---

a scribal assimilation to John 19:20. **23:39** *Railed on*: Gk. *eblasphēmei*, "slandered" or "denigrated." **23:42** *Lord*: better omitted (MS tradition). **23:43** *To day . . . paradise*: some Jewish texts reimagine paradise (the garden from Gen 2–3) as the heavenly dwelling of the souls of the righteous departed, but this understanding is rare in the NT, which usually emphasizes bodily resurrection (e.g., Luke 14:14). Some NT texts suggest that martyrs do not wait with everyone else to enjoy their eschatological afterlife (cf. Phil 1:23, where Paul ponders the possibility of dying while imprisoned for Christ; Rev 20:4–6). Perhaps Jesus graciously offers the dying criminal the immediate paradisical afterlife normally reserved for martyrs. Alternatively, Luke may be conflating an understanding of the immortal soul with an expectation of eschatological bodily resurrection. **23:44** *The sixth hour*: noon; for darkness at noon, see Amos 8:9 (cf. 1:78–79; 22:53). *The ninth hour*: 3 P.M. **23:45** *The veil . . . midst*: an ambiguous sign; see Mark 15:38 note. **23:46** *Father, into . . . spirit*: cf. Ps 31:5. *Gave up the ghost*: lit. "expired." **23:48** *Smote their breasts*: presumably in repentance (cf. 18:13). This verse forms an inclusive frame with v. 27, surrounding Jesus' crucifixion with statements of mourning. **23:49** *And all . . . off*: echoing Ps 38:11; cf. 22:54. *And all his acquaintance*: in the other synoptics, only Jesus' female followers witness his execution, the men having already fled. **23:50–56** Burial. Compare Matt 27:57–61; Mark 15:42–47 and notes; John 19:38–42. **23:50** *A counseller*: a member of the Sanhedrin; cf. 22:66; Mark 8:31 note. **23:54** *The preparation*: the day preceding the Sabbath.

24 Now upon the first day of the week, very early in the morning, they came unto the sepulchre, bringing the spices which they had prepared, and certain others with them. ²And they found the stone rolled away from the sepulchre. ³And they entered in, and found not the body of the Lord Jesus. ⁴And it came to pass, as they were much perplexed thereabout, behold, two men stood by them in shining garments: ⁵and as they were afraid, and bowed down their faces to the earth, they said unto them, Why seek ye the living among the dead? ⁶He is not here, but is risen: remember how he spake unto you when he was yet in Galilee, ⁷saying, The Son of man must be delivered into the hands of sinful men, and be crucified, and the third day rise again. ⁸And they remembered his words, ⁹and returned from the sepulchre, and told all these things unto the eleven, and to all the rest. ¹⁰It was Mary Magdalene, and Joanna, and Mary the mother of James, and other women that were with them, which told these things unto the apostles. ¹¹And their words seemed to them as idle tales, and they believed them not. ¹²Then arose Peter, and ran unto the sepulchre; and stooping down, he beheld the linen clothes laid by themselves, and departed, wondering in himself at that which was come to pass.

¹³And, behold, two of them went that same day to a village called Emmaus, which was from Jerusalem about threescore furlongs. ¹⁴And they talked together of all these things which had happened. ¹⁵And it came to pass, that, while they communed together and reasoned, Jesus himself drew near, and went with them. ¹⁶But their eyes were holden that they should not know him. ¹⁷And he said unto them, What manner of communications are these that ye have one to another, as ye walk, and are sad? ¹⁸And the one of them, whose name was Cleopas, answering said unto him, Art thou only a stranger in Jerusalem, and hast not known the things which are come to pass there in these days? ¹⁹And he said unto them, What things? And they said unto him, Concerning Jesus of Nazareth, which was a prophet mighty in deed and word before God and all the people: ²⁰and how the chief priests and our rulers delivered him to be condemned to death, and have crucified him. ²¹But we trusted that it had been he which should have redeemed Israel: and beside all this, to day is the third day since these things were done. ²²Yea, and certain women also of our company made us astonished, which were early at the sepulchre; ²³and when they found not his body, they came, saying, that they had also seen a vision

24:1–53 **Resurrection.** 24:1–12 Empty tomb. Compare Matt 28:1–10; Mark 16:1–8 and notes; John 20:1–10. **24:1** *First day*: Sunday. *And certain . . . them*: better omitted (MS tradition). **24:4** *Two men . . . garments*: later called angels (see v. 23). **24:5** *Why seek . . . dead*: recalling Jesus' teaching about resurrection in 20:38. **24:6–7** *Remember how . . . again*: cf. 9:22, 44. **24:10** *Mary Magdalene, and Joanna*: cf. 8:2–3 (and v. 2 note). *Mary the mother of James*: presumably Jesus' mother (cf. Acts 12:17 and note), now identified as mother of Jesus' brother James because Jesus has died. **24:13–35** On the road to Emmaus. Unique to Luke, this episode recalls a number of Genesis theophanies (e.g., 16:7–15; 18:1–33) and anticipates the story of Philip and the Ethiopian eunuch in Acts 8. **24:13** *Threescore furlongs*: Gk. "sixty stadia," about seven miles. **24:15** *Communed*: conversed. **24:17** *Walk, and are sad*: better "walk? And they stood still, sad" (MS tradition). **24:20–21** *And how . . . done*: recalling Jesus' prophecies from 9:22, 44; 18:32–33; cf. 24:7. Since these also include references to his resurrection, the disciples have information that should allow them to infer that Jesus has risen; because they do not, he rebukes them as fools (v. 25).

of angels, which said that he was alive. ²⁴And certain of them which were with us went to the sepulchre, and found it even so as the women had said: but him they saw not. ²⁵Then he said unto them, O fools, and slow of heart to believe all that the prophets have spoken: ²⁶ought not Christ to have suffered these things, and to enter into his glory? ²⁷And beginning at Moses and all the prophets, he expounded unto them in all the scriptures the things concerning himself.

²⁸And they drew nigh unto the village, whither they went: and he made as though he would have gone further. ²⁹But they constrained him, saying, Abide with us: for it is toward evening, and the day is far spent. And he went in to tarry with them. ³⁰And it came to pass, as he sat at meat with them, he took bread, and blessed it, and brake, and gave to them. ³¹And their eyes were opened, and they knew him; and he vanished out of their sight. ³²And they said one to another, Did not our heart burn within us, while he talked with us by the way, and while he opened to us the scriptures? ³³And they rose up the same hour, and returned to Jerusalem, and found the eleven gathered together, and them that were with them, ³⁴saying, The Lord is risen indeed, and hath appeared to Simon. ³⁵And they told what things were done in the way, and how he was known of them in breaking of bread.

³⁶And as they thus spake, Jesus himself stood in the midst of them, and saith unto them, Peace be unto you. ³⁷But they were terrified and affrighted, and supposed that they had seen a spirit. ³⁸And he said unto them, Why are ye troubled? and why do thoughts arise in your hearts? ³⁹Behold my hands and my feet, that it is I myself: handle me, and see; for a spirit hath not flesh and bones, as ye see me have. ⁴⁰And when he had thus spoken, he shewed them his hands and his feet. ⁴¹And while they yet believed not for joy, and wondered, he said unto them, Have ye here any meat? ⁴²And they gave him a piece of a broiled fish, and of an honeycomb. ⁴³And he took it, and did eat before them.

⁴⁴And he said unto them, These are the words which I spake unto you, while I was yet with you, that all things must be fulfilled, which were written in the law of Moses, and in the prophets, and in the psalms, concerning me. ⁴⁵Then opened he their understanding, that they might understand the scriptures, ⁴⁶and said unto them, Thus it is written, and thus it behoved Christ to suffer, and to rise from the

---

24:25 *Heart:* see 1:66 note.   **24:26** *Ought not . . . glory:* in light of Jesus' persistent teaching about status reversal (9:46–48; 13:30; 22:26; etc.) glory's emergence from suffering is to be expected. **24:30–31** *He took . . . opened:* echoing the accounts of the Last Supper (22:19–20) and especially of the miraculous feeding (9:12–17), which was followed by a revelation of Jesus' messianic identity (9:18–22). The connection between the breaking of bread and recognition of Jesus (vv. 35, 41–45) may speak to Luke's eucharistic theology. Just as importantly, recognition of him is tied closely to understanding Scripture (vv. 25–27, 32; cf. 44–45), as the disciples' eyes and Scripture are both "opened" (vv. 31–32; cf. 45).   **24:36–49** Another appearance. This episode has some points of contact with Matt 28:16–20 and John 20:19–29.   **24:37** *They were . . . spirit:* compare the appearances of angels in Luke 1:11–12, 28–29; 2:8–9; 24:4–5; cf. Mark 6:49.   **24:38** *Thoughts:* Gk. *dialogismoi,* "disputes" or "doubts."   **24:39–43** *Behold my . . . them:* Jesus is not a ghost, incorporeal soul, or angel (cf. Tob 12:19 and note), but a resurrected body. As such, he is able to appear and disappear at will (vv. 31, 36); see 1 Cor 15 for a discussion of the risen body's nature.   **24:41** *Believed not for joy:* i.e., it was too good to be true.   **24:42** *And of an honeycomb:* better omitted (MS tradition).

dead the third day: [47]and that repentance and remission of sins should be preached in his name among all nations, beginning at Jerusalem. [48]And ye are witnesses of these things. [49]And, behold, I send the promise of my Father upon you: but tarry ye in the city of Jerusalem, until ye be endued with power from on high.

[50]And he led them out as far as to Bethany, and he lifted up his hands, and blessed them. [51]And it came to pass, while he blessed them, he was parted from them, and carried up into heaven. [52]And they worshipped him, and returned to Jerusalem with great joy: [53]and were continually in the temple, praising and blessing God. Amen.

24:47 *That repentance . . . nations*: looking forward to Acts, but at the same time recalling Simeon's prophecy (2:29–32), which stresses God's prophetic promise to bring light to the Gentiles. *Remission*: Gk. *aphesis*, the key word with which Jesus characterized his own ministry at its inception (cf. 4:18 and note). Jesus now entrusts this ministry to the disciples.   **24:48** *Ye are witnesses*: the Greek echoes 21:13.   **24:49** *The promise . . . Father*: cf. 11:13. Luke goes into greater detail about this promise at the beginning of Acts (1:4–11). *Tarry ye . . . Jerusalem*: in the other canonical gospels, the disciples return to Galilee. *Power from on high*: in contrast to the power he had given them in 9:1. The reference is to the Spirit's descent in Acts 2.   **24:50–53** Ascension.   **24:50** *Bethany*: the village from which Jesus went up to Jerusalem (19:28–29) is now the locale from which he ascends to heaven.   **24:53** *Were continually . . . temple*: the disciples' continual presence as they await God's gift (v. 49) calls to mind Zacharias's temple service (cf. 1:8–10) as well as Simeon's and Anna's waiting at the temple for YHWH's redemption of Israel and the Gentile world (2:22–38). The first book of Luke's history thus ends as it begins, with expectation at the Jerusalem temple. Acts, its second book, narrates the gospel's expansion outward from Jerusalem, and especially from its temple (the site of Peter's first miracle in chap. 3), into the Mediterranean world. *Amen*: better omitted (MS tradition).

The Gospel According to St. John

THE reader coming to John from the Synoptics notices considerable differences. John's chronology diverges from theirs: Jesus' cleansing of the temple initiates rather than culminates his public ministry, which lasts for three years rather than one and alternates between Galilee and Jerusalem (with a stop in Samaria); the Synoptics' Jesus ministers for a single year and travels to Jerusalem only at his ministry's close. John omits almost all of Jesus' ethical and eschatological teaching, including his eccentric parables; it is replaced by extended dialogues and elaborate discourses meditating on Jesus' identity and calling for his auditors to accept him as God's life-giving emissary. These dialogues often revolve around the predicative "I am" sayings for which John is famous: for example, "I am the bread which came down from heaven" (6:41); "I am the light of the world" (8:12); "I am the resurrection, and the life" (11:25). They also feature the absolute "I am" sayings which, in light of Exod 3:13–16, seem to identify Jesus as YHWH (8:24, 28, 58; 13:19). The latter especially gesture at an elevated Christology largely foreign to the Synoptics, which John's prologue makes explicit: Jesus is God in the sense that he is God's word, God's expression of himself to the world he created.

Jesus' divinity in the Fourth Gospel necessitates a presentation of his death different from that provided by the first three. In the Synoptics, Jesus agonizes before his arrest, praying that he might avoid his destiny, and in Matthew and Mark his dying words accuse God of abandoning him: "My God, my God, why hast thou forsaken me?" (Matt 27:46; Mark 15:34). Such elements stand in stark tension with the Fourth Gospel's representation of Jesus as, in Ernst Käsemann's famous formulation, "God striding over the face of the earth," and so John changes them. After foretelling his impending death (12:23–26), John's Jesus explicitly rejects the agonizing prayer the Synoptics assign him: "Now is my soul troubled; and what shall I say? Father, save me from this hour: but for this cause came I unto this hour. Father, glorify thy name" (12:27–28). He goes on to insist that even if all his disciples abandon him—and in John they do not—"yet I am not alone, because the Father is with me" (16:32). It thus comes as no surprise that in the Fourth Gospel Jesus dies with equanimity rather than despair. His dying words are "It is finished" (19:30).

John's shocking presentation of Jesus' crucifixion as a glorification brings into sharp relief the theological implications of his reinterpretation of Jesus' death. While John's use of "glory" and "glorify" with reference to Jesus' resurrection is natural enough (e.g., 17:1–2, 5; cf. 11–13), he uses them of Jesus' death as well—for example, in the passage from chapter 12 quoted above (see also vv. 23–24).

Analogously, he employs for Jesus' crucifixion *hypsoō* ("lift up," 3:14; 8:28; 12:32), a Greek word normally meaning "exalt," which Acts more appropriately uses of Jesus' ascension to heaven (2:33). John's unusual employment of these terms carries substantial theological weight: for John, unlike the Synoptics, Jesus' death is not a disastrous tragedy that God's creative power must overcome by resurrection. The crucifixion is itself the first stage of the enfleshed word's glorious return to heaven. Jesus' "dying" words on the cross in John are not only composed but triumphant. They invite as a gloss "My mission is done! I'm headed home!"

Another difference between John and the Synoptics suggests a compositional context that helps explain the Fourth Gospel's other peculiarities. Matthew, Mark, and Luke rarely call anyone a "Jew." They employ the word only about fifteen times collectively, presumably because they found it virtually useless: since all of their main characters were Jewish, the label was superfluous. But in John the word appears more than sixty-five times, with "the Jews" repeatedly appearing as a kind of collective character hostile to Jesus. Among the Synoptic Gospels, Matthew alone refers to "the Jews" in a similar way—just once. When the chief priest and elders bribe the soldiers to say that Jesus' disciples had stolen his body from the grave, Matthew adds that the story "is commonly reported among the Jews until this day" (28:15). This shift in temporal perspective points to an explanation for John's usage of the term as well: the Fourth Gospel presupposes a split between "Jews" and "Christians" that would not occur until at least a generation after Jesus lived, and imagines Jesus ministering in this anachronistic context.

This willingness to recontextualize Jesus' ministry so radically may suggest a greater historical distance from the events recounted—that is, that John is a somewhat later composition than the other New Testament gospels (possibly very late in the first century C.E. or even early in the second). This gospel may include rather free adaptations of passages from one or more of the Synoptics; alternatively, or complementarily, it may have drawn on some of the same traditions as did the Synoptics themselves. It is a good guess that John also relies heavily on early Christian prophetic oracles spoken in the name of the risen Christ, attributing them to the character Jesus even though they reflect a theological and historical context incompatible with the earthly Jesus' ministry. This does not mean that John's gospel is radically ahistorical; it displays a clear concern to authorize itself by citing direct observation (see 21:24–25 and notes), and there is no reason to dismiss the possibility that some of the traditions it recounts—including those not found in the Synoptics—have a basis in eyewitness testimony. Accordingly, contemporary scholars with a historical bent are comfortable privileging John over the Synoptics on certain issues (e.g., the assignment to Jesus of a three-year ministry or the political motivation for the high priest's decision to arrest Jesus; see 11:47–50). Still, it is difficult to deny that the Fourth Gospel assumes and reflects a religious context that more closely resembles the early church's than Jesus' own: such context explains not only John's anachronistic representation of Jesus' opponents as "the Jews" but also his elevated Christology, which may be understood to reflect a later stage of theological reflection on Jesus' identity and death.

Such a context also helps explain a central literary feature of John's gospel: persistent dramatic irony. John's Jesus frequently speaks of himself in ways that his auditors—usually "the Jews" or their representatives—cannot grasp, but that would presumably be recognizable to John's "Christian" readers. In chapter 3, for example, Jesus tells Nicodemus, "a ruler of the Jews," "Except a man be born again, he cannot see the kingdom of God" (vv. 1, 3). Nicodemus takes Jesus literally ("How can a man be born when he is old? Can he enter the second time into his mother's womb, and be born?" v. 4), but Jesus is speaking metaphorically of a spiritual rebirth in which Nicodemus will not believe. Likewise in chapter 6 Jesus speaks of bread from heaven: his Jewish auditors ask to eat this bread (v. 34), but Jesus is again speaking metaphorically, this time of himself (vv. 35, 48). The discourse about bread is more complex than the one about birth, for Jesus transforms it into a scandalous image of cannibalism, identifying the bread with his "flesh" and commanding his listeners to "feed" on him (see 6:54 note) and to drink his blood as well (vv. 51–59). The "Jews" are perplexed (v. 52), but John's "Christian" readers probably recognized an allegory (albeit a crude one) of the Eucharist.

John's irony is open to a number of critiques. It is disturbingly mean-spirited, complicit in proffering a tendentious distinction between "Judaism" and "Christianity" which has been invoked throughout history to justify the ugly (and theologically untenable) idea that God has rejected Jews in favor of Christians. As John presents them, "the Jews" display a marked tendency toward narrow-minded and literalistic interpretation of Jesus' generously symbolic language, which always points at profound spiritual truth irreducible to the images of generation and consumption in which it is often couched. Those able to look past John's hostile deployment of irony against the stubborn "Jews" may still find it artificial and tedious, especially in comparison with the polysemous complexity of the synoptic parables, which resist reductive allegorical interpretation even on the few occasions Jesus offers it.

Our ethical or aesthetic response to Johannine irony all but determines our response to John's gospel, for dramatic irony is not merely one rhetorical device among others the evangelist employs; it is the rhetorical analogue of John's Christology. For John, Jesus is God's enfleshed *logos* (a Greek word itself meaning "word," as well as "reason"), which is to say that he is the human medium of God's expressed thought. Jesus' relationship to God as his "word" finds its reflection in the metaphorical language that Jesus himself employs. Just as Jesus demands that his auditors discern spiritual truth embedded within sometimes off-putting metaphors of reproduction, ingestion, and the like, so does the evangelist expect his readers to discern divine self-expression made flesh in the human Jesus. Or perhaps the analogy should be reversed. John's conception of Jesus as God's word made flesh may result from reflection on the kind of metaphorical language used by Jesus. Language, especially when it is metaphorically rich, conceals as well as reveals; it offers insight that discourse impoverished of metaphor cannot provide, but only at the cost of the auditor's self-conscious willingness to interpret the proffered figure of speech. Metaphorical language, then, promises a kind of communion between speaker and auditor that more straightforward discourse cannot offer, while at the same time signaling that its promise can never be fulfilled, for the auditor's obligation to interpret the speaker's words underscores an indissoluble disparity between speaker and listener, writer and reader, in a way that metaphorically impoverished language, which does not demand such interpretation, evades.

John's innovative representation of Jesus as God's word made flesh, as God's metaphorical self-expression, is a linguistically couched theological explanation of "the Jews'" incomprehension of Jesus' metaphorical discourse. Why don't "they" believe in Jesus? For the same reason "they" fail to comprehend or appreciate Jesus' rambling discourse about "living water" or "bread of life" or being "born again." These are metaphors, tactics of communicative desperation pointing to a hermeneutic distance between two parties that is difficult, if not impossible, ever totally to overcome. It is not enough simply to say that Jesus speaks metaphorically in John. Jesus is himself divine metaphor: God's word made flesh. Through him God attempts to overcome the abyss between himself and humanity, but, as John admits from the start, with only partial success (which may or may not be the same thing as failure): "He was in the world, and the world was made by him, and the world knew him not. He came unto his own, and his own received him not. But as many as received him, to them gave he power to become the sons of God, even to them that believe on his name" (1:10–12). The Fourth Gospel's persistent dramatic irony, the constant attention it draws to how its characters (especially "the Jews") fail to grasp what the ("Christian") reader may comprehend, is troubling on a number of levels. But perhaps most troubling of all is that it forces us to confront a fundamental difference between self and other that, John suggests, no "word," not even God's, can ever completely overcome.

Although a bit dated, Raymond Brown's Anchor Bible commentary on John is still a valuable resource: *The Gospel According to John,* 2 vols. (Garden City, NY: Doubleday, 1966–70). Its historical, theological, and literary-critical insights have influenced the notes that follow throughout.

THE GOSPEL ACCORDING TO
ST. JOHN

1 In the beginning was the Word, and the Word was with God, and the Word was God. ²The same was in the beginning with God. ³All things were made by him; and without him was not any thing made that was made. ⁴In him was life; and the life was the light of men. ⁵And the light shineth in darkness; and the darkness comprehended it not.

⁶There was a man sent from God, whose name was John. ⁷The same came for a witness, to bear witness of the Light, that all men through him might believe. ⁸He was not that Light, but was sent to bear witness of that Light. ⁹That was the true Light, which lighteth every man that cometh into the world.

¹⁰He was in the world, and the world was made by him, and the world knew him not. ¹¹He came unto his own, and his own received him not. ¹²But as many as received him, to them gave he power to become the sons of God, even to them

1:1–18 Prologue. The artful concision of the prologue's prose, combined with its deliberate development of key images ("light," creation, "word"), gives it a distinctively poetic quality. Many scholars believe it to be adapted from an ancient Christian hymn (perhaps with additional material inserted, e.g., at vv. 6–8, 13, and 15). John's prologue should be compared with the birth and infancy narratives of Matthew and Luke, which present a more constricted vision of Jesus' origins.   **1:1** *In the beginning*: echoing Gen 1:1. *The Word*: capitalized by KJV as a reference to Christ (cf. v. 14), like "Light" and "Son" below. It translates Gk. *logos*, which connotes at once the creative power of God, whose utterance brings everything into existence (cf. Gen 1:1–2:4); the Torah, the law God promulgated through Moses, and, more generally, the divine wisdom lying behind it (also associated with creation; cf. Prov 8:22–31); and the principle of order governing the cosmos (a technical meaning of *logos* in Hellenistic philosophy).   **1:3** *Were made*: Gk. *egeneto*, lit. "became" or "came into being" (also at vv. 10, 14); the rest of the verse reads "and without him nothing came into being that has come into being." The final phrase could also be taken as the beginning of the next verse: "What has come into being in him was life. . . ." Greek philosophy from Plato on assigns responsibility for creation to a divinity somehow distinct from the ultimate God, a tendency followed by Philo, Gnostic writings, and early Christian texts besides John (e.g., Col 1:16). *Him*: here and subsequently, the pronoun agrees with "word" and could be rendered "it."   **1:5** *Comprehended*: Gk. *katelaben*, also "seized" (i.e., with hostility).   **1:6** *There was*: Gk. *egeneto*; see v. 3 note. *John*: the Baptist.   **1:7** *Witness*: Gk. *martyria*, a key word in John. It and its cognates are variously translated "witness," "bear witness," "record," "bear record," "testimony," and "testify." *Believe*: the verbal form of Gk. *pistis*, usually translated "faith"; see Rom 1:8 note.   **1:8** *He was . . . of that Light*: on NT authors' anxiety to subordinate John to Jesus, see Mark 1:9–11 note.   **1:9** *That cometh . . . world*: the phrase may modify *light* rather than *man*. **1:11** *His own . . . his own*: the first possessive is neuter ("his own things"), the second masculine ("his own people"). *Received*: Gk. *parelabon*, the same root as "comprehended" (v. 5); cf. v. 12.   **1:12** *Sons*:

that believe on his name: ¹³which were born, not of blood, nor of the will of the flesh, nor of the will of man, but of God.

¹⁴And the Word was made flesh, and dwelt among us, (and we beheld his glory, the glory as of the only begotten of the Father,) full of grace and truth. ¹⁵John bare witness of him, and cried, saying, This was he of whom I spake, He that cometh after me is preferred before me: for he was before me. ¹⁶And of his fulness have all we received, and grace for grace. ¹⁷For the law was given by Moses, but grace and truth came by Jesus Christ. ¹⁸No man hath seen God at any time; the only begotten Son, which is in the bosom of the Father, he hath declared him.

¹⁹And this is the record of John, when the Jews sent priests and Levites from Jerusalem to ask him, Who art thou? ²⁰And he confessed, and denied not; but confessed, I am not the Christ. ²¹And they asked him, What then? Art thou Elias? And he saith, I am not. Art thou that prophet? And he answered, No. ²²Then said they unto him, Who art thou? that we may give an answer to them that sent us. What sayest thou of thyself? ²³He said, I am the voice of one crying in the wilderness, Make straight the way of the Lord, as said the prophet Esaias. ²⁴And they which were sent were of the Pharisees. ²⁵And they asked him, and said unto him, Why baptizest thou then, if thou be not that Christ, nor Elias, neither that prophet? ²⁶John answered them, saying, I baptize with water: but there standeth one among you, whom ye know not; ²⁷he it is, who coming after me is preferred before me, whose shoe's latchet I am not worthy to unloose. ²⁸These things were done in Bethabara beyond Jordan, where John was baptizing.

²⁹The next day John seeth Jesus coming unto him, and saith, Behold the Lamb of God, which taketh away the sin of the world. ³⁰This is he of whom I said, After me cometh a man which is preferred before me: for he was before me. ³¹And I

---

lit. "children."   **1:13** *Of man*: perhaps better "of a man," with reference to a man's decision to procreate.   **1:14** *Dwelt*: lit. "tented," alluding to God's glory inhabiting the tabernacle (and later temple) in the OT (Exod 40:34; 1 Kgs 8:10–11). *Only begotten*: Gk. *monogenēs*, "only son" (cf. v. 18; 3:16, 18). KJV is influenced by the Vulgate, which (mis)translates the word as Lat. *unigenitus* ("only begotten") in response to the Arian position that Jesus was a created being. *Grace and truth*: the combination "goodness/mercy and truth" is conventional in the OT (Exod 34:6; Ps 86:15; etc.).   **1:16** *Grace for grace*: *for* (Gk. *anti*) may imply substitution, addition ("grace on top of grace"), or correlation.   **1:17** *Came by*: lit. "came about by," paralleling the construction in vv. 3, 10.   **1:18** *No man . . . time*: cf. Exod 33:18–20. *The only begotten Son*: better "God the only son" (MS tradition; our translation).

1:19–2:11 John the Baptist, Jesus, and their disciples. Like Genesis' first creation story (1:1–2:4), this section is structured as a series of seven days (see 1:29, 35, 39 and note, 43, 2:1 and note), suggesting a parallel between Jesus' incipient ministry and the divine word's creativity. **1:19–1:34** John the Baptist. Compare Matt 3:1–17; Mark 1:2–11; Luke 3:1–22.   **1:19** *Levites*: see Luke 10:32 note.   **1:21** *Elias*: John's refusal to be identified with the eschatological Elijah (Mal 4:5–6) stands at odds with Matthew, Mark, and, to a lesser degree, Luke (who associates John with Elijah at 1:17, but elsewhere links Jesus with him; see Luke 7:11–17; 9:59–62 and notes). *That prophet*: the prophet like Moses (Deut 18:15–18).   **1:23** *As said . . . Esaias*: Isa 40:3.   **1:24** *Pharisees*: see Mark 2:16 note.   **1:27** *He it . . . unloose*: better "he who comes after me, whose shoe's latchet I am not worthy to unloose" (MS tradition).   **1:28** *Bethabara*: better "Bethany" (MS tradition), but located east of the Jordan River and so apparently not the place mentioned in 11:18. Scribes may have altered the name here to eliminate confusion.   **1:29** *Lamb of God*: the first of Jesus' several associations with the Passover lamb (cf. Exod 12:3–6). However, since the paschal lamb was not a sin offering, Lev 4:32–35

knew him not: but that he should be made manifest to Israel, therefore am I come baptizing with water. [32]And John bare record, saying, I saw the Spirit descending from heaven like a dove, and it abode upon him. [33]And I knew him not: but he that sent me to baptize with water, the same said unto me, Upon whom thou shalt see the Spirit descending, and remaining on him, the same is he which baptizeth with the Holy Ghost. [34]And I saw, and bare record that this is the Son of God.

[35]Again the next day after John stood, and two of his disciples; [36]and looking upon Jesus as he walked, he saith, Behold the Lamb of God! [37]And the two disciples heard him speak, and they followed Jesus. [38]Then Jesus turned, and saw them following, and saith unto them, What seek ye? They said unto him, Rabbi, (which is to say, being interpreted, Master,) where dwellest thou? [39]He saith unto them, Come and see. They came and saw where he dwelt, and abode with him that day: for it was about the tenth hour. [40]One of the two which heard John speak, and followed him, was Andrew, Simon Peter's brother. [41]He first findeth his own brother Simon, and saith unto him, We have found the Messias, which is, being interpreted, the Christ. [42]And he brought him to Jesus. And when Jesus beheld him, he said, Thou art Simon the son of Jona: thou shalt be called Cephas, which is by interpretation, A stone.

[43]The day following Jesus would go forth into Galilee, and findeth Philip, and saith unto him, Follow me. [44]Now Philip was of Bethsaida, the city of Andrew and Peter. [45]Philip findeth Nathanael, and saith unto him, We have found him, of whom Moses in the law, and the prophets, did write, Jesus of Nazareth, the son of Joseph. [46]And Nathanael said unto him, Can there any good thing come out of Nazareth? Philip saith unto him, Come and see. [47]Jesus saw Nathanael coming to him, and saith of him, Behold an Israelite indeed, in whom is no guile! [48]Nathanael saith unto him, Whence knowest thou me? Jesus answered and said unto him, Before that Philip called thee, when thou wast under the fig tree, I saw

---

may also (or alternatively) inform John's declaration. **1:32** *I saw . . . him*: John, like Luke, does not link the Spirit's descent with Jesus' baptism. *Abode*: Gk. *menō*, a key word in John (elsewhere rendered "remain," "dwell," "tarry," "endure," "be present," and "continue"). **1:35–51** Jesus calls his first disciples. Compare Matt 4:18–22; Mark 1:16–20; Luke 5:1–11. **1:38** *Rabbi*: the Fourth Gospel frequently includes transliterated Hebrew/Aramaic, usually explaining it. *Master*: teacher (so throughout). **1:39** *The tenth hour*: 4:00 P.M., so late in the third day (the Jewish day is measured from evening to evening). Verses 40–42 narrate what occurred on the fourth. **1:40** *One of the two . . . Andrew*: the other of Jesus' first disciples remains anonymous. (Perhaps this is the anonymous disciple who later becomes prominent; see 13:23 and note.) **1:41** *Messias, which . . . Christ*: Messias is the Hebrew/Aramaic word for "anointed" (Gk. *Christos*; i.e., Christ); see Mark 1:1 note. **1:42** *Jona*: better "John" (MS tradition). In Matt 16:16–18 (to which John's text has been assimilated), Peter's father is named Jona; that may be a different Greek form of his Hebrew name or may reflect a different tradition altogether. *A stone*: Gk. *petros*, whence "Peter." **1:43** *Would*: intended to. *Galilee*: a region of northern Palestine west of the Sea of Galilee and the Jordan River. **1:44** *Bethsaida*: not in Galilee (although John locates it there; cf. 12:21), but lying just to its east, in Gaulanitis. **1:45** *Nathanael*: not one of the Twelve. *Of whom . . . write*: if the references are to the prophet like Moses of Deut 18:15–18 (probable) and to the eschatological Elijah of Mal 4:5–6 (possible), then Jesus' disciples associate him with the figures with whom John refused to be identified (cf. v. 21). **1:46** *Can there . . . Nazareth*: this odd saying sounds proverbial, though no such proverb has been identified. **1:47** *Indeed*: lit. "truly." **1:48** *When thou . . . tree*: obscure, but "every man under his vine and under

thee. ⁴⁹Nathanael answered and saith unto him, Rabbi, thou art the Son of God; thou art the King of Israel. ⁵⁰Jesus answered and said unto him, Because I said unto thee, I saw thee under the fig tree, believest thou? thou shalt see greater things than these. ⁵¹And he saith unto him, Verily, verily, I say unto you, Hereafter ye shall see heaven open, and the angels of God ascending and descending upon the Son of man.

2 And the third day there was a marriage in Cana of Galilee; and the mother of Jesus was there: ²and both Jesus was called, and his disciples, to the marriage. ³And when they wanted wine, the mother of Jesus saith unto him, They have no wine. ⁴Jesus saith unto her, Woman, what have I to do with thee? mine hour is not yet come. ⁵His mother saith unto the servants, Whatsoever he saith unto you, do it. ⁶And there were set there six waterpots of stone, after the manner of the purifying of the Jews, containing two or three firkins apiece. ⁷Jesus saith unto them, Fill the waterpots with water. And they filled them up to the brim. ⁸And he saith unto them, Draw out now, and bear unto the governor of the feast. And they bare it. ⁹When the ruler of the feast had tasted the water that was made wine, and knew not whence it was: (but the servants which drew the water knew;) the governor of the feast called the bridegroom, ¹⁰and saith unto him, Every man at the beginning doth set forth good wine; and when men have well drunk, then that which is worse: but thou hast kept the good wine until now. ¹¹This beginning of miracles did Jesus in Cana of Galilee, and manifested forth his glory; and his disciples believed on him.

his fig tree" was an OT slogan of national prosperity (see 1 Kgs 4:25; Mic 4:4). **1:49** *Son of God . . . Israel*: the OT conventionally calls the Davidic king God's son (2 Sam 7:12–14; Ps 2:6–7; etc.). Perhaps Jesus' allusion to a slogan of national prosperity inspires Nathanael's declaration of his kingship, which even Jesus finds odd (v. 50). In light of the nationalistic gestures of vv. 48–49, it may be significant that Jesus invokes the vision that Jacob (Israel) experiences precisely as he leaves the promised land in exile. **1:51** *Ye shall see . . . man*: figuring Jesus' resurrection and eschatological advent by allusion to the ascending and descending angels in Jacob's vision (Gen 28:10–17). The echo recalls Jesus' insistence that Nathanael is an "Israelite . . . in whom is no guile [Gk. *dolos*]" (v. 47), for Jacob was full of guile (*dolos*) in his dealings with Esau just before he dreamed of the angels (see LXX Gen 27:35). *Son of man*: see Mark 2:10 note. **2:1–11** The wedding at Cana. **2:1** *The third day*: counted inclusively—one full day (the second) has passed between that on which Jesus intended to go to Galilee (1:43–51) and this. Compare Jesus' resurrection, in the synoptic tradition, on "the third day" (Sunday) after his crucifixion (Friday); e.g., Luke 24:7, 21. **2:4** *Woman*: while not as disrespectful in Greek as in English, Jesus' address of his mother in this way is peculiar. *What have . . . thee*: see Mark 1:24 note. *Mine hour*: enigmatic references to Jesus' *hour* or, less frequently, "time" appear throughout John. **2:6** *Six waterpots of stone*: cf. Exod 7:19–21, where Moses turns the water in the Egyptians' stone vessels to blood. *After the manner . . . Jews*: the vessels contained water for ritual purification (cf. Mark 7:4 note). *Containing two . . . apiece*: a firkin measures about eight gallons; thus Jesus provides a tremendous amount of wine, whose plenty was a conventional figure of eschatological celebration (cf. Jer 31:12; Amos 9:13–14; etc.). The wedding feast itself carries eschatological significance as well; see Mark 2:19 note. **2:8** *Governor of the feast*: probably the slave responsible for overseeing the banquet (but Sir 32:1 envisions a trusted guest selected to manage the party). **2:11** *Miracles*: Gk. *sēmeia*, lit. "signs" (so throughout). *In Cana . . . glory*: cf. 1:14; also compare the invitations to the disciples to "come and see" Jesus in Galilee (1:38–39, 43, 45–46).

[12]After this he went down to Capernaum, he, and his mother, and his brethren, and his disciples: and they continued there not many days. [13]And the Jews' passover was at hand, and Jesus went up to Jerusalem, [14]and found in the temple those that sold oxen and sheep and doves, and the changers of money sitting: [15]and when he had made a scourge of small cords, he drove them all out of the temple, and the sheep, and the oxen; and poured out the changers' money, and overthrew the tables; [16]and said unto them that sold doves, Take these things hence; make not my Father's house an house of merchandise. [17]And his disciples remembered that it was written, The zeal of thine house hath eaten me up.

[18]Then answered the Jews and said unto him, What sign shewest thou unto us, seeing that thou doest these things? [19]Jesus answered and said unto them, Destroy this temple, and in three days I will raise it up. [20]Then said the Jews, Forty and six years was this temple in building, and wilt thou rear it up in three days? [21]But he spake of the temple of his body. [22]When therefore he was risen from the dead, his disciples remembered that he had said this unto them; and they believed the scripture, and the word which Jesus had said.

[23]Now when he was in Jerusalem at the passover, in the feast day, many believed in his name, when they saw the miracles which he did. [24]But Jesus did not commit himself unto them, because he knew all men, [25]and needed not that any should testify of man: for he knew what was in man.

3 There was a man of the Pharisees, named Nicodemus, a ruler of the Jews: [2]the same came to Jesus by night, and said unto him, Rabbi, we know that thou art a teacher come from God: for no man can do these miracles that thou doest, except God be with him. [3]Jesus answered and said unto him, Verily, verily, I say unto thee, Except a man be born again, he cannot see the kingdom of God. [4]Nicodemus saith unto him, How can a man be born when he is old? can he enter the second time into his mother's womb, and be born? [5]Jesus answered, Verily, verily, I say unto thee, Except a man be born of water and of the Spirit, he cannot enter into the kingdom of God. [6]That which is born of the flesh is flesh; and that which is born of the Spirit is spirit. [7]Marvel not that I said unto thee, Ye must be

2:12–22 Cleansing the temple. Compare the Synoptics' later and shorter treatment of this scene: Matt 21:12–13; Mark 11:15–17; Luke 19:45–46. Perhaps reflection on Mal 3:1 in light of John the Baptist's ministry led the fourth evangelist to move it closer to John's introduction of Jesus. **2:12** *Capernaum*: a town on the northwest shore of the Sea of Galilee, which served as the center of Jesus' ministry.   **2:13** *Passover*: see Mark 14:1 note. This is the first of three in John (cf. 6:4; 11:55).   **2:14** *Temple*: Gk. *hieros*, referring to the temple's outer court (cf. v. 15); a different word is used in vv. 19–21. *Those that . . . money*: see Mark 11:15 note.   **2:17** *His disciples remembered*: after his resurrection (see v. 22). *The zeal . . . up*: Ps 69:9. *Hath eaten*: better "will eat" (MS tradition).   **2:19** *Destroy this . . . up*: in the synoptic tradition a similar saying is attributed to Jesus by his enemies (Matt 26:61; 27:40; Mark 14:58; 15:29).   **2:21** *The temple of his body*: Jesus' figurative substitution of his body for the temple recalls his earlier replacement of water for purification (v. 6) with wine.

2:23–3:21 Jesus and Nicodemus. 2:24 *Commit*: entrust; Gk. *episteuen* (cf. v. 23 [KJV "believed"]).   **3:3** *Again*: Gk. *anōthen*, also "from above." Jesus' metaphor of rebirth embraces this ambiguity, to which Nicodemus's literalistic interrogation offers unimaginative resistance. *Kingdom of God*: this common synoptic expression appears in John only in this episode.   **3:5** *Of water . . . Spirit*: the OT commonly speaks of God's spirit being poured out like water (e.g., Isa 32:15; Joel 2:28–29; cf.

born again. ⁸The wind bloweth where it listeth, and thou hearest the sound thereof, but canst not tell whence it cometh, and whither it goeth: so is every one that is born of the Spirit.

⁹Nicodemus answered and said unto him, How can these things be? ¹⁰Jesus answered and said unto him, Art thou a master of Israel, and knowest not these things? ¹¹Verily, verily, I say unto thee, We speak that we do know, and testify that we have seen; and ye receive not our witness. ¹²If I have told you earthly things, and ye believe not, how shall ye believe, if I tell you of heavenly things? ¹³And no man hath ascended up to heaven, but he that came down from heaven, even the Son of man which is in heaven. ¹⁴And as Moses lifted up the serpent in the wilderness, even so must the Son of man be lifted up: ¹⁵that whosoever believeth in him should not perish, but have eternal life.

¹⁶For God so loved the world, that he gave his only begotten Son, that whosoever believeth in him should not perish, but have everlasting life. ¹⁷For God sent not his Son into the world to condemn the world; but that the world through him might be saved. ¹⁸He that believeth on him is not condemned: but he that believeth not is condemned already, because he hath not believed in the name of the only begotten Son of God. ¹⁹And this is the condemnation, that light is come into the world, and men loved darkness rather than light, because their deeds were evil. ²⁰For every one that doeth evil hateth the light, neither cometh to the light, lest his deeds should be reproved. ²¹But he that doeth truth cometh to the light, that his deeds may be made manifest, that they are wrought in God.

²²After these things came Jesus and his disciples into the land of Judæa; and there he tarried with them, and baptized. ²³And John also was baptizing in Ænon near to Salim, because there was much water there: and they came, and were baptized. ²⁴For John was not yet cast into prison. ²⁵Then there arose a question between some of John's disciples and the Jews about purifying. ²⁶And they came unto John, and said unto him, Rabbi, he that was with thee beyond Jordan, to whom thou barest witness, behold, the same baptizeth, and all men come to him. ²⁷John answered and said, A man can receive nothing, except it be given him from heaven. ²⁸Ye yourselves bear me witness, that I said, I am not the Christ, but that I am sent before him. ²⁹He that hath the bride is the bridegroom: but the friend of the bridegroom, which standeth and heareth him, rejoiceth greatly because of

<hr>

Ezek 36:25–27), but an allusion to baptism is also possible (cf. 1 Cor 12:13).   **3:8** *Wind*: Gk. *pneuma*, rendered "spirit" elsewhere in this section.   **3:11–12** *We speak . . . heavenly things*: the momentary shift to plurals may suggest the dialogue's relevance to or even origination in discourse between the Evangelist's community of Jesus-believers and questioning "Jews."   **3:13** *Which is in heaven*: better omitted (MS tradition).   **3:14–15** *As Moses . . . life*: see Num 21:8–9.   **3:15** *Not perish, but*: better omitted (MS tradition).   **3:16** *For God . . . Son*: echoing the story of Abraham's sacrifice of Isaac (Gen 22:1–19, esp. vv. 2, 12).   **3:17** *Condemn*: Gk. *krinō*; throughout John, the same root is translated with forms of "condemn," "damn," and, more neutrally, "judge."   **3:20–21** *For every one . . . God*: cf. v. 2, where Nicodemus comes to Jesus by night.   **3:20** *Evil*: better "what is base" (a different Greek word is used in v. 19).

3:22–4:3 John the Baptist's decrease and Jesus' increase. 3:22 *And baptized*: only here in the NT is Jesus portrayed as baptizing (but cf. 4:2).   **3:23** *Ænon, near to Salim*: probably a site just west of the Jordan and north of Samaria. *And they . . . baptized*: i.e., "and people were coming and being baptized."   **3:25** *The Jews*: better "a Jew" (MS tradition). *About purifying*: presumably reflecting an understanding of baptism as ritual purification (cf. 2:6).   **3:29** *Bridegroom*: see Mark 2:19

the bridegroom's voice: this my joy therefore is fulfilled. ³⁰He must increase, but I must decrease.

³¹He that cometh from above is above all: he that is of the earth is earthly, and speaketh of the earth: he that cometh from heaven is above all. ³²And what he hath seen and heard, that he testifieth; and no man receiveth his testimony. ³³He that hath received his testimony hath set to his seal that God is true. ³⁴For he whom God hath sent speaketh the words of God: for God giveth not the Spirit by measure unto him. ³⁵The Father loveth the Son, and hath given all things into his hand. ³⁶He that believeth on the Son hath everlasting life: and he that believeth not the Son shall not see life; but the wrath of God abideth on him.

4 When therefore the Lord knew how the Pharisees had heard that Jesus made and baptized more disciples than John, ²(though Jesus himself baptized not, but his disciples,) ³he left Judæa, and departed again into Galilee.

⁴And he must needs go through Samaria. ⁵Then cometh he to a city of Samaria, which is called Sychar, near to the parcel of ground that Jacob gave to his son Joseph. ⁶Now Jacob's well was there. Jesus therefore, being wearied with his journey, sat thus on the well: and it was about the sixth hour. ⁷There cometh a woman of Samaria to draw water: Jesus saith unto her, Give me to drink. ⁸(For his disciples were gone away unto the city to buy meat.) ⁹Then saith the woman of Samaria unto him, How is it that thou, being a Jew, askest drink of me, which am a woman of Samaria? for the Jews have no dealings with the Samaritans. ¹⁰Jesus answered and said unto her, If thou knewest the gift of God, and who it is that saith to thee, Give me to drink; thou wouldest have asked of him, and he would have given thee living water. ¹¹The woman saith unto him, Sir, thou hast nothing to draw with, and the well is deep: from whence then hast thou that living water? ¹²Art thou

---

note. **3:30** *Decrease*: Gk. root *elasso-*, also used to describe the "worse" wine at Cana (2:10). **3:31–36** *He that . . . him*: after John claims to have heard and rejoiced at the bridegroom's voice (v. 29), his voice immediately begins to resemble Jesus' in vv. 1–21, thereby demonstrating Jesus' augmentation at John's expense (v. 30). **3:33** *Set to his seal*: the ancient equivalent of signing a legal document. **3:34** *For God . . . him*: i.e., the gift is limitless. **3:36** *Believeth not*: Gk. *apeithōn*, which normally means "disobeys." **4:1–3** *When therefore . . . Galilee*: although the Pharisees have so far merely questioned John (1:24–25) and Jesus (3:1–21), Jesus perceives danger. **4:1** *The Lord*: better "Jesus" (MS tradition).

4:4–42 The Samaritan woman. Especially since Jesus has just been called a bridegroom (3:29), the reader is prepared to recognize this episode's manipulations of the conventions of the OT type-scene in which the patriarch (or his representative) meets a future bride at a well (Gen 24:11–27; 29:1–14; Exod 2:15b–22). Instead of proposing, Jesus enters into an extended dialogue with the woman; their six exchanges cover a range of topics, from the religious to the intensely personal. **4:4** *He must . . . Samaria*: this is not geographically intelligible; it may allude to divine command. On Samaritans, see Matt 10:5 note. **4:5** *Sychar*: its exact location is debated, but the rest of the verse suggests that John identifies it with Shechem. *The parcel . . . Joseph*: see Gen 48:22 and note; cf. Gen 33:18–19; Josh 24:32. **4:6** *Jacob's well*: a well by this name was located near Mount Gerizim (see v. 20 note)—the well of Gen 29:1–11, which was in Mesopotamia. Perhaps an oral tradition about another well circulated in connection with Jacob's acquisition of land in Shechem (Gen 33:18–19); cf. Gen 21:22–34 (Abraham); 26:17–33 (Isaac). *Sixth hour*: noon. The normal time for drawing water would be in the morning or evening, so the woman (v. 7) may be trying to avoid others. **4:8** *Meat*: food. **4:10** *Living water*: the phrase normally means running water. The woman's unimaginative literalism (v. 11), like the disciples' (vv. 32–33), resembles Nicodemus's in chap. 3. **4:11** *Sir*: Gk. *kyrios*, also "lord." Context determines the best translation.

greater than our father Jacob, which gave us the well, and drank thereof himself, and his children, and his cattle? [13]Jesus answered and said unto her, Whosoever drinketh of this water shall thirst again: [14]but whosoever drinketh of the water that I shall give him shall never thirst; but the water that I shall give him shall be in him a well of water springing up into everlasting life. [15]The woman saith unto him, Sir, give me this water, that I thirst not, neither come hither to draw.

[16]Jesus saith unto her, Go, call thy husband, and come hither. [17]The woman answered and said, I have no husband. Jesus said unto her, Thou hast well said, I have no husband: [18]for thou hast had five husbands; and he whom thou now hast is not thy husband: in that saidst thou truly. [19]The woman saith unto him, Sir, I perceive that thou art a prophet. [20]Our fathers worshipped in this mountain; and ye say, that in Jerusalem is the place where men ought to worship. [21]Jesus saith unto her, Woman, believe me, the hour cometh, when ye shall neither in this mountain, nor yet at Jerusalem, worship the Father. [22]Ye worship ye know not what: we know what we worship: for salvation is of the Jews. [23]But the hour cometh, and now is, when the true worshippers shall worship the Father in spirit and in truth: for the Father seeketh such to worship him. [24]God is a Spirit: and they that worship him must worship him in spirit and in truth. [25]The woman saith unto him, I know that Messias cometh, which is called Christ: when he is come, he will tell us all things. [26]Jesus saith unto her, I that speak unto thee am he.

[27]And upon this came his disciples, and marvelled that he talked with the woman: yet no man said, What seekest thou? or, Why talkest thou with her? [28]The woman then left her waterpot, and went her way into the city, and saith to the men, [29]Come, see a man, which told me all things that ever I did: is not this the Christ? [30]Then they went out of the city, and came unto him.

[31]In the mean while his disciples prayed him, saying, Master, eat. [32]But he said unto them, I have meat to eat that ye know not of. [33]Therefore said the disciples one to another, Hath any man brought him ought to eat? [34]Jesus saith unto them, My meat is to do the will of him that sent me, and to finish his work. [35]Say not ye, There are yet four months, and then cometh harvest? behold, I say unto you, Lift up your eyes, and look on the fields; for they are white already to harvest. [36]And he that reapeth receiveth wages, and gathereth fruit unto life eternal: that both he that soweth and he that reapeth may rejoice together. [37]And herein is that saying true, One soweth, and another reapeth. [38]I sent you to reap that whereon ye bestowed no labour: other men laboured, and ye are entered into their labours.

4:12 *Which gave . . . cattle*: see Gen 29:1–11.   **4:14** *Springing up*: too idiomatic a translation to capture the Greek verb, which is not normally used of water: "jumping up" is better.   **4:20** *This mountain*: Mount Gerizim, although the shrine had been destroyed by Jesus' time. *Jerusalem*: "the place which the Lord your God shall choose out of all your tribes to put his name there" (Deut 12:5). By the time John writes, the Jerusalem temple had been destroyed.   **4:24** *God is a Spirit*: or "God is spirit."   **4:25** *I know . . . things*: see 1:41 note. In the NT, "anointed" normally has royal connotations, but prophets too could be anointed (cf. 1 Kgs 19:16) and the Samaritans probably anticipated the eschatological advent of the prophet like Moses from Deut 18:15–18 (cf. v. 19).   **4:26** *I . . . am he*: Gk. *egō eimi*; see Mark 6:50 note.   **4:27** *And marvelled . . . woman*: their private exchange was scandalous.   **4:31** *Prayed*: urged.   **4:34** *To finish his work*: anticipating Jesus' final words (19:30).   **4:35** *Lift up . . . harvest*: cf. Matt 9:37.   **4:37** *One soweth, . . . reapeth*: not an expression of community effort (contrast 1 Cor 3:5–9), but a vivid image of unfairness.   **4:38** *I sent . . . labours*: Jesus

³⁹And many of the Samaritans of that city believed on him for the saying of the woman, which testified, He told me all that ever I did. ⁴⁰So when the Samaritans were come unto him, they besought him that he would tarry with them: and he abode there two days. ⁴¹And many more believed because of his own word; ⁴²and said unto the woman, Now we believe, not because of thy saying: for we have heard him ourselves, and know that this is indeed the Christ, the Saviour of the world.

⁴³Now after two days he departed thence, and went into Galilee. ⁴⁴For Jesus himself testified, that a prophet hath no honour in his own country. ⁴⁵Then when he was come into Galilee, the Galilæans received him, having seen all the things that he did at Jerusalem at the feast: for they also went unto the feast.

⁴⁶So Jesus came again into Cana of Galilee, where he made the water wine. And there was a certain nobleman, whose son was sick at Capernaum. ⁴⁷When he heard that Jesus was come out of Judæa into Galilee, he went unto him, and besought him that he would come down, and heal his son: for he was at the point of death. ⁴⁸Then said Jesus unto him, Except ye see signs and wonders, ye will not believe. ⁴⁹The nobleman saith unto him, Sir, come down ere my child die. ⁵⁰Jesus saith unto him, Go thy way; thy son liveth. And the man believed the word that Jesus had spoken unto him, and he went his way. ⁵¹And as he was now going down, his servants met him, and told him, saying, Thy son liveth. ⁵²Then inquired he of them the hour when he began to amend. And they said unto him, Yesterday at the seventh hour the fever left him. ⁵³So the father knew that it was at the same hour, in the which Jesus said unto him, Thy son liveth: and himself believed, and his whole house. ⁵⁴This is again the second miracle that Jesus did, when he was come out of Judæa into Galilee.

5 After this there was a feast of the Jews; and Jesus went up to Jerusalem. ²Now there is at Jerusalem by the sheep market a pool, which is called in the Hebrew tongue Bethesda, having five porches. ³In these lay a great multitude of

---

requests that the disciples help him finish the job of evangelizing the Samaritans that the woman began (cf. vv. 39, 42). **4:42** *The Christ*: better omitted (MS tradition). *Saviour of the world*: cf. 3:17.

4:43–54 Healing a nobleman's son. While the healing (4:46–54) parallels Jesus' restoration of the centurion's son in Matt 8:5–13 and Luke 7:1–10, the dominical saying of v. 44 corresponds to that found in the synoptic tradition at Matt 13:57; Mark 6:4; Luke 4:24. John employs it to contrast the reception Jesus receives in Galilee (characterized by superficial excitement at "signs and wonders," 4:45, 48; cf. 2:23–25) with the Samaritans' more penetrating understanding of Jesus as the anointed eschatological prophet (4:19, 25 and note) who speaks challenging truth (4:29, 39–42). Jesus' "signs and wonders" actually realize the discourse about life he delivered to the Samaritan woman (see esp. vv. 50–51). **4:48** *Signs and wonders*: cf. Exod 7:3–4. **4:51** *Servants*: slaves (so frequently). **4:52** *Seventh hour*: 1 P.M. **4:54** *Second miracle*: like v. 46, v. 54 looks back to the miracle at Cana. Numbered miracles (lit. "signs") thus bookend 2:12–4:45 (2:1–11; 4:46–54).

5:1–47 The healing at Bethesda and subsequent discourse. The Synoptics include a very different account of Jesus healing a paralytic on the Sabbath and the controversy it engenders (Matt 9:1–8; Mark 2:1–12; Luke 5:17–26). **5:1** *A feast*: unidentified, but the feasts of Passover, Pentecost, and Tabernacles all required pilgrimage to Jerusalem. **5:2** *Market*: not in the Greek, but a word appears to have dropped out. Topographical and syntactical considerations suggest "gate" or "pool" as better guesses. *Bethesda*: various forms of this name occur in the MS tradition. Whatever it was called, the remains of a pool corresponding to the one described here have been discovered. It had one colonnade on each of its four sides and one on a partition down its middle, hence the *five porches*.

impotent folk, of blind, halt, withered, waiting for the moving of the water. [4]For an angel went down at a certain season into the pool, and troubled the water: whosoever then first after the troubling of the water stepped in was made whole of whatsoever disease he had. [5]And a certain man was there, which had an infirmity thirty and eight years. [6]When Jesus saw him lie, and knew that he had been now a long time in that case, he saith unto him, Wilt thou be made whole? [7]The impotent man answered him, Sir, I have no man, when the water is troubled, to put me into the pool: but while I am coming, another steppeth down before me. [8]Jesus saith unto him, Rise, take up thy bed, and walk. [9]And immediately the man was made whole, and took up his bed, and walked: and on the same day was the sabbath.

[10]The Jews therefore said unto him that was cured, It is the sabbath day: it is not lawful for thee to carry thy bed. [11]He answered them, He that made me whole, the same said unto me, Take up thy bed, and walk. [12]Then asked they him, What man is that which said unto thee, Take up thy bed, and walk? [13]And he that was healed wist not who it was: for Jesus had conveyed himself away, a multitude being in that place. [14]Afterward Jesus findeth him in the temple, and said unto him, Behold, thou art made whole: sin no more, lest a worse thing come unto thee. [15]The man departed, and told the Jews that it was Jesus, which had made him whole.

[16]And therefore did the Jews persecute Jesus, and sought to slay him, because he had done these things on the sabbath day. [17]But Jesus answered them, My Father worketh hitherto, and I work. [18]Therefore the Jews sought the more to kill him, because he not only had broken the sabbath, but said also that God was his Father, making himself equal with God. [19]Then answered Jesus and said unto them, Verily, verily, I say unto you, The Son can do nothing of himself, but what he seeth the Father do: for what things soever he doeth, these also doeth the Son likewise. [20]For the Father loveth the Son, and sheweth him all things that himself doeth: and he will shew him greater works than these, that ye may marvel. [21]For as the Father raiseth up the dead, and quickeneth them; even so the Son quickeneth whom he will. [22]For the Father judgeth no man, but hath committed all judgment unto the Son: [23]that all men should honour the Son, even as they honour the Father. He that honoureth not the Son honoureth not the Father which hath sent him. [24]Verily, verily, I say unto you, He that heareth my word, and believeth on him that sent me, hath everlasting life, and shall not come into condemnation; but is passed from death unto life. [25]Verily, verily, I say unto you,

---

5:3 *Impotent*: disabled. *Halt*: lame.   **5:3–4** *Waiting for . . . had*: better omitted (MS tradition) as a scribal gloss explaining the man's peculiar answer to Jesus' question in v. 7.   **5:5** *Infirmity*: Gk. root *asthene-*; cf. v. 3 ("impotent"). *Thirty and eight years*: the same period that the Israelites wandered in the wilderness, according to Deut 2:14.   **5:10** *Not lawful*: carrying burdens on the Sabbath is condemned in Neh 13:15, in Jer 17:21–27, and in rabbinic writings.   **5:14** *Behold, thou . . . thee*: Jesus presumes a connection between illness and sin (see Mark 2:5 note).   **5:16** *Persecute*: lit. "pursue." *And sought to slay him*: better omitted (MS tradition), perhaps as a scribal gloss prompted by "the more" in v. 18.   **5:17** *Hitherto*: until now—i.e., on the Sabbath.   **5:18** *The more*: in fact, this is the gospel's first reference to their seeking his death.   **5:21** *Quickeneth*: lit. "makes alive" (so throughout).

The hour is coming, and now is, when the dead shall hear the voice of the Son of God: and they that hear shall live. ²⁶For as the Father hath life in himself; so hath he given to the Son to have life in himself; ²⁷and hath given him authority to execute judgment also, because he is the Son of man. ²⁸Marvel not at this: for the hour is coming, in the which all that are in the graves shall hear his voice, ²⁹and shall come forth; they that have done good, unto the resurrection of life; and they that have done evil, unto the resurrection of damnation. ³⁰I can of mine own self do nothing: as I hear, I judge: and my judgment is just; because I seek not mine own will, but the will of the Father which hath sent me.

³¹If I bear witness of myself, my witness is not true. ³²There is another that beareth witness of me; and I know that the witness which he witnesseth of me is true. ³³Ye sent unto John, and he bare witness unto the truth. ³⁴But I receive not testimony from man: but these things I say, that ye might be saved. ³⁵He was a burning and a shining light: and ye were willing for a season to rejoice in his light. ³⁶But I have greater witness than that of John: for the works which the Father hath given me to finish, the same works that I do, bear witness of me, that the Father hath sent me. ³⁷And the Father himself, which hath sent me, hath borne witness of me. Ye have neither heard his voice at any time, nor seen his shape. ³⁸And ye have not his word abiding in you: for whom he hath sent, him ye believe not. ³⁹Search the scriptures; for in them ye think ye have eternal life: and they are they which testify of me. ⁴⁰And ye will not come to me, that ye might have life.

⁴¹I receive not honour from men. ⁴²But I know you, that ye have not the love of God in you. ⁴³I am come in my Father's name, and ye receive me not: if another shall come in his own name, him ye will receive. ⁴⁴How can ye believe, which receive honour one of another, and seek not the honour that cometh from God only? ⁴⁵Do not think that I will accuse you to the Father: there is one that accuseth you, even Moses, in whom ye trust. ⁴⁶For had ye believed Moses, ye would have believed me: for he wrote of me. ⁴⁷But if ye believe not his writings, how shall ye believe my words?

5:28 *Marvel not at this: for*: better "marvel not at this, namely that," a translation that underscores the decisive contrast between the material in vv. 19–25, at which "the Jews" are supposed to marvel (cf. v. 20), and the material of vv. 26–30, at which they are not. This difference corresponds to that between realized ("the hour is coming, and now is," v. 25) and future eschatology ("the hour is coming," v. 28). The marvel is that the Son offers in the present (vv. 24–25) the renewed life that will characterize the *eschaton* (vv. 28–29). This is the import of his two healings (4:43–54; 5:1–9). **5:29** *And shall . . . damnation*: cf. Dan 12:2. *Evil*: better "what is base." **5:31** *If I . . . true*: invoking a legal principle articulated in Deut 19:15 and echoed throughout the Bible (but contrast John 8:14): judgment must be founded on the testimony of more than one witness. Jesus here invokes four: John (vv. 32–35), his own "works" (v. 36), the Father (vv. 37–38), and Scripture (vv. 39–47). **5:35** *A burning and a shining light*: cf. Sir 48:1 (describing Elijah's speech). **5:37** *Ye have . . . shape*: recalling the accounts of the Sinai epiphany and its aftermath (Exod 19:9–25; Deut 4:12, 15; 5:23–27). **5:41** *Honour*: better "glory" (also in v. 44). **5:42** *Love of God*: either God's love for them or theirs for God. **5:45–46** *Even Moses . . . of me*: perhaps referring to Deut 18:15–22 (as at John 1:21, 45; 4:25), a passage that, like Jesus in vv. 43–44, draws a contrast between the Mosaic prophet who speaks in God's name and the false prophet speaking in another's.

6 After these things Jesus went over the sea of Galilee, which is the sea of Tiberias. ²And a great multitude followed him, because they saw his miracles which he did on them that were diseased. ³And Jesus went up into a mountain, and there he sat with his disciples. ⁴And the passover, a feast of the Jews, was nigh.

⁵When Jesus then lifted up his eyes, and saw a great company come unto him, he saith unto Philip, Whence shall we buy bread, that these may eat? ⁶And this he said to prove him: for he himself knew what he would do. ⁷Philip answered him, Two hundred pennyworth of bread is not sufficient for them, that every one of them may take a little. ⁸One of his disciples, Andrew, Simon Peter's brother, saith unto him, ⁹There is a lad here, which hath five barley loaves, and two small fishes: but what are they among so many? ¹⁰And Jesus said, Make the men sit down. Now there was much grass in the place. So the men sat down, in number about five thousand. ¹¹And Jesus took the loaves; and when he had given thanks, he distributed to the disciples, and the disciples to them that were set down; and likewise of the fishes as much as they would. ¹²When they were filled, he said unto his disciples, Gather up the fragments that remain, that nothing be lost. ¹³Therefore they gathered them together, and filled twelve baskets with the fragments of the five barley loaves, which remained over and above unto them that had eaten. ¹⁴Then those men, when they had seen the miracle that Jesus did, said, This is of a truth that prophet that should come into the world. ¹⁵When Jesus therefore perceived that they would come and take him by force, to make him a king, he departed again into a mountain himself alone.

¹⁶And when even was now come, his disciples went down unto the sea, ¹⁷and entered into a ship, and went over the sea toward Capernaum. And it was now dark, and Jesus was not come to them. ¹⁸And the sea arose by reason of a great wind that blew. ¹⁹So when they had rowed about five and twenty or thirty furlongs, they see Jesus walking on the sea, and drawing nigh unto the ship: and they

---

6:1–71 Jesus' miraculous feeding, walk on the sea, and discourse about bread. The first episode (vv. 1–15; cf. Matt 14:13–21; Mark 6:32–44; Luke 9:10–17) echoes Elisha's miraculous feeding (2 Kgs 4:42–44), as well as the story of manna in the wilderness (Exod 16; Num 11:1–15). Likewise, Jesus' subsequent walk on the water (vv. 16–21; cf. Matt 14:22–33; Mark 6:45–52) may figuratively correspond to the Israelites' crossing of the Red Sea (Exod 14). A brief transitional passage (vv. 22–24) is followed by Jesus' extended discourse (vv. 25–59), which is structured as a dialogue of six exchanges with the crowds, like those with the Samaritan woman in chap. 4. In addition, Jesus' elaborate discussion of the "bread of life" both recalls and advances the more limited discussion of "living water" in 4:10–15 (compare 4:14 and 6:27; 4:15 and 6:34; etc.). The chapter ends with the disciples' response to Jesus' discourse (vv. 60–71), culminating in Peter's confession (vv. 68–71; cf. Matt 16:13–20; Mark 8:27–30; Luke 9:18–21). **6:1** *After these . . . Galilee*: this notice is startlingly abrupt, for the Sea of Galilee is nowhere near Jerusalem, Jesus' previous location (cf. 5:1). However, 6:4 (another feast) indicates that significant time has passed. **6:6** *Prove*: or test. **6:7** *Pennyworth*: see Mark 14:5 note. **6:9** *Small fishes*: the Greek word refers to preserved fish. **6:11** *To the disciples, and the disciples*: better omitted (MS tradition) as scribal assimilation to the synoptic tradition. **6:14** *That prophet . . . world*: probably the Mosaic prophet (Deut 18:15–18). **6:15** *To make him a king*: odd, since they have just identified him as a prophet; but both inadequate interpretations serve as a foil to his self-identification at v. 20 (see note). **6:17** *Was not*: better "had not yet" (MS tradition). **6:19** *Furlongs*: Gk. *stadia*, so a distance of about three miles.

were afraid. [20]But he saith unto them, It is I; be not afraid. [21]Then they willingly received him into the ship: and immediately the ship was at the land whither they went.

[22]The day following, when the people which stood on the other side of the sea saw that there was none other boat there, save that one whereinto his disciples were entered, and that Jesus went not with his disciples into the boat, but that his disciples were gone away alone; [23](howbeit there came other boats from Tiberias nigh unto the place where they did eat bread, after that the Lord had given thanks:) [24]when the people therefore saw that Jesus was not there, neither his disciples, they also took shipping, and came to Capernaum, seeking for Jesus.

[25]And when they had found him on the other side of the sea, they said unto him, Rabbi, when camest thou hither? [26]Jesus answered them and said, Verily, verily, I say unto you, Ye seek me, not because ye saw the miracles, but because ye did eat of the loaves, and were filled. [27]Labour not for the meat which perisheth, but for that meat which endureth unto everlasting life, which the Son of man shall give unto you: for him hath God the Father sealed. [28]Then said they unto him, What shall we do, that we might work the works of God? [29]Jesus answered and said unto them, This is the work of God, that ye believe on him whom he hath sent. [30]They said therefore unto him, What sign shewest thou then, that we may see, and believe thee? what dost thou work? [31]Our fathers did eat manna in the desert; as it is written, He gave them bread from heaven to eat. [32]Then Jesus said unto them, Verily, verily, I say unto you, Moses gave you not that bread from heaven; but my Father giveth you the true bread from heaven. [33]For the bread of God is he which cometh down from heaven, and giveth life unto the world. [34]Then said they unto him, Lord, evermore give us this bread.

[35]And Jesus said unto them, I am the bread of life: he that cometh to me shall never hunger; and he that believeth on me shall never thirst. [36]But I said unto you, That ye also have seen me, and believe not. [37]All that the Father giveth me shall come to me; and him that cometh to me I will in no wise cast out. [38]For I came down from heaven, not to do mine own will, but the will of him that sent me. [39]And this is the Father's will which hath sent me, that of all which he hath given me I should lose nothing, but should raise it up again at the last day. [40]And this is the will of him that sent me, that every one which seeth the Son, and believeth on him, may have everlasting life: and I will raise him up at the last day.

6:20 *It is I*: Gk. *egō eimi*; see Mark 6:50 note.   **6:21** *Immediately the . . . went*: perhaps another miracle.   **6:23** *Tiberias*: on the southwestern shore of the Sea of Galilee.   **6:24** *Capernaum*: on its northwestern shore.   **6:27** *Meat*: food. *Perisheth*: Gk. *apollymenēn*; cf vv. 12, 39 (KJV "lost"). *Sealed*: see 3:33 note.   **6:28** *Work the works*: Gk. root *erga-*; cf. vv. 27 (KJV "labour"), 29–30.   **6:31** *Our fathers . . . desert*: see Exod 16; Num 11:1–15. *He gave . . . eat*: no OT text is quoted precisely, but cf. Exod 16:4, 15.   **6:32** *Moses gave . . . true bread from heaven*: in challenging their understanding of the citation (v. 31), Jesus alters both the subject and the tense of its verb.   **6:39** *Lose nothing*: the unexpected neuter here (*nothing* instead of "no one") and in v. 37 ("all that" instead of "everyone") may suggest an allegorical interpretation of the preserved fragments of bread (v. 12), but John elsewhere demonstrates

⁴¹The Jews then murmured at him, because he said, I am the bread which came down from heaven. ⁴²And they said, Is not this Jesus, the son of Joseph, whose father and mother we know? how is it then that he saith, I came down from heaven? ⁴³Jesus therefore answered and said unto them, Murmur not among yourselves. ⁴⁴No man can come to me, except the Father which hath sent me draw him: and I will raise him up at the last day. ⁴⁵It is written in the prophets, And they shall be all taught of God. Every man therefore that hath heard, and hath learned of the Father, cometh unto me. ⁴⁶Not that any man hath seen the Father, save he which is of God, he hath seen the Father. ⁴⁷Verily, verily, I say unto you, He that believeth on me hath everlasting life. ⁴⁸I am that bread of life. ⁴⁹Your fathers did eat manna in the wilderness, and are dead. ⁵⁰This is the bread which cometh down from heaven, that a man may eat thereof, and not die.

⁵¹I am the living bread which came down from heaven: if any man eat of this bread, he shall live for ever: and the bread that I will give is my flesh, which I will give for the life of the world. ⁵²The Jews therefore strove among themselves, saying, How can this man give us his flesh to eat? ⁵³Then Jesus said unto them, Verily, verily, I say unto you, Except ye eat the flesh of the Son of man, and drink his blood, ye have no life in you. ⁵⁴Whoso eateth my flesh, and drinketh my blood, hath eternal life; and I will raise him up at the last day. ⁵⁵For my flesh is meat indeed, and my blood is drink indeed. ⁵⁶He that eateth my flesh, and drinketh my blood, dwelleth in me, and I in him. ⁵⁷As the living Father hath sent me, and I live by the Father: so he that eateth me, even he shall live by me. ⁵⁸This is that bread which came down from heaven: not as your fathers did eat manna, and are dead: he that eateth of this bread shall live for ever. ⁵⁹These things said he in the synagogue, as he taught in Capernaum.

⁶⁰Many therefore of his disciples, when they had heard this, said, This is an hard saying; who can hear it? ⁶¹When Jesus knew in himself that his disciples murmured at it, he said unto them, Doth this offend you? ⁶²What and if ye shall see the Son of man ascend up where he was before? ⁶³It is the spirit that quickeneth; the flesh profiteth nothing: the words that I speak unto you, they are spirit,

---

a tendency to use neuters improperly (cf. 17:2, 24 notes).   **6:41** *Murmured*: cf. Exod 16:2, 7–9, 12. **6:42** *Is not . . . know*: in the Synoptics this question arises in a different context; see Matt 13:53–58; Mark 6:1–6a; Luke 4:16–30.   **6:45** *And they . . . God*: Isa 54:13.   **6:47** *On me*: better omitted (MS tradition).   **6:51–58** *I am . . . ever*: while the bread in vv. 25–50 seems to figure God's word or teaching (v. 45; cf. Deut 8:3), here it invites a eucharistic interpretation.   **6:51** *The bread . . . world*: recalling earlier references to the incarnation (cf. 1:14; 3:16–17) and perhaps also echoing early eucharistic liturgies (cf. 1 Cor 11:24–26).   **6:54** *Eateth*: Gk. *trōgō*, a word normally used of animals' feeding (cf. vv. 56, 57, 58b). Although KJV masks it, the imagery of consumption from this point on is shockingly crude, which helps explain the disciples' offended response (vv. 60–61) and their subsequent abandonment of Jesus (v. 66).   **6:55** *Meat indeed . . . drink indeed*: better "true food . . . true drink" (MS tradition).   **6:58** *Your fathers did eat manna*: better simply "the fathers ate" (MS tradition), using the standard verb for eating.   **6:60** *Hard*: Gk. *sklēros*, which connotes roughness and unpleasantness as well as difficulty.   **6:61** *His disciples murmured*: see v. 41 and note. *Offend you*: see Mark 4:17 note.   **6:62** *What*: not in the Greek, which instead offers half of a conditional. Jesus implies that if they cannot accept the incarnation in all its scandalous crudity (see vv. 51–58 and note), they will not be able to grasp the ascension.   **6:63** *The flesh profiteth nothing*: this claim stands in tension with the strong emphasis on Jesus' flesh in vv. 51–58. *Speak*: better "have spoken"

and they are life. [64]But there are some of you that believe not. For Jesus knew from the beginning who they were that believed not, and who should betray him. [65]And he said, Therefore said I unto you, that no man can come unto me, except it were given unto him of my Father. [66]From that time many of his disciples went back, and walked no more with him.

[67]Then said Jesus unto the twelve, Will ye also go away? [68]Then Simon Peter answered him, Lord, to whom shall we go? thou hast the words of eternal life. [69]And we believe and are sure that thou art that Christ, the Son of the living God. [70]Jesus answered them, Have not I chosen you twelve, and one of you is a devil? [71]He spake of Judas Iscariot the son of Simon: for he it was that should betray him, being one of the twelve.

7 After these things Jesus walked in Galilee: for he would not walk in Jewry, because the Jews sought to kill him. [2]Now the Jews' feast of tabernacles was at hand. [3]His brethren therefore said unto him, Depart hence, and go into Judæa, that thy disciples also may see the works that thou doest. [4]For there is no man that doeth any thing in secret, and he himself seeketh to be known openly. If thou do these things, shew thyself to the world. [5]For neither did his brethren believe in him. [6]Then Jesus said unto them, My time is not yet come: but your time is alway ready. [7]The world cannot hate you; but me it hateth, because I testify of it, that the works thereof are evil. [8]Go ye up unto this feast: I go not up yet unto this feast; for my time is not yet full come. [9]When he had said these words unto them, he abode still in Galilee. [10]But when his brethren were gone up, then went he also up unto the feast, not openly, but as it were in secret. [11]Then the Jews sought him at the feast, and said, Where is he? [12]And there was much murmuring among the people concerning him: for some said, He is a good man: others said, Nay; but he deceiveth the people. [13]Howbeit no man spake openly of him for fear of the Jews.

[14]Now about the midst of the feast Jesus went up into the temple, and taught. [15]And the Jews marvelled, saying, How knoweth this man letters, having never learned? [16]Jesus answered them, and said, My doctrine is not mine, but his that sent me. [17]If any man will do his will, he shall know of the doctrine, whether it

---

(MS tradition).   **6:69** *That Christ . . . God*: better "the holy one of God" (MS tradition).   **6:71** *Judas Iscariot . . . Simon*: better "Judas son of Simon Iscariot" (MS tradition; so subsequently). *Iscariot*: see Mark 3:19 note.

7:1–8:59 At the Feast of Tabernacles. An introduction (7:1–13) is followed by a lengthy discourse in which Jesus addresses and responds to various groups of "Jews" (7:14–8:59). It is interrupted by a brief discussion among the authorities, including Nicodemus, about how to respond to Jesus (7:45–53) and by the famous interpolated narrative of the woman caught in adultery (8:1–11). **7:1** *Jewry*: the Greek reads "Judea," the region around and containing Jerusalem.   **7:2** *Feast of tabernacles*: the harvest festival celebrated about six months after Passover, which also commemorated God's provisions during Israel's wilderness wanderings; cf. Lev 23:39–43; Deut 16:13–15. **7:8** *Not up yet*: better simply "not up" (MS tradition), which scribes presumably altered to eliminate Jesus' deception (v. 10).   **7:10** *As it were*: perhaps better omitted (MS tradition), with the same explanation as in v. 8 note.   **7:13** *For fear of the Jews*: "the people" (v. 12) are surely Jewish, and they included those who thought well of Jesus. Thus *the Jews* must refer to the Jewish leaders here and in v. 1. For the Evangelist's willingness to characterize *the Jews* as uniformly hostile to Jesus, even when doing so upsets his narrative's logic, cf. 8:31 and note.   **7:14** *Midst of the feast*: the celebration lasted one week.   **7:15** *Letters*: reading and writing.   **7:16** *Doctrine*: teaching (so throughout).

be of God, or whether I speak of myself. ¹⁸He that speaketh of himself seeketh his own glory: but he that seeketh his glory that sent him, the same is true, and no unrighteousness is in him. ¹⁹Did not Moses give you the law, and yet none of you keepeth the law? Why go ye about to kill me? ²⁰The people answered and said, Thou hast a devil: who goeth about to kill thee? ²¹Jesus answered and said unto them, I have done one work, and ye all marvel. ²²Moses therefore gave unto you circumcision; (not because it is of Moses, but of the fathers;) and ye on the sabbath day circumcise a man. ²³If a man on the sabbath day receive circumcision, that the law of Moses should not be broken; are ye angry at me, because I have made a man every whit whole on the sabbath day? ²⁴Judge not according to the appearance, but judge righteous judgment.

²⁵Then said some of them of Jerusalem, Is not this he, whom they seek to kill? ²⁶But, lo, he speaketh boldly, and they say nothing unto him. Do the rulers know indeed that this is the very Christ? ²⁷Howbeit we know this man whence he is: but when Christ cometh, no man knoweth whence he is. ²⁸Then cried Jesus in the temple as he taught, saying, Ye both know me, and ye know whence I am: and I am not come of myself, but he that sent me is true, whom ye know not. ²⁹But I know him: for I am from him, and he hath sent me. ³⁰Then they sought to take him: but no man laid hands on him, because his hour was not yet come. ³¹And many of the people believed on him, and said, When Christ cometh, will he do more miracles than these which this man hath done?

³²The Pharisees heard that the people murmured such things concerning him; and the Pharisees and the chief priests sent officers to take him. ³³Then said Jesus unto them, Yet a little while am I with you, and then I go unto him that sent me. ³⁴Ye shall seek me, and shall not find me: and where I am, thither ye cannot come. ³⁵Then said the Jews among themselves, Whither will he go, that we shall not find him? will he go unto the dispersed among the Gentiles, and teach the Gentiles? ³⁶What manner of saying is this that he said, Ye shall seek me, and shall not find me: and where I am, thither ye cannot come?

³⁷In the last day, that great day of the feast, Jesus stood and cried, saying, If any man thirst, let him come unto me, and drink. ³⁸He that believeth on me, as the scripture hath said, out of his belly shall flow rivers of living water. ³⁹(But this

7:17 *Of myself*: from myself. 7:18 *Of himself*: from himself. 7:20 *Hast a devil*: are possessed (cf. Matt 12:24; Mark 3:22; Luke 11:15). 7:22 *Not because . . . fathers*: Lev 12:3 mandates circumcision, but the command originates in the patriarchal narratives (Gen 17:9–14). 7:23 *Every whit whole*: if circumcision is mandated on the sabbath, then the healing of a man's entire body ought at least be permitted. (Healing on the sabbath was in fact permitted, but only when a life was threatened.) 7:26 *Rulers*: the same word used of Nicodemus in 3:1. *Very*: better omitted (MS tradition). 7:32 *Officers*: the temple security. 7:35 *The dispersed among the Gentiles*: Jews living outside Palestine. The word rendered *Gentiles* means "Greeks," but its reference is probably broader. When Jesus speaks of his departure (vv. 33–34), he alludes to his impending death and ascent to heaven, after which, ironically, he will be preached to diasporic Jews and to Gentiles. 7:37–38 *If any man . . . water*: alternatively, "if anyone thirsts, let him come to me, and let him who believes in me drink. As Scripture said, from his belly shall flow rivers of living water." 7:38 *Out of his belly . . . water*: the people's subsequent identification of Jesus with the prophet like Moses (v. 40, see note) may suggest a reference to Moses drawing water from the rock (Exod 17:6; cf. Ps 78:15–16), especially since other early Christian literature equates Jesus with this rock (cf. 1 Cor 10:4). Or perhaps the phrase refers to the eschatological imag-

spake he of the Spirit, which they that believe on him should receive: for the Holy Ghost was not yet given; because that Jesus was not yet glorified.) [40]Many of the people therefore, when they heard this saying, said, Of a truth this is the Prophet. [41]Others said, This is the Christ. But some said, Shall Christ come out of Galilee? [42]Hath not the scripture said, That Christ cometh of the seed of David, and out of the town of Bethlehem, where David was? [43]So there was a division among the people because of him. [44]And some of them would have taken him; but no man laid hands on him.

[45]Then came the officers to the chief priests and Pharisees; and they said unto them, Why have ye not brought him? [46]The officers answered, Never man spake like this man. [47]Then answered them the Pharisees, Are ye also deceived? [48]Have any of the rulers or of the Pharisees believed on him? [49]But this people who knoweth not the law are cursed. [50]Nicodemus saith unto them, (he that came to Jesus by night, being one of them,) [51]Doth our law judge any man, before it hear him, and know what he doeth? [52]They answered and said unto him, Art thou also of Galilee? Search, and look: for out of Galilee ariseth no prophet. [53]And every man went unto his own house.

8 Jesus went unto the mount of Olives. [2]And early in the morning he came again into the temple, and all the people came unto him; and he sat down, and taught them. [3]And the scribes and Pharisees brought unto him a woman taken in adultery; and when they had set her in the midst, [4]they say unto him, Master, this woman was taken in adultery, in the very act. [5]Now Moses in the law commanded us, that such should be stoned: but what sayest thou? [6]This they said,

---

ery of Zech 14:8, closely related to the Feast of Tabernacles (cf. Zech 14:16–19). The parenthetical explanation (v. 39) suggests a general allusion to the eschatological gift of God's Spirit, described in such OT passages as Ezek 11:19–20; 36:26–27; Joel 2:28.   **7:39** *Spirit, Ghost*: both Gk. *pneuma*. *Believe*: better "believed" (MS tradition). *Given*: added by KJV.   **7:40** *Many*: better "some" (MS tradition). *The Prophet*: probably referring to the prophet like Moses of Deut 18:15–18.   **7:41–42** *But some . . . Bethlehem*: the gospels betray tension between knowledge that Jesus' home was Nazareth in Galilee and the expectation (partly based on Mic 5:2) that the Christ would come from King David's hometown, Bethlehem in Judea. The infancy narratives in Matthew and Luke each resolve the tension differently, but John has no record of Jesus deriving from Bethlehem at all, and his decision to let stand the tension between knowledge and expectation may imply a critique of such attempts at harmonization. According to John, Christ is finally from neither Nazareth in Galilee nor Bethlehem, but from heaven (6:25–59).   **7:50** *By night*: better "before" (MS tradition).   **7:52** *Search, and . . . prophet*: or "search and see that no prophet arises from Galilee." They presumably direct Nicodemus to Scripture, but it is not clear what they expect him to find: the famous prophet Jonah hailed from a Galilean town (2 Kgs 14:25). This sloppiness may reflect John's lack of interest in theories about Jesus' geographic origins.   **8:1–11** The woman caught in adultery. This episode (including the transitional verse 7:53), reminiscent of the apocryphal tale of Susanna, is better omitted as an interpolation. Early and diverse MSS lack it, and several that do include it note its suspect authenticity. While the themes of judgment it shares with the previous episode (cf. 7:51–52) and with what follows (esp. 8:16) help explain why many locate it here, other MSS place it after 21:25, or after 7:44, or after 7:36, or even after Luke 21:38. It may have been a traditional story about Jesus that circulated independently, which early scribes incorporated into the gospels they copied. The notes will not comment on the many variant readings in the episode itself.   **8:1** *Mount of Olives*: a hill to the east of Jerusalem overlooking the city.   **8:5** *Moses in the law . . . stoned*: see Lev 20:10; Deut 22:22.

tempting him, that they might have to accuse him. But Jesus stooped down, and with his finger wrote on the ground, as though he heard them not. [7]So when they continued asking him, he lifted up himself, and said unto them, He that is without sin among you, let him first cast a stone at her. [8]And again he stooped down, and wrote on the ground. [9]And they which heard it, being convicted by their own conscience, went out one by one, beginning at the eldest, even unto the last: and Jesus was left alone, and the woman standing in the midst. [10]When Jesus had lifted up himself, and saw none but the woman, he said unto her, Woman, where are those thine accusers? hath no man condemned thee? [11]She said, No man, Lord. And Jesus said unto her, Neither do I condemn thee: go, and sin no more.

[12]Then spake Jesus again unto them, saying, I am the light of the world: he that followeth me shall not walk in darkness, but shall have the light of life. [13]The Pharisees therefore said unto him, Thou bearest record of thyself; thy record is not true. [14]Jesus answered and said unto them, Though I bear record of myself, yet my record is true: for I know whence I came, and whither I go; but ye cannot tell whence I come, and whither I go. [15]Ye judge after the flesh; I judge no man. [16]And yet if I judge, my judgment is true: for I am not alone, but I and the Father that sent me. [17]It is also written in your law, that the testimony of two men is true. [18]I am one that bear witness of myself, and the Father that sent me beareth witness of me. [19]Then said they unto him, Where is thy Father? Jesus answered, Ye neither know me, nor my Father: if ye had known me, ye should have known my Father also. [20]These words spake Jesus in the treasury, as he taught in the temple: and no man laid hands on him; for his hour was not yet come.

[21]Then said Jesus again unto them, I go my way, and ye shall seek me, and shall die in your sins: whither I go, ye cannot come. [22]Then said the Jews, Will he kill himself? because he saith, Whither I go, ye cannot come. [23]And he said unto them, Ye are from beneath; I am from above: ye are of this world; I am not of this world. [24]I said therefore unto you, that ye shall die in your sins: for if ye believe not that I am he, ye shall die in your sins. [25]Then said they unto him, Who art thou? And Jesus saith unto them, Even the same that I said unto you from the beginning. [26]I have many things to say and to judge of you: but he that sent me is true; and I speak to the world those things which I have heard of him. [27]They understood not that he spake to them of the Father. [28]Then said Jesus unto them, When ye have lifted up the Son of man, then shall ye know that I am he, and that I do nothing of myself; but as my Father hath taught me, I speak these things. [29]And he that

sent me is with me: the Father hath not left me alone; for I do always those things that please him. ³⁰As he spake these words, many believed on him.

³¹Then said Jesus to those Jews which believed on him, If ye continue in my word, then are ye my disciples indeed; ³²and ye shall know the truth, and the truth shall make you free. ³³They answered him, We be Abraham's seed, and were never in bondage to any man: how sayest thou, Ye shall be made free? ³⁴Jesus answered them, Verily, verily, I say unto you, Whosoever committeth sin is the servant of sin. ³⁵And the servant abideth not in the house for ever: but the Son abideth ever. ³⁶If the Son therefore shall make you free, ye shall be free indeed. ³⁷I know that ye are Abraham's seed; but ye seek to kill me, because my word hath no place in you. ³⁸I speak that which I have seen with my Father: and ye do that which ye have seen with your father. ³⁹They answered and said unto him, Abraham is our father. Jesus saith unto them, If ye were Abraham's children, ye would do the works of Abraham. ⁴⁰But now ye seek to kill me, a man that hath told you the truth, which I have heard of God: this did not Abraham.

⁴¹Ye do the deeds of your father. Then said they to him, We be not born of fornication; we have one Father, even God. ⁴²Jesus said unto them, If God were your Father, ye would love me: for I proceeded forth and came from God; neither came I of myself, but he sent me. ⁴³Why do ye not understand my speech? even because ye cannot hear my word. ⁴⁴Ye are of your father the devil, and the lusts of your father ye will do. He was a murderer from the beginning, and abode not in the truth, because there is no truth in him. When he speaketh a lie, he speaketh of his own: for he is a liar, and the father of it. ⁴⁵And because I tell you the truth, ye believe me not. ⁴⁶Which of you convinceth me of sin? And if I say the

---

(NRSV). **8:31** *To those Jews . . . him*: strangely, what may be the harshest polemic in the NT is directed at Jews who are said to believe in Jesus. Some speculate that the disturbing hostility in vv. 31–59 reflects resentment that the evangelist and his community felt toward apostates—Jews who adopted but later abandoned faith in Jesus, thus betraying them and, in a sense, Jesus himself. **8:33** *Were never . . . man*: contradicted by Exodus, and by Deuteronomy's reiterated commands that Israelites remember their slavery (e.g., Deut 6:20–21; 15:12–15). John characterizes these Jews as not only excessively literal but wrongheaded and obstinate as well. **8:34** *Servant of sin*: lit. "slave of sin"; cf. Rom 6:16–23. **8:38** *I speak . . . your father*: KJV seems to take this as Jesus' first suggestion that the Jews' father is the devil (cf. v. 44), but a better reading of the MS tradition and translation suggests a different construal: "I speak that which I have seen from the father. As for you, then, do that which you have heard from the father." **8:39** *If ye . . . Abraham*: better "if you are Abraham's children, you would be doing the works of Abraham" (MS tradition). **8:40** *This did not Abraham*: Jesus contrasts Abraham's hospitality to divine messengers (Gen 18:1–8) with the Jews' desire to kill him, God's representative from heaven. **8:41** *Ye do . . . father*: Jesus commands them to emulate Abraham or obey God (cf. vv. 38–40), and/or he anticipates his later accusation that their father is the devil (v. 44). *We be . . . God*: the reference to *fornication*, a biblical trope for idolatry, suggests that Jesus' auditors take his words as a charge of apostasy. By insisting that they have *one Father, even God*, they reassert their covenant relationship with YHWH (cf. Exod 4:22; Deut 32:6; etc.). **8:44** *He was . . . it*: Jesus alludes to two stories from the Primeval History commonly thought to feature the devil: Abel's murder by Cain (Gen 4:1–15), who was held to have been fathered by Satan rather than Adam (cf. 1 John 3:12–15 and v. 12 note), and Eve's deception by the serpent (Gen 3), who was held to be Satan himself (cf. 2 Cor 11:14 and note). *Abode*: lit. "stood." *Of his own*: alternatively "according to his own nature" (NRSV). **8:46** *Convinceth*: convicts.

truth, why do ye not believe me? [47]He that is of God heareth God's words: ye therefore hear them not, because ye are not of God.

[48]Then answered the Jews, and said unto him, Say we not well that thou art a Samaritan, and hast a devil? [49]Jesus answered, I have not a devil; but I honour my Father, and ye do dishonour me. [50]And I seek not mine own glory: there is one that seeketh and judgeth. [51]Verily, verily, I say unto you, If a man keep my saying, he shall never see death. [52]Then said the Jews unto him, Now we know that thou hast a devil. Abraham is dead, and the prophets; and thou sayest, If a man keep my saying, he shall never taste of death. [53]Art thou greater than our father Abraham, which is dead? and the prophets are dead: whom makest thou thyself? [54]Jesus answered, If I honour myself, my honour is nothing: it is my Father that honoureth me; of whom ye say, that he is your God: [55]yet ye have not known him; but I know him: and if I should say, I know him not, I shall be a liar like unto you: but I know him, and keep his saying. [56]Your father Abraham rejoiced to see my day: and he saw it, and was glad. [57]Then said the Jews unto him, Thou art not yet fifty years old, and hast thou seen Abraham? [58]Jesus said unto them, Verily, verily, I say unto you, Before Abraham was, I am. [59]Then took they up stones to cast at him: but Jesus hid himself, and went out of the temple, going through the midst of them, and so passed by.

9 And as Jesus passed by, he saw a man which was blind from his birth. [2]And his disciples asked him, saying, Master, who did sin, this man, or his parents, that he was born blind? [3]Jesus answered, Neither hath this man sinned, nor his parents: but that the works of God should be made manifest in him. [4]I must

---

8:48 *Thou art a Samaritan*: Jesus, like the Samaritans, denies the Jews' privileged relationship to YHWH (see Matt 10:5 note). *Devil*: Gk *daimōn* (cf. vv. 49, 52), in contrast to *diabolos* (v. 44). **8:54** *Honour . . . honour . . . honoureth*: lit. "glorify" . . . "glory" . . . "glorifies." **8:56** *Abraham rejoiced . . . glad*: Paul interprets Abraham's offspring ("seed") Isaac as Christ (see Rom 4:16–25; Gal 3:16). If John knew of this association, then he may be referring to Abraham's laughter when he learns of Isaac's impending birth (Gen 17:17), for *rejoiced* (Gk. *agalliaō*) contains the same root as the verb LXX uses of Abraham's laughing. (Although Abraham apparently laughs in disbelief, his amusement was traditionally seen in a more positive light.) **8:58** *Before Abraham . . . am*: the praise of God in Ps 90:2 similarly substitutes the present for the expected past tense. In Greek, though, the contrast here is even stronger: *I am* translates Gk. *egō eimi* (see vv. 24 and note, 28); *Abraham was* uses *gino- mai*, a verb that connotes coming into existence rather than existence itself. **8:59** *Took they up stones*: they apparently take Jesus' statement as blasphemy (cf. Mark 14:62–64); cf. Lev 24:16. *Hid himself*: cf. 7:10 (the Greek root of "in secret" and *hid* is the same). *Going through . . . by*: better omitted (MS tradition).

9:1–10:42 The healing of the blind man and the similitude of the shepherd. The initial narrative (chap. 9) juxtaposes the restored blind man's growing awareness of Jesus' divinity (he identifies Jesus as "a man . . . called Jesus" in v. 11, "a prophet" in v. 17, a "man . . . of God" in v. 33, "Son of man" in v. 35 [see note], and "Lord" in v. 38) to the Pharisees' willful blindness, culminating in their revilement (v. 28) and exclusion (v. 34) of the man who had honestly responded to their inquiries about Jesus. Jesus himself contrasts his insight with the Pharisees' refusal to see (vv. 39–41). Behind Jesus' subsequent discourse (10:1–42) lie many OT texts that describe God's care in pastoral terms (esp. Ezek 34, echoed throughout). The synoptic tradition frequently portrays Jesus as healing the blind (see esp. Matt 20:29–34; Mark 8:22–26; 10:46–52; Luke 18:35–43) and speaking metaphorically about sheep and shepherds, but this section has no sustained parallels with the other gospels. **9:2** *Who did sin . . . blind*: cf. Exod 20:5. **9:3** *Neither hath . . . him*: Jesus challenges the connection between illness and sin presumed in 5:14. **9:4** *I must*: better "we must" (MS tradition).

work the works of him that sent me, while it is day: the night cometh, when no man can work. ⁵As long as I am in the world, I am the light of the world. ⁶When he had thus spoken, he spat on the ground, and made clay of the spittle, and he anointed the eyes of the blind man with the clay, ⁷and said unto him, Go, wash in the pool of Siloam, (which is by interpretation, Sent.) He went his way therefore, and washed, and came seeing.

⁸The neighbours therefore, and they which before had seen him that he was blind, said, Is not this he that sat and begged? ⁹Some said, This is he: others said, He is like him: but he said, I am he. ¹⁰Therefore said they unto him, How were thine eyes opened? ¹¹He answered and said, A man that is called Jesus made clay, and anointed mine eyes, and said unto me, Go to the pool of Siloam, and wash: and I went and washed, and I received sight. ¹²Then said they unto him, Where is he? He said, I know not.

¹³They brought to the Pharisees him that aforetime was blind. ¹⁴And it was the sabbath day when Jesus made the clay, and opened his eyes. ¹⁵Then again the Pharisees also asked him how he had received his sight. He said unto them, He put clay upon mine eyes, and I washed, and do see. ¹⁶Therefore said some of the Pharisees, This man is not of God, because he keepeth not the sabbath day. Others said, How can a man that is a sinner do such miracles? And there was a division among them. ¹⁷They say unto the blind man again, What sayest thou of him, that he hath opened thine eyes? He said, He is a prophet.

¹⁸But the Jews did not believe concerning him, that he had been blind, and received his sight, until they called the parents of him that had received his sight. ¹⁹And they asked them, saying, Is this your son, who ye say was born blind? how then doth he now see? ²⁰His parents answered them and said, We know that this is our son, and that he was born blind: ²¹but by what means he now seeth, we know not; or who hath opened his eyes, we know not: he is of age; ask him: he shall speak for himself. ²²These words spake his parents, because they feared the Jews: for the Jews had agreed already, that if any man did confess that he was Christ, he should be put out of the synagogue. ²³Therefore said his parents, He is of age; ask him.

²⁴Then again called they the man that was blind, and said unto him, Give God the praise: we know that this man is a sinner. ²⁵He answered and said, Whether

---

9:5 *I am the light of the world*: Matt 5:14 identifies Jesus' disciples as "the light of the world." **9:6** *Spittle*: see Mark 7:33–34 and note. **9:7** *Siloam*: cf. Neh 3:15; Isa 8:6–8. The pool, fed by the Spring of Gihon, seems to have been in the southern part of Jerusalem. **9:17** *That*: alternatively "since." **9:22** *They feared . . . synagogue*: a clear anachronism, as Acts portrays Jesus' disciples long continuing to teach in synagogues and indeed in the temple itself. The threat of excommunication coheres with what we know about conflicts between proto-rabbinic Judaism and nascent Christianity that flared in the wake of Rome's destruction of Jerusalem in the late first century C.E., when John is believed to have been written. This episode locates Jesus in a situation more appropriate to Jesus-believers of a generation or two later than to Jesus' own historical context. It may update an authentic tradition involving Jesus healing a blind man, or it may have originated as a controversial healing performed by an early Christian in his name, which was subsequently recast as a story of Jesus himself. The latter origin might account for the odd pronominal slippage between "me" (i.e., Jesus) and "we" (i.e., Jesus' followers, the church) in v. 4 (see note) and Jesus' application to himself of a saying that Matthew applies to Jesus' followers (v. 5; see note). **9:24** *Give God the praise*: lit. "give glory to God," an oath that customarily

he be a sinner or no, I know not: one thing I know, that, whereas I was blind, now I see. ²⁶Then said they to him again, What did he to thee? how opened he thine eyes? ²⁷He answered them, I have told you already, and ye did not hear: wherefore would ye hear it again? will ye also be his disciples? ²⁸Then they reviled him, and said, Thou art his disciple; but we are Moses' disciples. ²⁹We know that God spake unto Moses: as for this fellow, we know not from whence he is. ³⁰The man answered and said unto them, Why herein is a marvellous thing, that ye know not from whence he is, and yet he hath opened mine eyes. ³¹Now we know that God heareth not sinners: but if any man be a worshipper of God, and doeth his will, him he heareth. ³²Since the world began was it not heard that any man opened the eyes of one that was born blind. ³³If this man were not of God, he could do nothing. ³⁴They answered and said unto him, Thou wast altogether born in sins, and dost thou teach us? And they cast him out.

³⁵Jesus heard that they had cast him out; and when he had found him, he said unto him, Dost thou believe on the Son of God? ³⁶He answered and said, Who is he, Lord, that I might believe on him? ³⁷And Jesus said unto him, Thou hast both seen him, and it is he that talketh with thee. ³⁸And he said, Lord, I believe. And he worshipped him. ³⁹And Jesus said, For judgment I am come into this world, that they which see not might see; and that they which see might be made blind. ⁴⁰And some of the Pharisees which were with him heard these words, and said unto him, Are we blind also? ⁴¹Jesus said unto them, If ye were blind, ye should have no sin: but now ye say, We see; therefore your sin remaineth.

10 Verily, verily, I say unto you, He that entereth not by the door into the sheepfold, but climbeth up some other way, the same is a thief and a robber. ²But he that entereth in by the door is the shepherd of the sheep. ³To him the porter openeth; and the sheep hear his voice: and he calleth his own sheep by name, and leadeth them out. ⁴And when he putteth forth his own sheep, he goeth before them, and the sheep follow him: for they know his voice. ⁵And a stranger will they not follow, but will flee from him: for they know not the voice of strangers. ⁶This parable spake Jesus unto them: but they understood not what things they were which he spake unto them.

⁷Then said Jesus unto them again, Verily, verily, I say unto you, I am the door of the sheep. ⁸All that ever came before me are thieves and robbers: but the sheep did not hear them. ⁹I am the door: by me if any man enter in, he shall be saved,

---

introduces admissions of culpability; cf. Josh 7:19; 1 Esd 9:8.   **9:28** *Thou art . . . disciples*: this clear-cut distinction is anachronistic (see v. 22 note).   **9:34** *Cast him out*: perhaps referring to excommunication (cf. v. 22).   **9:35** *God*: better "man" (MS tradition).   **9:36** *Lord*: see 4:11 note; "sir" is a better translation here and "Lord" only at v. 38.   **10:3** *By name*: apparently referring to a shepherd's pet names for choice sheep.   **10:4** *His own sheep*: better "all his own" (MS tradition).   **10:6** *Parable*: not Gk. *parabolē*, as in the Synoptics, but the meaning is probably the same; see Mark 4:2 note. Jesus offers divergent allegorical interpretations of this parable (vv. 7–16).   **10:8** *All that . . . robbers*: an impressive array of textual witnesses omit "before me"; it is possible that the words were later added to clarify Jesus' otherwise enigmatic statement, but it is somewhat more likely that they were omitted because of the theological problem they raise (potentially, the condemnation of the OT patriarchs and prophets). If the apostolic father Ignatius alludes to this passage when he calls Jesus the "door," he may be attempting to scale back Jesus' sweeping denunciation by specifying that the patriarchs and

and shall go in and out, and find pasture. [10]The thief cometh not, but for to steal, and to kill, and to destroy: I am come that they might have life, and that they might have it more abundantly. [11]I am the good shepherd: the good shepherd giveth his life for the sheep. [12]But he that is an hireling, and not the shepherd, whose own the sheep are not, seeth the wolf coming, and leaveth the sheep, and fleeth: and the wolf catcheth them, and scattereth the sheep. [13]The hireling fleeth, because he is an hireling, and careth not for the sheep. [14]I am the good shepherd, and know my sheep, and am known of mine. [15]As the Father knoweth me, even so know I the Father: and I lay down my life for the sheep. [16]And other sheep I have, which are not of this fold: them also I must bring, and they shall hear my voice; and there shall be one fold, and one shepherd. [17]Therefore doth my Father love me, because I lay down my life, that I might take it again. [18]No man taketh it from me, but I lay it down of myself. I have power to lay it down, and I have power to take it again. This commandment have I received of my Father.

[19]There was a division therefore again among the Jews for these sayings. [20]And many of them said, He hath a devil, and is mad; why hear ye him? [21]Others said, These are not the words of him that hath a devil. Can a devil open the eyes of the blind?

[22]And it was at Jerusalem the feast of the dedication, and it was winter. [23]And Jesus walked in the temple in Solomon's porch. [24]Then came the Jews round about him, and said unto him, How long dost thou make us to doubt? If thou be the Christ, tell us plainly. [25]Jesus answered them, I told you, and ye believed not: the works that I do in my Father's name, they bear witness of me. [26]But ye believe not, because ye are not of my sheep, as I said unto you. [27]My sheep hear my voice, and I know them, and they follow me: [28]and I give unto them eternal life; and they shall never perish, neither shall any man pluck them out of my hand. [29]My Father, which gave them me, is greater than all; and no man is able to pluck them out of my Father's hand. [30]I and my Father are one.

[31]Then the Jews took up stones again to stone him. [32]Jesus answered them, Many good works have I shewed you from my Father; for which of those works do ye stone me? [33]The Jews answered him, saying, For a good work we stone thee not; but for blasphemy; and because that thou, being a man, makest thyself God. [34]Jesus answered them, Is it not written in your law, I said, Ye are gods?

---

prophets, as well as the apostles and church, enter through it (*To the Philadelphians* 9.1).   **10:10** *Kill*: better "slaughter" (a Greek word normally used of killing animals).   **10:12–13** *The sheep. The hireling fleeth*: better omitted (MS tradition).   **10:16** *Other sheep*: probably Gentiles. *One fold*: lit. "one flock"; KJV seems to follow the Vulgate.   **10:22–42** Jesus at the Feast of the Dedication. Although the scene changes, Jesus' metaphorical discourse about sheep continues and its implications for his identity are explored under interrogation by "the Jews."   **10:22** *Feast of the Dedication*: Hanukkah, celebrating the Maccabean renewal of the temple (turned into a pagan shrine by Antiochus IV; 1 Macc 1:29–64); see 1 Macc 4:36–59.   **10:23** *Porch*: colonnade.   **10:24** *Make us to doubt*: lit. "carry away our soul/life"; the idiom may mean "hold us in suspense," but its exact significance and connotations are unknown.   **10:26** *As I said unto you*: better omitted (MS tradition).   **10:29** *My Father . . . all*: an alternative and possibly superior reading of the MS tradition yields "what my father gave to me is greater than all."   **10:34** *I said, Ye are gods*: Ps 82:6. Jesus seems to interpret the phrase with reference to prophets (see v. 35 note); other ancient exegetes understood it to refer to human judges or to

³⁵If he called them gods, unto whom the word of God came, and the scripture cannot be broken; ³⁶say ye of him, whom the Father hath sanctified, and sent into the world, Thou blasphemest; because I said, I am the Son of God? ³⁷If I do not the works of my Father, believe me not. ³⁸But if I do, though ye believe not me, believe the works: that ye may know, and believe, that the Father is in me, and I in him. ³⁹Therefore they sought again to take him: but he escaped out of their hand, ⁴⁰and went away again beyond Jordan into the place where John at first baptized; and there he abode. ⁴¹And many resorted unto him, and said, John did no miracle: but all things that John spake of this man were true. ⁴²And many believed on him there.

11 Now a certain man was sick, named Lazarus, of Bethany, the town of Mary and her sister Martha. ² (It was that Mary which anointed the Lord with ointment, and wiped his feet with her hair, whose brother Lazarus was sick.) ³Therefore his sisters sent unto him, saying, Lord, behold, he whom thou lovest is sick. ⁴When Jesus heard that, he said, This sickness is not unto death, but for the glory of God, that the Son of God might be glorified thereby. ⁵Now Jesus loved Martha, and her sister, and Lazarus. ⁶When he had heard therefore that he was sick, he abode two days still in the same place where he was. ⁷Then after that saith he to his disciples, Let us go into Judæa again. ⁸His disciples say unto him, Master, the Jews of late sought to stone thee; and goest thou thither again? ⁹Jesus answered, Are there not twelve hours in the day? If any man walk in the day, he stumbleth not, because he seeth the light of this world. ¹⁰But if a man walk in the night, he stumbleth, because there is no light in him. ¹¹These things said he: and after that he saith unto them, Our friend Lazarus sleepeth; but I go, that I may awake him out of sleep. ¹²Then said his disciples, Lord, if he sleep, he shall do

---

Israel.   **10:35** *Unto whom . . . came*: recalling a standard opening of OT prophetic books (e.g., Hos 1:1; Joel 1:1; Jonah 1:1). *Broken*: i.e., canceled.   **10:36** *Say ye . . . God*: Jesus is tendentiously interpreting his opponents' claim that he makes himself God (v. 33) in light of his own claim of divine parentage: if Scripture calls "gods" human figures to whom God's word merely comes (vv. 34–35), then no one should object if Jesus identifies himself as God's son (v. 30), for he is the word of God itself come into the world (cf. 1:1, 14). Since his opponents surely take offense at all of v. 30 ("I and my Father *are one*"), Jesus' argument misses the point, unless the unity he is claiming in vv. 30 and 38 is merely the concord between any faithful son and his father.   **10:36** *Sanctified*: Gk. *hēgiasen*, the same word used by LXX for the tabernacle's consecration (Num 7:1); Jesus' diction thus resonates within the discourse's Hanukkah setting (see v. 22 note).   **10:38** *Know, and believe*: better "know and understand" or "know and acknowledge" (MS tradition).   **10:40–42** *And went away . . . there*: Jesus' public ministry appropriately draws to a close with his return to the place where John the Baptist introduced him (1:19–36).

   11:1–12:11 The resurrection of Lazarus and the anointing at Bethany. Initiating a shift from Jesus' public ministry to his passion, Jesus' resurrection of his friend Lazarus (11:1–44) at once prompts the Jewish authorities to plot his murder (11:45–57; 12:9–11) and anticipates his final triumph over the impending death foreshadowed by Mary's ominous anointing (12:1–8).   **11:1** *Bethany*: although Jesus is currently staying at a Bethany (10:40; cf. 1:28 and note), Lazarus apparently lives in another town of the same name near Jerusalem, in the region of Judea (cf. vv. 7, 18). *Mary and her sister Martha*: see Luke 10:38–42.   **11:2** *It was . . . hair*: this event is narrated in 12:1–8, where Jesus interprets it as his anointing for burial (12:7). By forecasting it here, the evangelist signals that the defeat of death in the present episode is transitory.   **11:4** *This sickness . . . thereby*: cf. 9:3.   **11:10** *No light in him*: the ancients often explained vision as light emanating from the eye.   **11:12** *Do well*: recover (lit.

well. ¹³Howbeit Jesus spake of his death: but they thought that he had spoken of taking of rest in sleep. ¹⁴Then said Jesus unto them plainly, Lazarus is dead. ¹⁵And I am glad for your sakes that I was not there, to the intent ye may believe; nevertheless let us go unto him. ¹⁶Then said Thomas, which is called Didymus, unto his fellowdisciples, Let us also go, that we may die with him.

¹⁷Then when Jesus came, he found that he had lain in the grave four days already. ¹⁸Now Bethany was nigh unto Jerusalem, about fifteen furlongs off: ¹⁹and many of the Jews came to Martha and Mary, to comfort them concerning their brother. ²⁰Then Martha, as soon as she heard that Jesus was coming, went and met him: but Mary sat still in the house. ²¹Then said Martha unto Jesus, Lord, if thou hadst been here, my brother had not died. ²²But I know, that even now, whatsoever thou wilt ask of God, God will give it thee. ²³Jesus saith unto her, Thy brother shall rise again. ²⁴Martha saith unto him, I know that he shall rise again in the resurrection at the last day. ²⁵Jesus said unto her, I am the resurrection, and the life: he that believeth in me, though he were dead, yet shall he live: ²⁶and whosoever liveth and believeth in me shall never die. Believest thou this? ²⁷She saith unto him, Yea, Lord: I believe that thou art the Christ, the Son of God, which should come into the world.

²⁸And when she had so said, she went her way, and called Mary her sister secretly, saying, The Master is come, and calleth for thee. ²⁹As soon as she heard that, she arose quickly, and came unto him. ³⁰Now Jesus was not yet come into the town, but was in that place where Martha met him. ³¹The Jews then which were with her in the house, and comforted her, when they saw Mary, that she rose up hastily and went out, followed her, saying, She goeth unto the grave to weep there. ³²Then when Mary was come where Jesus was, and saw him, she fell down at his feet, saying unto him, Lord, if thou hadst been here, my brother had not died. ³³When Jesus therefore saw her weeping, and the Jews also weeping which came with her, he groaned in the spirit, and was troubled, ³⁴and said, Where have ye laid him? They said unto him, Lord, come and see. ³⁵Jesus wept. ³⁶Then said the Jews, Behold how he loved him! ³⁷And some of them said, Could not this man, which opened the eyes of the blind, have caused that even this man should not have died?

³⁸Jesus therefore again groaning in himself cometh to the grave. It was a cave, and a stone lay upon it. ³⁹Jesus said, Take ye away the stone. Martha, the sister of him that was dead, saith unto him, Lord, by this time he stinketh: for he hath been dead four days. ⁴⁰Jesus saith unto her, Said I not unto thee, that, if thou wouldest believe, thou shouldest see the glory of God? ⁴¹Then they took away the stone from the place where the dead was laid. And Jesus lifted up his eyes, and said, Father, I thank thee that thou hast heard me. ⁴²And I knew that thou hearest me always: but because of the people which stand by I said it, that they may

---

"be saved"). **11:16** *Didymus*: the Greek word for "twin," the meaning of the Aramaic root of "Thomas." He is initially faithless when confronting the possibility of Jesus' resurrection as well (20:24–29 and notes; cf. 14:1–5). **11:18** *Furlongs*: see 6:19 note. **11:27** *Thou art . . . God*: paralleling Peter's confession at 6:69. **11:33** *Groaned*: Gk. *embrimaomai*, which normally indicates anger; cf. v. 38; Mark 1:43, "scolded" (see note). If it connotes anger here as well, then the object of Jesus' rage is not clear:

believe that thou hast sent me. ⁴³And when he thus had spoken, he cried with a loud voice, Lazarus, come forth. ⁴⁴And he that was dead came forth, bound hand and foot with graveclothes: and his face was bound about with a napkin. Jesus saith unto them, Loose him, and let him go.

⁴⁵Then many of the Jews which came to Mary, and had seen the things which Jesus did, believed on him. ⁴⁶But some of them went their ways to the Pharisees, and told them what things Jesus had done. ⁴⁷Then gathered the chief priests and the Pharisees a council, and said, What do we? for this man doeth many miracles. ⁴⁸If we let him thus alone, all men will believe on him: and the Romans shall come and take away both our place and nation. ⁴⁹And one of them, named Caiaphas, being the high priest that same year, said unto them, Ye know nothing at all, ⁵⁰nor consider that it is expedient for us, that one man should die for the people, and that the whole nation perish not. ⁵¹And this spake he not of himself: but being high priest that year, he prophesied that Jesus should die for that nation; ⁵²and not for that nation only, but that also he should gather together in one the children of God that were scattered abroad. ⁵³Then from that day forth they took counsel together for to put him to death. ⁵⁴Jesus therefore walked no more openly among the Jews; but went thence unto a country near to the wilderness, into a city called Ephraim, and there continued with his disciples.

⁵⁵And the Jews' passover was nigh at hand: and many went out of the country up to Jerusalem before the passover, to purify themselves. ⁵⁶Then sought they for Jesus, and spake among themselves, as they stood in the temple, What think ye, that he will not come to the feast? ⁵⁷Now both the chief priests and the Pharisees had given a commandment, that, if any man knew where he were, he should shew it, that they might take him.

---

perhaps it is death itself.   **11:44** *Gravecloths*: strips of cloth in which corpses were commonly wrapped. The verse's imagery and diction (*bound, loose, let him go*) figure death as constricting. **11:45–57** Plotting against Jesus. In the Synoptics too the religious leaders plot to put Jesus to death, though their deliberations and the context differ significantly from those in John (cf. Matt 26:1–5; Mark 14:1–2; Luke 22:1–2).   **11:47** *Council*: Gk. *synedrion*, the Sanhedrin (see Mark 8:31 note). The presence of Pharisees is surprising: they are associated with Jesus' arrest, trial, and execution only rarely in John (here, 11:57; 12:19; 18:3) and never in the Synoptics (but see Matt 12:14; Mark 3:6; in Luke 13:31, Pharisees actually help Jesus evade arrest). Historically, though Jesus was known to have debated Pharisees in Galilee, they played no significant role in the events leading to his death in Jerusalem. John's perfunctory mention of them here is a manifestation of his tendency to portray "the Jews" as uniformly hostile to Jesus. *Miracles*: John has presented seven signs (cf. 2:11 note): changing water to wine (2:1–11), healing a nobleman's son (4:46–54), healing a paralytic (5:1–15), multiplying loaves (6:1–14), walking on water (6:16–21), healing a blind man (9:1–41), and resurrecting Lazarus (11:1–44).   **11:48** *All men . . . him*: they are worried about Jesus causing a disturbance during the upcoming Passover festival, when Jerusalem would be filled with pilgrims (cf. v. 55). *Our place*: probably the temple.   **11:49** *Caiaphas, being . . . year*: Caiaphas was high priest from ca. 18 to 36 C.E. **11:50** *For us*: better "for you" (MS tradition).   **11:52** *The children . . . abroad*: Gentile believers (cf. 10:16 and note) and diasporic Jews (cf. 7:35 and note).   **11:54** *Country*: region. *Ephraim*: unidentified, but 2 Sam 13:23 refers to an Ephraim near Baal-hazor (a town about twenty miles north of Jerusalem), the site where Absalom had Amnon assassinated (2 Sam 13:23–29).   **11:55** *Purify themselves*: see Num 9:10–14. The Sanhedrin plots against Jesus when its members are supposed to be purifying

12 Then Jesus six days before the passover came to Bethany, where Lazarus was which had been dead, whom he raised from the dead. ²There they made him a supper; and Martha served: but Lazarus was one of them that sat at the table with him. ³Then took Mary a pound of ointment of spikenard, very costly, and anointed the feet of Jesus, and wiped his feet with her hair: and the house was filled with the odour of the ointment. ⁴Then saith one of his disciples, Judas Iscariot, Simon's son, which should betray him, ⁵Why was not this ointment sold for three hundred pence, and given to the poor? ⁶This he said, not that he cared for the poor; but because he was a thief, and had the bag, and bare what was put therein. ⁷Then said Jesus, Let her alone: against the day of my burying hath she kept this. ⁸For the poor always ye have with you; but me ye have not always.

⁹Much people of the Jews therefore knew that he was there: and they came not for Jesus' sake only, but that they might see Lazarus also, whom he had raised from the dead. ¹⁰But the chief priests consulted that they might put Lazarus also to death; ¹¹because that by reason of him many of the Jews went away, and believed on Jesus.

¹²On the next day much people that were come to the feast, when they heard that Jesus was coming to Jerusalem, ¹³took branches of palm trees, and went forth to meet him, and cried, Hosanna: Blessed is the King of Israel that cometh in the name of the Lord. ¹⁴And Jesus, when he had found a young ass, sat thereon; as it is written, ¹⁵Fear not, daughter of Sion: behold, thy King cometh, sitting on an ass's colt. ¹⁶These things understood not his disciples at the first: but when Jesus was glorified, then remembered they that these things were written of him, and that they had done these things unto him. ¹⁷The people therefore that was with him when he called Lazarus out of his grave, and raised him from the dead, bare record. ¹⁸For this cause the people also met him, for that they heard that he had done this miracle. ¹⁹The Pharisees therefore said among themselves, Perceive ye how ye prevail nothing? behold, the world is gone after him.

---

themselves for Passover. **12:1–8** Anointing at Bethany. Compare Matt 26:6–13; Mark 14:3–9; Luke 7:36–50. **12:2** *Sat*: lit. "reclined." **12:3** *Spikenard*: see Mark 14:3 note. *Anointed the feet*: normally the head would be anointed. **12:5** *Pence*: see Mark 14:5 note. **12:6** *Had the bag*: held the company's money. *Bare*: i.e., "removed" (stole). **12:7** *Against the day . . . this*: better "so that she may keep this for the day of my burial" (MS tradition). **12:8** *The poor . . . you*: cf. Deut 15:11. **12:9–11** *Much people . . . Jesus*: forming an inclusive frame with 11:45–57 and thereby embedding the story of Jesus' anointing for burial within his enemies' murderous intrigues.
12:12–43 Jesus' entry into Jerusalem, where Gentiles seek him. Jesus' entry into Jerusalem (vv. 12–19; cf. Matt 21:1–11; Mark 11:1–10; Luke 19:28–40) concludes with the Pharisees' hyperbolic claim that "the whole world is gone after him" (v. 19). This introduces a surprising notice of Greeks seeking after Jesus (vv. 20–22). Jesus' subsequent discourse (vv. 23–33) culminates in his promise to "draw all men" to himself (v. 32). By locating this material immediately following Jesus' proclamation as king of Israel in the mold of Simon Maccabeus (v. 13; see Mark 11:7–9 note), the evangelist insists that Jesus' mission be understood as universal rather than national. **12:13** *Took branches . . . trees*: see Mark 11:8 note. *Hosanna, blessed . . . Lord*: better "Hosanna! Blessed is he who comes in the name of the Lord, even the king of Israel!" (KJV inverts the order of the two phrases.) The people quote from Ps 118 (vv. 25–26a); their addition of *the king of Israel* signals an interpretation of the psalm as a song of royal procession. *Hosanna*: a transliterated Hebrew phrase meaning "save now." **12:15** *Fear not . . . colt*: combining Zeph 3:16 and Zech 9:9.

²⁰And there were certain Greeks among them that came up to worship at the feast: ²¹the same came therefore to Philip, which was of Bethsaida of Galilee, and desired him, saying, Sir, we would see Jesus. ²²Philip cometh and telleth Andrew: and again Andrew and Philip tell Jesus. ²³And Jesus answered them, saying, The hour is come, that the Son of man should be glorified. ²⁴Verily, verily, I say unto you, Except a corn of wheat fall into the ground and die, it abideth alone: but if it die, it bringeth forth much fruit. ²⁵He that loveth his life shall lose it; and he that hateth his life in this world shall keep it unto life eternal. ²⁶If any man serve me, let him follow me; and where I am, there shall also my servant be: if any man serve me, him will my Father honour.

²⁷Now is my soul troubled; and what shall I say? Father, save me from this hour: but for this cause came I unto this hour. ²⁸Father, glorify thy name. Then came there a voice from heaven, saying, I have both glorified it, and will glorify it again. ²⁹The people therefore, that stood by, and heard it, said that it thundered: others said, An angel spake to him. ³⁰Jesus answered and said, This voice came not because of me, but for your sakes. ³¹Now is the judgment of this world: now shall the prince of this world be cast out. ³²And I, if I be lifted up from the earth, will draw all men unto me. ³³This he said, signifying what death he should die.

³⁴The people answered him, We have heard out of the law that Christ abideth for ever: and how sayest thou, The Son of man must be lifted up? who is this Son of man? ³⁵Then Jesus said unto them, Yet a little while is the light with you. Walk while ye have the light, lest darkness come upon you: for he that walketh in darkness knoweth not whither he goeth. ³⁶While ye have light, believe in the light, that ye may be the children of light. These things spake Jesus, and departed, and did hide himself from them.

³⁷But though he had done so many miracles before them, yet they believed not on him: ³⁸that the saying of Esaias the prophet might be fulfilled, which he

---

12:21 *The same . . . Galilee*: Philip's name was Greek, which may explain why these presumably proselytized Greeks came to him.   **12:23** *Answered them*: subsequent references to "the people" (vv. 29, 34), combined with the notice of v. 37, suggest that Jesus responds to his disciples' report of Gentile seekers with a public discourse. *The hour is come*: until now John had insisted that Jesus' hour has not yet arrived (2:4; 7:30; 8:20; cf. 7:6, 8).   **12:24** *Corn*: grain.   **12:25** *He that loveth . . . eternal*: cf. Matt 10:39; 16:25; Mark 8:35; Luke 9:23–24; 17:33. *Shall lose*: better "loses" (MS tradition). **12:27–30** *Now is . . . sakes*: this scene, which recalls the synoptic account of Jesus' agony in Gethsemane (cf. Matt 26:36–46; Mark 14:32–42; Luke 22:39–46), may polemically recast that tradition to emphasize Jesus' firmness of purpose as he confronts his impending death.   **12:29** *An angel spake to him*: cf. Luke 22:43–44 and note. If, as seems likely, the Lukan verses are inauthentic, they may be an imaginative scribal addition to the Gethsemane scene inspired by this reference to an angel in a parallel context.   **12:31** *The prince of this world*: Satan; see Luke 4:6 note.   **12:33** *Signifying*: the verbal form of Gk. *sēmeion*, "sign," which is usually rendered "miracle" in John (see 2:11 note). Jesus' crucifixion will be the ultimate "sign."   **12:34** *Christ abideth for ever*: see OT references to a king descended from David (i.e., *Christ*; see Mark 1:1 note) or a *Son of man* reigning forever (e.g., Ps 89:3–4; Dan 7:13–14).   **12:35** *Walk while . . . you*: reversing Isa 9:2.   **12:36** *Children of light*: see Luke 16:8 note. **12:37–43** The Jews' unbelief. Compare Matt 13:10–17; Mark 4:10–12; Luke 8:9–10. After the episode involving Gentiles seeking Jesus and the discourse it occasioned, the evangelist now offers an explanation of why Jesus' fellow Jews fail to believe in him.   **12:37** *But though . . . him*: echoing Deut 29:2–4.

spake, Lord, who hath believed our report? and to whom hath the arm of the Lord been revealed? ³⁹Therefore they could not believe, because that Esaias said again, ⁴⁰He hath blinded their eyes, and hardened their heart; that they should not see with their eyes, nor understand with their heart, and be converted, and I should heal them. ⁴¹These things said Esaias, when he saw his glory, and spake of him. ⁴²Nevertheless among the chief rulers also many believed on him; but because of the Pharisees they did not confess him, lest they should be put out of the synagogue: ⁴³for they loved the praise of men more than the praise of God.

⁴⁴Jesus cried and said, He that believeth on me, believeth not on me, but on him that sent me. ⁴⁵And he that seeth me seeth him that sent me. ⁴⁶I am come a light into the world, that whosoever believeth on me should not abide in darkness. ⁴⁷And if any man hear my words, and believe not, I judge him not: for I came not to judge the world, but to save the world. ⁴⁸He that rejecteth me, and receiveth not my words, hath one that judgeth him: the word that I have spoken, the same shall judge him in the last day. ⁴⁹For I have not spoken of myself; but the Father which sent me, he gave me a commandment, what I should say, and what I should speak. ⁵⁰And I know that his commandment is life everlasting: whatsoever I speak therefore, even as the Father said unto me, so I speak.

13 Now before the feast of the passover, when Jesus knew that his hour was come that he should depart out of this world unto the Father, having loved his own which were in the world, he loved them unto the end. ²And supper being ended, the devil having now put into the heart of Judas Iscariot, Simon's son, to betray him; ³Jesus knowing that the Father had given all things into his hands, and that he was come from God, and went to God; ⁴he riseth from supper, and

---

12:38 *Lord, who . . . revealed*: Isa 53:1.   **12:40** *He hath . . . them*: Isa 6:10. *Be converted*: lit. "turn." **12:41** *When*: better "because" (MS tradition). *Saw his glory*: referring to the prophet's vision in Isa 6, whose object the Evangelist understands as Jesus.   **12:42** *Chief rulers*: presumably members of the Sanhedrin. *Lest they . . . synagogue*: see 9:22 and note.   **12:43** *Praise*: Gk. *doxa*; cf. v. 41 (KJV "glory"). **12:44–50 Jesus' concluding proclamation.** This passage fits uncomfortably within the narrative context: Jesus had just hidden (v. 36); now he proclaims loudly (v. 44), with neither audience nor location specified. The proclamation actually functions as a concluding reflection on Jesus' public discourse and ministry in the first part of John's gospel. The second part is characterized by an intense focus on Jesus' private interactions with disciples, interrupted only by his death. **12:47** *Believe not*: better "does not keep them" (MS tradition).   **12:48–49** *He that . . . speak*: cf. Deut 18:18–19 (on the prophet like Moses).   **12:50** *And I . . . so I speak*: recalling the end of Moses' final address (Deut 32:45–47). **13:1–38 The Last Supper.** John's account differs notably from the Synoptics' and Paul's. Most significantly, it locates the Last Supper before the Passover (see v. 1), rather than construing it as a Passover meal (cf. Matt 26:17–19; Mark 14:12–16; Luke 22:7–13), and it does not present the supper as the institution of the Eucharist (cf. Matt 26:26–29; Mark 14:22–25; Luke 22:15–20; 1 Cor 11:23–26). The first difference points to an important disagreement in chronology between the Synoptics and John; see 19:31 and note.   **13:1** *Now before . . . end*: introducing the second part of John's gospel, which focuses on the events leading up to and succeeding Jesus' death, with *unto the end* (Gk. *eis telos*) foreshadowing Jesus' final words: "it is finished" (Gk. *tetelestai*).   **13:2–17** Jesus washes his disciples' feet. The Synoptics do not include it, but this episode echoes the dispute among the disciples recorded at Matt 20:20–28; Mark 10:35–45; Luke 22:24–27.   **13:2** *Supper being ended*: better "during supper" (MS tradition). *The devil . . . him*: John alone mentions this detail, but Luke agrees with his later claim that Satan entered Judas just before the betrayal (v. 27; cf. Luke 22:3).

laid aside his garments; and took a towel, and girded himself. ⁵After that he poureth water into a bason, and began to wash the disciples' feet, and to wipe them with the towel wherewith he was girded. ⁶Then cometh he to Simon Peter: and Peter saith unto him, Lord, dost thou wash my feet? ⁷Jesus answered and said unto him, What I do thou knowest not now; but thou shalt know hereafter. ⁸Peter saith unto him, Thou shalt never wash my feet. Jesus answered him, If I wash thee not, thou hast no part with me. ⁹Simon Peter saith unto him, Lord, not my feet only, but also my hands and my head. ¹⁰Jesus saith to him, He that is washed needeth not save to wash his feet, but is clean every whit: and ye are clean, but not all. ¹¹For he knew who should betray him; therefore said he, Ye are not all clean.

¹²So after he had washed their feet, and had taken his garments, and was set down again, he said unto them, Know ye what I have done to you? ¹³Ye call me Master and Lord: and ye say well; for so I am. ¹⁴If I then, your Lord and Master, have washed your feet; ye also ought to wash one another's feet. ¹⁵For I have given you an example, that ye should do as I have done to you. ¹⁶Verily, verily, I say unto you, The servant is not greater than his lord; neither he that is sent greater than he that sent him. ¹⁷If ye know these things, happy are ye if ye do them.

¹⁸I speak not of you all: I know whom I have chosen: but that the scripture may be fulfilled, He that eateth bread with me hath lifted up his heel against me. ¹⁹Now I tell you before it come, that, when it is come to pass, ye may believe that I am he. ²⁰Verily, verily, I say unto you, He that receiveth whomsoever I send receiveth me; and he that receiveth me receiveth him that sent me.

²¹When Jesus had thus said, he was troubled in spirit, and testified, and said, Verily, verily, I say unto you, that one of you shall betray me. ²²Then the disciples looked one on another, doubting of whom he spake. ²³Now there was leaning on

13:4 *Laid aside*: the same Greek verb used in chap. 10 of Jesus "laying down" his life (10:11, 15, 17, 18); "taken" (v. 12) similarly repeats the verb used there of Jesus "taking" his life again (10:17, 18). John's diction, together with the conventional use of garments to symbolize the body (both mortal and resurrected) clothing the soul (see 2 Cor 5:2 note), suggests that Jesus' washing of his disciples' feet symbolizes his abasing death in service of others. Recall also that Jesus associated Mary's anointing of his feet with his impending death (12:7).   **13:7** *Know hereafter*: although John often uses different Greek words for "know" interchangeably, it may be significant that in this verse he shifts from *oida* to *ginōskō*, which connotes recognition or acquaintance (also used at vv. 12, 28, 35).   **13:10** *He that is washed*: Gk *louō*, different from the word used elsewhere in the chapter; it commonly refers to washing the entire body and it or cognates are elsewhere in the NT associated with baptism (e.g., Acts 22:16; Titus 3:5). *Needeth not . . . feet*: perhaps implying that Peter is too fixated on the cleansing itself, rather than on the willingness to abase oneself in service that characterizes Jesus' slavish act.   **13:12** *Was set down*: lit. "reclined."   **13:16** *The servant . . . lord*: cf. Matt 10:24.   **13:17** *Happy*: or blessed. **13:18** *He that . . . against me*: Ps 41:9. *Eateth*: cf. 6:54–58 (see 6:54 note); a different verb is used in the LXX translation of Ps 49. The recollection of chap. 6's eucharistic imagery may suggest a eucharistic interpretation of the Last Supper, which John otherwise ignores. *Hath lifted up his heel*: a sign of hostility and disrespect that subverts Jesus' act of footwashing. Given the role of the devil in this scene (vv. 2, 27) and the common association of Genesis' serpent with Satan, there may be an allusion to Gen 3:15.   **13:19** *I am he*: Gk. *egō eimi*; see Mark 6:50 note.   **13:21–30** Jesus predicts his betrayal. Compare Matt 26:20–25; Mark 14:17–21; Luke 22:21–23.   **13:22** *Doubting of*: at a loss about. **13:23** *Leaning*: reclined. Since people in the ancient Mediterranean world reclined while dining, *was leaning on Jesus' bosom* probably means "reclined close to Jesus." Although the phrase surely connotes

Jesus' bosom one of his disciples, whom Jesus loved. [24]Simon Peter therefore beckoned to him, that he should ask who it should be of whom he spake. [25]He then lying on Jesus' breast saith unto him, Lord, who is it? [26]Jesus answered, He it is, to whom I shall give a sop, when I have dipped it. And when he had dipped the sop, he gave it to Judas Iscariot, the son of Simon. [27]And after the sop Satan entered into him. Then said Jesus unto him, That thou doest, do quickly. [28]Now no man at the table knew for what intent he spake this unto him. [29]For some of them thought, because Judas had the bag, that Jesus had said unto him, Buy those things that we have need of against the feast; or, that he should give something to the poor. [30]He then having received the sop went immediately out: and it was night.

[31]Therefore, when he was gone out, Jesus said, Now is the Son of man glorified, and God is glorified in him. [32]If God be glorified in him, God shall also glorify him in himself, and shall straightway glorify him. [33]Little children, yet a little while I am with you. Ye shall seek me: and as I said unto the Jews, Whither I go, ye cannot come; so now I say to you. [34]A new commandment I give unto you, That ye love one another; as I have loved you, that ye also love one another. [35]By this shall all men know that ye are my disciples, if ye have love one to another.

[36]Simon Peter said unto him, Lord, whither goest thou? Jesus answered him, Whither I go, thou canst not follow me now; but thou shalt follow me afterwards. [37]Peter said unto him, Lord, why cannot I follow thee now? I will lay down my life for thy sake. [38]Jesus answered him, Wilt thou lay down thy life for my sake? Verily, verily, I say unto thee, The cock shall not crow, till thou hast denied me thrice.

---

intimacy, its traditional visualization—the beloved disciple resting his head on Jesus' breast—is fancifully anachronistic. *One of . . . loved*: the so-called beloved disciple, a key figure from this point on in John's narrative. Although first introduced here as the disciple "whom Jesus loved," this anonymous, idealized figure should perhaps be identified with the unnamed disciple from 1:35–40. In any case, the mention of his physical proximity to Jesus at once recalls the earlier description of Jesus himself "in the bosom of the Father" (1:18) and presents this disciple as a foil to Judas, who leaves the meal in order to betray Jesus (13:30). The fourth evangelist will ultimately authorize his gospel by citing this anonymous disciple's testimony (21:20–24). Since the work has been attributed to John, some identify the beloved disciple as Zebedee's son by that name, or as another disciple named John not numbered among the Twelve (perhaps John the elder, who is mentioned in early extracanonical Christian writings). Others see him as Lazarus, whom Jesus is repeatedly said to have loved (11:3, 5, 36; cf. 11:11, with "friend" rendering the same Greek root elsewhere translated "love"), or as a figurative representation of the ideal follower of Jesus. **13:28** *No man . . . him*: in light of v. 26, it is strange that the ignorance extends even to Peter and the beloved disciple. **13:29** *Judas had the bag*: see 12:6 note. **13:32** *If God be glorified in him*: a large and diverse number of ancient witnesses omit this phrase. **13:33** *As I said unto the Jews*: cf. 7:33–34. **13:34** *A new commandment*: while Luke (22:20) and Paul (1 Cor 11:25) report that Jesus instituted a "new testament" (i.e., "covenant") at the Last Supper, John speaks only of a new commandment—one closely related to Lev 19:18. **13:36–38** Jesus predicts Peter's denial. Compare Matt 26:33–35; Mark 14:29–31; Luke 22:31–34. **13:37** *I will . . . sake*: Peter boldly casts himself in the role of the good shepherd who "giveth his life for the sheep" (10:11). The shepherding imagery resurfaces in the scene of Peter's redemption (21:15–19).

14 Let not your heart be troubled: ye believe in God, believe also in me. ²In my Father's house are many mansions: if it were not so, I would have told you. I go to prepare a place for you. ³And if I go and prepare a place for you, I will come again, and receive you unto myself; that where I am, there ye may be also. ⁴And whither I go ye know, and the way ye know. ⁵Thomas saith unto him, Lord, we know not whither thou goest; and how can we know the way? ⁶Jesus saith unto him, I am the way, the truth, and the life: no man cometh unto the Father, but by me. ⁷If ye had known me, ye should have known my Father also: and from henceforth ye know him, and have seen him. ⁸Philip saith unto him, Lord, shew us the Father, and it sufficeth us. ⁹Jesus saith unto him, Have I been so long time with you, and yet hast thou not known me, Philip? he that hath seen me hath seen the Father; and how sayest thou then, Shew us the Father? ¹⁰Believest thou not that I am in the Father, and the Father in me? the words that I speak unto you I speak not of myself: but the Father that dwelleth in me, he doeth the works. ¹¹Believe me that I am in the Father, and the Father in me: or else believe me for the very works' sake. ¹²Verily, verily, I say unto you, He that believeth on me, the works that I do shall he do also; and greater works than these shall he do; because I go unto my Father. ¹³And whatsoever ye shall ask in my name, that will I do, that the Father may be glorified in the Son. ¹⁴If ye shall ask any thing in my name, I will do it.

¹⁵If ye love me, keep my commandments. ¹⁶And I will pray the Father, and he shall give you another Comforter, that he may abide with you for ever; ¹⁷even the

14:1–17:26 Jesus' Farewell Discourse. On the farewell speech in biblical literature, see Acts 20:17–38 note. Perhaps nowhere in the NT are the seams of a composite discourse more evident than here. For instance, Jesus states "Hereafter I will not talk much with you. . . . Arise, let us go hence" (14:30–31), but then goes on to speak for three more chapters, with the departure announced at 14:31 occurring only at 18:1. Similarly, elements of the discourse stand in tension with the narrative of the Last Supper, to which it is appended: though in 13:36 Peter had asked Jesus "whither goest thou," in 16:5 Jesus asserts "none of you asketh me, Whither goest thou?" Despite its obvious junctions, the material has been combined into a thematically coherent whole. Note the careful and theologically meaningful parallelism between discussions of the Holy Spirit (i.e., "Comforter") at 14:15–17 and of the risen Christ at 14:18–21 (see notes), the artful balance between Jesus' and the disciples' love for one another (15:1–17) and the world's hatred for the disciples (15:18–16:4a), and the numerous variations on the theme of abiding/dwelling throughout.   **14:1–12** *Let not . . . Father*: Jesus initially and finally insists that he will go to his father's house (vv. 1–4, 12); but in response to Thomas's and Philip's questions, he complicates that idea by suggesting that he himself is the way to the father (vv. 5–7) and that the father and he actually dwell in one another (vv. 8–11).   **14:1** *Heart be troubled*: Jesus had this response when confronting Lazarus's death (11:33) and predicting his own deadly betrayal (13:21). *Ye believe . . . believe*: the verbs may be interpreted as indicatives or imperatives.   **14:2** *Mansions*: Gk. *monai*, the nominal form of *menein* (see 1:32 note), which appears at 14:10, 16, 17, 25; 15:5, 10 (twice), 16. Mansion here means "abode" (cf. v. 23). *If it . . . for you*: the Greek is unclear. A better reading of the MS tradition connects the two clauses with Gk. *hoti*, which here means either "because" or "that." Moreover, the entire condition could be understood as a question: "If it were not so, would I have told you . . . ?"   **14:4** *Whither I . . . way ye know*: better "you know the way to the place where I am going" (MS tradition). **14:7** *Known*: Gk. *ginōskō* (so throughout this verse; cf. vv. 9, 17, 20, 31), not *oida*, the verb used earlier in the chapter; see 13:7 note.   **14:10** *The works*: better "his works" (MS tradition).   **14:14** *Ask*: better "ask me" (MS tradition).   **14:16** *Comforter*: Gk. *paraklētos* (cf. v. 26; 15:26; 16:7), also "helper" or "encourager." This more active sense better explains why Jesus announces its coming right after demanding that his followers keep his commandments. *Abide*: better "be" (MS tradition).

Spirit of truth; whom the world cannot receive, because it seeth him not, neither knoweth him: but ye know him; for he dwelleth with you, and shall be in you. ¹⁸I will not leave you comfortless: I will come to you. ¹⁹Yet a little while, and the world seeth me no more; but ye see me: because I live, ye shall live also. ²⁰At that day ye shall know that I am in my Father, and ye in me, and I in you. ²¹He that hath my commandments, and keepeth them, he it is that loveth me: and he that loveth me shall be loved of my Father, and I will love him, and will manifest myself to him. ²²Judas saith unto him, not Iscariot, Lord, how is it that thou wilt manifest thyself unto us, and not unto the world? ²³Jesus answered and said unto him, If a man love me, he will keep my words: and my Father will love him, and we will come unto him, and make our abode with him. ²⁴He that loveth me not keepeth not my sayings: and the word which ye hear is not mine, but the Father's which sent me. ²⁵These things have I spoken unto you, being yet present with you. ²⁶But the Comforter, which is the Holy Ghost, whom the Father will send in my name, he shall teach you all things, and bring all things to your remembrance, whatsoever I have said unto you.

²⁷Peace I leave with you, my peace I give unto you: not as the world giveth, give I unto you. Let not your heart be troubled, neither let it be afraid. ²⁸Ye have heard how I said unto you, I go away, and come again unto you. If ye loved me, ye would rejoice, because I said, I go unto the Father: for my Father is greater than I. ²⁹And now I have told you before it come to pass, that, when it is come to pass, ye might believe. ³⁰Hereafter I will not talk much with you: for the prince of this world cometh, and hath nothing in me. ³¹But that the world may know that I love the Father; and as the Father gave me commandment, even so I do. Arise, let us go hence.

15 I am the true vine, and my Father is the husbandman. ²Every branch in me that beareth not fruit he taketh away: and every branch that beareth fruit, he purgeth it, that it may bring forth more fruit. ³Now ye are clean through

14:17 *Him*: lit. "it" (throughout the verse; also for *he*). **14:18–21** *I will . . . to him*: this passage reiterates vv. 15–17 (18 = 16, 19–20 = 17, 21 = 15), but replaces the Comforter with the risen Jesus, a theologically meaningful substitution. **14:18** *Comfortless*: lit. "orphans." KJV dilutes the metaphor in order to introduce a verbal connection with the "Comforter." **14:22** *Judas . . . not Iscariot*: probably Judas son of James, one of the Twelve according to Luke (6:16 and note). **14:23** *Words*: lit. "word." *We will . . . with him*: in the OT God frequently promises to dwell with Israel (e.g., Exod 29:45–46; Zech 2:10). **14:26** *He*: although the Greek phrase translated *Holy Ghost* by KJV is neuter, this Greek pronoun is masculine. **14:27** *Not as . . . you*: since "peace" was a common farewell, Jesus is saying that his departing utterance is not merely conventional but is an effective blessing. **14:27–31** *Let not . . . hence*: the inclusive frame with v. 1 (*let not your heart be troubled*), the reiteration of key themes from throughout the chapter (Jesus' departure and return [v. 28], the relationship between love and obedience [v. 31], etc.), and the transition from Jesus' discourse to his impending death (vv. 28–31) all combine to suggest that this passage originally concluded Jesus' farewell discourse, which was later supplemented by additional material. **14:28** *Because I said*: better simply "because" (MS tradition). **14:30** *Prince of this world*: see 12:31 and note. **14:31** *Arise, let us go hence*: the departure does not occur until 18:1. **15:1–6** *I am . . . burned*: conventional OT imagery, where the vine or vineyard symbolizes Israel and God acts as vinedresser (cf. Ps 80:8–16; Isa 5:1–7; etc.). John's development of the distinction between stem and branches is innovative. **15:2** *Purgeth*: i.e., prunes the vine; this Greek verb (*kathairō*) and the one translated *taketh away* share a root. **15:3** *Clean*: the adjectival

the word which I have spoken unto you. [4]Abide in me, and I in you. As the branch cannot bear fruit of itself, except it abide in the vine; no more can ye, except ye abide in me. [5]I am the vine, ye are the branches: He that abideth in me, and I in him, the same bringeth forth much fruit: for without me ye can do nothing. [6]If a man abide not in me, he is cast forth as a branch, and is withered; and men gather them, and cast them into the fire, and they are burned.

[7]If ye abide in me, and my words abide in you, ye shall ask what ye will, and it shall be done unto you. [8]Herein is my Father glorified, that ye bear much fruit; so shall ye be my disciples. [9]As the Father hath loved me, so have I loved you: continue ye in my love. [10]If ye keep my commandments, ye shall abide in my love; even as I have kept my Father's commandments, and abide in his love. [11]These things have I spoken unto you, that my joy might remain in you, and that your joy might be full. [12]This is my commandment, That ye love one another, as I have loved you. [13]Greater love hath no man than this, that a man lay down his life for his friends. [14]Ye are my friends, if ye do whatsoever I command you. [15]Henceforth I call you not servants; for the servant knoweth not what his lord doeth: but I have called you friends; for all things that I have heard of my Father I have made known unto you. [16]Ye have not chosen me, but I have chosen you, and ordained you, that ye should go and bring forth fruit, and that your fruit should remain: that whatsoever ye shall ask of the Father in my name, he may give it you. [17]These things I command you, that ye love one another.

[18]If the world hate you, ye know that it hated me before it hated you. [19]If ye were of the world, the world would love his own: but because ye are not of the world, but I have chosen you out of the world, therefore the world hateth you. [20]Remember the word that I said unto you, The servant is not greater than his lord. If they have persecuted me, they will also persecute you; if they have kept my saying, they will keep yours also. [21]But all these things will they do unto you for my name's sake, because they know not him that sent me. [22]If I had not come and spoken unto them, they had not had sin: but now they have no cloke for their sin. [23]He that

---

form of *kathairō* (see v. 2 note).   **15:4** *Abide*: a key motif in this chapter; see 1:32 note.   **15:5** *Bringeth forth*: Gk. *pherō* (cf. v. 16), elsewhere translated "bear."   **15:7–17** *If ye . . . another*: this section, which interprets the previous paragraph's parabolic discourse, is chiastically structured, with vv. 7 corresponding to 16b, 8 to 16a, 9 to 15, 10 to 14, and 11 to 13 (both of which emphasize comprehensiveness, of joy and love respectively). The correspondence is especially clear in the Greek, where the word for "friends" (vv. 14–15), *philoi*, has a root that can also mean "love" (vv. 9–10). The chiasmus centers around v. 12, Jesus' command that his disciples love one another, which the section's concluding verse emphatically repeats (v. 17). Love for the other represents the metaphorical fruit that Jesus' followers are to bear as a result of abiding in him as branches in a vine.   **15:8** *So shall ye*: better "and be" (MS tradition).   **15:11** *Remain*: better "be" (MS tradition).   **15:15** *Servants*: slaves (also in v. 20). *Made known*: a form of Gk. *ginōskō* (cf. v. 18; 16:3, 19), not *oida* (*knoweth*); see 13:7; 14:7 and notes.   **15:16** *Chosen*: Gk. root *leg-*, the same as "call" (v. 15).   **15:18–16:15** Impending persecution and the Spirit of truth. The material in this section thematically parallels Jesus' eschatological discourse in the Synoptic Gospels (cf. Matt 10:17–25; 24:9–22; Mark 13:9–20; Luke 21:12–24). The role of the encouraging Spirit (cf. Matt 10:19–20; Mark 13:11; Luke 21:15, where it is replaced by Jesus himself) is especially expanded.   **15:18** *Ye know*: the Greek form can be imperative or indicative.   **15:19** *Love*: Gk. *phileō*, which shares a root with "friends" (vv. 13–15).   **15:20** *The servant . . . lord*: see 13:16 (but contrast v. 15, "henceforth I call you not servants").   **15:22** *Cloke*: lit. "excuse" or "pretext."

hateth me hateth my Father also. [24]If I had not done among them the works which none other man did, they had not had sin: but now have they both seen and hated both me and my Father. [25]But this cometh to pass, that the word might be fulfilled that is written in their law, They hated me without a cause. [26]But when the Comforter is come, whom I will send unto you from the Father, even the Spirit of truth, which proceedeth from the Father, he shall testify of me: [27]and ye also shall bear witness, because ye have been with me from the beginning.

16 These things have I spoken unto you, that ye should not be offended. [2]They shall put you out of the synagogues: yea, the time cometh, that whosoever killeth you will think that he doeth God service. [3]And these things will they do unto you, because they have not known the Father, nor me. [4]But these things have I told you, that when the time shall come, ye may remember that I told you of them.

And these things I said not unto you at the beginning, because I was with you. [5]But now I go my way to him that sent me; and none of you asketh me, Whither goest thou? [6]But because I have said these things unto you, sorrow hath filled your heart. [7]Nevertheless I tell you the truth; It is expedient for you that I go away: for if I go not away, the Comforter will not come unto you; but if I depart, I will send him unto you. [8]And when he is come, he will reprove the world of sin, and of righteousness, and of judgment: [9]of sin, because they believe not on me; [10]of righteousness, because I go to my Father, and ye see me no more; [11]of judgment, because the prince of this world is judged.

[12]I have yet many things to say unto you, but ye cannot bear them now. [13]Howbeit when he, the Spirit of truth, is come, he will guide you into all truth: for he shall not speak of himself; but whatsoever he shall hear, that shall he speak: and he will shew you things to come. [14]He shall glorify me: for he shall receive of mine, and shall shew it unto you. [15]All things that the Father hath are mine: therefore said I, that he shall take of mine, and shall shew it unto you.

[16]A little while, and ye shall not see me: and again, a little while, and ye shall see me, because I go to the Father. [17]Then said some of his disciples among themselves, What is this that he saith unto us, A little while, and ye shall not see me: and again, a little while, and ye shall see me: and, Because I go to the Father?

15:25 *They hated . . . cause*: see Pss 35:19; 69:4.   **16:1** *Be offended*: see Mark 4:17 note.   **16:2** *Put you . . . synagogues*: see 9:22 note. *Time*: lit. "hour." *Doeth God service*: specifically, carries out religious functions.   **16:4** *The time*: better "their hour" (MS tradition and a more literal translation). *Because I . . . you*: while Jesus is present, he is the sole object of persecution.   **16:5** *None of . . . thou*: contradicted by 13:36. Jesus' idea seems to be that they are troubled not so much by his impending absence as by the persecution that he prophesied would occur (see v. 6).   **16:8** *Reprove the world of*: Gk. ambiguous; perhaps "prove the world wrong about" (NRSV) or "convict the world of."   **16:10** *Righteousness*: better "justice" (also in v. 8); the idea seems to be that Jesus' ascent to heaven will show him to have been executed unjustly.   **16:11** *Prince of this world*: see 12:31 note.   **16:13** *Of himself*: from himself. *Shew*: lit. "declare" (also in vv. 14–15, 25).   **16:15** *Shall take*: the same Greek word was rendered "receive" in v. 14. A better reading of the MS tradition puts it in the present tense.   **16:16** *Not see . . . see*: the Greek uses two different verbs for "see" here and in vv. 17, 19. The variation may be stylistic, or it may be meaningful (e.g., differentiating between mundane observation and spiritual or visionary insight). *Because I . . . Father*: better omitted (MS tradition).   **16:17** *And again . . . Father*:

¹⁸They said therefore, What is this that he saith, A little while? we cannot tell what he saith. ¹⁹Now Jesus knew that they were desirous to ask him, and said unto them, Do ye inquire among yourselves of that I said, A little while, and ye shall not see me: and again, a little while, and ye shall see me? ²⁰Verily, verily, I say unto you, That ye shall weep and lament, but the world shall rejoice: and ye shall be sorrowful, but your sorrow shall be turned into joy. ²¹A woman when she is in travail hath sorrow, because her hour is come: but as soon as she is delivered of the child, she remembereth no more the anguish, for joy that a man is born into the world. ²²And ye now therefore have sorrow: but I will see you again, and your heart shall rejoice, and your joy no man taketh from you. ²³And in that day ye shall ask me nothing. Verily, verily, I say unto you, Whatsoever ye shall ask the Father in my name, he will give it you. ²⁴Hitherto have ye asked nothing in my name: ask, and ye shall receive, that your joy may be full.

²⁵These things have I spoken unto you in proverbs: but the time cometh, when I shall no more speak unto you in proverbs, but I shall shew you plainly of the Father. ²⁶At that day ye shall ask in my name: and I say not unto you, that I will pray the Father for you: ²⁷for the Father himself loveth you, because ye have loved me, and have believed that I came out from God. ²⁸I came forth from the Father, and am come into the world: again, I leave the world, and go to the Father. ²⁹His disciples said unto him, Lo, now speakest thou plainly, and speakest no proverb. ³⁰Now are we sure that thou knowest all things, and needest not that any man should ask thee: by this we believe that thou camest forth from God. ³¹Jesus answered them, Do ye now believe? ³²Behold, the hour cometh, yea, is now come, that ye shall be scattered, every man to his own, and shall leave me alone: and yet I am not alone, because the Father is with me. ³³These things I have spoken unto you, that in me ye might have peace. In the world ye shall have tribulation: but be of good cheer; I have overcome the world.

---

see vv. 10 and 16; their contradiction helps explain the disciples' puzzlement. **16:21** *A woman . . . world*: childbirth is a conventional image of Israel's suffering in the Prophets (see Isa 26:17–19; Mic 4:9–10; etc.), but this dominical saying also recalls Eve's painful labor (Gen 3:16) and her delivery of Cain (Gen 4:1). **16:22** *I will . . . rejoice*: echoing Isa 66:14. **16:25** *In proverbs*: this phrase refers specifically to the birth imagery of v. 21, but should also be understood more broadly, as Jesus often uses symbolic language in John. **16:30** *Are we sure*: lit. "we know." *And needest . . . God*: perhaps referring to v. 19, where Jesus knows the disciples' question before they ask it. Matt 6:8 attributes analogous prescience to God. **16:32** *Ye shall be scattered*: probably echoing Zech 13:7, a passage Matthew (26:31, 56) and Mark (14:27, 49–50) also invoke in this context. While John's Jesus agrees with Matthew's and Mark's in predicting the disciples' flight and dispersion, unlike those gospels John does not report the disciples fleeing at Jesus' arrest, and the beloved disciple is said to remain with Jesus during his crucifixion (19:26–27). After finding the tomb empty the disciples all "went away again unto their own home" (20:10), but they are still united when the risen Jesus first appears (20:19). In Luke-Acts, the scattering of Jesus' followers from Jerusalem results from the persecution that later arose after Stephen's martyrdom (see Acts 8:1, 4; 11:19), not from Jesus' arrest. *His own*: i.e., his own home. *Yet I . . . with me*: this reads like a polemical response to the final words attributed by Matthew (27:46) and Mark (15:34) to the crucified Jesus, which accuse God of forsaking him. Jesus' final words in John will be quite different (see 19:30 and note). **16:33** *Shall have*: better "have" (MS tradition). *Tribulation*: cf. v. 21 (KJV "anguish").

17 These words spake Jesus, and lifted up his eyes to heaven, and said, Father, the hour is come; glorify thy Son, that thy Son also may glorify thee: ²as thou hast given him power over all flesh, that he should give eternal life to as many as thou hast given him. ³And this is life eternal, that they might know thee the only true God, and Jesus Christ, whom thou hast sent. ⁴I have glorified thee on the earth: I have finished the work which thou gavest me to do. ⁵And now, O Father, glorify thou me with thine own self with the glory which I had with thee before the world was.

⁶I have manifested thy name unto the men which thou gavest me out of the world: thine they were, and thou gavest them me; and they have kept thy word. ⁷Now they have known that all things whatsoever thou hast given me are of thee. ⁸For I have given unto them the words which thou gavest me; and they have received them, and have known surely that I came out from thee, and they have believed that thou didst send me. ⁹I pray for them: I pray not for the world, but for them which thou hast given me; for they are thine. ¹⁰And all mine are thine, and thine are mine; and I am glorified in them. ¹¹And now I am no more in the world, but these are in the world, and I come to thee. Holy Father, keep through thine own name those whom thou hast given me, that they may be one, as we are. ¹²While I was with them in the world, I kept them in thy name: those that thou gavest me I have kept, and none of them is lost, but the son of perdition; that the scripture might be fulfilled.

¹³And now come I to thee; and these things I speak in the world, that they might have my joy fulfilled in themselves. ¹⁴I have given them thy word; and the world hath hated them, because they are not of the world, even as I am not of the world. ¹⁵I pray not that thou shouldest take them out of the world, but that thou shouldest keep them from the evil. ¹⁶They are not of the world, even as I am not of the world. ¹⁷Sanctify them through thy truth: thy word is truth. ¹⁸As thou hast sent me into the world, even so have I also sent them into the world. ¹⁹And for their sakes I sanctify myself, that they also might be sanctified through the truth.

17:1–26 Jesus' final prayer. It has three foci: Jesus' and God's mutual glorification (vv. 1–8), the disciples (vv. 9–19), and those who come to faith through the disciples (vv. 20–26). **17:2** *That he . . . him*: lit. "in order that all that you have given to him, to them he may give eternal life." **17:3** *Know*: Gk. *ginōskō*, connoting acquaintance throughout this chapter. *Jesus Christ*: this name occurs elsewhere only in the prologue (1:17), which the current paragraph echoes throughout. **17:4** *I have . . . do*: foreshadowing Jesus' death; cf. 19:30. **17:5** *With thine . . . was*: KJV's repeated *with* obscures different expressions in Greek. Compare NRSV: "in your own presence with the glory that I had in your presence before the world existed." **17:6** *Manifested thy name*: compare Jesus' several references to himself as "I am," the divine name (4:26; 6:20; 8:24, 28, 58; 13:19; 18:5, 6, 8 and notes). **17:11** *Those whom*: better "which" (MS tradition), referring to the name. **17:12** *While I . . . have kept*: better "When I was with them, I kept them in your name, which you have given me. And I guarded them" (MS tradition). *Is lost, perdition*: in Greek, two forms of the same word. Better "none of them is destroyed, except the son of destruction." *Son of perdition* is a Semitic idiom meaning "one destined for destruction." In 2 Thess 2:3, it refers to a mysterious eschatological figure; here it seems to refer to Judas. *That the scripture might be fulfilled*: OT reference unclear, but see 13:18 and note. **17:15** *The evil*: or "the evil one," Satan (cf. 12:31; 14:30; 16:11). **17:17** *Thy truth*: better simply "truth" (MS tradition). **17:19** *Sanctify myself*: this odd phrase may allude to Jesus' willing death (cf. 10:17–18); for

²⁰Neither pray I for these alone, but for them also which shall believe on me through their word; ²¹that they all may be one; as thou, Father, art in me, and I in thee, that they also may be one in us: that the world may believe that thou hast sent me. ²²And the glory which thou gavest me I have given them; that they may be one, even as we are one: ²³I in them, and thou in me, that they may be made perfect in one; and that the world may know that thou hast sent me, and hast loved them, as thou hast loved me. ²⁴Father, I will that they also, whom thou hast given me, be with me where I am; that they may behold my glory, which thou hast given me: for thou lovedst me before the foundation of the world. ²⁵O righteous Father, the world hath not known thee: but I have known thee, and these have known that thou hast sent me. ²⁶And I have declared unto them thy name, and will declare it: that the love wherewith thou hast loved me may be in them, and I in them.

18 When Jesus had spoken these words, he went forth with his disciples over the brook Cedron, where was a garden, into the which he entered, and his disciples. ²And Judas also, which betrayed him, knew the place: for Jesus ofttimes resorted thither with his disciples. ³Judas then, having received a band of men and officers from the chief priests and Pharisees, cometh thither with lanterns and torches and weapons. ⁴Jesus therefore, knowing all things that should come upon him, went forth, and said unto them, Whom seek ye? ⁵They answered him, Jesus of Nazareth. Jesus saith unto them, I am he. And Judas also, which betrayed him, stood with them. ⁶As soon then as he had said unto them, I am he, they went backward, and fell to the ground. ⁷Then asked he them again, Whom seek ye? And they said, Jesus of Nazareth. ⁸Jesus answered, I have told you that I am he: if therefore ye seek me, let these go their way: ⁹that the saying might be fulfilled, which he spake, Of them which thou gavest me have I lost none. ¹⁰Then Simon Peter having a sword drew it, and smote the high priest's servant, and cut off his right ear. The servant's name was Malchus. ¹¹Then said Jesus unto Peter, Put up thy sword into

the sacrifice of animals to YHWH as their sanctification, see Deut 15:19–21.   **17:20** *Shall believe*: better simply "believe" (MS tradition).   **17:21** *One in us*: better simply "in us" (MS tradition). **17:23** *Made perfect*: Gk. *teleiō*, also "finished" (cf. v. 4). *In one*: or "into one."   **17:24** *Whom thou*: lit. "what thou."   **17:25** *Righteous*: or "just."   **17:26** *Declared*: lit. "made known"; "declare" in this verse shares a Greek root with "known" in v. 25.

18:1–19:42 Jesus' arrest, execution, and burial. 18:1–14 Jesus' arrest. Compare Matt 26:47–57; Mark 14:43–53; Luke 22:47–54a. Once the Synoptics' Jesus reaches the place of his arrest, he agonizes in prayer while the disciples doze (Matt 26:36–46; Mark 14:32–42; cf. Luke 22:39–46). John omits this episode, but the tradition lying behind it may be echoed (and polemically recast) at v. 11 (see note) and earlier at 12:27–30 (see note).   **18:1** *Brook*: i.e., wadi. *Cedron*: perhaps alluding to Solomon's words of warning to Shimei (1 Kgs 2:37) or to David's flight from Absalom (2 Sam 15:13–23), both of which mention the brook Kidron.   **18:3** *Band*: a cohort, consisting of several hundred soldiers. These are distinct from the "officers" (cf. 7:32 note) associated with the Jewish leaders. In John alone do Romans take part in Jesus' arrest (cf. 11:47–54, where the desire to placate Roman authorities motivates the plot against Jesus). *Chief priests and Pharisees*: in John alone are the Pharisees assigned responsibility for Jesus' arrest (cf. 11:47–54 and notes).   **18:5** *I am he*: Gk. *egō eimi* (also in v. 8); see Mark 6:50 note.   **18:6** *As soon . . . ground*: God's revelation often prompts such collapses (e.g., Dan 8:15–17; Rev 1:17). Some speculate that their prostration also fulfills Ps 56:9.   **18:8** *If therefore . . . way*: Jesus obeys his own commandment (15:12–13).   **18:9** *Of them . . . none*: cf. 6:39; 17:12 (neither is quoted precisely).   **18:10** *Simon Peter*: only John identifies Peter as the assailant or *Malchus* as the struck slave.

the sheath: the cup which my Father hath given me, shall I not drink it? [12]Then the band and the captain and officers of the Jews took Jesus, and bound him, [13]and led him away to Annas first; for he was father in law to Caiaphas, which was the high priest that same year. [14]Now Caiaphas was he, which gave counsel to the Jews, that it was expedient that one man should die for the people.

[15]And Simon Peter followed Jesus, and so did another disciple: that disciple was known unto the high priest, and went in with Jesus into the palace of the high priest. [16]But Peter stood at the door without. Then went out that other disciple, which was known unto the high priest, and spake unto her that kept the door, and brought in Peter. [17]Then saith the damsel that kept the door unto Peter, Art not thou also one of this man's disciples? He saith, I am not. [18]And the servants and officers stood there, who had made a fire of coals; for it was cold: and they warmed themselves: and Peter stood with them, and warmed himself.

[19]The high priest then asked Jesus of his disciples, and of his doctrine. [20]Jesus answered him, I spake openly to the world; I ever taught in the synagogue, and in the temple, whither the Jews always resort; and in secret have I said nothing. [21]Why askest thou me? ask them which heard me, what I have said unto them: behold, they know what I said. [22]And when he had thus spoken, one of the officers which stood by struck Jesus with the palm of his hand, saying, Answerest thou the high priest so? [23]Jesus answered him, If I have spoken evil, bear witness of the evil: but if well, why smitest thou me? [24]Now Annas had sent him bound unto Caiaphas the high priest.

[25]And Simon Peter stood and warmed himself. They said therefore unto him, Art not thou also one of his disciples? He denied it, and said, I am not. [26]One of the servants of the high priest, being his kinsman whose ear Peter cut off, saith, Did not I see thee in the garden with him? [27]Peter then denied again: and immediately the cock crew.

18:11 *The cup . . . it*: perhaps a polemical recasting of the prayer offered by Jesus before his arrest in the Synoptics, that God "take away this cup" (Mark 14:36; cf. Matt 26:39; Luke 22:42). *Cup*: see Mark 10:38 and note.   18:13 *Father in law . . . priest*: although John calls Caiaphas high priest here and at 11:49, Annas is also presented as holding that position (see vv. 19, 22); see Luke 3:2 and note.   18:14 *Now Caiaphas . . . people*: see 11:49–51.   18:15–27 Jesus before the high priest and Peter's denial. Compare Matt 26:58–75; Mark 14:54–72; Luke 22:54b–71.   18:15 *Another disciple*: identity uncertain, but two possibilities deserve consideration: (a) the anonymous disciple "whom Jesus loved" (see 13:23 note); (b) Judas, Jesus' betrayer (whose name the Evangelist now refuses to write). In favor of the first is the parallel with 20:2, where the "other disciple" accompanying Peter is the beloved disciple, as well as the beloved disciple's insistence on remaining with Jesus elsewhere in the Passion Narrative (19:26–27). In favor of the second is that the anonymous disciple is known to the high priest and allowed entry into his palace.   18:17 *I am not*: Gk. *ouk eimi* (also in v. 25), recalling and subverting Jesus' confession in vv. 5, 8.   18:18 *Servants and officers*: members of the group who had come to arrest Jesus; cf. vv. 3, 10, 26. *Peter stood with them*: because Judas "stood with" the same group (v. 5) as they carried "lanterns and torches" (v. 3), Peter is here figuratively assimilated to Jesus' betrayer at the moment he denies Jesus.   18:20 *The Jews always*: better "all the Jews" (MS tradition). *In secret . . . nothing*: cf. Isa 45:19; Jesus' words also recall Socrates' defense in Plato's *Apology*: "if anyone says that he has ever learned or heard something from me in private that all others did not also hear, know well that he does not speak the truth" (33b).   18:27 *The cock crew*: cf. 13:38.

²⁸Then led they Jesus from Caiaphas unto the hall of judgment: and it was early; and they themselves went not into the judgment hall, lest they should be defiled; but that they might eat the passover. ²⁹Pilate then went out unto them, and said, What accusation bring ye against this man? ³⁰They answered and said unto him, If he were not a malefactor, we would not have delivered him up unto thee. ³¹Then said Pilate unto them, Take ye him, and judge him according to your law. The Jews therefore said unto him, It is not lawful for us to put any man to death: ³²that the saying of Jesus might be fulfilled, which he spake, signifying what death he should die.

³³Then Pilate entered into the judgment hall again, and called Jesus, and said unto him, Art thou the King of the Jews? ³⁴Jesus answered him, Sayest thou this thing of thyself, or did others tell it thee of me? ³⁵Pilate answered, Am I a Jew? Thine own nation and the chief priests have delivered thee unto me: what hast thou done? ³⁶Jesus answered, My kingdom is not of this world: if my kingdom were of this world, then would my servants fight, that I should not be delivered to the Jews: but now is my kingdom not from hence. ³⁷Pilate therefore said unto him, Art thou a king then? Jesus answered, Thou sayest that I am a king. To this end was I born, and for this cause came I into the world, that I should bear witness unto the truth. Every one that is of the truth heareth my voice. ³⁸Pilate saith unto him, What is truth? And when he had said this, he went out again unto the Jews, and saith unto them, I find in him no fault at all. ³⁹But ye have a custom,

---

18:28–19:16 Jesus before Pilate. Compare Matt 27:1–2, 11–31; Mark 15:1–20; Luke 23:1–25. This episode is carefully structured into seven scenes, the transition between each marked by Pilate's exiting or entering the "hall of judgment" (18:33, 38b; 19:1 [implied], 4, 9, 12 [implied]). His physical movement mirrors his internal turmoil, as he unsuccessfully struggles to resist political pressure and finally orders Jesus' execution, despite being convinced of his innocence.   **18:28** *Hall of judgment*: see Mark 15:16 note. *Lest they . . . passover*: it is not clear what about this residence threatened defilement (leavened bread?), but the obscure reference to ritual underscores the supreme hypocrisy of the religious leaders.   **18:29** *Pilate*: Pontius Pilate, prefect of the Roman province of Judea, ca. 26–37 C.E.   **18:30** *If he . . . thee*: since Roman soldiers had helped arrest Jesus (see v. 3 and note), those delivering him for judgment may have expected Pilate already to know (as v. 33 suggests) that he was being accused of political insurrection. Their response to Pilate's question may also indicate their lack of concern with establishing that Jesus is guilty of anything in particular; they want Jesus eliminated because they fear his influence (cf. 11:48).   **18:31** *The Jews*: in this episode *the Jews* refers only to the group that brought Jesus from Caiaphas to (Gentile) Pilate. The Synoptics specify that crowds were involved, but John makes no mention of any Jews other than those coming from Caiaphas. (See v. 40 note; 19:6–7.) *It is . . . death*: this would explain why Caiaphas hands Jesus over to Pilate, but there is no independent evidence that Jewish authorities (i.e., the Sanhedrin) were denied the power to execute, and other NT passages (e.g., Acts 6:9–15; 7:54–60; cf. John 19:6) and Josephus (*Jewish Antiquities* 20.200) suggest the contrary. However, the interpretation of those texts is not certain and Rome may have monopolized this power in its provinces.   **18:32** *The saying of Jesus*: see 12:31–33. Crucifixion, which involves the victim's elevation from the ground, was a standard Roman form of execution.   **18:38** *What is truth?*: the question may suggest Pilate's curiosity about what Jesus said in v. 37, or it may express his flippant rejection of Jesus' statement there. It also thematizes his dilemma: does he affirm truth's value by insisting on the release of Jesus, whom he knows to be innocent (v. 38b), or does he disregard the truth by participating in the plot to execute an innocent man?   **18:39** *A custom . . . passover*: such a custom is not recorded outside the NT, and the synoptic tradition (Matt 27:15; Mark 15:6) refers to the procedure only as Pilate's normal practice. (Luke 23:17 is a scribal emendation.) Nonetheless, it is easy to imagine a Roman magistrate releasing a prominent prisoner in

that I should release unto you one at the passover: will ye therefore that I release unto you the King of the Jews? ⁴⁰Then cried they all again, saying, Not this man, but Barabbas. Now Barabbas was a robber.

19 Then Pilate therefore took Jesus, and scourged him. ²And the soldiers platted a crown of thorns, and put it on his head, and they put on him a purple robe, ³and said, Hail, King of the Jews! and they smote him with their hands. ⁴Pilate therefore went forth again, and saith unto them, Behold, I bring him forth to you, that ye may know that I find no fault in him. ⁵Then came Jesus forth, wearing the crown of thorns, and the purple robe. And Pilate saith unto them, Behold the man! ⁶When the chief priests therefore and officers saw him, they cried out, saying, Crucify him, crucify him. Pilate saith unto them, Take ye him, and crucify him: for I find no fault in him. ⁷The Jews answered him, We have a law, and by our law he ought to die, because he made himself the Son of God.

⁸When Pilate therefore heard that saying, he was the more afraid; ⁹and went again into the judgment hall, and saith unto Jesus, Whence art thou? But Jesus gave him no answer. ¹⁰Then saith Pilate unto him, Speakest thou not unto me? knowest thou not that I have power to crucify thee, and have power to release thee? ¹¹Jesus answered, Thou couldest have no power at all against me, except it were given thee from above: therefore he that delivered me unto thee hath the greater sin. ¹²And from thenceforth Pilate sought to release him: but the Jews cried out, saying, If thou let this man go, thou art not Cæsar's friend: whosoever maketh himself a king speaketh against Cæsar.

¹³When Pilate therefore heard that saying, he brought Jesus forth, and sat down in the judgment seat in a place that is called the Pavement, but in the Hebrew, Gabbatha. ¹⁴And it was the preparation of the passover, and about the sixth hour: and he saith unto the Jews, Behold your King! ¹⁵But they cried out,

---

order to mollify the people.   **18:40** *All*: better omitted (MS tradition) as a scribal attempt to assimilate John to the Synoptics, in which the crowds cry for Jesus' crucifixion (cf. Matt 27:20; Mark 15:11; Luke 23:4, 18). *Robber*: Gk. *lēstēs*, also a revolutionary bandit, which further underscores the hypocrisy of Caiaphas' representatives, who, respectful of Roman jurisdiction (v. 31), have delivered Jesus to Roman authorities on charges of anti-Roman insurrection (vv. 33, 35; cf. 11:47–54) but now request the release of an anti-Roman guerilla fighter to ensure Jesus' execution.   **19:1** *Scourged him*: i.e., "had him scourged."   **19:2** *Purple*: a color associated with royalty.   **19:3** *And said*: better "and came toward him and said" (MS tradition).   **19:4** *Fault*: perhaps better "grounds for complaint" (also in v. 6). **19:5** *Behold the man*: Pilate's words (famous in their Latin translation: *Ecce homo!*) echo Zech 6:12. That verse recalls the Davidic covenant (cf. 2 Sam 7:13), which Jesus-believers understood Christ to fulfill.   **19:7** *We have a law*: probably Lev 24:16. *He made . . . God*: see 10:30–36 and notes.   **19:8** *When Pilate . . . afraid*: according to Philo, Pilate at another time feared that a Jewish embassy might report to the emperor that he had disregarded the local customs of those he governed (*On the Embassy to Gaius* 301–2; Appendix, p. 981).   **19:9** *Whence art thou?*: Pilate's question may be understood as an inquiry about Jesus' possible divinity (cf. v. 7) or as evidence of his hunting for a jurisdictional excuse to evade his judicial responsibility; cf. Luke 23:6–7; Acts 23:34–35 and note.   **19:11** *Delivered*: Gk. *paradidōmi*, also "betray"—so used of Judas (6:64, 71; 18:2, 5); here the subject may be the people who delivered Jesus to Pilate (cf. 18:35).   **19:13** *Gabbatha*: "Elevated Place."   **19:14** *The preparation . . . hour*: noon (*the sixth hour*) on the day of Passover preparation was set as the time when the temple priests might begin to sacrifice the numerous lambs needed for the next day's feast (Exod 12:6, as interpreted). Recall that John the Baptist identifies Jesus as "the Lamb of God" (1:29, 36).   **19:15** *But they . . . Cæsar*: the shouted exchange between Pilate and "the Jews" recalls and reverses Jesus' royal

Away with him, away with him, crucify him. Pilate saith unto them, Shall I crucify your King? The chief priests answered, We have no king but Cæsar. [16]Then
delivered he him therefore unto them to be crucified. And they took Jesus, and
led him away.

[17]And he bearing his cross went forth into a place called the place of a skull,
which is called in the Hebrew Golgotha: [18]where they crucified him, and two
other with him, on either side one, and Jesus in the midst. [19]And Pilate wrote a
title, and put it on the cross. And the writing was, Jesus of Nazareth the King of
the Jews. [20]This title then read many of the Jews: for the place where Jesus was
crucified was nigh to the city: and it was written in Hebrew, and Greek, and Latin.
[21]Then said the chief priests of the Jews to Pilate, Write not, The King of the Jews;
but that he said, I am King of the Jews. [22]Pilate answered, What I have written
I have written.

[23]Then the soldiers, when they had crucified Jesus, took his garments, and
made four parts, to every soldier a part; and also his coat: now the coat was without seam, woven from the top throughout. [24]They said therefore among themselves, Let us not rend it, but cast lots for it, whose it shall be: that the scripture
might be fulfilled, which saith, They parted my raiment among them, and for my
vesture they did cast lots. These things therefore the soldiers did.

[25]Now there stood by the cross of Jesus his mother, and his mother's sister,
Mary the wife of Cleophas, and Mary Magdalene. [26]When Jesus therefore saw
his mother, and the disciple standing by, whom he loved, he saith unto his

---

acclamation upon his entry into Jerusalem (12:12–13). Moreover, their brazen claim to *have no king
but Cæsar* explicitly disavows the Davidic covenant (2 Sam 7:12–16, perhaps alluded to in v. 5 above;
see note).   **19:16** *Delivered*: see v. 11 and note. *Unto them*: this pronoun's grammatical referent is "the
Jews" (v. 14), even though Pilate's soldiers crucified Jesus (v. 23). The ambiguity is deliberate, as the
evangelist wants to establish that "the Jews" are responsible for Jesus' execution.   **19:17–42** Jesus'
crucifixion and burial. Compare Matt 27:32–66; Mark 15:21–47; Luke 23:26, 32–56.   **19:17** *Bearing his cross*: better "bearing the cross for himself" (MS tradition). This reading underscores John's
difference from the Synoptics, where Simon of Cyrene carries Jesus' cross. In Matthew and Mark,
Jesus goes to his death with helplessness and despair. (Luke's Jesus, like John's, is more stalwart.) It
may also assimilate Jesus more closely to Isaac at his sacrifice (see Gen 22:6). *Golgotha*: see Mark
15:22 note.   **19:19** *Title*: see Mark 15:26 note.   **19:20** *Written in Hebrew, and Greek, and Latin*: the
order of *Greek* and *Latin* is better reversed (MS tradition), so that the most widely understood language is mentioned last. The universalizing gesture recalls 12:32–33.   **19:23** *Coat*: Gk. *chitōn*, a long
garment worn underneath an outer mantle. LXX uses this word of the high priest's customary garment
(Exod 28:4; Lev 16:4); Exod 39:27 specifies that it was woven, and Josephus adds that it was woven in
one piece (*Jewish Antiquities* 3.161). The reference to this particular *coat* may therefore assimilate Jesus
to the high priest, a move not uncommon in the NT (see esp. Hebrews).   **19:24** *They parted . . . lots*:
Ps 22:18.   **19:25** *There stood . . . Magdalene*: the Synoptics concur that several women witnessed Jesus'
death (Matt 27:55–56; Mark 15:40; Luke 23:49). While Luke names none, Matthew and Mark agree
with John regarding the presence of Mary Magdalene and Jesus' mother, and each adds one whom
John omits. All three agree against John that the women observed Jesus' death from afar. *Mary, wife of
Cleophas*: better "Mary, wife of Clopas" (MS tradition), who is otherwise unknown. It is unclear whether
the name stands in apposition or addition to *his mother's sister*, although the latter seems more likely.
Mary Magdalene: a prominent follower of Jesus named alongside the Twelve in Luke 8:2 (see note).

mother, Woman, behold thy son! ²⁷Then saith he to the disciple, Behold thy mother! And from that hour that disciple took her unto his own home.

²⁸After this, Jesus knowing that all things were now accomplished, that the scripture might be fulfilled, saith, I thirst. ²⁹Now there was set a vessel full of vinegar: and they filled a spunge with vinegar, and put it upon hyssop, and put it to his mouth. ³⁰When Jesus therefore had received the vinegar, he said, It is finished: and he bowed his head, and gave up the ghost.

³¹The Jews therefore, because it was the preparation, that the bodies should not remain upon the cross on the sabbath day, (for that sabbath day was an high day,) besought Pilate that their legs might be broken, and that they might be taken away. ³²Then came the soldiers, and brake the legs of the first, and of the other which was crucified with him. ³³But when they came to Jesus, and saw that he was dead already, they brake not his legs: ³⁴but one of the soldiers with a spear pierced his side, and forthwith came there out blood and water. ³⁵And he that saw it bare record, and his record is true: and he knoweth that he saith true, that ye might believe. ³⁶For these things were done, that the scripture should be fulfilled, A bone of him shall not be broken. ³⁷And again another scripture saith, They shall look on him whom they pierced.

³⁸And after this Joseph of Arimathæa, being a disciple of Jesus, but secretly for fear of the Jews, besought Pilate that he might take away the body of Jesus: and Pilate gave him leave. He came therefore, and took the body of Jesus. ³⁹And there came also Nicodemus, which at the first came to Jesus by night, and brought a mixture of myrrh and aloes, about an hundred pound weight. ⁴⁰Then took they

19:26 *Woman*: Jesus invokes his mother in the same brusque way at the wedding at Cana (2:4). At that time he mentioned his "hour," now come (cf. 12:23–25); the two scenes are also connected by references to wine. **19:28** *Accomplished, fulfilled*: the same Greek verb (also "finished," v. 30). *That the scripture might be fulfilled*: Ps 69:21. **19:29** *Vinegar*: spoiled wine. *Hyssop*: a shrub not sturdy enough to carry a wet sponge, but used to mark the Israelites' doorposts with lamb's blood before the final plague in Egypt (Exod 12:22). Thus the evangelist's introduction of it furthers his symbolic identification of Jesus with the Passover lamb. **19:30** *It is finished*: Jesus' final words in John differ markedly from those in Mark (15:34) and Matthew (27:46). They emphasize Jesus' total control over his death and recall 4:34 (cf. 13:1 and note; 17:4). *Gave up*: Gk. *paradidōmi*; see vv. 11, 16 and notes. *The ghost*: his spirit. **19:31** *The preparation*: the day of preparation for the Sabbath (cf. v. 42; see Mark 15:42 and note). *For that . . . high day*: John understands the Passover feast during the year in question to have fallen on the Sabbath, the day after Jesus' death (see v. 14). The Synoptics likewise understand Jesus to have died on the day preceding the Sabbath (see Mark 15:42), but differ from John in making the Passover feast coincide with that day, rather than with the Sabbath itself (see note to 13:1–38). *Their legs . . . broken*: facilitating death, since broken legs could no longer push up to help sustain the body's weight on the cross or to ease breathing. **19:34** *Pierced*: better "poked at" or "stabbed at," probably in an attempt to confirm that Jesus was really dead; a different word in v. 37. *Blood and water*: cf. 7:37–39 (see notes), which links "living water" to the Spirit that will be given once Jesus is glorified. **19:35** *He that saw it*: presumably the beloved disciple (cf. vv. 25–27), whose testimony the evangelist will formally invoke to authorize his account (21:20–25). *Ye might believe*: better "ye also might believe" (MS tradition). **19:36** *A bone . . . broken*: Exod 12:46; Num 9:12, instructions about the proper presentation of the Passover lamb. (Ps 34:20 may also lie in the background.) This image brings the narrative of Jesus' ministry full circle (cf. 1:29, 36). *Broken*: or "crushed." **19:37** *They shall . . . pierced*: Zech 12:10. **19:38** *Arimathæa*: see Mark 15:43. *Being a disciple . . . Jews*: such secret disciples are denounced in 12:42–43. **19:39** *Nicodemus, which . . . night*: see 3:1–13. *Myrrh and aloes*: embalming spices; the amount (about seventy-five pounds avoirdupois) is appropriate to a royal burial. In John's

the body of Jesus, and wound it in linen clothes with the spices, as the manner of the Jews is to bury. ⁴¹Now in the place where he was crucified there was a garden; and in the garden a new sepulchre, wherein was never man yet laid. ⁴²There laid they Jesus therefore because of the Jews' preparation day; for the sepulchre was nigh at hand.

20 The first day of the week cometh Mary Magdalene early, when it was yet dark, unto the sepulchre, and seeth the stone taken away from the sepulchre. ²Then she runneth, and cometh to Simon Peter, and to the other disciple, whom Jesus loved, and saith unto them, They have taken away the Lord out of the sepulchre, and we know not where they have laid him. ³Peter therefore went forth, and that other disciple, and came to the sepulchre. ⁴So they ran both together: and the other disciple did outrun Peter, and came first to the sepulchre. ⁵And he stooping down, and looking in, saw the linen clothes lying; yet went he not in. ⁶Then cometh Simon Peter following him, and went into the sepulchre, and seeth the linen clothes lie, ⁷and the napkin, that was about his head, not lying with the linen clothes, but wrapped together in a place by itself. ⁸Then went in also that other disciple, which came first to the sepulchre, and he saw, and believed. ⁹For as yet they knew not the scripture, that he must rise again from the dead. ¹⁰Then the disciples went away again unto their own home.

¹¹But Mary stood without at the sepulchre weeping: and as she wept, she stooped down, and looked into the sepulchre, ¹²and seeth two angels in white sitting, the one at the head, and the other at the feet, where the body of Jesus had lain. ¹³And they say unto her, Woman, why weepest thou? She saith unto them, Because they have taken away my Lord, and I know not where they have laid him. ¹⁴And when she had thus said, she turned herself back, and saw Jesus standing, and knew not that it was Jesus. ¹⁵Jesus saith unto her, Woman, why weepest thou? whom seekest thou? She, supposing him to be the gardener, saith unto him, Sir,

---

tradition, Joseph and Nicodemus anoint Jesus' body on the day before the Sabbath; in Mark and Luke, by contrast, the female disciples who witness Jesus' death come to anoint his corpse on the first day after the Sabbath (Mark 16:1; Luke 23:54–24:1).   **19:42** *For the sepulchre . . . hand*: they bury him close to his place of execution to ensure interment is complete before the Sabbath begins.

20:1–29 The Risen Christ. 20:1–18 Mary Magdalene, Peter, and the beloved disciple at Jesus' tomb. Compare Matt 28:1–8; Mark 16:1–8; Luke 24:1–12. Of the canonical gospels, only John emphasizes the presence of Jesus' male disciples at the empty tomb. Indeed, Luke is the only other evangelist to mention it at all (24:12).   **20:2** *We know not*: the odd first-person plural (Mary alone visited Jesus' tomb) may indicate that the evangelist has incorporated a version of the story similar to that found in the Synoptics, in which multiple women discover Jesus' empty tomb.   **20:3** *Peter therefore . . . disciple*: competition between Peter and the beloved disciple recurs throughout John's closing chapters. Here (vv. 3–8) Peter leaves first, but the beloved disciple outruns him and views the tomb first, though he hesitates to enter. Peter then proceeds him into the tomb and gets a better view of it, but the beloved disciple, who enters second, is the first to believe.   **20:8** *He saw, and believed*: this climactic statement is preceded by multiple references to observing Jesus' burial clothes (vv. 5–7). The implication may be that the beloved disciple recognizes that Mary must have been mistaken, for no one taking Jesus' body would bother to undress it first.   **20:9** *The scripture . . . dead*: see 1 Cor 15:3 note.   **20:11** *Mary stood*: apparently she had followed the two men. The frantic race between Peter and the beloved disciple notwithstanding, Mary was the first to arrive at the tomb and now is the first to encounter the risen Christ.   **20:15** *The gardener*: the tomb was located in a garden

if thou have borne him hence, tell me where thou hast laid him, and I will take him away. [16]Jesus saith unto her, Mary. She turned herself, and saith unto him, Rabboni; which is to say, Master. [17]Jesus saith unto her, Touch me not; for I am not yet ascended to my Father: but go to my brethren, and say unto them, I ascend unto my Father, and your Father; and to my God, and your God. [18]Mary Magdalene came and told the disciples that she had seen the Lord, and that he had spoken these things unto her.

[19]Then the same day at evening, being the first day of the week, when the doors were shut where the disciples were assembled for fear of the Jews, came Jesus and stood in the midst, and saith unto them, Peace be unto you. [20]And when he had so said, he shewed unto them his hands and his side. Then were the disciples glad, when they saw the Lord. [21]Then said Jesus to them again, Peace be unto you: as my Father hath sent me, even so send I you. [22]And when he had said this, he breathed on them, and saith unto them, Receive ye the Holy Ghost: [23]whose soever sins ye remit, they are remitted unto them; and whose soever sins ye retain, they are retained.

[24]But Thomas, one of the twelve, called Didymus, was not with them when Jesus came. [25]The other disciples therefore said unto him, We have seen the Lord. But he said unto them, Except I shall see in his hands the print of the nails, and put my finger into the print of the nails, and thrust my hand into his side, I will not believe. [26]And after eight days again his disciples were within, and Thomas with them: then came Jesus, the doors being shut, and stood in the midst, and said, Peace be unto you. [27]Then saith he to Thomas, Reach hither thy finger, and behold my hands; and reach hither thy hand, and thrust it into my side: and be not faithless, but believing. [28]And Thomas answered and said unto him, My Lord and

---

(19:41).   **20:16** *Saith unto him*: better to add "in Hebrew" (MS tradition). Her recognition of Jesus only when he calls her by name recalls the discourse about the shepherd (10:1-21, esp. vv. 3, 14).   **20:17** *Touch me . . . to my Father*: the warning testifies to the unusual nature of Jesus' risen body (see Paul's technical discussion at 1 Cor 15:35-54 and notes). The risen Christ, for instance, does not look like the pre-risen one (vv. 14-15) and can apparently walk through closed doors (cf. vv. 19, 26). The Greek command translated "touch me not" may mean "do not hold onto me" (NRSV), which could imply that the disciples must instead await the sustained presence of the Comforter (Holy Ghost) that Jesus promised the Father would send in his name (14:1-26; 16:7). This reading is especially attractive in light of the subsequent episode. *My father . . . your God*: Jesus suggests that his disciples can now enjoy a filial relationship with God the Father similar to his own (cf. 1:12). The Spirit, which Jesus imparts in the subsequent episode, makes this relationship possible (cf. 3:5-8).   **20:19-23** Jesus commissions and imparts the Holy Spirit to his disciples. The material in this paragraph recalls Luke 24:36-43, Matthew's "Great Commission" (28:16-20), and the Pentecost narrative from Acts 2:1-13.   **20:19** *Assembled*: better omitted (MS tradition).   **20:21-22** *Peace be . . . Ghost*: fulfilling the words Jesus spoke in 14:26-28.   **20:22** *He breathed . . . Ghost*: recalling Gen 2:7 and perhaps suggesting that the disciples' commissioning initiates the re-creation of humanity. Just as John invokes Genesis' creation story to explain the word sent to earth incarnate (1:1-18 and notes), so does John's Jesus invoke the creation story to send out the disciples (v. 21).   **20:23** *Whose soever sins ye remit . . . retained*: cf. Matt 16:19; 18:18.   **20:25** *Except I . . . believe*: cf. 11:14-16. This disciple's desire "to probe the miraculous" (in Raymond Brown's words) opens him to the gospel's disparagements of those who rely on miracles (e.g., 2:23-25; 4:47-48). It also stands in tension with Jesus' command to Mary Magdalene (v. 17). **20:28** *My Lord and my God*: a phrase conventionally used of YHWH in the OT (1 Kgs 3:7; Ps 35:24; etc.). Despite his disrepute as a doubter, Thomas ultimately makes an unambiguous confession of Jesus'

my God. ²⁹Jesus saith unto him, Thomas, because thou hast seen me, thou hast believed: blessed are they that have not seen, and yet have believed.

³⁰And many other signs truly did Jesus in the presence of his disciples, which are not written in this book: ³¹but these are written, that ye might believe that Jesus is the Christ, the Son of God; and that believing ye might have life through his name.

21 After these things Jesus shewed himself again to the disciples at the sea of Tiberias; and on this wise shewed he himself. ²There were together Simon Peter, and Thomas called Didymus, and Nathanael of Cana in Galilee, and the sons of Zebedee, and two other of his disciples. ³Simon Peter saith unto them, I go a fishing. They say unto him, We also go with thee. They went forth, and entered into a ship immediately; and that night they caught nothing. ⁴But when the morning was now come, Jesus stood on the shore: but the disciples knew not that it was Jesus. ⁵Then Jesus saith unto them, Children, have ye any meat? They answered him, No. ⁶And he said unto them, Cast the net on the right side of the ship, and ye shall find. They cast therefore, and now they were not

divinity.   **20:29** *Because thou . . . have believed*: an explicit distinction is drawn between those who come to faith after having witnessed Jesus' ministry and resurrection and those who come to faith without such observation (especially the gospel's readers, whom the evangelist will address below; vv. 30–31). But the implicit comparison between Thomas and the beloved disciple (who comes to faith without having seen the risen Christ; v. 8) may point to a polemic against the Thomasine school of Christianity responsible for the noncanonical *Gospel of Thomas* (Appendix, pp. 1034–45), which seems to understand Jesus' resurrection figuratively, as his abiding presence in his remembered words (1–2). John's gospel—authorized by the beloved disciple himself (21:20–25)—equates this position with lack of faith.

20:30–21:25 Epilogue: the risen Jesus appears by the Sea of Tiberias. Many scholars regard chap. 21 as a later (and infelicitous) addition to the gospel, which would originally have ended with 20:30–31. The reference there to the "many other signs" Jesus did "which are not written in this book" supposedly inspired a scribe to append a story of the risen Jesus that presents an alternative version of the tradition Luke preserves at 5:1–11 and that also shares elements with Peter's walk on the water from Matt 14:28–33. While there is no evidence that John ever circulated without this concluding material, there may be internal clues that it is supplemental: after the special blessedness pronounced on those who "have not seen, and yet have believed" (20:29), another account of the risen Christ's appearances seems out of place; after Jesus' commission (20:21–23), it is surprising to find the disciples practicing their old ways of life in Galilee; and finally, after the disciples have already seen the risen Christ multiple times (20:19–20, 26), it is strange that they still cannot recognize him (21:4, 7). Yet despite such points of tension with earlier material, this section coheres with John's thematic interests, including those of chap. 20. Therefore, whether original or secondary, it may be best to view John's conclusion as an epilogue bounded by parallel passages emphasizing the multitude of Jesus' signs or deeds (20:30–31; 21:25) and finding its complement in the prologue of 1:1–18. The material in neither is perfectly integrated into John's larger narrative (note, for example, that 1:15 anticipates 1:30, and presupposes 1:19–29), but both highlight thematic concerns crucial to the gospel as a whole.   **20:30–31** *And many . . . name*: recalling and reversing 12:37–41, a passage that considers why "the Jews" did not come to faith as a result of Jesus' signs.   **20:31** *That ye might believe*: an equally sound reading of the MS tradition yields "that you might continue to believe," which would imply that the book's purpose is to nourish rather than inculcate faith.   **21:1** *Sea of Tiberias*: the setting of Jesus' miraculous feeding (6:1–15) and walk on the sea (6:16–24), both of which are echoed in the present chapter.   **21:4** *Jesus stood . . . Jesus*: cf. 6:16–21; 20:14–20.   **21:5** *Have ye any meat*: lit. "Do you have anything to eat?"; cf. 6:5 (the prelude to another meal of bread and fish).

able to draw it for the multitude of fishes. [7]Therefore that disciple whom Jesus loved saith unto Peter, It is the Lord. Now when Simon Peter heard that it was the Lord, he girt his fisher's coat unto him, (for he was naked,) and did cast himself into the sea. [8]And the other disciples came in a little ship; (for they were not far from land, but as it were two hundred cubits,) dragging the net with fishes. [9]As soon then as they were come to land, they saw a fire of coals there, and fish laid thereon, and bread. [10]Jesus saith unto them, Bring of the fish which ye have now caught. [11]Simon Peter went up, and drew the net to land full of great fishes, an hundred and fifty and three: and for all there were so many, yet was not the net broken. [12]Jesus saith unto them, Come and dine. And none of the disciples durst ask him, Who art thou? knowing that it was the Lord. [13]Jesus then cometh, and taketh bread, and giveth them, and fish likewise. [14]This is now the third time that Jesus shewed himself to his disciples, after that he was risen from the dead.

[15]So when they had dined, Jesus saith to Simon Peter, Simon, son of Jonas, lovest thou me more than these? He saith unto him, Yea, Lord; thou knowest that I love thee. He saith unto him, Feed my lambs. [16]He saith to him again the second time, Simon, son of Jonas, lovest thou me? He saith unto him, Yea, Lord; thou knowest that I love thee. He saith unto him, Feed my sheep. [17]He saith unto him the third time, Simon, son of Jonas, lovest thou me? Peter was grieved because he said unto him the third time, Lovest thou me? And he said unto him, Lord, thou knowest all things; thou knowest that I love thee. Jesus saith unto him, Feed my sheep. [18]Verily, verily, I say unto thee, When thou wast young, thou girdedst thyself, and walkedst whither thou wouldest: but when thou shalt be old, thou shalt stretch forth thy hands, and another shall gird thee, and carry thee

21:7 *For he was naked*: i.e., he was wearing only a loincloth. Or perhaps he was naked under *his fisher's coat*, which he tied securely around himself. *Cast himself . . . sea*: competition between the beloved disciple and Peter continues, as one first recognizes Jesus and the other does all he can to reach him first. **21:8** *Two hundred cubits*: about one hundred yards. **21:11** *Simon Peter . . . broken*: Gk. *helkuō*, "draw," is used in John only in 6:44; 12:32, where men are drawn to God and Jesus. This language, combined with the Synoptics' use of Peter's fishing to symbolize evangelism (cf. Matt 4:18–20; Mark 1:16–17; Luke 5:1–11), suggests that the present episode allegorically hints at the church's expansion and consolidation. *An hundred . . . broken*: the specific number may invoke universality. According to Jerome, Greek zoology knew of precisely 153 species of fish (*Commentary on Ezekiel*, at 47:6–12). This interpretation is supported by possible allusions to Ezek 47:9–10 and John 12:32. **21:13** *Jesus then . . . likewise*: recalling 6:11. **21:14** *Third time*: apparently not counting the appearance to Mary Magdalene. **21:15–19** *So when . . . me*: Jesus' triple command that Peter feed his sheep and the subsequent prophecy of his death recall not only his shepherding metaphor (10:1–21, esp. v. 11) but also Peter's invocation of it (13:37; see note). **21:15** *Son of Jonas*: better "son of John" (MS tradition; also subsequently); see 1:42 note. Jesus' use of Peter's patronymic expresses formality, in recognition of the distance placed between them by Peter's denial. *I love thee*: here and in v. 16, Peter and Jesus use different Greek words for love. Elsewhere in John these two verbs appear to be interchangeable, but in this passage Jesus may be asking Peter if he loves him with reverent devotion (Gk. *agapaō*), while Peter answers that he loves Jesus with friendly affection (*phileō*). **21:16** *Feed my sheep*: better "tend my sheep." **21:17** *The third time*: Jesus' triple question recalls and subverts Peter's triple denial. *Lovest thou me*: Jesus switches to Gk. *phileō*, the word consistently used by Peter. The variations in Jesus' reiterated commands that Peter shepherd his flock ("feed my lambs," "tend my sheep," "feed my sheep"; vv. 15–17) may gesture at the early church's diversity and the comprehensiveness of Peter's

whither thou wouldest not. ¹⁹This spake he, signifying by what death he should glorify God. And when he had spoken this, he saith unto him, Follow me.

²⁰Then Peter, turning about, seeth the disciple whom Jesus loved following; which also leaned on his breast at supper, and said, Lord, which is he that betrayeth thee? ²¹Peter seeing him saith to Jesus, Lord, and what shall this man do? ²²Jesus saith unto him, If I will that he tarry till I come, what is that to thee? follow thou me. ²³Then went this saying abroad among the brethren, that that disciple should not die: yet Jesus said not unto him, He shall not die; but, If I will that he tarry till I come, what is that to thee?

²⁴This is the disciple which testifieth of these things, and wrote these things: and we know that his testimony is true. ²⁵And there are also many other things which Jesus did, the which, if they should be written every one, I suppose that even the world itself could not contain the books that should be written. Amen.

ministerial responsibilities.   **21:19** *Signifying by what death . . . God*: it is often assumed that the evangelist alludes to Peter's crucifixion, in part because early Christian writers conventionally saw in OT images of outstretched hands allegories of Jesus' crucifixion. However, the earliest reference to Peter's martyrdom (*1 Clement* 5.4) does not specify how he died, and later traditions that he was crucified may actually be based on this verse. Jesus' death is also associated with glory—his own (7:39; 12:23) and God's (17:4–5). *Follow me*: recalling Jesus' earlier exchange with Peter (13:36–38). **21:20** *Which also . . . supper*: cf. 13:23 and note.   **21:21** *What shall this man do*: better "what about this man?"   **21:22** *He tarry till I come*: compare the more general saying in the Synoptics (Matt 16:28; Mark 9:1; Luke 9:27). The competition between Peter and the beloved disciple culminates in a contest over legacy: Peter will follow Jesus to a martyr's death, thereby giving glory to God (v. 19); the beloved disciple will live in order to give special testimony through this gospel (v. 24).   **21:24** *We know*: the sudden first-person plural may refer to scribes or redactors who in stages incorporated the oral and written testimony of the beloved disciple that they deemed trustworthy. Alternatively, it may function as a rhetorically heightened "I," thereby enhancing the authority of the author's/narrator's voice at the very moment it is identified as belonging to the beloved disciple (cf. 19:35, which is structurally similar but maintains a singular subject).   **21:25** *And there . . . that should be written*: cf. 20:30–31. *Amen*: better omitted (MS tradition) as a later liturgical addition.

THE
ACTS OF THE
APOSTLES†

1 The former treatise have I made, O Theophilus, of all that Jesus began both to do and teach, ²until the day in which he was taken up, after that he through the Holy Ghost had given commandments unto the apostles whom he had chosen: ³to whom also he shewed himself alive after his passion by many infallible proofs, being seen of them forty days, and speaking of the things pertaining to the kingdom of God: ⁴and, being assembled together with them, commanded them that they should not depart from Jerusalem, but wait for the promise of the Father, which, saith he, ye have heard of me. ⁵For John truly baptized with water; but ye shall be baptized with the Holy Ghost not many days hence.

⁶When they therefore were come together, they asked of him, saying, Lord, wilt thou at this time restore again the kingdom to Israel? ⁷And he said unto them, It is not for you to know the times or the seasons, which the Father hath put in his own power. ⁸But ye shall receive power, after that the Holy Ghost is come upon you: and ye shall be witnesses unto me both in Jerusalem, and in all Judæa, and in Samaria, and unto the uttermost part of the earth. ⁹And when he had spoken these things, while they beheld, he was taken up; and a cloud received him out of

† The introduction to the Gospel According to St. Luke serves also for Acts, Luke's companion volume. See pp. 124–30.

....

1:1–26 Introduction. Much of this material explicitly refers back to Luke.   **1:1–5** Prologue. **1:1** *The former treatise*: the Gospel of Luke. *Theophilus*: see Luke 1:3 and note.   **1:2** *Taken up*: in the NT Luke alone narrates Jesus' ascension (vv. 9–11; cf. Luke 24:51). His insistence on the risen Christ's absence from the early church opens up a space to be filled by the Holy Spirit, whose prominence in its ministry Acts emphasizes. *The apostles . . . chosen*: cf. Luke 6:13.   **1:3** *Passion*: suffering, a reference to Jesus' crucifixion; the only KJV appearance of this word. *Forty days*: a conventional expression for an extended length of time, as in Moses' stay on Sinai (Exod 24:18) or Jesus' wilderness temptations (Luke 4:2).   **1:4** *Which, saith . . . me*: Luke 11:13; 24:49.   **1:5** *John truly . . . Ghost*: cf. Luke 3:16.   **1:6–11** Ascension.   **1:6** *Restore again . . . Israel*: cf. Luke 1:32–33 and notes.   **1:7** *Power*: lit. "authority" (a different word is used in v. 8).   **1:8** *Ye shall . . . earth*: recalling Isa 49:6 and shifting focus away from expectation of Israel's eschatological restoration toward the church's global ministry, this statement lays out Acts' grand structure. *Receive power . . . you*: see 2:1–13. *Witnesses unto . . . Jerusalem*: see 2:14–8:3. *All Judæa . . . Samaria*: see 8:4–25. *The uttermost . . . earth*: referring

their sight. [10]And while they looked stedfastly toward heaven as he went up, behold, two men stood by them in white apparel; [11]which also said, Ye men of Galilee, why stand ye gazing up into heaven? this same Jesus, which is taken up from you into heaven, shall so come in like manner as ye have seen him go into heaven.

[12]Then returned they unto Jerusalem from the mount called Olivet, which is from Jerusalem a sabbath day's journey. [13]And when they were come in, they went up into an upper room, where abode both Peter, and James, and John, and Andrew, Philip, and Thomas, Bartholomew, and Matthew, James the son of Alphæus, and Simon Zelotes, and Judas the brother of James. [14]These all continued with one accord in prayer and supplication, with the women, and Mary the mother of Jesus, and with his brethren.

[15]And in those days Peter stood up in the midst of the disciples, and said, (the number of names together were about an hundred and twenty,) [16]Men and brethren, this scripture must needs have been fulfilled, which the Holy Ghost by the mouth of David spake before concerning Judas, which was guide to them that took Jesus. [17]For he was numbered with us, and had obtained part of this ministry. [18]Now this man purchased a field with the reward of iniquity; and falling headlong, he burst asunder in the midst, and all his bowels gushed out. [19]And it was known unto all the dwellers at Jerusalem; insomuch as that field is called in their proper tongue, Aceldama, that is to say, The field of blood. [20]For it is written in the book of Psalms, Let his habitation be desolate, and let no man dwell therein: and his bishoprick let another take. [21]Wherefore of these men which have companied with us all the time that the Lord Jesus went in and out among us, [22]beginning from the baptism of John, unto that same day that he was taken up from us, must one be ordained to be a witness with us of his resurrection. [23]And they appointed two, Joseph called Barsabas, who was surnamed Justus,

to the Gentile mission, the focus of 8:26–28:14.   **1:10** *Two men . . . apparel*: cf. Luke 24:4.   **1:11** *Ye men . . . go into heaven*: at once insisting on Jesus' absence and rejecting obsession with his anticipated return. Jesus will come back as he departed (cf. Luke 21:27 and note), but the apostles must not sit around waiting.   **1:12–26** Replacing Judas.   **1:12** *A sabbath day's journey*: i.e., not very distant (cf. Exod 16:29).   **1:13** *Peter, and . . . brother of James*: cf. Luke 6:12–16 and notes.   **1:14** *The women*: those mentioned in Luke 23:49–24:10.   **1:15** *Disciples*: better "brethren" (MS tradition), an ancient Christian self-designation that scribes presumably altered to avoid confusion with Jesus' "brethren" in v. 14. *Names*: i.e., "people," the first of several odd uses of "names" (Gk. *onomata*) in Acts' opening chapters. *An hundred and twenty*: 12 × 10; symbolically meaningful, since they are going to restore the Twelve whom Jesus originally chose.   **1:16–22** *Men and brethren . . . resurrection*: Peter's speech fulfills Jesus' command that he "strengthen [his] brethren" after his repentance (Luke 22:32), thereby confirming his rehabilitation.   **1:16** *Men and brethren*: lit. "men [who are] brothers." KJV frequently uses "men and . . ." to translate Gk. *andres* ("men") + noun in apposition, a common introductory address in classical oratory; see, e.g., 1:11; 2:14, 22; 7:2; 17:22; 19:35; and every occurrence of "men and brethren" in Acts. *This scripture . . . fulfilled*: probably Ps 41:9; cf. Mark 14:18; Luke 22:21.   **1:18–19** *Now this . . . blood*: Matt 27:3–10 recounts a different version of this story.   **1:18** *All his bowels gushed out*: Luke ironically assimilates Judas' death to Joab's traitorous murder of Amasa (2 Sam 20:9–10), the same OT passage he echoes in describing Judas' betrayal of Jesus (Luke 22:47). Now, however, God plays the role of Joab in killing the unsuspecting Judas. **1:19** *Proper tongue*: Aramaic.   **1:20** *Let his habitation . . . take*: Pss 69:25; 109:8. *Bishoprick*: an anachronistic translation of Gk. *episkopē*, which means "act of overseeing" and is perhaps better rendered "responsibility for overseeing"; but cf. 20:28 and note.   **1:22** *Be ordained to be*: lit. "become."

and Matthias. ²⁴And they prayed, and said, Thou, Lord, which knowest the hearts of all men, shew whether of these two thou hast chosen, ²⁵that he may take part of this ministry and apostleship, from which Judas by transgression fell, that he might go to his own place. ²⁶And they gave forth their lots; and the lot fell upon Matthias; and he was numbered with the eleven apostles.

2 And when the day of Pentecost was fully come, they were all with one accord in one place. ²And suddenly there came a sound from heaven as of a rushing mighty wind, and it filled all the house where they were sitting. ³And there appeared unto them cloven tongues like as of fire, and it sat upon each of them. ⁴And they were all filled with the Holy Ghost, and began to speak with other tongues, as the Spirit gave them utterance.

⁵And there were dwelling at Jerusalem Jews, devout men, out of every nation under heaven. ⁶Now when this was noised abroad, the multitude came together, and were confounded, because that every man heard them speak in his own language. ⁷And they were all amazed and marvelled, saying one to another, Behold, are not all these which speak Galilæans? ⁸And how hear we every man in our own tongue, wherein we were born? ⁹Parthians, and Medes, and Elamites, and the dwellers in Mesopotamia, and in Judæa, and Cappadocia, in Pontus, and Asia, ¹⁰Phrygia, and Pamphylia, in Egypt, and in the parts of Libya about Cyrene, and strangers of Rome, Jews and proselytes, ¹¹Cretes and Arabians, we do hear them speak in our tongues the wonderful works of God. ¹²And they were all amazed, and were in doubt, saying one to another, What meaneth this? ¹³Others mocking said, These men are full of new wine.

¹⁴But Peter, standing up with the eleven, lifted up his voice, and said unto them, Ye men of Judæa, and all ye that dwell at Jerusalem, be this known unto

---

1:24 *Whether*: which. **1:25** *Take part of*: better "take the place in" (MS tradition). *His own place*: i.e., hell, or perhaps the field he purchased. **1:26** *Gave forth their lots*: casting lots was a conventional way to determine God's will; cf. 1 Sam 14:41–42 and note. *Matthias*: he never again appears in Acts, perhaps subtly suggesting the fallacy of his election's basis—namely, the idea that an apostle was one whom John had baptized and who numbered among Jesus' original followers (vv. 21–22, 25). Paul, on whom Acts comes to focus, meets neither criterion, but Luke still calls him an apostle (Acts 14:4, 14).

2:1–41 **Gift of the Spirit.** This episode reverses the story of the tower of Babel (Gen 11:1–9). The spiritual manifestation it recounts may lie behind Paul's reference to the risen Christ appearing to "above five hundred brethren at once" (1 Cor 15:6). Compare also John 20:21–23. **2:1** *Pentecost*: lit. "the fiftieth," referring to the "Feast of Weeks," the harvest festival held fifty days after Passover. It came to be associated with God's covenants: *Jubilees* connects it to God's covenant with Noah (6.1–21); after the temple's destruction in 70 C.E., it commemorated the Mosaic covenant, as Exod 19:1 was thought to imply a fifty-day journey from Egypt to Mount Sinai. *With one accord*: better "together" (MS tradition). **2:2–3** *And suddenly . . . fire*: the manifestation displays conventional theophanic features (cf. Exod 19:18; 1 Kgs 19:11; Isa 66:15) and fulfills John the Baptist's prophecy (Luke 3:16; cf. Acts 1:5). **2:4** *Tongues*: i.e., languages (but the same Greek word as in v. 3). **2:5** *Dwelling at Jerusalem*: apparently residents (not the expected reference to pilgrims). **2:6** *When this was noised abroad*: lit. "when this sound [or voice] was made." **2:7** *Are not . . . Galilæans*: recalling Luke 22:59, where Peter's Galilean origins (and accent; see Mark 14:70) belie his denial of Jesus. Now, the disciples' status as parochial Galileans surprisingly speaking foreign languages gives Peter an opportunity to confess Jesus. **2:9–11** *Parthians, and . . . Arabians*: a list of nations covering much of the known world. **2:10** *Strangers*: visitors. *Proselytes*: Gentiles who had converted to Judaism, undergoing circumcision (if male) and observing the law. **2:13** *New wine*: i.e., the cheap stuff. **2:14–41** Peter's Pentecost

you, and hearken to my words: [15]for these are not drunken, as ye suppose, seeing it is but the third hour of the day. [16]But this is that which was spoken by the prophet Joel; [17]and it shall come to pass in the last days, saith God, I will pour out of my Spirit upon all flesh: and your sons and your daughters shall prophesy, and your young men shall see visions, and your old men shall dream dreams: [18]and on my servants and on my handmaidens I will pour out in those days of my Spirit; and they shall prophesy: [19]and I will shew wonders in heaven above, and signs in the earth beneath; blood, and fire, and vapour of smoke: [20]the sun shall be turned into darkness, and the moon into blood, before that great and notable day of the Lord come: [21]and it shall come to pass, that whosoever shall call on the name of the Lord shall be saved.

[22]Ye men of Israel, hear these words; Jesus of Nazareth, a man approved of God among you by miracles and wonders and signs, which God did by him in the midst of you, as ye yourselves also know: [23]him, being delivered by the determinate counsel and foreknowledge of God, ye have taken, and by wicked hands have crucified and slain: [24]whom God hath raised up, having loosed the pains of death: because it was not possible that he should be holden of it. [25]For David speaketh concerning him, I foresaw the Lord always before my face, for he is on my right hand, that I should not be moved: [26]therefore did my heart rejoice, and my tongue was glad; moreover also my flesh shall rest in hope: [27]because thou wilt not leave my soul in hell, neither wilt thou suffer thine Holy One to see corruption. [28]Thou hast made known to me the ways of life; thou shalt make me full of joy with thy countenance.

[29]Men and brethren, let me freely speak unto you of the patriarch David, that he is both dead and buried, and his sepulchre is with us unto this day. [30]Therefore being a prophet, and knowing that God had sworn with an oath to him, that of the fruit of his loins, according to the flesh, he would raise up Christ to sit on his throne; [31]he seeing this before spake of the resurrection of Christ, that his soul was not left in hell, neither his flesh did see corruption. [32]This Jesus hath God raised up, whereof we all are witnesses. [33]Therefore being by the right hand of God exalted, and having received of the Father the promise of the Holy Ghost, he hath shed forth this, which ye now see and hear. [34]For David is not ascended into the heavens: but he saith himself, The LORD said unto my Lord, Sit thou on my right hand, [35]until I make thy foes thy footstool. [36]Therefore let all the house

---

sermon.   **2:15** *Third hour*: 9 A.M.   **2:17–21** *And it . . . saved*: Joel 2:28–32, which Luke alters to underscore its eschatological implications.   **2:18** *Servants and . . . handmaidens*: male and female slaves (as often in Acts). *Of my Spirit*: from my Spirit.   **2:19** *Wonders in . . . beneath*: the OT phrase "signs and wonders" (e.g., Exod 7:3) recurs throughout Acts, sometimes with slight variation.   **2:23** *By the determinate counsel . . . God*: for Jesus' crucifixion as part of God's plan, see Luke 22:22.   **2:24** *Pains*: lit. "birth pangs." *Holden of it*: held in its power.   **2:25–28** *I foresaw . . . countenance*: Ps 16:8–11. **2:26** *Rest*: lit. "dwell as in a tabernacle"; cf. 2 Cor 5:1 and note.   **2:27** *Hell*: lit. "Hades" (also at v. 31); see Matt 11:23 note.   **2:29** *Freely*: Gk. *meta parrēsias*, "with outspokenness." *Parrēsia* is a key word in Acts, also translated "boldness" (as in chap. 4) or "confidence" (28:31). *The patriarch David . . . day*: therefore he does not refer to himself in the psalm.   **2:30** *Sworn with an oath*: 2 Sam 7:12–16. *According to . . . sit*: better "he would seat him" (MS tradition).   **2:31** *His soul*: better "he" (MS tradition). **2:33** *By the right hand*: or "at the right hand."   **2:34–35** *The LORD . . . footstool*: Ps 110:1; cf. Luke

of Israel know assuredly, that God hath made that same Jesus, whom ye have crucified, both Lord and Christ.

37Now when they heard this, they were pricked in their heart, and said unto Peter and to the rest of the apostles, Men and brethren, what shall we do? 38Then Peter said unto them, Repent, and be baptized every one of you in the name of Jesus Christ for the remission of sins, and ye shall receive the gift of the Holy Ghost. 39For the promise is unto you, and to your children, and to all that are afar off, even as many as the Lord our God shall call. 40And with many other words did he testify and exhort, saying, Save yourselves from this untoward generation. 41Then they that gladly received his word were baptized: and the same day there were added unto them about three thousand souls.

42And they continued stedfastly in the apostles' doctrine and fellowship, and in breaking of bread, and in prayers. 43And fear came upon every soul: and many wonders and signs were done by the apostles. 44And all that believed were together, and had all things common; 45and sold their possessions and goods, and parted them to all men, as every man had need. 46And they, continuing daily with one accord in the temple, and breaking bread from house to house, did eat their meat with gladness and singleness of heart, 47praising God, and having favour with all the people. And the Lord added to the church daily such as should be saved.

3 Now Peter and John went up together into the temple at the hour of prayer, being the ninth hour. 2And a certain man lame from his mother's womb was carried, whom they laid daily at the gate of the temple which is called Beautiful, to ask alms of them that entered into the temple; 3who seeing Peter and John about to go into the temple asked an alms. 4And Peter, fastening his eyes upon him with John, said, Look on us. 5And he gave heed unto them, expecting to receive something of them. 6Then Peter said, Silver and gold have I none; but such as I

20:42–43; see Mark 12:36 note.   **2:36** *God hath . . . Christ*: Peter's suggestion that God made Jesus "Lord and Christ" by resurrecting him (cf. Rom 1:3–4 and notes) stands in tension with Luke's infancy narrative, which states that Jesus was "Christ the Lord" at birth (Luke 2:11). It may point to Luke's reliance on an earlier source for Peter's sermon.   **2:38** *Be baptized . . . Christ*: a conventional turn of phrase (cf. 1 Cor 1:13), but in Acts' opening chapters, the power of the absent Lord operates through Jesus' name with exceptional frequency. *Remission*: Gk. *aphesis*, a keyword with which Jesus characterizes his ministry of liberation in Luke (see 4:18 and note). In Acts, "remission" or "forgiveness" (KJV alternates between the two translations) continues to be a standard way of describing what Jesus offers; cf. 5:31; 10:43; 26:18; etc.   **2:39** *The promise . . . call*: echoing Joel 2:32, the OT passage with which Peter's sermon began.   **2:40** *Untoward generation*: lit. "crooked generation," a biblical commonplace.   **2:41** *Gladly*: better omitted (MS tradition).   **2:42–4:35 The generous church.** Luke frames Peter's munificent healing of the lame beggar and its aftermath (3:1–4:31) within idealized portraits of the generous church to which the Pentecost event gave birth (2:42–47; 4:32–35). Acts' attention to material generosity (see also 4:36–5:11; 11:27–30; etc.) develops Luke's tendency to emphasize the economic implications of Jesus' message; see esp. Luke 4:18 note.   **2:42–47 Communal sharing.**   **2:42** *Doctrine*: teaching (so throughout).   **2:45** *Parted*: distributed.   **2:46** *Meat*: food (so throughout). *Singleness of heart*: an idiomatic phrase meaning "generosity" (see Matt 6:22 note).   **2:47** *To the church*: better "together" (MS tradition). *Such as . . . saved*: lit. "those being saved."   **3:1–4:31** Healing a lame man. This event and the opposition it meets repeat Jesus' healing of the paralytic near the beginning of his ministry (Luke 5:17–26). Luke presents the restoration as a lavish gift of alms to the lame beggar (Acts 3:2–6), thereby thematically linking the episode to its framing material (2:42–47; 4:32–37).   **3:1** *Ninth hour*: 3 P.M.   **3:4** *Fastening his eyes*: Gk. *atenizō*, rendered "looked steadfastly" in 1:10, where it signaled the redirection of

have give I thee: In the name of Jesus Christ of Nazareth rise up and walk. [7]And he took him by the right hand, and lifted him up: and immediately his feet and ancle bones received strength. [8]And he leaping up stood, and walked, and entered with them into the temple, walking, and leaping, and praising God. [9]And all the people saw him walking and praising God: [10]and they knew that it was he which sat for alms at the Beautiful gate of the temple: and they were filled with wonder and amazement at that which had happened unto him. [11]And as the lame man which was healed held Peter and John, all the people ran together unto them in the porch that is called Solomon's, greatly wondering.

[12]And when Peter saw it, he answered unto the people, Ye men of Israel, why marvel ye at this? or why look ye so earnestly on us, as though by our own power or holiness we had made this man to walk? [13]The God of Abraham, and of Isaac, and of Jacob, the God of our fathers, hath glorified his Son Jesus; whom ye delivered up, and denied him in the presence of Pilate, when he was determined to let him go. [14]But ye denied the Holy One and the Just, and desired a murderer to be granted unto you; [15]and killed the Prince of life, whom God hath raised from the dead; whereof we are witnesses. [16]And his name through faith in his name hath made this man strong, whom ye see and know: yea, the faith which is by him hath given him this perfect soundness in the presence of you all. [17]And now, brethren, I wot that through ignorance ye did it, as did also your rulers. [18]But those things, which God before had shewed by the mouth of all his prophets, that Christ should suffer, he hath so fulfilled.

[19]Repent ye therefore, and be converted, that your sins may be blotted out, when the times of refreshing shall come from the presence of the Lord; [20]and he shall send Jesus Christ, which before was preached unto you: [21]whom the heaven must receive until the times of restitution of all things, which God hath spoken by the mouth of all his holy prophets since the world began. [22]For Moses truly said unto the fathers, A prophet shall the Lord your God raise up unto you of your brethren, like unto me; him shall ye hear in all things whatsoever he shall say unto you. [23]And it shall come to pass, that every soul, which will not hear that prophet, shall be destroyed from among the people. [24]Yea, and all the proph-

the apostles' attention (cf. 1:11 note).   **3:6** *Name of Jesus*: the first of many references in this episode to Jesus' name (3:16; 4:7, 10, 12, 17, 18, 30).   **3:8** *Leaping up*: cf. Isa 35:6.   **3:11** *Porch*: colonnade.   **3:12** *Look ye so earnestly*: Gk. *atenizō*; see v. 4 note.   **3:13** *The God . . . Jacob*: the famous periphrastic appellation from Exod 3 (vv. 6, 15), another biblical passage featuring a divine name. *Son*: better "servant" (also in v. 26), as Peter echoes an Isaianic Servant Song (LXX Isa 52:13). *And denied him*: the verb Peter uses, emphatically repeated in the subsequent verse, brings to mind his own denial of Christ (Luke 22:54–62).   **3:15** *Prince*: alternatively "author."   **3:16** *By him*: or "by it," with reference to Jesus' name.   **3:17** *Wot*: know. *Through ignorance*: an excuse Peter cannot claim for his own denial.   **3:19** *Be converted*: lit. "turn again," i.e., toward God. *Times of refreshing*: the eschatological consummation.   **3:20** *Was preached*: better "was appointed" (MS tradition). **3:21** *Whom the heaven . . . things*: cf. 1:9–11. *Times of restitution*: another eschatological reference, alternatively rendered "times of restoration." *Since the world began*: lit. "from the ages."   **3:22–23** *A prophet . . . people*: quoting from Deut 18:15, 19; Lev 23:29.   **3:24** *All the prophets*: by insisting that *all the prophets* foretell the eschatological consummation (vv. 21, 24; cf. 18) and at the same time claiming that Moses prophetically figures Jesus' eschatological return from heaven as the appearance of *a prophet . . . like unto me* (v. 22), Luke creates a mise en abyme: all prophets (vv.

ets from Samuel and those that follow after, as many as have spoken, have likewise foretold of these days. [25]Ye are the children of the prophets, and of the covenant which God made with our fathers, saying unto Abraham, And in thy seed shall all the kindreds of the earth be blessed. [26]Unto you first God, having raised up his Son Jesus, sent him to bless you, in turning away every one of you from his iniquities.

4 And as they spake unto the people, the priests, and the captain of the temple, and the Sadducees, came upon them, [2]being grieved that they taught the people, and preached through Jesus the resurrection from the dead. [3]And they laid hands on them, and put them in hold unto the next day: for it was now eventide. [4]Howbeit many of them which heard the word believed; and the number of the men was about five thousand.

[5]And it came to pass on the morrow, that their rulers, and elders, and scribes, [6]and Annas the high priest, and Caiaphas, and John, and Alexander, and as many as were of the kindred of the high priest, were gathered together at Jerusalem. [7]And when they had set them in the midst, they asked, By what power, or by what name, have ye done this? [8]Then Peter, filled with the Holy Ghost, said unto them, Ye rulers of the people, and elders of Israel, [9]if we this day be examined of the good deed done to the impotent man, by what means he is made whole; [10]be it known unto you all, and to all the people of Israel, that by the name of Jesus Christ of Nazareth, whom ye crucified, whom God raised from the dead, even by him doth this man stand here before you whole. [11]This is the stone which was set at nought of you builders, which is become the head of the corner. [12]Neither is there salvation in any other: for there is none other name under heaven given among men, whereby we must be saved.

[13]Now when they saw the boldness of Peter and John, and perceived that they were unlearned and ignorant men, they marvelled; and they took knowledge of them, that they had been with Jesus. [14]And beholding the man which was healed standing with them, they could say nothing against it. [15]But when they had commanded them to go aside out of the council, they conferred among themselves, [16]saying, What shall we do to these men? for that indeed a notable miracle hath

---

21, 24) foretell the eschatological consummation, at which time a prophet like Moses will arise (v. 22), who as a prophet will foretell the eschatological consummation, at which time a prophet like Moses will arise who will foretell the eschatological consummation, and so on. This infinite eschatological deferral coheres with Luke's tendency to reject eschatological preoccupation; cf. Luke 17:20–37; Acts 1:11 and notes. **3:25** *In thy . . . blessed*: Gen 22:18; 26:4; cf. Gal 3:6–29. **4:1** *Captain of the temple*: i.e., captain of the temple guard. *Sadducees*: see Mark 12:18 note. **4:2** *Grieved*: disturbed. *Preached through . . . dead*: their message about Christ presupposed resurrection, which the Sadducees rejected (cf. Mark 12:18–27 and v. 18 note). **4:3** *In hold*: in custody. **4:5–6** *Their rulers . . . Jerusalem*: continuing the hostility they displayed toward Jesus in Luke; compare, e.g., vv. 16–17 and Luke 19:47–48. **4:6** *Annas the high priest, and Caiaphas*: see Luke 3:2 note. *John*: presumably Annas's son Jonathan, who succeeded Caiaphas as high priest. **4:10** *By him*: or "by it," i.e., his name. **4:11** *This is . . . corner*: Ps 118:22; cf. Luke 20:17. **4:13** *Unlearned*: unlettered or even illiterate. *Ignorant*: without expert knowledge. **4:15** *Council*: Gk. *synedrion*, the Sanhedrin (so throughout; see Mark 8:31 note). **4:16** *Miracle*: lit. "sign" (also in v. 22).

been done by them is manifest to all them that dwell in Jerusalem; and we cannot deny it. ¹⁷But that it spread no further among the people, let us straitly threaten them, that they speak henceforth to no man in this name.

¹⁸And they called them, and commanded them not to speak at all nor teach in the name of Jesus. ¹⁹But Peter and John answered and said unto them, Whether it be right in the sight of God to hearken unto you more than unto God, judge ye. ²⁰For we cannot but speak the things which we have seen and heard. ²¹So when they had further threatened them, they let them go, finding nothing how they might punish them, because of the people: for all men glorified God for that which was done. ²²For the man was above forty years old, on whom this miracle of healing was shewed.

²³And being let go, they went to their own company, and reported all that the chief priests and elders had said unto them. ²⁴And when they heard that, they lifted up their voice to God with one accord, and said, Lord, thou art God, which hast made heaven, and earth, and the sea, and all that in them is: ²⁵who by the mouth of thy servant David hast said, Why did the heathen rage, and the people imagine vain things? ²⁶The kings of the earth stood up, and the rulers were gathered together against the Lord, and against his Christ. ²⁷For of a truth against thy holy child Jesus, whom thou hast anointed, both Herod, and Pontius Pilate, with the Gentiles, and the people of Israel, were gathered together, ²⁸for to do whatsoever thy hand and thy counsel determined before to be done. ²⁹And now, Lord, behold their threatenings: and grant unto thy servants, that with all boldness they may speak thy word, ³⁰by stretching forth thine hand to heal; and that signs and wonders may be done by the name of thy holy child Jesus. ³¹And when they had prayed, the place was shaken where they were assembled together; and they were all filled with the Holy Ghost, and they spake the word of God with boldness.

³²And the multitude of them that believed were of one heart and of one soul: neither said any of them that ought of the things which he possessed was his own; but they had all things common. ³³And with great power gave the apostles witness of the resurrection of the Lord Jesus: and great grace was upon them all. ³⁴Neither was there any among them that lacked: for as many as were possessors of lands or houses sold them, and brought the prices of the things that were sold, ³⁵and laid them down at the apostles' feet: and distribution was made unto every man according as he had need.

4:19 *Whether it . . . ye:* perhaps echoing Socrates' famous words from Plato's *Apology*: "I have respect and affection for you, Athenians, but I shall obey God rather than you" (29d).   **4:24** *Lord:* see Luke 2:29 note. *Which hast . . . is:* cf. Exod 20:11; Ps 146:6.   **4:25–26** *Why did . . . Christ:* Ps 2:1–2, with KJV translating Gk. *christos* ("anointed") as *Christ* (see Mark 1:1 note).   **4:25** *By the . . . David:* the Greek is confused and uncertain. *Heathen:* lit. "nations" or "Gentiles."   **4:27** *Of a truth:* better to add "in this city" (MS tradition). *Child:* alternatively "servant" (also in v. 30). *Herod, and Pontius Pilate:* cf. Luke 23:8-12.   **4:31** *The place was shaken:* a theophenic sign recalling those of 2:2–3; cf. Exod 19:18; 1 Kgs 19:11.   **4:32–35** More communal sharing: cf. 2:42–47.   **4:33** *Great grace:* or "much favor"; Luke may mean they enjoyed God's favor, the people's, or both.

³⁶And Joses, who by the apostles was surnamed Barnabas, (which is, being interpreted, The son of consolation,) a Levite, and of the country of Cyprus, ³⁷having land, sold it, and brought the money, and laid it at the apostles' feet.

5 But a certain man named Ananias, with Sapphira his wife, sold a possession, ²and kept back part of the price, his wife also being privy to it, and brought a certain part, and laid it at the apostles' feet. ³But Peter said, Ananias, why hath Satan filled thine heart to lie to the Holy Ghost, and to keep back part of the price of the land? ⁴Whiles it remained, was it not thine own? and after it was sold, was it not in thine own power? why hast thou conceived this thing in thine heart? thou hast not lied unto men, but unto God. ⁵And Ananias hearing these words fell down, and gave up the ghost: and great fear came on all them that heard these things. ⁶And the young men arose, wound him up, and carried him out, and buried him.

⁷And it was about the space of three hours after, when his wife, not knowing what was done, came in. ⁸And Peter answered unto her, Tell me whether ye sold the land for so much? And she said, Yea, for so much. ⁹Then Peter said unto her, How is it that ye have agreed together to tempt the Spirit of the Lord? behold, the feet of them which have buried thy husband are at the door, and shall carry thee out. ¹⁰Then fell she down straightway at his feet, and yielded up the ghost: and the young men came in, and found her dead, and, carrying her forth, buried her by her husband. ¹¹And great fear came upon all the church, and upon as many as heard these things.

¹²And by the hands of the apostles were many signs and wonders wrought among the people; (and they were all with one accord in Solomon's porch. ¹³And of the rest durst no man join himself to them: but the people magnified them. ¹⁴And believers were the more added to the Lord, multitudes both of men and women.) ¹⁵Insomuch that they brought forth the sick into the streets, and laid them on beds and couches, that at the least the shadow of Peter passing by might overshadow some of them. ¹⁶There came also a multitude out of the cities round about unto Jerusalem, bringing sick folks, and them which were vexed with unclean spirits: and they were healed every one.

4:36–5:11 Examples of generosity, positive and negative. 4:36 *Joses*: the Greek form of "Joseph," which a better reading of the MS tradition provides. *Consolation*: or "encouragement," but Luke's etymology is obscure. *Levite*: a member of the priestly tribe. *Of the country*: lit. "by birth." *Cyprus*: an island in the eastern Mediterranean. **5:1–2** *A certain . . . feet*: in light of the customary practice (4:33–34), the couple implies a complete donation. The Jewish community at Qumran also condemned anyone caught lying about donated property (*Rule of the Community* 1QS VI, 22–25). **5:2** *Kept back*: Gk. *nosphizomai*, used in LXX for the trespass of Achan (Josh 7:1). **5:5** *Gave up the ghost*: lit. "expired" (also in v. 10). **5:11** *The church*: Gk. *ekklēsia*, Luke's first use of the word. ("Church" in 2:47 resulted from textual corruption.) See Matt 16:18 note.
   5:12–42 Further conflict with temple authorities. Despite the authorities' earlier warnings (4:18, 21), the apostles conduct their ministry in and around the temple (5:12–16), predictably provoking a hostile response (vv. 17–42). **5:12** *Solomon's porch*: see 3:11 and note. **5:13** *Of the rest . . . to them*: their temerity is reasonable in light of the apostles' transgression of the authorities' orders. *Magnified*: praised. **5:15** *The shadow . . . them*: cf. Luke 8:44 and Acts 19:12 for similar healings,

¹⁷Then the high priest rose up, and all they that were with him, (which is the sect of the Sadducees,) and were filled with indignation, ¹⁸and laid their hands on the apostles, and put them in the common prison. ¹⁹But the angel of the Lord by night opened the prison doors, and brought them forth, and said, ²⁰Go, stand and speak in the temple to the people all the words of this life. ²¹And when they heard that, they entered into the temple early in the morning, and taught. But the high priest came, and they that were with him, and called the council together, and all the senate of the children of Israel, and sent to the prison to have them brought. ²²But when the officers came, and found them not in the prison, they returned, and told, ²³saying, The prison truly found we shut with all safety, and the keepers standing without before the doors: but when we had opened, we found no man within.

²⁴Now when the high priest and the captain of the temple and the chief priests heard these things, they doubted of them whereunto this would grow. ²⁵Then came one and told them, saying, Behold, the men whom ye put in prison are standing in the temple, and teaching the people. ²⁶Then went the captain with the officers, and brought them without violence: for they feared the people, lest they should have been stoned. ²⁷And when they had brought them, they set them before the council: and the high priest asked them, ²⁸saying, Did not we straitly command you that ye should not teach in this name? and, behold, ye have filled Jerusalem with your doctrine, and intend to bring this man's blood upon us.

²⁹Then Peter and the other apostles answered and said, We ought to obey God rather than men. ³⁰The God of our fathers raised up Jesus, whom ye slew and hanged on a tree. ³¹Him hath God exalted with his right hand to be a Prince and a Saviour, for to give repentance to Israel, and forgiveness of sins. ³²And we are his witnesses of these things; and so is also the Holy Ghost, whom God hath given to them that obey him.

³³When they heard that, they were cut to the heart, and took counsel to slay them. ³⁴Then stood there up one in the council, a Pharisee, named Gamaliel, a doctor of the law, had in reputation among all the people, and commanded to put the apostles forth a little space; ³⁵and said unto them, Ye men of Israel, take heed to yourselves what ye intend to do as touching these men. ³⁶For before these days rose up Theudas, boasting himself to be somebody; to whom a number of men, about four hundred, joined themselves: who was slain; and all, as many as obeyed

associated with Jesus and Paul respectively.   **5:17** *Indignation*: alternatively "zeal" or "jealousy." **5:20** *This life*: cf. 3:15.   **5:21** *And all . . . Israel*: probably better "even all . . . ," a reference to the Sanhedrin.   **5:23** *Safety*: security.   **5:24** *The high priest*: better omitted (MS tradition). *They doubted . . . grow*: "they were much perplexed about them, wondering what this would come to" (RSV). **5:28** *Straitly*: strictly.   **5:29** *We ought . . . men*: see 4:19 and note.   **5:30** *Hanged on a tree*: viewing Jesus' crucifixion through the lens of Deut 21:22–23, an OT passage Paul also uses with reference to Jesus' death (Gal 3:13).   **5:31** *With his right hand*: or "at his right hand." *Prince*: cf. 3:15 and note. **5:33** *Cut to the heart*: i.e., "infuriated."   **5:34** *A Pharisee . . . people*: the Mishnah testifies to the renown of Hillel's grandson Gamaliel. On the Pharisees in Luke's writings, see Luke 5:26 note. *Forth a little space*: outside for a short time.   **5:36** *Theudas*: a prophetic leader who promised his followers he could part the Jordan River, presumably as a sign of national deliverance. Rome crushed the movement and put Theudas to death, sometime between 44 and 46 C.E. (see Josephus, *Jewish Antiquities* 20.97–98). This would have occurred several years after Gamaliel's address to the Sanhedrin, so

him, were scattered, and brought to nought. [37]After this man rose up Judas of Galilee in the days of the taxing, and drew away much people after him: he also perished; and all, even as many as obeyed him, were dispersed. [38]And now I say unto you, Refrain from these men, and let them alone: for if this counsel or this work be of men, it will come to nought: [39]but if it be of God, ye cannot overthrow it; lest haply ye be found even to fight against God. [40]And to him they agreed: and when they had called the apostles, and beaten them, they commanded that they should not speak in the name of Jesus, and let them go.

[41]And they departed from the presence of the council, rejoicing that they were counted worthy to suffer shame for his name. [42]And daily in the temple, and in every house, they ceased not to teach and preach Jesus Christ.

6 And in those days, when the number of the disciples was multiplied, there arose a murmuring of the Grecians against the Hebrews, because their widows were neglected in the daily ministration. [2]Then the twelve called the multitude of the disciples unto them, and said, It is not reason that we should leave the word of God, and serve tables. [3]Wherefore, brethren, look ye out among you seven men of honest report, full of the Holy Ghost and wisdom, whom we may appoint over this business. [4]But we will give ourselves continually to prayer, and to the ministry of the word. [5]And the saying pleased the whole multitude: and they chose Stephen, a man full of faith and of the Holy Ghost, and Philip, and Prochorus, and Nicanor, and Timon, and Parmenas, and Nicolas a proselyte of Antioch: [6]whom they set before the apostles: and when they had prayed, they laid their hands on them. [7]And the word of God increased; and the number of the disciples multiplied in Jerusalem greatly; and a great company of the priests were obedient to the faith. [8]And Stephen, full of faith and power, did great wonders and miracles among the people.

Luke's chronology seems to be confused.   **5:37** *After this . . . taxing*: Josephus likewise claims that the revolutionary Judas was active at the time of Quirinius's census (*Jewish Antiquities* 20.102). (This is presumably when Luke understands Jesus to have been born; see Luke 2:1 and note). *Much*: better omitted (MS tradition).   **5:38** *Come to naught*: lit. "be overthrown" (cf. v. 39).   **5:39** *Haply*: perhaps. *To fight against God*: Gk. *theomachoi*. The most famous "god fighter" is Pentheus, who imprisons Bacchus in Euripides' *Bacchae*. Since Luke later quotes this tragedy in a similar context (see Acts 26:14 note), there may be an allusion here to line 45, where Bacchus says that Pentheus "fights against god (*theomachei*) in me."   **5:40** *Beaten them*: presumably in accordance with Deut 25:1–3 (cf. 2 Cor 11:24 and note).   **5:41** *Rejoicing*: in accordance with Jesus' command in Luke 6:22–23.

6:1–8:4 Stephen's martyrdom. After narrating the appointment of seven administrators to supervise the church's charity (6:1–8), Luke focuses on a dispute between one named Stephen and a synagogue, resulting in his trial before the Sanhedrin (6:9–7:1). Stephen delivers a provocative defense (7:2–53), which results in his summary execution (7:54–8:1a) and a more sustained persecution of the church (8:1b–4).   **6:1** *A murmuring . . . Hebrews*: the church's Greek-speaking members complain about those speaking Aramaic. *Ministration*: the "distribution" of 4:35, which perhaps took the form of a daily stipend of food.   **6:2** *Reason*: lit. "pleasing"; cf. v. 5, "pleased" (same Gk. root). *Serve*: Gk. *diakoneō*, also "minister" (cf. vv. 1, 4; same Gk. root).   **6:6** *Laid their hands on them*: as Moses laid hands on Joshua (Num 27:18–23); cf. 1 Tim 4:14; 2 Tim 1:6.   **6:8** *Stephen, full . . . people*: this may be ironic. As soon as the Twelve demand that administrators (lit. "servants"; v. 2) be appointed so that they can continue their proclamation and prayer without mundane distractions, they find themselves eclipsed by two of these humble administrators, Stephen (chaps. 6–7) and Philip

⁹Then there arose certain of the synagogue, which is called the synagogue of the Libertines, and Cyrenians, and Alexandrians, and of them of Cilicia and of Asia, disputing with Stephen. ¹⁰And they were not able to resist the wisdom and the spirit by which he spake. ¹¹Then they suborned men, which said, We have heard him speak blasphemous words against Moses, and against God. ¹²And they stirred up the people, and the elders, and the scribes, and came upon him, and caught him, and brought him to the council, ¹³and set up false witnesses, which said, This man ceaseth not to speak blasphemous words against this holy place, and the law: ¹⁴for we have heard him say, that this Jesus of Nazareth shall destroy this place, and shall change the customs which Moses delivered us. ¹⁵And all that sat in the council, looking stedfastly on him, saw his face as it had been the face of an angel.

7 Then said the high priest, Are these things so? ²And he said, Men, brethren, and fathers, hearken; The God of glory appeared unto our father Abraham, when he was in Mesopotamia, before he dwelt in Charran, ³and said unto him, Get thee out of thy country, and from thy kindred, and come into the land which I shall shew thee. ⁴Then came he out of the land of the Chaldæans, and dwelt in Charran: and from thence, when his father was dead, he removed him into this land, wherein ye now dwell. ⁵And he gave him none inheritance in it, no, not so much as to set his foot on: yet he promised that he would give it to him for a possession, and to his seed after him, when as yet he had no child. ⁶And God spake on this wise, That his seed should sojourn in a strange land; and that they should bring them into bondage, and entreat them evil four hundred years. ⁷And the nation to whom they shall be in bondage will I judge, said God: and after that

---

(chap. 8), in apparent fulfillment of Luke 22:26: "he that is greatest among you, let him be as the younger; and he that is chief, as he that doth serve [Gk. *ho diakonōn*]." *Faith*: better "grace" (MS tradition). *Miracles*: lit. "signs." **6:9** *Synagogue, which . . . Libertines*: for *synagogue*, see Mark 1:21 note. KJV transliterates Luke's Greek transliteration of Lat. *libertini*, "freedmen." This synagogue was apparently founded by ex-slaves, with members predominantly from North Africa and Asia Minor. **6:11–14** *Then they . . . us*: their accusations resemble those made against Jesus in Mark (14:57–58, 63–64) and Matthew (26:60–61, 65). **6:13** *Blasphemous*: better omitted (MS tradition). **6:15** *As it . . . angel*: given the terror that angels inspire in Luke's writings (e.g., Luke 1:11–12; 2:9), this phrase probably implies intensity or fierceness—hardly tranquillity. **7:2–53** Stephen's defense. This précis of Israel's history of rebellion resembles accusatory historical summaries from, e.g., Pss 78, 106; Ezek 20. (Positive surveys of Israel's history are common as well; e.g., Heb 11; Sir 44–50.) Stephen's oration responds provocatively to the charges laid against him. In response to his supposed threat against the temple, he argues that the temple itself represents Israel's sinful error (vv. 44–50). In response to the claim that he shows contempt for the Mosaic law, Stephen argues that his accusers and their ancestors have themselves rejected Moses, the prophets, and the laws they promulgated (vv. 24–29, 35, 39–43, 52–53). **7:2–3** *Before he . . . shew thee*: according to Gen 11:31–12:1, God addressed these words to Abraham after he had already left Chaldea and arrived in Haran (*Charran*) with his father (but cf. Gen 15:7). Stephen's summary frequently fails to line up with the corresponding OT account, sometimes as a result of apparent error (e.g., v. 16; see note), sometimes because he privileges extrabiblical Jewish traditions (as here; cf. Philo, *On the Life of Abraham* 62; Josephus, *Jewish Antiquities* 1.154), sometimes as a result of tendentious biblical interpretation (e.g., vv. 42-43). **7:4** *He removed*: the subject is God. **7:5** *He gave . . . on*: echoing Deut 2:5. *Yet he . . . after him*: cf. Gen 17:8. **7:6–7** *His seed . . . judge*: Gen 15:13–14. **7:6** *Entreat them*: do them. *Four hundred years*: following Gen 15:13, rather than Exod 12:40–41.

shall they come forth, and serve me in this place. ⁸And he gave him the covenant of circumcision: and so Abraham begat Isaac, and circumcised him the eighth day; and Isaac begat Jacob; and Jacob begat the twelve patriarchs.

⁹And the patriarchs, moved with envy, sold Joseph into Egypt: but God was with him, ¹⁰and delivered him out of all his afflictions, and gave him favour and wisdom in the sight of Pharaoh king of Egypt; and he made him governor over Egypt and all his house. ¹¹Now there came a dearth over all the land of Egypt and Chanaan, and great affliction: and our fathers found no sustenance. ¹²But when Jacob heard that there was corn in Egypt, he sent out our fathers first. ¹³And at the second time Joseph was made known to his brethren; and Joseph's kindred was made known unto Pharaoh. ¹⁴Then sent Joseph, and called his father Jacob to him, and all his kindred, threescore and fifteen souls. ¹⁵So Jacob went down into Egypt, and died, he, and our fathers, ¹⁶and were carried over into Sychem, and laid in the sepulchre that Abraham bought for a sum of money of the sons of Emmor the father of Sychem.

¹⁷But when the time of the promise drew nigh, which God had sworn to Abraham, the people grew and multiplied in Egypt. ¹⁸till another king arose, which knew not Joseph. ¹⁹The same dealt subtilly with our kindred, and evil entreated our fathers, so that they cast out their young children, to the end they might not live. ²⁰In which time Moses was born, and was exceeding fair, and nourished up in his father's house three months: ²¹and when he was cast out, Pharaoh's daughter took him up, and nourished him for her own son. ²²And Moses was learned in all the wisdom of the Egyptians, and was mighty in words and in deeds.

²³And when he was full forty years old, it came into his heart to visit his brethren the children of Israel. ²⁴And seeing one of them suffer wrong, he defended him, and avenged him that was oppressed, and smote the Egyptian: ²⁵for he supposed his brethren would have understood how that God by his hand would deliver them: but they understood not. ²⁶And the next day he shewed himself unto them as they strove, and would have set them at one again, saying, Sirs, ye are brethren; why do ye wrong one to another? ²⁷But he that did his neighbour

---

7:7 *Shall they . . . place*: cf. Exod 3:12.   **7:8** *Covenant of circumcision*: cf. Gen 17:1–14. *Abraham begat . . . day*: Gen 21:1–4. *Isaac begat Jacob*: Gen 25:19–26. *Jacob begat . . . patriarchs*: see Gen 29:31–30:24. **7:9–16** *The patriarchs . . . of Sychem*: accurately summarizing the story of Joseph (Gen 37–50), until v. 16.   **7:11** *Dearth*: famine.   **7:12** *Corn*: grain.   **7:14** *Threescore and fifteen souls*: according to Gen 46:27, Exod 1:5, and Deut 10:22, only seventy went down to Egypt. However, in the LXX version of the first two of those passages the number is seventy-five.   **7:16** *That Abraham . . . Sychem*: according to Genesis, Jacob was buried with Abraham in the field of Machpelah, near Mamre (Gen 49:29–30; 50:13), Abraham having purchased the land for a tomb when Sarah died (Gen 23). The land in Shechem (*Sychem*) was actually purchased by Jacob for an altar (Gen 33:18–20), although Josh 24:32 reports that the bones of Joseph, carried out of Egypt during the Exodus (cf. Exod 13:19), were buried there once the Israelites settled in the promised land.   **7:17–44** *But when . . . seen*: Stephen's story of Moses supplements the Exodus account. Some added details appear in other ancient Jewish writings (such as Moses' being eloquent and learned in Egyptian wisdom [v. 22], in contrast with his self-assessment at Exod 4:10); others may represent ad hoc explanatory glosses (such as Moses' early awareness that God would use him to deliver Israel from Egypt in order to explain his slaying of the Egyptian; vv. 24–25) or structural embellishments (such as the division of Moses' life into three forty-year periods; vv. 23, 30, 36; cf. Deut 34:7).   **7:19** *Subtilly*: craftily. *Evil entreated*: did evil to.

wrong thrust him away, saying, Who made thee a ruler and a judge over us? ²⁸Wilt thou kill me, as thou diddest the Egyptian yesterday? ²⁹Then fled Moses at this saying, and was a stranger in the land of Madian, where he begat two sons.

³⁰And when forty years were expired, there appeared to him in the wilderness of mount Sina an angel of the Lord in a flame of fire in a bush. ³¹When Moses saw it, he wondered at the sight: and as he drew near to behold it, the voice of the Lord came unto him, ³²saying, I am the God of thy fathers, the God of Abraham, and the God of Isaac, and the God of Jacob. Then Moses trembled, and durst not behold. ³³Then said the Lord to him, Put off thy shoes from thy feet: for the place where thou standest is holy ground. ³⁴I have seen, I have seen the affliction of my people which is in Egypt, and I have heard their groaning, and am come down to deliver them. And now come, I will send thee into Egypt.

³⁵This Moses whom they refused, saying, Who made thee a ruler and a judge? the same did God send to be a ruler and a deliverer by the hand of the angel which appeared to him in the bush. ³⁶He brought them out, after that he had shewed wonders and signs in the land of Egypt, and in the Red sea, and in the wilderness forty years. ³⁷This is that Moses, which said unto the children of Israel, A prophet shall the Lord your God raise up unto you of your brethren, like unto me; him shall ye hear. ³⁸This is he, that was in the church in the wilderness with the angel which spake to him in the mount Sina, and with our fathers: who received the lively oracles to give unto us: ³⁹to whom our fathers would not obey, but thrust him from them, and in their hearts turned back again into Egypt, ⁴⁰saying unto Aaron, Make us gods to go before us: for as for this Moses, which brought us out of the land of Egypt, we wot not what is become of him. ⁴¹And they made a calf in those days, and offered sacrifice unto the idol, and rejoiced in the works of their own hands.

⁴²Then God turned, and gave them up to worship the host of heaven; as it is written in the book of the prophets, O ye house of Israel, have ye offered to me

---

7:29 *Then fled . . . saying*: cf. Exod 2:15 (Moses' motive is fear of Pharaoh). Stephen's version heightens the initial tension between Moses and the Israelites, which in vv. 39–41 erupts into the Israelites' outright rejection of him and God.   **7:30–36** *When forty . . . years*: Stephen's abbreviated summary of Exod 3–15 omits all references to Moses' own notable resistance to God.   **7:36** *He brought*: better "this man brought." KJV masks Stephen's rhetoric. The Greek begins each verse from 35 to 38 with an emphatic ("this") reference to Moses.   **7:37** *A prophet . . . me*: Deut 18:15, also quoted at 3:22. *Him shall ye hear*: better omitted (MS tradition).   **7:38** *Church in the wilderness*: following LXX usage, Stephen refers to the wandering Israelite congregation as Gk. *ekklēsia*, a word that the NT applies to the Jesus-believing community. Paul develops a typological equation between the church and Israel in the wilderness in 1 Cor 10:1–13. *With the angel . . . Sina*: cf. v. 53; Exodus does not mention angels in this context, but other ancient Jewish sources do (e.g., Gal 3:19; Heb 2:2; Josephus, *Jewish Antiquities* 15.136). The tradition presumably springs from Deut 33:2 (see note), whose LXX translation substitutes "angels" for the Hebrew word that KJV renders "saints." *Lively oracles*: living oracles; cf. Deut 32:45–47.   **7:39–41** *To whom . . . hands*: see Exod 32.   **7:40** *Wot*: know.   **7:42** *Then God . . . heaven*: compare the logic of Rom 1:18–32 (and earlier Jewish texts such as Wis 14:12–31), where God punishes idolaters by relinquishing them to depravity (here, further idolatry in the form of astral worship), forgoing corrective chastisement so that their liability will grow and their final punishment (here, the Babylonian captivity; v. 43) will be more severe. Normally, this sort of treatment is reserved for Gentiles (see Rom 2:4 note). *Book of the prophets*: i.e., the book of the twelve prophets.   **7:42–43** *O ye . . . Babylon*: Amos 5:25–27 (but "Damascus" is replaced with *Babylon* to make the

slain beasts and sacrifices by the space of forty years in the wilderness? ⁴³Yea, ye took up the tabernacle of Moloch, and the star of your god Remphan, figures which ye made to worship them: and I will carry you away beyond Babylon. ⁴⁴Our fathers had the tabernacle of witness in the wilderness, as he had appointed, speaking unto Moses, that he should make it according to the fashion that he had seen. ⁴⁵Which also our fathers that came after brought in with Jesus into the possession of the Gentiles, whom God drave out before the face of our fathers, unto the days of David; ⁴⁶who found favour before God, and desired to find a tabernacle for the God of Jacob. ⁴⁷But Solomon built him an house. ⁴⁸Howbeit the most High dwelleth not in temples made with hands; as saith the prophet, ⁴⁹Heaven is my throne, and earth is my footstool: what house will ye build me? saith the Lord: or what is the place of my rest? ⁵⁰Hath not my hand made all these things?

⁵¹Ye stiffnecked and uncircumcised in heart and ears, ye do always resist the Holy Ghost: as your fathers did, so do ye. ⁵²Which of the prophets have not your fathers persecuted? and they have slain them which shewed before of the coming of the Just One; of whom ye have been now the betrayers and murderers: ⁵³who have received the law by the disposition of angels, and have not kept it.

⁵⁴When they heard these things, they were cut to the heart, and they gnashed on him with their teeth. ⁵⁵But he, being full of the Holy Ghost, looked up stedfastly into heaven, and saw the glory of God, and Jesus standing on the right hand of God, ⁵⁶and said, Behold, I see the heavens opened, and the Son of man standing on the right hand of God. ⁵⁷Then they cried out with a loud voice, and stopped their ears, and ran upon him with one accord, ⁵⁸and cast him out of the city, and

---

prophecy refer to the Babylonian captivity), which Stephen understands to imply that Israel sacrificed to pagan gods (Moloch and Remphan) rather than to YHWH during the wilderness wanderings. **7:44** *Tabernacle of witness*: the LXX translation for the Hebrew phrase rendered in KJV as "tabernacle of the congregation" (Exod 27:21; 28:43; etc.). *Fashion*: pattern; cf. Exod 25:40. The connection between vv. 42–43 and 44–50 is tenuous: the earlier section implies that wandering Israel worshipped pagan deities instead of YHWH in the tabernacle, but the latter positively contrasts the God-ordained tent in which Israel worshipped YHWH in the wilderness with the later temple supposedly constructed on human initiative. Perhaps the distinction is that the tabernacle, though ordained by YHWH, is for worship of lesser divinities, while the temple is for worship of YHWH, even though God did not ordain or require it. **7:45** *Jesus*: the Greek form of Joshua. *Drave*: drove. **7:46** *Tabernacle*: Gk. *skēnōma*, better "abode"; a different but cognate word is used at v. 44. *For the God of Jacob*: better "for the house of Jacob" (MS tradition). "Abode for the house of Jacob" is strange, and the text may be corrupt, but the reference is certainly to the temple—specifically, the house David proposes to build for God's ark (2 Sam 7:1–3). YHWH rejects the offer (2 Sam 7:4–16). **7:47** *But Solomon . . . house*: see 1 Kgs 5–8 (cf. 1 Chr 17:12). In the Babylonian conquest (v. 43), this temple was destroyed. **7:49–50** *Heaven is . . . things*: Isa 66:1–2. **7:51** *Ye stiffnecked . . . ears*: common OT rebukes; cf. Exod 32:9; Lev 26:41; Jer 6:10; etc. **7:52** *Which of . . . them*: another common OT motif; see Luke 11:49 and note. *The Just One*: or "the righteous one." As the KJV capitalization implies, the phrase refers to Christ (cf. 3:14), as also, perhaps, at Rom 1:17 (see note). **7:53** *By the disposition of angels*: cf. v. 38 and note. **7:54–8:1a** Stephen's summary execution. As numerous echoes of Luke's gospel suggest, Luke assimilates Stephen's martyrdom to Jesus' execution. **7:54** *Cut to the heart*: infuriated. *They gnashed . . . teeth*: like Stephen's rebuke (vv. 51–52), their response is cast in conventional biblical imagery; cf. Job 16:9; Ps 35:16; etc. *On him*: at him. **7:55–56** *Looked up . . . hand of God*: cf. 1:10–11; Luke 22:69 (but here he is *standing* at God's right hand). **7:58** *And cast . . . stoned him*: his expulsion from the city recalls Luke 4:28–29. The OT specifies stoning as an appropriate punishment for certain serious infringements of the law, and executions were to occur outside city walls (Num

stoned him: and the witnesses laid down their clothes at a young man's feet, whose name was Saul. ⁵⁹And they stoned Stephen, calling upon God, and saying, Lord Jesus, receive my spirit. ⁶⁰And he kneeled down, and cried with a loud voice, Lord, lay not this sin to their charge. And when he had said this, he fell asleep. And Saul was consenting unto his death.

8 And at that time there was a great persecution against the church which was at Jerusalem; and they were all scattered abroad throughout the regions of Judæa and Samaria, except the apostles. ²And devout men carried Stephen to his burial, and made great lamentation over him. ³As for Saul, he made havock of the church, entering into every house, and haling men and women committed them to prison. ⁴Therefore they that were scattered abroad went every where preaching the word.

⁵Then Philip went down to the city of Samaria, and preached Christ unto them. ⁶And the people with one accord gave heed unto those things which Philip spake, hearing and seeing the miracles which he did. ⁷For unclean spirits, crying with loud voice, came out of many that were possessed with them: and many taken with palsies, and that were lame, were healed. ⁸And there was great joy in that city.

⁹But there was a certain man, called Simon, which beforetime in the same city used sorcery, and bewitched the people of Samaria, giving out that himself was some great one: ¹⁰to whom they all gave heed, from the least to the greatest, saying, This man is the great power of God. ¹¹And to him they had regard, because that of long time he had bewitched them with sorceries. ¹²But when they believed Philip preaching the things concerning the kingdom of God, and the name of Jesus Christ, they were baptized, both men and women. ¹³Then Simon himself believed also: and when he was baptized, he continued with Philip, and wondered, beholding the miracles and signs which were done.

¹⁴Now when the apostles which were at Jerusalem heard that Samaria had received the word of God, they sent unto them Peter and John: ¹⁵who, when they were come down, prayed for them, that they might receive the Holy Ghost: ¹⁶(for as yet he was fallen upon none of them: only they were baptized in the name of

---

15:35). Here the crowd rushes to judgment, executing Stephen before verdict and sentence have been rendered. *Saul*: an oblique introduction of the hero of Acts' second half, who will come to be known as Paul.   **7:59** *Lord Jesus . . . spirit*: cf. Luke 23:46.   **7:60** *Lord, lay not . . . charge*: cf. Luke 23:34, but see note. *Fell asleep*: died.   **8:1** *Scattered abroad . . . Samaria*: combined with v. 4, this notice recalls 1:8; thus Stephen's death leads to the fulfillment of Jesus' prophecy.   **8:3** *As for Saul . . . prison*: in his letters Paul admits to having persecuted the church (1 Cor 15:9; Gal 1:13; Phil 3:6; 1 Tim 1:13), but gives no details about what that entailed. *Made havock of*: destroyed. *Haling*: dragging away.

8:5–40 Philip's ministry in Samaria and beyond. Luke's focus shifts to Philip, another of the seven administrators (6:5).   **8:5** *The city of Samaria*: i.e., Sebaste, but alternatively "a city of Samaria" (MS tradition).   **8:7** *Taken with palsies*: paralyzed.   **8:9–25** Simon's rebuke. Although appearing only in this brief episode, Simon Magus (as he would later be called; see v. 9 note) acquired tremendous significance among proto-orthodox writers who, beginning with Irenaeus in the late second century, present him as a Christian poser and archheretic, the ancestral originator of virtually every form of the religion the proto-orthodox considered perverse. Luke authorizes none of this, representing Simon as making a presumptuous error and then repenting.   **8:9** *Used sorcery*: Gk. *mageuōn*, whence his traditional nickname Simon Magus. *Bewitched*: better "amazed" (also in v. 11).   **8:10** *The great power of God*: better "the power of God which is called great" (MS tradition).

the Lord Jesus.) [17]Then laid they their hands on them, and they received the Holy Ghost.

[18]And when Simon saw that through laying on of the apostles' hands the Holy Ghost was given, he offered them money, [19]saying, Give me also this power, that on whomsoever I lay hands, he may receive the Holy Ghost. [20]But Peter said unto him, Thy money perish with thee, because thou hast thought that the gift of God may be purchased with money. [21]Thou hast neither part nor lot in this matter: for thy heart is not right in the sight of God. [22]Repent therefore of this thy wickedness, and pray God, if perhaps the thought of thine heart may be forgiven thee. [23]For I perceive that thou art in the gall of bitterness, and in the bond of iniquity. [24]Then answered Simon, and said, Pray ye to the Lord for me, that none of these things which ye have spoken come upon me. [25]And they, when they had testified and preached the word of the Lord, returned to Jerusalem, and preached the gospel in many villages of the Samaritans.

[26]And the angel of the Lord spake unto Philip, saying, Arise, and go toward the south unto the way that goeth down from Jerusalem unto Gaza, which is desert. [27]And he arose and went: and, behold, a man of Ethiopia, an eunuch of great authority under Candace queen of the Ethiopians, who had the charge of all her treasure, and had come to Jerusalem for to worship, [28]was returning, and sitting in his chariot read Esaias the prophet. [29]Then the Spirit said unto Philip, Go near, and join thyself to this chariot. [30]And Philip ran thither to him, and heard him read the prophet Esaias, and said, Understandest thou what thou readest? [31]And he said, How can I, except some man should guide me? And he desired Philip that he would come up and sit with him. [32]The place of the scripture which he read was this, He was led as a sheep to the slaughter; and like a lamb dumb before his shearer, so opened he not his mouth: [33]in his humiliation his judgment was taken away: and who shall declare his generation? for his life is taken from the earth. [34]And the eunuch answered Philip, and said, I pray thee, of whom speaketh the prophet this? of himself, or of some other man? [35]Then Philip opened his mouth, and began at the same scripture, and preached unto him Jesus.

[36]And as they went on their way, they came unto a certain water: and the eunuch said, See, here is water; what doth hinder me to be baptized? [37]And Philip said, If thou believest with all thine heart, thou mayest. And he answered and said, I believe that Jesus Christ is the Son of God. [38]And he commanded the chariot to stand still: and they went down both into the water, both Philip and

---

8:17 *Then laid . . . Ghost*: perhaps a testimonial to the role played by the apostolic church in legitimizing ministries in the Mediterranean world: despite being baptized by Philip, Samaritans did not receive the Holy Spirit until the apostles from Jerusalem laid on hands. Paul too seems to recognize this authority, though possibly with some reservations (see Gal 2:1–10). It presumably came to an end during the Jewish War in the late 60s.   **8:18–19** *He offered . . . Ghost*: hence the term "simony."   **8:23** *Gall of bitterness . . . iniquity*: perhaps echoing Deut 29:18; Isa 58:6.   **8:26–40** The Ethiopian eunuch's conversion.   **8:26** *Gaza*: a city in southwest Palestine bordering Egypt.   **8:27** *Ethiopia*: referring to the region south of Egypt. *Candace*: Gk. *kandakē*, a transliterated Nubian word meaning "queen"; compare "Pharaoh king of Egypt" (7:10). *To Jerusalem for to worship*: he was either a diasporic Jew or a Gentile convert to Judaism.   **8:32–33** *He was led . . . earth*: Isa 53:7–8, from one of the Servant Songs.   **8:37** *And Philip . . . God*: better omitted (MS tradition). An early scribe apparently supplemented

the eunuch; and he baptized him. ³⁹And when they were come up out of the water, the Spirit of the Lord caught away Philip, that the eunuch saw him no more: and he went on his way rejoicing. ⁴⁰But Philip was found at Azotus: and passing through he preached in all the cities, till he came to Cæsarea.

9 And Saul, yet breathing out threatenings and slaughter against the disciples of the Lord, went unto the high priest, ²and desired of him letters to Damascus to the synagogues, that if he found any of this way, whether they were men or women, he might bring them bound unto Jerusalem. ³And as he journeyed, he came near Damascus: and suddenly there shined round about him a light from heaven: ⁴and he fell to the earth, and heard a voice saying unto him, Saul, Saul, why persecutest thou me? ⁵And he said, Who art thou, Lord? And the Lord said, I am Jesus whom thou persecutest: it is hard for thee to kick against the pricks. ⁶And he trembling and astonished said, Lord, what wilt thou have me to do? And the Lord said unto him, Arise, and go into the city, and it shall be told thee what thou must do. ⁷And the men which journeyed with him stood speechless, hearing a voice, but seeing no man. ⁸And Saul arose from the earth; and when his eyes were opened, he saw no man: but they led him by the hand, and brought him into Damascus. ⁹And he was three days without sight, and neither did eat nor drink.

¹⁰And there was a certain disciple at Damascus, named Ananias; and to him said the Lord in a vision, Ananias. And he said, Behold, I am here, Lord. ¹¹And the Lord said unto him, Arise, and go into the street which is called Straight, and inquire in the house of Judas for one called Saul, of Tarsus: for, behold, he prayeth, ¹²and hath seen in a vision a man named Ananias coming in, and putting his hand on him, that he might receive his sight. ¹³Then Ananias answered, Lord, I have heard by many of this man, how much evil he hath done to thy saints at Jerusalem: ¹⁴and here he hath authority from the chief priests to bind all that call on thy name. ¹⁵But the Lord said unto him, Go thy way: for he is a chosen vessel

---

Luke's account with a fragment from an ancient Christian baptismal liturgy.   **8:40** *Azotus*: north of Gaza, near the Mediterranean coast. *Cæsarea*: i.e., Caesarea Maritima, an important Mediterranean port city well north of Azotus. It was the seat of Roman government in Judea.

9:1–31 Saul's conversion. Compare 22:3–21; 26:9–18; and Paul's own account of his prophetic call in Gal 1:13–24, which differs significantly. In brief, Luke attempts to integrate Paul comfortably within the ecclesiastical institution whose development he has been narrating, while Paul himself emphasizes his independence from it. Moreover, Luke here and elsewhere in Acts shows Paul preaching to Jews first and turning to Gentiles only after the Jews reject his message, while Paul suggests that his primary mission is to the Gentiles.   **9:2** *Damascus*: a city in Syria. *This way*: lit. "the way," Luke's jargon for the church and its faith (cf. 19:9, 23; etc.).   **9:5** *I am . . . persecutest*: Paul's writings too can equate Jesus with the church; cf. 1 Cor 6:15–20 and notes; 12:12–26 and notes; etc.   **9:5–6** *It is . . . him*: better omitted (MS tradition) as a scribal assimilation of this version of Paul's conversion to that of chap. 26.   **9:8** *He saw no man*: better "he saw nothing" (MS tradition), i.e., he was blind. Paul himself claims to have seen Jesus during his call (Gal 1:15–16), but not to have been blinded by the vision. *But they . . . Damascus*: Paul mentions going to Arabia before heading to Damascus (Gal 1:17).   **9:10** *Ananias*: contrast Paul's insistence that after his call he "immediately . . . conferred not with flesh and blood" (Gal 1:16).   **9:13** *Saints*: "holy ones," a common self-designation of early Jesus-believers.

unto me, to bear my name before the Gentiles, and kings, and the children of Israel: ¹⁶for I will shew him how great things he must suffer for my name's sake. ¹⁷And Ananias went his way, and entered into the house; and putting his hands on him said, Brother Saul, the Lord, even Jesus, that appeared unto thee in the way as thou camest, hath sent me, that thou mightest receive thy sight, and be filled with the Holy Ghost. ¹⁸And immediately there fell from his eyes as it had been scales: and he received sight forthwith, and arose, and was baptized. ¹⁹And when he had received meat, he was strengthened.

Then was Saul certain days with the disciples which were at Damascus. ²⁰And straightway he preached Christ in the synagogues, that he is the Son of God. ²¹But all that heard him were amazed, and said; Is not this he that destroyed them which called on this name in Jerusalem, and came hither for that intent, that he might bring them bound unto the chief priests? ²²But Saul increased the more in strength, and confounded the Jews which dwelt at Damascus, proving that this is very Christ.

²³And after that many days were fulfilled, the Jews took counsel to kill him: ²⁴but their laying await was known of Saul. And they watched the gates day and night to kill him. ²⁵Then the disciples took him by night, and let him down by the wall in a basket. ²⁶And when Saul was come to Jerusalem, he assayed to join himself to the disciples: but they were all afraid of him, and believed not that he was a disciple. ²⁷But Barnabas took him, and brought him to the apostles, and declared unto them how he had seen the Lord in the way, and that he had spoken to him, and how he had preached boldly at Damascus in the name of Jesus. ²⁸And he was with them coming in and going out at Jerusalem. ²⁹And he spake boldly in the name of the Lord Jesus, and disputed against the Grecians: but they went about to slay him. ³⁰Which when the brethren knew, they brought him down to Cæsarea, and sent him forth to Tarsus. ³¹Then had the churches rest throughout all Judæa and Galilee and Samaria, and were edified; and walking in the fear of the Lord, and in the comfort of the Holy Ghost, were multiplied.

9:15 *To bear . . . Israel*: Paul claims that God called him simply to preach Christ "among the heathen" (Gal 1:16), but he elsewhere indicates that his mission to the Gentiles ultimately aims at Israel's salvation (Rom 11:13–14). **9:18** *There fell . . . scales*: in the ancient world, blindness was commonly thought to be caused by filmy substances covering the eyes (cf. Tob 2:10; 11:13; Pliny, *Natural History* 29.21). **9:22** *And confounded . . . Christ*: they could not refute his christological interpretation of biblical texts. **9:23–25** *And after . . . basket*: Paul reports the same story, but says he fled the Gentile authorities at Damascus, not the Jews (2 Cor 11:32–33 and note). **9:25** *The disciples*: better "his disciples" (MS tradition); Paul presumably has already acquired followers. **9:26** *When Saul . . . disciples*: contrast Paul's denial that he made any attempt to legitimize his credentials by showing himself to the apostles in Jerusalem (Gal 1:17). Paul admits to a Jerusalem journey, but insists it occurred at least three years after his call and that his stay there was brief (Gal 1:18–19). In Acts Paul's trip to Jerusalem took place only "many days" after he arrived in Damascus (v. 23) and involved an extended stay (v. 28). **9:27** *Barnabas*: see 4:36–37. **9:29** *And disputed*: lit. "and spoke and disputed." *Grecians*: Greek-speaking Jews. *They went . . . him*: Paul nowhere mentions this attempt on his life. **9:30** *Tarsus*: the leading city in Cilicia (a province in Asia Minor) and Paul's home (see v. 11). **9:31** *Then had . . . multiplied*: *churches* should be singular: "Then had the church rest . . . and was edified, and . . . was multiplied" (MS tradition). *Comfort*: or encouragement.

³²And it came to pass, as Peter passed throughout all quarters, he came down also to the saints which dwelt at Lydda. ³³And there he found a certain man named Æneas, which had kept his bed eight years, and was sick of the palsy. ³⁴And Peter said unto him, Æneas, Jesus Christ maketh thee whole: arise, and make thy bed. And he arose immediately. ³⁵And all that dwelt at Lydda and Saron saw him, and turned to the Lord.

³⁶Now there was at Joppa a certain disciple named Tabitha, which by interpretation is called Dorcas: this woman was full of good works and almsdeeds which she did. ³⁷And it came to pass in those days, that she was sick, and died: whom when they had washed, they laid her in an upper chamber. ³⁸And forasmuch as Lydda was nigh to Joppa, and the disciples had heard that Peter was there, they sent unto him two men, desiring him that he would not delay to come to them. ³⁹Then Peter arose and went with them. When he was come, they brought him into the upper chamber: and all the widows stood by him weeping, and shewing the coats and garments which Dorcas made, while she was with them. ⁴⁰But Peter put them all forth, and kneeled down, and prayed; and turning him to the body said, Tabitha, arise. And she opened her eyes: and when she saw Peter, she sat up. ⁴¹And he gave her his hand, and lifted her up, and when he had called the saints and widows, presented her alive. ⁴²And it was known throughout all Joppa; and many believed in the Lord. ⁴³And it came to pass, that he tarried many days in Joppa with one Simon a tanner.

10 There was a certain man in Cæsarea called Cornelius, a centurion of the band called the Italian band, ²a devout man, and one that feared God with all his house, which gave much alms to the people, and prayed to God alway. ³He saw in a vision evidently about the ninth hour of the day an angel of God coming in to him, and saying unto him, Cornelius. ⁴And when he looked on him, he was afraid, and said, What is it, Lord? And he said unto him, Thy prayers and thine alms are come up for a memorial before God. ⁵And now send men to Joppa, and call for one Simon, whose surname is Peter: ⁶he lodgeth with one Simon a tanner,

---

9:32–11:18 Peter's Gentile ministry. Luke begins this section with two brief healings: one in which Peter heals a man whose name suggests a Gentile identity (Aeneas, namesake of the Trojan hero claimed by Rome as its primary founder; 9:32–35) complementing another in which he resurrects a pious Jewish woman whose Aramaic name Luke draws attention to by translating it into Greek (9:36–43). He then launches into a complex narrative in which Peter converts the Roman centurion Cornelius (10:1–48) and reports back to the Jerusalem church (11:1–18), which legitimizes the conversion and concludes that God has reached out to Gentiles as well as to Jews (vv. 17–18).   **9:32** *Lydda*: a town northwest of Jerusalem, near the Plain of Sharon ("Saron," v. 35) that extends up the Mediterranean coast northwest of *Lydda* from Joppa (v. 36) to Caesarea (10:1).   **9:33** *Sick of the palsy*: paralyzed.   **9:34** *Arise, and make thy bed*: recalling Jesus' words to the paralytic in Luke 5:24.   **9:36** *Tabitha, Dorcas*: both names mean "Gazelle."   **9:37–42** *And it . . . Lord*: in its particulars, Peter's restoration of Dorcas recalls Jesus' resurrection of the synagogue leader Jairus's daughter (Luke 8:40–56).   **10:1** *Centurion*: an officer in the Roman army who oversaw several hundred soldiers.   **10:2** *A devout man . . . alway*: Cornelius along with his household (family and slaves) and other soldiers in his cohort (v. 7) worshipped YHWH and may even have attended synagogue, but were not circumcised and did not observe Jewish law. Acts gives the impression that Gentiles throughout the Mediterranean frequently associated themselves with Jewish communities in this limited way (cf. 13:26; 14:1; etc.).   **10:3** *Ninth hour*: 3 P.M. (also in v. 30). *Evidently*: clearly.

whose house is by the sea side: he shall tell thee what thou oughtest to do. ⁷And when the angel which spake unto Cornelius was departed, he called two of his household servants, and a devout soldier of them that waited on him continually; ⁸and when he had declared all these things unto them, he sent them to Joppa.

⁹On the morrow, as they went on their journey, and drew nigh unto the city, Peter went up upon the housetop to pray about the sixth hour: ¹⁰and he became very hungry, and would have eaten: but while they made ready, he fell into a trance, ¹¹and saw heaven opened, and a certain vessel descending unto him, as it had been a great sheet knit at the four corners, and let down to the earth: ¹²wherein were all manner of fourfooted beasts of the earth, and wild beasts, and creeping things, and fowls of the air. ¹³And there came a voice to him, Rise, Peter; kill, and eat. ¹⁴But Peter said, Not so, Lord; for I have never eaten any thing that is common or unclean. ¹⁵And the voice spake unto him again the second time, What God hath cleansed, that call not thou common. ¹⁶This was done thrice: and the vessel was received up again into heaven.

¹⁷Now while Peter doubted in himself what this vision which he had seen should mean, behold, the men which were sent from Cornelius had made inquiry for Simon's house, and stood before the gate, ¹⁸and called, and asked whether Simon, which was surnamed Peter, were lodged there. ¹⁹While Peter thought on the vision, the Spirit said unto him, Behold, three men seek thee. ²⁰Arise therefore, and get thee down, and go with them, doubting nothing: for I have sent them. ²¹Then Peter went down to the men which were sent unto him from Cornelius; and said, Behold, I am he whom ye seek: what is the cause wherefore ye are come? ²²And they said, Cornelius the centurion, a just man, and one that feareth God, and of good report among all the nation of the Jews, was warned from God by an holy angel to send for thee into his house, and to hear words of thee. ²³Then called he them in, and lodged them.

And on the morrow Peter went away with them, and certain brethren from Joppa accompanied him. ²⁴And the morrow after they entered into Cæsarea. And Cornelius waited for them, and had called together his kinsmen and near friends. ²⁵And as Peter was coming in, Cornelius met him, and fell down at his feet, and worshipped him. ²⁶But Peter took him up, saying, Stand up; I myself also am a man. ²⁷And as he talked with him, he went in, and found many that were come together. ²⁸And he said unto them, Ye know how that it is an unlawful thing for a man that is a Jew to keep company, or come unto one of another nation; but God hath shewed me that I should not call any man common or unclean. ²⁹Therefore came I unto you without gainsaying, as soon as I was sent for: I ask therefore for what intent ye have sent for me? ³⁰And Cornelius said, Four days ago I was fasting until this hour; and at the ninth hour I prayed in my house, and, behold, a man

---

10:6 *He shall tell . . . do*: better omitted (MS tradition). **10:9** *Sixth hour*: noon. **10:12** *Of the earth . . . beasts*: better omitted (MS tradition). *Creeping things*: reptiles. Better to add "of the earth" (MS tradition). **10:14** *Common or unclean*: i.e., animals God had forbidden Israel to eat; cf. Lev 11. Peter's exchange with God recalls Ezekiel's (Ezek 4:9–14). **10:30** *I was fasting . . . prayed*: Gk. obscure; better "from the fourth day until this hour I was praying a ninth-hour prayer" (MS tradition), but this makes little sense. Cornelius may mean that counting exactly four days ago from this very

stood before me in bright clothing, ³¹and said, Cornelius, thy prayer is heard, and thine alms are had in remembrance in the sight of God. ³²Send therefore to Joppa, and call hither Simon, whose surname is Peter; he is lodged in the house of one Simon a tanner by the sea side: who, when he cometh, shall speak unto thee. ³³Immediately therefore I sent to thee; and thou hast well done that thou art come. Now therefore are we all here present before God, to hear all things that are commanded thee of God.

³⁴Then Peter opened his mouth, and said, Of a truth I perceive that God is no respecter of persons: ³⁵but in every nation he that feareth him, and worketh righteousness, is accepted with him. ³⁶The word which God sent unto the children of Israel, preaching peace by Jesus Christ: (he is Lord of all:) ³⁷that word, I say, ye know, which was published throughout all Judæa, and began from Galilee, after the baptism which John preached; ³⁸how God anointed Jesus of Nazareth with the Holy Ghost and with power: who went about doing good, and healing all that were oppressed of the devil; for God was with him. ³⁹And we are witnesses of all things which he did both in the land of the Jews, and in Jerusalem; whom they slew and hanged on a tree: ⁴⁰him God raised up the third day, and shewed him openly; ⁴¹not to all the people, but unto witnesses chosen before of God, even to us, who did eat and drink with him after he rose from the dead. ⁴²And he commanded us to preach unto the people, and to testify that it is he which was ordained of God to be the Judge of quick and dead. ⁴³To him give all the prophets witness, that through his name whosoever believeth in him shall receive remission of sins.

⁴⁴While Peter yet spake these words, the Holy Ghost fell on all them which heard the word. ⁴⁵And they of the circumcision which believed were astonished, as many as came with Peter, because that on the Gentiles also was poured out the gift of the Holy Ghost. ⁴⁶For they heard them speak with tongues, and magnify God. Then answered Peter, ⁴⁷Can any man forbid water, that these should not be baptized, which have received the Holy Ghost as well as we? ⁴⁸And he commanded them to be baptized in the name of the Lord. Then prayed they him to tarry certain days.

11 And the apostles and brethren that were in Judæa heard that the Gentiles had also received the word of God. ²And when Peter was come up to Jerusalem, they that were of the circumcision contended with him, ³saying, Thou wentest in to men uncircumcised, and didst eat with them. ⁴But Peter rehearsed the matter from the beginning, and expounded it by order unto them, saying, ⁵I was in the city of Joppa praying: and in a trance I saw a vision, A certain vessel descend, as it had been a great sheet, let down from heaven by four corners; and it came

---

moment (i.e., 3 P.M.) he had been praying.   **10:32** *Who, when . . . thee*: better omitted (MS tradition). **10:34** *Is no respecter of persons*: shows no favoritism; cf. Deut 10:17, to which Paul also alludes in an identical context (Rom 2:11).   **10:39** *Hanged on a tree*: see 5:30 note.   **10:42** *Quick*: living.   **10:45** *They of the circumcision*: Jews.   **10:46** *Speak with tongues*: glossolalia, a gift Paul too associates with the Holy Spirit (1 Cor 12:10).   **10:47–48** *Can any man . . . Lord*: here, as in 8:14–17, the Spirit confirms a problematic conversion, which the apostolic church in Jerusalem will subsequently legitimize. **11:2** *They that . . . circumcision*: Jewish believers in Jesus (as in v. 45), though here Luke presumably has in mind an emerging faction in the Jerusalem church that resisted admitting uncircumcised

even to me: ⁶upon the which when I had fastened mine eyes, I considered, and saw fourfooted beasts of the earth, and wild beasts, and creeping things, and fowls of the air. ⁷And I heard a voice saying unto me, Arise, Peter; slay and eat. ⁸But I said, Not so, Lord: for nothing common or unclean hath at any time entered into my mouth. ⁹But the voice answered me again from heaven, What God hath cleansed, that call not thou common. ¹⁰And this was done three times: and all were drawn up again into heaven.

¹¹And, behold, immediately there were three men already come unto the house where I was, sent from Cæsarea unto me. ¹²And the spirit bade me go with them, nothing doubting. Moreover these six brethren accompanied me, and we entered into the man's house: ¹³and he shewed us how he had seen an angel in his house, which stood and said unto him, Send men to Joppa, and call for Simon, whose surname is Peter; ¹⁴who shall tell thee words, whereby thou and all thy house shall be saved. ¹⁵And as I began to speak, the Holy Ghost fell on them, as on us at the beginning. ¹⁶Then remembered I the word of the Lord, how that he said, John indeed baptized with water; but ye shall be baptized with the Holy Ghost. ¹⁷Forasmuch then as God gave them the like gift as he did unto us, who believed on the Lord Jesus Christ; what was I, that I could withstand God? ¹⁸When they heard these things, they held their peace, and glorified God, saying, Then hath God also to the Gentiles granted repentance unto life.

¹⁹Now they which were scattered abroad upon the persecution that arose about Stephen travelled as far as Phenice, and Cyprus, and Antioch, preaching the word to none but unto the Jews only. ²⁰And some of them were men of Cyprus and Cyrene, which, when they were come to Antioch, spake unto the Grecians, preaching the Lord Jesus. ²¹And the hand of the Lord was with them: and a great number believed, and turned unto the Lord.

Gentiles to full fellowship with Jewish believers (cf. 15:1; Gal 2:12; etc.).   **11:16** *John indeed . . . Ghost*: cf. 1:5.   **11:18** *Then hath . . . life*: assent to God's involvement in Cornelius's exceptional conversion does not represent a statement of policy on Gentile believers (for which see chap. 15).

11:19–12:25 Gentile support and Jewish persecution of the Jerusalem church. After a brief introduction of the Antioch church (11:19–26), Luke frames the story of Herod's persecution of the Jerusalem church's leaders (12:1–23), "because he saw it pleased the Jews" (v. 3), with references to the relief provided to Judean believers by the largely Gentile church at Antioch (11:27–30; 12:24–25). He thereby subtly suggests a change of orientation in the Jerusalem church, which begins to distinguish itself from the increasingly hostile "people of the Jews" (12:11) at the very moment its ties with the partly (largely?) Gentile congregation in Antioch are strengthened.   **11:19–26** The Antioch church. Luke follows his elaborate narrative of Peter evangelizing Cornelius's household with a brief mention of the Antioch church's multiethnic growth under Barnabas's and Paul's leadership. Historically, the development at Antioch and Paul's ministry to the Gentile world were far more significant to the Jesus movement's transformation from a small Jewish sect into a universal religion, and Luke knows this: he admits that it was in Antioch that the word "Christian" was coined (v. 26), for it was here that it first became clear that Jesus-believers were not merely Jewish sectarians. Moreover, it is in response not to the Gentile Cornelius's conversion (which was apparently exceptional in the southern Levant; cf. 15:3) but to the Antioch church's growth that the apostolic church in Jerusalem must develop a formal policy on Gentile inclusion (chap. 15).   **11:19** *Phenice*: Phoenicia, the Syrian coastland. *Cyprus*: see 4:36 note. *Antioch*: in the Roman province of Syria; one of the most important cities in the empire. **11:20** *Cyrene*: in North Africa. *Grecians*: Gk. *hellēnistai*, "Greek speakers"; here it refers to Gentiles, but

²²Then tidings of these things came unto the ears of the church which was in Jerusalem: and they sent forth Barnabas, that he should go as far as Antioch. ²³Who, when he came, and had seen the grace of God, was glad, and exhorted them all, that with purpose of heart they would cleave unto the Lord. ²⁴For he was a good man, and full of the Holy Ghost and of faith: and much people was added unto the Lord. ²⁵Then departed Barnabas to Tarsus, for to seek Saul: ²⁶and when he had found him, he brought him unto Antioch. And it came to pass, that a whole year they assembled themselves with the church, and taught much people. And the disciples were called Christians first in Antioch.

²⁷And in these days came prophets from Jerusalem unto Antioch. ²⁸And there stood up one of them named Agabus, and signified by the spirit that there should be great dearth throughout all the world: which came to pass in the days of Claudius Cæsar. ²⁹Then the disciples, every man according to his ability, determined to send relief unto the brethren which dwelt in Judæa: ³⁰which also they did, and sent it to the elders by the hands of Barnabas and Saul.

12 Now about that time Herod the king stretched forth his hands to vex certain of the church. ²And he killed James the brother of John with the sword. ³And because he saw it pleased the Jews, he proceeded further to take Peter also. (Then were the days of unleavened bread.) ⁴And when he had apprehended him, he put him in prison, and delivered him to four quaternions of soldiers to keep him; intending after Easter to bring him forth to the people.

⁵Peter therefore was kept in prison: but prayer was made without ceasing of the church unto God for him. ⁶And when Herod would have brought him forth, the same night Peter was sleeping between two soldiers, bound with two chains: and the keepers before the door kept the prison. ⁷And, behold, the angel of the Lord came upon him, and a light shined in the prison: and he smote Peter on the side, and raised him up, saying, Arise up quickly. And his chains fell off from his hands. ⁸And the angel said unto him, Gird thyself, and bind on thy sandals. And so he did. And he saith unto him, Cast thy garment about thee, and follow me. ⁹And he went out, and followed him; and wist not that it was true which was done by the angel; but thought he saw a vision. ¹⁰When they were past the first and the second ward, they came unto the iron gate that leadeth unto the city;

---

in 6:1 it referred to Jewish speakers of Greek. **11:25** *Then departed . . . Saul:* Luke tacitly admits the independence of Paul's ministry from the Jerusalem church, on which Paul vehemently insists in Gal 1:13–2:10: while the apostolic church sends Barnabas to Antioch, it plays no direct role in commissioning Paul. (Here, as in 9:27, Barnabas effectively mediates between them.) **11:26** *Christians:* Gk. *Christianoi* occurs in the NT only here, at 26:28, and at 1 Pet 4:16, always as a name by which outsiders refer to Jesus-believers. **11:28** *Dearth:* famine. *In the days of Claudius Cæsar:* Claudius was Roman emperor, 41–54 C.E. Josephus records a food shortage in Judea, dated to 46–48 C.E. (*Jewish Antiquities* 20.51–53, 101), and Luke may exaggerate it here. **11:29** *Send relief . . . Judæa:* though making no reference to a particular famine, Paul repeatedly discusses a collection of funds he was raising from Gentile congregations to assist the believers in Jerusalem (Rom 15:25–27; 1 Cor 16:1–4; 2 Cor 8–9; cf. Gal 2:10). **12:1** *Herod the king:* Herod Agrippa I ruled from 37 to 44 C.E. **12:3–4** *Because he . . . people:* recalling Jesus' persecution by Pilate, also carried out during the Passover holiday to please the populace (cf. Luke 23:13–25). **12:4** *Quaternions:* squadrons consisting of four soldiers. *Easter:* anachronistic; lit. "Passover." **12:9** *Wist:* knew.

which opened to them of his own accord: and they went out, and passed on through one street; and forthwith the angel departed from him.

[11]And when Peter was come to himself, he said, Now I know of a surety, that the Lord hath sent his angel, and hath delivered me out of the hand of Herod, and from all the expectation of the people of the Jews. [12]And when he had considered the thing, he came to the house of Mary the mother of John, whose surname was Mark; where many were gathered together praying. [13]And as Peter knocked at the door of the gate, a damsel came to hearken, named Rhoda. [14]And when she knew Peter's voice, she opened not the gate for gladness, but ran in, and told how Peter stood before the gate. [15]And they said unto her, Thou art mad. But she constantly affirmed that it was even so. Then said they, It is his angel. [16]But Peter continued knocking: and when they had opened the door, and saw him, they were astonished. [17]But he, beckoning unto them with the hand to hold their peace, declared unto them how the Lord had brought him out of the prison. And he said, Go shew these things unto James, and to the brethren. And he departed, and went into another place.

[18]Now as soon as it was day, there was no small stir among the soldiers, what was become of Peter. [19]And when Herod had sought for him, and found him not, he examined the keepers, and commanded that they should be put to death. And he went down from Judæa to Cæsarea, and there abode.

[20]And Herod was highly displeased with them of Tyre and Sidon: but they came with one accord to him, and, having made Blastus the king's chamberlain their friend, desired peace; because their country was nourished by the king's country. [21]And upon a set day Herod, arrayed in royal apparel, sat upon his throne, and made an oration unto them. [22]And the people gave a shout, saying, It is the voice of a god, and not of a man. [23]And immediately the angel of the Lord smote him, because he gave not God the glory: and he was eaten of worms, and gave up the ghost.

[24]But the word of God grew and multiplied. [25]And Barnabas and Saul returned from Jerusalem, when they had fulfilled their ministry, and took with them John, whose surname was Mark.

13 Now there were in the church that was at Antioch certain prophets and teachers; as Barnabas, and Simeon that was called Niger, and Lucius of Cyrene, and Manaen, which had been brought up with Herod the tetrarch, and Saul. [2]As they ministered to the Lord, and fasted, the Holy Ghost said, Separate

---

12:12 *John, whose . . . Mark*: presumably mentioned in Col 4:10 (where he is said to be Barnabas's nephew); 2 Tim 4:11; Phlm 24; 1 Pet 5:13. It is to him that the Second Gospel is attributed. **12:13** *Damsel*: slave. **12:15** *It is his angel*: i.e., guardian angel (cf. Matt 18:10 and note); they were sometimes imagined as doppelgangers of those they protected. **12:17** *James*: the brother of Jesus (cf. 1:14; Mark 6:3), who will emerge as a leader in the Jerusalem church (15:13; 21:18; cf. Gal 1:19; 2:9, 12). *Went into another place*: i.e., left Jerusalem. **12:20** *Tyre and Sidon*: cities in Phoenicia. *Desired*: requested, presumably through the influential courtier. **12:22–23** *It is . . . ghost*: Josephus provides a similar version of Herod's demise (*Jewish Antiquities* 19.343–52). **12:23** *Eaten of worms*: a conventional punishment for the hubristically impious in ancient Greek literature; cf. Herodotus 4.205; 2 Macc 9:4–28; etc. *Gave up the ghost*: lit. "expired."

13:1–14:28 Paul's first missionary journey. **13:1–3** Commissioning. **13:1** *Niger*: a transliteration of Gk. *Niger*, transliterating Lat. *niger*, "black." *Brought up*: raised (i.e., as a foster brother). *Herod the tetrarch*: Herod Antipas (see Luke 3:1), who ruled from 4 B.C.E. to 39 C.E. **13:4–12**

me Barnabas and Saul for the work whereunto I have called them. ³And when they had fasted and prayed, and laid their hands on them, they sent them away.

⁴So they, being sent forth by the Holy Ghost, departed unto Seleucia; and from thence they sailed to Cyprus. ⁵And when they were at Salamis, they preached the word of God in the synagogues of the Jews: and they had also John to their minister. ⁶And when they had gone through the isle unto Paphos, they found a certain sorcerer, a false prophet, a Jew, whose name was Bar-jesus: ⁷which was with the deputy of the country, Sergius Paulus, a prudent man; who called for Barnabas and Saul, and desired to hear the word of God. ⁸But Elymas the sorcerer (for so is his name by interpretation) withstood them, seeking to turn away the deputy from the faith. ⁹Then Saul, (who also is called Paul,) filled with the Holy Ghost, set his eyes on him, ¹⁰and said, O full of all subtilty and all mischief, thou child of the devil, thou enemy of all righteousness, wilt thou not cease to pervert the right ways of the Lord? ¹¹And now, behold, the hand of the Lord is upon thee, and thou shalt be blind, not seeing the sun for a season. And immediately there fell on him a mist and a darkness; and he went about seeking some to lead him by the hand. ¹²Then the deputy, when he saw what was done, believed, being astonished at the doctrine of the Lord.

¹³Now when Paul and his company loosed from Paphos, they came to Perga in Pamphylia: and John departing from them returned to Jerusalem. ¹⁴But when

---

Ministry at Cyprus.   13:4 *Seleucia*: Seleucia in Pieria, the Mediterranean port serving Antioch. **13:5** *Salamis*: on Cyprus's east coast. *They preached . . . Jews*: in Acts, Paul always begins by preaching in the synagogues, turning to Gentiles only after the Jewish community proves unreceptive or hostile. There is no hint of this procedure in Paul's letters. *John to their minister*: "John as their attendant" (John Mark; cf. 12:12, 25). From this point on he is known simply as John.   **13:6** *Paphos*: the city where the Roman proconsul (here "deputy of the country"; vv. 7, 12) was based. *Sorcerer*: Gk. *magos*, like Simon (cf. 8:9). Peter and Paul both begin their ministries outside of Jerusalem by confronting a magician, and both episodes emphasize the spiritual resistance the church meets at key moments of its expansion.   **13:7** *Sergius Paulus*: the proconsul, the first of many Roman officials in Acts who show themselves sympathetic to Paul. In this episode, the contrast between representative Roman and Jewish responses to Paul and his message is particularly stark. This scenario, repeated throughout Acts' second half, is probably not historically accurate, but rather represents an imaginative attempt on Luke's part to distinguish "Christians" from Jews (against whom the Romans had fought a bloody war in Judea perhaps just a few years before he wrote) and to emphasize that the former posed no threat to imperial peace.   **13:8** *Elymas the sorcerer . . . interpretation*: etymology obscure.   **13:9–11** *Then Saul . . . by the hand*: a complex culmination of Saul's transformation from Jewish opponent of the church to Christian evangelist of Gentiles: Saul, whose former blindness to God's will was emblematized in his own blindness just before his conversion, now himself blinds a Jewish magician to stop him from interfering with the Gentile leader's conversion. At the same moment Luke reveals Saul's Roman cognomen as "Paulus" (also the name of the Roman official he is evangelizing), never again referring to him as Saul. Paul's identity as an evangelist in Acts is therefore founded on a symbolic rejection of his Jewish past as misguided, even wicked, and on a symbolic identification with the Gentiles to whom he will minister in the future.   **13:10** *Child of the devil*: reversing the meaning of Bar-jesus (v. 6), "Son of Jesus" or "Son of Salvation" (see Matt 1:21 note).   **13:13–52** Ministry in Antioch of Pisidia. This section includes Paul's first sermon in Acts (vv. 16–41), which, like Stephen's (7:2–53), reviews Israel's history, but with an encouraging rather than condemning message. Paul's sermon also resembles Peter's (2:14–36) in its discussion of Jesus' resurrection, basing similar arguments on identical OT passages; cf. 13:30–37; 2:24–32.   **13:13** *Loosed*: set sail. *Perga*: a port city on the Cestrus River in Pamphylia, a Roman province in Asia Minor just west of Cilicia.

they departed from Perga, they came to Antioch in Pisidia, and went into the synagogue on the sabbath day, and sat down. ¹⁵And after the reading of the law and the prophets the rulers of the synagogue sent unto them, saying, Ye men and brethren, if ye have any word of exhortation for the people, say on.

¹⁶Then Paul stood up, and beckoning with his hand said, Men of Israel, and ye that fear God, give audience. ¹⁷The God of this people of Israel chose our fathers, and exalted the people when they dwelt as strangers in the land of Egypt, and with an high arm brought he them out of it. ¹⁸And about the time of forty years suffered he their manners in the wilderness. ¹⁹And when he had destroyed seven nations in the land of Chanaan, he divided their land to them by lot. ²⁰And after that he gave unto them judges about the space of four hundred and fifty years, until Samuel the prophet. ²¹And afterward they desired a king: and God gave unto them Saul the son of Cis, a man of the tribe of Benjamin, by the space of forty years. ²²And when he had removed him, he raised up unto them David to be their king; to whom also he gave testimony, and said, I have found David the son of Jesse, a man after mine own heart, which shall fulfil all my will. ²³Of this man's seed hath God according to his promise raised unto Israel a Saviour, Jesus: ²⁴when John had first preached before his coming the baptism of repentance to all the people of Israel. ²⁵And as John fulfilled his course, he said, Whom think ye that I am? I am not he. But, behold, there cometh one after me, whose shoes of his feet I am not worthy to loose.

²⁶Men and brethren, children of the stock of Abraham, and whosoever among you feareth God, to you is the word of this salvation sent. ²⁷For they that dwell at Jerusalem, and their rulers, because they knew him not, nor yet the voices of the prophets which are read every sabbath day, they have fulfilled them in condemning

13:14 *Antioch in Pisidia*: distinct from Antioch in Syria, the starting point of Paul and Barnabas's journey. Pisidian Antioch was actually located just north of Pisidia (a region of Galatia itself just north of Pamphylia). **13:16** *Paul stood . . . audience*: Jewish teachers usually sat while speaking (as Jesus does in Luke 4:20–27). Paul's posture, which may have been conventional in synagogues outside Palestine, resembles Greek oratorical practice. *And ye . . . God*: Gentiles in attendance; cf. v. 26. **13:17** *The God . . . it*: echoing Exod 6:6–7. **13:18** *Suffered he their manners*: i.e., "he put up with them," but MSS of more or less equal number and authority read "he nourished them." The same textual uncertainty affects LXX Deut 1:3, to which Paul alludes. **13:19** *Seven nations*: see Deut 7:1. *He divided . . . lot*: better "he gave their land as an inheritance" (MS tradition); see Josh 14:1–2. **13:20** *And after that*: lit. "and after those things." This phrase better follows the mention of *four hundred and fifty years* (MS tradition), yielding "and when he destroyed the seven nations in the land of Canaan, he gave their land as an inheritance, for about four hundred and fifty years. And after these things he gave them judges, until Samuel the prophet" (vv. 19–20). Perhaps to avoid the mistaken idea that Canaan's invasion alone lasted four hundred and fifty years, later scribes altered the text to produce the reading KJV translates (impossible in light of 1 Kgs 6:1). Many commentators today think the time span covers all the events narrated in vv. 17–19: four hundred years in Egypt (cf. 7:6 and note) and the traditional forty in the wilderness, with another ten thrown in for the conquest of Canaan (although Josh 14:7–10 suggests that the conquest took five years). **13:21** *They desired . . . Saul*: see 1 Sam 8:5–6; chaps. 9–10. *By the space of forty years*: it is not clear how Paul arrives at this number; the text of 1 Sam 13:1, which purports to give the length of Saul's reign, became corrupt very early on (see note) and LXX excises it. Josephus assigns contradictory lengths to Saul's rule, including forty years (*Jewish Antiquities* 6.378). **13:22** *He raised . . . king*: see 1 Sam 16:13. *I have . . . will*: cf. 1 Sam 13:14; Ps 89:20; LXX Isa 44:28. **13:23** *Promise*: see v. 34 and note. *Raised*: better "brought" (MS tradition). **13:25** *Whom think . . . he*: John does not say this in Luke, but see John 1:20; 3:28. *But, behold . . . loose*: Luke 3:16. **13:26** *To you*: better "to us" (MS tradition).

him. [28]And though they found no cause of death in him, yet desired they Pilate that he should be slain. [29]And when they had fulfilled all that was written of him, they took him down from the tree, and laid him in a sepulchre. [30]But God raised him from the dead: [31]and he was seen many days of them which came up with him from Galilee to Jerusalem, who are his witnesses unto the people. [32]And we declare unto you glad tidings, how that the promise which was made unto the fathers, [33]God hath fulfilled the same unto us their children, in that he hath raised up Jesus again; as it is also written in the second psalm, Thou art my Son, this day have I begotten thee. [34]And as concerning that he raised him up from the dead, now no more to return to corruption, he said on this wise, I will give you the sure mercies of David. [35]Wherefore he saith also in another psalm, Thou shalt not suffer thine Holy One to see corruption. [36]For David, after he had served his own generation by the will of God, fell on sleep, and was laid unto his fathers, and saw corruption: [37]but he, whom God raised again, saw no corruption.

[38]Be it known unto you therefore, men and brethren, that through this man is preached unto you the forgiveness of sins: [39]and by him all that believe are justified from all things, from which ye could not be justified by the law of Moses. [40]Beware therefore, lest that come upon you, which is spoken of in the prophets; [41]Behold, ye despisers, and wonder, and perish: for I work a work in your days, a work which ye shall in no wise believe, though a man declare it unto you.

[42]And when the Jews were gone out of the synagogue, the Gentiles besought that these words might be preached to them the next sabbath. [43]Now when the congregation was broken up, many of the Jews and religious proselytes followed Paul and Barnabas: who, speaking to them, persuaded them to continue in the grace of God.

[44]And the next sabbath day came almost the whole city together to hear the word of God. [45]But when the Jews saw the multitudes, they were filled with envy, and spake against those things which were spoken by Paul, contradicting and blaspheming. [46]Then Paul and Barnabas waxed bold, and said, It was necessary that the word of God should first have been spoken to you: but seeing ye put it from you, and judge yourselves unworthy of everlasting life, lo, we turn to the

---

13:29 *They took . . . sepulchre*: cf. Luke 23:50–53.   **13:31** *Of them . . . people*: in his letters, Paul includes himself among those who saw the risen Christ; cf. 1 Cor 15:8; Gal 1:15–16.   **13:33** *Thou art . . . thee*: Ps 2:7. Paul seems to suggest that Jesus became God's son at his resurrection; cf. 2:36 and note. According to Mark 1:11, which echoes the same OT verse, Jesus was declared (or became) God's son at baptism.   **13:34** *On this wise*: in this manner. *I will . . . David*: see Isa 55:3 and note. The divine guarantee refers to God's promise of eternal dominion to David (2 Sam 7:12–16), which Luke and others interpreted messianically (Acts 2:30 and note; 13:23; see Mark 10:47 note). **13:35** *Thou shalt . . . corruption*: Ps 16:10.   **13:36** *Fell on sleep . . . fathers*: echoing 1 Kgs 2:10. **13:39** *By him . . . things*: juxtaposing a typical Pauline understanding of Jesus' death and resurrection (cf. Rom 3:28; Gal 2:16; etc.) to a typical Lukan one ("forgiveness of sins" in v. 38; see 2:38 note).   **13:41** *Behold, ye . . . you*: Hab 1:5.   **13:42** *And when . . . besought*: better "and as they were leaving the synagogue, they besought" (MS tradition); the first *they* refers to Paul and Barnabas, and the second to the congregation as a whole.   **13:43** *Religious*: or "pious."   **13:46–47** *It was . . . earth*: in Rom 9–11 Paul explicitly rejects the theological proposition here attributed to him, namely that God has turned to the Gentiles in response to the Jews' rejection of the gospel.

Gentiles. [47]For so hath the Lord commanded us, saying, I have set thee to be a light of the Gentiles, that thou shouldest be for salvation unto the ends of the earth. [48]And when the Gentiles heard this, they were glad, and glorified the word of the Lord: and as many as were ordained to eternal life believed. [49]And the word of the Lord was published throughout all the region. [50]But the Jews stirred up the devout and honourable women, and the chief men of the city, and raised persecution against Paul and Barnabas, and expelled them out of their coasts. [51]But they shook off the dust of their feet against them, and came unto Iconium. [52]And the disciples were filled with joy, and with the Holy Ghost.

14 And it came to pass in Iconium, that they went both together into the synagogue of the Jews, and so spake, that a great multitude both of the Jews and also of the Greeks believed. [2]But the unbelieving Jews stirred up the Gentiles, and made their minds evil affected against the brethren. [3]Long time therefore abode they speaking boldly in the Lord, which gave testimony unto the word of his grace, and granted signs and wonders to be done by their hands. [4]But the multitude of the city was divided: and part held with the Jews, and part with the apostles. [5]And when there was an assault made both of the Gentiles, and also of the Jews with their rulers, to use them despitefully, and to stone them, [6]they were ware of it, and fled unto Lystra and Derbe, cities of Lycaonia, and unto the region that lieth round about: [7]and there they preached the gospel.

[8]And there sat a certain man at Lystra, impotent in his feet, being a cripple from his mother's womb, who never had walked: [9]the same heard Paul speak: who stedfastly beholding him, and perceiving that he had faith to be healed, [10]said with a loud voice, Stand upright on thy feet. And he leaped and walked. [11]And when the people saw what Paul had done, they lifted up their voices, saying in the speech of Lycaonia, The gods are come down to us in the likeness of men. [12]And they called Barnabas, Jupiter; and Paul, Mercurius, because he was the chief speaker.

[13]Then the priest of Jupiter, which was before their city, brought oxen and garlands unto the gates, and would have done sacrifice with the people. [14]Which

---

13:47 *I have . . . earth*: Isa 49:6; cf. Luke 2:32.   **13:48** *As many . . . believed*: perhaps the Bible's most unambiguous statement of the idea that God predestines individuals for salvation or damnation (cf. Rom 8:29–30), which has exercised the theological imaginations of Augustine, Calvin, and many others. **13:49** *Published*: disseminated.   **13:50** *Coasts*: territories.   **13:51** *Shook off . . . them*: in accordance with Luke 9:5; 10:11. *Iconium*: a Galatian city well east of Antioch.   **14:1–7** Ministry in Iconium. **14:2** *The unbelieving . . . brethren*: the political paradigm by which Luke explains Jesus' death (Jews prompting Gentile authorities to persecute the faithful) resurfaces here, and will recur throughout Acts, as it enables the author to emphasize that Christians pose no inherent threat to Roman peace and order (see 13:7 note). *Unbelieving*: or "disobedient."   **14:6** *Ware*: aware. *Lystra and Derbe*: cities south of Iconium; *Lycaonia* was the southern region of Galatia in which all three cities lay.   **14:8–20** Ministry in Lystra: replicating Peter's healing of the lame man at the temple gate (3:1–13).   **14:11** *The gods . . . men*: a common scenario in pagan myth. See especially the story of Philemon and Baucis (Ovid, *Metamorphoses* 8.618–724): in it Jupiter and Mercury, disguised as humans, visit an unsuspecting pious couple living in Phrygia, a region bordering nearby Pisidia.   **14:12** *Jupiter, Mercurius*: the Roman equivalents of the names in the Greek text: Zeus and Hermes (the divine messenger).

when the apostles, Barnabas and Paul, heard of, they rent their clothes, and ran in among the people, crying out, [15]and saying, Sirs, why do ye these things? We also are men of like passions with you, and preach unto you that ye should turn from these vanities unto the living God, which made heaven, and earth, and the sea, and all things that are therein: [16]who in times past suffered all nations to walk in their own ways. [17]Nevertheless he left not himself without witness, in that he did good, and gave us rain from heaven, and fruitful seasons, filling our hearts with food and gladness. [18]And with these sayings scarce restrained they the people, that they had not done sacrifice unto them.

[19]And there came thither certain Jews from Antioch and Iconium, who persuaded the people, and, having stoned Paul, drew him out of the city, supposing he had been dead. [20]Howbeit, as the disciples stood round about him, he rose up, and came into the city: and the next day he departed with Barnabas to Derbe.

[21]And when they had preached the gospel to that city, and had taught many, they returned again to Lystra, and to Iconium, and Antioch, [22]confirming the souls of the disciples, and exhorting them to continue in the faith, and that we must through much tribulation enter into the kingdom of God. [23]And when they had ordained them elders in every church, and had prayed with fasting, they commended them to the Lord, on whom they believed. [24]And after they had passed throughout Pisidia, they came to Pamphylia. [25]And when they had preached the word in Perga, they went down into Attalia: [26]and thence sailed to Antioch, from whence they had been recommended to the grace of God for the work which they fulfilled. [27]And when they were come, and had gathered the church together, they rehearsed all that God had done with them, and how he had opened the door of faith unto the Gentiles. [28]And there they abode long time with the disciples.

15 And certain men which came down from Judæa taught the brethren, and said, Except ye be circumcised after the manner of Moses, ye cannot be saved. [2]When therefore Paul and Barnabas had no small dissension and disputation with them, they determined that Paul and Barnabas, and certain other of them, should go up to Jerusalem unto the apostles and elders about this question. [3]And being brought on their way by the church, they passed through Phenice and Samaria, declaring the conversion of the Gentiles: and they caused great joy unto all the brethren. [4]And when they were come to Jerusalem, they were received of

---

14:14 *Rent their clothes*: compare the actions of the high priest at Jesus' trial when he hears analogous "blasphemy" from Jesus (Mark 14:63–64 and note). **14:15** *Of like passions*: i.e., of the same nature. *Living God*: cf. 1 Thess 1:9. *Which made . . . therein*: Ps 146:6. **14:16–17** *Who in times past . . . gladness*: Paul's analogous argument in Rom 1:18–32 (see notes) is harsher. There he claims YHWH actively gave over to various forms of depravity those who rejected the God of creation in favor of idols. **14:17** *Gave us*: better "gave you" (MS tradition). *Our hearts*: better "your hearts" (MS tradition). **14:19** *Having stoned Paul*: like Stephen (7:58); cf. 2 Cor 11:25. **14:21–28** Return to Antioch (more or less reversing the itinerary narrated in 13:1–14:19). **14:23** *Ordained them elders*: cf. 11:30. Among Paul's letters, only the possibly pseudepigraphical Pastorals mention "elders" (1 Tim 5:17–19; Titus 1:5–6). Acts' notice too may be anachronistic, reflecting a practice of the author's time rather than Paul's. **14:25** *Attalia*: a Mediterranean port city near Perga in Pamphylia.
  15:1–35 The Jerusalem council. Paul writes about the same meeting in Gal 2:1–10, but his version differs significantly. **15:1** *Except ye . . . saved*: this appears to have been the position of Paul's opponents in Galatia (see Gal 5:2–12 and notes). **15:3** *Declaring*: lit. "narrating," as in Luke 1:1.

the church, and of the apostles and elders, and they declared all things that God had done with them. ⁵But there rose up certain of the sect of the Pharisees which believed, saying, That it was needful to circumcise them, and to command them to keep the law of Moses.

⁶And the apostles and elders came together for to consider of this matter. ⁷And when there had been much disputing, Peter rose up, and said unto them, Men and brethren, ye know how that a good while ago God made choice among us, that the Gentiles by my mouth should hear the word of the gospel, and believe. ⁸And God, which knoweth the hearts, bare them witness, giving them the Holy Ghost, even as he did unto us; ⁹and put no difference between us and them, purifying their hearts by faith. ¹⁰Now therefore why tempt ye God, to put a yoke upon the neck of the disciples, which neither our fathers nor we were able to bear? ¹¹But we believe that through the grace of the Lord Jesus Christ we shall be saved, even as they.

¹²Then all the multitude kept silence, and gave audience to Barnabas and Paul, declaring what miracles and wonders God had wrought among the Gentiles by them. ¹³And after they had held their peace, James answered, saying, Men and brethren, hearken unto me: ¹⁴Simeon hath declared how God at the first did visit the Gentiles, to take out of them a people for his name. ¹⁵And to this agree the words of the prophets; as it is written, ¹⁶After this I will return, and will build again the tabernacle of David, which is fallen down; and I will build again the ruins thereof, and I will set it up: ¹⁷that the residue of men might seek after the Lord, and all the Gentiles, upon whom my name is called, saith the Lord, who doeth all these things. ¹⁸Known unto God are all his works from the beginning of the world. ¹⁹Wherefore my sentence is, that we trouble not them, which from among the Gentiles are turned to God: ²⁰but that we write unto them, that they abstain from pollutions of idols, and from fornication, and from things strangled, and from blood. ²¹For Moses of old time hath in every city them that preach him, being read in the synagogues every sabbath day.

15:7 *The Gentiles . . . believe*: Luke assimilates the ministries of Peter and Paul, but in Galatians Paul claims that the meeting revealed a fundamental distinction: "they saw that the gospel of the uncircumcision was committed unto me, as the gospel of the circumcision was unto Peter" (2:7).   **15:10** *A yoke . . . bear*: cf. Gal 5:1. The idea that the law was burdensome does not seem to have been widespread. On the contrary, Matthew suggests it was not strict enough (see esp. 5:17–48), although he describes as burdensome the Pharisaic regulations supplementing the law (23:2–4). Paul, himself a Pharisee, indicates he had no problems keeping the law faithfully (Phil 3:6) and has to urge his churches *not* to adopt the law (see esp. Galatians).   **15:11** *We believe . . . they*: Peter's argument is similar to one that Paul claims to have used against him sometime after the Jerusalem council, when Peter separated himself from Gentile believers at Antioch during a visit (Gal 2:15–16).   **15:14** *Simeon*: the Hebrew form of Simon.   **15:16–17** *After this . . . things*: Amos 9:11–12.   **15:17–18** *Who doeth . . . world*: better "who makes these things known from of old" (MS tradition).   **15:20** *Pollutions of idols*: i.e., eating meat from animals sacrificed to pagan gods. *Fornication*: sexual immorality. *Things strangled . . . blood*: i.e., meat not drained of blood (cf. Lev 17:10–14). Tertullian suggests that Gentile Christians kept this regulation at least until the end of the second century (*Apology* 9.13).   **15:21** *For Moses . . . day*: the import of James' closing statement may be that Moses already has many promoters, and so does not need the church to act as an advocate by demanding that Gentiles follow his law rigorously. Alternatively, he may mean that since Moses is widely known, Gentile believers will already be aware of the basic restrictions on diet and sex they are now obliged to follow and so not

²²Then pleased it the apostles and elders, with the whole church, to send chosen men of their own company to Antioch with Paul and Barnabas; namely, Judas surnamed Barsabas, and Silas, chief men among the brethren: ²³and they wrote letters by them after this manner; The apostles and elders and brethren send greeting unto the brethren which are of the Gentiles in Antioch and Syria and Cilicia: ²⁴forasmuch as we have heard, that certain which went out from us have troubled you with words, subverting your souls, saying, Ye must be circumcised, and keep the law: to whom we gave no such commandment: ²⁵it seemed good unto us, being assembled with one accord, to send chosen men unto you with our beloved Barnabas and Paul, ²⁶men that have hazarded their lives for the name of our Lord Jesus Christ. ²⁷We have sent therefore Judas and Silas, who shall also tell you the same things by mouth. ²⁸For it seemed good to the Holy Ghost, and to us, to lay upon you no greater burden than these necessary things; ²⁹that ye abstain from meats offered to idols, and from blood, and from things strangled, and from fornication: from which if ye keep yourselves, ye shall do well. Fare ye well.

³⁰So when they were dismissed, they came to Antioch: and when they had gathered the multitude together, they delivered the epistle: ³¹which when they had read, they rejoiced for the consolation. ³²And Judas and Silas, being prophets also themselves, exhorted the brethren with many words, and confirmed them. ³³And after they had tarried there a space, they were let go in peace from the brethren unto the apostles. ³⁴Notwithstanding it pleased Silas to abide there still. ³⁵Paul also and Barnabas continued in Antioch, teaching and preaching the word of the Lord, with many others also.

³⁶And some days after Paul said unto Barnabas, Let us go again and visit our brethren in every city where we have preached the word of the Lord, and see how they do. ³⁷And Barnabas determined to take with them John, whose surname was Mark. ³⁸But Paul thought not good to take him with them, who departed from them from Pamphylia, and went not with them to the work. ³⁹And the contention was so sharp between them, that they departed asunder one from the other: and so Barnabas took Mark, and sailed unto Cyprus; ⁴⁰and Paul chose Silas, and

view them as arbitrary or onerous. He may also imply that since throughout the empire knowledgeable Jews are likely to scrutinize Gentile Jesus-believers, the latter must make a meaningful gesture of obedience to the law. **15:22** *Silas*: Silvanus, whom Paul frequently mentions as a partner in ministry (2 Cor 1:19; 1 Thess 1:1; 2 Thess 1:1; cf. 1 Pet 5:12). **15:23–29** *The apostles . . . Fare ye well*: Paul does not mention this or any formal statement of policy emerging from the Jerusalem church, even when such a reference might be expected (e.g., in discussing whether Gentile believers should eat meat sacrificed to idols; see esp. 1 Cor 8–9). His own account suggests that the Jerusalem meeting was an informal affair (Gal 2:2) and indicates that the Jerusalem leaders only requested his congregations to "remember the poor" (see Gal 2:10 and note). **15:24** *Troubled you*: the phrase is used in an identical context at Gal 5:10, 12; 6:17. *Saying, Ye . . . law*: better omitted (MS tradition). **15:31** *Consolation*: Gk. *paraklēsis*, also "exhortation"; cf. v. 32. **15:33** *The apostles*: better "those who sent them" (MS tradition). **15:34** *Notwithstanding it . . . still*: better omitted (MS tradition).

15:36–18:22 Paul's second missionary journey. 15:36–41 Paul and Barnabas separate. **15:38** *Who departed . . . work*: cf. 13:13. **15:39** *The contention . . . other*: Gal 2:11–17 suggests another possible explanation: the division could have resulted from Barnabas's support of Peter's

departed, being recommended by the brethren unto the grace of God. ⁴¹And he went through Syria and Cilicia, confirming the churches.

16 Then came he to Derbe and Lystra: and, behold, a certain disciple was there, named Timotheus, the son of a certain woman, which was a Jewess, and believed; but his father was a Greek: ²which was well reported of by the brethren that were at Lystra and Iconium. ³Him would Paul have to go forth with him; and took and circumcised him because of the Jews which were in those quarters: for they knew all that his father was a Greek. ⁴And as they went through the cities, they delivered them the decrees for to keep, that were ordained of the apostles and elders which were at Jerusalem. ⁵And so were the churches established in the faith, and increased in number daily.

⁶Now when they had gone throughout Phrygia and the region of Galatia, and were forbidden of the Holy Ghost to preach the word in Asia, ⁷after they were come to Mysia, they assayed to go into Bithynia: but the Spirit suffered them not. ⁸And they passing by Mysia came down to Troas. ⁹And a vision appeared to Paul in the night; There stood a man of Macedonia, and prayed him, saying, Come over into Macedonia, and help us. ¹⁰And after he had seen the vision, immediately we endeavoured to go into Macedonia, assuredly gathering that the Lord had called us for to preach the gospel unto them.

¹¹Therefore loosing from Troas, we came with a straight course to Samothracia, and the next day to Neapolis; ¹²and from thence to Philippi, which is the chief city of that part of Macedonia, and a colony: and we were in that city abiding certain days. ¹³And on the sabbath we went out of the city by a river side, where prayer was wont to be made; and we sat down, and spake unto the women which resorted thither. ¹⁴And a certain woman named Lydia, a seller of purple, of the city of

refusal to eat with Gentile believers (Gal 2:13), which Paul strongly denounced.   **16:1–5** Ministry in Derbe and Lystra.   **16:1** *Timotheus:* Timothy, a missionary companion of Paul and coauthor of several of his letters.   **16:3** *And circumcised him:* flatly contradicting the position on Gentile circumcision articulated by Paul in his letters (e.g., 1 Cor 7:18–19; Gal 2:3; 5:2, 6), which he claims to have held even when it engendered persecution (Gal 5:11). Luke may be mistaken, or Paul may have made an exception to his normal policy, perhaps because Timothy's mother was Jewish. (But an exception on this basis still contradicts 1 Cor 7:18–19.)   **16:4** *The decrees . . . Jerusalem:* the letter of 15:23–29.   **16:6–40** Ministry in Philippi. The church at Philippi received one of Paul's extant letters.   **16:6** *Phrygia:* a region of the province of Asia, immediately to Galatia's west.   **16:7** *Mysia:* the northernmost region of Asia, southwest of the province of Bithynia and Pontus. *The Spirit:* better to add "of Jesus" (MS tradition).   **16:8** *Troas:* a city in northwest Asia, on the Aegean Sea.   **16:9** *Macedonia:* the Roman province across the Aegean from Troas, constituting the northern portion of Greece.   **16:10** *We endeavoured:* initiating the first of several passages in Acts narrated in the first person (vv. 10–17; cf. 20:5–15; 21:1–18; 27:1–28:16). The shift in voice may suggest that Acts' author was present at the events recounted, or (more likely) that he incorporated notes, itineraries, memoirs, etc. composed by members of Paul's traveling parties. At the same time, or perhaps alternatively, it represents a stylistic device heightening the narrative's vividness at certain key points.   **16:11** *Loosing:* setting sail. *Samothracia:* Samothrace, an island in the Aegean between *Troas* and *Neapolis,* a port city near Philippi. **16:12** *Colony:* Gk. *kolōnia,* transliterating Lat. *colonia,* a Roman settlement (cf. v. 21). Since the previous century, Roman veterans had been settled there after their military service was complete.   **16:13** *Where prayer . . . made:* i.e., where Jews gathered to worship.   **16:14** *Purple:* i.e., cloth dyed purple.

Thyatira, which worshipped God, heard us: whose heart the Lord opened, that she attended unto the things which were spoken of Paul. [15]And when she was baptized, and her household, she besought us, saying, If ye have judged me to be faithful to the Lord, come into my house, and abide there. And she constrained us.

[16]And it came to pass, as we went to prayer, a certain damsel possessed with a spirit of divination met us, which brought her masters much gain by soothsaying: [17]the same followed Paul and us, and cried, saying, These men are the servants of the most high God, which shew unto us the way of salvation. [18]And this did she many days. But Paul, being grieved, turned and said to the spirit, I command thee in the name of Jesus Christ to come out of her. And he came out the same hour.

[19]And when her masters saw that the hope of their gains was gone, they caught Paul and Silas, and drew them into the marketplace unto the rulers, [20]and brought them to the magistrates, saying, These men, being Jews, do exceedingly trouble our city, [21]and teach customs, which are not lawful for us to receive, neither to observe, being Romans. [22]And the multitude rose up together against them: and the magistrates rent off their clothes, and commanded to beat them. [23]And when they had laid many stripes upon them, they cast them into prison, charging the jailor to keep them safely: [24]who, having received such a charge, thrust them into the inner prison, and made their feet fast in the stocks.

[25]And at midnight Paul and Silas prayed, and sang praises unto God: and the prisoners heard them. [26]And suddenly there was a great earthquake, so that the foundations of the prison were shaken: and immediately all the doors were opened, and every one's bands were loosed. [27]And the keeper of the prison awaking out of his sleep, and seeing the prison doors open, he drew out his sword, and would have killed himself, supposing that the prisoners had been fled. [28]But Paul cried with a loud voice, saying, Do thyself no harm: for we are all here. [29]Then he called for a light, and sprang in, and came trembling, and fell down before Paul and Silas, [30]and brought them out, and said, Sirs, what must I do to be saved? [31]And they said, Believe on the Lord Jesus Christ, and thou shalt be saved, and thy house. [32]And they spake unto him the word of the Lord, and to all that were in his house. [33]And he took them the same hour of the night, and washed their stripes; and was baptized, he and all his, straightway. [34]And when he had brought them into his house, he set meat before them, and rejoiced, believing in God with all his house.

Thyatira: a city in Asia Minor. *Which worshipped God*: i.e., she was a Gentile who worshipped YHWH.   **16:16** *A spirit of divination*: lit. "a spirit [which was] a python." Because the serpent that Apollo was said to have killed at Delphi (cf. Ovid, *Metamorphoses* 1.438–47) was called *pythōn* in Greek, his oracular priestess there was known as the *pythia*, and the Greek word had the connotations drawn out by KJV. But at the time Luke wrote, the word could also refer to an oracular ventriloquist, and so it may hint at chicanery.   **16:17** *Unto us*: better "unto you" (MS tradition).   **16:18** *I command . . . hour*: recalling Jesus' exorcisms of demons that had insight into his identity (e.g., Luke 8:27–33).   **16:19** *Marketplace*: Gk. *agora*, the public square.   **16:21** *Customs, which . . . Romans*: Rome's attitudes toward and laws regarding foreign religions were more complex than this complaint suggests.   **16:22–23** *And the multitude . . . safely*: Paul refers to this mistreatment at Phil 1:30; 1 Thess 2:2; cf. 2 Cor 11:25.   **16:23** *Safely*: securely.   **16:25–40** *And at midnight . . . departed*: Paul and Silas's miraculous escape recalls and outdoes Peter's escape from Herod's jail (12:4–19): while Peter's ended with his jailors' execution (12:19), Paul saves his suicidal jailor's

³⁵And when it was day, the magistrates sent the serjeants, saying, Let those men go. ³⁶And the keeper of the prison told this saying to Paul, The magistrates have sent to let you go: now therefore depart, and go in peace. ³⁷But Paul said unto them, They have beaten us openly uncondemned, being Romans, and have cast us into prison; and now do they thrust us out privily? nay verily; but let them come themselves and fetch us out. ³⁸And the serjeants told these words unto the magistrates: and they feared, when they heard that they were Romans. ³⁹And they came and besought them, and brought them out, and desired them to depart out of the city. ⁴⁰And they went out of the prison, and entered into the house of Lydia: and when they had seen the brethren, they comforted them, and departed.

17 Now when they had passed through Amphipolis and Apollonia, they came to Thessalonica, where was a synagogue of the Jews: ²and Paul, as his manner was, went in unto them, and three sabbath days reasoned with them out of the scriptures, ³opening and alleging, that Christ must needs have suffered, and risen again from the dead; and that this Jesus, whom I preach unto you, is Christ. ⁴And some of them believed, and consorted with Paul and Silas; and of the devout Greeks a great multitude, and of the chief women not a few. ⁵But the Jews which believed not, moved with envy, took unto them certain lewd fellows of the baser sort, and gathered a company, and set all the city on an uproar, and assaulted the house of Jason, and sought to bring them out to the people. ⁶And when they found them not, they drew Jason and certain brethren unto the rulers of the city, crying, These that have turned the world upside down are come hither also; ⁷whom Jason hath received: and these all do contrary to the decrees of Cæsar, saying that there is another king, one Jesus. ⁸And they troubled the people and the rulers of the city, when they heard these things. ⁹And when they had taken security of Jason, and of the other, they let them go.

¹⁰And the brethren immediately sent away Paul and Silas by night unto Berea: who coming thither went into the synagogue of the Jews. ¹¹These were more noble than those in Thessalonica, in that they received the word with all readiness of

---

life by facilitating his conversion (16:27–34); while Peter's escape frustrates Herod (12:19), Paul's causes the Philippian magistrates to repent for mistreating him and his companions (16:37–39). **16:35** *Serjeants*: lit. "rod bearers" (Lat. *lictors*), the Roman officials responsible for enforcing magistrates' judgments. **16:37** *Romans*: i.e., Roman citizens, like many of Philippi's inhabitants (v. 21). At this time, only a fraction of the population Rome controlled were citizens, whom by law imperial magistrates could not beat, especially before guilt had been determined by means of a trial (hence their fear in v. 38). In the extant letters Paul never claims citizenship, and he says he received Roman beatings no less than three times (2 Cor 11:25 and note); if he was a citizen, then as Luke says, then he must often have chosen not to claim the privileges of citizenship (cf. 1 Cor 9:12). **17:1–15** Ministry in Thessalonica and Berea. Thessalonica was Macedonia's leading city. The church there received two of Paul's extant letters (although some scholars believe 2 Thessalonians to be pseudepigraphical). 1 Thess 1:5–2:16 discusses Paul's ministry in this city. **17:1** *Amphipolis and Apollonia*: on the road from Philippi to *Thessalonica*. **17:3** *Christ*: i.e., "the Christ" (twice in this verse), the anointed one or messiah. **17:5** *The Jews . . . people*: Paul may refer to this event in 1 Thess 2:14–16. *Which believed not*: better omitted (MS tradition). *Lewd*: lit. "wicked." *Gathered a company*: i.e., formed a mob. *Jason* had apparently hosted Paul and Silas (v. 7). **17:6** *Turned the world upside down*: the Greek phrase has political connotations: "destabilized the world" or "caused disturbances everywhere." **17:9** *Security*: bail. **17:10** *Berea*: well southwest of Thessalonica.

mind, and searched the scriptures daily, whether those things were so. ¹²Therefore many of them believed; also of honourable women which were Greeks, and of men, not a few. ¹³But when the Jews of Thessalonica had knowledge that the word of God was preached of Paul at Berea, they came thither also, and stirred up the people. ¹⁴And then immediately the brethren sent away Paul to go as it were to the sea: but Silas and Timotheus abode there still. ¹⁵And they that conducted Paul brought him unto Athens: and receiving a commandment unto Silas and Timotheus for to come to him with all speed, they departed.

¹⁶Now while Paul waited for them at Athens, his spirit was stirred in him, when he saw the city wholly given to idolatry. ¹⁷Therefore disputed he in the synagogue with the Jews, and with the devout persons, and in the market daily with them that met with him. ¹⁸Then certain philosophers of the Epicureans, and of the Stoicks, encountered him. And some said, What will this babbler say? other some, He seemeth to be a setter forth of strange gods: because he preached unto them Jesus, and the resurrection. ¹⁹And they took him, and brought him unto Areopagus, saying, May we know what this new doctrine, whereof thou speakest, is? ²⁰For thou bringest certain strange things to our ears: we would know therefore what these things mean. ²¹(For all the Athenians and strangers which were there spent their time in nothing else, but either to tell, or to hear some new thing.)

²²Then Paul stood in the midst of Mars' hill, and said, Ye men of Athens, I perceive that in all things ye are too superstitious. ²³For as I passed by, and beheld your devotions, I found an altar with this inscription, To the unknown god. Whom therefore ye ignorantly worship, him declare I unto you. ²⁴God that made

---

17:13 *People*: lit. "crowds"; cf. v. 5 (KJV "company").   **17:14** *As it were to*: better "as far as" (MS tradition). Paul and his companions presumably sailed southward along the Aegean coast to Athens, in Achaia. *But Silas . . . still*: cf. 1 Thess 3:1–2.   **17:16–34** Ministry in Athens. Athens was the cultural center of classical Greece, and Luke pays (ironic) homage to its great artistic (v. 16, see note), philosophical (vv. 18–21), and (less derisively) literary (v. 28) traditions.   **17:16** *His spirit was stirred*: i.e., to anger. *Wholly given to idolatry*: lit. "with idols throughout."   **17:17** *Devout persons*: i.e., God-fearing Gentiles. *Market*: Gk. *agora*, public square. *Them that met with him*: those happening upon him.   **17:18** *Epicureans, Stoicks*: two schools of Hellenistic philosophy associated with Athens. *Encountered*: or "conversed with." *Babbler*: lit. "seed gatherer," referring to one who haphazardly procures information or ideas from other sources and unintelligently combines them to produce a mediocre discourse. *Strange gods*: lit. "foreign deities" (Gk. *xenōn daimoniōn*), echoing Plato's *Apology*. (One of the accusations made against Socrates is that he "believes not in the gods in which the city believes, but in other strange deities [Gk. *daimonia kaina*]," 24b.) *The resurrection*: they presumably mistake Gk. *anastasis* ("resurrection") for a goddess, perhaps understanding her to be Jesus' mate.   **17:19** *Areopagus*: either "hill of Ares" (or "Mars' hill," as in v. 22), an area where orators declaimed, or the city's governing council named after this hill (cf. v. 34 and note).   **17:21** *Strangers*: Gk. *xenoi*, "visitors" or "resident aliens."   **17:22** *Too superstitious*: the Greek word contains the root *-daimon*, "god" (cf. v. 18); better "very reverent of deities," or simply "very religious."   **17:23** *Devotions*: Gk. *sebasmata*, "objects of worship"; cf. 2 Thess 2:4 ("that is worshipped"). *To the unknown god*: in the fourth century Jerome noted that "the altar's inscription was not, as Paul asserted, 'to the unknown god,' but 'to the gods of Asia, Europe, and Africa, gods unknown and foreign'" (*Commentary on Titus* 1.12). Other ancient sources attest that Athens had altars to "unknown deities," but it is unclear whether any was devoted to a single unknown god. *Declare I*: Gk. *katangellō*; KJV rendered its nominal form "preached" in v. 18. His earlier presentation of the gospel having proven unintelligible, Paul now couches his message in the idiom of Greek polytheism.

the world and all things therein, seeing that he is Lord of heaven and earth, dwelleth not in temples made with hands; ²⁵neither is worshipped with men's hands, as though he needed any thing, seeing he giveth to all life, and breath, and all things; ²⁶and hath made of one blood all nations of men for to dwell on all the face of the earth, and hath determined the times before appointed, and the bounds of their habitation; ²⁷that they should seek the Lord, if haply they might feel after him, and find him, though he be not far from every one of us: ²⁸for in him we live, and move, and have our being; as certain also of your own poets have said, For we are also his offspring. ²⁹Forasmuch then as we are the offspring of God, we ought not to think that the Godhead is like unto gold, or silver, or stone, graven by art and man's device. ³⁰And the times of this ignorance God winked at; but now commandeth all men every where to repent: ³¹because he hath appointed a day, in the which he will judge the world in righteousness by that man whom he hath ordained; whereof he hath given assurance unto all men, in that he hath raised him from the dead.

³²And when they heard of the resurrection of the dead, some mocked: and others said, We will hear thee again of this matter. ³³So Paul departed from among them. ³⁴Howbeit certain men clave unto him, and believed: among the which was Dionysius the Areopagite, and a woman named Damaris, and others with them.

18 After these things Paul departed from Athens, and came to Corinth; ²and found a certain Jew named Aquila, born in Pontus, lately come from Italy, with his wife Priscilla; (because that Claudius had commanded all Jews to depart

---

17:24 *Dwelleth not . . . hands*: cf. 7:48. The argument of vv. 24–27 also recalls a famous passage from the Roman Stoic philosopher Seneca: "Our hands need not be lifted toward heaven, nor need the keeper of a temple let us approach the ear of an idol, as if thus we would have a better chance of being heard. God is near you, is with you, is within you" (*Epistle* 41.1). **17:25** *Neither is worshipped . . . things*: recalling such biblical passages as Ps 50:8–13; 2 Macc 14:35. **17:26** *Blood*: better omitted (MS tradition), yielding "of one" or "of one man." *Hath determined . . . habitation*: perhaps referring to God's assignment of discrete geographical regions to particular peoples (Deut 32:8) and to the divinely determined times of their flourishing (e.g., Dan 11:2–45); alternatively, to the natural world, the earth being divided into different zones (some habitable and some not) and the year into different seasons (KJV "times"; cf. 14:17). **17:27** *The Lord*: better "God" (MS tradition). **17:28** *For we . . . offspring*: a quotation from the Stoic poet Aratus (*Phaenomena* 5), who flourished in the third century B.C.E. and studied in Athens. **17:29** *We ought not . . . device*: such an attitude is common in ancient Jewish literature (e.g., Isa 40:18–20; Wis 13:10), but is found in pagan writings as well (see 17:24 note). *Godhead*: lit. "deity." **17:30** *Winked at*: overlooked; cf. 14:16–17 and note. **17:31** *That man . . . dead*: Paul reintroduces Jesus and resurrection, which the Athenians had earlier misunderstood (v. 18 and note). **17:32** *When they . . . mocked*: bodily resurrection was a Jewish doctrine not easily compatible with Greco-Roman philosophical traditions, which tended to conceive of the afterlife in terms of a disembodied soul or, like the Epicureans, to reject it altogether. Analogous contempt for the idea of bodily resurrection among Gentile believers in Corinth may have motivated Paul's elaborate argument in 1 Cor 15. **17:34** *Areopagite*: i.e., a member of the Areopagus, Athens' governing council (see v. 19 note). Dionysius is said by later Christian writers to have been Athens' first bishop. Several hundred years after Acts, a Neoplatonic Christian theologian wrote a number of important treatises in his name. **18:1–17** Ministry in Corinth. The Corinthian church received two of Paul's extant letters. **18:1** *Corinth*: in the Peloponnese, west of Athens, Corinth was the center of Roman government in Achaia. **18:2** *Aquila, born . . . Priscilla*: Paul mentions this couple fondly at Rom 16:3–4; cf. 1 Cor 16:19; 2 Tim 4:19. *Claudius had commanded . . . Rome*: according to Suetonius, Claudius issued an edict (probably in 49 C.E.) to

from Rome:) and came unto them. ³And because he was of the same craft, he abode with them, and wrought: for by their occupation they were tentmakers. ⁴And he reasoned in the synagogue every sabbath, and persuaded the Jews and the Greeks. ⁵And when Silas and Timotheus were come from Macedonia, Paul was pressed in the spirit, and testified to the Jews that Jesus was Christ. ⁶And when they opposed themselves, and blasphemed, he shook his raiment, and said unto them, Your blood be upon your own heads; I am clean: from henceforth I will go unto the Gentiles.

⁷And he departed thence, and entered into a certain man's house, named Justus, one that worshipped God, whose house joined hard to the synagogue. ⁸And Crispus, the chief ruler of the synagogue, believed on the Lord with all his house; and many of the Corinthians hearing believed, and were baptized. ⁹Then spake the Lord to Paul in the night by a vision, Be not afraid, but speak, and hold not thy peace: ¹⁰for I am with thee, and no man shall set on thee to hurt thee: for I have much people in this city. ¹¹And he continued there a year and six months, teaching the word of God among them.

¹²And when Gallio was the deputy of Achaia, the Jews made insurrection with one accord against Paul, and brought him to the judgment seat, ¹³saying, This fellow persuadeth men to worship God contrary to the law. ¹⁴And when Paul was now about to open his mouth, Gallio said unto the Jews, If it were a matter of wrong or wicked lewdness, O ye Jews, reason would that I should bear with you: ¹⁵but if it be a question of words and names, and of your law, look ye to it; for I will be no judge of such matters. ¹⁶And he drave them from the judgment seat. ¹⁷Then all the Greeks took Sosthenes, the chief ruler of the synagogue, and beat him before the judgment seat. And Gallio cared for none of those things.

¹⁸And Paul after this tarried there yet a good while, and then took his leave of the brethren, and sailed thence into Syria, and with him Priscilla and Aquila; having shorn his head in Cenchrea: for he had a vow. ¹⁹And he came to Ephesus, and left them there: but he himself entered into the synagogue, and reasoned

---

this effect because the Jews were "constantly making disturbances at the instigation of Chrestus" (*Life of Claudius* 25, trans. Rolfe)—perhaps a reference to conflict between Jesus-believing and other Roman Jews about whether Jesus was "the Christ" (Gk. *Christos*, which the Roman historian may have mistaken for a similar-sounding common name).   **18:3** *Wrought*: worked; cf. 1 Cor 4:12; 1 Thess 2:9. **18:5** *Pressed in the spirit*: better "was occupied with the word" (MS tradition).   **18:6** *Blasphemed*: reviled or cursed. *Shook his raiment*: cf. Neh 5:13 and note. *Your blood . . . heads*: cf. 2 Sam 1:16; Ezek 33:4; Matt 27:25; etc.   **18:7** *Justus*: better "Titius Justus" (MS tradition).   **18:8** *Crispus*: probably mentioned at 1 Cor 1:14. He apparently resigned or was forced out of office on account of his faith in Christ (v. 17; cf. John 9:22).   **18:10** *I am with thee*: echoing God's assurances to numerous biblical heroes, including Jacob (Gen 31:3, 5), Moses (Exod 3:12), and Joshua (Josh 1:5).   **18:12** *Gallio*: the elder brother of Seneca (quoted at 17:24 note), proconsul in Achaia, 51–52 C.E. All other dates in Paul's career, including those of his letters, are estimated in relation to this fixed point. *Made insurrection*: or simply "rose up."   **18:14** *Wrong*: i.e., crime. *Lewdness*: villainy.   **18:17** *All the Greeks*: better "they all" (MS tradition), suggesting that the Jewish delegation led by Sosthenes became enraged at him because the suit had failed. *Cared for none of those things*: i.e., he didn't care.   **18:18–22** Return to Antioch via Ephesus.   **18:18** *Cenchrea*: a port near Corinth. *Having shorn . . . vow*: a Nazarite vow (cf. Num 6:2–21), which entailed letting one's hair grow, ceremonially cutting it, and making a concluding sacrifice. This sacrifice explains Paul's brief stop in Jerusalem (see v. 22 note).   **18:19** *Ephesus*: the leading city of the Roman province of Asia. In Paul's time it was an Aegean port on the Cayster River. (After the

with the Jews. ²⁰When they desired him to tarry longer time with them, he consented not; ²¹but bade them farewell, saying, I must by all means keep this feast that cometh in Jerusalem: but I will return again unto you, if God will. And he sailed from Ephesus. ²²And when he had landed at Cæsarea, and gone up, and saluted the church, he went down to Antioch.

²³And after he had spent some time there, he departed, and went over all the country of Galatia and Phrygia in order, strengthening all the disciples. ²⁴And a certain Jew named Apollos, born at Alexandria, an eloquent man, and mighty in the scriptures, came to Ephesus. ²⁵This man was instructed in the way of the Lord; and being fervent in the spirit, he spake and taught diligently the things of the Lord, knowing only the baptism of John. ²⁶And he began to speak boldly in the synagogue: whom when Aquila and Priscilla had heard, they took him unto them, and expounded unto him the way of God more perfectly. ²⁷And when he was disposed to pass into Achaia, the brethren wrote, exhorting the disciples to receive him: who, when he was come, helped them much which had believed through grace: ²⁸for he mightily convinced the Jews, and that publickly, shewing by the scriptures that Jesus was Christ.

19 And it came to pass, that, while Apollos was at Corinth, Paul having passed through the upper coasts came to Ephesus: and finding certain disciples, ²he said unto them, Have ye received the Holy Ghost since ye believed? And they said unto him, We have not so much as heard whether there be any Holy Ghost. ³And he said unto them, Unto what then were ye baptized? And they said, Unto John's baptism. ⁴Then said Paul, John verily baptized with the baptism of repentance, saying unto the people, that they should believe on him which should come after him, that is, on Christ Jesus. ⁵When they heard this, they were baptized in the name of the Lord Jesus. ⁶And when Paul had laid his hands upon them, the Holy Ghost came on them; and they spake with tongues, and prophesied. ⁷And all the men were about twelve.

---

port silted up, it was abandoned.)   **18:21** *I must . . . but*: better omitted (MS tradition) as a scribal interpolation (based on 20:16) to explain Paul's haste.   **18:22** *Cæsarea*: the port city nearest Jerusalem, which is located on a high ridge. "To go up to" and "to go down from Jerusalem" are such common expressions (cf. Luke 2:42; 18:31; 19:28) that the city's name can be omitted, as here (cf. 8:5).

18:23–20:38 Paul's third missionary journey. 18:23–28 Apollos in Ephesus and Corinth. **18:24** *Alexandria*: in Egypt; the center of Hellenistic literary culture, it had a large Jewish population. *Apollos*, like his contemporary Philo, was one of many learned Jews who were born there. **18:25** *Diligently*: Gk. *akribōs*, "accurately"; also in v. 26 (KJV "perfectly"). *The things of the Lord*: better "the things of Jesus" (MS tradition). Perhaps he knew Jesus only as a disciple of John. **18:26** *Aquila and Priscilla*: the names are better reversed (MS tradition), giving Aquila's wife Priscilla prominence. **18:28** *Shewing by . . . Christ*: perhaps referring to Apollos's skills as an allegorical exegete (cf. v. 24, "mighty in the scriptures"). **19:1–41** Paul's ministry in Ephesus. **19:1** *While Apollos . . . Corinth*: cf. 1 Cor 3:6. *Upper coasts*: interior. *Certain disciples*: i.e., of John the Baptist (v. 3), to whom Apollos also had been devoted (18:25). In both episodes, Luke tendentiously implies they were not so much members of a rival Jewish sect as marginal Christians. If the movement John the Baptist started was as widespread and long-lasting as Acts indicates, and especially if Jesus-believing missionaries were concerned to evangelize its adherents, the gospels' anxiety to demonstrate John's subservience to Jesus is easy to understand.   **19:4** *John verily . . . after him*: cf. Luke 3:3, 15–16.

⁸And he went into the synagogue, and spake boldly for the space of three months, disputing and persuading the things concerning the kingdom of God. ⁹But when divers were hardened, and believed not, but spake evil of that way before the multitude, he departed from them, and separated the disciples, disputing daily in the school of one Tyrannus. ¹⁰And this continued by the space of two years; so that all they which dwelt in Asia heard the word of the Lord Jesus, both Jews and Greeks. ¹¹And God wrought special miracles by the hands of Paul: ¹²so that from his body were brought unto the sick handkerchiefs or aprons, and the diseases departed from them, and the evil spirits went out of them.

¹³Then certain of the vagabond Jews, exorcists, took upon them to call over them which had evil spirits the name of the Lord Jesus, saying, We adjure you by Jesus whom Paul preacheth. ¹⁴And there were seven sons of one Sceva, a Jew, and chief of the priests, which did so. ¹⁵And the evil spirit answered and said, Jesus I know, and Paul I know; but who are ye? ¹⁶And the man in whom the evil spirit was leaped on them, and overcame them, and prevailed against them, so that they fled out of that house naked and wounded. ¹⁷And this was known to all the Jews and Greeks also dwelling at Ephesus; and fear fell on them all, and the name of the Lord Jesus was magnified. ¹⁸And many that believed came, and confessed, and shewed their deeds. ¹⁹Many of them also which used curious arts brought their books together, and burned them before all men: and they counted the price of them, and found it fifty thousand pieces of silver. ²⁰So mightily grew the word of God and prevailed.

²¹After these things were ended, Paul purposed in the spirit, when he had passed through Macedonia and Achaia, to go to Jerusalem, saying, After I have been there, I must also see Rome. ²²So he sent into Macedonia two of them that ministered unto him, Timotheus and Erastus; but he himself stayed in Asia for a season.

²³And the same time there arose no small stir about that way. ²⁴For a certain man named Demetrius, a silversmith, which made silver shrines for Diana, brought no small gain unto the craftsmen; ²⁵whom he called together with the workmen of like occupation, and said, Sirs, ye know that by this craft we have our wealth. ²⁶Moreover ye see and hear, that not alone at Ephesus, but almost throughout all Asia, this Paul hath persuaded and turned away much people, saying that they be no gods, which are made with hands: ²⁷so that not only this our craft is in danger

---

19:9 *School*: lecture hall; Paul is thus presented as an itinerant philosopher, a well-known figure in the Greco-Roman world. **19:11** *Miracles*: lit. "powers." **19:12** *From his body . . . of them*: see 5:15 note. **19:13** *Vagabond Jews, exorcists*: itinerant Jewish exorcists. *To call . . . Jesus*: cf. Luke 9:49–50. **19:14** *Chief of the priests*: Gk. *archiereus*; possibly the Jewish high priest, but there was none named *Sceva*. Since the term can also refer to a chief priest in the imperial cult (formalized adulation of the Roman emperor sponsored by provincial assemblies in the Greek east), Luke may be representing Sceva and his sons as apostates who embraced pagan worship. **19:16** *Overcame*: lit. "lorded over," recalling their failed invocation of "the Lord Jesus" (v. 13). **19:19** *Curious arts*: sorcery. **19:22** *Erastus*: cf. Rom 16:23; 2 Tim 4:20. **19:24** *Diana*: Gk. *Artemis*; KJV gives the Roman equivalent. The Ephesian temple of Artemis was one of the wonders of the ancient world. Some speculate that the *silver shrines* were miniature replicas of it. *Gain*: lit. "business." **19:26** *Not alone . . . hands*: this exaggerated complaint is echoed in Pliny's later concern about Christianity's proliferation (*Epistle* 10.96, ca. 110 C.E.; Appendix, pp. 987–89).

to be set at nought; but also that the temple of the great goddess Diana should be despised, and her magnificence should be destroyed, whom all Asia and the world worshippeth.

²⁸And when they heard these sayings, they were full of wrath, and cried out, saying, Great is Diana of the Ephesians. ²⁹And the whole city was filled with confusion: and having caught Gaius and Aristarchus, men of Macedonia, Paul's companions in travel, they rushed with one accord into the theatre. ³⁰And when Paul would have entered in unto the people, the disciples suffered him not. ³¹And certain of the chief of Asia, which were his friends, sent unto him, desiring him that he would not adventure himself into the theatre. ³²Some therefore cried one thing, and some another: for the assembly was confused; and the more part knew not wherefore they were come together. ³³And they drew Alexander out of the multitude, the Jews putting him forward. And Alexander beckoned with the hand, and would have made his defence unto the people. ³⁴But when they knew that he was a Jew, all with one voice about the space of two hours cried out, Great is Diana of the Ephesians. ³⁵And when the townclerk had appeased the people, he said, Ye men of Ephesus, what man is there that knoweth not how that the city of the Ephesians is a worshipper of the great goddess Diana, and of the image which fell down from Jupiter? ³⁶Seeing then that these things cannot be spoken against, ye ought to be quiet, and to do nothing rashly. ³⁷For ye have brought hither these men, which are neither robbers of churches, nor yet blasphemers of your goddess. ³⁸Wherefore if Demetrius, and the craftsmen which are with him, have a matter against any man, the law is open, and there are deputies: let them implead one another. ³⁹But if ye inquire any thing concerning other matters, it shall be determined in a lawful assembly. ⁴⁰For we are in danger to be called in question for this day's uproar, there being no cause whereby we may give an account of this concourse. ⁴¹And when he had thus spoken, he dismissed the assembly.

20 And after the uproar was ceased, Paul called unto him the disciples, and embraced them, and departed for to go into Macedonia. ²And when he had gone over those parts, and had given them much exhortation, he came into

---

19:27 *Be set at nought*: "come into disrepute" (RSV). *Her magnificence . . . destroyed*: better "she may even be deposed from her magnificence" (MS tradition; RSV).   **19:29** *Gaius and Aristarchus*: Paul mentions Gaius at Rom 16:23; 1 Cor 1:14; Aristarchus at Col 4:10; Phlm 24.   **19:31** *The chief of Asia*: Gk. *Asiarchoi*, either priests in the Roman imperial cult (the chief priests of v. 14; see note) or representatives in Asia's provincial assembly, which convened at Ephesus.   **19:33** *And they . . . forward*: the first part of the verse is better rendered "and some from the multitude instructed Alexander," but it is unclear who they were, what they told him, why the Jews wanted him to speak, or even whom he was going to defend (Paul? the Jewish community at Ephesus, by distinguishing it from the itinerant Paul and his companions?). Luke's baffling account reflects the situation's confusion.   **19:35** *Worshipper*: lit. "temple keeper." *The image . . . Jupiter*: lit. "that which fell from Zeus," presumably a statue (hence KJV "image") constructed from a meteorite. Compare Euripides' references to the image of Artemis fallen from heaven at Tauris (*Iphigenia in Tauris* 87–88, 1384–85).   **19:37** *Churches*: an anachronistic translation. (The Greek word refers to pagan temples.) *Your goddess*: better "our goddess" (MS tradition).   **19:38** *The law is open*: "courts are in session" (Fitzmyer). *Deputies*: proconsuls (cf. 13:7 and note), who had judicial authority. *Implead*: Gk. *enkaleō*, "bring charges against" (RSV).   **19:40** *Called in question*: Gk. *enkaleō*, "charged" (RSV; cf. v. 38).   **20:1–16** Ministry in Troas and journey to Miletus.   **20:1** *And embraced them, and departed*: better "and having exhorted them and said his good-byes, he departed" (MS tradition; our translation).

Greece, [3]and there abode three months. And when the Jews laid wait for him, as he was about to sail into Syria, he purposed to return through Macedonia. [4]And there accompanied him into Asia Sopater of Berea; and of the Thessalonians, Aristarchus and Secundus; and Gaius of Derbe, and Timotheus; and of Asia, Tychicus and Trophimus. [5]These going before tarried for us at Troas. [6]And we sailed away from Philippi after the days of unleavened bread, and came unto them to Troas in five days; where we abode seven days.

[7]And upon the first day of the week, when the disciples came together to break bread, Paul preached unto them, ready to depart on the morrow; and continued his speech until midnight. [8]And there were many lights in the upper chamber, where they were gathered together. [9]And there sat in a window a certain young man named Eutychus, being fallen into a deep sleep: and as Paul was long preaching, he sunk down with sleep, and fell down from the third loft, and was taken up dead. [10]And Paul went down, and fell on him, and embracing him said, Trouble not yourselves; for his life is in him. [11]When he therefore was come up again, and had broken bread, and eaten, and talked a long while, even till break of day, so he departed. [12]And they brought the young man alive, and were not a little comforted.

[13]And we went before to ship, and sailed unto Assos, there intending to take in Paul: for so had he appointed, minding himself to go afoot. [14]And when he met with us at Assos, we took him in, and came to Mitylene. [15]And we sailed thence, and came the next day over against Chios; and the next day we arrived at Samos, and tarried at Trogyllium; and the next day we came to Miletus. [16]For Paul had determined to sail by Ephesus, because he would not spend the time in Asia: for he hasted, if it were possible for him, to be at Jerusalem the day of Pentecost.

[17]And from Miletus he sent to Ephesus, and called the elders of the church. [18]And when they were come to him, he said unto them, Ye know, from the first day that I came into Asia, after what manner I have been with you at all seasons, [19]serving the Lord with all humility of mind, and with many tears, and temptations, which befell me by the lying in wait of the Jews: [20]and how I kept back nothing that was profitable unto you, but have shewed you, and have taught you

---

20:4 *Into Asia*: better omitted (MS tradition). *Sopater of Berea*: better to add "the son of Pyrrhus" (MS tradition). *Gaius of Derbe*: i.e., of Asia Minor; different from Gaius of Macedonia (19:29). *Tychicus*: cf. Eph 6:21; Col 4:7; 2 Tim 4:12; Titus 3:12. *Trophimus*: cf. 2 Tim 4:20. **20:6** *Days of unleavened bread*: Passover. **20:7–12** *And upon the first day . . . comforted*: as Dennis MacDonald has argued (see Appendix, pp. 1235–44), this episode, which seems to poke fun at Paul's long-windedness, may also rewrite Homer's story of Elpenor (*Odyssey* 10.552–60; 11.58–80; 12.8–15). Not only do the narrative details coincide, but while Elpenor is characteristically unlucky (11.76, 80), Eutychus's name means "lucky." **20:7** *Upon the first day . . . bread*: perhaps an early reference to a Sunday eucharistic celebration. *The disciples*: better "we" (MS tradition); also in v. 8 (KJV "they"). **20:9** *Loft*: story. **20:10** *Fell on him, and embracing him*: recalling the resurrections performed by Elijah (1 Kgs 17:21–22) and Elisha (2 Kgs 4:34–35). **20:13** *Assos*: an Aegean port near Troas. **20:14** *Mitylene*: a city on the island of Lesbos, just south of Assos. **20:15** *Chios, Samos*: islands in the eastern Aegean. *And tarried at Trogyllium*: better omitted (MS tradition). *Miletus*: an Aegean port city south of Ephesus. **20:16** *Pentecost*: see 2:1 note. **20:17–38** Paul addresses the Ephesian elders. Farewell speeches such as this are common in biblical and other ancient literature; compare Jacob's (Gen 49), Joshua's (Josh 23–24), Jesus' (John 14–17), etc. **20:17** *Elders*: cf. 14:23 and note. Later they are called "overseers" or "bishops" (see

publickly, and from house to house, ²¹testifying both to the Jews, and also to the Greeks, repentance toward God, and faith toward our Lord Jesus Christ. ²²And now, behold, I go bound in the spirit unto Jerusalem, not knowing the things that shall befall me there: ²³save that the Holy Ghost witnesseth in every city, saying that bonds and afflictions abide me. ²⁴But none of these things move me, neither count I my life dear unto myself, so that I might finish my course with joy, and the ministry, which I have received of the Lord Jesus, to testify the gospel of the grace of God.

²⁵And now, behold, I know that ye all, among whom I have gone preaching the kingdom of God, shall see my face no more. ²⁶Wherefore I take you to record this day, that I am pure from the blood of all men. ²⁷For I have not shunned to declare unto you all the counsel of God. ²⁸Take heed therefore unto yourselves, and to all the flock, over the which the Holy Ghost hath made you overseers, to feed the church of God, which he hath purchased with his own blood. ²⁹For I know this, that after my departing shall grievous wolves enter in among you, not sparing the flock. ³⁰Also of your own selves shall men arise, speaking perverse things, to draw away disciples after them. ³¹Therefore watch, and remember, that by the space of three years I ceased not to warn every one night and day with tears. ³²And now, brethren, I commend you to God, and to the word of his grace, which is able to build you up, and to give you an inheritance among all them which are sanctified. ³³I have coveted no man's silver, or gold, or apparel. ³⁴Yea, ye your-selves know, that these hands have ministered unto my necessities, and to them that were with me. ³⁵I have shewed you all things, how that so labouring ye ought to support the weak, and to remember the words of the Lord Jesus, how he said, It is more blessed to give than to receive.

³⁶And when he had thus spoken, he kneeled down, and prayed with them all. ³⁷And they all wept sore, and fell on Paul's neck, and kissed him, ³⁸sorrowing most of all for the words which he spake, that they should see his face no more. And they accompanied him unto the ship.

---

v. 28 and note). **20:24** *But none . . . myself*: a better reading of the MS tradition yields "but I do not count my life of any value to myself" (NRSV), though the Greek is obscure. *With joy*: better omitted (MS tradition). **20:26** *I am . . . men*: cf. 18:6. **20:27** *I have . . . you*: paralleling v. 20. **20:28** *Overseers*: Gk. *episkopoi*, usually "bishops" in KJV (cf. 1:20 and note; Phil 1:1 and note; etc.). The Pastoral Epistles seem to distinguish "elder" (1 Tim 4:14 and note; 5:17–19; Titus 1:5–6; cf. Acts 14:23 and note), "bishop" (1 Tim 3:1–7; Titus 1:7–9), and "deacon" (1 Tim 3:8–13) as different offices, but here the first two are conflated (cf. v. 17). KJV resolves the inconsistency by translating *episkopoi* as if it referred to a function rather than to a position. That may be appropriate in this verse, but in any case it is clear that the words translated "bishop," "elder," and "deacon" mean different things to different NT writers at different stages in the church's development. *Purchased*: or "acquired." **20:29** *Grievous*: or "fierce." **20:30** *Of your own selves . . . them*: cf. Luke 21:8. If the Pastoral Epistles are pseudepigraphical compositions countering dubious invocations of the deceased apostle's authority in support of ideas and practices that their later author(s) found objectionable, they may illuminate the Lukan Paul's vague reference to perversion in Pauline communities that emerged after the apostle's death. See, e.g., 1 Tim 4:1–3 and notes. **20:34** *These hands . . . me*: see 18:3 and note. **20:35** *It is . . . receive*: not found in the Gospels.

21 And it came to pass, that after we were gotten from them, and had launched, we came with a straight course unto Coos, and the day following unto Rhodes, and from thence unto Patara: ²and finding a ship sailing over unto Phenicia, we went aboard, and set forth. ³Now when we had discovered Cyprus, we left it on the left hand, and sailed into Syria, and landed at Tyre: for there the ship was to unlade her burden. ⁴And finding disciples, we tarried there seven days: who said to Paul through the Spirit, that he should not go up to Jerusalem. ⁵And when we had accomplished those days, we departed and went our way; and they all brought us on our way, with wives and children, till we were out of the city: and we kneeled down on the shore, and prayed. ⁶And when we had taken our leave one of another, we took ship; and they returned home again.

⁷And when we had finished our course from Tyre, we came to Ptolemais, and saluted the brethren, and abode with them one day. ⁸And the next day we that were of Paul's company departed, and came unto Cæsarea: and we entered into the house of Philip the evangelist, which was one of the seven; and abode with him. ⁹And the same man had four daughters, virgins, which did prophesy. ¹⁰And as we tarried there many days, there came down from Judæa a certain prophet, named Agabus. ¹¹And when he was come unto us, he took Paul's girdle, and bound his own hands and feet, and said, Thus saith the Holy Ghost, So shall the Jews at Jerusalem bind the man that owneth this girdle, and shall deliver him into the hands of the Gentiles. ¹²And when we heard these things, both we, and they of that place, besought him not to go up to Jerusalem. ¹³Then Paul answered, What mean ye to weep and to break mine heart? for I am ready not to be bound only, but also to die at Jerusalem for the name of the Lord Jesus. ¹⁴And when he would not be persuaded, we ceased, saying, The will of the Lord be done.

¹⁵And after those days we took up our carriages, and went up to Jerusalem. ¹⁶There went with us also certain of the disciples of Cæsarea, and brought with them one Mnason of Cyprus, an old disciple, with whom we should lodge. ¹⁷And when we were come to Jerusalem, the brethren received us gladly. ¹⁸And the day following Paul went in with us unto James; and all the elders were present. ¹⁹And when he had saluted them, he declared particularly what things God had wrought among the Gentiles by his ministry. ²⁰And when they heard it, they glorified the Lord, and said unto him, Thou seest, brother, how many thousands of Jews there are which believe; and they are all zealous of the law: ²¹and they are informed of thee, that thou teachest all the Jews which are among the Gentiles to forsake Moses, saying that they ought not to circumcise their children, neither to walk after the customs. ²²What is it therefore? the multitude must needs come

---

21:1–23:22 Paul in Jerusalem. 21:1–16 Journey to Jerusalem. Mirroring Jesus' final journey, Paul's also features predictions of the persecution he will suffer upon arrival. **21:1** *Unto Coos . . . Patara*: Cos and Rhodes are islands in the southern Aegean; *Patara* was a city on the southern coast of the Roman province Lycia, in Asia Minor. **21:7** *Ptolemais*: a port city somewhat south of Tyre. **21:8** *That were of Paul's company*: better omitted (MS tradition). *Unto Cæsarea . . . seven*: cf. 6:5; 8:40. **21:10** *Agabus*: cf. 11:27–28. **21:11** *So shall . . . Gentiles*: echoing Luke 18:32, one of Jesus' passion predictions. **21:14** *The will . . . done*: cf. Luke 22:42. **21:15–26** Paul visits the church at Jerusalem. **21:15** *Took up our carriages*: packed. **21:16** *Old disciple*: i.e., early disciple. **21:22** *The multitude . . .*

together: for they will hear that thou art come. [23]Do therefore this that we say to thee: We have four men which have a vow on them; [24]them take, and purify thyself with them, and be at charges with them, that they may shave their heads: and all may know that those things, whereof they were informed concerning thee, are nothing; but that thou thyself also walkest orderly, and keepest the law. [25]As touching the Gentiles which believe, we have written and concluded that they observe no such thing, save only that they keep themselves from things offered to idols, and from blood, and from strangled, and from fornication. [26]Then Paul took the men, and the next day purifying himself with them entered into the temple, to signify the accomplishment of the days of purification, until that an offering should be offered for every one of them.

[27]And when the seven days were almost ended, the Jews which were of Asia, when they saw him in the temple, stirred up all the people, and laid hands on him, [28]crying out, Men of Israel, help: This is the man, that teacheth all men every where against the people, and the law, and this place: and further brought Greeks also into the temple, and hath polluted this holy place. [29](For they had seen before with him in the city Trophimus an Ephesian, whom they supposed that Paul had brought into the temple.) [30]And all the city was moved, and the people ran together: and they took Paul, and drew him out of the temple: and forthwith the doors were shut. [31]And as they went about to kill him, tidings came unto the chief captain of the band, that all Jerusalem was in an uproar. [32]Who immediately took soldiers and centurions, and ran down unto them: and when they saw the chief captain and the soldiers, they left beating of Paul. [33]Then the chief captain came near, and took him, and commanded him to be bound with two chains; and demanded who he was, and what he had done. [34]And some cried one thing, some another, among the multitude: and when he could not know the certainty for the tumult, he commanded him to be carried into the castle. [35]And when he came upon the stairs, so it was, that he was borne of the soldiers for the violence of the people. [36]For the multitude of the people followed after, crying, Away with him.

[37]And as Paul was to be led into the castle, he said unto the chief captain, May I speak unto thee? Who said, Canst thou speak Greek? [38]Art not thou that Egyptian, which before these days madest an uproar, and leddest out into the wilderness four thousand men that were murderers? [39]But Paul said, I am a man which am a Jew of Tarsus, a city in Cilicia, a citizen of no mean city: and, I beseech thee,

---

for: better omitted (MS tradition).   **21:23** *Vow*: a Nazarite vow (cf. the shaven heads of v. 24), like the one Paul took in 18:18 (see note).   **21:24** *Purify thyself*: i.e., by sacrifice. *Be at charges with them*: cover the expenses for the offerings required at their vow's end (see Num 6:13–15). *Walketh orderly*: better "conform to" (i.e., the law).   **21:25** *As touching . . . fornication*: see 15:29. *That they observe . . . only*: better omitted (MS tradition).   **21:26** *To signify . . . them*: i.e., "to announce when their days of purification would be complete, at which time an offering would be made for each one of them." **21:27–22:1** Paul's arrest.   **21:31** *Chief captain of the band*: the military tribune commanding the cohort stationed at Jerusalem.   **21:34** *Castle*: fortress (so throughout).   **21:38** *That Egyptian . . . murderers*: Josephus notes that Felix, Roman procurator of Judea, violently suppressed this agitation, but that the Egyptian escaped (*Jewish Antiquities* 20.169–72; *Jewish War* 2.261–63). *Murderers*: lit. "dagger men"

suffer me to speak unto the people. ⁴⁰And when he had given him licence, Paul stood on the stairs, and beckoned with the hand unto the people. And when there was made a great silence, he spake unto them in the Hebrew tongue, saying, ¹Men, brethren, and fathers, hear ye my defence which I make now unto you. ²(And when they heard that he spake in the Hebrew tongue to them, they kept the more silence: and he saith,) ³I am verily a man which am a Jew, born in Tarsus, a city in Cilicia, yet brought up in this city at the feet of Gamaliel, and taught according to the perfect manner of the law of the fathers, and was zealous toward God, as ye all are this day. ⁴And I persecuted this way unto the death, binding and delivering into prisons both men and women. ⁵As also the high priest doth bear me witness, and all the estate of the elders: from whom also I received letters unto the brethren, and went to Damascus, to bring them which were there bound unto Jerusalem, for to be punished.

⁶And it came to pass, that, as I made my journey, and was come nigh unto Damascus about noon, suddenly there shone from heaven a great light round about me. ⁷And I fell unto the ground, and heard a voice saying unto me, Saul, Saul, why persecutest thou me? ⁸And I answered, Who art thou, Lord? And he said unto me, I am Jesus of Nazareth, whom thou persecutest. ⁹And they that were with me saw indeed the light, and were afraid; but they heard not the voice of him that spake to me. ¹⁰And I said, What shall I do, Lord? And the Lord said unto me, Arise, and go into Damascus; and there it shall be told thee of all things which are appointed for thee to do. ¹¹And when I could not see for the glory of that light, being led by the hand of them that were with me, I came into Damascus.

¹²And one Ananias, a devout man according to the law, having a good report of all the Jews which dwelt there, ¹³came unto me, and stood, and said unto me, Brother Saul, receive thy sight. And the same hour I looked up upon him. ¹⁴And he said, The God of our fathers hath chosen thee, that thou shouldest know his will, and see that Just One, and shouldest hear the voice of his mouth. ¹⁵For thou shalt be his witness unto all men of what thou hast seen and heard. ¹⁶And now why tarriest thou? arise, and be baptized, and wash away thy sins, calling on the name of the Lord.

¹⁷And it came to pass, that, when I was come again to Jerusalem, even while I prayed in the temple, I was in a trance; ¹⁸and saw him saying unto me, Make haste, and get thee quickly out of Jerusalem: for they will not receive thy testimony concerning me. ¹⁹And I said, Lord, they know that I imprisoned and beat in every synagogue them that believed on thee: ²⁰and when the blood of thy

---

(assassins).   **21:40** *The Hebrew tongue*: Aramaic.   **22:2–29** Paul's defense: the speech of vv. 3–21 constitutes the second of Acts' three accounts of Paul's conversion and commissioning (cf. 9:1–19; 26:9–18); they differ significantly.   **22:3** *At the feet of Gamaliel*: as Gamaliel's disciple (see 5:34 and note).   **22:5** *Estate of the elders*: a component of the Sanhedrin. *Brethren*: the Jewish community. **22:9** *And were afraid*: better omitted (MS tradition).   **22:14** *That Just One*: see 7:52 note.   **22:17–21** *And it . . . Gentiles*: chap. 9 does not report this, but Gal 1:15–16 presumably refers to something like it. Its occurrence in the temple (contrast Gal 1:17) recalls Simeon's recognition of God's salvation for all peoples in the infant Jesus at the temple (Luke 2:25–32). The escape from Jerusalem (vv. 18–21) recalls Paul's escape from Damascus (9:23–25) and may constitute an alternate version of that story.

martyr Stephen was shed, I also was standing by, and consenting unto his death, and kept the raiment of them that slew him. ²¹And he said unto me, Depart: for I will send thee far hence unto the Gentiles.

²²And they gave him audience unto this word, and then lifted up their voices, and said, Away with such a fellow from the earth: for it is not fit that he should live. ²³And as they cried out, and cast off their clothes, and threw dust into the air, ²⁴the chief captain commanded him to be brought into the castle, and bade that he should be examined by scourging; that he might know wherefore they cried so against him. ²⁵And as they bound him with thongs, Paul said unto the centurion that stood by, Is it lawful for you to scourge a man that is a Roman, and uncondemned? ²⁶When the centurion heard that, he went and told the chief captain, saying, Take heed what thou doest: for this man is a Roman. ²⁷Then the chief captain came, and said unto him, Tell me, art thou a Roman? He said, Yea. ²⁸And the chief captain answered, With a great sum obtained I this freedom. And Paul said, But I was free born. ²⁹Then straightway they departed from him which should have examined him: and the chief captain also was afraid, after he knew that he was a Roman, and because he had bound him.

³⁰On the morrow, because he would have known the certainty wherefore he was accused of the Jews, he loosed him from his bands, and commanded the chief priests and all their council to appear, and brought Paul down, and set him before them.

23 And Paul, earnestly beholding the council, said, Men and brethren, I have lived in all good conscience before God until this day. ²And the high priest Ananias commanded them that stood by him to smite him on the mouth. ³Then said Paul unto him, God shall smite thee, thou whited wall: for sittest thou to judge me after the law, and commandest me to be smitten contrary to the law? ⁴And they that stood by said, Revilest thou God's high priest? ⁵Then said Paul, I wist not, brethren, that he was the high priest: for it is written, Thou shalt not speak evil of the ruler of thy people.

⁶But when Paul perceived that the one part were Sadducees, and the other Pharisees, he cried out in the council, Men and brethren, I am a Pharisee, the son of a Pharisee: of the hope and resurrection of the dead I am called in question.

22:20 *Martyr*: lit. "witness." *Unto his death*: better omitted (MS tradition). **22:23** *Cast off . . . air*: symbolic objections to the conclusion of Paul's speech. **22:24** *Examined by scourging*: a common procedure for slaves. **22:25** *Bound him*: lit. "stretched him out." *Is it . . . uncondemned*: see 16:37 and note. **22:28** *With a great sum . . . freedom*: the military tribune's name, Claudius Lysias (23:26), indicates he had acquired citizenship (Gk. *politeia*, which KJV mistranslates "freedom") while the emperor Claudius ruled, for newly minted Roman citizens conventionally took the emperor's name. According to Dio Cassius 60.17.5–7, as Claudius's reign progressed, citizenship became more affordable and the old naming tradition was abandoned. The tribune's remark may thus be understood as his display of (as it turns out, misplaced) umbrage that Paul had recently become a citizen at small personal expense while he himself had to pay out a large sum of money. **22:30–23:11** Paul before the Sanhedrin. **22:30** *From his bands*: better omitted (MS tradition). **23:2** *Ananias*: high priest, ca. 47–59 C.E. *To smite him*: in contrast to the Romans (22:25–29), and perhaps recalling Jesus' beating in Luke 22:63. **23:3** *Whited*: whitewashed (cf. Ezek 13:10–15). **23:5** *Thou shalt not . . . people*: Exod 22:28. **23:6** *When Paul . . . question*: the inquiry not going well, Paul makes a statement seemingly designed to prompt the Sanhedrin's Pharisaic constituency to take his side. *Son of a Pharisee*: better "son of Pharisees" (MS tradition).

⁷And when he had so said, there arose a dissension between the Pharisees and the Sadducees: and the multitude was divided. ⁸For the Sadducees say that there is no resurrection, neither angel, nor spirit: but the Pharisees confess both. ⁹And there arose a great cry: and the scribes that were of the Pharisees' part arose, and strove, saying, We find no evil in this man: but if a spirit or an angel hath spoken to him, let us not fight against God. ¹⁰And when there arose a great dissension, the chief captain, fearing lest Paul should have been pulled in pieces of them, commanded the soldiers to go down, and to take him by force from among them, and to bring him into the castle. ¹¹And the night following the Lord stood by him, and said, Be of good cheer, Paul: for as thou hast testified of me in Jerusalem, so must thou bear witness also at Rome.

¹²And when it was day, certain of the Jews banded together, and bound themselves under a curse, saying that they would neither eat nor drink till they had killed Paul. ¹³And they were more than forty which had made this conspiracy. ¹⁴And they came to the chief priests and elders, and said, We have bound ourselves under a great curse, that we will eat nothing until we have slain Paul. ¹⁵Now therefore ye with the council signify to the chief captain that he bring him down unto you to morrow, as though ye would inquire something more perfectly concerning him: and we, or ever he come near, are ready to kill him. ¹⁶And when Paul's sister's son heard of their lying in wait, he went and entered into the castle, and told Paul.

¹⁷Then Paul called one of the centurions unto him, and said, Bring this young man unto the chief captain: for he hath a certain thing to tell him. ¹⁸So he took him, and brought him to the chief captain, and said, Paul the prisoner called me unto him, and prayed me to bring this young man unto thee, who hath something to say unto thee. ¹⁹Then the chief captain took him by the hand, and went with him aside privately, and asked him, What is that thou hast to tell me? ²⁰And he said, The Jews have agreed to desire thee that thou wouldest bring down Paul to morrow into the council, as though they would inquire somewhat of him more perfectly. ²¹But do not thou yield unto them: for there lie in wait for him of them more than forty men, which have bound themselves with an oath, that they will neither eat nor drink till they have killed him: and now are they ready, looking for a promise from thee. ²²So the chief captain then let the young man depart, and charged him, See thou tell no man that thou hast shewed these things to me.

²³And he called unto him two centurions, saying, Make ready two hundred soldiers to go to Cæsarea, and horsemen threescore and ten, and spearmen two hundred, at the third hour of the night; ²⁴and provide them beasts, that they may set Paul on, and bring him safe unto Felix the governor. ²⁵And he wrote a letter

---

23:9 *But if . . . God*: better "And what if a spirit or an angel spoke to him?" (MS tradition). The rhetorical question is designed to raise the Sadducees' ire, for they believed in neither angels nor spirits (v. 8). **23:12–22** The plot against Paul's life. **23:12** *Certain of*: better omitted (MS tradition). **23:15** *Or ever*: before.

23:23–26:32 Paul imprisoned in Caesarea. 23:23–35 Transfer to Caesarea. **23:23** *Two hundred soldiers . . . hundred*: a prodigious escort (about half the Jerusalem cohort). *The third hour of the night*: 9 P.M. **23:24** *Felix the governor*: Claudius Felix, Roman procurator of Judea, ca. 52–59 C.E. **23:25** *A letter*: its text (vv. 26–30) revises the events just narrated to give the impression that

after this manner: [26]Claudius Lysias unto the most excellent governor Felix sendeth greeting. [27]This man was taken of the Jews, and should have been killed of them: then came I with an army, and rescued him, having understood that he was a Roman. [28]And when I would have known the cause wherefore they accused him, I brought him forth into their council: [29]whom I perceived to be accused of questions of their law, but to have nothing laid to his charge worthy of death or of bonds. [30]And when it was told me how that the Jews laid wait for the man, I sent straightway to thee, and gave commandment to his accusers also to say before thee what they had against him. Farewell.

[31]Then the soldiers, as it was commanded them, took Paul, and brought him by night to Antipatris. [32]On the morrow they left the horsemen to go with him, and returned to the castle: [33]who, when they came to Cæsarea, and delivered the epistle to the governor, presented Paul also before him. [34]And when the governor had read the letter, he asked of what province he was. And when he understood that he was of Cilicia; [35]I will hear thee, said he, when thine accusers are also come. And he commanded him to be kept in Herod's judgment hall.

24 And after five days Ananias the high priest descended with the elders, and with a certain orator named Tertullus, who informed the governor against Paul. [2]And when he was called forth, Tertullus began to accuse him, saying, Seeing that by thee we enjoy great quietness, and that very worthy deeds are done unto this nation by thy providence, [3]we accept it always, and in all places, most noble Felix, with all thankfulness. [4]Notwithstanding, that I be not further tedious unto thee, I pray thee that thou wouldest hear us of thy clemency a few words. [5]For we have found this man a pestilent fellow, and a mover of sedition among all the Jews throughout the world, and a ringleader of the sect of the Nazarenes: [6]who also hath gone about to profane the temple: whom we took, and would have judged according to our law. [7]But the chief captain Lysias came upon us, and with great violence took him away out of our hands, [8]commanding his accusers to come unto thee: by examining of whom thyself mayest take knowledge of all these things, whereof we accuse him. [9]And the Jews also assented, saying that these things were so.

---

the tribune acted conscientiously from the beginning to protect a Roman citizen. **23:30** *How that . . . the man*: better "that there would be a plot against the man" (MS tradition). **23:31** *Antipatris*: a city between Jerusalem and Caesarea. **23:34–35** *He asked . . . thee*: Felix presumably seeks to confirm his jurisdictional authority (or obligation) to hear the case. Technically, Cilicia and Syria (in which Judea lay) were at this time one combined province. Had Paul originated from outside the province, Felix might have forwarded the case to his superior, the legate of Syria, or to another imperial delegate. **23:35** *Judgment hall*: Gk. *praitōrion* (see Mark 15:16 note). Herod's palace had long been the seat of Roman administration in Judea. **24:1–27** Paul's trial before Felix. **24:2** *Quietness*: lit. "peace." *Very worthy . . . done*: better "reforms are enacted" (MS tradition). **24:5** *The sect of the Nazarenes*: *sect* translates Gk. *hairesis*, a "school" or "party" within Judaism (cf. 5:17; 15:5), although v. 14 may imply that the word has a negative connotation (see note). Only here in the NT are Jesus-believers called *Nazarenes*, a term later used with special reference to Jewish Christians. **24:6–8** *And would . . . thee*: better omitted

¹⁰Then Paul, after that the governor had beckoned unto him to speak, answered, Forasmuch as I know that thou hast been of many years a judge unto this nation, I do the more cheerfully answer for myself: ¹¹because that thou mayest understand, that there are yet but twelve days since I went up to Jerusalem for to worship. ¹²And they neither found me in the temple disputing with any man, neither raising up the people, neither in the synagogues, nor in the city: ¹³neither can they prove the things whereof they now accuse me. ¹⁴But this I confess unto thee, that after the way which they call heresy, so worship I the God of my fathers, believing all things which are written in the law and in the prophets: ¹⁵and have hope toward God, which they themselves also allow, that there shall be a resurrection of the dead, both of the just and unjust. ¹⁶And herein do I exercise myself, to have always a conscience void of offence toward God, and toward men. ¹⁷Now after many years I came to bring alms to my nation, and offerings. ¹⁸Whereupon certain Jews from Asia found me purified in the temple, neither with multitude, nor with tumult. ¹⁹Who ought to have been here before thee, and object, if they had ought against me. ²⁰Or else let these same here say, if they have found any evil doing in me, while I stood before the council, ²¹except it be for this one voice, that I cried standing among them, Touching the resurrection of the dead I am called in question by you this day.

²²And when Felix heard these things, having more perfect knowledge of that way, he deferred them, and said, When Lysias the chief captain shall come down, I will know the uttermost of your matter. ²³And he commanded a centurion to keep Paul, and to let him have liberty, and that he should forbid none of his acquaintance to minister or come unto him.

²⁴And after certain days, when Felix came with his wife Drusilla, which was a Jewess, he sent for Paul, and heard him concerning the faith in Christ. ²⁵And as he reasoned of righteousness, temperance, and judgment to come, Felix trembled, and answered, Go thy way for this time; when I have a convenient season, I will call for thee. ²⁶He hoped also that money should have been given him of Paul, that he might loose him: wherefore he sent for him the oftener, and communed with him. ²⁷But after two years Porcius Festus came into Felix' room: and Felix, willing to shew the Jews a pleasure, left Paul bound.

(MS tradition).   **24:14** *Heresy*: Gk. *hairesis*, "sect" (see v. 5 note).   **24:15** *Both of the just and unjust*: presumably the unjust will be condemned.   **24:17** *I came . . . offerings*: i.e., the offering of 21:23–26, though perhaps also an allusion to the collection that Paul's letters repeatedly mention (Rom 15:25–27; 1 Cor 16:1–4).   **24:18** *Whereupon*: better "while I was bringing them" (MS tradition).   **24:21** *By you*: better "before you" (MS tradition).   **24:22** *Having more perfect knowledge*: or "knowing rather accurately"; comparative of Gk. *akribōs* (cf. 18:25–26 [KJV "diligently," "perfectly"]). *Know the uttermost*: decide by careful inspection.   **24:24** *Drusilla*: daughter of Herod Agrippa I (see 12:1 and note).   **24:26** *That he might loose him*: better omitted (MS tradition), though this may be what Luke is getting at.   **24:27** *Came into Felix' room*: replaced Felix as procurator. *To shew the Jews a pleasure*: to do them a favor (cf. 25:3, 9); cf. 12:1–3; Luke 23:13–25.

25 Now when Festus was come into the province, after three days he ascended from Cæsarea to Jerusalem. ²Then the high priest and the chief of the Jews informed him against Paul, and besought him, ³and desired favour against him, that he would send for him to Jerusalem, laying wait in the way to kill him. ⁴But Festus answered, that Paul should be kept at Cæsarea, and that he himself would depart shortly thither. ⁵Let them therefore, said he, which among you are able, go down with me, and accuse this man, if there be any wickedness in him.

⁶And when he had tarried among them more than ten days, he went down unto Cæsarea; and the next day sitting on the judgment seat commanded Paul to be brought. ⁷And when he was come, the Jews which came down from Jerusalem stood round about, and laid many and grievous complaints against Paul, which they could not prove. ⁸While he answered for himself, Neither against the law of the Jews, neither against the temple, nor yet against Cæsar, have I offended any thing at all. ⁹But Festus, willing to do the Jews a pleasure, answered Paul, and said, Wilt thou go up to Jerusalem, and there be judged of these things before me? ¹⁰Then said Paul, I stand at Cæsar's judgment seat, where I ought to be judged: to the Jews have I done no wrong, as thou very well knowest. ¹¹For if I be an offender, or have committed any thing worthy of death, I refuse not to die: but if there be none of these things whereof these accuse me, no man may deliver me unto them. I appeal unto Cæsar. ¹²Then Festus, when he had conferred with the council, answered, Hast thou appealed unto Cæsar? unto Cæsar shalt thou go.

¹³And after certain days king Agrippa and Bernice came unto Cæsarea to salute Festus. ¹⁴And when they had been there many days, Festus declared Paul's cause unto the king, saying, There is a certain man left in bonds by Felix: ¹⁵about whom, when I was at Jerusalem, the chief priests and the elders of the Jews informed me, desiring to have judgment against him. ¹⁶To whom I answered, It is not the manner of the Romans to deliver any man to die, before that he which is accused have the accusers face to face, and have licence to answer for himself concerning the crime laid against him. ¹⁷Therefore, when they were come hither, without any delay on the morrow I sat on the judgment seat, and commanded the man to be brought forth. ¹⁸Against whom when the accusers stood up, they brought none accusation

25:1–12 Paul before Festus. In danger of being returned to Jerusalem, Paul appeals to the emperor, a decision that enables him to "bear witness also in Rome" (23:11).   25:2 *High priest*: better "high priests" (MS tradition), though there was only one high priest at a time. (Luke has used the plural earlier; Luke 3:2).   25:3 *Desired favour against him*: asked as a favor to Paul's detriment.   25:5 *Any wickedness*: lit. "anything out of place."   25:6 *More than ten days*: better "not more than eight or ten days" (MS tradition).   25:11 *I appeal unto Cæsar*: while the legal framework of the imperial appeal process is not entirely clear, Luke plausibly understands a citizen arrested in the provinces to have the right to request that his case be adjudicated in Rome by the emperor.   25:12 *Hast thou*: or a statement, "thou hast."   25:13–26:32 Paul before Agrippa.   25:13 *King Agrippa and Bernice*: Marcus Julius Agrippa II was Herod Agrippa I's son (cf. 12:1–11, 20–23). In 53 C.E., he became the Roman client king overseeing the region Philip had controlled (see Luke 3:1 note), and later Nero expanded the territory he administered. Bernice was his sister (as was Drusilla, Felix's wife) and was believed to be his lover (Josephus, *Jewish Antiquities* 20.145; Juvenal, *Satire* 6.156–60).   25:16 *To die*: better omitted (MS tradition).

of such things as I supposed: [19]but had certain questions against him of their own superstition, and of one Jesus, which was dead, whom Paul affirmed to be alive. [20]And because I doubted of such manner of questions, I asked him whether he would go to Jerusalem, and there be judged of these matters. [21]But when Paul had appealed to be reserved unto the hearing of Augustus, I commanded him to be kept till I might send him to Cæsar. [22]Then Agrippa said unto Festus, I would also hear the man myself. To morrow, said he, thou shalt hear him.

[23]And on the morrow, when Agrippa was come, and Bernice, with great pomp, and was entered into the place of hearing, with the chief captains, and principal men of the city, at Festus' commandment Paul was brought forth. [24]And Festus said, King Agrippa, and all men which are here present with us, ye see this man, about whom all the multitude of the Jews have dealt with me, both at Jerusalem, and also here, crying that he ought not to live any longer. [25]But when I found that he had committed nothing worthy of death, and that he himself hath appealed to Augustus, I have determined to send him. [26]Of whom I have no certain thing to write unto my lord. Wherefore I have brought him forth before you, and specially before thee, O king Agrippa, that, after examination had, I might have somewhat to write. [27]For it seemeth to me unreasonable to send a prisoner, and not withal to signify the crimes laid against him.

26 Then Agrippa said unto Paul, Thou art permitted to speak for thyself. Then Paul stretched forth the hand, and answered for himself: [2]I think myself happy, king Agrippa, because I shall answer for myself this day before thee touching all the things whereof I am accused of the Jews: [3]especially because I know thee to be expert in all customs and questions which are among the Jews: wherefore I beseech thee to hear me patiently. [4]My manner of life from my youth, which was at the first among mine own nation at Jerusalem, know all the Jews; [5]which knew me from the beginning, if they would testify, that after the most straitest sect of our religion I lived a Pharisee. [6]And now I stand and am judged for the hope of the promise made of God unto our fathers: [7]unto which promise our twelve tribes, instantly serving God day and night, hope to come. For which hope's sake, king Agrippa, I am accused of the Jews. [8]Why should it be thought a thing incredible with you, that God should raise the dead?

[9]I verily thought with myself, that I ought to do many things contrary to the name of Jesus of Nazareth. [10]Which thing I also did in Jerusalem: and many of

---

25:19 *Superstition*: cf. 17:22 and note.   **25:20** *And because . . . Jerusalem*: vv. 3, 9 suggest a different reason.   **25:21** *Augustus*: Gk. *Sebastos* (also in v. 25), lit. "the Revered One" and the regular term for Lat. *augustus*, a common honorific for Roman emperors, first adopted by Octavian and here used of Nero.   **25:23** *Chief captains*: see 21:31 note.   **25:26** *My lord*: another conventional reference to the emperor. *After examination had*: after he has been examined.   **26:2–23** Paul's defense before Agrippa. This speech may be Luke-Acts' most literate: the Greek is precise and formal, the periodic sentences are intricate, and it records Jesus speaking to Paul in the language of the classical Hebrew prophets and of the Greek tragedians.   **26:4** *At the first*: lit. "from the beginning."   **26:5** *Most straitest*: "strictest," a form of *akribōs* (see 24:22 and note).   **26:6** *Promise*: i.e., the promise of resurrection; cf. 23:6–10; 24:21; 25:19. That promise is explicit in Dan 12:2–3 and, according to Luke's Jesus (Luke 20:37), implicit in Exod 3:6.   **26:7** *Instantly*: earnestly.   **26:9–18** *I verily thought . . . me*: in Paul's third account of his conversion, his persecution

the saints did I shut up in prison, having received authority from the chief priests; and when they were put to death, I gave my voice against them. [11]And I punished them oft in every synagogue, and compelled them to blaspheme; and being exceedingly mad against them, I persecuted them even unto strange cities.

[12]Whereupon as I went to Damascus with authority and commission from the chief priests, [13]at midday, O king, I saw in the way a light from heaven, above the brightness of the sun, shining round about me and them which journeyed with me. [14]And when we were all fallen to the earth, I heard a voice speaking unto me, and saying in the Hebrew tongue, Saul, Saul, why persecutest thou me? it is hard for thee to kick against the pricks. [15]And I said, Who art thou, Lord? And he said, I am Jesus whom thou persecutest. [16]But rise, and stand upon thy feet: for I have appeared unto thee for this purpose, to make thee a minister and a witness both of these things which thou hast seen, and of those things in the which I will appear unto thee; [17]delivering thee from the people, and from the Gentiles, unto whom now I send thee, [18]to open their eyes, and to turn them from darkness to light, and from the power of Satan unto God, that they may receive forgiveness of sins, and inheritance among them which are sanctified by faith that is in me.

[19]Whereupon, O king Agrippa, I was not disobedient unto the heavenly vision: [20]but shewed first unto them of Damascus, and at Jerusalem, and throughout all the coasts of Judæa, and then to the Gentiles, that they should repent and turn to God, and do works meet for repentance. [21]For these causes the Jews caught me in the temple, and went about to kill me. [22]Having therefore obtained help of God, I continue unto this day, witnessing both to small and great, saying none other things than those which the prophets and Moses did say should come: [23]that Christ should suffer, and that he should be the first that should rise from the dead, and should shew light unto the people, and to the Gentiles.

[24]And as he thus spake for himself, Festus said with a loud voice, Paul, thou art beside thyself; much learning doth make thee mad. [25]But he said, I am not mad, most noble Festus; but speak forth the words of truth and soberness. [26]For the king knoweth of these things, before whom also I speak freely: for I am persuaded that none of these things are hidden from him; for this thing was not done in a corner. [27]King Agrippa, believest thou the prophets? I know that thou believest. [28]Then Agrippa said unto Paul, Almost thou persuadest me to be a Christian.

---

of the church (vv. 9–11) appears much more severe than in the earlier versions (cf. 9:1–18; 22:3–21). **26:11** *Strange*: foreign. **26:13–15** *At midday . . . persecutest*: in the present context, Paul's claim to have seen the risen Christ bolsters the legitimacy of his belief in the resurrection of the dead. **26:14** *It is . . . pricks*: an allusion to Euripides, *Bacchae* 794–95, where the Greek proverb appears in an identical context (the disguised Bacchus/Dionysus is urging Pentheus not to neglect his worship). **26:16** *These things . . . seen*: better "of the things in which you have seen me" (MS tradition; NRSV). **26:17** *Delivering thee . . . thee*: cf. Jer 1:7–8. *The people*: i.e., the Jewish people (cf. v. 23). **26:18** *To open . . . light*: echoing Isa 42:6–7; cf. 49:6; Luke 2:32; Acts 13:47. *Inheritance among them . . . me*: with reference to the promise of resurrection made to the "fathers" (vv. 6–7), Paul here suggests that Gentiles too have access to the inherited promise through faith in Christ; cf. Gal 3:15–4:7. **26:20** *Meet for*: lit. "worthy of." **26:23** *The first . . . dead*: as in 1 Cor 15, Paul interprets Christ's resurrection as the beginning of the eschatological resurrection of the dead. *Light unto . . . Gentiles*: see v. 18 and note. **26:28** *Almost thou . . . Christian*: better "in a little [time] you persuade

²⁹And Paul said, I would to God, that not only thou, but also all that hear me this day, were both almost, and altogether such as I am, except these bonds.

³⁰And when he had thus spoken, the king rose up, and the governor, and Bernice, and they that sat with them: ³¹and when they were gone aside, they talked between themselves, saying, This man doeth nothing worthy of death or of bonds. ³²Then said Agrippa unto Festus, This man might have been set at liberty, if he had not appealed unto Cæsar.

27 And when it was determined that we should sail into Italy, they delivered Paul and certain other prisoners unto one named Julius, a centurion of Augustus' band. ²And entering into a ship of Adramyttium, we launched, meaning to sail by the coasts of Asia; one Aristarchus, a Macedonian of Thessalonica, being with us. ³And the next day we touched at Sidon. And Julius courteously entreated Paul, and gave him liberty to go unto his friends to refresh himself. ⁴And when we had launched from thence, we sailed under Cyprus, because the winds were contrary. ⁵And when we had sailed over the sea of Cilicia and Pamphylia, we came to Myra, a city of Lycia. ⁶And there the centurion found a ship of Alexandria sailing into Italy; and he put us therein. ⁷And when we had sailed slowly many days, and scarce were come over against Cnidus, the wind not suffering us, we sailed under Crete, over against Salmone; ⁸and, hardly passing it, came unto a place which is called The fair havens; nigh whereunto was the city of Lasea.

⁹Now when much time was spent, and when sailing was now dangerous, because the fast was now already past, Paul admonished them, ¹⁰and said unto them, Sirs, I perceive that this voyage will be with hurt and much damage, not only of the lading and ship, but also of our lives. ¹¹Nevertheless the centurion believed the master and the owner of the ship, more than those things which were spoken by Paul. ¹²And because the haven was not commodious to winter in, the more part advised to depart thence also, if by any means they might attain to Phenice, and there to winter; which is an haven of Crete, and lieth toward the south west and north west.

¹³And when the south wind blew softly, supposing that they had obtained their purpose, loosing thence, they sailed close by Crete. ¹⁴But not long after there

---

me that you are making me a Christian" (MS tradition). The sense of his statement is not altogether clear, but Festus's snide remark in v. 24 suggests that Agrippa too may speak sarcastically. For *Christian*, see 11:26 note.   **26:29** *Both almost, and altogether*: better "whether in little [time] or much." KJV obscures the connection with the previous verse. Thus "I would to God that whether in little [time] or much, not only you but also all who hear me this day would become as I am, except for these chains."

27:1–28:31 Paul's journey to Rome. 27:1–8 Departure.   **27:1** *Augustus' band*: the Augustan cohort (see 25:21 note).   **27:2** *Adramyttium*: a port in Asia Minor. *Aristarchus*: see 19:29; 20:4.   **27:3** *Entreated*: treated.   **27:4** *Under*: i.e., under the lee of (on the side protected from the wind; also in vv. 7, 16).   **27:5** *Myra*: a port used as a stopping point for Egyptian grain ships headed to Rome. It is presumably to one of these that they transfer (cf. v. 38).   **27:7** *Cnidus*: on the coast of Asia Minor, just north of Rhodes. *Salmone*: the cape at the eastern point of Crete.   **27:8** *Fair havens*: a harbor in southern Crete. *Lasea*: slightly inland from Fair Havens.   **27:9–44** Storm and shipwreck.   **27:9** *The fast*: the Day of Atonement, which occurs in early autumn (a stormy time on the Mediterranean).   **27:10** *Lading*: cargo.   **27:13** *Loosing*: setting sail.

arose against it a tempestuous wind, called Euroclydon. [15]And when the ship was caught, and could not bear up into the wind, we let her drive. [16]And running under a certain island which is called Clauda, we had much work to come by the boat: [17]which when they had taken up, they used helps, undergirding the ship; and, fearing lest they should fall into the quicksands, strake sail, and so were driven. [18]And we being exceedingly tossed with a tempest, the next day they lightened the ship; [19]and the third day we cast out with our own hands the tackling of the ship. [20]And when neither sun nor stars in many days appeared, and no small tempest lay on us, all hope that we should be saved was then taken away.

[21]But after long abstinence Paul stood forth in the midst of them, and said, Sirs, ye should have hearkened unto me, and not have loosed from Crete, and to have gained this harm and loss. [22]And now I exhort you to be of good cheer: for there shall be no loss of any man's life among you, but of the ship. [23]For there stood by me this night the angel of God, whose I am, and whom I serve, [24]saying, Fear not, Paul; thou must be brought before Cæsar: and, lo, God hath given thee all them that sail with thee. [25]Wherefore, sirs, be of good cheer: for I believe God, that it shall be even as it was told me. [26]Howbeit we must be cast upon a certain island.

[27]But when the fourteenth night was come, as we were driven up and down in Adria, about midnight the shipmen deemed that they drew near to some country; [28]and sounded, and found it twenty fathoms: and when they had gone a little further, they sounded again, and found it fifteen fathoms. [29]Then fearing lest we should have fallen upon rocks, they cast four anchors out of the stern, and wished for the day. [30]And as the shipmen were about to flee out of the ship, when they had let down the boat into the sea, under colour as though they would have cast anchors out of the foreship, [31]Paul said to the centurion and to the soldiers, Except these abide in the ship, ye cannot be saved. [32]Then the soldiers cut off the ropes of the boat, and let her fall off.

[33]And while the day was coming on, Paul besought them all to take meat, saying, This day is the fourteenth day that ye have tarried and continued fasting, having taken nothing. [34]Wherefore I pray you to take some meat: for this is for

---

27:14 *Euroclydon*: a transliteration of the Greek, which refers to a stormy, southeasterly wind, though a better reading of the MS tradition makes it a wind from the northeast. **27:16** *Clauda*: better "Cauda" (MS tradition), a small island south of Crete. *Come by the boat*: secure the skiff. **27:17** *Helps*: meaning unclear, but ships were often undergirded with cables to strengthen the hull. *Quicksands*: Gk. *Syrtis*, the name of an area of underwater sandbanks in shallow water off the coast of North Africa. **27:18** *Lightened the ship*: cf. Jonah 1:5. **27:19** *We*: better "they" (MS tradition). *Tackling*: tackle, i.e., rigging. **27:20** *Neither sun . . . appeared*: making it impossible to plot a course. **27:21** *Abstinence*: lit. "lack of appetite" (from seasickness, or perhaps apprehension; cf. v. 34). **27:21–26** *Sirs, ye . . . island*: Paul's situation reverses that of Jonah, the OT prophet whose presence threatens the ship when he flees God's call to prophesy to the Gentile city Nineveh. Paul, on the contrary, assures the crew that it will be saved from a storm because he is obeying God's call to witness to Gentiles in Rome (vv. 24–25). **27:27** *Adria*: in antiquity, the Adriatic Sea could be understood to stretch all the way south to North Africa. **27:29** *Wished*: or "prayed." **27:30–32** *And as the shipmen . . . off*: another reversal of the Jonah story. Jonah insists that the sailors throw him overboard to save their ship, and after resisting they ultimately accede (Jonah 1:11–16). Here, the crew wants to abandon ship, but Paul resists, insisting that they must remain for the ship to be saved. **27:30** *Under colour as though*: under the pretext that.

your health: for there shall not an hair fall from the head of any of you. ³⁵And when he had thus spoken, he took bread, and gave thanks to God in presence of them all: and when he had broken it, he began to eat. ³⁶Then were they all of good cheer, and they also took some meat. ³⁷And we were in all in the ship two hundred threescore and sixteen souls. ³⁸And when they had eaten enough, they lightened the ship, and cast out the wheat into the sea.

³⁹And when it was day, they knew not the land: but they discovered a certain creek with a shore, into the which they were minded, if it were possible, to thrust in the ship. ⁴⁰And when they had taken up the anchors, they committed themselves unto the sea, and loosed the rudder bands, and hoised up the mainsail to the wind, and made toward shore. ⁴¹And falling into a place where two seas met, they ran the ship aground; and the forepart stuck fast, and remained unmoveable, but the hinder part was broken with the violence of the waves. ⁴²And the soldiers' counsel was to kill the prisoners, lest any of them should swim out, and escape. ⁴³But the centurion, willing to save Paul, kept them from their purpose; and commanded that they which could swim should cast themselves first into the sea, and get to land: ⁴⁴and the rest, some on boards, and some on broken pieces of the ship. And so it came to pass, that they escaped all safe to land.

28 And when they were escaped, then they knew that the island was called Melita. ²And the barbarous people shewed us no little kindness: for they kindled a fire, and received us every one, because of the present rain, and because of the cold. ³And when Paul had gathered a bundle of sticks, and laid them on the fire, there came a viper out of the heat, and fastened on his hand. ⁴And when the barbarians saw the venomous beast hang on his hand, they said among themselves, No doubt this man is a murderer, whom, though he hath escaped the sea, yet vengeance suffereth not to live. ⁵And he shook off the beast into the fire, and felt no harm. ⁶Howbeit they looked when he should have swollen, or fallen down dead suddenly: but after they had looked a great while, and saw no harm come to him, they changed their minds, and said that he was a god.

⁷In the same quarters were possessions of the chief man of the island, whose name was Publius; who received us, and lodged us three days courteously. ⁸And it came to pass, that the father of Publius lay sick of a fever and of a bloody flux: to whom Paul entered in, and prayed, and laid his hands on him, and healed him. ⁹So when this was done, others also, which had diseases in the island, came, and were healed: ¹⁰who also honoured us with many honours; and when we departed, they laded us with such things as were necessary.

27:34 *For there . . . you*: see Luke 12:7; 21:18 and note. 27:35 *He took . . . eat*: replicating Jesus' gestures in Luke 9:16; 22:19; 24:30. 27:39 *Creek*: bay. 27:40 *And when . . . sea*: alternatively "and casting off the anchors, they left them in the sea" (RSV). *Hoised*: raised. 28:1–10 Paul on Malta. 28:1 *They*: better "we" (MS tradition), twice in this verse. *Melita*: Malta, an island south of Sicily. 28:2 *The barbarous people*: the inhabitants who did not speak Greek. 28:3 *Out of*: or "because of." 28:4 *Vengeance*: Gk. *dikē*, also "justice"; here understood as a god pursuing the guilty. 28:7 *Possessions*: i.e., property, an estate. *Publius*: a Roman name; he was likely a ranking provincial official. 28:8 *A bloody*

¹¹And after three months we departed in a ship of Alexandria, which has wintered in the isle, whose sign was Castor and Pollux. ¹²And landing at Syracuse, we tarried there three days. ¹³And from thence we fetched a compass, and came to Rhegium: and after one day the south wind blew, and we came the next day to Puteoli: ¹⁴where we found brethren, and were desired to tarry with them seven days: and so we went toward Rome. ¹⁵And from thence, when the brethren heard of us, they came to meet us as far as Appii forum, and The three taverns: whom when Paul saw, he thanked God, and took courage. ¹⁶And when we came to Rome, the centurion delivered the prisoners to the captain of the guard: but Paul was suffered to dwell by himself with a soldier that kept him.

¹⁷And it came to pass, that after three days Paul called the chief of the Jews together: and when they were come together, he said unto them, Men and brethren, though I have committed nothing against the people, or customs of our fathers, yet was I delivered prisoner from Jerusalem into the hands of the Romans. ¹⁸Who, when they had examined me, would have let me go, because there was no cause of death in me. ¹⁹But when the Jews spake against it, I was constrained to appeal unto Cæsar; not that I had ought to accuse my nation of. ²⁰For this cause therefore have I called for you, to see you, and to speak with you: because that for the hope of Israel I am bound with this chain. ²¹And they said unto him, We neither received letters out of Judæa concerning thee, neither any of the brethren that came shewed or spake any harm of thee. ²²But we desire to hear of thee what thou thinkest: for as concerning this sect, we know that every where it is spoken against.

²³And when they had appointed him a day, there came many to him into his lodging; to whom he expounded and testified the kingdom of God, persuading them concerning Jesus, both out of the law of Moses, and out of the prophets, from morning till evening. ²⁴And some believed the things which were spoken, and some believed not. ²⁵And when they agreed not among themselves, they departed, after that Paul had spoken one word, Well spake the Holy Ghost by Esaias the prophet unto our fathers, ²⁶saying, Go unto this people, and say, Hearing ye shall hear, and shall not understand; and seeing ye shall see, and not perceive: ²⁷for the heart of this people is waxed gross, and their ears are dull of

---

flux: dysentery.   **28:11–16** Paul's arrival at Rome.   **28:11** *Whose sign . . . Pollux*: whose figurehead was the Dioscuri, Castor and Pollux. Zeus's twin sons were traditional protectors of seafarers. **28:12** *Syracuse*: an important city on the east coast of Sicily.   **28:13** *Fetched a compass*: took a circuitous course. A better reading of the MS tradition provides a Greek word of uncertain meaning, apparently an idiomatic nautical term. *Rhegium*: on Italy's southern tip. *Puteoli*: well north of Rhegium, in the Bay of Naples.   **28:15** *Appii forum, The three taverns*: towns on the Appian Way, about forty and twenty miles from Rome, respectively.   **28:16** *The centurion . . . but*: better omitted (MS tradition). *Paul was . . . him*: i.e., he was put under house arrest.   **28:17–31** Paul's final address.   **28:17** *Chief*: leading men.   **28:20** *The hope of Israel*: perhaps a reference to the eschatological resurrection of the dead (cf. 23:6; 26:6 and note), which also implies Jesus' death and resurrection (see 26:23 and note). **28:22** *This sect*: see 24:5 note.   **28:25** *They departed . . . word*: i.e., as they were departing Paul spoke a final word. *Our*: better "your" (MS tradition).   **28:26–27** *Go unto this people . . . them*: Isa 6:9–10 (cf. Luke 8:10; Matt 13:14–15; Mark 4:12; John 12:39–40). Luke's Paul invokes the Isaianic

hearing, and their eyes have they closed; lest they should see with their eyes, and hear with their ears, and understand with their heart, and should be converted, and I should heal them. [28]Be it known therefore unto you, that the salvation of God is sent unto the Gentiles, and that they will hear it.

[29]And when he had said these words, the Jews departed, and had great reasoning among themselves. [30]And Paul dwelt two whole years in his own hired house, and received all that came in unto him, [31]preaching the kingdom of God, and teaching those things which concern the Lord Jesus Christ, with all confidence, no man forbidding him.

text to explain his successful mission to the Gentiles and Israel's rejection of the gospel, even though, as Luke is careful to specify (v. 24), not all Israel rejects it. In Rom 9–11 Paul alludes to the same OT passage in a similar context (11:8), arguing that Israel's partial rejection of the gospel that Gentiles embrace is part of God's eschatological plan to save "all Israel" (11:26).   **28:29** *And when . . . themselves*: better omitted (MS tradition).   **28:30–31** *And Paul . . . forbidding him*: Acts' ending is remarkably optimistic, especially since Luke presumably knows that Paul was executed by the imperial authorities in Rome (e.g., 20:22–25; 21:11). The tradition of Paul's martyrdom there is strong; some scholars speculate that Paul was put to death in the brief Neronian persecution of 64 C.E. (see Tacitus, *Annals* 15.44, Appendix p. 983–84). Perhaps Luke omits its mention out of a desire to avoid undercutting his portrayal of Christianity as a religious sect that, far from threatening Rome, actually enjoyed a favorable relationship with the empire in its early days, even receiving its special protection on occasion (cf. 23:10, 21–24; 27:42–43). In any case, the book ends with him bearing witness in Rome, and thus fulfilling divine prophecy (23:11; cf. 13:47).

The Pauline Collection

Paul's Ministry

ACTS and Paul's letters provide the only reliable information about his life. The letters, which should be privileged (although not uncritically) as primary sources, tell us that Paul had been a Pharisee who persecuted the church (e.g., Phil 3:5–6) before he had an experience that he interpreted as a prophetic call from God to preach Jesus to the Gentiles (Gal 1:13–16 and notes). After spending three years in Damascus and Arabia (Gal 1:17–18; Acts 9:19b–22 suggests a shorter stay), Paul fled that region, apparently in danger from the authorities (see 2 Cor 11:32–33; cf. Acts 9:23–25, which blames "the Jews"). After briefly visiting Jerusalem (Gal 1:18–20; cf. Acts 9:26–28) and possibly Tarsus (Acts 9:29–30), Paul began an extended ministry in Syria and Cilicia (fourteen years or more; cf. Gal 1:21; 2:1). It primarily focused on the mixed Jewish-Gentile congregation at Antioch (Acts 11:22–26) but also involved a regional missionary journey with Barnabas, sponsored by the Antioch church (Acts 13–14). Acts suggests that Gentiles were more receptive to the gospel Paul preached than Jews were, and Paul's letters themselves do not even mention an active attempt to evangelize Jews (on the contrary, see Rom 11:13–14; but cf. 2 Cor 11:24 and note).

Paul's mission to Gentiles became an issue of heated contention in the church at large. He did not demand their obedience to the Torah, but some believers quite reasonably thought that Gentiles turning from their pagan practices to worship YHWH and his son Jesus ought to keep the covenants God made with Israel through Abraham and Moses, by becoming circumcised and presumably observing God's other commandments as well (see Acts 15:1). Paul visited Jerusalem to present the opposing argument (Gal 2:1–2; Acts 15:2) and it was decided that Gentiles who turned to faith in Christ did not need to keep the law in its entirety, though they were subject to some obligations. (Paul and Acts disagree as to what these were; compare Gal 2:10 and Acts 15:20, 28–29.) Following this compromise, the dispute resurfaced in Antioch during Peter's visit to the church there (Gal 2:11–17), and possibly led to a breach between Paul and his partner in ministry Barnabas (see Gal 2:13–14 and notes; Acts 15:36–41 blames the break on a separate dispute). Paul subsequently left Antioch on a pair of missionary journeys through the region surrounding the Aegean Sea, establishing Gentile churches in cities throughout Asia Minor and on Greece's eastern coast. It was during this period that he composed his earliest extant letters.

Paul repeatedly addressed the question of whether Gentile converts should become circumcised and keep the law. He insisted that the answer was no, though his arguments may have subtly changed over time. His position on this issue never implied his rejection of Jews' special relationship with God, however (see Rom 9–11). On the contrary, in order to symbolize his Gentile congregations' solidarity with and spiritual dependency on the people of Israel (cf. Rom 11:13–32), Paul began collecting an offering for the Jerusalem church, a project he mentions in several letters (Rom 15:25–27; 1 Cor 16:1–4; 2 Cor 8–9). It probably represented his attempt to remain faithful to the compromise that had emerged from the earlier Jerusalem meeting (cf. Gal 2:10). When Paul traveled to Jerusalem to deliver this collection (Rom 15:25–33; Acts 20–21 understands the offering differently [see esp. 21:24 and note; cf. 24:17]), he was arrested—according to Acts, at the instigation of Asian Jews who mistakenly thought he had brought into the temple a Gentile whom they recognized from Ephesus (Acts 21:27–30). Paul remained imprisoned for the remaining years of his life, ultimately in expectation of a trial at Rome. He was incarcerated for a few days in Jerusalem, and then for two years in nearby Caesarea, and finally in Rome itself. Acts does not narrate his execution, but strongly suggests he perished in the city (e.g., 20:22–25; 21:11), two years after his arrival (see 28:30) or somewhat later. Early traditions confirm his execution at the hands of the imperial authorities, perhaps during Nero's persecution of the city's Christians in 64 C.E.

The Canonical Arrangement of Paul's Letters

The Pauline collection is the New Testament's second major division, with the book of Acts providing a narrative transition from the gospels' stories of Jesus to Paul's correspondence. The Pauline corpus is itself divided into three parts: letters to churches (Romans–2 Thessalonians), letters to individuals (1 Timothy–Philemon), and Hebrews, not written by Paul but sometimes thought to have been and exploring some of the same themes addressed by his letters. It serves as an appendix to the collection. The first two parts of the Pauline corpus are arranged roughly in order of decreasing length: Romans is the longest epistle to a church, 2 Thessalonians the shortest. Likewise, 1 Timothy is the longest letter to a delegate and Philemon the shortest.

A Chronology of the Epistles

To date individual Pauline Epistles or even to chart their order of composition is no mean feat. Most attempts to do so begin with Acts 18:12, which tells us that when Paul evangelized Corinth during his second missionary journey, Gallio (brother of the famous tragedian, philosopher, and statesman Seneca) served as proconsul of Achaia, the Roman province in which Corinth lay. An inscription informs us that Gallio held this position in 51–52 C.E., and this relatively fixed historical point enables us to construct a rough chronology of Paul's activities in Acts. We must try to fit the Pauline Epistles into that chronology.

Acts suggests that Paul evangelized Thessalonica soon before arriving in Corinth, for only brief stays in nearby Beroea and Athens intervened (17:1–33). 1 Thessalonians assumes that its recipients' conversion was recent (see, e.g., 1:9–10) and refers to news of that conversion having reached Achaia's inhabitants (1:7–8). We can therefore infer that Paul composed the letter during or just before his stay in Corinth around 51 or 52. It thus would be probably the earliest of Paul's Epistles and the earliest document in the entire New Testament. 2 Thessalonians gives the impression of having been written immediately after 1 Thessalonians, so it can tentatively be dated to about the same time.

An analogous procedure allows for approximate dating of the Corinthian correspondence. Paul wrote 1 Corinthians from Ephesus (16:8) and mentions in it his plan to send Timothy on to Macedonia before visiting that region personally (16:10, 5). Acts contains an account of Paul's ministry at Ephesus (chap. 19), which reports that Paul sent Timothy from Ephesus to Macedonia and then headed there himself (19:22; 20:1), so he apparently wrote 1 Corinthians during that sojourn in Ephesus. According to Acts' account, Paul ministered in Ephesus for two years (19:10) after evangelizing Corinth, with intervening trips to Jerusalem, Antioch, and finally Galatia and Phrygia (18:22–23). Allowing a reasonable amount of time for this travel yields a date of ca. 54–55 for the Ephesus ministry and the composition of 1 Corinthians. 2 Corinthians seems to be a composite document consisting of fragments from a number of letters that Paul sent the church at Corinth around the same time as 1 Corinthians, one of which might even be earlier than 1 Corinthians. Perhaps we should be satisfied with dating it (or rather the epistles lying behind it) to ca. 54–56. 1 Timothy may come from roughly the same period (ca. 55–56), for it purports to have been written by Paul soon after he left Ephesus for Macedonia (1 Tim 1:3), following Timothy's supposed return to Asia to oversee the Ephesian church in Paul's absence.

In Romans, Paul mentions an impending trip to Jerusalem in order to deliver the offering he had collected from his Gentile churches in the west (15:25–33). Acts narrates this trip (chap. 21), and estimating forward from the fixed point of Gallio's proconsulship we can speculate that it took place around 56–57. Romans can therefore be dated to this time. Incidentally, these passages confirm our dating of the Corinthian correspondence to a few years earlier, for in the letters to the Corinthian church Paul is still requesting donations for the offering whose delivery to Jerusalem Romans anticipates and Acts recounts (see 1 Cor 16:1–4; 2 Cor 8–9).

Other letters in the Pauline corpus are more difficult to date. Colossians, Philippians, Philemon, and 2 Timothy all claim to have been written from prison. Acts informs us of two prolonged incarcerations, both following Paul's arrest in Jerusalem during his trip to deliver the offering: first in nearby Caesarea (in the late 50s) and then, immediately after, in Rome (early 60s)—the second presumably culminating in Paul's martyrdom. Paul may also have been confined for a period during his ministry at Ephesus (see Philippians introduction), and any of the so-called prison epistles could conceivably have been written during any of these imprisonments, with a few limitations. Internal evidence in 2 Timothy (1:16–17) suggests that the letter was written in Rome. Since Philemon identifies the same people in Paul's company as Colossians (cf. Phlm 10, 24; Col 4:9–10, 14), it seems plausible that these two letters were written in tandem. More speculatively, we might include Ephesians with the pair, relying on its stylistic and thematic similarities to Colossians and the mention in both of Tychichus in Paul's company. So, it is a good guess that these three prison epistles were composed at roughly the same time, though we cannot identify them with any particular incarceration.

Galatians and Titus, the collection's remaining epistles, are notoriously difficult to date. Acts 18:23 may allude to Paul's founding of the Galatian church; if so this would have occurred immediately before his sojourn in Ephesus (ca. 54–55). But the allusion is far from certain, and Paul may have established the church at some other point in his ministry—for example, during his first missionary journey. Because Galatians itself (see 2:1–10) discusses the Jerusalem council narrated by Acts 15—a meeting that should probably be dated to ca. 48—it must have been composed after this time. Clues to its latest possible date are harder to discover. Since Galatians nowhere indicates that its writer is incarcerated, it was probably not written during Paul's final years, all of which were spent in custody. Moreover, Galatians makes no mention of the important Jerusalem offering that Paul was collecting from the Gentile churches he had founded. Since this offering symbolized Gentile and Jewish believers' ecclesiastical unity, which Galatians portrays as under threat, we might reasonably expect some reference to it were the collection under way at the time of the epistle's composition (as we find in 1 and 2 Corinthians and Romans). Some have even speculated that Paul decided to collect an offering for the Jerusalem church from the Gentile congregations he had established in the west as a response to his opponents in Galatia, who had apparently questioned the solidarity between his Gentile ministry and the largely Jewish congregation at Jerusalem. Building on such speculation, we might conjecture that Galatians was written soon before 1 and 2 Corinthians and Romans, in which the offering is first mentioned. This suggestion finds some confirmation in what appears to be a subtle clarification of Paul's thought in Romans on such issues raised in Galatians as God's covenant with Abraham and his faithfulness to Israel. So we are left with a span of time from ca. 48 to 54, with the latter years in that range appearing somewhat more likely.

Titus is the Pauline collection's greatest mystery, for it assumes a compositional context that corresponds to nothing mentioned in Acts or the other Pauline Epistles. Since Titus does not claim to have been written from prison, we might immediately assume that it was composed before the late 50s C.E. Nonetheless, largely as a result of its presumption that Paul evangelized Crete—a mission that neither Acts nor the other Paulines hint at—some have speculated that Paul was in fact not executed after the Roman incarceration reported by Acts. Instead, they argue, his trial must have ended favorably, leading to a release and another mission in the Aegean region and elsewhere, during which Paul established a Cretan church. Evidence supporting this possibility is scant, however, and the scenario flies in the face of Acts' clear suggestions that Paul's trip to Rome culminated in martyrdom. If Paul did write Titus, it is best to presume he did so before ca. 64, the likely date of his death, and that this letter simply makes reference to an episode from earlier in his career that no other reliable sources mention.

Many scholars would dispute much of this chronological reconstruction. Its most obvious vulnerability is its reliance on Acts, whose accuracy in recounting Paul's career should perhaps be viewed more skeptically. A reconstruction relying on relevant data from the Pauline Letters alone (or at least more exclusively) might look very different and would certainly be more tentative, since such data are few and far between. Determining the Pauline Epistles' dates and relative chronology is further complicated by the fact that Paul probably did not compose all of the

New Testament epistles attributed to him. Pseudepigraphy was common in antiquity, and to authors as diverse as Homer, Plato, Seneca, and Philo of Alexandria works were attributed that no one today believes these authors actually wrote. Such imitative writing was a natural outgrowth of Greco-Roman education, which focused on rhetoric and conventionally required students to imitate the styles and ideas of recognized masters; indeed, some pseudepigraphic compositions seem to have originated as school exercises. Moreover, students of a particular philosopher (e.g., Plato) or adherents to a philosophical tradition (e.g., the Peripatetic) frequently presented their own ideas in the form of treatises and epistles composed in the names of their schools' leading philosophers, and these were later taken for the masters' own compositions. The standard editions of the works of Plato and Aristotle include a number of works that fit into this category.

In light of the above, it comes as no surprise to learn that Pauline pseudepigrapha circulated in antiquity. For example, 3 Corinthians, a letter written in Paul's name, is today universally recognized as having been composed by a later Christian. Yet despite this modern consensus, certain Eastern Orthodox churches long regarded 3 Corinthians as canonical: it was included in some bibles and even boasts a commentary by the great fourth-century Syrian theologian and poet Ephraem. Paul's epistle to the Laodiceans is another important example. It was included in many late antique and medieval Latin Bibles, as well as in Wycliffe's translation, the first of the entire Bible into English. Since pseudepigraphy was common in Greco-Roman antiquity and since Pauline pseudepigrapha in particular were widespread, we might reasonably suspect that the New Testament accepted by most Christians today as canonical contains writings attributed to Paul that the apostle did not actually write. Titus, which assumes a compositional context that does not cohere with what we know of Paul's travels and ministry, is an especially likely candidate.

Christians in antiquity occasionally doubted whether Paul actually composed one or another of the canonical epistles attributed to him. For instance, Jerome felt it necessary to defend Philemon's authenticity in his prologue to the Vulgate translation. But serious and sustained inquiry into possible New Testament pseudepigraphy is a phenomenon more modern than ancient. Most influentially, the nineteenth-century biblical scholar Ferdinand Christian Bauer concluded that only Romans, 1 and 2 Corinthians, and Galatians were authentic, on the basis of his supposition that these Pauline Letters alone reflect conflict between Jewish (or Petrine) and Gentile (or Pauline) Christianity. Contemporary scholars, while deeply indebted to Bauer's concentrated focus on the doctrinal controversies to which Paul's letters respond, have largely rejected this paradigm and find too narrow its criteria for judging authenticity. Today, the authenticity of just six Pauline Epistles is seriously in doubt: Ephesians, Colossians, 2 Thessalonians, and the Pastoral Epistles (1 and 2 Timothy, and Titus). The status of the first three is vigorously debated; a broad consensus (though perhaps not a correct one) relegates the final three to pseudepigrapha.

Reasons for doubting the authenticity of the six disputed Pauline Epistles differ from letter to letter, and some are more persuasive than others. The introductions that follow trace the specific contours of the relevant debates. Any letter composed by a follower of Paul writing in his name is impossible to date confidently, as its true compositional context necessarily lies concealed beneath a pseudepigraphic veneer. Conventionally, scholars who believe that 2 Thessalonians, Ephesians, and Colossians are pseudepigraphic date them to the closing decades of the first century C.E. Those who believe that Paul did not compose the Pastoral Epistles tend to date them anywhere between the end of the first and beginning of the second century.

Epistle	Approximate Date of Composition, Assuming Authenticity	Complicating Factors
1 Thess	51–52	
2 Thess	51–52	If pseudepigraphic, late in the first century.
Galatians	48–54	Consideration of the Jerusalem offering may suggest a date toward the end of this range.
1 Corinthians	54–55	
2 Corinthians	54–56	If the epistle is a composite document, some sections may be earlier than 1 Corinthians.
1 Timothy	56	If pseudepigraphic, late in the first or early in the second century.
Romans	56–57	
Colossians	58–61	Assuming composition during Caesarean or Roman incarceration, and taking into consideration Colossae's destruction by earthquake and abandonment ca. 60–61. If pseudepigraphic, late in the first century. If written during imprisonment at Ephesus, ca. 55.
Philemon	58–62	Assuming composition during Caesarean or Roman incarceration. If written during imprisonment at Ephesus, ca. 55.
Ephesians	58–62	Assuming composition during Caesarean or Roman incarceration. If pseudepigraphic, late in the first century. If written during imprisonment at Ephesus, ca. 55.
Philippians	58–62	Assuming composition during Caesarean or Roman incarceration. If written during imprisonment at Ephesus, ca. 55.
2 Timothy	60–62	Inferring composition during Roman incarceration. If pseudepigraphic, late in the first or early in the second century.
Titus	?	If pseudepigraphic, late in the first or early in the second century.

One important implication of this chronology deserves special attention. Although Paul writes in the period following the events narrated by the gospels, all of his indubitably authentic epistles were composed before the gospels. Since Paul did not know the historical Jesus and could not have read the gospels, we cannot presume he was aware of any tradition about Jesus that these later texts preserve unless parallels between them and Paul's writings are strikingly clear (examples include the eschatological scenario outlined in 1 Thess 4:13–5:11 and Paul's discussion of divorce at 1 Cor 7:10–11). But such parallels occur infrequently and we must conclude either that Paul did not know much about Jesus' life and ministry or that he was not interested in addressing these topics in his correspondence (cf. 2 Cor 5:16). Jesus' crucifixion and resurrection, which Paul often mentions, seem to have been more important to him than Jesus' ethical teaching, miracles, and the like; but even on these topics Paul cannot be assimilated to the gospels. For instance, Paul never mentions Jesus' empty tomb, an important feature of all four gospels; and his elaborate treatment of resurrection in 1 Corinthians 15, which contrasts spiritual bodies with fleshly ones, may in fact be compatible with an assumption that Jesus' fleshly body remained decomposing in its tomb even after Jesus was "raised a spiritual body" (see 1 Cor 15:35–54 and notes).

Literary Character: The Many Voices of the Pauline Corpus

Paul's Epistles are not abstract treatises but real letters (or, for the potentially pseudepigraphical writings, careful imitations of real letters) written to particular groups of people at particular times in their communal association. Formally, the epistles resemble other correspondence in Greco-Roman antiquity. They begin with a salutation naming the sender and the recipient, as well as expressing a greeting (e.g., 1 Thess 1:1). A prayer of thanksgiving follows (1 Thess 1:2–3:13), providing a transition to the letter's body, in which the author offers instruction to the recipients (1 Thess 4:1–5:22). The letters close with a wish of peace (1 Thess 5:23–25), personal greetings (not actually personal in 1 Thess 5:26, but cf. Rom 16:1–16), and a benediction (1 Thess 5:28), sometimes preceded by a final command (1 Thess 5:27). As one might expect, this structure is not rigid. For example, 1 Thessalonians' thanksgiving is much longer than most, 2 Corinthians replaces the prayer of thanks with a more generic blessing (1:3–7), and Galatians omits it entirely. Nonetheless, an identifiable structure emerges from the study of Paul's Epistles, and it is similar to that found in other letters from Greco-Roman antiquity. A mundane letter from the first or second century C.E., which was written on a piece of papyrus that survived in Egypt's dry climate, is often cited for comparison:

> Irenaeus to Apollinarius his dearest brother many greetings. I pray continually for your health, and I myself am healthy. I want you to know that I reached land on the sixth of the month Epeiph and we uploaded our cargo on the eighteenth of the same month. I went up to Rome on the twenty-fifth of the same month and the place welcomed us as the god willed, and we are daily expecting our discharge, it so being that up till today nobody in the corn fleet

has been released. Many salutations to your wife and to Serenus and to all who love you, each by name. Goodbye. [Month of] Mesore 9.

(Trans. A. S. Hunt and C. C. Edgar, slightly modified)

In Irenaeus's letter the salutation precedes a brief prayer. The body follows, and is itself followed by a closing that includes personal greetings. The same elements are found in Paul's letters.

The status of Paul's Epistles as real letters has more than formal implications. Since Paul's letters are actual first-century dispatches, they function, all but literally, as voices in a conversation that we cannot hear in its totality. Paul wrote 1 Corinthians, for example, in response to reports about the church at Corinth that he had heard from "them which are of the house of Chloe" (1:11) as well as to a letter that the Corinthian church wrote to him (7:1). We have access to neither, nor to an earlier epistle Paul sent to Corinth (unless 2 Corinthians preserves a fragment; see 1 Cor 5:9 and note), which he is convinced the Corinthian church has misunderstood. We are therefore left with the task of reconstructing from Paul's written words alone—and not even all of his side of the correspondence—a complicated dialogue between him and the Corinthians that took place over a period of years, conducted by letter, by rumor, and in person. This task is not just daunting; it is impossible. We can make tentative guesses as to the conversation's contours and content, but there are surely aspects of it to which we will remain deaf.

Our ignorance about the conversations in which they participate often explains why we find some passages in Paul's letters difficult to comprehend. Many of 1 Corinthians' most obscure mysteries (e.g., Paul's invocation of angels as a reason for women not to pray without veils at 11:10, or his reference to baptism for the dead at 15:29) would likely have been transparent to the epistle's original audience: Paul can content himself with laconic references precisely because he assumes his readers' familiarity with what he is writing about.

An analogous line of reasoning suggests that we should adopt a posture of interpretive humility when approaching passages of Paul's Epistles that appear straightforward, for it is difficult to say how even a relatively uncomplicated assertion might have sounded in the context of an extended conversation. For example, when Paul moves from the abstract notion that God's wisdom is foolishness in the world's eyes (1 Cor 1:18–25) to a particular application of that idea, we must take care in gauging his discourse's tone: "For ye see your calling, brethren, how that not many wise men after the flesh, not many mighty, not many noble, are called: but God hath chosen the foolish things of the world to confound the wise; and God hath chosen the weak things of the world to confound the things which are mighty; and base things of the world, and things which are despised" (1 Cor 1:26–28). Paul may be making a commonplace observation about eschatological reversal with which he simply expects his readers to agree (cf. Mark 10:31); but he may be putting the Corinthians in their place by deliberately insulting them with the discourteous epithets "foolish," "weak," and "base." Or perhaps he is doing both. If we knew what they had written to Paul, and what he had heard of them from Chloe's people, we would be in a better position to judge; as it stands, we must admit our inability to hear Paul's words as they sounded to their original readers.

Although they are actual dispatches written and delivered to particular parties, Paul's Epistles have more in common with the philosophical letters of Plato and Epicurus or the *Moral Epistles* of Seneca than they do with Irenaeus's letter to Apollinarius. They are carefully argued, engaged with the relevant literary traditions (especially the Old Testament), and display a sophisticated style. Even if they were written only for their particular addressees, those recipients were often communities—that is, churches meeting in one or more homes (cf. Rom 16:5)—and so it is fitting that Paul's Epistles resemble ancient philosophical epistles, which even when addressed to particular individuals (as were Seneca's letters to Lucilius) were always intended for wider dissemination. The closest Pauline analogue to the philosophical epistle would be the Epistle to the Romans. It is in part a letter of introduction from Paul to an unfamiliar church he hopes to visit, but its elaborate theological argumentation transcends this rather mundane purpose. In it Paul takes the opportunity to articulate as clearly as he can his positions on a number of thorny theological issues, including the nature of God's covenant with Abraham, the relationship between sin and the law, and the implications of God's covenantal relationship with Israel for Jewish and non-Jewish believers in Christ.

In Romans Paul frequently adopts the so-called diatribal style, which characterizes much Hellenistic philosophical writing. It entails presenting an argument as an informal conversation between a dominant authorial voice and imaginary interlocutors whom the author introduces, thereby facilitating a lively presentation of dense philosophical reasoning. A passage from Seneca's *Epistle* 85, on the inviolability of virtue, is exemplary: "'What then? If a sword is held to the neck of a brave man, if his body is pierced again and again, . . . is he not afraid? Will you say that he is not feeling pain?' Yes, he feels pain (for no virtue strips a human being of his ability to feel), but he does not fear; he gazes upon his own pains from on high, unbeaten. You ask what kind of mind he has. Like the mind of those who comfort an ailing friend" (85.29). This brief section features two voices in conversation; although quotation marks signal the transition in Brad Inwood's translation, they are absent from the original Latin, which requires the reader to distinguish between voices by means of contextual clues alone. Indeed, even in Inwood's version, the presence of dialogue is not always explicit: where the interlocutor's voice is presented indirectly ("You ask what kind of mind he has"), the reader might not notice that a question is being attributed to the conversation partner. Seneca's argument here and throughout the epistle progresses as an informal conversation: in order to follow the train of thought it articulates, we must keep track of multiple voices engaging one another in lively dialogue.

In Romans 3, Paul employs a similar argumentative strategy in a dialogue somewhat more subtle than Seneca's. The apostle signals its initiation at Rom 2:17, by addressing a hypothetical Jewish teacher who will resurface a few verses later as an interlocutor questioning the dominant authorial voice about Jewish privilege and God's fairness. Romans 3 is not normally viewed as an example of Hellenistic diatribal argumentation, but sensitive early interpreters such as Origen observed a dialogic exchange in this chapter (see *Commentary on Romans* 3.9.8), and the manuscript tradition also evinces occasional use of scribal conventions designed to signal dramatic dialogue. This edition of KJV uses paragraph breaks to the same effect.

The diatribal style employed by Paul and contemporary popular philosophical writers tolerates a high level of argumentative complexity—complexity that may seem surprising in an author such as Paul, who is often judged to be rigidly dogmatic. These writers can skillfully manipulate informal dialogue to allow their discourses' dominant voices to articulate ever more qualified positions on subjects under consideration, and this is precisely what happens in Romans 3 and 6–7. Indeed, even when it might not be appropriate to divide a particular Pauline passage into distinct voices, the apostle's approach to his theme may still be dialogic in spirit.

In 1 Cor 11:2–16, for example, Paul challenges the Corinthians' practice of not requiring women to veil their heads when prophesying, but he begins with general praise of the recipients for remembering and practicing his teaching (v. 2). The encouragement may suggest that in the case of veiling, at least, the Corinthians have not so much rebelled against Paul's doctrine as misunderstood it. In other words, Paul objects to a conclusion about liturgical policy that his readers have reasonably drawn from something he himself had taught. Since his argument in 1 Corinthians 11 uses Gen 1:27 (awkwardly) to insist on veiling, a good guess is that the Corinthians' inference relied on teaching such as that preserved in Gal 3:27–28, where Paul invokes the same verse from Genesis to insist on gender dissolution: "For as many of you as have been baptized into Christ have put on Christ. There is neither Jew nor Greek, there is neither bond nor free, there is neither male and [KJV 'nor'; see note] female: for ye are all one in Christ Jesus."

In 1 Corinthians, Paul invokes Gen 1:27 in order to make a very different point about gender, one that implies female prophets should wear veils:

> A man indeed ought not to cover his head, forasmuch as he is the image and glory of God [cf. Gen 1:27]: but the woman is the glory of the man. For the man is not of the woman; but the woman of the man [cf. Gen 2:21–23]. Neither was the man created for the woman; but the woman for the man [cf. Gen 2:18]. For this cause ought the woman to have power on her head[.]
>
> (1 Cor 11:7–10)

Paul's exegesis is profoundly flawed, for Gen 1:27 actually says that "God created man in his own image, in the image of God created he him; *male and female* created he them" (emphasis added). According to the verse, men and women equally reflect the image of God. Paul, apparently recognizing this problem, immediately gives voice to an alternative perspective on the same material: "Nevertheless neither is the man without the woman, neither the woman without the man, in the Lord [cf. Gen 1:27; 2:24]. For as the woman is of the man, even so is the man also by the woman [i.e., men come from women's wombs]; but all things of God" (1 Cor 11:11–12). This is the final pronouncement on Genesis in Paul's argument, and it must be regarded as decisive, in light of both Gen 1:27 and 2:18–24; for even the later passage surely emphasizes God's creation of men and women over the incidental fact that God created Eve from Adam's rib. Moreover, the fact that every single man after Adam has come from a woman's body renders highly suspect the invocation of Eve's exceptional withdrawal from his side to support the dubious notion that women in general derive from men and therefore reflect God's glory only secondarily.

Paul's decision to leave off discussion of the Genesis story at this point amounts to granting the final exegetical word to an interpretation of the Bible that undermines the position he had been supporting. Paul does not abandon his assertion that female prophets should be veiled, but his argument becomes embarrassingly lame: "Judge in yourselves: is it comely that a woman pray unto God uncovered? Doth not even nature itself teach you, that, if a man have long hair, it is a shame unto him? But if a woman have long hair, it is a glory to her: for her hair is given her for a covering" (11:13–15). The reference to nature is confusing, if not actually confused (might Paul actually mean culture?), especially in comparison with the sophisticated invocations of natural law found in philosophers contemporary with Paul, like Seneca. The apostle mercifully puts to rest this flawed line of reasoning and ends discussion of the entire issue. Although he never explicitly abandons his conviction that women should prophesy only with veiled heads, he gives voice to an argument that effectively subverts his use of Genesis to support that conviction. His dialogic discussion proves to be so carefully qualified and complex that Paul cannot bring himself to close it with a demand that women stop prophesying unveiled. Such a demand would amount to a patently arbitrary conclusion to what he has written. Instead, his final words forbid contention about unveiled female prophets: "But if any man seem to be contentious, we have no such custom, neither the churches of God" (11:16)—that is, "however you decide to go forward, let's not have any fighting about it."

This is just one example of a passage where Paul's dialogic discourse evinces a complexity of argumentation that frustrates interpreters searching for rigid dogma and clear directives. Any number of others in the Pauline corpus similarly resist a simple reading, including his discussion of whether believers should eat meat sacrificed to idols in 1 Corinthians chapters 8 and 10, the contrast he draws between the new and old covenants in 2 Corinthians 3, and his meditation on God's covenant with Abraham in Romans 4. Anyone looking for easy answers should look elsewhere than in Paul, whose writings are thoroughly difficult, not only because they are composed as voices in a conversation whose other participants we can no longer hear, but also because Paul's own arguments are multivoiced; even when not going so far as introducing imaginary interlocutors, they articulate compelling objections to the main line of reasoning and thus force it to become ever more qualified, complex, and difficult to apprehend. Indeed, as 1 Corinthians 11 demonstrates, those competing voices can sometimes gain the upper hand, making it difficult or impossible to determine what the "main line of reasoning" actually is.

We ought not to assume that Paul is everywhere so flexible, however. While the dialogues his writings embody are often engagingly complex and surprisingly open-ended, Paul is capable of rigid dogmatism as well. He adopts an uncompromising position on Gentile circumcision, for example. In light of his insistence that "in Jesus Christ neither circumcision availeth any thing, nor uncircumcision"

(Gal 5:6, reiterated at 6:15), one might expect him to allow Gentile believers who desire to be circumcised to go ahead, insisting only that no Gentile be required or pressured to undergo the rite. Instead, he asserts that "if ye be circumcised, Christ shall profit you nothing" (Gal 5:2), thereby denying Gentile believers the option of becoming circumcised in faithful obedience to God's directive to Abraham. Paul can also be obnoxiously polemical. He is capable of sarcasm and even of out-and-out vitriol, as when he crudely wishes castration on those urging Gentile believers in Galatia to keep God's covenant with Abraham (Gal 5:12).

An exclusive focus on Paul's theological argumentation would give a false view of his letters. The Pauline Epistles are above all varied, containing moments of lovely rhetorical prose that borders on the lyrical, such as the paean to love of 1 Corinthians 13 and the beautiful prayer of thanksgiving occupying most of 1 Thessalonians 1–3. They also contain traditional liturgical material, such as the eucharistic liturgy (1 Cor 11:23–26) and Philippians' encomium of Christ (2:6–11). On a less elevated level, they contain lists, especially of vices and virtues, and a good deal of moral advice as well. Some of this is quite attractive (e.g., "Bear ye one another's burdens, and so fulfil the law of Christ," Gal 6:2); some is ugly ("Slaves [KJV 'servants'], be obedient to them that are your masters according to the flesh, with fear and trembling, in singleness of your heart, as unto Christ," Eph 6:5); and some is just plain strange ("ought the woman to have a power on her head because of the angels," 1 Cor 11:10). No matter how we look at them, Paul's letters turn out to contain multiple voices, especially if, as seems to be the case, Paul himself did not write all that the New Testament attributes to him. The Pauline corpus thus constitutes a discursive world wider than any other section of the New Testament. We can be grateful that the challenges of its exploration are matched by its pleasures.

The Epistle of Paul the Apostle
to the Romans

ROMANS seems to have been composed at the apex of Paul's ministry, soon before his planned visit to Jerusalem in the closing years of the 50s C.E., when he would present to the church there an offering he had spent years collecting from the Gentile congregations he founded and oversaw (see 15:25–33 and notes). Paul would be arrested in Jerusalem and ultimately sent to Rome for a trial, where he was all but certainly executed. Romans, therefore, is the last extant letter Paul wrote while his ministry was unimpeded. Depending on how a number of other epistles in the Pauline corpus are construed, it may be the latest indubitably authentic letter of Paul to survive.

Romans is certainly Paul's longest, most densely argued, and most influential epistle. Christians as diverse as Augustine and John Wesley claimed to have been converted by reading it, and Augustine relied heavily on Romans 7 when he constructed in his autobiographical *Confessions* what would become for fifteen centuries (until Freud) the West's standard psychological understanding of the self. Martin Luther's response to Romans was virtually the starting point of the Reformation, and William Tyndale's first English New Testament included, as by far its longest preface to a book, a translation of Luther's preface to Romans. In the early twentieth century, Karl Barth's brilliant commentary on the epistle ushered in a new era of theological inquiry, and more recently, Paul's insistence on the irrevocability of God's covenant with Israel in chapters 9–11 has guided contemporary Christians' tragically belated reappraisal of their traditions' and institutions' perverse attitudes toward Jews and Judaism.

In spite of its sweeping influence on later generations, Romans is also the Pauline epistle most thoroughly grounded in its first-century Greco-Roman context. This grounding is especially evident in the classical rhetorical techniques that Paul persistently employs and expects his readers to recognize. Readers as early as Origen (writing in the first half of the third century) have discovered in it examples of prosopopoeia (speech by an imagined character), as Paul adopts voices belonging to figures from ancient history or mythology (such as Eve and Medea in 7:7–25; see notes), or voices belonging to easily recognizable stereotyped personae (such as the hypocrite of 2:1–16). Moreover, large sections of the letter are written in the so-called diatribal style, also found in contemporary philosophical writers such as Seneca: lively dialogue between a commanding authorial voice and a rhetorically constructed interlocutor (e.g., 3:1–20; 3:27–4:2). Such conventional discourse ties Paul's letter firmly to its Greco-Roman rhetorical context, and readers familiar with ancient pagan philosophers such as Seneca and Plutarch will probably find themselves in a better position to follow Romans' argument than will readers familiar with the theological systems that later writers such as Augustine, Luther, and Barth based on it.

Of the audience to which Paul addresses Romans, almost nothing is known beyond what he tells us. We know it was a Christian community Paul had not founded, and one he had never before visited. His need to introduce his ministry and understanding of the gospel to people largely unfamiliar with him at least in part explains the exhaustiveness of this letter. Despite a number of scholars' elaborate arguments that the letter constitutes Paul's attempt to reconcile Jewish and Gentile constituents of an ethnically mixed Roman church, several passages clearly present the readers as Gentiles (e.g., 1:5–6, 13; 11:13), and Paul's ability to greet by name a handful of Jews in Romans' final chapter (16:3, 7, 11) does not undermine his construction of the audience as one consisting all but entirely of converted pagans. On the contrary, the letter's thematic development presupposes that Paul has in mind Gentile readers throughout: introducing himself as an apostle to the Gentiles (1:5) who expects to visit Gentile believers at Rome (1:11–15), Paul discusses God's plan for making Gentile sinners righteous (1:16–8:39), situates Gentiles' newfound righteousness in God's ancient plan for Israel (chaps. 9–11), and gives directions on exactly how righteous Gentiles should behave (chaps. 12–15).

In Romans Paul develops in a more sophisticated way ideas he had introduced in Galatians but had not fully worked out there, including the significance and implications of Abraham's faithful response to God's covenantal promise (Rom 4; cf. Gal 3:6–9, 14–18, 29), the role of the Mosaic law in light of the Abrahamic covenant's primacy (Rom 7; cf. Gal 3:15–26), and the complementarity of God's decision to reach out to Gentiles in Christ and his continued privileging of Israel (Rom 9–11; cf. Gal. 6:16). In developing these ideas, Paul draws on his considerable skills as a creative interpreter of Scripture: his reading of the Abraham story in chapter 4 is thoughtful and coherent, even if tendentious; his allusive rewriting of the story of Eve's deception and transgression in Rom 7:7–25 is subtle, surprising, and theologically rich; his use of the panorama of Scripture to explain God's commitment to Israel in chapters 9–11 is passionate and, with all its convolutions, reversals, and counterreversals, carefully attuned to the Hebrew Bible's portrayal of YHWH's tumultuous relationship with his people.

Many readers see in Romans 9–11's scripturally motivated insistence on God's unbreakable allegiance to Israel the highest expression of Pauline theology. Paul recognizes and tries to resolve an issue that simplistic forms of Christian supersessionism necessarily ignore: if God has broken faith with Israel in favor of the church, how can Christians trust he won't break faith with them as well? It is no accident that Romans 9–11 follows on the heels of the bold and comforting rhetoric of 8:31–39, a passage culminating in one of KJV's most exquisite sentences: "For I am persuaded, that neither death, nor life, nor angels, nor principalities, nor powers, nor things present, nor things to come, nor height, nor depth, nor any other creature, shall be able to separate us from the love of God, which is in Christ Jesus our Lord" (vv. 38–39). Paul recognizes that if God has abandoned Israel, then these words amount to nothing more than a pie-in-the-sky platitude, a self-delusive fantasy. The beautiful passage requires the subsequent argument of chapters 9–11 as its guarantee: if it is to be true, God's gift and calling must be irrevocable (11:29); as a consequence, all Israel, not just a meager remnant, must be saved (11:26). Despite Romans' profound influence on Christian thought, chapters 9–11 have been largely overlooked or perversely misconstrued by later generations, their relationship to the perpetually favorite 8:31–39 all but totally ignored. And this ignorance has had a tragic historical impact at least as significant as the epistle's combined influence on Augustine, Luther, Tyndale, Wesley, Barth, and countless others.

Any analysis foregrounding Romans' Gentile audience and giving due weight to chapters 9–11 will require a reappraisal of this influence. Many of Romans' crucial theological ideas, including Paul's bold tethering of righteousness to God's grace and to faith in (or the faith of) Jesus rather than to works of the law (cf. 3:20–28), have been abstracted from the epistle and incorporated into Christian theological systems constructed to address issues foreign to Paul's letter—especially religious legalism and its corollary, the conscientious individual tormented by an inability to adhere perfectly to religious and moral rules. Romans, however, reveals Paul to be essentially concerned with promoting the righteousness (including righteous behavior; see chaps. 12–13) of Gentile sinners who turn to Jesus, while at the same time to be fundamentally committed to maintaining Israel's pride of place in God's plan. Paul, then, must explain how the plan God accomplishes in Jesus both embraces Gentiles *qua* Gentiles and coheres with Jewish Scripture, including the story of Abraham, which defines God's people precisely in terms of their descent from the patriarch, thereby introducing the Jewish-Gentile distinction into the world. That is what Romans accomplishes. Whatever one thinks of later Christian theological systems founded on its ideas, it is important not to presume that they accurately represent Paul's position, for many of the concerns and commitments that this Jesus-believing Jew and self-styled "apostle of the Gentiles" (11:13) makes explicit in Romans are foreign to and perhaps ultimately incompatible with them.

There are a number of strong commentaries on Romans in English. Joseph A. Fitzmyer's Anchor Bible Commentary, *Romans: A New Translation with Introduction and Commentary* (New York: Doubleday, 1993), is particularly comprehensive, and Luke Timothy Johnson's more incisive *Reading Romans: A Literary and Theological Commentary* (New York: Crossroad, 1997) is valuable as well. A number of studies should also be consulted, especially Stanley K. Stowers, *A Rereading of Romans: Justice, Jews, and Gentiles* (New Haven: Yale University Press, 1994), and chapter 2 of Richard B. Hays, *Echoes of Scripture in the Letters of Paul* (New Haven: Yale University Press, 1989), both of which are excerpted in the Appendix, pp. 1436–48 and pp. 1255–73. This introduction and the annotations that follow incorporate observations and ideas from all these works.

THE EPISTLE OF PAUL THE APOSTLE TO THE

ROMANS

1 Paul, a servant of Jesus Christ, called to be an apostle, separated unto the gospel of God, ²(which he had promised afore by his prophets in the holy scriptures,) ³concerning his Son Jesus Christ our Lord, which was made of the seed of David according to the flesh; ⁴and declared to be the Son of God with power, according to the spirit of holiness, by the resurrection from the dead: ⁵by whom we have received grace and apostleship, for obedience to the faith among all nations, for his name: ⁶among whom are ye also the called of Jesus Christ: ⁷to all that be in Rome, beloved of God, called to be saints: Grace to you and peace from God our Father, and the Lord Jesus Christ.

⁸First, I thank my God through Jesus Christ for you all, that your faith is spoken of throughout the whole world. ⁹For God is my witness, whom I serve with my

---

1:1–15 Opening. Consisting of a salutation (vv. 1–7) and prayer of thanksgiving (vv. 8–15). Following Greco-Roman epistolary conventions, Romans (like all of Paul's letters) begins with the writer's name and title (vv. 1–6), followed by the name of the addressee and a greeting (v. 7). Probably because he is introducing himself to an unfamiliar church, Paul's self-description is longer here than in any of his other letters and includes an explanation of his gospel (vv. 2–4). Moreover, he carefully avoids presuming too much authority over his readers (vv. 11–12; contrast 1 Thess 3:10). The thanksgiving is a customary feature of Paul's letters, missing only in Galatians and Titus, and replaced by a blessing in 2 Corinthians.   **1:1** *Servant*: lit. "slave." The Greek words normally translated with forms of "serve" almost always refer to slavery. *Apostle*: Gk. *apostolos*, lit. "one sent out," i.e., an itinerant evangelist commissioned by a church (cf. Acts 13:1–3). *Separated*: see Gal 1:15 and note. *Gospel*: see Mark 1:1 note. **1:3** *Made*: better "born." *Seed of David*: Jesus is presented as the descendant God promised David in 2 Sam 7:12–16. Matthew (1:1–17) and Luke (3:23–31) analogously trace Jesus' descent from David through Mary's husband Joseph, even though their (divergent) genealogical speculations stand in some tension with their insistence on Jesus' virgin birth.   **1:4** *Declared*: alternatively "appointed" or "designated," suggesting that Jesus' resurrection divinized him. The OT calls Israel's anointed king *son of God* (e.g., in Ps 2; see notes, esp. at v. 7; cf. 2 Sam 7:14; Ps 89:26–27). Paul, then, implies that Jesus' resurrection enthrones him, appointing him king not merely of Israel but of "all nations" (v. 5). **1:5** *Grace*: Gk. *charis*, a gift or favor; cf. 15:15–16. *To the faith*: or "of faith." *Faith* is Gk. *pistis*, "faithfulness" or "loyalty"; KJV sometimes translates it "belief" (and its verbal form is usually "believe"), though it has a wider semantic range.   **1:7** *Saints*: a Christian self-designation meaning "holy/sanctified ones." *Grace to you and peace*: Paul's standard epistolary salutation. *Grace* here refers to divine favor. Heb. *shalom*, "well-being," might lie behind the reference to *peace*, but Paul may also suggest a distinction between God's peace and *pax Romana* ("Roman peace"), which contemporary political propaganda celebrated.   **1:9** *Serve*: Gk. *latreuō*, referring to cultic or, more broadly, religious service.

spirit in the gospel of his Son, that without ceasing I make mention of you always in my prayers; [10]making request, if by any means now at length I might have a prosperous journey by the will of God to come unto you. [11]For I long to see you, that I may impart unto you some spiritual gift, to the end ye may be established; [12]that is, that I may be comforted together with you by the mutual faith both of you and me. [13]Now I would not have you ignorant, brethren, that oftentimes I purposed to come unto you, (but was let hitherto,) that I might have some fruit among you also, even as among other Gentiles. [14]I am debtor both to the Greeks, and to the Barbarians; both to the wise, and to the unwise. [15]So, as much as in me is, I am ready to preach the gospel to you that are at Rome also.

[16]For I am not ashamed of the gospel of Christ: for it is the power of God unto salvation to every one that believeth; to the Jew first, and also to the Greek. [17]For therein is the righteousness of God revealed from faith to faith: as it is written, The just shall live by faith.

[18]For the wrath of God is revealed from heaven against all ungodliness and unrighteousness of men, who hold the truth in unrighteousness; [19]because that which may be known of God is manifest in them; for God hath shewed it unto them. [20]For the invisible things of him from the creation of the world are clearly seen, being understood by the things that are made, even his eternal power and Godhead; so that they are without excuse: [21]because that, when they knew God, they glorified him not as God, neither were thankful; but became vain in their imaginations, and their foolish heart was darkened. [22]Professing themselves to be wise, they became fools, [23]and changed the glory of the uncorruptible God into an image made like to corruptible man, and to birds, and four-footed beasts, and creeping things. [24]Wherefore God also gave them up to uncleanness through the lusts of their own hearts, to dishonour their own bodies between themselves:

1:11 *Gift*: Gk. *charisma*, related to *charis* (see v. 5 note) and here probably referring to an ability bestowed on believers by God; see 12:6–8 for a list of such gifts.   **1:12** *Comforted*: better "encouraged."   **1:13** *Brethren*: a common self-designation of Jesus-believers. *Let*: hindered. *Gentiles*: Gk. *ethnē*, also "nations" (cf. v. 5).   **1:14** *Barbarians*: non-Greeks.   **1:15** *So, as . . . ready*: alternatively "hence the eagerness in me."

1:16–17 Thesis. 1:16 *I am . . . gospel*: cf. Mark 8:38. *Of Christ*: better omitted (MS tradition). **1:17** *Righteousness*: Gk. root *dikaio-*, which KJV translates with forms of "righteous" and "just"; see Gal 2:16 note on "justified." *From faith to faith*: the phrase has a range of possible meanings, including that faith has different levels (cf. 2 Cor 2:16; 3:18); that faith is the basis and goal of Paul's gospel; or that Christ's faithfulness to God, exemplified in his willingness to die on the cross, brings about analogous faithfulness in the believer (cf. 3:22; see Gal 2:16 note on "faith of Jesus Christ"). *The just . . . faith*: Hab 2:4; alternatively "the righteous one will live from faith"—perhaps referring to Christ (cf. Acts 3:14, "the Just"), whose faithfulness to God was vindicated by resurrection.

1:18–32 God's anger against Gentiles. This section presupposes a Jewish myth (preserved in Wis 14:12–31) that Gentiles had rejected worship of God in order to venerate idols, causing God to give the Gentile world over to unrighteousness. Paul's argument is structured as a series of exchanges: creator for creation (vv. 20–21), wisdom for foolishness (v. 22), etc.   **1:18** *Hold*: i.e., hold back or restrain. **1:19** *In them*: or "among them."   **1:20** *The invisible things . . . excuse*: cf. Wis 13:1–9, which v. 25 also recalls.   **1:23** *Changed the glory . . . things*: echoing Ps 106:20; the reference here, as in the psalm, is to idols.   **1:24** *Lusts*: Gk. *epithymiai*, lit. "desires" (for food, wealth, etc. as well as sex); a different word is used in v. 27. In Greco-Roman philosophy, desire, in all its multitudinous forms, was the most troubling

²⁵who changed the truth of God into a lie, and worshipped and served the creature more than the Creator, who is blessed for ever. Amen.

²⁶For this cause God gave them up unto vile affections: for even their women did change the natural use into that which is against nature: ²⁷and likewise also the men, leaving the natural use of the woman, burned in their lust one toward another; men with men working that which is unseemly, and receiving in themselves that recompence of their error which was meet.

²⁸And even as they did not like to retain God in their knowledge, God gave them over to a reprobate mind, to do those things which are not convenient; ²⁹being filled with all unrighteousness, fornication, wickedness, covetousness, maliciousness; full of envy, murder, debate, deceit, malignity; whisperers, ³⁰backbiters, haters of God, despiteful, proud, boasters, inventors of evil things, disobedient to parents, ³¹without understanding, covenantbreakers, without natural affection, implacable, unmerciful: ³²who knowing the judgment of God, that they which commit such things are worthy of death, not only do the same, but have pleasure in them that do them.

2 Therefore thou art inexcusable, O man, whosoever thou art that judgest: for wherein thou judgest another, thou condemnest thyself; for thou that judgest doest the same things. ²But we are sure that the judgment of God is according to truth against them which commit such things. ³And thinkest thou this, O man, that judgest them which do such things, and doest the same, that thou shalt escape the judgment of God? ⁴Or despisest thou the riches of his goodness and forbearance

of human flaws: Philo calls it "treacherous, and the cause of all evils" (*Virtues* 100). **1:25** *Served*: see v. 9 note. **1:26** *Vile affections*: better "dishonorable passions." *Did change . . . nature*: a reference to homosexual acts, not to sexual orientation in the modern sense. While the Greco-Roman world widely denounced such acts between women, homosexual acts between men usually were condemned only under certain circumstances (e.g., in ancient Rome, if both men were freeborn). However, the penetrated partner was always liable to be accused of effeminacy. When Greco-Roman moralizers (including Jews like Philo) attack homosexual activity, they therefore present it as one vice among many (cf. vv. 28–32), often linking it with gluttony or greed: it does not manifest an idiosyncratic or perverted form of desire, but rather immoderate generic lust (cf. Dio Chrysostom 7.150–52; Philo, *Special Laws* 3.43; etc.). Gk. *para physin* (KJV "against nature") is therefore better rendered more literally as "beyond nature" (i.e., "beyond natural bounds"). **1:27** *Unseemly*: lit. "shameless." *Receiving in themselves . . . meet*: recapitulating vv. 18–27, which presents Gentiles' various desires (vv. 24, 26–27) as God's punishment for idolatry, before moving on to a more expansive list of destructive vices (vv. 28–32) to which God handed them over. *Meet*: necessary or due. **1:28** *Like*: Gk. *dokimazō*, lit. "approve"; the verb shares a root with *adokimos*, *reprobate*. *Convenient*: proper. **1:29** *Fornication*: better omitted (MS tradition). *Debate*: strife or contention. *Whisperers*: gossips. **1:30** *Backbiters*: slanderers. *Despiteful*: better "violently insolent." **1:31** *Implacable*: better omitted (MS tradition). **1:32** *Have pleasure in*: Gk. root *doke-*; see v. 28 note.

2:1–16 Condemnation of the pretentious. In the diatribal style, Paul addresses an imaginary character in order to rebuke him. Though interpreters usually have assumed that Paul admonishes a self-righteous Jew, nothing in the text warrants this reading. Paul turns to an imaginary Jewish teacher only at 2:17, and he marks this turn explicitly. Verses 1–16 resemble conventional diatribal apostrophes of (universally non-Jewish) hypocrites in Greco-Roman moralizing literature (cf. Seneca, *On the Blessed Life* 27.4; Epictetus, *Discourses* 2.21.11–12; etc.). **2:4** *Forbearance and longsuffering*: Jewish thought sometimes held that God delayed his punishment of Gentiles in order that their sins might accumulate, making them liable to more severe condemnation (cf. Dan 8:23; 2 Macc 6:14–16). Here Paul holds out the more optimistic possibility that God's patience gives Gentiles an opportunity

and longsuffering; not knowing that the goodness of God leadeth thee to repentance? [5]But after thy hardness and impenitent heart treasurest up unto thyself wrath against the day of wrath and revelation of the righteous judgment of God; [6]who will render to every man according to his deeds: [7]to them who by patient continuance in well doing seek for glory and honour and immortality, eternal life: [8]but unto them that are contentious, and do not obey the truth, but obey unrighteousness, indignation and wrath, [9]tribulation and anguish, upon every soul of man that doeth evil, of the Jew first, and also of the Gentile; [10]but glory, honour, and peace, to every man that worketh good, to the Jew first, and also to the Gentile: [11]for there is no respect of persons with God.

[12]For as many as have sinned without law shall also perish without law: and as many as have sinned in the law shall be judged by the law; [13](for not the hearers of the law are just before God, but the doers of the law shall be justified. [14]For when the Gentiles, which have not the law, do by nature the things contained in the law, these, having not the law, are a law unto themselves: [15]which shew the work of the law written in their hearts, their conscience also bearing witness, and their thoughts the mean while accusing or else excusing one another;) [16]in the day when God shall judge the secrets of men by Jesus Christ according to my gospel.

[17]Behold, thou art called a Jew, and restest in the law, and makest thy boast of God, [18]and knowest his will, and approvest the things that are more excellent, being instructed out of the law; [19]and art confident that thou thyself art a guide of the blind, a light of them which are in darkness, [20]an instructor of the foolish, a teacher of babes, which hast the form of knowledge and of the truth in the law. [21]Thou

---

to repent, which they squander (v. 5).   **2:5** *After*: in accordance with. *Against*: on.   **2:6** *Who will render . . . deeds*: quoting Ps 62:12 or Prov 24:12.   **2:7** *Immortality*: lit. "incorruption."   **2:9** *Soul of man*: in contrast to incorruptible spirit, which makes up the resurrected body, *soul* is subject to decay and destruction; cf. 1 Cor 15:44–49 and esp. v. 44 note.   **2:9, 10** *Gentile*: lit. "Greek."   **2:11** *Respect of persons*: favoritism; cf. Deut 10:17.   **2:12** *Without law*: Gk *anomōs*, "lawlessly" (KJV renders its nominal form "iniquity" at 6:19), so better "all who have sinned in a lawless manner shall perish in a manner befitting lawlessness" (Stowers). Paul here does not categorically distinguish Gentiles free of the law from Jews under it. (The verse's two sentences are complementary rather than antithetical.) On the contrary, all will be punished or rewarded with reference to the Jewish law, including Gentiles (cf. vv. 14–15, 26–27; 3:19–20).   **2:14** *When the Gentiles . . . themselves*: often taken as evidence of Paul's belief in natural law, to which Gentiles ignorant of biblical law would be accountable. But an alternative translation makes better sense in the context of Paul's argument: "When the Gentiles, who have not the law by nature, do the things contained in the law," with *by nature* meaning "by birth" or "by birthright" (cf. Gal 2:15). Paul, like many Hellenistic Jews, probably believes that the highest traditions of wisdom, knowledge, and justice in the Gentile world actually originated with Moses and reflect the divine law he promulgated.   **2:15** *Their thoughts . . . another*: better "their thoughts mutually accusing or defending them" (Fitzmyer). The parenthesis introduced by KJV at v. 13 has no basis in the Greek text. The segregation of v. 16 from v. 15 that it effects, in favor of a more direct link between vv. 12 and 16, is totally arbitrary.

2:17–29 Condemnation of a hypocritical Jewish teacher. Paul now apostrophizes a hypocritical Jewish instructor (not simply "the Jew") who teaches God's law—like Paul, especially to Gentiles (cf. vv. 19 and note, 24)—but does not obey it himself (cf. Matt 23:2–15). Paul's focus on the difference between name and reality (vv. 17, 28–29) owes much to conventional Greco-Roman popular philosophical discourse, which similarly rebukes rival philosophers (see, e.g., Epictetus, *Discourses* 2.19.19; 3.24.40–41).   **2:17** *Behold*: better "but if" (MS tradition). *Art called*: or "call yourself." *Makest thy . . . God*: cf. Jer 9:24.   **2:19** *A light . . . darkness*: Paul's echo of Isa 42:6–7 and 49:6 clarifies the implicit reference to Gentile instruction.   **2:20** *Form*: i.e., "embodiment."

therefore which teachest another, teachest thou not thyself? thou that preachest a man should not steal, dost thou steal? [22]Thou that sayest a man should not commit adultery, dost thou commit adultery? thou that abhorrest idols, dost thou commit sacrilege? [23]Thou that makest thy boast of the law, through breaking the law dishonourest thou God? [24]For the name of God is blasphemed among the Gentiles through you, as it is written.

[25]For circumcision verily profiteth, if thou keep the law: but if thou be a breaker of the law, thy circumcision is made uncircumcision. [26]Therefore if the uncircumcision keep the righteousness of the law, shall not his uncircumcision be counted for circumcision? [27]And shall not uncircumcision which is by nature, if it fulfil the law, judge thee, who by the letter and circumcision dost transgress the law? [28]For he is not a Jew, which is one outwardly; neither is that circumcision, which is outward in the flesh: [29]but he is a Jew, which is one inwardly; and circumcision is that of the heart, in the spirit, and not in the letter; whose praise is not of men, but of God.

3 What advantage then hath the Jew? or what profit is there of circumcision? [2]Much every way: chiefly, because that unto them were committed the oracles of God. [3]For what if some did not believe? shall their unbelief make the faith of God without effect?

[4]God forbid: yea, let God be true, but every man a liar; as it is written, That thou mightest be justified in thy sayings, and mightest overcome when thou art judged.

[5]But if our unrighteousness commend the righteousness of God, what shall we say? Is God unrighteous who taketh vengeance? (I speak as a man.)

[6]God forbid: for then how shall God judge the world?

2:21–22 *A man . . . sacrilege*: three of the Ten Commandments; cf. Exod 20:4–5, 14, 15.   **2:24** *The name . . . you*: a reference to Isa 52:5, in dialogic response to the Isaianic echo of v. 19.   **2:26** *Righteousness of the law*: lit. "just requirement of the law." Verses 26–27 suggest that God's law did not require Gentiles loyal to YHWH to be circumcised (an idea that may have been widespread, if Acts' reports of uncircumcised Gentiles participating in synagogue worship throughout the Mediterranean are trustworthy; 14:1–2; 17:4; cf. 10:2). This suggestion finds clear expression in the talmudic tradition that God required Gentiles to obey only the seven commandments that he gave to Noah, while Jews were to observe all scriptural law. Note the connection with vv. 11–16: in order for Paul's claim that God justly judges both Jews and Gentiles under the law to be meaningful, he must explain how God looks at (or overlooks) Gentiles' uncircumcised status, and metonymically, their neglect of the other scriptural laws that set Jews apart from Gentiles.   **2:27** *Uncircumcision . . . by nature*: i.e., those born Gentiles; cf. v. 14 note.   **2:28–29** *Outwardly . . . inwardly*: lit. "apparently" vs. "secretly," i.e., "for show" vs. "when no one is watching"; KJV spiritualizes Paul's dichotomy.   **2:29** *Circumcision is . . . heart*: an OT commonplace figuring sincere repentance, devotion to God and his law, or both; e.g., Deut 30:6; Jer 4:4.

    3:1–20 Dialogue with the Jewish teacher. In Greco-Roman philosophical discourse of the so-called diatribal style, the apostrophized persona can become an interlocutor. Verse 1 and every other paragraph through 9a should be assigned to the Jewish teacher, and vv. 2–3 along with every other paragraph through 20 to the authorial voice.   **3:2** *Oracles*: Gk. *logia*, probably God's scriptural promises.   **3:3** *What if . . . effect*: better "What if some were not faithful? Will their infidelity nullify God's faithfulness?"   **3:4** *Every man a liar*: echoing Ps 116:11. Mention of lying here and in v. 7 clarifies "infidelity" in v. 3 (KJV "unbelief"; see note): it is the Jewish teacher's blatant hypocrisy that undermines his mission to the Gentiles, with the result that they "blaspheme" God's name (2:19–24). *That thou . . . judged*: Ps 51:4 (words purportedly addressed to God by the penitent David after his affair with Bathsheba). *Sayings*: cf. v. 2 (KJV "oracles").   **3:5** *Taketh vengeance*: i.e., punishes us. *Man*: the period following this word is an editorial insertion; KJV lacks punctuation at this point.

⁷For if the truth of God hath more abounded through my lie unto his glory; why yet am I also judged as a sinner? ⁸And not rather, (as we be slanderously reported, and as some affirm that we say,) Let us do evil, that good may come? whose damnation is just.

⁹What then? are we better than they?

No, in no wise: for we have before proved both Jews and Gentiles, that they are all under sin; ¹⁰as it is written, There is none righteous, no, not one: ¹¹there is none that understandeth, there is none that seeketh after God. ¹²They are all gone out of the way, they are together become unprofitable; there is none that doeth good, no, not one. ¹³Their throat is an open sepulchre; with their tongues they have used deceit; the poison of asps is under their lips: ¹⁴whose mouth is full of cursing and bitterness: ¹⁵their feet are swift to shed blood: ¹⁶destruction and misery are in their ways: ¹⁷and the way of peace have they not known: ¹⁸there is no fear of God before their eyes. ¹⁹Now we know that what things soever the law saith, it saith to them who are under the law: that every mouth may be stopped, and all the world may become guilty before God. ²⁰Therefore by the deeds of the law there shall no flesh be justified in his sight: for by the law is the knowledge of sin.

²¹But now the righteousness of God without the law is manifested, being witnessed by the law and the prophets; ²²even the righteousness of God which is by faith of Jesus Christ unto all and upon all them that believe: for there is no difference: ²³for all have sinned, and come short of the glory of God; ²⁴being justified freely by his grace through the redemption that is in Christ Jesus: ²⁵whom God hath set forth to be a propitiation through faith in his blood, to declare his righteousness for the remission of sins that are past, through the forbearance of God;

3:7 *For*: better "but" (MS tradition). **3:8** *Whose*: those responsible for the slander. *Damnation*: judgment. **3:9** *Are we better*: a much-discussed Greek phrase; many commentators agree with KJV, but the most straightforward translation, "are we at a disadvantage," makes better sense in context. If God communicates his truth and righteousness to Gentiles despite Jewish missionaries' infidelity (vv. 3–4; cf. 2:19–24) but still insists on holding Jews accountable for that infidelity (vv. 5–8), then are not Jews at a disadvantage? **3:10–12** *There is . . . one*: Ps 14:1–3 (= Ps 53:1–3); cf. Eccl 7:20. **3:12** *Unprofitable*: worthless. **3:13** *Their throat . . . lips*: Pss 5:9; 140:3. **3:14** *Whose mouth . . . bitterness*: Ps 10:7. **3:15–17** *Their feet . . . known*: adapting Isa 59:7–8; cf. Prov 1:16. **3:18** *There is . . . eyes*: Ps 36:1. **3:20** *Therefore*: better "because." *There shall . . . sight*: Ps 143:2. *By the law . . . sin*: the law that ostensibly holds open the possibility of righteousness, for Gentiles (2:13–16) as for Jews, actually testifies to universal sinfulness (imparts *knowledge of sin*), as the preceding string of scriptural citations demonstrates. **3:21–4:2a Righteousness through faith for Jews and Gentiles.** Because 3:9b–20 undercut his earlier argument that God's law impartially justifies both Jews and Gentiles (chap. 2, esp. vv. 11–16, 25–29), Paul now changes tack: while still insisting on God's impartiality (3:29–30), he claims that Jews' and Gentiles' equal access to righteousness comes through the faith of Christ, which in that sense takes the place of the law (cf. 3:27). **3:21** *Without*: apart from (also in v. 28). **3:22** *By faith . . . believe*: cf. 1:17. *And upon all*: better omitted (MS tradition). **3:24** *Redemption*: Gk. *apolytrōsis*, the buying of a prisoner's or a slave's freedom (see Mark 10:45 note). **3:25** *Propitiation*: Gk. *hilastērion*, appeasement, especially of a divinity by means of expiatory sacrifice (cf., e.g., LXX Lev 16:11–28); *4 Maccabees* 6.28–29 and 17.22 describe martyrs' deaths in similar terms. *Through faith*: perhaps a separate clause (i.e., "a propitiation in his blood, through faith"), with *faith* referring either to the believer's faith in Christ or to Christ's faithfulness to God, exemplified in his willingness to die in order to satisfy God's wrath. On the ambiguity of "faith of Jesus" in Paul's writings, see Gal 2:16 note. *Remission*: or simply "passing over." *Forbearance of God*: cf. 2:4 and note.

²⁶to declare, I say, at this time his righteousness: that he might be just, and the justifier of him which believeth in Jesus.

²⁷Where is boasting then?

It is excluded.

By what law? of works?

Nay: but by the law of faith. ²⁸Therefore we conclude that a man is justified by faith without the deeds of the law. ²⁹Is he the God of the Jews only? is he not also of the Gentiles?

Yes, of the Gentiles also.

³⁰Seeing it is one God, which shall justify the circumcision by faith, and uncircumcision through faith.

³¹Do we then make void the law through faith?

God forbid: yea, we establish the law.

4 What shall we say then that Abraham our father, as pertaining to the flesh, hath found? ²For if Abraham were justified by works, he hath whereof to glory. But not before God. ³For what saith the scripture? Abraham believed God, and it was counted unto him for righteousness. ⁴Now to him that worketh is the reward not reckoned of grace, but of debt. ⁵But to him that worketh not, but believeth on him that justifieth the ungodly, his faith is counted for righteousness. ⁶Even as David also describeth the blessedness of the man, unto whom God imputeth righteousness without works, ⁷saying, Blessed are they whose iniquities are forgiven, and whose sins are covered. ⁸Blessed is the man to whom the Lord will not impute sin.

⁹Cometh this blessedness then upon the circumcision only, or upon the uncircumcision also? for we say that faith was reckoned to Abraham for righteousness. ¹⁰How was it then reckoned? when he was in circumcision, or in uncircumcision? Not in circumcision, but in uncircumcision. ¹¹And he received the sign of circumcision, a seal of the righteousness of the faith which he had yet being uncircumcised: that he might be the father of all them that believe, though they be not

---

3:26 *Him which believeth in Jesus*: lit. "the one from the faith of Jesus"; cf. v. 25 note.   **3:27** *Where is boasting then*: Paul's dialogue with the imaginary Jewish teacher resumes, with the interlocutor responding to the argument Paul presented in 3:9b–26. The first sentence of 3:27 and every other paragraph through "glory" in 4:2 belong to the Jewish teacher first apostrophized at 2:17. The remaining text, including 4:2's final clause, belongs to Paul's authorial voice.   **3:28** *Therefore we conclude*: better "for we reckon" (MS tradition).   **3:29** *Is he*: lit. "or is he." *Also*: KJV follows this word with a colon; the period is an editorial emendation.   **3:30** *Seeing it . . . God*: better "if indeed God is one" (MS tradition), alluding to the Shema (Deut 6:4 and note).   **4:1** *As pertaining to the flesh*: i.e., by descent.   **4:2** *Glory*: Gk. *kauchēma*; the same root was rendered "boast" at 2:17, 23; 3:27. KJV prefers "glory" (5:3; 15:17) and cognates of "joy" (5:2, 11) in contexts where the word's connotations are not straightforwardly negative.

4:2b–25 Abraham's faith. Paul interprets the Abraham story to argue that according to the law itself (cf. 3:31), Jews and Gentiles alike are justified by faith. This section develops in a somewhat different way ideas presented in Gal 3:6–18.   **4:2** *But not before God*: KJV actually connects this clause to the previous with a semicolon. We have altered the punctuation in light of the dialogue structuring this section of the epistle.   **4:3** *Abraham believed . . . righteousness*: Gen 15:6. *Counted*: Gk. *logizomai* (cf. v. 5), also translated with forms of "reckon" and "impute" (vv. 4, 6, 8, etc.).   **4:7–8** *Blessed are they . . . sin*: Ps 32:1–2.   **4:11** *He received . . . uncircumcised*: Abraham was circumcised in Gen 17, well after his initial faithful response to God's call, and LXX Gen 17:11 calls circumcision a

circumcised; that righteousness might be imputed unto them also: ¹²and the father of circumcision to them who are not of the circumcision only, but who also walk in the steps of that faith of our father Abraham, which he had being yet uncircumcised.

¹³For the promise, that he should be the heir of the world, was not to Abraham, or to his seed, through the law, but through the righteousness of faith. ¹⁴For if they which are of the law be heirs, faith is made void, and the promise made of none effect: ¹⁵because the law worketh wrath: for where no law is, there is no transgression. ¹⁶Therefore it is of faith, that it might be by grace; to the end the promise might be sure to all the seed; not to that only which is of the law, but to that also which is of the faith of Abraham; who is the father of us all, ¹⁷(as it is written, I have made thee a father of many nations,) before him whom he believed, even God, who quickeneth the dead, and calleth those things which be not as though they were. ¹⁸Who against hope believed in hope, that he might become the father of many nations; according to that which was spoken, So shall thy seed be. ¹⁹And being not weak in faith, he considered not his own body now dead, when he was about an hundred years old, neither yet the deadness of Sara's womb: ²⁰he staggered not at the promise of God through unbelief; but was strong in faith, giving glory to God; ²¹and being fully persuaded that, what he had promised, he was able also to perform. ²²And therefore it was imputed to him for righteousness. ²³Now it was not written for his sake alone, that it was imputed to him; ²⁴but for us also, to whom it shall be imputed, if we believe on him that raised up Jesus our Lord from the dead; ²⁵who was delivered for our offences, and was raised again for our justification.

5 Therefore being justified by faith, we have peace with God through our Lord Jesus Christ: ²by whom also we have access by faith into this grace wherein we stand, and rejoice in hope of the glory of God. ³And not only so, but we glory in tribulations also: knowing that tribulation worketh patience; ⁴and patience, experience; and experience, hope: ⁵and hope maketh not ashamed; because the love of God is shed abroad in our hearts by the Holy Ghost which is given unto us. ⁶For when we were yet without strength, in due time Christ died for the ungodly.

"sign" (KJV "token"). **4:13** *Promise*: Gk. *epangelia*, which contains the same root as *euangelion*, KJV "gospel." The idea that Abraham's offspring would be *heir of the world* is a traditional elaboration of Gen 12:2–3 (e.g., see Sir 44:19–21). **4:15** *For*: better "but" (MS tradition). *Where no . . . transgression*: cf. 7:7–12. **4:17** *I have . . . nations*: Gen 17:5. *Nations*: Gk. *ethnē*, elsewhere "Gentiles." **4:18** *So shall thy seed be*: Gen 15:5. *Seed*: heir. **4:19** *Considered not*: better "considered" (MS tradition), recognizing that Abraham trusts in God's promise though cognizant of his and Sarah's aged infertility. *Neither yet*: better "and." **4:20–21** *He staggered . . . perform*: Paul exaggerates Abraham's faith; cf. Gen 16:1–3 and see Gal 4:21–5:1 and notes. **4:24–25** *If we believe . . . justification*: trust in Christ's death and resurrection for justification finds its analogue in Abraham's righteousness-imputing trust (v. 3) in God's promise to generate an heir from his and Sarah's "dead bodies" (v. 19). Paul may understand this correspondence to verge on equivalence, for he identifies Abraham's "seed" as Christ in Gal 3:16–17.

   5:1–11 Gentiles' reconciliation with God. Terminology such as "ungodly" (v. 6), "sinners" (v. 8), and "enemies" of God (v. 10; cf. 1) indicates Paul's focus on Gentiles. **5:2** *Rejoice*: Gk. *kauchaomai*, lit. "boast"; cf. vv. 3 ("glory"), 11 ("joy"); see 4:2 note. *Hope of . . . God*: looking forward to the eschatological consummation, which a time of tribulation was supposed to precede (cf. vv. 3–4). **5:4** *Experience*: the Greek refers to testing that leads to approval. **5:5** *Shed abroad*: poured out. *Holy Ghost . . . us*: Paul views the Holy Spirit as "the firstfruits" of believers' eschatological transformation;

⁷For scarcely for a righteous man will one die: yet peradventure for a good man some would even dare to die. ⁸But God commendeth his love toward us, in that, while we were yet sinners, Christ died for us. ⁹Much more then, being now justified by his blood, we shall be saved from wrath through him. ¹⁰For if, when we were enemies, we were reconciled to God by the death of his Son, much more, being reconciled, we shall be saved by his life. ¹¹And not only so, but we also joy in God through our Lord Jesus Christ, by whom we have now received the atonement.

¹²Wherefore, as by one man sin entered into the world, and death by sin; and so death passed upon all men, for that all have sinned: ¹³(for until the law sin was in the world: but sin is not imputed when there is no law. ¹⁴Nevertheless death reigned from Adam to Moses, even over them that had not sinned after the similitude of Adam's transgression, who is the figure of him that was to come. ¹⁵But not as the offence, so also is the free gift. For if through the offence of one many be dead, much more the grace of God, and the gift by grace, which is by one man, Jesus Christ, hath abounded unto many. ¹⁶And not as it was by one that sinned, so is the gift: for the judgment was by one to condemnation, but the free gift is of many offences unto justification. ¹⁷For if by one man's offence death reigned by one; much more they which receive abundance of grace and of the gift of righteousness shall reign in life by one, Jesus Christ.) ¹⁸Therefore as by the offence of one judgment came upon all men to condemnation; even so by the righteousness of one the free gift came upon all men unto justification of life. ¹⁹For as by one man's disobedience many were made sinners, so by the obedience of one shall many be made righteous. ²⁰Moreover the law entered, that the offence might abound. But where sin abounded, grace did much more abound: ²¹that as sin hath reigned unto death,

cf. 8:23 and note; 2 Cor 1:22.   **5:9** *Justified by his blood*: contrast 4:25, which attributed justification to Christ's resurrection.   **5:10** *We shall . . . life*: i.e., we shall share in his resurrection at God's final judgment.   **5:11** *Atonement*: lit. "reconciliation" (cf. v. 10).

5:12–21 As Adam brings death, so Christ brings life. Compare 1 Cor 15:42–49. Augustine based his doctrine of original sin (the idea that all have inherited Adam's sin and guilt) in large part on this passage, especially on the phrase rendered "*for that* all have sinned" (v. 12). Its Greek original (*eph' hō*) and Latin translation (*in quo*) have various possible meanings, including "*in whom* all have sinned" (cf. Augustine, *Against Two Letters of the Pelagians* 4.4.7). But Paul's discussion of Adam focuses on death rather than sin, developing the previous section's emphasis on believers' eschatological participation in Christ's resurrection (vv. 9–10) by revealing its corollary, their current participation in Adam's death.   **5:12–14** *Wherefore, as . . . come*: Paul's linking of sin with Adam (*one man*) and death was conventional (e.g., Wis 2:23–24), founded on God's insistence that death would result from Adam's transgression of his command (Gen 2:17). But this standard association creates a problem: while Paul had earlier insisted that sin is revealed by the law (3:20; 4:15; cf. 7:7), Adam predates Moses' promulgation of God's law. Paul therefore concedes that *sin* was *not imputed* to people before the law (v. 13), but still insists its effect—namely death—was universally experienced (v. 14). In v. 20, Paul will suggest that the law exacerbates the problem of sin by disclosing its abundance; in 7:7–25 he imports the law into the story of the primeval transgression by assimilating God's command to the tenth commandment, "thou shalt not covet."   **5:14** *The figure . . . come*: cf. 1 Cor 15:21–22, 45–49.   **5:17** *Death reigned . . . life*: perhaps meant figuratively (cf. v. 21), or perhaps referring to death as a powerful demonic ruler (cf. 1 Cor 15:24–26) and to risen believers' authority in God's eschatological kingdom (cf. 1 Cor 6:2).   **5:18** *Therefore as . . . life*: KJV inserts *judgment came* and *the free gift came* to make sense of the difficult syntax; alternatively "Therefore, as by the offence of one, condemnation came to all, even so by the righteousness of one, justification of life came to all."   **5:20** *Moreover . . . more abound*: cf. vv. 12–14 and note; 1 Cor 15:56.   **5:21** *Unto death*: better "in death."

even so might grace reign through righteousness unto eternal life by Jesus Christ our Lord.

6 What shall we say then? Shall we continue in sin, that grace may abound? ²God forbid. How shall we, that are dead to sin, live any longer therein? ³Know ye not, that so many of us as were baptized into Jesus Christ were baptized into his death? ⁴Therefore we are buried with him by baptism into death: that like as Christ was raised up from the dead by the glory of the Father, even so we also should walk in newness of life. ⁵For if we have been planted together in the likeness of his death, we shall be also in the likeness of his resurrection: ⁶knowing this, that our old man is crucified with him, that the body of sin might be destroyed, that henceforth we should not serve sin. ⁷For he that is dead is freed from sin. ⁸Now if we be dead with Christ, we believe that we shall also live with him: ⁹knowing that Christ being raised from the dead dieth no more; death hath no more dominion over him. ¹⁰For in that he died, he died unto sin once: but in that he liveth, he liveth unto God. ¹¹Likewise reckon ye also yourselves to be dead indeed unto sin, but alive unto God through Jesus Christ our Lord.

¹²Let not sin therefore reign in your mortal body, that ye should obey it in the lusts thereof. ¹³Neither yield ye your members as instruments of unrighteousness unto sin: but yield yourselves unto God, as those that are alive from the dead, and your members as instruments of righteousness unto God. ¹⁴For sin shall not have dominion over you: for ye are not under the law, but under grace.

¹⁵What then? shall we sin, because we are not under the law, but under grace? God forbid. ¹⁶Know ye not, that to whom ye yield yourselves servants to obey, his servants ye are to whom ye obey; whether of sin unto death, or of obedience unto righteousness? ¹⁷But God be thanked, that ye were the servants of sin, but ye have obeyed from the heart that form of doctrine which was delivered you. ¹⁸Being then made free from sin, ye became the servants of righteousness. ¹⁹I speak after the manner of men because of the infirmity of your flesh: for as ye have yielded your members servants to uncleanness and to iniquity unto iniquity; even so now yield your members servants to righteousness unto holiness. ²⁰For when ye were the servants of sin, ye were free from righteousness. ²¹What fruit had ye then in those things whereof ye are now ashamed? for the end of those things is death. ²²But

6:1–23 Gentiles in Christ are free from sin and slaves of righteousness. This passage, with its focus on liberation from sin through participation in Jesus' death and resurrection, repeatedly echoes 1:18–32, where Paul described Gentiles' bondage to sin; cf. 6:13 and 1:18, 29 ("unrighteousness"); 6:12, 19 and 1:24 ("lusts" and "uncleanness"); 6:21 and 1:27 note ("shame"); etc. A dialogue returns (cf. vv. 1–2, 15–16), perhaps again with the Jewish teacher from 2:17–4:2, perhaps with a more generic interlocutive voice. (It is continued in chap. 7; cf. vv. 7, 13.) **6:1** *What shall . . . abound*: cf. 3:5–8. **6:3** *Baptized*: see Mark 1:4 note. Baptism became the early church's initiation ritual. **6:4** *Walk in newness of life*: while Paul stipulates that believers are assimilated to the risen Christ only in the eschatological future (vv. 5, 8), he still expects them to exemplify in morally transformed lives the divine power that raised Jesus from the dead (cf. vv. 11–13). **6:5** *Been planted*: or "grown." **6:6** *Serve sin*: lit. "be enslaved to sin" (cf. 1:1 note). **6:10** *Once*: i.e., once and for all. **6:13** *Instruments*: or "weapons". **6:17** *Doctrine*: "teaching," perhaps in implicit contrast with the hypocritical Jewish teacher (2:17–32, esp. vv. 20–21), whose legal instruction did not free even himself from sin. *Which was delivered you*: rather "to which you were given" (Gk. *paredothēte*). Paul thereby reverses his previous affirmations that God "gave up" (*paredōken*) Gentiles to "uncleanness" (1:24), "vile affections" (1:26), and "a reprobate mind" (1:28). **6:19** *Members*: parts of the body.

now being made free from sin, and become servants to God, ye have your fruit unto holiness, and the end everlasting life. [23]For the wages of sin is death; but the gift of God is eternal life through Jesus Christ our Lord.

7 Know ye not, brethren, (for I speak to them that know the law,) how that the law hath dominion over a man as long as he liveth? [2]For the woman which hath an husband is bound by the law to her husband so long as he liveth; but if the husband be dead, she is loosed from the law of her husband. [3]So then if, while her husband liveth, she be married to another man, she shall be called an adulteress: but if her husband be dead, she is free from that law; so that she is no adulteress, though she be married to another man. [4]Wherefore, my brethren, ye also are become dead to the law by the body of Christ; that ye should be married to another, even to him who is raised from the dead, that we should bring forth fruit unto God. [5]For when we were in the flesh, the motions of sins, which were by the law, did work in our members to bring forth fruit unto death. [6]But now we are delivered from the law, that being dead wherein we were held; that we should serve in newness of spirit, and not in the oldness of the letter.

[7]What shall we say then? Is the law sin?

God forbid. Nay, I had not known sin, but by the law: for I had not known lust, except the law had said, Thou shalt not covet. [8]But sin, taking occasion by the commandment, wrought in me all manner of concupiscence. For without the law sin was dead. [9]For I was alive without the law once: but when the commandment came, sin revived, and I died. [10]And the commandment, which was ordained to life, I found to be unto death. [11]For sin, taking occasion by the commandment,

---

7:1–25 The role of the law. 7:4 *Ye also . . . another*: Paul avoids the analogy that vv. 1–3 (following 6:16–23) led the reader to expect, namely that sin (first husband) has died so that believers (the wife), free from the law enforcing sin's power (marital law), can unite with Christ (second husband) (cf. 1 Cor 7:39). Instead, it is believers' death "by the body of Christ" that frees them to unite with Christ, whose death and supernatural resurrection, in which they vicariously share (cf. 6:3–11), disrupt the analogy's logic. **7:5** *Flesh*: a person's basest component—the substance he or she has in common with animals (1 Cor 15:39). It is weak (6:19), is subject to decay (1 Cor 15:50–54) and to sinful desire (7:18; cf. v. 25), and is often contrasted with spirit (8:1–17), a refined and potentially incorruptible material (1 Cor 15:42–49). *Motions*: lit. "passions" (see 1:26 and note).   **7:6** *That being dead*: better simply "being dead" (MS tradition); the participial phrase agrees with *we* rather than *the law*. *The letter*: also contrasted with *spirit* at 2:29; cf. 2 Cor 3:6.   **7:7–25** *Nay, I . . . sin*: as Paul describes the experience of being enslaved to sin, he employs the Greco-Roman rhetorical device of *prosopopoeia*, or speech by an imagined character. He does not write autobiographically, either about present struggles with sin (chaps. 6 and 8 preclude this possibility) or about his Pharisaic past (Phil 3:5–6 obviates such a reading). Paul instead imagines the experience of being captured by and enslaved to sin from the perspective of the biblical character Eve (see v. 11 and note), analogizing God's command that she and Adam refrain from the forbidden fruit of knowledge to the biblical commandment "thou shalt not covet." Paul's characterization of Eve draws both on Gen 3 and on conventional Greco-Roman literary depictions of mythological women overcome by base desires, such as Phaedra and Medea.   **7:7** *Thou shalt not covet*: Exod 20:17; Deut 5:21. Gk. *Ouk epithymēseis*, the verbal form of the noun previously rendered *lust*, actually refers to desire in general (see 1:24 note), although KJV often translates it with terms having overwhelmingly sexual connotations (e.g., v. 8, "concupiscence").   **7:10** *Ordained to life*: cf. Gen 2:17; 3:3, where God's command explicitly protects Adam's and Eve's lives. The phrase also recalls their freedom to eat of all the other trees in the garden (2:16; 3:2), including the tree of life (2:9), which was forbidden only after they transgressed (3:22–24).   **7:11** *Sin . . . deceived me*: echoing Eve (Gen 3:13, "the serpent

deceived me, and by it slew me. [12]Wherefore the law is holy, and the commandment holy, and just, and good.

[13]Was then that which is good made death unto me?

God forbid. But sin, that it might appear sin, working death in me by that which is good; that sin by the commandment might become exceeding sinful. [14]For we know that the law is spiritual: but I am carnal, sold under sin. [15]For that which I do I allow not: for what I would, that do I not; but what I hate, that do I. [16]If then I do that which I would not, I consent unto the law that it is good. [17]Now then it is no more I that do it, but sin that dwelleth in me. [18]For I know that in me (that is, in my flesh,) dwelleth no good thing: for to will is present with me; but how to perform that which is good I find not. [19]For the good that I would I do not: but the evil which I would not, that I do. [20]Now if I do that I would not, it is no more I that do it, but sin that dwelleth in me. [21]I find then a law, that, when I would do good, evil is present with me. [22]For I delight in the law of God after the inward man: [23]but I see another law in my members, warring against the law of my mind, and bringing me into captivity to the law of sin which is in my members. [24]O wretched man that I am! who shall deliver me from the body of this death? [25]I thank God through Jesus Christ our Lord. So then with the mind I myself serve the law of God; but with the flesh the law of sin.

8 There is therefore now no condemnation to them which are in Christ Jesus, who walk not after the flesh, but after the Spirit. [2]For the law of the Spirit of life in Christ Jesus hath made me free from the law of sin and death. [3]For what the law could not do, in that it was weak through the flesh, God sending his own Son in the likeness of sinful flesh, and for sin, condemned sin in the flesh: [4]that the righteousness of the law might be fulfilled in us, who walk not after the flesh, but after the Spirit. [5]For they that are after the flesh do mind the things of the flesh; but they that are after the Spirit the things of the Spirit. [6]For to be carnally minded is death; but to be spiritually minded is life and peace. [7]Because the carnal mind is enmity against God: for it is not subject to the law of God, neither indeed can be. [8]So then they that are in the flesh cannot please God.

---

beguiled me"); LXX uses the same Greek root.   **7:13** *That sin . . . sinful*: cf. 5:20.   **7:14** *Carnal*: lit. "of flesh" (so throughout). *Under sin*: i.e., as a slave to sin.   **7:15–24** *For that . . . am*: Paul assimilates sinful Eve to stock characterizations of women in Greco-Roman literature who are unable to control their desires: compare Euripides, *Medea* 1077–80 and *Hippolytus* 377–83; Epictetus, *Discourses* 1.28.6–8; and especially Medea's monologue in Ovid, *Metamorphoses* 7.17–21, which ends "I see what is better and I approve it, / but I follow what is worse."   **7:15** *Allow*: lit. "know."   **7:23** *Bringing me into captivity*: i.e., as a military victor enslaves a defeated enemy.   **7:24** *The body of this death*: or "this body of death."

8:1–39 God's Spirit liberates believers from sin. While 7:7–14 argues that the law is not responsible for Gentiles' slavery to sin, 7:15–25 insists that the law cannot free people from it. Chapter 8 now explains that it is God's spirit, to which believers have access through Christ, that liberates. **8:1** *Who walk . . . Spirit*: better omitted (MS tradition).   **8:2** *Me*: better "you" (MS tradition). *The law of sin*: cf. 7:21, 23.   **8:3** *His own son . . . flesh*: cf. 2 Cor 5:21.   **8:4** *Righteousness of the law*: lit. "just requirement of the law"; cf. 2:26. The spirit does not supersede the law but rather allows Gentiles to do what the law requires, and in this sense frees people from sin, whose power the law was impotent to break (vv. 2–3) and indeed indirectly or inadvertently sustained (5:20; cf. 7:8, 11–13).

⁹But ye are not in the flesh, but in the Spirit, if so be that the Spirit of God dwell in you. Now if any man have not the Spirit of Christ, he is none of his. ¹⁰And if Christ be in you, the body is dead because of sin; but the Spirit is life because of righteousness. ¹¹But if the Spirit of him that raised up Jesus from the dead dwell in you, he that raised up Christ from the dead shall also quicken your mortal bodies by his Spirit that dwelleth in you.

¹²Therefore, brethren, we are debtors, not to the flesh, to live after the flesh. ¹³For if ye live after the flesh, ye shall die: but if ye through the Spirit do mortify the deeds of the body, ye shall live. ¹⁴For as many as are led by the Spirit of God, they are the sons of God. ¹⁵For ye have not received the spirit of bondage again to fear; but ye have received the Spirit of adoption, whereby we cry, Abba, Father. ¹⁶The Spirit itself beareth witness with our spirit, that we are the children of God: ¹⁷and if children, then heirs; heirs of God, and joint-heirs with Christ; if so be that we suffer with him, that we may be also glorified together.

¹⁸For I reckon that the sufferings of this present time are not worthy to be compared with the glory which shall be revealed in us. ¹⁹For the earnest expectation of the creature waiteth for the manifestation of the sons of God. ²⁰For the creature was made subject to vanity, not willingly, but by reason of him who hath subjected the same in hope, ²¹because the creature itself also shall be delivered from the bondage of corruption into the glorious liberty of the children of God. ²²For we know that the whole creation groaneth and travaileth in pain together until now. ²³And not only they, but ourselves also, which have the firstfruits of the Spirit, even we ourselves groan within ourselves, waiting for the adoption, to wit, the redemption of our body.

²⁴For we are saved by hope: but hope that is seen is not hope: for what a man seeth, why doth he yet hope for? ²⁵But if we hope for that we see not, then do we with patience wait for it. ²⁶Likewise the Spirit also helpeth our infirmities: for we know not what we should pray for as we ought: but the Spirit itself maketh intercession for us with groanings which cannot be uttered. ²⁷And he that searcheth

8:9–17 *But ye . . . together*: this section contains numerous points of contact with Pauline discussions of baptism (cf. 6:3–4; 1 Cor 12:13; Gal 3:27–4:7), suggesting that Paul understands believers to receive God's spirit at baptism. **8:11** *Quicken*: make alive. **8:13** *Mortify*: put to death. **8:15** *Abba*: "Father" (Aramaic). *Abba, Father* also appears at Gal 4:6, whose context suggests it may have been part of a baptismal liturgy. Mark 14:36 attributes the same words to Jesus when he prays about his impending death (see note). **8:18–23** *For I . . . body*: Paul links believers' liberation from sin to the cosmos's freedom from decay. **8:19** *Creature*: creation (also in vv. 20–22). **8:20** *The creature . . . vanity*: perhaps alluding to the divine curse in Gen 3:17–18, with *vanity* meaning "futility." *Him who hath subjected*: the allusion to Genesis would suggest a reference to God, but some commentators propose Adam or Satan. **8:20–21** *In hope, because*: or "in the hope that." **8:22** *Groaneth and travaileth*: Paul imagines the creation in labor with God's children (cf. v. 29), although the reference to adoption in v. 23 (cf. v. 15) stands in tension with this imagery. **8:23** *They*: i.e., the creation as a whole. *Firstfruits*: see 1 Cor 15:20 and note. There Christ's resurrection guarantees believers' eschatological resurrection; here believers' possession of Christ's spirit is the guarantee (cf. 5:5 and note). *Redemption of our body*: see 3:24 note; here it is probably a reference to the eschatological transformation of believers' bodies into spirit (cf. 1 Cor 15:42–49). **8:24** *For what . . . for*: better "for who hopes for what he sees?" (MS tradition). **8:26** *The Spirit itself . . . uttered*: the immediate reference is probably to glossolalia (cf. 1 Cor 12:10), which Paul assimilates to the inarticulate groaning of creation in travail (cf. vv. 22–23). This is surprising, for there is evidence that speaking in tongues seems to have been normally viewed as a sign of elite spiritual glory (cf. 1 Cor 12–14; *Testament of Job* 48–50). *For us*: better omitted

the hearts knoweth what is the mind of the Spirit, because he maketh intercession for the saints according to the will of God. [28]And we know that all things work together for good to them that love God, to them who are the called according to his purpose. [29]For whom he did foreknow, he also did predestinate to be conformed to the image of his Son, that he might be the firstborn among many brethren. [30]Moreover whom he did predestinate, them he also called: and whom he called, them he also justified: and whom he justified, them he also glorified.

[31]What shall we then say to these things? If God be for us, who can be against us? [32]He that spared not his own Son, but delivered him up for us all, how shall he not with him also freely give us all things? [33]Who shall lay any thing to the charge of God's elect? It is God that justifieth. [34]Who is he that condemneth? It is Christ that died, yea rather, that is risen again, who is even at the right hand of God, who also maketh intercession for us. [35]Who shall separate us from the love of Christ? shall tribulation, or distress, or persecution, or famine, or nakedness, or peril, or sword? [36]As it is written, For thy sake we are killed all the day long; we are accounted as sheep for the slaughter. [37]Nay, in all these things we are more than conquerors through him that loved us. [38]For I am persuaded, that neither death, nor life, nor angels, nor principalities, nor powers, nor things present, nor things to come, [39]nor height, nor depth, nor any other creature, shall be able to separate us from the love of God, which is in Christ Jesus our Lord.

9 I say the truth in Christ, I lie not, my conscience also bearing me witness in the Holy Ghost, [2]that I have great heaviness and continual sorrow in my heart. [3]For I could wish that myself were accursed from Christ for my brethren, my kinsmen according to the flesh: [4]who are Israelites; to whom pertaineth the adoption, and the glory, and the covenants, and the giving of the law, and the service of

---

(MS tradition).   **8:28** *Are the called*: better "are called."   **8:29** *Conformed to . . . brethren*: a reference to the spiritual transformation of believers' bodies at the eschatological resurrection; cf. 1 Cor 15:20–23, 42–49.   **8:31–39** *What shall we . . . Lord*: the section's elevated rhetoric leads many commentators to refer to it as a hymn, and to suggest that Paul has not so much composed as compiled it of traditional material. In any case, it joyfully praises God's fidelity to Paul and his readers, insisting that nothing will ever come between them and God.   **8:32** *Give us all things*: All things (Gk. *ta panta*) is popular philosophical jargon for the entire universe (see 1 Cor 15:28 note), which will be restored and handed over to glorified believers at the end time; cf. vv. 19–21.   **8:34** *At the right hand of God*: cf. Ps 110:1. This is the only reference to Christ's exaltation in the undisputed Pauline epistles (but see Eph 1:20; Col 3:1). Paul often imagines the risen Christ as spiritually present within the body of believers (e.g., 1 Cor 6:15–18 and notes).   **8:36** *For thy sake . . . slaughter*: Ps 44:22.
8:38 *Nor principalities, nor powers*: hostile political authorities or demonic powers, which were sometimes believed to control them in Jewish apocalyptic thought, as in Rev 13 (see notes).

9:1–11:36 Israel's salvation. This extended meditation on God's eschatological plan for Israel follows naturally on the heels of 8:31–39, whose unreserved praise of God's fidelity raises the question of whether Israel's rejection of Christ indicates God has broken his covenant with it. This argument too progresses dialogically: see 9:14, 19, 30, 32; 10:14–15, 18–19; 11:1, 4, 7, 11, 12, 19.
9:1–5 Paul's concern for Israel.   **9:3** *Wish*: lit. "pray," with the prayer that follows recalling Moses' intercession for the Israelites at Exod 32:32.   **9:4** *Israelites*: the anachronistic term stresses continuity between contemporary Jews and scriptural Israel. *Adoption*: cf. 8:15, 23. The OT frequently speaks of Israel as or becoming God's children; see, e.g., Hos 1:10; 2:23, which Paul quotes at v. 25 (see note). *Glory*: God's presence among his people (Exod 16:10), especially in the tabernacle (Exod 29:43; 40:34–35) and later in the temple (1 Kgs 8:11; 2 Chr 7:1–3). *Service*: the temple cult.

God, and the promises; [5]whose are the fathers, and of whom as concerning the flesh Christ came, who is over all, God blessed for ever. Amen.

[6]Not as though the word of God hath taken none effect. For they are not all Israel, which are of Israel: [7]neither, because they are the seed of Abraham, are they all children: but, In Isaac shall thy seed be called. [8]That is, They which are the children of the flesh, these are not the children of God: but the children of the promise are counted for the seed. [9]For this is the word of promise, At this time will I come, and Sara shall have a son. [10]And not only this; but when Rebecca also had conceived by one, even by our father Isaac; [11](for the children being not yet born, neither having done any good or evil, that the purpose of God according to election might stand, not of works, but of him that calleth;) [12]it was said unto her, The elder shall serve the younger. [13]As it is written, Jacob have I loved, but Esau have I hated.

[14]What shall we say then? Is there unrighteousness with God? God forbid. [15]For he saith to Moses, I will have mercy on whom I will have mercy, and I will have compassion on whom I will have compassion. [16]So then it is not of him that willeth, nor of him that runneth, but of God that sheweth mercy. [17]For the scripture saith unto Pharaoh, Even for this same purpose have I raised thee up, that I might shew my power in thee, and that my name might be declared throughout all the earth. [18]Therefore hath he mercy on whom he will have mercy, and whom he will he hardeneth.

[19]Thou wilt say then unto me, Why doth he yet find fault? For who hath resisted his will? [20]Nay but, O man, who art thou that repliest against God? Shall the thing formed say to him that formed it, Why hast thou made me thus? [21]Hath not the potter power over the clay, of the same lump to make one vessel unto honour, and another unto dishonour? [22]What if God, willing to shew his wrath, and to make his power known, endured with much longsuffering the vessels of wrath fitted to destruction: [23]and that he might make known the riches of his glory on the vessels of mercy, which he had afore prepared unto glory, [24]even us, whom he hath called, not of the Jews only, but also of the Gentiles? [25]As he saith also in Osee, I will call them my people, which were not my people; and her

---

9:5 *Fathers*: the patriarchs Abraham, Isaac, and Jacob. *Of whom . . . came*: cf. 1:3.   **9:6–29** Redefining Israel. Paul tentatively proposes that God never intended the blessings of vv. 4–5 for "all Israel" (v. 6). Because God has acted throughout history to restrict Israel's bounds, it is not conterminous with Abraham's descendants, or Isaac's, or even Jacob's/Israel's (vv. 7, 12–13, 6); rather, it constitutes only a remnant of Jacob's faithful descendants, along with the church's Gentiles among whom they dwell (vv. 27–29, 24–26).   **9:6** *Taken none effect*: lit. "fallen down." Paul insists that God's scriptural word has not been invalidated. *Of Israel*: i.e., from Jacob (see Gen 32:28).   **9:7** *In Isaac . . . called*: as opposed to Ishmael (Gen 21:12).   **9:9** *At this time . . . son*: Gen 18:10, 14.   **9:12** *The elder . . . younger*: Gen 25:23.   **9:13** *Jacob have . . . hated*: Mal 1:2–3.   **9:15** *I will . . . have compassion*: Exod 33:19.   **9:16** *Runneth*: Paul develops the image of a footrace in 11:9–12 (see notes).   **9:17** *Even for . . . earth*: Exod 9:16.   **9:18** *Hardeneth*: recalling God's hardening of Pharoah's heart (e.g., Exod 4:21; 7:3; 14:4).   **9:20** *Shall the thing . . . thus*: cf. Isa 29:16; 45:9.   **9:21** *Hath not the potter . . . lump*: cf. Jer 18:6. *To make . . . dishonour*: cf. Wis 15:7. **9:22** *Vessels of wrath*: the Greek phrase derives from LXX Jer 50:25 (KJV "weapons of indignation"); cf. Isa 13:5.   **9:25–26** *I will call . . . God*: cf. Hos 1:9–10; 2:23. In their original context, these words refer to God's eschatological restoration of Israel, not to Gentile inclusion. The trajectory

beloved, which was not beloved. ²⁶And it shall come to pass, that in the place where it was said unto them, Ye are not my people; there shall they be called the children of the living God. ²⁷Esaias also crieth concerning Israel, Though the number of the children of Israel be as the sand of the sea, a remnant shall be saved: ²⁸for he will finish the work, and cut it short in righteousness: because a short work will the Lord make upon the earth. ²⁹And as Esaias said before, Except the Lord of Sabaoth had left us a seed, we had been as Sodoma, and been made like unto Gomorrha.

³⁰What shall we say then? That the Gentiles, which followed not after righteousness, have attained to righteousness, even the righteousness which is of faith. ³¹But Israel, which followed after the law of righteousness, hath not attained to the law of righteousness. ³²Wherefore? Because they sought it not by faith, but as it were by the works of the law. For they stumbled at that stumblingstone; ³³as it is written, Behold, I lay in Sion a stumblingstone and rock of offence: and whosoever believeth on him shall not be ashamed.

10 Brethren, my heart's desire and prayer to God for Israel is, that they might be saved. ²For I bear them record that they have a zeal of God, but not according to knowledge. ³For they being ignorant of God's righteousness, and going about to establish their own righteousness, have not submitted themselves unto the righteousness of God. ⁴For Christ is the end of the law for righteousness to every one that believeth.

⁵For Moses describeth the righteousness which is of the law, That the man which doeth those things shall live by them. ⁶But the righteousness which is of faith speaketh on this wise, Say not in thine heart, Who shall ascend into heaven? (that

---

of Paul's argument in Rom 9–11 suggests that he intends for his readers to observe the tension between his employment of Hosea's words and their original meaning.   **9:27–28** *Though the number . . . earth*: Isa 10:22–23, which Paul apparently applies to the relatively small number of Jews who have embraced the gospel, in contrast to the growing number of Gentile believers. In Isaiah, God's preservation of a *remnant* actually guarantees the future restoration of collective Israel (cf. 37:31), and Paul's understanding of the concept is ultimately the same.   **9:28** *For he . . . earth*: better "for the Lord will act upon the earth by accomplishing his word and cutting it short" (MS tradition; our translation), i.e., "by executing his word decisively and quickly" (cf. NRSV).   **9:29** *Except the Lord . . . Gomorrha*: Isa 1:9. *Sabaoth*: a transliteration of a Greek word itself transliterated from a Hebrew phrase, "of hosts." *Seed*: a term whose reference has been progressively narrowed in vv. 6–29, from all of Abraham's descendants (v. 7) to only Isaac's (vv. 8–9), to those of Jacob/Israel alone (vv. 10–13), and finally here to a meager remnant of Israelites.   **9:30–10:21** Jewish-Gentile reversal.   **9:30–31** *What shall . . . to the law of righteousness*: vv. 6–29 imply this reversal, whose cause Paul now explores.   **9:31** *Attained to the law of righteousness*: better "arrived at the law" (MS tradition; our translation).   **9:32** *By the works of the law*: better "by works" (MS tradition).   **9:33** *Behold, I . . . ashamed*: a combination of Isa 8:14 and 28:16, replacing the latter verse's "foundation stone" with the former's "stone of stumbling and . . . rock of offence" (cf. 1 Pet 2:6–8). The conflation suggests a paradox at the heart of the law: that which lies at the law's foundation (namely Christ, whom the NT conventionally figures as a cornerstone/copestone; see Mark 12:10; Eph 2:20; etc.) trips up those intent on attaining the righteousness it demands (vv. 31–32).   **10:4** *End of the law*: an ambiguous phrase (especially in Greek), which could mean either the law's foundational purpose or its termination. The two possibilities may inscribe another paradox: Christ, the law's purpose, brings the law to its end.   **10:5** *Moses describeth . . . them*: Lev 18:5.   **10:6** *Say not . . . heart*: quoting the introduction of Deut 9:4–6, which forbids Israel from presuming

is, to bring Christ down from above:) [7]or, Who shall descend into the deep? (that is, to bring up Christ again from the dead.) [8]But what saith it? The word is nigh thee, even in thy mouth, and in thy heart: that is, the word of faith, which we preach; [9]that if thou shalt confess with thy mouth the Lord Jesus, and shalt believe in thine heart that God hath raised him from the dead, thou shalt be saved. [10]For with the heart man believeth unto righteousness; and with the mouth confession is made unto salvation. [11]For the scripture saith, Whosoever believeth on him shall not be ashamed. [12]For there is no difference between the Jew and the Greek: for the same Lord over all is rich unto all that call upon him. [13]For whosoever shall call upon the name of the Lord shall be saved.

[14]How then shall they call on him in whom they have not believed? and how shall they believe in him of whom they have not heard? and how shall they hear without a preacher? [15]And how shall they preach, except they be sent? as it is written, How beautiful are the feet of them that preach the gospel of peace, and bring glad tidings of good things! [16]But they have not all obeyed the gospel. For Esaias saith, Lord, who hath believed our report? [17]So then faith cometh by hearing, and hearing by the word of God. [18]But I say, Have they not heard? Yes verily, their sound went into all the earth, and their words unto the ends of the world. [19]But I say, Did not Israel know? First Moses saith, I will provoke you to jealousy by them that are no people, and by a foolish nation I will anger you. [20]But Esaias is very bold, and saith, I was found of them that sought me not; I was made manifest unto them that asked not after me. [21]But to Israel he saith, All day long I have stretched forth my hands unto a disobedient and gainsaying people.

---

that God gave it the land on account of its righteousness.   **10:6–10** *Who shall ascend . . . salvation*: see Deut 30:11–14 (cf. Bar 3:29–30), large sections of which Paul here quotes, interjecting parenthetical glosses to impose a christological reading. Paul's patently arbitrary scriptural interpretation constitutes a third provocative paradox in his discourse about Christ's role in the law, for the passage from Deuteronomy explicitly rejects this kind of esoteric interpretation of God's words.   **10:11** *Whosoever believeth . . . ashamed*: Isa 28:16 again (cf. 9:33 and note).   **10:13** *Whosoever shall call . . . saved*: Joel 2:32.   **10:14–15** *How then . . . sent*: Paul inquires whether Israel's unbelief results from its ignorance of the gospel he preaches.   **10:15–18** *As it . . . world*: a string of citations suggesting that the gospel has been preached—proclaimed from the mountaintop, as it were (v. 15)—in Israel's Scriptures. This stands in some tension with Paul's previous discussion (9:30–10:13), which underscored the paradox and obscurity of Christ's role in the law. **10:15** *How beautiful . . . things*: Isa 52:7. *Preach the gospel . . . and*: better omitted (MS tradition). *Bring glad tidings*: Gk. root *euangel-*, the same as KJV "gospel."   **10:16** *Lord, who . . . report*: Isa 53:1. **10:17** *God*: better "Christ" (MS tradition).   **10:18** *Their sound . . . world*: quoting Ps 19 (v. 4), which insists that God's creation and law alike testify to God's glory.   **10:19–21** *First Moses . . . people*: three scriptural citations reiterating the troubling reversal Paul announced at the beginning of the section (9:30–31).   **10:19** *I will provoke . . . anger you*: Deut 32:21. *People, nation*: both Gk. *ethnos* (its plural is usually translated "Gentiles").   **10:20–21** *I was found . . . people*: Isa 65:1, 2.

11 I say then, Hath God cast away his people? God forbid. For I also am an Israelite, of the seed of Abraham, of the tribe of Benjamin. [2]God hath not cast away his people which he foreknew. Wot ye not what the scripture saith of Elias? how he maketh intercession to God against Israel, saying, [3]Lord, they have killed thy prophets, and digged down thine altars; and I am left alone, and they seek my life. [4]But what saith the answer of God unto him? I have reserved to myself seven thousand men, who have not bowed the knee to the image of Baal. [5]Even so then at this present time also there is a remnant according to the election of grace. [6]And if by grace, then is it no more of works: otherwise grace is no more grace. But if it be of works, then is it no more grace: otherwise work is no more work.

[7]What then? Israel hath not obtained that which he seeketh for; but the election hath obtained it, and the rest were blinded [8](according as it is written, God hath given them the spirit of slumber, eyes that they should not see, and ears that they should not hear;) unto this day. [9]And David saith, Let their table be made a snare, and a trap, and a stumblingblock, and a recompence unto them: [10]let their eyes be darkened, that they may not see, and bow down their back alway. [11]I say then, Have they stumbled that they should fall? God forbid: but rather through their fall salvation is come unto the Gentiles, for to provoke them to jealousy. [12]Now if the fall of them be the riches of the world, and the diminishing of them the riches of the Gentiles; how much more their fulness?

[13]For I speak to you Gentiles, inasmuch as I am the apostle of the Gentiles, I magnify mine office: [14]if by any means I may provoke to emulation them which are my flesh, and might save some of them. [15]For if the casting away of them be the reconciling of the world, what shall the receiving of them be, but life from the dead?

11:1–36 God has not rejected Israel. Paul addresses the crucial theological question implied by the Jewish-Gentile reversal he has been pondering (vv. 1–6) and then explains how Israel's unbelief fits into God's elaborate plan to save Jews and Gentiles alike (vv. 7–36). Paul returns to the idea of Israel's faithful remnant (cf. 9:6–29), but now insists that its survival does not suggest that God has excluded many of Jacob's descendants (cf. 9:6); rather, it guarantees God's eschatological faithfulness to all Israel (11:26).   **11:1** *Hath God . . . people*: cf. Ps 94:14.   **11:2** *Wot*: know.   **11:3** *Lord, they . . . life*: 1 Kgs 19:10, 14.   **11:4** *I have reserved . . . Baal*: 1 Kgs 19:18.   **11:6** *But if . . . more work*: better omitted (MS tradition).   **11:7–10** *What then . . . alway*: as numerous echoes of the earlier section suggest, Paul holds God responsible for the plight of Israel that he outlined in 9:30–10:13 (cf. 11:30–32). He is convinced that God has blinded Israel, obscuring from the majority of Jews Christ's central role in Scripture. This strange conviction generates the provocative scriptural paradoxes introduced in 9:30–10:13, as well as Paul's contradictory insistence in 10:14–21 that the law clearly bears witness to Christ: Christ is manifest in the Scriptures, but God intentionally hides him from Israel.   **11:7** *Israel hath not obtained . . . it*: recalling 9:30–31. *Blinded*: lit. "hardened"; cf. 9:18.   **11:8** *God hath given . . . day*: recalling Deut 29:4, and radically revising it with reference to Isa 6:9; 29:10.   **11:9–10** *Let their table . . . alway*: Ps 69:22–23. The *stumblingblock* recalls 9:33, where the same Greek root is translated "offence."   **11:11** *Through their fall*: a bizarre translation of Gk. *paraptōma*, "misstep" or "stumble" (also in v. 12), since Paul has just voiced outrage at the very idea that Israel would fall. He imagines a footrace between Israel and Gentiles, in which God trips Israel to give Gentiles the victory (cf. 9:16, 32–33), but not to make Israel fall down and prevent it from finishing the race (see 11:12 and note; cf. 9:6 and note). Paul probably alludes to the famous footrace of *Iliad* 23.700–97, where the goddess Athena trips Ajax to let Odysseus come in first but both are awarded splendid prizes.   **11:12** *Diminishing*: Gk. *hēttēma*, normally "loss" or "defeat," which better fits the context. *Fulness*: Gk. *plērōma*, which can refer to the completion of a race, as at Acts 13:25.   **11:13** *For*: better "but" (MS tradition).   **11:15** *Reconciling of the world*: cf. 2 Cor 5:18–21; here the reference is primarily to Gentile inclusion in the church. *Life from the dead*: Paul hints that Israel will be restored at the eschatological consummation, when the dead rise.

[16]For if the firstfruit be holy, the lump is also holy: and if the root be holy, so are the branches. [17]And if some of the branches be broken off, and thou, being a wild olive tree, wert grafted in among them, and with them partakest of the root and fatness of the olive tree; [18]boast not against the branches. But if thou boast, thou bearest not the root, but the root thee. [19]Thou wilt say then, The branches were broken off, that I might be graffed in. [20]Well; because of unbelief they were broken off, and thou standest by faith. Be not high-minded, but fear: [21]for if God spared not the natural branches, take heed lest he also spare not thee. [22]Behold therefore the goodness and severity of God: on them which fell, severity; but toward thee, goodness, if thou continue in his goodness: otherwise thou also shalt be cut off. [23]And they also, if they abide not still in unbelief, shall be graffed in: for God is able to graff them in again. [24]For if thou wert cut out of the olive tree which is wild by nature, and wert graffed contrary to nature into a good olive tree: how much more shall these, which be the natural branches, be graffed into their own olive tree?

[25]For I would not, brethren, that ye should be ignorant of this mystery, lest ye should be wise in your own conceits; that blindness in part is happened to Israel, until the fulness of the Gentiles be come in. [26]And so all Israel shall be saved: as it is written, There shall come out of Sion the Deliverer, and shall turn away ungodliness from Jacob: [27]for this is my covenant unto them, when I shall take away their sins. [28]As concerning the gospel, they are enemies for your sakes: but as touching the election, they are beloved for the fathers' sakes. [29]For the gifts and calling of God are without repentance. [30]For as ye in times past have not believed God, yet have now obtained mercy through their unbelief: [31]even so have these also now not believed, that through your mercy they also may obtain mercy. [32]For God hath concluded them all in unbelief, that he might have mercy upon all.

[33]O the depth of the riches both of the wisdom and knowledge of God! how unsearchable are his judgments, and his ways past finding out! [34]For who hath known the mind of the Lord? or who hath been his counseller? [35]Or who hath first given to him, and it shall be recompensed unto him again? [36]For of him, and through him, and to him, are all things: to whom be glory for ever. Amen.

11:16 *Firstfruit*: cf. 1 Cor 15:20 note. *Lump*: of dough. *Root*: for the comparison of Israel to a (cultivated) olive tree, see Jer 11:16–17; Hos 14:6.   **11:17** *Fatness*: i.e., oiliness (olive oil).   **11:18** *Boast*: compare Paul's earlier critiques of boasting, 2:17, 23; 3:27; 4:2.   **11:22** *Fell*: only here will Paul admit that Israel has fallen (cf. vv. 11–12 and notes), in a passage emphasizing God's mercy to it.   **11:25** *Mystery*: cf. 1 Cor 2:1 note. *Be wise . . . conceits*: cf. Prov 3:7; Isa 5:21. *Blindness*: or "hardening"; see v. 7 note. *Fulness*: cf. v. 12 and note; here the meaning is probably "complete number."   **11:26** *All Israel*: as opposed to the currently faithful "remnant" (v. 5).   **11:26–27** *There shall come . . . sins*: Isa 59:20–21, with a line from 27:9.   **11:26** *And shall*: better "he shall" (MS tradition), referring to the deliverer. **11:28** *Fathers*: "ancestors" or perhaps more narrowly "patriarchs," as in 9:5 (see note).   **11:29** *Without repentance*: on God's part, so "irrevocable."   **11:30** *Believed*: in vv. 30–32 this word and its cognates always render a Greek root (*peith-*) that normally means "obey."   **11:32** *Concluded*: shut together. **11:34** *For who hath known . . . counseller*: cf. Isa 40:13.   **11:35** *Who hath first given . . . again*: cf. Job 35:7; 41:11.   **11:36** *All things*: Gk. *ta panta*, Stoic philosophical jargon for the divine cosmos (cf. 8:32 and note). Paul's concluding doxology resembles traditional Stoic praise of nature, esp. Marcus Aurelius, *Meditations* 4.23: "All proceeds from you, all subsists in you, and to you all things return" (trans. Robin Hard).

12 I beseech you therefore, brethren, by the mercies of God, that ye present your bodies a living sacrifice, holy, acceptable unto God, which is your reasonable service. ²And be not conformed to this world: but be ye transformed by the renewing of your mind, that ye may prove what is that good, and acceptable, and perfect, will of God. ³For I say, through the grace given unto me, to every man that is among you, not to think of himself more highly than he ought to think; but to think soberly, according as God hath dealt to every man the measure of faith.

⁴For as we have many members in one body, and all members have not the same office: ⁵so we, being many, are one body in Christ, and every one members one of another. ⁶Having then gifts differing according to the grace that is given to us, whether prophecy, let us prophesy according to the proportion of faith; ⁷or ministry, let us wait on our ministering: or he that teacheth, on teaching; ⁸or he that exhorteth, on exhortation: he that giveth, let him do it with simplicity; he that ruleth, with diligence; he that sheweth mercy, with cheerfulness.

⁹Let love be without dissimulation. Abhor that which is evil; cleave to that which is good. ¹⁰Be kindly affectioned one to another with brotherly love; in honour preferring one another; ¹¹not slothful in business; fervent in spirit; serving the Lord; ¹²rejoicing in hope; patient in tribulation; continuing instant in prayer; ¹³distributing to the necessity of saints; given to hospitality. ¹⁴Bless them which persecute you: bless, and curse not. ¹⁵Rejoice with them that do rejoice, and weep with them that weep. ¹⁶Be of the same mind one toward another. Mind not high things, but condescend to men of low estate. Be not wise in your own conceits. ¹⁷Recompense to no man evil for evil. Provide things honest in the sight of all men. ¹⁸If it be possible, as much as lieth in you, live peaceably with all men. ¹⁹Dearly beloved, avenge not yourselves, but rather give place unto wrath: for it is written,

12:1–13:14 Proper behavior. 12:1–3 *I beseech . . . faith:* by echoing and reversing the condemnation of Gentile sin and pretension from 1:18–2:16, Paul introduces the ethical guidelines he presents in chaps. 12 and 13 as an antidote to Gentile depravity. **12:1** *Present your bodies . . . God:* in contrast to Gentiles' perverse use of their bodies in 1:26–27. *Service:* translating Gk. *latreia,* also "worship"; cf. 1:25 and note, where the verbal form refers to irrational idolatry. **12:2** *World:* lit. "age." *Renewing of your mind . . . God:* compare Gentiles' "reprobate mind" in 1:28, where "like" (see note) translates the same Greek word here rendered *prove.* **12:3** *Not to think . . . soberly:* in contrast to the pretentious Gentile whom Paul rebukes in 2:1–16. **12:4** *Members in one body:* Paul develops this image in 1 Cor 12:12–31, a passage preceded by a discussion of spiritual gifts (12:1–11) analogous to the one that follows here (vv. 6–8). **12:6** *Let us prophesy:* this and the similar exhortations in vv. 7 and 8 are KJV interpolations. **12:7** *Let us . . . ministering:* lit. "in ministering." *On teaching:* or "in teaching." **12:8** *On exhortation:* or "in exhortation." *Giveth:* in the sense of sharing. *Simplicity:* generosity (see Matt 6:22 note). **12:9–21** *Let love . . . good:* Paul draws especially on the OT wisdom tradition, as well as on the teachings of Jesus, to regulate believers' social relationships. **12:9** *Abhor that . . . good:* cf. Amos 5:15. **12:11** *Business:* diligence. **12:12** *Continuing instant:* always earnest. **12:13** *Given to:* lit. "pursuing" (Gk. *diōkontes*). **12:14** *Bless them . . . you:* perhaps echoing a saying of Jesus (cf. Matt 5:44; Luke 6:28). The word rendered "persecute" (*diōkontas;* see v. 13 note) can mean "harass." Whatever Paul has in mind, he does not refer to Roman persecution of Christians (as 13:1–7 makes clear), which began somewhat later. **12:16** *Condescend to men of low estate:* i.e., "accommodate yourselves to what is humble" or "associate with the lowly." *Be not . . . conceits:* see 11:25 and note. **12:17** *Recompense . . . for evil:* Prov 20:22; cf. Matt 5:38–39. *Provide things . . . men:* cf. LXX Prov 3:4. *Honest:* noble. **12:18** *Lieth in you:* is within your capacity. **12:19** *Avenge not yourselves:* Lev 19:18.

Vengeance is mine; I will repay, saith the Lord. [20]Therefore if thine enemy hunger, feed him; if he thirst, give him drink: for in so doing thou shalt heap coals of fire on his head. [21]Be not overcome of evil, but overcome evil with good.

13 Let every soul be subject unto the higher powers. For there is no power but of God: the powers that be are ordained of God. [2]Whosoever therefore resisteth the power, resisteth the ordinance of God: and they that resist shall receive to themselves damnation. [3]For rulers are not a terror to good works, but to the evil. Wilt thou then not be afraid of the power? do that which is good, and thou shalt have praise of the same: [4]for he is the minister of God to thee for good. But if thou do that which is evil, be afraid; for he beareth not the sword in vain: for he is the minister of God, a revenger to execute wrath upon him that doeth evil. [5]Wherefore ye must needs be subject, not only for wrath, but also for conscience sake. [6]For for this cause pay ye tribute also: for they are God's ministers, attending continually upon this very thing. [7]Render therefore to all their dues: tribute to whom tribute is due; custom to whom custom; fear to whom fear; honour to whom honour.

[8]Owe no man any thing, but to love one another: for he that loveth another hath fulfilled the law. [9]For this, Thou shalt not commit adultery, Thou shalt not kill, Thou shalt not steal, Thou shalt not bear false witness, Thou shalt not covet; and if there be any other commandment, it is briefly comprehended in this saying, namely, Thou shalt love thy neighbour as thyself. [10]Love worketh no ill to his neighbour: therefore love is the fulfilling of the law.

[11]And that, knowing the time, that now it is high time to awake out of sleep: for now is our salvation nearer than when we believed. [12]The night is far spent,

---

Vengeance is . . . Lord: Deut 32:35.   **12:20** *Therefore*: better "but" (MS tradition). *If thine . . . head*: see Prov 25:21–22 and note.   **13:1–7** *Let every soul . . . honour*: this paragraph has proven controversial, as it seems to demand obedience to even unjust political authorities. Luther commented on it that "Christians should not, under the pretense of Christian religion, refuse to obey men even if they are wicked" (*Commentary on Romans*, trans. J. Theodore Mueller).   **13:1** *The higher powers*: the government, i.e., Roman imperial authorities. Paul assumes that they support or even indirectly enforce the ethical guidelines he has laid out, which this section repeatedly echoes. Compare vv. 3–4a and 12:9, 17, 21; 13:4b–5 and 12:19. *Be subject* and *ordained* share a Greek root. *The powers . . . God*: a conventional idea; cf. Prov 8:15–16.   **13:2** *Damnation*: judgment.   **13:4** *He*: better "it" (throughout this verse), referring to "the power" (v. 3).   **13:6** *Tribute*: taxes. Paul here and in v. 7 goes further than Jesus in urging believers to subject themselves to Roman authorities (cf. Mark 12:17 and note).   **13:8** *Owe . . . any thing*: apparently contradicting v. 7, especially since Gk. *opheilete* (*owe*) echoes *opheilas* ("dues"). For an analogous conflict in Paul's ethical exhortation, see Gal 6:2 and 5. *Fulfilled the law*: see 8:4 and note.   **13:9** *Thou shalt not commit . . . covet*: quoting the second tablet of the Ten Commandments (Exod 20:13–17; Deut 5:17–21). The two-faced Jewish teacher of chap. 2 instructs Gentiles to obey some of the same commandments (vv. 21–22); Paul casts himself as the antidote to that hypocritical instruction, as a genuine and successful Jewish teacher of Gentiles. *Thou shalt not bear false witness*: better omitted (MS tradition). *Thou shalt not covet*: this commandment figured prominently in the discussion of slavery to sin (7:7–25). *Thou shalt love . . . thyself*: Lev 19:18 (cf. Rom 12:19 and note).   **13:10** *Love is . . . law*: cf. Matt 7:12. Gal 5:14 likewise asserts that Lev 19:18 sums up the law, and the synoptic tradition too privileges this verse from Leviticus over the rest of the law (with the exception of Deut 6:4–5); cf. Matt 22:34–40; Mark 12:28–34; Luke 10:25–28.   **13:11** *For now . . . believed*: i.e., the eschatological consummation is nearer now than when we came to faith.   **13:12–14** *The night . . . thereof*: cf. 1 Thess 5:2–10.

the day is at hand: let us therefore cast off the works of darkness, and let us put on the armour of light. [13]Let us walk honestly, as in the day; not in rioting and drunkenness, not in chambering and wantonness, not in strife and envying. [14]But put ye on the Lord Jesus Christ, and make not provision for the flesh, to fulfil the lusts thereof.

14 Him that is weak in the faith receive ye, but not to doubtful disputations. [2]For one believeth that he may eat all things: another, who is weak, eateth herbs. [3]Let not him that eateth despise him that eateth not; and let not him which eateth not judge him that eateth: for God hath received him. [4]Who art thou that judgest another man's servant? to his own master he standeth or falleth. Yea, he shall be holden up: for God is able to make him stand. [5]One man esteemeth one day above another: another esteemeth every day alike. Let every man be fully persuaded in his own mind. [6]He that regardeth the day, regardeth it unto the Lord; and he that regardeth not the day, to the Lord he doth not regard it. He that eateth, eateth to the Lord, for he giveth God thanks; and he that eateth not, to the Lord he eateth not, and giveth God thanks. [7]For none of us liveth to himself, and no man dieth to himself. [8]For whether we live, we live unto the Lord; and whether we die, we die unto the Lord: whether we live therefore, or die, we are the Lord's. [9]For to this end Christ both died, and rose, and revived, that he might be Lord both of the dead and living. [10]But why dost thou judge thy brother? or why dost thou set at nought thy brother? for we shall all stand before the judgment seat of Christ. [11]For it is written, As I live, saith the Lord, every knee shall bow to me, and every tongue shall confess to God. [12]So then every one of us shall give account of himself to God. [13]Let us not therefore judge one another any more: but judge this rather, that no man put a stumblingblock or an occasion to fall in his brother's way.

[14]I know, and am persuaded by the Lord Jesus, that there is nothing unclean of itself: but to him that esteemeth any thing to be unclean, to him it is unclean.

13:12 *Let us put . . . light*: while the specific reference to armor recognizes the spiritual hostility of this present world (cf. 2 Cor 4:4 and note), in the Pauline corpus the changing of clothes often figures moral transformation (cf. Eph 4:22–24; 6:13–17; Col 3:9–14), perhaps referring to a ceremonial change of garments at baptism (cf. Gal 3:27) or anticipating the new bodies that believers will *put on* at the eschatological resurrection (cf. 2 Cor 5:1–4). **13:13** *Honestly*: better "becomingly." *Chambering*: sexual license.
   14:1–15:13 "The strong" and "the weak." Paul directs the strong to accommodate the weak, those with beliefs that lead to fastidious behavior in consuming food and observing the calendar. For a similar discussion, see 1 Cor 8–10. **14:1** *Doubtful disputations*: "quarreling over opinions" (NRSV). **14:2** *One believeth . . . herbs*: the issue in question was presumably the extent to which believers should try to avoid meat sacrificed to idols (cf. 1 Cor 8 and notes). Some apparently went so far as to eat only vegetables. **14:4** *Servant*: house slave. *Holden up*: lit. "made to stand." **14:5** *One man . . . alike*: the practice to which Paul refers is unclear: scrupulous observance of Jewish holy days? superstitious avoidance of business on pagan holy days? something else entirely? **14:6** *And he that regardeth . . . it*: better omitted (MS tradition). **14:9** *Both died . . . revived*: better "died and lived" (MS tradition). **14:10** *Christ*: better "God" (MS tradition). **14:11** *As I . . . God*: Isa 45:23. **14:13** *Put a stumblingblock . . . way*: echoing the Greek of 9:33 more closely than KJV suggests: repeated words are *stumblingblock*/"stumblingstone," *occasion to fall*/rock "of offence," and *put*/"lays." In 9:33, God was laying down the stones to trip Israel. **14:14** *By the Lord Jesus*: perhaps referring to the tradition recorded at Matt 15:17–18 and Mark 7:18–19, to which v. 20 may be connected (see note).

¹⁵But if thy brother be grieved with thy meat, now walkest thou not charitably. Destroy not him with thy meat, for whom Christ died. ¹⁶Let not then your good be evil spoken of: ¹⁷for the kingdom of God is not meat and drink; but righteousness, and peace, and joy in the Holy Ghost. ¹⁸For he that in these things serveth Christ is acceptable to God, and approved of men. ¹⁹Let us therefore follow after the things which make for peace, and things wherewith one may edify another. ²⁰For meat destroy not the work of God. All things indeed are pure; but it is evil for that man who eateth with offence. ²¹It is good neither to eat flesh, nor to drink wine, nor any thing whereby thy brother stumbleth, or is offended, or is made weak. ²²Hast thou faith? have it to thyself before God. Happy is he that condemneth not himself in that thing which he alloweth. ²³And he that doubteth is damned if he eat, because he eateth not of faith: for whatsoever is not of faith is sin.

15 We then that are strong ought to bear the infirmities of the weak, and not to please ourselves. ²Let every one of us please his neighbour for his good to edification. ³For even Christ pleased not himself; but, as it is written, The reproaches of them that reproached thee fell on me. ⁴For whatsoever things were written aforetime were written for our learning, that we through patience and comfort of the scriptures might have hope. ⁵Now the God of patience and consolation grant you to be likeminded one toward another according to Christ Jesus: ⁶that ye may with one mind and one mouth glorify God, even the Father of our Lord Jesus Christ.

⁷Wherefore receive ye one another, as Christ also received us to the glory of God. ⁸Now I say that Jesus Christ was a minister of the circumcision for the truth of God, to confirm the promises made unto the fathers: ⁹and that the Gentiles might glorify God for his mercy; as it is written, For this cause I will confess to thee among the Gentiles, and sing unto thy name. ¹⁰And again he saith, Rejoice, ye Gentiles, with his people. ¹¹And again, Praise the Lord, all ye Gentiles; and laud him, all ye people. ¹²And again, Esaias saith, There shall be a root of Jesse, and he that shall rise to reign over the Gentiles; in him shall the Gentiles trust. ¹³Now the God of hope fill you with all joy and peace in believing, that ye may abound in hope, through the power of the Holy Ghost.

14:15 *But*: better "for" (MS tradition). *Meat*: food. *Charitably*: Gk. *kata agapēn*, using the same word translated "love" at 13:8, 10. **14:20** *All things . . . pure*: see Mark 7:19 note. *With offence*: alternatively "on account of a stumbling block" (see v. 13). **14:21** *Or is offended . . . weak*: better omitted (MS tradition). **14:22** *Happy*: or "blessed." *Alloweth*: lit. "approves." **14:23** *Damned*: condemned. **15:3** *The reproaches . . . me*: Ps 69:9. **15:4** *Patience*: or "endurance" (also in v. 5). **15:5** *Consolation*: or "encouragement." *According to*: i.e., "after the example of"; cf. vv. 7–9 and notes. **15:7** *Us*: better "you" (MS tradition). **15:8** *Now*: better "for" (MS tradition). **15:8–9** *Jesus Christ . . . mercy*: upholding God's integrity (*truth*, v. 8) only obligates Jesus to minister to the Jews, *to confirm the promises* God made to Israel (cf. 9:4; 11:29 and note). Nonetheless, Christ mercifully serves Gentiles too (v. 9), and Paul presents his service as an exemplary paradigm (cf. vv. 5–7) for the strong; cf. 14:14–21. **15:9** *For this cause . . . name*: Ps 18:49. **15:10** *Rejoice, ye . . . people*: Deut 32:43. **15:11** *Praise the . . . people*: Ps 117:1. **15:12** *There shall be . . . trust*: Isa 11:10. *Root of Jesse*: Jesse was David's father; Jesse's *root* (Gk. *riza*, also "shoot" or "offshoot") is synonymous with the "seed of David" (1:3–5; see notes). Paul thus brings his theological argument full circle before addressing practical matters concerning his planned visit to Rome and thence to Spain.

¹⁴And I myself also am persuaded of you, my brethren, that ye also are full of goodness, filled with all knowledge, able also to admonish one another. ¹⁵Nevertheless, brethren, I have written the more boldly unto you in some sort, as putting you in mind, because of the grace that is given to me of God, ¹⁶that I should be the minister of Jesus Christ to the Gentiles, ministering the gospel of God, that the offering up of the Gentiles might be acceptable, being sanctified by the Holy Ghost. ¹⁷I have therefore whereof I may glory through Jesus Christ in those things which pertain to God. ¹⁸For I will not dare to speak of any of those things which Christ hath not wrought by me, to make the Gentiles obedient, by word and deed, ¹⁹through mighty signs and wonders, by the power of the Spirit of God; so that from Jerusalem, and round about unto Illyricum, I have fully preached the gospel of Christ. ²⁰Yea, so have I strived to preach the gospel, not where Christ was named, lest I should build upon another man's foundation: ²¹but as it is written, To whom he was not spoken of, they shall see: and they that have not heard shall understand.

²²For which cause also I have been much hindered from coming to you. ²³But now having no more place in these parts, and having a great desire these many years to come unto you; ²⁴whensoever I take my journey into Spain, I will come to you: for I trust to see you in my journey, and to be brought on my way thitherward by you, if first I be somewhat filled with your company. ²⁵But now I go unto Jerusalem to minister unto the saints. ²⁶For it hath pleased them of Macedonia and Achaia to make a certain contribution for the poor saints which are at Jerusalem. ²⁷It hath pleased them verily; and their debtors they are. For if the Gentiles have been made partakers of their spiritual things, their duty is also to minister unto them in carnal things. ²⁸When therefore I have performed this, and have sealed to them this fruit, I will come by you into Spain. ²⁹And I am sure that, when I come unto you, I shall come in the fulness of the blessing of the gospel of Christ.

³⁰Now I beseech you, brethren, for the Lord Jesus Christ's sake, and for the love of the Spirit, that ye strive together with me in your prayers to God for me; ³¹that I may be delivered from them that do not believe in Judæa; and that my service which I have for Jerusalem may be accepted of the saints; ³²that I may

---

15:14-33 Paul's travel plans. Before sharing his plans and requesting financial support (vv. 20–32), Paul apologetically explains why he has written so boldly (vv. 14–19). **15:15** *As putting you in mind*: as a reminder. **15:16** *Minister, ministering*: the different Greek words thus rendered have cultic connotations. *The offering . . . Ghost*: Paul may be claiming that in a priestly role he offers sanctified Gentiles to God, or that his ministry allows Gentiles themselves to offer God worthy offerings (cf. 12:1). **15:19** *Illyricum*: a Roman province on the eastern Adriatic coast. **15:21** *To whom . . . understand*: Isa 52:15. **15:24** *I will come to you*: better omitted (MS tradition); the first part of v. 24 should modify the second clause of v. 23, even though an incomplete sentence results. *Be brought . . . you*: Paul subtly requests the Romans' financial support for his Spanish mission. **15:25–28** *But now . . . fruit*: for this offering, see 1 Cor 16:1–4; 2 Cor 8–9; cf. Gal 2:10 and note. **15:26** *Macedonia and Achaia*: regions covering the major part of the Greek peninsula. **15:27** *If the Gentiles . . . spiritual things*: cf. 11:13–24. **15:28** *Sealed to them this fruit*: when tenant farmers brought harvests to a landowner in antiquity, they used seals to identify their produce. **15:29** *Of the gospel*: better omitted (MS tradition). **15:31** *I may . . . Judæa*: Acts 21:27–36 reports a disturbance in Jerusalem during this trip that resulted in Paul's arrest and subsequent journey to Rome for trial, which presumably prevented his visit to Spain. *Be accepted . . . saints*: some speculate Paul feared that believers at Jerusalem would reject his

come unto you with joy by the will of God, and may with you be refreshed. ³³Now the God of peace be with you all. Amen.

16 I commend unto you Phebe our sister, which is a servant of the church which is at Cenchrea: ²that ye receive her in the Lord, as becometh saints, and that ye assist her in whatsoever business she hath need of you: for she hath been a succourer of many, and of myself also. ³Greet Priscilla and Aquila my helpers in Christ Jesus: ⁴who have for my life laid down their own necks: unto whom not only I give thanks, but also all the churches of the Gentiles. ⁵Likewise greet the church that is in their house. Salute my wellbeloved Epænetus, who is the firstfruits of Achaia unto Christ. ⁶Greet Mary, who bestowed much labour on us. ⁷Salute Andronicus and Junia, my kinsmen, and my fellowprisoners, who are of note among the apostles, who also were in Christ before me. ⁸Greet Amplias my beloved in the Lord. ⁹Salute Urbane, our helper in Christ, and Stachys my beloved. ¹⁰Salute Apelles approved in Christ. Salute them which are of Aristobulus' household. ¹¹Salute Herodion my kinsman. Greet them that be of the household of Narcissus, which are in the Lord. ¹²Salute Tryphena and Tryphosa, who labour in the Lord. Salute the beloved Persis, which laboured much in the Lord. ¹³Salute Rufus chosen in the Lord, and his mother and mine. ¹⁴Salute Asyncritus, Phlegon, Hermas, Patrobas, Hermes, and the brethren which are with them. ¹⁵Salute Philologus, and Julia, Nereus, and his sister, and Olympas, and all the saints which are with them. ¹⁶Salute one another with an holy kiss. The churches of Christ salute you.

¹⁷Now I beseech you, brethren, mark them which cause divisions and offences contrary to the doctrine which ye have learned; and avoid them. ¹⁸For they that are such serve not our Lord Jesus Christ, but their own belly; and by good words and fair speeches deceive the hearts of the simple. ¹⁹For your obedience is come

---

offering because of an unresolved conflict with Peter (cf. Gal 2:11–21). It apparently involved believers associated with James (Gal 2:12), who like Peter was closely identified with the Jerusalem church.
     16:1–20 Greetings and advice. 16:1 *Phebe . . . Cenchrea*: possibly she bore Paul's letter to Rome. Cenchrea, her church's home, was one of Corinth's ports. That she is called a *servant* (Gk. *diakonos*, translated "deacon" at Phil 1:1 and 1 Tim 3:8–13) may signal that she holds formal office in her church. In any case, Paul's praise of her as a "succourer of many" (v. 2) indicates how dependent on its female members the early church was. In the list of names from vv. 1–16, many are of women, and one of these is designated "apostle" (Junia, v. 7).   **16:3** *Priscilla and Aquila*: the only two named in vv. 1–16 who are otherwise known. According to Acts, Paul met and ministered with this couple in Corinth, where they had settled after Claudius expelled the Jews from Rome (18:1–2). They accompanied Paul to Asia (18:18–28; cf. 1 Cor 16:19) and apparently sometime later returned to Rome.   **16:5** *The church . . . house*: the church at Rome (as in other cities) would have consisted of various small congregations meeting at members' homes (cf. v. 23). *Firstfruits*: i.e., first convert. *Achaia*: better "Asia" (MS tradition).   **16:6** *On us*: better "on you" (MS tradition).   **16:7** *Kinsmen*: probably meaning "fellow Jews"; see also vv. 11, 21. *Apostles*: see 1:1 note.   **16:8** *Amplias*: better "Ampliatus" (MS tradition).   **16:10** *Them which . . . household*: his extended family, including slaves (also at v. 11).   **16:13** *His mother and mine*: she apparently treated Paul as a son.   **16:16** *Holy kiss*: a conventional greeting in the early church; cf. 1 Cor 16:20; 1 Pet 5:14; etc.   **16:17–18** *Mark them . . . simple*: the identity of these people is totally obscure, although in Phil 3:19 Paul uses similar language for opponents who seem to be urging Gentile believers to become circumcised (Phil 3:2–3). If the groups are related, perhaps the claim that they serve their belly refers to their emphasis on observing Jewish dietary law.   **16:18** *Simple*: lit. "innocent" (also in v. 19, though there it translates a different

abroad unto all men. I am glad therefore on your behalf: but yet I would have you wise unto that which is good, and simple concerning evil. ²⁰And the God of peace shall bruise Satan under your feet shortly. The grace of our Lord Jesus Christ be with you. Amen.

²¹Timotheus my workfellow, and Lucius, and Jason, and Sosipater, my kinsmen, salute you. ²²I Tertius, who wrote this epistle, salute you in the Lord. ²³Gaius mine host, and of the whole church, saluteth you. Erastus the chamberlain of the city saluteth you, and Quartus a brother. ²⁴The grace of our Lord Jesus Christ be with you all. Amen.

²⁵Now to him that is of power to stablish you according to my gospel, and the preaching of Jesus Christ, according to the revelation of the mystery, which was kept secret since the world began, ²⁶but now is made manifest, and by the scriptures of the prophets, according to the commandment of the everlasting God, made known to all nations for the obedience of faith: ²⁷to God only wise, be glory through Jesus Christ for ever. Amen.

Written to the Romans from Corinthus, and sent by Phebe servant of the church at Cenchrea.

Greek word). **16:19** *I am glad . . . behalf*: better "I therefore rejoice over you" (MS tradition). **16:20** *God of peace*: Paul's closing references to *peace* and then *grace* recall his salutation of "grace . . . and peace" (1:7). *Shall bruise . . . shortly*: cf. Gen 3:15; Satan is identified with the serpent. *Amen*: better omitted (MS tradition). **16:21–27 Closing. 16:21** *Timotheus*: see 1 Cor 4:17 note. *Jason*: perhaps the same figure mentioned in Acts 17:1–9. **16:22** *Who wrote this epistle*: Tertius apparently served as Paul's scribe. **16:23** *Gaius*: perhaps the Corinthian whom Paul claims to have baptized (1 Cor 1:14). *Erastus*: perhaps the figure mentioned in Acts 19:22; cf. 2 Tim 4:20. *Chamberlain*: Gk. *oikonomos*, probably translating Lat. *aedilis*. Aediles were treasurers responsible for managing city funds, as well as for sponsoring public works, and one named Erastus—probably the same—is credited by a contemporary Corinthian inscription with paving a city square. **16:24** *The grace . . . Amen*: better omitted (MS tradition). **16:25–27** *Now to him . . . Amen*: many ancient MSS omit the concluding doxology or locate it elsewhere in the text (e.g., after 14:23 or after 15:33); it thus may represent a later scribal addition. References to *power* (v. 25) and to the divine commandment *made known to all nations for the obedience to faith* (v. 26) recall Paul's salutation (1:1–7, esp. vv. 4–5). **16:25** *Revelation of the mystery*: cf. 11:25. **16:27** *Written to the Romans . . . Cenchrea*: better omitted (MS tradition).

The First Epistle of Paul the Apostle
to the Corinthians

PAUL founded the church at Corinth during his second missionary journey (Acts 18:1–17; cf. 1 Cor 4:15) and he corresponded with it regularly. He wrote 1 Corinthians from Ephesus (16:8–9), probably ca. 54–55 C.E. Throughout the epistle he offers advice on issues that the Corinthians had raised in a letter of their own (see 7:1 note), including marriage, divorce, and sex; eating meat sacrificed to idols; and ecstatic worship. Paul also addresses issues that seem to have originated in an unfavorable report from Corinth delivered by those "of the house of Chloe" (1:11). These include factionalism, sexual impropriety (committing incest, visiting prostitutes, etc.), the role and attire of women at church, and resurrection.

Paul's positions on all these issues have exercised a profound influence on Christianity. Perhaps more than any New Testament writing, 1 Corinthians is responsible for the church's traditional elevation of renunciation as the highest sexual ethic, a position not seriously challenged until the Reformation. More recently, Paul's resistance to speaking in tongues has been invoked to denigrate the pentecostal and charismatic movements that emerged in the twentieth century and exercise global influence today. And the institutionalized sexism characterizing a range of Christian denominations may find its origins—and certainly finds support—in 1 Corinthians' various directives concerning women, particularly in the requirement that women be veiled and keep silent in church (11:2–16; 14:34–35).

Because of its ubiquitous influence on Christianity, readers of 1 Corinthians run a high risk of confusing its effect with its character. This is unfortunate, because uncritical interpretation of this epistle through the lens of later Christianity robs it of much of its fascination and power. For instance, while Paul indubitably urges sexual renunciation in chapter 7 (in this he is rather typical of ancient writers—Jewish, Christian, or pagan), his asceticism finds its foundation not in a conventional commitment to subduing bodily appetites but rather in imminent eschatological expectation: believers should focus on pleasing the soon coming Lord, rather than a spouse and sexual partner. Paul's hesitance about speaking in tongues likewise has a surprising basis. Despite common construals of his argument, Paul is less concerned with the orderly worship conventional in many churches today than he is with making room for God to speak both spontaneously and intelligibly in the bedlam that apparently characterized early Christian gatherings (cf. 14:26–27). Paul nowhere denigrates ecstatic spirituality—indeed, he thanks God that he speaks in tongues more than the Corinthian believers themselves (14:18)—and he recognizes that an ecstatic community of worshippers is something awesome to behold (14:23 and note). But even in the midst of such impressive commotion, he wants to ensure that God's convincing prophetic voice is heard and understood, and for this reason he emphasizes spontaneous prophecy and translated tongues over uninterpreted glossolalia.

Finally, 1 Corinthians' overtly sexist gestures are less interesting than its profoundly ambivalent attitude toward the role of women in the church. Most obvious is the contradiction between 11:2–16 and 14:34–36. In the former passage, Paul assumes that women pray and prophesy publicly, and offers advice about how they should dress when doing so. In the latter, Paul forbids women from speaking in church, which he says would be shameful. Even if they have a question, "let them ask their husbands at home" (14:35). The latter passage stands in tension not only with 11:2–16 but also with the entire thrust of chapter 7: while 14:35 assumes that women in the church are married, throughout the earlier chapter Paul urges women to stay single.

Raising suspicions about the passage on textual grounds, several ancient witnesses place 14:34–35 after verse 40; it thus may have originated as an early marginal gloss composed by a scribe trying to assimilate Paul's teaching about women in 1 Corinthians to the directive of 1 Tim 2:11–14. This gloss would later have been incorporated into the text itself, in some copies after verse 33, in others after verse 40. The best way to deal with it, then, may be to excise it as a post-Pauline interpolation; but even this step does not resolve the ambivalence toward women's role in the church that Paul's letter reflects.

Chapter 11's argument that women should cover their heads during worship—surely an uncontroversial position in the Greco-Roman world—limps with a lameness that Paul himself seems to discern. At verses 11–12, he explicitly reverses the Genesis exegesis with which he initially supported his advice that women wear veils, seemingly recognizing the troubling implications of its mistaken inferences. (It rests on a faulty interpretation of Gen 1:27 and draws a conclusion that flies in the face of Gal 3:28, which invokes God's creation of humanity to dissolve gender, not to uphold traditional gender hierarchies.) After a confusing invocation of nature in verses 13–15, Paul abandons the subject entirely, forbidding contentiousness rather than veiling. Since Paul can come up with no strong argument supporting his aversion to unveiled women speaking in church, he contents himself with having made his views known and insisting that however the Corinthians go forward, they not fight about it.

1 Corinthians occupies a peculiar position in the New Testament canon. The letter opens a rare window onto the everyday life of early Greco-Roman Christianity, providing unique insight into what some first-generation believers thought about such mundane matters as what they should wear to church, how they might permissibly satisfy their sexual appetites, whether and whom they might marry, under what circumstances they might divorce, to what extent they might interact with outsiders, how conflicts with fellow believers should be resolved, and so on. Even if we assign 1 Corinthians no moral authority, its meandering discussions are worthwhile reading for their antiquarian interest alone.

Yet 1 Corinthians is more than an intriguing inventory of early Christian thought about routine matters such as sex, food, and fashion. It is at the same time a thematically unified treatise on the body of Christ. In this letter Christ's body must be understood simultaneously as the risen Christ himself, as the eucharistic meal, as the community of believers, and even as individual believers' transformed bodies assimilated to Christ's risen body at the eschatological resurrection. Paul's directives about the various issues he addresses consistently reflect his multivalent understanding of Christ's body. In the context of privileging intelligible prophecy over uninterpreted tongues, Paul observes that believers constitute one body—namely, Christ's—each forming a different part of it (chs. 12–14). Since Christ's body would be incomplete without all of its individual organs, the community ought not to dismiss its members' unassuming spiritual gifts in favor of a few ostentatious manifestations, especially tongues. In chapter 15, Paul assimilates the community of believers to Christ's body in a different way, explaining that at the eschatological resurrection believers' bodies will be transformed into spirit just as Christ's was when he rose from the dead.

Paul takes the equation of Christ's body with the believing community seriously throughout the epistle. This is especially clear in chapter 6, where he expresses perturbation at believers having sex with prostitutes—not out of a puritanical distaste for fornication, but rather out of his conviction that when a (male) believer penetrates a prostitute, he brings Christ's organ into contact with impurity. A complementary logic presumably underlies Paul's subsequent claim that unbelieving spouses are "sanctified" by their believing partners, and that the offspring of such unions are likewise holy (7:14). Paul invokes the body of Christ elsewhere as well, especially in his complex discussion of two interrelated issues: the consumption of meat sacrificed to idols and his treatment of the Eucharist (see esp. 10:14–22; 11:17–34). Here, too, Christ's body is a multivalent image, figuring the community of believers, the eucharistic host, and the spiritual presence of the risen Christ infusing them both.

Although its chief pleasures and importance are thematic, 1 Corinthians is also remarkable for its rhetoric, all the more so because of its explicit disavowal of rhetoric early on. In 2:4 Paul writes "my speech and my preaching was not with enticing words of man's wisdom, but in demonstration of the Spirit and of power" (2:4), but that claim culminates a section of the epistle abounding in rhetorical artistry (1:18–2:5), on display in the intricate structuring of 1:22–23 and especially 26–28 (see notes), the section's sometimes byzantine sentences (esp. v. 21), and its constant revelry in antithesis and paradox. Paul's repudiation of rhetoric turns out itself to be a rhetorical ploy highlighting the impressive rhetorical skill he has just demonstrated.

Paul's rhetorical skill is nowhere more evident than in his discussion of spiritual gifts—which perhaps comes as no surprise, since the point of this discussion is to privilege intelligible prophecy over inarticulate glossolalia. In chapter 12, Paul draws on the rhetorical commonplace of the body as a society but he turns this standard metaphor on its head. Writers and orators conventionally likened the elite to the most visibly important parts of the body, such as the head or the stomach (i.e., the parts without which the body would die), and equated the masses with its more dispensable members such as the limbs. As the limbs serve the head, so should the soldiers serve the general, the plebs the patricians, and so on. Only in this way would communal harmony be maintained. Paul adopts a different approach by focusing—shockingly—on the genitals (see 12:22–24). Our genitalia are vulnerable ("more feeble") and we hide them as if they were shameful; but at the same time they are indispensable ("necessary"), and our propensity to shield them from public gaze actually suggests that we honor them more than other parts of our bodies. Paul's discussion draws an implicit analogy from how individuals treat their genitals to how the community of believers should treat its "weaker" members (referring primarily to those with less desirable spiritual gifts, but the term "weak" has broader social connotations of which Paul was certainly aware—see 1:27–28 and notes). Paul, like his contemporaries, employs the trope of society as body in order to urge communal harmony (12:25), but the harmony he urges is not based on maintaining conventional hierarchical structures; on the contrary, it is founded on the community's powerful members recognizing the special dignity of brethren whom they might otherwise mistake as worthless.

Immediately after this intriguing variation on a rhetorical commonplace, Paul moves on to a more straightforward demonstration of his rhetorical skill, chapter 13's famous encomium of love, the most valuable spiritual gift of all. But that may be left to speak for itself, in KJV's rousing cadences.

Strong commentaries on 1 Corinthians abound: Anthony Thiselton's *The First Epistle to the Corinthians: A Commentary on the Greek Text* (Grand Rapids, MI.: Eerdmans, 2000) is especially thorough, and Hans Conzelmann's older commentary in the Hermeneia series, *1 Corinthians: A Commentary on the First Epistle to the Corinthians* (Philadelphia: Fortress, 1975) also contains a wealth of valuable information. This introduction and the notes that follow reveal their influence, as well as that of Dale Martin's *The Corinthian Body* (New Haven: Yale University Press, 1995) and Richard Hay's *First Corinthians* (Louisville, KY: John Knox, 1997), a pastoral but nonetheless perceptive commentary in the Interpretation series.

THE FIRST EPISTLE OF PAUL
THE APOSTLE TO THE
CORINTHIANS

1 Paul, called to be an apostle of Jesus Christ through the will of God, and Sosthenes our brother, ²unto the church of God which is at Corinth, to them that are sanctified in Christ Jesus, called to be saints, with all that in every place call upon the name of Jesus Christ our Lord, both theirs and ours: ³Grace be unto you, and peace, from God our Father, and from the Lord Jesus Christ.

⁴I thank my God always on your behalf, for the grace of God which is given you by Jesus Christ; ⁵that in every thing ye are enriched by him, in all utterance, and in all knowledge; ⁶even as the testimony of Christ was confirmed in you: ⁷so that ye come behind in no gift; waiting for the coming of our Lord Jesus Christ: ⁸who shall also confirm you unto the end, that ye may be blameless in the day of our Lord Jesus Christ. ⁹God is faithful, by whom ye were called unto the fellowship of his Son Jesus Christ our Lord.

¹⁰Now I beseech you, brethren, by the name of our Lord Jesus Christ, that ye all speak the same thing, and that there be no divisions among you; but that ye be perfectly joined together in the same mind and in the same judgment. ¹¹For it hath been declared unto me of you, my brethren, by them which are of the house of Chloe, that there are contentions among you. ¹²Now this I say, that every one of you saith, I am of Paul; and I of Apollos; and I of Cephas; and I of Christ. ¹³Is Christ divided? was Paul crucified for you? or were ye baptized in the name of Paul?

1:1–9 Salutation and thanksgiving. On the openings of Paul's letters, see note to Rom 1:1–15. **1:1** *Apostle*: see Rom 1:1 note. *Sosthenes*: otherwise unknown, although Acts 18:17 mentions a synagogue leader in Corinth by that name. **1:2** *Church*: see Rom 16:5 note. *Corinth*: a major city in the Roman province of Achaia, situated on the isthmus between mainland Greece and the Peloponnese. *Saints*: Gk. *hagioi*, the same root as "sanctified" (see Rom 1:7 and note). **1:3** *Grace be . . . peace*: see Rom 1:7 note. **1:4** *By*: lit. "in." **1:7** *Coming*: lit. "revelation."

1:10–17 Factions. Paul first gives the letter's thesis (v. 10) and then briefly explains the circumstances that have led him to write (vv. 11–17). **1:10** *Brethren*: a common self-designation of Jesus-believers. *Judgment*: alternatively "purpose." **1:11** *Chloe*: otherwise unknown. **1:12** *Every one . . . Christ*: these factions are obscure. Paul's final reference to a Christ party may rhetorically underscore the absurdity of such divisions in the church, Christ's body. *Apollos*: an eloquent and erudite biblical exegete from Alexandria, who spent time in Corinth (Acts 18:24–19:1). *Cephas*: Peter (see Gal 2:9 note). **1:13** *Baptized*: see Mark 1:4 note. Baptism became the early church's initiation ritual. *Name*

¹⁴I thank God that I baptized none of you, but Crispus and Gaius; ¹⁵lest any should say that I had baptized in mine own name. ¹⁶And I baptized also the household of Stephanas: besides, I know not whether I baptized any other. ¹⁷For Christ sent me not to baptize, but to preach the gospel: not with wisdom of words, lest the cross of Christ should be made of none effect.

¹⁸For the preaching of the cross is to them that perish foolishness; but unto us which are saved it is the power of God. ¹⁹For it is written, I will destroy the wisdom of the wise, and will bring to nothing the understanding of the prudent. ²⁰Where is the wise? where is the scribe? where is the disputer of this world? hath not God made foolish the wisdom of this world? ²¹For after that in the wisdom of God the world by wisdom knew not God, it pleased God by the foolishness of preaching to save them that believe. ²²For the Jews require a sign, and the Greeks seek after wisdom: ²³but we preach Christ crucified, unto the Jews a stumbling-block, and unto the Greeks foolishness; ²⁴but unto them which are called, both Jews and Greeks, Christ the power of God, and the wisdom of God. ²⁵Because the foolishness of God is wiser than men; and the weakness of God is stronger than men.

²⁶For ye see your calling, brethren, how that not many wise men after the flesh, not many mighty, not many noble, are called: ²⁷but God hath chosen the foolish things of the world to confound the wise; and God hath chosen the weak things of the world to confound the things which are mighty; ²⁸and base things of the world, and things which are despised, hath God chosen, yea, and things which are not, to bring to nought things that are: ²⁹that no flesh should glory in his presence. ³⁰But of him are ye in Christ Jesus, who of God is made unto us wisdom, and righ-

---

of Paul: believers were conventionally baptized in Jesus' name (cf. 6:11 and note; Matt 28:19; Acts 8:16; etc.). **1:14** *Crispus*: see Acts 18:8. *Gaius*: cf. Rom 16:23. **1:15** *I had baptized*: better "you were baptized" (MS tradition). **1:16** *Stephanas*: cf. 16:15. **1:16–17** *I know . . . gospel*: no longer sure how many Corinthians he did in fact baptize, Paul abandons the topic and turns to the subject of preaching, thereby introducing the first major section of his letter. **1:17** *Gospel*: see Mark 1:1 note. *Wisdom of words*: i.e., the rhetorical arts (see v. 20 note).
     1:18–2:5 God's wisdom and the world's foolishness. 1:18 *Preaching*: Gk. *logos*, lit. "word" (cf. v. 17). **1:19** *I will destroy . . . prudent*: cf. Isa 29:14. **1:20** *Where is the wise? Where is the scribe?*: echoing Isa 19:12; 33:18. *The wise*: Gk. *sophos*, probably alluding to the Greek-speaking itinerant orators and teachers called *sophistoi* ("sophists") who flourished in the first through third centuries C.E. *Scribe*: an expert in Jewish law (as in the Gospels). *Disputer*: a rhetorically trained debater; the term also calls to mind the factious Corinthian believers themselves (cf. vv. 10–12). *This world*: lit. "this age" (as often)—i.e., the present, as opposed to the eschatological consummation. **1:21** *After that*: since. **1:22–24** *The Jews . . . wisdom of God*: developing the threefold distinction between Greeks, Jews, and (Corinthian) believers to which v. 20 alluded (see note). **1:23** *Greeks*: better "Gentiles" (MS tradition). **1:26–28** *Not many . . . that are*: a lengthy (and discourteous) list of the Corinthians' limitations. Each element of v. 26's threefold insult ("not many wise men . . . mighty . . . noble") is taken up sequentially in the antitheses of vv. 27–28a ("foolish," "weak," "base . . . despised"), with the antithesis of v. 28b summing up the entire passage. **1:26** *After the flesh*: according to human standards. **1:27** *Confound*: lit. "put to shame." *Weak things . . . mighty*: Gk. *asthenē . . . ischyra*, which connote low and high social status. **1:28** *Base*: Gk. *agenē*, "lowborn," in opposition to v. 26's "noble" (Gk. *eugeneis*, lit. "wellborn"). **1:29** *Glory*: or *boast*," wherever "glory" is used as a verb.

teousness, and sanctification, and redemption: [31]that, according as it is written, He that glorieth, let him glory in the Lord.

2 And I, brethren, when I came to you, came not with excellency of speech or of wisdom, declaring unto you the testimony of God. [2]For I determined not to know any thing among you, save Jesus Christ, and him crucified. [3]And I was with you in weakness, and in fear, and in much trembling. [4]And my speech and my preaching was not with enticing words of man's wisdom, but in demonstration of the Spirit and of power: [5]that your faith should not stand in the wisdom of men, but in the power of God.

[6]Howbeit we speak wisdom among them that are perfect: yet not the wisdom of this world, nor of the princes of this world, that come to nought: [7]but we speak the wisdom of God in a mystery, even the hidden wisdom, which God ordained before the world unto our glory: [8]which none of the princes of this world knew: for had they known it, they would not have crucified the Lord of glory. [9]But as it is written, Eye hath not seen, nor ear heard, neither have entered into the heart of man, the things which God hath prepared for them that love him. [10]But God hath revealed them unto us by his Spirit: for the Spirit searcheth all things, yea, the deep things of God. [11]For what man knoweth the things of a man, save the spirit of man which is in him? even so the things of God knoweth no man, but the Spirit of God. [12]Now we have received, not the spirit of the world, but the spirit which is of God; that we might know the things that are freely given to us of God. [13]Which things also we speak, not in the words which man's wisdom teacheth, but which the Holy Ghost teacheth; comparing spiritual things with spiritual. [14]But the natural man receiveth not the things of the Spirit of God: for they are foolishness unto him: neither can he know them, because they are spiritually discerned. [15]But he that is spiritual

---

1:30 *Redemption*: see Rom 3:24 note.   **1:31** *He that . . . Lord*: cf. Jer 9:23–24.   **2:1** *Testimony*: better "mystery" (MS tradition), which in the NT can denote God's secret plan, revealed to the elect as it unfolds in Jesus' death, resurrection, and eschatological advent (cf. 15:50–55).   **2:4** *Enticing*: lit. "persuasive." *Man's*: better omitted (MS tradition). *Demonstration*: Gk. *apodeixis*, a rhetorical term referring to a demonstrative argument.   **2:5** *Faith*: see Rom 1:8 note.

2:6–3:4 God's secret wisdom. This section develops Paul's understanding of divinely revealed wisdom, which stands opposed to the worldly philosophical wisdom in which the Corinthians take pride.   **2:6** *Perfect*: better "mature," in light of 3:1–4. *Princes of this world*: cosmic spiritual powers (cf. 15:24–26), hostile political rulers, as v. 8 suggests, or both.   **2:7** *Mystery*: see v. 1 note.   **2:9** *Eye hath not seen . . . him*: cf. Isa 52:15; 64:4.   **2:11** *Spirit of man*: here meaning "inner self" or even "mind," an occasional use of Gk. *pneuma* in the NT; see Mark 2:8; Acts 19:21; etc.   **2:13** *Comparing spiritual things with spiritual*: this difficult clause should probably be understood concessively—i.e., as a man's spirit knows the things of man (v. 11a), so the Spirit of God knows the things of God (vv. 10b, 11b); since believers have God's Spirit rather than a worldly one (v. 12a), they know the things of God (v. 12b) and therefore speak what the Holy Spirit teaches, rather than human wisdom (v. 13a), even if their discourse (like Paul's here) compares things revealed by God's Spirit to those revealed by the human spirit (v. 13b).   **2:14** *Natural*: a mistranslation of Gk. *psychikos*, "characterized by or consisting of soul [*psychē*]," which introduces an antithesis foreign to Paul's thought. *Psychē* is less conducive to divine knowledge than the Spirit that "spiritual" (Gk. *pneumatikoi*) believers possess (vv. 12, 15; cf. 3:16; 6:11; 12:1–13; etc.). Comparison of vv. 14–15 with 15:44–49 (see notes) suggests that Paul understands *psychē* and *pneuma* as distinct substances, the former being base and the latter more refined. In consistently devaluing *psychē*, Paul may be opposing a Greco-Roman philosophical tendency (possibly embraced by the Corinthians) to view it as the highest material.

judgeth all things, yet he himself is judged of no man. ¹⁶For who hath known the mind of the Lord, that he may instruct him? But we have the mind of Christ.

3 And I, brethren, could not speak unto you as unto spiritual, but as unto carnal, even as unto babes in Christ. ²I have fed you with milk, and not with meat: for hitherto ye were not able to bear it, neither yet now are ye able. ³For ye are yet carnal: for whereas there is among you envying, and strife, and divisions, are ye not carnal, and walk as men? ⁴For while one saith, I am of Paul; and another, I am of Apollos; are ye not carnal?

⁵Who then is Paul, and who is Apollos, but ministers by whom ye believed, even as the Lord gave to every man? ⁶I have planted, Apollos watered; but God gave the increase. ⁷So then neither is he that planteth any thing, neither he that watereth; but God that giveth the increase. ⁸Now he that planteth and he that watereth are one: and every man shall receive his own reward according to his own labour. ⁹For we are labourers together with God: ye are God's husbandry, ye are God's building.

¹⁰According to the grace of God which is given unto me, as a wise masterbuilder, I have laid the foundation, and another buildeth thereon. But let every man take heed how he buildeth thereupon. ¹¹For other foundation can no man lay than that is laid, which is Jesus Christ. ¹²Now if any man build upon this foundation gold, silver, precious stones, wood, hay, stubble; ¹³every man's work shall be made manifest: for the day shall declare it, because it shall be revealed by fire; and the fire shall try every man's work of what sort it is. ¹⁴If any man's work abide which he hath built thereupon, he shall receive a reward. ¹⁵If any man's work shall be burned, he shall suffer loss: but he himself shall be saved; yet so as by fire. ¹⁶Know ye not that ye are the temple of God, and that the Spirit of God dwelleth in you? ¹⁷If any man defile the temple of God, him shall God destroy; for the temple of God is holy, which temple ye are.

¹⁸Let no man deceive himself. If any man among you seemeth to be wise in this world, let him become a fool, that he may be wise. ¹⁹For the wisdom of this world is foolishness with God. For it is written, He taketh the wise in their own craftiness.

2:15 *Judgeth . . . is judged*: Gk. *anakrinō*; cf. v. 14 (KJV "discerned"); in v. 13, "comparing" has the same root.   **2:16** *Who hath known . . . him*: cf. Isa 40:13.   **3:1** *Carnal*: Gk. *sarkinos* (also in vv. 3–4), the adjectival form of *sarx*, "flesh," which is a material baser even than soul—what humans have in common with animals (cf. 15:39).   **3:1–2** *Babes in . . . ye able*: Greco-Roman popular philosophical discourse commonly figures the distinction between immature and mature understanding as that between infant and adult nourishment; cf. Heb 5:12–14.   **3:2** *Meat*: solid food.   **3:3** *And divisions*: better omitted (MS tradition).   **3:4** *Carnal*: better "men" (MS tradition), in the sense of "merely human" (NRSV).

3:5–17 God's field and building. 3:5 *Who . . . who*: better "what . . . what" (MS tradition). *Ministers*: servants.   **3:6–7** *I have planted . . . increase*: perhaps recalling Jesus' agricultural parables, esp. Mark 4:26–29, which likewise downplays the farmer's role in bringing a crop to fruition. **3:8** *Are one*: reversing the claim in v. 7 that "neither is . . . any thing," the positive unity presuming the suppression of individualistic claims to significance; cf. 12:12–13; Gal 3:28. *Reward*: lit. "wage" (also in v. 14).   **3:9** *Labourers together with God*: in light of v. 7, better "together God's laborers." *Husbandry*: cultivated land.   **3:13** *The day . . . by fire*: the eschatological day of judgment, which Paul associates with fire in 2 Thess 1:7–8; cf. Isa 66:15–16.   **3:15** *By fire*: or "through fire," perhaps alluding to the prophetic image of "a brand plucked out of the fire" (Zech 3:2; cf. Amos 4:11), without implying purification.   **3:16** *Temple of God*: the building of vv. 9–12. *The Spirit . . . you*: as YHWH dwells in his sanctuary; cf. Exod 25:8; Matt 23:21; etc.   **3:17** *Defile, destroy*: both Gk. *phtheirō*, "ruin."

3:18–4:21 The Corinthians' boast and Paul's humiliation. 3:19 *He taketh . . . craftiness*:

²⁰And again, The Lord knoweth the thoughts of the wise, that they are vain. ²¹Therefore let no man glory in men. For all things are yours; ²²whether Paul, or Apollos, or Cephas, or the world, or life, or death, or things present, or things to come; all are yours; ²³and ye are Christ's; and Christ is God's.

4 Let a man so account of us, as of the ministers of Christ, and stewards of the mysteries of God. ²Moreover it is required in stewards, that a man be found faithful. ³But with me it is a very small thing that I should be judged of you, or of man's judgment: yea, I judge not mine own self. ⁴For I know nothing by myself; yet am I not hereby justified: but he that judgeth me is the Lord. ⁵Therefore judge nothing before the time, until the Lord come, who both will bring to light the hidden things of darkness, and will make manifest the counsels of the hearts: and then shall every man have praise of God.

⁶And these things, brethren, I have in a figure transferred to myself and to Apollos for your sakes; that ye might learn in us not to think of men above that which is written, that no one of you be puffed up for one against another. ⁷For who maketh thee to differ from another? and what hast thou that thou didst not receive? now if thou didst receive it, why dost thou glory, as if thou hadst not received it? ⁸Now ye are full, now ye are rich, ye have reigned as kings without us: and I would to God ye did reign, that we also might reign with you. ⁹For I think that God hath set forth us the apostles last, as it were appointed to death: for we are made a spectacle unto the world, and to angels, and to men. ¹⁰We are fools for Christ's sake, but ye are wise in Christ; we are weak, but ye are strong; ye are honourable, but we are despised. ¹¹Even unto this present hour we both hunger, and thirst, and are naked, and are buffeted, and have no certain dwellingplace; ¹²and labour, working with

---

Job 5:13.   **3:20** *The Lord . . . vain*: Ps 94:11.   **3:21** *All things are yours*: the well-known maxim of the Stoic wise man, who in his self-sufficiency emulates God: cf. Seneca, *On Benefits* 7.3: "It belongs to a great spirit [namely, the wise man's] . . . to utter these words of God: 'All these things are mine!'"; see also Cicero, *On the Ends of Goods and Evils* 3.75–76; Diogenes Laertius, *Lives of Eminent Philosophers* 7.125. Some of the Corinthians apparently used the maxim with reference to themselves (see 4:8 and note), leading Paul to relativize it in vv. 22–23.   **4:1** *Ministers*: servants (a different word is used in 3:5). *Stewards*: household managers, who were often slaves.   **4:3** *Man's judgment*: lit. "man's day," in contrast to the Day of the Lord (3:13).   **4:4** *By myself*: against myself.   **4:6** *In a figure transferred*: Gk. *meteschēmatisma*, lit. "changed the form of"; the verb could also be used of figurative language, as Paul uses it here (referring to the metaphors employed in 3:6–17). *Not to think . . . written*: better "the not beyond what is written" (MS tradition), which is quite obscure. Perhaps it refers to an otherwise unknown maxim: "so that you may learn [the meaning of] 'not beyond what is written.'" Alternatively, it may refer Scripture (whose citations Paul often introduces with "it is written"): "so that you may learn not [to go] beyond what is written" in Scripture.   **4:7** *Maketh thee . . . another*: alternatively "who distinguishes you"; i.e., "who sees anything different in you?" (RSV).   **4:8** *Now ye . . . kings*: Paul ironically repeats the Corinthians' self-assertions, which echo various claims about the "wise man" in Stoic (see Plutarch, *On the Tranquillity of the Mind* 472a) and other philosophical traditions (cf. Philo, *On the Life of Abraham* 261). Epictetus, for instance, claims that a Cynic philosopher will say to himself "Who, when he sees me, does not think he sees his own king and master?" (*Discourses* 3.22.49). *Now* may have the force of "already," implying that the Corinthians currently claim privileges reserved for the eschatological consummation (cf. 6:2–3).   **4:9** *Spectacle*: the image is of the condemned being paraded into an arena for public execution. It may have been a philosophical commonplace: Seneca uses it of the Stoic sage and republican hero Cato in *On Providence* 2.9–12.   **4:11–13** *Even unto . . . this day*: almost identical (in Greek) temporal references frame this catalogue of privations and hardships, which counters the Corinthians' self-aggrandizing boasts. Similar catalogues appear in 2 Corinthians (4:8–9; 6:4–5; 11:23–29; 12:10).

our own hands: being reviled, we bless; being persecuted, we suffer it: [13]being defamed, we intreat: we are made as the filth of the world, and are the offscouring of all things unto this day.

[14]I write not these things to shame you, but as my beloved sons I warn you. [15]For though ye have ten thousand instructors in Christ, yet have ye not many fathers: for in Christ Jesus I have begotten you through the gospel. [16]Wherefore I beseech you, be ye followers of me. [17]For this cause have I sent unto you Timotheus, who is my beloved son, and faithful in the Lord, who shall bring you into remembrance of my ways which be in Christ, as I teach every where in every church. [18]Now some are puffed up, as though I would not come to you. [19]But I will come to you shortly, if the Lord will, and will know, not the speech of them which are puffed up, but the power. [20]For the kingdom of God is not in word, but in power. [21]What will ye? shall I come unto you with a rod, or in love, and in the spirit of meekness?

5 It is reported commonly that there is fornication among you, and such fornication as is not so much as named among the Gentiles, that one should have his father's wife. [2]And ye are puffed up, and have not rather mourned, that he that hath done this deed might be taken away from among you. [3]For I verily, as absent in body, but present in spirit, have judged already, as though I were present, concerning him that hath so done this deed, [4]in the name of our Lord Jesus Christ, when ye are gathered together, and my spirit, with the power of our Lord Jesus Christ, [5]to deliver such an one unto Satan for the destruction of the flesh, that the spirit may be saved in the day of the Lord Jesus.

[6]Your glorying is not good. Know ye not that a little leaven leaveneth the whole lump? [7]Purge out therefore the old leaven, that ye may be a new lump, as ye are unleavened. For even Christ our passover is sacrificed for us: [8]therefore let us

4:12 *Being reviled, we bless*: recalling the dominical saying (Luke 6:28).   **4:13** *Intreat*: perhaps better "encourage."   **4:15** *Instructors*: Gk. *paidagōgoi*; see Gal 3:24 and note. *I have begotten you*: referring to Paul's founding of the Corinthian church.   **4:16** *Followers*: lit. "imitators."   **4:17** *Timotheus*: Paul's partner in ministry (cf. Acts 16:1–5; Rom 16:21; 2 Cor 1:1, 19; etc.), whom he expects to arrive at Corinth soon after this letter (16:10).

5:1–13 Outrageous sexual immorality. 5:1 *Commonly*: i.e., everywhere; an alternative meaning is "actually." *Fornication*: Gk. *porneia*, a generic term for sexual transgression. *So much as named*: better omitted (MS tradition). *Among the Gentiles*: compare Paul's bigoted attitude toward Gentiles at Gal 2:15. *His father's wife*: his stepmother; cf. Lev 18:8.   **5:2** *Puffed up*: the Corinthians apparently boast of their autonomy (cf. 3:21; 4:8 and notes), including their freedom from conventional moral restraints (compare "all things are lawful"; 6:12; 10:23 and notes).   **5:3–4** *For I . . . power of our Lord Jesus Christ*: Paul's language is conventional (cf. Col 2:5; 1 Thess 2:17), but his claim presupposes the mystical understanding of the community's spiritual unity articulated in 12:12–13. Paul imagines a gathering of Corinthian believers in which his own spirit—present with them like the Spirit of God (3:16)—and Jesus' power both play a role.   **5:5** *To deliver . . . Satan*: cf. LXX Job 2:6. Paul counsels excommunication of the offender (cf. v. 7), apparently assuming that his exclusion from the church will leave him vulnerable to satanic attack. *Destruction of the flesh*: probably physical suffering, such as Job experienced (Job 2:7), or even death (cf. 11:30 and note). But its goal is the man's eschatological salvation, which will involve his body's transformation from flesh subject to destruction into incorruptible spirit (cf. 15:42–53).   **5:7** *Purge out . . . us*: a reference to the removal of leaven from Jewish households on the first day of Passover, as legislated in Exod 12:15, 19; etc. *Our passover*: Passover lamb (cf. Exod 12:3–6). This is the only place in the undisputed Pauline Epistles where Paul explicitly compares Jesus' death to a sacrifice (but see Rom 3:25 and note; Eph 5:2), and even here the sacrificial analogy is subordinate to the moralizing interpretation of the Passover's ban on leaven. *For*

keep the feast, not with old leaven, neither with the leaven of malice and wicked-ness; but with the unleavened bread of sincerity and truth.

⁹I wrote unto you in an epistle not to company with fornicators: ¹⁰yet not alto-gether with the fornicators of this world, or with the covetous, or extortioners, or with idolaters; for then must ye needs go out of the world. ¹¹But now I have written unto you not to keep company, if any man that is called a brother be a fornicator, or covetous, or an idolater, or a railer, or a drunkard, or an extortioner; with such an one no not to eat. ¹²For what have I to do to judge them also that are without? do not ye judge them that are within? ¹³But them that are without God judgeth. Therefore put away from among yourselves that wicked person.

6 Dare any of you, having a matter against another, go to law before the unjust, and not before the saints? ²Do ye not know that the saints shall judge the world? and if the world shall be judged by you, are ye unworthy to judge the smallest matters? ³Know ye not that we shall judge angels? how much more things that per-tain to this life? ⁴If then ye have judgments of things pertaining to this life, set them to judge who are least esteemed in the church. ⁵I speak to your shame. Is it so, that there is not a wise man among you? no, not one that shall be able to judge between his brethren? ⁶But brother goeth to law with brother, and that before the unbeliev-ers. ⁷Now therefore there is utterly a fault among you, because ye go to law one with another. Why do ye not rather take wrong? why do ye not rather suffer yourselves to be defrauded? ⁸Nay, ye do wrong, and defraud, and that your brethren.

⁹Know ye not that the unrighteous shall not inherit the kingdom of God? Be not deceived: neither fornicators, nor idolaters, nor adulterers, nor effeminate, nor abus-ers of themselves with mankind, ¹⁰nor thieves, nor covetous, nor drunkards, nor revilers, nor extortioners, shall inherit the kingdom of God. ¹¹And such were some of you: but ye are washed, but ye are sanctified, but ye are justified in the name of the Lord Jesus, and by the Spirit of our God.

---

us: better omitted (MS tradition).   **5:9** *I wrote . . . epistle*: this letter has not survived, unless 2 Cor 6:14–7:1 preserves a fragment (see note).   **5:10** *Extortioners*: lit. "the rapacious" (also in v. 11).   **5:11** *Brother*: fellow believer.   **5:12** *To judge*: with judging.   **5:13** *Put away . . . person*: echoing a frequent Deuteronomic injunction (17:7; 19:19; 21:21; etc.).

6:1–11 Lawsuits among believers. It is a good guess that more affluent believers were using civil courts to railroad believers of lesser means (cf. Jas 2:6), as ecclesial conflict along socioeconomic lines seems to have been a persistent problem at Corinth (see 8:9 note).   **6:1** *The unjust*: unbelievers. **6:2** *Judge the world*: a common eschatological expectation (see Dan 7:22; Rev 20:4; Wis 3:8), which Paul uniquely extends to comprehend angels (v. 3).   **6:4** *Set them . . . church*: i.e., even judgment by the church's least esteemed would be preferable to that of outsiders. But the Greek could also be trans-lated as a question ("do you set?"), in which case *the least esteemed in the church* would refer to pagan outsiders.   **6:7** *Fault*: lit. "defeat."   **6:9** *Effeminate*: Gk. *malakoi*, lit. "soft," but connoting effeminacy. Most modern translations tendentiously limit its reference to sexual behavior, usually to homosexual-ity: e.g., "male prostitutes" (NRSV and NIV), "sexual perverts" (RSV, translating *malakoi* and the following term together), or "homosexual perversion" (NEB, also combining the terms). *Abusers of themselves with mankind*: Gk. *arsenokoitēs*, nowhere extant in earlier literature. Its meaning is unknown, but it combines the roots *arsēn* ("man") and *koitēs* ("intercourse"), leading to translations such as "sod-omites" (NRSV), "homosexual offenders" (NIV), and KJV's. However, the word's use in the handful of later texts in which it appears may suggest a reference to economic exploitation involving sex. **6:10** *Extortioners*: see 5:10 note.   **6:11** *Washed*: a reference to baptism.

¹²All things are lawful unto me, but all things are not expedient: all things are lawful for me, but I will not be brought under the power of any. ¹³Meats for the belly, and the belly for meats: but God shall destroy both it and them. Now the body is not for fornication, but for the Lord; and the Lord for the body. ¹⁴And God hath both raised up the Lord, and will also raise up us by his own power. ¹⁵Know ye not that your bodies are the members of Christ? shall I then take the members of Christ, and make them the members of an harlot? God forbid. ¹⁶What? know ye not that he which is joined to an harlot is one body? for two, saith he, shall be one flesh. ¹⁷But he that is joined unto the Lord is one spirit.

¹⁸Flee fornication. Every sin that a man doeth is without the body; but he that committeth fornication sinneth against his own body. ¹⁹What? know ye not that your body is the temple of the Holy Ghost which is in you, which ye have of God, and ye are not your own? ²⁰For ye are bought with a price: therefore glorify God in your body, and in your spirit, which are God's.

7 Now concerning the things whereof ye wrote unto me: It is good for a man not to touch a woman. ²Nevertheless, to avoid fornication, let every man have his own wife, and let every woman have her own husband. ³Let the husband render unto the wife due benevolence: and likewise also the wife unto the husband. ⁴The wife hath not power of her own body, but the husband: and likewise also the husband hath not power of his own body, but the wife. ⁵Defraud ye not one the other, except it be with consent for a time, that ye may give yourselves to fasting and prayer; and come together again, that Satan tempt you not for your incontinency. ⁶But I speak this by permission, and not of commandment. ⁷For I would that all men were even as I myself. But every man hath his proper gift of God, one after this manner, and another after that.

⁸I say therefore to the unmarried and widows, It is good for them if they abide even as I. ⁹But if they cannot contain, let them marry: for it is better to marry than to burn. ¹⁰And unto the married I command, yet not I, but the Lord, Let not

---

6:12–20 Sex with prostitutes. 6:12 *All things . . . me*: Paul twice quotes and counters what was probably a slogan of the Corinthians, which resembles assertions about the wise man in Greco-Roman philosophy; cf. 3:21; 4:8 and notes. **6:13** *Meats for . . . meats*: another quotation of the Corinthians, which Paul apparently understands as a claim of absolute license over one's body and proceeds to relativize. *Meats*: food in general. **6:15** *Members*: the Greek word refers to bodily organs and limbs. Paul develops the idea of the church as Christ's body in chap. 12. **6:16** *For two . . . flesh*: Gen 2:24. **6:17** *One spirit*: to be understood literally (cf. 5:3–4 and note). Sexual intercourse brings Christ's spiritual body into contact with impurity (v. 15), for God's Spirit, apparently imparted at baptism (v. 11; cf. 12:13), dwells within believers (v. 19; 3:16; cf. 12:4–11), who thereby become parts of his body ("ye are not your own," v. 19; cf. 12:12–27; 15:44–49). **6:18** *His own body*: both the believer's body and the body of Christ, the former being a member of the latter (v. 15). **6:19** *Your body . . . God*: recalling chap. 3 (vv. 16–17, 23). **6:20** *Bought with a price*: i.e., as a slave. *And in . . . God's*: better omitted (MS tradition).

7:1–40 Celibacy and marriage. 7:1 *Now concerning . . . me*: Paul now addresses various issues the Corinthians have raised, as opposed to rumors he has heard about them (cf. 1:11; 5:1), signaling transitions from one issue to the next with the phrase "now concerning/touching" (7:25; 8:1; 12:1; 16:1, 12). **7:3** *Due benevolence*: better simply "what is due" (MS tradition); i.e., "conjugal rights" (NRSV). **7:4** *Power of*: authority over. **7:5** *Defraud*: cf. 6:7; Paul's point is that sexual deprivation within marriage is illicit. *Fasting and*: better omitted (MS tradition). **7:6** *Permission*: concession. **7:7** *Even as I myself*: i.e., celibate. **7:9** *Contain*: control themselves. *Burn*: either with passion or in God's judgment (cf. 3:13, 15). **7:10** *Not I . . . Lord*: this and the subsequent verse refer to Jesus' prohibition of

the wife depart from her husband: ¹¹but and if she depart, let her remain unmarried, or be reconciled to her husband: and let not the husband put away his wife.

¹²But to the rest speak I, not the Lord: If any brother hath a wife that believeth not, and she be pleased to dwell with him, let him not put her away. ¹³And the woman which hath an husband that believeth not, and if he be pleased to dwell with her, let her not leave him. ¹⁴For the unbelieving husband is sanctified by the wife, and the unbelieving wife is sanctified by the husband: else were your children unclean; but now are they holy. ¹⁵But if the unbelieving depart, let him depart. A brother or a sister is not under bondage in such cases: but God hath called us to peace. ¹⁶For what knowest thou, O wife, whether thou shalt save thy husband? or how knowest thou, O man, whether thou shalt save thy wife?

¹⁷But as God hath distributed to every man, as the Lord hath called every one, so let him walk. And so ordain I in all churches. ¹⁸Is any man called being circumcised? let him not become uncircumcised. Is any called in uncircumcision? let him not be circumcised. ¹⁹Circumcision is nothing, and uncircumcision is nothing, but the keeping of the commandments of God. ²⁰Let every man abide in the same calling wherein he was called.

²¹Art thou called being a servant? care not for it: but if thou mayest be made free, use it rather. ²²For he that is called in the Lord, being a servant, is the Lord's freeman: likewise also he that is called, being free, is Christ's servant. ²³Ye are bought with a price; be not ye the servants of men. ²⁴Brethren, let every man, wherein he is called, therein abide with God.

²⁵Now concerning virgins I have no commandment of the Lord: yet I give my judgment, as one that hath obtained mercy of the Lord to be faithful. ²⁶I suppose therefore that this is good for the present distress, I say, that it is good for a man so to be. ²⁷Art thou bound unto a wife? seek not to be loosed. Art thou loosed from a wife? seek not a wife. ²⁸But and if thou marry, thou hast not sinned; and if a virgin marry, she hath not sinned. Nevertheless such shall have trouble in the flesh: but I spare you.

²⁹But this I say, brethren, the time is short: it remaineth, that both they that have wives be as though they had none; ³⁰and they that weep, as though they

---

divorce; see Matt 5:32 and note.   **7:11** *Put away*: divorce.   **7:12** *Speak I . . . Lord*: Paul admits that his advice contradicts Jesus' decree against divorce, which is absolute in Mark 10:11–12 and Luke 16:18, and relaxed only in cases involving adultery at Matt 5:32; 19:9.   **7:13** *Leave him*: Gk. *aphiēmi*, also "put away" (cf. vv. 11, 12).   **7:14** *The unbelieving husband . . . holy*: reversing the logic of 6:12–20, where Paul expressed concern lest a believer's sexual contact with an outsider pollute Christ's body. Here a sexual relationship sanctifies the outsider and offspring. *By the husband*: better "by the brother" (MS tradition), i.e., the believer.   **7:15** *Us*: better "you" (MS tradition).   **7:16** *What knowest . . . thy wife*: although marriage to a believer sanctifies the unbelieving partner (v. 14), he or she may not, in the end, be saved. The relationship between salvation and sanctification is obscure.   **7:18** *Become uncircumcised*: apparently alluding to a procedure aimed at reversing circumcision by stretching the foreskin; cf. *Testament of Moses* 8.3; 1 Macc 1:15.   **7:19** *Circumcision is . . . God*: cf. Gal 5:6; 6:15.   **7:21** *Servant*: lit. "slave" (see Rom 1:1 note). *Use it rather*: Gk. ambiguous; probably "use the opportunity," as vv. 22–23 suggest. "Make use of your present condition instead" is also possible (RSV footnote).   **7:22** *Freeman*: lit. "freedman," i.e., ex-slave.   **7:25** *Virgins*: unmarried women. Paul may have in mind women engaged to be married (cf. vv. 36–38). *Faithful*: trustworthy.   **7:26** *Present distress*: the imminent Day of the Lord. *So to be*: to be as he is.   **7:28** *In the flesh*: in mundane life. *But I spare you*: the force is "but I am trying to spare you this."   **7:29** *It remaineth, that*: "from now on, let" (RSV) or "as far as the

wept not; and they that rejoice, as though they rejoiced not; and they that buy, as though they possessed not; [31]and they that use this world, as not abusing it: for the fashion of this world passeth away.

[32]But I would have you without carefulness. He that is unmarried careth for the things that belong to the Lord, how he may please the Lord: [33]but he that is married careth for the things that are of the world, how he may please his wife. [34]There is difference also between a wife and a virgin. The unmarried woman careth for the things of the Lord, that she may be holy both in body and in spirit: but she that is married careth for the things of the world, how she may please her husband. [35]And this I speak for your own profit; not that I may cast a snare upon you, but for that which is comely, and that ye may attend upon the Lord without distraction.

[36]But if any man think that he behaveth himself uncomely toward his virgin, if she pass the flower of her age, and need so require, let him do what he will, he sinneth not: let them marry. [37]Nevertheless he that standeth stedfast in his heart, having no necessity, but hath power over his own will, and hath so decreed in his heart that he will keep his virgin, doeth well. [38]So then he that giveth her in marriage doeth well; but he that giveth her not in marriage doeth better. [39]The wife is bound by the law as long as her husband liveth; but if her husband be dead, she is at liberty to be married to whom she will; only in the Lord. [40]But she is happier if she so abide, after my judgment: and I think also that I have the Spirit of God.

8 Now as touching things offered unto idols, we know that we all have knowledge. Knowledge puffeth up, but charity edifieth. [2]And if any man think that he knoweth anything, he knoweth nothing yet as he ought to know. [3]But if any man love God, the same is known of him.

---

rest is concerned, let." **7:31** *Fashion*: Gk. *schēma*, "outward appearance" or "form." **7:34** *There is . . . careth*: better, continuing from v. 33, "and he is divided. And the unmarried woman as well as the virgin cares" (MS tradition). *Please*: the verb can have sexual connotations in the NT (cf. Mark 6:22), as here, where *please her husband* is contrasted with being *holy both in body and in spirit*. **7:35** *Comely*: "seemly" or "with good form"; this word (like "uncomely" in v. 36) is a compound of Gk. *schēma* (see v. 31 note), implying a contrast between "good form" and the transitory "form of this world." **7:36–38** *But if . . . better*: this passage apparently refers to engaged couples. Some scholars believe that it deals with innocent cohabitation (spiritual marriage); others that it concerns fathers arranging marriages for their daughters. **7:36** *She pass . . . age*: Gk. obscure, perhaps meaning "be past one's prime," or "be at one's sexual prime," or even "experience excessive passion." The Greek phrase may refer to the *man* or to the *virgin*. If the latter, perhaps Paul has in mind the beginning of menstruation, for in the Greco-Roman world prepubescent girls could be betrothed to older men, with the relationship's consummation delayed until the onset of puberty. **7:38** *Giveth her in marriage*: better "gives his virgin in marriage" (MS tradition), but Gk. *gamizō* can mean "marry" and should probably so be understood here, yielding "he who marries his virgin does well, but he who does not marry does better." **7:39** *The wife . . . will*: cf. Rom 7:2–4. *By the law*: better omitted (MS tradition), as a scribal assimilation to the analogous Romans passage. *Only in the Lord*: i.e., only to another believer. **7:40** *After*: in accordance with.

8:1–13 Meat sacrificed to idols. In a city like Corinth, where much meat sold at market would have originated as pagan sacrifices, the issue of whether believers might consume it would have been no small matter. **8:1** *Things offered unto idols*: Gk. *eidōlothyta*, a polemical term for what were conventionally known as *hierothyta*, "sacred sacrifices." *We all have knowledge*: probably a quotation from the Corinthians, which Paul immediately counters. *Knowledge*: Gk. *gnōsis*, which can refer to knowledge acquired by experience ("acquaintance"), sometimes with the connotation of religious knowledge mystically attained (e.g., 13:2; 14:6; 2 Cor 4:6; etc.). **8:3** *If any man . . . him*: cf. Gal 4:9,

⁴As concerning therefore the eating of those things that are offered in sacrifice unto idols, we know that an idol is nothing in the world, and that there is none other God but one. ⁵For though there be that are called gods, whether in heaven or in earth, (as there be gods many, and lords many,) ⁶but to us there is but one God, the Father, of whom are all things, and we in him; and one Lord Jesus Christ, by whom are all things, and we by him.

⁷Howbeit there is not in every man that knowledge: for some with conscience of the idol unto this hour eat it as a thing offered unto an idol; and their conscience being weak is defiled. ⁸But meat commendeth us not to God: for neither, if we eat, are we the better; neither, if we eat not, are we the worse. ⁹But take heed lest by any means this liberty of yours become a stumblingblock to them that are weak. ¹⁰For if any man see thee which hast knowledge sit at meat in the idol's temple, shall not the conscience of him which is weak be emboldened to eat those things which are offered to idols; ¹¹and through thy knowledge shall the weak brother perish, for whom Christ died? ¹²But when ye sin so against the brethren, and wound their weak conscience, ye sin against Christ. ¹³Wherefore, if meat make my brother to offend, I will eat no flesh while the world standeth, lest I make my brother to offend.

9 Am I not an apostle? am I not free? have I not seen Jesus Christ our Lord? are not ye my work in the Lord? ²If I be not an apostle unto others, yet doubtless I am to you: for the seal of mine apostleship are ye in the Lord. ³Mine answer to them that do examine me is this, ⁴Have we not power to eat and to drink? ⁵Have we not power to lead about a sister, a wife, as well as other apostles, and as the

---

also in the context of distinguishing the living God from idols. **8:4** *We know*: Gk. *oidamen*, not cognate with *gnōsis* in vv. 1–3 (see v. 1 note). *An idol . . . world*: a fundamental Jewish conviction (cf. Isa 46; Wis 14:12–31; etc.). *There is . . . one*: echoing the Shema, the major Jewish declaration of belief (Deut 6:4). **8:6** *In him*: alternatively "for him." **8:7** *With conscience*: better "with familiarity" (MS tradition). **8:8** *Meat commendeth . . . God*: recalling the Corinthian slogan quoted in 6:13 (see note). *Are we the better . . . are we the worse*: lit. "do we abound . . . do we lack." **8:9** *Take heed . . . weak*: Paul resisted the liberty the Corinthians claimed when they exercised it sexually (cf. 6:12–20); here he endorses it, although he urges self-restraint. *Liberty*: lit. "authority," with the connotation of "rights." *Weak*: Gk. *asthenēs*; for its socioeconomic connotations, see 1:27 note. Paul's insistence on applying the word to the party uncomfortable with eating sacrificial meat (vv. 7, 10–12) suggests that the faction is composed of (or significantly overlaps with) the Corinthian congregation's poorer members. These would also have been the ones who went hungry at the eucharistic celebration (see 11:20–22, 33–34 and notes) and those possessing less desirable spiritual gifts (see 12:22 and note). **8:10** *Emboldened*: Gk. *oikodomeō*, also "build up, edify" (cf. v. 1). Here it is used ironically. **8:12** *When ye . . . Christ*: the same logic underlies 6:15–20 (see notes). **8:13** *Meat*: food. *Flesh*: meat.

9:1–27 Paul's example. Paul offers his willingness to give up apostolic rights as a model of selflessness for the Corinthians of strong conscience, whom he urges to renounce for the benefit of the weak the right to eat meat sacrificed to idols (8:7–13; 10:23–11:1). Formally an apology (see v. 3 note), Paul's discourse in some ways resembles the Cynic philosopher's defense of his vocation in Epictetus (*Discourses* 3.22), perhaps suggesting that he means to portray his ministry as a variation on the mission of the itinerant philosopher, a well-known figure in the Greco-Roman world. **9:1** *An apostle . . . free*: a better reading of the MS tradition reverses *apostle* and *free*, more clearly connecting chap. 9 with Paul's preceding argument. *Have I . . . our Lord*: cf. Gal 1:15–16. **9:2** *Seal*: a mark of ownership, as from a signet ring. **9:3** *Answer*: Gk. *apologia*, a legal term meaning "defense," as in Plato's *Apology of Socrates*. **9:4** *Power*: Gk. *exousia* (cf. vv. 5, 12); the same word is translated "liberty" at 8:9 (see note).

brethren of the Lord, and Cephas? [6]Or I only and Barnabas, have not we power to forbear working? [7]Who goeth a warfare any time at his own charges? who planteth a vineyard, and eateth not of the fruit thereof? or who feedeth a flock, and eateth not of the milk of the flock? [8]Say I these things as a man? or saith not the law the same also? [9]For it is written in the law of Moses, Thou shalt not muzzle the mouth of the ox that treadeth out the corn. Doth God take care for oxen? [10]Or saith he it altogether for our sakes? For our sakes, no doubt, this is written: that he that ploweth should plow in hope; and that he that thresheth in hope should be partaker of his hope. [11]If we have sown unto you spiritual things, is it a great thing if we shall reap your carnal things? [12]If others be partakers of this power over you, are not we rather? Nevertheless we have not used this power; but suffer all things, lest we should hinder the gospel of Christ.

[13]Do ye not know that they which minister about holy things live of the things of the temple? and they which wait at the altar are partakers with the altar? [14]Even so hath the Lord ordained that they which preach the gospel should live of the gospel. [15]But I have used none of these things: neither have I written these things, that it should be so done unto me: for it were better for me to die, than that any man should make my glorying void. [16]For though I preach the gospel, I have nothing to glory of: for necessity is laid upon me; yea, woe is unto me, if I preach not the gospel! [17]For if I do this thing willingly, I have a reward: but if against my will, a dispensation of the gospel is committed unto me. [18]What is my reward then? Verily that, when I preach the gospel, I may make the gospel of Christ without charge, that I abuse not my power in the gospel.

[19]For though I be free from all men, yet have I made myself servant unto all, that I might gain the more. [20]And unto the Jews I became as a Jew, that I might gain the Jews; to them that are under the law, as under the law, that I might gain them that are under the law; [21]to them that are without law, as without law, (being not without law to God, but under the law to Christ,) that I might gain them that are without law. [22]To the weak became I as weak, that I might gain the weak: I am made all things to all men, that I might by all means save some. [23]And this I do for the gospel's sake, that I might be partaker thereof with you.

9:6 *Working*: i.e., for a living and with one's hands; cf. 4:12.   **9:7** *Goeth a warfare*: goes to war. *Charges*: the Greek refers to the money funding a soldier's provisions. *Planteth a vineyard . . . thereof*: recalling 3:5–9; cf. Deut 20:6. *Feedeth a flock . . . flock*: shepherding is a common biblical image for leadership; cf. Ezek 34; Mark 6:34; etc.   **9:9** *Thou shalt not . . . corn*: Deut 25:4. *Corn*: wheat.   **9:9–10** *Doth God . . . written*: compare Philo's justification for the allegorical interpretation of laws governing animal sacrifice: "the law is not concerned with creatures lacking reason, but rather with those having a mind and reason" (*On the Special Laws* 1.260).   **9:10** *And that . . . his hope*: better "and that he who threshes, in hope of partaking" (MS tradition).   **9:12** *Others*: perhaps referring to the "false apostles" of 2 Cor 11:13.   **9:13** *They which minister . . . with the altar*: cf. Num 18:8–32; Deut 18:1–5. *Minister*: Gk. *ergazomai*, which shares a root with "work," vv. 1, 6.   **9:14** *The Lord . . . of the gospel*: cf. Matt 10:7–10; Mark 6:8–11; Luke 9:3–5.   **9:17** *Dispensation*: lit. "stewardship"; see 4:1 and note. **9:20** *As under the law*: better to add "(although I myself am not under the law)" (MS tradition). **9:21** *Not without law . . . Christ*: better "not without God's law, but under Christ's" (MS tradition); cf. Matt 7:12; Rom 13:8–10; Gal 5:14 and notes.   **9:22** *The weak*: probably those uncomfortable

²⁴Know ye not that they which run in a race run all, but one receiveth the prize? So run, that ye may obtain. ²⁵And every man that striveth for the mastery is temperate in all things. Now they do it to obtain a corruptible crown; but we an incorruptible. ²⁶I therefore so run, not as uncertainly; so fight I, not as one that beateth the air: ²⁷but I keep under my body, and bring it into subjection: lest that by any means, when I have preached to others, I myself should be a castaway.

10 Moreover, brethren, I would not that ye should be ignorant, how that all our fathers were under the cloud, and all passed through the sea; ²and were all baptized unto Moses in the cloud and in the sea; ³and did all eat the same spiritual meat; ⁴and did all drink the same spiritual drink: for they drank of that spiritual Rock that followed them: and that Rock was Christ. ⁵But with many of them God was not well pleased: for they were overthrown in the wilderness. ⁶Now these things were our examples, to the intent we should not lust after evil things, as they also lusted.

⁷Neither be ye idolaters, as were some of them; as it is written, The people sat down to eat and drink, and rose up to play. ⁸Neither let us commit fornication, as some of them committed, and fell in one day three and twenty thousand. ⁹Neither let us tempt Christ, as some of them also tempted, and were destroyed of serpents. ¹⁰Neither murmur ye, as some of them also murmured, and were destroyed of the destroyer.

¹¹Now all these things happened unto them for ensamples: and they are written for our admonition, upon whom the ends of the world are come. ¹²Wherefore let him that thinketh he standeth take heed lest he fall. ¹³There hath no temptation taken you but such as is common to man: but God is faithful, who will not

---

eating meat sacrificed to idols; see 8:9 and note. *As*: better omitted (MS tradition).   **9:24–27** *Know ye . . . castaway*: such athletic metaphors are common in Greco-Roman philosophical writing, e.g., Seneca, *Epistle* 78:16: "How many blows in the face, in the entire body, do athletes receive! But they bear every torture out of desire for glory, and they suffer such things not only because they fight, but in order that they may do so: their training itself is torture. Let us too win all our contests, the prize for which is neither garland nor palm, nor the trumpet calling for silence before the proclamation of our name, but virtue, strength of character, and the peace created once and for all when fortune has been totally conquered in any contest."   **9:25** *Man that . . . mastery*: athlete. *Is temperate*: exercises self-control. *Crown*: garland, the conventional prize in ancient Greek sport.   **9:27** *Keep under*: lit. "give a black eye to," continuing the boxing metaphor. *Castaway*: lit. "not standing the test," with the connotation of "unsatisfactory."

    10:1–11:1 Meat sacrificed to idols (cont.). 10:1 *All our fathers . . . sea*: see Exod 13:21; 14:21. The elements from the Exodus narrative invoked by Paul in vv. 1–4 appear in identical order in Ps 105:39–41.   **10:2** *Baptized unto Moses*: allegorically interpreting the Israelites' crossing of the Red Sea (Exod 13:21–15:21).   **10:3** *Spiritual meat*: manna from heaven; see Exod 16:4. Like "drink" (v. 4), it is allegorically assimilated to the Eucharist (cf. vv. 16–17; 11:20–34).   **10:4** *They drank . . . them*: according to Jewish tradition, the water-producing rock of Exod 17:6 followed the wandering Israelites.   **10:5** *For they . . . wilderness*: see Num 14:29–30.   **10:6** *Examples*: Gk. *typoi*, "types," "patterns," or "figures"; cf. v. 11 (KJV "ensamples"). *As they also lusted*: see Num 11:4.   **10:7** *The people . . . play*: Exod 32:6; the Greek verb *paizō* (*play*) can have sexual connotations, which Paul picks up in v. 8.   **10:8** *As some . . . thousand*: see Num 25:1–9.   **10:9** *Tempt*: test. *Destroyed of serpents*: see Num 21:4–9.   **10:10** *As some . . . murmured*: Exod 16:7–8; Num 14:27, 36; 16:41; etc. *Destroyer*: employed by God to plague Egypt's firstborn (see Exod 12:23 and note). Divine plagues

suffer you to be tempted above that ye are able; but will with the temptation also make a way to escape, that ye may be able to bear it.

¹⁴Wherefore, my dearly beloved, flee from idolatry. ¹⁵I speak as to wise men; judge ye what I say. ¹⁶The cup of blessing which we bless, is it not the communion of the blood of Christ? The bread which we break, is it not the communion of the body of Christ? ¹⁷For we being many are one bread, and one body: for we are all partakers of that one bread.

¹⁸Behold Israel after the flesh: are not they which eat of the sacrifices partakers of the altar? ¹⁹What say I then? that the idol is any thing, or that which is offered in sacrifice to idols is any thing? ²⁰But I say, that the things which the Gentiles sacrifice, they sacrifice to devils, and not to God: and I would not that ye should have fellowship with devils. ²¹Ye cannot drink the cup of the Lord, and the cup of devils: ye cannot be partakers of the Lord's table, and of the table of devils. ²²Do we provoke the Lord to jealousy? are we stronger than he?

²³All things are lawful for me, but all things are not expedient: all things are lawful for me, but all things edify not. ²⁴Let no man seek his own, but every man another's wealth. ²⁵Whatsoever is sold in the shambles, that eat, asking no question for conscience sake: ²⁶for the earth is the Lord's, and the fulness thereof. ²⁷If any of them that believe not bid you to a feast, and ye be disposed to go; whatsoever is set before you, eat, asking no question for conscience sake. ²⁸But if any man say unto you, This is offered in sacrifice unto idols, eat not for his sake that shewed it, and for conscience sake: for the earth is the Lord's, and the fulness thereof: ²⁹conscience, I say, not thine own, but of the other: for why is my liberty judged of another man's conscience? ³⁰For if I by grace be a partaker, why am I evil spoken of for that for which I give thanks?

³¹Whether therefore ye eat, or drink, or whatsoever ye do, do all to the glory of God. ³²Give none offence, neither to the Jews, nor to the Gentiles, nor to the

---

punish Israel for its murmuring at Num 14:37; 16:46–50. **10:16–17** *The cup . . . that one bread*: the Eucharist. **10:19–20** *What say . . . with devils*: reiterating 8:4–6; cf. 8:10. **10:20** *They sacrifice . . . God*: cf. Deut 32:17. **10:21** *Ye cannot be . . . devils*: cf. Mal 1:7, 12. **10:22** *Provoke the Lord to jealousy*: cf. LXX Deut 32:21: "They provoked me to jealousy with what is not god and they provoked me to wrath with their idols." *Are we . . . he*: if idols provoke even God to passion ("jealousy" and "wrath"), how can believers claim immunity from their negative effects? Also recall 8:7–13, which attributes qualms about eating meat sacrificed to idols to those of "weak" conscience. **10:23** *All things are lawful for me*: better simply "all things are lawful" (twice; MS tradition). Paul again quotes the Corinthians' slogan; cf. 6:12 and note. **10:24** *Wealth*: in the general sense of "well-being." **10:25** *Shambles*: meat market. **10:26** *The earth . . . thereof*: Ps 24:1; cf. Deut 10:14. **10:27** *If any . . . sake*: Paul appears to recommend distinguishing between pagan religious and social functions (cf. vv. 19–22), but this distinction would be difficult to maintain: e.g., if a banquet's host were to offer Zeus a libation—a pagan analogue to "saying grace"—is the believer in attendance obligated to abstain? **10:28** *Offered in sacrifice unto idols*: better to substitute the neutral Gk. *hierothyton* ("a sacred sacrifice"; see 8:1 note) for the polemical Gk. *eidōlothyton* ("a sacrifice to idols") (MS tradition). *For the earth . . . thereof*: better omitted (MS tradition), as a scribal duplication of v. 26. **10:28–30** *Eat not . . . thanks*: while Paul again urges personal abstinence in situations where another's conscience might be wounded (cf. 8:7–13), he clarifies that this does not entail internalizing the other's "weak" (i.e., overly scrupulous) conscience. On the contrary, he seems to find such scruples narrow-minded. **10:30** *By grace*: alternatively "with thanksgiving," which better fits the context.

church of God: ³³even as I please all men in all things, not seeking mine own profit, but the profit of many, that they may be saved. ¹Be ye followers of me, even
11 as I also am of Christ.
²Now I praise you, brethren, that ye remember me in all things, and keep the ordinances, as I delivered them to you. ³But I would have you know, that the head of every man is Christ; and the head of the woman is the man; and the head of Christ is God. ⁴Every man praying or prophesying, having his head covered, dishonoureth his head. ⁵But every woman that prayeth or prophesieth with her head uncovered dishonoureth her head: for that is even all one as if she were shaven. ⁶For if the woman be not covered, let her also be shorn: but if it be a shame for a woman to be shorn or shaven, let her be covered. ⁷For a man indeed ought not to cover his head, forasmuch as he is the image and glory of God: but the woman is the glory of the man. ⁸For the man is not of the woman; but the woman of the man. ⁹Neither was the man created for the woman; but the woman for the man. ¹⁰For this cause ought the woman to have power on her head because of the angels.

¹¹Nevertheless neither is the man without the woman, neither the woman without the man, in the Lord. ¹²For as the woman is of the man, even so is the man also by the woman; but all things of God. ¹³Judge in yourselves: is it comely that a woman pray unto God uncovered? ¹⁴Doth not even nature itself teach you, that, if a man have long hair, it is a shame unto him? ¹⁵But if a woman have long hair, it is a glory to her: for her hair is given her for a covering. ¹⁶But if any man seem to be contentious, we have no such custom, neither the churches of God.

11:1 *Followers*: lit. "imitators."
11:2–16 Veiling women at church. 11:2 *I praise . . . to you*: this commendation suggests that the problem Paul now addresses stems from his readers' having embraced his teaching (possibly something akin to Gal 3:28), but applied it in a way that makes him uncomfortable. *Ordinances*: lit. "traditions." **11:3** *Head*: through this initial metaphorical use of *head*—meaning "archetype" or "origin" (cf. vv. 7–9)—Paul immediately locates the issue of head coverings in a broader theological context. **11:4** *Praying or prophesying*: kinds of public speaking at church meetings. *Head covered*: scholars debate the specific custom (if any) to which Paul refers, but cross-cultural analysis of ancient and modern veiling suggests that a woman's covered head figures the concealment of her sexuality (compare the bride's veiling and unveiling in contemporary Western and ancient Greek weddings), a significance at least in part motivating Paul's concern about the issue (see v. 10 and note). **11:7** *The image . . . God*: cf. Gen 1:27, which does not really support the hierarchical arrangement Paul proposes. Indeed, Gal 3:28 alludes to it in order to dissolve gender altogether. In vv. 11–12 Paul implicitly acknowledges his argument's exegetical and logical problems. **11:8** *But the woman of the man*: see Gen 2:21–22. **11:9** *Neither was . . . for the man*: see Gen 2:18. **11:10** *Have power . . . angels*: a cryptic statement, but Paul later suggests that angels are present during the Corinthians' communal worship. (At 13:1 he calls ecstatic utterances "tongues . . . of angels.") In light of the common Jewish conception of angels as sexually threatening (see Mark 12:25 note; Gen 6:1–4 and notes), Paul may understand veils to screen from angelic advances the women vulnerable during the spiritual openness of ecstatic worship. **11:13** *Judge in yourselves*: i.e., decide among yourselves. *Comely*: "good form" or "proper." **11:14–15** *Even nature . . . covering*: Greco-Roman (especially Stoic) philosophical argumentation makes sophisticated appeals to nature (in the sense of "cosmic order") to challenge arbitrary social convention, but Paul's invocation of it differs in no meaningful way from his earlier appeals to conventional propriety (vv. 5–6, 13). **11:16** *No such custom*: referring to contentiousness, not to women praying without veils.

¹⁷Now in this that I declare unto you I praise you not, that ye come together not for the better, but for the worse. ¹⁸For first of all, when ye come together in the church, I hear that there be divisions among you; and I partly believe it. ¹⁹For there must be also heresies among you, that they which are approved may be made manifest among you. ²⁰When ye come together therefore into one place, this is not to eat the Lord's supper. ²¹For in eating every one taketh before other his own supper: and one is hungry, and another is drunken. ²²What? have ye not houses to eat and to drink in? or despise ye the church of God, and shame them that have not? What shall I say to you? shall I praise you in this? I praise you not.

²³For I have received of the Lord that which also I delivered unto you, That the Lord Jesus the same night in which he was betrayed took bread: ²⁴and when he had given thanks, he brake it, and said, Take, eat: this is my body, which is broken for you: this do in remembrance of me. ²⁵After the same manner also he took the cup, when he had supped, saying, This cup is the new testament in my blood: this do ye, as oft as ye drink it, in remembrance of me. ²⁶For as often as ye eat this bread, and drink this cup, ye do shew the Lord's death till he come.

²⁷Wherefore whosoever shall eat this bread, and drink this cup of the Lord, unworthily, shall be guilty of the body and blood of the Lord. ²⁸But let a man examine himself, and so let him eat of that bread, and drink of that cup. ²⁹For he that eateth and drinketh unworthily, eateth and drinketh damnation to himself, not discerning the Lord's body. ³⁰For this cause many are weak and sickly among you, and many sleep. ³¹For if we would judge ourselves, we should not be judged. ³²But when we are judged, we are chastened of the Lord, that we should not be condemned with the world.

³³Wherefore, my brethren, when ye come together to eat, tarry one for another. ³⁴And if any man hunger, let him eat at home; that ye come not together unto condemnation. And the rest will I set in order when I come.

11:17–34 The Lord's Supper. 11:17 *I praise you not*: cf. v. 2.   **11:19** *There must be also heresies* [better "factions"] *among you*: Paul's statement, which stands in tension with v. 16 and with his earlier exhortations that the Corinthians avoid contention (1:10–17; 3:1–23), is probably founded on the conventional expectation that intense communal strife would precede the eschaton (Matt 10:34–36; Mark 13:12; 2 Pet 2:1).   **11:21–22** *In eating . . . in*: at Greco-Roman dinner parties those of low socioeconomic status commonly received a fare inferior to what the wealthy enjoyed, a practice Martial satirizes: "Since I am invited to dinner . . . / why am I not served the same dinner as you? . . . / A golden turtle-dove fills you with its excessive rump, / but I am dished-up a magpie that died in the cage" (3.60.1–2, 7–8). To Paul's dismay, the Corinthians' eucharistic celebration had come to resemble such banquets (see 8:9 note).   **11:23–26** *For I . . . come*: the earliest extant account of the eucharistic liturgy, which is also preserved in the Synoptic Gospels: Paul's version agrees with Luke (22:19–20) against Mark (14:22–25) and Matthew (26:26–29).   **11:23** *Received, took*: the verbs have the same Gk. root. *Delivered, betrayed*: both Gk. *paradidōmi*.   **11:24** *Take, eat*: better omitted (MS tradition). *Broken*: better omitted (MS tradition).   **11:25** *New testament*: new covenant; cf. 2 Cor 3:6. **11:29** *Unworthily*: better omitted (MS tradition). *Damnation*: Gk. *krima*, "condemnation," which shares a root with the words rendered *discerning*, "judge/judged" (vv. 31–32), and "condemned/condemnation" (vv. 32, 34). *Lord's*: better omitted (MS tradition). "Discerning the body" refers at once to distinguishing the Eucharist from normal meals and to recognizing the community's essential unity as Christ's body (see chap. 12).   **11:30** *Sleep*: have died.   **11:31** *Judge*: Gk. *diakrinō*, better "discern," as in v. 29 (see note).   **11:33** *Tarry one for another*: the poorer believers presumably were arriving late for the eucharistic celebration (probably because they worked long hours) and thereby missing out on the meal.

12 Now concerning spiritual gifts, brethren, I would not have you ignorant. [2]Ye know that ye were Gentiles, carried away unto these dumb idols, even as ye were led. [3]Wherefore I give you to understand, that no man speaking by the Spirit of God calleth Jesus accursed: and that no man can say that Jesus is the Lord, but by the Holy Ghost.

[4]Now there are diversities of gifts, but the same Spirit. [5]And there are differences of administrations, but the same Lord. [6]And there are diversities of operations, but it is the same God which worketh all in all. [7]But the manifestation of the Spirit is given to every man to profit withal. [8]For to one is given by the Spirit the word of wisdom; to another the word of knowledge by the same Spirit; [9]to another faith by the same Spirit; to another the gifts of healing by the same Spirit; [10]to another the working of miracles; to another prophecy; to another discerning of spirits; to another divers kinds of tongues; to another the interpretation of tongues: [11]but all these worketh that one and the selfsame Spirit, dividing to every man severally as he will.

[12]For as the body is one, and hath many members, and all the members of that one body, being many, are one body: so also is Christ. [13]For by one Spirit are we all baptized into one body, whether we be Jews or Gentiles, whether we be bond or free; and have been all made to drink into one Spirit. [14]For the body is not one member, but many. [15]If the foot shall say, Because I am not the hand, I am not of the body; is it therefore not of the body? [16]And if the ear shall say, Because I am not the eye, I am not of the body; is it therefore not of the body? [17]If the whole body were an eye, where were the hearing? If the whole were hearing, where were the smelling? [18]But now hath God set the members every one of them in the body, as it

12:1–31 *Spiritual gifts.* **12:4–6** *Now there . . . in all*: this passage was often invoked during the fourth-century Trinitarian controversy. **12:4** *Gifts*: Gk. *charismata*, "favors" or "benefits." **12:5** *Administrations*: Gk. *diakonia*, "services" or "offices." It shares a root with the verb "ministers" (cf. 3:5). **12:6** *Operations*: lit. "workings." **12:8–10** *To one . . . interpretation of tongues*: compare the similar lists at vv. 28–30; Rom 12:6–8. In 1 Corinthians tongues always come last. **12:9** *Faith*: presumably, because of its restricted possession, extraordinary faith; cf. 13:2. *Healings by the same Spirit*: better "healings by the one Spirit" (MS tradition). **12:10** *Discerning of*: distinguishing between. *Divers kinds of tongues*: glossolalia, i.e., speaking in tongues. **12:12** *As the body . . . Christ*: cf. 6:15–20 and notes; Rom 12:4–5. **12:13** *By one Spirit . . . free*: cf. Gal 3:27–28 and notes. Paul here neglects a reference to gender dissolution, perhaps in light of the problem addressed in 11:2–16. *Drink into*: better simply "drink" (MS tradition). **12:14–26** *For the body . . . rejoice with it*: Paul's comparison of the Corinthian church to Christ's body is not merely figurative; it is a mystical elaboration of his assertion that baptized believers who partake of the spirit constituting Christ's resurrected body become members of it (vv. 12–13; cf. 6:15–20; 10:17; 15:44–49). The comparison draws on a Greco-Roman rhetorical commonplace often employed to urge concord. Writers and orators conventionally likened the city or some other community to a body, emphasizing that its survival depended on organs performing their proper roles in the body's natural hierarchical structure. Livy 2.32.7–11: if the limbs, mouth, and teeth (i.e., *plebs*, the common folk) refuse to feed (i.e., revolt against) the stomach (i.e., *patres*, the elite), the entire body politic will waste away. Polyaenus 3.9.22: without the breast (i.e., phalanx), hands (i.e., light armed troops), or feet (i.e., cavalry), the body of the army is "limping and lame"; but without its head (i.e., general), "the whole thing is useless." Cicero, *On Duties* 3.22: if bodily members draw off one another's nourishment (i.e., if members of society seize one another's property for their own use), the "whole body would grow weak and die" (i.e., the social order would be overturned). As such examples indicate, the body-as-society theme called for social order by legitimizing the social and political status quo. Paul uses it to recommend order as well (v. 25), but he innovates by privileging not the status quo but the "feeble members," including the genitals (i.e., believers with spiritual gifts that the community finds less desirable; vv. 22–24). Paul's

hath pleased him. ¹⁹And if they were all one member, where were the body? ²⁰But now are they many members, yet but one body. ²¹And the eye cannot say unto the hand, I have no need of thee: nor again the head to the feet, I have no need of you. ²²Nay, much more those members of the body, which seem to be more feeble, are necessary: ²³and those members of the body, which we think to be less honourable, upon these we bestow more abundant honour; and our uncomely parts have more abundant comeliness. ²⁴For our comely parts have no need: but God hath tempered the body together, having given more abundant honour to that part which lacked: ²⁵that there should be no schism in the body; but that the members should have the same care one for another. ²⁶And whether one member suffer, all the members suffer with it; or one member be honoured, all the members rejoice with it.

²⁷Now ye are the body of Christ, and members in particular. ²⁸And God hath set some in the church, first apostles, secondarily prophets, thirdly teachers, after that miracles, then gifts of healings, helps, governments, diversities of tongues. ²⁹Are all apostles? are all prophets? are all teachers? are all workers of miracles? ³⁰Have all the gifts of healing? do all speak with tongues? do all interpret? ³¹But covet earnestly the best gifts: and yet shew I unto you a more excellent way.

13 Though I speak with the tongues of men and of angels, and have not charity, I am become as sounding brass, or a tinkling cymbal. ²And though I have the gift of prophecy, and understand all mysteries, and all knowledge; and though I have all faith, so that I could remove mountains, and have not charity, I am nothing. ³And though I bestow all my goods to feed the poor, and though I give my body to be burned, and have not charity, it profiteth me nothing.

⁴Charity suffereth long, and is kind; charity envieth not; charity vaunteth not itself, is not puffed up, ⁵doth not behave itself unseemly, seeketh not her own, is not easily provoked, thinketh no evil; ⁶rejoiceth not in iniquity, but rejoiceth in the truth; ⁷beareth all things, believeth all things, hopeth all things, endureth all things.

⁸Charity never faileth: but whether there be prophecies, they shall fail; whether there be tongues, they shall cease; whether there be knowledge, it shall vanish away. ⁹For we know in part, and we prophesy in part. ¹⁰But when that which is perfect is come, then that which is in part shall be done away. ¹¹When I was a child, I spake as a child, I understood as a child, I thought as a child: but when I became a man, I put away childish things. ¹²For now we see through a glass, darkly; but then face to

---

unique development of the metaphor demonstrates his concern lest those members feel excluded. **12:22** *More feeble*: Gk. *asthenestera*, "weaker" (cf. 8:9 and note). The distinction the Corinthians draw between those with more and less valuable spiritual gifts reflects the socioeconomic divisions in their congregation; cf. 11:21–22, 33–34 and notes. **12:23** *Those members . . . honourable*: referring to the genitals, as does *uncomely parts*. *Uncomely . . . comeliness*: "unpresentable . . . presentability" (also in v. 24). **12:24** *Have no need*: i.e., of such special treatment. *More abundant . . . lacked*: see 8:8 and note. **12:28** *Helps, governments*: acts of assistance, positions of leadership.

13:1–13 Love. 13:1 *Tongues of men . . . angels*: tongues were sometimes conceived of as angelic dialects. *Charity*: Gk. *agapē*, often translated "love." It has the broadest semantic range of the several Greek words meaning "love": it can be used of God's love for humanity or, as here, of one person's selfless love for another. **13:3** *To be burned*: better "in order that I may boast" (MS tradition). Paul boasts of his deprivations at 4:1–21; 2 Cor 11:30; 12:5, 9–10. **13:4** *Vaunteth not itself*: does not brag. **13:5** *Thinketh no evil*: or "calculates no wrongs." **13:8** *Faileth*: Gk. *piptei*, lit. "falls down." *Shall fail, shall vanish away*: both Gk. *katargeō*, later rendered "shall be done away" (v. 10) and "put away" (v. 11). **13:10** *When that . . . come*: i.e., the eschatological consummation. **13:12** *We see . . . darkly*: the glass

face: now I know in part; but then shall I know even as also I am known. ¹³And now abideth faith, hope, charity, these three; but the greatest of these is charity.

14 Follow after charity, and desire spiritual gifts, but rather that ye may prophesy. ²For he that speaketh in an unknown tongue speaketh not unto men, but unto God: for no man understandeth him; howbeit in the spirit he speaketh mysteries. ³But he that prophesieth speaketh unto men to edification, and exhortation, and comfort. ⁴He that speaketh in an unknown tongue edifieth himself; but he that prophesieth edifieth the church. ⁵I would that ye all spake with tongues, but rather that ye prophesied: for greater is he that prophesieth than he that speaketh with tongues, except he interpret, that the church may receive edifying.

⁶Now, brethren, if I come unto you speaking with tongues, what shall I profit you, except I shall speak to you either by revelation, or by knowledge, or by prophesying, or by doctrine? ⁷And even things without life giving sound, whether pipe or harp, except they give a distinction in the sounds, how shall it be known what is piped or harped? ⁸For if the trumpet give an uncertain sound, who shall prepare himself to the battle? ⁹So likewise ye, except ye utter by the tongue words easy to be understood, how shall it be known what is spoken? for ye shall speak into the air. ¹⁰There are, it may be, so many kinds of voices in the world, and none of them is without signification. ¹¹Therefore if I know not the meaning of the voice, I shall be unto him that speaketh a barbarian, and he that speaketh shall be a barbarian unto me. ¹²Even so ye, forasmuch as ye are zealous of spiritual gifts, seek that ye may excel to the edifying of the church.

¹³Wherefore let him that speaketh in an unknown tongue pray that he may interpret. ¹⁴For if I pray in an unknown tongue, my spirit prayeth, but my understanding is unfruitful. ¹⁵What is it then? I will pray with the spirit, and I will pray with the understanding also: I will sing with the spirit, and I will sing with the understanding also. ¹⁶Else when thou shalt bless with the spirit, how shall he that occupieth the room of the unlearned say Amen at thy giving of thanks, seeing he understandeth not what thou sayest? ¹⁷For thou verily givest thanks well, but the other is not edified. ¹⁸I thank my God, I speak with tongues more than ye all: ¹⁹yet in the church I had rather speak five words with my understanding, that by my voice I might teach others also, than ten thousand words in an unknown tongue.

²⁰Brethren, be not children in understanding: howbeit in malice be ye children, but in understanding be men. ²¹In the law it is written, With men of other tongues and other lips will I speak unto this people; and yet for all that will they not hear

---

(i.e., mirror) figures indirect prophetic knowledge in Plato, *Timaeus* 71b, which Paul may have in mind. *Darkly*: lit. "in a riddle," connoting obliqueness or ambiguity; cf. Num 12:6–8. *Now I . . . known*: cf. 8:1–3.   **13:13** *Faith, hope, charity*: a common Pauline triad; cf. Gal 5:5–6; Col 1:4–5; 1 Thess 1:3; 5:8.
14:1–40 Spiritual gifts (cont.): speaking in tongues. 14:1 *Rather*: especially.   **14:6** *Doctrine*: teaching (also in v. 26).   **14:9** *Easy to be understood*: intelligible.   **14:10** *Without signification*: more literally "without sound."   **14:11** *Barbarian*: one who does not speak Greek.   **14:14–15** *If I . . . pray with the understanding also*: Paul also alludes to unintelligible ecstatic prayer in Rom 8:26–27, but without reservations.   **14:16** *Room*: place.   **14:20** *Understanding*: Gk. *phrēn*, better "thinking"; a different word is used in v. 19. *Men*: lit. "perfect" or "full-grown" (cf. 2:6 and note).   **14:21** *With*

me, saith the Lord. ²²Wherefore tongues are for a sign, not to them that believe, but to them that believe not: but prophesying serveth not for them that believe not, but for them which believe. ²³If therefore the whole church be come together into one place, and all speak with tongues, and there come in those that are unlearned, or unbelievers, will they not say that ye are mad? ²⁴But if all prophesy, and there come in one that believeth not, or one unlearned, he is convinced of all, he is judged of all: ²⁵and thus are the secrets of his heart made manifest; and so falling down on his face he will worship God, and report that God is in you of a truth.

²⁶How is it then, brethren? when ye come together, every one of you hath a psalm, hath a doctrine, hath a tongue, hath a revelation, hath an interpretation. Let all things be done unto edifying. ²⁷If any man speak in an unknown tongue, let it be by two, or at the most by three, and that by course; and let one interpret. ²⁸But if there be no interpreter, let him keep silence in the church; and let him speak to himself, and to God. ²⁹Let the prophets speak two or three, and let the other judge. ³⁰If any thing be revealed to another that sitteth by, let the first hold his peace. ³¹For ye may all prophesy one by one, that all may learn, and all may be comforted. ³²And the spirits of the prophets are subject to the prophets. ³³For God is not the author of confusion, but of peace, as in all churches of the saints.

³⁴Let your women keep silence in the churches: for it is not permitted unto them to speak; but they are commanded to be under obedience, as also saith the law. ³⁵And if they will learn any thing, let them ask their husbands at home: for it is a shame for women to speak in the church. ³⁶What? came the word of God out from you? or came it unto you only?

³⁷If any man think himself to be a prophet, or spiritual, let him acknowledge that the things that I write unto you are the commandments of the Lord. ³⁸But if any man be ignorant, let him be ignorant. ³⁹Wherefore, brethren, covet to prophesy, and forbid not to speak with tongues. ⁴⁰Let all things be done decently and in order.

---

men . . . Lord: Isa 28:11–12.   **14:23** *Ye are mad*: Gk. *mainesthe*, which does not necessarily have negative connotations. It can signify divinely inspired prophetic frenzy, and probably should so be understood here. Paul's point becomes clear in vv. 24–25: outsiders visiting a church meeting characterized by such ecstatic utterances will be duly impressed (compare the roughly contemporary descriptions of the ecstatic Sybil in Virgil, *Aeneid* 6.42–51, 98–103, and of Phemonoe in Lucan 5.120–224). But outsiders at a meeting in which prophecy was prevalent would be convinced of their sins and prompted to worship God.   **14:25** *Falling down . . . truth*: cf. Isa 45:14.   **14:26** *Tongue . . . revelation*: the order of these terms is better reversed (MS tradition).   **14:27** *By course*: in turn.   **14:29** *Let the other judge*: the Greek is plural: "let the others judge."   **14:31** *Comforted*: or "encouraged."   **14:32** *The spirits . . . to the prophets*: i.e., those who prophesy can control their utterances.   **14:33** *As in all churches of the saints*: this phrase may also be taken as introducing vv. 34–36.   **14:34–35** *Let your women . . . church*: this passage may represent a scribal interpolation, and should perhaps be omitted (MS tradition; see introduction).   **14:34** *Under obedience*: Gk. *hypotassō*, also "subject" (cf. v. 32). *Saith the law*: Gen 3:16.   **14:38** *If any . . . ignorant*: better "if any man ignore this, he is ignored" (MS tradition).

15 Moreover, brethren, I declare unto you the gospel which I preached unto you, which also ye have received, and wherein ye stand; [2]by which also ye are saved, if ye keep in memory what I preached unto you, unless ye have believed in vain. [3]For I delivered unto you first of all that which I also received, how that Christ died for our sins according to the scriptures; [4]and that he was buried, and that he rose again the third day according to the scriptures: [5]and that he was seen of Cephas, then of the twelve: [6]after that, he was seen of above five hundred brethren at once; of whom the greater part remain unto this present, but some are fallen asleep. [7]After that, he was seen of James; then of all the apostles. [8]And last of all he was seen of me also, as of one born out of due time. [9]For I am the least of the apostles, that am not meet to be called an apostle, because I persecuted the church of God. [10]But by the grace of God I am what I am: and his grace which was bestowed upon me was not in vain; but I laboured more abundantly than they all: yet not I, but the grace of God which was with me. [11]Therefore whether it were I or they, so we preach, and so ye believed.

[12]Now if Christ be preached that he rose from the dead, how say some among you that there is no resurrection of the dead? [13]But if there be no resurrection of the dead, then is Christ not risen: [14]and if Christ be not risen, then is our preaching vain, and your faith is also vain. [15]Yea, and we are found false witnesses of God; because we have testified of God that he raised up Christ: whom he raised not up, if so be that the dead rise not. [16]For if the dead rise not, then is not Christ

---

15:1–58 Resurrection. Gk. *anastasis nekrōn* ("resurrection of the dead," vv. 12, 13) could be construed as referring to a zombie-like revivification of corpses—not a very attractive afterlife, especially in light of Greco-Roman philosophy's tendency to denigrate the body. Perhaps in response to such a misconception, Paul's argument aims to present embodied eschatological life in a way that resonates more appealingly within the context of his day's popular philosophy. **15:1** *Declare*: better "make known"; the Greek word contains the same root as "ignorant" in 14:38. **15:2** *Keep in memory*: or "hold firm." **15:3–7** *I delivered . . . apostles*: the earliest surviving detailed tradition about Jesus' resurrection. **15:3** *Delivered*: like *received*, a term referring to the transmission of traditional knowledge; cf. 11:23. *According to the scriptures*: the early church believed that numerous scriptures prophesied Jesus' death and resurrection, as the Gospels' Passion Narratives reveal. **15:5** *Was seen of*: Gk. *ōphthē*, "appeared to," the standard verb for manifestations of supernatural beings in LXX and NT; cf. LXX Gen 12:7; 17:1; Mark 9:4; Acts 9:17; etc. It is repeated in vv. 6–8. *Cephas*: Peter. In Matthew (28:9), John (20:11–18), and the spurious ending of Mark (16:9), Jesus first appears to women. Luke may allude to Peter's primacy as a resurrection witness (24:34), but does not emphasize it. *The twelve*: Jesus' specially chosen group of disciples (see Mark 3:13–19). The early church linked them with a diverse variety of traditions about Jesus' resurrection and its proper understanding (e.g., Luke 24:33–49; John 20:24–29). **15:6** *Five hundred . . . once*: perhaps referring to the Pentecost story recounted in Acts 2:1–13, which might have originated as an account of the risen Christ's appearance. *Fallen asleep*: dead. **15:7** *James*: Jesus' brother (Gal 1:19). The NT contains no other reference to this tradition, but it is preserved in a fragment of the *Gospel of the Hebrews* quoted by Jerome (*Of Illustrious Men* 2). **15:8** *He was . . . also*: see Gal 1:15–16. *One born . . . time*: "abortion" or "miscarriage." **15:9** *I persecuted . . . God*: see Gal 1:13 and note. **15:11** *Whether it . . . believed*: contrary to Paul's claim, early Christian writings about Jesus' resurrection are quite diverse, in their presentation both of who saw what when (compare, e.g., Matt 28:1–8; Mark 16:1–8; Luke 24:1–12; and John 20:1–18), and of the theological significance they impute to Jesus' resurrection (e.g., its degree of continuity with eschatological resurrection; compare v. 23 and Matt 27:52–53). **15:12** *Resurrection of the dead*: a traditional Jewish apocalyptic belief that in the Day of the Lord,

raised: ¹⁷and if Christ be not raised, your faith is vain; ye are yet in your sins. ¹⁸Then they also which are fallen asleep in Christ are perished. ¹⁹If in this life only we have hope in Christ, we are of all men most miserable.

²⁰But now is Christ risen from the dead, and become the firstfruits of them that slept. ²¹For since by man came death, by man came also the resurrection of the dead. ²²For as in Adam all die, even so in Christ shall all be made alive. ²³But every man in his own order: Christ the firstfruits; afterward they that are Christ's at his coming. ²⁴Then cometh the end, when he shall have delivered up the kingdom to God, even the Father; when he shall have put down all rule and all authority and power. ²⁵For he must reign, till he hath put all enemies under his feet. ²⁶The last enemy that shall be destroyed is death. ²⁷For he hath put all things under his feet. But when he saith, all things are put under him, it is manifest that he is excepted, which did put all things under him. ²⁸And when all things shall be subdued unto him, then shall the Son also himself be subject unto him that put all things under him, that God may be all in all.

²⁹Else what shall they do which are baptized for the dead, if the dead rise not at all? why are they then baptized for the dead? ³⁰And why stand we in jeopardy every hour? ³¹I protest by your rejoicing which I have in Christ Jesus our Lord, I die daily. ³²If after the manner of men I have fought with beasts at Ephesus, what advantageth it me, if the dead rise not? let us eat and drink; for to morrow we die.

God will raise the dead (to judge them); cf. Dan 12:1–3; Mark 12:18–27; etc.   **15:17** *Ye are . . . sins*: Rom 6 explores the link between Jesus' resurrection and believers' liberation from sin.   **15:18** *Which are . . . Christ*: believers who have died.   **15:20** *Firstfruits*: originally, the initial portion of a harvest, which was devoted to God (Exod 23:16, 19). Here and in v. 23 Paul uses the term figuratively, to present Jesus' resurrection as the initiation of the eschatological resurrection of the dead; cf. Matt 27:52–53 and note.   **15:21** *For since . . . death*: a reference to the story of the primeval transgression (see esp. Gen 3:19b).   **15:22** *As in Adam . . . alive*: Paul develops this typology in Rom 5:12–21.   **15:23** *His coming*: see Matt 24:3 and note.   **15:24–28** *Then cometh . . . in all*: a somewhat confusing passage in that it is often unclear whether the pronouns refer to God or to Christ. In any case, by the conclusion God alone remains standing.   **15:24** *All rule . . . power*: better "every ruler . . . power"; cf. 2:6 and note.   **15:25** *He hath put . . . feet*: alluding to Ps 110:1, an OT verse often applied in the NT to the risen Christ; cf. Mark 14:62 and note.   **15:26** *The last . . . death*: the destruction of death, which Paul conceives of as a demonic personality, corresponds to the resurrection of the dead; cf. vv. 54–55.   **15:27** *He hath put . . . feet*: alluding to Ps 8:6.   **15:28** *Subdued, subject*: rendering the same Greek verb elsewhere translated "put under." *All in all*: Gk. *ta panta en pasin*. Paul's equation of God with *ta panta* ("all things") recalls the Stoic penchant for divinizing the cosmos. (*Ta panta* is conventional Greco-Roman philosophical jargon for the universe.) The sentence's pantheistic implications may have led pious scribes to alter the phrase in order to mute its invocation of pagan philosophical ideas, for a large number of MSS eliminate the definite article *ta* to produce a somewhat more generic Greek idiom. But Paul links his understanding of the end time's culmination with the Stoic belief in an eschatological conflagration, when "God will expand until he absorbs the universe into himself" (Plutarch, *On Stoic Self-Contradictions* 1052c).   **15:29** *Baptized for the dead*: baptism functions as a guarantee of resurrection in Rom 6:3–5; here Paul refers to a practice of baptizing the dead by proxy in order to ensure their eschatological resurrection. Nothing more is known of it, but cf. 2 Macc 12:43–45.   **15:31** *By your rejoicing*: better "by my boast in you."   **15:32** *Fought with beasts*: combat in the arena is a common metaphor in Greco-Roman popular philosophical discourse (cf. 4:9 note). Here Paul probably refers figuratively to struggles with opponents at Ephesus (cf. 16:8–9). *Let us . . . die*: cf. Isa 22:13.

^{33}Be not deceived: evil communications corrupt good manners. ^{34}Awake to righteousness, and sin not; for some have not the knowledge of God: I speak this to your shame.

^{35}But some man will say, How are the dead raised up? and with what body do they come? ^{36}Thou fool, that which thou sowest is not quickened, except it die: ^{37}and that which thou sowest, thou sowest not that body that shall be, but bare grain, it may chance of wheat, or of some other grain: ^{38}but God giveth it a body as it hath pleased him, and to every seed his own body. ^{39}All flesh is not the same flesh: but there is one kind of flesh of men, another flesh of beasts, another of fishes, and another of birds. ^{40}There are also celestial bodies, and bodies terrestrial: but the glory of the celestial is one, and the glory of the terrestrial is another. ^{41}There is one glory of the sun, and another glory of the moon, and another glory of the stars: for one star differeth from another star in glory.

^{42}So also is the resurrection of the dead. It is sown in corruption; it is raised in incorruption: ^{43}it is sown in dishonour; it is raised in glory: it is sown in weakness; it is raised in power: ^{44}it is sown a natural body; it is raised a spiritual body. There is a natural body, and there is a spiritual body. ^{45}And so it is written, The first man Adam was made a living soul; the last Adam was made a quickening spirit. ^{46}Howbeit that was not first which is spiritual, but that which is natural; and afterward that which is spiritual. ^{47}The first man is of the earth, earthy: the second man is the Lord from heaven. ^{48}As is the earthy, such are they also that are earthy: and as is the heavenly, such are they also that are heavenly. ^{49}And as we have borne the image of the earthy, we shall also bear the image of the heavenly.

15:33–34 *Be not deceived . . . shame*: Paul's argument momentarily descends to an ad hominem attack. **15:33** *Evil communications . . . manners*: although it circulated independently as a proverb, this saying apparently originated in a comedy by the Athenian playwright Menander (ca. 342–ca. 292 B.C.E.). *Communications*: company or conversation. *Manners*: habits, customs, or even way of life. **15:34** *Awake to righteousness*: lit. "sober up rightly." **15:36** *Quickened*: made alive. **15:37** *Bare*: lit. "naked." Greco-Roman philosophical jargon commonly presents the body as something the self puts on or wears, and Paul therefore can use language of nakedness and clothing when discussing embodied eschatological existence; e.g., v. 49 and note; 2 Cor 4:16–5:10. **15:38** *His*: its. **15:39–41** *There is . . . in glory*: the order in which Paul lists creation's living constituents (men, beasts, birds, fish, heavenly bodies) reverses the order in which they were created in Gen 1:14–27. **15:39** *Fishes, birds*: their order should be reversed (MS tradition). **15:40** *Celestial bodies*: the Greco-Roman world often viewed the sun, moon, and stars as embodied divinities composed of refined substances such as fire, ether, or spirit (as opposed to base "flesh," a term now abandoned in favor of the more neutral "bodies"). Paul's argument consistently links resurrected bodies with heavenly bodies, on the basis of Dan 12:3 and other Jewish apocalyptic texts. **15:43** *Raised in glory*: recalling celestial bodies' "glory" in vv. 40–41. **15:44** *Natural*: Gk. *psychikon*, "consisting of soul" (see 2:14 note), mistranslated by KJV (so throughout). *There is . . . spiritual body*: better "If there is a body consisting of soul [*psychikon*], there is also a spiritual one" (MS tradition; our translation). **15:45** *Adam was made a living soul*: Gen 2:7. *Last Adam*: Christ; see v. 22. **15:47** *Of the earth*: see Gen 2:7. *The Lord*: better omitted (MS tradition). **15:48** *Heavenly*: Gk. *epouranios*; cf. vv. 40 [KJV "celestial"], 49. The man "from heaven" (v. 47) and the *heavenly* ones in his image constitute one of the classes of glorious "heavenly bodies" Paul discusses in vv. 40–41, as opposed to the kinds of fleshly bodies he enumerates in v. 39. **15:49** *Borne, bear*: the Greek word also means "worn." *We shall also bear*: alternatively "let us also bear" (MS tradition). *Image*: cf. Gen 1:26–27.

[50]Now this I say, brethren, that flesh and blood cannot inherit the kingdom of God; neither doth corruption inherit incorruption. [51]Behold, I shew you a mystery; We shall not all sleep, but we shall all be changed, [52]in a moment, in the twinkling of an eye, at the last trump: for the trumpet shall sound, and the dead shall be raised incorruptible, and we shall be changed. [53]For this corruptible must put on incorruption, and this mortal must put on immortality. [54]So when this corruptible shall have put on incorruption, and this mortal shall have put on immortality, then shall be brought to pass the saying that is written, Death is swallowed up in victory. [55]O death, where is thy sting? O grave, where is thy victory? [56]The sting of death is sin; and the strength of sin is the law. [57]But thanks be to God, which giveth us the victory through our Lord Jesus Christ. [58]Therefore, my beloved brethren, be ye stedfast, unmoveable, always abounding in the work of the Lord, forasmuch as ye know that your labour is not in vain in the Lord.

16 Now concerning the collection for the saints, as I have given order to the churches of Galatia, even so do ye. [2]Upon the first day of the week let every one of you lay by him in store, as God hath prospered him, that there be no gatherings when I come. [3]And when I come, whomsoever ye shall approve by your letters, them will I send to bring your liberality unto Jerusalem. [4]And if it be meet that I go also, they shall go with me.

[5]Now I will come unto you, when I shall pass through Macedonia: for I do pass through Macedonia. [6]And it may be that I will abide, yea, and winter with you, that ye may bring me on my journey whithersoever I go. [7]For I will not see you now by the way; but I trust to tarry a while with you, if the Lord permit. [8]But I will tarry at Ephesus until Pentecost. [9]For a great door and effectual is opened unto me, and there are many adversaries.

[10]Now if Timotheus come, see that he may be with you without fear: for he worketh the work of the Lord, as I also do. [11]Let no man therefore despise him: but conduct him forth in peace, that he may come unto me: for I look for him with the brethren. [12]As touching our brother Apollos, I greatly desired him to come unto you with the brethren: but his will was not at all to come at this time; but he will come when he shall have convenient time.

15:50 *Flesh and blood*: recalling the "flesh" associated with the creatures of v. 39. *Neither doth . . . incorruption*: cf. vv. 42, 53–54. **15:52** *The trumpet shall sound*: a common eschatological motif; cf. Matt 24:31; 1 Thess 4:16; etc. *We shall be changed*: cf. Phil 3:21; 2 Cor 3:18 suggests that the transformation has already begun. **15:54–55** *Death is swallowed up . . . thy victory*: Isa 25:8; Hos 13:14. **15:55** *O death . . . victory*: better "O death, where is thy victory? O death, where is thy sting?" (MS tradition). **15:56** *The sting . . . law*: death results from Adam's and Eve's transgression of the primeval commandment, which Paul can figure as "the law" (see Rom 7:7–13 and notes); cf. vv. 21–22 and notes.

16:1–4 The collection. Paul discusses the fund he was raising for believers in Jerusalem, a project he mentions throughout his letters (Rom 15:25–28; 2 Cor 8–9; cf. Gal 2:10 and note). **16:3** *Letters*: i.e., of introduction. *Liberality*: gift. **16:4** *They shall go with me*: this apparently happened; cf. Rom 15:25–28.

16:5–12 Travel plans. 16:5 *Macedonia*: the Roman imperial province north of Achaia (in which Corinth was located). **16:7** *Will not*: wish not to. *Now by the way*: just in passing. **16:8** *Ephesus*: in Asia, the province east of Achaia, across the Aegean. *Pentecost*: see Acts 2:1 note. **16:10** *If Timotheus come*: cf. 4:17.

[13]Watch ye, stand fast in the faith, quit you like men, be strong. [14]Let all your things be done with charity. [15]I beseech you, brethren, (ye know the house of Stephanas, that it is the firstfruits of Achaia, and that they have addicted themselves to the ministry of the saints,) [16]that ye submit yourselves unto such, and to every one that helpeth with us, and laboureth. [17]I am glad of the coming of Stephanas and Fortunatus and Achaicus: for that which was lacking on your part they have supplied. [18]For they have refreshed my spirit and yours: therefore acknowledge ye them that are such.

[19]The churches of Asia salute you. Aquila and Priscilla salute you much in the Lord, with the church that is in their house. [20]All the brethren greet you. Greet ye one another with an holy kiss.

[21]The salutation of me Paul with mine own hand. [22]If any man love not the Lord Jesus Christ, let him be Anathema Maranatha. [23]The grace of our Lord Jesus Christ be with you. [24]My love be with you all in Christ Jesus. Amen.

The first epistle to the Corinthians was written from Philippi by Stephanas, and Fortunatus, and Achaicus, and Timotheus.

16:13–24 Final comments and closing. 6:13 *Quit you like men*: be manly. **16:15** *House of Stephanas*: cf. 1:16. *Firstfruits*: first converts (cf. 15:20 note). *Addicted*: set. **16:17** *Fortunatus and Achaicus*: perhaps the people of Chloe mentioned in 1:11. *That which . . . supplied*: "they made up for your absence" (NRSV). **16:19** *Aquila and Priscilla*: see Rom 16:3 and note. **16:20** *Holy kiss*: a conventional greeting in the early church. **16:21** *With mine own hand*: indicating that Paul had dictated the letter to a scribe (Sosthenes? see 1:1) but adds the signature and coda himself. **16:22** *Anathema Maranatha*: these words should be separated by a full stop. The first transliterates a Greek word meaning "cursed," completing the sentence. The second transliterates an Aramaic phrase (itself transliterated into Greek) meaning "Our Lord, come," or perhaps "our Lord has come." **16:23** *The grace . . . you*: cf. 1:3. **16:24** *Amen. The first epistle . . . Timotheus*: better omitted (MS tradition).

The Second Epistle of Paul the Apostle
to the Corinthians

WRITTEN in the mid-50s C.E., around the same time as 1 Corinthians, 2 Corinthians is in some ways the most difficult of Paul's letters. First of all, it is the one whose compositional unity is most seriously in doubt: scholars argue that it incorporates passages from several of Paul's letters to the church at Corinth. This theory is not unappealing, for 2 Corinthians' discourse is at times so rambling, its changes of tone so sudden and so extreme, that even a reader committed to discovering formal unity may find Paul's line of thought irredeemably disjointed. In 2:12, for example, Paul begins a narrative involving Titus's expected return from Corinth, which breaks off after verse 14 in favor of a lengthy excursus on his own ministry (2:15–7:4), only to resume again with hardly a missed beat at 7:5. The unexpected shift in tone between 7:5–9:15 and chapters 10–13, from warm affection to bitter polemic, is likewise difficult to explain as part of a coherent rhetorical strategy, although this problem may be less intractable than the first.

Theories about 2 Corinthians' possible sources abound, some of them holding that Paul himself did not even write some sections of this letter. But many scholars believe that the epistle incorporates fragments from two other letters mentioned in Paul's Corinthian correspondence: one that Paul sent prior to 1 Corinthians (see 1 Cor 5:9), supposedly preserved at 2 Cor 6:14–7:1, and another, the "letter of tears," which Paul sent by Titus after he had written 1 Corinthians and then made a second, painful visit to Corinth in a futile attempt to resolve festering conflict between himself and the church there. Paul's letter of tears (cf. 2 Cor 2:4) apparently led to the rapprochement his earlier visit had failed to broker (see 2 Cor 7:8–13). This letter may be preserved in 2 Cor 2:14–6:13 and 7:2–4, or 10:1–13:10, or both. Some scholars believe only the latter section comes from it, with the former excerpting yet another of Paul's epistles to Corinth, a so-called first apology, also sent by Titus but just before Paul's painful visit. The rest of 2 Corinthians (1:1–2:13; 7:5–9:15; 13:11–13) would have been written after the reconciliation, and this material too might not all come from one letter. Chapters 8 and 9 urge Paul's readers to contribute to the offering he is collecting for the Jerusalem church, but the two chapters cover similar terrain and the latter seems to be directed not so much to believers at Corinth as to those living throughout Achaia, the province in which Corinth lay (see 9:2). On the basis of this and related observations, some have proposed that while chapter 8 was originally a part of Paul's letter of reconciliation to the Corinthian church, chapter 9 comes from a separate

A Possible Description of Paul's Corinthian Correspondence

Paul's first letter to Corinth	Partly preserved at 2 Cor 6:14–7:1	Mentioned at 1 Cor 5:9
Paul's second letter to Corinth	1 Corinthians	
Paul's third letter to Corinth: the "first apology"	Partly preserved at 2 Cor 2:14–6:13; 7:2–4	
Paul's fourth letter to Corinth: the "letter of tears"	Partly preserved at 2 Cor 10:1–13:10	Mentioned at 2 Cor 2:3–4
Paul's fifth letter to Corinth: the "letter of reconciliation"	Partly or fully preserved at 2 Cor 1:1–2:13; 7:5–8:24; 13:11–13	
Paul's "administrative letter" to believers in Achaia	Partly preserved at 2 Cor 9	

administrative letter, not addressed to the Corinthians but instead urging other Achaian communities to contribute to Paul's offering.

The table above presents one rather complex redactional scheme for 2 Corinthians, and not every element of it is equally compelling. Nonetheless, it seems safe to conclude that 2 Corinthians constitutes a string of passages from Paul's extensive correspondence with the Corinthians rather than a single sustained argument. But even if 2 Corinthians is a composite work, it nevertheless displays a broad thematic unity, which comes into sharp relief when it is read in conjunction with 1 Corinthians. Whereas that letter is concerned with the unity of the church, this one deals with the authority of Paul himself, the Corinthian church's founder and director, who must define and defend his own ministry with the same vigor and theological creativity with which he delineated the contours of Christ's body in the previous epistle.

2 Corinthians presents its readers with another special challenge, for it contains one of the most controversial passages in the entire Pauline corpus: the comparison of new and old covenants in chapter 3 that has supported a hermeneutic of Christian supersession which Paul, who never even uses the word "Christian" and in fact goes out of his way to identify himself as a Jew (11:22), certainly did not intend. KJV's decision to translate the Greek word *diathēkē* ("covenant") as "testament" (3:6, 14) participates in an interpretive tradition that reduces Paul's dialectic between old covenant and new to a contrast between the Old and New Testament, and by extension to an antithesis between Judaism and Christianity. But such readings, in addition to being anachronistic, fail to come to terms with the fact that Paul actually imports the term "new covenant" from Jer 31:31–34, an Old Testament passage echoed throughout chapter 3. These allusions indicate that he views the new covenant that Christ instituted (cf. 1 Cor 11:25) as a prophetic proclamation within the Jewish tradition (see also Gal 1:15–16; cf. Isa 49:6; Jer 1:5), rather than as the institution of a religion other than—let alone opposed to—Judaism. This does not deny Paul's critique of the Sinai covenant as transitory and

superficial—a critique arguably latent in the Old Testament prophets themselves (cf. Isa 55:3; Jer 32:38–41; Ezek 16:60; Amos 5:21–25; Mic 6:6–8)—or his audacions self-presentation as a prophet superior to Moses. But it does demand that the reader engage with the complexities of Paul's biblical hermeneutic, which emerge more clearly when 2 Corinthians is read within Paul's own ideological context, as opposed to later Christian ones.

Victor Paul Furnish's Anchor Bible commentary, *II Corinthians: A New Translation with Introduction and Commentary* (Garden City, N.Y.: Doubleday, 1984), is perceptive and thorough, as is Margaret Thrall's more recent two-volume work in the International Critical Commentary series, *A Critical and Exegetical Commentary on the Second Epistle to the Corinthians* (Edinburgh: T&T Clark, 1994–2000). This introduction and the notes that follow rely on both.

THE SECOND EPISTLE OF PAUL THE APOSTLE TO THE CORINTHIANS

1 Paul, an apostle of Jesus Christ by the will of God, and Timothy our brother, unto the church of God which is at Corinth, with all the saints which are in all Achaia: ²Grace be to you and peace from God our Father, and from the Lord Jesus Christ.

³Blessed be God, even the Father of our Lord Jesus Christ, the Father of mercies, and the God of all comfort; ⁴who comforteth us in all our tribulation, that we may be able to comfort them which are in any trouble, by the comfort wherewith we ourselves are comforted of God. ⁵For as the sufferings of Christ abound in us, so our consolation also aboundeth by Christ. ⁶And whether we be afflicted, it is for your consolation and salvation, which is effectual in the enduring of the same sufferings which we also suffer: or whether we be comforted, it is for your consolation and salvation. ⁷And our hope of you is stedfast, knowing, that as ye are partakers of the sufferings, so shall ye be also of the consolation.

⁸For we would not, brethren, have you ignorant of our trouble which came to us in Asia, that we were pressed out of measure, above strength, insomuch that we despaired even of life: ⁹but we had the sentence of death in ourselves, that we should not trust in ourselves, but in God which raiseth the dead: ¹⁰who delivered us from so great a death, and doth deliver: in whom we trust that he will yet deliver us; ¹¹ye also helping together by prayer for us, that for the gift bestowed upon us by the means of many persons thanks may be given by many on our behalf.

1:1–11 Salutation and blessing. On the openings of Paul's letters, see note to Rom 1:1–15. **1:1** *Apostle*: see Rom 1:1 note. *Timothy*: see 1 Cor 4:17 and note; 16:10. *Church*: see Rom 16:5 note. *At Corinth . . . Achaia*: see 1 Cor 1:2 note. *Saints*: see Rom 1:7 note. **1:2** *Grace be . . . peace*: see Rom 1:7 note. **1:3** *Comfort*: Gk. *paraklēsis*, also "encouragement" or "consolation" (see vv. 5–7). It and its cognate verb occur nine times in vv. 3–7. **1:4** *Tribulation*: Gk. *thlipsis*; this noun and its cognates are variously rendered in 2 Corinthians, with forms of "tribulation," "trouble" (later in this verse), "affliction," and "burden." **1:6** *Which is . . . salvation*: better "if we are consoled, it is for your consolation, which becomes effective when you endure the same sufferings which we also suffer" (MS tradition). **1:8** *Brethren*: a common self-designation of Jesus-believers. *Our trouble . . . Asia*: the life-threatening situation to which he refers is unknown. Some speculate it is an Ephesian incarceration not recorded by Acts; others, that it is the riot at Ephesus described in Acts 19:23–20:1. *That we . . . strength*: i.e., "that we were utterly pressed down, beyond our strength to bear." **1:10** *Doth deliver*: better "will deliver" (MS tradition).

¹²For our rejoicing is this, the testimony of our conscience, that in simplicity and godly sincerity, not with fleshly wisdom, but by the grace of God, we have had our conversation in the world, and more abundantly to you-ward. ¹³For we write none other things unto you, than what ye read or acknowledge; and I trust ye shall acknowledge even to the end; ¹⁴as also ye have acknowledged us in part, that we are your rejoicing, even as ye also are ours in the day of the Lord Jesus.

¹⁵And in this confidence I was minded to come unto you before, that ye might have a second benefit; ¹⁶and to pass by you into Macedonia, and to come again out of Macedonia unto you, and of you to be brought on my way toward Judæa. ¹⁷When I therefore was thus minded, did I use lightness? or the things that I purpose, do I purpose according to the flesh, that with me there should be yea yea, and nay nay? ¹⁸But as God is true, our word toward you was not yea and nay. ¹⁹For the Son of God, Jesus Christ, who was preached among you by us, even by me and Silvanus and Timotheus, was not yea and nay, but in him was yea. ²⁰For all the promises of God in him are yea, and in him Amen, unto the glory of God by us. ²¹Now he which stablisheth us with you in Christ, and hath anointed us, is God; ²²who hath also sealed us, and given the earnest of the Spirit in our hearts.

²³Moreover I call God for a record upon my soul, that to spare you I came not as yet unto Corinth. ²⁴Not for that we have dominion over your faith, but are helpers of your joy: for by faith ye stand. ¹But I determined this with myself, that I would not come again to you in heaviness. ²For if I make you sorry, who is he then that maketh me glad, but the same which is made sorry by me? ³And I wrote this same unto you, lest, when I came, I should have sorrow from them of

---

1:12–14 Thesis. Paul introduces his letter's central theme, a defense of his benevolence toward the Corinthian congregation.   **1:12** *Rejoicing*: lit. "boast" (also in v. 14). *In simplicity . . . wisdom*: cf. 1 Cor 1:18–2:16. *Had our conversation*: conducted ourselves. *To you-ward*: toward you.   **1:14** *The day . . . Jesus*: Christ's eschatological advent.

1:15–2:4 Paul's canceled visit. 1:15–16 *I was . . . Judæa*: compare the trip mentioned in 1 Cor 16:3–7; Paul's plans had slightly changed.   **1:15** *Benefit*: Gk. *charis*, "gift" or "grace" (cf. v. 2). **1:16** *Macedonia*: the Roman province just north of Achaia (in which lay Corinth).   **1:17** *Lightness*: levity. *According to the flesh*: according to worldly standards. *With me . . . nay*: referring to obsequious concurrence. Compare the flattery conventionally attributed to parasites in Roman comedy: "If anyone says no, I say no; if yes, yes. In short, I have ordered myself to agree in all matters" (Terence, *Eunuch* 252–53; cf. Plautus, *Menaechmi* 163).   **1:18** *Was*: better "is" (MS tradition).   **1:19** *Silvanus*: a Latin form of "Silas," one of Paul's ministry partners, who along with Timothy had helped establish the Corinthian church (Acts 18:1–17).   **1:20** *And in . . . us*: better "for this reason it is through him that we say the 'Amen' to the glory of God" (MS tradition; NRSV). *Amen* is conventionally uttered in assent, so the sentence is thematically related to vv. 18–20a.   **1:21** *Stablisheth*: Gk. *bebaiōn*, with the same root as "stedfast" (v. 7). The word can refer to guaranteeing the validity of a purchase; compare the financial metaphors of v. 22 (see note). *Anointed*: Gk. *chrisas*, whence derives *Christ* (see Mark 1:1 note). Paul may be assimilating himself to Christ, but in the OT anointing appears as a mark of consecration in a variety of contexts (e.g., Exod 29:7; 1 Sam 9:16; 1 Kgs 19:16).   **1:22** *Sealed*: i.e., "marked as his property." *Earnest*: installment, down payment.   **1:23** *Soul*: Gk. *psychē*, also "life." Paul is swearing by his own.   **1:24** *Not for that*: i.e., "it is not the case that." *Faith*: see Rom 1:8 note. *Are helpers . . . joy*: cf. v. 11, where the Corinthians are said to have helped Paul.   **2:1** *Come again*: Paul had apparently visited Corinth en route to Macedonia, but in order to avoid further discord decided he would not stop again on his way from Macedonia to Judea, as he had initially planned; cf. 1:15–16. *Heaviness*: Gk. *lypē*: it and its cognate verb are variously rendered in the subsequent verses as "sorry" (v. 2), "sorrow" (vv. 3, 7), "be grieved" (v. 4), and "caused grief" and "grieved" (v. 5). The word is countered by "joy" (1:24; 2:3; cf. 2:2, "glad"), recalling the opposition of "tribulation" and "comfort" (1:3–7).   **2:3** *I wrote this*

whom I ought to rejoice; having confidence in you all, that my joy is the joy of you all. [4]For out of much affliction and anguish of heart I wrote unto you with many tears; not that ye should be grieved, but that ye might know the love which I have more abundantly unto you.

[5]But if any have caused grief, he hath not grieved me, but in part: that I may not overcharge you all. [6]Sufficient to such a man is this punishment, which was inflicted of many. [7]So that contrariwise ye ought rather to forgive him, and comfort him, lest perhaps such a one should be swallowed up with overmuch sorrow. [8]Wherefore I beseech you that ye would confirm your love toward him. [9]For to this end also did I write, that I might know the proof of you, whether ye be obedient in all things. [10]To whom ye forgive any thing, I forgive also: for if I forgave any thing, to whom I forgave it, for your sakes forgave I it in the person of Christ; [11]lest Satan should get an advantage of us: for we are not ignorant of his devices.

[12]Furthermore, when I came to Troas to preach Christ's gospel, and a door was opened unto me of the Lord, [13]I had no rest in my spirit, because I found not Titus my brother: but taking my leave of them, I went from thence into Macedonia.

[14]Now thanks be unto God, which always causeth us to triumph in Christ, and maketh manifest the savour of his knowledge by us in every place. [15]For we are unto God a sweet savour of Christ, in them that are saved, and in them that perish: [16]to the one we are the savour of death unto death; and to the other the savour of life unto life. And who is sufficient for these things? [17]For we are not as many,

---

same: i.e., "I made this very point in my letter." **2:4** *I wrote . . . tears*: this "letter of tears" does not survive, unless it has been incorporated into 2 Corinthians itself, as 2:14–7:4 (perhaps omitting 6:14–7:1), as chaps. 10–13, or both.

2:5–11 Forgiving an insult. 2:5 *If any . . . all*: better "if anyone has caused grief, he has grieved not me, but to some extent—not to press the point too hard—you all." **2:6** *Such a man*: though sometimes linked with the offender of 1 Cor 5:1–8, context suggests that this man has hurt Paul personally, perhaps by slandering him.

2:12–13 An interrupted narrative. Paul begins to recount his trip from Corinth to Macedonia (via Troas), but breaks off suddenly after v. 13, to resume only at 7:5. Some scholars therefore view 2:14–7:4 as an interpolation, perhaps part of the "letter of tears" mentioned in 2:3–4. Paul would have written this letter soon after the painful visit alluded to in 1:15 and 2:1 (i.e., during his journey to Troas or ministry there; 2:12) and then sent it to Corinth by means of Titus, whose return with the church's response he anxiously awaited (v. 13; cf. 7:5–16). In this reading, 2 Corinthians' final redactor would have interrupted Paul's account of his anxious anticipation with the text of the letter on which his anxiety was focused. Other scholars hold that much of 2:14–7:4 actually excerpts another of Paul's letters to the Corinthians, sometimes called the "first apology," sent by way of Titus before his painful visit in a failed attempt to resolve the intensifying conflict. **2:12** *Troas*: a port on the northwest coast of Asia Minor. Acts 20:5–12 may give a version of this visit. *Gospel*: see Mark 1:1 note. **2:13** *Titus*: one of Paul's fellow missionaries, mentioned frequently in this letter and in Gal 2:1, 3.

2:14–5:21 Paul's ministry. This section constitutes a meditation on (and impassioned defense of) Paul's ministry. After introducing himself as a prisoner of Christ on display to the world (2:14–16), Paul explains the upright dealings and frankness of speech that have characterized his ministry (2:17–4:6), articulates a theological context in which to understand the suffering he experiences as an apostle and the hope to which he holds (4:7–5:10), and defines his ministry's principal goals (5:11–21). **2:14** *Causeth us to triumph*: Paul refers to being led in a triumphal procession. Roman imperial triumphs frequently culminated in prisoners' spectacular public executions, hence the subsequent imagery of death (vv. 15–16; cf. 1 Cor 4:9 and note). *Savour*: odor or aroma. Here and in the following verses, Paul figures himself as a burnt sacrifice to God (cf. Lev 1:9, 13, 17).

which corrupt the word of God: but as of sincerity, but as of God, in the sight of God speak we in Christ.

3 Do we begin again to commend ourselves? or need we, as some others, epis- tles of commendation to you, or letters of commendation from you? ²Ye are our epistle written in our hearts, known and read of all men: ³forasmuch as ye are manifestly declared to be the epistle of Christ ministered by us, written not with ink, but with the Spirit of the living God; not in tables of stone, but in fleshy tables of the heart. ⁴And such trust have we through Christ to God-ward: ⁵not that we are sufficient of ourselves to think any thing as of ourselves; but our suf- ficiency is of God; ⁶who also hath made us able ministers of the new testament; not of the letter, but of the spirit: for the letter killeth, but the spirit giveth life.

⁷But if the ministration of death, written and engraven in stones, was glorious, so that the children of Israel could not stedfastly behold the face of Moses for the glory of his countenance; which glory was to be done away: ⁸how shall not the min- istration of the spirit be rather glorious? ⁹For if the ministration of condemnation be glory, much more doth the ministration of righteousness exceed in glory. ¹⁰For even that which was made glorious had no glory in this respect, by reason of the glory that excelleth. ¹¹For if that which is done away was glorious, much more that which remaineth is glorious.

¹²Seeing then that we have such hope, we use great plainness of speech: ¹³and not as Moses, which put a vail over his face, that the children of Israel could not stedfastly look to the end of that which is abolished: ¹⁴but their minds were blinded: for until this day remaineth the same vail untaken away in the reading of the old testament; which vail is done away in Christ. ¹⁵But even unto this day, when Moses is read, the vail is upon their heart. ¹⁶Nevertheless when it shall turn

---

2:17 *Corrupt*: lit. "peddle."   **3:1** *As some others*: perhaps Paul's opponents; cf. 5:12; 10:2; 11:5 and note, 13; etc. *Epistles of commendation*: letters of introduction.   **3:3** *Ministered*: Gk. *diakonētheisa*, "cared for" or "seen to"; its cognate nouns are used in vv. 6–9. *Not in tables . . . heart*: alluding to Jer 31:31–34, which opposes a new covenant, whose laws will be inscribed in the hearts of God's people, to the Sinai covenant, inscribed on stone tablets (cf. Exod 34:1–28). *Tables*: tablets.   **3:4** *To God- ward*: toward God.   **3:6** *Able*: the Greek verb shares a root with "sufficient/sufficiency" in v. 5. *New testament*: better "new covenant," with reference to Jer 31:31. *Not of the letter . . . life*: later taken as a classic statement of Christian biblical hermeneutics, used by commentators throughout history to justify allegorical readings of virtually the whole OT.   **3:7** *Ministration of death*: cf. vv. 6 ("the letter killeth") and 9 ("ministration of condemnation"). Paul's tendency to associate God's primeval com- mandment with the Sinai covenant's laws (Rom 5:12–21), or even to conflate the two (Rom 7:7–13; cf. 1 Cor 15:54–56), helps explain his willingness to use for the latter language appropriate to the former. (The primeval commandment's violation indeed resulted in condemnation and death; see Gen 2:15– 3:24.) *The children . . . countenance*: see Exod 34:29–35. *Which glory . . . away*: Paul's suggestion that the Sinai covenant's glory was transitory (cf. vv. 11, 13) recalls the OT prophets' anticipation of an "everlasting covenant" between God and his people (Isa 55:3; Jer 32:40; Ezek 16:60; etc.).   **3:8** *Rather*: even more.   **3:12** *Plainness of speech*: frankness or boldness of speech.   **3:13** *That the chil- dren . . . abolished*: Exod 34:29–35 does not explain why Moses veiled his face; Paul presumably under- stands his own tendentious interpretation to "unveil" the episode (cf. vv. 14–15).   **3:14** *Old testament*: i.e., old covenant; as v. 15 indicates, Paul refers to the Pentateuch, which Moses supposedly wrote. *Which vail . . . Christ*: better "because it is done away in Christ" (cf. 4:4).   **3:16** *When it . . . away*: paraphrasing Exod 34:34, which indicates that the unexpressed subject of the Greek verb should be

to the Lord, the vail shall be taken away. [17]Now the Lord is that Spirit: and where the Spirit of the Lord is, there is liberty. [18]But we all, with open face beholding as in a glass the glory of the Lord, are changed into the same image from glory to glory, even as by the Spirit of the Lord.

4 Therefore seeing we have this ministry, as we have received mercy, we faint not; [2]but have renounced the hidden things of dishonesty, not walking in craftiness, nor handling the word of God deceitfully; but by manifestation of the truth commending ourselves to every man's conscience in the sight of God. [3]But if our gospel be hid, it is hid to them that are lost: [4]in whom the god of this world hath blinded the minds of them which believe not, lest the light of the glorious gospel of Christ, who is the image of God, should shine unto them. [5]For we preach not ourselves, but Christ Jesus the Lord; and ourselves your servants for Jesus' sake. [6]For God, who commanded the light to shine out of darkness, hath shined in our hearts, to give the light of the knowledge of the glory of God in the face of Jesus Christ.

[7]But we have this treasure in earthen vessels, that the excellency of the power may be of God, and not of us. [8]We are troubled on every side, yet not distressed; we are perplexed, but not in despair; [9]persecuted, but not forsaken; cast down, but not destroyed; [10]always bearing about in the body the dying of the Lord Jesus, that the life also of Jesus might be made manifest in our body. [11]For we which live are alway delivered unto death for Jesus' sake, that the life also of Jesus might be made manifest in our mortal flesh. [12]So then death worketh in us, but life in you. [13]We having the same spirit of faith, according as it is written, I believed, and therefore have I spoken; we also believe, and therefore speak; [14]knowing that he which raised up the Lord Jesus shall raise up us also by Jesus, and shall present us with you. [15]For all things are for your sakes, that the abundant grace might through the thanksgiving of many redound to the glory of God.

[16]For which cause we faint not; but though our outward man perish, yet the inward man is renewed day by day. [17]For our light affliction, which is but for a

---

"he" (Moses) rather than KJV's *it*.   **3:17** *Now the Lord is that Spirit*: i.e., "now 'the Lord' [in Exod 34:34] refers to the spirit."   **3:18** *But we all*: as opposed to only Moses in Exod 34:34. *Glass*: mirror; cf. 1 Cor 13:12 and note. *Are changed . . . Lord*: recalling the description of the body's eschatological transformation in 1 Cor 15:35–58.   **4:2** *Dishonesty*: lit. "shame." *In craftiness . . . deceitfully*: recalling the description of the serpent (Gen 3:1), to which Paul will later liken his opponents (11:3, 14).   **4:3** *Hid*: lit. "veiled".   **4:4** *God of this world*: Satan, commonly thought to exercise authority over the present world (cf. Luke 4:6). *Blinded the minds*: in Rom 11:7–10 it is God, rather than Satan, who blinds Israel to the gospel. *Christ, who . . . God*: cf. Col 1:15.   **4:5** *Servants*: lit. "slaves" (see Rom 1:1 note).   **4:6** *Commanded the light . . . darkness*: see Gen 1:3.   **4:7** *Earthen vessels*: in the OT earthenware can symbolize something of little value (Lam 4:2; cf. Ps 31:12; Jer 22:28). Greco-Roman popular philosophy figured the body as a vessel (of the soul or mind), a commonplace that Paul draws on here (cf. vv. 10–11, 16).   **4:8–11** *We are troubled . . . flesh*: throughout the Corinthian correspondence, Paul consistently defines himself as one who suffers in order to glorify Christ; cf. 1 Cor 4:9–13; 15:31–32; 2 Cor 2:14–16; 11:23–33; 12:7–10.   **4:13** *I believed . . . spoken*: Ps 116:10. In LXX, which Paul quotes, the psalmist cries "alleluia" despite his affliction.   **4:14** *By Jesus*: better "with Jesus" (MS tradition). *Present us with you*: "before God" or "before Jesus" must be understood, as 4:16–5:10 suggests a scenario of eschatological judgment (esp. 5:10).   **4:16** *Outward man . . . inward man*: cf. Rom 7:21–25. This antithesis relates to, but is more abstract than, the imagery of containment Paul

moment, worketh for us a far more exceeding and eternal weight of glory; [18]while we look not at the things which are seen, but at the things which are not seen: for the things which are seen are temporal; but the things which are not seen are eternal.

5 For we know that if our earthly house of this tabernacle were dissolved, we have a building of God, an house not made with hands, eternal in the heavens. [2]For in this we groan, earnestly desiring to be clothed upon with our house which is from heaven: [3]if so be that being clothed we shall not be found naked. [4]For we that are in this tabernacle do groan, being burdened: not for that we would be unclothed, but clothed upon, that mortality might be swallowed up of life. [5]Now he that hath wrought us for the selfsame thing is God, who also hath given unto us the earnest of the Spirit.

[6]Therefore we are always confident, knowing that, whilst we are at home in the body, we are absent from the Lord: [7](for we walk by faith, not by sight:) [8]we are confident, I say, and willing rather to be absent from the body, and to be present with the Lord. [9]Wherefore we labour, that, whether present or absent, we may be accepted of him. [10]For we must all appear before the judgment seat of Christ; that every one may receive the things done in his body, according to that he hath done, whether it be good or bad.

[11]Knowing therefore the terror of the Lord, we persuade men; but we are made manifest unto God; and I trust also are made manifest in your consciences. [12]For we commend not ourselves again unto you, but give you occasion to glory on our behalf, that ye may have somewhat to answer them which glory in appearance, and not in heart. [13]For whether we be beside ourselves, it is to God: or whether we be sober, it is for your cause. [14]For the love of Christ constraineth us; because we thus judge, that if one died for all, then were all dead: [15]and that he died for all, that they which live should not henceforth live unto themselves, but unto him which died for them, and rose again.

---

introduced in v. 7 and to which he will return in 5:1–5. It is the first of a series of dichotomies structuring 4:16–5:10. **5:1** *Tabernacle*: Hellenistic thought conventionally conceived of the body as a tent inhabited by the (immortal) soul or mind, an idea that surfaces, e.g., at 2 Pet 1:13–14; Wis 9:15. *Earthly . . . heavens*: this same dichotomy appears in Paul's discussion of the risen body (1 Cor 15:47–49). **5:2** *We groan*: cf. Rom 8:22–23, also in the context of eschatological expectation. *Clothed*: Greco-Roman philosophy conventionally figured the body as clothing the soul (e.g., Plato, *Phaedo* 87b–e). Jewish apocalyptic literature complementarily figured the resurrected body as a garment (e.g., *1 Enoch* 62.15–16), as Paul does here. **5:3** *Being clothed*: better "being stripped of clothing" (MS tradition). **5:4** *Not for that . . . life*: cf. 1 Cor 15:54. Paul distinguishes belief in an immortal soul that escapes the dying body (*be unclothed*) from belief in the body's resurrection (*be . . . clothed upon*), which denies death a permanent claim on any part of the self. **5:5** *Earnest of the Spirit*: see 1:22 and note. The gift of the Spirit guarantees resurrection, which entails the body's total transformation into spirit; cf. 1 Cor 15:42–50. **5:6–9** *Therefore we . . . him*: the opposition this section draws between Gk. *endēmeō* ("to be at home" [KJV "be present"], vv. 8–9) and *ekdēmeō* ("to be away from home" [KJV "be absent"], vv. 6, 8–9) develops the dichotomy of heavenly and earthly homes introduced in vv. 1–2. **5:9** *We labour*: lit. "we seek after honor." **5:10** *Receive*: i.e., receive back. **5:11** *Are made manifest*: Gk. *phaneroō*, translated "appear" in v. 10. **5:12** *Glory*: i.e., "boast," whenever "glory" is used as a verb. *Them which . . . heart*: this reference to Paul's opponents echoes 1 Sam 16:7. **5:13** *Be beside . . . God*: possibly a reference to some form of religious ecstasy;

¹⁶Wherefore henceforth know we no man after the flesh: yea, though we have known Christ after the flesh, yet now henceforth know we him no more. ¹⁷Therefore if any man be in Christ, he is a new creature: old things are passed away; behold, all things are become new. ¹⁸And all things are of God, who hath reconciled us to himself by Jesus Christ, and hath given to us the ministry of reconciliation; ¹⁹to wit, that God was in Christ, reconciling the world unto himself, not imputing their trespasses unto them; and hath committed unto us the word of reconciliation. ²⁰Now then we are ambassadors for Christ, as though God did beseech you by us: we pray you in Christ's stead, be ye reconciled to God. ²¹For he hath made him to be sin for us, who knew no sin; that we might be made the righteousness of God in him.

6 We then, as workers together with him, beseech you also that ye receive not the grace of God in vain. ²(For he saith, I have heard thee in a time accepted, and in the day of salvation have I succoured thee: behold, now is the accepted time; behold, now is the day of salvation.) ³Giving no offence in any thing, that the ministry be not blamed: ⁴but in all things approving ourselves as the ministers of God, in much patience, in afflictions, in necessities, in distresses, ⁵in stripes, in imprisonments, in tumults, in labours, in watchings, in fastings; ⁶by pureness, by knowledge, by longsuffering, by kindness, by the Holy Ghost, by love unfeigned, ⁷by the word of truth, by the power of God, by the armour of righteousness on the right hand and on the left, ⁸by honour and dishonour, by evil report and good report: as deceivers, and yet true; ⁹as unknown, and yet well known; as dying, and, behold, we live; as chastened, and not killed; ¹⁰as sorrowful, yet alway rejoicing; as poor, yet making many rich; as having nothing, and yet possessing all things.

¹¹O ye Corinthians, our mouth is open unto you, our heart is enlarged. ¹²Ye are not straitened in us, but ye are straitened in your own bowels. ¹³Now for a recompence in the same, (I speak as unto my children,) be ye also enlarged.

---

cf. 1 Cor 14. **5:17** *He is . . . creature*: the Greek provides an interjection that is better rendered "a new creature!" or "a new creation!"; cf. Isa 43:18–19; 65:17; 66:22. *Behold, all . . . new*: better "Behold, new things have come" (MS tradition). **5:18** *Ministry of reconciliation*: in opposition to the ministry of death and condemnation (3:7, 9). **5:21** *For he . . . in him*: describing Christ's identification with sinful humanity, which allows humanity to be made divinely righteous; cf. Rom 8:3–4.
  6:1–7:4 Appeals to the Corinthians. Having defended his ministry in 2:14–5:21, Paul now pleads with his readers to embrace him as a sincere servant of God (6:1–13; 7:2–4). Embedded within this appeal is a series of commands urging the Corinthians to separate themselves from pagan society (6:14–7:1). **6:1–10** *We then . . . things*: a single sentence in Greek, with vv. 3–10 modifying "we" (v. 1) and v. 2 serving as a parenthetical interjection. **6:2** *I have . . . succoured thee*: Isa 49:8. **6:4** *Necessities*: constraints or pressures. **6:5** *Tumults*: riots. *Watchings*: vigils. **6:7** *By the armour . . . left*: although KJV switches prepositions at the beginning of v. 6, the Greek begins using "by" only at this point. For the imagery of armor, see Rom 13:12 note. **6:8** *As*: the prepositional change from "by" to "as" suggests that these dichotomies constitute the *evil* and *good* reports: i.e., "we are reported as." **6:8, 9** *Yet*: added by KJV (twice). **6:9** *As chastened . . . killed*: echoing Ps 118:18. **6:10** *Possessing all things*: recalling the Corinthian slogan quoted at 1 Cor 3:21–22 (see note). **6:11** *Our mouth is open*: a biblical idiom emphasizing the importance of the words spoken; cf. Job 3:1; Sir 51:25. **6:12** *Straitened*: the Greek verb ("constricted") and its cognate noun are translated "distress" in 4:8 and 6:4. *Bowels*: entrails; a seat of affection, like "heart" (v. 11; 7:3). **6:13** *Be ye also enlarged*: i.e., "in your

¹⁴Be ye not unequally yoked together with unbelievers: for what fellowship hath righteousness with unrighteousness? and what communion hath light with darkness? ¹⁵And what concord hath Christ with Belial? or what part hath he that believeth with an infidel? ¹⁶And what agreement hath the temple of God with idols? for ye are the temple of the living God; as God hath said, I will dwell in them, and walk in them; and I will be their God, and they shall be my people. ¹⁷Wherefore come out from among them, and be ye separate, saith the Lord, and touch not the unclean thing; and I will receive you, ¹⁸and will be a Father unto you and ye shall be my sons and daughters, saith the Lord Almighty. ¹Having therefore 7 these promises, dearly beloved, let us cleanse ourselves from all filthiness of the flesh and spirit, perfecting holiness in the fear of God.

²Receive us; we have wronged no man, we have corrupted no man, we have defrauded no man. ³I speak not this to condemn you: for I have said before, that ye are in our hearts to die and live with you. ⁴Great is my boldness of speech toward you, great is my glorying of you: I am filled with comfort, I am exceeding joyful in all our tribulation.

⁵For, when we were come into Macedonia, our flesh had no rest, but we were troubled on every side; without were fightings, within were fears. ⁶Nevertheless God, that comforteth those that are cast down, comforted us by the coming of Titus; ⁷and not by his coming only, but by the consolation wherewith he was comforted in you, when he told us your earnest desire, your mourning, your fervent mind toward me; so that I rejoiced the more.

⁸For though I made you sorry with a letter, I do not repent, though I did repent: for I perceive that the same epistle hath made you sorry, though it were but for a season. ⁹Now I rejoice, not that ye were made sorry, but that ye sorrowed to repentance: for ye were made sorry after a godly manner, that ye might receive damage

---

hearts" (cf. v. 11). **6:14–7:1** *Be ye . . . God*: this series of commands interrupts the general appeal initiated at 6:1 and resuming at 7:2. Some scholars believe it interpolates material from yet another Pauline letter, perhaps the one mentioned in 1 Cor 5:9, whose call for separation from "the world" Paul must clarify and limit in 1 Cor 5:10–13. **6:14** *Unequally yoked*: LXX Lev 19:19 uses a related Greek word in a prohibition of cross-breeding livestock. Some therefore argue that Paul refers to marriage, but nothing in the present context invites such a narrow reading. **6:15** *Belial*: a transliterated Hebrew word used in the common biblical idiom "son of Belial." It denotes wickedness (Deut 13:13; Judg 19:22; etc.) and became a title for Satan in later Jewish literature. **6:16** *Ye are . . . living God*: cf. 1 Cor 3:16. *Ye*: better "we" (MS tradition). *I will . . . people*: Lev 26:12; Ezek 37:27. **6:17** *Wherefore come . . . you*: cf. Isa 52:11. **6:18** *And will be . . . Almighty*: invoking the language of God's covenant with David in 2 Sam 7:14. **7:2** *Receive us*: lit. "make room for us," resuming the plea of 6:13. **7:3–4** *I speak . . . tribulation*: these verses recall the themes with which 2 Corinthians opens, including comfort in the midst of affliction (1:1–11) and Paul's anxiety about conflict with the Corinthians (1:15–2:11). They serve as a transition to the resumption of the discourse broken off at 2:13.

7:5–16 Returning to earlier matters: the Corinthians' response to Paul's "letter of tears." **7:5** *For, when . . . Macedonia*: see 2:13. It is not clear to what trouble Paul refers, unless it is simply to anxious distress about the Corinthians' impending response to his "letter of tears." **7:8** *Made you sorry*: Gk. *lypeō* (or its cognate noun), twice in this verse and throughout vv. 9–11 ("sorry"/"sorrow"); see 2:1 note. *With a letter*: the "letter of tears" mentioned in 2:4. Paul suggests that the Corinthians' response to it amounted to repentance and reconciliation with him, but his defensive posture (2:17; 3:1; 4:2; 6:3; 7:2) presupposes active conflict, suggesting either that 2:14–7:4 was interpolated into 2

by us in nothing. [10]For godly sorrow worketh repentance to salvation not to be repented of: but the sorrow of the world worketh death. [11]For behold this selfsame thing, that ye sorrowed after a godly sort, what carefulness it wrought in you, yea, what clearing of yourselves, yea, what indignation, yea, what fear, yea, what vehement desire, yea, what zeal, yea, what revenge! In all things ye have approved yourselves to be clear in this matter.

[12]Wherefore, though I wrote unto you, I did it not for his cause that had done the wrong, nor for his cause that suffered wrong, but that our care for you in the sight of God might appear unto you. [13]Therefore we were comforted in your comfort: yea, and exceedingly the more joyed we for the joy of Titus, because his spirit was refreshed by you all. [14]For if I have boasted any thing to him of you, I am not ashamed; but as we spake all things to you in truth, even so our boasting, which I made before Titus, is found a truth. [15]And his inward affection is more abundant toward you, whilst he remembereth the obedience of you all, how with fear and trembling ye received him. [16]I rejoice therefore that I have confidence in you in all things.

8 Moreover, brethren, we do you to wit of the grace of God bestowed on the churches of Macedonia; [2]how that in a great trial of affliction the abundance of their joy and their deep poverty abounded unto the riches of their liberality. [3]For to their power, I bear record, yea, and beyond their power they were willing of themselves; [4]praying us with much intreaty that we would receive the gift, and take upon us the fellowship of the ministering to the saints. [5]And this they did, not as we hoped, but first gave their own selves to the Lord, and unto us by the will of God. [6]Insomuch that we desired Titus, that as he had begun, so he would also finish in you the same grace also. [7]Therefore, as ye abound in every thing, in faith, and utterance, and knowledge, and in all diligence, and in your love to us, see that ye abound in this grace also.

Corinthians (see note to 2:12–13) or that Paul now exaggerates the rapprochement for rhetorical effect.   **7:10** *Not to be repented of*: to be taken as modifying *repentance* in order to create an oxymoron: "repentance unrepented" or, perhaps better, "regrets unregretted" (because they bring about salvation).   **7:12** *For his cause that had done the wrong*: see 2:5–11. *Our care for you*: better "your devotion to us" (MS tradition; our translation).   **7:13** *Therefore we . . . we*: better "therefore we were comforted, and in our comfort we rejoiced exceedingly more" (MS tradition).   **7:15** *Inward affection*: the same Greek word was rendered "bowels" at 6:12 (see note).

8:1–9:15 Appeal for a contribution to the Jerusalem offering. Seizing the opportunity of their renewed profession of obedience, Paul urges the Corinthians (or the Corinthians in chap. 8 and other Achaian believers in chap. 9; see introduction) to contribute to his collection for the Jerusalem church, a project he mentions repeatedly in his letters (Rom 15:25–28; 1 Cor 16:1–4; cf. Gal 2:10 and note).   **8:1** *We do . . . wit of*: we make known to you.   **8:2** *Affliction*: Paul mentions Macedonian believers' affliction at Phil 1:29–30; 1 Thess 1:6; 2:14; 3:3–4; cf. Acts 16:11–17:15.   **8:3** *Power*: ability.   **8:4** *That we . . . saints*: better "for the favor and fellowship of this ministry to the saints" (MS tradition; our translation).   **8:6** *Grace*: Gk. *charis*, also "gift"; Paul uses the same word for the Corinthians' privilege of giving ("favor," v. 4; see note), for what they will give (vv. 6, 7, 19), for Christ's and God's gifts to them and other believers (8:1, 9; 9:8, 14), and for believers' gratitude to God for those gifts ("thanks," 8:16; 9:15). This verse assumes that Titus discussed the offering with the Corinthians during his recent visit, when he also delivered the "letter of tears" (see note to 2:12–13).   **8:7** *Your love to us*: better "our

[8]I speak not by commandment, but by occasion of the forwardness of others, and to prove the sincerity of your love. [9]For ye know the grace of our Lord Jesus Christ, that, though he was rich, yet for your sakes he became poor, that ye through his poverty might be rich. [10]And herein I give my advice: for this is expedient for you, who have begun before, not only to do, but also to be forward a year ago. [11]Now therefore perform the doing of it; that as there was a readiness to will, so there may be a performance also out of that which ye have. [12]For if there be first a willing mind, it is accepted according to that a man hath, and not according to that he hath not. [13]For I mean not that other men be eased, and ye burdened: [14]but by an equality, that now at this time your abundance may be a supply for their want, that their abundance also may be a supply for your want: that there may be equality: [15]as it is written, He that had gathered much had nothing over; and he that had gathered little had no lack.

[16]But thanks be to God, which put the same earnest care into the heart of Titus for you. [17]For indeed he accepted the exhortation; but being more forward, of his own accord he went unto you. [18]And we have sent with him the brother, whose praise is in the gospel throughout all the churches; [19]and not that only, but who was also chosen of the churches to travel with us with this grace, which is administered by us to the glory of the same Lord, and declaration of your ready mind: [20]avoiding this, that no man should blame us in this abundance which is administered by us: [21]providing for honest things, not only in the sight of the Lord, but also in the sight of men. [22]And we have sent with them our brother, whom we have oftentimes proved diligent in many things, but now much more diligent, upon the great confidence which I have in you. [23]Whether any do inquire of Titus, he is my partner and fellowhelper concerning you: or our brethren be inquired of, they are the messengers of the churches, and the glory of Christ. [24]Wherefore shew ye to them, and before the churches, the proof of your love, and of our boasting on your behalf.

9 For as touching the ministering to the saints, it is superfluous for me to write to you: [2]for I know the forwardness of your mind, for which I boast of you to them of Macedonia, that Achaia was ready a year ago; and your zeal hath provoked very many. [3]Yet have I sent the brethren, lest our boasting of you should be in vain in this behalf; that, as I said, ye may be ready: [4]lest haply if they of Macedonia come with me, and find you unprepared, we (that we say not, ye) should be ashamed in this same confident boasting. [5]Therefore I thought it necessary to exhort the brethren, that they would go before unto you, and make up before-

---

love to you" (MS tradition).   **8:9** *Our Lord . . . be rich*: cf. 5:21.   **8:10** *Who have begun . . . ago*: who have begun a year ago not only to do, but also to be willing.   **8:11** *Perform*: complete.   **8:15** *He that . . . lack*: Exod 16:18.   **8:17** *Being more forward*: better "having even more earnest care." The Greek adjective shares a root with "earnest care" in v. 16 and the same word is translated "diligent" (e.g., v. 22).   **8:18** *The brother*: identity unknown.   **8:19** *Grace*: i.e., "gift" (see v. 6 note), a reference to the collection. *Your*: better "our" (MS tradition).   **8:21** *Honest things . . . men*: see Rom 12:17 and note.   **8:22** *Our brother*: another unidentified believer.   **8:23** *Whether any . . . Christ*: Paul vouches for Titus and the two unnamed believers, apparently in order to guarantee the safety of the monetary gift (vv. 20–21) to be entrusted them by the Corinthians (v. 24); see 12:16 note. *Messengers*: lit. "apostles"; see Rom 1:1 note.   **9:2** *Forwardness*: readiness.

hand your bounty, whereof ye had notice before, that the same might be ready, as a matter of bounty, and not as of covetousness.

6But this I say, He which soweth sparingly shall reap also sparingly; and he which soweth bountifully shall reap also bountifully. 7Every man according as he purposeth in his heart, so let him give; not grudgingly, or of necessity: for God loveth a cheerful giver. 8And God is able to make all grace abound toward you; that ye, always having all sufficiency in all things, may abound to every good work: 9(as it is written, He hath dispersed abroad; he hath given to the poor: his righteousness remaineth for ever. 10Now he that ministereth seed to the sower both minister bread for your food, and multiply your seed sown, and increase the fruits of your righteousness;) 11being enriched in every thing to all bountifulness, which causeth through us thanksgiving to God. 12For the administration of this service not only supplieth the want of the saints, but is abundant also by many thanksgivings unto God; 13whiles by the experiment of this ministration they glorify God for your professed subjection unto the gospel of Christ, and for your liberal distribution unto them, and unto all men; 14and by their prayer for you, which long after you for the exceeding grace of God in you. 15Thanks be unto God for his unspeakable gift.

10 Now I Paul myself beseech you by the meekness and gentleness of Christ, who in presence am base among you, but being absent am bold toward you: 2but I beseech you, that I may not be bold when I am present with that

9:5 *Bounty, whereof . . . before*: better "blessing which was promised beforehand"—that is, the gift they had supposedly pledged during Titus's earlier trip.   9:7 *God loveth . . . giver*: LXX Prov 22:8; cf. Sir 35:9.   9:8 *All grace*: or "every gift."   9:9 *He hath dispersed . . . ever*: Ps 112:9.   9:10 *Now he . . . righteousness*: cf. Isa 55:10–11. *Minister . . . multiply . . . increase*: these three verbs should be in the future tense (MS tradition).   9:11 *Being*: i.e., "you all being." *Enriched . . . all bountifulness*: see 6:10 and note. *Bountifulness*: liberality.   9:13 *Experiment*: proof, testing.

10:1–13:10 Paul vs. the false apostles. This section features Paul's vehement response to the criticism of those at Corinth whom he calls "false apostles" (11:13), rival itinerant missionaries who have gained influence in his absence and, he believes, maligned him. Its strongly defensive tone, especially evident in Paul's paradoxical exultation of his own weakness, comes as a surprise after 7:5–9:15, where his reconciliation with the Corinthian community seemed assured (e.g., contrast 7:9–11 and 12:20–21). This alteration has led some to argue that 2 Corinthians' final four chapters constitute a fragment from an earlier letter, perhaps the "letter of tears" mentioned in 2:4, to which 2:14–6:13 or 7:2–4 (or both) might also belong. (Passages such as 12:14–21 and 13:10 would fit especially well in that context.) Clear points of contact between this section and the preceding material, including complementary references to Titus's recent visit (7:6–7, 13–14; 12:17–18) and hints at the Corinthians' suspicion that Paul and his crew plan to embezzle the offering they are collecting (8:20–23; 12:14–18), may make a rhetorical explanation for the change of tone as appealing as a redactional one, but scholars holding to the theory that the present section comes from Paul's letter of tears and the previous one from Paul's later letter of reconciliation have a compelling case. They suggest that the passionate appeal recorded here had resolved the Corinthians' suspicions about Paul's collection and therefore made possible the requests for donations that chaps. 8–9 preserve. If this section alone excerpts Paul's letter of tears and 2:14–6:13 and 7:2–4 comes from Paul's so-called first apology, an earlier letter he wrote to the Corinthians and sent by way of Titus just before his second painful visit there (see note to 2:12–13), then the repeated statements about Titus's recent visit to Corinth would refer to a trip on which Titus delivered Paul's first apology, not the one on which he delivered the letter of tears.

confidence, wherewith I think to be bold against some, which think of us as if we walked according to the flesh. ³For though we walk in the flesh, we do not war after the flesh: ⁴(for the weapons of our warfare are not carnal, but mighty through God to the pulling down of strong holds;) ⁵casting down imaginations, and every high thing that exalteth itself against the knowledge of God, and bringing into captivity every thought to the obedience of Christ; ⁶and having in a readiness to revenge all disobedience, when your obedience is fulfilled.

⁷Do ye look on things after the outward appearance? If any man trust to himself that he is Christ's, let him of himself think this again, that, as he is Christ's, even so are we Christ's. ⁸For though I should boast somewhat more of our authority, which the Lord hath given us for edification, and not for your destruction, I should not be ashamed: ⁹that I may not seem as if I would terrify you by letters. ¹⁰For his letters, say they, are weighty and powerful; but his bodily presence is weak, and his speech contemptible. ¹¹Let such an one think this, that, such as we are in word by letters when we are absent, such will we be also in deed when we are present.

¹²For we dare not make ourselves of the number, or compare ourselves with some that commend themselves: but they measuring themselves by themselves, and comparing themselves among themselves, are not wise. ¹³But we will not boast of things without our measure, but according to the measure of the rule which God hath distributed to us, a measure to reach even unto you. ¹⁴For we stretch not ourselves beyond our measure, as though we reached not unto you: for we are come as far as to you also in preaching the gospel of Christ: ¹⁵not boasting of things without our measure, that is, of other men's labours; but having hope, when your faith is increased, that we shall be enlarged by you according to our rule abundantly, ¹⁶to preach the gospel in the regions beyond you, and not to boast in another man's line of things made ready to our hand. ¹⁷But he that glorieth, let him glory in the Lord. ¹⁸For not he that commendeth himself is approved, but whom the Lord commendeth.

11 Would to God ye could bear with me a little in my folly: and indeed bear with me. ²For I am jealous over you with godly jealousy: for I have espoused you to one husband, that I may present you as a chaste virgin to Christ. ³But I fear, lest by any means, as the serpent beguiled Eve through his subtilty, so your minds should be corrupted from the simplicity that is in Christ. ⁴For if he that cometh

---

10:4 *Weapons*: Gk. *hopla*; cf. 6:7 (KJV "armour"). **10:5** *Imaginations*: the nominal form of the Greek word rendered "think" (vv. 2, 7, 11). **10:8** *Destruction*: the same Greek noun as "pulling down" (cf. v. 4), cognate with "casting down" (v. 5). **10:9** *That I . . . letters*: this clause's relationship with the previous verse is unclear. There may be no syntactical relationship at all, as it is possible to understand an elided "I say this" (in contrast with what "say they" in v. 10) to introduce it. **10:10** *His speech contemptible*: cf. 1 Cor 1:17–3:4. **10:13** *Without our measure*: better "beyond our measure" (also in v. 15). *Rule*: Gk. *kanōn*, which refers both to a standard of measurement and to a measured span (also in v. 15); cf. v. 16 (KJV "line"). **10:15–16** *Having hope . . . you*: Paul hopes the Corinthians will support his ministry. **10:17** *He that . . . Lord*: adapted from Jer 9:24; cf. 1 Cor 1:31. **11:2** *With godly jealousy*: or "with God's jealousy"; cf. Exod 20:5; Deut 4:24; etc. *I have espoused . . . husband*: cf. Hos 2:19–20. **11:3** *The serpent . . . subtilty*: cf. Gen 3:1–6, 13; the context of Paul's argument suggests that he equates Eve's transgression with adultery. Ancient Jewish interpretive traditions sexualized her sin, transforming the serpent of Genesis into a satanic seducer. *Simplicity that is in Christ*: better "sincere and pure devotion to Christ" (MS tradition; NRSV).

preacheth another Jesus, whom we have not preached, or if ye receive another spirit, which ye have not received, or another gospel, which ye have not accepted, ye might well bear with him. [5]For I suppose I was not a whit behind the very chiefest apostles. [6]But though I be rude in speech, yet not in knowledge; but we have been throughly made manifest among you in all things.

[7]Have I committed an offence in abasing myself that ye might be exalted, because I have preached to you the gospel of God freely? [8]I robbed other churches, taking wages of them, to do you service. [9]And when I was present with you, and wanted, I was chargeable to no man: for that which was lacking to me the brethren which came from Macedonia supplied: and in all things I have kept myself from being burdensome unto you, and so will I keep myself. [10]As the truth of Christ is in me, no man shall stop me of this boasting in the regions of Achaia. [11]Wherefore? because I love you not? God knoweth.

[12]But what I do, that I will do, that I may cut off occasion from them which desire occasion; that wherein they glory, they may be found even as we. [13]For such are false apostles, deceitful workers, transforming themselves into the apostles of Christ. [14]And no marvel; for Satan himself is transformed into an angel of light. [15]Therefore it is no great thing if his ministers also be transformed as the ministers of righteousness; whose end shall be according to their works.

[16]I say again, Let no man think me a fool; if otherwise, yet as a fool receive me, that I may boast myself a little. [17]That which I speak, I speak it not after the Lord, but as it were foolishly, in this confidence of boasting. [18]Seeing that many glory after the flesh, I will glory also. [19]For ye suffer fools gladly, seeing ye yourselves are wise. [20]For ye suffer, if a man bring you into bondage, if a man devour you, if a man take of you, if a man exalt himself, if a man smite you on the face. [21]I speak as concerning reproach, as though we had been weak.

Howbeit whereinsoever any is bold, (I speak foolishly,) I am bold also. [22]Are they Hebrews? so am I. Are they Israelites? so am I. Are they the seed of Abraham? so am I. [23]Are they ministers of Christ? (I speak as a fool) I am more; in labours more abundant, in stripes above measure, in prisons more frequent, in deaths oft. [24]Of the Jews five times received I forty stripes save one. [25]Thrice was

---

11:4 *Ye might . . . him*: lit. "you bear that well!" Paul's sarcastic praise echoes the frustration of v. 1. **11:5** *The very chiefest apostles*: here, as in 12:11, a sardonic reference to Paul's opponents, the "false apostles" (v. 13). **11:6** *But we . . . things*: better "on the contrary, we have thoroughly made it [i.e., our knowledge] manifest to you in everything" (MS tradition). **11:7–11** *Have I committed . . . knoweth*: Paul defends his practice of refusing support from the communities in which he ministers: cf. 1 Cor 9:1–18; 1 Thess 2:9; 2 Thess 3:7–8. See 12:16 note on a plausible context for this defense. Paul's emphasis on self-support ("abasing myself" [v. 7] probably refers to manual labor), and on the hardships he has suffered (vv. 16–33), reflects an image of the ideal philosopher that circulated in antiquity. (See 1 and 2 Thessalonians introduction.) **11:7** *Freely*: without charge. **11:9** *I was chargeable to*: i.e., "I burdened." **11:14** *Satan himself . . . light*: referring to a Jewish legend preserved in several extrabiblical texts, which equates the serpent of Gen 3 with Satan (cf. v. 3) and has him deceive Eve twice, the second time by assuming the appearance of a glorious angel (see *Life of Adam and Eve* 9.1; *Apocalypse of Moses* 29.12a). **11:19, 20** *Suffer*: the Greek verb was earlier translated "bear" (vv. 1, 4). **11:21** *I speak . . . weak*: Gk. obscure; probably "To my shame, I must say, we were too weak for that!" (i.e., to do the things mentioned in v. 20; RSV). **11:23** *Deaths*: mortally dangerous situations. **11:24** *Forty stripes save one*: following the injunction of Deut 25:1–3, the custom was to stop one short of the number to ensure that the limit of forty lashes was not accidentally transgressed. The frequency

I beaten with rods, once was I stoned, thrice I suffered shipwreck, a night and a day I have been in the deep; ²⁶in journeyings often, in perils of waters, in perils of robbers, in perils by mine own countrymen, in perils by the heathen, in perils in the city, in perils in the wilderness, in perils in the sea, in perils among false brethren; ²⁷in weariness and painfulness, in watchings often, in hunger and thirst, in fastings often, in cold and nakedness. ²⁸Beside those things that are without, that which cometh upon me daily, the care of all the churches. ²⁹Who is weak, and I am not weak? who is offended, and I burn not?

³⁰If I must needs glory, I will glory of the things which concern mine infirmities. ³¹The God and Father of our Lord Jesus Christ, which is blessed for evermore, knoweth that I lie not. ³²In Damascus the governor under Aretas the king kept the city of the Damascenes with a garrison, desirous to apprehend me: ³³and through a window in a basket was I let down by the wall, and escaped his hands.

12 It is not expedient for me doubtless to glory. I will come to visions and revelations of the Lord. ²I knew a man in Christ above fourteen years ago, (whether in the body, I cannot tell; or whether out of the body, I cannot tell: God knoweth;) such an one caught up to the third heaven. ³And I knew such a man, (whether in the body, or out of the body, I cannot tell: God knoweth;) ⁴how that he was caught up into paradise, and heard unspeakable words, which it is not lawful for a man to utter. ⁵Of such an one will I glory: yet of myself I will not glory, but in mine infirmities. ⁶For though I would desire to glory, I shall not be a fool; for I will say the truth: but now I forbear, lest any man should think of me above that which he seeth me to be, or that he heareth of me.

⁷And lest I should be exalted above measure through the abundance of the revelations, there was given to me a thorn in the flesh, the messenger of Satan to

---

with which the Jewish religious authorities disciplined Paul apparently testifies to his continued engagement with the synagogue (cf. Rom 9:1–5), despite what he understood to be his special mission to the Gentiles (Gal 1:16; 2:7–9).   **11:25** *Beaten with rods*: with the rods of a lictor, who attended and protected Roman magistrates; see Acts 16:19–24. *Once was I stoned*: cf. Acts 14:19. *Thrice I suffered shipwreck*: one is recorded in Acts 27:9–44, although it seems to have occurred after 2 Corinthians was composed.   **11:26** *Waters*: lit. "rivers." *The heathen*: Gentiles.   **11:27** *Watchings*: vigils.   **11:28** *Care of*: i.e., "anxiety about."   **11:29** *Weak*: Paul claims low social status; see 1 Cor 1:27 note. *Burn*: probably in the sense of burning with indignation. This verse recalls Paul's defense of the "weak" believers in Corinth (1 Cor 8–14).   **11:30** *Infirmities*: Gk. *astheneiai*, "weaknesses" (cf. 12:5, 9, 10), the cognate noun of "weak" (v. 29).   **11:32–33** *In Damascus . . . hands*: Aretas IV was a client king whom Rome installed in Nabataea, an Arabic kingdom southeast of Judea; he apparently also controlled Damascus for a time. Paul's narrative of cowardly flight reverses the Roman military tradition of presenting the *corona muralis* ("wall crown"; Lat.) to the first soldier who scaled the wall of an enemy city. This inversion makes a fitting conclusion to Paul's list of weaknesses of which he ironically boasts. (In Acts' version of this event, Paul escapes from Jews rather than Gentile authorities; see 9:19b–25.)   **12:1** *It is . . . glory*: better "it is necessary for me to boast, not expedient" (MS tradition).   **12:2** *A man*: presumably Paul himself. *Caught up . . . heaven*: Jewish apocalyptic literature commonly features heavenly journeys. *Third heaven*: the ancient Mediterranean world generally understood the heavens to be divided into a number of embedded spheres.   **12:4** *Into paradise*: Jewish apocalyptic texts often locate paradise in heaven (2 *Baruch* 4.6; cf. 2 *Enoch* 8.1), presumably assuming that after the events narrated in Gen 3 God preserved it there. In any case, Paul's entry into paradise stands in opposition to his representation of the false apostles as the satanic serpent deceiving Eve (11:3, 14) and orchestrating her exclusion from Eden (Gen 3:22–24).   **12:7** *And lest . . . revelations*: better, continuing the sentence begun in v. 6, "because of the revelations' extraordinary character. Therefore" (MS tradition; cf. NJB). *There was . . .*

buffet me, lest I should be exalted above measure. [8]For this thing I besought the Lord thrice, that it might depart from me. [9]And he said unto me, My grace is sufficient for thee: for my strength is made perfect in weakness. Most gladly therefore will I rather glory in my infirmities, that the power of Christ may rest upon me. [10]Therefore I take pleasure in infirmities, in reproaches, in necessities, in persecutions, in distresses for Christ's sake: for when I am weak, then am I strong.

[11]I am become a fool in glorying; ye have compelled me: for I ought to have been commended of you: for in nothing am I behind the very chiefest apostles, though I be nothing. [12]Truly the signs of an apostle were wrought among you in all patience, in signs, and wonders, and mighty deeds. [13]For what is it wherein ye were inferior to other churches, except it be that I myself was not burdensome to you? forgive me this wrong.

[14]Behold, the third time I am ready to come to you; and I will not be burdensome to you: for I seek not yours, but you: for the children ought not to lay up for the parents, but the parents for the children. [15]And I will very gladly spend and be spent for you; though the more abundantly I love you, the less I be loved. [16]But be it so, I did not burden you: nevertheless, being crafty, I caught you with guile. [17]Did I make a gain of you by any of them whom I sent unto you? [18]I desired Titus, and with him I sent a brother. Did Titus make a gain of you? walked we not in the same spirit? walked we not in the same steps?

[19]Again, think ye that we excuse ourselves unto you? we speak before God in Christ: but we do all things, dearly beloved, for your edifying. [20]For I fear, lest, when I come, I shall not find you such as I would, and that I shall be found unto you such as ye would not: lest there be debates, envyings, wraths, strifes, backbitings, whisperings, swellings, tumults: [21]and lest, when I come again, my God will

---

flesh: the so-called divine passive voice suggests that God has given Paul the mysterious satanic *thorn in the flesh* (a physical ailment of some sort?), which explains why God forbids its removal (vv. 8–9). God's collusion with Satan recalls the prologue to Job.   **12:10** *Necessities*: see 6:4 note. **12:11** *I ought . . . you*: cf. 3:1–3.   **12:13** *Except it . . . wrong*: cf. 11:7–11.   **12:14** *The third . . . come to you*: Paul founded the church at Corinth during this first visit. A second, painful visit (alluded to at 1:15 and 2:1), made to resolve the growing tension between him and the church he had founded, did not lead to rapprochement. Here Paul looks forward to visiting yet again. If 10:1–13:10 comes from the letter of tears (see note to 10:1–13:10), it is far from clear what sort of reception he would expect to meet (see 12:15); if it does not, then Paul must allude to the trip anticipated at 9:3–5, on which he would personally gather the offering collected from the Corinthians by Titus and the two unnamed brothers. **12:16** *Being crafty . . . guile*: Paul repeats a charge that assimilates him to the satanic serpent to which he likened his opponents (cf. 11:3–4, 14–15). Embedded within a defense of his and his partners' refusal to seek financial support from the Corinthians (vv. 13–18), this allegation may suggest that Paul was being accused of perpetrating a con: he made a show of refusing a stipend in order to gain the church's confidence and then collect a large offering (8:1–9:15)—purportedly for the believers in Jerusalem (cf. 1 Cor 16:3), but really for his and his cronies' pockets.   **12:18** *I desired Titus*: better "I encouraged Titus" (i.e., to visit you). Paul refers to this visit in 7:6–7, 13–14 (cf. 2:13); it differs from the one mentioned in 8:16–24. (If chaps. 10–13 are understood to be from Paul's letter of tears, then we must hypothesize yet another visit of Titus to Corinth on Paul's behalf.) *A brother*: identity unknown. **12:19** *Again*: better "all this time" (MS tradition). *We excuse*: Gk. *apologoumetha*; see 1 Cor 9:3 note. **12:20** *I fear*: introducing five object clauses: *lest, when I come*; *that I shall be found*; *lest there be*; "*lest, when I come again*" (v. 21); and "*that I shall bewail*" (v. 21). *Swellings*: i.e., with pride.

humble me among you, and that I shall bewail many which have sinned already, and have not repented of the uncleanness and fornication and lasciviousness which they have committed.

13 This is the third time I am coming to you. In the mouth of two or three witnesses shall every word be established. ²I told you before, and foretell you, as if I were present, the second time; and being absent now I write to them which heretofore have sinned, and to all other, that, if I come again, I will not spare: ³since ye seek a proof of Christ speaking in me, which to you-ward is not weak, but is mighty in you. ⁴For though he was crucified through weakness, yet he liveth by the power of God. For we also are weak in him, but we shall live with him by the power of God toward you.

⁵Examine yourselves, whether ye be in the faith; prove your own selves. Know ye not your own selves, how that Jesus Christ is in you, except ye be reprobates? ⁶But I trust that ye shall know that we are not reprobates. ⁷Now I pray to God that ye do no evil; not that we should appear approved, but that ye should do that which is honest, though we be as reprobates. ⁸For we can do nothing against the truth, but for the truth. ⁹For we are glad, when we are weak, and ye are strong: and this also we wish, even your perfection. ¹⁰Therefore I write these things being absent, lest being present I should use sharpness, according to the power which the Lord hath given me to edification, and not to destruction.

¹¹Finally, brethren, farewell. Be perfect, be of good comfort, be of one mind, live in peace; and the God of love and peace shall be with you. ¹²Greet one another with an holy kiss. ¹³All the saints salute you.

¹⁴The grace of the Lord Jesus Christ, and the love of God, and the communion of the Holy Ghost, be with you all. Amen.

The second epistle to the Corinthians was written from Philippi, a city of Macedonia, by Titus and Lucas.

12:21 *Fornication*: Gk. *porneia*, a generic term for sexual transgression.   **13:1** *In the mouth . . . established*: adapting Deut 19:15, on which Jesus draws in order to lay out a procedure for dealing with accusations between members of the church (Matt 18:16). Paul may be alluding to such a procedure, which he expects will vindicate him.   **13:3** *Which to you-ward*: who toward you.   **13:5** *Reprobates*: Gk. *adokimoi*, those who have been tested and found wanting; cf. *prove* (*dokimazō*) and "approved" (*dokimoi*, v. 7).   **13:7** *I*: better "we" (MS tradition).   **13:10** *Edification, and . . . destruction*: cf. 10:8 and note.

13:11–14 Closing. 13:11 *Be of good comfort*: cf. 1:3 and note.   **13:12** *Holy kiss*: see Rom 16:16 note.   **13:14** *The grace . . . all*: a Trinitarian formula analogous to 1 Cor 12:4–6; cf. Matt 28:19. *Amen. The second epistle . . . Lucas*: better omitted (MS tradition).

The Epistle of Paul the Apostle
to the Galatians

READERS of Galatians often mistakenly assume that it opposes the Christian gospel to the Jewish Torah. The second-century Christian teacher Marcion, for instance, placed it first in his collection of Paul's epistles, presenting it as the preeminent expression of what he believed to be a Pauline antithesis between god and God, the justice-obsessed creator who promulgated the Jewish law and the redeemer God revealed in Jesus, completely alien to the corrupt cosmic order. During the Reformation, Martin Luther saw in the allegory of two covenants from Gal 4:21–5:11 an antithesis between the New Testament and Old, equating the "Jerusalem which is above" with the church and associating "the Jerusalem which now is" with the "ornaments, temples, and ceremonies" legislated by the Jewish Torah (*Commentary on the Epistle to the Galatians*, at 4:25).

Although Luther's interpretation is perhaps more familiar to modern readers of Paul than Marcion's, it appears hardly less bizarre when Galatians is read within its own cultural and historical context. The letter's date is largely speculative, but most scholars believe that it was written during the early or middle 50s C.E. "Galatia" in the address probably refers to the region surrounding the city of Ancyra (modern Ankara) in Asia Minor, which Celts (Gk. *Galloi*; Latin *Galli*) had settled in the early third century B.C.E. Alternatively, "Galatia" may refer to the eponymous Roman province established by Augustus in the late first century B.C.E., which encompassed but expanded beyond that narrow geographical area. In either case, Paul's letter assumes that the churches he addresses (and likely founded) consist primarily of Hellenized Gentile converts to Christ, and the epistle proposes to settle an issue of special relevance to Gentile believers: must pagans who have turned away from "idols" and begun to worship YHWH, "the living and true God" (1 Thess 1:9), be circumcised and obey the Jewish law (5:2–12; cf. Acts 15)? In Galatians, Paul answers this question in the negative, refuting rival missionaries who have urged his Gentile converts to complete their conversion with circumcision, as well as rebuking the Galatians themselves for having entertained such an idea.

Paul's polemic is heated, and at times even ugly (see 5:12), but it is not directed at Jews, Judaism, or even really the law (despite the disparaging view of the law put forth in Gal 3:19–26, which Romans later clarifies and revises). It rather addresses Jesus-believers who preach a gospel that differs from Paul's own on the crucial issue of Gentile circumcision. Paul believes that Christ's act of redemption marks the beginning of the end time (Gal 1:4), and he is convinced that Gentile circumcision and law observance represent a dangerous denial of the radically new thing God is now doing through Christ: "neither is circumcision anything, nor uncircumcision, but a new creature" (Gal 6:15). Yet Paul, master dialectician that he is, does not view this innovation as really new: instead, it fulfills God's ancient covenant with Abraham, in whose story he finds God's promise that Gentiles will be blessed and declaration that Abraham is righteous, without reference to the law (3:6–8). For Paul, it is the Mosaic law that is new, inasmuch as it supplements an original Abrahamic covenant (3:17–18). To insist, as Luther did, that Galatians opposes a Christian "new covenant" to a Jewish "old" one closes off the complexity of Paul's argument, which presents the "faith of Christ" not as superseding the Mosaic law, but rather as fulfilling God's foundational covenant with Abraham, the father of Jews and of Gentile believers alike, according to Paul's reading of Genesis (Gal 3:7, 29).

One could argue that Galatians is not sufficiently nuanced to support the complex dialectical position that Paul stakes out. Paul might have agreed, for when he revisits in Romans some of the issues he here raises, his treatment of them is more subtle and sophisticated: he clarifies his awkward use of the Abraham story to support his opposition to Gentile circumcision (Rom 4; cf. Gal 3:15–18 note); he is careful to avoid denying the law's divine origins even as he limits its relevance (Rom 7:7–13; cf. Gal 3:19–26); he deftly closes off any notion that the church has replaced Israel as Abraham's descendents and God's chosen people (Rom 9–11; cf. Gal 4:25; 6:16). But though it may not represent the most finely tuned expression of Paul's theology, Galatians more than makes up for this shortcoming in the insight it offers into the fierce internecine struggles that characterized the early church and into Paul's own understanding of the prophetic role he was to play within this often divided community. Paul's mission to the Gentiles and its defense demanded, he understood, complex theological argumentation, which Galatians begins to present, but which come into full fruition later, in the Epistle to the Romans.

J. Louis Martyn's Anchor Bible commentary, *Galatians: A New Translation with Introduction and Commentary* (New York: Doubleday, 1997), is a valuable resource, as is Hans Dieter Betz's older commentary in the Hermeneia series, *Galatians: A Commentary on Paul's Letter to the Churches in Galatia* (Philadelphia: Fortress, 1979). Also outstanding is Richard Hays's commentary included in volume 11 of *The New Interpreter's Bible* (Nashville, TN: Abingdon Press, 2000), pp. 183–348. Hays's work is accessible but sophisticated, engaged with relevant contemporary research, and thoroughly persuasive. Its influence especially pervades this introduction and the annotations that follow.

THE EPISTLE OF PAUL
THE APOSTLE TO THE
GALATIANS

1 Paul, an apostle, (not of men, neither by man, but by Jesus Christ, and God the Father, who raised him from the dead;) [2]and all the brethren which are with me, unto the churches of Galatia: [3]Grace be to you and peace from God the Father, and from our Lord Jesus Christ, [4]who gave himself for our sins, that he might deliver us from this present evil world, according to the will of God and our Father: [5]to whom be glory for ever and ever. Amen.

[6]I marvel that ye are so soon removed from him that called you into the grace of Christ unto another gospel: [7]which is not another; but there be some that trouble you, and would pervert the gospel of Christ. [8]But though we, or an angel from heaven, preach any other gospel unto you than that which we have preached unto you, let him be accursed. [9]As we said before, so say I now again, If any man preach any other gospel unto you than that ye have received, let him be accursed.

[10]For do I now persuade men, or God? or do I seek to please men? for if I yet pleased men, I should not be the servant of Christ. [11]But I certify you, brethren, that the gospel which was preached of me is not after man. [12]For I neither received it of man, neither was I taught it, but by the revelation of Jesus Christ.

[13]For ye have heard of my conversation in time past in the Jews' religion, how

---

1:1–5 Salutation. On the openings of Paul's letters, see note to Rom 1:1–15. Galatians' differs from other salutations in that it includes a polemical definition of Paul's apostleship (v. 1), supplements his typical blessing of grace and peace with a confessional statement (vv. 3, 4), and omits a thanksgiving. **1:1** *Apostle*: see Rom 1:1 note. *God the father*: the phrase appears thrice in vv. 1–4 (with slight variation), forecasting Paul's argument that believers are God's children (cf. 3:26–4:11). **1:2** *Brethren*: a common self-designation of Jesus-believers. *Churches*: see Rom 16:5 note. **1:3** *Grace be . . . peace*: see Rom 1:7 note. **1:4** *World*: lit. "age," with the eschatological consummation expected.

1:6–9 The Galatians' apostasy. Instead of the conventional thanksgiving, Paul immediately reproaches his readers for heeding Jesus-believing missionaries who preach a gospel he considers perverse. **1:6** *Removed*: the Greek word can refer to transferring allegiance between philosophical schools. *Grace*: "favor" or "gift." *Gospel*: see Mark 1:1 note. **1:7** *Which is not another*: i.e., "which is really no gospel at all" (NIV). *Trouble*: cf. 5:10, 12; 6:17; Acts 15:24.

1:10–24 Apology, part 1: Paul's prophetic call. For a different version, see Acts 9:1–31. **1:10** *Servant*: lit. "slave" (see Rom 1:1 note). **1:13** *Conversation*: "way of life" or "behavior." *The Jews' religion*: Gk. *Ioudaismos*, which does not refer exclusively to a set of "religious" beliefs and practices.

that beyond measure I persecuted the church of God, and wasted it: [14]and profited in the Jews' religion above many my equals in mine own nation, being more exceedingly zealous of the traditions of my fathers. [15]But when it pleased God, who separated me from my mother's womb, and called me by his grace, [16]to reveal his Son in me, that I might preach him among the heathen; immediately I conferred not with flesh and blood: [17]neither went I up to Jerusalem to them which were apostles before me; but I went into Arabia, and returned again unto Damascus.

[18]Then after three years I went up to Jerusalem to see Peter, and abode with him fifteen days. [19]But other of the apostles saw I none, save James the Lord's brother. [20]Now the things which I write unto you, behold, before God, I lie not. [21]Afterwards I came into the regions of Syria and Cilicia; [22]and was unknown by face unto the churches of Judæa which were in Christ: [23]but they had heard only, That he which persecuted us in times past now preacheth the faith which once he destroyed. [24]And they glorified God in me.

2 Then fourteen years after I went up again to Jerusalem with Barnabas, and took Titus with me also. [2]And I went up by revelation, and communicated unto them that gospel which I preach among the Gentiles, but privately to them which were of reputation, lest by any means I should run, or had run, in vain. [3]But neither Titus, who was with me, being a Greek, was compelled to be circumcised: [4]and that because of false brethren unawares brought in, who came in privily to spy out our liberty which we have in Christ Jesus, that they might bring

---

Nor does Paul conceive of Judaism as a way of life belonging to others (cf. 2:15). He rather contrasts his present way of life as a Jew committed to Christ with his earlier life as one who persecuted the church (cf. Phil 3:5–9). *Persecuted the church*: unlike Acts (6:8–14; 7:58–8:3), Paul never specifies what such persecution entailed or why he carried it out, but the adjective "zealous" (v. 14) is often used in biblical narratives of pious violence aimed at maintaining Israel's ethnic and cultural distinctiveness (cf. Num 25:6–18; Sir 48:1–3, referring to 1 Kgs 18:38–40; 1 Macc 2:15–28). Paul thus may have persecuted the church for reasons similar to those motivating the rival missionaries to encourage Gentile believers to be circumcised.   **1:14** *Profited*: advanced. *Equals*: lit. "equals in age." *Traditions*: lit. "what has been handed down," in contrast to Paul's unmediated access to the gospel of Christ. Tradition was particularly important to the Pharisaic school of Judaism to which Paul had belonged; see Mark 2:16 note.   **1:15** *Who separated . . . womb*: by echoing Isa 49:1–6 and Jer 1:4–5, Paul presents his experience as a prophetic call to preach to Gentiles (rather than as a conversion).   **1:16** *The heathen*: "Gentiles" (so throughout).   **1:17** *Damascus*: northeast of Judea, in Syria. On Paul's time there, see 2 Cor 11:32–33.   **1:19** *James*: cf. Mark 6:3; he became a leader of the Jerusalem church (cf. Acts 12:17). **1:21** *Syria*: in which lay Antioch (cf. 2:1 note, 11). *Cilicia*: a region northwest of Syria.

2:1–10 Apology, part 2: Paul's second visit to Jerusalem. For a different version, see Acts 15:1–29.   **2:1** *Barnabas*: a co-leader of the Antioch church with Paul; see Acts 11:22–26. *Titus*: cf. 2 Cor 2:13; 7:6; 8:3–7, 16–24.   **2:2** *By revelation*: in response to a revelation. *But privately . . . reputation*: in contrast to the formal public conference that Acts 15 narrates. *Lest by any means . . . vain*: a driving conviction of Paul's mission—probably based on OT passages such as Isa 49:1–6; Zech 8:23; etc.—is that God's eschatological kingdom unites Gentiles with Jews (cf. 3:28; Rom 9–11; 1 Cor 12:13; etc.). Consequently, if leaders of the largely Jewish church at Jerusalem did not recognize as brethren the predominantly Gentile church at Antioch, Paul would have "run in vain" in the sense that his mission would have no eschatological significance.   **2:4–5** *And that . . . you*: KJV reproduces Paul's agitated and ungrammatical Greek, which omits a leading verb. **2:4** *False brethren*: a group of (presumably Jewish) Jesus-believers taking issue with Titus's lack of circumcision, which amounted to neglect of the responsibilities God laid out in his covenant with Abraham (Gen 17). According to Acts, Paul circumcises Timothy to avoid similar controversy (16:1–5 and notes; cf. Gal 5:11 note). *Spy out our liberty*: check to see if Titus was circumcised.

us into bondage: [5]to whom we gave place by subjection, no, not for an hour; that the truth of the gospel might continue with you. [6]But of these who seemed to be somewhat, (whatsoever they were, it maketh no matter to me: God accepteth no man's person:) for they who seemed to be somewhat in conference added nothing to me: [7]but contrariwise, when they saw that the gospel of the uncircumcision was committed unto me, as the gospel of the circumcision was unto Peter; [8](for he that wrought effectually in Peter to the apostleship of the circumcision, the same was mighty in me toward the Gentiles:) [9]and when James, Cephas, and John, who seemed to be pillars, perceived the grace that was given unto me, they gave to me and Barnabas the right hands of fellowship; that we should go unto the heathen, and they unto the circumcision. [10]Only they would that we should remember the poor; the same which I also was forward to do.

[11]But when Peter was come to Antioch, I withstood him to the face, because he was to be blamed. [12]For before that certain came from James, he did eat with the Gentiles: but when they were come, he withdrew and separated himself, fearing them which were of the circumcision. [13]And the other Jews dissembled likewise with him; insomuch that Barnabas also was carried away with their dissimulation. [14]But when I saw that they walked not uprightly according to the truth of the gospel, I said unto Peter before them all, If thou, being a Jew, livest after the manner

2:6 *These who . . . somewhat*: people of apparent importance. *Accepteth no man's person*: lit. "accepts no man's face," meaning "shows no favoritism." *Added nothing to me*: i.e., to my teaching. Paul's account again contradicts Acts, where the council stipulates several rules of Gentile behavior (15:28–29). **2:7–9** *When they . . . fellowship*: the Jerusalem apostles conclude that Paul's Gentile mission complements Peter's ministry to the Jews. Acts goes further by assimilating the ministries of Peter and Paul: God calls the former to evangelize the Gentiles (Acts 15:7; cf. 10:1–11:18), and the latter consistently preaches in a city's synagogue before turning to its Gentile population (13:5, 14; 14:1; etc.). **2:8** *Wrought effectually, was mighty*: both Gk. *energeō*. **2:9** *Cephas*: Peter (see John 1:42). *Cephas* is Aramaic for "rock," the meaning of Gk. *Petros* (cf. Mark 3:16 note). *John*: presumably the son of Zebedee. **2:10** *Remember the poor*: Paul would fulfill this demand by collecting money from his churches for the poor believers in Jerusalem (cf. Rom 15:25–27; 1 Cor 16:1–4; 2 Cor 8–9). The offering's status as a symbol of Jewish-Gentile communion in Christ helps explain why Paul assigns it so much importance in his letters. In Acts 15:29, the requirements placed on Gentile believers are more onerous.

2:11–21 Apology, part 3: conflict at Antioch. **2:11** *Withstood him to the face*: like God, Paul "accepts no man's face" (v. 6 note)—not even Peter's. **2:12** *Certain came from James*: assigning James responsibility for the conflict that emerges. The accusation suggests that James understood (or came to understand) the Jerusalem agreement (vv. 9–10) to imply that Gentiles and Jews constituted segregated constituencies within the church, a perspective Peter and Barnabas were willing to adopt. *He withdrew*: Gentile believers at Antioch may have eaten nonkosher food, perhaps including meat sacrificed to idols (cf. Rom 14; 1 Cor 8, 10). In any case, Jews in the Greco-Roman world sometimes hesitated to eat or even associate with Gentiles (Acts 10:28), whose influence could lead to transgressions of God's law (*Letter of Aristeas* 142) and contact with whom was itself sometimes thought to defile (*Jubilees* 22.16). *The circumcision*: a reference either to circumcised believers in general or to a faction in the Jerusalem church that resisted admitting uncircumcised Gentiles to full fellowship (cf. Acts 11:2). **2:13** *Dissembled*: Gk. *synypokrinomai*: which refers to playacting; the noun *dissimulation* has the same root. **2:14** *I said unto Peter*: the address to Peter probably continues through "sin" in v. 17 (see v. 18 note). The lack of any hint that Paul convinced Peter, Barnabas, or anyone else at Antioch implies that he lost the argument (contrast vv. 7–10, where he trumpets the Jerusalem leaders' agreement with him). The result may have been the termination of Paul's partnership with Barnabas, an event that Acts explains differently (see 15:36–41 and notes). *Livest after the manner of Gentiles*: either accusing Peter of being a wicked sinner (cf. v. 15) or merely

of Gentiles, and not as do the Jews, why compellest thou the Gentiles to live as do the Jews? ¹⁵We who are Jews by nature, and not sinners of the Gentiles, ¹⁶knowing that a man is not justified by the works of the law, but by the faith of Jesus Christ, even we have believed in Jesus Christ, that we might be justified by the faith of Christ, and not by the works of the law: for by the works of the law shall no flesh be justified. ¹⁷But if, while we seek to be justified by Christ, we ourselves also are found sinners, is therefore Christ the minister of sin? God forbid.

¹⁸For if I build again the things which I destroyed, I make myself a transgressor. ¹⁹For I through the law am dead to the law, that I might live unto God. ²⁰I am crucified with Christ: nevertheless I live; yet not I, but Christ liveth in me: and the life which I now live in the flesh I live by the faith of the Son of God, who loved me, and gave himself for me. ²¹I do not frustrate the grace of God: for if righteousness come by the law, then Christ is dead in vain.

3 O foolish Galatians, who hath bewitched you, that ye should not obey the truth, before whose eyes Jesus Christ hath been evidently set forth, crucified

---

suggesting that he is normally not so punctilious about guarding his Jewish distinctiveness. *Why*: better "how" (MS tradition). **2:15** *Sinners of the Gentiles*: lit. "Gentile sinners," expressing (perhaps ironically) the same prejudice underlying Peter's withdrawal in v. 12. **2:16** *Justified*: Gk. *dikaioō*, referring to a legal pronouncement that one is in the right, but also signifying being made righteous. KJV renders its nominal form "righteousness." In ancient Jewish literature, this word, its cognates, and their Hebrew equivalents can refer to God's eschatological vindication/rectification of Israel and of individual Israelites (LXX Isa 45:25; 50:7–8; *Rule of the Congregation* 1QS XI, 2ff.). Paul and his opponents share the conviction that God "justifies," disagreeing only on the implications of this for Torah observance. Paul believes that if God rectifies people through Christ, then that relativizes observance of the law: Gentiles need not follow it to be delivered from sin. His opponents would not concur that God's vindication of people through Christ precludes requiring Gentiles to obey God's law. The OT, after all, presents Israel's obedience to God's law as the appropriate faithful response to God's gracious acts of deliverance (e.g., Deut 6:20–25; chap. 26). *Works of the law*: not simply "works," as if Paul were combating the idea that salvation may be earned. He rather affirms the unity of Gentiles and Jews in the church—precisely the issue (he thought) his second Jerusalem visit had resolved. *Faith*: see Rom 1:8 note. *Faith of Jesus Christ*: ambiguous throughout, referring either to the believer's faithfulness to Christ or to Christ's faithfulness to God, exemplified in his willingness to die on the cross (cf. v. 20). *For by the works . . . justified*: see Ps 143:2, to which Paul adds *by the works of the law*. **2:17** *Minister*: the Greek word can refer to slaves serving food. Paul (sarcastically?) asks Peter if he thinks that Jewish believers who are discovered eating with Gentiles (*found sinners*) implicate Christ in their supposed sin. His shock at the idea (*God forbid*) may be partly based on Jesus' own willingness to eat with sinners (Matt 11:19; Mark 2:16; etc.). **2:17–18** *God forbid . . . transgressor*: the transition from first-person plural to singular signals that Paul's speech to Peter has ended, marking a shift from the earlier situation at Antioch to the current one at Galatia. Although notoriously obscure, v. 18 may claim that if Paul were suddenly to reverse himself and require Gentile converts to be circumcised, it would amount to confessing that his previous Gentile mission was an enormous transgression of God's law. It certainly suggests that sin lies not in communing with Gentiles, but in perpetuating obsolete distinctions. **2:19** *Through the law*: explained in 3:13. *Am dead*: lit. "died." **2:20** *I am . . . in me*: better "I have been crucified with Christ and I no longer live; rather Christ lives in me."

3:1–5:1 Reasons why Gentile believers ought not to become circumcised. **3:1–5** Argument 1: the Spirit. **3:1** *That ye . . . truth*: better omitted (MS tradition). *Before whose . . . you*: a

among you? ²This only would I learn of you, Received ye the Spirit by the works of the law, or by the hearing of faith? ³Are ye so foolish? having begun in the Spirit, are ye now made perfect by the flesh? ⁴Have ye suffered so many things in vain? if it be yet in vain. ⁵He therefore that ministereth to you the Spirit, and worketh miracles among you, doeth he it by the works of the law, or by the hearing of faith?

⁶Even as Abraham believed God, and it was accounted to him for righteousness. ⁷Know ye therefore that they which are of faith, the same are the children of Abraham. ⁸And the scripture, foreseeing that God would justify the heathen through faith, preached before the gospel unto Abraham, saying, In thee shall all nations be blessed. ⁹So then they which be of faith are blessed with faithful Abraham.

¹⁰For as many as are of the works of the law are under the curse: for it is written, Cursed is every one that continueth not in all things which are written in the book of the law to do them. ¹¹But that no man is justified by the law in the sight of God, it is evident: for, The just shall live by faith. ¹²And the law is not of faith: but, The man that doeth them shall live in them. ¹³Christ hath redeemed us from the curse of the law, being made a curse for us: for it is written, Cursed is every one that hangeth on a tree: ¹⁴that the blessing of Abraham might come on the Gentiles through Jesus Christ; that we might receive the promise of the Spirit through faith.

---

reference to Paul's preaching about Jesus (note "hearing" in vv. 2, 5; cf. 2:20; 6:17). **3:2** *The Spirit*: manifestations such as tongues and prophecy (v. 5; cf. 1 Cor 14), which were supposed to mark the onset of the end time (cf. Joel 2:28–29). **3:3** *Made perfect . . . flesh*: alluding to circumcision, which Gen 17:13 calls a "covenant . . . in your flesh" (see also Gal 6:12–13). Compare the story of Izates (Josephus, *Jewish Antiquities* 20.34–53, Appendix, pp. 977–79), introduced to Judaism by Ananias, who did not require circumcision. Another Jewish teacher (Eleazar) later urges Izates to complete his conversion by becoming circumcised. **3:4** *Suffered*: or "experienced." **3:5** *Ministereth*: better "supplies." **3:6–18** Argument 2: God's promise to Abraham. The argument unfolds in three stages: the promise to Abraham (vv. 6–9), the curse of the law (vv. 10–14), and the primacy of promise over curse (vv. 15–18). **3:6** *Abraham believed . . . righteousness*: see Gen 15:6. **3:8** *In thee . . . blessed*: Gen 12:3; 18:18; cf. 22:18. *Nations*: Gk. *ethnē*; elsewhere "heathen" or "Gentiles." **3:10** *Cursed is . . . them*: Deut 27:26; 28:58. A traditional interpretation holds that keeping the law is impossible and that everyone who tries falls under its curse willy-nilly, but this flies in the face of Phil 3:6, where Paul claims of himself that before turning to Christ, "touching the righteousness in the law" he was "blameless." Moreover, the law itself provides for atonement, even for unintentional and unknown transgressions. An alternative interpretation, observing Paul's conflation of two verses from Deuteronomy's extensive list of blessings for obedience to the law and curses for disobedience (27:11–28:68) and the self-evident suffering of Israel under Deuteronomy's curse—it had endured Roman rule for about a century—is that just as uncircumcised Gentile believers participate with Jews in Abraham's righteousness and blessing (vv. 6–9), so circumcised Jews (*as many as are of the works of the law*) participate with Gentiles in the curse resulting from disobedience to the law. **3:11** *But that . . . for*: KJV's introduction of the adversative "but" is unjustified, and the whole phrase may be better rendered "Since no man is justified by the law in the sight of God, it is evident that." *The just . . . faith*: Hab 2:4. **3:12** *The man . . . in them*: Lev 18:5. **3:13** *Redeemed*: a reference to buying a slave's freedom; compare "deliver" (1:4) and "bondage" (2:4). *Being made . . . us*: cf. 2 Cor 5:21. *Cursed is . . . tree*: Deut 21:23 (which concerns treatment of an executed criminal), here given a christological interpretation. **3:14** *That we . . . faith*: Paul's argument explains the basis on which

¹⁵Brethren, I speak after the manner of men; Though it be but a man's cove-nant, yet if it be confirmed, no man disannulleth, or addeth thereto. ¹⁶Now to Abraham and his seed were the promises made. He saith not, And to seeds, as of many; but as of one, And to thy seed, which is Christ. ¹⁷And this I say, that the covenant, that was confirmed before of God in Christ, the law, which was four hundred and thirty years after, cannot disannul, that it should make the promise of none effect. ¹⁸For if the inheritance be of the law, it is no more of promise: but God gave it to Abraham by promise.

¹⁹Wherefore then serveth the law? It was added because of transgressions, till the seed should come to whom the promise was made; and it was ordained by angels in the hand of a mediator. ²⁰Now a mediator is not a mediator of one, but God is one. ²¹Is the law then against the promises of God? God forbid: for if there had been a law given which could have given life, verily righteousness should have been by the law. ²²But the scripture hath concluded all under sin, that the promise by faith of Jesus Christ might be given to them that believe. ²³But before faith came, we were kept under the law, shut up unto the faith which should afterwards be revealed. ²⁴Wherefore the law was our schoolmaster to bring us unto Christ, that we might be justified by faith. ²⁵But after that faith is come, we are no longer under a schoolmaster.

²⁶For ye are all the children of God by faith in Christ Jesus. ²⁷For as many of you as have been baptized into Christ have put on Christ. ²⁸There is neither Jew

---

the Galatians have access to God's spirit without following his law; cf. vv. 1–5. **3:15–18** *Brethren, I . . . by promise*: Paul's privileging of God's promise to Abraham over the Mosaic covenant is not strictly relevant, for the commandment under consideration (circumcision; cf. 5:2–12; 6:12–15) is more prominent in the Abraham story (Gen 17) than in Mosaic law. When Paul revisits the issue in Rom 4, he contrasts not the Abrahamic and Mosaic covenants but rather the competing versions of the Abrahamic covenant in Genesis. **3:15** *Covenant*: Gk. *diathēkē*, also "testament" or "will"; once a human will is ratified, no one may annul or alter it. **3:16** *Promises*: Gk. *epangeliai*, which shares its root with "gospel." *He saith . . . one*: cf. LXX Gen 12:7; 13:15–16; 15:5; etc. The Greek word for "seed" (*sperma*) is collective, but Paul (perhaps influenced by an interpretive tradition equating David's "seed" in 2 Sam 7:12–14 with the eschatological messiah) argues from its singular form that Abraham's *seed* refers to Christ. **3:17** *In Christ*: better omitted (MS tradition). *Four hundred . . . after*: see Exod 12:40–41. **3:19–25** Argument 3: the Mosaic law's true purpose. **3:19** *Because of transgressions*: cf. vv. 22–25. *Ordained by angels . . . mediator*: ancient Jewish texts often highlight angels' role in the Sinai theophany; see Deut 33:2 and notes; Acts 7:53; *Jubilees* 1.27–2.1. The *media-tor* is Moses. **3:20** *God is one*: alluding to the Shema, Israel's fundamental declaration of faith (Deut 6:4). God made his promise to Abraham directly (cf. v. 18), but he promulgated the law through an intermediary, Moses; Paul therefore infers that the law does not perfectly reflect God's character or will. **3:22** *The scripture . . . believe*: Paul develops this idea more fully in Rom 3:9–31. *Concluded*: shut together; cf. v. 23 (KJV "shut up"). **3:23** *Unto*: Gk. *eis*, better "until." **3:24** *Schoolmaster*: Gk. *paidagōgos*, not a teacher but a household slave who accompanied boys to school and watched over them. *To bring us unto*: also "until" (see v. 23 and note). KJV adds *to bring us*. **3:26–4:11** Argument 4: believers become God's children at baptism. **3:26** *Children of God*: in contrast to wards of the *paidagōgos*. **3:27–28** *Baptized into Christ . . . Jesus*: Paul understands bap-tism to incorporate believers into Christ's body by imparting his spirit to them (see 1 Cor 12:11–13; cf. 6:15–20 and notes). On the basis of their shared possession of Christ's spirit they are *one in Christ*. **3:27** *Baptized*: see Mark 1:4 note. Baptism became the early church's initiation ritual. *Put on Christ*: perhaps the donning of a new garment at the close of the baptismal ceremony.

nor Greek, there is neither bond nor free, there is neither male nor female: for ye are all one in Christ Jesus. [29]And if ye be Christ's, then are ye Abraham's seed, and heirs according to the promise.

4 Now I say, That the heir, as long as he is a child, differeth nothing from a servant, though he be lord of all; [2]but is under tutors and governors until the time appointed of the father. [3]Even so we, when we were children, were in bondage under the elements of the world: [4]but when the fulness of the time was come, God sent forth his Son, made of a woman, made under the law, [5]to redeem them that were under the law, that we might receive the adoption of sons. [6]And because ye are sons, God hath sent forth the Spirit of his Son into your hearts, crying, Abba, Father. [7]Wherefore thou art no more a servant, but a son; and if a son, then an heir of God through Christ.

[8]Howbeit then, when ye knew not God, ye did service unto them which by nature are no gods. [9]But now, after that ye have known God, or rather are known of God, how turn ye again to the weak and beggarly elements, whereunto ye desire again to be in bondage? [10]Ye observe days, and months, and times, and years. [11]I am afraid of you, lest I have bestowed upon you labour in vain.

[12]Brethren, I beseech you, be as I am; for I am as ye are: ye have not injured me at all. [13]Ye know how through infirmity of the flesh I preached the gospel unto you at the first. [14]And my temptation which was in my flesh ye despised not, nor rejected; but received me as an angel of God, even as Christ Jesus. [15]Where is

---

3:28 *Neither male nor female*: a mistranslation; the Greek syntax, not parallel to the previous pairs, yields "neither male and female," echoing Gen 1:27 (compare the "new creature," 6:15). Gender dissolution relates to the question of whether Gentile believers must be circumcised, for privileging circumcision as a marker of covenant inclusion perpetuates eschatologically obsolete categories of gender as well as ethnicity.   **3:29** *Christ's*: "of Christ," with context suggesting that "of" indicates substance rather than possession (cf. vv. 27–28 and notes). *Abraham's seed*: on the basis of their baptismal participation in Christ (called Abraham's seed at v. 16), Gentile believers too become *Abraham's seed*.   **4:2** *Time appointed . . . father*: compare "fulness of time" (v. 4). Paul views Christ's advent eschatologically, as the beginning of the end time.   **4:3–6** *Even so . . . Father*: cf. Rom 8:1–17.   **4:3** *Elements of the world*: often held to be earth, water, air, and fire. Traditional Jewish belief held that pagan idolaters worshipped created cosmic elements, which they foolishly mistook for divinities; cf. Wis 13:1–9; Philo, *On the Contemplative Life* 3–4. Paul provocatively links the law with these elements, insisting that both hold people in bondage (vv. 3–5, 8–9).   **4:4** *Made*: lit. "born."   **4:5** *Redeem*: cf. 3:13 and note. *That we . . . sons*: this second purpose clause may depend on or be parallel to the first. *Adoption of* [i.e., "as"] *sons*: cf. 3:26.   **4:6** *Your hearts*: better "our hearts" (MS tradition). *Abba, Father*: see Rom 8:15 and note. Initiates may have said these words as part of a baptismal liturgy (cf. 3:27–28 and note).   **4:7** *Of God through Christ*: better "through God" (MS tradition).   **4:8** *Did service*: lit. "were enslaved."   **4:9** *Weak and beggarly*: on the weakness of pagan gods (idols), see Wis 13:18–19.   **4:10** *Ye observe . . . years*: Paul avoids terms referring to Jewish holidays (contrast Col 2:16: "holyday . . . new moon . . . sabbath") in favor of general religious language appropriate to pagan worship, thereby scandalously assimilating circumcision—the Jewish initiation rite that the Galatians were considering celebrating (5:2–6; 6:12; cf. 3:3)—to a pagan ritual, just as he had earlier associated the law commanding it with the cosmic elements that pagans mistake for divinities (v. 3 and note). Contrast Rom 3:1–6.   **4:11** *Afraid of*: fearful about. *Labour in vain*: echoing Isa 49:4.   **4:12–20** Argument 5: a personal appeal.   **4:12** *For I . . . are*: referring to Paul's willingness to forgo observing the law; cf. 2:11–14; 1 Cor 9:21. *Not injured me*: Gk. *adikeō*, lit. "done me no wrong"; it has the same root as the word rendered "justified" at 2:16 (see note) and elsewhere.   **4:13–14** *Infirmity of the flesh . . . my flesh*: cf. 2 Cor 12:7–9.   **4:14** *My temptation*: better "your

then the blessedness ye spake of? for I bear you record, that, if it had been possible, ye would have plucked out your own eyes, and have given them to me. [16]Am I therefore become your enemy, because I tell you the truth? [17]They zealously affect you, but not well; yea, they would exclude you, that ye might affect them. [18]But it is good to be zealously affected always in a good thing, and not only when I am present with you. [19]My little children, of whom I travail in birth again until Christ be formed in you, [20]I desire to be present with you now, and to change my voice; for I stand in doubt of you.

[21]Tell me, ye that desire to be under the law, do ye not hear the law? [22]For it is written, that Abraham had two sons, the one by a bondmaid, the other by a freewoman. [23]But he who was of the bondwoman was born after the flesh; but he of the freewoman was by promise. [24]Which things are an allegory: for these are the two covenants; the one from the mount Sinai, which gendereth to bondage, which is Agar. [25]For this Agar is mount Sinai in Arabia, and answereth to Jerusalem which now is, and is in bondage with her children. [26]But Jerusalem which is above is free, which is the mother of us all. [27]For it is written, Rejoice, thou barren that bearest not; break forth and cry, thou that travailest not: for the desolate

temptation" (MS tradition), i.e., to reject Paul.   **4:15** *Plucked out . . . eyes*: proverbial, meaning "made the utmost sacrifice."   **4:17** *Affect*: seek to obtain (also in v. 18). *They would . . . them*: they expect their exclusivity to attract the Galatians. The rival missionaries who encourage the Galatian believers to commit to circumcision and other forms of Torah observance (cf. 5:2–12) may be related to the group Paul labels "false brethren" (2:4) and/or to those "of the circumcision" (2:12).   **4:18** *Not only . . . you*: Paul does not as a rule oppose the churches he founds hosting missionaries in his absence; compare his attitude toward Apollos at 1 Cor 3:5–9.   **4:19** *Travail in birth again*: a reference to Paul's founding of these communities. He presents himself as their mother, with God conventionally imagined as the father (1:1–4; 3:26–4:7). His self-presentation rhetorically demonstrates the gender dissolution announced at 3:26.   **4:20** *Stand in doubt of*: am at a loss concerning. **4:21–5:1** Argument 6: the allegory of Sarah and Hagar. This scriptural exegesis develops the image of childbirth from 4:19. More significantly, its treatment of Abraham's major failure of faith in the Genesis narrative—his willingness to follow Sarah's suggestion and beget an heir with Hagar (Gen 16:1–3)—complements Paul's previous commendation of Abraham's faith (3:6–9) and progeny "by promise" (3:16–18). Paul's interpretation is fanciful, but his employment of allegory to explain problematic details in an authoritative text is thoroughly conventional in the Greco-Roman world.   **4:21** *The law*: here, Scripture in general, or else the Pentateuch in particular.   **4:22–23** *Abraham had . . . promise*: cf. Gen 16:15; 21:2.   **4:23** *After the flesh*: i.e., naturally, as in v. 29, but also echoing the reference to circumcision at 3:3 (see note). Paul thereby associates this Jewish rite with Hagar, Ishmael, and the covenant they represent. *By promise*: God promised that Sarah would conceive, despite her old age (Gen 17:15–19).   **4:24** *Are an allegory*: Gk. *allēgoroumena*, "mean something other than what they say." *The two covenants*: the Mosaic and Abrahamic, as elsewhere in Galatians. *Gendereth*: bears children. *Agar*: Hagar, Abraham's slave and the mother of his son Ishmael.   **4:25** *Mount Sinai in Arabia*: Paul probably relies on a Jewish tradition that Ishmael was patriarch of the Arabs to link him and his mother to the Mosaic covenant originating at Mount Sinai, traditionally located in Arabia. *To Jerusalem . . . children*: alluding to the Jerusalem church, from which the missionaries urging the Galatians to observe the law likely came; cf. 2:4, 12.   **4:26** *Jerusalem which is above*: the eschatological Jerusalem, a common image in the Bible (e.g., Isa 54:11–17; Rev 21) and Jewish apocalyptic literature. *Mother of us all*: better "our mother" (MS tradition), i.e., Sarah, Abraham's free wife who bore Isaac, "Abraham's seed" (cf. 3:29 and note).   **4:27** *Rejoice, thou . . . husband*: Isa 54:1. Paul's quotation links Isaiah's barren one who will conceive (to be equated with the restored Jerusalem of Isa 54:11–17) with Sarah, who bore Isaac when she was ninety years old (cf. Gen 17:17; 21:5). *Travailest* also recalls Paul's claim to be "in travail" with the Galatians (v. 19), thereby rhetorically

hath many more children than she which hath an husband. ²⁸Now we, brethren, as Isaac was, are the children of promise. ²⁹But as then he that was born after the flesh persecuted him that was born after the Spirit, even so it is now. ³⁰Nevertheless what saith the scripture? Cast out the bondwoman and her son: for the son of the bondwoman shall not be heir with the son of the freewoman. ³¹So then, brethren, we are not children of the bondwoman, but of the free. ¹Stand fast therefore in the liberty wherewith Christ hath made us free, and be not entangled again with the yoke of bondage.

²Behold, I Paul say unto you, that if ye be circumcised, Christ shall profit you nothing. ³For I testify again to every man that is circumcised, that he is a debtor to do the whole law. ⁴Christ is become of no effect unto you, whosoever of you are justified by the law; ye are fallen from grace. ⁵For we through the Spirit wait for the hope of righteousness by faith. ⁶For in Jesus Christ neither circumcision availeth any thing, nor uncircumcision; but faith which worketh by love. ⁷Ye did run well; who did hinder you that ye should not obey the truth? ⁸This persuasion cometh not of him that calleth you. ⁹A little leaven leaveneth the whole lump. ¹⁰I have confidence in you through the Lord, that ye will be none otherwise minded: but he that troubleth you shall bear his judgment, whosoever he be. ¹¹And I, brethren, if I yet preach circumcision, why do I yet suffer persecution?

---

assimilating him to Sarah and his addressees to Sarah's offspring.   **4:28** *We*: better "you" (MS tradition).   **4:29** *Persecuted*: a traditional interpretation of Gen 21:9 takes Ishmael's "playing" with Isaac as a form of harassment (see note).   **4:30** *Cast out . . . freewoman*: Gen 21:10. *The bondwoman and her son* allegorically correspond to the missionaries from Jerusalem and those among the Galatians they have persuaded, in contrast to Paul, *the freewoman*; cf. v. 27 note.   **5:1** *Stand fast . . . free*: better "with liberty hath Christ made us free. Stand fast therefore" (MS tradition). *Entangled again . . . bondage*: Paul once again provocatively associates the Jewish law with pagan practices; cf. 4:8–11.

5:2–12 Exhortation 1: against circumcision of Gentile believers. As Paul shifts from theological argumentation to moral exhortation (although the distinction is not absolute), he for the first time overtly addresses the issue that has generated the letter.   **5:2** *If ye . . . nothing*: it is important to recall that Paul is writing to Gentile believers (see, e.g., 4:8–11) who have rejected pagan practices to worship YHWH. Paul does not require Jewish believers to cease practicing circumcision. On the contrary, he is comfortable with the idea that a mission to Jews would look very different from his mission to Gentiles (see 2:7–10), and would presumably not preclude circumcision and observance of the law. (This sentiment lies behind 5:6 and 6:15 as well; cf. 1 Cor 7:19.) Paul would insist, though, that no believer—Jew or Gentile—is justified by the law, for God justifies all believers through the faith of Christ (cf. 2:16 and note; 3:23–24; etc.). His concern about Gentile believers becoming "entangled again with the yoke of bondage" (v. 1) stems from his judgment that doing so would imply Christ's insufficiency to justify them (vv. 3–4; cf. 2:21) and would deny the eschatologically new thing God is doing in Christ (cf. v. 5; 3:27–28; 6:15 and notes).   **5:3** *Testify again . . . law*: cf. 3:10–12.   **5:5** *For we . . . faith*: Paul's understanding of righteousness is ultimately eschatological: God will perfect it at the end time's consummation. See Rom 8:18–23 for a more elaborate expression of the ideas Paul gestures at here.   **5:9** *A little leaven . . . lump*: see Mark 8:15 and note. **5:11** *If I . . . persecution*: Paul's rival missionaries have apparently accused him of advocating Gentile circumcision in certain situations. (Compare Acts 16:1–5, where Paul circumcises Timothy "because of the Jews." Though not really an example of Gentile circumcision—Timothy's mother was Jewish—this situation, combined with Paul's acceptance of the practice among Jewish believers, might have given rise to such an accusation.) Paul's point may be that the accusation makes no sense, for if he advocates Gentile circumcision, why has he suffered harassment (KJV "persecution")

then is the offence of the cross ceased. [12]I would they were even cut off which trouble you.

[13]For, brethren, ye have been called unto liberty; only use not liberty for an occasion to the flesh, but by love serve one another. [14]For all the law is fulfilled in one word, even in this; Thou shalt love thy neighbour as thyself. [15]But if ye bite and devour one another, take heed that ye be not consumed one of another.

[16]This I say then, Walk in the Spirit, and ye shall not fulfil the lust of the flesh. [17]For the flesh lusteth against the Spirit, and the Spirit against the flesh: and these are contrary the one to the other: so that ye cannot do the things that ye would. [18]But if ye be led of the Spirit, ye are not under the law. [19]Now the works of the flesh are manifest, which are these; Adultery, fornication, uncleanness, lasciviousness, [20]idolatry, witchcraft, hatred, variance, emulations, wrath, strife, seditions, heresies, [21]envyings, murders, drunkenness, revellings, and such like: of the which I tell you before, as I have also told you in time past, that they which do such things shall not inherit the kingdom of God. [22]But the fruit of the Spirit is love, joy, peace, longsuffering, gentleness, goodness, faith, [23]meekness, temperance: against such there is no law. [24]And they that are Christ's have crucified the flesh with the affections and lusts. [25]If we live in the Spirit, let us also walk in the Spirit. [26]Let us not be desirous of vain glory, provoking one another, envying one another.

6 Brethren, if a man be overtaken in a fault, ye which are spiritual, restore such an one in the spirit of meekness; considering thyself, lest thou also be tempted. [2]Bear ye one another's burdens, and so fulfil the law of Christ.

---

regarding this controversial issue (e.g., 2:3–5; cf. 4:29)? (For an alternative interpretation, see 6:12 and note.)   **5:12** *Cut off*: the Greek word can refer to castration, yielding a vulgar pun.

5:13–6:10 Exhortation 2: temptations of the flesh. A major transition from and antithetical complication of Paul's earlier argument, which had associated "flesh" with circumcision (3:3) and observance of the Mosaic law (4:23) and had emphasized believers' freedom from those things (e.g., 3:13; 5:1). Now Paul changes tack, linking "flesh" with immorality (5:13, 16–17, 19) and betraying concern lest his readers understand their liberty in Christ as license. He goes so far as to urge them to forgo liberty and be slaves to one another, in order to fulfill the Mosaic law (5:13, 14).   **5:14** *Thou shalt love . . . thyself*: Lev 19:18; cf. Rom 13:9–10 and notes.   **5:15** *Bite and devour*: Greco-Roman philosophical rhetoric conventionally likens to animals people who are behaving badly.   **5:17** *So that . . . would*: better "so that you may not do whatever you want," with Paul again opposing an understanding of liberty in Christ as moral license.   **5:18** *If ye . . . law*: although Paul concedes that believers fulfill the law (v. 14), they do this *led of the spirit*; thus even when obeying the law's commands, they escape its authority (cf. Rom 8:1–17).   **5:19** *Now the works . . . manifest*: introducing a list of vices and of virtues (vv. 19–21, 22–23), which combine to assert that vice and virtue are self-evident (*manifest*), thereby denying the law its relevance: believers do not need it to forbid the latter and require the former. *Adultery*: better omitted (MS tradition). *Fornication*: Gk. *porneia*, a generic term for sexual transgression.   **5:20** *Variance, emulations*: rivalries, jealousies. *Heresies*: factionalism.   **5:21** *Murders*: better omitted (MS tradition). *Tell you before* [i.e., "forewarn you"], *told you in time past*: both the same Greek verb.   **5:23** *Temperance*: self-control.   **5:24** *Affections*: passions.   **6:1** *Lest thou . . . tempted*: i.e., to adopt a vainglorious demeanor of moral superiority.   **6:2** *Bear ye . . . burdens*: a commonplace in Greco-Roman popular philosophy; cf. Xenophon, *Memorabilia* 2.7.1, where Socrates says to Aristarchus, "Friends should share their burdens, for perhaps even we might relieve you somewhat." Paul here begins to articulate guidelines that believers must follow in a popular philosophical idiom foreign to the Mosaic law, calling these directives *the law of Christ*,

³For if a man think himself to be something, when he is nothing, he deceiveth himself. ⁴But let every man prove his own work, and then shall he have rejoicing in himself alone, and not in another. ⁵For every man shall bear his own burden.

⁶Let him that is taught in the word communicate unto him that teacheth in all good things. ⁷Be not deceived; God is not mocked: for whatsoever a man soweth, that shall he also reap. ⁸For he that soweth to his flesh shall of the flesh reap corruption; but he that soweth to the Spirit shall of the Spirit reap life everlasting. ⁹And let us not be weary in well doing: for in due season we shall reap, if we faint not. ¹⁰As we have therefore opportunity, let us do good unto all men, especially unto them who are of the household of faith.

¹¹Ye see how large a letter I have written unto you with mine own hand. ¹²As many as desire to make a fair shew in the flesh, they constrain you to be circumcised; only lest they should suffer persecution for the cross of Christ. ¹³For neither they themselves who are circumcised keep the law; but desire to have you circumcised, that they may glory in your flesh. ¹⁴But God forbid that I should glory, save in the cross of our Lord Jesus Christ, by whom the world is crucified unto me, and I unto the world. ¹⁵For in Christ Jesus neither circumcision availeth any thing, nor uncircumcision, but a new creature. ¹⁶And as many as walk according to this rule, peace be on them, and mercy, and upon the Israel of God.

---

a phrase found only here in his writings. **6:3** *If a man . . . deceiveth himself*: another Greco-Roman philosophical commonplace; cf. Plato, *Apology* 21b–d, 41b; etc.; Epictetus, *Discourses* 4.8.39. **6:4** *Prove*: Gk. *dokimazō*, also "examine"—self-examination being the sine qua non of Greco-Roman popular philosophy, ultimately harking back to the Delphic aphorism "know thyself." Epictetus, *Discourses* 4.7.40–41, provides an especially close parallel to this verse. **6:5** *Every man . . . burden*: that the future tense here is eschatological (cf. vv. 7–9) diminishes but does not eliminate the contradiction with v. 2. Paul's writings frequently display tension between communal responsibility and the individual's liability for his or her own deeds; cf. 1 Cor 6:12–20 and notes. **6:6** *Communicate unto him . . . things*: i.e., support financially. **6:7** *Whatsoever a man . . . reap*: proverbial; see, e.g., Prov. 22:8. **6:8** *Corruption*: a reference to the rotting of the flesh, as opposed to the spiritual body's eschatological resurrection to *life everlasting*; cf. 1 Cor 15:42, 50–54. **6:9** *In due season*: at the end time's consummation.

6:11–18 Final comments and closing. Distinctive in the indubitably authentic letters for the absence of personal greetings. **6:11** *How large a letter*: better "with what large letters." Paul has taken the pen from his scribe and writes the closing himself; cf. 1 Cor 16:21; Col 4:18; Phlm 19. The letters may have been *large* because Paul, like most Greco-Roman writers dependent on scribes, had poor penmanship. **6:12** *Flesh*: again linking flesh with circumcision. *Lest they . . . Christ*: Paul may presume that his opponents advocate Gentile circumcision not out of sincere conviction, but rather in order to establish that the community of Jesus-believers constitutes a legitimate Jewish sect as opposed to a newfangled foreign cult, which the Roman imperial authorities would likely find suspect and whose members they would be prone to harass. **6:13** *Neither they . . . law*: cf. 2:13–14. **6:14–15** *But God . . . creature*: the emphasis on eschatological renewal echoes the salutation's emphasis on eschatological liberation (cf. 1:4–5 and note to v. 4). **6:14** *By whom*: alternatively "by which." **6:15** *In Christ Jesus*: better omitted (MS tradition). *Availeth*: better "is" (MS tradition). *But a new creature*: the Greek phrase makes a syntactical break with what precedes. A better rendering would be "—a new creature" or even "—a new creation," with reference to God's eschatological promise in Isa 65:17–25. From Paul's perspective, the present world order, including his own identity, has been destroyed ("crucified," v. 14). The categories of both circumcised and uncircumcised are irrelevant to the new creation emerging in the church; cf. 3:27–28. **6:16** *And upon the Israel of God*:

¹⁷From henceforth let no man trouble me: for I bear in my body the marks of the Lord Jesus. ¹⁸Brethren, the grace of our Lord Jesus Christ be with your spirit. Amen.

Unto the Galatians written from Rome.

"Peace be upon Israel" is a well-known phrase from the Psalms (125:5; 128:6), but the meaning of Paul's variation is hotly debated. If he distinguishes *the Israel of God* from *as many as walk according to this rule*, the phrase refers to the Jewish people. This reading would anticipate Rom 11:25–32, where Paul expresses confidence that "all Israel shall be saved" (vv. 25–29) because of God's "mercy" (vv. 30–32). Alternatively, the phrase can be translated "even the Israel of God," with Paul identifying all believers who find their identity in the Abrahamic covenant—be they Jew or Gentile—as Israel; cf. 3:29 and note. In the context of Galatians' overarching argument, the latter interpretation makes more sense.   **6:17** *I bear . . . Jesus*: cf. 2 Cor 4:8–11; 11:23–25.   **6:18** *Unto the Galatians . . . Rome*: better omitted (MS tradition).

The Epistle of Paul the Apostle

to the Ephesians

T HE Epistle of Paul to the Ephesians is almost certainly not "to the Ephesians," and it may not be by Paul. The best reading of the manuscript tradition eliminates "which are at Ephesus" from verse 1 and the early Christian teacher Marcion refers to the letter as "To the Laodiceans" (perhaps inferring its identity with the epistle Paul mentions at Col 4:16). Textual uncertainty regarding its addressees may suggest that Ephesians originated as an encyclical, sent to various churches in Asia Minor and only later linked with the region's leading city.

Many scholars doubt that Ephesians is authentically Pauline for a number of reasons, including the following. First, all of Paul's other letters are sent to named addressees. If this is a Pauline encyclical, it is alone in not naming its recipient. Second, the style is unique in the Pauline corpus (with the exception of Colossians, which it emulates and whose authenticity is also in doubt), consisting of protracted sentences padded with synonymous expressions whose effect is to ornament rather than to clarify. Third, Ephesians seems to use Colossians as a source, reproducing significant portions of that epistle's text, which might imply that an author other than Paul used Colossians as a model to write Ephesians. Compare the following passages: Eph 1:1–2 and Col 1:1–2; Eph 1:7 and Col 1:14; Eph 2:5 and Col 2:13; Eph 3:2 and Col 1:25; Eph 3:9 and Col 1:26; Eph 4:16 and Col 2:19; Eph 4:32 and Col 3:13; Eph 5:5–6 and Col 3:5–6; Eph 5:19–20 and Col 3:16–17; Eph 6:1–4 and Col 3:20–21; Eph 6:5–9 and Col 3:22–4:1. In addition to these discrete points of contact, there are also important structural and thematic similarities. Fourth, the ideas this epistle presents stand in tension with what Paul elsewhere writes. In addition to the issues of Pauline consistency raised by Colossians (see introduction), Ephesians de-emphasizes eschatology: temporal language finds itself supplanted by spatial metaphors, and the writer seems to assume that the church will exist indefinitely (see 3:21 and note). Moreover, in Paul's undisputed epistles the apostle goes to excruciating lengths to explain the role of the law for faithful Gentiles, arguing that while it is not binding on them in the same way as it is on the Jews, it is still vital as the gospel's promise and foundation. In Ephesians, on the contrary, Paul can simply say that Christ "abolished in his flesh the enmity, even the law of commandments contained in ordinances; for to make in himself of twain one new man, so making peace" (2:15). This verse further indicates that Ephesians, unlike the indubitably authentic Paulines, presupposes the ecclesiastical solidarity between Jews and Gentiles that Paul fought for. In Ephesians this issue is less an urgent problem than an opportunity for abstract theological reflection on the spiritual unity of the church.

The examples could be multiplied, but need not be. Ephesians looks very much like a pseudepigraphical composition based on Colossians and presenting Pauline ideas, especially as Colossians expresses them, to a later generation of readers. Such readers may have been familiar with the controversies in which Paul had been embroiled, but evidently did not know them as conflicts requiring urgent resolution. Of course, this conclusion is not decisive, and scholars who hold to Ephesians' Pauline authorship propose reasonable explanations for each of its oddities. For example, it may closely resemble Colossians because Paul wrote the two epistles at the same time, not because it uses Colossians as a source. Moreover, despite its claim that Christ abolished the law, Ephesians quotes approvingly from the Decalogue (6:1–3), thereby maintaining the standard Pauline tension on this issue. If Paul wrote the letter, then he likely did so at the same time as Colossians, while imprisoned in Caesarea or Rome in the late 50s or early 60s, or perhaps in Ephesus in the mid-50s. If he did not, it is impossible to say exactly when Ephesians was composed. The first extant references to it appear around the mid-second century C.E., so certainly before then and perhaps as early as the previous century's final decade or two.

Ephesians concentrates on the church throughout, developing the Pauline comparison of the church to a body (Rom 12:4–8; 1 Cor 12) in order to emphasize the authoritative position of Christ within it: Christ is repeatedly proclaimed the church's head—most famously in the decidedly nonegalitarian conjugal imagery of chapter 5, but most vividly in chapter 1, where he is said to have been exalted to God's right hand in heaven and made "the head over all things to the church, which is his body, the fulness of him that filleth all in all" (1:22–23). The church, for its part, paradoxically enjoys a share in the authority that Christ exercises over it: in 2:6 the author declares that believers have been raised with Christ to sit with him in heaven, presumably to participate in the heavenly reign at God's right hand—the hand to which 1:22–23 made them subject. This dual vision of the church, as at once passively submissive to its Lord and cosmically commanding alongside him, finds a stylistic reflection in Ephesians' striking variations of tone, from straightforward moral exhortation to an ornate, quasipoetic discourse that scholars speculate has its roots in early Christian liturgy. The epistle's most memorable moments come when these two discursive registers merge: for example, in chapter 5, where Ephesians urges believing wives to submit to their husbands on the model of the church's humble submission to the loving authority of Christ its Lord, who "gave himself for it" (5:25); or in chapter 6, where, in the context of commanding children's obedience to parents and slaves' to masters, the writer urges believers metaphorically to don an elaborately described suit of divine armor, lest they fall prey to the wily devil's temptations. This brief epistle's expansive outlook, evident in both its stylistic variation and its thematic range, prompted hyperbolic praise from no less an authority than Samuel Taylor Coleridge, who called it "the divinest composition of man" and went on assert that "it embraces every doctrine of Christianity;—first those doctrines peculiar to Christianity, and then those precepts common to it with natural religion" (*Table Talk*, May 25, 1830).

A number of strong commentaries on Ephesians serve English readers, perhaps the best of which is Ernest Best's in the International Critical Commentary series, *A Critical and Exegetical Commentary on Ephesians* (Edinburgh: T&T Clark, 1998), although Markus Barth's older Anchor Bible commentary is also valuable, *Ephesians: A New Translation with Introduction and Commentary*, 2 vols. (Garden City, NY: Doubleday, 1974). This introduction and the annotations that follow rely on both.

THE EPISTLE OF PAUL THE
APOSTLE TO THE
EPHESIANS

1 Paul, an apostle of Jesus Christ by the will of God, to the saints which are at Ephesus, and to the faithful in Christ Jesus: [2]Grace be to you, and peace, from God our Father, and from the Lord Jesus Christ.

[3]Blessed be the God and Father of our Lord Jesus Christ, who hath blessed us with all spiritual blessings in heavenly places in Christ: [4]according as he hath chosen us in him before the foundation of the world, that we should be holy and without blame before him in love: [5]having predestinated us unto the adoption of children by Jesus Christ to himself, according to the good pleasure of his will, [6]to the praise of the glory of his grace, wherein he hath made us accepted in the beloved. [7]In whom we have redemption through his blood, the forgiveness of sins, according to the riches of his grace; [8]wherein he hath abounded toward us in all wisdom and prudence; [9]having made known unto us the mystery of his will, according to his good pleasure which he hath purposed in himself: [10]that in the dispensation of the fulness of times he might gather together in one all things in

1:1–23 Salutation, blessing, and thanksgiving. On the openings of Paul's letters, see note to Rom 1:1–15. Here a lengthy blessing (vv. 3–14) precedes the thanksgiving (vv. 15–23). **1:1** *Apostle*: see Rom 1:1 note. *Saints*: see Rom 1:7 note. *At Ephesus . . . the*: better simply "also" (MS tradition), suggesting that the letter may have been composed as an encyclical, perhaps originally sent to the churches of Asia Minor (whose leading city was Ephesus). **1:2** *Grace be . . . peace*: see Rom 1:7 note. **1:3–14** *Blessed be . . . glory*: one extended Greek sentence, whose tripartite structure reflects a chronological progression from past, to present, to future: vv. 3–5 emphasize believers' predestination from "before the foundation of the world" (v. 4); vv. 6–9 emphasize believers' present realization of that predestination, in redemption and forgiveness; vv. 10–14 emphasize the eschatological consummation of that present realization, which affects not only believers but the entire cosmos. **1:3** *In heavenly places*: which believers mystically occupy (cf. 2:5–6). **1:4** *Holy*: Gk. *hagioi*; cf. v. 1 (KJV "saints"). *In love*: this phrase might introduce the following verse—i.e., "in love having predestinated us . . ." **1:5** *Adoption of children*: cf. Rom 8:15; 9:4; Gal 4:5. **1:6** *Wherein he . . . accepted*: better "which he freely gave us" (MS tradition), with "freely gave" translating the verbal form of Gk. *charis*, or *grace. The beloved*: Christ; cf. Mark 1:11; 9:7; 2 Pet 1:17; etc. **1:7** *Redemption*: referring to the purchase of a prisoner's or slave's freedom, hence *riches of his grace*. In v. 14, "redemption" is a future promise. **1:9** *In himself*: lit. "in him," i.e., in Christ. **1:10** *Dispensation*: lit. "household administration" (NRSV "plan"). *He might gather . . . him*: contrast 1 Cor 15:28, where all things—including Christ—are subject to and gathered into God at the end time's consummation. *Gather together in one*: Gk. *anakephalaiōsasthai*, "sum up," which has as its root Gk. *kephalē* ("head"), often used of

Christ, both which are in heaven, and which are on earth; even in him: [11]in whom also we have obtained an inheritance, being predestinated according to the purpose of him who worketh all things after the counsel of his own will: [12]that we should be to the praise of his glory, who first trusted in Christ. [13]In whom ye also trusted, after that ye heard the word of truth, the gospel of your salvation: in whom also after that ye believed, ye were sealed with that holy Spirit of promise, [14]which is the earnest of our inheritance until the redemption of the purchased possession, unto the praise of his glory.

[15]Wherefore I also, after I heard of your faith in the Lord Jesus, and love unto all the saints, [16]cease not to give thanks for you, making mention of you in my prayers; [17]that the God of our Lord Jesus Christ, the Father of glory, may give unto you the spirit of wisdom and revelation in the knowledge of him: [18]the eyes of your understanding being enlightened; that ye may know what is the hope of his calling, and what the riches of the glory of his inheritance in the saints, [19]and what is the exceeding greatness of his power to us-ward who believe, according to the working of his mighty power, [20]which he wrought in Christ, when he raised him from the dead, and set him at his own right hand in the heavenly places, [21]far above all principality, and power, and might, and dominion, and every name that is named, not only in this world, but also in that which is to come: [22]and hath put all things under his feet, and gave him to be the head over all things to the church, [23]which is his body, the fulness of him that filleth all in all.

2 And you hath he quickened, who were dead in trespasses and sins; [2]wherein in time past ye walked according to the course of this world, according to the prince of the power of the air, the spirit that now worketh in the children of

Christ in Ephesians (cf. v. 22; 4:15; 5:23). **1:11** *Obtained an inheritance*: a logical implication of adoption (v. 5). **1:12** *First trusted*: or "earlier hoped." **1:13** *Gospel*: see Mark 1:1 note. *Sealed*: cf. 2 Cor 1:22 and note. **1:14** *Earnest*: down payment. **1:18** *Understanding*: better "heart" (MS tradition); see Luke 1:66 note. *That ye . . . saints*: cf. Deut 33:3–4. **1:19** *To us-ward*: toward us. **1:20** *Wrought*: Gk. *enērgēsen*, "worked"; cf. "working" (v. 19), its nominal form. *Set him . . . places*: recalling Ps 110:1; cf. Rom 8:34; Eph 1:3; 2:5–6. **1:21** *Far above . . . come*: cf. Phil 2:9. On the authorities listed, see Rom 8:38 and note; cf. 1 Cor 2:6; 15:24–26. *World*: lit. "age." **1:22** *Hath put . . . feet*: alluding to Ps 8:6; cf. 1 Cor 15:25–28, although Ephesians omits the straightforward subordination of Christ to God. **1:22–23** *The head . . . body*: cf. Rom 12:4–5; 1 Cor 12:12–27, though the identification of Christ as the church's head stands in tension with Paul's innovative egalitarian use of somatic imagery in 1 Cor 12 (see vv. 14–26 note). **1:23** *The fulness . . . in all*: in Stoic philosophy, God could be seen as coterminous with the cosmos (see 1 Cor 15:28 note). By applying this idea to Christ and juxtaposing it to an image of the church as his body (v. 22), the author presents the church as a cosmic entity.

2:1–3:21 Reconciliation. This section of the letter begins with a discussion of Gentiles' and Jews' reconciliation with God (2:1–10) before meditating on Jewish-Gentile reconciliation in the church (2:11–22). It considers the role Paul played in that reconciliation (3:1–13) and then offers a prayer that the readers may more fully comprehend God's love (3:14–21). **2:1** *Hath he quickened*: KJV inserts this verb (meaning "made alive") from v. 5 in order clearly to translate what is in Greek a single complex sentence (vv. 1–7). **2:2** *The course*: lit. "the age." *The prince . . . air*: the devil. In Hellenistic Jewish writings, spiritual beings, especially evil ones, conventionally reside in *the air*, a region above the earth and below the heavens, where Ephesians claims that Christ and believers dwell (1:20; 2:6).

disobedience: [3]among whom also we all had our conversation in times past in the lusts of our flesh, fulfilling the desires of the flesh and of the mind; and were by nature the children of wrath, even as others. [4]But God, who is rich in mercy, for his great love wherewith he loved us, [5]even when we were dead in sins, hath quickened us together with Christ, (by grace ye are saved;) [6]and hath raised us up together, and made us sit together in heavenly places in Christ Jesus: [7]that in the ages to come he might shew the exceeding riches of his grace in his kindness toward us through Christ Jesus. [8]For by grace are ye saved through faith; and that not of yourselves: it is the gift of God: [9]not of works, lest any man should boast. [10]For we are his workmanship, created in Christ Jesus unto good works, which God hath before ordained that we should walk in them.

[11]Wherefore remember, that ye being in time past Gentiles in the flesh, who are called Uncircumcision by that which is called the Circumcision in the flesh made by hands; [12]that at that time ye were without Christ, being aliens from the commonwealth of Israel, and strangers from the covenants of promise, having no hope, and without God in the world: [13]but now in Christ Jesus ye who sometimes were far off are made nigh by the blood of Christ. [14]For he is our peace, who hath made both one, and hath broken down the middle wall of partition between us; [15]having abolished in his flesh the enmity, even the law of commandments contained in ordinances; for to make in himself of twain one new man, so making peace; [16]and that he might reconcile both unto God in one body by the cross, having slain the enmity thereby: [17]and came and preached peace to you which were afar off, and to them that were nigh. [18]For through him we both have access by one Spirit unto the Father.

2:3 *Among whom . . . others*: this resembles anti-Gentile polemic (cf. 4:17–19; Rom 1:18–32; 1 Thess 4:5; etc.), but here, the Jewish authorial persona identifies himself, and indeed all people, with the unrestrained lust Jews conventionally associated with Gentiles. The universal sinfulness paves the way for the shared experience of salvation subsequently described. The implicit line of argumentation in vv. 1–7 thus resembles that in Rom 1:16–4:2, but it is briefer and less nuanced. *Had our conversation*: lived. 2:6 *And hath raised . . . Jesus*: cf. 1:3 and note, 20. Although this claim is qualified in the following verse, it is still surprising from Paul, who elsewhere discusses believers' resurrection as an eschatological expectation (e.g., Rom 6:1–14, esp. v. 4 and note), strongly opposing the idea that it has already taken place (2 Tim 2:18; cf. 1 Cor 4:8 and note; contrast Col 2:12–13 and note; 3:1). 2:8 *Through faith*: it is not clear to whose faith (or faithfulness; see Rom 1:8 note) the writer refers—Christ's, exemplified in his willingness to die (cf. 1:7) and, presumably, his trust that God would raise him (cf. 1:20–22), or believers'. In light of the emphasis on salvation as a gift from God, the former may be more likely. 2:9 *Not of works*: in Pauline writings, "works" tends to refer to "works of the law" (circumcision, Jewish dietary regulations, etc.), which some believers thought Gentiles obliged to fulfill (see Gal 2:16 note). 2:10 *That we . . . them*: forming an inclusive frame with vv. 1–2. 2:14 *Who hath made . . . us*: some scholars speculate that this obliquely refers to the fence that divided the areas in the Second Temple that Gentiles might visit from those that they might not, taking this passage as a theological interpretation of the temple's destruction in 70 C.E. (The reading is possible only if the epistle is pseudepigraphic; Paul died before the temple was destroyed.) 2:15 *Having abolished . . . ordinances*: an understanding of Christ's relationship to the law diametrically opposed to Matthew's (see esp. Matt 5:17–18) and going beyond the undisputed Pauline Epistles' as well. The latter insist that Gentile Jesus-believers must not become circumcised and keep the law, but not that the law is thereby abolished. *Twain*: two. *One new man*: compare Paul's references to the new creation, Gal 3:28; 6:15 (see notes). 2:16 *In one body*: an ambiguous phrase, referring to Christ's slain body as well as to the church, the body of Christ (1:22–23). 2:17 *And came . . . nigh*: alluding to Isa

¹⁹Now therefore ye are no more strangers and foreigners, but fellowcitizens with the saints, and of the household of God; ²⁰and are built upon the foundation of the apostles and prophets, Jesus Christ himself being the chief corner stone; ²¹in whom all the building fitly framed together groweth unto an holy temple in the Lord: ²²in whom ye also are builded together for an habitation of God through the Spirit.

3 For this cause I Paul, the prisoner of Jesus Christ for you Gentiles, ²if ye have heard of the dispensation of the grace of God which is given me to you-ward: ³how that by revelation he made known unto me the mystery; (as I wrote afore in few words, ⁴whereby, when ye read, ye may understand my knowledge in the mystery of Christ) ⁵which in other ages was not made known unto the sons of men, as it is now revealed unto his holy apostles and prophets by the Spirit; ⁶that the Gentiles should be fellowheirs, and of the same body, and partakers of his promise in Christ by the gospel: ⁷whereof I was made a minister, according to the gift of the grace of God given unto me by the effectual working of his power.

⁸Unto me, who am less than the least of all saints, is this grace given, that I should preach among the Gentiles the unsearchable riches of Christ; ⁹and to make all men see what is the fellowship of the mystery, which from the beginning of the world hath been hid in God, who created all things by Jesus Christ: ¹⁰to the intent that now unto the principalities and powers in heavenly places might be known by the church the manifold wisdom of God, ¹¹according to the eternal purpose which he purposed in Christ Jesus our Lord: ¹²in whom we have boldness and access with confidence by the faith of him. ¹³Wherefore I desire that ye faint not at my tribulations for you, which is your glory.

¹⁴For this cause I bow my knees unto the Father of our Lord Jesus Christ, ¹⁵of whom the whole family in heaven and earth is named, ¹⁶that he would grant you, according to the riches of his glory, to be strengthened with might by his Spirit

---

57:19 and, perhaps, 52:7.   **2:19** *Saints*: Gk. *hagioi*, lit. "holy ones," here referring to Israel (cf. v. 12 and 3:5–6, where "holy apostles and prophets" must refer to Jewish evangelists).   **2:20** *Apostles* could refer to Jesus-believing missionaries in general, or to Jesus' original twelve disciples, or to another group within the church. *Prophets* might refer to OT prophets or to believers with the gift of prophecy. *Chief corner stone*: a conventional image of Christ; see Rom 9:33 note.   **2:21** *Holy temple*: "household" (v. 19), "built" (v. 20), "building" (v. 21), "builded together," and "habitation" (v. 22) all contain the Greek root *oikos*, "house" or "dwelling." The wordplay lays the foundation for the author's comparison of the church to God's dwelling place, the temple—a metaphor also used in 1 Cor 3:16–17; 6:19.   **3:2** *Dispensation*: Gk. *oikonomia*, which also contains the root *oikos*; see 1:10 note. *To you-ward*: toward you.   **3:3** *Afore*: before. *In few words* refers to 2:11–22, as 3:6 makes clear.   **3:6** *Fellowheirs, and . . . gospel*: cf. Gal 3:26–29. The Greek words lying behind *fellowheirs, of the same body*, and *partakers* all contain the prefix *syn*-, "with" or "alongside."   **3:9** *Fellowship*: better "household administration" or "stewardship" (MS tradition). *The beginning . . . world*: lit. "the ages." *By Jesus Christ*: better omitted (MS tradition).   **3:10** *Known*: made known.   **3:11** *Purposed*: better "accomplished."   **3:12** *Boldness*: Gk. *parrēsia*, freedom or boldness in speech. *Of him*: alternatively "in him"; see 2:8 note.   **3:13** *Desire*: lit. "ask." *That ye*: or "that I." The request is ambiguous in Greek: it may be directed at God or at the readers. If the former, the writer may pray for himself or for his readers not to grow discouraged.   **3:14** *Of our . . . Christ*: better omitted (MS tradition).   **3:15** *The whole*: or "every." *Family*: Gk. *patria*, also "nation" or "people"; it shares a root with "father," v. 14.

in the inner man; [17]that Christ may dwell in your hearts by faith; that ye, being rooted and grounded in love, [18]may be able to comprehend with all saints what is the breadth, and length, and depth, and height; [19]and to know the love of Christ, which passeth knowledge, that ye might be filled with all the fulness of God.

[20]Now unto him that is able to do exceeding abundantly above all that we ask or think, according to the power that worketh in us, [21]unto him be glory in the church by Christ Jesus throughout all ages, world without end. Amen.

4 I therefore, the prisoner of the Lord, beseech you that ye walk worthy of the vocation wherewith ye are called, [2]with all lowliness and meekness, with longsuffering, forbearing one another in love; [3]endeavouring to keep the unity of the Spirit in the bond of peace. [4]There is one body, and one Spirit, even as ye are called in one hope of your calling; [5]one Lord, one faith, one baptism, [6]one God and Father of all, who is above all, and through all, and in you all.

[7]But unto every one of us is given grace according to the measure of the gift of Christ. [8]Wherefore he saith, When he ascended up on high, he led captivity captive, and gave gifts unto men. [9](Now that he ascended, what is it but that he also descended first into the lower parts of the earth? [10]He that descended is the same also that ascended up far above all heavens, that he might fill all things.) [11]And he gave some, apostles; and some, prophets; and some, evangelists; and some, pastors and teachers; [12]for the perfecting of the saints, for the work of the ministry, for the edifying of the body of Christ: [13]till we all come in the unity of the faith, and of the knowledge of the Son of God, unto a perfect man, unto the measure of the stature of the fulness of Christ: [14]that we henceforth be no more children, tossed to and fro, and carried about with every wind of doctrine, by the sleight of men, and cunning craftiness, whereby they lie in wait to deceive; [15]but speaking the truth in love, may grow up into him in all things, which is the head,

3:19 *Filled with . . . God*: cf. 1:23. **3:20** *Power*: Gk. *dynamis*, the nominal form of *able*. **3:21** *By*: better "and in" (MS tradition). *Throughout all . . . end*: a very loose translation; lit. "to all the generations, from the past to the future eternally."

4:1–6:20 The Gentiles' renewal and their resultant behavior. After a transitional exhortation to ecclesiastical unity (4:1–16), the author focuses on specific behaviors his converted Gentile readers must shun or embrace (4:17–6:9). Instruction about familial relationships, including those of masters and slaves, receives special emphasis. The section closes with the famous exhortation that the readers "put on the whole armour of God" (6:10–20), which develops OT imagery (e.g., Isa 11:5; 49:2; 52:7; 59:17; Hos 6:5; Wis 5:17–23). **4:1** *Vocation*: lit. "calling." **4:3** *Bond*: Gk. *syndesmos*, which shares its root with "prisoner" (v. 1). **4:5** *Baptism* (see Mark 1:4 note) became the early church's initiation ritual. **4:6** *In you all*: better "in all" (MS tradition); cf. 1:23 and note. **4:8** *When he . . . men*: echoing Ps 68:18. *Led captivity captive*: the abstract *captivity* must stand for the concrete "captives." **4:9** *He also . . . earth*: perhaps referring to Christ's descent to hell to evangelize its captives (cf. 1 Pet 3:19 and note); alternatively, *the lower parts of the earth* may describe Earth itself from the perspective of heaven, with *descended* referring to the incarnation (cf. 2:17; see Phil 2:6–11; John 3:13 for similar ideas and language). *First*: better omitted (MS tradition). **4:10** *Fill all things*: cf. 1:23 and note. **4:11** *He gave some*: "to be" must be understood. **4:12** *Perfecting*: "completing" or "equipping" (cf. NRSV). **4:13** *Unto a perfect man*: imagining the church maturing into the perfect person whose body it is, namely Christ (immediately identified as its head; vv. 15–16). *Stature*: or "age." **4:14** *Doctrine*: teaching.

even Christ: ¹⁶from whom the whole body fitly joined together and compacted by that which every joint supplieth, according to the effectual working in the measure of every part, maketh increase of the body unto the edifying of itself in love.

¹⁷This I say therefore, and testify in the Lord, that ye henceforth walk not as other Gentiles walk, in the vanity of their mind, ¹⁸having the understanding darkened, being alienated from the life of God through the ignorance that is in them, because of the blindness of their heart: ¹⁹who being past feeling have given themselves over unto lasciviousness, to work all uncleanness with greediness. ²⁰But ye have not so learned Christ; ²¹if so be that ye have heard him, and have been taught by him, as the truth is in Jesus: ²²that ye put off concerning the former conversation the old man, which is corrupt according to the deceitful lusts; ²³and be renewed in the spirit of your mind; ²⁴and that ye put on the new man, which after God is created in righteousness and true holiness.

²⁵Wherefore putting away lying, speak every man truth with his neighbour: for we are members one of another. ²⁶Be ye angry, and sin not: let not the sun go down upon your wrath: ²⁷neither give place to the devil. ²⁸Let him that stole steal no more: but rather let him labour, working with his hands the thing which is good, that he may have to give to him that needeth. ²⁹Let no corrupt communication proceed out of your mouth, but that which is good to the use of edifying, that it may minister grace unto the hearers. ³⁰And grieve not the holy Spirit of God, whereby ye are sealed unto the day of redemption. ³¹Let all bitterness, and wrath, and anger, and clamour, and evil speaking, be put away from you, with all malice: ³²and be ye kind one to another, tenderhearted, forgiving one another, even as God for Christ's sake hath forgiven you. ¹Be ye therefore followers of God, as dear children; ²and walk in love, as Christ also hath loved us, and hath given himself for us an offering and a sacrifice to God for a sweetsmelling savour.

³But fornication, and all uncleanness, or covetousness, let it not be once named among you, as becometh saints; ⁴neither filthiness, nor foolish talking, nor jesting, which are not convenient: but rather giving of thanks. ⁵For this ye know, that no whoremonger, nor unclean person, nor covetous man, who is an idolater, hath any inheritance in the kingdom of Christ and of God.

4:16 *Compacted*: held together. *That which . . . supplieth*: lit. "through every ligament of support." **4:17** *Other*: better omitted (MS tradition). **4:18** *Blindness*: or "hardness," in the sense of obduracy. **4:19** *Past feeling*: callous. *Have given themselves over*: cf. Rom 1:24, 26, 28, where God gives Gentiles up to such sinful behavior. **4:22** *Conversation*: way of life. *Is corrupt*: better "becomes corrupt" or even "rots." **4:25** *Putting away lying . . . neighbour*: echoing Zech 8:16–17. *Members one of another*: in the sense of belonging to the same body (e.g., vv. 15–16). **4:26** *Be ye . . . wrath*: cf. Ps 4:4. **4:28** *But rather . . . good*: for other Pauline exhortations to (manual) labor, see, e.g., 1 Thess 4:11; 2 Thess 3:6–12. **4:30** *Whereby ye are sealed*: see 2 Cor 1:22 and note. **5:1** *Followers*: lit. "imitators." **5:2** *An offering . . . savour*: using the language and imagery of OT descriptions of sacrifice to YHWH (e.g., Lev 1:9). Paul rarely describes Jesus' death using sacrificial imagery, and never elsewhere as explicitly as this (cf. Rom 3:25; 1 Cor 5:7 and notes). **5:3** *Fornication*: Gk. *porneia*, a generic term for sexual transgression. **5:4** *Filthiness*: indecency. *Jesting*: Gk. *eutrapelia*, "wittiness," but perhaps connoting ribaldry. *Convenient*: appropriate. *Giving of thanks*: Gk. *eucharistia*, a word that sounds similar to *eutrapelia*, which it replaces. **5:5** *This ye know*: better "know this" (MS tradition). *Whoremonger*: Gk. *pornos*, "sexually immoral person" (cognate with "fornication"; see v. 3 note). *Who is an idolater*:

⁶Let no man deceive you with vain words: for because of these things cometh the wrath of God upon the children of disobedience. ⁷Be not ye therefore partakers with them. ⁸For ye were sometimes darkness, but now are ye light in the Lord: walk as children of light: ⁹(for the fruit of the Spirit is in all goodness and righteousness and truth;) ¹⁰proving what is acceptable unto the Lord. ¹¹And have no fellowship with the unfruitful works of darkness, but rather reprove them. ¹²For it is a shame even to speak of those things which are done of them in secret. ¹³But all things that are reproved are made manifest by the light: for whatsoever doth make manifest is light. ¹⁴Wherefore he saith, Awake thou that sleepest, and arise from the dead, and Christ shall give thee light. ¹⁵See then that ye walk circumspectly, not as fools, but as wise, ¹⁶redeeming the time, because the days are evil. ¹⁷Wherefore be ye not unwise, but understanding what the will of the Lord is. ¹⁸And be not drunk with wine, wherein is excess; but be filled with the Spirit; ¹⁹speaking to yourselves in psalms and hymns and spiritual songs, singing and making melody in your heart to the Lord; ²⁰giving thanks always for all things unto God and the Father in the name of our Lord Jesus Christ; ²¹submitting yourselves one to another in the fear of God.

²²Wives, submit yourselves unto your own husbands, as unto the Lord. ²³For the husband is the head of the wife, even as Christ is the head of the church: and he is the saviour of the body. ²⁴Therefore as the church is subject unto Christ, so let the wives be to their own husbands in every thing. ²⁵Husbands, love your wives, even as Christ also loved the church, and gave himself for it; ²⁶that he might sanctify and cleanse it with the washing of water by the word, ²⁷that he might present it to himself a glorious church, not having spot, or wrinkle, or any such thing; but that it should be holy and without blemish. ²⁸So ought men to love their wives as their own bodies. He that loveth his wife loveth himself. ²⁹For no man ever yet hated his own flesh; but nourisheth and cherisheth it, even as the Lord

---

better "that is, an idolater" (MS tradition). This parenthetical aside suggests that polytheistic Gentiles are by definition sexually immoral, unclean, and covetous.   **5:8** *Children of light*: see Luke 16:8 note.   **5:9** *Spirit*: better "light" (MS tradition).   **5:11** *Reprove*: Gk. *elenchō*, "disclose" or "censure" (cf. v. 13); KJV introduces a pun with "proving" in v. 10 that is not present in the Greek.   **5:13** *Doth make . . . light*: lit. "whatever is made manifest is light"; though KJV's translation of a passive Greek participle as active is easier to understand, it is tendentious.   **5:14** *Awake thou . . . light*: it is not known what the author quotes. It may be an early Christian hymn using imagery of Isa 60:1. **5:15** *See then . . . circumspectly*: better "watch, then, carefully how you walk" (MS tradition).   **5:16** *Redeeming*: lit. "buying back." *The days are evil*: the notion that the present time is one of wickedness is found in a similar context at 1 Thess 5:1–11. There Paul commands his readers to live righteously in rejection of the present "night" and in solidarity with the coming eschatological "day." Here the author goes further, suggesting that believers' righteous behavior actually redeems the evil present. **5:18–19** *Be not . . . songs*: recalling LXX Prov 23:30–31: "Do not be drunk with wine, but converse with righteous men. . . ."   **5:21** *Fear of God*: better "fear of Christ" (MS tradition).   **5:22–6:9** *Wives, submit . . . him*: this section constitutes a household code or social code, a literary form found throughout Hellenistic moralizing writing (in the NT, at Col 3:18–25; 1 Pet 2:13–3:7; cf. Titus 2:1– 10). It consists of a list of directives governing how members of a given community, especially a family (including slaves), must behave toward each other.   **5:23** *The husband . . . wife*: cf. 1 Cor 11:2–16 (esp. v. 3), although Paul's tortured argument for women's subordination there is far more complex than the present assertion.   **5:24** *Is subject*: the same Gk. verb as "submit," v. 21.   **5:26** *Washing of water*: probably a reference to baptism.   **5:29** *The Lord*: better "Christ" (MS tradition).

the church: [30]for we are members of his body, of his flesh, and of his bones. [31]For this cause shall a man leave his father and mother, and shall be joined unto his wife, and they two shall be one flesh. [32]This is a great mystery: but I speak concerning Christ and the church. [33]Nevertheless let every one of you in particular so love his wife even as himself; and the wife see that she reverence her husband.

6 Children, obey your parents in the Lord: for this is right. [2]Honour thy father and mother; (which is the first commandment with promise;) [3]that it may be well with thee, and thou mayest live long on the earth. [4]And, ye fathers, provoke not your children to wrath: but bring them up in the nurture and admonition of the Lord.

[5]Servants, be obedient to them that are your masters according to the flesh, with fear and trembling, in singleness of your heart, as unto Christ; [6]not with eyeservice, as menpleasers; but as the servants of Christ, doing the will of God from the heart; [7]with good will doing service, as to the Lord, and not to men: [8]knowing that whatsoever good thing any man doeth, the same shall he receive of the Lord, whether he be bond or free. [9]And, ye masters, do the same things unto them, forbearing threatening: knowing that your Master also is in heaven; neither is there respect of persons with him.

[10]Finally, my brethren, be strong in the Lord, and in the power of his might. [11]Put on the whole armour of God, that ye may be able to stand against the wiles of the devil. [12]For we wrestle not against flesh and blood, but against principalities, against powers, against the rulers of the darkness of this world, against spiritual wickedness in high places. [13]Wherefore take unto you the whole armour of God, that ye may be able to withstand in the evil day, and having done all, to stand.

[14]Stand therefore, having your loins girt about with truth, and having on the breastplate of righteousness; [15]and your feet shod with the preparation of the gospel of peace; [16]above all, taking the shield of faith, wherewith ye shall be able to quench all the fiery darts of the wicked. [17]And take the helmet of salvation, and the sword of the Spirit, which is the word of God: [18]praying always with all prayer and supplication in the Spirit, and watching thereunto with all persever-

---

5:30 *Of his flesh . . . bones*: better omitted (MS tradition).   **5:31** *For this cause . . . flesh*: Gen 2:24. **5:33** *Reverence*: lit. "fear" (cf. v. 21).   **6:2–3** *Honour thy father . . . earth*: Exod 20:12; Deut 5:16.   **6:4** *Nurture*: Gk. *paideia*, which implies training or education.   **6:5** *Servants*: lit. "slaves" (so throughout the section); see Rom 1:1 note. *Masters*: lit. "lords" (*according to the flesh* distinguishes slave-owners from the Lord Jesus). *Singleness of your heart*: idiomatic, meaning "generosity."   **6:6** *Not with eyeservice*: less literally "not only while being watched" (NRSV).   **6:8** *Bond*: lit. "enslaved."   **6:9** *Your Master also*: better "their master and yours" (MS tradition), referring to the Lord (see v. 5 note). *Respect of persons*: favoritism.   **6:10** *Brethren*: a common self-designation of Jesus-believers.   **6:11** *Put on . . . God*: cf. 1 Thess 5:8 and note; see also Eph 4:24. *Be able*: Gk. *dynamai*, the root of the word rendered "be strong" in v. 10.   **6:12** *Against principalities . . . places*: see 1:21 and note. *The darkness . . . world*: better "this darkness" (MS tradition). *High places*: lit. "the heavens," where God, Christ (1:20–21), and believers (2:6) are also said to dwell.   **6:13** *The evil day*: see 5:16 and note. *Having done*: Gk. *katergazomai*, "to achieve" or "accomplish," but also "to subdue" or "conquer," perhaps suggesting that the writer momentarily looks forward to the happy result of believers' resistance: their standing with Christ in victory over evil spiritual powers at the eschatological consummation (cf. 1 Cor 15:24–26). **6:16** *The wicked*: or "the evil one," i.e., the devil.

ance and supplication for all saints; [19]and for me, that utterance may be given unto me, that I may open my mouth boldly, to make known the mystery of the gospel, [20]for which I am an ambassador in bonds: that therein I may speak boldly, as I ought to speak.

[21]But that ye also may know my affairs, and how I do, Tychicus, a beloved brother and faithful minister in the Lord, shall make known to you all things: [22]whom I have sent unto you for the same purpose, that ye might know our affairs, and that he might comfort your hearts.

[23]Peace be to the brethren, and love with faith, from God the Father and the Lord Jesus Christ. [24]Grace be with all them that love our Lord Jesus Christ in sincerity. Amen.

Written from Rome unto the Ephesians by Tychicus.

6:21–24 Closing. 6:21 *Tychicus*: mentioned at Acts 20:4 and as the bearer of Colossians (4:7–8). If Ephesians is pseudepigraphic, the reference probably attempts to connect it to Colossians. **6:22** *Comfort*: or "encourage." **6:23–24** *Peace be . . . sincerity*: the closing references to *grace* and *peace* recall 1:2. **6:24** *Sincerity*: lit. "incorruption." *Written from Rome . . . Tychicus*: better omitted (MS tradition).

The Epistle of Paul the Apostle

to the Philippians

AS the note at the end of Philippians indicates, Paul is traditionally believed to have written it in the early 60s while imprisoned in Rome, where he would soon be executed. Some scholars have proposed a slight modification to that theory, suggesting that Paul composed Philippians in the late 50s in Caesarea, where he was incarcerated before being sent to Rome for trial. Recently, however, a large number of scholars have argued for a very different compositional context, contending that Paul wrote the letter earlier in his career, while imprisoned in Ephesus. Neither Acts nor any of Paul's Epistles mention such an imprisonment, but the former makes it clear that Paul faced much hostility in Asia's leading city (19:23–40) and a few passages in 2 Corinthians may hint at an Ephesian incarceration (1:8–10; cf. 6:5; 11:23). The advantage of construing Philippians to have been written alongside the Corinthian correspondence during Paul's stay in Ephesus is twofold. First, it enables us to identify the impending trips mentioned in this letter: Paul plans to send Timothy to Philippi (2:19, 23; cf. Acts 19:22; 1 Cor 16:10) and hopes himself to visit as well (1:26; 2:24; cf. Acts 20:1; 1 Cor 16:5; 2 Cor 2:13; 7:5). Second, it situates Philippians in a compositional context closer to Galatians' (also likely written in the early or mid-50s), with which it shares a striking similarity: both refer to conflict between Paul and a group of presumably Jewish Jesus-believers who are urging his Gentile congregations to become circumcised and adopt other practices mandated by the Torah.

Wherever and whenever it was written, Paul's Epistle to the Philippians is unique in the Pauline corpus for its tone. Paul is often abrupt with the churches to which he writes, and his letters regularly evince an uncomfortable distance between author and audience—not simply geographical but emotional, doctrinal, and behavioral as well. In the present epistle, on the contrary, Paul writes to a church as to a partner in ministry, repeatedly mentioning its fellowship with and support of him. Indeed, while in other letters Paul underscores his refusal to seek financial assistance from the churches to which he writes (see 2 Cor 11:7–11 and note; 1 Thess 2:6), here he expresses gratitude for a gift the Philippians have sent him by way of Epaphroditus (4:18). Amicability characterizes not just Philippians' tone but also its subject matter: friendship is a crucial theme throughout—friendship within the Philippian community of believers as well as the Philippians' friendship with Paul. Recognizing this thematic thrust helps explain the letter's focus on mutual conformity of minds, a conventional way to figure friendship in the Greco-Roman world. Yet Paul very unconventionally makes Christ the foundation of this harmony: immediately after urging the Philippians to "be likeminded, having the same love, being of one accord, of one mind" (2:2), he urges conformity to the example of Christ ("Let this mind be in you, which was also in Christ Jesus," 2:5) and then proceeds to quote a hymn or encomium about Christ (2:6–11; see note). As the epistle progresses, the paradigm of Christ finds itself variously exemplified by Timothy (2:19–24), Epaphroditus (2:25–30), and finally Paul himself (chap. 3); reading closely, we find sundry parallels between Paul's discussions of these figures and the earlier section of the letter in which the encomium to Christ is embedded (2:1–18).

John Reumann's exhaustive Anchor Bible commentary, *Philippians: A New Translation with Introduction and Commentary* (New Haven, CT: Yale University Press, 2008), is a valuable resource. It informs this introduction and the notes that follow.

THE EPISTLE OF PAUL
THE APOSTLE TO THE
PHILIPPIANS

1 Paul and Timotheus, the servants of Jesus Christ, to all the saints in Christ Jesus which are at Philippi, with the bishops and deacons: [2]Grace be unto you, and peace, from God our Father, and from the Lord Jesus Christ.

[3]I thank my God upon every remembrance of you, [4]always in every prayer of mine for you all making request with joy, [5]for your fellowship in the gospel from the first day until now; [6]being confident of this very thing, that he which hath begun a good work in you will perform it until the day of Jesus Christ: [7]even as it is meet for me to think this of you all, because I have you in my heart; inasmuch as both in my bonds, and in the defence and confirmation of the gospel, ye all are partakers of my grace. [8]For God is my record, how greatly I long after you all in the bowels of Jesus Christ.

[9]And this I pray, that your love may abound yet more and more in knowledge and in all judgment; [10]that ye may approve things that are excellent; that ye may be sincere and without offence till the day of Christ; [11]being filled with the fruits of righteousness, which are by Jesus Christ, unto the glory and praise of God.

[12]But I would ye should understand, brethren, that the things which happened unto me have fallen out rather unto the furtherance of the gospel; [13]so that my bonds in Christ are manifest in all the palace, and in all other places; [14]and many

1:1–11 **Salutation and thanksgiving.** On the openings of Paul's letters, see note to Rom 1:1–15. **1:1** *Timotheus*: see 1 Cor 4:17 note. *Servants*: lit. "slaves" (as often in KJV). *Saints*: see Rom 1:7 note. *Philippi*: a city in the Roman province of Macedonia whose church Paul had founded; see Acts 16:6–40. *Bishops and deacons*: Gk. *episkopoi* and *diakonoi*, more literally "overseers and servants," who presumably led the Philippian church. It is not clear if these terms yet referred to particular ecclesiastical offices (see Acts 20:28 note). If they did, the responsibilities they entailed may not correspond to those of bishops and deacons later in the church's history. **1:2** *Grace be . . . peace*: see Rom 1:7 note. **1:5** *Gospel*: see Mark 1:1 note. **1:6** *Perform it until*: more literally "bring it to completion by" (NRSV). *The day . . . Christ*: the eschatological consummation (also in v. 11). **1:7** *Meet*: lit. "right." *Partakers*: Gk. *synkoinōnoi*, which shares a root with "fellowship" in v. 5. *Of my grace*: alternatively "with me of grace." **1:8** *Record*: witness. *Bowels*: entrails; a seat of affection, like "heart" in English (also at 2:1). **1:9** *Judgment*: in the sense of "discernment." **1:10** *Excellent*: Gk. *diapheronta*, connoting difference as well as superiority. **1:11** *Fruits of righteousness*: an OT phrase; cf. Amos 6:12.

1:12–26 **Paul's situation. 1:12** *Brethren*: a common self-designation of Jesus-believers. **1:13** *Palace*: Gk. *praitōrion*, transliterating Lat. *praetorium* and perhaps here referring to the residence of a region's imperial governor (cf. Mark 15:16 and note), or even to that of the emperor himself at Rome. It could also refer to the emperor's bodyguard. *And in all other places*: lit. "and in all the rest,"

of the brethren in the Lord, waxing confident by my bonds, are much more bold to speak the word without fear.

[15]Some indeed preach Christ even of envy and strife; and some also of good will: [16]the one preach Christ of contention, not sincerely, supposing to add affliction to my bonds: [17]but the other of love, knowing that I am set for the defence of the gospel. [18]What then? notwithstanding, every way, whether in pretence, or in truth, Christ is preached; and I therein do rejoice, yea, and will rejoice. [19]For I know that this shall turn to my salvation through your prayer, and the supply of the Spirit of Jesus Christ, [20]according to my earnest expectation and my hope, that in nothing I shall be ashamed, but that with all boldness, as always, so now also Christ shall be magnified in my body, whether it be by life, or by death. [21]For to me to live is Christ, and to die is gain. [22]But if I live in the flesh, this is the fruit of my labour: yet what I shall choose I wot not. [23]For I am in a strait betwixt two, having a desire to depart, and to be with Christ; which is far better: [24]nevertheless to abide in the flesh is more needful for you. [25]And having this confidence, I know that I shall abide and continue with you all for your furtherance and joy of faith; [26]that your rejoicing may be more abundant in Jesus Christ for me by my coming to you again.

[27]Only let your conversation be as it becometh the gospel of Christ: that whether I come and see you, or else be absent, I may hear of your affairs, that ye stand fast in one spirit, with one mind striving together for the faith of the gospel; [28]and in nothing terrified by your adversaries: which is to them an evident token of perdition, but to you of salvation, and that of God. [29]For unto you it is given in the behalf of Christ, not only to believe on him, but also to suffer for his sake; [30]having the same conflict which ye saw in me, and now hear to be in me.

---

i.e., in other places or among other soldiers.   **1:16–17** *The one . . . gospel*: the order of the two groups is better reversed (MS tradition).   **1:16** *Sincerely*: alternatively "purely" or "in holiness." *Supposing to add . . . bonds*: either by flaunting their freedom and thereby making Paul all the more aware of his own constraints, or perhaps by preaching so obnoxiously as to risk provoking the authorities' indignation at both themselves and Paul. *Add*: better "raise up" (MS tradition).   **1:17** *Defence*: Gk. *apologia*, referring to a legal defense.   **1:19** *This shall . . . salvation*: quoting LXX Job 13:16.   **1:20** *Boldness*: Gk. *parrēsia*, boldness of speech in particular.   **1:22** *This is . . . labour*: "this means fruitful labor for me" (NRSV); i.e., if he lives in the flesh he will continue in his role as an evangelist. *Wot*: know.   **1:23** *In a strait*: hard-pressed. *Depart*: a euphemism for "die." *And to be with Christ*: the eschatological scenarios Paul presents elsewhere, in contrast, involve the dead rising and uniting with Christ (1 Thess 4:13–18; cf. 1 Cor 15:12–58). While it is possible that Paul is being inconsistent, he may here envision a special afterlife for martyrs that offers immediate reward for the ultimate self-sacrifice: martyrs' souls depart to be with Christ until the eschatological consummation, when they are reunited with their bodies. (Cf. Rev 20:4–6, where martyrs are resurrected before the other dead to participate in Christ's millennial reign.)   **1:25** *Abide, continue*: the Greek verbs share a root. *Faith*: see Rom 1:8 note.   **1:26** *Your rejoicing . . . for me*: better "your boast . . . in me."

1:27–2:18 Exhortation to unified emulation of Christ. 1:27 *Let your conversation*: lit. "be citizens," i.e., live your communal life. *Mind*: lit. "soul" or even "life." *Striving*: Gk. *synathlountes*, participating in competition.   **1:29** *Given*: Gk. *charizomai*, the verbal form of *charis* ("grace," 1:2, 7; 4:23).   **1:30** *Conflict*: Gk. *agōn*, another athletic term (see v. 27 note).

2 If there be therefore any consolation in Christ, if any comfort of love, if any fellowship of the Spirit, if any bowels and mercies, [2]fulfil ye my joy, that ye be likeminded, having the same love, being of one accord, of one mind. [3]Let nothing be done through strife or vainglory; but in lowliness of mind let each esteem other better than themselves. [4]Look not every man on his own things, but every man also on the things of others.

[5]Let this mind be in you, which was also in Christ Jesus: [6]who, being in the form of God, thought it not robbery to be equal with God: [7]but made himself of no reputation, and took upon him the form of a servant, and was made in the likeness of men: [8]and being found in fashion as a man, he humbled himself, and became obedient unto death, even the death of the cross. [9]Wherefore God also hath highly exalted him, and given him a name which is above every name: [10]that at the name of Jesus every knee should bow, of things in heaven, and things in earth, and things under the earth; [11]and that every tongue should confess that Jesus Christ is Lord, to the glory of God the Father.

[12]Wherefore, my beloved, as ye have always obeyed, not as in my presence only, but now much more in my absence, work out your own salvation with fear and trembling. [13]For it is God which worketh in you both to will and to do of his good pleasure.

[14]Do all things without murmurings and disputings: [15]that ye may be blameless and harmless, the sons of God, without rebuke, in the midst of a crooked and perverse nation, among whom ye shine as lights in the world; [16]holding forth the word of life; that I may rejoice in the day of Christ, that I have not run in vain, neither laboured in vain. [17]Yea, and if I be offered upon the sacrifice and service of your faith, I joy, and rejoice with you all. [18]For the same cause also do ye joy, and rejoice with me.

2:1 *Consolation*: alternatively "encouragement." 2:2 *Being of . . . mind*: lit. "sharing a soul, thinking one thing." 2:5 *Let this mind*: recalling "likeminded" and "of one mind" (v. 2). 2:6–11 *Who, being . . . Father*: the elevated language of this artfully balanced discourse leads most scholars to conclude that Paul quotes a hymn or encomium about Christ, which the Philippian church would presumably have known. Its first three verses chart Christ's downward movement, from divinity to humanity to slavery to death; its final three, his exaltation and universal acclamation as Lord. 2:6 *Being in the form of God*: it is unclear whether Paul claims that the preexistent Christ is formally identical to God, but essentially distinct, or whether he makes a stronger claim of equality/identity. *Thought it . . . God*: KJV implies that even though Christ knew he had a right to insist on equality with God, he chose not to. An alternative translation makes Christ even more humble: "thought not equality with God something to be grasped." 2:7 *Made himself . . . reputation*: lit. "emptied himself." *Servant*: slave. 2:8 *Humbled*: Gk. root *tapeino-*, shared by "lowliness" (v. 3). *The death of the cross*: crucifixion was a humiliating form of public execution, involving prolonged exposure of the corpse; see Mark 8:34 note. 2:9 *Given*: cf. 1:29 note. 2:10–11 *That at . . . Father*: cf. Isa 45:23. 2:12 *With fear and trembling*: this is OT language; cf. Deut 2:25; Ps 2:11; etc. 2:13 *Worketh, to do of*: both the same Greek verb. 2:14 *Murmurings*: recalling the disobedience of Israel in the wilderness (e.g., Exod 16:7–9). 2:15 *Harmless*: "pure" or "innocent." *Sons of God*: lit. "children of God." *Without rebuke*: or "without blemish." *Crooked and perverse nation*: cf. Deut 32:5. *Nation*: or "generation." *Ye shine . . . world*: cf. Dan 12:3. 2:16 *Rejoice*: or "boast." *Laboured in vain*: echoing Isa 49:4; 65:23. 2:17 *Offered*: lit. "poured out" (as a libation); compare Christ's self-emptying (v. 7 note). The imagery recalls OT sacrificial legislation (e.g., Num 15:5; 28 passim; etc.). *Service*: Gk. *leitourgia*, cultic service.

[19]But I trust in the Lord Jesus to send Timotheus shortly unto you, that I also may be of good comfort, when I know your state. [20]For I have no man likeminded, who will naturally care for your state. [21]For all seek their own, not the things which are Jesus Christ's. [22]But ye know the proof of him, that, as a son with the father, he hath served with me in the gospel. [23]Him therefore I hope to send presently, so soon as I shall see how it will go with me. [24]But I trust in the Lord that I also myself shall come shortly.

[25]Yet I supposed it necessary to send to you Epaphroditus, my brother, and companion in labour, and fellowsoldier, but your messenger, and he that ministered to my wants. [26]For he longed after you all, and was full of heaviness, because that ye had heard that he had been sick. [27]For indeed he was sick nigh unto death: but God had mercy on him; and not on him only, but on me also, lest I should have sorrow upon sorrow. [28]I sent him therefore the more carefully, that, when ye see him again, ye may rejoice, and that I may be the less sorrowful. [29]Receive him therefore in the Lord with all gladness; and hold such in reputation: [30]because for the work of Christ he was nigh unto death, not regarding his life, to supply your lack of service toward me.

3 Finally, my brethren, rejoice in the Lord. To write the same things to you, to me indeed is not grievous, but for you it is safe. [2]Beware of dogs, beware of evil workers, beware of the concision. [3]For we are the circumcision, which worship God in the spirit, and rejoice in Christ Jesus, and have no confidence in the flesh. [4]Though I might also have confidence in the flesh. If any other man thinketh that he hath whereof he might trust in the flesh, I more: [5]circumcised the eighth

2:19–4:1 Examples of humility. Timothy (2:19–24), Epaphroditus (2:25–30), and finally Paul himself (3:1–21) each exemplify the humility and willingness to suffer and to serve others that Christ demonstrated (2:5–11) and Paul has just called for (1:27–2:4; 2:12–18). Timothy selflessly cares for the Philippians; Epaphroditus risked his life to serve Paul; Paul himself gave up a successful life as a Pharisee in order to follow Jesus (3:4–9), having accepted Christ's sufferings and death in anticipation of resurrection (3:10–21). These examples are contrasted with the rival missionaries at Philippi (see esp. 3:19 and note), who, like those in Galatia, seem to have been urging the Gentile church Paul founded to become circumcised and, perhaps, keep Jewish dietary law (3:2–4, 18–19; cf. Gal 5:2–12 and notes).   **2:19** *I trust*: lit. "I hope."   **2:20** *Likeminded*: Gk. *isopsychon*, lit. "of the same soul," which shares the root meaning "soul" with *eupsycheō*, "be of good comfort" (v. 19). *Naturally*: or "genuinely."   **2:22** *Proof*: the nominal form of "approve" (1:10). *Son*: lit. "child." *Served*: lit. "served as a slave."   **2:25** *Epaphroditus* seems to have been a representative sent by the Philippians to Paul to provide for his needs in prison; cf. 4:18.   **2:26** *Full of heaviness*: distressed.   **2:28** *Carefully*: diligently.   **2:29** *Reputation*: lit. "honor."   **2:30** *Not regarding*: better "risking" (MS tradition). *Your lack of service*: this does not seem to be a critique; cf. 4:10.   **3:1** *Finally*: lit. "as for the rest" (also at 4:8). *For you . . . safe*: it is in the interests of your safety.   **3:2** *Dogs*: if this was a traditional pejorative term for Gentiles (cf. Mark 7:27 and note), Paul's use of it here of missionaries urging Gentiles to become circumcised and keep the Jewish law would be ironic. *Evil workers*: in contrast to the "work of Christ" (2:30). *Concision*: the reference is to circumcision, as the following verse makes clear, but Paul polemically uses the LXX's term for cutting oneself in mourning, a pagan rite forbidden to Israelites (e.g., Lev 19:28; Deut 14:1; cf. 1 Kgs 18:28); cf. Gal 4:10 and note.   **3:3** *Worship*: Gk. *latreuō*, a verb that refers to cultic service. *God in the spirit*: better "by the spirit of God" (MS tradition). *Rejoice*: or

day, of the stock of Israel, of the tribe of Benjamin, an Hebrew of the Hebrews; as touching the law, a Pharisee; [6]concerning zeal, persecuting the church; touching the righteousness which is in the law, blameless.

[7]But what things were gain to me, those I counted loss for Christ. [8]Yea doubtless, and I count all things but loss for the excellency of the knowledge of Christ Jesus my Lord: for whom I have suffered the loss of all things, and do count them but dung, that I may win Christ, [9]and be found in him, not having mine own righteousness, which is of the law, but that which is through the faith of Christ, the righteousness which is of God by faith: [10]that I may know him, and the power of his resurrection, and the fellowship of his sufferings, being made conformable unto his death; [11]if by any means I might attain unto the resurrection of the dead.

[12]Not as though I had already attained, either were already perfect: but I follow after, if that I may apprehend that for which also I am apprehended of Christ Jesus. [13]Brethren, I count not myself to have apprehended: but this one thing I do, forgetting those things which are behind, and reaching forth unto those things which are before, [14]I press toward the mark for the prize of the high calling of God in Christ Jesus. [15]Let us therefore, as many as be perfect, be thus minded: and if in any thing ye be otherwise minded, God shall reveal even this unto you. [16]Nevertheless, whereto we have already attained, let us walk by the same rule, let us mind the same thing.

[17]Brethren, be followers together of me, and mark them which walk so as ye have us for an ensample. [18](For many walk, of whom I have told you often, and now tell you even weeping, that they are the enemies of the cross of Christ: [19]whose end is destruction, whose God is their belly, and whose glory is in their shame, who mind earthly things.) [20]For our conversation is in heaven; from whence also we look for the Saviour, the Lord Jesus Christ: [21]who shall change our vile body, that it may be fashioned like unto his glorious body, according to the working whereby 4 he is able even to subdue all things unto himself. [1]Therefore, my brethren dearly beloved and longed for, my joy and crown, so stand fast in the Lord, my dearly beloved.

"boast." **3:5** *Pharisee*: see Mark 2:16 note. **3:8** *Win*: lit. "gain"; cf. v. 7. **3:9** *Faith of Christ*: see Gal 2:16 note. *The righteousness . . . faith*: an allusive reference to the theological ideas elaborated in Romans and Galatians. **3:12** *Either*: or. **3:14** *High*: lit. "upward" (as an adverb). **3:15** *Perfect*: perhaps in the sense of "mature." **3:16** *Let us mind the same thing*: better omitted (MS tradition). **3:17** *Followers*: lit. "imitators." **3:19** *Whose God is their belly*: this accusation finds an intriguing parallel in Euripides' satyr play *Cyclops*, where an outrageously impious glutton claims to worship only himself and his own stomach (334–35). Paul may have in mind not so much his opponents' impiety as their concern to follow Jewish dietary practices; cf. Rom 16:17–18 and note. In any case, his description of them echoes and reverses the description of Christ at 2:5–11: instead of emptying themselves (cf. 2:7 and note), they worship their belly; instead of foregoing glory (cf. 2:6), they *glory in their shame*; in lieu of a heavenly trajectory (cf. 2:9–11), they *mind earthly things*. **3:20** *Conversation*: lit. "citizenship"; cf. 1:27 and note. *From whence . . . Christ*: referring to Christ's second coming; cf. 1 Thess 4:15–17. **3:21** *Who shall . . . glorious body*: see 1 Cor 15:35–58 and notes. *Be fashioned like*: lit. "be conformed to"; cf. "made conformable unto" in v. 10 and Christ "in the form of God" in 1:6. *To subdue . . . himself*: cf. 1 Cor 15:24–28. **4:1** *Crown*: the traditional prize for victors in Greek athletic competitions. Here an eschatological award is in view.

²I beseech Euodias, and beseech Syntyche, that they be of the same mind in the Lord. ³And I intreat thee also, true yokefellow, help those women which laboured with me in the gospel, with Clement also, and with other my fellowlabourers, whose names are in the book of life.

⁴Rejoice in the Lord alway: and again I say, Rejoice. ⁵Let your moderation be known unto all men. The Lord is at hand. ⁶Be careful for nothing; but in every thing by prayer and supplication with thanksgiving let your requests be made known unto God. ⁷And the peace of God, which passeth all understanding, shall keep your hearts and minds through Christ Jesus.

⁸Finally, brethren, whatsoever things are true, whatsoever things are honest, whatsoever things are just, whatsoever things are pure, whatsoever things are lovely, whatsoever things are of good report; if there be any virtue, and if there be any praise, think on these things. ⁹Those things, which ye have both learned, and received, and heard, and seen in me, do: and the God of peace shall be with you.

¹⁰But I rejoiced in the Lord greatly, that now at the last your care of me hath flourished again; wherein ye were also careful, but ye lacked opportunity. ¹¹Not that I speak in respect of want: for I have learned, in whatsoever state I am, therewith to be content. ¹²I know both how to be abased, and I know how to abound: every where and in all things I am instructed both to be full and to be hungry, both to abound and to suffer need. ¹³I can do all things through Christ which strengtheneth me. ¹⁴Notwithstanding ye have well done, that ye did communicate with my affliction.

¹⁵Now ye Philippians know also, that in the beginning of the gospel, when I departed from Macedonia, no church communicated with me as concerning giving and receiving, but ye only. ¹⁶For even in Thessalonica ye sent once and again unto my necessity. ¹⁷Not because I desire a gift: but I desire fruit that may abound to your account. ¹⁸But I have all, and abound: I am full, having received of Epaphroditus the things which were sent from you, an odour of a sweet smell, a sacrifice acceptable, wellpleasing to God. ¹⁹But my God shall supply all your need accord-

4:2–20 Final exhortations. 4:2 *Euodias, Syntyche*: otherwise unknown.   **4:3** *True yokefellow*: possibly a reference to Epaphroditus (apparently the letter's deliverer; cf. 2:25), whom Paul thereby authorizes to mediate a dispute between these two women, to an unknown person, or to someone named Syzygos ("Yokefellow"). *Laboured with*: Gk. *synēthlēsan*, "strove together" (see 1:27 note); *fellowlabourers* has a different root. *Clement*: otherwise unknown. *Book of life*: cf. Luke 10:20 and note.   **4:5** *Moderation*: alternatively "gentleness" or "forbearance."   **4:6** *Careful*: anxious.   **4:8** *Finally*: see 3:1 note. *Honest*: honorable. *Just*: or "righteous." *Lovely*: pleasing.   **4:10** *Your care . . . careful*: alternatively "your thought for me flourished again, about whom you did think."   **4:12** *Am instructed*: Gk. *myeō*, which refers to initiation into religious mysteries.   **4:13** *Christ*: better "him" or "the one" (MS tradition).   **4:14** *Communicate*: lit. "have fellowship" (also in v. 15).   **4:15** *The beginning . . . Macedonia*: for Paul's evangelization of Philippi, see Acts 16:12–40. *Church*: see Rom 16:5 note.   **4:16** *Thessalonica*: also in Macedonia, southwest of Philippi. According to Acts, Paul ministered there immediately after leaving Philippi (17:1–9). *Ye sent . . . necessity*: 1 Thess 2:6 suggests that Paul did not seek support from the Thessalonians during his time there. Apparently, the Philippian church was funding him.   **4:18** *I am full*: reversing the language of emptying from chap. 2 (vv. 7 and esp. 17). *An odour . . . God*: invoking OT sacrificial imagery; cf. Gen 8:21; Exod 29:18, 25; etc.

ing to his riches in glory by Christ Jesus. ²⁰Now unto God and our Father be glory for ever and ever. Amen.

²¹Salute every saint in Christ Jesus. The brethren which are with me greet you. ²²All the saints salute you, chiefly they that are of Cæsar's household. ²³The grace of our Lord Jesus Christ be with you all. Amen.

It was written to the Philippians from Rome by Epaphroditus.

4:21–23 Closing. 4:22 *Of Caesar's household*: the phrase could refer not only to members of the emperor's family but also to his slaves or freedmen. Since these were dispersed across the empire, it gives no clue as to where the epistle was composed. **4:23** *The grace . . . all*: recalling 1:2. *You all*: better "your spirit" (MS tradition). *Amen. It . . . Epaphroditus*: better omitted (MS tradition).

The Epistle of Paul the Apostle
to the Colossians

REFERENCES in chapter 2 to circumcision, Sabbath celebrations, and dietary restrictions suggest that the "philosophy and vain deceit" (2:8) against which Paul warns his readers is a form of mysticism that, if not straightforwardly Jewish, was at least heavily influenced by Jewish ideas. Therefore, while Colossians is often considered alongside Ephesians because of the two epistles' similarities of expression and thought, an equally meaningful comparison may be made with Galatians, where Paul vigorously exhorts Gentile Jesus-believers to resist supplementing their faithfulness to Christ with the adoption of Jewish religious practices. In the earlier epistle, Paul relies on a number of carefully formulated arguments, most of them exegetical, in urging his readers not to become circumcised and law observant; in this one, his strategy is more imaginative than rational. He portrays Christ on a cosmic scale, perhaps drawing on a preexisting hymn to depict him as responsible for the universe's creation and subsistence, superior to every other spiritual power in existence, the Father excluded (1:15–20). Taking a page from Galatians (3:27–28; cf. Col 3:10–11), he reminds his readers that they have been incorporated into this cosmic Christ at baptism: "Ye are complete in him, which is the head of all principality and power: . . . buried with him in baptism, wherein also ye are risen with him through the faith of the operation of God, who hath raised him from the dead" (2:10, 12). Paul calls their baptismal incorporation "the circumcision made without hands" (2:11), and he insists that this incorporation entails both forgiveness of sins and freedom from other divinities that might have demanded believers' allegiance in the past (2:13–15). His point is finally that baptized believers lack nothing: in Christ they are already circumcised, already triumphant over spiritual forces of wickedness. The religious practices that the Colossians are being urged to adopt, accordingly, are superfluous and futile, having merely "a shew of wisdom in will worship" (2:23). The Greek word KJV renders "will worship" seems to be a Pauline neologism referring to humanly willed devotion, contrived religious disciplines with no value against gratifying the flesh's desires. Paul is convinced that incorporation into Christ itself sufficiently empowers resistance to the flesh, and the second half of his letter consequently exhorts believers to proper behavior, ultimately focusing on how members of an extended family ought to behave toward one another.

Of all Paul's letters the authorship of Colossians may be the most hotly debated, with many scholars arguing that it is pseudepigraphical on the basis of the epistle's stylistic eccentricities (e.g., protracted sentences padded with synonymous expressions whose effect is to ornament rather than to clarify) and theological oddities, including Paul's claim that Christ is the head of his body the church and his assertion that believers have already risen with Christ. The former assertion departs from his more egalitarian development of the church as Christ's body in 1 Corinthians 12 (see notes), while the latter stands in tension with the care Paul elsewhere demonstrates to maintain an eschatological outlook on resurrection (Rom 6:3–8; cf. 2 Tim 2:18; etc.). Some have also thought that the claim made by Colossians' author to "fill up that which is behind of the afflictions of Christ in my flesh for his body's sake, which is the church" (1:24) seems excessively presumptuous coming from Paul himself, and is more easily imagined as having been penned by an ardent admirer writing in Paul's name sometime after his death. By probably a slight majority, however, most scholars conclude that the letter's theology is not incompatible with that of Paul's undisputed letters. Even if Colossians contains some surprising assertions, they are not unprecedented in the Pauline corpus. Romans 6's use of resurrection as a metaphor for the righteous comportment that Paul expects from believers baptized into Christ's death, for instance, anticipates Colossians' claim that believers have died and risen with Christ in baptism. As for the stylistic differences, skilled writers may be expected to employ different rhetorical tactics in different contexts, and the gilded language of Colossians' opening chapters well suits Paul's purpose of encouraging believers to imagine Christ's cosmic grandeur. In addition, it may draw on early Christian liturgical traditions whose language was more ornate than Paul's normal mode of expression.

Paul, then, likely wrote the Epistle to the Colossians. Since he claims to have composed it from prison, it may have been written in Caesarea or Rome, where Paul was incarcerated at the end of his career, from the late 50s to early 60s (cf. Acts 23:23–26:32; 28:11–31). Ephesus is also a possibility (see introduction to Philippians), which would suggest an earlier date of composition (mid-50s), perhaps closer to that of Galatians. In any case, Colossians seems to have been written around the same time as Philemon, since both mention the same people attending the apostle (see 4:9 note), although it is also possible that a sophisticated pseudepigrapher gave this epistle a veneer of Pauline authenticity by thus linking it to Paul's occasional letter to Philemon.

R. McL. Wilson's commentary in the International Critical Commentary series is strong, *A Critical and Exegetical Commentary on Colossians and Philemon* (London: T&T Clark, 2005). Also valuable is the Anchor Bible commentary by Markus Barth and Helmut Blanke, *Colossians: A New Translation with Introduction and Commentary* (New York: Doubleday, 1994). Both have influenced this introduction and the annotations that follow.

THE EPISTLE OF PAUL
THE APOSTLE TO THE
COLOSSIANS

1 Paul, an apostle of Jesus Christ by the will of God, and Timotheus our brother, ²to the saints and faithful brethren in Christ which are at Colosse: Grace be unto you, and peace, from God our Father and the Lord Jesus Christ.

³We give thanks to God and the Father of our Lord Jesus Christ, praying always for you, ⁴since we heard of your faith in Christ Jesus, and of the love which ye have to all the saints, ⁵for the hope which is laid up for you in heaven, whereof ye heard before in the word of the truth of the gospel; ⁶which is come unto you, as it is in all the world; and bringeth forth fruit, as it doth also in you, since the day ye heard of it, and knew the grace of God in truth: ⁷as ye also learned of Epaphras our dear fellowservant, who is for you a faithful minister of Christ; ⁸who also declared unto us your love in the Spirit.

⁹For this cause we also, since the day we heard it, do not cease to pray for you, and to desire that ye might be filled with the knowledge of his will in all wisdom and spiritual understanding; ¹⁰that ye might walk worthy of the Lord unto all pleasing, being fruitful in every good work, and increasing in the knowledge of God; ¹¹strengthened with all might, according to his glorious power, unto all patience and longsuffering with joyfulness; ¹²giving thanks unto the Father, which hath made us meet to be partakers of the inheritance of the saints in light: ¹³who hath delivered us from the power of darkness, and hath translated us into the kingdom of his dear Son: ¹⁴in whom we have redemption through his blood, even the forgiveness of sins:

1:1–14 Salutation and thanksgiving. On the openings of Paul's letters, see note to Rom 1:1–15. **1:1** *Apostle*: see Rom 1:1 note. *Timotheus*: see 1 Cor 4:17 note. **1:2** *Saints*: see Rom 1:7 note. *Brethren*: a common self-designation of Jesus-believers. *Colosse*: Colossae, a city in Asia Minor. *Grace be . . . peace*: see Rom 1:7 note. *And the . . . Christ*: better omitted (MS tradition). **1:4–5** *Your faith . . . heaven*: the triad of faith, hope, and love recurs throughout Paul's letters; see 1 Cor 13:13 and note. **1:4** *Faith*: see Rom 1:8 note. **1:5** *For*: because of. *The hope . . . heaven*: cf. 1 Cor 2:9. *Gospel*: see Mark 1:1 note. **1:6** *Fruit*: better to add "and increases" (MS tradition). **1:7** *Also*: better omitted (MS tradition), suggesting that *Epaphras* (cf. Phlm 23) founded the Colossian church; cf. 4:12–13. *Of Epaphras*: from Epaphras. *Fellowservant*: lit. "fellow slave." **1:10** *Unto all pleasing*: pleasing (the Lord) in every way. **1:12** *Us*: better "you" (MS tradition). **1:13** *Delivered*: Gk. *ryomai*, a word used by LXX to describe YHWH's rescue of Israel from Egypt (Exod 5:23; 12:27; etc.). "Redemption" in v. 14 may suggest a conscious allusion to the Exodus story. **1:14** *Redemption*: Gk. *apolytrōsis*, the purchase of a prisoner's or slave's freedom. (See Mark 10:45 note on its root, *lytron*.) *Through his blood*: better omitted (MS tradition).

¹⁵Who is the image of the invisible God, the firstborn of every creature: ¹⁶for by him were all things created, that are in heaven, and that are in earth, visible and invisible, whether they be thrones, or dominions, or principalities, or powers: all things were created by him, and for him: ¹⁷and he is before all things, and by him all things consist. ¹⁸And he is the head of the body, the church: who is the beginning, the firstborn from the dead; that in all things he might have the preeminence. ¹⁹For it pleased the Father that in him should all fulness dwell; ²⁰and, having made peace through the blood of his cross, by him to reconcile all things unto himself; by him, I say, whether they be things in earth, or things in heaven.

²¹And you, that were sometime alienated and enemies in your mind by wicked works, yet now hath he reconciled ²²in the body of his flesh through death, to present you holy and unblameable and unreproveable in his sight: ²³if ye continue in the faith grounded and settled, and be not moved away from the hope of the gospel, which ye have heard, and which was preached to every creature which is under heaven; whereof I Paul am made a minister; ²⁴who now rejoice in my sufferings for you, and fill up that which is behind of the afflictions of Christ in my flesh for his body's sake, which is the church: ²⁵whereof I am made a minister, according to the dispensation of God which is given to me for you, to fulfil the word of God; ²⁶even the mystery which hath been hid from ages and from generations, but now is made manifest to his saints: ²⁷to whom God would make known what is the riches of the glory of this mystery among the Gentiles; which is Christ in you, the hope of glory: ²⁸whom we preach, warning every man, and teaching every man in all wisdom; that we may present every man perfect in Christ Jesus: ²⁹whereunto I also labour, striving according to his working, which worketh in me mightily.

1:15–2:7 Christ's preeminence. **1:15–20** *Who is . . . heaven*: many scholars believe that this section constitutes a hymn quoted by the author, with alterations so extensive that its original form is unrecoverable. However, it may be possible to discern two strophes, each beginning with "who is" (vv. 15, 18b); compare "who" opening Phil 2:6–11, itself possibly a quoted hymn (see note); cf. 1 Tim 3:16 and note. **1:15** *The firstborn of every creature*: this passage played an important role in the fourth-century Arian controversies, when theologians disputed whether Christ was a creature. (It implies he was.) Here and in v. 16, Paul adapts Jewish traditions about the priority of God's wisdom in his creation; cf. Prov 8:22–31; Sir 24:1, 9. **1:16** *For by him . . . for him*: John 1:1–3 likewise assigns Christ a central role in creation (also see Heb 1:2). *Thrones, or . . . powers*: cf. Rom 8:38 and note; 1 Cor 2:6; 15:24–26; Eph 1:21; 6:12. *All things were . . . for him*: cf. Rom 11:36 and note. **1:18** *He is . . . church*: see Eph 1:22–23 and note. **1:19** *It pleased . . . dwell*: lit. "in him all the fullness was pleased to dwell," with *fulness* (Gk. *plērōma*) almost certainly referring to God's fullness (cf. 2:9; Eph 1:23 note). The term can refer to the aggregate of "aeons," "luminaries," and other spiritual authorities in the elaborate cosmogonies written by gnostics. Some scholars therefore have speculated that Paul polemically refers to these here and at v. 16, but this interpretation would require an earlier dating of the gnostic writings than our best evidence suggests. **1:20** *Having made . . . heaven*: cf. 2 Cor 5:17–19. **1:21** *Sometime*: at one time. **1:23** *To every creature*: or "in all creation." **1:24** *Fill up . . . sake*: cf. 2 Cor 1:5. *Behind of*: deficient in. Paul may suggest that Christ's suffering was insufficient to redeem, forgive, and reconcile the church, but that reading would stand in tension with vv. 14 and 20. Alternatively, *the afflictions of Christ* may refer to eschatological affliction analogous to Christ's suffering and expected to precede his return (cf. 2 Thess 2:1–12; Matt 24:9–31; etc.), which Paul understands his own suffering as helping to fulfill. **1:25** *Dispensation*: lit. "household admin-

2 For I would that ye knew what great conflict I have for you, and for them at Laodicea, and for as many as have not seen my face in the flesh; [2]that their hearts might be comforted, being knit together in love, and unto all riches of the full assurance of understanding, to the acknowledgement of the mystery of God, and of the Father, and of Christ; [3]in whom are hid all the treasures of wisdom and knowledge. [4]And this I say, lest any man should beguile you with enticing words. [5]For though I be absent in the flesh, yet am I with you in the spirit, joying and beholding your order, and the stedfastness of your faith in Christ. [6]As ye have therefore received Christ Jesus the Lord, so walk ye in him: [7]rooted and built up in him, and stablished in the faith, as ye have been taught, abounding therein with thanksgiving.

[8]Beware lest any man spoil you through philosophy and vain deceit, after the tradition of men, after the rudiments of the world, and not after Christ. [9]For in him dwelleth all the fulness of the Godhead bodily. [10]And ye are complete in him, which is the head of all principality and power: [11]in whom also ye are circumcised with the circumcision made without hands, in putting off the body of the sins of the flesh by the circumcision of Christ: [12]buried with him in baptism, wherein also ye are risen with him through the faith of the operation of God, who hath raised him from the dead. [13]And you, being dead in your sins and the uncircumcision of your flesh, hath he quickened together with him, having forgiven you all trespasses; [14]blotting out the handwriting of ordinances that was against us, which was contrary to us, and took it out of the way, nailing it to his

istration" or "stewardship." **2:1** *Conflict*: Gk. *agōn*, which shares its root with "striving" in 1:29. *Laodicea*: a city in Asia Minor neighboring Colossae. **2:2** *Comforted*: or "encouraged." *Acknowledgement*: or "knowledge." *Of God . . . Christ*: better "of God, of Christ" (MS tradition), i.e., "the knowledge of the mystery of God, [the knowledge] of Christ." **2:3** *In whom . . . knowledge*: echoing Prov 2:3–5; Isa 45:3. **2:5** *Though I . . . spirit*: cf. 1 Cor 5:3–4 and note. *Order*: Gk. *taxis*, often used specifically of a battle formation. *Stedfastness*: also with martial connotations (the word can refer to a formation's ability to function as a strong bulwark). **2:7** *Therein*: better omitted (MS tradition).

  2:8–23 Opposing false teaching. **2:8** *Spoil you*: "take you as spoils," i.e., "capture you." *Philosophy*: Gk. *philosophia*, which in Paul's time incorporated knowledge that most moderns would label "religious." Contemporary Jewish writers used *philosophy* as a term for Judaism in general and called discrete Jewish sects, such as the Pharisees, "philosophical schools." *Rudiments of the world*: or "elements of the world"; cf. Gal 4:3 and note, 9. In Colossians they seem to be associated with the spiritual powers mentioned at 1:16; 2:10, 15, and perhaps also with the angels of 2:18. **2:9** *The Godhead*: divinity. **2:10** *Ye are complete*: Gk. *plēroō*, "to make full," cognate with "fullness" in the previous verse; cf. 1:19 and note. *The head . . . power*: cf. Eph 1:10 and note. **2:11** *Ye are . . . hands*: figuring baptism as circumcision, as v. 12 makes clear. *Putting off*: i.e., "taking off"; cf. 1 Cor 15:37 note. *The body . . . flesh*: better "the body of flesh" (MS tradition), a phrase whose strangeness led later scribes to alter it. But for Paul, flesh is not equivalent to body; it characterizes only baser bodily forms. In 1 Cor 15, Paul insists that eschatologically resurrected believers have spiritual bodies, as opposed to bodies consisting of flesh and soul. The discarded "body of flesh" can therefore be explained with reference to the subsequent verse, where Paul emphasizes that believers have already risen with Christ at baptism. There may also be an allusion here to the removal of clothing at baptism; see 3:9–11; Gal 3:27 and notes. **2:12–13** *Buried with . . . trespasses*: see Rom 6:1–14 and notes, although there vv. 3–8 reserve resurrection for the eschatological future, while here it is enjoyed in the present; cf. Eph 2:6. **2:13** *Quickened*: made alive. *Forgiven you*: better "forgiven us" (MS tradition). **2:14** *The handwriting of ordinances*: Gk. *cheirographon* (*handwriting*) refers to a certificate of indebtedness, as in Tob 5:2–3. NRSV renders the entire phrase "the record . . . with its legal

cross; ¹⁵and having spoiled principalities and powers, he made a shew of them openly, triumphing over them in it.

¹⁶Let no man therefore judge you in meat, or in drink, or in respect of an holyday, or of the new moon, or of the sabbath days: ¹⁷which are a shadow of things to come; but the body is of Christ. ¹⁸Let no man beguile you of your reward in a voluntary humility and worshipping of angels, intruding into those things which he hath not seen, vainly puffed up by his fleshly mind, ¹⁹and not holding the Head, from which all the body by joints and bands having nourishment ministered, and knit together, increaseth with the increase of God.

²⁰Wherefore if ye be dead with Christ from the rudiments of the world, why, as though living in the world, are ye subject to ordinances, ²¹(touch not; taste not; handle not; ²²which all are to perish with the using;) after the commandments and doctrines of men? ²³Which things have indeed a shew of wisdom in will worship, and humility, and neglecting of the body; not in any honour to the satisfying of the flesh.

3 If ye then be risen with Christ, seek those things which are above, where Christ sitteth on the right hand of God. ²Set your affection on things above, not on things on the earth. ³For ye are dead, and your life is hid with Christ in God. ⁴When Christ, who is our life, shall appear, then shall ye also appear with him in glory.

⁵Mortify therefore your members which are upon the earth; fornication, uncleanness, inordinate affection, evil concupiscence, and covetousness, which is idolatry: ⁶for which things' sake the wrath of God cometh on the children of disobedience: ⁷in the which ye also walked some time, when ye lived in them. ⁸But now ye also put off all these; anger, wrath, malice, blasphemy, filthy communication out of

<hr />

demands." **2:15** *Spoiled*: lit. "stripped" or "stripped off himself." *He made . . . it*: the image is of a Roman triumphal parade; cf. 2 Cor 2:14 and note. *In it*: i.e., the cross (v. 14). As Rome's standard means of executing foreign or enslaved criminals and rebels, its assimilation to an image of triumphant victory is jarring. **2:16** *Meat*: food. *An holyday . . . days*: Jewish celebrations honoring YHWH (cf. 2 Chr 8:13; Neh 10:33; Hos 2:11); the beginning of the verse refers to Jewish dietary requirements. **2:17** *Which are . . . Christ*: this verse develops a philosophical commonplace originating with Plato, who figures ideal reality as a body casting shadows, which themselves figure the phenomenal world perceived by the senses (*Republic* 514a–518b). **2:18** *In a . . . angels*: alternatively "insisting on self-abasement and worship of angels" (NRSV). *Not*: better omitted (MS tradition). **2:19** *The Head*: Christ (cf. 1:18; 2:10). *Joints and bands*: ligaments and sinews. **2:20** *Why, as . . . ordinances*: Paul associates the Jewish regulations (v. 16) with the *rudiments of the world* (see v. 8 note). He makes a similar link in Galatians (see 4:3 note). *Ordinances* also harks back to v. 14, "handwriting of ordinances." **2:22** *Which all . . . using*: they are transient, consumed with their use. *After the . . . men*: echoing Isa 29:13; cf. Mark 7:6–7; etc. **2:23** *Will worship*: Gk. *ethelothrēskia* (will + worship), a word that first appears here in extant Greek literature; it probably refers to self-imposed worship. *Humility*: self-abasement. *Neglecting of the body*: a reference to ascetic practices. *Not in . . . flesh*: better "not of any value against gratifying the flesh."

3:1–4:6 Life in Christ. 3:1 *If ye . . . with Christ*: cf. 2:12; see Eph 2:6 and note. Here, too, the idea of present resurrection is eschatologically qualified: believers' "life is [currently] hid with Christ in God" (v. 3), to be revealed at his eschatological advent (v. 4). *Sitteth on . . . God*: see Ps 110:1; cf. Rom 8:34; Eph 1:20. **3:4** *Our*: better "your" (MS tradition). **3:5** *Mortify*: put to death. *Fornication*: Gk. *porneia*, a generic term for sexual transgression. *Concupiscence*: lit. "desire." *Covetousness, which is*

your mouth. [9]Lie not one to another, seeing that ye have put off the old man with his deeds; [10]and have put on the new man, which is renewed in knowledge after the image of him that created him: [11]where there is neither Greek nor Jew, circumcision nor uncircumcision, Barbarian, Scythian, bond nor free: but Christ is all, and in all.

[12]Put on therefore, as the elect of God, holy and beloved, bowels of mercies, kindness, humbleness of mind, meekness, longsuffering; [13]forbearing one another, and forgiving one another, if any man have a quarrel against any: even as Christ forgave you, so also do ye. [14]And above all these things put on charity, which is the bond of perfectness. [15]And let the peace of God rule in your hearts, to the which also ye are called in one body; and be ye thankful. [16]Let the word of Christ dwell in you richly in all wisdom; teaching and admonishing one another in psalms and hymns and spiritual songs, singing with grace in your hearts to the Lord. [17]And whatsoever ye do in word or deed, do all in the name of the Lord Jesus, giving thanks to God and the Father by him.

[18]Wives, submit yourselves unto your own husbands, as it is fit in the Lord. [19]Husbands, love your wives, and be not bitter against them. [20]Children, obey your parents in all things: for this is well pleasing unto the Lord. [21]Fathers, provoke not your children to anger, lest they be discouraged. [22]Servants, obey in all things your masters according to the flesh; not with eyeservice, as menpleasers; but in singleness of heart, fearing God: [23]and whatsoever ye do, do it heartily, as to the Lord, and not unto men; [24]knowing that of the Lord ye shall receive the reward of the inheritance: for ye serve the Lord Christ. [25]But he that doeth wrong shall receive for the wrong which he hath done: and there is no respect of persons.

4 [1]Masters, give unto your servants that which is just and equal; knowing that ye also have a Master in heaven.

[2]Continue in prayer, and watch in the same with thanksgiving; [3]withal praying also for us, that God would open unto us a door of utterance, to speak the mystery of Christ, for which I am also in bonds: [4]that I may make it manifest, as

---

idolatry: cf. Matt 6:24 and note.   **3:9–11** *Put off . . . in all*: Paul employs similar language and imagery at Gal 3:27–28; cf. 1 Cor 12:13. The imagery of exchanging clothing (which continues through v. 14) probably refers to donning the newly resurrected body (see, e.g., 2 Cor 5:2 note), thereby continuing Paul's discussion of being "risen with Christ," which began at v. 1. It may also refer to a new garment put on after baptism (see Gal 3:27), at which time believers were understood to have in a sense risen with Christ (see Col 2:12).   **3:10** *After . . . created him*: cf. Gen 1:27.   **3:11** *Barbarian*: one who does not speak Greek. *Scythian*: an inhabitant of the region northeast of the Black Sea. Greco-Roman authors conventionally used Scythians to signify extreme otherness, for their originally nomadic mode of existence was viewed as totally foreign to the culture of city-states that grew up around the eastern Mediterranean.   **3:12** *Bowels of mercies*: i.e., sincere compassion (KJV translates literally). *Humbleness*: cf. 2:18, 23, where (unlike here) "humility" seems to refer to ascetic self-abasement.   **3:13** *Quarrel*: or "complaint." *Christ*: better "the Lord" (MS tradition).   **3:15** *God*: better "Christ" (MS tradition). *Rule*: lit. "act as umpire" or "arbitrate." *In one body*: see 1:18, 24; cf. Rom 12:13–27 and notes.   **3:18–4:6** *Wives, submit . . . man*: a household code; see Eph 5:22–6:9 note.   **3:19** *Love*: Gk. *agapaō*; its nominal form is rendered "charity" in v. 14.   **3:20** *Unto*: better "in" (MS tradition).   **3:22–4:1** *Servants, obey . . . heaven*: see Eph 6:5–9 and notes.   **3:22** *Servants*: lit. "slaves" (see Rom 1:1 note).   **3:23** *Heartily*: lit. "from the soul."   **3:24** *Inheritance*: cf. 1:12.   **4:3** *Utterance*:

I ought to speak. ⁵Walk in wisdom toward them that are without, redeeming the time. ⁶Let your speech be alway with grace, seasoned with salt, that ye may know how ye ought to answer every man.

⁷All my state shall Tychicus declare unto you, who is a beloved brother, and a faithful minister and fellowservant in the Lord: ⁸whom I have sent unto you for the same purpose, that he might know your estate, and comfort your hearts; ⁹with Onesimus, a faithful and beloved brother, who is one of you. They shall make known unto you all things which are done here.

¹⁰Aristarchus my fellowprisoner saluteth you, and Marcus, sister's son to Barnabas, (touching whom ye received commandments: if he come unto you, receive him;) ¹¹and Jesus, which is called Justus, who are of the circumcision. These only are my fellowworkers unto the kingdom of God, which have been a comfort unto me. ¹²Epaphras, who is one of you, a servant of Christ, saluteth you, always labouring fervently for you in prayers, that ye may stand perfect and complete in all the will of God. ¹³For I bear him record, that he hath a great zeal for you, and them that are in Laodicea, and them in Hierapolis. ¹⁴Luke, the beloved physician, and Demas, greet you. ¹⁵Salute the brethren which are in Laodicea, and Nymphas, and the church which is in his house. ¹⁶And when this epistle is read among you, cause that it be read also in the church of the Laodiceans; and that ye likewise read the epistle from Laodicea. ¹⁷And say to Archippus, Take heed to the ministry which thou hast received in the Lord, that thou fulfil it.

¹⁸The salutation by the hand of me Paul. Remember my bonds. Grace be with you. Amen.

Written from Rome to the Colossians by Tychicus and Onesimus.

---

lit. "the word." **4:5** *Them that are without*: outsiders. *Redeeming the time*: see Eph 5:16 note. **4:6** *Seasoned with salt*: perhaps meaning "showing wisdom"; see Matt 5:13 and note.

4:7–18 Final comments and closing. **4:7** *Tychicus*: see Eph 6:21–22 and note to v. 21. **4:8** *He might . . . comfort*: better "you might know our circumstances, and he might comfort" (MS tradition; our translation). **4:9** *Onesimus*: the slave prompting Paul's letter to Philemon, his master. Aristarchus and Mark (v. 10), as well as Epaphras (v. 12), Luke and Demas (v. 14), and Archippus (v. 17) also receive mention in Philemon (vv. 2, 23–24), suggesting either that Paul composed the two epistles in tandem or that Colossians' true author gave the composition a veneer of authenticity by linking it with Paul's letter to Philemon. **4:10** *Marcus*: John Mark of Acts 12:12, 25; 15:37–39. *Sister's son*: lit. "cousin." Acts does not mention his being a relative of *Barnabas*, Paul's chief partner during much of his ministry. **4:11** *Jesus, which . . . Justus*: otherwise unknown. *Of the circumcision*: Jews. **4:12** *Epaphras*: see 1:7 note. *Labouring*: lit. "engaging in a contest." *Complete*: better "fully assured" (MS tradition). **4:13** *A great zeal*: better "much toil" (MS tradition). *Laodicea, Hierapolis*: cities near Colossae. **4:14** *Luke, the . . . Demas*: also mentioned at 2 Tim 4:10–11, where Demas is said to have abandoned Paul. **4:15** *Nymphas*: better "Nympha," the name of a woman (otherwise unknown). A *church* meets at "her" house (MS tradition); see Rom 16:5 note. **4:16** *The epistle from Laodicea*: a letter Paul had supposedly written to the church at Laodicea—no longer extant, unless it is Ephesians (see Ephesians introduction). **4:18** *The salutation . . . Paul*: see 1 Cor 16:21 note. *Grace be with you*: recalling 1:2. *Amen. Written . . . Onesimus*: better omitted (MS tradition).

The First Epistle of Paul the Apostle to the Thessalonians

ACTS 17:1–9 records Paul's tumultuous visit to Thessalonica, which resulted in the establishment of a church there. After moving on to nearby Berea and thence to Athens in Achaia, Paul arrives at Corinth, where he founds the church to which 1 and 2 Corinthians is addressed (Acts 17:10–18:18). Acts tells us that Paul there awaited Silas and Timothy, who remained in Macedonia, the province in which Thessalonica lay. 1 Thessalonians more or less coheres with this narrative. Paul writes that while in Athens he was overwhelmed with anxiety about how the Thessalonian believers were faring, and therefore sent Timothy to encourage them (3:1–3). Apparently, Timothy caught up with Paul again in Corinth, probably soon after Paul himself arrived there, and Paul immediately composed 1 Thessalonians in response to Timothy's report (cf. 3:6). Since Acts names Gallio as Achaian proconsul during Paul's stay in Corinth, 1 Thessalonians can be dated rather precisely: an inscription informs us that Gallio held office for one year, beginning in the late spring or early summer of 51 C.E. Thus 1 Thessalonians, written in 51 or 52, is the earliest book in the entire New Testament.

Despite its brevity, this early Pauline epistle is not only beautiful but varied and creative. The long and elaborate thanksgiving that opens it (chaps. 1–3) contains some of the apostle's most moving prose: for example, "Being affectionately desirous of you, we were willing to have imparted unto you, not the gospel of God only, but also our own souls, because ye were dear unto us" (2:8). Later, when Paul describes his response to Timothy's report about Thessalonica, he manages to convey palpable relief at learning of the Thessalonians' steadfastness and, at the same time, desperate longing to see them again so that he might encourage their faith: "Brethren, we were comforted over you in all our affliction and distress by your faith: for now we live, if ye stand fast in the Lord. For what thanks can we render to God again for you, for all the joy wherewith we joy for your sakes before our God; night and day praying exceedingly that we might see your face, and might perfect that which is lacking in your faith?" (3:7–10). KJV does not always translate Paul felicitously. When studying its version alongside Paul's own Greek, we might sometimes wonder how the English reader is supposed to reconstruct the apostle's argument from the translation it offers (e.g., see Rom 6:17 and note; Rom 11:11 and note; etc.). But even if KJV occasionally obscures Paul's logic, the diction and cadences of its English idiom effectively capture Paul's sometimes poignant rhetoric. The opening chapters of 1 Thessalonians, like the hymn to love of 1 Corinthians 13, take their place among KJV's most moving passages.

For all their affection for the Thessalonians, these opening chapters also feature an apologia of Paul's missionary work among them (2:1–12). The passage calls to mind similarly defensive self-presentations of "sophists," Greek-speaking itinerant orators and philosophical teachers who flourished as part of the Second Sophistic movement in the first through third centuries C.E. Likewise, Paul's emphasis on his exemplary self-support by manual labor (2:9–12; cf. 2 Thess 3:6–10) recalls an image of the ideal philosophical teacher that circulated in the Greco-Roman world: one who demonstrates "by manual labor the lessons which reason teaches, namely that it is necessary to work hard and to suffer pain in one's own body rather than to rely on another for support" (Musonius Rufus, Fragment 11). Abraham Malherbe in particular has emphasized the ways in which Paul adapts commonplaces from Greco-Roman philosophical writing throughout his correspondence, and this rhetorical strategy is on clear display in Paul's earliest extant letter.

Of course, 1 Thessalonians also draws on a body of discourse that those associated with the Second Sophistic movement undoubtedly would have found bizarre. In 4:13–5:11, Paul invokes Jewish apocalyptic eschatology to console and exhort his readers. Early in this section he claims to base his discussion on a "word of the Lord." Since much of what follows resembles material in the Synoptic Apocalypse (esp. Matt 24) and elsewhere in the Gospels as well, he likely passes on dominical traditions that independently found their way into the Gospels, though in a somewhat different form.

We should not view Paul as a passive participant in the process of preserving and transmitting Jesus' teaching. In 5:2 he quotes a saying attributed to Jesus in various New Testament books: "the day of the Lord so cometh as a thief in the night." The aphorism is usually invoked to encourage believers to guard carefully against the coming end, calling for moral uprightness that will ensure eschatological vindication on the day of judgment. Accordingly, Matthew's Jesus says that "if the goodman of the house had known in what watch the thief would come, he would have watched, and would not have suffered his house to be broken up. Therefore be ye also ready: for in such an hour as ye think not the Son of man cometh" (24:43–44). Paul offers a different application of the tradition, one suggesting that believers' moral discipline ought to be motivated not so much by anxious expectation of the coming Day of the Lord as by faithful allegiance to it: "Ye are all the children of light, and the children of the day: we are not of the night, nor of darkness. Therefore let us not sleep, as do others; but let us watch and be sober. For they that sleep sleep in the night; and they that be drunken are drunken in the night. But let us, who are of the day, be sober" (1 Thess 5:5–8). In Paul's discourse, the figure of the nocturnal thief finds itself subsumed within the overwhelming reality of the Day of the Lord itself, whose arrival will result in communal reunion and the establishment of Christ's eschatological reign (4:13–18 and notes). Believers should eagerly anticipate that day, like sunrise on a sleepless night, not anxiously guard against it, as if they were householders fearing a nighttime robber or misbehaving servants dreading the return of their absent lord (Matt 24:42–51). Believers ought to get out of bed, as it were, and dress as if the day had arrived, which is to say that they should live sober and upright lives (1 Thess 5:6–8). The moralizing exhortation offered by Matthew is analogous (24:48–51), but the First Gospel contextualizes it within a different vision of eschatological expectation.

Eschatology plays a crucial role in 2 Thessalonians as well, but Paul's discussion there diverges from that of 1 Thessalonians. In the first letter Christ's eschatological arrival is impending (4:15, 17); in the second Paul stresses its futurity, outlining a number of events that must come to pass before its arrival (2:3–12)—none of which 1 Thessalonians (or indeed any other of Paul's letters) mentions. Primarily on the basis of this incongruity, some hold that 2 Thessalonians is pseudepigraphical: they argue that like Revelation, to which it bears some resemblance (cf. Rev 13 and 2 Thess 2:3–12), it was written toward the end of the first century, when increasingly common imperial persecution of Christians supposedly renewed believers' interest in apocalyptic eschatology, with its emphasis on the divine vindication of righteous sufferers. On this reading, 2 Thessalonians protests with suspicious vehemence when it warns against forged letters circulating in Paul's name and insists on its own authenticity (e.g., 3:17).

In the end the argument fails to convince, because it demands an eschatological consistency not always present even within the same New Testament text (in Luke, for example, compare the warning against looking for the coming kingdom of God [17:20–37] and the exhortations to eschatological watchfulness [21:5–36]) and perhaps not present in the Pauline Epistles of undisputed authorship either. (The eschatological scenarios of 1 Cor 15 and 1 Thess 4:13–5:11 are not altogether consistent.) Most likely, Paul composed 2 Thessalonians soon after 1 Thessalonians to correct a misconception about the imminence of the Day of the Lord that his previous letter had inadvertently encouraged.

In 1 Thessalonians, Paul had written "Ye, brethren, are not in darkness, that that day should overtake you as a thief. Ye are all the children of light, and the children of the day" (5:4–5). Since much of 2 Thessalonians rejects the legitimacy of refusing to labor (see 3:6–15 and note), it may be that some of the Thessalonian believers inferred from Paul's discussion of eschatological anticipation that since the Day of the Lord was at hand, they ought no longer to pursue mundane activities such as work—an idea that may have had some traction even before Paul's initial letter (see 1 Thess 5:14 and note). It is even possible that 2 Thessalonians 2:1–2 amounts to a disavowal of the earlier letter's misinterpretation rather than a warning against Pauline forgeries: "We beseech you, brethren, . . . that ye be not soon shaken in mind, or be troubled, neither by spirit, nor by word, nor by letter as from us, as that the day of Christ is at hand." Paul may here suggest that his readers have so misconstrued the eschatological exhortation offered by 1 Thessalonians that they could not have been reading the letter he wrote, and in 2:3–12 he therefore introduces a timetable to underscore how much must happen before the Day of the Lord actually arrives. If this analysis of 2 Thessalonians' compositional context is correct, it becomes hard not to smile at the misconstrual of some modern scholars: ironically, they view the text as not authentically Pauline because of its supposed eschatological incompatibility with the very letter whose eschatology it attempts to amend.

Abraham Malherbe's Anchor Bible commentary on 1 and 2 Thessalonians, *The Letters to the Thessalonians: A New Translation with Introduction and Commentary* (New York: Doubleday, 2000), is an outstanding work of biblical scholarship. This introduction and the notes that follow are deeply indebted to it, and anyone desiring further information about these epistles should start by consulting it and its extensive bibliography.

THE FIRST EPISTLE OF PAUL
THE APOSTLE TO THE
THESSALONIANS

1 Paul, and Silvanus, and Timotheus, unto the church of the Thessalonians which is in God the Father and in the Lord Jesus Christ: Grace be unto you, and peace, from God our Father, and the Lord Jesus Christ.

²We give thanks to God always for you all, making mention of you in our prayers; ³remembering without ceasing your work of faith, and labour of love, and patience of hope in our Lord Jesus Christ, in the sight of God and our Father; ⁴knowing, brethren beloved, your election of God. ⁵For our gospel came not unto you in word only, but also in power, and in the Holy Ghost, and in much assurance; as ye know what manner of men we were among you for your sake. ⁶And ye became followers of us, and of the Lord, having received the word in much affliction, with joy of the Holy Ghost: ⁷so that ye were ensamples to all that believe in Macedonia and Achaia. ⁸For from you sounded out the word of the

1:1–3:13 Salutation and thanksgiving. On the openings of Paul's letters, see note to Rom 1:1–15. Although some see Paul's conventional prayer of thanksgiving ending at 1:10, it actually extends through chap. 3 (cf. 2:13; 3:9). Chapter 1 introduces the letter by recalling the Thessalonians' conversion as a result of Paul's preaching; 2:1–16 fleshes out that abbreviated recollection (vv. 1–12 focusing on Paul's ministry and 13–16 on the Thessalonians' response); 2:17–3:13 brings the thanksgiving to a close with a passionate expression of Paul's desire to return to Thessalonica. **1:1** *Silvanus, and Timotheus:* on Silvanus, see 2 Cor 1:19 note. On Timothy, see 1 Cor 4:17 note. Timothy and Silvanus also assist Paul in founding the church at Corinth (Acts 18:5; 2 Cor 1:19), and it is probably during their sojourn there, reported in Acts 18:1–17, that 1 and 2 Thessalonians were written. *Church:* see Rom 16:5 note. *Thessalonians:* Thessalonica was a major city in the Roman province of Macedonia. *Grace be . . . peace:* see Rom 1:7 note. *From God . . . Christ:* better omitted (MS tradition). **1:3** *Faith . . . love . . . hope:* a common Pauline triad, which reappears at 5:8 (see 1 Cor 13:13 note). Throughout this letter, Paul makes extensive use of rhetorical triads; cf. 2:5–6, 10, 11, 19; etc. *Faith:* see Rom 1:8 note. *Patience:* Gk. *hypomonē*, which throughout the Thessalonian correspondence may have a stronger meaning: "steadfast endurance." **1:4** *Brethren:* a common Christian self-designation. **1:5** *Gospel:* see Mark 1:1 note. *Came not . . . power:* cf. 1 Cor 4:20. *In much assurance:* or "in (our) full conviction." **1:6** *Followers:* lit. "imitators" (also in 2:14). *Affliction:* see Acts 17:1–9 for Luke's account of the harassment experienced by some associated with the Thessalonian church. **1:7** *Macedonia and Achaia:* the two Roman provinces constituting Greece. The former contains Berea, the latter Athens and Corinth—all cities which Paul visited soon after founding the church at Thessalonica (cf. Acts 17:10–18:18) and at which he presumably told the Thessalonians' story.

Lord not only in Macedonia and Achaia, but also in every place your faith to God-ward is spread abroad; so that we need not to speak any thing. [9]For they themselves shew of us what manner of entering in we had unto you, and how ye turned to God from idols to serve the living and true God; [10]and to wait for his Son from heaven, whom he raised from the dead, even Jesus, which delivered us from the wrath to come.

2 For yourselves, brethren, know our entrance in unto you, that it was not in vain: [2]but even after that we had suffered before, and were shamefully entreated, as ye know, at Philippi, we were bold in our God to speak unto you the gospel of God with much contention. [3]For our exhortation was not of deceit, nor of uncleanness, nor in guile: [4]but as we were allowed of God to be put in trust with the gospel, even so we speak; not as pleasing men, but God, which trieth our hearts. [5]For neither at any time used we flattering words, as ye know, nor a cloke of covetousness; God is witness: [6]nor of men sought we glory, neither of you, nor yet of others, when we might have been burdensome, as the apostles of Christ. [7]But we were gentle among you, even as a nurse cherisheth her children: [8]so being affectionately desirous of you, we were willing to have imparted unto you, not the gospel of God only, but also our own souls, because ye were dear unto us.

[9]For ye remember, brethren, our labour and travail: for labouring night and day, because we would not be chargeable unto any of you, we preached unto you the gospel of God. [10]Ye are witnesses, and God also, how holily and justly and unblameably we behaved ourselves among you that believe: [11]as ye know how we exhorted and comforted and charged every one of you, as a father doth his children, [12]that ye would walk worthy of God, who hath called you unto his kingdom and glory.

[13]For this cause also thank we God without ceasing, because, when ye received the word of God which ye heard of us, ye received it not as the word of men, but as it is in truth, the word of God, which effectually worketh also in you that believe. [14]For ye, brethren, became followers of the churches of God which in Judæa are in Christ Jesus: for ye also have suffered like things of your own countrymen, even as they have of the Jews: [15]who both killed the Lord Jesus, and their own prophets, and have persecuted us; and they please not God, and are contrary to

---

1:8 *To God-ward*: toward God.   **1:9–10** *How ye . . . come*: a summary of Paul's missionary preaching. Note its focus on pagan Gentiles converting to worship of YHWH and its emphasis on eschatological expectation.   **2:2** *But even . . . Philippi*: Acts 16:12–40 narrates Paul's rough treatment at *Philippi* (in Macedonia).   **2:4** *Allowed, trieth*: both Gk. *dokimazō*, "prove by testing." *Which trieth our hearts*: cf. Prov 17:3; Jer 11:20.   **2:6** *When we . . . Christ*: they might have demanded the Thessalonians' support and reverence; cf. 2 Cor 11:7–11. *Apostles*: see Rom 1:1 note.   **2:7** *Gentle*: better "infants" (MS tradition), though it results in a startling shift in metaphor. (See Gal 4:19 for an analogous metaphorical shift.)   **2:8** *Willing*: well pleased. *Souls*: better "lives" or "selves."   **2:9** *Labour and travail*: see Acts 18:3; 20:34; 1 Cor 4:12 for Paul's self-supporting labor. *Chargeable*: lit. "burdensome"; cf. v. 6.   **2:11** *Comforted*: or "encouraged."   **2:14** *For ye also . . . countrymen*: Paul may be referring to the events narrated in Acts 17:5–9, or to harassment that Thessalonian believers experienced after he departed (cf. 3:1–5).   **2:15** *Their own prophets*: better "the prophets" (MS tradition). For the motif of slain prophets, see, e.g., Neh 9:26; Jer 2:30. *And they*: lit. "and who," continuing the limiting clause.

all men: ¹⁶forbidding us to speak to the Gentiles that they might be saved, to fill up their sins alway: for the wrath is come upon them to the uttermost.

¹⁷But we, brethren, being taken from you for a short time in presence, not in heart, endeavoured the more abundantly to see your face with great desire. ¹⁸Wherefore we would have come unto you, even I Paul, once and again; but Satan hindered us. ¹⁹For what is our hope, or joy, or crown of rejoicing? Are not even ye in the presence of our Lord Jesus Christ at his coming? ²⁰For ye are our glory and joy.

3 Wherefore when we could no longer forbear, we thought it good to be left at Athens alone; ²and sent Timotheus, our brother, and minister of God, and our fellowlabourer in the gospel of Christ, to establish you, and to comfort you concerning your faith: ³that no man should be moved by these afflictions: for yourselves know that we are appointed thereunto. ⁴For verily, when we were with you, we told you before that we should suffer tribulation; even as it came to pass, and ye know. ⁵For this cause, when I could no longer forbear, I sent to know your faith, lest by some means the tempter have tempted you, and our labour be in vain.

⁶But now when Timotheus came from you unto us, and brought us good tidings of your faith and charity, and that ye have good remembrance of us always, desiring greatly to see us, as we also to see you: ⁷therefore, brethren, we were comforted over you in all our affliction and distress by your faith: ⁸for now we live, if ye stand fast in the Lord. ⁹For what thanks can we render to God again for you, for all the joy wherewith we joy for your sakes before our God; ¹⁰night and day praying exceedingly that we might see your face, and might perfect that which is lacking in your faith?

¹¹Now God himself and our Father, and our Lord Jesus Christ, direct our way unto you. ¹²And the Lord make you to increase and abound in love one toward

---

2:16 *Forbidding*: the participial phrase explains in what sense they "are contrary to all men" ("inasmuch as they forbid" is a possible translation), but Paul may also allude to the Greco-Roman stereotype of Jewish misanthropy (see, e.g., Tacitus, *Histories* 5.5; Appendix, p. 985). *Fill up . . . uttermost*: Jews sometimes believed that while God reprimanded them, he allowed Gentiles' sin to amass so that they might suffer more severe eschatological judgment (see Rom 2:4 note). Paul surprisingly applies this idea to Jews attempting to forbid Gentiles from hearing the gospel. *The wrath is come*: not referring to a specific act of divine retribution but anticipating the eschatological judgment. **2:17** *Being taken from you*: lit. "being orphaned away from you." **2:18** *But Satan hindered us*: Paul and Luke both make statements suggesting that Paul's travels were on occasion supernaturally hindered, but they usually hold God, not Satan, responsible (cf. Rom 1:10–13; 1 Cor 16:5–7; Acts 16:6–10). Paul may here have in mind divine-Satanic collusion (cf. 2 Cor 12:7–9 and note to v. 7). **2:19** *Crown of rejoicing*: the prize customarily awarded the winner of a Greek athletic competition; cf. 1 Cor 9:24–27 and note; Phil 3:12–14. *Are not . . . coming*: see 1 Cor 3:9–17 and notes for a similar idea. *His coming*: Gk. *parousia* (see Matt 24:3 note); cf. 3:13; 4:15; 5:23. **3:1–2** *We could . . . Timotheus*: Paul refers to the trip to Athens narrated in Acts 17:16–34. **3:2** *Minister of God, and our fellowlabourer*: better "a fellow labourer with God" (MS tradition). *Comfort*: Gk. *parakaleō*, or "encourage" (also in v. 7; 4:18; 5:11); translated "exhort" at 2:11; 4:1; 5:14 (cf. 2:3); and "beseech" at 4:10. **3:3** *Moved*: shaken, agitated. **3:4** *Suffer tribulation*: Gk. *thlibesthai*, the verbal form of "affliction(s)" in vv. 3, 7; 1:6. It is unclear to what afflictions Paul refers here and in v. 3; it is not necessarily to persecutions, and Paul may be implying that the Thessalonians are experiencing the kinds of eschatological tribulations predicted in Mark 13 and elsewhere. **3:5** *The tempter*: Satan. *Our labour be in vain*: echoing Isa 49:4. **3:10** *Night and . . . face*: Acts 20:1–2

another, and toward all men, even as we do toward you: [13]to the end he may sta-blish your hearts unblameable in holiness before God, even our Father, at the coming of our Lord Jesus Christ with all his saints.

4 Furthermore then we beseech you, brethren, and exhort you by the Lord Jesus, that as ye have received of us how ye ought to walk and to please God, so ye would abound more and more. [2]For ye know what commandments we gave you by the Lord Jesus.

[3]For this is the will of God, even your sanctification, that ye should abstain from fornication: [4]that every one of you should know how to possess his vessel in sanctification and honour; [5]not in the lust of concupiscence, even as the Gentiles which know not God: [6]that no man go beyond and defraud his brother in any mat-ter: because that the Lord is the avenger of all such, as we also have forewarned you and testified. [7]For God hath not called us unto uncleanness, but unto holiness. [8]He therefore that despiseth, despiseth not man, but God, who hath also given unto us his holy Spirit.

[9]But as touching brotherly love ye need not that I write unto you: for ye your-selves are taught of God to love one another. [10]And indeed ye do it toward all the brethren which are in all Macedonia: but we beseech you, brethren, that ye increase more and more; [11]and that ye study to be quiet, and to do your own business, and to work with your own hands, as we commanded you; [12]that ye may walk honestly toward them that are without, and that ye may have lack of nothing.

---

mentions a later trip back to Macedonia, suggesting that Paul did eventually see the Thessalonian church again.   **3:13** *Saints*: Gk. *hagioi*, cognate with *holiness;* see Rom 1:7 note.

4:1–5:22 Exhortation on various matters. After a brief introductory statement (4:1–2), Paul addresses in turn marriage (4:3–8), communal self-sufficiency (4:9–12), the eschatological resurrec-tion of the dead (4:13–18), and the Day of the Lord (5:1–11). He finally gives bits of behavioral advice (5:12–22), especially regarding labor (5:12–14a) and prophecy (5:19–22). Although the topics all relate to communal cohesion, their combination may owe more to Timothy's report about what the Thessa-lonians needed to hear (cf. 3:6) than to Paul's careful rhetorical structuring.   **4:1** *How ye . . . God*: better to add "(even as you do walk)" to the end of this phrase (MS tradition). *Abound more and more*: i.e., do even more what we have taught you.   **4:3** *Sanctification*: Gk. *hagiasmos*, "holiness"; cf. vv. 4, 7; 3:13 and note. *Fornication*: Gk. *porneia*, a generic term for sexual transgression.   **4:4** *Possess his vessel*: Gk. obscure; probably "take his own wife" (rabbinic writings refer to women as "vessels" when the context is sexual), but perhaps "control his own body" (in Greek, a body can be a "vessel," espe-cially in sexual contexts). Since the Greek word rendered "possess" (*ktasthai*) is used in an idiom for marriage (*ktasthai gynaika*, "take a woman/wife"), the former interpretation is more likely.   **4:5** *Even as . . . God*: on Paul's (and other ancient Jews') ideas about sexual promiscuity among Gentiles, see Rom 1:18–32 and notes.   **4:6** *Go beyond*: transgress. *In any matter*: lit. "in the matter," i.e., "in this matter." Paul prohibits adultery, urging each man to acquire his own wife honorably and not to *defraud* a fellow believer by taking his.   **4:8** *Hath also . . . us*: better "gives to you his Holy Spirit" (MS tradition).   **4:10** *Ye do . . . Macedonia*: Paul may refer to the Thessalonian church extending hospital-ity to believers from nearby cities passing through, or to its financial support of churches in other Macedonian locales, or to something else entirely.   **4:11** *Study*: Gk. *philotimeomai*, "have an ambi-tion"; it is conventionally used of seeking after public honor in a civic context. In a surprising rhetorical turn, Paul associates it with a quiet life, minding one's own business, and manual labor.   **4:12** *Hon-estly*: properly. *Them that are without*: unbelievers. *Have lack of nothing*: "have need of nothing" or of

¹³But I would not have you to be ignorant, brethren, concerning them which are asleep, that ye sorrow not, even as others which have no hope. ¹⁴For if we believe that Jesus died and rose again, even so them also which sleep in Jesus will God bring with him. ¹⁵For this we say unto you by the word of the Lord, that we which are alive and remain unto the coming of the Lord shall not prevent them which are asleep. ¹⁶For the Lord himself shall descend from heaven with a shout, with the voice of the archangel, and with the trump of God: and the dead in Christ shall rise first: ¹⁷then we which are alive and remain shall be caught up together with them in the clouds, to meet the Lord in the air: and so shall we ever be with the Lord. ¹⁸Wherefore comfort one another with these words.

5 But of the times and the seasons, brethren, ye have no need that I write unto you. ²For yourselves know perfectly that the day of the Lord so cometh as a thief in the night. ³For when they shall say, Peace and safety; then sudden destruction cometh upon them, as travail upon a woman with child; and they shall not escape. ⁴But ye, brethren, are not in darkness, that that day should overtake you as a thief. ⁵Ye are all the children of light, and the children of the day: we are not

---

"nobody." Compare Paul's manual self-support in 2:9. **4:13** *Them which are asleep*: believers who have died. *Even as . . . hope*: Paul is telling the Thessalonians not that they will grieve differently from the hopeless but that, in contrast with them, they will not grieve at all. (Compare the parallel construction in v. 5.) **4:14** *If we . . . him*: as in 1 Cor 15, Paul explains the eschatological implications of Jesus' resurrection, although here the context is more pastoral. **4:15** *This we . . . Lord*: close parallels between vv. 15–17 and Matt 16:28; 24:30–31 suggest Paul here refers to, applies, and supplements Jesus' eschatological teaching. Similar parallels pervade 5:1–11 (see notes), which may indicate that the phrase covers the subsequent paragraph as well. *Prevent*: precede. **4:16** *Trump*: a common eschatological motif (cf. 1 Cor 15:52; Matt 24:31), the trumpet recalls the apocalyptic vision of Isa 27:13, where its sound heralds the gathering of God's scattered people. **4:17** *Caught up . . . air*: the reference is not to the so-called rapture, which in popular evangelical discourse refers to the snatching away of Christians into heaven in advance of the eschatological afflictions outlined in the Synoptic Apocalypse and elsewhere in the NT—an idea that emerged only in the nineteenth century. On the contrary, Paul here suggests that the dead rise and immediately afterward the living join them: they are *caught up together with them in the clouds* and then all *meet the Lord in the air* as he descends from heaven (4:16). The celestial locale of this joyful reunion is not surprising in light of 1 Cor 15, where the eschatologically transformed bodies of believers (and of Jesus as well) are consistently associated with the heavens (vv. 40–41, 47–49). Nonetheless, Gk. *apantēsis* ("meet") can also mean "escort," as in Matt 25:6 (see 25:1 note), and can apply specifically to citizens escorting a foreign dignitary to their city (see Malherbe, *Letters to the Thessalonians* 276). Since Gk. *parousia* ("coming," v. 15) is itself a technical term for a royal dignitary's visit (see Matt 24:3 note), Paul likely imagines risen believers meeting Christ among the clouds in order to usher him back to earth, where he will confirm his reign (cf. Dan 7:13–14). **5:1** *The times and the seasons*: cf. Dan 2:21. **5:2** *As a thief*: the image, attributed to both the earthly (Matt 24:43; Luke 12:39) and the risen Jesus (Rev 3:3; 16:15), conventionally figures the Day of the Lord in the NT; also cf. 2 Pet 3:10. **5:3** *Peace and safety*: the two words were employed together in propaganda celebrating the Roman Empire and the peace it enforced (*pax Romana*), which the Day of the Lord threatens. *Travail*: labor pains; see Mark 13:8 note. **5:4–9** *But ye . . . Christ*: Paul develops the traditional image of the nocturnal thief in an unexpected way. Instead of calling on his readers to behave righteously in anxious anticipation of the coming day of judgment (contrast the passages cited in v. 2 note; Luke 21:34–36), he urges them to let their behavior demonstrate that they already belong to that day, rather than to "the night" which it will bring to an end (cf. Rom 13:11–14). **5:5** *Children of light*: a conventional apocalyptic self-designation (see Luke

of the night, nor of darkness. [6]Therefore let us not sleep, as do others; but let us watch and be sober. [7]For they that sleep sleep in the night; and they that be drunken are drunken in the night. [8]But let us, who are of the day, be sober, putting on the breastplate of faith and love; and for an helmet, the hope of salvation. [9]For God hath not appointed us to wrath, but to obtain salvation by our Lord Jesus Christ, [10]who died for us, that, whether we wake or sleep, we should live together with him. [11]Wherefore comfort yourselves together, and edify one another, even as also ye do.

[12]And we beseech you, brethren, to know them which labour among you, and are over you in the Lord, and admonish you; [13]and to esteem them very highly in love for their work's sake. And be at peace among yourselves. [14]Now we exhort you, brethren, warn them that are unruly, comfort the feebleminded, support the weak, be patient toward all men. [15]See that none render evil for evil unto any man; but ever follow that which is good, both among yourselves, and to all men.

[16]Rejoice evermore. [17]Pray without ceasing. [18]In every thing give thanks: for this is the will of God in Christ Jesus concerning you. [19]Quench not the Spirit. [20]Despise not prophesyings. [21]Prove all things; hold fast that which is good. [22]Abstain from all appearance of evil.

[23]And the very God of peace sanctify you wholly; and I pray God your whole spirit and soul and body be preserved blameless unto the coming of our Lord Jesus Christ. [24]Faithful is he that calleth you, who also will do it.

[25]Brethren, pray for us. [26]Greet all the brethren with an holy kiss. [27]I charge you by the Lord that this epistle be read unto all the holy brethren.

[28]The grace of our Lord Jesus Christ be with you. Amen.

The first epistle unto the Thessalonians was written from Athens.

16:8 note), here with a temporal nuance, suggesting that believers already belong to the coming Day of the Lord. **5:6** *Let us watch*: cf. Mark 13:35–37. *And be sober*: sobriety is typically conjoined with watchfulness in Greco-Roman moralizing philosophy and other ancient literature; cf. Luke 21:34–36; 1 Pet 5:8; Plutarch, *To an Uneducated Ruler* 781D. **5:8** *Putting on the breastplate . . . salvation*: in Eph 6:10–17 readers are also urged to arm themselves for apocalyptic battle, but there the armor is both offensive and defensive; see also Rom 6:13 and note; 13:12; 2 Cor 6:7; 10:4. **5:10** *Wake or sleep*: live or die (see 4:13 note). But Gk. *grēgoreō* (here *wake*) was earlier rendered "watch" (v. 6). In the eschatological discourse of 4:13–5:10, waking and sleeping have two related sets of connotations (compare 4:13–15 and 5:6–7). **5:14** *Unruly*: Gk. *ataktos*, "disorderly"; in 2 Thess 3:6–11 the same Greek word is thrice associated with believers who refuse to work (see notes). Paul may refer to the same problem here; cf. 2:9; 4:11–12 and notes. *Feebleminded*: fainthearted. **5:15** *See that . . . man*: see Rom 12:17 and note. **5:16** *Evermore*: at all times. **5:19–22** *Quench not . . . evil*: Paul's initial image of the Spirit's quenching plays on its common representation as a flame (Acts 2:3; cf. Matt 3:11; etc.), with the following verses providing an interpretive context for the image: the Thessalonian church must value the spiritual gift of prophecy (cf. 1 Cor 12:10; 14:1–12), but at the same time may not take for granted the authenticity of any given prophetic utterance. **5:22** *All appearance*: or "every form."

5:23–28 Closing. The framing references to the God of peace (v. 23) and to the grace Paul wishes the Thessalonians (v. 28) recall Paul's introductory wish of grace and peace (1:1). **5:23** *Your whole . . . body*: the division is emphatic (cf. Deut 6:5), unpacking *wholly*. **5:26** *Holy kiss*: see Rom 16:16 note. **5:27** *Holy*: better omitted (MS tradition). **5:28** *Amen. The first epistle . . . Athens*: better omitted (MS tradition).

THE SECOND EPISTLE OF PAUL
THE APOSTLE TO THE
THESSALONIANS†

1 Paul, and Silvanus, and Timotheus, unto the church of the Thessalonians in God our Father and the Lord Jesus Christ: [2]Grace unto you, and peace, from God our Father and the Lord Jesus Christ.

[3]We are bound to thank God always for you, brethren, as it is meet, because that your faith groweth exceedingly, and the charity of every one of you all toward each other aboundeth; [4]so that we ourselves glory in you in the churches of God for your patience and faith in all your persecutions and tribulations that ye endure: [5]which is a manifest token of the righteous judgment of God, that ye may be counted worthy of the kingdom of God, for which ye also suffer: [6]seeing it is a righteous thing with God to recompense tribulation to them that trouble you; [7]and to you who are troubled rest with us, when the Lord Jesus shall be revealed from heaven with his mighty angels, [8]in flaming fire taking vengeance on them that know not God, and that obey not the gospel of our Lord Jesus Christ: [9]who shall be punished with everlasting destruction from the presence of the Lord, and from the glory of his power; [10]when he shall come to be glorified in his saints, and to be admired in all them that believe (because our testimony among you was believed) in that day.

---

† The introduction to 1 Thessalonians serves also for its companion. See pp. 437–440.

1:1–12 Salutation and thanksgiving. 1:3 *Meet*: worthwhile; the same Greek root is translated "worthy" in vv. 5, 11. **1:4–7** *In all . . . troubled*: note the expanded emphasis on persecution, in contrast to the passing references in 1 Thess 1:6; 2:14; 3:3–4. At the time of the second letter, the Thessalonian believers may have been experiencing more harassment, of unknown source and nature. Or Paul here may simply underscore the affliction they have been experiencing as part of his strategy to emphasize the futurity of the Day of the Lord, which such tribulation must precede. **1:5** *Manifest token*: plain indication, clear proof. **1:6** *Trouble*: Gk. *thlibō* (also in v. 7); its nominal form is translated *tribulation* in this letter (cf. v. 4) and as "affliction" in 1 Thessalonians. **1:7** *Rest*: like "tribulation" in v. 6, this is a direct object of "recompense." **1:8** *In flaming fire*: fire is a conventional element in biblical theophanies, as well as an instrument of punishment; cf. Exod 19:18; Mark 9:43, 48; etc. *Vengeance*: Gk. *ekdikēsis*, which shares a root with "punished" (v. 9) and "righteous" (v. 6), implying just punishment. *Them that . . . Christ*: perhaps distinguishing Gentiles, "which know not God" (1 Thess 4:5), from Jews who do not embrace Paul's gospel. **1:9** *From the presence . . . power*: quoting LXX Isa 2:10, 19, 21. **1:10** *In all*: among all. *That believe*: better "that believed" (MS tradition).

¹¹Wherefore also we pray always for you, that our God would count you worthy of this calling, and fulfil all the good pleasure of his goodness, and the work of faith with power: ¹²that the name of our Lord Jesus Christ may be glorified in you, and ye in him, according to the grace of our God and the Lord Jesus Christ.

2 Now we beseech you, brethren, by the coming of our Lord Jesus Christ, and by our gathering together unto him, ²that ye be not soon shaken in mind, or be troubled, neither by spirit, nor by word, nor by letter as from us, as that the day of Christ is at hand. ³Let no man deceive you by any means: for that day shall not come, except there come a falling away first, and that man of sin be revealed, the son of perdition; ⁴who opposeth and exalteth himself above all that is called God, or that is worshipped; so that he as God sitteth in the temple of God, shewing himself that he is God.

⁵Remember ye not, that, when I was yet with you, I told you these things? ⁶And now ye know what withholdeth that he might be revealed in his time. ⁷For the mystery of iniquity doth already work: only he who now letteth will let, until he be taken out of the way. ⁸And then shall that Wicked be revealed, whom the Lord shall consume with the spirit of his mouth, and shall destroy with the brightness of his coming: ⁹even him, whose coming is after the working of Satan with all power and signs and lying wonders, ¹⁰and with all deceivableness of unrighteousness in them that perish; because they received not the love of the truth, that they might

2:1–3:15 Exhortation. 2:1–12 deals with the need to wait for the eschatological Day of the Lord; 2:13–3:5 continues that focus, but subtly modulates into a more general exhortation to faithfulness; 3:6–15 offers direction about how to deal with the "disorderly."   **2:1** *By*: lit. "concerning," both times in this verse. *Coming*: Gk. *parousia* (see Matt 24:3 note), as in 1 Thess 2:19; 3:13; 4:15; 5:23. *Our gathering together*: cf. 1 Thess 4:17. Such a gathering is a conventional eschatological expectation; see Matt 24:31 and note.   **2:2** *Be troubled*: "be worked up" (NRSV); a different Greek root is rendered "trouble" in chap. 1 (vv. 6, 7). *By letter . . . us*: the Thessalonian church had either received a letter written in Paul's name which he did not compose (cf. 3:17 and note), or they have so misconstrued (or been so misled as to the meaning of) 1 Thessalonians that Paul distances himself from their interpretation by suggesting he could not possibly be the author of what they have read. *Day of Christ*: better "day of the Lord" (MS tradition). *Is at hand*: or "is present," perhaps suggesting that the Thessalonians misconstrued 1 Thess 5:4–5.   **2:3** *Falling away*: Gk. *apostasia*, which may refer to political rebellion or to rebellion against God (e.g., LXX Josh 22:22); it sometimes corresponds to the English "apostasy" (cf. 1 Macc 2:15). *Man of sin*: better "man of lawlessness" (MS tradition). What Paul goes on to write about him resembles Rev 13. *Son of perdition*: see John 17:12 and note.   **2:4** *As God*: better omitted (MS tradition). *Sitteth in the temple . . . is God*: the language is conventional (cf. Isa 14:13–14; Ezek 28:1–10), but Paul may model the hubris of the son of perdition on that of the Roman emperor Caligula, who about a decade before Paul writes had ordered a statue of himself to be displayed in the Jewish temple, prompting the threat of Jewish rebellion against Rome (Josephus, *Jewish War* 2.184–85). Antiochus IV Epiphanes' desecration of the temple may also lie in the background (cf. Dan 8:13 and note; 1 Macc 1:54).   **2:6** *What withholdeth*: lit. "what restrains [him]."   **2:7** *Iniquity*: lit. "lawlessness," as in v. 3 (see note). *Letteth*: "restrains"; cf. v. 6 and note. Paul presents the restrainer both as a thing (v. 6) and as a person (v. 7), which lends support to an interpretation as old as Tertullian: Paul understands the (temporary) order and authority of the Roman Empire, embodied in its emperor, to restrain the "man of lawlessness." (Compare the attitude toward imperial authority expressed in Rom 13:1–7.)   **2:8** *That Wicked*: lit. "the lawless one," i.e., the man of lawlessness (see v. 3 and note). KJV capitalizes the term to clarify the reference. *Consume*: better "kill" (MS tradition). *Spirit of his mouth*: or "breath of his mouth"; cf. Isa 11:4; Matt 3:11 and note. *Brightness*: or "appearance."   **2:9** *Whose coming*: like Jesus, the man of lawlessness has a *parousia* (see v. 1 and note). *After*: according to.   **2:9–10** *With all power . . . perish*: see Mark 13:22 and note.   **2:10** *Deceivableness*: deceit. *In them*:

be saved. [11]And for this cause God shall send them strong delusion, that they should believe a lie: [12]that they all might be damned who believed not the truth, but had pleasure in unrighteousness.

[13]But we are bound to give thanks alway to God for you, brethren beloved of the Lord, because God hath from the beginning chosen you to salvation through sanctification of the Spirit and belief of the truth: [14]whereunto he called you by our gospel, to the obtaining of the glory of our Lord Jesus Christ. [15]Therefore, brethren, stand fast, and hold the traditions which ye have been taught, whether by word, or our epistle.

[16]Now our Lord Jesus Christ himself, and God, even our Father, which hath loved us, and hath given us everlasting consolation and good hope through grace, [17]comfort your hearts, and stablish you in every good word and work.

3 Finally, brethren, pray for us, that the word of the Lord may have free course, and be glorified, even as it is with you: [2]and that we may be delivered from unreasonable and wicked men: for all men have not faith. [3]But the Lord is faithful, who shall stablish you, and keep you from evil. [4]And we have confidence in the Lord touching you, that ye both do and will do the things which we command you. [5]And the Lord direct your hearts into the love of God, and into the patient waiting for Christ.

[6]Now we command you, brethren, in the name of our Lord Jesus Christ, that ye withdraw yourselves from every brother that walketh disorderly, and not after the tradition which he received of us. [7]For yourselves know how ye ought to follow us: for we behaved not ourselves disorderly among you; [8]neither did we eat any man's bread for nought; but wrought with labour and travail night and day, that we might not be chargeable to any of you: [9]not because we have not power, but to make ourselves an ensample unto you to follow us. [10]For even when we were with you, this we commanded you, that if any would not work, neither should he eat. [11]For we hear that there are some which walk among you disorderly, working not at all, but are busybodies. [12]Now them that are such we command and exhort by our Lord Jesus Christ, that with quietness they work, and eat their own bread. [13]But ye, brethren, be not weary in well doing. [14]And if any man obey not our word by this epistle, note that man, and have no company with him, that he may be ashamed. [15]Yet count him not as an enemy, but admonish him as a brother.

---

better "for them" (MS tradition).   **2:11** *Shall send*: better "sends" (MS tradition). *Strong delusion*: lit. "working of error" (RV).   **2:12** *Damned*: lit. "judged."   **2:13** *From the beginning*: better "as firstfruits" (MS tradition); see Rom 16:15; 1 Cor 15:20 note.   **2:15** *Whether by . . . epistle*: cf. vv. 2 (*epistle*) and 5 (*word*).   **2:16** *Consolation*: or "encouragement."   **2:17** *Comfort*: or "encourage," the verbal form of "consolation" in v. 16 (see note).   **3:1** *Have free course*: lit. "run."   **3:3** *Evil*: or "the evil one." **3:6–15** *Now we . . . brother*: the problem Paul here addresses (and to which he may allude at 1 Thess 5:14), of members of the church not working, may relate to some Thessalonians' belief that they are already living in the end times (see 2:2 note). With the form of this world passing away, mundane activities such as labor would no longer be appropriate—a conclusion possibly drawn from 1 Thess 5:4–8, as well as from statements that Paul might have made while preaching (cf. 2 Cor 5:17).   **3:6** *Disorderly*: see 1 Thess 5:14 note.   **3:7** *Follow*: lit. "imitate" (also in v. 9).   **3:8** *Wrought with labour and travail*: worked hard and toiled. *Chargeable*: see 1 Thess 2:9 note.   **3:9** *Power*: "authority," in the sense of "a right"; cf. 1 Cor 9:4–15.   **3:11** *Working not . . . busybodies*: an untranslatable pun on Gk. *ergazomenous* ("working") and *periergazomenous* ("being a busybody").

[16]Now the Lord of peace himself give you peace always by all means. The Lord be with you all. [17]The salutation of Paul with mine own hand, which is the token in every epistle: so I write. [18]The grace of our Lord Jesus Christ be with you all. Amen.

The second epistle to the Thessalonians was written from Athens.

3:16–18 Closing. 3:16 *The Lord . . . always*: recalling Num 6:26.   **3:17** *The salutation . . . write*: indicating that Paul has taken the pen from his scribe in order to add his authenticating signature (cf. 1 Cor 16:21 and note), perhaps in an attempt to distinguish this letter from pseudonymous writings already circulating in his name; see 2:2 and note.   **3:18** *Amen. The second epistle . . . Athens*: better omitted (MS tradition).

The Pastoral Epistles

IRST Timothy begins the second of the New Testament's three divisions of Pauline Epistles: the first nine, arranged in order of descending length, are all addressed to churches; the next four, similarly arranged, are addressed to individuals. In practice, most scholars segregate the letters to delegates even further, treating 1 and 2 Timothy and Titus as a discrete unit conventionally designated the Pastoral Epistles because of their focus on church management. A scholarly consensus holds them to be pseudepigraphic compositions from the late first or early second century. This judgment relies on a series of arguments that may be summarized as follows.

First, it is difficult to situate some events to which the Pastorals refer in the itinerary of Paul's ministry that Acts and the other Paulines allow us to reconstruct. The most obvious example would be Titus 1:5, which presupposes a mission to Crete for which neither any of Paul's other letters nor Acts offers evidence. (Acts 27:12 mentions that Paul made a very brief stop in Crete on his way to Rome, but says nothing of a ministry or church there.)

Second, peculiar diction and other stylistic features are seen as linking the three epistles together, while at the same time distinguishing them from the other Paulines. For instance, Gk. *eusebia* ("piety" or, as KJV prefers, "godliness") and its cognates appear more than a dozen times in the Pastorals, but nowhere else in Paul's letters. A related example is the Pastorals' tendency to use imagery of health and disease to describe teaching (e.g., 1 Tim 1:10 and note; 2 Tim 2:17).

Third, the Pastorals make multiple references to false teachings that may more closely resemble second-century "heresies" than those confronted by Paul in his other writings (see, e.g., 1 Tim 1:4 and note). Moreover, the Pastorals rely almost solely on vituperative polemic to combat such teachings. The other Paulines, while sometimes resorting to obloquy, rely primarily on theological and exegetical refutation of ideas deemed false and dangerous. (Compare the responses to false teaching about the resurrection at 2 Tim 2:16–18 and at 1 Cor 15, for example.)

Fourth, the Pastorals assume a more formal and elaborate ecclesiastical structure than do Paul's undisputed letters, and this structure resembles ecclesiastical hierarchies discussed in second-century Christian texts. (Compare 1 Tim 3:1–13 with *1 Clement* 42.4 and *Didache* 15.)

Finally, the Pastorals often find themselves at ideological odds with Paul's other writings. For instance, whereas Paul privileges celibacy (1 Cor 7:1–9, 25–26, 32–35, 38), the author of the Pastorals urges his readers to marry (1 Tim 3:2, 11–12; 5:14; Titus 1:6; etc.), even going so far as to assert that women will "be saved in childbearing" (1 Tim 2:15).

On its own, none of these arguments is particularly compelling, and we may consider them in order. First, no scholars believe that the outline of Paul's ministry which can be reconstructed from Acts and the undisputed epistles is anything approaching exhaustive, and so our inability easily to fit a handful of data into it does not undermine their historicity. Second, the stylistic arguments to which some scholars give weight are both somewhat naïve—failing to take into account that authors regularly adapt their style to particular compositional situations—and circular. If we start by segregating the Pastorals from the other Paulines and then look for distinguishing stylistic features to support that division, we can find them. But the same thing can be done with virtually any group of Paul's letters. For example, the Greek word *nomos* ("law") appears close to one hundred times in Romans and Galatians, yet only fourteen times in all the other Pauline epistles combined, with eight of those fourteen occurrences in 1 Corinthians alone. Scholars today, however, do not invoke this statistic to argue against Paul's composition of Romans, Galatians, and possibly 1 Corinthians, or to argue that he composed only those three letters and that all the others are pseudepigraphical (although F. C. Baur came close in the nineteenth century, arguing on a related basis that those letters and 2 Corinthians alone were assuredly authentic; see Luke Timothy Johnson, *The First and Second Letters to Timothy*, pp. 69, 45). Third, the Pastorals do not say enough about the false teachings to which they refer to allow us confidently to associate them with any discrete movements in early Christianity, either during Paul's ministry or after it. Fourth, Pauline epistles whose authenticity is not in doubt themselves allude in passing to precisely the ecclesiastical offices that the Pastorals discuss in detail (Rom 16:1 and note; Phil 1:1). There is no need to assume that it took generations for formal structures to develop in Paul's churches (see Acts 14:23) and it is not difficult to imagine Paul himself explaining in the Pastorals the qualifications for holding the positions he mentions elsewhere in his writings. Finally, the Pauline Letters recognized as authentic themselves lack rigorous ideological consistency (e.g., compare Gal 3:19–26 and Rom 7:7–13 on the law). Indeed, Paul may not be above contradicting himself within the course of a single letter (cf. 1 Cor 11:2–16; 14:34–35, but see note).

Scholars today increasingly recognize that the problems with the arguments against the Pastoral Epistles' Pauline authorship are serious, and admit that only their combined weight can begin to sustain the hypothesis of pseudepigraphy. What is perhaps less often admitted is the pressure of literary-historical context: the Pastoral Epistles, many find, simply make good sense when interpreted as being in dialogue with other second-century Christian writings, including those about or purporting to be by Paul. In response to gnostic traditions such as those preserved in *The Reality of the Rulers*, which authorizes its complex genealogical myth of cosmic powers by referring to Paul's Epistle to the Ephesians, the pseudepigraphic Pastorals show Paul decisively rejecting gnostic speculation about the mythical origins and genealogies of divine powers (1 Tim 1:4). In response to stories such as those preserved in the apocryphal *Acts of Paul and Thecla*, which offers Paul as a preacher of asceticism inspiring women to abandon the domestic world and become radical disciples of him and of Jesus, the Pastorals depict Paul utterly rejecting asceticism—he even urges Timothy to take a little wine to settle his stomach (1 Tim 5:23)—and restricting Christian women to the domestic sphere (1 Tim 2:11–15). The New Testament itself may betray an awareness of spurious letters of Paul (2 Thess 2:2; cf. 3:17) and a number of such compositions from later generations are extant (3 Corinthians, the Epistle to the Laodiceans, the correspondence between Paul and Seneca, etc.). The Pastorals may be among the many surviving examples of post-Pauline texts invoking the apostle's authority to support theological and ideological positions on such issues as the legitimacy of gnostic mythological speculation, asceticism, the role of women in the church, and the degree to which Christianity should complement or challenge Greco-Roman familial structures.

The ease with which the Pastorals can be interpreted within the context of second-century Christian debates is certainly intriguing, but invoking it as evidence of their late date of composition (and thus their pseudonymity) risks circular argumentation. Moreover, 2 Timothy fits just as well—if not better—into the literary-historical context of Paul's authentic oeuvre. Any interpretive decision to embrace the hypothesis of pseudonymity is neither comfortable nor certain, and the easy scholarly consensus that the Pastorals are late pseudepigraphical compositions rather than authentically Pauline is at best premature. The purpose of this introduction, and a main focus of the individual introductions and annotations that follow, is—to the extent possible in the space provided—to enable readers to come to their own tentative conclusions about how best to understand these fascinating texts. Consequently, information supporting both interpretive possibilities will be offered, and the critical appendix prints the *Acts of Paul and Thecla* (pp. 1020–27), the second-century text most clearly in dialogue with the Pastorals.

For a thorough discussion of the problems and history of the Pastoral Epistles' interpretation, see Luke Timothy Johnson's Anchor Bible Commentary, *The First and Second Letters to Timothy: A New Translation with Introduction and Commentary* (New York: Doubleday, 2001), pp. 13–131, whose influence may be detected throughout the introductions and annotations to the Pastoral Epistles.

The First Epistle of Paul the Apostle to Timothy

I T is difficult to discover literary coherence in 1 Timothy, which alternates throughout between personal exhortation to its addressee and instructions for managing the church at Ephesus (see note to 2:1–6:21a), sometimes with a spontaneity approaching randomness. Insofar as there is an overarching theme, it is articulated at 1:4, which urges Timothy to turn his attention to "godly household management in faith" (see note). The verse foreshadows the epistle's frequent concern with familial and ecclesiastical order, which turn out to be intimately related: "if a man know not how to rule his own house, how shall he take care of the church of God?" (3:5). This link is not surprising: the church at Ephesus would have met at one or more homes.

1 Timothy is interested in points of intersection between God's house and the Greco-Roman family, as its author repeatedly insists that the values of the former complement rather than challenge the benevolent patriarchalism ideally characterizing the latter. Along the way, the epistle provides an intriguing glimpse of the social world of the early church, revealing tantalizing bits of information about the institutions and communal tensions that emerged during its first fifty or hundred years of existence. 1 Timothy, for instance, adumbrates behavioral requirements for discrete positions of leadership; it insists on fair pay for ecclesiastical officers and their overall just treatment; it repeatedly urges the strict regulation of women's public speech, movement, and appearance; and it negotiates a complex compromise between the church's and individual families' responsibilities to care for those without means.

The letter contains no information about Paul's activities other than stating that he left Timothy at Ephesus to travel to Macedonia (1:3). According to Acts, Paul was at Ephesus for two years (19:10), apparently with Timothy (19:22), whence he departed for Macedonia (Acts 20:1–3)—perhaps leaving Timothy in Ephesus for a time as his delegate (he is not reported to be with Paul again until after the Macedonian trip; 20:4–5). 2 Corinthians also mentions what is presumably the same trip to Macedonia (1:16; 2:12–13; 7:5–6; cf. 1 Cor 16:5). If authentic, 1 Timothy could be associated with that excursion, or it may have been composed at virtually any other time during Paul's third missionary journey, which would have been an occasion for much travel and correspondence between Ephesus, Corinth, and Macedonia (the location of Thessalonica, Philippi, and other cities with churches that Paul established). These circumstances suggest a date of composition in the mid-50s C.E.

Traditionally, scholars arguing for its authenticity have dated the epistle to much later in Paul's career, speculating that he was released from Roman incarceration in the early 60s, renewed his ministry in the Aegean and beyond (during which period 1 Timothy is supposed to have been composed), and then was again arrested by Roman authorities, with his martyrdom following. Such a reconstruction has the advantage of allowing time for Paul's thought on such issues as celibacy and the role of women in the church to evolve, but it lacks compelling historical support; moreover, it stands in tension with Acts' strong hints that the Roman incarceration with which it concludes culminated in the apostle's execution (e.g., Acts 20:22–25; 21:11; see the introduction to Titus for more details on this hypothesis).

If 1 Timothy is a later pseudepigraphic composition, it probably seeks to authorize in Paul's name an institutional vision of emergent Christianity that was thought to represent a healthy development of Pauline teaching and practice. In accordance with Greco-Roman literary conventions, the author discreetly recedes behind the false front of a recognized master, attempting to emulate a respected sage's style and ideas while pursuing his own somewhat more modest philosophical, ideological, and rhetorical goals.

For more information on 1 Timothy, Luke Timothy Johnson's Anchor Bible commentary, *The First and Second Letters to Timothy: A New Translation with Introduction and Commentary* (New York: Doubleday, 2001), is the best place to start. Its influence can be discerned in this introduction and the notes that follow.

THE FIRST EPISTLE OF
PAUL THE APOSTLE TO
TIMOTHY

1 Paul, an apostle of Jesus Christ by the commandment of God our Saviour, and Lord Jesus Christ, which is our hope; ²unto Timothy, my own son in the faith: Grace, mercy, and peace, from God our Father and Jesus Christ our Lord.

³As I besought thee to abide still at Ephesus, when I went into Macedonia, that thou mightest charge some that they teach no other doctrine, ⁴neither give heed to fables and endless genealogies, which minister questions, rather than godly edifying which is in faith: so do. ⁵Now the end of the commandment is charity out of a pure heart, and of a good conscience, and of faith unfeigned: ⁶from which some having swerved have turned aside unto vain jangling; ⁷desiring to be teachers of the law; understanding neither what they say, nor whereof they affirm. ⁸But we know that the law is good, if a man use it lawfully; ⁹knowing this, that the law is not made for a righteous man, but for the lawless and disobedient, for the ungodly and for sinners, for unholy and profane, for murderers of fathers and murderers

1:1–20 Salutation, charge, and thanksgiving. On the openings of Paul's letters, see note to Rom 1:1–15. 1 Timothy's opening consists of a greeting (vv. 1–2) and exhortation (vv. 3–20), in which the conventional prayer of thanksgiving is embedded (vv. 12–17). **1:1** *Apostle*: see Rom 1:1 note. **1:2** *Timothy*: see 1 Cor 4:17 note. *Own*: lit. "legitimate," i.e., "genuine." *Grace, mercy . . . Lord*: a variation of Paul's standard salutation; see Rom 1:7 and note. **1:3** *Ephesus*: a city in Asia Minor; according to Acts 19, Paul founded a church there. *Macedonia*: the Roman province corresponding to northern Greece. **1:4** *Fables and endless genealogies*: if 1 Timothy is a second-century pseudepigraphic composition, the writer may be rejecting classic gnostic mythological speculation such as that found at the beginning of the *Apocryphon of John*. (Some ancient Christians embraced such speculation; see Ptolemy's Version of the Gnostic Myth, Appendix, pp. 1050–63.) But scholars have also seen the verse as warning against proto-rabbinic attempts to establish authoritative chains of transmission for oral traditions supplementing the Torah, or even against early Christian fabrications of Jesus' genealogy and legends about his miraculous birth, such as those in Matthew and Luke. *Minister*: provide for. *Edifying*: better "household management" (MS tradition), with the connotation of "ordering." *So do*: supplied by KJV to make the sentence grammatically coherent. **1:5** *Commandment*: Gk. *parangelia*, the nominal form of "charge" in v. 3. *Faith*: see Rom 1:8 note, though at times in the Pastorals "faith" appears to be more reified and less dynamic (e.g., see v. 2; 3:9). **1:6** *Vain jangling*: idle speech. **1:8** *But we . . . good*: cf. Rom 7:12, 14, 16. **1:9** *Knowing this*: the subject is "man" (v. 8); v. 9 thus explains how the law may be lawfully used. *Made*: Gk. *ketai*, lit. "laid down." *Lawless*: see Rom 2:12 and note. The suggestion in 1 Tim 1:7–10 that godless Gentiles (which this vice list clearly describes; cf. Rom 1:18–32 and notes) would benefit from the Jewish law fits the interpretation of Rom 1:18–2:16 proposed in

of mothers, for manslayers, [10]for whoremongers, for them that defile themselves with mankind, for menstealers, for liars, for perjured persons, and if there be any other thing that is contrary to sound doctrine; [11]according to the glorious gospel of the blessed God, which was committed to my trust.

[12]And I thank Christ Jesus our Lord, who hath enabled me, for that he counted me faithful, putting me into the ministry; [13]who was before a blasphemer, and a persecutor, and injurious: but I obtained mercy, because I did it ignorantly in unbelief. [14]And the grace of our Lord was exceeding abundant with faith and love which is in Christ Jesus. [15]This is a faithful saying, and worthy of all acceptation, that Christ Jesus came into the world to save sinners; of whom I am chief. [16]Howbeit for this cause I obtained mercy, that in me first Jesus Christ might shew forth all longsuffering, for a pattern to them which should hereafter believe on him to life everlasting. [17]Now unto the King eternal, immortal, invisible, the only wise God, be honour and glory for ever and ever. Amen.

[18]This charge I commit unto thee, son Timothy, according to the prophecies which went before on thee, that thou by them mightest war a good warfare; [19]holding faith, and a good conscience; which some having put away concerning faith have made shipwreck: [20]of whom is Hymenæus and Alexander; whom I have delivered unto Satan, that they may learn not to blaspheme.

2 I exhort therefore, that, first of all, supplications, prayers, intercessions, and giving of thanks, be made for all men; [2]for kings, and for all that are in authority; that we may lead a quiet and peaceable life in all godliness and honesty. [3]For

---

Rom 2:12 note. The provisional claims about Gentiles and the law that Paul makes in the early part of Romans are modified or even abrogated by the relationship between righteousness and faith in Christ articulated in Rom 3:21–4:2 (see note). The suggestion here that the law would benefit godless Gentiles is likewise nuanced by the claim that it *is not made for a righteous man*, which suggests that the law benefits those outside Christ, as opposed to those made righteous through him. *Ungodly*: impious. **1:10** *Whoremongers*: the sexually immoral. *Them that . . . mankind*: Gk. *arsenokoitēs*; see 1 Cor 6:9 note. *Menstealers*: i.e., slave dealers, especially those who sold into slavery people taken prisoner in war. *Is contrary to*: Gk. *antikeitai*, lit. "lies opposed to," containing the same root as "made" in v. 9 (see note). *Sound doctrine*: lit. "healthy teaching." Teaching is commonly described as "sound" or "healthy" in the Pastorals, a metaphorical usage also found in Greco-Roman popular philosophical writing. **1:11** *The glorious gospel . . . trust*: cf. Gal 2:7. *Gospel*: see Mark 1:1 note. **1:13** *Injurious*: Gk. *hybristēs*, "violently insolent," often connoting audacious assumption of divine prerogatives. *But I . . . unbelief*: compare Paul's statements in Rom 10:1–3 about the ignorant zeal of unbelieving Jews, to whom he expects God to show mercy (Rom 11:25–31, esp. v. 30). **1:15** *This is . . . saying*: identical formulae occur at 3:1; 4:9; 2 Tim 2:11; Titus 3:8. (KJV alternates between "true" and the more literal "faithful" as translations of Gk. *pistos*.) *Chief*: lit. "first"; cf. v. 16. **1:17** *Wise*: better omitted (MS tradition). **1:18** *This charge*: cf. v. 3. *The prophecies . . . thee*: probably a commission such as that narrated in Acts 13:1–4; cf. 1 Tim 4:14. **1:19** *Put away*: rejected. *Concerning faith . . . shipwreck*: "have suffered shipwreck in the faith" (NRSV). **1:20** *Hymenæus and Alexander*: mentioned in 2 Tim 2:17–18; 4:14. *Delivered unto Satan . . . blaspheme*: cf. 1 Cor 5:5 and note.

2:1–6:21 Ordering the Church. The letter's body consists of instruction on various matters, many of which relate to church order: prayer (2:1–7); gender roles in public worship (2:8–15); behavioral requirements for bishops (3:1–7) and for deacons (3:8–13); asceticism (4:1–5); treatment of the aged (5:1–2), of widows (5:3–16), and of elders current (5:17–21) and prospective (5:22, 24–25); the duties of slaves (6:1–2a); and avarice (6:2b–10, 17–19). This material is interspersed with personal exhortation to Timothy (3:14–16; 4:6–16; 5:23; 6:11–16, 20–21). **2:2** *For kings . . . honesty*: cf. Rom 13:1–7. *Godliness and honesty*: piety and reverence. Gk. *eusebeia* (*godliness*) is better

this is good and acceptable in the sight of God our Saviour; [4]who will have all men to be saved, and to come unto the knowledge of the truth. [5]For there is one God, and one mediator between God and men, the man Christ Jesus; [6]who gave himself a ransom for all, to be testified in due time. [7]Whereunto I am ordained a preacher, and an apostle, (I speak the truth in Christ, and lie not;) a teacher of the Gentiles in faith and verity.

[8]I will therefore that men pray every where, lifting up holy hands, without wrath and doubting. [9]In like manner also, that women adorn themselves in modest apparel, with shamefacedness and sobriety; not with broided hair, or gold, or pearls, or costly array; [10]but (which becometh women professing godliness) with good works. [11]Let the woman learn in silence with all subjection. [12]But I suffer not a woman to teach, nor to usurp authority over the man, but to be in silence. [13]For Adam was first formed, then Eve. [14]And Adam was not deceived, but the woman being deceived was in the transgression. [15]Notwithstanding she shall be saved in childbearing, if they continue in faith and charity and holiness with sobriety.

3 This is a true saying, If a man desire the office of a bishop, he desireth a good work. [2]A bishop then must be blameless, the husband of one wife, vigilant, sober, of good behaviour, given to hospitality, apt to teach; [3]not given to wine, no striker, not greedy of filthy lucre; but patient, not a brawler, not covetous; [4]one that ruleth well his own house, having his children in subjection with all gravity; [5](for if a man know not how to rule his own house, how shall he take care of the church of God?) [6]not a novice, lest being lifted up with pride he fall into the

---

rendered "piety" throughout the Pastorals.   **2:6** *Who gave . . . all*: contrast Mark 10:45, where "the Son of man" comes "to give his life a ransom for many." Likewise, Mark 4:10–12 stands in sharp contrast to 1 Tim 2:4. In vv. 4–6 (cf. 4:10) salvation appears to be universal, as in Col 1:19–20; cf. Rom 3:29–30; 11:25–32; 1 Cor 15:28.   **2:7** *I am ordained*: lit. "I am put" (cf. 1:12). *Preacher*: lit. "herald." *I speak . . . not*: Paul frequently protests his honesty; cf. Rom 9:1; 2 Cor 11:31; Gal 1:20.   **2:8** *Pray every where . . . doubting*: cf. Mark 11:23–24.   **2:9** *Shamefacedness*: modesty. *Sobriety*: "good judgment," "prudence," or even "discretion" (also in v. 15). *Not with broided hair . . . array*: sentiments about the need for modesty in female attire are common in Greco-Roman and Jewish literature. Ancient Jewish texts sometimes blame fallen angels (a common interpretation of the "sons of God" in Gen 6:1–4) for teaching women to adorn themselves in the ways here forbidden (e.g., *1 Enoch* 8.1). 1 Timothy's subsequent reference to Eve's deception by the fallen angel Satan (v. 14; see 2 Cor 11:14 and note) may suggest a grounding in such Jewish legends. *Broided*: plaited.   **2:11–12** *Let the woman . . . silence*: cf. 1 Cor 14:34–35, possibly a scribal interpolation influenced by this passage (see note there).   **2:13** *For Adam . . . Eve*: compare Paul's tortured argument in 1 Cor 11:7–12.   **2:14** *Adam was . . . transgression*: a reference to Gen 3:1–7 (cf. Rom 7:11), perhaps interpreted in light of apocryphal Jewish legends such as the one Paul mentions at 2 Cor 11:14 (see note); cf. v. 9 and note.   **2:15** *She shall be saved in childbearing*: presumably interpreting Gen 3:16, God's punishment of Eve's transgression.   **3:1** *This is a true saying*: this should perhaps be taken with the previous verse. *Desire the office of a bishop*: lit. "strive after the office of overseer." The scope of the overseer's ecclesiastical responsibilities during this period is obscure.   **3:2** *Blameless*: or "irreproachable"; a different Greek word is used in v. 10. *Husband of one wife*: lit. "the man of one woman" (also in v. 12). The directive probably prohibits remarriage, but it could refer to being faithful to one's wife, or even prohibit polygamy, although that practice was probably uncommon among the epistle's audience. *Vigilant, sober*: rather "temperate, prudent."   **3:3** *Striker*: one tending to fight. *Not greedy of filthy lucre*: better omitted (MS tradition). *Patient*: better "gentle." *Not covetous*: lit. "not loving money."   **3:4** *Gravity*: reverence.   **3:5** *Church*: see Rom 16:5 note.   **3:6** *Novice*: Gk. *neophytos*, lit. "newly planted," referring

condemnation of the devil. ⁷Moreover he must have a good report of them which are without; lest he fall into reproach and the snare of the devil.

⁸Likewise must the deacons be grave, not doubletongued, not given to much wine, not greedy of filthy lucre; ⁹holding the mystery of the faith in a pure conscience. ¹⁰And let these also first be proved; then let them use the office of a deacon, being found blameless. ¹¹Even so must their wives be grave, not slanderers, sober, faithful in all things. ¹²Let the deacons be the husbands of one wife, ruling their children and their own houses well. ¹³For they that have used the office of a deacon well purchase to themselves a good degree, and great boldness in the faith which is in Christ Jesus.

¹⁴These things write I unto thee, hoping to come unto thee shortly: ¹⁵but if I tarry long, that thou mayest know how thou oughtest to behave thyself in the house of God, which is the church of the living God, the pillar and ground of the truth. ¹⁶And without controversy great is the mystery of godliness: God was manifest in the flesh, justified in the Spirit, seen of angels, preached unto the Gentiles, believed on in the world, received up into glory.

4 Now the Spirit speaketh expressly, that in the latter times some shall depart from the faith, giving heed to seducing spirits, and doctrines of devils; ²speaking lies in hypocrisy; having their conscience seared with a hot iron; ³forbidding to marry, and commanding to abstain from meats, which God hath created to be

---

to a recent convert. *Condemnation of the devil*: either the condemnation Satan deserves or disciplinary deliverance into his hands (cf. 1:20 and note). **3:8** *Deacons*: Gk. *diakonoi*, "servants," which KJV normally renders "ministers" (e.g., Mark 10:43; Rom 13:4; 15:8). Here, as in vv. 1–7, a particular ecclesiastical office is being named, but the scope of its responsibilities is obscure. *Grave*: reverent (also in v. 11). *Greedy of filthy lucre*: lit. "shameful in pursuit of profit." **3:10** *Proved*: by testing, and so "approved." *Use the . . . deacon*: "serve as minister" (also in v. 13). **3:11** *Even so . . . grave*: lit. "in the same way must the women be reverent." The author likely refers not to ministers' wives but to female ministers. (Compare Rom 16:1–2 and note to v. 1, on Phebe.) *Sober*: perhaps better "temperate" (Gk. *nēphalios*, the word rendered "vigilant" in v. 2, not "sober"). **3:13** *Purchase to themselves a good degree*: acquire for themselves an excellent rank or standing. The writer may understand the office of minister (deacon) as a step below overseer (bishop) in a hierarchical sequence of ecclesiastical offices. That the requirements for overseers are more stringent than those for ministers suggests overseer is the more elite position. **3:15** *House of God . . . church*: see note on "edifying" at 1:4. **3:16** *God*: better "who" (MS tradition). The absence of an antecedent might suggest that the author quotes a fragment from a hymn; cf. Phil 2:6–11; Col 1:15–20 and notes. *Justified*: probably meaning "vindicated." *Angels*: Gk. *angeloi*, lit. "messengers"; especially in light of the subsequent clause, these may also be human. **4:1** *The Spirit speaketh*: a reference to prophetic utterances. *Seducing*: leading astray. *Seducing spirits* recalls the earlier discussion of Eve's deceit by Satan (2:14 and note). **4:2** *Conscience seared . . . iron*: Gk. *kautēriazō*; the resultant scar tissue lacks sensitivity. The conscience thus figured should be contrasted with the "good" (1:5, 19) and "pure" (3:9) conscience mentioned earlier. **4:3** *Forbidding to marry . . . meats*: the social and religious context of the asceticism rejected by the author is obscure, but reference to "the law" in 1:7–8 suggests a Jewish provenance, and Philo of Alexandria reports that some Jewish sects combined faithfulness to the law with rigorous ascetic practices. Paul himself privileged abstinence from marriage (1 Cor 7:1), though with qualifications; the more full-blown asceticism gestured at here is authorized by the character Paul in the second-century *Acts of Paul and Thecla* (see Appendix, pp. 1020–27). If the Pastorals are late, passages such as this, combined with the letters' emphasis on what might be labeled traditional "family values" (cf. 3:2, 4, 12), suggest that they were written in response to

received with thanksgiving of them which believe and know the truth. ⁴For every creature of God is good, and nothing to be refused, if it be received with thanksgiving: ⁵for it is sanctified by the word of God and prayer.

⁶If thou put the brethren in remembrance of these things, thou shalt be a good minister of Jesus Christ, nourished up in the words of faith and of good doctrine, whereunto thou hast attained. ⁷But refuse profane and old wives' fables, and exercise thyself rather unto godliness. ⁸For bodily exercise profiteth little: but godliness is profitable unto all things, having promise of the life that now is, and of that which is to come. ⁹This is a faithful saying and worthy of all acceptation. ¹⁰For therefore we both labour and suffer reproach, because we trust in the living God, who is the Saviour of all men, specially of those that believe.

¹¹These things command and teach. ¹²Let no man despise thy youth; but be thou an example of the believers, in word, in conversation, in charity, in spirit, in faith, in purity. ¹³Till I come, give attendance to reading, to exhortation, to doctrine. ¹⁴Neglect not the gift that is in thee, which was given thee by prophecy, with the laying on of the hands of the presbytery. ¹⁵Meditate upon these things; give thyself wholly to them; that thy profiting may appear to all. ¹⁶Take heed unto thyself, and unto the doctrine; continue in them: for in doing this thou shalt both save thyself, and them that hear thee.

5 Rebuke not an elder, but intreat him as a father; and the younger men as brethren; ²the elder women as mothers; the younger as sisters, with all purity.

---

this appropriation of Paul by other Christian groups valuing rigorous asceticism. **4:4** *Every creature . . . good*: recalling the refrain "it was good" in Gen 1 (esp. v. 31). "Sanctified by the word of God" (v. 5) may also refer to Gen 1's divine affirmations. **4:6** *Brethren*: a common self-designation of Jesus-believers. *Minister*: Gk. *diakonos* (see 3:8 note), here apparently used more generically than "deacon." *Whereunto thou hast attained*: lit. "which you have followed." **4:7** *Old wives' fables*: perhaps a dismissive rejection of the fables of 1:4 as "old wives' tales." Or the reference may be to the discourse of female teachers whom the author wants to silence (see 5:3–16 and notes). If the Pastorals are later pseudepigraphic compositions, *old wives' fables* may refer to traditions about Paul that female leaders in the church were publicly teaching. (On this reading, 2:8–15 also attempts to silence such teachers.) For examples of these traditions, see *The Acts of Paul and Thecla*, which emphasizes Paul's asceticism and his ministerial partnerships with women. **4:8** *For bodily . . . things*: contrasting (what the author understands as) piety with the ascetic practices outlined in v. 3. *Having promise of . . . of*: "holding promise for . . . for" (NRSV). *That which . . . come*: the eschatological resurrection. **4:10** *Suffer reproach*: better "struggle" (MS tradition). **4:12** *An example of*: i.e., "a model for." *Conversation*: conduct. *In spirit*: better omitted (MS tradition). **4:14** *Gift*: Gk. *charisma*, the word Paul uses at Rom 12:6 and throughout 1 Cor 12. Here the spiritual gift seems institutionalized, even hierarchically controlled. *Laying on of the hands*: cf. Num 27:18–23; Acts 6:3–6. *Presbytery*: Gk. *presbyterion*, the council of elders who presumably held authority in the Ephesian church. **4:15** *Meditate*: the same Greek root is translated "neglect not" in v. 14. *Give thyself wholly to them*: lit. "be in them." *Profiting*: progress or advancement. **5:1** *Elder*: Gk. *presbyteros*; but in contrast to 4:14 (see note) context suggests that the author here refers to an older man. He frames his directives on widows (vv. 3–16) within instruction about how to rebuke and reward the elderly, although in vv. 17–20 he again apparently refers to members of the presbytery. The fact that there would have been significant overlap between the Ephesian church's "elders" and its elderly members helps explain the slippage.

³Honour widows that are widows indeed. ⁴But if any widow have children or nephews, let them learn first to shew piety at home, and to requite their parents: for that is good and acceptable before God. ⁵Now she that is a widow indeed, and desolate, trusteth in God, and continueth in supplications and prayers night and day. ⁶But she that liveth in pleasure is dead while she liveth. ⁷And these things give in charge, that they may be blameless. ⁸But if any provide not for his own, and specially for those of his own house, he hath denied the faith, and is worse than an infidel.

⁹Let not a widow be taken into the number under threescore years old, having been the wife of one man, ¹⁰well reported of for good works; if she have brought up children, if she have lodged strangers, if she have washed the saints' feet, if she have relieved the afflicted, if she have diligently followed every good work. ¹¹But the younger widows refuse: for when they have begun to wax wanton against Christ, they will marry; ¹²having damnation, because they have cast off their first faith. ¹³And withal they learn to be idle, wandering about from house to house; and not only idle, but tattlers also and busybodies, speaking things which they ought not. ¹⁴I will therefore that the younger women marry, bear children, guide the house, give none occasion to the adversary to speak reproachfully. ¹⁵For some are already turned aside after Satan. ¹⁶If any man or woman that believeth have widows, let them relieve them, and let not the church be charged; that it may relieve them that are widows indeed.

5:3–16 *Honour widows . . . indeed*: this complex passage, framed by identical references to "widows indeed," exposes the early church's need to negotiate between the ecclesiastical community's responsibility to care for its members and families' responsibilities for their dependents. Read within the epistle's broader context, it may also reveal tension caused by female teachers in the church. Earlier restrictions on women's public speech (2:8–15; cf. 4:7) suggest that some believing women conspicuously exercised pedagogical authority, and many scholars believe that the *widows* here (as well as in the second-century epistles of Ignatius and Polycarp) constituted a discrete class of unmarried Christian women remunerated for teaching, prayer, and related ecclesiastical services. On this reading, 1 Timothy's author critiques this order of the faithful by disparaging its members' teaching as gossip (v. 13; cf. 4:7 and note) and many of them as ostentatious and lascivious (vv. 6, 11, 15; cf. 2:9). Furthermore, the class of widows is redefined to include only the elderly and destitute (v. 5); the younger (vv. 9, 14) and more affluent (v. 16) are excluded from its registry and instead encouraged to remarry and exercise authority within the home. Because this section contradicts Paul's strong statements in 1 Corinthians against widows' remarrying (see v. 14 and note), and it accords well with what we know about second-century Christianity, it seems to support the argument that the Pastorals are late pseudepigraphic compositions; but the conflicts can be resolved, and the passage also makes sense in the first-century context provided by Acts 6:1–4.   **5:3** *Honour*: Gk. *timaō*, which can include the idea of financial support; cf. Mark 7:10–13 and notes.   **5:4** *Nephews*: more accurately "grandchildren."   **5:5** *Desolate*: left alone.   **5:6** *Liveth in pleasure*: the Greek connotes voluptuousness and luxury. This condemnation of ostentatious living anticipates 6:6–10.   **5:7** *Give in charge*: command. *They*: the heads of family who are to care for widows, not the widows themselves. **5:9** *Taken into the number*: i.e., enrolled, presumably with reference to a list of widows deserving financial support.   **5:9–10** *Under threescore . . . work*: the requirements for enrolled widows recall those given for bishops and deacons (3:1–13).   **5:10** *Washed the saints' feet*: a sign of service and hospitality to those of the church, perhaps echoing the dominical injunction recorded in John 13:14. **5:11** *Will marry*: desire to marry.   **5:12** *Damnation*: condemnation. *First faith*: a misleading translation; better "initial commitment," i.e., to continual prayer (cf. v. 5).   **5:13** *Tattlers*: gossips.   **5:14** *I will . . . marry*: apparently contradicted by Paul in 1 Cor 7:1, 8, 29–35, 40 (but cf. 1 Cor 7:2, 9, 36–39). *The adversary*: Satan.   **5:16** *Man or woman . . . relieve them*: better "if any woman who believes has widows [as relatives], let her assist them" (MS tradition; our translation). *Charged*: lit. "burdened."

¹⁷Let the elders that rule well be counted worthy of double honour, especially they who labour in the word and doctrine. ¹⁸For the scripture saith, Thou shalt not muzzle the ox that treadeth out the corn. And, The labourer is worthy of his reward. ¹⁹Against an elder receive not an accusation, but before two or three witnesses. ²⁰Them that sin rebuke before all, that others also may fear. ²¹I charge thee before God, and the Lord Jesus Christ, and the elect angels, that thou observe these things without preferring one before another, doing nothing by partiality.

²²Lay hands suddenly on no man, neither be partaker of other men's sins: keep thyself pure. ²³Drink no longer water, but use a little wine for thy stomach's sake and thine often infirmities. ²⁴Some men's sins are open beforehand, going before to judgment; and some men they follow after. ²⁵Likewise also the good works of some are manifest beforehand; and they that are otherwise cannot be hid.

6 Let as many servants as are under the yoke count their own masters worthy of all honour, that the name of God and his doctrine be not blasphemed. ²And they that have believing masters, let them not despise them, because they are brethren; but rather do them service, because they are faithful and beloved, partakers of the benefit.

These things teach and exhort. ³If any man teach otherwise, and consent not to wholesome words, even the words of our Lord Jesus Christ, and to the doctrine which is according to godliness; ⁴he is proud, knowing nothing, but doting about questions and strifes of words, whereof cometh envy, strife, railings, evil

---

5:17 *Double honour*: double compensation (see v. 3 note). If the preceding section's intended effect was to eliminate from the church female teachers, the insistence here on (male) elders who teach being given higher pay makes sense not only ideologically but also practically, as more money would be available with which to compensate their increased teaching responsibilities. **5:18** *Thou shalt . . . corn* [i.e., wheat]: Deut 25:4. *The labourer . . . reward*: Luke 10:7. Perhaps a later author is quoting Luke as Scripture; or perhaps Paul invokes the same dominical saying that Luke records, linking it with a thematically similar passage from the Hebrew Bible. **5:19–20** *Against an elder . . . fear*: compare the directive of Matt 18:15–17, although there the guidelines regarding accusations apply to any accused believer. **5:19** *Before*: either "unless it is in the presence of" (cf. Matt 18:16) or "unless it is supported by" (cf. 2 Cor 13:1). *Two or three witnesses*: see Deut 19:15. **5:21** *The Lord*: better omitted (MS tradition). **5:22** *Lay hands . . . man*: presumably a warning to Timothy not to ordain an elder (cf. 4:14) before his character has been proven. **5:23** *Drink no . . . infirmities*: this piece of medical advice (common in the Greco-Roman world) interrupts a logical train of thought (vv. 22, 24–25), and its point is unclear. The author might be dissuading Timothy from the teetotaling asceticism that characterizes Paul in *The Acts of Paul and Thecla* (cf. 25), or he might have in mind the well-known Greco-Roman sentiment *in vino veritas* ("there's truth in wine"; cf. Pliny, *Natural History* 14.141), to which he would here allude with ironically deceptive subtlety, delicately suggesting that Timothy drink with the man he is considering for ordination in order to loosen him up so that he will reveal hidden sins that might disqualify him. **6:1–2** *Let as . . . benefit*: cf. Eph 6:5–9; Col 3:22–4:1. **6:1** *Servants*: lit. "slaves" (see Rom 1:1 note). *That the name . . . blasphemed*: echoing Isa 52:5. **6:2** *But rather . . . service*: lit. "but let them be enslaved the more." *Partakers of the benefit*: KJV suggests the masters partake of the slaves' benefaction, thereby recalling the status reversal announced in Luke 22:25–27. But the Greek could also mean that the masters "give a benefit" to the slaves, in the sense of reciprocating their service by supporting and advocating for them in the Greco-Roman patronage system (cf. Luke 22:25). **6:3** *Wholesome*: lit. "sound" or "healthy" (see 1:10 note). **6:4** *Proud*: perhaps instead "deluded." *Doting*: lit. "sick." *Strifes of words*: conflict about words. *Railings*: alternatively "blasphemies."

surmisings, [5]perverse disputings of men of corrupt minds, and destitute of the truth, supposing that gain is godliness: from such withdraw thyself. [6]But godliness with contentment is great gain. [7]For we brought nothing into this world, and it is certain we can carry nothing out. [8]And having food and raiment let us be therewith content. [9]But they that will be rich fall into temptation and a snare, and into many foolish and hurtful lusts, which drown men in destruction and perdition. [10]For the love of money is the root of all evil: which while some coveted after, they have erred from the faith, and pierced themselves through with many sorrows.

[11]But thou, O man of God, flee these things; and follow after righteousness, godliness, faith, love, patience, meekness. [12]Fight the good fight of faith, lay hold on eternal life, whereunto thou art also called, and hast professed a good profession before many witnesses. [13]I give thee charge in the sight of God, who quickeneth all things, and before Christ Jesus, who before Pontius Pilate witnessed a good confession; [14]that thou keep this commandment without spot, unrebukeable, until the appearing of our Lord Jesus Christ: [15]which in his times he shall shew, who is the blessed and only Potentate, the King of kings, and Lord of lords; [16]who only hath immortality, dwelling in the light which no man can approach unto; whom no man hath seen, nor can see: to whom be honour and power everlasting. Amen.

[17]Charge them that are rich in this world, that they be not highminded, nor trust in uncertain riches, but in the living God, who giveth us richly all things to enjoy; [18]that they do good, that they be rich in good works, ready to distribute, willing to communicate; [19]laying up in store for themselves a good foundation against the time to come, that they may lay hold on eternal life.

[20]O Timothy, keep that which is committed to thy trust, avoiding profane and

---

6:5 *Perverse disputings*: better "constant disputes" (MS tradition). *Gain is godliness*: better "piety is a means of gain." Calling into question the genuineness of an opponent's motivations is a standard polemical device (cf. Titus 1:11). *From such withdraw thyself*: better omitted (MS tradition).   **6:6** *But godliness . . . gain*: the Greek word order is emphatic: "But there is great gain: piety with contentment." *Contentment*: Gk. *autarkeia*, "self-sufficiency."   **6:7** *And it is certain*: better "because" (MS tradition); for the sentiment expressed in the verse, cf. LXX Eccl 5:15; Job 1:21.   **6:8** *Let us . . . content*: better "we shall be self-sufficient" (Gk. root *arke-*; cf. v. 6 and note).   **6:10** *The love . . . evil*: a commonplace in Greco-Roman popular philosophy. *Erred*: been led astray. *Sorrows*: or "pains."   **6:12** *Fight the good fight*: the Greek words rendered "fight" (root *agōn-*) connote athletic competition. *Profession*: or "confession" (cf. v. 13).   **6:13** *Quickeneth*: gives life to. *Who before . . . confession*: the only mention of Pilate in the Pauline Epistles (but cf. 1 Cor 2:8). The author perhaps refers to the tradition of Jesus "professing" before Pilate (see John 18:36–38). *Witnessed*: testified.   **6:14** *Unrebukeable*: irreproachable; see 3:2 note. *Appearing*: a reference to the eschatological advent.   **6:16** *Whom no man . . . see*: echoing Exod 33:20.   **6:17** *Trust*: lit. "hope." *The living*: better omitted (MS tradition).   **6:18** *Willing to communicate*: i.e., "generous," or possibly "sociable."   **6:19** *Against the time to come*: for the future. *Eternal life*: better "that which is life indeed" (MS tradition).

vain babblings, and oppositions of science falsely so called: ²¹which some professing have erred concerning the faith. Grace be with thee. Amen.

The first to Timothy was written from Laodicea, which is the chiefest city of Phrygia Pacatiana.

6:20 *Science*: Gk. *gnōsis*, "knowledge." The author takes a final swipe at the false teaching he has been rejecting, distinguishing it from the true traditions that Timothy, Paul's legitimate son (1:2 note), has been charged with guarding and the true life they offer (6:19 note). If 1 Timothy is late, the reference is likely to the second-century Christian group self-labeled "gnostics" and responsible for such texts as the *Apocryphon of John*. *Falsely so called*: contrast the opening's insistence on Timothy's status as Paul's "legitimate" or "genuine" son (1:2 and note).   **6:21** *Erred*: lit. "missed the mark." *Grace be with thee*: recalling 1:2. *With thee*: better "with you all" (MS tradition). *Amen. The first . . . Pacatiana*: better omitted (MS tradition).

The Second Epistle of Paul the Apostle to Timothy

SECOND Timothy is a far more intimate letter than its predecessor. Whereas 1 Timothy intersperses bits of personal exhortation within substantive formal discussions of church discipline, the present epistle bares Paul's soul to the delegate, revealing a movingly pessimistic assessment of Paul's own predicament and at the same time a deep concern about Timothy's commitment to Paul. The letter is purportedly written from prison, presumably in Rome (see 1:17), where according to Acts Paul was incarcerated for two years (28:16–31) in the early 60s C.E. The author mentions a "first *apologia* [legal defense]" (4:16; see note), which implies he awaits another hearing. Comments toward the letter's close indicate he expects not success but rather his imminent execution (4:6–7).

Just as unsettling, Paul sees his missionary network unraveling. The author writes that "all they which are in Asia be turned away from me," calling out prominent defectors by name (1:15). Even Demas, at one time a "fellowlabourer" with Paul (Phlm 24; cf. Col 4:14), has now forsaken him (2 Tim 4:10). The author expresses concern lest Timothy too turn away, presumably out of fear to associate with the apostle in the midst of mass desertion, out of shame in his imprisonment (1:6–8), or both. This concern, as well as intense loneliness, lies behind the request in 4:9 that Timothy visit Paul soon, a request desperately repeated at the epistle's close. Adding to his pain, as Paul sees his own missionary network dissolving, his enemies and opponent teachers are apparently experiencing success (3:1–6, 13; 4:3–4). To be sure, this bleak picture of the preoccupied apostle is qualified by Paul's faith in his opponents' future exposure as fools (3:9) and in his own eschatological vindication (e.g., 4:8). Likewise, his claims to be cold and lonely (4:10, 13, 16) are belied by numerous references to believers who continue to support him (1:16–17; 4:11, 21). All this suggests that Paul's beleaguered isolation is as much psychological as social, and it is precisely 2 Timothy's sustained view of the apostle's psyche that makes it such compelling reading.

The epistle shares much in common with the other Pastorals, including concern about false teachings and about the role of women, as well as discussions of a church leader's requisite qualities, but it contains much more personal information and omits problematic references to formal ecclesiastical structures. For these reasons and others, even scholars who argue that the Pastorals are pseudepigraphic recognize that 2 Timothy is in a somewhat different category from its partners, and is more likely to be authentic.

Another way to explain its differences from the other Pastorals is the hypothesis that 2 Timothy was composed in Paul's name as an imaginative testament or farewell discourse, which originally brought the collection of Pastoral Epistles to a close. (The Muratorian fragment, the oldest extant list of New Testament books, has 1 and 2 Timothy following Titus.) The classic model of the farewell discourse is Jacob's speech in Genesis 49, which spawned numerous ancient Jewish literary imitations, including the *Testaments of the Twelve Patriarchs*. Perhaps the most famous imitation is another Pauline testament, Paul's speech to the Ephesian elders in Acts 20:17–38. Such farewell discourses generally dwell on autobiographical details to prove the uprightness of the one departing, prophesy disastrous events that will occur after the departure (and that reflect the perceived situation of the author and his readers), and encourage those left behind to remain faithful to God. All these elements are found in 2 Timothy. If it constitutes an epistolary farewell discourse written in Paul's name, its dark tone may reflect a later author's assessment of Paul's legacy rather than Paul's assessment of his own situation: believers embracing the portrait of Paul found, say, in *The Acts of Paul and Thecla* are abandoning the apostle. By ostensibly commissioning Timothy to remain faithful to Paul's teaching in the face of opponents who preach a different gospel, the epistle encourages later generations to discern and preserve what its author takes to be the true Pauline tradition. More speculatively still, 2 Timothy's insistence that only Luke—the traditional author of Acts—remains with Paul (4:11) may signal its author's allegiance to Acts' portrait of Paul as the authoritative narrative of the apostle's life and mission, a belief the church gradually came to accept (with good reason, as Acts has a better claim to historicity than the apocryphal tales that circulated about Paul).

The hypothesis that 2 Timothy is a pseudepigraphic epistolary farewell discourse is attractive because it accounts for much of what is found in the epistle, including its apparent engagement with traditions about Paul preserved in *The Acts of Paul and Thecla*. But the hypothesis is speculative, and it is disingenuous to claim that the letter cannot reasonably and responsibly be interpreted as authentically Pauline. Once again we must confront the problem of literary-historical context: does it make more sense to read 2 Timothy as a genuinely bleak assessment of Paul's own situation as he awaits probable death in Rome, or to read it as a later pseudepigraphic composition reflecting on challenges to and developments of the Pauline tradition that the author who hides behind a pseudonym found troubling?

For more information on 2 Timothy, see Luke Timothy Johnson's Anchor Bible commentary, *The First and Second Letters to Timothy: A New Translation with Introduction and Commentary* (New York: Doubleday, 2001), which informs this introduction and the notes that follow.

THE SECOND EPISTLE OF PAUL
THE APOSTLE TO
TIMOTHY

1 Paul, an apostle of Jesus Christ by the will of God, according to the promise of life which is in Christ Jesus, ²to Timothy, my dearly beloved son: Grace, mercy, and peace, from God the Father and Christ Jesus our Lord.

³I thank God, whom I serve from my forefathers with pure conscience, that without ceasing I have remembrance of thee in my prayers night and day; ⁴greatly desiring to see thee, being mindful of thy tears, that I may be filled with joy; ⁵when I call to remembrance the unfeigned faith that is in thee, which dwelt first in thy grandmother Lois, and thy mother Eunice; and I am persuaded that in thee also.

⁶Wherefore I put thee in remembrance that thou stir up the gift of God, which is in thee by the putting on of my hands. ⁷For God hath not given us the spirit of fear; but of power, and of love, and of a sound mind. ⁸Be not thou therefore ashamed of the testimony of our Lord, nor of me his prisoner: but be thou partaker of the afflictions of the gospel according to the power of God; ⁹who hath saved us, and called us with an holy calling, not according to our works, but according to his

---

1:1–5 Salutation and thanksgiving. On the openings of Paul's letters, see note to Rom 1:1–15. This one consists of a greeting (vv. 1–2) and brief thanksgiving (vv. 3–5). **1:1** *Apostle*: see Rom 1:1 note. **1:2** *Timothy*: see 1 Cor 4:17 note. *Grace, mercy . . . Lord*: cf. 1 Tim 1:2 and note. **1:3** *Serve*: Gk. *latreuō*, which refers to religious or cultic service. *Forefathers*: the Greek word may also refer to one's parents, as in 1 Tim 5:4. In either case, the author claims strong continuity between his faith and that of previous generations. He makes the same claim for Timothy (v. 5). **1:5** *Faith*: see 1 Tim 1:5 note. *Which dwelt . . . Eunice*: on Timothy's mother, see Acts 16:1. *That in thee*: i.e., that it dwells in thee.

1:6–2:13 Exemplary models. The author introduces a number of models: Paul himself (1:6–12; 2:1–2) and Onesiphorus, his supporter (1:16–18); soldiers, athletes, and farmers (2:3–7); and finally Jesus (2:8–13). **1:6** *Stir up*: lit. "rekindle." *By the putting . . . hands*: in 1 Tim 4:14, the gift was linked to the presbytery's laying on of hands, which seemed to function as a kind of ordination (cf. 1 Tim 5:22 and note). Acts 16:3 reports Paul's commissioning of Timothy for ministry. **1:7** *Hath not given . . . fear*: the author may refer to the Holy Spirit, as KJV's insertion of *the* suggests, or may simply be saying that God has not given us "a fearful spirit," i.e., has not made us cowardly. **1:8** *The testimony . . . Lord*: cf. 1 Tim 6:13, where the Greek root *martyr-*, here rendered "testimony," is translated "witnessed." Paul's situation is assimilated to Jesus'. *According to the power of God*: as God empowers you. *Gospel*: see Mark 1:1 note. **1:9–10** *Who hath saved . . . gospel*: these verses may preserve a fragment of a hymn or other words of

own purpose and grace, which was given us in Christ Jesus before the world began, [10]but is now made manifest by the appearing of our Saviour Jesus Christ, who hath abolished death, and hath brought life and immortality to light through the gospel: [11]whereunto I am appointed a preacher, and an apostle, and a teacher of the Gentiles. [12]For the which cause I also suffer these things: nevertheless I am not ashamed: for I know whom I have believed, and am persuaded that he is able to keep that which I have committed unto him against that day.

[13]Hold fast the form of sound words, which thou hast heard of me, in faith and love which is in Christ Jesus. [14]That good thing which was committed unto thee keep by the Holy Ghost which dwelleth in us.

[15]This thou knowest, that all they which are in Asia be turned away from me; of whom are Phygellus and Hermogenes. [16]The Lord give mercy unto the house of Onesiphorus; for he oft refreshed me, and was not ashamed of my chain: [17]but, when he was in Rome, he sought me out very diligently, and found me. [18]The Lord grant unto him that he may find mercy of the Lord in that day: and in how many things he ministered unto me at Ephesus, thou knowest very well.

2 Thou therefore, my son, be strong in the grace that is in Christ Jesus. [2]And the things that thou hast heard of me among many witnesses, the same commit thou to faithful men, who shall be able to teach others also. [3]Thou therefore endure hardness, as a good soldier of Jesus Christ. [4]No man that warreth entangleth himself with the affairs of this life; that he may please him who hath chosen him to be a soldier. [5]And if a man also strive for masteries, yet is he not crowned, except he strive lawfully. [6]The husbandman that laboureth must be first partaker of the fruits. [7]Consider what I say; and the Lord give thee understanding in all things.

[8]Remember that Jesus Christ of the seed of David was raised from the dead according to my gospel: [9]wherein I suffer trouble, as an evil doer, even unto

---

liturgy. **1:9** *Before the world began*: more literally "before times eternal." **1:11** *Preacher*: herald. *Of the Gentiles*: better omitted (MS tradition). **1:12** *Believed*: or "trusted." *Able*: Gk. *dynatos*; its nominal form is rendered "power" in vv. 7–8. *Keep*: "guard" (also in v. 14). *Against that day*: "for that day" or "until that day," with reference to the eschatological consummation (also in v. 18). **1:13** *Form*: Gk. *hypotypōsis*, "model" or "exemplar." *Sound words*: see 1 Tim 1:10 note. *Of me*: from me. **1:14** *That good . . . keep*: cf. 1 Tim 6:20. **1:15–18** *This thou . . . well*: Phygellus is otherwise unknown, but *Onesiphorus* and *Hermogenes* appear as characters in *The Acts of Paul and Thecla*—the former offering hospitality to Paul, the latter as an opponent and false teacher. **1:15** *Asia*: the Roman province consisting of the western portion of Asia Minor. **1:18** *Unto me*: added by KJV. *Ephesus*: see 1 Tim 1:3 note. **2:1–7** *Thou therefore . . . things*: given the author's concern lest Timothy, Paul's "son," abandon him (1:8), as did Phygellus and Hermogenes (1:15), this section appears to function as a request that Timothy bravely make a public show of his faithfulness to the apostle, even if by doing so he might share in Paul's scorn. **2:1** *Be strong*: Gk. *endynamou*, which has the same root as words in 1:7–8, 12 (see note). **2:2** *Of me*: from me. **2:3** *Thou therefore endure hardness*: better "suffer hardship with me" (MS tradition; our translation). **2:4–6** *No man . . . fruits*: Paul uses the same three examples in 1 Cor 9 (vv. 7, 10, 24–27). **2:4** *Him who . . . soldier*: the one who recruited him. **2:5** *Strive for masteries . . . lawfully*: referring to an athlete in competition for a crown (the conventional prize in ancient Greek sport), who must play by the rules; cf. 1 Cor 9:24–27. **2:7** *Give thee*: better "shall give thee" (MS tradition). **2:8** *Remember that . . . dead*: KJV reverses the Greek's ordering of these two clauses—"remember Jesus Christ raised from the dead, from the seed of David"—and thus assimilates the sentence to Rom 1:3–4. **2:9** *Evil doer*: Gk. *kakourgos*, "criminal"; cf. Luke 23:32 (KJV

bonds; but the word of God is not bound. ¹⁰Therefore I endure all things for the elect's sakes, that they may also obtain the salvation which is in Christ Jesus with eternal glory. ¹¹It is a faithful saying: For if we be dead with him, we shall also live with him: ¹²if we suffer, we shall also reign with him: if we deny him, he also will deny us: ¹³if we believe not, yet he abideth faithful: he cannot deny himself.

¹⁴Of these things put them in remembrance, charging them before the Lord that they strive not about words to no profit, but to the subverting of the hearers. ¹⁵Study to shew thyself approved unto God, a workman that needeth not to be ashamed, rightly dividing the word of truth. ¹⁶But shun profane and vain babblings: for they will increase unto more ungodliness. ¹⁷And their word will eat as doth a canker: of whom is Hymenæus and Philetus; ¹⁸who concerning the truth have erred, saying that the resurrection is past already; and overthrow the faith of some. ¹⁹Nevertheless the foundation of God standeth sure, having this seal, The Lord knoweth them that are his. And, Let every one that nameth the name of Christ depart from iniquity.

²⁰But in a great house there are not only vessels of gold and of silver, but also of wood and of earth; and some to honour, and some to dishonour. ²¹If a man therefore purge himself from these, he shall be a vessel unto honour, sanctified, and meet for the master's use, and prepared unto every good work. ²²Flee also youthful lusts: but follow righteousness, faith, charity, peace, with them that call on the Lord out of a pure heart. ²³But foolish and unlearned questions avoid, knowing that they do gender strifes. ²⁴And the servant of the Lord must not strive; but be gentle unto all men, apt to teach, patient, ²⁵in meekness instructing those that oppose themselves; if God peradventure will give them repentance to the

---

"malefactors"). The strong term makes clear that imprisonment is a serious threat to Paul's reputation (cf. 1:8). **2:11** *It is . . . saying*: see 1 Tim 1:15 note. *If we . . . live with him*: cf. Rom 6:1–11. **2:12** *If we deny . . . deny us*: cf. Luke 12:9. **2:13** *Believe not*: Gk. *apisteō*, better "are not faithful," to complement the statement of Christ's abiding faithfulness (*pistos*).

2:14–4:5 Directives, especially regarding false teaching. 2:15 *Study*: Gk. *spoudason*, "take pains," repeated in 4:9, 21 (KJV "do diligence"). *Rightly dividing*: lit. "rightly cutting," which elsewhere refers to cutting a straight road through forested land. But the comparison of the opponents' word to cancer (v. 17) suggests a reference to cutting away infected tissue (see 1 Tim 1:10 note). **2:17** *Eat*: spread. *Canker*: gangrene or cancer. *Hymenæus*: mentioned at 1 Tim 1:20. *Philetus*: otherwise unknown. **2:18** *Erred*: see 1 Tim 6:21 and note. *The resurrection . . . already: The Acts of Paul and Thecla* attributes this teaching to Demas and Hermogenes, whom 2 Timothy mentions in unflattering terms (4:10; 1:15). It explains their position as follows: "the resurrection . . . has already taken place in the children and . . . we rise again, after having come to the knowledge of the true God" (14). This reference to children recalls the understanding of resurrection attributed to the Sadducees at Mark 12:18–27 (see notes); the emphasis on knowledge corresponds to a view of resurrection common in Valentinian and other gnostic writings (e.g., *Treatise on Resurrection* 49). Either or both are possible contexts here, as is the vaguer notion of "realized eschatology," which apparently characterized the views of some Corinthian believers rebuked by Paul (cf. 1 Cor 4:8 and note). **2:19** *Seal*: see 1 Cor 9:2 note. *Name of Christ*: better "name of the Lord" (MS tradition). **2:20** *Vessels of gold . . . dishonour*: cf. Rom 9:20–23. **2:21** *Sanctified*: this word metaphorically transforms the "great house" (v. 20) into the temple, identifying its master as God and its vessels as those dedicated for liturgical use. **2:22** *Lusts*: lit. "desires," not necessarily with sexual connotations (also at 4:3). **2:23** *Questions*: in the sense of "questionings" or "disputations." *Gender*: engender. **2:24** *Servant*: lit. "slave" (see Rom 1:1 note). *Strive*: fight. **2:25** *Oppose themselves*: put themselves in opposition.

acknowledging of the truth; ²⁶and that they may recover themselves out of the snare of the devil, who are taken captive by him at his will.

3 This know also, that in the last days perilous times shall come. ²For men shall be lovers of their own selves, covetous, boasters, proud, blasphemers, disobedient to parents, unthankful, unholy, ³without natural affection, trucebreakers, false accusers, incontinent, fierce, despisers of those that are good, ⁴traitors, heady, highminded, lovers of pleasures more than lovers of God; ⁵having a form of godliness, but denying the power thereof: from such turn away. ⁶For of this sort are they which creep into houses, and lead captive silly women laden with sins, led away with divers lusts, ⁷ever learning, and never able to come to the knowledge of the truth. ⁸Now as Jannes and Jambres withstood Moses, so do these also resist the truth: men of corrupt minds, reprobate concerning the faith. ⁹But they shall proceed no further: for their folly shall be manifest unto all men, as theirs also was.

¹⁰But thou hast fully known my doctrine, manner of life, purpose, faith, long-suffering, charity, patience, ¹¹persecutions, afflictions, which came unto me at Antioch, at Iconium, at Lystra; what persecutions I endured: but out of them all the Lord delivered me. ¹²Yea, and all that will live godly in Christ Jesus shall suffer persecution. ¹³But evil men and seducers shall wax worse and worse, deceiving, and being deceived. ¹⁴But continue thou in the things which thou hast learned and hast been assured of, knowing of whom thou hast learned them; ¹⁵and that from a child thou hast known the holy scriptures, which are able to

2:26 *That*: added by KJV; the Greek is better construed with this word omitted, as continuing the conditional statement from v. 25. *Recover themselves*: lit. "sober up again." *Taken captive*: Gk. *ezōgrē-menoi*, lit. "taken alive," sometimes with positive connotations (cf. LXX Josh 2:13; 6:25, where it means "save"). The idea may be that God will save the opponents from the devil.   **3:1** *In the last days . . . come*: a common eschatological expectation (cf. Mark 13; 2 Thess 2:1–12). The description of eschatological hardships here introduced corresponds to Timothy's current challenges (cf. vv. 6–7 and note; 4:3), suggesting that the time of the end has begun. *Perilous*: lit. "difficult."   **3:2** *Covetous*: lit. "lovers of money."   **3:3** *Trucebreakers*: lit. "without truce," in the sense of "irreconcilable." *Despisers of those that are good*: lit. "not loving the good."   **3:4** *Heady*: i.e., "headstrong," in the sense of "reckless." *Highminded*: conceited.   **3:6–7** *They which . . . truth*: again showing the Pastorals' concern with the role of women in the church (cf. 1 Tim 2:9–15; 4:7; 5:3–16). This passage polemically undermines the legitimacy of the teachers of women to which it refers, but its portrait of these teachers closely resembles the one in *The Acts of Paul and Thecla* of Paul himself, whose gospel of asceticism the young aristocratic woman Thecla enthusiastically hears and embraces.   **3:6** *Laden*: "piled high" (the same root is rendered "heap to" in 4:3).   **3:7** *Able*: Gk. root *dyna-* (cf. v. 15), the same root as "power" in v. 5; see 1:12 note.   **3:8** *Jannes and Jambres*: the names assigned by later Jewish tradition to Pharaoh's sorcerers (Exod 7:11–12, 22). *Withstood, resist*: the same Greek verb. *Reprobate*: Gk. *adikimos*, lit. "not approved" (cf. 2:15).   **3:9** *Proceed no further*: the same Greek phrase (although not negated) is translated "increase unto more" at 2:16. *As theirs also was*: cf. Exod 8:18–19.   **3:10** *Fully known*: more literally "closely followed."   **3:11** *Persecutions, afflictions . . . Lystra*: for Paul's afflictions at Antioch of Pisidia, see Acts 13:44–52; at Iconium, see Acts 14:1–7 and *The Acts of Paul and Thecla* 1–2, 14–21; at Lystra, see Acts 14:19–20.   **3:12** *Godly*: piously.   **3:13** *Seducers*: lit. "sorcerers" (often with the connotation of "swindler"), recalling the comparison of the opposing teachers to Jannes and Jambres (vv. 8–9). *Wax*: the same Greek verb as "proceed" in v. 9, which this verse seems to contradict.   **3:14** *Of whom*: plural in the Greek, i.e., "from what people."   **3:15** *From a child . . . scriptures*: presumably referring to training by Lois and Eunice (1:5).

make thee wise unto salvation through faith which is in Christ Jesus. [16]All scripture is given by inspiration of God, and is profitable for doctrine, for reproof, for correction, for instruction in righteousness: [17]that the man of God may be perfect, throughly furnished unto all good works.

4 I charge thee therefore before God, and the Lord Jesus Christ, who shall judge the quick and the dead at his appearing and his kingdom; [2]preach the word; be instant in season, out of season; reprove, rebuke, exhort with all longsuffering and doctrine. [3]For the time will come when they will not endure sound doctrine; but after their own lusts shall they heap to themselves teachers, having itching ears; [4]and they shall turn away their ears from the truth, and shall be turned unto fables. [5]But watch thou in all things, endure afflictions, do the work of an evangelist, make full proof of thy ministry.

[6]For I am now ready to be offered, and the time of my departure is at hand. [7]I have fought a good fight, I have finished my course, I have kept the faith: [8]henceforth there is laid up for me a crown of righteousness, which the Lord, the righteous judge, shall give me at that day: and not to me only, but unto all them also that love his appearing.

[9]Do thy diligence to come shortly unto me: [10]for Demas hath forsaken me, having loved this present world, and is departed unto Thessalonica; Crescens to Galatia, Titus unto Dalmatia. [11]Only Luke is with me. Take Mark, and bring him with thee: for he is profitable to me for the ministry. [12]And Tychicus have I sent to Ephesus. [13]The cloke that I left at Troas with Carpus, when thou comest, bring with thee, and the books, but especially the parchments.

[14]Alexander the coppersmith did me much evil: the Lord reward him according to his works: [15]of whom be thou ware also; for he hath greatly withstood our words.

3:16 *All scripture*: the Hebrew Scriptures (the NT was not yet in existence). *Given by . . . God*: lit. "breathed by God."   **3:17** *Perfect*: in the sense of "complete." Its Greek root is shared with *furnished*.   **4:1** *Quick*: living. *At*: better "by" (MS tradition).   **4:2** *Be instant*: "be urgent" (RSV).   **4:3** *The time will come*: another reference to eschatological hardships; cf. 3:1.   **4:4** *Fables*: cf. 1 Tim 1:4 and note; 4:7 and note; Titus 1:14.   **4:5** *Watch*: lit. "be sober." *Make full proof of*: lit. "fulfill."

4:6–18 Paul's lonely imprisonment. 4:6 *Now ready to be offered*: lit. "already being poured out as a libation"; cf. Phil 2:17 and note. *Departure*: i.e., from this life.   **4:7** *Fought a good fight*: a reference to athletic competition. *Course*: i.e., a footrace.   **4:8** *Crown*: see 2:5 note. *That day*: the eschatological consummation. *His appearing*: see 1 Tim 6:14 and note.   **4:10** *Demas*: Paul calls him and Luke "fellowlabourers" at Phlm 24; cf. Col 4:14. *The Acts of Paul and Thecla* presents Demas as a hypocrite, pretending to love Paul but really preaching an opposing gospel (1, 14). *Crescens*: otherwise unknown. *Galatia*: probably referring to the region surrounding the city of Ancyra (modern Ankara) in Asia Minor. *Titus*: one of Paul's ministry partners and the recipient of the third Pastoral Epistle, which locates him in Crete (Titus 1:5); he is mentioned at Gal 2:1, 3 and frequently in 2 Corinthians. *Dalmatia*: the southwestern region of the Roman province of Illyricum, north of Macedonia. Acts mentions no Pauline mission here, but cf. Rom 15:19.   **4:11** *Luke*: see Col 4:14; Phlm 24. Acts is traditionally attributed to him. *Take Mark . . . ministry*: Mark is with Paul at Col 4:10; cf. Phlm 24.   **4:12** *Tychicus*: see Acts 20:4; Eph 6:21–22; Col 4:7; Titus 3:12.   **4:13** *Troas*: a port city on the northwest coast of Asia Minor, visited by Paul at least twice (Acts 16:8–10; 20:5–12; cf. 2 Cor 2:12). *Carpus*: otherwise unknown. *Books, parchments*: materials for reading and writing.   **4:14** *Alexander the coppersmith*: cf. 1 Tim 1:20. *The Acts of Paul and Thecla* makes Hermogenes, one of Paul's false friends, a coppersmith (1). That text also has an Alexander, who tries to have his way with Thecla (26) and later arranges the spectacle of wild beasts in which she is sentenced to die (30). *The Lord . . . works*: cf. Ps

¹⁶At my first answer no man stood with me, but all men forsook me: I pray God that it may not be laid to their charge. ¹⁷Notwithstanding the Lord stood with me, and strengthened me; that by me the preaching might be fully known, and that all the Gentiles might hear: and I was delivered out of the mouth of the lion. ¹⁸And the Lord shall deliver me from every evil work, and will preserve me unto his heavenly kingdom: to whom be glory for ever and ever. Amen.

¹⁹Salute Prisca and Aquila, and the household of Onesiphorus. ²⁰Erastus abode at Corinth: but Trophimus have I left at Miletum sick. ²¹Do thy diligence to come before winter. Eubulus greeteth thee, and Pudens, and Linus, and Claudia, and all the brethren.

²²The Lord Jesus Christ be with thy spirit. Grace be with you. Amen.

The second epistle unto Timotheus, ordained the first bishop of the church of the Ephesians, was written from Rome, when Paul was brought before Nero the second time.

62:12; Prov 24:12.   **4:16** *Answer*: Gk. *apologia*, a legal defense. Paul makes several defense speeches in Acts (esp. 22:1–21; 24:10–21), but it is not clear whether he refers to any of these here. *I pray . . . not*: lit. "let it not."   **4:17** *Delivered out . . . Lion*: like Daniel (Dan 6:19–23; cf. Ps 22:21).

4:19–22 Closing. 4:19 *Prisca and Aquila*: see Rom 16:3 note.   **4:20** *Erastus*: cf. Acts 19:22; Rom 16:23 and note. *Corinth*: in Achaia, *Trophimus have . . . sick*: cf. Acts 20:4; 21:29; there *Trophimus* is associated with Asia and, more specifically, Ephesus (near Miletus).   **4:21** *Eubulus greeteth . . . brethren*: an apparent contradiction to v. 11, suggesting that Paul's isolation is psychological rather than social. The people named are otherwise unknown. *Brethren*: a common self-designation of Jesus-believers.   **4:22** *The Lord . . . you*: recalling 1:2. *Amen. The second epistle . . . time*: better omitted (MS tradition).

The Epistle of Paul to Titus

TITUS shares with 1 Timothy a focus on church administration, false teaching, and domestic order. Despite the close correspondence between Titus 1:5–9 and 1 Tim 3:1–13, both of which set out behavioral requirements for ecclesiastical officials (elder and bishop in Titus; bishop and deacon in 1 Timothy), the Epistle to Titus seems on the whole more interested in domestic than in ecclesiastical order (to the extent that the two may be distinguished in churches that met in homes). It carefully outlines behavioral standards not only for leaders but for all members—men and women, older and younger, free and enslaved (2:1–10)—and it specifies how believers are to live in the world: by submitting to governmental authority (3:1), being courteous to all (3:2), and pursuing good works (3:8).

Titus is the most difficult of the Pastorals to accept as authentically Pauline, and the problems its authorship raises deserve special consideration because of the light they shed on the concepts of ascribed authorship and pseudepigraphy, which are central to any informed discussion of the Pastoral Epistles and of other writings in the Pauline corpus as well. The letter presents itself as having been written to Titus after Paul left him in Crete (1:5), but neither Acts nor any of Paul's other letters refer to a mission to that Mediterranean island. Luke mentions Paul's brief layover in Crete at the end of Acts (27:7–13), but the shape of that episode all but excludes the possibility that he knew of a Pauline mission there. Consequently, some have proposed that Paul was not executed at Rome soon after Acts' close, despite that book's foreboding allusions to his impending death. Rather, he must have been released from prison, journeyed to Spain, and returned to the Aegean to continue ministering. During this time he would have established a church in Crete and composed the Epistle to Titus (and perhaps 1 Timothy as well); he must finally have returned to Rome, where he was executed under Nero. Yet the evidence to support this proposal is scant: Rom 15:24 mentions in passing Paul's planned visit to Spain, but Paul nowhere reports that his plan came to fruition. In Acts 13:47 God tells Paul he will "be for salvation unto the ends of the earth," an oracle that *1 Clement* 5.6–7 (ca. 96 C.E.) appears to echo: "after Paul preached in the east and in the west, he received the authentic glory of his faith [i.e., martyrdom], having taught the whole world righteousness, even going to the western frontier." Other evidence comes mainly from the second-century apocryphal Acts of Paul and other apostles, which are legendary compositions providing little to no reliable historical information about their characters. But no Spanish churches claimed that Paul founded them, and learned early Christian authorities such as Origen make no reference to a Pauline mission in the western Mediterranean.

If Paul did write Titus, then, it is probably best simply to assume that he established a church in Crete, unknown to Luke, during one of the missionary journeys that Luke does report.

But even a rather generous assumption such as this fails to resolve the problem of Titus 3:3–7, where Paul openly associates himself with the gross moral corruption he elsewhere attributes to Gentiles (e.g., Rom 1:18–32 and notes). Could the writer of Phil 3:6, who insists that before seeing the risen Christ he was "blameless" with regard to "righteousness under the law," also claim to have been "foolish, disobedient, deceived, serving divers lusts and pleasures. . . . But after that the kindness and love of God our Savior toward man appeared" (Titus 3:3–4)? In Gal 2:15, Paul reports having told Peter "we . . . are Jews by nature, and not sinners of the Gentiles." Accordingly, when Paul invokes language of moral turpitude, he tends to use not first-person pronouns but the second-person plural (e.g., Rom 6:16–22), attributing past sin to formerly pagan members of the churches to which he writes. When first-person pronouns do appear in such discussions, they are used to express rhetorical solidarity with his Gentile readers rather than personal confession (e.g., the rhetorical question of Rom 6:15; cf. 7:7–25 and note). Perhaps the only passage analogous to Titus 3:3–7 in the entire Pauline corpus is Eph 2:1–7 (esp. vv. 3–5), but Ephesians' authenticity is also in doubt. In any case, that passage too may be interpreted as a gesture of rhetorical solidarity with Gentile readers (see Eph 2:3 note): observe the slippage between "ye" and "we" and the emphasis on communality—"quickened us together," "raised us up together," "made us sit together," and so forth. If we take seriously Paul's shame at his persecution of the church expressed in 1 Tim 1:13 (cf. 1 Cor 15:9), perhaps we could imagine an authentic Pauline confession of sin in Titus; but even 1 Timothy is careful to specify that Paul acted out of ignorance, not wickedness (cf. Phil 3:6), and so the passage from Titus remains anomalous.

Some have argued Titus 3:1–7 contains traditional confessional material, which the author adopts without much critical reflection. They have made the same argument about 2:11–14; and 1:5b–9, which closely resembles 1 Tim 3:1–13, might similarly draw on an earlier tradition. On this account, large swaths of Titus were not composed by Paul, even if he "authored" the letter as a whole. A popular complementary hypothesis proposes that in writing the Epistle to Titus, Paul gave a secretary more compositional latitude than in the other epistles he authored. In other words, after laying out what he wanted to communicate, he allowed his scribe to choose the precise words, rhetorical strategies, and so on. Neither of these theories is objectionable on its face: we know that Paul introduced traditional material into his letters, sometimes explicitly signaling it (e.g., 1 Cor 15:3–7), sometimes not (e.g., "Abba, Father" in Rom 8:15; Gal 4:6; cf. Mark 14:36 note). We also know that he relied on a secretary (cf. Rom 16:22; 1 Cor 16:21 and notes), and scribes in the ancient world rarely functioned as mere dictation machines—their transcriptions often verged on what we would today call editing if not composing the text. The problem with these hypotheses lies not in their plausibility but rather in their undercutting of the very concept of authorship they purport to save. If Paul "wrote" Titus by uncritically assembling traditional materials or allowing a scribe such freedom of expression that the resulting composition is incompatible with his own general outlook, then in what meaningful sense does Pauline authorship differ from pseudepigraphy? Indeed, the former is reduced to the latter: one author writing in another's name. Because of these problems, and because Titus (like the other Pastorals) seems to fit comfortably in a late first- or early second-century C.E. context, it makes more sense to regard it as a later pseudepigraphical composition than to insist on its being an authentic Pauline epistle "written" by Paul only in a highly attenuated fashion.

So we end as we began with the Pastorals, which serve as a test case for the problems that critically engaged readers of all Greco-Roman literature must face when considering claims of authorship. Such questions are difficult—sometimes flatly impossible—to resolve, but on them much hangs. Do the Pastoral Epistles represent Paul's authentic voice, or do they invoke Paul in the context of later theological and ecclesiastical debates? Do they reflect the apostle's own views, or do they present what a later generation of believers was convinced he would have said if confronted with their problems? In short, are the epistles *by* Paul or are they *about* him and his legacy? For a long time scholarly consensus has uncritically privileged the latter position, but the question deserves to remain open.

Jerome D. Quinn's Anchor Bible commentary, *The Letter to Titus: A New Translation with Notes and Commentary and an Introduction to Titus, I and II Timothy, the Pastoral Epistles* (New York: Doubleday, 1990), is a good resource for anyone wanting to learn more about this work. It informs this introduction and the annotations that follow.

THE EPISTLE OF PAUL TO
TITUS

1 Paul, a servant of God, and an apostle of Jesus Christ, according to the faith of God's elect, and the acknowledging of the truth which is after godliness; ²in hope of eternal life, which God, that cannot lie, promised before the world began; ³but hath in due times manifested his word through preaching, which is committed unto me according to the commandment of God our Saviour; ⁴to Titus, mine own son after the common faith: Grace, mercy, and peace, from God the Father and the Lord Jesus Christ our Saviour.

⁵For this cause left I thee in Crete, that thou shouldest set in order the things that are wanting, and ordain elders in every city, as I had appointed thee: ⁶if any be blameless, the husband of one wife, having faithful children not accused of riot or unruly. ⁷For a bishop must be blameless, as the steward of God; not self-willed, not soon angry, not given to wine, no striker, not given to filthy lucre; ⁸but a lover of hospitality, a lover of good men, sober, just, holy, temperate; ⁹holding fast the faithful word as he hath been taught, that he may be able by sound doctrine both to exhort and to convince the gainsayers.

¹⁰For there are many unruly and vain talkers and deceivers, specially they of the circumcision: ¹¹whose mouths must be stopped, who subvert whole houses,

1:1–4 Salutation. On the openings of Paul's letters, see note to Rom 1:1–15. Titus omits a thanksgiving. **1:1** *Servant*: "slave" (see Rom 1:1 note). *Apostle*: see Rom 1:1 note. *Godliness*: piety. **1:2** *Before the world began*: see 2 Tim 1:9 note. **1:4** *Own*: see 1 Tim 1:2 and note. *Faith*: see 1 Tim 1:5 note. *Mercy*: better omitted (MS tradition); see Rom 1:7 note for *grace . . . and peace*.
1:5–3:11 Order in the household of God. 1:5 *Crete*: a large island in the eastern Mediterranean. There is no other NT mention of a Pauline mission or church there, although Acts reports a brief visit (27:7–13). *Ordain*: appoint. *Elders*: holders of an office in the church (cf. 1 Tim 4:14 and note; 5:17–20), the scope of whose responsibilities during this period is obscure. *Appointed*: "instructed" or "commanded." **1:6–9** *If any . . . gainsayers*: the requirements for elders and overseers (KJV "bishops") here are similar but not identical to those for overseers and ministers (KJV "deacons") in 1 Tim 3:1–13. They are somewhat less stringent, perhaps suggesting that the church at Crete was more desperate for leaders than that at Ephesus. (Verses 10–11 suggest that the situation was somewhat urgent.) **1:6** *Riot*: debauchery. **1:7** *Bishop*: see 1 Tim 3:1 note. *Steward*: household manager. *Striker*: one tending to fight. *Filthy lucre*: lit. "shameful pursuit of profit" (also in v. 11). **1:8** *Good men*: lit. "the good." *Sober*: prudent (also in 2:4, 5 [KJV "discreet"], 6, 12). **1:9** *That he . . . gainsayers*: more accurately "that he may be able both to exhort in healthy teaching and to reprove those who speak in opposition." *Sound doctrine*: healthy teaching (so throughout; see 1 Tim 1:10 note). **1:10** *They of the circumcision*: presumably Jewish-Christian missionaries, such as those mentioned in Galatians. **1:11** *Who subvert . . . not*:

teaching things which they ought not, for filthy lucre's sake. ¹²One of themselves, even a prophet of their own, said, The Cretians are alway liars, evil beasts, slow bellies. ¹³This witness is true. Wherefore rebuke them sharply, that they may be sound in the faith; ¹⁴not giving heed to Jewish fables, and commandments of men, that turn from the truth. ¹⁵Unto the pure all things are pure: but unto them that are defiled and unbelieving is nothing pure; but even their mind and conscience is defiled. ¹⁶They profess that they know God; but in works they deny him, being abominable, and disobedient, and unto every good work reprobate.

2 But speak thou the things which become sound doctrine: ²that the aged men be sober, grave, temperate, sound in faith, in charity, in patience. ³The aged women likewise, that they be in behaviour as becometh holiness, not false accusers, not given to much wine, teachers of good things; ⁴that they may teach the young women to be sober, to love their husbands, to love their children, ⁵to be discreet, chaste, keepers at home, good, obedient to their own husbands, that the word of God be not blasphemed. ⁶Young men likewise exhort to be sober minded. ⁷In all things shewing thyself a pattern of good works: in doctrine shewing uncorruptness, gravity, sincerity, ⁸sound speech, that cannot be condemned; that he that is of the contrary part may be ashamed, having no evil thing to say of you. ⁹Exhort servants to be obedient unto their own masters, and to please them well in all things; not answering again; ¹⁰not purloining, but shewing all good fidelity; that they may adorn the doctrine of God our Saviour in all things.

¹¹For the grace of God that bringeth salvation hath appeared to all men, ¹²teaching us that, denying ungodliness and worldly lusts, we should live soberly, righteously, and godly, in this present world; ¹³looking for that blessed hope, and the glorious appearing of the great God and our Saviour Jesus Christ; ¹⁴who gave himself for us, that he might redeem us from all iniquity, and purify unto himself a peculiar people, zealous of good works. ¹⁵These things speak, and exhort, and rebuke with all authority. Let no man despise thee.

---

recalling 2 Tim 3:6. *For filthy lucre's sake*: see 1 Tim 6:5 and note. **1:12–13** *One of themselves . . . true*: apparently a reference to Epimenides' famous paradox: Paul relies on the testimony of a Cretan to prove that all Cretans are liars. **1:12** *Slow bellies*: "lazy gluttons" (RSV). **1:13** *Witness*: testimony. **1:14** *Jewish fables*: compare the other *fables* mentioned in the Pastoral Epistles; 1 Tim 1:4 and note; 4:7; 2 Tim 4:4. **1:15** *Unto the pure . . . are pure*: recalling positions Paul articulates at, e.g., Rom 14:14, 20; 1 Cor 8; 10:23–30. **2:2–5** *That the aged men . . . blasphemed*: compare the directives concerning elder men and women in 1 Tim 5. **2:2–3** *Aged men . . . aged women*: translating the same Greek words as in 1 Tim 5:1–2, with the same ambiguity (see v. 1 note). The reference to pedagogical responsibilities, combined with the similarities between the behavior required here and of deacons in 1 Tim 3:8–13, suggests that these male and female elders occupy specific ecclesiastical positions. **2:2** *Grave*: reverent. **2:3** *Given*: lit. "enslaved." **2:5** *Keepers at home*: better "workers at home" (MS tradition). *Obedient to . . . blasphemed*: cf. 1 Tim 6:1, on slaves' obedience to masters. **2:7** *Gravity*: reverence. *Sincerity*: better omitted (MS tradition). **2:8** *Evil*: base or vulgar. *You*: better "us" (MS tradition). **2:9** *Servants*: lit. "slaves." *Answering again*: talking back. **2:10** *Fidelity*: Gk. *pistis*, usually translated "faith" or "faithfulness." **2:11** *For the grace . . . men*: better "for the grace of God that brings salvation to all men has appeared." **2:12** *Ungodliness*: impiety, with *godly* later in the verse meaning "piously." *World*: lit. "age." **2:13** *Looking for*: in the sense of "expecting." *The glorious . . . Christ*: a reference to the eschatological consummation. **2:14** *Gave himself . . . redeem us*: cf. 1 Tim 2:6 and note. *Redeem us . . . iniquity*: cf. Ps 130:8. *A peculiar people*: cf. Deut 14:2.

3 Put them in mind to be subject to principalities and powers, to obey magistrates, to be ready to every good work, [2]to speak evil of no man, to be no brawlers, but gentle, shewing all meekness unto all men. [3]For we ourselves also were sometimes foolish, disobedient, deceived, serving divers lusts and pleasures, living in malice and envy, hateful, and hating one another. [4]But after that the kindness and love of God our Saviour toward man appeared, [5]not by works of righteousness which we have done, but according to his mercy he saved us, by the washing of regeneration, and renewing of the Holy Ghost; [6]which he shed on us abundantly through Jesus Christ our Saviour; [7]that being justified by his grace, we should be made heirs according to the hope of eternal life.

[8]This is a faithful saying, and these things I will that thou affirm constantly, that they which have believed in God might be careful to maintain good works. These things are good and profitable unto men. [9]But avoid foolish questions, and genealogies, and contentions, and strivings about the law; for they are unprofitable and vain. [10]A man that is an heretick after the first and second admonition reject; [11]knowing that he that is such is subverted, and sinneth, being condemned of himself.

[12]When I shall send Artemas unto thee, or Tychicus, be diligent to come unto me to Nicopolis: for I have determined there to winter. [13]Bring Zenas the lawyer and Apollos on their journey diligently, that nothing be wanting unto them. [14]And let ours also learn to maintain good works for necessary uses, that they be not unfruitful.

[15]All that are with me salute thee. Greet them that love us in the faith. Grace be with you all. Amen.

It was written to Titus, ordained the first bishop of the church of the Cretians, from Nicopolis of Macedonia.

3:1 *Put them . . . magistrates:* cf. Rom 13:1–7.   **3:3–7** *For we . . . life:* cf. 1 Tim 1:13–16. This language is Pauline (cf. Rom 6:17–18; 1 Cor 6:9–11; Eph 2:2–9, which likewise uses the first-person plural, though its authenticity too is in doubt), but it seems unlikely that the author of the undisputed epistles would ascribe to himself these moral failures. The only personal fault Paul discusses with specificity is his harassment of the church, which he views as problematic (e.g., 1 Cor 15:8–9) but suggests was carried out with pure motives (Phil 3:6). At 1 Tim 1:13 the author also qualifies his confession of it, indicating that God forgave him because he acted in ignorance.   **3:3** *Sometimes:* at one time. *Hateful:* "despicable" (NRSV); *hating* translates a different root.   **3:5** *Washing of regeneration:* probably a reference to baptism.   **3:6** *Shed:* poured out; cf. Rom 5:5.   **3:7** *Justified:* see Gal 2:16 note. *We should . . . life:* cf. Rom 8:17.   **3:8** *Maintain:* "occupy themselves with" (also at v. 14).   **3:9** *Foolish questions:* cf. 1 Tim 6:4; 2 Tim 2:23. *Genealogies:* cf. 1 Tim 1:4 and note. *Strivings about the law:* conflicts about the law; cf. 1 Tim 1:7–9; 6:3–5.   **3:10** *An heretick:* an anachronistic translation of Gk. *hairetikos* ("factious"); cf. 1 Cor 11:19; Gal 5:20 and notes. *Reject:* or avoid.   **3:11** *Subverted:* perverted.

3:12–15 Personal directives and closing. 3:12 *Artemas:* otherwise unknown. *Tychicus:* see 2 Tim 4:12 note. *Nicopolis:* many cities shared this name; the later subscript (v. 15) provides one possibility.   **3:13** *Zenas:* otherwise unknown. *Apollos:* mentioned in 1 Corinthians and Acts as a Jesus-believing missionary; see 1 Cor 1:12 and note.   **3:14** *Ours:* i.e., our people.   **3:15** *Grace be with you all:* recalling 1:4. *Amen. It . . . Macedonia:* better omitted (MS tradition).

The Epistle of Paul to Philemon

THE situation addressed by Paul's epistle to Philemon has usually been understood as follows: Onesimus, Philemon's slave, runs away from his master and finds his way to Paul, who at the time is in prison—probably in Caesarea or Rome near the end of his career, but possibly earlier in Ephesus (see Philippians introduction). (In any case, Paul's mention of the same people present with him in Philemon's closing as in Colossians' suggests that the two letters were composed in the same place and at about the same time—unless a pseudepigrapher deliberately gave Colossians a veneer of authenticity by introducing this link to Paul's Epistle to Philemon.) Paul had been responsible for Philemon's conversion and now converts Onesimus as well. He found Onesimus useful, but nonetheless returns the escaped slave to his master with a letter asking Philemon to treat him kindly as a brother in Christ, requesting that he send Onesimus back, and hinting at an undisclosed additional favor as well. On the basis of verses 15–16, this veiled request is taken to be the manumission of Onesimus.

While this construal is not implausible, it lacks textual confirmation. First of all, the letter never states that Onesimus had run away, and Philemon may actually have sent him temporarily to serve Paul in prison (as the Philippians sent Epaphroditus to the incarcerated Paul; see Phil 2:25 and note). Paul does write of Onesimus that "if he hath wronged thee, or oweth thee ought, put that on mine account; . . . I will repay it" (vv. 18–19), and this "wrong" is often interpreted as Onesimus's flight, or else as some misdeed that prompted his escape to avoid punishment. But the offense is hypothetical, and Paul may be foreseeing and forestalling Philemon's anger at any number of things: for example, Onesimus's conversion, presumably without Philemon's permission; or Philemon's extended inability to make use of the slave, if Paul had kept Onesimus longer than his master intended. A more natural reading of Paul's request that Philemon send Onesimus back to him, combined with his confidence that Onesimus's owner will "also do more than I say" (v. 21), is as a hint that Philemon make permanent arrangements for Onesimus to serve Paul in prison (e.g., by formally transferring him to Paul's possession as an apprenticed slave).

Paul's coyness obscures the situation behind the letter: the apostle subtly pressures Philemon to accede to a request he is never so presumptuous as to articulate fully. Partly as a result of this vagueness, Philemon has developed a rich and varied tradition of interpretation, much of it focusing on its attitude toward slavery. In the late fourth century, John Chrysostom in his sermons on Philemon invoked the possibility that Onesimus was an escaped slave whom Paul had returned to his master in order to rebuke a faction in the church that was subverting the institution of slavery by removing bondservants from the custody of their masters (*Homilies on Philemon*, argument). Analogously, in the antebellum United States, Paul's willingness to return Onesimus was regularly cited to support the 1850 Fugitive Slave Act, a federal law that required local authorities in northern states to arrest and return to enslavement any black accused of being a fugitive, as well as imposing severe penalties on private citizens who aided escaped slaves. (Indeed, Philemon was invoked so often in this context that Frederick Douglass described the anticipated time of abolition as "the glorious coming future—when Doctors of Divinity shall find a better use for the Bible than in using it to prop up slavery, and a better employment of their time and talents than in finding analogies between Paul's Epistle to Philemon and the slave-catching bill," *Eulogy of the Late Hon. Wm. Jay*). On the other side of the debate, Paul's inferred request that Philemon free the slave Onesimus has often been invoked as evidence of God's supposed opposition to slavery. It perhaps goes without stating that this interpretive tradition ultimately says more about the desire of Philemon's readers to make Paul say something relevant to the institution of slavery than about the text of the letter itself.

   Joseph A. Fitzmyer's Anchor Bible commentary, *The Letter to Philemon: A New Translation with Introduction and Commentary* (New York: Doubleday, 2000), is helpful and informs this introduction and the notes that follow, as does the excellent treatment of Philemon in J. Albert Harrill's *Slaves in the New Testament: Literary, Social, and Moral Dimensions* (Minneapolis, MN: Fortress, 2004), 6–16, 165–96.

THE EPISTLE OF PAUL TO

PHILEMON

1 Paul, a prisoner of Jesus Christ, and Timothy our brother, unto Philemon our dearly beloved, and fellowlabourer, [2]and to our beloved Apphia, and Archippus our fellow-soldier, and to the church in thy house: [3]Grace to you, and peace, from God our Father and the Lord Jesus Christ.

[4]I thank my God, making mention of thee always in my prayers, [5]hearing of thy love and faith, which thou hast toward the Lord Jesus, and toward all saints; [6]that the communication of thy faith may become effectual by the acknowledging of every good thing which is in you in Christ Jesus. [7]For we have great joy and consolation in thy love, because the bowels of the saints are refreshed by thee, brother.

[8]Wherefore, though I might be much bold in Christ to enjoin thee that which is convenient, [9]yet for love's sake I rather beseech thee, being such an one as Paul the aged, and now also a prisoner of Jesus Christ. [10]I beseech thee for my son Onesimus, whom I have begotten in my bonds: [11]which in time past was to thee unprofitable, but now profitable to thee and to me: [12]whom I have sent again: thou therefore receive him, that is, mine own bowels: [13]whom I would have retained with me, that in thy stead he might have ministered unto me in the bonds of the gospel: [14]but

1–7 **Salutation and thanksgiving.** On the openings of Paul's letters, see note to Rom 1:1–15. **1** *Timothy*: see 1 Cor 4:17 note. *Philemon our dearly beloved*: Paul plays on Philemon's name, which in Greek means "beloved." **2** *Beloved Apphia*: better "Apphia our sister" (MS tradition), "sister" being a common self-designation of Jesus-believers (like "brother" in v. 16). She is otherwise unknown. *Archippus*: cf. Col 4:17. *And to the church in thy house*: the issue the letter addresses is essentially a private one, concerning Philemon's personal property (the slave Onesimus). Paul's decision to address it to the church meeting at Philemon's house (or Archippus's; the reference of *thy* is unclear) locates this issue in a communal context, and perhaps brings social pressure to bear on Philemon as he decides whether to accede to Paul's request. *Church*: see Rom 16:5 note. **3** *Grace to you, and peace*: see Rom 1:7 note. **5** *Faith*: see Rom 1:8 note. **6** *Communication*: Gk. *koinōnia*, lit. "fellowship," perhaps here meaning "sharing" (NRSV). *By the*: lit. "in the." *In you*: better "in us" (MS tradition). **7** *We have*: better "I had" (MS tradition). *Consolation*: or "encouragement." *Bowels*: entrails; a seat of affection, like "heart" in English (also in vv. 12, 20).

8–22 **Petition. 8** *Convenient*: proper. **9** *Beseech*: Gk. *parakaleō* (see v. 10); the nominal form is "consolation" in v. 7. **10** *My son . . . begotten*: Paul claims responsibility for converting him from paganism to worship of the one true God; cf. Gal 4:19 and note. **11** *Unprofitable, but now profitable*: Paul now plays on Onesimus's name (lit. "Beneficial" or "Profitable"). **12** *Thou therefore receive him*: better omitted (MS tradition). **13–14** *Whom I . . . willingly*: in effect, a request that Philemon return Onesimus back to Paul. **13** *Ministered unto*: served, as at table. *Gospel*: see Mark 1:1 note.

without thy mind would I do nothing; that thy benefit should not be as it were of necessity, but willingly. [15]For perhaps he therefore departed for a season, that thou shouldest receive him for ever; [16]not now as a servant, but above a servant, a brother beloved, specially to me, but how much more unto thee, both in the flesh, and in the Lord?

[17]If thou count me therefore a partner, receive him as myself. [18]If he hath wronged thee, or oweth thee ought, put that on mine account; [19]I Paul have written it with mine own hand, I will repay it: albeit I do not say to thee how thou owest unto me even thine own self besides. [20]Yea, brother, let me have joy of thee in the Lord: refresh my bowels in the Lord. [21]Having confidence in thy obedience I wrote unto thee, knowing that thou wilt also do more than I say. [22]But withal prepare me also a lodging: for I trust that through your prayers I shall be given unto you.

[23]There salute thee Epaphras, my fellowprisoner in Christ Jesus; [24]Marcus, Aristarchus, Demas, Lucas, my fellowlabourers.

[25]The grace of our Lord Jesus Christ be with your spirit. Amen.

Written from Rome to Philemon, by Onesimus a servant.

---

14 *Benefit*: lit. "goodness." **15** *Receive him for ever*: i.e., be eternally united with him in God's eschatological reign. **16** *Servant*: lit. "slave" (see Rom 1:1 note). *In the flesh*: in the human realm. **17** *Partner*: Gk. *koinōnos*, which shares its root with "communication" in v. 6 (see note). **19** *I Paul . . . repay it*: Paul presumably takes the pen from his scribe and adds this vow himself. *Thou owest . . . besides*: Paul claims responsibility for Philemon's conversion as well as Onesimus's (cf. v. 10). **21** *More than*: Gk. *hyper*; some, pointing to the echo of v. 16 (KJV "above a servant," better "more than [*hyper*] a slave"), see a veiled reference here to Onesimus's manumission. **22** *Withal*: in addition.

23–25 Closing. 23 *Epaphras*: see Col 1:7 and note; 4:12. **24** *Marcus, Aristarchus, Demas, Lucas*: all mentioned, along with Onesimus, at Colossians' ending (4:9–10, 14), suggesting either that Paul composed the two epistles in tandem or that a later pseudepigrapher gave Colossians a veneer of Pauline authenticity by linking it with Philemon, an obviously authentic letter of Paul (too incidental and idiosyncratic to have been composed by a later author writing in Paul's name). **25** *The grace . . . spirit*: recalling v. 3. *Amen. Written . . . servant*: better omitted (MS tradition).

The Epistle of Paul the Apostle
to the Hebrews

ALTHOUGH it serves as a kind of appendix to the Pauline corpus, Hebrews was not written by Paul, as even its earliest readers acknowledged. Origen, for instance, recognized that Hebrews' style was more sophisticated than Paul's and suggested that one of the apostle's disciples composed it—exactly who, he admitted, "God only knows." Modern scholars have gone further, noting that Hebrews' supersessionist theology, in particular its implication of the Jewish cult's total irrelevance in light of Christ's ultimate sacrifice, goes far beyond anything Paul ever wrote and seems antithetical to the unfailing confidence that Paul places in God's faithfulness to his covenants with Israel, especially in Romans 9–11.

In fact only Hebrews' title, probably a conjectural inference appended to the book by a later scribe, declares Pauline authorship. Thus Hebrews is not, properly speaking, pseudonymous; it is rather anonymous. The epistolary conclusion of chapter 13 resembles those of the Pauline Epistles, and some have speculated that it too is a later insertion added to suggest Paul's authorship, but Hebrews' conclusion may rather indicate that its author was influenced by Paul's writings, or even (as Origen surmised) that one of Paul's partners in ministry wrote the text—a suggestion particularly attractive if the Timothy mentioned in 13:23 is the well-known member of Paul's circle of missionaries. The postbiblical final sentence included by KJV names Timothy as its author—a strange guess in light of 13:23. Barnabas and Apollos have also been proposed, and with more likelihood, but Origen's final assessment still stands.

The epistle's unresolvable anonymity makes it all but impossible to date. The earliest text certain to have drawn on Hebrews is *1 Clement* (cf. *1 Clement* 36 and Heb 1:1–14), but *1 Clement* is itself difficult to date, with hypotheses ranging from ca. 70 C.E. to the mid-second century. Scholars have argued for a somewhat more compressed range for Hebrews, from ca. 60 to ca. 100, with a few outliers seeing it as earlier or later. Given Hebrews' persistent effort to disparage the temple cult in order by comparison to magnify Christ's sacrifice, one might expect some mention of the temple's destruction in 70 C.E., which brought the cult to an end. The book's silence on the matter therefore suggests a date earlier than 70.

The question of Hebrews' genre remains open as well. It has an epistolary conclusion but no salutation; moreover, its closing refers to the preceding text as a "word of exhortation" (13:22), a designation elsewhere used of orations (see Acts 13:15). A number of studies have demonstrated Hebrews' structural and stylistic parallels with ancient Jewish and Christian sermons, and so it seems plausible that the "epistle" to the Hebrews is actually the text of a sermon that its author sent away as a letter, although we have even fewer clues about to whom or where than about when. Even if we accept the title as authentic, it merely presumes a Jewish audience—it does not say where that audience was located. The title's presumption may be correct, for Hebrews engages intensely with the Jewish Scriptures; yet we must recall that Paul's letters too are often exegetically rigorous, even when explicitly addressed to Gentile communities.

Hebrews in fact alternates between exegesis and exhortation, with the latter focused especially on faith and faithfulness and the former establishing, on the basis of biblical interpretation, the superiority of Christ over the Jewish temple cult. Like Alexandrian scholars such as Philo Judaeus and the later Christian Origen, and indeed like Paul on occasion (cf. Col 2:17 and note), Hebrews' author reads Scripture through a Platonic lens. He or she believes in a world of pure ideas and forms, and is convinced that that world constitutes the ultimate reality, which relates to the phenomenal world perceived by the senses as does a physical object to the superficial shadow it casts. This analogy is fundamental to Platonic thought (see *Republic* 514a–518b), and was widely influential throughout Hellenistic popular philosophy. It exercised a particularly strong influence on Hebrews, not just in the passages in which it is explicitly invoked (8:5; 10:1; etc.) but also in the persistently disparaging comparisons drawn throughout the book between the true heavenly tabernacle and the mundane one modeled on it, and between Christ's ultimate sacrifice and the ineffectually repeated sacrifices of the temple priests.

The comparisons supported by Hebrews' Platonizing exegesis are tendentious in the extreme and profoundly disrespectful as well: in dismissing the temple cult as merely a dim and distorted reflection of a transcendent heavenly reality, Hebrews blatantly disparages a major feature of Second Temple Judaism. As troubling as it is, however, the execution of Hebrews' argument is often captivating. It is sustained and methodical (perhaps the longest sustained argument in the entire New Testament), slowly building by adducing more and more exegetical information to support its inexorable conclusion of Christ's superiority. And some of this exegesis is fascinating indeed, such as Hebrews' treatment of Melchizedek, the mysterious priestly figure from Genesis entirely unrelated to the cult that God would establish through Aaron and the Levites. In the mind of Hebrews' author, his sudden and baffling appearance in Genesis points to God's institution of a priestly order foreign to the one legislated in the Torah, an order that Christ fulfills.

The allegorical, or more specifically typological, Platonizing interpretation of the Old Testament that Hebrews executes will seem idiosyncratic to the modern reader, but it was thoroughly conventional in the ancient world, practiced not only by readers of the Bible but also by students of Homer, to take just one example. Ancient and medieval scholars employed it to resolve problems that inevitably arise when a given text is interpreted from an arbitrary ideological or theological perspective, or to advance an ideological program alien to the canonical literary works being invoked in its support. Hebrews is not only a model of this strategy's use but also one of the oldest extant examples of sustained Christian typological interpretation of the Old Testament; it is therefore a foundational document for an interpretive tradition in which most Christian biblical scholarship would participate until at least the Reformation.

This introduction and the notes that follow rely heavily on Harold Attridge's commentary for the Hermeneia series, *The Epistle to the Hebrews: A Commentary on the Epistle to the Hebrews* (Philadelphia: Fortress, 1999), which is a model of clear, concise, but still sophisticated and thorough biblical scholarship.

THE EPISTLE OF PAUL THE
APOSTLE TO THE
HEBREWS

1 God, who at sundry times and in divers manners spake in time past unto the fathers by the prophets, [2]hath in these last days spoken unto us by his Son, whom he hath appointed heir of all things, by whom also he made the worlds; [3]who being the brightness of his glory, and the express image of his person, and upholding all things by the word of his power, when he had by himself purged our sins, sat down on the right hand of the Majesty on high; [4]being made so much better than the angels, as he hath by inheritance obtained a more excellent name than they.

[5]For unto which of the angels said he at any time, Thou art my Son, this day have I begotten thee? And again, I will be to him a Father, and he shall be to me

1:1–4 Introduction. This artfully balanced sentence foreshadows the sophisticated rhetoric throughout Hebrews: two claims about the ancient past—one dealing with God's prophetic speech (v. 1); the other with Christ's role in creation (vv. 2b–3a)—interlocked with two balancing claims about the eschatological present, one dealing with God's speech through Christ (v. 2a) and the other with Christ's purification of sins and exaltation (vv. 3b–4). The contrast between new and old is Hebrews' driving opposition. **1:2** *In these last days*: better "at the end of these days" (MS tradition). *Whom he . . . things*: cf. Ps 2:8. *By whom . . . worlds*: for Christ's role in creation, see John 1:1–3; Col 1:16 and notes. **1:3** *Who being . . . glory*: echoing Wis 7:26 (about wisdom). *Express image*: lit. "imprint," especially of an image on a coin. *Person*: Gk. *hypostasis*, "sediment" or "foundation," and by extension "underlying reality" or "essence"; KJV anachronistically renders the technical sense it acquired during fourth-century Trinitarian debates. *By himself . . . sins*: better "made purification of sins" (MS tradition; our translation), alluding to sacrificial expiation; cf. Exod 29:36; 30:10; Luke 2:22–24; etc. NT texts other than Hebrews occasionally figure Jesus' death as such an expiation (e.g., John 1:29; Rom 3:25 and notes). *Sat down . . . high*: echoing Ps 110:1, on whose basis the NT regularly portrays the risen Christ as sitting at God's right hand (see Acts 2:25, 33–34; 5:31; Rom 8:34; etc.).

1:5–2:18 Jesus, superior to the angels, is the great high priest. This passage consists of a string of scriptural citations marshaled to corroborate the announcement in v. 4 of Christ's superiority to angels (1:5–14), a warning to the readers not to fall away (2:1–4), and an argument culminating in Christ's identification with the high priest (2:5–18). Although the first section has led to hypotheses about angel worship among Hebrews' original audience (cf. Col 2:18), claims of the exalted Christ's superiority to angels are common (cf. Phil 2:9–11, which likewise stresses Christ's "name"; Col 1:15–18; 1 Pet 3:22); thus the comparison may simply emphasize Jesus' magnificence. Christ's later comparison to Moses (3:1–6) probably serves the same purpose. **1:5** *Thou art . . . a Son*: Ps 2:7; 2 Sam 7:14. The Synoptics assign Ps 2:7 to the divine voice at Jesus' baptism (cf. Matt 3:17; Mark

a Son? ⁶And again, when he bringeth in the firstbegotten into the world, he saith, And let all the angels of God worship him. ⁷And of the angels he saith, Who maketh his angels spirits, and his ministers a flame of fire. ⁸But unto the Son he saith, Thy throne, O God, is for ever and ever: a sceptre of righteousness is the sceptre of thy kingdom. ⁹Thou hast loved righteousness, and hated iniquity; therefore God, even thy God, hath anointed thee with the oil of gladness above thy fellows. ¹⁰And, Thou, Lord, in the beginning hast laid the foundation of the earth; and the heavens are the works of thine hands: ¹¹they shall perish; but thou remainest; and they all shall wax old as doth a garment; ¹²and as a vesture shalt thou fold them up, and they shall be changed: but thou art the same, and thy years shall not fail. ¹³But to which of the angels said he at any time, Sit on my right hand, until I make thine enemies thy footstool? ¹⁴Are they not all ministering spirits, sent forth to minister for them who shall be heirs of salvation?

2 Therefore we ought to give the more earnest heed to the things which we have heard, lest at any time we should let them slip. ²For if the word spoken by angels was stedfast, and every transgression and disobedience received a just recompence of reward; ³how shall we escape, if we neglect so great salvation; which at the first began to be spoken by the Lord, and was confirmed unto us by them that heard him; ⁴God also bearing them witness, both with signs and wonders, and with divers miracles, and gifts of the Holy Ghost, according to his own will?

⁵For unto the angels hath he not put in subjection the world to come, whereof we speak. ⁶But one in a certain place testified, saying, What is man, that thou art mindful of him? or the son of man, that thou visitest him? ⁷Thou madest him a little lower than the angels; thou crownedst him with glory and honour, and didst set him over the works of thy hands: ⁸thou hast put all things in subjection under his feet. For in that he put all in subjection under him, he left nothing that is not

---

1:11; Luke 3:22), while Acts 13:33 invokes it in the context of his resurrection. 2 Cor 6:18 and Rev 21:7 use 2 Sam 7:14 to describe God's relationship with believers, but the speech in which it is embedded (2 Sam 7:8–16) becomes an important messianic prophecy in the NT (cf. Mark 10:47 and note; Acts 2:30; etc.). **1:6** *Firstbegotten*: lit. "firstborn." *And let . . . him*: LXX Deut 32:43; LXX Ps 97:7. If the first part of the verse refers to Jesus' birth, the citation might allude to a tradition similar to the one recounted in Luke 2:13–14. But "firstborn" is also used of the risen Christ (cf. Rom 8:29; Rev 1:5), a reference that would evoke a tradition such as that preserved in Phil 2:9–11. **1:7** *Who maketh . . . fire*: Ps. 104:4 (see note). Here too *spirits* is better rendered "winds," since the idea is that subordinate angels may be reduced to elements of nature subject to God's manipulation (cf. Exod 3:2; 14:19; etc.). **1:8–9** *Thy throne . . . fellows*: Ps 45:6–7. Hebrews' introduction of the quote identifies the Psalm's "God" with *the Son* (cf. Rom 9:5; John 1:1, 14; 20:28). **1:9** *Righteousness*: Gk. *dikaiosynē*, "justice"; a different word is used in v. 8. *Anointed*: kings in ancient Israel were traditionally anointed as a sign of their office. **1:10–12** *Thou, Lord . . . fail*: Ps 102:25–27, implicitly contrasting Christ, creator of the cosmos (cf. vv. 2–3), with the angels, earlier cast as elements of created nature (v. 7). **1:12** *Changed*: "like a garment" should be added (MS tradition). **1:13** *Sit on . . . footstool*: Ps 110:1; cf. v. 3 and note. **1:14** *Minister for*: or simply "serve." **2:1** *Let them slip*: lit. "flow away." **2:2** *The word . . . angels*: biblical law; see Gal 3:19 and note. *Stedfast*: Gk. *bebaios* (so throughout), a forensic term (like *just* and "bearing . . . witness" [v. 4]) that means "legally binding." **2:3** *Confirmed*: Gk. *bebaioō*, the verbal form of "stedfast" (see v. 2 and note). **2:4** *Gifts*: distributions. **2:6–8** *What is . . . feet*: Ps 8:4–6; though the lines are about humanity, their reference to the "son of man" (see Mark 2:10 note) invites application to Christ. **2:6** *Visitest*: alternatively "look after." **2:7** *And didst set . . . hands*: better omitted (MS tradition). **2:8** *For in that . . . things put under him*: cf. 1 Cor 15:27–28.

put under him. But now we see not yet all things put under him. [9]But we see Jesus, who was made a little lower than the angels for the suffering of death, crowned with glory and honour; that he by the grace of God should taste death for every man.

[10]For it became him, for whom are all things, and by whom are all things, in bringing many sons unto glory, to make the captain of their salvation perfect through sufferings. [11]For both he that sanctifieth and they who are sanctified are all of one: for which cause he is not ashamed to call them brethren, [12]saying, I will declare thy name unto my brethren, in the midst of the church will I sing praise unto thee. [13]And again, I will put my trust in him. And again, Behold I and the children which God hath given me. [14]Forasmuch then as the children are partakers of flesh and blood, he also himself likewise took part of the same; that through death he might destroy him that had the power of death, that is, the devil; [15]and deliver them who through fear of death were all their lifetime subject to bondage. [16]For verily he took not on him the nature of angels; but he took on him the seed of Abraham. [17]Wherefore in all things it behoved him to be made like unto his brethren, that he might be a merciful and faithful high priest in things pertaining to God, to make reconciliation for the sins of the people. [18]For in that he himself hath suffered being tempted, he is able to succour them that are tempted.

3 Wherefore, holy brethren, partakers of the heavenly calling, consider the Apostle and High Priest of our profession, Christ Jesus; [2]who was faithful to him that appointed him, as also Moses was faithful in all his house. [3]For this man was counted worthy of more glory than Moses, inasmuch as he who hath builded the house hath more honour than the house. [4]For every house is builded by some man; but he that built all things is God. [5]And Moses verily was faithful in all his house, as a servant, for a testimony of those things which were to be spoken after; [6]but Christ as a son over his own house; whose house are we, if we hold fast the confidence and the rejoicing of the hope firm unto the end.

[7]Wherefore (as the Holy Ghost saith, To day if ye will hear his voice, [8]harden not your hearts, as in the provocation, in the day of temptation in the wilderness:

2:10 *Captain*: Gk. *archēgos*, connoting both origination and leadership; hence "pioneer" (NRSV). 2:11 *One*: possibly God (cf. v. 10); but in light of what follows, it should perhaps be understood as "one man," referring to Abraham (v. 16; cf. 11:12 and note) or even to Adam. 2:12 *I will declare . . . thee*: Ps 22:22. *Church*: Gk. *ekklēsia*, used in LXX to refer to the assembly of Israel. 2:13 *I will . . . me*: LXX Isa 8:17–18. 2:15 *Fear of death*: many philosophers in the Greco-Roman tradition viewed the debilitating fear of death as man's essential crisis and offered rational arguments aimed at liberating people from it. 2:16 *He took not . . . nature*: lit. "he lays not hold." *Took on him* may be translated in the same way. 2:17 *High priest*: a number of ancient Jewish texts figure the messiah as an eschatological high priest (e.g., the figure of Melchizedek from *Melchizedek* 11Q13, and the "new priest" of *Testament of Levi* 18). *Make reconciliation*: rather "make expiation" or "make atonement," as in Lev 4:20, 26, 31; and esp. 16:15–16, 33–34, where the Yom Kippur sacrifice is described.

3:1–4:11 **Entering God's rest.** The complex interpretation of Ps 95 that this passage presents superficially resembles Paul's interpretation of Israel's wilderness wanderings in 1 Cor 10:1–22. 3:1 *Apostle*: lit. "one sent out." 3:2 *As also . . . house*: God's *house* is Israel, as the allusion to Num 12:7 suggests (cf. vv. 5–6). 3:6 *Firm unto the end*: better omitted (MS tradition). 3:7–11 *To day . . . rest*: Ps 95:7b–11, with alterations. KJV's relegation of this material to a parenthesis is unjustified. 3:8 *Provocation . . . temptation*: like KJV, LXX (which Hebrews quotes) at Ps 95:8 (see note)

⁹when your fathers tempted me, proved me, and saw my works forty years. ¹⁰Wherefore I was grieved with that generation, and said, They do alway err in their heart; and they have not known my ways. ¹¹So I sware in my wrath, They shall not enter into my rest.)

¹²Take heed, brethren, lest there be in any of you an evil heart of unbelief, in departing from the living God. ¹³But exhort one another daily, while it is called To day; lest any of you be hardened through the deceitfulness of sin. ¹⁴For we are made partakers of Christ, if we hold the beginning of our confidence stedfast unto the end; ¹⁵while it is said, To day if ye will hear his voice, harden not your hearts, as in the provocation. ¹⁶For some, when they had heard, did provoke: howbeit not all that came out of Egypt by Moses. ¹⁷But with whom was he grieved forty years? was it not with them that had sinned, whose carcases fell in the wilderness? ¹⁸And to whom sware he that they should not enter into his rest, but to them that believed not? ¹⁹So we see that they could not enter in because of unbelief.

4 Let us therefore fear, lest, a promise being left us of entering into his rest, any of you should seem to come short of it. ²For unto us was the gospel preached, as well as unto them: but the word preached did not profit them, not being mixed with faith in them that heard it. ³For we which have believed do enter into rest, as he said, As I have sworn in my wrath, if they shall enter into my rest: although the works were finished from the foundation of the world. ⁴For he spake in a certain place of the seventh day on this wise, And God did rest the seventh day from all his works. ⁵And in this place again, If they shall enter into my rest. ⁶Seeing therefore it remaineth that some must enter therein, and they to whom it was first preached entered not in because of unbelief: ⁷again, he limiteth a certain day, saying in David, To day, after so long a time; as it is said, To day if

translates the proper nouns "Meribah" and "Massah" (see Exod 17:1–7). **3:9** *Tempted me, proved me*: better "tested by proving" (MS tradition), with God's *works* the object of testing. **3:9–10** *Saw my works . . . generation*: Ps 95:9–10 says that God was angry for forty years (cf. Heb 3:17), not that the ancestors saw God's works for forty years. **3:11** *They shall . . . rest*: lit. "if they enter into my rest" (also at 4:3), a conditional oath with an implied main clause so terrible that it goes unsaid. The psalm's *rest* refers to the promised land (cf. Deut 12:9). **3:14** *Our confidence*: KJV adds "our" to Gk. *hypostasis* (see 1:3 note); thus Hebrews actually urges the readers to remain committed to Christ's "fundamental reality" in the present, although they will fully partake of Christ only in the eschatological future. **3:15** *While it is said*: "as it is said" (NRSV), introducing another quotation of Ps 95 (vv. 7–8). **3:16** *For some . . . Moses*: better translated as rhetorical questions (like vv. 17–18) based on Num 14: "For who, when they heard, provoked? Did not all of those who came out of Egypt by Moses?" (cf. Num 14:22). **3:17** *With whom . . . wilderness*: cf. Num 14:33. **3:18** *To whom . . . believed not*: cf. Num 14:11. **4:2** *Unto us . . . unto them*: Gk. *euēngelismenoi* (*was the gospel preached*) shares its root with "promise" in v. 1. The Hebrews author therefore claims that the promise of rest (i.e., the promised land; see 3:11 note) was a form of the gospel. Paul makes the same claim about another of God's promises to Abraham (see Gal 3:8–9). *Not being . . . it*: better "who were not united in faith with those who listened" (MS tradition). **4:3** *As I . . . rest*: Ps 95:11; cf. Heb 3:11 and note. **4:3–4** *Although the works . . . his works*: by quoting Gen 2:2, the Hebrews author substitutes God's work of creation for God's "work" sustaining Israel during its wilderness wanderings (cf. Ps 95:9, quoted at Heb 3:9). **4:5** *And in this place again*: i.e., Ps 95, quoting v. 11 yet again (see Heb 3:11 note). In the context of v. 4 and Gen 2:2, *rest* now signifies God's heavenly repose after creation. **4:6** *It was first preached*: better "the gospel was first preached"; see v. 2 note. **4:7** *Limiteth*: "sets" or "defines." The verse claims that "today" from Ps 95:7 refers to the Hebrews

ye will hear his voice, harden not your hearts. [8]For if Jesus had given them rest, then would he not afterward have spoken of another day. [9]There remaineth therefore a rest to the people of God. [10]For he that is entered into his rest, he also hath ceased from his own works, as God did from his. [11]Let us labour therefore to enter into that rest, lest any man fall after the same example of unbelief.

[12]For the word of God is quick, and powerful, and sharper than any twoedged sword, piercing even to the dividing asunder of soul and spirit, and of the joints and marrow, and is a discerner of the thoughts and intents of the heart. [13]Neither is there any creature that is not manifest in his sight: but all things are naked and opened unto the eyes of him with whom we have to do. [14]Seeing then that we have a great high priest, that is passed into the heavens, Jesus the Son of God, let us hold fast our profession. [15]For we have not an high priest which cannot be touched with the feeling of our infirmities; but was in all points tempted like as we are, yet without sin. [16]Let us therefore come boldly unto the throne of grace, that we may obtain mercy, and find grace to help in time of need.

5 For every high priest taken from among men is ordained for men in things pertaining to God, that he may offer both gifts and sacrifices for sins: [2]who can have compassion on the ignorant, and on them that are out of the way; for that he himself also is compassed with infirmity. [3]And by reason hereof he ought, as for the people, so also for himself, to offer for sins. [4]And no man taketh this honour unto himself, but he that is called of God, as was Aaron.

---

author's own time (a sudden maneuver, but anticipated by 3:13).   **4:8** *For if . . . day: Jesus* refers to Joshua—the two names are identical in Greek—who led Israel into the promised land. Josh 21:43–44 explicitly states "The Lord gave unto Israel all the land which he sware to give unto their fathers. . . . And the Lord gave them rest round about." Hebrews insists that the rest mentioned by God in Psalm 95 really had nothing to do with the promised land; it refers rather to God's heavenly repose, which his people may share (vv. 9–10; cf. note to v. 5).   **4:9** *Rest:* Gk. *sabbatismos,* lit. "Sabbath observance" (a different word was used previously), and therefore recalling Gen 2:3 (see note); Exod 20:8–11.

4:12–7:28 Christ the great high priest. This section consists of a brief transition (4:12–16) followed by an introductory exposition of its central theme (5:1–10). After an exhortational digression (5:11–6:12), the author returns to the argument that Christ is the true and perfect high priest (6:13–7:28).   **4:12–16** *For the word . . . need:* in this transitional section, the image of God's terrifying scrutiny (vv. 12–13) carries forward the warning of v. 11, but is immediately offset by an image of Christ the "great high priest" (v. 14), who with humane sympathy allows believers boldly to approach the divine throne (vv. 15–16).   **4:12** *The word . . . heart:* recalling Wis 18:15–16; cf. Isa 49:2; Rev 1:16. *Quick:* living.   **4:13** *With whom . . . do:* more literally "to whom our word is directed." The ambiguous phrase may mean "whom my discourse is about" or "who receives an account" (of our thoughts and intents).   **4:14** *Passed into:* lit. "passed through," perhaps imagining the high priest traversing the curtain to the sanctuary's innermost shrine (cf. Exod 26:31–34) to atone for the people at the mercy seat (Lev 16, esp. v. 2; cf. Heb 6:19–20; 9:24; 10:20).   **4:16** *Let us . . . grace:* recalling the exhortation in v. 11 and thereby connecting the image of God's throne with the idea of his heavenly repose. The *throne of grace* corresponds to the ark that the tabernacle's innermost chamber housed. It was at once an earthly representation of God's heavenly throne and the mercy seat upon which the high priest sprinkled atoning blood on Yom Kippur (see Exod 25:10–22 and notes; cf. Lev 16:14–15).   **5:2** *Have compassion on:* rather "deal gently with" (RSV) or even "moderate his anger toward." *Them that . . . way:* the errant; cf. 3:10 (KJV "err").   **5:3** *For the people . . . sins:* cf. Lev 16:6–19, describing the sacrifices to be performed on the Day of Atonement.   **5:4** *As was Aaron:* cf.

⁵So also Christ glorified not himself to be made an high priest; but he that said unto him, Thou art my Son, to day have I begotten thee. ⁶As he saith also in another place, Thou art a priest for ever after the order of Melchisedec. ⁷Who in the days of his flesh, when he had offered up prayers and supplications with strong crying and tears unto him that was able to save him from death, and was heard in that he feared; ⁸though he were a Son, yet learned he obedience by the things which he suffered; ⁹and being made perfect, he became the author of eternal salvation unto all them that obey him; ¹⁰called of God an high priest after the order of Melchisedec.

¹¹Of whom we have many things to say, and hard to be uttered, seeing ye are dull of hearing. ¹²For when for the time ye ought to be teachers, ye have need that one teach you again which be the first principles of the oracles of God; and are become such as have need of milk, and not of strong meat. ¹³For every one that useth milk is unskilful in the word of righteousness: for he is a babe. ¹⁴But strong meat belongeth to them that are of full age, even those who by reason of

6 use have their senses exercised to discern both good and evil. ¹Therefore leaving the principles of the doctrine of Christ, let us go on unto perfection; not laying again the foundation of repentance from dead works, and of faith toward God, ²of the doctrine of baptisms, and of laying on of hands, and of resurrection of the dead, and of eternal judgment. ³And this will we do, if God permit.

⁴For it is impossible for those who were once enlightened, and have tasted of the heavenly gift, and were made partakers of the Holy Ghost, ⁵and have tasted the good word of God, and the powers of the world to come, ⁶if they shall fall away, to renew them again unto repentance; seeing they crucify to themselves the

---

Exod 28:1; Lev 8:1–30.   **5:5** *Thou art . . . thee*: Ps 2:7, also quoted at 1:5.   **5:6** *Thou art . . . Melchisedec*: Ps 110:4 (see note); the same psalm is quoted at 1:13. This is the first of Hebrews' many citations of this verse.   **5:7** *Who in the days . . . death*: perhaps recalling the tradition of Jesus praying in Gethsemane (e.g., Mark 14:32–42), or his cry to God from the cross (Mark 15:34, 37; cf. Luke 23:46). *He feared*: a reference either to religious awe (as at 12:28 and perhaps 11:7) or to panic in the face of death.   **5:8** *Learned he . . . suffered*: drawing on a Greek adage (which rhymes in the original: *emathen aph' hōn epathen*).   **5:9** *Made perfect*: referring at once to Christ's resurrection/exaltation (thereby explaining how his prayer "was heard," v. 7) and to the completion of his preparation to become compassionate high priest (v. 10; cf. 4:15).   **5:12** *For the time*: "by this time" (RSV). *Become such . . . meat*: see 1 Cor 3:1–2 and note. *Strong meat*: solid food (also in v. 14).   **5:14** *Of full age*: Gk *teleios*, which shares its root with "made perfect" in v. 9. *Exercised*: Gk. *gegymnasmena*, referring to athletic training, an important component of a traditional Greek education.   **6:1** *Perfection*: or "maturity"; cf. 5:14 and note. *Dead works*: works bringing about death—i.e., sins (cf. 9:14). **6:2** *Baptisms*: Gk. *baptismoi*, an unusual plural, suggests not the ritual of baptism but a general reference to Christian ablutions. It is translated "washings" at 9:10.   **6:4–8** *For it . . . burned*: this section seems mainly to justify the author's subsequent assertion that the readers are not without hope of mending their ways (cf. v. 9). Tracking the imagery of consumption clarifies the logic: though they have not moved from milk to solid food (5:12–14), neither have they yet rejected the "heavenly gift" or "good word" that they have "tasted" (6:4–5).   **6:4** *It is impossible*: introducing a rationale for denying the possibility of repentance to apostates. The early church understood certain sins to be unforgivable (e.g., see Mark 3:29; 1 John 5:16), and many "Christians" in antiquity delayed baptism as long as feasible because they did not take for granted postbaptismal repentance of any serious transgressions (see Augustine, *Confessions* 1.17–18).   **6:5** *World*: lit. "age."   **6:6** *To themselves*: for them-

Son of God afresh, and put him to an open shame. [7]For the earth which drinketh in the rain that cometh oft upon it, and bringeth forth herbs meet for them by whom it is dressed, receiveth blessing from God: [8]but that which beareth thorns and briers is rejected, and is nigh unto cursing; whose end is to be burned. [9]But, beloved, we are persuaded better things of you, and things that accompany salvation, though we thus speak. [10]For God is not unrighteous to forget your work and labour of love, which ye have shewed toward his name, in that ye have ministered to the saints, and do minister. [11]And we desire that every one of you do shew the same diligence to the full assurance of hope unto the end: [12]that ye be not slothful, but followers of them who through faith and patience inherit the promises.

[13]For when God made promise to Abraham, because he could swear by no greater, he sware by himself, [14]saying, Surely blessing I will bless thee, and multiplying I will multiply thee. [15]And so, after he had patiently endured, he obtained the promise. [16]For men verily swear by the greater: and an oath for confirmation is to them an end of all strife. [17]Wherein God, willing more abundantly to shew unto the heirs of promise the immutability of his counsel, confirmed it by an oath: [18]that by two immutable things, in which it was impossible for God to lie, we might have a strong consolation, who have fled for refuge to lay hold upon the hope set before us: [19]which hope we have as an anchor of the soul, both sure and stedfast, and which entereth into that within the veil; [20]whither the forerunner is for us entered, even Jesus, made an high priest for ever after the order of Melchisedec.

7 For this Melchisedec, king of Salem, priest of the most high God, who met Abraham returning from the slaughter of the kings, and blessed him; [2]to whom also Abraham gave a tenth part of all; first being by interpretation King of righteousness, and after that also King of Salem, which is, King of peace; [3]without father, without mother, without descent, having neither beginning of days, nor end of life; but made like unto the Son of God; abideth a priest continually. [4]Now consider how great this man was, unto whom even the patriarch Abraham

---

selves.   **6:7–8** *The earth . . . burned*: agricultural imagery is conventionally employed to distinguish the faithful from the disobedient (e.g., Matt 7:16–20; Mark 4:1–20).   **6:8** *Thorns and briars*: echoing God's cursing of the earth in Gen 3:17–18. *End*: Gk. *telos*, which shares its root with "perfect" in 5:9 (see 5:14; 6:1 and notes).   **6:10** *Labour of*: better omitted (MS tradition).   **6:12** *Slothful*: the same Greek word as "dull" at 5:11, with which it forms an inclusive frame bracketing the exhortational digression. *Followers*: imitators.   **6:13–20** *For when . . . Melchisedec*: having allegorically interpreted the first of God's covenantal promises to Abraham—namely, the land (Gen 12:1; cf. Heb 3:7–4:11)—the author now addresses the second, offspring (Gen 12:2).   **6:14** *Surely blessing . . . multiply thee*: Gen 22:17; its context explains the reference to Abraham's patient endurance in v. 15. **6:16** *Confirmation*: see 2:2–3 and notes.   **6:17** *Confirmed*: rather "guaranteed" (a different root is translated "confirmation" in v. 16).   **6:18** *Two immutable things*: his counsel and his oath. *Who have fled . . . upon*: the image is of a fugitive seeking sanctuary by grabbing hold of a temple's altar (cf. 1 Kgs 2:28).   **6:19** *An anchor . . . veil*: a jarringly mixed metaphor, as the sure anchor suddenly penetrates the innermost shrine's veil (Exod 26:31–34), like the high priest on the Day of Atonement (Lev 16:2–3).   **6:20** *Whither the forerunner . . . Melchisedec*: see 4:14–16 and notes; cf. Ps 110:4. **7:1–2** *For this . . . all*: cf. Gen 14:18–20.   **7:2** *First being . . . peace*: both etymological interpretations of *Salem* were common.   **7:3** *Without father . . . continually*: because Genesis omitted information about his descent, Hebrews tendentiously concludes that Melchizedek is immortal, even divine. Other ancient Jewish texts speculate about this mysterious figure as well, including the

gave the tenth of the spoils. [5]And verily they that are of the sons of Levi, who receive the office of the priesthood, have a commandment to take tithes of the people according to the law, that is, of their brethren, though they come out of the loins of Abraham: [6]but he whose descent is not counted from them received tithes of Abraham, and blessed him that had the promises. [7]And without all contradiction the less is blessed of the better. [8]And here men that die receive tithes; but there he receiveth them, of whom it is witnessed that he liveth. [9]And as I may so say, Levi also, who receiveth tithes, payed tithes in Abraham. [10]For he was yet in the loins of his father, when Melchisedec met him.

[11]If therefore perfection were by the Levitical priesthood, (for under it the people received the law,) what further need was there that another priest should rise after the order of Melchisedec, and not be called after the order of Aaron? [12]For the priesthood being changed, there is made of necessity a change also of the law. [13]For he of whom these things are spoken pertaineth to another tribe, of which no man gave attendance at the altar. [14]For it is evident that our Lord sprang out of Juda; of which tribe Moses spake nothing concerning priesthood. [15]And it is yet far more evident: for that after the similitude of Melchisedec there ariseth another priest, [16]who is made, not after the law of a carnal commandment, but after the power of an endless life. [17]For he testifieth, Thou art a priest for ever after the order of Melchisedec.

[18]For there is verily a disannulling of the commandment going before for the weakness and unprofitableness thereof. [19]For the law made nothing perfect, but the bringing in of a better hope did; by the which we draw nigh unto God. [20]And inasmuch as not without an oath he was made priest: [21](for those priests were made without an oath; but this with an oath by him that said unto him, The Lord sware and will not repent, Thou art a priest for ever after the order of Melchisedec:) [22]by so much was Jesus made a surety of a better testament. [23]And they truly were many priests, because they were not suffered to continue by reason of death: [24]but this man, because he continueth ever, hath an unchangeable priesthood. [25]Wherefore he is able also to save them to the uttermost that come unto God by him, seeing he ever liveth to make intercession for them. [26]For such an high priest became us, who is holy, harmless, undefiled, separate from sinners, and made higher than the heavens; [27]who needeth not daily, as those high priests,

---

Qumran text *Melchizedek* 11Q13 and 2 *Enoch*.   **7:5** *They that . . . law*: cf. Num 18:21–24.   **7:6** *Him that . . . promises*: recalling 6:13–15.   **7:7** *Without all contradiction*: "it is beyond dispute that" (RSV). **7:8** *Witnessed that he liveth*: referring to his immortality (cf. v. 3).   **7:12** *Being changed . . . change*: Gk. *metatithēmi, metathesis*; the same root (negated) is present in "immutability" at 6:17, thereby implicitly contrasting the mutability of the priesthood and the law with the fixity of God's promises to Abraham.   **7:15** *After the similitude . . . priest*: echoing Ps 110:4, but replacing "order" with "similitude."   **7:16** *Is made*: has come into existence.   **7:17** *He testifieth*: better "it is testified of him" (MS tradition)—i.e., in Ps 110.   **7:18** *Weakness*: related to its status as "carnal" (v. 16) or fleshly (cf. Rom 8:3). *Unprofitableness*: uselessness.   **7:19** *But the bringing in . . . God*: cf. 6:19–20.   **7:20–21** *And inasmuch . . . Melchisedec*: recalling 6:13–18.   **7:21** *After the order of Melchisedec*: better omitted (MS tradition).   **7:22** *Testament*: Gk. *diathēkē* can mean "covenant" or, more specifically, (last will and) "testament"; KJV alternates between the two. Hebrews manipulates the ambiguity in 9:15–22.   **7:26** *Harmless*: lit. "without wickedness."   **7:27** *Daily, as . . . sacrifice*: Hebrews here

to offer up sacrifice, first for his own sins, and then for the people's: for this he did once, when he offered up himself. [28]For the law maketh men high priests which have infirmity; but the word of the oath, which was since the law, maketh the Son, who is consecrated for evermore.

8 Now of the things which we have spoken this is the sum: We have such an high priest, who is set on the right hand of the throne of the Majesty in the heavens; [2]a minister of the sanctuary, and of the true tabernacle, which the Lord pitched, and not man. [3]For every high priest is ordained to offer gifts and sacrifices: wherefore it is of necessity that this man have somewhat also to offer. [4]For if he were on earth, he should not be a priest, seeing that there are priests that offer gifts according to the law: [5]who serve unto the example and shadow of heavenly things, as Moses was admonished of God when he was about to make the tabernacle: for, See, saith he, that thou make all things according to the pattern shewed to thee in the mount. [6]But now hath he obtained a more excellent ministry, by how much also he is the mediator of a better covenant, which was established upon better promises.

[7]For if that first covenant had been faultless, then should no place have been sought for the second. [8]For finding fault with them, he saith, Behold, the days come, saith the Lord, when I will make a new covenant with the house of Israel and with the house of Judah: [9]not according to the covenant that I made with their fathers in the day when I took them by the hand to lead them out of the land of Egypt; because they continued not in my covenant, and I regarded them not, saith the Lord. [10]For this is the covenant that I will make with the house of Israel after those days, saith the Lord; I will put my laws into their mind, and write them in their hearts: and I will be to them a God, and they shall be to me a people: [11]and they shall not teach every man his neighbour, and every man his brother, saying, Know the Lord: for all shall know me, from the least to the greatest. [12]For I will be merciful to their unrighteousness, and their sins and their iniquities will I remember no more. [13]In that he saith, A new covenant, he hath made the first old. Now that which decayeth and waxeth old is ready to vanish away.

---

confuses the double sacrifice made by the high priest just once a year on Yom Kippur, first for his own sins and then for the people's (Lev 16:11–14, 15–16), with priests' twice-daily sacrifice to God (Exod 29:38–44; Num 28:3–8).   **7:28** *Infirmity*: Gk. *astheneia*, "weakness"; cf. v. 18. *Word of the oath . . . law*: a reference to Ps 110:4. *Consecrated*: lit. "perfected" (see 5:9).

8:1–10:39 The great high priest's sacrifice. This elaborate typological interpretation of the ancient Israelite tabernacle (and, implicitly, temple) cult culminates in an exhortational section beginning at 10:19.   **8:1** *Who is . . . heavens*: an allusion to Ps 110:1 (cf. Heb 1:3).   **8:2** *True tabernacle*: the heavenly model of the transportable tent that God instructed the Israelites to build; see Exod 25:40 (quoted in v. 5); 26:30; cf. Wis 9:8.   **8:5** *Shadow*: see Col 2:17 and note for this philosophical commonplace, which originated with Plato. *For, See . . . mount*: Exod 25:40.   **8:6** *A better covenant*: the idea of a new covenant comes from Jer 31:31–34, which Hebrews will quote (vv. 8–12); cf. Luke 22:20; 1 Cor 11:25; 2 Cor 3:6.   **8:7** *For if . . . second*: cf. 7:11.   **8:8–12** *Behold, the days . . . more*: Jer 31:31–34.   **8:11** *Neighbour*: better "fellow citizen" (MS tradition).   **8:12** *And their iniquities*: better omitted (MS tradition).   **8:13** *In that . . . away*: cf. 2 Cor 3, although Paul's

9 Then verily the first covenant had also ordinances of divine service, and a worldly sanctuary. [2]For there was a tabernacle made; the first, wherein was the candlestick, and the table, and the shewbread; which is called the sanctuary. [3]And after the second veil, the tabernacle which is called the Holiest of all; [4]which had the golden censer, and the ark of the covenant overlaid round about with gold, wherein was the golden pot that had manna, and Aaron's rod that budded, and the tables of the covenant; [5]and over it the cherubims of glory shadowing the mercyseat; of which we cannot now speak particularly.

[6]Now when these things were thus ordained, the priests went always into the first tabernacle, accomplishing the service of God. [7]But into the second went the high priest alone once every year, not without blood, which he offered for himself, and for the errors of the people: [8]the Holy Ghost this signifying, that the way into the holiest of all was not yet made manifest, while as the first tabernacle was yet standing: [9]which was a figure for the time then present, in which were offered both gifts and sacrifices, that could not make him that did the service perfect, as pertaining to the conscience; [10]which stood only in meats and drinks, and divers washings, and carnal ordinances, imposed on them until the time of reformation.

---

argument is more nuanced   **9:2** *Candlestick*: lampstand; cf. Exod 25:31–40; 37:17–24; 40:4, 24. *The table . . . shewbread*: the table (Exod 25:23–28; 37:10–15; 40:4, 22) displayed the bread (Exod 25:30; 40:22–23), on which see Lev 24:5–9.   **9:3** *Which is . . . all*: i.e., the tabernacle's innermost shrine, described at Exod 26:31–34, where it is called "the most holy place" (v. 34).   **9:4** *Censer*: the "altar to burn incense upon" of Exod 30:1–10 (v. 1; cf. 37:25–28); according to Exodus, it was located just outside the shrine curtained off (30:6; 40:5, 26–27), but Jewish texts other than Hebrews place it within the shrine (cf. 2 Baruch 6.7). *Ark of the covenant*: cf. Exod 25:10–15; 37:1–5; 40:3. Of the three items Hebrews says it contained, the Pentateuch specifies only *the tables of the covenant* within it (Exod 25:16; Deut 10:1–4) and other biblical texts insist "there was nothing in the ark save the two tables of stone, which Moses put there at Horeb" (1 Kgs 8:9; cf. 2 Chr 5:10). Exod 16:32–34 and Num 17:1–11 (esp. v. 10) apparently suggested to the Hebrews author that it also contained *the golden pot that had manna, and Aaron's rod that budded*.   **9:5** *Mercyseat*: see Exod 25:17–22 and notes.   **9:6** *Ordained*: lit. "prepared." *First tabernacle*: i.e., the area inside the tabernacle but outside its inner shrine (the "second" tabernacle; v. 7; cf. 2–3).   **9:7** *Once every year*: on the Day of Atonement; see Lev 16 (contrast 7:27 and note). *Errors*: Gk. *agnoēmata*, which refers to unintentional sins. Lev 16, in contrast, insists that the sacrifice covers all sins (vv. 16, 21, 30). In light of Heb 10:26, this alteration appears theologically meaningful.   **9:8** *Holiest of all*: not the Greek phrase thus rendered in v. 3 (see note), but a related term, translated as "sanctuary" in v. 2 and referring to the tabernacle in general, as opposed to its inner sanctum. KJV does not capture the shift in Hebrews' comparison away from the tabernacle's outer and inner sections (called "first" and "second" in vv. 2–3, 6–7) and toward a distinction between the mundane priestly cult described in the OT (*the first tabernacle* here) and the one overseen by Christ, the great high priest, in the heavenly sanctuary (v. 11).   **9:9** *Which was . . . perfect*: better "which is a figure for the present time, according to which (figure) both gifts and sacrifices are offered that cannot perfect the one who has done the service" (MS tradition; our translation). That is, the first tabernacle cult's failure to perfect the conscience points to the present success of Christ, the great high priest (vv. 11–12; see notes). Later scribes misunderstood the analogy, leading to textual corruption.   **9:10** *Meats*: foods. *And carnal ordinances*: better simply "carnal ordinances" (MS tradition); the phrase should follow *only*, with *in meats and drinks, and divers washings* understood as parenthetical examples of these ordinances.

[11]But Christ being come an high priest of good things to come, by a greater and more perfect tabernacle, not made with hands, that is to say, not of this building; [12]neither by the blood of goats and calves, but by his own blood he entered in once into the holy place, having obtained eternal redemption for us. [13]For if the blood of bulls and of goats, and the ashes of an heifer sprinkling the unclean, sanctifieth to the purifying of the flesh: [14]how much more shall the blood of Christ, who through the eternal Spirit offered himself without spot to God, purge your conscience from dead works to serve the living God?

[15]And for this cause he is the mediator of the new testament, that by means of death, for the redemption of the transgressions that were under the first testament, they which are called might receive the promise of eternal inheritance. [16]For where a testament is, there must also of necessity be the death of the testator. [17]For a testament is of force after men are dead: otherwise it is of no strength at all while the testator liveth. [18]Whereupon neither the first testament was dedicated without blood. [19]For when Moses had spoken every precept to all the people according to the law, he took the blood of calves and of goats, with water, and scarlet wool, and hyssop, and sprinkled both the book, and all the people, [20]saying, This is the blood of the testament which God hath enjoined unto you. [21]Moreover he sprinkled with blood both the tabernacle, and all the vessels of the ministry. [22]And almost all things are by the law purged with blood; and without shedding of blood is no remission.

[23]It was therefore necessary that the patterns of things in the heavens should be purified with these; but the heavenly things themselves with better sacrifices than these. [24]For Christ is not entered into the holy places made with hands, which are the figures of the true; but into heaven itself, now to appear in the presence of God for us: [25]nor yet that he should offer himself often, as the high priest entereth into the holy place every year with blood of others; [26]for then must he often have suffered since the foundation of the world: but now once in the end of the world hath he appeared to put away sin by the sacrifice of himself. [27]And

---

9:11 *To come*: better "that have come" (MS tradition). *Of this building*: better "of this creation." **9:12** *Goats and calves*: also in v. 13 and 10:4 ("bulls and . . . goats"); animals sacrificed on the Day of Atonement (see Lev 16). *Redemption*: Gk. *lytrōsis*, which shares its root with "ransom" in Mark 10:45; see note (cf. v. 15). *For us*: better omitted (KJV's addition). **9:13** *The ashes . . . unclean*: see Num 19 for the ritual. **9:14** *Without spot*: internalizing the requirement that sacrificial animals have bodies "without blemish" (e.g., Lev 1:3, 10). *Your*: better "our" (MS tradition). *Dead works*: see 6:1 note. **9:15** *Testament*: see 7:22 note. **9:17** *Of force*: Gk. *bebaios*, "legally binding"; cf. 2:2 note. **9:18** *Dedicated*: Gk. *enkekainistai*, alternatively "inaugurated." **9:19–20** *When Moses . . . you*: cf. Exod 24:6–8, supplemented with details from the cleansing ritual for those healed of leprosy (Lev 14:4–6) and perhaps from the sacrifice of the red heifer as well (Num 19:18). **9:21** *He sprinkled . . . ministry*: conflating the consecration of Aaron and his sons by the sprinkling of blood in Lev 8 (see esp. vv. 15, 19, 30) with the consecration of the tabernacle and its paraphernalia by the anointing with oil at Exod 40:9–11, and linking both to the covenant's inauguration (Exod 24:6–8). *He sprinkled*: lit. "he sprinkled in the same way." **9:22** *Remission*: i.e., of sins, a common NT usage. **9:24** *Christ is . . . us*: cf. 4:14–16 and notes. **9:25** *As the high priest . . . others*: i.e., to make the sacrifices of the Day of Atonement (Lev 16). **9:26** *End of the world*: lit. "end of the ages."

as it is appointed unto men once to die, but after this the judgment: [28]so Christ was once offered to bear the sins of many; and unto them that look for him shall he appear the second time without sin unto salvation.

10 For the law having a shadow of good things to come, and not the very image of the things, can never with those sacrifices which they offered year by year continually make the comers thereunto perfect. [2]For then would they not have ceased to be offered? because that the worshippers once purged should have had no more conscience of sins. [3]But in those sacrifices there is a remembrance again made of sins every year. [4]For it is not possible that the blood of bulls and of goats should take away sins. [5]Wherefore when he cometh into the world, he saith, Sacrifice and offering thou wouldest not, but a body hast thou prepared me: [6]in burnt offerings and sacrifices for sin thou hast had no pleasure. [7]Then said I, Lo, I come (in the volume of the book it is written of me,) to do thy will, O God. [8]Above when he said, Sacrifice and offering and burnt offerings and offering for sin thou wouldest not, neither hadst pleasure therein; which are offered by the law; [9]then said he, Lo, I come to do thy will, O God. He taketh away the first, that he may establish the second. [10]By the which will we are sanctified through the offering of the body of Jesus Christ once for all.

[11]And every priest standeth daily ministering and offering oftentimes the same sacrifices, which can never take away sins: [12]but this man, after he had offered one sacrifice for sins for ever, sat down on the right hand of God; [13]from henceforth expecting till his enemies be made his footstool. [14]For by one offering he hath perfected for ever them that are sanctified. [15]Whereof the Holy Ghost also is a witness to us: for after that he had said before, [16]This is the covenant that I will make with them after those days, saith the Lord, I will put my laws into their hearts and in their minds will I write them; [17]and their sins and iniquities will I remember no more. [18]Now where remission of these is, there is no more offering for sin.

[19]Having therefore, brethren, boldness to enter into the holiest by the blood of Jesus, [20]by a new and living way, which he hath consecrated for us, through the veil, that is to say, his flesh; [21]and having an high priest over the house of God; [22]let us draw near with a true heart in full assurance of faith, having our hearts sprinkled from an evil conscience, and our bodies washed with pure water. [23]Let

9:28 *Unto them . . . salvation*: alternatively "[he] will appear a second time, not to deal with sin but to save those who are eagerly waiting for him" (RSV).   **10:1** *Shadow*: see 8:5 note.   **10:5–7** *Sacrifice and . . . God*: LXX Ps 40:6–8; see notes.   **10:5** *Thou wouldest not*: "you did not will" (also in v. 8).   **10:7** *Volume*: scroll.   **10:12–13** *Sat down . . . footstool*: cf. Ps 110:1.   **10:15–17** *For after . . . more*: i.e., after he had said "This is . . . days" (Jer 31:33a), then the Lord said "I will . . . more" (Jer 31:33b–34).   **10:19** *Having therefore . . . holiest*: cf. 4:16.   **10:20** *Consecrated*: or "inaugurated"; cf. 9:18 and note. *Through the . . . flesh*: Jesus' sacrifice makes possible entrance into the heavenly tabernacle's inner sanctum (v. 19) and so is figuratively assimilated to the veil serving as that area's threshold (cf. 9:3; Exod 26:31–34).   **10:22** *Having our hearts . . . water*: cf. Ezek 36:25–26, but the language is multivalent and also evokes baptism as well as the various lustrations, anointings, and sprinklings of sacrificial blood discussed above, especially the blood sprinkled on the mercy seat

us hold fast the profession of our faith without wavering; (for he is faithful that promised;) [24]and let us consider one another to provoke unto love and to good works: [25]not forsaking the assembling of ourselves together, as the manner of some is; but exhorting one another: and so much the more, as ye see the day approaching.

[26]For if we sin wilfully after that we have received the knowledge of the truth, there remaineth no more sacrifice for sins, [27]but a certain fearful looking for of judgment and fiery indignation, which shall devour the adversaries. [28]He that despised Moses' law died without mercy under two or three witnesses: [29]of how much sorer punishment, suppose ye, shall he be thought worthy, who hath trodden under foot the Son of God, and hath counted the blood of the covenant, wherewith he was sanctified, an unholy thing, and hath done despite unto the Spirit of grace? [30]For we know him that hath said, Vengeance belongeth unto me, I will recompense, saith the Lord. And again, The Lord shall judge his people. [31]It is a fearful thing to fall into the hands of the living God.

[32]But call to remembrance the former days, in which, after ye were illuminated, ye endured a great fight of afflictions; [33]partly, whilst ye were made a gazingstock both by reproaches and afflictions; and partly, whilst ye became companions of them that were so used. [34]For ye had compassion of me in my bonds, and took joyfully the spoiling of your goods, knowing in yourselves that ye have in heaven a better and an enduring substance. [35]Cast not away therefore your confidence, which hath great recompence of reward. [36]For ye have need of patience, that, after ye have done the will of God, ye might receive the promise. [37]For yet a little while, and he that shall come will come, and will not tarry. [38]Now the just shall live by faith: but if any man draw back, my soul shall have no pleasure in him. [39]But we are not of them who draw back unto perdition; but of them that believe to the saving of the soul.

---

by the high priest on Yom Kippur (see 4:16 note).   **10:25** *The day*: i.e., of judgment.   **10:28** *Despised*: a related Greek word was translated "disannulling" at 7:18 (also with reference to the law) and "put away" at 9:26. *Died without mercy . . . witnesses*: cf. Deut 17:2–6, on the punishment for worshipping other gods.   **10:29** *Who hath trodden . . . grace*: the author presumably has apostasy in mind (cf. 6:4–6). *An unholy thing*: lit. "common."   **10:30** *Vengeance belongeth . . . people*: Deut 32:35, 36; cf. Rom 12:19.   **10:32** *Fight*: Gk. *athlēsis*, which refers to athletic competition.   **10:33** *Gazingstock*: public spectacle; cf. 1 Cor 4:9.   **10:34** *Of me in my bonds*: better "on those in bonds" (MS tradition; cf. 13:3). Later scribes, presuming Pauline authorship, turned the phrase into a reference to his imprisonment (e.g., Phil 1:7, 13). *Spoiling*: plunder. *In heaven*: better omitted (MS tradition). *Substance*: Gk. *hyparxis*, which shares its root with *goods*.   **10:37–38** *For yet . . . him*: alluding to Isa 26:20–21 and Hab 2:3–4, which Paul also quotes, though with a different interpretation (cf. Rom 1:17 and note; Gal 3:11). *Any man*: rather "he."   **10:38** *The just*: better "my just one" (MS tradition).   **10:39** *We are . . . soul*: more literally "we are not characterized by a drawing back unto destruction, but by faith which leads to the preservation of the soul" (Attridge, slightly emended).

11 Now faith is the substance of things hoped for, the evidence of things not seen. ²For by it the elders obtained a good report. ³Through faith we understand that the worlds were framed by the word of God, so that things which are seen were not made of things which do appear.

⁴By faith Abel offered unto God a more excellent sacrifice than Cain, by which he obtained witness that he was righteous, God testifying of his gifts: and by it he being dead yet speaketh. ⁵By faith Enoch was translated that he should not see death; and was not found, because God had translated him: for before his translation he had this testimony, that he pleased God. ⁶But without faith it is impossible to please him: for he that cometh to God must believe that he is, and that he is a rewarder of them that diligently seek him. ⁷By faith Noah, being warned of God of things not seen as yet, moved with fear, prepared an ark to the saving of his house; by the which he condemned the world, and became heir of the righteousness which is by faith.

⁸By faith Abraham, when he was called to go out into a place which he should after receive for an inheritance, obeyed; and he went out, not knowing whither he went. ⁹By faith he sojourned in the land of promise, as in a strange country, dwelling in tabernacles with Isaac and Jacob, the heirs with him of the same promise: ¹⁰for he looked for a city which hath foundations, whose builder and maker is God. ¹¹Through faith also Sara herself received strength to conceive seed, and was delivered of a child when she was past age, because she judged him faithful who had promised. ¹²Therefore sprang there even of one, and him as good as dead, so many as the stars of the sky in multitude, and as the sand which is by the sea shore innumerable.

11:1–12:29 Faith and endurance. Consisting of, first, a definition of faith (11:1) followed by an encomium of it (11:2–40) that amounts to a conventional synopsis of sacred history (see Acts 7:2–53 note), and second, an exhortation that the audience exercise faithful endurance (chap. 12). The material in chap. 11 is carefully structured. It focuses primarily on two OT heroes—Abraham (vv. 8–22) and Moses (vv. 23–31)—opening (vv. 2–7) and closing (vv. 32–40) with briefer résumés of the history preceding and following them. The entire chapter is bracketed by parallel references to the "good report" of the scriptural figures it discusses (vv. 2, 39). Moreover, its two main sections parallel one another precisely, each containing seven claims introduced by Gk. *pistei* (KJV "by faith" or "through faith"). Each set of seven has four developed statements about faithful deeds associated with its respective hero (vv. 8, 9, 11–12, 17–19; 23, 24–26, 27, 28), followed by three brief claims about the faithful acts of succeeding generations (vv. 20, 21, 22; 29, 30, 31).   **11:1** *Substance*: Gk. *hypostasis*; see 1:3 note.   **11:3** *Things which are . . . appear*: the statement presumes that a heavenly realm imperceptible to the senses provides the model for the created phenomenal cosmos, as it does for the tabernacle; cf. 8:5; 9:23.   **11:4** *Abel*: see Gen 4:1–15, though Abel's faith is not there mentioned. *He being dead yet speaketh*: see Gen 4:10.   **11:5** *Enoch*: see Gen 5:24. LXX reads "translated" for MT's "took" and specifies that Enoch pleased God.   **11:7** *By the which*: Noah's faith. *He condemned the world*: probably a reference to a tradition that before the flood (Gen 6:5–9:17), God instructed Noah to denounce the people of the world and call for their repentance (e.g., *Sibylline Oracles* 1.125–282).   **11:8** *Abraham . . . whither he went*: see Gen 12:1–4.   **11:9** *He sojourned . . . same promise*: cf. Gen 17:8.   **11:10** *A city . . . God*: perhaps the heavenly Jerusalem (12:22; cf. Rev 21:10–22:5), but in any case the heavenly reality lying behind the promised land (cf. vv. 15–16).   **11:11** *Also Sara . . . because she*: better "he also—and Sarah herself, being barren—received strength to sow seed when he was past age because he" (MS tradition); cf. Gen 17:15–21; 18:1–15; 21:1–7.   **11:12** *As good as dead*: cf. Rom 4:19. *The stars . . . innumerable*: cf. Gen 22:17.

¹³These all died in faith, not having received the promises, but having seen them afar off, and were persuaded of them, and embraced them, and confessed that they were strangers and pilgrims on the earth. ¹⁴For they that say such things declare plainly that they seek a country. ¹⁵And truly, if they had been mindful of that country from whence they came out, they might have had opportunity to have returned. ¹⁶But now they desire a better country, that is, an heavenly: wherefore God is not ashamed to be called their God: for he hath prepared for them a city.

¹⁷By faith Abraham, when he was tried, offered up Isaac: and he that had received the promises offered up his only begotten son, ¹⁸of whom it was said, That in Isaac shall thy seed be called: ¹⁹accounting that God was able to raise him up, even from the dead; from whence also he received him in a figure. ²⁰By faith Isaac blessed Jacob and Esau concerning things to come. ²¹By faith Jacob, when he was a dying, blessed both the sons of Joseph; and worshipped, leaning upon the top of his staff. ²²By faith Joseph, when he died, made mention of the departing of the children of Israel; and gave commandment concerning his bones.

²³By faith Moses, when he was born, was hid three months of his parents, because they saw he was a proper child; and they were not afraid of the king's commandment. ²⁴By faith Moses, when he was come to years, refused to be called the son of Pharaoh's daughter; ²⁵choosing rather to suffer affliction with the people of God, than to enjoy the pleasures of sin for a season; ²⁶esteeming the reproach of Christ greater riches than the treasures in Egypt: for he had respect unto the recompence of the reward. ²⁷By faith he forsook Egypt, not fearing the wrath of the king: for he endured, as seeing him who is invisible. ²⁸Through faith he kept the passover, and the sprinkling of blood, lest he that destroyed the firstborn should touch them. ²⁹By faith they passed through the Red sea as by dry land: which the Egyptians assaying to do were drowned. ³⁰By faith the walls of

---

11:13 *Having seen them afar off*: recalling Moses' distant vision of the promised land (Deut 32:49; 34:4). *And were persuaded of them*: better omitted (MS tradition). *Embraced*: lit. "greeted" or "welcomed." *And confessed . . . earth*: echoing Gen 17:8 and especially Abraham's confession at 23:4. *Earth*: Gk. *gē*, also "land." **11:15–16** *If they . . . heavenly*: i.e., if Abraham and his descendents merely longed for an earthly homeland in Canaan, they could easily have returned to their country of origin. That they did not indicates their desire for something more—for the heavenly fatherland. **11:17–22** *By faith . . . bones*: the examples of faith in this section all involve the patriarchs' expectation of continuity after death—in offspring, in resurrection, or both. **11:17** *Abraham, when . . . son*: see Gen 22:1–19. **11:18** *In Isaac . . . called*: Gen 21:12. **11:19** *Accounting that . . . dead*: a tendentious but not impossible reading of Gen 22. **11:20** *Isaac blessed . . . come*: see Gen 27:27–29, 39–40. **11:21** *Jacob, when . . . Joseph*: see Gen 48:8–20. *And worshipped . . . staff*: cf. LXX Gen 47:31, which apparently interprets the Hebrew word for "bed" as "staff." **11:22** *Joseph, when . . . bones*: see Gen 50:24–25, with the reference to *bones* perhaps alluding to an expectation of resurrection. *Died*: better "was dying." **11:23** *Was hid three months*: see Exod 2:2. *Proper*: rather "handsome." **11:24–25** *When he . . . season*: see Exod 2:10 for Moses' adoption by Pharaoh's daughter. Hebrews interprets his identification with the brutalized Israelites as a rejection of his status as an adopted Egyptian prince (Exod 2:11–15). **11:26** *Had respect*: paid attention to. **11:27** *Not fearing . . . king*: contradicting Exod 2:14. **11:28** *He kept . . . them*: see Exod 12:21–23. **11:29** *They passed . . . drowned*: see Exod 14:21–29. **11:30** *The walls . . . days*: see Josh 6:1–21.

Jericho fell down, after they were compassed about seven days. [31]By faith the harlot Rahab perished not with them that believed not, when she had received the spies with peace.

[32]And what shall I more say? for the time would fail me to tell of Gedeon, and of Barak, and of Samson, and of Jephthae; of David also, and Samuel, and of the prophets: [33]who through faith subdued kingdoms, wrought righteousness, obtained promises, stopped the mouths of lions, [34]quenched the violence of fire, escaped the edge of the sword, out of weakness were made strong, waxed valiant in fight, turned to flight the armies of the aliens. [35]Women received their dead raised to life again: and others were tortured, not accepting deliverance; that they might obtain a better resurrection: [36]and others had trial of cruel mockings and scourgings, yea, moreover of bonds and imprisonment: [37]they were stoned, they were sawn asunder, were tempted, were slain with the sword: they wandered about in sheepskins and goatskins; being destitute, afflicted, tormented; [38](of whom the world was not worthy:) they wandered in deserts, and in mountains, and in dens and caves of the earth.

[39]And these all, having obtained a good report through faith, received not the promise: [40]God having provided some better thing for us, that they without us should not be made perfect.

12 Wherefore seeing we also are compassed about with so great a cloud of witnesses, let us lay aside every weight, and the sin which doth so easily beset us, and let us run with patience the race that is set before us, [2]looking unto Jesus the author and finisher of our faith; who for the joy that was set before him endured the cross, despising the shame, and is set down at the right hand of the throne of God. [3]For consider him that endured such contradiction of sinners against himself, lest ye be wearied and faint in your minds.

11:31 *The harlot . . . peace*: see Josh 2; 6:22–25.   **11:32** *Gedeon, and . . . Jephthae*: see, respectively, Judg 6–8; 4–5; 13–16; 11–12. *David, Samuel*: see 1–2 Sam; 1 Kgs 1–2.   **11:32–38** *The prophets . . . earth*: the notes comment on only some items in this allusive anthology of notable acts of faithful prophets and others.   **11:33** *Stopped the mouths of lions*: see Dan 6:22.   **11:34** *Quenched the violence of fire*: see Dan 3.   **11:35** *Women received . . . again*: see 1 Kgs 17:17–24; 2 Kgs 4:18–37. *Others were tortured . . . resurrection*: recalling the martyrdoms in 2 Macc 7.   **11:36–38** *Others had . . . earth*: recalling the persecutions of the prophets—e.g., of Zechariah, who was stoned (2 Chr 24:21; cf. Matt 23:35); of Isaiah, who according to legend was sawn in half (*Martyrdom and Ascension of Isaiah* 5); and of Elijah, who fled destitute from Ahab and Jezebel (1 Kgs 19:1–8), hid in a cave (vv. 9–12), and had a "mantle" (v. 13; cf. 2 Kgs 2:8, 13–14), which LXX calls a "sheepskin."   **11:37** *Were tempted*: better omitted (MS tradition).   **12:1** *Witnesses*: Gk. *martyres*, which shares its root with "obtained a good report" (11:2, 39). Hebrews subverts the image, transforming those being witnessed by the readers into the readers' witnesses as they engage in a struggle analogous to an athletic competition. *Patience*: Gk. *hypomonē*, alternatively "endurance" (the nominal form of "endured" in vv. 2–3). **12:2** *Author*: Gk. *archēgos*, also "captain"; cf. 2:10 and note. *Is set . . . God*: echoing Ps 110:1. **12:3** *Contradiction*: here with the sense of "verbal hostility," probably in reference to traditions such as those recorded at Mark 14:63–65; 15:16–20, 29–32. *Against himself*: the MS tradition supports "against themselves," but this makes little sense in context and may reflect an early and widespread scribal alteration of the passage to suggest that hostile sinners ultimately injured not Jesus but them-

⁴Ye have not yet resisted unto blood, striving against sin. ⁵And ye have forgotten the exhortation which speaketh unto you as unto children, My son, despise not thou the chastening of the Lord, nor faint when thou art rebuked of him: ⁶for whom the Lord loveth he chasteneth, and scourgeth every son whom he receiveth. ⁷If ye endure chastening, God dealeth with you as with sons; for what son is he whom the father chasteneth not? ⁸But if ye be without chastisement, whereof all are partakers, then are ye bastards, and not sons. ⁹Furthermore we have had fathers of our flesh which corrected us, and we gave them reverence: shall we not much rather be in subjection unto the Father of spirits, and live? ¹⁰For they verily for a few days chastened us after their own pleasure; but he for our profit, that we might be partakers of his holiness. ¹¹Now no chastening for the present seemeth to be joyous, but grievous: nevertheless afterward it yieldeth the peaceable fruit of righteousness unto them which are exercised thereby.

¹²Wherefore lift up the hands which hang down, and the feeble knees; ¹³and make straight paths for your feet, lest that which is lame be turned out of the way; but let it rather be healed.

¹⁴Follow peace with all men, and holiness, without which no man shall see the Lord: ¹⁵looking diligently lest any man fail of the grace of God; lest any root of bitterness springing up trouble you, and thereby many be defiled; ¹⁶lest there be any fornicator, or profane person, as Esau, who for one morsel of meat sold his birthright. ¹⁷For ye know how that afterward, when he would have inherited the blessing, he was rejected: for he found no place of repentance, though he sought it carefully with tears.

¹⁸For ye are not come unto the mount that might be touched, and that burned with fire, nor unto blackness, and darkness, and tempest, ¹⁹and the sound of a trumpet, and the voice of words; which voice they that heard intreated that the word should not be spoken to them any more: ²⁰(for they could not endure that which was commanded, And if so much as a beast touch the mountain, it shall

---

selves.   **12:4** *Striving*: Gk. *antagōnizomai*, which shares its root with "race" in v. 1. The athletic analogy continues, but the image has changed from footrace to pugnacious sport. Such metaphors are common in Greco-Roman philosophical writing (see 1 Cor 9:24–27 and notes).   **12:5–6** *My son . . . receiveth*: Prov 3:11–12.   **12:5** *Chastening*: "discipline" (so subsequently).   **12:7** *If ye endure chastening*: better as an independent clause, "endure for the sake of discipline" (MS tradition; NRSV).   **12:9** *Spirits*: i.e., "our spirits" (in contrast to "our flesh").   **12:10** *After their own pleasure*: "as it seemed good to them." *That we . . . holiness*: cf. Lev 19:2.   **12:11** *Fruit of righteousness*: cf. Amos 6:12. *Exercised*: see 5:14 and note.   **12:12** *Lift up . . . knees*: recalling the encouragement of the weary in Isa 35:3–4.   **12:13** *Make straight . . . feet*: echoing LXX Prov 4:26.   **12:14** *Follow*: in the sense of "pursue."   **12:15** *Lest any root . . . you*: echoing Deut 29:18, where the "root" is related to idolatry.   **12:16** *Any fornicator . . . Esau*: Esau's marriages to foreign women (Gen 26:34–35) suggested licentiousness to ancient biblical commentators. *For one morsel . . . birthright*: see Gen 25:29–34.   **12:17** *Afterward, when . . . tears*: see Gen 27:30–40. This is Hebrews' third reference to the impossibility of repentance; cf. 6:4–6; 10:26–31.   **12:18** *The mount that*: better "that which" (MS tradition). *The mount* is a scribal interpolation clarifying the allusion to Sinai.   **12:18–19** *That burned . . . more*: combining traditional elements of God's manifestation at Horeb/Sinai during the giving of the law (cf. Exod 19:16; 20:19; Deut 4:11–12; 5:22–25), although the imagery recalls the plague of darkness as well (Exod 10:21).   **12:20** *They could not endure . . . dart*: see Exod 19:12–13.

be stoned, or thrust through with a dart: ²¹and so terrible was the sight, that Moses said, I exceedingly fear and quake:) ²²but ye are come unto mount Sion, and unto the city of the living God, the heavenly Jerusalem, and to an innumerable company of angels, ²³to the general assembly and church of the firstborn, which are written in heaven, and to God the Judge of all, and to the spirits of just men made perfect, ²⁴and to Jesus the mediator of the new covenant, and to the blood of sprinkling, that speaketh better things than that of Abel.

²⁵See that ye refuse not him that speaketh. For if they escaped not who refused him that spake on earth, much more shall not we escape, if we turn away from him that speaketh from heaven: ²⁶whose voice then shook the earth: but now he hath promised, saying, Yet once more I shake not the earth only, but also heaven. ²⁷And this word, Yet once more, signifieth the removing of those things that are shaken, as of things that are made, that those things which cannot be shaken may remain. ²⁸Wherefore we receiving a kingdom which cannot be moved, let us have grace, whereby we may serve God acceptably with reverence and godly fear: ²⁹for our God is a consuming fire.

13 Let brotherly love continue. ²Be not forgetful to entertain strangers: for thereby some have entertained angels unawares. ³Remember them that are in bonds, as bound with them; and them which suffer adversity, as being yourselves also in the body. ⁴Marriage is honourable in all, and the bed undefiled: but whoremongers and adulterers God will judge. ⁵Let your conversation be without covetousness; and be content with such things as ye have: for he hath said, I will never leave thee, nor forsake thee. ⁶So that we may boldly say, The Lord is my helper, and I will not fear what man shall do unto me.

⁷Remember them which have the rule over you, who have spoken unto you the word of God: whose faith follow, considering the end of their conversation. ⁸Jesus Christ the same yesterday, and to day, and for ever. ⁹Be not carried about with div-

---

Or thrust . . . dart: better omitted (MS tradition).   **12:21** *I exceedingly . . . quake*: cf. Deut 9:19, although there Moses' fear has a different cause.   **12:22** *Mount Sion*: the Temple Mount, but implying the heavenly temple.   **12:23** *General assembly*: i.e., a festive assembly. *Church of the firstborn*: see 2:12 note, although here also implying the community of Jesus-believers, which consists *of the firstborn* because believers inherit God's promises (see 9:15; cf. 12:16–17; etc.). *Written in heaven*: see Luke 10:20 note. *The spirits . . . perfect*: a conventional apocalyptic idea (cf. Rev 6:9–11). Although *made perfect* is here a euphemism for death, Hebrews contains several references to believers' perfection (cf. 6:1; 10:14).   **12:24** *The blood . . . Abel*: comparing Exod 24:6–8 and Gen 4:10 (cf. Heb 9:19–22; 11:4). **12:25** *They escaped not*: a reference to God's punishment of the exodus generation (see chap. 3). **12:26** *Whose voice . . . earth*: cf. Ps 68:8, another reference to the divine spectacle at Sinai. *Yet once . . . heaven*: cf. Hag 2:6. *Shake*: better "will shake" (MS tradition).   **12:27** *Which cannot be shaken*: i.e., the heavenly realm, of which the fragile material world is an inferior copy (cf. 8:2, 5; 9:24; etc.). Hebrews expects it to dissolve in the "consuming fire" of eschatological judgment (v. 29). **12:28** *Moved*: lit. "shaken." *Have grace*: or "give thanks."   **12:29** *Our God . . . fire*: cf. Deut 4:24.

13:1–25 Exhortational conclusion and epistolary postscript. 13:2 *Some have entertained angels unawares*: see Gen 18:1–19:14; Judg 13.   **13:4** *Marriage is honourable in all*: alternatively "let marriage be honorable before all." *But*: better "for" (MS tradition). *Whoremongers*: the sexually immoral.   **13:5** *Conversation*: way of life (also in v. 7). *Covetousness*: lit. "love of money." *I will never . . . forsake thee*: Josh 1:5.   **13:6** *The Lord . . . me*: Ps 118:6. *And I . . . me*: better "I will not fear. What shall man do to me?" (MS tradition).   **13:7** *Follow*: imitate. *End*: outcome.

ers and strange doctrines. For it is a good thing that the heart be established with grace; not with meats, which have not profited them that have been occupied therein. [10]We have an altar, whereof they have no right to eat which serve the tabernacle. [11]For the bodies of those beasts, whose blood is brought into the sanctuary by the high priest for sin, are burned without the camp. [12]Wherefore Jesus also, that he might sanctify the people with his own blood, suffered without the gate. [13]Let us go forth therefore unto him without the camp, bearing his reproach. [14]For here have we no continuing city, but we seek one to come. [15]By him therefore let us offer the sacrifice of praise to God continually, that is, the fruit of our lips giving thanks to his name. [16]But to do good and to communicate forget not: for with such sacrifices God is well pleased. [17]Obey them that have the rule over you, and submit yourselves: for they watch for your souls, as they that must give account, that they may do it with joy, and not with grief: for that is unprofitable for you.

[18]Pray for us: for we trust we have a good conscience, in all things willing to live honestly. [19]But I beseech you the rather to do this, that I may be restored to you the sooner.

[20]Now the God of peace, that brought again from the dead our Lord Jesus, that great shepherd of the sheep, through the blood of the everlasting covenant, [21]make you perfect in every good work to do his will, working in you that which is wellpleasing in his sight, through Jesus Christ; to whom be glory for ever and ever. Amen.

[22]And I beseech you, brethren, suffer the word of exhortation: for I have written a letter unto you in few words. [23]Know ye that our brother Timothy is set at liberty; with whom, if he come shortly, I will see you. [24]Salute all them that have the rule over you, and all the saints. They of Italy salute you. [25]Grace be with you all. Amen.

Written to the Hebrews from Italy by Timothy.

13:9 *Meats*: foods. The dietary conflict to which vv. 9–10 refer is hopelessly obscure. **13:11** *For the bodies . . . camp*: see Lev 16:27. **13:12** *Jesus also . . . gate*: cf. John 19:17, where Jesus "went forth" to the site of his execution (lit. "went out"; Gk. *exerchomai*, the same verb as in Heb 13:13). According to the OT, executions were to occur outside the city or camp (Num 15:35). **13:15** *Sacrifice of praise*: cf. Ps 107:22; etc. *Giving thanks to*: lit. "confessing." **13:16** *Communicate*: share. *With such sacrifices . . . pleased*: as opposed to the sacrifices offered at the earthly tabernacle (cf. v. 11). **13:17** *Obey them . . . for you*: this verse forms an inclusive frame with v. 7. **13:20–25** *Now the . . . all*: this section formally resembles the endings of the Pauline Epistles. **13:20** *Shepherd of the sheep*: the OT frequently likens God to a shepherd; e.g., Pss 23:1; 80:1; Jer 31:10. **13:21** *Work*: better "thing" (MS tradition). *In you*: better "in us" (MS tradition). **13:22** *Word of exhortation*: i.e., this discourse. In Acts 13:15 the same phrase designates a sermon. **13:23** *Our brother Timothy*: if this is the Timothy associated with Paul (see 1 Cor 4:17 note), the connection suggests that the author of Hebrews was a member of the Pauline circle of missionaries and ministers. **13:24** *Saints*: see Rom 1:7 note. *They of Italy*: either "they (now) in Italy" or Italians living abroad. The phrase therefore gives no evidence of Hebrews' place of composition. **13:25** *Amen. Written . . . Timothy*: better omitted (MS tradition).

The Catholic Epistles

THE seven texts known collectively as the Catholic Epistles constitute the New Testament's most heterogeneous collection of writings. They are not unified by attribution to a single author (as is the Pauline corpus), nor—since 1 John is not actually a letter—by a single generic mode (as are the four gospels and Acts). Moreover, the Catholic Epistles seem to have originated in several different geographical regions, and their proposed dates of composition range from perhaps as early as the mid-first century C.E. to possibly sometime in the mid-second.

In the mid-fourth century C.E., Eusebius and later Athanasius grouped these seven epistles together under the heading "Catholic," following earlier traditions that had identified one or another of them (and other writings as well) with that label. A later treatise attributed to Leontius of Byzantium offered a rationale for a practice that had become conventional by contrasting the "Catholic" with the Pauline Epistles, which are addressed to identifiable communities and individuals and which speak to particular situations: "they have been called 'catholic' since they were not written to a certain group of people [Gk. *pros hen ethnos*], as those of Paul, but generally to all [*katholou pros panta*]" (*On Sects* 2). Leontius's explanation is not altogether accurate. 1 John concentrates on a split within the particular community addressed by its author, even if the location of that community is not named. 1 Peter does name five provinces in Asia Minor to whose Christian communities it is addressed, all of which experience harassment and isolation as a result of their faith. 2 and 3 John are actually addressed to particular individuals, although the addressee is referred to by proper name only in the latter. Despite these complications, the seven "Catholic" epistles are for the most part addressed less specifically than the Pauline letters, and two of them (James and 2 Peter) perhaps assume a general audience, so the heading remains both a practical and not entirely unreasonable way to designate the non-Pauline epistles that the New Testament came to include.

Because of the disparate nature of the Catholic Epistles, it is difficult to speak meaningfully about them in the aggregate, but they do display a few common idiosyncrasies when compared with other New Testament writings. For example, James mentions Christ only twice, and consists entirely of ethical exhortation, while other New Testament books integrate moral advice into broader narrative and christological frameworks. Analogously, Jude aims exclusively at disparaging teachers whom its author opposes, while elsewhere in the New Testament such polemic finds itself integrated into broader theological, pastoral, or narrative discourses. Finally, 1 and 2 Peter, Jude, and 1 John all engage with ancient Jewish mythological elaborations that other New Testament writings tend to eschew (2 Cor 11:12–15 is an exception), with the first three expressing a particular interest in legendary expansions of the reference to the descent of the sons of God in Gen 6:1–4. 1 Peter even makes the esoteric claim that Christ preached to these supposedly fallen angels (3:19–20; see notes).

These examples and others not cited here suggest that the Catholic Epistles reflect approaches to what would become (or in some cases had already become) the Christian faith that differ more or less starkly from those encountered in other New Testament writings. Such differences are not particularly surprising: ancient Christianity was hardly homogeneous, even in individual Christian congregations (as the frequent conflicts in Paul's epistles demonstrate), and the Catholic Epistles' origins are both geographically and chronologically diverse. James and Jude, for instance, may have been composed in Palestine, a region from which surprisingly little first- and second-century Christian writing survives; and some scholars have dated 2 Peter as late as the mid-second century C.E., which would make it the latest text in the New Testament by several years. The peculiarities these letters display, then, reflect not only the general heterogeneity of the early church but also their diverse geographical and temporal origins.

Probably in part because of their peculiarities, the canonical status of all but two of the Catholic Epistles was debated in antiquity, and later voices too (most famously Martin Luther) have advocated the removal of some of them from the New Testament. In the modern era, even when such advocacy has been absent, these epistles have in interpretive practice been relegated to the New Testament's margins. But the Catholic Epistles' idiosyncrasies vis-à-vis other New Testament writings are balanced by their deep and productive engagement with them. 1 John, and to a lesser degree 2 and 3 John, draws carefully on the traditions codified in the Gospel of John to guide a community through a schism and related crises. James enters into implicit dialogue with Paul, drawing attention to potential problems in his yoking of righteousness with faith, especially in Romans and Galatians. 1 Peter seems to use Romans as a source, and 2 Peter alludes to Romans as well (see 3:9 note) before explicitly warning its readers against those who misinterpret Paul's writings.

Because several of the Catholic Epistles engage with Paul, they have sometimes been viewed as merely dim reflections of the apostle's brilliantly original theology, or, in the case of James, as an example of unimaginative and wrong-headed Judaizing resistance to vital Pauline ideas. Partly as a result of the influence of literary approaches to the Bible, most scholars instead now read the Catholic Epistles as independent, coherent, and frequently skillful rhetorical constructions. At the same time, intertextual relationships are not unimportant to literary critics, and it would be a mistake to discount how pervasively these works engage with other New Testament writings—sometimes straightforwardly invoking their support, at other times entering into more complicated conversations with them.

In the final analysis, the Catholic Epistles may be said to emblematize the tension between unity and diversity that characterized the early Christian movement Several testify to the gradual emergence of a handful of Christian traditions (especially those associated with Paul and John) into positions of ideological dominance, and while some of them seem comfortable with this growing influence, others express reservations. The Johannine epistles display no ambivalence about the traditions codified in the Fourth Gospel, and 1 Peter draws confidently on Paul's Epistle to the Romans as it exhorts its readers to remain faithful in the midst of harassment. But James seems to challenge a theological position commonly associated with Paul, and 2 Peter expresses analogous concern about how some believers interpret Paul's writings.

Readers of the Catholic Epistles as literature must attend to their originality, even to their strangeness in comparison with the rest of the New Testament, and of course they should acknowledge and respect such rhetorical coherence as the epistles display. But readers must also investigate their engagement with other ancient literary sources, including the Old Testament, extrabiblical Jewish texts, and the extant body of early Christian writing, much of which is included in the New Testament. These seven often neglected New Testament writings demand and reward maximal readings—readings that balance textual and intertextual concerns and that attend to historical and cultural context as well. Such are the interpretations that the following introductions and annotations aim to facilitate, and the reader informed by them will hopefully be equipped to resist the competing temptations of marginalizing the Catholic Epistles' sometimes peculiar voices and of forcibly assimilating them to more well-known New Testament works, by viewing them as dim reflections or even as misguided distortions of the latter.

The General Epistle of James

JAMES'S structure is rather free. A short salutation (1:1) is followed by a series of loosely connected exhortations (1:2–27), which are subsequently developed in several succinct essays (2:1–5:20). These essays deploy the Hebrew Bible (especially Lev 19, which is frequently quoted and echoed), sayings of Jesus, and popular Greco-Roman philosophical wisdom in order to urge and restrict certain kinds of behavior. James's language is vivid and terse; its sentences are typically short, frequently lack conjunctions, and often take the form of imperatives. The epistle relishes antinomy: the opposition articulated in 4:4, "friendship of the world is enmity with God," is the most sweeping example, but discrete dichotomies surface throughout—for example, between the affluent and the vulnerable, between merely hearing God's word and practicing it, and between blessing and cursing.

The James claiming to have written this epistle has traditionally been identified as Jesus' brother, an influential leader in the early Jerusalem church. In light of his documented concern that Jesus-believers remain faithful to the Jewish law (see Acts 15:13–21; 21:18–25), the identification makes sense, for the present epistle frequently urges its readers to follow God's law. James, in fact, actually urges adherence to the law in terms that recall and challenge Paul's theology. To cite only the most notable example, after insisting that readers keep the whole law (2:8–13), James seizes on Abraham as an example of righteousness by works rather than by faith alone (vv. 14–24). Paul, of course, famously employs the same Old Testament figure as the prototype of Gentiles justified by faith without works of the law, relying on Gen 15:6 to make his argument (Rom 4; Gal 3:6–14)—precisely the text James quotes in order to support an opposing claim.

James's engagement with Paul is the most revealing clue that this letter offers as to its provenance, but the evidence is open to competing interpretations. While it is possible that James responds to Paul's teaching, it is also possible that Paul developed his theology of righteousness through faith in dialogue with the present letter, or perhaps more likely in dialogue with James's teaching, which this letter letter would echo. This teaching may even have played a role in the conflict at Antioch reported by Paul in Gal 2:11–21, for he claims that the arrival of "certain [men] . . . from James" precipitated discord there between himself, Barnabas, and Peter regarding whether Jewish Jesus-believers should dine with Jesus-believing Gentiles (Gal 2:12).

The polemical edge of James's argument (2:14, 18–19, 24) suggests to most scholars that James responds to Paul, rather than vice versa, but at the same time many are surprised by how badly James seems to understand the apostle. Although introducing his treatment of faith's requisite qualification by works with a demand that his readers adhere to the entire Jewish law (2:8–11), James actually defines "works" very broadly, as ethical or altruistic endeavors (2:15–16) or even as simple obedience to God (2:20–21). Paul, on the other hand, always has in mind specific deeds commanded by the Jewish law, especially (but not exclusively) those signaling Jewish identity, such as circumcision, observance of liturgical festivals, or dietary regulations. Paul's coupling of righteousness with faith in Christ (or the faith of Christ; see Gal 2:16 note), in opposition to works of the Jewish law, emerged in the context of debate on a specific issue: whether Gentile believers in Jesus ought to be circumcised and obey the law. Paul himself, accordingly, was not interested in articulating the sweeping position that James here resists, namely that faith abstracted from charitable endeavors makes a faithful person righteous before God. On the contrary, even in Galatians, when he urges Gentile believers not to obey the law, Paul still insists that the ethical injunction of Lev 19:18 is obligatory (Gal 5:13–14) and ends by warning his readers that God will punish wicked behavior and reward righteous deeds (6:7–10).

Since James himself participated in the debate about Gentile circumcision, he presumably would have known and understood Paul's position. Accordingly, many scholars see in this epistle's deficient construal of Pauline theology evidence that James is a pseudepigraphic composition, the work of a Jewish Christian of the church's second generation writing after the debate about Gentile circumcision had been resolved. This later writer would have sought to resist the broader implications of Paul's thought which were then beginning to be explored, culminating in Augustine's interpretation of Pauline theology in the fourth and fifth centuries and later influencing Luther and the reformers. The understanding of Paul confronted by the Epistle of James therefore resembles that found in the late first-century C.E. text *1 Clement* 31–33, which draws on the arguments of Romans and Galatians not to insist that Gentiles need not become Jewish in order to be righteous, but rather to emphasize that righteousness is a free gift from God, which cannot be earned by pious or ethical endeavors but is attained only by faith abstracted from them. "Good works," for *1 Clement*, return simply as "adornments" of those who have already been made righteous by faith—an idea with which James would certainly disagree.

While the theory of pseudepigraphic composition is not unattractive, it may reflect a somewhat narrow construal of early Christianity, such as the one Martin Luther assumes in his preface to James and Jude, where he denies James's epistle apostolic authority because of its inconsistency with Paul. Luther to the contrary, the evident disagreement with Paul displayed in the Epistle of James may simply reflect the fact that Jesus' brother had a significant difference of opinion with Paul. (The New Testament elsewhere attests to conflict between Paul and the other apostles.) And the apparent distortion of Paul's ideas in the Epistle of James may reflect James's anticipation and response to a trajectory of Pauline thought that eventually would become popular, a trajectory that Paul himself may or may not have foreseen.

If James wrote the epistle, he probably wrote it in Palestine, where he was based, and must have done so before ca. 62 C.E., when he died, according to Josephus

(*Jewish Antiquities* 20.199–200; see Appendix, pp. 979–80). If the letter is pseude-pigraphic, its date of composition may be as late as the early second century C.E. Its place of composition was likely still Palestine, where James's reputation and authority were well established and a later writer's adoption of this authorial per-sona would have been most natural.

For more detailed exposition, consult Luke Timothy Johnson's excellent Anchor Bible commentary, *The Letter of James: A New Translation with Introduction and Commentary* (New York: Doubleday, 1995), which informs this introduction and the notes that follow.

THE GENERAL EPISTLE OF
JAMES

1 James, a servant of God and of the Lord Jesus Christ, to the twelve tribes which are scattered abroad, greeting.

²My brethren, count it all joy when ye fall into divers temptations; ³knowing this, that the trying of your faith worketh patience. ⁴But let patience have her perfect work, that ye may be perfect and entire, wanting nothing.

⁵If any of you lack wisdom, let him ask of God, that giveth to all men liberally, and upbraideth not; and it shall be given him. ⁶But let him ask in faith, nothing wavering. For he that wavereth is like a wave of the sea driven with the wind and tossed. ⁷For let not that man think that he shall receive any thing of the Lord. ⁸A double minded man is unstable in all his ways.

⁹Let the brother of low degree rejoice in that he is exalted: ¹⁰but the rich, in that he is made low: because as the flower of the grass he shall pass away. ¹¹For the sun is no sooner risen with a burning heat, but it withereth the grass, and the flower thereof falleth, and the grace of the fashion of it perisheth: so also shall the rich man fade away in his ways.

¹²Blessed is the man that endureth temptation: for when he is tried, he shall receive the crown of life, which the Lord hath promised to them that love him.

1:1 Salutation. Adhering to a conventional Greco-Roman epistolary pattern, James begins by identifying the writer, followed by a reference to the addressees and a greeting. *James*: here probably the brother of Jesus (see Gal 1:19 and note), the most well-known and authoritative person of that name in the early church. *Servant*: slave, as often in KJV. *The twelve tribes* refers either to Jesus-believing Jews *scattered abroad* throughout the Mediterranean world (Gk. *en tē diaspora*) or to the church understood as Israel eschatologically reconstituted (cf. Gal 6:16 and note).

1:2–27 Introductory exhortations. A rapid-fire series of lively exhortational statements connected one to another by verbal and thematic repetition, this section, as Luke Timothy Johnson observes, introduces a set of topics that James will later explore: testing (vv. 2–4, 12–13; cf. 5:7–11), faithful prayer (vv. 5–8; cf. 4:3; 5:12–18), the rich and the poor (vv. 9–11; cf. 2:1–13; 4:13–5:6), human desires vs. God's gifts (vv. 14–18; cf. 3:13–4:10), speech and God's word (vv. 19–21; cf. 3:1–12; 4:11–12), and enacted religion (vv. 22–27; cf. 2:14–26). **1:2** *Temptations*: or "tests" (also in vv. 12–14). **1:3** *Patience*: or "endurance" (also in v. 4). **1:5** *Lack*: Gk. *leipō*, translated "wanting" in v. 4. *Let him . . . him*: echoing the dominical saying of Matt 7:7; Luke 11:9. **1:6** *But let . . . wavering*: cf. Matt 21:21; Mark 11:23. **1:9–10** *Let the brother . . . made low*: cf. Matt 18:4; 23:12; Luke 14:11; 18:14, in all of which Gk. *tapeinoō* (here *made low*) is translated with forms of "abase" or "humble." The exhortation that the rich man rejoice in his humiliation may refer ironically to his impending eschatological judgment. **1:10–11** *As the flower . . . ways*: echoing Isa 40:7–8. **1:11** *The grace . . . it*: its beautiful appearance. **1:12** *Crown*: a wreath or garland awarded in the Greek world to victors

¹³Let no man say when he is tempted, I am tempted of God: for God cannot be tempted with evil, neither tempteth he any man: ¹⁴but every man is tempted, when he is drawn away of his own lust, and enticed. ¹⁵Then when lust hath conceived, it bringeth forth sin: and sin, when it is finished, bringeth forth death. ¹⁶Do not err, my beloved brethren. ¹⁷Every good gift and every perfect gift is from above, and cometh down from the Father of lights, with whom is no variableness, neither shadow of turning. ¹⁸Of his own will begat he us with the word of truth, that we should be a kind of firstfruits of his creatures.

¹⁹Wherefore, my beloved brethren, let every man be swift to hear, slow to speak, slow to wrath: ²⁰for the wrath of man worketh not the righteousness of God. ²¹Wherefore lay apart all filthiness and superfluity of naughtiness, and receive with meekness the engrafted word, which is able to save your souls.

²²But be ye doers of the word, and not hearers only, deceiving your own selves. ²³For if any be a hearer of the word, and not a doer, he is like unto a man beholding his natural face in a glass: ²⁴for he beholdeth himself, and goeth his way, and straightway forgetteth what manner of man he was. ²⁵But whoso looketh into the perfect law of liberty, and continueth therein, he being not a forgetful hearer, but a doer of the work, this man shall be blessed in his deed. ²⁶If any man among you seem to be religious, and bridleth not his tongue, but deceiveth his own heart, this man's religion is vain. ²⁷Pure religion and undefiled before God and the Father is this, To visit the fatherless and widows in their affliction, and to keep himself unspotted from the world.

of athletic competitions, or as a civic honor. The promise of an eschatological wreath of life to the one who endures testing contrasts with the previous depiction of the rich as withered and perishing vegetation. **1:13** *Neither tempteth he any man*: contradicting numerous biblical texts, including Gen 22:1, which James later invokes (2:21–23). The tension is perhaps mitigated by the emphasis on testing with evil intent, as opposed to testing in order to perfect, which the author does not find offensive (cf. vv. 2–4). **1:15** *Bringeth forth*: "gives birth to," also later in the verse, with the second occurrence translating a different Greek word. *Finished*: i.e., matures. **1:17** *Perfect gift*: Gk. *dōrēma teleion*: *teleion* (*perfect*) has the same root as "finished" (v. 15); two different words are used for *gift* in this verse. (The first may actually refer to the act of giving rather than to the object given.) *Father of lights*: i.e., creator of the stars. Their constancy of motion was admired in antiquity, and frequently explained with reference to divine direction (cf. Jude 13 note). *Shadow of turning*: better "variation or shadow due to change" (MS tradition; NRSV). **1:18** *Begat*: mistranslating one of the Greek verbs rendered "bringeth forth" in v. 15 (see note). Although just designated "Father of lights" (v. 17), God here gives birth. *Firstfruits*: see 1 Cor 15:20 and note. **1:19** *Wherefore*: better "you must know this" (MS tradition; NRSV), introducing the exhortation that follows. **1:21** *Superfluity of naughtiness*: abundance of wickedness. *Engrafted*: lit. "implanted," perhaps referring to insemination, in light of the previous imagery of childbirth (vv. 15, 18) and the common use of planting and sowing to figure sex. **1:23** *Glass*: mirror. Greco-Roman popular philosophical writings often invoke the mirror as a figure of self-reflection (e.g., Seneca, *Natural Questions* 1.17.4–5; Plutarch, *On Listening to Lectures* 42B). **1:25** *Law of liberty*: Hellenistic Jewish writers conventionally associated adherence to the law with freedom (i.e., from desire and vice); cf. 4 *Maccabees* 5.22–24. *A doer . . . deed*: recalling the dominical saying of Luke 11:28 (cf. Matt 7:24; Luke 6:47). **1:27** *The fatherless and widows*: objects of God's special concern in the OT; e.g., Deut 10:18; Ps 146:9; Mal 3:5.

2 My brethren, have not the faith of our Lord Jesus Christ, the Lord of glory, with respect of persons. [2]For if there come unto your assembly a man with a gold ring, in goodly apparel, and there come in also a poor man in vile raiment; [3]and ye have respect to him that weareth the gay clothing, and say unto him, Sit thou here in a good place; and say to the poor, Stand thou there, or sit here under my footstool: [4]are ye not then partial in yourselves, and are become judges of evil thoughts?

[5]Hearken, my beloved brethren, Hath not God chosen the poor of this world rich in faith, and heirs of the kingdom which he hath promised to them that love him? [6]But ye have despised the poor. Do not rich men oppress you, and draw you before the judgment seats? [7]Do not they blaspheme that worthy name by the which ye are called?

[8]If ye fulfil the royal law according to the scripture, Thou shalt love thy neighbour as thyself, ye do well: [9]but if ye have respect to persons, ye commit sin, and are convinced of the law as transgressors. [10]For whosoever shall keep the whole law, and yet offend in one point, he is guilty of all. [11]For he that said, Do not commit adultery, said also, Do not kill. Now if thou commit no adultery, yet if thou kill, thou art become a transgressor of the law. [12]So speak ye, and so do, as they that shall be judged by the law of liberty. [13]For he shall have judgment without mercy, that hath shewed no mercy; and mercy rejoiceth against judgment.

2:1–26 Authentic faith. This section explores material from 1:9–11 and 22–27. **2:1** *Have not . . . persons*: do not hold this faith together with acts of favoritism. *Faith of . . . Christ*: for the ambiguous construction, see Gal 2:16 note. In light of James's frequent echoes of dominical sayings, the reference here is probably to the faith taught by Jesus. *Respect of persons*: cf. Lev 19:15, where the phrase is used in a similar context. **2:2** *Assembly*: Gk. *synagōgē* (see Mark 1:21 note), which may suggest that James has Jewish Christians in mind (see 1:1 note). But the Greek word could also refer to a generic assembly. **2:3** *Sit here . . . footstool*: ironically echoing Ps 110:1, an OT text ubiquitously invoked by the early church as a prophecy of Christ's resurrection and eschatological victory. Compare the banqueting practices common in the Greco-Roman world, which Paul urges his readers to avoid (see 1 Cor 11:17–34 and notes, esp. vv. 20–22). **2:4** *Are ye . . . yourselves*: alternatively "have you not made distinctions among yourselves" (RSV). *Judges of evil thoughts*: i.e., "judges with evil thoughts." *Judges* (Gk. *kritai*) shares its root with *partial* (Gk. *diakrinō*). **2:5** *Hath not God . . . world*: a crucial passage for liberation theology, which emphasizes God's preference for the poor. *Heirs of the kingdom . . . him*: cf. Luke 6:20. **2:6** *Despised*: lit. "dishonored." *Draw you . . . seats*: drag you into court. The ability of the affluent to manipulate the legal system might also lie behind 1 Cor 6:1–11 (see note). **2:7** *Blaspheme that worthy name*: cf. Isa 52:5. *By the which . . . called*: better "which was invoked over you" (RSV), i.e., as a formal claim of possession. **2:8** *Royal law*: the law governing the kingdom mentioned in v. 5. *Thou shalt love . . . thyself*: Lev 19:18. Paul and the synoptic tradition agree that this verse sums up the law (cf. Rom 13:10 note). **2:9** *Convinced of the law*: convicted by the law, specifically by Lev 19:15. **2:10** *Whosoever shall keep . . . all*: cf. Gal 5 (esp. vv. 3, 13–14), where Paul distinguishes between keeping "the whole law," which Gentile believers are not obliged to do, and fulfilling the law by obeying Lev 19:18, which they are. This statement points to significant divergence between James's and Paul's understanding of the law's role, unless James addresses only Jewish believers in Christ (see 1:1; 2:2 and notes). **2:11** *Do not commit . . . kill*: quoting from the Decalogue, specifically LXX Deut 5:17–18, where the prohibition of adultery immediately precedes that of killing (cf. Exod 20:13–14). Matt 5:21–32 also juxtaposes discussions of what it means to keep these laws. **2:12** *The law of liberty*: see 1:25 and note; but the formulation may also point to a polemic against Paul, who in Galatians figures obedience to the law as slavery. In Gal 5:13–14 (see note to Gal 5:13–6:10), Paul presents fulfillment of the law as embodied in Lev 19:18 as

¹⁴What doth it profit, my brethren, though a man say he hath faith, and have not works? can faith save him? ¹⁵If a brother or sister be naked, and destitute of daily food, ¹⁶and one of you say unto them, Depart in peace, be ye warmed and filled; notwithstanding ye give them not those things which are needful to the body; what doth it profit? ¹⁷Even so faith, if it hath not works, is dead, being alone. ¹⁸Yea, a man may say, Thou hast faith, and I have works: shew me thy faith without thy works, and I will shew thee my faith by my works. ¹⁹Thou believest that there is one God; thou doest well: the devils also believe, and tremble. ²⁰But wilt thou know, O vain man, that faith without works is dead? ²¹Was not Abraham our father justified by works, when he had offered Isaac his son upon the altar? ²²Seest thou how faith wrought with his works, and by works was faith made perfect? ²³And the scripture was fulfilled which saith, Abraham believed God, and it was imputed unto him for righteousness: and he was called the Friend of God. ²⁴Ye see then how that by works a man is justified, and not by faith only. ²⁵Likewise also was not Rahab the harlot justified by works, when she had received the messengers, and had sent them out another way? ²⁶For as the body without the spirit is dead, so faith without works is dead also.

positively valued slavery; in Gal 3:23–4:7 adherence to the law is analogized to slavery more disparagingly. **2:14** *What doth it profit . . . him*: in light of the previous paragraph's insistence on faithfulness to the law, there may be another polemic against Paul here (which comes into sharper focus in vv. 21–26)—this time against his association of "righteousness" with the "faith of Christ" instead of with "works of the law" (Gal 2:16 and notes; cf. Rom 3:21–22; etc.). Paul, however, would likely agree with James's disparagement of faith divorced from deeds, and is even comfortable urging his readers to obey the law's ethical injunctions, especially when these injunctions are interpreted through the lens of Lev 19:18 (cf. Rom 13:8–10; Gal 5:13–14). Paul associates righteousness with the faith of Christ not to de-emphasize ethical endeavor—even ethical endeavor informed by the law—but rather to establish the unity of Jews and Gentiles in the church, insisting that both are made righteous by the faith of Christ rather than by circumcision and adherence to the Sinai covenant (e.g., Gal 2:16 and notes). James either misconstrues Paul or addresses a misunderstanding of Paul's teaching. (Such misunderstandings were apparently ubiquitous; cf. Rom 3:5–8; 1 Cor 5:9–13; 2 Pet 3:15–16.) **2:16** *Depart in peace*: wishes of peace are conventional in salutations, but James rejects the piety they suggest (cf. Judg 6:23; 18:6; Mark 5:34) as empty if not supported by action. *Be ye warmed and filled*: the passive voice expects that God will take care of the destitute.   **2:17** *Faith, if . . . alone*: cf. 1 John 3:17–18.   **2:18** *Thou hast faith, and I have works*: one expects precisely the opposite ("I have faith and you have works"), in light of the authorial voice's response in the rest of the verse and its subsequent opposition to the imaginary interlocutor's faith without works (vv. 19–20). James may simply mean "one person has faith; another has works."   **2:19** *There is one God*: better "God is one," alluding to the Shema (Deut 6:4), quoted by Jesus in the Synoptic Gospels alongside Lev 19:18 as the epitome of the law (Mark 12:28–31; cf. Matt 22:36–40; Luke 10:25–28). James likewise affirms adherence to both (cf. v. 8).   **2:20** *Dead*: better "barren" (MS tradition).   **2:21** *Was not Abraham . . . works*: cf. Rom 3:28, where Paul claims that "a man is justified by faith without the deeds of the law" and then goes on to quote Gen 15:6 from the Abraham cycle as proof (Rom 4:1–5; cf. Gal 3:6–18). He finally presents Abraham's conviction that God would grant him a son (Isaac) as an emblem of his faith (Rom 4:16–22). The points of contact between Paul's arguments and Jas 2:21–24 are striking, again suggesting that James stands in a polemical relationship with Paul. But it must be noted that for James and Paul "works" has a different meaning (see v. 14 note). *When he . . . altar*: see Gen 22.   **2:22** *Wrought with his works*: lit. "worked with his works."   **2:23** *Abraham believed . . . righteousness*: Gen 15:6. *He was called . . . God*: see 2 Chr 20:7; Isa 41:8.   **2:25** *Rahab*: see Josh 2:1–21. James's complementary discussion of a woman's exemplary works balances the

3 My brethren, be not many masters, knowing that we shall receive the greater condemnation. ²For in many things we offend all. If any man offend not in word, the same is a perfect man, and able also to bridle the whole body. ³Behold, we put bits in the horses' mouths, that they may obey us; and we turn about their whole body. ⁴Behold also the ships, which though they be so great, and are driven of fierce winds, yet are they turned about with a very small helm, whithersoever the governor listeth. ⁵Even so the tongue is a little member, and boasteth great things.

Behold, how great a matter a little fire kindleth! ⁶And the tongue is a fire, a world of iniquity: so is the tongue among our members, that it defileth the whole body, and setteth on fire the course of nature; and it is set on fire of hell. ⁷For every kind of beasts, and of birds, and of serpents, and of things in the sea, is tamed, and hath been tamed of mankind: ⁸but the tongue can no man tame; it is an unruly evil, full of deadly poison. ⁹Therewith bless we God, even the Father; and therewith curse we men, which are made after the similitude of God. ¹⁰Out of the same mouth proceedeth blessing and cursing. My brethren, these things ought not so to be. ¹¹Doth a fountain send forth at the same place sweet water and bitter? ¹²Can the fig tree, my brethren, bear olive berries? either a vine, figs? so can no fountain both yield salt water and fresh.

¹³Who is a wise man and endued with knowledge among you? let him shew out of a good conversation his works with meekness of wisdom. ¹⁴But if ye have bitter envying and strife in your hearts, glory not, and lie not against the truth. ¹⁵This

---

reference to the naked and hungry "brother or sister" (v. 15) whom the faithful must clothe and feed. In light of the evident polemic with Paul, Rahab's status as a Gentile may also be relevant: for Gentiles as for Abraham and his descendants, faith requires works.

3:1–12 The power of speech. This brief discourse, which develops the pronouncements of 1:19—and to a lesser degree all of vv. 19–21—and 26, combines a series of Greco-Roman popular philosophical commonplaces (only some of which the notes mention) with allusions to the Hebrew Bible in order to mount a conventional argument about the need to control one's mouth. **3:1** *Masters*: teachers. *We shall receive . . . condemnation*: recalling Jesus' statement about the scribes (Mark 12:40; cf. Luke 20:47). **3:2** *We offend all*: i.e., "we all offend," a Greco-Roman topos; e.g., Seneca, *On Clemency* 1.6.3 (*pecavimus omnes*); cf. Philo, *That God Is Unchangeable* 75. *If any man . . . body*: cf. Philo, *On the Posterity of Cain* 88. **3:3** *Behold*: better "and if" (MS tradition). *And we*: better "we also." **3:4** *Governor listeth*: pilot wills. The pilot steering his ship is a common image in Greco-Roman philosophical discourse. **3:5** *Matter*: Gk. *hylē* (alternatively "forest"). **3:6** *A world . . . that*: better "the tongue is placed among our members as a world of iniquity" (MS tradition; NRSV). *Course of nature*: more literally "wheel of becoming," i.e., life conceived of as a constant cycle of transitions. *Hell*: Gk. *geenna*; see Mark 9:43 note. Elsewhere in the NT the term surfaces only in the Synoptic Gospels' dominical sayings. This confirms James's familiarity with the Jesus traditions that the Synoptic Gospels employ, suggested by echoes of Jesus' words throughout. **3:7** *For every kind . . . mankind*: an allusion to Gen 1:26, 28. *Mankind*: Gk. *physis anthrōpinē*, echoing the earlier *kind* (*physis*). **3:8** *Unruly*: better "restless" (MS tradition). **3:9** *Which are made . . . God*: cf. Gen 1:27. **3:12** *Can the fig tree . . . figs*: the phrase recalls Matt 7:16–17, but Seneca also provides an exceptionally close parallel: "Good is born from evil no more than a fig from an olive tree" (*Moral Epistles* 87.25); cf. Sir 27:6. *Either*: or. *So can no fountain . . . fresh*: better "neither can salt water yield fresh" (MS tradition; cf. NRSV).

3:13–4:10 Human greed vs. divine generosity. This section develops the material from 1: 14–18. **3:13** *Conversation*: way of life. **3:14** *Glory*: boast. **3:15** *Sensual*: Gk. *psychikos*, referring to

wisdom descendeth not from above, but is earthly, sensual, devilish. [16]For where envying and strife is, there is confusion and every evil work. [17]But the wisdom that is from above is first pure, then peaceable, gentle, and easy to be intreated, full of mercy and good fruits, without partiality, and without hypocrisy. [18]And the fruit of righteousness is sown in peace of them that make peace. [1]From whence come wars and fightings among you? come they not hence, even of your lusts that war in your members? [2]Ye lust, and have not: ye kill, and desire to have, and cannot obtain: ye fight and war, yet ye have not, because ye ask not.

[3]Ye ask, and receive not, because ye ask amiss, that ye may consume it upon your lusts. [4]Ye adulterers and adulteresses, know ye not that the friendship of the world is enmity with God? whosoever therefore will be a friend of the world is the enemy of God. [5]Do ye think that the scripture saith in vain, The spirit that dwelleth in us lusteth to envy? [6]But he giveth more grace. Wherefore he saith, God resisteth the proud, but giveth grace unto the humble.

[7]Submit yourselves therefore to God. Resist the devil, and he will flee from you. [8]Draw nigh to God, and he will draw nigh to you. Cleanse your hands, ye sinners; and purify your hearts, ye double minded. [9]Be afflicted, and mourn, and weep: let your laughter be turned to mourning, and your joy to heaviness. [10]Humble yourselves in the sight of the Lord, and he shall lift you up.

[11]Speak not evil one of another, brethren. He that speaketh evil of his brother, and judgeth his brother, speaketh evil of the law, and judgeth the law: but if thou judge the law, thou art not a doer of the law, but a judge. [12]There is one lawgiver, who is able to save and to destroy: who art thou that judgest another?

---

a quality opposed to "spiritual," as in 1 Cor 15:44–50; Jude 19. *Devilish*: demonic.   **3:16** *Confusion*: Gk. *akatastasia*; its adjectival form is translated "unstable" at 1:8 and "restless" in 3:8 note.   **3:18** *Of them*: i.e., "by them," although "for them" is also possible. *Them that make peace*: perhaps echoing the dominical blessing of Matt 5:9.   **4:1** *Lusts*: lit. "pleasures" (also in v. 3); a different Greek word is used in v. 2.   **4:2** *Yet*: better omitted (MS tradition), severing the connection between what precedes and "ye have not." The new paragraph, focusing on prayer, properly begins with these words.   **4:2–3** *Ye have . . . receive not*: contrast Matt 7:7–8; Luke 11:9.   **4:3** *Amiss*: more literally "wickedly." *Consume it upon*: "spend it on" (RSV).   **4:4** *Adulterers and*: better omitted (MS tradition). The reference to *adulteresses* invokes the common OT image of Israel as YHWH's bride, whose idolatry was conventionally figured as adultery (e.g., Jer 3:6–10 and, more vividly, Ezek 16:8–43). James's point seems to be that the self-seeking prayer mentioned in v. 3 is appropriate to—or even itself amounts to—idolatry. *Friendship . . . of God*: recalling 2:23, where Abraham was called God's friend.   **4:5** *Do ye . . . envy*: better "do you think that the Scripture [quoted in the subsequent verse] speaks in vain? Does the spirit that he made to dwell in us lust enviously?" (MS tradition; our translation).   **4:6** *But he . . . grace*: Johnson's translation clarifies the train of thought: "rather, he gives a greater gift." *God resisteth . . . humble*: Prov 3:34. Again, the word rendered *grace* also means "gift" or "favor." *Humble* here and in v. 10 translates words cognate with those rendered "of low degree" and "made low" (at 1:9–10 and note). **4:8** *Draw nigh . . . hands*: an image of sacerdotal cleansing in anticipation of an approach to God's altar; cf. Exod 30:17–21.   **4:9** *Be afflicted . . . mourning*: recalling Jesus' words at Matt 5:4; Luke 6:21, 25. *Heaviness*: sadness.   **4:10** *Humble yourselves . . . up*: cf. 1:9–10 and note; 1 Pet 5:6.

4:11–5:6 Examples of pretension. This section explores several of the themes introduced in 1:2–27, including speech, wealth, and enacted religion.   **4:11** *Speak . . . of*: lit. "speak not against," but often connoting slander, here with Lev 19:16 lying in the background (see note). The slanderer *judgeth the law* in that he chooses what in it to obey and what to disregard; cf. 2:8–13.   **4:12** *Lawgiver*: better to add "and judge" (MS tradition). *Another*: better "your neighbor" (MS tradition).

¹³Go to now, ye that say, To day or to morrow we will go into such a city, and continue there a year, and buy and sell, and get gain: ¹⁴whereas ye know not what shall be on the morrow. For what is your life? It is even a vapour, that appeareth for a little time, and then vanisheth away. ¹⁵For that ye ought to say, If the Lord will, we shall live, and do this, or that. ¹⁶But now ye rejoice in your boastings: all such rejoicing is evil. ¹⁷Therefore to him that knoweth to do good, and doeth it not, to him it is sin.

5 Go to now, ye rich men, weep and howl for your miseries that shall come upon you. ²Your riches are corrupted, and your garments are motheaten. ³Your gold and silver is cankered; and the rust of them shall be a witness against you, and shall eat your flesh as it were fire. Ye have heaped treasure together for the last days. ⁴Behold, the hire of the labourers who have reaped down your fields, which is of you kept back by fraud, crieth: and the cries of them which have reaped are entered into the ears of the Lord of sabaoth. ⁵Ye have lived in pleasure on the earth, and been wanton; ye have nourished your hearts, as in a day of slaughter. ⁶Ye have condemned and killed the just; and he doth not resist you.

⁷Be patient therefore, brethren, unto the coming of the Lord. Behold, the husbandman waiteth for the precious fruit of the earth, and hath long patience for it, until he receive the early and latter rain. ⁸Be ye also patient; stablish your hearts: for the coming of the Lord draweth nigh. ⁹Grudge not one against another, brethren, lest ye be condemned: behold, the judge standeth before the door.

4:13 *Go to now*: i.e., "come now" (also in 5:1). **4:13–14** *To day or . . . the morrow*: cf. Luke 12:16–20. **4:14** *Ye know . . . morrow*: echoing Prov 27:1. *A vapour*: a conventional image for evildoers (e.g., *2 Baruch* 82.3). **4:15** *For that*: instead of that. **4:16** *Ye rejoice . . . rejoicing*: "You boast in your arrogance; all such arrogance" (NRSV). **5:1** *Ye rich . . . you*: cf. Luke 6:24. **5:2–3** *Your riches . . . cankered*: echoing the dominical saying recorded at Matt 6:19–20; Luke 12:33. **5:3** *Cankered*: corroded. *For the last days*: an ironic pun: the wealth supposed to bring security in one's latter days actually ensures eschatological judgment (cf. Luke 12:19–20). **5:4** *Hire*: wages. The treasure in storage should have gone to pay laborers, according to Lev 19:13. *Crieth: and . . . sabaoth*: recalling such OT passages as Gen 4:10; Exod 2:23; 3:7. *Sabaoth* transliterates a Greek transliteration of a Hebrew word meaning "of hosts" or "of armies." "Lord of hosts" is a conventional title for God in the OT, but the passage may echo Isa 5:9 in particular. **5:5** *Lived in pleasure . . . wanton*: the Greek words rendered *pleasure* and *wanton* denote luxury, indulgence, voluptuousness, and the like. *On the earth*: alternatively "on your land." *Ye have nourished . . . slaughter*: better "you have fattened your hearts on a day of slaughter" (MS tradition; our translation), alluding to such prophetic imagery as Jer 12:3; cf. Isa 34:2; Zech 11:4, 7. The idea is that the wealthy's luxurious living fattens them up for the metaphorical slaughter of God's eschatological judgment. **5:6** *Condemned*: this forensic verb recalls the condemnation of the wealthy at 2:6 (see note).

5:7–11 Patience. This section develops material from 1:2–4, 12–13. Its juxtaposition with the preceding section suggests that James understands his readers to be suffering at the hands of the wealthy. **5:7** *Be patient*: Gk. *makrothymeō*; forms of a different word, *hypomonē*, are translated "patience" at 1:3–4 and "endureth" in 1:12. In this section, "patience" usually has the more active sense of "forbearance." *Coming of the Lord*: see Matt 24:3 note. *Behold, the husbandman . . . it*: analogous agricultural metaphors abound in the NT; e.g., Mark 4:26–29; 1 Cor 9:7–10; 2 Tim 2:6. *Early and latter rain*: a common OT formulation for spring and fall; cf. Deut 11:14; Joel 2:23; etc. **5:9** *Grudge*: lit. "groan," with the sense of "grumble" or "murmur." *The judge . . . door*: in Matt 24:32–33 and Mark 13:28–29, a similar image of doors follows an agricultural metaphor; cf. Rev 3:20.

¹⁰Take, my brethren, the prophets, who have spoken in the name of the Lord, for an example of suffering affliction, and of patience. ¹¹Behold, we count them happy which endure. Ye have heard of the patience of Job, and have seen the end of the Lord; that the Lord is very pitiful, and of tender mercy.

¹²But above all things, my brethren, swear not, neither by heaven, neither by the earth, neither by any other oath: but let your yea be yea; and your nay, nay; lest ye fall into condemnation.

¹³Is any among you afflicted? let him pray. Is any merry? let him sing psalms. ¹⁴Is any sick among you? let him call for the elders of the church; and let them pray over him, anointing him with oil in the name of the Lord: ¹⁵and the prayer of faith shall save the sick, and the Lord shall raise him up; and if he have committed sins, they shall be forgiven him. ¹⁶Confess your faults one to another, and pray one for another, that ye may be healed. The effectual fervent prayer of a righteous man availeth much. ¹⁷Elias was a man subject to like passions as we are, and he prayed earnestly that it might not rain: and it rained not on the earth by the space of three years and six months. ¹⁸And he prayed again, and the heaven gave rain, and the earth brought forth her fruit.

¹⁹Brethren, if any of you do err from the truth, and one convert him; ²⁰let him know, that he which converteth the sinner from the error of his way shall save a soul from death, and shall hide a multitude of sins.

5:10 *Prophets*: OT prophets often suffered rejection and persecution—e.g., Elijah (see 1 Kgs 18–19) and Jeremiah (Jer 36:1–45:5).   **5:11** *Endure, patience*: forms of Gk. *hypomonē*, whereas "patient"/ "patience" in vv. 8 and 10 translate forms of *makrothymia* (see note to v. 7). The bitter complaints against God in the book of Job make him an unconvincing model of patient suffering under affliction, but James may have in mind a traditional portrayal preserved in such writings as the *Testament of Job*, where his patient endurance is indeed emphasized (e.g., 1.5; 26.5; 27.7). *The end of the Lord*: context suggests this means "the end that the Lord brought about" for Job—i.e., his dramatic reversal of fortune at Job 42:7–12.

5:12–20 Speech and prayer. This section returns to the matter of the proper use of one's tongue (cf. 1:19, 26; 3:1–12), developing the introductory material about prayer (1:5–8).   **5:12** *Swear not . . . earth*: cf. Matt 23:16–22; perhaps also alluding to Lev 19:12. *Let your yea . . . condemnation*: echoing the dominical saying of Matt 5:37.   **5:13** *Sing psalms*: perhaps overtranslating Gk. *psalletō*, "let him sing."   **5:14** *Elders of the church*: presumably, church leaders. *Anointing him with oil*: see Mark 6:13 and note. This passage is the scriptural basis for the Catholic sacrament of extreme unction. **5:15** *Prayer of faith*: distinguished from the prayer of 4:3.   **5:15–16** *The Lord . . . healed*: "raising up" is a common feature in the Synoptic Gospels' accounts of Jesus' healings, which James may here recall; e.g. Mark 2:9; 3:3; 5:41; and parallels. There may also be an allusion to eschatological resurrection.   **5:15** *If he . . . him*: see Mark 2:5 note.   **5:16** *Faults*: better "sins" (MS tradition).   **5:17** *He prayed . . . rain*: see 1 Kgs 17:1.   **5:17–18** *And it . . . fruit*: "After many days . . . in the third year," the Lord told Elijah he would bring rain (1 Kgs 18:1; cf. vv. 41–45; Luke 4:25).   **5:20** *He which . . . sins*: cf. Lev 19:17 and note. *Shall hide . . . sins*: it is not clear what this means, but the formulation was common; e.g., Prov 10:12; 1 Pet 4:8; *1 Clement* 49.5.

The First Epistle General of Peter

AMONG the Catholic Epistles, 1 Peter, like 1 John, is unusual in that its canonical authority avoided challenge in antiquity. Since antiquity the letter has enjoyed widespread influence, at least through the early modern era. To cite just one example, in his "Preface to the New Testament" (1522) Martin Luther identified it as a book of the highest doctrinal importance, placing 1 Peter in such notable company as the Gospel of John and the Pauline epistles to the Romans, Galatians, and Ephesians. In the nineteenth and early twentieth centuries, however, 1 Peter was increasingly marginalized. Like virtually every other book in the New Testament, it found its authorship challenged; specifically, it came to be seen as a second-rate imitation of Paul's writings, perhaps composed by a later author intent on laying a veneer of superficial theological accord over the conflicts that vexed Peter's and Paul's relationship (see Gal 2:11–14). In any case, the letter was deemed unworthy of serious inquiry on its own terms and treated mainly as evidence for the development of the second- or third-generation Pauline Christianity that the Pastoral Epistles also supposedly evinced.

Points of contact between 1 Peter and Paul's writings (in particular, Romans) are difficult to deny. Compare, for example, 1 Peter's treatment of spiritual gifts in 4:10–11 with Paul's in Rom 12:3–8 (cf. 1 Cor 12:4–11), its urging of obedience to governmental authority with Romans' (2:13–17; cf. Rom 13:1–7), and the linked citations of Isa 8:14, 28:16, and Hos 2:23 in 1 Pet 2:6–10 and Rom 9:25–33. Recently, however, scholars have downplayed 1 Peter's connections with Paul's writings, choosing instead to view the epistle as an important early Christian composition in its own right, even while recognizing that it may occasionally have pressed Pauline language and ideas into its service, as it certainly did the Old Testament, other ancient Jewish literature, and the teachings of Jesus.

1 Peter, after all, focuses on an issue that Paul rarely addresses in his extant epistles: persecution of the community of faith. In this emphasis it is closer to Revelation than to Paul, although 1 Peter, unlike the Apocalypse, carefully avoids implicating Roman authorities in the harassment confronting the communities to which it is addressed. The epistle's generally positive attitude toward political authority suggests that there was no government campaign aimed at extirpating Christianity, and in any case persecution at the time 1 Peter was written would not have been empire-wide and systematic, but rather regional and sporadic. In the communities to which the present letter is addressed it probably took the form of social exclusion and harassment by neighbors; if governmental authorities were

involved, as they seem to have been in the situations that Revelation imagines, they likely were compelled to intervene in response to accusations. Moreover, as the early second-century correspondence between Pliny and Trajan suggests (see Appendix, pp. 987–89), they may have been as concerned with limiting libelous charges as with restricting a potentially dangerous foreign cult.

It is instructive that 1 Peter consistently describes the harassment to which its readers were subject in terms of speech (2:12; 3:16; 4:4, 14; cf. 2:23). Chief among the insults leveled at them was "Christian" (4:16), a derogatory term in the first century C.E. that followers of Jesus would soon come to adopt as their preferred self-identification. One interpretation of this evidence proposes that 1 Peter's readers found themselves the victims of malicious rumors, perhaps of the sort that would surface later in the historical record—for example, that Christians participated in bizarre and suspicious nocturnal rites, practiced cannibalism, engaged in sexual orgies, and the like. Verbal harassment of this sort would not have been trivial. The isolation experienced by a minority religious community victimized by such gossip could threaten its survival, as the maligned might be ostracized and unable to find work. Moreover, the line between vicious rumor and legitimate accusation is a thin one, as demon-strated by the difficulty Pliny had in recognizing it, according to Trajan's reply to his letter.

The author of 1 Peter certainly takes seriously the harassment and isolation that the readers experience. The letter refers to its addressees twice as "strangers and sojourners"—that is, "resident aliens" (cf. 1:1, 17; 2:11 and notes)—vulnerable inhabitants of a foreign land who cannot count on the goodwill of their neighbors. It frequently compares their suffering to Christ's and exhorts them to respond to it as Christ did: "when he was reviled, [he] reviled not again" (2:23). Most importantly, it encourages communal solidarity in the midst of their suffering. 1 Peter urges a moral rigor (e.g., 1:13–16; 4:1–2) aimed at establishing clear boundaries between the community of faith and hostile outsiders (4:3–4); complementarily, it articulates clear guidelines as to how believers are to treat one another (2:18–3:7). Finally, like Revelation, 1 Peter looks forward to nonbelievers' eschatological punishment and to believers' ultimate vindication (4:5–6).

Peter probably did not compose this epistle: its Greek is far more polished than one would expect from a man identified elsewhere in the New Testament as "unlearned and ignorant" (Acts 4:13). More significantly, Rome's designation as "Babylon" (5:13) presupposes as the basis for the analogy its destruction of the second Jerusalem temple. But that took place in 70 C.E., well after the date when, according to a well-attested ancient Christian tradition, Peter was killed in Nero's persecution in Rome. 1 Peter is therefore likely a pseudepigraphic composition, written in the late first century as an encyclical to various congregations in Asia Minor. It was probably sent from Rome, where Peter was regarded as a particularly influential evangelist and leader and where Paul's Epistle to the Romans, on which 1 Peter draws, would certainly have been known. We should probably imagine a later Roman ecclesiastical leader adopting Peter's mantle and drawing on Petrine and other traditions preserved in his community to compose a letter in the master's name that would encourage harassed Christian communities in Asia Minor to remain faithful as they suffered.

For detailed exegesis of 1 Peter, see John H. Elliot's exhaustive Anchor Bible commentary, *1 Peter: A New Translation with Introduction and Commentary* (New York: Doubleday, 2000), which informs this introduction and the annotations that follow.

THE FIRST EPISTLE GENERAL OF
PETER

1 Peter, an apostle of Jesus Christ, to the strangers scattered throughout Pontus, Galatia, Cappadocia, Asia, and Bithynia, ²elect according to the foreknowledge of God the Father, through sanctification of the Spirit, unto obedience and sprinkling of the blood of Jesus Christ: Grace unto you, and peace, be multiplied.

³Blessed be the God and Father of our Lord Jesus Christ, which according to his abundant mercy hath begotten us again unto a lively hope by the resurrection of Jesus Christ from the dead, ⁴to an inheritance incorruptible, and undefiled, and that fadeth not away, reserved in heaven for you, ⁵who are kept by the power of God through faith unto salvation ready to be revealed in the last time. ⁶Wherein ye greatly rejoice, though now for a season, if need be, ye are in heaviness through manifold temptations: ⁷that the trial of your faith, being much more precious than of gold that perisheth, though it be tried with fire, might be found unto praise and honour and glory at the appearing of Jesus Christ: ⁸whom having not seen, ye love; in whom, though now ye see him not, yet believing, ye rejoice with joy unspeakable and full of glory: ⁹receiving the end of your faith, even the salvation of your souls. ¹⁰Of which salvation the prophets have inquired and searched diligently, who prophesied of the grace that should come unto you: ¹¹searching what, or what manner of time the Spirit of Christ which was in them did signify, when it testified beforehand the sufferings of Christ, and the glory that should follow. ¹²Unto whom it was revealed, that not unto themselves, but

---

1:1–12 Salutation and blessing. 1 Peter follows the same epistolary conventions as the Pauline letters (see note to Rom 1:1–15), although it replaces the usual thanksgiving with a blessing (cf. 2 Cor 1:1–11; Eph 1:1–23) and its diction is somewhat more ornate than Paul's usual salutations.   **1:1** *Apostle*: see Rom 1:1 and note. *Strangers*: or "resident aliens." *Pontus, Galatia . . . Bithynia*: regions covering all but the southern strip of Asia Minor.   **1:2** *Sprinkling of . . . Christ*: inaugurating a divine covenant (cf. Exod 24:3–8; Heb 9:18–21 and notes). This appropriation of OT imagery anticipates vv. 10–12. *Grace unto you, and peace*: see Rom 1:7 note.   **1:3–12** *Blessed be . . . into*: the blessing's tripartite division begins with an emphasis on the eschatological future (vv. 3–5) before moving backward to present trials (vv. 6–9) and then ancient prophecy (vv. 10–12).   **1:3** *Lively*: living. **1:6** *Heaviness*: grief. *Temptations*: alternatively "tests."   **1:7** *Trial*: lit. "proving," in the sense of "proving genuine" (as also *tried* later in the verse). *Appearing*: "revelation," as the same Greek root is translated in v. 13; cf. vv. 5, 12 ("revealed").   **1:8** *Seen*: better "known" (MS tradition).   **1:9** *End*: goal. *Salvation of your souls*: "saving of your lives" (cf. Mark 8:35–37 and 36–37 note), or even simply "your salvation," in accordance with 1 Peter's use of "soul" as a virtual synonym for "self" (cf. 1:22; 2:25; 4:19).

unto us they did minister the things, which are now reported unto you by them that have preached the gospel unto you with the Holy Ghost sent down from heaven; which things the angels desire to look into.

[13]Wherefore gird up the loins of your mind, be sober, and hope to the end for the grace that is to be brought unto you at the revelation of Jesus Christ; [14]as obedient children, not fashioning yourselves according to the former lusts in your ignorance: [15]but as he which hath called you is holy, so be ye holy in all manner of conversation; [16]because it is written, Be ye holy; for I am holy.

[17]And if ye call on the Father, who without respect of persons judgeth according to every man's work, pass the time of your sojourning here in fear: [18]for as much as ye know that ye were not redeemed with corruptible things, as silver and gold, from your vain conversation received by tradition from your fathers; [19]but with the precious blood of Christ, as of a lamb without blemish and without spot: [20]who verily was foreordained before the foundation of the world, but was manifest in these last times for you, [21]who by him do believe in God, that raised him up from the dead, and gave him glory; that your faith and hope might be in God.

[22]Seeing ye have purified your souls in obeying the truth through the Spirit unto unfeigned love of the brethren, see that ye love one another with a pure heart fervently: [23]being born again, not of corruptible seed, but of incorruptible, by the word of God, which liveth and abideth for ever. [24]For all flesh is as grass, and all the glory of man as the flower of grass. The grass withereth, and the flower thereof falleth away: [25]but the word of the Lord endureth for ever. And this is the word which by the gospel is preached unto you.

2 Wherefore laying aside all malice, and all guile, and hypocrisies, and envies, and all evil speakings, [2]as newborn babes, desire the sincere milk of the word, that ye may grow thereby: [3]if so be ye have tasted that the Lord is gracious. [4]To whom coming, as unto a living stone, disallowed indeed of men, but chosen of

---

1:12 *Unto us*: better "unto you" (MS tradition). *Which things . . . into*: the NT and other ancient Jewish literature frequently assert angelic ignorance and inferiority to humans (e.g., Mark 13:32; 1 Cor 6:3; Heb 1:14).

1:13–25 Exhortation to hope and brotherly love. Like the previous passage, this chapter moves back and forth from the past (vv. 14b–15a, 18–20), to the present (vv. 13a, 14a, 15b–17, 22–23), to the eschatological future (vv. 13b, 21, 24–25). It grounds the requirement to love one's brethren in the expectation of God's judgment (v. 17) and imaginatively links eschatological resurrection with moral transformation in the present (vv. 21–25). **1:13** *Gird up . . . mind*: "prepare your minds for action" (NRSV). *To the end*: perfectly, completely. **1:14** *Former lusts . . . ignorance*: this verse, like v. 18, marks the epistle's audience as converted Gentiles. (See Rom 1:18–32 and note for the mythological origins of the Gentile depravity here assumed.) *Lusts*: desires. **1:15** *Conversation*: conduct (also in v. 18). **1:16** *Be ye . . . am holy*: Lev 11:44–45; 19:2. **1:17** *Respect of persons*: favoritism. **1:18** *Redeemed*: or "ransomed" (see Mark 10:45 note). **1:19** *Precious blood . . . spot*: comparing Christ to the Passover lamb; cf. 1 Cor 5:7 note. For the perfection required of sacrificial offerings, see Lev 22:17–25. **1:20** *Foreordained*: according to the divine foreknowledge outlined in v. 2. **1:22** *Through the Spirit*: better omitted (MS tradition). **1:23** *Born again*: cf. John 3:3, 7. *For ever*: better omitted (MS tradition). **1:24–25** *All flesh . . . ever*: Isa 40:6–8. **1:25** *This is . . . you*: glossing "word" from the Isaiah quote.

2:1–10 The living stone. This section, featuring a chain of scriptural citations, develops an architectural image, with Christ figuring the cornerstone and the community of believers the building under construction. **2:2** *Sincere*: Gk. *adolos*, the opposite of *dolos*, "guile" (v. 1). *Thereby*: better to add "into salvation" (MS tradition). **2:3** *Tasted that . . . gracious*: echoing Ps 34:8. This psalm resurfaces in 3:10–12. *Gracious*: benevolent. **2:4** *Living stone, disallowed*: echoing Ps 118:22,

God, and precious, [5]ye also, as lively stones, are built up a spiritual house, an holy priesthood, to offer up spiritual sacrifices, acceptable to God by Jesus Christ. [6]Wherefore also it is contained in the scripture, Behold, I lay in Sion a chief corner stone, elect, precious: and he that believeth on him shall not be confounded. [7]Unto you therefore which believe he is precious: but unto them which be disobedient, the stone which the builders disallowed, the same is made the head of the corner, [8]and a stone of stumbling, and a rock of offence, even to them which stumble at the word, being disobedient: whereunto also they were appointed.

[9]But ye are a chosen generation, a royal priesthood, an holy nation, a peculiar people; that ye should shew forth the praises of him who hath called you out of darkness into his marvellous light: [10]which in time past were not a people, but are now the people of God: which had not obtained mercy, but now have obtained mercy.

[11]Dearly beloved, I beseech you as strangers and pilgrims, abstain from fleshly lusts, which war against the soul; [12]having your conversation honest among the Gentiles: that, whereas they speak against you as evildoers, they may by your good works, which they shall behold, glorify God in the day of visitation.

[13]Submit yourselves to every ordinance of man for the Lord's sake: whether it be to the king, as supreme; [14]or unto governors, as unto them that are sent by him for the punishment of evildoers, and for the praise of them that do well. [15]For so is the will of God, that with well doing ye may put to silence the ignorance of foolish men: [16]as free, and not using your liberty for a cloke of maliciousness, but as the servants of God. [17]Honour all men. Love the brotherhood. Fear God. Honour the king.

[18]Servants, be subject to your masters with all fear; not only to the good and gentle, but also to the froward. [19]For this is thankworthy, if a man for conscience toward God endure grief, suffering wrongfully. [20]For what glory is it, if, when ye be buffeted for your faults, ye shall take it patiently? but if, when ye do well, and

which v. 7 quotes. *Precious*: or "honored." **2:5** *Lively*: "living" (cf. v. 4). *Are built up*: alternatively "be built up." *An holy priesthood*: cf. Exod 19:6. **2:6** *Behold, I . . . confounded*: Isa 28:16. *Elect*: Gk. *eklekton*, "chosen" (cf. vv. 4, 9). **2:7** *Precious*: or "an honor." *Be disobedient*: better "believe not" (MS tradition). *The stone . . . corner*: Ps 118:22. *Head of the corner*: see Mark 12:10 note. **2:8** *A stone . . . offence*: Isa 8:14. *Even to them . . . disobedient*: better, beginning a new sentence, "they stumble, being disobedient to the word." **2:9** *A royal . . . nation*: recalling Exod 19:6. *Royal priesthood*: alternatively "a royal residence, a priesthood" (also in LXX Exod 19:6), with "royal residence" picking up the section's building imagery. *A peculiar people . . . praises*: more literally "a people for [God's] possession, that you should show forth the excellent deeds," alluding to LXX Isa 43:21; cf. Exod 19:5. *Who hath . . . light*: cf. Isa 9:2. **2:10** *Were not . . . have obtained mercy*: cf. Hos 2:23.
2:11–3:7 Obedience to authority. After a general call to commendable behavior (2:11–12), the author urges obedience to civil (2:13–17; cf. Rom 13:1–7) and domestic authority (2:18–3:7; cf. Eph 5:22–6:9; Col 3:18–4:1), the latter on the model of Christ's patient suffering as viewed through the lens of Isaiah's fourth Servant Song (52:13–53:12). **2:11** *Strangers and pilgrims*: Gk. *paroikous*, "sojourners" (cf. 1:17, "sojourning") and *parepidēmous*, "resident aliens" (see 1:1 note). *The soul*: or "life." **2:12** *Having your conversation honest*: "conducting yourself honorably" (NRSV). *Gentiles*: here, nonbelievers. *Visitation*: God's or Christ's, referring to the eschatological judgment and vindication of the elect. **2:13** *Ordinance*: or "institution." *The king*: probably the Roman emperor (also in v. 17). **2:16** *Servants*: lit. "slaves" (also in v. 18); see Rom 1:1 note. **2:17** *Brotherhood*: the community of believers. **2:18** *Froward*: lit. "crooked." **2:19** *For conscience toward God*: because conscious of God. **2:20** *Buffeted*: beaten.

suffer for it, ye take it patiently, this is acceptable with God. [21]For even hereunto were ye called: because Christ also suffered for us, leaving us an example, that ye should follow his steps: [22]who did no sin, neither was guile found in his mouth: [23]who, when he was reviled, reviled not again; when he suffered, he threatened not; but committed himself to him that judgeth righteously: [24]who his own self bare our sins in his own body on the tree, that we, being dead to sins, should live unto righteousness: by whose stripes ye were healed. [25]For ye were as sheep going astray; but are now returned unto the Shepherd and Bishop of your souls.

3 Likewise, ye wives, be in subjection to your own husbands; that, if any obey not the word, they also may without the word be won by the conversation of the wives; [2]while they behold your chaste conversation coupled with fear. [3]Whose adorning let it not be that outward adorning of plaiting the hair, and of wearing of gold, or of putting on of apparel; [4]but let it be the hidden man of the heart, in that which is not corruptible, even the ornament of a meek and quiet spirit, which is in the sight of God of great price. [5]For after this manner in the old time the holy women also, who trusted in God, adorned themselves, being in subjection unto their own husbands: [6]even as Sara obeyed Abraham, calling him lord: whose daughters ye are, as long as ye do well, and are not afraid with any amazement. [7]Likewise, ye husbands, dwell with them according to knowledge, giving honour unto the wife, as unto the weaker vessel, and as being heirs together of the grace of life; that your prayers be not hindered.

[8]Finally, be ye all of one mind, having compassion one of another, love as brethren, be pitiful, be courteous: [9]not rendering evil for evil, or railing for railing: but contrariwise blessing; knowing that ye are thereunto called, that ye should inherit a blessing. [10]For he that will love life, and see good days, let him refrain his tongue from evil, and his lips that they speak no guile: [11]let him eschew evil, and do good; let him seek peace, and ensue it. [12]For the eyes of the Lord are over the righteous, and his ears are open unto their prayers: but the face of the Lord is against them that do evil.

Acceptable: Gk. *charis*, translated "thankworthy" in v. 19.   **2:21** *Us . . . us*: better "you . . . you" (MS tradition).   **2:22** *Who did . . . mouth*: cf. Isa 53:9.   **2:23** *When he . . . again*: cf. Isa 53:3, 7. **2:24–25** *His own self . . . astray*: cf. Isa 53:4–6.   **2:24** *The tree*: i.e., the cross.   **2:25** *Bishop*: Gk. *episkopos*, lit. "overseer" (cf. 5:2 and note).   **3:1** *If any obey not the word*: 1 Cor 7:12–16 also provides advice for those married to unbelievers. *Conversation*: conduct (also in v. 2).   **3:2** *Chaste*: or, more generally, "pure."   **3:3** *Whose adorning . . . apparel*: see 1 Tim 2:9 note.   **3:6** *As Sara . . . lord*: see esp. Gen 18:12. *Are not afraid . . . amazement*: "do not fear any terror," echoing Prov 3:25.   **3:7** *Vessel*: see 1 Thess 4:4 and note.

3:8–22 Suffering according to the example of Christ. Looking back on believing slaves' exemplary suffering (2:18–25), this section advises all the readers to follow the model of Christ when experiencing harassment from outside the community. The initial demand that they "be . . . all of one mind" sums up the previous section's domestic exhortations, presenting them as a call for communal solidarity in the face of external hostility. (Compare 4:1–3 and Phil 2:1–11, where Paul urges his readers all to have the same mind and then goes on to describe Christ's humble suffering.)   **3:8** *Pitiful*: alternatively "tender-hearted" (NRSV). *Courteous*: better "humble-minded" (MS tradition).   **3:9** *Not rendering . . . contrariwise blessing*: recalling the portrayal of Jesus above (2:23), as well as his teaching (Luke 6:28); cf. Rom 12:17 and note.   **3:10–12** *He that . . . evil*: quoting LXX Ps 34:12–16.   **3:11** *Ensue*: pursue.

¹³And who is he that will harm you, if ye be followers of that which is good? ¹⁴But and if ye suffer for righteousness' sake, happy are ye: and be not afraid of their terror, neither be troubled; ¹⁵but sanctify the Lord God in your hearts: and be ready always to give an answer to every man that asketh you a reason of the hope that is in you with meekness and fear: ¹⁶having a good conscience; that, whereas they speak evil of you, as of evildoers, they may be ashamed that falsely accuse your good conversation in Christ. ¹⁷For it is better, if the will of God be so, that ye suffer for well doing, than for evil doing.

¹⁸For Christ also hath once suffered for sins, the just for the unjust, that he might bring us to God, being put to death in the flesh, but quickened by the Spirit: ¹⁹by which also he went and preached unto the spirits in prison; ²⁰which sometime were disobedient, when once the long suffering of God waited in the days of Noah, while the ark was a preparing, wherein few, that is, eight souls were saved by water. ²¹The like figure whereunto even baptism doth also now save us (not the putting away of the filth of the flesh, but the answer of a good conscience toward God,) by the resurrection of Jesus Christ: ²²who is gone into heaven, and is on the right hand of God; angels and authorities and powers being made subject unto him.

4 Forasmuch then as Christ hath suffered for us in the flesh, arm yourselves likewise with the same mind: for he that hath suffered in the flesh hath ceased from sin; ²that he no longer should live the rest of his time in the flesh to the lusts of men, but to the will of God. ³For the time past of our life may suffice us to have wrought the will of the Gentiles, when we walked in lasciviousness, lusts, excess of wine, revellings, banquetings, and abominable idolatries: ⁴wherein they think it strange that ye run not with them to the same excess of riot, speaking evil of you: ⁵who shall give account to him that is ready to judge the quick and the dead. ⁶For for this cause was the gospel preached also to them that are dead, that they might be judged according to men in the flesh, but live according to God in the spirit.

3:13 *Followers of*: better "zealous for" (MS tradition).   **3:14** *And if*: even if. *If ye . . . ye*: cf. Matt 5:10. **3:14–15** *Be not . . . hearts*: adapting Isa 8:12–13.   **3:15** *The Lord God*: better "Christ as Lord" (MS tradition). *Answer*: Gk. *apologia*, a term that refers to a forensic defense.   **3:16** *As of evildoers*: better omitted (MS tradition). *Conversation*: conduct.   **3:18** *Us*: better "you" (MS tradition). *Quickened*: made alive.   **3:19–20** *The spirits . . . Noah*: the angelic "sons of God" whose mingling with human women provoked the great flood (see Gen 6:1–4). *1 Enoch* 6–21 recounts their transgression, subsequent bondage, and God's instruction to Enoch that he preach condemnation to them. The present passage appears to Christianize that legendary expansion of the Genesis account.   **3:19** *Preached*: i.e., preached condemnation, in accordance with the Enochic parallel.   **3:20** *A preparing*: being prepared. *Eight souls*: eight lives; seven accompanied Noah on the ark (see Gen 8:18; cf. 10:1).   **3:21** *Us*: better "you" (MS tradition). *The answer . . . God*: better "a pledge to God of a good conscience," emphasizing the disposition of the initiate's will.   **3:22** *On the . . . God*: on the basis of Ps 110:1, ancient Christian literature conventionally locates the exalted Christ at God's right hand (e.g., Acts 5:31; Rom 8:34; etc.). *Angels and . . . him*: cf. 1 Cor 15:24–25.

4:1–11 Various exhortations. 4:1 *For us*: better omitted (MS tradition).   **4:2** *He no longer . . . God*: i.e., he should no longer live his life according to human desires, but rather by God's will. **4:3** *Of our life*: better omitted (MS tradition). *Us*: better omitted (MS tradition). *When we*: better "when you." *Lasciviousness*: licentiousness.   **4:5** *Quick*: living.   **4:6** *The gospel . . . spirit*: those who embraced the gospel and later died will rise again (cf. 1 Thess 4:13–18). *Be judged according to men in the flesh* obliquely refers to death as God's condemnation of human transgression, according to

⁷But the end of all things is at hand: be ye therefore sober, and watch unto prayer. ⁸And above all things have fervent charity among yourselves: for charity shall cover the multitude of sins. ⁹Use hospitality one to another without grudging. ¹⁰As every man hath received the gift, even so minister the same one to another, as good stewards of the manifold grace of God. ¹¹If any man speak, let him speak as the oracles of God; if any man minister, let him do it as of the ability which God giveth: that God in all things may be glorified through Jesus Christ, to whom be praise and dominion for ever and ever. Amen.

¹²Beloved, think it not strange concerning the fiery trial which is to try you, as though some strange thing happened unto you: ¹³but rejoice, inasmuch as ye are partakers of Christ's sufferings; that, when his glory shall be revealed, ye may be glad also with exceeding joy. ¹⁴If ye be reproached for the name of Christ, happy are ye; for the spirit of glory and of God resteth upon you: on their part he is evil spoken of, but on your part he is glorified. ¹⁵But let none of you suffer as a murderer, or as a thief, or as an evildoer, or as a busybody in other men's matters. ¹⁶Yet if any man suffer as a Christian, let him not be ashamed; but let him glorify God on this behalf. ¹⁷For the time is come that judgment must begin at the house of God: and if it first begin at us, what shall the end be of them that obey not the gospel of God? ¹⁸And if the righteous scarcely be saved, where shall the ungodly and the sinner appear? ¹⁹Wherefore let them that suffer according to the will of God commit the keeping of their souls to him in well doing, as unto a faithful Creator.

5 The elders which are among you I exhort, who am also an elder, and a witness of the sufferings of Christ, and also a partaker of the glory that shall be revealed: ²feed the flock of God which is among you, taking the oversight thereof, not by constraint, but willingly; not for filthy lucre, but of a ready mind; ³neither as being lords over God's heritage, but being ensamples to the flock. ⁴And when the chief Shepherd shall appear, ye shall receive a crown of glory that fadeth not away.

⁵Likewise, ye younger, submit yourselves unto the elder. Yea, all of you be subject one to another, and be clothed with humility: for God resisteth the proud, and giveth grace to the humble. ⁶Humble yourselves therefore under the mighty

---

Gen 2:17; 3:22–24 (cf. Rom 5:12–21).   **4:7** *The end of all things*: the eschatological consummation. *Watch unto prayer*: i.e., "be alert to facilitate prayer."   **4:8** *Charity shall cover . . . sins*: see Jas 5:20 note. *Shall cover*: better "covers" (MS tradition).   **4:10–11** *As every man . . . giveth*: cf. Rom 12:3–8; 1 Cor 12:4–11.   **4:11** *Praise*: lit. "glory."

4:12–19 Further encouragement in suffering. This is the letter's third extended treatment of suffering on the model of Christ's (cf. 2:18–25; 3:8–22).   **4:12** *Try*: test.   **4:14** *If ye . . . ye*: cf. Matt 5:11; Luke 6:22. *On their part . . . glorified*: better omitted (MS tradition).   **4:16** *Christian*: see Acts 11:26 note. *On this behalf*: better "in this name" (MS tradition).   **4:18** *If the righteous . . . appear*: quoting LXX Prov 11:31.

5:1–11 Final exhortations. 5:1 *Elders*: church leaders.   **5:2** *Feed*: lit. "tend." *Taking the oversight*: Gk. *episkopountes*, whose nominal form was rendered "bishop" at 2:25 (there with reference to Christ, but here to ecclesiastical leadership; see 1 Tim 3:1 and note). *Willingly*: better to add "according to God" (MS tradition). *Filthy lucre*: shameful profit.   **5:3** *God's heritage*: lit. "what is allotted to you." *Ensamples*: Gk. *typoi*, examples, which shares its root with "figure" in 3:21.   **5:4** *A crown . . . away*: see Jas 1:12 note.   **5:5** *Likewise, ye . . . elder*: for slippage between the use of "elder" to refer to ecclesiastical leadership and to age, see 1 Tim 5:1 note. *All of you . . . humility*: better "all of you must clothe yourselves with humility in your dealings with one another" (MS tradition; NRSV). *God resisteth . . . humble*: quoting LXX Prov 3:34; cf. Jas 4:6.   **5:6** *Humble yourselves . . .*

hand of God, that he may exalt you in due time: [7]casting all your care upon him; for he careth for you.

[8]Be sober, be vigilant; because your adversary the devil, as a roaring lion, walketh about, seeking whom he may devour: [9]whom resist stedfast in the faith, knowing that the same afflictions are accomplished in your brethren that are in the world. [10]But the God of all grace, who hath called us unto his eternal glory by Christ Jesus, after that ye have suffered a while, make you perfect, stablish, strengthen, settle you. [11]To him be glory and dominion for ever and ever. Amen.

[12]By Silvanus, a faithful brother unto you, as I suppose, I have written briefly, exhorting, and testifying that this is the true grace of God wherein ye stand. [13]The church that is at Babylon, elected together with you, saluteth you; and so doth Marcus my son. [14]Greet ye one another with a kiss of charity.

Peace be with you all that are in Christ Jesus. Amen.

---

time: cf. Matt 23:12; Luke 14:11; 18:14; Jas 4:10.   **5:8** *A roaring lion . . . devour*: perhaps echoing Ps 22:13.   **5:9** *In the world*: all over the world.   **5:10** *Called us*: better "called you" (MS tradition). *Make you . . . you*: better "will restore, establish, strengthen, provide a foundation for you" (MS tradition; our translation).   **5:11** *Glory and*: better omitted (MS tradition).

5:12–14 Closing. 5:12 *Silvanus*: presumably identifying Paul's colleague Silas (see 2 Cor 1:19 note) as the letter's bearer (probably as part of its pseudepigraphic veneer). Acts 15:22 may imply he had a relationship with Peter as well. *As I suppose*: as I account him.   **5:13** *The church . . . Babylon*: lit. "she that is in Babylon," but referring to the church in Rome, for which Babylon is a symbolic name (cf. Rev 17:9 and note). *Marcus my son*: Acts 12:12–17 implies Peter's relationship with John Mark, here figured as paternity.   **5:14** *Kiss of charity*: see Rom 16:16 and note. *Amen*: better omitted (MS tradition).

The Second Epistle General of Peter

SECOND Peter's pseudepigraphical status is almost entirely uncontroversial among critical scholars, and the book is usually dated quite late. Several features account for this broad consensus, the most crucial being 2 Peter's explicit concern to refute those insisting that prolonged delay of the Day of the Lord invalidates eschatological prophecy and expectation, and its identification of the letters written by Peter's contemporary Paul as Scripture. We might also note 2 Peter's dependence on Jude, from which it borrows extensively, although carefully eliminating the earlier epistle's potentially controversial references to apocryphal literature. If Peter actually wrote 2 Peter, then it is difficult to understand why this famous apostle would have relied on another epistle written by a relatively obscure leader in the early church. All these factors, but especially the first two, point to a date of composition well after the middle decades of the first century C.E., when Peter ministered. The letter was probably composed during the final decades of the first century, or else in the early decades of the second (although even later dates have been proposed), by a Christian scribe who viewed himself as standing in the stream of the Petrine tradition, and therefore as authorized to write in the master's name.

2 Peter presents itself as Peter's last testament (see esp. 1:12–15), a valedictory exhortation that Christians remain faithful to even those elements of apostolic doctrine whose credibility became increasingly strained as Jesus' ministry and teaching began to recede into the past. Foremost among these was the call for imminent expectation of the Day of the Lord, whose arrival in the lifetime of Jesus' original followers the synoptic tradition insists was promised by Jesus himself (Matt 16:28; Mark 9:1; Luke 9:27). 2 Peter suggests that such teaching ought to be preserved but not understood literally when it reminds readers that God's experience of time is not the same as theirs: "one day is with the Lord as a thousand years, and a thousand years as one day" (3:8). This "solution" to the problem of unfulfilled eschatological prophecy is tendentious, to be sure, as perhaps is the epistle's later statement that Paul was Peter's "beloved brother" (3:15), for the two figures are known from an earlier source to have experienced severe conflict (Gal 2:11–14). It is difficult to avoid the impression that 2 Peter aims to smooth over some of Jesus' apparently erroneous eschatological teaching, as well as an embarrassing dispute that characterized the relationship between a previous generation's most honored ecclesiastical leaders. This effort may have been undertaken with some urgency, for the epistle confronts those who are actively denying the validity of eschatological prophecy, and who perhaps do so claiming to follow Paul at the expense of other apostles.

It is impossible to identify with certainty the opponents whom 2 Peter addresses. Numerous targets have been proposed, including Epicureans, pagan-Christian syncretists, and gnostics. In favor of the last hypothesis (which is not incompatible with the second) is the opponents' apparent rejection of Old Testament prophecy (1:20–21), their willingness to slander angels (2:10), their claim to a saving knowledge of Christ (Gk. *epignōsis*, a key term among gnostic sectarians; 2:20), their denial of God's eschatological restoration of the cosmos (3:1–13), and finally the epistle's concern about controversial interpretations of Paul (3:15–17), on whose authority gnostic teaching frequently drew (see the introduction to the Pastoral Epistles). None of these factors is decisive, however, and it is admittedly more difficult to make the case that 2 Peter addresses gnostic teaching than that 1 Timothy or 1 John does (and neither of those arguments is uncontroversial). But if this letter responds to gnostic or proto-gnostic ideas, then its claim of Paul as Peter's beloved brother may best be understood as a polemical move suggesting that Paul's writings find their proper interpretation among the proto-orthodox rather than among gnosticizing Christians.

For more detailed analysis of 2 Peter, see Richard Bauckham's excellent Word Biblical Commentary, *Jude, 2 Peter* (Waco, TX: Word Books, 1983), which influences this introduction and the annotations that follow.

THE SECOND EPISTLE
GENERAL OF
PETER

1 Simon Peter, a servant and an apostle of Jesus Christ, to them that have obtained like precious faith with us through the righteousness of God and our Saviour Jesus Christ: ²Grace and peace be multiplied unto you through the knowledge of God, and of Jesus our Lord, ³according as his divine power hath given unto us all things that pertain unto life and godliness, through the knowledge of him that hath called us to glory and virtue: ⁴whereby are given unto us exceeding great and precious promises: that by these ye might be partakers of the divine nature, having escaped the corruption that is in the world through lust.

⁵And beside this, giving all diligence, add to your faith virtue; and to virtue knowledge; ⁶and to knowledge temperance; and to temperance patience; and to patience godliness; ⁷and to godliness brotherly kindness; and to brotherly kindness charity. ⁸For if these things be in you, and abound, they make you that ye shall neither be barren nor unfruitful in the knowledge of our Lord Jesus Christ. ⁹But he that lacketh these things is blind, and cannot see afar off, and hath forgotten that he was purged from his old sins. ¹⁰Wherefore the rather, brethren, give diligence to make your calling and election sure: for if ye do these things, ye shall never fall: ¹¹for so an entrance shall be ministered unto you abundantly into the everlasting kingdom of our Lord and Saviour Jesus Christ.

1:1–4 Salutation and reminder of God's gifts. Adhering to a conventional Greco-Roman epistolary pattern, 2 Peter begins by identifying the writer, followed by a reference to the addressees (here, rather vague) and a formal greeting (vv. 1–2). The epistle then reminds the readers of the gifts and promises of God that facilitate the virtue and holiness to which it goes on to call them (vv. 3–4). **1:1** *Simon*: better "Simeon" (MS tradition), transliterating the name's Semitic form, found elsewhere in the NT only at Acts 15:14. *Servant and an apostle*: see Rom 1:1 and notes. *Like precious . . . us*: "a faith as precious as ours" (NRSV). **1:2** *Grace and peace*: see Rom 1:7 and note. **1:3** *To*: or "by." **1:4** *The corruption . . . lust*: perhaps an allusion to Eve's transgression and its consequences (Gen 3); cf. Rom 7:7–25 and notes.

1:5–11 Exhortation to virtue. 1:5 *Beside this*: better "for this very reason" (NRSV). **1:6** *Temperance*: self-control. *Patience*: or "endurance." **1:8** *Barren*: or "idle." **1:9** *Cannot see far off*: is nearsighted. **1:11** *Ministered unto you abundantly*: "richly provided for you" (NRSV).

¹²Wherefore I will not be negligent to put you always in remembrance of these things, though ye know them, and be established in the present truth. ¹³Yea, I think it meet, as long as I am in this tabernacle, to stir you up by putting you in remembrance; ¹⁴knowing that shortly I must put off this my tabernacle, even as our Lord Jesus Christ hath shewed me. ¹⁵Moreover I will endeavour that ye may be able after my decease to have these things always in remembrance.

¹⁶For we have not followed cunningly devised fables, when we made known unto you the power and coming of our Lord Jesus Christ, but were eyewitnesses of his majesty. ¹⁷For he received from God the Father honour and glory, when there came such a voice to him from the excellent glory, This is my beloved Son, in whom I am well pleased. ¹⁸And this voice which came from heaven we heard, when we were with him in the holy mount. ¹⁹We have also a more sure word of prophecy; whereunto ye do well that ye take heed, as unto a light that shineth in a dark place, until the day dawn, and the day star arise in your hearts: ²⁰knowing this first, that no prophecy of the scripture is of any private interpretation. ²¹For the prophecy came not in old time by the will of man: but holy men of God spake as they were moved by the Holy Ghost.

2 But there were false prophets also among the people, even as there shall be false teachers among you, who privily shall bring in damnable heresies, even denying the Lord that bought them, and bring upon themselves swift destruction. ²And many shall follow their pernicious ways; by reason of whom the way of truth shall be evil spoken of. ³And through covetousness shall they with feigned words make merchandise of you: whose judgment now of a long time lingereth not, and their damnation slumbereth not.

⁴For if God spared not the angels that sinned, but cast them down to hell, and

---

1:12–15 Peter's testament. This section is framed by statements of hope that the readers will remember Peter's exhortation, even after his demise. **1:13** *Meet*: lit. "right." *As long . . . tabernacle*: see 2 Cor 5:1 note. **1:14** *Even as . . . me*: presumably a reference to a dominical tradition prophesying Peter's death, such as the one found at John 13:36; 21:18–19. (Similar traditions about Peter appear elsewhere in early Christian literature as well.)

1:16–2:10a Eschatology, prophecy, and judgment. The main argument of the letter begins by insisting on the eschatological coming of Christ (1:16–18), the authority of OT prophecy (1:19–21), and the inevitability of divine judgment (2:1–10a). The reference to false prophets in 2:1–3 suggests that the writer is responding to opponents who challenge the legitimacy of these convictions. The single sentence of 2:4–10a is closely related to Jude 4–7. **1:16** *Coming*: see Matt 24:3 note. **1:16–18** *Eyewitnesses of . . . mount*: compare the Synoptic Gospels' account of Jesus' transfiguration (Matt 17:1–8; Mark 9:2–8; Luke 9:28–36), although 2 Peter, like the *Apocalypse of Peter*, may understand it as an appearance of the risen Christ. (Here the tradition is invoked to establish that the risen Christ will return.) **1:19** *The day star*: Venus; see Rev 2:28 note. **1:20** *Of any private interpretation*: i.e., "a matter of private interpretation" (NRSV). **1:21** *In old time*: better "at any time." **2:1** *There were . . . people*: see, e.g., Jer 14:13–16; 27:9–18. *Even as . . . you*: see Matt 7:15–23 and note. *Damnable heresies*: rather "destructive opinions" (NRSV); Gk. *haireseis apōleias*, the latter word meaning "destruction" (as later in the verse). *That bought them*: cf. 1 Cor 6:20; 7:23. **2:2** *Pernicious*: better "licentious" (MS tradition). **2:3** *Make merchandise of*: exploit. *Damnation*: better "destruction" (as in v. 1; see note). **2:4** *Hell*: Gk. *Tartaros*, a realm beneath Hades (see Matt 11:23 note) and devoted to the punishment of the dead. Its use here suggests a parallel between the punishment of the "sons of God" from Gen 6:1–4 (see notes; cf. 1 Pet 3:19–20 and note) and the

delivered them into chains of darkness, to be reserved unto judgment; [5]and spared not the old world, but saved Noah the eighth person, a preacher of righteousness, bringing in the flood upon the world of the ungodly; [6]and turning the cities of Sodom and Gomorrha into ashes condemned them with an overthrow, making them an ensample unto those that after should live ungodly; [7]and delivered just Lot, vexed with the filthy conversation of the wicked: [8](for that righteous man dwelling among them, in seeing and hearing, vexed his righteous soul from day to day with their unlawful deeds;) [9]the Lord knoweth how to deliver the godly out of temptations, and to reserve the unjust unto the day of judgment to be punished: [10]but chiefly them that walk after the flesh in the lust of uncleanness, and despise government.

Presumptuous are they, selfwilled, they are not afraid to speak evil of dignities. [11]Whereas angels, which are greater in power and might, bring not railing accusation against them before the Lord. [12]But these, as natural brute beasts, made to be taken and destroyed, speak evil of the things that they understand not; and shall utterly perish in their own corruption; [13]and shall receive the reward of unrighteousness, as they that count it pleasure to riot in the day time. Spots they are and blemishes, sporting themselves with their own deceivings while they feast with you; [14]having eyes full of adultery, and that cannot cease from sin; beguiling unstable souls: an heart they have exercised with covetous practices; cursed children: [15]which have forsaken the right way, and are gone astray, following the way of Balaam the son of Bosor, who loved the wages of unrighteousness; [16]but was rebuked for his iniquity: the dumb ass speaking with man's voice forbad the madness of the prophet.

[17]These are wells without water, clouds that are carried with a tempest; to whom the mist of darkness is reserved for ever. [18]For when they speak great swelling words of vanity, they allure through the lusts of the flesh, through much wantonness, those that were clean escaped from them who live in error. [19]While they promise them liberty, they themselves are the servants of corruption: for of

---

Titans who, according to Greek mythology, were restrained in Tartarus (e.g., Hesiod, *Theogony* 711–45). **2:5** *Noah the eighth*: see 1 Pet 3:20 and note. *Preacher of righteousness*: see Heb 11:7 and note. **2:6–8** *Turning the cities . . . deeds*: see Gen 19. While the portrayal of Lot's character here is inconsistent with that in Genesis, his rescue from Sodom just before its destruction there too is analogized to God's rescue of the righteous Noah from the flood (see note to Gen 19:1–38). **2:7** *Filthy conversation . . . wicked*: more literally "licentious living of the lawless." **2:8** *Vexed*: tormented (a different Greek verb is used in v. 7). **2:9** *To reserve . . . punished*: alternatively "to keep the unjust under punishment until the day of judgment" (so NRSV)—apparently a reference to an interim punishment of the dead before their eschatological judgment. **2:10** *Government*: lit. "lordship." **2:10b–22 Disparaging the opposing teachers.** This section, which draws on Jude 8–13, denounces the opposing teachers as licentious apostates. **2:10–11** *Not afraid . . . Lord*: see Jude 8–9 and notes. **2:12** *As natural brute beasts*: the simile is picked up in vv. 16, 22. *Utterly perish*: better "become corrupt" (MS tradition; our translation). **2:13** *And shall receive*: better "suffering wrong as" (MS tradition). **2:14** *Adultery*: lit. "an adulteress." *An heart . . . cursed children*: both are objects of "having." **2:15–16** *Balaam the son . . . prophet*: see Num 22:21–35. **2:15** *Bosor*: in the OT, Balaam is known as Beor's son. **2:17** *Clouds that . . . ever*: better "mists driven by a storm; for them the deepest darkness has been reserved" (MS tradition; NRSV). **2:18** *Wantonness*: licentiousness. *Were clean*: better "hardly" (MS tradition). **2:19** *They promise them liberty*: presumably from the

whom a man is overcome, of the same is he brought in bondage. [20]For if after they have escaped the pollutions of the world through the knowledge of the Lord and Saviour Jesus Christ, they are again entangled therein, and overcome, the latter end is worse with them than the beginning. [21]For it had been better for them not to have known the way of righteousness, than, after they have known it, to turn from the holy commandment delivered unto them. [22]But it is happened unto them according to the true proverb, The dog is turned to his own vomit again; and the sow that was washed to her wallowing in the mire.

3 This second epistle, beloved, I now write unto you; in both which I stir up your pure minds by way of remembrance: [2]that ye may be mindful of the words which were spoken before by the holy prophets, and of the commandment of us the apostles of the Lord and Saviour: [3]knowing this first, that there shall come in the last days scoffers, walking after their own lusts, [4]and saying, Where is the promise of his coming? for since the fathers fell asleep, all things continue as they were from the beginning of the creation. [5]For this they willingly are ignorant of, that by the word of God the heavens were of old, and the earth standing out of the water and in the water: [6]whereby the world that then was, being overflowed with water, perished: [7]but the heavens and the earth, which are now, by the same word are kept in store, reserved unto fire against the day of judgment and perdition of ungodly men.

[8]But, beloved, be not ignorant of this one thing, that one day is with the Lord as a thousand years, and a thousand years as one day. [9]The Lord is not slack concerning his promise, as some men count slackness; but is longsuffering to us-ward, not willing that any should perish, but that all should come to repentance. [10]But the day of the Lord will come as a thief in the night; in the which the heavens shall pass away with a great noise, and the elements shall melt with fervent

unclean world, through their supposed knowledge of Christ (see v. 20), which leads some scholars to speculate that 2 Peter opposes gnostic or proto-gnostic Christians (as may the Pastoral Epistles and 1 John). The promised liberty may be from divine judgment, in light of their denial of the Day of the Lord (see chap. 3). **2:22** *The dog . . . again*: Prov 26:11. The following proverb finds parallels in sources as diverse as Heraclitus and the ancient Near Eastern *Tale of Ahiqar*.

3:1–16 The delayed Day of the Lord. This section defends against those who deny an eschatological consummation by arguing that God's judgment and renewal of the world are merely delayed. **3:1** *This second epistle*: probably a reference to 1 Peter, with which the present author associates his own letter, thereby perpetuating the pseudepigraphical fiction. **3:2** *That ye . . . prophets*: cf. 1 Pet 1:10–12. *The commandment . . . Saviour*: better "the commandment of the Lord and Savior through your apostles" (MS tradition; our translation). **3:4** *The fathers*: the biblical patriarchs, or else the first Christian generation. *Fell asleep*: died. **3:5** *Standing out . . . in the water*: probably a reference to the role of the primeval waters in the creation of the earth (cf. Gen 1:2, 6–10), and better rendered "established out of the water and amidst [or by means of] the water." **3:6** *Whereby the world . . . perished*: as God created the world by water and his word, so did he destroy the world by water and his word. The author recognizes Genesis's presentation of the flood as an act of anti-creation (see Gen 7:11 and note). **3:7** *The heavens . . . fire*: cf. Deut 32:22; Isa 66:15–16. The idea of an eschatological conflagration is common in postbiblical Jewish literature. **3:8** *One day . . . day*: adapting Ps 90:4. **3:9** *To us-ward*: better "toward you" (MS tradition). *Not willing . . . repentance*: cf. Rom 2:4 (and note), perhaps the passage lying behind the author's reference to Paul in v. 15. **3:10** *As a thief in the night*: better simply "as a thief"; see 1 Thess 5:2 note.

heat, the earth also and the works that are therein shall be burned up. [11]Seeing then that all these things shall be dissolved, what manner of persons ought ye to be in all holy conversation and godliness, [12]looking for and hasting unto the coming of the day of God, wherein the heavens being on fire shall be dissolved, and the elements shall melt with fervent heat? [13]Nevertheless we, according to his promise, look for new heavens and a new earth, wherein dwelleth righteousness.

[14]Wherefore, beloved, seeing that ye look for such things, be diligent that ye may be found of him in peace, without spot, and blameless. [15]And account that the longsuffering of our Lord is salvation; even as our beloved brother Paul also according to the wisdom given unto him hath written unto you; [16]as also in all his epistles, speaking in them of these things; in which are some things hard to be understood, which they that are unlearned and unstable wrest, as they do also the other scriptures, unto their own destruction.

[17]Ye therefore, beloved, seeing ye know these things before, beware lest ye also, being led away with the error of the wicked, fall from your own stedfastness. [18]But grow in grace, and in the knowledge of our Lord and Saviour Jesus Christ.

To him be glory both now and for ever. Amen.

Shall be burned up: better "will be discovered" (MS tradition). The dissolution of the elements will lay God's creation bare, leaving nowhere for the wicked to hide (cf. Rev 6:15–16 and notes). **3:13** *New heavens . . . earth*: cf. Isa 65:17; 66:22; Rev 21:1. **3:14–16** *Wherefore, beloved . . . destruction*: a reference to Paul's writings about God's delayed judgment (v. 15; cf. 9 and note) urging readers not to be influenced by perverse interpretations of them. **3:15** *Our beloved brother Paul*: some speculate that this friendly reference aims to smooth over the documented tension between Peter and Paul (Gal 2:11–14). **3:16** *As they . . . destruction*: the inclusion of Paul's letters among the *scriptures* suggests a date of composition well after Paul's (and Peter's) death. Many scholars see an allusion to second-century gnostic invocations of Pauline writings. (Gnostics, like the opponents whom 2 Peter addresses, denied the eschatological renewal of the cosmos, hoping instead for spiritual liberation from the corrupt material world.) *Wrest*: twist or distort.

3:17–18 Closing. A final exhortation that echoes the salutation precedes a brief benediction. **3:18** *Grow in grace . . . Christ*: cf. 1:2.

The First Epistle General of John

SINCE 1 John lacks a conventional salutation and closing, it is better classified as an essay than a letter. Its evident similarities to the Fourth Gospel explain why the New Testament attributes both to the same author; but though it is possible that the same person penned them, most scholars today account for their points of contact by hypothesizing common origination in a single network of early Christian churches, with 2 and 3 John (and, some believe, Revelation as well) deriving from this same extended Christian community. The Gospel of John would have been the community's fullest and most authoritative expression of its thought about Christ, which 1, 2, and 3 John liberally echo in various polemical contexts. This theory implies dates of composition for 1 John and the two remaining Johannine epistles (which actually are epistles) sometime after John's Gospel, perhaps slightly later than 100 C.E.

1 John informs us of a split within the Johannine community (2:19), and its author singles out a particular problem with the secessionists' doctrine: namely, that they do not believe "Jesus Christ is come in the flesh" (4:2–3; cf. 2:18–23). Exactly what this means is impossible to determine, but one hypothesis is particularly attractive. In the second century C.E., Christians who embraced a version of the gnostic myth understood Jesus to be divine in a very attenuated sense. Apparently drawing on a tradition included in the canonical gospels, they asserted that at Jesus' baptism a spiritual being called Christ descended into him in the form of a dove (Matt 3:16; Mark 1:10; Luke 3:21–22; cf. John 1:32–33) and that this same Spirit departed from Jesus immediately before his crucifixion (see, e.g., Ptolemy's version of the Valentinian gnostic myth in Irenaeus, *Against Heresies* 1.7.2; Appendix, p. 1062). Such a Christology eliminates the evident absurdity of a divinity being executed, but it clashes with an understanding of Christ's death as an atoning sacrifice—an understanding vital to the present work (see 1:7; 2:2 and notes)—as well as with the suggestion in John that Christ died as a passover sacrifice for the world (1:29, 36; 17:19; 19:14 and notes). If the spiritual Christ escaped its corporeal shell before Jesus' death, then it becomes difficult to comprehend that death as a cosmically effective sacrifice.

The existence of the gnostic myths preserved in Irenaeus's *Against Heresies* and other ancient works cannot be confirmed until the end of the second century C.E., at least several decades after 1 John's likely date of composition. Moreover, as mentioned above, 1 John concerns itself with those who have left the Johannine community and not with an independent, rival sects. Thus, rather than being a straightforward polemic against gnostic Christianity, this essay was apparently written in response to the departure of a group of believers who seem to have been inspired by some of the same theological ideas that would also come to animate gnostics. Those ideas were later systematized and elaborated as the gnostics composed, studied, and rewrote various versions of the so-called gnostic myth, many of which are extant today. (Later gnostic sects may have derived from the disaffected Johannine believers, but there is no direct evidence of such a link.)

These ideas might have appealed to some Johannine believers because they offered a neat resolution of the ambivalence that characterizes the Fourth Gospel's discourse about Christ's flesh. In John 6:51–58, for instance, Jesus orders his followers to consume his flesh and blood if they want to have life, but then, just a few verses later, goes on to insist, "It is the Spirit that gives life [KJV 'quickeneth']; the flesh profiteth nothing" (6:63). More broadly, John's prologue identifies Jesus as "the Word . . . made flesh" (1:14), but in the gospel's concluding resurrection stories Jesus can chastise his followers' attempts to examine or even touch his flesh in order to confirm his identity (20:24–29, cf. 16–17). Johannine secessionists would presumably have embraced the spiritual pole of these exegetical oppositions, and perhaps drew on the story of the divine spirit's possession of the man Jesus at the moment of his baptism to assert, as 1 John states they did, that Christ had not really "come in the flesh" at all. It may even be that the Fourth Gospel omits any reference to Jesus' baptism and neglects to narrate the Spirit's dove-like descent directly, instead assigning it to John the Baptist's testimony about Jesus (1:32–34), because its author knew of this particular interpretation and did not want the gospel used to authorize it.

1 John's engagement with proto-gnostic ideas is not confined to meditation on Christ's flesh. Its treatment of the story of Cain's murder of Abel (3:12; cf. Gen 4) also seems to reflect and respond to gnosticizing biblical exegesis. The author introduces this biblical story by contrasting the children of God with children of the devil (3:8–9) and explaining the wickedness of the latter as a failure to love their brethren (3:10–11). A rather sweeping conclusion is drawn from the story— "Whosoever hateth his brother is a murderer" (3:15)—followed by the suggestion that such hatred is evident in a refusal to share one's life and livelihood (3:17). This suggestion seems to look back to the author's denunciation of the secessionists' abandonment of their community.

Cain was regarded by gnostics and others as Satan's child (e.g., *Apocryphon of John* II 24.8–34), an imaginative elaboration of Eve's declaration at Cain's birth that she had "gotten a man from the Lord" (Gen 4:1). Some ancient exegetes took this as a claim by Eve to have copulated with God—but, recognizing its absurdity and struck by Cain's subsequent wickedness, they concluded she must unwittingly have been seduced by Satan. 1 John's invocation of the story of Cain and Abel in the context of a comparison between God's children and the devil's points to an awareness of this interpretive tradition, which was especially important to gnostics. That importance comes into relief when we examine a standard gnostic interpretation of Gen 4:25, where Eve says at Seth's birth that "God . . . hath appointed me another seed instead of Abel, whom Cain slew." Many gnostics took her statement about Seth as literally as they had her earlier claim about Cain, understanding a higher power to have been mystically involved in Seth's generation (see *Apocryphon of John* II 24.35–25.7). Tracing their own spiritual heritage through the righteous Seth to God, they sometimes called themselves "the seed of Seth" and, by implied opposition, traced the descent of all others from the devil through Cain. Though 1 John does not explicitly mention Seth, it does allude to Gen 4:25: "Whosoever is born of God doth not commit sin; for his seed remaineth in him: and he cannot sin, because he is born of God" (3:9).

The author of 1 John turns on its head this particular interpretation of the story of Cain, Abel, and Seth, which is attested in later gnostic writings and was presumably part of the secessionists' self-understanding as well. The secessionists with their gnosticizing Christology become children of Cain: having abandoned their brethren, they reenact Cain's hatred for his brother. Those who remain are likened to Abel insofar as they innocently suffer this hatred (see 3:12). But that analogy is only partial, for the author goes on to state, "We know that we have passed from death unto life, because we love the brethren" (3:14). In the context of the essay's exegesis of the Cain and Abel story, this appears to be a reference to the birth of Seth (alluded to in 3:9), whom, as noted above, Eve identifies as a divinely granted replacement for Abel. It is the Johannine believers, then, who are descended through Seth from God (though Seth himself is apparently unimportant to 1 John's author). The proto-gnostic secessionists, for their part, have descended through Cain from the devil.

Thus 1 John, despite its many similarities to the Gospel of John, ultimately complements that book rather than imitates it. Whereas the Fourth Gospel tends to direct its polemical edge at "the Jews," and frequently reflects the tension between synagogue and church that marked the emergence of Christianity as a religion distinct from Judaism (e.g., 9:22 and note, 28), 1 John's polemic is directed primarily at fellow believers in Jesus and looks forward to later debates among Christians about what dogma, practices, and traditions constituted authentic Christianity. During those debates, the proto-orthodox like Irenaeus would boldly define their own doctrine and praxis against heterogeneous "heretical" sects, which they frequently lumped together under the label "gnostics." The first tentative steps in this direction are evident in a handful of New Testament passages (e.g., 1 Tim 1:4; 6:20; see notes), but perhaps nowhere so pervasively as in 1 John, whose complex and imaginative response to proto-gnostic theology and biblical exegesis anticipates and in some ways surpasses the work of even the more sophisticated writers against heresy in later centuries.

For detailed exegesis of 1 John in particular, and of the Johannine epistles in general, see Raymond E. Brown's Anchor Bible commentary, *The Epistles of John: A New Translation with Introduction and Commentary* (Garden City, NY: Doubleday, 1982). Georg Strecker's Hermeneia commentary, *The Johannine Letters: A Commentary on 1, 2, and 3 John*, trans. Linda M. Maloney (Minneapolis, MN: Fortress, 1996), is also useful. Both have influenced the introductions and annotations for 1, 2, and 3 John.

THE FIRST EPISTLE GENERAL OF
JOHN

1 That which was from the beginning, which we have heard, which we have seen with our eyes, which we have looked upon, and our hands have handled, of the Word of life; [2](for the life was manifested, and we have seen it, and bear witness, and shew unto you that eternal life, which was with the Father, and was manifested unto us;) [3]that which we have seen and heard declare we unto you, that ye also may have fellowship with us: and truly our fellowship is with the Father, and with his Son Jesus Christ. [4]And these things write we unto you, that your joy may be full.

[5]This then is the message which we have heard of him, and declare unto you, that God is light, and in him is no darkness at all. [6]If we say that we have fellowship with him, and walk in darkness, we lie, and do not the truth: [7]but if we walk in the light, as he is in the light, we have fellowship one with another, and the blood of Jesus Christ his Son cleanseth us from all sin. [8]If we say that we have no sin, we deceive ourselves, and the truth is not in us. [9]If we confess our sins, he is faithful and just to forgive us our sins, and to cleanse us from all unrighteousness. [10]If we say that we have not sinned, we make him a liar, and his word is not in us.

1:1–4 Prologue. Although 1 John has traditionally been regarded as a letter, its introduction lacks the characteristic formulae with which Greco-Roman letters open. Instead, the language and imagery here frequently recall the prologue of John (1:1–18). The similarities are likely deliberate, with the use of "we" self-consciously associating its writer with the Fourth Gospel's authoritative witness (see John 21:24), which is invoked and interpreted throughout the document that follows. **1:1** *Which we . . . handled*: compare the similar emphasis on observable and tangible evidence at John's close (e.g., 20:16–31; 21:24–25). *Of the Word of life*: better "concerning the word of life," but the syntax is undeniably awkward. **1:2** *Shew*: more literally "declare" (cf. v. 3). *Eternal life*: a common promise to believers in John; e.g., 3:15–16, 36; 5:24; 6:40. **1:4** *Unto you . . . full*: better "that our joy may be full" (MS tradition); cf. John 3:29; 15:11; 16:24; 17:13.

1:5–2:11 Light and darkness. This section defines the "fellowship . . . with the Father" announced in the prologue. Its imagery, though conventional, particularly recalls a number of passages from John (e.g. 1:4–9; 3:19–21; 8:12; 9:4–5; 11:9–10; 12:35–36, 46). But 1 John associates God with the light, while John tends to use light as an image of Christ. **1:5** *God is . . . all*: this rhetorical device—stating something positively, and then immediately expressing the same idea negatively (or vice versa)—is characteristic of this author's style; cf. vv. 6, 8; 2:4, 7; etc. **1:6–7** *If we . . . another*: introducing an idea common in 1 John, as in John: that love of God (here *fellowship* with him) necessarily involves obedience to his commandments, especially the directive to love (here *have fellowship with*) one another (cf. John 14:15, 21; 15:9–12). It is precisely this commandment that the author will argue the secessionists have broken. **1:7** *The blood . . . sin*: assimilating Jesus' death to a sin offering, most likely that associated with the Day of Atonement described in Lev 16 (vv. 15–19; see esp. v. 30). **1:9** *If we . . . unrighteousness*: cf. Jas 5:16.

2 My little children, these things write I unto you, that ye sin not. And if any man sin, we have an advocate with the Father, Jesus Christ the righteous: ²and he is the propitiation for our sins: and not for ours only, but also for the sins of the whole world.

³And hereby we do know that we know him, if we keep his commandments. ⁴He that saith, I know him, and keepeth not his commandments, is a liar, and the truth is not in him. ⁵But whoso keepeth his word, in him verily is the love of God perfected: hereby know we that we are in him. ⁶He that saith he abideth in him ought himself also so to walk, even as he walked.

⁷Brethren, I write no new commandment unto you, but an old commandment which ye had from the beginning. The old commandment is the word which ye have heard from the beginning. ⁸Again, a new commandment I write unto you, which thing is true in him and in you: because the darkness is past, and the true light now shineth. ⁹He that saith he is in the light, and hateth his brother, is in darkness even until now. ¹⁰He that loveth his brother abideth in the light, and there is none occasion of stumbling in him. ¹¹But he that hateth his brother is in darkness, and walketh in darkness, and knoweth not whither he goeth, because that darkness hath blinded his eyes.

¹²I write unto you, little children, because your sins are forgiven you for his name's sake. ¹³I write unto you, fathers, because ye have known him that is from the beginning. I write unto you, young men, because ye have overcome the wicked one. I write unto you, little children, because ye have known the Father. ¹⁴I have written unto you, fathers, because ye have known him that is from the beginning. I have written unto you, young men, because ye are strong, and the word of God abideth in you, and ye have overcome the wicked one.

¹⁵Love not the world, neither the things that are in the world. If any man love

---

2:1 *Advocate*: Gk. *paraklētos*; cf. John 14:16 and note.   **2:2** *Propitiation*: atonement; see 1:7 note; cf. Heb 9:1–10:31. *The sins . . . world*: cf. John 1:29; 3:16–17; etc.   **2:3–6** *And hereby . . . walked*: see 1:6–7 note.   **2:6** *Abideth*: Gk. *menō*, a key word for 1 John, as it is for John (see 1:32 note).   **2:7** *Brethren*: better "beloved" (MS tradition). *No new . . . old commandment*: the *old commandment*, which is in fact also a *new commandment* (see v. 8), recalls John 13:34, whose "new commandment" to "love one another" is closely related to Lev 19:18. *Heard from the beginning*: better simply "heard" (MS tradition).   **2:8** *Again*: better "yet" or "on the other hand."   **2:9** *Brother*: fellow believer, as often in the NT.

2:12–17 Believers and the world. Various symbolic interpretations of the groups listed in this passage have been proposed. Origen and others saw an allusive reference to three stages of Christian maturity. Augustine saw Christians as a whole addressed by different titles: e.g., children, insofar as they are reborn through baptism; young men, insofar as they vigorously resist Satan. The author may also be addressing literal fathers, youth, children, and slaves (cf. Eph 5:22–6:9 and note).   **2:13** *Overcome the wicked one*: a reference to the devil's defeat, recalling John 12:31; 16:11, cf. 33. *I write*: the third appearance of this phrase should be in the past tense (MS tradition), as it is in v. 14. The variation is probably stylistic, but some have argued for a reference to an earlier writing, especially to John. *Little children*: Gk. *paidia*; in v. 12, the phrase translates *teknia*. It is possible that the Greek words refer to distinct groups of believers (*paidia* can also refer to young slaves, and the clauses accompanying the two words are quite different). On the other hand, the writer uses these words interchangeably in addressing his readers (*paidia* in v. 18; *teknia* in v. 28).   **2:15** *The world*: as frequently in the Fourth Gospel, here the world is conceptualized as a realm opposed to God (see, e.g.,

the world, the love of the Father is not in him. [16]For all that is in the world, the lust of the flesh, and the lust of the eyes, and the pride of life, is not of the Father, but is of the world. [17]And the world passeth away, and the lust thereof: but he that doeth the will of God abideth for ever.

[18]Little children, it is the last time: and as ye have heard that antichrist shall come, even now are there many antichrists; whereby we know that it is the last time. [19]They went out from us, but they were not of us; for if they had been of us, they would no doubt have continued with us: but they went out, that they might be made manifest that they were not all of us. [20]But ye have an unction from the Holy One, and ye know all things. [21]I have not written unto you because ye know not the truth, but because ye know it, and that no lie is of the truth. [22]Who is a liar but he that denieth that Jesus is the Christ? He is antichrist, that denieth the Father and the Son. [23]Whosoever denieth the Son, the same hath not the Father: [but] he that acknowledgeth the Son hath the Father also. [24]Let that therefore abide in you, which ye have heard from the beginning. If that which ye have heard from the beginning shall remain in you, ye also shall continue in the Son, and in the Father. [25]And this is the promise that he hath promised us, even eternal life.

[26]These things have I written unto you concerning them that seduce you. [27]But the anointing which ye have received of him abideth in you, and ye need not that any man teach you: but as the same anointing teacheth you of all things, and is truth, and is no lie, and even as it hath taught you, ye shall abide in him. [28]And now, little children, abide in him; that, when he shall appear, we may have confidence, and not be ashamed before him at his coming.

John 7:7; 15:18–19). The "wicked one" mentioned in vv. 13–14 is in John called the "prince of this world" (12:31 and note; 14:30; 16:11).   **2:16** *Life*: Gk. *bios*, also "livelihood," with reference to wealth or possessions.   **2:17** *The world passeth away*: cf. 1 Cor 7:29–31.

2:18–28 Truth and lies. Up to this point, the secessionists (v. 19) whom the writer wishes to denounce have figured only implicitly, as those who might make false claims (1:6, 8, 10; 2:4, 6, 9); here they are identified as antichrists whose false teaching heralds the eschatological consummation.   **2:18** *Antichrist*: a transliteration of Gk. *antichristos*, a term occurring in the NT only in this chapter (also at v. 22), in 4:3, and in 2 John 7. Its basic meaning is "one who replaces (or opposes) Christ." Other NT texts anticipate deceptive substitutes for Christ in the time preceding the eschatological consummation; see, e.g., Mark 13:5–6, 21–22 and parallels.   **2:20** *Unction*: anointing, a figure of consecration (cf. 2 Cor 1:21–22 and notes). On the basis of comparison with John 14:26, its association with knowledge here and in v. 27 may suggest that it symbolizes the Holy Spirit. Ancient Christian baptism sometimes involved anointing initiates with oil, and a reference to this practice would complement that symbolism (since baptism and the Holy Spirit are conceptually linked throughout the NT; see, e.g., Matt 3:11; John 1:33; 1 Cor 12:13), but the date at which baptismal anointing began is uncertain. *Ye know all things*: better "all of you have knowledge" (MS tradition; NRSV).   **2:22** *Denieth that . . . Christ*: see 4:2 and note for a possible explanation of this denial.   **2:23** *Whosoever denieth . . . also*: cf. John 5:23; 14:6–11; 15:23; etc.   **2:25** *Eternal life*: see 1:2 note.   **2:26** *Seduce*: Gk. *planaō*, more literally "deceive" (as in 3:7).   **2:27** *Ye shall abide*: better "abide" or "you all abide" (MS tradition).

²⁹If ye know that he is righteous, ye know that every one that doeth righteousness is born of him. ¹Behold, what manner of love the Father hath bestowed upon us, that we should be called the sons of God: therefore the world knoweth us not, because it knew him not. ²Beloved, now are we the sons of God, and it doth not yet appear what we shall be: but we know that, when he shall appear, we shall be like him; for we shall see him as he is. ³And every man that hath this hope in him purifieth himself, even as he is pure.

⁴Whosoever committeth sin transgresseth also the law: for sin is the transgression of the law. ⁵And ye know that he was manifested to take away our sins; and in him is no sin. ⁶Whosoever abideth in him sinneth not: whosoever sinneth hath not seen him, neither known him. ⁷Little children, let no man deceive you: he that doeth righteousness is righteous, even as he is righteous. ⁸He that committeth sin is of the devil; for the devil sinneth from the beginning. For this purpose the Son of God was manifested, that he might destroy the works of the devil. ⁹Whosoever is born of God doth not commit sin; for his seed remaineth in him: and he cannot sin, because he is born of God. ¹⁰In this the children of God are manifest, and the children of the devil: whosoever doeth not righteousness is not of God, neither he that loveth not his brother.

¹¹For this is the message that ye heard from the beginning, that we should love one another. ¹²Not as Cain, who was of that wicked one, and slew his brother. And wherefore slew he him? Because his own works were evil, and his brother's righteous. ¹³Marvel not, my brethren, if the world hate you. ¹⁴We know that we have passed from death unto life, because we love the brethren. He that loveth not his brother abideth in death. ¹⁵Whosoever hateth his brother is a murderer: and ye

2:29–3:17 Children of God and children of the devil. The author's initially abstract meditation on this symbolic opposition leads directly to a specific interpretation of Cain's murder of Abel in Genesis (see 3:15 note), the former traditionally thought to have been fathered by the devil (see 3:12 note). **2:29** *Born of him*: cf. John 1:12–13; 3:3–8. **3:1** *Sons of God*: better to add "and that is what we are" (MS tradition). *The world . . . him not*: John 1:10; cf. 15:21. **3:2** *Sons*: lit. "children." *It doth . . . is*: cf. 1 Cor 13:12; see also John 14:19; 17:24. The author probably has in mind the eschatological assimilation of believers' bodies to the risen Christ's, about which Paul speculates at length in 1 Cor 15 (see notes). **3:4** *Transgresseth also . . . of the law*: alternatively "acts lawlessly, for sin is lawlessness," which would describe sin as libertine immorality rather than as legal transgression. The same translation difficulty arises in Rom 2:12 (see note). **3:5** *Our*: better omitted (MS tradition). **3:6** *Whosoever abideth in him sinneth not*: contradicting 1:8. The author seems to have a flexible understanding of what it means to be sinless; cf. 5:16–18. **3:8** *For the devil . . . beginning*: in light of the deception mentioned in v. 7, this likely alludes to the devil's role in Eve's transgression of God's commandment (see Gen 3:13; cf. John 8:44 and note). **3:9** *His seed*: i.e., Christ, although the verse probably alludes to Gen 4:25 (see introduction). **3:11** *We should . . . another*: another reference to John 13:34 (see 1 John 2:7 and note); cf. John 15:12. **3:12** *Cain, who . . . brother*: the story of Cain and Abel (Gen 4) is also alluded to at John 8:44. In the context of a discussion of divine and satanic generation, the statement that Cain *was of that wicked one* probably alludes to a version of the story in which the devil fathered Cain. It survives in gnostic rewritings of Genesis and in later Jewish legend. *And wherefore . . . righteous*: this heavily moralizing interpretation goes far beyond the Genesis account, which is characteristically reticent about characters' motives. It may also depend on later rewritings of the story. **3:13** *The world hate you*: cf. John 15:18–19; 17:14. **3:14** *Passed from death unto life*: cf. John 5:24. *His brother*: better omitted (MS tradition). **3:15** *Whosoever hateth . . .*

know that no murderer hath eternal life abiding in him. [16]Hereby perceive we the love of God, because he laid down his life for us: and we ought to lay down our lives for the brethren. [17]But whoso hath this world's good, and seeth his brother have need, and shutteth up his bowels of compassion from him, how dwelleth the love of God in him?

[18]My little children, let us not love in word, neither in tongue; but in deed and in truth. [19]And hereby we know that we are of the truth, and shall assure our hearts before him. [20]For if our heart condemn us, God is greater than our heart, and knoweth all things. [21]Beloved, if our heart condemn us not, then have we confidence toward God. [22]And whatsoever we ask, we receive of him, because we keep his commandments, and do those things that are pleasing in his sight. [23]And this is his commandment, That we should believe on the name of his Son Jesus Christ, and love one another, as he gave us commandment. [24]And he that keepeth his commandments dwelleth in him, and he in him. And hereby we know that he abideth in us, by the Spirit which he hath given us.

4 Beloved, believe not every spirit, but try the spirits whether they are of God: because many false prophets are gone out into the world. [2]Hereby know ye the Spirit of God: Every spirit that confesseth that Jesus Christ is come in the flesh is of God: [3]and every spirit that confesseth not that Jesus Christ is come in the flesh is not of God: and this is that spirit of antichrist, whereof ye have heard that it should come; and even now already is it in the world. [4]Ye are of God, little children, and have overcome them: because greater is he that is in you, than he that is in the world. [5]They are of the world: therefore speak they of the world, and the world heareth them. [6]We are of God: he that knoweth God heareth us; he that

---

a murderer: this claim functions as a linchpin for the author's symbolic interpretation of the story. It suggests that Cain represents the secessionists, whose abandonment of the community (2:19) testifies to a hatred of their brethren, and that Abel represents the community, an innocent victim of that hatred (whose consequences were material, as 3:17 suggests). But the community is also associated with Seth, "another seed" that God "hath appointed . . . instead of Abel" (Gen 4:25; cf. 1 John 2:9), and thus it has "passed from death unto life" (3:14).   **3:16** *Of God*: better omitted (MS tradition). *He laid . . . brethren*: the antithesis of Cain's action. The formulation recalls John 15:12–13; cf. 10:11, 15, 17.   **3:17** *Good*: Gk. *bios* (see 2:16 note). *Bowels of compassion*: bowels are a conventional a seat of emotion, though not necessarily of *compassion*.

3:18–4:6 Truth and error. 3:20 *For if*: alternatively "as to whatever" or "whereinsoever" (RV), with the first clause of v. 20 continuing the previous verse's sentence and the second clause beginning a new one.   **3:21** *Confidence*: Gk. *parrēsia*, frankness or boldness of speech.   **3:22** *Whatsoever we . . . him*: cf. John 14:13–14; 15:7, 16; 16:23–27.   **3:23** *This is . . . another*: cf. John 6:29; 13:34; 15:12; 20:31.   **3:24** *He that . . . given us*: recalling John 14:15–26, which links the sending of God's spirit to the keeping of his commandments.   **4:1** *Believe not . . . God*: a common biblical injunction; cf. Deut 13:1–5; 18:20–22; 1 Cor 12:3; etc. *Many false prophets . . . world*: cf. Matt 7:15–23 and notes; 24:24; Mark 13:22; etc.   **4:2** *That Jesus . . . flesh*: presumably resisting a proto-gnostic Christology that radically separated the spiritual and divine Christ from the material and human Jesus, and that went so far as to question the reality of the latter (see Irenaeus, *Against Heresies* 1.7.2; Appendix, p. 1062; cf. 1.30.12–13).   **4:3** *That Jesus . . . flesh*: better simply "Jesus" (MS tradition). *This is . . . world*: Matt 24:24 and Mark 13:22 likewise combine anxiety about false prophets (cf. v. 1 above) and false Christs.   **4:4** *Ye are . . . world*: cf. John 16:33. Believers share in Christ's victory. *He that is in the world*: see 2:15 note.   **4:5–6** *They are . . . not us*: this passage suggests that the secessionists

is not of God heareth not us. Hereby know we the spirit of truth, and the spirit of error.

⁷Beloved, let us love one another: for love is of God; and every one that loveth is born of God, and knoweth God. ⁸He that loveth not knoweth not God; for God is love. ⁹In this was manifested the love of God toward us, because that God sent his only begotten Son into the world, that we might live through him. ¹⁰Herein is love, not that we loved God, but that he loved us, and sent his Son to be the propitiation for our sins. ¹¹Beloved, if God so loved us, we ought also to love one another. ¹²No man hath seen God at any time. If we love one another, God dwelleth in us, and his love is perfected in us.

¹³Hereby know we that we dwell in him, and he in us, because he hath given us of his Spirit. ¹⁴And we have seen and do testify that the Father sent the Son to be the Saviour of the world. ¹⁵Whosoever shall confess that Jesus is the Son of God, God dwelleth in him, and he in God. ¹⁶And we have known and believed the love that God hath to us.

God is love; and he that dwelleth in love dwelleth in God, and God in him. ¹⁷Herein is our love made perfect, that we may have boldness in the day of judgment: because as he is, so are we in this world. ¹⁸There is no fear in love; but perfect love casteth out fear: because fear hath torment. He that feareth is not made perfect in love. ¹⁹We love him, because he first loved us. ²⁰If a man say, I love God, and hateth his brother, he is a liar: for he that loveth not his brother whom he hath seen, how can he love God whom he hath not seen? ²¹And this commandment have we from him, That he who loveth God love his brother also.

5 Whosoever believeth that Jesus is the Christ is born of God: and every one that loveth him that begat loveth him also that is begotten of him. ²By this we know that we love the children of God, when we love God, and keep his commandments. ³For this is the love of God, that we keep his commandments: and his commandments are not grievous. ⁴For whatsoever is born of God overcometh the world: and this is the victory that overcometh the world, even our faith.

("they . . . of the world") experience greater missionary success than the author's community. Its explanation of that development recalls the frequent emphasis in John on the world's failure to hear or understand Jesus (e.g., 1:10–11; 8:21–27; cf. 17:14–21).   **4:6** *Spirit of truth*: cf. John 14:17; 15:26; 16:13. *Spirit of error*: the phrase appears nowhere else in the NT, but it is found in other ancient Jewish literature (*Testament of Judah* 14.8; 20.1, contrasted with the spirit of truth; 25.3) and may be related to the "counterfeit spirit" from the gnostic *Apocryphon of John* (II 29.10–30.11).
   4:7–5:4 God's love and the community's. **4:9** *In this . . . him*: cf. John 3:16–17.   **4:10** *Propitiation for our sins*: see 2:2 note.   **4:11** *If God . . . another*: cf. John 13:34; 15:12–13.   **4:12** *No man . . . time*: cf. John 1:18; 6:46.   **4:14** *The Father . . . world*: cf. John 3:17; 4:42; 12:47; etc.   **4:16** *To us*: alternatively "in us."   **4:17** *Boldness*: Gk. *parrēsia* (see 3:21 note).   **4:18** *Fear*: i.e., fear of God's judgment. *Hath torment*: or "has to do with punishment" (NRSV).   **4:19** *We love*: alternatively "let us love." *Him*: better omitted (MS tradition).   **4:21** *He who . . . also*: recalling Jesus' teaching in the synoptic tradition (Matt 22:34–40; Mark 12:28–34; cf. Luke 10:25–28), where he responds to a question about the "first commandment of all" by quoting both Deut 6:4–5 (calling for love of God) and Lev 19:18 (requiring love of one's neighbor).   **5:1** *Whoever believeth . . . God*: cf. John 1:12–13. *Born, begat, begotten*: all Gk. *gennaō*. (lit. "beget"), as in 5:18.   **5:3** *This is . . . keep his commandments*: cf. John 14:15, 21; 15:10. *His commandments . . . grievous*: cf. Matt 11:30.   **5:4** *Overcometh the world*: see 4:4 note.

⁵Who is he that overcometh the world, but he that believeth that Jesus is the Son of God? ⁶This is he that came by water and blood, even Jesus Christ; not by water only, but by water and blood. And it is the Spirit that beareth witness, because the Spirit is truth. ⁷For there are three that bear record in heaven, the Father, the Word, and the Holy Ghost: and these three are one. ⁸And there are three that bear witness in earth, the spirit, and the water, and the blood: and these three agree in one. ⁹If we receive the witness of men, the witness of God is greater: for this is the witness of God which he hath testified of his Son. ¹⁰He that believeth on the Son of God hath the witness in himself: he that believeth not God hath made him a liar; because he believeth not the record that God gave of his Son. ¹¹And this is the record, that God hath given to us eternal life, and this life is in his Son. ¹²He that hath the Son hath life; and he that hath not the Son of God hath not life. ¹³These things have I written unto you that believe on the name of the Son of God; that ye may know that ye have eternal life, and that ye may believe on the name of the Son of God.

¹⁴And this is the confidence that we have in him, that, if we ask any thing according to his will, he heareth us: ¹⁵and if we know that he hear us, whatsoever we ask, we know that we have the petitions that we desired of him.

¹⁶If any man see his brother sin a sin which is not unto death, he shall ask, and he shall give him life for them that sin not unto death. There is a sin unto death: I do not say that he shall pray for it. ¹⁷All unrighteousness is sin: and there is a sin not unto death.

5:5–13 Testimony to the Son. 5:6–8 *Water and . . . one*: see John 19:34–35 and notes; cf. 7:37–39, which links water with the Spirit.   **5:6** *Not by water only* probably refers to Jesus' baptism, not mentioned in the Fourth Gospel but especially important to some gnostic sects. The Valentinians, for instance, believed that it was at his baptism that Christ descended into Jesus in the form of a dove (see Matt 3:16; Mark 1:10; Luke 3:21–22; cf. John 1:32–34), later departing from him in advance of his crucifixion (Irenaeus, *Against Heresies* 1.7.2; see Appendix, p. 1062). In this light, *not by water only, but by water and blood* seems to be a polemical response to a proto-gnostic Christology that viewed Jesus' baptism as the crucial moment in his mission—the point when the divine being Christ tentatively united with the human being Jesus, only to disentangle itself just before his passion began (cf. 4:2 and note above). This Christology accounted for Jesus' powerful ministry but avoided the evident absurdity of a divine being suffering and dying. In the Johannine tradition, on the contrary, Jesus Christ is the divine word incarnate (John 1:14): divinity not housed in but intimately conjoined with man. Also, for the Johannine tradition the crucial moment of Jesus' ministry is his demise (see John 12:27–33; 19:30), when water flowed alongside blood from Jesus' corpse (John 19:34), a depiction that imaginatively assimilated and subordinated his baptism (which John never narrates or mentions) to his sacrificial death.   **5:7–8** *In heaven . . . earth*: better omitted (MS tradition), as a later Trinitarian scribal interpolation.   **5:9** *If we . . . greater*: cf. John 5:31–38; 8:14–18.   **5:10–11** *He that believeth on . . . his Son*: John 3:16 and 11:25–26 likewise link belief in Jesus with eternal life.   **5:13** *Unto you that believe on the name of the Son of God*: better simply "unto you" (MS tradition). *And that ye*: better "who" (MS tradition). This closing verse, like 1:1 above, recalls John 20:31, which states that gospel's purpose.

    5:14–21 Conclusion. 5:14–15 *And this . . . him*: see 3:21–22 and notes.   **5:16** *A sin unto death*: probably a lack of love for one's brethren (see 3:14), but other Christian writings understand different sins to be unforgiveable (see, e.g., Mark 3:28–30; Heb 6:4–6).

¹⁸We know that whosoever is born of God sinneth not; but he that is begotten of God keepeth himself, and that wicked one toucheth him not. ¹⁹And we know that we are of God, and the whole world lieth in wickedness. ²⁰And we know that the Son of God is come, and hath given us an understanding, that we may know him that is true, and we are in him that is true, even in his Son Jesus Christ. This is the true God, and eternal life.

²¹Little children, keep yourselves from idols. Amen.

5:18 *Himself*: better "him" (MS tradition), so that the verse refers to the injunction of v. 16, unless *he that is begotten of God* is to be understood here as Jesus. *That wicked one*: Satan.   **5:21** *Keep yourself from idols*: probably to be taken figuratively, as a command to separate from the world. *Amen*: better omitted (MS tradition).

The Second Epistle of John

FOR general background on the Johannine epistles, see the first paragraph of 1 John's introduction.

2 and 3 John were almost certainly composed by the same author, who may also have been responsible for 1 John, although the points of contact between 1 John and the others may merely evince their origination in a common theological and discursive milieu. The warnings against false teachers in verses 7–11 seem to refer to the secessionists that 1 John mentions (see notes), or perhaps to rival teachers who have siphoned off some Johannine believers from the community. Unlike 1 John, however, the present text does not offer a competing theology, or even denigrate the opponents exegetically; instead it simply disparages them as deceivers and urges its readers to deny them hospitality.

THE SECOND EPISTLE OF

JOHN

The elder unto the elect lady and her children, whom I love in the truth; and not I only, but also all they that have known the truth; ²for the truth's sake, which dwelleth in us, and shall be with us for ever. ³Grace be with you, mercy, and peace, from God the Father, and from the Lord Jesus Christ, the Son of the Father, in truth and love.

⁴I rejoiced greatly that I found of thy children walking in truth, as we have received a commandment from the Father. ⁵And now I beseech thee, lady, not as though I wrote a new commandment unto thee, but that which we had from the beginning, that we love one another. ⁶And this is love, that we walk after his commandments. This is the commandment, That, as ye have heard from the beginning, ye should walk in it.

⁷For many deceivers are entered into the world, who confess not that Jesus Christ is come in the flesh. This is a deceiver and an antichrist. ⁸Look to yourselves, that we lose not those things which we have wrought, but that we receive a full reward. ⁹Whosoever transgresseth, and abideth not in the doctrine of Christ, hath not God. He that abideth in the doctrine of Christ, he hath both the Father and the Son. ¹⁰If there come any unto you, and bring not this doctrine, receive him

1–3 **Salutation.** Adhering to a conventional Greco-Roman epistolary pattern, 2 John begins with the writer's identity, followed by that of the addressee and a greeting.   1 *The elder*: Gk. *presbyteros*, possibly referring to the holder of a particular ecclesiastical office (cf. 1 Tim 4:14; 5:1 and notes); the title could also function as a more general honorific. *Lady*: Gk. *kyria*, the feminine form of *kyrios*, "Lord." It probably figuratively names the church community to which the author writes, with the lady's *children* its individual members.   2 *Dwelleth*: Gk. *menō*, a key word for the Johannine epistles, as it is for John (see 1:32 note).   3 *Grace be . . . Christ*: compare the openings of the Pauline letters, esp. 1 Tim 1:2; 2 Tim 1:2. *With you*: better "with us" (MS tradition).

4–6 **Exhortation to mutual love.** This section recalls 1 John throughout. The notes that follow signal some of the most obvious echoes.   5 *Not as . . . another*: cf. 1 John 2:7 and note; 3:11, 23; 4:11.   6 *This is love . . . commandments*: cf. 1 John 5:2–3 and 3 note.

7–11 **Warning against false teaching.** Similarities between this section and 1 John's statements about the secessionists suggest that the author here is warning the readers about that group.   7 *Many deceivers . . . antichrist*: see 1 John 4:1–3 and notes. *Are entered*: better "have gone out" (MS tradition). *Antichrist*: see 1 John 2:18 note.   8 *We . . . we . . . we*: better "you all . . . you all . . . you all" (MS tradition).   9 *Transgresseth*: better "goes beyond" (MS tradition). *Doctrine*: teaching. *He that . . . Son*: see 1 John 2:23 and note; 4:15.   10–11 *If there . . . deeds*: the elder urges this church to withhold hospitality from opposing teachers, as Diotrephes urged his church to withhold hospitality from the elder (see 3 John 10 and note).   10 *Bid him God speed*: Gk. *chairō*, which can refer to a greeting or leave-taking; here the former is probably relevant.

not into your house, neither bid him God speed: [11]for he that biddeth him God speed is partaker of his evil deeds.

[12]Having many things to write unto you, I would not write with paper and ink: but I trust to come unto you, and speak face to face, that our joy may be full. [13]The children of thy elect sister greet thee. Amen.

12–13 Closing. 12 *Paper:* a sheet of papyrus. *I trust . . . full:* like many of Paul's letters, 2 John closes with mention of an anticipated visit; cf. 1 Cor 16:5–7; 2 Cor 13:1–3, 10. *Our joy . . . full:* cf. 1 John 1:4 and note. **13** *Thy elect sister:* i.e., the ecclesiastical community from which the author writes (see 1 note). *Amen:* better omitted (MS tradition).

The Third Epistle of John

F OR general background on the Johannine epistles, see the first paragraph of 1 John's introduction.

   2 and 3 John were almost certainly composed by the same author, who may also have been responsible for 1 John, although the points of contact between 1 John and the others may merely evince their origination in a common theological and discursive milieu. Like 2 John, 3 John is primarily concerned with hospitality. It is possible, but not certain, that Diotrephes (v. 9) is to be identified as one of the opponents mentioned in 1 and 2 John.

THE THIRD EPISTLE OF
JOHN

The elder unto the wellbeloved Gaius, whom I love in the truth.

²Beloved, I wish above all things that thou mayest prosper and be in health, even as thy soul prospereth. ³For I rejoiced greatly, when the brethren came and testified of the truth that is in thee, even as thou walkest in the truth. ⁴I have no greater joy than to hear that my children walk in truth.

⁵Beloved, thou doest faithfully whatsoever thou doest to the brethren, and to strangers; ⁶which have borne witness of thy charity before the church: whom if thou bring forward on their journey after a godly sort, thou shalt do well: ⁷because that for his name's sake they went forth, taking nothing of the Gentiles. ⁸We therefore ought to receive such, that we might be fellowhelpers to the truth.

⁹I wrote unto the church: but Diotrephes, who loveth to have the preeminence among them, receiveth us not. ¹⁰Wherefore, if I come, I will remember his deeds which he doeth, prating against us with malicious words: and not content therewith, neither doth he himself receive the brethren, and forbiddeth them that would, and casteth them out of the church.

¹¹Beloved, follow not that which is evil, but that which is good. He that doeth good is of God: but he that doeth evil hath not seen God. ¹²Demetrius hath good

1–4 **Salutation and prayer.** Beginning, as conventional for Greco-Roman letters, with the writer's identity, followed by that of the addressee (v. 1), 3 John lacks a formal greeting. As in many of Paul's epistles, a prayer immediately follows the salutation (vv. 2–4). **1** *Wellbeloved*: Gk. *agapētos*, later translated "beloved" (vv. 2, 5, 11), always with reference to Gaius (otherwise unknown). **2** *Wish*: alternatively "pray."

5–12 **Hospitality for itinerant preachers. 5** *Brethren*: fellow believers. *Strangers*: Gk. *xenoi*, implying those in need of hospitality. **6** *Charity*: Gk. *agapē*, "love," which shares its root with "beloved" (see v. 1 note). *Whom if . . . well*: you will do well if you send them on their way in a manner worthy of God. **7–8** *For his . . . truth*: the Synoptic Gospels require itinerant preachers to rely on the hospitality of those to whom they minster; cf. Matt 10:5–16; Mark 6:7–11; Luke 9:1–5. **7** *Gentiles*: presumably, non-Christians. **9** *I wrote . . . church*: probably to inform it of his impending arrival, as in v. 14; 2 John 12. *Who loveth . . . them*: perhaps suggesting that Diotrephes (otherwise unknown) occupied some ecclesiastical office. **10** *Neither doth . . . church*: the NT frequently displays concern about "false prophets," itinerant teachers preaching a gospel with which local church leaders disagree (cf. Matt 7:15–23 and note). Recall Paul's outrage at the Galatians' willingness to consider a gospel different from his own that rival missionaries preached (Gal 1:6–9; 5:7–12; etc.). The elder apparently looked to Diotrephes like such a false prophet, and he therefore prevented the church in which he served from offering hospitality (cf. 2 John 10–11). Some speculate that Diotrephes' hostility stemmed from his association with the secessionists whom 1 and 2 John resist. **11** *He that doeth good . . . seen God*: cf. 1 John 3:6, 10. **12** *Demetrius*: otherwise unknown. He may have been the

report of all men, and of the truth itself: yea, and we also bear record; and ye know that our record is true.

[13]I had many things to write, but I will not with ink and pen write unto thee: [14]but I trust I shall shortly see thee, and we shall speak face to face.

Peace be to thee. Our friends salute thee. Greet the friends by name.

---

bearer of this letter, an itinerant preacher for whom the elder requests hospitality from Gaius (rather than the inhospitable behavior of Diotrephes). *We also . . . true*: echoing John 19:35; 21:24.

13–14 Closing. See 2 John 12–13 and v. 12 note.

The General Epistle of Jude

SHORT, but packed with a vigorous vocabulary, was the description of Jude offered by the third-century Christian scholar Origen (*Commentary on Matthew* 10.17); indeed, although only twenty-five verses long, Jude contains fifteen words not found elsewhere in the New Testament. Most forceful are the terms reserved for the writer's opponents, those who have "crept in unawares," who "speak evil of dignities," and who are called "raging waves of the sea, foaming out their own shame." Exactly who these people were remains a mystery, but the epistle characterizes them as charismatic antinomian libertines, and some scholars argue that they engaged in deliberate provocation in order to demonstrate a spiritual autonomy realized in freedom from conventional moral constraint. Others have speculated that Jude rebukes adherents to one or another Greco-Roman philosophical school whose representatives were influencing his readers—for example, Cynics, who advocated that people reject conventional morality and instead live without shame in accordance with nature, or Epicureans, who argued that people should live their lives free from irrational fear of divine retribution. Such construals are possible, but the textual evidence cited in their support frequently amounts to conventional polemical disparagement, and in the end reveals little reliable information about those who are attacked.

This letter is attributed to James's (and Jesus') brother Jude (see v. 1 note). The attribution may be pseudepigraphical, in particular if verse 17 (see note) is interpreted to suggest a relatively late date of composition (late in the first or early in the second century C.E.). That verse is ambiguous, however, and so circumspect is the author's self-identification—Jude was already a fairly obscure figure in the early church, but here he does not even identify himself as Jesus' sibling—that it perhaps makes more sense to take the attribution at its face than to deny its authenticity. Why would a pseudepigrapher, presumably searching for an authoritative authorial persona, choose the name of someone as relatively unimportant as Jude, and then adopt so unassuming a demeanor besides? If Jude did write the letter, it must have been composed before the end of the first century C.E.

Whoever wrote it, Jude's epistle is largely exegetical. It consistently invokes biblical texts and traditional expansions of them, including noncanonical writings, in order to demonstrate how they all condemn the author's opponents. The exegesis, like the vocabulary, is dense and vigorous. It is also occasionally insightful: for example, in the connection it draws between the angelic-human coupling in Gen 6:1–4, which immediately precedes and perhaps precipitates God's destruction of the earth with a flood, and the attempt of the men of Sodom to rape the angelic visitors in Genesis 19, which occasions God's fiery destruction of the cities of the plain. It is no surprise that this brief but energetic letter strongly influenced another New Testament writing, 2 Peter, which draws on it throughout.

For more detailed exposition of this fascinating text, see Richard Bauckham's excellent Word Biblical Commentary, *Jude, 2 Peter* (Waco, TX: Word Books, 1983), which influences this introduction and the annotations that follow.

THE GENERAL EPISTLE OF
JUDE

Jude, the servant of Jesus Christ, and brother of James, to them that are sanctified by God the Father, and preserved in Jesus Christ, and called: ²Mercy unto
you, and peace, and love, be multiplied.

³Beloved, when I gave all diligence to write unto you of the common salvation,
it was needful for me to write unto you, and exhort you that ye should earnestly
contend for the faith which was once delivered unto the saints. ⁴For there are
certain men crept in unawares, who were before of old ordained to this condemnation, ungodly men, turning the grace of our God into lasciviousness, and denying the only Lord God, and our Lord Jesus Christ.

⁵I will therefore put you in remembrance, though ye once knew this, how that the
Lord, having saved the people out of the land of Egypt, afterward destroyed them
that believed not. ⁶And the angels which kept not their first estate, but left their own
habitation, he hath reserved in everlasting chains under darkness unto the judgment of the great day. ⁷Even as Sodom and Gomorrha, and the cities about them

1–2 Salutation. Adhering to a conventional Greco-Roman epistolary pattern, Jude begins by
identifying the writer, followed by a reference to the addressees (here, rather vague) and a formal
greeting. **1** *Jude the servant . . . brother of James*: James was a well-known leader in the early church
(cf. Acts 12:17; Gal 1:19), which is why the author identifies himself as his brother. Both Jude and
James were brothers of Jesus; cf. Mark 6:3; Gal 1:19. *Servant*: lit. "slave" (see Rom 1:1 note). *Sanctified*: better "beloved" (MS tradition). *Preserved in*: alternatively "kept for."

3–4 Purpose of the letter. 3 *When I . . . needful*: the author wanted to write about "our common salvation" (a better reading of the MS tradition), but felt constrained to urge his readers to
defend the authentic faith from false teachers. *Saints*: lit. "holy ones." **4** *Ordained*: lit. "assigned in
writing," referring to the various literary traditions that the letter goes on to invoke (see note to vv.
5–19). *Lasciviousness*: licentiousness. *The only . . . Christ*: better "our only master and Lord, Jesus
Christ" (MS tradition; NRSV).

5–19 Exegetical disparagement of opponents. The author invokes a number of textual or
traditional authorities (vv. 5–7, 9, 11–13, 14–15, 17–18), employing them to denigrate and vilify his
opponents, especially by associating those opponents with the various forms and figures of depravity condemned by the traditions invoked. **5** *Though ye . . . this*: better "though ye know all things
once for all" (RV). *Afterward destroyed . . . not*: see Num 14:20–23; 26:64–65. **6** *The angels . . .
day*: based on the reference to "sons of God" coupling with daughters of men in Gen 6:1–4, a fragmentary episode subject to interpretive expansion in a number of later Jewish texts, esp. *1 Enoch.*

in like manner, giving themselves over to fornication, and going after strange flesh, are set forth for an example, suffering the vengeance of eternal fire. [8]Likewise also these filthy dreamers defile the flesh, despise dominion, and speak evil of dignities.

[9]Yet Michael the archangel, when contending with the devil he disputed about the body of Moses, durst not bring against him a railing accusation, but said, The Lord rebuke thee. [10]But these speak evil of those things which they know not: but what they know naturally, as brute beasts, in those things they corrupt themselves.

[11]Woe unto them! for they have gone in the way of Cain, and ran greedily after the error of Balaam for reward, and perished in the gainsaying of Core. [12]These are spots in your feasts of charity, when they feast with you, feeding themselves without fear: clouds they are without water, carried about of winds; trees whose fruit withereth, without fruit, twice dead, plucked up by the roots; [13]raging waves of the sea, foaming out their own shame; wandering stars, to whom is reserved the blackness of darkness for ever.

[14]And Enoch also, the seventh from Adam, prophesied of these, saying, Behold, the Lord cometh with ten thousands of his saints, [15]to execute judgment upon all, and to convince all that are ungodly among them of all their ungodly deeds which they have ungodly committed, and of all their hard speeches which ungodly sinners have spoken against him. [16]These are murmurers, complainers, walking after their own lusts; and their mouth speaketh great swelling words, having men's persons in admiration because of advantage.

---

7 *Strange flesh*: lit. "other flesh"; as angels mated with human women in Gen 6:1–4, men from Sodom attempt to have sex with angels in Gen 19:1–11. *Vengeance*: lit. "justice."   **8** *Filthy*: a KJV interpolation. *Dreamers*: presumably people who draw on prophetic dreams to authorize doctrine and behavior that the author considers perverse; cf. Deut 13:5. *Dignities*: lit. "glories," probably referring to angels. The reason for this purported slander of angels is not clear. Perhaps to demonstrate spiritual autonomy?   **9** *Michael the archangel*: see Dan 10:13 note. *Contending, accusation*: the Greek words share the same root. *The Lord rebuke thee*: quoting Zech 3:2, but apparently referring to a lost passage from the *Assumption of Moses* in which that verse was quoted. In that passage, Michael and the devil would have disputed whether Moses, who was guilty of murder (see Exod 2:12), deserved a respectable burial.   **10** *Speak evil*: Gk. *blasphēmeō*, which shares its root with "railing" (v. 9). *Naturally*: i.e., "instinctively" (NRSV).   **11** *Cain*: see Gen 4:1–16. His inclusion here with Balaam and Korah, both of whom led Israel astray, may refer to the tradition in which Cain's attempt to convince his brother that God is unjust preceded his murder of Abel (see, e.g., *Targum Pseudo-Jonathan*). *Balaam* supposedly instigated Israel's idolatry at Peor (see Num 31:16; cf. 25:1–5). For the rebellion against Moses' leadership initiated by *Core* (Korah), see Num 16.   **12** *Spots*: alternatively "reefs" (i.e., submerged hazards). *Feasts of charity*: love feasts, i.e., communal celebratory meals. Compare the impiety some demonstrated at eucharistic feasts in Corinth (1 Cor 11:17–34 and notes). *Feeding themselves without fear*: alternatively "without fear, shepherding [only] themselves," a translation that assimilates the opponents to Israel's wicked shepherds from Ezek 34 (esp. v. 2). *Clouds they . . . winds*: cf. Prov 25:14. *Trees . . . without fruit*: better "autumnal trees without fruit." In Matt 7:16–20 a similar image describes false prophets.   **13** *Raging waves . . . shame*: echoing Isa 57:20. *Wandering stars*: planets or meteorites. They are ruled by rebellious angels, according to *1 Enoch* 18.13–16; 21.6; 86.1–3, while the stars, whose movements are regular, are governed by good angels (*1 Enoch* 82).   **14** *Enoch also, the seventh from Adam*: counting the generations listed in Gen 5:3–24. The words attributed to him, which run through the end of v. 15, come from the pseudepigraphical *1 Enoch* 1.9. *Of these*: or "to these." *Saints*: lit. "holy ones," here probably angels.   **15** *Convince*: alternatively "convict."   **16** *Lusts*: or "desires" (also in v. 18). *Great swelling*: "bombastic" (NRSV). *Having men's . . . advantage*: "flattering

¹⁷But, beloved, remember ye the words which were spoken before of the apostles of our Lord Jesus Christ; ¹⁸how that they told you there should be mockers in the last time, who should walk after their own ungodly lusts. ¹⁹These be they who separate themselves, sensual, having not the Spirit.

²⁰But ye, beloved, building up yourselves on your most holy faith, praying in the Holy Ghost, ²¹keep yourselves in the love of God, looking for the mercy of our Lord Jesus Christ unto eternal life. ²²And of some have compassion, making a difference: ²³and others save with fear, pulling them out of the fire; hating even the garment spotted by the flesh.

²⁴Now unto him that is able to keep you from falling, and to present you faultless before the presence of his glory with exceeding joy, ²⁵to the only wise God our Saviour, be glory and majesty, dominion and power, both now and ever. Amen.

---

people to their own advantage" (NRSV).   **17** *Remember ye . . . Christ*: scholars debate the meaning and implications of this verse, especially the identity of the *apostles*. If the verse harks back to the reminder of v. 5, then the term probably refers generically to "those sent out"—i.e., itinerant missionaries commissioned to spread the gospel. The author would thus be reminding the readers of eschatological warnings similar to those routinely issued by missionaries as part of their proclamation (see v. 18 note). But some see in *the words which were spoken before of the apostles of our Lord Jesus Christ* a more specific reference to the preaching of the Twelve (cf. Matt 10:1–15); and because this preaching is here located in the past, they argue that Jude was composed relatively late.   **18** *That they . . . lusts*: such eschatological warnings are common in the NT; cf. Matt 24:11; Mark 13:22; 1 Tim 4:1–2; etc. *Mockers*: the Greek word also connotes deception (cf. Matt 2:16, "mocked").   **19** *Separate themselves*: better "cause divisions" (MS tradition; NRSV). *Sensual*: Gk. *psychikoi*: the opposition here introduced, between *psychē* (lit. "soul") and *pneuma* ("spirit"), is formally identical to the one articulated by Paul in 1 Corinthians (see 2:14 note; 15:44–49).

   20–25 Concluding exhortation and doxology. 20 *Ghost*: Gk. *pneuma*, lit. "spirit."   **21** *Keep yourselves . . . life*: recalling v. 1 (see note).   **22–23** *And of some . . . flesh*: the text is corrupt, and its construal, translation, and interpretation necessarily conjectural. NRSV (slightly altered) offers "and have mercy on some who are wavering; save others by snatching them out of the fire; and have mercy on still others with fear, hating even the tunic defiled by their flesh."   **24–25** *Now unto him . . . Amen*: cf. Rom 16:25–27.   **25** *Wise*: better omitted (MS tradition). *Saviour*: better to add "through Jesus Christ our Lord." *Power*: better to add "before all time" (MS tradition).

The Revelation of St. John the Divine

REVELATION itself constitutes the final division of the New Testament. Generically an apocalypse, this book is akin to Daniel in the Old Testament, 2 Esdras in the Apocrypha, and several similar works that did not find their way into the Bible. Apocalyptic works characteristically feature divine revelations about future events granted to prophetic visionaries guided by angelic mediators. These revelations are frequently couched in bizarre symbolic imagery and usually reflect a dualistic outlook: they depict the cosmos as a grand battle between the forces of good and of evil, with the assumption that everyone lines up on one side or the other.

Revelation (Gk. *apokalypsis*, lit. "uncovering," from which the name of its genre derives) claims to have been written by a prophet named John, and there is no reason to doubt this. There is also no reason to identify Revelation's author with the Apostle John, or with the author of the Fourth Gospel, or with the author of any of the three Johannine epistles. "John" was a common name in antiquity, as it is today, and even ancient Christians were wary of linking Revelation's John with his New Testament namesakes. In the mid-third century C.E., for instance, Dionysius of Alexandria offered a brief rhetorical analysis of the book aiming to establish that it could not have been written by the apostle, to whom he attributed the Fourth Gospel and 1 John (qtd. in Eusebius, *Evangelical History* 7.25; see Appendix, pp. 1461–63). Most scholars today accept this conclusion. Dionysius at least nominally accepted Revelation's authority, but many ancient Christians did not, and the claims some made for its apostolic authorship, which Dionysius was resisting, may in fact have originated as bids to support the book's controversial inclusion in the canon.

Many scholars today believe that Revelation responds to a threat of persecution that Christians in Asia Minor faced or perceived toward the end of the first century C.E. Persecution at that time was regional and sporadic; only later in Roman history would it become widespread and systematic. If the contextual information provided in Pliny's correspondence with Emperor Trajan regarding Christians in Bithynia is relevant (*Epistles* 10.96–97; written ca. 112 C.E., a few decades later than Revelation—see Appendix, pp. 987–89), it may have been fuelled by local officials concerned lest Christians' refusal to worship the pagan gods endanger the prosperity of the community at large. A crucial aspect of such worship would have been participation in the Roman imperial cult, an expression of both religious piety and political loyalty expected of inhabitants of the Roman Empire. (It was especially prominent in cities of Asia Minor like those to which John addresses his book.) Pliny therefore required accused Christians to prove their innocence by invoking the gods and offering wine and incense to an image of Trajan.

Though Revelation's placement in such a context is only speculative, the fit is rather good. Revelation disparages pagan practices (9:20; 21:8; 22:15) and excoriates Christian leaders who, like Paul (cf. 1 Cor 8:1–13; 10:23–33), express flexibility on the issue of whether believers may consume meat from animals sacrificed to idols (e.g., 2:14, 20–23). It also displays ideological resistance to Rome throughout, focusing in particular on worship directed at the emperor (see esp. 13:11–18 and notes). The emperorship of Domitian (81–96 C.E.) saw an increased emphasis on the imperial cult, and external and internal evidence alike suggests that Revelation was composed during Domitian's rule. Irenaeus (late second century C.E.) as well as other early Christian writers date Revelation to the waning years of his reign. Moreover, John's insistence on comparing Rome to Babylon presupposes Rome's destruction of the second Jerusalem temple, which occurred in 70 C.E., and thus supports a date of composition in the first century's final decades.

Not coincidentally, it is during this same period that "Christianity" began to be seen as a religion distinct from Judaism. John twice refers to those "which say they are Jews, and are not, but are the synagogue of Satan" (2:9; cf. 3:9), probably because he conceives of the Jesus-believing communities to which he writes as the true Jews, but recognizes that this identity is contested. Indeed, the rage and frustration of John's vitriolic polemic against the "false Jews" probably react to the widespread view that they were Jewish while his own readers were adhering to an innovative religious tradition discontinuous with Judaism—a perspective that Pliny's correspondence likewise reflects.

Greco-Roman polytheists often found monotheistic Jews peculiar and their religious exclusivity offensive, but they recognized the antiquity of Jewish traditions and usually did not expect Jews to worship gods other than their own. To the extent that early "Christians" came to be seen as distinct from Jews, they lost this protected status. As a newfangled foreign cult whose primary ritual (the Eucharist) appeared cannibalistic, Christianity—with its worship of Christ to the exclusion of other gods (including the emperor)—appeared dangerous, even subversive. John's ability to attack the synagogue and his communities' persecutors in the same breath (2:9–10) may reflect the exclusion of Jesus-believers from synagogues in some of the cities to which he wrote, as Jewish congregations determined confession of Christ as Lord to be fundamentally incompatible with Judaism—a situation vividly dramatized by the Fourth Gospel (see John 9:22 and note). These believers, now seen as "Christians" rather than "Jews," would have become increasingly vulnerable to Roman intimidation if they refused to participate in pagan rituals. And it is possible that their refusal was denounced by members of the synagogues excluding them. According to Revelation, at least one believer has already been martyred (Antipas; 2:13) and John himself has been exiled to Patmos because of his faithful witness (1:9).

Revelation imagines God's decisive response to this oppression. It figures those who perpetrate it (Rome, its rulers, and its imperial cult) as satanic and subject to defeat and eternal torment by God. Those who suffer at their hands, on the contrary, experience only temporary affliction before the everlasting reward of eschatological existence in the renewed Jerusalem. But Revelation frequently complicates this dualistic scenario by juxtaposing its dramatic eschatological reversals in unexpected ways.

In chapter 19, for example, a heavenly voice announces a banquet celebrating the Lamb's wedding to his pure and faithful bride (a conventional image of Christ's eschatological union with his people and their faithful devotion to him; see Mark 2:19 note): "Blessed are they which are called unto the marriage supper of the Lamb" (19:9). Yet what follows is not the Lamb's joyous union with his bride but instead the sudden arrival of a rider on a white horse who conquers and destroys the nations he encounters (19:11–16). An angelic voice then calls the birds to gather for "the supper of the great God" at which they will "eat the flesh" of those the horseman has slaughtered (19:17–18). The expected Lamb is replaced by the violent horseman and his wedding celebration by a gruesome banquet.

This horseman is described in terms strongly reminiscent of the first horseman from 6:2, who also rides on a white horse and conquers whomever he encounters. But Revelation 19 implies that he is Christ by assigning him a trio of dominical titles: "Faithful and True" (19:11), "The Word of God" (19:13), and "King of kings and Lord of lords" (19:16). Perhaps not surprisingly, in light of these competing interpretive possibilities, emphasis ultimately falls on the inscrutability of the horseman's identity: "he had a name written, that no one knew, but he himself" (19:12). John's repeated thwarting of our expectations serves to underscore the ambiguity: the lamb is anticipated but a violent horseman appears, who would seem to be the threatening figure mentioned at 6:2 were it not for recurrent suggestions that this horseman is Christ, despite the difference between his demeanor and the Lamb's and despite his serving up a carrion banquet rather than the promised wedding feast. When all is said and done, we cannot be sure who exactly the horseman is.

This uncertainty raises a pressing theological question: does the horseman's violent arrival fulfill the prophesied eschatological banquet or supplant it? And that question implies another: should the righteous hope for the destruction of the wicked that the horseman accomplishes, or should they cringe at it? The provocative juxtaposition of incongruous images—wedding banquet and cannibalistic feast, meek lamb and violent horseman—in effect forces these questions on the reader, especially in combination with the chapter's insistence on the horseman's mysterious identity.

Some believe that such aesthetic and ideological tensions can be resolved by readings that stress Revelation's ubiquitous image of the slain Lamb, which first appears in 5:6 as an unexpected substitution for the lion of Judah (cf. 5:5). Richard Hays, for instance, sees in this image support for his view of Revelation as a fundamentally pacifistic work: "a work that places the Lamb that was slaughtered at the center of its praise and worship can hardly be used to validate violence and coercion" (*The Moral Vision of the New Testament* [1996]). But this line of interpretation fails to do justice to the complexity of Revelation's imagery. After all, the slaughtered Lamb of 5:6 is also a powerful ram (note its seven horns), and when it opens the scroll in the subsequent chapter it unleashes forces of destruction. Moreover, the first of these forces is represented by the horseman on his white steed (6:2), a violent figure which, we have seen, may supplant the image of the loving lamb in chapter 19. Locating the slaughtered Lamb at Revelation's aesthetic and ideological core might represent an attractive theological option, but it amounts to a denial of the book's dynamic and even unstable imagery—imagery with which any theological interpretation must come to terms.

Revelation's constantly shifting imagery is largely responsible for its reputation as a chaotic and incomprehensible text. George Bernard Shaw notoriously labeled it "the curious record of the visions of a drug addict," and D. H. Lawrence is reported to have said "the final proof of insanity is to have a theory about the Apocalypse." Closely read, however, Revelation reveals itself to be very carefully composed. Thus, the bizarre imagery it employs is almost all drawn from the Old Testament, as Revelation is easily the most densely allusive book in the entire Bible. One of the great pleasures in reading the Bible lies in recognizing and interpreting the complex intertextual relationships that Revelation constantly establishes with earlier biblical writings. The notes that follow aim to make this pleasure accessible by pointing to a large number, but by no means all of these allusions. Revelation is also a carefully structured book. That structure is too complex to summarize here and in any case no description of it is without controversy. But again, the notes should help the reader navigate it.

There is no denying that Revelation demands much of its reader. Yet its obscurities are rarely insoluble, and even the book's most mysterious passages (e.g., the identity of the beast's mark at 13:16–17) are frequently amenable to reasonable interpretation, if we are willing to read carefully and think analogically. To that end, those desiring fuller exposition of Revelation might begin by consulting David E. Aune's three-volume Word Biblical Commentary, *Revelation* (Dallas: Word Books, 1997; Nashville, TN: Thomas Nelson, 1997–98), or G. K. Beale's *The Book of Revelation: A Commentary on the Greek Text* (Grand Rapids, MI: Eerdmans, 1999), which is particularly useful in charting the book's frequent Old Testament allusions. Ben Witherington III's New Cambridge Bible Commentary, *Revelation* (Cambridge: Cambridge University Press, 2003), also contains some helpful observations. This introduction and the notes that follow have benefited from all three.

THE REVELATION

OF ST. JOHN THE DIVINE

1 The Revelation of Jesus Christ, which God gave unto him, to shew unto his servants things which must shortly come to pass; and he sent and signified it by his angel unto his servant John: ²who bare record of the word of God, and of the testimony of Jesus Christ, and of all things that he saw. ³Blessed is he that readeth, and they that hear the words of this prophecy, and keep those things which are written therein: for the time is at hand.

⁴John to the seven churches which are in Asia: Grace be unto you, and peace, from him which is, and which was, and which is to come; and from the seven Spirits which are before his throne; ⁵and from Jesus Christ, who is the faithful witness, and the first begotten of the dead, and prince of the kings of the earth. Unto him that loved us, and washed us from our sins in his own blood, ⁶and hath made us kings and priests unto God and his Father; to him be glory and dominion for ever and ever. Amen.

⁷Behold, he cometh with clouds; and every eye shall see him, and they also which pierced him: and all kindreds of the earth shall wail because of him. Even so, Amen.

⁸I am Alpha and Omega, the beginning and the ending, saith the Lord, which is, and which was, and which is to come, the Almighty.

1:1–3 **Opening.** These verses emphasize multiple levels of mediation between God and the audience: God reveals to Jesus, who reveals to an angel, who reveals to "his servant John," who writes (cf. vv. 11, 19), whose writing reveals to the reader, whose recitation reveals to auditors.   1:1 *Servants*: lit. "slaves" (so throughout). In the OT a prophet is conventionally called "God's servant/slave."   1:2 *Bare record*: Gk. *martyreō*, the verbal form of the word translated "testimony" later in this verse. The same root is elsewhere rendered "testify," "witness," and "martyr."   1:3 *Blessed is . . . therein*: the first of seven blessings; cf. 14:13; 16:15; 19:9; 20:6; 22:7, 14.

1:4–6 **Salutation.** A standard Greco-Roman epistolary greeting, giving first the writer's identity and then that of the addressees, followed by the salutation (here an extended wish of grace and peace recalling Paul's letters).   1:4 *Which is, and . . . come*: the Greek recalls LXX Exod 3:14–15. *Seven Spirits*: ancient Jewish literature often imagines seven angels attending God's throne (e.g., Tob 12:15; *1 Enoch* 20.1–8). The spirits correspond to those angels and are identical to "the angels of the seven churches" (v. 20), and possibly to those given the seven trumpets in 8:2.   1:5 *First begotten of the dead*: first to experience eschatological resurrection (cf. 1 Cor 15:20; Col 1:18). *Washed*: better "loosed" (MS tradition).   1:6 *Hath made . . . God*: cf. Exod 19:6. *Kings*: better "a kingdom" (MS tradition).

1:7–20 **The Son of Man.** 1:7 *Behold, he . . . clouds*: cf. Dan 7:13. *Every eye . . . wail*: echoing Zech 12:10–14. *Kindreds*: i.e., "tribes" (so throughout).   1:8 *Alpha and Omega*: the first and final letters of the Greek alphabet; cf. Isa 41:4; 44:6. *The beginning . . . ending*: better omitted (MS tradition) as an assimilation of this verse to 21:6 and 22:13. *The Almighty*: Gk. *pantokratōr* (so

⁹I John, who also am your brother, and companion in tribulation, and in the kingdom and patience of Jesus Christ, was in the isle that is called Patmos, for the word of God, and for the testimony of Jesus Christ. ¹⁰I was in the Spirit on the Lord's day, and heard behind me a great voice, as of a trumpet, ¹¹saying, I am Alpha and Omega, the first and the last: and, What thou seest, write in a book, and send it unto the seven churches which are in Asia; unto Ephesus, and unto Smyrna, and unto Pergamos, and unto Thyatira, and unto Sardis, and unto Philadelphia, and unto Laodicea. ¹²And I turned to see the voice that spake with me. And being turned, I saw seven golden candlesticks; ¹³and in the midst of the seven candlesticks one like unto the Son of man, clothed with a garment down to the foot, and girt about the paps with a golden girdle. ¹⁴His head and his hairs were white like wool, as white as snow; and his eyes were as a flame of fire; ¹⁵and his feet like unto fine brass, as if they burned in a furnace; and his voice as the sound of many waters. ¹⁶And he had in his right hand seven stars: and out of his mouth went a sharp two-edged sword: and his countenance was as the sun shineth in his strength.

¹⁷And when I saw him, I fell at his feet as dead. And he laid his right hand upon me, saying unto me, Fear not; I am the first and the last: ¹⁸I am he that liveth, and was dead; and, behold, I am alive for evermore, Amen; and have the keys of hell and of death. ¹⁹Write the things which thou hast seen, and the things which are, and the things which shall be hereafter; ²⁰the mystery of the seven stars which thou sawest in my right hand, and the seven golden candlesticks. The seven stars are the angels of the seven churches: and the seven candlesticks which thou sawest are the seven churches.

---

throughout). LXX employs this word to translate "Lord of hosts," a common Hebrew designation for YHWH.   **1:9** *Patience*: Gk. *hypomonē*, alternatively "endurance" or "perseverance" (so throughout). *Of Jesus Christ*: better "in Jesus" (MS tradition). *Patmos*: one of the Sporades islands, well offshore from Asia Minor in the Aegean.   **1:10** *In the Spirit*: in an ecstatic trance. *The Lord's day*: presumably Sunday, the day of Jesus' resurrection. If so, this is the earliest reference to it by that name. *As of a trumpet*: perhaps recalling the Sinai theophany (cf. Exod 19:16; 20:18).   **1:11** *I am . . . last: and*: better omitted (MS tradition). *The seven churches*: located in seven cities of Asia Minor, following the geographical order of a journey from Ephesus northward to Pergamum and then southeast to Laodicea.   **1:12** *Candlesticks*: lampstands (so throughout). They symbolize the seven churches (cf. v. 20) and recall both the perpetually burning lamp in God's tabernacle (Exod 27:20–21; Lev 24:2–4) and the vision of the seven lamps from Zech 4:1–5, 10b–14 (see notes).   **1:13** *One like . . . man*: quoting Dan 7:13, with details in the next two verses coming from Dan 7:9–10 (with reference to the "Ancient of days") and 10:6. Verses 13–15 also recall Ezekiel's opening vision of the divine chariot (esp. Ezek 1:7, 24), an important model for the vision of the divine throne in Rev 4–5. *Paps*: chest.   **1:16** *And he . . . strength*: the imagery of brilliance is heightened, as the seven candlesticks become seven stars and the Son of Man, earlier described as luminous (vv. 13–15), now resembles the sun itself. The sword coming from his mouth symbolizes God's prophetic word of judgment (cf. Isa 49:1–2; Wis 18:14–16).   **1:17** *Fell at his feet as dead*: a conventional response to overwhelming divine visions; cf. Ezek 1:28; Dan 8:17; etc.   **1:18** *Amen*: better omitted (MS tradition). *And have . . . death*: cf. Isa 22:22, where God vests Eliakim with authority over the house of David. The statement may also recall Jesus' claim about Peter in Matt 16:18–19, which was based on the Isaiah passage.

2 Unto the angel of the church of Ephesus write; These things saith he that holdeth the seven stars in his right hand, who walketh in the midst of the seven golden candlesticks; ²I know thy works, and thy labour, and thy patience, and how thou canst not bear them which are evil: and thou hast tried them which say they are apostles, and are not, and hast found them liars: ³and hast borne, and hast patience, and for my name's sake hast laboured, and hast not fainted. ⁴Nevertheless I have somewhat against thee, because thou hast left thy first love. ⁵Remember therefore from whence thou art fallen, and repent, and do the first works; or else I will come unto thee quickly, and will remove thy candlestick out of his place, except thou repent. ⁶But this thou hast, that thou hatest the deeds of the Nicolaitans, which I also hate. ⁷He that hath an ear, let him hear what the Spirit saith unto the churches; To him that overcometh will I give to eat of the tree of life, which is in the midst of the paradise of God.

⁸And unto the angel of the church in Smyrna write; These things saith the first and the last, which was dead, and is alive; ⁹I know thy works, and tribulation, and poverty, (but thou art rich) and I know the blasphemy of them which say they are Jews, and are not, but are the synagogue of Satan. ¹⁰Fear none of those things which thou shalt suffer: behold, the devil shall cast some of you into prison, that ye may be tried; and ye shall have tribulation ten days: be thou faithful unto death, and I will give thee a crown of life. ¹¹He that hath an ear, let him hear

2:1–3:22 Letters to the seven churches. Ancient Jewish literature frequently attributes letters to prophets; compare Elijah's letter in 2 Chr 21:12–15; Jeremiah's letters in Jer 29; the apocryphal Letter of Jeremiah; and the letter of Jeremiah's scribe Baruch in the pseudepigraphical *2 Baruch* 78–87. John's letters are carefully structured. Each is introduced by Christ's command to write to the appropriate church's angel before progressing to a typical formula of divine authorization, which usually describes Christ in terms drawn from chap. 1. Each next contains a section outlining Christ's knowledge of the church in question and then one devoted to admonition. Each closes with a command to listen and a promise of reward for those who overcome. **2:2** *Thou hast . . . liars*: see Matt 7:15–23 note. *Apostles*: lit. "those sent out," referring to itinerant preachers. **2:5** *Quickly*: better omitted (MS tradition). **2:6** *Nicolaitans*: no source independent of Revelation tells us anything about them, but "Nicolaitans" combines the Greek words for "victory" (*nikē*) and "people" (*laos*), which is significant in light of the letters' promise of reward for "him that overcometh" (Gk. *nikōnti*, v. 7). John's ironic contrast of the so-called victory people with true victors recalls Paul's sarcastic response to Corinthian boasts of liberty and the like in 1 Cor 4:8–13. **2:7** *Tree of life . . . God*: cf. Gen 2:9. For contemporary Jewish understandings of paradise, see Luke 23:43 note; 2 Cor 12:4 note. In Rev 22 (vv. 2, 14, 19 [see note]), the admission of the righteous to the tree of life— located in new Jerusalem—is a feature of the renewed cosmos. **2:9** *But thou art rich*: i.e., spiritually or morally (echoing Hos 12:8). *The blasphemy . . . Satan*: Gk. *blasphēmia* is better translated "slander," and *synagogue of Satan* ironically adapts LXX Num 16:3, which describes Israel as "the congregation [Gk. *synagōgē*] of the Lord." John may refer to Jews informing against Jesus-believers to Roman authorities. He apparently understands Jesus-believers in Smyrna to represent the authentic Jewish community there and other Jews to be apostate. This position, combined with excoriation of church leaders who (like Paul) permit the eating of meat sacrificed to idols (see vv. 14 and note, 20) and insistence on rigorous separation from the pagan world (as seen, e.g., in the condemnation of Roman currency; 13:16–18 and note), suggests a view of the Christian community more in line with proto-rabbinic understandings of religious identity than with Paul's. **2:10** *Ten days*: the round number signifying an indeterminate but limited time. *Crown*: a wreath conventionally awarded to victors in athletic competitions or as a civic honor in the Greek world; cf. 1 Cor 9:25; Jas 1:12; etc.

what the Spirit saith unto the churches; He that overcometh shall not be hurt of the second death.

¹²And to the angel of the church in Pergamos write; These things saith he which hath the sharp sword with two edges; ¹³I know thy works, and where thou dwellest, even where Satan's seat is: and thou holdest fast my name, and hast not denied my faith, even in those days wherein Antipas was my faithful martyr, who was slain among you, where Satan dwelleth. ¹⁴But I have a few things against thee, because thou hast there them that hold the doctrine of Balaam, who taught Balac to cast a stumblingblock before the children of Israel, to eat things sacrificed unto idols, and to commit fornication. ¹⁵So hast thou also them that hold the doctrine of the Nicolaitans, which thing I hate. ¹⁶Repent; or else I will come unto thee quickly, and will fight against them with the sword of my mouth. ¹⁷He that hath an ear, let him hear what the Spirit saith unto the churches; To him that overcometh will I give to eat of the hidden manna, and will give him a white stone, and in the stone a new name written, which no man knoweth saving he that receiveth it.

¹⁸And unto the angel of the church in Thyatira write; These things saith the Son of God, who hath his eyes like unto a flame of fire, and his feet are like fine brass; ¹⁹I know thy works, and charity, and service, and faith, and thy patience, and thy works; and the last to be more than the first. ²⁰Notwithstanding I have a few things against thee, because thou sufferest that woman Jezebel, which calleth herself a prophetess, to teach and to seduce my servants to commit fornication, and to eat things sacrificed unto idols. ²¹And I gave her space to repent of her fornication; and she repented not. ²²Behold, I will cast her into a bed, and them that commit adultery with her into great tribulation, except they repent of their deeds. ²³And I will kill her children with death; and all the churches shall

---

2:11 *Second death*: cf. 20:6, 14; 21:8.   **2:13** *Thy works, and*: better omitted (MS tradition). *Satan's seat*: reference obscure; possible candidates are Pergamum's great altar to Zeus (whose famous frieze depicts the Olympian gods' defeat of serpentine giants) or the grand temple of Augustus at Rome. *Antipas*: otherwise unknown. *Martyr*: lit. "witness"; see 1:2 note.   **2:14** *Doctrine*: teaching. *Balaam, who . . . Israel*: see Num 22–24, but the more resonant allusion is to Num 31:1–24 (esp. vv. 15–16), which implicates Balaam in the Israelites' idolatry at Peor (cf. Num 25). *Things sacrificed unto idols*: whether to eat meat from animals sacrificed to pagan gods was a serious concern for the Corinthian church as well, but Paul's approach to it is far more nuanced than John's (cf. 1 Cor 8:1–13; 10:1–11:1 and notes). *The doctrine of Balaam* may refer to the teaching of someone espousing a Pauline perspective on the issue. *Fornication*: sexual immorality, which conventionally figures idolatry in the OT (see Exod 34:15–16 and note). Here it recalls in particular Num 25:1–3, where the Israelites worship Baal at the invitation of the Moabite/Midianite women with whom they "commit whoredom."   **2:15** *Nicolaitans*: see v. 6 note. *Which I hate*: better "in the same way" (MS tradition).   **2:17** *Manna*: food miraculously supplied to the Israelites in the wilderness (Exod 16; Num 11). It is associated with eternal life at *Joseph and Aseneth* 16 (cf. John 6:31–58) and with the eschatological cosmic restoration at *Sibylline Oracles* 7.139–49. *White stone . . . written*: probably a magic amulet. Such talismans were conventionally inscribed with gods' names, and secret divine names were most powerful of all (cf. Statius, *Thebaid* 4.513–18).   **2:19** *Charity*: Gk. *agapē*, "love" (cf. v. 4). *And thy works; and the last . . . first*: better "and your last works are better than the first" (MS tradition).   **2:20** *A few things*: rather "this." *Jezebel*: polemically referring to a church leader as King Ahab's notorious wife, who is associated with idolatry and other wickedness (see 1 Kgs 16:31; 18–19; 21; 2 Kgs 9). *Commit Fornication . . . idols*: see 2:14 and notes.   **2:21** *Space*: lit. "time."   **2:22** *Bed*: i.e., sickbed.   **2:23** *Kill . . . with death*: LXX Ezek 33:27

know that I am he which searcheth the reins and hearts: and I will give unto every one of you according to your works. ²⁴But unto you I say, and unto the rest in Thyatira, as many as have not this doctrine, and which have not known the depths of Satan, as they speak; I will put upon you none other burden. ²⁵But that which ye have already hold fast till I come. ²⁶And he that overcometh, and keepeth my works unto the end, to him will I give power over the nations: ²⁷and he shall rule them with a rod of iron; as the vessels of a potter shall they be broken to shivers: even as I received of my Father. ²⁸And I will give him the morning star. ²⁹He that hath an ear, let him hear what the Spirit saith unto the churches.

3 And unto the angel of the church in Sardis write; These things saith he that hath the seven Spirits of God, and the seven stars; I know thy works, that thou hast a name that thou livest, and art dead. ²Be watchful, and strengthen the things which remain, that are ready to die: for I have not found thy works perfect before God. ³Remember therefore how thou hast received and heard, and hold fast, and repent. If therefore thou shalt not watch, I will come on thee as a thief, and thou shalt not know what hour I will come upon thee. ⁴Thou hast a few names even in Sardis which have not defiled their garments; and they shall walk with me in white: for they are worthy. ⁵He that overcometh, the same shall be clothed in white raiment; and I will not blot out his name out of the book of life, but I will confess his name before my Father, and before his angels. ⁶He that hath an ear, let him hear what the Spirit saith unto the churches.

⁷And to the angel of the church in Philadelphia write; These things saith he that is holy, he that is true, he that hath the key of David, he that openeth, and no man shutteth; and shutteth, and no man openeth; ⁸I know thy works: behold, I have set before thee an open door, and no man can shut it: for thou hast a little strength, and hast kept my word, and hast not denied my name. ⁹Behold, I will

---

uses the same Greek phrase to translate the idea of killing by plague; cf. LXX Num 14:12. *I am . . . works*: cf. Jer 11:20; 17:10. *Reins*: kidneys, traditionally a seat of the emotions.   **2:24** *As they speak*: i.e., "as they say," suggesting that *the depths of Satan* represents a slogan, or perhaps John's ironic distortion of one. ("Jezebel" may actually have claimed to teach "the deep things of God" [1 Cor 2:10].)   **2:26** *Power over the nations*: a share in Christ's eschatological sovereignty—what James and John request in Mark 10:37.   **2:27** *He shall rule . . . shivers*: Ps 2:9 (LXX reads "rule them" in place of MT's "break them").   **2:28** *The morning star*: Venus, but recalling the Davidic oracle at Num 24:17; cf. Rev 22:16.   **3:2** *Perfect*: lit. "fulfilled."   **3:3** *As a thief*: a conventional simile in the NT describing the arrival of the Day of the Lord; cf. Matt 24:43; Luke 12:39; 1 Thess 5:2, 4.   **3:4** *Names*: i.e., persons. *Not defiled . . . white*: white garments represent purity throughout Revelation.   **3:5** *I will not . . . angels*: recalling Exod 32:32–33; cf. Ps 69:28. In Dan 12:1–4, *the book of life* contains the names of the righteous living and dead, who will experience eternal life. This corresponds to Revelation's understanding of it (20:12–15).   **3:7–8** *He that hath . . . name*: cf. 1:18 and note. The risen Jesus' application of Isa 22:22 to himself may be set against the tradition preserved in Matt 16:19, where Jesus alludes to the same OT passage to grant Peter heaven's keys and the authority to bind and loose. Note John's reiterated insistence that "no man" can shut the door that Christ opens, and his explanation that Christ has opened the door for the Philadelphians because they had strength not to deny his name under threat of persecution—precisely what Peter lacked (Matt 26:69–75).   **3:7** *Shutteth*: Gk. *kleiō*, which shares its root with *key*.

make them of the synagogue of Satan, which say they are Jews, and are not, but do lie; behold, I will make them to come and worship before thy feet, and to know that I have loved thee. [10]Because thou hast kept the word of my patience, I also will keep thee from the hour of temptation, which shall come upon all the world, to try them that dwell upon the earth. [11]Behold, I come quickly: hold that fast which thou hast, that no man take thy crown. [12]Him that overcometh will I make a pillar in the temple of my God, and he shall go no more out: and I will write upon him the name of my God, and the name of the city of my God, which is new Jerusalem, which cometh down out of heaven from my God: and I will write upon him my new name. [13]He that hath an ear, let him hear what the Spirit saith unto the churches.

[14]And unto the angel of the church of the Laodiceans write; These things saith the Amen, the faithful and true witness, the beginning of the creation of God; [15]I know thy works, that thou art neither cold nor hot: I would thou wert cold or hot. [16]So then because thou art lukewarm, and neither cold nor hot, I will spue thee out of my mouth. [17]Because thou sayest, I am rich, and increased with goods, and have need of nothing; and knowest not that thou art wretched, and miserable, and poor, and blind, and naked: [18]I counsel thee to buy of me gold tried in the fire, that thou mayest be rich; and white raiment, that thou mayest be clothed, and that the shame of thy nakedness do not appear; and anoint thine eyes with eyesalve, that thou mayest see. [19]As many as I love, I rebuke and chasten: be zealous therefore, and repent. [20]Behold, I stand at the door, and knock: if any man hear my voice, and open the door, I will come in to him, and will sup with him, and he with me. [21]To him that overcometh will I grant to sit with me in my throne, even as I also overcame, and am set down with my Father in his throne. [22]He that hath an ear, let him hear what the Spirit saith unto the churches.

3:9 *Make them of*: lit. "give them from." *The synagogue of Satan*: see 2:9 note. *Worship*: better "bow down," a posture of humiliation and not necessarily veneration, unless it is to be read in light of v. 12, where the one who overcomes is permanently integrated into God's new temple (but see note). **3:10** *Temptation, try*: both (cognate) Greek words denote testing. John apparently refers here to the "great tribulation" (7:14; Matt 24:21) that Jesus-believers and other Jews expected to precede God's eschatological vindication of the elect and rectification of the cosmos (cf. Dan 12:1; Matt 24:4–31; Mark 13:5–27; Luke 21:8–28). Some eschatological texts (e.g., 2 Baruch 31.5–32.6) promise God's protection of his elect during this period. **3:12** *The name of my God*: cf. Exod 28:36–38 for the headgear inscribed with "holiness to the Lord" that Aaron must wear when he enters the sanctuary. *New Jerusalem . . . God* alludes to Isaiah's oracle of Jerusalem's redemption (62:1–12), which prophesies that both the city and its people will receive a "new name" (v. 2; cf. 12). The phrase also looks forward to the vision of new Jerusalem at Rev 21:9–22:5. Since there will be "no temple therein: for the Lord God Almighty and the Lamb are the temple of it" (21:22), the temple imagery here and elsewhere in Revelation should be interpreted symbolically. *New name*: compare Christ's undisclosed name at 19:12. **3:14** *The Amen*: echoing Isa 65:16 (see note). *The beginning . . . God*: cf. John 1:2–3; Col 1:15–16 and notes. **3:16** *Spue*: spew; perhaps an allusion to the well-known hot springs near Laodicea, whose lukewarm mineral water was good for bathing but unpleasant to drink. **3:17** *I am . . . naked*: inverting 2:9 (see note). **3:18** *Gold tried in the fire*: OT prophets use this metaphor for God's purification of his people (cf. Zech 13:9; Mal 3:3; etc.). **3:19** *As many . . . chasten*: cf. Prov 3:12. **3:20** *Behold . . . to him*: cf. vv. 7–8, but here Christ accuses the Laodiceans of shutting him out. **3:21** *Even as I . . . throne*: alluding to Ps 110:1; see Mark 14:62 note.

4 After this I looked, and, behold, a door was opened in heaven: and the first voice which I heard was as it were of a trumpet talking with me; which said, Come up hither, and I will shew thee things which must be hereafter. ²And immediately I was in the spirit: and, behold, a throne was set in heaven, and one sat on the throne. ³And he that sat was to look upon like a jasper and a sardine stone: and there was a rainbow round about the throne, in sight like unto an emerald. ⁴And round about the throne were four and twenty seats: and upon the seats I saw four and twenty elders sitting, clothed in white raiment; and they had on their heads crowns of gold. ⁵And out of the throne proceeded lightnings and thunderings and voices: and there were seven lamps of fire burning before the throne, which are the seven Spirits of God. ⁶And before the throne there was a sea of glass like unto crystal: and in the midst of the throne, and round about the throne, were four beasts full of eyes before and behind.

⁷And the first beast was like a lion, and the second beast like a calf, and the third beast had a face as a man, and the fourth beast was like a flying eagle. ⁸And the four beasts had each of them six wings about him; and they were full of eyes within: and they rest not day and night, saying, Holy, holy, holy, Lord God Almighty,

4:1–5:14 The vision of the heavenly throne and of the lamb. Primarily modeled on the opening vision of Ezekiel (1:4–3:15) and borrowing many of its elements, including the precious stones and the rainbow (4:3; cf. Ezek 1:16, 26–28), the lightning and thunderous voices emanating from the throne (4:5; cf. Ezek 1:13–14, 24), the sea of crystal (4:6; cf. Ezek 1:22, the crystal firmament), the four multieyed winged beasts (4:6–8; cf. Ezek 1:5–25), and the divine scroll (5:1; cf. Ezek 2:9–10). Daniel's vision of the Ancient of days' enthronement and the Son of Man's approach is also echoed (compare 5:9–10 and Dan 7:14; 5:11 and Dan 7:10; etc.). Revelation 4 and 5, focusing on God and the lamb respectively, are similarly structured: for instance, both culminate in descriptions of heavenly worship (4:8b–11; 5:8–12) and both include two hymns of praise (4:8b, 11; 5:9–10, 12).   **4:1** *The first voice . . . trumpet*: cf. 1:10–11.   **4:3** *Sardine stone*: carnelian.   **4:4** *Throne, seats*: both Gk. *thronos. Four and twenty elders*: perhaps inspired by the "seventy elders" of Exod 24:9–10; but since the elders function in a priestly capacity at 5:8 (see note), they presumably represent the twenty-four priestly courses responsible for service in God's temple (1 Chr 24:1–19). Complementarily, as twenty-four is two times the quantity of Israel's tribes, it may symbolize the Jewish and Gentile constituencies of the universal church.   **4:5** *Lightenings and . . . voices*: recalling the Sinai theophany (esp. Exod 19:16–19). *Lamps of fire*: better "flaming torches" (NRSV), which in ancient Greek conventionally figured astronomical phenomena (as at Rev 8:10); the seven burning torches thus may correspond to the seven stars equated with the seven angels/spirits at 1:20 (cf. 1:4 note).   **4:6** *Before the throne . . . crystal*: possibly representing God's creative power over chaos, conventionally figured as the sea in ancient Near Eastern literature (cf. Gen 1:1 note; Pss 74:12–17 and notes; 89:9–11 and note; etc.). Ezek 1:22, the basis for this image, refers to a "firmament . . . of the terrible crystal," alluding to God's creative division of the primeval waters in Gen 1:6–8. *Beasts*: lit. "living things" (Gk. *zōa*), the word used by LXX for the "living creatures" of Ezekiel's vision. ("Beast" is better restricted to *thērion*, a Greek word never used of Revelation's four living creatures.) Each creature here corresponds to one of the four faces possessed by Ezekiel's creatures (1:5–25). Though Irenaeus associated each with one of the four evangelists (*Against Heresies* 3.11.8), his influential interpretation says more about early Christian debates regarding canonicity than about Revelation. The beasts actually seem to symbolize God's awesome creation.   **4:8** *Six wings*: identifying the creatures with the seraphim from the throne vision of Isa 6:1–13. *Holy, holy . . . Almighty*: quoting Isa 6:3. Modern versions frequently treat this sentence as verse, as well as the rhetorically elevated discourse introduced by "saying" (and in one case "say") at 4:11; 5:9–10, 12, 13; 7:10, 12; 11:15, 17–18; 12:10–12; 15:3–4; 16:5–7; 18:2–3, 4–8, 10, 16–17, 19, 21–24; 19:1–3, 5, 6–8. Although the KJV translators did

which was, and is, and is to come. ⁹And when those beasts give glory and honour and thanks to him that sat on the throne, who liveth for ever and ever, ¹⁰The four and twenty elders fall down before him that sat on the throne, and worship him that liveth for ever and ever, and cast their crowns before the throne, saying, ¹¹Thou art worthy, O Lord, to receive glory and honour and power: for thou hast created all things, and for thy pleasure they are and were created.

5 And I saw in the right hand of him that sat on the throne a book written within and on the backside, sealed with seven seals. ²And I saw a strong angel proclaiming with a loud voice, Who is worthy to open the book, and to loose the seals thereof? ³And no man in heaven, nor in earth, neither under the earth, was able to open the book, neither to look thereon. ⁴And I wept much, because no man was found worthy to open and to read the book, neither to look thereon. ⁵And one of the elders saith unto me, Weep not: behold, the Lion of the tribe of Juda, the Root of David, hath prevailed to open the book, and to loose the seven seals thereof.

⁶And I beheld, and, lo, in the midst of the throne and of the four beasts, and in the midst of the elders, stood a Lamb as it had been slain, having seven horns and seven eyes, which are the seven Spirits of God sent forth into all the earth. ⁷And he came and took the book out of the right hand of him that sat upon the throne. ⁸And when he had taken the book, the four beasts and four and twenty elders fell down before the Lamb, having every one of them harps, and golden vials full of odours, which are the prayers of saints. ⁹And they sung a new song, saying, Thou art worthy to take the book, and to open the seals thereof: for thou wast slain, and hast redeemed us to God by thy blood out of every kindred, and tongue, and people, and nation; ¹⁰and hast made us unto our God kings and priests: and we shall reign on the earth.

---

not understand these passages as poetry, they all seem to represent hymnic praise or poetic laments. **4:9** *Liveth*: Gk. *zōnti* (also v. 10), a word cognate with "beasts" (see v. 6 note), suggesting a connection between God's eternal life and the contingent life of his creatures. **5:1** *Book*: or "scroll," presumably the same one as in Ezekiel's vision (Ezek 2:9–3:14). *Sealed with seven seals*: sealed seven times with a signet ring pressed in hot wax. **5:4** *I wept much*: compare Daniel's distress and his subsequent encouragement by one of the heavenly attendees (Dan 7:15–16). *No man . . . thereon*: perhaps an allusion to Isa 29:9–12. *And to read*: better omitted (MS tradition). **5:5** *Lion of . . . Juda*: cf. Gen 49:9–10. *Root of David*: see Isa 11:1, 10; Jer 23:5; etc. Both titles refer to a messianic descendent of David, understood by John to be Jesus; cf. Rom 15:12; Heb 7:14. *Prevailed*: or "overcome" (Gk. *nikeō*; cf. 2:6 note, 7, 11, 17, 26, etc.). **5:6** *A Lamb . . . slain*: this image of a sacrificed (passover?) lamb comes as a surprise since the lion of Judah was just announced, but the figure does combine meekness with power: the slaughtered Lamb is also a ram of seven horns. *Seven eyes . . . earth*: alluding to Zech 4:2, 10b; cf. Rev 4:5. **5:8** *Vials full of odours*: bowls full of incense. Priests offered incense to God alongside blood sacrifices (Lev 16:11–14), which suggests that the prayers here come from those who have been slaughtered for their faith (cf. 6:9 and note). *Saints*: lit. "holy ones" (so throughout). **5:9–14** *Thou art . . . and ever*: this section's hymns to the lamb (vv. 9–10, 12, 13) invoke elements of the judgment scene from Dan 7:9–14. **5:9** *New song*: see Ps 33:3 note. *Redeemed*: "purchased" or "ransomed" (as a slave). Exodus uses such language (e.g., 15:16) to describe God's deliverance of Israel from Egypt. *Us*: better "people" (MS tradition). **5:10** *Hast made us . . . priests*: cf. Exod 19:6. *Us*: better "them" (MS tradition). *Kings*: better "a kingdom" (MS tradition). *We*: better

[11]And I beheld, and I heard the voice of many angels round about the throne and the beasts and the elders: and the number of them was ten thousand times ten thousand, and thousands of thousands; [12]saying with a loud voice, Worthy is the Lamb that was slain to receive power, and riches, and wisdom, and strength, and honour, and glory, and blessing. [13]And every creature which is in heaven, and on the earth, and under the earth, and such as are in the sea, and all that are in them, heard I saying, Blessing, and honour, and glory, and power, be unto him that sitteth upon the throne, and unto the Lamb for ever and ever. [14]And the four beasts said, Amen. And the four and twenty elders fell down and worshipped him that liveth for ever and ever.

6 And I saw when the Lamb opened one of the seals, and I heard, as it were the noise of thunder, one of the four beasts saying, Come and see. [2]And I saw, and behold a white horse: and he that sat on him had a bow; and a crown was given unto him: and he went forth conquering, and to conquer.

[3]And when he had opened the second seal, I heard the second beast say, Come and see. [4]And there went out another horse that was red: and power was given to him that sat thereon to take peace from the earth, and that they should kill one another: and there was given unto him a great sword.

[5]And when he had opened the third seal, I heard the third beast say, Come and see. And I beheld, and lo a black horse; and he that sat on him had a pair of balances in his hand. [6]And I heard a voice in the midst of the four beasts say, A measure of wheat for a penny, and three measures of barley for a penny; and see thou hurt not the oil and the wine.

[7]And when he had opened the fourth seal, I heard the voice of the fourth beast say, Come and see. [8]And I looked, and behold a pale horse: and his name that sat on him was Death, and Hell followed with him. And power was given unto them over the fourth part of the earth, to kill with sword, and with hunger, and with death, and with the beasts of the earth.

[9]And when he had opened the fifth seal, I saw under the altar the souls of them that were slain for the word of God, and for the testimony which they held: [10]and they cried with a loud voice, saying, How long, O Lord, holy and true, dost

---

"they" (MS tradition).   **5:13** *Every creature . . . and ever*: cf. Phil 2:10–11.   **5:14** *Him that . . . and ever*: better omitted (MS tradition).

   6:1–8:1 The seven seals. Like the subsequent sounding of the seven trumpets, the first six seals are opened in rapid progression (chap. 6), followed by a digressive interlude (chap. 7) and then the opening of the seventh seal in 8:1. The four horsemen are based on the four chariots from Zech 6:1–8 (cf. Zech 1:7–17), but other OT texts lie in the background, especially the promises of divine judgment from Ezek 14:12–23 and Lev 26:18–39.   **6:1** *And see*: better omitted (MS tradition), also in vv. 3, 5, and 7. In each case, the command is issued to the horseman, not to John.   **6:6** *Penny*: corresponding to a day's wages (see Mark 14:5 note). The voice therefore commands excessive inflation of the price of grain, probably by means of famine.   **6:8** *Hell*: Gk. *hadēs*; see Matt 11:23 note. *With death*: see 2:23 note.   **6:9** *Altar*: not previously mentioned, but 5:8 suggested the incense altar's presence (cf. Exod 30:1–10 and Rev 8:3, where the altar is golden). The souls' location underneath it equates their deaths with sacrifices (see 5:8 and note; cf. Lev 4:7), as other ancient Jewish texts understand martyrs' deaths (e.g., *4 Maccabees* 6.28–29).   **6:10** *How long, O Lord*: a conventional refrain in biblical poetry; John may allude in particular to Ps 79:5, 10. *Lord*: Gk. *despotēs*, lit.

thou not judge and avenge our blood on them that dwell on the earth? ¹¹And white robes were given unto every one of them; and it was said unto them, that they should rest yet for a little season, until their fellowservants also and their brethren, that should be killed as they were, should be fulfilled.

¹²And I beheld when he had opened the sixth seal, and, lo, there was a great earthquake; and the sun became black as sackcloth of hair, and the moon became as blood; ¹³and the stars of heaven fell unto the earth, even as a fig tree casteth her untimely figs, when she is shaken of a mighty wind. ¹⁴And the heaven departed as a scroll when it is rolled together; and every mountain and island were moved out of their places. ¹⁵And the kings of the earth, and the great men, and the rich men, and the chief captains, and the mighty men, and every bondman, and every free man, hid themselves in the dens and in the rocks of the mountains; ¹⁶and said to the mountains and rocks, Fall on us, and hide us from the face of him that sitteth on the throne, and from the wrath of the Lamb: ¹⁷for the great day of his wrath is come; and who shall be able to stand?

7 And after these things I saw four angels standing on the four corners of the earth, holding the four winds of the earth, that the wind should not blow on the earth, nor on the sea, nor on any tree. ²And I saw another angel ascending from the east, having the seal of the living God: and he cried with a loud voice to the four angels, to whom it was given to hurt the earth and the sea, ³saying, Hurt not the earth, neither the sea, nor the trees, till we have sealed the servants of our God in their foreheads. ⁴And I heard the number of them which were sealed: and there were sealed an hundred and forty and four thousand of all the tribes of the children of Israel. ⁵Of the tribe of Juda were sealed twelve thousand. Of the

---

"master" (not *kyrios*, the word normally rendered "Lord").   **6:11** *White robes . . . season*: the white robes affirm their purity; but since the donning of new garments conventionally figures resurrection (see 2 Cor 5:2 and note), they also anticipate the martyrs' rising from the dead at God's eschatological rectification of the cosmos (see 20:4–6). *Until their fellowservants . . . fulfilled*: ancient Jewish literature commonly features a preordained number of the righteous (cf. 2 Esd 4:35–37 and notes; Rom 11:25, "fulness of the Gentiles"; etc.).   **6:12–14** *A great . . . places*: the clearest allusion is to Isa 34:4, but the passage draws on imagery of cosmic cataclysm from numerous prophetic texts, including Isa 13:10–13; 24:19–23; Ezek 32:6–8; Joel 2:10, 30–31; 3:15–16; Hab 3:6–11.   **6:15** *The kings . . . mountains*: recalling Isa 2:17–3:5. *Chief captains*: military leaders. *Bondman*: slave.   **6:16** *Said to . . . hide us*: cf. Hos 10:8.   **6:17** *For the great day . . . stand*: cf. Joel 2:11; Nah 1:5–6; Mal 4:5; etc. *His*: better "their" (MS tradition).   **7:1–17** *And after . . . eyes*: an elaborate digression answering the question of 6:17; 7:1–8 explains that before the scroll's seals were broken, God's protective seal was placed on his servants.   **7:1** *Four winds of the earth*: the four horsemen (cf. Zech 6:1–5).   **7:2** *Seal*: a mark from a signet ring, here to designate one's property. (Ezek 9 lies in the background, and ultimately Exod 12–13).   **7:3** *In their foreheads*: cf. 3:12 note.   **7:4** *An hundred . . . Israel*: the identities of this group (which returns at 14:1–5) and of the universal multitude (v. 9) have been much debated. For example, both may be the Christian church; both may be the full number of Christian martyrs (cf. 6:11); the 144,000 may be Christian martyrs and the more inclusive group may represent the church in its entirety; and the 144,000 may be Jews (or Jewish believers in Christ) and the larger group may represent the Christian community, including Jews and Gentiles. The last is the plainest interpretation of the chapter and is consistent with Paul's speculation that God's eschatological intervention must entail Israel's salvation (Rom 9–11), but it is difficult to reconcile with the group's reappearance at 14:1–5.   **7:5–8** *Of the tribe . . . thousand*: formally resembling the military census of Num 1 (cf.

tribe of Reuben were sealed twelve thousand. Of the tribe of Gad were sealed twelve thousand. [6]Of the tribe of Aser were sealed twelve thousand. Of the tribe of Nepthalim were sealed twelve thousand. Of the tribe of Manasses were sealed twelve thousand. [7]Of the tribe of Simeon were sealed twelve thousand. Of the tribe of Levi were sealed twelve thousand. Of the tribe of Issachar were sealed twelve thousand. [8]Of the tribe of Zabulon were sealed twelve thousand. Of the tribe of Joseph were sealed twelve thousand. Of the tribe of Benjamin were sealed twelve thousand.

[9]After this I beheld, and, lo, a great multitude, which no man could number, of all nations, and kindreds, and people, and tongues, stood before the throne, and before the Lamb, clothed with white robes, and palms in their hands; [10]and cried with a loud voice, saying, Salvation to our God which sitteth upon the throne, and unto the Lamb. [11]And all the angels stood round about the throne, and about the elders and the four beasts, and fell before the throne on their faces, and worshipped God, [12]saying, Amen: Blessing, and glory, and wisdom, and thanksgiving, and honour, and power, and might, be unto our God for ever and ever. Amen.

[13]And one of the elders answered, saying unto me, What are these which are arrayed in white robes? and whence came they? [14]And I said unto him, Sir, thou knowest. And he said to me, These are they which came out of great tribulation, and have washed their robes, and made them white in the blood of the Lamb. [15]Therefore are they before the throne of God, and serve him day and night in his temple: and he that sitteth on the throne shall dwell among them. [16]They shall hunger no more, neither thirst any more; neither shall the sun light on them, nor any heat. [17]For the Lamb which is in the midst of the throne shall feed them, and shall lead them unto living fountains of waters: and God shall wipe away all tears from their eyes.

Num 10:14–28; 13:1–16, also in military contexts). Levi is included (v. 7), although the priestly tribe was regularly omitted from OT lists (as from Num 1; cf. vv. 47–54). To compensate, the tribe of Joseph was counted as two, one under the name of each of his sons (Ephraim and Manasseh; cf. Num 1:32–35). But in Revelation's list, the tribe of Manasseh (v. 6) is accompanied by Joseph (v. 8) rather than Ephraim (omitted), and the tribe of Dan is missing as well. The rationale for these deviations is unclear, and the absence of Dan is especially strange. Some associate it with the tribe's reputation for violence and idolatry (cf. Gen 49:17; Deut 33:22; Judg 18); some ancient Christians more imaginatively connected the omission with Jer 8:16–17, which they supposed to prophesy that the Antichrist would be a Danite (see e.g., Irenaeus, *Against Heresies* 5.30.2). **7:9** *A great multitude . . . tongues*: echoing God's promise that all nations would be blessed by Abraham and his offspring (cf. Gen 18:18; 22:17–18; etc.). It finds its fulfillment in this vision of the universal multitude praising God for his salvation of the 144,000 Israelites. *Palms in their hands*: compare the celebration of Simon Maccabeus's capture of the Jerusalem citadel (1 Macc 13:51). **7:14** *Great tribulation*: see 3:10 and note. *Made them . . . Lamb*: this paradoxical image alludes to Christ's death understood as an atoning sacrifice (cf. Heb 9:1–10:18). Also compare Dan 11:35, where those who suffer eschatological tribulation are cleansed by the suffering itself, thereby becoming white. **7:15–17** *Serve him . . . waters*: alluding to Isa 25:8; 49:9–10 and anticipating the paradisiacal new Jerusalem of Rev 21:1–22:5 (see esp. 21:3–4, 6, 23; 22:1). As in 3:12, the reference to God's temple is not literal. God's sustained presence itself constitutes a temple (cf. 7:15; 21:22). **7:15** *Serve*: the Greek word refers to cultic service. **7:17** *Feed*: lit. "shepherd," another paradoxical metaphor describing the lamb. *Living*

8 And when he had opened the seventh seal, there was silence in heaven about the space of half an hour.

^{2}And I saw the seven angels which stood before God; and to them were given seven trumpets. ^{3}And another angel came and stood at the altar, having a golden censer; and there was given unto him much incense, that he should offer it with the prayers of all saints upon the golden altar which was before the throne. ^{4}And the smoke of the incense, which came with the prayers of the saints, ascended up before God out of the angel's hand. ^{5}And the angel took the censer, and filled it with fire of the altar, and cast it into the earth: and there were voices, and thunderings, and lightnings, and an earthquake. ^{6}And the seven angels which had the seven trumpets prepared themselves to sound.

^{7}The first angel sounded, and there followed hail and fire mingled with blood, and they were cast upon the earth: and the third part of trees was burnt up, and all green grass was burnt up.

^{8}And the second angel sounded, and as it were a great mountain burning with fire was cast into the sea: and the third part of the sea became blood; ^{9}and the third part of the creatures which were in the sea, and had life, died; and the third part of the ships were destroyed.

^{10}And the third angel sounded, and there fell a great star from heaven, burning as it were a lamp, and it fell upon the third part of the rivers, and upon the fountains of waters; ^{11}and the name of the star is called Wormwood: and the third part of the waters became wormwood; and many men died of the waters, because they were made bitter.

^{12}And the fourth angel sounded, and the third part of the sun was smitten, and the third part of the moon, and the third part of the stars; so as the third part of them was darkened, and the day shone not for a third part of it, and the night

---

fountains of waters: better "fountains of waters of life" (MS tradition).   **8:1** *Silence*: a conventional response before God's terrifying intervention and judgment (cf. Zeph 1:7; Zech 2:13; etc.), which here allows the saints' prayers to be heard (8:3–4).

8:2–11:18 The seven trumpets. After the prayers of the saints (8:2–6), the first six of the seven trumpets sound in rapid sequence (8:7–9:21), with an extended interlude (10:1–11:14) before the last at 11:15–18. Although the particular kinds of destruction heralded by the trumpets recall the Egyptian plagues (Exod 7–12), the scene as a whole is modeled on the destruction of Jericho in Josh 6, where seven priests bear seven trumpets and sound them on seven successive days, on the last of which Jericho falls. In Revelation metaphorical Babylon (most clearly at 17:5, 9 [see note]) is the target of God's judgment, as John's numerous echoes of Isaiah's and Jeremiah's oracles against the city make clear.   **8:2** *Seven angels*: see 1:4 and note.   **8:3–4** *Another angel . . . hand*: recalling 5:8 and 6:9–11 (see notes).   **8:5** *The angel . . . earth*: based on Ezek 10:1–7 and signaling God's judgment. The prayers of 6:9–10, deferred in 6:11, are now answered. *Voices, and . . . earthquake*: compare the Sinai theophany (Exod 19:16–19), which also features the sounding of trumpets.   **8:7** *Hail and . . . blood*: cf. Exod 9:22–25, the seventh Egyptian plague. *The earth*: better to add "and the third part of the earth was burnt up" (MS tradition). References to "the third part" (perhaps inspired by Ezek 5:2, 12) signal that the judgment is extensive, but not overwhelming.   **8:8** *A great . . . sea*: cf. Jer 51:25, on the destruction of Babylon. *The sea became blood*: cf. Exod 7:20–21, the first Egyptian plague.   **8:10** *A great star*: echoing Isa 14:12, which refers to the king of Babylon (cf. Isa 14:4).   **8:11** *Wormwood*: a bitter and potentially poisonous plant associated with God's judgment at Jer 9:15; 23:15; etc. *And many men . . . bitter*: cf. Exod 7:21, 24, continuing the second trumpet's correspondence with the first plague.   **8:12** *The sun . . .*

likewise. [13]And I beheld, and heard an angel flying through the midst of heaven, saying with a loud voice, Woe, woe, woe, to the inhabiters of the earth by reason of the other voices of the trumpet of the three angels, which are yet to sound!

9 And the fifth angel sounded, and I saw a star fall from heaven unto the earth: and to him was given the key of the bottomless pit. [2]And he opened the bottomless pit; and there arose a smoke out of the pit, as the smoke of a great furnace; and the sun and the air were darkened by reason of the smoke of the pit. [3]And there came out of the smoke locusts upon the earth: and unto them was given power, as the scorpions of the earth have power. [4]And it was commanded them that they should not hurt the grass of the earth, neither any green thing, neither any tree; but only those men which have not the seal of God in their foreheads. [5]And to them it was given that they should not kill them, but that they should be tormented five months: and their torment was as the torment of a scorpion, when he striketh a man. [6]And in those days shall men seek death, and shall not find it; and shall desire to die, and death shall flee from them. [7]And the shapes of the locusts were like unto horses prepared unto battle; and on their heads were as it were crowns like gold, and their faces were as the faces of men. [8]And they had hair as the hair of women, and their teeth were as the teeth of lions. [9]And they had breastplates, as it were breastplates of iron; and the sound of their wings was as the sound of chariots of many horses running to battle. [10]And they had tails like unto scorpions, and there were stings in their tails: and their power was to hurt men five months. [11]And they had a king over them, which is the angel of the bottomless pit, whose name in the Hebrew tongue is Abaddon, but in the Greek tongue hath his name Apollyon. [12]One woe is past; and, behold, there come two woes more hereafter.

[13]And the sixth angel sounded, and I heard a voice from the four horns of the golden altar which is before God, [14]saying to the sixth angel which had the trumpet, Loose the four angels which are bound in the great river Euphrates. [15]And the four

---

likewise: cf. Exod 10:21–23, the ninth Egyptian plague.   **8:13** *An angel*: better "an eagle" (MS tradition); cf. Hos 8:1. John may be referring to the fourth living creature (cf. 4:7). *Woe, woe . . . sound*: for the three woes, see 9:12; 11:14; 12:12.   **9:1** *A star fall*: lit. "a star fallen"; not Satan (Luke 10:18 to the contrary; see note), but rather the angel who also appears at 20:1—there to lock the abyss, here to open it. *The key*: held by Christ in 1:18. *Bottomless pit*: Gk. *abyssos*, also "the deep": the underworld, where demons (cf. Luke 8:31) and the dead (cf. Rom 10:7) were sometimes thought to dwell.   **9:3** *Locusts*: cf. Exod 10:4–6, 12–15, the eighth Egyptian plague. The vivid depiction of the creatures (vv. 2–10) is inspired by the plague of locusts in Joel (1:2–2:27).   **9:5** *Five months*: obscure, but perhaps measuring the annual period during which the land was vulnerable to locust swarms, or a locust's life span.   **9:10** *And there . . . was*: better "and stings, and in their tails is their power" (MS tradition).   **9:11** *Abaddon*: Hebrew for "destruction," used of the place of the dead (e.g., Job 26:6; 28:22; Ps 88:11); it thus came to name the evil angel associated with the netherworld (not necessarily Satan, though a Qumran text makes the identification). *Apollyon*: Greek for "destroyer." A popular etymology linked "Apollo" with Gk. *apollynai* ("to destroy"); cf. Aeschylus, *Agamemnon* 1080–82. Perhaps John polemically identifies the Olympian god of the sun (a patron divinity for Augustus and other Roman emperors) with this chthonic demon-king.   **9:13** *A voice . . . God*: probably the voice of the martyrs (cf. 6:9–10), whose prayers initiated the blowing of the seven trumpets (8:3–5). *Four horns*: cf. Exod 27:2.   **9:14** *The four angels . . . Euphrates*: alluding to God's threats to punish Israel with an army "from the north" (Jer 13:18–20), i.e., from "beyond the [Euphrates] river" (Isa 7:20; cf. 8:7–8; etc.), and his promise to do the same to Babylon (by means of Cyrus's invasion; see, e.g., Jer 50:3, 9, 41; 51:48; see Rev 16:12 note). Since the Euphrates formed the Roman Empire's eastern boundary, with

angels were loosed, which were prepared for an hour, and a day, and a month, and a year, for to slay the third part of men. ¹⁶And the number of the army of the horsemen were two hundred thousand thousand: and I heard the number of them. ¹⁷And thus I saw the horses in the vision, and them that sat on them, having breastplates of fire, and of jacinth, and brimstone: and the heads of the horses were as the heads of lions; and out of their mouths issued fire and smoke and brimstone. ¹⁸By these three was the third part of men killed, by the fire, and by the smoke, and by the brimstone, which issued out of their mouths. ¹⁹For their power is in their mouth, and in their tails: for their tails were like unto serpents, and had heads, and with them they do hurt. ²⁰And the rest of the men which were not killed by these plagues yet repented not of the works of their hands, that they should not worship devils, and idols of gold, and silver, and brass, and stone, and of wood: which neither can see, nor hear, nor walk: ²¹neither repented they of their murders, nor of their sorceries, nor of their fornication, nor of their thefts.

10 And I saw another mighty angel come down from heaven, clothed with a cloud: and a rainbow was upon his head, and his face was as it were the sun, and his feet as pillars of fire: ²and he had in his hand a little book open: and he set his right foot upon the sea, and his left foot on the earth, ³and cried with

---

Parthia just beyond, John may imagine an invasion of the Parthian army and its fearsome cavalry. **9:15** *For an hour . . . year*: better "for the hour, and day, and month, and year," referring to the time when the killing began rather than to how long it lasted. **9:16** *Two hundred thousand thousand*: two hundred million. **9:17** *Jacinth*: Gk. *hyakinthos*, apparently a blue gemstone. *Brimstone*: repeated associations of this cavalry with fire, brimstone, and smoke recall the destruction of Sodom and Gomorrah; cf. Gen 19:24–25, 28. **9:18** *These three*: better "these three plagues/calamities" (MS tradition). **9:19** *Their power*: better "the horses' power" (MS tradition). **9:20** *The works . . . walk*: echoing the disparagement of idols at, e.g., Deut 4:28; Pss 115:4–7; 135:15–17; Dan 5:4, 23. *Devils*: demons, which idols were sometimes thought to represent; cf. 1 Cor 10:19–20. **9:21** *Their murders . . . thefts*: the Bible frequently connects such vices to idolatry; cf. Rom 1:18–32; Wis 14:12–31. **10:1–11:14** A brief repose. After the disturbing intensification of divine violence announced by the six trumpets, John offers a moment of rest during which God's prophetic witnesses testify. Allusions to Amos (see 10:3, 7 and notes) point to a theological explanation for the relatively peaceful interlude: according to Amos 3:6–4:3, God is responsible for cities' violent conquest (3:6) but also reveals his plans to his prophets (3:7), who warn cities of what God will do and explain why he acts (3:8–4:3, esp. 3:8–9). Carefully read, however, the interlude goes beyond that explanation's mandate, offering a dialogic or even polemical response to the increasingly unrestrained divine violence that has characterized Revelation since the Lamb began to open the scroll (6:1). The scroll whose gradual unsealing brought escalating devastation (6:1–8:1) in this section finds itself resealed (10:4); in implicit response to God's release of "the destroyer" (9:11 and note), this section identifies God as creator (10:6); in contrast to the noted absence of repentance in the wake of God's massive carnage (cf. 9:20–21), in this section the prophetic witnesses' testimony, substantiated by relatively restrained divine violence, results in mass conversion (11:13 and note); etc. The focus on self-sacrificial prophetic witness (see John's prophetic commissioning in 10:8–11 and especially the two witnesses' testimony in 11:3–13) may imply an alternative to divinely inspired violence. **10:1** *Pillars of fire* suggests that this angel represents God's presence (cf. Exod 13:21), a suggestion confirmed by similarities between its description, Ezekiel's vision of "the likeness of the glory of the Lord" (1:27–28), and Daniel's vision of the Ancient of days (7:9; 10:6; cf. Rev 1:15–16). The *rainbow*, although inspired by the Ezekiel passage, recalls the restraint vowed by God in Gen 9:8–17. **10:2** *Little book*: the scroll of chap. 5, soon to be consumed by John (vv. 9–10). *He set . . . earth*: figuring God's dominance over his entire creation; cf. v. 6.

a loud voice, as when a lion roareth: and when he had cried, seven thunders uttered their voices. ⁴And when the seven thunders had uttered their voices, I was about to write: and I heard a voice from heaven saying unto me, Seal up those things which the seven thunders uttered, and write them not. ⁵And the angel which I saw stand upon the sea and upon the earth lifted up his hand to heaven, ⁶and sware by him that liveth for ever and ever, who created heaven, and the things that therein are, and the earth, and the things that therein are, and the sea, and the things which are therein, that there should be time no longer: ⁷but in the days of the voice of the seventh angel, when he shall begin to sound, the mystery of God should be finished, as he hath declared to his servants the prophets.

⁸And the voice which I heard from heaven spake unto me again, and said, Go and take the little book which is open in the hand of the angel which standeth upon the sea and upon the earth. ⁹And I went unto the angel, and said unto him, Give me the little book. And he said unto me, Take it, and eat it up; and it shall make thy belly bitter, but it shall be in thy mouth sweet as honey. ¹⁰And I took the little book out of the angel's hand, and ate it up; and it was in my mouth sweet as honey: and as soon as I had eaten it, my belly was bitter. ¹¹And he said unto me, Thou must prophesy again before many peoples, and nations, and tongues, and kings.

11 And there was given me a reed like unto a rod: and the angel stood, saying, Rise, and measure the temple of God, and the altar, and them that worship therein. ²But the court which is without the temple leave out, and measure it not; for it is given unto the Gentiles: and the holy city shall they tread under foot forty and two months. ³And I will give power unto my two witnesses, and they shall prophesy a thousand two hundred and threescore days, clothed in sackcloth. ⁴These are the two olive trees, and the two candlesticks standing

---

10:3 *As when a lion roareth*: cf. Amos 3:8. *Seven thunders . . . voices*: referring to the voices announcing the opening of each seal (cf. 6:1). See also Ps 29, which compares the Lord's voice to a thunderstorm and repeats "the voice of the Lord" seven times.   **10:4** *Seal up . . . not*: cf. Dan 12:4, 9.   **10:6** *There should . . . longer*: there will no longer be an interval of time, i.e., it will happen right away. This oath (which contradicts the one sworn in Dan 12:7) probably looks back to 6:10–11, indicating the completion of the number of martyrs.   **10:7** *The voice . . . sound*: i.e., the seventh trumpet. *The mystery . . . prophets*: cf. Amos 3:7; the mystery thus refers to God's eschatological design, as in Rom 11:25–27; 16:25–26; etc. (If v. 6 recalls 6:10–11, then there may be a more specific reference, to the number of martyrs or to the purpose of their suffering.)   **10:9–11** *Take it . . . kings*: based on Ezekiel's prophetic commissioning (Ezek 2:8–3:14).   **10:11** *He said*: better "they said" (MS tradition).   **11:1** *The angel stood, saying*: better "he was saying" (MS tradition).   **11:1–2** *Rise, and . . . months*: based on Ezek 40–42, this passage contextualizes the following narrative of the two witnesses in a scene of eschatological conflict between God's people and Gentiles oppressing God's city.   **11:2** *Forty and two months*: three and a half years, the length of the period of tribulation in Daniel (7:25; 12:7 and notes), which also corresponds to the length of time that the drought prophesied by Elijah (1 Kgs 17–18; cf. Rev 11:6 and note) was supposed to have lasted (cf. Luke 4:25; Jas 5:17).   **11:3** *Power*: a KJV interpolation. *Two witnesses*: cf. Deut 19:15, which specifies that at least two witnesses are required to sustain a conviction. *A thousand . . . days*: forty-two months; see v. 2 note. *Sackcloth*: garments made out of rough animal hair, worn often in mourning but also by prophets to exemplify self-effacing submission to God; cf. Isa 20:2; Zech 13:4; Mark 1:6.   **11:4** *Two olive trees . . . candlesticks*: see Zech 4:1–5, 10b–14 and v. 10 note. The reference to *candlesticks* perhaps connects these witnesses with God's

before the God of the earth. ⁵And if any man will hurt them, fire proceedeth out of their mouth, and devoureth their enemies: and if any man will hurt them, he must in this manner be killed. ⁶These have power to shut heaven, that it rain not in the days of their prophecy: and have power over waters to turn them to blood, and to smite the earth with all plagues, as often as they will.

⁷And when they shall have finished their testimony, the beast that ascendeth out of the bottomless pit shall make war against them, and shall overcome them, and kill them. ⁸And their dead bodies shall lie in the street of the great city, which spiritually is called Sodom and Egypt, where also our Lord was crucified. ⁹And they of the people and kindreds and tongues and nations shall see their dead bodies three days and an half, and shall not suffer their dead bodies to be put in graves. ¹⁰And they that dwell upon the earth shall rejoice over them, and make merry, and shall send gifts one to another; because these two prophets tormented them that dwelt on the earth. ¹¹And after three days and an half the Spirit of life from God entered into them, and they stood upon their feet; and great fear fell upon them which saw them. ¹²And they heard a great voice from heaven saying unto them, Come up hither. And they ascended up to heaven in a cloud; and their enemies beheld them. ¹³And the same hour was there a great earthquake, and the tenth part of the city fell, and in the earthquake were slain of men seven thousand: and the remnant were affrighted, and gave glory to the God of heaven. ¹⁴The second woe is past; and, behold, the third woe cometh quickly.

¹⁵And the seventh angel sounded; and there were great voices in heaven, saying, The kingdoms of this world are become the kingdoms of our Lord, and of his Christ; and he shall reign for ever and ever. ¹⁶And the four and twenty elders, which sat before God on their seats, fell upon their faces, and worshipped God, ¹⁷saying, We give thee thanks, O Lord God Almighty, which art, and wast, and art to come; because thou hast taken to thee thy great power, and hast reigned.

---

churches (cf. 1:20).   **11:5** *Fire proceedeth . . . enemies*: cf. Isa 11:4 and Jer 5:14, which liken God's judgment to deadly fire in the prophet's or messiah's mouth. The language also recalls Elijah's words in 2 Kgs 1:10.   **11:6** *To shut . . . prophecy*: recalling Elijah (1 Kgs 17:1). *Have power over . . . will*: recalling Moses and the ten plagues (Exod 7–12).   **11:7** *The beast . . . kill them*: recalling the fourth beast of Daniel (7:7–27, esp. v. 21).   **11:8** *The great city*: elsewhere in Revelation, "the great city" is Babylon (i.e., Rome), but here the label is applied to Jerusalem. *Sodom*: an example of perversion and injustice (cf. Gen 18:16–19:29). The OT prophets frequently liken Jerusalem to it (see, e.g., Isa 3:8–9; Jer 23:14; Ezek 16:46–51). *Egypt*: the paradigm of idolatry and oppression.   **11:9** *They of the people . . . graves*: cf. Ps 79:1–3. *Three days and an half*: cf. vv. 2–3 and notes for an analogous period of three and a half years. Here it recalls the interval between Jesus' death and resurrection.   **11:11** *The Spirit . . . feet*: cf. Ezek 37:10.   **11:12** *They ascended up to heaven*: like Elijah (2 Kgs 2:11) and, by tradition, Moses (see Mark 9:4 note), and of course Jesus (Luke 24:51; Acts 1:6–11).   **11:13** *A great earthquake . . . thousand*: in contrast to previous references to a "third part" suffering God's violence (8:7–12; 9:15, 18), here only a *tenth part* of the city is destroyed while the rest repents. In Isa 6:13, Amos 5:3, and elsewhere, a tenth of the population survives God's judgment; the reversal of this conventional ratio underscores the restraint God now exercises.   **11:15** *The seventh angel sounded*: the hymn that follows, praising God for exercising dominion over the earth (vv. 15–17) and for judging the dead (v. 18; cf. 20:12–13), suggests that the seventh trumpet marks the eschatological consummation. *Kingdoms . . . are become . . . kingdoms*: better "kingdom . . . is become . . . kingdom" (MS tradition).   **11:17** *And art to come*:

¹⁸And the nations were angry, and thy wrath is come, and the time of the dead, that they should be judged, and that thou shouldest give reward unto thy servants the prophets, and to the saints, and them that fear thy name, small and great; and shouldest destroy them which destroy the earth.

¹⁹And the temple of God was opened in heaven, and there was seen in his temple the ark of his testament: and there were lightnings, and voices, and thunderings, and an earthquake, and great hail. ¹And there appeared a great wonder in heaven; a woman clothed with the sun, and the moon under her feet, and upon her head a crown of twelve stars: ²and she being with child cried, travailing in birth, and pained to be delivered. ³And there appeared another wonder in heaven; and behold a great red dragon, having seven heads and ten horns, and seven crowns upon his heads. ⁴And his tail drew the third part of the stars of heaven, and did cast them to the earth: and the dragon stood before the woman which was ready to be delivered, for to devour her child as soon as it was

---

better omitted (MS tradition).   **11:18** *The nations were angry*: cf. Pss 2:1; 46:6. Gk. *ethnē* (*nations*) was rendered "Gentiles" in v. 2. *Shouldest destroy . . . earth*: echoing Jer 51:25.

11:19–15:4 Visions of conflict and judgment. This section consists of a series of visions that presents an overarching narrative symbolically describing the advent of Christ (11:19–12:13a) and the persecution of the church under Rome (12:13b–13:18), and culminating in a tableau of God's eschatological judgment (14:1–15:4). The events it depicts seem in part to overlap with the eschatological scenario developed in chaps. 6–11; but because 12:12 concludes the trio of woes announced in 8:13 (cf. 9:12; 11:14), this section may complete rather than coincide with the preceding material. Perhaps we should associate the entire section with the final trumpet's blare, understanding it to provide a mythic narrative of the events leading to the eschatological judgment that the trumpet introduces (11:15–18). The inclusive frame established by parallels between this section's final verses (15:1–4; see also v. 5) and the hymnic response to the seventh trumpet's blast (11:16–18; see also v. 19) support such a reading. However it relates to the previous section, the present one may be divided into seven parts, according to Beale: (a) the dragon's pursuit of the woman (11:19–12:17), (b) the first beast (13:1–10), (c) the second beast (13:11–18), (d) the 144,000 (14:1–5), (e) judgment announced (14:6–13), (f) judgment enacted (14:14–20), and (g) victory celebrated (15:1–4).   **11:19–12:17** The dragon's pursuit. This symbolic narrative has much in common with the myth of Python and Apollo, on which it is probably based see, e.g., Hyginus, *Fabulae* 140: "Python . . . was a huge dragon. . . . Death was fated to come to him from the offspring of Latona. At that time Jove lay with Latona. . . . When Juno found this out, she decreed that Latona should give birth at a place where the sun did not shine. When Python knew that Latona was pregnant by Jove, he followed her to kill her. But by the order of Jove the wind Aquilo carried Latona away, and bore her to Neptune. He protected her, but in order not to abrogate Juno's decree, he took her to the island Ortygia, and covered the island with waves. When Python did not find her, he returned to Parnassus. But Neptune brought the island of Ortygia up to a higher position; it was later called the island of Delos. There, Latona, clinging to an olive tree, bore Apollo and Diana, to whom Vulcan gave arrows as gifts. Four days after they were born, Apollo exacted vengeance for his mother. For he went to Parnassus and slew Python with his arrows" (trans. Mary Douglass, slightly altered).   **11:19** *Ark of his testament*: a sign of God's faithfulness to his covenant and of his presence with the community. (In the tabernacle/temple, the ark was hidden from sight within the inner sanctum; see Exod 26:31–35.)   **12:1** *Wonder*: lit. "sign." *The sun . . . stars*: cf. Gen 37:9–10, where the sun, moon, and zodiac figure the patriarch Jacob and his wife plus the twelve tribes' eponymous ancestors.   **12:2** *She being with child . . . delivered*: in the OT Prophets, Israel is frequently likened to a woman in travail (Jer 4:31; Mic 4:10; etc.).   **12:3** *Dragon*: Gk. *drakōn*, the word used by LXX to translate the Hebrew word for the sea monster rendered "leviathan"; cf. Ps 74:14; Isa 27:1 and notes. *Ten horns*: compare the beast from Dan 7:7, 24. *Crowns*: lit. "diadems" (a different word is used in 12:1).   **12:4** *His tail . . . earth*: cf. Dan 8:10, which itself echoes

born. ⁵And she brought forth a man child, who was to rule all nations with a rod of iron: and her child was caught up unto God, and to his throne. ⁶And the woman fled into the wilderness, where she hath a place prepared of God, that they should feed her there a thousand two hundred and threescore days.

⁷And there was war in heaven: Michael and his angels fought against the dragon; and the dragon fought and his angels, ⁸and prevailed not; neither was their place found any more in heaven. ⁹And the great dragon was cast out, that old serpent, called the Devil, and Satan, which deceiveth the whole world: he was cast out into the earth, and his angels were cast out with him. ¹⁰And I heard a loud voice saying in heaven, Now is come salvation, and strength, and the kingdom of our God, and the power of his Christ: for the accuser of our brethren is cast down, which accused them before our God day and night. ¹¹And they overcame him by the blood of the Lamb, and by the word of their testimony; and they loved not their lives unto the death. ¹²Therefore rejoice, ye heavens, and ye that dwell in them. Woe to the inhabiters of the earth and of the sea! for the devil is come down unto you, having great wrath, because he knoweth that he hath but a short time.

¹³And when the dragon saw that he was cast unto the earth, he persecuted the woman which brought forth the man child. ¹⁴And to the woman were given two wings of a great eagle, that she might fly into the wilderness, into her place, where she is nourished for a time, and times, and half a time, from the face of the serpent. ¹⁵And the serpent cast out of his mouth water as a flood after the woman, that he might cause her to be carried away of the flood. ¹⁶And the earth helped the woman, and the earth opened her mouth, and swallowed up the flood which the dragon cast out of his mouth. ¹⁷And the dragon was wroth with the woman, and went to make war with the remnant of her seed, which keep the commandments of God, and have the testimony of Jesus Christ.

Isa 14:13–14, commonly taken as a reference to Satan (see Isa 14:12 note). **12:5** *She brought . . . child*: cf. Isa 66:7. *Who was . . . iron*: cf. Ps 2:7–9; see Rev 2:27 and note. *Caught up . . . throne*: alluding to Jesus' resurrection/ascension; cf. Heb 12:2; 1 Pet 3:21–22; etc. **12:6** *Fled into the wilderness . . . there*: recalling God's protection of Israel during the wilderness wanderings. *A thousand . . . days*: see 11:3 note. **12:7** *War in heaven*: although vv. 7–9 are often viewed as a description of Satan's primeval expulsion from heaven, it is apparently the attempt of the dragon (identified with Satan in v. 9) to destroy the risen Christ that leads to his permanent exclusion. Thus Revelation, like Luke 10:18 but unlike other Jewish apocalyptic texts (e.g., *Life of Adam and Eve* 12–16) and the Qur'an (2:34; 15:28–39), presents Satan's expulsion as an eschatological rather than a primeval occurrence. This scenario could resolve the seeming contradiction in the OT's presentation of "Satan" (see Job 1:6 note) as a heavenly courtier who brings accusations before God (Job 1–2; Ps 109:6–7; Zech 3:1–2). *Michael*: see Dan 10:13 and note; 12:1. **12:9** *Old serpent . . . world*: recalling Gen 3; cf. 2 Cor 11:14 and note. **12:10** *Accuser*: see Job 1:6 note. **12:12** *The inhabiters . . . sea*: better "the earth and the sea" (MS tradition). **12:13** *Persecuted*: or "pursued." **12:14** *Two wings . . . eagle*: recalling OT metaphors describing God's deliverance of Israel from Egypt (Exod 19:4) and nourishment in the wilderness (Deut 32:10–11). *A time . . . time*: see Dan 7:25 and note; cf. Rev 11:2 note. **12:15** *Flood*: Gk. *potamos*, better "river" or perhaps "torrent" (twice, and also in v. 16). **12:16** *The earth . . . his mouth*: recalling numerous OT portrayals of God's defeat of the sea monster (to which the serpent is related; see v. 3 note), especially Isa 51:9–10, where its destruction is conflated with the parting of the Red Sea. **12:17** *Wroth*: indignant.

13 And I stood upon the sand of the sea, and saw a beast rise up out of the sea, having seven heads and ten horns, and upon his horns ten crowns, and upon his heads the name of blasphemy. ²And the beast which I saw was like unto a leopard, and his feet were as the feet of a bear, and his mouth as the mouth of a lion: and the dragon gave him his power, and his seat, and great authority. ³And I saw one of his heads as it were wounded to death; and his deadly wound was healed: and all the world wondered after the beast. ⁴And they worshipped the dragon which gave power unto the beast: and they worshipped the beast, saying, Who is like unto the beast? who is able to make war with him? ⁵And there was given unto him a mouth speaking great things and blasphemies; and power was given unto him to continue forty and two months. ⁶And he opened his mouth in blasphemy against God, to blaspheme his name, and his tabernacle, and them that dwell in heaven. ⁷And it was given unto him to make war with the saints, and to overcome them: and power was given him over all kindreds, and tongues, and nations. ⁸And all that dwell upon the earth shall worship him, whose names are not written in the book of life of the Lamb slain from the foundation of the world. ⁹If any man have an ear, let him hear. ¹⁰He that leadeth into captivity shall go into captivity: he that killeth with the sword must be killed with the sword. Here is the patience and the faith of the saints.

13:1 *I stood*: better "he stood" (MS tradition), referring to the dragon. *And saw*: better "and I saw" (MS tradition), introducing the second vision. *Out of the sea . . . blasphemy*: like the dragon it resembles (see 12:3), this beast recalls those of Dan 7:3–7; cf. Rev 11:7. *The name of blasphemy*: better "names of blasphemy" (MS tradition).   **13:2** *The dragon . . . authority*: Rev 17:9–10 associates this beast with Rome (see notes), so John suggests that Satan authorizes Roman rule. *Seat*: Gk. *thronos* (cf. 4:4 and note; 12:5).   **13:3** *One of his heads . . . healed*: a dark parody of Jesus' resurrection (Gk. *esphagmenēn*, translated *wounded*, is rendered "slain" when used of the lamb in v. 8 and also in 5:6, 9, 12), reflecting the widespread rumor that Nero, who committed suicide in 68 C.E., had been restored to life and was plotting to resume rule. Various figures claiming his identity arose for years after the emperor's death (cf. Suetonius, *Nero* 57; Tacitus, *Histories* 2.8–9; see Appendix, p. 987). Probably because of Nero's persecution of Christians in Rome (Tacitus, *Annals* 15.44; see Appendix, pp. 983–84), John presents him as the emblem of Roman blasphemy. *Wound*: Gk. *plēgē* (also v. 12), elsewhere translated "plague"; cf. 9:20; 11:6; etc.   **13:4** *Who is like . . . him*: echoing conventional OT assertions of God's unique omnipotence (see especially Ps 89:6–8, celebrating God's defeat of Leviathan). Their ironic deployment complements John's description of the beast as a perverse parody of the Lamb—it has multiple horns (13:1; cf. 5:6) and has been slain, resurrected (13:3), and enthroned by Satan (13:2; cf. 12:5). Adding to the irony, the Gk. verb *polemein, to make war* (also in v. 7), was used in 12:7 ("fought"), where Michael and his angels defeated the beast's sponsor.   **13:5–7** *Speaking great . . . them*: recalling the fourth beast's hostility toward God and those sided with him in Dan 7:8 (see note), 25.   **13:5** *Forty and two months*: see 11:2 note.   **13:6** *Tabernacle, and*: better simply "tabernacle" (MS tradition), equating the tabernacle with those dwelling in heaven. (The Greek words translated *tabernacle* and *dwell* are cognates.)   **13:7** *Power was . . . nations*: Dan 7:14 attributes this authority to the Son of Man.   **13:8** *The book of life*: see 3:5 note.   **13:10** *He that leadeth . . . killed with the sword*: the MS tradition is confused because scribes have attempted to clarify the epigrammatic phrases. A possible reading, taking into account the textual variations, is "If someone is for captivity, that one is led away captive; if someone is to be killed with a sword, that one is killed with a sword." The epigrams would thus allude to the fatalistic declarations of Jer 15:2 and 43:11. However, KJV's translation of the second phrase is also a viable reading, suggesting an additional allusion to the dominical saying at

[11]And I beheld another beast coming up out of the earth; and he had two horns like a lamb, and he spake as a dragon. [12]And he exerciseth all the power of the first beast before him, and causeth the earth and them which dwell therein to worship the first beast, whose deadly wound was healed. [13]And he doeth great wonders, so that he maketh fire come down from heaven on the earth in the sight of men, [14]and deceiveth them that dwell on the earth by the means of those miracles which he had power to do in the sight of the beast; saying to them that dwell on the earth, that they should make an image to the beast, which had the wound by a sword, and did live. [15]And he had power to give life unto the image of the beast, that the image of the beast should both speak, and cause that as many as would not worship the image of the beast should be killed. [16]And he causeth all, both small and great, rich and poor, free and bond, to receive a mark in their right hand, or in their foreheads: [17]and that no man might buy or sell, save he that had the mark, or the name of the beast, or the number of his name. [18]Here is wisdom. Let him that hath understanding count the number of the beast: for it is the number of a man; and his number is Six hundred threescore and six.

14 And I looked, and, lo, a Lamb stood on the mount Sion, and with him an hundred forty and four thousand, having his Father's name written in their foreheads. [2]And I heard a voice from heaven, as the voice of many waters, and as the voice of a great thunder: and I heard the voice of harpers harping with their harps: [3]and they sung as it were a new song before the throne, and before the four beasts, and the elders: and no man could learn that song but the hundred and forty and four thousand, which were redeemed from the earth. [4]These

---

Matt 26:52.   **13:12** *Causeth the earth . . . beast*: if the first beast represents Rome and its rulers (see vv. 2–3 and notes), then the second must represent the imperial cult (the worship of Roman emperors, a religious institution that was expanded under Domitian and was especially prevalent in Asia Minor) and other imperial propaganda.   **13:13** *Wonders*: lit. "signs" (also in v. 14 [KJV "miracles"]), perhaps recalling the numerous "signs" done by Moses on God's behalf (cf. Exod 4:8, 9, 17, 30; etc.). *Maketh fire . . . men*: attributed to Elijah (1 Kgs 18:38; 2 Kgs 1:9–14). The second beast is described in terms evocative of God's two witnesses (cf. 11:5).   **13:14** *He had power*: lit. "it was given to him" (also in v. 15).   **13:15** *Life*: lit. "breath," probably alluding to Gen 2:7. *That the image . . . speak*: compare Lucian's description of the charlatan Alexander rigging an icon of the god Asclepius to speak (*The False Prophet* 26). *Cause that . . . killed*: cf. Dan 3:1–7; the threat had special resonance for John's audience, since refusal to participate in the imperial cult could be viewed as seditious.   **13:16–17** *A mark . . . beast*: Ptolemy IV branded with the symbol of Dionysus those Alexandrian Jews who refused to participate in the official cult (see 3 *Maccabees* 2.27–29). John also alludes to money, for "no man might buy or sell" without the mark—i.e., the legends on Roman coins declaring the divinity of Rome and of its emperors (see Mark 12:14 note). The beast's mark thus symbolizes idolatrous money, with its location "in their right hands" and "in their foreheads" gesturing at its exchange and parodying the seal of God (cf. 7:2–3; 9:4; etc.).   **13:17–18** *The number . . . six*: gematria—the practice of finding hidden meaning by assigning numerical values to letters and summing (or otherwise manipulating) a word's or phrase's corresponding numbers—was widespread in the ancient world; many scholars speculate that 666 corresponds to a Hebrew transliteration of "Nero Caesar."   **14:1** *Mount Sion*: located in (or just outside) Jerusalem, but here either a heavenly Zion or the eschatological new Jerusalem. There is probably an allusion to Ps 2 (esp. vv. 6–7; see v. 6 note). *An hundred . . . foreheads*: see 7:3–4 and notes. *His Father's name*: better "his name and his father's name" (MS tradition).   **14:3** *Redeemed*: see 5:9 note (also at v. 4).

are they which were not defiled with women; for they are virgins. These are they which follow the Lamb whithersoever he goeth. These were redeemed from among men, being the firstfruits unto God and to the Lamb. [5]And in their mouth was found no guile: for they are without fault before the throne of God.

[6]And I saw another angel fly in the midst of heaven, having the everlasting gospel to preach unto them that dwell on the earth, and to every nation, and kindred, and tongue, and people, [7]saying with a loud voice, Fear God, and give glory to him; for the hour of his judgment is come: and worship him that made heaven, and earth, and the sea, and the fountains of waters. [8]And there followed another angel, saying, Babylon is fallen, is fallen, that great city, because she made all nations drink of the wine of the wrath of her fornication. [9]And the third angel followed them, saying with a loud voice, If any man worship the beast and his image, and receive his mark in his forehead, or in his hand, [10]the same shall drink of the wine of the wrath of God, which is poured out without mixture into the cup of his indignation; and he shall be tormented with fire and brimstone in the presence of the holy angels, and in the presence of the Lamb: [11]and the smoke of their torment ascendeth up for ever and ever: and they have no rest day nor night, who worship the beast and his image, and whosoever receiveth the mark of his name. [12]Here is the patience of the saints: here are they that keep the commandments of God, and the faith of Jesus. [13]And I heard a voice from heaven saying unto me, Write, Blessed are the dead which die in the Lord from henceforth: Yea, saith the Spirit, that they may rest from their labours; and their works do follow them.

[14]And I looked, and behold a white cloud, and upon the cloud one sat like unto the Son of man, having on his head a golden crown, and in his hand a sharp sickle. [15]And another angel came out of the temple, crying with a loud voice to him that sat on the cloud, Thrust in thy sickle, and reap: for the time is come for thee to reap; for the harvest of the earth is ripe. [16]And he that sat on the cloud thrust in his sickle on the earth; and the earth was reaped. [17]And another angel came out of the temple which is in heaven, he also having a sharp sickle. [18]And another angel came out from the altar, which had power over fire; and cried with

---

14:4 *Which were not defiled with women*: presumably a requirement of ancient Israelite soldiers in the OT (see 1 Sam 21:4–5; 2 Sam 11:8–11; cf. Deut 23:9–11); recall the military census of the 144,000 in 7:5–8 (see note). *Virgins*: in light of the Bible's figurative association of infidelity to God's covenant with sexual promiscuity (see 2:14 note; cf. 2 Cor 11:2). *Firstfruits*: cf. Jer 2:3 and note.   **14:5** *In their mouth . . . guile*: cf. Zeph 3:13. *Fault*: or "blemish." *Before the . . . God*: better omitted (MS tradition). **14:6** *Another angel*: the first mention of an angel since 12:7–9.   **14:6–7** *Having the everlasting gospel . . . come*: cf. Matt 24:14. The diverse multitude evangelized recalls the universal multitude introduced after the 144,000 in chap. 7 (see v. 9).   **14:8** *Babylon is . . . fornication*: conflating Isa 21:9 and Jer 51:7–8; cf. Hos 4:11–12.   **14:10** *Without mixture*: undiluted.   **14:10–11** *He shall . . . and ever*: cf. Isa 34:9–10 and note.   **14:12** *Here is . . . keep*: KJV translates a corrupt reading. The Greek is unclear, but it appears to define the saints' endurance as their ability to keep God's commandments and remain faithful to Jesus.   **14:14** *I looked . . . man*: closely echoing Dan 7:13. *Sickle*: God's judgment was conventionally figured as a harvest; see Mark 4:29 note. The harvest of grain (vv. 15–16) appears to represent the judgment of the righteous; the harvest of grapes (vv. 17–20), the condemnation of the wicked.   **14:15** *Thrust in thy sickle . . . ripe*: quoting Joel 3:13. *Ripe*: lit. "dried out," as wheat must be before harvesting.   **14:18** *Power over fire*: Jewish apocalyptic texts sometimes identify an angel overseeing fire (*Biblical Antiquities* 38.3; *Testament of Abraham* 12.14; 13.11) and assign supervisory angels to other natural elements as well (cf. *Jubilees* 2.2).

a loud cry to him that had the sharp sickle, saying, Thrust in thy sharp sickle, and gather the clusters of the vine of the earth; for her grapes are fully ripe. ¹⁹And the angel thrust in his sickle into the earth, and gathered the vine of the earth, and cast it into the great winepress of the wrath of God. ²⁰And the winepress was trodden without the city, and blood came out of the winepress, even unto the horse bridles, by the space of a thousand and six hundred furlongs.

15 And I saw another sign in heaven, great and marvellous, seven angels having the seven last plagues; for in them is filled up the wrath of God.
²And I saw as it were a sea of glass mingled with fire: and them that had gotten the victory over the beast, and over his image, and over his mark, and over the number of his name, stand on the sea of glass, having the harps of God. ³And they sing the song of Moses the servant of God, and the song of the Lamb, saying, Great and marvellous are thy works, Lord God Almighty; just and true are thy ways, thou King of saints. ⁴Who shall not fear thee, O Lord, and glorify thy name? for thou only art holy: for all nations shall come and worship before thee; for thy judgments are made manifest.

⁵And after that I looked, and, behold, the temple of the tabernacle of the testimony in heaven was opened: ⁶and the seven angels came out of the temple, having the seven plagues, clothed in pure and white linen, and having their breasts girded with golden girdles. ⁷And one of the four beasts gave unto the seven angels seven golden vials full of the wrath of God, who liveth for ever and ever. ⁸And the temple was filled with smoke from the glory of God, and from his power; and no man was able to enter into the temple, till the seven plagues of the seven angels were fulfilled.

14:19–20 *Great winepress . . . furlongs*: cf. Joel 3:13, but Isa 63:1–6 probably provides the model for this vivid image of God's wrath, which inspired the phrase "grapes of wrath" in "The Battle Hymn of the Republic." **14:20** *A thousand . . . furlongs*: lit. 1,600 stadia, about 180–200 miles. **15:1** *Seven angels . . . plagues*: anticipating the book's next major division. *Filled up*: lit. "finished." **15:2** *Sea of glass*: see 4:6 and note. *And over his mark*: better omitted (MS tradition). **15:3** *Song of Moses*: Exod 15:1–18, celebrating God's destruction of the Egyptians in the Red Sea; cf. Deut 32:1–43. **15:3–4** *Great and . . . manifest*: drawing on numerous OT texts—e.g., Pss 86:9–10; 111:2–4; Jer 10:7. **15:3** *Saints*: better "nations" (MS tradition).
   15:5–16:21 The seven final plagues. Anticipated in 15:1, the seven plagues, which recall Lev 26:14–39 (esp. v. 21, but see also vv. 18, 24, 28), partly parallel the events instigated by the seven trumpets: the first of each affects the earth (8:7; cf. 16:2); the second, the seas (8:8–9; cf. 16:3); the third, rivers and fountains (8:10–11; cf. 16:4–7); and the fourth, heavenly bodies (8:12–13; cf. 16:8–9); the fifth features darkness (9:1–3; cf. 16:10–11); the sixth involves a threat from the Euphrates (9:13–15; cf. 16:12); and the seventh includes severe storms and earthquakes (11:19; cf. 16:18). **15:5** *Temple*: better "sanctuary" (i.e., the temple's inner sanctum). *Tabernacle of testimony*: the OT tabernacle; *testimony* refers to the ark of the covenant (see Exod 16:34 and note; 26:31–35). **15:6** *Clothed in . . . girdles*: compare the Son of Man's attire at 1:13; cf. Dan 10:5. *White*: lit. "bright." *Linen*: alternatively "stone" (MS tradition), recalling the priestly ephod (Exod 28:17–20; cf. Ezek 28:13). **15:7** *Golden vials*: i.e., "golden bowls"; cf. 5:8. *Full of . . . God*: cf. Isa 51:17, 22. **15:8** *Filled with smoke . . . temple*: recalling the cloud (or "smoke"; cf. Isa 6:4) of God's glory that filled the

16

And I heard a great voice out of the temple saying to the seven angels, Go your ways, and pour out the vials of the wrath of God upon the earth.

²And the first went, and poured out his vial upon the earth; and there fell a noisome and grievous sore upon the men which had the mark of the beast, and upon them which worshipped his image.

³And the second angel poured out his vial upon the sea; and it became as the blood of a dead man: and every living soul died in the sea.

⁴And the third angel poured out his vial upon the rivers and fountains of waters; and they became blood. ⁵And I heard the angel of the waters say, Thou art righteous, O Lord, which art, and wast, and shalt be, because thou hast judged thus. ⁶For they have shed the blood of saints and prophets, and thou hast given them blood to drink; for they are worthy. ⁷And I heard another out of the altar say, Even so, Lord God Almighty, true and righteous are thy judgments.

⁸And the fourth angel poured out his vial upon the sun; and power was given unto him to scorch men with fire. ⁹And men were scorched with great heat, and blasphemed the name of God, which hath power over these plagues: and they repented not to give him glory.

¹⁰And the fifth angel poured out his vial upon the seat of the beast; and his kingdom was full of darkness; and they gnawed their tongues for pain, ¹¹and blasphemed the God of heaven because of their pains and their sores, and repented not of their deeds.

¹²And the sixth angel poured out his vial upon the great river Euphrates; and the water thereof was dried up, that the way of the kings of the east might be prepared. ¹³And I saw three unclean spirits like frogs come out of the mouth of the dragon, and out of the mouth of the beast, and out of the mouth of the false prophet. ¹⁴For they are the spirits of devils, working miracles, which go forth unto the kings of the earth and of the whole world, to gather them to the battle of that great day of God Almighty. ¹⁵Behold, I come as a thief. Blessed is he that watcheth, and keepeth his garments, lest he walk naked, and they see his shame. ¹⁶And he gathered them together into a place called in the Hebrew tongue Armageddon.

---

tabernacle (Exod 40:34–35) and temple (1 Kgs 8:10–11). **16:2** *Sore*: cf. Exod 9:9–11, the sixth Egyptian plague. **16:3** *Upon the sea . . . blood*: cf. Exod 7:17–21, the first plague (also in v. 4). **16:5** *Angel of the waters*: see 14:18 note. *Which art . . . be*: see 1:4 and note. *Wast, and shalt be*: better "was the holy one" (MS tradition). **16:7** *Another out of*: better omitted (MS tradition). **16:8** *Power*: lit. "it." **16:9** *They repented . . . glory*: recalling Pharaoh's refusal to relent in the face of the plagues in Exodus. **16:10** *Darkness*: cf. Exod 10:21–22, the ninth plague. **16:12** *The water . . . prepared*: recalling not only the crossing of the Red Sea (Exod 14), but also Jeremiah's oracles that figure Babylon's destruction (by Persia in 539 B.C.E.) as the drying up of the Euphrates (cf. Jer 50:38; 51:36). The Persian army's crossing of this river involved its draining (see Herodotus 1.191) and is presented as a new exodus at Isa 44:27–28. (The return of the exiles, which Cyrus's victory made possible, was also seen as a new exodus; see Isa 11:15–16 and v. 15 note; cf. 45:13.) See also Rev 9:14 note. **16:13** *Frogs*: cf. Exod 8:6, the second plague. *False prophet*: i.e., the second beast (13:11–18); cf. 19:20. **16:14** *Spirits of devils . . . world*: the plague of frogs was one of the two that Pharaoh's magicians could emulate (Exod 8:7). *Miracles*: lit. "signs." *To gather . . . Almighty*: cf. Zech 14, which prophesies a final battle between "the nations" and Israel. **16:15** *As a thief*: see 3:3 and note. **16:16** *Armageddon*: Mount Megiddo (or Megiddon, Zech 12:11). Megiddo, a plain north of Jerusalem, was the site of

[17]And the seventh angel poured out his vial into the air; and there came a great voice out of the temple of heaven, from the throne, saying, It is done. [18]And there were voices, and thunders, and lightnings; and there was a great earthquake, such as was not since men were upon the earth, so mighty an earthquake, and so great. [19]And the great city was divided into three parts, and the cities of the nations fell: and great Babylon came in remembrance before God, to give unto her the cup of the wine of the fierceness of his wrath. [20]And every island fled away, and the mountains were not found. [21]And there fell upon men a great hail out of heaven, every stone about the weight of a talent: and men blasphemed God because of the plague of the hail; for the plague thereof was exceeding great.

17 And there came one of the seven angels which had the seven vials, and talked with me, saying unto me, Come hither; I will shew unto thee the judgment of the great whore that sitteth upon many waters: [2]with whom the kings of the earth have committed fornication, and the inhabitants of the earth have been made drunk with the wine of her fornication.

[3]So he carried me away in the spirit into the wilderness: and I saw a woman sit upon a scarlet coloured beast, full of names of blasphemy, having seven heads and ten horns. [4]And the woman was arrayed in purple and scarlet colour, and decked with gold and precious stones and pearls, having a golden cup in her hand full of abominations and filthiness of her fornication: [5]and upon her forehead was a name written, Mystery, Babylon the great, the mother of harlots and abominations of the earth. [6]And I saw the woman drunken with the blood of the saints, and with the blood of the martyrs of Jesus: and when I saw her, I wondered with great admiration.

[7]And the angel said unto me, Wherefore didst thou marvel? I will tell thee the mystery of the woman, and of the beast that carrieth her, which hath the seven heads and ten horns. [8]The beast that thou sawest was, and is not; and shall

---

several battles between Israel and its enemies; cf. Judg 5:19; 2 Kgs 23:29; 2 Chr 35:20–22.   **16:17** *It is done*: alternatively "it has come about."   **16:18** *Voices, and . . . great earthquake*: cf. Isa 29:5–8 (esp. v. 6), whose context is also an eschatological battle. *Such as . . . great*: cf. Dan 12:1.   **16:20** *Every island . . . found*: another image of cosmic cataclysm; see 6:12–14 and note.   **16:21** *Great hail*: cf. Exod 9:23–25, the seventh plague (which also involved lightening and thunder; cf. v. 18 above); see also Isa 28:2. *Talent*: a variable unit of weight in antiquity; here, perhaps 100 lbs. (so NRSV).
 17:1–19:4 Babylon's fall. This section elaborates on the emptying of the seventh vial in 16:17–21.
 17:1–2 *Great whore . . . her fornication*: for the conceptual background, see Exod 34:15–16 and note. Of particular importance are the similarities between the harlot "Babylon" and "Jezebel" (2:20–23), which serve to assimilate the believers whom John rebukes in the introductory letters to the sinfully idolatrous Rome. The Greek words rendered *whore* and *fornication* share their root.   **17:1** *Sitteth upon many waters*: cf. Jer 51:13, which refers to Babylon (located on the Euphrates).   **17:2** *The kings . . . her fornication*: cf. Isa 23:17. *The wine of her fornication*: the drink is identified in v. 6.   **17:3** *A scarlet . . . horns*: the first beast (cf. 13:1); but now it is said to be red, like the dragon (12:3).   **17:4** *Arrayed in purple . . . hand*: Jer 4:30 similarly figures Israel. The whore's garish attire contrasts with the elegant garb of Revelation's heavenly characters (e.g., 15:6–7). *Golden cup in her hand*: cf. Jer 51:7. *Abominations*: a conventional OT description of idolatry, especially human sacrifice (e.g., 2 Kgs 16:3; 2 Chr 28:3; see v. 6 below).   **17:6** *With great admiration*: the Greek words translated *wondered*, *admiration*, and "marvel" (v. 7) all share the same root. *Admiration* may suggest that John was attracted to the whore, a possibility supported by the angel's rebuke in v. 7.   **17:8** *Was, and . . .*

ascend out of the bottomless pit, and go into perdition: and they that dwell on the earth shall wonder, whose names were not written in the book of life from the foundation of the world, when they behold the beast that was, and is not, and yet is. ⁹And here is the mind which hath wisdom. The seven heads are seven mountains, on which the woman sitteth. ¹⁰And there are seven kings: five are fallen, and one is, and the other is not yet come; and when he cometh, he must continue a short space. ¹¹And the beast that was, and is not, even he is the eighth, and is of the seven, and goeth into perdition. ¹²And the ten horns which thou sawest are ten kings, which have received no kingdom as yet; but receive power as kings one hour with the beast. ¹³These have one mind, and shall give their power and strength unto the beast. ¹⁴These shall make war with the Lamb, and the Lamb shall overcome them: for he is Lord of lords, and King of kings: and they that are with him are called, and chosen, and faithful.

¹⁵And he saith unto me, The waters which thou sawest, where the whore sitteth, are peoples, and multitudes, and nations, and tongues. ¹⁶And the ten horns which thou sawest upon the beast, these shall hate the whore, and shall make her desolate and naked, and shall eat her flesh, and burn her with fire. ¹⁷For God hath put in their hearts to fulfil his will, and to agree, and give their kingdom unto the beast, until the words of God shall be fulfilled. ¹⁸And the woman which thou sawest is that great city, which reigneth over the kings of the earth.

18 And after these things I saw another angel come down from heaven, having great power; and the earth was lightened with his glory. ²And he cried mightily with a strong voice, saying, Babylon the great is fallen, is fallen, and is become the habitation of devils, and the hold of every foul spirit, and a cage of every unclean and hateful bird. ³For all nations have drunk of the wine of the wrath of her fornication, and the kings of the earth have committed fornication

---

perdition: a parody of a phrase commonly applied to God (cf. 1:8; 4:8; 11:17; 16:5), as well as of Jesus' resurrection. *And yet is*: better "and will come" (MS tradition). **17:9** *Seven mountains*: clearly identifying the harlot Babylon as Rome, which was famous for its seven hills. **17:10** *And there are*: better "and they are." *Seven kings . . . space*: perhaps symbolically denoting the totality of Rome's dominion and all of its emperors, past, present, and future (though expecting that Rome's future rule will be abbreviated). The fourth beast from Dan 7:7–8 is likewise interpreted in terms of a kingdom and its kings; cf. Dan 7:19–27. **17:11** *Even he . . . perdition*: John understands the eighth king as Nero redivivus (see 13:3 note), a perverted risen Christ (see v. 8 and note). His emergence may find its inspiration in the ten horns/kings of Daniel's fourth beast (7:7, 24), three of which are eliminated to make room for another, a particularly heinous ruler (Dan 7:8, 24–25). *Is of*: perhaps in the sense of "belongs to" (NRSV); alternatively "descends from." **17:12** *Ten kings . . . beast*: cf. Dan 7:24–25, but the verse aptly describes Roman client kings, whose territory was under imperial rule and whose authority was limited. **17:14** *These shall . . . them*: cf. Dan 7:21–22. *Called, chosen*: the Greek words share a root. **17:15** *The waters . . . tongues*: cf. Isa 17:12–13. **17:16** *Shall make . . . fire*: cf. Ezek 23:25–29. **18:1–8** Fallen Babylon: an elaborate pastiche of OT fragments, taken mostly from the collection of oracles against Babylon at the end of Jeremiah (chaps. 50–51). **18:1** *The earth . . . glory*: cf. Ezek 43:2. **18:2** *Babylon the . . . fallen*: quoting Isa 21:9; cf. Jer 51:8; Rev 14:8. *The habitation . . . bird*: cf. Jer 51:37; Isa 13:21–22. *Foul*: better "unclean," as the same word is translated later in the verse. *Hold, cage*: both Gk. *phylakē*, "prison." **18:3** *All nations . . . delicacies*: again recalling Isa 23:17 (see Rev 17:2); cf. Jer 51:7.

with her, and the merchants of the earth are waxed rich through the abundance of her delicacies.

⁴And I heard another voice from heaven, saying, Come out of her, my people, that ye be not partakers of her sins, and that ye receive not of her plagues. ⁵For her sins have reached unto heaven, and God hath remembered her iniquities. ⁶Reward her even as she rewarded you, and double unto her double according to her works: in the cup which she hath filled fill to her double. ⁷How much she hath glorified herself, and lived deliciously, so much torment and sorrow give her: for she saith in her heart, I sit a queen, and am no widow, and shall see no sorrow. ⁸Therefore shall her plagues come in one day, death, and mourning, and famine; and she shall be utterly burned with fire: for strong is the Lord God who judgeth her.

⁹And the kings of the earth, who have committed fornication and lived deliciously with her, shall bewail her, and lament for her, when they shall see the smoke of her burning, ¹⁰standing afar off for the fear of her torment, saying, Alas, alas, that great city Babylon, that mighty city! for in one hour is thy judgment come.

¹¹And the merchants of the earth shall weep and mourn over her; for no man buyeth their merchandise any more: ¹²the merchandise of gold, and silver, and precious stones, and of pearls, and fine linen, and purple, and silk, and scarlet, and all thyine wood, and all manner vessels of ivory, and all manner vessels of most precious wood, and of brass, and iron, and marble, ¹³and cinnamon, and odours, and ointments, and frankincense, and wine, and oil, and fine flour, and wheat, and beasts, and sheep, and horses, and chariots, and slaves, and souls of men. ¹⁴And the fruits that thy soul lusted after are departed from thee, and all things which were dainty and goodly are departed from thee, and thou shalt find them no more at all. ¹⁵The merchants of these things, which were made rich by

---

Abundance: lit. "power." *Delicacies*: Gk. *strēnos*, "wantonness" (cognate with "lived deliciously," vv. 7, 9). **18:4** *Come out . . . people*: echoing Jer 50:8; 51:6, 45; cf. Isa 48:20; 52:11; etc. **18:5** *For her sins . . . iniquities*: cf. Jer 51:9. **18:6** *Reward her . . . you*: echoing Jer 50:29; cf. Ps 137:8; Jer 51:24. *Double unto her double*: repay her double (cf. Jer 16:18). **18:7** *She saith . . . sorrow*: compare Babylon's speech at Isa 47:7–8. **18:8** *Therefore shall . . . her*: combining images from Jer 50–51 (e.g., 50:13, 32; 51:30, 58). *One day* draws on Isaiah's oracle against Babylon (47:9). **18:9–19** Laments for Babylon: dirges from kings (vv. 9–10), merchants (vv. 11–17a), and shipmasters (vv. 17b–19), based on those for Tyre in Ezek 27. **18:9** *Kings of the earth*: God prompted them to destroy the city/whore in 17:16–17. **18:10** *Alas*: Gk. *ouai* (also in vv. 16, 19), earlier translated "woe" (8:13; 9:12; 11:14; 12:12). **18:12–13** *The merchandise . . . men*: a list based on that in Ezek 27:12–25; cf. Ezek 16:10–13. Such lists are common in Roman imperial literature (e.g., Pliny, *Natural History* 37.201–04; Statius, *Silvae* 5.1.210–16), where the variety of imported merchandise demonstrates the scope of Roman control over the Mediterranean. **18:12** *Thyine*: citron. **18:13** *Cinnamon*: better "cinnamon and amomum" (MS tradition). Amomum is a tropical aromatic plant. *Odours*: incense. *Beasts*: probably load-bearing animals. *Slaves*: lit. "bodies," an idiomatic way of referring to slaves. *And souls of men*: better "even souls of men." *Souls of men*, like "bodies," can refer to slaves (LXX uses the Greek phrase for "slaves" in Ezek 27:13). Thus the list's final clause ironically condemns the merchants' values by insisting on slaves' humanity. **18:14** *Dainty and goodly*: Gk. *ta lipara kai ta lampra*, "glitter and glamour" (REB), which both captures the Greek's connotation of brightness and preserves the alliteration. *Departed*: better "destroyed" (MS tradition); a different word is used earlier in the verse. *Thou*: better "they"

her, shall stand afar off for the fear of her torment, weeping and wailing, [16]and saying, Alas, alas, that great city, that was clothed in fine linen, and purple, and scarlet, and decked with gold, and precious stones, and pearls! [17]For in one hour so great riches is come to nought.

And every shipmaster, and all the company in ships, and sailors, and as many as trade by sea, stood afar off, [18]and cried when they saw the smoke of her burning, saying, What city is like unto this great city! [19]And they cast dust on their heads, and cried, weeping and wailing, saying, Alas, alas, that great city, wherein were made rich all that had ships in the sea by reason of her costliness! for in one hour is she made desolate. [20]Rejoice over her, thou heaven, and ye holy apostles and prophets; for God hath avenged you on her.

[21]And a mighty angel took up a stone like a great millstone, and cast it into the sea, saying, Thus with violence shall that great city Babylon be thrown down, and shall be found no more at all. [22]And the voice of harpers, and musicians, and of pipers, and trumpeters, shall be heard no more at all in thee; and no craftsman, of whatsoever craft he be, shall be found any more in thee; and the sound of a millstone shall be heard no more at all in thee; [23]and the light of a candle shall shine no more at all in thee; and the voice of the bridegroom and of the bride shall be heard no more at all in thee: for thy merchants were the great men of the earth; for by thy sorceries were all nations deceived. [24]And in her was found the blood of prophets, and of saints, and of all that were slain upon the earth.

19 And after these things I heard a great voice of much people in heaven, saying, Alleluia; Salvation, and glory, and honour, and power, unto the Lord our God: [2]for true and righteous are his judgments: for he hath judged the great whore, which did corrupt the earth with her fornication, and hath avenged the blood of his servants at her hand. [3]And again they said, Alleluia. And her smoke rose up for ever and ever. [4]And the four and twenty elders and the four beasts fell down and worshipped God that sat on the throne, saying, Amen; Alleluia.

[5]And a voice came out of the throne, saying, Praise our God, all ye his servants, and ye that fear him, both small and great. [6]And I heard as it were the voice of a great multitude, and as the voice of many waters, and as the voice of mighty thunderings, saying, Alleluia: for the Lord God omnipotent reigneth.

(MS tradition). **18:16** *Clothed in . . . pearls*: see 17:4 and note. **18:17** *Come to nought*: lit. "made desolate" (also in v. 19). **18:19** *Cast dust . . . heads*: a sign of mourning. **18:20** *Rejoice over . . . her*: cf. Jer 51:48. *Holy apostles*: better "saints and apostles" (MS tradition). *For God . . . her*: lit. "for God has judged your judgment on her" (or "for God has given judgment for you against her"; NRSV). The reference is to the martyrs' prayer in 6:10. **18:21** *A great millstone . . . all*: based on Jer 51:63–64. **18:22–23** *The voice . . . heard no more at all in thee*: combining images from such prophetic passages as Isa 24:8; Jer 25:10; Ezek 26:13; etc. **18:23** *Thy merchants . . . earth*: cf. Isa 23:8. *For by . . . deceived*: cf. Isa 47:9. **18:24** *In her . . . earth*: cf. Jer 51:49. **19:1** *Alleluia*: transliterating a Hebrew phrase meaning "praise YHWH" (as frequently in the Psalms). **19:2** *True and . . . judgments*: cf. Ps 19:9. *Which did . . . earth*: echoing LXX Jer 51:25. *Avenged*: Gk. *ekdikeō*, which shares its root with *righteous*. **19:3** *Her smoke . . . and ever*: see Isa 34:10.

19:5–21 The lamb's wedding. The announced wedding banquet (vv. 5–10) turns into a surprisingly grisly affair (vv. 11–21). **19:6** *Omnipotent*: Gk. *pantokratōr*, usually "Almighty" (see 1:8 note). *Reigneth*: the Greek verb here is in the past tense, as in the parallel passage 11:17. The meaning in

⁷Let us be glad and rejoice, and give honour to him: for the marriage of the Lamb is come, and his wife hath made herself ready. ⁸And to her was granted that she should be arrayed in fine linen, clean and white: for the fine linen is the righteousness of saints. ⁹And he saith unto me, Write, Blessed are they which are called unto the marriage supper of the Lamb. And he saith unto me, These are the true sayings of God. ¹⁰And I fell at his feet to worship him. And he said unto me, See thou do it not: I am thy fellowservant, and of thy brethren that have the testimony of Jesus: worship God: for the testimony of Jesus is the spirit of prophecy.

¹¹And I saw heaven opened, and behold a white horse; and he that sat upon him was called Faithful and True, and in righteousness he doth judge and make war. ¹²His eyes were as a flame of fire, and on his head were many crowns; and he had a name written, that no man knew, but he himself. ¹³And he was clothed with a vesture dipped in blood: and his name is called The Word of God. ¹⁴And the armies which were in heaven followed him upon white horses, clothed in fine linen, white and clean. ¹⁵And out of his mouth goeth a sharp sword, that with it he should smite the nations: and he shall rule them with a rod of iron: and he treadeth the winepress of the fierceness and wrath of Almighty God. ¹⁶And he hath on his vesture and on his thigh a name written, King of kings, and Lord of lords.

¹⁷And I saw an angel standing in the sun; and he cried with a loud voice, saying to all the fowls that fly in the midst of heaven, Come and gather yourselves together unto the supper of the great God; ¹⁸that ye may eat the flesh of kings, and the flesh of captains, and the flesh of mighty men, and the flesh of horses, and of them that sit on them, and the flesh of all men, both free and bond, both small and great. ¹⁹And I saw the beast, and the kings of the earth, and their armies, gathered together to make war against him that sat on the horse, and against his army. ²⁰And the beast was taken, and with him the false prophet that wrought miracles before him, with which he deceived them that had received the

---

both is "has begun to reign." **19:7** *Let us . . . ready*: cf. Isa 61:10. *Honour*: or "glory." *Marriage of the Lamb*: see Mark 2:19 note. *His wife*: later identified as new Jerusalem (21:2), the pure analogue of Babylon. More generally, the bride represents the community of the faithful, as the allegorical interpretation of her raiment in v. 8 indicates; cf. 2 Cor 11:2. **19:10** *I fell . . . brethren*: angels commonly refuse worship in ancient Jewish literature (e.g., Tob 12:15–22; *Ascension of Isaiah* 7.21). Here the motif is strategically employed to emphasize the radical difference between God (or Jesus) and his creatures, even at the moment when he is joined to them in intimate union. **19:11** *I saw . . . war*: the eschatological arrival of Christ unsettlingly resembles the advent of the first horseman, who also rode a white horse (6:2). *In righteousness he doth judge*: cf. Isa 11:4. **19:12** *His eyes . . . fire*: echoing Dan 10:6; cf. Rev 1:14; 2:18. *Crowns*: lit. "diadems," perhaps recalling those worn by the dragon (see 12:3 and note). *A name . . . himself*: see 2:17 and note. Despite this secrecy, two names are explicitly assigned to this figure (see vv. 13, 16) and he is called "Faithful and True" as well (v. 11). **19:13** *Clothed with . . . blood*: cf. Isa 63:2–3. *The Word of God*: cf. Wis 18:15–16. **19:14** *Clothed in . . . clean*: compare the bridal gown in v. 8. **19:15** *Out of . . . iron*: alluding to Isa 49:2 and Ps 2:9 (see Rev 2:27 note), probably combined with Isa 11:4. *He treadeth . . . God*: cf. Isa 63:2–3 (see Rev 14:19–20 and note). **19:17–18** *Saying to all . . . great*: based on the ghastly sacrificial feast described in Ezek 39:17–20. **19:17** *Supper of the great God*: better "great supper of God" (MS tradition). **19:19** *The beast . . . horse*: recalling 17:12–14. **19:20** *Miracles*: lit. "signs." *Lake of fire*: classical pagan descriptions of the netherworld commonly feature fiery bodies of water (cf. Plato, *Phaedo* 111d; Virgil, *Aeneid* 6.295–97, which seems to

mark of the beast, and them that worshipped his image. These both were cast alive into a lake of fire burning with brimstone. [21]And the remnant were slain with the sword of him that sat upon the horse, which sword proceeded out of his mouth: and all the fowls were filled with their flesh.

20 And I saw an angel come down from heaven, having the key of the bottomless pit and a great chain in his hand. [2]And he laid hold on the dragon, that old serpent, which is the Devil, and Satan, and bound him a thousand years, [3]and cast him into the bottomless pit, and shut him up, and set a seal upon him, that he should deceive the nations no more, till the thousand years should be fulfilled: and after that he must be loosed a little season.

[4]And I saw thrones, and they sat upon them, and judgment was given unto them: and I saw the souls of them that were beheaded for the witness of Jesus, and for the word of God, and which had not worshipped the beast, neither his image, neither had received his mark upon their foreheads, or in their hands; and they lived and reigned with Christ a thousand years. [5]But the rest of the dead lived not again until the thousand years were finished. This is the first resurrection. [6]Blessed and holy is he that hath part in the first resurrection: on such the second death hath no power, but they shall be priests of God and of Christ, and shall reign with him a thousand years.

[7]And when the thousand years are expired, Satan shall be loosed out of his prison, [8]and shall go out to deceive the nations which are in the four quarters of the earth, Gog and Magog, to gather them together to battle: the number of whom is as the sand of the sea. [9]And they went up on the breadth of the earth, and compassed the camp of the saints about, and the beloved city: and fire came down from God out of heaven, and devoured them. [10]And the devil that deceived them was cast into the lake of fire and brimstone, where the beast and the false prophet are, and shall be tormented day and night for ever and ever.

[11]And I saw a great white throne, and him that sat on it, from whose face the

describe rivers of magma; etc.). For everlasting punishment by fire in the Bible, see Isa 66:24; Matt 5:22; Mark 9:43, 48; etc. This fiery lake should probably be identified with the *abyssos* ("bottomless pit") of 20:1, since the Greek word can also refer to water (see 9:1 note).

20:1–21:1 The millennial reign and Christ's final victory. This section describes a thousand-year period of Christ's peaceful coreign with resurrected martyrs (v. 4), before Satan is released and decisively defeated and the dead are judged. **20:2–3** *Bound him . . . up*: the binding of Satan or wicked angels is a common motif in Jewish apocalyptic literature; cf. Mark 3:22–27; *1 Enoch* 10.4; *Jubilees* 10.7–11; etc. The bottomless pit was opened in 9:2. **20:4** *The souls . . . God*: cf. 6:9. *They lived and reigned*: for the eschatological reign of God's saints, see Dan 7:18, 22, 26–27. **20:6** *Priests of . . . him*: cf. Exod 19:6. *Shall reign . . . years*: the notion of a temporary kingdom preceding God's ultimate rule is not elsewhere attested in the NT (unless Paul alludes to it in 1 Cor 15:23–28), but it is a feature of other Jewish eschatological literature (e.g., 2 Esd 7:26–30; *1 Enoch* 91.12–17). **20:8** *Gog and Magog*: John represents this final battle between the Satan-inspired nations and God's people as that depicted in Ezek 38–39, which also follows on the heels of a resurrection (famously described as dry bones rising from the dead; chap. 37). **20:9** *The beloved city*: Jerusalem (cf. Jer 11:15; 12:7; Sir 24:11; etc.), whose geographic situation necessitates ascension. *Fire came . . . them*: cf. Ezek 38:22; 39:6; also see 2 Kgs 1:10–14. **20:11** *A great . . . it*: cf. Dan 7:9.

earth and the heaven fled away; and there was found no place for them. [12]And I saw the dead, small and great, stand before God; and the books were opened: and another book was opened, which is the book of life: and the dead were judged out of those things which were written in the books, according to their works. [13]And the sea gave up the dead which were in it; and death and hell delivered up the dead which were in them: and they were judged every man according to their works. [14]And death and hell were cast into the lake of fire. This is the second death. [15]And whosoever was not found written in the book of life was cast into the lake of fire.

21 [1]And I saw a new heaven and a new earth: for the first heaven and the first earth were passed away; and there was no more sea.

[2]And I John saw the holy city, new Jerusalem, coming down from God out of heaven, prepared as a bride adorned for her husband. [3]And I heard a great voice out of heaven saying, Behold, the tabernacle of God is with men, and he will dwell with them, and they shall be his people, and God himself shall be with them, and be their God. [4]And God shall wipe away all tears from their eyes; and there shall be no more death, neither sorrow, nor crying, neither shall there be any more pain: for the former things are passed away.

[5]And he that sat upon the throne said, Behold, I make all things new. And he said unto me, Write: for these words are true and faithful. [6]And he said unto me, It is done. I am Alpha and Omega, the beginning and the end. I will give unto him that is athirst of the fountain of the water of life freely. [7]He that overcometh shall inherit all things; and I will be his God, and he shall be my son. [8]But the fearful, and unbelieving, and the abominable, and murderers, and whoremongers, and sorcerers, and idolaters, and all liars, shall have their part in the lake which burneth with fire and brimstone: which is the second death.

[9]And there came unto me one of the seven angels which had the seven vials full of the seven last plagues, and talked with me, saying, Come hither, I will shew thee the bride, the Lamb's wife. [10]And he carried me away in the spirit to a

---

Earth and . . . them: recalling the astronomical and geological cataclysms described at, e.g., 8:10, 12; 16:20; but as 21:1 indicates, the cosmic transformation here initiated is far more radical.   **20:12** *Before God*: better "before the throne" (MS tradition). *The books were opened*: cf. Dan 7:10. *Another book . . . life*: see Dan 12:1–4, whose context is also a prophecy about resurrection.   **20:13** *The sea . . . them*: reflecting the distinction commonly drawn by ancient Greeks, Romans, and others between death at sea and death on land—the former seen as less desirable because it made burial impossible (cf. Seneca, *Natural Questions* 5.18.6–8; Propertius 3.7; etc.).   **20:14** *Death and hell . . . death*: as for Paul (see 1 Cor 15:26 and note), so for John the resurrection of the dead corresponds to death's destruction. *Second death*: better to add "the lake of fire" (MS tradition), clearly identifying the fiery lake with the second death.   **21:1** *A new . . . earth*: cf. Isa 65:17; 66:22. *No more sea*: perhaps because the sea conventionally symbolized chaos in ancient Near Eastern literature (see 4:6 note).
   21:2–22:5 New Jerusalem. 21:2 *John*: better omitted (MS tradition). *New Jerusalem*: cf. Isa 65:18. Earthly Jerusalem's heavenly prototype (cf. Gal 4:26; Heb 12:22; etc.) descends to replace it.   **21:3** *Heaven*: better "the throne" (MS tradition). *Behold, the . . . people*: cf. Ezek 37:27. *Tabernacle, dwell*: see 13:6 note. *People*: lit. "peoples."   **21:4** *God shall . . . death*: echoing Isa 25:8. *Neither sorrow . . . away*: cf. Isa 65:16–19.   **21:5** *Behold, I . . . new*: cf. Isa 43:18–19. *Faithful*: trustworthy.   **21:6** *It is done*: see 16:17 note. *Alpha and . . . end*: see 1:8 and note. *I will . . . freely*: echoing Isa 55:1.   **21:7** *He that overcometh*: recalling the conclusions of the seven epistles (2:7, 11, 17, 26; 3:5, 12, 21). *All things*: better "these things" (MS tradition). *I will be . . . son*: see Ps 2:7 and note. Here divine adoption is promised to all who "overcome."   **21:8** *Unbelieving*: or "unfaithful." *Whoremongers*: the sexually immoral (so throughout).   **21:10** *He carried . . . city*: based on Ezek 40:2 and introducing a number of

great and high mountain, and shewed me that great city, the holy Jerusalem, descending out of heaven from God, [11]having the glory of God: and her light was like unto a stone most precious, even like a jasper stone, clear as crystal; [12]and had a wall great and high, and had twelve gates, and at the gates twelve angels, and names written thereon, which are the names of the twelve tribes of the children of Israel: [13]on the east three gates; on the north three gates; on the south three gates; and on the west three gates. [14]And the wall of the city had twelve foundations, and in them the names of the twelve apostles of the Lamb.

[15]And he that talked with me had a golden reed to measure the city, and the gates thereof, and the wall thereof. [16]And the city lieth foursquare, and the length is as large as the breadth: and he measured the city with the reed, twelve thousand furlongs. The length and the breadth and the height of it are equal. [17]And he measured the wall thereof, an hundred and forty and four cubits, according to the measure of a man, that is, of the angel. [18]And the building of the wall of it was of jasper: and the city was pure gold, like unto clear glass. [19]And the foundations of the wall of the city were garnished with all manner of precious stones. The first foundation was jasper; the second, sapphire; the third, a chalcedony; the fourth, an emerald; [20]the fifth, sardonyx; the sixth, sardius; the seventh, chrysolite; the eighth, beryl; the ninth, a topaz; the tenth, a chrysoprasus; the eleventh, a jacinth; the twelfth, an amethyst. [21]And the twelve gates were twelve pearls; every several gate was of one pearl: and the street of the city was pure gold, as it were transparent glass.

[22]And I saw no temple therein: for the Lord God Almighty and the Lamb are the temple of it. [23]And the city had no need of the sun, neither of the moon, to

allusions to Ezekiel's final vision of a new Israel (chaps. 40–48). **21:11** *Having the glory of God*: cf. Ezek 43:2–5. *A stone . . . crystal*: perhaps recalling Ezek 28:13, which describes Eden. **21:12–13** *Twelve gates . . . west three gates*: as in Ezek 48:30–35. The reference to angels at the gates seems at variance with God's total pacification of the cosmos, but it recalls the angelic guard stationed at Eden in Gen 3:24 (cf. Ezek 28:14, 16). **21:14** *Twelve foundations . . . Lamb*: perhaps literalizing a common tradition in the early church; cf. Eph 2:20. **21:15** *He that talked . . . city*: cf. Ezek 40:3; Zech 2:1–2. **21:16** *Foursquare*: like various elements of Ezekiel's vision (cf. 41:13–15; 42:15–20; 48:15–20). Here the area envisioned is actually a cube. *Twelve thousand furlongs*: lit. 12,000 stadia, or about 1,400–1,500 miles. **21:17** *An hundred . . . cubits*: recalling the 144,000 children of Israel (7:4). The wall's measurement—about 216 feet—is hardly in keeping with the fantastic size of the city. Even as a measure of thickness, it seems far too low for a city occupying something like three billion cubic miles. (The walls of historical Babylon were about a third of this thickness [Herodotus 1.178], as were Ecbantana's, according to Judith [1:2].) A more appealing interpretation focuses on the word translated "cubit," Gk. *pēchus*, which originally meant "forearm." John finally describes the measurement as angelic rather than human (*according to the measure of a man, that is, of the angel*), thereby suggesting that it is unfathomable by readers' limited minds. After providing the mind-boggling but not totally incomprehensible size of new Jerusalem, John now offers a dimension the reader can readily grasp, only to reveal at the last moment that the comprehension was illusory. **21:18** *The building . . . jasper*: cf. Isa 54:11–12. **21:19** *Garnished with . . . stones*: echoing the description of the bride at Isa 61:10, here applied to the city representing her (see v. 2 above, where "adorned" translates the same word as *garnished*). **21:19–20** *The first . . . amethyst*: recalling the twelve precious stones on the ephod, each of which was engraved with one of the tribe's names (Exod 28:17–21; 39:10–14; cf. Ezek 28:13 and note). Here, the names are those of the apostles (cf. v. 14), while the tribes' names are on the gates (v. 12). **21:20** *Sardius*: carnelian. **21:22** *I saw . . . therein*: a polemical response to Ezekiel's vision of the new Israel, whose central feature was the temple. **21:23** *The city . . .*

shine in it: for the glory of God did lighten it, and the Lamb is the light thereof. [24]And the nations of them which are saved shall walk in the light of it: and the kings of the earth do bring their glory and honour into it. [25]And the gates of it shall not be shut at all by day: for there shall be no night there. [26]And they shall bring the glory and honour of the nations into it. [27]And there shall in no wise enter into it any thing that defileth, neither whatsoever worketh abomination, or maketh a lie: but they which are written in the Lamb's book of life.

22 And he shewed me a pure river of water of life, clear as crystal, proceeding out of the throne of God and of the Lamb. [2]In the midst of the street of it, and on either side of the river, was there the tree of life, which bare twelve manner of fruits, and yielded her fruit every month: and the leaves of the tree were for the healing of the nations. [3]And there shall be no more curse: but the throne of God and of the Lamb shall be in it; and his servants shall serve him: [4]and they shall see his face; and his name shall be in their foreheads. [5]And there shall be no night there; and they need no candle, neither light of the sun; for the Lord God giveth them light: and they shall reign for ever and ever.

[6]And he said unto me, These sayings are faithful and true: and the Lord God of the holy prophets sent his angel to shew unto his servants the things which must shortly be done. [7]Behold, I come quickly: blessed is he that keepeth the sayings of the prophecy of this book.

[8]And I John saw these things, and heard them. And when I had heard and seen, I fell down to worship before the feet of the angel which shewed me these things. [9]Then saith he unto me, See thou do it not: for I am thy fellowservant, and of thy brethren the prophets, and of them which keep the sayings of this book: worship God. [10]And he saith unto me, Seal not the sayings of the prophecy of this book: for the time is at hand. [11]He that is unjust, let him be unjust still: and he which is filthy, let him be filthy still: and he that is righteous, let him be righteous still: and he that is holy, let him be holy still. [12]And, behold, I come

---

lighten it: cf. Isa 60:19–20. The statement also recalls the first creation narrative, suggesting that the new cosmic order no longer requires "lights in the firmament of the heaven" (Gen 1:14). *Light*: better "lamp." **21:24** *Nations*: Gk. *ethnē*, also "Gentiles" (cf. v. 26). Verses 24–27 fulfill numerous OT prophecies of Gentiles' eschatological worship of YHWH (cf. Isa 45:20–24; Zech 2:11; 8:23; etc.). This verse alludes to Isa 60:3 in particular. *Of them which are saved*: better omitted (MS tradition). **21:25–26** *The gates . . . into it*: cf. Isa 60:11, with an echo of Zech 14:7. **21:27** *There shall . . . lie*: despite the entrance of Gentiles, there is no ritual or moral impurity. *Whatsoever*: better "whoever" (MS tradition). *Abomination*: see 17:4 note. **22:1–2** *River of water . . . nations*: based on the imagery of Ezek 47:1–12 (see notes); cf. Zech 14:8. The ultimate allusion is of course to Eden (Gen 2:8–14). **22:3** *There shall . . . curse*: alluding to LXX Zech 14:11, where Gk. *anathema*—related to *katathema*, here *curse*—translates Heb. *ḥerem* (KJV "utter destruction"): the sacred ban (see Deut 7:2 note) to which Jerusalem will no longer be subject. The edenic imagery suggests a secondary allusion to Gen 3:14–24. *Serve*: the Greek word refers to cultic service. **22:4** *They shall see his face*: recalling and contradicting Exod 33:20. **22:5** *There shall . . . giveth them light*: cf. Isa 60:19.

22:6–21 Conclusion. 22:6 *Faithful*: trustworthy. *The holy prophets*: better "the spirits of the prophets" (MS tradition); cf. 1 Cor 14:32. *Sent his angel*: recalling the angel mentioned in 1:1. *Must shortly be done* also echoes Revelation's first verse. **22:7** *Blessed is . . . book*: recalling 1:3. **22:8–9** *I fell . . . God*: see 19:10 and note. **22:10** *Seal not . . . hand*: recalling and reversing Dan 12:4, 9. **22:11** *He that is unjust . . . holy still*: probably an interpretive elaboration of Dan 12:10. *Be righteous*: better "do righteousness" (MS tradition). **22:12** *Behold, I . . . be*: echoing Isa 40:10; cf.

quickly; and my reward is with me, to give every man according as his work shall be. [13]I am Alpha and Omega, the beginning and the end, the first and the last. [14]Blessed are they that do his commandments, that they may have right to the tree of life, and may enter in through the gates into the city. [15]For without are dogs, and sorcerers, and whoremongers, and murderers, and idolaters, and whosoever loveth and maketh a lie.

[16]I Jesus have sent mine angel to testify unto you these things in the churches. I am the root and the offspring of David, and the bright and morning star. [17]And the Spirit and the bride say, Come. And let him that heareth say, Come. And let him that is athirst come. And whosoever will, let him take the water of life freely. [18]For I testify unto every man that heareth the words of the prophecy of this book, If any man shall add unto these things, God shall add unto him the plagues that are written in this book: [19]and if any man shall take away from the words of the book of this prophecy, God shall take away his part out of the book of life, and out of the holy city, and from the things which are written in this book. [20]He which testifieth these things saith, Surely I come quickly. Amen. Even so, come, Lord Jesus.

[21]The grace of our Lord Jesus Christ be with you all. Amen.

THE END.

62:11. *Reward is*: lit. "wages are." **22:13** *I am . . . last*: see 1:8 and note. **22:14** *That do his commandments*: better "who wash their robes" (MS tradition); cf. 7:14. *That they . . . life*: Revelation's ultimate blessing reverses the final consequence of the primeval transgression (cf. Gen 3:24). **22:16** *Unto you*: unto you all. *In the churches*: or possibly "for the churches," or "about the churches." In any case, the phrase refers to the seven to which John wrote and in which he expects his book to be read aloud (1:1–4). *The root . . . David*: see 5:5 and note. *The bright and morning star*: see 2:28 and note. **22:17** *Let him that is . . . freely*: cf. Isa 55:1. **22:18** *If any man . . . book*: cf. Deut 4:2. **22:19** *Book of life*: better "tree of life" (MS tradition). **22:21** *The grace . . . Amen*: better "the grace of the Lord Jesus be with everyone" (MS tradition). The closing resembles those of Paul's letters; cf. 1 Cor 16:23; Gal 6:18; etc.

THE APOCRYPHA

The First Book of Esdras

WHILE the Apocrypha generally contains material "extra" to the Old Testament, in the form either of Greek additions to its Hebrew books or of entirely separate works that recount the history of Israel in periods that it does not cover, 1 Esdras is the one apocryphal book that virtually replicates Old Testament texts. It reproduces 2 Chr 35–36, most of Ezra, and a dozen or so verses from Nehemiah to recount the history of Judea from the great Passover celebration under Josiah to the reforms and New Year celebration under Ezra (the Greek form of whose name is "Esdras"). Its only original element is the story of the bodyguards' debate in 3:1–5:6—a court tale in some ways reminiscent of Esther and Daniel, in other ways of ancient Near Eastern Wisdom literature. Just as interesting, but more mysterious, is the reordering of events as they are narrated in Ezra, suggesting that the organizing principle is not chronology but some other set of priorities. What those might be is obscure, but the almost complete suppression of Nehemiah, who oversaw the rebuilding of Jerusalem's walls, and the expanded role of Zerubbabel, responsible for the temple's restoration, may gesture at a particular agenda, as may 1 Esdras's shift from Ezra's focus on the city walls to a focus on the temple in 2:16–30 (cf. Ezra 4:7–24). It is likewise significant that 1 Esdras begins and ends with a religious celebration at the temple, each of which culminates a successful program of religious reforms: Josiah's great Passover (1:1–24) and the New Year's convocation under Ezra (9:37–55), the former initiating an extended period of exile, the latter emblematizing the pure new beginning that the returning exiles intend to make.

The text of 1 Esdras exists only in Greek and in ancient translations of that Greek. It differs significantly from the Septuagint's Ezra-Nehemiah (LXX 2 Esdras), and it is possible that it constitutes a later compilation and revision of that work, or an independent translation of the Hebrew original lying behind it. Alternatively, it may have been composed on the basis of a different Hebrew textual tradition. Largely because of its similarities to Esther and Daniel, most scholars date 1 Esdras to the second century B.C.E., along with the final editions of those two books. Josephus used it as a source for *Jewish Antiquities* toward the end the first century C.E., so it must have been composed before then. It is regarded as deuterocanonical in Greek and Russian Orthodox churches, but its status in the West has always been more marginal, and it was included only in an appendix to the Clementine Vulgate.

For detailed exegesis, the reader can consult Jacob M. Myers's Anchor Bible commentary, *I and II Esdras* (Garden City, NY: Doubleday, 1974), which informs this introduction and the notes that follow.

The First Book of Esdras

1 And Josias held the feast of the passover in Jerusalem unto his Lord, and offered the passover the fourteenth day of the first month; [2]having set the priests according to their daily courses, being arrayed in long garments, in the temple of the Lord. [3]And he spake unto the Levites, the holy ministers of Israel, that they should hallow themselves unto the Lord, to set the holy ark of the Lord in the house that king Solomon the son of David had built: [4]and said, Ye shall no more bear the ark upon your shoulders: now therefore serve the Lord your God, and minister unto his people Israel, and prepare you after your families and kindreds, [5]according as David the king of Israel prescribed, and according to the magnificence of Solomon his son: and standing in the temple according to the several dignity of the families of you the Levites, who minister in the presence of your brethren the children of Israel, [6]offer the passover in order, and make ready the sacrifices for your brethren, and keep the passover according to the commandment of the Lord, which was given unto Moses.

[7]And unto the people that was found there Josias gave thirty thousand lambs and kids, and three thousand calves: these things were given of the king's allowance, according as he promised, to the people, to the priests, and to the Levites. [8]And Helkias, Zacharias, and Syelus, the governors of the temple, gave to the priests for the passover two thousand and six hundred sheep, and three hundred calves. [9]And Jeconias, and Samaias, and Nathanael his brother, and Assabias, and Ochiel, and Joram, captains over thousands, gave to the Levites for the passover five thousand sheep, and seven hundred calves.

[10]And when these things were done, the priests and Levites, having the unleavened bread, stood in very comely order according to the kindreds, [11]and according to the several dignities of the fathers, before the people, to offer to the Lord, as it is written in the book of Moses: and thus did they in the morning. [12]And they roasted the passover with fire, as appertaineth: as for the sacrifices, they sod

---

1:1–33 The great Passover celebration and Josiah's death. Compare 2 Chr 35:1–27 and notes. As a prologue to the rebuilding of the temple the narrator recounts its last great celebration in the days of Josiah's ambitious religious reforms; see 2 Kgs 23:21–23. **1:1** *Josias*: king of Judah, ca. 639–609 B.C.E. KJV transliterates 1 Esdra's hellenized forms of Hebrew names throughout. The annotations that follow use the more familiar Hebrew versions, only occasionally glossing hellenized forms. (In most cases, the differences are not so great as to cause confusion.) **1:2** *Daily courses*: divisions of priestly work in the temple; see 1 Chr 24:1–31 and note. **1:5** *Several dignity*: the Greek may refer to an administrative unit, hence "groupings" (NRSV). **1:6** *Offer the passover*: sacrifice the Passover lamb. *Keep the passover . . . Moses*: see Exod 12:1–28. **1:11** *As it . . . morning*: Exod 12:6 requires an evening sacrifice. The error seems related to a misunderstanding of 2 Chr 35:12 (in particular, confusion of the Hebrew word there rendered "oxen" for a similar word meaning "morning"). **1:12** *Sod*: boiled.

them in brass pots and pans with a good savour, [13]and set them before all the people: and afterward they prepared for themselves, and for the priests their brethren, the sons of Aaron. [14]For the priests offered the fat until night: and the Levites prepared for themselves, and the priests their brethren, the sons of Aaron. [15]The holy singers also, the sons of Asaph, were in their order, according to the appointment of David, to wit, Asaph, Zacharias, and Jeduthun, who was of the king's retinue. [16]Moreover the porters were at every gate; it was not lawful for any to go from his ordinary service: for their brethren the Levites prepared for them.

[17]Thus were the things that belonged to the sacrifices of the Lord accomplished in that day, that they might hold the passover, [18]and offer sacrifices upon the altar of the Lord, according to the commandment of king Josias. [19]So the children of Israel which were present held the passover at that time, and the feast of sweet bread seven days. [20]And such a passover was not kept in Israel since the time of the prophet Samuel. [21]Yea, all the kings of Israel held not such a passover as Josias, and the priests, and the Levites, and the Jews, held with all Israel that were found dwelling at Jerusalem. [22]In the eighteenth year of the reign of Josias was this passover kept. [23]And the works of Josias were upright before his Lord with an heart full of godliness. [24]As for the things that came to pass in his time, they were written in former times, concerning those that sinned, and did wickedly against the Lord above all people and kingdoms, and how they grieved him exceedingly, so that the words of the Lord rose up against Israel.

[25]Now after all these acts of Josias it came to pass, that Pharaoh the king of Egypt came to raise war at Carchamis upon Euphrates: and Josias went out against him. [26]But the king of Egypt sent to him, saying, What have I to do with thee, O king of Judea? [27]I am not sent out from the Lord God against thee; for my war is upon Euphrates: and now the Lord is with me, yea, the Lord is with me hasting me forward: depart from me, and be not against the Lord. [28]Howbeit Josias did not turn back his chariot from him, but undertook to fight with him, not regarding the words of the prophet Jeremy spoken by the mouth of the Lord: [29]but joined battle with him in the plain of Magiddo, and the princes came against king Josias. [30]Then said the king unto his servants, Carry me away out of the battle; for I am very weak. And immediately his servants took him away out of the battle. [31]Then gat he up upon his second chariot; and being brought back to Jerusalem died, and was buried in his father's sepulchre. [32]And in all Jewry they mourned for Josias, yea, Jeremy the prophet lamented for Josias, and the chief men with the women made lamentation for him unto this day: and this was given out for an ordinance to be done continually in all the nation of Israel. [33]These things are written in the

---

1:15 *Jeduthun*: the Greek reads "Eddinus." Unless this is a hellenized deformation of *Jeduthun*, KJV imports the name from 2 Chr 35:15.   **1:19** *Sweet bread*: unleavened bread.   **1:23–24** *And the works . . . Israel*: not from 2 Chronicles, but apparently paraphrasing 2 Kgs 23:25–27.   **1:25** *Pharaoh*: identified as Necho at 2 Chr 35:20.   **1:28** *Jeremy*: in 2 Chr 35:21–22 God's warning is attributed to Necho. Piety probably inspired the emendation. Moreover, Jeremiah's oracle about Necho's subsequent defeat at the hands of Nebuchadnezzar (Jer 46:2–26) might have led the author to postulate an earlier prophecy of Necho's victory over Judah at the battle of Megiddo in 609 B.C.E.   **1:30** *I am very weak*: explained in 2 Chr 35:23.   **1:32** *Jewry*: Gk. *Ioudaia* (so throughout), often rendered "Judea" or "Judah."   **1:33** *The book . . . Judah*: none of the sources mentioned in vv. 33 or 42 are extant.

book of the stories of the kings of Judah, and every one of the acts that Josias did, and his glory, and his understanding in the law of the Lord, and the things that he had done before, and the things now recited, are reported in the book of the kings of Israel and Judea.

[34]And the people took Joachaz the son of Josias, and made him king instead of Josias his father, when he was twenty and three years old. [35]And he reigned in Judea and in Jerusalem three months: and then the king of Egypt deposed him from reigning in Jerusalem. [36]And he set a tax upon the land of an hundred talents of silver and one talent of gold. [37]The king of Egypt also made king Joacim his brother king of Judea and Jerusalem. [38]And he bound Joacim and the nobles: but Zaraces his brother he apprehended, and brought him out of Egypt.

[39]Five and twenty years old was Joacim when he was made king in the land of Judea and Jerusalem; and he did evil before the Lord. [40]Wherefore against him Nabuchodonosor the king of Babylon came up, and bound him with a chain of brass, and carried him unto Babylon. [41]Nabuchodonosor also took of the holy vessels of the Lord, and carried them away, and set them in his own temple at Babylon. [42]But those things that are recorded of him, and of his uncleanness and impiety, are written in the chronicles of the kings.

[43]And Joacim his son reigned in his stead: he was made king being eighteen years old; [44]and reigned but three months and ten days in Jerusalem; and did evil before the Lord. [45]So after a year Nabuchodonosor sent and caused him to be brought into Babylon with the holy vessels of the Lord; [46]and made Zedechias king of Judea and Jerusalem, when he was one and twenty years old; and he reigned eleven years: [47]and he did evil also in the sight of the Lord, and cared not for the words that were spoken unto him by the prophet Jeremy from the mouth of the Lord. [48]And after that king Nabuchodonosor had made him to swear by the name of the Lord, he forswore himself, and rebelled; and hardening his neck, and his heart, he transgressed the laws of the Lord God of Israel. [49]The governors also of the people and of the priests did many things against the laws, and passed all the pollutions of all nations, and defiled the temple of the Lord, which was sanctified in Jerusalem. [50]Nevertheless the God of their fathers sent by his messenger to call them back, because he spared them and his tabernacle also. [51]But they had his messengers in derision; and, look, when the Lord spake unto them, they made a sport of his prophets: [52]so far forth, that he, being wroth with his people for their great ungodliness, commanded the kings of the Chaldees to come up against them; [53]who slew their young men with the sword, yea, even within the compass of their holy temple, and spared neither young man nor maid, old man nor child, among

1:34–58 The fall of Jerusalem. Compare 2 Chr 36:1–21 and notes.   **1:34** *Joachaz*: the Greek actually reads "Jeconiah," but that seems to be an error; cf. 2 Kgs 23:30; 2 Chr 36:1.   **1:36** *Talents*: one talent weighed perhaps 75 lbs.   **1:38** *He bound*: the Greek reads "Joacim [i.e., Jehoiakim] bound" and assigns him responsibility for his brother's apprehension. KJV apparently follows 2 Chr 36:4. *Zaraces*: Zarius (apparently a hellenized deformation of "Jehoahaz"; cf. 2 Chr 36:4).   **1:40** *Nabuchodonosor*: Nebuchadnezzar II, king of Babylon, 605–562 B.C.E.   **1:41** *Holy vessels*: temple implements. **1:43** *Joacim*: apparently another error. It should read "Joacin" (i.e., "Jehoiachin"); cf. 2 Kgs 24:8; 2 Chr 36:9.   **1:47** *Cared not . . . Jeremy*: see Jer 37–38.   **1:49** *Passed*: surpassed.   **1:52** *Chaldees*: Babylonians.

them; for he delivered all into their hands. ⁵⁴And they took all the holy vessels of the Lord, both great and small, with the vessels of the ark of God, and the king's treasures, and carried them away into Babylon. ⁵⁵As for the house of the Lord, they burnt it, and brake down the walls of Jerusalem, and set fire upon her towers: ⁵⁶and as for her glorious things, they never ceased till they had consumed and brought them all to nought: and the people that were not slain with the sword he carried unto Babylon: ⁵⁷who became servants to him and his children, till the Persians reigned, to fulfil the word of the Lord spoken by the mouth of Jeremy: ⁵⁸until the land had enjoyed her sabbaths, the whole time of her desolation shall she rest, until the full term of seventy years.

2 In the first year of Cyrus king of the Persians, that the word of the Lord might be accomplished, that he had promised by the mouth of Jeremy; ²the Lord raised up the spirit of Cyrus the king of the Persians, and he made proclamation through all his kingdom, and also by writing, ³saying, Thus saith Cyrus king of the Persians; The Lord of Israel, the most high Lord, hath made me king of the whole world, ⁴and commanded me to build him an house at Jerusalem in Jewry. ⁵If therefore there be any of you that are of his people, let the Lord, even his Lord, be with him, and let him go up to Jerusalem that is in Judea, and build the house of the Lord of Israel: for he is the Lord that dwelleth in Jerusalem. ⁶Whosoever then dwell in the places about, let them help him, (those, I say, that are his neighbours,) with gold, and with silver, ⁷with gifts, with horses, and with cattle, and other things, which have been set forth by vow, for the temple of the Lord at Jerusalem.

⁸Then the chief of the families of Judea and of the tribe of Benjamin stood up; the priests also, and the Levites, and all they whose mind the Lord had moved to go up, and to build an house for the Lord at Jerusalem, ⁹and they that dwelt round about them, and helped them in all things with silver and gold, with horses and cattle, and with very many free gifts of a great number whose minds were stirred up thereto.

¹⁰King Cyrus also brought forth the holy vessels, which Nabuchodonosor had carried away from Jerusalem, and had set up in his temple of idols. ¹¹Now when Cyrus king of the Persians had brought them forth, he delivered them to Mithridates his treasurer: ¹²and by him they were delivered to Sanabassar the governor of Judea. ¹³And this was the number of them; A thousand golden cups, and a thousand of silver, censers of silver twenty nine, vials of gold thirty, and of silver two thousand four hundred and ten, and a thousand other vessels. ¹⁴So all the vessels of gold and of silver, which were carried away, were five thousand four hundred threescore and nine. ¹⁵These were brought back by Sanabassar, together with them of the captivity, from Babylon to Jerusalem.

¹⁶But in the time of Artaxerxes king of the Persians, Belemus, and Mithridates, and Tabellius, and Rathumus, and Beeltethmus, and Semellius the secretary, with

---

1:58 *Until the land . . . years*: cf. Jer 25:11–12; see also Lev 26:34–35.
    2:1–30 The return of the exiles. For vv. 1–15, cf. 2 Chr 36:22–23; Ezra 1:1–11 and notes; for vv. 16–30, cf. Ezra 4:7–24 and notes. The narrative moves forward seventy years, following Persia's conquest of Babylon.   **2:1** *Cyrus*: Cyrus II, who ruled Persia 559–530 B.C.E. and conquered Babylon in 539.   **2:13** *Vials*: bowls.   **2:16–30 But in the time . . . Persians**: this section is anachronistically

others that were in commission with them, dwelling in Samaria and other places, wrote unto him against them that dwelt in Judea and Jerusalem these letters following; [17]To king Artaxerxes our lord, Thy servants, Rathumus the storywriter, and Semellius the scribe, and the rest of their council, and the judges that are in Celosyria and Phenice. [18]Be it now known to the lord the king, that the Jews that are come up from you to us, being come into Jerusalem, (that rebellious and wicked city,) do build the marketplaces, and repair the walls of it, and do lay the foundation of the temple. [19]Now if this city and the walls thereof be made up again, they will not only refuse to give tribute, but also rebel against kings. [20]And forasmuch as the things pertaining to the temple are now in hand, we think it meet not to neglect such a matter, [21]but to speak unto our lord the king, to the intent that, if it be thy pleasure, it may be sought out in the books of thy fathers: [22]and thou shalt find in the chronicles what is written concerning these things, and shalt understand that that city was rebellious, troubling both kings and cities: [23]and that the Jews were rebellious, and raised always wars therein; for the which cause even this city was made desolate. [24]Wherefore now we do declare unto thee, O lord the king, that if this city be built again, and the walls thereof set up anew, thou shalt from henceforth have no passage into Celosyria and Phenice.

[25]Then the king wrote back again to Rathumus the storywriter, to Beeltethmus, to Semellius the scribe, and to the rest that were in commission, and dwellers in Samaria and Syria and Phenice, after this manner; [26]I have read the epistle which ye have sent unto me: therefore I commanded to make diligent search, and it hath been found that that city was from the beginning practising against kings; [27]and the men therein were given to rebellion and war: and that mighty kings and fierce were in Jerusalem, who reigned and exacted tributes in Celosyria and Phenice. [28]Now therefore I have commanded to hinder those men from building the city, and heed to be taken that there be no more done in it; [29]and that those wicked workers proceed no further to the annoyance of kings.

[30]Then king Artaxerxes his letters being read, Rathumus, and Semellius the scribe, and the rest that were in commission with them, removing in haste toward Jerusalem with a troop of horsemen and a multitude of people in battle array, began to hinder the builders; and the building of the temple in Jerusalem ceased until the second year of the reign of Darius king of the Persians.

---

imported from Ezra 4:7–24 (where it is likewise out of order), for Artaxerxes I ruled from 465 to 423 b.c.e., well after both Cyrus and Darius. In Ezra the passage focuses on the reconstruction of Jerusalem's walls rather than the temple, but 1 Esdras expands its lone references to the temple (2:30; Ezra 4:24; see also 1 Esd 2:18, 20; cf. Ezra 4:12, 14) in order to suggest a motivation for Zerubbabel's request in the subsequent episode.   **2:17** *Storywriter*: recorder (NRSV). *Celosyria and Phenice*: Coele-Syria and Phoenicia. The former probably refers to an area encompassing the southern part of the Mediterranean's easternmost seaboard, the latter refers to a smaller coastal region north of Judea. **2:30** *Artaxerxes his*: Artaxerxes'. *Darius*: Darius I, known as Darius the Great, ruled Persia from 522 to 486 b.c.e.

3 Now when Darius reigned, he made a great feast unto all his subjects, and unto all his household, and unto all the princes of Media and Persia, [2]and to all the governors and captains and lieutenants that were under him, from India unto Ethiopia, of an hundred twenty and seven provinces. [3]And when they had eaten and drunken, and being satisfied were gone home, then Darius the king went into his bedchamber, and slept, and soon after awaked.

[4]Then three young men, that were of the guard that kept the king's body, spake one to another; [5]Let every one of us speak a sentence: he that shall overcome, and whose sentence shall seem wiser than the others, unto him shall the king Darius give great gifts, and great things in token of victory: [6]as, to be clothed in purple, to drink in gold, and to sleep upon gold, and a chariot with bridles of gold, and an headtire of fine linen, and a chain about his neck: [7]and he shall sit next to Darius because of his wisdom, and shall be called Darius his cousin.

[8]And then every one wrote his sentence, sealed it, and laid it under king Darius his pillow; [9]and said that, when the king is risen, some will give him the writings; and of whose side the king and the three princes of Persia shall judge that his sentence is the wisest, to him shall the victory be given, as was appointed. [10]The first wrote, Wine is the strongest. [11]The second wrote, The king is strongest. [12]The third wrote, Women are strongest: but above all things Truth beareth away the victory.

[13]Now when the king was risen up, they took their writings, and delivered them unto him, and so he read them: [14]and sending forth he called all the princes of Persia and Media, and the governors, and the captains, and the lieutenants, and the chief officers; [15]and sat him down in the royal seat of judgment; and the writings were read before them. [16]And he said, Call the young men, and they shall declare their own sentences. So they were called, and came in. [17]And he said unto them, Declare unto us your mind concerning the writings.

Then began the first, who had spoken of the strength of wine; [18]and he said thus, O ye men, how exceeding strong is wine! it causeth all men to err that drink it: [19]it maketh the mind of the king and of the fatherless child to be all one; of the bondman and of the freeman, of the poor man and of the rich: [20]it turneth also every thought into jollity and mirth, so that a man remembereth neither sorrow nor debt: [21]and it maketh every heart rich, so that a man remembereth neither king nor governor; and it maketh to speak all things by talents: [22]and when they

---

3:1–4:63 The three bodyguards' debate. This section introduces Zerubbabel, rebuilder of the temple (see Hag 1:1–2; 2:2–4, 20–23; Zech 4:6–10), as the winner of a contest in which each of three bodyguards attempts to convince the king that what he names is strongest. Three morally ambivalent answers (wine, king, and women) give way to straightforward praise of truth as the third bodyguard, Zerubbabel (who actually gives two answers: women and then truth), wins the contest. For a prize, Zerubbabel asks that Darius honor his vow to rebuild the Jerusalem temple. The parenthetical identification of the third bodyguard as Zerubbabel (4:13) and the supplementary praise of truth (3:12b; 4:33b–41) are probably later additions to a story that circulated independently of 1 Esdras. **3:1–2** *Now when . . . provinces*: adapting Esth 1:1–3. **3:1** *Media*: part of the Persian Empire. **3:5** *Let every one . . . overcome*: perhaps better "let each of us say the one word which is strongest," i.e., "let each of us declare the most powerful thing in the world." **3:6** *Headtire*: turban. **3:7** *Darius his*: Darius's (also in v. 8). **3:16** *Declare*: explain. **3:17** *The strength of wine*: see Sir 31:27–31 for another meditation on wine's ambivalent power; Prov 23:29–35 condemns it outright. **3:21** *To speak . . . talents*: to speak in

are in their cups, they forget their love both to friends and brethren, and a little after draw out swords: ²³but when they are from the wine, they remember not what they have done. ²⁴O ye men, is not wine the strongest, that enforceth to do thus? And when he had so spoken, he held his peace.

4 Then the second, that had spoken of the strength of the king, began to say, ²O ye men, do not men excel in strength, that bear rule over sea and land, and all things in them? ³But yet the king is more mighty: for he is lord of all these things, and hath dominion over them; and whatsoever he commandeth them they do. ⁴If he bid them make war the one against the other, they do it: if he send them out against the enemies, they go, and break down mountains, walls, and towers. ⁵They slay and are slain, and transgress not the king's commandment: if they get the victory, they bring all to the king, as well the spoil, as all things else. ⁶Likewise for those that are no soldiers, and have not to do with wars, but use husbandry, when they have reaped again that which they had sown, they bring it to the king, and compel one another to pay tribute unto the king. ⁷And yet he is but one man: if he command to kill, they kill; if he command to spare, they spare; ⁸if he command to smite, they smite; if he command to make desolate, they make desolate; if he command to build, they build; ⁹if he command to cut down, they cut down; if he command to plant, they plant. ¹⁰So all his people and his armies obey him: furthermore he lieth down, he eateth and drinketh, and taketh his rest: ¹¹and these keep [watch] round about him, neither may any one depart, and do his own business, neither disobey they him in any thing. ¹²O ye men, how should not the king be mightiest, when in such sort he is obeyed? And he held his tongue.

¹³Then the third, who had spoken of women, and of the truth, (this was Zorobabel) began to speak. ¹⁴O ye men, it is not the great king, nor the multitude of men, neither is it wine, that excelleth; who is it then that ruleth them, or hath the lordship over them? are they not women? ¹⁵Women have borne the king and all the people that bear rule by sea and land. ¹⁶Even of them came they: and they nourished them up that planted the vineyards, from whence the wine cometh. ¹⁷These also make garments for men; these bring glory unto men; and without women cannot men be. ¹⁸Yea, and if men have gathered together gold and silver, or any other goodly thing, do they not love a woman which is comely in favour and beauty? ¹⁹And letting all those things go, do they not gape, and even with open mouth fix their eyes fast on her; and have not all men more desire unto her than unto silver or gold, or any goodly thing whatsoever?

²⁰A man leaveth his own father that brought him up, and his own country, and cleaveth unto his wife. ²¹He sticketh not to spend his life with his wife, and remembereth neither father, nor mother, nor country. ²²By this also ye must know that women have dominion over you: do ye not labour and toil, and give and bring all to the woman? ²³Yea, a man taketh his sword, and goeth his way to rob and to

---

highly exaggerated terms. **4:3** *The king . . . mighty*: the following discourse's emphasis on monarchs' absolute and arbitrary power recalls Samuel's diatribe against kings in 1 Sam 8:11–18, but the present passage is less pessimistic. **4:20** *A man . . . wife*: cf. Gen 2:24. **4:21** *He sticketh . . . wife*: alternatively "with his wife he ends his days" (NRSV). **4:22** *Women have . . . woman*: perhaps an ironic

steal, to sail upon the sea and upon rivers; ²⁴and looketh upon a lion, and goeth in the darkness; and when he hath stolen, spoiled, and robbed, he bringeth it to his love. ²⁵Wherefore a man loveth his wife better than father or mother. ²⁶Yea, many there be that have run out of their wits for women, and become servants for their sakes. ²⁷Many also have perished, have erred, and sinned, for women.

²⁸And now do ye not believe me? is not the king great in his power? do not all regions fear to touch him? ²⁹Yet did I see him and Apame the king's concubine, the daughter of the admirable Bartacus, sitting at the right hand of the king, ³⁰and taking the crown from the king's head, and setting it upon her own head; she also struck the king with her left hand. ³¹And yet for all this the king gaped and gazed upon her with open mouth: if she laughed upon him, he laughed also: but if she took any displeasure at him, the king was fain to flatter, that she might be reconciled to him again. ³²O ye men, how can it be but women should be strong, seeing they do thus?

³³Then the king and the princes looked one upon another: so he began to speak of the truth. ³⁴O ye men, are not women strong? great is the earth, high is the heaven, swift is the sun in his course, for he compasseth the heavens round about, and fetcheth his course again to his own place in one day. ³⁵Is he not great that maketh these things? therefore great is the truth, and stronger than all things. ³⁶All the earth calleth upon the truth, and the heaven blesseth it: all works shake and tremble at it, and with it is no unrighteous thing. ³⁷Wine is wicked, the king is wicked, women are wicked, all the children of men are wicked, and such are all their wicked works; and there is no truth in them; in their unrighteousness also they shall perish. ³⁸As for the truth, it endureth, and is always strong; it liveth and conquereth for evermore. ³⁹With her there is no accepting of persons or rewards; but she doeth the things that are just, and refraineth from all unjust and wicked things; and all men do well like of her works. ⁴⁰Neither in her judgment is any unrighteousness; and she is the strength, kingdom, power, and majesty, of all ages. Blessed be the God of truth. ⁴¹And with that he held his peace. And all the people then shouted, and said, Great is Truth, and mighty above all things.

⁴²Then said the king unto him, Ask what thou wilt more than is appointed in the writing, and we will give it thee, because thou art found wisest; and thou shalt sit next me, and shalt be called my cousin. ⁴³Then said he unto the king, Remember thy vow, which thou hast vowed to build Jerusalem, in the day when thou camest to thy kingdom, ⁴⁴and to send away all the vessels that were taken away out of Jerusalem, which Cyrus set apart, when he vowed to destroy Babylon, and to send them again thither. ⁴⁵Thou also hast vowed to build up the temple, which the Edomites burned when Judea was made desolate by the Chaldees. ⁴⁶And now, O lord the king, this is that which I require, and which I desire of

recasting of Gen 1:26.   **4:26** *Servants*: slaves (as often).   **4:39** *Accepting of persons*: favoritism.   **4:43** *Remember thy vow . . . kingdom*: a somewhat ironic request following Zerubbabel's praise of truth, for Darius is not reported to have made such a vow. Cyrus did, when he ascended to the throne (see 2:1–7). Perhaps Zerubbabel counts on Darius's mind being muddled by excessive feasting (3:3). If so, the strategy recalls the one used by Nathan and Bathsheba on David (1 Kgs 1:11–31 and notes).   **4:45** *Which the Edomites . . . Chaldees*: cf. Ps 137:7–8; Obad 8–18.

thee, and this is the princely liberality proceeding from thyself: I desire therefore that thou make good the vow, the performance whereof with thine own mouth thou hast vowed to the King of heaven.

[47]Then Darius the king stood up, and kissed him, and wrote letters for him unto all the treasurers and lieutenants and captains and governors, that they should safely convey on their way both him, and all those that go up with him to build Jerusalem. [48]He wrote letters also unto the lieutenants that were in Celosyria and Phenice, and unto them in Libanus, that they should bring cedar wood from Libanus unto Jerusalem, and that they should build the city with him. [49]Moreover he wrote for all the Jews that went out of his realm up into Jewry, concerning their freedom, that no officer, no ruler, no lieutenant, nor treasurer, should forcibly enter into their doors; [50]and that all the country which they hold should be free without tribute; and that the Edomites should give over the villages of the Jews which then they held: [51]yea, that there should be yearly given twenty talents to the building of the temple, until the time that it were built; [52]and other ten talents yearly, to maintain the burnt offerings upon the altar every day, (as they had a commandment to offer seventeen:) [53]and that all they that went from Babylon to build the city should have free liberty, as well they as their posterity, and all the priests that went away. [54]He wrote also concerning the charges, and the priests' vestments wherein they minister; [55]and likewise for the charges of the Levites, to be given them until the day that the house were finished, and Jerusalem builded up. [56]And he commanded to give to all that kept the city pensions and wages. [57]He sent away also all the vessels from Babylon, that Cyrus had set apart; and all that Cyrus had given in commandment, the same charged he also to be done, and sent unto Jerusalem.

[58]Now when this young man was gone forth, he lifted up his face to heaven toward Jerusalem, and praised the King of heaven, [59]and said, From thee cometh victory, from thee cometh wisdom, and thine is the glory, and I am thy servant. [60]Blessed art thou, who hast given me wisdom: for to thee I give thanks, O Lord of our fathers. [61]And so he took the letters, and went out, and came unto Babylon, and told it all his brethren. [62]And they praised the God of their fathers, because he had given them freedom and liberty [63]to go up, and to build Jerusalem, and the temple which is called by his name: and they feasted with instruments of musick and gladness seven days.

5 After this were the principal men of the families chosen according to their tribes, to go up with their wives and sons and daughters, with their menservants and maidservants, and their cattle. [2]And Darius sent with them a thousand horsemen, till they had brought them back to Jerusalem safely, and with musical

---

4:47–48 *Then Darius . . . Jerusalem*: cf. Neh 2:7–8, where Artaxerxes writes such a letter for Nehemiah.   **4:48** *Libanus*: Lebanon.   **4:54** *Charges*: support (also in v. 55).

5:1–73 The list of returned exiles. Verses 1–6 provide a transition from the narrative of the bodyguards' debate to the list of returning exiles drawn from Ezra and Nehemiah. For vv. 7–73, cf. Ezra 2:1–4:5 and notes. (In Ezra the exiles return while Cyrus, rather than Darius, is ruling; this discrepancy partially explains the anachronistic reference to Cyrus's reign in v. 73; see note.)

[instruments], tabrets and flutes. ³And all their brethren played, and he made them go up together with them.

⁴And these are the names of the men which went up, according to their families among their tribes, after their several heads. ⁵The priests, the sons of Phinees the son of Aaron: Jesus the son of Josedec, the son of Saraias, and Joacim the son of Zorobabel, the son of Salathiel of the house of David, out of the kindred of Phares of the tribe of Judah; ⁶who spake wise sentences before Darius the king of Persia in the second year of his reign, in the month Nisan, which is the first month.

⁷And these are they of Jewry that came up from the captivity, where they dwelt as strangers, whom Nabuchodonosor the king of Babylon had carried away unto Babylon. ⁸And they returned unto Jerusalem, and to the other parts of Jewry, every man to his own city, who came with Zorobabel, with Jesus, Nehemias, and Zacharias, and Reesaias, Enenius, Mardocheus, Beelsarus, Aspharasus, Reelius, Roimus, and Baana, their guides.

⁹The number of them of the nation, and their governors, sons of Phoros, two thousand an hundred seventy and two; the sons of Saphat, four hundred seventy and two: ¹⁰the sons of Ares, seven hundred fifty and six: ¹¹the sons of Phaath Moab, two thousand eight hundred and twelve: ¹²the sons of Elam, a thousand two hundred fifty and four: the sons of Zathui, nine hundred forty and five: the sons of Corbe, seven hundred and five: the sons of Bani, six hundred forty and eight: ¹³the sons of Bebai, six hundred twenty and three: the sons of Sadas, three thousand two hundred twenty and two: ¹⁴the sons of Adonikam, six hundred sixty and seven: the sons of Bagoi, two thousand sixty and six: the sons of Adin, four hundred fifty and four: ¹⁵the sons of Aterezias, ninety and two: the sons of Ceilan and Azetas, threescore and seven: the sons of Azuran, four hundred thirty and two: ¹⁶the sons of Ananias, an hundred and one: the sons of Arom, thirty two: and the sons of Bassa, three hundred twenty and three: the sons of Azephurith, an hundred and two: ¹⁷the sons of Meterus, three thousand and five: the sons of Bethlomon, an hundred twenty and three: ¹⁸they of Netophah, fifty and five: they of Anathoth, an hundred fifty and eight: they of Bethsamos, forty and two: ¹⁹they of Kiriathiarius, twenty and five: they of Caphira and Beroth, seven hundred forty and three: they of Pira, seven hundred: ²⁰they of Chadias and Ammidioi, four hundred twenty and two: they of Cirama and Gabdes, six hundred twenty and one: ²¹they of Macalon, an hundred twenty and two: they of Betolius, fifty and two: the sons of Nephis, an hundred fifty and six: ²²the sons of Calamolalus and Onus, seven hundred twenty and five: the sons of Jerechus, two hundred forty and five: ²³the sons of Annaas, three thousand three hundred and thirty.

²⁴The priests: the sons of Jeddu, the son of Jesus, among the sons of Sanasib, nine hundred seventy and two: the sons of Meruth, a thousand fifty and two: ²⁵the sons of Phassaron, a thousand forty and seven: the sons of Carme, a thousand and seventeen. ²⁶The Levites: the sons of Jessue, and Cadmiel, and Banuas, and

---

5:2 *Tabret*: diminutive of "tabor."   5:5 *Joacim the son of Zorobabel*: this is confusing, for Zerubbabel comes from the tribe of Judah and therefore cannot be the father of a priest (who by definition would be a Levite). Moreover, 1 Chr 3:19 lists Zerubbabel's sons, and Joakim is not among them.   5:7–46 *And*

Sudias, seventy and four. [27]The holy singers: the sons of Asaph, an hundred twenty and eight. [28]The porters: the sons of Salum, the sons of Jatal, the sons of Talmon, the sons of Dacobi, the sons of Teta, the sons of Sami, in all an hundred thirty and nine. [29]The servants of the temple: the sons of Esau, the sons of Asipha, the sons of Tabaoth, the sons of Ceras, the sons of Sud, the sons of Phaleas, the sons of Labana, the sons of Graba, [30]the sons of Acua, the sons of Uta, the sons of Cetab, the sons of Agaba, the sons of Subai, the sons of Anan, the sons of Cathua, the sons of Geddur, [31]the sons of Airus, the sons of Daisan, the sons of Noeba, the sons of Chaseba, the sons of Gazera, the sons of Azia, the sons of Phinees, the sons of Azara, the sons of Bastai, the sons of Asana, the sons of Meani, the sons of Naphisi, the sons of Acub, the sons of Acipha, the sons of Assur, the sons of Pharacim, the sons of Basaloth, [32]the sons of Meeda, the sons of Coutha, the sons of Charea, the sons of Charcus, the sons of Aserer, the sons of Thomoi, the sons of Nasith, the sons of Atipha. [33]The sons of the servants of Solomon: the sons of Azaphion, the sons of Pharira, the sons of Jeeli, the sons of Lozon, the sons of Isdael, the sons of Sapheth, [34]the sons of Hagia, the sons of Phacareth, the sons of Sabi, the sons of Sarothie, the sons of Masias, the sons of Gar, the sons of Addus, the sons of Suba, the sons of Apherra, the sons of Barodis, the sons of Sabat, the sons of Allom. [35]All the ministers of the temple, and the sons of the servants of Solomon, were three hundred seventy and two.

[36]These came up from Thermeleth and Thelersas, Charaathalar leading them, and Aalar; [37]neither could they shew their families, nor their stock, how they were of Israel: the sons of Ladan, the son of Ban, the sons of Necodan, six hundred fifty and two. [38]And of the priests that usurped the office of the priesthood, and were not found: the sons of Obdia, the sons of Accoz, the sons of Addus, who married Augia one of the daughters of Berzelus, and was named after his name. [39]And when the description of the kindred of these men was sought in the register, and was not found, they were removed from executing the office of the priesthood: [40]for unto them said Nehemias and Atharias, that they should not be partakers of the holy things, till there arose up an high priest clothed with doctrine and truth.

[41]So of Israel, from them of twelve years old and upward, they were all in number forty thousand, beside menservants and womenservants two thousand three hundred and sixty. [42]Their menservants and handmaids were seven thousand three hundred forty and seven: the singing men and singing women, two hundred forty and five: [43]four hundred thirty and five camels, seven thousand thirty and six horses, two hundred forty and five mules, five thousand five hundred twenty and five beasts used to the yoke. [44]And certain of the chief of their families, when they came to the temple of God that is in Jerusalem, vowed to set up the house again in his own place according to their ability, [45]and to give into the

---

these . . . villages: the list displays only a few minor differences from Ezra 2 (cf. Neh 7:6–73). **5:40** Nehemias and Atharias: Ezra 2:63, on which this verse draws, does not mention Nehemiah; its "Tirshatha" (hellenized as Atharias) is a Persian title given to the governor, which the author of 1 Esdras apparently mistook for a person's name. Because it is a title given to Nehemiah at Neh 8:9, a scribe may have written his name in a marginal gloss at Ezra 2:63, leading the author of 1 Esdras to import it into his text here. Doctrine and truth: i.e., Urim and Thummim, the sacred lots (compare LXX and MT

holy treasury of the works a thousand pounds of gold, five thousand of silver, and an hundred priestly vestments. ⁴⁶And so dwelt the priests and the Levites and the people in Jerusalem, and in the country, the singers also and the porters; and all Israel in their villages.

⁴⁷But when the seventh month was at hand, and when the children of Israel were every man in his own place, they came all together with one consent into the open place of the first gate which is toward the east. ⁴⁸Then stood up Jesus the son of Josedec, and his brethren the priests, and Zorobabel the son of Salathiel, and his brethren, and made ready the altar of the God of Israel, ⁴⁹to offer burnt sacrifices upon it, according as it is expressly commanded in the book of Moses the man of God. ⁵⁰And there were gathered unto them out of the other nations of the land, and they erected the altar upon his own place, because all the nations of the land were at enmity with them, and oppressed them; and they offered sacrifices according to the time, and burnt offerings to the Lord both morning and evening. ⁵¹Also they held the feast of tabernacles, as it is commanded in the law, and offered sacrifices daily, as was meet: ⁵²and after that, the continual oblations, and the sacrifice of the sabbaths, and of the new moons, and of all holy feasts. ⁵³And all they that had made any vow to God began to offer sacrifices to God from the first day of the seventh month, although the temple of the Lord was not yet built.

⁵⁴And they gave unto the masons and carpenters money, meat, and drink, with cheerfulness. ⁵⁵Unto them of Sidon also and Tyre they gave carrs, that they should bring cedar trees from Libanus, which should be brought by floats to the haven of Joppe, according as it was commanded them by Cyrus king of the Persians.

⁵⁶And in the second year and second month after his coming to the temple of God at Jerusalem began Zorobabel the son of Salathiel, and Jesus the son of Josedec, and their brethren, and the priests, and the Levites, and all they that were come unto Jerusalem out of the captivity: ⁵⁷and they laid the foundation of the house of God in the first day of the second month, in the second year after they were come to Jewry and Jerusalem. ⁵⁸And they appointed the Levites from twenty years old over the works of the Lord. Then stood up Jesus, and his sons and brethren, and Cadmiel his brother, and the sons of Madiabun, with the sons of Joda the son of Eliadun, with their sons and brethren, all Levites, with one accord setters forward of the business, labouring to advance the works in the house of God. So the workmen built the temple of the Lord.

⁵⁹And the priests stood arrayed in their vestments with musical instruments and trumpets; and the Levites the sons of Asaph had cymbals, ⁶⁰singing songs of thanksgiving, and praising the Lord, according as David the king of Israel had ordained. ⁶¹And they sung with loud voices songs to the praise of the Lord, because his mercy and glory is for ever in all Israel. ⁶²And all the people sounded trumpets, and shouted with a loud voice, singing songs of thanksgiving unto the Lord for the rearing up of the house of the Lord. ⁶³Also of the priests and Levites, and of the chief of their families, the ancients who had seen the former house came to the building of this with weeping and great crying. ⁶⁴But many with trumpets and joy

Exod 28:30; see 1 Sam 14:41–42 note).   **5:50** *His*: its.   **5:51** *Feast of tabernacles . . . law*: Lev 23:39–42.   **5:55** *Carrs*: carriages; but the Greek, which deviates from Ezra 3:7's "oil," is obscure. *Joppe*: Joppa.

shouted with loud voice, ⁶⁵insomuch that the trumpets might not be heard for the weeping of the people: yet the multitude sounded marvellously, so that it was heard afar off.

⁶⁶Wherefore when the enemies of the tribe of Judah and Benjamin heard it, they came to know what that noise of trumpets should mean. ⁶⁷And they perceived that they that were of the captivity did build the temple unto the Lord God of Israel. ⁶⁸So they went to Zorobabel and Jesus, and to the chief of the families, and said unto them, We will build together with you. ⁶⁹For we likewise, as ye, do obey your Lord, and do sacrifice unto him from the days of Azbazareth the king of the Assyrians, who brought us hither.

⁷⁰Then Zorobabel and Jesus and the chief of the families of Israel said unto them, It is not for us and you to build together an house unto the Lord our God. ⁷¹We ourselves alone will build unto the Lord of Israel, according as Cyrus the king of the Persians hath commanded us. ⁷²But the heathen of the land lying heavy upon the inhabitants of Judea, and holding them strait, hindered their building; ⁷³and by their secret plots, and popular persuasions and commotions, they hindered the finishing of the building all the time that king Cyrus lived: so they were hindered from building for the space of two years, until the reign of Darius.

6 Now in the second year of the reign of Darius, Aggeus and Zacharias the son of Addo, the prophets, prophesied unto the Jews in Jewry and Jerusalem in the name of the Lord God of Israel, which was upon them. ²Then stood up Zorobabel the son of Salathiel, and Jesus the son of Josedec, and began to build the house of the Lord at Jerusalem, the prophets of the Lord being with them, and helping them. ³At the same time came unto them Sisinnes the governor of Syria and Phenice, with Sathrabuzanes and his companions, and said unto them, ⁴By whose appointment do ye build this house and this roof, and perform all the other things? and who are the workmen that perform these things? ⁵Nevertheless the elders of the Jews obtained favour, because the Lord had visited the captivity; ⁶and they were not hindered from building, until such time as signification was given unto Darius concerning them, and an answer received.

⁷The copy of the letters which Sisinnes, governor of Syria and Phenice, and Sathrabuzanes, with their companions, rulers in Syria and Phenice, wrote and sent unto Darius: To king Darius, greeting: ⁸Let all things be known unto our lord the king, that being come into the country of Judea, and entered into the city of Jerusalem, we found in the city of Jerusalem the ancients of the Jews that were of the captivity, ⁹building an house unto the Lord, great and new, of hewn and

---

5:69–71 *For we . . . us*: 2 Kgs 17:24–41 helps explain this exchange.   5:69 *Azbazareth*: conceivably a hellenized deformation of Ezra 4:2's Esarhaddon, who ruled Assyria 681–669 B.C.E.; but 2 Kgs 17:3–5 seems to identify Shalmaneser (727–722 B.C.E.) as the Assyrian monarch who ordered the resettlement.   5:72 *Holding them strait*: besieging them.   5:73 *They hindered . . . lived*: the anachronistic reference to a delay while Cyrus ruled comes from Ezra 4:4–5, but the claim that it lasted only two years, until the reign of Darius, is impossible, since Cambyses ruled for almost a decade between them (530–522 B.C.E.).

6:1–7:15 **The completion of the temple.** Compare Ezra 4:24b–6:22 and notes.   6:1 *Aggeus and Zacharias*: Haggai and Zechariah; see Hag 1:1–4; 2:1–4; Zech 4:8–10; 6:15.   6:8 *Ancients*: Gk.

costly stones, and the timber already laid upon the walls. ¹⁰And those works are done with great speed, and the work goeth on prosperously in their hands, and with all glory and diligence is it made. ¹¹Then asked we these elders, saying, By whose commandment build ye this house, and lay the foundations of these works? ¹²Therefore to the intent that we might give knowledge unto thee by writing, we demanded of them who were the chief doers, and we required of them the names in writing of their principal men. ¹³So they gave us this answer, We are the servants of the Lord which made heaven and earth. ¹⁴And as for this house, it was builded many years ago by a king of Israel great and strong, and was finished. ¹⁵But when our fathers provoked God unto wrath, and sinned against the Lord of Israel which is in heaven, he gave them over into the power of Nabuchodonosor king of Babylon, of the Chaldees; ¹⁶who pulled down the house, and burned it, and carried away the people captives unto Babylon. ¹⁷But in the first year that king Cyrus reigned over the country of Babylon, Cyrus the king wrote to build up this house. ¹⁸And the holy vessels of gold and of silver, that Nabuchodonosor had carried away out of the house at Jerusalem, and had set them in his own temple, those Cyrus the king brought forth again out of the temple at Babylon, and they were delivered to Zorobabel and to Sanabassarus the ruler, ¹⁹with commandment that he should carry away the same vessels, and put them in the temple at Jerusalem; and that the temple of the Lord should be built in his place. ²⁰Then the same Sanabassarus, being come hither, laid the foundations of the house of the Lord at Jerusalem; and from that time to this being still a building, it is not yet fully ended. ²¹Now therefore, if it seem good unto the king, let search be made among the records of king Cyrus: ²²and if it be found that the building of the house of the Lord at Jerusalem hath been done with the consent of king Cyrus, and if our lord the king be so minded, let him signify unto us thereof.

²³Then commanded king Darius to seek among the records at Babylon: and so at Ecbatana the palace, which is in the country of Media, there was found a roll wherein these things were recorded. ²⁴In the first year of the reign of Cyrus, king Cyrus commanded that the house of the Lord at Jerusalem should be built again, where they do sacrifice with continual fire: ²⁵whose height shall be sixty cubits, and the breadth sixty cubits, with three rows of hewn stones, and one row of new wood of that country; and the expenses thereof to be given out of the house of king Cyrus: ²⁶and that the holy vessels of the house of the Lord, both of gold and silver, that Nabuchodonosor took out of the house at Jerusalem, and brought to Babylon, should be restored to the house at Jerusalem, and be set in the place where they were before.

²⁷And also he commanded that Sisinnes the governor of Syria and Phenice, and Sathrabuzanes, and their companions, and those which were appointed rulers in Syria and Phenice, should be careful hot to meddle with the place, but suffer Zorobabel, the servant of the Lord, and governor of Judea, and the elders of the Jews, to build the house of the Lord in that place. ²⁸I have commanded also to

---

presbyteroi, "elders" (so throughout; cf. v. 5).   **6:19** His: its.   **6:20** Still a building: in the process of construction.   **6:25** Sixty cubits: about ninety feet.   **6:28** I have commanded: introducing a quotation

have it built up whole again; and that they look diligently to help those that be of the captivity of the Jews, till the house of the Lord be finished: ²⁹and out of the tribute of Celosyria and Phenice a portion carefully to be given these men for the sacrifices of the Lord, that is, to Zorobabel the governor, for bullocks, and rams, and lambs; ³⁰and also corn, salt, wine, and oil, and that continually every year without further question, according as the priests that be in Jerusalem shall signify to be daily spent: ³¹that offerings may be made to the most high God for the king and for his children, and that they may pray for their lives. ³²And he commanded that whosoever should transgress, yea, or make light of any thing afore spoken or written, out of his own house should a tree be taken, and he thereon be hanged, and all his goods seized for the king. ³³The Lord therefore, whose name is there called upon, utterly destroy every king and nation, that stretcheth out his hand to hinder or endamage that house of the Lord in Jerusalem. ³⁴I Darius the king have ordained that according unto these things it be done with diligence.

7 Then Sisinnes the governor of Celosyria and Phenice, and Sathrabuzanes, with their companions, following the commandments of king Darius, ²did very carefully oversee the holy works, assisting the ancients of the Jews and governors of the temple. ³And so the holy works prospered, when Aggeus and Zacharias the prophets prophesied. ⁴And they finished these things by the commandment of the Lord God of Israel, and with the consent of Cyrus, Darius, and Artaxerxes, kings of Persia. ⁵And thus was the holy house finished in the three and twentieth day of the month Adar, in the sixth year of Darius king of the Persians. ⁶And the children of Israel, the priests, and the Levites, and others that were of the captivity, that were added unto them, did according to the things written in the book of Moses. ⁷And to the dedication of the temple of the Lord they offered an hundred bullocks, two hundred rams, four hundred lambs; ⁸and twelve goats for the sin of all Israel, according to the number of the chief of the tribes of Israel. ⁹The priests also and the Levites stood arrayed in their vestments, according to their kindreds, in the services of the Lord God of Israel, according to the book of Moses: and the porters at every gate.

¹⁰And the children of Israel that were of the captivity held the passover the fourteenth day of the first month, after that the priests and the Levites were sanctified. ¹¹They that were of the captivity were not all sanctified together: but the Levites were all sanctified together. ¹²And so they offered the passover for all them of the captivity, and for their brethren the priests, and for themselves. ¹³And the children of Israel that came out of the captivity did eat, even all they that had separated themselves from the abominations of the people of the land, and sought the Lord. ¹⁴And they kept the feast of unleavened bread seven days, making merry before the Lord, ¹⁵for that he had turned the counsel of the king of Assyria toward them, to strengthen their hands in the works of the Lord God of Israel.

---

of Darius's commands, as v. 34 makes clear.   **7:4** *Artaxerxes*: another anachronistic reference to Artaxerxes (see 2:16–30 and note), and an oddly positive one in light of the earlier passage, but it anticipates 8:1–9:36.   **7:5** *In the three . . . Persians*: February-March 516 B.C.E.   **7:11** *Sanctified*: purified, in advance of the Passover, although purification was not always required (see Num 9:6–14; cf. 2 Chr 30:18–19).   **7:15** *King of Assyria*: Darius, actually the Persion emperor; but see Ezra 6:22 note.

8 And after these things, when Artaxerxes the king of the Persians reigned, came Esdras the son of Saraias, the son of Ezerias, the son of Helchiah, the son of Salum, [2]the son of Sadduc, the son of Achitob, the son of Amarias, the son of Ezias, the son of Memeroth, the son of Zaraias, the son of Savias, the son of Boccas, the son of Abisum, the son of Phinees, the son of Eleazar, the son of Aaron the chief priest. [3]This Esdras went up from Babylon, as a scribe, being very ready in the law of Moses, that was given by the God of Israel. [4]And the king did him honour: for he found grace in his sight in all his requests. [5]There went up with him also certain of the children of Israel, of the priests, of the Levites, of the holy singers, porters, and ministers of the temple, unto Jerusalem, [6]in the seventh year of the reign of Artaxerxes, in the fifth month, this was the king's seventh year; for they went from Babylon in the first day of the first month, and came to Jerusalem, according to the prosperous journey which the Lord gave them. [7]For Esdras had very great skill, so that he omitted nothing of the law and commandments of the Lord, but taught all Israel the ordinances and judgments.

[8]Now the copy of the commission, which was written from Artaxerxes the king, and came to Esdras the priest and reader of the law of the Lord, is this that followeth; [9]King Artaxerxes unto Esdras the priest and reader of the law of the Lord sendeth greeting: [10]having determined to deal graciously, I have given order, that such of the nation of the Jews, and of the priests and Levites, being within our realm, as are willing and desirous, should go with thee unto Jerusalem. [11]As many therefore as have a mind thereunto, let them depart with thee, as it hath seemed good both to me and my seven friends the counsellers; [12]that they may look unto the affairs of Judea and Jerusalem, agreeably to that which is in the law of the Lord; [13]and carry the gifts unto the Lord of Israel to Jerusalem, which I and my friends have vowed, and all the gold and silver that in the country of Babylon can be found, to the Lord in Jerusalem, [14]with that also which is given of the people for the temple of the Lord their God at Jerusalem: and that silver and gold may be collected for bullocks, rams, and lambs, and things thereunto appertaining; [15]to the end that they may offer sacrifices unto the Lord upon the altar of the Lord their God, which is in Jerusalem. [16]And whatsoever thou and thy brethren will do with the silver and gold, that do, according to the will of thy God. [17]And the holy vessels of the Lord, which are given thee for the use of the temple of thy God, which is in Jerusalem, thou shalt set before thy God in Jerusalem. [18]And whatsoever thing else thou shalt remember for the use of the temple of thy God, thou shalt give it out of the king's treasury.

[19]And I king Artaxerxes have also commanded the keepers of the treasures in Syria and Phenice, that whatsoever Esdras the priest and the reader of the law of the most high God shall send for, they should give it him with speed, [20]to the sum of an hundred talents of silver, likewise also of wheat even to an hundred cors, and an hundred pieces of wine, and other things in abundance. [21]Let all things

8:1–9:55 Ezra's reforms. For 8:1–9:36, cf. Ezra 7:1–10:44 and notes; for 9:37–55, cf. Neh 7:73b– 8:12 and notes. Here the narrative moves forward, probably by about forty years. This section contains Ezra's prayer of confession (8:74–90) in which the nation's betrayal of God, recounted in 1:34–58, is finally given full recognition, in words and immediately thereafter in deeds of repentance. **8:3** *Ready*: "skilled" (NRSV). **8:11** *Seven friends the counsellors*: cf. Esth 1:14. **8:20** *An hundred cors . . . wine*:

be performed after the law of God diligently unto the most high God, that wrath come not upon the kingdom of the king and his sons. ²²I command you also, that ye require no tax, nor any other imposition, of any of the priests, or Levites, or holy singers, or porters, or ministers of the temple, or of any that have doings in this temple, and that no man have authority to impose any thing upon them.

²³And thou, Esdras, according to the wisdom of God ordain judges and justices, that they may judge in all Syria and Phenice all those that know the law of thy God; and those that know it not thou shalt teach. ²⁴And whosoever shall transgress the law of thy God, and of the king, shall be punished diligently, whether it be by death, or other punishment, by penalty of money, or by imprisonment.

²⁵Then said Esdras the scribe, Blessed be the only Lord God of my fathers, who hath put these things into the heart of the king, to glorify his house that is in Jerusalem: ²⁶and hath honoured me in the sight of the king, and his counsellers, and all his friends and nobles. ²⁷Therefore was I encouraged by the help of the Lord my God, and gathered together men of Israel to go up with me.

²⁸And these are the chief according to their families and several dignities, that went up with me from Babylon in the reign of king Artaxerxes: ²⁹of the sons of Phinees, Gerson: of the sons of Ithamar, Gamael: of the sons of David, Lettus the son of Sechenias: ³⁰of the sons of Pharez, Zacharias: and with him were counted an hundred and fifty men: ³¹of the sons of Pahath Moab, Eliaonias, the son of Zaraias, and with him two hundred men: ³²of the sons of Zathoe, Sechenias the son or Jezelus, and with him three hundred men: of the sons of Adin, Obeth the son of Jonathan, and with him two hundred and fifty men: ³³of the sons of Elam, Josias son of Gotholias, and with him seventy men: ³⁴of the sons of Saphatias, Zaraias son of Michael, and with him threescore and ten men: ³⁵of the sons of Joab, Abadias son of Jezelus, and with him two hundred and twelve men: ³⁶of the sons of Banid, Assalimoth son of Josaphias, and with him an hundred and threescore men: ³⁷of the sons of Babi, Zacharias son of Bebai, and with him twenty and eight men: ³⁸of the sons of Astath, Johannes son of Acatan, and with him an hundred and ten men: ³⁹of the sons of Adonikam, the last, and these are the names of them, Eliphalet, Jeuel, and Samaias, and with them seventy men: ⁴⁰of the sons of Bago, Uthi the son of Istalcurus, and with him seventy men.

⁴¹And these I gathered together to the river called Theras, where we pitched our tents three days: and then I surveyed them. ⁴²But when I had found there none of the priests and Levites, ⁴³then sent I unto Eleazar, and Iduel, and Masman, ⁴⁴and Alnathan, and Mamaias, and Joribus, and Nathan, Eunatan, Zacharias, and Mosollamon, principal men and learned. ⁴⁵And I bade them that they should go unto Saddeus the captain, who was in the place of the treasury: ⁴⁶and commanded them that they should speak unto Daddeus, and to his brethren, and to the treasurers in that place, to send us such men as might execute the priests' office in the house of the Lord. ⁴⁷And by the mighty hand of our Lord they brought unto

perhaps about 650 bushels of wheat and 600 gallons of wine.   **8:25** *Then said Esdras*: marking the shift to a first-person narrative (sometimes called "Ezra's Memoir") that continues through v. 90.   **8:28–40** *And these . . . men*: the list parallels, but is not identical to, that in Ezra 8:1–14.   **8:41** *Theras*: apparently a variant of Ahava (see Ezra 8:15 and note).   **8:45–46** *Saddeus, Daddeus*: the same

us skilful men of the sons of Moli the son of Levi, the son of Israel, Asebebia, and his sons, and his brethren, who were eighteen. ⁴⁸And Asebia, and Annuus, and Osaias his brother, of the sons of Channuneus, and their sons, were twenty men. ⁴⁹And of the servants of the temple whom David had ordained, and the principal men for the service of the Levites, to wit, the servants of the temple, two hundred and twenty, the catalogue of whose names were shewed.

⁵⁰And there I vowed a fast unto the young men before our Lord, to desire of him a prosperous journey both for us and them that were with us, for our children, and for the cattle: ⁵¹for I was ashamed to ask the king footmen, and horsemen, and conduct for safeguard against our adversaries. ⁵²For we had said unto the king, that the power of the Lord our God should be with them that seek him, to support them in all ways. ⁵³And again we besought our Lord as touching these things, and found him favourable unto us.

⁵⁴Then I separated twelve of the chief of the priests, Esebrias, and Assanias, and ten men of their brethren with them: ⁵⁵and I weighed them the gold, and the silver, and the holy vessels of the house of our Lord, which the king, and his council, and the princes, and all Israel, had given. ⁵⁶And when I had weighed it, I delivered unto them six hundred and fifty talents of silver, and silver vessels of an hundred talents, and an hundred talents of gold, ⁵⁷and twenty golden vessels, and twelve vessels of brass, even of fine brass, glittering like gold. ⁵⁸And I said unto them, Both ye are holy unto the Lord, and the vessels are holy, and the gold and the silver is a vow unto the Lord, the Lord of our fathers. ⁵⁹Watch ye, and keep them till ye deliver them to the chief of the priests and Levites, and to the principal men of the families of Israel, in Jerusalem, into the chambers of the house of our God. ⁶⁰So the priests and the Levites, who had received the silver and the gold and the vessels, brought them unto Jerusalem, into the temple of the Lord.

⁶¹And from the river Theras we departed the twelfth day of the first month, and came to Jerusalem by the mighty hand of our Lord, which was with us: and from the beginning of our journey the Lord delivered us from every enemy, and so we came to Jerusalem. ⁶²And when we had been there three days, the gold and silver that was weighed was delivered in the house of our Lord on the fourth day unto Marmoth the priest the son of Iri. ⁶³And with him was Eleazar the son of Phinees, and with them were Josabad the son of Jesu and Moeth the son of Sabban, Levites: all was delivered them by number and weight. ⁶⁴And all the weight of them was written up the same hour. ⁶⁵Moreover they that were come out of the captivity offered sacrifice unto the Lord God of Israel, even twelve bullocks for all Israel, fourscore and sixteen rams, ⁶⁶threescore and twelve lambs, goats for a peace offering, twelve; all of them a sacrifice to the Lord. ⁶⁷And they delivered the king's commandments unto the king's stewards, and to the governors of Celosyria and Phenice; and they honoured the people and the temple of God.

⁶⁸Now when these things were done, the rulers came unto me, and said, ⁶⁹The nation of Israel, the princes, the priests and Levites, have not put away from them the strange people of the land, nor the pollutions of the Gentiles, to wit, of the

person. The MS tradition gives a range of variations for this name, which corresponds to Ezra 8:17's Iddo. **8:68** *The rulers*: the leading men in Judea. **8:69** *Strange*: alien (so throughout).

Canaanites, Hittites, Pheresites, Jebusites, and the Moabites, Egyptians, and Edomites. [70]For both they and their sons have married with their daughters, and the holy seed is mixed with the strange people of the land; and from the beginning of this matter the rulers and the great men have been partakers of this iniquity.

[71]And as soon as I had heard these things, I rent my clothes, and the holy garment, and pulled off the hair from off my head and beard, and sat me down sad and very heavy. [72]So all they that were then moved at the word of the Lord God of Israel assembled unto me, whilst I mourned for the iniquity: but I sat still full of heaviness until the evening sacrifice. [73]Then rising up from the fast with my clothes and the holy garment rent, and bowing my knees, and stretching forth my hands unto the Lord, [74]I said, O Lord, I am confounded and ashamed before thy face; [75]for our sins are multiplied above our heads, and our ignorances have reached up unto heaven. [76]For ever since the time of our fathers we have been and are in great sin, even unto this day. [77]And for our sins and our fathers' we with our brethren and our kings and our priests were given up unto the kings of the earth, to the sword, and to captivity, and for a prey with shame, unto this day. [78]And now in some measure hath mercy been shewed unto us from thee, O Lord, that there should be left us a root and a name in the place of thy sanctuary; [79]and to discover unto us a light in the house of the Lord our God, and to give us food in the time of our servitude. [80]Yea, when we were in bondage, we were not forsaken of our Lord; but he made us gracious before the kings of Persia, so that they gave us food; [81]yea, and honoured the temple of our Lord, and raised up the desolate Sion, that they have given us a sure abiding in Jewry and Jerusalem.

[82]And now, O Lord, what shall we say, having these things? for we have transgressed thy commandments, which thou gavest by the hand of thy servants the prophets, saying, [83]that the land, which ye enter into to possess as an heritage, is a land polluted with the pollutions of the strangers of the land, and they have filled it with their uncleanness. [84]Therefore now shall ye not join your daughters unto their sons, neither shall ye take their daughters unto your sons. [85]Moreover ye shall never seek to have peace with them, that ye may be strong, and eat the good things of the land, and that ye may leave the inheritance of the land unto your children for evermore. [86]And all that is befallen is done unto us for our wicked works and great sins: for thou, O Lord, didst make our sins light, [87]and didst give unto us such a root: but we have turned back again to transgress thy law, and to mingle ourselves with the uncleanness of the nations of the land. [88]Mightest not thou be angry with us to destroy us, till thou hadst left us neither root, seed, nor name? [89]O Lord of Israel, thou art true: for we are left a root this day. [90]Behold, now are we before thee in our iniquities, for we cannot stand any longer by reason of these things before thee.

[91]And as Esdras in his prayer made his confession, weeping, and lying flat upon the ground before the temple, there gathered unto him from Jerusalem a very great multitude of men and women and children: for there was great weeping among the multitude. [92]Then Jechonias the son of Jeelus, one of the sons of Israel, called out, and said, O Esdras, we have sinned against the Lord God, we

---

8:82 *Thy commandments . . . prophets*: 1 Esdras presumably sees Moses as the fountainhead of prophecy, for what follows in vv. 83–85 recalls directives from Leviticus and Deuteronomy (e.g., Deut 7:1–4).

have married strange women of the nations of the land, and now is all Israel aloft. ⁹³Let us make an oath to the Lord, that we will put away all our wives, which we have taken of the heathen, with their children, ⁹⁴like as thou hast decreed, and as many as do obey the law of the Lord. ⁹⁵Arise, and put in execution: for to thee doth this matter appertain, and we will be with thee: do valiantly. ⁹⁶So Esdras arose, and took an oath of the chief of the priests and Levites of all Israel to do after these things; and so they sware.

9 Then Esdras rising from the court of the temple went to the chamber of Joanan the son of Eliasib, ²and remained there, and did eat no meat nor drink water, mourning for the great iniquities of the multitude. ³And there was a proclamation in all Jewry and Jerusalem to all them that were of the captivity, that they should be gathered together at Jerusalem: ⁴and that whosoever met not there within two or three days, according as the elders that bare rule appointed, their cattle should be seized to the use of the temple, and himself cast out from them that were of the captivity.

⁵And in three days were all they of the tribe of Judah and Benjamin gathered together at Jerusalem the twentieth day of the ninth month. ⁶And all the multitude sat trembling in the broad court of the temple because of the present foul weather. ⁷So Esdras arose up, and said unto them, Ye have transgressed the law in marrying strange wives, thereby to increase the sins of Israel. ⁸And now by confessing give glory unto the Lord God of our fathers, ⁹and do his will, and separate yourselves from the heathen of the land, and from the strange women.

¹⁰Then cried the whole multitude, and said with a loud voice, Like as thou hast spoken, so will we do. ¹¹But forasmuch as the people are many, and it is foul weather, so that we cannot stand without, and this is not a work of a day or two, seeing our sin in these things is spread far: ¹²therefore let the rulers of the multitude stay, and let all them of our habitations that have strange wives come at the time appointed, ¹³and with them the rulers and judges of every place, till we turn away the wrath of the Lord from us for this matter. ¹⁴Then Jonathan the son of Azael and Ezechias the son of Theocanus accordingly took this matter upon them: and Mosollam and Levis and Sabbatheus helped them. ¹⁵And they that were of the captivity did according to all these things. ¹⁶And Esdras the priest chose unto him the principal men of their families, all by name: and in the first day of the tenth month they sat together to examine the matter. ¹⁷So their cause that held strange wives was brought to an end in the first day of the first month.

¹⁸And of the priests that were come together, and had strange wives, there were found; ¹⁹of the sons of Jesus the son of Josedec, and his brethren; Matthelas, and Eleazar, and Joribus, and Joadanus. ²⁰And they gave their hands to put away their wives, and to offer rams to make reconcilement for their errors. ²¹And of the sons of Emmer; Ananias, and Zabdeus, and Eanes, and Sameius, and Hiereel, and Azarias. ²²And of the sons of Phaisur; Elionas, Massias, Ismael, and Nathanael, and Ocidelus, and Talsas. ²³And of the Levites; Jozabad, and Semis, and Colius, who was called Calitas, and Patheus, and Judas, and Jonas. ²⁴Of the

8:92 *Is all Israel aloft*: better "there is hope for Israel" (MS tradition).   8:93 *Put away*: lit. "throw out," i.e., divorce.   9:2 *Meat*: food.   9:4 *Seized to . . . temple*: lit. "seized for sacrifice," i.e., subject to the sacred ban (see Deut 7:2 and note).   9:5 *The twentieth day . . . month*: in the winter.

holy singers; Eleazurus, Bacchurus. ²⁵Of the porters; Sallumus, and Tolbanes. ²⁶Of them of Israel, of the sons of Phoros; Hiermas, and Eddias, and Melchias, and Maelus, and Eleazar, and Asibias, and Baanias. ²⁷Of the sons of Ela; Matthanias, Zacharias, and Hierielus, and Hieremoth, and Aedias. ²⁸And of the sons of Zamoth; Eliadas, Elisimus, Othonias, Jarimoth, and Sabatus, and Sardeus. ²⁹Of the sons of Bebai; Johannes, and Ananias, and Josabad, and Amatheis. ³⁰Of the sons of Mani; Olamus, Mamuchus, Jedeus, Jasubus, Jasael, and Hieremoth. ³¹And of the sons of Addi: Naathus, and Moosias, Lacunus, and Naidus, and Mathanias, and Sesthel, Balnuus, and Manasseas. ³²And of the sons of Annas: Elionas, and Aseas, and Melchias, and Sabbeus, and Simon Chosameus. ³³And of the sons of Asom; Altaneus, and Matthias, and Bannaia, Eliphalat, and Manasses, and Semei. ³⁴And of the sons of Maani; Jeremias, Momdis, Omaerus, Juel, Mabdai, and Pelias, and Anos, Carabasion, and Enasibus, and Mamnitanaimus, Eliasis, Bannus, Eliali, Samis, Selemias, Nathanias: and of the sons of Ozora; Sesis, Esril, Azaelus, Samatus, Zambis, Josephus. ³⁵And of the sons of Ethma; Mazitias, Zabadaias, Edes, Juel, Banaias. ³⁶All these had taken strange wives, and they put them away with their children.

³⁷And the priests and Levites, and they that were of Israel, dwelt in Jerusalem, and in the country, in the first day of the seventh month: so the children of Israel were in their habitations. ³⁸And the whole multitude came together with one accord into the broad place of the holy porch toward the east: ³⁹and they spake unto Esdras the priest and reader, that he would bring the law of Moses, that was given of the Lord God of Israel. ⁴⁰So Esdras the chief priest brought the law unto the whole multitude from man to woman, and to all the priests, to hear the law in the first day of the seventh month. ⁴¹And he read in the broad court before the holy porch from morning unto midday, before both men and women; and all the multitude gave heed unto the law. ⁴²And Esdras the priest and reader of the law stood up upon a pulpit of wood, which was made for that purpose. ⁴³And there stood up by him Mattathias, Sammus, Ananias, Azarias, Urias, Ezecias, Balasamus, upon the right hand: ⁴⁴and upon his left hand stood Phaldaius, Misael, Melchias, Lothasubus, and Nabarias.

⁴⁵Then took Esdras the book of the law before the multitude: for he sat honourably in the first place in the sight of them all. ⁴⁶And when he opened the law, they stood all straight up. So Esdras blessed the Lord God most High, the God of hosts, Almighty. ⁴⁷And all the people answered, Amen; and lifting up their hands they fell to the ground, and worshipped the Lord. ⁴⁸Also Jesus, Anus, Sarabias, Adinus, Jacubus, Sabateas, Auteas, Maianeas, and Calitas, Azarias, and Joazabdus, and Ananias, Biatas, the Levites, taught the law of the Lord, making them withal to understand it.

⁴⁹Then spake Attharates unto Esdras the chief priest and reader, and to the Levites that taught the multitude, even to all, saying, ⁵⁰This day is holy unto the Lord; (for they all wept when they heard the law:) ⁵¹go then, and eat the fat, and

---

9:37–38 *First day . . . accord*: they gather together on the first day of the new year in accordance with Lev 23:23–25 (see notes); Num 29:1.   **9:38** *The broad place . . . east*: "in the open square before the east gate of the temple" (NRSV).   **9:49** *Attharates*: another hellenized deformation of Tirshatha, "governor," which 1 Esdras again takes for a proper name (see 5:40 note). Neh 8:9, on which this verse is

drink the sweet, and send part to them that have nothing; [52]for this day is holy unto the Lord: and be not sorrowful; for the Lord will bring you to honour. [53]So the Levites published all things to the people, saying, This day is holy to the Lord; be not sorrowful. [54]Then went they their way, every one to eat and drink, and make merry, and to give part to them that had nothing, and to make great cheer; [55]because they understood the words wherein they were instructed, and for the which they had been assembled.

---

based, identifies Nehemiah as the governor. 1 Esdras eliminates him from its account of Ezra's reading of the law. **9:53** *Published all . . . people*: better "commanded all the people" (MS tradition; NRSV). **9:55** *For the which*: a strained translation; 1 Esdras properly ends with the simple claim that "they were assembled." The conclusion's apparent abruptness (especially when compared with Neh 8:13) may indicate that 1 Esdras is incomplete, originally having incorporated more of Nehemiah's text. As it stands, however, the book ends as it begins, with a religious convocation at the temple.

The Second Book of Esdras

STUDENTS of the Apocrypha will easily discern what the Old Testament's readers may just as easily miss, namely the importance of Ezra (a.k.a. Esdras) to the ancient Jewish literary tradition. The few chapters in the Hebrew Bible devoted to this figure—really only half a book, since Ezra-Nehemiah was originally a single work—have until recently received relatively little attention. In contrast, the KJV Apocrypha's first two books are named after Ezra and 2 Esdras amasses a number of ancient Jewish and Christian traditions that originally circulated independently, presumably under Ezra's pseudonymous authority. Some of those traditions assign Ezra a significance rivaling Moses' (e.g., 2:33; chap. 14 passim).

Hardly anything about 2 Esdras is straightforward, least of all its title. In the Vulgate, 2 Esdras is called 4 Esdras (1 Esdras = KJV Ezra; 2 Esdras = KJV Nehemiah; 3 Esdras = KJV 1 Esdras), but many Latin manuscripts complicate the matter by labeling KJV Ezra-Nehemiah as 1 Esdras and then dividing 4 Esdras into three distinct works (chaps. 1–2 = 2 Esdras; chaps. 3–14 = 4 Esdras; chaps. 15–16 = 5 Esdras). The KJV translators do not recognize this division, but all modern scholars accept it. Chapters 3–14 constitute an originally Jewish work, now conventionally designated 4 Ezra, to which Christian additions came to be appended (chaps. 1–2, now called 5 Ezra, and chaps. 15–16, now called 6 Ezra).

The textual tradition of 2 Esdras is no less confusing. Unlike every other book of the Apocrypha, this one is not found in the Septuagint, and so KJV translates the Latin text preserved in the Clementine Vulgate. The Latin appears to be a translation from Greek, but most scholars believe that behind 4 Ezra, at least, lay a Hebrew original. Thus KJV's 2 Esdras is in large part an English translation of a Latin translation of a Greek translation of a Hebrew original. To make matters worse, the text KJV translates was missing a lengthy passage from chapter 7 (see v. 35 note), which was not discovered in Latin until the nineteenth century (although a translation of an Arabic version, published in 1711, included the missing verses). KJV's 2 Esdras therefore suffers from a lacuna of approximately seventy verses. The Latin translation of 2 Esdras remains an important textual witness, but modern scholars supplement it with readings from other early translations of the Greek, especially the Syriac, Georgian, and Ethiopian, as well as a brief Coptic fragment. (These so-called 'oriental versions' contain the missing section and lack chapters 1–2 and 15–16.) The annotations below note several (although by no means all) places where KJV deviates from the best reading of the Latin text, which is based on A. Frederik J. Klijn's critical edition, *Der Lateinische Text der Apokalypse des Esra* (Berlin: Akademie-Verlag, 1983), and they occasionally signal variations vis-à-vis other versions as well. The fragment omitted by KJV may be found in the Appendix (pp. 996–1000).

As mentioned above, 4 Ezra is a Jewish work, certainly written after the temple's destruction in 70 C.E. (presupposed by the book's figurative equation of Rome with Babylon) and before the earliest definite allusion to it in the late second century. Generically an apocalypse (see the introduction to Revelation), this book presents Ezra's seven visions of the angel Uriel, with whom he vigorously debates God's justice while gradually coming to accept his eschatological plan, despite persistent awe at the extensive suffering it entails. 4 Ezra culminates in a dramatic scene that both recalls and trumps the Pentateuch's gestures at self-authorization (e.g., Exod 24:12; 31:18; 34:1–4, 27–28): not only does the inspired Ezra recall from memory and dictate the twenty-four books of the Hebrew Bible, thereby restoring the Scriptures destroyed in Babylon's sack of Jerusalem, but he dictates seventy additional books as well—esoteric writings addressed only to the wise, foremost among which is presumably 4 Ezra itself. 5 and 6 Ezra are later Christian works, probably composed in Greek in the second or third century C.E. They allude to writings from the Old and New Testaments and are conversant with ancient Christian ideas (e.g., God's privileging of the church over Israel) and with historical events datable to the third century.

The history of 2 Esdras's interpretation and influence is delightfully idiosyncratic, as Alastair Hamilton's study of its reception demonstrates (*The Apocryphal Apocalypse* [Oxford: Clarendon Press, 1999]). "Menstruous women shall bring forth monsters" (5:8) was often quoted in late sixteenth- and early seventeenth-century medical texts to argue that conception during menstruation caused birth defects. Rodrigo da Castro's *De universa mulierum medicina* (Hamburg, 1603), for instance, says of "copulation in the time of menstruation" that "those who are born from this are either maimed or deformed or humpbacked or defective in body and spirit. For that reason Esdras said 'menstruous women shall bring forth monsters.'" Somewhat earlier, in the thirteenth century, Roger Bacon invoked 2 Esdras 6:42–46 in his *Opus maius* to argue that six-sevenths of the earth was land and only one-seventh water, and this piece of exegesis found its way via Pierre d'Ailly's *Ymago mundi* (1480) to Christopher Columbus, who relied on it in his successful appeal to the Spanish monarchs Ferdinand and Isabella to underwrite his proposed voyage to the Indies. In the wake of Columbus's failure and Europe's subsequent discovery of the "New World," the American Indians were widely understood to be the lost tribes of Israel from 2 Esdras 13:40–45—a passage frequently cited in debates about European policies toward indigenous Americans. A variation of this tradition survives today in the beliefs of the Latter-day Saints.

Despite its widespread influence, 2 Esdras has never enjoyed fully canonical status. The Vulgate included a Latin translation, but Jerome dismissed 2 Esdras as a book of dreams in his prologue to Ezra and deprecated it elsewhere as well. In large part, his disparagement is based on recognition that Jews did not accept the book as scriptural, but he seems also to have been aware that he did not possess a reliable text and to have been doubtful about its content. Throughout late antiquity and the Middle Ages, Jerome's strictures often carried the day. Many bibles did not include 1 or 2 Esdras, and those that did frequently offered caveats noting the books' apocryphal status. When the humanists and Reformers challenged the Apocrypha's canonicity, the Catholic Church's official response did not include a defense of 1 or 2 Esdras or the Prayer of Manasses: the Canons and Decrees of the Council of Trent mentioned none of these books, even while insisting on the canonical status of the other apocryphal texts. The Sixtine Vulgate (1590), intended by Pope Sixtus V to make available a version of the Scriptures adhering to the council's directives, omitted them, but many thought that it had gone too far. Pope Clement VIII's far more influential revision, published two years later (the Clementine Vulgate), restored 1 and 2 Esdras and the Prayer of Manasses, though relegating them to an appendix. Despite an analogous debate in Britain, the Church of England maintained its officially positive stance toward the Apocrypha and 2 Esdras was included in the King James Version.

For detailed exposition of 2 Esdras, the reader can consult Michael Edward Stone's Hermeneia commentary, *Fourth Ezra: A Commentary on the Book of Fourth Ezra* (Minneapolis: Fortress, 1990), as well as Jacob M. Myers's Anchor Bible commentary, *1 and 2 Esdras* (Garden City, NY: Doubleday, 1974). Theodore A. Bergren's notes in *The New Oxford Annotated Bible*, ed. Michael D. Cougan, 3rd ed. (Oxford: Oxford University Press, 2001) are also strong. All inform this introduction and the annotations that follow.

The Second Book of Esdras

1 The second book of the prophet Esdras, the son of Saraias, the son of Azarias, the son of Helchias, the son of Sadamias, the son of Sadoc, the son of Achitob, ²the son of Achias, the son of Phinees, the son of Heli, the son of Amarias, the son of Aziei, the son of Marimoth, the son of Arna, the son of Ozias, the son of Borith, the son of Abisei, the son of Phinees, the son of Eleazar, ³the son of Aaron, of the tribe of Levi; which was captive in the land of the Medes, in the reign of Artaxerxes king of the Persians.

⁴And the word of the Lord came unto me, saying, ⁵Go thy way, and shew my people their sinful deeds, and their children their wickedness which they have done against me; that they may tell their children's children: ⁶because the sins of their fathers are increased in them: for they have forgotten me, and have offered unto strange gods. ⁷Am not I even he that brought them out of the land of Egypt, from the house of bondage? but they have provoked me unto wrath, and despised my counsels. ⁸Pull thou off then the hair of thy head, and cast all evil upon them, for they have not been obedient unto my law, but it is a rebellious people. ⁹How long shall I forbear them, unto whom I have done so much good? ¹⁰Many kings have I destroyed for their sakes; Pharaoh with his servants and all his power have I smitten down. ¹¹All the nations have I destroyed before them, and in the east I have scattered the people of two provinces, even of Tyrus and Sidon, and have slain all their enemies.

¹²Speak thou therefore unto them, saying, Thus saith the Lord, ¹³I led you through the sea, and in the beginning gave you a large and safe passage; I gave you Moses for a leader, and Aaron for a priest. ¹⁴I gave you light in a pillar of fire, and great wonders have I done among you; yet have ye forgotten me, saith the Lord.

¹⁵Thus saith the Almighty Lord, The quails were as a token for you; I gave you tents for your safeguard: nevertheless ye murmured there, ¹⁶and triumphed not

---

1:1–2:48 5 Ezra. This originally independent document is a later addition to 4 Ezra (chaps. 3–14), replete with Christian theology emphasizing God's rejection of Israel as a result of its persistent disobedience and his subsequent embrace of Gentiles. It echoes OT and pseudepigraphical literature throughout (although the annotations that follow do not flag the latter), as well as NT writings. **1:1** *Second*: better omitted (MS tradition). *Esdras*: Ezra; for his genealogy in vv. 1–3, compare Ezra 7:1–5 and 1 Esd 8:1–2. **1:3** *Artaxerxes*: either Artaxerxes I, who ruled the Persian Empire (of which Media was an important part) 465–423 B.C.E., or Artaxerxes II, who reigned 405–359 B.C.E. **1:4** *The word . . . me*: a conventional introduction of prophetic oracles (like "thus saith the Lord," v. 12); cf. Isa 38:4; Jer 1:4 and passim; Hos 1:1; etc. **1:6** *Strange*: foreign. **1:8** *Pull thou . . . head*: a figure of mourning. God often orders prophets to perform provocative symbolic acts; cf. Ezek 12:1–7; Hos 1–3; etc. **1:10** *Pharaoh with his servants . . . down*: see Exod 14 (also at v. 13). **1:11** *In the east . . . Sidon*: an uncertain reference; context suggests an episode in a version of the Exodus story different from the Bible's. **1:14** *Light . . . fire*: see Exod 13:21–22. **1:15** *Quails*: see Exod 16:11–13. *Token*: sign (so throughout). *Tents*: the temporary shelters mentioned at Lev 23:42–43. **1:15–20** *Nevertheless ye . . .*

in my name for the destruction of your enemies, but ever to this day do ye yet murmur. [17]Where are the benefits that I have done for you? when ye were hungry and thirsty in the wilderness, did ye not cry unto me, [18]saying, Why hast thou brought us into this wilderness to kill us? it had been better for us to have served the Egyptians, than to die in this wilderness. [19]Then had I pity upon your mournings, and gave you manna to eat; so ye did eat angels' bread. [20]When ye were thirsty, did I not cleave the rock, and waters flowed out to your fill? for the heat I covered you with the leaves of the trees. [21]I divided among you a fruitful land, I cast out the Canaanites, the Pherezites, and the Philistines, before you: what shall I yet do more for you? saith the Lord.

[22]Thus saith the Almighty Lord, When ye were in the wilderness, in the river of the Amorites, being athirst, and blaspheming my name, [23]I gave you not fire for your blasphemies, but cast a tree in the water, and made the river sweet. [24]What shall I do unto thee, O Jacob? thou, Juda, wouldest not obey me: I will turn me to other nations, and unto those will I give my name, that they may keep my statutes. [25]Seeing ye have forsaken me, I will forsake you also; when ye desire me to be gracious unto you, I shall have no mercy upon you. [26]Whensoever ye shall call upon me, I will not hear you: for ye have defiled your hands with blood, and your feet are swift to commit manslaughter. [27]Ye have not as it were forsaken me, but your own selves, saith the Lord.

[28]Thus saith the Almighty Lord, Have I not prayed you as a father his sons, as a mother her daughters, and a nurse her young babes, [29]that ye would be my people, and I should be your God; that ye would be my children, and I should be your father? [30]I gathered you together, as a hen gathereth her chickens under her wings: but now, what shall I do unto you? I will cast you out from my face. [31]When ye offer unto me, I will turn my face from you: for your solemn feast-days, your new moons, and your circumcisions, have I forsaken. [32]I sent unto you my servants the prophets, whom ye have taken and slain, and torn their bodies in pieces, whose blood I will require of your hands, saith the Lord.

[33]Thus saith the Almighty Lord, Your house is desolate, I will cast you out as the wind doth stubble. [34]And your children shall not be fruitful; for they have despised my commandment, and done the thing that is evil before me. [35]Your houses will I give to a people that shall come; which not having heard of me yet shall believe me; to whom I have shewed no signs, yet they shall do that I have commanded them. [36]They have seen no prophets, yet they shall call their sins to remembrance, and acknowledge them. [37]I take to witness the grace of the people to come, whose little ones rejoice in gladness: and though they have not seen me with bodily eyes, yet in spirit they believe the thing that I say.

---

fill: see Exod 15:22–16:36.   **1:19** *Angels' bread*: see Ps 78:25.   **1:20** *I covered you . . . trees*: presumably referring to Exod 15:27.   **1:21** *I divided . . . before you*: presumably referring to the events Joshua narrates.   **1:22** *River of the Amorites*: better "bitter river" (MS tradition), referring to Exod 15:22–26.   **1:24–25** *What shall . . . you also*: this seems to reflect Christian supersessionist theology, which surfaces occasionally in the NT (e.g., Acts 13:46) and became increasingly prominent as Christianity developed into a religion independent of Judaism. See also vv. 35–37; 2:10; etc.   **1:28** *Prayed*: "entreated" (NRSV).   **1:30–33** *I gathered . . . desolate*: cf. Isa 1:7–15; Matt 23:30–38.   **1:33** *I will cast . . . stubble*: a common image of divine judgment; e.g., Ps 1:4; Isa 40:24; Jer 13:24 (about Jerusalem).   **1:37** *Grace*: better "gratitude."

³⁸And now, brother, behold what glory; and see the people that cometh from the east: ³⁹unto whom I will give for leaders, Abraham, Isaac, and Jacob, Oseas, Amos, and Micheas, Joel, Abdias, and Jonas, ⁴⁰Nahum, and Abacuc, Sophonias, Aggeus, Zachary, and Malachy, which is called also an angel of the Lord.

2 Thus saith the Lord, I brought this people out of bondage, and I gave them my commandments by my servants the prophets; whom they would not hear, but despised my counsels. ²The mother that bare them saith unto them, Go your way, ye children; for I am a widow and forsaken. ³I brought you up with gladness; but with sorrow and heaviness have I lost you: for ye have sinned before the Lord your God, and done that thing that is evil before him. ⁴But what shall I now do unto you? I am a widow and forsaken: go your way, O my children, and ask mercy of the Lord. ⁵As for me, O father, I call upon thee for a witness over the mother of these children, which would not keep my covenant, ⁶that thou bring them to confusion, and their mother to a spoil, that there may be no offspring of them. ⁷Let them be scattered abroad among the heathen, let their names be put out of the earth: for they have despised my covenant.

⁸Woe be unto thee, Assur, thou that hidest the unrighteous in thee! O thou wicked people, remember what I did unto Sodom and Gomorrha; ⁹whose land lieth in clods of pitch and heaps of ashes: even so also will I do unto them that hear me not, saith the Almighty Lord.

¹⁰Thus saith the Lord unto Esdras, Tell my people that I will give them the kingdom of Jerusalem, which I would have given unto Israel. ¹¹Their glory also will I take unto me, and give these the everlasting tabernacles, which I had prepared for them. ¹²They shall have the tree of life for an ointment of sweet savour; they shall neither labour, nor be weary. ¹³Go, and ye shall receive: pray for few days unto you, that they may be shortened: the kingdom is already prepared for you: watch. ¹⁴Take heaven and earth to witness; for I have broken the evil in pieces, and created the good: for I live, saith the Lord.

¹⁵Mother, embrace thy children, and bring them up with gladness, make their feet as fast as a pillar: for I have chosen thee, saith the Lord. ¹⁶And those that be dead will I raise up again from their places, and bring them out of the graves: for I have known my name in Israel. ¹⁷Fear not, thou mother of the children: for I

1:38 *Brother*: better "father" (MS tradition). *The people . . . east*: apparently a group different from that mentioned in vv. 35–37; perhaps returning exiles, as opposed to Gentile converts (cf. Bar 4:36–37; 5:5). 1:39–40 *Abraham, Isaac . . . Malachy*: the three patriarchs and the twelve prophets of the eponymous Book of the Twelve.   1:40 *Angel of the Lord*: i.e., the Lord's messenger, a play on the Hebrew meaning of "Malachi" (see Mal 1:1 note).   2:1 *I brought . . . counsels*: cf. Jer 7:25–26.   2:2–7 *The mother . . . covenant*: the *mother* probably figures Jerusalem, as in Bar 4:12–16, which this passage recalls.   2:3 *Heaviness*: sadness (so throughout). *Before him*: better "before me" (MS tradition). 2:5 *Father*: the reference depends on how one reads vv. 5–7. If they continue God's declaration beginning in v. 1 and ending with v. 9, then God calls Ezra "father" (cf. 1:38 note). If vv. 5–7 constitute Ezra's response to God's oracle in vv. 1–4, then he is calling God "father" (cf. 1:28–29). *Over*: in the sense of "in addition to."   2:8 *Assur*: Assyria. *Sodom and Gomorrha*: see Gen 19.   2:11 *Everlasting tabernacles*: presumably a reference to resurrected existence (see 2 Cor 5:1–8 and notes); cf. vv. 16, 31.   2:12 *Tree of life*: see Gen 3:22–24; Rev 22:2, 14. *They shall neither . . . weary*: reversing Adam's curse at Gen 3:19.   2:14 *Take heaven . . . Lord*: echoing Deut 30:19.   2:15 *As a pillar*: better "as a dove" (MS tradition), and understood to modify *bring them up with gladness*: "Bring them up with gladness, as does a dove. Strengthen their feet" (NRSV).   2:16 *In Israel*: better "in them" (MS tradition).

have chosen thee, saith the Lord. [18]For thy help will I send my servants Esay and Jeremy, after whose counsel I have sanctified and prepared for thee twelve trees laden with divers fruits, [19]and as many fountains flowing with milk and honey, and seven mighty mountains, whereupon there grow roses and lilies, whereby I will fill thy children with joy.

[20]Do right to the widow, judge for the fatherless, give to the poor, defend the orphan, clothe the naked, [21]heal the broken and the weak, laugh not a lame man to scorn, defend the maimed, and let the blind man come into the sight of my clearness. [22]Keep the old and young within thy walls. [23]Wheresoever thou findest the dead, take them and bury them, and I will give thee the first place in my resurrection.

[24]Abide still, O my people, and take thy rest, for thy quietness shall come. [25]Nourish thy children, O thou good nurse; stablish their feet. [26]As for the servants whom I have given thee, there shall not one of them perish; for I will require them from among thy number. [27]Be not weary: for when the day of trouble and heaviness cometh, others shall weep and be sorrowful, but thou shalt be merry and have abundance. [28]The heathen shall envy thee, but they shall be able to do nothing against thee, saith the Lord. [29]My hands shall cover thee, so that thy children shall not see hell.

[30]Be joyful, O thou mother, with thy children; for I will deliver thee, saith the Lord. [31]Remember thy children that sleep, for I shall bring them out of the sides of the earth, and shew mercy unto them: for I am merciful, saith the Lord Almighty. [32]Embrace thy children until I come and shew mercy unto them: for my wells run over, and my grace shall not fail.

[33]I Esdras received a charge of the Lord upon the mount Oreb, that I should go unto Israel; but when I came unto them, they set me at nought, and despised the commandment of the Lord. [34]And therefore I say unto you, O ye heathen, that hear and understand, look for your Shepherd, he shall give you everlasting rest; for he is nigh at hand, that shall come in the end of the world. [35]Be ready to the reward of the kingdom, for the everlasting light shall shine upon you for evermore. [36]Flee the shadow of this world, receive the joyfulness of your glory: I testify my Saviour openly. [37]O receive the gift that is given you, and be glad, giving thanks unto him that hath called you to the heavenly kingdom. [38]Arise up and stand, behold the number of those that be sealed in the feast of the Lord; [39]which

---

2:18 *Esay and Jeremy*: Isaiah and Jeremiah, presumably resurrected (cf. v. 16). *Twelve trees . . . fruits*: cf. Rev 22:2.   **2:19** *Flowing with milk and honey*: a conventional description of the promised land (cf. Exod 3:8, 17; Lev 20:24; etc.).   **2:20–23** *Do right . . . bury them*: acts of piety; cf. Isa 1:17; Matt 15:30–31; Tob 1:16–19; etc.   **2:21** *Clearness*: alternatively "brightness."   **2:26** *Servants*: slaves (so throughout). *Require*: seek.   **2:28** *Heathen*: as opposed to Christians; in v. 34, in contrast, "heathen" is opposed to Jews.   **2:29** *Hell*: Lat. *Gehenna*; cf. Mark 9:43 note.   **2:31** *Sleep*: a euphemism for "lie dead."   **2:33** *Mount Oreb*: Mount Horeb/Sinai, thereby suggesting a parallel between Ezra and Moses.   **2:35–36** *The everlasting light . . . world*: cf. Isa 60:1–3, 19–20.   **2:36** *Shadow of this world*: the language is Platonic; see Col 2:17 note. *World* (Lat. *saeculum*) might better be translated "age" (so often). *Saviour*: a reference to Christ (so also "Son of God," v. 47).   **2:38** *Behold the number . . . Lord*: cf. Rev 7:3–4. *Feast*: a common image for God's eschatological reign; cf. Mark 2:19 note.

are departed from the shadow of the world, and have received glorious garments of the Lord. ⁴⁰Take thy number, O Sion, and shut up those of thine that are clothed in white, which have fulfilled the law of the Lord. ⁴¹The number of thy children, whom thou longedst for, is fulfilled: beseech the power of the Lord, that thy people, which have been called from the beginning, may be hallowed.

⁴²I Esdras saw upon the mount Sion a great people, whom I could not number, and they all praised the Lord with songs. ⁴³And in the midst of them there was a young man of a high stature, taller than all the rest, and upon every one of their heads he set crowns, and was more exalted; which I marvelled at greatly. ⁴⁴So I asked the angel, and said, Sir, what are these? ⁴⁵He answered and said unto me, These be they that have put off the mortal clothing, and put on the immortal, and have confessed the name of God: now are they crowned, and receive palms. ⁴⁶Then said I unto the angel, What young person is it that crowneth them, and giveth them palms in their hands? ⁴⁷So he answered and said unto me, It is the Son of God, whom they have confessed in the world. Then began I greatly to commend them that stood so stiffly for the name of the Lord. ⁴⁸Then the angel said unto me, Go thy way, and tell my people what manner of things, and how great wonders of the Lord thy God, thou hast seen.

3 In the thirtieth year after the ruin of the city I was in Babylon, and lay troubled upon my bed, and my thoughts came up over my heart: ²for I saw the desolation of Sion, and the wealth of them that dwelt at Babylon. ³And my spirit was sore moved, so that I began to speak words full of fear to the most High, and said, ⁴O Lord, who bearest rule, thou spakest at the beginning, when thou didst plant the earth, and that thyself alone, and commandedst the people, ⁵and gavest a body unto Adam without soul, which was the workmanship of thine hands, and didst breathe into him the breath of life, and he was made living before thee. ⁶And thou leddest him into paradise, which thy right hand had

---

2:39–40 *Glorious garments . . . clothed in white*: signaling resurrected existence (cf. Mark 9:3; 16:5 and notes; see also v. 45 below) and, complementarily, purity (cf. Rev 3:4 and note).   **2:40** *Thy number*: Rom 11:25 mentions a set number of Gentiles that will be saved; Rev 6:11, a set number of martyrs. Verse 42 paradoxically suggests that the predetermined number of the saved cannot be counted.   **2:42** *Upon the mount . . . songs*: cf. Rev 14:1–3.   **2:43** *Crowns*: see Rev 2:10 and note. **2:44** *The angel*: better "an angel."   **2:45** *Put off . . . immortal*: cf. 2 Cor 5:1–8 and notes. *Palms*: signifying victory; cf. 1 Macc 13:51; 2 Macc 10:7.

3:1–36 Introduction to 4 Ezra: Ezra questions God's judgment.   3:1 *In the thirtieth year . . . city*: i.e., thirty years after Babylon's destruction of Jerusalem in 586 B.C.E. Ezra actually lived much later, at the end of the exile. *I was in Babylon*: better "I was in Babylon—I, Salathiel, who am also called Ezra" (Lat. MS tradition; so NRSV). It is not clear on what basis Ezra is assigned the alias. Salathiel (in Hebrew "Shealtiel") is Zerubbabel's father, according to Ezra-Nehemiah (Ezra 3:2; 5:2; Neh 12:1), but that does not explain the identification. Some invoke etymology: *shealtiel* could be interpreted as "I asked God," which is what Ezra will do.   **3:2** *Sion*: Zion (as at 2:40, 42), here referring to Jerusalem.   **3:4** *Lord, who bearest rule*: "Sovereign Lord" (NRSV; so throughout). *Thou spakest at the beginning*: i.e., at the creation (Gen 1:1–2:3), when God spoke the cosmos into existence. *The people*: many versions, ancient and modern, emend the text to "dust" or "word" in order to preserve logical sequencing in vv. 4–5. However, the author may be distinguishing the creation and commissioning of humanity in Gen 1:26–30 from the creation of the particular human beings Adam and Eve

planted, before ever the earth came forward. ⁷And unto him thou gavest commandment to love thy way: which he transgressed, and immediately thou appointedst death in him and in his generations, of whom came nations, tribes, people, and kindreds, out of number. ⁸And every people walked after their own will, and did wonderful things before thee, and despised thy commandments. ⁹And again in process of time thou broughtest the flood upon those that dwelt in the world, and destroyedst them. ¹⁰And it came to pass in every of them, that as death was to Adam, so was the flood to these. ¹¹Nevertheless one of them thou leftest, namely, Noah with his household, of whom came all righteous men.

¹²And it happened, that when they that dwelt upon the earth began to multiply, and had gotten them many children, and were a great people, they began again to be more ungodly than the first. ¹³Now when they lived so wickedly before thee, thou didst choose thee a man from among them, whose name was Abraham. ¹⁴Him thou lovedst, and unto him only thou shewedst thy will: ¹⁵and madest an everlasting covenant with him, promising him that thou wouldest never forsake his seed. ¹⁶And unto him thou gavest Isaac, and unto Isaac also thou gavest Jacob and Esau. As for Jacob, thou didst choose him to thee, and put by Esau: and so Jacob became a great multitude.

¹⁷And it came to pass, that when thou leddest his seed out of Egypt, thou broughtest them up to the mount Sinai. ¹⁸And bowing the heavens, thou didst set fast the earth, movedst the whole world, and madest the depths to tremble, and troubledst the men of that age. ¹⁹And thy glory went through four gates, of fire, and of earthquake, and of wind, and of cold; that thou mightest give the law unto the seed of Jacob, and diligence unto the generation of Israel. ²⁰And yet tookest thou not away from them a wicked heart, that thy law might bring forth fruit in them. ²¹For the first Adam bearing a wicked heart transgressed, and was overcome; and so be all they that are born of him. ²²Thus infirmity was made permanent; and the law (also) in the heart of the people with the malignity of the root; so that the good departed away, and the evil abode still.

²³So the times passed away, and the years were brought to an end: then didst thou raise thee up a servant, called David: ²⁴whom thou commandedst to build a

---

and their subsequent transgression in Gen 2–3, which is treated in vv. 5–7 below.   **3:7** *Commandment to love thy way*: better "your one commandment" (Lat. MS tradition). *And in his genrations . . . number*: see Rom 5:12–21 and notes.   **3:8** *Wonderful*: better "impious" or "ungodly" (Lat. MS tradition). *Thy commandments*: better "you, and you did not prevent them" (Lat. MS tradition).   **3:9** *The flood*: see Gen 6–9.   **3:10** *Every*: every one.   **3:12** *More ungodly than the first*: perhaps an allusion to the story of the tower of Babel (Gen 11:1–9).   **3:13** *From among them*: Abraham descended from the Babylonians (see Gen 11:27–32 and notes), who are mockingly represented in Gen 11:1–9.   **3:14** *Thy will*: better "the end of times secretly at night" (Lat. MS tradition), perhaps with reference to Gen 15:12–21.   **3:15** *Covenant*: see Gen 15:18; cf. Gen 17.   **3:16** *As for Jacob . . . Esau*: echoing Mal 1:2–3; cf. Gen 25:19–27:40.   **3:17** *Thou leddest . . . Sinai*: see Exod 1–19.   **3:18–19** *Bowing the heavens . . . cold*: references to phenomena associated with God's descent to Sinai to deliver the law (see Exod 19:16–18).   **3:18** *Didst set fast*: other versions read "shook."   **3:19** *Diligence*: the same Latin word was rendered "commandment" in v. 7.   **3:21–22** *The first Adam . . . still*: compare Paul's speculation in Romans about Adam and the implications of the primeval transgression (5:12–21; 7:1–25 and notes); also cf. v. 7 above and 4:30–31.   **3:22** *So that*: the Latin simply reads "and."   **3:24** *Whom thou commandedst . . . therein*: David is made responsible for building Jerusalem (see 2 Sam 5:9;

city unto thy name, and to offer incense and oblations unto thee therein. ²⁵When this was done many years, then they that inhabited the city forsook thee, ²⁶and in all things did even as Adam and all his generations had done: for they also had a wicked heart: ²⁷and so thou gavest thy city over into the hands of thine enemies.

²⁸Are their deeds then any better that inhabit Babylon, that they should therefore have the dominion over Sion? ²⁹For when I came thither, and had seen impieties without number, then my soul saw many evildoers in this thirtieth year, so that my heart failed me. ³⁰For I have seen how thou sufferest them sinning, and hast spared wicked doers: and hast destroyed thy people, and hast preserved thine enemies, and hast not signified it. ³¹I do not remember how this way may be left: Are they then of Babylon better than they of Sion? ³²Or is there any other people that knoweth thee beside Israel? or what generation hath so believed thy covenants as Jacob? ³³And yet their reward appeareth not, and their labour hath no fruit: for I have gone here and there through the heathen, and I see that they flow in wealth, and think not upon thy commandments. ³⁴Weigh thou therefore our wickedness now in the balance, and theirs also that dwell in the world; and so shall thy name no where be found but in Israel. ³⁵Or when was it that they which dwell upon the earth have not sinned in thy sight? or what people have so kept thy commandments? ³⁶Thou shalt find that Israel by name hath kept thy precepts; but not the heathen.

4 And the angel that was sent unto me, whose name was Uriel, gave me an answer, ²and said, Thy heart hath gone too far in this world, and thinkest thou to comprehend the way of the most High? ³Then said I, Yea, my lord.

And he answered me, and said, I am sent to shew thee three ways, and to set forth three similitudes before thee: ⁴whereof if thou canst declare me one, I will shew thee also the way that thou desirest to see, and I shall shew thee from whence the wicked heart cometh. ⁵And I said, Tell on, my lord. Then said he unto me, Go thy way, weigh me the weight of the fire, or measure me the blast of the wind, or call me again the day that is past. ⁶Then answered I and said, What man is able to do that, that thou shouldest ask such things of me? ⁷And he said unto me, If I should ask thee how great dwellings are in the midst of the sea, or

---

1 Chr 11:7–8), but the origination of the temple cult alluded to here is elsewhere attributed to his son Solomon (cf. 2 Sam 7:12–13; 1 Kgs 6–7; 1 Chr 17:11–12; etc.). It is conceivable that the text refers to the altar David built on Araunah's threshing floor (2 Sam 24:15–25). **3:27** *Thou gavest . . . enemies*: see 2 Kgs 24–25. **3:28** *Are their deeds*: better introduced by "and I said in my heart" (Lat. MS tradition). **3:29** *In this thirtieth year*: other versions read "in these thirty years" (so NRSV). **3:30–31** *Hast not signified . . . left*: better "have not shown to anyone in what manner your way may be abandoned" (Lat. MS tradition). The Syriac version more intelligibly substitutes "comprehended" for "abandoned" (so NRSV). **3:34** *And so . . . Israel*: better "and it will be found which way the turn of the scale will incline" (Lat. MS tradition; NRSV). **3:36** *Israel by name*: the Latin does not mention "Israel" but rather has "people by name," i.e., "individual people."

4:1–5:20 The first vision. Uriel responds to Ezra's questions by insisting on the limits of Ezra's comprehension (cf. Job 38–41) and by assuring him that the eschatological consummation will vindicate God's judgment. Ezra is hardly appeased, and his persistent queries suggest doubt about the relevance of God's future intervention to his and his community's present plight. **4:3** *Similtudes*: Lat. *similitudines*, "analogies"; a Hebrew word meaning "riddle" may ultimately lie behind it. **4:7** *How great*:

how many springs are in the beginning of the deep, or how many springs are above the firmament, or which are the outgoings of paradise: ⁸peradventure thou wouldest say unto me, I never went down into the deep, nor as yet into hell, neither did I ever climb up into heaven. ⁹Nevertheless now have I asked thee but only of the fire and wind, and of the day wherethrough thou hast passed, and of things from which thou canst not be separated, and yet canst thou give me no answer of them. ¹⁰He said moreover unto me, Thine own things, and such as are grown up with thee, canst thou not know; ¹¹how should thy vessel then be able to comprehend the way of the Highest, and, the world being now outwardly corrupted, to understand the corruption that is evident in my sight? ¹²Then said I unto him, It were better that we were not at all, than that we should live still in wickedness, and to suffer, and not to know wherefore.

¹³He answered me, and said, I went into a forest into a plain, and the trees took counsel, ¹⁴and said, Come, let us go and make war against the sea, that it may depart away before us, and that we may make us more woods. ¹⁵The floods of the sea also in like manner took counsel, and said, Come, let us go up and subdue the woods of the plain, that there also we may make us another country. ¹⁶The thought of the wood was in vain, for the fire came and consumed it. ¹⁷The thought of the floods of the sea came likewise to nought, for the sand stood up and stopped them. ¹⁸If thou wert judge now betwixt these two, whom wouldest thou begin to justify? or whom wouldest thou condemn? ¹⁹I answered and said, Verily it is a foolish thought that they both have devised, for the ground is given unto the wood, and the sea also hath his place to bear his floods.

²⁰Then answered he me, and said, Thou hast given a right judgment, but why judgest thou not thyself also? ²¹For like as the ground is given unto the wood, and the sea to his floods: even so they that dwell upon the earth may understand nothing but that which is upon the earth: and he that dwelleth above the heavens may only understand the things that are above the height of the heavens. ²²Then answered I and said, I beseech thee, O Lord, let me have understanding: ²³for it was not my mind to be curious of the high things, but of such as pass by us daily, namely, wherefore Israel is given up as a reproach to the heathen, and for what cause the people whom thou hast loved is given over unto ungodly nations, and why the law of our forefathers is brought to nought, and the written covenants come to none effect, ²⁴and we pass away out of the world as grasshoppers, and our life is astonishment and fear, and we are not worthy to obtain mercy. ²⁵What will he then do unto his name whereby we are called? of these things have I asked.

---

how many. *Which are . . . paradise*: other versions read "which are the exits of Hades, or which are the entrances of paradise?" (so NRSV). On Hades, see Matt 11:23 note.   **4:11** *Vessel*: body, i.e., "self." *The world . . . sight*: Lat. obscure; Klijn tentatively offers this reading: "one already worn out by the corrupt age understand incorruption?"   **4:12** *Then said I*: other versions introduce the verse with "when I heard this, I fell on my face" (so NRSV).   **4:13–17** *I went . . . them*: compare the fable at Judg 9:8–15.   **4:21** *He that*: alternatively "those who."   **4:22** *Let me have*: Lat. obscure and probably corrupt; other versions read "why have I been endowed with the power of" (NRSV).   **4:23** *Such as pass by us daily*: recalling Uriel's reference in v. 9 to "the day wherethrough thou hast passed." Ezra turns the angel's analogy on its head.   **4:24** *Grasshoppers*: connoting insignificance; cf. Num 13:33; Isa 40:22. *Astonishment and fear*: better "like a mist" (Lat. MS tradition); cf. Hos 13:3; Wis 2:4. **4:25** *His name . . . called*: a reference to the conventional notion that God's reputation is tied up in

²⁶Then answered he me, and said, The more thou searchest, the more thou shalt marvel; for the world hasteth fast to pass away, ²⁷and cannot comprehend the things that are promised to the righteous in time to come: for this world is full of unrighteousness and infirmities. ²⁸But as concerning the things whereof thou askest me, I will tell thee; for the evil is sown, but the destruction thereof is not yet come. ²⁹If therefore that which is sown be not turned upside down, and if the place where the evil is sown pass not away, then cannot it come that is sown with good. ³⁰For the grain of evil seed hath been sown in the heart of Adam from the beginning, and how much ungodliness hath it brought up unto this time? and how much shall it yet bring forth until the time of threshing come? ³¹Ponder now by thyself, how great fruit of wickedness the grain of evil seed hath brought forth. ³²And when the ears shall be cut down, which are without number, how great a floor shall they fill?

³³Then I answered and said, How, and when shall these things come to pass? wherefore are our years few and evil? ³⁴And he answered me, saying, Do not thou hasten above the most Highest: for thy haste is in vain to be above him, for thou hast much exceeded. ³⁵Did not the souls also of the righteous ask question of these things in their chambers, saying, How long shall I hope on this fashion? when cometh the fruit of the floor of our reward? ³⁶And unto these things Uriel the archangel gave them answer, and said, Even when the number of seeds is filled in you: for he hath weighed the world in the balance. ³⁷By measure hath he measured the times, and by number hath he numbered the times; and he doth not move nor stir them, until the said measure be fulfilled.

³⁸Then answered I and said, O Lord that bearest rule, even we all are full of impiety. ³⁹And for our sakes peradventure it is that the floors of the righteous are not filled, because of the sins of them that dwell upon the earth. ⁴⁰So he answered me, and said, Go thy way to a woman with child, and ask of her when she hath fulfilled her nine months, if her womb may keep the birth any longer within her. ⁴¹Then said I, No, Lord, that can she not. And he said unto me, In the grave the chambers of souls are like the womb of a woman: ⁴²for like as a woman that travaileth maketh haste to escape the necessity of the travail: even so do these places haste to deliver those things that are committed unto them. ⁴³From the beginning, look, what thou desirest to see, it shall be shewed thee.

⁴⁴Then answered I and said, If I have found favour in thy sight, and if it be possible, and if I be meet therefore, ⁴⁵shew me then whether there be more to come

Israel's fate; cf. Exod 32:11–12; Josh 7:9; etc. **4:26** *The more thou searchest . . . marvel*: more literally "if you exist, you will see, and if you live, you will often marvel" (so NRSV). **4:27** *Comprehend*: lit. "bear" or "carry." **4:28** *But as concerning . . . thee*: Lat. obscure. **4:29** *Turned upside down*: better "reaped" (Lat. MS tradition). *It*: Lat. "the field." **4:32** *Cut down*: better "sown" (Lat. MS tradition). *Floor*: i.e., threshing floor (Lat. *area*, rendered "time of threshing" in v. 30; cf. 35). **4:34** *For thy . . . exceeded*: the Latin text is corrupt. A conjectural emendation yields "for you hurry for yourself, but the Highest hurries on account of many" (so NRSV). **4:36** *Uriel*: better "Jeremiel" (Lat. MS tradition), another angel, whose answer to the righteous souls Uriel reports. *When the number . . . you*: better "when the number of those like yourselves is completed" (Lat. MS tradition, emended); cf. Rev 6:9–11. **4:39** *And for . . . filled*: alternatively "it is perhaps on account of us that the time of threshing is delayed for the righteous" (NRSV); see v. 32 and note. **4:41–42** *In the grave . . . them*: alluding to the eschatological resurrection of the dead; cf. vv. 35–37. **4:43** *From the beginning*: this phrase

than is past, or more past than is to come. ⁴⁶What is past I know, but what is for to come I know not. ⁴⁷And he said unto me, Stand up upon the right side, and I shall expound the similitude unto thee.

⁴⁸So I stood, and saw, and, behold, an hot burning oven passed by before me: and it happened, that when the flame was gone by I looked, and, behold, the smoke remained still. ⁴⁹After this there passed by before me a watery cloud, and sent down much rain with a storm; and when the stormy rain was past, the drops remained still. ⁵⁰Then said he unto me, Consider with thyself; as the rain is more than the drops, and as the fire is greater than the smoke; but the drops and the smoke remain behind: so the quantity which is past did more exceed. ⁵¹Then I prayed, and said, May I live, thinkest thou, until that time? or what shall happen in those days? ⁵²He answered me, and said, As for the tokens whereof thou askest me, I may tell thee of them in part: but as touching thy life, I am not sent to shew thee; for I do not know it.

5 Nevertheless as concerning the tokens, behold, the days shall come, that they which dwell upon earth shall be taken in a great number, and the way of truth shall be hidden, and the land shall be barren of faith. ²But iniquity shall be increased above that which now thou seest, or that thou hast heard long ago. ³And the land, that thou seest now to have root, shalt thou see wasted suddenly. ⁴But if the most High grant thee to live, thou shalt see after the third trumpet that the sun shall suddenly shine again in the night, and the moon thrice in the day: ⁵and blood shall drop out of wood, and the stone shall give his voice, and the people shall be troubled: ⁶and even he shall rule, whom they look not for that dwell upon the earth, and the fowls shall take their flight away together: ⁷and the Sodomitish sea shall cast out fish, and make a noise in the night, which many have not known: but they shall all hear the voice thereof. ⁸There shall be a confusion also in many places, and the fire shall be oft sent out again, and the wild beasts shall change their places, and menstruous women shall bring forth monsters: ⁹and salt waters shall be found in the sweet, and all friends shall destroy one another; then shall wit hide itself, and understanding withdraw itself into his secret chamber, ¹⁰and shall be sought of many, and yet not be found: then shall unrighteousness and incontinency be multiplied upon earth. ¹¹One land also shall ask another, and say, Is righteousness that maketh a man righteous gone through thee? And it shall say, No. ¹²At the same time shall men hope, but nothing obtain: they shall labour, but their ways shall not prosper. ¹³To shew thee such tokens I have leave; and if thou

---

should modify the previous sentence, yielding "that are committed unto them from the beginning." **4:48** *An hot burning oven . . . still*: cf. Gen 15:17.   **4:51** *What shall happen*: alternatively "who will be alive" (Lat. MS tradition; NRSV).   **5:1** *Taken in a great number*: Lat. unclear; other versions read "taken with great terror" (so NRSV).   **5:3** *Have root . . . suddenly*: Lat. obscure, but it seems to suggest "rule will be a place of confused tracks, and they will see it desolate" (so NRSV).   **5:4** *Trumpet*: the text is uncertain. *The sun . . . day*: this and many of the other phenomena mentioned in vv. 4–12 conventionally portend the eschatological consummation; cf. Jer 4:25; Joel 2:10; 3:15; Hab 2:11; Luke 19:40; etc. *Thrice*: better omitted (Lat. MS tradition).   **5:5** *Troubled*: better to add "and the courses [of the stars?] will be thrown into disorder" (Lat. MS tradition).   **5:7** *Sodomitish sea*: Dead Sea. **5:9–10** *Then shall wit hide . . . found*: cf. Job 28:12–22; Bar 3:15–31. *Wit*: Lat. *sensus*, "perception,"

wilt pray again, and weep as now, and fast seven days, thou shalt hear yet greater things. [14]Then I awaked, and an extreme fearfulness went through all my body, and my mind was troubled, so that it fainted. [15]So the angel that was come to talk with me held me, comforted me, and set me up upon my feet.

[16]And in the second night it came to pass, that Salathiel the captain of the people came unto me, saying, Where hast thou been? and why is thy countenance so heavy? [17]Knowest thou not that Israel is committed unto thee in the land of their captivity? [18]Up then, and eat bread, and forsake us not, as the shepherd that leaveth his flock in the hands of cruel wolves. [19]Then said I unto him, Go thy ways from me, and come not nigh me. And he heard what I said, and went from me. [20]And so I fasted seven days, mourning and weeping, like as Uriel the angel commanded me.

[21]And after seven days so it was, that the thoughts of my heart were very grievous unto me again, [22]and my soul recovered the spirit of understanding, and I began to talk with the most High again, [23]and said, O Lord that bearest rule, of every wood of the earth, and of all the trees thereof, thou hast chosen thee one only vine: [24]and of all lands of the whole world thou hast chosen thee one pit: and of all the flowers thereof one lily: [25]and of all the depths of the sea thou hast filled thee one river: and of all builded cities thou hast hallowed Sion unto thyself: [26]and of all the fowls that are created thou hast named thee one dove: and of all the cattle that are made thou hast provided thee one sheep: [27]and among all the multitudes of peoples thou hast gotten thee one people: and unto this people, whom thou lovedst, thou gavest a law that is approved of all. [28]And now, O Lord, why hast thou given this one people over unto many? and upon the one root hast thou prepared others, and why hast thou scattered thy only one people among many? [29]And they which did gainsay thy promises, and believed not thy covenants, have trodden them down. [30]If thou didst so much hate thy people, yet shouldest thou punish them with thine own hands.

[31]Now when I had spoken these words, the angel that came to me the night afore was sent unto me, [32]and said unto me, Hear me, and I will instruct thee; hearken to the thing that I say, and I shall tell thee more. [33]And I said, Speak on, my Lord.

Then said he unto me, Thou art sore troubled in mind for Israel's sake: lovest thou that people better than he that made them? [34]And I said, No, Lord: but of very grief have I spoken: for my reins pain me every hour, while I labour to comprehend the way of the most High, and to seek out part of his judgment. [35]And he

---

"thought," or "reason."   **5:16** *Salathiel*: better "Phaltiel" (Lat. MS tradition), otherwise unknown. **5:18** *As the shepherd . . . wolves*: cf. Ezek 34.   **5:19** *Come not nigh me*: better to add "for seven days" (Lat. MS tradition).

5:21–6:34 The second vision. The dialogue does not much advance in this section: Ezra and Uriel put forward more or less the same positions as in the first vision's narrative—Ezra questioning God's judgment, Uriel urging him to anticipate God's eschatological intervention.   **5:23–27** *O Lord . . . one people*: the metaphors here conventionally describe Israel in the OT; cf. Pss 74:19; 80:8–15; etc. **5:24** *Pit*: the Latin text is evidently corrupt; other versions suggest "region."   **5:28** *Upon the one root . . . others*: the Latin text is corrupt; other versions suggest "dishonored the one root beyond the others" (NRSV).   **5:29** *And believed . . . down*: better "have trodden down those who believed your covenants" (Lat. MS tradition).   **5:34** *Very*: true. *Reins*: kidneys (like "heart" in English, a conventional seat of

said unto me, Thou canst not. And I said, Wherefore, Lord? whereunto was I born then? or why was not my mother's womb then my grave, that I might not have seen the travail of Jacob, and the wearisome toil of the stock of Israel? ³⁶And he said unto me, Number me the things that are not yet come, gather me together the drops that are scattered abroad, make me the flowers green again that are withered, ³⁷open me the places that are closed, and bring me forth the winds that in them are shut up, shew me the image of a voice: and then I will declare to thee the thing that thou labourest to know.

³⁸And I said, O Lord that bearest rule, who may know these things, but he that hath not his dwelling with men? ³⁹As for me, I am unwise: how may I then speak of these things whereof thou askest me? ⁴⁰Then said he unto me, Like as thou canst do none of these things that I have spoken of, even so canst thou not find out my judgment, or in the end the love that I have promised unto my people. ⁴¹And I said, Behold, O Lord, yet art thou nigh unto them that be reserved till the end: and what shall they do that have been before me, or we [that be now], or they that shall come after us? ⁴²And he said unto me, I will liken my judgment unto a ring: like as there is no slackness of the last, even so there is no swiftness of the first. ⁴³So I answered and said, Couldest thou not make those that have been made, and be now, and that are for to come, at once; that thou mightest shew thy judgment the sooner? ⁴⁴Then answered he me, and said, The creature may not haste above the maker; neither may the world hold them at once that shall be created therein.

⁴⁵And I said, As thou hast said unto thy servant, that thou, which givest life to all, hast given life at once to the creature that thou hast created, and the creature bare it: even so it might now also bear them that now be present at once. ⁴⁶And he said unto me, Ask the womb of a woman, and say unto her, If thou bringest forth children, why dost thou it not together, but one after another? pray her therefore to bring forth ten children at once. ⁴⁷And I said, She cannot: but must do it by distance of time. ⁴⁸Then said he unto me, Even so have I given the womb of the earth to those that be sown in it in their times. ⁴⁹For like as a young child may not bring forth the things that belong to the aged, even so have I disposed the world which I created.

⁵⁰And I asked, and said, Seeing thou hast now given me the way, I will proceed to speak before thee: for our mother, of whom thou hast told me that she is young, draweth now nigh unto age. ⁵¹He answered me, and said, Ask a woman that beareth children, and she shall tell thee. ⁵²Say unto her, Wherefore are not they

---

emotion).   **5:35** *Whereunto was I . . . Israel*: echoing the initial complaint of Job (chap. 3).   **5:36–37** *Number me . . . know*: recalling God's response to Job in chaps. 38–41.   **5:40** *In the end the love*: better "the goal of the love" (Lat. MS tradition).   **5:41** *Them that . . . end*: i.e., those who will survive until the eschatological consummation. *End*: Lat. *finis*, also "goal" (see v. 40 note). *And what . . . me*: Paul addresses this same question in 1 Thess 4:13–18.   **5:45** *As thou . . . present at once*: an alternative translation, with a clause (erroneously omitted by the Latin) restored from the other versions, reads "How have you said to your servant that, since you give life, you will give life at once to the creation created by you? If they will live at once and the creation will sustain it, it will be able even now to bear those that are present at once." The initial question alludes to eschatological resurrection (see 4:41–42), in light of which Ezra has understood 5:42.   **5:49** *The things . . . aged*: better "nor a woman who has become old" (Lat. MS tradition).   **5:50** *For our mother . . . age*: better construed as a question: "for is our mother, about whom you told me that she is still young, already

whom thou hast now brought forth like those that were before, but less of stature? [53]And she shall answer thee, They that be born in the strength of youth are of one fashion, and they that are born in the time of age, when the womb faileth, are otherwise. [54]Consider thou therefore also, how that ye are less of stature than those that were before you. [55]And so are they that come after you less than ye, as the creatures which now begin to be old, and have passed over the strength of youth.

[56]Then said I, Lord, I beseech thee, if I have found favour in thy sight, shew thy servant by whom thou visitest thy creature. [1]And he said unto me, In the beginning, when the earth was made, before the borders of the world stood, or ever the winds blew, [2]before it thundered and lightened, or ever the foundations of paradise were laid, [3]before the fair flowers were seen, or ever the moveable powers were established, before the innumerable multitude of angels were gathered together, [4]or ever the heights of the air were lifted up, before the measures of the firmament were named, or ever the chimneys in Sion were hot, [5]and ere the present years were sought out, and or ever the inventions of them that now sin were turned, before they were sealed that have gathered faith for a treasure: [6]then did I consider these things, and they all were made through me alone, and through none other: by me also they shall be ended, and by none other.

[7]Then answered I and said, What shall be the parting asunder of the times? or when shall be the end of the first, and the beginning of it that followeth? [8]And he said unto me, From Abraham unto Isaac, when Jacob and Esau were born of him, Jacob's hand held first the heel of Esau. [9]For Esau is the end of the world, and Jacob is the beginning of it that followeth. [10]The hand of man is betwixt the heel and the hand: other question, Esdras, ask thou not.

[11]I answered then and said, O Lord that bearest rule, if I have found favour in thy sight, [12]I beseech thee, shew thy servant the end of thy tokens, whereof thou shewedst me part the last night. [13]So he answered and said unto me, Stand up upon thy feet, and hear a mighty sounding voice. [14]And it shall be as it were a great motion; but the place where thou standest shall not be moved. [15]And therefore when it speaketh be not afraid: for the word is of the end, and the foundation of the earth is understood. [16]And why? because the speech of these things trembleth and is moved: for it knoweth that the end of these things must be changed.

---

approaching old age?" **5:54** *Ye are . . . you*: Gen 6:4, Num 13:32–33, and Amos 2:9 all assume the existence of giants in previous generations. The idea of a gradual decline of human potency is conventional in the ancient Mediterranean world (see, e.g., Hesiod's myth of the four ages in *Works and Days* 106–201). **5:56** *Lord, I . . . creature*: Ezra addresses the Lord via Uriel, through whom God answers in the first person (cf. 6:6). *Creature*: creation. **6:3** *Moveable powers*: better "powers of motions" (Lat. MS tradition). "Motions" may refer to earthquakes, but the phrase may also refer to angels, or to something else entirely. **6:4** *The chimneys . . . hot*: better "the footstool of Zion was considered" (Lat. MS tradition). **6:5** *Inventions*: contrivances or "imaginations" (NRSV). *Turned*: lit. "estranged." **6:8** *Jacob's hand . . . Esau*: see Gen 25:26. **6:10** *The hand . . . hand*: this accurate rendition of the Latin (which is probably corrupt) makes no sense; other versions read "the beginning of a person is the hand, and the end of a person is the heel" (so NRSV), or something similar. **6:14–15** *And it . . . speaketh*: a better reading of the Latin MS tradition yields a more awkward sentence, which Stone renders as "and it will be if the place where you are standing is greatly shaking while (the voice) is speaking with you." **6:15–16** *Is understood . . . changed*: better "will be understood,

¹⁷And it happened, that when I had heard it I stood up upon my feet, and hearkened, and, behold, there was a voice that spake, and the sound of it was like the sound of many waters. ¹⁸And it said, Behold, the days come, that I will begin to draw nigh, and to visit them that dwell upon the earth, ¹⁹and will begin to make inquisition of them, what they be that have hurt unjustly with their unrighteousness, and when the affliction of Sion shall be fulfilled; ²⁰and when the world, that shall begin to vanish away, shall be finished, then will I shew these tokens: the books shall be opened before the firmament, and they shall see all together: ²¹and the children of a year old shall speak with their voices, the women with child shall bring forth untimely children of three or four months old, and they shall live, and be raised up. ²²And suddenly shall the sown places appear unsown, the full storehouses shall suddenly be found empty: ²³and the trumpet shall give a sound, which when every man heareth, they shall be suddenly afraid. ²⁴At that time shall friends fight one against another like enemies, and the earth shall stand in fear with those that dwell therein, the springs of the fountains shall stand still, and in three hours they shall not run. ²⁵Whosoever remaineth from all these that I have told thee shall escape, and see my salvation, and the end of your world. ²⁶And the men that are received shall see it, who have not tasted death from their birth: and the heart of the inhabitants shall be changed, and turned into another meaning. ²⁷For evil shall be put out, and deceit shall be quenched. ²⁸As for faith, it shall flourish, corruption shall be overcome, and the truth, which hath been so long without fruit, shall be declared.

²⁹And when he talked with me, behold, I looked by little and little upon him before whom I stood. ³⁰And these words said he unto me; I am come to shew thee the time of the night to come. ³¹If thou wilt pray yet more, and fast seven days again, I shall tell thee greater things by day than I have heard. ³²For thy voice is heard before the most High: for the Mighty hath seen thy righteous dealing, he hath seen also thy chastity, which thou hast had ever since thy youth. ³³And therefore hath he sent me to shew thee all these things, and to say unto thee, Be of good comfort, and fear not. ³⁴And hasten not with the times that are past, to think vain things, that thou mayest not hasten from the latter times.

since the speech concerns it. It will tremble and be shaken, for it knows that its end must be altered" (Lat. MS tradition). **6:17** *Like the sound . . . waters*: cf. Ezek 1:24–25; 43:2; Rev 1:15; etc. **6:20** *Finished*: lit. "sealed." *Tokens* has the same Latin root. *The books*: presumably the book of life; see Rev 3:5 note. **6:21** *The children . . . raised up*: taking the principle articulated at 5:54–55 to an extreme, in order to signal the onset of the eschatological restoration. **6:23** *The trumpet . . . sound*: see 1 Thess 4:16 note. **6:24** *Shall friends . . . enemies*: cf. Mic 7:5–6, which some ancients read as a prophecy of eschatological strife. *In three hours*: for three hours. **6:25** *Your*: better "my" (Lat. MS tradition). **6:26** *The men . . . who have not tasted death*: in particular, Enoch (Gen 5:24), Elijah (2 Kgs 2:11), and, according to legend, Moses (see Mark 9:4 note). **6:29** *I looked . . . stood*: other versions read "little by little the place where I was standing began to rock to and fro" (NRSV). **6:30** *The time . . . come*: the text is confused. NRSV translates the Syriac version: "I have come to show you these things this night." But that reading may not be correct. **6:34** *Hasten from the latter times*: the text is uncertain and the meaning unclear.

³⁵And it came to pass after this, that I wept again, and fasted seven days in like manner, that I might fulfil the three weeks which he told me. ³⁶And in the eighth night was my heart vexed within me again, and I began to speak before the most High. ³⁷For my spirit was greatly set on fire, and my soul was in distress.

³⁸And I said, O Lord, thou spakest from the beginning of the creation, even the first day, and saidst thus; Let heaven and earth be made; and thy word was a perfect work. ³⁹And then was the spirit, and darkness and silence were on every side; the sound of man's voice was not yet formed. ⁴⁰Then commandedst thou a fair light to come forth of thy treasures, that thy work might appear.

⁴¹Upon the second day thou madest the spirit of the firmament, and commandedst it to part asunder and to make a division betwixt the waters, that the one part might go up, and the other remain beneath.

⁴²Upon the third day thou didst command that the waters should be gathered in the seventh part of the earth: six parts hast thou dried up, and kept them, to the intent that of these some being planted of God and tilled might serve thee. ⁴³For as soon as thy word went forth the work was made. ⁴⁴For immediately there was great and innumerable fruit, and many and divers pleasures for the taste, and flowers of unchangeable colour, and odours of wonderful smell: and this was done the third day.

⁴⁵Upon the fourth day thou commandedst that the sun should shine, and the moon give her light, and the stars should be in order: ⁴⁶and gavest them a charge to do service unto man, that was to be made.

⁴⁷Upon the fifth day thou saidst unto the seventh part, where the waters were gathered, that it should bring forth living creatures, fowls and fishes: and so it came to pass. ⁴⁸For the dumb water and without life brought forth living things at the commandment of God, that all people might praise thy wondrous works. ⁴⁹Then didst thou ordain two living creatures, the one thou calledst Enoch, and

6:35–9:25 The third vision. This long and complex section begins with Ezra recounting God's creation (6:38–53; cf. Gen 1:1–2:3) in order to pose a penetrating question: if God has privileged Israel among Adam's descendents, then why does Israel suffer at the hands of heathen nations rather than ruling the world as God promised (6:54–59)? That leads to a lengthy discourse about God's eschatological judgment, which Uriel indicates will set right the injustice Ezra has pointed out (7:1–35). Ezra then grows concerned about fate of those who have transgressed God's law—virtually everyone, he is convinced (7:36–8:19a)—and his concern culminates in a prayer of confession on behalf of his community (8:19b–36). The prayer has no effect (8:37–41), but Ezra continues pressing for God's mercy (8:42–45) until Uriel tells him to stop (8:46–62). Ezra then asks when God will judge the world and receives a rather conventional response (8:63–9:13), at which point he again expresses his concern about the massive condemnation that God's eschatological judgment will entail (9:14–16). Uriel insists that the world deserves what it receives (9:17–20), but assures Ezra that a remnant will survive (9:21–22) and then tells him to prepare for the next vision (9:23–25).   **6:35** *Three weeks*: only one other period of seven days has been described (see 5:20), but cf. Dan 10:2–3.   **6:41** *Spirit of the firmament*: perhaps referring to an angel guarding the firmament, or else understanding the firmament to consist of Lat. *spiritum*, which can refer to a highly refined, breathy substance (like Gk. *pneuma*; see 1 Cor 2:14 note; 15:44–49).   **6:42** *The waters . . . thee*: Christopher Columbus seized on this verse, as well as other ancient writings, to support the geographical theories on which he based his exploratory navigations.   **6:44** *Unchangeable*: better "inimitable" (Lat. MS tradition).   **6:49** *Enoch*:

the other Leviathan; [50]and didst separate the one from the other: for the seventh part (namely, where the water was gathered together) might not hold them both. [51]Unto Enoch thou gavest one part, which was dried up the third day, that he should dwell in the same part, wherein are a thousand hills: [52]but unto Leviathan thou gavest the seventh part, namely, the moist; and hast kept him to be devoured of whom thou wilt, and when.

[53]Upon the sixth day thou gavest commandment unto the earth, that before thee it should bring forth beasts, cattle, and creeping things: [54]and after these, Adam also, whom thou madest lord of all thy creatures: of him come we all, and the people also whom thou hast chosen.

[55]All this have I spoken before thee, O Lord, because thou madest the world for our sakes. [56]As for the other people, which also come of Adam, thou hast said that they are nothing, but be like unto spittle: and hast likened the abundance of them unto a drop that falleth from a vessel. [57]And now, O Lord, behold, these heathen, which have ever been reputed as nothing, have begun to be lords over us, and to devour us. [58]But we thy people (whom thou hast called thy firstborn, thy only begotten, and thy fervent lover) are given into their hands. [59]If the world now be made for our sakes, why do we not possess an inheritance with the world? how long shall this endure?

7 And when I had made an end of speaking these words, there was sent unto me the angel which had been sent unto me the nights afore: [2]and he said unto me, Up, Esdras, and hear the words that I am come to tell thee. [3]And I said, Speak on, my God. Then said he unto me, The sea is set in a wide place, that it might be deep and great. [4]But put the case the entrance were narrow, and like a river; [5]who then could go into the sea to look upon it, and to rule it? if he went not through the narrow, how could he come into the broad? [6]There is also another thing; A city is builded, and set upon a broad field, and is full of all good things: [7]the entrance thereof is narrow, and is set in a dangerous place to fall, like as if there were a fire on the right hand, and on the left a deep water: [8]and one only path between them both, even between the fire and the water, so small that there could but one man go there at once. [9]If this city now were given unto a man for an inheritance, if he never shall pass the danger set before it, how shall he receive this inheritance? [10]And I said, It is so, Lord.

Then said he unto me, Even so also is Israel's portion. [11]Because for their sakes I made the world: and when Adam transgressed my statutes, then was decreed that now is done. [12]Then were the entrances of this world made narrow, full of sorrow and travail: they are but few and evil, full of perils, and very painful.

---

better "Behemoth" (Lat. MS tradition); also in v. 51. 4 Ezra associates Behemoth and *Leviathan* with monsters that the creator God defeats in ancient Near Eastern cosmogonies such as the Babylonian Creation Epic and a handful preserved in the Bible (e.g., Ps 74:14–17). In Job, on the contrary, they represent God's wild and majestic creation (40:15–41:34). **6:55** *Thou madest*: better introduced by "you have said" (Lat. MS tradition), probably referring to God's words in Gen 1:26. **6:56** *Thou hast said . . . vessel*: cf. LXX Isa 40:15, 17. **6:58** *Fervent lover*: better "imitator, dear one" (Lat. MS tradition). **6:59** *An inheritance with the world*: i.e., "our world as an inheritance" (NRSV). **7:3** *My God*: lit. "my lord," probably a term of respect rather than a recognition of divinity. However, at various points in

¹³For the entrances of the elder world were wide and sure, and brought immortal fruit. ¹⁴If then they that live labour not to enter these strait and vain things, they can never receive those that are laid up for them. ¹⁵Now therefore why disquietest thou thyself, seeing thou art but a corruptible man? and why art thou moved, whereas thou art but mortal? ¹⁶Why hast thou not considered in thy mind this thing that is to come, rather than that which is present?

¹⁷Then answered I and said, O Lord that bearest rule, thou hast ordained in thy law, that the righteous should inherit these things, but that the ungodly should perish. ¹⁸Nevertheless the righteous shall suffer strait things, and hope for wide: for they that have done wickedly have suffered the strait things, and yet shall not see the wide.

¹⁹And he said unto me, There is no judge above God, and none that hath understanding above the Highest. ²⁰For there be many that perish in this life, because they despise the law of God that is set before them. ²¹For God hath given strait commandment to such as came, what they should do to live, even as they came, and what they should observe to avoid punishment. ²²Nevertheless they were not obedient unto him; but spake against him, and imagined vain things; ²³and deceived themselves by their wicked deeds; and said of the most High, that he is not; and knew not his ways: ²⁴but his law have they despised, and denied his covenants: in his statutes have they not been faithful, and have not performed his works. ²⁵And therefore, Esdras, for the empty are empty things, and for the full are the full things.

²⁶Behold, the time shall come, that these tokens which I have told thee shall come to pass, and the bride shall appear, and she coming forth shall be seen, that now is withdrawn from the earth. ²⁷And whosoever is delivered from the foresaid evils shall see my wonders. ²⁸For my son Jesus shall be revealed with those that be with him, and they that remain shall rejoice within four hundred years. ²⁹After these years shall my son Christ die, and all men that have life. ³⁰And the world shall be turned into the old silence seven days, like as in the former judgments: so that no man shall remain. ³¹And after seven days the world, that yet awaketh not, shall be raised up, and that shall die that is corrupt. ³²And the earth shall restore those that are asleep in her, and so shall the dust those that dwell in

this book Ezra and God address one another through the angel.   **7:13** *Elder world*: before Adam's transgression. *Immortal fruit*: fruit from "the tree of life" (Gen 2:9; 3:22).   **7:14** *Strait*: constricted, and therefore difficult.   **7:17** *Thou hast ordained . . . perish*: perhaps referring to Deut 8:1 and/or to Ps 37:9, 11.   **7:19** *There is . . . understanding above*: better "you are not a judge higher than God, nor more understanding than" (Lat. MS tradition).   **7:20** *For there . . . despise*: better "for let many perish rather than despise" (Lat. MS tradition).   **7:22** *Imagined vain things*: cf. Ps 2:1.   **7:23** *Said of . . . is not*: cf. Ps 14:1.   **7:26** *And she . . . that*: better "(that is, the city appearing) and shall be seen, who" (Lat. MS tradition). The text is confused, however, and different versions offer different readings. **7:28** *My son Jesus*: ancient Christian scribes transcribing the Latin text equated an originally unidentified messianic figure with Jesus. Other versions omit Jesus' name, referring more generally to an anointed son or servant (i.e., a messiah; see Mark 1:1 note).   **7:29** *My son Christ*: another Christian interpolation in the Latin; other versions again offer a vaguer messianic reference.   **7:30** *Judgments*: better "beginnings" (Lat. MS tradition), referring to the time before God's creative discourse in Gen 1:1–2:3.   **7:32–35** *The earth . . . no rule*: referring to the eschatological resurrection of the dead and

silence, and the secret places shall deliver those souls that were committed unto them. ³³And the most High shall appear upon the seat of judgment, and misery shall pass away, and the long suffering shall have an end: ³⁴but judgment only shall remain, truth shall stand, and faith shall wax strong: ³⁵and the work shall follow, and the reward shall be shewed, and the good deeds shall be of force, and wicked deeds shall bear no rule.

³⁶Then said I, Abraham prayed first for the Sodomites, and Moses for the fathers that sinned in the wilderness: ³⁷and Jesus after him for Israel in the time of Achan: ³⁸and Samuel and David for the destruction: and Solomon for them that should come to the sanctuary: ³⁹and Helias for those that received rain; and for the dead, that he might live: ⁴⁰and Ezechias for the people in the time of Sennacherib: and many for many. ⁴¹Even so now, seeing corruption is grown up, and wickedness increased, and the righteous have prayed for the ungodly; wherefore shall it not be so now also?

⁴²He answered me, and said, This present life is not the end where much glory doth abide; therefore have they prayed for the weak. ⁴³But the day of doom shall be the end of this time, and the beginning of the immortality for to come, wherein corruption is past, ⁴⁴intemperance is at an end, infidelity is cut off, righteousness is grown, and truth is sprung up. ⁴⁵Then shall no man be able to save him that is destroyed, nor to oppress him that hath gotten the victory.

⁴⁶I answered then and said, This is my first and last saying, that it had been better not to have given the earth unto Adam: or else, when it was given him, to have restrained him from sinning. ⁴⁷For what profit is it for men now in this present time to live in heaviness, and after death to look for punishment? ⁴⁸O thou Adam, what hast thou done? for though it was thou that sinned, thou art not fallen alone, but we all that come of thee. ⁴⁹For what profit is it unto us, if there be promised us an immortal time, whereas we have done the works that bring death? ⁵⁰And that there is promised us an everlasting hope, whereas ourselves being most wicked are made vain? ⁵¹And that there are laid up for us dwellings of health and safety, whereas we have lived wickedly? ⁵²And that the glory of the most High is kept to defend them which have led a wary life, whereas we have walked in the most wicked ways of all? ⁵³And that there should be shewed a paradise, whose fruit

God's judgment of them. **7:33** *Misery*: better "mercy" (Lat. MS tradition). **7:35** *The good deeds . . . no rule*: better "righteous deeds shall awake, and unrighteous deeds shall not sleep" (Lat. MS tradition; NRSV). This verse is followed by a lengthy passage missing from the texts of the Vulgate available to KJV translators, but present in the other versions. The passage's NRSV translation is included in the Appendix (2 Esdras 7:36–105; pp. 996–1000). It offers a detailed description of God's judgment, including discussion about why there are so few righteous people in the world, and ends with Uriel responding in the negative to Ezra's question about whether the godly will be able to intercede for their unrighteous loved ones on judgment day. Verse 36 in KJV (now also known as v. 106, with the rest of the chapter renumbered accordingly) picks up with Ezra objecting to the angel's answer. **7:36–40** *Abraham prayed . . . Sennacherib*: see Gen 18:16–33 (Abraham); Exod 32:7–14 (Moses); Josh 7:6–26 (Jesus/Joshua); 1 Sam 7:8–11; cf. 12:23 (Samuel); 2 Sam 24:15–25 (David); 1 Kgs 8:22–30 (Solomon); 1 Kgs 17:17–24; 18:41–45 (Helias/Elijah); 2 Kgs 19:8–37 (Ezechias/Hezekiah). **7:43** *Doom*: judgment. **7:48** *Fallen*: Lat. *casus*, which can refer to suffering a misfortune, a meaning supported by the other versions. **7:53** *A paradise . . . for ever*: see Rev 22:1–2 and note.

endureth for ever, wherein is security and medicine, since we shall not enter into it? ⁵⁴(For we have walked in unpleasant places.) ⁵⁵And that the faces of them which have used abstinence shall shine above the stars, whereas our faces shall be blacker than darkness? ⁵⁶For while we lived and committed iniquity, we considered not that we should begin to suffer for it after death.

⁵⁷Then answered he me, and said, This is the condition of the battle, which man that is born upon the earth shall fight; ⁵⁸that, if he be overcome, he shall suffer as thou hast said: but if he get the victory, he shall receive the thing that I say. ⁵⁹For this is the life whereof Moses spake unto the people while he lived, saying, Choose thee life, that thou mayest live. ⁶⁰Nevertheless they believed not him, nor yet the prophets after him, no nor me which have spoken unto them. ⁶¹That there should not be such heaviness in their destruction, as shall be joy over them that are persuaded to salvation.

⁶²I answered then, and said, I know, Lord, that the most High is called merciful, in that he hath mercy upon them which are not yet come into the world, ⁶³and upon those also that turn to his law; ⁶⁴and that he is patient, and long suffereth those that have sinned, as his creatures; ⁶⁵and that he is bountiful, for he is ready to give where it needeth; ⁶⁶and that he is of great mercy, for he multiplieth more and more mercies to them that are present, and that are past, and also to them which are to come. ⁶⁷For if he shall not multiply his mercies, the world would not continue with them that inherit therein. ⁶⁸And he pardoneth; for if he did not so of his goodness, that they which have committed iniquities might be eased of them, the ten thousandth part of men should not remain living. ⁶⁹And being judge, if he should not forgive them that are cured with his word, and put out the multitude of contentions, ⁷⁰there should be very few left peradventure in an innumerable multitude.

8 And he answered me, saying, The most High hath made this world for many, but the world to come for few. ²I will tell thee a similitude, Esdras; As when thou askest the earth, it shall say unto thee, that it giveth much mould whereof earthen vessels are made, but little dust that gold cometh of: even so is the course of this present world. ³There be many created, but few shall be saved.

⁴So answered I and said, Swallow then down, O my soul, understanding, and devour wisdom. ⁵For thou hast agreed to give ear, and art willing to prophesy: for thou hast no longer space than only to live. ⁶O Lord, if thou suffer not thy servant, that we may pray before thee, and thou give us seed unto our heart, and culture to our understanding, that there may come fruit of it; how shall each man live that is

7:55 *Shine above the stars*: cf. Dan 12:3. **7:59** *Choose thee life . . . live*: Deut 30:19. **7:61** *That are persuaded to salvation*: "whose salvation is assured" (NRSV). **7:65** *Is ready . . . needeth*: better "he would rather give than take away" (Lat. MS tradition; NRSV). **7:67** *Inherit*: in the archaic sense of "dwell." **7:69** *Cured*: better "created" (Lat. MS tradition). *Contentions*: better "acts of contempt" (Lat. MS tradition). **7:70** *There should . . . in*: "there would probably be left only very few of" (NRSV). **8:5** *For thou . . . prophesy*: the Latin appears to be corrupt. NRSV translates the Syriac version: "For not of your own will did you come into the world, and against your will you depart." *For thou hast no longer . . . live*: "for you have been given only a short time to live" (NRSV). **8:6** *If thou suffer not*: better "above us, would that you would suffer" (Lat. MS tradition). *Culture*: cultivation. *How shall . . . a man*: rather "by which everyone corrupt, who has borne the rank of a man, shall be able to live" (Lat.

corrupt, who beareth the place of a man? [7]For thou art alone, and we all one workmanship of thine hands, like as thou hast said. [8]For when the body is fashioned now in the mother's womb, and thou givest it members, thy creature is preserved in fire and water, and nine months doth thy workmanship endure thy creature which is created in her. [9]But that which keepeth and is kept shall both be preserved: and when the time cometh, the womb preserved delivereth up the things that grew in it. [10]For thou hast commanded out of the parts of the body, that is to say, out of the breasts, milk to be given, which is the fruit of the breasts, [11]that the thing which is fashioned may be nourished for a time, till thou disposest it to thy mercy. [12]Thou broughtest it up with thy righteousness, and nurturedst it in thy law, and reformedst it with thy judgment. [13]And thou shalt mortify it as thy creature, and quicken it as thy work. [14]If therefore thou shalt destroy him which with so great labour was fashioned, it is an easy thing to be ordained by thy commandment, that the thing which was made might be preserved.

[15]Now therefore, Lord, I will speak; touching man in general, thou knowest best; but touching thy people, for whose sake I am sorry; [16]and for thine inheritance, for whose cause I mourn; and for Israel, for whom I am heavy; and for Jacob, for whose sake I am troubled; [17]therefore will I begin to pray before thee for myself and for them: for I see the falls of us that dwell in the land. [18]But I have heard the swiftness of the judge which is to come. [19]Therefore hear my voice, and understand my words, and I shall speak before thee.

This is the beginning of the words of Esdras, before he was taken up: and I said, [20]O Lord, thou that dwellest in everlastingness, which beholdest from above things in the heaven and in the air; [21]whose throne is inestimable; whose glory may not be comprehended; before whom the hosts of angels stand with trembling, [22](whose service is conversant in wind and fire,) whose word is true, and sayings constant; whose commandment is strong, and ordinance fearful; [23]whose look drieth up the depths, and indignation maketh the mountains to melt away; which the truth witnesseth: [24]O hear the prayer of thy servant, and give ear to the petition of thy creature. [25]For while I live I will speak, and so long as I have understanding I will answer. [26]O look not upon the sins of thy people; but on them which serve thee in truth. [27]Regard not the wicked inventions of the heathen, but

---

MS tradition). **8:7** *Thou art alone*: cf. Deut 4:35. *Like as . . . said*: see 3:5. **8:9** *But that . . . preserved*: lit. "but that which preserves and that which is preserved both are preserved." **8:13** *Mortify . . . quicken*: put to death . . . bring to life. **8:14** *If therefore . . . preserved*: better "if then you will with a light command destroy what with so great labor was fashioned by your command, to what purpose was it made?" (Lat. MS tradition; NRSV). **8:19** *Before he was taken up*: presumably based on a tradition that Ezra did not die but was translated to heaven like Enoch and Elijah; cf. 6:26 and note; 14:9 and 48 note. **8:20–36** *O Lord . . . works*: this confessional prayer, reminiscent of other postexilic penitentiary prayers (e.g., Ezra 9:5–15; Neh 9:6–37; Dan 9:3–19; and others found in the Apocrypha), is conventionally called the "Confession of Ezra." It circulated independently of 4 Ezra and was probably used in ancient Christian liturgy. Its imagery is conventional throughout, with numerous parallels to other biblical texts (e.g., compare v. 23 and Ps 97:5; Isa 51:10). **8:20** *Which beholdest . . . air*: the Latin reads "whose eyes are exalted [*or* whose are the highest heavens] and whose upper chambers are in the air" (NRSV). **8:22** *Conversant in*: alternatively "transformed into."

the desire of those that keep thy testimonies in afflictions. [28]Think not upon those that have walked feignedly before thee: but remember them, which according to thy will have known thy fear. [29]Let it not be thy will to destroy them which have lived like beasts; but to look upon them that have clearly taught thy law. [30]Take thou no indignation at them which are deemed worse than beasts; but love them that alway put their trust in thy righteousness and glory. [31]For we and our fathers do languish of such diseases: but because of us sinners thou shalt be called merciful. [32]For if thou hast a desire to have mercy upon us, thou shalt be called merciful, to us namely, that have no works of righteousness. [33]For the just, which have many good works laid up with thee, shall out of their own deeds receive reward. [34]For what is man, that thou shouldest take displeasure at him? or what is a corruptible generation, that thou shouldest be so bitter toward it? [35]For in truth there is no man among them that be born, but he hath dealt wickedly; and among the faithful there is none which hath not done amiss. [36]For in this, O Lord, thy righteousness and thy goodness shall be declared, if thou be merciful unto them which have not the confidence of good works.

[37]Then answered he me, and said, Some things hast thou spoken aright, and according unto thy words it shall be. [38]For indeed I will not think on the disposition of them which have sinned before death, before judgment, before destruction: [39]but I will rejoice over the disposition of the righteous, and I will remember also their pilgrimage, and the salvation, and the reward, that they shall have. [40]Like as I have spoken now, so shall it come to pass. [41]For as the husbandman soweth much seed upon the ground, and planteth many trees, and yet the thing that is sown good in his season cometh not up, neither doth all that is planted take root: even so is it of them that are sown in the world; they shall not all be saved.

[42]I answered then and said, If I have found grace, let me speak. [43]Like as the husbandman's seed perisheth, if it come not up, and receive not thy rain in due season; or if there come too much rain, and corrupt it: [44]even so perisheth man also, which is formed with thy hands, and is called thine own image, because thou art like unto him, for whose sake thou hast made all things, and likened him unto the husbandman's seed. [45]Be not wroth with us, but spare thy people, and have mercy upon thine own inheritance: for thou art merciful unto thy creature.

[46]Then answered he me, and said, Things present are for the present, and things to come for such as be to come. [47]For thou comest far short that thou shouldest be able to love my creature more than I: but I have ofttimes drawn nigh

---

8:27 *Testimonies*: better "covenants" (Lat. MS tradition).   8:31 *Do languish of such diseases*: better "have passed our lives in ways subject to death" (Lat. MS tradition).   8:34 *What is man . . . it*: echoing Ps 8:4.   8:37–39 *Some things . . . have*: a response to vv. 26–30.   8:38 *Disposition*: more literally "making" (also in v. 39). *Before death . . . destruction*: better "or about their death, or judgment, or destruction" (Lat. MS tradition).   8:39 *Pilgrimage*: a metaphor for death.   8:41 *His*: its. 8:43–44 *Like as . . . seed*: Klijn's Latin text, slightly emended, makes it clear that Ezra challenges the appropriateness of Uriel's simile: "Since a farmer's seed, if it does not come up because it does not receive your rain in due season, or if it rots because of an abundance of rain—man who is created by your hands and called your image, since he for whom you have created all things is similar [to you], did you also make him similar to a farmer's seed?"   8:45 *Be not wroth with us*: better "no, Lord above us" (Lat. MS tradition).   8:47 *But I . . . unrighteous*: better "but you have frequently

unto thee, and unto it, but never to the unrighteous. [48]In this also thou art marvellous before the most High: [49]in that thou hast humbled thyself, as it becometh thee, and hast not judged thyself worthy to be much glorified among the righteous. [50]For many great miseries shall be done to them that in the latter time shall dwell in the world, because they have walked in great pride. [51]But understand thou for thyself, and seek out the glory for such as be like thee. [52]For unto you is paradise opened, the tree of life is planted, the time to come is prepared, plenteousness is made ready, a city is builded, and rest is allowed, yea, perfect goodness and wisdom. [53]The root of evil is sealed up from you, weakness and the moth is hid from you, and corruption is fled into hell to be forgotten: [54]sorrows are passed, and in the end is shewed the treasure of immortality. [55]And therefore ask thou no more questions concerning the multitude of them that perish. [56]For when they had taken liberty, they despised the most High, thought scorn of his law, and forsook his ways. [57]Moreover they have trodden down his righteous, [58]and said in their heart, that there is no God; yea, and that knowing they must die. [59]For as the things aforesaid shall receive you, so thirst and pain are prepared for them: for it was not his will that men should come to nought: [60]but they which be created have defiled the name of him that made them, and were unthankful unto him which prepared life for them. [61]And therefore is my judgment now at hand. [62]These things have I not shewed unto all men, but unto thee, and a few like thee.

Then answered I and said, [63]Behold, O Lord, now hast thou shewed me the multitude of the wonders, which thou wilt begin to do in the last times: but at what time, thou hast not shewed me. [1]He answered me then, and said, Measure thou the time diligently in itself: and when thou seest part of the signs past, which I have told thee before, [2]then shalt thou understand, that it is the very same time, wherein the Highest will begin to visit the world which he made. [3]Therefore when there shall be seen earthquakes and uproars of the people in the world: [4]then shalt thou well understand, that the most High spake of those things from the days that were before thee, even from the beginning. [5]For like as all that is made in the world hath a beginning and an end, and the end is manifest: [6]even so the times also of the Highest have plain beginnings in wonders and powerful works, and endings in effects and signs. [7]And every one that shall be saved, and shall be able to escape by his works, and by faith, whereby ye have believed, [8]shall be preserved from the said perils, and shall see my salvation in my land, and within my borders: for I have sanctified them for me from the beginning. [9]Then shall they be in pitiful case, which now have abused my ways: and they that have cast them away despitefully shall dwell in torments. [10]For such as in their life have

drawn yourself near the unrighteous. Never do that!" (Lat. MS tradition). He presumably rebukes Ezra for frequently identifying with sinners. **8:52** *Paradise opened . . . planted*: the imagery comes from Gen 2:15–3:24. **8:53** *Weakness and . . . forgotten*: better "illness has been banished from you all and death has been hidden. Hades and corruption have fled into oblivion" (Lat. MS tradition; so NRSV). **8:58** *Said . . . God*: cf. Ps 14:1. **9:3** *World*: better to add "intrigues of nations, wavering of leaders, confusion of princes" (Lat. MS tradition; NRSV). The signs of the end given in this verse are conventional; cf. Mark 13:3–37 and notes. **9:5** *Hath a beginning . . . manifest*: Lat. obscure; other versions read "the beginning is evident, and the end manifest" (so NRSV). **9:9** *In pitiful case*: better

received benefits, and have not known me; [11]and they that have lothed my law, while they had yet liberty, and, when as yet place of repentance was open unto them, understood not, but despised it; [12]the same must know it after death by pain. [13]And therefore be thou not curious how the ungodly shall be punished, and when: but inquire how the righteous shall be saved, whose the world is, and for whom the world is created.

[14]Then answered I and said, [15]I have said before, and now do speak, and will speak it also hereafter, that there be many more of them which perish, than of them which shall be saved: [16]like as a wave is greater than a drop. [17]And he answered me, saying, Like as the field is, so is also the seed; as the flowers be, such are the colours also; such as the workman is, such also is the work; and as the husbandman is himself, so is his husbandry also: for it was the time of the world. [18]And now when I prepared the world, which was not yet made, even for them to dwell in that now live, no man spake against me. [19]For then every one obeyed: but now the manners of them which are created in this world that is made are corrupted by a perpetual seed, and by a law which is unsearchable rid themselves. [20]So I considered the world, and, behold, there was peril because of the devices that were come into it. [21]And I saw, and spared it greatly, and have kept me a grape of the cluster, and a plant of a great people. [22]Let the multitude perish then, which was born in vain; and let my grape be kept, and my plant; for with great labour have I made it perfect.

[23]Nevertheless, if thou wilt cease yet seven days more, (but thou shalt not fast in them, [24]but go into a field of flowers, where no house is builded, and eat only the flowers of the field; taste no flesh, drink no wine, but eat flowers only;) [25]and pray unto the Highest continually, then will I come and talk with thee.

[26]So I went my way into the field which is called Ardath, like as he commanded me; and there I sat among the flowers, and did eat of the herbs of the field, and the meat of the same satisfied me. [27]After seven days I sat upon the grass, and my heart was vexed within me, like as before: [28]and I opened my mouth, and began to talk before the most High, and said, [29]O Lord, thou that shewest thyself unto us, thou wast shewed unto our fathers in the wilderness, in a place where no man treadeth, in a barren place, when they came out of Egypt. [30]And thou spakest, saying, Hear me,

---

"amazed" (Lat. MS tradition).   **9:13** *And when:* in the Latin, this phrase is at the end of the verse. **9:17** *The workman . . . work:* better "the work . . . product" (Lat. MS tradition; NRSV). *Husbandry:* better "threshing floor" (Lat. MS tradition).   **9:17–19** *For it . . . themselves:* better "for there was a time in this age, even then when I was making preparations for those who now exist, before the world came into existence which they would inhabit, and no one opposed me then, for no one existed; but now those who have been created in this world, which is supplied both with an unfailing table and an inexhaustible law [or pasture], have become corrupt in their ways" (Lat. MS tradition; so NRSV). The final words of the correct reading echo Gen 6:11–12, verses that explain why God destroyed the world with a flood.   **9:20** *Behold:* better to insert "it was destroyed; and I considered my earth, and behold" (Lat. MS tradition).   **9:21** *Greatly:* better "hardly with strength" (Lat. MS tradition); i.e., "with great difficulty" (NRSV). *Grape of the cluster:* echoing Mic 7:1; but in light of the echo of Gen 6:11–12 in v. 19, perhaps also recalling Noah, the first vintner (see Gen 9:20). *A plant . . . people:* this phrase evokes Isaianic language about Israel (Isa 60:21; 61:3).

9:26–10:59 The fourth vision. 9:26 *Ardath:* otherwise unknown. *Meat:* food.   **9:30–31** *Hear me . . . for ever:* this "quotation" is patterned on injunctions from Deuteronomy; e.g., 5:1; 6:4; 9:1.

O Israel; and mark my words, thou seed of Jacob. ³¹For, behold, I sow my law in you, and it shall bring fruit in you, and ye shall be honoured in it for ever. ³²But our fathers, which received the law, kept it not, and observed not thy ordinances: and though the fruit of thy law did not perish, neither could it, for it was thine: ³³yet they that received it perished, because they kept not the thing that was sown in them. ³⁴And, lo, it is a custom, when the ground hath received seed, or the sea a ship, or any vessel meat or drink, that, that being perished wherein it was sown or cast into, ³⁵that thing also which was sown, or cast therein, or received, doth perish, and remaineth not with us: but with us it hath not happened so. ³⁶For we that have received the law perish by sin, and our heart also which received it. ³⁷Notwithstanding the law perisheth not, but remaineth in his force.

³⁸And when I spake these things in my heart, I looked back with mine eyes, and upon the right side I saw a woman, and, behold, she mourned and wept with a loud voice, and was much grieved in heart, and her clothes were rent, and she had ashes upon her head. ³⁹Then let I my thoughts go that I was in, and turned me unto her, ⁴⁰and said unto her, Wherefore weepest thou? why art thou so grieved in thy mind? ⁴¹And she said unto me, Sir, let me alone, that I may bewail myself, and add unto my sorrow, for I am sore vexed in my mind, and brought very low. ⁴²And I said unto her, What aileth thee? tell me. ⁴³She said unto me, I thy servant have been barren, and had no child, though I had an husband thirty years. ⁴⁴And those thirty years I did nothing else day and night, and every hour, but make my prayer to the Highest. ⁴⁵After thirty years God heard me thine handmaid, Looked upon my misery, considered my trouble, and gave me a son: and I was very glad of him, so was my husband also, and all my neighbours: and we gave great honour unto the Almighty. ⁴⁶And I nourished him with great travail. ⁴⁷So when he grew up, and came to the time that he should have a wife, I made a feast.

10 And it so came to pass, that when my son was entered into his wedding chamber, he fell down, and died. ²Then we all overthrew the lights, and all my neighbours rose up to comfort me: so I took my rest unto the second day at night. ³And it came to pass, when they had all left off to comfort me, to the end I might be quiet; then rose I up by night, and fled, and came hither into this field, as thou seest. ⁴And I do now purpose not to return into the city, but here to stay, and neither to eat nor drink, but continually to mourn and to fast until I die.

⁵Then left I the meditations wherein I was, and spake to her in anger, saying, ⁶Thou foolish woman above all other, seest thou not our mourning, and what happeneth unto us? ⁷How that Sion our mother is full of all heaviness, and much humbled, mourning very sore? ⁸And now, seeing we all mourn and are sad, for we are all in heaviness, art thou grieved for one son? ⁹For ask the earth, and she shall tell thee, that it is she which ought to mourn for the fall of so many that

9:34–35 *That being perished . . . us*: better "when it comes about that what was sown or what was launched or what was put in is destroyed, destroyed those things are, but the things into which they were put remain" (Lat. MS tradition).   9:38 *Her clothes . . . head*: signs of mourning.   9:45 *After thirty years . . . son*: adhering to the conventional biblical pattern of God ending a prolonged infertility with a joyful birth; compare Sarah (Gen 18:11–15; 21:1–3), Rachel (Gen 30:1–2, 22–23), Hannah (1 Sam 1:1–20), etc.; cf. Isa 54:1. The tragedy is therefore exceptionally shocking because it violates

grow upon her. ¹⁰For out of her came all at the first, and out of her shall all others come, and, behold, they walk almost all into destruction, and a multitude of them is utterly rooted out. ¹¹Who then should make more mourning than she, that hath lost so great a multitude; and not thou, which art sorry but for one?

¹²But if thou sayest unto me, My lamentation is not like the earth's, because I have lost the fruit of my womb, which I brought forth with pains, and bare with sorrows; ¹³but the earth not so: for the multitude present in it according to the course of the earth is gone, as it came: ¹⁴then say I unto thee, Like as thou hast brought forth with labour; even so the earth also hath given her fruit, namely, man, ever since the beginning unto him that made her. ¹⁵Now therefore keep thy sorrow to thyself, and bear with a good courage that which hath befallen thee. ¹⁶For if thou shalt acknowledge the determination of God to be just, thou shalt both receive thy son in time, and shalt be commended among women. ¹⁷Go thy way then into the city to thine husband.

¹⁸And she said unto me, That will I not do: I will not go into the city, but here will I die. ¹⁹So I proceeded to speak further unto her, and said, ²⁰Do not so, but be counselled by me: for how many are the adversities of Sion? be comforted in regard of the sorrow of Jerusalem. ²¹For thou seest that our sanctuary is laid waste, our altar broken down, our temple destroyed; ²²our psaltery is laid on the ground, our song is put to silence, our rejoicing is at an end, the light of our candlestick is put out, the ark of our covenant is spoiled, our holy things are defiled, and the name that is called upon us is almost profaned: our children are put to shame, our priests are burnt, our Levites are gone into captivity, our virgins are defiled, and our wives ravished; our righteous men carried away, our little ones destroyed, our young men are brought in bondage, and our strong men are become weak; ²³and, which is the greatest of all, the seal of Sion hath now lost her honour; for she is delivered into the hands of them that hate us. ²⁴And therefore shake off thy great heaviness, and put away the multitude of sorrows, that the Mighty may be merciful unto thee again, and the Highest shall give thee rest and ease from thy labour.

²⁵And it came to pass, while I was talking with her, behold, her face upon a sudden shined exceedingly, and her countenance glistered, so that I was afraid of her, and mused what it might be. ²⁶And, behold, suddenly she made a great cry very fearful: so that the earth shook at the noise of the woman. ²⁷And I looked, and, behold, the woman appeared unto me no more, but there was a city builded, and a large place shewed itself from the foundations: then was I afraid, and cried with a loud voice, and said, ²⁸Where is Uriel the angel, who came unto me at the first? for he hath caused me to fall into many trances, and mine end is turned into corruption, and my prayer to rebuke.

²⁹And as I was speaking these words, behold, he came unto me, and looked upon me. ³⁰And, lo, I lay as one that had been dead, and mine understanding was taken from me: and he took me by the right hand, and comforted me, and set me

the expected happy ending.   **10:22** *Psaltery*: harp. *Spoiled*: plundered (so throughout).   **10:23** *Seal of Sion*: reference uncertain, but cf. Jer 22:24–25.   **10:27** *Builded*: being built (also in v. 42). The image is of the eschatological Jerusalem's construction; cf. Rev 21:2–22:5 and the OT texts alluded to there,

upon my feet, and said unto me, [31]What aileth thee? and why art thou so disquieted? and why is thine understanding troubled, and the thoughts of thine heart? [32]And I said, Because thou hast forsaken me, and yet I did according to thy words, and I went into the field, and, lo, I have seen, and yet see, that I am not able to express. [33]And he said unto me, Stand up manfully, and I will advise thee. [34]Then said I, Speak on, my lord, in me; only forsake me not, lest I die frustrate of my hope. [35]For I have seen that I knew not, and hear that I do not know. [36]Or is my sense deceived, or my soul in a dream? [37]Now therefore I beseech thee that thou wilt shew thy servant of this vision.

[38]He answered me then, and said, Hear me, and I shall inform thee, and tell thee wherefore thou art afraid: for the Highest will reveal many secret things unto thee. [39]He hath seen that thy way is right: for that thou sorrowest continually for thy people, and makest great lamentation for Sion. [40]This therefore is the meaning of the vision which thou lately sawest: [41]thou sawest a woman mourning, and thou begannest to comfort her: [42]but now seest thou the likeness of the woman no more, but there appeared unto thee a city builded. [43]And whereas she told thee of the death of her son, this is the solution: [44]this woman, whom thou sawest, is Sion: and whereas she said unto thee, (even she whom thou seest as a city builded,) [45]whereas, I say, she said unto thee, that she hath been thirty years barren: those are the thirty years wherein there was no offering made in her. [46]But after thirty years Solomon builded the city, and offered offerings: and then bare the barren a son. [47]And whereas she told thee that she nourished him with labour: that was the dwelling in Jerusalem. [48]But whereas she said unto thee, That my son coming into his marriage chamber happened to have a fall, and died: this was the destruction that came to Jerusalem. [49]And, behold, thou sawest her likeness, and because she mourned for her son, thou begannest to comfort her: and of these things which have chanced, these are to be opened unto thee. [50]For now the most High seeth that thou art grieved unfeignedly, and sufferest from thy whole heart for her, so hath he shewed thee the brightness of her glory, and the comeliness of her beauty: [51]and therefore I bade thee remain in the field where no house was builded: [52]for I knew that the Highest would shew this unto thee. [53]Therefore I commanded thee to go into the field, where no foundation of any building was. [54]For in the place wherein the Highest beginneth to shew his city, there can no man's building be able to stand.

[55]And therefore fear not, let not thine heart be affrighted, but go thy way in, and see the beauty and greatness of the building, as much as thine eyes be able to see: [56]and then shalt thou hear as much as thine ears may comprehend. [57]For thou art blessed above many other, and art called with the Highest; and so are but few. [58]But to morrow at night thou shalt remain here; [59]and so shall the

---

esp. Zech 2:1–5; Ezek 40–48.   **10:34** *In me*: better omitted (Lat. MS tradition).   **10:35** *That . . . that*: better "what . . . what" (Lat. MS tradition).   **10:45** *The thirty years*: better "the three years" (Lat. MS tradition; also in the subsequent verse), but the text is probably corrupt. Other versions offer "three thousand," although that calculation is mysterious.   **10:48** *Have a fall*: suffer a misfortune, as at 7:48 (see note).   **10:49** *Comfort her . . . thee*: better "comfort her about the things which happened. These were the things to be opened [i.e., disclosed] to you" (Lat. MS tradition).

Highest shew thee visions of the high things, which the most High will do unto
them that dwell upon earth in the last days. So I slept that night and another, like
as he commanded me.

11 Then saw I a dream, and, behold, there came up from the sea an eagle,
which had twelve feathered wings, and three heads. [2]And I saw, and,
behold, she spread her wings over all the earth, and all the winds of the air blew
on her, and were gathered together. [3]And I beheld, and out of her feathers there
grew other contrary feathers; and they became little feathers and small. [4]But her
heads were at rest: the head in the midst was greater than the other, yet rested it
with the residue. [5]Moreover I beheld, and, lo, the eagle flew with her feathers,
and reigned upon earth, and over them that dwelt therein. [6]And I saw that all
things under heaven were subject unto her, and no man spake against her, no,
not one creature upon earth. [7]And I beheld, and, lo, the eagle rose upon her tal-
ons, and spake to her feathers, saying, [8]Watch not all at once: sleep every one in
his own place, and watch by course: [9]but let the heads be preserved for the last.

[10]And I beheld, and, lo, the voice went not out of her heads, but from the midst
of her body. [11]And I numbered her contrary feathers, and, behold, there were eight
of them. [12]And I looked, and, behold, on the right side there arose one feather, and
reigned over all the earth; [13]and so it was, that when it reigned, the end of it came,
and the place thereof appeared no more: so the next following stood up, and
reigned, and had a great time: [14]and it happened, that when it reigned, the end of it
came also, like as the first, so that it appeared no more. [15]Then came there a voice
unto it, and said, [16]Hear thou that hast borne rule over the earth so long: this I say
unto thee, before thou beginnest to appear no more, [17]there shall none after thee
attain unto thy time, neither unto the half thereof. [18]Then arose the third, and
reigned as the other before, and appeared no more also. [19]So went it with all the
residue one after another, as that every one reigned, and then appeared no more.

[20]Then I beheld, and, lo, in process of time the feathers that followed stood up
upon the right side, that they might rule also; and some of them ruled, but within
a while they appeared no more: [21]for some of them were set up, but ruled not.
[22]After this I looked, and, behold, the twelve feathers appeared no more, nor the

11:1–12:51 The fifth vision. Modeled on Dan 7 (see 11:39–40 and notes below; 12:11–12), and
identifying Daniel's fourth beast (normally associated with Alexander the Great's empire; see Dan
7:7 note) as an eagle (the insignia of the Roman legions), Ezra's fifth vision seems to allude to the
Roman Empire. Specific details of its interpretation are debated, but some elements seem fairly
clear: (a) The second feather/wing (11:12–17; 12:15) corresponds to Augustus, who ruled Rome 27
B.C.E.–14 C.E.). (b) The three heads (11:23, 29–35; 12:22–28) correspond to the Flavian emperors,
Vespasian (69–79 C.E.), Titus (79–81; under his command, a decade before he became emperor,
the Roman legions destroyed Jerusalem), and Domitian (81–96; his cruelty was infamous). (c) Starting with Julius Caesar and ending with Domitian, Rome had twelve emperors, corresponding to
the twelve wings (11:1; 12:14). (Numbering the Flavians among them may not be appropriate,
since they are separately represented as the eagle's heads; in that case, "twelve" would be
obscure.) (d) The little feathers/wings and the "contrary" feathers/wings presumably figure would-
be usurpers of imperial power and foreign rulers revolting from Roman dominion. **11:2** *And
were gathered together*: other versions read "and clouds were gathered around it." **11:3** *Feathers*:
Lat. *pinnae*, also "wings," apparently the relevant meaning throughout the section (cf. vv. 1, 22).

two little feathers: ²³and there was no more upon the eagle's body, but three heads that rested, and six little wings. ²⁴Then saw I also that two little feathers divided themselves from the six, and remained under the head that was upon the right side: for the four continued in their place. ²⁵And I beheld, and, lo, the feathers that were under the wing thought to set up themselves, and to have the rule. ²⁶And I beheld, and, lo, there was one set up, but shortly it appeared no more. ²⁷And the second was sooner away than the first. ²⁸And I beheld, and, lo, the two that remained thought also in themselves to reign: ²⁹and when they so thought, behold, there awaked one of the heads that were at rest, namely, it that was in the midst; for that was greater than the two other heads. ³⁰And then I saw that the two other heads were joined with it. ³¹And, behold, the head was turned with them that were with it, and did eat up the two feathers under the wing that would have reigned. ³²But this head put the whole earth in fear, and bare rule in it over all those that dwelt upon the earth with much oppression; and it had the governance of the world more than all the wings that had been. ³³And after this I beheld, and, lo, the head that was in the midst suddenly appeared no more, like as the wings. ³⁴But there remained the two heads, which also in like sort ruled upon the earth, and over those that dwelt therein. ³⁵And I beheld, and, lo, the head upon the right side devoured it that was upon the left side.

³⁶Then I heard a voice, which said unto me, Look before thee, and consider the thing that thou seest. ³⁷And I beheld, and lo as it were a roaring lion chased out of the wood: and I saw that he sent out a man's voice unto the eagle, and said, ³⁸Hear thou, I will talk with thee, and the Highest shall say unto thee, ³⁹Art not thou it that remainest of the four beasts, whom I made to reign in my world, that the end of their times might come through them? ⁴⁰And the fourth came, and overcame all the beasts that were past, and had power over the world with great fearfulness, and over the whole compass of the earth with much wicked oppression; and so long time dwelt he upon the earth with deceit. ⁴¹For the earth hast thou not judged with truth. ⁴²For thou hast afflicted the meek, thou hast hurt the peaceable, thou hast loved liars, and destroyed the dwellings of them that brought forth fruit, and hast cast down the walls of such as did thee no harm. ⁴³Therefore is thy wrongful dealing come up unto the Highest, and thy pride unto the Mighty. ⁴⁴The Highest also hath looked upon the proud times, and, behold, they are ended, and his abominations are fulfilled. ⁴⁵And therefore appear no more, thou eagle, nor thy horrible wings, nor thy wicked feathers, nor thy malicious heads, nor thy hurtful claws, nor all thy vain body: ⁴⁶that all the earth may be refreshed, and may return, being delivered from thy violence, and that she may hope for the judgment and mercy of him that made her.

11:22 *Two little feathers*: i.e., two of the eight contrary feathers/wings mentioned in vv. 3, 11.   **11:39** *The four beasts*: see Dan 7.   **11:40** *Overcame all the beasts . . . deceit*: recalling Dan 7:23–24.   **11:42** *Peaceable*: better to add "you have hated those who tell the truth" (Lat. MS tradition).   **11:45** *Feathers*:

12 And it came to pass, whiles the lion spake these words unto the eagle, I saw, [2]and, behold, the head that remained and the four wings appeared no more, and the two went unto it, and set themselves up to reign, and their kingdom was small, and full of uproar. [3]And I saw, and, behold, they appeared no more, and the whole body of the eagle was burnt, so that the earth was in great fear: then awaked I out of the trouble and trance of my mind, and from great fear, and said unto my spirit, [4]Lo, this hast thou done unto me, in that thou searchest out the ways of the Highest. [5]Lo, yet am I weary in my mind, and very weak in my spirit; and little strength is there in me, for the great fear wherewith I was affrighted this night. [6]Therefore will I now beseech the Highest, that he will comfort me unto the end.

[7]And I said, Lord that bearest rule, if I have found grace before thy sight, and if I am justified with thee before many others, and if my prayer indeed be come up before thy face; [8]comfort me then, and shew me thy servant the interpretation and plain difference of this fearful vision, that thou mayest perfectly comfort my soul. [9]For thou hast judged me worthy to shew me the last times.

[10]And he said unto me, This is the interpretation of the vision: [11]The eagle, whom thou sawest come up from the sea, is the kingdom which was seen in the vision of thy brother Daniel. [12]But it was not expounded unto him, therefore now I declare it unto thee. [13]Behold, the days will come, that there shall rise up a kingdom upon earth, and it shall be feared above all the kingdoms that were before it. [14]In the same shall twelve kings reign, one after another: [15]whereof the second shall begin to reign, and shall have more time than any of the twelve. [16]And this do the twelve wings signify, which thou sawest.

[17]As for the voice which thou heardest speak, and that thou sawest not to go out from the heads, but from the midst of the body thereof, this is the interpretation: [18]That after the time of that kingdom there shall arise great strivings, and it shall stand in peril of falling: nevertheless it shall not then fall, but shall be restored again to his beginning.

[19]And whereas thou sawest the eight small under feathers sticking to her wings, this is the interpretation: [20]That in him there shall arise eight kings, whose times shall be but small, and their years swift. [21]And two of them shall perish, the middle time approaching: four shall be kept until their end begin to approach: but two shall be kept unto the end.

[22]And whereas thou sawest three heads resting, this is the interpretation: [23]In his last days shall the most High raise up three kingdoms, and renew many things therein, and they shall have the dominion of the earth, [24]and of those that dwell therein, with much oppression, above all those that were before them: therefore are they called the heads of the eagle. [25]For these are they that shall accomplish his wickedness, and that shall finish his last end.

---

lit. "little feathers/wings." **12:2** *And the four wings*: better omitted (Lat. MS tradition). **12:7** *Before many others*: i.e., more than many others. **12:8** *Plain difference*: Lat. *distinctio*, i.e., distinction or significance. **12:11** *Brother*: countryman. The reference is to Daniel's vision of the fourth beast in Dan 7. **12:23** *Kingdoms*: other versions read "kings." *Therein*: lit. "in it [the eagle/kingdom]" (also in v. 24).

²⁶And whereas thou sawest that the great head appeared no more, it signifieth that one of them shall die upon his bed, and yet with pain. ²⁷For the two that remain shall be slain with the sword. ²⁸For the sword of the one shall devour the other: but at the last shall he fall through the sword himself.

²⁹And whereas thou sawest two feathers under the wings passing over the head that is on the right side; ³⁰it signifieth that these are they, whom the Highest hath kept unto their end: this is the small kingdom and full of trouble, as thou sawest.

³¹And the lion, whom thou sawest rising up out of the wood, and roaring, and speaking to the eagle, and rebuking her for her unrighteousness with all the words which thou hast heard; ³²this is the anointed, which the Highest hath kept for them and for their wickedness unto the end: he shall reprove them, and shall upbraid them with their cruelty. ³³For he shall set them before him alive in judgment, and shall rebuke them, and correct them. ³⁴For the rest of my people shall he deliver with mercy, those that have been preserved upon my borders, and he shall make them joyful until the coming of the day of judgment, whereof I have spoken unto thee from the beginning.

³⁵This is the dream that thou sawest, and these are the interpretations. ³⁶Thou only hast been meet to know this secret of the Highest. ³⁷Therefore write all these things that thou hast seen in a book, and hide them: ³⁸and teach them to the wise of the people, whose hearts thou knowest may comprehend and keep these secrets. ³⁹But wait thou here thyself yet seven days more, that it may be shewed thee, whatsoever it pleaseth the Highest to declare unto thee. And with that he went his way.

⁴⁰And it came to pass, when all the people saw that the seven days were past, and I not come again into the city, they gathered them all together, from the least unto the greatest, and came unto me, and said, ⁴¹What have we offended thee? and what evil have we done against thee, that thou forsakest us, and sittest here in this place? ⁴²For of all the prophets thou only art left us, as a cluster of the vintage, and as a candle in a dark place, and as a haven or ship preserved from the tempest. ⁴³Are not the evils which are come to us sufficient? ⁴⁴If thou shalt forsake us, how much better had it been for us, if we also had been burned in the midst of Sion? ⁴⁵For we are not better than they that died there. And they wept with a loud voice.

Then answered I them, and said, ⁴⁶Be of good comfort, O Israel; and be not heavy, thou house of Jacob: ⁴⁷for the Highest hath you in remembrance, and the Mighty hath not forgotten you in temptation. ⁴⁸As for me, I have not forsaken you, neither am I departed from you: but am come into this place, to pray for the desolation of Sion, and that I might seek mercy for the low estate of your sanctuary.

12:26 *One of them . . . pain*: Vespasian died of an illness.   **12:27–28** *For the two . . . himself*: Titus died of an illness, like his father, but rumors circulated accusing his younger brother Domitian of poisoning him, or of speeding his demise by withdrawing medical care. Domitian himself was assassinated.   **12:32** *This is . . . cruelty*: the text is obscure. NRSV (slightly altered) offers the following, supplementing a Latin text similar to Klijn's with a clause from the Syriac: "this is the anointed [i.e., messiah], whom the Most High has kept until the end of days, who will arise from the offspring of David, and will come and speak with them. He will denounce them for their ungodliness and for their wickedness, and will display before them their contemptuous dealings."   **12:33** *Correct*: better "destroy" (Lat. MS tradition).   **12:34** *Upon*: throughout.   **12:37–38** *Write all . . . secrets*: see Dan 12:3–4; cf. Isa 8:16.   **12:42** *Cluster of the vintage*: see 9:21 and note. *Or*: better "for a" (Lat. MS tradition).   **12:47** *Temptation*: better "struggle" (Lat. MS tradition).

⁴⁹And now go your way home every man, and after these days will I come unto you. ⁵⁰So the people went their way into the city, like as I commanded them: ⁵¹but I remained still in the field seven days, as the angel commanded me; and did eat only in those days of the flowers of the field, and had my meat of the herbs.

13 And it came to pass after seven days, I dreamed a dream by night: ²and, lo, there arose a wind from the sea, that it moved all the waves thereof. ³And I beheld, and, lo, that man waxed strong with the thousands of heaven: and when he turned his countenance to look, all the things trembled that were seen under him. ⁴And whensoever the voice went out of his mouth, all they burned that heard his voice, like as the earth faileth when it feeleth the fire.

⁵And after this I beheld, and, lo, there was gathered together a multitude of men, out of number, from the four winds of the heaven, to subdue the man that came out of the sea. ⁶But I beheld, and, lo, he had graved himself a great mountain, and flew up upon it. ⁷But I would have seen the region or place whereout the hill was graven, and I could not.

⁸And after this I beheld, and, lo, all they which were gathered together to subdue him were sore afraid, and yet durst fight. ⁹And, lo, as he saw the violence of the multitude that came, he neither lifted up his hand, nor held sword, nor any instrument of war: ¹⁰but only I saw that he sent out of his mouth as it had been a blast of fire, and out of his lips a flaming breath, and out of his tongue he cast out sparks and tempests. ¹¹And they were all mixed together; the blast of fire, the flaming breath, and the great tempest; and fell with violence upon the multitude which was prepared to fight, and burned them up every one, so that upon a sudden of an innumerable multitude nothing was to be perceived, but only dust and smell of smoke: when I saw this I was afraid.

¹²Afterward I saw the same man come down from the mountain, and call unto him another peaceable multitude. ¹³And there came much people unto him, whereof some were glad, some were sorry, some of them were bound, and other some brought of them that were offered: then was I sick through great fear, and I awaked, and said, ¹⁴Thou hast shewed thy servant these wonders from the beginning, and hast counted me worthy that thou shouldest receive my prayer: ¹⁵shew me now yet the interpretation of this dream. ¹⁶For as I conceive in mine understanding, woe unto them that shall be left in those days! and much more woe unto them that are not left behind! ¹⁷For they that were not left were in heaviness. ¹⁸Now understand I the things that are laid up in the latter days, which shall happen unto them, and to those that are left behind. ¹⁹Therefore are they come

13:1–13:58 The sixth vision. Also drawing on Daniel (and other biblical texts), this vision, like the fifth, focuses on the eschatological victory of God and his messiah over enemy nations. 13:3 *That man . . . heaven*: better "that man flew together with the clouds of heaven" (Lat. MS tradition). Verses 2–3 are based on Dan 7:2, 13. 13:4 *As the earth faileth*: better "as wax melts" (Lat. MS tradition), an image conventionally used in meditations on God's judgment; cf. Pss 68:2; 97:5; Mic 1:4; etc. 13:5 *There was . . . sea*: recalling the final battle of Ezek 38–39 and numerous other biblical texts, esp. Zech 14:2–4. 13:6 *He had graved . . . upon it*: cf. Dan 2:34, 45. 13:7 *Whereout*: from where. 13:10–11 *He sent . . . smoke*: cf. Isa 11:4. For the violent power of God's word or breath, see also 2 Thess 2:8; Wis 12:9; 18:15. 13:13 *Other some . . . offered*: cf. Isa 66:18–21. 13:16 *Be left*: i.e., remain alive. 13:18–19 *Now understand I . . . into*: better "because they now

into great perils and many necessities, like as these dreams declare. ²⁰Yet is it easier for him that is in danger to come into these things, than to pass away as a cloud out of the world, and not to see the things that happen in the last days.

And he answered unto me, and said, ²¹The interpretation of the vision shall I shew thee, and I will open unto thee the thing that thou hast required. ²²Whereas thou hast spoken of them that are left behind, this is the interpretation: ²³He that shall endure the peril in that time hath kept himself: they that be fallen into danger are such as have works, and faith toward the Almighty. ²⁴Know this therefore, that they which be left behind are more blessed than they that be dead.

²⁵This is the meaning of the vision: Whereas thou sawest a man coming up from the midst of the sea: ²⁶the same is he whom God the Highest hath kept a great season, which by his own self shall deliver his creature: and he shall order them that are left behind. ²⁷And whereas thou sawest, that out of his mouth there came as a blast of wind, and fire, and storm; ²⁸and that he held neither sword, nor any instrument of war, but that the rushing in of him destroyed the whole multitude that came to subdue him; this is the interpretation: ²⁹Behold, the days come, when the most High will begin to deliver them that are upon the earth. ³⁰And he shall come to the astonishment of them that dwell oh the earth. ³¹And one shall undertake to fight against another, one city against another, one place against another, one people against another, and one realm against another.

³²And the time shall be when these things shall come to pass, and the signs shall happen which I shewed thee before, and then shall my Son be declared, whom thou sawest as a man ascending. ³³And when all the people hear his voice, every man shall in their own land leave the battle they have one against another. ³⁴And an innumerable multitude shall be gathered together, as thou sawest them, willing to come, and to overcome him by fighting. ³⁵But he shall stand upon the top of the mount Sion. ³⁶And Sion shall come, and shall be shewed to all men, being prepared and builded, like as thou sawest the hill graven without hands. ³⁷And this my Son shall rebuke the wicked inventions of those nations, which for their wicked life are fallen into the tempest; ³⁸and shall lay before them their evil thoughts, and the torments wherewith they shall begin to be tormented, which are like unto a flame: and he shall destroy them without labour by the law which is like unto fire.

³⁹And whereas thou sawest that he gathered another peaceable multitude unto him; ⁴⁰those are the ten tribes, which were carried away prisoners out of their

understand the things that are reserved for the last days, and they will not encounter them. But on account of this, woe also to those who are left behind, for they will see" (Lat. MS tradition; NRSV, altered).   **13:23** *That shall endure . . . Almighty*: better "who brings danger in that time, that one will guard those who fall into danger, who have works and faith toward the Almighty" (Lat. MS tradition).   **13:28** *But that . . . subdue him*: better "for he destroyed the attack of that multitude which came to blot him out" (Lat. MS tradition).   **13:31** *One shall undertake . . . realm against another*: cf. Isa 19:2.   **13:32** *My Son*: see 7:28 note.   **13:37** *Which for . . . tempest*: better "which was symbolized by the tempest" (Lat. MS tradition; NRSV).   **13:40–45** *Those are . . . Arsareth*: the myth of Israel's so-called lost tribes survives in a number of ancient texts. This passage in particular was invoked in early speculation about the origins of Native Americans, whom many Europeans believed to constitute remnants of Israel's lost tribes. Such theories remain central to the beliefs of contemporary Latter-day Saints.   **13:40** *Ten*: other versions read "nine and a half" or "nine," but ten is the

own land in the time of Osea the king, whom Salmanasar the king of Assyria led away captive, and he carried them over the waters, and so came they into another land. ⁴¹But they took this counsel among themselves, that they would leave the multitude of the heathen, and go forth into a further country, where never mankind dwelt, ⁴²that they might there keep their statutes, which they never kept in their own land. ⁴³And they entered into Euphrates by the narrow passages of the river. ⁴⁴For the most High then shewed signs for them, and held still the flood, till they were passed over. ⁴⁵For through that country there was a great way to go, namely, of a year and a half: and the same region is called Arsareth. ⁴⁶Then dwelt they there until the latter time; and now when they shall begin to come, ⁴⁷the Highest shall stay the springs of the stream again, that they may go through: therefore sawest thou the multitude with peace. ⁴⁸But those that be left behind of thy people are they that are found within my borders. ⁴⁹Now when he destroyeth the multitude of the nations that are gathered together, he shall defend his people that remain. ⁵⁰And then shall he shew them great wonders.

⁵¹Then said I, O Lord that bearest rule, shew me this: Wherefore have I seen the man coming up from the midst of the sea? ⁵²And he said unto me, Like as thou canst neither seek out nor know the things that are in the deep of the sea: even so can no man upon earth see my Son, or those that be with him, but in the daytime. ⁵³This is the interpretation of the dream which thou sawest, and whereby thou only art here lightened. ⁵⁴For thou hast forsaken thine own way, and applied thy diligence unto my law, and sought it. ⁵⁵Thy life hast thou ordered in wisdom, and hast called understanding thy mother. ⁵⁶And therefore have I shewed thee the treasures of the Highest: after other three days I will speak other things unto thee, and declare unto thee mighty and wondrous things.

⁵⁷Then went I forth into the field, giving praise and thanks greatly unto the most High because of his wonders, which he did in time; ⁵⁸and because he governeth the same, and such things as fall in their seasons: and there I sat three days.

14 And it came to pass upon the third day, I sat under an oak, and, behold, there came a voice out of a bush over against me, and said, Esdras, Esdras. ²And I said, Here am I, Lord. And I stood up upon my feet.

³Then said he unto me, In the bush I did manifestly reveal myself unto Moses, and talked with him, when my people served in Egypt: ⁴and I sent him, and led my people out of Egypt, and brought him up to the mount of Sinai, where I held

number of tribes normally assigned to the Northern Kingdom, whose deportation to Assyria the verse goes on to describe (see 2 Kgs 17:1–6 and notes). *Osea:* Hoshea. *Salmanasar:* Shalmaneser, king of Assyria (727–722 B.C.E.). **13:44** *Held still . . . passed over:* recalling Exod 14; Josh 3. **13:45** *Arsareth:* this may have derived from a Hebrew phrase meaning "another land." **13:48** *Those that . . . borders:* Klijn's text, supplemented by the Syriac version, reads "those who are left of your people, who are found within my holy borders, shall be saved" (NRSV). **13:53** *Lightened:* enlightened. **13:55** *And hast called . . . mother:* cf. Prov 7:4. **13:57** *In time:* better "from time to time" (so NRSV).

14:1–48 The seventh vision. Analogizing Ezra to Moses, this vision focuses on his divinely inspired reinscription of the Torah. Several elements of this story of Scripture's legendary restoration by Ezra find parallels in rabbinic writings. **14:1–2** *And, behold . . . Lord:* cf. Exod 3:1–4 (v. 3 below calls attention to the echo). **14:4** *Brought him . . . season:* see Exod 19:20; 32:1; 34:28; etc.

him by me a long season, ⁵and told him many wondrous things, and shewed him the secrets of the times, and the end; and commanded him, saying, ⁶These words shalt thou declare, and these shalt thou hide. ⁷And now I say unto thee, ⁸That thou lay up in thy heart the signs that I have shewed, and the dreams that thou hast seen, and the interpretations which thou hast heard: ⁹for thou shalt be taken away from all, and from henceforth thou shalt remain with my Son, and with such as be like thee, until the times be ended. ¹⁰For the world hath lost his youth, and the times begin to wax old. ¹¹For the world is divided into twelve parts, and the ten parts of it are gone already, and half of a tenth part: ¹²and there remaineth that which is after the half of the tenth part. ¹³Now therefore set thine house in order, and reprove thy people, comfort such of them as be in trouble, and now renounce corruption, ¹⁴let go from thee mortal thoughts, cast away the burdens of man, put off now the weak nature, ¹⁵and set aside the thoughts that are most heavy unto thee, and haste thee to flee from these times. ¹⁶For yet greater evils than those which thou hast seen happen shall be done hereafter. ¹⁷For look how much the world shall be weaker through age, so much the more shall evils increase upon them that dwell therein. ¹⁸For the truth is fled far away, and leasing is hard at hand: for now hasteth the vision to come, which thou hast seen.

¹⁹Then answered I before thee, and said, ²⁰Behold, Lord, I will go, as thou hast commanded me, and reprove the people which are present: but they that shall be born afterward, who shall admonish them? thus the world is set in darkness, and they that dwell therein are without light. ²¹For thy law is burnt, therefore no man knoweth the things that are done of thee, or the works that shall begin. ²²But if I have found grace before thee, send the Holy Ghost into me, and I shall write all that hath been done in the world since the beginning, which were written in thy law, that men may find thy path, and that they which will live in the latter days may live.

²³And he answered me, saying, Go thy way, gather the people together, and say unto them, that they seek thee not for forty days. ²⁴But look thou prepare thee many box trees, and take with thee Sarea, Dabria, Selemia, Ecanus, and Asiel, these five which are ready to write swiftly; ²⁵and come hither, and I shall light a candle of understanding in thine heart, which shall not be put out, till the things be performed which thou shalt begin to write. ²⁶And when thou hast done, some things shalt thou publish, and some things shalt thou shew secretly to the wise: to morrow this hour shalt thou begin to write.

14:6 *These words . . . hide*: a declaration by God not recorded in the Pentateuch; but cf. Deut 29:29. The passage distinguishes not between the written Torah and oral tradition (a distinction also traditionally traced back to Moses on Sinai), but rather between open and esoteric teaching. **14:9** *Thou shalt . . . thee*: see 6:26 and note; 8:19b. **14:11** *World*: age. **14:13** *Such of them . . . trouble*: better "their lowly, and instruct those that are wise" (Lat. MS tradition, supplemented by other versions). **14:15** *Heavy*: lit. "troubling." **14:18** *Leasing*: falsehood. *The vision*: better "the eagle" (Lat. MS tradition). **14:21** *Thy law is burnt*: see 4:23. **14:23** *Forty days*: recalling Moses' time on Mount Sinai, when he originally received the law; cf. Exod 24:18; 34:28. **14:24** *Box trees*: other versions refer to writing implements (so NRSV). **14:25** *Till the things . . . write*: i.e., until what you will

²⁷Then went I forth, as he commanded, and gathered all the people together, and said, ²⁸Hear these words, O Israel. ²⁹Our fathers at the beginning were strangers in Egypt, from whence they were delivered: ³⁰and received the law of life, which they kept not, which ye also have transgressed after them. ³¹Then was the land, even the land of Sion, parted among you by lot: but your fathers, and ye yourselves, have done unrighteousness, and have not kept the ways which the Highest commanded you. ³²And forasmuch as he is a righteous judge, he took from you in time the thing that he had given you. ³³And now are ye here, and your brethren among you. ³⁴Therefore if so be that ye will subdue your own understanding, and reform your hearts, ye shall be kept alive, and after death ye shall obtain mercy. ³⁵For after death shall the judgment come, when we shall live again: and then shall the names of the righteous be manifest, and the works of the ungodly shall be declared. ³⁶Let no man therefore come unto me now, nor seek after me these forty days.

³⁷So I took the five men, as he commanded me, and we went into the field, and remained there. ³⁸And the next day, behold, a voice called me, saying, Esdras, open thy mouth, and drink that I give thee to drink. ³⁹Then opened I my mouth, and, behold, he reached me a full cup, which was full as it were with water, but the colour of it was like fire. ⁴⁰And I took it, and drank: and when I had drunk of it, my heart uttered understanding, and wisdom grew in my breast, for my spirit strengthened my memory: ⁴¹and my mouth was opened, and shut no more. ⁴²The Highest gave understanding unto the five men, and they wrote the wonderful visions of the night that were told, which they knew not: and they sat forty days, and they wrote in the day, and at night they ate bread. ⁴³As for me, I spake in the day, and I held not my tongue by night. ⁴⁴In forty days they wrote two hundred and four books.

⁴⁵And it came to pass, when the forty days were fulfilled, that the Highest spake, saying, The first that thou hast written publish openly, that the worthy and unworthy may read it: ⁴⁶but keep the seventy last, that thou mayest deliver them only to such as be wise among the people: ⁴⁷for in them is the spring of understanding, the fountain of wisdom, and the stream of knowledge. ⁴⁸And I did so.

---

begin to write is finished.   **14:33** *Your brethren among you*: Lat. obscure.   **14:38–41** *Open thy mouth . . . shut no more*: cf. Ezek 3:1–4.   **14:42** *The wonderful visions . . . not*: better "what was dictated, using notations which they did not know" (Lat. MS tradition). The reference is to the recalled law, not to Ezra's visions, and the passage alludes to a tradition that Ezra adopted the Aramaic alphabet for his restored edition of the Pentateuch, thereby introducing the square script still used for Hebrew today.   **14:44** *Two hundred and four*: better "ninety-four" (Lat. MS tradition), leaving twenty-four to be published openly (cf. v. 46; in other versions the number is actually specified at v. 45). (By a traditional count, the Jewish Scriptures contain twenty-four books.) The remaining seventy are presumably apocalyptic treatises such as 4 Ezra itself.   **14:48** *And I did so*: other versions add "in the seventh year of the sixth week, five thousand years and three months and twelve days after creation. At that time Ezra was caught up, and taken to the place of those who are like him, after he had written all these things. And he was called the scribe of the knowledge of the Most High for ever and ever" (NRSV).

15 Behold, speak thou in the ears of my people the words of prophecy, which I will put in thy mouth, saith the Lord: [2]and cause them to be written in paper: for they are faithful and true. [3]Fear not the imaginations against thee, let not the incredulity of them trouble thee, that speak against thee. [4]For all the unfaithful shall die in their unfaithfulness.

[5]Behold, saith the Lord, I will bring plagues upon the world; the sword, famine, death, and destruction. [6]For wickedness hath exceedingly polluted the whole earth, and their hurtful works are fulfilled. [7]Therefore saith the Lord, [8]I will hold my tongue no more as touching their wickedness, which they profanely commit, neither will I suffer them in those things, in which they wickedly exercise themselves: behold, the innocent and righteous blood crieth unto me, and the souls of the just complain continually. [9]And therefore, saith the Lord, I will surely avenge them, and receive unto me all the innocent blood from among them. [10]Behold, my people is led as a flock to the slaughter: I will not suffer them now to dwell in the land of Egypt: [11]but I will bring them with a mighty hand and a stretched out arm, and smite Egypt with plagues, as before, and will destroy all the land thereof.

[12]Egypt shall mourn, and the foundation of it shall be smitten with the plague and punishment that God shall bring upon it. [13]They that till the ground shall mourn: for their seeds shall fail through the blasting and hail, and with a fearful constellation. [14]Woe to the world and them that dwell therein! [15]For the sword and their destruction draweth nigh, and one people shall stand up to fight against another, and swords in their hands. [16]For there shall be sedition among men, and invading one another; they shall not regard their kings nor princes, and the course of their actions shall stand in their power. [17]A man shall desire to go into a city, and shall not be able. [18]For because of their pride the cities shall be troubled, the houses shall be destroyed, and men shall be afraid. [19]A man shall have no pity upon his neighbour, but shall destroy their houses with the sword, and spoil their goods, because of the lack of bread, and for great tribulation.

[20]Behold, saith God, I will call together all the kings of the earth to reverence me, which are from the rising of the sun, from the south, from the east, and Libanus; to turn themselves one against another, and repay the things that they have done to them. [21]Like as they do yet this day unto my chosen, so will I do also, and recompense in their bosom. Thus saith the Lord God; [22]My right hand shall not spare the sinners, and my sword shall not cease over them that shed innocent blood upon the earth. [23]The fire is gone forth from his wrath, and hath

---

15:1–16:78 6 Ezra. Like 5 Ezra above (chaps. 1–2), this series of prophetic oracles, many of which evidently refer to events from the third century C.E., is apparently a later Christian supplement to 4 Ezra. **15:3** *Imaginations*: plots. **15:5** *The sword . . . destruction*: recalling Isa 51:19; Jer 14:12; compare the imaginative elaboration of the conventional list at Rev 6:1–8. **15:8** *The innocent . . . continually*: cf. Gen 4:10; Rev 6:9–10. **15:11** *I will bring . . . thereof*: cf. Deut 4:34; 26:8; etc. **15:13** *Blasting*: blight. **15:15–16** *One people . . . one another*: see Mark 13:7–8 note. **15:16** *And the course . . . power*: better omitted (MS tradition). **15:17–18** *A man . . . afraid*: cf. Mark 13:14–16. **15:20** *To reverence me*: an erroneous reading, though the correct one is uncertain: "to stir me" or "to come to me" are both possible (MS tradition). *Libanus*: Lebanon. **15:23** *The fire . . .*

consumed the foundations of the earth, and the sinners, like the straw that is kindled. [24]Woe to them that sin, and keep not my commandments! saith the Lord. [25]I will not spare them: go your way, ye children, from the power, defile not my sanctuary. [26]For the Lord knoweth all them that sin against him, and therefore delivereth he them unto death and destruction. [27]For now are the plagues come upon the whole earth, and ye shall remain in them: for God shall not deliver you, because ye have sinned against him.

[28]Behold an horrible vision, and the appearance thereof from the east: [29]where the nations of the dragons of Arabia shall come out with many chariots, and the multitude of them shall be carried as the wind upon earth, that all they which hear them may fear and tremble. [30]Also the Carmanians raging in wrath shall go forth as the wild boars of the wood, and with great power shall they come, and join battle with them, and shall waste a portion of the land of the Assyrians. [31]And then shall the dragons have the upper hand, remembering their nature; and if they shall turn themselves, conspiring together in great power to persecute them, [32]then these shall be troubled, and keep silence through their power, and shall flee. [33]And from the land of the Assyrians shall the enemy besiege them, and consume some of them, and in their host shall be fear and dread, and strife among their kings.

[34]Behold clouds from the east and from the north unto the south, and they are very horrible to look upon, full of wrath and storm. [35]They shall smite one upon another, and they shall smite down a great multitude of stars upon the earth, even their own star; and blood shall be from the sword unto the belly, [36]and dung of men unto the camel's hough. [37]And there shall be great fearfulness and trembling upon earth: and they that see the wrath shall be afraid, and trembling shall come upon them. [38]And then shall there come great storms from the south, and from the north, and another part from the west. [39]And strong winds shall arise from the east, and shall open it; and the cloud which he raised up in wrath, and the star stirred to cause fear toward the east and west wind, shall be destroyed. [40]The great and mighty clouds shall be lifted up full of wrath, and the star, that they may make all the earth afraid, and them that dwell therein; and they shall pour out over every high and eminent place an horrible star, [41]fire, and hail, and

---

kindled: kindling engulfed by fire is a common image of judgment and destruction in the Bible; cf. Isa 5:24; Obad 18. Also see v. 61; 1:33.   **15:25** *From the power*: better "who are apostate" or "faithless" (MS tradition).   **15:27** *Plagues*: Lat. *mala*, "evils" (also in v. 49).   **15:28–33** *Behold . . . kings*: perhaps referring to battles in the early 260s c.e. between the Sasanid Persian Empire and the Arab Septimus Odaenathus, an ostensibly pro-Roman ruler from the Syrian city Palmyra who helped wrest the Greek east from Sasanid control. He was subsequently assassinated (or perhaps simply murdered), as v. 33 seems to acknowledge.   **15:29** *The multitude . . . wind*: better "from the day that they set out, their hissing shall be" (MS tradition; NRSV, slightly altered).   **15:30** *Carmanians*: inhabitants of the eponymous province in the Sasanid Empire. *Land of the Assyrians*: Syria.   **15:34–45** *Behold clouds . . . in fear*: this passage probably represents the chaotic years of the mid-third century c.e., when the Roman Empire suffered devastating invasions from the Germans, Goths, Persians, and others. **15:35** *Belly*: better to add "of a horse" (MS tradition); cf. Rev 14:20.   **15:36** *Dung of men*: better "to the thigh of a man and" (MS tradition). *Hough*: hock.   **15:39** *And strong winds . . . destroyed*: the text of this verse is confused and uncertain.   **15:40** *Make all the earth afraid*: better "destroy all the earth"

flying swords, and many waters, that all fields may be full, and all rivers, with the abundance of great waters. [42]And they shall break down the cities and walls, mountains and hills, trees of the wood, and grass of the meadows, and their corn. [43]And they shall go stedfastly unto Babylon, and make her afraid. [44]They shall come to her, and besiege her, the star and all wrath shall they pour out upon her: then shall the dust and smoke go up unto the heaven, and all they that be about her shall bewail her. [45]And they that remain under her shall do service unto them that have put her in fear.

[46]And thou, Asia, that art partaker of the hope of Babylon, and art the glory of her person: [47]woe be unto thee, thou wretch, because thou hast made thyself like unto her; and hast decked thy daughters in whoredom, that they might please and glory in thy lovers, which have alway desired to commit whoredom with thee! [48]Thou hast followed her that is hated in all her works and inventions: therefore saith God, [49]I will send plagues upon thee; widowhood, poverty, famine, sword, and pestilence, to waste thy houses with destruction and death. [50]And the glory of thy power shall be dried up as a flower, when the heat shall arise that is sent over thee. [51]Thou shalt be weakened as a poor woman with stripes, and as one chastised with wounds, so that the mighty and lovers shall not be able to receive thee. [52]Would I with jealousy have so proceeded against thee, saith the Lord, [53]if thou hadst not always slain my chosen, exalting the stroke of thine hands, and saying over their dead, when thou wast drunken, [54]Set forth the beauty of thy countenance? [55]The reward of thy whoredom shall be in thy bosom, therefore shalt thou receive recompence. [56]Like as thou hast done unto my chosen, saith the Lord, even so shall God do unto thee, and shall deliver thee into mischief. [57]Thy children shall die of hunger, and thou shalt fall through the sword: thy cities shall be broken down, and all thine shall perish with the sword in the field. [58]They that be in the mountains shall die of hunger, and eat their own flesh, and drink their own blood, for very hunger of bread, and thirst of water. [59]Thou as unhappy shalt come through the sea, and receive plagues again. [60]And in the passage they shall rush on the idle city, and shall destroy some portion of thy land, and consume part of thy glory, and shall return to Babylon that was destroyed. [61]And thou shalt be cast down by them as stubble, and they shall be

---

(MS tradition). **15:42** *Corn*: grain. **15:43–45** *They shall go . . . fear*: cf. Rev 18. **15:45** *Put her in fear*: better "destroyed her" (MS tradition). **15:46–48** *And thou . . . inventions*: equating Asia Minor with the daughter of the whore identified as Babylon in Rev 17:1–6. The historical occasion for this ugly denunciation (which continues until the end of the chapter) seems to be the region's return to Roman authority under the Palmyran ruler Odaenathus (see vv. 28–33 and note). **15:49** *I will send . . . death*: echoing Rev 18:7–8. **15:51** *Stripes*: wounds from a whip. **15:52** *Jealousy*: zeal. **15:53** *Saying over*: alternatively "talking about." (Some MSS actually read "deriding.") Verse 54, which is better taken as a command than as a question, would then be addressed (sarcastically) to the whore Asia (rather than representing Asia's words spoken over the corpses of God's chosen). **15:58** *They that . . . mountains*: i.e., those who fled from the chaotic city; see vv. 17–19; cf. Mark 13:14; etc. *Eat their own flesh . . . water*: a conventional divine punishment; cf. Lev 26:29; Deut 28:53; Jer 19:9. **15:59** *Thou as unhappy . . . again*: better "unhappy above all others, you shall come and suffer fresh miseries" (MS tradition; NRSV). **15:60** *In the passage they*: "as they pass by they" (NRSV), apparently referring to invading armies. *Idle*: better "hateful" (MS tradition).

unto thee as fire; ⁶²and shall consume thee, and thy cities, thy land, and thy mountains; all thy woods and thy fruitful trees shall they burn up with fire. ⁶³Thy children shall they carry away captive, and, look, what thou hast, they shall spoil it, and mar the beauty of thy face.

16 Woe be unto thee, Babylon, and Asia! woe be unto thee, Egypt, and Syria! ²Gird up yourselves with cloths of sack and hair, bewail your children, and be sorry; for your destruction is at hand. ³A sword is sent upon you, and who may turn it back? ⁴A fire is sent among you, and who may quench it? ⁵Plagues are sent unto you, and what is he that may drive them away? ⁶May any man drive away an hungry lion in the wood? or may any one quench the fire in stubble, when it hath begun to burn? ⁷May one turn again the arrow that is shot of a strong archer? ⁸The mighty Lord sendeth the plagues, and who is he that can drive them away? ⁹A fire shall go forth from his wrath, and who is he that may quench it? ¹⁰He shall cast lightnings, and who shall not fear? he shall thunder, and who shall not be afraid? ¹¹The Lord shall threaten, and who shall not be utterly beaten to powder at his presence? ¹²The earth quaketh, and the foundations thereof; the sea ariseth up with waves from the deep, and the waves of it are troubled, and the fishes thereof also, before the Lord, and before the glory of his power: ¹³for strong is his right hand that bendeth the bow, his arrows that he shooteth are sharp, and shall not miss, when they begin to be shot into the ends of the world. ¹⁴Behold, the plagues are sent, and shall not return again, until they come upon the earth. ¹⁵The fire is kindled, and shall not be put out, till it consume the foundation of the earth. ¹⁶Like as an arrow which is shot of a mighty archer returneth not backward: even so the plagues that shall be sent upon earth shall not return again. ¹⁷Woe is me! woe is me! who will deliver me in those days?

¹⁸The beginning of sorrows and great mournings; the beginning of famine and great death; the beginning of wars, and the powers shall stand in fear; the beginning of evils! what shall I do when these evils shall come? ¹⁹Behold, famine and plague, tribulation and anguish, are sent as scourges for amendment. ²⁰But for all these things they shall not turn from their wickedness, nor be alway mindful of the scourges. ²¹Behold, victuals shall be so good cheap upon earth, that they shall think themselves to be in good case, and even then shall evils grow upon earth, sword, famine, and great confusion. ²²For many of them that dwell upon earth shall perish of famine; and the other, that escape the hunger, shall the sword destroy. ²³And the dead shall be cast out as dung, and there shall be no man to comfort them: for the earth shall be wasted, and the cities shall be cast down. ²⁴There shall be no man left to till the earth, and to sow it. ²⁵The trees shall give fruit, and who shall gather them? ²⁶The grapes shall ripen, and who

16:1–78 *Woe be unto thee . . . consumed therewith*: for the most part, this material consists of general oracles about eschatological cosmic cataclysms and divine judgment. **16:2** *Cloths of sack and hair*: attire for mourning. **16:5** *Plagues*: evils (also in vv. 8, 14, 37, 39; see 15:27 note). **16:7–16** *May one . . . again*: the idea of God's arrow affecting the foundations of the cosmos recalls the flood in Genesis, which is presented as God's removal of creation's underpinnings (e.g., Gen 7:11 and note) and culminates in God's symbolic hanging of his bow in the sky, pointed away from the earth (Gen 9:13 and note). Here God takes up his bow again to destroy the world. **16:21** *So good cheap*: so

shall tread them? for all places shall be desolate of men: [27]so that one man shall desire to see another, and to hear his voice. [28]For of a city there shall be ten left, and two of the field, which shall hide themselves in the thick groves, and in the clefts of the rocks. [29]As in an orchard of olives upon every tree there are left three or four olives; [30]or as when a vineyard is gathered, there are left some clusters of them that diligently seek through the vineyard: [31]even so in those days there shall be three or four left by them that search their houses with the sword. [32]And the earth shall be laid waste, and the fields thereof shall wax old, and her ways and all her paths shall grow full of thorns because no man shall travel therethrough. [33]The virgins shall mourn, having no bridegrooms; the women shall mourn having no husbands; their daughters shall mourn, having no helpers. [34]In the wars shall their bridegrooms be destroyed, and their husbands shall perish of famine.

[35]Hear now these things, and understand them, ye servants of the Lord. [36]Behold the word of the Lord, receive it: believe not the gods of whom the Lord spake. [37]Behold, the plagues draw nigh, and are not slack. [38]As when a woman with child in the ninth month bringeth forth her son, within two or three hours of her birth great pains compass her womb, which pains, when the child cometh forth, they slack not a moment: [39]even so shall not the plagues be slack to come upon the earth, and the world shall mourn, and sorrows shall come upon it on every side. [40]O my people, hear my word: make you ready to the battle, and in those evils be even as pilgrims upon the earth. [41]He that selleth, let him be as he that fleeth away: and he that buyeth, as one that will lose: [42]he that occupieth merchandise, as he that hath no profit by it: and he that buildeth, as he that shall not dwell therein: [43]he that soweth, as if he should not reap: so also he that planteth the vineyard, as he that shall not gather the grapes: [44]they that marry, as they that shall get no children; and they that marry not, as the widowers. [45]And therefore they that labour, labour in vain: [46]for strangers shall reap their fruits, and spoil their goods, overthrow their houses, and take their children captives, for in captivity and famine shall they get children. [47]And they that occupy their merchandise with robbery, the more they deck their cities, their houses, their possessions, and their own persons: [48]the more will I be angry with them for their sin, saith the Lord. [49]Like as a whore envieth a right honest and virtuous woman: [50]so shall righteousness hate iniquity, when she decketh herself, and shall accuse

affordable. **16:28** *For of a city . . . left*: echoing Amos 5:3. *And in the clefts of the rocks*: cf. Rev 6:15–16 and notes. **16:29–31** *As in an orchard . . . sword*: echoing Isa 17:5–6. **16:32** *Man*: better "sheep" (MS tradition). **16:36** *Believe not . . . spake*: cf. Deut 32:37; Isa 42:17; etc. **16:38–39** *As when . . . side*: the Bible conventionally likens eschatological tribulations to labor pains; see Mark 13:8 note and cf. 4:40–43 above. **16:39** *Shall mourn, and sorrows*: better "shall groan, and pains" (continuing the childbirth imagery). **16:42** *Occupieth merchandise*: does business. **16:44** *They that marry, as . . . widowers*: compare Paul's advice about marriage in 1 Cor 7, similarly offered in view of what Paul calls the "present distress" (v. 26)—i.e., the imminent eschatological consummation. However, this passage seems to privilege celibacy even in marriage, a practice that 1 Cor 7 prohibits (vv. 3–5) but that many later Christians viewed as admirable self-control (see Augustine, *The Good of Marriage* 9–11). **16:46** *Get*: beget. **16:47** *And they . . . robbery*: better "those who conduct business

her to her face, when he cometh that shall defend him that diligently searcheth out every sin upon earth. [51]And therefore be ye not like thereunto, nor to the works thereof. [52]For yet a little, and iniquity shall be taken away out of the earth, and righteousness shall reign among you. [53]Let not the sinner say that he hath not sinned: for God shall burn coals of fire upon his head, which saith before the Lord God and his glory, I have not sinned. [54]Behold, the Lord knoweth all the works of men, their imaginations, their thoughts, and their hearts: [55]which spake but the word, Let the earth be made; and it was made: Let the heaven be made; and it was created. [56]In his word were the stars made, and he knoweth the number of them. [57]He searcheth the deep, and the treasures thereof; he hath measured the sea, and what it containeth. [58]He hath shut the sea in the midst of the waters, and with his word hath he hanged the earth upon the waters. [59]He spreadeth out the heavens like a vault; upon the waters hath he founded it. [60]In the desert hath he made springs of water, and pools upon the tops of the mountains, that the floods might pour down from the high rocks to water the earth. [61]He made man, and put his heart in the midst of the body, and gave him breath, life, and understanding. [62]Yea, and the Spirit of Almighty God, which made all things, and searcheth out all hidden things in the secrets of the earth, [63]surely he knoweth your inventions, and what ye think in your hearts, even them that sin, and would hide their sin, [64]Therefore hath the Lord exactly searched out all your works, and he will put you all to shame. [65]And when your sins are brought forth, ye shall be ashamed before men, and your own sins shall be your accusers in that day. [66]What will ye do? or how will ye hide your sins before God and his angels? [67]Behold, God himself is the judge, fear him: leave off from your sins, and forget your iniquities, to meddle no more with them for ever: so shall God lead you forth, and deliver you from all trouble.

[68]For, behold, the burning wrath of a great multitude is kindled over you, and they shall take away certain of you, and feed you, being idle, with things offered unto idols. [69]And they that consent unto them shall be had in derision and in reproach, and trodden under foot. [70]For there shall be in every place, and in the next cities, a great insurrection upon those that fear the Lord. [71]They shall be like mad men, sparing none, but still spoiling and destroying those that fear the Lord. [72]For they shall waste and take away their goods, and cast them out of their houses. [73]Then shall they be known, who are my chosen; and they shall be tried as the gold in the fire.

do so only to have it plundered" (MS tradition; NRSV). **16:53** *God shall burn . . . head*: cf. Prov 25:22. **16:55–61** *Which spake . . . understanding*: this précis of God's creation draws on Gen 1:1–2:3, 7, as well as on other biblical descriptions of the natural cosmos and its formation, such as Ps 147:4 (at v. 56); Job 38:16 (at v. 57); etc. **16:66** *Angels*: better "glory" (MS tradition). **16:68–73** *For, behold . . . fire*: perhaps alluding to the persecution of Christians under the Roman emperor Decius in the mid-third century C.E. **16:68** *Feed you . . . idols*: prohibited for Jews and later for Christians (see Exod 34:15; Acts 15:29; but cf. 1 Cor 8–10 for Paul's characteristically complicated advice on the subject). **16:73** *Then shall . . . fire*: drawing on Zech 13:9.

⁷⁴Hear, O ye my beloved, saith the Lord: behold, the days of trouble are at hand, but I will deliver you from the same. ⁷⁵Be ye not afraid, neither doubt; for God is your guide, ⁷⁶and the guide of them who keep my commandments and precepts, saith the Lord God: let not your sins weigh you down, and let not your iniquities lift up themselves. ⁷⁷Woe be unto them that are bound with their sins, and covered with their iniquities, like as a field is covered over with bushes, and the path thereof covered with thorns, that no man may travel through! ⁷⁸It is left undressed, and is cast into the fire to be consumed therewith.

Tobit

T HE book of Tobit explores the conditions of exile. Not only are its main characters all Jews exiled in Media (or an angel disguised as one, in the case of Raphael), but the book begins with its protagonist recounting the deportation of the Northern Kingdom's population to Assyria, and closes with the same character prophesying the Southern Kingdom's impending exile, as well as predicting the return to the promised land. Many of the story's themes were concerns of ancient exilic and diasporic Jewish populations, including faithfulness to one's traditions in a setting hostile to them (cf. Dan 1:8–20) and endogamous marriage (cf. Ezra 9–10). Tobit complements its meditation on national exile by grappling with personal exile as well, in the form of the isolation and mockery that Tobit experiences when he adheres to his values, and of Sarah's perpetual virginity, violently enforced by her demonic captor. Both figures act as models for pious exilic Jews struggling to preserve their traditions and communities as they longed for return to the promised land, a longing given plaintive expression in the hymns, prayers, and prophecies that bring Tobit to a close. Likewise, both pose a complementary question of theodicy: will God abandon his people to isolation and harassment in a foreign land? No, Tobit suggests, although in the midst of intense suffering, alienation, and anxiety it may be impossible to discern God's supportive presence and providential plan.

Tobit is a remarkably packed book, for we might consider many other elements besides the major concern of exile. With no real idea of an afterlife, the book looks coolly at various aspects of death, including unburied corpses left out like rubbish, suicide contemplated by those who feel they can endure no longer, and the peaceful passing of the elderly in bed, surrounded by family. It is also a central work in the development of the biblical treatment of supernatural beings, giving major roles to the angel Raphael and the demon Asmodeus. It shows great interest in wisdom material, skillfully integrating proverbial passages into its narrative throughout. Likewise, it is intensely focused on expressions of personal piety such as giving alms and prayer, with all of its central human characters praying effectually at crucial points in the story.

Tobit is probably best described as a romance, but its quest narrative, prominent angels and demons, and unabashed fictiveness (in the opening verses, Tobit claims to have been alive both when Jereboam led the Northern Kingdom's succession and two hundred years later, when the Northern Kingdom fell to Assyria) have led to comparisons with the fairy-tale genre. In fact, Tobit does seem to be a literary retelling of an international folktale, for it integrates two commonly joined folktale motifs: the grateful dead and the bride of the monster (see 1:10–22 and note). But Tobit's literary influences are varied: it contains numerous references to the popular ancient Near Eastern Tale of Ahiqar, and may owe something to the *Odyssey* as well. In addition it models its protagonist on a number of famous biblical characters, most notably Daniel and Job, and also includes material reflecting biblical doxology, Wisdom literature, and law.

Fragments of Tobit written in Hebrew and Aramaic were found among the Dead Sea Scrolls. Although the earliest complete version of the work survives in Greek, it was probably translated from one of these Semitic languages. Tobit was likely written sometime in the period following the exile, perhaps in the late third or early second century B.C.E., in which case it would look back imaginatively on the struggles of that earlier time. Its interest in the experience and conditions of exile suggests a diasporic setting, but that inference is entirely speculative. Tobit survives in two major recensions, that preserved in the Codex Sinaiticus and that in the Codices Vaticani and Alexandrini. Unlike most modern English bibles, KJV translates the latter; though shorter than the version preserved in the Codex Sinaiticus (which was discovered only in the mid-nineteenth century), it is basically the same work.

For detailed exposition of Tobit, the reader can consult Carey A. Moore's Anchor Bible commentary, *Tobit: A New Translation with Introduction and Commentary* (New York: Doubleday, 1996), which influences this introduction and the annotations that follow.

Tobit

1 The book of the words of Tobit, son of Tobiel, the son of Ananiel, the son of Aduel, the son of Gabael, of the seed of Asael, of the tribe of Nephthali; ²who in the time of Enemessar king of the Assyrians was led captive out of Thisbe, which is at the right hand of that city, which is called properly Nephthali in Galilee above Aser.

³I Tobit have walked all the days of my life the way of truth and justice, and I did many almsdeeds to my brethren, and my nation, who came with me to Nineve, into the land of the Assyrians. ⁴And when I was in mine own country, in the land of Israel, being but young, all the tribe of Nephthali my father fell from the house of Jerusalem, which was chosen out of all the tribes of Israel, that all the tribes should sacrifice there, where the temple of the habitation of the most High was consecrated and built for all ages. ⁵Now all the tribes which together revolted, and the house of my father Nephthali, sacrificed unto the heifer Baal. ⁶But I alone went often to Jerusalem at the feasts, as it was ordained unto all the people of Israel by an everlasting decree, having the firstfruits and tenths of increase, with that which was first shorn; and them gave I at the altar to the priests the children of Aaron. ⁷The first tenth part of all increase I gave to the sons of Aaron, who ministered at Jerusalem: another tenth part I sold away, and went, and spent it every year at Jerusalem: ⁸and the third I gave unto them to whom it was meet, as

1:1–9 **Tobit's life before exile.** Tobit narrates his own story, first (vv. 1–2) describing his family background and his provenance, and then (vv. 3–9) recounting his preexilic pious life. **1:1** *Tobit*: a hellenized form of Tobi, "My Good," short for Tobijah, "the Lord Is My Good." **1:2** *Enemessar*: probably a corruption of Shalmaneser V (king of Assyria, 727–722 B.C.E.). However, his predecessor, Tiglath-pileser III (ruled 745–727 B.C.E.), deported the tribe of Naphtali to Assyria (see 2 Kgs 15:29). *Nephthali*: i.e., Kedesh Naphtali (see Josh 20:7). **1:3** *And my nation . . . Assyrians*: Sargon II (721–705 B.C.E) defeated and exiled the rest of the Northern Kingdom in 722/1 B.C.E. **1:4** *Father*: forefather. *Which was chosen . . . there*: see Deut 12:4–12. **1:5** *All the tribes . . . Baal*: a reference to the Northern tribes' secession under Jeroboam and his institution of the shrine at Dan, northeast of the territory of Naphtali (see 1 Kgs 12), which occurred several generations earlier. **1:6** *As it was . . . decree*: on the festivals requiring pilgrimage to the city, see, e.g., Deut 16:1–17. Tobit's tithing in vv. 6–8 basically conforms to Deut 14:22–29; 26:1–15.

1:10–22 **Tobit's good deeds.** Tobit's piety is further marked by the care he takes to bury the dead. On the need to do so promptly, see Deut 21:23; cf. 2 Sam 21:12–14. Behind the plot set in motion by this pious act may lie the folktale motifs of "the grateful dead" and "the bride of the monster" (combined in a number of folkloric traditions, most famously in Hans Christian Andersen's "The Traveling Companion," a literary retelling of a story he heard as a child): a man who goes out of his way to bury a corpse is unwittingly rewarded by assistance from a traveling companion who turns out to be the spirit of the dead man ("the grateful dead" motif). The companion helps the burier win the hand of a princess ensnared by enchantment ("the bride of the monster"). While Tobit and his son Tobias split the role of the burier, Raphael plays the traveling companion; Sarah, the princess;

Debora my father's mother had commanded me, because I was left an orphan by my father. ⁹Furthermore, when I was come to the age of a man, I married Anna of mine own kindred, and of her I begat Tobias.

¹⁰And when we were carried away captives to Nineve, all my brethren and those that were of my kindred did eat of the bread of the Gentiles. ¹¹But I kept myself from eating; ¹²because I remembered God with all my heart. ¹³And the most High gave me grace and favour before Enemessar, so that I was his purveyor. ¹⁴And I went into Media, and left in trust with Gabael, the brother of Gabrias, at Rages a city of Media, ten talents of silver.

¹⁵Now when Enemessar was dead, Sennacherib his son reigned in his stead; whose estate was troubled, that I could not go into Media. ¹⁶And in the time of Enemessar I gave many alms to my brethren, and gave my bread to the hungry, ¹⁷and my clothes to the naked: and if I saw any of my nation dead, or cast about the walls of Nineve, I buried him. ¹⁸And if the king Sennacherib had slain any, when he was come, and fled from Judea, I buried them privily; (for in his wrath he killed many;) but the bodies were not found, when they were sought for of the king. ¹⁹And when one of the Ninevites went and complained of me to the king, that I buried them, and hid myself; understanding that I was sought for to be put to death, I withdrew myself for fear. ²⁰Then all my goods were forcibly taken away, neither was there any thing left me, beside my wife Anna and my son Tobias.

²¹And there passed not five and fifty days, before two of his sons killed him, and they fled into the mountains of Ararath; and Sarchedonus his son reigned in his stead; who appointed over his father's accounts, and over all his affairs, Achiacharus my brother Anael's son. ²²And Achiacharus intreating for me, I returned to Nineve. Now Achiacharus was cupbearer, and keeper of the signet, and steward, and overseer of the accounts: and Sarchedonus appointed him next unto him: and he was my brother's son.

2 Now when I was come home again, and my wife Anna was restored unto me, with my son Tobias, in the feast of Pentecost, which is the holy feast of the seven weeks, there was a good dinner prepared me, in the which I sat down to eat. ²And when I saw abundance of meat, I said to my son, Go and bring what poor

---

and Asmodeus, the princess's enchanter.   **1:10–13** *All my brethren . . . purveyor*: compare Daniel's refusal to partake of unclean food and God's subsequent blessing of him (Dan 1:8–20). **1:13** *Favour*: lit. "a comely appearance," strengthening the parallel with Daniel (cf. Dan 1:13–15). *Purveyor*: buyer.   **1:14** *Media*: where those deported from the Northern Kingdom were settled (cf. 2 Kgs 17:6). *Ten Talents*: a significant amount.   **1:15** *Sennacherib his son*: Sennacherib (king of Assyria, 705–681 B.C.E.) in fact ruled immediately after Sargon II. *Whose estate was troubled, that*: better "and the roads were unsafe."   **1:18** *When he . . . Judea*: cf. 2 Kgs 19:35–36.   **1:21** *Two of his sons . . . Ararath*: see 2 Kgs 19:37. *Sarchedonus*: Esarhaddon (ruled 681–669 B.C.E.). *Achiacharus*: Tobit's author has transformed the sage Ahiqar from the Tale of Ahiqar into an Israelite and a relative of Tobit. In that ancient Near Eastern story, which the author assumes is familiar to the reader, the protagonist adopts his nephew Nadim, educates him, and then is betrayed by him to the king Esarhaddon; accused of treachery, Ahiqar has to hide to save his life (see 2:10; 11:18; 14:10 and notes). **1:22** *Signet*: a ring used for sealing official documents, and thus a symbol of authority.

2:1–14 Tobit loses his sight. Tobit continues to suffer because of his piety. The parallel with Job is most obvious in the rebuke of Tobit's wife Anna in 2:14 (cf. Job 2:9).   **2:1** *Pentecost*: see Acts 2:1 note. *Sat down*: lit. "reclined" (at table), the customary posture for dining.

man soever thou shalt find out of our brethren, who is mindful of the Lord; and, lo, I tarry for thee. [3]But he came again, and said, Father, one of our nation is strangled, and is cast out in the marketplace. [4]Then before I had tasted of any meat, I started up, and took him up into a room until the going down of the sun. [5]Then I returned, and washed myself, and ate my meat in heaviness, [6]remembering that prophecy of Amos, as he said, Your feasts shall be turned into mourning, and all your mirth into lamentation. [7]Therefore I wept: and after the going down of the sun I went and made a grave, and buried him. [8]But my neighbours mocked me, and said, This man is not yet afraid to be put to death for this matter: who fled away; and yet, lo, he burieth the dead again.

[9]The same night also I returned from the burial, and slept by the wall of my courtyard, being polluted, and my face was uncovered: [10]and I knew not that there were sparrows in the wall, and mine eyes being open, the sparrows muted warm dung into mine eyes, and a whiteness came into mine eyes; and I went to the physicians, but they helped me not: moreover Achiacharus did nourish me, until I went into Elymais. [11]And my wife Anna did take women's works to do. [12]And when she had sent them home to the owners, they paid her wages, and gave her also besides a kid. [13]And when it was in my house, and began to cry, I said unto her, From whence is this kid? is it not stolen? render it to the owners; for it is not lawful to eat any thing that is stolen. [14]But she replied upon me, It was given for a gift more than the wages. Howbeit I did not believe her, but bade her render it to the owners: and I was abashed at her. But she replied upon me, Where are thine alms and thy righteous deeds? behold, thou and all thy works are known.

3 Then I being grieved did weep, and in my sorrow prayed, saying, [2]O Lord, thou art just, and all thy works and all thy ways are mercy and truth, and thou judgest truly and justly for ever. [3]Remember me, and look on me, punish me not for my sins and ignorances, and the sins of my fathers, who have sinned before thee: [4]for they obeyed not thy commandments: wherefore thou hast delivered us for a spoil, and unto captivity, and unto death, and for a proverb of reproach to all the nations among whom we are dispersed. [5]And now thy judgments are many and true: deal with me according to my sins and my fathers': because we have not kept thy commandments, neither have walked in truth before thee. [6]Now therefore

---

2:6 *Your feasts . . . lamentation*: Amos 8:10.   2:9 *Being polluted*: a surprising claim, since he had eaten a meal in the house before. Perhaps narrative contingency explains the inconsistency: the Pentecost meal is a fitting setting for Tobit's poignant quotation of Amos, but sleeping outdoors is necessary for him to be blinded by bird droppings. (Num 9:6–10 also may be interpreted as permitting the celebration of the Pentecost festival, despite uncleanness.)   2:10 *Muted*: defecated. *Until I*: the text should be emended to "until he." *Elymais*: i.e., Elam, northwest of Persia.   2:14 *Was abashed*: lit. "blushed," but it is not clear whether with shame or rage.

3:1–6 **Tobit prays for death.** There are two further parallels with Job: Tobit's concern lest he be caught up in the sins of others (cf. Job 1:5) and the expression of his wish for extinction (Job 3; 7:15–16; etc.). The prayers of Tobit and subsequently of Sarah—like almost all the prayers and blessings in this book—contain conventional doxological language, especially as found in the Psalms.   3:3 *Ignorances*: anything Tobit had done unwittingly or had unintentionally neglected to do.   3:5 *Deal with me . . . thee*: despite parallels with Job, Tobit does not persist in declaring his innocence.

deal with me as seemeth best unto thee, and command my spirit to be taken from me, that I may be dissolved, and become earth: for it is profitable for me to die rather than to live, because I have heard false reproaches, and have much sorrow: command therefore that I may now be delivered out of this distress, and go into the everlasting place: turn not thy face away from me.

⁷It came to pass the same day, that in Ecbatane a city of Media Sara the daughter of Raguel was also reproached by her father's maids; ⁸because that she had been married to seven husbands, whom Asmodeus the evil spirit had killed, before they had lain with her. Dost thou not know, said they, that thou hast strangled thine husbands? thou hast had already seven husbands, neither wast thou named after any of them. ⁹Wherefore dost thou beat us for them? if they be dead, go thy ways after them, let us never see of thee either son or daughter. ¹⁰When she heard these things, she was very sorrowful, so that she thought to have strangled herself; and she said, I am the only daughter of my father, and if I do this, it shall be a reproach unto him, and I shall bring his old age with sorrow unto the grave.

¹¹Then she prayed toward the window, and said, Blessed art thou, O Lord my God, and thine holy and glorious name is blessed and honourable for ever: let all thy works praise thee for ever. ¹²And now, O Lord, I set mine eyes and my face toward thee, ¹³and say, Take me out of the earth, that I may hear no more the reproach. ¹⁴Thou knowest, Lord, that I am pure from all sin with man, ¹⁵and that I never polluted my name, nor the name of my father, in the land of my captivity: I am the only daughter of my father, neither hath he any child to be his heir, neither any near kinsman, nor any son of his alive, to whom I may keep myself for a wife: my seven husbands are already dead; and why should I live? but if it please not thee that I should die, command some regard to be had of me, and pity taken of me, that I hear no more reproach.

¹⁶So the prayers of them both were heard before the majesty of the great God. ¹⁷And Raphael was sent to heal them both, that is, to scale away the whiteness of Tobit's eyes, and to give Sara the daughter of Raguel for a wife to Tobias the son of Tobit; and to bind Asmodeus the evil spirit; because she belonged to Tobias by right of inheritance. The selfsame time came Tobit home, and entered into his house, and Sara the daughter of Raguel came down from her upper chamber.

3:6 *Become earth*: cf. Gen 3:19. *Everlasting place*: a euphemism for the grave.

   3:7–17 Sarah and Asmodeus. Here, at the point where the narrative switches from first to third person, its patterning is made explicit. First, Sarah, in her plight, matches Tobit by praying for death, and then the omniscient narrator reveals the providential plot that will save them both. The two figures are finally united by simultaneous movement out of seclusion, Tobit returning home and Sarah coming downstairs.   **3:8** *Married to . . . her*: recalling Gen 38:6–11. *Asmodeus*: perhaps derived ultimately from the Zoroastrian *aeshma daeva* ("the demon of anger"). *Neither wast thou . . . them*: since the marriages were not consummated, she had not become known as their wife.   **3:10** *Strangled*: hanged. **3:15** *Near kinsman*: an allusion to the levirate law; see 6:12 and note. *Son of his*: distinct from the *child to be his heir*, and thus presumably referring to a more distant relative rather than to an immediate descendant. The emphasis on Raguel's lack of a male heir makes relevant another piece of biblical legislation: the law restricting whom daughters inheriting from their fathers may marry (Num 36). **3:17** *Raphael*: that the angel's name was commonly taken to mean "God has healed" is significant, in light of the narrative that follows (see esp. 12:14). *She belonged . . . inheritance*: i.e., she is a relation of Tobias (although neither she nor he yet know it), whom the levirate law obliged to marry her.

4 In that day Tobit remembered the money which he had committed to Gabael in Rages of Media, ²and said with himself, I have wished for death; wherefore do I not call for my son Tobias, that I may signify to him of the money before I die?

³And when he had called him, he said, My son, when I am dead, bury me; and despise not thy mother, but honour her all the days of thy life, and do that which shall please her, and grieve her not. ⁴Remember, my son, that she saw many dangers for thee, when thou wast in her womb; and when she is dead, bury her by me in one grave.

⁵My son, be mindful of the Lord our God all thy days, and let not thy will be set to sin, or to transgress his commandments: do uprightly all thy life long, and follow not the ways of unrighteousness. ⁶For if thou deal truly, thy doings shall prosperously succeed to thee, and to all them that live justly. ⁷Give alms of thy substance; and when thou givest alms, let not thine eye be envious, neither turn thy face from any poor, and the face of God shall not be turned away from thee. ⁸If thou hast abundance, give alms accordingly: if thou have but a little, be not afraid to give according to that little: ⁹for thou layest up a good treasure for thyself against the day of necessity. ¹⁰Because that alms do deliver from death, and suffer not to come into darkness. ¹¹For alms is a good gift unto all that give it in the sight of the most High.

¹²Beware of all whoredom, my son, and chiefly take a wife of the seed of thy fathers, and take not a strange woman to wife, which is not of thy father's tribe: for we are the children of the prophets, Noe, Abraham, Isaac, and Jacob: remember, my son, that our fathers from the beginning, even that they all married wives of their own kindred, and were blessed in their children, and their seed shall inherit the land. ¹³Now therefore, my son, love thy brethren, and despise not in thy heart thy brethren, the sons and daughters of thy people, in not taking a wife of them: for in pride is destruction and much trouble, and in lewdness is decay and great want: for lewdness is the mother of famine.

¹⁴Let not the wages of any man, which hath wrought for thee, tarry with thee, but give him it out of hand: for if thou serve God, he will also repay thee: be circumspect, my son, in all things thou doest, and be wise in all thy conversation. ¹⁵Do that to no man which thou hatest: drink not wine to make thee drunken: neither let drunkenness go with thee in thy journey.

¹⁶Give of thy bread to the hungry, and of thy garments to them that are naked; and according to thine abundance give alms; and let not thine eye be envious, when thou givest alms. ¹⁷Pour out thy bread on the burial of the just, but give

---

4:1–21 Tobit's instructions to his son take the form of a testament (compare Jacob's testament in Gen 49). They are replete with echoes of OT legislation, Wisdom literature, and doxology, some of which are noted below. **4:3** *Honour her . . . life*: the fifth commandment (Exod 20:12; Deut 5:16). **4:9–10** *For thou . . . darkness*: this advice is vividly dramatized in Luke's parable of the Unjust Steward (16:1–9, esp. v. 9), although here evasion of premature death is at issue (*against the day of necessity*) rather than immortality. **4:12** *Our fathers . . . kindred*: for endogamy among the patriarchs, see Gen 20:12; 24:3–4; 27:46–28:2. For Noah's endogamous marriage, see *Jubilees* 4.33. *Their seed . . . land*: Gen 13:15; 17:8. **4:13** *In pride is destruction*: echoing Prov 16:18. *Lewdness*: in the archaic sense of "lack of skill"; the Greek reads "uselessness" (idleness). **4:14** *Let not . . . hand*: cf. Lev 19:13; Deut 24:15. *Conversation*: comportment. **4:15** *Do that . . . hatest*: cf. Matt 7:12 and note. *Drink not wine . . . journey*: cf. Prov 23:29–35. **4:17** *Thy bread*: apparently offerings for the dead, although they are prohibited in the Pentateuch (Deut 26:14; cf. Sir 7:33 and note).

nothing to the wicked. [18]Ask counsel of all that are wise, and despise not any counsel that is profitable. [19]Bless the Lord thy God alway, and desire of him that thy ways may be directed, and that all thy paths and counsels may prosper: for every nation hath not counsel; but the Lord himself giveth all good things, and he humbleth whom he will, as he will; now therefore, my son, remember my commandments, neither let them be put out of thy mind.

[20]And now I signify this to thee, that I committed ten talents to Gabael the son of Gabrias at Rages in Media. [21]And fear not, my son, that we are made poor: for thou hast much wealth, if thou fear God, and depart from all sin, and do that which is pleasing in his sight.

5 Tobias then answered and said, Father, I will do all things which thou hast commanded me: [2]but how can I receive the money, seeing I know him not? [3]Then he gave him the handwriting, and said unto him, Seek thee a man which may go with thee, whiles I yet live, and I will give him wages: and go and receive the money.

[4]Therefore when he went to seek a man, he found Raphael that was an angel. [5]But he knew not; and he said unto him, Canst thou go with me to Rages? and knowest thou those places well? [6]To whom the angel said, I will go with thee, and I know the way well: for I have lodged with our brother Gabael. [7]Then Tobias said unto him, Tarry for me, till I tell my father. [8]Then he said unto him, Go, and tarry not. So he went in and said to his father, Behold, I have found one which will go with me. Then he said, Call him unto me, that I may know of what tribe he is, and whether he be a trusty man to go with thee. [9]So he called him, and he came in, and they saluted one another. [10]Then Tobit said unto him, Brother, shew me of what tribe and family thou art. [11]To whom he said, Dost thou seek for a tribe or family, or an hired man to go with thy son? Then Tobit said unto him, I would know, brother, thy kindred and name. [12]Then he said, I am Azarias, the son of Ananias the great, and of thy brethren.

[13]Then Tobit said, Thou art welcome, brother; be not now angry with me, because I have inquired to know thy tribe and thy family; for thou art my brother, of an honest and good stock: for I know Ananias and Jonathas, sons of that great Samaias, as we went together to Jerusalem to worship, and offered the firstborn, and the tenths of the fruits; and they were not seduced with the error of our brethren: my brother, thou art of a good stock. [14]But tell me, what wages shall I give thee? wilt thou a drachm a day, and things necessary, as to mine own son? [15]Yea, moreover, if ye return safe, I will add something to thy wages. [16]So they

5:1–22 Tobias hires Raphael for the journey. 5:3 The handwriting: the Greek refers to a certificate of indebtedness. 5:4 When he . . . angel: although divinities commonly masquerade as humans in ancient Mediterranean literature, Raphael's role as incognito traveling companion of the hero's maturing son may owe something in particular to Athena's role as disguised companion of Telemachus during his journeys in the opening books of Homer's Odyssey. 5:12 Azarias: Heb. Azariah, meaning "the Lord helped." Ananias: Heb. Hananiah, meaning "the Lord has had mercy." The false names are classic examples of dramatic irony, as are Tobit's prayer in v. 16 and his comforting words to Anna in v. 21. 5:14 Wilt thou: do you agree to. Drachm: Gk. drachma, a silver coin of significant value.

were well pleased. Then said he to Tobias, Prepare thyself for the journey, and God send you a good journey. And when his son had prepared all things for the journey, his father said, Go thou with this man, and God, which dwelleth in heaven, prosper your journey, and the angel of God keep you company. So they went forth both, and the young man's dog with them.

¹⁷But Anna his mother wept, and said to Tobit, Why hast thou sent away our son? is he not the staff of our hand, in going in and out before us? ¹⁸Be not greedy [to add] money to money: but let it be as refuse in respect of our child. ¹⁹For that which the Lord hath given us to live with, doth suffice us. ²⁰Then said Tobit to her, Take no care, my sister; he shall return in safety, and thine eyes shall see him. ²¹For the good angel will keep him company, and his journey shall be prosperous, and he shall return safe. ²²Then she made an end of weeping.

6 And as they went on their journey, they came in the evening to the river Tigris, and they lodged there. ²And when the young man went down to wash himself, a fish leaped out of the river, and would have devoured him. ³Then the angel said unto him, Take the fish. And the young man laid hold of the fish, and drew it to land. ⁴To whom the angel said, Open the fish, and take the heart and the liver and the gall, and put them up safely. ⁵So the young man did as the angel commanded him; and when they had roasted the fish, they did eat it: then they both went on their way, till they drew near to Ecbatane. ⁶Then the young man said to the angel, Brother Azarias, to what use is the heart and the liver and the gall of the fish? ⁷And he said unto him, Touching the heart and the liver, if a devil or an evil spirit trouble any, we must make a smoke thereof before the man or the woman, and the party shall be no more vexed. ⁸As for the gall, it is good to anoint a man that hath whiteness in his eyes, and he shall be healed.

⁹And when they were come near to Rages, ¹⁰the angel said to the young man, Brother, to day we shall lodge with Raguel, who is thy cousin; he also hath one only daughter, named Sara; I will speak for her, that she may be given thee for a wife. ¹¹For to thee doth the right of her appertain, seeing thou only art of her kindred. ¹²And the maid is fair and wise: now therefore hear me, and I will speak to her father; and when we return from Rages we will celebrate the marriage: for I know that Raguel cannot marry her to another according to the law of Moses, but he shall be guilty of death, because the right of inheritance doth rather appertain to thee than to any other.

5:17 *The staff . . . us*: i.e., our support and our guide.   **5:18** *Refuse in . . . child*: the Greek is more vivid—lit. "our child's offscourings."

6:1–17 Tobias catches the fish that will defeat Asmodeus.   **6:2** *Would have devoured him*: Codex Sinaiticus has the fish try to swallow Tobias's foot, and "foot" may be a euphemism for penis (see Ruth 3:4 note). The fish's assault would then foreshadow Asmodeus's threat to Sarah's would-be husband on their wedding night, and Tobias's landing it (v. 3) would foreshadow his victory over the demon.   **6:9** *Near to Rages*: Ecbatana, where they are staying (v. 5), is nowhere near Rages, despite the proximity the narrative assumes.   **6:12** *According to the law . . . death*: the law in question is the levirate law described in Deut 25:5–10, where a death penalty is not mentioned. Also relevant is Num 36:1–12 (esp. v. 8), which specifies that a daughter receiving an inheritance from her father (Sarah has no siblings; see 3:15) must marry a member of her father's tribe, so that it may maintain control

¹³Then the young man answered the angel, I have heard, brother Azarias, that this maid hath been given to seven men, who all died in the marriage chamber. ¹⁴And now I am the only son of my father, and I am afraid, lest, if I go in unto her, I die, as the other before: for a wicked spirit loveth her, which hurteth no body, but those which come unto her: wherefore I also fear lest I die, and bring my father's and my mother's life, because of me, to the grave with sorrow: for they have no other son to bury them. ¹⁵Then the angel said unto him, Dost thou not remember the precepts which thy father gave thee, that thou shouldest marry a wife of thine own kindred? wherefore hear me, O my brother; for she shall be given thee to wife; and make thou no reckoning of the evil spirit; for this same night shall she be given thee in marriage. ¹⁶And when thou shalt come into the marriage chamber, thou shalt take the ashes of perfume, and shalt lay upon them some of the heart and liver of the fish, and shalt make a smoke with it: ¹⁷and the devil shall smell it, and flee away, and never come again any more: but when thou shalt come to her, rise up both of you, and pray to God which is merciful, who will have pity on you, and save you: fear not, for she is appointed unto thee from the beginning; and thou shalt preserve her, and she shall go with thee. Moreover I suppose that she shall bear thee children. Now when Tobias had heard these things, he loved her, and his heart was effectually joined to her.

7 And when they were come to Ecbatane, they came to the house of Raguel, and Sara met them: and after they had saluted one another, she brought them into the house. ²Then said Raguel to Edna his wife, How like is this young man to Tobit my cousin! ³And Raguel asked them, From whence are ye, brethren? To whom they said, We are of the sons of Nephthalim, which are captives in Nineve. ⁴Then he said to them, Do ye know Tobit our kinsman? And they said, We know him. Then said he, Is he in good health? ⁵And they said, He is both alive, and in good health: and Tobias said, He is my father. ⁶Then Raguel leaped up, and kissed him, and wept, ⁷and blessed him, and said unto him, Thou art the son of an honest and good man. But when he had heard that Tobit was blind, he was sorrowful, and wept. ⁸And likewise Edna his wife and Sara his daughter wept. Moreover they entertained them cheerfully; and after that they had killed a ram of the flock, they set store of meat on the table.

Then said Tobias to Raphael, Brother Azarias, speak of those things of which thou didst talk in the way, and let this business be dispatched. ⁹So he communicated the matter with Raguel: and Raguel said to Tobias, Eat and drink, and make merry: ¹⁰for it is meet that thou shouldest marry my daughter: nevertheless I will declare unto thee the truth. ¹¹I have given my daughter in marriage to seven men, who died

---

of the inheritance.   **6:14** *I am afraid . . . come unto her*: cf. Gen 38:11. *Bring my father's . . . sorrow*: echoing Sarah's prayer in 3:10. Tobias's resistance to marrying Sarah ironically assimilates him to her.   **6:15** *Make thou no reckoning of*: do not have a thought about.   **6:16** *Ashes of perfume*: "embers of incense" (NRSV).

7:1–18 The wedding of Tobias and Sarah.   **7:9–10** *Eat and drink . . . daughter*: in light of what Raguel expects to happen if Tobias does marry Sarah, this may macabrely echo Isa 22:13: "let us eat

that night they came in unto her: nevertheless for the present be merry. But Tobias said, I will eat nothing here, till we agree and swear one to another. ¹²Raguel said, Then take her from henceforth according to the manner, for thou art her cousin, and she is thine, and the merciful God give you good success in all things.

¹³Then he called his daughter Sara, and she came to her father, and he took her by the hand, and gave her to be wife to Tobias, saying, Behold, take her after the law of Moses, and lead her away to thy father. And he blessed them; ¹⁴and called Edna his wife, and took paper, and did write an instrument of covenants, and sealed it. ¹⁵Then they began to eat. ¹⁶After Raguel called his wife Edna, and said unto her, Sister, prepare another chamber, and bring her in thither. ¹⁷Which when she had done as he had bidden her, she brought her thither: and she wept, and she received the tears of her daughter, and said unto her, ¹⁸Be of good comfort, my daughter; the Lord of heaven and earth give thee joy for this thy sorrow: be of good comfort, my daughter.

8 And when they had supped, they brought Tobias in unto her. ²And as he went, he remembered the words of Raphael, and took the ashes of the perfumes, and put the heart and the liver of the fish thereupon, and made a smoke therewith. ³The which smell when the evil spirit had smelled, he fled into the utmost parts of Egypt, and the angel bound him. ⁴And after that they were both shut in together, Tobias rose out of the bed, and said, Sister, arise, and let us pray that God would have pity on us.

⁵Then began Tobias to say, Blessed art thou, O God of our fathers, and blessed is thy holy and glorious name for ever; let the heavens bless thee, and all thy creatures. ⁶Thou madest Adam, and gavest him Eve his wife for an helper and stay: of them came mankind: thou hast said, It is not good that man should be alone; let us make unto him an aid like unto himself. ⁷And now, O Lord, I take not this my sister for lust, but uprightly: therefore mercifully ordain that we may become aged together. ⁸And she said with him, Amen. ⁹So they slept both that night.

And Raguel arose, and went and made a grave, ¹⁰saying, I fear lest he also be dead. ¹¹But when Raguel was come into his house, ¹²he said unto his wife Edna, Send one of the maids, and let her see whether he be alive: if he be not, that we may bury him, and no man know it. ¹³So the maid opened the door, and went in, and found them both asleep, ¹⁴and came forth, and told them that he was alive.

¹⁵Then Raguel praised God, and said, O God, thou art worthy to be praised with all pure and holy praise; therefore let thy saints praise thee with all thy creatures; and let all thine angels and thine elect praise thee for ever. ¹⁶Thou art to be praised, for thou hast made me joyful; and that is not come to me which I suspected; but thou hast dealt with us according to thy great mercy. ¹⁷Thou art to be praised, because thou hast had mercy of two that were the only begotten children

---

and drink; for tomorrow we shall die." **7:12** *Manner*: Gk. *krisis*, "judgment" or "decree," which is explained in the reference to the "law of Moses" (v. 13). On the laws in question, see 6:12 note. **7:14** *Instrument of covenants*: the Greek refers to a marriage contract.

8:1–18 The exorcism of Asmodeus. **8:3** *The utmost parts of Egypt*: the desert country of south Egypt, in accordance with demons' supposed preference for dry places (see Matt 12:43 and note). **8:6** *Stay*: support. *It is not good . . . unto himself*: Gen 2:18.

of their fathers: grant them mercy, O Lord, and finish their life in health with joy and mercy. [18]Then Raguel bade his servants to fill the grave.

[19]And he kept the wedding feast fourteen days. [20]For before the days of the marriage were finished, Raguel had said unto him by an oath, that he should not depart till the fourteen days of the marriage were expired; [21]and then he should take the half of his goods, and go in safety to his father; and should have the rest when I and my wife be dead.

9 Then Tobias called Raphael, and said unto him, [2]Brother Azarias, take with thee a servant, and two camels, and go to Rages of Media to Gabael, and bring me the money, and bring him to the wedding. [3]For Raguel hath sworn that I shall not depart. [4]But my father counteth the days; and if I tarry long, he will be very sorry. [5]So Raphael went out, and lodged with Gabael, and gave him the handwriting: who brought forth bags which were sealed up, and gave them to him. [6]And early in the morning they went forth both together, and came to the wedding: and Tobias blessed his wife.

10 Now Tobit his father counted every day: and when the days of the journey were expired, and they came not, [2]then Tobit said, Are they detained? or is Gabael dead, and there is no man to give him the money? [3]Therefore he was very sorry. [4]Then his wife said unto him, My son is dead, seeing he stayeth long; and she began to bewail him, and said, [5]Now I care for nothing, my son, since I have let thee go, the light of mine eyes. [6]To whom Tobit said, Hold thy peace, take no care, for he is safe. [7]But she said, Hold thy peace, and deceive me not; my son is dead. And she went out every day into the way which they went, and did eat no meat on the daytime, and ceased not whole nights to bewail her son Tobias, until the fourteen days of the wedding were expired, which Raguel had sworn that he should spend there.

Then Tobias said to Raguel, Let me go, for my father and my mother look no more to see me. [8]But his father in law said unto him, Tarry with me, and I will send to thy father, and they shall declare unto him how things go with thee. [9]But Tobias said, No; but let me go to my father. [10]Then Raguel arose, and gave him Sara his wife, and half his goods, servants, and cattle, and money: [11]and he blessed them, and sent them away, saying, The God of heaven give you a prosperous journey, my children. [12]And he said to his daughter, Honour thy father and thy mother in law, which are now thy parents, that I may hear good report of thee.

8:18 *Then Raguel . . . grave*: recalling Tobit's burial of the dead earlier in the story and signaling that his pious deeds, despite the initial hardships they occasioned, have finally been rewarded.
    8:19–10:12 Tobias's celebration and Tobit's distress. The two scenes are ironically juxtaposed: Tobias is delayed because of a wedding celebration, but Tobit and his wife suspect disaster. **9:2–4** *Brother Azarias . . . sorry*: Tobias's words recall Saul's to his servant at 1 Sam 9:5, though Tobias's are far more authoritative, especially when contrasted with his earlier deference to Azarias. **9:5** *The handwriting*: see 5:3 note. **10:4–7** *Then his wife . . . her son Tobias*: compare Tobit and Anna's exchange just before Tobias departed (5:17–22). There, in response to Tobit's encouragement, Anna "made an end of weeping" (5:22); now, depressed and resentful, she will not be consoled (10:7). **10:8** *Tarry with me*: Raguel's excessive hospitality recalls that of the father of the Levite's concubine in Judg 19:1–10, who also seemed reluctant (though ominously so) to let his daughter depart with her husband. **10:12** *Honour thy father . . . parents*: again, the fifth commandment (cf. 4:3).

And he kissed her. Edna also said to Tobias, The Lord of heaven restore thee, my dear brother, and grant that I may see thy children of my daughter Sara before I die, that I may rejoice before the Lord: behold, I commit my daughter unto thee of special trust; wherefore do not entreat her evil.

11 After these things Tobias went his way, praising God that he had given him a prosperous journey, and blessed Raguel and Edna his wife, and went on his way till they drew near unto Nineve. ²Then Raphael said to Tobias, Thou knowest, brother, how thou didst leave thy father: ³let us haste before thy wife, and prepare the house. ⁴And take in thine hand the gall of the fish. So they went their way, and the dog went after them.

⁵Now Anna sat looking about toward the way for her son. ⁶And when she espied him coming, she said to his father, Behold, thy son cometh, and the man that went with him.

⁷Then said Raphael, I know, Tobias, that thy father will open his eyes. ⁸Therefore anoint thou his eyes with the gall, and being pricked therewith, he shall rub, and the whiteness shall fall away, and he shall see thee.

⁹Then Anna ran forth, and fell upon the neck of her son, and said unto him, Seeing I have seen thee, my son, from henceforth I am content to die. And they wept both. ¹⁰Tobit also went forth toward the door, and stumbled: but his son ran unto him, ¹¹and took hold of his father: and he strake of the gall on his father's eyes, saying, Be of good hope, my father. ¹²And when his eyes began to smart, he rubbed them; ¹³and the whiteness pilled away from the corners of his eyes: and when he saw his son, he fell upon his neck. ¹⁴And he wept, and said, Blessed art thou, O God, and blessed is thy name for ever; and blessed are all thine holy angels: ¹⁵for thou hast scourged, and hast taken pity on me: for, behold, I see my son Tobias. And his son went in rejoicing, and told his father the great things that had happened to him in Media.

¹⁶Then Tobit went out to meet his daughter in law at the gate of Nineve, rejoicing, and praising God: and they which saw him go marvelled, because he had received his sight. ¹⁷But Tobit gave thanks before them, because God had mercy on him. And when he came near to Sara his daughter in law, he blessed her, saying, Thou art welcome, daughter: God be blessed, which hath brought thee unto us, and blessed be thy father and thy mother. And there was joy among all his brethren which were at Nineve. ¹⁸And Achiacharus, and Nasbas his brother's son, came: ¹⁹and Tobias' wedding was kept seven days with great joy.

Restore: bring back. *Entreat her evil*: lit. "cause her grief."
    11:1–19 The restoration of Tobit's sight prefigures the manifestation of God's providential plan to the story's characters.   **11:4** *The dog went after them*: Tobias's dog, also mentioned at the journey's outset (5:16), reminds many readers of Odysseus's faithful dog Argos; perhaps for that reason Jerome in his Latin translation adds the detail that when Tobias's dog returned to Tobit's home, "it rejoiced by wagging its tail" (11:9; cf. Homer, *Odyssey* 17.302).   **11:9** *Seeing I . . . die*: echoing Jacob's words to Joseph in Gen 46:30.   **11:11** *Strake of*: smeared.   **11:13** *Pilled*: peeled.   **11:18** *Nasbas*: in the Tale of Ahiqar, Ahiqar's (i.e., Achiacharus's) nephew is Nadim; cf. 1:21 and note.

12 Then Tobit called his son Tobias, and said unto him, My son, see that the man have his wages, which went with thee, and thou must give him more. [2]And Tobias said unto him, O father, it is no harm to me to give him half of those things which I have brought: [3]for he hath brought me again to thee in safety, and made whole my wife, and brought me the money, and likewise healed thee. [4]Then the old man said, It is due unto him. [5]So he called the angel, and he said unto him, Take half of all that ye have brought, and go away in safety.

[6]Then he took them both apart, and said unto them, Bless God, praise him, and magnify him, and praise him for the things which he hath done unto you in the sight of all that live. It is good to praise God, and exalt his name, and honourably to shew forth the works of God; therefore be not slack to praise him. [7]It is good to keep close the secret of a king, but it is honourable to reveal the works of God. Do that which is good, and no evil shall touch you. [8]Prayer is good with fasting and alms and righteousness. A little with righteousness is better than much with unrighteousness. It is better to give alms than to lay up gold: [9]for alms doth deliver from death, and shall purge away all sin. Those that exercise alms and righteousness shall be filled with life: [10]but they that sin are enemies to their own life.

[11]Surely I will keep close nothing from you. For I said, It was good to keep close the secret of a king, but that it was honourable to reveal the works of God. [12]Now therefore, when thou didst pray, and Sara thy daughter in law, I did bring the remembrance of your prayers before the Holy One: and when thou didst bury the dead, I was with thee likewise. [13]And when thou didst not delay to rise up, and leave thy dinner, to go and cover the dead, thy good deed was not hid from me: but I was with thee. [14]And now God hath sent me to heal thee and Sara thy daughter in law. [15]I am Raphael, one of the seven holy angels, which present the prayers of the saints, and which go in and out before the glory of the Holy One.

[16]Then they were both troubled, and fell upon their faces: for they feared. [17]But he said unto them, Fear not, for it shall go well with you; praise God therefore. [18]For not of any favour of mine, but by the will of our God I came; wherefore praise him for ever. [19]All these days I did appear unto you; but I did neither eat nor drink, but ye did see a vision. [20]Now therefore give God thanks: for I go up to him that sent me; but write all things which are done in a book. [21]And when they arose, they saw him no more. [22]Then they confessed the great and wonderful works of God, and how the angel of the Lord had appeared unto them.

12:1–22 The revelation of Raphael's identity. Integrated into this section of the narrative is a didactic passage echoing biblical Wisdom literature (vv. 6–11) and framed by declarations that it is honorable to reveal God's works. This teaching contains several points of contact with the narrative's events, and Raphael draws attention to a number of them. **12:3** *Whole*: healthy. **12:6** *Then he* [Raphael] *took them both apart*: although the narrative calls little attention to it, commentators note the distance Raphael places between himself and the story's female characters (see also 11:3), perhaps to remove the temptation that overcame Asmodeus; see 1 Cor 11:10 and note. **12:9** *Alms doth deliver from death*: see 4:9–10 and note. **12:15** *The seven holy angels*: cf. Rev 1:4 and note. *Which present . . . saints*: cf. Rev 8:4. **12:19** *I did appear . . . vision*: angels supposedly did not eat (cf. Judg 13:16; Luke 24:36–43, where the risen Jesus eats to demonstrate his physicality). **12:20** *But write . . . book*: epiphanies often include such a command; cf. Jer 30:2; Hab 2:2; Rev 1:11, 19; etc.

13 Then Tobit wrote a prayer of rejoicing, and said, Blessed be God that liveth for ever, and blessed be his kingdom. ²For he doth scourge, and hath mercy: he leadeth down to hell, and bringeth up again: neither is there any that can avoid his hand.

³Confess him before the Gentiles, ye children of Israel: for he hath scattered us among them. ⁴There declare his greatness, and extol him before all the living: for he is our Lord, and he is the God our Father for ever. ⁵And he will scourge us for our iniquities, and will have mercy again, and will gather us out of all nations, among whom he hath scattered us. ⁶If ye turn to him with your whole heart, and with your whole mind, and deal uprightly before him, then will he turn unto you, and will not hide his face from you. Therefore see what he will do with you, and confess him with your whole mouth, and praise the Lord of might, and extol the everlasting King. In the land of my captivity do I praise him, and declare his might and majesty to a sinful nation. O ye sinners, turn and do justice before him: who can tell if he will accept you, and have mercy on you? ⁷I will extol my God, and my soul shall praise the King of heaven, and shall rejoice in his greatness.

⁸Let all men speak, and let all praise him for his righteousness. ⁹O Jerusalem, the holy city, he will scourge thee for thy children's works, and will have mercy again on the sons of the righteous. ¹⁰Give praise to the Lord, for he is good: and praise the everlasting King, that his tabernacle may be builded in thee again with joy, and let him make joyful there in thee those that are captives, and love in thee for ever those that are miserable. ¹¹Many nations shall come from far to the name of the Lord God with gifts in their hands, even gifts to the King of heaven; all generations shall praise thee with great joy. ¹²Cursed are all they which hate thee, and blessed shall all be which love thee for ever. ¹³Rejoice and be glad for the children of the just: for they shall be gathered together, and shall bless the Lord of the just. ¹⁴O blessed are they which love thee, for they shall rejoice in thy peace: blessed are they which have been sorrowful for all thy scourges; for they shall rejoice for thee, when they have seen all thy glory, and shall be glad for ever. ¹⁵Let my soul bless God the great King. ¹⁶For Jerusalem shall be built up with sapphires, and emeralds, and precious stone: thy walls and towers and battlements with pure gold. ¹⁷And the streets of Jerusalem shall be paved with

13:1–18 Tobit's Prayer is a highly polished composition, perhaps originally used in a Jewish liturgy known by Tobit's author. Like other prayers in Tobit, its language is conventional, often recalling the Psalms and other biblical literature, but unlike them it lacks specific references to the narrative's events. Instead it gestures at thematic links between them and the collective exilic experience on which it meditates, implying an analogy between the suffering and deliverance of Tobit and Sarah and that of Israel in exile and restoration. **13:2** *Hell:* Gk. *hadēs* (see Matt 11:23 note). Some see a reference here to the belief in eschatological resurrection, an attractive possibility in light of the image of an eschatologically renewed Jerusalem that closes the prayer (vv. 16–17). But it is also possible that *leadeth down to hell, and bringeth up again* is symbolic (cf. Ezek 37:1–14 and notes). **13:3–7** *Confess him . . . greatness:* recalling the prophecies of Israel's exile and return in Deuteronomy (e.g., 4:27–31; 30:1–5) and elsewhere. **13:11** *Many nations . . . heaven:* cf. Zech 8:20–23; 14:16. **13:16–17** *For Jerusalem . . . Ophir:* for related images of the eschatologically renewed Jerusalem,

beryl and carbuncle and stones of Ophir. ¹⁸And all her streets shall say, Alleluia; and they shall praise him, saying, Blessed be God, which hath extolled it for ever.

14 So Tobit made an end of praising God. ²And he was eight and fifty years old when he lost his sight, which was restored to him after eight years: and he gave alms, and he increased in the fear of the Lord God, and praised him.

³And when he was very aged, he called his son, and the six sons of his son, and said to him, My son, take thy children; for, behold, I am aged, and am ready to depart out of this life. ⁴Go into Media, my son, for I surely believe those things which Jonas the prophet spake of Nineve, that it shall be overthrown; and that for a time peace shall rather be in Media; and that our brethren shall lie scattered in the earth from that good land: and Jerusalem shall be desolate, and the house of God in it shall be burned, and shall be desolate for a time; ⁵and that again God will have mercy on them, and bring them again into the land, where they shall build a temple, but not like to the first, until the time of that age be fulfilled; and afterward they shall return from all places of their captivity, and build up Jerusalem gloriously, and the house of God shall be built in it for ever with a glorious building, as the prophets have spoken thereof. ⁶And all nations shall turn, and fear the Lord God truly, and shall bury their idols. ⁷So shall all nations praise the Lord, and his people shall confess God, and the Lord shall exalt his people; and all those which love the Lord God in truth and justice shall rejoice, shewing mercy to our brethren.

⁸And now, my son, depart out of Nineve, because that those things which the prophet Jonas spake shall surely come to pass. ⁹But keep thou the law and the commandments, and shew thyself merciful and just, that it may go well with thee. ¹⁰And bury me decently, and thy mother with me; but tarry no longer at Nineve. Remember, my son, how Aman handled Achiacharus that brought him up, how out of light he brought him into darkness, and how he rewarded him again: yet Achiacharus was saved, but the other had his reward: for he went down into darkness. Manasses gave alms, and escaped the snares of death which they

---

see Isa 54:11–14; Rev 21:2–22:5.   **13:17** *Ophir*: an unidentified nation renowned in the Bible for exporting gold, jewels, and the like.   **13:18** *Alleluia*: see Ps 104:35 note.

14:1–15 Tobit's testament. Actually Tobit's second testament (see chap. 4) or farewell discourse. (For the conventions of this genre, see the introduction to 2 Timothy.) Its prophecies of Jerusalem's destruction, the Southern Kingdom's exile, the exiles' return, and the reconstruction of the temple recall the book's opening (1:1–9), which similarly emphasizes national exile and the centrality of the temple cult. But this closing, like the prayer that immediately precedes it, blends historical matters with eschatological ones—in particular, the new Jerusalem at which all nations shall worship.   **14:4** *Which Jonas . . . Nineve*: Codex Sinaiticus attributes the prophecy not to Jonah but to Nahum. The eponymous biblical book constitutes an extended oracle of Nineveh's doom. *And Jerusalem . . . time*: a reference to Babylon's conquest of the Southern Kingdom, destruction of Jerusalem and its temple, and ultimate deportation of the population. Jerusalem fell in 586 B.C.E.   **14:10** *Aman*: unknown; Codex Sinaiticus gives a form of Nasbas (Nadim; see 1:21–22; 11:18 and notes). *Rewarded him again*: i.e., "repaid him." *Manasses*: this reference is obscure. Since Tobit seems to continue speaking of Ahiqar, it is possible that "Manasses" is a hellenized corruption of an Aramaic

had set for him: but Aman fell into the snare, and perished. ¹¹Wherefore now, my son, consider what alms doeth, and how righteousness doth deliver.

When he had said these things, he gave up the ghost in the bed, being an hundred and eight and fifty years old; and he buried him honourably. ¹²And when Anna his mother was dead, he buried her with his father. But Tobias departed with his wife and children to Ecbatane to Raguel his father in law, ¹³where he became old with honour, and he buried his father and mother in law honourably, and he inherited their substance, and his father Tobit's. ¹⁴And he died at Ecbatane in Media, being an hundred and seven and twenty years old. ¹⁵But before he died he heard of the destruction of Nineve, which was taken by Nabuchodonosor and Assuerus: and before his death he rejoiced over Nineve.

---

word (referring to Ahiqar) that means "his benefactor." **14:11** *Gave up the ghost*: lit. "his life left him." **14:15** *Nabuchodonosor and Assuerus*: in fact Nabopolassar (father of Nebuchadnezzar II) destroyed Nineveh, the capital of Assyria, in cooperation with Cyaxares of Media in 612 B.C.E.; Ahasuerus, who appears in Esther and is commonly identified with one or another Persian ruler, likewise had nothing to do with Nineveh's destruction.

Judith

JUDITH declares itself to be more story than history from its opening verse, which makes Nebuchadnezzar Assyria's ruler rather than Babylon's and identifies the city from which he reigns as Nineveh—destroyed several years before the book's events supposedly take place. Judith's geography is hardly less confused than its history: even when the action occurs in presumably familiar Judea, most of the cities (and characters) named turn out to be unidentifiable. The book's numerous "errors" are so glaring that they could only have been planted deliberately, inviting the reader to approach the story as edifying fiction rather than as a record of actual events. More specifically, Judith's salvation of her nation from the army commanded by Nebuchadnezzar's general Holofernes purportedly takes place in 587 B.C.E. (see 1:13 note), precisely when the Southern Kingdom actually fell to Babylon. Judith, then, anticipates a trope of contemporary science fiction by offering an alternative history: it takes place in a kind of parallel universe, with both similarities to and crucial differences from our own. Most significantly, in Judith's world the faithfulness of an independent heroine saves Judah from the devastation it experienced at the hands of Babylon in the universe that Judith's readers inhabit. In this book the nation's devastation is only a vague memory (5:18–19; 8:19; cf. 4:3) or an unrealized threat.

The most ancient version of Judith that survives is apparently a Greek translation of an original Hebrew composition, no longer extant. The book was composed during Hellenistic times, perhaps as late as the Maccabean period, in the mid- to late second century B.C.E. Its inclusion in the Septuagint suggests that some Greek-speaking Jews viewed it as Scripture, but it was not included in the Hebrew Bible; many ancient Christians—including such authorities as Origen and Athanasius—followed the lead of Palestinian Jews in rejecting it. Its exclusion from the canon is an interesting phenomenon, particularly in contrast to the inclusion of Esther and Ruth, both of which have much in common with Judith. Some speculate that specific elements such as the book's generally positive view of Samaritans, or approval of an Ammonite's conversion, or even its supposed historical inaccuracy might have rendered it unacceptable to the scholars responsible for the shape of the Hebrew Bible, but similar "problem passages" may be found in any number of canonical books. The decisive factor in relegating Judith to the margins may instead be its peculiar representation of feminine power. Certainly, the story is designed to set masculine weakness against female strength, as its overall structure strikingly reveals. For most of the book's first half, the masculine world of Nebuchadnezzar and Holofernes controls everything and military strength rules all. Then, with Judith's entrance into the narrative at the beginning of chapter 8, beauty takes over and eventually overcomes, as one woman's arm annihilates the whole army of Holofernes. The decisive image is presented at 14:6, where Achior, the man who has come out of the warrior world of Holofernes, faints at the sight of the general's head, which Judith has cut off.

This image is not just shocking but complex. Judith, who has been an object of men's ogling ever since she discarded her widow's garb to dress beautifully for Holofernes, had armed herself with Holofernes' own sword and decapitated him in the bed in which he had intended to have his way with her (a heroic act designed to recall David's slaughter of Goliath). Now, back in Bethulia, she holds his head out for her countrymen to gaze on (13:15) and causes Achior to see it as well (14:6). She has become the warrior and Holofernes the object of the gaze, a reversal signaled by Judith's swift transformation into a general who concocts a military strategy to defeat Holofernes' now leaderless army. Judith may start out as a conventional heroine drawing on the traditional feminine weapons of beauty, seduction, and deceit, but she ultimately transcends that stereotype to become a surprisingly masculine hero, as the book's final insistence on her perpetual chastity underscores: Judith will submit to no man's authority, only to the authority of God. Without a Mordecai to guide her, and with no Boaz into whose arms to fall, Judith points to a female independence that strongly patriarchal societies are likely to find disturbing. Perhaps the location of the book's action in a kind of parallel universe amounts to tacit recognition by the author that there is really no place for Judith in the world in which most other biblical narratives are set.

For detailed exposition of Judith, the reader can consult Carey A. Moore's Anchor Bible commentary, *Judith: A New Translation with Introduction and Commentary* (Garden City, NY: Doubleday, 1985), which influences this introduction and the annotations that follow.

Judith

1 In the twelfth year of the reign of Nabuchodonosor, who reigned in Nineve, the great city; in the days of Arphaxad, which reigned over the Medes in Ecbatane, ²and built in Ecbatane walls round about of stones hewn three cubits broad and six cubits long, and made the height of the wall seventy cubits, and the breadth thereof fifty cubits: ³and set the towers thereof upon the gates of it, an hundred cubits high, and the breadth thereof in the foundation threescore cubits: ⁴and he made the gates thereof, even gates that were raised to the height of seventy cubits, and the breadth of them was forty cubits, for the going forth of his mighty armies, and for the setting in array of his footmen: ⁵even in those days king Nabuchodonosor made war with king Arphaxad in the great plain, which is the plain in the borders of Ragau. ⁶And there came unto him all they that dwelt in the hill country, and all that dwelt by Euphrates, and Tigris, and Hydaspes, and the plain of Arioch the king of the Elymeans, and very many nations of the sons of Chelod, assembled themselves to the battle.

⁷Then Nabuchodonosor king of the Assyrians sent unto all that dwelt in Persia, and to all that dwelt westward, and to those that dwelt in Cilicia, and Damascus, and Libanus, and Antilibanus, and to all that dwelt upon the sea coast, ⁸and to those among the nations that were of Carmel, and Galaad, and the higher Galilee, and the great plain of Esdrelom, ⁹and to all that were in Samaria and the cities thereof, and beyond Jordan unto Jerusalem, and Betane, and Chellus, and Kades, and the river of Egypt, and Taphnes, and Ramesse, and all the land of Gesem, ¹⁰until ye come beyond Tanis and Memphis, and to all the inhabitants of Egypt, until ye come to the borders of Ethiopia. ¹¹But all the inhabitants of the land made light of the commandment of Nabuchodonosor king of the Assyrians, neither went they with him to the battle; for they were not afraid of him: yea, he was before them as one man, and they sent away his ambassadors from them without effect, and with disgrace. ¹²Therefore Nabuchodonosor was very angry

---

1:1–16 Nebuchadnezzar defeats Arphaxad without the support of the western nations. This section not only gives the (supposedly) historical setting for the story but also emphasizes the overwhelming strength of the forces that will turn on Israel.   **1:1** *In the twelfth year . . . Ecbatane*: Nebuchadnezzar II ruled Babylon 515/4–562 B.C.E. (Alongside Media, Babylon destroyed Nineveh, Assyria's capital city, in 612.) *Arphaxad* is unidentifiable and probably a fictional character.   **1:2** *Cubits*: a cubit was about eighteen inches.   **1:5** *Ragau*: Rages, another city in Media.   **1:6** *Hydaspes*: unlike the Tigris and Euphrates, in Mesopotamia, this river was in India. *Elymeans*: inhabitants of Elam, south of Media. *Sons of Chelod*: i.e., Chaldeans, or Babylonians.   **1:7–10** *Persia . . . Ethiopia*: the nations listed here cover much of the Middle East and Africa.   **1:11** *All the inhabitants . . . land*: i.e., the western region, as far south as Egypt and as far north as Cilicia (see v. 12; 2:6, 19, etc.). *Without effect*: empty-handed.

with all this country, and sware by his throne and kingdom, that he would surely be avenged upon all those coasts of Cilicia, and Damascus, and Syria, and that he would slay with the sword all the inhabitants of the land of Moab, and the children of Ammon, and all Judea, and all that were in Egypt, till ye come to the borders of the two seas.

¹³Then he marched in battle array with his power against king Arphaxad in the seventeenth year, and he prevailed in his battle: for he overthrew all the power of Arphaxad, and all his horsemen, and all his chariots, ¹⁴and became lord of his cities, and came unto Ecbatane, and took the towers, and spoiled the streets thereof, and turned the beauty thereof into shame. ¹⁵He took also Arphaxad in the mountains of Ragau, and smote him through with his darts, and destroyed him utterly that day. ¹⁶So he returned afterward to Nineve, both he and all his company of sundry nations, being a very great multitude of men of war, and there he took his ease, and banqueted, both he and his army, an hundred and twenty days.

2 And in the eighteenth year, the two and twentieth day of the first month, there was talk in the house of Nabuchodonosor king of the Assyrians, that he should, as he said, avenge himself on all the earth. ²So he called unto him all his officers, and all his nobles, and communicated with them his secret counsel, and concluded the afflicting of the whole earth out of his own mouth. ³Then they decreed to destroy all flesh, that did not obey the commandment of his mouth.

⁴And when he had ended his counsel, Nabuchodonosor king of the Assyrians called Holofernes the chief captain of his army, which was next unto him, and said onto him, ⁵Thus saith the great king, the lord of the whole earth, Behold, thou shalt go forth from my presence, and take with thee men that trust in their own strength, of footmen an hundred and twenty thousand; and the number of horses with their riders twelve thousand. ⁶And thou shalt go against all the west country, because they disobeyed my commandment. ⁷And thou shalt declare unto them, that they prepare for me earth and water: for I will go forth in my wrath against them, and will cover the whole face of the earth with the feet of mine army, and I will give them for a spoil unto them: ⁸so that their slain shall fill their valleys and brooks, and the river shall be filled with their dead, till it overflow: ⁹and I will lead them captives to the utmost parts of all the earth. ¹⁰Thou therefore shalt go forth,

---

1:12 *The two seas*: obscure; many commentators infer the Mediterranean and the Red Sea.   **1:13** *The seventeenth year*: i.e., of Nebuchadnezzar's reign: 587/6, the year that Nebuchadnezzar in fact laid siege to Jerusalem before destroying it and its temple—perhaps suggesting that Judith be read as an alternative history.   **1:14** *And turned . . . shame*: a significant phrase, since the rest of the book shows how beauty, in the form of Judith, turns Nebuchadnezzar's empire into shame.   **1:15** *Darts*: spears.

2:1–3:10 Holofernes invades the western nations. This is a swift-moving narrative, reinforcing the reader's perception of the power of Nebuchadnezzar's forces. Its reckless handling of geographical detail is striking.   **2:1** *Earth*: better "land" (also in v. 2, as at 1:11; see note).   **2:4** *Holofernes*: a fictional figure.   **2:5** *The lord . . . strength*: Nebuchadnezzar's speech is shot through with impious arrogance, often appropriating biblical language normally reserved for God: here he speaks of himself in terms appropriate to YHWH (cf. Pss 24:1; 47:2; etc.) and values hubristic self-reliance in his warriors (cf. Isa 12:2; 26:4; etc.). His impiety peaks at 3:8.   **2:7** *Prepare for me . . . water*: a symbolic gesture of capitulation required by Persian kings of nations they dominated (cf. Herodotus 6.48).   **2:8** *Their slain . . . overflow*: echoing God's threat in Ezek 35:8.

and take beforehand for me all their coasts: and if they will yield themselves unto thee, thou shalt reserve them for me till the day of their punishment. [11]But concerning them that rebel, let not thine eye spare them; but put them to the slaughter, and spoil them wheresoever thou goest. [12]For as I live, and by the power of my kingdom, whatsoever I have spoken, that will I do by mine hand. [13]And take thou heed that thou transgress none of the commandments of thy lord, but accomplish them fully, as I have commanded thee, and defer not to do them.

[14]Then Holofernes went forth from the presence of his lord, and called all the governors and captains, and the officers of the army of Assur; [15]and he mustered the chosen men for the battle, as his lord had commanded him, unto an hundred and twenty thousand, and twelve thousand archers on horseback; [16]and he ranged them, as a great army is ordered for the war. [17]And he took camels and asses for their carriages, a very great number; and sheep and oxen and goats without number for their provision: [18]and plenty of victual for every man of the army, and very much gold and silver out of the king's house.

[19]Then he went forth and all his power to go before king Nabuchodonosor in the voyage, and to cover all the face of the earth westward with their chariots, and horsemen, and their chosen footmen. [20]A great number also of sundry countries came with them like locusts, and like the sand of the earth: for the multitude was without number.

[21]And they went forth of Nineve three days' journey toward the plain of Bectileth, and pitched from Bectileth near the mountain which is at the left hand of the upper Cilicia. [22]Then he took all his army, his footmen, and horsemen, and chariots, and went from thence into the hill country; [23]and destroyed Phud and Lud, and spoiled all the children of Rasses, and the children of Ismael, which were toward the wilderness at the south of the land of the Chellians. [24]Then he went over Euphrates, and went through Mesopotamia, and destroyed all the high cities that were upon the river Arbonai, till ye come to the sea. [25]And he took the borders of Cilicia, and killed all that resisted him, and came to the borders of Japheth, which were toward the south, over against Arabia. [26]He compassed also all the children of Madian, and burned up their tabernacles, and spoiled their sheepcotes. [27]Then he went down into the plain of Damascus in the time of wheat harvest, and burnt up all their fields, and destroyed their flocks and herds, also he spoiled their cities, and utterly wasted their countries, and smote all their young men with the edge of the sword.

[28]Therefore the fear and dread of him fell upon all the inhabitants of the sea coasts, which were in Sidon and Tyrus, and them that dwelt in Sur and Ocina, 3 and all that dwelt in Jemnaan; and they that dwelt in Azotus and Ascalon feared him greatly. [1]So they sent ambassadors unto him to treat of peace,

---

2:10 *Coasts*: regions.   2:12 *Whatsoever I . . . hand*: again echoing God's words in Ezekiel (24:14).   2:14 *Assur*: Assyria (so throughout).   2:21–27 *And they . . . sword*: apparently Holofernes marches with Nebuchadnezzar's army west from Assyria to Cilicia (although the journey could not be accomplished in three days), and then south to Syria, bringing destruction in his wake. But the geography is perplexing, and many of the locations are unidentifiable.   2:26 *Tabernacles*: tents. *Sheepcotes*: sheepfolds.   2:28 *Inhabitants*

saying, [2]Behold, we the servants of Nabuchodonosor the great king lie before thee; use us as shall be good in thy sight. [3]Behold, our houses, and all our places, and all our fields of wheat, and flocks, and herds, and all the lodges of our tents, lie before thy face; use them as it pleaseth thee. [4]Behold, even our cities and the inhabitants thereof are thy servants; come and deal with them as seemeth good unto thee. [5]So the men came to Holofernes, and declared unto him after this manner.

[6]Then came he down toward the sea coast, both he and his army, and set garrisons in the high cities, and took out of them chosen men for aid. [7]So they and all the country round about received them with garlands, with dances, and with timbrels. [8]Yet he did cast down their frontiers, and cut down their groves: for he had decreed to destroy all the gods of the land, that all nations should worship Nabuchodonosor only, and that all tongues and tribes should call upon him as god. [9]Also he came over against Esdraelon near unto Judea, over against the great strait of Judea. [10]And he pitched between Geba and Scythopolis, and there he tarried a whole month, that he might gather together all the carriages of his army.

4 Now the children of Israel, that dwelt in Judea, heard all that Holofernes the chief captain of Nabuchodonosor king of the Assyrians had done to the nations, and after what manner he had spoiled all their temples, and brought them to nought. [2]Therefore they were exceedingly afraid of him, and were troubled for Jerusalem, and for the temple of the Lord their God: [3]for they were newly returned from the captivity, and all the people of Judea were lately gathered together: and the vessels, and the altar, and the house, were sanctified after the profanation. [4]Therefore they sent into all the coasts of Samaria, and the villages, and to Bethoron, and Belmen, and Jericho, and to Choba, and Esora, and to the valley of Salem: [5]and possessed themselves beforehand of all the tops of the high mountains, and fortified the villages that were in them, and laid up victuals for the provision of war: for their fields were of late reaped.

[6]Also Joacim the high priest, which was in those days in Jerusalem, wrote to them that dwelt in Bethulia, and Betomestham, which is over against Esdraelon toward the open country, near to Dothaim, [7]charging them to keep the passages of the hill country: for by them there was an entrance into Judea, and it was easy to stop them that would come up, because the passage was strait, for two men at the most. [8]And the children of Israel did as Joacim the high priest had commanded them, with the ancients of all the people of Israel, which dwelt at Jerusalem.

---

of the sea coasts: Phoenicians and Philistines.   **3:2** *Servants*: Gk. *paides*, slaves (so throughout).   **3:8** *Frontiers*: i.e., borders; the Syriac version reads "shrines." *Groves*: see 1 Kgs 14:15 note. *That all nations . . . god*: this resembles monarchical ideology of ancient Egypt and of Egypt's later Hellenic rulers.   **3:9–10** *He came . . . Scythopolis*: Holofernes now marches east from the Mediterranean coast to Judea.   **3:9** *Unto Judea*: better "unto Dothan" (MS tradition).

4:1–15 Judea asks for God's help.   4:3 *They were . . . captivity*: the chronology is as confused as the geography. The exile began when the events of Judith are supposed to have taken place (see 1:13 note), and the return occurred much later, after Persia had conquered the Babylonian Empire.   **4:6** *Bethulia*: the center of action in Judith; like many cities in this book's Judea, it is unidentified and probably fictitious.   **4:7** *Keep the passages*: hold the passes.   **4:8** *The ancients*: Gk. *gerousia*, a council of elders, though none is elsewhere attested for this period.

⁹Then every man of Israel cried to God with great fervency, and with great vehemency did they humble their souls: ¹⁰both they, and their wives, and their children, and their cattle, and every stranger and hireling, and their servants bought with money, put sackcloth upon their loins. ¹¹Thus every man and woman, and the little children, and the inhabitants of Jerusalem, fell before the temple, and cast ashes upon their heads, and spread out their sackcloth before the face of the Lord: also they put sackcloth about the altar, ¹²and cried to the God of Israel all with one consent earnestly, that he would not give their children for a prey, and their wives for a spoil, and the cities of their inheritance to destruction, and the sanctuary to profanation and reproach, and for the nations to rejoice at.

¹³So God heard their prayers, and looked upon their afflictions: for the people fasted many days in all Judea and Jerusalem before the sanctuary of the Lord Almighty. ¹⁴And Joacim the high priest, and all the priests that stood before the Lord, and they which ministered unto the Lord, had their loins girt with sackcloth, and offered the daily burnt offerings, with the vows and free gifts of the people, ¹⁵and had ashes on their mitres, and cried unto the Lord with all their power, that he would look upon all the house of Israel graciously.

5 Then was it declared to Holofernes, the chief captain of the army of Assur, that the children of Israel had prepared for war, and had shut up the passages of the hill country, and had fortified all the tops of the high hills, and had laid impediments in the champaign countries: ²wherewith he was very angry, and called all the princes of Moab, and the captains of Ammon, and all the governors of the sea coast, ³and he said unto them, Tell me now, ye sons of Chanaan, who this people is, that dwelleth in the hill country, and what are the cities that they inhabit, and what is the multitude of their army, and wherein is their power and strength, and what king is set over them, or captain of their army; ⁴and why have they determined not to come and meet me, more than all the inhabitants of the west?

⁵Then said Achior, the captain of all the sons of Ammon, Let my lord now hear a word from the mouth of thy servant, and I will declare unto thee the truth concerning this people, which dwelleth near thee, and inhabiteth the hill countries: and there shall no lie come out of the mouth of thy servant. ⁶This people are descended of the Chaldeans: ⁷and they sojourned heretofore in Mesopotamia, because they would not follow the gods of their fathers, which were in the land of Chaldea. ⁸For

4:10 *Sackcloth*: a sign of mourning or repentance, like the ashes cast upon their heads in v. 11. The image of cattle (and the altar in v. 11) wearing sackcloth is hard to interpret—perhaps meant to be humorous, or to underscore how dire the situation is (cf. Jonah 3:8). **4:13** *So God . . . afflictions*: recalling Exod 3:7. **4:14** *The daily burnt offerings*: see Exod 29:38–42. *The vows and free gifts*: "the votive offerings, and free will offerings" (NRSV); cf. Lev 22:17–30. **4:15** *Mitres*: turbans. **5:1–6:21 Achior tries to persuade Holofernes not to attack and is turned over to Israel.** Achior recounts Israel's history from Abraham through the captivity and return. **5:1** *Laid impediments . . . countries*: laid traps in the plains. **5:2** *Moab*: southeast of Judah; like *Ammon*, to its northeast, and *the sea coast* (i.e., Philistia) to its southwest, a frequent enemy. **5:3** *Sons of Chanaan*: sons of Canaan, i.e., indigenous inhabitants of the land that God promised Israel. **5:6** *Descended of the Chaldeans*: cf. Gen 11:27–31. **5:7–8** *Because they . . . many days*: this detail is not in Genesis, although it is found in one form or another in many later retellings of the Abraham story (e.g.,

they left the way of their ancestors, and worshipped the God of heaven, the God whom they knew: so they cast them out from the face of their gods, and they fled into Mesopotamia, and sojourned there many days. [9]Then their God commanded them to depart from the place where they sojourned, and to go into the land of Chanaan: where they dwelt, and were increased with gold and silver, and with very much cattle. [10]But when a famine covered all the land of Chanaan, they went down into Egypt, and sojourned there, while they were nourished, and became there a great multitude, so that one could not number their nation. [11]Therefore the king of Egypt rose up against them, and dealt subtilly with them, and brought them low with labouring in brick, and made them slaves. [12]Then they cried unto their God, and he smote all the land of Egypt with incurable plagues: so the Egyptians cast them out of their sight. [13]And God dried the Red sea before them, [14]and brought them to mount Sina, and Cades-Barne, and cast forth all that dwelt in the wilderness. [15]So they dwelt in the land of the Amorites, and they destroyed by their strength all them of Esebon, and passing over Jordan they possessed all the hill country. [16]And they cast forth before them the Chanaanite, the Pherezite, the Jebusite, and the Sychemite, and all the Gergesites, and they dwelt in that country many days.

[17]And whilst they sinned not before their God, they prospered, because the God that hateth iniquity was with them. [18]But when they departed from the way which he appointed them, they were destroyed in many battles very sore, and were led captives into a land that was not theirs, and the temple of their God was cast to the ground, and their cities were taken by the enemies. [19]But now are they returned to their God, and are come up from the places where they were scattered, and have possessed Jerusalem, where their sanctuary is, and are seated in the hill country; for it was desolate. [20]Now therefore, my lord and governor, if there be any error in this people, and they sin against their God, let us consider that this shall be their ruin, and let us go up, and we shall overcome them. [21]But if there be no iniquity in their nation, let my lord now pass by, lest their Lord defend them, and their God be for them, and we become a reproach before all the world.

[22]And when Achior had finished these sayings, all the people standing round about the tent murmured, and the chief men of Holofernes, and all that dwelt by the sea side, and in Moab, spake that he should kill him. [23]For, say they, we will not be afraid of the face of the children of Israel: for, lo, it is a people that have no strength nor power for a strong battle. [24]Now therefore, lord Holofernes, we will go up, and they shall be a prey to be devoured of all thine army.

Jubilees 11.16–17; 12.1–21) and may have emerged as an imaginative explanation of why Genesis seems to recount two separate migrations of Abraham (11:31; 12:1–3), only the latter of which is divinely prompted.   **5:10** *Famine*: see Gen 42:5. Verses 10–13 recapitulate Gen 42–50 and Exod 1–15.   **5:14–16** *Brought them . . . many days*: summarizing, from a military perspective, the rest of the Pentateuch and Joshua.   **5:18–19** *When they . . . desolate*: apparently referring to Babylon's defeat of Judah, the exile of its population (see 2 Kgs 24–25), and the exiles' return under the

6 And when the tumult of men that were about the council was ceased, Holofernes the chief captain of the army of Assur said unto Achior and all the Moabites before all the company of other nations, ²And who art thou, Achior, and the hirelings of Ephraim, that thou hast prophesied among us as to day, and hast said, that we should not make war with the people of Israel, because their God will defend them? and who is God but Nabuchodonosor? ³He will send his power, and will destroy them from the face of the earth, and their God shall not deliver them: but we his servants will destroy them as one man; for they are not able to sustain the power of our horses. ⁴For with them we will tread them under foot, and their mountains shall be drunken with their blood, and their fields shall be filled with their dead bodies, and their footsteps shall not be able to stand before us, for they shall utterly perish, saith king Nabuchodonosor, lord of all the earth: for he said, None of my words shall be in vain. ⁵And thou, Achior, an hireling of Ammon, which hast spoken these words in the day of thine iniquity, shalt see my face no more from this day, until I take vengeance of this nation that came out of Egypt. ⁶And then shall the sword of mine army, and the multitude of them that serve me, pass through thy sides, and thou shalt fall among their slain, when I return. ⁷Now therefore my servants shall bring thee back into the hill country, and shall set thee in one of the cities of the passages: ⁸and thou shalt not perish, till thou be destroyed with them. ⁹And if thou persuade thyself in thy mind that they shall not be taken, let not thy countenance fall: I have spoken it, and none of my words shall be in vain.

¹⁰Then Holofernes commanded his servants, that waited in his tent, to take Achior, and bring him to Bethulia, and deliver him into the hands of the children of Israel. ¹¹So his servants took him, and brought him out of the camp into the plain, and they went from the midst of the plain into the hill country, and came unto the fountains that were under Bethulia. ¹²And when the men of the city saw them, they took up their weapons, and went out of the city to the top of the hill: and every man that used a sling kept them from coming up by casting of stones against them. ¹³Nevertheless having gotten privily under the hill, they bound Achior, and cast him down, and left him at the foot of the hill, and returned to their lord. ¹⁴But the Israelites descended from their city, and came unto him, and loosed him, and brought him into Bethulia, and presented him to the governors of the city: ¹⁵which were in those days Ozias the son of Micha, of the tribe of Simeon, and Chabris the son of Gothoniel, and Charmis the son of Melchiel. ¹⁶And they called together all the ancients of the city, and all their youth ran together, and their women, to the assembly, and they set Achior in the midst of

Persian ruler Cyrus (see Ezra-Nehemiah). **6:2** *Hirelings of Ephraim*: i.e., "mercenaries of Ephraim"; Ephraim, one of Israel's tribes and eponymous regions, sometimes stands for the entire Northern Kingdom or its territories. Holofernes accuses Achior of being on the enemy's payroll. *Who is God but Nabuchodonosor*: perversely echoing 2 Sam 22:32; Ps 18:31. **6:4** *Their mountains . . . bodies*: again echoing language of YHWH; cf. Isa 34:3; Ezek 32:6. **6:5** *Hireling of Ammon*: i.e., Ammonite mercenary Holofernes's (cf. 5:5; 6:2 and note). *Shalt see . . . Egypt*: a deliciously ironic detail in light of 14:6, as is Holofernes' prediction that Achior will fall among the slain Israelites (v. 6). **6:6** *Multitude*: the Latin and Syriac versions here read "spear." **6:7** *Passages*: mountain passes; cf. 4:6–7. **6:11** *Fountains*: springs. **6:13** *Gotten privily*: slipped in. **6:16** *Ancients*: elders.

all their people. Then Ozias asked him of that which was done. ¹⁷And he answered and declared unto them the words of the council of Holofernes, and all the words that he had spoken in the midst of the princes of Assur, and whatsoever Holofernes had spoken proudly against the house of Israel.

¹⁸Then the people fell down and worshipped God, and cried unto God, saying, ¹⁹O Lord God of heaven, behold their pride, and pity the low estate of our nation, and look upon the face of those that are sanctified unto thee this day. ²⁰Then they comforted Achior, and praised him greatly. ²¹And Ozias took him out of the assembly unto his house, and made a feast to the elders; and they called on the God of Israel all that night for help.

7 The next day Holofernes commanded all his army, and all his people which were come to take his part, that they should remove their camp against Bethulia, to take aforehand the ascents of the hill country, and to make war against the children of Israel. ²Then their strong men removed their camps in that day, and the army of the men of war was an hundred and seventy thousand footmen, and twelve thousand horsemen, beside the baggage, and other men that were afoot among them, a very great multitude. ³And they camped in the valley near unto Bethulia, by the fountain, and they spread themselves in breadth over Dothaim even to Belmaim, and in length from Bethulia unto Cyamon, which is over against Esdraelom.

⁴Now the children of Israel, when they saw the multitude of them, were greatly troubled, and said every one to his neighbour, Now will these men lick up the face of the earth; for neither the high mountains, nor the valleys, nor the hills, are able to bear their weight. ⁵Then every man took up his weapons of war, and when they had kindled fires upon their towers, they remained and watched all that night. ⁶But in the second day Holofernes brought forth all his horsemen in the sight of the children of Israel which were in Bethulia, ⁷and viewed the passages up to the city, and came to the fountains of their waters, and took them, and set garrisons of men of war over them, and he himself removed toward his people.

⁸Then came unto him all the chief of the children of Esau, and all the governors of the people of Moab, and the captains of the sea coast, and said, ⁹Let our lord now hear a word, that there be not an overthrow in thine army. ¹⁰For this people of the children of Israel do not trust in their spears, but in the height of the mountains wherein they dwell, because it is not easy to come up to the tops of their mountains. ¹¹Now therefore, my lord, fight not against them in battle array, and there shall not so much as one man of thy people perish. ¹²Remain in thy camp, and keep all the men of thine army, and let thy servants get into their hands the fountain of water, which issueth forth of the foot of the mountain: ¹³for all the inhabitants of Bethulia have their water thence; so shall thirst kill them, and they shall give up their city, and we and our people shall go up to the tops of the mountains that are near, and will camp upon them, to watch that none go out of the city. ¹⁴So they and their wives and their children shall be consumed with famine,

---

7:1–32 The siege of Bethulia. 7:1 *Remove their camp against*: strike camp and advance on. 7:8 *Children of Esau*: the Edomites, another frequent enemy of Israel. 7:9 *Overthrow*: lit. "frac-

and before the sword come against them, they shall be overthrown in the streets where they dwell. [15]Thus shalt thou render them an evil reward; because they rebelled, and met not thy person peaceably.

[16]And these words pleased Holofernes and all his servants, and he appointed to do as they had spoken. [17]So the camp of the children of Ammon departed, and with them five thousand of the Assyrians, and they pitched in the valley, and took the waters, and the fountains of the waters of the children of Israel. [18]Then the children of Esau went up with the children of Ammon, and camped in the hill country over against Dothaim: and they sent some of them toward the south, and toward the east, over against Ekrebel, which is near unto Chusi, that is upon the brook Mochmur; and the rest of the army of the Assyrians camped in the plain, and covered the face of the whole land; and their tents and carriages were pitched to a very great multitude.

[19]Then the children of Israel cried unto the Lord their God, because their heart failed, for all their enemies had compassed them round about, and there was no way to escape out from among them. [20]Thus all the company of Assur remained about them, both their footmen, chariots, and horsemen, four and thirty days, so that all their vessels of water failed all the inhabitants of Bethulia. [21]And the cisterns were emptied, and they had not water to drink their fill for one day; for they gave them drink by measure. [22]Therefore their young children were out of heart, and their women and young men fainted for thirst, and fell down in the streets of the city, and by the passages of the gates, and there was no longer any strength in them.

[23]Then all the people assembled to Ozias, and to the chief of the city, both young men, and women, and children, and cried with a loud voice, and said before all the elders, [24]God be judge between us and you: for ye have done us great injury, in that ye have not required peace of the children of Assur. [25]For now we have no helper: but God hath sold us into their hands, that we should be thrown down before them with thirst and great destruction. [26]Now therefore call them unto you, and deliver the whole city for a spoil to the people of Holofernes, and to all his army. [27]For it is better for us to be made a spoil unto them, than to die for thirst: for we will be his servants, that our souls may live, and not see the death of our infants before our eyes, nor our wives nor our children to die. [28]We take to witness against you the heaven and the earth, and our God and Lord of our fathers, which punisheth us according to our sins and the sins of our fathers, that he do not according as we have said this day. [29]Then there was great weeping with one consent in the midst of the assembly; and they cried unto the Lord God with a loud voice.

[30]Then said Ozias to them, Brethren, be of good courage, let us yet endure five days, in the which space the Lord our God may turn his mercy toward us; for he will not forsake us utterly. [31]And if these days pass, and there come no help unto us, I will do according to your word. [32]And he dispersed the people, every one to

---

ture," perhaps referring to a casualty. **7:22** *Out of heart*: terrified. **7:24–28** *God be judge . . . this day*: recalling Israel's panic at various points after the people escaped from Egypt, especially at Exod 17:1–3 and Num 20:2–5, when they lacked water. **7:27** *Our souls may live*: "our lives will be spared" (NRSV).

their own charge; and they went unto the walls and towers of their city, and sent the women and children into their houses: and they were very low brought in the city.

8 Now at that time Judith heard thereof, which was the daughter of Merari, the son of Ox, the son of Joseph, the son of Oziel, the son of Elcia, the son of Ananias, the son of Gedeon, the son of Raphaim, the son of Acitho, the son of Eliu, the son of Eliab, the son of Nathanael, the son of Samael, the son of Salasadai, the son of Israel. ²And Manasses was her husband, of her tribe and kindred, who died in the barley harvest. ³For as he stood overseeing them that bound sheaves in the field, the heat came upon his head, and he fell on his bed, and died in the city of Bethulia: and they buried him with his fathers in the field between Dothaim and Balamo. ⁴So Judith was a widow in her house three years and four months. ⁵And she made her a tent upon the top of her house, and put on sackcloth upon her loins, and ware her widow's apparel. ⁶And she fasted all the days of her widowhood, save the eves of the sabbaths, and the sabbaths, and the eves of the new moons, and the new moons, and the feasts and solemn days of the house of Israel. ⁷She was also of a goodly countenance, and very beautiful to behold: and her husband Manasses had left her gold, and silver, and menservants, and maidservants, and cattle, and lands; and she remained upon them. ⁸And there was none that gave her an ill word; for she feared God greatly.

⁹Now when she heard the evil words of the people against the governor, that they fainted for lack of water; for Judith had heard all the words that Ozias had spoken unto them, and that he had sworn to deliver the city unto the Assyrians after five days; ¹⁰then she sent her waiting woman, that had the government of all things that she had, to call Ozias and Chabris and Charmis, the ancients of the city.

¹¹And they came unto her, and she said unto them, Hear me now, O ye governors of the inhabitants of Bethulia: for your words that ye have spoken before the people this day are not right, touching this oath which ye made and pronounced between God and you, and have promised to deliver the city to our enemies, unless within these days the Lord turn to help you. ¹²And now who are ye that have tempted God this day, and stand instead of God among the children of men? ¹³And now try the Lord Almighty, but ye shall never know any thing. ¹⁴For ye cannot find the depth of the heart of man, neither can ye perceive the things that he thinketh: then how can ye search out God, that hath made all these things, and know his mind, or comprehend his purpose? Nay, my brethren, provoke not the Lord our God to anger. ¹⁵For

---

7:32 *Low brought*: dejected.

8:1–9:14 Judith promises to deliver her people and prays. Like earlier speeches by Nebuchadnezzar (2:5–13) and Holofernes (6:2–9), Judith's here (8:11–27) and in the prayer that follows (chap. 9) echoes biblical discourse throughout, but piously rather than perversely (unless there is something perverse about her prayer for successful deceit), as the select OT allusions noted below indicate.   **8:1** *Judith*: her name means "female Jew." *Israel*: i.e., Jacob (see Gen 32:28; 35:10).   **8:5** *She made . . . house*: in her mourning, she refuses the comfort of her home.   **8:6** *Save the eves . . . Israel*: the celebratory context made fasting inappropriate.   **8:12** *Who are . . . God*: echoing Deut 6:16, "Ye shall not tempt the Lord your God, as ye tempted him in Massah," where Moses twice proved God's faithfulness by producing water from a rock (Exod 17:1–7; Num 20:2–13), and in the second instance was punished for doing so.   **8:13** *Try*: better "you are trying," although the verb may mean "scrutinize," in which case the imperative could stand.   **8:14** *Provoke not . . . anger*: cf. Deut 4:25; 9:18; etc.

if he will not help us within these five days, he hath power to defend us when he will, even every day, or to destroy us before our enemies. [16]Do not bind the counsels of the Lord our God: for God is not as man, that he may be threatened; neither is he as the son of man, that he should be wavering. [17]Therefore let us wait for salvation of him, and call upon him to help us, and he will hear our voice, if it please him. [18]For there arose none in our age, neither is there any now in these days, neither tribe, nor family, nor people, nor city, among us, which worship gods made with hands, as hath been aforetime. [19]For the which cause our fathers were given to the sword, and for a spoil, and had a great fall before our enemies. [20]But we know none other god, therefore we trust that he will not despise us, nor any of our nation. [21]For if we be taken so, all Judea shall lie waste, and our sanctuary shall be spoiled; and he will require the profanation thereof at our mouth. [22]And the slaughter of our brethren, and the captivity of the country, and the desolation of our inheritance, will he turn upon our heads among the Gentiles, wheresoever we shall be in bondage; and we shall be an offence and a reproach to all them that possess us. [23]For our servitude shall not be directed to favour: but the Lord our God shall turn it to dishonour.

[24]Now therefore, O brethren, let us shew an example to our brethren, because their hearts depend upon us, and the sanctuary, and the house, and the altar, rest upon us. [25]Moreover let us give thanks to the Lord our God, which trieth us, even as he did our fathers. [26]Remember what things he did to Abraham, and how he tried Isaac, and what happened to Jacob in Mesopotamia of Syria, when he kept the sheep of Laban his mother's brother. [27]For he hath not tried us in the fire, as he did them, for the examination of their hearts, neither hath he taken vengeance on us: but the Lord doth scourge them that come near unto him, to admonish them.

[28]Then said Ozias to her, All that thou hast spoken hast thou spoken with a good heart, and there is none that may gainsay thy words. [29]For this is not the first day wherein thy wisdom is manifested; but from the beginning of thy days all the people have known thy understanding, because the disposition of thine heart is good. [30]But the people were very thirsty, and compelled us to do unto them as we have spoken, and to bring an oath upon ourselves, which we will not break. [31]Therefore now pray thou for us, because thou art a godly woman, and the Lord will send us rain to fill our cisterns, and we shall faint no more.

[32]Then said Judith unto them, Hear me, and I will do a thing, which shall go throughout all generations to the children of our nation. [33]Ye shall stand this night in the gate, and I will go forth with my waiting woman: and within the days that ye have promised to deliver the city to our enemies the Lord will visit Israel by mine hand. [34]But inquire not ye of mine act: for I will not declare it unto you, till the things be finished that I do. [35]Then said Ozias and the princes unto her,

8:15 *He hath power . . . to destroy us*: cf. Job 1:21; 2:10.   8:16 *God is not as man . . . wavering*: cf. Num 23:19; 1 Sam 15:29.   8:19 *Had a great fall*: apparently referring to the conquest of the Southern Kingdom by Babylon in 586 B.C.E. (the putative date of the events of the current story).   8:21 *At our mouth*: better "from our blood," meaning "he will make us pay for it with our blood" (MS tradition).   8:22 *Turn upon our heads*: i.e., "bring upon our heads" (NRSV). *To all them*: before all them.   8:25 *Trieth*: Gk. *peirazō*, "tempt" (also in v. 26; cf. v. 12; a different word is used in v. 13).   8:26 *Remember what . . . brother*: see Gen 22 (Abraham and Isaac); 29–30 (Jacob).   8:27 *Examination*: from the same

Go in peace, and the Lord God be before thee, to take vengeance on our enemies. ³⁶So they returned from the tent, and went to their wards.

9 Then Judith fell upon her face, and put ashes upon her head, and uncovered
the sackcloth wherewith she was clothed; and about the time that the
incense of that evening was offered in Jerusalem in the house of the Lord Judith
cried with a loud voice, and said,

²O Lord God of my father Simeon, to whom thou gavest a sword to take vengeance of the strangers, who loosened the girdle of a maid to defile her, and discovered the thigh to her shame, and polluted her virginity to her reproach; for
thou saidst, It shall not be so; and yet they did so: ³wherefore thou gavest their
rulers to be slain, so that they dyed their bed in blood, being deceived, and smot-
est the servants with their lords, and the lords upon their thrones; ⁴and hast
given their wives for a prey, and their daughters to be captives and all their spoils
to be divided among thy dear children; which were moved with thy zeal, and
abhorred the pollution of their blood, and called upon thee for aid: O God, O my
God, hear me also a widow.

⁵For thou hast wrought not only those things, but also the things which fell out
before, and which ensued after; thou hast thought upon the things which are
now, and which are to come. ⁶Yea, what things thou didst determine were ready
at hand, and said, Lo, we are here: for all thy ways are prepared, and thy judgments are in thy foreknowledge.

⁷For, behold, the Assyrians are multiplied in their power; they are exalted with
horse and man; they glory in the strength of their footmen; they trust in shield,
and spear, and bow, and sling; and know not that thou art the Lord that breakest
the battles: the Lord is thy name. ⁸Throw down their strength in thy power, and
bring down their force in thy wrath: for they have purposed to defile thy sanctuary, and to pollute the tabernacle where thy glorious name resteth, and to cast
down with sword the horn of thy altar.

⁹Behold their pride, and send thy wrath upon their heads: give into mine hand,
which am a widow, the power that I have conceived. ¹⁰Smite by the deceit of my
lips the servant with the prince, and the prince with the servant: break down
their stateliness by the hand of a woman. ¹¹For thy power standeth not in multitude, nor thy might in strong men; for thou art a God of the afflicted, an helper
of the oppressed, an upholder of the weak, a protector of the forlorn, a saviour of
them that are without hope. ¹²I pray thee, I pray thee, O God of my father, and
God of the inheritance of Israel, Lord of the heavens and earth, Creator of the
waters, King of every creature, hear thou my prayer: ¹³and make my speech and

---

Greek root as "try" in v. 13 (see note).   **9:2** *Simeon*: see Gen 34.   **9:3** *So that . . . deceived*: rather
"and their bed, which was ashamed of the deceit they had practiced, was stained with blood"
(NRSV). The reference seems to be to Simeon and Levi's slaughter of the Shechemite men who
had just been circumcised.   **9:5** *Thought upon*: intended (the same Gk. root as "conceived" in
v. 9; see note).   **9:7** *The Lord that breakest the battles*: echoing LXX Exod 15:3.   **9:8** *Horn of thy
altar*: see 1 Kgs 1:50 note.   **9:9** *The power . . . conceived*: i.e., "power for what I have intended."
9:10 *By the hand of a woman*: echoing Judg 4:9.   **9:11** *Helper . . . protector . . . saviour*: two of
these terms and a cognate are used in the LXX version of Moses' Song of the Sea (Exod 15:2).

deceit to be their wound and stripe, who have purposed cruel things against thy covenant, and thy hallowed house, and against the top of Sion, and against the house of the possession of thy children. ¹⁴And make every nation and tribe to acknowledge that thou art the God of all power and might, and that there is none other that protecteth the people of Israel but thou.

10 Now after that she had ceased to cry unto the God of Israel, and had made an end of all these words, ²she rose where she had fallen down, and called her maid, and went down into the house, in the which she abode in the sabbath days, and in her feast days, ³and pulled off the sackcloth which she had on, and put off the garments of her widowhood, and washed her body all over with water, and anointed herself with precious ointment, and braided the hair of her head, and put on a tire upon it, and put on her garments of gladness, wherewith she was clad during the life of Manasses her husband. ⁴And she took sandals upon her feet, and put about her her bracelets, and her chains, and her rings, and her earrings, and all her ornaments, and decked herself bravely, to allure the eyes of all men that should see her. ⁵Then she gave her maid a bottle of wine, and a cruse of oil, and filled a bag with parched corn, and lumps of figs, and with fine bread; so she folded all these things together, and laid them upon her.

⁶Thus they went forth to the gate of the city of Bethulia, and found standing there Ozias, and the ancients of the city, Chabris and Charmis. ⁷And when they saw her, that her countenance was altered, and her apparel was changed, they wondered at her beauty very greatly, and said unto her, ⁸The God, the God of our fathers, give thee favour, and accomplish thine enterprizes to the glory of the children of Israel, and to the exaltation of Jerusalem. Then they worshipped God. ⁹And she said unto them, Command the gates of the city to be opened unto me, that I may go forth to accomplish the things whereof ye have spoken with me. So they commanded the young men to open unto her, as she had spoken. ¹⁰And when they had done so, Judith went out, she, and her maid with her; and the men of the city looked after her, until she was gone down the mountain, and till she had passed the valley, and could see her no more.

¹¹Thus they went straight forth in the valley: and the first watch of the Assyrians met her, ¹²and took her, and asked her, Of what people art thou? and whence comest thou? and whither goest thou? And she said, I am a woman of the Hebrews, and am fled from them: for they shall be given you to be consumed: ¹³and I am coming before Holofernes the chief captain of your army, to declare words of truth; and I will shew him a way, whereby he shall go, and win all the hill country, without losing the body or life of any one of his men. ¹⁴Now when the men heard her words, and beheld her countenance, they wondered greatly at her beauty, and said unto her, ¹⁵Thou hast saved thy life, in that thou hast hasted to come down to the presence of our lord: now therefore come to his tent, and some of us shall conduct thee, until they have delivered thee to his hands. ¹⁶And when thou standest before

---

9:13 *Stripe*: a wound from a whip.

10:1–11:23 **Judith captivates Holofernes.** This section introduces a major thematic concern of the second half of the book, the triumph of beauty. 10:3 *Tire*: headdress. 10:4 *Bravely*: finely.

him, be not afraid in thine heart, but shew unto him according to thy word; and he will entreat thee well. [17]Then they chose out of them an hundred men to accompany her and her maid; and they brought her to the tent of Holofernes. [18]Then was there a concourse throughout all the camp: for her coming was noised among the tents, and they came about her, as she stood without the tent of Holofernes, till they told him of her. [19]And they wondered at her beauty, and admired the children of Israel because of her, and every one said to his neighbour, Who would despise this people, that have among them such women? surely it is not good that one man of them be left, who being let go might deceive the whole earth. [20]And they that lay near Holofernes went out, and all his servants, and they brought her into the tent. [21]Now Holofernes rested upon his bed under a canopy, which was woven with purple, and gold, and emeralds, and precious stones. [22]So they shewed him of her; and he came out before his tent with silver lamps going before him. [23]And when Judith was come before him and his servants, they all marvelled at the beauty of her countenance; and she fell down upon her face, and did reverence unto him: and his servants took her up.

11 Then said Holofernes unto her, Woman, be of good comfort, fear not in thine heart: for I never hurt any that was willing to serve Nabuchodonosor, the king of all the earth. [2]Now therefore, if thy people that dwelleth in the mountains had not set light by me, I would not have lifted up my spear against them: but they have done these things to themselves. [3]But now tell me wherefore thou art fled from them, and art come unto us: for thou art come for safeguard; be of good comfort, thou shalt live this night, and hereafter: [4]for none shall hurt thee, but entreat thee well, as they do the servants of king Nabuchodonosor my lord.

[5]Then Judith said unto him, Receive the words of thy servant, and suffer thine handmaid to speak in thy presence, and I will declare no lie to my lord this night. [6]And if thou wilt follow the words of thine handmaid, God will bring the thing perfectly to pass by thee; and my lord shall not fail of his purposes, [7]as Nabuchodonosor king of all the earth liveth, and as his power liveth, who hath sent thee for the upholding of every living thing: for not only men shall serve him by thee, but also the beasts of the field, and the cattle, and the fowls of the air, shall live by thy power under Nabuchodonosor and all his house. [8]For we have heard of thy wisdom and thy policies, and it is reported in all the earth, that thou only art excellent in all the kingdom, and mighty in knowledge, and wonderful in feats of war.

[9]Now as concerning the matter, which Achior did speak in thy council, we have heard his words; for the men of Bethulia saved him, and he declared unto them all that he had spoken unto thee. [10]Therefore, O lord and governor, reject not his word; but lay it up in thine heart, for it is true: for our nation shall not be punished, neither can the sword prevail against them, except they sin against

---

10:16 *Entreat*: treat.   10:19 *Deceive*: different Greek roots are used in 9:3 and 13. NRSV offers "beguile."   11:2 *Set light by me*: slighted me.   11:3 *Thou art come for safeguard*: lit. "you have come to salvation."   11:6 *If thou . . . purposes*: nicely ironic, especially if *my lord* is understood as referring to YHWH. Such irony pervades Judith and Holofernes' exchanges (see v. 3, for example).   11:7 *Upholding*: setting straight. *Not only . . . house*: cf. Dan 2:38.

their God. ¹¹And now, that my lord be not defeated and frustrate of his purpose, even death is now fallen upon them, and their sin hath overtaken them, wherewith they will provoke their God to anger, whensoever they shall do that which is not fit to be done: ¹²for their victuals fail them, and all their water is scant, and they have determined to lay hands upon their cattle, and purposed to consume all those things, that God hath forbidden them to eat by his laws: ¹³and are resolved to spend the firstfruits of the corn, and the tenths of wine and oil, which they had sanctified, and reserved for the priests that serve in Jerusalem before the face of our God; the which things it is not lawful for any of the people so much as to touch with their hands. ¹⁴For they have sent some to Jerusalem, because they also that dwell there have done the like, to bring them a licence from the senate. ¹⁵Now when they shall bring them word, they will forthwith do it, and they shall be given thee to be destroyed the same day. ¹⁶Wherefore I thine handmaid, knowing all this, am fled from their presence; and God hath sent me to work things with thee, whereat all the earth shall be astonished, and whosoever shall hear it. ¹⁷For thy servant is religious, and serveth the God of heaven day and night: now therefore, my lord, I will remain with thee, and thy servant will go out by night into the valley, and I will pray unto God, and he will tell me when they have committed their sins: ¹⁸and I will come and shew it unto thee: then thou shalt go forth with all thine army, and there shall be none of them that shall resist thee. ¹⁹And I will lead thee through the midst of Judea, until thou come before Jerusalem; and I will set thy throne in the midst thereof; and thou shalt drive them as sheep that have no shepherd, and a dog shall not so much as open his mouth at thee: for these things were told me according to my foreknowledge, and they were declared unto me, and I am sent to tell thee.

²⁰Then her words pleased Holofernes and all his servants; and they marvelled at her wisdom, and said, ²¹There is not such a woman from one end of the earth to the other, both for beauty of face, and wisdom of words. ²²Likewise Holofernes said unto her, God hath done well to send thee before the people, that strength might be in our hands, and destruction upon them that lightly regard my lord. ²³And now thou art both beautiful in thy countenance, and witty in thy words: surely if thou do as thou hast spoken, thy God shall be my God, and thou shalt dwell in the house of king Nabuchodonosor, and shalt be renowned through the whole earth.

12 Then he commanded to bring her in where his plate was set; and bade that they should prepare for her of his own meats, and that she should drink of his own wine. ²And Judith said, I will not eat thereof, lest there be an offence: but provision shall be made for me of the things that I have brought.

11:12 *Cattle*: the Greek word can refer to beasts of burden (as at Luke 10:34), which would not normally be eaten.   11:14 *Senate*: Gk. *gerousia* (see 4:8 note).   11:23 *Witty*: lit. "good"; i.e., she speaks well.

12:1–13:10 **Holofernes' banquet and assassination.** The most obvious parallels are with Jael's assassination of Sisera (Judg 4:17–22) and Ehud's of Eglon (Judg 3:15–25), but there are also echoes of David's slaying of Goliath (1 Sam 17:48–51).   12:2 *Lest there . . . brought*: this detail, like Judith's midnight prayer (vv. 5–8), aids the con: she presents herself as punctiliously religious, especially by observing the dietary requirements that she has falsely accused her fellow Israelites of

³Then Holofernes said unto her, If thy provision should fail, how should we give thee the like? for there be none with us of thy nation. ⁴Then said Judith unto him, As thy soul liveth, my lord, thine handmaid shall not spend those things that I have, before the Lord work by mine hand the things that he hath determined.

⁵Then the servants of Holofernes brought her into the tent, and she slept till midnight, and she arose when it was toward the morning watch, ⁶and sent to Holofernes, saying, Let my lord now command that thine handmaid may go forth unto prayer. ⁷Then Holofernes commanded his guard that they should not stay her: thus she abode in the camp three days, and went out in the night into the valley of Bethulia, and washed herself in a fountain of water by the camp. ⁸And when she came out, she besought the Lord God of Israel to direct her way to the raising up of the children of her people. ⁹So she came in clean, and remained in the tent, until she did eat her meat at evening.

¹⁰And in the fourth day Holofernes made a feast to his own servants only, and called none of the officers to the banquet. ¹¹Then said he to Bagoas the eunuch, who had charge over all that he had, Go now, and persuade this Hebrew woman which is with thee, that she come unto us, and eat and drink with us. ¹²For, lo, it will be a shame for our person, if we shall let such a woman go, not having had her company; for if we draw her not unto us, she will laugh us to scorn.

¹³Then went Bagoas from the presence of Holofernes, and came to her, and he said, Let not this fair damsel fear to come to my lord, and to be honoured in his presence, and drink wine, and be merry with us, and be made this day as one of the daughters of the Assyrians, which serve in the house of Nabuchodonosor. ¹⁴Then said Judith unto him, Who am I now, that I should gainsay my lord? surely whatsoever pleaseth him I will do speedily, and it shall be my joy unto the day of my death. ¹⁵So she arose, and decked herself with her apparel and all her woman's attire, and her maid went and laid soft skins on the ground for her over against Holofernes, which she had received of Bagoas for her daily use, that she might sit and eat upon them.

¹⁶Now when Judith came in and sat down, Holofernes his heart was ravished with her, and his mind was moved, and he desired greatly her company; for he waited a time to deceive her, from the day that he had seen her. ¹⁷Then said Holofernes unto her, Drink now, and be merry with us. ¹⁸So Judith said, I will drink now, my lord, because my life is magnified in me this day more than all the days since I was born. ¹⁹Then she took and ate and drank before him what her maid had prepared. ²⁰And Holofernes took great delight in her, and drank much more wine than he had drunk at any time in one day since he was born.

---

transgressing. **12:10** *A feast . . . banquet*: i.e., a private dinner. **12:12** *Having had her company*: "having intercourse with her" (NRSV). *Draw*: the Greek verb can mean "to drag," as by the hair, or "to allure." **12:16** *Holofernes his*: Holofernes's (also at 13:9 and 15:11). *Moved*: shaken. *Deceive*: i.e., seduce. **12:18** *My life . . . born*: i.e., "today is the greatest day of my whole life" (NRSV).

13 Now when the evening was come, his servants made haste to depart, and Bagoas shut his tent without, and dismissed the waiters from the presence of his lord; and they went to their beds: for they were all weary, because the feast had been long. ²And Judith was left alone in the tent, and Holofernes lying along upon his bed: for he was filled with wine. ³Now Judith had commanded her maid to stand without her bedchamber, and to wait for her coming forth, as she did daily: for she said she would go forth to her prayers, and she spake to Bagoas according to the same purpose. ⁴So all went forth, and none was left in the bedchamber, neither little nor great. Then Judith, standing by his bed, said in her heart, O Lord God of all power, look at this present upon the works of mine hands for the exaltation of Jerusalem. ⁵For now is the time to help thine inheritance, and to execute mine enterprizes to the destruction of the enemies which are risen against us.

⁶Then she came to the pillar of the bed, which was at Holofernes' head, and took down his fauchion from thence, ⁷and approached to his bed, and took hold of the hair of his head, and said, Strengthen me, O Lord God of Israel, this day. ⁸And she smote twice upon his neck with all her might, and she took away his head from him, ⁹and tumbled his body down from the bed, and pulled down the canopy from the pillars; and anon after she went forth, and gave Holofernes his head to her maid; ¹⁰and she put it in her bag of meat: so they twain went together according to their custom unto prayer: and when they passed the camp, they compassed the valley, and went up the mountain of Bethulia, and came to the gates thereof.

¹¹Then said Judith afar off to the watchmen at the gate, Open, open now the gate: God, even our God, is with us, to shew his power yet in Jerusalem, and his forces against the enemy, as he hath even done this day. ¹²Now when the men of her city heard her voice, they made haste to go down to the gate of their city, and they called the elders of the city. ¹³And then they ran all together, both small and great, for it was strange unto them that she was come: so they opened the gate, and received them, and made a fire for a light, and stood round about them. ¹⁴Then she said to them with a loud voice, Praise, praise God, praise God, [I say,] for he hath not taken away his mercy from the house of Israel, but hath destroyed our enemies by mine hands this night.

¹⁵So she took the head out of the bag, and shewed it, and said unto them, Behold the head of Holofernes, the chief captain of the army of Assur, and behold the canopy, wherein he did lie in his drunkenness; and the Lord hath smitten him by the hand of a woman. ¹⁶As the Lord liveth, who hath kept me in

---

13:2 *Holofernes lying . . . wine:* apparently his excessive drink (see 12:20) made him unable to consummate the seduction he had planned. *He was filled with wine:* more literally "he was drenched with wine." **13:4** *This present:* the present moment. **13:6** *Fauchion:* sword. KJV's foreign diction parallels that of the Greek text, which here employs a Persian loanword. **13:10** *Bag of meat:* the provisions she had brought (cf. 10:5; 12:2–4). *They twain:* they both.

13:11–14:10 Judith's return and Achior's conversion. Achior, like Ruth, converts in violation of Deut 23:3: "An Ammonite or Moabite shall not enter into the congregation of the Lord" (cf. 5:5 above).

my way that I went, my countenance hath deceived him to his destruction, and yet hath he not committed sin with me, to defile and shame me.

¹⁷Then all the people were wonderfully astonished, and bowed themselves, and worshipped God, and said with one accord, Blessed be thou, O our God, which hast this day brought to nought the enemies of thy people. ¹⁸Then said Ozias unto her, O daughter, blessed art thou of the most high God above all the women upon the earth; and blessed be the Lord God, which hath created the heavens and the earth, which hath directed thee to the cutting off of the head of the chief of our enemies. ¹⁹For this thy confidence shall not depart from the heart of men, which remember the power of God for ever. ²⁰And God turn these things to thee for a perpetual praise, to visit thee in good things, because thou hast not spared thy life for the affliction of our nation, but hast revenged our ruin, walking a straight way before our God. And all the people said, So be it, so be it.

14 Then said Judith unto them, Hear me now, my brethren, and take this head, and hang it upon the highest place of your walls. ²And so soon as the morning shall appear, and the sun shall come forth upon the earth, take ye every one his weapons, and go forth every valiant man out of the city, and set ye a captain over them, as though ye would go down into the field toward the watch of the Assyrians; but go not down. ³Then they shall take their armour, and shall go into their camp, and raise up the captains of the army of Assur, and they shall run to the tent of Holofernes, but shall not find him: then fear shall fall upon them, and they shall flee before your face. ⁴So ye, and all that inhabit the coast of Israel, shall pursue them, and overthrow them as they go. ⁵But before ye do these things, call me Achior the Ammonite, that he may see and know him that despised the house of Israel, and that sent him to us, as it were to his death.

⁶Then they called Achior out of the house of Ozias; and when he was come, and saw the head of Holofernes in a man's hand in the assembly of the people, he fell down on his face, and his spirit failed. ⁷But when they had recovered him, he fell at Judith's feet, and reverenced her, and said, Blessed art thou in all the tabernacle of Juda, and in all nations, which hearing thy name shall be astonished. ⁸Now therefore tell me all the things that thou hast done in these days. Then Judith declared unto him in the midst of the people all that she had done, from the day that she went forth until that hour she spake unto them. ⁹And when she had left off speaking, the people shouted with a loud voice, and made a joyful noise in their city. ¹⁰And when Achior had seen all that the God of Israel had done, he believed in God greatly, and circumcised the flesh of his foreskin, and was joined unto the house of Israel unto this day.

13:18 *O daughter . . . earth*: recalling Deborah's blessing of Jael (Judg 5:24). *Blessed be the Lord God . . . enemies*: echoing Melchizedek's blessing of Abraham after his defeat of the coalition of kings holding Lot (Gen 14:19–20). **14:5** *Know*: recognize (i.e., verify). **14:7** *In all the tabernacle of Juda*: alternatively "in every tent of Judah" (NRSV), echoing Judg 5:24.

¹¹And as soon as the morning arose, they hanged the head of Holofernes upon the wall, and every man took his weapons, and they went forth by bands unto the straits of the mountain. ¹²But when the Assyrians saw them, they sent to their leaders, which came to their captains and tribunes, and to every one of their rulers. ¹³So they came to Holofernes' tent, and said to him that had the charge of all his things, Waken now our lord: for the slaves have been bold to come down against us to battle, that they may be utterly destroyed. ¹⁴Then went in Bagoas, and knocked at the door of the tent; for he thought that he had slept with Judith. ¹⁵But because none answered, he opened it, and went into the bedchamber, and found him cast upon the floor dead, and his head was taken from him. ¹⁶Therefore he cried with a loud voice, with weeping, and sighing, and a mighty cry, and rent his garments. ¹⁷After he went into the tent where Judith lodged: and when he found her not, he leaped out to the people, and cried, ¹⁸These slaves have dealt treacherously; one woman of the Hebrews hath brought shame upon the house of king Nabuchodonosor: for, behold, Holofernes lieth upon the ground without a head. ¹⁹When the captains of the Assyrians' army heard these words, they rent their coats, and their minds were wonderfully troubled, and there was a cry and a very great noise throughout the camp.

15 And when they that were in the tents heard, they were astonished at the thing that was done. ²And fear and trembling fell upon them, so that there was no man that durst abide in the sight of his neighbour, but rushing out all together, they fled into every way of the plain, and of the hill country. ³They also that had camped in the mountains round about Bethulia fled away. Then the children of Israel, every one that was a warrior among them, rushed out upon them.

⁴Then sent Ozias to Betomasthem, and to Bebai, and Chobai, and Cola, and to all the coasts of Israel, such as should tell the things that were done, and that all should rush forth upon their enemies to destroy them. ⁵Now when the children of Israel heard it, they all fell upon them with one consent, and slew them unto Chobai: likewise also they that came from Jerusalem, and from all the hill country, (for men had told them what things were done in the camp of their enemies,) and they that were in Galaad, and in Galilee, chased them with a great slaughter, until they were past Damascus and the borders thereof. ⁶And the residue, that dwelt at Bethulia, fell upon the camp of Assur, and spoiled them, and were greatly enriched. ⁷And the children of Israel that returned from the slaughter had that which remained; and the villages and the cities, that were in the mountains and in the plain, gat many spoils: for the multitude was very great.

⁸Then Joacim the high priest, and the ancients of the children of Israel that dwelt in Jerusalem, came to behold the good things that God had shewed to Israel, and to see Judith, and to salute her. ⁹And when they came unto her, they blessed her with one accord, and said unto her, Thou art the exaltation of Jerusalem, thou art the great glory of Israel, thou art the great rejoicing of our nation: ¹⁰thou hast done all these things by thine hand: thou hast done much good to

14:11–15:13 **The flight of the Assyrians.** 14:11 *Straits*: passes. 15:2 *Durst*: dared. 15:7 *Gat*:

Israel, and God is pleased therewith: blessed be thou of the Almighty Lord for evermore. And all the people said, So be it. [11]And the people spoiled the camp the space of thirty days: and they gave unto Judith Holofernes his tent, and all his plate, and beds, and vessels, and all his stuff: and she took it, and laid it on her mule; and made ready her carts, and laid them thereon. [12]Then all the women of Israel ran together to see her, and blessed her, and made a dance among them for her: and she took branches in her hand, and gave also to the women that were with her. [13]And they put a garland of olive upon her and her maid that was with her, and she went before all the people in the dance, leading all the women: and all the men of Israel followed in their armour with garlands, and with songs in their mouths.

16 Then Judith began to sing this thanksgiving in all Israel, and all the people sang after her this song of praise. [2]And Judith said,

> Begin unto my God with timbrels, sing unto my Lord with
>   cymbals: tune unto him a new psalm: exalt him, and call upon
>   his name.
> [3]For God breaketh the battles: for among the camps in the midst
>   of the people he hath delivered me out of the hands
>   of them that persecuted me.
> [4]Assur came out of the mountains from the north, he came with
>   ten thousands of his army, the multitude whereof stopped the
>   torrents, and their horsemen have covered the hills.
> [5]He bragged that he would burn up my borders, and kill my young
>   men with the sword, and dash the sucking children against the
>   ground, and make mine infants as a prey, and my virgins as a
>   spoil.
> [6]But the Almighty Lord hath disappointed them by the hand of a
>   woman.
> [7]For the mighty one did not fall by the young men, neither did the
>   sons of the Titans smite him, nor high giants set upon him: but
>   Judith the daughter of Merari weakened him with the beauty
>   of her countenance.

got.   **15:11** *Thirty days*: Judith had spent the four preceding days with Holofernes (12:10); thus the combined total of thirty-four days equals the length of Bethulia's siege before Judith intervened (cf. 7:20).   **15:12** *Branches*: Gk. *thyrsoi*, the "ivy-wreathed branches" (NRSV) that female followers of Dionysus, Greek god of wine, conventionally carried while in frenzies. (According to Greek mythology, Pentheus was dismembered by women in such a frenty; cf. Euripides, *Bacchae* 1043–1152, esp. 1054–55.) The garland (v. 13) similarly invokes a Greek practice: the awarding of wreaths to victors in Greek contests.
  16:1–25 The song of Judith and celebrations in Jerusalem. Judith's song (vv. 2–17) recalls the Song of the Sea (Exod 15:1–18) and the Song of Deborah (Judg 5).   **16:2** *Begin*: i.e., "begin a song."   **16:3** *God breaketh the battles*: see 9:7 note.   **16:7** *Sons of the Titans*: a reference to the myth of the Olympian gods' war against the previous generation of divinities, the Titans—a popular subject of ancient epic poetry. (The only extant example is Hesiod, *Theogony* 617–720.) *Giants*: a reference to another popular Greek myth, the giants' attempt to dethrone the Olympian gods (cf. Horace, *Odes* 3.4.42–80). The language raises Judith's song to the level of epic poetry and, by implication, her

⁸For she put off the garment of her widowhood for the exaltation
of those that were oppressed in Israel, and anointed her face
with ointment, and bound her hair in a tire, and took a linen
garment to deceive him.
⁹Her sandals ravished his eyes, her beauty took his mind prisoner,
and the fauchion passed through his neck.
¹⁰The Persians quaked at her boldness, and the Medes were
daunted at her hardiness.
¹¹Then my afflicted shouted for joy, and my weak ones cried
aloud; but they were astonished: these lifted up their voices,
but they were overthrown.
¹²The sons of the damsels have pierced them through, and
wounded them as fugitives' children: they perished by the
battle of the Lord.

¹³I will sing unto the Lord a new song: O Lord, thou art great and
glorious, wonderful in strength, and invincible.
¹⁴Let all creatures serve thee: for thou spakest, and they were
made, thou didst send forth thy spirit, and it created them, and
there is none that can resist thy voice.
¹⁵For the mountains shall be moved from their foundations with
the waters, the rocks shall melt as wax at thy presence: yet
thou art merciful to them that fear thee.
¹⁶For all sacrifice is too little for a sweet savour unto thee, and all
the fat is not sufficient for thy burnt offering: but he that
feareth the Lord is great at all times.
¹⁷Woe to the nations that rise up against my kindred! the Lord
Almighty will take vengeance of them in the day of judgment,
in putting fire and worms in their flesh; and they shall feel
them, and weep for ever.

¹⁸Now as soon as they entered into Jerusalem, they worshipped the Lord; and as soon as the people were purified, they offered their burnt offerings, and their free offerings, and their gifts. ¹⁹Judith also dedicated all the stuff of Holofernes, which the people had given her, and gave the canopy, which she had taken out of his bedchamber, for a gift unto the Lord. ²⁰So the people continued feasting in Jerusalem before the sanctuary for the space of three months, and Judith remained with them.

²¹After this time every one returned to his own inheritance, and Judith went to Bethulia, and remained in her own possession, and was in her time honourable in all the country. ²²And many desired her, but none knew her all the days of her life, after that Manasses her husband was dead, and was gathered to his people. ²³But she increased more and more in honour, and waxed old in her husband's

---

deed to the level of epic heroism.   **16:10** *Persians, Medes*: legendarily powerful nations.   **16:12**
Sons of the damsels: i.e., young boys.   **16:13–17** *I will sing . . . ever*: Judith's doxology echoes the
Psalms and other biblical poetry; e.g., Pss 33:3; 97:5; 104:30; Isa 66:24.   **16:22** *Knew*: had sexual

house, being an hundred and five years old, and made her maid free: so she died in Bethulia: and they buried her in the cave of her husband Manasses. ²⁴And the house of Israel lamented her seven days: and before she died, she did distribute her goods to all them that were nearest of kindred to Manasses her husband, and to them that were the nearest of her kindred. ²⁵And there was none that made the children of Israel any more afraid in the days of Judith, nor a long time after her death.

---

relations with.   **16:24** *Before she died . . . husband*: she wills her property in accordance with Num 27:11; thus she is faithful to God in death, as in life.   **16:25** *There was none . . . afraid*: "No one ever again spread terror among the Israelites" (NRSV).

The Rest of the Chapters of
the Book of Esther

THE additions are preserved in the Greek translation of Esther and included by Protestants in the Apocrypha because, as the KJV superscript explains, they are extant in no Hebrew, Aramaic, or other Semitic version independent of the Greek. In fact, there are two Greek versions of Esther: the so-called B-text from the Septuagint, itself the freest translation of any Septuagint book, and the A-text, possibly a translation of a different Hebrew version, possibly a revision of the version in the Septuagint. Both include the additions; KJV translates the former.

There is no evidence that any of these additions was part of the original Hebrew Esther, although A, C, D, and F may originally have been composed in a Semitic language. (B and E, on the contrary, were likely composed in Greek.) Those translated into Greek were presumably part of the Hebrew text that the Septuagint version's colophon (11:1) claims Lysimachus translated no later than the mid-first century B.C.E. (see note). More certainly, four (B, C, D, and E) were in existence by late in the first century C.E., when Josephus drew on them in *Jewish Antiquities*. The additions' supplementarity is confirmed by their frequent contradictions with OT Esther, which are occasionally signaled in the annotations that follow.

The additions seem to perform two primary functions. One is to strengthen the piety of the story. OT Esther is notoriously the one biblical book not even to mention God's name, and these additions are integral to the Septuagint's transformation of that book into a more conventional work of religious prose. Not content merely to supplement the story with pious material frequently echoing other biblical texts, the Greek translator also inserted references to God in places where none stand in the extant Hebrew text (at Esth 2:20; 4:8; 6:1, 13) and made many other alterations as well. The additions' second function is to add dramatic detail to the narrative—for example, by quoting in delightfully pompous Greek the royal decrees that OT Esther is content merely to mention, or by filling out scenes that OT Esther narrates with somewhat more restraint, most notably the heroine's entrance into the presence of the king.

KJV's ordering of the additions follows Jerome's Latin Vulgate, where all but one were lifted from their place in the Greek text and treated as appendices to the OT book. The confusing result is that the reader confronts the last addition first (10:4–11:1), for it already followed OT Esther's close in the Septuagint; rather than displacing it, Jerome marked it as spurious. Then comes the first addition, and then the second, and so on. Scholars now conventionally label the additions A to F according to the order in which they appear in the Greek text. The annotations that follow adopt that scheme and assume that F will be read last.

For more information on the Esther additions, the reader can consult Carey A. Moore's Anchor Bible commentary, *Daniel, Esther, and Jeremiah: The Additions* (Garden City, NY: Doubleday, 1977), which informs this introduction and the annotations that follow.

The Rest of the Chapters

of the

Book of Esther,

Which Are Found Neither in the Hebrew,
nor in the Chaldee

[4]Then Mardocheus said, God hath done these things. [5]For I remember a dream which I saw concerning these matters, and nothing thereof hath failed. [6]A little fountain became a river, and there was light, and the sun, and much water: this river is Esther, whom the king married, and made queen: [7]and the two dragons are I and Aman. [8]And the nations were those that were assembled to destroy the name of the Jews: [9]and my nation is this Israel, which cried to God, and were saved: for the Lord hath saved his people, and the Lord hath delivered us from all those evils, and God hath wrought signs and great wonders, which have not been done among the Gentiles. [10]Therefore hath he made two lots, one for the people of God, and another for all the Gentiles. [11]And these two lots came at the hour, and time, and day of judgment, before God among all nations. [12]So God remembered his people, and justified his inheritance. [13]Therefore those days shall be unto them in the month Adar, the fourteenth and fifteenth day of the same month, with an assembly, and joy, and with gladness before God, according to the generations for ever among his people.

11 In the fourth year of the reign of Ptolemeus and Cleopatra, Dositheus, who said he was a priest and Levite, and Ptolemeus his son, brought this epistle of Phurim, which they said was the same, and that Lysimachus the son of Ptolemeus, that was in Jerusalem, had interpreted it.

10:4–11:1 Addition F: the interpretation of Mordecai's dream and colophon. In narrative time this passage comes at the very end of Esther, following Esth 10:3 and interpreting the dream given at 11:2–11 below (see notes). **10:10** *Lots*: recalling the lots cast in Esth 9:24, after which the holiday Purim was named. **10:13** *Adar*: February-March. **11:1** *In the fourth year . . . interpreted it*: the colophon to LXX Esther. The reference to Ptolemeus and Cleopatra is ambiguous, for there were several Egyptian kings of that name with wives named Cleopatra. The *fourth year of the reign* could therefore be ca. 114, 78, or 49 B.C.E. *Epistle of Phurim*: Esther mentions a letter about Purim at 9:29, but here this phrase appears to refer to the entire book. The colophon thereby constitutes an interpretive guide suggesting that Esther be read as an encyclical encouraging Purim's celebration. (The letters that open 2 Maccabees have much the same function, urging that that book be interpreted as promoting Hanukkah.) *The same*: "authentic" (NRSV). The explicit attributions to

[PLACED IN THE GREEK BEFORE CHAP. I. I OF THE HEBREW]

²In the second year of the reign of Artaxerxes the great, in the first day of the month Nisan, Mardocheus the son of Jairus, the son of Semei, the son of Cisai, of the tribe of Benjamin, had a dream; ³who was a Jew, and dwelt in the city of Susa, a great man, being a servitor in the king's court. ⁴He was also one of the captives, which Nabuchodonosor the king of Babylon carried from Jerusalem with Jechonias king of Judea; and this was his dream: ⁵Behold a noise of a tumult, with thunder, and earthquakes, and uproar in the land: ⁶and, behold, two great dragons came forth ready to fight, and their cry was great. ⁷And at their cry all nations were prepared to battle, that they might fight against the righteous people. ⁸And lo a day of darkness and obscurity, tribulation and anguish, affliction and great uproar, upon the earth. ⁹And the whole righteous nation was troubled, fearing their own evils, and were ready to perish. ¹⁰Then they cried unto God, and upon their cry, as it were from a little fountain, was made a great flood, even much water. ¹¹The light and the sun rose up, and the lowly were exalted, and devoured the glorious.

¹²Now when Mardocheus, who had seen this dream, and what God had determined to do, was awake, he bare this dream in mind, and until night by all means was desirous to know it.

12 And Mardocheus took his rest in the court with Gabatha and Tharra, the two eunuchs of the king, and keepers of the palace. ²And he heard their devices, and searched out their purposes, and learned that they were about to lay hands upon Artaxerxes the king; and so he certified the king of them. ³Then the king examined the two eunuchs, and after that they had confessed it, they were strangled. ⁴And the king made a record of these things, and Mardocheus also wrote thereof. ⁵So the king commanded Mardocheus to serve in the court, and for this he rewarded him. ⁶Howbeit Aman the son of Amadathus the Agagite,

---

Dositheus (*who said* he was a priest; which *they said* was the same) may suggest some doubt in the translator's mind about the legitimacy of the text Dositheus brought, possibly because he knew of a different version of Esther—one closer to that included in the Hebrew Bible. *Interpreted*: translated (into Greek).

11:2−12:6 Addition A: Mordecai's dream and exposure of the plot against Artaxerxes. In narrative time this passage precedes Esth 1:1, with 12:1−6 doubling Esth 2:21−23. By employing cosmogonic and eschatological imagery, it elevates the court intrigues of the OT version to a grander stage.   **11:2** *The second year . . . great*: i.e., a year earlier than the time at the beginning of OT Esther (see 1:3). *Artaxerxes*: Ahasuerus in OT Esther (see 1:1 and note). *Nisan*: March-April. *Mardocheus*: the LXX equivalent of OT Esther's Mordecai (see 2:5 note). On the implications of his genealogy, see Esth 2:5 note.   **11:3** *Susa*: see Esth 1:2 note. *Being a servitor*: i.e., "serving."   **11:4** *One of the captives . . . Judea*: see Esth 2:6 note.   **11:5** *A noise . . . land*: cf. Isa 29:1−8, esp. v. 6.   **11:6** *Two great dragons*: such monsters figure primeval chaos in ancient Near Eastern cosmogonic myths, including passages from the Bible (e.g., Pss 74:12−17; 89:9−12; Isa 51:9−10).   **11:8** *A day . . . great uproar*: cf. Joel 2:2, 10−11; Zeph 1:15; etc.   **11:9** *Their own evils*: "the evils that threatened them" (NRSV).   **12:1** *Gabatha and Tharra*: compare the conspirators of Esth 2:21−23, Bigthan and Teresh.   **12:5** *So the king . . . court*: Mardocheus already was serving, according to 11:3.   **12:6** *Aman*: Haman; see Esth 3:1 note. *Agagite*: so Esth 3:1, where LXX—like the text Greek here—has *bougaios* (derivation and meaning obscure). Later in the additions Haman is referred to as a Macedonian (16:10).

who was in great honour with the king, sought to molest Mardocheus and his people because of the two eunuchs of the king.

[PLACED IN THE GREEK AFTER CHAP. 3. 13 OF THE HEBREW]

13 The copy of the letters was this: The great king Artaxerxes writeth these things to the princes and governors that are under him from India unto Ethiopia, in an hundred and seven and twenty provinces. [2]After that I became lord over many nations, and had dominion over the whole world, not lifted up with presumption of my authority, but carrying myself alway with equity and mildness, I purposed to settle my subjects continually in a quiet life, and making my kingdom peaceable, and open for passage to the utmost coasts, to renew peace, which is desired of all men. [3]Now when I asked my counsellers how this might be brought to pass, Aman, that excelled in wisdom among us, and was approved for his constant good will and stedfast fidelity, and had the honour of the second place in the kingdom, [4]declared unto us, that in all nations throughout the world there was scattered a certain malicious people, that had laws contrary to all nations, and continually despised the commandments of kings, so as the uniting of our kingdoms, honourably intended by us, cannot go forward. [5]Seeing then we understand that this people alone is continually in opposition unto all men, differing in the strange manner of their laws, and evil affected to our state, working all the mischief they can, that our kingdom may not be firmly established: [6]therefore have we commanded, that all they that are signified in writing unto you by Aman, who is ordained over the affairs, and is next unto us, shall all, with their wives and children, be utterly destroyed by the sword of their enemies, without all mercy and pity, the fourteenth day of the twelfth month Adar of this present year: [7]that they, who of old and now also are malicious, may in one day with violence go into the grave, and so ever hereafter cause our affairs to be well settled, and without trouble.

[PLACED IN THE GREEK AFTER CHAP. 4. 17 OF THE HEBREW]

[8]Then Mardocheus thought upon all the works of the Lord, and made his prayer unto him, [9]saying, O Lord, Lord, the King Almighty: for the whole world

---

Because . . . king: contradicting Esth 3:5–6.
13:1–7 Addition B: the king's decree. In narrative time this passage follows Esth 3:13. Almost certainly composed in Greek, this decree is a highly rhetorical piece, and its pomposity is nicely captured by KJV's long, syntactically complex sentences. The impulse toward imperial unity that ostensibly motivates the pronouncement closely resembles that lying behind Antiochus's prohibition of Jewish religious practices in 1 Macc 1:41–51 (see esp. v. 41). **13:1** *An hundred . . . provinces*: see Esth 1:1 note. **13:2** *Coasts*: territories. **13:5** *Continually in opposition unto all men*: a common charge against Jews in antiquity, based on a misinterpretation of their cultural exclusivity and their resistance to conventional syncretistic approaches toward religion. *Affected*: disposed. **13:6** *Next*: lit. "second father"; cf. Gen 45:8. *Fourteenth*: apparently an error—elsewhere the date is given as the thirteenth; cf. 16:20; Esth 3:13; 8:12; 9:1.
13:8–14:19 Addition C: the prayers of Mordecai and Esther. In narrative time this passage follows Esth 4:17. Like Addition F, it enhances the piety of OT Esther. Both prayers are marked by

is in thy power, and if thou hast appointed to save Israel, there is no man that can gainsay thee: [10]for thou hast made heaven and earth, and all the wondrous things under the heaven. [11]Thou art Lord of all things, and there is no man that can resist thee, which art the Lord. [12]Thou knowest all things, and thou knowest, Lord, that it was neither in contempt nor pride, nor for any desire of glory, that I did not bow down to proud Aman. [13]For I could have been content with good will for the salvation of Israel to kiss the soles of his feet. [14]But I did this, that I might not prefer the glory of man above the glory of God: neither will I worship any but thee, O God, neither will I do it in pride.

[15]And now, O Lord God and King, spare thy people: for their eyes are upon us to bring us to nought; yea, they desire to destroy the inheritance, that hath been thine from the beginning. [16]Despise not the portion, which thou hast delivered out of Egypt for thine own self. [17]Hear my prayer, and be merciful unto thine inheritance: turn our sorrow into joy, that we may live, O Lord, and praise thy name: and destroy not the mouths of them that praise thee, O Lord.

[18]All Israel in like manner cried most earnestly unto the Lord, because their death was before their eyes.

14 Queen Esther also, being in fear of death, resorted unto the Lord: [2]and laid away her glorious apparel, and put on the garments of anguish and mourning: and instead of precious ointments, she covered her head with ashes and dung, and she humbled her body greatly, and all the places of her joy she filled with her torn hair. [3]And she prayed unto the Lord God of Israel, saying, O my Lord, thou only art our King: help me, desolate woman, which have no helper but thee: [4]for my danger is in mine hand. [5]From my youth up I have heard in the tribe of my family, that thou, O Lord, tookest Israel from among all people, and our fathers from all their predecessors, for a perpetual inheritance, and thou hast performed whatsoever thou didst promise them. [6]And now we have sinned before thee: therefore hast thou given us into the hands of our enemies, [7]because we worshipped their gods: O Lord, thou art righteous. [8]Nevertheless it satisfieth them not, that we are in bitter captivity: but they have stricken hands with their idols, [9]that they will abolish the thing that thou with thy mouth hast ordained, and destroy thine inheritance, and stop the mouth of them that praise thee, and quench the glory of thy house, and of thine altar, [10]and open the mouths of the heathen to set forth the praises of the idols, and to magnify a fleshly king for ever.

---

continuous repetition of "God" and "Lord," not merely invoking but urgently insisting on the presence of the divine name so conspicuously absent from the OT book.   **13:12** *That I . . . Aman*: see Esth 3:2 and note.   **13:14** *That I might not . . . O God*: recalling some Jews' response to Antiochus's decree; cf. Dan 3:12–18; 1 Macc 2:19–22; 2 Macc 7:30; etc.   **13:15** *The inheritance*: i.e., Israel; cf. Exod 34:9; Deut 9:26, 29; etc. (also at v. 17; 14:5, 9).   **13:16** *Portion*: cf. Deut 32:9. *Delivered out of Egypt*: see Exod 1–15.   **14:2** *All the places of her joy*: more literally "every place of joyful adornment," i.e., her head and neck.   **14:3** *O my Lord . . . thee*: cf. Ps 89:18; Isa 33:22.   **14:6–7** *We have sinned . . . righteous*: recalling such postexilic national confessions as Ezra 9:6–7; Neh 9:26–27, 33–35; Sg Three 6–8; etc.   **14:8** *Stricken hands with*: "covenanted with" (NRSV).   **14:9** *Thy house . . . altar*: the Jerusalem temple was destroyed at the time Esther is purportedly

¹¹O Lord, give not thy sceptre unto them that be nothing, and let them not laugh at our fall; but turn their device upon themselves, and make him an example, that hath begun this against us. ¹²Remember, O Lord, make thyself known in time of our affliction, and give me boldness, O King of the nations, and Lord of all power. ¹³Give me eloquent speech in my mouth before the lion: turn his heart to hate him that fighteth against us, that there may be an end of him, and of all that are likeminded to him: ¹⁴but deliver us with thine hand, and help me that am desolate, and which have no other helper but thee.

¹⁵Thou knowest all things, O Lord; thou knowest that I hate the glory of the unrighteous, and abhor the bed of the uncircumcised, and of all the heathen. ¹⁶Thou knowest my necessity: for I abhor the sign of my high estate, which is upon mine head in the days wherein I shew myself, and that I abhor it as a menstruous rag, and that I wear it not when I am private by myself, ¹⁷and that thine handmaid hath not eaten at Aman's table, and that I have not greatly esteemed the king's feast, nor drunk the wine of the drink offerings. ¹⁸Neither had thine handmaid any joy since the day that I was brought hither to this present, but in thee, O Lord God of Abraham. ¹⁹O thou mighty God above all, hear the voice of the forlorn, and deliver us out of the hands of the mischievous, and deliver me out of my fear.

15 And upon the third day, when she had ended her prayer, she laid away her mourning garments, and put on her glorious apparel. ²And being gloriously adorned, after she had called upon God, who is the beholder and saviour of all things, she took two maids with her: ³and upon the one she leaned, as carrying herself daintily; ⁴and the other followed, bearing up her train. ⁵And she was ruddy through the perfection of her beauty, and her countenance was cheerful and very amiable: but her heart was in anguish for fear. ⁶Then having passed through all the doors, she stood before the king, who sat upon his royal throne, and was clothed with all his robes of majesty, all glittering with gold and precious stones; and he was very dreadful.

⁷Then lifting up his countenance that shone with majesty, he looked very fiercely upon her: and the queen fell down, and was pale, and fainted, and bowed herself upon the head of the maid that went before her. ⁸Then God changed the spirit of the king into mildness, who in a fear leaped from his throne, and took her in his arms, till she came to herself again, and comforted her with loving

---

praying (see 2 Kgs 25:9, 13–17), but had been rebuilt by the time of the prayer's composition. **14:13** *The lion*: referring to Artaxerxes. **14:15** *Abhor the bed . . . heathen*: OT Esther raises no objection to marrying a Gentile, but Esther here turns from concern for her people to a defense of her own miscegenation, ultimately claiming that "necessity" alone prompts her to marry the foreign king (v. 16). Her views adhere to the strain of postexilic Jewish thought about intermarriage reflected in Ezra 9–10. **14:16** *The sign of my high estate*: i.e., the crown (cf. Esth 1:11; 2:17); her refusal to name it dramatizes her abhorrence. **14:17** *Hath not eaten . . . offerings*: i.e., have observed Jewish dietary regulations and avoided food devoted to pagan gods; cf. Dan 1:8–17.

15:1–16 Addition D: Esther appears before the king. In narrative time this passage continues directly from Addition C above. It imaginatively elaborates on Esth 5:1–2, making explicit God's

words, and said unto her, ⁹Esther, what is the matter? I am thy brother, be of good cheer: ¹⁰thou shalt not die, though our commandment be general: come near. ¹¹And so he held up his golden sceptre, and laid it upon her neck, ¹²and embraced her, and said, Speak unto me. ¹³Then said she unto him, I saw thee, my lord, as an angel of God, and my heart was troubled for fear of thy majesty. ¹⁴For wonderful art thou, lord, and thy countenance is full of grace. ¹⁵And as she was speaking, she fell down for faintness. ¹⁶Then the king was troubled, and all his servants comforted her.

[PLACED IN THE GREEK AFTER CHAP. 8. 12 OF THE HEBREW]

16 The great king Artaxerxes unto the princes and governors of an hundred and seven and twenty provinces from India unto Ethiopia, and unto all our faithful subjects, greeting.

²Many, the more often they are honoured with the great bounty of their gracious princes, the more proud they are waxen, ³and endeavour to hurt not our subjects only, but not being able to bear abundance, do take in hand to practise also against those that do them good: ⁴and take not only thankfulness away from among men, but also lifted up with the glorious words of lewd persons, that were never good, they think to escape the justice of God, that seeth all things, and hateth evil. ⁵Oftentimes also fair speech of those, that are put in trust to manage their friends' affairs, hath caused many that are in authority to be partakers of innocent blood, and hath enwrapped them in remediless calamities: ⁶beguiling with the falsehood and deceit of their lewd disposition the innocency and goodness of princes.

⁷Now ye may see this, as we have declared, not so much by ancient histories, as ye may, if ye search what hath been wickedly done of late through the pestilent behaviour of them that are unworthily placed in authority. ⁸And we must take care for the time to come, that our kingdom may be quiet and peaceable for all men, ⁹both by changing our purposes, and always judging things that are evident with more equal proceeding. ¹⁰For Aman, a Macedonian, the son of Amadatha, being indeed a stranger from the Persian blood, and far distant from our goodness, and as a stranger received of us, ¹¹had so far forth obtained the favour that we shew toward every nation, as that he was called our father, and was continually honoured of all men, as the next person unto the king.

¹²But he, not bearing his great dignity, went about to deprive us of our kingdom and life: ¹³having by manifold and cunning deceits sought of us the destruction, as well of Mardocheus, who saved our life, and continually procured our good, as also of blameless Esther, partaker of our kingdom, with their whole

---

role in the narrative (esp. v. 8).   **15:10** *Thou shalt not die . . . general*: cf. Esth 4:11.   **15:13–14** *I saw thee . . . grace*: she describes the king as he appeared in v. 6 in terms almost fit for a divinity, thereby suggesting that God's transformation of him (v. 8) amounted to his humbling.

16:1–24 Addition E: the king's second decree, in favor of the Jews. In narrative time this passage follows Esth 8:12. Highly rhetorical, like Addition B, it was almost certainly composed in Greek.   **16:4** *They think . . . evil*: in a sign of the extreme piety of these additions, even Artaxerxes

nation. [14]For by these means he thought, finding us destitute of friends, to have translated the kingdom of the Persians to the Macedonians. [15]But we find that the Jews, whom this wicked wretch hath delivered to utter destruction, are no evildoers, but live by most just laws: [16]and that they be children of the most high and most mighty living God, who hath ordered the kingdom both unto us and to our progenitors in the most excellent manner.

[17]Wherefore ye shall do well not to put in execution the letters sent unto you by Aman the son of Amadatha. [18]For he, that was the worker of these things, is hanged at the gates of Susa with all his family: God, who ruleth all things, speedily rendering vengeance to him according to his deserts.

[19]Therefore ye shall publish the copy of this letter in all places, that the Jews may freely live after their own laws. [20]And ye shall aid them, that even the same day, being the thirteenth day of the twelfth month Adar, they may be avenged on them, who in the time of their affliction shall set upon them. [21]For Almighty God hath turned to joy unto them the day, wherein the chosen people should have perished.

[22]Ye shall therefore among your solemn feasts keep it an high day with all feasting: [23]that both now and hereafter there may be safety to us, and the well affected Persians; but to those which do conspire against us a memorial of destruction. [24]Therefore every city and country whatsoever, which shall not do according to these things, shall be destroyed without mercy with fire and sword, and shall be made not only unpassable for men, but also most hateful to wild beasts and fowls for ever.

---

recognizes and praises the God of the Jews (see also vv. 16, 18, 21). **16:14** *Translated*: transferred. The charge of treason is signaled earlier in the additions; see 12:6, which hints that Haman was a co-conspirator with the two eunuchs. **16:17** *The letters sent unto you by Aman*: see Esth 3:12–15. **16:22** *Ye shall . . . feasting*: this *high day* is Purim (see Esth 9:20–32).

The Wisdom of Solomon

THIS text offers a carefully crafted fusion of Jewish and Greek thinking about the nature of wisdom. It was composed in Greek by a hellenized Jew writing sometime between ca. 220 B.C.E. and 50 C.E. Perhaps it was written in Alexandria, whose Jewish community produced similar writings in this time period. If so, the text's animosity toward the villains of Exodus might have been a veiled attack on the pagan Egyptians of the author's own day. While Wisdom's form owes much to the Hebrew poetic tradition (see introduction to Sirach), its Greek style is good as well (Jerome praised its eloquence highly), as befits the book's ambitious aim to bridge the exclusivity of the Torah and the universality of Greek philosophical thought. Indeed, although its exegesis is sustained and subtle, Wisdom never mentions biblical characters or events by name, preferring to refer to them in ostensibly general terms that grant the scriptural stories it invokes an air of typicality, as if to suggest their universal philosophical relevance. While this book is addressed to the "judges of the earth" (1:1), it is hard to imagine how readers without a thorough knowledge of the Jewish Scriptures so allusively mentioned could have ever appreciated or even understood it. It therefore was probably written with a Jewish audience in mind, perhaps to urge its readers toward an appreciation of the philosophical lessons contained in their own cultural inheritance, as well as to suggest broad compatibility between Jewish traditions and Greek thought. Wisdom is hardly the only Hellenistic literary work that looks like such an attempt. It has much in common with the writings of Josephus and of Philo of Alexandria, to name just two examples.

The Wisdom of Solomon is fascinating on a number of levels. The reader is initially struck by its exegetical sophistication: for instance, it constructs insightful readings of Exodus by carefully tracing ironic correspondences between God's punishment of Egypt and protection of Israel. On a different exegetical note, this pseudepigraphical composition deftly attributes itself to the legendary king Solomon by "autobiographically" elaborating on discrete elements of his history as preserved in older biblical texts. Leaving exegesis aside, the excursus on "idolatry" in chapters 13–15—part speculative exploration on the origins of ancient Mediterranean paganism, part polemical diatribe blaming this religious tradition for every transgression imaginable—offers important insight into what many ancient Jews (including Paul; see Rom 1:18–32 and notes) thought about their neighbors' religious beliefs and practices. Perhaps Wisdom's most impressive feature, however, is the breadth of knowledge it displays. As the annotations that follow only begin to suggest, this book is deeply engaged with Greek literature and philosophy as well as with traditional Jewish biblical exegesis, containing almost as many parallels with Platonic and Stoic writings as with other biblical texts and their traditional interpretations.

Wisdom is ultimately more than a compendium of passages of interest. The book is a carefully structured whole: an opening address to the world's rulers in which the righteous and unrighteous are contrasted (chaps. 1–6) gives way to an ostensibly autobiographical account of an Israelite king's encounter with Wisdom (chaps. 7–9). This leads in turn to an extended treatment of Israel's history, ultimately focusing on its exodus from unjust and foolishly idolatrous Egypt (chaps. 10–19, with an excursus on idolatry in chaps. 13–15). Binding the whole work together is the thematic opposition of life and death—most clearly on display in the contrast between Israel and Egypt that dominates the book's latter half, but evident elsewhere as well. For instance, while adhering to the Platonic philosophical tradition's conception of an immortal soul (see 8:19–20 and v. 19 note; 9:15), Wisdom nonetheless conceives of the soul's immortality in a non-Platonic way: as a divine bestowal of life on the wise rather than as a property of the soul itself (2:23; 3:1–9). Conversely, Wisdom makes death the progenitor of folly, as evident in such disparate passages as the exploration of the brutally nihilistic philosophy of the unrighteous (1:16–2:24) and the author's speculation that idolatry, the apex of folly, originated in a bereaved man's pathetic obsession with his dead child (14:15–21).

For more information, the reader can consult David Winston's Anchor Bible commentary, *The Wisdom of Solomon: A New Translation with Introduction and Commentary* (Garden City, NY: Doubleday, 1979), which does an excellent job of tracing Wisdom's erudite engagement with ancient Jewish and Greek literature. It and Winston's thorough annotations (revised by Thomas H. Tobin) in *The HarperCollins Study Bible*, ed. Harold W. Attridge, revised ed. (San Francisco: HarperCollins, 2006), inform this introduction and the notes that follow.

The Wisdom of Solomon

1 Love righteousness, ye that be judges of the earth: think of the Lord with a good (heart,) and in simplicity of heart seek him.

^{2}For he will be found of them that tempt him not; and sheweth himself unto such as do not distrust him.

^{3}For froward thoughts separate from God: and his power, when it is tried, reproveth the unwise.

^{4}For into a malicious soul wisdom shall not enter; nor dwell in the body that is subject unto sin.

^{5}For the holy spirit of discipline will flee deceit, and remove from thoughts that are without understanding, and will not abide when unrighteousness cometh in.

^{6}For wisdom is a loving spirit; and will not acquit a blasphemer of his words: for God is witness of his reins, and a true beholder of his heart, and a hearer of his tongue.

^{7}For the Spirit of the Lord filleth the world: and that which containeth all things hath knowledge of the voice.

^{8}Therefore he that speaketh unrighteous things cannot be hid: neither shall vengeance, when it punisheth, pass by him.

^{9}For inquisition shall be made into the counsels of the ungodly: and the sound of his words shall come unto the Lord for the manifestation of his wicked deeds.

^{10}For the ear of jealousy heareth all things: and the noise of murmurings is not hid.

1:1–6:25 Wisdom the source of immortality. Beginning and closing with an address to the world's rulers, the first part of this work explores and defines the ways in which Wisdom protects the righteous and condemns the unrighteous. Giving the ungodly a chance to speak and reveal their own emptiness, it sets their worldly wisdom against the immortality that the wisdom of the righteous guarantees. **1:1–16 Exhortation to wisdom.** Comparable to the Stoic concept of spirit (Gk. *pneuma*) that pervades, sustains, and structures all that exists, Wisdom is here identified as the true generative resource of the world. **1:1** *Judges*: rulers. *Heart*: a seat of intellection and volition, in addition to emotion (so throughout). *Simplicity*: lit. "singleness," sometimes connoting generosity, but here perhaps sincerity (so NRSV). **1:2** *Tempt*: test; cf. Deut 6:16. **1:5** *The holy spirit of discipline*: "a holy and disciplined spirit" (NRSV). *Will not abide*: "will be ashamed" (NRSV), rendering the same Greek verb as "reproveth" in v. 3. **1:6** *Reins* [kidneys]: see note on "heart" at 1:1. **1:7** *The Spirit . . . things*: assimilating God's spirit to the Stoic concept of *pneuma* (see note to 1:1–16). *Hath knowledge of the voice*: "knows what is said" (NRSV). **1:8** *Vengeance*: better "justice." **1:10** *The ear of jealousy*: i.e., God's jealousy; cf. Exod 20:5; 34:14; etc. (unless the correct translation is "the zealous ear"). *Murmurings*: the word traditionally associated with rebellion against God, especially

¹¹Therefore beware of murmuring, which is unprofitable; and refrain your tongue from backbiting: for there is no word so secret, that shall go for nought: and the mouth that belieth slayeth the soul. ¹²Seek not death in the error of your life: and pull not upon yourselves destruction with the works of your hands. ¹³For God made not death: neither hath he pleasure in the destruction of the living. ¹⁴For he created all things, that they might have their being: and the generations of the world were healthful; and there is no poison of destruction in them, nor the kingdom of death upon the earth: ¹⁵For righteousness is immortal: ¹⁶But ungodly men with their works and words called it to them: for when they thought to have it their friend, they consumed to nought, and made a covenant with it, because they are worthy to take part with it.

2 For the ungodly said, reasoning with themselves, but not aright, Our life is short and tedious, and in the death of a man there is no remedy: neither was there any man known to have returned from the grave. ²For we are born at all adventure: and we shall be hereafter as though we had never been: for the breath in our nostrils is as smoke, and a little spark in the moving of our heart: ³Which being extinguished, our body shall be turned into ashes, and our spirit shall vanish as the soft air, ⁴And our name shall be forgotten in time, and no man shall have our works in remembrance, and our life shall pass away as the trace of a cloud, and shall be dispersed as a mist, that is driven away with the beams of the sun, and overcome with the heat thereof. ⁵For our time is a very shadow that passeth away; and after our end there is no returning: for it is fast sealed, so that no man cometh again. ⁶Come on therefore, let us enjoy the good things that are present: and let us speedily use the creatures like as in youth.

---

during the Israelites' wilderness wanderings (e.g., Exod 16:7–12). **1:11** *Backbiting*: slander. *Belieth*: tells lies about others. **1:13–14** *God made . . . earth*: so Gen 1–3. **11:14** *No poison of destruction in them*: unless one counts the tree of knowledge (see Gen 2:17).

2:1–2:24 The philosophy of the unrighteous. In response to the preceding exhortation, this section gives, ostensibly in their own words, the counterview of the ungodly who put themselves under the power of death (2:1–20). **1:16** *It*: i.e., destruction or death. *Consumed to nought*: melted away. **2:2** *At all adventure*: without premeditation, and thus "by chance." **2:6** *Let us enjoy . . . present*: a common idea in ancient literature; cf. Isa 22:13 and, most famously, Horace, *Ode* 1.11.8, *carpe diem, quam minimum credula postero* ("seize today, trusting as little as possible in tomorrow"). *Creatures*: creation.

⁷Let us fill ourselves with costly wine and ointments: and let no flower of the spring pass by us:

⁸Let us crown ourselves with rosebuds, before they be withered:

⁹Let none of us go without his part of our voluptuousness: let us leave tokens of our joyfulness in every place: for this is our portion, and our lot is this.

¹⁰Let us oppress the poor righteous man, let us not spare the widow, nor reverence the ancient gray hairs of the aged.

¹¹Let our strength be the law of justice: for that which is feeble is found to be nothing worth.

¹²Therefore let us lie in wait for the righteous; because he is not for our turn, and he is clean contrary to our doings: he upbraideth us with our offending the law, and objecteth to our infamy the transgressions of our education.

¹³He professeth to have the knowledge of God: and he calleth himself the child of the Lord.

¹⁴He was made to reprove our thoughts.

¹⁵He is grievous unto us even to behold: for his life is not like other men's, his ways are of another fashion.

¹⁶We are esteemed of him as counterfeits: he abstaineth from our ways as from filthiness: he pronounceth the end of the just to be blessed, and maketh his boast that God is his father.

¹⁷Let us see if his words be true: and let us prove what shall happen in the end of him.

¹⁸For if the just man be the son of God, he will help him, and deliver him from the hand of his enemies.

¹⁹Let us examine him with despitefulness and torture, that we may know his meekness, and prove his patience.

²⁰Let us condemn him with a shameful death: for by his own saying he shall be respected.

²¹Such things they did imagine, and were deceived: for their own wickedness hath blinded them.

²²As for the mysteries of God, they knew them not: neither hoped they for the wages of righteousness, nor discerned a reward for blameless souls.

²³For God created man to be immortal, and made him to be an image of his own eternity.

2:8 *Let us crown . . . withered*: another conventional motif; cf. Horace, *Ode* 2.3.13–16.   **2:9** *Voluptuousness*: revelry.   **2:12** *Let us . . . righteous*: recalling Prov 1:11. *He is not for our turn*: we have no use for him. *Objecteth*: denounces.   **2:17** *Prove*: test.   **2:18** *If the just man . . . enemies*: cf. Matt 27:43.   **2:20** *Respected*: Gk. *episkopē*, lit. "watched over" (elsewhere "visitation"; see 8:7, 13; 14:11). It may mean protected (so NRSV) or punished (cf. 14:11).   **2:23** *Made him . . . eternity*: see Gen 1:27.

²⁴Nevertheless through envy of the devil came death into the world: and they that do hold of his side do find it.

3 But the souls of the righteous are in the hand of God, and there shall no torment touch them.

²In the sight of the unwise they seemed to die: and their departure is taken for misery,

³And their going from us to be utter destruction: but they are in peace.

⁴For though they be punished in the sight of men, yet is their hope full of immortality.

⁵And having been a little chastised, they shall be greatly rewarded: for God proved them, and found them worthy for himself.

⁶As gold in the furnace hath he tried them, and received them as a burnt offering.

⁷And in the time of their visitation they shall shine, and run to and fro like sparks among the stubble.

⁸They shall judge the nations, and have dominion over the people, and their Lord shall reign for ever.

⁹They that put their trust in him shall understand the truth: and such as be faithful in love shall abide with him: for grace and mercy is to his saints, and he hath care for his elect.

¹⁰But the ungodly shall be punished according to their own imaginations, which have neglected the righteous, and forsaken the Lord.

¹¹For whoso despiseth wisdom and nurture, he is miserable, and their hope is vain, their labours unfruitful, and their works unprofitable:

¹²Their wives are foolish, and their children wicked:

¹³Their offspring is cursed.

Wherefore blessed is the barren that is undefiled, which hath not known the sinful bed: she shall have fruit in the visitation of souls.

2:24 *Through envy . . . world*: referring to legendary expansions on Gen 2–3 such as that preserved in the *Life of Adam and Eve*, which portrays Satan, expelled from heaven as a result of his refusal to worship God's image in man, becoming envious of the first couple in the garden and therefore tempting Eve to transgress God's commandment. This traditional elaboration of Genesis influenced such later works as the Qur'an (e.g., 7:11–22) and Milton's *Paradise Lost*. *Hold of his side*: belong to his party.

3:1–4:20 The justice of God. A section that explores the problem of the suffering of the righteous, focusing first on their general trials (3:1–13a) and then on the specific issues of childlessness (3:13b–4:6) and early death (4:7–20). **3:6** *Gold in the furnace*: a common OT image; e.g., Zech 13:9; Mal 3:3. **3:7** *The time of their visitation*: i.e., divine judgment (also at v. 13). **3:7–8** *They shall shine . . . people*: common eschatological expectations; cf. Dan 7:22; 12:3. **3:7** *Like sparks . . . stubble*: cf. Joel 2:5; Zech 12:6. **3:9** *Saints*: holy ones.

¹⁴And blessed is the eunuch, which with his hands hath wrought
no iniquity, nor imagined wicked things against God: for unto
him shall be given the special gift of faith, and an inheritance
in the temple of the Lord more acceptable to his mind.
¹⁵For glorious is the fruit of good labours: and the root of wisdom
shall never fall away.
¹⁶As for the children of adulterers, they shall not come to their
perfection, and the seed of an unrighteous bed shall be rooted
out.
¹⁷For though they live long, yet shall they be nothing regarded:
and their last age shall be without honour.
¹⁸Or, if they die quickly, they have no hope, neither comfort in the
day of trial.
¹⁹For horrible is the end of the unrighteous generation.

4 ¹Better it is to have no children, and to have virtue: for the memorial thereof is immortal: because it is known with God, and
with men.
²When it is present, men take example at it; and when it is gone,
they desire it: it weareth a crown, and triumpheth for ever,
having gotten the victory, striving for undefiled rewards.
³But the multiplying brood of the ungodly shall not thrive, nor
take deep rooting from bastard slips, nor lay any fast
foundation.
⁴For though they flourish in branches for a time; yet standing not
fast, they shall be shaken with the wind, and through the force
of winds they shall be rooted out.
⁵The imperfect branches shall be broken off, their fruit unprofit-
able, not ripe to eat, yea, meet for nothing.
⁶For children begotten of unlawful beds are witnesses of wicked-
ness against their parents in their trial.

⁷But though the righteous be prevented with death, yet shall he be
in rest.
⁸For honourable age is not that which standeth in length of time,
nor that is measured by number of years.
⁹But wisdom is the gray hair unto men, and an unspotted life is
old age.
¹⁰He pleased God, and was beloved of him: so that living among
sinners he was translated.

3:14 *Eunuch*: the promise of blessing for the castrated recalls Isa 56:3–5 (see note to 56:1–8),
which abrogates Deut 23:1. **3:16** *Children of adulterers*: their curse recalls Deut 23:2, which denies
children born of illicit unions a place in the congregation; also cf. Sir 23:25. **4:1** *The memorial
thereof is immortal*: cf. Ps 112:6. **4:2** *Weareth a crown*: crowns were conventionally awarded to victors of Greek athletic and other competitions. **4:3** *Slips*: transplanted shoots. **4:7** *Be prevented
with death*: "die early" (NRSV). **4:10–15** *He pleased . . . chosen*: referring to Enoch (see Gen 5:24).
This book's peculiar omission of proper names encourages the reader to view the biblical characters
alluded to as generalized archetypes. It also recalls the penchant displayed in Hellenistic literature for

¹¹Yea, speedily was he taken away, lest that wickedness should alter his understanding, or deceit beguile his soul.
¹²For the bewitching of naughtiness doth obscure things that are honest; and the wandering of concupiscence doth undermine the simple mind.
¹³He, being made perfect in a short time, fulfilled a long time:
¹⁴For his soul pleased the Lord: therefore hasted he to take him away from among the wicked.
¹⁵This the people saw, and understood it not, neither laid they up this in their minds, That his grace and mercy is with his saints, and that he hath respect unto his chosen.
¹⁶Thus the righteous that is dead shall condemn the ungodly which are living; and youth that is soon perfected the many years and old age of the unrighteous.
¹⁷For they shall see the end of the wise, and shall not understand what God in his counsel hath decreed of him, and to what end the Lord hath set him in safety.
¹⁸They shall see him, and despise him; but God shall laugh them to scorn: and they shall hereafter be a vile carcase, and a reproach among the dead for evermore.
¹⁹For he shall rend them, and cast them down headlong, that they shall be speechless; and he shall shake them from the foundation; and they shall be utterly laid waste, and be in sorrow; and their memorial shall perish.
²⁰And when they cast up the accounts of their sins, they shall come with fear: and their own iniquities shall convince them to their face.

5 Then shall the righteous man stand in great boldness before the face of such as have afflicted him, and made no account of his labours.
²When they see it, they shall be troubled with terrible fear, and shall be amazed at the strangeness of his salvation, so far beyond all that they looked for.
³And they repenting and groaning for anguish of spirit shall say within themselves, This was he, whom we had sometimes in derision, and a proverb of reproach:
⁴We fools accounted his life madness, and his end to be without honour:

obscure allusions discernible only by attentive and erudite readers.   **4:11** *Yea, speedily . . . soul*: cf. Isa 57:1.   **4:18** *God shall laugh them to scorn*: cf. Pss 2:4; 37:13.   **4:19** *Their memorial shall perish*: cf. Ps 9:6.   **4:20** *Convince*: convict; cf. Jer 2:19.
   5:1–23 The final judgment. This section contrasts the vindication of the righteous with the condemnation of the unrighteous, who in vv. 3–13 regret their earlier arrogance (2:1–20).

⁵How is he numbered among the children of God, and his lot is among the saints!

⁶Therefore have we erred from the way of truth, and the light of righteousness hath not shined unto us, and the sun of righteousness rose not upon us.

⁷We wearied ourselves in the way of wickedness and destruction: yea, we have gone through deserts, where there lay no way: but as for the way of the Lord, we have not known it.

⁸What hath pride profited us? or what good hath riches with our vaunting brought us?

⁹All those things are passed away like a shadow, and as a post that hasted by;

¹⁰And as a ship that passeth over the waves of the water, which when it is gone by, the trace thereof cannot be found, neither the pathway of the keel in the waves;

¹¹Or as when a bird hath flown through the air, there is no token of her way to be found, but the light air being beaten with the stroke of her wings, and parted with the violent noise and motion of them, is passed through, and therein afterwards no sign where she went is to be found;

¹²Or like as when an arrow is shot at a mark, it parteth the air, which immediately cometh together again, so that a man cannot know where it went through:

¹³Even so we in like manner, as soon as we were born, began to draw to our end, and had no sign of virtue to shew; but were consumed in our own wickedness.

¹⁴For the hope of the ungodly is like dust that is blown away with the wind; like a thin froth that is driven away with the storm; like as the smoke which is dispersed here and there with a tempest, and passeth away as the remembrance of a guest that tarrieth but a day.

¹⁵But the righteous live for evermore; their reward also is with the Lord, and the care of them is with the most High.

¹⁶Therefore shall they receive a glorious kingdom, and a beautiful crown from the Lord's hand: for with his right hand shall he cover them, and with his arm shall he protect them.

¹⁷He shall take to him his jealousy for complete armour, and make the creature his weapon for the revenge of his enemies.

¹⁸He shall put on righteousness as a breastplate, and true judgment instead of an helmet.

5:7 *We have gone . . . way*: cf. Ps 107:40.   5:8 *Vaunting*: pretentious boasting.   5:9 *Post*: messenger.   5:10–11 *As a ship . . . is to be found*: elaborating Job 9:26.   5:14 *Dust*: alternatively "thistledown"; cf. Job 21:18. *Froth*: better "frost" (MS tradition). *As the smoke*: cf. Ps 68:2.   5:17–20 *He shall take to him . . . sword*: cf. Isa 59:16–17.   5:17 *Jealousy*: zeal. *Creature*: creation.

¹⁹He shall take holiness for an invincible shield.
²⁰His severe wrath shall he sharpen for a sword, and the world
    shall fight with him against the unwise.
²¹Then shall the right aiming thunderbolts go abroad; and from
    the clouds, as from a well drawn bow, shall they fly to the mark.
²²And hailstones full of wrath shall be cast as out of a stone bow,
    and the water of the sea shall rage against them, and the floods
    shall cruelly drown them.
²³Yea, a mighty wind shall stand up against them, and like a storm
    shall blow them away: thus iniquity shall lay waste the whole
    earth, and ill dealing shall overthrow the thrones of the mighty.

6 Hear therefore, O ye kings, and understand; learn, ye that be
    judges of the ends of the earth.
²Give ear, ye that rule the people, and glory in the multitude of
    nations.
³For power is given you of the Lord, and sovereignty from the
    Highest, who shall try your works, and search out your
    counsels.
⁴Because, being ministers of his kingdom, ye have not judged
    aright, nor kept the law, nor walked after the counsel of God;
⁵Horribly and speedily shall he come upon you: for a sharp
    judgment shall be to them that be in high places.
⁶For mercy will soon pardon the meanest: but mighty men shall
    be mightily tormented.
⁷For he which is Lord over all shall fear no man's person, neither
    shall he stand in awe of any man's greatness: for he hath made
    the small and great, and careth for all alike.
⁸But a sore trial shall come upon the mighty.
⁹Unto you therefore, O kings, do I speak, that ye may learn
    wisdom, and not fall away.
¹⁰For they that keep holiness holily shall be judged holy: and they
    that have learned such things shall find what to answer.
¹¹Wherefore set your affection upon my words; desire them, and
    ye shall be instructed.
¹²Wisdom is glorious, and never fadeth away: yea, she is easily
    seen of them that love her, and found of such as seek her.

5:21 *Go abroad*: go forth.   **5:22** *Stone bow*: catapult.   **5:23** *Yea, a mighty wind . . . away*: this verse
forms an inclusive frame with v. 14; cf. Isa 41:16.
    6:1–25 The need to search for wisdom. This section closes the first part of the work with
an exhortation (paralleling 1:1–16) that rulers seek and embrace wisdom. Verses 22–25 form a
bridge to the next part, as the narrator prepares to reveal Wisdom's mysteries. The address to the
world's rulers here may allude specifically to the growing power of Rome.   **6:4** *Nor kept . . . God*:
cf. Rom 2:14 note.   **6:6** *Meanest*: lowliest.   **6:12** *She is . . . seek her*: because in Greek (as in
Hebrew) "wisdom" is a feminine noun (*sophia*), it is conventionally personified as a woman.

¹³She preventeth them that desire her, in making herself first known unto them.

¹⁴Whoso seeketh her early shall have no great travail: for he shall find her sitting at his doors.

¹⁵To think therefore upon her is perfection of wisdom: and whoso watcheth for her shall quickly be without care.

¹⁶For she goeth about seeking such as are worthy of her, sheweth herself favourably unto them in the ways, and meeteth them in every thought.

¹⁷For the very true beginning of her is the desire of discipline; and the care of discipline is love;

¹⁸And love is the keeping of her laws; and the giving heed unto her laws is the assurance of incorruption;

¹⁹And incorruption maketh us near unto God:

²⁰Therefore the desire of wisdom bringeth to a kingdom.

²¹If your delight be then in thrones and sceptres, O ye kings of the people, honour wisdom, that ye may reign for evermore.

²²As for wisdom, what she is, and how she came up, I will tell you, and will not hide mysteries from you: but will seek her out from the beginning of her nativity, and bring the knowledge of her into light, and will not pass over the truth.

²³Neither will I go with consuming envy; for such a man shall have no fellowship with wisdom.

²⁴But the multitude of the wise is the welfare of the world: and a wise king is the upholding of the people.

²⁵Receive therefore instruction through my words, and it shall do you good.

7 I myself also am a mortal man, like to all, and the offspring of him that was first made of the earth,

---

6:13 *Preventeth*: anticipates.   **6:14** *Seeketh her early*: cf. Prov 8:17.   **6:17–20** *The very true beginning . . . kingdom*: a six-part syllogism, in which one statement leads to another, climaxing at v. 20, which binds together the love of wisdom and divine sovereignty.   **6:24** *Welfare*: alternatively "salvation." *Upholding*: stability.

7:1–9:18 Solomon's love of wisdom. This second part of the work contains the core of its teaching: it explores the origins of Wisdom, her attributes, and her prime role in the organization of the universe, finally leading, in chap. 9, to an extended prayer for wisdom. It is ostensibly autobiographical, elaborating and alluding to elements of Solomon's story recorded elsewhere in the Bible: the purported author of the work first identifies himself and stresses his common humanity (7:1–6), and then recounts his own search for Wisdom (7:7–21), his appreciation of her nature (7:22–8:1), his love for her (8:2–8), his understanding of her benefits (8:9–16), and his recognition that she is essentially a gift of God (8:17–21), before recounting his prayer for her (chap. 9).   **7:1** *Him that . . . earth*: Adam (Gen 2:7).

²And in my mother's womb was fashioned to be flesh in the time
     of ten months, being compacted in blood, of the seed of man,
     and the pleasure that came with sleep.
³And when I was born, I drew in the common air, and fell upon
     the earth, which is of like nature, and the first voice which I
     uttered was crying, as all others do.
⁴I was nursed in swaddling clothes, and that with cares.
⁵For there is no king that had any other beginning of birth.
⁶For all men have one entrance into life, and the like going out.

⁷Wherefore I prayed, and understanding was given me: I called
     upon God, and the spirit of wisdom came to me.
⁸I preferred her before sceptres and thrones, and esteemed riches
     nothing in comparison of her.
⁹Neither compared I unto her any precious stone, because all gold
     in respect of her is as a little sand, and silver shall be counted
     as clay before her.
¹⁰I loved her above health and beauty, and chose to have her
     instead of light: for the light that cometh from her never goeth
     out.
¹¹All good things together came to me with her, and innumerable
     riches in her hands.
¹²And I rejoiced in them all, because wisdom goeth before them:
     and I knew not that she was the mother of them.
¹³I learned diligently, and do communicate her liberally: I do not
     hide her riches.
¹⁴For she is a treasure unto men that never faileth: which they
     that use become the friends of God, being commended for the
     gifts that come from learning.
¹⁵God hath granted me to speak as I would, and to conceive as is
     meet for the things that are given me: because it is he that
     leadeth unto wisdom, and directeth the wise.
¹⁶For in his hand are both we and our words; all wisdom also, and
     knowledge of workmanship.
¹⁷For he hath given me certain knowledge of the things that are,
     namely, to know how the world was made, and the operation of
     the elements:

7:2 *Ten months*: in antiquity the period of human gestation could be reckoned as ten lunar
months. *Compacted in blood . . . man*: this description follows Aristotle, who believed that semen
acts on menstrual blood to form a fetus in a process analogous to curdling (see *Generation of
Animals* 739b21).   7:3 *Which is of like nature*: alternatively "which suffers the same from all."
7:7–12 *I prayed . . . mother of them*: amplifying 1 Kgs 3:3–15 and 2 Chr 1:1–13 (as does chap. 9).
7:13 *Communicate*: share.   7:15 *As I would*: alternatively "with judgment" (NRSV). *Conceive*: in
the sense of "think." *As is meet for*: worthily of.   7:17–20 *For he . . . roots*: elaborating 1 Kgs
4:33.   7:17 *Elements*: probably referring to earth, water, air, and fire; see Gal 4:3 and note.

¹⁸The beginning, ending, and midst of the times: the alterations
of the turning of the sun, and the change of seasons:
¹⁹The circuits of years, and the positions of stars:
²⁰The natures of living creatures, and the furies of wild beasts:
the violence of winds, and the reasonings of men: the diversities of plants, and the virtues of roots:
²¹And all such things as are either secret or manifest, them I know.

²²For wisdom, which is the worker of all things, taught me: for in
her is an understanding spirit, holy, one only, manifold, subtil,
lively, clear, undefiled, plain, not subject to hurt, loving the thing
that is good, quick, which cannot be letted, ready to do good,
²³Kind to man, stedfast, sure, free from care, having all power,
overseeing all things, and going through all understanding,
pure, and most subtil, spirits.
²⁴For wisdom is more moving than any motion: she passeth and
goeth through all things by reason of her pureness.
²⁵For she is the breath of the power of God, and a pure influence
flowing from the glory of the Almighty: therefore can no
defiled thing fall into her.
²⁶For she is the brightness of the everlasting light, the unspotted
mirror of the power of God, and the image of his goodness.
²⁷And being but one, she can do all things: and remaining in
herself, she maketh all things new: and in all ages entering
into holy souls, she maketh them friends of God, and prophets.
²⁸For God loveth none but him that dwelleth with wisdom.
²⁹For she is more beautiful than the sun, and above all the order
of stars: being compared with the light, she is found before it.
³⁰For after this cometh night: but vice shall not prevail against wisdom.

8 ¹Wisdom reacheth from one end to another mightily: and sweetly
doth she order all things.

²I loved her, and sought her out from my youth, I desired to make
her my spouse, and I was a lover of her beauty.
³In that she is conversant with God, she magnifieth her nobility:
yea, the Lord of all things himself loved her.
⁴For she is privy to the mysteries of the knowledge of God, and a
lover of his works.

7:20 *Virtues of roots*: i.e., their medicinal properties.   **7:22** *For in her*: introducing Wisdom's twenty-one attributes. *One only*: unique. *Quick*: sharp or keen. *Letted*: hindered.   **7:23** *Going through . . . spirits*: "penetrating through all spirits that are intelligent, pure, and altogether subtle" (NRSV).
7:24 *She passeth . . . things*: again assimilating wisdom to the Stoic *pneuma*, which was conceived of as a refined and subtle substance that interpenetrated everything and thereby made the cosmos cohere.   **7:25** *Influence*: in the technical sense of an ethereal effluence or divine emanation that affects the cosmos, and thus compatible with the Stoic concept of *pneuma*.   **8:3** *Is conversant*: Gk.

⁵If riches be a possession to be desired in this life; what is richer
than wisdom, that worketh all things?

⁶And if prudence work; who of all that are is a more cunning
workman than she?

⁷And if a man love righteousness, her labours are virtues: for she
teacheth temperance and prudence, justice and fortitude:
which are such things, as men can have nothing more profitable in their life.

⁸If a man desire much experience, she knoweth things of old, and
conjectureth aright what is to come: she knoweth the subtilties
of speeches, and can expound dark sentences: she foreseeth
signs and wonders, and the events of seasons and times.

⁹Therefore I purposed to take her to me to live with me, knowing
that she would be a counseller of good things, and a comfort in
cares and grief.

¹⁰For her sake I shall have estimation among the multitude, and
honour with the elders, though I be young.

¹¹I shall be found of a quick conceit in judgment, and shall be
admired in the sight of great men.

¹²When I hold my tongue, they shall bide my leisure, and when I
speak, they shall give good ear unto me: if I talk much, they
shall lay their hands upon their mouth.

¹³Moreover by the means of her I shall obtain immortality, and
leave behind me an everlasting memorial to them that come
after me.

¹⁴I shall set the people in order, and the nations shall be subject
unto me.

¹⁵Horrible tyrants shall be afraid, when they do but hear of me; I
shall be found good among the multitude, and valiant in war.

¹⁶After I am come into mine house, I will repose myself with her:
for her conversation hath no bitterness; and to live with her
hath no sorrow, but mirth and joy.

¹⁷Now when I considered these things in myself, and pondered them
in my heart, how that to be allied unto wisdom is immortality;

¹⁸And great pleasure it is to have her friendship; and in the works
of her hands are infinite riches; and in the exercise of conference with her, prudence; and in talking with her, a good
report; I went about seeking how to take her to me.

¹⁹For I was a witty child, and had a good spirit.

---

symbiōsin, lit. "lives with" (cf. v. 9).   **8:8** *Subtilties*: lit. "twists." *Dark sentences*: "riddles"
(NRSV). *Events*: in the sense of "outcomes."   **8:11** *Of a quick conceit*: lit. "sharp."   **8:16** *Conversation*: "companionship" (NRSV).   **8:18** *Conference*: company or society.   **8:19** *Witty*: naturally clever. *And had a good spirit*: more literally "and a good soul fell to my lot" (NRSV); vv.
19–20 amount to an explicit statement of the Platonic doctrine of the soul's preexistence.

²⁰Yea rather, being good, I came into a body undefiled.
²¹Nevertheless, when I perceived that I could not otherwise obtain her, except God gave her me; and that was a point of wisdom also to know whose gift she was; I prayed unto the Lord, and besought him, and with my whole heart I said,

9 O God of my fathers, and Lord of mercy, who hast made all things with thy word,
²And ordained man through thy wisdom, that he should have dominion over the creatures which thou hast made,
³And order the world according to equity and righteousness, and execute judgment with an upright heart:
⁴Give me wisdom, that sitteth by thy throne; and reject me not from among thy children:
⁵For I thy servant and son of thine handmaid am a feeble person, and of a short time, and too young for the understanding of judgment and laws.
⁶For though a man be never so perfect among the children of men, yet if thy wisdom be not with him, he shall be nothing regarded.
⁷Thou hast chosen me to be a king of thy people, and a judge of thy sons and daughters:
⁸Thou hast commanded me to build a temple upon thy holy mount, and an altar in the city wherein thou dwellest, a resemblance of the holy tabernacle, which thou hast prepared from the beginning.
⁹And wisdom was with thee: which knoweth thy works, and was present when thou madest the world, and knew what was acceptable in thy sight, and right in thy commandments.
¹⁰O send her out of thy holy heavens, and from the throne of thy glory, that being present she may labour with me, that I may know what is pleasing unto thee.
¹¹For she knoweth and understandeth all things, and she shall lead me soberly in my doings, and preserve me in her power.
¹²So shall my works be acceptable, and then shall I judge thy people righteously, and be worthy to sit in my father's seat.
¹³For what man is he that can know the counsel of God? or who can think what the will of the Lord is?

9:1–18 *O God . . . wisdom*: Solomon's prayer for wisdom elaborates 1 Kgs 3:6–9; 2 Chr 1:8–10. **9:2** *Ordained man . . . thou hast made*: see Gen 1:26–28. **9:5** *I thy servant . . . handmaid*: cf. Ps 116:16. The subservience is more prominent in the Greek: "I your slave and son of your slave girl." *Too young*: the Greek reads "rather small," perhaps connoting youth but certainly signaling deficiency. **9:8** *Thou hast commanded . . . dwellest*: cf. 2 Sam 7:12–13; 1 Chr 17:11–12. Solomon's construction of the temple in Jerusalem is reported at 1 Kgs 5–8 and 2 Chr 2–7. *A resemblance . . . beginning*: cf. Exod 25:9, 40; Heb 8:2; etc. **9:9** *Wisdom was . . . world*: cf. Prov 3:19–20; 8:22–31. **9:12** *My father's seat*: King David's throne. **9:13–17** *What man . . . from above*: cf. 1 Cor 2:10–13 and notes.

¹⁴For the thoughts of mortal men are miserable, and our devices
    are but uncertain.
¹⁵For the corruptible body presseth down the soul, and the earthy
    tabernacle weigheth down the mind that museth upon many
    things.
¹⁶And hardly do we guess aright at things that are upon earth,
    and with labour do we find the things that are before us: but
    the things that are in heaven who hath searched out?
¹⁷And thy counsel who hath known, except thou give wisdom, and
    send thy Holy Spirit from above?
¹⁸For so the ways of them which lived on the earth were reformed,
    and men were taught the things that are pleasing unto thee,
    and were saved through wisdom.

10 She preserved the first formed father of the world, that was
        created alone, and brought him out of his fall,
²And gave him power to rule all things.
³But when the unrighteous went away from her in his anger, he
    perished also in the fury wherewith he murdered his brother.
⁴For whose cause the earth being drowned with the flood, wisdom
    again preserved it, and directed the course of the righteous in
    a piece of wood of small value.
⁵Moreover, the nations in their wicked conspiracy being con-
    founded, she found out the righteous, and preserved him
    blameless unto God, and kept him strong against his tender
    compassion toward his son.
⁶When the ungodly perished, she delivered the righteous man,
    who fled from the fire which fell down upon the five cities.
⁷Of whose wickedness even to this day the waste land that
    smoketh is a testimony, and plants bearing fruit that never
    come to ripeness: and a standing pillar of salt is a monument
    of an unbelieving soul.

9:15 *Earthy tabernacle*: cf. 2 Cor 5:1 and note.
    10:1–19:22 Wisdom in Israel's history. The third and most complex part of the work is devel-
oped around the experience of Israel and Egypt during the exodus. Its excursion on idolatry (chaps.
13–15) offers a reflection on the major sin of which the Egyptians were guilty.
    10:1–21 Wisdom in history. This section summarizes biblical history from the creation of
Adam to Israel's exodus from Egypt in such a way as to emphasize the role of Wisdom in its progression. The full rhetorical stress on Wisdom is lost in KJV: in Greek, the emphatic pronoun *hautē*, "it
was she who," introduces vv. 1, 5, 6, 10, 13, and 15.   **10:1** *The first . . . world*: Adam (see Gen 2–3).
10:3 *The unrighteous*: Cain (see Gen 4).   **10:4** *For whose cause*: Cain, the first murderer, both
initiates and personifies the violence that ultimately leads to the great deluge (see esp. Gen 6:11).
The righteous: Noah (see Gen 6–9).   **10:5** *The nations . . . being confounded*: referring to the story
of the tower of Babel (see Gen 11:1–9). *The righteous*: Abraham; the rest of the verse refers to his
near-sacrifice of Isaac (see Gen 22).   **10:6** *The righteous man*: Lot, who escaped the destruction
of the cities of the plain (see Gen 19).   **10:7** *An unbelieving soul*: Lot's wife (see Gen 19:26).

⁸For regarding not wisdom, they gat not only this hurt, that they knew not the things which were good; but also left behind them to the world a memorial of their foolishness: so that in the things wherein they offended they could not so much as be hid.

⁹But wisdom delivered from pain those that attended upon her.

¹⁰When the righteous fled from his brother's wrath, she guided him in right paths, shewed him the kingdom of God, and gave him knowledge of holy things, made him rich in his travails, and multiplied the fruit of his labours.

¹¹In the covetousness of such as oppressed him she stood by him, and made him rich.

¹²She defended him from his enemies, and kept him safe from those that lay in wait, and in a sore conflict she gave him the victory; that he might know that godliness is stronger than all.

¹³When the righteous was sold, she forsook him not, but delivered him from sin: she went down with him into the pit,

¹⁴And left him not in bonds, till she brought him the sceptre of the kingdom, and power against those that oppressed him: as for them that had accused him, she shewed them to be liars, and gave him perpetual glory.

¹⁵She delivered the righteous people and blameless seed from the nation that oppressed them.

¹⁶She entered into the soul of the servant of the Lord, and withstood dreadful kings in wonders and signs;

¹⁷Rendered to the righteous a reward of their labours, guided them in a marvellous way, and was unto them for a cover by day, and a light of stars in the night-season;

¹⁸Brought them through the Red sea, and led them through much water:

¹⁹But she drowned their enemies, and cast them up out of the bottom of the deep.

²⁰Therefore the righteous spoiled the ungodly, and praised thy holy name, O Lord, and magnified with one accord thine hand, that fought for them.

²¹For wisdom opened the mouth of the dumb, and made the tongues of them that cannot speak eloquent.

10:8 *Gat*: got.   **10:10** *The righteous*: Jacob; vv. 10–12 summarize the Jacob cycle (see Gen 27–33). **10:12** *A sore conflict*: with the angel; see Gen 32:24–31.   **10:13** *The righteous*: Joseph; vv. 13–14 summarize the Joseph story (Gen 37–50).   **10:15** *The righteous people*: Israel. *Righteous* and *blameless* hark back to v. 5, about Abraham.   **10:16** *The servant of the Lord*: Moses; vv. 16–20 summarize the story of Israel's exodus from Egypt as recounted in Exod 1–15.   **10:17** *Guided them . . . the night-season*: see Exod 13:21–22.   **10:18–19** *Brought them . . . deep*: see Exod 14.   **10:20** *The righteous spoiled the ungodly*: Israel despoiled the Egyptians (Exod 12:35–36). *Praised thy holy name . . . them*: see Exod 15.   **10:21** *Them that cannot speak*: i.e., infants (recalling Ps 8:2).

11 ¹She prospered their works in the hand of the holy prophet.
²They went through the wilderness that was not inhabited, and
pitched tents in places where there lay no way.

³They stood against their enemies, and were avenged of their
adversaries.

⁴When they were thirsty, they called upon thee, and water was
given them out of the flinty rock, and their thirst was
quenched out of the hard stone.

⁵For by what things their enemies were punished, by the same
they in their need were benefited.

⁶For instead of a fountain of a perpetual running river troubled
with foul blood,

⁷For a manifest reproof of that commandment, whereby the
infants were slain, thou gavest unto them abundance of water
by a means which they hoped not for:

⁸Declaring by that thirst then how thou hadst punished their
adversaries.

⁹For when they were tried, albeit but in mercy chastised, they
knew how the ungodly were judged in wrath and tormented,
thirsting in another manner than the just.

¹⁰For these thou didst admonish and try, as a father: but the
other, as a severe king, thou didst condemn and punish.

¹¹Whether they were absent or present, they were vexed alike.

¹²For a double grief came upon them, and a groaning for the
remembrance of things past.

¹³For when they heard by their own punishments the other to be
benefited, they had some feeling of the Lord.

¹⁴For whom they rejected with scorn, when he was long before
thrown out at the casting forth of the infants, him in the end,
when they saw what came to pass, they admired.

11:1–12:27 Wisdom guides Israel in the wilderness. First, Wisdom uses water in contrasting ways to support the righteous Israelites and punish the unrighteous Egyptians, according to the measure-for-measure doctrine spelled out at 11:16. For Egypt, the Nile's water was turned into blood, while for Israel the rock brought forth lifesaving water (11:1–14). Then, in two passages, the parallel treatment of the Egyptians (11:15–12:2) and the Canaanites (12:3–18) is developed: God showed mercy toward both in chastising them for their offenses (11:23; 12:10), but neither repented, and God's treatment of both is intended to teach a lesson to Israel (12:19–22). Finally, the punishment of Egypt is described as the supreme example of measure-for-measure retribution (12:23–27). **11:1** *The holy prophet*: again, Moses. **11:3** *They stood . . . adversaries*: see, e.g., Exod 17:8–13. **11:4** *Water was given . . . stone*: see Exod 17:1–7; Num 20:2–13. **11:6** *A fountain . . . blood*: the first plague (see Exod 7:14–24). **11:7** *That commandment . . . slain*: see Exod 1:15–16. **11:8** *Declaring*: demonstrating. **11:9** *Thirsting . . . the just*: better omitted (MS tradition). **11:10** *These thou . . . as a father*: echoing Deut 8:5. **11:11** *Whether they were absent or present*: i.e., whether the Egyptians were with the Israelites in Egypt or were chasing them as they departed. **11:13** *Had some feeling of*: perceived. **11:14** *Whom they . . . infants*: i.e., Moses, who was hidden in the reeds when the Israelite children were killed (see Exod 2:1–10).

¹⁵But for the foolish devices of their wickedness, wherewith being deceived they worshipped serpents void of reason, and vile beasts, thou didst send a multitude of unreasonable beasts upon them for vengeance;

¹⁶That they might know, that wherewithal a man sinneth, by the same also shall he be punished.

¹⁷For thy Almighty hand, that made the world of matter without form, wanted not means to send among them a multitude of bears, or fierce lions,

¹⁸Or unknown wild beasts, full of rage, newly created, breathing out either a fiery vapour, or filthy scents of scattered smoke, or shooting horrible sparkles out of their eyes:

¹⁹Whereof not only the harm might dispatch them at once, but also the terrible sight utterly destroy them.

²⁰Yea, and without these might they have fallen down with one blast, being persecuted of vengeance, and scattered abroad through the breath of thy power: but thou hast ordered all things in measure and number and weight.

²¹For thou canst shew thy great strength at all times when thou wilt; and who may withstand the power of thine arm?

²²For the whole world before thee is as a little grain of the balance, yea, as a drop of the morning dew that falleth down upon the earth.

²³But thou hast mercy upon all; for thou canst do all things, and winkest at the sins of men, because they should amend.

²⁴For thou lovest all the things that are, and abhorrest nothing which thou hast made: for never wouldest thou have made any thing, if thou hadst hated it.

²⁵And how could any thing have endured, if it had not been thy will? or been preserved, if not called by thee?

²⁶But thou sparest all: for they are thine, O Lord, thou lover of souls.

12 ¹For thine incorruptible Spirit is in all things.

²Therefore chastenest thou them by little and little that offend, and warnest them by putting them in remembrance wherein they have offended, that leaving their wickedness they may believe on thee, O Lord.

³For it was thy will to destroy by the hands of our fathers both those old inhabitants of thy holy land,

---

11:15 *Thou didst send . . . vengeance*: referring to the plagues (of frogs, gnats, locusts, etc.—the kinds of animals whose images the Egyptians supposedly worshipped). **11:17** *That made . . . without form*: see Gen 1:2. **11:22** *A little grain . . . earth*: for the imagery, see Isa 40:15. **11:23** *Winkest at*: overlook. *Because they should amend*: better "so that they may repent" (NRSV). **11:26** *Souls*: alternatively "the living" (NRSV). **12:3–5** *Both those . . . and also those*: the translation is misleading, as the text does not here refer to separate groups of people. **12:3** *Those old inhabitants . . . land*: the

⁴Whom thou hatedst for doing most odious works of witchcrafts, and wicked sacrifices;

⁵And also those merciless murderers of children, and devourers of man's flesh, and the feasts of blood,

⁶With their priests out of the midst of their idolatrous crew, and the parents, that killed with their own hands souls destitute of help:

⁷That the land, which thou esteemedst above all other, might receive a worthy colony of God's children.

⁸Nevertheless even those thou sparedst as men, and didst send wasps, forerunners of thine host, to destroy them by little and little.

⁹Not that thou wast unable to bring the ungodly under the hand of the righteous in battle, or to destroy them at once with cruel beasts, or with one rough word:

¹⁰But executing thy judgments upon them by little and little, thou gavest them place of repentance, not being ignorant that they were a naughty generation, and that their malice was bred in them, and that their cogitation would never be changed.

¹¹For it was a cursed seed from the beginning; neither didst thou for fear of any man give them pardon for those things wherein they sinned.

¹²For who shall say, What hast thou done? or who shall withstand thy judgment? or who shall accuse thee for the nations that perish, whom thou hast made? or who shall come to stand against thee, to be revenged for the unrighteous men?

¹³For neither is there any God but thou that careth for all, to whom thou mightest shew that thy judgment is not unright.

¹⁴Neither shall king or tyrant be able to set his face against thee for any whom thou hast punished.

¹⁵Forsomuch then as thou art righteous thyself, thou orderest all things righteously: thinking it not agreeable with thy power to condemn him that hath not deserved to be punished.

Canaanites. **12:5–6** *Murderers of children . . . help*: referring to (and graphically imagining) sacrifices to the god Molech, as mentioned in numerous places in the OT; see Lev 18:21 and note. **12:5** *Man's flesh*: lit. "human entrails." **12:8** *Wasps*: or "hornets"; see Exod 23:28 and note. **12:10** *They were a naughty generation*: "their origin was evil" (NRSV) or "their nature was evil" (NRSV footnote). **12:11** A *cursed seed from the beginning*: see Gen 9:25–27. **12:12** *To be revenged*: to advocate.

¹⁶For thy power is the beginning of righteousness, and because thou art the Lord of all, it maketh thee to be gracious unto all.

¹⁷For when men will not believe that thou art of a full power, thou shewest thy strength, and among them that know it thou makest their boldness manifest.

¹⁸But thou, mastering thy power, judgest with equity, and orderest us with great favour: for thou mayest use power when thou wilt.

¹⁹But by such works hast thou taught thy people that the just man should be merciful, and hast made thy children to be of a good hope that thou givest repentance for sins.

²⁰For if thou didst punish the enemies of thy children, and the condemned to death, with such deliberation, giving them time and place, whereby they might be delivered from their malice:

²¹With how great circumspection didst thou judge thine own sons, unto whose fathers thou hast sworn, and made covenants of good promises?

²²Therefore, whereas thou dost chasten us, thou scourgest our enemies a thousand times more, to the intent that, when we judge, we should carefully think of thy goodness, and when we ourselves are judged, we should look for mercy.

²³Wherefore, whereas men have lived dissolutely and unrighteously, thou hast tormented them with their own abominations.

²⁴For they went astray very far in the ways of error, and held them for gods, which even among the beasts of their enemies were despised, being deceived, as children of no understanding.

²⁵Therefore unto them, as to children without the use of reason, thou didst send a judgment to mock them.

²⁶But they that would not be reformed by that correction, wherein he dallied with them, shall feel a judgment worthy of God.

²⁷For, look, for what things they grudged, when they were punished, that is, for them whom they thought to be gods; [now] being punished in them, when they saw it, they acknowledged him to be the true God, whom before they denied to know; and therefore came extreme damnation upon them.

12:17 *Boldness*: "rashness" or even "insolence."   **12:27** *For them . . . punished in them*: i.e., punished by plagues of creatures that they had worshipped; see 11:15 note.

13 Surely vain are all men by nature, who are ignorant of God, and could not out of the good things that are seen know him that is: neither by considering the works did they acknowledge the workmaster;

²But deemed either fire, or wind, or the swift air, or the circle of the stars, or the violent water, or the lights of heaven, to be the gods which govern the world.

³With whose beauty if they being delighted took them to be gods; let them know how much better the Lord of them is: for the first author of beauty hath created them.

⁴But if they were astonished at their power and virtue, let them understand by them, how much mightier he is that made them.

⁵For by the greatness and beauty of the creatures proportionably the maker of them is seen.

⁶But yet for this they are the less to be blamed: for they peradventure err, seeking God, and desirous to find him.

⁷For being conversant in his works they search him diligently, and believe their sight: because the things are beautiful that are seen

⁸Howbeit neither are they to be pardoned.

⁹For if they were able to know so much, that they could aim at the world; how did they not sooner find out the Lord thereof?

¹⁰But miserable are they, and in dead things is their hope, who called them gods, which are the works of men's hands, gold and silver, to shew art in, and resemblances of beasts, or a stone good for nothing, the work of an ancient hand.

¹¹Now a carpenter that felleth timber, after he hath sawn down a tree meet for the purpose, and taken off all the bark skilfully round about, and hath wrought it handsomely, and made a vessel thereof fit for the service of man's life;

¹²And after spending the refuse of his work to dress his meat, hath filled himself;

¹³And taking the very refuse among those which served to no use, being a crooked piece of wood, and full of knots, hath carved it diligently, when he had nothing else to do, and formed it by

---

13:1–15:19 Idolatry: its nature, origins, and consequences. In good biblical tradition, the book mounts an extensive polemic against idolatry: an attack first on nature worship (13:1–9) and then on the worship of wooden images (13:10–14:11), leading to a euhemeristic exploration of idolatry's origins and a tendentious discussion of its consequences (14:12–31). After a contrasting excursus on worship of the true God (15:1–6), the focus quickly returns to idolatry: an attack on the crafting of clay idols as a profit-making enterprise (15:7–13) is followed by a final exposé of idolatry's general folly, which serves as a transition back to the historical narrative (15:14–19). **13:1** *Workmaster*: "artisan" (NRSV); the Greek word used here describes Wisdom at 8:6. **13:6** *Peradventure*: perhaps. **13:7** *Being conversant in*: dwelling among. **13:9** *Aim at*: conjecture about. **13:12** *Spending the refuse . . . meat*: using the discarded wood as fuel for fire.

the skill of his understanding, and fashioned it to the image of a man;

[14]Or made it like some vile beast, laying it over with vermilion, and with paint colouring it red, and covering every spot therein;

[15]And when he had made a convenient room for it, set it in a wall, and made it fast with iron:

[16]For he provided for it that it might not fall, knowing that it was unable to help itself; for it is an image, and hath need of help:

[17]Then maketh he prayer for his goods, for his wife and children, and is not ashamed to speak to that which hath no life.

[18]For health he calleth upon that which is weak: for life prayeth to that which is dead: for aid humbly beseecheth that which hath least means to help: and for a good journey he asketh of that which cannot set a foot forward:

[19]And for gaining and getting, and for good success of his hands, asketh ability to do of him, that is most unable to do any thing.

14 Again, one preparing himself to sail, and about to pass through the raging waves, calleth upon a piece of wood more rotten than the vessel that carrieth him.

[2]For verily desire of gain devised that, and the workman built it by his skill.

[3]But thy providence, O Father, governeth it: for thou hast made a way in the sea, and a safe path in the waves;

[4]Shewing that thou canst save from all danger: yea, though a man went to sea without art.

[5]Nevertheless thou wouldest not that the works of thy wisdom should be idle, and therefore do men commit their lives to a small piece of wood, and passing the rough sea in a weak vessel are saved.

[6]For in the old time also, when the proud giants perished, the hope of the world governed by thy hand escaped in a weak vessel, and left to all ages a seed of generation.

[7]For blessed is the wood whereby righteousness cometh.

[8]But that which is made with hands is cursed, as well it, as he that made it: he, because he made it; and it, because, being corruptible, it was called god.

[9]For the ungodly and his ungodliness are both alike hateful unto God.

[10]For that which is made shall be punished together with him that made it.

13:19 *Gaining and getting:* "money-making and work" (NRSV). **14:2** *That:* the ship. **14:4** *Without art:* without skill. **14:6** *In the old time:* the time of the great deluge (see Gen 6–9). The following reference to *the proud giants* recalls Gen 6:4, and the *weak vessel* is Noah's ark.

¹¹Therefore even upon the idols of the Gentiles shall there be a visitation: because in the creature of God they are become an abomination, and stumblingblocks to the souls of men, and a snare to the feet of the unwise.

¹²For the devising of idols was the beginning of spiritual fornication, and the invention of them the corruption of life.

¹³For neither were they from the beginning, neither shall they be for ever.

¹⁴For by the vain glory of men they entered into the world, and therefore shall they come shortly to an end.

¹⁵For a father afflicted with untimely mourning, when he hath made an image of his child soon taken away, now honoured him as a god, which was then a dead man, and delivered to those that were under him ceremonies and sacrifices.

¹⁶Thus in process of time an ungodly custom grown strong was kept as a law, and graven images were worshipped by the commandments of kings.

¹⁷Whom men could not honour in presence, because they dwelt far off, they took the counterfeit of his visage from far, and made an express image of a king whom they honoured, to the end that by this their forwardness they might flatter him that was absent, as if he were present.

¹⁸Also the singular diligence of the artificer did help to set forward the ignorant to more superstition.

¹⁹For he, peradventure willing to please one in authority, forced all his skill to make the resemblance of the best fashion.

²⁰And so the multitude, allured by the grace of the work, took him now for a god, which a little before was but honoured as a man.

²¹And this was an occasion to deceive the world: for men, serving either calamity or tyranny, did ascribe unto stones and stocks the incommunicable name.

²²Moreover this was not enough for them, that they erred in the knowledge of God; but whereas they lived in the great war of ignorance, those so great plagues called they peace.

²³For whilst they slew their children in sacrifices, or used secret ceremonies, or made revellings of strange rites;

²⁴They kept neither lives nor marriages any longer undefiled: but either one slew another traiterously, or grieved him by adultery.

14:11 *Creature:* creation. **14:12** *Spiritual fornication: spiritual* is added by KJV; see Rom 1:18–32 and notes. **14:17** *Forwardness:* zeal. **14:21** *Calamity:* mishap or misfortune. *Stocks:* tree trunks. *The incommunicable name:* or "the name that ought not to be shared" (NRSV); cf. Isa 42:8.

²⁵So that there reigned in all men without exception blood, manslaughter, theft, and dissimulation, corruption, unfaithfulness, tumults, perjury,

²⁶Disquieting of good men, forgetfulness of good turns, defiling of souls, changing of kind, disorder in marriages, adultery, and shameless uncleanness.

²⁷For the worshipping of idols not to be named is the beginning, the cause, and the end, of all evil.

²⁸For either they are mad when they be merry, or prophesy lies, or live unjustly, or else lightly forswear themselves.

²⁹For insomuch as their trust is in idols, which have no life; though they sweat falsely, yet they look not to be hurt.

³⁰Howbeit for both causes shall they be justly punished: both because they thought not well of God, giving heed unto idols, and also unjustly swore in deceit, despising holiness.

³¹For it is not the power of them by whom they swear: but it is the just vengeance of sinners, that punisheth always the offence of the ungodly.

15 But thou, O God, art gracious and true, longsuffering, and in mercy ordering all things.

²For if we sin, we are thine, knowing thy power: but we will not sin, knowing that we are counted thine.

³For to know thee is perfect righteousness: yea, to know thy power is the root of immortality.

⁴For neither did the mischievous invention of men deceive us, nor an image spotted with divers colours, the painter's fruitless labour;

⁵The sight whereof enticeth fools to lust after it, and so they desire the form of a dead image, that hath no breath.

⁶Both they that make them, they that desire them, and they that worship them, are lovers of evil things, and are worthy to have such things to trust upon.

⁷For the potter, tempering soft earth, fashioneth every vessel with much labour for our service: yea, of the same clay he maketh both the vessels that serve for clean uses, and likewise also all such as serve to the contrary: but what is the use of either sort, the potter himself is the judge.

14:26 *Changing of kind*: perhaps a reference to homosexual activity; cf. Rom 1:26 and note. *Shameless uncleanness*: licentiousness.   **14:28** *They are mad . . . merry*: in orgiastic revelry.   **14:31** *Just vengeance of sinners*: "just penalty for those who sin" (NRSV).   **15:1–2** *Thou, O God . . . are thine*: cf. Exod 34:6–9, in the context of the Sinai covenant's renewal.   **15:7** *Vessels that serve . . . the contrary*:

⁸And employing his labours lewdly, he maketh a vain god of the
    same clay, even he which a little before was made of earth
    himself, and within a little while after returneth to the same,
    out of the which he was taken, when his life which was lent
    him shall be demanded.
⁹Notwithstanding his care is, not that he shall have much
    labour, nor that his life is short: but striveth to excel gold-
    smiths and silversmiths, and endeavoureth to do like the
    workers in brass, and counteth it his glory to make counter-
    feit things.
¹⁰His heart is ashes, his hope is more vile than earth, and his life
    of less value than clay:
¹¹Forasmuch as he knew not his Maker, and him that inspired
    into him an active soul, and breathed in a living spirit.
¹²But they counted our life a pastime, and our time here a market
    for gain: for, say they, we must be getting every way, though it
    be by evil means.
¹³For this man, that of earthly matter maketh brittle vessels
    and graven images, knoweth himself to offend above all
    others.

¹⁴And all the enemies of thy people, that hold them in subjec-
    tion, are most foolish, and are more miserable than very
    babes.
¹⁵For they counted all the idols of the heathen to be gods: which
    neither have the use of eyes to see, nor noses to draw breath,
    nor ears to hear, nor fingers of hands to handle; and as for
    their feet, they are slow to go.
¹⁶For man made them, and he that borrowed his own spirit
    fashioned them: but no man can make a god like unto
    himself.
¹⁷For being mortal, he worketh a dead thing with wicked hands:
    for he himself is better than the things which he worshippeth:
    whereas he lived once, but they never.
¹⁸Yea, they worshipped those beasts also that are most hateful: for
    being compared together, some are worse than others.
¹⁹Neither are they beautiful, so much as to be desired in respect
    of beasts: but they went without the praise of God and his
    blessing.

cf. Rom 9:21. **15:8** *Lewdly*: perversely. *Even he . . . demanded*: cf. Gen 3:19. **15:9** *Notwith-standing his care . . . short*: i.e., "but he does not consider that his life will be full of toil and brief." **15:11** *Inspired into him . . . spirit*: combining the Platonic doctrine of preexistent souls with Gen 2:7. **15:12** *Getting*: providing for ourselves or profiting. **15:15** *Which neither . . . go*: cf. Pss 115:5–7; 135:16–17.

16

Therefore by the like were they punished worthily, and by the multitude of beasts tormented.

[2] Instead of which punishment, dealing graciously with thine own people, thou preparedst for them meat of a strange taste, even quails to stir up their appetite:

[3] To the end that they, desiring food, might for the ugly sight of the beasts sent among them lothe even that, which they must needs desire; but these, suffering penury for a short space, might be made partakers of a strange taste.

[4] For it was requisite, that upon them exercising tyranny should come penury, which they could not avoid: but to these it should only be shewed how their enemies were tormented.

[5] For when the horrible fierceness of beasts came upon these, and they perished with the stings of crooked serpents, thy wrath endured not for ever:

[6] But they were troubled for a small season, that they might be admonished, having a sign of salvation, to put them in remembrance of the commandment of thy law.

[7] For he that turned himself toward it was not saved by the thing that he saw, but by thee, that art the Saviour of all.

[8] And in this thou madest thine enemies confess, that it is thou who deliverest from all evil:

[9] For them the bitings of grasshoppers and flies killed, neither was there found any remedy for their life: for they were worthy to be punished by such.

[10] But thy sons not the very teeth of venomous dragons overcame: for thy mercy was ever by them, and healed them.

[11] For they were pricked, that they should remember thy words; and were quickly saved, that not falling into deep forgetfulness, they might be continually mindful of thy goodness.

16:1–19:22 God's support of Israel against idolatrous Egypt. Returning to the historical narrative, this section contrasts God's dealings with Israel and Egypt: while the Egyptians hungered, Israel had quail (16:1–4); while the Egyptians were slain by locusts and flies, Israel was saved from serpents (16:5–14); while thunderstorms rained on Egypt, manna rained on Israel (16:15–29); while Egypt suffered darkness, Israel had light and was led by a pillar of fire (17:1–18:4); Egypt's firstborn were killed while Israel was protected and its later punishment at God's hand was interrupted (18:5–25); and while Israel passed safely through the Red Sea, the Egyptians were drowned (19:1–9). A retrospective glance at God's faithfulness to Israel and Egypt's wickedness and punishment brings the book to a close (19:10–22).   **16:1** *By the multitude of beasts tormented*: many of the plagues of Exod 7:14–12:32 involved animals and affected Egypt's food supply.   **16:2** *Meat of a strange taste*: foreign or exotic food (see Exod 16, although the focus in this section seems to be on the *quails* in particular; Exod 16:12–13; cf. Num 11:31–32).   **16:3** *To the end . . . desire*: i.e., in order that the Egyptians might lose their appetite even for necessary sustenance, God having afflicted them with disgusting pests (which occupied even their kitchens; Exod 8:3).   **16:5** *They perished . . . serpents*: see Num 21:6–9.   **16:9** *Grasshoppers and flies*: see Exod 8:20–32; 10:1–20.   **16:10** *Dragons*: serpents.

¹²For it was neither herb, nor mollifying plaister, that restored
    them to health: but thy word, O Lord, which healeth all things.
¹³For thou hast power of life and death: thou leadest to the gates
    of hell, and bringest up again.
¹⁴A man indeed killeth through his malice: and the spirit, when it
    is gone forth, returneth not; neither the soul received up
    cometh again.

¹⁵But it is not possible to escape thine hand.
¹⁶For the ungodly, that denied to know thee, were scourged by the
    strength of thine arm: with strange rains, hails, and showers,
    were they persecuted, that they could not avoid, and through
    fire were they consumed.
¹⁷For, which is most to be wondered at, the fire had more force in
    the water, that quencheth all things: for the world fighteth for
    the righteous.
¹⁸For sometime the flame was mitigated, that it might not burn up
    the beasts that were sent against the ungodly; but themselves
    might see and perceive that they were persecuted with the
    judgment of God.
¹⁹And at another time it burneth even in the midst of water above
    the power of fire, that it might destroy the fruits of an unjust
    land.

²⁰Instead whereof thou feddest thine own people with angels'
    food, and didst send them from heaven bread prepared without
    their labour, able to content every man's delight, and agreeing
    to every taste.
²¹For thy sustenance declared thy sweetness unto thy children,
    and serving to the appetite of the eater, tempered itself to
    every man's liking.
²²But snow and ice endured the fire, and melted not, that they
    might know that fire burning in the hail, and sparkling in the
    rain, did destroy the fruits of the enemies.
²³But this again did even forget his own strength, that the righ-
    teous might be nourished.
²⁴For the creature that serveth thee, who art the Maker, increas-
    eth his strength against the unrighteous for their punishment,

16:12 *Mollifying plaister:* poultice. **16:13** *Hell:* Gk. *hadēs* (see Matt 11:23 note). **16:16**
Strange rains . . . consumed: for the plague of hail and fire, see Exod 9:13–35. **16:17** *The fire . . .*
all things: see Exod 9:24, which also lies behind vv. 19 and 22. *The world:* i.e., nature. **16:18**
For sometime . . . the ungodly: this verse apparently imagines that the plagues occurred at the
same time. **16:20** *Angels' food:* manna (see Exod 16; Ps 78:25). **16:23** *This again . . . strength:*
i.e., the fire "forgot its native power" (NRSV). The author seems to presume that lightning
fell along with the manna, but did not destroy it (see v. 27). **16:24** *The creature:* creation.

and abateth his strength for the benefit of such as put their trust in thee. ²⁵Therefore even then was it altered into all fashions, and was obedient to thy grace, that nourisheth all things, according to the desire of them that had need: ²⁶That thy children, O Lord, whom thou lovest, might know, that it is not the growing of fruits that nourisheth man: but that it is thy word, which preserveth them that put their trust in thee. ²⁷For that which was not destroyed of the fire, being warmed with a little sunbeam, soon melted away: ²⁸That it might be known, that we must prevent the sun to give thee thanks, and at the dayspring pray unto thee. ²⁹For the hope of the unthankful shall melt away as the winter's hoar frost, and shall run away as unprofitable water.

17 For great are thy judgments, and cannot be expressed: therefore unnurtured souls have erred. ²For when unrighteous men thought to oppress the holy nation; they being shut up, in their houses, the prisoners of darkness, and fettered with the bonds of a long night, lay [there] exiled from the eternal providence. ³For while they supposed to lie hid in their secret sins, they were scattered under a dark veil of forgetfulness, being horribly astonished, and troubled with [strange] apparitions. ⁴For neither might the corner that held them keep them from fear: but noises [as of waters] falling down sounded about them, and sad visions appeared unto them with heavy countenances. ⁵No power of the fire might give them light: neither could the bright flames of the stars endure to lighten that horrible night. ⁶Only there appeared unto them a fire kindled of itself, very dreadful: for being much terrified, they thought the things which they saw to be worse than the sight they saw not. ⁷As for the illusions of art magick, they were put down, and their vaunting in wisdom was reproved with disgrace. ⁸For they, that promised to drive away terrors and troubles from a sick soul, were sick themselves of fear, worthy to be laughed at. ⁹For though no terrible thing did fear them; yet being scared with beasts that passed by, and hissing of serpents,

---

16:26 *It is not . . . thee*: cf. Deut 8:3.   **16:27** *Melted away*: see Exod 16:21.   **16:28** *Prevent*: anticipate, rise in advance of.   **17:1** *Unnurtured*: uneducated.   **17:2** *Prisoners of darkness*: see Exod 10:21–29, which the description that follows imaginatively elaborates, perhaps seizing on the suggestive detail that the darkness could be felt (v. 21). The imagery in this section has much in common with the conventional "descent to Hades" motif (see, e.g., Homer, *Odyssey* 11 and Virgil, *Aeneid* 6).   **17:3** *Supposed to*: thought they would.   **17:4** *Corner*: the Greek refers to the innermost part of a house.   **17:7** *The illusions . . . down*: i.e., their magic was defeated (cf. Exod 7:11–12, 22; 8:7, 18–19; 9:11).

¹⁰They died for fear, denying that they saw the air, which could of
    no side be avoided.

¹¹For wickedness, condemned by her own witness, is very timo-
    rous, and being pressed with conscience, always forecasteth
    grievous things.

¹²For fear is nothing else but a betraying of the succours which
    reason offereth.

¹³And the expectation from within, being less, counteth the
    ignorance more than the cause which bringeth the torment.

¹⁴But they sleeping the same sleep that night, which was indeed
    intolerable, and which came upon them out of the bottoms of
    inevitable hell,

¹⁵Were partly vexed with monstrous apparitions, and partly
    fainted, their heart failing them: for a sudden fear, and not
    looked for, came upon them.

¹⁶So then whosoever there fell down was straitly kept, shut up in a
    prison without iron bars.

¹⁷For whether he were husbandman, or shepherd, or a labourer in
    the field, he was overtaken, and endured that necessity, which
    could not be avoided: for they were all bound with one chain of
    darkness.

¹⁸Whether it were a whistling wind, or a melodious noise of birds
    among the spreading branches, or a pleasing fall of water
    running violently,

¹⁹Or a terrible sound of stones cast down, or a running that could
    not be seen of skipping beasts, or a roaring voice of most
    savage wild beasts, or a rebounding echo from the hollow
    mountains; these things made them to swoon for fear.

²⁰For the whole world shined with clear light, and none were
    hindered in their labour:

²¹Over them only was spread an heavy night, an image of that
    darkness which should afterwards receive them: but yet were
    they unto themselves more grievous than the darkness.

18 Nevertheless thy saints had a very great light, whose voice they
    hearing and not seeing their shape, because they also had not
    suffered the same things, they counted them happy.

²But for that they did not hurt them now, of whom they had been
    wronged before, they thanked them, and besought them
    pardon for that they had been enemies.

17:10 *Denying that they saw the air*: Gk. *aēr* (here *air*) can also mean "haze"; the sense may be that they refused to look at the gloomy mist.   **17:13** *The expectation . . . torment*: perhaps this means that those who lack hope prefer to remain ignorant of what causes their torment because they do not believe that it can ever be removed.   **17:14** *Hell*: see 16:13 note.   **17:17** *Field*: lit. "wilderness" or "desert."   **18:1–2** *Nevertheless thy saints . . . enemies*: at this point, the author's refusal to employ proper names

³Instead whereof thou gavest them a burning pillar of fire, both to be a guide of the unknown journey, and an harmless sun to entertain them honourably.

⁴For they were worthy to be deprived of light, and imprisoned in darkness, who had kept thy sons shut up, by whom the uncorrupt light of the law was to be given unto the world.

⁵And when they had determined to slay the babes of the saints, one child being cast forth, and saved, to reprove them, thou tookest away the multitude of their children, and destroyedst them altogether in a mighty water.

⁶Of that night were our fathers certified afore, that assuredly knowing unto what oaths they had given credence, they might afterwards be of good cheer.

⁷So of thy people was accepted both the salvation of the righteous, and destruction of the enemies.

⁸For wherewith thou didst punish our adversaries, by the same thou didst glorify us, whom thou hadst called.

⁹For the righteous children of good men did sacrifice secretly, and with one consent made a holy law, that the saints should be alike partakers of the same good and evil, the fathers now singing out the songs of praise.

¹⁰But on the other side there sounded an ill according cry of the enemies; and a lamentable noise was carried abroad for children that were bewailed.

¹¹The master and the servant were punished after one manner; and like as the king, so suffered the common person.

¹²So they all together had innumerable dead with one kind of death; neither were the living sufficient to bury them: for in one moment the noblest offspring of them was destroyed.

¹³For whereas they would not believe any thing by reason of the enchantments; upon the destruction of the firstborn, they acknowledged this people to be the sons of God.

---

becomes confusing, for it is difficult to distinguish between the Egyptians and the Israelites. In v. 1, the second "they" refers to Israel; the others, to Egypt. In v. 2, the first and second "they" refer to the Israelites; the third and fourth, to the Egyptians. For the Israelites' light during the plague of darkness, see Exod 10:23. **18:3** *Burning pillar of fire*: see Exod 13:21. **18:4** *Uncorrupt*: imperishable. **18:5** *Slay the babes of the saints*: see Exod 1:15–16. *One child . . . saved*: Moses (see Exod 2:1–9). *Thou tookest . . . children*: see Exod 11; 12:29–32. The following descriptions of the (literal) plagues afflicting Egypt and Israel resemble conventional Greco-Roman plague narratives; see, e.g., Thucydides 2.47–54; Lucretius 6.1138–1286; Seneca, *Oedipus* 110–201. *And destroyedst them . . . water*: Exod 14:21–31. **18:6** *Of that night . . . cheer*: referring to Israel's guided preparations for the first Passover (Exod 12:1–28). **18:7** *Accepted*: better "expected." **18:9** *Sacrifice secretly*: i.e., slaughter the Passover lambs. *Now*: alternatively "already"—i.e., the ancestors were already celebrating the Passover that would later commemorate their experience. The conflation of event memorialized and commemoration thereof is an important element of Exodus's Passover narrative. **18:10** *Ill according*: discordant. *Carried abroad*: i.e., heard throughout the country; see Exod 12:30. **18:13** *By reason of the enchantments*: apparently a reference to the Egyptian magicians' ability to emulate some of Moses'

¹⁴For while all things were in quiet silence, and that night was in
the midst of her swift course,

¹⁵Thine Almighty word leaped down from heaven out of thy royal
throne, as a fierce man of war into the midst of a land of
destruction,

¹⁶And brought thine unfeigned commandment as a sharp sword,
and standing up filled all things with death; and it touched the
heaven, but it stood upon the earth.

¹⁷Then suddenly visions of horrible dreams troubled them sore,
and terrors came upon them unlooked for.

¹⁸And one thrown here, and another there, half dead, shewed the
cause of his death.

¹⁹For the dreams that troubled them did foreshew this, lest they
should perish, and not know why they were afflicted.

²⁰Yea, the tasting of death touched the righteous also, and there
was a destruction of the multitude in the wilderness: but the
wrath endured not long.

²¹For then the blameless man made haste, and stood forth to
defend them; and bringing the shield of his proper ministry,
even prayer, and the propitiation of incense, set himself against
the wrath, and so brought the calamity to an end, declaring
that he was thy servant.

²²So he overcame the destroyer, not with strength of body, nor
force of arms, but with a word subdued he him that punished,
alleging the oaths and covenants made with the fathers.

²³For when the dead were now fallen down by heaps one upon
another, standing between, he stayed the wrath, and parted
the way to the living.

²⁴For in the long garment was the whole world, and in the four
rows of the stones was the glory of the fathers graven, and thy
Majesty upon the diadem of his head.

²⁵Unto these the destroyer gave place, and was afraid of them: for
it was enough that they only tasted of the wrath.

19

As for the ungodly, wrath came upon them without mercy unto
the end: for he knew before what they would do;

²how that having given them leave to depart, and sent them
hastily away, they would repent and pursue them.

miracles (see Exod 7:11, 22; 8:7), unless those miracles are themselves being called "enchantments."
18:15–16 *Thine Almighty word . . . sword*: cf. 5:17–20; 9:4, 10. The parallels with chap. 9, where Wisdom likewise departs from God's throne, may suggest an equation of wisdom with God's word (Gk.
logos; cf. John 1:1 note).   **18:20** *The tasting of death touched the righteous also*: see Num 16:41–50.
18:21 *The blameless man*: Aaron.   **18:22** *Destroyer*: better "multitude" (MS tradition), presumably a
reference to the peoples' rebellion. NRSV adopts a conjectural reading: "[God's] wrath."   **18:24** *Long
garment . . . head*: the high priest's vestments (see Exod 28), which were often symbolically interpreted.

³For whilst they were yet mourning and making lamentation at the graves of the dead, they added another foolish device, and pursued them as fugitives, whom they had intreated to be gone. ⁴For the destiny, whereof they were worthy, drew them unto this end, and made them forget the things that had already happened, that they might fulfil the punishment which was wanting to their torments: ⁵And that thy people might pass a wonderful way: but they might find a strange death. ⁶For the whole creature in his proper kind was fashioned again anew, serving the peculiar commandments that were given unto them, that thy children might be kept without hurt: ⁷As namely, a cloud shadowing the camp; and where water stood before, dry land appeared; and out of the Red sea a way without impediment; and out of the violent stream a green field: ⁸Wherethrough all the people went that were defended with thy hand, seeing thy marvellous strange wonders. ⁹For they went at large like horses, and leaped like lambs, praising thee, O Lord, who hadst delivered them.

¹⁰For they were yet mindful of the things that were done while they sojourned in the strange land, how the ground brought forth flies instead of cattle, and how the river cast up a multitude of frogs instead of fishes. ¹¹But afterwards they saw a new generation of fowls, when, being led with their appetite, they asked delicate meats. ¹²For quails came up unto them from the sea for their contentment. ¹³And punishments came upon the sinners not without former signs by the force of thunders: for they suffered justly according to their own wickedness, insomuch as they used a more hard and hateful behaviour toward strangers. ¹⁴For the Sodomites did not receive those, whom they knew not when they came: but these brought friends into bondage, that had well deserved of them.

19:3 *Pursued them . . . gone*: see Exod 14.   **19:4** *The destiny . . . happened*: cf. v. 1; see Exod 14:8–9.   **19:6** *Creature*: creation; see note to Exod 13:17–14:31 on the crossing of the parted Red Sea as a renewal of creation.   **19:7** *A cloud shadowing the camp*: see Exod 13:21–22. There is a secondary reference in this verse to Gen 1:6–8, where the primeval waters are separated above the sky (i.e., clouds) and below it. *Where water . . . field*: cf. Gen 1:9–13.   **19:9** *Praising thee . . . them*: see Exod 15:1–18.   **19:11** *A new generation of fowls*: see Exod 16:12–13. *Delicate meats*: delicious food.   **19:13** *Former signs*: forewarning. *Signs by the force of thunders*: see Exod 19:16–25.   **19:14** *The Sodomites*: lit. "others," but the reference is clearly to the abuse of strangers by the inhabitants of Sodom (see Gen 19:1–11). *These brought friends . . . them*: referring to Egypt's enslavement of Joseph's descendants, generations after the Pharoah had welcomed his extended family (Gen 45:17–20; 47:5–6; Exod 1:8–11).

¹⁵And not only so, but peradventure some respect shall be had of
those, because they used strangers not friendly:
¹⁶But these very grievously afflicted them, whom they had received
with feastings, and were already made partakers of the same
laws with them.
¹⁷Therefore even with blindness were these stricken, as those
were at the doors of the righteous man: when, being compassed about with horrible great darkness, every one sought
the passage of his own doors.
¹⁸For the elements were changed in themselves by a kind of
harmony, like as in a psaltery notes change the name of the
tune, and yet are always sounds; which may well be perceived
by the sight of the things that have been done.
¹⁹For earthly things were turned into watery, and the things, that
before swam in the water, now went upon the ground.
²⁰The fire had power in the water, forgetting his own virtue: and
the water forgat his own quenching nature.
²¹On the other side, the flames wasted not the flesh of the corruptible living things, though they walked therein; neither
melted they the icy kind of heavenly meat, that was of nature
apt to melt.
²²For in all things, O Lord, thou didst magnify thy people, and
glorify them, neither didst thou lightly regard them: but didst
assist them in every time and place.

19:15 *Some respect shall be had of those*: alternatively "those shall have some kind of visitation," i.e.,
will be subject to divine punishment of some sort. **19:17** *As those . . . righteous man*: see Gen 19:11.
The *righteous man* is Lot. **19:18** *For the elements . . . sounds*: the translation is conjectural, but the
point seems to be that music involves variation in unity. **19:20–21** *The fire . . . melt*: cf. 16:16–29
and v. 23 note. **19:20** *Virtue*: power. **19:21** *On the other side*: on the contrary. *The icy kind of heavenly meat*: manna (see Exod 16:14). **19:22** *Magnify*: exalt or praise. *Lightly regard*: neglect.

The Wisdom of Jesus the Son of Sirach, or, Ecclesiasticus

ECCLESIASTICUS sits squarely in the Old Testament wisdom tradition. Also known as Sirach, or the Wisdom of Sirach, it is a work whose total effect is appreciably less than the sum of its parts. Some of the parts are very good indeed—most famously, the magnificent section on the history of Israel, which spans chapters 44–49 and is rounded off in chapter 50 by a hymn of praise for the high priest Simon II, the author's older contemporary. In the course of this hymn, Sirach presents a rhapsodic vision of the priest officiating at a temple ceremony. There are also, at the beginning of the book and in chapter 24, celebrations of the origins, power, and beauty of Wisdom that match and develop the eighth chapter of the Old Testament book of Proverbs. Also occasionally striking are passages of a more limited scope, such as 22:11–12, which unfavorably compares the fool to the dead. But Sirach as a whole is rather prolix and inchoate. One of the longest books in the Bible, it seldom makes its points briefly, or with the kind of edge that is frequently found in Proverbs or Ecclesiastes, which it echoes throughout. (A handful of these and other Old Testament allusions are cited in the notes that follow.) Moreover, it apparently lacks any structural coherence beyond the simple grouping together of sayings with broadly similar themes.

So it may be partly on aesthetic terms that Sirach was excluded from the Jewish canon. It was written in Hebrew, ca. 180 B.C.E., perhaps in Jerusalem; its author was Yeshua ben Sira (i.e., Jesus, son of Sirach). Two generations later, ca. 132 B.C.E., it was translated into Greek by Ben Sira's grandson living in Egypt. The Hebrew text subsequently ceased to be copied, but the book was preserved in the Greek translation and other languages as well. Owing to finds at Cairo in the late nineteenth century and at Qumran and Masada in the mid-twentieth, about two-thirds of the Hebrew text has now been recovered. KJV's translation is based entirely on a Greek text, however, and as a translation of a translation—despite its competence and overall attractiveness—it inevitably misses many instances of the original wordplay and other verbal effects so important in ancient Near Eastern Wisdom literature (a few of which are pointed out in the annotations below). Because nineteenth- and twentieth-century discoveries have increased our knowledge of Sirach's text to a degree largely unmatched by other apocryphal books, these annotations also provide a more generous (though by no means exhaustive) sample of its textual variants than do those to other works in the KJV Apocrypha (2 Esdras excluded).

Sirach's theme is largely the one announced in Proverbs, that fear of the Lord is the source of wisdom: indeed, the phrase "fear of God" occurs more than fifty times in the book. Sirach employs the classical form for Hebrew wisdom literature, common in Job, Proverbs, and Ecclesiastes—the poetic bicola: that is, discrete sense units of usually two lines each, often built around some form of syntactic parallelism and bound together by thematic complementarity, as well as by alliteration, assonance, or some other sound effect. (KJV, like most early editions, generally sets these out as single verses and marks each unit only by punctuation.) As in Proverbs, the wisdom that this book urges is as often practical and bound to a particular cultural context (about how to behave at banquets, for example, or how to choose a wife) as it is ethical or spiritual. Moreover, despite its conventional tendency to feminize wisdom, the book intensifies the strain of misogyny that runs through Old Testament Wisdom literature. Ben Sira even goes so far as to say that a wicked man is better than a good woman (see 42:14 and note).

The book's original purpose may have been to counter the increasing influence of Hellenism on Ben Sira's fellow Jews; in social and political contexts in which they saw their religion threatened and marginalized, it would have guided them in forms of behavior that they might practice in order to function effectively but without compromising their faith. It is therefore an essentially conservative work designed to appeal, as Ben Sira's grandson himself says, to those who are prepared to live according to Old Testament law.

For detailed exposition of Sirach, the reader should consult the Anchor Bible commentary *The Wisdom of Ben Sira: A New Translation*, with translation and notes by Patrick W. Skehan and introduction and commentary by Alexander A. Di Lella (Garden City, NY: Doubleday, 1987). It frequently informs this introduction and the annotations that follow. The section headings below often follow those provided by Harold C. Washington in the *New Oxford Annotated Bible* (Oxford: Oxford University Press, 2001).

THE WISDOM OF JESUS THE SON OF SIRACH, OR, ECCLESIASTICUS

A Prologue made by an uncertain Author

This Jesus was the son of Sirach, and grandchild to Jesus of the same name with him: this man therefore lived in the latter times, after the people had been led away captive, and called home again, and almost after all the prophets. Now his grandfather Jesus, as he himself witnesseth, was a man of great diligence and wisdom among the Hebrews, who did not only gather the grave and short sentences of wise men, that had been before him, but himself also uttered some of his own, full of much understanding and wisdom. When as therefore the first Jesus died, leaving this book almost perfected, Sirach his son receiving it after him left it to his own son Jesus, who, having gotten it into his hands, compiled it all orderly into one volume, and called it Wisdom, intituling it both by his own name, his father's name, and his grandfather's; alluring the hearer by the very name of Wisdom to have a greater love to the study of this book. It containeth therefore wise sayings, dark sentences, and parables, and certain particular ancient godly stories of men that pleased God; also his prayer and song; moreover, what benefits God had vouchsafed his people, and what plagues he had heaped upon their enemies. This Jesus did imitate Solomon, and was no less famous for wisdom and learning, both being indeed a man of great learning, and so reputed also.

The Prologue of the Wisdom of Jesus, the Son of Sirach

Whereas many and great things have been delivered unto us by the law and the prophets, and by others that have followed their steps, for the which things Israel ought to be commended for learning and wisdom; and whereof not only the readers must needs become skilful themselves, but also they that desire to learn be able to profit them which are without, both by speaking and writing: my

A Prologue made by an uncertain author. A spurious prologue, which probably originated in the fourth or fifth century C.E. and was at one point falsely attributed to Athanasius.

The Prologue of the Wisdom of Jesus, the Son of Sirach. *Others that . . . steps*: i.e., "the others that followed them," referring to the Writings in the conventional tripartite division of the Hebrew Bible (preceded by the Law and the Prophets). *Them which are without*: outsiders, i.e.,

grandfather Jesus, when he had much given himself to the reading of the law, and the prophets, and other books of our fathers, and had gotten therein good judgment, was drawn on also himself to write something pertaining to learning and wisdom; to the intent that those which are desirous to learn, and are addicted to these things, might profit much more in living according to the law. Wherefore let me intreat you to read it with favour and attention, and to pardon us, wherein we may seem to come short of some words, which we have laboured to interpret. For the same things uttered in Hebrew, and translated into another tongue, have not the same force in them; and not only these things, but the law itself, and the prophets, and the rest of the books, have no small difference, when they are spoken in their own language. For in the eight and thirtieth year coming into Egypt, when Euergetes was king, and continuing there some time, I found a book of no small learning: therefore I thought it most necessary for me to bestow some diligence and travail to interpret it; using great watchfulness and skill in that space to bring the book to an end, and set it forth for them also, which in a strange country are willing to learn, being prepared before in manners to live after the law.

1 All wisdom cometh from the Lord, and is with him for ever.
² Who can number the sand of the sea, and the drops of rain, and the days of eternity?
³ Who can find out the height of heaven, and the breadth of the earth, and the deep, and wisdom?
⁴ Wisdom hath been created before all things, and the understanding of prudence from everlasting.
⁵ The word of God most high is the fountain of wisdom; and her ways are everlasting commandments.
⁶ To whom hath the root of wisdom been revealed? or who hath known her wise counsels?
⁷ [Unto whom hath the knowledge of wisdom been made manifest? and who hath understood her great experience?]
⁸ There is one wise and greatly to be feared, the Lord sitting upon his throne.
⁹ He created her, and saw her, and numbered her, and poured her out upon all his works.
¹⁰ She is with all flesh according to his gift, and he hath given her to them that love him.

Gentiles. *Good judgment*: rather "sufficient proficiency." *Eight and . . . king*: 132 B.C.E., during the reign of Ptolemy VII Euergetes.

1:1–30 Wisdom is the fear of the Lord. Consisting of two sections: the first (vv. 1–10) insists on the divine origin of Wisdom (cf. Prov 8:22–31); the second (vv. 11–30) demonstrates that the fear of God is the beginning of wisdom. The latter section was perhaps an alphabetical acrostic in the original Hebrew, for it has the same number of lines as letters in the Hebrew alphabet. If so, it forms an inclusive frame with Sirach's closing acrostic (51:13–30). **1:3** *Who can find out . . . wisdom*: cf. Job 38:16–18. **1:5** *The word . . . commandments*: better omitted (MS tradition). **1:6** *Wise counsels*: rather "subtleties." **1:7** *[Unto whom . . . experience]*: better omitted (MS tradition). **1:9** *Her*: Wisdom is conventionally figured as a woman, because the Greek word for "wisdom" (*sophia*), like the Hebrew, is feminine.

¹¹ The fear of the Lord is honour, and glory, and gladness, and a
crown of rejoicing.

¹² The fear of the Lord maketh a merry heart, and giveth joy, and
gladness, and a long life.

¹³ Whoso feareth the Lord, it shall go well with him at the last,
and he shall find favour in the day of his death.

¹⁴ To fear the Lord is the beginning of wisdom: and it was
created with the faithful in the womb.

¹⁵ She hath built an everlasting foundation with men, and she
shall continue with their seed.

¹⁶ To fear the Lord is fulness of wisdom, and filleth men with her
fruits.

¹⁷ She filleth all their house with things desirable, and the
garners with her increase.

¹⁸ The fear of the Lord is a crown of wisdom, making peace and
perfect health to flourish; both which are the gifts of God:
and it enlargeth their rejoicing that love him.

¹⁹ Wisdom raineth down skill and knowledge of understanding,
and exalteth them to honour that hold her fast.

²⁰ The root of wisdom is to fear the Lord, and the branches
thereof are long life.

²¹ The fear of the Lord driveth away sins: and where it is present,
it turneth away wrath.

²² A furious man cannot be justified; for the sway of his fury shall
be his destruction.

²³ A patient man will bear for a time, and afterward joy shall
spring up unto him.

²⁴ He will hide his words for a time, and the lips of many shall
declare his wisdom.

²⁵ The parables of knowledge are in the treasures of wisdom: but
godliness is an abomination to a sinner.

²⁶ If thou desire wisdom, keep the commandments, and the Lord
shall give her unto thee.

²⁷ For the fear of the Lord is wisdom and instruction: and faith
and meekness are his delight.

²⁸ Distrust not the fear of the Lord when thou art poor: and come
not unto him with a double heart.

²⁹ Be not an hypocrite in the sight of men, and take good heed
what thou speakest.

³⁰ Exalt not thyself, lest thou fall, and bring dishonour upon thy
soul, and so God discover thy secrets, and cast thee down in

1:14 *To fear . . . wisdom*: cf. Ps 111:10; Prov 9:10; etc.   **1:15–17** *She hath built . . . increase*: recalling the imagery of Prov 9:1–6.   **1:17** *Garners*: granaries.   **1:21** *The fear . . . wrath*: better omitted (MS tradition).   **1:22** *The sway of his fury shall be*: alternatively "anger tips the scale to" (NRSV).   **1:25** *Parables*: see Mark 4:2 note.   **1:27** *The fear . . . delight*: cf. Prov 15:33.   **1:28** *When thou art poor*: better

the midst of the congregation, because thou camest not in truth to the fear of the Lord, but thy heart is full of deceit.

2 My son, if thou come to serve the Lord, prepare thy soul for temptation.
²Set thy heart aright, and constantly endure, and make not haste in time of trouble.
³Cleave unto him, and depart not away, that thou mayest be increased at thy last end.
⁴Whatsoever is brought upon thee take cheerfully, and be patient when thou art changed to a low estate.
⁵For gold is tried in the fire, and acceptable men in the furnace of adversity.
⁶Believe in him, and he will help thee; order thy way aright, and trust in him.
⁷Ye that fear the Lord, wait for his mercy; and go not aside, lest ye fall.
⁸Ye that fear the Lord, believe him; and your reward shall not fail.
⁹Ye that fear the Lord, hope for good, and for everlasting joy and mercy.
¹⁰Look at the generations of old, and see; did ever any trust in the Lord, and was confounded? or did any abide in his fear, and was forsaken? or whom did he ever despise, that called upon him?
¹¹For the Lord is full of compassion and mercy, longsuffering, and very pitiful, and forgiveth sins, and saveth in time of affliction.

¹²Woe be to fearful hearts, and faint hands, and the sinner that goeth two ways!
¹³Woe unto him that is fainthearted! for he believeth not; therefore shall he not be defended.
¹⁴Woe unto you that have lost patience! and what will ye do when the Lord shall visit you?
¹⁵They that fear the Lord will not disobey his word; and they that love him will keep his ways.
¹⁶They that fear the Lord will seek that which is wellpleasing unto him; and they that love him shall be filled with the law.
¹⁷They that fear the Lord will prepare their hearts, and humble their souls in his sight,
¹⁸Saying, We will fall into the hands of the Lord, and not into the hands of men: for as his majesty is, so is his mercy.

omitted (MS tradition). **1:30** *Heart*: a seat of intellection, in addition to emotion (so throughout). **2:1–18 Trusting God. 2:1** *Temptation*: test. **2:5** *Adversity*: lit. "abasement." **2:10** *Did ever . . . upon him*: cf. Pss 22:4–5; 37:25. **2:11** *The Lord . . . sins*: cf. Exod 34:6; Ps 103:8. **2:14** *When the Lord shall visit you*: a reference to divine judgment. **2:18** *We will fall . . . mercy*: echoing David's words in 2 Sam 24:14.

3 Hear me your father, O children, and do thereafter, that ye may be safe.
[2] For the Lord hath given the father honour over the children, and hath confirmed the authority of the mother over the sons.
[3] Whoso honoureth his father maketh an atonement for his sins:
[4] And he that honoureth his mother is as one that layeth up treasure.
[5] Whoso honoureth his father shall have joy of his own children; and when he maketh his prayer, he shall be heard.
[6] He that honoureth his father shall have a long life; and he that is obedient unto the Lord shall be a comfort to his mother.
[7] He that feareth the Lord will honour his father, and will do service unto his parents, as to his masters.
[8] Honour thy father and mother both in word and deed, that a blessing may come upon thee from them.
[9] For the blessing of the father establisheth the houses of children; but the curse of the mother rooteth out foundations.
[10] Glory not in the dishonour of thy father; for thy father's dishonour is no glory unto thee.
[11] For the glory of a man is from the honour of his father; and a mother in dishonour is a reproach to the children.
[12] My son, help thy father in his age, and grieve him not as long as he liveth.
[13] And if his understanding fail, have patience with him; and despise him not when thou art in thy full strength.
[14] For the relieving of thy father shall not be forgotten; and instead of sins it shall be added to build thee up.
[15] In the day of thine affliction it shall be remembered; thy sins also shall melt away, as the ice in the fair warm weather.
[16] He that forsaketh his father is as a blasphemer; and he that angereth his mother is cursed of God.

[17] My son, go on with thy business in meekness; so shalt thou be beloved of him that is approved.
[18] The greater thou art, the more humble thyself, and thou shalt find favour before the Lord.
[19] Many are in high place, and of renown: but mysteries are revealed unto the meek.
[20] For the power of the Lord is great, and he is honoured of the lowly.
[21] Seek not out the things that are too hard for thee, neither search the things that are above thy strength.

3:1–16 Honoring parents. 3:2 *The Lord . . . sons*: see Exod 20:12; Deut 5:16. The Greek verb for "honor" (*doxazō*, also in vv. 4, 6, and 20) has the same root as "glory" (vv. 10, 11). A different word is used for "honor" in vv. 3, 5, 8, and 11.   **3:8** *Thy father and mother . . . from them*: better "thy father . . . from him" (MS tradition).   **3:16** *He that . . . God*: cf. Exod 21:17; Lev 20:9; Deut 27:16 and note; etc.
3:17–24 Humility. 3:19 *Many are . . . meek*: better omitted (MS tradition).   **3:21–23** *Seek not . . . understand*: compare the insistence in Deut 30:11–14 that God's essential commandments are accessible rather than esoteric.   **3:21** *Seek not . . . strength*: a conventional idea in biblical literature; cf.

²²But what is commanded thee, think thereupon with reverence; for
it is not needful for thee to see with thine eyes the things that
are in secret.

²³Be not curious in unnecessary matters: for more things are
shewed unto thee than men understand.

²⁴For many are deceived by their own vain opinion; and an evil
suspicion hath overthrown their judgment.

²⁵Without eyes thou shalt want light: profess not the knowledge
therefore that thou hast not.

²⁶A stubborn heart shall fare evil at the last; and he that loveth
danger shall perish therein.

²⁷An obstinate heart shall be laden with sorrows; and the wicked
man shall heap sin upon sin.

²⁸In the punishment of the proud there is no remedy; for the plant
of wickedness hath taken root in him.

²⁹The heart of the prudent will understand a parable; and an
attentive ear is the desire of a wise man.

³⁰Water will quench a flaming fire; and alms maketh an atonement for sins.

³¹And he that requiteth good turns is mindful of that which
may come hereafter; and when he falleth, he shall find a stay.

4 ¹My son, defraud not the poor of his living, and make not the
needy eyes to wait long.

²Make not an hungry soul sorrowful; neither provoke a man in his
distress.

³Add no more trouble to an heart that is vexed; and defer not to
give to him that is in need.

⁴Reject not the supplication of the afflicted; neither turn away thy
face from a poor man.

⁵Turn not away thine eye from the needy, and give him none
occasion to curse thee:

⁶For if he curse thee in the bitterness of his soul, his prayer shall
be heard of him that made him.

⁷Get thyself the love of the congregation, and bow thy head to a
great man.

Ps 131:1.   **3:22** *With reverence*: this phrase, along with *to see with thine eyes*, should be omitted (MS
tradition).

3:25–29 Stubbornness. 3:25 *Without eyes . . . hast not*: some MSS omit this verse; others place
it after v. 27.   **3:26** *Stubborn* [lit. "hard"] *heart*: the same Greek phrase as "obstinate heart" in v. 27;
cf. Exod 4:21; 7:14; etc.

3:30–4:10 Caring for the destitute. For relevant biblical legislation, see esp. Deut 15:7–11 and
Exod 22:21–23.   **4:5** *Turn not away . . . thee*: cf. Prov 28:27.

⁸Let it not grieve thee to bow down thine ear to the poor, and give
 him a friendly answer with meekness.
⁹Deliver him that suffereth wrong from the hand of the oppressor;
 and be not fainthearted when thou sittest in judgment.
¹⁰Be as a father unto the fatherless, and instead of an husband
 unto their mother: so shalt thou be as the son of the most
 High, and he shall love thee more than thy mother doth.

¹¹Wisdom exalteth her children, and layeth hold of them that seek
 her.
¹²He that loveth her loveth life; and they that seek to her early
 shall be filled with joy.
¹³He that holdeth her fast shall inherit glory; and wheresoever she
 entereth, the Lord will bless.
¹⁴They that serve her shall minister to the Holy One: and them
 that love her the Lord doth love.
¹⁵Whoso giveth ear unto her shall judge the nations: and he that
 attendeth unto her shall dwell securely.
¹⁶If a man commit himself unto her, he shall inherit her; and his
 generations shall hold her in possession.
¹⁷For at the first she will walk with him by crooked ways, and
 bring fear and dread upon him, and torment him with her
 discipline, until she may trust his soul, and try him by her
 laws.
¹⁸Then will she return the straight way unto him, and comfort
 him, and shew him her secrets.
¹⁹But if he go wrong, she will forsake him, and give him over to
 his own ruin.

²⁰Observe the opportunity, and beware of evil; and be not
 ashamed when it concerneth thy soul.
²¹For there is a shame that bringeth sin; and there is a shame
 which is glory and grace.
²²Accept no person against thy soul, and let not the reverence of
 any man cause thee to fall.
²³And refrain not to speak, when there is occasion to do good, and
 hide not thy wisdom in her beauty.
²⁴For by speech wisdom shall be known; and learning by the word
 of the tongue.

4:8–9 *Let it not grieve . . . judgment*: for critiques of unfair legal judgment, see Ps 82:2–4; Amos
5:10–15; etc.
   4:11–19 Wisdom's tests and rewards. 4:11 *Exalteth*: the Hebrew version reads "teaches."
4:14–15 *Them that love . . . nations*: cf. Prov 8:15–17.
   4:20–31 Good shame and bad. 4:20 *When it concerneth thy soul*: KJV translates literally;
NRSV paraphrases: "to be yourself." **4:22** *Accept no person . . . soul*: "do not show partiality [also in
v. 27] to your soul's harm," in context suggesting that partiality springs from an inappropriate sense

²⁵In no wise speak against the truth; but be abashed of the error of thine ignorance.

²⁶Be not ashamed to confess thy sins; and force not the course of the river.

²⁷Make not thyself an underling to a foolish man; neither accept the person of the mighty.

²⁸Strive for the truth unto death, and the Lord shall fight for thee.

²⁹Be not hasty in thy tongue, and in thy deeds slack and remiss.

³⁰Be not as a lion in thy house, nor frantick among thy servants.

³¹Let not thine hand be stretched out to receive, and shut when thou shouldest repay.

5 Set not thy heart upon thy goods; and say not, I have enough for my life.

²Follow not thine own mind and thy strength, to walk in the ways of thy heart:

³And say not, Who shall controul me for my works? for the Lord will surely revenge thy pride.

⁴Say not, I have sinned, and what harm hath happened unto me? for the Lord is longsuffering, he will in no wise let thee go.

⁵Concerning propitiation, be not without fear to add sin unto sin:

⁶And say not, His mercy is great; he will be pacified for the multitude of my sins: for mercy and wrath come from him, and his indignation resteth upon sinners.

⁷Make no tarrying to turn to the Lord, and put not off from day to day: for suddenly shall the wrath of the Lord come forth, and in thy security thou shalt be destroyed, and perish in the day of vengeance.

⁸Set not thine heart upon goods unjustly gotten; for they shall not profit thee in the day of calamity.

⁹Winnow not with every wind, and go not into every way: for so doth the sinner that hath a double tongue.

¹⁰Be stedfast in thy understanding; and let thy word be the same.

¹¹Be swift to hear; and let thy life be sincere; and with patience give answer.

¹²If thou hast understanding, answer thy neighbour; if not, lay thy hand upon thy mouth.

¹³Honour and shame is in talk: and the tongue of man is his fall.

---

of shame.   **4:30** *Frantick*: Gk. *phantasiokopōn*, "indulgent of fantasies," probably referring to excessive suspicion.

    5:1–8 Presumption. 5:3 *For my works*: better omitted (MS tradition).   **5:4** *The Lord is longsuffering*: cf. Exod 34:6; Num 14:18; etc.   **5:7** *In thy security . . . vengeance*: better simply "you will perish in the time of vengeance" (MS tradition).

    5:9–6:4 Inconstancy and incontinence. 5:9 *Winnow not . . . tongue*: privileging expediency undermines integrity.   **5:11** *And let . . . sincere*: better omitted (MS tradition).

¹⁴Be not called a whisperer, and lie not in wait with thy tongue: for a foul shame is upon the thief, and an evil condemnation upon the double tongue.

¹⁵Be not ignorant of any thing in a great matter or a small.

6 ¹Instead of a friend become not an enemy; for [thereby] thou shalt inherit an ill name, shame, and reproach: even so shall a sinner that hath a double tongue.

²Extol not thyself in the counsel of thine own heart; that thy soul be not torn in pieces as a bull [straying alone.]

³Thou shalt eat up thy leaves, and lose thy fruit, and leave thyself as a dry tree.

⁴A wicked soul shall destroy him that hath it, and shall make him to be laughed to scorn of his enemies.

⁵Sweet language will multiply friends: and a fair speaking tongue will increase kind greetings.

⁶Be in peace with many; nevertheless have but one counseller of a thousand.

⁷If thou wouldest get a friend, prove him first, and be not hasty to credit him.

⁸For some man is a friend for his own occasion, and will not abide in the day of thy trouble.

⁹And there is a friend, who being turned to enmity and strife will discover thy reproach.

¹⁰Again, some friend is a companion at the table, and will not continue in the day of thy affliction.

¹¹But in thy prosperity he will be as thyself, and will be bold over thy servants.

¹²If thou be brought low, he will be against thee, and will hide himself from thy face.

¹³Separate thyself from thine enemies, and take heed of thy friends.

¹⁴A faithful friend is a strong defence: and he that hath found such an one hath found a treasure.

¹⁵Nothing doth countervail a faithful friend, and his excellency is invaluable.

¹⁶A faithful friend is the medicine of life; and they that fear the Lord shall find him.

¹⁷Whoso feareth the Lord shall direct his friendship aright: for as he is, so shall his neighbour be also.

5:14 A *whisperer*: a slanderer; the Hebrew version reads "double-tongued" (NRSV).   **5:15** *Be not ignorant of any thing*: other versions (including the Hebrew) read "cause no harm" (NRSV).   **6:2** *Extol not . . . alone*: other versions (including the Hebrew) read "do not fall into the grip of passion, or you may be torn apart as by a bull" (NRSV).   **6:3** *Thou shalt eat up . . . tree*: systematically reversing Ps 1:3.

6:5–17 False friendship and true. 6:7 *Prove*: test.   **6:9** *Discover*: reveal.   **6:15** *Doth countervail*: is worth more than.   **6:17** *As he . . . also*: recalling the "golden rule" (Lev 19:18; etc.).

¹⁸My son, gather instruction from thy youth up: so shalt thou find
  wisdom till thine old age.

¹⁹Come unto her as one that ploweth and soweth, and wait for her
  good fruits: for thou shalt not toil much in labouring about
  her, but thou shalt eat of her fruits right soon.

²⁰She is very unpleasant to the unlearned: he that is without
  understanding will not remain with her.

²¹She will lie upon him as a mighty stone of trial; and he will cast
  her from him ere it be long.

²²For wisdom is according to her name, and she is not manifest
  unto many.

²³Give ear, my son, receive my advice, and refuse not my
  counsel,

²⁴And put thy feet into her fetters, and thy neck into her chain.

²⁵Bow down thy shoulder, and bear her, and be not grieved with
  her bonds.

²⁶Come unto her with thy whole heart, and keep her ways with all
  thy power.

²⁷Search, and seek, and she shall be made known unto thee: and
  when thou hast got hold of her, let her not go.

²⁸For at the last thou shalt find her rest, and that shall be turned
  to thy joy.

²⁹Then shall her fetters be a strong defence for thee, and her
  chains a robe of glory.

³⁰For there is a golden ornament upon her, and her bands are
  purple lace.

³¹Thou shalt put her on as a robe of honour, and shalt put her
  about thee as a crown of joy.

³²My son, if thou wilt, thou shalt be taught: and if thou wilt apply
  thy mind, thou shalt be prudent.

³³If thou love to hear, thou shalt receive understanding; and if
  thou bow thine ear, thou shalt be wise.

³⁴Stand in the multitude of the elders; and cleave unto him that is
  wise.

³⁵Be willing to hear every godly discourse; and let not the parables
  of understanding escape thee.

6:18–37 Embracing Wisdom. 6:21 *Mighty stone of trial*: i.e., a "heavy stone" (NRSV). **6:22** *For wisdom is according to her name*: LXX here uses *sophia* (whence KJV "wisdom") for Hebrew *musar* (usually translated "discipline" or "instruction"; cf. Prov. 1:2, 3, 7; 23:23). But the same Hebrew letters may represent a different root, which means "be removed or withdrawn," whence KJV *not manifest*—a pun unfortunately lost in translation. **6:28** *Thou shalt find her rest*: cf. Matt 11:29. **6:30** *There is*: the Hebrew version reads "her yoke is." **6:30–31** *A golden ornament . . . crown of joy*: her attire recalls the high priest's vestments (see Exod 28:22–28; 29:5–6), as well as the "ribband of blue" Israelites were to wear in remembrance of God's commandments (Num 15:37–40). **6:35** *Parables of understanding*:

³⁶And if thou seest a man of understanding, get thee betimes unto him, and let thy foot wear the steps of his door.

³⁷Let thy mind be upon the ordinances of the Lord, and meditate continually in his commandments: he shall establish thine heart, and give thee wisdom at thine own desire.

7 Do no evil, so shall no harm come unto thee.
²Depart from the unjust, and iniquity shall turn away from thee.
³My son, sow not upon the furrows of unrighteousness, and thou shalt not reap them sevenfold.
⁴Seek not of the Lord pre-eminence, neither of the king the seat of honour.
⁵Justify not thyself before the Lord; and boast not of thy wisdom before the king.
⁶Seek not to be judge, being not able to take away iniquity; lest at any time thou fear the person of the mighty, and lay a stumblingblock in the way of thy uprightness.
⁷Offend not against the multitude of a city, and then thou shalt not cast thyself down among the people.
⁸Bind not one sin upon another; for in one thou shalt not be unpunished.
⁹Say not, God will look upon the multitude of my oblations, and when I offer to the most high God, he will accept it.
¹⁰Be not fainthearted when thou makest thy prayer, and neglect not to give alms.
¹¹Laugh no man to scorn in the bitterness of his soul: for there is one which humbleth and exalteth.
¹²Devise not a lie against thy brother; neither do the like to thy friend.
¹³Use not to make any manner of lie; for the custom thereof is not good.
¹⁴Use not many words in a multitude of elders, and make not much babbling when thou prayest.
¹⁵Hate not laborious work, neither husbandry, which the most High hath ordained.
¹⁶Number not thyself among the multitude of sinners, but remember that wrath will not tarry long.
¹⁷Humble thy soul greatly: for the vengeance of the ungodly is fire and worms.

---

i.e., "wise proverbs" (NRSV).   **6:36** *Betimes*: quickly.   **6:37** *Let thy mind . . . commandments*: echoing Josh 1:8; cf. Ps 1:2–3.
  7:1–17 Avoiding unrighteousness and presumption. 7:6 *Being not able*: alternatively "lest you are unable." **7:11** *Humbleth and exalteth*: echoing 1 Sam 2:7. **7:13** *Use not*: lit. "do not desire" or "do not will." **7:14** *Make not . . . prayest*: cf. Matt 6:7. **7:15** *Neither husbandry . . . ordained*: see Gen 2:15; 3:19, 23. **7:17** *Vengeance*: punishment. *Fire and worms*: cf. Isa 66:24; the Hebrew version simply reads "what awaits humans is worms" (trans. Skehan), referring to decomposition rather than to torment in hell.

[18]Change not a friend for any good by no means; neither a faithful
   brother for the gold of Ophir.

[19]Forego not a wise and good woman; for her grace is above gold.

[20]Whereas thy servant worketh truly, entreat him not evil, nor the
   hireling that bestoweth himself wholly for thee.

[21]Let thy soul love a good servant, and defraud him not of liberty.

[22]Hast thou cattle? have an eye to them: and if they be for thy
   profit, keep them with thee.

[23]Hast thou children? instruct them, and bow down their neck
   from their youth.

[24]Hast thou daughters? have a care of their body, and shew not
   thyself cheerful toward them.

[25]Marry thy daughter, and so shalt thou have performed a weighty
   matter; but give her to a man of understanding.

[26]Hast thou a wife after thy mind? forsake her not; but give not
   thyself over to a light woman.

[27]Honour thy father with thy whole heart, and forget not the
   sorrows of thy mother.

[28]Remember that thou wast begotten of them; and how canst thou
   recompense them the things that they have done for thee?

[29]Fear the Lord with all thy soul, and reverence his priests.

[30]Love him that made thee with all thy strength, and forsake not
   his ministers.

[31]Fear the Lord, and honour the priest; and give him his portion,
   as it is commanded thee; the firstfruits, and the trespass
   offering, and the gift of the shoulders, and the sacrifice of
   sanctification, and the first-fruits of the holy things.

[32]And stretch thine hand unto the poor, that thy blessing may be
   perfected.

[33]A gift hath grace in the sight of every man living; and for the
   dead detain it not.

[34]Fail not to be with them that weep, and mourn with them that
   mourn.

[35]Be not slow to visit the sick: for that shall make thee to be beloved.

7:18–28 Household admonitions. 7:18 *Good*: lit. "money"; some MSS substitute *adiaphoron*, a
technical term from Greek philosophy referring to "indifferent things" (i.e., things neither good nor
bad in themselves). *Ophir*: see Tob 13:17 note.   **7:19** *Forego*: Gk. *astochei*, lit. "miss the mark of"
(i.e., fail to acquire); the Hebrew version has "dismiss." *Woman*: better "wife." *Her grace is above gold*:
cf. Prov 31:10.   **7:20** *Entreat*: treat.   **7:21** *Good*: better "wise" or "intelligent" (MS tradition).
Defraud him not of liberty: perhaps a reference to legislation demanding manumission of slaves after
six years' service (e.g., Exod 21:2).   **7:24** *Body*: i.e., chastity (so NRSV).   **7:26** *Light*: lit. "hated."
7:27 *Sorrows*: lit. "pangs of childbirth."
    7:29–36 Obligations of piety. Gifts to priests (vv. 29–31) and to the poor (vv. 32–36).   **7:31** *As
it is commanded thee*: see Num 18:8–19; etc.   **7:33** *For the dead detain it not*: perhaps referring to
offerings to the dead (cf. Tob 4:17), although they were prohibited (see Deut 26:14) and the author
later seems to mock the practice (30:18). Alternatively, the clause might refer to funereal provisions

³⁶ Whatsoever thou takest in hand, remember the end, and thou
   shalt never do amiss.

8 Strive not with a mighty man, lest thou fall into his hands.
² Be not at variance with a rich man, lest he overweigh thee:
   for gold hath destroyed many, and perverted the hearts of kings.
³ Strive not with a man that is full of tongue, and heap not wood
   upon his fire.
⁴ Jest not with a rude man, lest thy ancestors be disgraced.
⁵ Reproach not a man that turneth from sin, but remember that we
   are all worthy of punishment.
⁶ Dishonour not a man in his old age: for even some of us wax old.
⁷ Rejoice not over thy greatest enemy being dead, but remember
   that we die all.
⁸ Despise not the discourse of the wise, but acquaint thyself with
   their proverbs: for of them thou shalt learn instruction, and
   how to serve great men with ease.
⁹ Miss not the discourse of the elders: for they also learned of their
   fathers, and of them thou shalt learn understanding, and to
   give answer as need requireth.
¹⁰ Kindle not the coals of a sinner, lest thou be burnt with the
   flame of his fire.
¹¹ Rise not up [in anger] at the presence of an injurious person, lest
   he lie in wait to entrap thee in thy words.
¹² Lend not unto him that is mightier than thyself; for if thou
   lendest him, count it but lost.
¹³ Be not surety above thy power: for if thou be surety, take care to
   pay it.
¹⁴ Go not to law with a judge; for they will judge for him according
   to his honour.
¹⁵ Travel not by the way with a bold fellow, lest he become grievous
   unto thee: for he will do according to his own will, and thou
   shalt perish with him through his folly.
¹⁶ Strive not with an angry man, and go not with him into a
   solitary place: for blood is as nothing in his sight; and where
   there is no help, he will overthrow thee.
¹⁷ Consult not with a fool; for he cannot keep counsel.

(cf. Tob 1:17), or merely be hyperbolic.   **7:36** *Remember the end*: lit. "remember your end" (i.e., your death).

8:1–19 Dealing with the wicked and powerful, with an excursus demanding attention to those experienced in such delicate matters (vv. 8–9).   **8:3** *A man . . . tongue*: a loudmouth.   **8:7** *Thy greatest enemy being dead*: better "the dead" (MS tradition).   **8:9** *Miss*: Gk. *astochei*; see 7:19 note.   **8:11–16** *Rise not up . . . overthrow thee*: much of this material is apparently derived from the series of maxims in Prov 22:24–27.   **8:11** *[In anger]*: better omitted. *Injurious*: Gk. *hybristos*, referring to wanton—even violent—arrogance.   **8:14** *Honour*: i.e., reputation.

¹⁸Do no secret thing before a stranger; for thou knowest not what
he will bring forth.

¹⁹Open not thine heart to every man, lest he requite thee with a
shrewd turn.

9 Be not jealous over the wife of thy bosom, and teach her not an
evil lesson against thyself.

²Give not thy soul unto a woman to set her foot upon thy
substance.

³Meet not with an harlot, lest thou fall into her snares.

⁴Use not much the company of a woman that is a singer, lest thou
be taken with her attempts.

⁵Gaze not on a maid, that thou fall not by those things that are
precious in her.

⁶Give not thy soul unto harlots, that thou lose not thine
inheritance.

⁷Look not round about thee in the streets of the city, neither
wander thou in the solitary places thereof.

⁸Turn away thine eye from a beautiful woman, and look not upon
another's beauty; for many have been deceived by the beauty of
a woman; for herewith love is kindled as a fire.

⁹Sit not at all with another man's wife, nor sit down with her in
thine arms, and spend not thy money with her at the wine; lest
thine heart incline unto her, and so through thy desire thou
fall into destruction.

¹⁰Forsake not an old friend; for the new is not comparable to him:
a new friend is as new wine; when it is old, thou shalt drink it
with pleasure.

¹¹Envy not the glory of a sinner: for thou knowest not what shall
be his end.

¹²Delight not in the thing that the ungodly have pleasure in; but
remember they shall not go unpunished unto their grave.

¹³Keep thee far from the man that hath power to kill; so shalt
thou not doubt the fear of death: and if thou come unto him,
make no fault, lest he take away thy life presently: remember

---

8:19 *Lest he . . . turn*: more literally "and let him not return your favor" or "requite you with thanks," perhaps hinting at malicious use of the secret. The Hebrew version reads "or you may drive away your happiness" (NRSV). **9:1–9 Warnings about women. 9:1** *Teach her . . . thyself*: i.e., by being needlessly jealous, you will encourage her to be unfaithful. **9:2** *Substance*: strength. **9:3** *Harlot*: the Greek more accurately refers to a courtesan. **9:4** *Use not*: do not become accustomed to. **9:5** *By those things . . . her*: better "on the penalties you incur for her"; cf. Deut 22:28–29. **9:7** *Look not round . . . thereof*: Prov 7:6–23 may be in the background. **9:8** *Another's beauty*: i.e., the beauty of a woman belonging to another man. **9:9** *Nor sit down . . . money with her*: rather "nor indulge in feasting with her." *Through thy desire*: the Hebrew version reads "in blood," referring to the husband's vengeance or to legal penalties for adultery (e.g., Lev 20:10). **9:10–16 Admonitions concerning companions. 9:13** *Doubt*: be apprehensive about.

that thou goest in the midst of snares, and that thou walkest
upon the battlements of the city.

¹⁴As near as thou canst, guess at thy neighbour, and consult with
the wise.

¹⁵Let thy talk be with the wise, and all thy communication in the
law of the most High.

¹⁶And let just men eat and drink with thee; and let thy glorying be
in the fear of the Lord.

¹⁷For the hand of the artificer the work shall be commended; and
the wise ruler of the people for his speech.

¹⁸A man of an ill tongue is dangerous in his city; and he that is
rash in his talk shall he hated.

10 ¹A wise judge will instruct his people; and the government of a
prudent man is well ordered.

²As the judge of the people is himself, so are his officers; and
what manner of man the ruler of the city is, such are all they
that dwell therein.

³An unwise king destroyeth his people; but through the prudence
of them which are in authority the city shall be inhabited.

⁴The power of the earth is in the hand of the Lord, and in due
time he will set over it one that is profitable.

⁵In the hand of God is the prosperity of man; and upon the person
of the scribe shall he lay his honour.

⁶Bear not hatred to thy neighbour for every wrong; and do nothing
at all by injurious practices.

⁷Pride is hateful before God and man: and by both doth one
commit iniquity.

⁸Because of unrighteous dealings, injuries, and riches got by
deceit, the kingdom is translated from one people to another.

⁹Why is earth and ashes proud? There is not a more wicked thing
than a covetous man: for such an one setteth his own soul to
sale; because while he liveth he casteth away his bowels.

¹⁰The physician cutteth off a long disease; and he that is to day a
king to morrow shall die.

¹¹For when a man is dead, he shall inherit creeping things, beasts,
and worms.

Upon the battlements of the city: i.e., in an exposed position.   **9:14** *Guess at*: i.e., endeavor to understand.   **9:15** *In*: about.
　　9:17–10:18 Rulers and their pride. 10:3 *Shall be inhabited*: i.e., its population will increase.
10:5 *Scribe*: the Hebrew version refers here to a ruler (so Skehan).   **10:9** *Earth and ashes*: cf. Gen
3:19. *There is . . . sale*: better omitted (MS tradition). *Because while . . . bowels*: the Hebrew version
reads "even in life the human body decays" (NRSV).   **10:10** *The physician . . . disease*: rather "'a
long disease,' the physician says in jest." The Hebrew version may tentatively be translated as "a long

¹²The beginning of pride is when one departeth from God, and his heart is turned away from his Maker.

¹³For pride is the beginning of sin, and he that hath it shall pour out abomination: and therefore the Lord brought upon them strange calamities, and overthrew them utterly.

¹⁴The Lord hath cast down the thrones of proud princes, and set up the meek in their stead.

¹⁵The Lord hath plucked up the roots of the proud nations, and planted the lowly in their place.

¹⁶The Lord overthrew countries of the heathen, and destroyed them to the foundations off the earth.

¹⁷He took some of them away, and destroyed them, and hath made their memorial to cease from the earth.

¹⁸Pride was not made for men, nor furious anger for them that are born of a woman.

¹⁹They that fear the Lord are a sure seed, and they that love him an honourable plant: they that regard not the law are a dishonourable seed; they that transgress the commandments are a deceivable seed.

²⁰Among brethren he that is chief is honourable; so are they that fear the Lord in his eyes.

²¹The fear of the Lord goeth before the obtaining of authority: but roughness and pride is the losing thereof.

²²Whether he be rich, noble, or poor, their glory is the fear of the Lord.

²³It is not meet to despise the poor man that hath understanding; neither is it convenient to magnify a sinful man.

²⁴Great men, and judges, and potentates, shall be honoured; yet is there none of them greater than he that feareth the Lord.

²⁵Unto the servant that is wise shall they that are free do service: and he that hath knowledge will not grudge when he is reformed.

²⁶Be not overwise in doing thy business; and boast not thyself in the time of thy distress.

²⁷Better is he that laboureth, and aboundeth in all things, than he that boasteth himself, and wanteth bread.

²⁸My son, glorify thy soul in meekness, and give it honour according to the dignity thereof.

---

disease baffles the physician" (NRSV).   **10:16** *Countries of the heathen*: or "lands of the nations."
   10:19–11:6 Authentic honor. 10:19 *They that fear . . . deceivable seed*: better "Whose offspring are worthy of honor? Human offspring. Whose offspring are worthy of honor? Those who fear the Lord. Whose offspring are unworthy of honor? Human offspring. Whose offspring are unworthy of honor? Those who break the commandments" (MS tradition; NRSV).   **10:21** *The fear . . . thereof*: better omitted (MS tradition).   **10:23–24** *It is not meet . . . Lord*: recalling Eccl 9:13–17.   **10:23** *Convenient*: appropriate.   **10:25** *Will not grudge . . . reformed*: better "will not murmur" (MS tradition; our translation).   **10:26** *Be not overwise*: perhaps meaning "do not make a display of your

29 Who will justify him that sinneth against his own soul? and who will honour him that dishonoureth his own life?

30 The poor man is honoured for his skill, and the rich man is honoured for his riches.

31 He that is honoured in poverty, how much more in riches? and he that is dishonourable in riches, how much more in poverty?

11 ¹Wisdom lifteth up the head of him that is of low degree, and maketh him to sit among great men.

2 Commend not a man for his beauty; neither abhor a man for his outward appearance.

3 The bee is little among such as fly; but her fruit is the chief of sweet things.

4 Boast not of thy clothing and raiment, and exalt not thyself in the day of honour: for the works of the Lord are wonderful, and his works among men are hidden.

5 Many kings have sat down upon the ground; and one that was never thought of hath worn the crown.

6 Many mighty men have been greatly disgraced; and the honourable delivered into other men's hands.

7 Blame not before thou hast examined the truth: understand first, and then rebuke.

8 Answer not before thou hast heard the cause: neither interrupt men in the midst of their talk.

9 Strive not in a matter that concerneth thee not; and sit not in judgment with sinners.

10 My son, meddle not with many matters: for if thou meddle much, thou shalt not be innocent; and if thou follow after, thou shalt not obtain, neither shalt thou escape by fleeing.

11 There is one that laboureth, and taketh pains, and maketh haste, and is so much the more behind.

12 Again, there is another that is slow, and hath need of help, wanting ability, and full of poverty; yet the eye of the Lord looked upon him for good, and set him up from his low estate,

13 And lifted up his head from misery; so that many that saw it marvelled at him.

14 Prosperity and adversity, life and death, poverty and riches, come of the Lord.

wisdom" (so NRSV).   **10:30** *Skill:* or "knowledge."   **11:5** *One that . . . crown:* this phrase perhaps glances at David's unlikely origins (see Ps 78:70–71).
    11:7–28 Divine providence and judgment. After a brief introduction on the need to understand a situation fully before evaluating it (vv. 7–9), Ben Sira addresses God's provisions (vv. 10–19) and his judgment and rewards (vv. 20–28). The section's final verse forms an inclusive frame with its introduction.   **11:8** *Answer not . . . cause:* cf. Prov 18:13.   **11:14** *Prosperity . . . of the Lord:*

¹⁵Wisdom, knowledge, and understanding of the law, are of the
    Lord: love, and the way of good works, are from him.
¹⁶Error and darkness had their beginning together with sinners:
    and evil shall wax old with them that glory therein.
¹⁷The gift of the Lord remaineth with the godly, and his favour
    bringeth prosperity for ever.
¹⁸There is that waxeth rich by his wariness and pinching, and this
    is the portion of his reward:
¹⁹Whereas he saith, I have found rest, and now will eat continually
    of my goods; and yet he knoweth not what time shall come upon
    him, and that he must leave those things to others, and die.

²⁰Be stedfast in thy covenant, and be conversant therein, and wax
    old in thy work.
²¹Marvel not at the works of sinners; but trust in the Lord, and
    abide in thy labour: for it is an easy thing in the sight of the
    Lord on the sudden to make a poor man rich.
²²The blessing of the Lord is in the reward of the godly, and
    suddenly he maketh his blessing to flourish.
²³Say not, What profit is there of my service? and what good things
    shall I have hereafter?
²⁴Again, say not, I have enough, and possess many things, and
    what evil can come to me hereafter?
²⁵In the day of prosperity there is a forgetfulness of affliction: and in
    the day of affliction there is no more remembrance of prosperity.
²⁶For it is an easy thing unto the Lord in the day of death to
    reward a man according to his ways.
²⁷The affliction of an hour maketh a man forget pleasure: and in
    his end his deeds shall be discovered.
²⁸Judge none blessed before his death: for a man shall be known in
    his children.

²⁹Bring not every man into thine house: for the deceitful man
    hath many trains.
³⁰Like as a partridge taken [and kept] in a cage, so is the heart of
    the proud; and like as a spy, watcheth he for thy fall:
³¹For he lieth in wait, and turneth good into evil, and in things
    worthy praise will lay blame upon thee.

---

cf. 1 Sam 2:7.   **11:15–16** *Wisdom, knowledge . . . glory therein*: better omitted (MS tradition).
11:18 *Wariness and pinching*: alternatively "diligence and greed," suggesting acquisition through
labor.   **11:19** *I have found rest . . . die*: cf. Luke 12:19–20.   **11:20** *Thy covenant*: the Greek could
refer simply to a contract or agreement, or, more specifically, to the Mosaic covenant. *Be conversant
therein*: or "attend to it."   **11:28** *Judge none . . . death*: echoing a famous Greek sentiment, "Call no
man happy until he is dead" (cf. Herodotus 1.32; Aeschylus, *Agamemnon* 928–29). *In his children*:
the Hebrew version reads "by how he ends" (NRSV).
   11:29–12:18 Selecting associates. 11:29 *Trains*: tricks.   **11:30** *Like as a partridge . . . cage*:
perhaps used as decoys by bird hunters, as described by Aristotle (*History of Animals* 614a).

³²Of a spark of fire a heap of coals is kindled: and a sinful man
   layeth wait for blood.
³³Take heed of a mischievous man, for he worketh wickedness;
   lest he bring upon thee a perpetual blot.
³⁴Receive a stranger into thine house, and he will disturb thee,
   and turn thee out of thine own.

12 When thou wilt do good, know to whom thou doest it; so shalt
   thou be thanked for thy benefits.
²Do good to the godly man, and thou shalt find a recompence; and
   if not from him, yet from the most High.
³There can no good come to him that is always occupied in evil,
   nor to him that giveth no alms.
⁴Give to the godly man, and help not a sinner.
⁵Do well unto him that is lowly, but give not to the ungodly: hold
   back thy bread, and give it not unto him, lest he overmaster
   thee thereby: for [else] thou shalt receive twice as much evil
   for all the good thou shalt have done unto him.
⁶For the most High hateth sinners, and will repay vengeance unto
   the ungodly, and keepeth them against the mighty day of their
   punishment.
⁷Give unto the good, and help not the sinner.

⁸A friend cannot be known in prosperity: and an enemy cannot be
   hidden in adversity.
⁹In the prosperity of a man enemies will be grieved: but in his
   adversity even a friend will depart.
¹⁰Never trust thine enemy: for like as iron rusteth, so is his
   wickedness.
¹¹Though he humble himself, and go crouching, yet take good
   heed and beware of him, and thou shalt be unto him as if thou
   hadst wiped a lookingglass, and thou shalt know that his rust
   hath not been altogether wiped away.
¹²Set him not by thee, lest, when he hath overthrown thee, he
   stand up in thy place; neither let him sit at thy right hand, lest
   he seek to take thy seat, and thou at the last remember my
   words, and be pricked therewith.
¹³Who will pity a charmer that is bitten with a serpent, or any
   such as come nigh wild beasts?
¹⁴So one that goeth to a sinner, and is defiled with him in his sins,
   who will pity?

11:32 *A sinful man . . . blood*: echoing Prov 1:11.   12:4 *Give to the godly man . . . sinner*: contrast the
dominical injunction in Matt 5:42; Luke 6:30.   12:5 *But give not . . . done unto him*: Jesus' words in
Matt 7:6 also address this concern.   12:6 *And keepeth . . . punishment*: better omitted (MS tradition).
12:9 *Of a man . . . grieved*: the Hebrew version reads "a man's enemies are friendly" (so NRSV); cf. Prov
19:4.   12:11 *Lookingglass*: mirror; the author draws an analogy between suspecting an enemy and
wiping a mirror, both actions that aid perception.   12:13–14 *Who will pity . . . who will pity*: for the

¹⁵For a while he will abide with thee, but if thou begin to fall, he will not tarry. ¹⁶An enemy speaketh sweetly with his lips, but in his heart he imagineth how to throw thee into a pit: he will weep with his eyes, but if he find opportunity, he will not be satisfied with blood. ¹⁷If adversity come upon thee, thou shalt find him there first; and though he pretend to help thee, yet shall he undermine thee. ¹⁸He will shake his head, and clap his hands, and whisper much, and change his countenance.

13 He that toucheth pitch shall be defiled therewith; and he that hath fellowship with a proud man shall be like unto him. ²Burden not thyself above thy power while thou livest; and have no fellowship with one that is mightier and richer than thyself: for how agree the kettle and the earthen pot together? for if the one be smitten against the other, it shall be broken. ³The rich man hath done wrong, and yet he threateneth withal: the poor is wronged, and he must intreat also. ⁴If thou be for his profit, he will use thee; but if thou have nothing, he will forsake thee. ⁵If thou have any thing, he will live with thee: yea, he will make thee bare, and will not be sorry for it. ⁶If he have need of thee, he will deceive thee, and smile upon thee, and put thee in hope; he will speak thee fair, and say, What wantest thou? ⁷And he will shame thee by his meats, until he have drawn thee dry twice or thrice, and at the last he will laugh thee to scorn: afterward, when he seeth thee, he will forsake thee, and shake his head at thee. ⁸Beware that thou be not deceived, and brought down in thy jollity. ⁹If thou be invited of a mighty man, withdraw thyself, and so much the more will he invite thee. ¹⁰Press thou not upon him, lest thou be put back; stand not far off, lest thou be forgotten. ¹¹Affect not to be made equal unto him in talk, and believe not his many words: for with much communication will he tempt thee, and smiling upon thee will get out thy secrets: ¹²But cruelly he will lay up thy words, and will not spare to do thee hurt, and to put thee in prison.

---

analogy, see Ps 58:3–5.   **12:16** *An enemy . . . blood*: recalling Joseph's deception by his brothers (Gen 37:18–33).

13:1–23 Associating with the wealthy. Continuing the previous section's exploration of proper companionship, this section focuses specifically on the dangers of associating with the rich. **13:3** *Hath done wrong . . . withal*: adds insult to injury. *Intreat*: implore.   **13:4** *If thou be for his profit*: if you can be of use to him.   **13:7** *Meats*: food (so throughout).   **13:9** *If thou . . . thee*: cf.

¹³Observe, and take good heed, for thou walkest in peril of thy overthrowing: when thou hearest these things, awake in thy sleep.

¹⁴Love the Lord all thy life, and call upon him for thy salvation.

¹⁵Every beast loveth his like, and every man loveth his neighbour.

¹⁶All flesh consorteth according to kind, and a man will cleave to his like.

¹⁷What fellowship hath the wolf with the lamb? so the sinner with the godly.

¹⁸What agreement is there between the hyena and a dog? and what peace between the rich and the poor?

¹⁹As the wild ass is the lion's prey in the wilderness: so the rich eat up the poor.

²⁰As the proud hate humility: so doth the rich abhor the poor.

²¹A rich man beginning to fall is held up of his friends: but a poor man being down is thrust also away by his friends.

²²When a rich man is fallen, he hath many helpers: he speaketh things not to be spoken, and yet men justify him: the poor man slipped, and yet they rebuked him too; he spake wisely, and could have no place.

²³When a rich man speaketh, every man holdeth his tongue, and, look, what he saith, they extol it to the clouds: but if the poor man speak, they say, What fellow is this? and if he stumble, they will help to overthrow him.

²⁴Riches are good unto him that hath no sin, and poverty is evil in the mouth of the ungodly.

²⁵The heart of a man changeth his countenance, whether it be for good or evil: and a merry heart maketh a cheerful countenance.

²⁶A cheerful countenance is a token of a heart that is in prosperity; and the finding out of parables is a wearisome labour of the mind.

14 ¹Blessed is the man that hath not slipped with his mouth, and is not pricked with the multitude of sins.

²Blessed is he whose conscience hath not condemned him, and who is not fallen from his hope in the Lord.

³Riches are not comely for a niggard: and what should an envious man do with money?

⁴He that gathereth by defrauding his own soul gathereth for others, that shall spend his goods riotously.

⁵He that is evil to himself, to whom will he be good? he shall not take pleasure in his goods.

Prov 25:6–7; Luke 14:7–11. **13:13–14** *When thou . . . salvation*: better omitted (MS tradition). **13:17** *The wolf with the lamb*: cf. Isa 11:6.
  13:24–14:19 The use of wealth. 13:25–26 *A merry heart . . . prosperity*: cf. Prov 15:13. **14:3** *Envious*: "miserly" (NRSV), also in vv. 6 (i.e., "is miserly toward"), 8.

⁶There is none worse than he that envieth himself; and this is a recompence of his wickedness.

⁷And if he doeth good, he doeth it unwillingly; and at the last he will declare his wickedness.

⁸The envious man hath a wicked eye; he turneth away his face, and despiseth men.

⁹A covetous man's eye is not satisfied with his portion; and the iniquity of the wicked drieth up his soul.

¹⁰A wicked eye envieth [his] bread, and he is a niggard at his table.

¹¹My son, according to thy ability do good to thyself, and give the Lord his due offering.

¹²Remember that death will not be long in coming, and that the covenant of the grave is not shewed unto thee.

¹³Do good unto thy friend before thou die, and according to thy ability stretch out thy hand and give to him.

¹⁴Defraud not thyself of the good day, and let not the part of a good desire overpass thee.

¹⁵Shalt thou not leave thy travails unto another? and thy labours to be divided by lot?

¹⁶Give, and take, and sanctify thy soul; for there is no seeking of dainties in the grave.

¹⁷All flesh waxeth old as a garment: for the covenant from the beginning is, Thou shalt die the death.

¹⁸As of the green leaves on a thick tree, some fall, and some grow; so is the generation of flesh and blood, one cometh to an end, and another is born.

¹⁹Every work rotteth and consumeth away, and the worker thereof shall go withal.

²⁰Blessed is the man that doth meditate good things in wisdom, and that reasoneth of holy things by his understanding.

²¹He that considereth her ways in his heart shall also have understanding in her secrets.

14:7 *Unwillingly*: more literally "obliviously."   **14:9** *The iniquity of the wicked*: lit. (his own) "wicked iniquity."   **14:10** *Wicked eye*: i.e., "a miser" (see Matt 6:23 note).   **14:11–19** *My son . . . withal*: this section often echoes Ecclesiastes (cf. 5:17–19; 6:2–3; 9:9–10; etc.).   **14:12** *The grave*: Gk. *hadēs* (see Matt 11:23 note).   **14:15** *Travails, labours*: both words refer to the product of one's work. **14:16** *Sanctify*: better "beguile" (MS tradition), the same Greek verb that Eve uses to describe the serpent's treachery in LXX Gen 3:13. Recognizing that avoiding death is no longer possible (see v. 17 and note), the author encourages the same kind of seductive self-indulgence as the serpent. **14:17** *All flesh . . . garment*: cf. Ps 102:26. *Thou shalt die the death*: quoting LXX Gen 2:17.   **14:18** *As of the green leaves . . . born*: a conventional simile; cf. Homer, *Iliad* 6.146–49; Horace, *Ars poetica* 60–62; etc.
     14:20–15:10 Pursuing wisdom. 14:20 *Good things in*: better simply "on" (MS tradition). *Of holy things*: better omitted (MS tradition). The verse recalls Ps 1:2, substituting wisdom for God's law.

²²Go after her as one that traceth, and lie in wait in her ways.

²³He that prieth in at her windows shall also hearken at her doors.

²⁴He that doth lodge near her house shall also fasten a pin in her walls.

²⁵He shall pitch his tent nigh unto her, and shall lodge in a lodging where good things are.

²⁶He shall set his children under her shelter, and shall lodge under her branches.

²⁷By her he shall be covered from heat, and in her glory shall he dwell.

15 ¹He that feareth the Lord will do good; and he that hath the knowledge of the law shall obtain her.

²And as a mother shall she meet him, and receive him as a wife married of a virgin.

³With the bread of understanding shall she feed him, and give him the water of wisdom to drink.

⁴He shall be stayed upon her, and shall not be moved; and shall rely upon her, and shall not be confounded.

⁵She shall exalt him above his neighbours, and in the midst of the congregation shall she open his mouth.

⁶He shall find joy and a crown of gladness, and she shall cause him to inherit an everlasting name.

⁷But foolish men shall not attain unto her, and sinners shall not see her.

⁸For she is far from pride, and men that are liars cannot remember her.

⁹Praise is not seemly in the mouth of a sinner, for it was not sent him of the Lord.

¹⁰For praise shall be uttered in wisdom, and the Lord will prosper it.

¹¹Say not thou, It is through the Lord that I fell away: for thou oughtest not to do the things that he hateth.

¹²Say not thou, He hath caused me to err: for he hath no need of the sinful man.

¹³The Lord hateth all abomination; and they that fear God love it not.

¹⁴He himself made man from the beginning, and left him in the hand of his counsel;

¹⁵If thou wilt, to keep the commandments, and to perform acceptable faithfulness.

14:22 *Traceth*: tracks.   14:24 *Pin*: tent peg, as v. 25 makes clear.   15:1 *Do good*: lit. "do it," i.e., pursue wisdom.   15:2 *Wife married of a virgin*: "young bride" (NRSV).   15:3 *With the bread . . . drink*: compare Wisdom's words in Prov 9:5.

15:11–16:23 Freedom and accountability. 15:14–15 *He himself . . . faithfulness*: recalling

¹⁶He hath set fire and water before thee: stretch forth thy hand
   unto whether thou wilt.

¹⁷Before man is life and death; and whether him liketh shall be
   given him.

¹⁸For the wisdom of the Lord is great, and he is mighty in power,
   and beholdeth all things:

¹⁹And his eyes are upon them that fear him, and he knoweth every
   work of man.

²⁰He hath commanded no man to do wickedly, neither hath he
   given any man licence to sin.

16 Desire not a multitude of unprofitable children, neither delight in
   ungodly sons.

²Though they multiply, rejoice not in them, except the fear of the
   Lord be with them.

³Trust not thou in their life, neither respect their multitude: for
   one that is just is better than a thousand; and better it is to die
   without children, than to have them that are ungodly.

⁴For by one that hath understanding shall the city be replenished:
   but the kindred of the wicked shall speedily become desolate.

⁵Many such things have I seen with mine eyes, and mine ear hath
   heard greater things than these.

⁶In the congregation of the ungodly shall a fire be kindled; and in
   a rebellious nation wrath is set on fire.

⁷He was not pacified toward the old giants, who fell away in the
   strength of their foolishness.

⁸Neither spared he the place where Lot sojourned, but abhorred
   them for their pride.

⁹He pitied not the people of perdition, who were taken away in
   their sins:

¹⁰Nor the six hundred thousand footmen, who were gathered
   together in the hardness of their hearts.

¹¹And if there be one stiffnecked among the people, it is marvel if
   he escape unpunished: for mercy and wrath are with him; he is
   mighty to forgive, and to pour out displeasure.

¹²As his mercy is great, so is his correction also: he judgeth a man
   according to his works.

Gen 2:4–17.   **15:16** *Unto whether thou wilt*: for whichever you want.   **15:17** *Before man is life and death*: see Deut 30:19. *Whether him liketh*: whichever pleases him.   **16:1–4** *Desire not . . . desolate*: an excursus on useless children.   **16:6** *In the congregation . . . on fire*: see Num 11:1 and chap. 16 (esp. v. 35).   **16:7** *The old giants*: see Gen 6:1–4 and note.   **16:8** *Neither spared . . . pride*: see Gen 19.   **16:9** *The people . . . sins*: presumably, *the people* were the indigenous inhabitants of the promised land; see Lev 18:24–25; Deut 7:1–2; etc.   **16:10** *The six hundred thousand footmen*: the Israelites who escaped from Egypt (see Exod 12:37). *Hardness of their hearts*: an ironic description, since

¹³The sinner shall not escape with his spoils: and the patience of the godly shall not be frustrate.

¹⁴Make way for every work of mercy: for every man shall find according to his works.

¹⁵The Lord hardened Pharaoh, that he should not know him, that his powerful works might be known to the world.

¹⁶His mercy is manifest to every creature; and he hath separated his light from the darkness with an adamant.

¹⁷Say not thou, I will hide myself from the Lord: shall any remember me from above? I shall not be remembered among so many people: for what is my soul among such an infinite number of creatures?

¹⁸Behold, the heaven, and the heaven of heavens, the deep, and the earth, and all that therein is, shall be moved when he shall visit.

¹⁹The mountains also and foundations of the earth shall be shaken with trembling, when the Lord looketh upon them.

²⁰No heart can think upon these things worthily: and who is able to conceive his ways?

²¹It is a tempest which no man can see: for the most part of his works are hid.

²²Who can declare the works of his justice? or who can endure them? for his covenant is afar off, and the trial of all things is in the end.

²³He that wanteth understanding will think upon vain things: and a foolish man erring imagineth follies.

²⁴My son, hearken unto me, and learn knowledge, and mark my words with thy heart.

²⁵I will shew forth doctrine in weight, and declare his knowledge exactly.

²⁶The works of the Lord are done in judgment from the beginning; and from the time he made them he disposed the parts thereof.

²⁷He garnished his works for ever, and in his hand are the chief of them unto all generations: they neither labour, nor are weary, nor cease from their works.

²⁸None of them hindereth another, and they shall never disobey his word.

---

in Exodus it was Pharaoh's heart that was hardened (e.g., 7:13; 8:15; etc.).   **16:15–16** *The Lord . . . an adamant*: better omitted (MS tradition).   **16:19** *The mountains . . . upon them*: conventional imagery; cf. Judg 5:4–5; Ps 18:7; etc.   **16:22** *Endure*: await. *His covenant*: probably a reference to death; cf. 14:12, 17. *And the trial . . . end*: better omitted (MS tradition).   **16:23** *Vain*: lit. "these," i.e., "such are the thoughts of one devoid of understanding" (NRSV).

16:24–17:14 God's creation and law. 16:25 *Doctrine in weight*: teaching precisely measured. **16:27** *The chief of them*: their rulers—probably a reference to the sun and the moon (Gen 1:16, 18).

²⁹After this the Lord looked upon the earth, and filled it with his blessings.

³⁰With all manner of living things hath he covered the face thereof; and they shall return into it again.

17 The Lord created man of the earth, and turned him into it again. ²He gave them few days, and a short time, and power also over the things therein.

³He endued them with strength by themselves, and made them according to his image,

⁴And put the fear of man upon all flesh, and gave him dominion over beasts and fowls.

⁵[They received the use of the five operations of the Lord, and in the sixth place he imparted them understanding, and in the seventh, speech, an interpreter of the cogitations thereof.]

⁶Counsel, and a tongue, and eyes, ears, and a heart, gave he them to understand.

⁷Withal he filled them with the knowledge of understanding, and shewed them good and evil.

⁸He set his eye upon their hearts, that he might shew them the greatness of his works.

⁹He gave them to glory in his marvellous acts for ever, that they might declare his works with understanding.

¹⁰And the elect shall praise his holy name.

¹¹Beside this he gave them knowledge, and the law of life for an heritage.

¹²He made an everlasting covenant with them, and shewed them his judgments.

¹³Their eyes saw the majesty of his glory, and their ears heard his glorious voice.

¹⁴And he said unto them, Beware of all unrighteousness; and he gave every man commandment concerning his neighbour.

¹⁵Their ways are ever before him, and shall not be hid from his eyes.

¹⁶Every man from his youth is given to evil; neither could they make to themselves fleshy hearts for stony.

16:29–30 *After this . . . thereof*: cf. Gen 1:20–25.   **17:1** *The Lord . . . again*: see Gen 2:7; 3:19. **17:2** *He gave . . . time*: see, e.g., Job 14:1–2.   **17:2–4** *And power . . . fowls*: see Gen 1:26–28; 9:2. **17:5** *[They received . . . thereof]*: better omitted (MS tradition).   **17:7** *Shewed them good and evil*: recalling God's warning about the tree of the knowledge (cf. Gen 2:16–17).   **17:9–10** *He gave . . . name*: better "and they shall praise his holy name in order that they may declare the greatness of his works" (MS tradition).   **17:11** *Law of life*: see Deut 30:15–20.   **17:12** *Everlasting covenant*: the law promulgated at Mount Sinai, as the following verse makes clear.   **17:13** *Their eyes . . . his glorious voice*: see Exod 19:16–19; 20:18; Deut 4:11–15; etc.   **17:14** *He gave . . . neighbour*: i.e., commandments five through ten of the Decalogue (Exod 20:12–17); also cf. Lev 19:18.

17:15–32 Judgment and repentance. 17:16 *Every man . . . stony*: better omitted (MS tradition).

¹⁷For in the division of the nations of the whole earth he set a
ruler over every people; but Israel is the Lord's portion:

¹⁸Whom, being his firstborn, he nourisheth with discipline, and
giving him the light of his love doth not forsake him.

¹⁹Therefore all their works are as the sun before him, and his eyes
are continually upon their ways.

²⁰None of their unrighteous deeds are hid from him, but all their
sins are before the Lord.

²¹But the Lord being gracious, and knowing his workmanship,
neither left nor forsook them, but spared them.

²²The alms of a man is as a signet with him, and he will keep the
good deeds of man as the apple of the eye, and give repentance
to his sons and daughters.

²³Afterwards he will rise up and reward them, and render their
recompence upon their heads.

²⁴But unto them that repent, he granted them return, and comforted those that failed in patience.

²⁵Return unto the Lord, and forsake thy sins, make thy prayer
before his face, and offend less.

²⁶Turn again to the most High, and turn away from iniquity; for
he will lead thee out of darkness into the light of health, and
hate thou abomination vehemently.

²⁷Who shall praise the most High in the grave, instead of them
which live and give thanks?

²⁸Thanksgiving perisheth from the dead, as from one that is not:
the living and sound in heart shall praise the Lord.

²⁹How great is the lovingkindness of the Lord our God, and his
compassion unto such as turn unto him in holiness!

³⁰For all things cannot be in men, because the son of man is not
immortal.

³¹What is brighter than the sun? yet the light thereof faileth: and
flesh and blood will imagine evil.

³²He vieweth the power of the height of heaven; and all men are
but earth and ashes.

18

He that liveth for ever created all things in general. ²The Lord only is righteous, and there is none other but he, ³who governeth the world with the palm of his hand, and all things obey his will: for he is the King of all, by his power dividing holy things among them from profane.

17:17 *In the division . . . people*: Deut 32:8–9. **17:18** *Whom . . . forsake him*: better omitted (MS tradition). **17:21** *But the Lord . . . spared them*: better omitted (MS tradition). **17:22** *Signet*: i.e., signet ring, traditionally held to be of great value; cf. Gen 38:18; Jer 22:24–25. **17:23** *And render . . . heads*: drawing on Joel 3:4, 7. **17:26** *For he . . . health*: better omitted (MS tradition). **17:30** *The son of man*: i.e., a human being. **17:32** *Earth and ashes*: see 10:9 and note.
  18:1–14 God's compassion. 18:2–3 *And there . . . profane*: better omitted (MS tradition).

⁴To whom hath he given power to declare his works? and who
shall find out his noble acts?

⁵Who shall number the strength of his majesty? and who shall
also tell out his mercies?

⁶As for the wondrous works of the Lord, there may nothing be
taken from them, neither may any thing be put unto them,
neither can the ground of them be found out.

⁷When a man hath done, then he beginneth; and when he leaveth
off, then he shall be doubtful.

⁸What is man, and whereto serveth he? what is his good, and
what is his evil?

⁹The number of a man's days at the most are an hundred years.

¹⁰As a drop of water unto the sea, and a gravel stone in comparison of the sand; so are a thousand years to the days of eternity.

¹¹Therefore is God patient with them, and poureth forth his
mercy upon them.

¹²He saw and perceived their end to be evil; therefore he multiplied his compassion.

¹³The mercy of man is toward his neighbour; but the mercy of the
Lord is upon all flesh: he reproveth, and nurtureth, and
teacheth, and bringeth again, as a shepherd his flock.

¹⁴He hath mercy on them that receive discipline, and that diligently seek after his judgments.

¹⁵My son, blemish not thy good deeds, neither use uncomfortable
words when thou givest any thing.

¹⁶Shall not the dew asswage the heat? so is a word better than a gift.

¹⁷Lo, is not a word better than a gift? but both are with a gracious
man.

¹⁸A fool will upbraid churlishly, and a gift of the envious consumeth the eyes.

¹⁹Learn before thou speak, and use physick or ever thou be sick.

²⁰Before judgment examine thyself, and in the day of visitation
thou shalt find mercy.

²¹Humble thyself before thou be sick, and in the time of sins shew
repentance.

²²Let nothing hinder thee to pay thy vow in due time, and defer
not until death to be justified.

18:8 *What is man*: a question the Bible occasionally poses; see Job 7:17; 15:14; Ps 8:4; etc. **18:9**
The number . . . years: cf. Ps 90:10. **18:13** *The mercy of the Lord is upon all flesh*: cf. Ps 145:9. *As a*
shepherd: cf. Ps 23; Ezek 34:11–16; etc.
   18:15–19:3 Various admonitions, on giving, self-examination, vows, and self-control.
18:18 *Envious*: see 14:3 note.   **18:19** *Use physick . . . sick*: "before you fall ill, take care of your
health" (NRSV).   **18:22** *Be justified*: be made right (i.e., fulfill the vow); cf. Deut 23:21; Eccl 5:4–5.

²³Before thou prayest, prepare thyself; and be not as one that tempteth the Lord.

²⁴Think upon the wrath that shall be at the end, and the time of vengeance, when he shall turn away his face.

²⁵When thou hast enough, remember the time of hunger: and when thou art rich, think upon poverty and need.

²⁶From the morning until the evening the time is changed, and all things are soon done before the Lord.

²⁷A wise man will fear in every thing, and in the day of sinning he will beware of offence: but a fool will not observe time.

²⁸Every man of understanding knoweth wisdom, and will give praise unto him that found her.

²⁹They that were of understanding in sayings became also wise themselves, and poured forth exquisite parables.

³⁰Go not after thy lusts, but refrain thyself from thine appetites.

³¹If thou givest thy soul the desires that please her, she will make thee a laughingstock to thine enemies that malign thee.

³²Take not pleasure in much good cheer, neither be tied to the expence thereof.

³³Be not made a beggar by banqueting upon borrowing, when thou hast nothing in thy purse: for thou shalt lie in wait for thine own life, and be talked on.

19 ¹A labouring man that is given to drunkenness shall not be rich: and he that contemneth small things shall fall by little and little.

²Wine and women will make men of understanding to fall away: and he that cleaveth to harlots will become impudent.

³Moths and worms shall have him to heritage, and a bold man shall be taken away.

⁴He that is hasty to give credit is lightminded; and he that sinneth shall offend against his own soul.

⁵Whoso taketh pleasure in wickedness shall be condemned: but he that resisteth pleasures crowneth his life.

⁶He that can rule his tongue shall live without strife; and he that hateth babbling shall have less evil.

⁷Rehearse not unto another that which is told unto thee, and thou shalt fare never the worse.

18:23 *Prayest*: better "make a vow." *Tempteth*: tests; cf. Deut 6:16.   18:26 *Are soon done*: move quickly.   18:27 *But a fool . . . time*: better omitted (MS tradition).   18:33 *For thou . . . talked on*: better omitted (MS tradition).   19:1 *Is given to drunkenness*: the Hebrew version reads "does this" (referring to 18:32–33).   19:3 *Bold*: Gk. *tolmēros*, which shares its root with "impudent" (v. 2).

19:4–17 Speaking carefully. 19:5–6 *But he . . . without strife*: better omitted (MS tradition).   **19:6** *Babbling*: Gk. *lalia*, "chat" or even "loquacity" (so throughout; cf. NRSV).

⁸Whether it be to friend or foe, talk not of other men's lives; and
    if thou canst without offence, reveal them not.

⁹For he heard and observed thee, and when time cometh he will
    hate thee.

¹⁰If thou hast heard a word, let it die with thee; and be bold, it
    will not burst thee.

¹¹A fool travaileth with a word, as a woman in labour of a child.

¹²As an arrow that sticketh in a man's thigh, so is a word within a
    fool's belly.

¹³Admonish a friend, it may be he hath not done it: and if he have
    done it, that he do it no more.

¹⁴Admonish thy friend, it may be he hath not said it: and if he
    have, that he speak it not again.

¹⁵Admonish a friend: for many times it is a slander, and believe
    not every tale.

¹⁶There is one that slippeth in his speech, but not from his heart;
    and who is he that hath not offended with his tongue?

¹⁷Admonish thy neighbour before thou threaten him; and not
    being angry, give place to the law of the most High.

¹⁸The fear of the Lord is the first step to be accepted [of him,]
    and wisdom obtaineth his love.

¹⁹The knowledge of the commandments of the Lord is the doc-
    trine of life: and they that do things that please him shall
    receive the fruit of the tree of immortality.

²⁰The fear of the Lord is all wisdom; and in all wisdom is the
    performance of the law, and the knowledge of his
    omnipotency.

²¹If a servant say to his master, I will not do as it pleaseth thee;
    though afterward he do it, he angereth him that nourisheth him.

²²The knowledge of wickedness is not wisdom, neither at any time
    the counsel of sinners prudence.

²³There is a wickedness, and the same an abomination; and there
    is a fool wanting in wisdom.

²⁴He that hath small understanding, and feareth God, is better
    than one that hath much wisdom, and transgresseth the law of
    the most High.

19:8 *If thou canst . . . not*: more literally "unless it would be a sin for you, do not reveal it" (NRSV);
cf. Lev 5:1.   **19:10** *Bold*: courageous (a different word is used in v. 3).   **19:14** *Friend*: better "neighbor" (MS tradition), as in v. 17.   **19:17** *Admonish thy neighbour . . . High*: cf. Lev 19:17–18. *Not being
angry*: better omitted (MS tradition).

   19:18–30 The wise and the crafty. 19:18–19 *The fear . . . immortality*: better omitted
(MS tradition).   **19:20–21** *And the knowledge . . . nourisheth him*: better omitted (MS
tradition).   **19:23** *Wickedness*: better "subtlety" (MS tradition), reading the same Greek verb
as in v. 25.   **19:24** *Wisdom*: better "intelligence."

²⁵There is an exquisite subtilty, and the same is unjust; and there is one that turneth aside to make judgment appear; and there is a wise man that justifieth in judgment.

²⁶There is a wicked man that hangeth down his head sadly; but inwardly he is full of deceit,

²⁷Casting down his countenance, and making as if he heard not: where he is not known, he will do thee a mischief before thou be aware.

²⁸And if for want of power he be hindered from sinning, yet when he findeth opportunity he will do evil.

²⁹A man may be known by his look, and one that hath understanding by his countenance, when thou meetest him.

³⁰A man's attire, and excessive laughter, and gait, shew what he is.

20 There is a reproof that is not comely: again, some man holdeth his tongue, and he is wise.

²It is much better to reprove, than to be angry secretly: and he that confesseth his fault shall be preserved from hurt.

³How good is it, when thou art reproved, to shew repentance! for so shalt thou escape wilful sin.

⁴As is the lust of an eunuch to deflower a virgin; so is he that executeth judgment with violence.

⁵There is one that keepeth silence, and is found wise: and another by much babbling becometh hateful.

⁶Some man holdeth his tongue, because he hath not to answer: and some keepeth silence, knowing his time.

⁷A wise man will hold his tongue till he see opportunity: but a babbler and a fool will regard no time.

⁸He that useth many words shall be abhorred; and he that taketh to himself authority therein shall be hated.

⁹There is a sinner that hath good success in evil things; and there is a gain that turneth to loss.

¹⁰There is a gift that shall not profit thee; and there is a gift whose recompence is double.

¹¹There is an abasement because of glory; and there is that lifteth up his head from a low estate.

¹²There is that buyeth much for a little, and repayeth it sevenfold.

¹³A wise man by his words maketh himself beloved: but the graces of fools shall be poured out.

19:25 *Turneth aside to make judgment appear*: the Greek is difficult; NRSV (slightly altered) has "abuses favors to gain a verdict" (cf. NJB). *And there is a wise . . . judgment*: better omitted (MS tradition).
  20:1–32 Wise speech and prudent disposal of resources. Proverbs on speech (vv. 1–8, 18–32) frame a set on prudent generosity (vv. 9–17).   **20:3** *How good . . . sin*: better omitted (MS tradition).   **20:4** *With violence*: alternatively "under compulsion."   **20:5** *There is one . . . hateful*: cf. Prov 17:28.   **20:13** *By his words*: the Hebrew version reads "by only few words" (NRSV). *Graces*:

¹⁴The gift of a fool shall do thee no good when thou hast it;
   neither yet of the envious for his necessity: for he looketh to
   receive many things for one.
¹⁵He giveth little, and upbraideth much; he openeth his mouth
   like a crier; to day he lendeth, and to morrow will he ask it
   again: such an one is to be hated of God and man.
¹⁶The fool saith, I have no friends, I have no thank for all my
   good deeds, and they that eat my bread speak evil of me.
¹⁷How oft, and of how many shall he be laughed to scorn! for he
   knoweth not aright what it is to have; and it is all one unto him
   as if he had it not.

¹⁸To slip upon a pavement is better than to slip with the tongue:
   so the fall of the wicked shall come speedily.
¹⁹An unseasonable tale will always be in the mouth of the unwise.
²⁰A wise sentence shall be rejected when it cometh out of a fool's
   mouth; for he will not speak it in due season.

²¹There is that is hindered from sinning through want: and when
   he taketh rest, he shall not be troubled.
²²There is that destroyeth his own soul through bashfulness, and
   by accepting of persons overthroweth himself.
²³There is that for bashfulness promiseth to his friend, and
   maketh him his enemy for nothing.

²⁴A lie is a foul blot in a man, yet it is continually in the mouth of
   the untaught.
²⁵A thief is better than a man that is accustomed to lie: but they
   both shall have destruction to heritage.
²⁶The disposition of a liar is dishonourable, and his shame is ever
   with him.

²⁷A wise man shall promote himself to honour with his words: and
   he that hath understanding will please great men.
²⁸He that tilleth his land shall increase his heap: and he that
   pleaseth great men shall get pardon for iniquity.
²⁹Presents and gifts blind the eyes of the wise, and stop up his
   mouth that he cannot reprove.
³⁰Wisdom that is hid, and treasure that is hoarded up, what profit
   is in them both?

---

probably meaning "favors" or "courtesies." **20:14** *When thou . . . necessity*: better omitted (MS
tradition). **20:17** *For he . . . had it not*: better omitted (MS tradition). **20:19** *An unseasonable . . .
unwise*: better "an ungracious person is like an unseasonable tale, always in the mouth of the
unwise" (cf. NRSV). **20:22** *By accepting of persons*: i.e., by showing favor; alternatively "by a foolish face" (MS tradition). **20:27** *To honour*: better omitted. **20:28** *Get pardon*: lit. "atone."

³¹Better is he that hideth his folly than a man that hideth his wisdom.

³²Necessary patience in seeking the Lord is better than he that leadeth his life without a guide.

21

My son, hast thou sinned? do so no more, but ask pardon for thy former sins.

²Flee from sin as from the face of a serpent: for if thou comest too near it, it will bite thee: the teeth thereof are as the teeth of a lion, slaying the souls of men.

³All iniquity is as a twoedged sword, the wounds whereof cannot be healed.

⁴To terrify and do wrong will waste riches: thus the house of proud men shall be made desolate.

⁵A prayer out of a poor man's mouth reacheth to the ears of God, and his judgment cometh speedily.

⁶He that hateth to be reproved is in the way of sinners: but he that feareth the Lord will repent from his heart.

⁷An eloquent man is known far and near; but a man of understanding knoweth when he slippeth.

⁸He that buildeth his house with other men's money is like one that gathereth himself stones for the tomb of his burial.

⁹The congregation of the wicked is like tow wrapped together; and the end of them is a flame of fire to destroy them.

¹⁰The way of sinners is made plain with stones, but at the end thereof is the pit of hell.

¹¹He that keepeth the law of the Lord getteth the understanding thereof: and the perfection of the fear of the Lord is wisdom.

¹²He that is not wise will not be taught: but there is a wisdom which multiplieth bitterness.

¹³The knowledge of a wise man shall abound like a flood: and his counsel is like a pure fountain of life.

¹⁴The inner parts of a fool are like a broken vessel, and he will hold no knowledge as long as he liveth.

¹⁵If a skilful man hear a wise word, he will commend it, and add unto it: but as soon as one of no understanding heareth it, it displeaseth him, and he casteth it behind his back.

¹⁶The talking of a fool is like a burden in the way: but grace shall be found in the lips of the wise.

20:32 *Necessary patience . . . guide*: better omitted (MS tradition).
    21:1–10 Warnings against sin. 21:2–3 *Serpent . . . lion . . . twoedged sword*: all three images are conventional, though the first calls to mind Gen 3:1–5 in particular.   **21:7** *He*: i.e., the eloquent man.   **21:10** *Hell*: Gk. *hadēs* (see Matt 11:23 note).
    21:11–28 The wise and the foolish. A group of proverbs that set wise behavior against folly. **21:11** *Getteth the understanding thereof*: probably a mistranslation; "controls his thoughts" is better (so NRSV).   **21:12** *Wise . . . wisdom*: better "clever . . . cleverness" (also in v. 20).

¹⁷They inquire at the mouth of the wise man in the congregation,
     and they shall ponder his words in their heart.
¹⁸As is a house that is destroyed, so is wisdom to a fool: and the
     knowledge of the unwise is as talk without sense.
¹⁹Doctrine unto fools is as fetters on the feet, and like manacles
     on the right hand.
²⁰A fool lifteth up his voice with laughter; but a wise man doth
     scarce smile a little.
²¹Learning is unto a wise man as an ornament of gold, and like a
     bracelet upon his right arm.
²²A foolish man's foot is soon in his [neighbour's] house: but a
     man of experience is ashamed of him.
²³A fool will peep in at the door into the house: but he that is well
     nurtured will stand without.
²⁴It is the rudeness of a man to hearken at the door: but a wise
     man will be grieved with the disgrace.
²⁵The lips of talkers will be telling such things as pertain not unto
     them: but the words of such as have understanding are weighed
     in the balance.
²⁶The heart of fools is in their mouth: but the mouth of the wise
     is in their heart.
²⁷When the ungodly curseth Satan, he curseth his own soul.
²⁸A whisperer defileth his own soul, and is hated wheresoever he
     dwelleth.

22 A slothful man is compared to a filthy stone, and every one will
     hiss him out to his disgrace.
²A slothful man is compared to the filth of a dunghill: every man
     that takes it up will shake his hand.

³An evil nurtured son is the dishonour of his father that begat him:
     and a [foolish] daughter is born to his loss.
⁴A wise daughter shall bring an inheritance to her husband: but
     she that liveth dishonestly is her father's heaviness.
⁵She that is bold dishonoureth both her father and her husband,
     but they both shall despise her.
⁶A tale out of season [is as] musick in mourning: but stripes and
     correction of wisdom are never out of time.

21:19 *Doctrine*: Gk. *paideia*, "education" or "learning" (as in v. 21); compare its verbal form in v. 23, "well nurtured."   **21:22** *Ashamed of*: ashamed before. *Him*: probably the neighbor, into whose house the *man of experience* hesitates to enter.   **21:27** *Satan*: perhaps better understood generically as "an adversary" (see Job 1:6 note).
     22:1–18 The lazy, evil children, and the foolish. 22:3 *[Foolish]*: a word absent from the Greek. The misogynistic author may simply be asserting that daughters are less desirable than sons; but in light of v. 4, KJV may be right in understanding "foolish" here (i.e., "of the same sort as the son").   **22:4** *Shall bring an inheritance to her husband*: better "shall inherit a husband." *Dishonestly*: lit. "shamefully." *Heaviness*: sadness.   **22:5** *Dishonoureth*: lit. "shames."   **22:6** *Stripes*: wounds from a whip; cf. Prov 13:24;

⁷Whoso teacheth a fool is as one that glueth a potsherd together, and as he that waketh one from a sound sleep.

⁸He that telleth a tale to a fool speaketh to one in a slumber: when he hath told his tale, he will say, What is the matter?

⁹If children live honestly, and have wherewithal, they shall cover the baseness of their parents.

¹⁰But children, being haughty, through disdain and want of nurture do stain the nobility of their kindred.

¹¹Weep for the dead, for he hath lost the light: and weep for the fool, for he wanteth understanding: make little weeping for the dead, for he is at rest: but the life of the fool is worse than death.

¹²Seven days do men mourn for him that is dead; but for a fool and an ungodly man, all the days of his life.

¹³Talk not much with a fool, and go not to him that hath no understanding: beware of him, lest thou have trouble, and thou shalt never be defiled with his fooleries: depart from him, and thou shalt find rest, and never be disquieted with madness.

¹⁴What is heavier than lead? and what is the name thereof, but a fool?

¹⁵Sand, and salt, and a mass of iron, is easier to bear, than a man without understanding.

¹⁶As timber girt and bound together in a building cannot be loosed with shaking: so the heart that is stablished by advised counsel shall fear at no time.

¹⁷A heart settled upon a thought of understanding is as a fair plaistering on the wall of a gallery.

¹⁸Pales set on a high place will never stand against the wind: so a fearful heart in the imagination of a fool cannot stand against any fear.

¹⁹He that pricketh the eye will make tears to fall: and he that pricketh the heart maketh it to shew her knowledge.

²⁰Whoso casteth a stone at the birds frayeth them away: and he that upbraideth his friend breaketh friendship.

²¹Though thou drewest a sword at thy friend, yet despair not: for there may be a returning [to favour.]

²²If thou hast opened thy mouth against thy friend, fear not; for there may be a reconciliation: except for upbraiding, or pride, or disclosing of secrets, or a treacherous wound: for, for these things every friend will depart.

23:13–14. **22:9–10** *If children . . . kindred*: better omitted (MS tradition). **22:13** *Fooleries*: lit. "shaking" (the image is of an animal shaking off dirt). **22:14–15** *What is heavier . . . understanding*: cf. Prov 27:3. **22:18** *Pales*: stakes for fences.
22:19–26 Fidelity in friendship. 22:19 *Knowledge*: better "perception." **22:20** *Frayeth*: frightens.

²³Be faithful to thy neighbour in his poverty, that thou mayest
  rejoice in his prosperity: abide stedfast unto him in the time of
  his trouble, that thou mayest be heir with him in his heritage:
  for a mean estate is not always to be contemned: nor the rich
  that is foolish to be had in admiration.
²⁴As the vapour and smoke of a furnace goeth before the fire; so
  reviling before blood.
²⁵I will not be ashamed to defend a friend; neither will I hide
  myself from him.
²⁶And if any evil happen unto me by him, every one that heareth
  it will beware of him.

²⁷Who shall set a watch before my mouth, and a seal of wisdom
  upon my lips, that I fall not suddenly by them, and that my
  tongue destroy me not?

23 ¹O Lord, Father and Governor of all my whole life, leave me not
  to their counsels, and let me not fall by them.

²Who will set scourges over my thoughts, and the discipline of
  wisdom over mine heart? that they spare me not for mine
  ignorances, and it pass not by my sins:
³Lest mine ignorances increase, and my sins abound to my
  destruction, and I fall before mine adversaries, and mine
  enemy rejoice over me, whose hope is far from thy mercy.
⁴O Lord, Father and God of my life, give me not a proud look, but
  turn away from thy servants always a haughty mind.
⁵Turn away from me vain hopes and concupiscence, and thou
  shalt hold him up that is desirous always to serve thee.
⁶Let not the greediness of the belly nor lust of the flesh take hold of
  me; and give not over me thy servant into an impudent mind.

⁷Hear, O ye children, the discipline of the mouth: he that keepeth
  it shall never be taken in his lips.
⁸The sinner shall be left in his foolishness: both the evil speaker
  and the proud shall fall thereby.

22:23 *For a mean estate . . . admiration*: better omitted (MS tradition).
  22:27–23:6 A prayer for self-discipline. The prayer falls into two parts, preparing for the two
sections that follow: the first (22:27–23:1) asks for protection against self-destructive speech (developed
in 23:7–15); the second (23:2–6) asks for protection against lust (developed in 23:16–28). **22:27** *Who
shall set . . . me not*: cf. Pss 39:1; 141:3. **23:3** *To my destruction*: better omitted (MS tradition). *Whose
hope . . . mercy*: better omitted (MS tradition). **23:4** *Proud look*: more literally "a rising of eyes,"
probably referring to a look of lust (cf. Matt 5:28). *But turn . . . mind*: better omitted (MS tradition).
23:5 *Vain hopes and*: better omitted (MS tradition). *And thou . . . thee*: better omitted (MS tradition). **23:6** *Thy servant*: better omitted (MS tradition).
  23:7–15 Careful speech. Compare Matt 5:33–37. **23:7–8** *In his lips . . . foolishness*: *In his lips*
should be taken with v. 8, a better reading of whose first half yields "the sinner shall be taken by his

⁹Accustom not thy mouth to swearing; neither use thyself to the naming of the Holy One.

¹⁰For as a servant that is continually beaten shall not be without a blue mark: so he that sweareth and nameth God continually shall not be faultless.

¹¹A man that useth much swearing shall be filled with iniquity, and the plague shall never depart from his house: if he shall offend, his sin shall be upon him: and if he acknowledge not his sin, he maketh a double offence: and if he swear in vain, he shall not be innocent, but his house shall be full of calamities.

¹²There is a word that is clothed about with death: God grant that it be not found in the heritage of Jacob; for all such things shall be far from the godly, and they shall not wallow in their sins.

¹³Use not thy mouth to intemperate swearing, for therein is the word of sin.

¹⁴Remember thy father and thy mother, when thou sittest among great men. Be not forgetful before them, and so thou by thy custom become a fool, and wish that thou hadst not been born, and curse the day of thy nativity.

¹⁵The man that is accustomed to opprobrious words will never be reformed all the days of his life.

¹⁶Two sorts of men multiply sin, and the third will bring wrath: a hot mind is as a burning fire, it will never be quenched till it be consumed: a fornicator in the body of his flesh will never cease till he hath kindled a fire.

¹⁷All bread is sweet to a whoremonger, he will not leave off till he die.

¹⁸A man that breaketh wedlock, saying thus in his heart, Who seeth me? I am compassed about with darkness, the walls cover me, and no body seeth me; what need I to fear? the most High will not remember my sins:

¹⁹Such a man only feareth the eyes of men, and knoweth not that the eyes of the Lord are ten thousand times brighter than the sun, beholding all the ways of men, and considering the most secret parts.

²⁰He knew all things ere ever they were created; so also after they were perfected he looked upon them all.

²¹This man shall be punished in the streets of the city, and where he suspecteth not he shall be taken.

---

lips" (MS tradition).   **23:9** *Swearing*: i.e., oaths.   **23:11** *Plague*: scourge. *If he acknowledge not his sin*: better "if he disregard his oath."   **23:12** *A word . . . death*: blasphemy (see Lev 24:16).   **23:13** *Intemperate swearing*: more literally "lewd stupidity." NRSV paraphrases: "coarse, foul language."
   23:16–28 Fornication and adultery. 23:16 *In the body of his flesh*: probably a reference to incest.   **23:18** *Who seeth . . . seeth me*: cf. Job 24:15.

²²Thus shall it go also with the wife that leaveth her husband, and
bringeth in an heir by another.
²³For first, she hath disobeyed the law of the most High; and
secondly, she hath trespassed against her own husband; and
thirdly, she hath played the whore in adultery, and brought
children by another man.
²⁴She shall be brought out into the congregation, and inquisition
shall be made of her children.
²⁵Her children shall not take root, and her branches shall bring
forth no fruit.
²⁶She shall leave her memory to be cursed, and her reproach shall
not be blotted out.
²⁷And they that remain shall know that there is nothing better
than the fear of the Lord, and that there is nothing sweeter
than to take heed unto the commandments of the Lord.
²⁸It is great glory to follow the Lord, and to be received of him is
long life.

24 Wisdom shall praise herself, and shall glory in the midst of her
people.
²In the congregation of the most High shall she open her mouth,
and triumph before his power.

³I came out of the mouth of the most High, and covered the earth
as a cloud.
⁴I dwelt in high places, and my throne is in a cloudy pillar.
⁵I alone compassed the circuit of heaven, and walked in the
bottom of the deep.
⁶In the waves of the sea, and in all the earth, and in every people
and nation, I got a possession.
⁷With all these I sought rest: and in whose inheritance shall I abide?

⁸So the Creator of all things gave me a commandment, and he
that made me caused my tabernacle to rest, and said, Let thy
dwelling be in Jacob, and thine inheritance in Israel.
⁹He created me from the beginning before the world, and I shall
never fail.
¹⁰In the holy tabernacle I served before him; and so was I estab-
lished in Sion.
¹¹Likewise in the beloved city he gave me rest, and in Jerusalem
was my power.

23:23 *Disobeyed the law*: see Exod 20:14; Deut 5:18.   **23:24** *Inquisition shall . . . children*: the
Greek may rather refer to the punishment of her children (cf. v. 25; Deut 23:2).   **23:25** *Her children . . . fruit*: cf. Hos 9:16.   **23:28** *It is . . . life*: better omitted (MS tradition).
    24:1–34 Praise of Wisdom. This chapter recalls the praise of Wisdom in chap. 1, as well as
Prov 8:22–9:12.   **24:4** *Cloudy pillar*: identifying Wisdom as the pillar of cloud in Exodus (13:21), an
identification also made by Philo (*Who Is the Heir?* 203–4).   **24:8** *He that . . . rest*: see Exod 33:7–11.

¹²And I took root in an honourable people, even in the portion of the Lord's inheritance.

¹³I was exalted like a cedar in Libanus, and as a cypress tree upon the mountains of Hermon.

¹⁴I was exalted like a palm tree in En-gaddi, and as a rose plant in Jericho, as a fair olive tree in a pleasant field, and grew up as a plane tree by the water.

¹⁵I gave a sweet smell like cinnamon and aspalathus, and I yielded a pleasant odour like the best myrrh, as galbanum, and onyx, and sweet storax, and as the fume of frankincense in the tabernacle.

¹⁶As the turpentine tree I stretched out my branches, and my branches are the branches of honour and grace.

¹⁷As the vine brought I forth pleasant savour, and my flowers are the fruit of honour and riches.

¹⁸I am the mother of fair love, and fear, and knowledge, and holy hope: I therefore, being eternal, am given to all my children which are named of him.

¹⁹Come unto me, all ye that be desirous of me, and fill yourselves with my fruits.

²⁰For my memorial is sweeter than honey, and mine inheritance than the honeycomb.

²¹They that eat me shall yet be hungry, and they that drink me shall yet be thirsty.

²²He that obeyeth me shall never be confounded, and they that work by me shall not do amiss.

²³All these things are the book of the covenant of the most high God, even the law which Moses commanded for an heritage unto the congregations of Jacob.

²⁴Faint not to be strong in the Lord; that he may confirm you, cleave unto him: for the Lord Almighty is God alone, and beside him there is no other Saviour.

²⁵He filleth all things with his wisdom, as Phison and as Tigris in the time of the new fruits.

²⁶He maketh the understanding to abound like Euphrates, and as Jordan in the time of the harvest.

24:12 *Even in the portion . . . inheritance*: cf. Deut 32:9; Jer 10:16; etc. 24:13 *Libanus*: Lebanon, whose cedars were proverbially lofty and strong; cf. Pss 92:12; 104:16–17; etc. *Hermon*: in Syria. 24:14 *En-gaddi*: En-gedi, an oasis west of the Dead Sea. 24:15 *Cinnamon and . . . myrrh*: compare the perfume described in Exod 30:23–30, used for anointing the temple, its paraphernalia, and its personnel. *Galbanum . . . frankincense*: incense used in temple rituals (see Exod 30:34–35). 24:16 *Turpentine*: Terebinth. 24:18 *I am the mother . . . him*: better omitted (MS tradition). 24:19 *Come unto me . . . fruits*: echoing Isa 55:1. 24:20 *My memorial . . . honeycomb*: cf. Ps 19:10, on divine judgment. 24:21 *Yet be hungry . . . yet be thirsty*: "hunger for more . . . thirst for more" (NRSV). 24:23 *Book of the covenant*: cf. Exod 24:7. *The law . . . Jacob*: Deut 33:4. 24:24 *Faint not . . . Saviour*: better omitted (MS tradition). 24:25 *Phison*: the Pison River, mentioned in Gen 2:10–14 (see note).

²⁷He maketh the doctrine of knowledge appear as the light, and as
    Geon in the time of vintage.
²⁸The first man knew her not perfectly: no more shall the last find
    her out.
²⁹For her thoughts are more than the sea, and her counsels
    profounder than the great deep.

³⁰I also came out as a brook from a river, and as a conduit into a
    garden.
³¹I said, I will water my best garden, and will water abundantly my
    garden bed: and, lo, my brook became a river, and my river
    became a sea.
³²I will yet make doctrine to shine as the morning, and will send
    forth her light afar off.
³³I will yet pour out doctrine as prophecy, and leave it to all ages
    for ever.
³⁴Behold that I have not laboured for myself only, but for all them
    that seek wisdom.

25 In three things I was beautified, and stood up beautiful both
    before God and men: the unity of brethren, the love of neigh-
    bours, a man and a wife that agree together.
²Three sorts of men my soul hateth, and I am greatly offended at
    their life: a poor man that is proud, a rich man that is a liar,
    and an old adulterer that doateth.

³If thou hast gathered nothing in thy youth, how canst thou find
    any thing in thine age?
⁴O how comely a thing is judgment for gray hairs, and for ancient
    men to know counsel!
⁵O how comely is the wisdom of old men, and understanding and
    counsel to men of honour!
⁶Much experience is the crown of old men, and the fear of God is
    their glory.

⁷There be nine things which I have judged in mine heart to be
    happy, and the tenth I will utter with my tongue: A man that hath
    joy of his children; and he that liveth to see the fall of his enemy:
⁸Well is him that dwelleth with a wife of understanding, and that
    hath not slipped with his tongue, and that hath not served a
    man more unworthy than himself:

24:27 *Geon*: Gihon, another river named in Gen 2:10–14.   **24:33** *I will . . . prophecy*: cf. Joel 2:28.
   25:1–12 Marriage, wisdom in old age, and ten blessed things. 25:8 *Wife of understanding*: other versions (including the Hebrew) add "and the one who does not plow with ox and
ass together" (NRSV), an action forbidden in Deut 22:10; cf. Lev 19:19. (See 2 Cor 6:14
and note for another possible instance of applying this idea to objectionable marriages.)

⁹Well is him that hath found prudence, and he that speaketh in
the ears of them that will hear:

¹⁰O how great is he that findeth wisdom! yet is there none above
him that feareth the Lord.

¹¹But the love of the Lord passeth all things for illumination: he
that holdeth it, whereto shall he be likened?

¹²The fear of the Lord is the beginning of his love: and faith is the
beginning of cleaving unto him.

¹³[Give me] any plague, but the plague of the heart: and any
wickedness, but the wickedness of a woman:

¹⁴And any affliction, but the affliction from them that hate me:
and any revenge, but the revenge of enemies.

¹⁵There is no head above the head of a serpent; and there is no
wrath above the wrath of an enemy.

¹⁶I had rather dwell with a lion and a dragon, than to keep house
with a wicked woman.

¹⁷The wickedness of a woman changeth her face, and darkeneth
her countenance like sackcloth.

¹⁸Her husband shall sit among his neighbours; and when he
heareth it shall sigh bitterly.

¹⁹All wickedness is but little to the wickedness of a woman: let the
portion of a sinner fall upon her.

²⁰As the climbing up a sandy way is to the feet of the aged, so is a
wife full of words to a quiet man.

²¹Stumble not at the beauty of a woman, and desire her not for
pleasure.

²²A woman, if she maintain her husband, is full of anger, impu-
dence, and much reproach.

²³A wicked woman abateth the courage, maketh an heavy countenance and a wounded heart: a woman that will not comfort
her husband in distress maketh weak hands and feeble knees.

²⁴Of the woman came the beginning of sin, and through her we
all die.

²⁵Give the water no passage; neither a wicked woman liberty to
gad abroad.

25:9 *Prudence*: other versions read "a friend."   **25:11** *Love*: better "fear" (MS tradition).   **25:12**
The fear . . . him: better omitted (MS tradition).

   25:13–26:27 Wicked and virtuous women. 25:13 *Plague*: wound.   **25:15** *Head*: other versions
read "poison" (twice in this verse). The Greek seems to mistranslate.   **25:16** *I had rather dwell . . .
woman*: for analogous comparisons, see Prov 21:19; 25:24.   **25:17** *Sackcloth*: better "a bear" (MS tradition).   **25:18** *When he heareth it*: i.e., what they say about his wife.   **25:22** *Maintain*: provide for.
25:23 *Comfort her husband in distress*: more literally "bless her husband" or "make her husband happy."
25:24 *Of the woman . . . die*: a reference to Eve's transgression (Gen 3; cf. 1 Tim 2:14).   **25:25** *Gad*:

²⁶If she go not as thou wouldest have her, cut her off from thy flesh, and give her a bill of divorce, and let her go.

26 Blessed is the man that hath a virtuous wife, for the number of his days shall be double.
²A virtuous woman rejoiceth her husband, and he shall fulfil the years of his life in peace.
³A good wife is a good portion, which shall be given in the portion of them that fear the Lord.
⁴Whether a man be rich or poor, if he have a good heart toward the Lord, he shall at all times rejoice with a cheerful countenance.

⁵There be three things that mine heart feareth; and for the fourth I was sore afraid: the slander of a city, the gathering together of an unruly multitude, and a false accusation: all these are worse than death.
⁶But a grief of heart and sorrow is a woman that is jealous over another woman, and a scourge of the tongue which communicateth with all.
⁷An evil wife is a yoke shaken to and fro: he that hath hold of her is as though he held a scorpion.
⁸A drunken woman and a gadder abroad causeth great anger, and she will not cover her own shame.
⁹The whoredom of a woman may be known in her haughty looks and eyelids.

¹⁰If thy daughter be shameless, keep her in straitly, lest she abuse herself through overmuch liberty.
¹¹Watch over an impudent eye: and marvel not if she trespass against thee.
¹²She will open her mouth, as a thirsty traveller when he hath found a fountain, and drink of every water near her: by every hedge will she sit down, and open her quiver against every arrow.
¹³The grace of a wife delighteth her husband, and her discretion will fatten his bones.
¹⁴A silent and loving woman is a gift of the Lord; and there is nothing so much worth as a mind well instructed.
¹⁵A shamefaced and faithful woman is a double grace, and her continent mind cannot be valued.
¹⁶As the sun when it ariseth in the high heaven; so is the beauty of a good wife in the ordering of her house.

---

wander idly.   **25:26** *And give . . . go*: better omitted (MS tradition) as an explanatory gloss.   **26:4** *Whether a man . . . he shall*: rather "whether rich or poor, his good heart shall."   **26:6** *A woman*: a wife (also in vv. 8, 9, 14, 15).   **26:12** *She will open . . . near her*: better "as a thirsty traveler opens his mouth and drinks from any water near him" (NRSV). *Hedge*: better "peg" or "stake," a euphemism for penis.   **26:13** *Discretion*: better "knowledge" or "skill"; cf. Prov 31:10–31.   **26:14** *And loving*: better omitted (MS tradition).   **26:15** *Shamefaced*: modest (so throughout). *And faithful*: better

¹⁷As the clear light is upon the holy candlestick; so is the beauty
of the face in ripe age.
¹⁸As the golden pillars are upon the sockets of silver; so are the
fair feet with a constant heart.

¹⁹My son, keep the flower of thine age sound; and give not thy
strength to strangers.
²⁰When thou hast gotten a fruitful possession through all the field,
sow it with thine own seed, trusting in the goodness of thy stock.
²¹So thy race which thou leavest shall be magnified, having the
confidence of their good descent.

²²An harlot shall be accounted as spittle; but a married woman is
a tower against death to her husband.
²³A wicked woman is given as a portion to a wicked man: but a
godly woman is given to him that feareth the Lord.
²⁴A dishonest woman contemneth shame: but an honest woman
will reverence her husband.
²⁵A shameless woman shall be counted as a dog; but she that is
shamefaced will fear the Lord.
²⁶A woman that honoureth her husband shall be judged wise of
all; but she that dishonoureth him in her pride shall be
counted ungodly of all.
²⁷A loud crying woman and a scold shall be sought out to drive
away the enemies.

²⁸There be two things that grieve my heart; and the third maketh me
angry: a man of war that suffereth poverty; and men of understanding that are not set by; and one that returneth from righteousness to sin; the Lord prepareth such an one for the sword.

²⁹A merchant shall hardly keep himself from doing wrong; and an
huckster shall not be freed from sin.

27 ¹Many have sinned for a small matter; and he that seeketh for
abundance will turn his eyes away.
²As a nail sticketh fast between the joinings of the stones; so doth
sin stick close between buying and selling.
³Unless a man hold himself diligently in the fear of the Lord, his
house shall soon be overthrown.

omitted (MS tradition).   **26:17** *Holy candlestick*: holy lampstand, a temple implement (see Exod
25:31–37).   **26:18** *The golden pillars . . . silver*: another reference to the temple; cf. Exod 26:32.
26:19–27 *My son . . . enemies*: missing in some ancient authorities and perhaps an interpolation.
Their several textual variations are not given here.
26:28–27:15 Various proverbs. An introductory proverb (26:28) is followed by meditations on sin in commerce (26:29–27:3), on revelation of character through speech (27:4–7),
on righteousness and sin (27:8–10), and on foolish chatter (27:11–15).   **26:28** *Not set by*:
looked on with contempt.   **27:1** *Will turn his eyes away*: i.e., will not be scrupulous.

⁴As when one sifteth with a sieve, the refuse remaineth; so the
    filth of man in his talk.
⁵The furnace proveth the potter's vessels; so the trial of man is in
    his reasoning.
⁶The fruit declareth if the tree have been dressed; so is the
    utterance of a conceit in the heart of man.
⁷Praise no man before thou hearest him speak: for this is the trial
    of men.

⁸If thou followest righteousness, thou shalt obtain her, and put
    her on, as a glorious long robe.
⁹The birds will resort unto their like; so will truth return unto
    them that practise in her.
¹⁰As the lion lieth in wait for the prey; so sin for them that work
    iniquity.

¹¹The discourse of a godly man is always with wisdom; but a fool
    changeth as the moon.
¹²If thou be among the indiscreet, observe the time; but be
    continually among men of understanding.
¹³The discourse of fools is irksome, and their sport is in the
    wantonness of sin.
¹⁴The talk of him that sweareth much maketh the hair stand
    upright; and their brawls make one stop his ears.
¹⁵The strife of the proud is bloodshedding, and their revilings are
    grievous to the ear.

¹⁶Whoso discovereth secrets loseth his credit; and shall never find
    friend to his mind.
¹⁷Love thy friend, and be faithful unto him: but if thou bewrayest
    his secrets, follow no more after him.
¹⁸For as a man hath destroyed his enemy; so hast thou lost the
    love of thy neighbour.
¹⁹As one that letteth a bird go out of his hand, so hast thou let thy
    neighbour go, and shalt not get him again.
²⁰Follow after him no more, for he is too far off; he is as a roe
    escaped out of the snare.
²¹As for a wound, it may be bound up; and after reviling there may
    be reconcilement: but he that bewrayeth secrets is without hope.

²²He that winketh with the eyes worketh evil: and he that
    knoweth him will depart from him.

27:5 *Reasoning*: alternatively "discussion."   27:6 *Conceit*: thought.
    27:16–28:26 Social conflict. This section addresses the betrayal of secrets (27:16–21),
treachery (27:22–27), revenge and forgiveness (27:28–28:7), verbal strife (28:8–12), slander
(28:13–16), and "the tongue" (28:17–26).   **27:17** *Bewrayest*: betray.   **27:22** *Winketh with
the eyes*: blinking conventionally signals treachery; cf. Ps 35:19; Prov 6:12–14; etc.

²³When thou art present, he will speak sweetly, and will admire thy words: but at the last he will writhe his mouth, and slander thy sayings.

²⁴I have hated many things, but nothing like him; for the Lord will hate him.

²⁵Whoso casteth a stone on high casteth it on his own head; and a deceitful stroke shall make wounds.

²⁶Whoso diggeth a pit shall fall therein: and he that setteth a trap shall be taken therein.

²⁷He that worketh mischief, it shall fall upon him, and he shall not know whence it cometh.

²⁸Mockery and reproach are from the proud; but vengeance, as a lion, shall lie in wait for them.

²⁹They that rejoice at the fall of the righteous shall be taken in the snare; and anguish shall consume them before they die.

³⁰Malice and wrath, even these are abominations; and the sinful man shall have them both.

28 ¹He that revengeth shall find vengeance from the Lord, and he will surely keep his sins [in remembrance.]

²Forgive thy neighbour the hurt that he hath done unto thee, so shall thy sins also be forgiven when thou prayest.

³One man beareth hatred against another, and doth he seek pardon from the Lord?

⁴He sheweth no mercy to a man, which is like himself: and doth he ask forgiveness of his own sins?

⁵If he that is but flesh nourish hatred, who will intreat for pardon of his sins?

⁶Remember thy end, and let enmity cease; [remember] corruption and death, and abide in the commandments.

⁷Remember the commandments, and bear no malice to thy neighbour: [remember] the covenant of the Highest, and wink at ignorance.

⁸Abstain from strife, and thou shalt diminish thy sins: for a furious man will kindle strife.

⁹A sinful man disquieteth friends, and maketh debate among them that be at peace.

¹⁰As the matter of the fire is, so it burneth: and as a man's strength is, so is his wrath; and according to his riches his anger riseth;

27:23 *Writhe his mouth*: i.e., "twist his speech" (NRSV). *Slander thy sayings*: more literally "trip you up by your own words" (cf. NRSV). **27:25–27** *Whoso casteth . . . cometh*: the imagery is conventional; cf. Ps 7:15–16; Prov 26:27; etc. **28:2** *Forgive thy neighbour . . . prayest*: cf. Matt 6:14–15; 18:23–35; etc. **28:5** *Intreat for pardon of*: make atonement for. **28:7** *Bear no malice to thy neighbour*: cf. Lev 19:17–18. *Wink at*: overlook. *Ignorance*: alternatively "mistakes". **28:8** *A furious man will kindle strife*: cf. Prov 15:18. **28:10** *Matter*: fuel. For this verse's imagery, see Prov 26:21.

and the stronger they are which contend, the more they will be
inflamed.

¹¹An hasty contention kindleth a fire: and an hasty fighting
sheddeth blood.

¹²If thou blow the spark, it shall burn: if thou spit upon it, it shall
be quenched: and both these come out of thy mouth.

¹³Curse the whisperer and doubletongued: for such have destroyed
many that were at peace.

¹⁴A backbiting tongue hath disquieted many, and driven them
from nation to nation: strong cities hath it pulled down, and
overthrown the houses of great men.

¹⁵A backbiting tongue hath cast out virtuous women, and deprived
them of their labours.

¹⁶Whoso hearkeneth unto it shall never find rest, and never dwell
quietly.

¹⁷The stroke of the whip maketh marks in the flesh: but the
stroke of the tongue breaketh the bones.

¹⁸Many have fallen by the edge of the sword: but not so many as
have fallen by the tongue.

¹⁹Well is he that is defended from it, and hath not passed through
the venom thereof; who hath not drawn the yoke thereof, nor
hath been bound in her bands.

²⁰For the yoke thereof is a yoke of iron, and the bands thereof are
bands of brass.

²¹The death thereof is an evil death, the grave were better than it.

²²It shall not have rule over them that fear God, neither shall they
be burned with the flame thereof.

²³Such as forsake the Lord shall fall into it; and it shall burn in
them, and not be quenched; it shall be sent upon them as a
lion, and devour them as a leopard.

²⁴Look that thou hedge thy possession about with thorns, and
bind up thy silver and gold,

²⁵And weigh thy words in a balance, and make a door and bar for
thy mouth.

²⁶Beware thou slide not by it, lest thou fall before him that lieth in
wait.

The stronger . . . inflamed: this clause should be moved to come immediately after *burneth*. NRSV (slightly altered) renders it as "in proportion to the obstinacy, so will strife burn."   **28:17** *The stroke of the tongue breaketh the bones*: cf. Prov 25:15.   **28:19** *Venom*: rather "wrath."   **28:20** *Yoke of iron*: echoing Jer 28:14.   **28:24** *With thorns*: "and make a door and bar for thy mouth," from v. 25, should be moved to follow here (MS tradition).

29 He that is merciful will lend unto his neighbour; and he that strengtheneth his hand keepeth the commandments.
²Lend to thy neighbour in time of his need, and pay thou thy neighbour again in due season.
³Keep thy word, and deal faithfully with him, and thou shalt always find the thing that is necessary for thee.
⁴Many, when a thing was lent them, reckoned it to be found, and put them to trouble that helped them.
⁵Till he hath received, he will kiss a man's hand; and for his neighbour's money he will speak submissly: but when he should repay, he will prolong the time, and return words of grief, and complain of the time.
⁶If he prevail, he shall hardly receive the half, and he will count as if he had found it: if not, he hath deprived him of his money, and he hath gotten him an enemy without cause: he payeth him with cursings and railings; and for honour he will pay him disgrace.
⁷Many therefore have refused to lend for other men's ill dealing, fearing to be defrauded.

⁸Yet have thou patience with a man in poor estate, and delay not to shew him mercy.
⁹Help the poor for the commandment's sake, and turn him not away because of his poverty.
¹⁰Lose thy money for thy brother and thy friend, and let it not rust under a stone to be lost.
¹¹Lay up thy treasure according to the commandments of the most High, and it shall bring thee more profit than gold.
¹²Shut up alms in thy storehouses: and it shall deliver thee from all affliction.
¹³It shall fight for thee against thine enemies better than a mighty shield and strong spear.

¹⁴An honest man is surety for his neighbour: but he that is impudent will forsake him.
¹⁵Forget not the friendship of thy surety, for he hath given his life for thee.
¹⁶A sinner will overthrow the good estate of his surety:
¹⁷And he that is of an unthankful mind will leave him [in danger] that delivered him.

29:1–28 Lending and borrowing. This section treats making loans (vv. 1–7), giving alms (vv. 8–13), standing as surety (vv. 14–20), and not relying on the hospitality of others (vv. 21–28). **29:1–2** *He that is . . . need*: see, e.g., Exod 22:25–27; Lev 25:35–37; Deut 15:7–8. **29:4** *Reckoned it to be found*: i.e., considered it a windfall (so NRSV; also in v. 6). **29:5** *Submissly*: submissively. **29:6** *If he prevail*: i.e., the lender. **29:7** *For other men's ill dealing*: better "not for reason of evil" (MS tradition). **29:12** *In thy storehouses*: cf. Matt 19:21. **29:14** *Surety*: guarantor.

[18]Suretiship hath undone many of good estate, and shaken them
as a wave of the sea: mighty men hath it driven from their
houses, so that they wandered among strange nations.
[19]A wicked man transgressing the commandments of the Lord
shall fall into suretiship: and he that undertaketh and followeth
other men's business for gain shall fall into suits.
[20]Help thy neighbour according to thy power, and beware that
thou thyself fall not into the same.

[21]The chief thing for life is water, and bread, and clothing, and an
house to cover shame.
[22]Better is the life of a poor man in a mean cottage, than delicate
fare in another man's house.
[23]Be it little or much, hold thee contented, that thou hear not the
reproach of thy house.
[24]For it is a miserable life to go from house to house: for where
thou art a stranger, thou darest not open thy mouth.
[25]Thou shalt entertain, and feast, and have no thanks: moreover,
thou shalt hear bitter words:
[26]Come, thou stranger, and furnish a table, and feed me of that
thou hast ready.
[27]Give place, thou stranger, to an honourable man; my brother
cometh to be lodged, and I have need of mine house.
[28]These things are grievous to a man of understanding; the
upbraiding of houseroom, and reproaching of the lender.

30

He that loveth his son causeth him oft to feel the rod, that he
may have joy of him in the end.
[2]He that chastiseth his son shall have joy in him, and shall rejoice
of him among his acquaintance.
[3]He that teacheth his son grieveth the enemy: and before his
friends he shall rejoice of him.
[4]Though his father die, yet he is as though he were not dead: for
he hath left one behind him that is like himself.
[5]While he lived, he saw and rejoiced in him: and when he died, he
was not sorrowful.
[6]He left behind him an avenger against his enemies, and one that
shall requite kindness to his friends.

[7]He that maketh too much of his son shall bind up his wounds;
and his bowels will be troubled at every cry.

Sirach is more lenient regarding surety than is Proverbs (e.g., 6:1–5; 22:26–27). **29:23** *House*: better "sojourning" (MS tradition).
   30:1–13 Bringing up children. 30:1–2 *He that loveth . . . acquaintance*: cf. Prov 13:24;

⁸An horse not broken becometh headstrong: and a child left to
   himself will be wilful.
⁹Cocker thy child, and he shall make thee afraid: play with him,
   and he will bring thee to heaviness.
¹⁰Laugh not with him, lest thou have sorrow with him, and lest
   thou gnash thy teeth in the end.
¹¹Give him no liberty in his youth, and wink not at his follies.
¹²Bow down his neck while he is young, and beat him on the sides
   while he is a child, lest he wax stubborn, and be disobedient
   unto thee, and so bring sorrow to thine heart.
¹³Chastise thy son, and hold him to labour, lest his lewd behaviour be an offence unto thee.

¹⁴Better is the poor, being sound and strong of constitution, than
   a rich man that is afflicted in his body.
¹⁵Health and good estate of body are above all gold, and a strong
   body above infinite wealth.
¹⁶There is no riches above a sound body, and no joy above the joy
   of the heart.
¹⁷Death is better than a bitter life or continual sickness.
¹⁸Delicates poured upon a mouth shut up are as messes of meat
   set upon a grave.
¹⁹What good doeth the offering unto an idol? for neither can it eat
   nor smell: so is he that is persecuted of the Lord.
²⁰He seeth with his eyes and groaneth, as an eunuch that
   embraceth a virgin and sigheth.

²¹Give not over thy mind to heaviness, and afflict not thyself in
   thine own counsel.
²²The gladness of the heart is the life of man, and the joyfulness
   of a man prolongeth his days.
²³Love thine own soul, and comfort thy heart, remove sorrow far
   from thee: for sorrow hath killed many, and there is no profit
   therein.
²⁴Envy and wrath shorten the life, and carefulness bringeth age
   before the time.
²⁵A cheerful and good heart will have a care of his meat and diet.

23:13–14; etc.   **30:9** *Cocker*: indulge.   **30:11** *Wink not at*: do not overlook.
30:13 *Hold him to labour*: the Hebrew version reads "make his yoke heavy" (NRSV).
   30:14–25 Health and happiness. The first part (vv. 14–20) explores the benefits of robust health;
the second (vv. 21–25), the benefits of a good disposition.   **30:15** *Good estate of body*: NRSV nicely
translates the Greek as "fitness."   **30:18** *Delicates*: lit. "good things," with the *mouth shut up* on account
of illness. *Messes of meat . . . grave*: see 7:33 and note.   **30:19** *For neither . . . smell*: cf. Deut 4:28; Ps
115:4–7; etc.   **30:23** *Love*: better "beguile" (MS tradition); see 14:16 note.   **30:24** *Carefulness*: anxiety.   **30:25** *A cheerful . . . diet*: lit. "a cheerful and good heart at table will take interest in its food."

31

Watching for riches consumeth the flesh, and the care thereof driveth away sleep.

2 Watching care will not let a man slumber, as a sore disease breaketh sleep.

3 The rich hath great labour in gathering riches together; and when he resteth, he is filled with his delicates.

4 The poor laboureth in his poor estate; and when he leaveth off, he is still needy.

5 He that loveth gold shall not be justified, and he that followeth corruption shall have enough thereof.

6 Gold hath been the ruin of many, and their destruction was present.

7 It is a stumblingblock unto them that sacrifice unto it, and every fool shall be taken therewith.

8 Blessed is the rich that is found without blemish, and hath not gone after gold.

9 Who is he? and we will call him blessed: for wonderful things hath he done among his people.

10 Who hath been tried thereby, and found perfect? then let him glory. Who might offend, and hath not offended? or done evil, and hath not done it?

11 His goods shall be established, and the congregation shall declare his alms.

12 If thou sit at a bountiful table, be not greedy upon it, and say not, There is much meat on it.

13 Remember that a wicked eye is an evil thing: and what is created more wicked than an eye? therefore it weepeth upon every occasion.

14 Stretch not thine hand whithersoever it looketh, and thrust it not with him into the dish.

15 Judge of thy neighbour by thyself: and be discreet in every point.

16 Eat, as it becometh a man, those things which are set before thee; and devour not, lest thou be hated.

17 Leave off first for manners' sake; and be not unsatiable, lest thou offend.

18 When thou sittest among many, reach not thine hand out first of all.

31:1–11 The proper use of wealth. **31:1** *Watching*: sleeplessness. **31:3** *Delicates*: luxuries. **31:5** *Shall have enough thereof*: other versions (including the Hebrew) read "will be led astray by it" (NRSV). **31:7** *That sacrifice unto it*: better "who are enthusiastic about it" (MS tradition). **31:9–11** *Who is he? . . . alms*: the rhetorical questions imply that the righteous wealthy were rare—a notion that Jesus takes to an extreme at, e.g., Mark 10:23–25.

31:12–32:13 Feasting and drink. Sections on etiquette in dining (31:12–24; 32:1–13) frame a meditation on temperance in drinking (31:25–31). **31:12** *If thou sit . . . meat on it*: Prov 23:1–3 offers similar advice, although in a darker context. **31:13** *Wicked eye*: connoting greed; see Matt 6:23 and note.

¹⁹A very little is sufficient for a man well nurtured, and he fetcheth not his wind short upon his bed.

²⁰Sound sleep cometh of moderate eating: he riseth early, and his wits are with him: but the pain of watching, and choler, and pangs of the belly, are with an unsatiable man.
²¹And if thou hast been forced to eat, arise, go forth, vomit, and thou shalt have rest.
²²My son, hear me, and despise me not, and at the last thou shalt find as I told thee: in all thy works be quick, so shall there no sickness come unto thee.
²³Whoso is liberal of his meat, men shall speak well of him; and the report of his good housekeeping will be believed.
²⁴But against him that is a niggard of his meat the whole city shall murmur; and the testimonies of his niggardness shall not be doubted of.

²⁵Shew not thy valiantness in wine; for wine hath destroyed many.
²⁶The furnace proveth the edge by dipping: so doth wine the hearts of the proud by drunkenness.
²⁷Wine is as good as life to a man, if it be drunk moderately: what life is then to a man that is without wine? for it was made to make men glad.
²⁸Wine measurably drunk and in season bringeth gladness of the heart, and cheerfulness of the mind:
²⁹but wine drunken with excess maketh bitterness of the mind, with brawling and quarrelling.
³⁰Drunkenness increaseth the rage of a fool till he offend: it diminisheth strength, and maketh wounds.
³¹Rebuke not thy neighbour at the wine, and despise him not in his mirth: give him no despiteful words, and press not upon him with urging him [to drink.]

32 If thou be made the master [of a feast,] lift not thyself up, but be among them as one of the rest; take diligent care for them, and so sit down.
²And when thou hast done all thy office, take thy place, that thou mayest be merry with them, and receive a crown for thy well ordering of the feast.

31:19 *Well nurtured*: well educated or well brought up (cf. 21:19 note). *Fetcheth not his wind short*: does not breathe hard.   31:20 *Watching*: sleeplessness. *Choler*: i.e., cholera.   31:22 *Quick*: adroit; other versions (including the Hebrew) read "moderate."   31:23 *Good housekeeping*: more literally "beauty" (i.e., excellence).   31:25–31 *Shew not . . . drink*: Proverbs also warns against drunkenness; e.g., 20:1; 23:29–35.   31:26 *Dipping*: i.e., into water, to temper the hot steel. *Of the proud by drunkenness*: better "of the insolent when they fight" (MS tradition; cf. NRSV).   31:27 *For it . . . glad*: recalling Ps 104:15.   31:28 *Measurably*: moderately.   31:31 *Despiteful*: reproachful. *With urging him [to drink]*: the Greek reads "with formal demands," leaving their exact nature unclear.   32:2 *Office*: duties. *Receive a crown*:

³Speak, thou that art the elder, for it becometh thee, but with
    sound judgment; and hinder not musick.
⁴Pour not out words where there is a musician, and shew not forth
    wisdom out of time.
⁵A concert of musick in a banquet of wine is as a signet of car-
    buncle set in gold.
⁶As a signet of an emerald set in a work of gold, so is the melody
    of musick with pleasant wine.

⁷Speak, young man, if there be need of thee: and yet scarcely
    when thou art twice asked.
⁸Let thy speech be short, comprehending much in few words; be
    as one that knoweth and yet holdeth his tongue.
⁹If thou be among great men, make not thyself equal with them;
    and when ancient men are in place, use not many words.

¹⁰Before the thunder goeth lightning; and before a shamefaced
    man shall go favour.
¹¹Rise up betimes, and be not the last; but get thee home without
    delay.
¹²There take thy pastime, and do what thou wilt: but sin not by
    proud speech.
¹³And for these things bless him that made thee, and hath replen-
    ished thee with his good things.

¹⁴Whoso feareth the Lord will receive his discipline; and they that
    seek him early shall find favour.
¹⁵He that seeketh the law shall be filled therewith: but the
    hypocrite will be offended thereat.
¹⁶They that fear the Lord shall find judgment, and shall kindle
    justice as a light.
¹⁷A sinful man will not be reproved, but findeth an excuse accord-
    ing to his will.
¹⁸A man of counsel will be considerate; but a strange and proud
    man is not daunted with fear, even when of himself he hath
    done without counsel.
¹⁹Do nothing without advice; and when thou hast once done,
    repent not.

---

a sign of honor. (Crowns were customarily awarded to victors in ancient Greek competitions.)
32:3–9 *Speak, thou . . . many words*: drinking banquets (Gk. *symposia*) were conventional occasions for learned discourse in the Greco-Roman world; this section's advice assumes such a setting. **32:11** *Betimes*: early. **32:12** *There*: at the feast. **32:13** *Replenished*: lit. "intoxicated." (The Greek word shares its root with "drunkenness" at 31:30.)
    32:14–33:6 The man who fears God and the sinful man. 32:16 *Justice*: Gk. *dikaiōmata*, just deeds. **32:17** *Excuse*: better "judgment" or "opinion." **32:18** *Strange*: foreign, though the Hebrew version reads "insolent." *Even when . . . without counsel*: better omitted (MS tradition).

²⁰Go not in a way wherein thou mayest fall, and stumble not among the stones.

²¹Be not confident in a plain way.

²²And beware of thine own children.

²³In every good work trust thy own soul; for this is the keeping of the commandments.

²⁴He that believeth in the Lord taketh heed to the commandment; and he that trusteth in him shall fare never the worse.

33 ¹There shall no evil happen unto him that feareth the Lord; but in temptation even again he will deliver him.

²A wise man hateth not the law; but he that is an hypocrite therein is as a ship in a storm.

³A man of understanding trusteth in the law; and the law is faithful unto him, as an oracle.

⁴Prepare what to say, and so thou shalt be heard: and bind up instruction, and then make answer.

⁵The heart of the foolish is like a cartwheel; and his thoughts are like a rolling axletree.

⁶A stallion horse is as a mocking friend, he neigheth under every one that sitteth upon him.

⁷Why doth one day excel another, when as all the light of every day in the year is of the sun?

⁸By the knowledge of the Lord they were distinguished: and he altered seasons and feasts.

⁹Some of them hath he made high days, and hallowed them, and some of them hath he made ordinary days.

¹⁰And all men are from the ground, and Adam was created of earth.

¹¹In much knowledge the Lord hath divided them, and made their ways diverse.

¹²Some of them hath he blessed and exalted, and some of them hath he sanctified, and set near himself: but some of them hath he cursed and brought low, and turned out of their places.

¹³As the clay is in the potter's hand, to fashion it at his pleasure: so man is in the hand of him that made him, to render to them as liketh him best.

¹⁴Good is set against evil, and life against death: so is the godly against the sinner, and the sinner against the godly.

¹⁵So look upon all the works of the most High; and there are two and two, one against another.

32:22 *Children*: other versions (including the Hebrew) read "paths." **32:23** *Trust*: other versions (including the Hebrew) read "guard." **32:24** *Taketh heed to the commandment*: the Hebrew version reads "preserves himself." **33:1** *Temptation*: trial. **33:4** *Bind up instruction*: cf. Isa 8:16.

33:7–15 Antitheses in creation. 33:8 *By the knowledge . . . feasts*: see Gen 1:14; 2:3; Deut 16:1–15; etc. **33:10** *Adam was created of earth*: see Gen 2:7. **33:13** *As the clay . . . best*: cf. Rom 9:20–22 and notes.

¹⁶I awaked up last of all, as one that gathereth after the grapegatherers: by the blessing of the Lord I profited, and filled my
winepress like a gatherer of grapes.
¹⁷Consider that I laboured not for myself only, but for all them
that seek learning.
¹⁸Hear me, O ye great men of the people, and hearken with your
ears, ye rulers of the congregation.

¹⁹Give not thy son and wife, thy brother and friend, power over
thee while thou livest, and give not thy goods to another: lest it
repent thee, and thou intreat for the same again.
²⁰As long as thou livest and hast breath in thee, give not thyself
over to any.
²¹For better it is that thy children should seek to thee, than that
thou shouldest stand to their courtesy.
²²In all thy works keep to thyself the preeminence: leave not a
stain in thine honour.
²³At the time when thou shalt end thy days, and finish thy life,
distribute thine inheritance.

²⁴Fodder, a wand, and burdens, are for the ass; and bread, correction, and work, for a servant.
²⁵If thou set thy servant to labour, thou shalt find rest: but if thou
let him go idle, he shall seek liberty.
²⁶A yoke and a collar do bow the neck: so are tortures and torments for an evil servant.
²⁷Send him to labour, that he be not idle; for idleness teacheth
much evil.
²⁸Set him to work, as is fit for him: if he be not obedient, put on
more heavy fetters.
²⁹But be not excessive toward any; and without discretion do nothing.
³⁰If thou have a servant, let him be unto thee as thyself, because
thou hast bought him with a price.
³¹If thou have a servant, entreat him as a brother: for thou hast
need of him, as of thine own soul: if thou entreat him evil, and
he run from thee, which way wilt thou go to seek him?

34 The hopes of a man void of understanding are vain and false:
and dreams lift up fools.

33:16–18 The author's diligence. 33:16 *I awaked up:* better "I stayed awake," in the sense of
keeping watch. *As one . . . grapegatherers:* cf. Lev 19:10. *Profited:* lit. "came first."
    33:19–31 Property and slaves. 33:20 *Give not thyself over to any:* do not trade yourself to anyone,
perhaps meaning "do not cede your position to anyone." **33:21** *Stand to their courtesy:* lit. "look to the
hands of your sons." **33:24** *Wand:* a stick for beating. **33:29** *Discretion:* lit. "judgment," perhaps referring to respect for a slave's rights (see, e.g., Exod 21:1–11, 20–21, 26–27). **33:30** *With a price:* lit. "with
blood." Skehan captures the sense: "your life's blood went into his purchase." **33:31** *Entreat:* treat.

²Whoso regardeth dreams is like him that catcheth at a shadow,
  and followeth after the wind.
³The vision of dreams is the resemblance of one thing to another,
  even as the likeness of a face to a face.
⁴Of an unclean thing what can be cleansed? and from that thing
  which is false what truth can come?
⁵Divinations, and soothsayings, and dreams, are vain: and the
  heart fancieth, as a woman's heart in travail.
⁶If they be not sent from the most High in thy visitation, set not
  thy heart upon them.
⁷For dreams have deceived many, and they have failed that put
  their trust in them.
⁸The law shall be found perfect without lies: and wisdom is
  perfection to a faithful mouth.

⁹A man that hath travelled knoweth many things; and he that
  hath much experience will declare wisdom.
¹⁰He that hath no experience knoweth little: but he that hath
  travelled is full of prudence.
¹¹When I travelled, I saw many things; and I understand more
  than I can express.
¹²I was ofttimes in danger of death: yet I was delivered because of
  these things.

¹³The spirit of those that fear the Lord shall live: for their hope is
  in him that saveth them.
¹⁴Whoso feareth the Lord shall not fear nor be afraid: for he is his
  hope.
¹⁵Blessed is the soul of him that feareth the Lord: to whom doth
  he look? and who is his strength?
¹⁶For the eyes of the Lord are upon them that love him, he is their
  mighty protection and strong stay, a defence from heat, and a
  cover from the sun at noon, a preservation from stumbling,
  and an help from falling.
¹⁷He raiseth up the soul, and lighteneth the eyes: he giveth health,
  life, and blessing.

34:1–8 Empty dreams. Compare Deut 13:1–5. **34:5** *Divinations, and soothsayings*: prohibited in Lev 19:26; Deut 18:10–11. **34:6** *If they . . . visitation*: a necessary exception (divine dreams are ubiquitous in the Bible), but a perplexing one, since those trusting in dreams presumably believe, as a rule, that God speaks through them.

34:9–12 The author's experience. 34:9 *A man that hath travelled*: better "an educated man" (MS tradition).

34:13–17 The blessing of the Godfearer. 34:13 *The spirit . . . saveth them*: perhaps recalling Isa 38:16–17. **34:14** *Feareth . . . fear . . . afraid*: translating three different Greek roots, with the first also appearing in v. 15. **34:16** *For the eyes . . . him*: echoing Ps 33:18. *He is . . . falling*: conventional biblical imagery; cf. Gen 15:1; Ps 61:3–4; etc. **34:17** *Lighteneth the eyes*: signaling refreshment (cf. 1 Sam 14:27, 29).

¹⁸He that sacrificeth of a thing wrongfully gotten, his offering is
   ridiculous; and the gifts of unjust men are not accepted.
¹⁹The most High is not pleased with the offerings of the wicked;
   neither is he pacified for sin by the multitude of sacrifices.
²⁰Whoso bringeth an offering of the goods of the poor doeth as
   one that killeth the son before his father's eyes.

²¹The bread of the needy is their life: he that defraudeth him
   thereof is a man of blood.
²²He that taketh away his neighbour's living slayeth him; and he
   that defraudeth the labourer of his hire is a bloodshedder.
²³When one buildeth, and another pulleth down, what profit have
   they then but labour?
²⁴When one prayeth, and another curseth, whose voice will the
   Lord hear?
²⁵He that washeth himself after the touching of a dead body, if he
   touch it again, what availeth his washing?
²⁶So is it with a man that fasteth for his sins, and goeth again, and
   doeth the same: who will hear his prayer? or what doth his
   humbling profit him?

35 He that keepeth the law bringeth offerings enough: he that
   taketh heed to the commandment offereth a peace offering.
²He that requiteth a good turn offereth fine flour; and he that
   giveth alms sacrificeth praise.
³To depart from wickedness is a thing pleasing to the Lord; and to
   forsake unrighteousness is a propitiation.
⁴Thou shalt not appear empty before the Lord.
⁵For all these things [are to be done] because of the
   commandment.
⁶The offering of the righteous maketh the altar fat, and the sweet
   savour thereof is before the most High.
⁷The sacrifice of a just man is acceptable, and the memorial
   thereof shall never be forgotten.
⁸Give the Lord his honour with a good eye, and diminish not the
   firstfruits of thine hands.
⁹In all thy gifts shew a cheerful countenance, and dedicate thy
   tithes with gladness.
¹⁰Give unto the most High according as he hath enriched thee;
   and as thou hast gotten, give with a cheerful eye.

34:18–35:11 *Sacrifices.* For God's disgust at insincere sacrifices, see Isa 1:11–15; Amos 5:21–24;
cf. Ps 51:16–19; etc.   35:1 *The commandment*: for legislation governing peace offerings, see Lev 3.
35:2 *Fine flour*: on grain offerings, see Lev 2. *Sacrificeth praise*: a reference to offerings of thanksgiving, legislated at Lev 7:12–14.   35:4–11 *Thou shalt not . . . as much*: clarifying that the previous
discussion did not imply the insignificance of actual offerings.   35:4 *Thou shalt not . . . Lord*: quoting Exod 23:15; Deut 16:16.   35:8 *Good eye*: connoting generosity (likewise "cheerful eye," v. 10), as
the evil eye connoted stinginess (see 14:10; 31:13 and notes). *Firstfruits*: for their offering, see Lev
2:12–16.   35:9 *Tithes*: God required the tenth part of one's produce (see Lev 27:30–33 and notes).

¹¹For the Lord recompenseth, and will give thee seven times as much.

¹²Do not think to corrupt with gifts; for such he will not receive: and trust not to unrighteous sacrifices; for the Lord is judge, and with him is no respect of persons.

¹³He will not accept any person against a poor man, but will hear the prayer of the oppressed.

¹⁴He will not despise the supplication of the fatherless; nor the widow, when she poureth out her complaint.

¹⁵Do not the tears run down the widow's cheeks? and is not her cry against him that causeth them to fall?

¹⁶He that serveth the Lord shall be accepted with favour, and his prayer shall reach unto the clouds.

¹⁷The prayer of the humble pierceth the clouds: and till it come nigh, he will not be comforted; and will not depart, till the most High shall behold to judge righteously, and execute judgment.

¹⁸For the Lord will not be slack, neither will the Mighty be patient toward them, till he have smitten in sunder the loins of the unmerciful, and repaid vengeance to the heathen; till he have taken away the multitude of the proud, and broken the sceptre of the unrighteous;

¹⁹Till he have rendered to every man according to his deeds, and to the works of men according to their devices; till he have judged the cause of his people, and made them to rejoice in his mercy.

²⁰Mercy is seasonable in the time of affliction, as clouds of rain in the time of drought.

36 Have mercy upon us, O Lord God of all, and behold us: ²And send thy fear upon all the nations that seek not after thee.

³Lift up thy hand against the strange nations, and let them see thy power.

⁴As thou wast sanctified in us before them; so be thou magnified among them before us.

⁵And let them know thee, as we have known thee, that there is no God but only thou, O God.

⁶Shew new signs, and make other strange wonders: glorify thy hand and thy right arm, that they may set forth thy wondrous works.

⁷Raise up indignation, and pour out wrath: take away the adversary, and destroy the enemy.

⁸Make the time short, remember the covenant, and let them declare thy wonderful works.

35:12–20 God's justice. 35:12–15 *Do not think . . . fall*: see Deut 10:17–18 in particular, although many OT passages call for protection of the poor, orphans, and widows. **35:13** *He will not accept . . . man*: alternatively "he will not show partiality to the poor" (NRSV). *The oppressed*: more literally "the one done wrong." **35:18** *And broken . . . unrighteous*: cf. Isa 14:5. **35:19** *Judged the cause*: i.e., decided the case (in a legal proceeding); cf. Isa 51:22 for the image.

36:1–17 Prayer for Israel's restoration. 36:2 *That seek not after thee*: better omitted (MS tradition), perhaps as a gloss based on Ps 79:6. **36:3** *Strange*: foreign. **36:8** *Covenant*: lit. "oath."

⁹Let him that escapeth be consumed by the rage of the fire; and
     let them perish that oppress the people.
¹⁰Smite in sunder the heads of the rulers of the heathen, that say,
     There is none other but we.
¹¹Gather all the tribes of Jacob together, and inherit thou them, as
     from the beginning.
¹²O Lord, have mercy upon the people that is called by thy name,
     and upon Israel, whom thou hast named thy firstborn.
¹³O be merciful unto Jerusalem, thy holy city, the place of thy rest.
¹⁴Fill Sion with thine unspeakable oracles, and thy people with
     thy glory.
¹⁵Give testimony unto those that thou hast possessed from the
     beginning, and raise up prophets that have been in thy name.
¹⁶Reward them that wait for thee, and let thy prophets be found
     faithful.
¹⁷O Lord, hear the prayer of thy servants, according to the
     blessing of Aaron over thy people, that all they which dwell
     upon the earth may know that thou art the Lord, the eternal
     God.

¹⁸The belly devoureth all meats, yet is one meat better than another.
¹⁹As the palate tasteth divers kinds of venison: so doth an heart of
     understanding false speeches.
²⁰A froward heart causeth heaviness: but a man of experience will
     recompense him.

²¹A woman will receive every man, yet is one daughter better than
     another.
²²The beauty of a woman cheereth the countenance, and a man
     loveth nothing better.
²³If there be kindness, meekness, and comfort, in her tongue,
     then is not her husband like other men.
²⁴He that getteth a wife beginneth a possession, a help like unto
     himself, and a pillar of rest.
²⁵Where no hedge is, there the possession is spoiled: and he that
     hath no wife will wander up and down mourning.

36:11 *Gather all . . . together*: a conventional expectation; cf. Isa 11:11–12; Jer 31:8–10; etc. *Inherit thou them*: perhaps better "give them their inheritance" (NRSV).   **36:12** *Called by thy name . . . firstborn*: cf. Exod 4:22; Deut 28:10; etc.   **36:14** *Unspeakable oracles*: better "praise of divine deeds" (MS tradition). *People*: other versions (including the Hebrew) read "temple."
     36:18–37:18 Discernment. A brief section suggesting an analogy between gastronomical discrimination and moral discernment (36:18–20) introduces a series of related meditations, on how to discern a good wife (36:21–26), a good friend (37:1–6), and a good counselor (37:7–18).   **36:24** *Beginneth a possession*: acquires. *A help like unto himself*: the Greek quotes LXX Gen 2:18: "an help meet for him."   **36:25** *Wander up and down mourning*: the Hebrew version reads "become a fugi-

²⁶Who will trust a thief well appointed, that skippeth from city to city? so [who will believe] a man that hath no house, and lodgeth wheresoever the night taketh him?

37 Every friend saith, I am his friend also: but there is a friend, which is only a friend in name.

²Is it not a grief unto death, when a companion and friend is turned to an enemy?

³O wicked imagination, whence camest thou in to cover the earth with deceit?

⁴There is a companion, which rejoiceth in the prosperity of a friend, but in the time of trouble will be against him.

⁵There is a companion, which helpeth his friend for the belly, and taketh up the buckler against the enemy.

⁶Forget not thy friend in thy mind, and be not unmindful of him in thy riches.

⁷Every counseller extolleth counsel; but there is some that counselleth for himself.

⁸Beware of a counseller, and know before what need he hath; for he will counsel for himself; lest he cast the lot upon thee,

⁹And say unto thee, Thy way is good: and afterward he stand on the other side, to see what shall befall thee.

¹⁰Consult not with one that suspecteth thee: and hide thy counsel from such as envy thee.

¹¹Neither consult with a woman touching her of whom she is jealous; neither with a coward in matters of war; nor with a merchant concerning exchange; nor with a buyer of selling; nor with an envious man of thankfulness; nor with an unmerciful man touching kindness; nor with the slothful for any work; nor with an hireling for a year of finishing work; nor with an idle servant of much business: hearken not unto these in any matter of counsel.

¹²But be continually with a godly man, whom thou knowest to keep the commandments of the Lord, whose mind is according to thy mind, and will sorrow with thee, if thou shalt miscarry.

¹³And let the counsel of thine own heart stand: for there is no man more faithful unto thee than it.

¹⁴For a man's mind is sometime wont to tell him more than seven watchmen, that sit above in an high tower.

---

tive and a vagabond," quoting the description of Cain in Gen 4:12.   **36:26** *Well appointed*: lit. "girt up for exercise," i.e., unencumbered.   **37:3** *Wicked imagination . . . deceit*: cf. Gen 6:5 and note.   **37:6** *Thy mind . . . riches*: the Hebrew version reads "battle . . . spoils," continuing the martial imagery.   **37:7** *Counsel*: i.e., his own advice. *For himself*: i.e., in his own interests (so NRSV).   **37:8** *Cast the . . . thee*: better "cast the lot against thee." Skehan translates as "take chances against your interest."

¹⁵And above all this pray to the most High, that he will direct thy
way in truth.

¹⁶Let reason go before every enterprize, and counsel before every
action.

¹⁷The countenance is a sign of changing of the heart.

¹⁸Four manner of things appear: good and evil, life and death: but
the tongue ruleth over them continually.

¹⁹There is one that is wise and teacheth many, and yet is unprofit-
able to himself.

²⁰There is one that sheweth wisdom in words, and is hated: he
shall be destitute of all food.

²¹For grace is not given him from the Lord; because he is deprived
of all wisdom.

²²Another is wise to himself; and the fruits of understanding are
commendable in his mouth.

²³A wise man instructeth his people; and the fruits of his under-
standing fail not.

²⁴A wise man shall be filled with blessing; and all they that see
him shall count him happy.

²⁵The days of the life of man may be numbered: but the days of
Israel are innumerable.

²⁶A wise man shall inherit glory among his people, and his name
shall be perpetual.

²⁷My son, prove thy soul in thy life, and see what is evil for it, and
give not that unto it.

²⁸For all things are not profitable for all men, neither hath every
soul pleasure in every thing.

²⁹Be not unsatiable in any dainty thing, nor too greedy upon meats:

³⁰For excess of meats bringeth sickness, and surfeiting will turn
into choler.

³¹By surfeiting have many perished; but he that taketh heed
prolongeth his life.

38 Honour a physician with the honour due unto him for the uses
which ye may have of him: for the Lord hath created him.

²For of the most High cometh healing, and he shall receive
honour of the king.

³The skill of the physician shall lift up his head: and in the sight
of great men he shall be in admiration.

37:16 *Reason:* alternatively "discussion." **37:17–18** *The countenance . . . appear:* better "four portions arise as a sign of the heart's changing" (MS tradition); cf. Deut 30:19.
    37:19–31 The wise man and moderation. **37:19** *Wise:* Gk. *panourgos,* better "clever"; a dif-
ferent word (*sophos*) is used elsewhere in this section. **37:25–26** *The days . . . perpetual:* i.e., a wise
man will enjoy immortality in the memory of his countrymen. **37:27** *Prove:* test.

⁴The Lord hath created medicines out of the earth; and he that is wise will not abhor them.

⁵Was not the water made sweet with wood, that the virtue thereof might be known?

⁶And he hath given men skill, that he might be honoured in his marvellous works.

⁷With such doth he heal [men,] and taketh away their pains.

⁸Of such doth the apothecary make a confection; and of his works there is no end; and from him is peace over all the earth.

⁹My son, in thy sickness be not negligent: but pray unto the Lord, and he will make thee whole.

¹⁰Leave off from sin, and order thine hands aright, and cleanse thy heart from all wickedness.

¹¹Give a sweet savour, and a memorial of fine flour; and make a fat offering, as not being.

¹²Then give place to the physician, for the Lord hath created him: let him not go from thee, for thou hast need of him.

¹³There is a time when in their hands there is good success.

¹⁴For they shall also pray unto the Lord, that he would prosper that, which they give for ease and remedy to prolong life.

¹⁵He that sinneth before his Maker, let him fall into the hand of the physician.

¹⁶My son, let tears fall down over the dead, and begin to lament, as if thou hadst suffered great harm thyself; and then cover his body according to the custom, and neglect not his burial.

¹⁷Weep bitterly, and make great moan, and use lamentation, as he is worthy, and that a day or two, lest thou be evil spoken of: and then comfort thyself for thy heaviness.

¹⁸For of heaviness cometh death, and the heaviness of the heart breaketh strength.

¹⁹In affliction also sorrow remaineth: and the life of the poor is the curse of the heart.

²⁰Take no heaviness to heart: drive it away, and remember the last end.

²¹Forget it not, for there is no turning again: thou shalt not do him good, but hurt thyself.

²²Remember my judgment: for thine also shall be so; yesterday for me, and to day for thee.

38:1–15 In praise of physicians.   38:5 *Water made sweet with wood*: see Exod 15:23–25. 38:9 *Make thee whole*: heal you.   38:10 *Leave off . . . wickedness*: on the connection between illness and sin, see Mark 2:5 note.   38:11 *Give a sweet savour . . . flour*: echoing Lev 2:1–2. *As not being*: Gk. obscure (as KJV's translation suggests). It may mean "as not living," i.e., as at the door of death and so totally dependent on God for preservation. The Hebrew version offers "as much as you can afford" (NRSV).   38:15 *Let him . . . physician*: the Hebrew version reads "will be defiant toward the physician" (NRSV), forming an inclusive frame with v. 1.

38:16–23 Mourning the dead. 38:21 *Turning again*: i.e., returning from death.   38:22 *Remember my judgment . . . thee*: the words of the one who died.

23 When the dead is at rest, let his remembrance rest; and be
      comforted for him, when his spirit is departed from him.

24 The wisdom of a learned man cometh by opportunity of leisure:
      and he that hath little business shall become wise.
25 How can he get wisdom that holdeth the plough, and that
      glorieth in the goad, that driveth oxen, and is occupied in their
      labours, and whose talk is of bullocks?
26 He giveth his mind to make furrows; and is diligent to give the
      kine fodder.
27 So every carpenter and workmaster, that laboureth night and
      day: and they that cut and grave seals, and are diligent to make
      great variety, and give themselves to counterfeit imagery, and
      watch to finish a work:
28 The smith also sitting by the anvil, and considering the iron
      work, the vapour of the fire wasteth his flesh, and he fighteth
      with the heat of the furnace: the noise of the hammer and the
      anvil is ever in his ears, and his eyes look still upon the pattern
      of the thing that he maketh; he setteth his mind to finish his
      work, and watcheth to polish it perfectly.
29 So doth the potter sitting at his work, and turning the wheel
      about with his feet, who is alway carefully set at his work, and
      maketh all his work by number;
30 He fashioneth the clay with his arm, and boweth down his
      strength before his feet; he applieth himself to lead it over; and
      he is diligent to make clean the furnace:
31 All these trust to their hands: and every one is wise in his work.
32 Without these cannot a city be inhabited: and they shall not
      dwell where they will, nor go up and down:
33 They shall not be sought for in publick counsel, nor sit high in the
      congregation: they shall not sit on the judges' seat, nor understand
      the sentence of judgment: they cannot declare justice and
      judgment; and they shall not be found where parables are spoken.
34 But they will maintain the state of the world, and [all] their desire
      is in the work of their craft.

39   But he that giveth his mind to the law of the most High, and is
        occupied in the meditation thereof, will seek out the wisdom of
        all the ancient, and be occupied in prophecies.

38:24–39:11 **Craftsmen contrasted with scribes.** This section has much in common with
the *Teaching of Khety*, a popular pharaonic Egyptian work that compares artisans and other manual
laborers unfavorably to scribes. But Sirach lacks Khety's emphasis on the wretchedness of those
who work with their hands.   **38:26** *Kine*: cows.   **38:27** *Grave*: engrave. *Counterfeit imagery*: making lifelike images.   **38:30** *Lead it over*: glaze it.   **38:32** *Go up and down*: lit. "walk around."

²He will keep the sayings of the renowned men: and where subtil parables are, he will be there also.

³He will seek out the secrets of grave sentences, and be conversant in dark parables.

⁴He shall serve among great men, and appear before princes: he will travel through strange countries; for he hath tried the good and the evil among men.

⁵He will give his heart to resort early to the Lord that made him, and will pray before the most High, and will open his mouth in prayer, and make supplication for his sins.

⁶When the great Lord will, he shall be filled with the spirit of understanding: he shall pour out wise sentences, and give thanks unto the Lord in his prayer.

⁷He shall direct his counsel and knowledge, and in his secrets shall he meditate.

⁸He shall shew forth that which he hath learned, and shall glory in the law of the covenant of the Lord.

⁹Many shall commend his understanding; and so long as the world endureth, it shall not be blotted out; his memorial shall not depart away, and his name shall live from generation to generation.

¹⁰Nations shall shew forth his wisdom, and the congregation shall declare his praise.

¹¹If he die, he shall leave a greater name than a thousand: and if he live, he shall increase it.

¹²Yet have I more to say, which I have thought upon; for I am filled as the moon at the full.

¹³Hearken unto me, ye holy children, and bud forth as a rose growing by the brook of the field:

¹⁴And give ye a sweet savour as frankincense, and flourish as a lily, send forth a smell, and sing a song of praise, bless the Lord in all his works.

¹⁵Magnify his name, and shew forth his praise with the songs of your lips, and with harps, and in praising him ye shall say after this manner:

¹⁶All the works of the Lord are exceeding good, and whatsoever he commandeth shall be accomplished in due season.

¹⁷And none may say, What is this? wherefore is that? for at time convenient they shall all be sought out: at his commandment

---

39:2–3 *Where subtil parables . . . dark parables*: cf. Prov 1:5–6.   **39:2** *Keep*: preserve.   **39:5** *Resort early*: lie awake before dawn.   **39:11** *Die . . . live*: the order of these verbs is better reversed (MS tradition). *He shall increase it*: Gk. obscure.

39:12–35 In praise of God's works. 39:17 *At his commandment . . . of waters*: see Gen 1:9–10.

the waters stood as an heap, and at the words of his mouth the receptacles of waters.

¹⁸At his commandment is done whatsoever pleaseth him; and none can hinder, when he will save.

¹⁹The works of all flesh are before him, and nothing can be hid from his eyes.

²⁰He seeth from everlasting to everlasting; and there is nothing wonderful before him.

²¹A man need not to say, What is this? wherefore is that? for he hath made all things for their uses.

²²His blessing covered the dry land as a river, and watered it as a flood.

²³As he hath turned the waters into saltness: so shall the heathen inherit his wrath.

²⁴As his ways are plain unto the holy; so are they stumblingblocks unto the wicked.

²⁵For the good are good things created from the beginning: so evil things for sinners.

²⁶The principal things for the whole use of man's life are water, fire, iron, and salt, flour of wheat, honey, milk, and the blood of the grape, and oil, and clothing.

²⁷All these things are for good to the godly: so to the sinners they are turned into evil.

²⁸There be spirits that are created for vengeance, which in their fury lay on sore strokes; in the time of destruction they pour out their force, and appease the wrath of him that made them.

²⁹Fire, and hail, and famine, and death, all these were created for vengeance;

³⁰Teeth of wild beasts, and scorpions, serpents, and the sword, punishing the wicked to destruction.

³¹They shall rejoice in his commandment, and they shall be ready upon earth, when need is; and when their time is come, they shall not transgress his word.

³²Therefore from the beginning I was resolved, and thought upon these things, and have left them in writing.

³³All the works of the Lord are good: and he will give every needful thing in due season.

³⁴So that a man cannot say, This is worse than that: for in time they shall all be well approved.

³⁵And therefore praise ye the Lord with the whole heart and mouth, and bless the name of the Lord.

39:23 *Waters*: better "watered land," referring to Sodom and Gomorrah (Gen 13:10; cf. 19:24–26). **39:25** *Evil things*: the Hebrew version reads "good things and bad" (NRSV). **39:28** *Spirits*: alternatively "winds." *Sore strokes*: scourges.

40 Great travail is created for every man, and an heavy yoke is upon the sons of Adam, from the day that they go out of their mother's womb, till the day that they return to the mother of all things.

2 Their imagination of things to come, and the day of death, [trouble] their thoughts, and [cause] fear of heart;

3 From him that sitteth on a throne of glory, unto him that is humbled in earth and ashes;

4 From him that weareth purple and a crown, unto him that is clothed with a linen frock.

5 Wrath, and envy, trouble, and unquietness, fear of death, and anger, and strife, and in the time of rest upon his bed his night sleep, do change his knowledge.

6 A little or nothing is his rest, and afterward he is in his sleep, as in a day of keeping watch, troubled in the vision of his heart, as if he were escaped out of a battle.

7 When all is safe, he awaketh, and marvelleth that the fear was nothing.

8 [Such things happen] unto all flesh, both man and beast, and that is sevenfold more upon sinners.

9 Death, and bloodshed, strife, and sword, calamities, famine, tribulation, and the scourge;

10 These things are created for the wicked, and for their sakes came the flood.

11 All things that are of the earth shall turn to the earth again: and that which is of the waters doth return into the sea.

12 All bribery and injustice shall be blotted out: but true dealing shall endure for ever.

13 The goods of the unjust shall be dried up like a river, and shall vanish with noise, like a great thunder in rain.

14 While he openeth his hand he shall rejoice; so shall transgressors come to nought.

15 The children of the ungodly shall not bring forth many branches; but are as unclean roots upon a hard rock.

16 The weed growing upon every water and bank of a river shall be pulled up before all grass.

17 Bountifulness is as a most fruitful garden, and mercifulness endureth for ever.

18 To labour, and to be content with that a man hath, is a sweet life: but he that findeth a treasure is above them both.

40:1–17 Anxiety. This section contrasts the anxiety that is a part of the human condition (vv. 1–7) with that which sinners experience when they anticipate divine retribution (vv. 8–17). **40:5** *Change his knowledge*: i.e., "confuse his thinking." **40:10** *For their sakes came the flood*: see Gen 6:5–8, 11–13. **40:11** *All things . . . again*: cf. Gen 3:19. *That which . . . sea*: cf. Eccl 1:7.

40:18–27 Pleasures. 40:18 *To labour . . . hath*: the Hebrew version reads "wealth and wages"

¹⁹Children and the building of a city continue a man's name: but a blameless wife is counted above them both.

²⁰Wine and musick rejoice the heart: but the love of wisdom is above them both.

²¹The pipe and the psaltery make sweet melody: but a pleasant tongue is above them both.

²²Thine eye desireth favour and beauty: but more than both corn while it is green.

²³A friend and companion never meet amiss: but above both is a wife with her husband.

²⁴Brethren and help are against time of trouble: but alms shall deliver more than them both.

²⁵Gold and silver make the foot stand sure: but counsel is esteemed above them both.

²⁶Riches and strength lift up the heart: but the fear of the Lord is above them both: there is no want in the fear of the Lord, and it needeth not to seek help.

²⁷The fear of the Lord is a fruitful garden, and covereth him above all glory.

²⁸My son, lead not a beggar's life; for better it is to die than to beg.

²⁹The life of him that dependeth on another man's table is not to be counted for a life; for he polluteth himself with other men's meat: but a wise man well nurtured will beware thereof.

³⁰Begging is sweet in the mouth of the shameless: but in his belly there shall burn a fire.

41 O death, how bitter is the remembrance of thee to a man that liveth at rest in his possessions, unto the man that hath nothing to vex him, and that hath prosperity in all things: yea, unto him that is yet able to receive meat!

²O death, acceptable is thy sentence unto the needy, and unto him whose strength faileth, that is now in the last age, and is vexed with all things, and to him that despaireth, and hath lost patience!

³Fear not the sentence of death, remember them that have been before thee, and that come after; for this is the sentence of the Lord over all flesh.

(NRSV). **40:19** *Name*: other versions (including the Hebrew) add "but better than either is the one who finds wisdom. Cattle and orchards make one prosperous" (NRSV). **40:20** *Wisdom*: the Hebrew version reads "friends" or "lovers." **40:21** *Psaltery*: harp. **40:22** *Corn while it is green*: more literally "the first green of a crop." **40:23** *A wife with her husband*: the Hebrew version reads "a sensible wife" (NRSV), echoing Prov 19:14. **40:24** *Against*: for.

40:28–41:4 Death for the needy and prosperous. 40:29 *Nurtured*: instructed or educated. **41:1** *Receive meat*: perhaps meaning "digest a meal."

⁴And why art thou against the pleasure of the most High? there is
no inquisition in the grave, whether thou have lived ten, or an
hundred, or a thousand years.

⁵The children of sinners are abominable children, and they that
are conversant in the dwelling of the ungodly.
⁶The inheritance of sinners' children shall perish, and their
posterity shall have a perpetual reproach.
⁷The children will complain of an ungodly father, because they
shall be reproached for his sake.
⁸Woe be unto you, ungodly men, which have forsaken the law of the
most high God! for if ye increase, it shall be to your destruction:
⁹And if ye be born, ye shall be born to a curse: and if ye die, a
curse shall be your portion.
¹⁰All that are of the earth shall turn to earth again: so the ungodly
shall go from a curse to destruction.
¹¹The mourning of men is about their bodies: but an ill name of
sinners shall be blotted out.
¹²Have regard to thy name; for that shall continue with thee above
a thousand great treasures of gold.
¹³A good life hath but few days: but a good name endureth for ever.

¹⁴My children, keep discipline in peace: for wisdom that is hid,
and a treasure that is not seen, what profit is in them both?
¹⁵A man that hideth his foolishness is better than a man that
hideth his wisdom.
¹⁶Therefore be shamefaced according to my word: for it is not
good to retain all shamefacedness; neither is it altogether
approved in every thing.
¹⁷Be ashamed of whoredom before father and mother: and of a lie
before a prince and a mighty man;
¹⁸Of an offence before a judge and ruler; of iniquity before a congregation and people; of unjust dealing before thy partner and friend;
¹⁹And of theft in regard of the place where thou sojournest, and in
regard of the truth of God and his covenant; and to lean with
thine elbow upon the meat; and of scorning to give and take;

41:4 *There is . . . years:* i.e., the question of how long one has lived does not arise in the grave (on
"grave," see 14:12 note); cf. Eccl 6:3–6.
    41:5–13 The legacy of the ungodly and the virtuous. 41:8 *For if . . . destruction:* better
omitted (MS tradition).   **41:9** *Be born:* better "reproduce" (both times in this verse).   **41:11** *The
mourning . . . blotted out:* the Hebrew version reads "the human body is a fleeting thing, but a virtuous name will never be blotted out" (NRSV).
    41:14–42:8 Appropriate and inappropriate shame.   41:16. *Neither is . . . every thing:*
better "neither is everything approved by all in faith" (MS tradition). The Hebrew version
more intelligibly reads "nor is every kind of abashment to be approved" (NRSV).   **41:17** *Whoredom:* sexual immorality.   **41:19** *Sojournest:* i.e., "dwell." *And in regard . . . covenant:* the Hebrew
version reads "and of breaking an oath or agreement" (NRSV). *To lean . . . meat:* possibly, to
reach for food. *Scorning to give and take:* better "of contumely in receiving and giving."

²⁰And of silence before them that salute thee; and to look upon an harlot;

²¹And to turn away thy face from thy kinsman; or to take away a portion or a gift; or to gaze upon another man's wife;

²²Or to be overbusy with his maid, and come not near her bed; or of upbraiding speeches before friends; and after thou hast given, upbraid not;

²³Or of iterating and speaking again that which thou hast heard; and of revealing of secrets.

²⁴So shalt thou be truly shamefaced, and find favour before all men.

42 Of these things be not thou ashamed, and accept no person to sin thereby:

²Of the law of the most High, and his covenant; and of judgment to justify the ungodly;

³Of reckoning with thy partners and travellers; or of the gift of the heritage of friends;

⁴Of exactness of balance and weights; or of getting much or little;

⁵And of merchants' indifferent selling; of much correction of children; and to make the side of an evil servant to bleed.

⁶Sure keeping is good, where an evil wife is; and shut up, where many hands are.

⁷Deliver all things in number and weight; and put all in writing that thou givest out, or receivest in.

⁸Be not ashamed to inform the unwise and foolish, and the extreme aged that contendeth with those that are young: thus shalt thou be truly learned, and approved of all men living.

⁹The father waketh for the daughter, when no man knoweth; and the care for her taketh away sleep: when she is young, lest she pass away the flower of her age; and being married, lest she should be hated;

¹⁰In her virginity, lest she should be defiled and gotten with child in her father's house; and having an husband, lest she should misbehave herself; and when she is married, lest she should be barren.

41:20 *Salute*: greet. **42:1** *Accept no . . . thereby*: do not let your relationship with anyone lead you into sin. **42:3** *Reckoning*: keeping accounts. *Gift of the heritage*: leaving one's inheritance, or part of it. **42:4** *Of exactness . . . weights*: a common concern in the Bible; cf. Lev 19:35–36; Prov 11:1; 16:11; etc. **42:5** *Merchants' indifferent selling*: the sense is of profiting in one's dealings with merchants. It is sometimes understood as aggressive haggling. **42:6** *Sure keeping*: lit. "a seal." **42:8** *Inform*: instruct.

42:9–14 Fathers' anxiety regarding their daughters. 42:9 *Lest she . . . age*: i.e., in case she is not married. **42:10** *In her virginity . . . house*: for the father's responsibility for his daughter's

¹¹Keep a sure watch over a shameless daughter, lest she make thee
a laughingstock to thine enemies, and a byword in the city, and
a reproach among the people, and make thee ashamed before
the multitude.
¹²Behold not every body's beauty, and sit not in the midst of women.
¹³For from garments cometh a moth, and from women wickedness.
¹⁴Better is the churlishness of a man than a courteous woman, a
woman, I say, which bringeth shame and reproach.

¹⁵I will now remember the works of the Lord, and declare the
things that I have seen: In the words of the Lord are his works.
¹⁶The sun that giveth light looketh upon all things, and the work
thereof is full of the glory of the Lord.
¹⁷The Lord hath not given power to the saints to declare all his
marvellous works, which the Almighty Lord firmly settled, that
whatsoever is might be established for his glory.
¹⁸He seeketh out the deep, and the heart, and considereth their
crafty devices: for the Lord knoweth all that may be known,
and he beholdeth the signs of the world.
¹⁹He declareth the things that are past, and for to come, and
revealeth the steps of hidden things.
²⁰No thought escapeth him, neither any word is hidden from him.
²¹He hath garnished the excellent works of his wisdom, and he is
from everlasting to everlasting: unto him may nothing be
added, neither can he be diminished, and he hath no need of
any counseller.
²²O how desirable are all his works! and that a man may see even
to a spark.
²³All these things live and remain for ever for all uses, and they
are all obedient.
²⁴All things are double one against another: and he hath made
nothing imperfect.
²⁵One thing establisheth the good of another: and who shall be
filled with beholding his glory?

virginity, see Deut 22:13–19, 28–29.   **42:11** *Shameless*: more literally "headstrong."   **42:12** *Behold not . . . women*: Gk. obscure; the Hebrew version reads "do not let her parade her beauty before any man, or spend her time among married women" (NRSV).   **42:14** *Churlishness of a man . . . courteous woman*: the Greek is stronger: "evil of a man . . . good deeds of a woman."
42:15–43:33 Praise of God and his creation. After an introduction (42:15–25), the section focuses first on astronomy (43:1–10), then on meteorology (43:11–22), and finally on oceanography (43:23–25), before concluding (43:26–33). The creation is thereby described from its highest elevations to its lowest depths (cf., for example, Sg Three 35–68). The language is frequently conventional, and echoes of other biblical texts are common (for example, cf. v. 18 and Job 38:16; Prov 15:11; v. 19 and Isa 41:22–23; v. 21 and Isa 40:13; and compare Job 38–41 throughout); they are generally not cited in the notes.   **42:17** *Saints*: lit. "holy ones," probably angels.   **42:21** *Garnished*: alternatively "ordered."   **42:22** *And that . . . spark*: Gk. obscure; the translation is conjectural.
42:25 *Be filled with*: get enough of.

43 The pride of the height, the clear firmament, the beauty of
   heaven, with his glorious shew;

2The sun when it appeareth, declaring at his rising a marvellous
   instrument, the work of the most High:

3At noon it parcheth the country, and who can abide the burning
   heat thereof?

4A man blowing a furnace is in works of heat, but the sun burneth
   the mountains three times more; breathing out fiery vapours,
   and sending forth bright beams, it dimmeth the eyes.

5Great is the Lord that made it; and at his commandment it
   runneth hastily.

6He made the moon also to serve in her season for a declaration
   of times, and a sign of the world.

7From the moon is the sign of feasts, a light that decreaseth in her
   perfection.

8The month is called after her name, increasing wonderfully in
   her changing, being an instrument of the armies above,
   shining in the firmament of heaven;

9The beauty of heaven, the glory of the stars, an ornament giving
   light in the highest places of the Lord.

10At the commandment of the Holy One they will stand in their
   order, and never faint in their watches.

11Look upon the rainbow, and praise him that made it; very
   beautiful it is in the brightness thereof.

12It compasseth the heaven about with a glorious circle, and the
   hands of the most High have bended it.

13By his commandment he maketh the snow to fall apace, and
   sendeth swiftly the lightnings of his judgment.

14Through this the treasures are opened: and clouds fly forth as fowls.

15By his great power he maketh the clouds firm, and the hailstones are broken small.

16At his sight the mountains are shaken, and at his will the south
   wind bloweth.

17The noise of the thunder maketh the earth to tremble: so doth
   the northern storm and the whirlwind: as birds flying he
   scattereth the snow, and the falling down thereof is as the
   lighting of grasshoppers:

18The eye marvelleth at the beauty of the whiteness thereof, and
   the heart is astonished at the raining of it.

19The hoarfrost also as salt he poureth on the earth, and being
   congealed, it lieth on the top of sharp stakes.

43:1–10 *The pride . . . in their watches:* describing the firmament and its lights (see Gen 1:6–8, 14–19).
43:7 *Decreaseth in her perfection:* i.e., wanes as soon as it becomes full.   **43:8** *Being an instrument . . .*
heaven: imagining the moon as a signal for the celestial hosts.   **43:16** *At his sight . . . bloweth:* this

²⁰When the cold north wind bloweth, and the water is congealed into ice, it abideth upon every gathering together of water, and clotheth the water as with a breastplate.
²¹It devoureth the mountains, and burneth the wilderness, and consumeth the grass as fire.
²²A present remedy of all is a mist coming speedily: a dew coming after heat refresheth.

²³By his counsel he appeaseth the deep, and planteth islands therein.
²⁴They that sail on the sea tell of the danger thereof; and when we hear it with our ears, we marvel thereat.
²⁵For therein be strange and wondrous works, variety of all kinds of beasts and whales created.

²⁶By him the end of them hath prosperous success, and by his word all things consist.
²⁷We may speak much, and yet come short: wherefore in sum, he is all.
²⁸How shall we be able to magnify him? for he is great above all his works.
²⁹The Lord is terrible and very great, and marvellous is his power.
³⁰When ye glorify the Lord, exalt him as much as ye can; for even yet will he far exceed: and when ye exalt him, put forth all your strength, and be not weary; for ye can never go far enough.
³¹Who hath seen him, that he might tell us? and who can magnify him as he is?
³²There are yet hid greater things than these be, for we have seen but a few of his works.
³³For the Lord hath made all things; and to the godly hath he given wisdom.

44 Let us now praise famous men, and our fathers that begat us. ²The Lord hath wrought great glory by them through his great power from the beginning.
³Such as did bear rule in their kingdoms, men renowned for their power, giving counsel by their understanding, and declaring prophecies:
⁴Leaders of the people by their counsels, and by their knowledge, of learning meet for the people, wise and eloquent in their instructions:
⁵Such as found out musical tunes, and recited verses in writing:

passage should follow "tremble" in v. 17 (MS tradition). **43:21** *It*: the subject of this verse's verbs is perhaps better construed as "he," i.e., God. **43:26** *The end . . . success*: better "his angel succeeds" (MS tradition).
44:1–15 Praise of Israel's heroes: introduction. Such surveys of Israel's history are common in the Bible (see Acts 7:2–53 note). **44:4** *Learning meet for the people*: lit. "learning of the people,"

⁶Rich men furnished with ability, living peaceably in their habitations:
⁷All these were honoured in their generations, and were the glory
of their times.
⁸There be of them, that have left a name behind them, that their
praises might be reported.
⁹And some there be, which have no memorial; who are perished,
as though they had never been; and are become as though they
had never been born; and their children after them.
¹⁰But these were merciful men, whose righteousness hath not
been forgotten.
¹¹With their seed shall continually remain a good inheritance,
and their children are within the covenant.
¹²Their seed standeth fast, and their children for their sakes.
¹³Their seed shall remain for ever, and their glory shall not be
blotted out.
¹⁴Their bodies are buried in peace; but their name liveth for evermore.
¹⁵The people will tell of their wisdom, and the congregation will
shew forth their praise.

¹⁶Enoch pleased the Lord, and was translated, being an example
of repentance to all generations.

¹⁷Noah was found perfect and righteous; in the time of wrath he
was taken in exchange [for the world;] therefore was he left as
a remnant unto the earth, when the flood came.
¹⁸An everlasting covenant was made with him, that all flesh
should perish no more by the flood.

¹⁹Abraham was a great father of many people: in glory was there
none like unto him;
²⁰Who kept the law of the most High, and was in covenant with
him: he established the covenant in his flesh; and when he was
proved, he was found faithful.
²¹Therefore he assured him by an oath, that he would bless the
nations in his seed, and that he would multiply him as the dust
of the earth, and exalt his seed as the stars, and cause them to
inherit from sea to sea, and from the river unto the utmost
part of the land.

---

whatever that means. (NRSV offers "the people's lore.")   **44:11** *And their children . . . covenant*: the Hebrew version reads "and their inheritance with their children's children."   **44:12** *Standeth fast*: better construed as "stands fast in the covenants," importing the final words of v. 11.

44:16–23 Enoch, Noah, and the patriarchs. 44:16 *Enoch pleased . . . generations*: several ancient manuscripts lack this verse, and some scholars view it as an interpolation. *Enoch*: see Gen 5:24. *Repentance*: cf. Philo, *Questions on Genesis* 1.86; he seems to interpret Enoch's translation to heaven as a conversion from a life of the senses to one of the intellect.   **44:17** *Noah*: see Gen 6:5–9:29. *Perfect and righteous*: see Gen 6:9; 7:1.   **44:18** *An everlasting covenant . . . flood*: see Gen 9:8–17. **44:19** *A great father of many people*: see Gen 17:4–5.   **44:20** *In covenant . . . flesh*: see Gen 17. **44:20–21** *And when . . . land*: see Gen 22:1–18.   **44:21** *The river*: the Euphrates (see Gen 15:18).

²²With Isaac did he establish likewise [for Abraham his father's sake] the blessing of all men, and the covenant,

²³And made it rest upon the head of Jacob. He acknowledged him in his blessing, and gave him an heritage, and divided his portions; among the twelve tribes did he part them.

45 And he brought out of him a merciful man, which found favour in the sight of all flesh, even Moses, beloved of God and men, whose memorial is blessed.

²He made him like to the glorious saints, and magnified him, so that his enemies stood in fear of him.

³By his words he caused the wonders to cease, and he made him glorious in the sight of kings, and gave him a commandment for his people, and shewed him part of his glory.

⁴He sanctified him in his faithfulness and meekness, and chose him out of all men.

⁵He made him to hear his voice, and brought him into the dark cloud, and gave him commandments before his face, even the law of life and knowledge, that he might teach Jacob his covenants, and Israel his judgments.

⁶He exalted Aaron, an holy man like unto him, even his brother, of the tribe of Levi.

⁷An everlasting covenant he made with him, and gave him the priesthood among the people; he beautified him with comely ornaments, and clothed him with a robe of glory.

⁸He put upon him perfect glory; and strengthened him with rich garments, with breeches, with a long robe, and the ephod.

⁹And he compassed him with pomegranates, and with many golden bells round about, that as he went there might be a sound, and a noise made that might be heard in the temple, for a memorial to the children of his people;

¹⁰With an holy garment, with gold, and blue silk, and purple, the work of the embroiderer, with a breastplate of judgment, and with Urim and Thummim;

¹¹With twisted scarlet, the work of the cunning workman, with precious stones graven like seals, and set in gold, the work of the jeweller, with a writing engraved for a memorial, after the number of the tribes of Israel.

44:22 *With Isaac . . . covenant*: see Gen 26:3–5.   **44:23** *His blessing*: see Gen 27:28–29. *An heritage*: see Gen 25:29–34. *And divided . . . them*: see Gen 48:21–49:28.

45:1–26 Moses, Aaron, and Phinehas. 45:2 *Saints*: see 42:17 note.   **45:3** *By his words . . . cease*: see Exod 8:11–13, 29–31; 9:33; etc. *Made him . . . kings*: see Exod 5:1–10:29. *Gave him a commandment for his people*: probably a reference to Moses' role as legislator, or perhaps to his role in bringing to Israel God's directions about the first Passover (see Exod 11:1–13:16). *Shewed him part of his glory*: see Exod 33:18–23.   **45:4** *Meekness*: see Num 12:3.   **45:5** *He made . . . before his face*: see Exod 34:27–35.   **45:7** *An everlasting covenant . . . people*: see Exod 28:1. *Comely ornaments*: for

¹²He set a crown of gold upon the mitre, wherein was engraved
     Holiness, an ornament of honour, a costly work, the desires of
     the eyes, goodly and beautiful.
¹³Before him there were none such, neither did ever any stranger
     put them on, but only his children and his children's children
     perpetually.
¹⁴Their sacrifices shall be wholly consumed every day twice
     continually.
¹⁵Moses consecrated him, and anointed him with holy oil: this
     was appointed unto him by an everlasting covenant, and to his
     seed, so long as the heavens should remain, that they should
     minister unto him, and execute the office of the priesthood,
     and bless the people in his name.
¹⁶He chose him out of all men living to offer sacrifices to the
     Lord, incense, and a sweet savour, for a memorial, to make
     reconciliation for his people.
¹⁷He gave unto him his commandments, and authority in the
     statutes of judgments, that he should teach Jacob the testimo-
     nies, and inform Israel in his laws.
¹⁸Strangers conspired together against him, and maligned him in
     the wilderness, even the men that were of Dathan's and Abiron's
     side, and the congregation of Core, with fury and wrath.
¹⁹This the Lord saw, and it displeased him, and in his wrathful
     indignation were they consumed: he did wonders upon them,
     to consume them with the fiery flame.
²⁰But he made Aaron more honourable, and gave him an heritage,
     and divided unto him the firstfruits of the increase; especially
     he prepared bread in abundance:
²¹For they eat of the sacrifices of the Lord, which he gave unto
     him and his seed.
²²Howbeit in the land of the people he had no inheritance, neither
     had he any portion among the people: for the Lord himself is
     his portion and inheritance.

²³The third in glory is Phinees the son of Eleazar, because he had
     zeal in the fear of the Lord, and stood up with good courage of
     heart when the people were turned back, and made reconcilia-
     tion for Israel.

---

the details of Aaron's vestments, see Exod 28:1–43 and notes.   **45:13** *Stranger*: Gk. *allogenēs*, one of
another descent.   **45:14** *Their sacrifices . . . continually*: see Num 28:3–8.   **45:15** *Moses consecrated him . . . oil*: see Lev 8.   **45:16** *Incense, and . . . people*: cf. Lev 2:2, 9; 4:20; etc.   **45:17** *He
gave . . . laws*: cf. Lev 10:11.   **45:18–19** *Strangers conspired . . . flame*: see Num 16.   **45:18** *Strangers*: Gk. *allotrioi*, outsiders.   **45:20–22** *And gave him . . . portion and inheritance*: see Num 18:8–
32; v. 22 almost quotes Num 18:20.   **45:23–24** *Phinees the son . . . for ever*: see Num 25:1–13.

²⁴Therefore was there a covenant of peace made with him, that he should be the chief of the sanctuary and of his people, and that he and his posterity should have the dignity of the priesthood for ever: ²⁵According to the covenant made with David son of Jesse, of the tribe of Juda, that the inheritance of the king should be to his posterity alone: so the inheritance of Aaron should also be unto his seed.

²⁶God give you wisdom in your heart to judge his people in righteousness, that their good things be not abolished, and that their glory may endure for ever.

46 Jesus the son of Nave was valiant in the wars, and was the successor of Moses in prophecies, who according to his name was made great for the saving of the elect of God, and taking vengeance of the enemies that rose up against them, that he might set Israel in their inheritance. ²How great glory gat he, when he did lift up his hands, and stretched out his sword against the cities! ³Who before him so stood to it? for the Lord himself brought his enemies unto him. ⁴Did not the sun go back by his means? and was not one day as long as two? ⁵He called upon the most high Lord, when the enemies pressed upon him on every side; and the great Lord heard him. ⁶And with hailstones of mighty power he made the battle to fall violently upon the nations, and in the descent [of Beth-horon] he destroyed them that resisted, that the nations might know all their strength, because he fought in the sight of the Lord, and he followed the Mighty One.

⁷In the time of Moses also he did a work of mercy, he and Caleb the son of Jephunne, in that they withstood the congregation, and withheld the people from sin, and appeased the wicked murmuring.

45:25 *The covenant . . . alone*: see 2 Sam 7:12–16.   **45:26** *God give you*: apparently addressed to later priests. The Hebrew version introduces the verse with "and now bless the Lord who has crowned you with glory" (NRSV).
   46:1–20 Joshua, Caleb, the judges, and Samuel. 46:1 *Son of Nave*: Joshua's LXX patronymic. In the Hebrew Bible he is "son of Nun." *According to his name*: "Jesus," the equivalent of the Hebrew name Joshua, means "the Lord saves."   **46:2** *How great glory . . . cities*: for his military victories, see Josh 6–12.   **46:3** *For the Lord . . . him*: better "for he waged the wars of the Lord" (MS tradition; NRSV).   **46:4** *Did not the sun . . . means*: see Josh 10:12–14.   **46:6** *Hailstones of mighty power . . . resisted*: see Josh 10:11.   **46:7** *He and Caleb . . . murmuring*: see Num 14:6–9.

⁸And of six hundred thousand people on foot, they two were
  preserved to bring them into the heritage, even unto the land
  that floweth with milk and honey.
⁹The Lord gave strength also unto Caleb, which remained with
  him unto his old age: so that he entered upon the high places
  of the land, and his seed obtained it for an heritage:
¹⁰That all the children of Israel might see that it is good to follow
  the Lord.

¹¹And concerning the judges, every one by name, whose heart
  went not a whoring, nor departed from the Lord, let their
  memory be blessed.
¹²Let their bones flourish out of their place, and let the name of
  them that were honoured be continued upon their children.

¹³Samuel, the prophet of the Lord, beloved of his Lord, established a kingdom, and anointed princes over his people.
¹⁴By the law of the Lord he judged the congregation, and the Lord
  had respect unto Jacob.
¹⁵By his faithfulness he was found a true prophet, and by his word
  he was known to be faithful in vision.
¹⁶He called upon the mighty Lord, when his enemies pressed
  upon him on every side, when he offered the sucking lamb.
¹⁷And the Lord thundered from heaven, and with a great noise
  made his voice to be heard.
¹⁸And he destroyed the rulers of the Tyrians, and all the princes
  of the Philistines.
¹⁹And before his long sleep he made protestations in the sight of
  the Lord and his anointed, I have not taken any man's goods,
  so much as a shoe: and no man did accuse him.
²⁰And after his death he prophesied, and shewed the king his end,
  and lifted up his voice from the earth in prophecy, to blot out
  the wickedness of the people.

47 And after him rose up Nathan to prophesy in the time of David.
  ²As is the fat taken away from the peace offering, so was David
  chosen out of the children of Israel.
³He played with lions as with kids, and with bears as with lambs.

46:8 *They two . . . milk and honey*: see Num 14:8, 24, 30.   **46:9** *The Lord . . . heritage*: see Josh 14:13–14.   **46:11** *Whose heart went not a whoring*: probably a reference to idolatry (cf. Exod 34:15–16; etc.).   **46:13** *The prophet*: better "beloved" (MS tradition). *Established a kingdom . . . people*: see 1 Sam 10:1, 20–26; 16:13.   **46:15** *By his faithfulness . . . vision*: see 1 Sam 3:19–20.   **46:16–18** *He called . . . Philistines*: see 1 Sam 7:7–14, although *the Tyrians* (v. 18) are not there mentioned. (The Hebrew version substitutes "enemy.")   **46:19** *I have not taken . . . him*: see 1 Sam 12:3–4.   **46:20** *After his death he prophesied*: see 1 Sam 28:8–19.

  47:1–25 David and Solomon. 47:1 *Nathan*: see, e.g., 2 Sam 7:1–17; 12:1–15.   **47:2** *The fat . . . peace offering*: see Lev 3:3–5.   **47:3–7** *He played . . . this day*: see 1 Sam 17:1–18:8.

⁴Slew he not a giant, when he was yet but young? and did he not take away reproach from the people, when he lifted up his hand with the stone in the sling, and beat down the boasting of Goliath?

⁵For he called upon the most high Lord; and he gave him strength in his right hand to slay that mighty warrior, and set up the horn of his people.

⁶So the people honoured him with ten thousands, and praised him in the blessings of the Lord, in that he gave him a crown of glory.

⁷For he destroyed the enemies on every side, and brought to nought the Philistines his adversaries, and brake their horn in sunder unto this day.

⁸In all his works he praised the Holy One most high with words of glory; with his whole heart he sung songs, and loved him that made him.

⁹He set singers also before the altar, that by their voices they might make sweet melody, and daily sing praises in their songs.

¹⁰He beautified their feasts, and set in order the solemn times until the end, that they might praise his holy name, and that the temple might sound from morning.

¹¹The Lord took away his sins, and exalted his horn for ever: he gave him a covenant of kings, and a throne of glory in Israel.

¹²After him rose up a wise son, and for his sake he dwelt at large.

¹³Solomon reigned in a peaceable time, and was honoured; for God made all quiet round about him, that he might build an house in his name, and prepare his sanctuary for ever.

¹⁴How wise wast thou in thy youth, and, as a flood, filled with understanding!

¹⁵Thy soul covered the whole earth, and thou filledst it with dark parables.

¹⁶Thy name went far unto the islands; and for thy peace thou wast beloved.

¹⁷The countries marvelled at thee for thy songs, and proverbs, and parables, and interpretations.

¹⁸By the name of the Lord God, which is called the Lord God of Israel, thou didst gather gold as tin, and didst multiply silver as lead.

47:5 *Horn*: a symbol of power (also in vv. 7, 11).   47:8 *He sung songs*: several psalms were ascribed to David.   47:9–10 *He set . . . morning*: see 1 Chr 16:4–6; 23:1–6, 24–32.   47:11 *The Lord took away his sins*: see 2 Sam 12:13. The *sins* here are David's affair with Bathsheba and the subsequent murder of her husband to cover up her pregnancy (2 Sam 11–12). *He gave . . . kings*: see 2 Sam 7:12–16. 47:12 *At large*: more literally "in a broad space," referring to the extent of territory he controlled (see 1 Kgs 4:20–21).   47:13 *God made . . . ever*: see 1 Kgs 5:4–5. For Solomon's construction and dedication of the temple, see 1 Kgs 6:1–9:9.   47:14–17 *How wise . . . proverbs, and parables*: see 1 Kgs 4:29–34.   47:15 *Dark*: riddling.   47:18 *Thou didst gather . . . lead*: for Solomon's outlandish

¹⁹Thou didst bow thy loins unto women, and by thy body thou
    wast brought into subjection.
²⁰Thou didst stain thy honour, and pollute thy seed: so that thou
    broughtest wrath upon thy children, and wast grieved for thy
    folly.
²¹So the kingdom was divided, and out of Ephraim ruled a
    rebellious kingdom.
²²But the Lord will never leave off his mercy, neither shall any of
    his works perish, neither will he abolish the posterity of his
    elect, and the seed of him that loveth him he will not take
    away: wherefore he gave a remnant unto Jacob, and out of him
    a root unto David.

²³Thus rested Solomon with his fathers, and of his seed he left
    behind him Roboam, even the foolishness of the people, and
    one that had no understanding, who turned away the people
    through his counsel. There was also Jeroboam the son of Nebat,
    who caused Israel to sin, and shewed Ephraim the way of sin:
²⁴And their sins were multiplied exceedingly, that they were
    driven out of the land.
²⁵For they sought out all wickedness, till the vengeance came
    upon them.

48 Then stood up Elias the prophet as fire, and his word burned like
    a lamp.
²He brought a sore famine upon them, and by his zeal he dimin-
    ished their number.
³By the word of the Lord he shut up the heaven, and also three
    times brought down fire.
⁴O Elias, how wast thou honoured in thy wondrous deeds! and
    who may glory like unto thee!
⁵Who didst raise up a dead man from death, and his soul from
    the place of the dead, by the word of the most High:
⁶Who broughtest kings to destruction, and honourable men from
    their bed:

---

wealth, see 1 Kgs 10:14–29, esp. vv. 21, 27.   **47:19–20** *Thou didst bow . . . folly*: see 1 Kgs 11:1–13.
47:21 *The kingdom was divided*: see 1 Kgs 12. *Ephraim*: the Northern Kingdom (here called by the
name of its main tribe).   **47:22** *But the Lord . . . David*: God's continued faithfulness to Solomon's posterity is based on the covenant he made with David in 2 Sam 7:12–16.   **47:23** *Roboam*:
Rehoboam. The Hebrew version does not mention his name, though the line that KJV renders *the
foolishness of the people, and one that had no understanding* hints at it with a pun. *Who turned . . .
counsel*: see 1 Kgs 11:43–12:19. *Jeroboam the son . . . sin*: see 1 Kgs 12:25–33.   **47:24** *They were
driven out of the land*: see 2 Kgs 17:5–18 for the Northern Kingdom's deportation to Assyria.
    48:1–16 Elijah and Elisha. 48:1 *Lamp*: torch.   **48:3** *By the word . . . heaven*: see 1 Kgs 17:1.
Three times brought down fire: see 1 Kgs 18:38 and 2 Kgs 1:9–12.   **48:5** *Who didst raise up . . . death*:
see 1 Kgs 17:17–24.   **48:6** *Who broughtest kings to destruction*: see 1 Kgs 21:20–21. *From their bed*:

7Who heardest the rebuke of the Lord in Sinai, and in Horeb the
    judgment of vengeance:
8Who anointedst kings to take revenge, and prophets to succeed
    after him:
9Who wast taken up in a whirlwind of fire, and in a chariot of
    fiery horses:
10Who wast ordained for reproofs in their times, to pacify the
    wrath of the Lord's judgment, before it brake forth into fury,
    and to turn the heart of the father unto the son, and to restore
    the tribes of Jacob.
11Blessed are they that saw thee, and slept in love: for we shall
    surely live.

12Elias it was, who was covered with a whirlwind: and Eliseus was
    filled with his spirit: whilst he lived, he was not moved with
    the presence of any prince, neither could any bring him into
    subjection.
13No word could overcome him; and after his death his body
    prophesied.
14He did wonders in his life, and at his death were his works
    marvellous.
15For all this the people repented not, neither departed they from
    their sins, till they were spoiled and carried out of their land,
    and were scattered through all the earth: yet there remained a
    small people, and a ruler in the house of David:
16Of whom some did that which was pleasing to God, and some
    multiplied sins.

17Ezekias fortified his city, and brought in water into the midst
    thereof: he digged the hard rock with iron, and made wells for
    waters.
18In his time, Sennacherib came up, and sent Rabsaces, and lifted
    up his hand against Sion, and boasted proudly.
19Then trembled their hearts and hands, and they were in pain, as
    women in travail.

i.e., to destruction from their bed, with reference to 2 Kgs 1:2–17.   **48:7** *Who heardest . . . vengeance*: see 1 Kgs 19:8–18.   **48:8** *Who anointedst . . . him*: see 1 Kgs 19:15–17 and note.   **48:9** *Who wast taken up . . . horses*: see 2 Kgs 2:11.   **48:10** *Who wast ordained . . . Jacob*: referring to Elijah's anticipated eschatological role; see esp. Mal 4:5–6, which Sirach quotes.   **48:11** *Slept in love: slept* is a euphemism for "lay dead," but a better reading of the MS tradition yields "have been adorned with your love."   **48:12** *Eliseus*: Elisha. *Filled with his spirit*: see 2 Kgs 2:8–15. *He was not moved . . . subjection*: for his attitude toward royal authority, see, e.g., 2 Kgs 3:9–15.   **48:13** *After his death his body prophesied*: see 2 Kgs 13:20–21.   **48:15** *Till they . . . earth*: see 2 Kgs 18:11–12.
   48:17–25 Hezekiah and Isaiah. 48:17 *Ezekias*: Hezekiah. *Fortified his city . . . for waters*: see 2 Kgs 20:20.   **48:18–21** *In his time . . . them*: see 2 Kgs 18:13–19:37.   **48:18** *Rabsaces*: Rabshakeh.

²⁰But they called upon the Lord which is merciful, and stretched out
their hands toward him: and immediately the Holy One heard
them out of heaven, and delivered them by the ministry of Esay.
²¹He smote the host of the Assyrians, and his angel destroyed them.
²²For Ezekias had done the thing that pleased the Lord, and was
strong in the ways of David his father, as Esay the prophet,
who was great and faithful in his vision, had commanded him.

²³In his time the sun went backward, and he lengthened the king's life.
²⁴He saw by an excellent spirit what should come to pass at the
last, and he comforted them that mourned in Sion.
²⁵He shewed what should come to pass for ever, and secret things
or ever they came.

49 The remembrance of Josias is like the composition of the perfume that is made by the art of the apothecary: it is sweet as
honey in all mouths, and as musick at a banquet of wine.
²He behaved himself uprightly in the conversion of the people,
and took away the abominations of iniquity.
³He directed his heart unto the Lord, and in the time of the
ungodly he established the worship of God.

⁴All, except David and Ezekias and Josias, were defective; for they
forsook the law of the most High, even the kings of Juda failed.
⁵Therefore he gave their power unto others, and their glory to a
strange nation.
⁶They burnt the chosen city of the sanctuary, and made the
streets desolate, according to the prophecy of Jeremias.
⁷For they entreated him evil, who nevertheless was a prophet,
sanctified in his mother's womb, that he might root out, and
afflict, and destroy; and that he might build up also, and plant.

⁸It was Ezekiel who saw the glorious vision, which was shewed
him upon the chariot of the cherubims.
⁹For he made mention of the enemies under the figure of the rain,
and directed them that went right.

¹⁰And of the twelve prophets let the memorial be blessed, and let
their bones flourish again out of their place: for they comforted
Jacob, and delivered them by assured hope.

48:20 *Esay*: Isaiah.   **48:22** *Ezekias had done . . . father*: see 2 Kgs 18:3.   **48:23** *The sun . . . life*: see
2 Kgs 20:8–11.   **48:24–25** *He saw . . . came*: alluding to such passages in Isaiah as 40:1–11; 42:9.
    49:1–13 Josiah, the prophets, and the restorers of the temple. 49:1 *Josias*: Josiah. *Apoth-
ecary*: lit. "perfumer."   **49:2–3** *He behaved . . . God*: for Josiah's religious reforms, see 2 Kgs 22:1–
23:30.   **49:5–6** *He gave . . . desolate*: referring to the Babylonian conquest and captivity; see 2 Kgs
24–25.   **49:6** *According to . . . Jeremias*: cf. Jer 36, esp. vv. 3, 29.   **49:7** *Who nevertheless . . . plant*:
see Jer 1:5–10.   **49:8** *The glorious vision . . . cherubims*: see Ezek 1:4–28.   **49:9** *For he . . . right*:
Gk. obscure; the Hebrew version reads "He also referred to Job, who always held fast to the way of
righteousness" (trans. Skehan), probably alluding to Ezek 14:14, 20.   **49:10** *The twelve prophets*: i.e.,

¹¹How shall we magnify Zorobabel? even he was as a signet on the
   right hand:

¹²So was Jesus the son of Josedec: who in their time builded the
   house, and set up an holy temple to the Lord, which was
   prepared for everlasting glory.

¹³And among the elect was Neemias, whose renown is great, who
   raised up for us the walls that were fallen, and set up the gates
   and the bars, and raised up our ruins again.

¹⁴But upon the earth was no man created like Enoch; for he was
   taken from the earth.

¹⁵Neither was there a man born like unto Joseph, a governor of his
   brethren, a stay of the people, whose bones were regarded of
   the Lord.

¹⁶Sem and Seth were in great honour among men, and so was
   Adam above every living thing in the creation.

50 Simon the high priest, the son of Onias, who in his life repaired
   the house again, and in his days fortified the temple:

²And by him was built from the foundation the double height, the
   high fortress of the wall about the temple:

³In his days the cistern to receive water, being in compass as the
   sea, was covered with plates of brass:

⁴He took care of the temple that it should not fall, and fortified
   the city against besieging:

⁵How was he honoured in the midst of the people in his coming
   out of the sanctuary!

⁶He was as the morning star in the midst of a cloud, and as the
   moon at the full:

---

those from the OT Book of the Twelve (Hosea–Malachi)   **49:11–13** *How shall we . . . again*: all the
figures mentioned here played a crucial role in Judah's return from exile.   **49:11** *Zorobabel*: Zerubbabel; see Ezra 3:2. *As a signet . . . hand*: see Hag 2:23.   **49:12** *Jesus*: Jeshua/Joshua; see Ezra 3:2;
Hag 1:12; 2:2; Zech 3:1.   **49:13** *Neemias*: Nehemiah; the eponymous OT book recounts his quest to
rebuild Jerusalem's walls.
   49:14–16 Enoch, Joseph, Shem, and Seth. 49:14 *Enoch*: see Gen 5:24.   **49:15** *Joseph*: for
his story, see Gen 37–50. *Whose bones . . . Lord*: see Gen 50:25–26; Exod 13:19; Josh 24:32.   **49:16**
Sem and Seth: Shem was Noah's first son (see Gen 5:32); Seth was born to Adam and Eve after Cain
murdered Abel (see Gen 5:3).
   50:1–24 Simon the high priest. 50:1 *Simon* served as high priest ca. 219–196 B.C.E. and was
presumably an older contemporary of the author.   **50:1–4** *Who in his life . . . besieging*: Josephus
(*Jewish Antiquities* 12.141) seems to confirm a restoration of the temple during Simon's tenure; but
it is surely significant that this description combines the heroic missions of Ezra (to rebuild the
temple) and of Nehemiah (to rebuild the Jerusalem wall), to whom Sirach thereby assimilates Simon.
50:5 *Coming out of the sanctuary*: several details suggest that vv. 5–21 depict Simon presiding over
commemoration of the Day of Atonement (cf. Lev 16; 23:26–32; Num 29:7–11), though some commentators think that the daily offering is being described (cf. Exod 29:38–42; Lev 6:8–13; Num 28:3–
8; and esp. the later description of it in *Mishnah Tamid* 6.3–7.3). *Sanctuary*: lit. "house of the veil"—i.e.,
the temple, whose inner sanctum was behind a curtain and was entered only by the high priest and but

⁷As the sun shining upon the temple of the most High, and as the
rainbow giving light in the bright clouds:

⁸And as the flower of roses in the spring of the year, as lilies by
the rivers of waters, and as the branches of the frankincense
tree in the time of summer:

⁹As fire and incense in the censer, and as a vessel of beaten gold
set with all manner of precious stones:

¹⁰And as a fair olive tree budding forth fruit, and as a cypress tree
which groweth up to the clouds.

¹¹When he put on the robe of honour, and was clothed with the
perfection of glory, when he went up to the holy altar, he made
the garment of holiness honourable.

¹²When he took the portions out of the priests' hands, he himself
stood by the hearth of the altar, compassed with his brethren
round about, as a young cedar in Libanus; and as palm trees
compassed they him round about.

¹³So were all the sons of Aaron in their glory, and the oblations of
the Lord in their hands, before all the congregation of Israel.

¹⁴And finishing the service at the altar, that he might adorn the
offering of the most high Almighty,

¹⁵He stretched out his hand to the cup, and poured of the blood of
the grape, he poured out at the foot of the altar a sweetsmelling savour unto the most high King of all.

¹⁶Then shouted the sons of Aaron, and sounded the silver trumpets, and made a great noise to be heard, for a remembrance
before the most High.

¹⁷Then all the people together hasted, and fell down to the earth
upon their faces to worship their Lord God Almighty, the most
High.

¹⁸The singers also sang praises with their voices, with great
variety of sounds was there made sweet melody.

¹⁹And the people besought the Lord, the most High, by prayer
before him that is merciful, till the solemnity of the Lord was
ended, and they had finished his service.

²⁰Then he went down, and lifted up his hands over the whole
congregation of the children of Israel, to give the blessing of
the Lord with his lips, and to rejoice in his name.

---

once a year, on the Day of Atonement (see Lev 16:12–17).   **50:11** *Robe of honour . . . garment of holiness*: presumably the special garments worn by the high priest on the Day of Atonement (see Lev 16:4
and note). Perhaps it is because they, unlike regular vestments, were made of simple linen that Simon's
officiating in them *made the garment of holiness honourable.*   **50:12–15** *When he . . . of all*: for this
part of the ritual, see Lev 16:18–19.   **50:12** *Libanus*: Lebanon.   **50:20** *To rejoice in his name*: according to some scholars, the high priest uttered the divine name only once a year on the Day of Atonement, but the restrictions on the use of "YHWH" are debated (see, e.g., the presumably common
priestly blessing at Num 6:22–27).

²¹And they bowed themselves down to worship the second time, that they might receive a blessing from the most High.

²²Now therefore bless ye the God of all, which only doeth wondrous things every where, which exalteth our days from the womb, and dealeth with us according to his mercy. ²³He grant us joyfulness of heart, and that peace may be in our days in Israel for ever: ²⁴That he would confirm his mercy with us, and deliver us at his time!

²⁵There be two manner of nations which my heart abhorreth, and the third is no nation: ²⁶They that sit upon the mountain of Samaria, and they that dwell among the Philistines, and that foolish people that dwell in Sichem. ²⁷Jesus the son of Sirach of Jerusalem hath written in this book the instruction of understanding and knowledge, who out of his heart poured forth wisdom. ²⁸Blessed is he that shall be exercised in these things; and he that layeth them up in his heart shall become wise. ²⁹For if he do them, he shall be strong to all things: for the light of the Lord leadeth him, who giveth wisdom to the godly. Blessed be the Lord for ever. Amen, Amen.

A Prayer of Jesus the son of Sirach.

51 I will thank thee, O Lord and King, and praise thee, O God my Saviour: I do give praise unto thy name: ²For thou art my defender and helper, and hast preserved my body from destruction, and from the snare of the slanderous tongue, and from the lips that forge lies, and hast been mine helper against mine adversaries: ³And hast delivered me, according to the multitude of thy mercies and greatness of thy name, from the teeth of them that were ready to devour me, and out of the hands of such as sought after my life, and from the manifold afflictions which I had; ⁴From the choking of fire on every side, and from the midst of the fire which I kindled not;

50:25–29 Epilogue. 50:26 *Samaria*: the Hebrew and Latin versions read "Seir," an alternative designation for Edom or Idumea, the land inhabited by Edomites. *Philistines*: traditional enemies of Israel *Sichem*: Shechem, in Samaria (on which, see Matt 10:5 note). **50:29** *Who giveth . . . Amen, Amen*: better omitted (MS tradition).

51:1–12 Appendix 1: prayer of thanksgiving. The language is highly conventional; only a few of its frequent echoes of other biblical texts are noted below. Following this prayer the Hebrew version includes an antiphonal hymn resembling Ps 136. **51:2** *The snare . . . lies*: cf. Ps 120:2.

⁵From the depth of the belly of hell, from an unclean tongue, and
   from lying words.

⁶By an accusation to the king from an unrighteous tongue my soul
   drew near even unto death, my life was near to the hell beneath.

⁷They compassed me on every side, and there was no man to help
   me: I looked for the succour of men, but there was none.

⁸Then thought I upon thy mercy, O Lord, and upon thy acts of
   old, how thou deliverest such as wait for thee, and savest them
   out of the hands of the enemies.

⁹Then lifted I up my supplication from the earth, and prayed for
   deliverance from death.

¹⁰I called upon the Lord, the Father of my Lord, that he would not
   leave me in the days of my trouble, and in the time of the
   proud, when there was no help.

¹¹I will praise thy name continually, and will sing praise with
   thanksgiving; and so my prayer was heard:

¹²For thou savedst me from destruction, and deliveredst me from
   the evil time: therefore will I give thanks, and praise thee, and
   bless thy name, O Lord.

¹³When I was yet young, or ever I went abroad, I desired wisdom
   openly in my prayer.

¹⁴I prayed for her before the temple, and will seek her out even to
   the end.

¹⁵Even from the flower till the grape was ripe hath my heart
   delighted in her: my foot went the right way, from my youth up
   sought I after her.

¹⁶I bowed down mine ear a little, and received her, and gat much
   learning.

¹⁷I profited therein, therefore will I ascribe the glory unto him
   that giveth me wisdom.

¹⁸For I purposed to do after her, and earnestly I followed that
   which is good; so shall I not be confounded.

¹⁹My soul hath wrestled with her, and in my doings I was exact: I
   stretched forth my hands to the heaven above, and bewailed
   my ignorances of her.

²⁰I directed my soul unto her, and I found her in pureness: I have
   had my heart joined with her from the beginning, therefore
   shall I not be forsaken.

51:5 *Hell*: see Matt 11:23 note (also at v. 6).   **51:6** *My soul . . . beneath*: cf. Ps 88:3.   **51:10** *I called . . .
my Lord*: the Hebrew version reads "I cried out, 'Lord, you are my Father'" (NRSV). The Greek may
reflect scribal assimilation to Mark 12:36–37 and parallels.
   51:13–30 Appendix 2: the author's acquisition of wisdom. The Hebrew version is an alphabetical acrostic: each successive verse begins with the next letter of the Hebrew alphabet.   **51:13** *Or ever*:
before. *I desired . . . prayer*: recalling Solomon (see 1 Kgs 3:6–12).   **51:20** *Had my heart joined with*:

²¹My heart was troubled in seeking her: therefore have I gotten a good possession.

²²The Lord hath given me a tongue for my reward, and I will praise him therewith.

²³Draw near unto me, ye unlearned, and dwell in the house of learning.

²⁴Wherefore are ye slow, and what say ye of these things, seeing your souls are very thirsty?

²⁵I opened my mouth, and said, Buy her for yourselves without money.

²⁶Put your neck under the yoke, and let your soul receive instruction: she is hard at hand to find.

²⁷Behold with your eyes, how that I have had but little labour, and have gotten unto me much rest.

²⁸Get learning with a great sum of money, and get much gold by her.

²⁹Let your soul rejoice in his mercy, and be not ashamed of his praise.

³⁰Work your work betimes, and in his time he will give you your reward.

---

i.e., "acquired understanding of." **51:21** *My heart . . . her*: more literally "my stomach was stirred to seek her out" (i.e., "I hungered for her"). **51:22** *The Lord . . . reward*: cf. Isa 50:4. **51:24** *Wherefore are . . . thirsty*: better "why do you say that you lack these things, and that your souls thirst so greatly?" (MS tradition). **51:26–27** *Put your neck . . . rest*: cf. Matt 11:28–30. **51:28** *Get learning . . . her*: other versions read "hear but a little of my instruction and through me you will acquire silver and gold" (NRSV). **51:30** *Betimes*: early.

Baruch, with the *Epistle of Jeremiah*

IN many Septuagint manuscripts Baruch follows Jeremiah, purporting to be the work of the prophet's secretary who accompanied him into exile (see Jer 43:1–7). It consists of four independent sections, all more or less unified by the theme of exile, which probably originated in different times and contexts. Though the oldest version of Baruch survives in Greek, the first two sections were almost certainly composed in Hebrew, and scholars debate whether the latter two as well were originally written in Hebrew and translated later. Arguments about the date and provenance of the book (or, more precisely, of its various sections) are mainly speculative, but errors in the historical introduction, which was probably composed by the final editor, suggest that Baruch was compiled by someone unfamiliar with the exile's early history, probably because he or she lived in a much later period, perhaps in the second century B.C.E. Baruch's individual components were presumably written sometime before that.

In various Septuagint manuscripts the pseudepigraphic Epistle of Jeremiah (actually a homily against idolatry) follows Baruch, but in others it comes after Lamentations. In the Vulgate, as in KJV, it is appended to Baruch, but it is nonetheless an independent work, as KJV's titular superscription recognizes. Although the oldest extant version survives in Greek, some of the work's oddities are most easily explained as translation errors from a hypothetical Hebrew original (see 6:54 and note, for example). Its heavy reliance on earlier biblical texts suggests a relatively late date of composition, as does its assertion that exiles will remain in Babylon for an extended period of time (the round figure "seven generations" at 6:3), which appears to be a correction of Jer 29:10's competing claim that they will return after only seventy years. The modification was probably made by a later writer who knew of large diasporic communities remaining in Babylon long after Jeremiah's seventy years had elapsed. A Greek fragment of the Epistle of Jeremiah from ca. 100 B.C.E. found among the Dead Sea Scrolls, taken together with the allusion to the work in 2 Maccabees (see 2:2 and note), mandates a date of composition before the first century B.C.E.—most likely in the second or third century, but perhaps as early as the late fourth.

For detailed exposition of these works, see Carey A. Moore's Anchor Bible commentary, *Daniel, Esther, and Jeremiah: The Additions* (Garden City, NY: Doubleday, 1977), which informs this introduction and the annotations that follow.

Baruch

1 And these are the words of the book, which Baruch the son of Nerias, the son of Maasias, the son of Sedecias, the son of Asadias, the son of Chelcias, wrote in Babylon. ²In the fifth year, and in the seventh day of the month, what time as the Chaldeans took Jerusalem, and burnt it with fire. ³And Baruch did read the words of this book in the hearing of Jechonias the son of Joachim king of Juda, and in the ears of all the people that came to hear the book, ⁴and in the hearing of the nobles, and of the kings' sons, and in the hearing of the elders, and of all the people, from the lowest unto the highest, even of all them that dwelt at Babylon by the river Sud.

⁵Whereupon they wept, fasted, and prayed before the Lord. ⁶They made also a collection of money according to every man's power: ⁷and they sent it to Jerusalem unto Joachim the high priest, the son of Chelcias, son of Salom, and to the priests, and to all the people which were found with him at Jerusalem, ⁸at the same time when he received the vessels of the house of the Lord, that were carried out of the temple, to return them into the land of Juda, the tenth day of the month Sivan, namely, silver vessels, which Sedecias the son of Josias king of Juda had made, ⁹after that Nabuchodonosor king of Babylon had carried away Jechonias,

---

1:1–14 Historical introduction. A contextual setting (vv. 1–9) is followed by a letter accompanying the offering and temple vessels (vv. 10–14), which urges that Baruch be read during communal worship. Full of factual errors and ambiguities, this introduction seems to reimagine in an alternative historical context the events detailed in Ezra 1, which took place after Persia had conquered Babylon in 539 B.C.E. **1:1** *Baruch*: see Jer 36:4 note. *In Babylon*: Jer 43:6–7 suggests that Baruch went not to Babylon but rather to Egypt, with Jeremiah. **1:2** *Fifth year*: the count is presumably from Jerusalem's destruction in 586 B.C.E. *Chaldeans*: Babylonians. **1:3** *Jechonias*: Jehoiachin (see Jer 22:24; 24:1 notes), king of Judah at the time of the first Babylonian invasion. For his surrender and deportation to Babylon, see 2 Kgs 24:10–12, 15. 2 Kings concludes with his release from prison and elevation to the Babylonian king's court (25:27–30), which would have occurred after the events narrated here; thus his presence in Baruch's audience is confusing. **1:4–5** *All them . . . wept*: recalling Ps 137:1. **1:4** *Sud*: unidentified; possibly a corruption of "Ahava" (see Ezra 8:15–31; 1 Esd 8:41 note). **1:6–7** *They made . . . Jerusalem*: compare the collection preceding the return authorized by Cyrus (Ezra 1:5–6). **1:7** *Joachim the high priest*: otherwise unattested. **1:8** *When he . . . to return them*: recalling the prophecy of Jer 28:3, but contradicting the account of the vessels' much later return in Ezra 1:7–11. *Sivan*: May–June. **1:8–9** *Namely, silver vessels . . . unto Babylon*: this account assumes that Zedekiah (KJV's *Sedecias*, who was put in place by Babylon after Jehoiachin was removed; see 2 Kgs 24:17) commissioned new vessels to replace those carried off in the plunder of 597 (see 2 Kgs 24:13–16). Their commissioning was presumably inferred from the report that the temple was again plundered about a decade later, under Zedekiah's rule (see 2 Kgs 25:8–17). **1:9** *Nabuchodonosor*: Nebuchadnezzar (see Jer 21:2

and the princes, and the captives, and the mighty men, and the people of the land, from Jerusalem, and brought them unto Babylon.

[10]And they said, Behold, we have sent you money to buy you burnt offerings, and sin offerings, and incense, and prepare ye manna, and offer upon the altar of the Lord our God; [11]and pray for the life of Nabuchodonosor king of Babylon, and for the life of Balthasar his son, that their days may be upon earth as the days of heaven: [12]and the Lord will give us strength, and lighten our eyes, and we shall live under the shadow of Nabuchodonosor king of Babylon, and under the shadow of Balthasar his son, and we shall serve them many days, and find favour in their sight. [13]Pray for us also unto the Lord our God, for we have sinned against the Lord our God; and unto this day the fury of the Lord and his wrath is not turned from us. [14]And ye shall read this book which we have sent unto you, to make confession in the house of the Lord, upon the feasts and solemn days.

[15]And ye shall say, To the Lord our God belongeth righteousness, but unto us the confusion of faces, as it is come to pass this day, unto them of Juda, and to the inhabitants of Jerusalem, [16]and to our kings, and to our princes, and to our priests, and to our prophets, and to our fathers: [17]for we have sinned before the Lord, [18]and disobeyed him, and have not hearkened unto the voice of the Lord our God, to walk in the commandments that he gave us openly: [19]since the day that the Lord brought our forefathers out of the land of Egypt, unto this present day, we have been disobedient unto the Lord our God, and we have been negligent in not hearing his voice. [20]Wherefore the evils cleaved unto us, and the curse, which the Lord appointed by Moses his servant at the time that he brought our fathers out of the land of Egypt, to give us a land that floweth with milk and honey, like as it is to see this day. [21]Nevertheless we have not hearkened unto the voice of the Lord our God, according unto all the words of the prophets, whom he sent unto us: [22]but every man followed the imagination of his own wicked heart, to serve strange gods, and to do evil in the sight of the Lord our God.

---

note).   **1:10** *Manna*: probably reflecting an error in translating from Hebrew into Greek. The original reference may have been to "grain offerings" (so NRSV). *Upon the altar . . . God*: see Jer 41:5 and note.   **1:11–12** *Pray for the life . . . sight*: recalling Jeremiah's advice in Jer 29:7.   **1:11** *Balthasar*: Belshazzar (see Dan 5:1 note), who in fact was not Nebuchadnezzar's son.   **1:12** *Lighten our eyes*: see 3:14 and note.

1:15–3:8 Confession. The confession comes in two parts, the first (1:15–2:5) composed from the perspective of the resident Judeans (cf. 1:15, 20) and the second (2:6–3:8) from the perspective of the exilic community (cf. 2:13–14), with 2:6 marking the transition between them (see note). The two parts frequently echo one another (compare 2:7 and 2:1–2; 2:8 and 1:22; 2:10 and 1:18; 2:11 and 1:19–20; etc.), and the parallels unite the two communities in humility before God. The entire section is based primarily on Dan 9:7–19, with frequent echoes of Jeremiah (e.g., compare 1:17–21 and Jer 7:23–26), the covenantal curses from Deut 28:15–68, and other OT texts. Indeed, virtually every phrase and idea in this section finds its source or inspiration somewhere in the OT.   **1:15** *To the Lord . . . righteousness*: i.e., "the Lord God is in the right" (NRSV; also at 2:6). *Confusion of faces*: the same Greek phrase is translated "open shame" at 2:6.   **1:20** *The curse*: see Deut 28:15–68, the source of the "plagues" mentioned in 2:2–5 (e.g., Deut 28:13, 37, 53). *He brought . . . honey*: conventional language; cf. Deut 26:8–9; Jer 32:21–22; etc.   **1:22** *Strange*: alien.

2 Therefore the Lord hath made good his word, which he pronounced against us, and against our judges that judged Israel, and against our kings, and against our princes, and against the men of Israel and Juda, [2]to bring upon us great plagues, such as never happened under the whole heaven, as it came to pass in Jerusalem, according to the things that were written in the law of Moses; [3]that a man should eat the flesh of his own son, and the flesh of his own daughter. [4]Moreover he hath delivered them to be in subjection to all the kingdoms that are round about us, to be as a reproach and desolation among all the people round about, where the Lord hath scattered them. [5]Thus we were cast down, and not exalted, because we have sinned against the Lord our God, and have not been obedient unto his voice.

[6]To the Lord our God appertaineth righteousness: but unto us and to our fathers open shame, as appeareth this day. [7]For all these plagues are come upon us, which the Lord hath pronounced against us. [8]Yet have we not prayed before the Lord, that we might turn every one from the imaginations of his wicked heart. [9]Wherefore the Lord watched over us for evil, and the Lord hath brought it upon us: for the Lord is righteous in all his works which he hath commanded us. [10]Yet we have not hearkened unto his voice, to walk in the commandments of the Lord, that he hath set before us.

[11]And now, O Lord God of Israel, that hast brought thy people out of the land of Egypt with a mighty hand, and high arm, and with signs, and with wonders, and with great power, and hast gotten thyself a name, as appeareth this day: [12]O Lord our God, we have sinned, we have done ungodly, we have dealt unrighteously in all thine ordinances. [13]Let thy wrath turn from us: for we are but a few left among the heathen, where thou hast scattered us. [14]Hear our prayers, O Lord, and our petitions, and deliver us for thine own sake, and give us favour in the sight of them which have led us away: [15]that all the earth may know that thou art the Lord our God, because Israel and his posterity is called by thy name.

[16]O Lord, look down from thy holy house, and consider us: bow down thine ear, O Lord, to hear us. [17]Open thine eyes, and behold; for the dead that are in the graves, whose souls are taken from their bodies, will give unto the Lord neither praise nor righteousness: [18]but the soul that is greatly vexed, which goeth stooping and feeble, and the eyes that fail, and the hungry soul, will give thee praise and righteousness, O Lord.

[19]Therefore we do not make our humble supplication before thee, O Lord our God, for the righteousness of our fathers, and of our kings. [20]For thou hast sent out thy wrath and indignation upon us, as thou hast spoken by thy servants the

---

2:1 *Which he pronounced against us*: "with which he threatened us" (also in v. 7). *Judges*: i.e., rulers. **2:2** *Plagues*: calamities (so throughout). **2:6** *To the Lord . . . day*: this verse repeats 1:15 almost verbatim (see note) but replaces references to the resident Judeans with *us and . . . our fathers*, namely the exilic community (see 2:13–14). **2:8** *That we . . . one*: alternatively "by turning away, each of us" (NRSV). **2:15** *Israel*: i.e., Jacob. **2:17** *The dead . . . righteousness*: this reflects a conventional view of death in the OT; cf. Pss 30:9; 88:10–12; Isa 38:18; etc. *Graves*: Gk. *hadēs* (also at 3:11, 19); see Matt 11:23 note. *Souls*: Gk. *pneuma*, "spirit" or, as here, "breath." ("Soul" in KJV normally translates *psychē*, which can simply mean life.) To "give righteousness" to the Lord means to "ascribe righteousness" (so NRSV) or even to "vindicate." **2:18** *Soul*: Gk. *psychē*, here meaning "person," both times in this verse.

prophets, saying, [21] Thus saith the Lord, Bow down your shoulders to serve the king of Babylon: so shall ye remain in the land that I gave unto your fathers. [22]But if ye will not hear the voice of the Lord, to serve the king of Babylon, [23]I will cause to cease out of the cities of Juda, and from without Jerusalem, the voice of mirth, and the voice of joy, the voice of the bridegroom, and the voice of the bride: and the whole land shall be desolate of inhabitants.

[24]But we would not hearken unto thy voice, to serve the king of Babylon: therefore hast thou made good the words that thou spakest by thy servants the prophets, namely, that the bones of our kings, and the bones of our fathers, should be taken out of their places. [25]And, lo, they are cast out to the heat of the day, and to the frost of the night, and they died in great miseries by famine, by sword, and by pestilence. [26]And the house which is called by thy name hast thou laid waste, as it is to be seen this day, for the wickedness of the house of Israel and the house of Juda.

[27]O Lord our God, thou hast dealt with us after all thy goodness, and according to all that great mercy of thine, [28]as thou spakest by thy servant Moses in the day when thou didst command him to write thy law before the children of Israel, saying, [29]If ye will not hear my voice, surely this very great multitude shall be turned into a small number among the nations, where I will scatter them. [30]For I knew that they would not hear me, because it is a stiffnecked people: but in the land of their captivities they shall remember themselves, [31]and shall know that I am the Lord their God: for I will give them an heart, and ears to hear: [32]and they shall praise me in the land of their captivity, and think upon my name, [33]and return from their stiff neck, and from their wicked deeds: for they shall remember the way of their fathers, which sinned before the Lord. [34]And I will bring them again into the land which I promised with an oath unto their fathers, Abraham, Isaac, and Jacob, and they shall be lords of it: and I will increase them, and they shall not be diminished. [35]And I will make an everlasting covenant with them to be their God, and they shall be my people: and I will no more drive my people of Israel out of the land that I have given them.

3 O Lord Almighty, God of Israel, the soul in anguish, the troubled spirit, crieth unto thee. [2]Hear, O Lord, and have mercy; for thou art merciful: and have pity upon us, because we have sinned before thee. [3]For thou endurest for ever, and we perish utterly. [4]O Lord Almighty, thou God of Israel, hear now the prayers of the dead Israelites, and of their children, which have sinned before thee, and not hearkened unto the voice of thee their God: for the which cause these plagues

---

2:21 *Bow down . . . fathers*: cf. Jer 27:11–12.   2:23 *I will cause . . . inhabitants*: echoing Jer 7:34; 16:9; 33:10–11.   2:24–25 *That the bones . . . night*: see Jer 8:1–2; 36:30.   2:26 *The house . . . name*: the temple. *Hast thou . . . day*: the Greek reads "you have made as it is today" (NRSV).   2:29 *If ye . . . them*: cf. Deut 28:62.   2:30 *Stiffnecked*: stubborn. *In the land . . . themselves*: cf. 1 Kgs 8:47. 2:31 *Shall know . . . hear*: cf. Deut 29:4; Jer 24:7.   2:34–35 *I will bring them . . . given them*: cf. Lev 26:42–45; Jer 32:37, 40–41. On the *everlasting covenant* (v. 35), see also Jer 31:31–34.   3:4 *The dead Israelites*: this odd phrase—in light of 2:17, all but nonsensical—probably reflects an error made by the Greek translator, who confused two similar Hebrew roots meaning "men" and "dead"; or it might

cleave unto us. ⁵Remember not the iniquities of our forefathers: but think upon thy power and thy name now at this time. ⁶For thou art the Lord our God, and thee, O Lord, will we praise. ⁷And for this cause thou hast put thy fear in our hearts, to the intent that we should call upon thy name, and praise thee in our captivity: for we have called to mind all the iniquity of our forefathers, that sinned before thee. ⁸Behold, we are yet this day in our captivity, where thou hast scattered us, for a reproach and a curse, and to be subject to payments, according to all the iniquities of our fathers, which departed from the Lord our God.

⁹Hear, Israel, the commandments of life: give ear to understand wisdom.

¹⁰How happeneth it, Israel, that thou art in thine enemies' land, that thou art waxen old in a strange country, that thou art defiled with the dead,

¹¹That thou art counted with them that go down into the grave?

¹²Thou hast forsaken the fountain of wisdom.

¹³For if thou hadst walked in the way of God, thou shouldest have dwelled in peace for ever.

¹⁴Learn where is wisdom, where is strength, where is understanding; that thou mayest know also where is length of days, and life, where is the light of the eyes, and peace.

¹⁵Who hath found out her place? or who hath come into her treasures?

¹⁶Where are the princes of the heathen become, and such as ruled the beasts upon the earth;

¹⁷They that had their pastime with the fowls of the air, and they that hoarded up silver and gold, wherein men trust, and made no end of their getting?

¹⁸For they that wrought in silver, and were so careful, and whose works are unsearchable,

---

figuratively represent the exiled community's misery.　　**3:7** *Called to mind*: better "turned away from our hearts" (MS tradition).　　**3:8** *A reproach . . . payments*: cf. Jer 42:18. *Payments* here presumably are punishments (so NRSV). *According to all . . . fathers*: for the principle, see Exod 20:5–6.

　　3:9–4:4 Hymn to Wisdom. The regular thematic parallelism suggests that this section is poetic. Distinct from what has come before, it implies that the exile is now a long-standing situation (see 3:10). The poem frequently echoes Wis 9, Job 28, and many other passages from the Bible's Wisdom literature. It employs three Greek synonyms for wisdom: *phronēsis*, in 3:9, 14, 28; *synesis*, in 3:14, 23 (rendered "understanding" at 3:32); and *sophia*, in v. 12. Their respective senses are, roughly, "discretion," "understanding," and "wisdom."　　**3:9** *Hear, Israel . . . wisdom*: this verse combines echoes of Deuteronomy's injunctions to obey God's laws (4:1; 5:1; 6:3) and Proverbs' encouragement to attend to wisdom (2:2; 5:1).　　**3:10** *Waxen old in a strange country*: this contradicts the time frame suggested by 1:2.　　**3:11** *Thou art counted . . . grave*: cf. Ps 55:15; 88:4.　　**3:12** *Thou hast forsaken . . . wisdom*: echoing Jer 2:13.　　**3:13–14** *If thou . . . and peace*: recalling Prov 3:16–17.　　**3:14** *Light of the eyes*: refreshment; see 1 Sam 14:27 and note.　　**3:15–31** *Who hath found out . . . path*: recalling Job 28:12–22.　　**3:17** *Pastime with the fowls of the air*: falconry, a sport of the elite.　　**3:18** *They that wrought in silver*: i.e., silversmiths, but "those who acquired silver" is a possible reading of the MS tradition. *Careful*: anxious.

¹⁹They are vanished and gone down to the grave, and others are
come up in their steads.

²⁰Young men have seen light, and dwelt upon the earth: but the
way of knowledge have they not known,

²¹Nor understood the paths thereof, nor laid hold of it: their
children were far off from that way.

²²It hath not been heard of in Chanaan, neither hath it been seen
in Theman.

²³The Agarenes that seek wisdom upon earth, the merchants of
Meran and of Theman, the authors of fables, and searchers out
of understanding; none of these have known the way of
wisdom, or remember her paths.

²⁴O Israel, how great is the house of God! and how large is the
place of his possession!

²⁵Great, and hath none end; high, and unmeasurable.

²⁶There were the giants famous from the beginning, that were of
so great stature, and so expert in war.

²⁷Those did not the Lord choose, neither gave he the way of
knowledge unto them:

²⁸But they were destroyed, because they had no wisdom, and
perished through their own foolishness.

²⁹Who hath gone up into heaven, and taken her, and brought her
down from the clouds?

³⁰Who hath gone over the sea, and found her, and will bring her
for pure gold?

³¹No man knoweth her way, nor thinketh of her path.

³²But he that knoweth all things knoweth her, and hath found her
out with his understanding: he that prepared the earth for
evermore hath filled it with fourfooted beasts:

³³He that sendeth forth light, and it goeth, calleth it again, and it
obeyeth him with fear.

³⁴The stars shined in their watches, and rejoiced: when he calleth
them, they say, Here we be; and so with cheerfulness they
shewed light unto him that made them.

³⁵This is our God, and there shall none other be accounted of in
comparison of him.

3:20 *Young men . . . earth*: referring to the birth of newer generations (so NRSV).   3:22 *Chanaan*: Canaan. *Theman*: Teman, a city in Edom, apparently famous for wisdom (cf. Jer 49:7).   3:23 *Agarenes*: lit. "sons of Hagar," i.e., Ishmaelites. (For their nomadism, see Gen 37:25.) *Meran*: obscure, but perhaps a corruption of Medan, an Arabian city, or of Midian, also in Arabia. *Theman* might here refer to another Arabian city, Tema.   3:24 *House of God*: i.e., the created world.   3:26–28 *There were . . . foolishness*: see Gen 6:1–4 and notes.   3:29–31 *Who hath gone up . . . path*: alluding to Deut 30:11–14, but radically revising the meaning of that passage; cf. Rom 10:6–10 and note.   3:32–36 *But he . . . knowledge*: cf. Job 28:23–28.   3:33 *Light*: lightning; cf. Job 38:35. *With fear*: lit. "trembling" or "quaking."   3:34–35 *The stars . . . of him*: recalling Isa 40:25–26.

³⁶He hath found out all the way of knowledge, and hath given it unto Jacob his servant, and to Israel his beloved.

³⁷Afterward did he shew himself upon earth, and conversed with men.

4 ¹This is the book of the commandments of God, and the law that endureth for ever: all they that keep it shall come to life; but such as leave it shall die.

²Turn thee, O Jacob, and take hold of it: walk in the presence of the light thereof, that thou mayest be illuminated.

³Give not thine honour to another, nor the things that are profitable unto thee to a strange nation.

⁴O Israel, happy are we: for things that are pleasing to God are made known unto us.

⁵Be of good cheer, my people, the memorial of Israel.

⁶Ye were sold to the nations, not for [your] destruction: but because ye moved God to wrath, ye were delivered unto the enemies.

⁷For ye provoked him that made you by sacrificing unto devils, and not to God.

3:36 *Hath given . . . beloved:* echoing Sir 24:8. **3:37** *Did he shew . . . men:* the ancient Christian tradition treating this verse as a prophetic reference to Christ's incarnation and the more modern dismissal of the verse as a later Christian interpolation are both belied by the Greek, which refers more naturally to Wisdom: "she showed herself." The echo of Sir 24:8 in v. 36 makes especially apt a comparison here with Sir 24:9–12, for those verses speak of wisdom resting in Israel and taking root among its inhabitants. *Conversed:* lived with. **4:1** *This is:* rather "she is," equating Wisdom with the Torah (cf. Sir 24:23). *They that . . . die:* cf. Deut 30:15–20. **4:2** *Walk in the presence . . . illuminated:* cf. Prov 6:23; Isa 2:5; etc. **4:4** *O Israel . . . us:* cf. Wis 9:18.

4:5–5:9 Poem of encouragement. This section, like the previous, features regular thematic parallelism. It is reminiscent of Isaiah throughout (esp. chaps. 40–55), and at 4:36–5:9 it closely follows the pseudepigraphic *Psalm of Solomon* 11:3–8:

> Stand on a high place, Jerusalem, and look at your children,
>   from the east and the west assembled together by the Lord.
> From the north they come in the joy of their God;
>   from far distant islands God has assembled them.
> He flattened high mountains into level ground for them;
>   the hills fled at their coming.
> The forests shaded them as they passed by;
>   God made every fragrant tree to grow for them.
> So that Israel might proceed under the supervision of the glory of their God.
> Jerusalem, put on (the) clothes of your glory,
>   prepare the robe of your holiness,
> for God has spoken well of Israel forevermore.
> May the Lord do what he has spoken about Israel and Jerusalem;
>   may the Lord lift up Israel in the name of his glory.
> May the mercy of the Lord be upon Israel forevermore. (Trans. R. B. Wright)

The section has two speakers: the psalmist and Jerusalem personified. First the psalmist addresses the exiles (4:5–9a); then Jerusalem addresses Israel's neighbors (4:9b–16); next Jerusalem addresses the exiles (4:17–29); and finally the psalmist addresses Jerusalem (4:30–5:9). **4:6** *Ye were sold:* echoing Isa 50:1; 52:3. **4:7–8** *By sacrificing . . . brought you up:* cf. Deut

⁸Ye have forgotten the everlasting God, that brought you up; and
　　ye have grieved Jerusalem, that nursed you.
⁹For when she saw the wrath of God coming upon you, she said,

　　Hearken, O ye that dwell about Sion: God hath brought upon
　　　me great mourning;
¹⁰for I saw the captivity of my sons and daughters, which the
　　Everlasting brought upon them.
¹¹With joy did I nourish them; but sent them away with weeping
　　and mourning.
¹²Let no man rejoice over me, a widow, and forsaken of many, who
　　for the sins of my children am left desolate; because they
　　departed from the law of God.
¹³They knew not his statutes, nor walked in the ways of his
　　commandments, nor trod in the paths of discipline in his
　　righteousness.
¹⁴Let them that dwell about Sion come, and remember ye the
　　captivity of my sons and daughters, which the Everlasting hath
　　brought upon them.
¹⁵For he hath brought a nation upon them from far, a shameless
　　nation, and of a strange language, who neither reverenced old
　　man, nor pitied child.
¹⁶These have carried away the dear beloved children of the widow,
　　and left her that was alone desolate without daughters.

¹⁷But what can I help you?
¹⁸For he that brought these plagues upon you will deliver you
　　from the hands of your enemies.
¹⁹Go your way, O my children, go your way: for I am left desolate.
²⁰I have put off the clothing of peace, and put upon me the sack-
　　cloth of my prayer: I will cry unto the Everlasting in my days.
²¹Be of good cheer, O my children, cry unto the Lord, and he shall
　　deliver you from the power and hand of the enemies.
²²For my hope is in the Everlasting, that he will save you; and joy
　　is come unto me from the Holy One, because of the mercy
　　which shall soon come unto you from the Everlasting our
　　Saviour.
²³For I sent you out with mourning and weeping: but God will give
　　you to me again with joy and gladness for ever.
²⁴Like as now the neighbours of Sion have seen your captivity: so
　　shall they see shortly your salvation from our God, which shall

---

32:17–18.   **4:12** *A widow . . . desolate*: this imagery, which surfaces throughout the section, recalls
Isa 49:21; 51:18–20; 54:1–4; etc.   **4:15** *He hath brought . . . child*: cf. Deut 28:49–50.   **4:20** *I have
put off . . . prayer*: reversing the imagery applied to Jerusalem at Isa 52:1–2.   **4:23** *I sent . . . for ever*:
again invoking imagery from Isaiah (35:10; 51:11); also cf. Ps 126:6.   **4:24** *So shall . . . Everlasting*:

come upon you with great glory, and brightness of the Everlasting.

²⁵My children, suffer patiently the wrath that is come upon you from God: for thine enemy hath persecuted thee; but shortly thou shalt see his destruction, and shalt tread upon his neck.

²⁶My delicate ones have gone rough ways, and were taken away as a flock caught of the enemies.

²⁷Be of good comfort, O my children, and cry unto God: for ye shall be remembered of him that brought these things upon you.

²⁸For as it was your mind to go astray from God: so, being returned, seek him ten times more.

²⁹For he that hath brought these plagues upon you shall bring you everlasting joy again with your salvation.

³⁰Take a good heart, O Jerusalem: for he that gave thee that name will comfort thee.

³¹Miserable are they that afflicted thee, and rejoiced at thy fall.

³²Miserable are the cities which thy children served: miserable is she that received thy sons.

³³For as she rejoiced at thy ruin, and was glad of thy fall: so shall she be grieved for her own desolation.

³⁴For I will take away the rejoicing of her great multitude, and her pride shall be turned into mourning.

³⁵For fire shall come upon her from the Everlasting, long to endure; and she shall be inhabited of devils for a great time.

³⁶O Jerusalem, look about thee toward the east and behold the joy that cometh unto thee from God.

³⁷Lo, thy sons come, whom thou sentest away, they come gathered together from the east to the west by the word of the Holy One, rejoicing in the glory of God.

5 ¹Put off, O Jerusalem, the garment of thy mourning and affliction, and put on the comeliness of the glory that cometh from God for ever.

²Cast about thee a double garment of the righteousness which cometh from God; and set a diadem on thine head of the glory of the Everlasting.

---

cf. Isa 60:1–3. **4:25** *Tread upon his neck*: an image from Deuteronomy (33:29; see note); cf. Isa 51:23. **4:27** *Be of good comfort, O my children*: echoing Isa 40:1. **4:30** *He that gave thee that name*: rather "the one who named you," probably in the sense of periphrastic references to Jerusalem, especially those invoking God's name, such as "The city of the Lord" and "The Zion of the Holy One of Israel" (Isa 60:14). Also see Isa 62:2–4; cf. Bar 5:4. **4:32** *Which thy children served*: lit. "in which your children were enslaved." *She*: Babylon. **4:35** *Fire shall come upon her*: Jeremiah frequently prophesies Babylon's burning; e.g., 50:32; 51:30. *She shall be inhabited . . . time*: cf. Isa 13:19–22. **4:36–37** *Look about thee . . . God*: cf. Isa 43:5–6; Zech 8:7–8. **5:1–2** *Put off . . . Everlasting*: recalling and subverting 4:20 (see note); cf. Isa 52:1; 61:10. **5:2** *A double garment*: referring

³For God will shew thy brightness unto every country under
heaven.
⁴For thy name shall be called of God for ever, The peace of
righteousness, and The glory of God's worship.
⁵Arise, O Jerusalem, and stand on high, and look about toward
the east, and behold thy children gathered from the west unto
the east by the word of the Holy One, rejoicing in the remembrance of God.
⁶For they departed from thee on foot, and were led away of their
enemies: but God bringeth them unto thee exalted with glory,
as children of the kingdom.
⁷For God hath appointed that every high hill, and banks of long
continuance, should be cast down, and valleys filled up, to
make even the ground, that Israel may go safely in the glory
of God.
⁸Moreover even the woods and every sweetsmelling tree shall
overshadow Israel by the commandment of God.
⁹For God shall lead Israel with joy in the fight of his glory with
the mercy and righteousness that cometh from him.

THE EPISTLE OF JEREMY

6 A copy of an epistle, which Jeremy sent unto them which were to be led captives into Babylon by the king of the Babylonians, to certify them, as it was
commanded him of God.

²Because of the sins which ye have committed before God, ye shall be led away
captives into Babylon by Nabuchodonosor king of the Babylonians. ³So when ye
be come unto Babylon, ye shall remain there many years, and for a long season,
namely, seven generations: and after that I will bring you away peaceably from
thence. ⁴Now shall ye see in Babylon gods of silver, and of gold, and of wood,
borne upon shoulders, which cause the nations to fear. ⁵Beware therefore that ye
in no wise be like to strangers, neither be ye afraid of them, when ye see the mul-

---

to a cloak.   **5:6** *As children of the kingdom*: better "as the throne of the king" (MS tradition).
5:7 *Every high hill . . . God*: echoing Isa 40:4–5. *Banks of long continuance*: "everlasting hills" (NRSV).
5:9 *God shall lead . . . glory*: recalling the imagery of radiance at Isa 60:1–5.
    6:1–73 Epistle of Jeremiah. This homily against idolatry, misleadingly called a letter in v. 1,
depends on a number of OT passages that decry the practice; see esp. Ps 115:3–8; 135:6–7; Isa
44:9–20; 46:5–7; Jer 10:2–5. It also resembles the excursus on idolatry in Wis 13:1–15:9. Parallels
with these texts are frequent, and are not cited in the notes that follow. The epistle is punctuated
by a refrain insisting that idols ought not to be mistaken for gods (vv. 16, 23, 29, 40, 44, 49, 52, 56,
65, 69), which divides the work into eleven separate sections after its superscription (v. 1) and
introduction (vv. 2–7).   **6:1** *A copy . . . Babylonians*: the superscription models this *epistle* on
those that Jeremiah sent to the exiles in Babylonia (Jer 29:4–28). *Certify them*: inform them certainly.   **6:3** *For a long . . . generations*: although Jeremiah insisted the exile would be protracted
(cf. Jer 32:14), he foresaw a period of only seventy years (see Jer 25:12; 29:10).   **6:5** *Strangers*:

titude before them and behind them, worshipping them. [6]But say ye in your hearts, O Lord, we must worship thee. [7]For mine angel is with you, and I myself caring for your souls.

[8]As for their tongue, it is polished by the workman, and they themselves are gilded and laid over with silver; yet are they but false, and cannot speak. [9]And taking gold, as it were for a virgin that loveth to go gay, they make crowns for the heads of their gods. [10]Sometimes also the priests convey from their gods gold and silver, and bestow it upon themselves. [11]Yea, they will give thereof to the common harlots, and deck them as men with garments, [being] gods of silver, and gods of gold, and wood. [12]Yet cannot these gods save themselves from rust and moths, though they be covered with purple raiment. [13]They wipe their faces because of the dust of the temple, when there is much upon them. [14]And he that cannot put to death one that offendeth him holdeth a sceptre, as though he were a judge of the country. [15]He hath also in his right hand a dagger and an axe: but cannot deliver himself from war and thieves. [16]Whereby they are known not to be gods: therefore fear them not.

[17]For like as a vessel that a man useth is nothing worth when it is broken; even so it is with their gods: when they be set up in the temple, their eyes be full of dust through the feet of them that come in. [18]And as the doors are made sure on every side upon him that offendeth the king, as being committed to suffer death: even so the priests make fast their temples with doors, with locks, and bars, lest their gods be spoiled with robbers. [19]They light them candles, yea, more than for themselves, whereof they cannot see one. [20]They are as one of the beams of the temple, yet they say their hearts are gnawed upon by things creeping out of the earth; and when they eat them and their clothes, they feel it not. [21]Their faces are blacked through the smoke that cometh out of the temple. [22]Upon their bodies and heads sit bats, swallows, and birds, and the cats also. [23]By this ye may know that they are no gods: therefore fear them not.

[24]Notwithstanding the gold that is about them to make them beautiful, except they wipe off the rust, they will not shine: for neither when they were molten did they feel it. [25]The things wherein there is no breath are bought for a most high price. [26]They are borne upon shoulders, having no feet, whereby they declare unto men that they be nothing worth. [27]They also that serve them are ashamed: for if they fall to the ground at any time, they cannot rise up again of themselves: neither, if one set them upright, can they move of themselves: neither, if they be bowed down, can they make themselves straight: but they set gifts before them, as unto dead men. [28]As for the things that are sacrificed unto them, their priests

---

foreigners. **6:7** *Mine angel is with you*: echoing Exod 23:23, but apparently assuming something akin to the notion of guardian angels (see Matt 18:10 and note). *I myself*: alternatively "he is." **6:9** *Loveth to go gay*: "loves ornaments" (NRSV). **6:11** *Common harlots*: lit. "prostitutes on the roof," although this is obscure. **6:12** *Moths*: Gk. *brōmata*, which appears to refer more generally to corrosion; the same root is rendered "rust" in Matt 6:19 (see note). **6:18** *As being committed to suffer death*: "as though under sentence of death" (NRSV). **6:20** *They say . . . earth*: obscure.

sell and abuse; in like manner their wives lay up part thereof in salt; but unto the poor and impotent they give nothing of it. ²⁹Menstruous women and women in childbed eat their sacrifices: by these things ye may know that they are no gods: fear them not.

³⁰For how can they be called gods? because women set meat before the gods of silver, gold, and wood. ³¹And the priests sit in their temples, having their clothes rent, and their heads and beards shaven, and nothing upon their heads. ³²They roar and cry before their gods, as men do at the feast when one is dead. ³³The priests also take off their garments, and clothe their wives and children. ³⁴Whether it be evil that one doeth unto them, or good, they are not able to recompense it: they can neither set up a king, nor put him down. ³⁵In like manner, they can neither give riches nor money: though a man make a vow unto them, and keep it not, they will not require it. ³⁶They can save no man from death, neither deliver the weak from the mighty. ³⁷They cannot restore a blind man to his sight, nor help any man in his distress. ³⁸They can shew no mercy to the widow, nor do good to the fatherless. ³⁹Their gods of wood, and which are overlaid with gold and silver, are like the stones that be hewn out of the mountain: they that worship them shall be confounded.

⁴⁰How should a man then think and say that they are gods, when even the Chaldeans themselves dishonour them? ⁴¹Who if they shall see one dumb that cannot speak, they bring him, and intreat Bel that he may speak, as though he were able to understand. ⁴²Yet they cannot understand this themselves, and leave them: for they have no knowledge. ⁴³The women also with cords about them, sitting in the ways, burn bran for perfume: but if any of them, drawn by some that passeth by, lie with him, she reproacheth her fellow, that she was not thought as worthy as herself, nor her cord broken. ⁴⁴Whatsoever is done among them is false: how may it then be thought or said that they are gods?

⁴⁵They are made of carpenters and goldsmiths: they can be nothing else than the workmen will have them to be. ⁴⁶And they themselves that made them can never continue long; how should then the things that are made of them be gods?

6:28 *In salt*: to preserve it.   6:29 *Menstruous women . . . childbed*: i.e., the priests' wives, even when in states of what Israelites took to be ritual impurity; cf. Lev 12:2–4; 15:24 note and 33. 6:30 *Women set . . . gods*: i.e., priestesses officiate before them.   6:31–32 *The priests . . . dead*: with a few exceptions, Leviticus bars YHWH's priests from such practices, which are appropriate to mourners of the dead rather than to those serving the living God (21:1–6, 10–11). In addition, cultic mourning was associated with the worship of some pagan divinities (cf. Ezek 8:14 and note) whose death and rebirth figured the seasonal cycle.   6:33 *Their garments*: i.e., belonging to the idols.   6:34 *They can neither set up . . . down*: for the conventional idea that God distributes political power, see Rom 13:1 and note.   6:35 *They can neither give riches nor money*: in contrast to YHWH; cf. 1 Sam 2:7. *Though a man . . . require it*: in contrast to YHWH; cf. Deut 23:21.   6:36 *They can save . . . death*: again in contrast to YHWH; cf. Deut 32:39.   6:37–38 *They cannot restore . . . fatherless*: reversing the praise of YHWH in Ps 146:8–9.   6:40 *How should . . . them*: KJV misleadingly joins the two independent clauses. NRSV is more accurate: "Why then must anyone think that they are gods, or call them gods? Besides, even the Chaldeans themselves dishonor them." The section break should actually come between the two sentences.   6:41 *Bel*: see Bel 3 note.   6:43 *The women . . . broken*: apparently the practice attrib-

[47] For they left lies and reproaches to them that come after. [48] For when there cometh any war or plague upon them, the priests consult with themselves, where they may be hidden with them. [49] How then cannot men perceive that they be no gods, which can neither save themselves from war, nor from plague?

[50] For seeing they be but of wood, and overlaid with silver and gold, it shall be known hereafter that they are false: [51] and it shall manifestly appear to all nations and kings that they are no gods, but the works of men's hands, and that there is no work of God in them. [52] Who then may not know that they are no gods?

[53] For neither can they set up a king in the land, nor give rain unto men. [54] Neither can they judge their own cause, nor redress a wrong, being unable: for they are as crows between heaven and earth. [55] Whereupon when fire falleth upon the house of gods of wood, or laid over with gold or silver, their priests will flee away, and escape; but they themselves shall be burned asunder like beams. [56] Moreover they cannot withstand any king or enemies: how can it then be thought or said that they be gods?

[57] Neither are those gods of wood, and laid over with silver or gold, able to escape either from thieves or robbers. [58] Whose gold, and silver, and garments wherewith they are clothed, they that are strong do take, and go away withal: neither are they able to help themselves. [59] Therefore it is better to be a king that sheweth his power, or else a profitable vessel in an house, which the owner shall have use of, than such false gods; or to be a door in an house, to keep such things safe as be therein, than such false gods; or a pillar of wood in a palace, than such false gods. [60] For sun, moon, and stars, being bright, and sent to do their offices, are obedient. [61] In like manner the lightning when it breaketh forth is easy to be seen; and after the same manner the wind bloweth in every country. [62] And when God commandeth the clouds to go over the whole world, they do as they are bidden. [63] And the fire sent from above to consume hills and woods doeth as it is commanded: but these are like unto them neither in shew nor power. [64] Wherefore it is neither to be supposed nor said that they are gods, seeing they are able neither to judge causes, nor to do good unto men. [65] Knowing therefore that they are no gods, fear them not.

[66] For they can neither curse nor bless kings: [67] neither can they shew signs in the heavens among the heathen, nor shine as the sun, nor give light as the moon. [68] The beasts are better than they: for they can get under a covert, and help themselves. [69] It is then by no means manifest unto us that they are gods: therefore fear them not.

[70] For as a scarecrow in a garden of cucumbers keepeth nothing: so are their gods of wood, and laid over with silver and gold. [71] And likewise their gods of wood, and laid over with silver and gold, are like to a whitethorn in an orchard,

uted to the Babylonians by Herodotus (1.199). The references to *cords* are obscure.   **6:47** *For they . . . after*: i.e., the artisans left the false gods to later generations.   **6:53** *Neither can . . . land*: see v. 34 and note. *Nor give rain*: in contrast to YHWH; see Deut 11:14.   **6:54** *Crows*: some propose another LXX translation error, speculating that similar Hebrew phrases meaning "as crows" and "as clouds" (arguably a more appropriate image) were confused.   **6:70** *Keepeth*: protects.   **6:71** *Whitethorn*: hawthorn; for the

that every bird sitteth upon; as also to a dead body, that is cast into the dark. [72]And ye shall know them to be no gods by the bright purple that rotteth upon them: and they themselves afterward shall be eaten, and shall be a reproach in the country. [73]Better therefore is the just man that hath none idols: for he shall be far from reproach.

---

proverbially worthless bramble, cf. Judg 9:14–15 and note to v. 7; 2 Kgs 14:9. **6:72** *Bright purple*: royal attire; the Greek actually reads "purple and marble," which may represent a translation error. (The same Hebrew word can mean "marble" and "linen.")

The Song of the Three Holy Children

O NE of the Apocrypha's three "additions" to Daniel, this "song," probably written originally in Hebrew, was placed between 3:23 and 24, perhaps sometime in the first or second century B.C.E. It ultimately found its way into both major Greek versions of the book (the Septuagint and Theodotion, which the church has traditionally privileged and which KJV translates here), but there is no evidence that the Song (or any of the other Daniel additions) was ever a part of the version that the Masoretic Text preserves, on which KJV relies for Daniel in the Old Testament. The evident purpose of this insertion is to fill out the otherwise perfunctory descriptions of the three youths who survived the furnace. Here, as elsewhere in the Apocrypha, the faith and piety of a biblical story's heroes receive emphasis.

There are four discrete parts to the Song: a prayer, a narrative, and a hymn that itself consists of two poems (called "ode" and "psalm" in the notes that follow). While the narrative adds vivid details to Daniel's account of the youths' ordeal, the other parts consist of rather general confessions and doxologies, which may have originated in postexilic liturgical settings.

For more information about all three of the Daniel additions, the reader can consult Carey A. Moore's Anchor Bible commentary, *Daniel, Esther, and Jeremiah: The Additions* (Garden City, NY: Doubleday, 1977). Amy-Jill Levine's introductions and notes in *The New Oxford Annotated Bible*, ed. Michael D. Coogan, 3rd ed. (Oxford: Oxford University Press, 2001) are also strong. Both thoroughly inform this introduction and the annotations that follow.

The Song of the Three Holy Children

which followeth in the third Chapter of DANIEL after this place,—*fell down bound into the midst of the burning fiery furnace*—verse 23. That which followeth is not in the Hebrew, to wit, *And they walked*—unto these words, *Then Nebuchadnezzar*—verse 24.

¹And they walked in the midst of the fire, praising God, and blessing the Lord. ²Then Azarias stood up, and prayed on this manner; and opening his mouth in the midst of the fire, said, ³Blessed art thou, O Lord God of our fathers: thy name is worthy to be praised and glorified for evermore: ⁴for thou art righteous in all the things that thou hast done to us: yea, true are all thy works, thy ways are right, and all thy judgments truth. ⁵In all the things that thou hast brought upon us, and upon the holy city of our fathers, even Jerusalem, thou hast executed true judgment: for according to truth and judgment didst thou bring all these things upon us because of our sins. ⁶For we have sinned and committed iniquity, departing from thee. ⁷In all things have we trespassed, and not obeyed thy commandments, nor kept them, neither done as thou hast commanded us, that it might go well with us. ⁸Wherefore all that thou hast brought upon us, and every thing that thou hast done to us, thou hast done in true judgment. ⁹And thou didst deliver us into the hands of lawless enemies, most hateful forsakers of God, and to an unjust king, and the most wicked in all the world. ¹⁰And now we cannot open our mouths, we are become a shame and reproach to thy servants, and to them that worship thee.

1–22 Prayer of Azariah. This prayer, a national lament akin to such poems as Pss 44 and 79, has little to do with the actual predicament of the three youths. Indeed, while Azariah claims that he and his fellow martyrs suffer justly because God punishes them for transgressing his commandments (see vv. 6–8; the confession recalls postexilic prayers such as Ezra 9:6–7; Neh 9:26–27, 33; Tob 3:2–6), the three young men are sent into the fiery furnace precisely because of their refusal to transgress God's prohibition against idolatry (Dan 3:12–18). The prayer resonates with traditional biblical language and imagery; almost every phrase finds a precedent in the Psalms, the Prophets, etc. A handful of these echoes are noted below. **1** *They*: Hananiah, Mishael, and Azariah, whose Aramaic names are Shadrach, Meshach, and Abednego; see Dan 1:7. **2** *Azarias*: in LXX the three sing together, as the title suggests. **4** *Thou art righteous . . . things*: cf. Dan 9:14. **6** *For we . . . iniquity*: cf. Dan 9:5, 15. **9** *An unjust king . . . world*: in Daniel the king is Nebuchadnezzar, but the author of this addition (like the author of Daniel itself) probably saw his harassment of faithful Jews (cf. Dan 3:13–23) as paralleling the oppressive policies of the Seleucid ruler Antiochus IV Epiphanes; cf. 1 Macc 1:20–64. **10** *Servants*: lit. "slaves" (so throughout).

¹¹Yet deliver, us not up wholly, for thy name's sake, neither disannul thou thy covenant: ¹²and cause not thy mercy to depart from us, for thy beloved Abraham's sake, for thy servant Isaac's sake, and for thy holy Israel's sake; ¹³to whom thou hast spoken and promised, that thou wouldest multiply their seed as the stars of heaven, and as the sand that lieth upon the sea shore. ¹⁴For we, O Lord, are become less than any nation, and be kept under this day in all the world because of our sins. ¹⁵Neither is there at this time prince, or prophet, or leader, or burnt offering, or sacrifice, or oblation, or incense, or place to sacrifice before thee, and to find mercy. ¹⁶Nevertheless in a contrite heart and an humble spirit let us be accepted. ¹⁷Like as in the burnt offerings of rams and bullocks, and like as in ten thousands of fat lambs: so let our sacrifice be in thy sight this day, and grant that we may wholly go after thee: for they shall not be confounded that put their trust in thee. ¹⁸And now we follow thee with all our heart, we fear thee, and seek thy face. ¹⁹Put us not to shame: but deal with us after thy lovingkindness, and according to the multitude of thy mercies. ²⁰Deliver us also according to thy marvellous works, and give glory to thy name, O Lord: and let all them that do thy servants hurt be ashamed; ²¹and let them be confounded in all their power and might, and let their strength be broken; ²²and let them know that thou art Lord, the only God, and glorious over the whole world.

²³And the king's servants, that put them in, ceased not to make the oven hot with rosin, pitch, tow, and small wood; ²⁴so that the flame streamed forth above the furnace forty and nine cubits. ²⁵And it passed through, and burned those Chaldeans it found about the furnace. ²⁶But the angel of the Lord came down into the oven together with Azarias and his fellows, and smote the flame of the fire out of the oven; ²⁷and made the midst of the furnace as it had been a moist whistling wind, so that the fire touched them not at all, neither hurt nor troubled them.

²⁸Then the three, as out of one mouth, praised, glorified, and blessed God in the furnace, saying,

²⁹Blessed art thou, O Lord God of our fathers: and to be
praised and exalted above all for ever.
³⁰And blessed is thy glorious and holy name: and to be
praised and exalted above all for ever.

11 *Neither disannul thou thy covenant*: cf. Lev 26:44.   13 *Thou wouldst multiply . . . shore*: see Gen 15:5; 22:17; 26:4; Exod 32:13; etc.   14 *For we . . . nation*: cf. Deut 28:62.   15 *Neither is . . . prophet*: cf. Ps 74:9.   16 *In a contrite heart . . . accepted*: recalling Ps 51:17; Mic 6:7–8.   22 *And let . . . world*: cf. Ps 83:18.

23–27 **Narrative.** This passage appears to be an imaginative expansion of the sparse and mysterious report of the young men's ordeal at Dan 3:21–25.   23 *Rosin*: Gk. *naphtha*, petroleum (see 2 Macc 1:36 note). *Small wood*: i.e., kindling.   24 *Forty and nine cubits*: more than 70 feet.   25 *Chaldeans*: Babylonians.

28–34 **Hymn part 1: ode.** Formally this ode resembles Ps 136 (as does the psalm that follows in vv. 35–68), which also repeats the same refrain in the second half of each verse throughout.

³¹Blessed art thou in the temple of thine holy glory: and to
be praised and glorified above all for ever.
³²Blessed art thou that beholdest the depths, and sittest
upon the cherubims: and to be praised and exalted
above all for ever.
³³Blessed art thou on the glorious throne of thy kingdom:
and to be praised and glorified above all for ever.
³⁴Blessed art thou in the firmament of heaven: and above all
to be praised and glorified for ever.

³⁵O all ye works of the Lord, bless ye the Lord: praise and
exalt him above all for ever.
³⁶O ye heavens, bless ye the Lord: praise and exalt him
above all for ever.
³⁷O ye angels of the Lord, bless ye the Lord: praise and exalt
him above all for ever.
³⁸O all ye waters that be above the heaven, bless ye the Lord:
praise and exalt him above all for ever.
³⁹O all ye powers of the Lord, bless ye the Lord: praise and
exalt him above all for ever.
⁴⁰O ye sun and moon, bless ye the Lord: praise and exalt
him above all for ever.
⁴¹O ye stars of heaven, bless ye the Lord: praise and exalt
him above all for ever.
⁴²O every shower and dew, bless ye the Lord: praise and
exalt him above all for ever.
⁴³O all ye winds, bless ye the Lord: praise and exalt him
above all for ever.
⁴⁴O ye fire and heat, bless ye the Lord: praise and exalt him
above all for ever.
⁴⁵O ye winter and summer, bless ye the Lord: praise and
exalt him above all for ever.
⁴⁶O ye dews and storms of snow, bless ye the Lord: praise
and exalt him above all for ever.

Verses 29–30 virtually replicate the introduction of Tobit's prayer (cf. 8:5).   **32** *Sittest upon the cherubims*: see Exod 25:17–22.   **34** *Firmament*: cf. Gen 1:6.

35–68 Hymn part 2: psalm. This psalm is addressed directly to God's works; its content evokes Ps 148, its form Ps 136 (see note to vv. 28–34). The psalm's calls for praise descend gradually from the heavens (vv. 36–41) through the atmosphere (vv. 42–51) to the earth below (vv. 52–54), and then to the waters (vv. 55–56), before demanding that the creatures inhabiting the terrestrial realms praise the Lord as well (vv. 57–66). (In LXX, the order of vv. 47–48 and 49–50 is reversed to make the thematic development more logical.)   **38** *Waters that be above the heaven*: see Gen 1:7.   **39** *Powers of the Lord*: probably God's angelic army (cf. Neh 9:6).

⁴⁷O ye nights and days, bless ye the Lord: praise and exalt
    him above all for ever.

⁴⁸O ye light and darkness, bless ye the Lord: praise and exalt
    him above all for ever.

⁴⁹O ye ice and cold, bless ye the Lord: praise and exalt him
    above all for ever.

⁵⁰O ye frost and snow, bless ye the Lord: praise and exalt
    him above all for ever.

⁵¹O ye lightnings and clouds, bless ye the Lord: praise and
    exalt him above all for ever.

⁵²O let the earth bless the Lord: praise and exalt him above
    all for ever.

⁵³O ye mountains and little hills, bless ye the Lord: praise
    and exalt him above all for ever.

⁵⁴O all ye things that grow on the earth, bless ye the Lord:
    praise and exalt him above all for ever.

⁵⁵O ye fountains, bless ye the Lord: praise and exalt him
    above all for ever.

⁵⁶O ye seas and rivers, bless ye the Lord: praise and exalt
    him above all for ever.

⁵⁷O ye whales, and all that move in the waters, bless ye the
    Lord: praise and exalt him above all for ever.

⁵⁸O all ye fowls of the air, bless ye the Lord: praise and exalt
    him above all for ever.

⁵⁹O all ye beasts and cattle, bless ye the Lord: praise and
    exalt him above all for ever.

⁶⁰O ye children of men, bless ye the Lord: praise and exalt
    him above all for ever.

⁶¹O Israel, bless ye the Lord: praise and exalt him above all
    for ever.

⁶²O ye priests of the Lord, bless ye the Lord: praise and exalt
    him above all for ever.

⁶³O ye servants of the Lord, bless ye the Lord: praise and
    exalt him above all for ever.

⁶⁴O ye spirits and souls of the righteous, bless ye the Lord:
    praise and exalt him above all for ever.

⁶⁵O ye holy and humble men of heart, bless ye the Lord:
    praise and exalt him above all for ever.

⁶⁶O Ananias, Azarias, and Misael, bless ye the Lord: praise
    and exalt him above all for ever: for he hath delivered
    us from hell, and saved us from the hand of death, and
    delivered us out of the midst of the furnace and burn-

---

57 *Whales*: Gk. *kētē*, large fish or sea monsters, perhaps alluding to Leviathan (cf. Job 41).   **66** *Hell*:

ing flame: even out of the midst of the fire hath he
delivered us.

[67] O give thanks unto the Lord, because he is gracious: for
his mercy endureth for ever.

[68] O all ye that worship the Lord, bless the God of gods,
praise him, and give him thanks: for his mercy endureth
for ever.

Gk. *hadēs* (see Matt 11:23 note).   **67–68** *O give thanks . . . for ever*: formal resemblance to Ps 136 turns
into virtual identity at this poem's conclusion; compare that psalm's opening and closing verses (1–3, 26).

The History of Susanna

ONE of the three "additions" to Daniel in the two Greek versions of that book, Susanna was placed at the end of Daniel 13 in the Septuagint, but before the book in the so-called Theodotion version—the one preferred from very early times by the church and the basis of KJV's translation. The latter placing is the more logical, given that this story—one of several extant Daniel legends not preserved in the Hebrew Bible—concerns Daniel's youth.

This early detective story combines elements of at least two folktale motifs: the faithful wife falsely accused but finally vindicated and the wise child who rectifies an unjust verdict. In addition, it resembles the episode of Joseph and Potiphar's wife from Genesis 39, providing a second biblical rewriting of that vivid tale. (See also the rape of Tamar and murder of Amnon; 2 Sam 13:1–39 and notes.) In its original form, the wise youth may not have been identified as Daniel; perhaps only later, sometime in the second or first century B.C.E., was the narrative seized on as an appealing way to exemplify the youthful wisdom attributed to this hero at Dan 1:17; 5:12; and so on. In any case the true center of this story is Susanna, who piously defends her chastity against the perverse advances and unjust accusations of hypocritical religious leaders serving their own lust rather than God's law.

Although no Semitic text of Susanna exists, it, like Bel and the Dragon, was likely composed in Aramaic; the significant differences between the Septuagint and Theodotion versions (some of which are noted in the following annotations) may reflect variations in the Aramaic versions translated, or, perhaps, editorial activity on the ancient translators' part.

The History of Susanna

set apart from the beginning of *Daniel*, because it is not in the Hebrew,
as neither the narration of *Bel and the Dragon*.

There dwelt a man in Babylon, called Joacim: ²and he took a wife, whose name was Susanna, the daughter of Chelcias, a very fair woman, and one that feared the Lord. ³Her parents also were righteous, and taught their daughter according to the law of Moses. ⁴Now Joacim was a great rich man, and had a fair garden joining unto his house: and to him resorted the Jews; because he was more honourable than all others. ⁵The same year were appointed two of the ancients of the people to be judges, such as the Lord spake of, that wickedness came from Babylon from ancient judges, who seemed to govern the people. ⁶These kept much at Joacim's house: and all that had any suits in law came unto them.

⁷Now when the people departed away at noon, Susanna went into her husband's garden to walk. ⁸And the two elders saw her going in every day, and walking; so that their lust was inflamed toward her. ⁹And they perverted their own mind, and turned away their eyes, that they might not look unto heaven, nor remember just judgments. ¹⁰And albeit they both were wounded with her love, yet durst not one shew another his grief. ¹¹For they were ashamed to declare their lust, that they desired to have to do with her. ¹²Yet they watched diligently from day to day to see her. ¹³And the one said to the other, Let us now go home: for it is dinner time. ¹⁴So when they were gone out, they parted the one from the other, and turning back again they came to the same place; and after that they had asked one another the cause, they acknowledged their lust: then appointed they a time both together, when they might find her alone.

¹⁵And it fell out, as they watched a fit time, she went in as before with two maids only, and she was desirous to wash herself in the garden: for it was hot. ¹⁶And there was no body there save the two elders, that had hid themselves, and watched her. ¹⁷Then she said to her maids, Bring me oil and washing balls, and shut the garden

---

1–27 Susanna falsely accused. Among the many notable differences between LXX and the text translated by KJV is the former's omission of vv. 15–18, 20–21, and 24–27. In addition, LXX seems to be missing its initial verses, for it begins with the second clause of v. 6. **3** *Taught their daughter . . . Moses*: she demonstrates her knowledge of appropriate legal procedure in vv. 43–44 (see note). **5** *Ancients*: elders. *That wickedness . . . people*: the exact quote is unidentified, but see Jer 23:14–15. Another possibility is Jer 29:21–23: an ancient interpretive tradition identified the two elders as the prophets Ahab and Zedekiah, condemned by that passage as adulterers and liars. **15** *She was . . . garden*: the scene of temptation calls to mind the story of the primeval transgression in Eden (Gen 3), as well as David's lust for the bathing Bathsheba (2 Sam 11:1–5). **17** *Washing balls*:

doors, that I may wash me. ¹⁸And they did as she bade them, and shut the garden doors, and went out themselves at privy doors to fetch the things that she had commanded them: but they saw not the elders, because they were hid.

¹⁹Now when the maids were gone forth, the two elders rose up, and ran unto her, saying, ²⁰Behold, the garden doors are shut, that no man can see us, and we are in love with thee; therefore consent unto us, and lie with us. ²¹If thou wilt not, we will bear witness against thee, that a young man was with thee: and therefore thou didst send away thy maids from thee. ²²Then Susanna sighed, and said, I am straitened on every side: for if I do this thing, it is death unto me: and if I do it not, I cannot escape your hands. ²³It is better for me to fall into your hands, and not do it, than to sin in the sight of the Lord. ²⁴With that Susanna cried with a loud voice: and the two elders cried out against her. ²⁵Then ran the one, and opened the garden door. ²⁶So when the servants of the house heard the cry in the garden, they rushed in at a privy door, to see what was done unto her. ²⁷But when the elders had declared their matter, the servants were greatly ashamed: for there was never such a report made of Susanna.

²⁸And it came to pass the next day, when the people were assembled to her husband Joacim, the two elders came also full of mischievous imagination against Susanna to put her to death; ²⁹and said before the people, Send for Susanna, the daughter of Chelcias, Joacim's wife. And so they sent. ³⁰So she came with her father and mother, her children, and all her kindred. ³¹Now Susanna was a very delicate woman, and beauteous to behold. ³²And these wicked men commanded to uncover her face, (for she was covered) that they might be filled with her beauty. ³³Therefore her friends and all that saw her wept.

³⁴Then the two elders stood up in the midst of the people, and laid their hands upon her head. ³⁵And she weeping looked up toward heaven: for her heart trusted in the Lord. ³⁶And the elders said, As we walked in the garden alone, this woman came in with two maids, and shut the garden doors, and sent the maids away. ³⁷Then a young man, who there was hid, came unto her, and lay with her. ³⁸Then we that stood in a corner of the garden, seeing this wickedness, ran unto them. ³⁹And when we saw them together, the man we could not hold: for he was stronger than we, and opened the door, and leaped out. ⁴⁰But having taken this woman, we asked who the young man was, but she would not tell us: these things do we testify. ⁴¹Then the assembly believed them, as those that were the elders and judges of the people: so they condemned her to death.

---

soap, although the Greek refers to unguent.   **18** *Privy doors* lit. "side doors" (also in v. 26).   **20** *In love*: more literally "in desire" or "in lust."   **22** *Straitened*: constrained. *It is death for me*: OT legislation regarding adultery sentenced the guilty parties to death (see Lev 20:10; Deut 22:22), but Susanna may here be speaking figuratively.   **23** *It is . . . Lord*: recalling Joseph's words to Potiphar's wife at Gen 39:9.   **25** *Opened the garden door*: to support their story of Susanna's escaped lover. **27** Here, as often, *servants* (Gk. *douloi*) are more literally "slaves."

28–44 Susanna's trial. LXX omits vv. 42–43 and has other differences as well.   **28** *Imagination*: designs.   **30** *Her father . . . kindred*: that Joacim is not mentioned suggests he believed the elders.   **32** *Covered*: veiled. Her unveiling is an act of mortification, a discreet version of God's more vulgar threats in the allegory of the unfaithful wife at Ezek 16 (vv. 35–39). (LXX implies that she was violently disrobed rather than unveiled.)   **34** *Laid their hands upon her head*: cf. Lev 24:14.

⁴²Then Susanna cried out with a loud voice, and said, O everlasting God, that knowest the secrets, and knowest all things before they be: ⁴³thou knowest that they have borne false witness against me, and, behold, I must die; whereas I never did such things as these men have maliciously invented against me. ⁴⁴And the Lord heard her voice.

⁴⁵Therefore when she was led to be put to death, the Lord raised up the holy spirit of a young youth, whose name was Daniel: ⁴⁶who cried with a loud voice, I am clear from the blood of this woman. ⁴⁷Then all the people turned them toward him, and said, What mean these words that thou hast spoken? ⁴⁸So he standing in the midst of them, said, Are ye such fools, ye sons of Israel, that without examination or knowledge of the truth ye have condemned a daughter of Israel? ⁴⁹Return again to the place of judgment: for they have borne false witness against her.

⁵⁰Wherefore all the people turned again in haste, and the elders said unto him, Come, sit down among us, and shew it us, seeing God hath given thee the honour of an elder. ⁵¹Then said Daniel unto them, Put these two aside one far from another, and I will examine them. ⁵²So when they were put asunder one from another, he called one of them, and said unto him, O thou that art waxen old in wickedness, now thy sins which thou hast committed aforetime are come to light: ⁵³for thou hast pronounced false judgment, and hast condemned the innocent, and hast let the guilty go free; albeit the Lord saith, The innocent and righteous shalt thou not slay. ⁵⁴Now then, if thou hast seen her, tell me, Under what tree sawest thou them companying together? Who answered, Under a mastick tree. ⁵⁵And Daniel said, Very well; thou hast lied against thine own head; for even now the angel of God hath received the sentence of God to cut thee in two. ⁵⁶So he put him aside, and commanded to bring the other, and said unto him, O thou seed of Chanaan, and not of Juda, beauty hath deceived thee, and lust hath perverted thine heart. ⁵⁷Thus have ye dealt with the daughters of Israel, and they for fear companied with you: but the daughter of Juda would not abide your wickedness. ⁵⁸Now therefore tell me, Under what tree didst thou take them companying together? Who answered, Under a holm tree. ⁵⁹Then said Daniel unto him,

---

42 *That knowest the secrets*: see Dan 2:22; cf. Ps 44:21. In LXX, the prayer occurs earlier (in v. 35). **43–44** *Thou knowest . . . voice*: her prayer in these circumstances necessarily evokes the legal strictures of Deut 19:16–21, which are followed as the story progresses. **45–64 Susanna's vindication.** Whereas here Daniel is motivated by the holy spirit (cf. Dan 4:9; 5:11), in LXX an angel of the Lord intervenes, as in Dan 9:21; 10:5–6. **46** *I am clear . . . woman*: cf. Matt 27:24. Unlike Pilate, however, Daniel acts to save the victim of perverted justice. **48** *Without examination*: they have not even bothered to cross-examine the accusers, thereby neglecting the formal procedure (laid out in Deut 19:18) to which Susanna's prayer alluded (vv. 43–44). **53** *The innocent and the righteous . . . slay*: Exod 23:7. **54** *Mastick*: Gk. *schinon*; the name puns on the verb used by Daniel in v. 55, "cut in two" (*schisei*); cf. v. 58 note. **55** *Cut thee in two*: perhaps an allusion to Solomon's famous judicial deception (1 Kgs 3:16–28). **56** *Seed of Chanaan* [Canaan]: see Gen 9:20–27. **57** *Daughters of Israel . . . daughter of Juda*: the Northern Kingdom (Israel) had fallen to Assyria and been resettled long before Babylon conquered the Southern Kingdom (Judah), leading southerners to doubt not only their neighbors' religious uprightness but their ethnic and moral purity as well (cf. 2 Kgs 17; Hos 4:15; etc.). **58** *Holm*: Gk. *prinos*, punning on *prisai* (v. 59), translated "cut in two."

Well; thou hast also lied against thine own head: for the angel of God waiteth with the sword to cut thee in two, that he may destroy you. [60] With that all the assembly cried out with a loud voice, and praised God, who saveth them that trust in him. [61] And they arose against the two elders, (for Daniel had convicted them of false witness by their own mouth;) [62] and according to the law of Moses they did unto them in such sort as they maliciously intended to do to their neighbour: and they put them to death. Thus the innocent blood was saved the same day. [63] Therefore Chelcias and his wife praised God for their daughter Susanna, with Joacim her husband, and all the kindred, because there was no dishonesty found in her.

[64] From that day forth was Daniel had in great reputation in the sight of the people.

59 *The angel . . . sword*: perhaps another echo of the story of the primeval transgression; cf. Gen 3:24. **62** *According to the law . . . neighbour*: see Deut 19:19. *They put them to death*: LXX is much more graphic, specifying that they were thrown into a ravine and consumed by fire from the angel of the Lord.

The History of the Destruction of Bel and the Dragon

BEL and the Dragon consists of two separate stories, both describing confrontations between Daniel and Babylonian idols. What binds them together is the motif of eating: surreptitious eating by the priests of Bel, fatal eating by the "dragon," and divinely ordained sustenance for Daniel in the den of lions who are supposed to consume him.

These selections from the substantial collection of Daniel legends not found in the eponymous Old Testament book were likely written in Aramaic in the second or third century B.C.E. and later became appended to at least some early versions of Daniel—though not the one preserved in the Masoretic Text, which KJV translates. There are several intriguing theories about their origins. They may constitute narrative expansions of Jer 51:34–35, 44. Alternatively, they may have been composed to dramatize the mockery of idols found in such texts as Isa 44:9–20; 46:1–2, 6–8; and, more extensively, Wis 13:1–15:9. Finally, some find the destruction of the "dragon" (really a snake; see v. 23 note) and that of serpentine Tiamat in the Babylonian Creation Epic uncannily similar, speculating that verses 23–27, at least, amount to a parodic recasting of that classic Babylonian myth (analogous to, albeit less ambitious than, the first creation account in Genesis).

Like the other Daniel additions, KJV translates not the Septuagint but the so-called Theodotion text, which was the church's chosen version of Daniel from very early times. There are a number of significant differences between the two, but both agree in placing Bel and the Dragon at the end of Daniel, as a kind of appendix.

Bel and the Dragon

cut off from the end of *Daniel*.

A nd king Astyages was gathered to his fathers, and Cyrus of Persia received his kingdom. ²And Daniel conversed with the king, and was honoured above all his friends. ³Now the Babylonians had an idol, called Bel, and there were spent upon him every day twelve great measures of fine flour, and forty sheep, and six vessels of wine. ⁴And the king worshipped it, and went daily to adore it: but Daniel worshipped his own God. And the king said unto him, Why dost not thou worship Bel? ⁵Who answered and said, Because I may not worship idols made with hands, but the living God, who hath created the heaven and the earth, and hath sovereignty over all flesh. ⁶Then said the king unto him, Thinkest thou not that Bel is a living god? seest thou not how much he eateth and drinketh every day? ⁷Then Daniel smiled, and said, O king, be not deceived: for this is but clay within, and brass without, and did never eat or drink any thing. ⁸So the king was wroth, and called for his priests, and said unto them, If ye tell me not who this is that devoureth these expences, ye shall die. ⁹But if ye can certify me that Bel devoureth them, then Daniel shall die: for he hath spoken blasphemy against Bel. And Daniel said unto the king, Let it be according to thy word. ¹⁰(Now the priests of Bel were threescore and ten, beside their wives and children.) And the king went with Daniel into the temple of Bel.

¹¹So Bel's priests said, Lo, we go out: but thou, O king, set on the meat, and make ready the wine, and shut the door fast, and seal it with thine own signet; ¹²and to morrow when thou comest in, if thou findest not that Bel hath eaten up all, we will suffer death; or else Daniel, that speaketh falsely against us. ¹³And they little regarded it: for under the table they had made a privy entrance, whereby they entered in continually, and consumed those things. ¹⁴So when they were gone forth, the king set meats before Bel. Now Daniel had commanded his servants to bring ashes, and those they strewed throughout all the temple in the

1–22 Daniel and the statue of Bel. There are a number of differences between this and the LXX version; most notably, here in v. 22 Daniel destroys Bel; in LXX, the king does. (Compare also Herodotus's description of Bel's temple and very different account of its plunder at 1.183; the account in Strabo 16.1.5 specifies that it was destroyed.) **1** *Cyrus of Persia*: Cyrus II; see Dan 5:31 note. He began to rule Persia in 559 B.C.E.; defeated his grandfather Astyages, king of the Medes, in 550; and died in 530. **2** *Conversed with*: "was a companion to" (NRSV). **3** *Bel*: a title of Marduk, the chief Babylonian god; cf. Isa 46:1–2; Jer 50:2; Babylonian Creation Epic (Appendix to OT, p. 1689). **5** *Idols made with hands*: cf. Isa 2:8; Acts 19:26; Wis 14:8; etc. **8** *Wroth*: indignant. **11** *Set on the meat*: lay out the food. **13** *Little regarded it*: were unconcerned. *Privy*: secret.

presence of the king alone: then went they out, and shut the door, and sealed it with the king's signet, and so departed. [15]Now in the night came the priests with their wives and children, (as they were wont to do,) and did eat and drink up all.

[16]In the morning betime the king arose, and Daniel with him. [17]And the king said, Daniel, are the seals whole? And he said, Yea, O king, they be whole. [18]And as soon as he had opened the door, the king looked upon the table, and cried with a loud voice, Great art thou, O Bel, and with thee is no deceit at all. [19]Then laughed Daniel, and held the king that he should not go in, and said, Behold now the pavement, and mark well whose footsteps are these. [20]And the king said, I see the footsteps of men, women, and children. And then the king was angry, [21]and took the priests with their wives and children, who shewed him the privy doors, where they came in, and consumed such things as were upon the table. [22]Therefore the king slew them, and delivered Bel into Daniel's power, who destroyed him and his temple.

[23]And in that same place there was a great dragon, which they of Babylon worshipped. [24]And the king said unto Daniel, Wilt thou also say that this is of brass? lo, he liveth, he eateth and drinketh; thou canst not say that he is no living god: therefore worship him. [25]Then said Daniel unto the king, I will worship the Lord my God: for he is the living God. [26]But give me leave, O king, and I shall slay this dragon without sword or staff. The king said, I give thee leave. [27]Then Daniel took pitch, and fat, and hair, and did seethe them together, and made lumps thereof: this he put in the dragon's mouth, and so the dragon burst in sunder: and Daniel said, Lo, these are the gods ye worship.

[28]When they of Babylon heard that, they took great indignation, and conspired against the king, saying, The king is become a Jew, and he hath destroyed Bel, he hath slain the dragon, and put the priests to death. [29]So they came to the king, and said, Deliver us Daniel, or else we will destroy thee and thine house. [30]Now when the king saw that they pressed him sore, being constrained, he delivered Daniel unto them: [31]who cast him into the lions' den: where he was six days. [32]And in the den there were seven lions, and they had given them every day two carcases, and two sheep: which then were not given to them, to the intent they might devour Daniel.

[33]Now there was in Jewry a prophet, called Habbacuc, who had made pottage, and had broken bread in a bowl, and was going into the field, for to bring it to the

---

16 *Betime*: early. **22** *Delivered Bel . . . temple*: as the Babylonians had destroyed YHWH's temple (2 Kgs 25:9).

23–42 Daniel and the snake. This section combines three stories: the destruction of the snake (vv. 23–27); Daniel in the lions' den, a parallel version of Dan 6:10–28 (vv. 28–32, 40–42); and, inset into the latter, another story about the prophet Habakkuk (vv. 33–39). **23** *Dragon*: Gk. *drakōn*, which can also refer to a serpent. **27** *Seethe*: boil. **28** *The king is become a Jew*: compare the decree issued at the end of the lions' den story in Daniel (6:25–27). **29** *House*: family. **31** *Six days*: in the OT account, he is in the den for only one night (Dan 6:16–20). **32** *Carcases*: the Greek word refers to human corpses. **33** *Jewry*: Judea. *Habbacuc*: the OT prophet, who may have prophesied a few years before Babylon's conquest of the Southern Kingdom. This story imagines Habakkuk remaining in Judea at the time of the exile, as did Jeremiah. *Pottage*: stew.

reapers. [34]But the angel of the Lord said unto Habbacuc, Go, carry the dinner that thou hast into Babylon unto Daniel, who is in the lions' den. [35]And Habbacuc said, Lord, I never saw Babylon; neither do I know where the den is. [36]Then the angel of the Lord took him by the crown, and bare him by the hair of his head, and through the vehemency of his spirit set him in Babylon over the den. [37]And Habbacuc cried, saying, O Daniel, Daniel, take the dinner which God hath sent thee. [38]And Daniel said, Thou hast remembered me, O God: neither hast thou forsaken them that seek thee and love thee. [39]So Daniel arose, and did eat: and the angel of the Lord set Habbacuc in his own place again immediately.

[40]Upon the seventh day the king went to bewail Daniel: and when he came to the den, he looked in, and, behold, Daniel was sitting. [41]Then cried the king with a loud voice, saying, Great art thou, O Lord God of Daniel, and there is none other beside thee. [42]And he drew him out, and cast those that were the cause of his destruction into the den: and they were devoured in a moment before his face.

34 *Go, carry the dinner . . . Daniel*: not only does God miraculously keep the lions from eating Daniel, but he also ensures that Daniel himself is well fed in the den.   **36** *Crown*: i.e., of his head; for this mode of prophetic transport, cf. Ezek 8:3. *Through the vehemency of his spirit*: alternatively "with the speed of wind."   **41** *Great art thou . . . thee*: recalling his earlier praise of Bel (v. 18).   **42** *Cast those . . . face*: cf. Dan 6:24.

The Prayer of Manasses

ACCORDING to 2 Chr 33:11–13, Manasseh, the wicked king of Judah, while in exile composed a prayer asking forgiveness for his sins. The Old Testament account mentions two literary works that include this prayer, the "book of the kings of Israel" and the "sayings of the seers" (2 Chr 33:18–19), neither of which survives. The moving penitential prayer that follows is a pseud-epigraphical composition meant to fill that gap.

The Prayer frequently recalls Psalm 51, the most famous of the so-called peni-tential psalms, and echoes other biblical texts as well. Its strong resemblance to postexilic literary confessions (especially the Song of the Three Holy Children) suggests that it was created in the second or first century B.C.E., if not later. It may have been composed in a Semitic language, or it may have been written originally in Greek.

It is included in the Odes, a book of the Septuagint that follows the Psalms in some manuscripts, but it appears elsewhere in other bibles (e.g., after 2 Chroni-cles in many medieval Vulgate manuscripts, and in an appendix along with 1 and 2 Esdras in the Clementine Vulgate [1590], the most important Catholic Bible published in the wake of the Council of Trent). It is also preserved in the third-century C.E. *Didascalia Apostolorum*, which survives in its entirety only in Syriac, and the Syriac version of the Prayer is in fact the earliest one extant. It differs from the Greek, which KJV translates, at various points, a few of which are remarked in the annotations that follow.

For more information, the reader can consult the heavily annotated transla-tion, with extensive introduction, in J. H. Charlesworth, *Old Testament Pseud-epigrapha* (Garden City, NY: Doubleday, 1986), 2.625–37, which informs this introduction and the annotations that follow.

The Prayer of Manasses
King of Juda

When he was Holden Captive
in Babylon

O Lord, Almighty God of our fathers, Abraham, Isaac, and Jacob, and of their righteous seed; who hast made heaven and earth, with all the ornament thereof; who hast bound the sea by the word of thy commandment; who hast shut up the deep, and sealed it by thy terrible and glorious name; whom all men fear, and tremble before thy power; for the majesty of thy glory cannot be borne, and thine angry threatening toward sinners is importable: but thy merciful promise is unmeasurable and unsearchable; for thou art the most high Lord, of great compassion, longsuffering, very merciful, and repentest of the evils of men.

Thou, O Lord, according to thy great goodness hast promised repentance and forgiveness to them that have sinned against thee: and of thine infinite mercies hast appointed repentance unto sinners, that they may be saved. Thou therefore, O Lord, that art the God of the just, hast not appointed repentance to the just, as to Abraham, and Isaac, and Jacob, which have not sinned against thee; but thou hast appointed repentance unto me that am a sinner: for I have sinned above the number of the sands of the sea. My transgressions, O Lord, are multiplied: my

O Lord . . . seed: because the Prayer displays regular thematic parallelism, many modern translations versify it; e.g., "O Lord, Almighty God of our fathers / Abraham, Isaac, and Jacob, and of their righteous seed / etc." Who hast made . . . glorious name: alluding to the opening verses of Genesis, as well as to alternative biblical creation accounts such as Ps 74:12–17; 89:9–12; Isa 51:9–10. Ornament: Gk. kosmos, which connotes both beauty and order. Deep: Gk. abyssos, "bottomless pit." The same Greek word translates Heb. tehom in LXX Gen 1:2 (see note), which the Syriac version uses here as a loanword, thereby alluding to the ancient Near Eastern cosmogonic myth of the creator god's triumph over primeval chaos (e.g., the Babylonian Creation Epic; see Appendix to OT, p. 1689). All men: the Greek reads "all things." Importable: unbearable, irresistible. Of great compassion . . . merciful: echoing Ps 86:15; cf. LXX Joel 2:13. Repentest of the evils of men: this seems to suggest that God's mercy to sinners stems from his own responsibility for human evil—responsibility he accepts as the cosmic creator. I have sinned . . . sea: see 2 Kgs 21:1–16; 2 Chr 33:2–9. Above the number of the sands of the sea ironically recalls God's promises to the righteous patriarchs just mentioned (Gen 22:17; 26:4; 32:12; Exod 32:13; etc.). My transgressions . . . my transgressions are multiplied: the

transgressions are multiplied, and I am not worthy to behold and see the height of heaven for the multitude of mine iniquities. I am bowed down with many iron bands, that I cannot lift up mine head, neither have any release: for I have provoked thy wrath, and done evil before thee: I did not thy will, neither kept I thy commandments: I have set up abominations, and have multiplied offences.

Now therefore I bow the knee of mine heart, beseeching thee of grace. I have sinned, O Lord, I have sinned, and I acknowledge mine iniquities: wherefore, I humbly beseech thee, forgive me, O Lord, forgive me, and destroy me not with mine iniquities. Be not angry with me for ever, by reserving evil for me; neither condemn me into the lower parts of the earth. For thou art the God, even the God of them that repent; and in me thou wilt shew all thy goodness: for thou wilt save me, that am unworthy, according to thy great mercy. Therefore I will praise thee for ever all the days of my life: for all the powers of the heavens do praise thee, and thine is the glory for ever and ever. Amen.

---

repetition dramatizes the multiplication. These words are not in the Syriac version, although subsequent repetitions are (*I have sinned, O Lord, I have sinned* and *Forgive me, O Lord, forgive me*). *Multitude of mine iniquities*: the Syriac adds "I have no strength so that I can lift up my eyes. And now, O Lord, I am justly afflicted, and as I deserve I am harassed; for already I am ensnared" (trans. Charlesworth). *Many iron bands*: according to 2 Chr 33:11, Manasseh was taken "captive in manacles, and bound with fetters" (see note). *Neither have any release*: the Syriac reads "for I do not deserve to lift up my eyes and look and see the height of heaven, because of the multitude of the iniquity of my wicked deeds" (trans. Charlesworth). *I did not . . . commandments*: the Syriac version omits this phrase. *Set up abominations*: probably a reference to idolatry, which the Syriac version makes explicit. *The lower parts of the earth*: the realm of the dead; cf. Ezek 26:20; 31:14; etc. *Powers of the heaven*: the heavenly hosts (cf. Neh 9:6).

The First Book of the Maccabees

I N order to appreciate what kind of history 1 Maccabees is, and to understand its purposes and design, we must set it against its companion volume, 2 Maccabees. Both deal with the same historical period, when Jews resisted the Seleucid rulers' attempts to hellenize Judea. 1 Maccabees covers the whole sweep of the forty or so years from Mattathias's launch of the revolt in 167 B.C.E. to 134, when John Hyrcanus became high priest. The book may have been written during the later years of John's rule, which ended in 104; it was certainly written before 63 B.C.E., because its overwhelmingly positive view of Rome would have been unimaginable after Pompey's conquest of Jerusalem in that year. Although the oldest extant version is in Greek, it is probably a translation of a work written originally in Hebrew; 2 Maccabees, in contrast, was composed in Greek, in a highly literary style.

Also in contrast to 2 Maccabees is this book's totally committed support for the cause of the Hasmoneans. (On the family name, see note to 2:1–28.) Here recent Jewish history is Hasmonean history, exemplified in the attitude taken toward the pietist martyrs who die in the early days of the revolt (see 2:29–38 and note; cf. 2:42 note). While for the author of 2 Maccabees their fate is a vital element in the unfolding of God's retributive design, 1 Maccabees presents it as a wasting of God's resources. Unlike these pietists, the Hasmonean forces, under Mattathias and his sons, react flexibly and heroically to the crisis precipitated by Antiochus IV Epiphanes' decree, as emphasized by this work's frequent allusions to major figures of Old Testament history. In 2 Maccabees Scripture is also cited, but with no special focus on its heroes. And in place of the frequent supernaturalism of 2 Maccabees, this book contains a number of highly rhetorical and even poetic passages celebrating the achievements of its Hasmonean heroes. It is not, however, a parochial account of Judea's war with the Seleucid Empire. 1 Maccabees offers a wide view of the Mediterranean world, showing how the Hasmoneans leveraged the support of surrounding kings and empires—in particular the growing power of Rome.

As history, 1 Maccabees is restrained and precise, except for conventionally exaggerated enumerations of armed forces and occasionally erroneous geography (which often seems to be the fault of the Greek translator or later scribes, rather than of the book's author). It is an important and reliable source of information for the period of Judean history it covers, as well as for the Seleucid Empire. Many readers notice that 1 Maccabees' literary artifice becomes less conspicuous as the book progresses: biblical allusions are rarer, as are the highly rhetorical celebrations and laments that frequently appear in its early chapters. One explanation of the book's stylistic evolution is that 1 Maccabees finds itself progressively burdened with the responsibility of getting its history right. As its subject matter slowly forces it to shift from offering a relatively straightforward story of conflict between Judea and the Seleucid Empire to presenting a quite complex account of internal conflict among the Seleucid royalty and elites, it increasingly becomes focused on accurate and intelligible reportage, thereby excluding, or at least marginelizing, more belletristic literary pretensions.

But 1 Maccabees should not be idealized as a historical account, for in at least one respect it patently refuses to acknowledge the complexity of the events it narrates: it tends to downplay the internal religious and political tensions that marked the Hasmonean period in Judea. Throughout the book, the complex and diverse motives of Jewish opposition to the Hasmoneans are dismissed with such blanket labels as "wicked" and "ungodly"; even those who agree with their resistance to the Seleucid decrees but favor passive resistance here find themselves quickly co-opted into the Hasmoneans' armed struggle (see 2:29–43 and v. 42 note). In the tradition of the biblical accounts of Israel's kings and of Jesus, however, 1 Maccabees is joined by a companion volume that presents some of the same information from a somewhat different ideological and theological perspective—one more sympathetic to at least some of the constituencies that this volume is content to marginalize.

For more detailed exposition of 1 Maccabees, the reader can consult Jonathan A. Goldstein's Anchor Bible commentary, *I Maccabees: A New Translation, with Introduction and Commentary* (Garden City, NY: Doubleday, 1976), which frequently informs this introduction and the notes that follow.

The First Book of the Maccabees

1 And it happened, after that Alexander son of Philip, the Macedonian, who came out of the land of Chettiim, had smitten Darius king of the Persians and Medes, that he reigned in his stead, the first over Greece, ²and made many wars, and won many strong holds, and slew the kings of the earth, ³and went through to the ends of the earth, and took spoils of many nations, insomuch that the earth was quiet before him; whereupon he was exalted, and his heart was lifted up. ⁴And he gathered a mighty strong host, and ruled over countries, and nations, and kings, who became tributaries unto him. ⁵And after these things he fell sick, and perceived that he should die. ⁶Wherefore he called his servants, such as were honourable, and had been brought up with him from his youth, and parted his kingdom among them, while he was yet alive. ⁷So Alexander reigned twelve years, and then died. ⁸And his servants bare rule every one in his place. ⁹And after his death they all put crowns upon themselves; so did their sons after them many years: and evils were multiplied in the earth. ¹⁰And there came out of them a wicked root, Antiochus surnamed Epiphanes, son of Antiochus the king, who had been an hostage at Rome, and he reigned in the hundred and thirty and seventh year of the kingdom of the Greeks.

¹¹In those days went there out of Israel wicked men, who persuaded many, saying, Let us go and make a covenant with the heathen that are round about us: for

1:1–10 **The death of Alexander.** A brief glance backward, noting Alexander's conquest of Persia, his rule over much of the known world, his death, and the dissolution of his empire. **1:1** *Alexander . . . the Macedonian*: Alexander the Great (356–323 B.C.E.); soon after becoming king of Macedon in the autumn of 336, he was recognized as leader of the League of Corinth, an alliance of Greek states established by his father. *Chettiim*: a Greek transliteration of a Hebrew word, which originally referred to Cyprus (so "Kittim," Gen 10:4; see note) but here is used of all Greece. *Darius king . . . Medes*: Darius III Artashata, the final ruler of the Achaemenid Empire (336–330 B.C.E.). **1:3** *He was . . . lifted up*: signaling his hubris, and perhaps more specifically alluding to his self-designation as son of Zeus Ammon. **1:4** *Host*: army. **1:6** *And parted . . . alive*: in fact, Alexander's empire was divided after his death as various generals sought to control it. **1:10** *Antiochus surnamed Epiphanes*: Antiochus IV, ruler of the Seleucid Empire, 175–164 B.C.E. (a fragment of the territory that Alexander controlled; at this time it contained Cilicia and Syria, and stretched as far east as central Asia, including Persia). He had been held hostage in Rome as a condition of the treaty of Apamea (188 B.C.E.), established after Rome had thwarted his father's attempt to extend the Seleucid Empire as far west as Thrace. He became king after the assassination of his elder brother, Seleucus IV Philopator. *Epiphanes* may mean "illustrious" or, more grandly, "god manifest." *The hundred . . . Greeks*: 175 B.C.E. The years in this text are calculated from the founding of the Seleucid monarchy. (All dates given are approximate.)

1:11–15 **Hellenization in Judea.** For another account of the hellenizing process, see 2 Macc 4:7–20. **1:11** *Wicked men*: hellenizers, trying to introduce Greek customs. Throughout the text, they are disparaged with the labels *wicked* and "ungodly." *Let us go . . . about us*: in violation of God's

since we departed from them we have had much sorrow. ¹²So this device pleased them well. ¹³Then certain of the people were so forward herein, that they went to the king, who gave them licence to do after the ordinances of the heathen: ¹⁴whereupon they built a place of exercise at Jerusalem according to the customs of the heathen: ¹⁵and made themselves uncircumcised, and forsook the holy covenant, and joined themselves to the heathen, and were sold to do mischief.

¹⁶Now when the kingdom was established before Antiochus, he thought to reign over Egypt, that he might have the dominion of two realms. ¹⁷Wherefore he entered into Egypt with a great multitude, with chariots, and elephants, and horsemen, and a great navy, ¹⁸and made war against Ptolemee king of Egypt: but Ptolemee was afraid of him, and fled; and many were wounded to death. ¹⁹Thus they got the strong cities in the land of Egypt, and he took the spoils thereof. ²⁰And after that Antiochus had smitten Egypt, he returned again in the hundred forty and third year, and went up against Israel and Jerusalem with a great multitude, ²¹and entered proudly into the sanctuary, and took away the golden altar, and the candlestick of light, and all the vessels thereof, ²²and the table of the shewbread, and the pouring vessels, and the vials, and the censers of gold, and the veil, and the crowns, and the golden ornaments that were before the temple, all which he pulled off. ²³He took also the silver and the gold, and the precious vessels: also he took the hidden treasures which he found. ²⁴And when he had taken all away, he went into his own land, having made a great massacre, and spoken very proudly. ²⁵Therefore there was great mourning in Israel, in every place where they were; ²⁶so that the princes and elders mourned, the virgins and young men were made feeble, and the beauty of women was changed. ²⁷Every bridegroom took up lamentation, and she that sat in the marriage chamber was in heaviness. ²⁸The land also was moved for the inhabitants thereof, and all the house of Jacob was covered with confusion.

²⁹And after two years fully expired the king sent his chief collector of tribute unto the cities of Juda, who came unto Jerusalem with a great multitude, ³⁰and spake peaceable words unto them, but all was deceit: for when they had given him credence, he fell suddenly upon the city, and smote it very sore, and destroyed

---

commandments (see Exod 34:11–16; Deut 7:1–5).   **1:12** *Device*: plan.   **1:13** *Heathen*: alternatively "Gentiles" (so throughout).   **1:14** *Place of exercise*: Gk. *gymnasion*, a center of Greek education.   **1:15** *Made themselves uncircumcised*: see 1 Cor 7:18 note. *Were sold to*: better "sold themselves to."

1:16–28 Antiochus desecrates the temple. Compare 2 Macc 5:1–23; Dan 11:21–39 and notes.   **1:18** *Ptolemee*: Ptolemy VI Philometer, who ruled the Egyptian fragment of Alexander's divided empire, ca. 176–145 B.C.E.   **1:20** *After that . . . Egypt*: Rome in fact forced Antiochus to abandon his attempt on Egypt and Dan 11:30 suggests that this humiliation prompted his desecration of the sanctuary. *The hundred forty and third year*: 169 B.C.E.   **1:21–23** *The golden altar . . . found*: the temple's accoutrements are described in Exod 25–30; for a brief list, see Exod 39:33–41.   **1:22** *Vials*: bowls.   **1:25–28** *Therefore there . . . confusion*: the regular thematic parallelism suggests that the lament is poetic, and many modern translations versify it.   **1:26** *Princes*: rulers (as often).   **1:27** *Was in heaviness*: lit. "mourned."   **1:28** *House of Jacob*: Israel.

1:29–40 The sack of Jerusalem. Compare 2 Macc 5:24–26.   **1:29** *His chief collector of tribute*: scholars conjecture that this represents a Greek mistranslation of a Hebrew phrase meaning "chief of the Mysians" (identified as Apollonius by 2 Macc 5:24). Mysia was a region in northwest

much people of Israel. ³¹And when he had taken the spoils of the city, he set it on fire, and pulled down the houses and walls thereof on every side. ³²But the women and children took they captive, and possessed the cattle. ³³Then builded they the city of David with a great and strong wall, and with mighty towers, and made it a strong hold for them. ³⁴And they put therein a sinful nation, wicked men, and fortified themselves therein. ³⁵They stored it also with armour and victuals, and when they had gathered together the spoils of Jerusalem, they laid them up there, and so they became a sore snare: ³⁶for it was a place to lie in wait against the sanctuary, and an evil adversary to Israel. ³⁷Thus they shed innocent blood on every side of the sanctuary, and defiled it: ³⁸insomuch that the inhabitants of Jerusalem fled because of them: whereupon the city was made an habitation of strangers, and became strange to those that were born in her; and her own children left her. ³⁹Her sanctuary was laid waste like a wilderness, her feasts were turned into mourning, her sabbaths into reproach, her honour into contempt. ⁴⁰As had been her glory, so was her dishonour increased, and her excellency was turned into mourning.

⁴¹Moreover king Antiochus wrote to his whole kingdom, that all should be one people, ⁴²and every one should leave his laws: so all the heathen agreed according to the commandment of the king. ⁴³Yea, many also of the Israelites consented to his religion, and sacrificed unto idols, and profaned the sabbath. ⁴⁴For the king had sent letters by messengers unto Jerusalem and the cities of Juda, that they should follow the strange laws of the land, ⁴⁵and forbid burnt offerings, and sacrifice, and drink offerings, in the temple; and that they should profane the sabbaths and festival days: ⁴⁶and pollute the sanctuary and holy people: ⁴⁷set up altars, and groves, and chapels of idols, and sacrifice swine's flesh, and unclean beasts: ⁴⁸that they should also leave their children uncircumcised, and make their souls abominable with all manner of uncleanness and profanation: ⁴⁹to the end they might forget the law, and change all the ordinances. ⁵⁰And whosoever would not do according to the commandment of the king, he said, he should die. ⁵¹In the selfsame manner wrote he to his whole kingdom, and appointed overseers over all the people, commanding the cities of Juda to sacrifice, city by city. ⁵²Then many of the people were gathered unto them, to wit, every one that

---

Asia Minor that sent mercenaries to aid the Seleucids. **1:33** *Builded*: in the sense of "fortified." *City of David*: Jerusalem. **1:35** *Victuals*: provisions. **1:36–40** *For it . . . mourning*: the regular parallelism again suggests poetry; cf. Pss 74 and 79, which also lament foreign occupation and devastation of the temple. **1:38** *Strangers . . . strange*: foreigners . . . foreign (so throughout). **1:39** *Her feasts were turned into mourning*: cf. Amos 8:10.

1:41–64 Apostasy and martyrdom. Compare 2 Macc 6–7. This section narrates Antiochus's attempt to eradicate the Jews' distinctive religious practices (vv. 41–53), a misguided attempt to promote unity by forcing cultural assimilation. It then provides a general description of the Jewish resistance that followed (vv. 54–64; contrast the more vivid and extensive account in 2 Maccabees). The decree itself is not quoted but summarized by a hostile narrator. **1:47** *Groves*: KJV suggests a connection with the sacred posts or trees associated with Canaanite worship (cf. Deut 7:5; 12:3; 16:21–17:1 and notes), but the Greek word refers more generally to a piece of land dedicated to a god. *Chapels*: shrines or temples. *Sacrifice swine's flesh*: customary in pagan rituals, but abhorrent to Jews; cf. Lev 11:7.

forsook the law; and so they committed evils in the land; [53]and drove the Israelites into secret places, even wheresoever they could flee for succour.

[54]Now the fifteenth day of the month Casleu, in the hundred forty and fifth year, they set up the abomination of desolation upon the altar, and builded idol altars throughout the cities of Juda on every side; [55]and burnt incense at the doors of their houses, and in the streets. [56]And when they had rent in pieces the books of the law which they found, they burnt them with fire. [57]And wheresoever was found with any the book of the testament, or if any consented to the law, the king's commandment was, that they should put him to death. [58]Thus did they by their authority unto the Israelites every month, to as many as were found in the cities. [59]Now the five and twentieth day of the month they did sacrifice upon the idol altar, which was upon the altar of God. [60]At which time according to the commandment they put to death certain women, that had caused their children to be circumcised. [61]And they hanged the infants about their necks, and rifled their houses, and slew them that had circumcised them. [62]Howbeit many in Israel were fully resolved and confirmed in themselves not to eat any unclean thing. [63]Wherefore they chose rather to die, that they might not be defiled with meats, and that they might not profane the holy covenant: so then they died. [64]And there was very great wrath upon Israel.

2 In those days arose Mattathias the son of John, the son of Simeon, a priest of the sons of Joarib, from Jerusalem, and dwelt in Modin. [2]And he had five sons, Joannan, called Caddis: [3]Simon, called Thassi: [4]Judas, who was called Maccabeus: [5]Eleazar, called Avaran: and Jonathan, whose surname was Apphus.

[6]And when he saw the blasphemies that were committed in Juda and Jerusalem, [7]he said, Woe is me! wherefore was I born to see this misery of my people, and of the holy city, and to dwell there, when it was delivered into the hand of the enemy, and the sanctuary into the hand of strangers? [8]Her temple is become as a man without glory. [9]Her glorious vessels are carried away into captivity, her infants are slain in the streets, her young men with the sword of the enemy. [10]What nation hath not had a part in her kingdom, and gotten of her spoils? [11]All her ornaments are taken away; of a free woman she is become a bond-slave. [12]And, behold, our sanctuary, even our beauty and our glory, is laid waste, and the Gentiles have profaned it. [13]To what end therefore shall we live any longer?

1:53 *The Israelites*: this name is given only to the faithful.　**1:54** *Casleu*: November-December. *The hundred forty and fifth year*: 167 B.C.E. *Abomination of desolation*: see Dan 8:13 and note.　**1:57** *Book of the testament*: i.e., "book of the covenant" (a reference to the Torah, as is "books of the law," v. 56).

　2:1–28 The resistance of Mattathias and his sons. Compare 2 Macc 5:27. Verses 1–5 introduce the members of the Hasmonean family (for the family's name, see Josephus, *Jewish Antiquities* 12.265) who will play central roles in subsequent portions of the book: Mattathias (chap. 2), Judas (chaps. 3–8), Jonathan (chaps. 9–12), and Simon (chaps. 13–16). The significances of their surnames are obscure, but "Maccabeus" (v. 4) perhaps means "like a hammer." The lament of Mattathias (vv. 6–14) is followed by an account of the beginnings of their resistance (vv. 15–28).　**2:1** *Modin*: a mountain town northwest of Jerusalem.　**2:7–13** *Woe is me . . . any longer*: a poetic lament (versified by modern translations) that recalls, by turns, Lamentations (e.g., compare v. 11 with Lam 1:1)

[14]Then Mattathias and his sons rent their clothes, and put on sackcloth, and mourned very sore.

[15]In the mean while the king's officers, such as compelled the people to revolt, came into the city Modin, to make them sacrifice. [16]And when many of Israel came unto them, Mattathias also and his sons came together. [17]Then answered the king's officers, and said to Mattathias on this wise, Thou art a ruler, and an honourable and great man in this city, and strengthened with sons and brethren: [18]now therefore come thou first, and fulfil the king's commandment, like as all the heathen have done, yea, and the men of Juda also, and such as remain at Jerusalem: so shalt thou and thy house be in the number of the king's friends, and thou and thy children shall be honoured with silver and gold, and many rewards.

[19]Then Mattathias answered and spake with a loud voice, Though all the nations that are under the king's dominion obey him, and fall away every one from the religion of their fathers, and give consent to his commandments: [20]yet will I and my sons and my brethren walk in the covenant of our fathers. [21]God forbid that we should forsake the law and the ordinances. [22]We will not hearken to the king's words, to go from our religion, either on the right hand, or the left.

[23]Now when he had left speaking these words, there came one of the Jews in the sight of all to sacrifice on the altar which was at Modin, according to the king's commandment. [24]Which thing when Mattathias saw, he was inflamed with zeal, and his reins trembled, neither could he forbear to shew his anger according to judgment: wherefore he ran, and slew him upon the altar. [25]Also the king's commissioner, who compelled men to sacrifice, he killed at that time, and the altar he pulled down. [26]Thus dealt he zealously for the law of God, like as Phinees did unto Zambri the son of Salom. [27]And Mattathias cried throughout the city with a loud voice, saying, Whosoever is zealous of the law, and maintaineth the covenant, let him follow me. [28]So he and his sons fled into the mountains, and left all that ever they had in the city.

[29]Then many that sought after justice and judgment went down into the wilderness, to dwell there: [30]both they, and their children, and their wives, and their cattle; because afflictions increased sore upon them.

---

and Pss 44, 74, 79. **2:14** *Rent their clothes . . . sackcloth*: customary habits of mourning. **2:17** *On this wise*: in this manner. **2:18** *The king's friends*: "friend of the king" was an official Seleucid title, applied to a member of the king's council. **2:22** *To go . . . left*: echoing Deut 5:32; 17:20; 28:14; etc. *Religion*: Gk. *latreia*, "service," a term suggesting that Mattathias and his family will serve God rather than Antiochus. **2:23–26** *Now when . . . Salom*: as the text itself underscores, this stylized scene assimilates Mattathias to Phinehas (see Num 25:6–13). **2:24** *Reins*: kidneys (figuratively, heart), considered a seat of emotion. *Neither could . . . anger*: more literally "he poured forth his anger." *According to judgment*: on the basis of legislation recorded at Deut 13:6–11; 17:2–7. **2:25** *The altar he pulled down*: again in accordance with divine law (cf. Exod 34:13; Deut 7:5; 12:3). In light of the communal resistance that his zeal prompts (vv. 27–30), an allusion to Gideon's destruction of the altar of Baal is also possible (see Judg 6:25–35).

2:29–38 A massacre. Compare 2 Macc 6:11. The narrative invites an unfavorable comparison between the actions of those who refuse to fight on the Sabbath and the active resistance of

³¹Now when it was told the king's servants, and the host that was at Jerusalem, in the city of David, that certain men, who had broken the king's commandment, were gone down into the secret places in the wilderness, ³²they pursued after them a great number, and having overtaken them, they camped against them, and made war against them on the sabbath day. ³³And they said unto them, Let that which ye have done hitherto suffice; come forth, and do according to the commandment of the king, and ye shall live. ³⁴But they said, We will not come forth, neither will we do the king's commandment, to profane the sabbath day. ³⁵So then they gave them the battle with all speed. ³⁶Howbeit they answered them not, neither cast they a stone at them, nor stopped the places where they lay hid; ³⁷but said, Let us die all in our innocency: heaven and earth shall testify for us, that ye put us to death wrongfully. ³⁸So they rose up against them in battle on the sabbath, and they slew them, with their wives and children, and their cattle, to the number of a thousand people.

³⁹Now when Mattathias and his friends understood hereof, they mourned for them right sore. ⁴⁰And one of them said to another, If we all do as our brethren have done, and fight not for our lives and laws against the heathen, they will now quickly root us out of the earth. ⁴¹At that time therefore they decreed, saying, Whosoever shall come to make battle with us on the sabbath day, we will fight against him; neither will we die all, as our brethren that were murdered in the secret places.

⁴²Then came there unto him a company of Assideans, who were mighty men of Israel, even all such as were voluntarily devoted unto the law. ⁴³Also all they that fled for persecution joined themselves unto them, and were a stay unto them. ⁴⁴So they joined their forces, and smote sinful men in their anger, and wicked men in their wrath: but the rest fled to the heathen for succour. ⁴⁵Then Mattathias and his friends went round about, and pulled down the altars: ⁴⁶and what children soever they found within the coast of Israel uncircumcised, those they circumcised valiantly. ⁴⁷They pursued also after the proud men, and the work prospered in their hand. ⁴⁸So they recovered the law out of the hand of the Gentiles, and out of the hand of kings, neither suffered they the sinner to triumph.

⁴⁹Now when the time drew near that Mattathias should die, he said unto his sons, Now hath pride and rebuke gotten strength, and the time of destruction, and the wrath of indignation: ⁵⁰now therefore, my sons, be ye zealous for the law, and give your lives for the covenant of your fathers. ⁵¹Call to remembrance what acts our fathers did in their time; so shall ye receive great honour and an everlast-

---

Mattathias, by indicating that the former fled "down into the wilderness" (v. 29) while Mattathias and his sons fled upward "into the mountains" (v. 28).   **2:36** *Stopped*: obstructed.   **2:37** *Shall testify*: the Greek verb is in the present tense.

2:39–70 The death of Mattathias.   **2:42** *Assideans*: Hasideans (Heb. "pious ones"). This obscure group played an important role in the Maccabean revolt. Many scholars conjecture that those of the previous section belonged to it, and that their massacre precipitated the group's later alliance with Mattathias.   **2:43** *Stay*: support.   **2:46** *Coast*: territory. *Valiantly*: lit. "in strength," which here probably means "forcibly" (so NRSV, NJB, etc.).   **2:47** *The proud men*: presumably the king's officers (cf. 1:21, 24, where Antiochus is said to have behaved "proudly" in Judea).   **2:49–68** *Now hath . . .*

ing name. ⁵²Was not Abraham found faithful in temptation, and it was imputed unto him for righteousness? ⁵³Joseph in the time of his distress kept the commandment, and was made lord of Egypt. ⁵⁴Phinees our father in being zealous and fervent obtained the covenant of an everlasting priesthood. ⁵⁵Jesus for fulfilling the word was made a judge in Israel. ⁵⁶Caleb for bearing witness before the congregation received the heritage of the land. ⁵⁷David for being merciful possessed the throne of an everlasting kingdom. ⁵⁸Elias for being zealous and fervent for the law was taken up into heaven. ⁵⁹Ananias, Azarias, and Misael, by believing were saved out of the flame. ⁶⁰Daniel for his innocency was delivered from the mouth of lions. ⁶¹And thus consider ye throughout all ages, that none that put their trust in him shall be overcome. ⁶²Fear not then the words of a sinful man: for his glory shall be dung and worms. ⁶³To day he shall be lifted up, and to morrow he shall not be found, because he is returned into his dust, and his thought is come to nothing. ⁶⁴Wherefore, ye my sons, be valiant, and shew yourselves men in the behalf of the law; for by it shall ye obtain glory.

⁶⁵And, behold, I know that your brother Simon is a man of counsel, give ear unto him alway: he shall be a father unto you. ⁶⁶As for Judas Maccabeus, he hath been mighty and strong, even from his youth up: let him be your captain, and fight the battle of the people. ⁶⁷Take also unto you all those that observe the law, and avenge ye the wrong of your people. ⁶⁸Recompense fully the heathen, and take heed to the commandments of the law.

⁶⁹So he blessed them, and was gathered to his fathers. ⁷⁰And he died in the hundred forty and sixth year, and his sons buried him in the sepulchres of his fathers at Modin, and all Israel made great lamentation for him.

3 Then his son Judas, called Maccabeus, rose up in his stead. ²And all his brethren helped him, and so did all they that held with his father, and they fought with cheerfulness the battle of Israel. ³So he gat his people great honour, and put on a breastplate as a giant, and girt his warlike harness about him, and he made battles, protecting the host with his sword. ⁴In his acts he was like a lion, and like a lion's whelp roaring for his prey. ⁵For he pursued the wicked, and sought them out, and burnt up those that vexed his people. ⁶Wherefore the

---

law: Mattathias's farewell discourse is patterned on Jacob's farewell to his sons in Gen 49. Many modern versions present it as verse. **2:52** *Was not Abraham . . . righteousness*: see Gen 15:6; 22. **2:53** *Joseph . . . commandment*: see Gen 39, where Joseph resists the temptation to commit adultery with Potiphar's wife. *Was made lord of Egypt*: see Gen 41:37–57. **2:54** *Phinees*: see Num 25:6–13. **2:55** *Jesus*: Joshua; see Josh 1:1–9 for his commission. **2:56** *Caleb*: see Num 13–14; Deut 1:36. **2:57** *David*: God promises him an eternal dynasty (see 2 Sam 7:12–16), but it is not clear how that promise is related to his *being merciful*. (A Hebrew word meaning "pious" may lie behind it.) **2:58** *Elias*: Elijah, who *was taken up into heaven* in 2 Kgs 2:9–12. For his zeal, see, e.g., 1 Kgs 18:20–40. **2:59** *Ananias, Azarias, and Misael*: Hananiah, Azariah, and Mishael (Shadrach, Abednego, and Meshach; see Dan 1:7; 3:8–30). **2:60** *Daniel*: see Dan 6. **2:62** *Dung and worms*: see 2 Macc 9:5–12. **2:65–66** *I know . . . people*: the reversal of primogeniture (Simon was born before Judas; see vv. 3–4) recalls Jacob's deathbed blessing of Joseph's sons in Gen 48. **2:70** *The hundred forty and sixth year*: 166 B.C.E.

3:1–4:35 Judas's successful resistance. The material in this section roughly corresponds to 2 Macc 8.

wicked shrunk for fear of him, and all the workers of iniquity were troubled, because salvation prospered in his hand. [7]He grieved also many kings, and made Jacob glad with his acts, and his memorial is blessed for ever. [8]Moreover he went through the cities of Juda, destroying the ungodly out of them, and turning away wrath from Israel: [9]so that he was renowned unto the utmost part of the earth, and he received unto him such as were ready to perish.

[10]Then Apollonius gathered the Gentiles together, and a great host out of Samaria, to fight against Israel. [11]Which thing when Judas perceived, he went forth to meet him, and so he smote him, and slew him: many also fell down slain, but the rest fled. [12]Wherefore Judas took their spoils, and Apollonius' sword also, and therewith he fought all his life long.

[13]Now when Seron, a prince of the army of Syria, heard say that Judas had gathered unto him a multitude and company of the faithful to go out with him to war; [14]he said, I will get me a name and honour in the kingdom; for I will go fight with Judas and them that are with him, who despise the king's commandment. [15]So he made him ready to go up, and there went with him a mighty host of the ungodly to help him, and to be avenged of the children of Israel. [16]And when he came near to the going up of Beth-horon, Judas went forth to meet him with a small company: [17]who, when they saw the host coming to meet them, said unto Judas, How shall we be able, being so few, to fight against so great a multitude and so strong, seeing we are ready to faint with fasting all this day? [18]Unto whom Judas answered, It is no hard matter for many to be shut up in the hands of a few; and with the God of heaven it is all one, to deliver with a great multitude, or a small company: [19]for the victory of battle standeth not in the multitude of an host; but strength cometh from heaven. [20]They come against us in much pride and iniquity to destroy us, and our wives and children, and to spoil us: [21]but we fight for our lives and our laws. [22]Wherefore the Lord himself will overthrow them before our face: and as for you, be ye not afraid of them.

[23]Now as soon as he had left off speaking, he leapt suddenly upon them, and so Seron and his host was overthrown before him. [24]And they pursued them from the going down of Beth-horon unto the plain, where were slain about eight hundred men of them; and the residue fled into the land of the Philistines.

3:1–26 The succession and early victories of Judas Maccabeus. This section includes, in vv. 3–9, what may be a poem celebrating Judas. **3:7** *Jacob*: Israel. **3:8** *Wrath*: i.e., God's. **3:9** *Such as were ready to perish*: lit. "those who were perishing." Compare David's company at 1 Sam 22:2. **3:10** *Apollonius*: governor of Samaria (cf. Josephus, *Jewish Antiquities* 12.261, 287), perhaps also to be identified with the "chief collector of tribute" mentioned at 1:29 (see note). **3:12** *Apollonius' sword*: reminiscent of David's despoiling of Goliath (1 Sam 17:51, 54). *Therewith he . . . long*: David too used Goliath's sword later in his career (see 1 Sam 21:8–9). **3:16** *The going up of Beth-horon*: a course from the Mediterranean coast to the town of Beth-horon (cf. v. 24), on the way to Jerusalem. **3:18–22** *Unto whom . . . of them*: Judas addresses the troops before battle in accordance with the instructions to the priest in Deuteronomy (20:2–4). For analogous speeches, see vv. 58–60; 4:8–11; etc. His speech here recalls Jonathan's at 1 Sam 14:6. **3:18** *The God of heaven*: as often in 1 Maccabees, KJV introduces a direct reference to God that the Greek text, which simply reads "heaven," piously avoids. **3:24** *The land of the Philistines*: a reference to the southern coastal region. Only nominally Philistine, this Gentile territory's cities were thoroughly hellenized.

²⁵Then began the fear of Judas and his brethren, and an exceeding great dread, to fall upon the nations round about them: ²⁶insomuch as his fame came unto the king, and all nations talked of the battles of Judas.

²⁷Now when king Antiochus heard these things, he was full of indignation: wherefore he sent and gathered together all the forces of his realm, even a very strong army. ²⁸He opened also his treasure, and gave his soldiers pay for a year, commanding them to be ready whensoever he should need them. ²⁹Nevertheless, when he saw that the money of his treasures failed, and that the tributes in the country were small, because of the dissension and plague, which he had brought upon the land in taking away the laws which had been of old time; ³⁰he feared that he should not be able to bear the charges any longer, nor to have such gifts to give so liberally as he did before: for he had abounded above the kings that were before him. ³¹Wherefore, being greatly perplexed in his mind, he determined to go into Persia, there to take the tributes of the countries, and to gather much money. ³²So he left Lysias, a nobleman, and one of the blood royal, to oversee the affairs of the king from the river Euphrates unto the borders of Egypt: ³³and to bring up his son Antiochus, until he came again. ³⁴Moreover he delivered unto him the half of his forces, and the elephants, and gave him charge of all things that he would have done, as also concerning them that dwelt in Juda and Jerusalem: ³⁵to wit, that he should send an army against them, to destroy and root out the strength of Israel, and the remnant of Jerusalem, and to take away their memorial from that place; ³⁶and that he should place strangers in all their quarters, and divide their land by lot. ³⁷So the king took the half of the forces that remained, and departed from Antioch, his royal city, the hundred forty and seventh year; and having passed the river Euphrates, he went through the high countries.

³⁸Then Lysias chose Ptolemee the son of Dorymenes, and Nicanor, and Gorgias, mighty men of the king's friends: ³⁹and with them he sent forty thousand footmen, and seven thousand horsemen, to go into the land of Juda, and to destroy it, as the king commanded. ⁴⁰So they went forth with all their power, and came and pitched by Emmaus in the plain country. ⁴¹And the merchants of the country, hearing the fame of them, took silver and gold very much, with servants, and came into the camp to buy the children of Israel for slaves: a power also of Syria and of the land of the Philistines joined themselves unto them.

3:27–37 Antiochus orders an invasion. The narrator presents what was at this point only a minor guerilla war in one of his provinces as a major irritant to Antiochus.   **3:29** *Plague*: in the general sense of "calamity." *Which he . . . time*: despite this suggestion that his decree (see 1:41–50) caused problems elsewhere in the empire, it is not clear that it had much effect outside of Judea and its environs.   **3:32** *Nobleman*: lit. "a man of repute." *One of the blood royal*: "of royal lineage" (NRSV), but "relation of the king" (like "friend of the king"; see 2:18 note) was an honorific in the Seleucid court. *From the river . . . Egypt*: i.e., from as far east as the western border of Babylon to as far west as the eastern border of Egypt.   **3:36** *Quarters*: territories.   **3:37** *Antioch*: in Syria. *The hundred forty and seventh year*: 165 B.C.E. *High countries*: i.e., the Persian plateau.

3:38–60 Judas prepares his army for battle. 3:40 *Power*: Gk. *dynamis*, "force" (also in v. 41; cf. v. 42). *Emmaus*: northwest of Jerusalem.

⁴²Now when Judas and his brethren saw that miseries were multiplied, and that the forces did encamp themselves in their borders; (for they knew how the king had given commandment to destroy the people, and utterly abolish them;) ⁴³they said one to another, Let us restore the decayed estate of our people, and let us fight for our people and the sanctuary. ⁴⁴Then was the congregation gathered together, that they might be ready for battle, and that they might pray, and ask mercy and compassion. ⁴⁵Now Jerusalem lay void as a wilderness, there was none of her children that went in or out: the sanctuary also was trodden down, and aliens kept the strong hold; the heathen had their habitation in that place; and joy was taken from Jacob, and the pipe with the harp ceased.

⁴⁶Wherefore the Israelites assembled themselves together, and came to Maspha, over against Jerusalem; for in Maspha was the place where they prayed aforetime in Israel. ⁴⁷Then they fasted that day, and put on sackcloth, and cast ashes upon their heads, and rent their clothes, ⁴⁸and laid open the book of the law, wherein the heathen had sought to paint the likeness of their images. ⁴⁹They brought also the priests' garments, and the firstfruits, and the tithes: and the Nazarites they stirred up, who had accomplished their days. ⁵⁰Then cried they with a loud voice toward heaven, saying, What shall we do with these, and whither shall we carry them away? ⁵¹For thy sanctuary is trodden down and profaned, and thy priests are in heaviness, and brought low. ⁵²And, lo, the heathen are assembled together against us to destroy us: what things they imagine against us, thou knowest. ⁵³How shall we be able to stand against them, except thou, O God, be our help?

⁵⁴Then sounded they with trumpets, and cried with a loud voice. ⁵⁵And after this Judas ordained captains over the people, even captains over thousands, and over hundreds, and over fifties, and over tens. ⁵⁶But as for such as were building houses, or had betrothed wives, or were planting vineyards, or were fearful, those he commanded that they should return, every man to his own house, according to the law. ⁵⁷So the camp removed, and pitched upon the south side of Emmaus. ⁵⁸And Judas said, Arm yourselves, and be valiant men, and see that ye be in readiness against the morning, that ye may fight with these nations, that are assembled together against us to destroy us and our sanctuary: ⁵⁹for it is better for us to die in battle, than to behold the calamities of our people and our sanctuary. ⁶⁰Nevertheless, as the will of God is in heaven, so let him do.

3:45 *Now Jerusalem . . . the harp ceased:* because of the regular thematic parallelism, many modern versions print this verse as poetry.   **3:46** *Maspha:* Mizpah, a few miles north of Jerusalem. *For in Maspha . . . Israel:* cf. Judg 20:1; 1 Sam 7:3–14.   **3:48** *Wherein the heathen . . . images:* better "to inquire into those matters about which the Gentiles consulted the likenesses of their gods [i.e., idols]" (MS tradition; NRSV).   **3:49** *Nazarites:* people who took a special vow to God; see Num 6:2–21. *Who had accomplished their days:* cf. Num 6:13.   **3:50–53** *What shall . . . help:* many modern versions print this as poetry.   **3:51** *Are in heaviness:* mourn.   **3:52** *The heathen . . . imagine against us:* echoing Ps 2:1.   **3:54** *Sounded they with trumpets:* in accordance with Num 10:2, 9.   **3:55** *Ordained captains . . . tens:* recalling Exod 18:25.   **3:56** *According to the law:* Deut 20:5–8.   **3:58** *Against:* early in.

4 Then took Gorgias five thousand footmen, and a thousand of the best horsemen, and removed out of the camp by night; [2]to the end he might rush in upon the camp of the Jews, and smite them suddenly. And the men of the fortress were his guides. [3]Now when Judas heard thereof, he himself removed, and the valiant men with him, that he might smite the king's army which was at Emmaus, [4]while as yet the forces were dispersed from the camp. [5]In the mean season came Gorgias by night into the camp of Judas: and when he found no man there, he sought them in the mountains: for said he, These fellows flee from us. [6]But as soon as it was day, Judas shewed himself in the plain with three thousand men, who nevertheless had neither armour nor swords to their minds. [7]And they saw the camp of the heathen, that it was strong and well harnessed, and compassed round about with horsemen; and these were expert of war.

[8]Then said Judas to the men that were with him, Fear ye not their multitude, neither be ye afraid of their assault. [9]Remember how our fathers were delivered in the Red sea, when Pharaoh pursued them with an army. [10]Now therefore let us cry unto heaven, if peradventure the Lord will have mercy upon us, and remember the covenant of our fathers, and destroy this host before our face this day: [11]that so all the heathen may know that there is one who delivereth and saveth Israel.

[12]Then the strangers lifted up their eyes, and saw them coming over against them. [13]Wherefore they went out of the camp to battle; but they that were with Judas sounded their trumpets. [14]So they joined battle, and the heathen being discomfited fled into the plain. [15]Howbeit all the hindmost of them were slain with the sword: for they pursued them unto Gazera, and unto the plains of Idumea, and Azotus, and Jamnia, so that there were slain of them upon a three thousand men. [16]This done, Judas returned again with his host from pursuing them, [17]and said to the people, Be not greedy of the spoils, inasmuch as there is a battle before us, [18]and Gorgias and his host are here by us in the mountain: but stand ye now against our enemies, and overcome them, and after this ye may boldly take the spoils.

[19]As Judas was yet speaking these words, there appeared a part of them looking out of the mountain: [20]who when they perceived that the Jews had put their host to flight, and were burning the tents; for the smoke that was seen declared what was done: [21]when therefore they perceived these things, they were sore afraid, and seeing also the host of Judas in the plain ready to fight, [22]they fled every one into the land of strangers. [23]Then Judas returned to spoil the tents, where they got much gold, and silver, and blue silk, and purple of the sea, and

---

4:1–25 Judas's victory at Emmaus. 4:2 *Fortress*: the stronghold mentioned at 1:33. **4:5** *Mean season*: meantime. **4:6** *To their minds*: as they would have liked. **4:9** *Our fathers . . . army*: see Exod 14:26–30. **4:11** *That so . . . Israel*: echoing God's words in Exodus (10:2; 14:4; etc.). **4:15** *Gazera*: Gezer, just west of Emmaus. *Idumea*: the region on Judea's southern border. *Azotus*: Ashdod, near the Mediterranean coast in the land of the Philistines. *Jamnia*: north of Azotus. *Upon a*: as many as. **4:18** *Gorgias and . . . mountain*: for the movements of this contingent of Gorgias's force, see vv. 1–5. **4:22** *The land of strangers*: the nearby land of the Philistines. **4:23** *Purple of the sea*: cloth colored purple by dye made from shellfish. Considered luxurious, it was conventionally

great riches. ²⁴After this they went home, and sung a song of thanksgiving, and praised the Lord in heaven: because it is good, because his mercy endureth for ever. ²⁵Thus Israel had a great deliverance that day.

²⁶Now all the strangers that had escaped came and told Lysias what had happened: ²⁷who, when he heard thereof, was confounded and discouraged, because neither such things as he would were done unto Israel, nor such things as the king commanded him were come to pass. ²⁸The next year therefore following Lysias gathered together threescore thousand choice men of foot, and five thousand horsemen, that he might subdue them. ²⁹So they came into Idumea, and pitched their tents at Bethsura, and Judas met them with ten thousand men. ³⁰And when he saw that mighty army, he prayed and said, Blessed art thou, O Saviour of Israel, who didst quell the violence of the mighty man by the hand of thy servant David, and gavest the host of strangers into the hands of Jonathan the son of Saul, and his armourbearer; ³¹shut up this army in the hand of thy people Israel, and let them be confounded in their power and horsemen: ³²make them to be of no courage, and cause the boldness of their strength to fall away, and let them quake at their destruction: ³³cast them down with the sword of them that love thee, and let all those that know thy name praise thee with thanksgiving.

³⁴So they joined battle; and there were slain of the host of Lysias about five thousand men, even before them were they slain. ³⁵Now when Lysias saw his army put to flight, and the manliness of Judas' soldiers, and how they were ready either to live or die valiantly, he went into Antiochia, and gathered together a company of strangers, and having made his army greater than it was, he purposed to come again into Judea.

³⁶Then said Judas and his brethren, Behold, our enemies are discomfited: let us go up to cleanse and dedicate the sanctuary. ³⁷Upon this all the host assembled themselves together, and went up into mount Sion. ³⁸And when they saw the sanctuary desolate, and the altar profaned, and the gates burned up, and shrubs growing in the courts as in a forest, or in one of the mountains, yea, and the priests' chambers pulled down; ³⁹they rent their clothes, and made great lamentation, and cast ashes upon their heads, ⁴⁰and fell down flat to the ground upon their faces, and blew an alarm with the trumpets, and cried toward heaven.

⁴¹Then Judas appointed certain men to fight against those that were in the fortress, until he had cleansed the sanctuary. ⁴²So he chose priests of blameless conver-

---

worn by royalty.   **4:24** *Praised the Lord . . . for ever*: KJV introduces "Lord" (see 3:18 note), but NRSV translates more literally, and more clearly: "they sang . . . praises to Heaven—'for he is good, for his mercy endures for ever' [Ps 136:1]."

4:26–35 Judas defeats Lysias at Bethsura. This completes the first round of the war.   **4:27** *Would*: wished.   **4:28** *The next year*: 164 B.C.E.   **4:29** *Bethsura*: Beth-zur, a town south of Jerusalem.   **4:30** *The mighty man*: Goliath; see 1 Sam 17. *Gavest the host . . . armourbearer*: see 1 Sam 14:1–23.   **4:35** *Antiochia*: Antioch. *Gathered together*: the Greek word refers to the recruitment of mercenaries.

4:36–61 Rededication of the temple. Compare 2 Macc 10:1–9.   **4:37** *Mount Sion*: Mount Zion, here referring to the Temple Mount.   **4:41** *Fortress*: see 1:33; 4:2.   **4:42** *Conversation*: way of

sation, such as had pleasure in the law: ⁴³who cleansed the sanctuary, and bare out the defiled stones into an unclean place. ⁴⁴And when as they consulted what to do with the altar of burnt offerings, which was profaned; ⁴⁵they thought it best to pull it down, lest it should be a reproach to them, because the heathen had defiled it: wherefore they pulled it down, ⁴⁶and laid up the stones in the mountain of the temple in a convenient place, until there should come a prophet to shew what should be done with them. ⁴⁷Then they took whole stones according to the law, and built a new altar according to the former; ⁴⁸and made up the sanctuary, and the things that were within the temple, and hallowed the courts. ⁴⁹They made also new holy vessels, and into the temple they brought the candlestick, and the altar of burnt offerings, and of incense, and the table. ⁵⁰And upon the altar they burned incense, and the lamps that were upon the candlestick they lighted, that they might give light in the temple. ⁵¹Furthermore they set the loaves upon the table, and spread out the veils, and finished all the works which they had begun to make.

⁵²Now on the five and twentieth day of the ninth month, which is called the month Casleu, in the hundred forty and eighth year, they rose up betimes in the morning, ⁵³and offered sacrifice according to the law upon the new altar of burnt offerings, which they had made. ⁵⁴Look, at what time and what day the heathen had profaned it, even in that was it dedicated with songs, and citherns, and harps, and cymbals. ⁵⁵Then all the people fell upon their faces, worshipping and praising the God of heaven, who had given them good success. ⁵⁶And so they kept the dedication of the altar eight days, and offered burnt offerings with gladness, and sacrificed the sacrifice of deliverance and praise. ⁵⁷They decked also the forefront of the temple with crowns of gold, and with shields; and the gates and the chambers they renewed, and hanged doors upon them. ⁵⁸Thus was there very great gladness among the people, for that the reproach of the heathen was put away. ⁵⁹Moreover Judas and his brethren with the whole congregation of Israel ordained, that the days of the dedication of the altar should be kept in their season from year to year by the space of eight days, from the five and twentieth day of the month Casleu, with mirth and gladness.

⁶⁰At that time also they builded up the mount Sion with high walls and strong towers round about, lest the Gentiles should come and tread it down, as they had done before. ⁶¹And they set there a garrison to keep it, and fortified Bethsura to preserve it; that the people might have a defence against Idumea.

---

life.   **4:43** *Defiled stones*: presumably *defiled* by the "abomination of desolation" (1:54 and note).   **4:46** *Until there . . . them*: see 9:27 note.   **4:47** *According to the law*: see Exod 20:25; Deut 27:6.   **4:49–51** *They made . . . veils*: see 1:21–23 and note.   **4:51** *And finished . . . make*: echoing Exod 40:33, where "Moses finished the work" of erecting and equipping the tabernacle.   **4:52** *On the five . . . year*: three years after the temple's desecration, as v. 54 makes clear (see 1:54). *Betimes*: early.   **4:53** *According to the law*: presumably referring to legislation directing daily sacrifices and offerings (see Exod 29:38–42).   **4:54** *Citherns*: stringed instruments.   **4:56** *Eight days*: following the precedent of earlier temple dedications; cf. 1 Kgs 8:65–66; 2 Chr 29:17. Compare also the length of time devoted to the Feast of Tabernacles (Lev 23:33–43), to which Hanukkah (see v. 59 note) is related in 2 Macc 1:9, 18; 10:6.   **4:59** *The days . . . gladness*: instituting Hanukkah. This passage seems to be modeled on the institution of Purim in Esth 9:21–22.   **4:61** *Against Idumea*: whence the Seleucid force had invaded (v. 29).

5 Now when the nations round about heard that the altar was built, and the sanctuary renewed as before, it displeased them very much. ²Wherefore they thought to destroy the generation of Jacob that was among them, and thereupon they began to slay and destroy the people. ³Then Judas fought against the children of Esau in Idumea at Arabattine, because they besieged Israel: and he gave them a great overthrow, and abated their courage, and took their spoils. ⁴Also he remembered the injury of the children of Bean, who had been a snare and an offence unto the people, in that they lay in wait for them in the ways. ⁵He shut them up therefore in the towers, and encamped against them, and destroyed them utterly, and burned the towers of that place with fire, and all that were therein. ⁶Afterward he passed over to the children of Ammon, where he found a mighty power, and much people, with Timotheus their captain. ⁷So he fought many battles with them, till at length they were discomfited before him; and he smote them. ⁸And when he had taken Jazar, with the towns belonging thereto, he returned into Judea.

⁹Then the heathen that were at Galaad assembled themselves together against the Israelites that were in their quarters, to destroy them; but they fled to the fortress of Dathema, ¹⁰and sent letters unto Judas and his brethren, The heathen that are round about us are assembled together against us to destroy us: ¹¹and they are preparing to come and take the fortress whereunto we are fled, Timotheus being captain of their host. ¹²Come now therefore, and deliver us from their hands, for many of us are slain: ¹³yea, all our brethren that were in the places of Tobie are put to death: their wives and their children also they have carried away captives, and borne away their stuff; and they have destroyed there about a thousand men.

¹⁴While these letters were yet reading, behold, there came other messengers from Galilee with their clothes rent, who reported on this wise, ¹⁵and said, They of Ptolemais, and of Tyrus, and Sidon, and all Galilee of the Gentiles, are assembled together against us to consume us. ¹⁶Now when Judas and the people heard

5:1–68 **War with neighboring nations.** Compare 2 Macc 10:14–38. The opening two verses provide the context for the war—namely, the persecution of Jews in surrounding countries. Several of the place-names are obscure, and they may reflect an archaizing tendency. The wars are with the Idumaeans and Ammonites (vv. 3–8), and then with Gentile inhabitants of Galilee and Gilead (vv. 9–44). After Judas's return to Jerusalem (vv. 45–54) comes an account of the defeat of presumptuous Jewish commanders and unsuccessful attacks on hellenized cities in the south (vv. 55–68). The central portion of the narrative, in which Judas defeats his enemies in Gilead and then leads the Jews across the Jordan, implicitly compares the hero of 1 Maccabees to Moses, as numerous parallels with the Pentateuch make clear.   **5:3** *Children of Esau*: Edomites. *Arabattine*: Gk. *Akrabattēne*, suggesting a connection with the "ascent of Akrabbim" (see Num 34:4; Josh 15:3; etc.), but the exact site is unknown.   **5:4** *Children of Bean*: perhaps related to Beon in the Transjordan (cf. Num 32:3).   **5:6** *Children of Ammon*: Ammonites, whose country was also east of the Jordan River. *Timotheus*: perhaps to be identified with the Syrian leader mentioned in 2 Macc 8:30–32, suggesting Seleucid involvement in these conflicts.   **5:8** *Jazar*: Jazer, a town or region in the Transjordan.   **5:9** *Galaad*: Gilead, a name for the area east of the Jordan inhabited by Israelites (see Josh 22:9). *Dathema*: unidentified.   **5:13** *Places of Tobie*: apparently the land of Tob mentioned in Judg 11:3, 5, which lay adjacent to Gilead.   **5:14** *Reading*: being read. *Galilee*: a region north and west of the Jordan. *On this wise*: in this manner.   **5:15** *Ptolemais, Tyrus, Sidon*: Phoenician cities on the Mediterranean coast. *Galilee of the Gentiles*: see Isa 9:1

these words, there assembled a great congregation together, to consult what they should do for their brethren, that were in trouble, and assaulted of them. ¹⁷ Then said Judas unto Simon his brother, Choose thee out men, and go and deliver thy brethren that are in Galilee, for I and Jonathan my brother will go into the country of Galaad. ¹⁸ So he left Joseph the son of Zacharias, and Azarias, captains of the people, with the remnant of the host in Judea to keep it. ¹⁹ Unto whom he gave commandment, saying, Take ye the charge of this people, and see that ye make not war against the heathen until the time that we come again. ²⁰ Now unto Simon were given three thousand men to go into Galilee, and unto Judas eight thousand men for the country of Galaad.

²¹ Then went Simon into Galilee, where he fought many battles with the heathen, so that the heathen were discomfited by him. ²² And he pursued them unto the gate of Ptolemais; and there were slain of the heathen about three thousand men, whose spoils he took. ²³ And those that were in Galilee, and in Arbattis, with their wives and their children, and all that they had, took he away with him, and brought them into Judea with great joy.

²⁴ Judas Maccabeus also and his brother Jonathan went over Jordan, and travelled three days' journey in the wilderness, ²⁵ where they met with the Nabathites, who came unto them in a peaceable manner, and told them every thing that had happened to their brethren in the land of Galaad: ²⁶ and how that many of them were shut up in Bosora, and Bosor, and Alema, Casphor, Maked, and Carnaim; (all these cities are strong and great:) ²⁷ and that they were shut up in the rest of the cities of the country of Galaad, and that against to morrow they had appointed to bring their host against the forts, and to take them, and to destroy them all in one day.

²⁸ Hereupon Judas and his host turned suddenly by the way of the wilderness unto Bosora; and when he had won the city, he slew all the males with the edge of the sword, and took all their spoils, and burned the city with fire. ²⁹ From whence he removed by night, and went till he came to the fortress. ³⁰ And betimes in the morning they looked up, and, behold, there was an innumerable people bearing ladders and other engines of war, to take the fortress: for they assaulted them. ³¹ When Judas therefore saw that the battle was begun, and that the cry of the city went up to heaven, with trumpets, and a great sound, ³² he said unto his host, Fight this day for your brethren. ³³ So he went forth behind them in three companies, who sounded their trumpets, and cried with prayer. ³⁴ Then the host of Timotheus, knowing that it was Maccabeus, fled from him: wherefore he smote them with a great slaughter; so that there were killed of them that day about eight thousand men. ³⁵ This done, Judas turned aside to Maspha; and after he had assaulted it, he took it, and slew all the males therein, and received the

---

and note.   **5:23** *Arbattis*: unidentified.   **5:25** *Nabathites*: Nabateans, who inhabited the southern region east of the Jordan and Dead Sea, well south of Gilead. They were traders and traveled widely. **5:26** *Bosora, and . . . Carnaim*: all cities in Gilead, as v. 27 makes clear.   **5:27** *Against*: in preparation for.   **5:29** *The fortress*: at Dathema (see v. 9).   **5:30** *Betimes*: early.   **5:35** *Maspha*: perhaps Mizpeh of Gilead (see Judg 11:29), but some MSS read "Alema" and Josephus names yet another

spoils thereof, and burnt it with fire. [36]From thence went he, and took Casphon, Maged, Bosor, and the other cities of the country of Galaad.

[37]After these things gathered Timotheus another host, and encamped against Raphon beyond the brook. [38]So Judas sent men to espy the host, who brought him word, saying, All the heathen that be round about us are assembled unto them, even a very great host. [39]He hath also hired the Arabians to help them, and they have pitched their tents beyond the brook, ready to come and fight against thee. Upon this Judas went to meet them.

[40]Then Timotheus said unto the captains of his host, When Judas and his host come near the brook, if he pass over first unto us, we shall not be able to withstand him; for he will mightily prevail against us: [41]but if he be afraid, and camp beyond the river, we shall go over unto him, and prevail against him. [42]Now when Judas came near the brook, he caused the scribes of the people to remain by the brook: unto whom he gave commandment, saying, Suffer no man to remain in the camp, but let all come to the battle. [43]So he went first over unto them, and all the people after him: then all the heathen, being discomfited before him, cast away their weapons, and fled unto the temple that was at Carnaim. [44]But they took the city, and burned the temple with all that were therein. Thus was Carnaim subdued, neither could they stand any longer before Judas.

[45]Then Judas gathered together all the Israelites that were in the country of Galaad, from the least unto the greatest, even their wives, and their children, and their stuff, a very great host, to the end they might come into the land of Judea. [46]Now when they came unto Ephron, (this was a great city in the way as they should go, very well fortified) they could not turn from it, either on the right hand or the left, but must needs pass through the midst of it. [47]Then they of the city shut them out, and stopped up the gates with stones. [48]Whereupon Judas sent unto them in peaceable manner, saying, Let us pass through your land to go into our own country, and none shall do you any hurt; we will only pass through on foot: howbeit they would not open unto him. [49]Wherefore Judas commanded a proclamation to be made throughout the host, that every man should pitch his tent in the place where he was. [50]So the soldiers pitched, and assaulted the city all that day and all that night, till at the length the city was delivered into his hands: [51]who then slew all the males with the edge of the sword, and rased the city, and took the spoils thereof, and passed through the city over them that were slain.

[52]After this went they over Jordan into the great plain before Bethsan. [53]And Judas gathered together those that came behind, and exhorted the people

place.   **5:36** *Casphon, Maged:* "Casphor, Maked" of v. 26 (see note).   **5:37** *Raphon:* another city in Gilead. 2 Macc 8:30–32 seems to locate the battle there. *Brook:* i.e., wadi.   **5:42** *Scribes of the people:* perhaps officers responsible for keeping the troops' rolls (see 2 Chr 26:11 for a precedent).   **5:43** *Temple:* lit. "dedicated land," referring to a shrine to the Syrian goddess Atargatis (see 2 Macc 12:26).   **5:46** *Ephron:* a few miles east of the Jordan River.   **5:48** *Let us pass . . . on foot:* recalling Moses' requests to Edom (Num 20:17) and to the Amorites (Num 21:22). Moses and the Israelites conquer the Amorites (Num 21:23–25), as Judas here conquers Ephron.   **5:52** *After this went they over Jordan:* in this way, Judas trumps Moses, who died before he was able to lead his people over the Jordan (Deut 34:1–5). The scene may be intended to fulfill Isaiah's prophecies of a new exodus (e.g., 35:10; 52:10–11). *Bethsan:* a.k.a. Skythopolis, just west of the Jordan River.   **5:53** *Those that came behind:* the stragglers.

all the way through, till they came into the land of Judea. ⁵⁴So they went up to mount Sion with joy and gladness, where they offered burnt offerings, because not one of them were slain until they had returned in peace.

⁵⁵Now what time as Judas and Jonathan were in the land of Galaad, and Simon his brother in Galilee before Ptolemais, ⁵⁶Joseph the son of Zacharias, and Azarias, captains of the garrisons, heard of the valiant acts and warlike deeds which they had done. ⁵⁷Wherefore they said, Let us also get us a name, and go fight against the heathen that are round about us. ⁵⁸So when they had given charge unto the garrison that was with them, they went toward Jamnia. ⁵⁹Then came Gorgias and his men out of the city to fight against them. ⁶⁰And so it was, that Joseph and Azarias were put to flight, and pursued unto the borders of Judea: and there were slain that day of the people of Israel about two thousand men. ⁶¹Thus was there a great overthrow among the children of Israel, because they were not obedient unto Judas and his brethren, but thought to do some valiant act. ⁶²Moreover these men came not of the seed of those, by whose hand deliverance was given unto Israel. ⁶³Howbeit the man Judas and his brethren were greatly renowned in the sight of all Israel, and of all the heathen, wheresoever their name was heard of; ⁶⁴insomuch as the people assembled unto them with joyful acclamations.

⁶⁵Afterward went Judas forth with his brethren, and fought against the children of Esau in the land toward the south, where he smote Hebron, and the towns thereof, and pulled down the fortress of it, and burned the towers thereof round about. ⁶⁶From thence he removed to go into the land of the Philistines, and passed through Samaria. ⁶⁷At that time certain priests, desirous to shew their valour, were slain in battle, for that they went out to fight unadvisedly. ⁶⁸So Judas turned to Azotus in the land of the Philistines, and when he had pulled down their altars, and burned their carved images with fire, and spoiled their cities, he returned into the land of Judea.

6 About that time king Antiochus travelling through the high countries heard say, that Elymais in the country of Persia was a city greatly renowned for riches, silver, and gold; ²and that there was in it a very rich temple, wherein were coverings of gold, and breastplates, and shields, which Alexander, son of Philip, the Macedonian king, who reigned first among the Grecians, had left there. ³Wherefore he came and sought to take the city, and to spoil it; but he was not

---

5:57 *Let us . . . name*: their decision to disobey Judas's command (cf. v. 19) ominously echoes the words of the builders of the tower of Babel (Gen 11:4). **5:61** *Thus was . . . act*: their presumption recalls that of the Israelites in Num 14:39–45, as do the subsequent actions of the priests (see v. 67). **5:62** *Came not . . . Israel*: i.e., they were not from the Hasmonean family. **5:63** *The man Judas . . . heard of*: recalling Exod 11:3, about the fame of "the man Moses." **5:65** *Hebron*: a city south of Jerusalem. **5:66** *Samaria*: the geography makes no sense, for Samaria is far to the north of Hebron. Josephus offers Marisa (*Jewish Antiquities* 12.353), a city roughly between Hebron and the land of the Philistines. **5:68** *Pulled down . . . cities*: in accordance with Deuteronomy's decrees, like the actions of his father (see 2:25 and note).

6:1–17 The death of Antiochus Epiphanes. Compare 2 Macc 9:1–29. **6:1** *Elymais*: Elam, northwest of Persia. It was a region rather than a city, and 2 Macc 9:2 identifies the site of the

able, because they of the city, having had warning thereof, ⁴rose up against him in battle: so he fled, and departed thence with great heaviness, and returned to Babylon. ⁵Moreover there came one who brought him tidings into Persia, that the armies, which went against the land of Judea, were put to flight: ⁶and that Lysias, who went forth first with a great power, was driven away of the Jews; and that they were made strong by the armour, and power, and store of spoils, which they had gotten of the armies, whom they had destroyed: ⁷also that they had pulled down the abomination, which he had set up upon the altar in Jerusalem, and that they had compassed about the sanctuary with high walls, as before, and his city Bethsura.

⁸Now when the king heard these words, he was astonished and sore moved: whereupon he laid him down upon his bed, and fell sick for grief, because it had not befallen him as he looked for. ⁹And there he continued many days: for his grief was ever more and more, and he made account that he should die. ¹⁰Wherefore he called for all his friends, and said unto them, The sleep is gone from mine eyes, and my heart faileth for very care. ¹¹And I thought with myself, Into what tribulation am I come, and how great a flood of misery is it, wherein now I am! for I was bountiful and beloved in my power. ¹²But now I remember the evils that I did at Jerusalem, and that I took all the vessels of gold and silver that were therein, and sent to destroy the inhabitants of Judea without a cause. ¹³I perceive therefore that for this cause these troubles are come upon me, and, behold, I perish through great grief in a strange land.

¹⁴Then called he for Philip, one of his friends, whom he made ruler over all his realm, ¹⁵and gave him the crown, and his robe, and his signet, to the end he should bring up his son Antiochus, and nourish him up for the kingdom. ¹⁶So king Antiochus died there in the hundred forty and ninth year. ¹⁷Now when Lysias knew that the king was dead, he set up Antiochus his son (whom he had brought up, being young,) to reign in his stead, and his name he called Eupator.

¹⁸About this time they that were in the tower shut up the Israelites round about the sanctuary, and sought always their hurt, and the strengthening of the heathen. ¹⁹Wherefore Judas, purposing to destroy them, called all the people together to besiege them. ²⁰So they came together, and besieged them in the hundred and fiftieth year, and he made mounts for shot against them, and other engines. ²¹Howbeit certain of them that were besieged got forth, unto whom some ungodly men of Israel joined themselves: ²²and they went unto the king, and said, How long will it be ere thou execute judgment, and avenge our breth-

attempted plunder as nearby Persepolis. **6:4** *Heaviness*: sadness. **6:10** *Friends*: see 3:38 note. **6:15** *Signet*: ring used for sealing official documents, and thus a symbol of authority. **6:16** *The hundred forty and ninth year*: 163 B.C.E. **6:17** *Eupator*: "of a noble father." Antiochus V Eupator reigned until 162 B.C.E.

6:18–63 War with Antiochus Eupator. Compare 2 Macc 11:1–14. The siege of the fortress in Jerusalem (vv. 18–31) is followed by defeat at the battle of Bathzacharias (vv. 32–47), the Syrian siege of the temple (vv. 48–54), and a treaty between the two forces (vv. 55–63). **6:18** *They that were in the tower*: the Jerusalem fortress was still under Seleucid control (see 4:41). **6:20** *The hundred and fiftieth year*: 162 B.C.E. *Mounts for shot*: "siege towers" (NRSV).

ren? 23 We have been willing to serve thy father, and to do as he would have us, and to obey his commandments; 24for which cause they of our nation besiege the tower, and are alienated from us: moreover as many of us as they could light on they slew, and spoiled our inheritance. 25Neither have they stretched out their hand against us only, but also against all their borders. 26And, behold, this day are they besieging the tower at Jerusalem, to take it: the sanctuary also and Beth-sura have they fortified. 27 Wherefore if thou dost not prevent them quickly, they will do greater things than these, neither shalt thou be able to rule them.

28Now when the king heard this, he was angry, and gathered together all his friends, and the captains of his army, and those that had charge of the horse. 29 There came also unto him from other kingdoms, and from isles of the sea, bands of hired soldiers. 30So that the number of his army was an hundred thousand footmen, and twenty thousand horsemen, and two and thirty elephants exercised in battle. 31 These went through Idumea, and pitched against Bethsura, which they assaulted many days, making engines of war; but they of Bethsura came out, and burned them with fire, and fought valiantly.

32Upon this Judas removed from the tower, and pitched in Bathzacharias, over against the king's camp. 33 Then the king rising very early marched fiercely with his host toward Bathzacharias, where his armies made them ready to battle, and sounded the trumpets. 34And to the end they might provoke the elephants to fight, they shewed them the blood of grapes and mulberries. 35Moreover they divided the beasts among the armies, and for every elephant they appointed a thousand men, armed with coats of mail, and with helmets of brass on their heads; and beside this, for every beast were ordained five hundred horsemen of the best. 36 These were ready at every occasion: wheresoever the beast was, and whithersoever the beast went, they went also, neither departed they from him. 37And upon the beasts were there strong towers of wood, which covered every one of them, and were girt fast unto them with devices: there were also upon every one two and thirty strong men, that fought upon them, beside the Indian that ruled him. 38As for the remnant of the horsemen, they set them on this side and that side at the two parts of the host, giving them signs what to do, and being harnessed all over amidst the ranks. 39Now when the sun shone upon the shields of gold and brass, the mountains glistered therewith, and shined like lamps of fire.

40So part of the king's army being spread upon the high mountains, and part on the valleys below, they marched on safely and in order. 41 Wherefore all that heard the noise of their multitude, and the marching of the company, and the rattling of the harness, were moved: for the army was very great and mighty.

6:24 *Are alienated from us*: i.e., "have become our enemies." *Spoiled*: plundered.   6:32 *Bathzacharias*: Beth-zechariah, in between Jerusalem and Beth-zur to the south.   6:34 *Shewed them . . . mulberries*: for reasons unknown—to rouse their appetites? to prepare them for blood in battle? to intoxicate them and thereby remove their natural fear?   6:37 *Two and thirty*: an impossible number; the text may have suffered corruption by a scribe mistakenly importing the number of elephants from v. 30. *The Indian that ruled him*: the elephant driver.   6:38 *Giving them . . . ranks*: Gk. obscure.   6:41 *Moved*: in the

⁴²Then Judas and his host drew near, and entered into battle, and there were slain of the king's army six hundred men.

⁴³Eleazar also, surnamed Savaran, perceiving that one of the beasts, armed with royal harness, was higher than all the rest, and supposing that the king was upon him, ⁴⁴put himself in jeopardy, to the end he might deliver his people, and get him a perpetual name: ⁴⁵wherefore he ran upon him courageously through the midst of the battle, slaying on the right hand and on the left, so that they were divided from him on both sides. ⁴⁶Which done, he crept under the elephant, and thrust him under, and slew him: whereupon the elephant fell down upon him, and there he died. ⁴⁷Howbeit the rest of the Jews seeing the strength of the king, and the violence of his forces, turned away from them.

⁴⁸Then the king's army went up to Jerusalem to meet them, and the king pitched his tents against Judea, and against mount Sion. ⁴⁹But with them that were in Bethsura he made peace: for they came out of the city, because they had no victuals there to endure the siege, it being a year of rest to the land. ⁵⁰So the king took Bethsura, and set a garrison there to keep it. ⁵¹As for the sanctuary, he besieged it many days: and set there artillery with engines and instruments to cast fire and stones, and pieces to cast darts and slings. ⁵²Whereupon they also made engines against their engines, and held them battle a long season. ⁵³Yet at the last, their vessels being without victuals, (for that it was the seventh year, and they in Judea, that were delivered from the Gentiles, had eaten up the residue of the store;) ⁵⁴there were but a few left in the sanctuary, because the famine did so prevail against them, that they were fain to disperse themselves, every man to his own place.

⁵⁵At that time Lysias heard say, that Philip (whom Antiochus the king, whiles he lived, had appointed to bring up his son Antiochus, that he might be king,) ⁵⁶was returned out of Persia and Media, and the king's host also that went with him, and that he sought to take unto him the ruling of the affairs. ⁵⁷Wherefore he went in all haste, and said to the king and the captains of the host and the company, We decay daily, and our victuals are but small, and the place we lay siege unto is strong, and the affairs of the kingdom lie upon us: ⁵⁸now therefore let us be friends with these men, and make peace with them, and with all their nation; ⁵⁹and covenant with them, that they shall live after their laws, as they did before: for they are therefore displeased, and have done all these things, because we abolished their laws. ⁶⁰So the king and the princes were content: wherefore he sent unto them to make peace; and they accepted thereof. ⁶¹Also the king and the princes made an oath unto them: whereupon they went out of the strong hold. ⁶²Then the king entered into mount Sion; but when he saw the strength of

---

sense of "shaken." **6:44** *To the end . . . perpetual name*: the author obliges, despite the failure of Eleazar Savaran (see 2:5, where he is surnamed "Avaran") to kill the king and the Jews' subsequent flight (v. 47). Once again, desire for fame leads to defeat (cf. 5:57–60). **6:49** *A year . . . land*: every seventh year (see v. 53) the land was to lie fallow, as ordained in Lev 25:2–7. The Seleucids also suffer from the resulting lack of provisions (v. 57). **6:51** *Artillery*: "siege towers" (NRSV). **6:54** *Fain*: glad under the circumstances. **6:59** *As they did before*: i.e., before Antiochus Epiphanes' pronouncement (see 1:41–50).

the place, he brake his oath that he had made, and gave commandment to pull down the wall round about. ⁶³Afterward departed he in all haste, and returned unto Antiochia, where he found Philip to be master of the city: so he fought against him, and took the city by force.

7 In the hundred and one and fiftieth year Demetrius the son of Seleucus departed from Rome, and came up with a few men unto a city of the sea coast, and reigned there. ²And as he entered into the palace of his ancestors, so it was, that his forces had taken Antiochus and Lysias, to bring them unto him. ³Wherefore, when he knew it, he said, Let me not see their faces. ⁴So his host slew them.

Now when Demetrius was set upon the throne of his kingdom, ⁵there came unto him all the wicked and ungodly men of Israel, having Alcimus (who was desirous to be high priest) for their captain: ⁶and they accused the people to the king, saying, Judas and his brethren have slain all thy friends, and driven us out of our own land. ⁷Now therefore send some man whom thou trustest, and let him go and see what havock he hath made among us, and in the king's land, and let him punish them with all them that aid them.

⁸Then the king chose Bacchides, a friend of the king, who ruled beyond the flood, and was a great man in the kingdom, and faithful to the king. ⁹And him he sent with that wicked Alcimus, whom he made high priest, and commanded that he should take vengeance of the children of Israel. ¹⁰So they departed, and came with a great power into the land of Judea, where they sent messengers to Judas and his brethren with peaceable words deceitfully. ¹¹But they gave no heed to their words; for they saw that they were come with a great power.

¹²Then did there assemble unto Alcimus and Bacchides a company of scribes, to require justice. ¹³Now the Assideans were the first among the children of Israel that sought peace of them: ¹⁴for said they, One that is a priest of the seed of Aaron is come with this army, and he will do us no wrong. ¹⁵So he spake unto them peaceably, and sware unto them, saying, We will procure the harm neither of you nor your friends. ¹⁶Whereupon they believed him: howbeit he took of them threescore men, and slew them in one day, according to the words which he wrote, ¹⁷The flesh of thy saints have they cast out, and their blood have they shed round about Jerusalem, and there was none to bury them. ¹⁸Wherefore the fear and dread of them fell upon all the people, who said, There is neither truth nor righteousness in them; for they have broken the covenant and oath that they made.

7:1–25 The ascension of Demetrius. 7:1 *The hundred and one and fiftieth year*: 161 B.C.E. *Demetrius the son . . . Rome*: Demetrius I Soter ruled the Seleucid Empire ca. 162–150 B.C.E. He was the son of Seleucus IV Philopator, who was Antiochus Epiphanes' elder brother. When Seleucus was made king, he required Demetrius to take Antiochus's place as a Roman hostage (see 1:10 note). Demetrius later escaped Rome, as recounted in Polybius 31.12–15. *A city of the sea coast*: Tripolis (2 Macc 14:1), on the Mediterranean coast south of Antioch, where the palace (v. 2) was located. **7:8** *Beyond the flood*: lit. "Beyond the River," the name of a province west of the Euphrates; see Ezra 4:11 note. **7:13** *Assideans*: see 2:42 note. **7:16** *Howbeit he . . . day*: perhaps he concluded he could not trust them as a result of their earlier alliance with the Hasmoneans (see 2:42). *Which he wrote*: referring to Ps 79:2–3 (quoted in v. 17), which the author believes that this massacre fulfilled and, it seems, that Alcimus himself wrote (unless the Greek is to be construed as "which was written"; so

¹⁹After this removed Bacchides from Jerusalem, and pitched his tents in Bezeth, where he sent and took many of the men that had forsaken him, and certain of the people also, and when be had slain them, he cast them into the great pit. ²⁰Then committed he the country to Alcimus, and left with him a power to aid him: so Bacchides went to the king. ²¹But Alcimus contended for the high priesthood. ²²And unto him resorted all such as troubled the people, who, after they had gotten the land of Juda into their power, did much hurt in Israel. ²³Now when Judas saw all the mischief that Alcimus and his company had done among the Israelites, even above the heathen, ²⁴he went out into all the coasts of Judea round about, and took vengeance of them that had revolted from him, so that they durst no more go forth into the country. ²⁵On the other side, when Alcimus saw that Judas and his company had gotten the upper hand, and knew that he was not able to abide their force, he went again to the king, and said all the worst of them that he could.

²⁶Then the king sent Nicanor, one of his honourable princes, a man that bare deadly hate unto Israel, with commandment to destroy the people. ²⁷So Nicanor came to Jerusalem with a great force; and sent unto Judas and his brethren deceitfully with friendly words, saying, ²⁸Let there be no battle between me and you; I will come with a few men, that I may see you in peace. ²⁹He came therefore to Judas, and they saluted one another peaceably. Howbeit the enemies were prepared to take away Judas by violence. ³⁰Which thing after it was known to Judas, to wit, that he came unto him with deceit, he was sore afraid of him, and would see his face no more. ³¹Nicanor also, when he saw that his counsel was discovered, went out to fight against Judas beside Capharsalama: ³²where there were slain of Nicanor's side about five thousand men, and the rest fled into the city of David.

³³After this went Nicanor up to mount Sion, and there came out of the sanctuary certain of the priests and certain of the elders of the people, to salute him peaceably, and to shew him the burnt sacrifice that was offered for the king. ³⁴But he mocked them, and laughed at them, and abused them shamefully, and spake proudly, ³⁵and sware in his wrath, saying, Unless Judas and his host be now delivered into my hands, if ever I come again in safety, I will burn up this house: and with that he went out in a great rage. ³⁶Then the priests entered in, and stood before the altar and the temple, weeping, and saying, ³⁷Thou, O Lord,

---

NRSV). **7:19** *Bezeth*: Beth-zaith, just north of Beth-zur. *Pit*: lit. "cistern." **7:21** *Alcimus contended for the high priesthood*: he is in an untenable position. Declared high priest by Demetrius, he would have had little legitimacy in the temple restored by the anti-Seleucid leader Judas. Despite the civil authority granted him, as well as the forces he commanded (v. 20), he must have appeared a patently illegitimate ruler, which explains why Judas immediately regains "the upper hand" and Alcimus returns to Antioch (v. 25).

7:26–50 The battle of Adasa. 7:26 *Nicanor*: perhaps not the figure mentioned in 3:38, but rather the Nicanor who Polybius says fled Rome with Demetrius (see v. 1 note), unless somehow the two are the same. **7:31** *Capharsalama*: unidentified. **7:33** *To shew . . . king*: i.e., to make it clear that (from these priests' perspective, at least) the battle for religious and cultural autonomy did not amount to a quest for political independence from Syria (cf. Ezra 6:10). **7:37–38** *Thou, O Lord . . . longer*: the parallelism suggests poetry. The description of the temple echoes any number of biblical

didst choose this house to be called by thy name, and to be a house of prayer and petition for thy people: ³⁸be avenged of this man and his host, and let them fall by the sword: remember their blasphemies, and suffer them not to continue any longer.

³⁹So Nicanor went out of Jerusalem, and pitched his tents in Beth-horon where an host out of Syria met him. ⁴⁰But Judas pitched in Adasa with three thousand men, and there he prayed, saying, ⁴¹O Lord, when they that were sent from the king of the Assyrians blasphemed, thine angel went out, and smote an hundred fourscore and five thousand of them. ⁴²Even so destroy thou this host before us this day, that the rest may know that he hath spoken blasphemously against thy sanctuary, and judge thou him according to his wickedness.

⁴³So the thirteenth day of the month Adar the hosts joined battle: but Nicanor's host was discomfited, and he himself was first slain in the battle. ⁴⁴Now when Nicanor's host saw that he was slain, they cast away their weapons, and fled. ⁴⁵Then they pursued after them a day's journey, from Adasa unto Gazera, sounding an alarm after them with their trumpets. ⁴⁶Whereupon they came forth out of all the towns of Judea round about, and closed them in; so that they, turning back upon them that pursued them, were all slain with the sword, and not one of them was left. ⁴⁷Afterwards they took the spoils, and the prey, and smote off Nicanor's head, and his right hand, which he stretched out so proudly, and brought them away, and hanged them up toward Jerusalem. ⁴⁸For this cause the people rejoiced greatly, and they kept that day a day of great gladness. ⁴⁹Moreover they ordained to keep yearly this day, being the thirteenth of Adar. ⁵⁰Thus the land of Juda was in rest a little while.

8 Now Judas had heard of the fame of the Romans, that they were mighty and valiant men, and such as would lovingly accept all that joined themselves unto them, and make a league of amity with all that came unto them; ²and that they were men of great valour. It was told him also of their wars and noble acts which they had done among the Galatians, and how they had conquered them, and brought them under tribute; ³and what they had done in the country of Spain, for the winning of the mines of the silver and gold which is there; ⁴and that by their policy and patience they had conquered all the place, though it were very far from them; and the kings also that came against them from the uttermost

---

passages (e.g., Deut 12:5; 1 Kgs 8:29; Isa 56:7), as does the prayer for vengeance (e.g., Isa 37:6–7). **7:39** *Beth-horon*: see 3:16 note. **7:40** *Adasa*: southeast of Beth-horon, on the way to Jerusalem. **7:41** *The king . . . them*: see 2 Kgs 18–19. Judas invokes the same OT story in preparation for a different battle with Nicanor at 2 Macc 8:19. **7:43** *Adar*: February-March. **7:45** *Gazera*: Gezer, to the west. **7:49** *They ordained . . . Adar*: known as Nicanor's Day, the holiday is no longer celebrated.

    8:1–32 The embassy to Rome. A eulogy of Rome, focusing primarily on its military conquests (vv. 1–13), but with brief discussion of its political institutions and cultural character (vv. 14–16) analogous to Polybius's more extensive treatment (see book 6). It is followed by an account of the Hasmoneans' alliance with the growing Mediterranean power (vv. 17–32). **8:2** *Galatians*: Gk. *Galatai*, which can be used of both the Galatians (Celts settled in Asia Minor) and the inhabitants of Gaul (Celts living in western Europe). Rome decisively defeated the latter in 191 B.C.E. and the former in 189. **8:3–4** *What they . . . discomfited them*: referring to the Second Punic War (218–201 B.C.E.). **8:4** *The kings . . . earth* may be a confused reference to the invasion of the great Carthaginian general

part of the earth, till they had discomfited them, and given them a great over-throw, so that the rest did give them tribute every year: ⁵beside this, how they had discomfited in battle Philip, and Perseus, king of the Citims, with others that lifted up themselves against them, and had overcome them: ⁶how also Antiochus the great king of Asia, that came against them in battle, having an hundred and twenty elephants, with horsemen, and chariots, and a very great army, was dis-comfited by them; ⁷and how they took him alive, and covenanted that he and such as reigned after him should pay a great tribute, and give hostages, and that which was agreed upon, ⁸and the country of India, and Media, and Lydia, and of the goodliest countries, which they took of him, and gave to king Eumenes: ⁹more-over how the Grecians had determined to come and destroy them; ¹⁰and that they, having knowledge thereof, sent against them a certain captain, and fighting with them slew many of them, and carried away captives their wives and their children, and spoiled them, and took possession of their lands, and pulled down their strong holds, and brought them to be their servants unto this day: ¹¹it was told him besides, how they destroyed and brought under their dominion all other kingdoms and isles that at any time resisted them; ¹²but with their friends and such as relied upon them they kept amity: and that they had conquered kingdoms both far and nigh, insomuch as all that heard of their name were afraid of them: ¹³also that, whom they would help to a kingdom, those reign; and whom again they would, they displace: finally, that they were greatly exalted: ¹⁴yet for all this none of them wore a crown, or was clothed in purple, to be magnified thereby: ¹⁵moreover how they had made for themselves a senate house, wherein three hundred and twenty men sat in council daily, consulting alway for the people, to the end they might be well ordered: ¹⁶and that they committed their government to one man every year, who ruled over all their country, and that all were obedi-ent to that one, and that there was neither envy nor emulation among them.

¹⁷In consideration of these things, Judas chose Eupolemus the son of John, the son of Accos, and Jason the son of Eleazar, and sent them to Rome, to make a league of amity and confederacy with them, ¹⁸and to intreat them that they would take the yoke from them; for they saw that the kingdom of the Grecians did oppress Israel with servitude. ¹⁹They went therefore to Rome, which was a very great journey, and came into the senate, where they spake and said, ²⁰Judas Maccabeus with his brethren, and the people of the Jews, have sent us unto you,

Hannibal during the Second Punic War.   **8:5** *Philip, and Perseus*: Macedonian monarchs, defeated by Rome in 197 and 168 B.C.E. respectively.   **8:6** *Antiochus the great*: Antiochus III, who ruled 223–187 B.C.E. The subsequent verses contain some historical errors, but evoke the humiliating terms of the treaty of Apamea (see 1:10 note).   **8:8** *Eumenes*: Eumenes II of Pergamum (another kingdom carved out of Alexander's empire), who ruled 197–159 B.C.E.   **8:9–10** *How the Grecians . . . day*: anachronistically referring to Lucius Mummius's defeat of the Achaean Confederacy and his famous looting of Corinth (146 B.C.E., after the events here narrated).   **8:14** *Was clothed in purple*: see 4:23 note.   **8:15** *Three hundred and twenty . . . daily*: other sources give the number as three hundred; the senate convened at the discretion of the presiding magistrate, not *daily*.   **8:16** *Committed their gov-ernment to one man*: i.e., the consul, who was elected annually (in fact, two consuls, equal in author-ity, served at the same time).   **8:18** *Kingdom of the Grecians*: a reference to the Greek origins and

to make a confederacy and peace with you, and that we might be registered your confederates and friends. ²¹So that matter pleased the Romans well.

²²And this is the copy of the epistle which the senate wrote back again in tables of brass, and sent to Jerusalem, that there they might have by them a memorial of peace and confederacy: ²³Good success be to the Romans, and to the people of the Jews, by sea and by land for ever: the sword also and enemy be far from them. ²⁴If there come first any war upon the Romans or any of their confederates throughout all their dominion, ²⁵the people of the Jews shall help them, as the time shall be appointed, with all their heart: ²⁶neither shall they give any thing unto them that make war upon them, or aid them with victuals, weapons, money, or ships, as it hath seemed good unto the Romans; but they shall keep their covenants without taking any thing therefore. ²⁷In the same manner also, if war come first upon the nation of the Jews, the Romans shall help them with all their heart, according as the time shall be appointed them: ²⁸neither shall victuals be given to them that take part against them, or weapons, or money, or ships, as it hath seemed good to the Romans; but they shall keep their covenants, and that without deceit. ²⁹According to these articles did the Romans make a covenant with the people of the Jews. ³⁰Howbeit if hereafter the one party or the other shall think meet to add or diminish any thing, they may do it at their pleasures, and whatsoever they shall add or take away shall be ratified. ³¹And as touching the evils that Demetrius doeth to the Jews, we have written unto him, saying, Wherefore hast thou made thy yoke heavy upon our friends and confederates the Jews? ³²If therefore they complain any more against thee, we will do them justice, and fight with thee by sea and by land.

9 Furthermore when Demetrius heard that Nicanor and his host were slain in battle, he sent Bacchides and Alcimus into the land of Judea the second time, and with them the chief strength of his host: ²who went forth by the way that leadeth to Galgala, and pitched their tents before Masaloth, which is in Arbela, and after they had won it, they slew much people. ³Also the first month of the hundred fifty and second year they encamped before Jerusalem: ⁴from whence they removed, and went to Berea, with twenty thousand footmen and two thousand horsemen. ⁵Now Judas had pitched his tents at Eleasa, and three thousand chosen men with him: ⁶who seeing the multitude of the other army to

---

orientation of the Seleucid Empire. **8:22** *Tables of brass*: bronze tablets. **8:25** *As the time shall be appointed*: "as the occasion may indicate" (NRSV; also in v. 27). The treaty does not oblige either party to assist the other militarily. **8:30** *Howbeit if . . . ratified*: the Greek makes clear that the treaty can be emended only with both parties' mutual consent, not by either at will. **8:31–32** *And as touching . . . by land*: though the treaty did exist, the historicity of these two verses is dubious. Rome never came to Judea's assistance in its ongoing war against the Seleucids, and Josephus's account of the treaty does not mention any promise to intervene (see *Jewish Antiquities* 12.415–19).

9:1–22 The death of Judas. The geography in this section is quite confused; the text may have suffered corruption in translation from Hebrew or in later copying. **9:2** *Galgala*: Gilgal, but probably an error for Galilee, a region far to Jerusalem's north. *Arbela* seems to have been a Galilean city, but *Masaloth* is obscure; it may mistakenly transliterate as a proper name a Hebrew word referring to a road. **9:3** *The hundred fifty and second year*: 160 B.C.E. **9:4** *Berea*: just northwest of Jerusalem. **9:5** *Eleasa*:

be so great were sore afraid; whereupon many conveyed themselves out of the host, insomuch as there abode of them no more but eight hundred men.

⁷When Judas therefore saw that his host slipt away, and that the battle pressed upon him, he was sore troubled in mind, and much distressed, for that he had no time to gather them together. ⁸Nevertheless unto them that remained he said, Let us arise and go up against our enemies, if peradventure we may be able to fight with them. ⁹But they dehorted him, saying, We shall never be able: let us now rather save our lives, and hereafter we will return with our brethren, and fight against them: for we are but few. ¹⁰Then Judas said, God forbid that I should do this thing, and flee away from them: if our time be come, let us die manfully for our brethren, and let us not stain our honour.

¹¹With that the host of Bacchides removed out of their tents, and stood over against them, their horsemen being divided into two troops, and their slingers and archers going before the host, and they that marched in the foreward were all mighty men. ¹²As for Bacchides, he was in the right wing: so the host drew near on the two parts, and sounded their trumpets. ¹³They also of Judas' side, even they sounded their trumpets also, so that the earth shook at the noise of the armies, and the battle continued from morning till night. ¹⁴Now when Judas perceived that Bacchides and the strength of his army were on the right side, he took with him all the hardy men, ¹⁵who discomfited the right wing, and pursued them unto the mount Azotus. ¹⁶But when they of the left wing saw that they of the right wing were discomfited, they followed upon Judas and those that were with him hard at the heels from behind: ¹⁷whereupon there was a sore battle, insomuch as many were slain on both parts. ¹⁸Judas also was killed, and the remnant fled.

¹⁹Then Jonathan and Simon took Judas their brother, and buried him in the sepulchre of his fathers in Modin, ²⁰moreover they bewailed him, and all Israel made great lamentation for him, and mourned many days, saying, ²¹How is the valiant man fallen, that delivered Israel! ²²As for the other things concerning Judas and his wars, and the noble acts which he did, and his greatness, they are not written: for they were very many.

²³Now after the death of Judas the wicked began to put forth their heads in all the coasts of Israel, and there arose up all such as wrought iniquity. ²⁴In those days also was there a very great famine, by reason whereof the country revolted, and went with them. ²⁵Then Bacchides chose the wicked men, and made them lords of the country. ²⁶And they made inquiry and search for Judas' friends, and brought them unto Bacchides, who took vengeance of them, and used them despitefully. ²⁷So was there a great affliction in Israel, the like whereof was not since the time that a prophet was not seen among them.

---

unidentified.   **9:9** *Dehorted*: discouraged.   **9:15** *Azotus*: Ashdod, but it is a city, not a mountain, and somewhat removed from the site of battle (see 4:15 and note).   **9:21** *How is the valiant man fallen*: echoing the beginning of David's lament for Saul and Jonathan (2 Sam 1:19–27).   **9:22** *As for . . . many*: recalling (and trumping) the closing of accounts of individual monarchs' reigns in 1 and 2 Kings; e.g., 1 Kgs 11:41; 14:19, 29.

9:23–31 Jonathan succeeds his brother.   **9:23** *Coasts*: territories.   **9:26** *Used them despitefully*: lit. "mocked them."   **9:27** *Since the time . . . them*: cf. 4:46; 14:41. This seems to anticipate the

²⁸For this cause all Judas' friends came together, and said unto Jonathan, ²⁹Since thy brother Judas died, we have no man like him to go forth against our enemies, and Bacchides, and against them of our nation that are adversaries to us. ³⁰Now therefore we have chosen thee this day to be our prince and captain in his stead, that thou mayest fight our battles. ³¹Upon this Jonathan took the governance upon him at that time, and rose up instead of his brother Judas.

³²But when Bacchides gat knowledge thereof, he sought for to slay him. ³³Then Jonathan, and Simon his brother, and all that were with him, perceiving that, fled into the wilderness of Thecoe, and pitched their tents by the water of the pool Asphar. ³⁴Which when Bacchides understood, he came near to Jordan with all his host upon the sabbath day. ³⁵Now Jonathan had sent his brother John, a captain of the people, to pray his friends the Nabathites, that they might leave with them their carriage, which was much. ³⁶But the children of Jambri came out of Medaba, and took John, and all that he had, and went their way with it.

³⁷After this came word to Jonathan and Simon his brother, that the children of Jambri made a great marriage, and were bringing the bride from Nadabatha with a great train, as being the daughter of one of the great princes of Canaan. ³⁸Therefore they remembered John their brother, and went up, and hid themselves under the covert of the mountain: ³⁹where they lifted up their eyes, and looked, and, behold, there was much ado and great carriage: and the bridegroom came forth, and his friends and brethren, to meet them with drums, and instruments of musick, and many weapons. ⁴⁰Then Jonathan and they that were with him rose up against them from the place where they lay in ambush, and made a slaughter of them in such sort, as many fell down dead, and the remnant fled into the mountain, and they took all their spoils. ⁴¹Thus was the marriage turned into mourning, and the noise of their melody into lamentation. ⁴²So when they had avenged fully the blood of their brother, they turned again to the marsh of Jordan.

⁴³Now when Bacchides heard hereof, he came on the sabbath day unto the banks of Jordan with a great power. ⁴⁴Then Jonathan said to his company, Let us go up now and fight for our lives, for it standeth not with us to day, as in time past: ⁴⁵for, behold, the battle is before us and behind us, and the water of Jordan on this side and that side, the marsh likewise and wood, neither is there place for us to turn aside. ⁴⁶Wherefore cry ye now unto heaven, that ye may be delivered from the hand of your enemies. ⁴⁷With that they joined battle, and Jonathan stretched forth his hand to smite Bacchides, but he turned back from him.

---

rabbinic idea that God's voice had been silent since Malachi, the last of the biblical prophets, leaving only *bat qol*, the "daughter of the voice," a mode of revelation that was neither as impressive nor as authoritative as God's prophetic inspiration. On the basis of such passages as Mal 4:5 and Deut 18:15–19, some Jews expected God's prophetic voice to sound again only at the eschatological consummation.

9:32–42 The death of John and Jonathan's revenge. **9:33** *Wilderness of Thecoe*: desert of Tekoa, to Jerusalem's southeast. **9:35** *John*: Joannan (see 2:2), the eldest son of Mattathias. *Nabathites*: Nabateans, who had aided the Hasmoneans before (see 5:25). *Carriage*: baggage. **9:36** *Children of Jambri*: perhaps a Nabatean clan. *Medaba*: several miles east of the Dead Sea's northernmost part. **9:37** *Nadabatha*: unidentified. **9:41** *Was the marriage . . . lamentation*: echoing Amos 8:10; cf. 1 Macc 1:39.

⁴⁸Then Jonathan and they that were with him leapt into Jordan, and swam over unto the farther bank: howbeit the other passed not over Jordan unto them. ⁴⁹So there were slain of Bacchides' side that day about a thousand men.

⁵⁰Afterward returned Bacchides to Jerusalem, and repaired the strong cities in Judea: the fort in Jericho, and Emmaus, and Beth-horon, and Bethel, and Thamnatha, Pharathoni, and Taphon, these did he strengthen with high walls, with gates, and with bars. ⁵¹And in them he set a garrison, that they might work malice upon Israel. ⁵²He fortified also the city Bethsura, and Gazara, and the tower, and put forces in them, and provision of victuals. ⁵³Besides, he took the chief men's sons in the country for hostages, and put them into the tower at Jerusalem to be kept.

⁵⁴Moreover in the hundred fifty and third year, in the second month, Alcimus commanded that the wall of the inner court of the sanctuary should be pulled down; he pulled down also the works of the prophets. ⁵⁵And as he began to pull down, even at that time was Alcimus plagued, and his enterprises hindered: for his mouth was stopped, and he was taken with a palsy, so that he could no more speak any thing, nor give order concerning his house. ⁵⁶So Alcimus died at that time with great torment. ⁵⁷Now when Bacchides saw that Alcimus was dead, he returned to the king: whereupon the land of Judea was in rest two years.

⁵⁸Then all the ungodly men held a council, saying, Behold, Jonathan and his company are at ease, and dwell without care: now therefore we will bring Bacchides hither, who shall take them all in one night. ⁵⁹So they went and consulted with him. ⁶⁰Then removed he, and came with a great host, and sent letters privily to his adherents in Judea, that they should take Jonathan and those that were with him: howbeit they could not, because their counsel was known unto them. ⁶¹Wherefore they took of the men of the country, that were authors of that mischief, about fifty persons, and slew them.

⁶²Afterward Jonathan, and Simon, and they that were with him, got them away to Bethbasi, which is in the wilderness, and they repaired the decays thereof, and made it strong. ⁶³Which thing when Bacchides knew, he gathered together all his host, and sent word to them that were of Judea. ⁶⁴Then went he and laid siege against Bethbasi; and they fought against it a long season, and made engines of war. ⁶⁵But Jonathan left his brother Simon in the city, and went forth himself into the country, and with a certain number went he forth. ⁶⁶And he smote Odonarkes and his brethren, and the children of Phasiron in their tent. ⁶⁷And when he began to smite them, and came up with his forces, Simon and his company went out of

---

9:43–57 **The death of Alcimus.**   9:50 *The fort . . . Taphon*: these are the *strong cities in Judea*. 9:54 *The hundred fifty and third year*: 159 B.C.E. *The wall . . . sanctuary*: the wall enclosing that part of the temple which only priests were permitted to enter. Alcimus's motives for destroying it are obscure, although it is surely significant that he was high priest at the time (7:5, 21; cf. Josephus, *Jewish Antiquities* 12.413). *The works of the prophets*: presumably referring to Haggai and Zechariah, who prophetically urged the temple's reconstruction (see Ezra 6:14–15).   9:55 *Palsy*: paralysis.

9:58–73 **Jonathan's victories.** The end of the war.   9:61 *They*: presumably Jonathan's constituency   9:62 *Bethbasi*: several miles south of Jerusalem.   9:66 *Odonarkes, Phasiron*: presumably local supporters of Bacchides (cf. v. 63); their killing seems to have been intended to distract him.

the city, and burned up the engines of war, ⁶⁸and fought against Bacchides, who was discomfited by them, and they afflicted him sore: for his counsel and travail was in vain. ⁶⁹Wherefore he was very wroth at the wicked men that gave him counsel to come into the country, insomuch as he slew many of them, and purposed to return into his own country. ⁷⁰Whereof when Jonathan had knowledge, he sent ambassadors unto him, to the end he should make peace with him, and deliver them the prisoners. ⁷¹Which thing he accepted, and did according to his demands, and sware unto him that he would never do him harm all the days of his life.

⁷²When therefore he had restored unto him the prisoners that he had taken aforetime out of the land of Judea, he returned and went his way into his own land, neither came he any more into their borders. ⁷³Thus the sword ceased from Israel: but Jonathan dwelt at Machmas, and began to govern the people; and he destroyed the ungodly men out of Israel.

10 In the hundred and sixtieth year Alexander, the son of Antiochus surnamed Epiphanes, went up and took Ptolemais: for the people had received him, by means whereof he reigned there. ²Now when king Demetrius heard thereof, he gathered together an exceeding great host, and went forth against him to fight. ³Moreover Demetrius sent letters unto Jonathan with loving words, so as he magnified him. ⁴For said he, Let us first make peace with him, before he join with Alexander against us: ⁵else he will remember all the evils that we have done against him, and against his brethren and his people. ⁶Wherefore he gave him authority to gather together an host, and to provide weapons, that he might aid him in battle: he commanded also that the hostages that were in the tower should be delivered him.

⁷Then came Jonathan to Jerusalem, and read the letters in the audience of all the people, and of them that were in the tower: ⁸who were sore afraid, when they heard that the king had given him authority to gather together an host. ⁹Whereupon they of the tower delivered their hostages unto Jonathan, and he delivered them unto their parents. ¹⁰This done, Jonathan settled himself in Jerusalem, and began to build and repair the city. ¹¹And he commanded the workmen to build the walls and the mount Sion round about with square stones for fortification; and they did so. ¹²Then the strangers, that were in the fortresses which Bacchides had built, fled away; ¹³insomuch as every man left his place, and went into his own country. ¹⁴Only at Bethsura certain of those that had forsaken the law and the commandments remained still: for it was their place of refuge.

9:70 *The prisoners*: cf. v. 26.   **9:73** *The sword ceased from Israel*: the period of his peaceful rule lasted about seven years, until Demetrius's aggressions (see 10:67–73). *Machmas*: Michmash, north of Jerusalem, the site of the early victories of Saul, Israel's first king, over the Philistines (see 1 Sam 13–14). *Govern*: more literally "judge," a word that assimilates Jonathan to Israel's early charismatic deliverers.
   10:1–47 Alexander Balas and Demetrius vie for Jonathan's support.   10:1 *The hundred and sixtieth year*: 152 B.C.E. *Alexander, the son . . . Epiphanes*: Alexandar I Balas was a pretender to the throne, his filiation to Antiochus being very doubtful. In 158 he claimed to be king, in 153 he won the support of Rome (which was none too trusting of Demetrius, who had escaped Roman custody before seizing power; see 7:1 note), and he established his authority in the following year by taking the important Phoenician city *Ptolemais*. He died in 145.   **10:3** *Loving words*: lit. "peaceable words."   **10:6** *The hostages . . . tower*: see 9:53.   **10:11** *Mount Sion*: probably the Temple Mount

¹⁵Now when king Alexander had heard what promises Demetrius had sent unto Jonathan: when also it was told him of the battles and noble acts which he and his brethren had done, and of the pains that they had endured, ¹⁶he said, Shall we find such another man? now therefore we will make him our friend and confederate. ¹⁷Upon this he wrote a letter, and sent it unto him, according to these words, saying, ¹⁸King Alexander to his brother Jonathan sendeth greeting: ¹⁹We have heard of thee, that thou art a man of great power, and meet to be our friend. ²⁰Wherefore now this day we ordain thee to be the high priest of thy nation, and to be called the king's friend; (and therewithal he sent him a purple robe and a crown of gold:) and require thee to take our part, and keep friendship with us. ²¹So in the seventh month of the hundred and sixtieth year, at the feast of the tabernacles, Jonathan put on the holy robe, and gathered together forces, and provided much armour.

²²Whereof when Demetrius heard, he was very sorry, and said, ²³What have we done, that Alexander hath prevented us in making amity with the Jews to strengthen himself? ²⁴I also will write unto them words of encouragement, and promise them dignities and gifts, that I may have their aid. ²⁵He sent unto them therefore to this effect: King Demetrius unto the people of the Jews sendeth greeting: ²⁶Whereas ye have kept covenants with us, and continued in our friendship, not joining yourselves with our enemies, we have heard hereof, and are glad. ²⁷Wherefore now continue ye still to be faithful unto us, and we will well recompense you for the things ye do in our behalf, ²⁸and will grant you many immunities, and give you rewards. ²⁹And now do I free you, and for your sake I release all the Jews, from tributes, and from the customs of salt, and from crown taxes, ³⁰and from that which appertaineth unto me to receive for the third part of the seed, and the half of the fruit of the trees, I release it from this day forth, so that they shall not be taken of the land of Judea, nor of the three governments which are added thereunto out of the country of Samaria and Galilee, from this day forth for evermore. ³¹Let Jerusalem also be holy and free, with the borders thereof, both from tenths and tributes. ³²And as for the tower which is at Jerusalem, I yield up my authority over it, and give it to the high priest, that he may set in it such men as he shall choose to keep it.

³³Moreover I freely set at liberty every one of the Jews, that were carried captives out of the land of Judea into any part of my kingdom, and I will that all my officers remit the tributes even of their cattle. ³⁴Furthermore I will that all the feasts, and sabbaths, and new moons, and solemn days, and the three days before

---

(see 4:37 note), but possibly referring to all Jerusalem. **10:15–20** *Now when . . . with us*: Alexander appeals to Jonathan against Demetrius, just as Judas had earlier appealed to Rome against Demetrius (cf. 8:17–32); in the next section, Demetrius in turn will appeal to Jonathan against Alexander—a remarkable reversal. 1 Maccabees thereby presents the Hasmonean state as a power broker equal to Rome! **10:19** *Meet*: "fit," or even "worthy." **10:21** *Feast of the tabernacles*: see Lev 23:33–43. **10:23** *Prevented*: anticipated. **10:30** *Seed*: i.e., "grain." *Three governments*: i.e., "three districts" (NRSV), identified at 11:34. *Samaria and Galilee*: north of Judea proper. **10:31** *Both from tenths and tributes*: better "and its tithes and taxes," perhaps meaning that Syria would take no share of the money collected for support of the priests and temple.

the feast, and the three days after the feast, shall be all days of immunity and freedom for all the Jews in my realm. ³⁵Also no man shall have authority to meddle with them, or to molest any of them in any matter. ³⁶I will further, that there be enrolled among the king's forces about thirty thousand men of the Jews, unto whom pay shall be given, as belongeth to all the king's forces. ³⁷And of them some shall be placed in the king's strong holds, of whom also some shall be set over the affairs of the kingdom, which are of trust: and I will that their overseers and governors be of themselves, and that they live after their own laws, even as the king hath commanded in the land of Judea. ³⁸And concerning the three governments that are added to Judea from the country of Samaria, let them be joined with Judea, that they may be reckoned to be under one, nor bound to obey other authority than the high priest's. ³⁹As for Ptolemais, and the land pertaining thereto, I give it as a free gift to the sanctuary at Jerusalem for the necessary expences of the sanctuary.

⁴⁰Moreover I give every year fifteen thousand shekels of silver out of the king's accounts from the places appertaining. ⁴¹And all the overplus, which the officers payed not in as in former time, from henceforth shall be given toward the works of the temple. ⁴²And beside this, the five thousand shekels of silver, which they took from the uses of the temple out of the accounts year by year, even those things shall be released, because they appertain to the priests that minister. ⁴³And whosoever they be that flee unto the temple at Jerusalem, or be within the liberties thereof, being indebted unto the king, or for any other matter, let them be at liberty, and all that they have in my realm. ⁴⁴For the building also and repairing of the works of the sanctuary expences shall be given of the king's accounts. ⁴⁵Yea, and for the building of the walls of Jerusalem, and the fortifying thereof round about, expences shall be given out of the king's accounts, as also for the building of the walls in Judea.

⁴⁶Now when Jonathan and the people heard these words, they gave no credit unto them, nor received them, because they remembered the great evil that he had done in Israel; for he had afflicted them very sore. ⁴⁷But with Alexander they were well pleased, because he was the first that entreated of true peace with them, and they were confederate with him always.

⁴⁸Then gathered king Alexander great forces, and camped over against Demetrius. ⁴⁹And after the two kings had joined battle, Demetrius' host fled: but Alexander followed after him, and prevailed against them. ⁵⁰And he continued the battle very sore until the sun went down: and that day was Demetrius slain.

⁵¹Afterward Alexander sent ambassadors to Ptolemee king of Egypt with a message to this effect: ⁵²Forasmuch as I am come again to my realm, and am set

10:34 *Immunity and freedom*: i.e., freedom from public burdens.   10:37 *Be set over . . . trust*: "be put in positions of trust in the kingdom" (NRSV).   10:39 *Ptolemais*: Alexander had just taken the city (v. 1), so Demetrius must be promising Jonathan that if he dislodge his rival, he may keep possession of it.   10:40 *Fifteen thousand shekels of silver*: a very large sum.   10:41 *Overplus*: surplus. *Which the officers . . . time*: Gk. obscure.   10:43 *Liberties*: domains.   10:47 *That entreated . . . them*: "to speak peaceable words to them" (NRSV).
    10:48–66 Alexander Balas defeats Demetrius and honors Jonathan.   10:51 *Ptolemee*: see

in the throne of my progenitors, and have gotten the dominion, and overthrown Demetrius, and recovered our country; [53](for after I had joined battle with him, both he and his host was discomfited by us, so that we sit in the throne of his kingdom:) [54]now therefore let us make a league of amity together, and give me now thy daughter to wife: and I will be thy son in law, and will give both thee and her gifts according to thy dignity.

[55]Then Ptolemee the king gave answer, saying, Happy be the day wherein thou didst return into the land of thy fathers, and satest in the throne of their kingdom. [56]And now will I do to thee, as thou hast written: meet me therefore at Ptolemais, that we may see one another; for I will marry my daughter to thee according to thy desire.

[57]So Ptolemee went out of Egypt with his daughter Cleopatra, and they came unto Ptolemais in the hundred threescore and second year: [58]where king Alexander meeting him, gave unto him his daughter Cleopatra, and celebrated her marriage at Ptolemais with great glory, as the manner of kings is.

[59]Now king Alexander had written unto Jonathan, that he should come and meet him. [60]Who thereupon went honourably to Ptolemais, where he met the two kings, and gave them and their friends silver and gold, and many presents, and found favour in their sight. [61]At that time certain pestilent fellows of Israel, men of a wicked life, assembled themselves against him, to accuse him: but the king would not hear them. [62]Yea more than that, the king commanded to take off his garments, and clothe him in purple: and they did so. [63]Also he made him sit by himself, and said unto his princes, Go with him into the midst of the city, and make proclamation, that no man complain against him of any matter, and that no man trouble him for any manner of cause. [64]Now when his accusers saw that he was honoured according to the proclamation, and clothed in purple, they fled all away. [65]So the king honoured him, and wrote him among his chief friends, and made him a duke, and partaker of his dominion. [66]Afterward Jonathan returned to Jerusalem with peace and gladness.

[67]Furthermore in the hundred threescore and fifth year came Demetrius son of Demetrius out of Crete into the land of his fathers: [68]whereof when king Alexander heard tell, he was right sorry, and returned into Antioch. [69]Then Demetrius made Apollonius the governor of Celosyria his general, who gathered together a great host, and camped in Jamnia, and sent unto Jonathan the high priest, saying, [70]Thou alone liftest up thyself against us, and I am laughed to scorn for thy sake, and reproached: and why dost thou vaunt thy power against us

---

1:18 note.   **10:57** *Cleopatra*: Cleopatra Thea (not the famous Ptolemaic Cleopatra VII, consort of Julius Caesar and Mark Antony, who flourished about a century later). *The hundred threescore and second year*: 150 B.C.E.   **10:65** *Wrote*: enrolled. *Made him . . . dominion*: "made him a general and provincial governor."

10:67–89 Jonathan defeats Demetrius II's forces at Ashdod and Joppa.   10:67 *The hundred threescore and fifth year*: 147 B.C.E. *Demetrius son of Demetrius*: Demetrius II Nicator ruled ca. 145–140 B.C.E. and again 129–125 (beyond the scope of 1 Maccabees), after he was released from Parthian captivity (see 14:1–2 and notes).   **10:69** *Then Demetrius . . . general*: i.e., *Apollonius, governor of Celosyria* (a province of the Seleucid Empire encompassing much of the Mediterranean's

in the mountains? ⁷¹Now therefore, if thou trustest in thine own strength, come down to us into the plain field, and there let us try the matter together: for with me is the power of the cities. ⁷²Ask and learn who I am, and the rest that take our part, and they shall tell thee that thy foot is not able to stand before our face; for thy fathers have been twice put to flight in their own land. ⁷³Wherefore now thou shalt not be able to abide the horsemen and so great a power in the plain, where is neither stone nor flint, nor place to flee unto.

⁷⁴So when Jonathan heard these words of Apollonius, he was moved in his mind, and choosing ten thousand men he went out of Jerusalem, where Simon his brother met him for to help him. ⁷⁵And he pitched his tents against Joppe: but they of Joppe shut him out of the city, because Apollonius had a garrison there. ⁷⁶Then Jonathan laid siege unto it: whereupon they of the city let him in for fear: and so Jonathan won Joppe. ⁷⁷Whereof when Apollonius heard, he took three thousand horsemen, with a great host of footmen, and went to Azotus as one that journeyed, and therewithal drew him forth into the plain, because he had a great number of horsemen, in whom he put his trust. ⁷⁸Then Jonathan followed after him to Azotus, where the armies joined battle. ⁷⁹Now Apollonius had left a thousand horsemen in ambush. ⁸⁰And Jonathan knew that there was an ambushment behind him; for they had compassed in his host, and cast darts at the people, from morning till evening. ⁸¹But the people stood still, as Jonathan had commanded them: and so the enemies' horses were tired.

⁸²Then brought Simon forth his host, and set them against the footmen, (for the horsemen were spent,) who were discomfited by him, and fled. ⁸³The horsemen also, being scattered in the field, fled to Azotus, and went into Bethdagon, their idol's temple, for safety. ⁸⁴But Jonathan set fire on Azotus, and the cities round about it, and took their spoils; and the temple of Dagon, with them that were fled into it, he burned with fire. ⁸⁵Thus there were burned and slain with the sword well nigh eight thousand men. ⁸⁶And from thence Jonathan removed his host, and camped against Ascalon, where the men of the city came forth, and met him with great pomp. ⁸⁷After this returned Jonathan and his host unto Jerusalem, having many spoils. ⁸⁸Now when king Alexander heard these things, he honoured Jonathan yet more, ⁸⁹and sent him a buckle of gold, as the use is to be given to such as are of the kings' blood: he gave him also Accaron with the borders thereof in possession.

easternmost seaboard, including Judea), defected to Demetrius.   **10:72** *Twice put . . . land*: see 6:32–47 (Judas's defeat at Beth-zechariah) and 9:1–22 (Judas's defeat and death, probably in Galilee; see notes).   **10:75** *Joppe*: Joppa, a Mediterranean port north of Jamnia.   **10:77** *As one that journeyed*: as if he were traveling through. *Drew him forth*: advanced.   **10:80** *Cast darts*: or "shot arrows" (NRSV).   **10:83** *Beth-dagon, their idol's temple*: for the Philistine god Dagon's temple at Ashdod (Azotus), see 1 Sam 5:2–5. The horsemen hope that Jonathan will honor the right of sanctuary conventionally granted to those taking refuge in temples (cf. v. 43; 1 Kgs 2:28–34).   **10:86** *Ascalon*: in the land of the Philistines.   **10:89** *Of the kings' blood*: see 3:32 note. *Accaron*: Ekron, another city in the same region. *The borders thereof*: "its environs" (NRSV).

11 And the king of Egypt gathered together a great host, like the sand that lieth upon the sea shore, and many ships, and went about through deceit to get Alexander's kingdom, and join it to his own. ²Whereupon he took his journey into Syria in peaceable manner, so as they of the cities opened unto him, and met him: for king Alexander had commanded them so to do, because he was his father in law. ³Now as Ptolemee entered into the cities, he set in every one of them a garrison of soldiers to keep it. ⁴And when he came near to Azotus, they shewed him the temple of Dagon that was burnt, and Azotus and the suburbs thereof that were destroyed, and the bodies that were cast abroad, and them that he had burnt in the battle; for they had made heaps of them by the way where he should pass. ⁵Also they told the king whatsoever Jonathan had done, to the intent he might blame him: but the king held his peace. ⁶Then Jonathan met the king with great pomp at Joppe, where they saluted one another, and lodged. ⁷Afterward Jonathan, when he had gone with the king to the river called Eleutherus, returned again to Jerusalem.

⁸·King Ptolemee therefore, having gotten the dominion of the cities by the sea unto Seleucia upon the sea coast, imagined wicked counsels against Alexander. ⁹Whereupon he sent ambassadors unto king Demetrius, saying, Come, let us make a league betwixt us, and I will give thee my daughter whom Alexander hath, and thou shalt reign in thy father's kingdom: ¹⁰for I repent that I gave my daughter unto him, for he sought to slay me. ¹¹Thus did he slander him, because he was desirous of his kingdom. ¹²Wherefore he took his daughter from him, and gave her to Demetrius, and forsook Alexander, so that their hatred was openly known. ¹³Then Ptolemee entered into Antioch, where he set two crowns upon his head, the crown of Asia, and of Egypt.

¹⁴In the mean season was king Alexander in Cilicia, because those that dwelt in those parts had revolted from him. ¹⁵But when Alexander heard of this, he came to war against him: whereupon king Ptolemee brought forth his host, and met him with a mighty power, and put him to flight. ¹⁶So Alexander fled into Arabia, there to be defended; but king Ptolemee was exalted: ¹⁷for Zabdiel the Arabian took off Alexander's head, and sent it unto Ptolemee. ¹⁸King Ptolemee also died the third day after, and they that were in the strong holds were slain one of another. ¹⁹By this means Demetrius reigned in the hundred threescore and seventh year.

²⁰At the same time Jonathan gathered together them that were in Judea, to take the tower that was in Jerusalem: and he made many engines of war against it. ²¹Then certain ungodly persons, who hated their own people, went unto the

---

11:1–19 War between Alexander and Ptolemy. 11:1 *To get . . . his own*: Josephus, *Jewish Antiquities* 13.103–7 makes Alexander the deceiver. The author of 1 Maccabees evidently knows of such a version of events but does not find it credible (cf. vv. 10–11). **11:7** *Eleutherus*: well north of Joppa, and perhaps to be understood as the southern border of Syria; cf. 12:30. **11:8** *Seleucia*: the Mediterranean port city serving inland Antioch. **11:14** *Cilicia*: the region northwest of Syria. **11:18** *King Ptolemee also died*: according to other ancient sources, of wounds received in the battle. **11:19** *The hundred threescore seventh year*: 145 B.C.E.

11:20–53 Alliance between Demetrius II and Jonathan. 11:20 *The tower that was in Jerusalem*:

king, and told him that Jonathan besieged the tower. ²²Whereof when he heard, he was angry, and immediately removing, he came to Ptolemais, and wrote unto Jonathan, that he should not lay siege to the tower, but come and speak with him at Ptolemais in great haste. ²³Nevertheless Jonathan, when he heard this, commanded to besiege it still: and he chose certain of the elders of Israel and the priests, and put himself in peril; ²⁴and took silver and gold, and raiment, and divers presents besides, and went to Ptolemais unto the king, where he found favour in his sight. ²⁵And though certain ungodly men of the people had made complaints against him, ²⁶yet the king entreated him as his predecessors had done before, and promoted him in the sight of all his friends, ²⁷and confirmed him in the high priesthood, and in all the honours that he had before, and gave him pre-eminence among his chief friends. ²⁸Then Jonathan desired the king, that he would make Judea free from tribute, as also the three governments, with the country of Samaria; and he promised him three hundred talents.

²⁹So the king consented, and wrote letters unto Jonathan of all these things after this manner: ³⁰King Demetrius unto his brother Jonathan, and unto the nation of the Jews, sendeth greeting: ³¹We send you here a copy of the letter which we did write unto our cousin Lasthenes concerning you, that ye might see it. ³²King Demetrius unto his father Lasthenes sendeth greeting: ³³We are determined to do good to the people of the Jews, who are our friends, and keep covenants with us, because of their good will toward us. ³⁴Wherefore we have ratified unto them the borders of Judea, with the three governments of Apherema and Lydda and Ramathem, that are added unto Judea from the country of Samaria, and all things appertaining unto them, for all such as do sacrifice in Jerusalem, instead of the payments which the king received of them yearly aforetime out of the fruits of the earth and of trees. ³⁵And as for other things that belong unto us, of the tithes and customs pertaining unto us, as also the salt pits, and the crown taxes, which are due unto us, we discharge them of them all for their relief. ³⁶And nothing hereof shall be revoked from this time forth for ever. ³⁷Now therefore see that thou make a copy of these things, and let it be delivered unto Jonathan, and set upon the holy mount in a conspicuous place.

³⁸After this, when king Demetrius saw that the land was quiet before him, and that no resistance was made against him, he sent away all his forces, every one to his own place, except certain bands of strangers, whom he had gathered from the isles of the heathen: wherefore all the forces of his fathers hated him. ³⁹Moreover there was one Tryphon, that had been of Alexander's part afore, who, seeing that all the host murmured against Demetrius, went to Simalcue the Arabian, that brought up Antiochus the young son of Alexander, ⁴⁰and lay sore upon him to deliver him this young Antiochus, that he might reign in his father's stead: he

---

still in Seleucid control (cf. 10:6–9, 32).   **11:24** *Divers*: various.   **11:26** *Entreated*: treated (as often). **11:28** *Three governments*: see 10:30 note. *Three hundred talents*: a very large sum.   **11:31** *Cousin*: lit. "relative"; see 3:32 note. *Lasthenes* (unidentified) was apparently Demetrius's elder, as he is called "father" in v. 32; scholars speculate that he was the current governor of Coele-Syria.   **11:32–36** *King Demetrius . . . for ever*: cf. 10:25–45; the letter concedes much of what Demetrius I had earlier offered when he was trying to woo Jonathan to side with him against Alexander.   **11:38** *Except certain*

told him therefore all that Demetrius had done, and how his men of war were at enmity with him, and there he remained a long season. ⁴¹In the mean time Jonathan sent unto king Demetrius, that he would cast those of the tower out of Jerusalem, and those also in the fortresses: for they fought against Israel. ⁴²So Demetrius sent unto Jonathan, saying, I will not only do this for thee and thy people, but I will greatly honour thee and thy nation, if opportunity serve. ⁴³Now therefore thou shalt do well, if thou send me men to help me; for all my forces are gone from me. ⁴⁴Upon this Jonathan sent him three thousand strong men unto Antioch: and when they came to the king, the king was very glad of their coming. ⁴⁵Howbeit they that were of the city gathered themselves together into the midst of the city, to the number of an hundred and twenty thousand men, and would have slain the king. ⁴⁶Wherefore the king fled into the court, but they of the city kept the passages of the city, and began to fight. ⁴⁷Then the king called to the Jews for help, who came unto him all at once, and dispersing themselves through the city slew that day in the city to the number of an hundred thousand. ⁴⁸Also they set fire on the city, and gat many spoils that day, and delivered the king. ⁴⁹So when they of the city saw that the Jews had got the city as they would, their courage was abated: wherefore they made supplication to the king, and cried, saying, ⁵⁰Grant us peace, and let the Jews cease from assaulting us and the city. ⁵¹With that they cast away their weapons, and made peace; and the Jews were honoured in the sight of the king, and in the sight of all that were in his realm; and they returned to Jerusalem, having great spoils.

⁵²So king Demetrius sat on the throne of his kingdom, and the land was quiet before him. ⁵³Nevertheless he dissembled in all that ever he spake, and estranged himself from Jonathan, neither rewarded he him according to the benefits which he had received of him, but troubled him very sore.

⁵⁴After this returned Tryphon, and with him the young child Antiochus, who reigned, and was crowned. ⁵⁵Then there gathered unto him all the men of war, whom Demetrius had put away, and they fought against Demetrius, who turned his back and fled. ⁵⁶Moreover Tryphon took the elephants, and won Antioch. ⁵⁷At that time young Antiochus wrote unto Jonathan, saying, I confirm thee in the high priesthood, and appoint thee ruler over the four governments, and to be one of the king's friends. ⁵⁸Upon this he sent him golden vessels to be served in, and gave him leave to drink in gold, and to be clothed in purple, and to wear a golden buckle. ⁵⁹His brother Simon also he made captain from the place called The ladder of Tyrus unto the borders of Egypt.

bands . . . heathen: a reference to foreign mercenaries; cf. 1:29; 5:39 and notes.   **11:41–42** *He would cast . . . serve*: the mutual recognition of Demetrius and Jonathan (vv. 20–37) had not led to an agreement about the Jerusalem tower, still a Seleucid stronghold.   **11:45** *The city*: Antioch.   **11:46** *Passages*: or "streets" (NRSV).

11:54–74 Alliance between Jonathan and Antiochus VI Epiphanes and renewed hostilities with Demetrius II. 11:54 *Antiochus*: Typhon asserted the right to rule of Antiochus VI Epiphanes, child of Alexander Balas and Cleopatra Thea, in 145 B.C.E., and then murdered him three years later (see 13:31 and note).   **11:57** *Confirm thee . . . friends*: cf. vv. 27–30; 10:20.   **11:59** *Made captain*: probably meaning "appointed as governor." *The ladder of Tyrus*: a point on Phoenicia's

⁶⁰Then Jonathan went forth, and passed through the cities beyond the water, and all the forces of Syria gathered themselves unto him for to help him: and when he came to Ascalon, they of the city met him honourably. ⁶¹From whence he went to Gaza, but they of Gaza shut him out; wherefore he laid siege unto it, and burned the suburbs thereof with fire, and spoiled them. ⁶²Afterward, when they of Gaza made supplication unto Jonathan, he made peace with them, and took the sons of their chief men for hostages, and sent them to Jerusalem, and passed through the country unto Damascus.

⁶³Now when Jonathan heard that Demetrius' princes were come to Cades, which is in Galilee, with a great power, purposing to remove him out of the country, ⁶⁴he went to meet them, and left Simon his brother in the country. ⁶⁵Then Simon encamped against Bethsura, and fought against it a long season, and shut it up: ⁶⁶but they desired to have peace with him, which he granted them, and then put them out from thence, and took the city, and set a garrison in it. ⁶⁷As for Jonathan and his host, they pitched at the water of Gennesar, from whence betimes in the morning they gat them to the plain of Nasor. ⁶⁸And, behold, the host of strangers met them in the plain, who, having laid men in ambush for him in the mountains, came themselves over against him. ⁶⁹So when they that lay in ambush rose out of their places, and joined battle, all that were of Jonathan's side fled; ⁷⁰insomuch as there was not one of them left, except Mattathias the son of Absalom, and Judas the son of Calphi, the captains of the host. ⁷¹Then Jonathan rent his clothes, and cast earth upon his head, and prayed. ⁷²Afterwards turning again to battle, he put them to flight, and so they ran away. ⁷³Now when his own men that were fled saw this, they turned again unto him, and with him pursued them to Cades, even unto their own tents, and there they camped. ⁷⁴So there were slain of the heathen that day about three thousand men: but Jonathan returned to Jerusalem.

12 Now when Jonathan saw that the time served him, he chose certain men, and sent them to Rome, for to confirm and renew the friendship that they had with them. ²He sent letters also to the Lacedemonians, and to other places, for the same purpose. ³So they went unto Rome, and entered into the senate, and said, Jonathan the high priest, and the people of the Jews, sent us unto you, to the end ye should renew the friendship, which ye had with them, and league, as in former time. ⁴Upon this the Romans gave them letters unto the governors of every place, that they should bring them into the land of Judea peaceably.

⁵And this is the copy of the letters which Jonathan wrote to the Lacedemonians: ⁶Jonathan the high priest, and the elders of the nation, and the priests, and

---

coast, south of Tyre and north of Ptolemais.   **11:60** *Beyond the water*: lit. "beyond the river," i.e., the Euphrates; see 7:8 note.   **11:61** *Gaza*: south of Ascalon, near the coast in the land of the Philistines.   **11:62** *Damascus*: in Syria.   **11:65** *Bethsura*: Beth-zur was still held by Seleucid supporters; cf. 10:14.   **11:67** *Water of Gennesar*: Lake Genessaret, i.e., the Sea of Galilee. *Nasor*: better "Hazor" (MS tradition), north of the Sea of Galilee.   **11:70** *Except Mattathias . . . host*: including the men they commanded.   **11:71** *Rent his clothes . . . prayed*: compare the actions of Joshua after the initial failure to take Jericho (Josh 7:6).

12:1–23 The letter to the Spartans. 12:2 *Lacedemonians*: lit. "Spartans" (so throughout). Sparta, Lacedaemon's leading city, became especially influential after Rome's defeat of the Achaean

the other people of the Jews, unto the Lacedemonians their brethren send greeting: [7]There were letters sent in times past unto Onias the high priest from Darius, who reigned then among you, to signify that ye are our brethren, as the copy here underwritten doth specify. [8]At which time Onias entreated the ambassador that was sent honourably, and received the letters, wherein declaration was made of the league and friendship. [9]Therefore we also, albeit we need none of these things, for that we have the holy books of scripture in our hands to comfort us, [10]have nevertheless attempted to send unto you for the renewing of brotherhood and friendship, lest we should become strangers unto you altogether: for there is a long time passed since ye sent unto us. [11]We therefore at all times without ceasing, both in our feasts, and other convenient days, do remember you in the sacrifices which we offer, and in our prayers, as reason is, and as it becometh us to think upon our brethren: [12]and we are right glad of your honour. [13]As for ourselves, we have had great troubles and wars on every side, forsomuch as the kings that are round about us have fought against us. [14]Howbeit we would not be troublesome unto you, nor to others of our confederates and friends, in these wars: [15]for we have help from heaven that succoureth us, so as we are delivered from our enemies, and our enemies are brought under foot. [16]For this cause we chose Numenius the son of Antiochus, and Antipater the son of Jason, and sent them unto the Romans, to renew the amity that we had with them, and the former league. [17]We commanded them also to go unto you, and to salute you, and to deliver you our letters concerning the renewing of our brotherhood. [18]Wherefore now ye shall do well to give us an answer thereto.

[19]And this is the copy of the letters which Oniares sent. [20]Areus king of the Lacedemonians to Onias the high priest, greeting: [21]It is found in writing, that the Lacedemonians and Jews are brethren, and that they are of the stock of Abraham: [22]now therefore, since this is come to our knowledge, ye shall do well to write unto us of your prosperity. [23]We do write back again to you, that your cattle and goods are ours, and ours are yours. We do command therefore our ambassadors to make report unto you on this wise.

[24]Now when Jonathan heard that Demetrius' princes were come to fight against him with a greater host than afore, [25]he removed from Jerusalem, and met them in the land of Amathis: for he gave them no respite to enter his country. [26]He sent spies also unto their tents, who came again, and told him that they were appointed to come upon them in the night season. [27]Wherefore so soon as the sun was

---

Confederacy (see 8:9–10 note).   **12:7** *Onias . . . Darius:* the evidently corrupt text (see v. 19 note; cf. v. 20) makes certainty impossible, but *Onias* is probably Onias I, high priest, ca. 300 B.C.E., and *Darius* should read "Arius" (see v. 20), king of Sparta, ca. 309–265 B.C.E.   **12:11** *As reason is:* more literally "as we ought."   **12:19** *Which Oniares sent:* the corruption of Onias's name (apparently conflated with Arius's), combined with the obviously mistaken assertion (cf. v. 20), suggests scribal error. The text should probably read "which Arius sent Onais," or something of the sort.   **12:21** *In writing:* perhaps better "in a writing." The genealogical connection so vaguely cited is probably nothing more than a diplomatically expedient fiction.   **12:23** *On this wise:* in this manner.

12:24–38 Victories of Jonathan and Simon. 12:25 *Amathis:* Hamath, south of Antioch, on the Orontes River. *Respite:* i.e., of hostilities.   **12:26** *Appointed:* or "in formation."

down, Jonathan commanded his men to watch, and to be in arms, that all the night long they might be ready to fight: also he sent forth centinels round about the host. ²⁸But when the adversaries heard that Jonathan and his men were ready for battle, they feared, and trembled in their hearts, and they kindled fires in their camp. ²⁹Howbeit Jonathan and his company knew it not till the morning: for they saw the lights burning. ³⁰Then Jonathan pursued after them, but overtook them not: for they were gone over the river Eleutherus. ³¹Wherefore Jonathan turned to the Arabians, who were called Zabadeans, and smote them, and took their spoils. ³²And removing thence, he came to Damascus, and so passed through all the country. ³³Simon also went forth, and passed through the country unto Ascalon, and the holds there adjoining, from whence he turned aside to Joppe, and won it. ³⁴For he had heard that they would deliver the hold unto them that took Demetrius' part; wherefore he set a garrison there to keep it.

³⁵After this came Jonathan home again, and calling the elders of the people together, he consulted with them about building strong holds in Judea, ³⁶and making the walls of Jerusalem higher, and raising a great mount between the tower and the city, for to separate it from the city, that so it might be alone, that men might neither sell nor buy in it. ³⁷Upon this they came together to build up the city, forasmuch as part of the wall toward the brook on the east side was fallen down, and they repaired that which was called Caphenatha. ³⁸Simon also set up Adida in Sephela, and made it strong with gates and bars.

³⁹Now Tryphon went about to get the kingdom of Asia, and to kill Antiochus the king, that he might set the crown upon his own head. ⁴⁰Howbeit he was afraid that Jonathan would not suffer him, and that he would fight against him; wherefore he sought a way how to take Jonathan, that he might kill him. So he removed, and came to Bethsan. ⁴¹Then Jonathan went out to meet him with forty thousand men chosen for the battle, and came to Bethsan. ⁴²Now when Tryphon saw that Jonathan came with so great a force, he durst not stretch his hand against him; ⁴³but received him honourably, and commended him unto all his friends, and gave him gifts, and commanded his men of war to be as obedient unto him, as to himself. ⁴⁴Unto Jonathan also he said, Why hast thou put all this people to so great trouble, seeing there is no war betwixt us? ⁴⁵Therefore send them now home again, and choose a few men to wait on thee, and come thou with me to Ptolemais, for I will give it thee, and the rest of the strong holds and forces, and all that

12:27 *Centinels*: sentinels.   **12:29** *Knew it not . . . burning*: like the fires that Demetrius's forces had lit to disguise their retreat, the narrative itself initially conceals their flight.   **12:31** *The Arabians . . . Zabadeans*: the motives for Jonathan's attack are not clear. Arabs had provided mercenary assistance to the Seleucids when Antiochus IV Epiphanes ruled (see 5:39 note), but Jonathan is himself now fighting for a Seleucid emperor. Some speculate that the Zabadeans played a role in the death of Alexander I Balsas, whom Jonathan supported, because "Zabdiel the Arabian" killed him (11:16–17).   **12:33** *Holds*: strongholds.   **12:36** *For to separate it . . . in it*: i.e., to cut it off from any source of provisions (cf. 13:49).   **12:37** *The brook on the east side*: the Wadi Kidron. *Caphenatha*: presumably the name of part of the wall, or of a neighborhood adjacent to a given section of the wall.   **12:38** *Adida in Sephela*: near Joppa, on the route there from Jerusalem.
    12:39–53 The betrayal and capture of Jonathan. 12:39 *Tryphon*: having seized power in

have any charge: as for me, I will return and depart: for this is the cause of my coming. ⁴⁶So Jonathan believing him did as he bade him, and sent away his host, who went into the land of Judea. ⁴⁷And with himself he retained but three thousand men, of whom he sent two thousand into Galilee, and one thousand went with him. ⁴⁸Now as soon as Jonathan entered into Ptolemais, they of Ptolemais shut the gates, and took him, and all them that came with him they slew with the sword. ⁴⁹Then sent Tryphon an host of footmen and horsemen into Galilee, and into the great plain, to destroy all Jonathan's company. ⁵⁰But when they knew that Jonathan and they that were with him were taken and slain, they encouraged one another, and went close together, prepared to fight. ⁵¹They therefore that followed upon them, perceiving that they were ready to fight for their lives, turned back again. ⁵²Whereupon they all came into the land of Judea peaceably, and there they bewailed Jonathan, and them that were with him, and they were sore afraid; wherefore all Israel made great lamentation. ⁵³Then all the heathen that were round about them sought to destroy them: for said they, They have no captain, nor any to help them: now therefore let us make war upon them, and take away their memorial from among men.

13 Now when Simon heard that Tryphon had gathered together a great host to invade the land of Judea, and destroy it, ²and saw that the people was in great trembling and fear, he went up to Jerusalem, and gathered the people together, ³and gave them exhortation, saying, Ye yourselves know what great things I, and my brethren, and my father's house, have done for the laws and the sanctuary, the battles also and troubles which we have seen, ⁴by reason whereof all my brethren are slain for Israel's sake, and I am left alone. ⁵Now therefore be it far from me, that I should spare mine own life in any time of trouble: for I am no better than my brethren. ⁶Doubtless I will avenge my nation, and the sanctuary, and our wives, and our children: for all the heathen are gathered to destroy us of very malice.

⁷Now as soon as the people heard these words, their spirit revived. ⁸And they answered with a loud voice, saying, Thou shalt be our leader instead of Judas and Jonathan thy brother. ⁹Fight thou our battles, and whatsoever thou commandest us, that will we do. ¹⁰So then he gathered together all the men of war, and made haste to finish the walls of Jerusalem, and he fortified it round about. ¹¹Also he sent Jonathan the son of Absalom, and with him a great power, to Joppe: who casting out them that were therein remained there in it.

¹²So Tryphon removed from Ptolemais with a great power to invade the land of Judea, and Jonathan was with him in ward. ¹³But Simon pitched his tents at Adida, over against the plain. ¹⁴Now when Tryphon knew that Simon was risen

Antiochus VI Epiphanes' name (11:39, 54), he now wants to rule in his own.   **12:50** *Went close together*: drew into close formation.

   13:1–11 Simon succeeds Jonathan. 13:4 *All my brethren . . . alone*: recalling the refrain of Elijah (1 Kgs 18:22; 19:10, 14).   **13:6** *All the heathen . . . malice*: perhaps echoing Zech 12:3.

   13:12–30 The death of Jonathan. Jonathan is nowhere eulogized in the manner of his brothers Judas (3:1–9) or Simon (14:4–15, 25–45), perhaps because of his constant willingness to negotiate

up instead of his brother Jonathan, and meant to join battle with him, he sent messengers unto him, saying, [15] Whereas we have Jonathan thy brother in hold, it is for money that he is owing unto the king's treasure, concerning the business that was committed unto him. [16] Wherefore now send an hundred talents of silver, and two of his sons for hostages, that when he is at liberty he may not revolt from us, and we will let him go. [17] Hereupon Simon, albeit he perceived that they spake deceitfully unto him, yet sent he the money and the children, lest peradventure he should procure to himself great hatred of the people: [18] who might have said, Because I sent him not the money and the children, therefore is Jonathan dead. [19] So he sent them the children and the hundred talents: howbeit Tryphon dissembled, neither would he let Jonathan go.

[20] And after this came Tryphon to invade the land, and destroy it, going round about by the way that leadeth unto Adora: but Simon and his host marched against him in every place, wheresoever he went. [21] Now they that were in the tower sent messengers unto Tryphon, to the end that he should hasten his coming unto them by the wilderness, and send them victuals. [22] Wherefore Tryphon made ready all his horsemen to come that night: but there fell a very great snow, by reason whereof he came not. So he departed, and came into the country of Galaad. [23] And when he came near to Bascama, he slew Jonathan, who was buried there. [24] Afterward Tryphon returned and went into his own land.

[25] Then sent Simon, and took the bones of Jonathan his brother, and buried them in Modin, the city of his fathers. [26] And all Israel made great lamentation for him, and bewailed him many days. [27] Simon also built a monument upon the sepulchre of his father and his brethren, and raised it aloft to the sight, with hewn stone behind and before. [28] Moreover he set up seven pyramids, one against another, for his father, and his mother, and his four brethren. [29] And in these he made cunning devices, about the which he set great pillars, and upon the pillars he made all their armour for a perpetual memory, and by the armour ships carved, that they might be seen of all that sail on the sea. [30] This is the sepulchre which he made at Modin, and it standeth yet unto this day.

[31] Now Tryphon dealt deceitfully with the young king Antiochus, and slew him. [32] And he reigned in his stead, and crowned himself king of Asia, and brought a great calamity upon the land. [33] Then Simon built up the strong holds in Judea, and fenced them about with high towers, and great walls, and gates, and bars, and laid up victuals therein. [34] Moreover Simon chose men, and sent to king Demetrius, to the end he should give the land an immunity, because all that Tryphon did was to spoil. [35] Unto whom king Demetrius answered and wrote after this manner: [36] King Demetrius unto Simon the high priest, and friend of kings,

with the Seleucids, which ultimately led to his capture (12:44–48). **13:15** *For money . . . him*: it is unclear to what Tryphon refers, but in any case he is dissimulating. **13:20** *Adora*: south of Jerusalem. **13:22** *Galaad*: Gilead. **13:23** *Bascama*: unidentified. **13:28** *Seven pyramids . . . brethren*: the seventh monument must be for himself. **13:29** *In these*: better "for these," referring either to the pyramids' setting (so NRSV) or to their ornamentation.

13:31–53 Simon captures the Jerusalem citadel. **13:31** *Young king Antiochus*: he was still a boy when murdered; according to Livy (*Periocha* 55), Tryphon bribed doctors to trump up a reason

as also unto the elders and nation of the Jews, sendeth greeting: [37] The golden crown, and the scarlet robe, which ye sent unto us, we have received: and we are ready to make a stedfast peace with you, yea, and to write unto our officers, to confirm the immunities which we have granted. [38] And whatsoever covenants we have made with you shall stand; and the strong holds, which ye have builded, shall be your own. [39] As for any oversight or fault committed, unto this day, we forgive it, and the crown tax also, which ye owe us: and if there were any other tribute paid in Jerusalem, it shall no more be paid. [40] And look who are meet among you to be in our court, let them be enrolled, and let there be peace betwixt us.

[41] Thus the yoke of the heathen was taken away from Israel in the hundred and seventieth year. [42] Then the people of Israel began to write in their instruments and contracts, In the first year of Simon the high priest, the governor and leader of the Jews. [43] In those days Simon camped against Gaza, and besieged it round about; he made also an engine of war, and set it by the city, and battered a certain tower, and took it. [44] And they that were in the engine leaped into the city; whereupon there was a great uproar in the city: [45] insomuch as the people of the city rent their clothes, and climbed upon the walls with their wives and children, and cried with a loud voice, beseeching Simon to grant them peace. [46] And they said. Deal not with us according to our wickedness, but according to thy mercy. [47] So Simon was appeased toward them, and fought no more against them, but put them out of the city, and cleansed the houses wherein the idols were, and so entered into it with songs and thanksgiving. [48] Yea, he put all uncleanness out of it, and placed such men there as would keep the law, and made it stronger than it was before, and built therein a dwelling place for himself.

[49] They also of the tower in Jerusalem were kept so strait, that they could neither come forth, nor go into the country, nor buy, nor sell: wherefore they were in great distress for want of victuals, and a great number of them perished through famine. [50] Then cried they to Simon, beseeching him to be at one with them: which thing he granted them; and when he had put them out from thence, he cleansed the tower from pollutions: [51] and entered into it the three and twentieth day of the second month, in the hundred seventy and first year, with thanksgiving, and branches of palm tress, and with harps, and cymbals, and with viols, and hymns, and songs: because there was destroyed a great enemy out of Israel. [52] He ordained also that that day should be kept every year with gladness. Moreover the hill of the temple that was by the tower he made stronger than it was, and there he dwelt himself with his company. [53] And when Simon saw that John his son was a valiant man, he made him captain of all the hosts; and he dwelt in Gazara.

---

to operate on the king and kill him in the process.   **13:41** *The hundred and seventieth year*: 142 B.C.E.   **13:42** *Instruments*: formal documents.   **13:43** *Engine of war*: siege tower.   **13:46** *Deal not . . . mercy*: cf. Dan 9:18.   **13:49** *Strait*: constrained.   **13:51** *The hundred seventy and first year*: 141 B.C.E.   **13:52** *He ordained . . . year*: another short-lived holiday (cf. 7:49 and note).

14 Now in the hundred threescore and twelfth year king Demetrius gathered his forces together, and went into Media, to get him help to fight against Tryphon. ²But when Arsaces, the king of Persia and Media, heard that Demetrius was entered within his borders, he sent one of his princes to take him alive: ³who went and smote the host of Demetrius, and took him, and brought him to Arsaces, by whom he was put in ward. ⁴As for the land of Judea, that was quiet all the days of Simon; for he sought the good of his nation in such wise, as that evermore his authority and honour pleased them well. ⁵And as he was honourable in all his acts, so in this, that he took Joppe for an haven, and made an entrance to the isles of the sea, ⁶and enlarged the bounds of his nation, and recovered the country, ⁷and gathered together a great number of captives, and had the dominion of Gazara, and Bethsura, and the tower, out of the which he took all uncleanness, neither was there any that resisted him. ⁸Then did they till their ground in peace, and the earth gave her increase, and the trees of the field their fruit. ⁹The ancient men sat all in the streets, communing together of good things, and the young men put on glorious and warlike apparel. ¹⁰He provided victuals for the cities, and set in them all manner of munition, so that his honourable name was renowned unto the end of the world. ¹¹He made peace in the land, and Israel rejoiced with great joy: ¹²for every man sat under his vine and his fig tree, and there was none to fray them: ¹³neither was there any left in the land to fight against them: yea, the kings themselves were overthrown in those days. ¹⁴Moreover he strengthened all those of his people that were brought low: the law he searched out; and every contemner of the law and wicked person he took away. ¹⁵He beautified the sanctuary, and multiplied the vessels of the temple.

¹⁶Now when it was heard at Rome, and as far as Sparta, that Jonathan was dead, they were very sorry. ¹⁷But as soon as they heard that his brother Simon was made high priest in his stead, and ruled the country, and the cities therein: ¹⁸they wrote unto him in tables of brass, to renew the friendship and league which they had made with Judas and Jonathan his brethren: ¹⁹which writings were read before the congregation at Jerusalem.

²⁰And this is the copy of the letters that the Lacedemonians sent; The rulers of the Lacedemonians, with the city, unto Simon the high priest, and the elders, and priests, and residue of the people of the Jews, our brethren, send greeting: ²¹The ambassadors that were sent unto our people certified us of your glory and honour: wherefore we were glad of their coming, ²²and did register the things

---

14:1–49 The reign of Simon. 14:1 *The hundred threescore and twelfth year*: 140 B.C.E. **14:2** *Arsaces*: better known as Mithridates I, who ruled the Parthian empire ca. 171–138 B.C.E., a time of significant expansion—much of it at the Seleucid Empire's expense. (Based in northeastern Persia, the Parthian kingdom was established in the third century B.C.E. when that region broke free of Seleucid dominance.) Demetrius presumably thought he could liberate some of Parthia's recently conquered territories and enlist their support in his war with Antiochus VI Epiphanes. **14:4–15** *As for the land . . . temple*: many modern versions print this encomium as poetry. It contains several echoes of biblical language; a few are mentioned in the notes below. **14:4** *In such wise*: in such a manner. **14:5** *Haven*: harbor. **14:8–9** *Then did they . . . warlike apparel*: recalling such OT passages as Lev 26:3–4; Ezek 34:27; Zech 8:4, 12. **14:12** *Every man . . . tree*: an OT slogan of national prosperity (see 1 Kgs 4:25; Mic 4:4; etc.). *Fray*: frighten. **14:14** *Contemner*: despiser. **14:18** *Tables of brass*:

that they spake in the council of the people in this manner; Numenius son of Antiochus, and Antipater son of Jason, the Jews' ambassadors, came unto us to renew the friendship they had with us. [23]And it pleased the people to entertain the men honourably, and to put the copy of their ambassage in publick records, to the end the people of the Lacedemonians might have a memorial thereof: furthermore we have written a copy thereof unto Simon the high priest. [24]After this Simon sent Numenius to Rome with a great shield of gold of a thousand pound weight, to confirm the league with them.

[25]Whereof when the people heard, they said, What thanks shall we give to Simon and his sons? [26]For he and his brethren and the house of his father have established Israel, and chased away in fight their enemies from them, and confirmed their liberty. [27]So then they wrote it in tables of brass, which they set upon pillars in mount Sion: and this is the copy of the writing; The eighteenth day of the month Elul, in the hundred threescore and twelfth year, being the third year of Simon the high priest, [28]at Saramel in the great congregation of the priests, and people, and rulers of the nation, and elders of the country, were these things notified unto us. [29]Forasmuch as oftentimes there have been wars in the country, wherein for the maintenance of their sanctuary, and the law, Simon the son of Mattathias, of the posterity of Jarib, together with his brethren, put themselves in jeopardy, and resisting the enemies of their nation did their nation great honour: [30](for after that Jonathan, having gathered his nation together, and been their high, priest, was added to his people, [31]their enemies purposed to invade their country, that they might destroy it, and lay hands on the sanctuary: [32]at which time Simon rose up, and fought for his nation, and spent much of his own substance, and armed the valiant men of his nation, and gave them wages, [33]and fortified the cities of Judea, together with Bethsura, that lieth upon the borders of Judea, where the armour of the enemies had been before; but he set a garrison of Jews there: [34]moreover he fortified Joppe, which lieth upon the sea, and Gazara, that bordereth upon Azotus, where the enemies had dwelt before: but he placed Jews there, and furnished them with all things convenient for the reparation thereof.)

[35]The people therefore, seeing the acts of Simon, and unto what glory he thought to bring his nation, made him their governor and chief priest, because he had done all these things, and for the justice and faith which he kept to his nation, and for that he sought by all means to exalt his people. [36]For in his time things prospered in his hands, so that the heathen were taken out of their country, and they also that were in the city of David in Jerusalem, who had made themselves a tower, out of which they issued, and polluted all about the sanctuary, and did much hurt in the holy place: [37]but he placed Jews therein, and fortified it for the safety of the country and the city, and raised up the walls of Jerusalem. [38]King Demetrius also confirmed him in the high priesthood accord-

---

bronze tablets.   **14:23** *Ambassage*: diplomatic message.   **14:27** *The eighteenth day . . . year*: August–September 140 B.C.E.   **14:28** *Saramel*: probably reflecting the original translator's misunderstanding of a Hebrew phrase meaning "the court of God's people."   **14:30** *Was added to his people*: died

ing to those things, ³⁹and made him one of his friends, and honoured him with great honour. ⁴⁰For he had heard say, that the Romans had called the Jews their friends and confederates and brethren; and that they had entertained the ambassadors of Simon honourably; ⁴¹also that the Jews and priests were well pleased that Simon should be their governor and high priest for ever, until there should arise a faithful prophet; ⁴²moreover that he should be their captain, and should take charge of the sanctuary, to set them over their works, and over the country, and over the armour, and over the fortresses, that, I say, he should take charge of the sanctuary; ⁴³beside this, that he should be obeyed of every man, and that all the writings in the country should be made in his name, and that he should be clothed in purple, and wear gold: ⁴⁴also that it should be lawful for none of the people or priests to break any of these things, or to gainsay his words, or to gather an assembly in the country without him, or to be clothed in purple, or wear a buckle of gold: ⁴⁵and whosoever should do otherwise, or break any of these things, he should be punished.

⁴⁶Thus it liked all the people to deal with Simon, and to do as hath been said. ⁴⁷Then Simon accepted hereof, and was well pleased to be high priest, and captain and governor of the Jews and priests, and to defend them all. ⁴⁸So they commanded that this writing should be put in tables of brass, and that they should be set up within the compass of the sanctuary in a conspicuous place; ⁴⁹also that the copies thereof should be laid up in the treasury, to the end that Simon and his sons might have them.

15 Moreover Antiochus son of Demetrius the king sent letters from the isles of the sea unto Simon the priest and prince of the Jews, and to all the people; ²the contents whereof were these: King Antiochus to Simon the high priest and prince of his nation, and to the people of the Jews, greeting: ³Forasmuch as certain pestilent men have usurped the kingdom of our fathers, and my purpose is to challenge it again, that I may restore it to the old estate, and to that end have gathered a multitude of foreign soldiers together, and prepared ships of war; ⁴my meaning also being to go through the country, that I may be avenged of them that have destroyed it, and made many cities in the kingdom desolate: ⁵now therefore I confirm unto thee all the oblations which the kings before me granted thee, and whatsoever gifts besides they granted. ⁶I give thee leave also to coin money for thy country with thine own stamp. ⁷And as concerning Jerusalem and the sanctuary, let them be free; and all the armour that thou hast made, and fortresses that thou hast built, and keepest in thine hands, let them remain unto thee. ⁸And if any thing be, or shall be, owing to the king, let it be forgiven thee from this time forth for evermore. ⁹Furthermore, when we have obtained our kingdom, we will honour thee, and thy nation, and thy temple, with great honour, so that your honour shall be known throughout the world.

(cf. 2:69).   **14:41** *Until there . . . prophet*: see 9:27 note.   **14:43** *All the writings . . . name*: cf. 13:42 and note.   **14:46** *Liked*: pleased.

15:1–14 Antiochus VII Sidetes wages war against Tryphon.   **15:1** *Antiochus son of Demetrius the king*: Antiochus VII Sidetes reigned from 138 (when he defeated Tryphon, against whom he is here planning an expedition) to 129 B.C.E.   **15:5** *Oblations*: lit. "remissions," i.e., of taxes.

¹⁰In the hundred threescore and fourteenth year went Antiochus into the land of his fathers: at which time all the forces came together unto him, so that few were left with Tryphon. ¹¹Wherefore being pursued by king Antiochus, he fled unto Dora, which lieth by the sea side: ¹²for he saw that troubles came upon him all at once, and that his forces had forsaken him. ¹³Then camped Antiochus against Dora, having with him an hundred and twenty thousand men of war, and eight thousand horsemen. ¹⁴And when he had compassed the city round about, and joined ships close to the town on the sea side, he vexed the city by land and by sea, neither suffered he any to go out or in.

¹⁵In the mean season came Numenius and his company from Rome, having letters to the kings and countries; wherein were written these things: ¹⁶Lucius, consul of the Romans, unto king Ptolemee, greeting: ¹⁷The Jews' ambassadors, our friends and confederates, came unto us to renew the old friendship and league, being sent from Simon the high priest, and from the people of the Jews: ¹⁸and they brought a shield of gold of a thousand pound. ¹⁹We thought it good therefore to write unto the kings and countries, that they should do them no harm, nor fight against them, their cities, or countries, nor yet aid their enemies against them. ²⁰It seemed also good to us to receive the shield of them.

²¹If therefore there be any pestilent fellows, that have fled from their country unto you, deliver them unto Simon the high priest, that he may punish them according to their own law. ²²The same things wrote he likewise unto Demetrius the king, and Attalus, to Ariarathes, and Arsaces, ²³and to all the countries, and to Sampsames, and the Lacedemonians, and to Delus, and Myndus, and Sicyon, and Caria, and Samos, and Pamphylia, and Lycia, and Halicarnassus, and Rhodus, and Phaselis, and Cos, and Side, and Aradus, and Gortyna, and Cnidus, and Cyprus, and Cyrene. ²⁴And the copy hereof they wrote to Simon the high priest.

²⁵So Antiochus the king camped against Dora the second day, assaulting it continually, and making engines, by which means he shut up Tryphon, that he could neither go out nor in. ²⁶At that time Simon sent him two thousand chosen men to aid him; silver also, and gold, and much armour. ²⁷Nevertheless he would not receive them, but brake all the covenants which he had made with him afore, and became strange unto him. ²⁸Furthermore he sent unto him Athenobius, one of his friends, to commune with him, and say, Ye withhold Joppe and Gazara, with the tower that is in Jerusalem, which are cities of my realm. ²⁹The borders thereof ye have wasted, and done great hurt in the land, and got the dominion of many places within my kingdom. ³⁰Now therefore deliver the cities which ye have

---

15:10 *The hundred threescore and fourteenth year*: 138 B.C.E.   **15:11** *Dora*: on the Mediterranean coast, south of Ptolemais.

15:15–24 The letter from Rome.   15:16 *Lucius, consul of the Romans*: apparently Lucius Caecilius Metellus Calvus, consul in 142 B.C.E. This passage looks back to 14:16–24, reporting the belated result of Numenius's mission to Rome following Jonathan's death. Some scholars believe that it was originally placed after 14:24 but was moved through scribal error. *Ptolemee*: Ptolemy VIII Eugertes II, who ruled Egypt 170–116 B.C.E.   **15:22** *The same thing . . . Arsaces*: i.e., the letter was an encyclical. *Attalus, to Ariarathes, and Arsaces*: rulers of Pergamum, Cappadocia, and Parthia, respectively.   **15:23** *All the countries*: those listed in this verse are in Greece and Asia Minor.

15:25–41 Antiochus Sidetes initiates hostilities with Simon.   15:27 *Strange unto*: "alien-

taken, and the tributes of the places, whereof ye have gotten dominion without the borders of Judea: [31]or else give me for them five hundred talents of silver; and for the harm that ye have done, and the tributes of the cities, other five hundred talents: if not, we will come and fight against you.

[32]So Athenobius the king's friend came to Jerusalem: and when he saw the glory of Simon, and the cupboard of gold and silver plate, and his great attendance, he was astonished, and told him the king's message. [33]Then answered Simon, and said unto him, We have neither taken other men's land, nor holden that which appertaineth to others, but the inheritance of our fathers, which our enemies had wrongfully in possession a certain time. [34]Wherefore we, having opportunity, hold the inheritance of our fathers. [35]And whereas thou demandest Joppe and Gazara, albeit they did great harm unto the people in our country, yet will we give an hundred talents for them. Hereunto Athenobius answered him not a word; [36]but returned in a rage to the king, and made report unto him of these speeches, and of the glory of Simon, and of all that he had seen: whereupon the king was exceeding wroth.

[37]In the mean time fled Tryphon by ship unto Orthosias. [38]Then the king made Cendebeus captain of the sea coast, and gave him an host of footmen and horsemen, [39]and commanded him to remove his host toward Judea: also he commanded him to build up Cedron, and to fortify the gates, and to war against the people; but as for the king himself, he pursued Tryphon. [40]So Cendebeus came to Jamnia, and began to provoke the people, and to invade Judea, and to take the people prisoners, and slay them. [41]And when he had built up Cedron, he set horsemen there, and an host of footmen, to the end that issuing out they might make outroads upon the ways of Judea, as the king had commanded him.

16 Then came up John from Gazara, and told Simon his father what Cendebeus had done. [2]Wherefore Simon called his two eldest sons, Judas and John, and said unto them, I, and my brethren, and my father's house, have ever from our youth unto this day fought against the enemies of Israel; and things have prospered so well in our hands, that we have delivered Israel oftentimes. [3]But now I am old, and ye, by God's mercy, are of a sufficient age: be ye instead of me and my brother, and go and fight for our nation, and the help from heaven be with you.

[4]So he chose out of the country twenty thousand men of war with horsemen, who went out against Cendebeus, and rested that night at Modin. [5]And when as they rose in the morning, and went into the plain, behold, a mighty great host both of footmen and horsemen came against them: howbeit there was a water brook betwixt them. [6]So he and his people pitched over against them: and when he saw that the people were afraid to go over the water brook, he went first over

---

ated from" or "hostile to." **15:31** *Five hundred talents*: a sizeable sum. **15:37** *Orthosias*: just north of Tripolis on the Mediterranean coast. According to other sources, Tryphon's flight continued beyond Orthosias and ultimately led to his death, although accounts of how he died differ. **15:39** *Cedron*: just southeast of Jamnia, near the Mediterranean coast. **15:41** *Make outroads*: "make raids" (NRSV).

16:1–10 The succession and victory of John Hyrcanus. 16:1 *Then came up John from Gazar*: see 13:53. *John*: John Hyrcanus, who ruled Judea 135–104 B.C.E. **16:5** *Water brook*: wadi. **16:6** *He went . . . after him*: perhaps recalling Israel's crossing of the Jordan to conquer the promised land under the leadership of Joshua (Josh 1, 3), immediately after he succeeded Moses.

himself, and then the men seeing him passed through after him. ⁷That done, he divided his men, and set the horsemen in the midst of the footmen: for the enemies' horsemen were very many. ⁸Then sounded they with the holy trumpets: whereupon Cendebeus and his host were put to flight, so that many of them were slain, and the remnant gat them to the strong hold. ⁹At that time was Judas John's brother wounded; but John still followed after them, until he came to Cedron, which Cendebeus had built. ¹⁰So they fled even unto the towers in the fields of Azotus; wherefore he burned it with fire: so that there were slain of them about two thousand men. Afterward he returned into the land of Judea in peace.

¹¹Moreover in the plain of Jericho was Ptolemeus the son of Abubus made captain, and he had abundance of silver and gold: ¹²for he was the high priest's son in law. ¹³Wherefore his heart being lifted up, he thought to get the country to himself, and thereupon consulted deceitfully against Simon and his sons to destroy them. ¹⁴Now Simon was visiting the cities that were in the country, and taking care for the good ordering of them; at which time he came down himself to Jericho with his sons, Mattathias and Judas, in the hundred threescore and seventeenth year, in the eleventh month, called Sabat: ¹⁵where the son of Abubus receiving them deceitfully into a little hold, called Docus, which he had built, made them a great banquet: howbeit he had hid men there. ¹⁶So when Simon and his sons had drunk largely, Ptolemee and his men rose up, and took their weapons, and came upon Simon into the banqueting place, and slew him, and his two sons, and certain of his servants. ¹⁷In which doing he committed a great treachery, and recompensed evil for good.

¹⁸Then Ptolemee wrote these things, and sent to the king, that he should send him an host to aid him, and he would deliver him the country and cities. ¹⁹He sent others also to Gazara, to kill John: and unto the tribunes he sent letters to come unto him, that he might give them silver, and gold, and rewards. ²⁰And others he sent to take Jerusalem, and the mountain of the temple. ²¹Now one had run afore to Gazara, and told John that his father and brethren were slain, and, quoth he, Ptolemee hath sent to slay thee also. ²²Hereof when he heard, he was sore astonished: so he laid hands on them that were come to destroy him, and slew them; for he knew that they sought to make him away.

²³As concerning the rest of the acts of John, and his wars, and worthy deeds which he did, and the building of the walls which he made, and his doings, ²⁴behold, these are written in the chronicles of his priesthood, from the time he was made high priest after his father.

16:11–24 The murder of Simon and his sons. After the possible recollection of Joshua in the previous section (see v. 6 and note), it is ironic that here a national betrayal occurs precisely at Jericho (see Josh 2, 6), especially since that betrayal ultimately leads to Jerusalem's siege (see v. 20 note). 1 Maccabees therefore begins and ends with different acts of national betrayal that invite foreign oppression (cf. 1:11–15): like the Deuteronomistic History, it blames Israel for its own national tragedies. **16:14** *The hundred threescore and seventeenth year*: 134 B.C.E. *Sabat*: February-March. **16:15** *Docus*: rather "Dok." **16:20** *Others he . . . temple*: Antiochus would soon lay siege to Jerusalem, forcing Hyrcanus into a not altogether favorable treaty (Josephus, *Jewish Antiquities* 13.236–49). **16:23–24** *As concerning . . . priesthood*: like the close of the section focusing on Judas (9:22; see note), this conclusion recalls the endings of accounts of individual monarchs' reigns in 1 and 2 Kings. But unlike the earlier OT allusion, there is no one-upmanship here.

The Second Book of the Maccabees

A S explained in the introduction to 1 Maccabees, this companion book is in some sense its antagonist, a rival account of the last great period of Jewish nationalism in the biblical era. It was written by one who, though not an outright opponent of the Hasmoneans, boldly emphasizes the role of others in the fight to retain Jewish national and religious sovereignty—especially martyrs such as Eleazar, the anonymous seven sons and their mother, and Razis. It is surely significant that while 1 Maccabees unflatteringly contrasts the martyrs' willingness to die lest they violate the Sabbath with the Hasmoneans' readiness to fight heroically even on the day of rest (2:29–44), the present book subtly assimilates Judas Maccabeus to such martyrs by suggesting that he shares the beliefs motivating their willing deaths (see 12:43–45 and note). More important even than the martyrs in 2 Maccabees is the role of providence, which frequently intervenes to ensure the Seleucids' defeat through the manifestation of bellicose apparitions. The book's numerous examples of ironic retribution more subtly evince God's intervention: throughout 2 Maccabees wicked characters receive their comeuppance in poetically justified ways, as Heliodorus has to be carried out of the temple after he had pompously entered it for plunder, the blasphemous Nicanor has his tongue fed piecemeal to birds, and so on.

The sustained maintenance of this thematic pattern of ironic retribution bespeaks 2 Maccabees' careful literary design, evidence of which also surfaces in its style. It is written in a highly literate Greek—some classicists even find it pompous. Moreover, the narrative has a distinctly pathetic quality, which is so striking that some have labeled the work "tragic historiography." Consider, to cite just two examples, the vivid depiction of Jerusalem in mourning as it awaits Heliodorus's plunder of the temple (3:14–23) and the portrait of Razis, who rips out his entrails in the presence of his enemies and cries for God to restore them at the eschatological resurrection (14:37–46). Both descriptions provoke in the reader intense emotional responses—pity and awe, respectively. But these and similar episodes are so flamboyantly provocative that readers are as likely to be repulsed by as attracted to the characters with whom they are ostensibly invited to empathize. How well this "tragic" work of history is able to control the emotions aroused by its powerful narratives remains an open question.

2 Maccabees is an abridgement of a five-book work by Jason of Cyrene. This fact complicates analysis of the book's style and aim; and because Jason's unabridged work no longer survives, many questions can never be answered. But if we can believe the prologue (2:19–32), where the epitomizer claims credit for the work's ease of style and its selection of subjects, as well as for its adornments, at least

some of its distinctive literary qualities are probably the responsibility of its final editor. 2 Maccabees' narrative is preceded by two letters to the Jewish community in Alexandria urging it to celebrate Hanukkah, which commemorated the temple's rededication under Judas Maccabeus, and some speculate that the entire document was assembled—perhaps by Jason's abridger—as a propagandistic attempt to promote the faithful celebration of this innovative holiday among Egyptian Jews.

Unlike its companion, 2 Maccabees does not seem to be a Greek translation from Hebrew or any other language (with the exception of the prefatory letters, which may have been originally composed in Hebrew or Aramaic). It must have been written after 161 B.C.E., the final year it narrates, and before 63 B.C.E., because its attitude toward Rome is generally positive (see the introduction to 1 Maccabees). If the multiple points of contact between 1 and 2 Maccabees demonstrate that they drew on the same sources, as many scholars now believe, their presentation of such contrasting versions of Judea's liberation from Seleucid oppression becomes all the more intriguing. As often, the Bible incorporates conflicting accounts of key moments in sacred history, thereby belying the notion that historiography is ever anything other than "revisionary."

For fuller exposition of 2 Maccabees, see Jonathan A. Goldstein's Anchor Bible commentary, *II Maccabees* (Garden City, NY: Doubleday, 1983), which thoroughly informs the annotations that follow, as do Mary Chilton Callaway's notes in the *New Oxford Annotated Bible*, ed. Michael D. Coogan, 3rd ed. (Oxford: Oxford University Press, 2001).

The Second Book of the Maccabees

1 The brethren, the Jews that be at Jerusalem and in the land of Judea, wish unto the brethren, the Jews that are throughout Egypt, health and peace: ²God be gracious unto you, and remember his covenant that he made with Abraham, Isaac, and Jacob, his faithful servants; ³and give you all an heart to serve him, and to do his will, with a good courage and a willing mind; ⁴and open your hearts in his law and commandments, and send you peace, ⁵and hear your prayers, and be at one with you, and never forsake you in time of trouble. ⁶And now we be here praying for you.

⁷What time as Demetrius reigned, in the hundred threescore and ninth year, we the Jews wrote unto you in the extremity of trouble that came upon us in those years, from the time that Jason and his company revolted from the holy land and kingdom, ⁸and burned the porch, and shed innocent blood: then we prayed unto the Lord, and were heard; we offered also sacrifices and fine flour, and lighted the lamps, and set forth the loaves. ⁹And now see that ye keep the feast of tabernacles in the month Casleu.

¹⁰In the hundred fourscore and eighth year, the people that were at Jerusalem and in Judea, and the council, and Judas, sent greeting and health unto Aristobulus, king Ptolemeus' master, who was of the stock of the anointed priests, and to

1:1–2:18 Two letters concerning Hanukkah. Both are directed to the Jewish community of Egypt. The first (1:1–9) is usually considered to be an authentic festal letter giving the community to which it is addressed notice of Hanukkah's coming celebration. (Compare the announcements of Hezekiah's Passover in 2 Chr 30:1–9 and of Purim in Esth 9:20–32.) Notably, it makes no reference to the Hasmoneans, even though its subject is a commemoration of a Hasmonean victory. The second (1:10–2:18), also a festal letter, purports to have been written by Judas Maccabeus, but is usually thought to be a later forgery, perhaps composed because Hanukkah had still failed to take root among the Alexandrian Jews. Its full explanation of events contrasts with the first letter's more allusive references, perhaps signaling its address to an audience more distant historically from the events whose celebration it was urging.   **1:1** *Health and peace*: more literally "a good peace."   **1:2** *His covenant*: see Gen 15:18; 17:1–21; etc.   **1:7** *Demetrius*: Demetrius II Nicator; see 1 Macc 10:67 note. *The hundred threescore and ninth year*: 143 B.C.E. For the dating of events in this book, see 1 Macc 1:10 note. *Jason*: see 4:7–22.   **1:8** *Porch*: temple entrance; for its burning, see 1 Macc 4:38. For the shedding of *innocent blood*, see 1 Macc 1:60–61; 2 Macc 5:12–14; etc. *We offered . . . loaves*: acts performed in the rededication of the temple (see 1 Macc 4:36–58).   **1:9** *The feast . . . Casleu*: the festival of Hanukkah (cf. 1 Macc 4:59), which was related to the Feast of Tabernacles, celebrated earlier in the year (see 2 Macc 10:6). *Casleu*: November-December.   **1:10** *The hundred fourscore and eighth year*: 124 B.C.E.; but this is better construed as the date of the first letter than of the second, with the paragraph break coming after "year." *Council*: Gk. *gerousia*, a council of elders. *Aristobulus, king Ptolemeus' master*: probably referring to the Alexandrian Jewish scholar (second century

the Jews that were in Egypt: [11]Insomuch as God hath delivered us from great perils, we thank him highly, as having been in battle against a king. [12]For he cast them out that fought within the holy city. [13]For when the leader was come into Persia, and the army with him that seemed invincible, they were slain in the temple of Nanea by the deceit of Nanea's priests. [14]For Antiochus, as though he would marry her, came into the place, and his friends that were with him, to receive money in name of a dowry. [15]Which when the priests of Nanea had set forth, and he was entered with a small company into the compass of the temple, they shut the temple as soon as Antiochus was come in: [16]and opening a privy door of the roof, they threw stones like thunderbolts, and struck down the captain, hewed them in pieces, smote off their heads, and cast them to those that were without. [17]Blessed be our God in all things, who hath delivered up the ungodly.

[18]Therefore whereas we are now purposed to keep the purification of the temple upon the five and twentieth day of the month Casleu, we thought it necessary to certify you thereof, that ye also might keep it, as the feast of the tabernacles, and of the fire, which was given us when Neemias offered sacrifice, after that he had builded the temple and the altar. [19]For when our fathers were led into Persia, the priests that were then devout took the fire of the altar privily, and hid it in an hollow place of a pit without water, where they kept it sure, so that the place was unknown to all men. [20]Now after many years, when it pleased God, Neemias, being sent from the king of Persia, did send of the posterity of those priests that had hid it to the fire: but when they told us they found no fire, but thick water; [21]then commanded he them to draw it up, and to bring it; and when the sacrifices were laid on, Neemias commanded the priests to sprinkle the wood and the things laid thereupon with the water. [22]When this was done, and the time came that the sun shone, which afore was hid in the cloud, there was a great fire kindled, so that every man marvelled. [23]And the priests made a prayer

B.C.E.), whose works survive only in a handful of quotations. He is here identified as teacher of Ptolemy VI Philometor (see 1 Macc 1:18 note), perhaps because he had dedicated a book to him. **1:13** *Come into Persia*: this trip seems to correspond to the one narrated at 9:1–2; cf. 1 Macc 6:1–4. *Nanea*: a Syrian fertility goddess. Conventional ancient syncretism assimilated her to Aphrodite or Artemis. **1:14** *Antiochus*: Antiochus IV Epiphanes (see 1 Macc 1:10 note). *Friends*: see 1 Macc 2:18 note. **1:16** *Privy*: secret. *Captain*: Gk. *hēgemōn*, translated "leader" in v. 13, also with reference to Antiochus. KJV can be read as claiming that someone besides Antiochus died in this attack, presumably in order to avoid contradiction with the alternative account of his death later in the book (2 Macc 9:1–29; cf. 1 Macc 6:1–17). The present letter, however, suggests that Antiochus dies in Nanea's temple as divine retribution (*like thunderbolts*) for his own assault on Jerusalem and its temple. **1:18** *The purification of the temple*: the Hanukkah festival; its associations with *fire* (the lighting of the menorah, a multibranched candelabrum, is its central ritual) are explained in v. 19. *As the feast . . . altar*: Zerubbabel, not Nehemiah, oversaw the rebuilding of the temple and offered an initial sacrifice after the altar's reconstruction that seems to lie behind this reference (Ezra 3:1–5). The letter apparently conflates the two figures. **1:19** *When our fathers were led into Persia*: the Babylonian captivity (see 2 Kgs 24:13–16). Babylon is called *Persia* because it was subsumed within the Persian Empire. **1:20** *Neemias*: the eponymous biblical book narrates Nehemiah's commission by Artaxerxes (2:1–8) and subsequent return to Judea, but only here is the story of the preserved fire recounted. *Thick water*: viscous liquid, i.e., oil.

whilst the sacrifice was consuming, I say, both the priests, and all the rest, Jonathan beginning, and the rest answering thereunto, as Neemias did.

²⁴And the prayer was after this manner; O Lord, Lord God, Creator of all things, who art fearful and strong, and righteous, and merciful, and the only and gracious King, ²⁵the only giver of all things, the only just, almighty, and everlasting, thou that deliverest Israel from all trouble, and didst choose the fathers, and sanctify them: ²⁶receive the sacrifice for thy whole people Israel, and preserve thine own portion, and sanctify it. ²⁷Gather those together that are scattered from us, deliver them that serve among the heathen, look upon them that are despised and abhorred, and let the heathen know that thou art our God. ²⁸Punish them that oppress us, and with pride do us wrong. ²⁹Plant thy people again in thy holy place, as Moses hath spoken. ³⁰And the priests sung psalms of thanksgiving.

³¹Now when the sacrifice was consumed, Neemias commanded the water that was left to be poured on the great stones. ³²When this was done, there was kindled a flame: but it was consumed by the light that shined from the altar. ³³So when this matter was known, it was told the king of Persia, that in the place, where the priests that were led away had hid the fire, there appeared water, and that Neemias had purified the sacrifices therewith. ³⁴Then the king, inclosing the place, made it holy, after he had tried the matter. ³⁵And the king took many gifts, and bestowed thereof on those whom he would gratify. ³⁶And Neemias called this thing Naphthar, which is as much as to say, a cleansing: but many men call it Nephi.

2 It is also found in the records, that Jeremy the prophet commanded them that were carried away to take of the fire, as it hath been signified: ²and how that the prophet, having given them the law, charged them not to forget the commandments of the Lord, and that they should not err in their minds, when they see images of silver and gold, with their ornaments. ³And with other such speeches exhorted he them, that the law should not depart from their hearts.

⁴It was also contained in the same writing, that the prophet, being warned of God, commanded the tabernacle and the ark to go with him, as he went forth

---

1:23 *Consuming:* being consumed. *Jonathan:* obscure, but perhaps a mistake for the Levite Mattaniah, who is said to have begun a prayer (see Neh 11:17) and whose name in Hebrew has a meaning similar to that of "Jonathan" ("gift of the Lord" and "the Lord gave," respectively); alternatively, it could refer to the figure included in the succession of high priests at Neh 12:11, although that Jonathan served well after Nehemiah. **1:24–29** *O Lord . . . hath spoken:* the prayer's language and imagery are biblically resonant; cf. Gen 18:19; Isa 49:25–26; etc. **1:26** *Thine own portion:* i.e., Israel (see Deut 32:9). **1:27** *Gather those . . . among the heathen:* a common motif in exilic and postexilic biblical writings (see, e.g., Ps 147:2), often with eschatological connotations (e.g., Jer 23:8). *Serve:* Gk. root *doul-,* which refers to enslavement. *Heathen:* alternatively "Gentiles" (so throughout). **1:29** *As Moses hath spoken:* see Deut 30:5. **1:34** *Tried:* "investigated" (NRSV). **1:36** *Naphthar, which . . . Nephi:* the etymology is confused, but Gk. *naphtha* seems to have been a (Persian?) loanword for petroleum. **2:1** *In the records . . . fire:* references to protective burial of the ark and other temple implements appear in pseudepigraphical literature associated with Jeremiah and his scribe Baruch (e.g., *2 Baruch* 6; *4 Baruch* 3.8–11). (The tradition presumably arose because 2 Kings' report of the Babylonian plundering of the temple makes no reference to the ark; see 24:13 and note). These texts do not mention the fire's preservation or many other details recounted in this letter (vv. 4–8). The "writing" (v. 4), assuming it did exist, has not survived, though similar traditions are preserved in texts that have. **2:2** *The prophet . . . ornaments:* see Bar (Ep Jer) 6:4–6.

into the mountain, where Moses climbed up, and saw the heritage of God. ⁵And when Jeremy came thither, he found an hollow cave, wherein he laid the tabernacle, and the ark, and the altar of incense, and so stopped the door. ⁶And some of those that followed him came to mark the way, but they could not find it. ⁷Which when Jeremy perceived, he blamed them, saying, As for that place, it shall be unknown until the time that God gather his people again together, and receive them unto mercy. ⁸Then shall the Lord shew them these things, and the glory of the Lord shall appear, and the cloud also, as it was shewed under Moses, and as when Solomon desired that the place might be honourably sanctified.

⁹It was also declared, that he being wise offered the sacrifice of dedication, and of the finishing of the temple. ¹⁰And as when Moses prayed unto the Lord, the fire came down from heaven, and consumed the sacrifices: even so prayed Solomon also, and the fire came down from heaven, and consumed the burnt offerings. ¹¹And Moses said, Because the sin offering was not to be eaten, it was consumed. ¹²So Solomon kept those eight days.

¹³The same things also were reported in the writings and commentaries of Neemias; and how he founding a library gathered together the acts of the kings, and the prophets, and of David, and the epistles of the kings concerning the holy gifts. ¹⁴In like manner also Judas gathered together all those things that were lost by reason of the war we had, and they remain with us. ¹⁵Wherefore if ye have need thereof, send some to fetch them unto you.

¹⁶Whereas we then are about to celebrate the purification, we have written unto you, and ye shall do well, if ye keep the same days. ¹⁷We hope also, that the God, that delivered all his people, and gave them all an heritage, and the kingdom, and the priesthood, and the sanctuary, ¹⁸as he promised in the law, will shortly have mercy upon us, and gather us together out of every land under heaven into the holy place: for he hath delivered us out of great troubles, and hath purified the place.

¹⁹Now as concerning Judas Maccabeus, and his brethren, and the purification of the great temple, and the dedication of the altar, ²⁰and the wars against Antiochus

2:4 *The mountain . . . God*: Mount Nebo; see Deut 32:49.   **2:5** *Stopped*: "sealed" (NRSV).   **2:7** *It shall be unknown*: like the site of Moses' burial (see Deut 34:6).   **2:8** *The glory . . . Moses*: see Exod 40:34–38 (at the tabernacle's inauguration). *When Solomon . . . sanctified*: see 1 Kgs 8:10–11; 2 Chr 5:13–14.   **2:9** *He being wise . . . temple*: see 1 Kgs 8:62–64.   **2:10** *As when . . . offerings*: see Lev 9:24 (Moses); 2 Chr 7:1 (Solomon).   **2:11** *Because the sin offering . . . consumed*: presumably referring to Lev 10:16–20, but the Greek is not altogether clear.   **2:12** *Those eight days*: see 1 Kgs 8:65–66; 2 Chr 7:8–9.   **2:13** *The same things . . . Neemias*: perhaps referring to Ezra 3:1–4 or 1 Esd 5:47–50. *Commentaries*: lit. "memoirs." (Some of Ezra-Nehemiah is, in fact, written in the first person.) *Founding a library*: the leaders of the returning exiles (especially Ezra) seem to have taken important steps toward establishing a Hebrew biblical canon (see Neh 8:1–18 and note), and this otherwise unattested claim may distortedly reflect that development. *Acts of the kings . . . David*: lit. "the books about the kings and of the prophets and of David" (the last perhaps referring to the Psalms). *The epistles . . . gifts*: apparently referring to the letter of Artaxerxes preserved at Ezra 7:11–26 (see esp. vv. 15–20); cf. 1 Esd 8:9–24.   **2:14** *Judas gathered . . . with us*: i.e., Judas preserved writings that Antiochus tried to destroy as part of his strategy to eliminate Jewish religious distinctiveness (cf. 1 Macc 1:56–57).   **2:17** *Sanctuary*: lit. "sanctification."

2:19–32 Prologue. After the prefatory documentary material, the writer, adhering to Greco-Roman historiographical convention (see Luke 1:1–4 and note), offers a prologue to his work,

Epiphanes, and Eupator his son, ²¹and the manifest signs that came from heaven unto those that behaved themselves manfully to their honour for Judaism: so that, being but a few, they overcame the whole country, and chased barbarous multitudes, ²²and recovered again the temple renowned all the world over, and freed the city, and upheld the laws which were going down, the Lord being gracious unto them with all favour: ²³all these things, I say, being declared by Jason of Cyrene in five books, we will assay to abridge in one volume. ²⁴For considering the infinite number, and the difficulty which they find that desire to look into the narrations of the story, for the variety of the matter, ²⁵we have been careful, that they that will read may have delight, and that they that are desirous to commit to memory might have ease, and that all into whose hands it comes might have profit.

²⁶Therefore to us, that have taken upon us this painful labour of abridging, it was not easy, but a matter of sweat and watching; ²⁷even as it is no ease unto him that prepareth a banquet, and seeketh the benefit of others: yet for the pleasuring of many we will undertake gladly this great pains; ²⁸leaving to the author the exact handling of every particular, and labouring to follow the rules of an abridgment. ²⁹For as the master builder of a new house must care for the whole building; but he that undertaketh to set it out, and paint it, must seek out fit things for the adorning thereof: even so I think it is with us. ³⁰To stand upon every point, and go over things at large, and to be curious in particulars, belongeth to the first author of the story: ³¹but to use brevity, and avoid much labouring of the work, is to be granted to him that will make an abridgment. ³²Here then will we begin the story: only adding thus much to that which hath been said, that it is a foolish thing to make a long prologue, and to be short in the story itself.

3 Now when the holy city was inhabited with all peace, and the laws were kept very well, because of the godliness of Onias the high priest, and his hatred of wickedness, ²it came to pass that even the kings themselves did honour the place, and magnify the temple with their best gifts; ³insomuch that Seleucus king of Asia of his own revenues bare all the costs belonging to the service of the sacrifices. ⁴But one Simon of the tribe of Benjamin, who was made governor of the

---

explaining that it abridges a much longer history.   **2:21** *Manifest signs*: Gk. *epiphaneia*, an ironic pun on Antiochus IV's added name, Epiphanes (see 1 Macc 1:10 note). *Overcame*: more literally "plundered."   **2:23** *Cyrene*: in North Africa.   **2:24** *The infinite number*: more literally "the flow of numbers," i.e., "the flood of statistics involved" (NRSV).   **2:26** *Watching*: staying awake.   **2:29** *Set it out*: the Greek verb refers to encaustic painting. The comparison is between one who builds and one who decorates a house.

3:1–40 The defeat of Heliodorus. To trace the providential shape of his history, the writer begins by narrating an earlier miracle connected with the Second Temple (alluded to in Dan 11:20). The supernatural horseman who appears in v. 25 is the first of a number of such apparitions in this book.   **3:1** *Onias*: Onias III served ca. 190–171 B.C.E.   **3:3** *Seleucus king of Asia*: Seleucus IV Philopator ruled the Seleucid Empire, 187–175 B.C.E. (see 1 Macc 1:10 note).   **3:4** *Simon of the tribe of Benjamin*: unless we prefer a reading of the MS tradition that assigns Simon to the Levite "clan Bilgah," this stands in tension with 4:23–24, where his brother becomes high priest and therefore must have belonged to the tribe of Levi. Perhaps Simon's identification as a Benjaminite is designed to recall the Benjaminite Saul's analogous massacre of the priests at the shrine at Nob (by the hand of Doeg the Edomite) in the context of his power struggle with David (1 Sam 22:6–19).

temple, fell out with the high priest about disorder in the city. ⁵And when he could not overcome Onias, he gat him to Apollonius the son of Thraseas, who then was governor of Celosyria and Phenice, ⁶and told him that the treasury in Jerusalem was full of infinite sums of money, so that the multitude of their riches, which did not pertain to the account of the sacrifices, was innumerable, and that it was possible to bring all into the king's hand. ⁷Now when Apollonius came to the king, and had shewed him of the money whereof he was told, the king chose out Heliodorus his treasurer, and sent him with a commandment to bring him the foresaid money. ⁸So forthwith Heliodorus took his journey, under a colour of visiting the cities of Celosyria and Phenice, but indeed to fulfil the king's purpose.

⁹And when he was come to Jerusalem, and had been courteously received of the high priest of the city, he told him what intelligence was given of the money, and declared wherefore he came, and asked if these things were so indeed. ¹⁰Then the high priest told him that there was such money laid up for the relief of widows and fatherless children: ¹¹and that some of it belonged to Hircanus son of Tobias, a man of great dignity, and not as that wicked Simon had misinformed: the sum whereof in all was four hundred talents of silver, and two hundred of gold: ¹²and that it was altogether impossible that such wrongs should be done unto them, that had committed it to the holiness of the place, and to the majesty and inviolable sanctity of the temple, honoured over all the world. ¹³But Heliodorus, because of the king's commandment given him, said, That in any wise it must be brought into the king's treasury.

¹⁴So at the day which he appointed he entered in to order this matter: wherefore there was no small agony throughout the whole city. ¹⁵But the priests, prostrating themselves before the altar in their priests' vestments, called unto heaven upon him that made a law concerning things given to be kept, that they should safely be preserved for such as had committed them to be kept. ¹⁶Then whoso had looked the high priest in the face, it would have wounded his heart: for his countenance and the changing of his colour declared the inward agony of his mind. ¹⁷For the man was so compassed with fear and horror of the body, that it was manifest to them that looked upon him, what sorrow he had now in his heart. ¹⁸Others ran flocking out of their houses to the general supplication, because the place was like to come into contempt. ¹⁹And the women, girt with sackcloth under their breasts, abounded in the streets, and the virgins that were kept in ran, some to the gates, and some to the walls, and others looked out of the windows. ²⁰And all, holding their hands toward heaven, made supplication. ²¹Then it would have pitied a man to see the falling down of the multitude of all sorts, and the fear of the high priest,

Disorder in the city: better "the administration of the city market" (MS tradition; NRSV). **3:5** *Celosyria*: see 1 Macc 10:69 and note. *Phenice*: Phoenicia, the Mediterranean coastal territory just north of Palestine. **3:7** *His treasurer*: the Greek is not so specific; more accurately "who was in charge of his affairs" (NRSV). **3:8** *Colour*: pretext. **3:11** *Not as . . . misinformed*: i.e., the money was not as much as Simon had said, nor did it consist of unallocated public funds (cf. v. 6). **3:13** *Wise*: case. **3:15** *That they should safely be preserved*: rather "that he would safely preserve them." **3:18** *To the*: i.e., "to make a." **3:19** *Sackcloth*: customarily worn by those in mourning. *Kept in*: not allowed in public. **3:21** *Falling down*:

being in such an agony. ²²They then called upon the Almighty Lord to keep the things committed of trust safe and sure for those that had committed them. ²³Nevertheless Heliodorus executed that which was decreed.

²⁴Now as he was there present himself with his guard about the treasury, the Lord of spirits, and the Prince of all power, caused a great apparition, so that all that presumed to come in with him were astonished at the power of God, and fainted, and were sore afraid. ²⁵For there appeared unto them an horse with a terrible rider upon him, and adorned with a very fair covering, and he ran fiercely, and smote at Heliodorus with his forefeet, and it seemed that he that sat upon the horse had complete harness of gold. ²⁶Moreover two other young men appeared before him, notable in strength, excellent in beauty, and comely in apparel, who stood by him on either side, and scourged him continually, and gave him many sore stripes. ²⁷And Heliodorus fell suddenly unto the ground, and was compassed with great darkness: but they that were with him took him up, and put him into a litter. ²⁸Thus him, that lately came with a great train and with all his guard into the said treasury, they carried out, being unable to help himself with his weapons: and manifestly they acknowledged the power of God: ²⁹for he by the hand of God was cast down, and lay speechless without all hope of life. ³⁰But they praised the Lord, that had miraculously honoured his own place: for the temple, which a little afore was full of fear and trouble, when the Almighty Lord appeared, was filled with joy and gladness.

³¹Then straightways certain of Heliodorus' friends prayed Onias, that he would call upon the most High to grant him his life, who lay ready to give up the ghost. ³²So the high priest, suspecting lest the king should misconceive that some treachery had been done to Heliodorus by the Jews, offered a sacrifice for the health of the man. ³³Now as the high priest was making an atonement, the same young men in the same clothing appeared and stood beside Heliodorus, saying, Give Onias the high priest great thanks, insomuch as for his sake the Lord hath granted thee life: ³⁴and seeing that thou hast been scourged from heaven, declare unto all men the mighty power of God. And when they had spoken these words, they appeared no more.

³⁵So Heliodorus, after he had offered sacrifice unto the Lord, and made great vows unto him that had saved his life, and saluted Onias, returned with his host to the king. ³⁶Then testified he to all men the works of the great God, which he had seen with his eyes. ³⁷And when the king asked Heliodorus, who might be a fit man to be sent yet once again to Jerusalem, he said, ³⁸If thou hast any enemy or traitor, send him thither, and thou shalt receive him well scourged, if he escape with his life: for in that place, no doubt, there is an especial power of God. ³⁹For he that dwelleth in heaven hath his eye on that place, and defendeth it; and he beateth and destroyeth them that come to hurt it. ⁴⁰And the things concerning Heliodorus, and the keeping of the treasury, fell out on this sort.

---

prostration.   **3:25** *Harness*: armor (so throughout).   **3:31** *Most High*: see Mark 5:7 note.

4 This Simon now, of whom we spake afore, having been a bewrayer of the money, and of his country, slandered Onias, as if he had terrified Heliodorus, and been the worker of these evils. ²Thus was he bold to call him a traitor, that had deserved well of the city, and tendered his own nation, and was so zealous of the laws. ³But when their hatred went so far, that by one of Simon's faction murders were committed, ⁴Onias seeing the danger of this contention, and that Apollonius, as being the governor of Celosyria and Phenice, did rage, and increase Simon's malice, ⁵he went to the king, not to be an accuser of his countrymen, but seeking the good of all both publick and private: ⁶for he saw that it was impossible that the state should continue quiet, and Simon leave his folly, unless the king did look thereunto.

⁷But after the death of Seleucus, when Antiochus, called Epiphanes, took the kingdom, Jason the brother of Onias laboured underhand to be high priest, ⁸promising unto the king by intercession three hundred and threescore talents of silver, and of another revenue eighty talents: ⁹beside this, he promised to assign an hundred and fifty more, if he might have licence to set him up a place for exercise, and for the training up of youth in the fashions of the heathen, and to write them of Jerusalem by the name of Antiochians. ¹⁰Which when the king had granted, and he had gotten into his hand the rule, he forthwith brought his own nation to the Greekish fashion. ¹¹And the royal privileges granted of special favour to the Jews by the means of John the father of Eupolemus, who went ambassador to Rome for amity and aid, he took away; and putting down the governments which were according to the law, he brought up new customs against the law: ¹²for he built gladly a place of exercise under the tower itself, and brought the chief young men under his subjection, and made them wear a hat. ¹³Now such was the height of Greek fashions, and increase of heathenish manners, through the exceeding profaneness of Jason, that ungodly wretch, and no high priest; ¹⁴that the priests had no courage to serve any more at the altar, but despising the temple, and neglecting the sacrifices, hastened to be partakers of the unlawful allowance in the place of exercise, after the game of Discus called them forth; ¹⁵not setting by the honours of their fathers, but liking the glory of the Grecians best of all. ¹⁶By reason whereof sore calamity came upon them: for they had them to be their enemies and avengers, whose cus-

4:1–17 Hellenizing Jerusalem. Cf. 1 Macc 1:11–15. 4:1 *Bewrayer*: betrayer. 4:2 *Tendered*: protected. 4:4 *Apollonius*: apparently, son of Menestheus (v. 21), not son of Thraseas (3:5). 4:7 *Antiochus, called Epiphanes*: see 1 Macc 1:10 note. 4:9 *A place . . . heathen*: see 1 Macc 1:14 note. *To write . . . Antiochians*: though the precise meaning of this phrase is obscure, it seems to promise to assimilate Jerusalem to Antioch, the Seleucid Empire's Hellenistic capital; cf. 9:15 for an analogous assimilation. 4:10 *He*: Jason. 4:11 *Royal privileges . . . Jews*: Josephus (*Jewish Antiquities* 12.138–46) provides a letter from Antiochus III the Great enumerating these privileges. *Eupolemus, who . . . aid*: 1 Macc 8:17–32 recounts his mission. 4:12 *The tower*: Gk. *akropolis*, "castle"; this is evidently not the Jerusalem citadel central to 1 Maccabees, for that structure was built later (see 1 Macc 1:33), but v. 27 (see note) suggests that it was a Seleucid stronghold of some sort. *Brought the chief young men . . . hat*: the Greek involves a pun: *hypotassōn hypo petason*, "subjecting them to/setting them under the broad-brimmed Greek hat"—a hat conventionally worn by Greek adolescents. 4:14 *Unlawful allowance*: reference obscure. *The game . . . forth*: "the signal for the discus-throwing" (NRSV). 4:15 *Setting by*: esteeming.

tom they followed so earnestly, and unto whom they desired to be like in all things. [17]For it is not a light thing to do wickedly against the laws of God: but the time following shall declare these things.

[18]Now when the game that was used every fifth year was kept at Tyrus, the king being present, [19]this ungracious Jason sent special messengers from Jerusalem, who were Antiochians, to carry three hundred drachms of silver to the sacrifice of Hercules, which even the bearers thereof thought fit not to bestow upon the sacrifice, because it was not convenient, but to be reserved for other charges. [20]This money then, in regard of the sender, was appointed to Hercules' sacrifice; but because of the bearers thereof, it was employed to the making of gallies.

[21]Now when Apollonius the son of Menestheus was sent into Egypt for the coronation of king Ptolemeus Philometor, Antiochus, understanding him not to be well affected to his affairs, provided for his own safety: whereupon he came to Joppe, and from thence to Jerusalem: [22]where he was honourably received of Jason, and of the city, and was brought in with torchlight, and with great shoutings: and so afterward went with his host unto Phenice.

[23]Three years afterward Jason sent Menelaus, the aforesaid Simon's brother, to bear the money unto the king, and to put him in mind of certain necessary matters. [24]But he being brought to the presence of the king, when he had magnified him for the glorious appearance of his power, got the priesthood to himself, offering more than Jason by three hundred talents of silver. [25]So he came with the king's mandate, bringing nothing worthy the high priesthood, but having the fury of a cruel tyrant, and the rage of a savage beast. [26]Then Jason, who had undermined his own brother, being undermined by another, was compelled to flee into the country of the Ammonites. [27]So Menelaus got the principality: but as for the money that he had promised unto the king, he took no good order for it, albeit Sostratus the ruler of the castle required it: [28]for unto him appertained the gathering of the customs. Wherefore they were both called before the king. [29]Now Menelaus left his brother Lysimachus in his stead in the priesthood; and Sostratus left Crates, who was governor of the Cyprians.

4:18–50 The murder of Onias. Although Jason performs a series of actions aimed at securing Antiochus's support (vv. 18–22), Menelaus manages to get himself appointed high priest in his stead (vv. 23–29). When he robs the temple to remunerate Antiochus for the appointment, Onias denounces him and is promptly murdered (vv. 30–35; Dan 9:26 and 11:22 also seem to refer to the assassination; see notes). This murder, combined with sacrileges that his brother committed under his authority, leads to a trial, but a well-placed bribe results in Antiochus's last-minute intercession on Menelaus's behalf (vv. 36–50).   **4:19** *Three hundred drachms*: perhaps a modest sum. *Hercules*: the Greek demigod in whose name the games of Tyre in Phoenicia were held. *Convenient*: proper. **4:20** *Gallies*: triremes (warships).   **4:21** *Ptolemeus Philometor*: see 1 Macc 1:18 note. *Not to be . . . affairs*: "to have become hostile to his [Antiochus's] government" (NRSV). *Joppe*: Joppa, a Mediterranean seaport about thirty miles northwest of Jerusalem.   **4:23** *To bear the money*: promised in vv. 8–9.   **4:24** *For the glorious appearance of his power*: alternatively "with the appearance of authority." **4:26** *His own brother*: Onias (see v. 7). The present verse again hints at God's ironic retribution (cf. 1:14–16 and notes).   **4:27** *Principality*: position of leadership. *Took no good order for it*: did not pay it regularly. *Castle*: Gk. *akropolis* (see v. 12 note).   **4:29** *Cyprians*: a mercenary contingent from

³⁰While those things were in doing, they of Tarsus and Mallos made insurrection, because they were given to the king's concubine, called Antiochis. ³¹Then came the king in all haste to appease matters, leaving Andronicus, a man in authority, for his deputy. ³²Now Menelaus, supposing that he had gotten a convenient time, stole certain vessels of gold out of the temple, and gave some of them to Andronicus, and some he sold into Tyrus and the cities round about. ³³Which when Onias knew of a surety, he reproved him, and withdrew himself into a sanctuary at Daphne, that lieth by Antiochia. ³⁴Wherefore Menelaus, taking Andronicus apart, prayed him to get Onias into his hands; who being persuaded thereunto, and coming to Onias in deceit, gave him his right hand with oaths; and though he were suspected by him, yet persuaded he him to come forth of the sanctuary: whom forthwith he shut up without regard of justice. ³⁵For the which cause not only the Jews, but many also of other nations, took great indignation, and were much grieved for the unjust murder of the man.

³⁶And when the king was come again from the places about Cilicia, the Jews that were in the city, and certain of the Greeks that abhorred the fact also, complained because Onias was slain without cause. ³⁷Therefore Antiochus was heartily sorry, and moved to pity, and wept, because of the sober and modest behaviour of him that was dead. ³⁸And being kindled with anger, forthwith he took away Andronicus his purple, and rent off his clothes, and leading him through the whole city unto that very place, where he had committed impiety against Onias, there slew he the cursed murderer. Thus the Lord rewarded him his punishment, as he had deserved.

³⁹Now when many sacrileges had been committed in the city by Lysimachus with the consent of Menelaus, and the bruit thereof was spread abroad, the multitude gathered themselves together against Lysimachus, many vessels of gold being already carried away. ⁴⁰Whereupon the common people rising, and being filled with rage, Lysimachus armed about three thousand men, and began first to offer violence; one Auranus being the leader, a man far gone in years, and no less in folly. ⁴¹They then seeing the attempt of Lysimachus, some of them caught stones, some clubs, others taking handfuls of dust, that was next at hand, cast them all together upon Lysimachus, and those that set upon them. ⁴²Thus many of them they wounded, and some they struck to the ground, and all of them they forced to flee, but as for the church robber himself, him they killed beside the treasury. ⁴³Of these matters therefore there was an accusation laid against Menelaus.

Cyprus, a large island off the Mediterranean coast. **4:30** *Tarsus and Mallos*: cities in Cilicia (in southwest Asia Minor). Antiochis would receive their taxation revenue. (Compare 1 Macc 10:39, where Demetrius offers Jonathan revenue for the temple's support from Ptolemais.) **4:32** *Stole certain vessels . . . about*: thereby raising money to pay his debt. (The gift to Andronicus is apparently a bribe, lest he disclose how Menelaus raised the money.) **4:33** *And withdrew*: more literally "having first withdrawn" to the temple of Apollo and his sister Artemis at *Daphne, a sanctuary* where supplicants were supposed to be inviolate (cf. 1 Kgs 2:28–34). Onias foresaw that his exposure of the corruption would bring reprisal. *Antiochia*: Antioch, the "city" mentioned in v. 36. **4:34** *Shut up*: i.e., "got out of the way" (cf. NRSV). **4:38** *Purple*: clothes dyed purple, considered luxurious, were conventionally worn by royalty. **4:39** *The city*: Jerusalem. **4:42** *Church robber*: temple robber

⁴⁴Now when the king came to Tyrus, three men that were sent from the senate pleaded the cause before him: ⁴⁵but Menelaus, being now convicted, promised Ptolemee the son of Dorymenes to give him much money, if he would pacify the king toward him. ⁴⁶Whereupon Ptolemee taking the king aside into a certain gallery, as it were to take the air, brought him to be of another mind: ⁴⁷insomuch that he discharged Menelaus from the accusations, who notwithstanding was cause of all the mischief: and those poor men, who, if they had told their cause, yea, before the Scythians, should have been judged innocent, them he condemned to death. ⁴⁸Thus they that followed the matter for the city, and for the people, and for the holy vessels, did soon suffer unjust punishment. ⁴⁹Wherefore even they of Tyrus, moved with hatred of that wicked deed, caused them to be honourably buried. ⁵⁰And so through the covetousness of them that were of power Menelaus remained still in authority, increasing in malice, and being a great traitor to the citizens.

5 About the same time Antiochus prepared his second voyage into Egypt: ²and then it happened, that through all the city, for the space almost of forty days, there were seen horsemen running in the air, in cloth of gold, and armed with lances, like a band of soldiers, ³and troops of horsemen in array, encountering and running one against another, with shaking of shields, and multitude of pikes, and drawing of swords, and casting of darts, and glittering of golden ornaments, and harness of all sorts. ⁴Wherefore every man prayed that that apparition might turn to good.

⁵Now when there was gone forth a false rumour, as though Antiochus had been dead, Jason took at the least a thousand men, and suddenly made an assault upon the city; and they that were upon the walls being put back, and the city at length taken, Menelaus fled into the castle: ⁶but Jason slew his own citizens without mercy, not considering that to get the day of them of his own nation would be a most unhappy day for him; but thinking they had been his enemies, and not his countrymen, whom he conquered. ⁷Howbeit for all this he obtained not the principality, but at the last received shame for the reward of his treason, and fled again into the country of the Ammonites. ⁸In the end therefore he had an unhappy return, being accused before Aretas the king of the Arabians, fleeing from city to city, pursued of all men, hated as a forsaker of the laws, and being had in abomination as an open enemy of his country and countrymen, he was cast out into Egypt. ⁹Thus he that had driven many out of their country perished in a strange land, retiring to the Lacedemonians, and thinking there to find succour by reason of his kindred: ¹⁰and he that had cast out many unburied had none to mourn for him, nor any solemn funerals at all, nor sepulchre with his fathers.

(i.e., Lysimachus).   **4:44** *Senate*: Gk. *gerousia*, council of elders.   **4:47** *Scythians*: see Col 3:11 note.   **4:48** *Followed the matter for*: lit. "spoke publicly on behalf of."
   5:1–27 The death of Jason and the temple's desecration. Compare 1 Macc 1:16–2:28. **5:1** *Second voyage into Egypt*: apparently the invasion reported in 1 Macc 1:16–20 (see notes); cf. Dan 11:29–35.   **5:6** *To get the day of*: to win a victory against. (KJV preserves the Greek pun.)   **5:7** *The country of the Ammonites*: east of the Jordan river.   **5:8** *Return*: outcome. *Aretas the king of the Arabians*: king of Nabatea.   **5:9** *Lacedemonians*: Spartans. *His kindred*: see 1 Macc 12:21 and note.

[11]Now when this that was done came to the king's ear, he thought that Judea had revolted: whereupon removing out of Egypt in a furious mind, he took the city by force of arms, [12]and commanded his men of war not to spare such as they met, and to slay such as went up upon the houses. [13]Thus there was killing of young and old, making away of men, women, and children, slaying of virgins and infants. [14]And there were destroyed within the space of three whole days fourscore thousand, whereof forty thousand were slain in the conflict; and no fewer sold than slain. [15]Yet was he not content with this, but presumed to go into the most holy temple of all the world; Menelaus, that traitor to the laws, and to his own country, being his guide: [16]and taking the holy vessels with polluted hands, and with profane hands pulling down the things that were dedicated by other kings to the augmentation and glory and honour of the place, he gave them away. [17]And so haughty was Antiochus in mind, that he considered not that the Lord was angry for a while for the sins of them that dwelt in the city, and therefore his eye was not upon the place. [18]For had they not been formerly wrapped in many sins, this man, as soon as he had come, had forthwith been scourged, and put back from his presumption, as Heliodorus was, whom Seleucus the king sent to view the treasury. [19]Nevertheless God did not choose the people for the place's sake, but the place for the people's sake. [20]And therefore the place itself, that was partaker with them of the adversity that happened to the nation, did afterward communicate in the benefits sent from the Lord: and as it was forsaken in the wrath of the Almighty, so again, the great Lord being reconciled, it was set up with all glory.

[21]So when Antiochus had carried out of the temple a thousand and eight hundred talents, he departed in all haste unto Antiochia, weening in his pride to make the land navigable, and the sea passable by foot: such was the haughtiness of his mind. [22]And he left governors to vex the nation: at Jerusalem, Philip, for his country a Phrygian, and for manners more barbarous than he that set him there; [23]and at Garizim, Andronicus; and besides, Menelaus, who worse than all the rest bare an heavy hand over the citizens, having a malicious mind against his countrymen the Jews. [24]He sent also that detestable ringleader Apollonius with an army of two and twenty thousand, commanding him to slay all those that were in their best age, and to sell the women and the younger sort: [25]who coming to Jerusalem, and pretending peace, did forbear till the holy day of the sabbath, when taking the Jews keeping holy day, he commanded his men to arm themselves. [26]And so he slew all them that were gone to the celebrating of the sabbath, and running through the city with weapons slew great multitudes. [27]But Judas Maccabeus with nine others, or thereabout, withdrew himself into the wilderness, and lived in the mountains after the manner of beasts, with his company, who fed on herbs continually, lest they should be partakers of the pollution.

5:14 *Sold*: i.e., into slavery.   **5:17** *The Lord was angry for a while*: cf. Isa 54:7–8.   **5:20** *Communicate*: share.   **5:21** *Weening*: thinking. *To make . . . foot*: massive disruption of waterways was a conventional act of royal hubris in ancient Greek literature; cf. Herodotus 7.22–37. *Haughtiness*: lit. "elevation," perhaps recalling such biblical prophecies against haughty rulers as Isa 14:12–14; 37:24–25.   **5:22** *Phrygian*: Phrygia was a region in central Asia Minor.   **5:23** *Garizim*: Gerizim, a mountain in Samaria that here may stand for the surrounding territory. *Andronicus*: not the man of this name executed earlier (see 4:38).   **5:24–26** *He sent . . . multitudes*: 1 Macc 1:29–32 also recounts this event.   **5:27** *But Judas Maccabeus . . . pollution*: compare the violent resistance to

6 Not long after this the king sent an old man of Athens to compel the Jews to depart from the laws of their fathers, and not to live after the laws of God: [2]and to pollute also the temple in Jerusalem, and to call it the temple of Jupiter Olympius; and that in Garizim, of Jupiter the Defender of strangers, as they did desire that dwelt in the place. [3]The coming in of this mischief was sore and grievous to the people: [4]for the temple was filled with riot and revelling by the Gentiles, who dallied with harlots, and had to do with women within the circuit of the holy places, and besides that brought in things that were not lawful. [5]The altar also was filled with profane things, which the law forbiddeth. [6]Neither was it lawful for a man to keep sabbath days or ancient feasts, or to profess himself at all to be a Jew. [7]And in the day of the king's birth every month they were brought by bitter constraint to eat of the sacrifices; and when the feast of Bacchus was kept, the Jews were compelled to go in procession to Bacchus, carrying ivy. [8]Moreover there went out a decree to the neighbour cities of the heathen, by the suggestion of Ptolemee, against the Jews, that they should observe the same fashions, and be partakers of their sacrifices: [9]and whoso would not conform themselves to the manners of the Gentiles should be put to death.

Then might a man have seen the present misery. [10]For there were two women brought, who had circumcised their children; whom when they had openly led round about the city, the babes hanging at their breasts, they cast them down headlong from the wall. [11]And others, that had run together into caves near by, to keep the sabbath day secretly, being discovered to Philip, were all burnt together, because they made a conscience to help themselves for the honour of the most sacred day.

[12]Now I beseech those that read this book, that they be not discouraged for these calamities, but that they judge those punishments not to be for destruction, but for a chastening of our nation. [13]For it is a token of his great goodness, when wicked doers are not suffered any long time, but forthwith punished. [14]For not as with other nations, whom the Lord patiently forbeareth to punish, till they be come to the fulness of their sins, so dealeth he with us, [15]lest that, being come to the height of sin, afterwards he should take vengeance of us. [16]And therefore he never withdraweth his mercy from us: and though he punish with adversity, yet doth he never forsake his people. [17]But let this that we have spoken be for a warning unto us. And now will we come to the declaring of the matter in few words.

---

participation in pagan rites by Mattathias, who then flees to the hills with his sons, including Judas (see 1 Macc 2:15–28).

6:1–7:42 Persecution and martyrdom. Compare 1 Macc 1:41–53; 2:29–38. These chapters constitute the earliest extant martyrologies, edifying stories of faithful believers who suffer vicious (and often vividly depicted) tortures before they die at the hands of their depraved persecutors. The genre to which they gave rise became particularly popular among ancient Christians.

6:1–17 The martyrdom of faithful Jews. 6:1 *An old man of Athens*: old man might refer to an Athenian senator (so NRSV), but other construals are possible. **6:2** *That in Garizim*: i.e, the Samaritan temple. **6:7** *Ivy*: sacred to Bacchus (Dionysus), Greek god of wine and revelry. **6:8** *Heathen*: rather "Greeks" (also for "Gentiles" in v. 9). *Ptolemee*: presumably the figure mentioned in 4:45–46. **6:11** *They made . . . themselves*: "their piety kept them from defending themselves" (NRSV); cf. 1 Macc 2:29–38 and note. **6:14–16** *For not . . . his people*: see Rom 2:4 note.

¹⁸Eleazar, one of the principal scribes, an aged man, and of a well favoured countenance, was constrained to open his mouth, and to eat swine's flesh. ¹⁹But he, choosing rather to die gloriously, than to live stained with such an abomination, spit it forth, and came of his own accord to the torment, ²⁰as it behoved them to come, that are resolute to stand out against such things, as are not lawful for love of life to be tasted. ²¹But they that had the charge of that wicked feast, for the old acquaintance they had with the man, taking him aside, besought him to bring flesh of his own provision, such as was lawful for him to use, and make as if he did eat of the flesh taken from the sacrifice commanded by the king; ²²that in so doing he might be delivered from death, and for the old friendship with them find favour. ²³But he began to consider discreetly, and as became his age, and the excellency of his ancient years, and the honour of his gray head, whereunto he was come, and his most honest education from a child, or rather the holy law made and given by God: therefore he answered accordingly, and willed them straightways to send him to the grave. ²⁴For it becometh not our age, said he, in any wise to dissemble, whereby many young persons might think that Eleazar, being fourscore years old and ten, were now gone to a strange religion; ²⁵and so they through mine hypocrisy, and desire to live a little time and a moment longer, should be deceived by me, and I get a stain to mine old age, and make it abominable. ²⁶For though for the present time I should be delivered from the punishment of men: yet should I not escape the hand of the Almighty, neither alive, nor dead. ²⁷Wherefore now, manfully changing this life, I will shew myself such an one as mine age requireth, ²⁸and leave a notable example to such as be young to die willingly and courageously for the honourable and holy laws.

And when he had said these words, immediately he went to the torment: ²⁹they that led him changing the good will they bare him a little before into hatred, because the foresaid speeches proceeded, as they thought, from a desperate mind. ³⁰But when he was ready to die with stripes, he groaned, and said, It is manifest unto the Lord, that hath the holy knowledge, that whereas I might have been delivered from death, I now endure sore pains in body by being beaten: but in soul am well content to suffer these things, because I fear him.

³¹And thus this man died, leaving his death for an example of a noble courage, and a memorial of virtue, not only unto young men, but unto all his nation.

7 It came to pass also, that seven brethren with their mother were taken, and compelled by the king against the law to taste swine's flesh, and were tormented with scourges and whips. ²But one of them that spake first said thus,

6:18−31 The martyrdom of Eleazar. This event is recounted in more detail in the pseudepigraphical *4 Maccabees* 5−7. Commentators often observe that Eleazar resembles Socrates in Plato's *Apology*, speculating that the author deliberately patterned Eleazar after the Greek philosopher. **6:18** *Scribes*: experts in Jewish law. *Swine's flesh*: see Lev 11:7. **6:19** *The torment*: Gk. *tympanon*, here a specific (though unknown) instrument of torture. **6:21** *Eat of . . . sacrifice*: see 1 Macc 1:47 and note. **6:23** *The grave*: Gk. *hadēs* (see Matt 11:23 and note). **6:27** *Changing*: i.e., exchanging, "giving up" (NRSV). **6:30** *Stripes*: wounds from a whip.

7:1−42 The martyrdom of the seven sons and their mother. Recounted in more detail in *4 Maccabees* 8−18, the episode here emphasizes that the nation's intense suffering is self-inflicted

What wouldest thou ask or learn of us? we are ready to die, rather than to transgress the laws of our fathers. ³Then the king, being in a rage, commanded pans and caldrons to be made hot: ⁴which forthwith being heated, he commanded to cut out the tongue of him that spake first, and to cut off the utmost parts of his body, the rest of his brethren and his mother looking on. ⁵Now when he was thus maimed in all his members, he commanded him being yet alive to be brought to the fire, and to be fried in the pan: and as the vapour of the pan was for a good space dispersed, they exhorted one another with the mother to die manfully, saying thus, ⁶The Lord God looketh upon us, and in truth hath comfort in us, as Moses in his song, which witnessed to their faces, declared, saying, And he shall be comforted in his servants.

⁷So when the first was dead after this manner, they brought the second to make him a mocking stock: and when they had pulled off the skin of his head with the hair, they asked him, Wilt thou eat, before thou be punished throughout every member of thy body? ⁸But he answered in his own language, and said, No. Wherefore he also received the next torment in order, as the former did. ⁹And when he was at the last gasp, he said, Thou like a fury takest us out of this present life, but the King of the world shall raise us up, who have died for his laws, unto everlasting life.

¹⁰After him was the third made a mocking stock: and when he was required, he put out his tongue, and that right soon, holding forth his hands manfully, ¹¹and said courageously, These I had from heaven; and for his laws I despise them; and from him I hope to receive them again. ¹²Insomuch that the king, and they that were with him, marvelled at the young man's courage, for that he nothing regarded the pains.

¹³Now when this man was dead also, they tormented and mangled the fourth in like manner. ¹⁴So when he was ready to die he said thus, It is good, being put to death by men, to look for hope from God to be raised up again by him: as for thee, thou shalt have no resurrection to life.

¹⁵Afterward they brought the fifth also, and mangled him. ¹⁶Then looked he unto the king, and said, Thou hast power over men, thou art corruptible, thou doest what thou wilt; yet think not that our nation is forsaken of God; ¹⁷but abide a while, and behold his great power, how he will torment thee and thy seed.

¹⁸After him also they brought the sixth, who being ready to die said, Be not deceived without cause: for we suffer these things for ourselves, having sinned

---

rather than God's doing. This key point is developed in the speeches of the sixth and seventh sons (vv. 18–19, 30–38). **7:4** *And to cut off*: better "and, scalping him in Scythian fashion, to cut off." Herodotus (4.64) vividly describes the gruesome procedure. **7:5** *As the vapour . . . dispersed*: i.e., as they smelled the burning flesh. **7:6** *Hath comfort in us*: better "relents toward us" (also later in the verse). *And he . . . servants*: Deut 32:36 (see note). **7:8** *His own language*: more literally "the language of his fathers." His use of Hebrew instead of Greek is itself an act of resistance. **7:9** *Shall raise . . . life*: referring to the doctrine of bodily resurrection, alluded to at Dan 12:2 (see note), which this text may echo, and assumed throughout most of the NT. See also vv. 11, 14, 22–23, etc. **7:14** *Thou shalt have no resurrection to life*: many conceptions of eschatological resurrection assume that divine judgment will follow on its heels (cf. Rev 20:12–15), but here, the resurrection is itself the judgment: the just are raised and the wicked are not (cf. v. 36). **7:17** *How he . . . seed*: see 9:5–28; for the death of

against our God: therefore marvellous things are done unto us. [19]But think not thou, that takest in hand to strive against God, that thou shalt escape unpunished. [20]But the mother was marvellous above all, and worthy of honourable memory: for when she saw her seven sons slain within the space of one day, she bare it with a good courage, because of the hope that she had in the Lord. [21]Yea, she exhorted every one of them in her own language, filled with courageous spirits; and stirring up her womanish thoughts with a manly stomach, she said unto them, [22]I cannot tell how ye came into my womb; for I neither gave you breath nor life, neither was it I that formed the members of every one of you; [23]but doubtless the Creator of the world, who formed the generation of man, and found out the beginning of all things, will also of his own mercy give you breath and life again, as ye now regard not your own selves for his laws' sake.

[24]Now Antiochus, thinking himself despised, and suspecting it to be a reproachful speech, whilst the youngest was yet alive, did not only exhort him by words, but also assured him with oaths, that he would make him both a rich and a happy man, if he would turn from the laws of his fathers; and that also he would take him for his friend, and trust him with affairs. [25]But when the young man would in no case hearken unto him, the king called his mother, and exhorted her that she would counsel the young man to save his life. [26]And when he had exhorted her with many words, she promised him that she would counsel her son. [27]But she bowing herself toward him, laughing the cruel tyrant to scorn, spake in her country language on this manner: O my son, have pity upon me that bare thee nine months in my womb, and gave thee suck three years, and nourished thee, and brought thee up unto this age, and endured the troubles of education. [28]I beseech thee, my son, look upon the heaven and the earth, and all that is therein, and consider that God made them of things that were not; and so was mankind made likewise. [29]Fear not this tormentor, but, being worthy of thy brethren, take thy death, that I may receive thee again in mercy with thy brethren.

[30]Whiles she was yet speaking these words, the young man said, Whom wait ye for? I will not obey the king's commandment: but I will obey the commandment of the law that was given unto our fathers by Moses. [31]And thou, that hast been the author of all mischief against the Hebrews, shalt not escape the hands of God. [32]For we suffer because of our sins. [33]And though the living Lord be angry with us a little while for our chastening and correction, yet shall he be at one again with his servants. [34]But thou, O godless man, and of all other most wicked, be not lifted up without a cause, nor puffed up with uncertain hopes, lifting up thy hand against the servants of God: [35]for thou hast not yet escaped the judgment of Almighty God, who seeth all things. [36]For our brethren, who now have suffered a short pain, are dead under God's covenant of everlasting life: but thou, through the judgment of God, shalt receive just punishment for thy pride.

Antiochus's son Antiochus V Eupator, see 1 Macc 7:1–4. **7:21** *Stomach*: valor. **7:22** *I cannot tell . . . of you*: echoing Jer 1:5. **7:28** *God made . . . not*: an early statement of the concept of creation *ex nihilo* ("out of nothing"), an idea that later interpreters imported into Gen 1. But rather than being an abstract claim about God's creative activity, here it is is part of an analogy that sets creation—one instance of which is childbirth—against resurrection, the mother's true concern (see v. 29; cf. vv. 10–11). **7:33** *At one*: rec-

[37]But I, as my brethren, offer up my body and life for the laws of our fathers, beseeching God that he would speedily be merciful unto our nation; and that thou by torments and plagues mayest confess, that he alone is God; [38]and that in me and my brethren the wrath of the Almighty, which is justly brought upon all our nation, may cease.

[39]Then the king, being in a rage, handled him worse than all the rest, and took it grievously that he was mocked. [40]So this man died undefiled, and put his whole trust in the Lord. [41]Last of all after the sons the mother died.

[42]Let this be enough now to have spoken concerning the idolatrous feasts, and the extreme tortures.

8 Then Judas Maccabeus, and they that were with him, went privily into the towns, and called their kinsfolks together, and took unto them all such as continued in the Jews' religion, and assembled about six thousand men. [2]And they called upon the Lord, that he would look upon the people that was trodden down of all; and also pity the temple profaned of ungodly men; [3]and that he would have compassion upon the city, sore defaced, and ready to be made even with the ground; and hear the blood that cried unto him, [4]and remember the wicked slaughter of harmless infants, and the blasphemies committed against his name; and that he would shew his hatred against the wicked.

[5]Now when Maccabeus had his company about him, he could not be withstood by the heathen: for the wrath of the Lord was turned into mercy. [6]Therefore he came at unawares, and burnt up towns and cities, and got into his hands the most commodious places, and overcame and put to flight no small number of his enemies. [7]But specially took he advantage of the night for such privy attempts, insomuch that the bruit of his manliness was spread every where.

[8]So when Philip saw that this man increased by little and little, and that things prospered with him still more and more, he wrote unto Ptolemeus, the governor of Celosyria and Phenice, to yield more aid to the king's affairs. [9]Then forthwith choosing Nicanor the son of Patroclus, one of his special friends, he sent him with no fewer than twenty thousand of all nations under him, to root out the whole generation of the Jews; and with him he joined also Gorgias a captain, who in matters of war had great experience. [10]So Nicanor undertook to make so much money of the captive Jews, as should defray the tribute of two thousand talents, which the king was to pay to the Romans. [11]Wherefore immediately he sent to the cities upon the sea coast, proclaiming a sale of the captive Jews, and promising

---

onciled.   **7:38** *That in me . . . cease*: perhaps suggesting that the martyrdoms be viewed as atonement for the community's sins (as in early Christian writers; e.g., in the *Acts of Perpetua and Felicitas*, the soon-to-be-martyred Perpetua successfully intercedes for her dead brother Dinocrates, who is suffering in the afterlife). Alternatively, it may suggest that these deaths hasten the completion of God's limited punishment of his people (see 6:14–16 and note).

8:1–36 The rise of Judas Maccabeus and Nicanor's defeat. On Nicanor's defeat (vv. 8–36), cf. 1 Macc 3:38–4:25.   **8:3** *Hear the blood . . . him*: echoing Gen 4:10.   **8:6–7** *Therefore he . . . every where*: for an account of these victories, see 1 Macc 3:10–26.   **8:6** *Commodious*: opportune or "strategic" (NRSV).   **8:10** *The tribute . . . Romans*: a stipulation of the treaty of Apamea (see 1 Macc

that they should have fourscore and ten bodies for one talent, not expecting the vengeance that was to follow upon him from the Almighty God.

^{12}Now when word was brought unto Judas of Nicanor's coming, and he had imparted unto those that were with him that the army was at hand, ^{13}they that were fearful, and distrusted the justice of God, fled, and conveyed themselves away. ^{14}Others sold all that they had left, and withal besought the Lord to deliver them, being sold by the wicked Nicanor before they met together: ^{15}and if not for their own sakes, yet for the covenants he had made with their fathers, and for his holy and glorious name's sake, by which they were called. ^{16}So Maccabeus called his men together unto the number of six thousand, and exhorted them not to be stricken with terror of the enemy, nor to fear the great multitude of the heathen, who came wrongfully against them; but to fight manfully, ^{17}and to set before their eyes the injury that they had unjustly done to the holy place, and the cruel handling of the city, whereof they made a mockery, and also the taking away of the government of their forefathers: ^{18}for they, said he, trust in their weapons and boldness; but our confidence is in the Almighty God, who at a beck can cast down both them that come against us, and also all the world.

^{19}Moreover he recounted unto them what helps their forefathers had found, and how they were delivered, when under Sennacherib an hundred fourscore and five thousand perished. ^{20}And he told them of the battle that they had in Babylon with the Galatians, how they came but eight thousand in all to the business, with four thousand Macedonians, and that the Macedonians being perplexed, the eight thousand destroyed an hundred and twenty thousand because of the help that they had from heaven, and so received a great booty.

^{21}Thus when he had made them bold with these words, and ready to die for the laws and the country, he divided his army into four parts; ^{22}and joined with himself his own brethren, leaders of each band, to wit, Simon, and Joseph, and Jonathan, giving each one fifteen hundred men. ^{23}Also he appointed Eleazar to read the holy book: and when he had given them this watchword, The help of God; himself leading the first band, he joined battle with Nicanor. ^{24}And by the help of the Almighty they slew above nine thousand of their enemies, and wounded and maimed the most part of Nicanor's host, and so put all to flight; ^{25}and took their money that came to buy them, and pursued them far: but lacking time they returned: ^{26}for it was the day before the sabbath, and therefore they would no longer pursue them.

^{27}So when they had gathered their armour together, and spoiled their enemies, they occupied themselves about the sabbath, yielding exceeding praise and thanks to the Lord, who had preserved them unto that day, which was the beginning of mercy distilling upon them. ^{28}And after the sabbath, when they had given part of the spoils to the maimed, and the widows, and orphans, the residue they divided among themselves and their servants. ^{29}When this was done, and they had made

---

1:10 note). **8:18** *For they . . . God*: cf. 1 Sam 17:45; Ps 20:7. *Beck*: nod. **8:19** *How they . . . perished*: see 2 Kgs 19:35. **8:20** *The battle . . . Galatians*: presumably referring to an otherwise unknown battle in which Jewish soldiers fought against Galatians (the term can refer to the inhabitants of Gaul or to Celts settled in Asia Minor) as part of the Seleucid army, alongside a Macedonian contingent. **8:23** *Eleazar*: another of Judas's brothers. *Holy book*: presumably the Torah. **8:28** *The maimed . . . orphans*:

a common supplication, they besought the merciful Lord to be reconciled with his servants for ever.

[30]Moreover of those that were with Timotheus and Bacchides, who fought against them, they slew above twenty thousand, and very easily got high and strong holds, and divided among themselves many spoils more, and made the maimed, orphans, widows, yea, and the aged also, equal in spoils with themselves. [31]And when they had gathered their armour together, they laid them up all carefully in convenient places, and the remnant of the spoils they brought to Jerusalem. [32]They slew also Philarches, that wicked person, who was with Timotheus, and had annoyed the Jews many ways. [33]Furthermore at such time as they kept the feast for the victory in their country they burnt Callisthenes, that had set fire upon the holy gates, who had fled into a little house; and so he received a reward meet for his wickedness.

[34]As for that most ungracious Nicanor, who had brought a thousand merchants to buy the Jews, [35]he was through the help of the Lord brought down by them, of whom he made least account; and putting off his glorious apparel, and discharging his company, he came like a fugitive servant through the midland unto Antioch, having very great dishonour, for that his host was destroyed. [36]Thus he, that took upon him to make good to the Romans their tribute by means of the captives in Jerusalem, told abroad, that the Jews had God to fight for them, and therefore they could not be hurt, because they followed the laws that he gave them.

9 About that time came Antiochus with dishonour out of the country of Persia. [2]For he had entered the city called Persepolis, and went about to rob the temple, and to hold the city; whereupon the multitude running to defend themselves with their weapons put them to flight; and so it happened, that Antiochus being put to flight of the inhabitants returned with shame. [3]Now when he came to Ecbatane, news was brought him what had happened unto Nicanor and Timotheus. [4]Then swelling with anger, he thought to avenge upon the Jews the disgrace done unto him by those that made him flee. Therefore commanded he his chariot man to drive without ceasing, and to dispatch the journey, the judgment of God now following him. For he had spoken proudly in this sort, That he would come to Jerusalem, and make it a common buryingplace of the Jews.

[5]But the Lord Almighty, the God of Israel, smote him with an incurable and invisible plague: for as soon as he had spoken these words, a pain of the bowels that was remediless came upon him, and sore torments of the inner parts; [6]and that most justly: for he had tormented other men's bowels with many and strange torments. [7]Howbeit he nothing at all ceased from his bragging, but still was filled

---

the survivors of the persecution (also in v. 30).   **8:29** *To be . . . for ever*: recalling the martyr's prayer at 7:33 (see note).   **8:30–34** *Moreover of those . . . wickedness*: according to 1 Maccabees, Timotheus's defeat took place later (see 5:37–44; cf. 2 Macc 10:24–38), as did Bacchides' (9:23–73).   **8:31** *Their armour*: i.e., the enemy's armor. They separate it from the other spoils with the intent of using it themselves.   **8:32** *Philarches, . . . with Timotheus*: better "the commander of Timothy's forces, a most wicked man" (NRSV).   **8:34** *Most ungracious*: lit. "thrice cursed."   **8:35** *Midland*: inland country.

9:1–29 The death of Antiochus Epiphanes. Compare 1 Macc 6:1–17.   **9:3** *Ecbatane*: far northwest of Persepolis.   **9:5** *Plague*: blow.   **9:7** *Carried violently*: a description of the rushing chariot.

with pride, breathing out fire in his rage against the Jews, and commanding to haste the journey: but it came to pass that he fell down from his chariot, carried violently; so that having a sore fall, all the members of his body were much pained. [8]And thus he that a little afore thought he might command the waves of the sea, (so proud was he beyond the condition of man) and weigh the high mountains in a balance, was now cast on the ground, and carried in an horse litter, shewing forth unto all the manifest power of God. [9]So that the worms rose up out of the body of this wicked man, and whiles he lived in sorrow and pain, his flesh fell away, and the filthiness of his smell was noisome to all his army. [10]And the man, that thought a little afore he could reach to the stars of heaven, no man could endure to carry for his intolerable stink. [11]Here therefore, being plagued, he began to leave off his great pride, and to come to the knowledge of himself by the scourge of God, his pain increasing every moment.

[12]And when he himself could not abide his own smell, he said these words, It is meet to be subject unto God, and that a man that is mortal should not proudly think of himself, as if he were God. [13]This wicked person vowed also unto the Lord, who now no more would have mercy upon him, saying thus, [14]that the holy city (to the which he was going in haste, to lay it even with the ground, and to make it a common buryingplace,) he would set at liberty: [15]and as touching the Jews, whom he had judged not worthy so much as to be buried, but to be cast out with their children to be devoured of the fowls and wild beasts, he would make them all equals to the citizens of Athens: [16]and the holy temple, which before he had spoiled, he would garnish with goodly gifts, and restore all the holy vessels with many more, and out of his own revenue defray the charges belonging to the sacrifices: [17]yea, and that also he would become a Jew himself, and go through all the world that was inhabited, and declare the power of God.

[18]But for all this his pains would not cease: for the just judgment of God was come upon him: therefore despairing of his health, he wrote unto the Jews the letter underwritten, containing the form of a supplication, after this manner: [19]Antiochus, king and governor, to the good Jews his citizens wisheth much joy, health, and prosperity: [20]If ye and your children fare well, and your affairs be to your contentment, I give very great thanks to God, having my hope in heaven. [21]As for me, I was weak, or else I would have remembered kindly your honour and good will. Returning out of Persia, and being taken with a grievous disease, I thought it necessary to care for the common safety of all: [22]not distrusting mine health, but having great hope to escape this sickness. [23]But considering that even my father, at what time he led an army into the high countries, appointed a suc-

---

9:8 *Command the waves . . . balance:* language conventionally used of YHWH in the Bible (Ps 89:9; Isa 40:12; etc.); also cf. 5:21 and note. **9:9** *The worms . . . noisome:* see Acts 12:22–23 and note. **9:10** *He could reach . . . heaven:* assimilating Antiochus's downfall to the fall of Lucifer in Isa 14:12–20 (see v. 20 note). **9:11** *Plagued:* better "broken in spirit" (NRSV). **9:15** *Athens:* a representative Greek city-state. **9:18** *Underwritten:* quoted below (in vv. 19–27). **9:23** *High countries:* the Persian

cessor, [24]to the end that, if any thing fell out contrary to expectation, or if any tidings were brought that were grievous, they of the land, knowing to whom the state was left, might not be troubled: [25]again, considering how that the princes that are borderers and neighbours unto my kingdom wait for opportunities, and expect what shall be the event, I have appointed my son Antiochus king, whom I often committed and commended unto many of you, when I went up into the high provinces; to whom I have written as followeth: [26]therefore I pray and request you to remember the benefits that I have done unto you generally, and in special, and that every man will be still faithful to me and my son. [27]For I am persuaded that he understanding my mind will favourably and graciously yield to your desires.

[28]Thus the murderer and blasphemer having suffered most grievously, as he entreated other men, so died he a miserable death in a strange country in the mountains. [29]And Philip, that was brought up with him, carried away his body, who also fearing the son of Antiochus went into Egypt to Ptolemeus Philometor.

10 Now Maccabeus and his company, the Lord guiding them, recovered the temple and the city: [2]but the altars which the heathen had built in the open street, and also the chapels, they pulled down. [3]And having cleansed the temple they made another altar, and striking stones they took fire out of them, and offered a sacrifice after two years, and set forth incense, and lights, and shewbread. [4]When that was done, they fell flat down, and besought the Lord that they might come no more into such troubles; but if they sinned any more against him, that he himself would chasten them with mercy, and that they might not be delivered unto the blasphemous and barbarous nations. [5]Now upon the same day that the strangers profaned the temple, on the very same day it was cleansed again, even the five and twentieth day of the same month, which is Casleu. [6]And they kept eight days with gladness, as in the feast of the tabernacles, remembering that not long afore they had held the feast of the tabernacles, when as they wandered in the mountains and dens like beasts. [7]Therefore they bare branches, and fair boughs, and palms also, and sang psalms unto him that had given them good success in cleansing his place. [8]They ordained also by a common statute and decree, That every year those days should be kept of the whole nation of the Jews. [9]And this was the end of Antiochus, called Epiphanes.

---

plateau. **9:25** *Event*: i.e., outcome (of his illness). *To whom . . . followeth*: i.e., an attached letter (whose text is not included). **9:27** *Understanding my mind*: better "following my intent." **9:28** *Entreated*: treated. **9:29** *Who also . . . Antiochus*: apparently an allusion to the events recorded at 1 Macc 6:55–63 (though no journey to Egypt is mentioned there). *Ptolemeus Philometor*: Ptolemy VI Philometor, who ruled Egypt ca. 175–145 B.C.E.

10:1–9 Rededication of the temple. Compare 1 Macc 4:36–61 and notes. **10:2** *Chapels*: lit. lands dedicated (i.e., to a god). **10:3** *Striking stones . . . them*: contradicting the miraculous account given in 1:19–36. **10:6** *Feast of the tabernacles*: see Lev 23:33–43. *Remembering that . . . beasts*: this explains why the feast of Hanukkah resembled the Feast of Tabernacles held earlier in the year (see 1:9 and note): Judas and his company were unable to observe it properly, and so incorporated some of its elements into their celebration of the temple's rededication, which itself became a national holiday (see v. 8). **10:7** *Bare branches . . . also*: see Lev 23:40.

¹⁰Now will we declare the acts of Antiochus Eupator, who was the son of this wicked man, gathering briefly the calamities of the wars. ¹¹So when he was come to the crown, he set one Lysias over the affairs of his realm, and appointed him chief governor of Celosyria and Phenice. ¹²For Ptolemeus, that was called Macron, choosing rather to do justice unto the Jews for the wrong that had been done unto them, endeavoured to continue peace with them. ¹³Whereupon being accused of the king's friends before Eupator, and called traitor at every word, because he had left Cyprus, that Philometor had committed unto him, and departed to Antiochus Epiphanes, and seeing that he was in no honourable place, he was so discouraged, that he poisoned himself and died.

¹⁴But when Gorgias was governor of the holds, he hired soldiers, and nourished war continually with the Jews: ¹⁵and therewithal the Idumeans, having gotten into their hands the most commodious holds, kept the Jews occupied, and receiving those that were banished from Jerusalem, they went about to nourish war. ¹⁶Then they that were with Maccabeus made supplication, and besought God that he would be their helper; and so they ran with violence upon the strong holds of the Idumeans, ¹⁷and assaulting them strongly, they won the holds, and kept off all that fought upon the wall, and slew all that fell into their hands, and killed no fewer than twenty thousand.

¹⁸And because certain, who were no less than nine thousand, were fled together into two very strong castles, having all manner of things convenient to sustain the siege, ¹⁹Maccabeus left Simon and Joseph, and Zaccheus also, and them that were with him, who were enough to besiege them, and departed himself unto those places which more needed his help. ²⁰Now they that were with Simon, being led with covetousness, were persuaded for money, (through certain of those that were in the castle,) and took seventy thousand drachms, and let some of them escape. ²¹But when it was told Maccabeus what was done, he called the governors of the people together, and accused those men, that they had sold their brethren for money, and set their enemies free to fight against them. ²²So he slew those that were found traitors, and immediately took the two castles. ²³And having good success with his weapons in all things he took in hand, he slew in the two holds more than twenty thousand.

²⁴Now Timotheus, whom the Jews had overcome before, when he had gathered a great multitude of foreign forces, and horses out of Asia not a few, came as though he would take Jewry by force of arms. ²⁵But when he drew near, they that were with Maccabeus turned themselves to pray unto God, and sprinkled earth upon their heads, and girded their loins with sackcloth, ²⁶and fell down at the

---

10:10–38 War with neighboring nations and Timotheus's defeat. This section has several points of contact with 1 Macc 5. **10:10** *Antiochus Eupator*: see 1 Macc 6:17 note. **10:12** *Ptolemeus*: see 4:45–46; 6:8. **10:11** *He set . . . Phenice*: 1 Maccabees credits this appointment to Antiochus Epiphanes (3:32–33). **10:13** *Because he . . . Epiphanes*: this event occurred during Antiochus Epiphanes' invasion of Egypt in the time of Ptolemy IV Philomotor's reign (see 1 Macc 1:16–19): while governing the Egyptian territory of Cyprus, Ptolemeus Macron had defected to the Seleucid Empire. **10:14** *Gorgias*: initially one of Lysias's generals, according to 1 Macc 3:3. *Holds*: places (presumably in Judea and its environs, as opposed to the broader region overseen by Lysias). **10:15** *Idumeans*: they occupied a region just south of Judea. **10:24** *Timotheus, whom . . . before*: see 8:30, though the earlier passage may actually refer to the events narrated here (see note). *Jewry*: lit. "Judea."

foot of the altar, and besought him to be merciful to them, and to be an enemy to their enemies, and an adversary to their adversaries, as the law declareth. [27]So after the prayer they took their weapons, and went on further from the city: and when they drew near to their enemies, they kept by themselves.

[28]Now the sun being newly risen, they joined both together; the one part having together with their virtue their refuge also unto the Lord for a pledge of their success and victory: the other side making their rage leader of their battle. [29]But when the battle waxed strong, there appeared unto the enemies from heaven five comely men upon horses, with bridles of gold, and two of them led the Jews, [30]and took Maccabeus betwixt them, and covered him on every side with their weapons, and kept him safe, but shot arrows and lightnings against the enemies: so that being confounded with blindness, and full of trouble, they were killed. [31]And there were slain of footmen twenty thousand and five hundred, and six hundred horsemen. [32]As for Timotheus himself, he fled into a very strong hold, called Gazara, where Chereas was governor. [33]But they that were with Maccabeus laid siege against the fortress courageously four days. [34]And they that were within, trusting to the strength of the place, blasphemed exceedingly, and uttered wicked words. [35]Nevertheless upon the fifth day early twenty young men of Maccabeus' company, inflamed with anger because of the blasphemies, assaulted the wall manly, and with a fierce courage killed all that they met withal. [36]Others likewise ascending after them, whiles they were busied with them that were within, burnt the towers, and kindling fires burnt the blasphemers alive; and others broke open the gates, and, having received in the rest of the army, took the city, [37]and killed Timotheus, that was hid in a certain pit, and Chereas his brother, with Apollophanes. [38]When this was done, they praised the Lord with psalms and thanksgiving, who had done so great things for Israel, and given them the victory.

11 Not long after this, Lysias the king's protector and cousin, who also managed the affairs, took sore displeasure for the things that were done. [2]And when he had gathered about fourscore thousand with all the horsemen, he came against the Jews, thinking to make the city an habitation of the Gentiles, [3]and to make a gain of the temple, as of the other chapels of the heathen, and to set the high priesthood to sale every year: [4]not at all considering the power of God, but puffed up with his ten thousands of footmen, and his thousands of horsemen, and his fourscore elephants. [5]So he came to Judea, and drew near to Bethsura,

---

10:26 *To be merciful . . . their adversaries*: see Exod 23:22.   **10:32** *Gazara*: Gezer, about twenty miles northwest of Jerusalem.

11:1–38 The defeat of Lysias and subsequent peace. Contrast the account in 1 Macc 4:26–35, where Lysias's first expedition takes place significantly earlier—in the reign of Antiochus IV Epiphanes, not of Antiochus V Eupator—and before even the rededication of the temple. The dates in vv. 30 and 33 (and perhaps 21 and 38 as well, but more problematically) seem to confirm the earlier setting, though the chronology here is probably too jumbled to resolve by simple transposition to an earlier historical context. The section closes with four letters regarding the peace agreed to by Judas and Lysias: from Lysias to the Jews (vv. 16–21), from Antiochus to Lysias (vv. 22–26), from Antiochus to the Jews (vv. 27–33), and from Roman ambassadors to the Jews (vv. 34–38).   **11:1** *Protector*: guardian (see 1 Macc 3:33).   **11:2** *Gentiles*: rather "Greeks" (also at v. 24).   **11:3** *Chapels*: see 10:2 note.   **11:5** *Bethsura*: Beth-zur, but rather than being *five furlongs* (more than half a mile)

which was a strong town, but distant from Jerusalem about five furlongs, and he laid sore siege unto it.

⁶Now when they that were with Maccabeus heard that he besieged the holds, they and all the people with lamentation and tears besought the Lord that he would send a good angel to deliver Israel. ⁷Then Maccabeus himself first of all took weapons, exhorting the others that they would jeopard themselves together with him to help their brethren: so they went forth together with a willing mind. ⁸And as they were at Jerusalem, there appeared before them on horseback one in white clothing, shaking his armour of gold. ⁹Then they praised the merciful God all together, and took heart, insomuch that they were ready not only to fight with men, but with most cruel beasts, and to pierce through walls of iron.

¹⁰Thus they marched forward in their armour, having an helper from heaven: for the Lord was merciful unto them. ¹¹And giving a charge upon their enemies like lions, they slew eleven thousand footmen, and sixteen hundred horsemen, and put all the other to flight. ¹²Many of them also being wounded escaped naked; and Lysias himself fled away shamefully, and so escaped. ¹³Who, as he was a man of understanding, casting with himself what loss he had had, and considering that the Hebrews could not be overcome, because the Almighty God helped them, he sent unto them, ¹⁴and persuaded them to agree to all reasonable conditions, and promised that he would persuade the king that he must needs be a friend unto them. ¹⁵Then Maccabeus consented to all that Lysias desired, being careful of the common good; and whatsoever Maccabeus wrote unto Lysias concerning the Jews, the king granted it.

¹⁶For there were letters written unto the Jews from Lysias to this effect: Lysias unto the people of the Jews sendeth greeting: ¹⁷John and Absalon, who were sent from you, delivered me the petition subscribed, and made request for the performance of the contents thereof. ¹⁸Therefore what things soever were meet to be reported to the king, I have declared them, and he hath granted as much as might be. ¹⁹If then ye will keep yourselves loyal to the state, hereafter also will I endeavour to be a means of your good. ²⁰But of the particulars I have given order both to these, and the other that came from me, to commune with you. ²¹Fare ye well. The hundred and eight and fortieth year, the four and twentieth day of the month Dioscorinthius.

²²Now the king's letter contained these words: King Antiochus unto his brother Lysias sendeth greeting: ²³Since our father is translated unto the gods, our will is, that they that are in our realm live quietly, that every one may attend upon his own affairs. ²⁴We understand also that the Jews would not consent to our father, for to be brought unto the custom of the Gentiles, but had rather keep their own manner of living: for the which cause they require of us, that we should suffer them to live after their own laws. ²⁵Wherefore our mind is, that this nation shall

---

from Jerusalem, it is about fifteen miles south of the city.   **11:7** *Jeopard:* put in jeopardy (so throughout).   **11:12** *Naked:* i.e., of armor.   **11:13** *Casting with himself:* weighing in his mind.   **11:17** *Subscribed:* written below (although its text is not included here).   **11:20** *These:* i.e., John and Absalon.   **11:21** *The hundred . . . Dioscorinthius:* only the year (164 B.C.E.) is clear, as the Greeks called

be in rest, and we have determined to restore them their temple, that they may live according to the customs of their forefathers. ²⁶Thou shalt do well therefore to send unto them, and grant them peace, that when they are certified of our mind, they may be of good comfort, and ever go cheerfully about their own affairs.

²⁷And the letter of the king unto the nation of the Jews was after this manner: King Antiochus sendeth greeting unto the council, and the rest of the Jews: ²⁸If ye fare well, we have our desire: we are also in good health. ²⁹Menelaus declared unto us, that your desire was to return home, and to follow your own business: ³⁰wherefore they that will depart shall have safe conduct till the thirtieth day of Xanthicus with security. ³¹And the Jews shall use their own kind of meats and laws, as before; and none of them any manner of ways shall be molested for things ignorantly done. ³²I have sent also Menelaus, that he may comfort you. ³³Fare ye well. In the hundred forty and eighth year, and the fifteenth day of the month Xanthicus.

³⁴The Romans also sent unto them a letter containing these words: Quintus Memmius and Titus Manlius, ambassadors of the Romans, send greeting unto the people of the Jews. ³⁵Whatsoever Lysias the king's cousin hath granted, therewith we also are well pleased. ³⁶But touching such things as he judged to be referred to the king, after ye have advised thereof, send one forthwith, that we may declare as it is convenient for you: for we are now going to Antioch. ³⁷Therefore send some with speed, that we may know what is your mind. ³⁸Farewell. This hundred and eight and fortieth year, the fifteenth day of the month Xanthicus.

12 When these covenants were made, Lysias went unto the king, and the Jews were about their husbandry. ²But of the governors of several places, Timotheus, and Apollonius the son of Genneus, also Hieronymus, and Demophon, and beside them Nicanor the governor of Cyprus, would not suffer them to be quiet, and live in peace. ³The men of Joppe also did such an ungodly deed: they prayed the Jews that dwelt among them to go with their wives and children into

---

no month Dioscorinthius; presumably, this letter was sent before the king's. **11:27** *Council*: Gk. *gerousia*, "council of elders." **11:30** *The thirtieth day of Xanthicus*: March-April 164 B.C.E. **11:31** *The Jews . . . done*: Antiochus thus rescinds his father's policy of forced assimilation. **11:34–38** *The Romans . . . Xanthicus*: this letter suggests that Roman ambassadors acted as mediators between the Jews and Antiochus in negotiating the peace, but the earlier letters indicate that the terms of the peace had already been finalized. Verse 36 is especially perplexing, for it invites the Jews to comment on matters that Lysias had referred to the king and promises to relay those comments to him, even though those matters had already been decided (see v. 18). Moreover, the Roman letter was purportedly written on the same day as the king's own letter to the Jews confirming the peace whose terms the Roman ambassadors claim to be able to influence (v. 38; cf. 33). Such inconsistencies have led many scholars to question the authenticity of this section's final letter, although other explanations are possible (e.g., that the Roman ambassadors are offering to intercede with Antiochus about particulars that Lysias expects to be resolved locally; see v. 20). The inconsistencies might also be resolved by textual emendations, which find limited support in the MS tradition: at v. 18 "he hath" is occasionally replaced by "I have," and at v. 38 some MSS offer different dates.

12:1–45 Judas's victories. This chapter roughly parallels 1 Macc 5, but with significant differences. **12:2** *Timotheus*: he had already been defeated and supposedly killed (see 10:24–38); either the author is confused or there were two figures by that name. *Apollonius the son of Genneus*: not the Apollonius mentioned earlier (cf. 4:21). *Nicanor the governor of Cyprus*: a Nicanor was defeated

the boats which they had prepared, as though they had meant them no hurt. [4]Who accepted of it according to the common decree of the city, as being desirous to live in peace, and suspecting nothing: but when they were gone forth into the deep, they drowned no less than two hundred of them. [5]When Judas heard of this cruelty done unto his countrymen, he commanded those that were with him to make them ready. [6]And calling upon God the righteous Judge, he came against those murderers of his brethren, and burnt the haven by night, and set the boats on fire, and those that fled thither he slew. [7]And when the town was shut up, he went backward, as if he would return to root out all them of the city of Joppe. [8]But when he heard that the Jamnites were minded to do in like manner unto the Jews that dwelt among them, [9]he came upon the Jamnites also by night, and set fire on the haven and the navy, so that the light of the fire was seen at Jerusalem two hundred and forty furlongs off.

[10]Now when they were gone from thence nine furlongs in their journey toward Timotheus, no fewer than five thousand men on foot and five hundred horsemen of the Arabians set upon him. [11]Whereupon there was a very sore battle; but Judas' side by the help of God got the victory; so that the Nomades of Arabia, being overcome, besought Judas for peace, promising both to give him cattle, and to pleasure him otherwise. [12]Then Judas, thinking indeed that they would be profitable in many things, granted them peace: whereupon they shook hands, and so they departed to their tents.

[13]He went also about to make a bridge to a certain strong city, which was fenced about with walls, and inhabited by people of divers countries; and the name of it was Caspis. [14]But they that were within it put such trust in the strength of the walls and provision of victuals, that they behaved themselves rudely toward them that were with Judas, railing and blaspheming, and uttering such words as were not to be spoken. [15]Wherefore Judas with his company, calling upon the great Lord of the world, who without any rams or engines of war did cast down Jericho in the time of Joshua, gave a fierce assault against the walls, [16]and took the city by the will of God, and made unspeakable slaughters, insomuch that a lake two furlongs broad near adjoining thereunto, being filled full, was seen running with blood.

[17]Then departed they from thence seven hundred and fifty furlongs, and came to Characa unto the Jews that are called Tubieni. [18]But as for Timotheus, they found him not in the places: for before he had dispatched any thing, he departed from thence, having left a very strong garrison in a certain hold. [19]Howbeit Dositheus and Sosipater, who were of Maccabeus' captains, went forth, and slew

---

earlier (see 8:8–36), perhaps the same man mentioned here.   **12:6** *Haven*: harbor (so throughout).   **12:8** *Jamnites*: from Jamnia, near the Mediterranean coast several miles south from Joppa.   **12:9** *Two hundred and forty furlongs*: about thirty miles.   **12:10** *Nine furlongs*: just over a mile.   **12:11** *Nomades*: nomads. *Pleasure*: lit. "aid."   **12:12** *Shook hands*: the Greek refers to a pledge of faith.   **12:13** *Went also . . . walls*: Gk. obscure. *Divers*: various (also at v. 27). *Caspis*: perhaps to be identified with Casphor in Gilead (see 1 Macc 5:26).   **12:15** *Cast down . . . Joshua*: see Josh 6.   **12:16** *Two furlongs*: a quarter mile.   **12:17** *Seven hundred and fifty furlongs*: nearly a hundred miles. *Characa*: unidentified; the Greek may simply be a noun referring to a palisaded camp rather than a name. *Tubieni*: probably the inhabitants of Tob (see 1 Macc 5:13

those that Timotheus had left in the fortress, above ten thousand men. ²⁰And Maccabeus ranged his army by bands, and set them over the bands, and went against Timotheus, who had about him an hundred and twenty thousand men of foot, and two thousand and five hundred horsemen. ²¹Now when Timotheus had knowledge of Judas' coming, he sent the women and children and the other baggage unto a fortress called Carnion: for the town was hard to besiege, and uneasy to come unto, by reason of the straitness of all the places. ²²But when Judas his first band came in sight, the enemies, being smitten with fear and terror through the appearing of him that seeth all things, fled amain, one running this way, another that way, so as that they were often hurt of their own men, and wounded with the points of their own swords. ²³Judas also was very earnest in pursuing them, killing those wicked wretches, of whom he slew about thirty thousand men.

²⁴Moreover Timotheus himself fell into the hands of Dositheus and Sosipater, whom he besought with much craft to let him go with his life, because he had many of the Jews' parents, and the brethren of some of them, who, if they put him to death, should not be regarded. ²⁵So when he had assured them with many words that he would restore them without hurt, according to the agreement, they let him go for the saving of their brethren.

²⁶Then Maccabeus marched forth to Carnion, and to the temple of Atargatis, and there he slew five and twenty thousand persons. ²⁷And after he had put to flight and destroyed them, Judas removed the host toward Ephron, a strong city, wherein Lysias abode, and a great multitude of divers nations, and the strong young men kept the walls, and defended them mightily: wherein also was great provision of engines and darts. ²⁸But when Judas and his company had called upon Almighty God, who with his power breaketh the strength of his enemies, they won the city, and slew twenty and five thousand of them that were within. ²⁹From thence they departed to Scythopolis, which lieth six hundred furlongs from Jerusalem. ³⁰But when the Jews that dwelt there had testified that the Scythopolitans dealt lovingly with them, and entreated them kindly in the time of their adversity; ³¹they gave them thanks, desiring them to be friendly still unto them: and so they came to Jerusalem, the feast of the weeks approaching.

³²And after the feast, called Pentecost, they went forth against Gorgias the governor of Idumea, ³³who came out with three thousand men of foot and four hundred horsemen. ³⁴And it happened that in their fighting together a few of the Jews were slain. ³⁵At which time Dositheus, one of Bacenor's company, who was on horseback, and a strong man, was still upon Gorgias, and taking hold of his coat drew him by force; and when he would have taken that cursed man alive, a

note).   **12:20** *Them over the bands*: i.e., "men in command of the divisions" (NRSV).   **12:21** *Carnion*: Carnaim; see 1 Macc 5:26. *Straitness of all the places*: "narrowness of all the approaches" (NRSV). **12:22** *Judas his*: Judas's. *The appearing of him . . . things*: another divine apparition. *Amain*: at full speed.   **12:24** *Should not be regarded*: "would be shown no consideration" (cf. NRSV).   **12:26** *Atargatis*: a Syrian divinity.   **12:27** *Ephron*: a few miles east of the Jordan River.   **12:29** *Skythopolis*: just west of the Jordan River. *Six hundred furlongs*: about seventy-five miles.   **12:31** *Feast of the weeks*: Pentecost (v. 32); see Lev 23:15–21.   **12:32** *Gorgias*: cf. 8:9; 10:14.   **12:35** *Dositheus, one of Bacenor's company*: probably a different figure from the Dositheus mentioned in vv. 19, 24. *Was still upon*: was holding on

horseman of Thracia coming upon him smote off his shoulder, so that Gorgias fled unto Marisa.

³⁶Now when they that were with Gorgias had fought long, and were weary, Judas called upon the Lord, that he would shew himself to be their helper and leader of the battle. ³⁷And with that he began in his own language, and sung psalms with a loud voice, and rushing unawares upon Gorgias' men, he put them to flight. ³⁸So Judas gathered his host, and came into the city of Odollam. And when the seventh day came, they purified themselves, as the custom was, and kept the sabbath in the same place.

³⁹And upon the day following, as the use had been, Judas and his company came to take up the bodies of them that were slain, and to bury them with their kinsmen in their fathers' graves. ⁴⁰Now under the coats of every one that was slain they found things consecrated to the idols of the Jamnites, which is forbidden the Jews by the law. Then every man saw that this was the cause wherefore they were slain. ⁴¹All men therefore praising the Lord, the righteous Judge, who had opened the things that were hid, ⁴²betook themselves unto prayer, and besought him that the sin committed might wholly be put out of remembrance. Besides, that noble Judas exhorted the people to keep themselves from sin, forsomuch as they saw before their eyes the things that came to pass for the sins of those that were slain. ⁴³And when he had made a gathering throughout the company to the sum of two thousand drachms of silver, he sent it to Jerusalem to offer a sin offering, doing therein very well and honestly, in that he was mindful of the resurrection: ⁴⁴for if he had not hoped that they that were slain should have risen again, it had been superfluous and vain to pray for the dead. ⁴⁵And also in that he perceived that there was great favour laid up for those that died godly, it was an holy and good thought. Whereupon he made a reconciliation for the dead, that they might be delivered from sin.

13 In the hundred forty and ninth year it was told Judas, that Antiochus Eupator was coming with a great power into Judea, ²and with him Lysias his protector, and ruler of his affairs, having either of them a Grecian power of footmen, an hundred and ten thousand, and horsemen five thousand and three hundred, and elephants two and twenty, and three hundred chariots armed with hooks.

---

to. *Thracia*: Thrace. *Marisa*: more than twenty miles southwest of Jerusalem. **12:38** *Odollam*: Adullam, a few miles northeast of Marisa. *They purified . . . was*: cf. Num 31:19–24. **12:39** *Use*: need. **12:40** *Under the coats . . . slain*: 1 Macc 5:65–68 explains the deaths differently. **12:43–45** *And when . . . sin*: this passage is sometimes cited as support for the doctrine of purgatory. It presents a surprising theology, for atonement on behalf of the dead was an innovative concept in Judaism at this time. (For a later NT parallel, see 1 Cor 15:29 and note.) Perhaps the author is imposing a tendentious interpretation on Judas's actions, designed to assimilate him to the heroic martyrs of chaps. 6–7 who were encouraged by a belief in bodily resurrection that Judas himself may not have shared. He may have intended the sin offering ritually to atone for the guilt that the idolaters' transgression brought on the surviving community; cf. Lev 4:13–21; Josh 7 (where Achan's transgression leads to Israel's defeat). **12:43** *Gathering*: collection.

13:1–8 The death of Menelaus. Another retribution narrative, making explicit the poetic justice of God's punishment of Menelaus for his acts of sacrilege. **13:1** *The hundred forty and ninth year*: 163 B.C.E. *Power*: force. **13:2** *Hooks*: for mowing down infantry.

³Menelaus also joined himself with them, and with great dissimulation encouraged Antiochus, not for the safeguard of the country, but because he thought to have been made governor. ⁴But the King of kings moved Antiochus' mind against this wicked wretch, and Lysias informed the king that this man was the cause of all mischief, so that the king commanded to bring him unto Berea, and to put him to death, as the manner is in that place. ⁵Now there was in that place a tower of fifty cubits high, full of ashes, and it had a round instrument, which on every side hanged down into the ashes. ⁶And whosoever was condemned of sacrilege, or had committed any other grievous crime, there did all men thrust him unto death. ⁷Such a death it happened that wicked man to die, not having so much as burial in the earth; and that most justly: ⁸for inasmuch as he had committed many sins about the altar, whose fire and ashes were holy, he received his death in ashes.

⁹Now the king came with a barbarous and haughty mind to do far worse to the Jews, than had been done in his father's time. ¹⁰Which things when Judas perceived, he commanded the multitude to call upon the Lord night and day, that if ever at any other time, he would now also help them, being at the point to be put from their law, from their country, and from the holy temple: ¹¹and that he would not suffer the people, that had even now been but a little refreshed, to be in subjection to the blasphemous nations. ¹²So when they had all done this together, and besought the merciful Lord with weeping and fasting, and lying flat upon the ground three days long, Judas, having exhorted them, commanded they should be in a readiness. ¹³And Judas, being apart with the elders, determined, before the king's host should enter into Judea, and get the city, to go forth and try the matter in fight by the help of the Lord.

¹⁴So when he had committed all to the Creator of the world, and exhorted his soldiers to fight manfully, even unto death, for the laws, the temple, the city, the country, and the commonwealth, he camped by Modin: ¹⁵and having given the watchword to them that were about him, Victory is of God; with the most valiant and choice young men he went in into the king's tent by night, and slew in the camp about four thousand men, and the chiefest of the elephants, with all that were upon him. ¹⁶And at last they filled the camp with fear and tumult, and departed with good success. ¹⁷This was done in the break of the day, because the protection of the Lord did help him.

¹⁸Now when the king had taken a taste of the manliness of the Jews, he went about to take the holds by policy, ¹⁹and marched toward Bethsura, which was a

---

13:4 *Berea*: a city in Syria.   **13:5** *A round instrument . . . ashes*: "a rim running around it that on all sides inclines precipitously into the ashes" (NRSV). However this contrivance worked, suffocation by ashes was a conventional Persian means of execution (see Ctesias, *Persica*, frags. 48, 51–52; etc.). **13:8** *Many sins about the altar*: see 4:32; 5:15–16.
13:9–26 Judas defeats Antiochus's army. Compare 1 Macc 6:18–63. The author's abridgment of Jason of Cyrene's history is especially evident here: vv. 22–26 reads like a list of details rather than a proper narrative, but the precipitous flow of verbs perhaps gives the impression of historical events speeding toward their divinely ordained conclusion.   **13:14** *Modin*: the mountain town whence the Hasmoneans hailed (cf. 1 Macc 2:1), about twenty miles northwest of Jerusalem.   **13:18** *Policy*:

strong hold of the Jews: but he was put to flight, failed, and lost of his men: ²⁰for Judas had conveyed unto them that were in it such things as were necessary. ²¹But Rhodocus, who was in the Jews' host, disclosed the secrets to the enemies; therefore he was sought out, and when they had gotten him, they put him in prison. ²²The king treated with them in Bethsura the second time, gave his hand, took theirs, departed, fought with Judas, was overcome; ²³heard that Philip, who was left over the affairs in Antioch, was desperately bent, confounded, intreated the Jews, submitted himself, and sware to all equal conditions, agreed with them, and offered sacrifice, honoured the temple, and dealt kindly with the place, ²⁴and accepted well of Maccabeus, made him principal governor from Ptolemais unto the Gerrhenians; ²⁵came to Ptolemais: the people there were grieved for the covenants; for they stormed, because they would make their covenants void: ²⁶Lysias went up to the judgment seat, said as much as could be in defence of the cause, persuaded, pacified, made them well affected, returned to Antioch. Thus it went touching the king's coming and departing.

14 After three years was Judas informed, that Demetrius the son of Seleucus, having entered by the haven of Tripolis with a great power and navy, ²had taken the country, and killed Antiochus, and Lysias his protector. ³Now one Alcimus, who had been high priest, and had defiled himself wilfully in the times of their mingling with the Gentiles, seeing that by no means he could save himself, nor have any more access to the holy altar, ⁴came to king Demetrius in the hundred and one and fiftieth year, presenting unto him a crown of gold, and a palm, and also of the boughs which were used solemnly in the temple: and so that day he held his peace. ⁵Howbeit, having gotten opportunity to further his foolish enterprize, and being called into counsel by Demetrius, and asked how the Jews stood affected, and what they intended, he answered thereunto: ⁶those of the Jews that be called Assideans, whose captain is Judas Maccabeus, nourish war, and are seditious, and will not let the realm be in peace. ⁷Therefore I, being deprived of mine ancestors' honour, I mean the high priesthood, am now come hither: ⁸first, verily for the unfeigned care I have of things pertaining to the king; and secondly, even for that I intend the good of mine own countrymen: for all our nation is in no small misery through the unadvised dealing of them aforesaid. ⁹Wherefore, O king, seeing thou knowest all these things, be careful for the country, and our nation, which is pressed on every side, according to the clemency that thou readily

stratagem (so throughout).   **13:22** *Treated*: negotiated.   **13:23** *Was desperately bent*: an allusion to Philip's rebellion. *Confounded*: i.e., Philip was confounded.   **13:24** *Gerrhenians*: Judas is made governor of a region stretching from southern Phoenicia (where *Ptolemais* was located) all the way south to Gerar, and incorporating Judea.

   14:1–25 Peace between Judas and Nicanor. For vv. 1–14, cf. 1 Macc 7:1–6; 25–26; for vv. 15–25, cf. 1 Macc 7:27–29a.   **14:1** *Demetrius the son of Seleucus*: see 1 Macc 7:1 note. *Tripolis*: south of Antioch, on the Mediterranean coast. *Power*: force.   **14:3** *Alcimus, who . . . priest*: Josephus (*Jewish Antiquities* 12.387) reports that he served after Menelaus. *Mingling with the Gentiles*: presumably in the period of forced hellenization; but Gk. *epimeixia* ("mingling") may also be construed as "peace." An alternate reading of the MS tradition is "interruption of communication" or "absence of intercourse" (so NRSV), probably referring to the rebellion.   **14:4** *The hundred and one and fiftieth year*: 161 B.C.E.   **14:6** *Assideans*: see 1 Macc 2:42 note. 1 Macc 7:12–18 narrates Alcimus's betrayal of them.   **14:9** *Careful*:

shewest unto all. ¹⁰For as long as Judas liveth, it is not possible that the state should be quiet.

¹¹This was no sooner spoken of him, but others of the king's friends, being maliciously set against Judas, did more incense Demetrius. ¹²And forthwith calling Nicanor, who had been master of the elephants, and making him governor over Judea, he sent him forth, ¹³commanding him to slay Judas, and to scatter them that were with him, and to make Alcimus high priest of the great temple. ¹⁴Then the heathen, that had fled out of Judea from Judas, came to Nicanor by flocks, thinking the harm and calamities of the Jews to be their welfare.

¹⁵Now when the Jews heard of Nicanor's coming, and that the heathen were up against them, they cast earth upon their heads, and made supplication to him that had established his people for ever, and who always helpeth his portion with manifestation of his presence. ¹⁶So at the commandment of the captain they removed straightways from thence, and came near unto them at the town of Dessau. ¹⁷Now Simon, Judas' brother, had joined battle with Nicanor, but was somewhat discomfited through the sudden silence of his enemies. ¹⁸Nevertheless Nicanor, hearing of the manliness of them that were with Judas, and the courageousness that they had to fight for their country, durst not try the matter by the sword. ¹⁹Wherefore he sent Posidonius, and Theodotus, and Mattathias, to make peace.

²⁰So when they had taken long advisement thereupon, and the captain had made the multitude acquainted therewith, and it appeared that they were all of one mind, they consented to the covenants, ²¹and appointed a day to meet in together by themselves: and when the day came, and stools were set for either of them, ²²Judas placed armed men ready in convenient places, lest some treachery should be suddenly practised by the enemies: so they made a peaceable conference. ²³Now Nicanor abode in Jerusalem, and did no hurt, but sent away the people that came flocking unto him. ²⁴And he would not willingly have Judas out of his sight: for he loved the man from his heart. ²⁵He prayed him also to take a wife, and to beget children: so he married, was quiet, and took part of this life.

²⁶But Alcimus, perceiving the love that was betwixt them, and considering the covenants that were made, came to Demetrius, and told him that Nicanor was not well affected toward the state; for that he had ordained Judas, a traitor to his realm, to be the king's successor. ²⁷Then the king being in a rage, and provoked with the accusations of the most wicked man, wrote to Nicanor, signifying that he was much displeased with the covenants, and commanding him that he should send Maccabeus prisoner in all haste unto Antioch.

²⁸When this came to Nicanor's hearing, he was much confounded in himself, and took it grievously that he should make void the articles which were agreed

---

concerned.   **14:12** *Nicanor*: he had been defeated in chap. 8.   **14:15** *Cast earth . . . supplication*: see 10:25. *His portion*: see 1:26 note.   **14:16** *Dessau*: unidentified, unless it is an alternative form of "Adasa," a site of battle between Judas and Nicanor (see 1 Macc 7:40–45).   **14:17** *Was somewhat . . . enemies*: NRSV translates "had been temporarily checked because of the sudden consternation created by the enemy."

14:26–46 Nicanor's oath and the death of Razis. For vv. 26–36, see 1 Macc 7:29b–38.

upon, the man being in no fault. ²⁹But because there was no dealing against the king, he watched his time to accomplish this thing by policy. ³⁰Notwithstanding, when Maccabeus saw that Nicanor began to be churlish unto him, and that he entreated him more roughly than he was wont, perceiving that such sour behaviour came not of good, he gathered together not a few of his men, and withdrew himself from Nicanor. ³¹But the other, knowing that he was notably prevented by Judas' policy, came into the great and holy temple, and commanded the priests, that were offering their usual sacrifices, to deliver him the man. ³²And when they sware that they could not tell where the man was whom he sought, ³³he stretched out his right hand toward the temple, and made an oath in this manner: If ye will not deliver me Judas as a prisoner, I will lay this temple of God even with the ground, and I will break down the altar, and erect a notable temple unto Bacchus.

³⁴After these words he departed. Then the priests lifted up their hands toward heaven, and besought him that was ever a defender of their nation, saying in this manner; ³⁵Thou, O Lord of all things, who hast need of nothing, wast pleased that the temple of thine habitation should be among us: ³⁶therefore now, O holy Lord of all holiness, keep this house ever undefiled, which lately was cleansed, and stop every unrighteous mouth.

³⁷Now was there accused unto Nicanor one Razis, one of the elders of Jerusalem, a lover of his countrymen, and a man of very good report, who for his kindness was called a father of the Jews. ³⁸For in the former times, when they mingled not themselves with the Gentiles, he had been accused of Judaism, and did boldly jeopard his body and life with all vehemency for the religion of the Jews. ³⁹So Nicanor, willing to declare the hate that he bare unto the Jews, sent above five hundred men of war to take him: ⁴⁰for he thought by taking him to do the Jews much hurt. ⁴¹Now when the multitude would have taken the tower, and violently broken into the outer door, and bade that fire should be brought to burn it, he being ready to be taken on every side fell upon his sword; ⁴²choosing rather to die manfully, than to come into the hands of the wicked, to be abused otherwise than beseemed his noble birth: ⁴³but missing his stroke through haste, the multitude also rushing within the doors, he ran boldly up to the wall, and cast himself down manfully among the thickest of them. ⁴⁴But they quickly giving back, and a space being made, he fell down into the midst of the void place. ⁴⁵Nevertheless, while there was yet breath within him, being inflamed with anger, he rose up; and though his blood gushed out like spouts of water, and his wounds were grievous, yet he ran through the midst of the throng; and standing upon a steep rock, ⁴⁶when as his blood was now quite gone, he plucked out his bowels, and taking them in both his hands, he cast them upon the throng, and calling upon the Lord of life and spirit to restore him those again, he thus died.

14:30 *Entreated*: treated. **14:33** *Bacchus*: see 6:7 note. **14:38** *Mingled not*: Gk. *ameixia*, the same word as the alternate reading in v. 3 (see note). **14:41** *The tower*: reference unclear.

15 But Nicanor, hearing that Judas and his company were in the strong places about Samaria, resolved without any danger to set upon them on the sabbath day. [2]Nevertheless the Jews that were compelled to go with him said, O destroy not so cruelly and barbarously, but give honour to that day, which he, that seeth all things, hath honoured with holiness above other days. [3]Then the most ungracious wretch demanded, if there were a Mighty One in heaven, that had commanded the sabbath day to be kept. [4]And when they said, There is in heaven a living Lord, and mighty, who commanded the seventh day to be kept: [5]then said the other, And I also am mighty upon earth, and I command to take arms, and to do the king's business. Yet he obtained not to have his wicked will done.

[6]So Nicanor in exceeding pride and haughtiness determined to set up a publick monument of his victory over Judas and them that were with him. [7]But Maccabeus had ever sure confidence that the Lord would help him: [8]wherefore he exhorted his people not to fear the coming of the heathen against them, but to remember the help which in former times they had received from heaven, and now to expect the victory and aid, which should come unto them from the Almighty. [9]And so comforting them out of the law and the prophets, and withal putting them in mind of the battles that they won afore, he made them more cheerful. [10]And when he had stirred up their minds, he gave them their charge, shewing them therewithal the falsehood of the heathen, and the breach of oaths. [11]Thus he armed every one of them, not so much with defence of shields and spears, as with comfortable and good words: and beside that, he told them a dream worthy to be believed, as if it had been so indeed, which did not a little rejoice them.

[12]And this was his vision: That Onias, who had been high priest, a virtuous and a good man, reverend in conversation, gentle in condition, well spoken also, and exercised from a child in all points of virtue, holding up his hands prayed for the whole body of the Jews. [13]This done, in like manner there appeared a man with gray hairs, and exceeding glorious, who was of a wonderful and excellent majesty. [14]Then Onias answered, saying, This is a lover of the brethren, who prayeth much for the people, and for the holy city, to wit, Jeremias the prophet of God. [15]Whereupon Jeremias holding forth his right hand gave to Judas a sword of gold, and in giving it spake thus, [16]Take this holy sword, a gift from God, with the which thou shalt wound the adversaries.

[17]Thus being well comforted by the words of Judas, which were very good, and able to stir them up to valour, and to encourage the hearts of the young men, they

15:1–16 **Judas's vision.** The appearance of Onias in this vision recalls chaps. 3–4. **15:3** *Demanded*: asked. **15:4** *There is . . . kept*: see Exod 20:8–11. **15:9** *The law and the prophets*: i.e., Scripture. **15:11** *Comfortable*: encouraging. **15:12–16** *That Onias . . . adversaries*: this passage has been used to support the Christian doctrine of the intercession of the saints. **15:12** *Conversation*: way of life. *Exercised*: trained. **15:15–16** *Jeremias holding forth . . . adversaries*: perhaps recalling and reinterpreting the oracle at Jer 50:35–37. For a contemporary encouraging reference to Jeremiah in a similar context, see Dan 9:2, 24 (and notes), where an oracle from Jeremiah is understood to prophesy the end of the Babylonian captivity.

15:17–36 The defeat and death of Nicanor. Compare 1 Macc 7:39–50. In this last of the many

determined not to pitch camp, but courageously to set upon them, and manfully to try the matter by conflict, because the city and the sanctuary and the temple were in danger. ¹⁸For the care that they took for their wives, and their children, their brethren, and kinsfolks, was in least account with them: but the greatest and principal fear was for the holy temple. ¹⁹Also they that were in the city took not the least care, being troubled for the conflict abroad. ²⁰And now, when as all looked what should be the trial, and the enemies were already come near, and the army was set in array, and the beasts conveniently placed, and the horsemen set in wings, ²¹Maccabeus seeing the coming of the multitude, and the divers preparations of armour, and the fierceness of the beasts, stretched out his hands toward heaven, and called upon the Lord that worketh wonders, knowing that victory cometh not by arms, but even as it seemeth good to him, he giveth it to such as are worthy: ²²therefore in his prayer he said after this manner; O Lord, thou didst send thine angel in the time of Ezekias king of Judea, and didst slay in the host of Sennacherib an hundred fourscore and five thousand: ²³wherefore now also, O Lord of heaven, send a good angel before us for a fear and dread unto them; ²⁴and through the might of thine arm let those be stricken with terror, that come against thy holy people to blaspheme. And he ended thus.

²⁵Then Nicanor and they that were with him came forward with trumpets and songs. ²⁶But Judas and his company encountered the enemies with invocation and prayer. ²⁷So that fighting with their hands, and praying unto God with their hearts, they slew no less than thirty and five thousand men: for through the appearance of God they were greatly cheered.

²⁸Now when the battle was done, returning again with joy, they knew that Nicanor lay dead in his harness. ²⁹Then they made a great shout and a noise, praising the Almighty in their own language. ³⁰And Judas, who was ever the chief defender of the citizens both in body and mind, and who continued his love toward his countrymen all his life, commanded to strike off Nicanor's head, and his hand with his shoulder, and bring them to Jerusalem. ³¹So when he was there, and had called them of his nation together, and set the priests before the altar, he sent for them that were of the tower, ³²and shewed them vile Nicanor's head, and the hand of that blasphemer, which with proud brags he had stretched out against the holy temple of the Almighty. ³³And when he had cut out the tongue of that ungodly Nicanor, he commanded that they should give it by pieces unto the fowls, and hang up the reward of his madness before the temple. ³⁴So every man praised toward the heaven the glorious Lord, saying, Blessed be he that hath kept his own place undefiled. ³⁵He hanged also Nicanor's head upon the tower, an evident and manifest sign unto all of the help of the Lord. ³⁶And they ordained all with a common decree in no case to let that day pass without solem-

---

examples of God's retributive justice, the tongue of the blasphemer is fed to the birds. **15:19** *Not the least*: i.e., "no little." **15:21** *Divers*: varied. *The Lord that worketh wonders*: cf. Pss 72:18; 86:10; 136:4. **15:22** *Thou didst send . . . thousand*: see 2 Kgs 19:35; cf. 2 Macc 8:19. **15:31** *The tower*: the Jerusalem citadel mentioned throughout 1 Maccabees. At this point, the Seleucids still held it. **15:36** *Common decree*: a decree agreed on by a public vote.

nity, but to celebrate the thirteenth day of the twelfth month, which in the Syrian tongue is called Adar, the day before Mardocheus' day.

³⁷ Thus went it with Nicanor: and from that time forth the Hebrews had the city in their power. And here will I make an end. ³⁸And if I have done well, and as is fitting the story, it is that which I desired: but if slenderly and meanly, it is that which I could attain unto. ³⁹For as it is hurtful to drink wine or water alone; and as wine mingled with water is pleasant, and delighteth the taste: even so speech finely framed delighteth the ears of them that read the story. And here shall be an end.

THE END OF THE APOCRYPHA

Syrian tongue: Aramaic. *Adar*: February-March. *Mardocheus' day*: Mordecai's day, the festival of Purim; see Esth 9:26–32.

15:37–39 Epilogue. 15:38 *Slenderly and meanly*: i.e., in cheap and mediocre fashion.

nity, but to celebrate the nineteenth day of the twelfth month, which in the Syrian tongue is called Adar, the day before Mardochian, day.

Thus went it with Nicanor: and from that time the Hebrews had the city in their power. And here will I make an end. [38] And if I have done well, and as is fitting the story, it is that which I desired: but if slenderly and meanly, it is that which I could attain unto. [39] For as it is hurtful to drink wine or water alone; and as wine mingled with water is pleasant, and delighteth the taste: even so speech finely framed delighteth the ears of them that read the story. And here shall be an end.

THE END OF THE APOCRYPHA

CONTEXT, RECEPTION, CRITICISM

Part I. Historical Contexts

BACKGROUNDS

JOSEPHUS

Initially a leader of the Judean forces opposing Rome during the Jewish War (66–70 C.E.), Josephus (37–ca. 100 C.E.) was captured (or surrendered) in Galilee, defected, and subsequently relocated to Rome, where he enjoyed the Flavian emperors' patronage. Somewhat like Paul, Josephus was a Pharisee concerned with presenting Judaism to the Gentile world. His works include the *Jewish Antiquities*. Written in Greek, it ambitiously traces the history of the Jewish people from their mythical origins until the time of the Jewish War. The following excerpts provide important background for readers of the New Testament. In the first (18.11–25), Josephus discusses different Jewish religious or philosophical schools, several of which figure in New Testament writings. The second (20.34–53) offers an anecdote giving evidence of Jewish attitudes toward circumcising Gentile converts, an issue which the early church also debated (cf. Acts 15 and Galatians). The third and the fourth excerpts deal with John the Baptist (18.116–119) and James the brother of Jesus (20.197, 199–203); the latter includes Josephus's sole undoubtedly authentic reference to Jesus.

[Jewish Philosophies] (from *Jewish Antiquities*, book 18)[†]

11 The Jews had for a great while three sects of philosophy peculiar to themselves; the sect of the Essenes, and the sect of the Sadducees, and the third sort of opinions was that of those called Pharisees; of which sects, although I have already spoken in the second book of the Jewish War,[1] yet will I a little touch upon them now.
12 Now, for the Pharisees, they live meanly, and despise delicacies in diet; and they follow the conduct of reason; and what that prescribes to them as good for them, they do; and they think they ought earnestly to strive to observe reason's dictates for practice. They also pay a respect to such as are advanced in years; nor are they so bold as to contradict them in anything which they have introduced;
13 and when they determine that all things are done by fate, they do not take away

---

† All selections are from *The Works of Flavius Josephus*, trans. William Whiston (London: George Routledge and Sons, n.d.), 423–24, 429–30, 467–68, 475–76 (occasionally altered).
   1. *Jewish War* 2.119–166.

the freedom from men of acting as they think fit; since their notion is, that it hath pleased God to make a temperament; whereby what he wills is done, but so that the will of men can act virtuously or viciously. **14** They also believe that souls have an immortal vigour in them, and that under the earth there will be rewards or punishments, according as they have lived virtuously or viciously in this life; and the latter are to be detained in an everlasting prison, but that the former shall have power to revive and live again; **15** on account of which doctrines, they are able greatly to persuade the body of the people; and whatsoever they do about divine worship, prayers, and sacrifices, they perform them according to their direction; insomuch that the cities gave great attestations to them on account of their entire virtuous conduct, both in the actions of their lives and their discourses also.

16 But the doctrine of the Sadducees is this: That souls die with the bodies; nor do they regard the observation of anything besides what the law enjoins them;[2] for they think it an instance of virtue to dispute with those teachers of philosophy whom they frequent; **17** but this doctrine is received but by a few, yet by those still of the greatest dignity; but they are able to do almost nothing of themselves; for when they become magistrates, as they are unwillingly and by force sometimes obliged to be, they come over to the notions of the Pharisees, because the multitude would not otherwise bear them.

18 The doctrine of the Essenes[3] is this: That all things are best ascribed to God. They teach the immortality of souls, and esteem that the rewards of righteousness are to be earnestly striven for: **19** and when they send what they have dedicated to God into the temple, they do not offer sacrifices,[4] because they have more pure lustrations of their own; on which account they are excluded from the common court of the temple, but offer their sacrifices themselves; yet is their course of life better than that of other men; and they entirely direct their attention to husbandry. **20** It also deserves our admiration, how much they exceed all other men that lay claim to virtue, and this in righteousness: and indeed to such a degree, that as it hath never appeared among any other men, neither Greeks nor barbarians, no, not for a little time, so hath it endured a long while among them. This is demonstrated by that institution of theirs, which will not suffer anything to hinder them from having all things in common:[5] so that a rich man enjoys no more of his own wealth than he who hath nothing at all. There are about four thousand men that live in this way, **21** and neither marry wives, nor are desirous to keep servants; as thinking the latter tempts men to be unjust, and the former gives the handle to domestic quarrels; but as they live by themselves, they minister one to another. They also appoint certain stewards to receive the

2. The Sadducees accepted only the Torah as authoritative (in contrast to the Pharisees, who also embraced legal traditions preserved orally).

3. Josephus also discusses the Essenes at *Jewish War* 2.120–161; cf. Philo, *That Every Good Person is Free* 75–91, on which this passage may draw. Many modern scholars attribute the Dead Sea Scrolls (excerpted below; pp. 989–96) to members of an Essene community.

4. It seems by what Josephus says here, that these Essenes did not use to go to the Jewish festivals at Jerusalem, or to offer sacrifices there, which may be one great occasion why they are never mentioned in the ordinary books of the New Testament [translator's note].

5. Cf. Acts 2:44–45; 4:32–5:11.

incomes of their revenues, and of the fruits of the ground; 22 such as are good men and priests, who are to get their corn and their food ready for them. * * *

23 But of the fourth sect of Jewish philosophy, Judas the Galilean was the author. These men agree in all other things with the Pharisaic notions; but they have an inviolable attachment to liberty; and they say that God is to be their only ruler and Lord. They also do not value dying any kinds of death, nor indeed do they heed the deaths of their relations and friends, nor can any such fear make them call any man Lord; 24 and since this immovable resolution of theirs is well known to a great many, I shall speak no further about that matter; nor am I afraid that anything I have said of them should be disbelieved, but rather fear, that what I have said is beneath the resolution they show when they undergo pain; 25 and it was in Gessius Florus's time that the nation began to grow mad with this distemper, who was our procurator, and who occasioned the Jews to go wild with it by the abuse of his authority, and to make them revolt from the Romans: and these are the sects of Jewish philosophy.

[Circumcision of Gentile Converts]
(from *Jewish Antiquities*, book 20)

34 Now, during the time Izates abode at Charax-Spasini, a certain Jewish merchant, whose name was Ananias, got among the women that belonged to the king, and taught them to worship God according to the Jewish religion. 35 He, moreover, by their means became known to Izates; and persuaded him, in like manner, to embrace that religion; he also, at the earnest entreaty of Izates, accompanied him when he was sent for by his father to come to Adiabene; it also happened that Helena, about the same time, was instructed by a certain other Jew, and went over to them. 36 But, when Izates had taken the kingdom, and was come to Adiabene,[1] and there saw his brethren and other kinsmen in bonds, he was displeased at it; 37 and as he thought it was an instance of impiety either to slay or imprison them, but still thought it a hazardous thing for to let them have their liberty, with the remembrance of the injuries that had been offered them, he sent some of them and their children for hostages to Rome, to Claudius Cæsar, and sent the others to Artabanus, the king of Parthia, with the like intentions.

38 And when he perceived that his mother was highly pleased with the Jewish customs, he made haste to change, and to embrace them entirely; and as he supposed that he could not be thoroughly a Jew unless he were circumcised, he was ready to have it done. 39 But when his mother understood what he was about, she endeavoured to hinder him from doing it, and said to him that this thing would bring him into danger: and that as he was a king, he would thereby bring himself into great odium among his subjects, when they should understand that he was so fond of rites that were to them strange and foreign; and that they would never bear to be ruled over by a Jew. 40 This it was that she said to him, and for the present persuaded him to forbear. And when he had related what she

---

1. In northern Mesopotamia.

said to Ananias, he confirmed what his mother had said; and when he had also threatened to leave him, unless he complied with him, he went away from him; **41** and said he was afraid lest such an action being once become public to all, he should himself be in danger of punishment for having been the king's instructor in actions that were of ill reputation; and he said, that he might worship God without being circumcised, even though he did resolve to follow the Jewish law entirely; which worship of God was of a superior nature to circumcision. **42** He added, that God would forgive him, though he did not perform the operation, while it was omitted out of necessity, and for fear of his subjects. So the king at that time complied with these persuasions of Ananias. **43** But afterwards, as he had not quite left off his desire of doing this thing, a certain other Jew that came out of Galilee, whose name was Eleazar, and who was esteemed very skilful in the learning of his country, persuaded him to do the thing; **44** for as he entered into his palace to salute him, and found him reading the law of Moses, he said to him, 'Thou dost not consider, O king! that thou unjustly breakest the principal of those laws,[2] and art injurious to God himself [by omitting to be circumcised;] for thou oughtest not only to read them, but chiefly to practise what they enjoin thee. **45** How long wilt thou continue uncircumcised? but, if thou hast not yet read the law about circumcision, and dost not know how great impiety thou art guilty of by neglecting it, read it now.' **46** When the king had heard what he said, he delayed no longer, but retired to another room, and sent for a surgeon, and did what he was commanded to do. He then sent for his mother, and Ananias his tutor, and informed them that he had done the thing: **47** upon which they were presently struck with astonishment and fear, and that to a great degree, lest the thing should be openly discovered and censured, and the king should hazard the loss of his kingdom, while his subjects would not bear to be governed by a man who was so zealous in another religion; and lest they should themselves run some hazard, because they would be supposed the occasion of his so doing. **48** But it was God himself who hindered what they feared from taking effect; for he preserved both Izates himself and his sons when they fell into many dangers, and procured their deliverance when it seemed to be impossible, and demonstrated thereby, that the fruit of piety does not perish as to those that have regard to him, and fix their faith upon him only: —but these events we shall relate hereafter.

49 But as to Helena, the king's mother, when she saw that the affairs of Izates's kingdom were in peace, and that her son was a happy man, and admired among all men, and even among foreigners, by the means of God's providence over him, she had a mind to go to the city of Jerusalem, in order to worship at that temple of God which was so very famous among all men, and to offer her thank-offerings there. So she desired her son to give her leave to go thither: **50** upon which he gave his consent to what she desired very willingly, and made great preparations for her dismission, and gave her a great deal of money, and she went down to the city Jerusalem, her son conducting her on her journey a great way. **51** Now her coming was of very great advantage to the people of Jerusalem; for whereas a famine[3] did

2. E.g., Gen 17:10–14.
3. Cf. Acts 11:28 and note.

oppress them at that time, and many people died for want of what was necessary to procure food withal, queen Helena sent some of her servants to Alexandria with money to buy a great quantity of corn, and others of them to Cyprus, to bring a cargo of dried figs; **52** and as soon as they were come back, and had brought those provisions, which was done very quickly, she distributed food to those that were in want of it, and left a most excellent memorial behind her of this benefaction, which she bestowed on our whole nation; **53** and when her son Izates was informed of this famine, he sent a great sum of money to the principal men in Jerusalem.

[John the Baptist] (from *Jewish Antiquities*, book 18)

116 Now, some of the Jews thought that the destruction of Herod's army came from God, and that very justly, as a punishment of what he did against John, that was called the Baptist; **117** for Herod slew him, who was a good man, and commanded the Jews to exercise virtue, both as to righteousness towards one another, and piety towards God, and so to come to baptism;[1] for that the washing [with water] would be acceptable to him, if they made use of it, not for the pardon of some sins but for the purification of the body: supposing still that the soul was thoroughly purified beforehand by righteousness. **118** Now, when [many] others came to crowd about him, for they were greatly pleased by hearing his words, Herod, who feared lest the great influence John had over the people might put it into his power and inclination to raise a rebellion (for they seemed ready to do anything he should advise), thought it best, by putting him to death, to prevent any mischief he might cause, and not bring himself into difficulties, by sparing a man who might make him repent of it when it should be too late. **119** Accordingly he was sent a prisoner, out of Herod's suspicious temper, to Macherus, the castle I before mentioned, and was there put to death.[2] Now the Jews had an opinion that the destruction of this army was sent as a punishment upon Herod, and a mark of God's displeasure against him.

[James the Brother of Jesus] (from *Jewish Antiquities*, book 20)

197 And now Cæsar, upon hearing of the death of Festus, sent Albinus into Judea as procurator;[1] * * * **199** but this younger Ananus, who, as we have told you already, took the high priesthood, was a bold man in his temper, and very insolent; he was also of the sect of the Sadducees, who were very rigid in judging offenders, above all the rest of the Jews, as we have already observed;[2] **200** when, therefore, Ananus was of this disposition, he thought he had now a proper opportunity [to exercise his authority.] Festus was now dead, and Albinus was but upon the road;

1. Cf. Matt 3:1–10; Mark 1:1–6; Luke 3:1–14.
2. Cf. Mark 6:14–29 and parallels.
1. Cf. *Jewish War* 2.272. Porcius Festus had been made Procurator by Nero in ca. 60 C.E; Lucceius Albinus succeeded him in ca. 62.
2. Cf. *Jewish Antiquities* 13.294.

so he assembled the sanhedrin of the judges, and brought before them the brother of Jesus, who was called Christ,[3] whose name was James, and some others, and when he had formed an accusation against them as breakers of the law, he delivered them to be stoned: **201** but as for those who seemed the most equitable of the citizens, and such as were the most uneasy at the breach of the laws, they disliked what was done; they also sent to the king [Agrippa],[4] desiring him to send to Ananus that he should act so no more, for what he had already done was not to be justified: **202** nay, some of them went also to meet Albinus, as he was upon his journey from Alexandria, and informed him that it was not lawful for Ananus to assemble a sanhedrin without his consent: **203** —whereupon Albinus complied with what they had said, and wrote in anger to Ananus, and threatened that he would bring him to punishment for what he had done; on which king Agrippa took the high priesthood from him, when he had ruled but three months, and made Jesus, the son of Damneus, high priest.

PHILO

Philo (ca. 20 B.C.E.–ca. 50 C.E.) was an influential member of the large Jewish community in Alexandria. Like Josephus, Paul, and other Hellenistic Jews, he participates in a long tradition of Jewish writing in Greek language and genres; but Philo seems to have been the first to rigorously apply to the Old Testament the allegorical mode of interpretation (which Greek philosophers had long used in reading Homer), in order to understand it in terms amenable to Greek philosophy—a strategy that Paul too occasionally adopted (e.g., Gal 4:21–26). In 40 C.E. Philo participated in a delegation from the Alexandrian Jewish community to the Roman emperor Gaius Caligula in order to protest the provincial government's failure to intervene during recent anti-Jewish riots. The following excerpt from *The Embassy to Gaius*, Philo's book about the mission, quotes King Herod Agrippa I's letter to Caligula, which recounts an earlier conflict between the inhabitants of Jerusalem and Pontius Pilate, the Roman governor of Judea at the time of Jesus' death during the reign of the emperor Tiberius. It addresses both Pilate's character and the complex negotiations and compromises required to maintain stable Roman rule in Judea.

3. Contrast *Jewish Antiquities* 18.63–64, where Christian scribes have elaborately embellished what must originally have been a similar statement about Jesus:

> "Now, there was about this time, Jesus, a wise man, if it be lawful to call him a man, for he was a doer of wonderful works,—a teacher of such men as receive the truth with pleasure. He drew over to him both many of the Jews, and many of the Gentiles. He was [the] Christ; and when Pilate, at the suggestion of the principal men amongst us, had condemned him to the cross, those that loved him at the first did not forsake him, for he appeared to them alive again the third day, as the divine prophets had foretold these and ten thousand other wonderful things concerning him; and the tribe of Christians, so named from him, are not extinct at this day."

4. See Acts 25:13 note.

[Pontius Pilate and Roman Rule in Judea]†

298 "What again did your other grandfather, Tiberius Cæsar, do? does not he appear to have adopted an exactly similar line of conduct? At all events, during the three and twenty years that he was emperor, he preserved the form of worship in the temple as it had been handed down from the earliest times, without abrogating or altering the slightest particular of it.

299 "Moreover, I have it in my power to relate one act of ambition on his part, though I suffered an infinite number of evils when he was alive; but nevertheless the truth is considered dear, and much to be honoured by you. Pilate was one of the emperor's lieutenants, having been appointed governor of Judæa. He, not more with the object of doing honour to Tiberius than with that of vexing the multitude, dedicated some gilt shields in the palace of Herod, in the holy city; which had no form nor any other forbidden thing represented on them except some necessary inscription, which mentioned these two facts, the name of the person who had placed them there, and the person in whose honour they were so placed there. **300** But when the multitude heard what had been done, and when the circumstance became notorious, then the people, putting forward the four sons of the king,[1] who were in no respect inferior to the kings themselves, in fortune or in rank, and his other descendants, and those magistrates who were among them at the time, entreated him to alter and to rectify the innovation which he had committed in respect of the shields; and not to make any alteration in their national customs, which had hitherto been preserved without any interruption, without being in the least degree changed by any king or emperor.

301 "But when he steadfastly refused this petition (for he was a man of a very inflexible disposition, and very merciless as well as very obstinate), they cried out: 'Do not cause a sedition; do not make war upon us; do not destroy the peace which exists. The honour of the emperor is not identical with dishonour to the ancient laws; let it not be to you a pretence for heaping insult on our nation. Tiberius is not desirous that any of our laws or customs shall be destroyed. And if you yourself say that he is, show us either some command from him, or some letter, or something of the kind, that we, who have been sent to you as ambassadors, may cease to trouble you, and may address our supplications to your master.'

302 "But this last sentence exasperated him in the greatest possible degree, as he feared lest they might in reality go on an embassy to the emperor, and might impeach him with respect to other particulars of his government, in respect of his corruption, and his acts of insolence, and his rapine, and his habit of insulting people, and his cruelty, and his continual murders of people untried and uncondemned, and his never ending, and gratuitous, and most grievous inhumanity. **303** Therefore, being exceedingly angry, and being at all times a man of most ferocious passions, he was in great perplexity, neither venturing to take down

---

† From *The Works of Philo Judaeus, the Contemporary of Josephus*, vol. 4., trans. C. D. Yonge (London: Henry G. Bohn, 1855), 164–67.

1. Cf. Josephus, *Jewish War* 2.169ff.

what he had once set up, nor wishing to do any thing which could be acceptable to his subjects, and at the same time being sufficiently acquainted with the firmness of Tiberius on these points. And those who were in power in our nation, seeing this, and perceiving that he was inclined to change his mind as to what he had done, but that he was not willing to be thought to do so, wrote a most supplicatory letter to Tiberius. 304 And he, when he had read it, what did he say of Pilate, and what threats did he utter against him! But it is beside our purpose at present to relate to you how very angry he was, although he was not very liable to sudden anger; since the facts speak for themselves; 305 for immediately, without putting any thing off till the next day, he wrote a letter, reproaching and reviling him in the most bitter manner for his act of unprecedented audacity and wickedness, and commanding him immediately to take down the shields and to convey them away from the metropolis of Judæa to Cæsarea, on the sea which had been named Cæsarea Augusta, after his grandfather, in order that they might be set up in the temple of Augustus. And accordingly, they were set up in that edifice. And in this way he provided for two matters: both for the honour due to the emperor, and for the preservation of the ancient customs of the city.

306 "Now the things set up on that occasion were shields, on which there was no representation of any living thing whatever engraved. But now the thing proposed to be erected is a colossal statue.[2] Moreover, then the erection was in the dwelling-house of the governor; but they say, that which is now contemplated is to be in the inmost part of the temple, in the very holy of holies itself, into which, once in the year, the high priest enters, on the day called the great fast, to offer incense, and on no other day, being then about in accordance with our national law also to offer up prayers for a fertile and ample supply of blessings, and for peace to all mankind. 307 And if any one else, I will not say of the Jews, but even of the priests, and those not of the lowest order, but even those who are in the rank next to the first, should go in there, either with him or after him, or even if the very high priest himself should enter in thither on two days in the year, or three or four times on the same day, he is subjected to inevitable death for his impiety, 308 so great are the precautions taken by our lawgiver with respect to the holy of holies, as he determined to preserve it alone inaccessible to and untouched by any human being.

"How many deaths then do you not suppose that the people, who have been taught to regard this place with such holy reverence, would willingly endure rather than see a statue introduced into it? I verily believe that they would rather slay all their whole families, with their wives and children, and themselves last of all, in the ruins of their houses and families, and Tiberius knew this well. 309 And what did your great-grandfather, the most excellent of all emperors that ever lived upon the earth, he who was the first to have the appellation of Augustus given him, on account of his virtue and good fortune; he who diffused peace in every direction over earth and sea, to the very furthest extremities of the world? 310 Did not he, when he had heard a report of the peculiar characteristics of our temple, and that there is in it no image or representation made by

2. Caligula had ordered a statue of himself placed in the temple; cf. *Embassy to Gaius*, 184–96 and Tacitus, *Histories* 5.9 (excerpted below, pp. 985–86).

hands, no visible likeness of Him who is invisible, no attempt at any imitation of his nature, did not he, I say, marvel at and honour it? for as he was imbued with something more than a mere smattering of philosophy, inasmuch as he had deeply feasted on it, and continued to feast on it every day, he partly retraced in his recollection all the precepts of philosophy which his mind had previously learnt, and partly also he kept his learning alive by the conversation of the literary men who were always about him; for at his banquets and entertainments, the greatest part of the time was devoted to learned conversation, in order that not only his friends' bodies but their minds also might be nourished.

TACITUS

The popular image of the Roman emperors as a cruel and depraved lot comes largely from the brilliant imperial historian and daring Latin stylist Tacitus (ca. 56–ca. 120 C.E.), and perhaps no Tacitean passage bears more responsibility for this stereotype than the first excerpted here. It describes Nero's brutal persecution of Roman Christians in 64 C.E. (which may have claimed the lives of Paul and Peter)—according to Tacitus, a lame attempt on the emperor's part to deflect suspicion away from himself for causing a fire that had recently devastated the city. This passage also provides the earliest reference to Christ by a pagan writer. The second excerpt presents a fairly typical view of how Greco-Roman writers understood Jewish religious culture. The third briefly recounts Roman rule in Judea, from Pompey's conquest in 63 B.C.E. to the procuratorship of Felix, which ended a few years before the Jewish War broke out in 66 C.E.

[Nero's Persecution of Christians in Rome]
(from *Annals*, book 15)[†]

44 Such indeed were the precautions of human wisdom. The next thing was to seek means of propitiating the gods, and recourse was had to the Sibylline books, by the direction of which prayers were offered to Vulcanus, Ceres, and Proserpina. Juno, too, was entreated by the matrons, first, in the Capitol, then on the nearest part of the coast, whence water was procured to sprinkle the temple and image of the goddess. And there were sacred banquets and nightly vigils celebrated by married women. But all human efforts, all the lavish gifts of the emperor, and the propitiations of the gods, did not banish the sinister belief that the conflagration was the result of an order. Consequently, to get rid of the report, Nero fastened the guilt and inflicted the most exquisite tortures on a class hated for their abominations, called Christians by the populace. Christus, from whom the name had its origin, suffered the extreme penalty during the reign of Tiberius at the hands of one of our procurators, Pontius Pilatus, and a most mischievous

† From *The Annals of Tacitus*, trans. Alfred John Church and William Jackson Brodribb (London: Macmillan and Co., 1884), 304–05 (occasionally altered).

superstition, thus checked for the moment, again broke out not only in Judæa, the first source of the evil, but even in Rome, where all things hideous and shameful from every part of the world find their centre and become popular. Accordingly, an arrest was first made of all who pleaded guilty; then, upon their information, an immense multitude was convicted, not so much of the crime of firing the city, as of hatred against mankind.[1] Mockery of every sort was added to their deaths. Covered with the skins of beasts, they were torn by dogs and perished, or were nailed to crosses, or were doomed to the flames and burnt, to serve as a nightly illumination, when daylight had expired.

Nero offered his gardens for the spectacle, and was exhibiting a show in the circus, while he mingled with the people in the dress of a charioteer or stood aloft on a car. Hence, even for criminals who deserved extreme and exemplary punishment, there arose a feeling of compassion; for it was not, as it seemed, for the public good, but to glut one man's cruelty, that they were being destroyed.

[A Gentile's View of Jewish Beliefs and Practices] (from *Histories*, book 5)[†]

4 Moses, wishing to secure for the future his authority over the nation, gave them a novel form of worship, opposed to all that is practised by other men. Things sacred with us with them have no sanctity, while they allow what with us is forbidden. In their holy place they have consecrated an image of the animal by whose guidance they found deliverance from their long and thirsty wanderings.[1] They slay the ram, seemingly in derision of Hammon,[2] and they sacrifice the ox, because the Egyptians worship it as Apis. They abstain from swine's flesh, in consideration of what they suffered when they were infected by the leprosy to which this animal is liable. By their frequent fasts they still bear witness to the protracted starvation of a former time, and the Jewish bread, made without leaven, is retained as a memorial of the harvests which they plundered. We are told that the rest of the seventh day was adopted, because this day brought with it a termination of their toils; afterwards, under the seductions of indolence, they gave up the seventh year also to inaction. But others say that it is an observance in honour of Saturn, either from the primitive elements of their faith having been transmitted from the Idæi, who are said to have shared the flight of that God, and to have founded the race,[3] or from the circumstance that of the seven stars which rule the destinies of men Sat-

1. Cf. Tacitus, *Histories* 5.5 (p. 985 below).
   † This and the following selection come from *The History of Tacitus*, trans. Alfred John Church and William Jackson Brodribb (London: Macmillan and Co., 1864), 266–68, 270–71.
   1. In the previous section Tacitus states that a herd of wild asses led Moses to the rock that provided water during the exodus (cf. Exod 17:1–7). Christians too were later accused of worshipping an ass.
   2. Ammon, an Egyptian god depicted with features of a ram.
   3. Cf. *Histories* 5.2: "Some say that the Jews were fugitives from the island of Crete, who settled on the nearest coast of Africa about the time when Saturn was driven from his throne by the power of Jupiter. They look for evidence in the name. There is a famous mountain in crete called Ida; the neighbouring tribe, the Idæi, came to be called Judæi by a barbarous lengthening of the national name."

urn moves in the highest orbit and with the mightiest power, and that many of the heavenly bodies complete their revolutions and courses in multiples of seven.

5 This worship, however introduced, is upheld by its antiquity; all their other customs, which are at once perverse and disgusting, owe their strength to their very badness. The most degraded out of other races, scorning their national beliefs, brought to them their contributions and presents.[4] This augmented the wealth of the Jews; and there was the fact, that among themselves they are inflexibly honest and ever ready to show compassion, though they regard the rest of mankind with all the hatred of enemies. They sit apart at meals, they sleep apart, and though, as a nation, they are singularly prone to lust, they abstain from intercourse with foreign women; among themselves nothing is unlawful. They have made a practice of circumcision, wishing to be known by some distinguishing mark. Those who come over to their religion adopt the practice, and have this lesson first instilled into them, to disown their country, and set at nought parents, children, and brethren. Still they provide for the increase of their numbers. It is a crime among them to kill any newly born infant. They hold that the souls of all who perish in battle or by the hands of the executioner are immortal. Hence a passion for propagating their race and a contempt for death. They are wont to bury rather than to burn their dead, following in this the Egyptian custom; they pay the same attentions to the departed, and they hold the same belief about the lower world. Quite different is their faith about things divine. The Egyptians worship many animals and images of monstrous form; the Jews have purely mental conceptions of Deity, as one in essence. They call those profane who make representations of God in human shape out of perishable materials. They believe that Being to be supreme and eternal, not to be represented, and incapable of decay. They therefore do not allow any images to stand in their cities, much less in their temples. This flattery is not paid to their kings, nor this honour to our Emperors. From the fact, however, that their priests used to chant to the music of flutes and cymbals, and to wear garlands of ivy, and that a golden vine was found in the temple, some have thought that they worshipped Father Liber,[5] the conqueror of the East, though their institutions do not by any means harmonize with the theory; for Liber established a festive and cheerful worship, while the Jewish religion is tasteless and mean.

[A Brief History of Roman Rule in Judea]
(from *Histories*, book 5)

9 Cneius Pompeius was the first of our countrymen to subdue the Jews.[1] Availing himself of the right of conquest, he entered the temple. Thus it became commonly known that the place stood empty with no similitude of Gods within, and that the shrine had nothing to reveal. The walls of Jerusalem were destroyed, the temple was left standing. After these provinces had fallen, in the course of our civil wars, into the hands of Marcus Antonius, Pacorus, King of the Parthians,

---

4. Apparently referring to proselytes' and diasporic Jews' contributions to the temple (cf. Josephus, *Jewish War* 7.218).

5. Another name for Bacchus or Dionysus, god of wine.

1. Pompey conquered the region in 63 B.C.E.

seized Judæa.[2] He was slain by Publius Ventidius, and the Parthians were driven back over the Euphrates.[3] Caius Sosius reduced the Jews to subjection.[4] The royal power, which had been bestowed by Antony on Herod, was augmented by the victorious Augustus. On Herod's death,[5] one Simon, without waiting for the approbation of the Emperor, usurped the title of King. He was punished by Quintilius Varus then governor of Syria, and the nation, with its liberties curtailed, was divided into three provinces under the sons of Herod. Under Tiberius all was quiet. But when the Jews were ordered by Caligula to set up his statue in the temple,[6] they preferred the alternative of war. The death of the Emperor put an end to the disturbance. The kings were either dead, or reduced to insignificance, when Claudius entrusted the province of Judæa to the Roman equestrians, or to his own freedmen, one of whom, Antonius Felix, indulging in every kind of barbarity and lust, exercised the power of a king in the spirit of a slave.[7] He had married Drusilla, the granddaughter of Antony and Cleopatra, and so was the grandson-in-law, as Claudius was the grandson, of Antony.

SUETONIUS

The first excerpt by Suetonius (ca. 70–ca. 130 C.E.) from his biography of Nero mentions the same persecution as the passage from Tacitus's *Annals* included above (pp. 983–84), although in a very different rhetorical and ideological context. The second gives evidence of a legend that Nero would rise again, which Revelation imaginatively transforms (see Rev 13:3 and note).

[Nero's Persecution of Christians in Rome][†]

16 He devised a new form for the buildings of the city and in front of the houses and apartments he erected porches, from the flat roofs of which fires could be fought; and these he put up at his own cost. He had also planned to extend the walls as far as Ostia[1] and to bring the sea from there to Rome by a canal.

During his reign many abuses were severely punished and put down, and no fewer new laws were made: a limit was set to expenditures; the public banquets were confined to a distribution of food; the sale of any kind of cooked foods in the taverns was forbidden, with the exception of legumes and vegetables, whereas before every

2. This occurred in 40 B.C.E.
3. This occurred in 38 B.C.E.
4. The region was reconquered by Roman and allied forces in 37 B.C.E., at which point Herod the Great was installed.
5. Herod died in 4 B.C.E.
6. This occurred in 40 C.E.
7. Felix served as procurator of Judea, 52–60 C.E.; he figures prominently in Acts 23–26.
† This and the following selection come from *Suetonius*, vol. 2, trans. J. C. Rolfe; Loeb Classical Library (London: William Heinemann, 1914), 111, 185, 187 (occasionally altered).
1. The port at the mouth of the Tiber that served Rome.

sort of dainty was exposed for sale. Punishment was inflicted on the Christians, a class of men given to a new and mischievous superstition. He put an end to the diversions of the chariot drivers, who from immunity of long standing claimed the right of ranging at large and amusing themselves by cheating and robbing the people. The pantomimic actors and their partisans were banished from the city.

[Nero's Anticipated Resurrection]

57 He met his death in the thirty-second year of his age, on the anniversary of the murder of Octavia,[1] and such was the public rejoicing that the people put on liberty-caps[2] and ran about all over the city. Yet there were some who for a long time decorated his tomb with spring and summer flowers, and now produced his statues on the rostra in the fringed toga, and now his edicts, as if he were still alive and would shortly return and deal destruction to his enemies. Nay more, Vologaesus, king of the Parthians, when he sent envoys to the senate to renew his alliance, earnestly begged this too, that honour be paid to the memory of Nero. In fact, twenty years later, when I was a young man, a person of obscure origin appeared, who gave out that he was Nero, and the name was still in such favour with the Parthians that they supported him vigorously and surrendered him with great reluctance.

PLINY

Letters 10.96 and 97 from the epistolary corpus the younger Pliny (ca. 61–ca. 112 C.E.) date to the final two or three years of his life, during his service as governor of the province Bithynia in Asia Minor. This brief exchange between the Roman senator and the emperor Trajan is probably the most important early pagan record of ancient Christian beliefs and practices, as well as of Roman suspicions of them.

[Correspondence with Emperor Trajan Regarding Alleged Christians]†

To the Emperor Trajan

1 It is a rule, Sir, which I inviolably observe, to refer myself to you in all my doubts; for who is more capable of guiding my uncertainty or informing my ignorance? Having never been present at any trials of the Christians, I am unacquainted with the method and limits to be observed either in examining or punishing them. **2**

---

1. Claudia Octavia, Nero's stepsister and first wife, whom he ordered killed in 62 C.E. Nero died in 68.
2. The caps customarily worn by manumitted slaves.
    † From Pliny, *Letters*, vol. 2, trans. William Melmoth, rev. W. M. L. Hutchinson, Loeb Classical Library (London: William Heinemann, 1915), 401, 403, 405, 407.

Whether any difference is to be made on account of age, or no distinction allowed between the youngest and the adult; whether repentance admits to a pardon, or if a man has been once a Christian it avails him nothing to recant; whether the mere profession of Christianity, albeit without crimes, or only the crimes associated therewith are punishable—in all these points I am greatly doubtful.

In the meanwhile, the method I have observed towards those who have been denounced to me as Christians is this: 3 I interrogated them whether they were Christians; if they confessed it I repeated the question twice again, adding the threat of capital punishment; if they still persevered, I ordered them to be executed. For whatever the nature of their creed might be, I could at least feel no doubt that contumacy and inflexible obstinacy deserved chastisement. 4 There were others also possessed with the same infatuation, but being citizens of Rome, I directed them to be carried thither.[1]

These accusations spread (as is usually the case) from the mere fact of the matter being investigated and several forms of the mischief came to light. 5 A placard was put up, without any signature, accusing a large number of persons by name. Those who denied they were, or had ever been, Christians, who repeated after me an invocation to the gods, and offered adoration, with wine and frankincense, to your image, which I had ordered to be brought for that purpose, together with those of the gods, and who finally cursed Christ—none of which acts, it is said, those who are really Christians can be forced into performing— these I thought it proper to discharge. 6 Others who were named by that informer at first confessed themselves Christians, and then denied it; true, they had been of that persuasion but they had quitted it, some three years, others many years, and a few as much as twenty-five years ago. They all worshipped your statue and the images of the gods, and cursed Christ.

7 They affirmed, however, the whole of their guilt, or their error, was, that they were in the habit of meeting on a certain fixed day before it was light, when they sang in alternate verses a hymn to Christ, as to a god, and bound themselves by a solemn oath, not to any wicked deeds, but never to commit any fraud, theft or adultery, never to falsify their word, nor deny a trust when they should be called upon to deliver it up; after which it was their custom to separate, and then reassemble to partake of food—but food of an ordinary and innocent kind. Even this practice, however, they had abandoned after the publication of my edict, by which, according to your orders, I had forbidden political associations. 8 I judged it so much the more necessary to extract the real truth, with the assistance of torture, from two female slaves, who were styled deaconesses: but I could discover nothing more than depraved and excessive superstition.

I therefore adjourned the proceedings, and betook myself at once to your counsel. 9 For the matter seemed to me well worth referring to you,—especially considering the numbers endangered. Persons of all ranks and ages, and of both sexes are, and will be, involved in the prosecution. For this contagious superstition is not confined to the cities only, but has spread through the villages and rural districts; it seems possible, however, to check and cure it. 10 'Tis certain at least that the temples, which had been almost deserted, begin now to be fre-

---

1. Cf. Acts 25:11–12.

quented; and the sacred festivals, after a long intermission, are again revived; while there is a general demand for sacrificial animals, which for some time past have met with but few purchasers. From hence it is easy to imagine what multitudes may be reclaimed from this error, if a door be left open to repentance.

Trajan to Pliny

The method you have pursued, my dear Pliny, in sifting the cases of those denounced to you as Christians is extremely proper. It is not possible to lay down any general rule which can be applied as the fixed standard in all cases of this nature. No search should be made for these people; when they are denounced and found guilty they must be punished; with the restriction, however, that when the party denies himself to be a Christian, and shall give proof that he is not (that is, by adoring our gods) he shall be pardoned on the ground of repentance, even though he may have formerly incurred suspicion. Informations without the accuser's name subscribed must not be admitted in evidence against anyone, as it is introducing a very dangerous precedent, and by no means agreeable to the spirit of the age.

THE COMMUNITY RULE[†]

The Community Rule seems to have functioned as a constitution for a Jewish sectarian (probably Essene; see pp. 976–77 above for Josephus's description) community founded perhaps as early as the first or second century B.C.E. and located just northwest of the Dead Sea at Qumran. This community was most likely decimated in the Jewish War (66–70 C.E.), but a large collection of its writings has survived. The text excerpted below suggests it had organized itself around principles similar to those on which the earliest Christian communities ordered their life together. For example, the Community Rule's guidelines for congregational assemblies (see column VI) recall 1 Corinthians (see especially 14:26–35); its demands for communal possession of property at the beginning of column V and the end of column VI recall Acts' opening chapters (e.g., 2:44–45; 4:32); more broadly, its dualistic outlook (see especially columns III–IV) recalls the Johannine writings, and occasionally Paul's epistles too (e.g., Rom 7:14–8:9). The annotations that follow signal only a handful of intriguing parallels. Here, as often, the Dead Sea Scrolls offer valuable contextual information that helps us to understand the emergence of Christianity from first-century Judaism, as a minor Jewish sect on the path to becoming a major world religion.

I [The Master shall teach the sai]nts to live(?) {according to the Book} (4Q255, 257) of the Community [Rul]e, that they may seek God with a whole heart and

[†] From *The Complete Dead Sea Scrolls in English*, trans. Geza Vermes, rev. ed. (London: Penguin, 2004), 98–107. (Parenthetical references signal the various manuscripts found at Qumran on which Vermes bases his translation. The primary manuscript is designated 1QS. Boldfaced roman numerals refer to columns of text in the manuscripts.)

soul, and do what is good and right before Him as He commanded by the hand of Moses and all His servants the Prophets; that they may love all that He has chosen and hate all that He has rejected; that they may abstain from all evil and hold fast to all good; that they may practise truth, righteousness, and justice upon earth and no longer stubbornly follow a sinful heart and lustful eyes, committing all manner of evil. He shall admit into the Covenant of Grace all those who have freely devoted themselves to the observance of God's precepts, that they may be joined to the counsel of God and may live perfectly before Him in accordance with all that has been revealed concerning their appointed times, and that they may love all the sons of light, each according to his lot in God's design, and hate all the sons of darkness, each according to his guilt in God's vengeance.

All those who freely devote themselves to His truth shall bring all their knowledge, powers and possessions into the Community of God, that they may purify their knowledge in the truth of God's precepts and order their powers according to His ways of perfection and all their possessions according to His righteous counsel. They shall not depart from any command of God concerning their times; they shall be neither early nor late for any of their appointed times, they shall stray neither to the right nor to the left of any of His true precepts. All those who embrace the Community Rule shall enter into the Covenant before God to obey all His commandments so that they may not abandon Him during the dominion of Belial[1] because of fear or terror or affliction.

On entering the Covenant, the Priests and Levites shall bless the God of salvation and all His faithfulness, and all those entering the Covenant shall say after them, 'Amen, Amen!'

Then the Priests shall recite the favours of God manifested in His mighty deeds and shall declare all His merciful grace to Israel, and the Levites shall recite the iniquities of the children of Israel, all their guilty rebellions and sins during the dominion of Belial. And after them, all those entering the Covenant shall confess and say: 'We have strayed! We have [disobeyed!] We and our fathers before us have sinned and acted wickedly in walking [counter to the precepts] of truth and righteousness. [And God has] judged us and our fathers also; II but He has bestowed His bountiful mercy on us from everlasting to everlasting.' And the Priests shall bless all the men of the lot of God who walk perfectly in all His ways, saying: 'May He bless you with all good and preserve you from all evil! May He lighten your heart with life-giving wisdom and grant you eternal knowledge! May He raise His merciful face towards you for everlasting bliss!'

And the Levites shall curse all the men of the lot of Belial, saying: 'Be cursed because of all your guilty wickedness! May He deliver you up for torture at the hands of the vengeful Avengers! May He visit you with destruction by the hand of all the Wreakers of Revenge! Be cursed without mercy because of (4Q256) the darkness of your deeds! Be damned in the shadowy place of everlasting fire! May God not heed when you call on Him, nor pardon you by blotting out your sin! May He raise His angry face towards you for vengeance! May there be no "Peace"

1. Satan.

for you in the mouth of those who hold fast to the Fathers!' And after the blessing and the cursing, all those entering the Covenant shall say, 'Amen, Amen!'

And the Priests and Levites shall continue, saying: 'Cursed be the man who enters this Covenant while walking among the idols of his heart, who sets up before himself his stumbling-block of sin so that he may backslide! Hearing the words of this Covenant, he blesses himself in his heart and says, "Peace be with me, even though I walk in the stubbornness of my heart" (Deut. xxix, 18–19), whereas his spirit, parched (for lack of truth) and watered (with lies), shall be destroyed without pardon. God's wrath and His zeal for His precepts shall consume him in everlasting destruction. All the curses of the Covenant shall cling to him and God will set him apart for evil. He shall be cut off from the midst of all the sons of light, and because he has turned aside from God on account of his idols and his stumbling-block of sin, his lot shall be among those who are cursed for ever.' And after them, all those entering the Covenant shall answer and say, 'Amen, Amen!'

Thus shall they do, year by year, for as long as the dominion of Belial endures. The Priests shall enter first, ranked one after another according to the perfection of their spirit; then the Levites; and thirdly, all the people one after another in their Thousands, Hundreds, Fifties, and Tens, that every Israelite may know his place in the Community of God according to the everlasting design. No man shall move down from his place nor move up from his allotted position. For according to the holy design, they shall all of them be in a Community of truth and virtuous humility, of loving-kindness and good intent one towards the other, and (they shall all of them be) sons of the everlasting Company.

No man [shall be in the] Community of His truth who refuses to enter [the Covenant of] God so that he may walk in the stubbornness of his heart, for III his soul detests the wise teaching of just laws. He shall not be counted among the upright for he has not persisted in the conversion of his life. His knowledge, powers, and possessions shall not enter the Council of the Community, for whoever ploughs the mud of wickedness returns defiled (?). He shall not be justified by that which his stubborn heart declares lawful, for seeking the ways of light he looks towards darkness. He shall not be reckoned among the perfect; he shall neither be purified by atonement, nor cleansed by purifying waters, nor sanctified by seas and rivers, nor washed clean with any ablution. Unclean, unclean shall he be. For as long as he despises the precepts of God he shall receive no instruction in the Community of His counsel.

For it is through the spirit of true counsel concerning the ways of man that all his sins shall be expiated, that he may contemplate the light of life. He shall be cleansed from all his sins by the spirit of holiness uniting him to His truth, and his iniquity shall be expiated by the spirit of uprightness and humility. And when his flesh is sprinkled with purifying water and sanctified by cleansing water, it shall be made clean by the humble submission of his soul to all the precepts of God. Let him then order his steps {to walk} (4Q255) perfectly in all the ways commanded by God concerning the times appointed for him, straying neither to the right nor to the left and transgressing none of His words, and he shall be accepted by virtue of a pleasing atonement before God and it shall be to him a Covenant of the everlasting Community.

The Master shall instruct all the sons of light and shall teach them the nature of all the children of men according to the kind of spirit which they possess, the signs identifying their works during their lifetime, their visitation for chastisement, and the time of their reward.

From the God of Knowledge comes all that is and shall be. Before ever they existed He established their whole design, and when, as ordained for them, they come into being, it is in accord with His glorious design that they accomplish their task without change. The laws of all things are in His hand and He provides them with all their needs.

He has created man to govern the world, and has appointed for him two spirits in which to walk until the time of His visitation: the spirits of truth and injustice. Those born of truth spring from a fountain of light, but those born of injustice spring from a source of darkness. All the children of righteousness are ruled by the Prince of Light and walk in the ways of light, but all the children of injustice are ruled by the Angel of Darkness and walk in the ways of darkness. The Angel of Darkness leads all the children of righteousness astray, and until his end, all their sin, iniquities, wickedness, and all their unlawful deeds are caused by his dominion in accordance with the mysteries of God. Every one of their chastisements, and every one of the seasons of their distress, shall be brought about by the rule of his persecution; for all his allotted spirits seek the overthrow of the sons of light.[2]

But the God of Israel and His Angel of Truth will succour all the sons of light. For it is He who created the spirits of Light and Darkness and founded every action upon them and established every deed [upon] their [ways]. And He loves the one **IV** everlastingly and delights in its works for ever; but the counsel of the other He loathes and for ever hates its ways.

These are their ways in the world for the enlightenment of the heart of man, and so that all the paths of true righteousness may be made straight before him, and so that the fear of the laws of God may be instilled in his heart: a spirit of humility, patience, abundant charity, unending goodness, understanding, and intelligence; (a spirit of) mighty wisdom which trusts in all the deeds of God and leans on His great loving-kindness; a spirit of discernment in every purpose, of zeal for just laws, of holy intent with steadfastness of heart, of great charity towards all the sons of truth, of admirable purity which detests all unclean idols, of humble conduct sprung from an understanding of all things, and of faithful concealment of the mysteries of truth. These are the counsels of the spirit to the sons of truth in this world.

And as for the visitation of all who walk in this spirit, it shall be healing, great peace in a long life, and fruitfulness, together with every everlasting blessing and eternal joy in life without end, a crown of glory and a garment of majesty in unending light.[3]

---

2. This paragraph has multiple points of contact with the NT, especially with Johannine writings; e.g., see John 8:12; 12:35–36; 14:17; 15:26; 16:13; 1 John 3:8–10; 4:6.

3. For this paragraph and the preceding, cf. 1 Cor 13:4–7; Gal 5:22–23; and similar lists in the Pauline collection and other NT epistles.

But the ways of the spirit of falsehood are these: greed, and slackness in the search for righteousness, wickedness and lies, haughtiness and pride, falseness and deceit, cruelty and abundant evil, ill-temper and much folly and brazen insolence, abominable deeds (committed) in a spirit of lust, and ways of lewdness in the service of uncleanness, a blaspheming tongue, blindness of eye and dullness of ear, stiffness of neck and heaviness of heart, so that man walks in all the ways of darkness and guile.

And the visitation of all who walk in this spirit shall be a multitude of plagues by the hand of all the destroying angels, everlasting damnation by the avenging wrath of the fury of God, eternal torment and endless disgrace together with shameful extinction in the fire of the dark regions. The times of all their generations shall be spent in sorrowful mourning and in bitter misery and in calamities of darkness until they are destroyed without remnant or survivor.[4]

The nature of all the children of men is ruled by these (two spirits), and during their life all the hosts of men have a portion of their divisions and walk in (both) their ways. And the whole reward for their deeds shall be, for everlasting ages, according to whether each man's portion in their two divisions is great or small. For God has established the spirits in equal measure until the final age, and has set everlasting hatred between their divisions. Truth abhors the works of injustice, and injustice hates all the ways of truth. And their struggle is fierce in all their arguments for they do not walk together. But in the mysteries of His understanding, and in His glorious wisdom, God has ordained an end for injustice, and at the time of the visitation He will destroy it for ever. Then truth, which has wallowed in the ways of wickedness during the dominion of injustice until the appointed time of judgement, shall arise in the world for ever. God will then purify every deed of man with His truth; He will refine for Himself the human frame by rooting out all spirit of injustice from the bounds of his flesh. He will cleanse him of all wicked deeds with the spirit of holiness; like purifying waters He will shed upon him the spirit of truth (to cleanse him) of all abomination and injustice. And he shall be plunged into the spirit of purification, that he may instruct the upright in the knowledge of the Most High and teach the wisdom of the sons of heaven to the perfect of way. For God has chosen them for an everlasting Covenant and all the glory of Adam shall be theirs. There shall be no more lies and all the works of injustice shall be put to shame.[5]

Until now the spirits of truth and injustice struggle in the hearts of men and they walk in both wisdom and folly. According to his portion of truth so does a man hate injustice, and according to his inheritance in the realm of injustice so is he wicked and so hates truth. For God has established the two spirits in equal measure until the determined end, and until the Renewal, and He knows the reward of their deeds from all eternity. He has allotted them to the children of men that they may know good [and evil, and] that the destiny of all the living may be according to the spirit within [them at the time] of the visitation.

4. For this paragraph and the preceding, cf. 1 Cor 6:9–10; Gal 5:19–21; and similar lists in the Pauline collection and other NT epistles.
5. The eschatological purification of the "human frame" described in this paragraph in some ways resembles 1 Cor 15:20–58.

V *And this is the Rule for the men of the Community who have freely pledged them-*
selves to be converted from all evil and to cling to all His commandments according
to His will

They shall separate from the congregation of the men of injustice and shall
unite, with respect to the Law and possessions, under the authority of the sons of
Zadok,[6] the Priests who keep the Covenant, and of the multitude of the men of
the Community who hold fast to the Covenant. Every decision concerning doctrine, property, and justice shall be determined by them.[7]

They shall practise truth and humility in common, and justice and uprightness
and charity and modesty in all their ways. No man shall walk in the stubbornness
of his heart so that he strays after his heart and eyes and evil inclination, but he
shall circumcise in the Community the foreskin of evil inclination and of stiffness of neck that they may lay a foundation of truth for Israel, for the Community of the everlasting Covenant. They shall atone for all those in Aaron who
have freely pledged themselves to holiness, and for those in Israel who have freely
pledged themselves to the House of Truth, and for those who join them to live in
community and to take part in the trial and judgement and condemnation of all
those who transgress the precepts.

On joining the Community, this shall be their code of behaviour with respect
to all these precepts.

Whoever approaches the Council of the Community shall enter the Covenant
of God in the presence of all who have freely pledged themselves. He shall undertake by a binding oath to return with all his heart and soul to every commandment of the Law of Moses in accordance with all that has been revealed of it
to the sons of Zadok, the Priests, Keepers of the Covenant and Seekers of His
will, and to the multitude of the men of their Covenant who together have freely
pledged themselves to His truth and to walking in the way of His delight. And he
shall undertake by the Covenant to separate from all the men of injustice who walk
in the way of wickedness.

For they are not reckoned in His Covenant. They have neither inquired nor
sought after Him concerning His laws that they might know the hidden things
in which they have sinfully erred; and matters revealed they have treated with
insolence. Therefore Wrath shall rise up to condemn, and Vengeance shall be
executed by the curses of the Covenant, and great chastisements of eternal destruction shall be visited on them, leaving no remnant. They shall not enter the water
to partake of the pure Meal of the men of holiness, for they shall not be cleansed
unless they turn from their wickedness: for all who transgress His word are
unclean. Likewise, no man shall consort with him in regard to his work or property lest he be burdened with the guilt of his sin. He shall indeed keep away from
him in all things: as it is written, *Keep away from all that is false* (Exod. xxiii, 7).
No member of the Community shall follow them in matters of doctrine and justice,

6. Zadok was priest during the reigns of David and Solomon. See 2 Sam 8:17; 15:24–29; 1 Kgs
4:2; etc.

7. References to common property, which also surface at the middle of section I and at the
end of section VI, recall Acts 2:44–45; 4:32; etc.

or eat or drink anything of theirs, or take anything from them except for a price; as it is written, *Keep away from the man in whose nostrils is breath, for wherein is he counted?* (Isa. ii, 22). For all those not reckoned in His Covenant are to be set apart, together with all that is theirs. None of the men of holiness shall lean upon works of vanity: for they are all vanity who know not His Covenant, and He will blot from the world all them that despise His word. All their deeds are defilement before Him, and all their property unclean.

But when a man enters the Covenant to walk according to all these precepts that he may be joined to the holy Congregation, they shall examine his spirit in community with respect to his understanding and practice of the Law, under the authority of the sons of Aaron who have freely pledged themselves in the Community to restore His Covenant and to heed all the precepts commanded by Him, and of the multitude of Israel who have freely pledged themselves in the Community to return to His Covenant. They shall inscribe them in order, one after another, according to their understanding and their deeds, that every one may obey his companion, the man of lesser rank obeying his superior. And they shall examine their spirit and deeds yearly, so that each man may be advanced in accordance with his understanding and perfection of way, or moved down in accordance with his distortions. They shall rebuke one another in truth, humility, and charity. Let no man address his companion with anger, or ill-temper, or obdu[racy, or with envy prompted by (4Q258)] the spirit of wickedness. Let him not hate him [because of his uncircumcised] heart, but let him rebuke him on the very same day lest **VI** he incur guilt because of him. And furthermore, let no man accuse his companion before the Congregation without having admonished him in the presence of witnesses.

These are the ways in which all of them shall walk, each man with his companion, wherever they dwell. The man of lesser rank shall obey the greater in matters of work and money. They shall eat in common and bless in common and deliberate in common.

Wherever there are ten men of the Council of the Community there shall not lack a Priest among them. And they shall all sit before him according to their rank and shall be asked their counsel in all things in that order. And when the table has been prepared for eating, and the new wine for drinking, the Priest shall be the first to stretch out his hand to bless the firstfruits of the bread and new wine.

And where the ten are, there shall never lack a man among them who shall study the Law continually, day and night, concerning the right conduct of a man with his companion. And the Congregation shall watch in community for a third of every night of the year, to read the Book and to study the Law and to bless together.

This is the Rule for an Assembly of the Congregation

Each man shall sit in his place: the Priests shall sit first, and the elders second, and all the rest of the people according to their rank. And thus shall they be questioned concerning the Law, and concerning any counsel or matter coming before the Congregation, each man bringing his knowledge to the Council of the Community.

No man shall interrupt a companion before his speech has ended, nor speak before a man of higher rank; each man shall speak in his turn. And in an Assembly of the Congregation no man shall speak without the consent of the Congregation, nor indeed of the Guardian of the Congregation. Should any man wish to speak to the Congregation, yet not be in a position to question the Council of the Community, let him rise to his feet and say: 'I have something to say to the Congregation.' If they command him to speak, he shall speak.[8]

Every man, born of Israel, who freely pledges himself to join the Council of the Community shall be examined by the Guardian at the head of the Congregation concerning his understanding and his deeds. If he is fitted to the discipline, he shall admit him into the Covenant that he may be converted to the truth and depart from all injustice; and he shall instruct him in all the rules of the Community. And later, when he comes to stand before the Congregation, they shall all deliberate his case, and according to the decision of the Council of the Congregation he shall either enter or depart. After he has entered the Council of the Community he shall not touch the pure Meal of the Congregation until one {full} (4Q256) year is completed, and until he has been examined concerning his spirit and deeds; nor shall he have any share of the property of the Congregation. Then when he has completed one year within the Community, the Congregation shall deliberate his case with regard to his understanding and observance of the Law. And if it be his destiny, according to the judgement of the Priests and the multitude of the men of their Covenant, to enter the company of the Community, his property and earnings shall be handed over to the Bursar of the Congregation who shall register it to his account and shall not spend it for the Congregation. He shall not touch the Drink of the Congregation until he has completed a second year among the men of the Community. But when the second year has passed, he shall be examined, and if it be his destiny, according to the judgement of the Congregation, to enter the Community, then he shall be inscribed among his brethren in the order of his rank for the Law, and for justice, and for the pure Meal; his property shall be merged and he shall offer his counsel and judgement to the Community.

2 ESDRAS (from chap. 7)[†]

[The angel said to me:] 36 "The pit[1] of torment shall appear, and opposite it shall be the place of rest; and the furnace of hell[2] shall be disclosed, and opposite it the paradise of delight. 37 Then the Most High will say to the nations that have

8. The guidelines for behavior at congregational assemblies are similar to those given in 1 Cor 14:26–35.

† Verses 36–105 were missing from the Latin text of the apocryphal book that KJV translated (see introduction to 2 Esdras and 7:35 note). The translation printed here is from the New Revised Standard Version of the Bible. All notes are from the NRSV.

1. Syr Ethiop: Lat *place*.

2. Lat Syr Ethiop *Gehenna*.

been raised from the dead, 'Look now, and understand whom you have denied, whom you have not served, whose commandments you have despised. 38 Look on this side and on that; here are delight and rest, and there are fire and torments.' Thus he will[3] speak to them on the day of judgment— 39 a day that has no sun or moon or stars, 40 or cloud or thunder or lightning, or wind or water or air, or darkness or evening or morning, 41 or summer or spring or heat or winter[4] or frost or cold, or hail or rain or dew, 42 or noon or night, or dawn or shining or brightness or light, but only the splendor of the glory of the Most High, by which all shall see what has been destined. 43 It will last as though for a week of years. 44 This is my judgment and its prescribed order; and to you alone I have shown these things."

45 I answered and said, "O sovereign Lord, I said then and[5] I say now: Blessed are those who are alive and keep your commandments! 46 But what of those for whom I prayed? For who among the living is there that has not sinned, or who is there among mortals that has not transgressed your covenant? 47 And now I see that the world to come will bring delight to few, but torments to many. 48 For an evil heart has grown up in us, which has alienated us from God,[6] and has brought us into corruption and the ways of death, and has shown us the paths of perdition and removed us far from life—and that not merely for a few but for almost all who have been created."

49 He answered me and said, "Listen to me, Ezra,[7] and I will instruct you, and will admonish you once more. 50 For this reason the Most High has made not one world but two. 51 Inasmuch as you have said that the righteous are not many but few, while the ungodly abound, hear the explanation for this.

52 "If you have just a few precious stones, will you add to them lead and clay?"[8] 53 I said, "Lord, how could that be?" 54 And he said to me, "Not only that, but ask the earth and she will tell you; defer to her, and she will declare it to you. 55 Say to her, 'You produce gold and silver and bronze, and also iron and lead and clay; 56 but silver is more abundant than gold, and bronze than silver, and iron than bronze, and lead than iron, and clay than lead.' 57 Judge therefore which things are precious and desirable, those that are abundant or those that are rare?"

58 I said, "O sovereign Lord, what is plentiful is of less worth, for what is more rare is more precious."

59 He answered me and said, "Consider within yourself[9] what you have thought, for the person who has what is hard to get rejoices more than the person who has what is plentiful. 60 So also will be the judgment[1] that I have promised; for I will rejoice over the few who shall be saved, because it is they who have

3. Syr Ethiop Arab 1: Lat *you shall.*
4. Or *storm.*
5. Syr: Lat *And I answered, "I said then, O Lord, and.*
6. Cn [conjecture]: Lat Syr Ethiop *from these.*
7. Syr Arab 1 Georg: Lat Ethiop lack *Ezra.*
8. Arab 1: Meaning of Lat Syr Ethiop uncertain.
9. Syr Ethiop Arab 1: Meaning of Lat uncertain.
1. Syr Arab 1: Lat *creation.*

made my glory to prevail now, and through them my name has now been honored. *61* I will not grieve over the great number of those who perish; for it is they who are now like a mist, and are similar to a flame and smoke—they are set on fire and burn hotly, and are extinguished."

62 I replied and said, "O earth, what have you brought forth, if the mind is made out of the dust like the other created things? *63* For it would have been better if the dust itself had not been born, so that the mind might not have been made from it. *64* But now the mind grows with us, and therefore we are tormented, because we perish and we know it. *65* Let the human race lament, but let the wild animals of the field be glad; let all who have been born lament, but let the cattle and the flocks rejoice. *66* It is much better with them than with us; for they do not look for a judgment, and they do not know of any torment or salvation promised to them after death. *67* What does it profit us that we shall be preserved alive but cruelly tormented? *68* For all who have been born are entangled in[2] iniquities, and are full of sins and burdened with transgressions. *69* And if after death we were not to come into judgment, perhaps it would have been better for us."

70 He answered me and said, "When the Most High made the world and Adam and all who have come from him, he first prepared the judgment and the things that pertain to the judgment. *71* But now, understand from your own words—for you have said that the mind grows with us. *72* For this reason, therefore, those who live on earth shall be tormented, because though they had understanding, they committed iniquity; and though they received the commandments, they did not keep them; and though they obtained the law, they dealt unfaithfully with what they received. *73* What, then, will they have to say in the judgment, or how will they answer in the last times? *74* How long the Most High has been patient with those who inhabit the world!—and not for their sake, but because of the times that he has foreordained."

75 I answered and said, "If I have found favor in your sight, O Lord, show this also to your servant: whether after death, as soon as everyone of us yields up the soul, we shall be kept in rest until those times come when you will renew the creation, or whether we shall be tormented at once?"

76 He answered me and said, "I will show you that also, but do not include yourself with those who have shown scorn, or number yourself among those who are tormented. *77* For you have a treasure of works stored up with the Most High, but it will not be shown to you until the last times. *78* Now concerning death, the teaching is: When the decisive decree has gone out from the Most High that a person shall die, as the spirit leaves the body to return again to him who gave it, first of all it adores the glory of the Most High. *79* If it is one of those who have shown scorn and have not kept the way of the Most High, who have despised his law and hated those who fear God— *80* such spirits shall not enter into habitations, but shall immediately wander about in torments, always grieving and sad, in seven ways. *81* The first way, because they have scorned the law of the Most High. *82* The second way, because they cannot now make a good repentance so

---

2. Syr *defiled with.*

that they may live. 83 The third way, they shall see the reward laid up for those who have trusted the covenants of the Most High. 84 The fourth way, they shall consider the torment laid up for themselves in the last days. 85 The fifth way, they shall see how the habitations of the others are guarded by angels in profound quiet. 86 The sixth way, they shall see how some of them will cross over[3] into torments. 87 The seventh way, which is worse[4] than all the ways that have been mentioned, because they shall utterly waste away in confusion and be consumed with shame,[5] and shall wither with fear at seeing the glory of the Most High in whose presence they sinned while they were alive, and in whose presence they are to be judged in the last times.

88 "Now this is the order of those who have kept the ways of the Most High, when they shall be separated from their mortal body.[6] 89 During the time that they lived in it,[7] they laboriously served the Most High, and withstood danger every hour so that they might keep the law of the Lawgiver perfectly. 90 Therefore this is the teaching concerning them: 91 First of all, they shall see with great joy the glory of him who receives them, for they shall have rest in seven orders. 92 The first order, because they have striven with great effort to overcome the evil thought that was formed with them, so that it might not lead them astray from life into death. 93 The second order, because they see the perplexity in which the souls of the ungodly wander and the punishment that awaits them. 94 The third order, they see the witness that he who formed them bears concerning them, that throughout their life they kept the law with which they were entrusted. 95 The fourth order, they understand the rest that they now enjoy, being gathered into their chambers and guarded by angels in profound quiet, and the glory waiting for them in the last days. 96 The fifth order, they rejoice that they have now escaped what is corruptible and shall inherit what is to come; and besides they see the straits and toil[8] from which they have been delivered, and the spacious liberty that they are to receive and enjoy in immortality. 97 The sixth order, when it is shown them how their face is to shine like the sun, and how they are to be made like the light of the stars, being incorruptible from then on. 98 The seventh order, which is greater than all that have been mentioned, because they shall rejoice with boldness, and shall be confident without confusion, and shall be glad without fear, for they press forward to see the face of him whom they served in life and from whom they are to receive their reward when glorified. 99 This is the order of the souls of the righteous, as henceforth is announced;[9] and the previously mentioned are the ways of torment that those who would not give heed shall suffer hereafter."

---

3. Cn [conjecture]: Meaning of Lat uncertain.
4. Lat Syr Ethiop *greater*.
5. Syr Ethiop: Meaning of Lat uncertain.
6. Lat *the corruptible vessel*.
7. Syr Ethiop: Meaning of Latin uncertain.
8. Syr Ethiop: Lat *fullness*.
9. Syr: Meaning of Lat uncertain.

100 Then I answered and said, "Will time therefore be given to the souls, after they have been separated from the bodies, to see what you have described to me?"

101 He said to me, "They shall have freedom for seven days, so that during these seven days they may see the things of which you have been told, and afterwards they shall be gathered in their habitations."

102 I answered and said, "If I have found favor in your sight, show further to me, your servant, whether on the day of judgment the righteous will be able to intercede for the ungodly or to entreat the Most High for them— *103* fathers for sons or sons for parents, brothers for brothers, relatives for their kindred, or friends for those who are most dear."

104 He answered me and said, "Since you have found favor in my sight, I will show you this also. The day of judgment is decisive[1] and displays to all the seal of truth. Just as now a father does not send his son, or a son his father, or a master his servant, or a friend his dearest friend, to be ill[2] or sleep or eat or be healed in his place, *105* so no one shall ever pray for another on that day, neither shall anyone lay a burden on another;[3] for then all shall bear their own righteousness and unrighteousness."

VIRGIL

At least since the time of Constantine (see his *Speech to the Assembly of the Saints*), Christians have interpreted the fourth eclogue of Virgil (70 B.C.E.–19 C.E.), perhaps composed around 40 B.C.E., as a prophecy of Christ's birth. It is largely on the strength of this tradition that Dante makes Virgil his guide in the *Commedia* and portrays the Roman poet Statius as claiming to have converted upon reading Virgil's poem. Modern scholars rightly reject any attempt to read the eclogue in a Judeo-Christian eschatological context, but there is no consensus on the identification of the child whose birth it seems to prophesy, or even if the child should be identified at all and not merely taken as the leading symbol of the cosmic regeneration attending the figured nativity. While the poem's imagery of rebirth certainly resonates with a number of biblical texts (its focus on the birth of an extraordinary infant recalls Isaiah 7:14 and the opening chapters of Luke, for example), such imagery is not uncommon in Roman literary and visual art celebrating the emperor Augustus's reign as a time of prosperity and optimism that brought to an end decades of civil war. Virgil's poem is thus finally important to readers of the New Testament not because it speaks of the Christian Messiah, nor even because later writers believed that it did, but rather because it shows how ancient pagan authors writing around the same time as those that composed the New Testament employed similar ideas and imagery in very different ideological contexts.

---

1. Lat *bold*.
2. Syr Ethiop Arm: Lat *to understand*.
3. Syr Ethiop: Lat lacks *on that . . . another*.

Eclogue 4[†]

1 Sicilian[1] Muses, let us sing a somewhat loftier strain. Not all do the orchards please and the lowly tamarisks. If our song is of the woodland, let the woodland be worthy of a consul.

4 Now is come the last age of the song of Cumae; the great line of the centuries begins anew. Now the Virgin[2] returns, the reign of Saturn returns; now a new generation descends from heaven on high. Only do thou, pure Lucina,[3] smile on the birth of the child, under whom the iron brood shall first cease, and a golden race spring up throughout the world! Thine own Apollo now is king!

11 And in thy consulship, Pollio,[4] yea in thine, shall this glorious age begin, and the mighty months commence their march; under thy sway, any lingering traces of our guilt shall become void, and release the earth from its continual dread. He shall have the gift of divine life, shall see heroes mingled with gods, and shall himself be seen of them, and shall sway a world to which his father's virtues have brought peace.

18 But for thee, child, shall the earth untilled pour forth, as her first pretty gifts, straggling ivy with foxglove everywhere, and the Egyptian bean blended with the smiling acanthus. Uncalled, the goats shall bring home their udders swollen with milk, and the herds shall fear not huge lions; unasked, thy cradle shall pour forth flowers for thy delight. The serpent, too, shall perish, and the false poison-plant shall perish; Assyrian spice shall spring up on every soil.

26 But soon as thou canst read of the glories of heroes and thy father's deeds, and canst know what valour is, slowly shall the plain yellow with the waving corn, on wild brambles shall hang the purple grape, and the stubborn oak shall distil dewy honey. Yet shall some few traces of olden sin lurk behind, to call men to essay the sea in ships, to gird towns with walls, and to cleave the earth with furrows. A second Tiphys shall then arise, and a second Argo to carry chosen heroes; a second warfare, too, shall there be, and again shall a great Achilles[5] be sent to Troy.

37 Next, when now the strength of years has made thee man, even the trader shall quit the sea, nor shall the ship of pine exchange wares; every land shall bear

---

† Prose translation from *Virgil*, vol. 1, trans. H. Rushton Fairclough, Loeb Classical Library (London: William Heinemann, 1916), 29, 31, 33. (Boldfaced numbers correspond to line numbers in the Latin poem.)

1. Called Sicilian because Virgil's model in pastoral poetry, Theocritus, was a Sicilian [translator's note].

2. That is, the golden age; the Virgin, Justice, was the final divinity to abandon the earth in the iron age; cf. Virgil, *Georgics* 2.474; Ovid, *Metamorphoses* 1.148.

3. Roman goddess of childbirth.

4. Gaius Asinius Pollio, a patron and friend of Virgil, was consul in 40 B.C.E. In that year he helped negotiate the treaty of Brundisium, which temporarily halted Rome's civil war by dividing its imperial territories among Octavian (later known as Augustus), Antony, and Lepidus.

5. The greatest of the Greek warriors who fought (and died) in the Trojan War. Tiphys, a generation earlier, piloted the *Argo*, which carried Jason and other heroes and demigods on the quest for the golden fleece.

all fruits. The earth shall not feel the harrow, nor the vine the pruning-hook; the sturdy ploughman, too, shall now loose his oxen from the yoke. Wool shall no more learn to counterfeit varied hues, but of himself the ram in the meadows shall change his fleece, now to sweetly blushing purple, now to a saffron yellow; of its own will shall scarlet clothe the grazing lambs.

46 "Ages such as these, glide on!" cried to their spindles the Fates, voicing in unison the fixed will of Destiny!

48 Enter on thy high honours—the hour will soon be here—O thou dear off-spring of the gods, mighty seed of a Jupiter to be! Behold the world bowing with its massive dome—earth and expanse of sea and heaven's depth! Behold, how all things exult in the age that is at hand! O that then the last days of a long life may still linger for me, with inspiration enough to tell of thy deeds! Not Thracian Orpheus, not Linus[6] shall vanquish me in song, though his mother be helpful to the one, and his father to the other, Calliope to Orpheus, and fair Apollo[7] to Linus. Even Pan,[8] were he to contend with me and Arcady be judge, even Pan, with Arcady for judge, would own himself defeated.

60 Begin, baby boy, to know thy mother with a smile—to thy mother ten months have brought the weariness of travail. Begin, baby boy! Him on whom his parents have not smiled, no god honours with his table, no goddess with her bed![9]

PLUTARCH

The following excerpt from the *Life of Alexander* by the Greek biographer and philosopher Plutarch (ca. 50–120 C.E.) raises the possibility that Zeus was Alexander the Great's father. Plutarch's biography thereby participates in a tradition of ascribing divine parentage to extraordinary figures, much like the narratives of Jesus' birth in Matthew and Luke.

[The Birth of Alexander the Great][†]

2 As for the lineage of Alexander, on his father's side he was a descendant of Heracles through Caranus, and on his mother's side a descendant of Aeacus

---

6. The greatest of the Greek mythological musicians; they sang their poetic compositions.
7. God of poetry and the arts; Calliope was the muse of epic poetry.
8. God of flocks and shepherds, credited with inventing the shepherd's flute; his main seat of worship was Arcadia (Arcady), which was also a conventional setting of pastoral poetry.
9. *I.e.* such a child can never win the rewards bestowed on a hero, such as Hercules (*cf.* Homer, *Odyssey*, XI. 601) [translator's note].
† From Plutarch, *Lives*, vol. 7, trans. Bernadotte Perrin, Loeb Classical Library (1919; reprint, Cambridge, MA: Harvard University Press, 1967), 225, 227, 229.

through Neoptolemus;[1] this is accepted without any question. And we are told that Philip, after being initiated into the mysteries of Samothrace at the same time with Olympias, he himself being still a youth and she an orphan child, fell in love with her and betrothed himself to her at once with the consent of her brother, Arymbas. Well, then, the night before that on which the marriage was consummated, the bride dreamed that there was a peal of thunder and that a thunder-bolt fell upon her womb,[2] and that thereby much fire was kindled, which broke into flames that travelled all about, and then was extinguished. At a later time, too, after the marriage, Philip dreamed that he was putting a seal upon his wife's womb; and the device of the seal, as he thought, was the figure of a lion. The other seers, now, were led by the vision to suspect that Philip needed to put a closer watch upon his marriage relations; but Aristander of Telmessus said that the woman was pregnant, since no seal was put upon what was empty, and pregnant of a son whose nature would be bold and lion-like. Moreover, a serpent was once seen lying stretched out by the side of Olympias as she slept, and we are told that this, more than anything else, dulled the ardour of Philip's attentions to his wife, so that he no longer came often to sleep by her side, either because he feared that some spells and enchantments might be practised upon him by her, or because he shrank from her embraces in the conviction that she was the partner of a superior being.

But concerning these matters there is another story to this effect: all the women of these parts were addicted to the Orphic rites and the orgies of Dionysus from very ancient times (being called Klodones and Mimallones[3]), and imitated in many ways the practices of the Edonian women and the Thracian women about Mount Haemus, from whom, as it would seem, the word "threskeuein" came to be applied to the celebration of extravagant and superstitious ceremonies. Now Olympias, who affected these divine possessions more zealously than other women, and carried out these divine inspirations in wilder fashion, used to provide the revelling companies with great tame serpents, which would often lift their heads from out the ivy and the mystic winnowing-baskets,[4] or coil themselves about the wands and garlands of the women, thus terrifying the men.

3 However, after his vision, as we are told, Philip sent Chaeron of Megalopolis to Delphi, by whom an oracle was brought him from Apollo, who bade him sacrifice to Ammon[5] and hold that god in greatest reverence, but told him he was to lose that one of his eyes which he had applied to the chink in the door when he espied the god, in the form of a serpent, sharing the couch of his wife. Moreover,

1. The son of Achilles, who was the best of the Greek warriors in the Trojan War. Heracles, or Hercules, was probably the greatest hero of classical mythology.
2. In Greek mythology, the thunderbolt was wielded by Zeus, king of the Olympian gods.
3. Names used in Macedonia, the northern Greek kingdom ruled by Philip, for female worshippers of Dionysus.
4. Broad baskets used to separate the chaff from the wheat; sacred to Dionysus (as was ivy), they were carried on the head at his festivals.
5. A deity worshipped in Egypt that came to be identified with Zeus.

Olympias, as Eratosthenes says, when she sent Alexander forth upon his great expedition, told him, and him alone, the secret of his begetting, and bade him have purposes worthy of his birth. Others, on the contrary, say that she repudiated the idea, and said: "Alexander must cease slandering me to Hera."[6]

PHILOSTRATUS

The life of the first-century itinerant Pythagorean philosopher and holy man Apollonius, written by the sophist Philostratus (latter decades of second century—ca. 245 C.E.), bears obvious affinities to the New Testament gospels, and several parallels between them are noted in the excerpts that follow. Taken as a whole, these parallels underscore the conventionality of Jesus' ministry in the Greco-Roman world; but they may at the same time represent Philostratus's adaptation of increasingly popular Christian literary forms to pagan religious and philosophical contexts.

[The Birth and Youth of Apollonius]
(from *Life of Apollonius*, book 1)[†]

4 Apollonius' home, then, was Tyana, a Greek city amidst a population of Cappadocians. His father was of the same name, and the family was ancient and directly descended from the first settlers. It excelled in wealth the surrounding families, though the district is a rich one. To his mother, just before he was born, there came an apparition of Proteus, who changes his form so much in Homer, in the guise of an Egyptian demon. She was in no way frightened, but asked him what sort of child she would bear. And he answered: "Myself." "And who are you?" she asked. "Proteus," answered he, "the god of Egypt." Well, I need hardly explain to readers of the poets the quality of Proteus and his reputation as regards wisdom; how versatile he was, and for ever changing his form, and defying capture, and how he had the reputation of knowing both past and future. And we must bear Proteus in mind all the more, when my advancing story shows its hero to have been more of a prophet than Proteus, and to have triumphed over many difficulties and dangers in the moment when they beset him most closely.

5 Now he is said to have been born in a meadow, hard by which there has been now erected a sumptuous temple to him; and let us not pass by the manner of his birth. For just as the hour of his birth was approaching, his mother was warned in a dream to walk out into the meadow and pluck the flowers; and in due course she

6. The sister and wife of Zeus.

† This and the following selections come from Philostratus, *The Life of Apollonius of Tyana*, trans. F. C. Conybeare, 2 vols., Loeb Classical Library (London: William Heinemann, 1912, 1921), 1:11, 13, 15, 17, 27, 29, 315, 317, 319, 389, 391, 393, 397, 457, 459; 2:273, 275, 277, 279, 281, 283, 285, 357, 359, 361, 363, 365, 399, 401, 403, 405.

came there and her maids attended to the flowers, scattering themselves over the meadow, while she fell asleep lying on the grass. Thereupon the swans who fed in the meadow set up a dance around her as she slept, and lifting their wings, as they are wont to do, cried out aloud all at once, for there was somewhat of a breeze blowing in the meadow. She then leaped up at the sound of their song and bore her child, for any sudden fright is apt to bring on a premature delivery. But the people of the country say that just at the moment of the birth, a thunderbolt seemed about to fall to earth and then rose up into the air and disappeared aloft; and the gods thereby indicated, I think, the great distinction to which the sage was to attain, and hinted in advance how he should transcend all things upon earth and approach the gods, and signified all the things that he would achieve.

6 Now there is near Tyana a well sacred to Zeus, the god of oaths, so they say, and they call it the well of Asbama. Here a spring rises cold, but bubbles up like a boiling cauldron. This water is favourable and sweet to those who keep their oaths, but to perjurers it brings hot-footed justice; for it attacks their eyes and hands and feet, and they fall the prey of dropsy and wasting disease; and they are not even able to go away, but are held on the spot and bemoan themselves at the edge of the spring, acknowledging their perjuries. The people of the country, then, say that Apollonius was a son of Zeus, but the sage called himself the son of Apollonius.[1]

7 On reaching the age when children are taught their letters, he showed great strength of memory and power of application; and his tongue affected the Attic dialect,[2] nor was his accent corrupted by the race he lived among. All eyes were turned upon him, for he was, moreover, conspicuous for his beauty. When then he reached his fourteenth year, his father brought him to Tarsus, to Euthydemus the teacher from Phoenicia. Now Euthydemus was a good rhetorician, and began his education; but, though he was attached to his teacher, he found the atmosphere of the city harsh and strange and little conducive to the philosophic life, for nowhere are men more addicted than here to luxury: jesters and full of insolence are they all; and they attend more to their fine linen than the Athenians did to wisdom; and a stream called the Cydnus runs through their city, along the banks of which they sit like so many water-fowl. Hence the words which Apollonius addresses to them in his letter: "Be done with getting drunk upon your water." He therefore transferred his teacher, with his father's consent, to the town of Aegae, which was close by, where he found a peace congenial to one who would be a philosopher, and a more serious school of study and a temple of Asclepius,[3] where that god reveals himself in person to men.

* * *

11 * * * [H]e inculcated the wise rule, that in our sacrifices or dedications we should not go beyond the just mean, in the following way. On one occasion

---

1. Compare Jesus' divine parenthood (e.g., Luke 1:26–35).
2. That is, the dialect spoken in Attica, the region whose leading city was Athens, Greece's cultural capital.
3. God of medicine.

several people had flocked to the temple, not long after the expulsion of the Cilician, and he took the occasion to ask the priest the following questions.[4] "Are then," he said, "the gods just?" "Why, of course, most just," answered the priest. "Well, and are they wise?" "And what," said the other, "can be wiser than the godhead?" "But do they know the affairs of men, or are they without experience of them?" "Why," said the other, "this is just the point in which the gods excel mankind, for the latter, because of their frailty, do not understand their own concerns, whereas the gods have the privilege of understanding the affairs both of men and of themselves." "All your answers," said Apollonius, "are excellent, O Priest, and very true. Since then, they know everything, it appears to me that a person who comes to the house of God and has a good conscience, should put up the following prayer: 'O ye gods, grant unto me that which I deserve.' For," he went on, "the holy, O Priest, surely deserve to receive blessings, and the wicked the contrary. Therefore the gods, as they are beneficent, if they find anyone who is healthy and whole and unscarred by vice, will send him away, surely, after crowning him, not with golden crowns, but with all sorts of blessings; but if they find a man branded with sin and utterly corrupt, they will hand him over and leave him to justice, after inflicting their wrath upon him all the more, because he dared to invade their temples without being pure." And at the same moment he looked towards Asclepius, and said: "O Asclepius, the philosophy you teach is secret and congenial to yourself, in that you suffer not the wicked to come hither, not even if they pour into your lap all the wealth of India and Sardis. For it is not out of reverence for the divinity that they sacrifice these victims and kindle these fires, but in order to purchase a verdict, which you will not concede to them in your perfect justice." And much similar wisdom he delivered himself of in this temple, while he was still a youth.

[Apollonius Exorcises a Youth and Heals Several People] (from *Life of Apollonius*, book 3)[1]

38 This discussion was interrupted by the appearance among the sages[2] of the messenger bringing in certain Indians who were in want of succour. And he brought forward a poor woman who interceded in behalf of her child, who was, she said, a boy of sixteen years of age, but had been for two years possessed by a devil. Now the character of the devil was that of a mocker and a liar. Here one of the sages asked, why she said this, and she replied: "This child of mine is extremely good-looking, and therefore the devil is amorous of him and will not allow him to retain his reason, nor will he permit him to go to school, or to learn archery, nor even to remain at home, but drives him out into desert places. And the boy does not even retain his own voice, but speaks in a deep hollow tone, as

4. Cf. Luke 2:46–47, where the young Jesus discourses with the teachers in the temple.
1. This story recalls Mark 9:14–29.
2. Indian wise men, to whom Apollonius (also a "sage") has journeyed.

men do; and he looks at you with other eyes rather than with his own. As for myself I weep over all this, and I tear my cheeks, and I rebuke my son so far as I well may; but he does not know me. And I made up my mind to repair hither, indeed I planned to do so a year ago; only the demon discovered himself, using my child as a mask, and what he told me was this, that he was the ghost of a man, who fell long ago in battle, but that at death he was passionately attached to his wife. Now he had been dead for only three days when his wife insulted their union by marrying another man, and the consequence was that he had come to detest the love of women, and had transferred himself wholly into this boy. But he promised, if I would only not denounce him to yourselves, to endow the child with many noble blessings. As for myself, I was influenced by these promises; but he has put me off and off for such a long time now, that he has got sole control of my household, yet has no honest or true intentions." Here the sage asked afresh, if the boy was at hand; and she said not, for, although she had done all she could to get him to come with her, the demon had threatened her with steep places and precipices and declared that he would kill her son, "in case," she added, "I haled him hither for trial." "Take courage," said the sage, "for he will not slay him when he has read this." And so saying he drew a letter out of his bosom and gave it to the woman; and the letter, it appears, was addressed to the ghost and contained threats of an alarming kind.

39 There also arrived a man who was lame. He already thirty years old was a keen hunter of lions; but a lion had sprung upon him and dislocated his hip so that he limped with one leg. However when they massaged with their hands his hip, the youth immediately recovered his upright gait. And another man had had his eyes put out, and he went away having recovered the sight of both of them. Yet another man had his hand paralysed, but left their presence in full possession of the limb.[3] And a certain woman had suffered in labour already seven times, but was healed in the following way through the intercession of her husband. He bade the man, whenever his wife should be about to bring forth her next child, to enter her chamber carrying in his bosom a live hare; then he was to walk once round her and at the same moment to release the hare; for that the womb would be expelled together with the fœtus, unless the hare was at once driven out.

[Apollonius Exorcises Another Youth]
(from *Life of Apollonius*, book 4)][1]

20 Now while he was discussing the question of libations, there chanced to be present in his audience a young dandy who bore so evil a reputation for licentiousness, that his conduct had once been the subject of coarse street-corner songs. His home was Corcyra, and he traced his pedigree to Alcinous the Phaeacian who entertained Odysseus. Apollonius then was talking about libations, and

3. Cf. Mark 3:1–6; 8:22–26; 10:46–52.
1. This story recalls Mark 5:1–20.

was urging them not to drink out of a particular cup, but to reserve it for the gods, without ever touching it or drinking out of it. But when he also urged them to have handles on the cup, and to pour the libation over the handle, because that is the part of the cup at which men are least likely to drink, the youth burst out into loud and coarse laughter, and quite drowned his voice. Then Apollonius looked up at him and said: "It is not yourself that perpetrates this insult, but the demon, who drives you on without your knowing it." And in fact the youth was, without knowing it, possessed by a devil; for he would laugh at things that no one else laughed at, and then he would fall to weeping for no reason at all, and he would talk and sing to himself. Now most people thought that it was the boisterous humour of youth which led him into such excesses; but he was really the mouth-piece of a devil, though it only seemed a drunken frolic in which on that occasion he was indulging. Now when Apollonius gazed on him, the ghost in him began to utter cries of fear and rage, such as one hears from people who are being branded or racked; and the ghost swore that he would leave the young man alone and never take possession of any man again. But Apollonius addressed him with anger, as a master might a shifty, rascally, and shameless slave and so on, and he ordered him to quit the young man and show by a visible sign that he had done so. "I will throw down yonder statue," said the devil, and pointed to one of the images which was in the king's portico, for there it was that the scene took place. But when the statue began by moving gently, and then fell down, it would defy anyone to describe the hubbub which arose thereat and the way they clapped their hands with wonder. But the young man rubbed his eyes as if he had just woke up, and he looked towards the rays of the sun, and won the consideration of all who now had turned their attention to him; for he no longer showed himself licentious, nor did he stare madly about, but he had returned to his own self, as thoroughly as if he had been treated with drugs; and he gave up his dainty dress and summery garments and the rest of his sybaritic way of life, and he fell in love with the austerity of philosophers, and donned their cloak, and stripping off his old self modelled his life in future upon that of Apollonius.

[Apollonius Calls for the Purification of the Acropolis] (from *Life of Apollonius*, book 4)[1]

22 He also corrected the following abuse at Athens. The Athenians ran in crowds to the theatre beneath the Acropolis to witness human slaughter, and the passion for such sports was stronger there than it is in Corinth today; for they would buy for large sums adulterers and fornicators and burglars and cutpurses and kidnappers and such-like rabble, and then they took them and armed them and set them to fight with one another. Apollonius then attacked these practices, and when the Athenians invited him to attend their assembly, he refused to enter a place so impure and reeking with gore. And this he said in an epistle to them; he said that he was surprised "that the goddess had not already quitted the Acropolis,

1. This story recalls Jesus' cleansing of the temple (Mark 11:15–19).

when you shed such blood under her eyes. For I suspect that presently, when you are conducting the pan-Athenaic procession,[2] you will no longer be content with bulls, but will be sacrificing hecatombs of men to the goddess. And thou, O Dionysus, dost thou after such bloodshed frequent their theatre? And do the wise among the Athenians pour libations to thee there? Nay do thou depart, O Dionysus. Holier and purer is thy Cithaeron."[3]

Such were the more serious of the subjects which I have found he treated of at that time in Athens in his philosophic discourses.

[Apollonius Raises a Girl from the Dead]
(from *Life of Apollonius*, book 4)[1]

45 Here too is a miracle which Apollonius worked: A girl had died just in the hour of her marriage, and the bridegroom was following her bier lamenting as was natural his marriage left unfulfilled, and the whole of Rome was mourning with him, for the maiden belonged to a consular family.[2] Apollonius then witnessing their grief, said: "Put down the bier, for I will stay the tears that you are shedding for this maiden." And withal he asked what was her name. The crowd accordingly thought that he was about to deliver such an oration as is commonly delivered as much to grace the funeral as to stir up lamentation; but he did nothing of the kind, but merely touching her and whispering in secret some spell over her, at once woke up the maiden from her seeming death; and the girl spoke out loud, and returned to her father's house, just as Alcestis did when she was brought back to life by Hercules.[3] And the relations of the maiden wanted to present him with the sum of 150,000 sesterces, but he said that he would freely present the money to the young lady by way of a dowry. Now whether he detected some spark of life in her, which those who were nursing her had not noticed,—for it is said that although it was raining at the time, a vapour went up from her face—or whether life was really extinct, and he restored it by the warmth of his touch, is a mysterious problem which neither I myself nor those who were present could decide.

2. The Panathenaea, an annual festival held in Athens to celebrate its patron goddess Athena.

3. A mountain range in the northwest border of Attica, sacred to Dionysus, god of wine and revelry.

1. This story recalls Mark 5:35–43.

2. In the Roman Republic, the two consuls were the highest civil and military authorities; the consulship continued into the empire, though consuls' authority became largely symbolic.

3. The Greek hero rescued Alcestis from Hades after she willingly died to save her husband.

[Apollonius on Trial before Emperor Domitian]
(from *Life of Apollonius*, book 8)[1]

1 Let us now repair to the law-court to listen to the sage pleading his cause; for it is already sunrise and the doors are thrown open to admit the celebrities. And the companions of the Emperor say that he had taken no food that day, because, I imagine, he was so absorbed in examining the documents of the case. For they say he was holding in his hands a roll of writing of some sort, sometimes reading it with anger, and sometimes more calmly. And we must needs figure him as one who was angry with the law for having invented such things as courts of justice.

2 But Apollonius, as we meet him in this conjuncture seems to regard the trial as a dialectical discussion, rather than as a race to be run for his life; and this we may infer from the way he behaved before he entered the court. For on his way thither he asked the secretary who was conducting him, where they were going; and when the latter answered that he was leading him to the court, he said: "Whom am I going to plead against?" "Why," said the other, "against your accuser, of course, and the Emperor[2] will be judge." "And," said Apollonius, "who is going to be judge between myself and the Emperor? For I shall prove that he is wronging philosophy." "And what concern," said the other, "has the Emperor for philosophy, even if he does happen to do her wrong?" "Nay, but philosophy," said Apollonius, "is much concerned about the Emperor, that he should govern as he should." The secretary commended this sentiment, for indeed he was already favourably disposed to Apollonius, as he proved from the very beginning. "And how long will your pleading last by the water-clock's reckoning? For I must know this before the trial begins." "If," said Apollonius, "I am allowed to plead as long as the necessities of the suit require me to, the whole of the Tiber[3] might run through the meter before I should have done; but if I am only to answer all the questions put to me, then it depends on the cross-examiner how long I shall be making my answers." "You have cultivated," remarked the other, "contrary talents when you thus engage to talk about one and the same matter both with brevity and with prolixity." "They are not contrary talents," said Apollonius, "but resemble one another; for an expert in the one would never be far to seek in the other. And moreover there is a mean composed of the two, which I should not myself allege to be a third, but a first requisite of a pleader; and for my own part I am sure that silence constitutes a fourth excellence much required in a law-court." "Anyhow," said the other, "it will do you no good nor anyone else who stands in great peril." "And yet," said Apollonius, "it was of great service to Socrates of Athens, when he was prosecuted." "And what good did it do him," said the other, "seeing that

---

1. The account of Apollonius's trial is similar to the accounts of Jesus before Pontius Pilate in the NT gospels, insofar as all reveal the holy man's moral superiority and the Roman judge's hypocrisy (cf. esp. Matt 27:1–2, 11–26; John 18:28–19:16).
2. Domitian, Roman emperor 81–96 C.E.
3. The river on which Rome lies.

he died just because he would say nothing?" "He did not die," said Apollonius, "though the Athenians thought he did."

*   *   *

4 * * * The court was fitted up as if for an audience listening to a panegyrical discourse; and all the illustrious men of the city were present at the trial, because the Emperor was intent upon proving before as many people as possible that Apollonius was an accomplice of Nerva and his friends.[4] Apollonius, however, ignored the Emperor's presence so completely as not even to glance at him; and when his accuser upbraided him for want of respect, and bade him turn his eyes upon the god of all mankind, Apollonius raised his eyes to the ceiling, by way of giving a hint that he was looking up to Zeus, and that he regarded the recipient of such profane flattery as worse than he who administered it. Whereupon the accuser began to bellow and spoke somewhat as follows: "'Tis time, my sovereign, to apportion the water, for if you allow him to talk as long as he chooses, he will choke us. Moreover I have a roll here which contains the heads of the charges against him, and to these he must answer, so let him defend himself against them one by one."

5 The Emperor approved this plan of procedure and ordered Apollonius to make his defence according to the informer's advice; however, he dropped out other accusations, as not worth discussion, and confined himself to four questions which he thought were embarrassing and difficult to answer. "What induces you," he said, "Apollonius, to dress yourself differently from everybody else, and to wear this peculiar and singular garb?" "Because," said Apollonius, "the earth which feeds me also clothes me, and I do not like to bother the poor animals." The Emperor next asked the question: "Why is it that men call you a god?" "Because," answered Apollonius, "every man that is thought to be good, is honoured by the title of god." I have shown in my narrative of India how this tenet passed into our hero's philosophy.[5] The third question related to the plague in Ephesus; "What motived," he said, "or suggested your prediction to the Ephesians that they would suffer from a plague?"[6] "I used," he said, "O my sovereign, a lighter diet than others, and so I was the first to be sensible of the danger; and, if you like, I will enumerate the causes of pestilences." But the Emperor, fearful, I imagine, lest Apollonius should reckon among the causes of such epidemics his own wrong-doing, and his incestuous marriage,[7] and his other misdemeanours, replied: "Oh, I do not want any such answer as that." And when he came to the fourth question which related to Nerva and his friends, instead of hurrying straight on to it, he allowed a certain interval to elapse, and after long reflection, and with the air of one who felt dizzy, he put his question in a way which surprised them all; for they expected him to throw off all disguise and blurt out the names of the persons in question without any reserve, complaining loudly and

4. According to Philostratus, Domitian exiled Nerva, Orfitus, and Rufus for plotting against him (7.8), but his history may be confused.

5. See 3.18 (not included here).

6. See 4.4, 10 (not included here).

7. See 7.7 (not included here).

bitterly of the sacrifice;[8] but instead of putting the question in this way, he beat about the bush, and said: "Tell me, you went out of your house on a certain day, and you travelled into the country, and sacrificed the boy—I would like to know for whom?" And Apollonius as if he were rebuking a child replied: "Good words, I beseech you; for if I did leave my house, I was in the country; and if this was so, then I offered the sacrifice: and if I offered it, then I ate of it. But let these assertions be proved by trustworthy witnesses." Such a reply on the part of the sage aroused louder applause than beseemed the court of an Emperor; and the latter deeming the audience to have borne witness in favour of the accused, and also not a little impressed himself by the answers he had received, for they were both firm and sensible, said: "I acquit you of the charges; but you must remain here until we have had a private interview." Thereat Apollonius was much encouraged and said: "I thank you indeed, my sovereign, but I would fain tell you that by reason of these miscreants your cities are in ruin, and the islands full of exiles, and the mainland of lamentations, and your armies of cowardice, and the senate of suspicion. Accord me also, if you will, opportunity to speak; but if not, then send some one to take my body, for my soul you cannot take. Nay, you cannot take even my body,

"For thou shalt not slay me, since I tell thee I am not mortal." [*Iliad* 22.13]

And with these words he vanished from the court, which was the best thing he could do under the circumstances, for the Emperor clearly intended not to question him sincerely about the case, but about all sorts of irrelevant matters. For he took great credit to himself for not having put Apollonius to death, nor was the latter anxious to be drawn into such discussions. And he thought that he would best effect his end if he left no one in ignorance of his true nature, but allowed it to be known to all to be such that he had it in him never to be taken prisoner against his own will. * * *

* * *

8 * * * But the effect upon the despot of his quitting the court in a manner so godlike and inexplicable was quite other than that which the many expected; for they expected him to make a terrific uproar and institute a hunt for the man, and to send forth proclamations over his empire to arrest him wherever they should find him. But he did nothing of the kind, as if he set himself to defeat men's expectations; or because he now at last realised that as against the sage he had no resources of his own. But whether he acted from contempt, let us conjecture from what ensued, for he will be seen to have been confounded with astonishment rather than filled with contempt.

9 For he had to hear another case after that of Apollonius, an action brought, I think, in connexion with a will by some city against a private individual; and he had forgotten not only the names of the parties, but also the matter at issue in the suit; for his questions were without meaning and his answers were not even relevant to the cause,—all which argued the degree of astonishment and perplex-

8. Apollonius had been accused of sacrificing a boy and performing an extispicium for the conspirators (7.11).

ity under which the despot laboured, the more so because his flatterers had persuaded him that nothing could escape his memory.

[Apollonius Rejoins His Friends after His Miraculous Escape] (from *Life of Apollonius*, book 8)[1]

10 Such was the condition to which Apollonius reduced the despot, making him
a plaything of his philosophy who had been the terror of Hellenes and barbarians; and before midday he left the court, and at dusk appeared to Demetrius and
Damis at Dicaearchia. And this accounts for his having instructed Damis to go
by land to Dicaearchia, without waiting to hear his defence. For he had given no
previous notice of his intentions, but had merely told the man who was mostly in
his intimacy to do what best accorded with his plans.

   11 Now Damis had arrived the day before and had talked with Demetrius about
the preliminaries of the trial; and the account filled the latter, when he listened to
it, with more apprehension than you might expect of a listener when Apollonius was
in question. The next day also he asked him afresh about the same particulars, as he
wandered with him along the edge of the sea, which figures in the fables told about
Calypso;[2] for they were almost in despair of their master coming to them, because
the tyrant's hand was hard upon all; yet out of respect for Apollonius' character they
obeyed his instructions. Discouraged, then, they sat down in the chamber of the
nymphs, where there is the cistern of white marble, which contains a spring of
water which neither overflows its edges, nor recedes, even if water be drawn from it.
They were talking about the quality of the water in no very serious manner; and
presently, owing to the anxiety they felt about the sage, brought back their conversation to the circumstances which preceded the trial.

   12 Damis' grief had just broken out afresh, and he had made some such
exclamation as the following: "Shall we ever behold, O ye gods, our noble and
good companion?" when Apollonius, who had heard him,—for as a matter of
fact he was already present in the chamber of the nymphs,—answered: "Ye shall
see him, nay, ye have already seen him." "Alive?" said Demetrius, "For if you
are dead, we have anyhow never ceased to lament you." Where upon Apollonius
stretched out his hand and said: "Take hold of me, and if I evade you, then I am
indeed a ghost come to you from the realm of Persephone,[3] such as the gods of
the under-world reveal to those who are dejected with much mourning. But if I
resist your touch, then you shall persuade Damis also that I am both alive and
that I have not abandoned my body." They were no longer able to disbelieve, but
rose up and threw themselves on his neck and kissed him, and asked him about
his defence. For while Demetrius was of opinion that he had not even made his
defence,—for he expected him to be destroyed without any wrong being proved

---

   1. Cf. Luke 24:13–49 (esp. vv. 38–39); John 20:24–29.
   2. The nymph Calypso entertained Odysseus on the mythical island of Ogygia (*Odyssey*
7.240–66, etc.), often placed by ancient authorities in the Ionian sea. Philostratus seems to
imagine the island lying to Italy's west, off the shore of Campania.
   3. The underworld; Persephone was the wife of Hades, lord of the dead.

against him,—Damis thought that he had made his defence, but perhaps more quickly than was expected; for he never dreamed that he had made it only that day. But Apollonius said: "I have made my defence, gentlemen, and have gained my cause; and my defence took place this very day not so long ago, for it lasted on even to midday." "How then," said Demetrius, "have you accomplished so long a journey in so small a fraction of the day?" And Apollonius replied: "Imagine what you will, flying goat or wings of wax excepted,[4] so long as you ascribe it to the intervention of a divine escort."

"Well," said Demetrius, "I have always thought that your actions and words were providentially cared for by some god, to whom you owe your present preservation, nevertheless pray tell us about the defence you made, what it consisted of and what the accusation had to say against you, and about the temper of the judge, and what questions he put, and what he allowed to pass of your pleas and what not." * * * "You shall learn everything, but not in this place; for it is already growing late in the evening, and it is time for us to proceed to the town; and it is pleasant too to talk as you go along the road, for conversation assists you on your way like an escort. Let us then start and discuss your questions as we go along, and I will certainly tell you of to-day's events in the court. For you both of you know the circumstances which preceded the trial, the one of you because he was present, and the other because I am sure, by Zeus, he has not heard it once only, but again and again, if I know you well, my Demetrius. But I will relate to you what you do not know as yet, beginning with my being summoned into the Emperor's presence, into which I was ushered naked." And he proceeded to detail to them his own words, and above all at the end of them the citation: "For thou shalt not kill me," and he told them exactly how he vanished from the seat of judgment.

[Apollonius's Death, Ascension, and Continuing Appearances]
(from *Life of Apollonius*, book 8)

29 The memoirs then of Apollonius of Tyana which Damis the Assyrian composed, end with the above story; for with regard to the manner in which he died, if he did actually die, there are many stories, though Damis has repeated none. But as for myself I ought not to omit even this, for my story should, I think, have its natural ending. Neither has Damis told us anything about the age of our hero; but there are some who say that he was eighty, others that he was over ninety, others again who say that his age far exceeded a hundred. He was fresh in all his body and upright, when he died, and more agreeable to look at than in his youth. For there is a certain beauty even in wrinkles, which was especially conspicuous in his case, as is clear from the likenesses of him which are preserved in the

---

4. An allusion to two famous mythological escapes: when Phrixus was to be sacrificed, he and his sister Helle rode away through the air (or the sea) on the ram with the golden fleece; and when the craftsman Daedalus was held against his will on Crete, he devised wings of wax and feathers so that he and his son Icarus could fly away.

temple at Tyana, and from accounts which praise the old age of Apollonius more than was once praised the youth of Alcibiades.[1]

30 Now there are some who relate that he died in Ephesus, tended by two maid servants; for the freedmen of whom I spoke at the beginning of my story were already dead. One of these maids he emancipated, and was blamed by the other one for not conferring the same privilege upon her, but Apollonius told her that it was better for her to remain the other's slave, for that that would be the beginning of her well-being. Accordingly after his death this one continued to be the slave of the other, who for some insignificant reason sold her to a merchant, from whom she was purchased. Her new master, although she was not good-looking, nevertheless fell in love with her; and being a fairly rich man, made her his legal wife and had legitimate children by her.

Others again say that he died in Lindus, where he entered the temple of Athena and disappeared within it. Others again say that he died in Crete in a much more remarkable manner than the people of Lindus relate. For they say that he continued to live in Crete, where he became a greater centre of admiration than ever before, and that he came to the temple of Dictynna late at night. Now this temple is guarded by dogs, whose duty it is to watch over the wealth deposited in it, and the Cretans claim that they are as good as bears or any other animals equally fierce. None the less, when he came, instead of barking, they approached him and fawned upon him, as they would not have done even with people they knew familiarly. The guardians of the shrine arrested him in consequence, and threw him in bonds as a wizard and a robber, accusing him of having thrown to the dogs some charmed morsel. But about midnight he loosened his bonds, and after calling those who had bound him, in order that they might witness the spectacle, he ran to the doors of the temple, which opened wide to receive him;[2] and when he had passed within they closed afresh, as if they had been shut, and there was heard a chorus of maidens singing from within the temple, and their song was this. "Hasten thou from earth, hasten thou to Heaven, hasten." In other words: "Do thou go upwards from earth."[3]

31 And even after his death he continued to preach that the soul is immortal; but although he taught this account of it to be correct, yet he discouraged men from meddling in such high subjects. For there came to Tyana a youth who did not shrink from acrimonious discussions, and would not accept truth in argument.[4] Now Apollonius had already passed away from among men, but people still wondered at his passing, and no one ventured to dispute that he was immortal. This being so, the discussions were mainly about the soul, for a band of youths were there passionately addicted to wisdom. The young man in question, however, would on no account allow the tenet of the immortality of the soul, and said: "I myself, gentlemen, have done nothing now for over nine months but pray to Apollonius that he would reveal to me the truth about the soul; but he is so utterly dead that he will not appear to me in response to my entreaties, nor give me any reason

1. Athenian statesman (ca. 451/50–404/03 B.C.E), famous for his beauty, among other things.
2. Compare Peter's (Acts 12:3–19) and Paul's (Acts 16:22–34) miraculous liberations from prison.
3. Compare Jesus' ascension to heaven (Luke 24:50–51; Acts 1:6–11).
4. Compare Thomas's resistance to belief in Jesus' resurrection (John 20:24–29).

to consider him immortal." Such were the young man's words on that occasion, but on the fifth day following, after discussing the same subject, he fell asleep where he was talking with them, and of the young men who were studying with him, some were reading books, and others were industriously drawing geometrical figures on the ground, when on a sudden, like one possessed, he leapt up from an uneasy sleep, streaming with perspiration, and cried out: "I believe thee." And, when those who were present asked him what was the matter; "Do you not see," said he, "Apollonius the sage, how that he is present with us and is listening to our discussion, and is reciting wondrous verses about the soul?" "But where is he?" they asked, "For we cannot see him anywhere, although we would rather do so than possess all the blessings of mankind." And the youth replied: "It would seem that he is come to converse with myself alone concerning the tenets which I would not believe. Listen therefore to the inspired argument which he is delivering:

> "The soul is immortal, and 'tis no possession of thine own,
> But of Providence,
> "And after the body is wasted away,
> Like a swift horse freed from its traces,
> "It lightly leaps forward and mingles itself with the light air,
> "Loathing the spell of harsh and painful servitude which it has endured.
> "But for thee, what use is there in this? Some day when thou art no more
> Thou shalt believe it.
> "So why, as long as thou art among living beings,
> Dost thou explore these mysteries?"

Here we have a clear utterance of Apollonius, established like an oracular tripod, to convince us of the mysteries of the soul, to the end that cheerfully, and with due knowledge of our own true nature, we may pursue our way to the goal appointed by the Fates. With any tomb, however, or cenotaph of the sage I never met, that I know of, although I have traversed most of the earth, and have listened everywhere to stories of his divine quality.[5] And his shrine at Tyana is singled out and honoured with royal officers: for neither have the Emperors denied to him the honours of which they themselves were held worthy.

---

5. Compare Jesus' empty tomb and the frequent reports of his postmortem appearances (e.g., Matt 28:5–10, 16–20).

EARLY DEVELOPMENTS

PAPIAS

Only a handful of fragments survive from *Expositions of the Sayings of the Lord* by Papias (ca. 60–ca. 130 C.E.). Quoted in the fourth century by Eusebius, they give evidence of very early Christian attitudes toward apostolic authority, offer important information about Revelation and its ancient interpretation, and contain the earliest extant statements—surprisingly defensive—about the Gospels. Papias admits to preferring "information from a living . . . voice" to books, but he nonetheless goes on to defend the Gospel of Mark against the charge that it lacks clear order. While his statement about Matthew is more difficult to explain, it seems plausible that some people claimed that it too seemed confused and that Papias attributes its supposed incoherence to incompetent translation from a Semetic original. Alternatively, or complementarily, Papias may want to account for why what looked like different versions of Matthew circulated in his day (one of which might have been the *Gospel according to the Hebrews*, which Eusebius mentions just after quoting Papias).

The surviving fragments from Papias's book raise a number of questions. Is Papias referring to the gospels we know today as Matthew and Mark, or to different versions of these works? (He himself assumes that numerous versions of Matthew circulated.) Is he passing on genuine traditions about them, or merely inferring from their contents compositional origins that would ensure apostolic authority despite their apparent lack of order, their disagreement with one another or with John (which there is some evidence Papias knew), and their textual discrepancies? If Papias does relate a genuine tradition—perhaps one he learned from an authoritative elder—is this tradition historically accurate? This final question is especially pressing because New Testament Matthew gives no evidence of having been translated from a Semitic language. More fundamentally, the fragments' translation is itself contested at key points, so that it is sometimes difficult to discern exactly what Papias is claiming, let alone why and on what grounds he claims it. Despite the light they shine on early Christian attitudes toward the Gospels, the fragments from Papias are important not so much because they solve problems related to the Gospels' origins and authority as because they reveal that Christians have been wrestling with these problems from the very beginning.

[The Origins of the Gospels]†

FRAGMENT 3[1] (HOLMES)

1 Five books of Papias are in circulation, which are titled *Expositions of the Sayings of the Lord*. Irenaeus also mentions these as the only works written by him, saying something like this:

† From "Fragments of Papias," in *The Apostolic Fathers*, ed. and trans. Michael W. Holmes, 3rd ed. (Grand Rapids, MI: Baker Academic, 2007), 732–41.

1. SOURCE: Eusebius, *Church History* 3.39. TEXT: G. Bardy, *Eusèbe de Césarée: Histoire ecclésiastique*, vol. 1, *Livres I–IV*, SC 31 (Paris: Cerf, 1952), 153–57 [translator's note].

"Papias, a man of the early period, who was a hearer of John and a companion of Polycarp, bears witness to these things in writing in the fourth of his books. For there are five books composed by him."

2 So says Irenaeus. Yet Papias himself, in the preface to his discourses, indicates that he was by no means a hearer or eyewitness of the holy apostles, but shows by the language he uses that he received the matters of the faith from those who had known them:

3 "I will not hesitate to set down for you, along with my interpretations, everything I carefully learned then from the elders and carefully remembered, guaranteeing their truth. For unlike most people I did not enjoy those who have a great deal to say, but those who teach the truth. Nor did I enjoy those who recall someone else's commandments, but those who remember the commandments given by the Lord to the faith and proceeding from the truth itself. 4 And if by chance someone who had been a follower of the elders should come my way, I inquired about the words of the elders—what Andrew or Peter said, or Philip or Thomas or James or John or Matthew or any other of the Lord's disciples, and whatever Aristion and the elder John, the Lord's disciples, were saying. For I did not think that information from books would profit me as much as information from a living and abiding voice."

5 Here it is worth noting that he lists twice the name of John. The first he mentions in connection with Peter and James and Matthew and the rest of the apostles, clearly meaning the Evangelist, but he classes the other John with others outside the number of the apostles by changing the wording and putting Aristion before him, and he distinctly calls him "elder." 6 Moreover, by these remarks he confirms the truth of the story told by those who have said that there were two men in Asia who had the same name, and that there are two tombs in Ephesus, each of which even today is said to be John's. It is important to notice this, for it is probably the second, unless one prefers the first, who saw the Revelation that circulates under the name of John. 7 And Papias, of whom we are now speaking, acknowledges that he had received the words of the apostles from those who had followed them, but he says that he was himself a hearer of Aristion and John the Elder. In any event he frequently mentions them by name and includes their traditions in his writings as well. Let these statements of ours not be wasted on the reader.

8 It is worthwhile to add to the statements of Papias given above some other sayings of his, in which he records some other remarkable things as well, which came down to him, as it were, from tradition. 9 That Philip the apostle resided in Hierapolis with his daughters has already been stated,[2] but now it must be pointed out that Papias, their contemporary, recalls that he heard an amazing story from Philip's daughters. For he reports that in his day a man rose from the dead, and again another amazing story involving Justus, who was surnamed Barsabbas: he drank a deadly poison and yet by the grace of the Lord suffered nothing unpleasant. 10 The book of Acts records that after the ascension of the Savior the holy apostles put forward this Justus with Matthias and prayed for the choice by lot to fill out their number in place of the traitor Judas; the passage

2. Cf. Eusebius, *Church History* 3.31.3 [translator's note].

runs as follows: "And they put forward two, Joseph, called Barsabbas, who was surnamed Justus, and Matthias; and they prayed and said . . ." [Acts 1:23–24]. **11** The same writer has recorded other accounts as having come to him from unwritten tradition, certain strange parables of the Lord and teachings of his and some other statements of a more mythical character. **12** Among other things he says that after the resurrection of the dead there will be a period of a thousand years when the kingdom of Christ will be set up in material form on this earth.[3] These ideas, I suppose, he got through a misunderstanding of the apostolic accounts, not realizing that the things recorded in figurative language were spoken by them mystically. **13** For he certainly appears to be a man of very little intelligence, as one may say judging from his own words. Yet he was the reason that so many ecclesiastical writers after him held the same opinion, on the grounds that he was a man of the early period—like Irenaeus, for example, and anyone else who has expressed similar ideas.

14 In his writing he also passes along other accounts of the sayings of the Lord belonging to Aristion, who has been mentioned above, and the traditions of John the Elder, to which we refer those interested. For our present purpose we must add to his statements already quoted above a tradition concerning Mark, who wrote the Gospel, that has been set forth in these words:

15 "And the elder used to say this: 'Mark, having become Peter's interpreter, wrote down accurately everything he remembered, though not in order, of the things either said or done by Christ. For he neither heard the Lord nor followed him, but afterward, as I said, followed Peter, who adapted his teachings as needed[4] but had no intention of giving an ordered account of the Lord's sayings. Consequently Mark did nothing wrong in writing down some things as he remembered them, for he made it his one concern not to omit anything that he heard or to make any false statement in them.'"

Such, then, is the account given by Papias with respect to Mark. **16** But with respect to Matthew the following is said:

"So Matthew composed the oracles[5] in the Hebrew language and each person interpreted them as best he could."

17 The same writer utilized testimonies from the first letter of John and, likewise, from that of Peter. And he has related another account about a woman accused of many sins before the Lord, which the *Gospel according to the Hebrews* contains.[6] And these things we must take into account, in addition to what has already been stated.

---

3. Cf. Rev 20:1–7. Eusebius tentatively attributes Revelation to John the Elder, from whom Papias learned (see §§4 and 6 above).

4. "As needed" (Gk. *pros tas chreias*) is alternatively rendered "in the form of useful anecdotes."

5. "Composed the oracles" (Gk. *ta logia synetaxato*) is alternatively rendered "put the sayings in an ordered arrangement," translating a Greek verb that shares a root with "order/ordered account" (*taxis/syntaxis*) in the previous section.

6. This account must be a version of the story included at John 8:1–11 (see note).

THE ACTS OF PAUL AND THECLA[†]

In the late second or early third century C.E. Tertullian disparaged The *Acts of Paul and Thecla* as a forgery and, referring to 1 Corinthians 14:34–35, condemned its apparent authorization of women's teaching and baptizing (*On Baptism* 17). His brief discussion suggests that this work and the legendary accounts it contains circulated rather early in Christian history and that their ideological implications were evident from the start. The Pastoral Epistles (1 and 2 Timothy and Titus), which may themselves be post-Pauline pseudepigraphic compositions, perhaps contended with The *Acts of Paul and Thecla* (or with the traditions it employs) by offering a more conservative interpretation of the apostle's legacy that emphasized the feminine domesticity which Thecla here rejects.

---

1 As Paul was going up to Iconium after the flight from Antioch, his fellow-travellers were Demas and Ermogenes,[1] full of hypocrisy; and they were importunate with Paul, as if they loved him. But Paul, looking only to the goodness of Christ, did them no harm, but loved them exceedingly, so that he made the oracles of the Lord sweet to them in the teaching both of the birth and the resurrection of the Beloved; and he gave them an account, word for word, of the great things of Christ, how He had been revealed to him.

2 And a certain man, by name Onesiphorus,[2] hearing that Paul had come to Iconium, went out to meet him with his children Silas and Zeno, and his wife Lectra, in order that he might entertain him: for Titus had informed him what Paul was like in appearance: for he had not seen him in the flesh, but only in the spirit. **3** And he went along the road to Lystra, and stood waiting for him, and kept looking at the passersby according to the description of Titus. And he saw Paul coming, a man small in size, bald-headed, bandy-legged, well-built, with eyebrows meeting, rather long-nosed, full of grace. For sometimes he seemed like a man, and sometimes he had the countenance of an angel. **4** And Paul, seeing Onesiphorus, smiled; and Onesiphorus said: Hail, O servant of the blessed God! And he said: Grace be with thee and thy house. And Demas and Ermogenes were jealous, and showed greater hypocrisy; so that Demas said: Are not we of the blessed God, that thou hast not thus saluted us? And Onesiphorus said: I do not see in you the fruit of righteousness; but if such you be, come you also into my house and rest yourselves.

5 And Paul having gone into the house of Onesiphorus, there was great joy, and bending of knees, and breaking of bread, and the word of God about self-control and the resurrection; Paul saying: Blessed are the pure in heart, for they shall see God [Matt 5:8]: blessed are they that have kept the flesh chaste, for they

---

† From *Acts of Paul and Thecla*, trans. Alexander Walker, in *The Ante-Nicene Fathers*, vol. 8 (1885; reprint, Peabody, MA: Hendrickson, 1994), 487–91.

1. For Demas, cf. Col 4:14; 2 Tim 4:10; Phlm 24; for Hermogenes, cf. 2 Tim 1:15.

2. For Onesiphorus, cf. 2 Tim 1:16–18; 4:19.

shall become a temple of God [1 Cor 6:18–19]: blessed are they that control themselves, for God shall speak with them: blessed are they that have kept aloof from this world, for they shall be called upright: blessed are they that have wives as not having them, for they shall receive God for their portion [1 Cor 7:29]: blessed are they that have the fear of God, for they shall become angels of God: **6** blessed are they that have kept the baptism, for they shall rest beside the Father and the Son: blessed are the merciful, for they shall obtain mercy [Matt 5:7], and shall not see the bitter day of judgment: blessed are the bodies of the virgins, for they shall be well pleasing to God, and shall not lose the reward of their chastity; for the word of the Father shall become to them a work of salvation against the day of His Son, and they shall have rest for ever and ever.[3]

7 And while Paul was thus speaking in the midst of the church in the house of Onesiphorus, a certain virgin Thecla, the daughter of Theocleia, betrothed to a man named Thamyris, sitting at the window close by, listened night and day to the discourse of virginity and prayer, and did not look away from the window, but paid earnest heed to the faith, rejoicing exceedingly. And when she still saw many women going in beside Paul, she also had an eager desire to be deemed worthy to stand in the presence of Paul, and to hear the word of Christ; for never had she seen his figure, but heard his word only.

8 And as she did not stand away from the window, her mother sends to Thamyris; and he comes gladly, as if already receiving her in marriage. And Theocleia said: I have a strange story to tell thee, Thamyris; for assuredly for three days and three nights Thecla does not rise from the window, neither to eat nor to drink; but looking earnestly as if upon some pleasant sight, she is so devoted to a foreigner teaching deceitful and artful discourses, that I wonder how a virgin of such modesty is so painfully put about. **9** Thamyris, this man will overturn the city of the Iconians, and thy Thecla too besides; for all the women and the young men go in beside him, being taught to fear God and to live in chastity. Moreover also my daughter, tied to the window like a spider, lays hold of what is said by Paul with a strange eagerness and awful emotion; for the virgin looks eagerly at what is said by him, and has been captivated. But do thou go near and speak to her, for she has been betrothed to thee.

10 And Thamyris going near, and kissing her, but at the same time also being afraid of her overpowering emotion, said: Thecla, my betrothed, why dost thou sit thus? and what sort of feeling holds thee overpowered? Turn round to thy Thamyris, and be ashamed. Moreover also her mother said the same things: Why dost thou sit thus looking down, my child, and answering nothing, but like a mad woman? And they wept fearfully, Thamyris indeed for the loss of a wife, and Theocleia of a child, and the maid-servants of a mistress: there was accordingly much confusion in the house of mourning.[4] And while these things were thus going on, Thecla did not turn round, but kept attending earnestly to the word of Paul.

3. Some MSS. add the following beatitudes: Blessed are they that tremble at the words of God, for they shall be comforted: blessed are they that have received the wisdom of Jesus Christ, for they shall be called the sons of the Most High: blessed are they that through love of Christ have come out from conformity with the world, for they shall judge the angels, and shall be blessed at the right hand of the Father [translator's note].

4. Or, a great outpouring of lamentation in the house [translator's note].

11 And Thamyris starting up, went forth into the street, and kept watching those going in to him and coming out. And he saw two men bitterly contending with each other; and he said: Men, tell me who this is among you, leading astray the souls of young men, and deceiving virgins, so that they do not marry, but remain as they are. I promise, therefore, to give you money enough if you tell me about him; for I am the first man of the city. **12** And Demas and Ermogenes said to him: Who this is, indeed, we do not know; but he deprives young men of wives, and maidens of husbands, saying, There is for you a resurrection in no other way, unless you remain chaste, and pullute not the flesh, but keep it chaste. **13** And Thamyris said to them: Come into my house, and rest yourselves. And they went to a sumptuous dinner, and much wine, and great wealth, and a splendid table; and Thamyris made them drink, from his love to Thecla, and his wish to get her as his wife. And Thamyris said during the dinner: Ye men, what is his teaching, tell me, that I also may know; for I am no little distressed about Thecla, because she thus loves the stranger, and I am prevented from marrying.

14 Demas and Ermogenes said: Bring him before the governor Castelios on the charge of persuading the multitudes to embrace the new teaching of the Christians, and he will speedily destroy him, and thou shalt have Thecla as thy wife. And we shall teach thee that the resurrection of which this man speaks has taken place, because it has already taken place in the children which we have;[5] and we rose again when we came to the knowledge of the true God.

15 And Thamyris, hearing these things, being filled with anger and rage, rising up early, went to the house of Onesiphorus with archons and public officers, and a great crowd with batons, saying: Thou hast corrupted the city of the Iconians, and her that was betrothed to me, so that she will not have me: let us go to the governor Castelios. And all the multitude said: Away with the magician; for he has corrupted all our wives, and the multitudes have been persuaded to change their opinions.

16 And Thamyris, standing before the tribunal, said with a great shout: O proconsul, this man, who he is we know not, who makes virgins averse to marriage; let him say before thee on what account he teaches these things. And Demas and Ermogenes said to Thamyris: Say that he is a Christian, and thus thou wilt do away with him. But the proconsul stayed his intention, and called Paul, saying: Who art thou, and what dost thou teach? for they bring no small charges against thee. **17** And Paul lifted up his voice, saying: Since I am this day examined as to what I teach, listen, O proconsul: A living God, a God of retributions, a jealous God, a God in need of nothing, consulting for the salvation of men, has sent me that I may reclaim them from corruption and uncleanness, and from all pleasure, and from death, that they may not sin. Wherefore God sent His own Son, whom I preach, and in whom I teach men to rest their hope, who alone has had compassion upon a world led astray, that they may be no longer under judgment, O proconsul, but may have faith, and the fear of God, and the knowledge of holiness, and the love of truth. If, therefore, I teach what has been revealed to me by God, wherein do I do wrong? And the proconsul having heard, ordered Paul to be bound, and sent to prison, until, said he, I, being at leisure, shall hear him more attentively.

5. I.e., we rise again in our children [translator's note; cf. 2 Tim 2:18].

18 And Thecla by night having taken off her bracelets, gave them to the gate-keeper; and the door having been opened to her, she went into the prison; and having given the jailor a silver mirror, she went in beside Paul, and, sitting at his feet, she heard the great things of God. And Paul was afraid of nothing, but ordered his life in the confidence of God. And her faith also was increased, and she kissed his bonds.

19 And when Thecla was sought for by her friends, and Thamyris, as if she had been lost, was running up and down the streets, one of the gatekeeper's fellow-slaves informed him that she had gone out by night. And having gone out, they examined the gatekeeper; and he said to them: She has gone to the foreigner into the prison. And having gone, they found her, as it were, enchained by affection. And having gone forth thence, they drew the multitudes together, and informed the governor of the circumstance. **20** And he ordered Paul to be brought to the tribunal; but Thecla was wallowing on the ground in the place where he sat and taught her in the prison; and he ordered her too to be brought to the tribunal. And she came, exulting with joy. And the crowd, when Paul had been brought, vehemently cried out: He is a magician! away with him! But the proconsul gladly heard Paul upon the holy works of Christ. And having called a council, he summoned Thecla, and said to her: Why dost thou not obey Thamyris, according to the law of the Iconians? But she stood looking earnestly at Paul. And when she gave no answer, her mother cried out, saying: Burn the wicked wretch; burn in the midst of the theatre her that will not marry, in order that all the women that have been taught by this man may be afraid.

21 And the governor was greatly moved; and having scourged Paul, he cast him out of the city, and condemned Thecla to be burned. And immediately the governor went away to the theatre, and all the crowd went forth to the spectacle of Thecla. But as a lamb in the wilderness looks round for the shepherd, so she kept searching for Paul. And having looked upon the crowd, she saw the Lord sitting in the likeness of Paul, and said: As I am unable to endure my lot, Paul has come to see me. And she gazed upon him with great earnestness, and he went up into heaven. **22** But the maid-servants and virgins brought the faggots, in order that Thecla might be burned. And when she came in naked, the governor wept, and wondered at the power that was in her. And the public executioners arranged the faggots for her to go up on the pile. And she, having made the sign of the cross, went up on the faggots; and they lighted them. And though a great fire was blazing, it did not touch her; for God, having compassion upon her, made an underground rumbling, and a cloud overshadowed them from above, full of water and hail; and all that was in the cavity of it was poured out, so that many were in danger of death. And the fire was put out, and Thecla saved.

23 And Paul was fasting with Onesiphorus and his wife, and his children, in a new tomb, as they were going from Iconium to Daphne. And when many days were past, the fasting children said to Paul: We are hungry, and we cannot buy loaves; for Onesiphorus had left the things of the world, and followed Paul, with all his house. And Paul, having taken off his cloak, said: Go, my child, buy more loaves, and bring them. And when the child was buying, he saw Thecla their neighbour, and was astonished, and said: Thecla, whither art thou going? And she said: I have been saved from the fire, and am following Paul. And the boy said:

Come, I shall take thee to him; for he is distressed about thee, and is praying six days. **24** And she stood beside the tomb where Paul was with bended knees, and praying, and saying: O Saviour Christ, let not the fire touch Thecla, but stand by her, for she is Thine. And she, standing behind him, cried out: O Father, who hast made the heaven and the earth, the Father of Thy holy Son, I bless Thee that Thou hast saved me that I may see Paul. And Paul, rising up, saw her, and said: O God, that knowest the heart, the Father of our Lord Jesus Christ, I bless Thee that Thou, having heard me, hast done quickly what I wished.

25 And they had five loaves, and herbs, and water; and they rejoiced in the holy works of Christ. And Thecla said to Paul: I shall cut my hair, and follow thee whithersoever thou mayst go. And he said: It is a shameless age, and thou art beautiful. I am afraid lest another temptation come upon thee worse than the first, and that thou withstand it not, but be cowardly. And Thecla said: Only give me the seal in Christ [2 Cor 1:22; Eph 1:13; 4:30], and temptation shall not touch me. And Paul said: Thecla, wait with patience, and thou shalt receive the water.

26 And Paul sent away Onesiphorus and all his house to Iconium; and thus, having taken Thecla, he went into Antioch. And as they were going in, a certain Syriarch, Alexander by name,[6] seeing Thecla, became enamoured of her, and tried to gain over Paul by gifts and presents. But Paul said: I know not the woman whom thou speakest of, nor is she mine. But he, being of great power, himself embraced her in the street. But she would not endure it, but looked about for Paul. And she cried out bitterly, saying: Do not force the stranger; do not force the servant of God. I am one of the chief persons of the Iconians; and because I would not have Thamyris, I have been cast out of the city. And taking hold of Alexander, she tore his cloak, and pulled off his crown, and made him a laughing-stock. **27** And he, at the same time loving her, and at the same time ashamed of what had happened, led her before the governor; and when she had confessed that she had done these things, he condemned her to the wild beasts. And the women were struck with astonishment, and cried out beside the tribunal: Evil judgment! impious judgment! And she asked the governor, that, said she, I may remain pure until I shall fight with the wild beasts. And a certain Tryphæna, whose daughter was dead, took her into keeping, and had her for a consolation.

28 And when the beasts were exhibited, they bound her to a fierce lioness; and Tryphæna accompanied her. But the lioness, with Thecla sitting upon her, licked her feet; and all the multitude was astonished. And the charge on her inscription was: Sacrilegious. And the women cried out from above: An impious sentence has been passed in this city! And after the exhibition, Tryphæna again receives her. For her daughter Falconilla had died, and said to her in a dream: Mother, thou shalt have this stranger Thecla in my place, in order that she may pray concerning me, and that I may be transferred to the place of the just.

29 And when, after the exhibition, Tryphæna received her, at the same time indeed she grieved that she had to fight with the wild beasts on the day following; and at the same time, loving her as much as her daughter Falconilla, she said: My second child Thecla, come and pray for my child, that she may live for ever; for

6. Cf. 1 Tim 1:19–20; 2 Tim 4:14–15.

this I saw in my sleep. And she, nothing hesitating, lifted up her voice, and said: God most high, grant to this woman according to her wish, that her daughter Falconilla may live for ever. And when Thecla had thus spoken, Tryphæna lamented, considering so much beauty thrown to the wild beasts.

30 And when it was dawn, Alexander came to take her, for it was he that gave the hunt,[7] saying: The governor is sitting, and the crowd is in uproar against us. Allow me to take away her that is to fight with the wild beasts. And Tryphæna cried aloud, so that he even fled, saying: A second mourning for my Falconilla has come upon my house, and there is no one to help; neither child, for she is dead, nor kinsman, for I am a widow. God of Thecla, help her!

31 And immediately the governor sends an order that Thecla should be brought. And Tryphæna, taking her by the hand, said: My daughter Falconilla, indeed, I took away to the tomb; and thee, Thecla, I am taking to the wild-beast fight. And Thecla wept bitterly, saying: O Lord, the God in whom I believe, to whom I have fled for refuge, who deliveredst me from the fire, do Thou grant a recompense to Tryphæna, who has had compassion on Thy servant, and because she has kept me pure. **32** Then a tumult arose, and a cry of the people, and the women sitting together, the one saying: Away with the sacrilegious person! the others saying: Let the city be raised against this wickedness. Take off all of us, O proconsul! Cruel sight! evil sentence!

33 And Thecla, having been taken out of the hand of Tryphæna, was stripped, and received a girdle, and was thrown into the arena, and lions and bears and a fierce lioness were let loose upon her; and the lioness having run up to her feet, lay down; and the multitude of the women cried aloud. And a bear ran upon her; but the lioness, meeting the bear, tore her to pieces. And again a lion that had been trained against men, which belonged to Alexander, ran upon her; and she, the lioness, encountering the lion, was killed along with him. And the women made great lamentation, since also the lioness, her protector, was dead.

34 Then they send in many wild beasts, she standing and stretching forth her hands, and praying. And when she had finished her prayer, she turned and saw a ditch full of water, and said: Now it is time to wash myself. And she threw herself in, saying: In the name of Jesus Christ I am baptized on my last day. And the women seeing, and the multitude, wept, saying: Do not throw thyself into the water; so that also the governor shed tears, because the seals were going to devour such beauty. She then threw herself in in the name of Jesus Christ; but the seals having seen the glare of the fire of lightning, floated about dead. And there was round her, as she was naked, a cloud of fire; so that neither could the wild beasts touch her, nor could she be seen naked.

35 And the women, when other wild beasts were being thrown in, wailed. And some threw sweet-smelling herbs, others nard, others cassia, others amomum, so that there was abundance of perfumes. And all the wild beasts that had been thrown in, as if they had been withheld by sleep, did not touch her; so that Alexander said to the governor: I have bulls exceedingly terrible; let us bind to them her that is to fight with the beasts. And the governor, looking gloomy, turned, and

7. I.e., the exhibition of wild beasts [translator's note].

said: Do what thou wilt. And they bound her by the feet between them, and put red-hot irons under the privy parts of the bull, so that they, being rendered more furious, might kill her. They rushed about, therefore; but the burning flame consumed the ropes, and she was as if she had not been bound. **36** But Tryphæna fainted standing beside the arena, so that the crowd said: Queen Tryphæna is dead. And the governor put a stop to the games, and the city was in dismay. And Alexander entreated the governor, saying: Have mercy both on me and the city, and release this woman. For if Cæsar hear of these things, he will speedily destroy the city also along with us, because his kinswoman Queen Tryphæna has died beside the theater gates.

37 And the governor summoned Thecla out of the midst of the wild beasts, and said to her: Who art thou? and what is there about thee, that not one of the wild beasts touches thee? And she said: I indeed am a servant of the living God; and as to what there is about me, I have believed in the Son of God, in whom He is well pleased [Matt 3:17; Mark 1:11; Luke 3:22]; wherefore not one of the beasts has touched me. For He alone is the end of salvation, and the basis of immortal life; for He is a refuge to the tempest-tossed, a solace to the afflicted, a shelter to the despairing; and, once for all, whoever shall not believe on Him, shall not live for ever.

38 And the governor having heard this, ordered her garments to be brought, and to be put on. And Thecla said: He that clothed me naked among the wild beasts, will in the day of judgment clothe thee with salvation. And taking the garments, she put them on. The governor therefore immediately issued an edict, saying: I release to you the God-fearing Thecla, the servant of God. And the women shouted aloud, and with one mouth returned thanks to God, saying: There is one God, the God of Thecla; so that the foundations of the theatre were shaken by their voice. **39** And Tryphæna having received the good news, went to meet the holy Thecla, and said: Now I believe that the dead are raised; now I believe that my child lives. Come within, and I shall assign to thee all that is mine. She therefore went in along with her, and rested eight days, having instructed her in the word of God, so that most even of the maid-servants believed. And there was great joy in the house.

40 And Thecla kept seeking Paul; and it was told her that he was in Myra of Lycia. And taking young men and maidens, she girded herself; and having sewed the tunic so as to make a man's cloak, she came to Myra, and found Paul speaking the word of God. And Paul was astonished at seeing her, and the crowd with her, thinking that some new trial was coming upon her. And when she saw him, she said: I have received the baptism, Paul; for He that wrought along with thee for the Gospel has wrought in me also for baptism. **41** And Paul, taking her, led her to the house of Hermæus, and hears everything from her, so that those that heard greatly wondered, and were comforted, and prayed over Tryphæna. And she rose up, and said: I am going to Iconium. And Paul said: Go, and teach the word of God. And Tryphæna sent her much clothing and gold, so that she left to Paul many things for the service of the poor.

42 And she went to Iconium. And she goes into the house of Onesiphorus, and fell upon the pavement where Paul used to sit and teach her, and wept, saying:

God of myself and of this house, where Thou didst make the light to shine upon me, O Christ Jesus, the Son of the living God, my help in the fire, my help among the wild beasts, Thou art glorified for ever. Amen. **43** And she found Thamyris dead, but her mother alive. And having sent for her mother, she said: Theocleia, my mother, canst thou believe that the Lord liveth in the heavens? For whether thou desirest wealth, God gives it to thee through me; or thy child, I am standing beside thee. And having thus testified, she departed to Seleucia.[8] * * *

MARCION

Marcion of Sinope (in Pontus), born in the late first century C.E., is one of the most important figures of early Christianity. He constructed a revisionist history of Christian origins in order to resolve the tension he observed in Paul's writings between faithfulness to and freedom from the Old Testament law. Marcion concluded that a Jewish conspiracy had distorted the Christian gospel of grace. Though Paul himself (unlike all the other apostles) was not involved, this conspiracy nonetheless managed to corrupt his writings, perversely transforming Christ into a representative of the Old Testament creator when in fact Paul had proclaimed that an alien god had graciously sent Christ to save people, without any obligation entailed by creation of or covenant with humanity. Marcion's views were rejected by the proto-orthodox— indeed, emerging orthodoxy seems to have defined itself in part as a rejection of Marcionite Christianity—and so Marcion founded an independent ecclesiastical structure, whose growth rivaled that of orthodox Christianity for centuries. Having discarded the Old Testament, he promulgated what was probably the first Christian canon, which consisted of a version of Luke's Gospel and of the Epistles of Paul, all expurgated of positive references (interpolations, Marcion insisted) to the Old Testament and its god. Many scholars today believe that the New Testament canon originated as a proto-orthodox response to Marcionite scripture. While Marcion's rejection of the Old Testament creator god is reminiscent of gnostic writings, the similarities between his and gnostic thought do not go much deeper than that. Marcion was instead a radical Pauline reformer whose commitment to Paul, somewhat like that of Martin Luther centuries later, led him to dismiss certain apostolic writings as excessively devoted to the Old Testament law.

We know about Marcion only from reports by orthodox writers who rejected his views and from possible fragments of a book he wrote titled *Antitheses*. The following excerpts include testimonies against Marcion by Irenaeus (late second century) and Tertullian (early third century), as well as Adolf von Harnack's fragmentary and hypothetical reconstruction of Marcion's *Antitheses*.

---

8. After this point in the text the MSS differ widely, preserving several distinct conclusions. Bernhard Pick prints the following: "and enlightened many by the word of God; then she rested in a glorious sleep" (*The Apocryphal Acts of Paul, Peter, John, Andrew and Thomas* [Chicago: Open Court; London: Kegan Paul, 1909], 32; cf. J. K. Elliott, *The Apocryphal New Testament* [Oxford: Clarendon, 1993], 372).

[Testimony of Irenaeus Against Marcion][†]
(*Against Heresies* 1.27)

1. Cerdo was one who took his system from the followers of Simon,[1] and came to live at Rome in the time of Hyginus, who held the ninth place in the episcopal succession from the apostles downwards. He taught that the God proclaimed by the law and the prophets was not the Father of our Lord Jesus Christ. For the former was known, but the latter unknown; while the one also was righteous, but the other benevolent.

2. Marcion of Pontus succeeded him, and developed his doctrine. In so doing, he advanced the most daring blasphemy against Him who is proclaimed as God by the law and the prophets, declaring Him to be the author of evils, to take delight in war, to be infirm of purpose, and even to be contrary to Himself. But Jesus being derived from that father who is above the God that made the world, and coming into Judæa in the times of Pontius Pilate the governor, who was the procurator of Tiberius Cæsar, was manifested in the form of a man to those who were in Judæa, abolishing the prophets and the law, and all the works of that God who made the world, whom also he calls Cosmocrator. Besides this, he mutilates the Gospel which is according to Luke, removing all that is written respecting the generation of the Lord, and setting aside a great deal of the teaching of the Lord, in which the Lord is recorded as most clearly confessing that the Maker of this universe is His Father. He likewise persuaded his disciples that he himself was more worthy of credit than are those apostles who have handed down the Gospel to us, furnishing them not with the Gospel, but merely a fragment of it. In like manner, too, he dismembered the Epistles of Paul, removing all that is said by the apostle respecting that God who made the world, to the effect that He is the Father of our Lord Jesus Christ, and also those passages from the prophetical writings which the apostle quotes, in order to teach us that they announced beforehand the coming of the Lord.

3. Salvation will be the attainment only of those souls which had learned his doctrine; while the body, as having been taken from the earth, is incapable of sharing in salvation. In addition to his blasphemy against God Himself, he advanced this also, truly speaking as with the mouth of the devil, and saying all things in direct opposition to the truth,—that Cain, and those like him, and the Sodomites, and the Egyptians, and others like them, and, in fine, all the nations who walked in all sorts of abomination, were saved by the Lord, on His descending into Hades, and on their running unto Him, and that they welcomed Him into their kingdom. But the serpent which was in Marcion declared that Abel, and Enoch, and Noah, and those other righteous men who sprang[2] from the patriarch Abraham, with all

---

† From Irenaeus, *Against Heresies*, trans. Alexander Roberts and James Donaldson, in *The Ante-Nicene Fathers*, vol. 1 (1885; reprint, Peabody, MA: Hendrickson, 1994), 352–53. All notes are the translators'.

1. The figure from Acts 8:8–25.

2. We here follow the amended version proposed by the Benedictine editor [in the text published by Migne].

the prophets, and those who were pleasing to God, did not partake in salvation. For since these men, he says, knew that their God was constantly tempting them, so now they suspected that He was tempting them, and did not run to Jesus, or believe His announcement: and for this reason he declared that their souls remained in Hades.

4. But since this man is the only one who has dared openly to mutilate the Scriptures, and unblushingly above all others to inveigh against God, I purpose specially to refute him, convicting him out of his own writings; and, with the help of God, I shall overthrow him out of those discourses of the Lord and the apostles, which are of authority with him, and of which he makes use.[3] At present, however, I have simply been led to mention him. * * *

[Testimony of Tertullian Against Marcion][†]
(from *Against Marcion*, Book 1)

19 * * * Marcion's special and principal work is the separation of the law and the gospel; and his disciples will not deny that in this point they have their very best pretext for initiating and confirming themselves in his heresy. These are Marcion's *Antitheses*, or contradictory propositions, which aim at committing the gospel to a variance with the law, in order that from the diversity of the two documents which contain them, they may contend for a diversity of gods also. Since, therefore, it is this very opposition between the law and the gospel which has suggested that the God of the gospel is different from the God of the law, it is clear that, before the said separation, that god could not have been known who became known from the argument of the separation itself. He therefore could not have been revealed by Christ, who came before the separation, but must have been devised by Marcion, the author of the breach of peace between the gospel and the law. Now this peace, which had remained unhurt and unshaken from Christ's appearance to the time of Marcion's audacious doctrine, was no doubt maintained by that way of thinking, which firmly held that the God of both law and gospel was none other than the Creator, against whom after so long a time a separation has been introduced by the heretic of Pontus.

20 This most patent conclusion requires to be defended by us against the clamours of the opposite side. For they allege that Marcion did not so much innovate on the rule (of faith) by his separation of the law and the gospel, as restore it after it had been previously adulterated. O Christ, most enduring Lord, who didst bear so many years with this interference with Thy revelation, until Marcion forsooth came to Thy rescue! Now they adduce the case of Peter himself, and the others, who were pillars of the apostolate, as having been blamed by Paul for not walking uprightly, according to the truth of the gospel [Gal 2:11–17]—that very Paul indeed, who, being yet in the mere rudiments of grace, and

---

3. A promise never fulfilled.

† From Tertullian, *Against Marcion*, trans. Peter Holmes, in *The Ante-Nicene Fathers*, vol. 3 (1885; reprint, Peabody, MA: Hendrickson, 1994), 285–86 (slightly altered).

trembling, in short, lest he should have run or were still running in vain, then for the first time conferred with those who were apostles before himself [Gal 2:1–3]. Therefore because, in the eagerness of his zeal against Judaism as a neophyte, he thought that there was something to be blamed in their conduct—even the promiscuousness of their conversation—but afterwards was himself to become in his practice all things to all men, that he might gain all—to the Jews, as a Jew, and to them that were under the law, as under the law [1 Cor 9:20–21],—you would have his censure, which was merely directed against conduct destined to become acceptable even to their accuser, suspected of prevarication against God on a point of public doctrine.[1] Touching their public doctrine, however, they had, as we have already said, joined hands in perfect concord, and had agreed also in the division of their labour in their fellowship of the gospel, as they had indeed in all other respects: "Whether it were I or they, so we preach" [1 Cor 15:11]. When, again, he mentioned "certain false brethren as having crept in unawares," who wished to remove the Galatians into another gospel [Gal 1:6, 7; 2:4], he himself shows that that adulteration of the gospel was not meant to transfer them to the faith of another god and christ, but rather to perpetuate the teaching of the law; because he blames them for maintaining circumcision, and observing times, and days, and months, and years, according to those Jewish ceremonies which they ought to have known were now abrogated, according to the new dispensation purposed by the Creator Himself, who of old foretold this very thing by His prophets [Gal 4:10–11; 5:1–6]. Thus He says by Isaiah: Old things have passed away. "Behold, I will do a new thing" [Isa 43:18–19]. And in another passage: "I will make a new covenant, not according to the covenant that I made with their fathers, when I brought them out of the land of Egypt" [Jer 31:31–32]. In like manner by Jeremiah: Make to yourselves a new covenant, "circumcise yourselves to the Lord, and take away the foreskins of your heart" [4:4]. It is this circumcision, therefore, and this renewal, which the apostle insisted on, when he forbade those ancient ceremonies concerning which their very founder announced that they were one day to cease; thus by Hosea: "I will also cause all her mirth to cease, her feast-days, her new moons, and her Sabbaths, and all her solemn feasts" [2:11]. So likewise by Isaiah: "The new moons, and Sabbaths, the calling of assemblies, I cannot bear; your holy days, and fasts, and feast-days, my soul hateth" [Isa 1:13, 14]. Now, if even the Creator had so long before discarded all these things, and the apostle was now proclaiming them to be worthy of renunciation, the very agreement of the apostle's meaning with the decrees of the Creator proves that none other God was preached by the apostle than He whose purposes he now wished to have recognised, branding as false both apostles and brethren, for the express reason that they were pushing back the gospel of Christ the Creator from the new condition which the Creator had foretold, to the old one which He had discarded.

---

1. Tertullian's argument is confusing, if not simply confused. He seems to dismiss as doctrinally irrelevant Paul's famous rebuke of Peter in Gal 2 on multiple but mutually exclusive grounds.

21 Now if it was with the view of preaching a new god that he was eager to abrogate the law of the old God, how is it that he prescribes no rule about the new god, but solely about the old law, if it be not because faith in the Creator was still to continue, and His law alone was to come to an end?—just as the Psalmist had declared: "Let us break their bands asunder, and cast away their cords from us. Why do the heathen rage, and the people imagine a vain thing? The kings of the earth stand up, and the rulers take counsel together against the Lord, and against His Anointed" [Ps 2:1–3]. And, indeed, if another god were preached by Paul, there could be no doubt about the law, whether it were to be kept or not, because of course it would not belong to the new lord, the enemy of the law. The very newness and difference of the god would take away not only all question about the old and alien law, but even all mention of it. But the whole question, as it then stood, was this, that although the God of the law was the same as was preached in Christ, yet there was a disparagement of His law. Permanent still, therefore, stood faith in the Creator and in His Christ; manner of life and discipline alone fluctuated. Some disputed about eating idol sacrifices, others about the veiled dress of women, others again about marriage and divorce, and some even about the hope of the resurrection;[2] but about God no one disputed. Now, if this question also had entered into dispute, surely it would be found in the apostle, and that too as a great and vital point. No doubt, after the time of the apostles, the truth respecting the belief of God suffered corruption, but it is equally certain that during the life of the apostles their teaching on this great article did not suffer at all; so that no other teaching will have the right of being received as apostolic than that which is at the present day proclaimed in the churches of apostolic foundation. You will, however, find no church of apostolic origin but such as reposes its Christian faith in the Creator. But if the churches shall prove to have been corrupt from the beginning, where shall the pure ones be found? Will it be amongst the adversaries of the Creator? Show us, then, one of your churches, tracing its descent from an apostle, and you will have gained the day. Forasmuch then as it is on all accounts evident that there was from Christ down to Marcion's time no other God in the rule of sacred truth than the Creator, the proof of our argument is sufficiently established, in which we have shown that the god of our heretic first became known by his separation of the gospel and the law. Our previous position is accordingly made good, that no god is to be believed whom any man has devised out of his own conceits; except indeed the man be a prophet, and then his own conceits would not be concerned in the matter. If Marcion, however, shall be able to lay claim to this inspired character, it will be necessary for it to be shown. There must be no doubt or paltering. For all heresy is thrust out by this wedge of the truth, that Christ is proved to be the revealer of no God else but the Creator.

---

2. All of these were matters of dispute in the Corinthian church according to 1 Corinthians.

The Antitheses†

1. The Creator was known to Adam and to the following generations, but the Father of Christ is unknown, as Christ himself said of him in these words: "No one has known the Father except the Son" [Luke 10:22].

2. The Creator did not even know where Adam was, so he cried, "Where are you?" [Gen. 3:9]. But Christ knew even the thoughts of men [cf. Luke 5:22; 6:8; 9:47].

3. Joshua conquered the land with violence and terror; but Christ forbade all violence and preached mercy and peace.

4. The God of Creation did not restore the sight of the blinded Isaac, but our Lord, because he is good, opened the eyes of many blind men [Luke 7:21].

5. Moses intervened unbidden in the brothers' quarrel, chiding the offender, "Why do you strike your neighbor?" But he was rejected by him with the words, "Who made you master or judge over us?" [Exod. 2:13–14]. Christ, on the contrary, when someone asked him to settle a question of inheritance between him and his brother, refused his assistance even in so honest a cause—because he is the Christ of the Good, not of the Just God—and said, "Who made me a judge over you?" [Luke 12:13 f.].

6. At the time of the Exodus from Egypt, the God of Creation commanded Moses, "Be ready, your loins girded, your feet shod, staffs in your hands, knapsacks on your shoulders, and carry off gold and silver and everything that belongs to the Egyptians" [cf. Exod. 3:22; 12:11; 11:2; 12:35]. But our Lord, the good, said to his disciples as he sent them into the world: "Have no sandals on your feet, nor knapsack, nor two tunics, nor coppers in your belts" [cf. Luke 9:3].

7. The prophet of the God of Creation, when the people was engaged in battle, climbed to the mountain peak and extended his hands to God, imploring that he kill as many as possible in the battle [cf. Exod. 17:8 ff.]. But our Lord, the good, extended his hands [on the cross] not to kill men, but to save them.

8. In the Law it is said, "An eye for an eye, a tooth for a tooth" [Exod. 21:24; Deut. 19:21]. But the Lord, being good, says in the Gospel: "If anyone strikes you on the cheek, offer him the other as well" [cf. Luke 6:29].

9. In the Law it is said, "A coat for a coat" [?]. But the good Lord says, "If anyone takes your coat, give him your tunic as well" [Luke 6:29].

10. The prophet of the God of Creation, in order to kill as many as possible in battle, kept the sun from going down until he finished annihilating those who

---

† From Marcion, *Antitheses*, in Adolf von Harnack, *Marcion: Das Evangelium vom fremden Gott*, 2nd ed. (1924; reprint, Darmstadt: Wissenshaftliche Buchgesellshaft, 1960), 89–92, as translated in Wayne A. Meeks and John T. Fitzgerald, *The Writings of St. Paul*, 2nd ed. (New York: Norton, 2007), 286–88. The following paragraph in this note and much of the bracketed material throughout the selection are provided by Meeks and Fitzgerald.

The epigrammatic antitheses reproduced here are those which Adolf von Harnack reconstructed. It is not certain that all go back to Marcion; several are quoted in a form attributed to Marcion's disciple Megethius in the fourth-century Dialogues of Adamantius. As Harnack showed, "The Antitheses" contained, besides such epigrams, a more systematic theological part, which is impossible to reconstruct.

made war on the people [Josh. 10:12 ff.]. But the Lord, being good, says, "Let not the sun go down on your anger" [Eph. 4:26].

11. David, when he besieged Zion, was opposed by the blind who sought to prevent his entry, and he had them killed [2 Sam 5:6 ff.]. But Christ came freely to help the blind.

12. The Creator, at the request of Elijah, sent the plague of fire [2 Kings 1:9–12]; Christ however forbids the disciples to beseech fire from heaven [Luke 9:51 ff.].

13. The prophet of the God of Creation commanded bears to come from the thicket and devour the children who had opposed him [2 Kings 2:24]; the good Lord, however, says, "Let the children come to me and do not forbid them, for of such is the Kingdom of Heaven" [Luke 18:16].

14. Elisha, prophet of the Creator, healed only one of the many Israelite lepers, and that a Syrian, Naaman [2 Kings 5:1 ff.]. But Christ, though himself "the alien," healed an Israelite, whose own Lord did not want him healed [Luke 7:1 ff.]. Elisha used material for the healing, namely water, and seven times; but Christ healed through a single, bare word. Elisha healed only one leper; Christ healed ten, and this contrary to the Law [Luke 17:11 ff.] . . .

15. The prophet of the Creator says: "My bow is strung and my arrows are sharp against them" [Isa. 5:28]; the Apostle says, "Put on the armor of God, that you may quench the fiery arrows of the Evil One" [Eph. 6:11, 16].

16. The Creator says, "Hear and hear, but do not understand" [Isa. 6:9]; Christ on the contrary says, "He who has ears to hear, let him hear" [Luke 8:8, etc.].

17. The Creator says, "Cursed is everyone who hangs on the tree" [Deut. 21:23], but Christ suffered the death of the cross [cf. Gal. 3:13 f.].

18. The Jewish Christ was designated by the Creator solely to restore the Jewish people from the Diaspora; but our Christ was commissioned by the good God to liberate all mankind.

19. The Good is good toward all men; the Creator, however, promises salvation only to those who are obedient to him. The Good redeems those who believe in him, but he does not judge those who are disobedient to him; the Creator, however, redeems his faithful and judges and punishes the sinners.

20. Cursing characterizes the Law; blessing, the faith.

21. The Creator commands to give to one's brothers [e.g., Lev. 25:35 ff.] Christ, however, to all who ask [Luke 6:30].

22. In the Law the Creator said, "I make rich and poor" [cf. Prov. 22:2]; Jesus calls the poor blessed [Luke 6:20].

23. In the Law of the Just [God] fortune is given to the rich and misfortune to the poor; but Christ calls [only] the poor blessed.

24. In the Law God says, "Love him who loves you and hate your enemy" [cf. Lev. 19:18 and Matt. 5:43]; our Lord, the good, says: "Love your enemies and pray for those who persecute you" [cf. Luke 6:27; Matt. 5:44].

25. The Creator established the Sabbath [Gen. 2:3; Exod. 20:8 ff.]; Christ abolishes it [cf. Luke 6:1 ff.].

26. The Creator rejects the tax collectors as non-Jews and profane men; Christ accepts the tax collectors [Luke 5:27 ff.].

27. The Law forbids touching a woman with a flow of blood [Lev. 15:19 ff.]; Christ not only touches her, but heals her [Luke 8:43 ff.].

28. Moses permits divorce [Deut. 24:1], Christ forbids it [Luke 16:18; 1 Cor. 7:10 f.].

29. The Christ [of the Old Testament] promises to the Jews the restoration of their former condition by return of their land and, after death, a refuge in Abraham's bosom in the underworld. Our Christ will establish the Kingdom of God, an eternal and heavenly possession.

30. Both the place of punishment and that of refuge of the Creator are placed in the underworld for those who obey the Law and the Prophets. But Christ and the God who belongs to him have a heavenly place of rest and a haven, of which the Creator never spoke.

THE GOSPEL ACCORDING TO THOMAS

A collection of dominical sayings formally similar to the hypothetical document Q and composed sometime before 200 C.E. *The Gospel of Thomas* includes several *logia* whose versions the New Testament gospels also preserve, as well as many not found in the Synoptics or John. Its relationship to the historical Jesus and the New Testament is complex and obscure. It probably uses the Synoptic Gospels as a source, but at times it seems to preserve Jesus' sayings in forms more primitive than (and thus, presumably, independent of) those found in Matthew, Mark, and Luke (e.g., 9). Although much of *Thomas* must have originated in early Christian prophetic oracles or the imagination of its author(s), it is also possible that the work transmits a few authentic dominical sayings that the New Testament omits altogether (e.g., 98, whose calculated inappropriateness is reminiscent of Jesus in the Synoptics).

The Gospel of Thomas was likely composed in Syria or Mesopotamia, where the apostle to whom it is pseudepigraphically attributed was held in high esteem. Other writings associated with Thomas were produced there, and together they bear witness to a school of Christian thought in some ways similar to classic and Valentian Gnosticism, especially in its understanding of the divine nature of the authentic self and of the self's salvation through detachment from the material world. But *The Gospel of Thomas* and related writings lack any specific reference to the distinctive gnostic myth (a version of which Ptolemy preserves [see below, pp. 1050–63]) and also neglect revisionary interpretation of Genesis—two hallmarks of gnostic thought. Some scholars therefore speculate that *Thomas* was simply part of the standard scriptural canon used by second- and third-century Mesopotamian Christians, not rejected by church leaders as heretical until after Mani (the founder of Manichaeism, a religion that competed with Christianity for adherents) adopted its model of divine twinship and encouraged his followers to read it as scripture. In any case, *The Gospel of Thomas* survived only in brief fragments until a complete Coptic translation of the Greek work surfaced in the codices found at Nag Hammadi in 1945, of which the following is Beate Blatz's translation.

(from Nag Hammadi Codex II, pp. 32–51)[†]

These are the secret words which the living Jesus spoke, and which Didymus Judas Thomas wrote down (1) And he said: He who shall find the interpretation of these words shall not taste of death.[1]

(2) Jesus said: He who seeks, let him not cease seeking until he finds; and when he finds he will be troubled, and when he is troubled he will be amazed, and he will reign over the All.[2]

(3) Jesus said: If those who lead you say to you: See, the kingdom is in heaven, then the birds of the heaven will go before you; if they say to you: It is in the sea, then the fish will go before you. But the kingdom is within you, and it is outside of you. When you know yourselves, then you will be known, (p. 33) and you will know that you are the sons of the living Father. But if you do not know yourselves, then you are in poverty, and you are poverty.[3]

(4) Jesus said: The man aged in days will not hesitate to ask a little child of seven days about the place of life, and he shall live; for there are many first who shall be last, and they will become a single one.[4]

(5) Jesus said: Recognise what is before you, and what is hidden from you will be revealed to you; for there is nothing hidden that will not be made manifest.[5]

(6) His disciples asked him (and) said to him: Do you want us to fast? And how shall we pray (and) give alms? What diet should we observe? Jesus said: Do not lie, and what you abhor, do not do; for all things are manifest in the sight of heaven; for there is nothing hidden which will not be revealed, and there is nothing covered which will remain without being uncovered.[6]

(7) Jesus said: Blessed is the lion which the man eats, and the lion will become man; and cursed is the man whom the lion eats, and the lion will become man.

(8) And he said: Man is like a wise fisherman who cast his net into the sea; he drew it up from the sea full of small fish; among them he found a large good fish, the wise fisherman; he threw all the small fish (p. 34) into the sea; he chose the large fish without difficulty. He who has ears to hear, let him hear![7]

(9) Jesus said: Look, the sower went out, he filled his hand (and) cast (the seed). Some fell upon the road; the birds came, they gathered them. Others fell upon the rock, and struck no root in the ground, nor did they produce any ears.

† Trans. Beate Blatz, from *New Testament Apocrypha*, vol. 1., ed. Wilhelm Schneemelcher and R. McL. Wilson, 2nd ed. (Cambridge: James Clarke & Co., 1992), 117–33. All notes are the translator's (substantially abbreviated).
1. Cf. Jn. 8:51; log. 18; log. 19.
2. Cf. Mt. 7:7–8; Lk. 11:9–10.
3. Cf. Lk. 17:21b; Mt. 5:45.
4. Cf. Mt. 11:25 par.; Mk. 10:31 par.
5. Cf. Mk. 4:22 par.
6. Cf. Mt. 6:1–18; Eph. 4:25 (Col. 3:9); Mk. 4:22 par.
7. Cf. Mt. 13:47–50. On the 'awakening formula' at the end of the logion cf. Mk. 4:9 par.; Rev. 2:7.

And others fell on the thorns; they choked the seed and the worm ate them. And others fell on the good earth, and it produced good fruit; it yielded sixty per measure and a hundred and twenty per measure.[8]

(10) Jesus said: I have cast a fire upon the world, and see, I watch over it until it is ablaze.[9]

(11) Jesus said: This heaven will pass away, and the one above it will pass away; and those who are dead are not alive, and those who are living will not die. In the days when you ate of what is dead, you made of it what is living. When you come to be light, what will you do? On the day when you were one, you became two. But when you have become two, what will you do?[1]

(12) The disciples said to Jesus: We know that you will depart from us; who is it who will be great over us? Jesus said to them: Wherever you have come, you will go to James the Just, for whose sake heaven and earth came into being.[2]

(13) Jesus said to his disciples: Compare me, tell me whom I am like. Simon Peter said to him: You are like a righteous angel. Matthew said to him: (p. 35) You are like a wise philosopher. Thomas said to him: Master, my mouth is wholly incapable of saying whom you are like. Jesus said: I am not your master, for you have drunk, you have become drunk from the bubbling spring which I have caused to gush forth (?). And he took him, withdrew, (and) spoke to him three words. Now when Thomas came (back) to his companions, they asked him: What did Jesus say to you? Thomas said to them: If I tell you one of the words which he said to me, you will take up stones (and) throw them at me; and a fire will come out of the stones (and) burn you up.[3]

(14) Jesus said to them: If you fast, you will put a sin to your charge; and if you pray, you will be condemned; and if you give alms, you will do harm to your spirits. And if you go into any land and walk about in the regions, if they receive you, eat what is set before you; heal the sick among them. For what goes into your mouth will not defile you; but what comes out of your mouth, that is what will defile you.[4]

(15) Jesus said: When you see him who was not born of woman, fall down upon your faces and worship him; that one is your Father.

(16) Jesus said: Perhaps men think that I am come to cast peace upon the world; and they do not know that I am come to cast dissensions upon the earth, fire, sword, war. For there will be five who (p. 36) are in a house: three shall be against two and two against three, the father against the son and the son against the father, and they shall stand as solitaries.[5]

(17) Jesus said: I will give you what no eye has seen and what no ear has heard and what no hand has touched and what has not entered into the heart of man.[6]

---

8. Cf. Mk. 4:3–9 par.
9. Cf. Lk. 12:49.
1. Cf. Mk. 13:31 par.
2. Cf. Mk. 9:33–37 par.
3. Cf. Mk. 8:27–30 par.; Mt. 23:8; Jn. 13:13; Jn. 4:10ff.
4. Cf. Mt. 6:1–6, 16–18; Lk. 10:8; Mk. 7:18f. par.
5. Cf. Mt. 10:34–36; Lk. 12:49–53.
6. Cf. 1 Cor. 2:9.

(18) The disciples said to Jesus: Tell us how our end will be. Jesus said: Since you have discovered the beginning, why do you seek the end? For where the beginning is, there will the end be. Blessed is he who shall stand at the beginning (in the beginning), and he shall know the end, and shall not taste death.

(19) Jesus said: Blessed is he who was before he came into being. If you become disciples to me (and) listen to my words, these stones will minister to you. For you have five trees in Paradise which do not change, either in summer or in winter, and their leaves do not fall. He who knows them shall not taste of death.[7]

(20) The disciples said to Jesus: Tell us what the kingdom of heaven is like. He said to them: It is like a grain of mustard-seed, the smallest of all seeds; but when it falls on tilled ground, it puts forth a great branch and becomes shelter for the birds of heaven.[8]

(21) Mariham said to Jesus: Whom are your disciples like? He said: They are like (p. 37) little children who have settled in a field which does not belong to them. When the owners of the field come, they will say: Leave us our field. They are naked before them, in order to leave it to them and give them (back) their field. Therefore I say: If the master of the house knows that the thief is coming, he will keep watch before he comes, and will not let him dig through into his house of his kingdom to carry off his things. You, then, be watchful over against the world; gird your loins with great strength, that the robbers may find no way to come at you. For the advantage for which you look, they will find. May there be among you a man of understanding! When the fruit ripened, he came quickly, his sickle in his hand, and reaped it. He who has ears to hear, let him hear.[9]

(22) Jesus saw some infants who were being suckled. He said to his disciples: These infants being suckled are like those who enter the kingdom. They said to him: If we then become children, shall we enter the kingdom? Jesus said to them: When you make the two one, and when you make the inside as the outside, and the outside as the inside, and the upper as the lower, and when you make the male and the female into a single one, so that the male is not male and the female not female, and when you make eyes in place of an eye, and a hand in place of a hand, and a foot in place of a foot, an image in place of an image, then shall you enter [the kingdom].[1]

(23) (p.38) Jesus said: I shall choose you, one out of a thousand and two out of ten thousand, and they shall stand as a single one.

(24) His disciples said: Teach us about the place where you are, for it is necessary for us to seek it. He said to them: He who has ears, let him hear! There is light within a man of light, and he lights the whole world. If he does not shine, there is darkness.[2]

7. Cf. Mk. 9:1 par.
8. Cf. Mk. 4:30–32 par.
9. Cf. Lk. 12:39f. par.; Mk. 13:33ff. par.; Mk. 4:29.
1. Cf. Mk. 10:13–16 par.; Mt. 18:3.
2. Cf. Mt. 6:22f. par.; Jn. 7:34ff. Cf. also log. 2; log. 77.

(25) Jesus said: Love your brother as your soul; watch over him like the apple of your eye.[3]

(26) Jesus said: You see the mote which is in your brother's eye; but you do not see the beam which is in your own eye. When you cast out the beam from your own eye, then you will see (clearly) to cast out the mote from your brother's eye.[4]

(27) <Jesus> said: If you do not fast to the world, you will not find the kingdom; if you do not keep the Sabbath as Sabbath, you will not see the Father.[5]

(28) Jesus said: I stood in the midst of the world, and I appeared to them in the flesh. I found them all drunk; I found none among them thirsting, and my soul was afflicted for the sons of men; for they are blind in their heart, and they do not see that they came empty into the world, (and) empty they seek to leave the world again. But now they are drunk. When they have thrown off their wine, they will repent.

(29) Jesus said: If the flesh came into existence because of the spirit, it is a marvel. But if the spirit (came into existence) because of the body, it is a marvel of marvels. But as for me, I wonder at this, (p. 39) how this great wealth made its home in this poverty.[6]

(30) Jesus said: Where there are three gods, they are gods; where there are two or one, I am with him.[7]

(31) Jesus said: No prophet is accepted in his own village; no doctor heals those who know him.[8]

(32) Jesus said: A city that is built on a high mountain and fortified cannot fall, nor can it be hidden.[9]

(33) Jesus said: What you hear with your ear (and) with the other ear, proclaim it on your roof-tops. For no one lights a lamp to set it under a bushel, or to put it in a hidden place; but he sets it on the lamp-stand, that all who go in and come out may see its light.[1]

(34) Jesus said: If a blind man leads a blind man, they both fall into a pit.[2]

(35) Jesus said: It is not possible for anyone to go into the strong man's house (and) take it by force, unless he binds his hands; then will he plunder his house.[3]

(36) Jesus said: Be not anxious from morning to evening and from evening to morning about what you shall put on.[4]

(37) His disciples said: On what day will you be revealed to us, and on what day shall we see you? Jesus said: When you unclothe yourselves and are not ashamed, and take your garments and lay them beneath your feet like the little children

---

3. Cf. Mk. 12:31 par.
4. Cf. Mt. 7:3–5 par.
5. Cf. Jn. 14:9.
6. Cf. log. 87; log. 112.
7. Cf. Mt. 18:20.
8. Cf. Mk. 6:4 par.; Jn. 4:44.
9. Cf. Mt. 5:14.
1. Cf. Mt. 10:27 par.; Mk. 4:21 par.
2. Cf. Lk. 6:39 par.
3. Cf. Mk. 3:27 par.
4. Cf. Mt. 6:25ff. par.

(and) trample on them, then [you will (p. 40) see] the Son of the Living One, and you will not be afraid.[5]

(38) Jesus said: Many times have you desired to hear these words which I speak to you, and you have no other from whom to hear them. Days will come when you will seek me (and) you will not find me.[6]

(39) Jesus said: The Pharisees and the scribes have taken the keys of knowledge (and) have hidden them. They did not go in, and those who wished to go in they did not allow. But you, be wise as serpents and innocent as doves.[7]

(40) Jesus said: A vine has been planted outside of the Father; and since it is not established, it will be plucked out with its roots (and) will perish.[8]

(41) Jesus said: He who has in his hand, to him shall be given; and he who has not, from him shall be taken even the little that he has.[9]

(42) Jesus said: Become passers-by!

(43) His disciples said to him: Who are you, that you say these things to us? <Jesus said to them:> From what I say to you, do you not know who I am? But you have become like the Jews; for they love the tree (and) hate its fruit, and they love the fruit (and) hate the tree.[1]

(44) Jesus said: He who blasphemes against the Father will be forgiven, and he who blasphemes against the Son will be forgiven; but he who blasphemes against the Holy Spirit will not be forgiven, either on earth or in heaven.[2]

(45) Jesus said: Grapes are not harvested from thorn-bushes, nor are figs gathered from hawthorns, [f]or they yield no fruit. (p. 41) [A go]od man brings forth good from his treasure; a bad man brings forth evil things from his evil treasure, which is in his heart, and he says evil things, for out of the abundance of his heart he brings forth evil things.[3]

(46) Jesus said: From Adam to John the Baptist there is among the children of women none higher than John the Baptist, for his eyes were not destroyed (?). But I have said: Whoever among you becomes small will know the kingdom and will be higher than John.[4]

(47) Jesus said: It is not possible for a man to ride two horses or stretch two bows; and it is not possible for a servant to serve two masters, unless he honours the one and insults the other. No one drinks old wine and immediately desires to drink new wine. And new wine is not poured into old wineskins, lest they burst; nor is old wine poured into a new wineskin, lest it spoil. An old patch is not sewn on a new garment, for a rent would result.[5]

5. Cf. Jn. 14:22; 1 Jn. 3:2; log. 22; Mt. 16:16.
6. Cf. Mt. 13:16f. par.; Mk. 2:20 par.; Lk. 17:22; Jn. 7:33ff.; 13:33.
7. Cf. Lk. 11:52; Mt. 23:13; Mt. 10:16.
8. Cf. Mt. 15:13.
9. Cf. Mk. 4:25 par.
1. Cf. Jn. 8:25; Lk. 6:43f. par.
2. Cf. Mk. 3:28f. par.
3. Cf. Lk. 6:44ff. par.
4. Cf. Mt. 11:11; Lk. 7:28.
5. Cf. Mt. 6:24; Lk. 16:13; Mk. 2:21f. par.

(48) Jesus said: If two make peace with one another in this one house, they will say to the mountain: Be removed, and it will be removed.[6]

(49) Jesus said: Blessed are the solitary and the elect, for you will find the kingdom; for you came forth from it, (and) you will return to it again.[7]

(50) Jesus said: If they say to you: Whence have you come?, say to them: We have come from the light, the place where the light came into being of itself. It [established itself] (p. 42), and it revealed itself in their image. If they say to you: Who are you?, say: We are his sons, and we are the elect of the living Father. If they ask you: What is the sign of your Father in you?, say to them: It is movement and rest.

(51) His disciples said to him: On what day will the rest of the dead come into being, and on what day will the new world come? He said to them: What you await has come, but you do not know it.[8]

(52) His disciples said to him: Twenty-four prophets spoke in Israel, and they all spoke of you. He said to them: You have abandoned the living one before your eyes, and spoken about the dead.[9]

(53) His disciples said to him: Is circumcision useful or not? He said to them: If it were useful, their father would beget them from their mother (already) circumcised. But the true circumcision in the Spirit has proved useful in every way.[1]

(54) Jesus said: Blessed are the poor, for yours is the kingdom of heaven.[2]

(55) Jesus said: He who does not hate his father and his mother cannot be a disciple to me. And (he who does not) hate his brothers and sisters and take up his cross like me, will not be worthy of me.[3]

(56) Jesus said: He who has known the world has found a corpse; and he who has found a corpse, the world is not worthy of him.

(57) Jesus said: The kingdom of the Father is like a man who had [good] seed. His enemy came by night (p. 43) and sowed weeds among the good seed. The man did not allow them to pull up the weeds. He said to them: Lest you go to pull up the weeds, (and) pull up the wheat with it. For on the day of the harvest the weeds will be manifest; they will be pulled up and burned.[4]

(58) Jesus said: Blessed is the man who has suffered; he has found life.

(59) Jesus said: Look upon the Living One so long as you live, that you may not die and seek to see him, and be unable to see him.[5]

(60) <They saw> a Samaritan carrying a lamb, who was going to Judaea. He said to his disciples: (What will) this man (do) with the lamb? They said to him:

6. Cf. Mk. 11:23 par.
7. Cf. log. 4; log. 16; log. 23; log. 50; log. 75.
8. Cf. Mk. 9:13 par.; Lk. 21:7; Mt. 17:11f.
9. Cf. Lk. 24:5; Jn. 5:39f.; 8:53.
1. Cf. Rom. 2:25, 29; 3:1f.
2. Cf. Lk. 6:20 par.
3. Cf. Mt. 10:37f. par.
4. Cf. Mt. 13:24–30.
5. Cf. Jn. 8:21.

Kill it and eat it. He said to them: While it is alive he will not eat it, but (only) when he kills it (and) it becomes a corpse. They said to him: Otherwise he cannot do it. He said to them: You also, seek a place for yourselves in rest, that you may not become a corpse and be eaten.

(61) Jesus said: Two will rest upon a bed; one will die, the other live. Salome said: Who are you, man, whose son? You have mounted my bed and eaten from my table. Jesus said to her: I am he who comes forth from the one who is equal; I was given of the things of my Father. <Salome said:> I am your disciple. <Jesus said to her:> Therefore I say: If he is equal, he is full of light; but if he is divided, he will be full of darkness.[6]

(62) Jesus said: I speak my mysteries to those [who are worthy (p. 44) of my] mysteries. What your right hand does, let not your left hand know what it does.[7]

(63) Jesus said: There was a rich man who had many possessions. He said: I will use my possessions to sow and reap and plant, to fill my barns with fruit, that I may have need of nothing. These were his thoughts in his heart; and in that night he died. He who has ears, let him hear.[8]

(64) Jesus said: A man had guests; and when he had prepared the dinner, he sent his servant to invite the guests. He went to the first, and said to him: My master invites you. He said: I have money with some merchants; they are coming to me this evening. I will go and give them my orders. I ask to be excused from the dinner. He went to another (and) said to him: My master has invited you. He said to him: I have bought a house, and I am asked for a day. I shall not have time. He went to another (and) said to him: My master invites you. He said to him: My friend is about to be married, and I am to arrange the dinner. I shall not be able to come. I ask to be excused from the dinner. He went to another; he said to him: My master invites you. He said to him: I have bought a farm; I am going to collect the rent. I shall not be able to come. I ask to be excused. The servant came back (and) said to his master: Those whom you invited to the dinner have asked to be excused. The master said to his servant: Go out to the roads; bring those whom you find, that they may dine. Traders and merchants [shall] not [enter] the places of my Father.[9]

(65) (p. 45)He said: A good man had a vineyard; he leased it to tenants, that they might work in it (and) he receive the fruits from them. He sent his servant, that the tenants might give him the fruits of the vineyard. They seized his servant, beat him, (and) all but killed him. The servant went away (and) told his master. His master said: Perhaps <they> did not know <him>. He sent another servant; the tenants beat the other also. Then the master sent his son. He said: Perhaps they will have respect for my son. Those tenants, since they knew that he was the heir of the vineyard, they seized him and killed him. He who has ears, let him hear.[1]

6. Cf. Lk. 17:34; Mt. 11:27 par.
7. Cf. Mt. 6:3.
8. Cf. Lk. 12:16–21.
9. Cf. Lk. 14:16–24 par.
1. Cf. Mk. 12:1–12 par.

(66) Jesus said: Show me the stone which the builders rejected; it is the cornerstone.[2]

(67) Jesus said: He who knows the all, (but) fails (to know) himself, misses everything.[3]

(68) Jesus said: Blessed are you when you are hated and persecuted, and they will find no place where you have been persecuted.[4]

(69) Jesus said: Blessed are those who have been persecuted in their heart; these are they who have known the Father in truth. Blessed are the hungry, for the belly of him who desires will be filled.[5]

(70) Jesus said: If you have gained this within you, what you have will save you. If you do not have this in [you], what you do not have in you [will] kill you.

(71) Jesus said: I will des[troy this] house, and none shall be able to build it [again].[6]

(72) (p. 46) [A man said] to him: Speak to my brothers, that they may divide my father's possessions with me. He said to him: O man, who made me a divider? He turned to his disciples. He said to them: I am not a divider, am I?[7]

(73) Jesus said: The harvest is indeed great, but the labourers are few. But pray the Lord, that he send forth labourers into the harvest.[8]

(74) He said: Lord, there are many about the well, but no one in the well.

(75) Jesus said: There are many standing at the door, but it is the solitary who will enter the bridal chamber.

(76) Jesus said: The kingdom of the Father is like a merchant who had a load (of goods) and found a pearl. That merchant was wise. He sold the load and bought for himself the pearl alone. You also, seek after his treasure which does not fail (but) endures, where moth does not come near to devour nor worm to destroy.[9]

(77) Jesus said: I am the light that is above them all. I am the all; the all came forth from me, and the all attained to me. Cleave a (piece of) wood, I am there. Raise up a stone, and you will find me there.[1]

(78) Jesus said: Why did you come out into the field? To see a reed shaken by the wind? And to see a man clothed in soft raiment? [Look, your] kings and your great men, (p. 47) these are the ones who wear soft clothing, and they [will] not be able to know the truth.[2]

(79) A woman in the crowd said to him: Blessed is the womb which bore you, and the breasts which nourished you. He said to [her]: Blessed are those who have heard the word of the Father (and) have kept it in truth. For there will be

---

2. Cf. Ps. 118:22; Mk. 12:10 par.
3. Cf. Mk. 8:36 par.; log. 2.
4. Cf. Mt. 5:11 par.; log. 69.
5. Cf. Mt. 5:8, 10 par.; Mt. 5:6 par.
6. Cf. Mk. 14:58 par.; 15:29 par.; Jn. 2:19.
7. Cf. Lk. 12:13f.
8. Cf. Mt. 9:37f. par.
9. Cf. Mt. 13:45f.; Mt. 6:20 par.
1. Cf. Jn. 8:12. In POx 1 the second part of logion 77 is attached to logion 30.
2. Cf. Mt. 11:7f. par.

days when you will say: Blessed is the womb which has not conceived, and the breasts which have not given suck.[3]

(80) Jesus said: He who has known the world has found the body; and he who has found the body, the world is not worthy of him.

(81) Jesus said: He who has become rich, let him become king, and he who has power, let him renounce (it).[4]

(82) Jesus said: He who is near to me is near the fire, and he who is far from me is far from the kingdom.[5]

(83) Jesus said: The images are revealed to man, and the light which is in them is hidden in the image of the light of the Father. He will reveal himself, and his image is hidden by his light.

(84) Jesus said: When you see your likeness, you rejoice. But when you see your images which came into existence before you, which neither die nor are made manifest, how much will you bear?

(85) Adam came into being out of a great power and a great wealth, and he was not worthy of you; for if he had been worthy, [he would] not [have tasted] of death.

(86) Jesus said: [The foxes] (p. 48) [have] the[ir holes] and the birds have [their] nest, but the Son of Man has no place to lay his head and rest.[6]

(87) Jesus said: Wretched is the body which depends on a body, and wretched is the soul which depends on these two.[7]

(88) Jesus said: The angels and the prophets will come to you, and they will give you what is yours. You also, give them what is in your hands, and say to yourselves: On what day will they come to take what is theirs?[8]

(89) Jesus said: Why do you wash the outside of the cup? Do you not understand that he who made the inside is also he who made the outside?[9]

(90) Jesus said: Come to me, for my yoke is easy and my lordship is gentle, and you will find rest for yourselves.[1]

(91) They said to him: Tell us who you are, that we may believe in you. He said to them: You test the face of the sky and of the earth, and him who is before you you have not known, and you do not know (how) to test this moment.[2]

(92) Jesus said: Seek, and you will find; but the things you asked me in those days and I did not tell you then, now I desire to tell them, but you do not ask about them.[3]

3. Cf. Lk. 11:27f.; 23:29; Mt. 24:19 par.
4. Cf. log. 110; log. 111.
5. Cf. Mk. 12:34; Lk. 12:49; Mt. 3:11.
6. Cf. Mt. 8:20 par.
7. Cf. log. 29; log. 112.
8. Cf. Mt. 16:27 par.
9. Cf. Mt. 23:25f. par.
1. Cf. Mt. 11:28–30.
2. Cf. Mt. 16:1–3 par; log. 5.
3. Cf. Mt. 7:7 par.

(93) <Jesus said:> Do not give what is holy to the dogs, lest they cast it on the dung-heap. Do not cast the pearls to the swine, lest they make it [. . .].[4]

(94) Jesus [said:] He who seeks will find, [and he who knocks], to him will be opened.[5]

(95) [Jesus said:] If you have money, (p. 49) do not lend at interest, but give [. . .] to him from whom you will not receive it back.[6]

(96) Jesus [said:] The kingdom of the Father is like a woman. She took a little leaven, [hid] it in dough, (and) made large loaves of it. He who has ears, let him hear.[7]

(97) Jesus said: The kingdom of the [Father] is like a woman carrying a jar full of meal. While she was walking [on a] distant road, the handle of the jar broke (and) the meal poured out behind her on the road. She was unaware; she had not noticed the misfortune. When she came to her house, she put the jar down (and) found it empty.

(98) Jesus said: The kingdom of the Father is like a man who wanted to kill a powerful man. He drew the sword in his house and drove it into the wall, that he might know that his hand would be strong (enough). Then he slew the powerful man.

(99) The disciples said to him: Your brothers and your mother are standing outside. He said to them: Those here who do the will of my Father, these are my brothers and my mother; they are the ones who will enter into the kingdom of my Father.[8]

(100) They showed Jesus a gold piece and said to him: Caesar's men demand tribute from us. He said to them: What belongs to Caesar, give to Caesar; what belongs to God, give to God; and what is mine, give it to me.[9]

(101) <Jesus said:> He who does not hate his father and his mother like me cannot be a [disciple] to me. And he who does [not] love [his father] and his mother like me cannot be a [disciple] to me. For my mother [. . .] (p. 50), but [my] true [mother] gave me life.[1]

(102) Jesus said: Woe to the Pharisees, for they are like a dog lying in the manger of the cattle; for he neither eats nor does he let the cattle eat.[2]

(103) Jesus said: Blessed is the man who knows [in which] part (of the night) the robbers are coming, that he may rise and gather his [. . .] and gird up his loins before they come in.[3]

(104) They said [to him]: Come, let us pray today and fast. Jesus said: What then is the sin that I have done, or in what have I been overcome? But when the bridegroom comes out from the bridal chamber, then let them fast and pray.[4]

---

4. Cf. Mt. 7:6.
5. Cf. Mt. 7:7 par; log. 2; log. 92.
6. Cf. Mt. 5:42 par.; Lk. 6:34f.
7. Cf. Mt. 13:33 par.
8. Cf. Mk. 3:31–35 par.
9. Cf. Mk. 12:13–17 par.
1. Cf. Mt. 10:37–39 par.; 16:24 par.; log. 55.
2. Cf. Mt. 23:13ff. par.
3. Cf. Lk. 12:35ff. par.
4. Cf. Mt. 9:14f. par.; log. 6; log. 14.

(105) Jesus said: He who knows father and mother will be called the son of a harlot.

(106) Jesus said: When you make the two one, you will become sons of man, and when you say: Mountain, move away, it will move away.[5]

(107) Jesus said: The kingdom is like a shepherd who had a hundred sheep; one of them, the biggest, went astray; he left (the) ninety-nine (and) sought after the one until he found it. After he had laboured, he said to the sheep: I love you more than the ninety-nine.[6]

(108) Jesus said: He who drinks from my mouth will become like me, and I will become like him, and the hidden things will be revealed to him.[7]

(109) Jesus said: The kingdom is like a man who had in his field a [hidden] treasure, of which he knew nothing. And [after] he died he left it to his [son. The] son also did not know; he took (p. 51) the field and sold it. The man who bought it came (and) as he was ploughing [found] the treasure. He began to lend money at interest to whomever he wished.[8]

(110) Jesus said: He who has found the world (and) become rich, let him renounce the world.

(111) Jesus said: The heavens will be rolled up and likewise the earth in your presence, and the living one, (come forth) from the Living One, will not see death or <fear>, because Jesus says: He who finds himself, of him the world is not worthy.[9]

(112) Jesus said: Woe to the flesh that depends on the soul; woe to the soul that depends on the flesh.[1]

(113) His disciples said to him: On what day will the kingdom come? <Jesus said:> It will not come while people watch for it; they will not say: Look, here it is, or: Look, there it is; but the kingdom of the father is spread out over the earth, and men do not see it.[2]

(114) Simon Peter said to them: Let Mariham go out from among us, for women are not worthy of the life. Jesus said: Look, I will lead her that I may make her male, in order that she too may become a living spirit resembling you males. For every woman who makes herself male will enter into the kingdom of heaven.[3]

The Gospel according to Thomas

---

5. Cf. log. 22; log. 48; Mt. 21:20ff. par.
6. Cf. Mt. 18:12–14 par.
7. Cf. Jn. 7:37; log. 13.
8. Cf. Mt. 13:44.
9. Cf. Isa. 34:4; log. 2; log. 56.
1. Cf. log. 87.
2. Cf. Lk. 17:20–21, 23 par.; log. 3; log. 51.
3. Cf. log. 22.

VALENTINUS

The brilliant Christian theologian and teacher Valentinus (ca. 100–ca. 175 C.E.) was educated in Alexandria, an important center of Hellenistic learning and culture. As a young man he moved to Rome, where he involved himself so vigorously in ecclesiastical affairs that he apparently expected to be appointed bishop (i.e., pope). He never won this appointment, and the report of his ambition may be exaggerated, but the situation points to Valentinus's close association with proto-orthodox Christianity.

The fragmentary remains of Valentinus's own ponderous works bear witness to his use of the gnostic myth. The second-century proto-orthodox writer Irenaeus of Lyons preserves a version of this myth attributed to him, as well as a more elaborate version propagated by his pupil Ptolemy, both of which he disparages. Valentinian Gnosticism is thoroughly Christianized, however, and Valentinus and his students may have understood themselves to be adapting highly complex classic gnostic mythological and mystical speculation to a theological framework amenable to proto-orthodox Christianity. After all, Valentinus's followers did not originally coalesce into a rival religious sect, but rather came together as philosophical study groups. (The language of Ptolmey especially can be technically philosophical.) Like other Christian philosophical schools (such as the famous school at Alexandria headed by such luminaries as Clement and Origen), Valentinians seem to have attended proto-orthodox churches and then met separately, under the tutelage of like-minded Christian theologians, to discuss mystical interpretations of the church's Scripture and doctrine as explored through imaginative allegorical exegesis. Only in the late second century would Valentinians begin to establish their own ecclesiastical structures, which seem to have persisted, despite increasing hostility from the proto-orthodox and a lack of governmental sanction once the Roman Empire began to involve itself in intra-Christian disputes, until as late as the seventh century C.E.

This section includes two excerpts from Valentinus's sermon titled *The Gospel of Truth*, a Coptic version of which survives among the Nag Hammadi codices, as well as Ptolemy's version of the Valentinian gnostic myth, preserved by Irenaeus in *Against Heresies*.

The Gospel of Truth†
(from Nag Hammadi codex 1, pp. 16–43)

II. DISCOVERY OF THE FATHER

The Crucified Jesus is God within

It is to the perfect[1] that this, the proclamation of the one they search for, has made itself known, through the mercies of the father. By this the hidden mystery Jesus Christ shed light upon those who were, because of forgetfulness, in darkness. He

---

† From *The Gnostic Scriptures*, trans. Bentley Layton, Anchor Bible Reference Library (Garden City, NY: Doubleday, 1987), 254–56, 262–63. (Bracketed biblical references come from Layton's marginal notes, with some alterations; the section headings are also Layton's, as are all notes.)

1. "The perfect": the elect, who have been chosen for salvation.

enlightened them and gave them a way, and the way is the truth, about which he instructed them [John 14:6]. For this reason error became angry at him and persecuted him. She was constrained by him, and became inactive. He was nailed to a tree[2] and became fruit of the father's acquaintance. Yet it did not cause ruin because it was eaten. Rather, to those who ate of it, it gave the possibility that whoever he discovered within himself might be joyful in the discovery of him. And as for him, they discovered him within them—the inconceivable uncontained, the father, who is perfect, who created the entirety [Col 1:16].

Existence within the Father

Because the entirety was within him and the entirety was in need of him[3]—since he had retained within himself its completion, which he had not given unto the entirety—the father was not grudging; for what envy is there between him and his own members? For if **19** this realm had [. . .] them, they would not be able to [. . .] the father, retaining their completion within himself, in that it [was] given them in the form of return to him and acquaintance and completion. It is he who created the entirety, and the entirety is in him [Col 1:16]. And the entirety was in need of him: just as someone who is unknown to certain people might wish to become known, and so become loved, by them. For what did the entirety need if not acquaintance with the father?

The Savior as Teacher

He became a guide,[4] at peace and occupied with classrooms. He came forward and uttered the word as a teacher. The self-appointed wise people came up to him, testing him, but he refuted them, for they were empty; and they despised him, for they were not truly intelligent. After them all, came also the little ones, to whom belongs acquaintance with the father. Once they were confirmed and had learned about the outward manifestations of the father they gained acquaintance, they were known; they were glorified, they gave glory.

III. PREDESTINATION TO SALVATION

The Book of the Living

In their hearts appeared the living book of the living [Rev 13:8], which is written in the father's thought and intellect. **p. 20** And since the foundation of the entirety it had been among his incomprehensibles: and no one had been able to take it up [Rev 5:2–3], inasmuch as it was ordained that whoever should take it up would be put to death. Nothing would have been able to appear among those who believed in salvation, had not that book come forward.

2. "A tree": Christian jargon for the cross, but here also contrasted with the tree of acquaintance with good and evil, Gen 2:17, which in the non-gnostic reading "caused ruin" to Eve and Adam.

3. "In need of him": had a lack of him.

4. Or "pedagogue," a trained slave who accompanied schoolchildren to the classroom and supervised their conduct.

The Crucifixion and Publication of the Book

Therefore the merciful and faithful Jesus became patient and accepted the sufferings even unto taking up that book [Heb 2:17; Rev 5:7]; inasmuch as he knew that his death would mean life for many [Matt 20:28]. Before a will[5] is opened, the extent of the late property owner's fortune remains a secret; just so, the entirety was concealed. Since the father of the entirety is invisible—and the entirety derives from him, from whom every way emanated—Jesus appeared, wrapped himself in that document, was nailed to a piece of wood, and published the father's edict upon the cross [Col 2:14]. O, such a great lesson! Drawing himself down unto death, clothed in eternal life, having put off the corrupt rags,[6] he put on incorruptibility [1 Cor 15:53], a thing that no one can take from him. Having entered upon the empty ways of fear, he escaped the clutches of those who had been stripped naked by forgetfulness, for he was acquaintance and completion, and read out [their] contents **p. 21** [. . .]. When [. . .] instruct whoever might learn. And those who would learn, [namely] the living enrolled in the book of the living, learn about themselves, recovering themselves from the father, and returning to him.

Predestination of the Elect

Inasmuch as the completion of the entirety is in the father, the entirety must go to him. Then upon gaining acquaintance, all individually receive what belongs to them, and draw it to themselves.[7] For whoever does not possess acquaintance is in need, and what that person needs is great, inasmuch as the thing that such a person needs is what would complete the person. Inasmuch as the completion of the entirety resides in the father, and the entirety must go to him and all receive their own, he inscribed these things in advance, having prepared them for assignment to those who (eventually) emanated from him.

Calling of the Elect

Those whose names he foreknew were called at the end [Rom 8:29], as persons having acquaintance. It is the latter whose names the father called. For one whose name has not been spoken does not possess acquaintance. How else would a person hear, if that person's name had not been read out [John 10:3; Rom 10:14]? For whoever lacks acquaintance until the end, is a modeled form of forgetfulness, and will perish along with it. Otherwise, why do these contemptible persons have no **p. 22** name? Why do they not possess the faculty of speech?

Response to the Call

So that whoever has acquaintance is from above: and if called, hears, replies, and turns to the one who is calling; and goes to him. And he knows how that one is called.[8] Having acquaintance, that person does the will of the one who has called;

---

5. Or "testament."
6. "Corrupt rags": it was a Platonist cliché that the human body is the garment of the soul.
7. "And draw it to themselves": or "and he draws them to himself."
8. Or "he knows how he is called."

wishes to please him; and gains repose. One's name becomes one's own. Those who gain acquaintance in this way know whence they have come and whither they will go [John 3:8]; they know in the manner of a man who, after having been intoxicated, has recovered from his intoxication: having returned into himself, he has caused his own to stand at rest.[9]

He has brought many back from error, going before them unto their ways from which they had swerved after accepting error because of the depth of him who surrounds every way, while nothing surrounds him. It was quite amazing that they were in the father without being acquainted with him and that they alone were able to emanate, inasmuch as they were not able to perceive and recognize the one in whom they were.

Contents of the Book

For had not his will emanated from him ⟨ . . . ⟩[1] For he revealed it to bestow an acquaintance in harmony with all its emanations, that is to say, acquaintance with the living book, an acquaintance which at the end appeared to the **p. 23** aeons[2] in the form of [passages of text from] it.

When it is manifest, they speak: they are not places for use of the voice, nor are they mute texts for someone to read out and so think of emptiness; rather, they are texts of truth, which speak and know only themselves. And each text is a perfect truth—like a book that is perfect and consists of texts written in unity, written by the father for the aeons: so that through its passages of text the aeons might become acquainted with the father.

*   *   *

VIII. THE FATHER AND THE SON

The Father's Name

Now, the name of the father is the son. It is he who in the beginning named what emanated from him, remaining always the same. And he begot him as a son [Heb 1:5] and gave him his name, which he possessed [John 17:11]. It is he in whose vicinity the father has all things: he has the name, and he has the son. The latter can be seen; but the name is invisible, for it alone is the mystery of the invisible, which comes into ears that are wholly full of it, because of him. And yet the father's name is not spoken. Rather, it is manifest in a son. Thus, great is the name!

Who, then, can utter his name, the great name, but him alone who possesses the name—and the children of the name in whom the father's name reposed and who in turn reposed in his name! Inasmuch as the father is unengendered, it is he who alone bore him unto himself, as a name, before he had put the aeons in order, so that the name of the father might be supreme over them as lord. And this is the

---

9. To "stand at rest" is philosophical jargon for the state of permanence, nonchange, and real being, as opposed to what exists in instability, change, and becoming.

1. One or more words are inadvertently omitted here.

2. Or "eternal realms." In gnostic myth, the aeons are emanations of the first principle and compose the structure of the spiritual universe, which contains only aeons.

p. 39 true name, confirmed by his command in perfect power. For this name does not result from words and acts of naming, but rather his name is invisible.

He alone gave him a name, for he alone saw him, and it was he alone who was able to name him: for what does not exist has no name—indeed, what would a nonexistent be named?—but what exists, exists along with its name. And he alone is acquainted with him and ⟨ . . . ⟩³ for him alone to give him a name. He is the father: his name is the son. So he did not hide it within action, rather it existed. The son alone gave names. So the name belongs to the father, just as the name of the father is the son, the beloved. For where would he find a name except from the father?

Yet perhaps someone will say to another, "Who could name one that preexisted before him? Do not children get names **p. 40** from their parents?" First, we must consider the question of what sort of thing a name is. For he is the true name. Thus it is he who is the name from the father; for it is he who exists as the most lordly name. Accordingly, he did not get the name on loan—unlike others, all of whom individually get their names according as they are created [cf. Gen 2:19–20]. But this one is the most lordly name. There is no other being that bestowed it upon him. Rather, he is unnameable and indescribable until such time as the perfect alone has spoken of him. And it is the latter who is able to speak his name and see him.

So when it pleased him that his uttered name should be his son, and when he who had emanated from the depth gave him his name he spoke of his secrets, knowing that the father is without evil. Precisely for this reason he produced him—so that he might speak concerning the place from which he had emanated and his realm of repose, **p. 41** and that he might glorify the fullness, the greatness of his name, and the father's sweetness.

PTOLEMY

[A Version of the Valentinian Gnostic Myth]
(From Irenaeus, *Against Heresies*, book 1)†

1.1 [The disciples of Ptolemy] affirm that there is in certain high places unseen and unnamed I know not what perfect Æon, existing before all, whom they call sometimes Proarche, the First Beginning, sometimes Propator, the First Father, sometimes Bythos, that is, the Deep; that he is likewise invisible and incomprehensible; and that being incomprehensible and invisible, eternal also and unbegotten, he abode in great tranquillity and calm through boundless ages;

That there exists with him also, Thought, the same whom they likewise denominate Grace and Silence; and that at some unknown time it occurred to the said Bythos to put forth from himself what should be a beginning of all things; and

---

3. The Coptic text is corrupt; one or more words may be inadvertently omitted here.

† From Irenaeus, *Five Books of S. Irenaeus: Against Heresies*, trans. John Keble, A Library of Fathers of the Holy Catholic Church (London: James Parker and Co., 1872), 3–24 (ocassionally altered).

that this which he was minded to put forth, being as it were seed, he deposited as in a womb with the partner of his being Silence;

That she, having received this seed and become pregnant, brought forth Mind, who is similar to him that begat him and alone comprehends the greatness of his Father, to which Mind they also give the name of Only-begotten, and Father, and principle of all things; and that there was produced together with him Truth; and that this is the first and aboriginal quaternion of Pythagoras,[1] which also they style the root of all things, namely, the Deep, and Silence, and, after them, Mind and Truth;

Further, that the Only Begotten, having become aware of the purposes for which he was produced, did himself also produce the Word and the Life, thus becoming the Father of all who should be after him and the principle and formative power of the whole Pleroma;[2] next, that from the Word and the Life were produced, as in marriage, the Man and the Church; and that this was the aboriginal Ogdoas or Eight, the root and substance of all things, having according to them, four names: the Deep, the Mind, the Word, and the Man, each of these being both male and female, as follows: First, the Great Father, they said, was united as in marriage to his own Thought; next the Only-begotten, that is, the Mind, to the Truth; afterwards the Word to the Life; and the Man to the Church;

1.2 Moreover, that these Æons, as they were produced for the Father's glory, so wishing also themselves to glorify the Father by something of their own, produced offspring as in marriage; first, that the Word and the Life, after the Man and the Church, brought into being other ten Æons, whose names they say are these: the Profound, and Commixture; the Undecaying, and Union; the Self-originated, and Pleasure; the Unmoved, and Incorporation; the Only-begotten, and the Blessed One. These are the ten additional Æons, who they say were produced by the Word and Life. They add that the Man also for his part with the Church produced twelve Æons, on whom they bestow these names: the Comforter, and Faith; the Paternal One, and Hope; the Maternal One, and Love; the Ever-Intelligent, and Understanding; the Ecclesiastical One, and Blessedness; the Desired, and Wisdom.

1.3 These are the 30 Æons of their false doctrine, kept hitherto in silence and unknown. This is the invisible and spiritual Fullness they talk of, with its threefold division into sets respectively of eight, and ten, and twelve beings. And they affirm this to have been the reason why the Saviour (for they are not willing to call Him Lord) for 30 years did nothing openly [Luke 3:23], declaring this mystery of the Æons. Yea, and in the parable of the labourers which were sent into the vineyard [Matt 20:1–16] they say it is most evident that these 30 Æons are indicated, in that some are sent about the first hour, some about the third, others about the sixth, others again the ninth, and a further sent about the eleventh. Now the aforesaid hours, being added together, make up the number thirty,

1. That is, $1+2+3+4=10$, which could be depicted as a triangle with one unit on top, two just below, and so forth.

2. A Greek word meaning "fullness" (as it is rendered in 1.3 below) and referring to the spiritual universe in the Valentinian gnostic system.

for $1+3+6+9+11=30$. And the Hours, they affirm, signify the Æons. And these, they add, are the great and wonderful and unutterable mysteries, the fruit of which they themselves only bear, as also of any among the many sayings of Scripture which one haply may be able to accommodate and cause to appear like their invention.

2.1 To proceed. Their First Father they affirm to be known unto none but the Only-Begotten who sprang from him, that is, to the Mind; to all the rest, they say, he remains invisible and incomprehensible. But the Mind alone, according to them, having delight in the contemplation of the Father and rejoicing in the thought of His immeasurable greatness, was purposing to communicate to the other Æons also the greatness of the Father, how vast his duration and extent, how he was unoriginated and incomprehensible and incapable of being beheld. But Silence restrained him, by the will of the Father, because he was minded to bring them all to imagine and long for some mode of searching out their First Father, such as we have described him. And thus all the other Æons continued alike in a kind of silence, longing to behold the first originator of their seed and to acquaint themselves with the Root which has no beginning.

2.2 Only the last and youngest Æon of the Family of twelve, produced by the Man and the Church, that is, Wisdom,[3] surged forward and was affected in some way without intercourse with her partner, the Desired—a kind of thing which had begun in the case of the Mind, and Truth, but in its result affected only this perverted Æon (perverted, in pretence, by Love, but in reality by Presumption)—on account of her not having communion with the Perfect Father, as the Mind also had. Now the Passion which this Æon conceived was searching after the Father. For she would fain, they say, comprehend His greatness. Next, they add, not being able—because it was a thing impossible which she was attempting—she was in a very intense inward strife, because of the vastness of that Deep and the unsearchable nature of the Father and her yearning after him. Which things continually urging her onward, she would at length have been absorbed by His delightsomeness and resolved into His whole being, had she not met with that power which supports and guards all things, excepting only the greatness which is unspeakable. And to this power they give the name also of Horos, that is, Order, or Limit. And by this that youngest Æon, they say, was restrained and steadied; and having hardly returned to herself and become convinced that the Father is incomprehensible, she put off her former intention, together with the impression which had come upon her from that astounding wonder!

2.3 And some of them make a kind of legend of that which befel Wisdom and her recovery, as though she having attempted a thing impossible and inconceivable brought forth a substance without form, even as it was natural for her, being a female, to bring forth. And on considering her offspring, they add, she was first of all vexed because of the imperfect birth, then affrighted lest her being itself might prove incapable of perfection;[4] and upon that she was beside herself and in despair, enquiring the cause and how she might conceal what happened;

---

3. Gk. *Sophia*, a feminine noun. (Each pair of aeons has a masculine and feminine member.)
4. Gk. obscure. She may also fear lest her offspring die or lest her own existence come to an end.

and that being sore beset with these passions, she took a turn and endeavoured to hasten back to the Father, and having ventured a certain way failed through weakness and became a suppliant to the Father; and that she was joined in her supplication by the other Æons, especially by the Mind.

This, they say, was the first origin of the substance of matter, namely, out of that ignorance and grief, and fear, and astonishment.

2.4 Moreover, the Father, with a view to these things, produces the aforesaid Order, or Limit, by the Only Begotten, in his own image, unpaired, with nothing of the weaker sex about him. (For so they affirm the Father to exist, sometimes in concert with Silence, sometimes above male and female alike). And this being, called Order, they denominate also the Cross, and the Redeemer, and the Assertor of Liberty, and Assigner of Boundaries, and Maintainer of Causes. And by means of this Order, they say, Wisdom was purified and confirmed and restored to her place as one of a pair of Æons. That is, desire having been separated from her, with the passion which accompanied it, she herself remains within the Pleroma; but [they say] that this her mental produce, with all passion, is by the aforesaid Order put apart in a state of privation and being turned out of the Pleroma, continues indeed a spiritual substance, having a certain natural energy such as belongs to an Æon but without form or kind, as not comprehending any thing. And therefore they call it an imbecile and feminine fruit (of wisdom).

2.5 But after the separation of the Offspring to a region without the Pleroma of the Æons and the restoration of the mother to her place as one of a pair, the Only-Begotten, as they say, again produced another pair according to the purpose of the Father, that none of the Æons might suffer as she had done—another pair, Christ and the Holy Ghost, to fix and consolidate the Pleroma. And so by these the worlds [or Æons] were framed [Heb 11:3]. For that Christ for his part instructed them that they were sufficiently acquainted already with the nature of their own Communion and the Idea of the Unbegotten; and that[5] he declared among them the mode of coming to more knowledge of the Father: that He is incomprehensible and inconceivable and can neither be seen nor heard any further than He is known through the Only Begotten [Matt 11:27]; also that the principal eternal duration to the other Æons is the original incomprehensible nature of the Father, but to him who is the Father's offspring and Son it is His being comprehensible by him which indeed is what makes him His equal. These then were the proceedings among them of the newly produced Æon, Christ.

2.6 The one Spirit, again, the Holy one, for his part instructed them to give thanks for being all made mutually equal and guided them to the true rest.

And so they say the Æons were constituted equal in form and in purpose, having all become Minds; and all, Words; and all, Men; and all, Christs; and the females in like manner, all, Truths; and all, Lives; and Spirits; and Churches.

And it is added, that hereupon all things being confirmed and come to perfect rest with great joy say hymns to the First Father, taking their share in high festal gladness.

And [they say] that on account of this benefit with one will and mind the whole Pleroma of Æons, Christ and the Spirit consenting, and their Father setting his

---

5. *For that Christ . . . and that*: the Greek text is corrupt and thus the translation is incoherent.

seal—each, I say, of the Æons severally contributed whatever he had most beautiful and blooming in himself; and having put in each his share, and fitly combined the same, and harmoniously united them, they produced a most perfect Emanation to the honour and glory of Him who is the Deep, the beauty and star of their Pleroma, even their perfect fruit, Jesus, who was also called Saviour, and Christ, and the Word, as a son is called after his father, and All, because he is of them all.

Moreover, that as body-guards to themselves, to their own honour, they produced also Angels of the same nature with him.

3.1 These then are the transactions spoken of by them as taking place within the Pleroma: first, what became subject to passion and well nigh lost itself as it were in a vast and intricate matter, trying to search out the Father; next, the composition, equivalent to six Æons in one, of him who is called Order, and the Cross, and the Redeemer, and the Assertor of liberty, and the Assigner of bounds, and Maintainers of causes; then the production, by their Father, upon second thoughts of the first Christ, with the Holy Spirit, subsequent to that of the Æons; lastly, how the second Christ, whom they denominate also Saviour, was put together and framed by way of contribution from them all.

But all this, they say, is not openly uttered, being all cannot receive such knowledge; however, our Saviour has mysteriously indicated it in parables to such as have power to understand it [Matt 19:11; Mark 4:10–12]. As for instance: the thirty Æons, they say, are indicated by the thirty years of which we made mention before, wherein, as they observe, our Saviour did nothing openly; as also by the Parable of the Labourers in the Vineyard. Paul also, as they affirm, most evidently names these Æons in many places, and hath moreover observed the Order in which they follow one another when he says, Unto all the generations of the Age of all Ages: (literally, of the Æon of all Æons) [Eph 3:21]. Nay, and that we too, in the Eucharist, when we utter the clause, 'World without end' (literally, unto the Æon of all Æons) give signification of those Æons. In a word, wheresoever mention is made of Age or Ages they will have it referred to the aforesaid Æons.

3.2 They add that the origination of their band of twelve Æons is signified by our Lord's being twelve years old when He conversed with the Doctors of the Law [Luke 2:42–50]; and by His choice of the Apostles, in that there were twelve of them [Matt 10:2; Mark 3:14; Luke 6:13]. Again, that the other eighteen Æons are manifested by the circumstance of His abiding eighteen months, as they say, with His Disciples, after He rose from the dead. Also, that by the two first letters of His Name, the I and the H, those eighteen Æons are clearly enough indicated; and the ten Æons in like manner they say are signified by the letter I, which stands first in His Name.[6] And this was the cause why our Saviour said, "one iota, or one tittle, must not pass away, till all be fulfilled" [Matt 5:18].

3.3 As to the calamity which befel the twelfth Æon, they say it was darkly implied in the apostasy of Judas, who was twelfth among the Apostles, as also by His having suffered in the twelfth month. For they will have it that He preached for one year only after His Baptism [Luke 4:19].

---

6. The Greek letter I (iota) conventionally represented the number 10; the Greek letter H (eta) represented 8.

They add that in the case of the woman with an issue of blood, this is most evidently set forth in that she, having suffered twelve years [Matt 9:20; Mark 5:25; Luke 8:43], was healed by the presence of Our Saviour upon touching the hem of His Garment; and that this was why Our Saviour said, "Who touched me?" informing His Disciples of the mysterious event among the Æons, the healing of that Æon which had become subject to Passion. For the woman who had suffered for twelve years being in fact that Power, when its substance was being drawn out and melting away without limit (as they affirm), had she not touched that which He wore—that is, the Truth which makes one of the first quaternion, and of which the hem of His Garment is the symbol—would have been resolved into that which was the ground of her being. She was stayed, however, and rested from her calamity because the Power which went out of Him (and this they will have to be Order or Limit) healed her and withdrew the calamity from her.

3.4 Again, their doctrine that Our Saviour proceeding from all is in a certain sense all, they affirm, to be signified by the expression, "Every male that openeth the Womb" [Exod 13:2; Luke 2:23]; and that He, being All,[7] opened the womb of her who is the thought, or Imagination, of that afflicted Æon, the womb, I say, of her who was banished from the Pleroma—the same whom they also denominate the second Ogdoad, whereof we shall give an account a little below. And Paul also evidently for no other reason, as they affirm, used the expression, "And He is all" [Col 3:11], and again, "All things are to Him, and of Him are all things" [Rom 11:36], and again, "In Him dwelleth all The Fullness (Pleroma) of the Godhead" [Col 2:9], and this following, "That He summed up all things in Christ, by God" [Eph 1:10]—these they expounded to the same effect, and if there be any thing else of the like sound.

3.5 Next, as concerning him whom they call Order, or Limit—to whom they give so many names, affirming that he has two modes of operation, the one apt to establish, the other to divide, and that in respect of his establishing and consolidating he is the Cross, but in respect of his dividing and distinguishing, he is Order, or Limit—the operation of the same Order, they say, our Saviour signified as follows: that is to say, first his work of consolidating when He says, "He that taketh not up his cross and followeth Me, cannot become My Disciple" [Matt 10:38; Luke 14:27]; and, "Take up the cross and follow Me" [Mark 10:21, according to some MSS]; and, his distinguishing work again, where it is said, "I came not to send peace, but a sword" [Matt 10:34; Luke 12:51]. John also, according to them, indicated the same by the words, "The fan is in His Hand, and He shall throughly purge the floor, and shall gather the wheat into His garner, but the chaff He will burn with fire unquenchable" [Matt 3:12; Luke 3:17]. Now in this speech also they said there was signified the operation of Order or Limit. For that "Fan" they expound to be the Cross, who, they add, consumes also all material things, as fire the chaff, but purges those who are saved, as the fan does the wheat. Moreover they affirm that Paul the Apostle also makes mention of this Cross in the text, "For the Word of the Cross is to them that perish foolishness; but to us which are saved, it is the Power of God" [1 Cor 1:18]. And again, "God

---

7. "Every" and "all" translate the same Greek word.

forbid that I should glory, save in the Cross of Jesus, by whom the world is crucified unto me, and I unto the world" [Gal 6:14].

* * *

4.1 Now the transactions outside the Pleroma, stated by them, are as follows.

The conception of the Wisdom which is above, to which also they give the
name of Achamoth,[8] being excluded, with all Passion, from the Pleroma and
abiding in certain shadows and void places did there of necessity, as they affirm,
effervesce, being turned out of the Light and the Pleroma, without form or kind,
as an abortion, because she had not comprehended anything. Hereupon, they
add, the superior Christ pitying her and overshadowing her by the intervention of
him who is the Cross did of his own power bring her into form—such form as
implies resemblance to him in substance only and not in knowledge. And having
done this he has turned back, withdrawing his power, and left her to herself, in
order that perceiving her calamity, in that she was separated from the Pleroma,
she might aim at the things which are more excellent, having a kind of savour of
incorruption left in her by Christ and the Holy Spirit. And that this is why she is
called by both names, namely, Wisdom, from her parent (for that which produced
her is called Wisdom), and the Holy Ghost, from the spirit which attends on Christ.

Further, [they say] that having received form and consciousness but being
presently left void of the Invisible Word who was with her (that is, Christ) she set
herself to search out the Light which had forsaken her but was unable to attain
unto it because she was forbidden by the power of Order (or Limit). And that at
this point of time Order, checking her in her onward impulse, uttered the word
IAO, from which the Holy Name, Yahweh they say, had its origin. And that she,
unable to pass by the said Order because of her being entangled with her affliction and thus left alone outside, sank under every part of her affliction, manifold
and various as it was, and so had to endure first grief, because she could not attain
to her end, then fear of the Life forsaking her, even as the Light had done, and
besides these perplexity, and the whole together in ignorance. And not as her
mother, the first Wisdom, who is also an Æon, did she simply endure alternation
in her passions, but even absolute contrariety, another tendency also having
befallen her, that of conversion to him who gave her life.

4.2 This, they say, was the composition and being of matter, out of which this
world was formed. For on the one hand from this her conversion the whole soul
of the world and of its Fabricator took its origin; on the other, from her tears was
produced all liquid substance; from her laughter, all that is luminous; from her
grief and perplexity, the bodily elements of the world. Since she was now in tears
and grief, as they affirm, on account of her being left alone in the darkness and
void, once while having lit upon an imagination of the light which had left her, she
relaxed into a smile; and then again on the contrary she was smitten with fear;
and another time she was in utter perplexity and amazement.

* * *

8. Derived from a Hebrew word for wisdom.

4.5 Their Mother, then, having travelled through her whole calamity and only just begun to surmount it, betook herself, as they say, to supplication of the Light which had left her, that is, of the Christ. But he, having returned to the Pleroma, shrank, I suppose, from the trouble of descending a second time and rather sent out to her the Comforter, that is the Saviour—the Father having yielded unto him all his power and delivered every thing to be under his authority [Matt 11:27; Luke 10:22]—and the Æons too in like manner, that in him all things should be created, visible and invisible, Thrones, Deities, Dominions [Col 1:16]. He is sent forth to her with the Angels which were formed at the same time with him.

Thereupon Achamoth, reverencing him, as they say, first put on a veil out of bashfulness; but afterwards beholding him with all his rich show of fruit, hastened towards him, receiving power to do so by his manifestation. He, they say, reduced her into form with such formation as implies perfect knowledge and acheived the healing of her passions. He separated them from her; he did not entirely neglect them (to annihilate them being impossible, because now they were habitual and strong), but he put them apart by themselves, then mingled and consolidated them and changed them from incorporal accidents into matter still incorporeal. Next accordingly he wrought in them aptitude and a peculiar nature, that they might enter into combinations and bodies, so that two substances might come into being: the one bad, liable to the Passions; the other intelligent, capable of conversion. And for this cause, they say that our Saviour was virtually the Framer of the Universe.

Moreover [they say] that Achamoth being delivered from her trouble and obtaining with that joy the contemplation of the lights that were with Him, that is, of the Angels, his companions, and smitten with longing for them, became pregnant (so they teach) with offspring after their image, a spiritual offspring, formed after the resemblance of those who were the body-guards of our Saviour.

5.1 Having now therefore these three ingredients given her, by their account (the first proceeding from Passion, which was matter; the second from a tendency to recovery, which was the animal[9] part; the third that which she bore, that is, the spiritual part), she next applied herself to the forming thereof. However, the spiritual part she was unable herself to reduce into form, being herself of the same substance with it. But she betook herself to the formation of the animal substance which arose from her tendency to recovery and so brought to light the instructions she had received from the Saviour.

Now her first formation out of the animal substance, they say, was the Father and King of all things, both of such as are of the same substance with himself, that is, the animal, the same which they call also things on the right hand; and of those also which owe their origin to passion and matter, the same which they say are on the left. For all things akin to himself,[1] they say, he formed, unconsciously moved thereto by his Mother—whence also they give him the names of Metropator,[2] and Unfathered, and Artificer, and Father, affirming him to be Father of

---

9. I.e., "animate," characterized by *anima* (Gk. psychē), soul.
1. Or "after himself" [translator's note].
2. I.e., "Mother-father."

things on the right, that is, animal, but of those on the left, that is, material, Artificer, and of all taken together, King.

For the aforesaid Enthymesis[3] [or Achamoth], they say, desired to do all to the honour of the Æons and therefore made certain images of them—or rather the Saviour did so by her. And she reserved herself to be in the image of the invisible Father, she not being known by the Demiurgus [or Artificer] while he was to represent the only-begotten Son,[4] and the images of the other Æons were to be the Archangels and Angels formed by him.

5.2 He [the Demiurgus] then, by their account, became Father and God of things outside the Pleroma, being maker of all, both animal and material. For that he separated those two substances before confused and brought the incorporeal into bodily shape and so framed both heavenly and earthly things and became their Artificer, whether material or animal, on the right hand or on the left, light or heavy, of upward or of downward tendency. He furnished seven Heavens, above which, they say, is the Demiurgus himself. And therefore they call him the Hebdomad, but his mother Achamoth the Ogdoad, she thus keeping entire the number of the original and first Ogdoad belonging to the Pleroma.

Further, as to these seven heavens,[5] which, they say, are endowed with understanding, they suppose them to be a kind of Angels, and the Demiurgus too himself an angel like unto God. As they say also that Paradise, being above the third heaven, is virtually a fourth angel, and that Adam obtained I know not what from it in consequence of his abode therein.

5.3 Moreover, they say that the Demiurgus fancied himself to be framing these things of himself, but that in reality he made them by virtue which came out from Achamoth, so that Heaven was made by him, he not knowing heaven; and man was moulded, he not knowing man; and Earth manifested, while he was unacquainted with Earth. And throughout in like manner they say he was ignorant of the substantial forms of what he was making, and of his mother herself, and fancied that he himself alone was all. And the cause of this his imagination, they affirm, was his mother, whose will it had been so to train him up to be head and principle of his own proper substance and director of this whole work, which mother of his they call also the Ogdoad, and Wisdom, and Earth, and Jerusalem, and the Holy Spirit, and in the masculine, Lord. Her home, they say, is in the intermediate space so that she abides above the Demiurgus but beneath or outside the Pleroma until the consummation.

5.4 The material substance, then, being, as they say, made out of three passions or affections, fear, and grief, and perplexity, they will have it that the partakers of animal life owe their subsistence partly to fear and partly to an effort after recovery; that from this effort the Demiurgus had his birth, but from fear, all other being that has animal life, as the souls of irrational creatures, and of beasts, and men; wherefore that he, wanting energy to discern any spiritual things, considered himself alone to be God, and said by his Prophets, "I am God, beside Me there is

3. A Greek word meaning "thinking."
4. I.e., Mind (1.1).
5. Cf. 2 Cor 12:2 and note.

none" [Isa 45:21; 46:9]. From grief again they teach that the spiritual powers of wickedness proceeded; that hence the Devil had his origin, whom also they call the Ruler of this world, his demons too, and his angels, and all that spiritually exists on the side of wickedness. The Demiurgus however they call the son of that Mother of theirs, but the Ruler of this world, a creature of the Demiurgus. And [they teach] that the Ruler of the world knows the things above him because he is a spirit of wickedness, but the Demiurgus knows them not, as having merely an animal existence.

The abode of their Mother they say is the super celestial region, that is, in the intermediate space; of the Demiurgus, in the heavenly, that is, in the series of seven heavens; of the Ruler of the world, in this world of ours.

Further, that from that astonishment and extreme perplexity as from the meaner passions, the corporeal elements of the world, as we stated before, had their origin: Earth, upon the stay of that amazement; Water, upon the exciting of Fear; air, upon the fixing (or condensation) of grief. Fire, they say, existed in them all to be a cause of death and decay, even as ignorance was secretly mingled in those three passions.

5.5 Thus having formed the world, he created also the earthly man, not however out of this dry earth, but out of its invisible substance, taking his material from that which is continually exhaled and flowing [from the grosser being]. And into this earthly man, as they carefully distinguish, he breathed the animal man. And this, they say, was the man formed after his image and similitude [Gen 1:26]: the material man being after his image, like but not consubstantial with his God; while the animal man was after his likeness, for which cause also his substance is called the Spirit of Life, coming of a spiritual efflux [from Him] [Gen 2:7]. But afterwards, they say, the coat of skins was put on him [Gen 3:21]; and this, they say, is the frail flesh, the object of sense.

5.6 But the offspring of their Mother Achamoth, whereof she became pregnant in her contemplation of the Angels which waited on the Saviour, being of the same substance with the Mother-spiritual was unknown even to the Demiurgus, as they affirm. And they say it was secretly lodged in him without his consciousness, in order that by him having been sown in the soul which he made,[6] and in this material body, and having therein, like an unborn babe, received growth, it might be made ready to admit the perfect Word.

That spiritual Man therefore was unknown, as they say, to the Demiurgus, who was sown by Wisdom in the natural man at the moment of his breathing into his nostrils, and that through an ineffable Providence. For as he knew not his Mother, so neither did he know her seed. And this same seed they affirm also to be the Church, corresponding to the Church above.

And with this they maintain their inward being to be completed, as though they had their animal soul from the Demiurgus, their body from the dust of the Earth, and their fleshly part from its matter, while the spiritual Man comes from their Mother Achamoth.

6.1 There being then three principles: the material, first of all, which they call also that on the left hand, necessarily, as they affirm, perishes, as being incapable

---

6. I.e., the animal (animate) man of 5.5.

of receiving any breath of incorruption; but the animal principle, which they denominate likewise that on the right hand, as being midway between the spiritual and material, departs in that direction towards which it makes itself incline. As to the spiritual part, they say it is sent forth in order that being here joined to the animal it may be fashioned, sharing the discipline thereof in its conversation here. And this they say is the salt and the light of the world [Matt 5:13, 14]. For the animal principle had need of outward and sensible discipline of various kinds. By such, they say, the world itself was framed, and what is more, that the Saviour came to the aid of this, the animal part, it having also free will, that he might save it.

For of those whom he was to save, they affirm, he took on him the firstfruits: from Achamoth assuming the spiritual principle, from the Demiurgus the animal Christ wherewith he clothed himself; and by that peculiar dispensation putting on a body which had an animal being, but was constructed by unspeakable art so as to be both visible and palpable and capable of suffering. They add that he took not on him any thing at all material, matter not being capable of salvation.

As to the end of the world, they say it will be when the whole spiritual creation is formed and perfected in knowledge, meaning those of mankind who are spiritual, who have the perfect knowledge concerning God and are initiated by Achamoth into her mysteries. And these, they imagine, are themselves.

6.2 For mere animal lessons are the discipline of mere animal men, of those who are established by bare faith and works and possess not the perfect knowledge. And this account they give of us who belong to the Church, which is the reason why they also affirm good conduct to be necessary for us, since otherwise we cannot be saved. As to themselves, they maintain that not by any course of conduct but because they are by nature spiritual they shall in any case and by all means be saved. For as the earthly cannot attain salvation (not being as they say capable of it) so again the spiritual, which they will have to be themselves, never can admit corruption, whatsoever actions they may be engaged in. For even as gold deposited in mud does not cast off its beauty, but keeps its proper nature, the mud having no power to damage the gold at all, just so they affirm of themselves that whatever kind of material actions they may be concerned in, they are not at all damaged themselves, nor do they cast away their spiritual subsistence.

6.3 For which cause also the most perfect among them do all forbidden things without fear, such things whereof the scriptures are positive that they who do them shall not inherit God's Kingdom [Gal 5:21].[7] Thus, in the first place, they eat indifferently of things sacrificed to idols, not esteeming themselves at all stained thereby. And at every holiday amusement of the Gentiles, taking place in honour of the idols, they are first to assemble, some of them not even abstaining from that murderous spectacle, hated by God and man, of combats with wild beasts and of single fight. Others again, who are the slaves of all fleshly pleasures, even unto loathing, say that "The carnal things are for the carnal, and the spiri-

---

7. The status of Irenaeus' report in 6.3 and 6.4 is suspect. It is unclear to what extent he reports sound information about Valentinian Christians, to what extent he presents reasonable (though not necessarily correct) inferences drawn from sound information, and to what extent he simply concocts defamatory charges.

tual things for the spiritual, being so assigned." Some of them privately corrupt the women who are instructed by them in this doctrine, as many times certain have confessed, together with the rest of their error—such I mean as had been seduced by one or other of them and had afterwards returned to the Church of God. Others even publicly casting off all shame, whatsoever women they have a fancy for they force away from their husbands and account their own wives. A third sort again, pretending at first to live in all honour, as with sisters, in process of time have been exposed, the sister becoming pregnant by the brother.

6.4 Yea, and they have many other abominable and godless practices. And while they run down us, who keep ourselves through the fear of God from sinning so much as in thought or word for being unlearned and knowing nothing, themselves they magnify above measure under the names of Perfect and Seeds of Election. For we, they affirm, receive Grace to be used only, and therefore it will be taken from us. But they have their grace as a possession of their own, it having come down from above, from the Unspeakable and Unnameable Combination; and therefore it will be added unto them.

For which cause, they add, it is right for them in every way to be always practising the mystery of Combination. And of this they convince the foolish, their words being literally such as these: "Whosoever being merely in the world hath not loved a woman so as that she should give way to him is not of the Truth and shall not proceed unto the Truth; but he that, being of the world, is overcome by a woman shall not proceed unto the Truth, because he is overcome by desire of woman."[8] For this cause accordingly they call us "good sort of natural men,"[9] and say that we are "of the world," and that we "have need of continence and of good conduct," that we may come thereby into the intermediate space; but they, 'Spiritual' and 'Perfect,' as they are called, have no such need. For it is not any conduct which brings men into the Pleroma, but that seed which is sent out from thence in an infant state and is here brought to perfection.

7.1 Now when the whole seed is made perfect, Achamoth their mother, they say, is to pass from the Intermediate Place and to enter within the Pleroma and to receive her Spouse the Saviour, him who was made up of all, that there may be a Combination of the Saviour and of Wisdom, who is Achamoth. And this, they say, is the meaning of the "Bridegroom," and "Bride," the Bridechamber being the whole Pleroma.[1]

Next, [they say] that all spiritual persons putting off their animal souls and becoming intellectual spirits are to enter within the Pleroma, incomprehensibly and invisibly, and to be assigned as the Brides to the Angels which are about the Saviour; and that the Demiurge also for his part is to pass into the region of his mother, Wisdom, that is, in the intermediate state; that the souls also of the righteous will themselves be refreshed in the place of the middle state, for nothing animal finds place within the Pleroma.

---

8. The distinction between being *in* the world (Valentinian Christians) and being *of* the world (other christians) harks back to John 17:16.
9. The Greek reads *psychikos*, "animate" or "consisting of soul."
1. Other Valentinian writings elaborate this imagery; a Valentinian ritual may lie behind it.

Moreover, that when all this has so taken place, the fire which lurks in the world is to shine forth and be kindled, and destroying all Matter, is itself to be spent together with it and to come to an end of its existence—so they say. But the Demiurge knew none of these things, as they assert, before the coming of the Saviour.

7.2 And there are some who say that he also produced a Christ, a son of his own, of animal nature however; that concerning him he spake by the Prophets. And that this was he who passed through Mary, as water passes through a pipe; and that to him at his baptism descended that other, that Saviour from the Pleroma, made up of all [the Æons], in the form of a Dove [Matt 3:16; Mark 1:10; Luke 3:22; John 1:32]. And there was in him also the same spiritual seed of Achamoth. Our Lord therefore they affirm to have been composed of these four, keeping the pattern of the original and first Quaternion: viz. of the Spiritual being, which was from Achamoth; and of the animal, which was from the Demiurge; and of the ordering of events, that which was framed with unspeakable art; and of the Saviour, which part was the Dove that descended upon Him. And that as to this part he remained impassive (for he could not suffer, being incomprehensible and invisible); and therefore, they say, it was taken away when he was brought before Pilate, I mean the Spirit of Christ which had been lodged in him.[2] But neither, by their statement, did the seed suffer, which he had from his mother; for this also, the spiritual part of him, is impassive and invisible even to the Demiurge himself. It remains that what suffered, according to them, was the animal Christ and he who by the ordering of events was mysteriously framed, that his Mother might exhibit by him the pattern of the Christ who is above, of him who was extended upon the Cross and who gave to Achamoth her essential form. For all things here, they say, are types of the things there.

7.3 Now the souls which had the seed of Achamoth were better, they say, than the rest. Wherefore also the Demiurge loves them more than the rest, not knowing the reason but accounting such to be from himself. And so, they add, he ordained them to be some Prophets, some Priests, some Kings (and many things by virtue of this seed they expound to be spoken by the Prophets) as though those souls were of a higher nature. And his Mother too they affirm to have uttered many things concerning that superior world, partly however through him and partly through the souls that were made by him. And they proceed to divide the Prophecies: one thing, as they will have it, being uttered by the Mother; another by the seed aforesaid; a third by the Demiurge. Yea, and that Jesus also in like manner uttered some things by virtue of the Saviour, some of his Mother, some of the Demiurge, as we shall explain in the progress of our argument.

7.4 Further, the Demiurge, they say, as being ignorant of the things above him, although not insensible to what was thus uttered, yet thought little of them, imagining now one cause and now another—either the prophesying Spirit (as though it had also a sort of movement of its own), or man, or the adhesion of the inferior beings—and he continued in this ignorance until the coming of the Lord. But when the Saviour was come, they say that from Him he learned all things, approaching Him, and that with a willing mind, with all his power; and that he is the centurion in the Gospel, who says to our Saviour, "For I too have

2. This was sometimes how Matt 27:46 and Mark 15:34 were interpreted.

under my own authority soldiers and slaves, and whatsoever I command, they do" [Matt 8:9; Luke 7:8]; but that he will himself accomplish the ordering of events the world until the appointed time, and that chiefly because of his care of the church, partly however through his having come to the knowledge of the reward prepared for him, that is, his being to pass into the region of his Mother.

7.5 Of men, moreover, they constitute three sorts, Spiritual, Earthly, Animal— such as were Cain, Abel, Seth—and from these the three Natures, having passed from individuals into classes. And the earthly, they say, goes into corruption; and the Animal, if it choose the better part, rests in the place of the middle state, but if the worse, it also will go to its like. But the spiritual beings, whatsoever Achamoth may have sown from that time even until now in righteous souls are first educated and fully nurtured here, as having been sent out in an infantile state; but hereafter are to have perfection vouchsafed to them and to be assigned as Brides to the Angels of the Saviour. This is their doctrine; and they add that their souls will have thoroughly rested the while of necessity in the middle state with the Demiurge. And the souls too themselves they again subdivide, saying some are naturally good, some naturally bad—the good being these, which are filled to receive that seed, while those which are naturally bad never could exhibit that seed in themselves.

TOLEDOTH YESHU[†] (The Generations of Jesus)

The date of this strange version of the story of Jesus is notoriously difficult to determine. Some of its traditions are undoubtedly ancient, as they are reported by the anti-Christian polemicist Celsus in the second century c.e. This has led a handful of scholars to postulate a connection between the *Toledoth Yeshu* and the *Gospel According to the Hebrews* mentioned by early Christian authorities as a work read by Jewish Christians. Such links are speculative, to be sure, especially since the latter is not extant and the manuscripts of the former are all relatively late. It is more likely that the *Toledoth Yeshu*, at least in the form in which it survives today, is a late antique or medieval Jewish composition—a satirical and polemical anti-gospel written in the context of increasing Christian persecution of Jews.

The *Toledoth* survives in many different versions; the following is an excerpt from a translation of the Hebrew Codex in the University Library of Strasburg.

Chap. II

1 Now the rule of all Israel was in the hand of a woman, and her name was Helene.

2 And in the temple was the foundation-stone which, being interpreted, is Jah-founded-it, and this is the stone which Jacob anointed with oil; and on it were graven the letters of the Ineffable Name.

† From Hugh J. Schonfield, *According to the Hebrews* (London: Duckworth, 1937), 39–47. Scriptural citations are provided by Schonfield.

3 And whosoever learned them could do whatsoever he would.

4 But whereas the wise men feared that the young men of Israel would learn them, and thereby destroy the world, they took steps that it should not be possible to learn them.

5 Dogs of brass were bound to two pillars of iron at the gate of the place of burnt-offerings, so that whosoever entered and learnt the letters, as soon as he went forth the dogs bayed at him: if he then looked at them the letters went forth from his mind.

6 Then came Jesus and learned them, and wrote upon parchment and cut open his thigh and laid the parchment with those letters therein; so that the cutting of his flesh pained him not. And he restored the flesh to its place.

7 And as he went forth the dogs of the pillars bayed at him, and the letters went forth from his mind.

8 He went into his house, and cut into his flesh with a knife, and lifted out the writing and learnt the letters.

9 Then went he forth and gathered together three hundred and ten of the young men of Israel.

10 He saith unto them, See ye them which say concerning me, a bastard and son of a woman in her separation;[1] they desire greatness for themselves and seek to exercise lordship in Israel.

11 Have ye not seen that all the prophets prophesied concerning the Messiah of God, and I am the Messiah.

12 And concerning me Isaiah prophesied, and said, Behold, the virgin shall conceive, and bear a son, and shall call his name Immanuel [Isa 7:14].

13 And, again, David my ancestor prophesied concerning me, and said, The Lord said unto me, Thou art my son; this day have I begotten thee [Ps 2:7].

14 He begat me without a male lying with (my mother); yet they call me a bastard.

15 And again he prophesied, Why do the heathen rage, and the people imagine a vain thing? The kings of the earth set themselves, and the rulers take counsel together, against the Lord, and against his anointed [Ps 2:1–2].

16 I am the Messiah, and them that withstand me are the children of whoredoms, for so saith the scripture, For they be the children of whoredoms [Hos 2:4].

17 Then answered him the young men, If thou art the Messiah, show unto us a sign.

18 He saith unto them, What sign seek ye of me that I should do for you?

19 Straightway they brought unto him a lame man, that never yet had stood upon his feet. He spake over him the letters, and he rose up upon his feet.

20 In that hour they all worshipped him, and said, This is the Messiah.

21 Again he performed for them another sign.

22 They brought unto him a leper, and he spake over him the letters, and he was healed.

---

1. That is, the bastard son of a menstrous woman—which is precisely what Jesus is, according to the *Toledoth's* opening.

23 There joined themselves unto him the insurgents of his people [Dan 11:14].

Chap. III

1 Now when the wise men saw that all were believing in him, straightway they bound him fast and led him before Helene the queen, under whose hand was the land of Israel.

2 They said unto her, This man is a sorcerer, and he deceiveth the world.

3 Jesus answering her, saith, The prophets aforetime prophesied concerning me, And there shall come forth a rod out of the stem of Jesse, and I am he [Isa 11:1]. But concerning them the scripture saith, Blessed is the man that walketh not in the counsel of the ungodly [Ps 1:1].

4 She saith unto them, Is it in your law, what he saith?

5 They say, It is in our law, but it was not spoken concerning him: for it is written, And that prophet which shall presume to speak a word in my name, which I have not commanded him to speak, or that shall speak in the name of other gods, even that prophet shall die [Deut 18:20]. And thou shalt put away the evil from among you [Deut 19:19].

6 But the Messiah whom we expect, with him are other signs, and he shall smite the earth with the rod of his mouth [Isa 11:4]. But with this bastard the signs are not present.

7 Jesus said unto her, Lady, I am he, and I revive the dead.

8 She sent for faithful men bringing with them a dead body. He spake the letters and the dead revived.

9 In that hour the queen trembled, and said, It is a great sign.

10 She rebuked the wise men, and they went forth from her presence shamefaced, and they were sore distressed.

11 The insurgents increased and were with him, and there was a great schism in Israel.

12 Jesus went forth to Upper Galilee. And the wise men assembled and came before the queen, and said unto her, Lady, he practiseth sorcery and therewith he leadeth the world astray.

13 Therefore she sent horsemen on his account, and they found him as he was misleading the men of Upper Galilee, and saying to them, I am the son of God of whom it is written in your law.

14 The horsemen rose up therefore to take him, but the men of Upper Galilee would not suffer them, and began to fight.

15 Jesus saith unto them, Fight not, but trust ye in the power of my Father which is in heaven.

16 Now the men of Galilee were making birds of clay. And he spake the letters of the Ineffable Name and they flapped their wings. The same hour they fell down before him.

17 He said unto them, Bring ye me a millstone: they rolled it to the sea shore. And he spake the letters, and set it upon the face of the waters, and sat thereon as one sitteth in a boat, and went and floated upon the face of the waters.

18 And they that were sent saw it and wondered.

19 And Jesus said unto the horsemen, Go unto your mistress, and tell her what ye have seen. Then the spirit lifted him up from the face of the waters and brought him to the dry land.

20 So the horsemen departed and reported all these things to the queen. And the queen trembled and was greatly amazed.

21 And she sent and gathered together the elders of Israel, and said unto them, Ye say that he is a sorcerer, yet daily he reneweth great signs.

22 Then said they to her, Lady, lay not his affairs to heart. Send messengers and bring him now and his reproach shall be made plain.

23 In the same hour she sent messengers, and there were joined with him his wicked company, and they came with him before the queen.

24 Then went the elders of Israel and took a certain man whose name was Judas Iscariot, and brought him into the house of the holy of holies; and he learned the letters of the Ineffable Name which were engraved on the foundation stone, and wrote them upon a small parchment, cut open his thigh and spake the Ineffable Name that it pained not even as Jesus had done at the first.

25 As soon as Jesus with his company had returned before the queen, and she had bidden the wise men attend, Jesus answered and said, Of me it was prophesied and said, For dogs compassed me about [Ps 22:16].

26 When the wise men entered and Judas Iscariot with them, they began vehemently to accuse him, and he them, until he said to the queen, Of me it was said, I will ascend unto heaven [Isa 14:13]; and it is written, For he shall receive me. Selah [Ps 49:15].

27 Then lifted he up his hands as the wings of an eagle and did fly, and the world was amazed before him, How is he able to fly between heaven and earth!

28 Then said the elders of Israel to Judas Iscariot, Do thou make mention of the letters and ascend after him.

29 And straightway he did so, and flew in the heavens, and the world was amazed, How are they able to fly like eagles!

30 Until Iscariot gripped him and flew in the heavens; but he was not able to force him down to the earth, neither one the other by means of the Ineffable Name; for the Ineffable Name was with each of them.

31 Now when Judas saw that it was so, he acted foully and polluted Jesus, so that he became unclean and fell to the earth, and Judas also with him. And for this deed they weep bitterly on their night, yea, for the deed that Judas did to him.

32 In that hour they seized him, and said unto Helene (the queen) . . . Let him be destroyed . . . [2] Let him tell us who smote him.

33 And they covered his head with a garment and smote him with pomegranate staves, and as he knew not a word, it was seen that the Ineffable Name had departed from him.

34 Now as he was fast in their hands, he answered and said to his fellows before the queen, Concerning me it was said, Who will rise up for me against the

2. Text defective [translator's note].

the evil-doers? [Ps 94:16]. And of them he said, The proud waters [Ps 124:5]. Yea, of them he said, They have made their faces harder than a rock [Jer 5:3].

35 When the queen heard this she threatened the insurgents, and said to the wise men of Israel, See, he is in your hands.

36 And they went forth from the presence of the queen, and brought him into the synagogue of Tiberias, and bound him to a pillar of the ark.

37 Then gathered together the company of fools and impious ones which believed on his words, and desired to deliver him from the elders. But they could not, and there was great strife between them.

38 Now when he saw that he had no power to escape, he said, Give me a little water. They gave him vinegar in a copper vessel.

39 He answered and spake with a loud voice, Did not David prophesy concerning me, and say, In my thirst they gave me vinegar to drink [Ps 69:21].

40 On his head they set a crown of thorns, and the insurgents lamented sore, and there began a fight between them, brother with brother, father with son; but the wise men vanquished the insurgents.

41 Then answered he, and said, Of me was it prophesied and said, I gave my back to the smiters, and my cheeks to them that plucked off the hair [Isa 50:6]. And again concerning these the scripture saith, Draw near hither, ye sons of the sorceress [Isa 57:3]. But of me it was said, And we did esteem him stricken, smitten of God and afflicted [Isa 53:4]. And of me he said, The Messiah shall be cut off, and shall have nothing [Dan 9:26].

42 And when the insurgents heard this, they began to stone them with stones, and there was great strife between them.

43 And the elders were confounded, and the insurgents caused him to escape from them, and his three hundred and ten disciples brought him into the region of Antioch, and he abode there until the eve of the passover.

Part II. Exegesis

PRECRITICAL EXEGESIS
ORIGEN

Origen (ca. 185–ca. 251) was born into a Christian family in Alexandria, where he received both a classical and a Christian education. As a young man he was placed in charge of the Alexandrian catechetical school, which seems to have functioned at least in part as a school for advanced theological study modeled after pagan philosophical academies of the time. Perhaps because of a controversy surrounding his ordination, around 231 Origen emigrated to Caesaria, where he continued to preach, teach, and write. He died as a result of torture inflicted during Decius's persecution.

Origen was one of the outstanding intellectuals of antiquity and the sheer quantity of his output is unparalleled, amounting to several thousand books. His writing focused primarily on biblical interpretation and included the *Hexapla*, a work of Old Testament textual criticism whose philological rigor was not surpassed until the Renaissance and Reformation. Only a portion of Origen's corpus survives, in part because it was too abundant to copy, but his condemnation by important Christian intellectuals in the fourth, fifth, and sixth centuries also discouraged its preservation. Dogmatic interpretations of his theologically speculative writings prompted many who were committed to an orthodoxy defined by creeds formulated after Origen's death to denounce his writings as heretical.

The following is a series of excerpts from book 10 of Origen's commentary on John that address discrepancies between the Fourth Gospel and the Synoptics.

[Discrepancies Between the Gospels]†
(from *Commentary on John*, book 10)

1. * * * The book begins at the words: "After this He went down to Capernaum, He and His mother and His brothers and His disciples, and there they abode not many days" [John 2:12]. The other three Evangelists say that the Lord, after His conflict with the devil, departed into Galilee. Matthew [4:11–13] and Luke [4:13–16, 31] represent that he was first at Nazara, and then left them and came and dwelt in Capernaum. Matthew and Mark also state a certain reason why He

---

† From Origen, *Commentary on John*, trans. Allan Menzies, in *The Ante-Nicene Fathers*, vol. 9 (1896–97; reprint, Peabody, MA: Hendrickson, 1994), 381–85, 391–95.

departed thither, namely, that He had heard that John was cast into prison [Matt 4:12–13; Mark 1:13–15, 21]. * * * Luke gives what He said at Nazara, and how those in the synagogue were enraged at Him and cast Him out of the city and brought Him to the brow of the hill on which their cities were built, to cast Him down headlong, and how going through the midst of them the Lord went His way [4:16–30]; and with this he connects the statement, "And He came down to Capernaum, a city of Galilee, and He was teaching them on the Sabbath day" [4:31].

2. The truth of these matters must lie in that which is seen by the mind. If the discrepancy between the Gospels is not solved, we must give up our trust in the Gospels, as being true and written by a divine spirit, or as records worthy of credence, for both these characters are held to belong to these works. Those who accept the four Gospels, and who do not consider that their apparent discrepancy is to be solved anagogically (by mystical interpretation), will have to clear up the difficulty, raised above, about the forty days of the temptation, a period for which no room can be found in any way in John's narrative; and they will also have to tell us when it was that the Lord came to Capernaum. If it was after the six days of the period of His baptism, the sixth being that of the marriage at Cana of Galilee, then it is clear that the temptation never took place, and that He never was at Nazara, and that John was not yet delivered up. Now, after Capernaum, where He abode not many days, the passover of the Jews was at hand, and He went up to Jerusalem, where He cast the sheep and oxen out of the temple, and poured out the small change of the bankers [John 2:12–15]. In Jerusalem, too, it appears that Nicodemus, the ruler and Pharisee, first came to Him by night, and heard what we may read in the Gospel [John 3:1–21]. "After these things, Jesus came, and His disciples, into the land of Judæa, and there He tarried with them and baptized, at the same time at which John also was baptizing in Ænon near Salim, because there were many waters there, and they came and were baptized; for John was not yet cast into prison" [John 3:22–24]. On this occasion, too, there was a questioning on the part of John's disciples with the Jews about purification, and they came to John, saying of the Saviour, "Behold, He baptizeth, and all come to Him" [John 3:26]. They had heard words from the Baptist, the exact tenor of which it is better to take from Scripture itself [John 3:27–36]. Now, if we ask when Christ was first in Capernaum, our respondents, if they follow the words of Matthew, and of the other two, will say, After the temptation, when, "leaving Nazareth, He came and dwelt in Capernaum by the sea" [Matt 4:12–13; Mark 1:14, 21; Luke 4:14, 31]. But how can they show both the statements to be true, that of Matthew and Mark, that it was because He heard that John was delivered up that He departed into Galilee, and that of John, found there, after a number of other transactions, subsequent to His stay at Capernaum, after His going to Jerusalem, and His journey from there to Judæa, that John was not yet cast into prison, but was baptizing in Ænon near Salim [2:12–13; 3:22–24]? There are many other points on which the careful student of the Gospels will find that their narratives do not agree; and these we shall place before the reader, according to our power, as they occur. The student, staggered at the consideration of these things, will either renounce the attempt to find all the Gospels true, and not venturing to conclude that all our information about our Lord is untrustworthy, will choose at random one of them to be his guide; or he will accept the four, and will consider that their truth is not to be sought for in the outward and material letter.

3. We must, however, try to obtain some notion of the intention of the Evangelists in such matters, and we direct ourselves to this. Suppose there are several men who, by the spirit, see God, and know His words addressed to His saints, and His presence which He vouchsafes to them, appearing to them at chosen times for their advancement. There are several such men, and they are in different places, and the benefits they receive from above vary in shape and character. And let these men report, each of them separately, what he sees in spirit about God and His words, and His appearances to His saints, so that one of them speaks of God's appearances and words and acts to one righteous man in such a place, and another about other oracles and great works of the Lord, and a third of something else than what the former two have dealt with. And let there be a fourth, doing with regard to some particular matter something of the same kind as these three. And let the four agree with each other about something the Spirit has suggested to them all, and let them also make brief reports of other matters besides that one; then their narratives will fall out something on this wise: God appeared to such a one at such a time and in such a place, and did to him thus and thus; as if He had appeared to him in such a form, and had led him by the hand to such a place, and then done to him thus and thus. The second will report that God appeared at the very time of the foresaid occurrences, in a certain town, to a person who is named, a second person, and in a place far removed from that of the former account, and he will report a different set of words spoken at the same time to this second person. And let the same be supposed to be the case with the third and with the fourth. And let them, as we said, agree, these witnesses who report true things about God, and about His benefits conferred on certain men, let them agree with each other in some of the narratives they report. He, then, who takes the writings of these men for history, or for a representation of real things by a historical image, and who supposes God to be within certain limits in space, and to be unable to present to several persons in different places several visions of Himself at the same time, or to be making several speeches at the same moment, he will deem it impossible that our four writers are all speaking truth. To him it is impossible that God, who is in certain limits in space, could at the same set time be saying one thing to one man and another to another, and that He should be doing a thing and the opposite thing as well, and, to put it bluntly, that He should be both sitting and standing, should one of the writers represent Him as standing at the time, and making a certain speech in such a place to such a man, while a second writer speaks of Him as sitting.

4. In the case I have supposed where the historians desire to teach us by an image what they have seen in their mind, their meaning would be found, if the four were wise, to exhibit no disagreement; and we must understand that with the four Evangelists it is not otherwise. They made full use for their purpose of things done by Jesus in the exercise of His wonderful and extraordinary power; they use in the same way His sayings, and in some places they tack on to their writing, with

language apparently implying things of sense, things made manifest to them in a purely intellectual way. I do not condemn them if they even sometimes dealt freely with things which to the eye of history happened differently, and changed them so as to subserve the mystical aims they had in view; so as to speak of a thing which happened in a certain place, as if it had happened in another, or of what took place at a certain time, as if it had taken place at another time, and to introduce into what was spoken in a certain way some changes of their own. They proposed to speak the truth where it was possible both materially and spiritually, and where this was not possible it was their intention to prefer the spiritual to the material. The spiritual truth was often preserved, as one might say, in the material falsehood. As, for example, we might judge of the story of Jacob and Esau [Gen 27]. Jacob says to Isaac, "I am Esau thy firstborn son," and spiritually he spoke the truth, for he already partook of the rights of the first-born, which were perishing in his brother, and clothing himself with the goatskins he assumed the outward semblance of Esau, and was Esau all but the voice praising God, so that Esau might afterward find a place to receive a blessing. For if Jacob had not been blessed as Esau, neither would Esau perhaps have been able to receive a blessing of his own. And Jesus too is many things, according to the conceptions of Him, of which it is quite likely that the Evangelists took up different notions; while yet they were in agreement with each other in the different things they wrote. Statements which are verbally contrary to each other, are made about our Lord, namely, that He was descended from David and that He was not descended from David. The statement is true, "He was descended from David," as the Apostle says, "born of the seed of David according to the flesh" [Rom 1:3], if we apply this to the bodily part of Him; but the self-same statement is untrue if we understand His being born of the seed of David of His diviner power; for He was declared to be the Son of God with power [Rom 1:4]. And for this reason too, perhaps, the sacred prophecies speak of Him now as a servant, and now as a Son. They call Him a servant on account of the form of a servant which he wore, and because He was of the seed of David, but they call Him the Son of God according to His character as first-born. Thus it is true to call Him man and to call Him not man; man, because He was capable of death; not man, on account of His being diviner than man. Marcion, I suppose, took sound words in a wrong sense, when he rejected His birth from Mary, and declared that as to His divine nature He was not born of Mary, and hence made bold to delete from the Gospel the passages which have this effect. And a like fate seems to have overtaken those who make away with His humanity and receive His deity alone; and also those opposites of these who cancel His deity and confess Him as a man to be a holy man, and the most righteous of all men. And those who hold the doctrine of Dokesis,[1] not remembering that He humbled Himself even unto death and became obedient even to the cross [Phil 2:8], but only imagining in Him the absence of suffering, the superiority to all such accidents, they do what they can to deprive us of the man who is more just than all men, and are left with a figure which cannot save them, for as by one man came death, so also by one man is the justification of life. We could not have received

---

1. That is, that Jesus only appeared to have a human body and to live and die as a man.

such benefit as we have from the Logos had He not assumed the man, had He remained such as He was from the beginning with God the Father, and had He not taken up man, the first man of all, the man more precious than all others, purer than all others and capable of receiving Him. But after that man we also shall be able to receive Him, to receive Him so great and of such nature as He was, if we prepare a place in proportion to Him in our soul. So much I have said of the apparent discrepancies in the Gospels, and of my desire to have them treated in the way of spiritual interpretation.

* * *

6. These examples may be serviceable to illustrate statements not only about the Saviour, but about the disciples too, for here also there is some discrepancy of statement. For there is a difference in thought perhaps between Simon who is found by his own brother Andrew, and who is addressed "Thou shalt be called Cephas" [John 1:42], and him who is seen by Jesus when walking by the sea of Galilee, along with his brother, and addressed conjointly with that brother, "Come after Me, and I will make you fishers of men" [Matt 4:18–19; Mark 1:16–17; cf. Luke 5:1–10]. There was some fitness in the fact that the writer who goes more to the root of the matter and tells of the Word becoming flesh, and hence does not record the human generation of the Word who was in the beginning with God, should not tell us of Simon's being found at the seashore and called away from there, but of his being found by his brother who had been staying with Jesus at the tenth hour, and of his receiving the name Cephas in connection with his being thus found out. If he was seen by Jesus when walking by the sea of Galilee, it would scarcely be on a later occasion that he was addressed, "Thou art Peter and upon this rock I will build My church" [Matt 16:18]. With John again the Pharisees know Jesus to be baptizing with His disciples [John 4:1–2], adding this to His other great activities; but the Jesus of the three does not baptize at all. John the Baptist, too, with the Evangelist of the same name, goes on a long time without being cast into prison. With Matthew, on the contrary, he is put in prison almost at the time of the temptation of Jesus, and this is the occasion of Jesus retiring to Galilee, to avoid being put in prison. But in John there is nothing at all about John's being put in prison.[2] Who is so wise and so able as to learn all the things that are recorded about Jesus in the four Evangelists, and both to understand each incident by itself, and have a connected view of all His sojournings and words and acts at each place? * * *

* * *

15. * * * It is to be noted that John makes this transaction of Jesus with those He found selling oxen and sheep and doves in the temple His second work [2:13–17]; while the other Evangelists narrate a similar incident almost at the end and in connection with the story of the passion [Matt 21:10–13; Mark 11:15–17; Luke 19:45–46]. * * * It is further to be observed that what is recorded by the three as having taken place in connection with the Lord's going up to Jerusalem, when

2. See §2 above.

He did these things in the temple [Matt 21:1–9; Mark 11:1–10; Luke 19:28–38], is narrated in a very similar manner by John as taking place long after this, after another visit to Jerusalem different from this one [John 12:12–15]. * * * Three of the Gospels place these incidents, which we supposed to be the same as those narrated by John, in connection with one visit of the Lord to Jerusalem. While John, on the other hand, places them in connection with two visits which are widely separated from each other and between which were various journeys of the Lord to other places. I conceive it to be impossible for those who admit nothing more than the history in their interpretation to show that these discrepant statements are in harmony with each other. If any one considers that we have not given a sound exposition, let him write a reasoned rejoinder to this declaration of ours.

16. We shall, however, expound according to the strength that is given to us the reasons which move us to recognize here a harmony; and in doing so we entreat Him who gives to every one that asks and strives acutely to enquire, and we knock that by the keys of higher knowledge the hidden things of Scripture may be opened to us [cf. Matt 7:7]. And first, let us fix our attention on the words of John, beginning, "And Jesus went up to Jerusalem" [2:13]. Now Jerusalem, as the Lord Himself teaches in the Gospel according to Matthew, "is the city of the great King" [5:35]. It does not lie in a depression, or in a low situation, but is built on a high mountain, and there are mountains round about it [Ps 125:2], * * * and thither the tribes of the Lord went up, a testimony for Israel [Ps 122:3–4]. But that city also is called Jerusalem, to which none of those upon the earth ascends, nor goes in; but every soul that possesses by nature some elevation and some acuteness to perceive the things of the mind is a citizen of that city. And it is possible even for a dweller in Jerusalem to be in sin (for it is possible for even the acutest minds to sin), should they not turn round quickly after their sin, when they have lost their power of mind and are on the point not only of dwelling in one of those strange cities of Judæa, but even of being inscribed as its citizens. Jesus goes up to Jerusalem, after bringing help to those in Cana of Galilee, and then going down to Capernaum, that He may do in Jerusalem the things which are written. He found in the temple, certainly, which is said to be the house of the Father of the Saviour, that is, in the church or in the preaching of the ecclesiastical and sound word, some who were making His Father's house a house of merchandise. And at all times Jesus finds some of this sort in the temple. For in that which is called the church, which is the house of the living God, the pillar and ground of the truth [1 Tim 3:15], when are there not some money-changers sitting who need the strokes of the scourge Jesus made of small cords, and dealers in small coin who require to have their money poured out and their tables overturned? When are there not those who are inclined to merchandise, but need to be held to the plough and the oxen, that having put their hand to it and not turning round to the things behind them, they may be fit for the kingdom of God [Luke 9:62]? When are there not those who prefer the mammon of unrighteousness [cf. Luke 16:9–13] to the sheep which give them the material for their true adornment? And there are always many who look down on what is sincere and pure and unmixed with any bitterness or gall [cf. Acts 8:23], and who, for

the sake of miserable gain, betray the care of those tropically called doves. When, therefore, the Saviour finds in the temple, the house of His Father, those who are selling oxen and sheep and doves, and the changers of money sitting, He drives them out, using the scourge of small cords which He has made, along with the sheep and oxen of their trade, and pours out their stock of coin, as not deserving to be kept together, so little is it worth. He also overturns the tables in the souls of such as love money, saying even to those who sell doves, "Take these things hence," that they may no longer traffic in the house of God. But I believe that in these words He indicated also a deeper truth, and that we may regard these occurrences as a symbol of the fact that the service of that temple was not any longer to be carried on by the priests in the way of material sacrifices, and that the time was coming when the law could no longer be observed, however much the Jews according to the flesh desired it. For when Jesus casts out the oxen and sheep, and orders the doves to be taken away, it was because oxen and sheep and doves were not much longer to be sacrificed there in accordance with Jewish practices. And possibly the coins which bore the stamp of material things and not of God were poured out by way of type [cf. Matt 22:15–22; Mark 12:13–17; Luke 20:20–27]; because the law which appears so venerable, with its letter that kills [cf. 2 Cor 3:6], was, now that Jesus had come and had used His scourge to the people, to be dissolved and poured out, the sacred office (episcopate) being transferred to those from the Gentiles who believed, and the kingdom of God being taken away from the Jews and given to a nation bringing forth the fruits of it [Matt 21:43]. But it may also be the case that the natural temple is the soul skilled in reason, which, because of its inborn reason, is higher than the body; to which Jesus ascends from Capernaum, the lower-lying place of less dignity, and in which, before Jesus' discipline is applied to it, are found tendencies which are earthly and senseless and dangerous, and things which have the name but not the reality of beauty, and which are driven away by Jesus with His word plaited out of doctrines of demonstration and of rebuke, to the end that His Father's house may no longer be a house of merchandize but may receive, for its own salvation and that of others, that service of God which is performed in accordance with heavenly and spiritual laws. The ox is symbolic of earthly things, for he is a husbandman. The sheep, of senseless and brutal things, because it is more servile than most of the creatures without reason. Of empty and unstable thoughts, the dove. Of things that are thought good but are not, the small change. If any one objects to this interpretation of the passage and says that it is only pure animals that are mentioned in it, we must say that the passage would otherwise have an unlikely air. The occurence is necessarily related according to the possibilities of the story. It could not have been narrated that a herd of any other animals than pure ones had found access to the temple, nor could any have been sold there but those used for sacrifice. The Evangelist makes use of the known practice of the merchants at the times of the Jewish feasts; they did bring in such animals to the outer court; this practice, with a real occurrence he knew of, were his materials. Any one, however, who cares to do so may enquire whether it is in agreement with the position held by Jesus in this world, since He was reputed to be the Son of a carpenter, to venture upon such an act as to drive out a crowd of merchants from the temple? They had come up to the feast to sell to a great number of the people, the sheep, several myriads in number, which they were to sacrifice according to their fathers' houses. To the richer Jews they had oxen to sell, and there were doves for those who had vowed such animals, and many no doubt bought these with a view to their good cheer at the festival. And did not Jesus do an unwarrantable thing when He poured out the money of the money-changers, which was their own, and overthrew their tables? And who that received a blow from the scourge of small cords at the hands of One held in but slight esteem, was driven out of the temple, would not have attacked Him and raised a cry and avenged himself with his own hand, especially when there was such a multitude present who might all feel themselves insulted by Jesus in the same way? To think, moreover, of the Son of God taking the small cords in His hands and plaiting a scourge out of them for this driving out from the temple, does it not bespeak audacity and temerity and even some measure of lawlessness? One refuge remains for the writer who wishes to defend these things and is minded to treat the occurrence as real history, namely, to appeal to the divine nature of Jesus, who was able to quench, when He desired to do so, the rising anger of His foes, by divine grace to get the better of myriads, and to scatter the devices of tumultuous men; for "the Lord scatters the counsels of the nations and brings to naught devices of the peoples, but the counsel of the Lord abideth for ever" [Ps 33:10–11]. Thus the occurrence in our passage, if it really took place, was not second in point of the power it exhibits to any even of the most marvellous works Christ wrought, and claimed no less by its divine character the faith of the beholders. One may show it to be a greater work than that done at Cana of Galilee in the turning of water into wine; for in that case it was only soulless matter that was changed, but here it was the soul and will of thousands of men. It is, however, to be observed that at the marriage the mother of Jesus is said to be there, and Jesus to have been invited and His disciples, but that no one but Jesus is said to have descended to Capernaum. His disciples, however, appear afterwards as present with Him; they remembered that "the zeal of thine house shall devour me" [John 2:17]. And perhaps Jesus was in each of the disciples as He ascended to Jerusalem, whence it is not said, Jesus went up to "Jerusalem and His disciples," but He went down to Capernaum, "He and His mother and His brothers and His disciples" [John 2:12].

AUGUSTINE

Augustine (354–430) was born in the North African city of Thagaste. He received a Roman education in literature and rhetoric that would have prepared him for a career in the law courts. Augustine's mother was a devout Christian, but as a youth and young man her son never really shared her faith. Indeed, he found Scripture "quite unworthy of comparison with the stately prose of Cicero" (*Confessions* 3.5). Augustine eventually joined the Manichees, a quasi-Christian religious sect that rejected the Old Testament and much of the New; they espoused a highly dualistic cosmology that Augustine found attractive.

In 384 he moved to Milan, where he taught rhetoric and heard Bishop Ambrose preach. At first he regarded Ambrose as merely an excellent orator, but soon he was enticed by his allegorical approach to the Bible and came to believe that Scripture's rough exterior often veils mysterious spiritual meanings. Augustine's newfound regard for Scripture was central to his well-known conversion experience. He was baptized by Ambrose in 387 and returned to Africa four years later where he was ordained a priest and subsequently consecreated bishop of Hippo.

Augustine's thought, more than any other ancient Christian's, has been central to the development of Western Catholic and Protestant theology. Augustine's exploration of the literary relationship between the Gospels in the first selection (a series of excerpts from *The Harmony of the Gospels*) anticipates modern study of the Synoptic Problem, although most modern scholars would find Augustine's relentless harmonization an intellectual dead end. The second selection, Homily 24 on John, exemplifies the allegorical method of interpretation popular in antiquity and the Middle Ages.

The Harmony of the Gospels[†]
(From Book 1)

3. Now, those four evangelists whose names have gained the most remarkable circulation over the whole world, and whose number has been fixed as four,—it may be for the simple reason that there are four divisions of that world through the universal length of which they, by their number as by a kind of mystical sign, indicated the advancing extension of the Church of Christ,—are believed to have written in the order which follows: first Matthew, then Mark, thirdly Luke, lastly John. Hence, too, [it would appear that] these had one order determined among them with regard to the matters of their personal knowledge and their preaching [of the gospel], but a different order in reference to the task of giving the written narrative. As far, indeed, as concerns the acquisition of their own knowledge and the charge of preaching, those unquestionably came first in order who were actually followers of the Lord when He was present in the flesh, and who heard Him speak and saw Him act; and [with a commission received] from His lips they were despatched to preach the gospel. But as respects the task of composing that record of the gospel which is to be accepted as ordained by divine authority, there were (only) two, belonging to the number of those whom the Lord chose before the passover, that obtained places,—namely, the first place and the last. For the first place in order was held by Matthew, and the last by John. And thus the remaining two, who did not belong to the number referred to, but who at the same time had become followers of the Christ who spoke in these others, were supported on either side by the same, like sons who were to be embraced, and who in this way were set in the midst between these twain.

---

† From Augustine, *The Harmony of the Gospels*, trans. S. D. F. Salmond, in *The Nicene and Post-Nicene Fathers*, First Series, vol. 6 (1888; reprint, Peabody, MA: Hendrickson, 1994), 78–81, 117–19, 160, 191–93.

4. Of these four, it is true, only Matthew is reckoned to have written in the Hebrew language; the others in Greek. And however they may appear to have kept each of them a certain order of narration proper to himself, this certainly is not to be taken as if each individual writer chose to write in ignorance of what his predecessor had done, or left out as matters about which there was no information things which another nevertheless is discovered to have recorded. But the fact is, that just as they received each of them the gift of inspiration, they abstained from adding to their several labours any superfluous conjoint compositions. For Matthew is understood to have taken it in hand to construct the record of the incarnation of the Lord according to the royal lineage, and to give an account of most part of His deeds and words as they stood in relation to this present life of men. Mark follows him closely, and looks like his attendant and epitomizer. For in his narrative he gives nothing in concert with John apart from the others: by himself separately, he has little to record; in conjunction with Luke, as distinguished from the rest, he has still less; but in concord with Matthew, he has a very large number of passages. Much, too, he narrates in words almost numerically and identically the same as those used by Matthew, where the agreement is either with that evangelist alone, or with him in connection with the rest. On the other hand, Luke appears to have occupied himself rather with the priestly lineage and character of the Lord. For although in his own way he carries the descent back to David, what he has followed is not the royal pedigree, but the line of those who were not kings. That genealogy, too, he has brought to a point in Nathan the son of David [Luke 3:31], which person likewise was no king. It is not thus, however, with Matthew. For in tracing the lineage along through Solomon the king [Matt 1:6], he has pursued with strict regularity the succession of the other kings; and in enumerating these, he has also conserved that mystical number of which we shall speak hereafter.

5. For the Lord Jesus Christ, who is the one true King and the one true Priest, the former to rule us, and the latter to make expiation for us, has shown us how His own figure bore these two parts together, which were only separately commended [to notice] among the Fathers. This becomes apparent if (for example) we look to that inscription which was affixed to His cross—"King of the Jews:" in connection also with which, and by a secret instinct, Pilate replied, "What I have written, I have written" [John 19:19–22]. For it had been said aforetime in the Psalms, "Destroy not the writing of the title."[1] The same becomes evident, so far as the part of priest is concerned, if we have regard to what He has taught us concerning offering and receiving. For thus it is that He sent us beforehand a prophecy respecting Himself, which runs thus, "Thou art a priest for ever, after the order of Melchisedek" [Ps 110:4]. And in many other testimonies of the divine Scriptures, Christ appears both as King and as Priest. Hence, also, even David himself, whose son He is, not without good reason, more frequently declared to be than he is said to be Abraham's son, and whom Matthew and Luke have both alike held by,—the one viewing him as the person from whom, through Solomon, His lineage can be traced down, and the other taking him for the person

---

1. Superscription to Ps 75; see note there.

to whom, through Nathan, His genealogy can be carried up,—did represent the part of a priest, although he was patently a king, when he ate the shew-bread. For it was not lawful for any one to eat that, save the priests only [1 Sam 21:6; Matt 12:3–4]. To this it must be added that Luke is the only one who mentions how Mary was discovered by the angel, and how she was related to Elisabeth, who was the wife of Zacharias the priest. And of this Zacharias the same evangelist has recorded the fact, that the woman whom he had for wife was one of the daughters of Aaron, which is to say she belonged to the tribe of the priests [Luke 1:5].

6. Whereas, then, Matthew had in view the kingly character, and Luke the priestly, they have at the same time both set forth pre-eminently the humanity of Christ: for it was according to His humanity that Christ was made both King and Priest. To Him, too, God gave the throne of His father David, in order that of His kingdom there should be none end [Luke 1:32]. And this was done with the purpose that there might be a mediator between God and men, the man Christ Jesus [1 Tim 2:5], to make intercession for us. Luke, on the other hand, had no one connected with him to act as his summarist in the way that Mark was attached to Matthew. And it may be that this is not without a certain solemn significance. For it is the right of kings not to miss the obedient following of attendants; and hence the evangelist, who had taken it in hand to give an account of the kingly character of Christ, had a person attached to him as his associate who was in some fashion to follow in his steps. But inasmuch as it was the priest's wont to enter all alone into the holy of holies, in accordance with that principle, Luke, whose object contemplated the priestly office of Christ, did not have any one to come after him as a confederate, who was meant in some way to serve as an epitomizer of his narrative.

7. These three evangelists, however, were for the most part engaged with those things which Christ did through the vehicle of the flesh of man, and after the temporal fashion. But John, on the other hand, had in view that true divinity of the Lord in which He is the Father's equal, and directed his efforts above all to the setting forth of the divine nature in his Gospel in such a way as he believed to be adequate to men's needs and notions. Therefore he is borne to loftier heights, in which he leaves the other three far behind him; so that, while in them you see men who have their conversation in a certain manner with the man Christ on earth, in him you perceive one who has passed beyond the cloud in which the whole earth is wrapped, and who has reached the liquid heaven from which, with clearest and steadiest mental eye, he is able to look upon God the Word, who was in the beginning with God, and by whom all things were made [John 1:2–3]. And there, too, he can recognise Him who was made flesh in order that He might dwell amongst us [John 1:14]; [that Word of whom we say,] that He assumed the flesh, not that He was changed into the flesh. For had not this assumption of the flesh been effected in such a manner as at the same time to conserve the unchangeable Divinity, such a word as this could never have been spoken,— namely, "I and the Father are one" [John 10:30]. For surely the Father and the flesh are not one. And the same John is also the only one who has recorded that witness which the Lord gave concerning Himself, when He said: "He that hath seen

me, hath seen the Father also" [14:9]; and, "I am in the Father, and the Father is in me" [14:10]; "that they may be one, even as we are one" [17:22]; and, "Whatsoever the Father doeth, these same things doeth the Son likewise" [5:19]. And whatever other statements there may be to the same effect, calculated to betoken, to those who are possessed of right understanding, that divinity of Christ in which He is the Father's equal, of all these we might almost say that we are indebted for their introduction into the Gospel narrative to John alone. For he is like one who has drunk in the secret of His divinity more richly and somehow more familiarly than others, as if he drew it from the very bosom of his Lord on which it was his wont to recline when He sat at meat [cf. John 13:23].

* * *

10. Those sacred chariots of the Lord [i.e., the four Gospels], however, in which He is borne throughout the earth and brings the peoples under His easy yoke and His light burden, are assailed with calumnious charges by certain persons who, in impious vanity or in ignorant temerity, think to rob of their credit as veracious historians those teachers by whose instrumentality the Christian religion has been disseminated all the world over, and through whose efforts it has yielded fruits so plentiful that unbelievers now scarcely dare so much as to mutter their slanders in private among themselves, kept in check by the faith of the Gentiles and by the devotion of all the peoples. Nevertheless, inasmuch as they still strive by their calumnious disputations to keep some from making themselves acquainted with the faith, and thus prevent them from becoming believers, while they also endeavour to the utmost of their power to excite agitations among others who have already attained to belief, and thereby give them trouble; and further, as there are some brethren who, without detriment to their own faith, have a desire to ascertain what answer can be given to such questions, either for the advantage of their own knowledge or for the purpose of refuting the vain utterances of their enemies, with the inspiration and help of the Lord our God (and would that it might prove profitable for the salvation of such men), we have undertaken in this work to demonstrate the errors or the rashness of those who deem themselves able to prefer charges, the subtilty of which is at least sufficiently observable, against those four different books of the gospel which have been written by these four several evangelists. And in order to carry out this design to a successful conclusion, we must prove that the writers in question do not stand in any antagonism to each other. For those adversaries are in the habit of adducing this as the palmary allegation in all their vain objections, namely, that the evangelists are not in harmony with each other.

(From Book 2)

27. If now the question is asked, as to which of the words we are to suppose the most likely to have been the precise words used by John the Baptist, whether those recorded as spoken by him in Matthew's Gospel [see Matt 3], or those in Luke's [see Luke 3:1–18], or those which Mark has introduced, among the few sentences which he mentions to have been uttered by him [see Mark 1:1–11], while he omits notice of all the rest, it will not be deemed worth while creating any difficulty for oneself in a matter of that kind, by any one who wisely understands that the real requisite in order to get at the knowledge of the truth is just to make sure of the things really meant, whatever may be the precise words in which they happen to be expressed. For although one writer may retain a certain order in the words, and another present a different one, there is surely no real contradiction in that. Nor, again, need there be any antagonism between the two, although one may state what another omits. For it is evident that the evangelists have set forth these matters just in accordance with the recollection each retained of them, and just according as their several predilections prompted them to employ greater brevity or richer detail on certain points, while giving, nevertheless, the same account of the subjects themselves.

28. Thus, too, in what more pertinently concerns the matter in hand, it is sufficiently obvious that, since the truth of the Gospel, conveyed in that word of God which abides eternal and unchangeable above all that is created, but which at the same time has been disseminated throughout the world by the instrumentality of temporal symbols, and by the tongues of men, has possessed itself of the most exalted height of authority, we ought not to suppose that any one of the writers is giving an unreliable account, if, when several persons are recalling some matter either heard or seen by them, they fail to follow the very same plan, or to use the very same words, while describing, nevertheless, the self-same fact. Neither should we indulge such a supposition, although the order of the words may be varied; or although some words may be substituted in place of others, which nevertheless have the same meaning; or although something may be left unsaid, either because it has not occurred to the mind of the recorder, or because it becomes readily intelligible from other statements which are given; or although, among other matters which (may not bear directly on his immediate purpose, but which) he decides on mentioning rather for the sake of the narrative, and in order to preserve the proper order of time, one of them may introduce something which he does not feel called upon to expound as a whole at length, but only to touch upon in part; or although, with the view of illustrating his meaning, and making it thoroughly clear, the person to whom authority is given to compose the narrative makes some additions of his own, not indeed in the subject-matter itself, but in the words by which it is expressed; or although, while retaining a perfectly reliable comprehension of the fact itself, he may not be entirely successful, however he may make that his aim, in calling to mind and reciting anew with the most literal accuracy the very words which he heard on the occasion. Moreover, if any one affirms that the evangelists ought certainly to have had that kind of capacity imparted to them by the power of the Holy Spirit, which would secure them against all variation the one from the other, either in the kind of words, or in their order, or in their number, that person fails to perceive, that just in proportion as the authority of the evangelists [under their existing conditions] is made pre-eminent, the credit of all other men who offer true statements of events ought to have been established on a stronger basis by their instrumentality: so that when several parties happen to narrate the same circumstance, none of them can by any means be rightly charged with untruthfulness if he differs from the other only in such a way as can be defended on the ground of the antecedent example of the evangelists themselves. For as we are not at liberty either to suppose or to say that any one of the evangelists has stated what is false, so it will be apparent that any other writer is as little chargeable with untruth, with whom, in the process of recalling anything for narration, it has fared only in a way similar to that in which it is shown to have fared with those evangelists. And just as it belongs to the highest morality to guard against all that is false, so ought we all the more to be ruled by an authority so eminent, to the effect that we should not suppose ourselves to come upon what must be false, when we find the narratives of any writers differ from each other in the manner in which the records of the evangelists are proved to contain variations. At the same time, in what most seriously concerns the faithfulness of doctrinal teaching, we should also understand that it is not so much in mere words, as rather truth in the facts themselves, that is to be sought and embraced; for as to writers who do not employ precisely the same modes of statement, if they only do not present discrepancies with respect to the facts and the sentiments themselves, we accept them as holding the same position in veracity.

29. With respect, then, to those comparisons which I have instituted between the several narratives of the evangelists, what do these present that must be considered to be of a contradictory order? Are we to regard in this light the circumstance that one of them has given us the words, "whose shoes I am not worthy to bear" [Matt 3:11], whereas the others speak of the "unloosing of the latchet of the shoe" [Mark 1:7; Luke 3:16; John 1:27]? For here, indeed, the difference seems to be neither in the mere words, nor in the order of the words, nor in any matter of simple phraseology, but in the actual matter of fact, when in the one case the "bearing of the shoe" is mentioned, and in the other the "unloosing of the shoe's latchet." Quite fairly, therefore, may the question be put, as to what it was that John declared himself unworthy to do—whether to bear the shoes, or to unloose the shoe's latchet. For if only the one of these two sentences was uttered by him, then that evangelist will appear to have given the correct narrative who was in a position to record what was said; while the writer who has given the saying in another form, although he may not indeed have offered an [intentionally] false account of it, may at any rate be taken to have made a slip of memory, and will be reckoned thus to have stated one thing instead of another. It is only seemly, however, that no charge of absolute unveracity should be laid against the evangelists, and that, too, not only with regard to that kind of unveracity which comes by the positive telling of what is false, but also with regard to that which arises through forgetfulness. Therefore, if it is pertinent to the matter to deduce one sense from the words "to bear the shoes," and another sense from the words "to unloose the shoe's latchet," what should one suppose the correct interpretation to be put on the facts, but that John did give utterance to both these sentences, either on two different occasions or in one and the same connection? For he might very well have expressed himself thus, "whose shoe's latchet I am not worthy to unloose, and whose shoes I am not worthy to bear:" and then one of the evangelists may have reproduced the one portion of the saying, and the rest of them the other; while, notwithstanding this, all of them have really given a veracious narrative. But further, if, when he spoke of the shoes of the Lord, John meant nothing more

than to convey the idea of His supremacy and his own lowliness, then, whichever of the two sayings may have actually been uttered by him, whether that regarding the unloosing of the latchet of the shoes, or that respecting the bearing of the shoes, the self-same sense is still correctly preserved by any writer who, while making mention of the shoes in words of his own, has expressed at the same time the same idea of lowliness, and thus has not made any departure from the real mind [of the person of whom he writes]. It is therefore a useful principle, and one particularly worthy of being borne in mind, when we are speaking of the concord of the evangelists, that there is no divergence [to be supposed] from truth, even when they introduce some saying different from what was actually uttered by the person concerning whom the narrative is given, provided that, notwithstanding this, they set forth as his mind precisely what is also so conveyed by that one among them who reproduces the words as they were literally spoken. For thus we learn the salutary lesson, that our aim should be nothing else than to ascertain what is the mind and intention of the person who speaks.

* * *

31. Thereafter Matthew proceeds thus: "And Jesus, when He was baptized, went up straightway out of the water; and, lo, the heavens were opened unto Him, and He saw the Spirit of God descending like a dove, and lighting upon Him; and, lo, a voice from heaven saying, This is my beloved Son, in whom I am well pleased" [3:16–17]. This incident is also recorded in a similar manner by two of the others, namely Mark and Luke. But at the same time, while preserving the sense intact, they use different modes of expression in reproducing the terms of the voice which came from heaven. For although Matthew tells us that the words were, "This is my beloved Son," while the other two put them in this form, "Thou art my beloved Son" [Mark 1:11; Luke 3:22], these different methods of speech serve but to convey the same sense, according to the principle which has been discussed above. For the heavenly voice gave utterance only to one of these sentences; but by the form of words thus adopted, namely, "This is my beloved Son," it was the evangelist's intention to show that the saying was meant to intimate specially to the hearers there [and not to Jesus] the fact that He was the Son of God. With this view, he chose to give the sentence, "Thou art my beloved Son," this turn, "This is my beloved Son," as if it were addressed directly to the people. For it was not meant to intimate to Christ a fact which He knew already; but the object was to let the people who were present hear it, for whose sakes indeed the voice itself was given. * * *

* * *

129. Matthew goes on with his narrative in the following terms: "And when He was come into Jerusalem, all the city was moved, saying, Who is this? And the multitude said, This is Jesus, the prophet of Nazareth of Galilee. And Jesus went into the temple of God, and cast out all them that sold and bought in the temple;" and so on, down to where we read, "But ye have made it a den of thieves" [Matt 21:10–13]. This account of the multitude of sellers who were cast out of the temple is given by all the evangelists; but John introduces it in a remarkably different order [Mark 11:15–17; Luke 19:45–46; cf. John 2:1–16]. For, after recording the testimony borne by John the Baptist to Jesus, and mentioning that He went into Galilee at the time when He turned the water into wine, and after he has also noticed the sojourn of a few days in Capharnaum, John proceeds to tell us that He went up to Jerusalem at the season of the Jews' passover, and when He had made a scourge of small cords, drove out of the temple those who were selling in it. This makes it evident that this act was performed by the Lord not on a single occasion, but twice over; but that only the first instance is put on record by John, and the last by the other three.

(From Book 3)

28. First, however, Matthew makes a digression with the purpose of telling the story of Judas' end, which is related only by him. * * * [He concludes with] "Then was fulfilled that which was spoken by Jeremy the prophet, saying, And they took the thirty pieces of silver, the price of Him that was valued, whom the children of Israel did value, and gave them for the potter's field, as the Lord appointed me" [Matt 27:3–10].

29. Now, if any one finds a difficulty in the circumstance that this passage is not found in the writings of the prophet Jeremiah, and thinks that damage is thus done to the veracity of the evangelist, let him first take notice of the fact that this ascription of the passage to Jeremiah is not contained in all the codices of the Gospels, and that some of them state simply that it was spoken *"by the prophet."* It is possible, therefore, to affirm that those codices deserve rather to be followed which do not contain the name of Jeremiah. For these words were certainly spoken by a prophet, only that prophet was Zechariah. In this way the supposition is, that those codices are faulty which contain the name of Jeremiah, because they ought either to have given the name of Zechariah or to have mentioned no name at all, as is the case with a certain copy, merely stating that it was spoken *"by the prophet, saying,"* which prophet would assuredly be understood to be Zechariah. However, let others adopt this method of defence, if they are so minded. For my part, I am not satisfied with it; and the reason is, that a majority of codices contain the name of Jeremiah, and that those critics who have studied the Gospel with more than usual care in the Greek copies, report that they have found it to stand so in the more ancient Greek exemplars. I look also to this further consideration, namely, that there was no reason why this name should have been added [subsequently to the true text], and a corruption thus created; whereas there was certainly an intelligible reason for erasing the name from so many of the codices. For venturesome inexperience might readily have done that, when perplexed with the problem presented by the fact that this passage could not be found in Jeremiah.

30. How, then, is the matter to be explained, but by supposing that this has been done in accordance with the more secret counsel of that providence of God by which the minds of the evangelists were governed? For it may have been the case, that when Matthew was engaged in composing his Gospel, the word Jeremiah occurred to his mind, in accordance with a familiar experience, instead of Zechariah. Such an inaccuracy, however, he would most undoubtedly have corrected (having his attention called to it, as surely would have been the case, by some who might have read it while he was still alive in the flesh), had he not reflected that [perhaps] it was not without a purpose that the name of the one prophet had been suggested instead of the other in the process of recalling the circumstances (which process of recollection was also directed by the Holy Spirit), and that this might not have occurred to him had it not been the Lord's purpose to have it so written. If it is asked, however, why the Lord should have so determined it, there is this first and most serviceable reason, which deserves our most immediate consideration, namely, that some idea was thus conveyed of the marvellous manner in which all the holy prophets, speaking in one spirit, continued in perfect unison with each other in their utterances,—a circumstance certainly much more calculated to impress the mind than would have been the case had all the words of all these prophets been spoken by the mouth of a single individual. The same consideration might also fitly suggest the duty of accepting unhesitatingly whatever the Holy Spirit has given expression to through the agency of these prophets, and of looking upon their individual communications as also those of the whole body, and on their collective communications as also those of each separately. If, then, it is the case that words spoken by Jeremiah are really as much Zechariah's as Jeremiah's, and, on the other hand, that words spoken by Zechariah are really as much Jeremiah's as they are Zechariah's, what necessity was there for Matthew to correct his text when he read over what he had written, and found that the one name had occurred to him instead of the other? Was it not rather the proper course for him to bow to the authority of the Holy Spirit, under whose guidance he certainly felt his mind to be placed in a more decided sense than is the case with us, and consequently to leave untouched what he had thus written, in accordance with the Lord's counsel and appointment, with the intent to give us to understand that the prophets maintain so complete a harmony with each other in the matter of their utterances that it becomes nothing absurd, but, in fact, a most consistent thing for us to credit Jeremiah with a sentence originally spoken by Zechariah? For if, in these days of ours, a person, desiring to bring under our notice the words of a certain individual, happens to mention the name of another by whom the words were not actually uttered,[2] but who at the same time is the most intimate friend and associate of the man by whom they were really spoken; and if forthwith recollecting that he has given the one name instead of the other, he recovers himself and corrects the mistake, but does it nevertheless in some such way as this, "After all, what I said was not amiss"; what would we take to be meant by this, but just that there subsists so perfect a unison of sentiment between the two parties—that is to say, the man whose words the individual in question intended to repeat, and the second person whose name occurred to him at the time instead of that of the other—that it comes much to the same thing to represent the words to have been spoken by the former as to say that they were uttered by the latter? How much more, then, is this a usage which might well be understood and most particularly commended to our attention in the case of the holy prophets, so that we might accept the books

2. Reading *a quo non dicta sint*. Most of the MSS. omit the *non* ["not"; translator's note].

composed by the whole series of them, as if they formed but a single book written by one author, in which no discrepancy with regard to the subjects dealt with should be supposed to exist, as none would be found, and in which there would be a more remarkable example of consistency and veracity than would have been the case had a single individual, even the most learned, been the enunciator of all these sayings? Therefore, while there are those, whether unbelievers or merely ignorant men, who endeavour to find an argument here to help them in demonstrating a want of harmony between the holy evangelists, men of faith and learning, on the other hand, ought rather to bring this into the service of proving the unity which characterizes the holy prophets.

31. I have also another reason (the fuller discussion of which must be reserved, I think, for another opportunity, in order to prevent the present discourse from extending to larger limits than may be allowed by the necessity which rests upon us to bring this work to a conclusion) to offer in explanation of the fact that the name of Jeremiah has been permitted, or rather directed, by the authority of the Holy Spirit, to stand in this passage instead of that of Zechariah. It is stated in Jeremiah that he bought a field from the son of his brother, and paid him money for it [32:7–9]. That sum of money is not given, indeed, under the name of the particular price which is found in Zechariah, namely, thirty pieces of silver [Zech 11:12–13]; but, on the other hand, there is no mention of the buying of the field in Zechariah. Now, it is evident that the evangelist has interpreted the prophecy which speaks of the thirty pieces of silver as something which has received its fulfilment only in the Lord's case, so that it is made to stand for the price set upon Him. But again, that the words which were uttered by Jeremiah on the subject of the purchase of the field have also a bearing upon the same matter, may have been mystically signified by the selection thus made in introducing [into the evangelical narrative] the name of Jeremiah, who spoke of the purchase of the field, instead of that of Zechariah, to whom we are indebted for the notice of the thirty pieces of silver. In this way, on perusing first the Gospel, and finding the name of Jeremiah there, and then, again, on perusing Jeremiah, and failing there to discover the passage about the thirty pieces of silver, but seeing at the same time the section about the purchase of the field, the reader would be taught to compare the two paragraphs together, and get at the real meaning of the prophecy, and learn how it also stands in relation to this fulfilment of prophecy which was exhibited in the instance of our Lord. For [it is also to be remarked that] Matthew makes the following addition to the passage cited, namely, "Whom the children of Israel did value; and gave them the potter's field, as the Lord appointed me" [27:9–10]. Now, these words are not to be found either in Zechariah or in Jeremiah. Hence we must rather take them to have been inserted with a nice and mystical meaning by the evangelist, on his own responsibility,—the Lord having given him to understand, by revelation, that a prophecy of the said tenor had a real reference to this occurrence, which took place in connection with the price set upon Christ. Moreover, in Jeremiah, the evidence of the purchase of the field is ordered to be cast into an earthen vessel [32:14]. In like manner, we find in the Gospel that the money paid for the Lord was used for the purchase of a potter's field, which field also was to be employed as a burying-place for strangers. And it may be that all

this was significant of the permanence of the repose of those who sojourn like strangers in this present world, and are buried with Christ by baptism. For the Lord also declared to Jeremiah, that the said purchase of the field was expressive of the fact that in that land [of Judæa] there would be a remnant of the people delivered from their captivity [32:15, 37–44]. I judged it proper to give some sort of sketch of these things, as I was calling attention to the kind of significance which a really careful and painstaking study should look for in these testimonies of the prophets, when they are reduced to a unity and compared with the evangelical narrative. These, then, are the statements which Matthew has introduced with reference to the traitor Judas.

Sermon on John 6:1–14[†]

1. The miracles which our Lord Jesus Christ performed are indeed divine works, and, from visible things and events, they encourage the human mind to come to some understanding of God. God, after all, is not the kind of substance that can be seen with the eyes, and his miracles, by which he governs the whole world and administers every creature, have grown cheap in our estimation through their regularity, so that almost no one bothers to pay attention to the wonderful and stupendous action of God in every grain of seed. So with his usual kindheartedness he kept back some things for himself, to perform them at a suitable time apart from the usual course and order of nature, so that wonders that were not greater than the daily ones, but just more out of the ordinary, would amaze people who had ceased to value those that occur every day.

Governing the whole cosmos, after all, is a greater marvel than satisfying five thousand men on five loaves of bread, and yet nobody marvels at it; people marvel at the latter because it is uncommon. Who, after all, even now feeds the whole world but the one who creates the crops from a few grains? So, on this occasion, the Lord acted as God. Just as he multiplies a few grains into the crops, so too did he multiply the five loaves in his hands. For there was power in the hands of Christ. Those five loaves were seeds of a kind, not indeed committed to the earth but seeds which were multiplied by the one who made the earth.

Something therefore was brought to the attention of the senses whereby the mind would be alerted, something displayed before the eyes whereby the understanding could be exercised, so that we might marvel at the invisible God through his visible works; and so, being thus raised up to faith and purified through faith, we might even long to see in an invisible manner the one we recognized through things visible as invisible.

2. It is not enough all the same just to observe this truth in the miracles of Christ. Let us question the miracles themselves about what they are telling us about Christ. For, if properly understood, they have their own language. In fact,

† From Augustine, *Homilies on the Gospel of John 1–40*, trans. Edmund Hill, *The Works of Saint Augustine: A Translation for the 21st Century*, part 3, vol. 12 (Hyde Park, NY: New City Press, 2009), 423–29. All notes are the translator's.

because Christ is himself the Word of God, even the deeds of the Word are a word for us. So then, let us inquire about this miracle, since we have heard that it was great, and ask how deep is its meaning; let us not just delight in its appearance; let us also scan its depths. After all, there is an inner meaning to the outer form that fills us with wonder.

We have seen, we have looked upon something great, something outstanding and altogether divine, which could only be done by God; the deed has led us to admire the doer. But if, for example, we were to look at the beautiful letters on the pages of some book, we would not be satisfied with admiring the scribe's skilful fingers in producing such a regular, neat and even script, without also reading what he was saying to us with it. Well, in the same way anyone who just takes a look at this deed is delighted by its beauty and filled with admiration for the craftsman; anyone though who takes the trouble to understand it is after a fashion reading it. Pictures, after all, are looked at in one way, letters in another. When you see a picture, that is all there is to it, to see it and admire it; when you see letters, that is not all there is to it, because you are being urged also to read them.

Even if you do not know how to read some letters when you see them, you say, do you not, "What are we to suppose is written here?" You inquire what it is, when you have already seen something; the person you ask to help you understand what you have seen will show you something else, something more. He has eyes of one sort, you of another. Do you not both see the marks on the page in the same way? But you do not both know the signs in the same way. So you, then, see them and admire; he sees, admires, reads and understands. Because, then, we have seen this miracle and admired it, let us read it and come to understand it.

3. The Lord is on the mountain;[1] let us more fully understand that the Lord on the mountain means the Word on high. Accordingly what was done on the mountain is not like something down to earth or lowly, not something to step over and to pass by casually, but to which we should raise our eyes.

He saw the crowds, he realized they were hungry, he fed them out of the kindness of his heart, not just in virtue of his goodness but of his power as well. What use, after all, would goodness alone have been, where there was no bread on which to feed the hungry multitudes? Unless power had been joined to goodness, that crowd would have remained fasting and hungry. Finally, even the disciples, who were with the Lord and who were hungry, wanted to feed the crowds,[2] so that they would not remain with empty stomachs, but they had nothing to feed them with. The Lord asked them where they might buy enough bread to feed the crowds. And scripture adds, *But he said this by way of testing him,* namely the disciple Philip, to whom he addressed the question; *for he himself knew what he was going to do* (John 6:6).

So what was the point of testing the disciple, if not to show up his ignorance? And perhaps by demonstrating the disciple's ignorance, he was signifying

1. See John 6:3.
2. See Mark 6:35–36, and the parallel passages in Matt and Luke.

something. What this is, in fact, will be obvious when the actual sacrament[3] of the five loaves begins to talk to us and to indicate what it signifies; I mean, we shall see then why the Lord, on this occasion, wished to manifest the disciple's ignorance by asking him about something that he already knew. For sometimes we ask a question about something we do not know, wishing to hear the answer in order to learn; sometimes we ask about what we do know, wishing to find out whether the one we are asking also knows the answer. The Lord of course knew both things; he knew the answer to his question, being quite aware, after all, of what he was going to do; and in the same way he knew that Philip did not know. So why else did he ask, if not to show up the man's ignorance? And why he did this, as I have just said, we shall shortly understand.

4. Andrew said, *There is a lad here who has five loaves, and two fish; but what are these for so many* (John 6:9)? When Philip was questioned, he had said that 200 denarii would not be enough to buy bread to feed such a huge crowd; whereupon a boy with five barley loaves and two fish was there. *Jesus said, Make the people sit down. There was plenty of grass there, and almost five thousand people sat down. The Lord Jesus, then, took the loaves, gave thanks,* directed them, the loaves were broken and set before those sitting down to eat—no longer just five loaves, but what had been added by the one who created the increase. *And the same for the fish as much as was sufficient* (John 6:10–11). It is too little that such a crowd was given its fill; there were even fragments left over, and he ordered these to be collected, so that they should not be wasted; and *they filled twelve baskets with the fragments* (John 6:13).

5. Let us run through this briefly. The five loaves are to be understood as the five books of Moses; it is right that they were not wheat loaves but barley, because they belong to the Old Testament. You know, of course, that barley was created in a way that makes it hard to get at the kernel; for the kernel is clothed with a hairy husk, and it is tenacious and clinging, so that it is stripped with great effort. Such is the letter of the Old Testament, clothed in the husks of material, this-worldly symbols;[4] but if one does get to its kernel or heart, it nourishes and satisfies.

So then, some boy brought five loaves and two fish; if we inquire who this boy may have been, perhaps he was the people of Israel; he carried the bread as a child and did not eat it. The things he carried, after all, were a burden when they were all wrapped up; once opened, they were nourishing.

But the two fish, it seems, represent for us those two eminent Old Testament figures, who were anointed to sanctify and to govern the people, the priest and the king. And the one whom they prefigured eventually came in mystery; the one who finally came was concealed by the barley husk and revealed in the barley kernel. He came, one man bearing in himself each of these roles, of priest and of king; that of priest insofar as he offered himself to God as victim for our sakes; that of king, insofar as we are ruled by him; and then what was carried all wrapped up was opened.

---

3. *Sacramentum* in the full Augustinian sense of a sacred, significant action or thing. That usually applies to what is found in the scriptures.

4. Rather more succinctly, *carnalium sacramentorum* in the Latin.

Let thanks be given to him, for he realized in himself everything that was promised through the Old Testament. And he gave orders to break the bread; by being broken the loaves were multiplied. Nothing could be more true: to how many more books have those five books of Moses—by being commented upon, by being broken open, and explained—given rise! But the ignorance of the first people, the people of whom it is said, *As long as Moses is read, there is a veil placed over their hearts* (2 Cor 3:15), was wrapped up in that barley. And the veil, in fact, had not yet been taken away, because Christ had not yet come; the veil of the temple had not yet been torn to ribbons as he was hanging on the cross.[5] So it is because the people's ignorance was embodied in the law that the Lord—by testing him—showed up the ignorance of the disciple.

6. No detail, therefore is pointless, everything has a meaning, but someone has to understand what that is. For instance, even the number of the people who ate signified the people which was established under the law. Why, after all, were there five thousand of them, if not because they were under the law, the law which is explained in the five books of Moses? That is why the sick were laid out by those five porticoes and were not cured.[6] But the one who cured the sick man there fed the crowds here on five loaves. That is also why they were reclining on the grass; theirs was a wisdom of the flesh, and they were taking their ease in the things of the flesh. *All flesh, you see, is grass* (Isa 40:6).

But what are those fragments, but that which this people could not eat? Let them be seen as more mysterious truths which the crowd cannot grasp. What remains, then, but to entrust these more mysterious things—which the multitude cannot grasp—to the intelligence, to those capable of also teaching others, such as the apostles were? That is why twelve baskets were filled.

This deed was both amazing because it was extraordinary and useful because it was spiritual. Those who saw it at that time were amazed; we on the other hand are not amazed when we hear the account of it. It was done, I mean, for them to see, while it has been written down for us to hear. What their eyes could do for them, faith is able to do for us. We discern with our minds what we have not been able to see with our eyes, and we have an advantage over them because about us it was said, *Blessed are those who do not see, and yet believe* (John 20:29). I must add, though, that maybe we have also understood what that crowd did not understand; and we have truly been fed, because we have been able to get at the kernel of the barley.

7. Finally, what did the people who saw all this think about it? *When the people*, it says, *had seen what a sign he had done, they started saying, This man is truly a prophet* (John 6:14). They may have still been thinking of Christ as a prophet because they were reclining on the grass.[7] But he was the Lord of the prophets, the one who inspired the prophets, the one who sanctified the prophets; even so he was also a prophet, since Moses had been told, *I will raise up for them a*

---

5. See Matt 27:51.
6. See John 5:2–9.
7. That is, because they were still thinking according to the flesh. So they were thinking he was a prophet in the same way and the same sense as the Old Testament prophets.

prophet like yourself (Deut 18:18), like him as regards the flesh, not as regards dignity; and that this promise of the Lord's might be understood as referring to Christ, it is openly stated and explained in the Acts of the Apostles.[8] And the Lord said about himself, *A prophet is not without honor, except in his own country* (Mark 6:4). The Lord is a prophet, and the Lord is the Word of God, and no prophet prophesies without the Word of God; the Word of God is with the prophets, and the Word of God is a prophet. Previous ages were thought worthy of inspired prophets and prophets filled by the Word of God; we have been thought worthy of a prophet who is the very Word of God.

Christ however is a prophet, the Lord of prophets, in the same way as Christ is an angel, the Lord of angels. For he was also called the *angel of great counsel* (Isa 9:6 LXX). And yet what does the prophet Isaiah say in another place? *That not an ambassador nor an angel, but he himself will come and save them* (Isa 63:9 LXX); that is, to save them he will not send an ambassador, will not send an angel, but will come in person. Who will come? The angel himself. Certainly not acting through an angel, except insofar as this one is an angel in such a way as to be also the Lord of angels. In Latin, in fact, angels are heralds. If Christ had had nothing to announce, he would not be called an angel. He exhorted us to believe, and by faith to lay hold of eternal life; he announced something present, foretold something to come in the future. Insofar as he announced something present, he was an angel; insofar as he foretold something to come, he was a prophet; insofar as *the Word was made flesh* (John 1:14), he was, of both angels and prophets, the Lord.

TERTULLIAN

Little is known about the Christian apologist and theologian Tertullian (ca. 160–ca. 240). He was born in or around Carthage and lived much of his life in North Africa. It is possible, though by no means certain, that he is to be identified with a contemporary jurist of the same name. Sometime after converting to Christianity as an adult, Tertullian found himself attracted to the New Prophesy, a charismatic Christian movement later known as Montanism. This precipitated his break with the proto-orthodox church, but it does not seem to have had serious doctrinal implications. Indeed, Tertullian composed treatises lambasting a number of "heresies" against which emergent orthodoxy defined itself (including one against Marcion, excerpted above) and his writings were valued highly by later orthodox Christians writing in Latin, such as Augustine. The following is an exegetical argument from *Flight in Time of Persecution*, Tertullian's short treatise about whether Christians might flee a city in advance of persecution or if such flight would betray their faith—a pressing pastoral issue of his time.

---

8. See Acts 3:22.

On Flight in Time of Persecution[†]

2. If, because injustice is not from God, but from the devil, and persecution consists of injustice (for what more unjust than that the bishops of the true God, that all the followers of the truth, should be dealt with after the manner of the vilest criminals?), persecution therefore seems to proceed from the devil, by whom the injustice which constitutes persecution is perpetrated, we ought to know, as you have neither persecution without the injustice of the devil, nor the trial of faith without persecution, that the injustice necessary for the trial of faith does not give a warrant for persecution, but supplies an agency; that in reality, in reference to the trial of faith, which is the reason of persecution, the will of God goes first, but that as the instrument of persecution, which is the way of trial, the injustice of the devil follows. For in other respects, too, injustice in proportion to the enmity it displays against righteousness affords occasion for attestations of that to which it is opposed as an enemy, that so righteousness may be perfected in injustice, as strength is perfected in weakness. For the weak things of the world have been chosen by God to confound the strong, and the foolish things of the world to confound its wisdom [1 Cor 1:27]. Thus even injustice is employed, that righteousness may be approved in putting unrighteousness to shame. Therefore, since the service is not of free-will, but of subjection (for persecution is the appointment of the Lord for the trial of faith, but its ministry is the injustice of the devil, supplied that persecution may be got up), we believe that persecution comes to pass, no question, by the devil's agency, but not by the devil's origination. Satan will not be at liberty to do anything against the servants of the living God unless the Lord grant leave, either that He may overthrow Satan himself by the faith of the elect which proves victorious in the trial, or in the face of the world show that apostatizers to the devil's cause have been in reality His servants. You have the case of Job, whom the devil, unless he had received authority from God, could not have visited with trial, not even, in fact, in his property, unless the Lord had said, "Behold, all that he has I put at your disposal; but do not stretch out your hand against himself" [Job 1:12]. In short, he would not even have stretched it out, unless afterwards, at his request, the Lord had granted him this permission also, saying, "Behold, I deliver him to you; only preserve his life" [Job 2:6]. So he asked in the case of the apostles likewise an opportunity to tempt them, having it only by special allowance, since the Lord in the Gospel says to Peter, "Behold, Satan asked that he might sift you as grain; but I have prayed for you, that your faith fail not" [Luke 22:31–32]; that is, that the devil should not have power granted him sufficient to endanger his faith. Whence it is manifest that both things belong to God, the shaking of faith as well as the shielding of it, when both are sought from Him—the shaking by the devil, the shielding by the Son. And certainly, when the Son of God has faith's protection absolutely committed to Him, beseeching it of the Father, from whom He receives all power in heaven and on

---

[†] Trans. S. Thelwall, in *The Ante-Nicene Fathers*, vol. 4 (1885; reprint, Peabody, MA: Hendrickson, 1994), 117–21.

earth, how entirely out of the question is it that the devil should have the assailing of it in *his* own power! But in the prayer prescribed to us, when we say to our Father, "Lead us not into temptation" [Matt 6:13] (now what greater temptation is there than persecution?), we acknowledge that that comes to pass by His will whom we beseech to exempt us from it. For this is what follows, "But deliver us from the wicked one," that is, do not lead us into temptation by giving us up to the wicked one, for then are we delivered from the power of the devil, when we are not handed over to him to be tempted. Nor would the devil's legion have had power over the herd of swine unless they had got it from God [Mark 5:11–13 and parallels]; so far are they from having power over the sheep of God. I may say that the bristles of the swine, too, were then counted by God, not to speak of the hairs of holy men. The devil, it must be owned, seems indeed to have power—in this case really his own—over those who do not belong to God, the nations being once for all counted by God as a drop of the bucket, and as the dust of the threshing-floor, and as the spittle of the mouth, and so thrown open to the devil as, in a sense, a free possession. But against those who belong to the household of God he may not do ought as by any right of his own, because the cases marked out in Scripture show when—that is, for what reasons—he may touch them. For either, with a view to their being approved, the power of trial is granted to him, challenged or challenging, as in the instances already referred to, or, to secure an opposite result, the sinner is handed over to him, as though he were an executioner to whom belonged the inflicting of punishment, as in the case of Saul. "And the Spirit of the LORD," says Scripture, "departed from Saul, and an evil spirit from the LORD troubled and stifled him" [1 Sam 16:14]; or the design is to humble, as the apostle tells us, that there was given him a stake, the messenger of Satan, to buffet him [2 Cor 12:7]; and even this sort of thing is not permitted in the case of holy men, unless it be that at the same time strength of endurance may be perfected in weakness. For the apostle likewise delivered Phygellus and Hermogenes over to Satan, that by chastening they might be taught not to blaspheme [1 Tim 1:20; 2 Tim 1:15]. You see, then, that the devil receives more suitably power even from the servants of God; so far is he from having it by any right of his own.

3. Seeing therefore, too, these cases occur in persecutions more than at other times, as there is then among us more of proving or rejecting, more of abasing or punishing, it must be that their general occurrence is permitted or commanded by Him at whose will they happen even partially; by Him, I mean, who says, "I am He who make peace and create evil" [Isa 45:7],—that is, war, for that is the antithesis of peace. But what other war has our peace than persecution? If in its issues persecution emphatically brings either life or death, either wounds or healing, you have the author, too, of this. "I will smite and heal, I will make alive and put to death" [Deut 32:39]. "I will burn them," He says, "as gold is burned; and I will try them," He says, "as silver is tried" [Zech 13:9], for when the flame of persecution is consuming us, then the stedfastness of our faith is proved. These will be the fiery darts of the devil [Eph 6:16], by which faith gets a ministry of burning and kindling; yet by the will of God. As to this I know not who can doubt, unless it be persons with frivolous and frigid faith, which seizes upon those who with trembling assemble together in the church. For you say, seeing

we assemble without order, and assemble at the same time, and flock in large numbers to the church, the heathen are led to make inquiry about us, and we are alarmed lest we awaken their anxieties. Do ye not know that God is Lord of all? And if it is God's will, then you shall suffer persecution; but if it is not, the heathen will be still. Believe it most surely, if indeed you believe in that God without whose will not even the sparrow, which a penny can buy, falls to the ground [Matt 10:29]. But we, I think, are better than many sparrows.

4. Well, then, if it is evident from whom persecution proceeds, we are able at once to satisfy your doubts, and to decide from these introductory remarks alone, that men should not flee in it. For if persecution proceeds from God, in no way will it be our duty to flee from what has God as its author; a twofold reason opposing: for what proceeds from God ought not on the one hand to be avoided, and it cannot be evaded on the other. It ought not to be avoided, because it is good; for everything must be good on which God has cast His eye. And with this idea has perhaps this statement been made in Genesis, "And God saw because it is good" [Gen 1:4, 10, 12, etc.]; not that He would have been ignorant of its goodness unless He had seen it, but to indicate by this expression that it was good because it was viewed by God. There are many events indeed happening by the will of God, and happening to somebody's harm. Yet for all that, a thing is therefore good because it is of God, as divine, as reasonable; for what is divine, and not reasonable and good? What is good, yet not divine? But if to the universal apprehension of mankind this seems to be the case, in judging, man's faculty of apprehension does not predetermine the nature of things, but the nature of things his power of apprehension. For every several nature is a certain definite reality, and it lays it on the perceptive power to perceive it just as it exists. Now, if that which comes from God is good indeed in its natural state (for there is nothing from God which is not good, because it is divine, and reasonable), but seems evil only to the human faculty, all will be right in regard to the former; with the latter the fault will lie. In its real nature a very good thing is chastity, and so is truth, and righteousness; and yet they are distasteful to many. Is perhaps the real nature on this account sacrificed to the sense of perception? Thus persecution in its own nature too is good, because it is a divine and reasonable appointment; but those to whom it comes as a punishment do not feel it to be pleasant. You see that as proceeding from Him, even that evil has a reasonable ground, when one in persecution is cast out of a state of salvation, just as you see that you have a reasonable ground for the good also, when one by persecution has his salvation made more secure. Unless, as it depends on the Lord, one either perishes irrationally, or is irrationally saved, he will not be able to speak of persecution as an evil, which, while it is under the direction of reason, is, even in respect of its evil, good. So, if persecution is in every way a good, because it has a natural basis, we on valid grounds lay it down, that what is good ought not to be shunned by us, because it is a sin to refuse what is good; besides that, what has been looked upon by God can no longer indeed be avoided, proceeding as it does from God, from whose will escape will not be possible. Therefore those who think that they should flee, either reproach God with doing what is evil, if they flee from persecution as an evil (for no one avoids what is good); or they count themselves stronger than God:

so they think, who imagine it possible to escape when it is God's pleasure that such events should occur.

5. But, says some one, I flee, the thing it belongs to me to do, that I may not perish, if I deny; it is for Him on His part, if He chooses, to bring me, when I flee, back before the tribunal. First answer me this: Are you sure you will deny if you do not flee, or are you not sure? For if you are sure, you have denied already, because by presupposing that you will deny, you have given yourself up to that about which you have made such a presupposition; and now it is vain for you to think of flight, that you may avoid denying, when in intention you have denied already. But if you are doubtful on that point, why do you not, in the incertitude of your fear wavering between the two different issues, presume that you are able rather to act a confessor's part, and so add to your safety, that you may not flee, just as you presuppose denial to send you off a fugitive? The matter stands thus—we have either both things in our own power, or they wholly lie with God. If it is ours to confess or to deny, why do we not anticipate the nobler thing, that is, that we shall confess? If you are not willing to confess, you are not willing to suffer; and to be unwilling to confess is to deny. But if the matter is wholly in God's hand, why do we not leave it to His will, recognising His might and power in that, just as He can bring us back to trial when we flee, so is He able to screen us when we do not flee; yes, and even living in the very heart of the people? Strange conduct, is it not, to honour God in the matter of flight from persecution, because He can bring you back from your flight to stand before the judgment-seat; but in regard of witness-bearing, to do Him high dishonour by despairing of power at His hands to shield you from danger? Why do you not rather on this, the side of constancy and trust in God, say, I do my part; I depart not; God, if He choose, will Himself be my protector? It beseems us better to retain our position in submission to the will of God, than to flee at our own will. Rutilius, a saintly martyr, after having ofttimes fled from persecution from place to place, nay, having bought security from danger, as he thought, by money, was, notwithstanding the complete security he had, as he thought, provided for himself, at last unexpectedly seized, and being brought before the magistrate, was put to the torture and cruelly mangled,—a punishment, I believe, for his fleeing,—and thereafter he was consigned to the flames, and thus paid to the mercy of God the suffering which he had shunned. What else did the Lord mean to show us by this example, but that we ought not to flee from persecution because it avails us nothing if God disapproves?

6. Nay, says some one, he fulfilled the command, when he fled from city to city. For so a certain individual, but a fugitive likewise, has chosen to maintain, and others have done the same who are unwilling to understand the meaning of that declaration of the Lord, that they may use it as a cloak for their cowardice, although it has had its persons as well as its times and reasons to which it specially applies. "When they begin," He says, "to persecute you, flee from city to city" [Matt 10:23]. We maintain that this belongs specially to the persons of the apostles, and to their times and circumstances, as the following sentences will show, which are suitable only to the apostles: "Do not go into the way of the Gentiles, and into a city of the Samaritans do not enter: but go rather to the lost sheep of the house of Israel" [Matt 10:5–6]. But to us the way of the Gentiles is also open, as in it we in fact were found, and to the very last we walk; and no city has been excepted. So we preach throughout all the world; nay, no special care even for Israel has been laid upon us, save as also we are bound to preach to all nations. Yes, and if we are apprehended, we shall not be brought into Jewish councils, nor scourged in Jewish synagogues [Matt 10:17], but we shall certainly be cited before Roman magistrates and judgment-seats. So, then, the circumstances of the apostles even required the injunction to flee, their mission being to preach first to the lost sheep of the house of Israel [Matt 15:24]. That, therefore, this preaching might be fully accomplished in the case of those among whom this behoved first of all to be carried out—that the sons might receive bread before the dogs [Matt 15:26–27; Mark 7:27–28], for that reason He commanded them to flee then for a time—not with the object of eluding danger, under the plea strictly speaking which persecution urges (rather He was in the habit of proclaiming that they would suffer persecutions, and of teaching that these must be endured); but in order to further the proclamation of the Gospel message, lest by their being at once put down, the diffusion of the Gospel too might be prevented. Neither were they to flee to any city as if by stealth, but as if everywhere about to proclaim their message; and for this, everywhere about to undergo persecutions, until they should fulfil their teaching. Accordingly the Saviour says, "Ye will not go over all the cities of Israel" [Matt 10:23]. So the command to flee was restricted to the limits of Judea. But no command that shows Judea to be specially the sphere for preaching applies to us, now that the Holy Spirit has been poured out upon all flesh. Therefore Paul and the apostles themselves, mindful of the precept of the Lord, bear this solemn testimony before Israel, which they had now filled with their doctrine—saying, "It was necessary that the word of God should have been first delivered to you; but seeing ye have rejected it, and have not thought yourselves worthy of eternal life, lo, we turn to the Gentiles" [Acts 13:46]. And from that time they turned their steps away, as those who went before them had laid it down, and departed into the way of the Gentiles, and entered into the cities of the Samaritans; so that, in very deed, their sound went forth into all the earth, and their words to the end of the world [Ps 19:4]. If, therefore, the prohibition against setting foot in the way of the Gentiles, and entering into the cities of the Samaritans, has come to an end, why should not the command to flee, which was issued at the same time, have come also to an end? Accordingly, from the time when, Israel having had its full measure, the apostles went over to the Gentiles, they neither fled from city to city, nor hesitated to suffer. Nay, Paul too, who had submitted to deliverance from persecution by being let down from the wall [2 Cor 11:32–33; cf. Acts 9:23–25], as to do so was at this time a matter of command, refused in like manner now at the close of his ministry, and after the injunction had come to an end, to give in to the anxieties of the disciples, eagerly entreating him that he would not risk himself at Jerusalem, because of the sufferings in store for him which Agabus had foretold; but doing the very opposite, it is thus he speaks, "What do ye, weeping and disquieting my heart? For I could wish not only to suffer bonds, but also to die at Jerusalem, for the name of my Lord Jesus Christ." And so they all said, "Let the will of the Lord be done" [Acts 21:13–14]. What was the will of the Lord? Certainly no longer to flee from persecution. Otherwise they who had wished him rather to avoid persecution, might also have adduced that prior will of the Lord, in which He had commanded flight. Therefore, seeing even in the days of the apostles themselves, the command to flee was temporary, as were those also relating to the other things at the same time enjoined, that [command] cannot continue with us which ceased with our teachers, even although it had not been issued specially for them; or if the Lord wished it to continue, the apostles did wrong who were not careful to keep fleeing to the last.

7. Let us now see whether also the rest of our Lord's ordinances accord with a lasting command of flight. In the first place, indeed, if persecution is from God, what are we to think of our being ordered to take ourselves out of its way, by the very party who brings it on us? For if He wanted it to be evaded, He had better not have sent it, that there might not be the appearance of His will being thwarted by another will. For He wished us either to suffer persecution or to flee from it. If to flee, how to suffer? If to suffer, how to flee? In fact, what utter inconsistency in the decrees of One who commands to flee, and yet urges to suffer, which is the very opposite! "Him who will confess Me, I also will confess before My Father" [Matt 10:32]. How will he confess, fleeing? How flee, confessing? "Of him who shall be ashamed of Me, will I also be ashamed before My Father" [Mark 8:38; Luke 9:26]. If I avoid suffering, I am ashamed to confess. "Happy they who suffer persecution for My name's sake" [Matt 5:11]. Unhappy, therefore, they who, by running away, will not suffer according to the divine command. "He who shall endure to the end shall be saved" [Matt 10:22]. How then, when you bid me flee, do you wish me to endure to the end? If views so opposed to each other do not comport with the divine dignity, they clearly prove that the command to flee had, at the time it was given, a reason of its own, which we have pointed out. But it is said, the Lord, providing for the weakness of some of His people, nevertheless, in His kindness, suggested also the haven of flight to them. For He was not able even without flight—a protection so base, and unworthy, and servile—to preserve in persecution such as He knew to be weak! Whereas in fact He does not cherish, but ever rejects the weak, teaching first, not that we are to fly from our persecutors, but rather that we are not to fear them. "Fear not them who are able to kill the body, but are unable to do ought against the soul; but fear Him who can destroy both body and soul in hell" [Matt 10:28]. And then what does He allot to the fearful? "He who will value his life more than Me, is not worthy of Me; and he who takes not up his cross and follows Me, cannot be My disciple" [Luke 14:26–27]. Last of all, in the Revelation, He does not propose flight to the "fearful" but a miserable portion among the rest of the outcast, in the lake of brimstone and fire, which is the second death [Rev 21:8].

8. He sometimes also fled from violence Himself, but for the same reason as had led Him to command the apostles to do so: that is, he wanted to fulfil His ministry of teaching;[1] and when it was finished, I do not say He stood firm, but He had no desire even to get from His Father the aid of hosts of angels: finding

---

1. Cf. Luke 4:29–30 and John 7:1–10, although in neither case is the motive Tertullian offers given.

fault, too, with Peter's sword. He likewise acknowledged, it is true, that His "soul was troubled, even unto death" [Matt 26:38; Mark 14:34], and the flesh weak [Matt 26:41; Mark 14:38]; with the design, (however,) first of all, that by having, as His own, trouble of soul and weakness of the flesh, He might show you that both the substances in Him were truly human; lest, as certain persons have now brought it in, you might be led to think either the flesh or the soul of Christ different from ours;[2] and then, that, by an exhibition of their states, you might be convinced that they have no power at all of themselves without the spirit. And for this reason He puts first "the willing spirit," that, looking to the natures respectively of both the substances, you may see that you have in you the spirit's strength as well as the flesh's weakness; and even from this may learn what to do, and by what means to do it, and what to bring under what,—the weak, namely, under the strong, that you may not, as is now your fashion, make excuses on the ground of the weakness of the flesh, forsooth, but put out of sight the strength of the spirit. He also asked of His Father, that if it might be, the cup of suffering should pass from Him [Matt 26:39]. So ask you the like favour; but as He did, holding your position,—merely offering supplication, and adding, too, the other words: "but not what I will, but what Thou wilt." But when you run away, how will you make this request? taking, in that case, into your own hands the removal of the cup from you, and instead of doing what your Father wishes, doing what you wish yourself.

9. The teaching of the apostles was surely in everything according to the mind of God: they forgot and omitted nothing of the Gospel. Where, then, do you show that they renewed the command to flee from city to city? In fact, it was utterly impossible that they should have laid down anything so utterly opposed to their own examples as a command to flee, while it was just from bonds, or the islands in which, for confessing, not fleeing from the Christian name, they were confined, they wrote their letters to the Churches. Paul bids us support the weak [1 Thess 5:14], but most certainly it is not when they flee. For how can the absent be supported by you? By bearing with them? Well, he says that people must be supported, if anywhere they have committed a fault through the weakness of their faith, just as (he enjoins) that we should comfort the fainthearted; he does not say, however, that they should be sent into exile. But when he urges us not to give place to evil [Eph 4:27], he does not offer the suggestion that we should take to our heels, he only teaches that passion should be kept under restraint; and if he says that the time must be redeemed, because the days are evil [Eph 5:16], he wishes us to gain a lengthening of life, not by flight, but by wisdom. Besides, he who bids us shine as sons of light [1 Thess 5:5], does not bid us hide away out of sight as sons of darkness. He commands us to stand stedfast [1 Cor 15:58], certainly not to act an opposite part by fleeing; and to be girt, not to play the fugitive or oppose the Gospel. He points out weapons, too, which persons who intend to run away would not require. And among these he notes the shield too, that ye may be able to quench the darts of the devil [Eph 6:16], when doubtless ye resist him, and sustain his assaults in their utmost force. Accordingly John also teaches that we must lay down our lives for the brethren [1 John 3:16]; much more, then, we must do it for the Lord. This cannot be fulfilled by those who flee. Finally,

2. Cf. Irenaeus, *Against Heresies* 1.6.1; 1.7.2 (above, pp. 1059–60, 1062).

mindful of his own Revelation, in which he had heard the doom of the fearful, (and so) speaking from personal knowledge, he warns us that fear must be put away. "There is no fear," says he, "in love; but perfect love casteth out fear; because fear has torment"—the fire of the lake, no doubt [cf. Rev 21:8]. "He that feareth is not perfect in love" [1 John 4:18]—to wit, the love of God. And yet who will flee from persecution, but he who fears? Who will fear, but he who has not loved? Yes; and if you ask counsel of the Spirit, what does He approve more than that utterance of the Spirit? For, indeed, it incites all almost to go and offer themselves in martyrdom, not to flee from it; so that we also make mention of it.[3] If you are exposed to public infamy, says he, it is for your good; for he who is not exposed to dishonour among men is sure to be so before the Lord. Do not be ashamed; righteousness brings you forth into the public gaze. Why should you be ashamed of gaining glory? The opportunity is given you when you are before the eyes of men. So also elsewhere: seek not to die on bridal beds, nor in miscarriages, nor in soft fevers, but to die the martyr's death, that He may be glorified who has suffered for you.

THOMAS AQUINAS

The systematizing impulse that comes to full fruition in the magisterial *Summa Theologica* by Thomas Aquinas (ca. 1225–1274) is already on display in the *Catena Aurea* (*Golden Chain*), his compendium of patristic exegesis on the Gospels written in the early 1260s. Such compendia are common in late antiquity and the Middle Ages. The form's potential to bring traditional authorities into meaningful dialogue made it especially attractive to scholastics like Thomas, who believed that authoritative voices of the past—pagan and Christian—could be harmonized to produce a coherent and robust orthodox theology. Thomas's catena is more carefully constructed than most and it can be fruitfully read in at least two ways: as a simple compilation of earlier exegesis, or as a complex conversation between learned authorities regarding difficult exegetical problems, from which a thoughtful reader can dialectically infer the true interpretation.

Catena Aurea [on Matthew 27:51–56][†]

51. And, behold, the veil of the temple was rent in twain from the top to the bottom; and the earth did quake, and the rocks rent;

---

3. Tertullian quotes two Montanist prophecies. (Montanus was a 2nd-century Christian in Asia Minor who, along with Maximilla and Priscilla, claimed to have received authoritative personal revelations from the Holy Spirit.)

† From *Catena Aurea*, trans. John Henry Newman, vol. 1 (Oxford: John Henry Parker, 1842), 962–67. (Aquinas of course quotes numerous earlier Christian authorities, including in this section Origen [see headnote on p. 1068], Augustine [see headnote on pp. 1075–76], John Chrysostom [see note on p. 1358], Jerome [see note on p. 1395], Hilary of Poitiers [4th century], Pope Leo I [the Great, 5th century], Remigius of Auxerre [9th century], and Rabanus Maurus of Mainz [9th century].)

52. And the graves were opened; and many bodies of the saints which slept arose,

53. And came out of the graves after his resurrection, and went into the holy city, and appeared unto many.

54. Now when the centurion, and they that were with him, watching Jesus, saw the earthquake, and those things that were done, they feared greatly, saying, Truly this was the Son of God.

55. And many women were there beholding afar off, which followed Jesus from Galilee, ministering unto him:

56. Among which was Mary Magdalene, and Mary the mother of James and Joses, and the mother of Zebedee's children.

ORIGEN: Great things were done at the moment that Jesus cried with a great voice. AUG[USTINE]: The wording sufficiently shews that the veil was rent just when He gave up the ghost. If he had not added, *And, lo!* but had merely said, *And the veil of the temple was rent*, it would have been uncertain whether Matthew and Mark had not inserted it here out of its place as they recollected, and Luke had observed the right order, who having said, *And the sun was darkened*, adds, *And the veil of the temple was rent in twain* [Luke 23:45]; or, on the contrary, Luke had returned to what they had inserted in its place. ORIGEN: It is understood that there were two veils; one veiling the Holy of Holies, the other, the outer part of the tabernacle or temple. In the Passion then of our Lord and Saviour, it was the outer veil which was rent from the top to the bottom, that by the rending of the veil from the beginning to the end of the world, the mysteries might be published which had been hid with good reason until the Lord's coming. *But when that which is perfect is come* [1 Cor 13:10], then the second veil also shall be taken away, that we may see the things that are hidden within, to wit, the true Ark of the Testament, and behold the Cherubim and the rest in their real nature. HIL-ARY [of Poitiers]: Or, The veil of the temple is rent, because from this time the nation was dispersed, and the honour of the veil is taken away with the guardian-ship of the protecting Angel. LEO [I]: The sudden commotion in the elements is a sufficient sign in witness of His venerable Passion, *The earth quaked, and the rocks rent, and the graves were opened.* JEROME: It is not doubtful to any what these great signs signify according to the letter, namely, that heaven and earth and all things should bear witness to their crucified Lord. HILARY: *The earth quaked*, because it was unequal to contain such a body; *the rocks rent*, for the Word of God that pierces all strong and mighty things, and the virtue of the eter-nal Power had penetrated them; *the graves were opened*, for the bands of death were loosed. *And many bodies of the saints which slept arose*, for illumining the darkness of death, and shedding light upon the gloom of Hades, He robbed the spirits of death. CHRYS[OSTOM]: When He remained on the cross they had said tauntingly, *He saved others, himself he cannot save.* But what He would not do for Himself, that He did and more than that for the bodies of the Saints. For if it was a great thing to raise Lazarus after four days, much more was it that they who had long slept should now shew themselves alive; this is indeed a proof of the resurrection to come. But that it might not be thought that that which was done was an appearance merely, the Evangelist adds, *And came out of the graves after his resurrection, and went into the holy city, and appeared unto many.* JEROME: As Lazarus rose from the dead, so also did many bodies of the Saints rise again to shew forth the Lord's resurrection; yet notwithstanding that the graves were opened, they did not rise again before the Lord rose, that He might be the first-born of the resurrection from the dead. *The holy city* in which they were seen after they had risen may be understood to mean either the heavenly Jerusalem, or this earthly, which once had been holy. For the city of Jerusalem was called Holy on account of the Temple and the Holy of Holies, and to distinguish it from other cities in which idols were worshipped. When it is said, *And appeared unto many,* it is signified that this was not a general resurrection which all should see, but special, seen only by such as were worthy to see it. REMIG[ius]; But some one will ask, what became of those who rose again when the Lord rose. We must believe that they rose again to be witnesses of the Lord's resurrection. Some have said that they died again, and were turned to dust, as Lazarus and the rest whom the Lord raised. But we must by no means give credit to these men's sayings, since if they were to die again, it would be greater torment to them, than if they had not risen again. We ought therefore to believe without hesitation that they who rose from the dead at the Lord's resurrection, ascended also into heaven together with Him.

ORIGEN: These same mighty works are still done every day; the veil of the temple is rent for the Saints, in order to reveal the things that are contained within. The earth quakes, that is, all flesh because of the new word and new things of the New Testament. The rocks are rent, i. e. the mystery of the Prophets, that we may see the spiritual mysteries hid in their depths. The graves are the bodies of sinful souls, that is, souls dead to God; but when by God's grace these souls have been raised, their bodies which before were graves, become bodies of Saints, and appear to go out of themselves, and follow Him who rose again, and walk with Him in newness of life; and such as are worthy to have their conversation in heaven enter into the Holy City at divers times, and appear unto many who see their good works.

AUG: It is no contradiction here that Matthew says, that *The centurion and they that were with him, watching Jesus, feared when they saw the earthquake, and the things that were done;* while Luke says, that he wondered at the giving up the ghost with a loud voice [Luke 23:46–47]. For when Matthew adds, *the things that were done,* this gives full scope for Luke's expression, that he wondered at the Lord's death, for this among the rest was wonderful. JEROME: Observe, that in the very midst of the offence of His passion the Centurion acknowledges the Son of God, while Arius[1] in the Church proclaims Him a creature. RABAN[US MAURUS]: Whence with good reason by the Centurion is denoted the faith of the Church, which, when the veil of heavenly mysteries had been rent by the Lord's death, immediately asserts Jesus to be both very Man, and truly Son of God, while the Synagogue held its peace. LEO: From this example then of the Centurion let the substance of the earth tremble in the punishment of its Redeemer, let the rocks of unbelieving minds be rent, and those who were pent up in these sepulchres of mortality leap

---

1. Arius of Alexander (ca. 250–336) taught that Christ was created by God the Father. He was declared to be a heretic at the Council of Nicea in 325.

forth, bursting the bonds that would detain them; and let them shew themselves in the Holy City, i.e. the Church of God, as signs of the Resurrection to come; and thus let that take place in the heart, which we must believe takes place in the body.

JEROME: It was a Jewish custom, and held no disgrace, according to the manners of the people of old, for women to minister of their substance, food, and clothing to their teachers. This Paul says, that he refused, because it might occasion scandal among the Gentiles. They ministered to the Lord of their substance, that He might reap their carnal things, of whom they reaped spiritual things. Not that the Lord needed food of the creature, but that He might set an example for the teacher, that He should be content to receive food and clothing from His disciples. But let us see what sort of attendants He had; *Among whom was Mary Magdalene, and Mary the mother of James and Joseph, and the mother of Zebedee's children.* ORIGEN: In Mark the third is called Salome. CHRYS: These women thus watching the things that are done are the most compassionate, the most sorrowful. They had followed Him ministering, and remained by Him in danger, showing the highest courage, for when the disciples fled they remained. JEROME: 'See,' says Helvidius,[2] 'Jacob and Joseph are the sons of Mary the Lord's mother, whom the Jews call the brethren of Christ [Mark 6:3]. He is also called James the less, to distinguish him from James the greater, who was the son of Zebedee.' And he urges that 'it were impious to suppose that His mother Mary would be absent, when the other women were there; or that we should have to invent some other third unknown person of the name of Mary, and that too when John's Gospel witnesses that His mother was present.' O blind folly! O mind perverted to its own destruction! Hear what the Evangelist John says: *There stood by the cross of Jesus, his mother, and his mother's sister, Mary the wife of Cleophas, and Mary Magdalene* [John 19:25]. No one can doubt that there were two Apostles called James; the son of Zebedee, and the son of Alpheus. This unknown James the less, whom Scripture mentions as the son of Mary, if he is an Apostle, is the son of Alpheus; if he is not an Apostle, but a third unknown James, how can he be supposed to be the Lord's brother, and why should he be styled 'The Less,' to distinguish him from 'The Greater?' For The Greater and The Less are epithets which distinguish two persons, but not three. And that the James, the Lord's brother, was an Apostle, is proved by Paul, *Other of the Apostles saw I none, save James the Lord's brother* [Gal 1:19]. But that you should not suppose this James to be the son of Zebedee, read the Acts, where he was put to death by Herod [Acts 12:1–2]. The conclusion then remains, that this Mary, who is described as the mother of James the less, was wife of Alpheus, and sister of Mary the Lord's mother,[3] called by John, Mary the wife of Cleophas. But should you incline to think them two different persons, because in one place she is called Mary the mother of James the less, and in another place Mary the wife of Cleophas, you will learn the Scripture custom of calling the same man by different names; as Raguel Moses'

---

2. A contemporary of Jerome who argued against Mary's perpetual virginity.

3. Since James, son of Alpheus is thus Jesus' cousin, they can imprecisely be refferred to as brothers, which is how Jerome understands Gal 1:19 (cf. Mark 6:3).

father-in-law is called Jethro [cf. Exod 2:18–21; 3:1]. In like manner then, Mary the wife of Cleophas is called the wife of Alpheus, and the mother of James the less. For if she had been the Lord's mother, the Evangelist would here, as in all other places, have called her so, and not described her as the mother of James, when he meant to designate the mother of the Lord. But even if Mary the wife of Cleophas, and Mary the mother of James and Joses, were different persons, it is still certain, that Mary the mother of James and Joses was not the Lord's mother. Aug: We might have supposed that some of the women *stood afar off*, as three Evangelists say, and others *near the cross*, as John says, had not Matthew and Mark reckoned Mary Magdalen among those that stood afar off, while John puts her among those that stood near [John 19:25]. This is reconciled if we understand the distance at which they were to be such that they might be said to be near, because they were in His sight; but far off in comparison of the crowd who stood nearer with the centurion and soldiers. We might also suppose that they who were there together with the Lord's mother, began to depart after He had commended her to the disciple, that they might extricate themselves from the crowd, and looked on from a distance at the other things which were done, so that the Evangelists, who speak of them after the Lord's death, speak of them as standing afar off.

THOMAS HOBBES

The English political philosopher Thomas Hobbes (1588–1679) published his masterpiece *Leviathan* in 1651. Famous for its innovative use of social contract theory to explain the state's sovereign power and to urge absolute obedience to it, this lengthy treatise, written in the wake of a century of European religious wars, argues for so radical a subordination of religious to political authority that readers today continue to find it shocking. Hobbes frequently engages the Bible, usually with great sophistication. In the excerpts below, he provocatively argues that Scripture's authority derives from the Sovereign and that the New Testament itself prohibits virtually all civil disobedience, even that based on religious principles. (Hobbes explicitly rejects an understanding of martyrdom equivalent to the one Tertullian proposed in *Flight in Time of Persecution*, and may productively be read alongside the selection from that treatise above [pp. 1091–98].)

[The Authority of Scripture Dependent on the Sovereign]†
(from *Leviathan*, chap. 33)

The question of the Authority of the Scriptures stated

It is a question much disputed between the divers sects of Christian Religion, *From whence the Scriptures derive their Authority*; which question is also propounded sometimes in other terms, as, *How wee know them to be the Word of God*, or, *Why we beleeve them to be so*: And the difficulty of resolving it, ariseth chiefly

---

† From *Leviathan*, ed. C. B. Macpherson (London: Penguin, 1985), 425–27, 525–31. The spelling and punctuation follow the 1651 edition. Marginal headings are Hobbes's own.

from the impropernesse of the words wherein the question it self is couched. For it is beleeved on all hands, that the first and originall *Author* of them is God; and consequently the question disputed, is not that. Again, it is manifest, that none can know they are Gods Word, (though all true Christians beleeve it,) but those to whom God himself hath revealed it supernaturally; and therefore the question is not rightly moved, of our *Knowledge* of it. Lastly, when the question is propounded of our *Beleefe*; because some are moved to beleeve for one, and others for other reasons, there can be rendred no one generall answer for them all. The question truly stated is, *By what Authority they are made Law.*

As far as they differ not from the Laws of Nature, there is no doubt, but they are the Law of God, and carry their Authority with them, legible to all men that have the use of naturall reason: but this is no other Authority, then that of all other Morall Doctrine consonant to Reason; the Dictates whereof are Laws, not *made*, but *Eternall.* *Their Authority and Interpretation*

If they be made Law by God himselfe, they are of the nature of written Law, which are Laws to them only to whom God hath so sufficiently published them, as no man can excuse himself, by saying, he knew not they were his.

He therefore, to whom God hath not supernaturally revealed, that they are his, nor that those that published them, were sent by him, is not obliged to obey them, by any Authority, but his, whose Commands have already the force of Laws; that is to say, by any other Authority, then that of the Common-wealth, residing in the Soveraign, who only has the Legislative power. Again, if it be not the Legislative Authority of the Common-wealth, that giveth them the force of Laws, it must bee some other Authority derived from God, either private, or publique: if private, it obliges onely him, to whom in particular God hath been pleased to reveale it. For if every man should be obliged, to take for Gods Law, what particular men, on pretence of private Inspiration, or Revelation, should obtrude upon him, (in such a number of men, that out of pride, and ignorance, take their own Dreams, and extravagant Fancies, and Madnesse, for testimonies of Gods Spirit; or out of ambition, pretend to such Divine testimonies, falsely, and contrary to their own consciences,) it were impossible that any Divine Law should be acknowledged. If publique, it is the Authority of the *Common-wealth*, or of the *Church*. But the Church, if it be one person, is the same thing with a Common-wealth of Christians; called a *Common-wealth*, because it consisteth of men united in one person, their Soveraign; and a *Church*, because it consisteth in Christian men, united in one Christian Soveraign. But if the Church be not one person, then it hath no authority at all; it can neither command, nor doe any action at all; nor is capable of having any power, or right to any thing; nor has any Will, Reason, nor Voice; for all these qualities are personall. Now if the whole number of Christians be not contained in one Common-wealth, they are not one person; nor is there an Universall Church that hath any authority over them; and therefore the Scriptures are not made Laws, by the Universall Church: or if it bee one Common-wealth, then all Christian Monarchs, and States are private persons, and subject to bee judged, deposed, and punished by an Universall Soveraigne of all Christendome. So that the question of the Authority of the Scriptures, is reduced to this, *Whether Christian Kings, and the Soveraigne Assemblies in Christian Commonwealths, be absolute in their own Territories, immediately under God; or subject to*

*one Vicar of Christ, constituted over the Universall Church; to bee judged, con-
demned, deposed, and put to death, as hee shall think expedient, or necessary for
the common good.*

Which question cannot bee resolved, without a more particular consideration
of the Kingdome of God; from whence also, wee are to judge of the Authority of
Interpreting the Scripture. For, whosoever hath a lawfull power over any Writing, to make it Law, hath the power also to approve, or disapprove the interpretation of the same.

[The Authority Christ Left to Churches]
(from *Leviathan*, chap. 42)

*An argument
thereof, the
Power of
Christ
himself:*

I have shewn already (in the last Chapter,) that the Kingdome of Christ is not of
this world: therefore neither can his Ministers (unlesse they be Kings,) require
obedience in his name. For if the Supreme King, have not his Regall Power in this
world; by what authority can obedience be required to his Officers? As my Father
sent me, (so saith our Saviour) I send you [John 20:21]. But our Saviour was sent
to perswade the Jews to return to, and to invite the Gentiles, to receive the Kingdome of his Father, and not to reign in Majesty, no not, as his Fathers Lieutenant,
till the day of Judgment.

*From the
name of
Regeneration:*

The time between the Ascension, and the generall Resurrection, is called, not
a Reigning, but a Regeneration; that is, a Preparation of men for the second and
glorious coming of Christ, at the day of Judgment; as appeareth by the words of
our Saviour, *Mat. 19.28. You that have followed me in the Regeneration, when the
Son of man shall sit in the throne of his glory, you shall also sit upon twelve
Thrones*; And of St. Paul (*Ephes. 6.15.) Having your feet shod with the Preparation
of the Gospell of Peace.*

*From the
comparison
of it, with
Fishing,
Leaven, Seed*

And is compared by our Saviour, to Fishing; that is, to winning men to obedience, not by Coercion, and Punishing; but by Perswasion: and therefore he said not
to his Apostles, hee would make them so many Nimrods, *Hunters of men* [Gen
10:9]; *but Fishers of men* [Matt 4:19 and parallels]. It is compared also to Leaven; to
Sowing of Seed, and to the Multiplication of a grain of Mustard-seed [Matt 13:24–
34 and parallels]; by all which Compulsion is excluded; and consequently there can
in that time be no actual Reigning. The work of Christs Ministers, is Evangelization; that is, a Proclamation of Christ, and a preparation for his second comming;
as the Evangelization of John Baptist, was a preparation to his first coming.

*From the
nature of
Faith:*

Again, the Office of Christs Ministers in this world, is to make men Beleeve,
and have Faith in Christ: But Faith hath no relation to, nor dependence at all
upon Compulsion, or Commandement; but onely upon certainty, or probability of
Arguments drawn from Reason, or from something men beleeve already. Therefore the Ministers of Christ in this world, have no Power by that title, to Punish
any man for not Beleeving, or for Contradicting what they say; they have I say
no Power by that title of Christs Ministers, to Punish such: but if they have
Soveraign Civill Power, by politick institution, then they may indeed lawfully

2 Cor. 1. 24 Punish any Contradiction to their laws whatsoever: And St. Paul, of himselfe and other the then Preachers of the Gospell, saith in expresse words; *Wee have no Dominion over your Faith, but are Helpers of your Joy.*

Another Argument, that the Ministers of Christ in this present world have no right of Commanding, may be drawn from the lawfull Authority which Christ hath left to all Princes, as well Christians, as Infidels. St. Paul saith (*Col. 3.20.*) *Children obey your Parents in all things; for this is well pleasing to the Lord.* And ver. 22. *Servants obey in all things your Masters according to the flesh, not with eye-service, as men-pleasers, but in singlenesse of heart, as fearing the Lord*: This is spoken to them whose Masters were Infidells; and yet they are bidden to obey them *in all things.* And again, concerning obedience to Princes. (*Rom.* 13. the first 6. verses) exhorting *to be subject to the Higher Powers,* he saith, *that all Power is ordained of God*; and *that we ought to be subject to them, not onely for* fear of incurring their *wrath, but also for conscience sake.* And St. *Peter,* (1 Epist. chap. 2. ver. 13, 14, 15.) *Submit your selves to every Ordinance of Man, for the Lords sake, whether it bee to the King, as Supreme, or unto Governours, as to them that be sent by him for the punishment of evill doers, and for the praise of them that doe well; for so is the will of God.* And again St. Paul (*Tit.* 3.1.) *Put men in mind to be subject to Principalities, and Powers, and to obey Magistrates.* These Princes, and Powers, whereof St. Peter, and St. Paul here speak, were all Infidels: much more therefore we are to obey those Christians, whom God hath ordained to have Soveraign Power over us. How then can wee be obliged to obey any Minister of Christ, if he should command us to doe any thing contrary to the Command of the King, or other Soveraign Representant of the Common-wealth, whereof we are members, and by whom we look to be protected? It is therefore manifest, that Christ hath not left to his Ministers in this world, unlesse they be also endued with Civill Authority, any authority to Command other men.

From the Authority Christ hath left to Civill Princes

But what (may some object) if a King, or a Senate, or other Soveraign Person forbid us to beleeve in Christ? To this I answer, that such forbidding is of no effect, because Beleef, and Unbeleef never follow mens Commands. Faith is a gift of God, which Man can neither give, nor take away by promise of rewards, or menaces of torture. And if it be further asked, What if wee bee commanded by our lawfull Prince, to say with our tongue, wee beleeve not; must we obey such command? Profession with the tongue is but an externall thing, and no more then any other gesture whereby we signifie our obedience; and wherein a Christian, holding firmely in his heart the Faith of Christ, hath the same liberty which the Prophet Elisha allowed to Naaman the Syrian. Naaman was converted in his heart to the God of Israel; For hee saith (2 *Kings* 5.17.) *Thy servant will hence-forth offer neither burnt offering, nor sacrifice unto other Gods but unto the Lord. In this thing the Lord pardon thy servant, that when my Master goeth into the house of Rimmon to worship there, and he leaneth on my hand, and I bow my selfe in the house of Rimmon; when I bow my selfe in the house of Rimmon, the Lord pardon thy servant in this thing.* This the Prophet approved, and bid him *Goe in peace.* Here Naaman beleeved in his heart; but by bowing before the Idol Rimmon, he denyed the true God in effect, as much as if he had done it with his lips. But then what shall we answer to our Saviours saying, *Whosoever denyeth me before men, I will deny him before my Father which is in Heaven* [Matt 10:33 and parallels]? This we

What Christians may do to avoid persecution

may say, that whatsoever a Subject, as Naaman was, is compelled to in obedience to his Soveraign, and doth it not in order to his own mind, but in order to the laws of his country, that action is not his, but his Soveraigns; nor is it he that in this case denyeth Christ before men, but his Governour, and the law of his countrey. If any man shall accuse this doctrine, as repugnant to true, and unfeigned Christianity; I ask him, in case there should be a subject in any Christian Common-wealth, that should be inwardly in his heart of the Mahometan Religion, whether if his Soveraign command him to bee present at the divine service of the Christian Church, and that on pain of death, he think that Mahometan obliged in conscience to suffer death for that cause, rather than to obey that command of his lawful Prince. If he say, he ought rather to suffer death, then he authorizeth all private men, to disobey their Princes, in maintenance of their Religion, true, or false: if he say, he ought to bee obedient, then he alloweth to himself, that which hee denyeth to another, contrary to the words of our Saviour, *Whatsoever you would that men should doe unto you, that doe yee unto them* [Matt 7:12]; and contrary to the Law of Nature, (which is the indubitable everlasting Law of God) *Do not to another, that which thou wouldest not he should doe unto thee.*

Of Martyrs   But what then shall we say of all those Martyrs we read of in the History of the Church, that they have needlessely cast away their lives? For answer hereunto, we are to distinguish the persons that have been for that cause put to death; whereof some have received a Calling to preach, and professe the Kingdome of Christ openly; others have had no such Calling, nor more has been required of them than their owne faith. The former sort, if they have been put to death, for bearing witnesse to this point, that Jesus Christ is risen from the dead, were true Martyrs; For a *Martyr* is, (to give the true definition of the word) a Witnesse of the Resurrection of Jesus the Messiah; which none can be but those that conversed with him on earth, and saw him after he was risen: For a Witnesse must have seen what he testifieth, or else his testimony is not good. And that none but such, can properly be called Martyrs of Christ, is manifest out of the words of St. Peter, *Act.* 1.21, 22. *Wherefore of these men which have companyed with us all the time that the Lord Jesus went in and out amongst us, beginning from the Baptisme of John unto that same day hee was taken up from us, must one be ordained to be a Martyr* (that is a Witnesse) *with us of his Resurrection*: Where we may observe, that he which is to bee a Witnesse of the truth of the Resurrection of Christ, that is to say, of the truth of this fundamentall article of Christian Religion, that Jesus was the Christ, must be some Disciple that conversed with him, and saw him before, and after his Resurrection; and consequently must be one of his originall Disciples: whereas they which were not so, can Witnesse no more, but that their antecessors said it, and are therefore but Witnesses of other mens testimony; and are but second Martyrs, or Martyrs of Christs Witnesses.

He, that to maintain every doctrine which he himself draweth out of the History of our Saviours life, and of the Acts, or Epistles of the Apostles; or which he beleeveth upon the authority of a private man, wil oppose the Laws and Authority of the Civill State, is very far from being a Martyr of Christ, or a Martyr of his Martyrs. 'Tis one Article onely, which to die for, meriteth so honorable a name;

and that Article is this, that *Jesus is the Christ*; that is to say, He that hath redeemed us, and shall come again to give us salvation, and eternall life in his glorious Kingdome. To die for every tenet that serveth the ambition, or profit of the Clergy, is not required; nor is it the Death of the Witnesse, but the Testimony it self that makes the Martyr: for the word signifieth nothing else, but the man that beareth Witnesse, whether he be put to death for his testimony, or not.

Also he that is not sent to preach this fundamentall article, but taketh it upon him of his private authority, though he be a Witnesse, and consequently a Martyr, either primary of Christ, or secundary of his Apostles, Disciples, or their Successors; yet is he not obliged to suffer death for that cause; because being not called thereto, tis not required at his hands; nor ought hee to complain, if he loseth the reward he expecteth from those that never set him on work. None therefore can be a Martyr, neither of the first, nor second degree, that have not a warrant to preach Christ come in the flesh; that is to say, none, but such as are sent to the conversion of Infidels. For no man is a Witnesse to him that already beleeveth, and therefore needs no Witnesse; but to them that deny, or doubt, or have not heard it. Christ sent his Apostles, and his Seventy Disciples, with authority to preach; he sent not all that beleeved: And he sent them to unbeleevers; *I send you* (saith he) *as sheep amongst wolves* [Luke 10:3; cf. Matt 10:16], not as sheep to other sheep.

CRITICAL EXEGESIS

HERMANN SAMUEL REIMARUS

For obvious reasons, the German classical philologist and philosopher Hermann Samuel Reimarus (1694–1768) never published his *Apology for Rational Worshippers of God*, but his daughter gave a copy of the manuscript to the influential dramatist and philosopher Gotthold Ephraim Lessing. During the decade following Reimarus's death, Lessing published several sections of it (which he called "fragments") in a series he edited as librarian for the Duke of Brunswick at Wolfenbüttel, with an additional section published in 1787, a few years after his own death. Lessing attributed the fragments to an unknown author and they were not publicly associated with Reimarus until the early nineteenth century. Their elevation of reason as the sole arbiter of truth marks them as standard Enlightenment fare, but their bold application of this principle to biblical interpretation and the sheer rigor of their arguments made them especially influential. Albert Schweitzer plausibly claimed that "before Reimarus, no one had attempted to form a historical conception of the life of Jesus." What follows is an excerpt from the sixth Fragment that Lessing published, on the resurrection narratives.

[Contradictions in the Gospels' Resurrection Accounts]†

§19

* * * Now, let us see if the other evangelists' testimony of Jesus' resurrection is more consistent. If the evangelists and all the apostles were still alive they could not object to our undertaking this investigation and doubting their testimony because of our findings. The matter is quite extraordinary and supernatural: they can produce nobody from their ranks who saw Jesus rise, they alone are witnesses of it, and if we consider the matter carefully today we can produce only two who claim to have seen Jesus themselves; the other two were not with him but simply repeat hearsay. And the others are merely cited as witnesses in the testimony of these witnesses. Yet we are supposed to base a whole doctrinal structure on the testimony of these few disciples of Jesus. And what is more remarkable, according to their reports Jesus' disciples in the beginning did not themselves want to believe it and some of them continued to doubt the reality of his resurrection until the period of his final days on earth. When Mary Magdalene and the other women asserted to the apostles that they had seen a vision of angels and, indeed, that they had seen Jesus himself, had spoken with him and touched him, they did not believe it [Mark 16:11]. Their words seemed an idle tale to them [Luke 24:11 ff.]. Peter hurried out to the tomb and saw there only the linen cloths, but he was amazed as to how it had happened [John 20:6]. When the two traveling disciples told the other apostles how Jesus had walked and spoken with them on the road and had then disappeared, they did not believe them either [Mark 16:12–13]. When Jesus had already appeared to all his disciples Thomas still would not believe their words until he had put his hands into Jesus' nail prints and side [John 20:24, 25]. Indeed, when Jesus appeared to them in Galilee (according to John's report the third time that Jesus had manifested himself to all the apostles) there were still some among them who doubted [Matt 28:16–17]. Now, if all the apostles who of course had seen and heard Jesus' earlier miracles and proclamations and who now saw him often clearly and distinctly with their own eyes, talked and ate with him, felt and touched him, were still skeptical and doubtful about such an important event, how much less should we be reproached today for being doubtful and skeptical since we cannot experience all these things with our own senses but must accept it seventeen hundred years later from the reports of a few witnesses? And the only reasonable thing left for us to do, since our own experience is lacking, is to see if the surviving testimonies agree. Or do the evangelists and apostles perhaps wish to tell us in their caution (and it always seems this way), "We have investigated Jesus' resurrection as carefully as any unbeliever and doubter can do, so you may now definitely trust us and need not undertake a fresh investigation nor have any reservations"? Certainly this would be an unreasonable demand. They themselves doubted their

† From *Reimarus: Fragments*, Part II, ed. Charles H. Talbert, trans. Ralph S. Fraser (1970; reprint, Eugene, OR: Wipf & Stock, 2009), 172–77, 185–87. Cross-references, all notes, and scriptural citations (with occasional alterations) are supplied by Talbert and Fraser.

master's annunciation, miracles, and visible and obvious appearance, and should we not have the right to put to the test the truth of their written reports to the extent that we see whether their testimony agrees? No; we have in our hands too many prior proofs that betray to us how their new doctrine was composed after Jesus' death that we need not pay close attention to the main points upon which their whole system is based.

§20

The first thing that we notice concerning the consistency of the four evangelists is that their stories diverge from each other in almost each and every point of the affair, and each one reads differently. Although this does not straightway show a contradiction, still it certainly does not make a unanimous story, especially since the difference is expressed in the most important elements of the event. And I am definitely assured that if today in court four witnesses were heard in a case and their testimony was as different in all respects as is that of our four evangelists', the conclusion would at least have to be made that no case could be constructed on such conflicting testimony. Here it is a question of the truth of Jesus' resurrection, and insofar as it is to be judged by the mere testimony of witnesses, a unanimity of their testimony is necessary as to who saw him, where and how often, what he said and did in the meantime, and finally, what became of him. But how does the testimony read among the four evangelists? (1) In John's story Mary Magdalene goes alone to the tomb; in Matthew, Mary Magdalene and the other Mary; in Mark, Mary Magdalene, Mary the mother of James, and Salome; in Luke, Mary Magdalene, Johanna, and Mary the mother of James, and others with them. (2) Matthew merely says that Mary went out to inspect the tomb; Mark, that they might come out and embalm him; Luke, that they carried the spices which they had prepared; John says nothing at all about why Mary went out. (3) According to Matthew, Mark, and Luke this Mary had gone only once to the tomb and had straightway seen an angel; but in John's story she goes out twice, the first time without having seen an angel, since she runs back and tells Peter, "They have taken away the Lord" [John 20:13], and the second time when she returns and then sees the angel. (4) Peter and John are also supposed to have run out early to the tomb, as John reports; but the other evangelists do not say a word about it. (5) The angel's words in Matthew and Mark tell them not to be afraid, Jesus had risen, they should announce it to the disciples, he would precede them into Galilee. But in Luke there is none of this; instead, "Remember how he told you while he was still in Galilee, that the Son of man must be delivered into the hands of sinful men, and be crucified, and on the third day rise" [Luke 24:6–7]. In John the angel says nothing at all except this to Mary: "Woman, why are you weeping?" [John 20:13]. (6) Jesus' words to Mary Magdalene on the road read this way in Matthew, "Hail! . . . Do not be afraid; go and tell my brethren to go to Galilee, and there they will see me" [Matt. 28:9–10]. In contrast, John says he told Mary Magdalene, "Woman, why are you weeping? . . . Mary . . . Do not hold me, for I have not yet ascended to the Father; but go to my brethren and say to them, I am ascending to my Father and your Father, to my God and your God" [John 20:15, 16, 17]. (7) Matthew and

John make no mention of Jesus' appearing to the two disciples on the road to Emmaus, as Mark[1] and Luke do. (8) Matthew does not say anything about Jesus' appearing to his disciples in Jerusalem, merely that this had happened once in Galilee and that some of the disciples doubted it was he [Matt. 28:16, 17, without parallel]. On the other hand, Mark and Luke know nothing of the manifestation in Galilee, merely of the one in Jerusalem [Luke 24:36–49; Mark 16:14 ff.]. But John remembers two appearances in Jerusalem, a week apart; he relates the one in Galilee as the third, with completely different circumstances [John 20:19 ff., 26 ff.; 21]. (9) The speeches that Jesus is supposed to have made to the disciples vary greatly among the evangelists, but it would be too lengthy to demonstrate this in all its details. Still, it is especially to be noted that in Luke's story Jesus does not say that they should baptize the converted as Matthew and Mark[2] report, but simply that they should preach repentance and the forgiveness of sins. However, in John Jesus tells the disciples nothing at all about either preaching or baptism. Rather, he says to Peter alone, "If you love me, feed my sheep" [John 21:17]. (10) Mark and Luke, who themselves did not see Jesus, report his ascension [Luke 24:50–53; Mark 16:19]. But John and Matthew, disciples who claim to have seen Jesus themselves, are utterly silent on this important point. In their reports Jesus speaks with his disciples, then nothing more is said about where he was, and their story is at an end. To be sure, John still has so much on his heart to tell concerning things that Jesus did that there would not be enough room in all the world if these things would be written in books; but I think that the few lines about his ascension would have found their bit of space and could have served a better purpose than all the monstrous hyperbole.

§21

Witnesses who differ so greatly in the most important points of their testimony would not be recognized in any secular court as valid and legal (even if it were merely a matter of a little money belonging to someone) to the extent that the judge could rely upon their story and base his decision on it. How then can anyone want the whole world and all mankind to base their religion, faith, and hope of salvation at all times and in all places upon the testimony of four such varying witnesses? But even with the differences between their stories it does not stop; they unquestionably contradict one another in many passages and make many a futile martyr of good commentators who attempt to make this tetrachordon[3] emit a more harmonious sound. I shall give only ten such obvious contradictions, ignoring the fact that there are many more.

* * *

1. Reimarus alludes to Mark 16:12–13 which he accepts as an authentic part of the Gospel.
   2. Again the reference is to the spurious ending of Mark (16:16). [Cf. Matt 28:19.]
   3. "A musical instrument with four strings; here the four evangelists are meant" [Lessing].

§26

The fifth contradiction is between John and Luke. Luke [24:1–12] reports that just as Mary Magdalene and the others entered the tomb and wondered about the whereabouts of Jesus' corpse two angels appeared to them and announced Jesus' resurrection, upon which these women hurried away and announced the news to the eleven (that is, as the other evangelists add, they were to tell the disciples and especially Peter according to the command of the angels). As a result Peter would have hurried out to the tomb, looked into it, found nothing but the grave cloths, and left filled with wonder at the event. From this it is clear that the angels appeared to Mary even before Peter had gone out to the tomb and that these very angels announced Jesus' resurrection to Mary and she in turn to Peter. But John [20:1–18] says that he and Peter got from Mary merely the news that the body had been taken away; they heard nothing of Jesus' resurrection from her, nor did she herself know anything about it. With considerable detail he tells it thus: Mary found the stone rolled away from the tomb, hurried to the two of them and said that someone had removed Jesus' corpse from the tomb and she did not know where it might have been put; then he and Peter hurried to the tomb as quickly as possible, found the linen and napkin lying there empty, and thus believed what Mary had told them, namely, that human hands had removed the corpse (for they would not yet have known that Jesus must rise from the dead); then they left again, but Mary stayed weeping before the tomb and behold, as she looked inside she saw two youths, one at the head and the other at the foot, who asked her, "Woman, why are you weeping?" When she answered, "They have taken away my Lord, and I do not know where they have laid him," Jesus himself stood behind her and revealed himself to her. From this it is clear that Mary Magdalene herself did not yet know that Jesus had risen when she ran to Peter, and that no angel must have appeared to her at that time; similarly, that Peter and John also knew nothing of the resurrection when they hurried to the tomb; and that they also did not learn of it at the tomb; that Mary, moreover, did not learn of it from the angels but from Jesus himself, all of which contradicts Luke's account in three ways. But so that nobody will here offer the general excuse with which people have tried to make so many discrepancies agree (namely, that Peter had been twice at the tomb, for example) I shall show from the circumstances that in the accounts of both evangelists it was one and the same trip that Peter made to the tomb:

1) Luke 24:12,[4] Peter ran to the tomb; ἔδραμεν.
   John 20:4, Peter and John ran; ἔτρεχον.
2) Luke 24:12, Peter looked inside; παρακύψας.
   John 20:5, John looked inside; παρακύψας.
3) Luke 24:12, Peter saw only the cloths lying there; βλέπει τὰ ὀθόνια κείμενα μόνα.

4. This verse is not found in D [a 5th-century MS], the greater number of old Latin witnesses, and Marcion. It is omitted in Nestle's text [a standard critical edition of the Greek NT] and in the RSV.

John 20:6, 7, Peter saw the cloths lying, and the napkin not with the cloths; θεωρεῖ τὰ ὀθόνια κείμενα καὶ τὸ σουδάριον οὐ μετὰ τῶν ὀθονίων κείμενον.

4) Luke 24:12, Peter went home; ἀπῆλθεν πρὸς ἑαυτόν.
John 20:10, Peter and John returned home; ἀπῆλθον πάλιν πρὸς ἑαυτούς.

The matter also shows that Peter cannot have been at the tomb a second time, for example, after Mary had come again and announced the resurrection to him. For such a frequent and successive running in and out on the part of Peter and Mary, along with the viewing of the tomb and the conversation with the angels and Jesus would have consumed so much time that Peter could not have gone out through the gate and back again before high noon, which is quite the opposite of the circumstances and behavior of Jesus' disciples. For at that time they were still in hiding and did not go out publicly among the people, staying behind locked doors together in one room, fearing the Jews. Now, if Peter went out to the tomb only once and quite early upon hearing Mary's message, how can it agree with the fact that according to Luke's story Mary had heard the resurrection announced earlier by the angels? Or indeed, that she had even seen and spoken with Jesus himself on the way back according to Matthew, and had also received his command to tell the news to the disciples and especially to Peter? Or that she nevertheless said nothing to the disciples and Peter, according to John's account, only that someone had taken the Lord from the tomb and it is not known where they have laid him? Or indeed, that only after this she saw the angels and even then did not find out from them that Jesus was alive, but found it out from Jesus himself?

DAVID FRIEDRICH STRAUSS

David Friedrich Strauss (1808–1874) viewed the gospels as self-consciously mythical narratives, rejecting the naturalistic explanations of their miracles popularized by earlier scholars. (For example, Heinrich Paulus had famously argued that Jesus' walk on water was merely a stroll on the beach, which his disciples mistook for a supernatural event because an early morning mist clouded the shore.) Strauss's *The Life of Jesus Critically Examined* (originally published in two volumes, 1835–36) applies this hermeneutical perspective with such rigor and exhaustion that Albert Schweitzer called it "one of the most perfect things in the whole range of learned literature. In over fourteen hundred pages he has not a superfluous phrase; his analysis descends to the minutest details, but he does not lose his way among them." It is hard to avoid the impression that George Eliot, Strauss's English translator, envisioned Casaubon's unfinished and unfocused *Key to All Mythologies* in *Middlemarch* (1871–72) as a foil to the exhaustive but compelling tome excerpted here.

§15. Definition of the Evangelical Mythus and Its Distinctive Characteristics[†]

The precise sense in which we use the expression *mythus*, applied to certain parts of the gospel history, is evident from all that has already been said; at the same time the different kinds and gradations of the mythi which we shall meet with in this history may here by way of anticipation be pointed out.

We distinguish by the name *evangelical mythus* a narrative relating directly or indirectly to Jesus, which may be considered not as the expression of a fact, but as the product of an idea of his earliest followers: such a narrative being mythical in proportion as it exhibits this character. The mythus in this sense of the term meets us, in the Gospel as elsewhere, sometimes in its pure form, constituting the substance of the narrative, and sometimes as an accidental adjunct to the actual history.

The pure mythus in the Gospel will be found to have two sources, which in most cases contributed simultaneously, though in different proportions, to form the mythus. The one source is, as already stated, the Messianic ideas and expectations existing according to their several forms in the Jewish mind before Jesus, and independently of him; the other is that particular impression which was left by the personal character, actions, and fate of Jesus, and which served to modify the Messianic idea in the minds of his people. The account of the Transfiguration [Mark 9:2–8 and parallels], for example, is derived almost exclusively from the former source; the only amplification taken from the latter source being—that they who appeared with Jesus on the Mount spake of his decease. On the other hand, the narrative of the rending of the veil of the temple at the death of Jesus [Mark 15:37–38 and parallels] seems to have had its origin in the hostile position which Jesus, and his church after him, sustained in relation to the Jewish temple worship. Here already we have something historical, though consisting merely of certain general features of character, position, etc.; we are thus at once brought upon the ground of the historical mythus.

The historical mythus has for its groundwork a definite individual fact which has been seized upon by religious enthusiasm, and twined around with mythical conceptions culled from the idea of the Christ. This fact is perhaps a saying of Jesus such as that concerning "fishers of men" or the barren fig-tree, which now appear in the Gospels transmuted into marvellous histories [cf. Luke 5:1–11; Mark 11:12–14, 20–21 and parallels]: or, it is perhaps a real transaction or event taken from his life; for instance, the mythical traits in the account of the baptism were built upon such a reality. Certain of the miraculous histories may likewise have had some foundation in natural occurrences, which the narrative has either exhibited in a supernatural light, or enriched with miraculous incidents.

All the species of imagery here enumerated may justly be designated as mythi, even according to the modern and precise definition of George,[1] inasmuch as the

---

† From *The Life of Jesus Critically Examined*, 4th German ed., trans. George Eliot, 2nd ed. (New York: Macmillan, 1892), 86–92, 507–19.
1. J. F. L. George, *Mythus und Sage* (Berlin, 1837).

unhistorical which they embody—whether formed gradually by tradition, or created by an individual author—is in each case the product of an *idea*. But for those parts of the history which are characterized by indefiniteness and want of connexion, by misconstruction and transformation, by strange combinations and confusion,—the natural results of a long course of oral transmission; or which, on the contrary, are distinguished by highly coloured and pictorial representations, which also seem to point to a traditionary origin;—for these parts the term *legendary* is certainly the more appropriate.

Lastly. It is requisite to distinguish equally from the mythus and the legend, that which, as it serves not to clothe an idea on the one hand, and admits not of being referred to tradition on the other, must be regarded as *the addition of the author*, as purely individual, and designed merely to give clearness, connexion, and climax, to the representation.

It is to the various forms of the unhistorical in the Gospels that this enumeration exclusively refers: it does not involve the renunciation of the *historical* which they may likewise contain.

§ 16. Criteria by Which to Distinguish the Unhistorical in the Gospel Narrative

Having shown the possible existence of the mythical and the legendary in the Gospels, both on extrinsic and intrinsic grounds, and defined their distinctive characteristics, it remains in conclusion to inquire how their actual presence may be recognised in individual cases?

The mythus presents two phases: in the first place it is not history; in the second it is fiction, the product of the particular mental tendency of a certain community. These two phases afford the one a negative, the other a positive criterion, by which the mythus is to be recognised.

I. *Negative.* That an account is not historical—that the matter related could not have taken place in the manner described is evident,

First. When the narration is irreconcilable with the known and universal laws which govern the course of events. Now according to these laws, agreeing with all just philosophical conceptions and all credible experience, the absolute cause never disturbs the chain of secondary causes by single arbitrary acts of interposition, but rather manifests itself in the production of the aggregate of finite casualities, and of their reciprocal action. When therefore we meet with an account of certain phenomena or events of which it is either expressly stated or implied that they were produced immediately by God himself (divine apparitions—voices from heaven and the like), or by human beings possessed of supernatural powers (miracles, prophecies), such an account is *in so far* to be considered as not historical. And inasmuch as, in general, the intermingling of the spiritual world with the human is found only in unauthentic records, and is irreconcilable with all just conceptions; so narratives of angels and of devils, of their appearing in human shape and interfering with human concerns, cannot possibly be received as historical.

Another law which controls the course of events is the law of succession, in accordance with which all occurrences, not excepting the most violent convulsions and the most rapid changes, follow in a certain order of sequence of increase and decrease. If therefore we are told of a celebrated individual that he attracted already at his birth and during his childhood that attention which he excited in his manhood; that his followers at a single glance recognized him as being all that he actually was; if the transition from the deepest despondency to the most ardent enthusiasm after his death is represented as the work of a single hour; we must feel more than doubtful whether it is a real history which lies before us. Lastly, all those psychological laws, which render it improbable that a human being should feel, think, and act in a manner directly opposed to his own habitual mode and that of men in general, must be taken into consideration. As for example, when the Jewish Sanhedrim are represented as believing the declaration of the watch at the grave that Jesus was risen, and instead of accusing them of having suffered the body to be stolen away whilst they were asleep, bribing them to give currency to such a report. By the same rule it is contrary to all the laws belonging to the human faculty of memory, that long discourses, such as those of Jesus given in the fourth Gospel, could have been faithfully recollected and reproduced.

It is however true that effects are often far more rapidly produced, particularly in men of genius and by their agency, than might be expected; and that human beings frequently act inconsequently, and in opposition to their general modes and habits; the two last mentioned tests of the mythical character must therefore be cautiously applied, and in conjunction only with other tests.

Secondly. An account which shall be regarded as historically valid, must neither be inconsistent with itself, nor in contradiction with other accounts.

The most decided case falling under this rule, amounting to a positive contradiction, is when one account affirms what another denies. Thus, one gospel represents the first appearance of Jesus in Galilee as subsequent to the imprisonment of John the Baptist [Luke 4:14–15; cf. 3:19–20], whilst another Gospel remarks, long after Jesus had preached both in Galilee and in Judea, that "John was not yet cast into prison" [John 3:24].

When on the contrary, the second account, without absolutely contradicting the first, differs from it, the disagreement may be merely between the incidental particulars of the narrative; such as *time*, (the clearing of the Temple [cf. Mark 11:15–19 and John 2:13–17]) *place*, (the original residence of the parents of Jesus [Matt 1:18–2:23 assumes Bethlehem; Luke 2:1–6 assumes Nazareth]) *number*, (the Gadarenes [cf. Matt 8:28 and Mark 5:1–2], the angels at the sepulchre [Matt 28:1–8 and Luke 24:1–6]) *names*, (Matthew and Levi [cf. Matt 9:9 and Mark 2:14]) or it may concern the essential substance of the history. In the latter case, sometimes the character and circumstances in one account differ altogether from those in another. Thus, according to one narrator, the Baptist recognizes Jesus as the Messiah destined to suffer [John 1:29, 34–36]; according to the other, John takes offence at his suffering condition [Matt 3:13–15]. Sometimes an occurrence is represented in two or more ways, of which one only can be consistent with the reality; as when in one account Jesus calls his first disciples from their nets whilst fishing on the sea of Galilee [Matt 4:18–22; Mark 1:16–20], and in the other meets them in Judea on his way to Galilee [John 1:35–51]. We may class under the same head instances where events or discourses are represented as having occurred on two distinct occasions, whilst they are so similar that it is impossible to resist the conclusion that both the narratives refer to the same event or discourse.

It may here be asked: is it to be regarded as a contradiction if one account is wholly silent respecting a circumstance mentioned by another? In itself, apart from all other considerations, the argumentum ex silentio is of no weight; but it is certainly to be accounted of moment when, at the same time, it may be shown that had the author known the circumstance he could not have failed to mention it, and also that he must have known it had it actually occurred.

II. *Positive.*   The positive characters of legend and fiction are to be recognized sometimes in the form, sometimes in the substance of a narrative.

If the form be poetical, if the actors converse in hymns, and in a more diffuse and elevated strain than might be expected from their training and situations, such discourses, at all events, are not to be regarded as historical. The absence of these marks of the unhistorical do not however prove the historical validity of the narration, since the mythus often wears the most simple and apparently historical form: in which case the proof lies in the substance.

If the contents of a narrative strikingly accords with certain ideas existing and prevailing within the circle from which the narrative proceeded, which ideas themselves seem to be the product of preconceived opinions rather than of practical experience, it is more or less probable, according to circumstances, that such a narrative is of mythical origin. The knowledge of the fact, that the Jews were fond of representing their great men as the children of parents who had long been childless, cannot but make us doubtful of the historical truth of the statement that this was the case with John the Baptist; knowing also that the Jews saw predictions everywhere in the writings of their prophets and poets, and discovered types of the Messiah in all the lives of holy men recorded in their Scriptures; when we find details in the life of Jesus evidently sketched after the pattern of these prophecies and prototypes, we cannot but suspect that they are rather mythical than historical.

The more simple characteristics of the legend, and of additions by the author, after the observations of the former section, need no further elucidation.

Yet each of these tests, on the one hand, and each narrative on the other, considered apart, will rarely prove more than the possible or probable unhistorical character of the record. The concurrence of several such indications, is necessary to bring about a more definite result. The accounts of the visit of the Magi [Matt 2:1–12], and of the murder of the innocents at Bethlehem [Matt 2:16–23], harmonize remarkably with the Jewish Messianic notion, built upon the prophecy of Balaam, respecting the star which should come out of Jacob [Num 24:17]; and with the history of the sanguinary command of Pharaoh [Exod 1:15–22]. Still this would not alone suffice to stamp the narratives as mythical. But we have also the corroborative facts that the described appearance of the star is contrary to the physical, the alleged conduct of Herod to the psychological laws; that Josephus, who gives in other respects so circumstantial an account of Herod, agrees with all other historical authorities in being silent concerning the Bethlehem massacre; and that the visit of the Magi together with the flight into Egypt related in the one Gospel [Matt 2:1–15], and the presentation in the temple related in another Gospel [Luke 2:22–39], mutually exclude one another. Wherever, as in this instance, the several criteria of the mythical character concur, the result is certain, and certain in proportion to the accumulation of such grounds of evidence.

It may be that a narrative, standing alone, would discover but slight indications, or perhaps, might present no one distinct feature of the mythus; but it is connected with others, or proceeds from the author of other narratives which exhibit unquestionable marks of a mythical or legendary character; and consequently suspicion is reflected back from the latter, on the former. Every narrative, however miraculous, contains some details which might in themselves be historical, but which, in consequence of their connexion with the other supernatural incidents, necessarily become equally doubtful.

In these last remarks we are, to a certain extent, anticipating the question which is, in conclusion, to be considered: viz., whether the mythical character is restricted to those features of the narrative, upon which such character is actually stamped; and whether a contradiction between two accounts invalidate one account only, or both? That is to say, what is the precise boundary line between the historical and the unhistorical?—the most difficult question in the whole province of criticism.

In the first place, when two narratives mutually exclude one another, one only is thereby proved to be unhistorical. If one be true the other must be false, but though the one be false the other may be true. Thus, in reference to the original residence of the parents of Jesus, we are justified in adopting the account of Luke which places it at Nazareth, to the exclusion of that of Matthew, which plainly supposes it to have been at Bethlehem; and, generally speaking, when we have to choose between two irreconcilable accounts, in selecting as historical that which is the least opposed to the laws of nature, and has the least correspondence with certain national or party opinions. But upon a more particular consideration it will appear that, since one account is false, it is possible that the other may be so likewise: the existence of a mythus respecting some certain point, shows that the imagination has been active in reference to that particular subject; (we need only refer to the genealogies;) and the historical accuracy of either of two such accounts cannot be relied upon, unless substantiated by its agreement with some other well authenticated testimony.

Concerning the different parts of one and the same narrative: it might be thought for example, that though the appearance of an angel, and his announcement to Mary that she should be the Mother of the Messiah [Luke 1:26–38], must certainly be regarded as unhistorical, still, that Mary should have indulged this hope before the birth of the child, is not in itself incredible. But what should have excited this hope in Mary's mind? It is at once apparent that that which is credible in itself is nevertheless unhistorical when it is so intimately connected with what is incredible that, if you discard the latter, you at the same time remove the basis on which the former rests. Again, any action of Jesus represented as a miracle, when divested of the marvellous, might be thought to exhibit a perfectly natural occurrence; with respect to some of the miraculous histories, the expulsion of devils for instance, this might with some limitation, be possible. But for this reason alone: in these instances, a cure, so instantaneous, and effected by a few words merely, as it is described in the Gospels, is not psychologically incredible; so that, the essential in these narratives remains untouched. It is different in the case of the healing of a man born blind. A natural cure could not have been effected otherwise than by a gradual process; the narrative states the cure to have been immediate; if therefore the history be understood to record a natural occurrence, the most essential particular is incorrectly represented, and consequently all security for the truth of the otherwise natural remainder is gone, and the real fact cannot be discovered without the aid of arbitrary conjecture.

The following examples will serve to illustrate the mode of deciding in such cases. According to the narrative, as Mary entered the house and saluted her cousin Elizabeth, who was then pregnant, the babe leaped in her womb, she was filled with the Holy Ghost, and she immediately addressed Mary as the mother of the Messiah [Luke 1:39–45]. This account bears indubitable marks of an unhistorical character. Yet, it is not, in itself, impossible that Mary should have paid a visit to her cousin, during which everything went on quite naturally. The fact is however that there are psychological difficulties connected with this journey of the betrothed; and that the visit, and even the relationship of the two women, seem to have originated entirely in the wish to exhibit a connexion between the mother of John the Baptist, and the mother of the Messiah. Or when in the history of the transfiguration it is stated, that the men who appeared with Jesus on the Mount were Moses and Elias: and that the brilliancy which illuminated Jesus was supernatural [Matt 17:1–8; Mark 9:2–8; Luke 9:28–36]; it might seem here also that, after deducting the marvellous, the presence of two men and a bright morning beam might be retained as the historical facts. But the legend was predisposed, by virtue of the current idea concerning the relation of the Messiah to these two prophets, not merely to make any two men (whose persons, object and conduct, if they were not what the narrative represents them, remain in the highest degree mysterious) into Moses and Elias, but to create the whole occurrence; and in like manner not merely to conceive of some certain illumination as a supernatural effulgence (which, if a natural one, is much exaggerated and misrepresented), but to create it at once after the pattern of the brightness which illumined the face of Moses on Mount Sinai.

Hence is derived the following rule. Where not merely the particular nature and manner of an occurrence is critically suspicious, its external circumstances represented as miraculous and the like; but where likewise the essential substance and groundwork is either inconceivable in itself, or is in striking harmony with some Messianic idea of the Jews of that age, then not the particular alleged course and mode of the transaction only, but the entire occurrence must be regarded as unhistorical. Where on the contrary, the form only, and not the general contents of the narration, exhibits the characteristics of the unhistorical, it is at least possible to suppose a kernel of historical fact; although we can never confidently decide whether this kernel of fact actually exists, or in what it consists; unless, indeed, it be discoverable from other sources. In legendary narratives, or narratives embellished by the writer, it is less difficult,—by divesting them of all that betrays itself as fictitious imagery, exaggeration, etc.—by endeavouring to abstract from them every extraneous adjunct and to fill up every hiatus—to succeed, proximately at least, in separating the historical groundwork.

The boundary line, however, between the historical and the unhistorical, in records, in which as in our Gospels this latter element is incorporated, will ever remain fluctuating and unsusceptible of precise attainment. Least of all can it be expected that the first comprehensive attempt to treat these records from a critical point of view should be successful in drawing a sharply defined line of demarcation. In the obscurity which criticism has produced, by the extinction of all lights hitherto held historical, the eye must accustom itself by degrees to discriminate objects with precision; and at all events the author of this work, wishes especially to guard himself in those places where he declares he knows not what happened, from the imputation of asserting that he knows that nothing happened.

§ 102. The Miraculous Multiplication of the Loaves and Fishes

As, in the histories last considered, Jesus determined and mitigated the motions of irrational and even of inanimate existences; so, in the narratives which we are about to examine, he exhibits the power of multiplying not only natural objects, but also productions of nature which had been wrought upon by art.

That Jesus miraculously multiplied prepared articles of food, feeding a great multitude of men with a few loaves and fishes, is narrated to us with singular unanimity by all the Evangelists (Matt. xiv. 13 ff.; Mark vi. 30 ff.; Luke ix. 10 ff.; John vi. 1 ff.). And if we believe the two first, Jesus did not do this merely once; for in Matt. xv. 32 ff.; Mark viii. 1 ff. we read of a second multiplication of loaves and fishes, the circumstances of which are substantially the same as those of the former. It happens somewhat later; the place is rather differently described, and the length of time during which the multitude stayed with Jesus is differently stated; moreover, and this is a point of greater importance, the proportion between the stock of food and the number of men is different, for, on the first occasion, five thousand men are satisfied with five loaves and two fishes, and, on the second, four thousand with seven loaves and a few fishes; on the first twelve baskets are filled with the fragments, on the second only seven. Notwithstanding this, not only is the substance of the two histories exactly the same—the satisfying of a multitude of people with disproportionately small means of nourishment; but also the description of the scene in the one, entirely corresponds in its principal features to that in the other. In both instances, the locality is a solitary region in the vicinity of the Galilean sea; Jesus is led to perform the miracle because the people have lingered too long with him; he manifests a wish to feed the people from his own stores, which the disciples regard as impossible; the stock of food at his disposal consists of loaves and fishes; Jesus makes the people sit down, and, after giving thanks, distributes the provisions to them through the medium of the disciples; they are completely satisfied, and yet a disproportionately great quantity of fragments is afterwards collected in baskets; lastly, in the one case as in the other, Jesus after thus feeding the multitude, crosses the sea.

This repetition of the same event creates many difficulties. The chief of these is suggested by the question: Is it conceivable that the disciples, after they had themselves witnessed how Jesus was able to feed a great multitude with a small quantity of provision, should nevertheless on a second occasion of the same kind, have totally forgotten the first, and have asked, *Whence should we have so much bread in the wilderness as to feed so great a multitude?* To render such an obliviousness on the part of the disciples probable, we are reminded that they had, in just as incomprehensible a manner, forgotten the declarations of Jesus concerning his approaching sufferings and death, when these events occurred; but it is equally a pending question, whether after such plain predictions from Jesus, his death could in fact have been so unexpected to the disciples. It has been supposed that a longer interval had elapsed between the two miracles, and that during this there had occurred a number of similar cases, in which Jesus did not think fit to afford miraculous assistance: but, on the one hand, these are pure fictions; on the other, it would remain just as inconceivable as ever, that the striking similarity of the circumstances preceding the second feeding of the multitude to those preceding the first, should not have reminded even one of the disciples of that former event. Paulus[1] therefore is right in maintaining, that had Jesus once already fed the multitude by a miracle, the disciples, on the second occasion, when he expressed his determination not to send the people away fasting, would confidently have called upon him for a repetition of the former miracle.

In any case then, if Jesus on two separate occasions fed a multitude with disproportionately small provision, we must suppose, as some critics have done, that many features in the narrative of the one incident were transferred to the other, and thus the two, originally unlike, became in the course of oral tradition more and more similar; the incredulous question of the disciples especially having been uttered only on the first occasion, and not on the second. It may seem to speak in favour of such an assimilation, that the fourth Evangelist, though in his numerical statement he is in accordance with the first narrative of Matthew and Mark, yet has, in common with the second, the circumstances that the scene opens with an address of Jesus and not of the disciples, and that the people come to Jesus on a mountain. But if the fundamental features be allowed to remain,— the wilderness, the feeding of the people, the collection of the fragments,—it is still, even without that question of the disciples, sufficiently improbable that the scene should have been repeated in so entirely similar a manner. If, on the contrary, these general features be renounced in relation to one of the histories, it is no longer apparent, how the veracity of the evangelical narratives as to the *manner* in which the second multiplication of loaves and fishes took place can be

1. Heinrich Eberhard Gottlob Paulus; Strauss cites both his *Philologisch-kritischer und historischer Commentar über das Neue Testament* (Lübeck, 1804–08) and his *Exegetisches Handbuch über die drei ersten Evangelien* (Heidelberg, 1830–33).

questioned on all points, and yet their statement as to the *fact* of its occurrence be maintained as trustworthy, especially as this statement is confined to Matthew and his imitator Mark.

Hence later critics have, with more or less decision, expressed the opinion, that here one and the same fact has been doubled, through a mistake of the first Evangelist, who was followed by the second. They suppose that several narratives of the miraculous feeding of the multitude were current which presented divergencies from each other, especially in relation to numbers, and that the author of the first gospel, to whom every additional history of a miracle was a welcome prize, and who was therefore little qualified for the critical reduction of two different narratives of this kind into one, introduced both into his collection. This fully explains how on the second occasion the disciples could again express themselves so incredulously: namely, because in the tradition whence the author of the first gospel obtained the second history of a miraculous multiplication of loaves and fishes, it was the first and only one, and the Evangelist did not obliterate this feature because, apparently, he incorporated the two narratives into his writing just as he read or heard them. Among other proofs that this was the case, may be mentioned the constancy with which he and Mark, who copied him, not only in the account of the events, but also in the subsequent allusion to them (Matt. xvi. 9 f.; Mark viii. 19 f.), call the baskets in the first feeding, κόφινοι, in the second σπυρίδες.[2] * * * A similar instance of duplication occurs in the Pentateuch in relation to the histories of the feeding of the Israelites with quails, and of the production of water out of the rock, the former of which is narrated both in Exod. xvi. and Num. xi., the latter in Exod. xvii. and again in Num. xx., in each instance with an alteration in time, place, and other circumstances. Meanwhile, all this yields us only the negative result that the double narratives of the first gospels cannot have been founded on two separate events. To determine which of the two is historical, or whether either of them deserves that epithet, must be the object of a special inquiry.

*   *   *

But how are we to represent such a miracle to ourselves, and in what stage of the event must it be placed? In relation to the latter point, three opinions are possible, corresponding to the number of the groups that act in our narrative; for the multiplication may have taken place either in the hands of Jesus, or in those of the disciples who dispensed the food, or in those of the people who received it. The last idea appears, on the one hand, puerile even to extravagance, if we are to imagine Jesus and the apostles distributing, with great carefulness, that there might be enough for all, little crumbs which in the hands of the recipients swelled into considerable pieces: on the other hand, it would have been scarcely a possible task, to get a particle, however small, for every individual in a multitude of five thousand men, out of five loaves, which, according to Hebrew custom, and particularly as they were carried by a boy, cannot have been very large;

---

2. "Baskets" and "large baskets" or "creels," respectively.

and still less out of two fishes. Of the two other opinions I think, with Olshausen,[3] the one most suitable is that which supposes that the food was augmented under the creative hands of Jesus, and that he time after time dispensed new quantities to the disciples. We may then endeavour to represent the matter to ourselves in two ways: first we may suppose that as fast as one loaf or fish was gone, a new one came out of the hands of Jesus, or secondly, that the single loaves and fishes grew, so that as one piece was broken off, its loss was repaired, until on a calculation the turn came for the next loaf or fish. The first conception appears to be opposed to the text, which as it speaks of fragments ἐκ τῶν πέντε ἄρτων, *of the five loaves* (John vi. 13), can hardly be held to presuppose an increase of this number; thus there remains only the second, by the poetical description of which Lavater has done but a poor service to the orthodox view.[4] For this miracle belongs to the class which can only appear in any degree credible so long as they can be retained in the obscurity of an indefinite conception: no sooner does the light shine on them, so that they can be examined in all their parts, than they dissolve like the unsubstantial creations of the mist. Loaves, which in the hands of the distributors expand like wetted sponges,—broiled fish, in which the severed parts are replaced instantaneously, as in the living crab gradually,—plainly belong to quite another domain than that of reality.

What gratitude then do we not owe to the rationalistic interpretation, if it be true that it can free us, in the easiest manner, from the burden of so unheard-of a miracle? If we are to believe Dr. Paulus, the Evangelists had no idea that they were narrating anything miraculous, and the miracle was first conveyed into their accounts by expositors. What they narrate is, according to him, only thus much: that Jesus caused his small store of provisions to be distributed, and that in consequence of this the entire multitude obtained enough to eat. Here, in any case, we want a middle term, which would distinctly inform us, how it was possible that, although Jesus had so little food to offer, the whole multitude obtained enough to eat. A very natural middle term however is to be gathered, according to Paulus, out of the historical combination of the circumstances. As, on a comparison with John vi. 4, the multitude appear to have consisted for the greater part of a caravan on its way to the feast, they cannot have been quite destitute of provisions, and probably a few indigent persons only had exhausted their stores. In order then to induce the better provided to share their food with those who were in want, Jesus arranged that they should have a meal, and himself set the example of imparting what he and his disciples could spare from their own little store; this example was imitated, and thus the distribution of bread by Jesus having led to a general distribution, the whole multitude were satisfied. It is true that this natural middle term must be first mentally interpolated into the text; as, however, the supernatural middle term which is generally received is just as little stated expressly, and both alike depend upon inference, the reader can hardly do otherwise than decide for the natural one. Such is the reasoning of Dr. Paulus: but the alleged identity in the relation of the two middle terms to the text does not in fact exist. For while the natural expla-

3. Hermann Olshausen, *Biblischer Commentar über sämtliche Schriften des Neuen Testaments* (Königsberg, 1837–62).

4. Johann Caspar Lavater, *Jesus Messias* (Zurich, 1780).

nation requires us to suppose a new distributing subject (the better provided among the multitude), and a new distributed object (their provisions), together with the act of distributing these provisions: the supranatural explanation contents itself with the subject actually present in the text (Jesus and his disciples), with the single object there given (their little store), and the described distribution of this; and only requires us to supply from our imagination the means by which this store could be made sufficient to satisfy the hunger of the multitude, namely its miraculous augmentation under the hands of Jesus (or of his disciples). How can it be yet maintained that neither of the two middle terms is any more suggested by the text than the other? That the miraculous multiplication of the loaves and fishes is not expressly mentioned, is explained by the consideration that the event itself is one of which no clear conception can be formed, and therefore it is best conveyed by the result alone. But how will the natural theologian account for nothing being said of the distribution, called forth by the example of Jesus, on the part of those among the multitude who had provisions? It is altogether arbitrary to insert that distribution between the sentences, *He gave them to the disciples, and the disciples to the multitude* (Matt. xiv. 19), and, *they did all eat and were filled* (v. 20); while the words, καὶ τοὺς δύο ἰχθύας ἐμέρισε πᾶσι, *and the two fishes divided he among them all* (Mark vi. 41), plainly indicate that only the two fishes—and consequently only the five loaves—were the object of distribution for all. * * *

Here, then, the natural explanation once more fails to fulfil its task: the text retains its miracle, and if we have reason to think this incredible, we must inquire whether the narrative of the text deserves credence. The agreement of all the four Evangelists is generally adduced in proof of its distinguished credibility: but this agreement is by no means so perfect. There are minor differences, first between Matthew and Luke; then between these two and Mark, who in this instance again embellishes; and lastly, between the synoptists collectively and John, in the following points: according to the synoptists, the scene of the event is a *desert place*, according to John, a *mountain*; according to the former, the scene opens with an address from the disciples, according to John, with a question from Jesus (two particulars in which, as we have already remarked, the narrative of John approaches that of the second feeding in Matthew and Mark); lastly, the words which the three first Evangelists put into the mouth of the disciples indefinitely, the fourth in his individualizing manner ascribes to Philip and Andrew, and the same Evangelist also designates the bearer of the loaves and fishes as a *boy* (παιδάριον). These divergencies however may be passed over as less essential, that we may give our attention only to one, which has a deeper hold. While, namely, according to the synoptical accounts, Jesus had been long teaching the people and healing their sick, and was only led to feed them by the approach of evening, and the remark of the disciples that the people needed refreshment: in John, the first thought of Jesus, when he lifts up his eyes and sees the people gathering round him, is that which he expresses in his question to Philip: *Whence shall we buy bread that these may eat?* or rather, as he asked this merely to *prove* Philip, well knowing himself *what he would do*, he at once forms the resolution of feeding the multitude in a miraculous manner. But how could the design of feeding the people arise in Jesus immediately on their approach? They did not come to him for this, but for the sake of his teaching and his curative power. He must therefore have conceived this design entirely of his own accord, with a view to establish his miraculous power by so signal a demonstration. But did he ever thus work a miracle without any necessity, and even without any inducement,—quite arbitrarily, and merely for the sake of working a miracle? I am unable to describe strongly enough how impossible it is that eating should here have been the first thought of Jesus, how impossible that he could thus obtrude his miraculous repast on the people. Thus in relation to this point, the synoptical narrative, in which there is a reason for the miracle, must have the preference to that of John, who, hastening towards the miracle, overlooks the requisite motive for it, and makes Jesus create instead of awaiting the occasion for its performance. An eye-witness could not narrate thus; and if, therefore, the account of that gospel to which the greatest authority is now awarded, must be rejected as unhistorical; so, with respect to the other narratives, the difficulties of the fact itself are sufficient to cast a doubt on their historical credibility, especially if in addition to these negative grounds we can discover positive reasons which render it probable that our narrative had an unhistorical origin.

Such reasons are actually found both within the evangelical history itself, and beyond it in the Old Testament history, and the Jewish popular belief. In relation to the former source, it is worthy of remark, that in the synoptical gospels as well as in John, there are more or less immediately appended to the feeding of the multitude by Jesus with literal bread, figurative discourses of Jesus on bread and leaven: namely, in the latter, the declarations concerning the bread of heaven, and the bread of life which Jesus gives (John vi. 27 ff.); in the former, those concerning the false leaven of the Pharisees and Sadducees, that is, their false doctrine and hypocrisy. (Matt. xvi. 5 ff.; Mark viii. 14 ff.; comp. Luke xii. 1); and on both sides, the figurative discourse of Jesus is erroneously understood of literal bread. It would not then be a very strained conjecture, that as in the passages quoted we find the disciples and the people generally, understanding literally what Jesus meant figuratively; so the same mistake was made in the earliest Christian tradition. If, in figurative discourses, Jesus had sometimes represented himself as him who was able to give the true bread of life to the wandering and hungering people, perhaps also placing in opposition to this, the leaven of the Pharisees: the legend, agreeably to its realistic tendency, may have converted this into the fact of a miraculous feeding of the hungry multitude in the wilderness by Jesus. The fourth Evangelist makes the discourse on the bread of heaven arise out of the miracle of the loaves: but the relation might very well have been the reverse, and the history owe its origin to the discourse, especially as the question which introduces John's narrative, *Whence shall we buy bread that these may eat?* may be more easily conceived as being uttered by Jesus on the first sight of the people, if he alluded to feeding them with the word of God (comp. John iv. 32 ff.), to appeasing their spiritual hunger (Matt. v. 6), in order to exercise ($\pi\varepsilon\iota\rho\acute{\alpha}\zeta\omega\nu$) the higher understanding of his disciples, than if he really thought of the satisfaction of their bodily hunger, and only wished to try whether his disciples would in this case confide in his miraculous power. The synoptical narrative is less suggestive of such a view; for the figurative discourse on the leaven could not by itself originate the history of the miracle. Thus the gospel of John stands alone with reference to the above mode of derivation, and it is more agreeable to the character of this gospel to conjecture that it has applied the narrative of a miracle presented by tradition to the production of figurative discourses in the Alexandrian taste, than to suppose that it has preserved to us the original discourses out of which the legend spun that miraculous narrative.

If then we can discover, beyond the limits of the New Testament, very powerful causes for the origination of our narrative, we must renounce the attempt to construct it out of materials presented by the gospels themselves. And here the fourth Evangelist, by putting into the mouth of the people a reference to the manna, that bread of heaven which Moses gave to the fathers in the wilderness (v. 31), reminds us of one of the most celebrated passages in the early history of the Israelites (Exod. xvi.), which was perfectly adapted to engender the expectation that its antitype would occur in the Messianic times; and we in fact learn from rabbinical writings, that among those functions of the first Goël[5] which were to be revived in the second, a chief place was given to the impartation of bread from heaven. If the Mosaic manna presents itself as that which was most likely to be held a type of the bread miraculously augmented by Jesus; the fish which Jesus also multiplied miraculously, may remind us that Moses gave the people, not only a substitute for bread in the manna, but also animal food in the quails (Exod. xvi. 8, xii. 13; Num. xi. 4 ff.). On comparing these Mosaic narratives with our evangelical ones, there appears a striking resemblance even in details. The locality in both cases is the wilderness; the inducement to the miracle here as there, is fear lest the people should suffer from want in the wilderness, or perish from hunger; in the Old Testament history, this fear is expressed by the people in loud murmurs, in that of the New Testament, it results from the shortsightedness of the disciples, and the benevolence of Jesus. The direction of the latter to his disciples that they should give the people food, a direction which implies that he had already formed the design of feeding them miraculously, may be paralleled with the command which Jehovah gave to Moses to feed the people with manna (Exod. xvi. 4), and with quails (Exod. xvi. 12; Num. xi. 18–20). But there is another point of similarity which speaks yet more directly to our present purpose. As, in the evangelical narrative, the disciples think it an impossibility that provision for so great a mass of people should be procured in the wilderness, so, in the Old Testament history, Moses replies doubtingly to the promise of Jehovah to satisfy the people with flesh (Num. xi. 21 f.). To Moses, as to the disciples, the multitude appears too great for the possibility of providing sufficient food for them; as the latter ask, whence they should have so much bread in the wilderness, so Moses asks ironically whether they should slay the flocks and the herds (which they had not). And as the disciples object, that not even the most impoverishing expenditure on their part would thoroughly meet the demand, so Moses, clothing the idea in another form, had declared, that to satisfy the people as Jehovah promised, an impossibility must happen (the fish of the sea be gathered together for them); objections which Jehovah there, as here Jesus, does not regard, but issues the command that the people should prepare for the reception of the miraculous food.

---

5. Redeemer (Hebrew); i.e., Moses.

But though these two cases of a miraculous supply of nourishment are thus analogous, there is this essential distinction, that in the Old Testament, in relation both to the manna and the quails, it is a miraculous procuring of food not previously existing which is spoken of, while in the New Testament it is a miraculous augmentation of provision already present, but inadequate; so that the chasm between the Mosaic narrative and the evangelical one is too great for the latter to have been derived immediately from the former. If we search for an intermediate step, a very natural one between Moses and the Messiah is afforded by the prophets. We read of Elijah, that through him and for his sake, the little store of meal and oil which he found in the possession of the widow of Zarephath was miraculously replenished, or rather was made to suffice throughout the duration of the famine (1 Kings xvii. 8–16). This species of miracle is developed still further, and with a greater resemblance to the evangelical narrative, in the history of Elisha (2 Kings iv. 42 ff.). As Jesus fed five thousand men in the wilderness with five loaves and two fishes, so this prophet, during a famine, fed a hundred men with twenty loaves, (which like those distributed by Jesus in John, are called barley loaves,) together with some ground corn (בְּכַרְמֶל, LXX. παλάθας); a disproportion between the quantity of provisions and the number of men, which his servant, like the disciples in the other instance, indicates in the question: *What! should I set this before a hundred men?* Elisha, like Jesus, is not diverted from his purpose, but commands the servant to give what he has to the people; and as in the New Testament narrative great stress is laid on the collection of the remaining fragments, so in the Old Testament it is specially noticed at the close of this story, that notwithstanding so many had eaten of the store, there was still an overplus. The only important difference here is, that on the side of the evangelical narrative, the number of the loaves is smaller, and that of the people greater; but who does not know that in general the legend does not easily imitate, without at the same time surpassing, and who does not see that in this particular instance it was entirely suited to the position of the Messiah, that his miraculous power, compared with that of Elisha, should be placed, as it regards the need of natural means, in the relation of five to twenty, but as it regards the supernatural performance, in that of five thousand to one hundred? Paulus indeed, in order to preclude the inference, that as the two narratives in the Old Testament are to be understood mythically, so also is the strikingly similar evangelical narrative, extends to the former the attempt at a natural explanation which he has pursued with the latter, making the widow's cruse of oil to be replenished by the aid of the scholars of the prophets, and the twenty loaves suffice for one hundred men by means of a praiseworthy moderation; a mode of explanation which is less practicable here than with the New Testament narrative, in proportion as, by reason of the greater remoteness of these anecdotes, they present fewer critical (and, by reason of their merely mediate relation to Christianity, fewer dogmatical) motives for maintaining their historical veracity.

Nothing more is wanting to complete the mythical derivation of this history of the miraculous feeding of the multitude, except the proof, that the later Jews also believed of particularly holy men, that by their means a small amount of provision was made sufficient, and of this proof the disinterested industry of Dr. Paulus as a collector, has put us in possession. He adduces a rabbinical statement that in the time of a specially holy man, the small quantity of shew-bread more than sufficed for the supply of the priests. To be consequent, this commentator should try to explain this story also naturally,—by the moderation of the priests, for instance: but it is not in the canon, hence he can unhesitatingly regard it as a fable, and he only so far admits its striking similarity to the evangelical narrative as to observe, that in consequence of the Jewish belief in such augmentations of food, attested by that rabbinical statement, the New Testament narrative may in early times have been understood by judaizing Christians in the same (miraculous) sense. But our examination has shown that the evangelical narrative was designedly composed so as to convey this sense, and if this sense was an element of the popular Jewish legend, then is the evangelical narrative without doubt a product of that legend.

FRIEDRICH NIETZSCHE

Unlike most eighteenth- and nineteenth-century German intellectuals who directed their attention to Jesus and the Gospels, the brilliant classical philologist and philosopher Friedrich Nietzsche (1844–1900) was largely uninterested in their historical truth or falsity. He was rather concerned with the ideological implications of the gospel story, and with understanding and critiquing its determinative effect on the development of Western morality. The following comes from the first essay of Nietzsche's polemical critique, *Genealogy of Morals*, originally published in 1887.

[The Genealogy of Christian Morality]†

Essay 1, § 7

The reader will have already surmised with what ease the priestly mode of valuation can branch off from the knightly aristocratic mode, and then develop into the very antithesis of the latter: special impetus is given to this opposition, by every occasion when the castes of the priests and warriors confront each other with mutual jealousy and cannot agree over the prize. The knightly-aristocratic "values" are based on a careful cult of the physical, on a flowering, rich, and even effervescing healthiness, that goes considerably beyond what is necessary for maintaining life, on war, adventure, the chase, the dance, the tourney—on everything, in fact, which is contained in strong, free, and joyous action. The priestly-aristocratic mode of valuation is—we have seen—based on other hypotheses: it is bad enough for this class when it is a question of war! Yet the priests are, as is notorious, *the worst enemies*—why? Because they are the weakest. Their weakness

---

† From Friedrich Nietzsche, *The Genealogy of Morals: A Polemic*, trans. Horace B. Samuel, in *The Complete Works of Friedrich Nietzsche*, ed. Oscar Levy, vol. 13 (Edinburgh: T. N. Foulis, 1913), 29–33.

causes their hate to expand into a monstrous and sinister shape, a shape which is most crafty and most poisonous. The really great haters in the history of the world have always been priests, who are also the cleverest haters—in comparison with the cleverness of priestly revenge, every other piece of cleverness is practically negligible. Human history would be too fatuous for anything were it not for the cleverness imported into it by the weak—take at once the most important instance. All the world's efforts against the "aristocrats," the "mighty," the "masters," the "holders of power," are negligible by comparison with what has been accomplished against those classes by *the Jews*—the Jews, that priestly nation which eventually realised that the one method of effecting satisfaction on its enemies and tyrants was by means of a radical transvaluation of values, which was at the same time an act of the *cleverest revenge*. Yet the method was only appropriate to a nation of priests, to a nation of the most jealously nursed priestly revengefulness. It was the Jews who, in opposition to the aristocratic equation (good = aristocratic = beautiful = happy = loved by the gods), dared with a terrifying logic to suggest the contrary equation, and indeed to maintain with the teeth of the most profound hatred (the hatred of weakness) this contrary equation, namely, "the wretched are alone the good; the poor, the weak, the lowly, are alone the good; the suffering, the needy, the sick, the loathsome, are the only ones who are pious, the only ones who are blessed, for them alone is salvation—but you, on the other hand, you aristocrats, you men of power, you are to all eternity the evil, the horrible, the covetous, the insatiate, the godless; eternally also shall you be the unblessed, the cursed, the damned!" We know who it was who reaped the heritage of this Jewish transvaluation.[1] In the context of the monstrous and inordinately fateful initiative which the Jews have exhibited in connection with this most fundamental of all declarations of war, I remember the passage which came to my pen on another occasion (*Beyond Good and Evil*, Aph. 195)—that it was, in fact, with the Jews that the *revolt of the slaves* begins in the sphere *of morals*; that revolt which has behind it a history of two millennia, and which at the present day has only moved out of our sight, because it—has achieved victory.

Essay 1, § 8

But you understand this not? You have no eyes for a force which has taken two thousand years to achieve victory?—There is nothing wonderful in this: all *lengthy* processes are hard to see and to realise. But *this* is what took place: from the trunk of that tree of revenge and hate, Jewish hate,—that most profound and sublime hate, which creates ideals and changes old values to new creations, the like of which has never been on earth,—there grew a phenomenon which was equally incomparable, *a new love*, the most profound and sublime of all kinds of love;— and from what other trunk could it have grown? But beware of supposing that this love has soared on its upward growth, as in any way a real negation of that thirst for revenge, as an antithesis to the Jewish hate! No, the contrary is the truth! This love grew out of that hate, as its crown, as its triumphant crown, circling wider

---

1. That is, Jesus, and later, Christians.

and wider amid the clarity and fulness of the sun, and pursuing in the very kingdom of light and height its goal of hatred, its victory, its spoil, its strategy, with the
same intensity with which the roots of that tree of hate sank into everything
which was deep and evil with increasing stability and increasing desire. This Jesus
of Nazareth, the incarnate gospel of love, this "Redeemer" bringing salvation and
victory to the poor, the sick, the sinful—was he not really temptation in its most
sinister and irresistible form, temptation to take the tortuous path to those very
Jewish values and those very Jewish ideals? Has not Israel really obtained the final
goal of its sublime revenge, by the tortuous paths of this "Redeemer," for all that
he might pose as Israel's adversary and Israel's destroyer? Is it not due to the black
magic of a really *great* policy of revenge, of a far-seeing, burrowing revenge, both
acting and calculating with slowness, that Israel himself must repudiate before all
the world the actual instrument of his own revenge and nail it to the cross, so that
all the world—that is, all the enemies of Israel—could nibble without suspicion at
this very bait? Could, moreover, any human mind with all its elaborate ingenuity
invent a bait that was more truly *dangerous*? Anything that was even equivalent in
the power of its seductive, intoxicating, defiling, and corrupting influence to that
symbol of the holy cross, to that awful paradox of a "god on the cross," to that
mystery of the unthinkable, supreme, and utter horror of the self-crucifixion of a
god for the *salvation of man*? It is at least certain that *sub hoc signo*[2] Israel, with its
revenge and transvaluation of all values, has up to the present always triumphed
again over all other ideals, over all more aristocratic ideals.

WILHELM WREDE

In *The Messianic Secret* (1901), Wilhelm Wrede (1859–1906) argues that Mark's overarching narrative and thematic framework is not historigraphical but rather a theological construction of the early church designed to resolve a crucial problem: why did no
one—including his original followers—recognize Jesus as Messiah until after his crucifixion? Although Wrede understood his work to offer important insight into the historical Jesus (i.e., that Jesus never claimed to be Messiah but was only proclaimed as
such after his followers came to believe he rose from the dead), its lasting import has
been to pave the way for analysis of the Gospels focused not so much on their relationship to the Jesus of history as on their literary artifice, their theological tendencies, and
the social situations of the communities in and for which they were composed.

---

2. Under this sign (Latin). Nietzsche alludes to the famous vision of the Roman emperor
Constantine: a cross with the inscription: *in hoc signo vinces* ("in this sign you will conquer");
see Eusebius, *Life of Constantine* 1.126–29.

The Messianic Secret[†]

THE SELF-CONCEALMENT OF THE MESSIAH

The Injunctions to Keep the Messianic Secret

I list the relevant passages together, arranged under five headings.

1. *Prohibitions addressed to the demons*

1.25: But Jesus rebuked him (*eptimēsen autō*), saying, "Be silent (*phimō-theti*), and come out of him".

1.34: and he would not permit the demons to speak, because they knew him.

3.12: And he strictly ordered them not to make him known.

2. *Prohibitions following (other) miracles*

1.43–45 (The leper): And he sternly charged him (*embrimēsamenos*), and sent him away at once, and said to him, "See (*hora*) that you say nothing to any one; but (*alla*) go, show yourself to the priest, and offer for your cleansing what Moses commanded, for a proof to the people". But he went out and began to talk freely about it and to spread the news . . .

5.43 (Jairus's daughter): And he strictly charged them that no one should know this.

cf. v. 37: And he allowed no one to follow him except Peter and James and John the brother of James . . .

v. 40: But he put them all outside, and took the child's father and mother and those who were with him, and went in where the child was.

7.36 (The deaf mute): And he charged them to tell no one; but the more he charged them, the more zealously (*mallon perissoteron*) they proclaimed it.

cf. v. 33: And taking him aside from the multitude privately, he put his fingers into his ears . . .

8.26 (The blind man of Bethsaida). And he sent him away to his home, saying, "Do not even enter the village." (v. 1, "and tell nobody in the village".)[1]

cf. v. 23: And he took the blind man by the hand, and led him out of the village; and when he had spit on his eyes . . .

3. *Prohibitions after Peter's confession*

8.30 (directly after the Confession): And he charged them to tell no one about him.

9.9 (after the Transfiguration): And as they were coming down the mountain, he charged them to tell no one what they had seen, until the Son of man should have risen from the dead.

---

† From *The Messianic Secret*, trans. J. C. G. Greig (Greenwood, SC: Attic Press, 1971), 34–52, 67–68, 80–81, 129–32, 213–20, 227–30. Except as indicated, all notes are Wrede's.

1. There are other variants too. The interpretation is in any event the correct one.

cf. vv. 2, 3: And after six days Jesus took with him Peter and James and
   John, and led them up a high mountain apart (*kat' idian*) by themselves
   (*monous*); and he was transfigured before them . . .

4. *Intentional preservation of his incognito*

7.24: And from there he arose and went away to the region of Tyre and
   Sidon. And he entered a house, and would not have anyone know it; yet
   he could not be hid.
9.30f.: They went on from there and passed through Galilee. And he would
   not have anyone know it; for he was teaching his disciples, saying to
   them, "The Son of man will be delivered . . ."

5. *A prohibition to speak which did not originate with Jesus*

10.47f. (The blind man of Jericho): And when he heard that it was Jesus of
   Nazareth, he began to cry out and say, "Jesus, Son of David, have mercy
   on me!" And many rebuked him, telling him to be silent; . . .

The passages in section 4 and 5 above actually do not contain any prohibitions
by Jesus. No explanation for their being added will be necessary. It will be
equally self-evident why the passages both about Jesus' confidants and about taking the sick aside have also been introduced. Their features are unmistakably
connected with Jesus' words of command; by themselves they are enough to indicate that matters are at issue which are not for the public ear. We are not therefore to think of the isolation of the sick for their own sake, despite the *kat' idian*
even in the account of the Transfiguration.

In numerous Markan miracle stories the command to be silent is ineffective
(2.1ff.; 3.1ff.; etc.). In the story of the Gadarene (Gerasene) demoniac even the
demons are not asked to keep silence after their messianic salutation. Rather do
we have (5.19) Jesus saying: "Go home to your friends, and tell them how much
the Lord has done for you, and how much he has had mercy on you."

The form of the commands is quite stereotyped. A peculiarity of the passage in 9.9
is the remark about the Resurrection. Otherwise, striking are points of two sorts.

1. The commands are sharp and definite. The repeated use of *epitiman* [to
rebuke] in itself characterises this stringency; the sense of scolding or severe
rebuke must be perceived in this. The *polla* [many times] is in addition an especial mark of emphatic admonition. In the story of the leper it will be proper to
link this up with the emotion of anger (*embrimēsamenos*). I simply don't in the
slightest believe that it is to be explained from the peculiar circumstances of this
story, as has variously been attempted. In Mt 9.30 the same term *embrimasthai*
appears in the story of the two blind men.

2. Nowhere is a motive expressed for these instructions. This is particularly
noteworthy. Only in 9.30 is Jesus' intention of going through Galilee incognito
accounted for by his teaching his disciples about his passion. This point I shall to
begin with leave aside.

Exegetes have not reached a generally agreed exposition of these passages
and, one may add, have not reached an exposition which gives the impression of

certainty. If one contemplates the particular and general explanations offered, an extremely variegated picture is disclosed. This does not exclude the possibility that *one* of them is the right one, but it can also mean that no understanding at all has been arrived at.

First and foremost it must be reckoned extremely probable that all the various commands in Mark have the same sense. For every disinterested reader this is the first impression. The continuous repetition of the feature is by itself enough to press this upon one, but the lack of a motivation intensifies it. Why would the narrator give no hints if he was thinking now of one and now of another reason? What reader could guess his opinion? Or did he sometimes no longer have any consciousness of any reason? If so, then he ought in other instances to be all the more explicit. That from start to finish he had conceived of no reason is, however, an impossibility. One can therefore only suppose that he assumed the reader would read all these remarks with an idea which he did not first need to communicate to him. The two sayings about the incognito of Jesus (7.24, 9.30) are included in this. They sound too much related to be separated from the prohibitions. On the other hand, it may be questionable whether the rebuke by the "many" in 10.48 does not have its own special significance. Consequently it is the explanation which exhibits a unity of conception that is most conclusive.

For this reason we must above all start from the fact that everywhere the preservation of the *messianic* secret is contemplated. It is true that this is explicitly stated only in the commands given to the demons and in the passage 8.30 and perhaps 9.9. But what other meaning is to be attached to the rebukes following the raising of the dead and the healing miracles? The remaining passages make nothing more obvious than that Jesus demands silence on the presupposition that his miracle would at once permit a conclusion about what his secret nature was, and his dignity. Thus at least the earliest readers of the Gospel must have understood it, and thus Mark himself and specifically Mark must have intended it. For after all the miracles do count in Christianity in its most primitive period as witnesses for the nature and meaning of Christ. Quite certainly, however, the evangelist made no distinction between his own viewpoint and a viewpoint of the contempories of Jesus. I do not even need to appeal to the fact that he as well as Matthew, Luke and John will have been of the opinion that Jesus' miracles encountered a general and fervent expectation of the Messiah. Thus neither is it adequate to represent each individual miracle as an isolated mystery withheld from the crowd. Mark always reckons with the impression the miracle-worker makes through his miracles. After the stilling of the storm it is asked: Who is this who can do these things?

Accordingly all those explanations at once fall to the ground which can illuminate only individual passages. For they presuppose a plurality or an alternation of motivations for the prohibitions Jesus utters.

Jesus is supposed to have prohibited the demons from speaking about his messiahship because he did not wish to be acknowledged by such unclean mouths or in "unconventional" fashion. It may be asked whether this is an explanation in Mark's mind at all. It certainly cannot be used for the prohibition that follows the raising of the dead girl, or the healing of the deaf mute.

Just as improbable is the idea that here and there, say at 7.36 or 8.26, the prohibition has the purpose of repelling the claims of the crowd on Jesus to perform miracles as he wanted to have peace or wanted to devote himself to his disciples. For the period when, according to Mark, Jesus lets one miracle follow upon another a new explanation must be found therefore, and for the homage of the demons perhaps yet another.

Thus reasons of situation or locality are also hardly of importance. In areas with a pagan population Jesus wanted to remain concealed (7.24) and there too he commands the person possessed to broadcast his experience (5.19); in Galilee he performs miracles before all the people, friend and foe, and in Galilee too he avoids the public, 9.30. Nothing is easier than to conjure up reasons for Jesus' proceeding this way or that in one particular locality or another. But it is hard to prove that Mark was aware of these reasons.

The somewhat more far-reaching view that Jesus shunned the reputation of a wonder-worker in order not to be diverted from his true calling or in order not to evoke a false and valueless acknowledgement of a moralistic religious flavour again does not fit the stories of demons any more than it does 8.30 and 9.9, quite apart from the fact that a category like "moralistic and religious" is less familiar to Mark than say to Klostermann and B. Weiss,[2] and that the wholesale performance of miracles as reported by Mark is a strange proceeding if from one wonder alone such consequences are feared.

* * *

The most widespread view derives Jesus' reserve from considerations relating to his vocation. Above all much is said of his educational aim. He is afraid of materialistic views of the Messiah among his disciples if he gives them too early an idea for which they are not yet mature. Above all he is afraid of a political exploitation of his dignity, both in the case of the disciples and in the case of the people, amounting to national demonstrations and ultimately messianic revolution. For the people and the disciples, it is said, did not have his idea of the Messiah but the Jewish, that is a political, one.

Under the one designation of education we have here actually a variety of things tied up. Materialistic ideas of the Messiah such as the disciples are said to have are not of necessity political and national ones and while in relation to the disciples concern for the gradual and unadulterated development of their inner life becomes the main concern, in regard to the people Jesus seems to have thought less about provision for their religious development than about the possible endangering of his own life's work. Enough, however, of this.

It is remarkable that most people so quickly act as if content with this explanation. It seems to be regarded as something axiomatic that Jesus had resort to silence if he nourished the fears with which he is credited. But why should this be axiomatic? Was there no other and more natural way? It seems to me that it would have been a better way if Jesus had spoken, at least to the disciples. Why

2. August Klosterman and Bernhard Weiss, biblical scholars contemporary with Wrede [editors' note].

does he not simply say that the political messiahship is "no go" and that he has as little to do with that as with their materialistic expectation? But be this as it may, there are at all events moments in Mark's account where the explanation simply breaks down.

The fact that up to the confession of Peter Jesus simply shuts himself off from his disciples may be understood in this way as can the repulse of the loud cries of the demons, and even the continued preservation of the secret from the people after Peter has spoken may not be all that much of an enigma. But why did Jesus alter his behaviour at the entry into Jerusalem and why does he let himself quietly become the object of a messianic ovation, and indeed not without some initiative on his own part? Nobody has yet properly explained this, for not even the assumption that word of Jesus' messiahship got around at that period is an adequate explanation for this attitude. This would, after all, have been the best way of unleashing that enthusiasm for political messiahship against which he is supposed to have been so much on his guard.

It remains entirely obscure why once the Transfiguration is past Jesus commands silence *until his resurrection* (9.9). An educational intention can no longer be the dominant one here and to avoid Jewish misunderstanding till the resurrection would amount to a renunciation of the messianic claim in the last resort for his earthly ministry. Our question is not whether a special motivation renders the remark in 9.9 comprehensible, but we *are* concerned with how much what is assumed can do by way of explanation of all the passages. In the same way the excuse that the saying has been inaccurately transmitted or is not genuine is not to be sustained. It suffices that Mark has it!

And once again we must think up a new explanation for the prohibitions after the miracles. If we are to say that Jesus was afraid of messianic demonstrations when he performed his miracles and that this fear guided his actions, then he would not on a single occasion have been able to do cures in front of crowds, and as Bruno Bauer has said,[3] he would have done best to do absolutely nothing. That is to say, the prohibitions are incomprehensible.

Not seldom another idea is also linked with the "educational motive". It is said that Jesus feared the Romans would jeopardise his work were he known too early as the Messiah. Taken by itself this notion is also dealt with by our last remark on the miracles. But what, according to the accounts, can lead to such an idea at all, if Jesus wished to be Messiah only in the unpolitical sense? Would it be the fact that the Roman authorities did not intervene against Jesus on their own initiative but at the instigation of the Jewish leaders?

I turn again with a similar question to the chief point, the supposed educational intention of Jesus. More important than the fact that exegetes and critics have troubled themselves little about obvious objections in this connection, seems in my view the other fact that they have never asked themselves at all whence they derived this idea.

There may well be doubts about whether a prophetic nature like Jesus, with its inner self-assurance and decisiveness, and with its consciousness of having a

3. *Kritik der Evangelien* [*und Geschichte ihres Usprungs*, 4 vols. (Berlin, 1850–52)], IV, p. 101.

mission, and with its urge to express the thoughts dwelling in his mind regardless of the consequences, would be so constituted psychologically as to confront men in the condescending manner of the pastor or with the sophisticated approach of the educator. One may, however, be permitted to suppose that gradually and in a very natural way the picture of Jesus has undergone a sizeable transformation into the pastoral mode, albeit a noble version of the pastoral. But this consideration is certainly not going to be followed up here. On the other hand, we cannot in any circumstances avoid considering whether Mark offers us something relevant to an educational activity on the part of Jesus, if Markan texts are being interpreted with this idea in mind. And here I confess to having decided doubts.

The attempt has indeed even been made, to elevate the idea of the education of the disciples into a dominant standpoint for Mark.

But the attempt has not been successful, and it is actually comprehensible only if one looks at the Gospel through very modern eyes.

It goes without saying that there are many points in it which can be easily associated with an idea of education: the disciples are called, sent out, receive instruction and teaching, parables are explained to them and they are permitted to hear prophecies. But of a procedure such as would take account of development and would lead from stage to stage or would meet existing weaknesses half-way—that would in fact deserve the name of education—nothing is to be seen. It can be surmised only by those who consider it right to fill in the gaps between the extant data with subjective notions of their own or link up what the narrator has not linked up in any recognisable way. The teacher is not necessarily the educator. The teacher can almost be the opposite of the educator. Where do we find passages in Mark which clearly delineate the educational point of view? We find ourselves having to inflate every answer of Jesus to a question of the disciples into a form of education. It is necessary to overlook the fact that according to Mark the form of speaking in parables which Jesus used was the very thing *not* chosen in order to come to the aid of those of weak understanding, and we have to forget that Jesus when his disciples don't understand him as a rule does *nothing* to make himself comprehensible to them. All in all, concepts like "taking account of a development in their knowledge from within" and "education for independent knowledge" fall outside the orbit of Mark from the start. The only thing that can give the view an appearance of correctness is that a development seems discernible in the disciples' knowledge and that Jesus frequently asks, "Have you *not yet* understood?" There will later be an opportunity of showing that in both connections the explanation is to be found in an entirely different quarter from the idea of education. For the present I assert that the interpretation of the commands relating to the secret is not rendered axiomatic by this idea because the idea is lacking in Mark.

But the same thing will also hold good if in the matter of "Jesus' educational intention" we are thinking of his fear about the awakening of political messianic enthusiasm. Did Mark ever think at all, or ever know anything, to the effect that Jesus deliberately eschewed such a belief in the Messiah? The reader will give a superior smile at the scepticism in this question, for everybody makes use of this idea. But the question must be opened up.

Let us imagine a reader of Mark who has never heard anything of Jesus' story. He will at once notice that the question of messiahship is of importance, but that he should on the basis of the Gospel hit upon the notion of a dual idea of the Messiah, namely a spiritual one nurtured by Jesus and a popular political one, is completely impossible. The narrator has not touched upon it by any direct allusion; Jesus does not express himself about it and blames neither disciples nor people in this connection; to all appearances he does not struggle either within himself or in relation to the outside world against a false expectation of the Messiah. We do not notice the people failing to come near Jesus on this account. If we hear about a contrast between the views of the people and Jesus' own assessment of himself, this contrast none the less lies only in the fact that the people take him to be Baptist returned to life again, the promised Elijah or one of the prophets, that is to say, *not* the Messiah. Can this all be understood if the Evangelist, so far as the question of the messiahship is at issue, is thinking of the opposition to the political view of the messiahship as the mainspring behind the whole behaviour of Jesus. He betrays such a variety of things to us, when all is said, for example about his christological views and about the way in which the opponents of Jesus thought. He regards it as necessary to instruct his gentile Christian readers, even about Jewish customs of purification (7.3ff.), explicitly. And yet here he is silent as if this contrast to the messianic expectation of the Jews were self-explanatory!

* * *

We now summarise the results of these observations. Exegetes have been unable to explain Jesus' command, which was repeated again and again up to the very last, to keep silent about his messianic dignity. For they have not been able to find a likely *motivation* which is conceivable for the historical Jesus and which can be applied to all the individual situations. In this connection they have used views to interpret the Markan accounts, possession of which by the evangelist has not, to say no more, been demonstrated. Basically, however, they have gone to little pains about Mark himself at all. It has been the custom simply to leave him out of account and imagine oneself directly in the life of Jesus. But yet all the while this information only comes to us from *Mark*.

This circumstance is, to be sure, no compelling proof that the accounts about Jesus' commands are unhistorical. But at this point already it does seem very strange that the assertion could be made that in the whole gospel story there could hardly very well be more trustworthy information than this. And the suspicion here rather forces itself upon us that they could be unhistorical, and then perhaps with this presupposition of unhistoricity it might be possible to provide the explanation which was not to be gained with a contrary assumption.

And in fact the accounts *are* unhistorical, each and every one of them.

In the first place this is clear in the resistance to the homage of the demons. If the demons did not greet Jesus as Messiah then equally he cannot have resisted their greeting. These features fall to the ground with their presuppositions.

A second argument has already frequently been adumbrated. The Gospel not only reports expressly that Jesus was widely known as a wonder-worker and it does not simply describe numerous wonders in this sense. Even the miracle stories in which the prohibitions are found themselves rest on this view. The leper, Jairus, the deaf mute and the blind man only come into contact with Jesus *because* his miraculous power is common talk. This is therefore a presupposition on the basis of which the prohibitions which follow the miracles can be criticised. If Jesus considered his miracles signs of his messiahship then he cannot have taken offence at the conclusion that he was Messiah; that is to say, the prohibitions attached to individual miracles become incomprehensible if, as everything seems to suggest, they were otherwise meant in a messianic sense. If, on the other hand, Jesus did not think at all that his miracles would admit of conclusions about his messiahship the prohibitions none the less again become incomprehensible, for (1) why does he light upon the idea of commanding silence in these particular individual instances, an idea which otherwise he does not have, and (2) how can he think it possible to render innocuous by his prohibitions the extremely extensive publicity attaching to his activity?

Thirdly, a series of questions arises from the miracle stories themselves, where we find the prohibitions.

* * *

Here first and foremost the story of Jairus's daughter is very clear. The death of the girl has become known and the mourning has begun round her. Jesus then accomplishes her resuscitation in the presence of the few witnesses, but could the miracle be concealed from the crowd by removal of the people? Later on everybody would inevitably see that the girl was alive and would have to conclude that her resurrection was owed to Jesus who had been fetched in as a wonderworker. In consequence a prohibition by Jesus would be completely without point and, because it was completely pointless, from the historical standpoint it is senseless. We may add that *every* view of the prohibition meets with this objection.

Exactly the same has to be said of the healing of the deaf-mute. Jesus simply could not in any circumstances have happened upon the idea that he could hinder the healing coming to public notice by isolation of the sick person and subsequent instructions.

In the case of the healing of the blind man the command not to go into the town does seem to promise more success for in this way the blind man will be kept at a sizeable distance from the people who brought him to Jesus but at the same time he is sent to his own house. We must then ask if his house did not lie in the town. Nothing is said of this; and the idea is remote although exegetes readily shove it in. How then is the sufferer to reach his house without going near the town and how is he to remain concealed from the people in his house? This too does not seem to have the air of historicity about it.

In the story of the leper, concealment of the miracle-worker seems more conceivable, for here nothing is said of those known and related to the sick person; and the instruction that he should show himself to the priest and bring the prescribed sacrifice for purification is in particular capable of bearing the appearance of an effective means of diverting attention from Jesus. For this and this alone will be the point of this demand: Jesus, that is Mark's Jesus, wishes to hide himself behind the pronouncement of the priest.[4] Of course for this very reason

---

4. Legalistic tendencies are not to my mind in question. The *eis marturion autois* [for a testimony to them] means that the people are to have in the priest's pronouncement a declaration that the sick man is clean which will satisfy them.

Jesus' procedure recounted here will lead to great consternation in another direction. Along with this it is worth mentioning that the prohibition is closely linked with a feature which itself seems little worthy of credence. The leper disregards Jesus' words and broadcasts the miracle as if in defiance of him. This is a peculiar way of behaving towards his benefactor, and is certainly no testimony at all to the authority of Jesus. The feature recurs, however, at 7.36 and there seems to be another parallel when in 7.24 we read "And he entered a house and would not have anyone know it; yet *he could not be hid*". This formula speaks clearly.

*   *   *

The Meaning of the Secret

In the history of Jesus we have so far found no motive which provides us with a satisfactory and intelligible explanation for his conscious concealment of himself as it is described in Mark. But neither have we been able to establish any more clearly that *Mark* found his explanation for the attitude of Jesus, which is equally delineated in many individual stories, in the conditions, relationships and events characteristic of the historical life of Jesus. I would go further and assert that *a historical motive is really absolutely out of the question; or, to put it positively, that the idea of the messianic secret is a theological idea.*

A relatively little-heeded passage provides us with the key to this approach. For me at least it has undoubtedly been the proper starting-point for getting to know this whole series of ideas and to this extent I regard it as one of the most important sayings written down by Mark. It is the command Jesus gives after the Transfiguration, 9.9. "And as they were coming down the mountain, he charged them to tell no one what they had seen, *until the Son of man should have risen from the dead.*" From this saying it is deduced that the Transfiguration is regarded as a sort of anticipation or preview of the resurrection of Jesus, or as a prophecy of his return in glory, and in this way the meaning of the saying is again explained. The true meaning of the vision in which Jesus' confidants participated would, however, have been discernible only after the resurrection, and thus they were not to talk about it till then.

This interpretation of the event as a prophetic picture of what was to come may not be wrong, but does it lead to clarity about why Jesus gives an express command? If the meaning of the Transfiguration was to be discerned only later then it seems more or less harmless if people heard about it earlier. Moreover, according to Mark, Jesus did speak directly for all to hear in advance, about his coming in glory, 8.38, cf. 34. Why then should the event on the mountain remain a secret?

There is, however, something else much more important than this.

This view separates the command of Jesus from its parallels, and provides it with a motivation of which one would not think in any single one of the other cases. One cannot, however, get away from the impression that this passage is of the same kind as the others. Exegetes have again and again perceived this too. This is to say that here too the issue must be the preservation of the messianic secret. No exegete would ever have had any doubts about this had not the command occurred with the indication of a time-limit ("until the Son of man shall have risen from the dead"). For the text itself does indeed speak expressly of messiahship.

To be sure the story of the Transfiguration does show, as the pseudo-Petrine epistle says,[5] the *megaleiotēs,* i.e. the glory or majesty of Jesus; that is, it shows something supramundane which has no place in the earthly life of Jesus. But here there is no kind of contrast to the messiahship. This will become self-evident as our investigation proceeds. But we hear quite expressly about the messiahship when the voice from heaven cries, "This is my beloved son; listen to him". Whatever the appearance of Moses and Elijah may mean, this testimony from heaven which forms the conclusion of the scene at least can only be regarded as a sort of interpretation of the whole affair, and it is axiomatic that the commandment to keep silence about what has been *seen* also embraces this that has been *heard.* It is then in fact clear that the contents of this command basically coincide with those of the others.

Why, then, should the addition of the resurrection hinder us from thinking about the preservation of the secrecy of the *messianic title?* Only let us be bold in grasping the idea towards which the matter is leading us. Our conclusion is that *during his earthly life Jesus' messiahship is absolutely a secret and is supposed to be such; no one apart from the confidants of Jesus is supposed to learn about it; with the resurrection, however, its disclosure ensues.*

This is in fact the crucial idea, the underlying point of Mark's entire approach.

* * *

Let us now sum up. It emerges that seen by itself Jesus' being and everything connected with it is in the nature of the case a secret—not merely a secret of his consciousness but, so to speak, an objective secret. Now it does not, of course, follow from this in the least that this secret has to remain a secret for ever during the earthly life of Jesus and that he is himself consistently resolved on *keeping* it secret. Rather is this idea to be regarded as quite incomprehensible, as far as we have so far carried the discussion. Meanwhile let us merely establish that the concealment of the messiahship in Mark is accompanied by a theological, non-historical view of the messiahship, is connected with this view, and gains a particular meaning as a result of this view.

My final question is, What sort of things are thought of *individually* as the contents of the secret, or, more plainly, as items to be kept secret? On this the following may be said.

Secret is in the first place the messiahship of Jesus or his being Son of God.

Secret is the wonder-working which is the characteristic of messiahship and would betray it.

Secret is the whole teaching of Jesus because it is completely hidden from the crowd.

---

5. II Peter 1.16 on the Transfiguration reads: *epoptai genēthentes tēs ekeinou megaleiotētos* [were eyewitnesses of his majesty].

Secret in particular is the meaning of the parables, as it is only disclosed to the disciples, and even to them not without interpretation.

These are specifications of varied scope and value. Moreover, the notions of the secret of the person and the secret of the doctrine in a certain sense overlap. For that Jesus is God's son can be, and actually *is*, also conceived as the content of the teaching.

There is, however, still a special point deserving particular mention.

Also secret in a pre-eminent sense is the necessity of Jesus' suffering, dying and rising. This already follows from one of the passages previously considered.

In 9.30 Mark says that Jesus finally wanted to hide his presence in Galilee, and adds in verse 31 "*for* he was teaching his disciples, saying to them, 'The Son of man will be delivered into the hands of men, and they will kill him; and when he is killed, after three days he will rise'".

Here expositors do not normally grasp this idea as pointedly as they might. We cannot in fact simply rest content with Jesus' wishing to be alone with his disciples, so that he could dedicate himself wholly to them, and *thus particularly* prepare them for the approaching suffering. Here it is not a question of the teaching in general but simply of the particular *content*. But if Jesus wishes to remain concealed *because* he is imparting this teaching, which after all is what Mark says, the point lies in the fact that this very teaching too and in a special sense is a *mustērion* [mystery or secret]. On this account it requires to be kept secret and can have no witnesses. For this reason, therefore, Jesus is intent upon preserving his incognito in Galilee.

This idea may strike us as very odd effect for we may object that in order to discuss the secret of his suffering in the restricted circle of his confidants Jesus required to withdraw himself with his disciples only now and then, but that nobody would have hindered him from doing this and he hardly even needed to do it anyway. Nevertheless the narrator's idea is that Jesus conceals himself in Galilee because he is passing on to the disciples the secret of his death and resurrection. We must, however, reject every attempt to make this more historically imaginable by reading between the lines, e.g. by the interpretation that Jesus must have been afraid of being so besieged as not to have the necessary time and leisure left over for the instruction of the disciples. This attempt takes away from the peculiar character of the idea before us.

It will be of value to supplement what this passage has so far yielded. It is not hard, in the light of well-known early Christian standpoints, to see that the suffering, dying and rising of Jesus are considered as a distinctive mystery.

* * *

MARK IN RETROSPECT

Mark as an Author

Present-day investigation of the Gospels is entirely governed by the idea that Mark in his narrative had more or less clearly before his eyes the actual circumstances of the life of Jesus, even if not without gaps. It presupposes that he is *thinking from the standpoint of the life of Jesus,* and is motivating the individual features of his story in accordance with the actual circumstances of this life and in accordance with the actual thoughts and feelings of Jesus, and is linking together the events he describes in the historical psychological sense.

This is its criterion for the investigation and criticism of the Gospel in particular. It does, to be sure, assume chronological displacements and inaccuracies in matters of fact, alterations in the wording of pronouncements ascribed to Jesus and even an accretion of later dogmatic views. But everywhere it operates with the psychological necessities and probabilities which existed in the given situations for the persons taking part. This is where it finds its motivation, supplementing the information by the consequences which might naturally be expected to follow from them, and so clothing the skeleton of dry data with flesh.

This view and this procedure must be recognised as wrong in principle. It must frankly be said that *Mark no longer has a real view of the historical life of Jesus.*

In this I am not at all intending to pass judgement on the historical character of the materials I have not examined. These may be entirely disregarded here. What we have inspected more closely is an adequate basis for our verdict.

It is axiomatic that Mark has a whole series of historical ideas, or ideas in a historical form.

Jesus came on the scene as a teacher first and foremost in Galilee. He is surrounded by a circle of disciples and goes around with them and gives instruction to them. Among them some are his special confidants. A larger crowd sometimes joins itself to the disciples. Jesus likes to speak in parables. Alongside his teaching there is his working of miracles. This is sensational and he is mobbed. He was specially concerned with those whose illnesses took the form of demon possession. In so far as he encountered the people he did not despise associating with publicans and sinners. He takes up a somewhat free attitude towards the Law. He encounters the opposition of the Pharisees and the Jewish authorities. They lie in wait for him and try to entrap him. In the end they succeed after he has not only walked on Judaean soil but even entered Jerusalem. He suffers and is condemned to death. The Roman authorities co-operate in this.

We may say that these will be the main features. To them may be added indeed many a detail as to the miracles, the discourses and the locations, and it may be possible to abstract features of significance from them. But for Mark's *view* and thus for his presentation as a whole this is not of importance. For in these questions of detail we are concerned not with actual factors and dominant characteristics of history. In so far as these come under consideration, almost all the ideas are quite general and undefined. On no account can we say that with them a concrete picture of his life is given. We only get the external framework or as I see it a few trivial sketches.

But the real texture of the presentation becomes apparent only when to the warp of these general historical ideas is added a strong thread of thoughts that are dogmatic in quality. In part they merge with the historical motifs and in part they stand alongside and between them.

The person of Jesus is dogmatically conceived. He is the bearer of a definite dignity bestowed by God, or, which comes to the same thing, he is a higher supernatural being. Jesus acts with divine power and he knows the future in advance. The motives for his actions do not derive from human peculiarity, human objectives and human necessities. The one pervasive motive rather takes the form of a divine decree lying above and beyond human comprehension. This he seeks to realise in his actions and his suffering. The teaching of Jesus is correspondingly supernatural. His knowledge is such as no man can possess on his own account but he conceals it and conceals his own being because from the beginning his gaze is directed to the point of the whole story, i.e. the resurrection, which is the event that will make manifest for men what is secret. For he is known in the world beyond and already on earth he has a link with that world when he proves his power to the spirits or sees the heavens opening.

But the other main factors of the story are also theologically or dogmatically conceived. The disciples are by nature receivers of the highest revelation and are naturally and indeed by a higher necessity lacking in understanding. The people are by nature non-recipients of revelation, and the actual enemies of Jesus from the beginning are as it were essentially full of evil and contrariety and so far as men come into it bring about the end but thereby also the glory.

These motifs and not just the historical ones represent what actually motivates and determines the shape of the narrative in Mark. They give it its colouring. The interest naturally depends on them and the actual thought of the author is directed towards them. It therefore remains true to say that as a whole the Gospel no longer offers a historical *view* of the real life of Jesus. Only pale residues of such a view have passed over into what is a suprahistorical view for faith. In this sense the Gospel of Mark belongs to the history of dogma.

Exegesis of Mark must therefore take this into account. For in the last resort the formal nature of its presentation of history rests on this. In this respect I shall single out only two features as characteristic.

If one considers together the *different portions* of the account one discovers that in general no internal sequence is provided. Several stories are indeed often held together by the same situation, by a chronological or other type of remark; smaller sections complete in themselves can be isolated; and we even get references back to something said earlier, such as in 6.52, 8.17ff. But on the whole one portion stands next to the other with a piecemeal effect. There is naturally a connection, but it is the connection of ideas and not of historical developments. It could indeed be conceived that Mark might have given a sort of historical life to the dogmatic or semi-dogmatic ideas which he presents formally as historical motifs and that in his own way he might have thought historically in them. For a painfully naïve author of antiquity this is, of course, extremely improbable, and in any event Mark does not do it. We saw that he did not establish any connection between the many kinds of prohibition, the different prophecies about death and resurrection and the various expressions of incomprehension on the part of the disciples. In actual fact he did not think through from one point in his presentation to the next.

It follows from this that we must not draw conclusions from what he says which he has not himself drawn, or establish connections which are not manifest. B.

---

6. *Das Markusevangelium* [*und seine synoptischen Parallelen* (Berlin, 1872)], p. 213.

Weiss on one occasion remarks[6] on the statement in 6.14, according to which Jesus' name was also known at the court of Herod, that this was the result of the previous mission of the disciples which had directed attention to Jesus in much wider circles. This remark certainly does not merit special censure, for such connections are made in dozens in the gospels, nor is the example specially glaring. But it is all the more typical for that. At the bottom of such connections there lies a false overall view of the type of authorship that we have in Mark. Not by a single syllable does he indicate that he desires to see two facts brought into connection which he happens to tell one after the other. For this reason it is not legitimate to manufacture such a connection.

* * *

THE CONCEALMENT OF THE MESSIAHSHIP
UP TO THE RESURRECTION

The Hidden Messiah in Judaism

* * *

We now have a Christian approach the near relationship of which to ours can hardly be denied.[7] This is the idea that *Jesus becomes messiah only with the Resurrection.*

The comparison presses itself upon us for the very reason that the resurrection in both cases is the decisive item. But in these circumstances negative consideration of the earthly life of Jesus is closely related to this. On the one hand the conclusion must be formed that Jesus during his earthly activity was as yet not the messiah but on the other hand we have it that he did not wish to be the messiah as yet and did not as yet count as such. In the light of this the Resurrection is in the one instance the revelation, and in the other the realisation, of the messiahship. The impression that these ideas belong together is a strong one from the start.

The point demands exhaustive consideration. Let us for the sake of argument simply designate the idea that Jesus *becomes* messiah only after his earthly life by the expression "future messiahship".

The Secret and the Future Messiah

In his sermon at Pentecost in Acts 2.36 Peter says that God has *made* the Jesus whom the Jews crucified *both Lord and Christ.* In this it is implied that this has been done through his being raised from the dead. This saying quite by itself would prove that there was in primitive Christianity a view in accordance with which Jesus was not the messiah in his earthly life. I shall avoid the expression "was not *fully* the messiah". In his earthly life, to be sure, Jesus lacks only one thing in order to be the messiah: namely the sovereign dignity and power. But this one thing is the *whole* thing. It is precisely what makes the concept of messiah what it is, as Christianity received it from Judaism. The Resurrection showed

7. Wrede has just discussed Justin Martyr, *Dialogue with Trypho* 8 and 110 [editors' note].

that Jesus from now on had attained to this dignity and power, and did not merely show it, but put it into effect. From now on therefore the messiah can be expected. He exists and therefore he can come.

It has rightly been pointed out that Paul gives evidence of having an analagous view. Jesus is "designated Son of God in power" (Ro. 1.4) "by his resurrection from the dead". It is all one whether Paul was able to call the earthly Jesus too "Son of God". If he did, this would only derive from the fact that in his premundane existence he already possessed the sonship, the *einai isa theō* [being equal to God]. In reality the one who became man has already shed the existence which characterises the Son of God.[8] And thus according to Paul too he *becomes* something, as a result of the resurrection, which as a man he in no sense was. The well-known passage in the letter to the Philippians, 2.6ff., says this plainly too. The human existence in which Jesus is devoid and empty of all dignity and lordship that was his due is removed as a result of his exaltation, and thereby he receives the name above all names, that of "Lord", but with it naturally also the substance, which is lordship over everyone and everything.

The way the New Testament speaks of his future appearance is also significant. We do not hear of his coming again, but simply of his coming. In all the eschatological discourses of the Gospel nothing is said differently of the Christ than what is said of the expected kingdom. The term is *erchesthai* [it/he will come].[9] Further, *parousia* does not mean "return" but always "arrival". The wrong translation should be strictly avoided, in order not to eliminate an important peculiarity of New Testament language. The entire usage manifestly rests upon the idea that the "return" is the first and only messianic appearance. Jesus has been there but the messiah is yet to come. But this is not to say that he only *becomes* messiah when he arrives. He has been messiah since the resurrection.

It is useful to remember the alteration introduced in the subsequent period. Justin already distinguishes everywhere between a *prōtē* [first] and a *deutera parousia* [second coming] of Christ. The one is *adoxos* [without glory] but the other is *endoxos* [glorious].[1] It is the double coming which is a distinctively Christian doctrine over against Judaism. It too is of course already found in Scripture. The two goats in Lev. 16 are the type of the two *parousiai*, Dial. ch. 40. But even already in Ignatius the new linguistic usage is observable, and by the phrase *parousia tou sotēros* [coming of the savior] his appearance in the flesh is understood.[2, 3]

These alterations in terminology are characteristic. However the matter is not always entirely covered by terminology. The terminology is to an extent second-

8. Sonship in the true sense depends for the Christians too on their abandonment of their carnal life (Ro. 8.23). Only thereby are they conformed to the "image of the Son", that is, to his mode of being (8.29).

9. Lk 17.30 *apokaluptesthai* [it/he is revealed].

1. Dial. [*Dialogue with Trypho*] ch. 49.

2. Ad Philad. 9.

3. Justin uses alongside *parousia* also *epiphaneia* [manifestation] (Apol. 1.44) or *phanerōsis tou Christou* [disclosure of Christ] in this way. Moreover the transformation in usage is already to be seen in the writings of the N. T., cf. e.g. *epiphaneia* in 2 Tim. 1.10.

ary; the substance is what matters. But this is already fully there, for example, in the Gospel of John. Jesus *is* manifestly already the messiah in his historical life. Whatever the future coming of Christ may mean,[4] the fact that he *has* come, appearing in the flesh, does not fall behind this in importance. The verdict that he *was* the messiah is precisely as necessary as the other, that he *has* revealed God and his truth and *has* accomplished everything necessary for salvation.

The development in the view of the messiah Jesus which we here perceive, is very easily comprehensible.

The view that Jesus only becomes messiah after his death is assuredly not merely an old one, but the oldest of which we have any knowledge. Had the earthly life of Jesus been looked upon from the start as the actual life of the messiah, it would have been only with difficulty that, by way of supplement to this, the idea could have been hit upon of regarding the resurrection as the formal beginning of the messiahship and the appearance in glory as the *single* coming of the messiah.

We may add here another consideration. Who was able to find the essence of the messiahship realised even only partially in the earthly life of Jesus, according to Jewish ideas? These Jewish ideas were, after all, hardly capable of being stretched to the point where an itinerant teacher and healer whose life gave no signs of lordship and glory could be regarded as the real messiah. The most that is conceivable is that the activity or personality of Jesus might already have awakened during his lifetime the question or presentiment, the hope or perhaps the belief that he had been chosen by God to be the messiah. But once again this would simply be as much as to say that as yet he was not messiah. Those who regard Peter's confession as a historical fact must draw the same conclusion from this too. For at all events it proves that despite all the preceding miraculous activity the people until then found nothing in Jesus which was a compelling indication of his messiahship, and even for the disciples, despite all their veneration for their master, the same thing must have held good for a very long time.

This oldest view of the messiahship of Jesus underwent more and more change as time went on. The decisive factor in this is not that the earthly Jesus was *called* messiah or that it was said that God *had sent* the messiah. This would still be capable of being taken to mean that he whom we can now expect as messiah was there. But the whole thing is rather a question of the facts of Jesus' past life gaining a new emphasis and a different aspect.

Here the clearest example is the death of Jesus, an event which originally must have represented the sharpest contrast to every hope focused on Jesus. Those who regarded this death as a saving death thereby recognised that what was past and had happened did not merely provide an earnest for future happenings but really had already produced something of substance. Despite what was said above, this is already true of Paul. To be sure it is not right to say that in Paul yearning for the future came to take second place to the perception of an already experienced salvation and we should not say that he emphasises faith more than he does hope. For there are other reasons for the emphasis on faith, and it can be shown that all the pronouncements of Paul on an already accomplished salvation

4. 1 Jn 2.28, *parousia.*

do contain within them an allusion to the future. But this much is correct, that however much in his case too all thoughts are pressing towards the end, his hope is based just as much on what God *has* done in Christ, and on that past fact that he *has* died.

But alongside his death much else in the earthly life of Jesus became significant and necessary and indispensable, whether it was only an accretion that went along with reminiscence or was already originally contained within that reminiscence. It is not merely the endowment of Jesus with the Holy Spirit and his supernatural birth which belong here but in the last resort the miracles too,[5] as the signs and testimonies of his power and glory, together with everything which proved that prophecy had been fulfilled in him. For the mere fact that a feature of his life, even a subordinate one, had been prophesied, transformed its quality.

Parallel to some extent with this growing significance of the life of Jesus there went an occlusion of the first hope. Belief in a directly imminent *parousia*, though not indeed in the *parousia* itself, recedes into the background.

Thus the verdict that Jesus *was* the messiah more and more gained a content of its own and an independent significance. There arose a new and *specifically Christian* concept of the messiah which cannot be sufficiently definitely distinguished from the older one. It is a concept of a very complex kind. To a great extent it came into existence as a result of the fact that a plethora of new predicates became attached to the inherited concept of the messiah, as a result of which even the old predicates took on a new look; or else it came into existence because anything essential known about the life of *Jesus*, or regarded as known about it, was attached to the concept of the messiah itself.

At all events the dating of the messiahship from the Resurrection is not an idea of Jesus' but one of the community. Experience of the appearances of the Risen One is presupposed in this. This can be denied only by those who think it possible for Jesus to have prophesied his immediate resurrection.

* * *

Certain it is, that the messiahship beginning with the Resurrection does not demand the idea of the concealed messiahship. It does not necessarily exclude the possibility that Jesus called himself messiah on earth, but still less does it exclude the possibility that the earthly Jesus simply was not thought of as messiah. As against this the secret messiah in my opinion presupposes the future messiah and thereby shows itself to be the later view.

Thus if the secret messiahship really is an idea of the community which arose after the life of Jesus I cannot see how it should have arisen if everyone already knew and reported that Jesus had openly given himself out as messiah on earth. Traditions can assuredly be corrected and in the process even be transformed into their opposite but in such cases a particular motive is usually at work. But what would have prompted making the messiahship of Jesus a matter for secrecy

5. Even if already in Jesus' lifetime they might be supposed to have awakened thoughts about his messianic destiny, these were nevertheless evaluated messianically in another sense, later.

in contradiction to the original idea, in other words simply denying in retrospect Jesus' messianic claims on earth?

Let us try to picture this supposition. The explanation could probably be sought only in the idea that Jesus really revealed himself to the disciples alone. They received from him secret disclosures and thus to them too only the main thing was known, namely the messiahship. Accordingly it was withheld from the people. It would amount to the *indirect* self-disclosure of this idea; and it would then have to have attained an independent significance.

This development has little to be said for it. Let us suppose that the starting point, this dogmatic separation of the disciples and the people, is established. Let us also leave out of account that Mark, where he speaks about the concealment of the messiahship, certainly does not put the contrast between the disciples and the people all that prominently in the foreground. But it remains incomprehensible how *if it actually existed* the conviction should have been so lightly set aside or disregarded that Jesus came forward publicly with the messianic claim. It would not be immaterial that he already wished in his lifetime to be what the Resurrection showed him to be. Furthermore it is again important that the secret is supposed to be preserved until the Resurrection. In accordance with the supposition under discussion, which emphasises the concealment of the messiahship *from the people*, the meaning would have to be that Jesus as a result of the resurrection would now become manifest *to the people*. This idea is not found and assuredly this is not by accident. In itself it is inept; no early Christian thought[6] that the resurrection would bring a special revelation to the people. Thus if the resurrection is regarded as the terminus of the secret this tells against all the deductions we have taken into account. For the resurrection forms the terminus not because of the crowd but because now we have the event which is decisive for Jesus' messianic being itself.

Thus hardly any possibility remains other than the suggestion that the idea of the secret arose at a time when as yet there was no knowledge of any messianic claim on the part of Jesus on earth; which is as much as to say at a time when the resurrection was regarded as the beginning of the messiahship.

At that time, to be sure, the title messiah must really still have had a futuristic sense—reckoned from the life of Jesus onwards. Otherwise the secret messiahship could not have developed out of the future messiahship, which is in fact what happened. It did not merely arise *after* the future messiahship but out of it.

Naturally this would occur only once the original idea was already materially losing ground, that is, when already in the life of Jesus hints about his future standing, and characteristics and utterances about his messiahship were being found. For this is a further necessary presupposition which follows directly from the idea of the secret itself. The concealment includes the idea that there was something to conceal.

The carrying back of the messiahship into the life of Jesus was a very natural process, but Jesus himself must have awaited the moment of glorification. He must

---

6. Acts 10.40ff. says that God through the resurrection made Jesus manifest "not to all the people" but "to us who were chosen by God as witnesses".

have lived for it. In his activity too he must already have betrayed something of his coming greatness and thus in a certain sense have been the messiah. This above all was precisely the light in which his life had to be regarded if the experience of the resurrection really was the focal point of the ideas, and this it was. His previous life was only worthy of the Easter morning if the splendour of this day itself shone back upon it. But it was still plainly known that he had only later become the messiah. Hence if in contemplating his life one wished to say that he *was* the messiah there was just as much motivation for going back on this in part. But the tension between the two ideas was eased when it was asserted that he really was messiah already on earth and naturally also knew this but did not as yet say so and did not yet wish to be it; and even if his activities were entirely adapted to the awakening of belief in his messiahship nevertheless he did everything he could not to betray it for only the future was to be the bringer of revelation.

In this it may have been important that the resurrection was not regarded merely as God's establishment of his dignity but at the same time as the public intimation of this. It was the *phanerōsis* [disclosure] of *doxa* [glory] (Jn 21.1, 14; Mk 16.14). The *revelation* was then axiomatically preceded by the secret or concealment. But nothing certain can be said about this. However it will at all events be noted that the idea of secrecy and secret knowledge played a role in religion at that time in the most varied connections. It is doubly easy to understand how the idea we are discussing came to be formed in such a period.

To my mind this is the origin of the idea which we have shown to be present in Mark. It is, so to speak, a transitional idea and *it can be characterised as the after-effect of the view that the resurrection is the beginning of the messiahship at a time when the life of Jesus was already being filled materially with messianic content.* Or else it proceeded from the impulse to make the earthly life of Jesus messianic, but one inhibited by the older view, which was still potent.

Perhaps a difficulty will be found in the fact that Mark does not content himself with suggesting that Jesus kept quiet about his dignity, but rather reports that he diligently and strictly forbade talking about it, and expressly took steps to prevent its disclosure. However, even if one believed that Jesus did not wish that disclosure, there is nothing odd about this powerful expression of the idea. Moreover, in the idea of *mustērion* there usually lies the stimulation to discover the mystery. It may have been the original idea that Jesus was not known as messiah, and only the later idea that he *wanted* to be unknown.

What I have just been saying should be regarded as a tentative solution. I am not asserting that I have provided a proof to remove every obscurity. It may perhaps be reckoned that this whole field of ideas is illuminated too little by written sources for us to make any completely certain progress. Can we after all say no more than that we are making an overall survey of the possible modes of explanation? I do not underestimate the aptness of this question; but I do believe that my attempt has a good solid basis in the strong similarity of the two ideas that we have compared.

If my deductions are correct, then they are significant for the assessment of Jesus' historical life itself. If our view could only arise where nothing is known of an open messianic claim on Jesus' part, then we would seem to have in it *a positive historical testimony for the idea that Jesus actually did not give himself out as messiah*. But this question cannot be fully worked out here.

ALBERT SCHWEITZER

Albert Schweitzer (1875–1965) was a groundbreaking organist and musicologist, a physician and medical missionary to Africa, and one of the most important New Testament scholars of the twentieth century. His *Quest of the Historical Jesus: A Critical Study of Its Progress from Reimarus to Wrede* (1906) argues that Jesus can be adequately understood only within the context of ancient Jewish apocalyptic eschatology. His book today is often cited for its exposure of earlier scholarship on the historical Jesus as naïve, but even more compelling is the argument of its penultimate chapter, part of which is excerpted here. Formulated in response to Wrede's *Messianic Secret* (representative of the title's "thoroughgoing scepticism"), it provocatively posits that the Gospels' narrative framework is historical precisely insofar as it is incoherent: we cannot and must not rationalize the behavior of Jesus, who after all believed against reason that he was the Jewish Messiah that would usher in the imminent end of the age.

The Quest of the Historical Jesus[†]

Thoroughgoing Scepticism and Eschatology

The whole history of "Christianity" down to the present day, that is to say, the real inner history of it, is based on the delay of the Parousia, the non-occurrence of the Parousia, the abandonment of eschatology, the progress and completion of the "de-eschatologising" of religion which has been connected therewith. It should be noted that the non-fulfilment of Matt. x. 23 is the first postponement of the Parousia. We have therefore here the first significant date in the "history of Christianity"; it gives to the work of Jesus a new direction, otherwise inexplicable.

* * *

The prediction of the Parousia of the Son of Man is not the only one which remained unfulfilled. There is the prediction of sufferings which is connected with it. To put it more accurately, the prediction of the appearing of the Son of Man in Matt. x. 23 runs up into a prediction of sufferings, which, working up to a climax, forms the remainder of the discourse at the sending forth of the disciples. This prediction of sufferings has as little to do with objective history as the prediction of the Parousia. Consequently, none of the Lives of Jesus, which follow the lines of a natural psychology, from Weisse down to Oskar Holtzmann,

† From *The Quest of the Historical Jesus*, trans. W. Montgomery (New York: Macmillan, 1962), 360–64, 370–82, 398–403. All notes are Schweitzer's.

can make anything of it.[1] They either strike it out, or transfer it to the last "gloomy epoch" of the life of Jesus, regard it as an unintelligible anticipation, or put it down to the account of "primitive theology," which serves as a scrap-heap for everything for which they cannot find a place in the "historical life of Jesus."

In the texts it is quite evident that Jesus is not speaking of sufferings after His death, but of sufferings which will befall them as soon as they have gone forth from Him. The death of Jesus is not here pre-supposed, but only the Parousia of the Son of Man, and it is implied that this will occur just after these sufferings and bring them to a close. If the theology of the primitive Church had remoulded the tradition, as is always being asserted, it would have made Jesus give His followers directions for their conduct after His death. That we do not find anything of this kind is the best proof that there can be no question of a remoulding of the Life of Jesus by primitive theology. How easy it would have been for the Early Church to scatter here and there through the discourses of Jesus directions which were only to be applied after His death! But the simple fact is that it did not do so.

The sufferings of which the prospect is held out at the sending forth are doubly, trebly, nay four times over, unhistorical. In the first place—and this is the only point which modern historical theology has noticed—because there is not a shadow of a suggestion in the outward circumstances of anything which could form a natural occasion for such predictions of, and exhortations relating to, sufferings. In the second place—and this has been overlooked by modern theology because it had already declared them to be unhistorical in its own characteristic fashion, viz. by striking them out—because they were not fulfilled. In the third place—and this has not entered into the mind of modern theology at all— because these sayings were spoken in the closest connexion with the promise of the Parousia and are placed in the closest connexion with that event. In the fourth place, because the description of that which is to befall the disciples is quite without any basis in experience. A time of general dissension will begin, in which brothers will rise up against brothers, and fathers against sons and children against their parents to cause them to be put to death (Matt. x. 21). And the disciples "shall be hated of all men for His name's sake." Let them strive to hold out to the "end," that is, to the coming of the Son of Man, in order that they may be saved (Matt. x. 22).

But why should they suddenly be hated and persecuted for the name of Jesus, seeing that this name played no part whatever in their preaching? That is simply inconceivable. The relation of Jesus to the Son of Man, the fact, that is to say, that it is He who is to be manifested as Son of Man, must therefore in some way or other become known in the interval; not, however, through the disciples, but by some other means of revelation. A kind of supernatural illumination will suddenly make known all that Jesus has been keeping secret regarding the Kingdom

---

1. The most logical attitude in regard to it is Bousset's, who proposes to treat the mission and everything connected with it as a "confused and unintelligible" tradition [Bernhard Weiss, *The Life of Jesus* (1882), trans. John Walter Hope (Edinburgh, 1883); Oskar Holtzmann, *The Life of Jesus* (1901), trans. J. T. Bealby and Maurice A. Canney (London, 1904); Wilhelm Bousset, *Jesus* (1904), trans. Janet Penrose Trevelyan (New York, 1906)].

of God and His position in the Kingdom. This illumination will arise as suddenly and without preparation as the spirit of strife.

And as a matter of fact Jesus predicts to the disciples in the same discourse that to their own surprise a supernatural wisdom will suddenly speak from their lips, so that it will be not they but the Spirit of God who will answer the great ones of the earth. As the Spirit is for Jesus and early Christian theology something concrete which is to descend upon the elect among mankind only in consequence of a definite event—the outpouring of the Spirit which, according to the prophecy of Joel, should precede the day of judgment—Jesus must have anticipated that this would occur during the absence of the disciples, in the midst of the time of strife and confusion.

To put it differently; the whole of the discourse at the sending forth of the Twelve, taken in the clear sense of the words, is a prediction of the events of the "time of the end," events which are immediately at hand, in which the supernatural eschatological course of history will break through into the natural course. The expectation of sufferings is therefore doctrinal and unhistorical, as is, precisely in the same way, the expectation of the pouring forth of the Spirit uttered at the same time. The Parousia of the Son of Man is to be preceded according to the Messianic dogma by a time of strife and confusion—as it were, the birth-throes of the Messiah—and the outpouring of the Spirit. It should be noticed that according to Joel ii. and iii. the outpouring of the Spirit, along with the miraculous signs, forms the prelude to the judgment; and also, that in the same context, Joel iii. 13, the judgment is described as the harvest-day of God.[2] Here we have a remarkable parallel to the saying about the harvest in Matt. ix. 38, which forms the introduction to the discourse at the sending forth of the disciples.

There is only one point in which the predicted course of eschatological events is incomplete: the appearance of Elias is not mentioned.

Jesus could not prophesy to the disciples the Parousia of the Son of Man without pointing them, at the same time, to the pre-eschatological events which must

---

2. Cf. Rev. xiv. 15 and 16. The most remarkable parallel to the discourse at the sending forth of the disciples is offered by the Syriac Apocalypse of Baruch: "Behold, the days come, when the time of the world shall be ripe, and the harvest of the sowing of the good and of the evil shall come, when the Almighty shall bring upon the earth and upon its inhabitants and upon their rulers confusion of spirit and terror that makes the heart stand still; and they shall hate one another and provoke one another to war; and the despised shall have power over them of reputation, and the mean shall exalt themselves over them that are highly esteemed. And the many shall be at the mercy of the few . . . and all who shall be saved and shall escape the before-mentioned (dangers) . . . shall be given into the hands of my servant, the Messiah." (Cap. lxx. 2, 3, 9. Following the translation of E. Kautzsch.)

The connexion between the ideas of harvest and of judgment was therefore one of the stock features of the apocalyptic writings. And as the Apocalypse of Baruch dates from the period about A.D. 70, it may be assumed that this association of ideas was also current in the Jewish apocalyptic of the time of Jesus. Here is a basis for understanding the secret of the Kingdom of God in the parables of sowing and reaping historically and in accordance with the ideas of the time. What Jesus did was to make known to those who understood Him that the coming earthly harvest was the last, and was also the token of the coming heavenly harvest. The eschatological interpretation is immensely strengthened by these parallels.

first occur. He must open to them a part of the secret of the Kingdom of God, viz. the nearness of the harvest, that they might not be taken by surprise and caused to doubt by these events.

Thus this discourse is historical as a whole and down to the smallest detail precisely because, according to the view of modern theology, it must be judged unhistorical. It is, in fact, full of eschatological dogma. Jesus had no need to instruct the disciples as to what they were to teach; for they had only to utter a cry. But concerning the events which should supervene, it was necessary that He should give them information. Therefore the discourse does not consist of instruction, but of predictions of sufferings and of the Parousia.

That being so, we may judge with what right the modern psychological theology dismisses the great Matthaean discourses off-hand as mere "composite structures." Just let any one try to show how the Evangelist when he was racking his brains over the task of making a "discourse at the sending forth of the disciples," half by the method of piecing it together out of traditional sayings and "primitive theology," and half by inventing it, lighted on the curious idea of making Jesus speak entirely of inopportune and unpractical matters; and of then going on to provide the evidence that they never happened.

The foretelling of the sufferings that belong to the eschatological distress is part and parcel of the preaching of the approach of the Kingdom of God, it embodies the secret of the Kingdom. It is for that reason that the thought of suffering appears at the end of the Beatitudes and in the closing petition of the Lord's Prayer. For the πειρασμός [temptation] which is there in view is not an individual psychological temptation, but the general eschatological time of tribulation, from which God is besought to exempt those who pray so earnestly for the coming of the Kingdom, and not to expose them to that tribulation by way of putting them to the test.

There followed neither the sufferings, nor the outpouring of the Spirit, nor the Parousia of the Son of Man. The disciples returned safe and sound and full of a proud satisfaction; for one promise had been realised—the power which had been given them over the demons.

But from the moment when they rejoined Him, all His thoughts and efforts were devoted to getting rid of the people in order to be alone with them (Mark vi. 30–33). Previously, during their absence, He had, almost in open speech, taught the multitude concerning the Baptist, concerning that which was to precede the coming of the Kingdom, and concerning the judgment which should come upon the impenitent, even upon whole towns of them (Matt. xi. 20–24), because, in spite of the miracles which they had witnessed, they had not recognised the day of grace and diligently used it for repentance. At the same time He had rejoiced before them over all those whom God had enlightened that they might see what was going forward; and had called them to His side (Matt. xi. 25–30).

And now suddenly, the moment the disciples return, His one thought is to get away from the people. They, however, follow Him and overtake Him on the shores of the lake. He puts the Jordan between Himself and them by crossing to Bethsaida. They also come to Bethsaida. He returns to Capernaum. They do the same. Since in Galilee it is impossible for Him to be alone, and He absolutely must be alone, He "slips away" to the north. Once more modern theology was right: He really does flee; not, however, from hostile Scribes, but from the people, who dog His footsteps in order to await in His company the appearing of the Kingdom of God and of the Son of Man—to await it in vain.

* * *

The Baptist and Jesus are not, therefore, borne upon the current of a general eschatological movement. The period offers no events calculated to give an impulse to eschatological enthusiasm. They themselves set the times in motion by acting, by creating eschatological facts. It is this mighty creative force which constitutes the difficulty in grasping historically the eschatology of Jesus and the Baptist. Instead of literary artifice speaking out of a distant imaginary past, there now enter into the field of eschatology men, living, acting men. It was the only time when that ever happened in Jewish eschatology.

There is silence all around. The Baptist appears, and cries: "Repent, for the Kingdom of Heaven is at hand." Soon after that comes Jesus, and in the knowledge that He is the coming Son of Man lays hold of the wheel of the world to set it moving on that last revolution which is to bring all ordinary history to a close. It refuses to turn, and He throws Himself upon it. Then it does turn; and crushes Him. Instead of bringing in the eschatological conditions, He has destroyed them. The wheel rolls onward, and the mangled body of the one immeasurably great Man, who was strong enough to think of Himself as the spiritual ruler of mankind and to bend history to His purpose, is hanging upon it still. That is His victory and His reign.

These considerations regarding the distinctive character of the Synoptic eschatology were necessary in order to explain the significance of the sending forth of the disciples and the discourse which Jesus uttered upon that occasion. Jesus' purpose is to set in motion the eschatological development of history, to let loose the final woes, the confusion and strife, from which shall issue the Parousia, and so to introduce the supra-mundane phase of the eschatological drama. That is His task, for which He has authority here below. That is why He says in the same discourse, "Think not that I am come to send peace on the earth; I am not come to send peace, but a sword" (Matt. x. 34).

It was with a view to this initial movement that He chose His disciples. They are not His helpers in the work of teaching; we never see them in that capacity, and He did not prepare them to carry on that work after His death. The very fact that He chooses just twelve shows that it is a dogmatic idea which He has in mind. He chooses them as those who are destined to hurl the firebrand into the world, and are afterwards, as those who have been the comrades of the unrecognised Messiah, before He came to His Kingdom, to be His associates in ruling and judging it.[3]

---

3. Jesus promises them expressly that at the appearing of the Son of Man they shall sit upon twelve thrones, judging the twelve tribes of Israel (Matt. xix. 28). It is to their part in the judgment that belong also the authority to bind and to loose which He entrusts to them—first to Peter personally (Matt. xvi. 19) and afterwards to all the Twelve (Matt. xviii. 18)—in such a way, too, that their present decisions will be somehow or other binding at the Judgment. Or

But what was to be the fate of the future Son of Man during the Messianic woes of the last times? It appears as if it was appointed for Him to share the persecution and the suffering. He says that those who shall be saved must take their cross and follow Him (Matt. x. 38), that His followers must be willing to lose their lives for His sake, and that only those who in this time of terror confess their allegiance to Him, shall be confessed by Him before His heavenly Father (Matt. x. 32). Similarly, in the last of the Beatitudes, He had pronounced those blessed who were despised and persecuted for His sake (Matt. v. 11, 12). As the future bearer of the supreme rule He must go through the deepest humiliation. There is danger that His followers may doubt Him. Therefore, the last words of His message to the Baptist, just at the time when He had sent forth the Twelve, is, "Blessed is he whosoever shall not be offended in me" (Matt. xi. 6).

If He makes a point of familiarising others with the thought that in the time of tribulation they may even lose their lives, He must have recognised that this possibility was still more strongly present in His own case. It is possible that in the enigmatic saying about the disciples fasting "when the bridegroom is taken away from them" (Mark ii. 20), there is a hint of what Jesus expected. In that case suffering, death, and resurrection must have been closely united in the Messianic consciousness from the first. So much, however, is certain, viz. that the thought of suffering formed part, at the time of the sending forth the disciples, of the mystery of the Kingdom of God and of the Messiahship of Jesus, and that in the form that Jesus and all the elect were to be brought low in the $\pi\epsilon\iota\rho\alpha\sigma\mu\acute{o}\varsigma$ at the time of the death-struggle against the evil world-power which would arise against them; brought down, it might be, even to death. It mattered as little in His own case as in that of others whether at the time of the Parousia He should be one of those who should be metamorphosed, or one who had died and risen again. The question arises, however, how this self-consciousness of Jesus could remain concealed. It is true the miracles had nothing to do with the Messiahship, since no one expected the Messiah to come as an earthly miracle-worker in the present age. On the contrary, it would have been the greatest of miracles if any one had recognised the Messiah in an earthly miracle-worker. How far the cries of the demoniacs who addressed Him as Messiah were intelligible by the people must remain an open question. What is clear is that His Messiahship did not become known in this way even to His disciples.

does the "upon earth" refer only to the fact that the Messianic Last Judgment will be held on earth? "I give unto thee the Keys of the Kingdom of Heaven, and whatsoever thou shalt bind on earth shall be bound in heaven, and whatsoever thou shalt loose on earth shall be loosed in heaven" (Matt. xvi. 19). Why should these words not be historical? Is it because in the same context Jesus speaks of the "church" which He will found upon the Rock-disciple? But if one has once got a clear idea from Paul, 2 Clement, the Epistle to the Hebrews, and the Shepherd of Hermas, what the pre-existing "church" was which was to appear in the last times, it will no longer appear impossible that Jesus might have spoken of the church against which the gates of hell shall not prevail. Of course, if the passage is given an uneschatological reference to the Church as we know it, it loses all real meaning and becomes a treasure-trove to the Roman Catholic exegete, and a terror to the Protestant.

And yet in all His speech and action the Messianic consciousness shines forth. One might, indeed, speak of the acts of His Messianic consciousness. The Beatitudes, nay, the whole of the Sermon on the Mount, with the authoritative "I" for ever breaking through, bear witness to the high dignity which He ascribed to Himself. Did not this "I" set the people thinking?

What must they have thought when, at the close of this discourse, He spoke of people who, at the Day of Judgment, would call upon Him as Lord, and appeal to the works that they had done in His name, and who yet were destined to be rejected because He would not recognise them (Matt. vii. 21–23)?

What must they have thought of Him when He pronounced those blessed who were persecuted and despised for His sake (Matt. v. 11, 12)? By what authority did this man forgive sins (Mark ii. 5 ff.)?

In the discourse at the sending forth of the disciples the "I" is still more prominent. He demands of men that in the trials to come they shall confess Him, that they shall love Him more than father or mother, bear their cross after Him, and follow Him to the death, since it is only for such that He can entreat His Heavenly Father (Matt. x. 32 ff.). Admitting that the expression "Heavenly Father" contained no riddle for the listening disciples, since He had taught them to pray "Our Father which art in Heaven," we have still to ask who was He whose yea or nay should prevail with God to determine the fate of men at the Judgment?

And yet they found it hard, nay impossible, to think of Him as Messiah. They guessed Him to be a prophet; some thought of Elias, some of John the Baptist risen from the dead, as appears clearly from the answer of the disciples at Caesarea Philippi. The Messiah was a supernatural personality who was to appear in the last times, and who was not expected upon earth before that.

At this point a difficulty presents itself. How could Jesus be Elias for the people? Did they not hold John the Baptist to be Elias? Not in the least! Jesus was the first and the only person who attributed this office to him. And, moreover, He declares it to the people as something mysterious, difficult to understand—"If ye can receive it, this is Elias, which was for to come. He that hath ears to hear, let him hear" (Matt. xi. 14, 15). In making this revelation He is communicating to them a piece of supernatural knowledge, opening up a part of the mystery of the Kingdom of God. Therefore He uses the same formula of emphasis as when making known in parables the mystery of the Kingdom of God (Mark iv.).

The disciples were not with Him at this time, and therefore did not learn what was the rôle of John the Baptist. When a little later, in descending from the mount of transfiguration He predicted to the three who formed the inner circle of His followers the resurrection of the Son of Man, they came to Him with difficulties about the rising from the dead—how could this be possible when, according to the Pharisees and Scribes, Elias must first come?—whereupon Jesus explains to them that the preacher of repentance whom Herod had put to death had been Elias (Mark ix. 11–13).

Why did not the people take the Baptist to be Elias? In the first place no doubt because he did not describe himself as such. In the next place because he did no miracle! He was only a natural man without any evidence of supernatural power, only a prophet. In the third place, and that was the decisive point, he had himself pointed forward to the coming of Elias. He who was to come, he whom he preached, was not the Messiah, but Elias.

He describes him, not as a supernatural personality, not as a judge, not as one who will be manifested at the unveiling of the heavenly world, but as one who in his work shall resemble himself, only much greater—one who, like himself, baptizes, though with the Holy Spirit. Had it ever been represented as the work of the Messiah to baptize?

Before the Last Judgment, so it was inferred from Joel, the great outpouring of the Spirit was to take place; before the Last Judgment, so taught Malachi, Elias was to come. Until these events had occurred the manifestation of the Son of Man was not to be looked for. Men's thoughts were fixed, therefore, not on the Messiah, but upon Elias and the outpouring of the Spirit. The Baptist in his preaching combines both ideas, and predicts the coming of the Great One who shall "baptize with the Holy Spirit," *i.e.* who brings about the outpouring of the Spirit. His own preaching was only designed to secure that at His coming that Great One should find a community sanctified and prepared to receive the Spirit.

When he heard in the prison of one who did great wonders and signs, he desired to learn with certainty whether this was "he who was to come." If this question is taken as referring to the Messiahship the whole narrative loses its meaning, and it upsets the theory of the Messianic secret, since in this case at least one person had become aware, independently, of the office which belonged to Jesus, not to mention all the ineptitudes involved in making the Baptist here speak in doubt and confusion. Moreover, on this false interpretation of the question the point of Jesus' discourse is lost, for in this case it is not clear why He says to the people afterwards, "If ye can receive it, John himself is Elias." This revelation presupposes that Jesus and the people, who had heard the question which had been addressed to Him, also gave it its only natural meaning, referring it to Jesus as the bearer of the office of Elias.

That even the first Evangelist gives the episode a Messianic setting by introducing it with the words "When John heard in the prison of the works of the Christ" does not alter the facts of the body of the narrative. The sequel directly contradicts the introduction. And this interpretation fully explains the evasive answer of Jesus, in which exegesis has always recognised a certain reserve without ever being able to make it intelligible why Jesus did not simply send him the message, "Yes, I am he"—whereto, however, according to modern theology, He would have needed to add, "but another kind of Messiah from him whom you expect."

The fact was, the Baptist had put Him in an extremely difficult position. He could not answer that He was Elias if He held Himself to be the Messiah; on the other hand He could not, and would not, disclose to him, and still less to the messengers and the listening multitude, the secret of His Messiahship. Therefore He sends this obscure message, which only contains a confirmation of the facts which John had already heard and closes with a warning, come what may, not to be offended in Him. Of this the Baptist was to make what he could.

It mattered, in fact, little how John understood the message. The time was much more advanced than he supposed; the hammer of the world's clock had risen to strike the last hour. All that he needed to know was that he had no cause to doubt.

In revealing to the people the true office of the Baptist, Jesus unveiled to them almost the whole mystery of the Kingdom of God, and nearly disclosed the secret of His Messiahship. For if Elias was already present, was not the coming of the Kingdom close at hand? And if John was Elias, who was Jesus? . . . There could only be one answer: the Messiah. But this seemed impossible, because Messiah was expected as a supernatural personality. The eulogy on the Baptist is, historically regarded, identical in content with the prediction of the Parousia in the discourse at the sending forth of the disciples. For after the coming of Elias there must follow immediately the judgment and the other events belonging to the last time. Now we can understand why in the enumeration of the events of the last time in the discourse to the Twelve the coming of Elias is not mentioned.

We see here, too, how, in the thought of Jesus, Messianic doctrine forces its way into history and simply abolishes the historic aspect of the events. The Baptist had not held himself to be Elias, the people had not thought of attributing this office to him; the description of Elias did not fit him at all, since he had done none of those things which Elias was to do: and yet Jesus makes him Elias, simply because He expected His own manifestation as Son of Man, and before that it was necessary that Elias must first have come. And even when John was dead Jesus still told the disciples that in him Elias had come, although the death of Elias was not contemplated in the eschatological doctrine, and was in fact unthinkable. But Jesus must somehow drag or force the eschatological events into the framework of the actual occurrences.

Thus the conception of the "dogmatic element" in the narrative widens in an unsuspected fashion. And even what before seemed natural becomes on a closer examination doctrinal. The Baptist is made into Elias solely by the force of Jesus' Messianic consciousness.

A short time afterwards, immediately upon the return of the disciples, He spoke and acted before their eyes in a way which presupposed the Messianic secret. The people had been dogging his steps; at a lonely spot on the shores of the lake they surrounded Him, and He "taught them about many things" (Mark vi. 30–34). The day was drawing to a close, but they held closely to Him without troubling about food. In the evening, before sending them away, He fed them.

Weisse, long ago, had constantly emphasised the fact that the feeding of the multitude was one of the greatest historical problems, because this narrative, like that of the transfiguration, is very firmly riveted to its historical setting and, therefore, imperatively demands explanation. How is the historical element in it to be got at? Certainly not by seeking to explain the apparently miraculous in it on natural lines, by representing that at the bidding of Jesus people brought out the baskets of provisions which they had been concealing, and, thus importing into the tradition a natural fact which, so far from being hinted at in the narrative, is actually excluded by it.

Our solution is that the whole is historical, except the closing remark that they were all filled. Jesus distributed the provisions which He and His disciples had with them among the multitude so that each received a very little, after He had first offered thanks. The significance lies in the giving of thanks and in the fact that they had received from Him consecrated food. Because He is the future Messiah, this meal becomes without their knowledge the Messianic feast. With the morsel of bread which He gives His disciples to distribute to the people He consecrates them as partakers in the coming Messianic feast, and gives them the guarantee that they, who had shared His table in the time of His obscurity, would also share it in the time of His glory. In the prayer He gave thanks not only for the food, but also for the coming Kingdom and all its blessings. It is the counterpart of the Lord's prayer, where He so strangely inserts the petition for daily bread between the petitions for the coming of the Kingdom and for deliverance from the πειρασμός.

The feeding of the multitude was more than a love-feast, a fellowship-meal. It was from the point of view of Jesus a sacrament of salvation.

We never realise sufficiently that in a period when the judgment and the glory were expected as close at hand, one thought arising out of this expectation must have acquired special prominence—how, namely, in the present time a man could obtain a guarantee of coming scatheless through the judgment, of being saved and received into the Kingdom, of being signed and sealed for deliverance amid the coming trial, as the Chosen People in Egypt had a sign revealed to them from God by means of which they might be manifest as those who were to be spared. But once we do realise this, we can understand why the thought of signing and sealing runs through the whole of the apocalyptic literature. It is found as early as the ninth chapter of Ezekiel. There, God is making preparation for judgment. The day of visitation of the city is at hand. But first the Lord calls unto "the man clothed with linen who had the writer's ink-horn by his side" and said unto him, "Go through the midst of the city, through the midst of Jerusalem, and set a mark upon the foreheads of the men that sigh and that cry for all the abominations that be done in the midst thereof." Only after that does He give command to those who are charged with the judgment to begin, adding, "But come not near any man upon whom is the mark" (Ezek. ix. 4 and 6).

In the fifteenth of the Psalms of Solomon, the last eschatological writing before the movement initiated by the Baptist, it is expressly said in the description of the judgment that "the saints of God bear a sign upon them which saves them."

In the Pauline theology very striking prominence is given to the thought of being sealed unto salvation. The apostle is conscious of bearing about with him in his body "the marks" of Jesus (Gal. vi. 17), the "dying" of Jesus (2 Cor. iv. 10). This sign is received in baptism, since it is a baptism "into the death of Christ"; in this act the recipient is in a certain sense really buried with Him, and thenceforth walks among men as one who belongs, even here below, to risen humanity (Rom. vi. 1 ff.). Baptism is the seal, the earnest of the spirit, the pledge of that which is to come (2 Cor. i. 22; Eph. i. 13, 14, iv. 30).

This conception of baptism as a "salvation" in view of that which was to come goes down through the whole of ancient theology. Its preaching might really be summed up in the words, "Keep your baptism holy and without blemish."

In the Shepherd of Hermas even the spirits of the men of the past must receive "the seal, which is the water" in order that they may "bear the name of God upon them." That is why the tower is built over the water, and the stones which are brought up out of the deep are rolled through the water (Vis. iii. and Sim. ix. 16).

In the Apocalypse of John the thought of the sealing stands prominently in the foreground. The locusts receive power to hurt those only who have not the seal of God on their foreheads (Rev. ix. 4, 5). The beast (Rev. xiii. 16 ff.) compels men to bear his mark; only those who will not accept it are to reign with Christ (Rev. xx. 4). The chosen hundred and forty-four thousand bear the name of God and the name of the Lamb upon their foreheads (Rev. xiv. 1).

"Assurance of salvation" in a time of eschatological expectation demanded some kind of security for the future of which the earnest could be possessed in the present. And with this the pre-destinarian thought of election was in complete accord. If we find the thought of being sealed unto salvation previously in the Psalms of Solomon, and subsequently in the same signification in Paul, in the Apocalypse of John, and down to the Shepherd of Hermas, it may be assumed in advance that it will be found in some form or other in the so strongly eschatological teaching of Jesus and the Baptist.

It may be said, indeed, to dominate completely the eschatological preaching of the Baptist, for this preaching does not confine itself to the declaration of the nearness of the Kingdom, and the demand for repentance, but leads up to an act to which it gives a special reference in relation to the forgiveness of sins and the outpouring of the spirit. It is a mistake to regard baptism with water as a "symbolic act" in the modern sense, and make the Baptist decry his own wares by saying, "I baptize only with water, but the other can baptize with the Holy Spirit." He is not contrasting the two baptisms, but connecting them—he who is baptized by him has the certainty that he will share in the outpouring of the Spirit which shall precede the judgment, and at the judgment shall receive forgiveness of sins, as one who is signed with the mark of repentance. The object of being baptized by him is to secure baptism with the Spirit later. The forgiveness of sins associated with baptism is proleptic, it is to be realised at the judgment. The Baptist himself did not forgive sin.[4] If he had done so, how could such offence have been taken when Jesus claimed for Himself the right to forgive sins in the present (Mark ii. 10)?

The baptism of John was therefore an eschatological sacrament pointing forward to the pouring forth of the spirit and to the judgment, a provision for "salvation." Hence the wrath of the Baptist when he saw Pharisees and Sadducees crowding to his baptism: "Ye generation of vipers, who hath warned you to flee from the wrath to come? Bring forth now fruits meet for repentance" (Matt. iii. 7, 8). By the reception of baptism, that is, they are saved from the judgment.

4. That the baptism of John was essentially an act which gave a claim to something future may be seen from the fact that Jesus speaks of His sufferings and death as a special baptism, and asks the sons of Zebedee whether they are willing, for the sake of gaining the thrones on His right hand and His left, to undergo this baptism. If the baptism of John had had no real sacramental significance it would be unintelligible that Jesus should use this metaphor.

As a cleansing unto salvation it is a divine institution, a revealed means of grace. That is why the question of Jesus, whether the baptism of John was from heaven or from men, placed the Scribes at Jerusalem in so awkward a dilemma (Mark xi. 30).

The authority of Jesus, however, goes farther than that of the Baptist. As the Messiah who is to come He can give even here below to those who gather about Him a right to partake in the Messianic feast, by this distribution of food to them; only, they do not know what is happening to them and He cannot solve the riddle for them. The supper at the Lake of Gennesareth was a veiled eschatological sacrament. Neither the disciples nor the multitude understood what was happening, since they did not know who He was who thus made them His guests.[5] This meal must have been transformed by tradition into a miracle, a result which may have been in part due to the references to the wonders of the Messianic feast which were doubtless contained in the prayers, not to speak of the eschatological enthusiasm which then prevailed universally. Did not the disciples believe that on the same evening, when they had been commanded to take Jesus into their ship at the mouth of the Jordan, to which point He had walked along the shore— did they not believe that they saw Him come walking towards them upon the waves of the sea? The impulse to the introduction of the miraculous into the narrative came from the unintelligible element with which the men who surrounded Jesus were at this time confronted.

The Last Supper at Jerusalem had the same sacramental significance as that at the lake. Towards the end of the meal Jesus, after giving thanks, distributes the bread and wine. This had as little to do with the satisfaction of hunger as the distribution to the Galilaean believers. The act of Jesus is an end in itself, and

---

5. The thought of the Messianic feast is found in Isaiah lv, 1 ff. and lxv. 12 ff. It is very strongly marked in Isa. xxv. 6–8, a passage which perhaps dates from the time of Alexander the Great.

In Enoch xxiv. and xxv. the conception of the Messianic feast is connected with that of the tree of life which shall offer its fruits to the elect upon the mountain of the King. Similarly in the Testament of Levi, cap. xviii. 11.

The decisive passage is in Enoch lxii. 14. After the Parousia of the Son of Man, and after the Judgment, the elect who have been saved "shall eat with the Son of Man, shall sit down and rise up with Him to all eternity."

Jesus' references to the Messianic feast are therefore not merely images, but point to a reality. In Matt. viii. 11 and 12 He prophesies that many shall come from the East and from the West to sit at meat with Abraham, Isaac, and Jacob. In Matt. xxii. 1–14 the Messianic feast is pictured as a royal marriage, in Matt. xxv. 1–13 as a marriage feast.

The Apocalypse is dominated by the thought of the feast in all its forms. In Rev. ii. 7 it appears in connexion with the thought of the tree of life; in ii. 17 it is pictured as a feeding with manna; in iii. 21 it is the feast which the Lord will celebrate with His followers; in vii. 16, 17 there is an allusion to the Lamb who shall feed His own so that they shall no more hunger or thirst; chapter xix. describes the marriage feast of the Lamb.

The Messianic feast therefore played a dominant part in the conception of blessedness from Enoch to the Apocalypse of John. From this we can estimate what sacramental significance a guarantee of taking part in that feast must have had. The meaning of the celebration was obvious in itself, and was made manifest in the conduct of it. The sacramental effect was wholly independent of the apprehension and comprehension of the recipient. Therefore, in this also the meal at the lake-side was a true sacrament.

the significance of the celebration consists in the fact that it is He Himself who makes the distribution. In Jerusalem, however, they understood what was meant, and He explained it to them explicitly by telling them that He would drink no more of the fruit of the vine until He drank it new in the Kingdom of God. The mysterious images which He used at the time of the distribution concerning the atoning significance of His death do not touch the essence of the celebration, they are only discourses accompanying it.

On this interpretation, therefore, we may think of Baptism and the Lord's Supper as from the first eschatological sacraments in the eschatological movement which later detached itself from Judaism under the name of Christianity. That explains why we find them both in Paul and in the earliest theology as sacramental acts, not as symbolic ceremonies, and find them dominating the whole Christian doctrine. Apart from the assumption of the eschatological sacraments, we can only make the history of dogma begin with a "fall" from the earlier purer theology into the sacramental magical, without being able to adduce a single syllable in support of the idea that after the death of Jesus Baptism and the Lord's Supper existed even for an hour as symbolical actions—Paul, indeed, makes this supposition wholly impossible.

In any case the adoption of the baptism of John in Christian practice cannot be explained except on the assumption that it was the sacrament of the eschatological community, a revealed means of securing "salvation" which was not altered in the slightest by the Messiahship of Jesus. How else could we explain the fact that baptism, without any commandment of Jesus, and without Jesus' ever having baptized, was taken over, as a matter of course, into Christianity, and was given a special reference to the receiving of the Spirit?

It is no use proposing to explain it as having been instituted as a symbolical repetition of the baptism of Jesus, thought of as "an anointing to the Messiahship." There is not a single passage in ancient theology to support such a theory. And we may point also to the fact that Paul never refers to the baptism of Jesus in explaining the character of Christian baptism, never, in fact, makes any distinct reference to it. And how could baptism, if it had been a symbolical repetition of the baptism of Jesus, ever have acquired this magic-sacramental sense of "salvation"?

Nothing shows more clearly than the dual character of ancient baptism, which makes it the guarantee both of the reception of the Spirit and of deliverance from the judgment, that it is nothing else than the eschatological baptism of John with a single difference. Baptism with water and baptism with the Spirit are now connected not only logically, but also in point of time, seeing that since the day of Pentecost the period of the outpouring of the Spirit is present. The two portions of the eschatological sacrament which in the Baptist's preaching were distinguished in point of time—because he did not expect the outpouring of the Spirit until some future period—are now brought together, since one eschatological condition—the baptism with the Spirit—is now present. The "Christianising" of baptism consisted in this and in nothing else; though Paul carried it a stage farther when he formed the conception of baptism as a mystic partaking in the death and resurrection of Jesus.

Thus the thoroughgoing eschatological interpretation of the Life of Jesus puts into the hands of those who are reconstructing the history of dogma in the earliest times an explanation of the conception of the sacraments, of which they had been able hitherto only to note the presence as an x of which the origin was undiscoverable, and for which they possessed no equation by which it could be evaluated. If Christianity as the religion of historically revealed mysteries was able to lay hold upon Hellenism and overcome it, the reason of this was that it was already in its purely eschatological beginnings a religion of sacraments, a religion of eschatological sacraments, since Jesus had recognised a Divine institution in the baptism of John, and had Himself performed a sacramental action in the distribution of food at the Lake of Gennesareth and at the Last Supper.

This being so, the feeding of the multitude also belongs to the dogmatic element in the history. But no one had previously recognised it as what it really was, an indirect disclosure of the Messianic secret, just as no one had understood the full significance of Jesus' description of the Baptist as Elias.

* * *

Results

Those who are fond of talking about negative theology can find their account here. There is nothing more negative than the result of the critical study of the Life of Jesus.

The Jesus of Nazareth who came forward publicly as the Messiah, who preached the ethic of the Kingdom of God, who founded the Kingdom of Heaven upon earth, and died to give His work its final consecration, never had any existence. He is a figure designed by rationalism, endowed with life by liberalism, and clothed by modern theology in an historical garb.

This image has not been destroyed from without, it has fallen to pieces, cleft and disintegrated by the concrete historical problems which came to the surface one after another, and in spite of all the artifice, art, artificiality, and violence which was applied to them, refused to be planed down to fit the design on which the Jesus of the theology of the last hundred and thirty years had been constructed, and were no sooner covered over than they appeared again in a new form. * * *

Whatever the ultimate solution may be, the historical Jesus of whom the criticism of the future, taking as its starting-point the problems which have been recognised and admitted, will draw the portrait, can never render modern theology the services which it claimed from its own half-historical, half-modern, Jesus. He will be a Jesus, who was Messiah, and lived as such, either on the ground of a literary fiction of the earliest Evangelist, or on the ground of a purely eschatological Messianic conception.

In either case, He will not be a Jesus Christ to whom the religion of the present can ascribe, according to its long-cherished custom, its own thoughts and ideas, as it did with the Jesus of its own making. Nor will He be a figure which can be made by a popular historical treatment so sympathetic and universally intelligible to the multitude. The historical Jesus will be to our time a stranger and an enigma.

The study of the Life of Jesus has had a curious history. It set out in quest of the historical Jesus, believing that when it had found Him it could bring Him straight into our time as a Teacher and Saviour. It loosed the bands by which He had been riveted for centuries to the stony rocks of ecclesiastical doctrine, and rejoiced to see life and movement coming into the figure once more, and the historical Jesus advancing, as it seemed, to meet it. But He does not stay; He passes by our time and returns to His own. What surprised and dismayed the theology of the last forty years was that, despite all forced and arbitrary interpretations, it could not keep Him in our time, but had to let Him go. He returned to His own time, not owing to the application of any historical ingenuity, but by the same inevitable necessity by which the liberated pendulum returns to its original position.

The historical foundation of Christianity as built up by rationalistic, by liberal, and by modern theology no longer exists; but that does not mean that Christianity has lost its historical foundation. The work which historical theology thought itself bound to carry out, and which fell to pieces just as it was nearing completion, was only the brick facing of the real immovable historical foundation which is independent of any historical comfirmation or justification.

Jesus means something to our world because a mighty spiritual force streams forth from Him and flows through our time also. This fact can neither be shaken nor confirmed by any historical discovery. It is the solid foundation of Christianity.

The mistake was to suppose that Jesus could come to mean more to our time by entering into it as a man like ourselves. That is not possible. First because such a Jesus never existed. Secondly because, although historical knowledge can no doubt introduce greater clearness into an existing spiritual life, it cannot call spiritual life into existence. History can destroy the present; it can reconcile the present with the past; can even to a certain extent transport the present into the past; but to contribute to the making of the present is not given unto it.

*　*　*

We modern theologians are too proud of our historical method, too proud of our historical Jesus, too confident in our belief in the spiritual gains which our historical theology can bring to the world. The thought that we could build up by the increase of historical knowledge a new and vigorous Christianity and set free new spiritual forces, rules us like a fixed idea, and prevents us from seeing that the task which we have grappled with and in some measure discharged is only one of the intellectual preliminaries of the great religious task. We thought that it was for us to lead our time by a roundabout way through the historical Jesus, as we understood Him, in order to bring it to the Jesus who is a spiritual power in the present. This roundabout way has now been closed by genuine history.

There was a danger of our thrusting ourselves between men and the Gospels, and refusing to leave the individual man alone with the sayings of Jesus.

There was a danger that we should offer them a Jesus who was too small, because we had forced Him into conformity with our human standards and human psychology. To see that, one need only read the Lives of Jesus written since the [eighteen-]sixties, and notice what they have made of the great imperious sayings of the Lord, how they have weakened down His imperative world-contemning demands upon individuals, that He might not come into conflict with our ethical ideals, and might tune His denial of the world to our acceptance of it. Many of the greatest sayings are found lying in a corner like explosive shells from which the charges have been removed. No small portion of elemental religious power needed to be drawn off from His sayings to prevent them from conflicting with our system of religious world-acceptance. We have made Jesus hold another language with our time from that which He really held.

In the process we ourselves have been enfeebled, and have robbed our own thoughts of their vigour in order to project them back into history and make them speak to us out of the past. It is nothing less than a misfortune for modern theology that it mixes history with everything and ends by being proud of the skill with which it finds its own thoughts—even to its beggarly pseudo-metaphysic with which it has banished genuine speculative metaphysic from the sphere of religion—in Jesus, and represents Him as expressing them. It had almost deserved the reproach: "he who putteth his hand to the plough, and looketh back, is not fit for the Kingdom of God" [Luke 9:62].

It was no small matter, therefore, that in the course of the critical study of the Life of Jesus, after a resistance lasting for two generations, during which first one expedient was tried and then another, theology was forced by genuine history to begin to doubt the artificial history with which it had thought to give new life to our Christianity, and to yield to the facts, which, as Wrede strikingly said, are sometimes the most radical critics of all. History will force it to find a way to transcend history, and to fight for the lordship and rule of Jesus over this world with weapons tempered in a different forge.

We are experiencing what Paul experienced. In the very moment when we were coming nearer to the historical Jesus than men had ever come before, and were already stretching out our hands to draw Him into our own time, we have been obliged to give up the attempt and acknowledge our failure in that paradoxical saying: "If we have known Christ after the flesh yet henceforth know we Him no more" [2 Cor 5:16]. And further we must be prepared to find that the historical knowledge of the personality and life of Jesus will not be a help, but perhaps even an offence to religion.

But the truth is, it is not Jesus as historically known, but Jesus as spiritually arisen within men, who is significant for our time and can help it. Not the historical Jesus, but the spirit which goes forth from Him and in the spirits of men strives for new influence and rule, is that which overcomes the world.

It is not given to history to disengage that which is abiding and eternal in the being of Jesus from the historical forms in which it worked itself out, and to introduce it into our world as a living influence. It has toiled in vain at this undertaking. As a water-plant is beautiful so long as it is growing in the water, but once torn from its roots, withers and becomes unrecognisable, so it is with the historical Jesus when He is wrenched loose from the soil of eschatology, and the attempt is made to conceive Him "historically" as a Being not subject to temporal conditions. The abiding and eternal in Jesus is absolutely independent of historical knowledge and can only be understood by contact with His spirit which is still at work in the world. In proportion as we have the Spirit of Jesus we have the true knowledge of Jesus.

Jesus as a concrete historical personality remains a stranger to our time, but His spirit, which lies hidden in His words, is known in simplicity, and its influence is direct. Every saying contains in its own way the whole Jesus. The very strangeness and unconditionedness in which He stands before us makes it easier for individuals to find their own personal standpoint in regard to Him.

Men feared that to admit the claims of eschatology would abolish the significance of His words for our time; and hence there was a feverish eagerness to discover in them any elements that might be considered not eschatologically conditioned. When any sayings were found of which the wording did not absolutely imply an eschatological connexion there was a great jubilation—these at least had been saved uninjured from the coming *débâcle*.

But in reality that which is eternal in the words of Jesus is due to the very fact that they are based on an eschatological worldview, and contain the expression of a mind for which the contemporary world with its historical and social circumstances no longer had any existence. They are appropriate, therefore, to any world, for in every world they raise the man who dares to meet their challenge, and does not turn and twist them into meaninglessness, above his world and his time, making him inwardly free, so that he is fitted to be, in his own world and in his own time, a simple channel of the power of Jesus.

Modern Lives of Jesus are too general in their scope. They aim at influencing, by giving a complete impression of the life of Jesus, a whole community. But the historical Jesus, as He is depicted in the Gospels, influenced individuals by the individual word. They understood Him so far as it was necessary for them to understand, without forming any conception of His life as a whole, since this in its ultimate aims remained a mystery even for the disciples.

Because it is thus preoccupied with the general, the universal, modern theology is determined to find its world-accepting ethic in the teaching of Jesus. Therein lies its weakness. The world affirms itself automatically; the modern spirit cannot but affirm it. But why on that account abolish the conflict between modern life, with the world-affirming spirit which inspires it as a whole, and the world-negating spirit of Jesus? Why spare the spirit of the individual man its appointed task of fighting its way through the world-negation of Jesus, of contending with Him at every step over the value of material and intellectual goods—a conflict in which it may never rest? For the general, for the institutions of society, the rule is: affirmation of the world, in conscious opposition to the view of Jesus, on the ground that the world has affirmed itself! This general affirmation of the world, however, if it is to be Christian, must in the individual spirit be Christianised and transfigured by the personal rejection of the world which is preached in the sayings of Jesus. It is only by means of the tension thus set up that religious energy can be communicated to our time. There was a danger that modern theology, for the sake of peace, would deny the world-negation in the sayings of Jesus, with which Protestantism was out of sympathy, and thus unstring the bow and make Protestantism a mere sociological instead of a religious force. There was perhaps also a danger of inward insincerity, in the fact that it refused to admit to itself and others that it maintained its affirmation of the world in opposition to the sayings of Jesus, simply because it could not do otherwise.

For that reason it is a good thing that the true historical Jesus should overthrow the modern Jesus, should rise up against the modern spirit and send upon earth, not peace, but a sword. He was not teacher, not a casuist; He was an imperious ruler. It was because He was so in His inmost being that He could think of Himself as the Son of Man. That was only the temporally conditioned expression of the fact that He was an authoritative ruler. The names in which men expressed their recognition of Him as such, Messiah, Son of Man, Son of God, have become for us historical parables. We can find no designation which expresses what He is for us.

He comes to us as One unknown, without a name, as of old, by the lake-side, He came to those men who knew Him not. He speaks to us the same word: "Follow thou me!" and sets us to the tasks which He has to fulfil for our time. He commands. And to those who obey Him, whether they be wise or simple, He will reveal Himself in the toils, the conflicts, the sufferings which they shall pass through in His fellowship, and, as an ineffable mystery, they shall learn in their own experience Who He is.

RUDOLF BULTMANN

Rudolf Bultmann (1884–1976), probably the most important New Testament scholar of the twentieth century, produced important work on the synoptic tradition, Paul, and the Gospel of John. Like Strauss, he found the category of myth especially useful for understanding the New Testament; but writing in the shadow of Schweitzer's insistence on the New Testament's unsettlingly irrational apocalyptic-eschatological outlook, Bultmann came to believe that its continuing relevance demanded its demythologization, and he was convinced that the New Testament's most profound theological writers (Paul and the author of the Fourth Gospel) had already set this process in motion. In the following excerpt from his two-volume *Theology of the New Testament* (1948–52), Bultmann suggests that the Fourth Gospel demythologizes at the same time traditional Jewish eschatology and a hypothetical gnostic Redeemer myth (in which a representative of the transcendent God arrives on earth to remind the spiritual of their divine nature and heavenly destiny). The result is a universal proclamation with urgent existential import.

The "Krisis" of the World: [The Christology of John's Gospel]†

§ 45. *The Sending of the Son*

1. *Within this world of death life appeared* (I Jn. 1:2), into the world of darkness came the light (1:5; 3:19)—it came by *the coming of the Son of God* into the world. Jesus is he. Though he came after the Baptist in time, he nevertheless was prior to him (1:15, 30). He even claims that he was before Abraham (8:58); yes, even more: that he was before the foundation of the world (17:5, 24). It is he in whom the Christian Congregation believes as the one "who is from the beginning" (I Jn. 2:13f.). In him the "Word" which in the beginning was with God became flesh (1:1f., 14) and came into its (his) own property—i.e. into the world, which belongs to it, and hence to him, as the one through whom it came into being (1:9–11).

To what extent are such statements, which speak of Jesus in mythological form as the pre-existent Son of God who became man, to be understood in the actual mythological sense? That can only be answered in the course of more detailed interpretation. At any rate, the beginning of the first Epistle, intending to say the same thing as the prologue to the Gospel, significantly speaks of the *life* that in the beginning was with the Father, and has audibly, visibly, and tangibly appeared (in Jesus, of course—that goes without saying). It speaks of this *life* as "*that which* was in the beginning," as a thing and not as a person (I Jn. 1:1f.). At any rate, it is clear that in the person of Jesus the transcendent divine reality became audible, visible, and tangible in the realm of the earthly world. Jesus is "the Christ, the Son of God, he who is coming into the world" (11:27).

In all that he is, says, and does, he is not to be understood as a figure of this world, but his appearing in the world is to be conceived as an *embassage from without, an arrival from elsewhere.* Jesus is he "whom the Father consecrated and sent into the world" (10:36). That the Father sent him is testified by his works (5:16); this (his sending) is what is to be believed (6:29; 11:42; 17:8) or acknowledged (17:25); for eternal life is this: to "know thee the only true God, and Jesus Christ whom thou hast sent" (17:3). So God's name accordingly is: "the Father who sent me" (six times) or simply: "(he) who sent me" (nineteen times). (Both expressions, as crystallized participial phrases, might better be translated with nouns: "my Commissioner, the Father," and "my Commissioner.") And so the congregation confesses: "And we have seen and testify that the Father has sent his Son as the Savior of the world" (I Jn. 4:14). The counterpart of his sending is his "coming" or his "having come." The sending and the coming may, of course, be combined in the same statement. Being the envoy, he did not come on his own initiative: "for I went forth from God and have come (hither). For I am not here (ἐλήλυθα, perfect) of my own accord, but he sent me" (8:42, tr.; *cf.* 7:28f.; 17:8). Repeated time and again are statements that he "came into the world" (3:19; 9:39; 11:27; 12:46;

† From *Theology of the New Testament*, trans. Kendrick Grobel, vol. 2 (New York: Charles Scribner's Sons, 1955), 33–49, 56–69. Except as indicated, all notes are Bultmann's.

16:28; 18:37), or that he "came from the Father (or God)"—(8:42; 13:3; 16:27f., 30; 17:8), or simply that he "has come" (5:43; 7:28; 8:14; 10:10; 12:47; 15:22). This is just the thing that his own have come to know and to acknowledge (17:8) and is what faith confesses (11:27), while "the Jews" know not whence he comes (8:14) or have a false notion about his origin (7:28f.), and the false teachers deny that Jesus Christ has come "in the flesh" (I Jn. 4:2; II Jn. 7). In more vividly mythological formulation it is also possible to say that he came down from heaven (3:13; 6:33, 38, 41f.).

His coming is the Revelation of the divine reality in the world; this aspect of his coming is emphasized by *the correspondence of his departure to his coming.* By his coming, that is, he does not become a phenomenon of the world, a figure within world-history. He is here, so to speak, only as a guest; the hour is coming when he must depart (13:1; *cf.* 1:14 "he tented among us" tr.). He came and will go again (8:14):

> "I came from the Father and have come into the world;
> Again, I am leaving the world and going to the Father."

(16:28; *cf.* 13:3; 14:12, 28; 16:5, 10, 17). The time of his sojourn on earth is but short, and when he is gone he will be sought in vain (7:33; 8:21; *cf.* 13:33). As he came down from heaven—mythological language again—he will ascend again thither where he previously was (6:62; *cf.* 3:13). He will be "elevated" (3:14; 12:32, 34; *cf.* 8:28); he will be "glorified" (12:23; 13:31f.; 17:1; *cf.* 7:39; 12:16), glorified with the "glory" that he had had in pre-existence with the Father (17:5, 24). His coming and his going belong together as a unit, the unity of his activity as Revealer; this is indicated by the fact that both his coming and his going (3:19 and 12:31) can be termed the judgment and by the fact that both his exaltation and his sending can be regarded as the basis for the gift of eternal life (3:14 and 3:16).

2. The sending of the Son is *the deed of God's love*: "In this the love of God was made manifest among us, that God sent his only Son into the world, so that we might live through him" (I Jn. 4:9). "For God so loved the world that he gave his only Son, that whoever believes in him should not perish but have eternal life" (3:16).* * *

The intent of this sending is therefore fulfilled in those who believe in Jesus as the Son sent from God: they receive the love of God—"we have come to know and to believe the love God has for us" (I Jn. 4:16 tr.; *cf.* Jn. 17:26; I Jn. 2:5; 3:17; 4:7–12), while he who loves the world is not embraced by the love of God (I Jn. 2:15, understanding the genitive, with KJ, as subjective, not objective).

The fact that the love of God is the basis for the sending of the Son is expressed by the way in which *the purpose of his sending or coming* is given. He came into the world only "to bear witness to the 'truth'" (18:37), or, meaning the same thing, he came into the world as "light," in order "that whoever believes in me may not remain in 'darkness'" (12:46). Again, it means the same when Jesus says he came "that they may have life and have abundance" (10:10 tr.), or when the author says God "gave" him in order that "whoever believes in him might not perish but have eternal life" (3:16), or that God sent him into the world "so that we might live through him" (I Jn. 4:9), or that he sent him as "the expiation for our sins" (I

Jn. 4:10, if this sentence is not a redactional gloss). In altogether general formulation it is also said that God sent him "that the world might be saved by him" (3:17).

Jesus, accordingly, can be called *"the savior of the world"* (4:42; I Jn. 4:14). While in this term he is accorded the specifically Hellenistic title of the salvation-bringer, the meaning of his sending is more frequently expressed by the title that comes out of the Jewish and earliest Christian tradition: Messiah; whereas the Kyrios-title is completely missing. * * *

Jesus is the *Messiah* (1:41; 4:25) or "the Christ" (which in both passages is explicitly pointed out to be the translation of "Messiah"). * * *

3. What is expressed by all these titles is that Jesus is the eschatological salvation-bringer, that *his coming is the eschatological event.* By his coming the predictions of Moses and the prophets are fulfilled (1:45; *cf.* 5:39, 46). To the Samaritan woman who expects enlightenment from the Messiah, Jesus answers, "I who speak to you am he" (4:25f.). The Jewish expectation that the Messiah, as the "second redeemer," will bestow bread from heaven as Moses, the "first redeemer," did of yore is fulfilled by Jesus who bestows the true bread of heaven (6:31f.). When he calls his coming "my day" which Abraham rejoiced to see (8:56), that means that his coming is "the Messiah's day" which was part of the Jewish and earliest Christian expectation.

But the assertion that his coming-and-going, which constitute a unity as we have seen (see 1 in this §), is the eschatological event is primarily made in those sentences where his coming or going is termed *the judgment of the world:*

> "And this is the judgment, that the light has come into the world,
> and men loved darkness rather than light" (3:19).

> "For judgment I came into this world,
> that those who do not see may see,
> and that those who see may become blind" (9:39).

The historizing of eschatology already introduced by Paul is radically carried through by John in his understanding of κρίσις and κρίμα as both having the double sense "judgment" and "sunderance." The judgment takes place in just the fact that upon the encounter with Jesus the sunderance between faith and unfaith, between the sighted and the blind, is accomplished (3:19; 9:39). He who believes is not judged (i.e. not condemned), but he who does not believe remains in darkness, remains under the wrath of God, and is thereby judged (i.e. condemned):

> "He who believes in him is not condemned,
> he who does not believe is condemned already" (3:18).

Right now, while Jesus' word is sounding forth, the "sunderance" which is also "judgment" is taking place:

> "He who hears my word and believes him who sent me,
> has eternal life; he does not come into judgment (=condemnation),
> but has passed from death to life."

". . . the hour is coming, and now is,
when the dead will hear the voice of the Son of God,
and those who hear will live" (5:24f.).

In sending Jesus into the world the Father gave him authority to raise the dead
and hold judgment (5:21f., 26f.). Therefore, he who believes in him already has life:

"He who believes in the Son has eternal life;
he who does not obey the Son shall not see life,
but the wrath of God rests (i.e. remains) upon him" (3:36; *cf.* 6:47; I Jn. 5:12).

Jesus declares:

"I am the resurrection and the life;
he who believes in me, though he die, yet shall he live,
and whoever lives and believes in me shall never die" (11:25f.; *cf.* 8:51).

The judgment, then, is no dramatic cosmic event, but takes place in the response
of men to the word of Jesus. As it accordingly may be said that Jesus came into the
world for judgment (9:39), so it can also be said that God sent him not to judge but
to save (3:17). He can say that he judges no one (8:15), and again can say that he
judges nevertheless (8:16; 5:30). It is not he who is the actual judge, but the word
that he speaks:

"If any one hears my sayings and does not keep them,
I do not judge him
For I did not come to judge the world
but to save the world.
He who rejects me and does not receive my sayings
has a judge;
the word that I have spoken will be his judge" (12:47f.).

A later ecclesiastical redaction has here added "on the last day," "correcting" the text by introducing the traditional futuristic eschatology, just as it
did in 6:39, 40, 44 by inserting the refrain "but (or "and") I will raise him
up at the last day." This is a sentence which has an organic place in 6:54
within the passage 6:51b–58, which likewise was inserted by ecclesiastical
redaction; in this passage the bread of life, which in the preceding discourse is Jesus himself, is equated with the Sacrament of the Lord's Supper
and the latter is understood (in Ignatius' sense) as the "medicine of immortality." Even more jarring than these additions, if that be possible, is the
insertion of 5:28f., where in direct contradiction of v. 25 the "hour" of the
resurrection is transferred from the present to the future. * * *

The theme of whole sections is that Jesus' coming-and-going is the "judgment"
of the world (3:1–21, 31–36; 4:43–46; 7:15–24; 8:13–20). A concrete scene,

6:60–71, depicts the "sundering" which takes place through his word: at his "hard saying" true and false disciples are put asunder, they separate themselves. Moreover, the sundering accomplished by Jesus' ministry is underscored by the author's dividing his portrayal of this ministry into two parts: chs. 2–12 portray Jesus' revealing-activity to the world, and chs. 13–17 (or 13–20) his revealing-activity to the community of believers.

The historizing of eschatology[1] also finds expression in the fact that the world is oblivious to what is happening. In its sight there is only a disturbance, a commotion that leads to "divisions" (7:43; 9:16; 10:19). It has no inkling that in these "divisions" a decision and a sunderance are being reflected. This obliviousness grimly demonstrates that the world is judged—condemned. While for it the hour of the passion is the hour of triumph and joy (16:20) because in it the "ruler of the world" seems to be in command (14:30), in reality this hour is just the opposite: the judgment of the world and judgment over its "ruler" (12:31; 16:11).

§ 46. The Offense of the Incarnation of the Word

1. How does God's Son come into the world? As a human being. The theme of the whole Gospel of John is the statement: "The word became flesh" (1:14). This statement is defended by I and II John against the false teachers. These are evidently Christian Gnostics who deny the identity of the Son of God with the human Jesus either by asserting that their union was only temporary or by flatly rejecting the reality of the human Jesus and docetically regarding the human form of the Son of God as only a seeming body. John's answer to them is: every spirit that does not confess that Jesus Christ came in the flesh, that does not confess Jesus (the man as the Son of God) is not "from God"; indeed, such false doctrine is nothing less than the work of Antichrist (I Jn. 4:2f.; II Jn. 7).

* * *

The Revealer appears not as *man-in-general*, i.e. not simply as a bearer of human *nature*, but as a *definite human being in history*: Jesus of Nazareth. His humanity is genuine humanity: "the word became flesh." Hence, John has no theory about the pre-existent one's miraculous manner of entry into the world nor about the manner of his union with the man Jesus. He knows neither the legend of the virgin birth[2] nor that of Jesus' birth in Bethlehem—or if he knows of them, he will have nothing to do with them. Jesus comes from Nazareth, and this fact, offensive to "the Jews," is emphasized (1:45; 7:52) rather than deprecated. "The Jews," knowing Jesus' place of origin and his parents (7:27f.; 6:42), are not in error as to the facts, but err in denying the claim of this Jesus of Nazareth

---

1. A specific example of John's de-mythologizing of eschatology is his interpretation of the mythical figure, Antichrist. In I Jn. 2:18, 4:3 the appearing of false teachers is interpreted as the coming of the Antichrist. It is even said: "now many antichrists have come!"

2. In some Latin witnesses to the text of Jn. 1:13 *"qui . . . natus est"* (who . . . was born) is found instead of "who . . . were born"; this is certainly a "correcting" of the original text.

to be the Revealer of God. They err not in the matter upon which they judge but in making a judgment at all κατὰ σάρκα (according to the "flesh"—according to external appearances).

Neither does the Revealer appear as a mystagogue communicating teachings, formulas, and rites as if he himself were only a means to an end who could sink into unimportance to any who had received his "Gnosis." Though Jesus says in departing from the earth, "I have manifested thy name to the men whom thou gavest me out of the world" (17:6; cf. v. 26), still he has imparted no information about God at all, any more than he has brought instruction about the origin of the world or the fate of the self. He does not *communicate anything*, but *calls men to himself.* Or when he promises a gift, he is, himself, that gift: he himself is the bread of life that he bestows (6:35); he himself is the light (8:12); he himself is life (11:25; 14:6).

Jesus, the Son of God who has become man, is a genuine man—which again does not mean that in his personality the divine became visible so as to fill men with enthusiasm and touch their feelings or to fascinate and overwhelm them. If that were the case, the divine would then be conceived of simply as the human exalted and intensified. But according to John, the divine is the very counter-pole to the human, with the result that it is a paradox, an offense, that the Word became flesh. As a matter of fact, the divinity of the figure of Jesus in John is completely lacking in visibility, and the disciples' relation to him as "friends" (15:14f.) is by no means conceived of as a personal relation of human friendship. It is the farewell discourses especially that strive to teach this distinction by making clear that the disciples will not achieve the right relation to him until he has departed from them—indeed, that he is not in the full sense the Revealer until he has been lifted up and glorified (see especially 14:28; 16:7).

*   *   *

3. Jesus *performs miracles*, a fact that is sometimes mentioned in general terms (2:23; 3:2; 4:45; 7:3, 31; 10:41; 11:47; 12:37; 20:30) and sometimes is depicted in accounts of specific miracles (2:1–12; 4:46–54; 5:1–9; 6:1–25; 9:1–7; 11:1–44). The term used for these miracles is σημεῖα ("signs" and, secondarily, "miracles"), and in John this word retains its true meaning of "sign." The "signs" reveal Jesus' glory (2:11; cf. 9:3; 11:4), and the disbelief that refuses to be convinced by so many miracles is reproved (12:37). On the other hand, however, Jesus says in rebuke: "Unless you see signs and wonders you will not believe" (4:48). And the risen Jesus addresses to Thomas the reproving word: "Do you believe now because you have seen me? Blessed are those who see (me) not and yet believe" (20:29 tr.). It is an indication of disbelief when "the Jews" ask: "Then what sign do you do, that we may see, and believe you? What work do you perform?" (6:30; cf. 2:18). They ask for a miracle analogous to the manna-miracle of Moses, and have no understanding of the work Jesus is performing. The fact that their question chronologically follows the sign of the bread-miracle makes it clear that the meaning of the sign does not lie in the miraculous occurrence. In fact, this had already been said in v. 26: "You seek me, not because you saw signs, but because you ate some of the loaves and were filled" (6:26 tr.).

As "signs" the miracles of Jesus are ambiguous. Like Jesus' words, they are misunderstandable. Of course, they are remarkable occurrences, but that only makes them indicators that the activity of the Revealer is a disturbance of what is familiar to the world. They point to the fact that the Revelation is no worldly occurrence, but an other-worldly one. They are pictures, symbols. The wine-miracle, an epiphany (2:1–12) symbolizes what occurs in all Jesus' work: the revelation of his "glory"—not the glory of a miracle-worker, but that of him by whom the gift of "grace and truth" is made. The cure of the official's son (4:46–54) and the healing of the lame man at the pool (5:1–9), both miraculous, are "signs" only in the general sense that they point to the Revealer's work as of life-promoting kind. But the bread-miracle (6:1–15), the cure of the blind man (9:1–7), and the raising of Lazarus (11:1–44) have specific symbolic meaning: they represent the Revelation as food, light, and life, respectively. It can hardly be decided whether the walking on the water is appended to the multiplication of the loaves only by the force of tradition or whether it is meant to convey that the Revealer and the Revelation are not subject to the laws of natural life.

We have already seen how 6:26 and 30 indicate that the "signs," though they are miraculous occurrences, do not furnish Jesus with legitimating credentials. The remark that the faith of the many, which rests upon the miracles, is no trust-worthy faith (2:23–25) indicates the same thing. John's whole presentation shows, rather, that if the miracles are not understood as signs, they are an offense! The healing of the lame man and the cure of the blind man both elicit enmity and persecution, and the raising of Lazarus brings Jesus to the cross. The miracles may be for many the first shock that leads them to pay heed to Jesus and so begin to have faith—for this purpose, miracles are, so to speak, conceded; neverthe-less, for the leaders of the people, the representatives of "the world," the miracles are the offense that leads them to condemn him to death (11:47; *cf.* 12:18f.).

4. Just because the miracles are "signs" which require understanding, they also provide the possibility of *misunderstanding*. After the bread-miracle which raises the question whether he is "the prophet who is to come into the world" (6:14), the crowd wants to make him king (6:15) because it expects material ben-efits of him (6:26). His brothers want to take him to Jerusalem to the Feast of Tabernacles so that he may make himself conspicuous there, saying: "For no man works in secret if he seeks to be known openly. If you do these things, show your-self to the world" (7:4). They do not understand the way in which the Revelation works. They do not understand that from the world's standpoint the Revelation must always be a "hidden thing" (*cf.* "in secret" 7:4) and that it nevertheless occurs "openly"—not, however, with demonstrative obtrusiveness but with the unobtru-siveness of everyday events. What is true of the miracles is true of all that Jesus does: it is not understood. Even the disciples understand the cleansing of the tem-ple no more than "the Jews" do. Not until after the resurrection does its meaning dawn upon them (2:17); likewise with the entry into Jerusalem (12:16). Peter does not grasp the meaning of the foot-washing (13:4ff.).

As Jesus' actions are *misunderstood*, so are *his words* so long as they are conceived in the categories of worldly thought. "The Jews" cannot but grossly misunderstand the saying about the destruction and rebuilding of the temple (2:20). As Nicodemus is able to understand re-birth only in the external natural sense (3:4), so the woman of Samaria misunderstands the saying about "living water" first to mean running water and then to mean miraculous water (4:11, 15). The disciples cannot conceive what food Jesus means as his secret nourishment (4:33), nor can "the Jews" guess what the bread from heaven is that Jesus bestows (6:34). Jesus' saying about his departure is misunderstood as an intention to go to the Dispersion (7:35f.) or even to kill himself (8:22). The disciples misunderstand the sentence addressed to Judas: "What you are going to do, do quickly" (13:27f.). And Thomas cannot cope with the statement that the disciples know the way which Jesus will take (14:4). The disciples do not understand the "little while" used by Jesus of his approaching departure and return (16:17f.). They do not see why Jesus does not wish to manifest himself to the world (14:22). The incomprehension of the crowd is symbolically illustrated by the fact that some misunderstand the heavenly voice in answer to Jesus' prayer as thunder and others understand it as the angel voice which it is, but without perceiving that it is really speaking not to Jesus but to them (12:28–38).

In all these misunderstandings the offense of the assertion, "the word became flesh" finds expression. This offense lies in the fact that the Revealer appears as a man whose claim to be the Son of God is one which he cannot, indeed, must not, prove to the world. For the Revelation is judgment upon the world and is necessarily felt as an attack upon it and an offense to it, so long as the world refuses to give up its norms. Until it does so, the world inevitably misunderstands the words and deeds of the Revealer, or they remain a riddle for it (10:6; 16:25, 29), even though Jesus has said everything openly all along (18:20). The world's inner incapacity to understand comes most crassly to expression in the demand, "If you are the Christ, tell us plainly." Jesus, of course, had been telling them for a long time, so he can only answer, "I told you, and you do not believe" (10:24f.). Evidently he is to the world a foreigner whose language it does not understand. Why not? Not because he is not a real man, but because he, a mere man, demands credence for his claim to be the Revealer: "Why do you not understand what I say? Because you cannot hear my word" (8:43 tr.). Why do "the Jews," who know him and his home town, nevertheless not know who he is nor where he comes from? Because they do not know God (7:28)! So, on the one hand, Jesus can say that he does not bear witness for himself; if he did, his testimony would not be true (5:31f.). On the other hand, he is constantly bearing witness for himself by claiming to be the Revealer, and can assert that his testimony is true when he does so (8:14). Each statement is true, according to which point of view is adopted: such a testimony as the world demands, a legitimation, he cannot and must not give. But there is a testimony which consists of his claim to be the Revealer, a claim which denies the world's competence to judge; in the world's opinion this cannot be considered true testimony (8:13). But this testimony he must bear.

The offense of the assertion, "the word became flesh," comes most clearly to light in the *direct contradiction of Jesus' claim.* It can only appear as an insane blasphemy that he, a man, makes himself equal to God, and the authorities seek to kill him (5:17f.). His claim calls forth the accusation that he is demon-possessed and a "Samaritan" (8:51f.). So does his assertion that whoever keeps his word will not see death (8:51f.). And when he claims that he is older than Abraham (8:57), they want to stone him (8:59). His assertion that he and the Father are one fills them with such indignation that once more they want to stone him (10:30f.). In short, his "hard word" is intolerable to hear. And his persistence in his claim results in the apostasy of all but a few of his very disciples (6:66). What a scandal (σκάνδαλον) his cross will one day be to men, he hints in the words: "Does this (his "hard word") scandalize you? What, then, if you see the Son of Man ascending where he was at first?" (6:61f., tr.)—a saying of remarkably double meaning, for the world will, of course, perceive only the outward form of his "ascending": his crucifixion. John at the end brings this *skandalon* drastically into view when he has Pilate present the scourged and thorn-crowned Jesus to the crowd with the words, "Behold the man!" (19:5 KJ) and, "Behold your king!" (19:14 KJ). Here and in the inscription over the cross (19:19) the paradoxical stumbling-block of Jesus' claim is presented in a symbol of tremendous irony.

5. By his presentation of Jesus' work as the incarnate Son of God John has singularly developed and deepened Mark's theory of the *Messiah-secret*. Over the figure of Jesus there hangs a mystery, even though—or rather just because—he quite openly says who he is and what claim he makes. For to the world he is still in spite of all publicity the hidden Messiah, not because he conceals anything or commands anything to be kept secret, but because the world does not see with seeing eyes (12:40). His hiddenness is the very *consequence* of his self-revelation; his revealing of himself is the very thing that makes "those who see" become "blind" (9:39).

His work as a whole, which forms a unity framed by his coming and his departure, *is both revelation and offense*. His departure or "exaltation" (i.e. upon the cross) not only belongs to the whole as its culmination but is that which makes the whole what it is: both revelation and offense. The possibility considered by Jesus in the meditation which is John's substitute for the Gethsemane scene of the synoptic tradition, "What shall I say? 'Father, save me from this hour'?" Jesus immediately rejects: "No, for this purpose I have come to this hour" (12:27). In his passion the meaning of the sending of Jesus is fulfilled. And by his conceiving and accepting it as the fulfilment of the mission enjoined upon him by the Father (14:31), it becomes the hour of exaltation, the hour of glorification. Seen from the vantage-point of this fulfilment the whole work of the man Jesus is a revelation of the divine glory. Whereas in the Gospel of Mark we can recognize the historical process by which the unmessianic life of Jesus was retrospectively made messianic, in John the inner appropriateness of that process is made clear. This is expressed by the evangelist by means of the petition of Jesus which follows the deliberation mentioned above: "Father, glorify thy name" (12:28) and by the heavenly voice which answers this prayer, "I have glorified it, and I will glorify it again" (12:28). Hence, the glorification of God's name which begins with Jesus' exaltation by crucifixion and the glorification of God's name by the ministry of the earthly Jesus (17:4) are a unity. Neither exists without the other; each exists only through the other. But the glorification of the name of God is also the glorification of Jesus himself, and Jesus' other prayer, "Father, the hour has come; glorify thy Son" (17:1), corresponds to this one ("Father, glorify thy name"). And the motive for this prayer—"that the Son may glorify thee"—makes the unity of God's glory and Jesus' glory evident. And when the motive is further developed in the words "since thou has given him power over all flesh" (17:2), the unity of his glory after the exaltation with that before it is once again made clear. Both unities are once more expressed in the words which pronounce the granting of this prayer:

> "Now is the Son of man glorified,
>   and in him God is glorified;
> if God is glorified in him,
>   God will also glorify him in himself
> and glorify him at once" (13:31f.).[3]

In the "now" of the "hour" when the Son of God departs from the world the past and the future are bound together, as it were. And since not until the future will the past be made into what it really is (*viz.*, the revelation of the "glory"), the disciples can only be glad that Jesus is going away (14:28; 16:7).

Faith in Jesus, then, is faith in the exalted Jesus, but not as if he were a heavenly being who had stripped off the garment of earthly-human existence as the Gnostic Redeemer was conceived to do. Rather, the exalted Jesus is at the same time the earthly man Jesus; the "glorified one" is still always he who "became flesh." In other words, Jesus' life on earth does not become an item of the historical past, but constantly remains present reality. The historical figure of Jesus, i.e. his human history, retains its significance of being the revelation of his "glory" and thereby of God's. It is the eschatological occurrence. Of course, this is not visible to the world, for the exalted Jesus does not reveal himself to it (14:22)—indeed he cannot, for it cannot receive the Spirit of truth which gives knowledge to those who believe (14:17; 16:13f.). But those who believe can now look back upon Jesus' earthly life and say, "We have beheld his glory" (1:14). What, then, is the picture of that life at which faith arrives?

§ 47. The Revelation of the Glory

* * *

3. If Jesus' death on the cross is already his exaltation and glorification, *his resurrection* cannot be an event of special significance. No resurrection is needed to destroy the triumph which death might be supposed to have gained in the cruci-

---

3. In the text of John as we now have it this passage precedes the prayer by some chapters. But the original arrangement has been disturbed. This section, 13:31f., must be the sequel to ch. 17; see my *Kommentar* [*Das Evangelium des Johannes* (Göttingen, 1941)], pp. 350f. [*The Gospel of John: A Commentary*, trans. G. R. Beasley-Murray (Philadelphia: Westminster Press, 1971)].

fixion. For the cross itself was already triumph over the world and its ruler. The hour of the passion is κρίσις (of the world) and means the fall of the "ruler of this world" and his condemnation (12:31; 16:11). As a conqueror over whom the "ruler of the world" has no power, Jesus strides on to meet his passion (14:30). There is not a word in John of the idea that not until the resurrection and exaltation after his death was Jesus made lord of all cosmic and demonic powers (cf., for example, Phil. 2:11; Eph. 1:20f.; I Pet. 3:21f.; Pol. Phil. 2:1). For the Father did not delay the gift of life-creating power to him until the resurrection but gave it to him from the outset: "he has granted the Son also to have life in himself" (5:26). It is as he who is the resurrection and the life, or the way, the truth and the life (11:25; 14:6) that he encounters men and calls the believer into life now (5:24f.; 11:25f.), as the raising of Lazarus demonstrates (ch. 11). That is why we also fail to find in Jesus' words in John the prediction of his "rising" or "being raised" as we know it from the synoptics. The evangelist himself mentions it only in an aside (2:22): "When therefore he was raised from the dead, his disciples remembered. . . ." But as a substitute for it we find in 12:16: "but when Jesus had been glorified, then they remembered" . . . (tr.). "To rise" (ἀναστῆναι) occurs only in a redactional gloss at 20:9 and "to be raised" (ἐγερθῆναι) only in the redactional epilogue (21:4). Both terms are completely lacking in the Epistles of John.

It is not surprising that the evangelist, following the tradition, narrates some *Easter-stories*. The question is, what do they mean to him? The original close of the Gospel (20:31) just after the Easter-stories says, "Now Jesus also did many other signs." Evidently, then, the resurrection appearances just like the miracles of Jesus are reckoned among his "signs." They symbolize the fulfilment of the prediction of 16:22: "So you have sorrow now, but I will see you again and your hearts will rejoice" (cf. 16:16). So far as they are actual occurrences—and the evangelist need not have doubted their reality—they resemble the miracles in that ultimately they are not indispensable; in fact, there ought to be no need for them, but they were granted as a concession to man's weakness. The Thomas-story is used to make this idea clear: his wish to see the risen Jesus in the body, even to touch him, is granted. But in the same moment he is reprimanded: "Because you have seen me have you come to faith? Blessed are those who though they do not see me yet believe" (20:29 tr.). It is hard to believe that the evangelist closes his representation of Jesus with this as his last word without a deep intention behind it. In it lies a criticism of the small faith which asks for tangible demonstrations of the Revealer. It also contains a warning against taking the Easter-stories for more than they are able to be: signs and pictures of the Easter faith—or, perhaps still better, confessions of faith in it.

The same conclusion can be drawn from the promises made in the farewell discourses. Parallel to the Easter-promise ("but I will see you again," 16:22, already mentioned above, within the whole passage 16:16–24) is another, 14:18; "I will not leave you desolate; I will come to you." This is the promise of his "coming," i.e. his parousia. But when it continues: "Yet a little while, and the world will see me no more, but you will see me; because I live, you will live also," the promise of the parousia is merging into the Easter-promise. What this means is that Jesus' resurrection and parousia are identical to John. Not only that, but parallel to these parallel promises stands a third, the promise of the Spirit (the Paraclete 14:15;

16:33), i.e. the promise of Pentecost. Hence, for John Easter, Pentecost, and the parousia are not three separate events, but one and the same. Consequently, the terminology appropriate to Easter again and again mingles with that appropriate to the parousia—reunion with him is mentioned in 14:19; 16:16, 19, 20; the fact that he lives, 14:9; his appearing to the disciples, 14:21f. But out of the traditional parousia-expectation these themes occur: his coming, 14:3, 18, 23, 28; and the phrases characteristic of eschatology, "in that day" 14:20; 16:23, 26 and "the hour is coming," 16:25. And into the midst of these the promise of the Spirit is thrust: 14:15–17, 26; 15:26; 16:7–11, 13–15. But the one event that is meant by all these is not an external occurrence, but an inner one: the victory which Jesus wins when faith arises in man by the overcoming of the offense that Jesus is to him. The victory over the "ruler of the world" which Jesus has won, is the fact that now there exists a faith which recognizes in Jesus the Revelation of God. The declaration, "I have overcome the world" (16:33), has its parallel in the believer's confession: "this is the victory that overcomes the world: our faith. Who is it that overcomes the world but he who believes that Jesus is the Son of God?" (I Jn. 5:4f.). In the short dialogue between Judas and Jesus it is explicitly stated that this is a matter of inward occurrence: "Lord, how is it that you will manifest yourself to us, and not to the world?" Jesus answers, "If a man loves me, he will keep my word, and my Father will love him, and we will come to him and make our home with him" (14:22f.). The same is said of the sending of the Spirit—"the Spirit of truth, whom the world cannot receive, because it neither sees him nor knows him; you know him, for he dwells with you, and will be in you" (14:17).

If, as John maintains, Jesus' original coming is already the $\kappa\rho\acute{\iota}\sigma\iota\varsigma$ (judgment), then it is evident that for him the parousia is not an impending cosmic drama. Accordingly, John contains none of the synoptic parousia-predictions of the coming of the Son of Man in the glory of his Father, on the clouds of heaven, or the like (Mk. 8:38; 13:26f., etc.).

* * *

§48. The Revelation as the Word

1. We have still to ask what the works are that Jesus accomplishes and that "bear witness" to him (5:36; 10:25). Are they *the* "signs," the miracles which Mt. 11:2 calls the "works of the Christ" (tr.)? No, at least not in the sense of being an unambiguous legitimation. For, as we have seen, they are ambiguous signs whose meaning can only be found in faith. In that respect they resemble Jesus' words, which are just as ambiguous and open to misunderstanding. In fact the miracles in John are neither more nor less than words, *verba visibilia*. Otherwise, it would be incomprehensible how Jesus' ministry could be called in retrospect a "doing of signs" (12:37; 20:30), whereas in the actual account of his ministry the "signs" are secondary in importance to the "words"—and the farewell prayer, looking back, describes Jesus' ministry as the passing on of the *words* God gave him.

That is the fact—the *works of Jesus* (or, seen collectively as a whole: his work) *are his words.* When Jesus says, "The works which the Father has given me to accomplish, these very works which I am doing, bear me witness that the Father has sent me" (5:36 tr.), the words of the preceding discussion (5:19ff.) indicate what the true works of Jesus are: "judging" and "making alive." They also indicate how these works are accomplished: by Jesus' word. Numerous formulations indicate that to John deed and word are identical.

8:28: "then you will know that I am he and that on my own authority I *do* nothing; but as the Father taught me, that I *speak*."

14:10: "The *words* that I *say* to you I do not speak on my own authority; but the Father who dwells in me *is doing* his *works*" (tr.).

15:22, 24: "If I had not come and *spoken* to them, they would not have sin . . . If I had not done among them the *works* . . . they would not have sin." In addition *cf.* in 8:38 the interchange between "speak" and "do"; in 17:4, 8, 14 the equivalence of "work," "words" (ῥήματα) and "word" (λόγος). There is a corresponding interchange between "see" and "hear" in 8:38, etc.; on which see below. 10:38 and 14:11 seem to contradict our assertion that the works are not added to the words to substantiate them but are nothing but the words themselves. Both times we read: "even though you do not believe *me*, believe the *works*" (in one case "for the sake of the works"). Does not "me" mean "my works"? But 14:11 is the continuation of 14:10, and together they indicate that the "works" of v. 11 are neither more nor less than the "words" of v. 10. When Jesus thus points away from himself to his working, that can only mean that he is rejecting an authoritarian faith which will meekly accept what is said *about* Jesus. In its place he is demanding a faith that understands Jesus' words as *personal address* aimed at the believer—i.e. as Jesus' "working" upon him. This is the sense in which Jesus refuses the demand of "the Jews" that he openly say whether or not he is the Messiah (10:24f.). The answer to that they ought to gather from his works—or workings—which bear witness for him.

The identity of work and word can be further seen in what is said of the effect of the word. "The words that I have spoken to you are spirit and life," (6:68). This is followed by Peter's confession: "You have the words of eternal life." Whoever believes the word of Jesus and Him who sent him, has eternal life, has stepped over from death into life (5:24). Whoever keeps his word will never see death (8:51). *His word therefore bestows life.* And neither more nor less than that is meant when it is said that his word leads to knowledge and hence to freedom (8:31f.). His word cleanses and consecrates (15:3; 17:17). Therein, of course, the word is *also the judge* over unbelief:

"If any one hears my words and does not keep them,
    I do not judge him . . .
He who rejects me and does not receive my words has a judge:
    the word that I have spoken judges him" (12:47f. Blt.).

2. Now what of *the content of Jesus' word* or words? *What Jesus saw or heard with the Father* he speaks. (Or, as a consequence of identifying word and deed, John may also say that he "shows" it or "does" it.) This is in accord with the final sentence of the prologue: "No one has ever seen God; the only Son, who is in the bosom of the Father, he has made him known" (1:18; *cf.* 6:46).

Jesus testifies or speaks what he saw with his Father (3:11; 8:38) or what he saw and heard (3:32) or simply what he heard (8:26, 40; 15:15; *cf.* 5:30— the same thing is said of the Spirit in 16:13). He speaks what the Father taught him to speak (8:28, *cf.* 7:17), or commanded him to speak (12:49). He speaks the words that the Father gave him (17:8). He does what he sees the Father do, what the Father shows him (5:19f.). Expressed also in a very general way: he reveals the Father's name (17:6, 26). It makes no difference whether the present tense is used of what the Son sees and hears (5:19f., 30), or a past tense of what he saw and heard (all the other passages), any more than there is a difference between "all that the Father *gives* me" (6:37) and "my Father who *has given* them to me" (10:29).

But the astonishing thing about it is that Jesus' words never convey anything specific or concrete that he has seen with the Father. Not once does he communicate matters or events to which he had been a witness by either eye or ear. Never is the heavenly world the theme of his words. Nor does he communicate cosmogonic or soteriological mysteries like the Gnostic Redeemer. His theme is always just this one thing: that the Father sent him, that he came as the light, the bread of life, witness for the truth, etc.; that he will go again, and that one must believe in him. So it is clear that the mythological statements have lost their mythological meaning. Jesus is not presented in literal seriousness as a pre-existent divine being who came in human form to earth to reveal unprecedented secrets. Rather, the mythological terminology is intended to express the absolute and decisive significance of his word—the mythological notion of pre-existence is made to serve the idea of the Revelation. His word does not arise from the sphere of human observation and thought, but comes from beyond. It is a word free of all human motivation, a word determined from outside himself, just as men's speech and deeds can only be determined from outside themselves when they oppose themselves to his word as enemies—determined in the latter case, of course, by the devil (8:38, 41). Therefore his word is not subject to men's scrutiny or control. It is an authoritative word which confronts the hearer with a life-and-death decision.

The same thing is meant by the solemn affirmation that Jesus does or says nothing on his own authority. Such statements have the purpose of underlining the authority of Jesus, whose words, although spoken by a man, still are not human words: "No man ever spoke like this man" (7:46). To a certain extent, the word of the Old Testament prophets is analogous in that they also do not speak by their own authority but are inspired by God. But the analogy also uncovers the difference: Jesus' words are not *from time to time* inspired, but he speaks and acts *constantly* from within his one-ness with God. Unlike the prophets' words, Jesus' words do not thrust the concrete historical situation of the People into the light of God's demand with its promise or threat; they do not open men's eyes to what some present moment demands. Rather, the encounter with Jesus' words and person casts man into decision in his bare, undifferentiated situation of being human. None of the prophets was of absolute importance; one followed upon another. No new revealer follows Jesus; in him the Revelation of God is once for all given to the world, and this Revelation is inexhaustible. For whatever new knowledge may yet be given the Church by the Spirit, it will all be only a reminder of what Jesus said (14:26)—or, as Jesus says, "he will select from what is mine and declare it to you" (16:14 tr.).

Thus comes to light the deeper meaning of that peculiar fluctuation of expression between "speak" and "do" and between "word" and "work." Jesus' words communicate no definable content at all except that they are words of life, words of God. That is, they are words of life, words of God, not because of their content, but because of *whose* words they are. They are something special and decisive not in and by their timeless content, but in and by the act of being uttered—and that is why they are just as much "works" as "words": Whatever Jesus does is a speaking, whatever he says is a doing. His actions speak, his words act.

For that very reason practically all the words of Jesus in John are *assertions about himself* and no definite complex of ideas can be stated as their content and claimed to be the "teaching" of Jesus. Hence the radical difference between Jesus' preaching in John and that in the synoptics; John took over only a minimal quantity of the traditional words of Jesus. His words are assertions about himself. But that does not mean christological instruction, or teaching about the metaphysical quality of his person. On the contrary, to understand them in that way would be to misunderstand them; for it would be a failure to understand that his "words" are "deeds." Anyone so understanding him would have to let himself be referred to Jesus' deeds, as were "the Jews" who required of him a clear statement whether he were the Messiah or not (10:24f.).

His words are utterances about himself; *for his word is identical with himself.* What is said of his word is also said of himself: his words are "life," they are "truth" (6:63; 17:17); but so is he himself—"I am the way, and the truth, and the life" (14:6). Whoever hears his word and believes Him who sent him has Life (5:24), but that is what he himself is—"I am the resurrection and the life; he who believes in me, though he die, yet shall he live" (11:25). His words (12:48; 17:8), his "testimony" (3:11, 32f.), must be "accepted" ($\lambda\alpha\mu\beta\acute{\alpha}\nu\epsilon\iota\nu$)—so must he (1:12; 5:43; *cf.* 13:20). To reject him ($\mathring{\alpha}\theta\epsilon\tau\epsilon\hat{\iota}\nu$) is identical with not accepting his words (12:48). That his own "abide" in him and he in them means the same thing as that his words "abide" in them (15:4–7). He is the judge (5:22, 27)—so is his word (12:48). No wonder, then, that the evangelist can confer upon him for his pre-existent period the mythological title: *Word* (Logos)!

*   *   *

His words are utterances about himself. Accordingly, all the Revelation that he brings is concentrated in the great *"I-am" statements.*

> "The bread of life—it is I.
> He who comes to me shall not hunger, and he who believes in me shall
>   never thirst" (6:35 *cf.* 6:51a Blt.).
> "The light of the world—it is I.

He who follows me shall not walk in darkness but shall have the light
   of life" (8:12 Blt. tr.).
"The door is I" (10:9 Blt.). "The good shepherd is I" (10:11, 14 Blt.).
"The resurrection and the life are I" (11:25 Blt.).
"The way, the truth, and the life are I" (14:6 Blt.).
"The true vine is I" (15:1, 5).

In fact, Jesus can pronounce this "It is I" absolutely, without any real subject:
"unless you believe that it is I, you will die in your sins" (8:24 Blt.) and: "when you
have lifted up the Son of man, then you will know that it is I" (8:28 Blt.). What is
to be supplied as the real subject in place of "it"? Obviously nothing definite or
specific, but something of this sort: "all that I say is I"—or perhaps better: "he
upon whom life and death, being and non-being depend"—"he for whom all the
world is waiting as the bringer of salvation." For let it be observed that in these
"I"-statements the "I" is a predicate nominative and not the subject.[4] The meaning
is always: "in *me* the thing mentioned (bread of life, light, etc.) is present; it is I."

All these figures of speech—that of the bread and the light, the door and the
way, the shepherd and the vine—mean what John, without using a figure, calls
life and truth. That is, they all mean that which man must have and longs to have
in order to be able truly to exist. With his "It is I" Jesus therefore presents himself
as the one for whom the world is waiting, the one who satisfies all longing. This
is symbolically represented in the scene at the well in Samaria. The woman of
Samaria says, "I know that Messiah is coming . . . when he comes he will show
us all things." To which Jesus replies: "I who speak to you am he" (4:25f.). He
similarly answers the healed blind man's question who the Son of Man is: "You
have both seen him and it is he who is speaking to you" (9:37 tr.). The world's
longing takes form in the concept of the *salvation-bringer* in his various forms,
with his various titles. So the titles of the salvation-bringer from both the Jewish
and the Hellenistic tradition are conferred in John upon Jesus. Jesus is he in
whom the old hope is fulfilled; his coming is the eschatological event. But all the
traditional titles are insufficient, as is suggested by the title which occurs in
Peter's confession: "and we have come to believe and to know that you are the
Holy One of God" (6:69 tr.). Only one other time does this title occur in the New
Testament: in the demon's confession at Mk. 1:24; it has no tradition (at least no
recognizable one), for though Jesus is called "the holy one" at I Jn. 2:20 and Rev.
3:7, in these passages it is not a title but means simply "he who is holy." The title
designates Jesus as the absolutely transcendent one whose place is at the side of
God and who stands over against the world as the representative of God. At the
same time, however, the reader is probably expected to hear in it the etymological overtone: holy—hallow (ἅγιος—ἁγιάζειν) and to remember that Jesus is he

4. In Greek there is no change in the person of the verb between "I *am* he" and "it *is* I"—
both are ἐγώ εἰμι (contrast, for instance, in both KJ and RSV Jn. 4:26 with Mk. 6:50—both
translate ἐγώ εἰμι). The context must determine which is meant. See Bultmann's *Kommentar*
p. 167, note 2, on these and two other meanings of the Greek formula "I am." (Tr.).

"whom the father hallowed and sent into the world" (10:36) and he who hallows himself for his own (17:19).

3. Thus it turns out in the end that Jesus as the Revealer of God *reveals nothing but that he is the Revealer.* And that amounts to saying that it is he for whom the world is waiting, he who brings in his own person that for which all the longing of man yearns: life and truth as the reality out of which man can exist, light as the complete transparence of existence in which questions and riddles are at an end. But how is he that and how does he bring it? In no other way than that he says that he is it and says that he brings it—he, a man with his human word, which, without legitimation, demands faith. John, that is, in his Gospel presents only the fact (*das Dass*) of the Revelation without describing its content (*ihr Was*).

* * * He does not give content to the Revelation by filling it with rational or speculative insights, nor by reproducing the message preached by the synoptic Jesus. Consequently, it was natural enough for investigators to declare John a mystic. For the negation of all definable Revelation-content has a counterpart in mysticism: the soul's experience, the content of which goes beyond any possibility of expression. But John is no mystic. The mystic formulas adopted by him he wishes to be understood in the sense of his Revelation-idea. Any interest in disciplining the soul or cultivating experiences of the soul ("mystical experiences") is lacking. The negative predications of God characteristic of mysticism are missing. And the negation of the world in John does not have the same meaning that it has in mysticism. That is, it does not have the ontological meaning of describing God's mode of being by the *via negationis*.[5] John's negation of the world does mean the condemnation of man, because John sees the "world" as a historical force—*viz.*, as the world constituted of men in rebellion against God. Therefore, his negating of the world means the rejecting and condemning of man's presumptuous independence and of the norms and evaluations emanating therefrom.

But if the Revelation is to be presented neither as the communication of a definite teaching nor as the kindling of a mystical experience of the soul, then all that can be presented is the bare fact of it. This fact, however, does not remain empty. For the Revelation is represented as the shattering and negating of all human self-assertion and all human norms and evaluations. And, precisely by virtue of being such negation, the Revelation is the affirmation and fulfilment of human longing for life, for true reality. That the Revelation is this positive thing can only be seen by such a faith as overcomes the "offense" and subjects itself to that negation, acknowledging its own blindness in order to receive sight (9:39). Then it becomes clear that the man called to have faith can ask for no credentials, no legitimation, no "testimony" (μαρτυρία) to the validity of the word of the Revelation.

Jesus cannot legitimate himself, cannot present "testimony" in the sense in which such is demanded by the world. The "Scriptures" do indeed bear witness to Jesus (5:39) but their meaning has been perverted by "the Jews." God, too, bears him witness (5:31f.), but this witness is not accepted by the world because it does not know God (5:37; 7:28; 8:19, 55; 16:3). And how does God bear him

---

5. Literally, "way of negation" (Latin): a description of God in terms of what God is not [editors' note].

witness? Through Jesus' own "works" (5:36f.)! But these works, as we have seen, are identical with his word—identical, that is, with his claim to be the Revealer. The testimony, therefore, is identical with that which is to be substantiated! Hence, contradictory statements can stand in the Gospel, one of which says that Jesus does not bear witness to himself (5:31ff.) and the other that he does (8:14, 18). He bears witness to himself with his "It is I." But only by faith is this testimony understood as testimony: "He who accepts his testimony has affixed his seal that God is true" (3:33 tr.). "He who believes in the Son of God has the testimony in himself. He who does not believe God has made him a liar . . ." (I Jn. 5:10). The paradox is that the word of Jesus does not find its substantiation by a backward movement from the attesting word to the thing attested—as it might if the thing itself were confirmable irrespective of the word—but finds it only in a faith-prompted acceptance of the word. This is also what is meant by the following saying: "if any man's will is to do his will, (i.e. God's) he shall know whether the (sc. my) teaching is from God or whether I am speaking on my own authority" (7:17). For "doing the will of God" here is not meant morally, as if the sentence were urging men to begin with ethics and promising that from it an understanding for dogmatics would of itself arise. No, the will of God demands nothing more nor less than faith (6:29). Only in faith is the attested matter seen, only in faith is the witness recognized as legitimate. In other words, the object of faith makes itself accessible to nothing but faith. But whoever, having such faith, "has the testimony in himself," thereby has Life itself: "And this is the confirmation: the fact that God gave us eternal life" (I Jn. 5:11 tr.).

Now it also becomes clear that the Revealer is nothing but a definite historical man, Jesus of Nazareth. Why this specific man? That is a question that must not, may not, be answered—for to do so would destroy the offense which belongs ineradicably to the Revelation. This Jesus had to meet men in a definite form, of course, but John confines himself to letting only that about Jesus become visible which was an "offense." If he presupposes that a traditional picture of Jesus and his proclamation lives on in the congregations for which he is writing, he, at any rate, wishes that picture to be understood in the light of his Revelation-idea. That would mean that he sees the meaning of the synoptic message of Jesus to be that ultimately it is the shattering and negating of the "world's" understanding of itself. In any case, he does not consider the task of the Church's proclamation to be the transmitting of the historical tradition about Jesus. The testimony of the Church is the testimony of the Spirit that was given it. The Spirit, as the "other Counselor," is Jesus' substitute (14:16). And when the Spirit "reminds" believers of all that Jesus said (14:26), this reminding is not an evocation of the past by historical reproduction. Rather, it is that which makes present the eschatological occurrence which with him burst into the world (16:8–11). When it is said that the Spirit "will guide you into the whole truth" (16:13 Blt.), that means that the Spirit teaches the believer by the light of this occurrence to understand each particular present hour.

HANS CONZELMANN

This technical but illuminating study of Luke-Acts (*Der Mitte der Zeit*, lit. "The Middle of Time" [1954]; English translation, *The Theology of St. Luke*) by Hans Conzelmann (1915–1989) is one of the first works of biblical scholarship to employ the technique of redaction criticism. Conzelmann's careful attention to the third evangelist's subtle alterations of his sources (primarily Mark) enables him to uncover and explore a previously unacknowledged theological tendency displayed by Luke-Acts, namely its careful division of sacred history into three periods—the law and the prophets, Christ's ministry, and then the church's—and its concomitant emphasis on the delay of the Parousia (Christ's second coming).

[The Middle of Time in Luke-Acts]†

Part One: Geographical Elements in the Composition of Luke's Gospel

A. PROLOGUE: JOHN THE BAPTIST

(a) THE PLACE

In the much-discussed passage iii, 1, there is geographical as well as chronological material. We are not so much concerned with determining the separate regions as with the fact that Samaria and Peræa are missing. Klostermann in discussing this passage reminds us that in official language the mention of Samaria would not be necessary. Yet it is questionable whether this can be assumed in the case of Luke. In any case his official terminology is not exact (as the use of ἡγεμών shows). Is there perhaps a connection between the omission of Samaria and other statements? We must bear this in mind as a possibility. The same applies to Peræa. This region is missing not only here, but consistently in the whole book, even where it appears in Luke's sources.

As regards iii, 3–20, the question of the relation between the desert and the Jordan as the scene of John's ministry is clearly answered by Luke in opposition to Mark (and Q?): first he is in the desert, then he appears by the Jordan. The alteration of the locality compared with the source is part of the author's editorial work, whether out of regard for the statement in the prologue or as a result of reflection on the relation between desert and water. The expression ἦλθεν εἰς πᾶσαν τὴν περίχωρον τοῦ Ἰορδάνου [He came into all the country about Jordan] suggests the idea of itinerant preaching, and all the more so, in that it has no support in the parallel passages. It is true that Matthew makes a statement which seems very similar, but it has in fact a characteristic difference: all the region round about Jordan comes to him. Matthew therefore presupposes a fixed locality by the Jordan, as Matt. iii, 6 shows. If the similarity of expression is derived from a source, namely Q, which is quite possible, as the sequel of the story of the Baptist shows,

---

† From *The Theology of St. Luke*, trans. Geoffrey Buswell (New York: Harper & Row, 1960), 18–27, 95–97, 120–132. Except as indicated, all notes are Conzelmann's.

then this variation attains greater significance as being the result of deliberate editing.

On the literary side, it should be noted that Luke omits Mark i, 5, but he presupposes the verse in v. 3 as well as later in v. 21. What is it that Luke objects to? Evidently the statement of where those who come to John have come from. He replaces it by the motif of the 'whole people', which is peculiar to him; even the term 'Judæa' is too narrow for him (or it may be an example of a 'wider' use of the concept, as many think). As will become plain later from the demarcation of the area of Jesus' ministry, the reference to the Baptist's connection with the Jordan serves a special purpose in Luke, viz., the clear demarcation of their two spheres of activity. Later, Luke will omit Mark x, 1. According to Luke, after his Baptism Jesus has no more contact with the Jordan or even with its surroundings. It is true that according to Luke Jesus does in fact come to Jericho, but it is questionable whether Luke knew that this town was in the region of the Jordan. As we shall see later, his acquaintance with Palestine is in many respects imperfect; and from the LXX, of which he made great use, Luke would find nothing to tell him that Jericho was situated in the neighbourhood of the Jordan. One might even wonder whether he avoids mentioning the Jordan because it is the river associated with John.

The alternative gives rise to a discrepancy in respect of the quotation. Luke is evidently prepared to allow this, in order to implement his idea that the Jordan is the region of the Baptist, the region of the old era, whereas the ministry of Jesus lies elsewhere. In any case 'Judæa', when connected with John, is consistently omitted in contrast with the parallel passages. People do not come to him from Judæa and Jerusalem.

The purpose of this separation from the ministry of Jesus is seen when one compares Luke iii, 21 and iv, 1, 14 with Mark.[1] The distinction of locality corresponds to a fundamental distinction, for John does not proclaim the Kingdom of God, as is made plain in xvi, 16 as a point of principle.

Thus the locality of the Baptist becomes remarkably vague. Luke can associate him neither with Judæa nor with Galilee, for these are both areas of Jesus' activity. Yet on the other hand there has to be some connection, so the Baptist is placed on the border [i.e., the Jordan river]. It is obvious that Luke has no exact knowledge of the area, and this is why he can make such a straightforward symbolical use of localities.

He creates a further discrepancy by introducing a motif of his own: in place of the Pharisees and Sadducees he puts the ὄχλοι [multitude]. This might be derived from Mark i, 5, but with variations. Verses 7, 10 and 20 show how consistently this has been done, and in vii, 29 Luke attributes to Jesus the statement that 'all' were baptized.

In other words, all the people are baptized, but their leaders without exception refuse to be baptized [3:21; 7:29]. In this way Luke creates a peculiar variant of

---

1. Luke omits the information as to where Jesus came from. Chapter iv, 1 stresses the final departure from the Jordan and iv, 14 mentions Galilee as the destination. Apart from iv, 1 (and the omission in iii, 21) this is the first mention of Galilee. Therefore John has nothing to do with this region, although Luke knows that John and Jesus are under the same ruler (ix, 8 ff.). Is the disappearance of Peræa from the story of Jesus connected with this demarcation?

the idea of the people of God within Israel. We have therefore right at the beginning two distinct groups (in Luke's view, of course, actual historical groups) forming the background to the ministry of Jesus.

The explanatory remark in iii, 15 is to be regarded as an editorial comment by Luke. The verse corresponds both formally and as regards meaning to v. 21.

The reference to the imprisonment in iii, 19 f. divides the section concerning John from the section concerning Jesus in the sense of drawing a distinction between the epochs of salvation, for which xvi, 16 provides the clue. Now the way is open for the story of Jesus. The fact that the activity of the two still overlaps cannot be entirely eliminated, but Luke deprives it of any real significance. According to iii, 21 f. Jesus is baptized as one of the people, like everyone else. Luke excludes any suggestion that John plays an important part in the incident. This is in keeping with his whole conception of the significance of John.

* * *

(b) THE SIGNIFICANCE OF JOHN THE BAPTIST ACCORDING TO LUKE

In the pre-Lucan tradition John is understood from the standpoint of the dawn of the new eschatological age. He is more than a prophet, he is the forerunner, he is Elijah. Here Mark and Matthew use traditions which Luke himself has preserved for us, so it is all the more striking that Luke's own pronouncements point in another direction. It is true that he does not set out his views coherently, but he indicates it whenever he speaks of John by what he omits and by what he adds.[2]

In the tradition John the Baptist stands on the dividing line between the old and the new epoch. He not only announces the imminent Kingdom of God, but is himself a sign of its arrival. This is what is implied by the interpretation of his figure (not only of his teaching) as that of the forerunner, under the influence of the apocalyptic expectation of Elijah. This is implied by the position which Mark gives him at the opening of the Gospel.[3]

Luke uses the existing material, but transforms it in a characteristic way. Nowhere in his writings is a figure from the past brought into direct connection with the future eschatological events. On the contrary, existing interpretations are rejected. Instead of being directly linked with the eschatological events, the figure is given a definite place in a continuous story of salvation, the end of which is not yet in sight. John no longer marks the arrival of the new aeon, but the division between two epochs in the one continuous story, such as is described in Luke xvi, 16. The eschatological events do not break out after John, but a new stage in the process of salvation is reached, John himself still belonging to the earlier of the two epochs which meet at this point. This transformation of the tradition concerning John affects all the different sources, and therefore is to be attributed to Luke himself.

2. We are not taking the prologue into consideration here. The view it contains is expressed in i, 17 and i, 76.

3. In the Acts of the Apostles there is in this connection a specific use of ἀρχή-ἄρχεσθαι [beginning, to begin] which corresponds to Mark i, 1; both in Acts x, 37 and in Acts xiii, 24 the preaching of John is mentioned not for its content; but for its function as an eschatological sign.

As we have already said, Luke xvi, 16 provides the key to the topography of redemptive history. According to this passage, there is no preparation before Jesus for the proclamation of the Kingdom of God, that is, of the 'Gospel' in Luke's sense.[4] A statement such as Matthew iii, 2 is impossible in Luke. Of course it does not follow that because the preaching of the Kingdom by John is disputed, the preaching of repentance is also disputed. On the contrary, this is his real task. What is more, it is this that persists on into the new epoch. To the traditional verse Luke xvi, 16 there is immediately added the obviously editorial statement of v. 17. Thus even if the original sense of this verse pointed to a break, to the supersession of the old aeon by the new, Luke makes it point at the same time to a continuity: until now there was 'only' the law and the Prophets, but from now on there is 'also' the preaching of the Kingdom. Therefore the preaching of repentance is continued by Jesus. It is John's role to prepare the way for this by preaching and baptism, and his great merit is that he refused to claim for himself the Messianic role. At the same time, however, this makes plain John's limitations: it is only through the proclamation of the Kingdom that John's preaching, and only through the Spirit that John's baptism, are raised to a level appropriate to the new epoch.

Apart from the prologue Luke recognizes no typological correspondence between John the Baptist and Jesus. One might even wonder whether he did not deliberately exclude any indications of it.[5] The fact is that two epochs meet at this point, and although they have a connection, they have to be all the more clearly distinguished because even in the new epoch it is a question of a continuation of the one redemptive history. Yet John has to be described in the categories of the old epoch, as a 'precursor', as Elijah, or as a sign of the 'arrival'.[6] If his baptism is described as a baptism of repentance, the accent does not lie so much on the fact of its being an advance over earlier times, as on how it falls short compared with Christian baptism with the Spirit. To what extent this distinction concerns the author is shown by the continued reference to the problem in Acts (i, 5; xi, 16; xviii, 24–xix, 7). We have already mentioned the motif which is of importance for the composition of redemptive history, viz., that all the people submit to John's baptism.[7]

Thus John has a clearly defined function in the centre of the story of salvation. As it is his ministry rather than his person that serves as a preparation for Jesus, he is subordinate to the work of Jesus in the same way as is the whole epoch of the Law.

---

4. One cannot appeal against this view to the word εὐαγγελίζεσθαι [lit., "to announce good news"] in Luke iii, 18. In this context it means simply 'to preach'. In Luke John is thought of as quite unconnected with the message of the Kingdom. The *praeparatio* is not conceived by Luke in eschatological categories, as in the other Synoptics, but is seen in the simple fact of the preaching of repentance, which is valued therefore not because it is a sign, but because of its content.

5. Why does he omit the account of John's death? Perhaps in order to avoid a possible typological parallel. Why does he emphasize so strongly in another passage that John is dead and cannot return?

6. In Luke's view there is only one prelude to the Parousia: the Resurrection of Jesus. And even this is separated from the Parousia by a long interval.

7. Luke finds in this the explanation as to why Jesus himself does not baptize. John has performed it extensively—and a new stage of baptism presupposes the sending of the Spirit. Is the omission of the confession of sin (in contrast to Mark i, 5) linked with the fact that baptism is connected with the earlier period?

Luke recognizes neither earthly precursors of the Parousia nor those appearing from heaven. In iii, 16 he even omits ὀπίσω μου [after me]. John is great, but not in the Kingdom of God. In addition to this fact, we must also consider Luke's view of Moses and Elijah. Again it plainly contradicts the prologue, where in i, 17 John is linked with Elijah. Luke's own view stands out here particularly clearly. Luke can find apologetic on behalf of the Baptist in his sources. Yet in respect of these two figures he is quite independent, but consistent, as a result of his eschatology.

The apologetic note is strengthened; cf. the addition in iii, 15, and the contrast brought out in passages such as Acts i, 5, xi, 16 and xiii, 23 ff. Luke's sources use the precursor motif in their apologetic: John is not the Messiah but 'only' the preparer of the way. He may be Elijah. Luke's argument, however, is the reverse of this: John is not the precursor, for there is no such thing, but he is the last of the prophets (cf. the omission from Mark i, 7 already mentioned). Luke ix, 8 informs us that John is dead and appears no more. Nothing definite is said about Elijah: but this applies only in the actual historical situation, that is to say, in the case of Herod. He does not wish to commit himself to do anything about John. We have to distinguish between what Luke makes Herod say and what he himself thinks. The argument concerning John presupposes the general doctrine that before the Parousia there is no resurrection apart from that of Jesus, no return to earth of figures from the past. As far as Elijah and Moses are concerned, Luke answers the undecided question in the story of the Transfiguration, ix, 28–36. With their appearances here the role of both of them is completed. Luke emphasizes, by way of correcting his source, that this is in fact their role: they come as heavenly messengers to Jesus, but only to him, not publicly. According to Luke they do not even speak in the hearing of the three disciples. Therefore it is foolish to look for precursors; the Kingdom does not come μετὰ παρατηρήσεως [with observation; Luke 17:20], it comes suddenly. In Luke's view evidently this element of surprise is a refutation of the apocalyptic idea of the precursor. Luke xvii, 30 ff. is relevant to this. Any suggestion of a false interpretation has to be removed. As a consequence therefore Mark ix, 9–12 is omitted. The Elijah-motif is excluded also from the account of Jesus' death, hence the absence of Mark xv, 35.

The tension between tradition and the adaptation of it can be seen in Luke vii, 18–35. Verses 28–30 presumably contain the author's interpretation, although perhaps influenced by the source. In the tradition John was more than a prophet; now he becomes the greatest prophet. This agrees with xvi, 16. He is included within the saving events, for it is God's will that men should be baptized, but not that one should think of John in an eschatological sense. The people fulfil God's will, whilst the leaders keep themselves apart; in this way John gives support to the claim made by Christians that they are Israel.[8]

Already before Luke one of the main themes of the tradition concerning John is that he marks a division in the story of salvation, so now Luke proceeds to build up his scheme of successive epochs (xvi, 16). Acts x, 37 and xiii, 25 show how he does it. Because of the emphasis on the separation of the epochs, the fact that

8. In anticipation we may say that as a result of this the leaders are thought of as a merely secular factor, along with all those who support them. Luke xx, 1–8 is closely related to vii, 18 ff.

the ministry of John and that of Jesus overlap to a certain extent in time is lost sight of. This is shown by the statement in Luke iii, 19 f., which contains nothing new and yet provides the key to Luke's composition. It is true that it is not in the 'right' place from the historical or the literary point of view. Yet this position is not the result of following a source, so we must conclude that it has been fixed by the author. These verses form the dividing line between the section about John and that about Jesus, and their purpose apparently is, in view of the temporal overlap, to make clear the fundamental separation.

The exit of John has no particular significance, and we learn of his death incidentally in ix, 9. His fate is that of the prophets [Luke 11:47; Acts 7:52], and is not an eschatological event.

The account of John's preaching completes the picture. By the insertion of this special section we are given the pattern of his preaching:

(1) The threat of judgement, which provides the motive for
(2) The challenge to repent and be converted (which to Luke's mind are separate conceptions).
(3) Exhortation.

In Matthew John's teaching has a definitely Christological bearing. In Luke it is directed to conversion, baptism and exhortation. The Christological reference, on the other hand, is made relatively independent by the insertion of v. 15, and thus acquires a more polemical and apologetic flavour.

To sum up, we may say that Luke employs geographical factors for the purpose of setting out his fundamental conception, and that he modifies his sources to a considerable extent. This modification takes the form of a conscious editorial process of omissions, additions, and alterations in the wording of the sources. It is plain that his purpose is to keep separate the respective localities of John and of Jesus. As far as the outline of Jesus' life is concerned, it is the beginning of his own ministry that marks the 'arché' [beginning] not, as in Mark, the appearance of John. It is not until now that the region of Galilee is mentioned, Luke having omitted it from Mark i, 9.

Part Two: Luke's Eschatology

I. THE PROBLEM

We are not concerned with the eschatology of Jesus or with that of the primitive Christian community, but with the eschatological conceptions which Luke sets out, and which underlie his description of the life of Jesus and of the work of the Spirit in the life of the Church.

If we wish to see the peculiar features of his conception, we have to reckon of course with discrepancies between the ideas in his sources and his own ideas. It is these very discrepancies that help us to understand which motifs are peculiar to Luke. For example, in the quotation from Joel in the story of Pentecost (Acts ii, 17 ff.), the Spirit is thought of as a sign of the End, in the source and also in Luke, but the interpretation is different in each case. In their original sense the 'last days' have not yet been expanded into a longer epoch, which is what happens in Luke's conception of the Spirit and of the Church, according to which the outpouring of the Spirit is no longer itself the start of the Eschaton, but the beginning of a longer epoch, the period of the Church. It is true that this is the last epoch in the course of redemptive history, but this very fact represents a change in the understanding of the 'last days'. The Spirit Himself is no longer the eschatological gift, but the substitute in the meantime for the possession of ultimate salvation; He makes it possible for believers to exist in the continuing life of the world and in persecution, and He gives the power for missionary endeavour and for endurance. This change in the understanding of eschatology can be seen in the way in which Luke, by his description of history, depicts the nature of the Church, its relation to the world, and the course of the mission in its progress step by step, and in the way in which he repeatedly describes the Spirit as the power behind this whole process. As far as the history of tradition is concerned, this means that Luke employs for his reconstruction of history the traditional material, which is stamped with the view that the last days have already arrived.

Wellhagen traces the 'weakening' of the 'primitive eschatological theme' through the various aspects, the view of the Church, e.g., of the Spirit, and of the ministry.[9] Everywhere he sees as the basic theme that of the mission and of the Church, and rightly affirms that this represents a slackening of the eschatological expectation and a shift of emphasis in view of the continuance of the Church in the world. But when his investigations are complete, the task of understanding the specifically Lucan form of eschatology as a phenomenon in its own context remains. For this task literary criticism and form analysis are necessary, although there is practically no analysis of the text in Wellhagen.

According to him, this 'weakening' is something which 'happens' to Luke in the same way as to the Church of his time in general: in principle the early expectation is preserved, but in reality it is weakened. But this leaves unexplained the deliberate intention with which Luke recasts his sources, and also the fact that he does not preserve the early expectation, but eliminates it. We see the extent of this recasting if we make a comprehensive comparison with the sources, particularly with the Marcan passages. Such a comparison shows that it is not an adequate explanation of Luke's alterations to see them merely as 'development', but that it is a question of a definite theological attitude to the problem of eschatology. Luke in fact replaces the early expectation by a comprehensive scheme of a different kind. In Wellhagen eschatology, redemptive history and the Church are unrelated, held together merely by a view of the Church which only serves to blur the problems. The fact that these themes are ranged alongside each other, however, raises the question, whether the author was not aware of the problem of their relationship. This is primarily a question that concerns the text, but it is one that has to be asked. We shall see that a connection is in fact established between the different themes.

Luke's eschatology, compared with the original conception of the imminence of the Kingdom, is a secondary construction based on certain considerations which with the passage of time cannot be avoided. It is obvious what gives rise to these reflections—the delay of the Parousia. The original idea presupposes that what is hoped for is near, which means that the hope cannot be reconciled with

9. Julius Wellhagen, *Anden och riket* (Stockholm, 1941) [editors' note].

a delay, as otherwise the connection with the present would be lost. The same is true of Jewish apocalyptic, for here also out of affliction there arises the hope of an early deliverance, but with the passage of time the hope necessarily becomes 'apocalyptic'. This explains the analogy between the Jewish and the Christian development. The primitive Christian hope, which at first had an immediate bearing, suffers a similar fate to its Jewish predecessor: salvation is delayed. Thus the way is open for accepting the old apocalyptic ideas.

Eschatology as an imminent hope belonging to the present cannot by its very nature be handed down by tradition. It is only the ideas concerning what is hoped for, not the hope itself, that can be transmitted. It is well known that all the stages in the contrast between the beginning of eschatology and the growth of apocalyptic ideas can be found both separately and merging into one another; this is because from the outset the eschatological hope has to be expressed in concepts, and on the other hand in all the speculative development the connection with concrete reality is never lost. If we trace the 'development' from Luke's sources to his own outline, we see not so much phases in a temporal development as the basic elements in the structure of eschatological thought. Of course time itself is a factor in the development, in so far as the delay of the Parousia plays a vital part in the transformation of the hope.

* * *

4. LUKE xvii, 20 ff.

We will now turn to the expositions of the theme of the Last Things. We shall not repeat in full the many discussions of the famous ἐντός [within or among].* * * Instead we shall consider the relation of this teaching to Luke's whole conception of eschatology, and also the special problems which Luke raises.

We have already indicated the questions which are of concern to Luke, and which prompt him to a reconsideration of the whole complex of eschatological ideas, and which also influence his particular account of the course and the nature of the Last Things.

We have noted previously distinct signs of a change of attitude to eschatology, but there is one question that has not been definitely answered: is this change a process, a part of the general development within the Church, of the problem of which Luke himself was scarcely aware? Are we therefore to form the same opinion of Luke as of his predecessor Mark, who retains the early expectation, but yet shows traces of a change of attitude, or is Luke perhaps aware of the problematic situation in which he stands? Does he lay before us a new outline, and thus provide a solution which will not demand further revision in the course of time?

The answer emerges from the fact that the problem which determines Luke's treatment of his material, which is for the most part derived from tradition, is imported by Luke himself into his material and also from the fact that this material itself is transformed in its general structure and in individual sayings in the light of this problem, by means of corrections and omissions.

The basic question, that concerning the time, appears on four occasions: Luke xvii, 20; xix, 11; xxi, 7, and Acts i, 6. On one occasion—Acts i, 7—it is dismissed on grounds of principle. On three occasions it is the subject of detailed teaching; in chapters xvii and xxi the apocalyptic theme is directly dealt with. Chapter xix, vv. 11 ff., gives the answer—a denial of the general supposition—in the form of a parable. Throughout, it is linked with the problem of Jerusalem. It is true that in chapter xvii this link is indicated only by the context of the report of the journey (xvii, 11), but in other passages it is stated explicitly: in xix, 11 by the editorial form of the question, in chapter xxi by the connection with the Temple theme, and in Acts i, 6 f. by the connection with the command to remain in the city (v. 4). The order of the arrangement should be noted. Chapter xvii, vv. 20 ff. provides the answer to the question of the Pharisee, one which is commonly asked but which, according to Luke, is asked by a man who agrees with the Christians in acknowledging belief in the resurrection; the teaching after xix, 11 is directed to the disciples in view of their special question about the relation between Jerusalem and the End; there is a corresponding situation in Acts i; and finally, Luke xxi is addressed to all according to Luke. As regards the fundamental issue, there are three things that are excluded: apocalyptic calculations in general, the connection with the fate of Jerusalem, and calculations based on the Resurrection of Jesus.

The problem of the exegesis of Luke xvii, 20 ff., has been clearly stated by J. Weiss: is the Kingdom a present or a future entity? If one thinks of it as belonging entirely to the future, then what is the meaning of the statement that it is ἐντὸς ὑμῶν [within/among you]? If one thinks of it as present, then what is the nature of this presence supposed to be? Is it present in the person of Jesus, in the Church, in certain events, or in an immanent, organic development? The exegesis of this passage brings to light the central problem not only of the Synoptic eschatology, but also that of the eschatology of Jesus which has to be reconstructed from it. Too little consideration is given to the particular features of Luke's conception.

The futurist interpretation is as follows: it is not the Kingdom that is present, but the preliminary signs of it. The external manifestation is not disputed, but calculating when it will take place is contested. This is a correct observation, which must now be linked with the problem of the Parousia in Luke. There is of course a definite reason for the rejection of calculations, viz., the denial of the early expectation. The real problem in the passage is the juxtaposition of the statement 'ἐντὸς' and the detailed account of the course of the Last Things which follows immediately. In view of the analogous passage xix, 11, it cannot really be disputed that Luke means by the Kingdom a future entity. The spiritualizing interpretation according to which the Kingdom is present in the Spirit and in the Church is completely misleading, for Luke sets these two factors strictly within his scheme of the periods of history: during the time of Jesus' earthly life they are not yet present, but the Messianic manifestations are present and visible (iv, 18 ff.). In them salvation has come to light and has become effective. It is the message of the Kingdom that is present, which in Luke is distinguished from the Kingdom itself. He knows nothing of an immanent development on the basis of the preaching of the Kingdom.

It should not be overlooked that it is only here and in xxii, 18 that the 'coming' of the Kingdom is mentioned, and here it is not spoken of by way of positive proclamation, but in a critical attitude which brings out its limitations. The main declaration is not that the Kingdom is coming, but that the Kingdom is being preached by Jesus and made manifest in his ministry. The 'coming' itself belongs to the future, and is separated by a long interval from this manifestation. It is not that a development leading up to the Kingdom has begun with Jesus, but that in Him salvation has 'appeared', so that from now on one can see it and be assured of it.

Although this passage has to be linked with the aspect of Jesus' ministry, its specific significance can only be seen within the pattern of Christology and of redemptive history. The basis is Luke's conception of the period of Jesus as the middle epoch, described as the period of salvation within the whole course of redemptive history. This does not exclude, but includes, the future hope and the purely transcendent version of the concept of the Kingdom. The fact that the great objective description of the future follows immediately upon v. 21 is not the result of a merely accidental accumulation of traditions that have been thrown together. We see here the essence of Luke's plan: the further the Parousia recedes into the distance, the better can it be described from an objective point of view, but at the same time its connection with the present has to be brought out all the more clearly, if the expectation is not to turn into mere speculation, and become an end in itself. It is this that Luke wants to prevent. His struggle is essentially an anti-apocalyptic one. This is proved by the repeated treatment of the question of the time of the Parousia—and by the rejection of the question as such.

Turning to certain details, we may consider first the extent of the immediate context, according to Luke. The fact that Jesus is addressing a different audience in v. 22 does not signify a transition to a new theme, as though the account of the 'Kingdom' as an immanent entity was now followed by the description of the Parousia as a future occurrence, but it denotes the explanation—in secret—of what has been said. A comparison with Luke xxi, where the same teaching is given in public, shows that the fact that it is here given in secret is of no fundamental significance. It merely serves to mark what follows as interpretation. The change of audience might also be required because it helps the author to set out what follows as a continuous speech. There are of course certain passages (e.g. xviii, 1 ff.) which by their very nature can be addressed only to the disciples.

The section xviii, 1–8 provides a commentary on the petition 'Thy Kingdom come', a petition which is fulfilled at the Parousia. This helps us to see the structure of xvii, 24–37: vv. 26–30 show how men will behave, and vv. 31 f. show the attitude that is required. Verses 24 and 37 deal with how and where the Parousia will take place. The remaining verses serve to emphasize the teaching of the verses we have mentioned.

The image in v. 24 underlines the warning in v. 23. The lightning stands for suddenness, not * * * the impossibility of misunderstanding. 'Days' is a technical eschatological term. In the present context the plural indicates that the Eschaton is no longer imagined as one complete event, but as a succession of events distinct from one another. * * *

What then is the meaning of ἐντός? The answer to this question is not as important as is often supposed. Whether we take the word to mean 'intra' or 'inter', it does not vitally affect Luke's conception of eschatology. It is clear that the Kingdom itself is not an immanent, spiritual entity. It is a fundamental fact that the account of the Last Things, which is far fuller than in the sources, corresponds to the increased emphasis on its transcendence. Here we see what is for Luke the typical parallel between sayings about the nature of the Kingdom, which have no reference to time, and sayings about temporal events. He has reached the goal of his apologetic: the Kingdom has appeared in Christ, although its presence is not now immanent in the Church.

But the Church possesses a picture that can never be lost, because it possesses the account of Jesus. By virtue of this it can endure in the world. In xviii, 1–8 we see the practical aim of the teaching. From now on the time of the Parousia can no longer present to the Church a problem on which it might come to grief, for in view of the information in vv. 20 f., it becomes impossible even to ask about it.

5. LUKE xxi

We can deal briefly with the literary critical problem. The attempts of English critics in particular to reconstruct a non-Marcan source in addition to Mark, which would also provide a complete eschatological outline, cannot be considered successful. They misunderstand both the extent and the individuality of Luke's revision. The divergences from Mark prove to be the result of editorial work, in which a definite plan can be traced.

The description of the setting in vv. 5–7 is definitely editorial. Luke abandons the symbolism of Mark's setting, according to which Jesus speaks from the Mount of Olives 'over against' the Temple, and transfers the speech to the Temple, before an audience which has been listening to Jesus each day. This is in keeping with Luke's scheme, according to which there are before the Last Supper only two places in which Jesus is found: in the Temple by day, and on the Mount of Olives by night (xxi, 37 f.). This scheme is part of Luke's editorial work.

In v. 7 the expression ταῦτα γενέσθαι [shall these things be], which is in contrast to Mark's συντελεῖσθαι πάντα [all these things shall be fulfilled, 13:4], comes from the editor. Mark's saying has the sense of eschatological fulfilment, but Luke is concerned in what follows with events which do not belong to the Eschaton.

In v. 8 Luke avoids the word βασιλεία [kingdom]. Of course he cannot dispute that Jesus did in fact say that the Kingdom was near at hand, therefore he avoids the phrase and prevents a wrong interpretation of it by replacing βασιλεία by καιρός [time]. The references to time in v. 9, πρῶτον [first] and οὐκ εὐθέως [not by and by], and in v. 12, πρὸ δὲ τούτων [before all these], prove to be elements in a whole conception, which is based on the Marcan text. The latter is not broken up and completely re-composed, but in particular instances Luke reveals his different arrangement by corrections such as these, although as a result earlier material is not mentioned until later, and vice versa.

Mark is already using traditional material, and even in him a certain postponement of the Parousia can be traced [Mark 13:8; cf. Luke 21:10]. His aim already is to correct an apocalyptic tradition which is predominantly Jewish. In particular he has to transform the sayings about the fate of the Temple, which he does by deliberately placing it within the context of the Last Things.[1]

---

1. The disciples have understood correctly that Jesus is speaking of the End, and they ask concerning the time, that of the whole eschatological event. If this is meant as a correction of a widespread apocalyptic tendency in the community, then v. 4 must have been formulated as such by Mark.

In the first part of his exposition there are two references to time, οὔπω τὸ τέλος [the end shall not be yet] in v. 7, and ἀρχὴ ὠδίνων ταῦτα [these are the beginnings of sorrows] in v. 8. The first gives a clear indication of the aim which Mark is pursuing, whether it is a Jewish or a Christian expectation that he is correcting. He shares the general expectation that there will be a time of war, but he makes the correction: οὔπω τὸ τέλος evidently because the idea of the Messianic war has no place in the Christian expectation, but only the supernatural advent of the Messiah. There is, however, some connection: ἀρχὴ ὠδίνων ταῦτα. The next mention of time is in v. 10, which envisages a fairly long period of missionary activity.[2]

We must now consider what use Luke makes of Mark. Once again in his great synopsis we see that the imminence of the End has ceased to play any vital part in Luke. What is merely hinted at in Mark has become in Luke a definite idea, as our analysis will show.

The new form of v. 7—after the alteration of the setting, which reveals a changed attitude to the Temple—excludes the eschatological interpretation of the fate of the Temple which is fundamental in Mark. The importance of this apparently insignificant alteration will become clear later. In v. 8 the stock phrase of the early expectation is introduced by way of amplification. Then there come the extensive, but again apparently insignificant, corrections in the chronological arrangement, of which there is a foreshadowing in v. 9. Luke does his work of amplification systematically. He inserts πρῶτον [first] and brings out the meaning of Mark's οὔπω [not yet], but in the following passage he simply breaks down Mark's structure. Instead of the conjunctional γάρ [for] he provides a new opening: τότε ἔλεγει [then he said, v.10], which in this context means that up to now the principle has been stated but that now there follows a systematic exposition. This, however, cannot be achieved simply by a carefully planned construction of the description, for it is prevented by the connection with Mark's text. Thus the events of v. 12, which Luke places before the conflict of the nations (v. 10) and the cosmic upheavals of v. 11, have to be introduced by πρὸ δὲ τούτων [before all these]. Mark's statement in v. 8, ἀρχὴ ὠδίνων [beginning of sorrows], must now of course disappear, as according to Luke the events of v. 12, the persecution of the Church, mark the beginning. As a consequence of the recasting, Mark xiii, 10 also disappears, with its now superfluous πρῶτον. The universal proclamation is achieved in the present, as the second part of Luke's writings shows. Luke therefore sees the persecution only as the prelude to the Last Things. It is in keeping with this that the situation in the present is described, and the word of comfort inserted in v. 18. Here again we can see the change of attitude: in v. 14 the simple 'Be not anxious' is given a psychological import, so that it becomes a conscious attitude towards oneself. It is not the Spirit Himself who speaks, but man, although of course it is given him what he is to speak. The aim, as in chapter xvii (and xviii, 1) is the exhortation to ὑπομονή [endurance], in other words, to adjustment to a long period of persecution, for such is the existence of the Church in the world.

2. Matthew transposes the verse and achieves a more compact train of thought.

Whereas Mark goes on to give a fuller description of the eschatological events, Luke now gives a polemical excursus about matters which are mistakenly included among the eschatological events, namely the destruction of Jerusalem and the Temple. In this way eschatology is lifted out of any historical context, and is removed from all events which take place within history. Thus the apocalyptic allusion in Mark xiii, 14 disappears, because one cannot 'read' of such a thing (N.B. Luke's concept of Scripture) and because it has nothing to do with the Eschaton.

Verses 21b, 22, 25b, 26a and 28 can be considered as examples of Lucan interpretation. The section vv. 34–6 with its 'Pauline' terminology may have been composed by Luke or taken over by him, but in any case it makes clear what is his own aim and also how he uses existing material. We can see Luke's editorial activity also in the omissions: Mark xiii, 21–3, 24 are omitted, and in Bultmann's view v. 20 is altered in the light of events.[3]

Luke recognizes that there are signs—cf. v. 11 (note, however, the alterations compared with Mark); but, as xvii, 21 reminds us, they do not signify that the coming is imminent, but they point to a long period which comes first. The Kingdom is announced for a long time—and then it comes like lightning. A systematic account of this preliminary period can be given. The coming itself is not included in the description. By combining the various chronological references, we arrive at the following picture:

    (*a*) the period of persecution, with which the exhortation, i.e. vv. 14 ff., is
         concerned. Luke places great emphasis upon this.

Not until then do

    (*b*) the period of political dissolution, and
    (*c*) the period of cosmic dissolution,

follow, by which the End is gradually ushered in.

However, as it is not the sequence of events as such that is most important, but the instructions addressed to the *ecclesia pressa* [oppressed church], we are given a criticism of the prevailing errors. We find this already in Mark, but here it is considerably expanded, and at the same time elements which are still eschatological in Mark are excluded (cf. vv. 20 ff.).[4]

Verse 19 emphasizes more strongly than Mark that deliverance is the result of patience (Mark still thinks of the End in an immediate eschatological sense, whereas Luke introduces into the conception a preliminary period, therefore he can omit εἰς τέλος [unto the end]). The addition in v. 18 is in keeping with this; it is a variation of a traditional logion (Luke xii, 7/Matt. x, 30), and now points to the future resurrection as a comfort for the martyr. Verse 16 ('some shall be put to death') completes the picture. The account is transferred from an eschatological background to that of the Church. Time after time we meet the same

3. Rudolf Bultmann, *The History of the Synoptic Tradition*, trans. John Marsh (New York: Harper and Row, 1963) [editors' note].

4. Even the exhortation in vv. 14 ff. has a stronger psychological colouring. What is referred to in v. 13 is not the confession of faith, which serves as 'a testimony' in the eschatological sense to the one who is addressed, but the testimony which the one who confesses receives from God. It is not necessary yet to take 'testimony' in a technical sense.

readjustment from an immediate eschatology to martyrdom as a present fact in which the eschatological prospect provides consolation. The saying in v. 18, which in itself speaks of the general providence of God, is now addressed to those who are killed in the persecution.

We shall omit for the time being the passage concerning Jerusalem. As these events no longer belong to the context of eschatology, a further significant theme disappears, that of the merciful shortening of the sufferings (cf. Mark xiii, 19 f.). We have already mentioned that Mark xiii, 21–3 are omitted. It is Luke's aim to relegate the Parousia to a still greater distance. The times of the Gentiles (v. 24) have not yet come; it is only the time of the Jewish dispersion, and the End will not come until after the cosmic upheaval (vv. 25 f.). In Mark the cosmic signs and the Parousia form one complex of events, but in Luke they are separated.

In v. 27 we find the last of the chronological references, in this case simply the same as in Mark, but its significance is modified by the change of context. If we summarize once again all Luke's statements, the following structure emerges: persecution, the distress of nations, cosmic signs and the end of the nations, and finally the Parousia. Verse 28 then contains instructions for the Christian, which refer especially to the period of the cosmic signs—not to the 'beginning', as in Mark—just as the teaching in vv. 14 ff. has a special reference to the epoch of persecution. Until then the important thing is not to allow oneself to be bewildered. It should be noted that the cosmic upheaval does not affect the elect; on the contrary, it brings them liberation. The present meaning of vv. 29–31 emerges from the context. As they now stand, they provide a fuller explanation of v. 28: now, in the last crisis of the world, believers can lift up their heads. It is not until now that one can rightly say 'the Kingdom is at hand'. This is the key to all Luke's sayings about the nearness of the Kingdom.

Whilst the separate events before the Parousia are described in considerable detail, the description of the Parousia itself is cut down—cf. Luke xxi, 27 with Mark xiii, 26 f. It is true that the description of the appearing of the Son of Man is the same word for word, but in Luke the escort of angels is omitted. This is in keeping with Luke's conception of angels, according to which they are subject only to God, not to the Son (Luke also omits Mark i, 13; cf. Luke ix, 26 and Mark viii, 38). At the Parousia they seem to stay in Heaven and form the background when the Son of Man sits in judgement (Luke xii, 8 f.; xv, 10; cf. the stress on τοῦ θεοῦ [of God]).

In connection with the timing of the Parousia, Mark xiii, 32, is omitted, for although the Son knows the day and the hour, it is not for us to know.[5]

In v. 32 Luke omits ταῦτα [these things], as a result of which the saying does not refer to the matters that have just been mentioned, but to the whole of the

5. The same view is present in Acts i, 6, where one cannot infer from harmonizing it with the Marcan passage that Jesus did not know; similarly there is no indication of any differentiation by Luke between the knowledge possessed by Jesus while on earth and that possessed by the Exalted Lord. According to Luke, Jesus has a knowledge of the Last Things while still on earth; otherwise he could not give all this instruction. For according to Luke, knowledge of the Last Things is not part of Scriptural prophecy, which extends only to the coming of the Spirit.

Divine plan. 'This generation' means here humanity in general, whereas in Mark it is doubtful who is meant, especially if one also considers Mark ix, 1. The saying is no longer a declaration that the End is near at hand.

Again there follows, as the climax of the account, as we have already mentioned, the practical application and exhortation. As the verses are closely linked with vv. 32 f., they too no doubt need to be seen in the light of the hortatory theme, i.e. less as promise than as warning: this generation will not escape the judgement. Here again the summons to endurance forms the climax and the conclusion, as in v. 19 above and also xviii, 1.

Summary

The main motif in the recasting to which Luke subjects his source, proves to be the delay of the Parousia, which leads to a comprehensive consideration of the nature and course of the Last Things. Whereas originally the imminence of the End was the most important factor, now other factors enter. The delay has to be explained, and this is done by means of the idea of God's plan which underlies the whole structure of Luke's account.[6] Corresponding to this there is also the greater emphasis on the suddenness of the irruption. The hortatory nature of the context is obvious. As the End is still far away, the adjustment to a short time of waiting is replaced by a 'Christian life' of long duration, which requires ethical regulation and is no longer dependent upon a definite termination. The virtue of ὑπομονή [endurance] comes to the fore. The appeal is no longer based on the time, but on the fact of a future Judgement. The ethical teaching is coloured by the fact that persecution now prevails. Endurance is viewed from the standpoint of martyrdom, although the specific terminology of martyrdom has not yet been developed. The longer the time of waiting, the greater the impact of suffering, which makes the expected End 'endlessly' remote.

In line with the modification we have described, there is in Luke a shift of emphasis from the imminent End to the general idea of the resurrection of the dead, independent of any fixed time. In Luke xxi it is merely hinted at—because of both the theme and the source—but there is a suggestion of it. Where Luke is freely composing, it comes to the fore.

We see also how, by removing the End to a greater distance, a more reflective attitude emerges, as a result of which the individual events are separated. This development is parallel to the other development, by which the past is broken up into its separate component parts. Thus we see how the whole story of salvation, as well as the life of Jesus in particular, is now objectively set out and described according to its successive stages.

---

6. The Qumran sect is faced with a similar problem: 1 Q p Hab, VII, 7 ff.: 'For still the vision is for an appointed time; it hastens to the period and does not lie. This means that the last period extends over and above all that the prophets said; for the mysteries of God are marvellous.' This gives rise to the same summons as in Luke—to the 'men of truth, the doers of the law, whose hands do not grow slack from the service of the truth, when the last period is stretched out over them. For all the periods of God will come to their fixed term, as he decreed for them in the mysteries of his wisdom.' (Translation by M. Burrows, *The Dead Sea Scrolls*, 1955, p. 368.)

BRIGITTE KAHL

No Longer Male:
Masculinity Struggles Behind Galatians 3.28?[†]

There is not Jew nor Greek, there is not slave nor free, there is not male and female,
for you all are one in Christ Jesus (Gal. 3.28).

Feminist and liberation oriented readings rather commonly have treated the baptismal formula of Gal. 3.26–28 as a kind of *ET*, a lovely lonely alien unhappily trapped in the hostile matter of a Pauline letter. While testifying to an egalitarian life practice in the congregations before, besides, and against Paul, it is considered to fit only loosely into the specific context of Galatians: Paul mainly quotes the baptismal unity of Jew and Greek as he wants to dissuade the Galatian Gentiles from getting circumcised as Jews. The emancipatory message, however, of slave/free and male/female becoming one in Christ—if it is emancipatory at all—is mostly irrelevant to the rest of the Galatian debate and to the patriarchal mindset of Paul in general.

There are, however, weighty reasons to perceive Gal. 3.28 in its threefold dimension as tightly interwoven with the textual and theological structure of Galatians as a whole. In fact, Paul's most famous and controversial statement on the border-transgressing unity of nation/culture/religion (Jew–Greek), of class/social status (slave–free), and of biological sex (male–female) can be seen not only as a coherent part, but as the very climax of his intense wrestling with the Galatians—even if he quotes it from the tradition and if the thought pattern of reunifying difference was well known in the wider cultural context of the Hellenistic world.[1] Pre-Pauline in origin, the baptismal formula nevertheless is genuinely Pauline in its present rhetorical embedding and literary shape. Using the socio-literary context of Galatians as the primary interpretational framework thus may not only shed new light on the meaning of Gal. 3.26–28, but also considerably challenge the common notion of Paul's overall 'conservatism' regarding gender issues and slavery—without converting him into a present-day feminist or liberation thinker. In the framework of this article I will focus on a specific aspect of the gender problem.

What does Paul tell the Galatians, if he declares biological sex ($\ἄρσεν$ and $\θῆλυ$) in 3.28 as no longer existent and one in Christ? Another question needs to be answered right away: Why actually is Paul fighting so fiercely against circumcision in the messianic communities in Galatia? Maybe one has to start by just observing the un-precise nature of this question. Definitely there were no women tempted to let themselves be circumcised. The problem is an exclusively male one. * * * This is a first point of entry.

† From Brigitte Kahl, "No Longer Male: Masculinity Struggles Behind Galatians 3.28?" *Journal for the Study of the New Testament* 79 (2000): 37–49. All notes are Kahl's.

1. [Cf.] 1 Cor. 12.13, Col. 3.9–11, 2 *Clem.* 12.2, *Gos. Thom.* 22, *Gospel of the Egyptians* 3.91.

Male and Female as Key Concepts of Galatians

Apart from Gal. 3.28 the terms male (ἄρσεν) and female (θῆλυ) as such recur nowhere else in Galatians. But this does not prove yet that the gender related part of the baptismal formula is foreign to Paul's debate with the Galatians. If it really did not matter, why did he not leave the male/female pair out as occurs in parallel quotations in 1 Cor. 12.13 and Col. 3.11? Rather, as a closer look at the word material and the textual structures of the letter shows, the re-conceptualization of male and female in general, and of male in particular, is right at the core of Paul's messianic argument, even if it might well be that the apostle was not fully aware of the practical implications of his own theology himself. Texts may be wiser than their authors.

If one analyses the vocabulary of Galatians, a remarkable emphasis on male/female-related issues emerges:

1. The semantic field which already the first creation account (Gen. 1.27–28 LXX) and the flood story (Gen. 6.19–7.3 LXX) build up around the terms ἄρσεν/θῆλυ is focused on procreation. It comprises terms like fatherhood, motherhood, sonship, brotherhood, genealogy, kinship, inheritance, birth and so on. All these terms and concepts are absolutely dominant in Galatians 3–4, where the essential points of Paul's theological argument are developed by re-reading the 'family-stories' of Genesis. Similarly, as Philip Esler has shown, family and kinship imagery is central to Gal. 5.13–6.10 as well.[2] This semantic coherence is a first indication that Gal. 3.28c is firmly integrated into the letter as a whole.

2. Ever since Gen. 17.10–14 LXX physical maleness (ἄρσεν or ἀρσενικός) is the object of circumcision. Nobody would question that circumcision is the most burning problem of Galatians. How then could masculinity as its primary referent stay so completely outside the scholarly debate, rather than being discussed as, maybe, one of the secret storm-centers of Paul's heated controversy with his Galatian brothers?

3. In terms of vocabulary, masculinity indeed appears to be another strong focus of Galatians. Hardly any other New Testament document is so densely populated by male body-language as this letter: the terms foreskin, circumcision/circumcise, and sperm occur 22 times, including the stunning polemical reference to castration in 5.12. Even the gospel itself is linked to male anatomy, with Paul coining the two rather striking phrases 'gospel of the foreskin' and 'gospel of the circumcision' (2.7), which are repeated nowhere else in the New Testament. Whereas the Latin Vulgate still rendered the precise meaning as 'evangelium praeputii/circumcisionis' subsequent translations mostly have tried to conceal this 'naked maleness' of Paul's theological language by using more indirect and non-gendered terms like 'gospel for the Gentiles/Jews' (NIV, GNB [New International Version, Good News Bible]) or at least 'gospel for the uncircumcised/circumcised'

---

2. P. F. Esler, 'Family Imagery and Christian Identity in Gal. 5.13 to 6.10', in H. Moxnes (ed.), *Constructing Early Christian Families: Family as Social Reality and Metaphor* (London: Routledge, 1997), pp. 121–49 (122).

(NRSV). Unfortunately, they thereby have contributed to making the male body as a major site of theological struggle in Galatians invisible.

To conclude: A first analytical reading of Galatians not only shows that male and female are key concepts of Galatians; it also indicates a remarkable emphasis on masculinity. In terms of word statistics Galatians could be perceived as the most 'phallocentric' document of the New Testament. This inherent masculinity of a primarily 'male correspondence' has to be taken seriously. Otherwise the liberating message (if there is one) will remain unreadable. Paul addresses primarily the Galatian brothers. The sisters should not be mixed into this dialogue too hastily.

Decentering the Male—No More Fathers (Galatians 3)

Belonging to Abraham's seed and thus to Israel from Gen. 17 onwards has been defined in a decisive way by the male line of descent (= fathers begetting sons), which is physically marked by circumcision. This whole logic of belonging and not-belonging, which rests primarily on maleness in terms of physical father-hood, is completely subverted in Gal. 3:

In vv. 6–7 Abraham is identified as essentially the faithful one. Thus those out of faith become accepted as the 'real' children of Abraham. One could see Abraham's seed redefined in a double way: It is firstly marked, so to say, by the exclusive 'gene $\pi i \sigma \tau \iota \varsigma$/faith'. This 'genetic' narrowing down produces openness: Now all faithful are legitimately integrated into Abraham's genealogy. But this is not yet sufficient. Paul once again redefines Abraham's seed, now reducing it to the one and only 'sperm Christ' (3.16). This turn to a messianic, strictly christocentric spermatology has a triple effect:

(a) It transforms all who through baptism are clothed/identified with Christ into Abraham's seed/sperm: Gal. 3.29 ('And if you are of Christ, then of Abraham's seed') is the rhetorical target and climax of the baptismal formula.

(b) 'In Christ' (3.28) thus constitutes a space of bodily belonging to Abraham's offspring/heirs and therefore to Israel, which is no longer defined by physical fatherhood. This radical decentering of maleness could be seen as one of the most 'natural' reasons why physical maleness ($\H{\alpha}\rho\sigma\epsilon\nu$) cannot any longer bear the identity marker of circumcision for those who enter into the messianic communities from the Gentile side.

(c) In a patriarchal setting the male line of descent constitutes the backbone of an 'orderly', that is vertically and exclusively structured genealogy, which inscribes the most fundamental hierarchies and in/out relationships of the social body. The superiority of the father defines not only the inferiority of son vs. father, but also female vs. male, slave vs. master, second-born vs. firstborn, Gentiles vs. children of Israel. 'In Christ', thus (i.e. without the basic father-son structure) the genealogy of Abraham gets horizontalized and inclusive in a radical way: It is becoming open for the 'others', the Gentiles/Greeks next to 'us', the Jews. And it is no longer comprised of hierarchical relations. Fatherhood is replaced by brotherhood, with the exception of God the father (3.26–4.7). That is the wider horizon of the question, why circumcision as a specifically male marker of gendered and ethno-religious exclusivity/hierarchy is no longer decisive for newcomers.

The 'phallocentricity' of Galatians turns out to be articulated in the most rigor-ously anti-phallocratic way.

Recentering the Female: Only Mothers Left (Galatians 4)

The establishment of a faith-based genealogy and a christomonist spermat(he)ology in ch. 3 has created a concept of inclusive Jewishness that makes the bio-logical fathers practically a-functional. Inevitably, this fundamental subversion of maleness (ἄρσεν) must change the perception and position of the female counterpart as well. If male (in its procreative role) is no longer male as it used to be—what happens to the female (θῆλυ)?

Apparently, the counter-patriarchal logic of his theology immediately starts to re-shape the language Paul uses. It is somehow striking to see that Gal. 4 is dominated by mother and birth terminology. In one single chapter we come across the mother of Jesus (4.4), the mothers Hagar and Sarah (4.21–31), the mother Jerusalem (4.26), the barren and forsaken mothers of Isaiah who get many children without a male (ἀνήρ) (Isa. 54.1 = Gal. 4.27).

Most confusing, however, is the 'mother Paul', whom we meet in 4.19 as she/he is painfully trying to rebirth his/her Galatian children in the shape (μορφή) of Christ. With only a few exceptions this striking 'transgendering' Pauline self-description in terms of symbolic birth-labor has usually been ignored—it does not fit into any of the standard Pauline interpretations and stereotypes. But pre-cisely Gal. 4.19 could be a key to understanding the meaning of sex/gender-unity in Gal. 3.28 and in Galatians as a whole.

The term mother (μήτηρ) itself occurs only once in 4.26, but after Paul has appeared on the Galatian stage as a troubled mother, practically every single fol-lowing verse of the chapter deals with the relationship of children/sons to a female parent. One could describe the whole passage 4.19–31 as a motherly exhortation of children who are about to forget who they are. The mother's voice is serious, even angry while telling the allegory of the two mothers Hagar and Sarah: 'I wish I were present with you now and could change my tone, for I am perplexed about you . . .' (4.20).

The focus of the allegory is once more the Galatians' identity as 'children of the promise' and 'heirs of Abraham' (4.28, 30). Both terms refer back to the debate about Abraham's fore-fatherhood in ch. 3. But this time the definition rests on the female part alone: Abraham's heirs are qualified exclusively by their mother, the free woman rather than the slave woman (4.30–31). While I cannot go into the debate of the free-slave polarity at this point, the effect of the allegory in terms of male and female is quite clear: The human fathers do not count any longer—only the divine one (3.26–4.7). But motherhood is retained, even if it is defined in a-typical or non-biological terms. Different from what has happened to the male in Gal. 3, the female is dramatically re-centered in Gal. 4 as the 'mother-chapter' of Paul.

One in Christ: Apocalyptic Subversion and Confusion
of One and Other (Galatians 5–6)

What concrete imagery has Paul in mind if he speaks about male and female becoming one in Christ? His emphasis on the 'mothers' makes it unlikely that he thinks of something like an ungendered, a-sexual reality or a male-defined monosex, into which the female becomes transformed. To understand the way Paul deals with the opposite pairs of male/female, Jew/Greek, slave/free, J. Louis Martyn's observations about the cosmic dichotomies in apocalyptic thinking seem to be most helpful.[3] Martyn argues that Paul in his apocalyptic revelation of the messianic event (cf. Gal. 1.15–16) has 'seen' the end of the στοιχεῖα τοῦ κόσμου, the elements of the world, which are mentioned in Gal. 4.3, 9 as universally enslaving. These 'elements', according to Martyn, are the universal polarities that the Greeks and others thought to be the basis of the cosmos, structuring reality in binary oppositional pairs like air vs. earth, fire vs. water, but also Law vs. non-Law, circumcision vs. non-circumcision, slave vs. free and female vs. male and so on. Paul presupposes that this bi-polar order of the 'world' (κόσμος) has been broken down through the cross. As a result, neither circumcision nor foreskin count any longer, but only a new creation (6.14–15).

I would like to take up Martyn's argument, but go beyond it with regard to the hierarchical and exclusivist aspects implied in the elemental 'table of opposites'. The 'one' (i.e. male) was not just considered different/opposite, but also superior to the 'other' (i.e. female). Aristotle could define the elements fire and water as dominant and related to man, higher, active, lighter, whereas water and earth as inferior were related to woman, lower, passive, heavier.[4] This may be helpful to decipher the Galatian oneness/difference puzzle. Declaring the end of polarity in terms of the new creation, Paul does not proclaim the erasure of sexual (or any other) difference, but the end of the social hierarchies and exclusions (re)produced by it. The oneness of the new creation attacks the old age by constantly undermining the hierarchical structuring of difference either as repressive sameness (= the other made similar to the one, e.g. all males to be circumcised) or as imperial oneness (= the one, e.g. Jew, superior to the other). Paul's concept of oneness in Christ according to Gal. 3.28 thus is a liberating vision of egalitarian inclusiveness; it rejects hierarchy but not difference as such.

This apocalyptic-messianic rethinking of oneness inevitably creates a new battlefield with new polarities; this is the site of Paul's highly dialectic and polemic socio-rhetorical strategy. Watching Paul's self-transformation into an apostolic mother, seeing him define Abraham's fatherhood through motherhood is at first confusing. All throughout Gal. 3–4 we have observed how male/female

---

3. Martyn, *Galatians: A New Translation with Introduction and Commentary*, Anchor Bible 33A (New York: Doubleday, 1997), pp. 100–101, 393–406.

4. In the table of opposites which is attributed to the Pythagoreans and quoted by Aristotle in his *Metaphysics* 986a, the following hierarchical polarities are given: limit, odd, one, right, male, rest, straight, light, good, square are opposed and superior to absence of limit, even, many, left, female, motion, curved, dark, bad, oblong.

identities were reversed and distorted. In a way, this confusion seems to be at the core of Paul's subversive rhetoric as a whole. The semantic universe of the old age with its established polarities and hierarchies of male/female, slave/free, Jew/Gentile, one/other collapses. Words get a different meaning.[5]

This 'semantic confusion' in a very fundamental way raises the question of whether Paul's usage of 'male' language basically serves to reinforce a patriarchal definition of male and female—or to subvert it. If, for example, 'one in Christ' in Gal. 3.28 in its Greek original refers grammatically to a masculine being ($\varepsilon \tilde{\iota} \varsigma$ [the masculine form of "one"]), does that mean that Paul wants to (re)introduce male as normative? As we have seen, the 'one' new identity 'in Christ' is decisively marked by the female line of descent, another 'confusion' of a seemingly male core concept with a decisively female dimension. Does Paul maybe speak about messianic 'oneness' in male terms as he indeed primarily addresses men—but not in order to confirm, but rather to undermine their established notions of maleness?

Following this line of thought, it would be perfectly consistent that the apostolic male, trying to re-shape the Galatian community in the image of Christ, appears as a female him/herself in 4.19. What at first sight seems to be the voice of a patriarchal Pauline rule demanding obedience, in an ironic twist becomes the birth-cry of a woman in labor pains. In the same way, just a few verses before, Paul's apparently 'authoritarian' demand to become like him turns out to mean the imitation of 'unmanly' weakness, which reflects the ultimate weakness of the cross and undermines all the dominance-oriented norms of the honor and shame code both on the individual/social and on a cosmological level (4.12–14). At first sight Paul constantly evokes patriarchal patterns, hierarchies, polarities. At a closer look he systematically subverts them in his semantic 'labor' that reflects the messianic subversion of the old age still present by the new creation already decisive.

Messianic Conversion of One and Other: One-an-other (Galatians 5–6; 1–2)

While, very generally speaking, one could describe Paul's subversive rhetorical strategy in the more systematic part of Gal. 3–4 as a way of 'confusing the hierarchies', the historical and parenetic sections of Gal. 1–2 and 5–6 seem to focus on a new life practice that transforms and 'converts' the hierarchical oppositions into patterns of active mutuality and solidarity.

The question of oneness in Christ in Galatians is fundamentally related to the basics of Israel's creed, that is the exclusive oneness of God and of Abraham's seed as the one chosen people of God.[6] But as this messianic oneness of God's

5. Similar 'confusions' may be observed in many other places, e.g. in the Sarah-Hagar allegory (4.21–31) where all the 'right' people appear on the 'wrong' side of the table of opposites.

6. The topic on 'oneness' in Gal. 3.28 is another element of semantic and theological coherence throughout the whole letter: it points back to the 'one sperm' and the 'oneness of God' in 3.16 and 3.20, and forward to the 'one' commandment of love as fulfillment of the whole Torah (5.14).

people is no longer based on the marital union of male and female becoming 'one flesh' (Gen. 2.24) nor on uniformity in observing the Law, how is it 'embodied'? Does it materialize itself solely in the 'theo-poetic' realm of a subversive, transformative language? Is it a matter of 'grace alone' in the sense of a faith reality detached from social practice, as a common Protestant (mis)reading of Paul's theology of justification has suggested?

Probably Paul would have had great difficulties in imagining faith, grace, and word as things that do not become a 'corporate' reality in the life practice of the messianic congregations. Messianic oneness of Jew and Greek, slave and free, male and female for him is essentially 'embodied' in 'faith working through love' (5.6). Love of the neighbor is the 'one' commandment that fulfils the Law (5.14), but as such it does not only confirm the notion of Israel's socio-religious oneness being centered in the Torah, it also fundamentally transforms it by subverting the established hierarchies of 'one' and 'other': all throughout the parenetic section of Galatians this 'oneness' of the new creation of Israel's God is shown as the movement of the 'ones' going down to the level of the lowly and excluded 'others' of all kinds, to be in solidarity and community with them, to become 'others' themselves.

One of the most striking examples of this paradigm is the subversion and 'conversion' of the hierarchical polarity of slave and free. After Paul has established 'our' identity as children 'not of the slave woman, but of the free woman' in 4.31, this freedom a few verses later is explained precisely as doing slave service to one another—through love (5.13). In similar ways authority and teaching are to be exercised mutually and reciprocally (6.1–6). Thus the 'household of faith' (6.10) is clearly lacking any patriarchal head. The massive occurrence of the term ἀλλήλων (one another, from ἄλλος-ἄλλος)—no less than seven times in 5.13, 15, 17, 26; 6.2—points in the same direction. Oneness as opposed to otherness is redefined and re-enacted in the messianic-apocalyptic congregations as 'one-an-otherness', which has its focus in the other, rather than the one/self.

This wrestling with the transformation of an exclusive, hierarchical concept and practice of unity/oneness towards a horizontal inclusiveness shapes the introductory chapters 1–2 as well. The most important result of the Jerusalem meeting for Paul is community (κοινωνία). It is established when the 'ones' in Jerusalem who represent the 'gospel of the circumcision' extend the 'right hand of community' towards the otherness of Paul's 'gospel of the foreskin' (2.1–9). Oneness-in-difference is acknowledged. It will be practiced by the 'other side', the Gentile communities, as remembering of the poor in Jerusalem, that is material solidarity (2.10). And it failed, when the 'ones'—the Jerusalem authorities—destroyed the table community between Jews and Gentiles at Antioch (2.11–14).

One could see this as another major reason why the male Galatians have to retain their foreskin in a community where circumcision is still the dominant identity marker. Oneness and difference are reconciled by 'bearing one another's burdens' (6.2), not by creating physical sameness of Jews and non-Jews.

No Longer Male: Gender Trouble in Galatia?

After all it is hard to believe that there was no gender trouble in Galatia. Reconciling oneness and otherness as one-an-otherness almost necessarily must have confronted the male members of the Galatian congregations with specific problems of their masculine identity. Surely it was the biological, procreative role of both sexes—male and female—which Paul had invalidated, but nevertheless the male part of the congregation must have felt that they were the 'natural' loser of that theology. Bearing one another's burdens: Didn't this primarily mean that men became unbearably and confusingly burdened with female tasks, identities, and inferiorities? Did free people doing slave service for one another maybe include even men serving women? * * * Why had Paul defined the Jewish/Gentile fathers as irrelevant for the Jewish messianic identity of the 'children', while retaining metaphorical motherhood? And what about physical maleness: All of their new messianic identity was Jewish—after abandoning their former gods and socio-religious contexts, after entering into the story and history of Israel and its One God alone. But being a Jewish male, different from being a Jewish female, definitely also meant being circumcised. No truly Jewish man had his foreskin. Why were they forced to be physically, in a way, like women, that is uncircumcised? Were they considered to be not real Jews—or maybe not 'real men'?

It seems highly probable that the tensions in Galatia were not only related to problems of socio-cultural dislocation, unclear ethical norms, status inconsistency, issues of honor and shame in general, but that all these problems had a specific gender/masculinity related compound. The male Galatians' wish to get circumcised then would indicate a profound desire to return to a less confusing understanding of what it meant to be a Jew, free and, on top of all that, a man.

If this were true, then Paul did not do much to confirm or comfort the frustrated masculinity of his Galatian brothers. His 'queer' appearance as a mother in labor, his 'matriarchal' reconstruction of Abraham's genealogy, his shamefully 'unmanly' boasting of weakness as something to be imitated (4.12–15), his rejection of male honor and image games (5.26; 6.12), his nasty remark concerning castration, his model of a 'household of faith' without patriarchal authority (6.10)—all this which is firmly tied to his understanding of the cross as subversion of the old order by God's new creation (6.12–15) adds even more challenge. No wonder we see already a few decades after Paul his successors in the pastoral letters and elsewhere working very hard to bring the relationship of male and female in Christ back to somewhat more 'orderly' patriarchal household norms.

INTERDISCIPLINARY APPROACHES

PAUL RICOEUR

Listening to the Parables of Jesus†

To preach today on the Parables of Jesus looks like a lost cause. Have we not already heard these stories at Sunday School? Are they not childish stories, unworthy of our claims to scientific knowledge, in particular in a University Chapel? Are not the situations which they evoke typical of a rural existence which our urban civilization has made nearly ununderstandable? And the symbols, which in the old days awakened the imagination of simple-minded people, have not these symbols become dead metaphors, as dead as the leg of the chair? More than that, is not the wearing out of these images, borrowed from the agricultural life, the most convincing proof of the general erosion of Christian symbols in our modern culture?

To preach today on the Parables of Jesus—or rather to preach the Parables—is indeed a wager: the wager that in spite of all contrary arguments, it is still possible to listen to the Parables of Jesus in such a way that we are once more astonished, struck, renewed, and put in motion. It is this wager which led me to try to preach the Parables and not only to study them in a *scholarly* way, as a text among other texts.

The first thing that may strike us is that the Parables are radically profane stories. There are no gods, no demons, no angels, no miracles, no time before time, as in the creation stories, not even founding events as in the Exodus account. Nothing like that, but precisely people like us: Palestinian landlords traveling and renting their fields, stewards and workers, sowers and fishers, fathers and sons; in a word, ordinary people doing ordinary things: selling and buying, letting down a net into the sea, and so on. Here resides the initial paradox: on the one hand, these stories are—as a critic said—narratives of normalcy—but on the other hand, it is the Kingdom of God that is said to be like this. The paradox is that the *extraordinary* is *like* the *ordinary*.

Some other sayings of Jesus speak of the Kingdom of Heaven: among them, the eschatological sayings, and they seem to point toward something Wholly-Other, to something beyond, as different from our history as heaven is from earth. Therefore, the first thing which may amaze us is that at the very moment we were expecting the language of the myth, the language of the sacred, the language of

† From *The Philosophy of Paul Ricoeur: An Anthology of His work,* ed. Charles E. Reagan and David Stewart (Boston: Beacon Press, 1978), 239–45.

One of the most prominent philosophers of the twentieth century, Paul Ricouer (1913–2005) served as professor of philosophical theology at the University of Chicago for much of his career, though he also taught elsewhere in the United States and in France (his country of origin). This sermon on Jesus' parables displays his lifelong interest in biblical hermeneutics.

mysteries, we receive the language of our history, the language of the profane, the language of open drama.

And it is this contrast between the kind of thing *about* which it is spoken—the Kingdom of Heaven—and the kind of thing *to* which it is compared which may put in motion our search. It is not the religious man in us, it is not the sacred man in us, but precisely the profane man, the secular man who is summoned.

The second step, beyond this first shock, will be to ask what makes sense in the Parables. If it is true—as contemporary exegesis shows—that the Kingdom of God is not compared to the man who . . . to the woman who . . . to the yeast which . . . but to *what happens* in the story, we have to look more closely at the short story itself, to identify what may be paradigmatic in it. It is here that we run the risk of sticking too closely to the sociological aspects which I evoked at the beginning when I said that the situations described in the Parables are those of agricultural activity and of rural life. What makes sense is not the situations as such, but, as a recent critique has shown, it is the *plot*, it is the structure of the drama, its composition, its culmination, its denouement.

If we follow this suggestion, we are immediately led to look at the critical moments, at the decisive turning points in the short dramas. And what do we find? Let us read once more the shortest, the most condensed of all the Parables: Matthew 13, verse 44. Three critical moments emerge: *finding* the treasure, *selling* everything else, *buying* the field. The same threefold division may be found in the two following Parables: Matthew 13:45–46, 47–49.

If we attempt, now, to let these three critical moments expand, so to say, in our imagination, in our feeling, in our thought, they begin to *mean much more* than the apparent practical, professional, economical, commercial transactions told by the story. *Finding* something . . . This simple expression encompasses all the kinds of *encounters* which make of our life the contrary of an acquisition by skill or by violence, by work or by cunning. Encounter of people, encounter of death, encounter of tragic situations, encounter of joyful events. Finding the other, finding ourselves, finding the world, recognizing those whom we had not even noticed, and those whom we don't know too well and whom we don't know at all. Unifying all these kinds of finding, does not the parable point toward a certain fundamental relation to time? Toward a fundamental way of being in time? I mean, this mode which deserves to be called the Event par excellence. Something happens. Let us be prepared for the newness of what is new. Then we shall "find."

But the art of the parable is to link dialectically *finding* to two other critical turning points. The man who found the treasure went and sold everything he had and *bought* it. Two new critical points, which we could call after a modern commentator, himself taught by Heidegger:[1] Reversal and Decision. Decision does not even come second. Before Decision; Reversal. And all those who have

1. Martin Heidegger (1889–1976), German existentialist philosopher.

read some religious texts other than biblical, and even some texts other than religious, know how much has been invested in this word "conversion," which means much more than making a new choice, but which implies a shift in the direction of the look, a reversal in the vision, in the imagination, in the heart, before all kinds of good intentions and all kinds of good decisions and good actions. Doing appears as the conclusive act, engendered by the Event and by the Reversal. First, encountering the Event, then changing one's heart, then doing accordingly. This succession is full of sense: the Kingdom of God is compared to the chain of these three acts: letting the Event blossom, looking in another direction, and doing with all one's strength in accordance with the new vision.

Of course, all the Parables are not built in a mechanical way along the same pattern. If this were the case, they would lose for that very reason the power of surprise. But each of them develops and, so to say, dramatizes one of the other of these three critical terms.

Look at the so-called parables of Growth: Matthew 13:31–33. This unexpected growth of the mustard seed, this growth beyond all proportion, draws our attention in the same direction as finding. The natural growth of the seed and the unnatural size of the growth speak of something which happens to us, invades us, overwhelms us, beyond our control and our grasp, beyond our willing and our planning. Once more the Event comes as a gift.

Some other Parables which have not been read this morning will lay the stress on the Reversal. Thus the Prodigal Son changes his mind, reverts his glance, his regard, whereas it is the father who waits, who expects, who welcomes, and the Event of the encounter proceeds from the conjunction of this Reversal and this Waiting.

In some other Parables, the emphasis will fall on the decision, on the doing, even on the good deed, as in the Parable of the Good Samaritan. But, reduced to the last critical turn, the Parable seems to be nothing more than a moral fable, a mere call to "do the same." Thus reduced to a moral teaching, the Parable ceases to be a Parable of the Kingdom to become an allegory of charitable action. We have to replace it within the inclusion of the Parables of Event, Reversal, and Decision, if the moral fable is to speak once more as a Parable.

Having made, in that way, this second step and recognized the dramatic structure, the articulation of the plot which makes sense, we are ready for a new discovery, for a new surprise. If we ask: "And finally, what is the Kingdom of Heaven," we must be prepared to receive the following answer. The Gospel says nothing about the Kingdom of Heaven, except that it is *like* . . . It does not say what it *is*, but what it *looks like*. This is hard to hear. Because all our scientific training tends to use images only as provisory devices and to replace *images* by *concepts*. We are invited here to proceed the other way. And to think according to a mode of thought which is not metaphorical for the sake of rhetoric, but for the sake of what it has to say. Only *analogy* approximates what is wholly practical. The Gospel is not alone to speak in that way. We have elsewhere heard Hosea speaking of Yahweh as the Husband, of Israel as the Wife, of the Idols as the Lovers. No translation in abstract language is offered, only the violence of a language which, from the beginning to the end, *thinks through* the Metaphor and never *beyond*. The power of this language is that it abides to the end *within* the tension created by the images.

What are the implications of this disquieting discovery that Parables allow no translation in conceptual language? At first sight, this state of affairs exposes the weakness of this mode of discourse. But for a second glance, it reveals the unique strength of it. How is it possible? Let us consider that with the Parables we have not to do with a unique story dramatically expanded in a long discourse, but with a full range of short Parables gathered together in the Unifying form of the Gospel. This fact means something. It means that the Parables make a whole, that we have to grasp them as a whole and to understand each one in the light of the other. The Parables make sense together. They constitute a network of intersignification, if I dare say so. If we assume this hypothesis, then our disappointment— the disappointment which a scientific mind perceives when it fails to draw a coherent idea, an equivocal concept from this bundle of metaphors—our disappointment may become amazement. Because there is now more in the Parables taken together than in any conceptual system about God and his action among us. There is more to *think through* the richness of the images than in the coherence of a simple concept. What confirms this feeling is the fact that we can draw from the Parables nearly all the kinds of theologies which have divided Christianity through the centuries. If you isolate the Parable of the Lost Coin, if you interrupt the dynamism of the story and extract from it a frozen concept, then you get the kind of doctrine of predestination which pure Calvinism advocated. But if you pick the Parable of the Prodigal Son and extract from it the frozen concept of personal conversion, then you get a theology based on the absolutely free will of man, as in the doctrine that the Jesuits opposed to the Calvinists, or the Protestant Liberals to the Orthodox Protestants.

Therefore, it is not enough to say that the Parables say nothing directly concerning the Kingdom of God. *We must say in more positive terms, that taken all together, they say more than any rational theology.* At the very moment that they call for theological clarification, they start shattering the theological simplifications which we attempt to put in their place. This challenge to rational theology is nowhere more obvious than in the Parable of the Good Seed spoiled by the darnel sowed among the wheat. The farmer's servants went to their master and said, "Sir, was it not good seed that you sowed in your field? Then where has the darnel come from?" Such is the question of the philosopher when he discusses theoretically the so-called problem of evil. But the only answer which we get is itself metaphorical: "This is an enemy's doing." And you may come through several kinds of theologies in agreement with that enigmatic answer. Because there is more to think about in the answer said in a parabolic way than any kind of theory.

Let me propose one more step, a step which I hope will increase our surprise, our amazement. Many people will be tempted to say, "Well, we have no difficulty dropping all systems, including rational or rationalizing theologies." Then, if all theories are wrong, let us look at the Parables as mere practical teaching, as moral or maybe political teaching. If Parables are not pieces of dogmatic theology, let us look at them as pieces of practical theology. This proposal sounds better at first sight than the first one. Is it not said that to listen to the word is to put it into practice? This obviously is true. But what does that mean, to put in practice the Parables?

I fear that a too-zealous attempt to draw immediate application from the Parables for private ethics or for political morality must necessarily miss the target. We immediately surmise that such an indiscreet zeal quickly transposes the Parables into trivial advice, into moral platitudes. And we kill them more surely by trivial moralizing than by transcendent theologizing.

The Parables obviously teach, but they don't teach in an ordinary way. There is, indeed, something in the Parables which we have as yet overlooked and which they have in common with the Proverbs used by Jesus according to the Synoptics. This trait is easy to identify in the Proverbs. It is the use of paradox and hyperbole, in such aphorism and antithetical formulae as: "Whoever seeks to gain his life will lose it, but whoever loses his life will preserve it." As one commentator says, the paradox is so acute in this overturning of fates that it jolts the imagination from its vision of a continuous sequence between one situation and another. Our project of making a totality continuous with our own existence is defeated. For who can plan his future according to the project of losing "in order to win"? Nevertheless, these are not ironical nor skeptical words of wisdom. In spite of everything, life is granted by the very means of this paradoxical path. The same has to be said of hyperbolic orders like: "Love your enemies, do good to those who hate you." Like paradox, hyperbole is intended to jolt the hearer from the project of making his life something continuous. But whereas humor or detachment would remove us from reality entirely, hyperbole leads back to the heart of existence. The challenge to the conventional wisdom is at the same time a way of life. We are first disoriented before being reoriented.

Does not the same happen with the Parables? Is their way of teaching different from that of reorientation by disorientation? We have not been aware enough of the paradoxes and the hyperbole implied in those short stories. In most of them there is an element of extravagance which alerts us and summons our attention.

Consider the extravagance of the landlord in the Parable of the Wicked Husbandman, who after having sent his servants, sent his son. What Palestinian property owner living abroad would be foolish enough to act like this landlord? Or what can we say about the host in the Parable of the Great Feast who looks for substitute guests in the streets? Would we not say that he was unusual? And in the Parable of the Prodigal Son, does not the father overstep all bounds in greeting his son? What employer would pay the employees of the eleventh hour the same wages as those hired first?

The Parables of Growth are no less implausible. Here it is the hyperbole of the proverb that is at work. What small seed would yield a huge tree where birds can nest? The contrast is hardly less in the Parable of the Leaven. As to the Parable of the Sower, it is constructed on the same contrast. If it points to eschatological plenitude, it is because the yield of grain in the story surpasses by far all reality.

The most paradoxical and most outlandish Parables, as far as their realism is concerned, are those which Joachim Jeremias has grouped under the titles "The Imminence of Catastrophe" and "It may be Too Late."[2] The schema of *occasion*, which only presents itself *one time* and after which it is *too late*, includes a dramatization of what in ordinary experience we call seizing the occasion, but this dramatization is both paradoxical and hyperbolic; paradoxical because it runs counter to actual experience where there will always be another chance, and hyperbolic because it exaggerates the experience of the unique character of the momentous decisions of existence.

At what village wedding has anyone slammed the door on the frivolous maidens who do not consider the future (and who are, after all, as carefree as the lilies of the field)? It is said that "these are Parables of Crisis." Of course, but the hour of testing and the "selective sorting" is signified by a crisis in the story which intensifies the surprise, the scandal, and sometimes provokes disapproval as when the denouement is "unavoidably tragic."

Let me draw the conclusion which seems to emerge from this surprising strategy of discourse used by Jesus when he told the Parables to the disciples and to the mob. To listen to the Parables of Jesus, it seems to me, is to let one's imagination be opened to the new possibilities disclosed by the extravagance of these short dramas. If we look at the Parables as at a word addressed first to our imagination rather than to our will, we shall not be tempted to reduce them to mere didactic devices, to moralizing allegories. We will let their poetic power display itself within us.

But, was not this poetic discussion already at work, when we read the Parable of the Pearl and the Parable of Event, Reversal, and Decision? Decision, we said, moral decision comes third. Reversal precedes. But the Event opens the path. The poetic power of the Parable is the power of the Event. Poetic means more than poetry as a literary genre. Poetic means creative. And it is in the heart of our imagination that we let the Event happen, before we may convert our heart and tighten our will.

Listen, therefore, to the Parables of Jesus (Matthew 13:31–32 and 45–46):

And another parable he put before them, saying, "The Kingdom of heaven is like a grain of mustard seed which a man took and sowed in his field; it is the smallest of all seeds, but when it has grown it is the greatest of shrubs and becomes a tree, so that the birds of the air come and make nests in its branches.

"Again, the kingdom of heaven is like a merchant in search of fine pearls, who, on finding one pearl of great value, went and sold all that he had and bought it."

---

2. See *The Parables of Jesus*, trans. S. H. Hooke (London: S.C.M. Press, 1954).

FRANK KERMODE

[Being and Becoming in John's Prologue]†

Some of the problems arising from the differences between the Fourth Gospel and the three Synoptic Gospels were discussed in the Introduction to the New Testament. There are also, of course, problems arising from its resemblance to those other Gospels. Indeed there is a long list of questions calling for answers from historical critics, and it is fair to say that the answers are always changing, and the list of questions always lengthening. Earlier in the present century there were those who strongly believed John to have been related to a particular form of Gnosticism, the Mandean. This belief was abandoned after the discovery of the Dead Sea Scrolls, which were the work of Jewish writers before the time of John, and which anticipated some of his characteristic imagery and habits of thought. John is now seen to derive from a tradition that is fundamentally Jewish, however influenced by Hellenistic ideas. Such considerations and others, such as the accuracy of his Palestinian topography, have induced most scholars to reject the view that John's was a late theological reworking of the material, lacking direct contact with the original tradition. It is now commonly thought that the Fourth Gospel has sources as old as, though largely independent of, those available to the Synoptics.

Although in certain historical respects John clearly differs from the other Gospels, and although one needs to take some account of this fact when studying his practice as a writer, such considerations affect the present essay only obliquely. Literary critics can reasonably avoid many of the arguments which orthodox biblical criticism cannot. There is, for example, a protracted discussion concerning which verses of the Prologue—a feature unique to John—are original, and which are interpolations. Literary critics may not feel disposed to substitute for the poem as it now stands some hypothetical predecessor that fits better their views on John's theology or his historical situation. They may attach much importance to the long existence of the Gospel in its present form and wish to see it in its immemorial contexts as a member of a set of gospels, as part of a Testament, and as part of the Bible. They may suppose that its career in these contexts has conferred upon it a certain cohesiveness and integral force that are dispersed when the book is detached from its neighbors, distributed among redactors, and purged of supposedly intrusive elements.

They are therefore likely to assume a real and intelligible relation between the Prologue and the narrative it introduces. They will not be troubled by fine theological differences between this poem and the Gospel as a whole, or postulate a

† From Frank Kermode, "John," in *The Literary Guide to the Bible*, ed. Robert Alter and Frank Kermode (Cambridge, MA: Harvard University Press, 1987), 440–48. Except as indicated, all notes are Kermode's.

In the 1970s Frank Kermode (1919–2010), one of the most important contemporary literary critics writing in English, began applying to the Gospels his formidable skills and refined sensibilities as a literary scholar. His work on the New Testament, along with Robert Alter's on the Old, led many biblical scholars to begin approaching the Bible as a collection of artful and sophisticated writings, inspiring a brief literary turn in the discipline.

different author for each, or maintain that the incorporation of the Prologue in the Gospel has been none too neatly achieved, or explain what the Prologue originally consisted of before the meddling began. For declining, whether from indifference or incapacity, to take part in such exercises they may be condemned as "precritical," that is, ignorant of the scientific advances made in biblical criticism over the past two hundred years. But there is a case for preferring the label "postcritical." In deciding not to be hindered by this immensely powerful tradition of largely disintegrative commentary, one hopes, without forgetting its importance, to regain some of the advantages of the precritical commentators who knew nothing about the Higher Criticism.[1] For example, Chrysostom, sixteen centuries ago, remarked at the outset of his commentary on John that when we read this Gospel, we are not after all conversing with a particular person, so there is no point in asking where he lived or what sort of education he had.[2] Chrysostom gives his attention to other matters; not for him those arduous modern inquiries into sources Jewish and Greek and into the beliefs and needs of some hypothetical community. He is content to study what God says in the words that are there in front of him, as they strike him in his own life, in his own time. Augustine remarked, with much relevance, that we understand this difficult work only according to our restricted capacities[3]—restricted not only by what we are but also by when we are.

It would of course be foolish to deny what detailed study of the text has made obvious: some of it has gone awry. For example, 14:31 indicates a closure but the discourse continues; the pericope of the woman taken in adultery doesn't belong; some transitional verses are carelessly introduced; possibly some chapters are not in the original order. The last chapter is obviously not from the same hand as its predecessors. But it must also be said that long continuance has endowed the book as it stands with a certain unchallengeable integrity. It is substantially as it has been for many ages, and during most of its history people thought of it as inerrant, coherent, and urgently applicable to readers in their own situation and according to their powers of reading, which might include the skill of reading poetry—a skill calling for close attention to the words as they stand in the text rather than attention to their hypothetical antecedents. All the evangelists insist, by proceeding as they do, that we take an interest in stories, and we neglect that insistence when we take the stories apart with the purpose of deciding which of them is earliest, closest to actual historical events. There is a sense in which the critic who attends to the story rather than to some lost narrative it perhaps replaced is attending to the first requirement of the Gospels. In much the same way biblical poems need to be read as poems before they are disassembled or treated simply as clues to a theology.

It may be helpful here to glance at Luther, an important though "transitional" commentator, a herald of the critical though in many ways still of the precritical world. Luther tells us, with suitable expressions of contempt, that in popish times

---

1. Historical-critical analysis that focuses on the sources used by the authors of the Bible [editors' note].

2. *Patrologiae Graecae Cursus Completus*, ed. J.-P. Migne, LIX (Paris, 1862), 29.

3. *Patrologiae Latinae Cursus Completus*, ed. J.-P. Migne, XXXV (Paris, 1841), 1569.

it had been the custom to write the words "In the beginning was the Word" on a piece of paper, place the paper in a quill or other container, and "hang it around one's neck or somewhere else; or to read these words as a protective charm against thunder and storms." What folly! If faith is wanting, there is no power in words. They were not provided for magical purposes, and our business is merely to believe them; we may then get our wish, not through incantations and spells but "in and through faith."[4]

Luther, we see, is well aware that the words are mysterious; indeed he says they are beyond the reach of human understanding without the aid of faith. But their efficacy is not inherent in them; it lies in something beyond, to which they merely point. Thus he wishes poetry away. Yet his commentary cannot altogether dispense with it, as we see from the curious figures he uses to express the relation between God and the Word. God, he says, is as it were pregnant with the Word; and then, shifting the figure, he adds, like a man's heart when it is filled with love or anger. "There was in God a Speech or Word which occupies all of God," he says more plainly.[5] But Luther's business is less with such musings than with the correction of heretics, from Cerinthus (against whom he supposed the Gospel to have been written) to the ruling pope. He is a theologian; he will employ reason, aided by faith, to ask what beyond themselves is signified by the words. That the Prologue should have the qualities of a poem, *carmen* (itself related to charm and incantation), is a superstition or accident to be discoursed away.

Calvin is yet more prosaic. Following Erasmus, he wishes to translate *logos* not as *verbum* but as *sermo*, "speech": "In the beginning was the Speech, and the Speech was with God, and the Speech was God." Philologically there is something to be said for this version, and Calvin likes it because "as Speech is said to be among men the image of mind, so it is not inappropriate to apply this to God, and to say that he reveals himself to us by his *Speech*.[6] *Sermo* is as far from *carmen* and incantation as papistical magic from human rationality. It brings the Word out of dangerous poetry into rational discourse. Reason, dimmed though it was by the Fall, had the task of establishing the coeternality of the Speech and God because the doctrine of the Trinity depends on it, and that doctrine must not be thought to have anything to do with charm or magic. So Calvin is severe on Augustine, who on this text allowed himself to indulge the Platonic fancy that God first created the forms.[7] That was a philosophical-poetic irrelevance with which Calvin would have nothing to do.

Calvin, incidentally, was a little troubled by the tense of the verb *to be* in the first verse. Does its *was* suggest that the state of affairs alluded to did not continue, that it was so only for a time? This is, in fact, an ancient problem. Chrysostom, as it happens, dealt firmly with it, and his precritical explanation has much appeal to readers of poetry. "It is not the expression *was* alone that denotes eternity," he says, "but that One was in the beginning." Used of men, he adds, the

4. Luther, *Works*, ed. Jaroslav Pelikan, XXII (New York, 1957), 3.

5. Ibid., p. 10.

6. *Commentaires de Jean Calvin sur le Nouveau Testament*, ed. M. Reveillard, II (Geneva, 1968), 12.

7. That is, the perfect and immutable transcendent Forms which are the source of all knowledge and of which all particular phenomena are reflections [editors' note].

word *being* only distinguishes present time (as when we say "for the time being"), but when used of God it signifies eternity; just so, *was*, when used of our nature, signifies past time, indeed limited past time; it *was* but it stopped being; but when used in respect of God it signifies eternity.[8] What could be more apposite than this affirmation that *was* is here and throughout the Prologue a word specially and peculiarly illuminated, taken out of ordinary usage, by its immediate and mysterious context? And that context is extensive. God in the Old Testament and his Son in the New have special rights over the verb *to be*; for them to say "I am" is to assert divinity. And we may remind ourselves of the sentence with which Jesus ends the discussion concerning his stature in relation to that of Abraham: "Before Abraham was, I am" (8:58). In the Greek the words translated as "Before Abraham was" really mean "Before Abraham *became*" (came into being).

The words for "being" and "becoming" are, of course, as common in Greek as they are in English. When we think about their function in John's proem (and about their shaping influence on what follows) we must hold on to Chrysostom's insight: the initial context gives them a peculiar coded force. No doubt the implications of these special senses will in the end be theological; but the means are poetic.

The normal view of historical-critical exegetes is that in the first eighteen verses of John there are intrusions; premature splicings of subsequent narrative into a Prologue that probably existed before they did. The verses in question are 6–9 and 12–13; 6–9 are often said to be the original opening of the book before it was attached to the proem, displaced when the proem was, as it were, stuck on top. And for those who look at the matter in this way the next question is what sort of a document the original hymn was. From what "conceptual grid" does it come? It may have some resemblance to the *Hermetica*:[9] should we therefore treat it as of Hellenistic origin? How does it relate to Philo, how to the Dead Sea Scrolls? Perhaps it is Jewish after all, but, as Kümmel supposes, the expression of a peculiarly Jewish form of *gnōsis*, related to the old Wisdom literature but opposed to the docetic element in other forms of Gnosticism?[1] These are real questions, but they are not of the kind I am competent, or wish, to ask. They are all concerned with origins, or with the relation between the text and a conjectural external order, the order of religious and intellectual history at large. The assumption is contrary to that of Chrysostom: if you discover what John *could* originally have intended you can reorganize his book to make it conform more closely to that possible intention. The notion that nobody ever thought anything that had not been thought before is curiously strong in biblical studies; it is an illegitimate inference from a much more defensible position, that there are linguistic and cultural constraints on what can be intended. These are controversial matters, but my claim here is merely that we may properly ask what the poem in its internal relations—in its language and also in its connection with the subsequent narrative—means to us, now, reading it as Augustine said we have to, in

---

8. Chrysostom, *Patrologiae Graecae*, LIX, 40.

9. Philosophical and esoteric writings of late antiquity attributed to the god Hermes Trismegistus [editors' note].

1. W. G. Kümmel, *Introduction to the New Testament*, 17th rev. ed. (1973), trans. Howard Clark Kee (London, 1975), p. 228.

accordance with our restricted capacities. To do that we must treat verses 6–9 and 12–13 as part of the poem.

*   *   *

Commentators ancient and modern would agree that the poem is what might be called a "threshold" poem. It is concerned with what *was* (in Chrysostom's sense, eternally) and how that which *was* crossed over into *becoming.* So the key words of the poem, its axis, are *was* and *became,* in Greek *ēn* and *egeneto,* common words used in an uncommon way. The first sentence of the book asks us to remember the opening words of the whole Bible, verse 1 of Genesis (known in Hebrew simply as "In the Beginning"); it tells how things became, at the behest, at the Word, of the God who is and was from the beginning. This beginning, the one that concerns John, is an older beginning than that of Genesis. *Was* is thrice repeated: the Word *was,* it *was* with God, it *was* God. It is traditional to explain that *was* is here used in three distinct grammatical senses: as denoting existence, relationship, and predication. This triplicity strongly reinforces the special sense of the word; its multidimensional quality, the variety of its aspects which are ignored in ordinary speech, is emphasized, and it is as it were abstracted from such speech. It draws attention to itself in the way of poetry. It stands for the condition of the eternal at the threshold of that which is not eternal but *becomes*—the eternal on the point of an unheard-of participation in that which cannot be eternal because it is created, because it has or will become. It is in contrast with this becoming on the other side of the threshold that the uniqueness of this *was* is affirmed.

The second verse is strongly placed on the *was* side of the threshold, strongly echoes the *was* of the first verse. But the third verse shows us the other side of the threshold: "All things were made by him, and without him was not anything made that was made." "Were made" translates *egeneto* ("became"); "was not" is also *egeneto* ("became not one thing"); and the final phrase, "that was made," is another form of the same verb ("not one thing that has become"). So we have three "becomings" to set against the triple *was* of eternity.

Some scholars argue that the last bit of verse 3 should really be the opening of verse 4, the change having been made for doctrinal reasons, perhaps to disarm Arian heretics.[2] However—as sometimes happens in poetry—the phrase can equally well belong to either or both verses. If the words "that which has become" are taken with verse 4 we have, instead of "In him was life," the more complicated proposition, "that which has become was in him life," which brings together *become* and *was* in a vivid antithesis representing the created and the creator, itself a threshold. It was life in no other way save in him; that measured the extent of its being, its degree of freedom from becoming. The issue is philosophical but the method is the method of poetry.

"The life was the light of men": *was* now means both "was" and "is." Why is "life" identified with "light"? When the life-creating Word was spoken in Genesis, the first being created was light: "God said, Let there be light: and there was

---

2. Those who argued that Christ was God's creation rather than part of the Godhead [editors' note].

light." The light shines in the darkness as in Genesis the light *was* when ordered to be, when the earth was without form and only about to become. The darkness is still the darkness of that primitive chaos which, as later thinkers remarked, had only the potentiality of becoming. The pronouns of verses 3 and 4 do not let us know whether their antecedent is "God" or "the Word"; and that is poetry, for it is right that they should not at this point be separated by grammar. The Word and God, like light and life, are, at any rate in the poem, indivisible.

At this point we might almost suppose the poem to be over, for an apparently unconnected narrative begins: "There was a man sent from God, whose name was John." *Egeneto anthrōpos:* "there became, there came into existence, a man . . ." So the narrative actually begins—comes into being—with a verb that has already been given special weight by John, as it had in the Greek version of Genesis, which he is remembering. John the Baptist is at once firmly labeled as belonging to *becoming.* He was witness to the light (= the Word that *was*) but he *was not (ouk ēn)* that light now coming into the world. Verse 10 tells us that light *was* in the world; the positive form surely remembers the negative form applied in verse 8 to John.

It may well be that these verses were meant to limit the influence of John the Baptist or cut the ground from under the feet of some surviving Baptist sect. It remains true that the newly arrived John is here firmly associated with the *becoming* end of the axis; insofar as the form *was* can be used of him it must be used in the negative. Hence his introduction by means of *ouk ēn;* it is what he is *not* that links the narrative to the poem. And as the hymn continues it goes on distinguishing between the positivity of *was* and the negativity of the world upon whose threshold the Word stood. He, the Word, *was* in the world which *became* ("was made," *egeneto,* v. 10) through him but which failed to recognize him. That world was his own (v. 11)—his own property, of his own making—and his own (his own people) received him not. In other words, Being is treated as an alien by that which it caused to become. In these verses one may find something of that incantatory buildup of semantic pressure that Robert Alter distinguishes as a characteristic of some ancient Hebrew poetry.[3] For the general pathos of the first "verset," to use Alter's term—the creation denies its creator—grows more specific, and "his own" in the second part means "his own people," the neuter giving way to the masculine plural. And then in verse 12 exceptions are mentioned, those who did receive him and so earned the right to *become* sons of God and so to *be.* And this process is related semantically and in other ways to the paradigmatic moment of becoming, namely birth; but this is a different birth, a birth into being, a birth from above, of the spirit and not of the flesh.

It is now that we reach the most remarkable moment of the poem. We have met a paradoxical style of becoming (of birth) which is actually a form of being— one must be born not out of the stuff of becoming, but into being. In verse 14 the paradox is inverted, and we have the violent conceit of the incarnation, *being* surrendering to *becoming:* "The Word was made flesh." And here for the first

---

3. Robert Alter, *The Art of Biblical Poetry* (New York, 1985), and his essay "The Character-istics of Ancient Hebrew Poetry" in *The Literary Guide to the Bible,* ed. Robert Alter and Frank Kermode (Cambridge, Mass., 1987), pp. 611–24.

time we find *egeneto* associated with the Word, for the Word which *was*, in that very special poetic sense, now *became*—became flesh. Such a union of being and becoming must be transient, which is why in the expression "dwelt among us" the Greek verb really means something like "pitched his tent," "camped," as Wisdom did in Ecclesiasticus 24:8. It may well strike the layman as strange that there is a good deal of argument as to whether this verse is really part of the poem.

Like Wisdom again, the Word is known by its glory—*doxa*, a word of many senses in John as elsewhere, though John uses it as a poet might, exploiting its ambiguity. The glory of the Word is distinguished from the world's glory; for example, in 5:41 Jesus says he receives not honor (*doxa*) from men, and in 5:44 that it is impossible for men to believe if they receive *doxa* from one another but do not seek the *doxa* that comes from God. There are other instances, as we shall see. The word *doxa* contains within itself antithetical senses, as antithetical as *ēn* and *egeneto*, the world of the dying generations. *Doxa* is related to the verb *dokeō*, which means "to seem" or "to appear"—it can be a glory by means of which being shines out amidst becoming, or it can be a mere semblance, an attempt on the part of becoming to simulate that true glory.

Here John cuts again to the Baptist, now bearing witness: "This [man] was he of whom I spake" ("was" when we expect "is," perhaps to remind us of the special status of *was* in the poem). The verse is generally regarded as intrusive, a renewed polemic against the followers of John who made excessive claims for him. But its language is the language of the hymn carried over into the incipient narrative: "the one coming after me has *become* before me, because he *was* before me," or rather "because before me he *was*" [author's translation]. In the order of becoming, and only there, does the Word made flesh *appear* to be the follower; by right of the eternal *was* he takes precedence over all that merely becomes. If this is an attack on false claims made for John it is still made in these high terms. It does not matter whether the voice speaking in verse 16 is that of the character John or of the hymn singer. Both know where the fullness of being resides, and that the grace received is superadded to such grace as was formerly available, for instance under Moses and the Law. The whole narrative, its past and its future, must fall under the rule of the great antithesis of being and becoming, be governed by the presence of the *was* in the *become*, the light in the darkness.

All will agree that the hymn ends and gives way to the narrative when, after a clean break, John is questioned about his status ("And this is the record of John, when the Jews sent priests and Levites from Jerusalem to ask him, Who art thou?" v. 19). His relationship to Jesus, first expressed in terms of the metaphysical plot of the hymn, is now given a narrative explanation. John repeatedly affirms his role as witness to the Word. He makes the first announcement of Jesus' paschal and eschatological role: "Behold the Lamb of God" (v. 29), and at once repeats the disclaimer of verse 15: he has become before me because he *was*.

The threshold quality, the liminality of the poem is now deepened into myth, and the myth is dressed in representations of actuality. Jordan is an archetypal threshold. Crossing over its water is baptism; the dove that descends is a figure not only of the spirit from above but also of that *pneuma* that brooded over the formless waste of waters in the beginning, at the great threshold between darkness and light. The ladder by which the angels will descend and reascend (as

Jesus tells Nathaniel) is another bridge between chaos and spirit. Being can cross over or descend into becoming; it will participate in becoming until it reaches its end, a death which restores it to its former unencumbered state. Yeats remarked that Being was "a property of the dead, / A something incompatible with life"[4]— the thought is similar, except that for John the "something" is the *true* life ("true" is another of his heavily loaded words), whereas the life with which Yeats says Being is incompatible is in fact a form of death. So the liminal antitheses of the poem extend themselves into the book as a whole.

WERNER H. KELBER

[The Gospel of Mark as Written Parable][†]

The Gospel as Written Parable

If the gospel is viewed as having arisen out of a process of decontextualization, transformation, and reintegration, we have thereby sketched the history of its textuality but not its new literary identity. The issue here is the gospel's constructive unity. Into what literary form did Mark organize language? What is the formal, artistic principle determining the linguistic gestalt of the gospel? The conventional designation for this concern is genre criticism. Its objective is to probe authorial compliance with the larger, transpersonal imperatives of literary culture. One may in fairness say that genres are hardly ever fully objectified in any given text. The purpose of genre definitions ought not to be the positing of immutable verities and classical certainties, but experimentation with heuristic tools that allow a holistic grasp of the gospel or any other text. If in the following we find fault with four prominent genre models—tragedy, comedy, aretalogy, biography—we do not wish to dismiss their usefulness altogether. Our critique notwithstanding, each model casts the gospel in a different, illuminating perspective.

Resuming earlier studies on tragic aspects in Mark, Gilbert G. Bilezikian has developed a cogent argument for the gospel's affinity with Greek tragedy.[1] For Mark "action represents the substance of the gospel,"[2] and the dynamic progression of action is played out according to the classic pattern of complication-crisis-denouement. In this Mark is said to have followed, by cultural osmosis more than by conscious design, the structural formula recommended by Aristotle for tragic composition in his *Poetics*.[3] The first half of the gospel produces complication, with the disciples' blindness being "the most pathetic aspect."[4] Peter's confession

---

4. William Butler Yeats, "Blood and the Moon" (1929) [editors' note].

† From *The Oral and the Written Gospel* (1983; Bloomington: Indiana University Press, 1997), 117–31, 136–39. Except as indicated, all notes are Kelber's.

1. Gilbert G. Bilezikian, *The Liberated Gospel: A Comparison of the Gospel of Mark and Greek Tragedy* (Grand Rapids: Baker Book House, 1977).

2. Ibid., p. 53.

3. Ibid., pp. 51–55.

4. Ibid., p. 62.

near Caesarea Philippi marks the critical turning point, and the remainder of the story narrates the hero's downfall. There is much to be said for Bilezikian's thesis that the dramatic movement is sustained by the disciples' deteriorating relations with Jesus, but it is not entirely clear how the gospel's revolutionary dynamics can be built on Aristotle's plot structure. Amos Wilder's often quoted caveat that "Greek and traditional humanistic categories are inadequate as measuring rods"[5] for early Christian literature may not be valid in all instances, but it does apply to Mark's gospel. All canonical gospels contain an element that "rebels against order imposed from the past. This element is most visible in Mark."[6] If Mark is the gospel that dramatizes renewal of the world by subverting its foundation, is it amenable to the formal category of Greek tragedy? Are we blunting the shock effects emanating from the gospel by dignifying it with a cultured, classical designation? How does the gospel's open-endedness conform with the formal closure of Greek tragedy? Does Mark intend "to proclaim the universal relevance of a very Jewish story by telling it in the manner of a Greek tragedy,"[7] or does he perhaps narrate his Jewish story in a form more directly compatible with Jesus the Jew?

Dan O. Via has offered the most penetrating genre analysis of the gospel up to date.[8] While Bilezikian followed the narrative sequence, Via deconstructed the text into a series of textemes.[9] Examining a variety of structural relations of actions, functions, and sequels, he finds the paradigm of death and resurrection, the rhythm of upset and recovery, reverberating on all levels. Since death and resurrection stand at the heart of the comic form, comedy is the generic source from which the text is generated. It is out of a special sense of appreciation for Via's work that the following five issues are being raised. First, if one is dedicated to the proposition that "the New Testament kerygma [sic] belongs to the structure of comedy,"[1] which, moreover, is said to be "a deep, generative structure of the human mind,"[2] why go through the motion and recapitulate the case for Mark? Second, Via admits that "Mark does not really exploit the comic side of these patterns."[3] While "the comic genre . . . generated the Gospel of Mark,"[4] the text in fact belongs to the genre of "tragicomedy" in the modern sense. Tragicomedy, apart from maintaining the life-through-death pattern of comedy, emphasizes the global presence of death and confronts us with uncertainties about Jesus, and, one might add, about ourselves.[5] If tragicomedy is what really matters, is there not a more appropriate category that takes account of Markan uncertain-

---

5. Amos N. Wilder, *The Language of the Gospel: Early Christian Rhetoric* (New York: Harper & Row, 1964), p. 44. Bilezikian is conscious of the issue (*Liberated Gospel*, pp. 19, n. 27; 29).

6. William A. Beardslee, *Literary Criticism of the New Testament*, GBS (Philadelphia: Fortress Press, 1970), p. 28.

7. Bilezikian, *Liberated Gospel*, p. 31.

8. Dan O. Via, *Kerygma and Comedy in the New Testament: A Structuralist Approach to Hermeneutic* (Philadelphia: Fortress Press, 1975).

9. The smallest meaningful units of a text (a word created by analogy with *phoneme* and *morpheme*) [editors' note].

1. Via, *Kerygma and Comedy*, p. 49.

2. Ibid., p. 93.

3. Ibid., p. 101.

4. Ibid., p. 93.

5. Ibid., pp. 99–103.

ties, metaphorical language, and reversal of roles and expectations? Third, in reflecting on Rom. 9:30ff., a Pauline discourse on righteousness through faith versus righteousness by law, Via suggests that "the narrative form is tragic, the last word being Israel's disobedience."[6] Yet what does this say for Mark who dares end his narrative with the aborted transmission of the message of life? That ending cannot be taken lightly as regards the gospel's genre. Fourth, one wonders whether Via has satisfactorily answered the crucial question with which he has challenged other scholars: why did Mark produce a narrative? To say that the gospel "came to be written because . . . the death and resurrection of Jesus reverberated in the mind of Mark and activated the comic genre,"[7] begs the question. If one believes, as Via does, that both Mark and Paul belong to comedy,[8] why then did this same comic genre in one case produce a narrative, but not in the other? Fifth, there is the question of the application of structuralism to biblical texts, an issue that admittedly deserves a more detailed response than is possible here. Herbert Schneidau * * * has proposed a differentiation between cybernetic and kerygmatic language.[9] Cybernetic, mythic, and frequently oral communication confirms and repeats structure. Kerygmatic and frequently biblical communication disconfirms and subverts structure.[1] Structuralist interpretation is most aptly applied to cybernetic language and least successfully to kerygmatic language. In Mark's case one wonders whether a text born out of linguistic disorientation and reflecting a deep sense of alienation is adequately grasped by fitting it into stable grids and schemata.

In a joint project undertaken by Moses Hadas and Morton Smith the gospel was found to conform to the ancient genre of aretalogy.[2] The latter was broadly defined as a form of religious biography in which the hero is characterized by the gift of miracle working and impressive teaching, and often suffers martyrdom at the hands of a tyrant. For two reasons New Testament scholars have been reluctant to endorse this proposal. First, the very existence of a literary genre of aretalogy is subject to doubt. As Howard C. Kee has noted,[3] the paradigmatic model of aretalogy, that is, Plato's portrait of Socrates, lacks miracles, and the most fully developed aretalogy, Philostratus's *Life of Apollonius of Tyana*, is without martyrdom. Second, the inclination among New Testament scholars was and is to apply the designation of aretalogy strictly to a source of miracle stories, usually understood to have been written for the purpose of religious propaganda. It is in this restricted sense that Gerd Theissen has recently sought to find the generic

6. Ibid., p. 50.

7. Ibid., p. 93.

8. Ibid., pp. 77–90.

9. [Herbert N.] Schneidau, *Sacred Discontent*[: *The Bible and the Western Tradition* (Berkeley: University of California Press, 1976)], pp. 286–306; idem, "For Interpretation," *Missouri Review* 1 (1978): 70–88, esp. 79.

1. The terms kerygmatic versus cybernetic correspond to our use of mythoclastic [myth destroying] versus mythopoetic [myth creating].

2. Moses Hadas and Morton Smith, *Heroes and Gods: Spiritual Biographies in Antiquity* (New York: Harper & Row, 1965).

3. Howard Clark Kee, "Aretalogy and Gospel," *JBL* 92 (1973): 402–22; idem, *Aretalogies, Hellenistic 'Lives,' and the Sources of Mark*, Protocol of the Colloquy 12 (Berkeley, Calif.: Center for Hermeneutical Studies, 1975).

key to Mark in aretalogy.[4] He proceeded from the thesis that acclamation is the intended goal of all synoptic miracle stories. This element, he observed, is either absent in Mark or overshadowed by misunderstanding and secrecy. The pre-passion narrative, largely made up of a string of exclusive miracle stories, is thus put in a state of suspense from which it is not released until the centurion's Son of God confession (15:39). It is his climactic confession that rounds out the areta-logical overarching structure (*aretalogischer Spannungsbogen*) and generates an inclusive aretalogical composition. One may wonder, however, whether the mir-acles are allowed to function as an overarching structure, if one observes with Paul Achtemeier,[5] Hans D. Betz,[6] Helmut Koester,[7] and James Robinson[8] that they have been subjected to critical transformations.[9] In the oral-textual per-spectives we have been developing, the issue may be formulated from a different angle. If the process of textualization injects a controversial, metaphorical ele-ment into the heroic stories, sharpens the mythoclastic function of the didactic stories, and, as we shall see, introduces a parabolic hermeneutic, one must question whether this thrust toward the mythoclastic and parabolic is compati-ble with the elevation of the most heroic and mythopoetic form to the position of genre determinant.

Johannes Weiss, one of the first scholars to propose the gospel's relation to the genre of ancient biographies,[1] has at the same time articulated two major objec-tions: the authorial absence from the text, and the lack of birth and childhood stories.[2] Similar questions must be raised in regard to Clyde W. Votaw's more elaborate effort to link the gospel with the biographical accounts of philosopher teachers such as Socrates, or miracle workers like Apollonius.[3] For Philip L. Shuler the gospel is an encomium,[4] a laudatory biographical genre, the principal

4. Gerd Theissen, *Urchristliche Wundergeschichten: Ein Beitrag zur formgeschichtlichen Erforschung der synoptischen Evangelien* (Gütersloh: Gerd Mohn, 1974), pp. 211–21.

5. [Paul J.] Achtemeier, "Imperfect Union[: Reflections on Gerd Theissen, *Urchristliche Wundergeschichten*," *Semeia* 11 (1978)], 63.

6. Hans Dieter Betz, "Jesus as Divine Man," in *Jesus and the Historian: Festschrift for E. C. Colwell*, ed. F. Thomas Trotter (Philadelphia: Westminster Press, 1968), pp. 114–33.

7. Helmut Koester, "One Jesus and Four Primitive Gospels," in *Trajectories through Early Christianity* (Philadelphia: Fortress Press, 1971), pp. 187–93.

8. James M. Robinson, "The Problem of History in Mark, Reconsidered," *Union Seminary Quarterly Review* 20 (1965): 131–47; reissued in idem, *Problem of History in Mark [and Other Marcan Studies* (Philadelphia: Fortress Press, 1982)].

9. Achtemeier (*Mark* [Philadelphia: Fortress Press, 1975], p. 78) suggests that "Mark contin-ued the process of adapting and interpreting the miracle stories." Betz ("Jesus as Divine Man," p. 121) argues that the miracle tradition underwent "a total transformation when it came into the hands of Mark." According to Koester ("One Jesus," p. 189, n. 105), the miracles "were subjected to the principle of the cross." On Robinson's view ("Problem of History," p. 137), Mark "blunted the proclivities of collections of miracle stories."

1. Johannes Weiss, *Das älteste Evangelium* (Göttingen: Vandenhoeck & Ruprecht, 1907), pp. 6–29.

2. Ibid., pp. 9, 14.

3. Clyde Weber Votaw, *The Gospels and Contemporary Biographies in the Greco-Roman World* (Philadelphia: Fortress Press, 1970).

4. Philip L. Shuler, *The Synoptic Gospels and the Problem of Genre* (Ph.D. diss., McMaster University, 1975).

purpose of which was "to present a portrait of a person in such a way as either to call forth praise from an audience or to persuade an audience of his praiseworthiness."[5] While there is what Shuler calls a *bios factor* present in Mark, encomium is too genteel and bland a category. Charles H. Talbert has come closer to Mark's generic identity by defining the gospel as a biography that aims "to dispel a false image of the teacher and to provide a true model to follow."[6] But the manner of dispelling a traditional model of Jesus and the precise mechanism of reverting roles and expectations moves this gospel toward the parabolic.

Recently a number of scholars have detected a parabolic dimension in the gospels, and especially in Mark. In the latest edition of *Traditions in Conflict*, Theodore Weeden noted cryptically that "the evangelist intended a parabolic effect."[7] Frederick H. Borsch in a popular book on gospels and gospel traditions concluded that the narration of Jesus' life and death "became the consummate parable of the new faith."[8] Robert Tannehill brilliantly traced the narrative role of the disciples in Mark, in effect offering a parabolic interpretation.[9] John R. Donahue, S. J., deserves major credit for a creative reading of the gospel as "a narrative parable of the meaning of the life and death of Jesus."[1] He clearly spelled out the connection between the gospel's leading motif of the mystery of the kingdom and its parabolic nature: it is by shaking conventions and shattering expectations that the gospel beckons toward the mystery of the kingdom of God. John Dominic Crossan, reflecting on the transition from Jesus to tradition, suggested that Rudolf Bultmann's thesis of the Proclaimer becoming the Proclaimed ought to be redefined in terms of the parabler becoming parable: "Jesus announced the kingdom of God in parables, but the primitive church announced Jesus as Christ, the Parable of God."[2] In this connection Crossan specified my own reading of Mark 1–13 in *The Kingdom in Mark* as a genuinely parabolic one.[3] Ricoeur, as noted in an epigraph to this chapter, has wondered whether the role of the exclusive parable in the space of intersignification may not contribute to the meaning of gospel as parable.[4] In a comprehensive structuralist analysis of the spatial world of Mark, Elizabeth Struthers Malbon argued that the narrative was a parable-myth, powered

5. Ibid., p. 169.

6. Charles H. Talbert, *What Is a Gospel? The Genre of the Canonical Gospels* (Philadelphia: Fortress Press, 1977), p. 94.

7. [Theodore J.] Weeden, *Mark[: Traditions in Conflict* (Philadelphia: Fortress Press)], p. viii.

8. Frederick Houk Borsch, *God's Parable* (Philadelphia: Westminster Press, 1975), p. 98.

9. [Robert C.] Tannehill, "The Disciples in Mark[: The Function of a Narrative Role," *Journal of Religion* 57 (1977): 386–405].

1. John R. Donahue, S. J., "Jesus as Parable of God in the Gospel of Mark," *Interpretation* 32 (1978): 369–86.

2. John Dominic Crossan, *The Dark Interval: Towards a Theology of Story* (Niles, Ill.: Argus Communications, 1975), p. 124, cf. also 10; idem, *In Parables: The Challenge of the Historical Jesus* (New York: Harper & Row, 1973), p. xiv; idem, *Finding Is the First Act: Trove Folktales and Jesus' Treasure Parable*, Semeia Studies 8 (Philadelphia: Fortress Press; Missoula, Mont.: Scholars Press, 1979), pp. 106–7. [See Rudolf Bultmann, *Theology of the New Testament*, trans. Kendrick Grobel (New York: Scribner, 1951), vol. 1, p. 33.]

3. Crossan, *Dark Interval*, p. 126.

4. [Paul] Ricoeur, "Biblical Hermeneutics," [*Semeia* 4 (1975):] 103.

by the reversal of expectations.[5] Amos Wilder long ago sensed that "some of the parables present the larger story in microcosm."[6] Today the matter is expressed more forthrightly, as exemplified by Schneidau, who suggested that the gospels, insofar as they emphasize the difficulty of receiving their message, share the kerygmatic function of parabolic speech: "The parable, therefore, is the typifying form of the Gospel."[7]

It is curious that none of the above scholars, the present writer included, have bothered to consult the gospel about *its* thought on parables. As is well known, the evangelist develops what has been called a parable theory in chapter 4. How is Mark's thesis related to contemporary parable hermeneutics, and what, if anything, does it contribute to the gospel's generic identity?

The intriguingly difficult verses 4:10–12 contain the germ of Mark's so-called parabolic theory. In response to a question concerning parables Jesus states that "to those about him with the twelve" (4:10; au. trans.) the mystery has been given that pertains to the kingdom of God, whereas "to those on the outside" (*ekeinois de tois exō*) everything is "in parables" (4:11). One immediately observes an insider-outsider dichotomy. Insiders are admitted into the mystery of the kingdom, while outsiders are barred from it. The latter are depicted as people who, while seeing and hearing, nonetheless are lacking in comprehension (4:12). Theirs is a situation of everything being "in parables." As often observed, the meaning of parables here has been slanted toward riddle. Parabolic speech, on this riddling notion, casts hearers into outsiders by withholding understanding from them.

This, then, is the heart of the so-called theory on parables: parabolic discourse is the carrier of a cryptic message that casts to the outside those who cannot fathom it, while confirming as insiders those to whom it is revealed.

How did Mark arrive at a parabolic hermeneutic that espouses esoteric teaching with deeply alienating effects? The observation that he derived it from Isa. 6:9–10 (= Mark 4:12) merely begs the question. One must rather ask what encouraged him to link Isaiah's pessimistic verdict about those who see but don't perceive, hear but don't understand, with parabolic discourse.

John C. Meagher has recently explained the Markan theme of esoteric teaching in parables as a strategic device aimed at overcoming contradictions that arose between Jesus' own message and its history of tradition.[8] The historical Jesus, he suggested, was generally known to have spoken parables for the purpose of illumination, not obscuration. After the resurrection, when the tradition about him conflicted with his own pre-resurrectional message, parables were turned into riddles. Consequently, Jesus could be said to have preached all that tradition reported about him because he had taught in a form accessible only to a few, and opaque to others. Esoteric teaching is therefore a continuity-affirming device that reconciles Jesus with the post-resurrectional situation. Meagher's thesis is predicated on two major assumptions that are subject to question. There is first the issue of parabolic herme-

5. Elizabeth Struthers Malbon, "Narrative Space and Mythic Meaning: A Structural Exegesis of the Gospel of Mark" (Ph.D. diss., Florida State University, 1980).

6. Wilder, *Language of Gospel*, p. 67.

7. Schneidau, "For Interpretation," p. 84.

8. John C. Meagher, *Clumsy Construction in Mark's Gospel: A Critique of Form- and Redaktionsgeschichte*, Toronto Studies in Theology 3 (New York and Toronto: Edwin Mellen Press, 1979).

neutics. The author states flatly: "Parables are normally instruments of clarification, illustration, illumination, not obfuscation."[9] Parable scholarship has learned much since Adolf Jülicher,[1] above all that parables are not "normally" means of clarification. Whence this confidence in a Jesus who was "generally known to have taught openly and clearly"?[2] There is secondly the issue of Mark's distortion of parables, his redactional "clumsiness," and tradition-historical conclusions drawn from it. That the evangelist has misconstrued the linguisticality of parables is a charge running through much of nineteenth and twentieth century Markan scholarship, but it is, we will show below, unacceptable. Meagher issues an important warning against overestimating the evangelist's literary skills and ambitions. Mark is not the sterling literary genius he appears to be in some recent scholarship. Still, "clumsiness" is hardly an acceptable intellectual category for approaching a text. What is more, to proceed from redactional "clumsiness" toward sorting out stages in the tradition is hazardous in the extreme. The proposition that esoteric teaching served to conform Jesus with conflicting traditions about him remains as unconvincing as the remarkably similar theory by William Wrede who suggested that the Messianic Secret was meant to reconcile an unmessianic life of Jesus with a messianizing tradition.[3] The more obvious linguistic consideration is to associate esoteric teaching in parables not with redactional clumsiness, but with the very hermeneutics of parables.

Contemporary parable scholarship is in a position to appreciate the Markan hermeneutic of esoteric teaching and parabolic alienation, and the corresponding casting of audience into insider and outsider roles. We have noted in the preceding chapter that it is the nature of parables to deviate from literal meaning, evade the event character of oral speech, suspend meaning, and disrupt oral synthesis— all features which complicate and impede the hermeneutical process. In emphasizing the riddling, alienating function of parables, Mark has thus seized upon a hermeneutical potential inherent in parabolic discourse. By the same token, the very parabolic speech that delays comprehension and relegates hearers to the outside may strengthen oral synthesis and locate hearers on the inside. As also noted before, parabolist and audience partake in social contextuality that can facilitate an instantaneous transaction of the hermeneutical process. In that case, speaker and hearers have come to share inside knowledge hidden from those who have now become outsiders. The parable functions as carrier of secrecy. In emphasizing the initiation of the twelve into insider roles, Mark has thus again exploited inherent parabolic potentiality.

We have arrived at an important preliminary conclusion. The features that constitute Mark's so-called parable theory—esoteric teaching and corresponding alienation, and the complementary roles of insiders versus outsiders—reflect genuine implications of parabolic discourse. What we find is neither clumsiness nor misunderstanding, but a developed hermeneutical reflection on parabolic language. Madeleine Boucher has expressed the matter most perceptively:

9. Ibid., p. 86.

1. In the nineteenth century, Jülicher argued against understanding parables as allegorical; he viewed each as making a single point [editors' note].

2. Meagher, *Clumsy Construction*, p. 93.

3. William Wrede, *The Messianic Secret*, Eng. trans. J. C. G. Greig (London: James Clarke & Co., 1971) [see Appendix, pp. 1129–49].

The charge made in much of the scholarly literature since the nineteenth century that Mark has distorted the parable as a verbal construct is simply unfounded. Mark has not taken clear, straightforward speech, the parable, and transformed it into obscure, esoteric speech, the allegory. He has rather taken what is essential to the parable, the double-meaning effect, and made it the starting point of a theological theme concerning the audience's resistance to hearing the word.[4]

Mark is not, of course, a philosopher of language who lectures on a theory of parables. Rather he narrates a story that displays notable sensitivity toward parabolic hermeneutic. The precise question, then, is that of the narrative implications of the so-called parable theory. Jesus' parabolic discourse, it is made very clear to the disciples, concerns the kingdom of God (4:10–11). The mystery of the kingdom draws parabolic speech. What is noteworthy at this point is that the theme of kingdom is not exclusively tied to, let alone exhausted by, exclusive parabolic speech. Mark's whole gospel is the proclamation of the kingdom of God. Initiation into the mystery of the kingdom requires that the disciples follow Jesus' way to the very end. But if consciousness of the kingdom is inseparable from the way of Jesus, all aspects of his life and death are pointers toward the kingdom's mystery. The Markan space of intersignification, as noted above, slants individual forms of speech toward the metaphorical, and produces, we now conclude, a thoroughgoing metaphorical text. Mark's gospel in its entirety points beyond itself to the mystery of the kingdom of God. The first criterion for parable, that of metaphoricity, is thereby met by the gospel of Mark.

The metaphorical character of the text may induce us to take seriously statements that tend to extend the concept of the parabolic across the gospel's narrative. When in Mark 4:34 it is narrated that Jesus "did not speak to them without a parable, but privately to his own disciples he explained everything (*panta*)," one must not immediately dismiss this as a redactional oversight. It could well mean that everything Jesus says signifies the kingdom's mystery to which the disciples are privileged insiders. There is Markan justification for stretching parabolic dynamics across the gospel. When, moreover, it is argued that to ousiders "everything (*ta panta*) is in parables" (4:11), the concept of the parabolic and the creation of outsiders is applied once again to the whole story.[5] At this point it can no longer be claimed that Mark argues a particular theory on parables. In effect, what is articulated is the parabolic nature of Jesus' story. Jesus' life and death, as narrated by Mark, transpires according to the hermeneutical process of parable. It functions *ad malam partem* [on the bad side] as an impenetrable riddle, and *ad bonam partem* [on the good side] as revelation into the mystery of the kingdom of God.

In turning to the second criterion for parable, that of *extravagance*, one suspects a connection with the insider-outsider dichotomy. At least this feature is

---

4. [Madeleine] Boucher, [*The*] *Mysterious Parable*[: *A Literary Study*, Catholic Biblical Quarterly Monograph Series 6 (Washington, D.C.: Catholic Biblical Association of America, 1977)], p. 83.

5. Friedrich Hauck, *"parabole," Theological Dictionary of the New Testament* V: 758.

the principal narrative candidate in Mark 4:10–12. For the most part, Markan scholarship observed the placement of the disciples onto the inside track, and the author's peculiar reluctance, or inability, to carry out their appointed narrative role. Meagher, for example, observed that the gospel "tends to have the crowds see and hear quite well, while the inner circle has difficulties—nearly the opposite of the policy strangely advanced in chapter 4."[6] Not only has Mark mistakenly connected esoteric teaching with parables, but esoteric teaching is itself "curiously inconsistent with the Gospel at large."[7] In the same vein, Heikki Räisänen proposed that Markan redaction deliberately foiled a parabolic interpretation that came to him from tradition.[8] Since crowds, apparently the outsiders, are depicted in a neutral, or even enlightened posture, whereas the insiders' role of the twelve is virtually turned into its opposite, Räisänen concluded that Mark adopted a parable theory (4:10–12) for the purpose of relativizing it via the thoroughgoing motif of discipleship misunderstanding.[9]

It is, however, Räisänen, Meagher, and many other scholars—not Mark—who have prevented the parabolic story from running its due course. Insensitive to parabolic extravagance and obsessed with the logic of "normality," they could not see the wood for the trees. Indeed the very feature that they considered out of step with parabolic logic, the rapidly increasing blindness of the inner circle, is the key to the parabolic narrative. If Mark is as rigorous a parabolic thinker as we claim, he cannot narrate the insider-outsider syndrome in such a way as to allow easy and direct identification. The insider-outsider dichotomy, we noted, is a constitutive feature of parabolic language. But a genuinely parabolic story aims at defying the structure of expectancy, even the expected structure of parable! That it is the nature of the parable to turn on itself was keenly discerned by Schneidau:

> A parable is always a parable or, more exactly, the existence of parables is itself a parable. Whatever its messages and whatever utilitarian purposes these suggest and incur, the form itself enacts a further parabolic dramatization of the evanescent nature of any "message," or more precisely, of the uncertainties of interpreting it.[1]

Lest parable be converted into myth, its very own logic requires a parabolic dramatization.

If one recognizes in Jesus' announcement of the kingdom (1:14–15) the high point of the introduction, then the call of the first disciples (1:16–20) marks the formal opening of the narrative proper.[2] With Jesus' calling upon the four to follow him, the dominant theme of discipleship gets under way, and a structure of expectancy is initiated. The subsequent story strengthens this expectancy by letting

6. Meagher, *Clumsy Construction*, p. 87.
7. Ibid.
8. Heikki Räisänen, *Die Parabeltheorie im Markusevangelium*, Schriften der Finnischen Exegetischen Gesellschaft 26 (Helsinki: Länsi-Suomi, 1973).
9. Ibid., pp. 27–47.
1. Schneidau, "For Interpretation," p. 85.
2. Leander E. Keck, "The Introduction to Mark's Gospel," NTS 12 (1966): 352–70.

those who follow Jesus be privy to prominent aspects of his mission of the king-dom: exorcism and teaching with authority (1:21–28), healing (1:29–31), the purpose of journeying (1:38), the shattering novelty of the mission and its colli-sion with a world of traditional values (2:13–17, 18–22, 23–28), as well as the ecumenical proportion of the movement (3:7–12). In an act of far-reaching sig-nificance Jesus "makes" the twelve, singling out three by special names (3:13–19). The twelve and especially the three have been appointed to official leadership. Since the three were among the first to be called, the structure of expectancy is reinforced. They can be expected to follow Jesus and to absorb the information indispensable for their functioning as apostolic representatives. There is one crack in the structure of expectancy: Judas is marked as traitor (3:19).

With apostolic leadership firmly established, the author brings the parabolic dimension into narrative focus. The first time Jesus speaks "in parables" (3:23), he does so in condemnation of the Jerusalem scribes who accused him of demonic possession. When the relatives, who consider Jesus mentally deranged, arrive (3:20–21), he relegates them to the outside by identifying those inside the house sitting "about him" (3:34: *tous peri auton*) as the true family of God. By intercon-necting the two episodes (3:20–22, 23–30, 31–35), the author strengthens the view that inasmuch as scribes and blood relatives are united in their objection to Jesus, both are cast to the outside. Hence, the very first reference to parabolic speech sets into motion the insider-outsider dichotomy.

No sooner is the insider-outsider scheme confirmed than "those about him (4:10: *hoi peri auton*) with the twelve" are declared participants in the mystery of the kingdom of God (4:11a). In addition to delegating the twelve to the inside, Jesus articulates a most carefully drawn up characterization of the outsiders (4:11b–12). With this placement of the twelve into the role of privileged insiders, the structure of expectancy is completed. But at that very point the insider-outsider scheme is also disclosed as being part of a parabolic process. Indeed, no sooner are the twelve confirmed as insiders over against outsiders than Jesus questions their grasp of parables (4:13). How does lack of comprehension con-form with their insider position? The answer is that the very moment the struc-ture of expectancy has been completed and shown to be subject to parabolic logic, the parabolic reversal of roles is ever so slightly set into motion.

Subsequently (4:35–8:21) "Mark shows how Jesus unites the community in a sacrificial existence."[3] In a series of boat trips the Markan Jesus opens the fron-tier toward Gentile land, connecting it with Jewish land. Two pivotal feedings (6:34–44; 8:1–10) are designed to initiate the disciples into the Jewish-Gentile fellowship. But the logic of his voyages finds no congenial response among them. On the first voyage (4:35–41) they become panic-stricken. Both purpose and goal of the trip elude their comprehension. During the second trip to the Gentiles (6:45–52) they once again fail to overcome adversity and to reach the shore on their own strength. Thereafter their condition is described as one of ignorance about the loaves (= the first feeding) and of hardness of heart (6:52).

---

3. [Ulrich E.] Simon, *Story and Faith* [*in the Biblical Narrative* (London: SPCK, 1975)], p. 75.

The motif of ignorance replays an outsider characteristic (6:52: *ou gar synhēkan* [for they did not understand]; 4:12: *mē synhiōsin* [they may not understand]), and hardness of heart, applied earlier and later to opponents (3:5; 10:5), reinforces the impression of the disciples' drift toward the outside. On the final voyage (8:13–21) the decisive step is taken of conferring the entire catalogue of outsider characteristics upon the disciples: lack of understanding, hardness of heart, blindness and deafness (8:17–18). At this point, the systematic application of all outsider characteristics to the insiders has resulted in the overthrow of the structure of expectancy.

But is the reversal sustained? Jesus' final question, "Do you not yet understand?" (8:21) leaves the door open for repentance, a distinct possibility for outsiders (4:12c). Is the gospel narrating a genuinely parabolic story, or does it defuse the paradox and reconcile us with the initial narrative expectation?

Jesus' threefold passion predictions (Mark 8:31; 9:31; 10:33–34) emphasize the irrefutability of his impending death. But as the necessity of the Son of man's suffering is accentuated, so is the failure of the disciples to adopt his model of discipleship. Each passion pronouncement is followed by a glaring case of misconception on the part of the disciples. Peter, the leader, stands exposed as Jesus' satanic adversary (8:33); the disciples are convicted of lack of perception and fear (9:32); James and John, among the first to be called, are found asking for positions of power (10:35–46). The disciples' failure to come to terms with Jesus' suffering is compounded by the apparent obtuseness of the triumvirate regarding the resurrection (9:9–10). A false sense of presence makes Peter, together with James and John, misjudge the proleptic nature of the transfiguration (9:2–8). Unable to perform an exorcism, the disciples default on an obligation that they had earlier been able to discharge successfully (9:14–29; cf. 6:7, 13). Contrary to Jesus' wishes, they obstruct the work of an accomplished exorcist (9:38–41) and rebuke children (10:13–16; cf. 9:36–37). The author, it seems, spares little effort to sharpen the conflict between Jesus and the disciples, and to consolidate thereby the outsider position of the latter. Seeing they do not see, and hearing they do not hear. At the same time, the author has them thoroughly prepared for the Jerusalem events, and he sustains their relation with Jesus into the passion. The reader's (or hearer's) expectation for a final turnabout is thus very much kept alive.

The last time Jesus speaks "in parable," he addresses the parable of the *Wicked Tenants* (12:1–11) to the temple authorities (11:27; 12:12). As his first speech "in parables" (3:23) was designed to set into motion the insider-outsider dynamic, so does his last parable speech likewise cast hearers to the outside. The tenants of the vineyard are turned outside, while the beloved Son, who was killed and thrown outside (12:8), becomes the insider. The implication of the parable is grasped by the temple authorities, the perceived insiders. Although the exclusive parable does not implicate the disciples, it is made to function according to the parabolic logic of the gospel's inclusive parabolic narrative.

In the Jerusalem speech (13:5b–37) Jesus initiates the very disciples whom he had called first into the meaning of the final events. Tannehill has recently suggested that the speech "anticipates a continuing role for the disciples beyond the disaster of chapter 14,"[4] and Norman Petersen has gone even further by stating that Peter, James, John, and Andrew "will be representatives of Jesus up to the time of the parousia."[5] This seems a curious argument to come from literary critics. How can one make assumptions about the role of narrativized persons in the world outside the narrative world without letting the story come to its completion? Petersen correctly states that in accord with the Markan story line "we are compelled to assume that they [the disciples] understood it [Jesus' speech] no more than anything else."[6] Unless there is forthcoming evidence to the contrary, Jesus explains everything to the disciples, who hear but fail to perceive. That there is "lack of any mention"[7] of the disciples' response to the speech is, however, not quite correct. Tannehill points to known connections between the eschatological speech and passion motifs.[8] The speech climaxes in the admonition to endurance (13:13) and vigilance (13:33–37). These are virtues required during passion. But when in the Gethsemane story (14:32–42) the motif cluster of waking-coming-finding-sleeping is resumed, the disciples fail to wake, and sleep instead. Despite Jesus' speech, they consolidate their role as outsiders, consistently undermining hope that they could function as future leaders. Nor can it be said that Jesus' words must come to pass or else his authority is invalidated. In the story world, his words fall on the deaf ears of the disciples; they are disobeyed, not disconfirmed. The hardness of heart of the inner circle does not discredit the authority of Jesus. Nor does Jesus ever promise the actualization of a reunion with the disciples. He merely promises to go ahead of them to Galilee (14:28). They have been informed of the return to Galilee, as they were told everything else pertaining to the mystery of the kingdom. It is up to the disciples to follow the leader and his words.

If the hopes of the gospel's recipients have been kept alive into the passion story, it is there that they are decisively crushed. Far from experiencing a change of heart, the disciples, under the leadership of Peter, play out their roles of outsiders to the bitter end. Peter contradicts Jesus' prediction of the discipleship failure (14:26–29), all the disciples promise to suffer with Jesus (14:30–31), the triumvirate falters at Gethsemane (14:32–42), one disciple betrays Jesus (14:10–11, 43–46), all desert him at the moment of arrest (14:50), and Peter, the last hope, denies Jesus while the latter makes his fateful confession before the high priest (14:53–72).

After the disappearance of the disciples the three women act as vital intermediaries between Jesus and the disciples (16:1–8). This one last time hopes are aroused that the women might repair the broken connection, transmit the mes-

---

4. Tannehill, "The Disciples in Mark," p. 402.

5. [Norman R.] Petersen, *Literary Criticism for New Testament Critics* [Guides to Biblical Scholarship (Philadelphia: Fortress Press, 1978)], p. 70.

6. Ibid.

7. Ibid.

8. Tannehill, "The Disciples in Mark," p. 402; cf. also F. Dewar, "Chapter 13 and the Passion Narrative in Mark," *Theology* 64 (1961): 99–107; R. H. Lightfoot, *The Gospel Message of St. Mark* (New York and London: Oxford University Press, 1950), pp. 41–60; Werner H. Kelber, "The Hour of the Son of Man and the Temptation of the Disciples," in [*The*] *Passion in Mark* [(Philadelphia: Fortress Press, 1976)], pp. 41–60.

sage of life, and facilitate the disciples' rehabilitation. But inasmuch as the narrative kindles such hopes, it does everything to wreck them. While the women are indeed commissioned to carry the message of the resurrection to the disciples, they fail to deliver it. Overcome by trembling, astonishment, and fear, they flee (16:8: *ephygon*), as earlier all the disciples had fled (14:50: *ephygon pantes*). As a result, the disciples, who had been absent at the crucifixion and have remained ignorant of the resurrection, never learn that the signal has been given for the reunion with the resurrected one. They are thereby effectively eliminated as apostolic representatives of the risen Lord. With their demise the structure of expectancy is finally and irrevocably reversed, and the narrative has found its proper, parabolic ending. If it is assumed that the "projected meeting in Galilee is the only moment of all those in Mark's narrative world when the disciples could come out from under the cloud of ignorance—when the plot of Mark's narrative could be resolved,"[9] one has dulled the gospel's extravagance and trivialized its oddness. One has, in short, remained undisturbed by parabolic disorientation. The obvious conclusion to be drawn from the open ending is that it is meant to be inconclusive. "The parable," Robert W. Funk states flatly, "does not have a conclusion."[1] This is so because the parable, far from inviting us to settle for familiar, classical perspectives, shocks us out of them toward a new and unfamiliar logic.

Textuality as Agent of Alienation and Liberation

At crucial points of linguistic transit the dynamics of the medium enter into the recorded message to an extent that medium and message become intersecting phenomena. The reasons are intricate and far from being fully explored. But in a general sense, this interpenetration of narrative and medium features is intelligible. When a tradition that was contingent on and grew up in oral speech shifts its mode of communication, it may have to argue its linguistic existence and assignment vis-à-vis the conventional medium and its authorities. One may thus find inscribed in the newly mediated story a rationale for its own medium history. In the early synoptic tradition the oral medium had been sanctioned by Jesus himself. His was a message inherently bound up with speaking. Prophetic and apostolic speakers carried his words and words about him to audiences. In this predominantly oral milieu a writer's reflexive and distancing appropriation of Jesus' words and deeds marked a linguistic and theological departure that may have required justification. It is for this reason that Mark's gospel is not merely concerned with the life and death of Jesus, but also with writing about it.

Mark as a writer, we saw, had to maneuver himself into an outside position vis-à-vis oral tradition. He could not have plotted the gospel without exercising reserve toward the oral metaphysics of presence and contemporizing. Distance from orality gave him the new perspective. Characteristically, the story he wrote favored the outsider and narrated the epistemological paradox of proximity versus

9. Petersen, *Literary Criticism for New Testament Critics*, p. 77.

1. Robert W. Funk, *Language, Hermeneutic, and Word of God: The Problem of Language in the New Testament and Contemporary Theology* (New York: Harper & Row, 1966; reprint: Missoula, Mont.: Scholars Press, 1979), p. 196.

distance. There is a tendency for the power of perception of at least some characters to increase in proportion to their distance from Jesus. Those within constant
earshot of the teacher do not hear well. Crowds, which do not partake in Jesus'
traveling, tend to have a better comprehension. Outsiders such as the Greek
woman (6:24–30) and a blind man (10:46–52) become models of faith and discipleship. The Roman centurion, distanced to an extreme by his discharge of duty,
nonetheless more clearly than anyone else in the narrative perceives Jesus as the
Son of God. His, not Peter's, is the true confession of Jesus the Crucified. Jesus
himself is an outsider who contradicts his own tradition and the expectations of
his followers, and in the end is thrown out of the vineyard. That the outsider is a
secret insider is both a medium experience and the narrative truth of the gospel.

Mark, the writer, chose the written medium, not to recapitulate oral messages,
but to transform them. By this logic, his literary production is inherently linked
with alienation from living words. Notably, the story that came to be written down
is dominated by a sense of distancing. But it is an alienation hardly comprehensible as apocalyptic world-weariness or gnostic aloofness. Mark's estrangement is
from the standard-bearers of oral transmission. In narrating the exclusion of family, the rejection of the prophets, the growing and incorrigible incomprehension of
the disciples, and in making the story culminate in the definitive rupture of oral
communication, the author has narrated the justification for his own written narrative. The story self-authenticates its new, redemptive medium over against the
prevailing authorities of oral transmission. It is a story in which its own medium
history is deeply implicated.

Technically, Mark dissociates heterogeneous units from live contextuality,
reconstructing them into a new unity. The textual medium alters oral language
and its norms, and thereby reconceptualizes the way one perceives christology, the
kingdom, and authority. Mark's story reorients basic assumptions held about Jesus
and his message. It disconnects the kingdom from central place and traditional
expectations, and projects a vision of its incomparable mystery. It is no longer an
orally present actuality, but is now connected with the textual recapitulation of
Jesus' life and above all death. The gospel's Jesus does not enter into mimetic relations with any oral model. He speaks with unprecedented authority. Markan christology even defies the scheme of promise and fulfillment. The redemption Jesus
offers is at odds with the anticipations of friend and foe alike. The freedom he
gives is inseparable from dislocations. The depth of alienation that dominates this
gospel is in direct proportion to the profundity of its revelation. That "new wine is
for fresh wineskins" (2:22) is technically Mark's medium experience and dramatically his deep theological conviction.

Mark, the storywriter, suffers and accomplishes the death of living words for
the purpose of inaugurating the life of textuality. Linguistic and narrative perspectives concur in acknowledging death as the key to life. The protagonist's arduous and paradoxical journey from life to death to life again may thus be conceived
as a narrative manifestation of the medium experience of drifting away from oral
life in the exercise of writing for life.

For a language that asserts itself by distanciation from the received mode of communication, parable is the ultimate metaphor. The parabolic strategy of reorientation
by disorientation that marks this gospel's linguistic genesis has likewise etched itself

into its story line. Medium and message are connected by a compelling parabolic logic. It is this logic that shapes the gospel's narrative, disorienting away from oral authorities and reorienting toward the textually recaptured Jesus, and all along gesturing toward the mystery of God's kingdom. There is a deep sense, therefore, in which the gospel as a novel language project narrates the story of its own story.

DENNIS R. MACDONALD

Luke's Eutychus and Homer's Elpenor: Acts 20:7–12 and *Odyssey* 10–12[†]

According to Acts 20:7–12, a young man named Eutychus, sitting on a third story windowsill, dozed off and fell to his death because of Paul's longwinded preaching. Paul then raised him back to life.

> 7. On the first day of the week, when we convened to break bread, Paul spoke to them, and because he wanted to leave the next day, he prolonged his speech until midnight. 8. There were plenty of lamps in the upper room where we were gathered. 9. A certain young man named Eutychus was seated at the window and was carried off by a deep sleep, because of Paul's having spoken for so long. Carried off by sleep, he fell from the third story and was lifted up dead. 10. Paul went down, laid upon him, embraced him, and said, "Don't raise a ruckus! His soul (*psuchê*) is in him." 11. Paul went back upstairs, broke bread, and once he had eaten and had spoken for a long time, until dawn, he left. 12. Then they fetched the lad, alive, and were not a little relieved.

On the surface, the text seems quite straightforward, but a closer reading discloses several peculiarities. Here are but a few.

1. The change of narrator. The passage begins in the first person plural, e.g. "**we** convened," but switches to the third person in vs. 9. The narrator retains the third person throughout the story and reverts to the first person in vs. 13: "But going ahead to the ship, we set sail for Assos." Such changes of voice from first to third and back to first person are common in ancient texts, but Luke could easily have maintained the first person plural throughout and for some reason chose not to do so.

2. The presence of the lamps. In a story otherwise spare of details, one is surprised to read "There were plenty of lamps in the upper room" (20:8). Some interpreters have suggested that the excessive smoke from the lamps made Eutychus want to sit near the window and ultimately caused him to fall asleep, or that the lamps explain how Paul knew the lad had dropped out of sight, or that by mentioning the abundance of lamps Luke indicated that the celebration of the Eucharist was joyous. According to other scholars, Luke fended off charges that Christian

† From "Luke's Eutychus and Homer's Elpenor: Acts 20:7–12 and *Odyssey* 10–12," *Journal of Higher Criticism* (1994): 4–24. Except as indicated, all notes are MacDonald's.

meetings were held in the dark for lewd purposes. These lamps puzzled ancient readers too. A scribe of the western textual tradition thought it more reasonable to supply the room with fenestration instead of illumination, and thus changed *lampades* ("lamps") to *hupolampades* ("little windows").

3. Eutychus's condition after the fall. Several interpreters have taken Paul's declaration in vs. 10, "His soul is in him," to imply that the fall did not actually kill Eutychus but merely stunned him. When Paul embraced him, the apostle detected a spark of life. Vs. 9, however, says unambiguously that the boy died (*êrthê nekros*). But if Eutychus died, what then does Luke mean that his soul was in him? At first glance, it would seem reasonable to suppose that when Paul embraced the corpse he revived it, but the text does not declare Eutychus alive until several hours later.

4. Eutychus's revival. Paul left the body where he had found it, went upstairs to eat and speak until daybreak, and then walked off for Assos (20:13). Only after Paul left did the believers in Troas raise the lad to life. This ending obviously bothered the scribe responsible for a variant reading that attributes the healing to Paul himself. In Codex Bezae, vs. 12 begins, "and while they were saying their farewells, **he** fetched (*êgagen*) the young man, alive."

F. F. Bruce speaks for many interpreters: "Luke probably intends us to understand that his life returned to him when Paul embraced him. But it may have been a few hours before Eutychus recovered consciousness."[1] Such an interpretation, though not impossible, stretches the apparent meaning of vs. 12, which implies that only after Paul had left for Assos was the lad actually revived. Had Luke wished merely to claim that Eutychus then regained consciousness, he surely would not have used the word *zônta* ("alive"). What is more, although already in vs. 10 Paul tells his audience not to lament, not until vs. 12 does Luke state that the believers took comfort in his reviving (*paraklêthêsan*), presumably because not until then did they observe any change in Eutychus's condition. Commentators have attempted to remove vs. 11 or to reverse the order of vss. 11–12 to avoid the awkward delay in Eutychus's revival.[2]

---

1. [F. F. Bruce,] *Commentary* [*on the Book of Acts*, New International Commentary on the New Testament (Grand Rapids, MI: Eerdmans, 1954)], 408.

2. Hans Conzelmann attributed vs. 11 to Luke's redaction of the story ([*The*] *Acts* [*of the Apostles*, Hermeneia (Philadelphia: Fortress, 1987)], 169–70. Albert C. Clark preferred the reading in D and relocated the ending of vs. 12 (*êgagen ton neaniskon zônta kai pareklêthêsan ou metriôs*), so that it follows Paul's statement that Eutychus's soul was in him (*The Acts of the Apostles* [Oxford: Oxford University Press, 1933, reprint = 1970], 130 and 377).

A parallel to this story in Luke 8:49–56, which the author borrowed from Mark 5:35–43, suggests that Luke may well have intended the delay to be taken seriously. In the story of Jairus's daughter, Jesus declared that "she is not dead but sleeping." Those who heard this laughed at him, "because they knew that she had died." Only later, when Jesus took her hand and spoke to her, did she actually revive. Here, as in Acts 20:10–12, the declaration that the child was not truly dead had nothing to do with the child's actual physical condition. Both Jairus's daughter and Eutychus had died (Mark 5:35, *apethanen*; Luke 8:49, *tethnêken*; 8:53, *apethanen*; Acts 20:89, *nekros*) and remained dead until raised up. Jesus raised Jairus's daughter almost at once, but believers in Troas did not raise Eutychus for several hours.

5. Theological and literary motivation. This is the only episode told of Paul's visit to Troas, nothing is said concerning the content of his preaching, Eutychus appears nowhere else in Acts, and apart from the "breaking of bread" and Paul's ability to perform miracles, no major Lukan theme occurs here. In comparison with most of Acts, this story seems to be an unintegrated, elliptical mess.

* * *

I propose a * * * solution to the peculiarities in Acts 20:7–12 * * * apparently never before advanced, namely, that Luke attempted, somewhat infelicitously, to recast the story of Elpenor found in Books 10–12 of *The Odyssey*. Elpenor, the youngest of Odysseus's crew, asleep on a roof, fell to his death in the middle of the night. Odysseus was unaware of the tragedy until Elpenor's soul came to meet him from the netherworld. Later, Odysseus gave Elpenor's corpse the requisite lamentation and burial. Because of the popularity of Odysseus's visit to the netherworld in *Odyssey* Book 11, the famous nekyia, Luke could assume that his more educated readers would have recognized the similarities between the stories.[3] Luke apparently recast Homer's story in order to contrast Elpenor's lethal fall from Circe's roof with Eutychus's good fortune at having died in the presence of a wonder-working apostle. Here at last we have a reason for the lamps, the fall, the delay of the revivification.

After having spent a year with the goddess Circe on her island home of Aeaea, Odysseus insisted on continuing his journey back to Ithaca. Circe provided a lavish dinner prior to the disembarkation, and Odysseus spent the night with her, learning the magic he would need to summon from the dead the blind seer Tiresias who could tell him how to find his way home. At break of day, Odysseus woke his crew from their deep, dinner-induced sleep in order to sail at once for their rendezvous with the dead. All sailed off but Elpenor. Odysseus speaks:

> There was one, Elpenor, the youngest (*neôtatos*) of all, not over valiant (*alki-mos*) in war nor sound of understanding, who had laid him down apart from his comrades in the sacred house of Circe, seeking the cool air, for he was heavy with wine. He heard the noise and the bustle of his comrades as they moved about, and suddenly sprang up, and forgot to go to the long ladder that he might come down again, but fell headlong from the roof (*tegeos pesen*), and his neck was broken away from the spine, and his spirit (*psuchên*) went down to the house of Hades. (*Odyssey* 10.552–60)[4]

Odysseus's ship took him to the edge of the world, where, in near total darkness, he performed bloody necromantic rites in order to attract the souls of the dead, especially that of Tiresias. To Odysseus's horror, the first soul (*psuchê*) to

3. Several ancient authors refer to Elpenor as though his story were common knowledge: Apollodorus, *Epitome* 7.17; Pliny, *Natural History* 15.119; Theophrastus, *Enquiry into Plants* 5.8.3; Pausanius 10.29.8; Hyginus, *Fabulae* 125; Martial 11.82; Juvenal 15.22; and Ovid, *Ibis* 485–86, and *Tristia* 3.4.19. [Nekyia, a name given to *Odyssey* 11, refers more generally to a rite of summoning ghosts to question them.]

4. Cf. *Iliad* 23.69–92. Unless otherwise indicated, all translations of classical Greek and Latin literature are those found in the Loeb Classical Library.

meet him was that of Elpenor, who told the hero how he had died and begged him to burn his corpse in full armor and to bury his ashes with due rites.

> Leave me not behind thee unwept and unburied as thou goest thence, and turn not away from me, lest haply I bring the wrath of the gods upon thee. Nay, burn me with my armour, all that is mine, and heap up a mound for me on the shore of the grey sea, in memory of an unhappy man, that men yet to be may learn of me. Fulfil this my prayer, and fix upon the mound my oar wherewith I rowed in life when I was among my comrades. (11.72–78)

Odysseus promised.

Indeed, after he had won his traveling instructions from Tiresias, had seen a host of the dead—including his mother, Achilles, Agamemnon, and Heracles—and had witnessed the punishments of the wicked, Odysseus returned to Aeaea where he beached the ship at night. Odysseus tells king Alcinous of the Phaea-cians what happened next.

> As soon as early Dawn appeared, the rosy-fingered, then I sent forth my com-rades to the house of Circe to fetch the body of the dead Elpenor. Straight-way then we cut billets of wood and gave him burial where the headland runs furthest out to sea, sorrowing and shedding big tears. But when the dead man was burned, and the armour of the dead, we heaped up a mound and dragged on to it a pillar, and on the top of the mound we planted his shapely oar. (12.8–15)

Because of his strategic location immediately prior to, at the beginning of, and immediately following one of Homer's most memorable and controversial epi-sodes, Elpenor became an ancient household word,[5] even in Christian households. Clement of Alexandria, writing at the end of the second century cited the example of Elpenor's fall in order to discourage drunkenness and assumed that his readers would recognize the tale: "just as Elpenor 'broke his neck' (*Odyssey* 10.560) when he fell down because he was drunk."[6]

---

5. A tragedian named Timotheus (4th c. BCE) wrote a play entitled *Elpenor*. By the third century residents of an Italian coastal village proudly took visitors to Elpenor's tomb (Theo-phrastus, *Enquiry into Plants* 5.8.3; cf. Pliny, *Natural History* 15.119). Ovid three times referred to Elpenor as though the reader would know his tale. In the *Metamorphoses* one reads that Elpenor was given to the bottle and was turned into pork by Circe (14.252; cf. Juvenal 15.22); in the *Ibis* Ovid mentions the lad's fatal, drunken fall (485–86); in the Tristia: "poor (*miser*) Elpenor who fell from the high roof met his king a crippled shade" (3.4.19–20). Plutarch rec-ords a scholarly discussion in which a teacher of literature says, "of all the souls (*psuchôn*) that Homer named in the episode of the Dead (*Nekuia*) . . . that of Elpenor had not yet joined those in Hades, his corpse (*nekron*) not yet having had its burial, but wandered about in a kind of no man's land" (*Quaestiones convivales* 740e). Elpenor seems also to have been commonly known to the readers addressed by Athenaeus, Apollodorus, and Martial.

6. *Paedagogos* 2.2.34.2. Lucian quoted part of Odysseus's question to Elpenor in *Odyssey* 11.93, and called the line "the well-known words" (*Wisdom of Nigrinus* 17).

Before comparing Homer's Elpenor with Luke's Eutychus, I should emphasize that many ancient authors, including some of Luke's contemporaries, modeled fictional characters after the fallen youth in *The Odyssey.* * * *

* * *

Writing about 170–180 CE, Luke's contemporary, Apuleius of Madauros, wrote a large Latin novel about the peregrinations of a certain Lucius who, by accidental magic, had turned himself into an ass. One of Apuleius's stories, told by a thief, narrates the death of a lad named Alcimus ("valiant"), the very property—the very Greek word—that Homer denied to Elpenor. Alcimus, too, was foolish, died from a fall from a tall house at night, and was not properly buried. Thus Apuleius calls him unlucky, like "unfortunate" Elpenor. The thief speaks:

> Alcimus, despite his cautious plans, could not attract the approving nod of Fortune. He had broken into the cottage of an old woman who was asleep, and had gone to the bedroom upstairs. Although he should have squeezed her throat and strangled her to death at once, he chose first to toss her possessions out through a fairly wide window, item by item—for us to pick up, of course. He had already diligently heaved out everything else, but he was unwilling to pass up even the bed on which the poor old lady was sleeping; so he rolled her off the cot and pulled out the bedclothes, evidently planning to throw them out the window too. But the wicked woman groveled at his knees and pleaded with him. "Please, my son," she said, "why are you giving a miserable old lady's poor shabby junk to her rich neighbours, whose house is outside that window?"
>
> That clever speech cunningly deceived Alcimus, who believed that she was telling the truth. He was doubtless afraid that what he had already thrown out and what he was going to throw out later would be gift to someone else's household and not his comrades, since he was now convinced of his mistake. Therefore he leaned out of the window in order to take a careful survey of the situation, and especially to estimate the fortunes of that house next door which she had mentioned. As he was making this energetic and not very prudent attempt, that old sinner gave him a shove; although it was weak, it caught him suddenly and unexpectedly, while he hung balanced there and was preoccupied with his spying. She sent him head over heels. Not to mention the considerable altitude, he fell on a huge rock lying beside the house, shattering and scattering his ribcage. Vomiting streams of blood from deep within, he told us what had happened and then departed from life without much suffering. We buried him as we had our other comrade, and so gave Lamachus a worthy squire. (*Metamorphoses* 4.12)

The burial of Alcimus was no burial at all, but the wrapping of his corpse in a linen cloth and a watery grave at sea (4.11). Observe the following similarities:

ELPENOR	ALCIMUS
Soldier at night	Thief at night
Not valiant (*alkimos*) and not foolish	Alcimus ("Valiant") but foolish
At home of Circe the witch	At home of an old woman
Falls from roof and dies	Falls out of window and dies
"Unfortunate"	"Could not attract the approving nod of Fortune"
Body not buried, but later buried near the sea	Body not buried, wrapped and thrown in the sea

I have found several other examples of the rewriting of the Elpenor story,[7] but the ones presented thus far should suffice to demonstrate his popularity in ancient literature. Apuleius's Alcimus is the most useful for our purposes, for it suggests that the author expected his readers who were familiar with Homer to derive additional pleasure from the story by comparing it with the Elpenor incident in *The Odyssey*. I suggest that Luke had the same expectation.

As we have seen, Luke's tale is a third-person narration nested in a first-person-plural narration of Paul's voyage from Achaea to Troas. He stayed there seven days, and just prior to leaving he and his companions convened to "break bread." Odysseus, too, told in the first person how his crew had sailed to Circe's island, stayed there for a year, and enjoyed a lavish banquet just before departing (*Odyssey* 10.476–79). According to Homer, Elpenor fell asleep when "darkness came on," when his comrades bedded in Circe's "darkened halls" (*megara skioenta*, 10.479). Paul's upper room, however, was full of lamps. Luke's care to mention these lamps probably derives from a desire not only to contrast the upper room with Circe's dark, mysterious home, but also to exculpate Paul for Eutychus's death. The lad did not die for want of light but for want of attentiveness.

Acts 20:9 contains several verbal resonances with Homer.

Odyssey 10.522: *Elpênôr de tis eske neôtatos* ("There was one, Elpenor, the youngest of all")

Acts 20:9: *kathezomenos de tis neanias onomati Eutuchos epi tês thuridos* ("A certain young man named Eutychus was seated at the window.")

Both phrases name the lad, call him a young man (*neanias/neôtatos*), and contain the words *de tis*. Furthermore, neither Elpenor nor Eutychus had been mentioned before in their host narratives.

Homer states that Odysseus's crew gave way to "sweet sleep" (*glukon upnon*, 10.549); Luke's Eutychus was overcome by "deep sleep" (*upnô bathei* and *apo tou upnou*, 20:9). Homer supplies a reasonable motivation for Elpenor's location on top of the roof. After a long day of eating and drinking, his head abuzz with wine,

7. For example, Lucan, *Pharsalia* 6.413–830; Silius Italicus, *Punica* 13.400–68; and Heliodorus, *Aethiopica* 6.14.

he needed fresh air. Luke, on the other hand, does not disclose why Eutychus perched on the windowsill, but a reader familiar with *The Odyssey* might well have assumed that he, too, wanted ventilation in a room full of lamps. Elpenor died when he woke up from his sleep; Eutychus when he dozed off.

Luke's description of Eutychus's fall likewise echoes *The Odyssey*.

Odyssey 10.559 (=11.64): *katantikru tegeos pesen* ("he fell down from the roof")

Acts 20:9: *epesen apo tou tristegou katô* ("he fell down from the third story")

Both lines contain *pesen* or *epesen* (third-person-singular aorist of *piptô*, "fall"), a form of *kata* (*katantikru* and *katô*, "down"), and some variation of the word *tegos* ("roof"), in the genitive case (*tegeos* and *tristegou*).

Luke's choice of *tristegon*, "third story," here is particularly suggestive. It is a hapax[8] not only in Luke-Acts, but also in the New Testament and in contemporary Christian literature. The related words *stegos, stegê, tegos* ("roof,"), from which *tristegon* derives, appear in Luke's writings only in Luke 7:6, where *stegê* derives from Q (cf. Matt 8:8). Insofar as Luke prefers *dôma* when referring to a roof,[9] Luke's *tristegon* may have derived from the *tegos* in Homer.

Because Elpenor's fall escaped Odysseus's attention, his body remained unburied until the crew returned from the netherworld. This delay of burial might account for the peculiar delay between Paul's stating that Eutychus's soul was in him and the lad's actual revival. Twice Homer says that the soul (*psuchê*) of Elpenor immediately rushed off to Hades (10.560 and 11.65). When Odysseus conjured up souls from the netherworld, it was Elpenor's that first greeted him (*Prôtê de psuchê Elpênoros*). On seeing him, Odysseus sobbed: "I wept, and my heart had compassion on him" (11.55). Believers in Troas, on the other hand, had no reason to lament, for unlike Elpenor's soul, immediately and forever banished to Hades, Eutychus's soul returned to him thanks to Paul's extraordinary powers. Even so, the boy did not yet return to life. This would happen the next morning when those left in Troas lift him up.

In the netherworld, Elpenor's soul asked Odysseus to return to Circe's island to mourn and to bury his corpse (11.59–78), and the king of Ithaca did so the following day, at dawn:

> As soon as early Dawn appeared, the rosy-fingered, then I sent forth my comrades to the house of Circe to fetch the body of the dead Elpenor. Straightway then we cut billets of wood and gave him burial where the headland runs furthest out to sea, sorrowing and shedding big tears. But when the dead man was burned, and the armour of the dead, we heaped up a mound and dragged on to it a pillar, and on the top of the mound we planted his shapely oar. (*Odyssey* 12.8–15)

---

8. A word or phrase occurring only once in a body of writings [editors' note].

9. Luke 5:19 (where he substitutes *dôma* for Mark's *stegê*), 12:3 (Q), 17:31 (from Mark), and Acts 10:9.

Both here and in Acts 20:11–12 the resolution of the victim's plight does not occur until dawn. Odysseus can only mourn and bury his dead comrade; Paul's God raises Elpenor's counterpart back to life. Furthermore, Odysseus himself did not fetch Elpenor's corpse, his comrades did, "sorrowing and shedding big tears" (12.12). Similarly, Paul did not revive Eutychus's corpse, his converts did, "and were not a little relieved." Compare the following lines.

> *Odyssey* 12.10: *oisemenai nekron, Elpênora tethnêôta* ("to fetch the body of the dead Elpenor")

> Acts 20:12: *êgagon de ton paida zônta* (cf. 20:9: *êrthê nekros*) ("they fetched the lad, living")

The following columns summarize the arguments made above.

ODYSSEY 10–12	ACTS 20:7–12
1. Odysseus and crew leave Troy and sail back to Achaea	Paul and crew stop at Troy, having left Achaea to sail back to Jerusalem
2. First person plural (most of book 10)	First person plural (20:1–8)
3. After a sojourn, a meal (10.466–77)	After a sojourn, a meal (20:6, 7, 11)
4. Circe's "dark halls" (10.479)	There were plenty of lamps in the upper room (20:8)
5. "sweet sleep" (*glukon upnon*, 10.548)	deep sleep (*upnô bathei*, 20:9)
6. Switch to third person (10.552)	Switch to third person (20:9)
7. There was one, Elpenor, the youngest of all lying on the roof (*Elpênôr de tis eske neôtatos*, 10.552)	A certain young man named Eutychus was seated at a window (*kathezomenos de tis neanias onomati Eutuchos epi tês thuridos*, 20:9)
8. Elpenor fell from a roof (*katantikru tegeos pesen*, 10.559=11.64)	Eutychus fell from the third story (*epesen apo tou tristegou katô*, 20:9)
9. Elpenor's soul (*psuchê*) goes to Hades (10.560=11.65)	Eutychus's soul (*psuchê*) stays in him (20:10)
10. Delay in burying Elpenor until dawn of the next day (12.1–15)	Delay in raising Eutychus until dawn of the next day (20:11)
11. Associates fetch the body (*oisemenai nekron, Elpênora tethnêôta*, 12.10)	Associates revive the body (*êgagon de ton paida zônta*, 20:12)

The parallels between these stories are more lexical, more detailed, and more sequential than the rewritings of the Elpenor story by Plato, Plutarch, Virgil, and Apuleius discussed earlier.

The literary critic Gérard Genette would call Luke's manipulation of the Elpenor story a "hypertextual transvaluation,"[1] a common literary strategy for replacing the values or perspectives of an earlier, targeted text (the "hypotext") with alternative values or perspectives. For such a strategy to succeed, the hypertext must display, even if obscurely, its relationship to the hypotext. Obviously, the strategy has not succeeded with modern readers of Acts; no previous study of the text has suggested this relationship. Furthermore, evidence of ancient readings provide little encouragement that they understood the Homeric background either.[2]

On the other hand, two additional aspects of the story in Acts indicate that Luke advertised its Homeric hypertextuality, even though his readers failed to perceive it: the location of the story in Troas and the name Eutychus.

Troas, of course, is ancient Troy. To be sure, the city of Troy during Luke's day was not precisely on the location of the ancient city, but it was nearby, and the two were repeatedly identified with each other. No educated ancient would have been numb to Troy's rich mythological and Homeric associations, including the nostos [homecoming] of Odysseus and Elpenor back to Achaea from the Troad. By placing the story of Eutychus in Troy, Luke seems to be hinting that one should read it in light of Troy's legacy.[3]

The most important hypertextual clue, however, is the name Eutychus. Homer repeatedly emphasizes Elpenor's bad fortune. He simply forgot that he was sleeping on a roof, died, and was not missed by the crew: "we had left his corpse behind us in the hall of Circe, unwept and unburied" (11.53–54). The young soldier survived the Trojan war, Laestrygonian cannibals, and Polyphemus, only to step off Circe's roof to his doom. Elpenor himself states that he was the victim of "an evil fate" (*aisa kakê*, 11.61) and calls himself "an unhappy man" (*andros dustênoio*, 10.76). Odysseus too addresses him as "unfortunate" (*ô dustêne*, 11.80). When Ovid referred to this story, his single adjective for the lad was *miser*, "wretched," "unhappy."[4] Eutychus, on the other hand, means "lucky." Although usually one must avoid putting too much stock in the meanings of personal names used in Acts, such onomastics were commonplace in Greek literature, as early as Homer himself. When Apuleius wished to call attention to his rewriting

---

1. *Palimpsestes: la littérature au second degré* (Paris: Editions de Seuil, 1982).

2. Codex Bezae in 20:4 replaces the name Tychicus (*Tuchikos*) with Eutychus (*Eutuchos*), thereby making the lad one of Paul's sailing companions from Achaea. This correlates with Elpenor's sailing with Odysseus from Troy to Achaea. It is more likely, however, that the variant Eutychus in 20:4 was due to scribal error. *The Acts of Paul* makes Eutychus into Nero's cupbearer, Patroclus, the name of another famous Homeric hero, the associate and perhaps lover of Achilles. Nothing else in *The Acts of Paul*, however, demonstrates awareness of the Homeric backdrop to the story.

3. The very fact that Luke records this story in Troas is surprising insofar as Luke had said nothing earlier about such converts, not even during Paul's earlier visit there (16:8–11, cf. 2 Cor 2:12).

4. *Tristia* 3.4.19.

of the Elpenor story he did so by naming his character Alcimus ("Valiant") and declaring from the outset his bad luck: he "could not attract the approving nod of Fortune." In light of the other similarities between the two stories, the selection of the name Eutychus hardly seems accidental. Eutychus had the "good fortune" (*eutuchia*) to have died when Paul was nearby to revive him.

If the hypothesis advanced here is correct—namely, that the story in Acts 20:7–12 is a hypertextual transvaluation of Homer's Elpenor—it bears weighty implications for our understanding of Acts as a whole. First, Luke apparently expected his primary audience (Theophilus, say) to have been sufficiently aware of *The Odyssey* in order to decode the Eutychus story as a clever transformation of a classical tale. Luke was writing for a sophisticated reader.

Second, other passages of Acts, especially other we-passages, may also play off against the Homeric epics or other Greek mythology. For example, the story of Paul and Silas dragged off to prison for exorcising a slave girl and their subsequent prison break has parallels in *The Bacchae* of Euripides. Tiresias' prophecy to Odysseus concerning his death might compare with Agabus's prophecy to Paul about his death.[5] One also must not overlook the famous shipwreck scene in Acts 27–28 and the story of the serpent at Malta. Odysseus too faces dreadful monsters on islands and outlives them.[6]

Third, if the story of Elpenor lies behind that of Eutychus, it would add support to those who suggest that Acts ought not be read as an historical record but as an historical novel.[7] One misses the point in the Eutychus tale if one insists that Luke intended the reader to view it as an historical event. Rather, Luke's "Lucky" in Troas is an alternative to Homer's unlucky Elpenor on his way home from Troy.

WAYNE A. MEEKS

The Polyphonic Ethics of the Apostle Paul[†]

In *Ethics and the Limits of Philosophy* Bernard Williams has reminded us that moral conviction is not the same thing as certainty, nor can it be reduced to naked existential decision. What is required for a robust ethical life, writes Williams, is "moral confidence," and moral confidence "is basically a social phenomenon."[1] The study of the work of Paul acquires a new accent if we consider his letters in light of the ques-

---

5. Vernon K. Robbins "By Land and By Sea: The We-Passages and Ancient Sea Voyages," in *Perspectives on Luke-Acts*, ed. Charles H. Talbert (Danville, VA: Association of Baptist Professors of Religion, 1978), 232.

6. A closer parallel, however, might be the story of Mopsus and the serpent in Apollonius Rhodius, *Argonautica* 4.1502–36. See also *Palatine Anthology* 7.290.

7. E.g., Richard I. Pervo, *Profit with Delight: The Literary Genre of the Acts of the Apostles* (Philadelphia: Fortress, 1987).

† "The Polyphonic Ethics of the Apostle Paul," *Annual of the Society of Christian Ethics* (1988): 17–29. Except as indicated, all notes are Meeks's.

1. Bernard Williams, *Ethics and the Limits of Philosophy* (Cambridge, Mass., and London: Harvard University Press, 1985).

tion suggested by Williams's argument: What is the social process by which a religious movement like that of the early Christians undertakes to instill moral confidence in its members? By far the most common thing that we see happening in Paul's letters is his attempt to form moral communities: to instruct, admonish, cajole, remind, rebuke, reform, and argue the new converts to this strange new cult into behaving in ways "worthy," as he puts it, "of the God who called you." We may say, then, that the letters of Paul were preeminently instruments of resocialization and evidence of a larger process of resocialization. That process (Paul's word for it is *oikodomē*) was forming and reforming moral intuitions; its aim was to create moral confidence—the confidence that obtains when worldview and ethos match.

However, viewing Paul's work from this perspective functions to sharpen the misgivings that arise as, with the results of recent biblical criticism in mind, we contemplate the multiplicity of voices we hear in the letters of Paul. The discovery of these several voices is actually one of the successes of modern biblical criticism, but it is so troubling that many worried critics believe it indicates a failure of the method. Was Paul a schizophrenic? Or an unprincipled religious entrepreneur? Or did he merely change his mind as time passed? Did his thought evolve, or did he vacillate? How can we rescue a coherent Paul from all those contingencies to which he seems to have bent his message? What *is* the constant theological message that emerges from Paul's apparently dialectical thinking?

Perhaps our habit of searching for coherence and constancy in the substance of the message—our expectation of some univocal instruction or fixed pattern—misleads us in our effort to apprehend Paul's purpose and assess his contribution. It may be that the manyness of the voices is essential to the form of communication Paul has chosen. In order to demonstrate the plausibility of such a position, I would like to draw upon the insights of Mikhail Bakhtin, the polymath Russian literary critic and philosopher whose late rediscovery has been causing such a stir in literary circles.[2] Bakhtin was convinced that human identity is essentially dialogical and that only through dialogue do enduring values emerge. He interpreted the history of Western literature as a struggle toward a style in which genuine dialogue—not just dialectical monologues, which are quite a different thing—could come to expression. Bakhtin argued that the appropriate style was found at last by Dostoevsky, who invented "a fundamentally new novelistic genre," the polyphonic novel, characterized by "a plurality of independent and unmerged voices and consciousnesses, a genuine polyphony of fully valid voices."[3]

I have two theses, one of which I shall try to argue; the other I shall only assert. The first thesis is that the style of moral argument that Paul adopts is not so much dialectical as polyphonic. The second thesis is a corollary of the first: if we turn to Paul to find a paradigm of the appropriate way to do Christian ethics, we must examine not only the *result* of the Pauline polyphony (which would be the focus of attention if his ethical style were really dialectical) but also, and more importantly, the process itself, the *transaction*.

2. Katerina Clark and Michael Holquist, *Mikhail Bakhtin* (Cambridge, Mass., and London: Harvard University Press, 1984).

3. Mikhail Bakhtin, *Problems of Dostoevsky's Poetics*, ed. and trans. Caryl Emerson, Theory and History of Literature no. 8 (Minneapolis: University of Minnesota Press, 1984).

In order to try to persuade you of this thesis and its corollary, I will conduct a case study in two parts. The first part examines Paul's answer to the Corinthian Christians who wrote asking him whether it was permissible to eat meat that might have been obtained from some pagan temple. His answer is found in 1 Corinthians, Chapters 8–10. The second part of the case study will review Paul's own revision of that answer into a generalized paradigm for other Christians who find themselves in a different time, place, or situation. That revision is found in Romans 14:1–15:13.

Issue: Eidōlothyta in Corinth

The story behind 1 Corinthians 8–10 will be familiar to many of you. The Corinthian Christians have sent a delegation to Paul, bearing a letter asking several questions about things that were evidently under dispute in the Christian house-assemblies in that city. Among them is the question whether it is all right to eat meat purchased at public markets or served at private dinners in non-Christian settings. Those who say "Yes" take their stand on something that all Christians, they say, "know": there is no God but one and (therefore) the "idols" in the world have no reality. Hence eating food obtained from the temples and shrines is what we would call a purely secular and social act.

On the other side there are some Christians at Corinth who do not share this cheerful view of the cultic world around them. The images represent to them something quite real and quite dangerous; to partake in any way, however indirect, in the cults of those images is "idolatry."

Paul's reply is anything but straightforward. Indeed, some commentators have found it so disjointed that they want to argue it has been patched together by a clumsy editor from fragments of different letters. Others have found a single goal toward which Paul's zig-zag mental path was leading; deciphering his dialectic, they provide us with the clear maxim that Paul's roundabout diplomacy has obscured. But what if the point is not to arrive at a clear and simple rule to fit this and all similar occasions, but rather to let all the legitimate voices be heard and to encourage all the vociferous speakers to become listeners, too, and then to act within that polyphonic world?

What voices can we in fact hear in these three much-disputed chapters? First there is an ambiguous "we": "We know that we all have knowledge" (8:1); "We know that there is no 'idol' in the world and that there is no God but one" (8:4). This, surely, is the voice of one of the factions in the dispute. Most commentators now take these and similar assertions throughout 1 Corinthians to be "slogans" used by the disputants and here quoted by Paul. Note that, if this is the case, the disputants claim to speak for everyone: "We *all* have knowledge." One of the counter-statements that Paul will make is to deny that claim that there is but one valid voice: "But the knowledge is *not* in all," he says (8:7). Yet initially he joins his own voice with that would-be dominant one: "*We* know . . ." (8:1). Bakhtin, I think, would take this as a strategy of the author to maintain control and thus as failure to advance to real dialogue. It is important, however, to see just what the strategy accomplishes here. By joining his voice with that of the dominant and perhaps most articulate party, Paul gains leverage on them: that "we" can now implicate those speakers in statements that follow logically from their asserted knowledge but relativize their assumed superiority: "Food does not commend *us* to God: neither if *we* do not eat do *we* lack nor if *we* eat do *we* excel" (8:8). And that twist of the "we" softens them up for a sharp separation of voices in the imperatives of the next verse: "Watch out lest this 'authority' of *yours* become a stumbling block for the weak." The plural "you" is replaced in the next sentences by the sharper, apostrophic singular "you" before the encompassing plural returns in verse 12, paving the way for the equally sharp and personal "I" that appears in 8:13–9:27 and repeatedly in chapter 10. Paul thus uses the familiar diatribal style to pull the "we" apart. Accepting at the outset the claim and desire of this "we" to speak for "all," Paul gives voices to those implicitly excluded by the "we," exposing a hidden contradiction. He converts the attempted monologue into a dialogue.

In this way Paul makes room for a second voice, one that does not in fact ever speak for itself: the voice of those who have been excluded from the "all" of the self-defined "knowing" Christians (8:7), the voice of those who are "weak" (8:7, 9, 11), but whom Paul immediately personifies and individualizes as "the brother for whom Christ died" (8:11). Here again, perhaps, Bakhtin would find Paul a less masterful dialogist than Dostoevsky. Would it not be better if he had quoted slogans of the "weak" as well as of the "gnostics"? Does he not, by speaking *about* them and *for* them, connive in their continued weakness? Or is it the case that the "weak in conscience" were also weak in eloquence? Did those who "knew" so much, and who most likely commanded the greater resources of wealth and influence,[4] also possess the skills of rhetoric the Corinthian Christians seem to have admired so much? Or did Paul fear that insidious negating power that weakness as weakness can sometimes claim, at which he hints in 10:29 and more broadly in Romans—that *ressentiment*[5] that Nietzsche by his exaggerations has indelibly stigmatized for us? For whatever reason, deliberate or unconscious, strategic or principled, Paul speaks *for* and *about* the weaker party and, moreover, lends them not only his own voice, but other voices as well, as we shall see. The result, while falling short of the "dialogism" that Bakhtin prizes, nevertheless is effective. A company of voices makes the case of the weak more powerfully than they could have made it themselves.

The third voice that speaks is a formal and neutral voice that by the matter-of-factness of its indicative statements signals its claim to be authoritative. It corrects, and itself brooks no correction. "Knowledge inflates; love constructs. If anyone thinks he knows something, he has not yet come to know as he ought to know. But if any one loves God, this person *is known* by him" (8:2f.). "But the knowledge is not in all" (8:7). "Food does not commend us to God" (8:8). And so on. Of course it is Paul, or Paul and Sosthenes, who speaks. Yet formally these statements are quite

4. Gerd Theissen, "Die Starken und Schwachen in Korinth," *Evangelische Theologie* 35 (1975): 155–72; English translation in Gerd Theissen, *The Social Setting of Pauline Christianity; Essays on Corinth*, ed. and tr. with intro by John H. Schütz (Philadelphia: Fortress Press, 1982), 121–43.

5. Resentment (French), an important concept and term in what Nietzsche views as the emergence of a priestly "slave ethics"; see especially *The Genealogy of Morals* (1887) [editors' note].

carefully distinguished from those in which Paul emphasizes his own speaking by the personal pronouns or, as in chapter 7, by his *legō*, "I say." These statements are deliberately impersonal observations; they thus claim the force of reported facts or of maxims or axioms. What is the function of this impersonal voice in relation to the others? As I said, it corrects and challenges, indeed contradicts the "we" who know so much, by speaking as a generalized other who knows more. Yet the contradictions are not simple or absolute. For example, after the sharp challenge to the asserted knowledge in verses 2–3, verse 4 returns to the point of view of the first voice—"we know that there is no 'idol' in the world"—and, by its first-person plural, embraces it again in spite of the intervening contradiction.

The fourth voice is related to the third and can be distinguished from it, if at all, only by its more formal accent. For example, verses 5–6:

> (but) For us there is one God, the Father,
> > from whom is the universe and to whom we are destined,
> and one Lord, Jesus Christ,
> > through whom comes the universe and through whom we exist.

Here early Christian tradition speaks. And it resonates with much older overtones: (1) the "one God" and "one Lord" obviously echo and reconfess the classic Jewish confession of the *šhema*[6] and imply the Jewish polemic against polytheism, from II Isaiah on; (2) yet the phrases "from whom is the universe and to whom we are destined" are echoes of popular intellectual religion, originating in Stoic pantheism; so that diaspora Judaism's long dialogue with and adjustment to Hellenistic culture are taken up into early Christianity's own self-identifying and self-involving language and modified to make them the Christians' own. Their own—for the second member of the couplet decisively transforms both the Jewish and the broad culture's theologies.

The fifth voice is Paul's own. Paul speaks, explicitly in his own voice, in two ways: as authoritative apostle and as personal example. Many of the imperatives in the three chapters are Paul's own authoritative formulations specific to the occasion. For example the rules formulated in 10:25–11:1, "Everything sold in the public market eat without asking questions of conscience," and so on. Naturally some of these authoritative directives merge with the third or fourth voices. For example, the "Flee from idolatry!" of 10:14 is a widespread early Christian rule, formally codified in Acts 15:29 and parallels, but here Paul makes it his own (note the *legō* of the following verse) and asserts it on behalf of the unheard "weak" Christians.

More important in these particular chapters than the apostolic directives as such, but depending on them for its force, is the apostolic example (8:13–9:27; 10:31–11:1). It has taken New Testament commentators an embarrassingly long time to recognize how integral this example is to the argument of chaps. 8–10, but once seen the connections are obvious. The leitmotifs of chapter 9 are freedom and authority (*exousia*). Paul has already pinpointed the use of *exousia* to the detriment of the weak as the central issue (8:9). Now he dramatizes the issue by meta-

---

6. The first Hebrew word ("hear") of the profession of faith in Deut 6:4–9 [editors' note].

phors from the extreme case of authority and its lack: free person and slave. We have to say that when Paul talks about himself, he talks in a very complicated way. The example is elaborately rigged to trip the expectations of the reader. Paul begins by insisting upon his own apostolic freedom and authority—to have a wife as traveling companion and to be paid for his efforts. He hammers out his claim with one rhetorical question after another: "Am I not free? Am I not an apostle? Have I not seen Jesus our Lord? . . . Do we not have authority to eat and drink? . . . If others share this authority of yours, do we not even more?" This crescendo of questions calls upon other examples and incorporates the warranting voices of Scripture and tradition into Paul's own argument. Yet all this is only in order to say that he would rather die than *use* this well-grounded right. His one source of pride (*kauchēma*) is not the authority, but his freedom not to exercise it (9:15–18). In the following verses he comes daringly close to self-parody, for the free person who makes himself slave of everyone has been since Aristophanes a common and contemptuous description of the demagogue. The voice of Paul speaking of himself is thus, in this instance and in several others (notably 2 Cor. 10–13), an ironic voice. Moreover, as Dale Martin has shown, Paul will be heard differently by different groups at Corinth.[7]

Voice number six belongs to the Scripture and traditions of Israel. These chapters are one of the places in the Pauline corpus where this voice is strongest. Its contributions to the polyphony are by no means simple; indeed this voice is itself perhaps more an antiphonal chorus than a solo. It speaks on both sides of the dialogue, and in several ways. A quotation from a psalm, for example, can provide a warrant for a rule, as in 10:25–26: "Anything sold in the market eat without making discriminations of conscience—*for* 'To the Lord belong the earth and its fullness.'" Again, a quotation (with the tense of its main verb altered) provides an interpretive naming of the present situation: "What they sacrifice, they sacrifice to demons and not to God" (10:20, cf, Deut. 32:17). Earlier and more generally, reference to the scripturally-recorded story of Israel has established the horizon of interpretation by identifying the readers with Israel: "*Our* fathers all . . ." (10:1–4). Finally, as so often in Christian as in Jewish monitory literature, Scripture provides specific behavioral "types" or *exempla*, as here in 10:1–13 and 18–20.

The little homily that Paul uses in 10:1–13 provides us with one of the most illuminating instances of real polyphony in the letter. For the homily, centered on Exodus 32:6, does more than is strictly needed for Paul's argument here. That is why commentators so often find this chapter confusing—and too quickly assume that Paul is confused. It is as if Scripture's voice has a certain willfulness, rather like the aging uncle who, once having wedged into the conversation, will tell us the whole too-familiar story, however far it takes us from the point under discussion. So Paul, in order to quote Scripture about idolatry, must cite the classic text, "They sat down to eat and drink and rose up to play," and then ring all the

---

7. Dale B. Martin, "Slave of Christ, Slave of All: Paul's Metaphor of Slavery and 1 Corinthians 9" (Ph.D. dissertation, Yale University, 1988), upon which much of the discussion in this paragraph depends.

traditional changes on both "eat and drink" and "play."[8] Yet this apparently rambling voice has a function here. The wide, speculative, almost playful midrash on the several possible meanings of *paizein* [to play] and the several disasters of Israel's wilderness sojourn exemplifies the multiple forms and consequences of "idolatry." The midrash thus sketches out a broad interpretive horizon within which Paul's specific admonitions and advice on the Corinthians' problem are to be read.

Finally, alongside these traditions peculiar to Israel, the rhetorical commonplaces of popular moralizing pepper Paul's discourse, here as elsewhere. For example, in 9:24–27 the familiar "agon-motif"[9] describes the wise person's progress toward perfection by rationally subduing the body. Construed as a principle, it is not a point we would find easy to fit into place if we were constructing Paul's theological ethics. Yet this cultural commonplace would perhaps strike home with special force to the sophisticated know-it-alls of the Corinthian church, who evidently were concerned not to let superstitious taboos cut them off from the ordinary social occasions of urban high culture. And in and through Paul that culture does speak; that world—however darkly Paul could occasionally consign it to "the god of this world"—has its own valid expression in the Christian polyphony. Self-control was a notion on which Jew, Greek, and Christian could agree.

I hope that by simply describing these seven voices I have demonstrated the major point I have to make. That is, even in this instance where Paul has been asked to give his authoritative directive as founder and apostle, and where he speaks with full consciousness of his apostolic authority, he does so through the curious indirection of polyphony. He gives voice to the speakers of the dispute— reflects back their speaking and himself speaks with as well as to them. At the same time he introduces other voices, from other times and a wider community of discourse, that, when heard, alter the to-and-fro of the dispute into a much more complex conversation. It is by no means a conversation without boundaries; Paul guides firmly and rounds off with rhetorical finesse—some would even say, he manipulates his speakers. At the end, the kind of behavior and the kind of attitude he wants to encourage is clear enough. Yet if we were to reduce his admonitions to rules or to ends, we would have lost something essential of that *oikodomē*, that construction of moral community, that is happening here. A strong-minded editor could have made Paul's argument much more straightforward, but with reduction of the polyphony, much of the moral force would have been lost.

The claim that Paul's polyphony has a moral force that some other form of discourse, say a simple, apodictic command, would not have may seem excessively strong. I think the claim is justified, however, if we remember again what Williams said about the social dimension of moral confidence. What Paul is undertaking to do in this part of his letter is not merely to secure a particular outcome in the case under discussion. It is rather to help the participants to

---

8. Wayne A. Meeks, "'And Rose Up to Play': Midrash and Paraenesis in 1 Corinthians 10:1–22," *Journal for the Study of the New Testament* 16 (1982): 64–78.

9. V. C. Pflitzner, *Paul and the Agon Motif, Novum Testamentum* Supplements 16 (Leiden: E. J. Brill, 1967); Abraham J. Malherbe, "The Beasts at Ephesus," *Journal of Biblical Literature* 87 (1968): 71–80.

become more competent moral agents, that is, to help them to achieve a peculiar form of moral confidence that befits their status as believers in Jesus Christ and members of his "body." To have moral confidence is to know what one is doing. The dominant group at Corinth thought they knew exactly what they were doing, but by forcing them to listen to other voices, Paul undertakes to expand their knowledge to include such things as what Israel learned about "idolatry" through its Scripture, its traditions, and its long experience in hostile environments; what the Apostle has learned by revelation and experience; what all the Christian communities have come to understand as foundational beliefs; and finally what the "weak" members of the community think and feel. What the "weak" thought they knew, we cannot find out precisely, but in the letter they hear a number of things that they might have said, besides having to hear the strong group again but in a new context, with Paul and Scripture and tradition speaking sometimes with the one side, sometimes the other, sometimes not quite with either. The linguistic field that constitutes knowledge relevant to the Christian life is at every moment exceedingly complex, embracing as it does Israel's Scripture, traditions both old and not so old, cultural commonplaces that persist unless specifically overturned, prophetic and apostolic pronouncements, and so on. The groups in dispute at Corinth, if they listen well to Paul's letter, will come to command a larger sector of that ever-expanding field. In what sense then will they be more competent moral agents as a result? Certainly not because they will find decisions easier to make; more likely the contrary. Rather, they will possess a more supple and articulate store of pertinent knowledge. Their moral confidence will have advanced from a shallow self-confidence that purchases its security by excluding inconvenient considerations and inconvenient people, toward a confidence resting on the grace that makes dialogue possible.

Transformation of a Paradigm: Romans 14:1–15:13

Paul's admonitions to "the strong" and "the weak" in chapters 14 and 15 of his letter to the Romans can be particularly instructive for us who seek to interpret him, because he is interpreting himself. And he does two things that we also would like to do. First, he is trying to exemplify the kind of behavior that ought to follow from the vision of God's action in Christ that Paul's gospel proclaims. This is the way faith acts. Second, he is tacitly exploring the way his experience with one specific problem in one Christian congregation, in its peculiar time, place, and contingent circumstances, may contribute to the moral formation of other Christians in quite different circumstances. For, without saying so, Paul has here taken up again and transformed what he said to the Corinthians about idol-offered food.

I will not discuss the details of Rom 14:1–15:13, fascinating though I find them.[1] I want only to point to some of the most important modulations Paul makes of the

---

1. Wayne A. Meeks, "Judgment and the Brother: Romans 14:1–15:13," in Gerald F. Hawthorne with Otto Betz, eds., *Tradition and Interpretation in the New Testament: Essays in Honor of E. Earle Ellis* (Grand Rapids: William B. Eerdmans; Tübingen: J. C. B. Mohr [Paul Siebeck], 1987), 290–300.

voices that spoke in 1 Corinthians 8–10 as he adapts them to speak to the Roman Christians. First, he generalizes. The term *eidōlothyta*, "idol-sacrificed food," does not appear in Romans, and indeed the whole question of idolatry is unmentioned in this context. Rather, the question is whether some food is "profane" (*koinos*), whether one day is different from another. Now to be sure, the way Paul characterizes the issue between "strong" and "weak" embraces concerns that are specific to Judaism. This may be, as many commentators have argued, because Paul has reason to believe that tensions between Jews and Gentiles were a problem within the Christian communities in Rome. What is more certain is that the relation between Jew and Gentile in the church is Paul's principal theme in this letter; he is preoccupied with it, whether or not his audience is, and therefore it is the context within which he looks back upon the "idolatry" issue at Corinth.

Nevertheless, it is very important to see that "the weak" cannot be simply identified with "Jewish Christians" nor "the strong" with "Gentile Christians." Moreover, though the pertinence of his language to questions about *kashrut*[2] and Sabbath is obvious, Paul does not use those terms, nor any halakic language. That is, he takes pains to state the issue in terms general enough that a former Jew is not necessarily on one side and a former Gentile on the other. Thus 14:2 speaks of those who "eat everything" and those who "eat (only) vegetables," and 14:20 suggests that "it is good neither to eat meat nor to drink wine" if such things would trip up a brother. To be sure, there is a certain degree of rhetorical hyperbole in these sentences, but it is nevertheless significant that Paul chooses expressions that are broader than either the *eidōlothyta* of Corinth or food purity-rules. Similarly in the other kind of example that he gives in 14:5–6, Sabbath observance is perhaps the most obvious instance of someone who "judges one day in contradistinction from another," but that need not be the only case. Anyone who has read Theophrastus's or Plutarch's description of the superstitious person will see that there were many reasons for a pagan to judge one day more auspicious or more dangerous than another, and some of those concerns could (and doubtless did) persist in people who were converted to Christianity. Thus, throughout the argument, Paul is describing concerns that every diaspora Jew faced, but using language general enough to include Gentiles, too.

Second, the dialectic between the two mutually distrustful positions becomes more definite in Romans. While "weakness of conscience" is mentioned in Corinthians, the knowing disparagers of the weak are not called "strong." Here they are. The two sides are now explicitly "the strong" (*hoi dynatoi*) and "the powerless" (*adynatoi*) or "weak with respect to faith" (*asthenountes tē pistei*). The latter characterization, which appears at the very beginning of Paul's admonitions, is especially striking. "Conscience" is nowhere mentioned in this part of Romans, though there are some verbal expressions that are functionally equivalent. Rather, the weakness has to do with "faith," which is, of course, one of Paul's central themes throughout the letter. In 1 Corinthians Paul asks that consideration be given to the voice of consciences that are imperfect because they were formed by their recent experience of pagan religion. Here, he asks for the acceptance of those persons whose ways of seeing their fellows and their world have been inadequately

2. Jewish dietary laws [editors' note].

"transformed," whose "minds" have been only weakly "renovated" (12:2) by faith. By replacing the word common to popular morality, "conscience," with the word he has loaded with specifically Christian meaning, Paul puts the issue more squarely into the center of what he has been talking about through the whole letter.

Third, the mutual or reciprocal obligation of the weak toward the strong as well as the strong toward the weak—which Paul was groping to express in 1 Corinthians 10:29f.—here becomes explicit. The whole argument is framed by two parallel, imperatival statements, in 14:1, "the person who is weak in faith receive," and 15:7, "therefore receive one another." The imperatives are identical, but their objects are not, and the differences reflect the movement of the intervening argument. Paul begins by assuming an unequal relationship; the "strong" are urged to "accept" those who are "weak with respect to faith." However, 14:2 already introduces a series of statements in antithetical form, which introduce a pattern of reciprocity. That reciprocity is underscored by the "receive one another" that sums up the argument. Paul is aware of the insidious tyranny of the weak-minded that Nietzsche so much feared and that we know all too well from the life of our own churches (not to mention the politics of the free-market religious entrepreneurs).

Finally, Paul in Romans makes the Christological model more explicit: for example, in 15:7 he advises, "Receive one another as also Christ received you" (compare 1 Cor. 11:1), and in the following verses, he offers with scriptural backing the complex example of Christ's service of circumcision, both confirming the promise to the fathers and extending mercy to the Gentiles. The crucifixion and resurrection of Jesus the Messiah reveals the impartial righteousness of the one God, "himself just and justifying" (3:26) without respect of human distinctions. The debate over the eating of meat at Corinth has helped Paul to see what he here explains to the Roman Christians: those acts of judging one another that divide the people of God run directly contrary to the universal judgment of the one God. Until the strong accept the weak and the weak the strong, the liberated and the scrupulous each other, they do not yet understand the implication of the fact that "Christ has received us."

Some Conclusions

The voices that spoke in Corinth echo in Rome. The dialogue, however, has changed; the polyphony is different. The new context requires a new speech. All the more, Paul's polyphony comes to us in altered contexts. Not only is our context different from his—we are neither in Rome nor Corinth, we are not in the first century but the twentieth, and so on—but Paul is now in a different context. Each of these letters comes to us not as a self-contained unit, with the oral explanations and supplementations by Stephanas and friends or by Phoebe, but as part of a canon of Scripture larger than Paul's own, set within a long and often conflicting tradition.

One of the primary functions of this double setting within canon and tradition—the *intratextuality* of our normative texts, as George Lindbeck calls it[3]—is to contain the multiplicity of voices. From the time of Irenaeus, at the latest, one of the

3. See George A. Lindbeck, *The Nature of Doctrine: Religion and Theology in a Postliberal Age* (Louisville, KY: Westminster John Knox Press, 1984) [editors' note].

most effective ways of limiting the divisive potential of Scripture's diversity was by reading all of it within one master story: from creation to incarnation to judgment, from Adam to Abraham to Moses to Christ. But there have been other ways as well: for example, by hearing all the voices (or all those one chose to listen to) as answering questions asked by Aristotle or by Kant. Much of the recent unhappiness about the theological consequences of historical biblical research has arisen because the latter has tended to dissolve each of the strategies by which the Bible was made to speak univocally. Polyphony has become cacophony.

Cacophony is rightly to be feared. If what the Bible has to say is no more focused than the noise of Punk Rock, then it will have no normative force at all. My plea is only that we not assume that the alternative is to filter out all but a single way of speaking. To return to my examples, it is certainly possible to analyze Paul's advice to the Corinthians in terms of rules or goals or principles.[4] Yet focusing on Paul's deontology or his teleology obscures for us the specific process of ethical formation that ought to have taken place in Corinth if his letter was competently and effectively heard there. Even to say that Paul's rules and goals are best understood within the context of his implicit Christological narrative,[5] while a step in the right direction, may have the effect of narrowing prematurely the scope of the things we ought to listen to in the texts.

Thus in the present ethical debate, insofar as I understand it, I find myself siding with such writers as Stanley Hauerwas and Jeffrey Stout[6] in their attacks on foundationalism. Yet I fear that "narrative ethics" threatens already to become a slogan that either must be stretched beyond all ordinary senses of narrative or else will unduly limit the elements of the biblical account to which we need to pay attention.[7] Certainly I do not intend to suggest that "polyphony" is a better slogan that ought simply to replace "narrative." Perhaps "polyphony" is best understood as a "self-consuming metaphor."

I have argued that Paul had a special purpose in view when he chose to write to the Corinthians in such a multivocal way and when he repeated that indirect way of speaking, with significant alterations, in his sample, self-introductory letter to the Roman Christians. He was not just long-winded; nor did he have any trouble making up his mind. He employed this polyphonic style because the kind of ethic demanded by the action of God in the crucified and risen Messiah is one in which all these voices get a hearing. Acknowledgment of that event had for Paul broken open the limitation of Israel's hopes to Israel alone, but it would also break open the inevitable presumption of Gentile Christians to own God's salvation in disregard of Israel. God's judgments are too unsearchable (Rom. 11:33) for any single voice to presume to pronounce them.

4. Sally Barker Purvis, "Problems and Possibilities in Paul's Ethics of Community" (Ph.D. dissertation, Yale University, 1987).

5. Ibid.

6. See, e.g., Hauerwas, *Character and the Christian Life: A Study in Theological Ethics* (San Antonio: Trinity University Press, 1975), and Stout, *Ethics After Babel* (Boston: Beacon Press, 1988) [editors' note].

7. Paul Nelson, *Narrative and Morality: A Theological Inquiry* (University Park and London: Pennsylvania University Press, 1987).

Time fails me to do more than hint at the hermeneutical implications that I think may be discerned in cases like these. What is at work here is something more than the intertextual character of all discourse, particularly the discourse of people like Paul and ourselves who live in pluralist cultures,[8] although historically it was only within such a nexus of cultural fusion that the Pauline polyphony could be voiced. What we may learn from Paul is that the development of a coherent and distinctively Christian pattern of moral discernment is a continual process, simultaneously interpretive and social. Social, because personal and social identities, the normative community and the community of norms, are dialectically related. Interpretive, because Christianity transforms but does not annihilate the norms it inherits. Our fundamental ethical question—How can we have moral confidence when our world is constantly changing beneath us?—is a question that Paul, in Rom. 9–11, faced as radically as any of us can. If God by manifesting his grace in the crucifixion of his Son has shocked the sensibilities of those most loyal to the revelation God himself had previously given, how can one trust such a God not to play equally astonishing tricks on us in the future? Paul says "Yes" both to the reliability of God and to his unpredictability. The polyphonic ethic undertakes at the same time to make sure that the community continues to hear and heed the norms and stories voiced in the past and at the same time engages in the transformative, interpretive work that is required to discern also what may be valid in the new voices from outside and from the future.

The openness of the polyphonic ethic is an eschatological dimension. In describing Paul's eschatologically-aimed polyphony, I can hardly do better than to quote Dostoevsky's description of Shakespeare's poetics: "Reality in its entirety is not to be exhausted by what is immediately at hand, for an overwhelming part of this reality is contained in the form of a still *latent, unuttered future Word*."[9]

RICHARD B. HAYS

Intertextual Echo in Romans[†]

HAS THE WORD OF GOD FALLEN?

The reader who has attended carefully to the echoes of Scripture in the first eight chapters of Romans will hardly be taken by surprise when Paul at last in Romans 9–11 undertakes an explicit discussion of the fate of Israel. This is not some excursus or appendix peripheral to the letter's theme; it is the heart of the matter, around which scriptural echoes have rumbled since Rom. 1:16–17. The psalmist's complaint that the people of God are "sheep to be slaughtered" modulates immediately into

8. Richard B. Hays to Wayne A. Meeks, letter, November 17, 1987.

9. Fyodor M. Dostoevsky, *The Notebooks of F. M. Dostoevsky* (Moscow, 1935), quoted by Bakhtin, *Dostoevsky's Poetics*, 90. Emphasis original.

† From *Echoes of Scripture in the Letters of Paul* (New Haven: Yale University Press, 1989), 63–83, 206–9. Except as indicated, all notes are Hays's.

Paul's lament over the Jewish people ("my brothers, my kinsmen according to the flesh") in Rom. 9:1–5: "my grief is great and unceasing is the anguish in my heart." If suffering is the vocation of the church as well as the destiny of Israel in exile, the distinction between Israel and church is not sharply drawn for Paul. What was predicated of Israel can now be predicated of the church. There is one crucial distinction, however: Israel has refused to believe the gospel of Jesus Christ. If indeed nothing can separate "us" from the love of God in Christ Jesus our Lord (Rom. 8:39), what is to be said of Israel? Are they included or excluded by Paul's "us"? Has Israel been separated from the love of God? Does their refusal to accept Jesus Christ as Lord exclude them from the sphere of God's mercy? This is the explosive question that Paul confronts in Romans 9–11.

Despite the difficulty of interpreting many of its individual statements, Romans 9–11 has a clearly recognizable overall structure, broadly analogous to the structure of a lament psalm:

> 9:1–5: Lament over Israel.
> 9:6–29: Has God's word failed? Defense of God's elective purpose.
> 9:30–10:21: Paradox: Israel failed to grasp the word of faith attested by God in
>   Scripture.
> 11:1–32: Has God abandoned his people? No, all Israel will be saved.
> 11:33–36: Doxological conclusion.

The density of scriptural citation and allusion increases dramatically in these chapters, as Paul seeks to show that Israel's unbelief, though paradoxical, is neither unexpected nor final. As Paul reads Scripture, he finds not only manifold prefigurations of God's mercy to the Gentiles but also promises of Israel's ultimate restoration. The purpose of Romans 9–11—as of the letter in its entirety—is to show that God's dealing with Israel and the nations in the present age is fully consistent with God's modus operandi in the past and with his declared purposes. Both the narrative of God's past action and his prophetic promises for the future are found in Scripture. Thus, Romans 9–11 is an extended demonstration of the congruity between God's word in Scripture and God's word in Paul's gospel.

If there is no such congruity, then the word of God has "fallen" (Rom. 9:6), and the God with whom we have to do is either untrustworthy or impotent. The fact that Paul stares this horrifying prospect in the face and wrestles with it at such length is a significant measure both of the discontinuity between Scripture and gospel—why else such hermeneutical exertion?—and of Paul's tenacious integrity in holding to the proposition that unless the Law and the Prophets really do bear witness to the gospel there is no gospel at all.

The intertextual linkages in Romans 9–11, then, are structural girders, not filigrees. If Paul's reading of Scripture in these chapters is flimsy, then there is little hope for his proclamation to stand.

"In Isaac Shall Be Called for You a Seed"

To prove that the word of God has not fallen, Paul first seeks to establish that Scripture has always told stories that illustrate the selective character of God's grace. God's will is disclosed through these stories as *hē kat' eklogēn prothesis tou theou* (God's purpose that operates according to election) (Rom. 9:11). Paul begins the argument by appealing once again to the Genesis narrative about Abraham, this time quoting Gen. 21:12, "In Isaac shall be called for you a seed" (Rom. 9:7b). The quotation, adduced in support of the claim that "not all the children of Abraham are 'seed'" (Rom. 9:7a), is followed by a pesher-style commentary (i.e., a commentary that cites a text line by line and glosses each line with a brief explanation): "That is, not the children of the flesh are children of God, but the children of the promise are reckoned as 'seed'" (Rom. 9:8). Why is Isaac identified with promise rather than flesh? The answer is given by the tidy prooftext of Rom. 9:9, quoting loosely from Gen. 18:10, 14 to show that Isaac's birth was specifically *promised* to Abraham: "According to this time I will come, and there will be for Sarah a son." This quotation reinforces the link between *Isaac* and *promise*, a link supporting the more general claim that God singled out Isaac from among Abraham's children as the special bearer of election.

Thus, Gen. 18:10, 14 becomes the first of many passages tied by Paul in Romans 9 into an intricate intertextual web suspended from Gen. 21:12. The key terms of this programmatic quotation ("In Isaac shall be *called* for you a *seed*") are recapitulated in quotations from Hosea and Isaiah (in Rom. 9:25–29) that create an *inclusio* [inclusive frame] encompassing verses 6–29. Within this unit, Paul brings forward a series of scriptural illustrations of God's selectivity: Abraham, Sarah, and Isaac (vv. 7–9); Jacob and Esau (vv. 10–13); Moses and Pharaoh (vv. 15–18); the potter and the clay (vv. 20–23). While the first two texts appeal to the patriarchal narratives to show God's elective will in action, the latter two illustrations serve to defend God's right to do as he pleases with his own creation, thus answering once again the recurrent rhetorical question about God's justice (Rom. 9:14: "What then shall we say? Is there injustice with God?").

The metaphor of the potter and the clay—evoking complex echoes from numerous scriptural antecedents[1]—alludes powerfully to a parable of Paul's precursor Jeremiah:

> So I went down to the potter's house, and there he was working at his wheel. And the vessel he was making of clay was spoiled [LXX: "fell"; cf. Rom. 11:11, 22] in the potter's hand, and he reworked it into another vessel, as it seemed good to the potter to do. Then the word of the Lord came to me: "O house of Israel, can I not do with you as this potter has done? says the Lord.

---

1. In addition to Jer. 18:3–6, we can hear echoes here of Job 9:12, 10:8–9; Isa. 29:16, 45:9, 64:8; Sir. 33:10–13. (I am indebted to Maggi Despot for bringing some of these references to my attention.) A detailed investigation of these subtexts would demonstrate the complexity of the intertextual matrix from which Paul's metaphor emerges.

Behold, like the clay in the potter's hand, so are you in my hand, O house of
Israel." (Jer. 18:3–6)

The potter/clay image must not be read simply as a rebuke to silence impertinent
questions, nor is the effect of the allusion—unmarked by Paul—limited to the
obvious immediate purpose of establishing God's absolute power to do whatever
he chooses (like the five hundred pound gorilla); it also resonates deeply with
Paul's wider argument about God's dealings with Israel. The parable suggests that
the potter's power is not destructive but creative: the vessel may fall, but the potter
reshapes it. The parable, spoken in prophetic judgment upon Israel, is simultaneously a summons to repentance and a reassurance of the benevolent sovereignty
of God, persistently enacted in his love for his people Israel even in and through
the pronouncement of judgment. Thus, the allusion to Jeremiah 18 in Rom.
9:20–21, like other allusions and echoes earlier in the text, anticipates the resolution of Paul's argument in Romans 11. The reader who recognizes the allusion
will not slip into the error of reading Rom. 9:14–29 as an excursus on the doctrine of the predestination of individuals to salvation or damnation, because the
prophetic subtexts keep the concern with which the chapter began—the fate of
Israel—sharply in focus.

Paul's development of the potter metaphor concludes with a reference to God's
preparation of "vessels of mercy." Then, abandoning the metaphor in midsentence
and speaking directly of Christian believers, Paul describes these vessels as
"*called* . . . not only from the Jews but also from the Gentiles" (Rom. 9:24). With
the word *called*, he picks up the motif of vocation sounded in the Genesis quotation with which the unit began (Rom. 9:7), and this motif becomes the hook on
which the quotations from Hosea are hung: "as indeed he says in Hosea, 'Him who
was "not my people" I will *call* [*kalesō*] "my people," and her who was "not beloved"
I will call "beloved."' . . . 'And in the place where it was said to them, "You are not
my people," there sons of the living God shall be *called* [*klēthēsontai*]'" (Rom. 9:25–
26, paraphrasing Hos. 2:25 and quoting Hos. 2:1 LXX).

The extraordinary feature of Paul's appeal to this text is not the freedom with
which he paraphrases the wording of Hos. 2:25 (2:23 in most English translations)—
including his introduction of the link-word *call* into the passage—but the revisionary interpretation that he places on the prophecy. In its original setting, Hosea's
prophecy promises the restoration of a sinful and wayward Israel (i.e., the northern
kingdom) to covenant relationship with God. Though God provisionally disowns
Israel through a dramatic reversal of the covenant promise ("for you are not my
people and I am not your God" [Hos. 1:9b, cf. Exod. 6:7]), he ultimately will supersede Israel's covenant violation through his own steadfast love, symbolized by
Hosea's faithfulness to the harlot Gomer: "And I will betroth you to me for ever; I
will betroth you to me in righteousness [*dikaiosynē*] and in justice, in steadfast
love, and in mercy. I will betroth you to me in faithfulness [*pistei*]; and you shall
know the Lord" (Hos. 2:21–22 LXX). Where Hosea clings to the poignant hope of
Israel's privileged place despite her "harlotry," Paul deconstructs the oracle and
dismantles Israel's privilege; with casual audacity he rereads the text as a prophecy
of God's intention to embrace the Gentiles as his own people.

This hermeneutical coup is so smoothly executed that Gentile Christian readers might miss its innovative boldness—and therefore its potential scandal to Jewish readers. Paul is *not* arguing by analogy that just as God extended mercy to Israel even when Israel was unworthy so also he will extend grace to the Gentiles. Instead, Paul is arguing that God was speaking through the prophet Hosea to declare his intention to call Gentiles to be his own people. It is as though the light of the gospel shining through the text has illuminated a latent sense so brilliant that the opaque original sense has vanished altogether.

Or has it? If the quotation is a warrant for the claim made in Rom. 9:24 that God has "called us *not only from the Jews* but also from the Gentiles," then a real ambiguity exists in Paul's use of it. On the one hand, the Gentiles are historically the ones who have no claim on being called God's people, in direct contrast to the Jews (cf. Rom. 9:1–5); thus, in the first instance, Paul is reading the prophecy as a promise of Gentile inclusion among God's people (cf. Eph. 2:11–13 and 1 Pet. 2:9–10 for analogous formulations from a Christian point of view). However, the whole argument of Romans 9–11 presupposes that, *para doxan* [contrary to expectation], the Jews have in fact stumbled or been broken off so that it is now they who are "not my people," despite their birthright. In the scandalous inversions implied by the analogies of Romans 9, it is the Jewish people who stand in the role of Ishmael, the role of Esau, and even the role of Pharaoh. It is they who have experienced hardening and rejection, so that their contemporary situation is exactly analogous to the situation of the unfaithful Israel addressed by Hosea. But if that is so, then may they not also be included in the number of the non-people whom God calls and loves? This is exactly the conclusion toward which Paul works in chapter 11 with his discussion of the regrafting of the broken branches and his declaration of the mystery that after the full number of the Gentiles comes in, "all Israel shall be saved" (Rom. 11:25–26). Thus, if in Romans 9 and 10 Paul deconstructs Scripture's witness to Israel's favored status, Romans 11 dialectically deconstructs the deconstructive reading, subverting any Gentile Christian pretension to a position of hermeneutical privilege.

For that reason, some ambiguity hovers about the citation from Isaiah that Paul juxtaposes (Rom. 9:27–28) to his revisionary reading of Hosea. Turning from a prophecy that he construes as an oracle concerning Gentiles, Paul now cites a prophecy about Israel. The introductory formula is a peculiar one, however: "But Isaiah cries out *hyper* Israel" (Rom. 9:27a). Though the preposition *hyper* can sometimes mean "concerning" (equivalent to *peri*; cf. 2 Cor. 1:8), in the idiom of the Greek New Testament it more typically means "on behalf of, for the sake of." If the latter sense were followed, Isaiah's cry might be heard not as a threat, but as a voice of hope: "But Isaiah cries out for the sake of Israel, 'If [*ean*] the number of the sons of Israel[2] be as the sand of the sea, a remnant *will* be saved.'" (The rendering *"only* a remnant will be saved," found in many English versions,[3] is an

2. This phrase, taken not from Isaiah but from Hos. 2:1 LXX, serves as an artful transition to the quotation of Isa. 10:22.

3. E.g., RSV, New English Bible, Jerusalem Bible, New International Version, Today's English Version [Good News Bible].

interpretive paraphrase with no textual basis in any Greek manuscript.) Indeed, if we remember that Paul is adducing prooftexts in support of his claim that God has called vessels of mercy from among Jews and Gentiles alike (Rom. 9:24), it makes much better sense to read the Isaiah prophecy as a positive word of hope rather than as a word of condemnation: the quotation from Hosea proves that God calls Gentiles, and the quotation from Isaiah proves that he calls Jews.[4] This reading would also be fully consistent with Paul's use of the remnant motif in Romans 11, where he employs the notion of the remnant to prove that God has *not* rejected his people.

Finally, in Rom. 9:29, Paul echoes the other key term of the Gen. 21:12 quotation, *seed*, by citing another prophecy of Isaiah that draws together the images of remnant and seed: "If the Lord of hosts had not left [*egkatelipen*] us a seed [*sperma*], we would have become like Sodom, and we would have been likened to Gomorrah." This reference to the elect remnant/seed closes an intertextual circle opened in 9:7 and concludes Paul's demonstration from Scripture that the selective operation of God's will is a truth deeply imbedded in Israel's canonical texts. Only the presence of the seed distinguishes Israel from the archetypal targets of God's wrath.

Has God Abandoned His People?

Romans 11 brings to a climax Paul's wrestling with the question of Israel's status before God. The rhetorical question of Rom. 11:1 articulates the anxious concern that has generated the whole argument: "I say then, has God abandoned his people?" Paul curiously warrants his emphatic denial of this possibility (*mē genoito* [by no means!]) with autobiographical information ("I also am an Israelite, from the seed of Abraham, the tribe of Benjamin"). One would not suppose that Paul's ethnic affiliation could prevent God from abandoning his people; presumably, the implication is that Paul, as a Jew, should never be suspected of suggesting such an appalling idea. (Perhaps he is also anticipating the argument of the following verses by putting himself forward as a notable representative of the "remnant chosen by grace" [Rom. 11:5].) Then, more substantively, he resorts to the language of Scripture to make his point: "God has not abandoned his people [*ouk apōsato ho theos ton laon autou*] whom he foreknew" (Rom. 11:2a). Because Paul supports this climactic affirmation by appealing directly to the story of Elijah (Rom. 11:2b–5), it is easy to overlook that the affirmation is itself an echo of two other scriptural passages, whose original contexts frame Romans 11 instructively.

In 1 Samuel 12, the people, having incurred Samuel's disapproval by asking for a king, implore him to intercede for them: "Pray for your servants to the Lord your God, that we may not die; for we have added to all our sins this evil, to ask for ourselves a king" (1 Sam. 12:19). Samuel responds with a speech that would sound strangely apropos if it were found in Paul's mouth addressing his Jewish kin:

---

4. In both cases, the calling that Paul envisions is a calling through the gospel of Jesus Christ. There is no doctrine in Paul of separate but equal covenants for Jews and Christians; the remnant that will be saved is composed of Jewish Christians, like Paul himself.

Fear not; you have done all this evil, yet do not turn aside from following the Lord, but serve the Lord with all your heart. . . . For the Lord will not cast away his people [*ouk apōsetai kyrios ton laon autou*], for his great name's sake, because the Lord has gently received [*proselabeto;* cf. Rom. 14:3, 15:7] you as a people for himself. Moreover, as for me, far be it from me that I should sin against the Lord by ceasing to pray for you [cf. Rom. 9:3, 10:1]. (1 Sam. 12:20–23)

Does Samuel's speech sound in sympathetic harmony behind Rom. 11:2? If so, Paul has changed *kyrios* to *theos,* to make it clear that he is speaking of Yahweh, the God of Israel, not of Kyrios Christos, and he has shifted Samuel's future tense verb into the aorist ("has not cast off," rather than "will not cast off"), to make it clear that he is speaking of an accomplished not-abandonment rather than an anticipated one.

"God will not cast off his people." Exactly the same sentence is found in Ps. 94:14 (93:14 LXX). Here no narrative context is indicated, but the following lines play the theme of which Romans 9–11 is a variation:

> For the Lord will not cast off his people
> [*ouk apōsetai kyrios ton laon autou*],
> And he will not leave [*egkataleipsei*] his heritage,
> Until righteousness [*dikaiosynē*] returns for judgment.

The verb *egkataleipō,*[5] appearing in the line immediately following the psalm line that Paul echoes in Rom. 11:2, is the same verb that occurs in Isa. 1:9, quoted in Rom. 9:29, and it is etymologically connected with the verb *kataleipō* and the noun *leimma,* used in Rom. 11:4–5 to describe the remnant left by God's elective grace. The interplay of these words can be approximated in English only through recourse to a metaphor from the book trade: "God will not *remainder* his heritage. . . . He has caused seven thousand[6] to *remain* who have not bowed the knee to Baal. . . . So too at the present time there is a *remnant.*" Paul's allusion in Rom.

5. This verb, another standard element of the lament psalm vocabulary, is taken up prominently in early Christian interpretations of Jesus' death and resurrection as a fulfillment of the suffering-vindication pattern in these Psalms. See especially Mark 15:34 ("My God, my God, why have you forsaken [*egkatelipes*] me?"), quoting Ps. 22:1 (Ps. 21:2 LXX); and Acts 2:27 ("You will not abandon [*egkataleipseis*] my life to Hades"), quoting Ps. 16:10 (Ps. 15:10 LXX).

6. [Karl] Barth (*Church Dogmatics* II. 2 [trans. G. W. Bromiley et al. (Edinburgh: T. & T. Clark, 1957)], 270) calls attention to the fact that in 1 Kings 20:15—following hard upon God's promise (1 Kings 19:18) to leave seven thousand in Israel who have not fallen into idolatry—the number of "all the people of Israel" is given as seven thousand! Barth remarks: "It is these seven thousand men, and not the unfaithful majority, who represent Israel as such. By 'leaving them' God holds fast to Israel as such, and it is decided that He has not rejected His people. When therefore . . . the solitary Elijah is consoled by reference to these seven thousand men, he does not stand alone, but as the holder of his commission he is invisibly surrounded by these seven thousand. . . . Even in his loneliness he stands effectively before God for the whole of Israel, for Israel as such. In just the same way Paul does not stand alone. . . . He can and must, therefore, appeal to his existence as a Jew and as a Gentile missionary as a valid proof that God has not rejected his people." (I am grateful to Sherry Jordan for calling my attention to this passage.)

11:2a to Psalm 94 adumbrates the remnant theme that appears in the following sentences. This foreshadowing effect is formally identical to the pattern observed with regard to the use of Psalm 143 in Rom. 3:20 * * *: an unvoiced element of the explicitly cited text subliminally generates the next movement of the discourse.

It is difficult to say whether Paul intended to create resonances with 1 Sam. 12:22 and Ps. 94:14 when he wrote straightforwardly that "God has not cast off his people." But whether he intended it or not, the language through which his trust in God found voice was the language of Scripture. It would be inadequate to say that Scripture was *langue* and Paul's discourse *parole*,[7] as though Scripture were merely a pool of lexemes from which Paul draws; rather, Scripture's poetry and narratives materially govern his confession. Scripture's *parole*, already spoken, rebounds and is heard once again in Paul's discourse. Consequently, Paul's sentences carry the weight of meanings acquired through earlier narrative and liturgical utterance. This allusive evocation of earlier declarations of God's faithfulness to Israel covertly undergirds the burden of Paul's overt argument.

Rejoice, Gentiles, with his People

The reading of Romans that has emerged from our examination of the letter's scriptural echoes is confirmed by the conclusion of the letter-body in Rom. 15:7–13, a passage that functions as a *peroratio*, a summation of the letter's themes.

Receive one another, therefore, just as Christ has received [*proselabeto*; cf. 1 Sam. 12:22] you, for the glory of God. For I am saying that Christ became a servant of the circumcision for the sake of the truthfulness of God [*hyper aletheias theou*; cf. Rom. 3:4, 7], in order to confirm the promises given to the fathers [cf. Rom. 4:16] and in order that the Gentiles might glorify God for his mercy, just as it is written,
    Therefore I will praise you among the Gentiles,
    and I will sing to your name. [Ps. 18:49, 2 Sam. 22:50]
And again he says,
    Rejoice, Gentiles, with his people. [Deut. 32:43]
And again,
    Praise the Lord, all you Gentiles,
    And let all peoples praise him. [Ps. 117:1]
And again Isaiah says,
    There shall be a root of Jesse,
    And one who rises to rule the Gentiles;
    Upon him Gentiles shall hope. [Isa. 11:10]
May the God of hope fill you with all joy and peace in believing, in order that you might abound in hope in the power of the Holy Spirit.

---

7. The structuralist distinction drawn by the Swiss linguist Ferdinand de Saussure between *langue* (language), referring to the entire language as a system of signs, and *parole* (speech), referring to the individual utterances of a particular subject [editors' note].

Why does Paul place this florilegium at the end of his letter to the Romans? Clearly, he has saved his clinchers for the end. After much allusive and labored argumentation, Paul finally draws back the curtain and reveals a collection of passages that explicitly embody his vision for a church composed of Jews and Gentiles glorifying God together. Commentators often note that Paul has offered here one quotation from the Pentateuch, one from the Prophets, and two from the Writings, all strung together by the catchword *ethnē* [peoples], all pointing to the eschatological consummation in which Gentiles join in the worship of Israel's God: truly the Law and the Prophets are brought forward here as witnesses. As Käsemann remarks, "The Old Testament foreshadowed this message. The recipients of the letter must recognize this agreement with Scripture. An apology could hardly have a more magnificent conclusion."[8] There is no sleight of hand here: Paul rests his case on the claim that his churches, in which Gentiles do in fact join Jews in praising God, must be the eschatological fulfillment of the scriptural vision. If so, then God's Gentile-embracing righteousness, proclaimed in Paul's gospel, really is "promised beforehand through his prophets in holy texts" (Rom. 1:2), and Paul has successfully made his case in defense of the justice of God. That is why these particular quotations are a fitting culmination of the letter's argument.

Even here, however, where the significance of the passages for Paul's case is evident, we will miss important intertextual echoes if we ignore the loci from which the quotations originate. Both of the psalm passages refer not only to Gentiles, but also to God's mercy (*eleos*; Ps. 17:51 LXX, Ps. 116:2 LXX), the attribute for which the Gentiles are said in Rom. 15:9 to glorify God. In neither instance does Paul quote the part of the text that mentions mercy, but the appearance of the word in these passages is hardly a case of blind luck. Paul has presumably selected these passages precisely because they bring references to God's mercy into conjunction with references to praise of God among the Gentiles. In all likelihood, Paul's own discursive formulation in Rom. 15:9a is influenced directly by the Psalm vocabulary. One way of putting this point is to say that Rom. 15:9a is an allusion to the passages quoted in 15:9b and 15:11, an allusion to an original context slightly wider than the explicit quotations.

Ps. 18:49–50, in addition to its references to Gentiles and mercy, voices other themes that echo tantalizingly in Romans. In verse 50, God is described as

> Magnifying the saving deeds [*sotērias*] of his king
> And performing mercy [*eleos*] for his Messiah [*Christō*],
> For David and his seed [*spermati*] forever.

A reader who remembered these phrases would hear in them an echo creating a satisfying *inclusio* with the letter's opening proclamation about God's son, who was promised in holy texts, "who came from the seed [*spermatos*] of David, . . . Jesus Messiah [*Christou*]," who commissioned Paul to preach the obedience of faith among all the Gentiles (Rom. 1:3–5). Indeed, given a messianic reading of

8. [Ernst] Käsemann, [*Commentary on*] *Romans* [trans. G. W. Bromiley (Grand Rapids, MI: Eerdmans, 1980)], 387.

the psalm, it is hard to avoid the impression that the "I" who speaks in the verse that Paul quotes must be the Messiah himself, whom Paul would of course identify as Jesus, who now is pictured as praising God among the Gentiles. The quotation, after all, is introduced as a supporting prooftext for a description of something that Christ did (Rom. 15:8), and Paul has just quoted in Rom. 15:3 another psalm (69:9) in which he understands Christ to be the speaker: "The reproaches of those who reproached you fell upon me." Thus, the picture evoked by Paul's quotation of Psalm 18 is very much like the picture painted in Heb. 2:10–13: Jesus stands amidst the congregation of his brothers, singing praise to God. Paul, of course, emphasizes for his purposes not the solidarity of Jesus with the congregation but the fact that the congregation is made up of Gentiles.

The quotation from Deut. 32:43, then, adds a crucial element to the portrait. "Rejoice, Gentiles, *with his people*." The Gentiles do not stand alone around Christ; they are being summoned to join *with* Israel in rejoicing. Here Paul's agreement with the LXX is crucial. The Hebrew text reads, "Gentiles, praise his people," an admonition very different from what Paul finds in the LXX. For Paul's purposes it is wonderfully useful to find a text in which Moses, in his great climactic song at the end of Deuteronomy, includes Gentiles in the company of the people of God.

Similarly, the final text in Paul's catena also envisions a gathering of Gentiles and Jews around the Messiah. The full force of Paul's citation of Isa. 11:10 becomes apparent only when the reader recollects Isa. 11:11–12: "And it shall be in that day that the Lord will purpose to show his hand to be zealous for the remnant of the people that is left [*to kataleiphthen hypoloipon tou laou*] .... And he will lift up a sign for the Gentiles, and he will gather the lost ones of Israel, and he will gather the dispersed ones of Judah from the four corners of the earth." Paul quotes only an excerpt that prophesies Gentiles placing their hope in the "root of Jesse," but the quotation also works as an allusion to Isaiah's vision of God's eschatological kingdom in which the lost ones of Israel rejoin these Gentiles in being gathered at the feet of the one whom God has raised up. This allusion in turn forges an intertextual link back to the remnant theme of Romans 11.

As in Romans 9–11, these scriptures project an inversion of the order suggested by Paul's earlier claim that the gospel is the power of salvation to the Jew first and then subsequently to the Greek. Here the Gentiles seem to come in first; that is the anomaly that Paul must explain. Isaiah sings in the background, however. If Gentiles come, can Israel be far behind?

"THE RIGHTEOUSNESS FROM FAITH SAYS"

In surveying the scriptural texts that sound within Paul's discourse in Romans, we have observed an extraordinary—indeed, almost monotonous—thematic consistency. In Romans, Paul cites Scripture not as a repository of miscellaneous wisdom on various topics but as an insistent witness of one great truth: God's righteousness, which has now embraced Gentiles among the people of God, includes the promise of God's unbroken faithfulness to Israel. Virtually every text that Paul cites or alludes to is made to circle around this one theme. It is as though the letter were a great parabola that picks up echoes of Scripture and reflects them all onto a single focal point.

Only after we have followed the trajectory of these echoes and concentrated our attention on the theme to which they incessantly lead can we hope to make some sense out of Rom. 10:5–10, the baffling text with which we began our inquiry in the previous chapter. In an apparently capricious act of interpretation, the reader will recall, Paul seizes Moses' admonition to Israel, warning them to obey the Law without rationalization or excuse (Deut. 30:11–14), and turns it into an utterance of The Righteousness from Faith, a character who contravenes the manifest sense of Moses' words by transmuting them into a cryptic prophecy of the Christian gospel as preached by Paul.

Such a reading looks on the face of it like a wild and disingenuous piece of exegesis, so much so that embarrassed Christian commentators have with surprising frequency—and perhaps not without a certain disingenuousness of their own—attempted to deny that Paul is actually interpreting Scripture at all. For example, W. Sanday and A. C. Headlam, in their Romans commentary in the International Critical Commentary series—throughout much of the twentieth century the most influential English-language commentary on Romans—argue that "the Apostle does not intend to base any argument on the quotation from the O.T., but only selects the language as being familiar, suitable, and proverbial, in order to express what he wishes to say."[9] More recent critical opinion, however, has tended to acknowledge that Paul is indeed interpreting Scripture; most studies of the passage have either sought to establish some historical background against which Paul's reading looks intelligible[1]—or to explain on theological grounds why Paul's use of the text is legitimate.[2] These studies have turned up some helpful insights, which may be most usefully integrated if we reexamine Romans 10 in light of our foregoing observations about the effects of intertextual echo in Romans.

The Place of Rom. 9:30–10:21 within the Argument

The movement of the discourse through Romans 9–11 is, as we have previously indicated, easy to chart in broad outline. After first expressing dismay over his own people's evident unbelief in the gospel message, which they ought by rights to embrace (9:1–5), Paul argues that their unbelief is not to be construed as evidence that God's word has failed, because God has always dealt with humanity through a dialectic of rejection and election (9:6–29). In 9:30–10:21, Paul gives a

9. William Sanday and Arthur C. Headlam, *A Critical and Exegetical Commentary on the Epistle to the Romans* (ICC; Edinburgh: T. & T. Clark, 1906), 289.

1. M. Jack Suggs, "'The Word Is Near You': Romans 10:6–10 within the Purpose of the Letter," in W. R. Farmer, C. F. D. Moule, and R. R. Niebuhr, eds., *Christian History and Interpretation: Studies Presented to John Knox* (Cambridge: Cambridge University Press, 1967), 289–312; J. D. G. Dunn, "'Righteousness from the Law' and 'Righteousness from Faith': Paul's Interpretation of Scripture in Romans 10:1–10," in G. F. Hawthorne and O. Betz, eds., *Tradition and Interpretation in the New Testament: Essays in Honor of E. Earle Ellis for His Sixtieth Birthday* (Grand Rapids, MI: Eerdmans, 1987), 216–28.

2. Barth, *Church Dogmatics* II.2, 245–47; [E. Earle] Ellis, *Paul's Use of the Old Testament* [(Edinburgh: Oliver and Boyd, 1957)], 123; [C. E. B.] Cranfield, [*A Critical and Exegetical Commentary on the Epistle to the*] *Romans*, [6th ed., 2 vols. (ICC; Edinburgh: T. & T. Clark, 1975–79),] 2.552–56; Käsemann, *Romans*, 283–92.

fuller account of the anomaly that gives rise to these reflections: "Gentiles who did not pursue righteousness have grasped[3] righteousness, the righteousness from faith, but Israel, pursuing a Law of righteousness, did not attain to the Law" (9:30–31). The remainder of this section of the discourse (9:32–10:21) elaborates this paradox, reflecting on how it came to be, explaining what went wrong. This phase of the argument ends by recapitulating the paradox through Paul's remarkable misreading of Isa. 65:1–2: he splits the oracle down the middle, interpreting the first verse ("I have been found by those who did not seek me; I have become manifest to those who did not ask for me") innovatively as a reference to Gentile Christians, and the second verse ("All day long I have stretched out my hands to a disobedient and contrary people"), quite properly, as a reference to Israel. The image of God's persistently outstretched hands, however, foreshadows the final turn of Paul's dialectic, in which God's grace has the last word. In chapter 11, Paul affirms that God remains faithful to his people Israel despite their unbelief and that he will in the end effect their eschatological redemption as he had always promised. In short, Rom. 9:30–10:21 has a parenthetical place in the logic of the argument. While Rom. 9:6–29 and 11:1–32 affirm the unshakeable efficacy of God's word and God's elective will, Rom. 9:30–10:21 pauses in midcourse to describe how Israel has temporarily swerved off the track during an anomalous interval preceding the consummation of God's plan.

Paul's strange interpretation of Deut. 30:12–14 must fit somehow into this train of thought. In other words, this text must for Paul somehow support an explanation—or at least a description—of how Israel and the Gentiles came to switch roles in the drama of election, how Israel, despite its advantages and its intentional pursuit of the "Law of righteousness," failed to grasp the Law's real message. In order to see how Paul's reading of Deuteronomy serves this purpose, it is necessary to set the quotation in context with some care.

The Telos of the Law

In Rom. 9:31–32 Paul describes Israel as failing to attain the Law, despite their concern for works. One hoary interpretive tradition in Christian theology holds that they failed to attain the Law in the sense that they were unable to perform all the commandments perfectly. In the present discussion, however, Paul makes no such claim. The problem is not that they are unable to do what the Law requires: the problem is that they pursue obedience not *ek pisteōs* (through faith) but *ex ergōn* (through works). This suggests that the aim of the Law is actually not perfect performance of works at all, but something else.

Paul contends that his Jewish brothers and sisters have zeal for God, but it is poorly informed zeal. They seek to establish their own righteousness because they are ignorant of the righteousness of God (which, of course, equals the righteousness of faith; cf. 9:30), to which they do not submit—understandably, since they do not know about it (Rom. 10:1–3). But what is this righteousness of God? The answer is given in Rom. 10:4: "For Christ is the *telos* of the Law, for righteousness to everyone who believes." The conjunction *gar* (for) in 10:4 is

---

3. The verb *katelaben* can include the idea of intellectual comprehension: cf. its use in John 1:5.

a crucial logical connective. This sentence explains what was said in the fore-going sentence: the real aim of the Law, the righteousness of God, *is* Jesus Christ. Strongly established Christian tradition, especially in the Reformation churches, has construed this statement to mean that Christ is the termination of the Law, but this interpretation makes no sense at all in the context of Romans.[4] Paul has already written that the Law and the Prophets bear witness to the righteousness of God (3:21) and that his gospel of righteousness through faith confirms rather than abolishes the Law (3:31), demonstrating through the story of Abraham (Romans 4) that the Law teaches faith-righteousness. What more could he say to make his point clear? The sum and substance of the Torah, according to the whole argument of this letter, is righteousness through faith. That is what Israel failed to grasp, and that is what God's act in Christ now makes evident—to Paul—beyond all possible doubt.

Therefore, Rom. 10:5 and 10:6 must not stand in antithesis to one another. Paul is not playing "the righteousness from the Law" (10:5) off against "the righteousness from faith" (10:6). He is using these terms synonymously, quoting Moses in both verses to support his interpretation. The quotation from Lev. 18:5 ("The person who does these things shall live by them") appears in the argument not because Paul wants to disparage "doing"; indeed, Paul has already argued a few paragraphs earlier (8:1–11) that those who receive the Spirit through Jesus Christ are now enabled to fulfill the righteous intent (*dikaiōma*) of the Law (8:4) and to submit (*hypotassō*) to God's Law.[5] The quotation from Lev. 18:5 appears because of its promise of life for those who heed the Law, a promise fully consonant with the message of Deuteronomy 30 (see especially Deut. 30:15). The efforts of some commentators to drive a wedge between these two texts as though they represented radically different conceptions of righteousness have wrought disastrous consequences for Christian theology.[6]

4. The detailed study of [Robert] Badenas, *Christ the End of the Law*[: *Romans 10:4 in Pauline Perspective* (Journal for the Study of the New Testament, Supplement series 10; Sheffield: JSOT Press, 1985)], has made a compelling case for the "teleological" interpretation of *telos* as "goal" or "completion." Cranfield (*Romans*, 2.515–20) had already reached a similar conclusion. See also the nuanced discussion of Paul Meyer, "Romans 10:4 and the End of the Law," in J. L. Crenshaw and S. Sandmel, eds., *The Divine Helmsman: Studies on God's Control of Human Events, Presented to Lou H. Silberman* (New York: KTAV, 1980), 59–78. The burden of proof lies strongly on any interpreter who reads *telos* as "termination."

5. Indeed, Rom. 10:3b ("they did not submit [*hypetagēsan*] to the righteousness of God") can be explicated by cross-reference to Rom. 8:7 ("The mindset of the flesh is inimical towards God, for it does not submit [*hypotassetai*] to the Law of God"). The apparent equivalence in these formulations between "righteousness of God" and "Law of God" is theologically noteworthy.

6. The use of Lev. 18:5 in Gal. 3:12 is an entirely different matter. As in so many other particulars, Paul argues very differently in Romans from the way that he had argued earlier in Galatians. Whether it is possible, as Barth thinks (*Church Dogmatics* II. 2, p. 245), to reinterpret Gal. 3:12 in light of this reading of Romans 10 is a question too complicated to address here. Likewise, a full exegesis of Rom. 10:5–6 must take into account Phil. 3:9, which juxtaposes "my own righteousness derived from Law" to the righteousness that comes "through the faithfulness of Christ, the righteousness from God based upon faith." Whatever the interpreter decides to do about synthesizing Paul's apparently divergent statements about the Law in the various letters, the harmonizing impulse must not override the internal logic of the argument in Romans 10.

The exegetical debate is technical and convoluted, but a paraphrase of the passage (Rom. 10:1–6a, 8–9, omitting for the moment the strange comments in 6b–7) can clarify the interpretation proposed here:

> Brothers, the desire of my heart and my prayer to God for the sake of the Jewish people is that they may be saved. For I bear them witness that they have zeal for God, though it is ill-informed. For, because they are ignorant of the righteousness of God and because they seek to establish their own righteousness, they do not submit to the righteousness of God. What is it that they do not know about the righteousness of God? Just this: that Christ is the *telos* of the Torah, for righteousness to everyone who believes. How can I say that Christ is the *telos* of the Torah? Let me prove it by citing two passages from Torah. Moses writes concerning the righteousness that is from the Torah, that "The person who does these things will live by them" [Lev. 18:5]. What things does he mean? In another place, as Moses writes, this righteousness from faith [equivalent to righteousness from Torah equivalent to righteousness of God] speaks like this: . . . "The word is near you, in your mouth and in your heart" [Deut. 30:14]. What "word" does Moses mean? He is referring to the word of faith, which we also now preach, because if you confess with *your mouth* that Jesus is Lord and believe *in your heart* that God raised him from the dead, you will be saved, i.e., you will find life, just as Moses promised in Lev. 18:5, because you will be obeying the true message of the Law.

Only when the passage is interpreted in this way does its coherence become clear.

There is a sad irony here. Paul agonized over the fact that his Jewish contemporaries failed to understand that Israel's Law pointed to the righteousness of faith; now, Christians make the same tragic error when they fail to acknowledge that the Law and the Prophets bear witness to the righteousness of God and when they think that Torah and Christ are antithetical. It is the same hermeneutical mistake, viewed from the two different sides of the schism that it created.

"In Your Mouth and In Your Heart"

All of this preliminary discussion was necessary in order to establish the conceptual framework within which Paul's peculiar handling of Deut. 30:12–14 must be understood. Paul's fundamental claim is that the Torah proclaims the Christian kerygma. We have seen throughout our consideration of Romans that he reads Israel's Scripture under the guidance of this hermeneutical presupposition, and that his readings of the text frequently achieve their effects through an intricate play of intertextual echoes. Nowhere is this peculiarly poetic mode of interpretation more boldly evident than in Rom. 10:5–10.

When Paul places his Deuteronomy quotation in the mouth of The Righteousness from Faith, he has already provided the decisive clue to his understanding of the text: he is reading Deuteronomy in light of the same hermeneutical framework developed through his interpretations of Hab. 2:4 ("The righteous one shall live by faith") and Gen. 15:6 ("Abraham believed God, and it was reckoned to him for righteousness"). Moses' speech in Deuteronomy, no less than these other biblical texts, will be read as an expression of faith-righteousness.

In contrast to the Habakkuk and Genesis passages, however, there is no reference to faith or to righteousness in Deuteronomy 30. How then does Paul achieve the reading that he proposes? He does it through tinkering with the text in order to create an impressionistic textual triple-exposure.

First, he opens the quotation with a phrase extracted from Deut. 8:17, 9:4: "Do not say in your heart." This simple formulation replaces Deut. 30:11, which emphasizes a point uncongenial to Paul, the fact that Moses is speaking about the accessibility of the commandments of the Law: "This commandment which I am commanding you today is not grievous, nor is it far from you. It is not in heaven." Paul tacitly omits these words and replaces them with the briefer formula from earlier in the text of Deuteronomy.

This textual substitution does not, however, merely serve the negative purpose of deleting material uncongenial to Paul's case; it also at the same time introduces echoes that ring in harmony with the positive position that he is developing. Both Deut. 8:17 and 9:4, recalling God's gracious deliverance of them from Egypt and his provision for them in the wilderness, admonish Israel against complacency after they enter the land. The former text reads (in the LXX), "Do not say in your heart, 'My strength and the might of my hand have accomplished for me this great mighty deed.' You shall remember the Lord your God, for he gives you the strength to do a mighty deed, even in order that he might establish his covenant, which the Lord swore with your fathers, as today" (Deut. 8:17–18). The second text, occurring just a few sentences later, stirs even more echoes for the reader who listens carefully:

> Do not say in your heart, when the Lord your God drives these nations [*ethnē*] out before you, "Because of my righteousness the Lord has brought me in to inherit this good land." . . . Not on account of your righteousness nor on account of the holiness of your heart will you go in to inherit their land, but on account of the impiety of these nations the Lord will destroy them from before you, even in order that he might establish his covenant, which he swore with your fathers, Abraham and Isaac and Jacob. And you shall know today that not on account of your righteousness is the Lord your God giving you this good land to inherit, because you are a stiffnecked people. (Deut. 9:4–6)

Paul, it seems, has deftly chosen the words "Do not say in your heart" to introduce the discourse of The Righteousness from Faith because these words evoke an earlier word of God to Israel, in which the Lord God warns them against the presumption of their own righteousness and reminds these "stiffnecked" people that the initiative in deliverance and covenant-making is his, not theirs. The message is so apt for Paul's argument in Romans that we are left wondering why he did not go ahead and quote these words rather than delving into his problematical exegesis of Deut. 30:12–14. In fact, however, he leaves his readers only the subtlest allusion to Deuteronomy 8 and 9. Any reader who knows where the words come from will surely smile in recognition of the point; most readers will miss the point altogether.

Perhaps Paul passed up the shot because it was too easy. To make his case by quoting "Do not say in your heart, 'It is because of my righteousness'" would be to end the argument prematurely. He spins a more complex effect by citing the tag phrase from Deut. 9:4—perhaps counting on the reader to finish the sentence— but then shifting ground to a new text in which he also hears faith-righteousness speaking.

The choice of Deut. 30:12–14, with its blunt insistence on doing the command-ments, is daring and perhaps deliberately provocative. It would not be easy to find another text in the Old Testament that looks less promising for Paul's purposes. In Deuteronomy, the questions, "Who will go up into heaven for us and receive it for us?" and "Who will cross for us to the other side of the sea and receive it for us?" serve as foils for Moses' assertion of the nearness of the Law. It has already been given to Israel "in the book of this Law" (Deut. 30:10), so there is no need for speculative excurses and inquiries. Yet even here, Paul argues, the speaker is The Righteousness from Faith. His subversive exegesis commands our attention for several reasons.

Adopting an uncharacteristic exegetical format, Paul offers a running line-by-line pesher commentary on the passage. Formally, the method is similar to the exegesis found in the Qumran biblical commentaries (e.g., lQpHab), where the biblical text is treated as a cryptically encoded allegory of the community's own history, apocalyptically interpreted. Materially, however, the commentary in Rom. 10:6–7 takes a distinctive turn as Paul fancifully supposes that the imagi-nary questers are looking high and low for Christ. They may suppose that they are looking for "the commandment" of the Law (Deut. 30:11), but since Christ is the *telos* of the Law, Paul portrays them as looking for Christ, whether they know it or not. The absurdity of the undertaking is stressed: Christ has already come down from heaven, already been raised up from the dead. God has already done the work in Christ's incarnation and resurrection and needs no help from well-intentioned spiritual questers. The futility of the undertaking mirrors the futility of Israel's seeking to establish their own righteousness and not submitting to God's.

As all commentators notice, Paul's citation of Deut. 30:13 diverges widely from any known textual tradition. Whereas both the MT and the LXX speak of cross-ing the sea to find the commandment, Paul's citation reads, "Who will go down into the abyss?" This is the sort of divergence from the scriptural text that encour-aged Sanday and Headlam to venture the opinion that Paul was not really inter-preting Deuteronomy 30. In fact, however, this deviant quotation is not just a careless Pauline paraphrase; it is the third layer of the triple exposure that I men-tioned earlier, a textual overlay that is decidedly interpretive in effect. M. Jack Suggs has demonstrated convincingly that Paul's formulation reflects conventions associated with the personified figure of Sophia in Jewish Wisdom tradition.[7]

7. Suggs, "The Word Is Near You," 306–12.

Suggs adduces a number of texts in which heaven and the abyss are symbols of the inaccessibility of Wisdom. For example, in Sir. 24:5 Sophia speaks:

> Alone I have made the circuit of the vault of heaven
> And have walked in the depths of the abyss.

This same tradition appears tellingly in Bar. 3:29–30, which allusively transfers the language of Deut. 30:12–14 onto the figure of Wisdom:

> Who has gone up into heaven and taken her,
> and brought her down from the clouds?
> Who has gone over the sea and found her,
> and will buy her for pure gold?

Paul's filtered citation of Deuteronomy echoes these Wisdom traditions, in which Wisdom is identified with Israel's Torah (cf. Bar. 4:1). Paul's variation on Deut. 30:13 signals to the reader that the text must be heard not only in polyphony with Deut. 8:17 and 9:4 but also with Bar. 3:29–30 and other traditional texts about elusive Wisdom (cf. Job 28:12–14). Suggs is probably correct to suggest that this intertextual fusion serves Paul's christological interpretation of Deut. 30:12–14: "The tension between Gospel and Law is resolved by the identification of Christ with Wisdom-Torah. The apostle hopes in this way to rescue his gospel from the stigma of absolute opposition to the law. . . . The righteousness based on faith does not annul the law but brings it to its true goal, for 'the word of faith which we preach' is Jesus Christ, incarnate wisdom, *telos nomou* [goal of (the) law]." The only trouble with Suggs' insightful argument is that he underplays the allusive character of Paul's textual transformation: he assumes that Paul's transmutation of the Deuteronomy text would have a self-evident argumentative force in the defense of his gospel. In fact, however, only a very subtle reader would make the connections that Suggs makes and draw the appropriate theological conclusions. Paul does not explicitly argue that Christ is to be identified with Wisdom and therefore also with Torah. This fusion occurs in the cave of echo, not at the overt discursive level.

Paul centers his reading of Deut. 30:12–14 on the theme of the *nearness* of the word, rather than on the imperative to do the commandments. He omits from his quotation not only the introductory sentence (Deut. 30:11) but also the last clause of Deut. 30:14: "so that you can do it." With these strategic excisions, his reading of the text drives toward a climax in Rom. 10:8. After the comical portrayal of questers who fret about where to find Christ, Paul states positively what The Righteousness from Faith actually does say: "But what does it say? 'Near you is the word, in your mouth and in your heart'; that is, the word of faith which we preach." Thus, Paul provocatively reads Deuteronomy 30:11–14 not as a summons to do what the plain superficial sense of the Law requires, but as a summons to discern the true content of the word (*rēma* [that which God has spoken]), which has always been the word of the righteousness of faith. The word that was near to Israel in the Law is identical with the word that is now near in the Christian kerygma.

This revisionary reading of Deut. 30:14, employing the pesher style, treats each phrase of the precursor text as a shorthand cipher for an element of the Christian confession. Paul works out his interpretation in Rom. 10:8–9 by expanding each key term of Deut. 30:14. The result can be diagrammed as follows:

(Rom. 10:8a, quoting Deut. 30:14)	(Rom. 10:8b–9)
But what does it say?	That is
The word is near you,	the *word* of faith which we preach.
	Because if you confess
in your *mouth*	with your *mouth*
	that Jesus is Lord,
	and if you believe
and in your *heart*	in your *heart*
	that God raised him from the dead,
	you will be saved.

Paul is not merely echoing Deuteronomy. This is an instance of line-by-line rereading, asserting explicitly that the latent sense of the Torah text is now expressed overtly in the gospel.

Thus, Paul's interpretation presupposes what it argues and argues what it presupposes: that the real meaning of Deuteronomy 30 is disclosed not in lawkeeping but in Christian preaching. The argument, at its explicit level, rests on sheer force of assertion. Implicitly, however, the intertextual echoes created by Paul's evocation of Deut. 9:4 and of the Wisdom tradition suggest hauntingly that Paul's reading is less arbitrary than it sounds. From Deuteronomy, Paul echoes the idea that the covenant depends on grace from start to finish rather than on Israel's own righteousness. Echoing Job, Baruch, and Sirach, Paul hints at the notion that the word of God spoken in the Law is identical with the Wisdom of God, who "appeared upon earth and lived among men" (Bar. 3:37)—not as Torah, as Israel's sages affirmed, but in the person of Jesus Messiah.

The Word as Metaphor

> Where shall the word be found, where will the word
> Resound? Not here, there is not enough silence.
>
> —T. S. ELIOT, "ASH WEDNESDAY"

This account of the effects of intertextual echo in Rom. 10:5–10 should not be read as a defense of Paul's exegesis. It is, rather, an account of the devices whereby a historically outrageous reading gains poetic plausibility. (Whether this intertextual plausibility ought, normatively speaking, to confer upon the reading theological legitimacy is a question beyond the scope of our present deliberations. Readers interested in this issue are referred to the final chapter of this book.) What Paul has in fact done is, simply, to read the text of Deuteronomy 30 as a *metaphor* for Christian proclamation. This particular metaphorical reading seems especially jarring to modern historically sensitive readers. Paul's interpretation of this passage, however, is neither more nor less fanciful than many other scriptural interpretations in Romans. When Paul reads Habakkuk as a proclaimer of justification by faith or interprets Hosea's prophecy to the northern kingdom of Israel as an adumbration of God's calling of Gentiles, the same sort of metaphorical shift takes place: Paul is reading the ancient scriptural text as a trope, which speaks by indirection about his own message and ministry. Romans 10 differs from other cases only in articulating more explicitly the hermeneutical warrant that implicitly authorizes all of Paul's intertextual excursions: the word of God, now present in the Christian gospel, is the same word of God that was always present to Israel in Torah. It was so close to them that they had no need to go looking for it; yet they were unable to hear it.

The function, then, of Rom. 10:5–10 is to intensify the paradox of Israel's unbelief. Paul exposits Deuteronomy in such a way that its latent sense is alleged to be identical with the manifest claims of his own proclamation. The nearness of the word stands in ironic juxtaposition to Israel's deafness. The same people of Israel to whom Moses proclaims the nearness of the word, whose hearts God promises to circumcise (Deut. 30:6), are also the "perverse generation" (Deut. 32:20) who so stir God's anger that Moses pronounces on them the judgment cited by Paul in Rom. 10:19:

> I will make you jealous of those who are not a nation;
> With a senseless nation I will make you angry.

Paul later explains his hope that even this stirring of the Jews to jealousy against Gentile converts will be subsumed into God's design for saving Israel (11:11–14, where the verb *parazēloun* [provoke to jealousy] should be heard as an echo of Deut. 32:21). In Romans 10, however, Paul meditates on the mystery of Israel's culpable unresponsiveness to the word in their midst. Behind the quotation of Deut. 32:21 in Rom. 10:19 lingers the—metaleptically suppressed—echo of God's verdict on Israel in Deut. 32:20 (LXX):

> I will turn my face away from them,
> And I will show what will happen to them
>   in the last times [*ep' eschatōn*].
> Because they are a perverse generation,
> Sons in whom there is no faith [*pistis*].

Part III. Poetic Reimaginings

LYRIC

THE DREAM OF THE ROOD†

Listen, I will tell the best of visions,
that came to me in the middle of the night,
when voice-bearers dwelled in rest.
    It seemed to me that I saw a more wonderful tree
lifted in the air, wound round with light,   5
the brightest of beams. That beacon was entirely
cased in gold; beautiful gems stood
at the corners of the earth, likewise there were five
upon the cross-beam. All those fair through creation
gazed on the angel of the Lord there. There was certainly no gallows of
     the wicked;   10
but the holy spirits beheld it there,
men over the earth and all this glorious creation.
Wondrous was the victory-tree, and I stained with sins,
wounded with guilts. I saw the tree of glory,
honoured with garments, shining with joys,   15
covered with gold; gems had
covered magnificently the tree of the forest.
    Nevertheless, I was able to perceive through that gold
the ancient hostility of wretches, so that it first began
to bleed on the right side. I was all drenched with sorrows.   20
I was frightened by the beautiful vision; I saw that urgent beacon
change its covering and colours: sometimes it was soaked with wetness,
stained with the coursing of blood; sometimes adorned with treasure.

---

† Translated by Elaine Treharne, from, *Old and Middle English c. 890–c. 1450: An Anthology*, ed. Elaine Treharne, 3rd ed. (Chichester, West Sussex: Wiley-Blackwell, 2010), 120–27.
    The anonymous Old English "Dream of the Rood" is one of the earliest extant English poems: parts of it were inscribed (in runes) in the eighth-century Ruthwell Cross, an elaborately carved stone monument that stands eighteen feet tall and is now housed in Scotland's Ruthwell church (although there is some debate about whether that inscription is original to the sculpture or a somewhat later addition). It is also one of the strangest English poems, as it retells the story of Christ's crucifixion from a rather surprising perspective—that of the cross itself. (*Rood*, an obsolete word for a wooden staff, was conventionally used of Christ's cross.)

Yet as I lay there a long while
I beheld sorrowful the tree of the Saviour,   25
until I heard it utter a sound;
it began to speak words, the best of wood:
    'That was very long ago, I remember it still,
that I was cut down from the edge of the wood,
ripped up by my roots. They seized me there, strong enemies,   30
made me a spectacle for themselves there, commanded me to raise up
        their criminals.
Men carried me there on their shoulders, until they set me on a hill,[1]
enemies enough fastened me there. I saw then the Saviour of mankind
hasten with great zeal, as if he wanted to climb up on me.
There I did not dare, against the word of the Lord,   35
bow or break, when I saw the
corners of the earth tremble.[2] I might have
felled all the enemies; even so, I stood fast.
He stripped himself then, young hero—that was God almighty—
strong and resolute; he ascended on the high gallows,   40
brave in the sight of many, when he wanted to ransom mankind.
I trembled when the warrior embraced me; even then I did not dare to
        bow to earth,
fall to the corners of the earth, but I had to stand fast.
I was reared a cross. I raised up the powerful King,
the Lord of heaven; I did not dare to bend.   45
They pierced me with dark nails; on me are the wounds visible,
the open wounds of malice; I did not dare to injure any of them.
They mocked us both together. I was all drenched with blood
poured out from that man's side after he had sent forth his spirit.[3]
    I have experienced on that hillside many   50
cruelties of fate. I saw the God of hosts
violently stretched out. Darkness had
covered with clouds the Ruler's corpse,
the gleaming light. Shadows went forth
dark under the clouds.[4] All creation wept,
lamented the King's fall. Christ was on the cross.   55
    Yet there eager ones came from afar
to that noble one; I beheld all that.
I was all drenched with sorrow; nevertheless I bowed down to the hands
        of the men,
humble, with great eagerness. There they took almighty God,   60
lifted him from that oppressive torment. The warriors forsook me then

1. The "hill" is Golgotha or Calvary on which Christ was crucified [translator's note; see Mark 15:22
and parallels].
2. Cf. Matt 27:51.
3. Cf. John 19:33–34.
4. Cf. Mark 15:33 and parallels.

standing covered with moisture; I was all wounded with arrows.
They laid the weary-limbed one down there, they stood at the head of
 his body,
they beheld the Lord of heaven there, and he himself rested there a while,
weary after the great battle. They began to fashion a tomb for him,   65
warriors in the sight of the slayer; they carved that from bright stone,
they set the Lord of victories in there.[5] They began to sing the sorrow-song
 for him,
wretched in the evening-time; then they wanted to travel again,
weary from the glorious Lord. He rested there with little company.
  Nevertheless, weeping, we[6] stood there a good while   70
in a fixed position, after the voice departed up
of the warriors. The corpse grew cold,
the fair life-dwelling. Then men began to fell us
all to the ground: that was a terrible fate.
Men buried us in a deep pit; nevertheless the Lord's thanes,   75
friends,[7] discovered me there,
adorned me with gold and silver.
  Now you might hear, my beloved hero,
that I have experienced the work of evil-doers,
grievous sorrows. Now the time has come   80
that I will be honoured far and wide
by men over the earth and all this glorious creation;
they will pray to this beacon. On me the Son of God
suffered for a while; because of that I am glorious now,
towering under the heavens, and I am able to heal   85
each one of those who is in awe of me.
Formerly I was made the hardest of punishments,
most hateful to the people, before I opened for them,
for the voice-bearers, the true way of life.
Listen, the Lord of glory, the Guardian of the kingdom of heaven,   90
then honoured me over the forest trees,
just as he, almighty God, also honoured
his mother, Mary herself, for all men,
over all womankind.[8]
  Now I urge you, my beloved man,   95
that you tell men about this vision:
reveal with words that it is the tree of glory
on which almighty God suffered
for mankind's many sins
and Adam's ancient deeds.   100

5. Cf. Matt 27:57–60.
6. "We" are the three crosses: that of Christ and those of the two thieves crucified with him [translator's note; cf. Mark 15:27 and parallels].
7. Helena, mother of Constantine, and Saint Cyriac [supposedly] discovered the Cross in the fourth century [translator's note].
8. Cf. Luke 1:42.

Death he tasted there; nevertheless, the Lord rose again
with his great might to help mankind.
He ascended into heaven. He will come again
to this earth to seek mankind
on doomsday, the Lord himself,   105
almighty God, and his angels with him,
so that he will then judge, he who has the power of judgement,
each one of them, for what they themselves have
earned here earlier in this transitory life.
Nor may any of them be unafraid there   110
because of the words which the Saviour will speak:
he will ask in front of the multitude where the person might be
who for the Lord's name would
taste bitter death, just as he did before on that tree.
But then they will be fearful and little think   115
what they might begin to say to Christ.
Then there will be no need for any of those to be very afraid
who bear before them in the breast the best of trees.
But by means of the rood each soul
who thinks to dwell with the Ruler   120
must seek the kingdom from the earthly way.'
    I prayed to the tree with a happy spirit then,
with great zeal, there where I was alone
with little company. My spirit was
inspired with longing for the way forward; I experienced in all   125
many periods of longing. It is now my life's hope
that I might seek the tree of victory
alone more often than all men,
to honour it well. My desire for that is
great in my mind, and my hope of protection is   130
directed to the cross. I do not have many wealthy
friends on earth; but they have gone forward from here,
passed from the joys of this world, sought for themselves the King of glory;
they live now in heaven with the High Father,
they dwell in glory. And I myself hope   135
each day for when the Lord's cross,
that I looked at here on earth,
will fetch me from this transitory life,
and then bring me where there is great bliss,
joy in heaven, where the Lord's people   140
are set in feasting, where there is unceasing bliss;
and he will then set me where I might afterwards
dwell in glory fully with the saints
to partake of joy. May the Lord be a friend to me,
he who here on earth suffered previously   145
on the gallows-tree for the sins of man.

He redeemed us, and gave us life,
a heavenly home. Hope was renewed
with dignity and with joy for those who suffered burning there.
The Son was victorious in that undertaking,[9]   150
powerful and successful, when he came with the multitudes,
a troop of souls, into God's kingdom,
the one Ruler almighty, to the delight of angels
and all the saints who were in heaven before,
who dwelled in glory, when their Ruler came,   155
almighty God, to where his native land was.

WILLIAM DUNBAR

Done Is a Battell on the Dragon Blak[†]

1

Done is a battell on the dragon blak,
Our campioun Chryst confoundit hes his force,
The yettis of hell ar brokin with a crak,
The signe triumphall rasit is of the croce.
The divillis trymmillis with hiddous voce,   5
The saulis ar borrowit and to the blis can go.
Chryst with his blud our ransonis dois indoce:
Surrexit dominus de sepulchro.

2

Dungin is the deidly dragon, Lucifer,
The crewall serpent with the mortall stang,   10
The auld kene tegir, with his teith on char,

9. "That undertaking" refers to the Harrowing of Hell, when Christ rescued the souls who had been condemned to hell following the centuries after the Fall of Man. This apocryphal event took place in the days between Christ's Crucifixion and Resurrection [translator's note; the tradition is based on 1 Pet 3:18–20; 4:6].
† From *William Dunbar: Selected Poems,* ed. Priscilla Bawcutt (London: Longman, 1996), 77–79. Except as indicated, all glosses are Bawcutt's. Willam Dunbar (ca. 1465–ca. 1530), Scottish poet and Catholic priest.
1. *Done]* Completed.
2. *campioun]* Champion. *confoundit]* Overthrown.
3. *yettis]* Gates. *crak]* Explosion. [Lines 3–6 recount Christ's Harrowing of Hell. See note 9 above.]
5. *divillis]* Devils. *trymmillis]* Tremble. *voce]* Voice.
6. *saulis]* Souls. *borrowit]* Redeemed.
7. *ransonis]* Ransoms. *indoce]* Endorse.
8] [Latin for] the lord has risen from the tomb [see Luke 24:34].
9. *Dungin]* Beaten.
10. *Crewall]* Cruel. [*serpent]* See Rev 12:9; 20:2–3 and notes.] *mortall stang]* Deadly sting.

Quhilk in a wait hes lyne for us so lang,
Thinking to grip us in his clowis strang.
The mercifull lord wald nocht that it wer so.
He maid him for to felye of that fang: 15
Surrexit dominus de sepulchro.

3

He for our saik that sufferit to be slane
And lyk a lamb in sacrifice wes dicht,
Is lyk a lyone rissin up agane
And as a gyane raxit him on hicht.   20
Sprungin is Aurora, radius and bricht,
On loft is gone the glorius Appollo,
The blisfull day departit fro the nycht:
Surrexit dominus de sepulchro.

4

The grit victour agane is rissin on hicht,   25
That for our querrell to the deth wes woundit.
The sone that wox all paill now schynis bricht,
And, dirknes clerit, our fayth is now refoundit.
The knell of mercy fra the hevin is soundit,
The Cristin ar deliverit of thair wo,   30
The Jowis and thair errour ar confoundit:
Surrexit dominus de sepulchro.

5

The fo is chasit, the battell is done ceis,
The presone brokin, the jevellouris fleit and flemit,

11. *kene tegir]* Fierce tiger. [The image recalls 1 Pet 5:8.] *on char]* Bared.
12. *wait]* Ambush. *lyne]* Lain.
13. *clowis]* Claws.
14. *wald nocht]* Did not wish.
15. *felye . . . fang]* Be deprived of that prey.
18. *dicht]* Prepared.
20] And as a giant stretched himself on high. [The line echoes Vulg. Ps 19:5: "He rejoiced as a giant to finish his race."]
21. *Sprungin]* Risen. *radius]* Radiant.
22. *On loft]* On high. [*Appollo]* The sun.]
23. *departit]* Separated.
26. *querrell]* Cause.
27. *sone]* Sun. *wox]* Grew. [The line recalls Mark 15:33 and parallels.]
28. *dirknes clerit]* Darkness cleared away. *refoundit]* Re-established.
29. *knell]* Peal of bells.
30. *Cristin]* Christians.
31. *Jowis]* Jews. *errour]* Erroneous belief.
33. *done ceis]* Finished.
34. *jevellouris]* Gaolers. *fleit]* Terrified. *flemit]* Put to flight.

The weir is gon, confermit is the peis,   35
The fetteris lowsit and the dungeoun temit,
The ransoun maid, the presoneris redemit,
The feild is win, ourcumin is the fo,
Dispulit of the tresur that he yemit:
Surrexit dominus de sepulchro.   40

JOHN DONNE[†]

La Corona[1]

1.

Deign[2] *at my hands this crown of prayer and praise,*
Weav'd in my low, devout melancholy,
Thou which of good hast, yea, art treasury,
All changing unchang'd Ancient of Days.[3]
But do not, with a vile crown of frail bays,[4]   5
Reward my muse's white sincerity,
But what thy thorny crown gain'd, that give me,
A crown of glory, which doth flower always.
The ends crown our works, but thou crown'st our ends,
So at our end begins our endless rest.   10
This first last end, now zealously possess'd,
With a strong sober thirst, my soul attends.
'Tis time that voice and heart be lifted high,
Salvation to all that will is nigh.

2. Annunciation.[5]

Salvation to all that will is nigh:
That All, which always is all everywhere,

35. *weir*] War. *gon*] Ended. *confermit*] Formally ratified. *peis*] Peace.
36. *lowsit*] Loosened. *temit*] Emptied.
37. *redemit*] Redeemed.
38. *feild*] Battle. *win*] Won. *ourcumin*] Overcome.
39] Deprived of the treasure that he guarded. [The line recalls Mark 3:27 (see note) and parallels.]
† The following selection comes from *John Donne's Poetry*, ed. Donald R. Dickson, Norton Critical Edition (New York: Norton, 2007), 133–36. Except as indicated, all notes are Dickson's. John Donne (ca. 1571–1631), English poet and Anglican priest.
1. As the title indicates, these seven sonnets form a sequence in which the last line of each poem is repeated as the first line of the next, thus forming a crown or *corona*.
2. Think it worthy to accept (*OED*).
3. A name emphasizing God's eternal being, from Daniel 7:9.
4. The poet's laurel crown.
5. Gabriel's announcement to Mary that she would bear a child [see Luke 1:26–38].

Which cannot sin, and yet all sins must bear,
Which cannot die, yet cannot choose but die,
Lo, faithful Virgin, yields himself to lie   5
In prison, in thy womb; and though he there
Can take no sin, nor thou give, yet he'll wear,
Taken from thence, flesh, which death's force may try.[6]
Ere by the spheres time was created, thou
Wast in his mind, who is thy son and brother;   10
Whom thou conceiv'st, conceiv'd; yea thou art now
Thy Maker's maker, and thy Father's mother,
Thou hast light in dark, and shutt'st in little room,
Immensity,[7] cloister'd in thy dear womb.

3. Nativity.

Immensity, cloister'd in thy dear womb,
Now leaves his well-belov'd imprisonment.
There he hath made himself to his intent
Weak enough, now into our world to come.
But oh, for thee, for him, hath th'inn no room?   5
Yet lay him in this stall, and from th'Orient,
Stars and wise men will travel to prevent[8]
Th'effect of Herod's jealous, general doom.[9]
Seest thou, my soul, with thy faith's eyes, how he
Which fills all place, yet none holds him, doth lie?   10
Was not his pity towards thee wondrous high,
That would have need to be pitied by thee?
Kiss him, and with him into Egypt go,
With his kind mother, who partakes thy woe.

4. Temple.[1]

With his kind mother, who partakes thy woe,
Joseph, turn back; see where your child doth sit,
Blowing, yea blowing out those sparks of wit,
Which himself on those doctors did bestow.
The Word[2] but lately could not speak, and lo,   5
It suddenly speaks wonders: Whence comes it,
That all which was, and all which should be writ,
A shallow seeming child should deeply know?

6. Attempt to conquer.
7. Infinite being.
8. Come before, anticipate.
9. Herod's slaughter of the innocents (Matthew 2: [13–]16).
1. At the age of twelve Jesus stayed behind (after Mary and Joseph left) to answer questions posed by the doctors at the Temple (Luke 2:41–49).
2. Logos [Greek], identified with Jesus in John 1:14.

His Godhead was not soul to his manhood,[3]
Nor had time mellow'd him to this ripeness;   10
But as to'one which hath long tasks, thinks good
With the sun to begin his business,
He in his age's morning thus began,
By miracles exceeding power of man.

5. *Crucifying.*

By miracles exceeding power of man,
He faith in some, envy in some begat,
For, what meek spirits admire, ambitious hate.
In both affections many to him ran.
But oh, the worst are most, they will and can,   5
Alas, and do, unto th'immaculate,
Whose creature fate is, now prescribe a fate,
Measuring self-life's infinity t'a span,[4]
Nay to an inch. Lo, where condemned he
Bears his own cross, with pain, yet by and by   10
When it bears him, he must bear more and die.
Now thou art lifted up, draw me to thee,
And at thy death, giving such liberal dole,[5]
Moist, with one drop of thy blood, my dry soul.

6. *Resurrection.*

Moist with one drop of thy blood, my dry soul
Shall (though she now be in extreme degree
Too stony hard, and yet too fleshly)[6] be
Freed by that drop, from being starv'd, hard or foul,
And life, by thy death abled, shall control   5
Death, whom thy death slew; nor shall to me
Fear of first or last death bring misery,
If in thy life-book[7] my name thou enroll.
Flesh in that last long sleep is not putrefi'd,
But made that there, of which, and for which 'twas;[8]   10
Nor can by other means be glorified.
May then sin's sleep, and death's, soon from me pass,

3. Christ was fully God and fully man with a human soul in a human body.
4. The length of a human life; a *span* was the distance from the tip of the thumb to the tip of the little finger (*OED*).
5. An allotted portion.
6. The heart of stone that must be turned to flesh is a common trope; see Ezekiel 11:19: "And I will give them one heart, and I will put a new spirit within you; and I will take the stony heart out of their flesh, and will give them an heart of flesh."
7. See Rev 3:5 and note [editors' note].
8. Genesis 3:19: "Dust thou art, and unto dust shalt thou return."

That wak'd from both, I again risen may
Salute the last, and everlasting day.

7. Ascension.

Salute the last and everlasting day,
Joy at th'uprising of this sun, and son,
Ye whose true tears, or tribulation
Hath purely wash'd, or burnt your drossy clay.
Behold, the highest, parting hence away,   5
Lightens the dark clouds, which he treads upon;[9]
Nor doth he by ascending show alone,
But first he, and he first, enters the way.
O strong ram,[1] which hast batter'd heaven for me,
Mild lamb, which with thy blood hast mark'd the path,   10
Bright torch, which shin'st, that I the way may see,
Oh, with thine own blood quench thine own just wrath;
And if thy Holy Spirit my muse did raise,
Deign at my hands this crown of prayer and praise.

GEORGE HERBERT[†]

The Agonie[1]

Philosophers have measured mountains,
Fathom'd the depth of seas, of states, and kings,
Walk'd with a staffe to heav'n, and traced fountains:
    But there are two vast, spacious things,
The which to measure it doth more behove: 5
Yet few there are that sound them; Sinne and Love.

Who would know Sinne, let him repair
Unto Mount Olivet; there shall he see
A man so wrung with pains, that all his hair,
    His skinne, his garments, bloudie be.[2]   10
Sinne is that presse[3] and vice, which forceth pain

---

9. Cf. Acts 1:9 [editors' note].
1. Christ is typologically associated with the ram in the thicket, sacrificed by Abraham in place of Isaac (Genesis 22:13).
† The following selections come from *The Poetical Works of George Herbert*, ed. Robert Aris Willmott (Boston: Little, Brown and Company, 1855), 37, 40–41, 218. George Herbert, English poet (born in Wales) and Anglican priest (1593–1633).
1. See Mark 14:32–42 and parallels, a scene traditionally called Christ's Agony.
2. Cf. Luke 22:44.
3. Cf. Isa 63:3.

To hunt his cruell food through ev'ry vein.

Who knows not Love, let him assay,
And taste that juice, which on the crosse a pike
Did set again abroach;[4] then let him say   15
    If ever he did taste the like.
Love is that liquor sweet and most divine,
Which my God feels as bloud, but I as wine.

Sepulchre

O blessed bodie! whither art thou thrown?
No lodging for thee, but a cold hard stone?[5]
So many hearts on earth, and yet not one
                    Receive thee?

Sure there is room within our hearts good store;   5
For they can lodge transgressions by the score:
Thousands of toyes dwell there, yet out of doore
                    They leave thee.

But that which shews them large shews them unfit.
Whatever sinne did this pure rock commit,   10
Which holds thee now?   Who hath indited it
                    Of murder?

Where our hard hearts have took up stones to brain thee,[6]
And missing this, most falsely did arraigne thee;[7]
Onely these stones in quiet entertain thee,   15
                    And order.

And as of old the law, by heav'nly art,
Was writ in stone; so thou, which also art
The letter of the word, find'st no fit heart
                    To hold thee.[8]   20

Yet do we still persist as we began,
And so should perish, but that nothing can,
Though it be cold, hard, foul, from loving man
                    Withhold thee.

4. Cf. John 19:34. The eucharistic imagery in the rest of the stanza recalls John 6:53–56; 7:37–39.
5. A conflation of Luke 2:7 and 23:53.
6. Cf. John 10:31.
7. A reference to Jesus' trial before Pilate (Mark 15:1–15 and parallels).
8. Cf. 2 Cor 3:1–3 and notes.

Marie Magdalene[9]

When blessed Marie wip'd her Saviours feet,
(Whose precepts she had trampled on before,)
And wore them for a jewell on her head,
   Shewing his steps should be the street
   Wherein she thenceforth evermore   5
With pensive humblenesse would live and tread:

She being stain'd herself, why did she strive
To make Him clean who could not be defil'd?
Why kept she not her tears for her own faults,
   And not his feet? Though we could dive   10
   In tears like seas, our sinnes are pil'd
Deeper then they in words, and works, and thoughts.

Deare soul, she knew who did vouchsafe and deigne
To bear her filth, and that her sinnes did dash
Ev'n God himself: wherefore she was not loth,   15
   As she had brought wherewith to stain,
   So to bring in wherewith to wash;
And yet, in washing one, she washed both.

RICHARD CRASHAW

On St. Peter cutting off Malchus his eare[†]

Well, Peter, dost thou wield thy active sword;[1]
Well for thyselfe, I meane, not for thy Lord.
To strike at eares is to take heed there bee
No witnesse, Peter, of thy perjury.[2]

And He answered them nothing[3]

O mighty Nothing! unto thee,
Nothing, wee owe all things that bee.

9. Herbert participates in a tradition of identifying the sinful woman who washed Jesus' feet (Luke 7:36–50) with Mary Magdalene, one of Jesus' disciples (Luke 8:1–3; 23:55–24:10).
† The following epigrams come from *The Complete Works of Richard Crashaw*, vol. 2, ed. Alexander B. Grosart (London: Robson and Sons, 1873), 64, 108, 144, 164. Richard Crashaw, English poet, Anglican priest, and eventual convert to catholicism (ca. 1612–1649).
1. Cf. John 18:10.
2. Cf. John 18:25–27; compare Emily Dickinson's "He forgot - and I - remembered" and Elizabeth Bishop's "Roosters," both on the same theme (below, pp. 1301–02, 1321–25).
3. Cf. Matt 27:12.

God spake once when hee all things made,[4]
Hee sav'd all when hee Nothing said.
The world was made of Nothing then;   5
'Tis made by Nothing now againe.

To Pontius washing his blood-stained hands[5]

Is murther no sin? or a sin so cheape
            That thou need'st heape
A rape upon't? Till thy adult'rous touch
   Taught her these sullied cheeks, this blubber'd face,
She was a nimph,[6] the meadowes knew none such;   5
   Of honest parentage, of unstain'd race;
The daughter of a faire and well-fam'd fountaine
As ever silver-tipt the side of shady mountaine.

See how she weeps, and weeps, that she appeares
           Nothing but teares: 10
Each drop's a teare that weeps for her own wast.
   Harke how at every touch she does complaine her;
Harke how she bids her frighted drops make hast,
   And with sad murmurs chides the hands that stain her.
Leave, leave, for shame; or else, good judge, decree   15
What water shal wash this when this hath washèd thee.

On our crucified Lord naked and bloody[7]

Th' have left thee naked, Lord: O that they had!
This garment too I would they had deny'd.
Thee with thyselfe they have too richly clad,
Opening the purple wardrobe of thy side.[8]
   O never could bee found garments too good   5
   For thee to weare, but these of thine own blood.

4. Cf. Gen 1:3, 6, 9.
5. See Matt 27:24.
6. A nymph—in classical mythology, a lesser female divinity typically associated with a specific natural feature (spring, tree, mountain, etc.).
7. See Mark 15:16–20 and parallels.
8. Cf. John 19:34.

HENRY VAUGHAN

The Night[†]

John 2. 3[1]

Through that pure *Virgin-shrine*,
That sacred vail drawn o'r thy glorious noon
That men might look and live as Glo-worms shine,
   And face the Moon:
  Wise *Nicodemus* saw such light   5
As made him know his God by night.

Most blest believer he!
Who in that land of darkness and blinde eyes
Thy long expected healing wings could see,
   When thou didst rise,[2]   10
  And what can never more be done,
Did at mid-night speak with the Sun!

O who will tell me, where
He found thee at that dead and silent hour!
What hallow'd solitary ground did bear   15
   So rare a flower,
  Within whose sacred leafs did lie
The fulness of the Deity.

No mercy-seat[3] of gold,
No dead and dusty *Cherub*, nor carv'd stone,   20
But his own living works did my Lord hold
   And lodge alone;
  Where *trees* and *herbs* did watch and peep
And wonder, while the *Jews* did sleep.

Dear night! this worlds defeat;   25
The stop to busie fools; cares check and curb;
The day of Spirits; my souls calm retreat
   Which none disturb!
  Christs progress, and his prayer time;[4]
The hours to which high Heaven doth chime.   30

---

† From *The Works of Henry Vaughan*, vol. 2, ed. Leonard Cyril Martin (Oxford: Clarendon Press, 1914), 522–23. Henry Vaughan, Welsh poet (1622–1695).
1. The epigraph is apparently in error. In John 3:2 the Pharisee Nicodemus comes to Jesus "by night" in order to converse with him.
2. Echoing Mal 4:2.
3. Cf. Exod 25:17–22; 1 Kgs 8:6–9.
4. Vaughan himself cites Mark 1:35 and Luke 21:37 in a note in the 1655 edition.

Gods silent, searching flight:
When my Lords head is fill'd with dew, and all
His locks are wet with the clear drops of night;
     His still, soft call;
His knocking time;[5] The souls dumb watch,   35
When Spirits their fair kinred catch.

          Were all my loud, evil days
Calm and unhaunted as is thy dark Tent,
Whose peace but by some *Angels* wing or voice
     Is seldom rent;   40
Then I in Heaven all the long year
Would keep, and never wander here.

          But living where the Sun
Doth all things wake, and where all mix and tyre
Themselves and others, I consent and run   45
     To ev'ry myre,
And by this worlds ill-guiding light,
Erre more then I can do by night.

          There is in God (some say)
A deep, but dazling darkness; As men here   50
Say it is late and dusky, because they
     See not all clear;
O for that night! where I in him
Might live invisible and dim.

JOHN MILTON

Sonnet XIX[†]

When I consider how my light is spent,[1]
     Ere half my days, in this dark world[2] and wide,
     And that one talent which is death to hide
Lodged with me useless,[3] though my soul more bent
To serve therewith my Maker, and present   5
     My true account, lest he returning chide,

5. Echoing Song 5:2.
† From *Milton's Selected Poetry and Prose*, ed. Jason P. Rosenblatt, Norton Critical Edition (New York: Norton, 2010), 87–88. John Milton (1608–1674), English poet and radical Protestant nonconformist.
1. Perhaps subtly echoing Matt 25:1–13 or Luke 12:35–40.
2. Milton became blind in his forties.
3. See Matt 25:18, 26; Matthew's parable of the Talents (25:14–30; cf. Luke 19:11–27) lies behind this sonnet.

"Doth God exact day-labor, light denied?"[4]
I fondly[5] ask; but Patience to prevent
That murmur soon replies: "God doth not need
    Either man's work or his own gifts; who best
    Bear his mild yoke,[6] they serve him best. His state   10
Is kingly: thousands at his bidding speed
    And post o'er land and ocean without rest;
    They also serve who only stand and wait."[7]

WILLIAM BLAKE

The Everlasting Gospel[†]

[m][1]

I will tell you what Joseph of Arimathea[2]
Said to my Fairy:[3] was not it very queer?
'Pliny and Trajan![4] What! are you here?
Come before Joseph of Arimathea.

---

4. Recalling the parable of the Workers in the Vineyard (Matt 20:1–16), also echoed in the final verse. The sonnet thus mediates between the two Mathean parables.
5. Foolishly.
6. Echoing Matt 11:28–30.
7. Cf. Matt 20:3–7.
† From *The Poetical Works of William Blake*, ed. John Sampson (London: Oxford University Press, 1914), 139, 146–158.
    Several fragments scattered throughout a notebook of the English poet and artist William Blake (1757–1827) commonly referred to as the Rossetti MS (because Dante Gabriel Rossetti acquired it and was first to transcribe, edit, and publish the works it included) seem to belong to a long poem that Blake left incomplete at the time of his death. One of the fragments is titled "The Everlasting Gospel" and this was probably the name Blake intended for the entire work. The fragments have been frequently edited, and we print here John Sampson's version, which is amended in light of a contemporary consensus among Blake scholars as to the fragments' shape and likely order of composition. We also label the fragments according to Geoffrey Keynes's scheme (*The Complete Writings of William Blake* (rev edn; London: Oxford University Press, 1966), which has become conventional. Punctuation (wholly lacking in the MS) is Sampson's, and he in other ways as well normalizes the text to a significant degree.
    Following David Erdman (*The Complete Poetry and Prose of William Blake* [newly rev edn; Berkeley: University of California Press, 2008]), David Fuller (*William Blake: Selected Poetry and Prose* [rev edn; New York: Pearson, 2008]), and others, we present six fragments from the notebook as the text of "The Everlasting Gospel" (k, f, i, e, l, h), with another two as a prefix (m and n). Fragment d was sown into the notebook and we include it as an appendix, as well as one other couplet, g, which was written below f in the MS and followed by a catch phrase apparently linking it to a lost section of the poem. An additional fragment (j) is simply an earlier version of k and so not included at all. Finally, three fragments not from the Rossetti MS but associated with the poem (including one paragraph in prose) are entirely omitted. They are widely available elsewhere, including in David Owen's hypertext edition of the poem: http://www.english.uga.edu/wblake/EverlastingGospel/egtp.html.
1. These lines were written in the margins of one of the notebook pages.
2. Cf. Mark 15:43–46 and parallels.
3. Blake frequently figures his muse as a fairy.
4. An allusion to the correspondence of Pliny and Trajan about the persecution of Christians in Bithynia (see Appendix, pp. 987–89).

Listen patient, and when Joseph has done
'Twill make a fool laugh, and a fairy fun.'

[*n*]⁵

What can be done with such desperate fools
Who follow after the heathen schools?
I was standing by when Jesus died;
What I[6] call'd humility, they call'd pride.

[*k*]⁷

The Everlasting Gospel

Was Jesus humble? or did He
Give any proofs of humility?
Boast of high things with humble tone,
And give with charity a stone?
When but a child He ran away,   5
And left His parents in dismay.
When they had wander'd three days long
These were the words upon His tongue:
'No earthly parents I confess:
I am doing My Father's business.'[8]   10
When the rich learnèd Pharisee
Came to consult Him secretly,
Upon his heart with iron pen
He wrote 'Ye must be born again.'[9]
He was too proud to take a bribe;   15
He spoke with authority, not like a Scribe.[1]
He says with most consummate art
'Follow Me, I am meek and lowly of heart,[2]
As that is the only way to escape
The miser's net and the glutton's trap.   20
He who loves his enemies betrays his friends.
This surely is not what Jesus intends;[3]
But the sneaking pride of heroic schools,

---

5. These lines were written adjacent to k in the notebook and Sampson includes them as ll. 21–25 of that section. But Blake did not signal his intent to include them there and more recent editors treat them as a separate section. We follow this practice, excising them from k and renumbering k's lines accordingly.

6. Joseph of Arimathea?
7. Sampson labels this fragment γ.
8. Cf. Luke 2:40–52; Mark 3:31–35 and parallels.
9. Cf. John 3:1–9.
1. Cf. Matt 7:29; Mark 1:22; Luke 4:32.
2. Cf. Matt 11:28–29.
3. Cf. Matt 5:43–44.

And the Scribes' and Pharisees' virtuous rules;
For He acts with honest, triumphant pride,   25
And this is the cause that Jesus died.
He did not die with Christian ease,
Asking pardon of His enemies:[4]
If He had, Caiaphas[5] would forgive;
Sneaking submission can always live.   30
He had only to say that God was the Devil,
And the Devil was God, like a Christian civil;
Mild Christian regrets to the Devil confess
For affronting him thrice in the wilderness;[6]
He had soon been bloody Caesar's elf,   35
And at last he would have been Caesar himself,
Like Dr. Priestly and Bacon and Newton—[7]
Poor spiritual knowledge is not worth a button!
For thus the Gospel Sir Isaac confutes:
'God can only be known by His attributes;   40
And as for the indwelling of the Holy Ghost,
Or of Christ and His Father, it's all a boast
And pride, and vanity of the imagination,
That disdains to follow this world's fashion.'
To teach doubt and experiment   45
Certainly was not what Christ meant.
What was He doing all that time,
From twelve years old[8] to manly prime?
Was He then idle, or the less
About His Father's business?   50
Or was His wisdom held in scorn
Before His wrath began to burn
In miracles throughout the land,
That quite unnerv'd Lord Caiaphas's hand?[9]
If He had been Antichrist,[1] Creeping Jesus,   55
He'd have done anything to please us;
Gone sneaking into synagogues,
And not us'd the Elders and Priests like dogs;

4. Lines 27–28 anticipate the peculiar interpretation of Luke's version of Christ's death on the cross (23:33–46) in ll. 79ff.
5. The high priest during Jesus' ministry, who was partly responsible for his execution (Matt 26:3–4; John 11:47–50).
6. Cf. Matt 4:1–11 and parallels.
7. Joseph Priestly (1733–1804), Francis Bacon (1561–1626), and Isaac Newton (1642–1727) were all important English scientists.
8. Cf. Luke 2:41–52.
9. Sampson prints "the Seraph band," apparently an erroneous transcription from Blake's notebook.
1. Cf. 1 John 2:18 and note.

But humble as a lamb or ass[2]
Obey'd Himself to Caiaphas.   60
God wants not man to humble himself:
That is the trick of the Ancient Elf.
This is the race that Jesus ran:
Humble to God, haughty to man,
Cursing the Rulers before the people   65
Even to the Temple's highest steeple,[3]
And when He humbled Himself to God
Then descended the cruel rod.
'If Thou humblest Thyself, Thou humblest Me.
Thou also dwell'st in Eternity.   70
Thou art a Man: God is no more:
Thy own Humanity learn to adore,
For that is My spirit of life.
Awake, arise to spiritual strife,
And Thy revenge abroad display   75
In terrors at the last Judgement Day.
God's mercy and long suffering
Is but the sinner to judgement to bring.
Thou on the Cross for them shalt pray—[4]
And take revenge at the Last Day.'   80
Jesus replied, and thunders hurl'd:
'I never will pray for the world.[5]
Once I did so when I pray'd in the Garden;
I wish'd to take with Me a bodily pardon.'[6]
Can that which was of woman born,   85
In the absence of the morn,
When the Soul fell into sleep,
And Archangels round it weep,
Shooting out against the light
Fibres of a deadly night,   90
Reasoning upon its own dark fiction,
In doubt which is self-contradiction?
Humility is only doubt,
And does the sun and moon blot out,
Rooting over with thorns and stems   95
The buried soul and all its gems.

2. The NT sometimes equates Jesus with a sacrificial lamb (John 1:29; Rev 5:6; etc.). For the ass, see Matt 21:1–9.
3. Cf. Mark 11:27–13:4 and parallels.
4. Cf. Luke 23:34.
5. Cf. John 17:9.
6. Cf. Mark 14:32–42 and parallels.

This life's dim[7] windows of the soul
Distorts the Heavens from pole to pole,
And leads you to believe a lie
When you see with, not thro', the eye   100
That was born in a night, to perish in a night,
When the soul slept in the beams of light.

[*f*][8]

Was Jesus chaste? or did He
Give any lessons of chastity?
The Morning blushèd fiery red:
Mary was found in adulterous bed;
Earth groan'd beneath, and Heaven above   5
Trembled at discovery of Love
Jesus was sitting in Moses' chair.[9]
They brought the trembling woman there.
Moses commands she be ston'd to death.
What was the sound of Jesus' breath?   10
He laid His hand on Moses' law;[1]
The ancient Heavens, in silent awe,
Writ with curses from pole to pole,
All away began to roll.
The Earth trembling and naked lay   15
In secret bed of mortal clay;
On Sinai felt the Hand Divine
Pulling back the bloody shrine;
And she heard the breath of God,
As she heard by Eden's flood: 20
'Good and Evil are no more![2]
Sinai's trumpets[3] cease to roar!
Cease, finger of God, to write![4]
The Heavens are not clean in Thy sight.
Thou art good, and Thou alone;[5]   25
Nor may the sinner cast one stone.
To be good only, is to be
A Devil[6] or else a Pharisee.

7. Sampson prints "five," apparently an erroneous transcription from Blake's notebook.
8. Sampson labels this fragment ξ.
9. Cf. Matt 23:2 and note.
1. Cf. John 8:1–11.
2. A reference to the creation and/or to the time before Eve acquired knowledge of good and evil (see Gen 1–3).
3. The trumpets that sounded at God's giving of the Law (Exod 19:13, 16, 19; 20:18).
4. Cf. Exod 31:18; there is also a reference to John 8:8.
5. Cf. Mark 10:18 and parallels.
6. Sampson prints "God," but the MS shows that Blake crossed "God" out and wrote "Devil."

Thou Angel of the Presence Divine,[7]
That didst create this Body of Mine,   30
Wherefore hast thou writ these laws
And created Hell's dark jaws?
My Presence I will take from thee:
A cold leper thou shalt be.
Tho' thou wast so pure and bright   35
That Heaven was impure in thy sight,
Tho' thy oath turn'd Heaven pale,
Tho' thy covenant built Hell's jail,
Tho' thou didst all to chaos roll
With the Serpent for its soul,[8]   40
Still the breath Divine does move,
And the breath Divine is Love.
Mary, fear not! Let me see
The seven devils that torment thee.[9]
Hide not from My sight thy sin,   45
That forgiveness thou may'st win.
Has no man condemnèd thee?'
'No man, Lord.' 'Then what is he
Who shall accuse thee? Come ye forth,
Fallen fiends of heavenly birth,   50
That have forgot your ancient love,
And driven away my trembling Dove.
You shall bow before her feet;
You shall lick the dust for meat;[1]
And tho' you cannot love, but hate,   55
Shall be beggars at Love's gate.
What was thy love? Let Me see it;
Was it love or dark deceit?'
'Love too long from me has fled;
'Twas dark deceit, to earn my bread;   60
'Twas covet, or 'twas custom, or
Some trifle not worth caring for;
That they may call a shame and sin
Love's temple that God dwelleth in,[2]
And hide in secret hidden shrine   65
The naked Human Form Divine,
And render that a lawless thing
On which the Soul expands its wing.

7. Cf. Exod 14:19.
8. For God's imprisonment of the serpent (Satan), see Rev 20:1–3. OT poetry associating chaos with serpentine monsters that God subdues as he creates is also relevant (see Ps 74:12–17 and notes).
9. Equating the woman caught in adultery with Mary Magdalene (see Luke 8:2).
1. Cf. Gen 3:14, with the serpent commonly interpreted as Satan, a fallen angel (cf. l. 95 below).
2. Cf. 1 Cor 6:19.

But this, O Lord, this was my sin,
When first I let these devils in,   70
In dark pretence to chastity
Blaspheming Love, blaspheming Thee,
Thence rose secret adulteries,
And thence did covet also rise.
My sin Thou hast forgiven me;   75
Canst Thou forgive my blasphemy?
Canst Thou return to this dark hell,
And in my burning bosom dwell?
And canst Thou die that I may live?
And canst Thou pity and forgive?'   80
Then roll'd the shadowy Man away
From the limbs of Jesus, to make them His prey,
An ever devouring appetite,
Glittering with festering venoms bright;
Crying 'Crucify this cause of distress,   85
Who don't keep the secrets of holiness!
All[3] mental powers by diseases we bind;
But He heals the deaf, the dumb, and the blind.[4]
Whom God has afflicted for secret ends,
He comforts and heals and calls them friends.'[5]   90
But, when Jesus was crucified,
Then was perfected His galling pride.
In three nights He devour'd His prey,
And still He devours the body of clay;
For dust and clay is the Serpent's meat,   95
Which never was made for Man to eat.

[i][6]

Was Jesus gentle, or did He
Give any marks of gentility?
When twelve years old He ran away,
And left His parents in dismay.
When after three days' sorrow found,   5
Loud as Sinai's trumpet-sound:
'No earthly parents I confess—
My Heavenly Father's business!
Ye understand not what I say,
And, angry, force Me to obey.[7]   10

---

3. Sampson prints "the," apparently an erroneous transcription from Blake's notebook.
4. Cf. Mark 7:37; Luke 7:22.
5. Cf. Matt 11:19 and parallel.
6. Sampson labels this fragment β.
7. Cf. Luke 2:40–52; Mark 3:31–35 and parallels.

Obedience is a duty then,
And favour gains with God and men.
John from the wilderness loud cried;[8]
Satan gloried in his pride.
'Come,' said Satan, 'come away,   15
I'll soon see if you'll obey!
John for disobedience bled,[9]
But you can turn the stones to bread.
God's high king and God's high priest
Shall plant their glories in your breast,   20
If Caiaphas you will obey,
If Herod you with bloody prey
Feed with the sacrifice, and be
Obedient, fall down, worship me.'[1]
Thunders and lightnings broke around,   25
And Jesus' voice in thunders' sound:
'Thus I seize the spiritual prey.
Ye smiters with disease, make way.
I come your King and God to seize,
Is God a smiter with disease?'   30
The God of this world[2] rag'd in vain:
He bound old Satan in His chain,[3]
And, bursting forth, His furious ire
Became a chariot of fire.[4]
Throughout the land He took His course,   35
And trac'd diseases to their source.
He curs'd the Scribe and Pharisee,
Trampling down hypocrisy.[5]
Where'er His chariot took its way,
There Gates of Death let in the Day,   40
Broke down from every chain and bar;
And Satan in His spiritual war
Dragg'd at His chariot-wheels: loud howl'd[6]
The God of this world: louder roll'd
The chariot-wheels, and louder still   45
His voice was heard from Zion's Hill,[7]
And in His hand the scourge shone bright;

8. Cf. Mark 1:2–4 and parallels.
9. Cf. Mark 6:14–29 and parallel.
1. Cf. Matt 4:1–11 and parallels.
2. Satan (cf. 2 Cor 4:4 and note; John 12:31).
3. Cf. Rev 20:1–3.
4. Cf. 2 Kgs 2:11.
5. Cf. Matt 23:1–36 and parallels.
6. Compare Achilles' dragging of Hector around the walls of Troy after killing him (*Iliad* 22.395–404).
7. The Temple Mount. For the following lines, see John 2:13–17.

He scourg'd the merchant Canaanite
From out the Temple of His Mind,
And in his body tight does bind   50
Satan and all his hellish crew;
And thus with wrath He did subdue
The serpent bulk of Nature's dross,
Till He had nail'd it to the Cross.
He took on sin in the Virgin's womb   55
And put it off on the Cross and tomb
To be worshipp'd by the Church of Rome.[8]

[e][9]

The Vision of Christ that thou dost see
Is my vision's greatest enemy.
Thine has a great hook nose like thine;
Mine has a snub nose like to mine.
Thine is the Friend of all Mankind;   5
Mine speaks in parables to the blind.[1]
Thine loves the same world that mine hates;
Thy heaven doors are my hell gates.
Socrates taught what Meletus[2]
Loath'd as a nation's bitterest curse,   10
And Caiaphas was in his own mind
A benefactor to mankind.
Both read the Bible day and night,
But thou read'st black where I read white.

[l][3]

I am sure this Jesus will not do,
Either for Englishman or Jew.

[h][4]

This was spoken by my Spectre to Voltaire,[5] Bacon, & c.

Did Jesus teach doubt? or did He
Give any lessons of philosophy,

---

8. The Catholic church.
9. Sampson labels this fragment α.
1. Cf. Mark 4:10–12 and parallels.
2. Meletus, whose accusation that Socrates was corrupting Athens' youth led to the philosopher's trial and execution. Cf. Blake, *Jerusalem* (plate 93): "Anytus Melitus & Lycon thought Socrates a very pernicious man. So Caiaphas thought Jesus."
3. Sampson labels this fragment θ. It appears in the margin of the MS by the conclusion of fragment k.
4. Sampson labels this fragment δ.
5. French deist and philosopher (1694–1778), repeatedly attacked by Blake.

Charge Visionaries with deceiving,
Or call men wise for not believing? . . .

[d][6]

Was Jesus born of a Virgin pure
With narrow soul and looks demure?
If He intended to take on sin
The Mother should an harlot been,
Just such a one as Magdalen,   5
With seven devils in her pen.[7]
Or were Jew virgins still more curs'd,
And more sucking devils nurs'd?
Or what was it which He took on
That He might bring salvation?   10
A body subject to be tempted,
From neither pain nor grief exempted;
Or such a body as might not feel
The passions that with sinners deal?
Yes, but they say He never fell.   15
Ask Caiaphas; for he can tell.—
'He mock'd the Sabbath, and He mock'd
The Sabbath's God, and He unlock'd
The evil spirits from their shrines,
And turn'd fishermen to divines;[8]   20
O'erturn'd the tent of secret sins,
And its golden cords and pins,
In the bloody shrine of war
Pour'd around from star to star,—[9]
Halls of justice, hating vice,   25
Where the Devil combs his lice.
He turn'd the devils into swine[1]
That He might tempt the Jews to dine;
Since which, a pig has got a look
That for a Jew may be mistook.   30
"Obey your parents."[2]—What says He?
"Woman, what have I to do with thee?[3]
No earthly parents I confess:
I am doing My Father's business."[4]

6. Sampson labels this fragment ε.
7. Cf. Luke 8:2.
8. Cf. Mark 1:16–20 and parallels.
9. Cf. John 2:13–17.
1. Cf. Mark 5:11–14 and parallels.
2. Cf. Exod 20:12; Deut 5:16.
3. John 2:4.
4. Cf. Luke 2:49.

He scorn'd Earth's parents, scorn'd Earth's God,   35
And mock'd the one and the other's rod;
His seventy Disciples sent
Against Religion and Government—[5]
They by the sword of Justice fell,
And Him their cruel murderer tell.   40
He left His father's trade to roam,
A wand'ring vagrant without home;
And thus He others' labour stole,
That He might live above control.
The publicans and harlots He   45
Selected for His company,
And from the adulteress turn'd away
God's righteous law, that lost its prey.'[6]

[g]

Seeing this False Christ, in fury and passion
I made my voice heard all over the nation.
What are those . . .

EMILY DICKINSON

["Sown in dishonor"!][†]

"Sown in dishonor"![1]
Ah! Indeed!
May *this* "dishonor" be?
If I were half so fine myself
I'd notice nobody!   5

"Sown in corruption"![2]
Not so fast!
Apostle is askew!
Corinthians 1. 15. narrates
A circumstance or two!   10

---

5. Cf. Luke 10:1–20.
6. Cf. John 8:1–11.
† The following selections come from *The Poems of Emily Dickinson: Reading Edition*, ed. R. W. Franklin (Cambridge, MA: Harvard University Press, 1999), 75, 99, 101, 105, 111–12, 180, 240–41, 299, 477, 627. Emily Dickinson (1830–1886), American poet.
1. 1 Cor 15:43.
2. 1 Cor 15:42.

[I shall know why - when Time is over]

I shall know why - when Time is over -
And I have ceased to wonder why -
Christ will explain each separate anguish
In the fair schoolroom of the sky -

He will tell me what "Peter" promised -   5
And I - for wonder at his woe[3]-
I shall forget the drop of anguish
That scalds me now - that scalds me now!

[Dying! Dying in the night!]

Dying! Dying in the night!
Wont somebody bring the light
So I can see which way to go
Into the everlasting snow?

And "Jesus"! Where is *Jesus* gone?   5
They said that Jesus - always came -
Perhaps he does'nt know the House -
This way, Jesus, Let him pass!

Somebody run to the great gate
And see if Dollie's[4] coming! Wait!   10
I hear her feet opon the stair!
Death wont hurt - now Dollie's here!

[He forgot - and I - remembered]

He forgot - and I - remembered -
'Twas an everyday affair -
Long ago as Christ and Peter -
"Warmed them" at the "Temple fire".

"Thou wert with him" - quoth "the Damsel"?   5
"*No*" - said Peter - 'twas'nt me[5] -

---

3. Cf. Mark 14:29–31, 66–72 and parallels. The quotation marks around *Peter* ironically invoke Matt 16:18 as well.
4. Perhaps a nickname for Susan Dickinson, Emily's sister-in-law; perhaps Emily's poetic alter ego.
5. The versions of Peter's denial from Luke (22:54–62) and John (18:15–18, 25–27) seem most relevant. Compare Richard Crashaw's "On St. Peter cutting off Malchus his eare" and Elizabeth Bishop's "Roosters" (pp. 1286, 1321–25), both on the same theme.

Jesus merely "looked" at Peter -
Could I do aught else - to Thee?

[You're right - "the way *is* narrow"]

You're right - "the way *is* narrow" -
And "difficult the Gate" -
And "few there be" - Correct again -
That "enter in - thereat"[6] -

'Tis* Costly - So are *purples!*[7]   5
'Tis just the price of *Breath* -
With but the "Discount" of *the Grave* -
Termed by the *Brokers* - "*Death*"!

And after *that* - there's Heaven -
The *Good* man's - "*Dividend*" -   10
And *Bad* men - "go to Jail"[8] -
I guess -

[Do People moulder equally]

Do People moulder equally,
They bury, in the Grave?
I do believe a species
As positively live

As I, who testify it   5
Deny that I - am dead -
And fill my Lungs, for Witness -
From Tanks - above my Head -

I say to you, said Jesus,
That there be standing here -
A sort, that shall not taste of Death[9] -   10
If Jesus was sincere -

I need no further Argue -
The statement of the Lord

6. The stanza quotes from Matt 7:13–14.
7. Cf. Matt 13:46.
8. Cf. Matt 25:14–30.
9. Cf. Mark 9:1 and parallels.

Is not a controvertible -   15
He told me, Death was dead[1] -

[He gave away his Life]

He gave away his Life -
To Us - Gigantic Sum -
A trifle - in his own esteem -
But magnified - by Fame[2]

Until it burst the Hearts   5
That fancied they could hold -
When swift it slipped it's limit -
And on the Heavens - unrolled -

'Tis Our's - to wince - and weep -
And wonder - and decay   10
By Blossom's gradual process -
He chose - Maturity -

And quickening - as we sowed -
Just obviated Bud -
And when We turned to note the Growth -   15
Broke - perfect - from the Pod[3] -

[One Crucifixion is recorded - only]

One Crucifixion is recorded - only -
How many be
Is not affirmed of Mathematics -
Or History -

One Calvary - exhibited to stranger -   5
As many be
As Persons - or Peninsulas -
Gethsemane[4] -

Is but a Province - in the Being's Centre -
Judea -   10

1. Cf. 1 Cor 15:54; Rev 20:14.
2. Cf. Phil 2:5–11.
3. Compare the imagery from 1 Cor 15:35–49.
4. Like Calvary, a place associated with Christ's passion; see Mark 14:32 and parallels; Luke 23:33.

For Journey - or Crusade's Achieving -
Too near -

Our Lord - indeed - made Compound Witness -
And yet -
There's newer - nearer Crucifixion   15
Than That -

[Of Paul and Silas it is said][5]

Of Paul and Silas it is said
They were in Prison laid
But when they went to take them out
They were not there instead.

Security the same insures   5
To our assaulted minds -
The staple must be optional
That an Immortal binds.

["Remember Me" implored the Thief][6]

"Remember Me" implored the Thief -
Oh Magnanimity!
My Visitor in Paradise
I give thee guaranty.

That Courtesy will fair remain   5
When the Delight is Dust
With which we cite this mightiest case
Of compensated Trust.

Of All, we are allowed to hope
But Affidavit stands   10
That this was due, where some, we fear,
Are unexpected friends -

[One crown that no one seeks][7]

One crown that no one seeks
And yet the highest head

5. See Acts 16:23–27.
6. See Luke 23:39–43.
7. See John 19:1–5; cf. Mark 15:9–20 and parallels.

It's isolation coveted
It's stigma deified

While Pontius Pilate lives   5
In whatsoever hell
That coronation pierces him
He recollects it well.

[Proud of my broken heart, since thou did'st break it]

Proud of my broken heart, since thou did'st break it,
Proud of the pain I did not feel till thee,

Proud of my night, since thou with moons dost slake it,
Not to partake thy passion, *my* humility.

Thou can'st not boast, like Jesus, drunken without companion   5
Was the strong cup of anguish brewed for the Nazarene[8]

Thou can'st not pierce tradition with the peerless puncture,
See! I usurped *thy* crucifix to honor mine!

CHRISTINA ROSSETTI

Good Friday[†]

Am I a stone, and not a sheep,
   That I can stand, O Christ, beneath Thy cross,
   To number drop by drop Thy Blood's slow loss,
And yet not weep?

Not so those women loved   5
   Who with exceeding grief lamented Thee;
   Not so fallen Peter weeping bitterly;
Not so the thief was moved;

Not so the Sun and Moon
   Which hid their faces in a starless sky,   10

---

8. Cf. Mark 14:32–42, esp. v. 36 and parallels.
† The following selections come from *The Poetical Works of Christina Georgina Rossetti* (London: Macmillan and Co., Ltd., 1904), 174–76, 234. Christina Rossetti, English poet (1830–1894).

A horror of great darkness at broad noon[1]—
    I, only I.

Yet give not o'er,
    But seek Thy sheep, true Shepherd of the flock;[2]
Greater than Moses, turn and look once more   15
    And smite a rock.[3]

St. Barnabas

'Now when we had discovered Cyprus, we
left it on the left hand.'—*Acts* xxi. 3.
'We sailed under Cyprus, because the
winds were contrary.'—*Acts* xxvii. 4.

St. Barnabas, with John his sister's son,
    Set sail for Cyprus; leaving in their wake
    That Chosen Vessel who for Jesus' sake
Proclaimed the Gentiles and the Jews at one.
Divided while united,[4] each must run   5
    His mighty course not hell should overtake;
    And pressing toward the mark must own the ache
Of love, and sigh for heaven not yet begun.
For saints in life-long exile yearn to touch
    Warm human hands, and commune face to face;   10
    But these we know not ever met again:
Yet once St. Paul at distance overmuch
    Just sighted Cyprus; and once more in vain
    Neared it and passed;—not there his landing-place.

GERARD MANLEY HOPKINS[†]

The Caged Skylark[1]

As a dare-gale skylark scanted in a dull cage
    Man's mounting spirit in his bone-house, mean house, dwells—

---

1. For lines 5–11, see, e.g., Matt 26:75; 27:45; John 20:11.
2. Cf. Matt 18:12–14 and parallel.
3. Cf. Exod 17:1–7; Num 20:2–13.
4. According to Acts 15:36–41, Paul and Barnabas divided over a conflict about whether to take John Mark with them on their voyage (he had abandoned them before; Acts 13:13). Gal 2:11–14 suggests that they disagreed over the relations between Gentiles and Jews within the Church, an alternative that is also relevant to Rossetti's poem.
† The following selections come from *Poems of Gerard Manley Hopkins*, ed. Robert Bridges (London: Humphrey Milford, 1908), 31, 47. Gerard Manley Hopkins, English poet and Catholic priest (1844–1889).
1. A symbolic meditation on the NT doctrine of bodily resurrection (see 1 Cor 15 and notes; cf. Thomas Hardy, "A Drizzling Easter Morning," p. 1309 below).

That bird beyond the remembering his free fells;
This in drudgery, day-labouring-out life's age.

Though aloft on turf or perch or poor low stage,   5
    Both sing sometimes the sweetest, sweetest spells,
    Yet both droop deadly sómetimes in their cells
Or wring their barriers in bursts of fear or rage.

Not that the sweet-fowl, song-fowl, needs no rest—
Why, hear him, hear him babble and drop down to his nest,   10
    But his own nest, wild nest, no prison.

Man's spirit will be flesh-bound when found at best,
But uncumbered: meadow-down is not distressed
    For a rainbow footing it nor he for his bónes rísen.

The Candle Indoors[2]

Some candle clear burns somewhere I come by.
I muse at how its being puts blissful back
With yellowy moisture mild night's blear-all black,
Or to-fro tender trambeams truckle at the eye.
By that window what task what fingers ply,   5
I plod wondering, a-wanting, just for lack
Of answer the eagerer a-wanting Jessy or Jack
There God to aggrándise, God to glorify.—

Come you indoors, come home; your fading fire
Mend first and vital candle in close heart's vault:[3]   10
You there are master, do your own desire;
What hinders? Are you beam-blind, yet to a fault
In a neighbour deft-handed?[4] Are you that liar
And cast by conscience out, spendsavour salt?[5]

2. The poem develops ideas and imagery from Matt 5:14–16.
3. Cf. Matt 25:1–13.
4. Cf. Matt 7:3–5.
5. Cf. Matt 5:13.

THOMAS HARDY

The Respectable Burgher[†]

On "The Higher Criticism"[1]

Since Reverend Doctors now declare
That clerks and people must prepare
To doubt if Adam ever were;
To hold the flood a local scare;
To argue, though the stolid stare,   5
That everything had happened ere
The prophets to its happening sware;
That David was no giant-slayer,
Nor one to call a God-obeyer
In certain details we could spare,   10
But rather was a debonair
Shrewd bandit, skilled as banjo-player:
That Solomon sang the fleshly Fair,
And gave the Church no thought whate'er;
That Esther with her royal wear,   15
And Mordecai, the son of Jair,
And Joshua's triumphs, Job's despair,
And Balaam's ass's bitter blare;
Nebuchadnezzar's furnace-flare,
And Daniel and the den affair,   20
And other stories rich and rare,
Were writ to make old doctrine wear
Something of a romantic air:
That the Nain widow's only heir,
And Lazarus with cadaverous glare   25
(As done in oils by Piombo's[2] care)
Did not return from Sheol's lair:
That Jael set a fiendish snare,
That Pontius Pilate acted square,
That never a sword cut Malchus' ear   30
And (but for shame I must forbear)
That —— —— did not reappear! . . .
—Since thus they hint, nor turn a hair,

[†] From Thomas Hardy, *Wessex Poems and Other Verses: Poems of the Past and the Present* (London: Macmillan and Co., Ltd., 1908), 425–27. Thomas Hardy, English novelist and poet (1840–1928).
[1]. Historical-critical investigation of biblical and other ancient literature, as opposed to textual criticism ("lower criticism"), which is concerned with establishing texts by collating and comparing manuscripts and other evidence.
[2]. Sebastian Luciani, known as del Piombo (ca. 1485–1547), an Italian Renaissance painter; his famous alterpiece *The Raising of Lazarus* was acquired in 1824 by the National Gallery in London.

All churchgoing will I forswear,
And sit on Sundays in my chair,   35
And read that moderate man Voltaire.[3]

A Drizzling Easter Morning[†]

And he is risen? Well, be it so. . . .
And still the pensive lands complain,
And dead men wait as long ago,
As if, much doubting, they would know
What they are ransomed from, before   5
They pass again their sheltering door.

I stand amid them in the rain,
While blusters vex the yew and vane;
And on the road the weary wain
Plods forward, laden heavily;   10
And toilers with their aches are fain
For endless rest—though risen is he.

WILLIAM BUTLER YEATS[‡]

The Magi[1]

Now as at all times I can see in the mind's eye,
In their stiff, painted clothes, the pale unsatisfied ones
Appear and disappear in the blue depth of the sky
With all their ancient faces like rain-beaten stones,
And all their helms of silver hovering side by side,   5
And all their eyes still fixed, hoping to find once more,
Being by Calvary's turbulence[2] unsatisfied,
The uncontrollable mystery on the bestial floor.[3]

3. French deist, satirist, philosopher, and historian (1694–1778).
† From Thomas Hardy, *Late Lyrics and Earlier* (London, Macmillan and Co., Ltd., 1922), 204.
‡ The following selections come from *W. B. Yeats: The Poems*, ed. Richard J. Finneran, new ed. (New York: Macmillan, 1983), 126, 187, 249, 341. William Butler Yeats (1865–1939), Irish poet.
1. See Matt 2:1–12. Compare T. S. Eliot's "Journey of the Magi" (pp. 1311–12).
2. The Magi are imagined among the witnesses of Jesus' crucifixion (see esp. Matt 27:51).
3. "The bestial floor" at once looks back to the manger of Christ's nativity (Luke 2:7) and forward to the figurative birth of the Antichrist (see below "The Second Coming," ll. 21–22).

The Second Coming

Turning and turning in the widening gyre
The falcon cannot hear the falconer;
Things fall apart; the centre cannot hold;
Mere anarchy is loosed upon the world,
The blood-dimmed tide is loosed, and everywhere   5
The ceremony of innocence is drowned;
The best lack all conviction, while the worst
Are full of passionate intensity.

Surely some revelation is at hand;
Surely the Second Coming is at hand.   10
The Second Coming! Hardly are those words out
When a vast image out of *Spiritus Mundi*[4]
Troubles my sight: somewhere in sands of the desert
A shape with lion body and the head of a man,
A gaze blank and pitiless as the sun,   15
Is moving its slow thighs, while all about it
Reel shadows of the indignant desert birds.
The darkness drops again; but now I know
That twenty centuries of stony sleep
Were vexed to nightmare by a rocking cradle,   20
And what rough beast, its hour come round at last,
Slouches towards Bethlehem to be born?

The Mother of God[5]

The three-fold terror of love; a fallen flare
Through the hollow of an ear;
Wings beating about the room;
The terror of all terrors that I bore
The Heavens in my womb.   5

Had I not found content among the shows
Every common woman knows,
Chimney corner, garden walk,
Or rocky cistern where we tread the clothes
And gather all the talk?   10

4. The Spirit of the World (Latin).
5. See Luke 1:26–28; 2:22–35 (esp. v. 35).

What is this flesh I purchased with my pains,
This fallen star my milk sustains,
This love that makes my heart's blood stop
Or strikes a sudden chill into my bones
And bids my hair stand up?

A Stick of Incense

Whence did all that fury come,
From empty tomb or Virgin womb?
St Joseph thought the world would melt
But liked the way his finger smelt.

T. S. ELIOT[†]

Journey of the Magi[1]

'A cold coming we had of it,
Just the worst time of the year
For a journey, and such a long journey:
The ways deep and the weather sharp,
The very dead of winter.'   5
And the camels galled, sore-footed, refractory,
Lying down in the melting snow.
There were times we regretted
The summer palaces on slopes, the terraces,
And the silken girls bringing sherbet.   10
Then the camel men cursing and grumbling
And running away, and wanting their liquor and women,
And the night-fires going out, and the lack of shelters,
And the cities hostile and the towns unfriendly
And the villages dirty and charging high prices: 15
A hard time we had of it.
At the end we preferred to travel all night,
Sleeping in snatches,
With the voices singing in our ears, saying
That this was all folly.   20

---

† From T. S. Eliot, *The Complete Poems and Plays, 1909–1950* (New York: Harcourt, Brace & World, 1952), 68–69. A poet and literary critic, T. S. Eliot (1888–1965) emigrated from the United States to England in his twenties, soon before his first published poem, "The Love Song of J. Alfred Prufrock," appeared in print.
1. See Matt 2:1–12. Compare W. B. Yeats's "The Magi" (p. 1309 above).

Then at dawn we came down to a temperate valley,
Wet, below the snow line, smelling of vegetation;
With a running stream and a water-mill beating the darkness,
And three trees on the low sky,
And an old white horse galloped away in the meadow.   25
Then we came to a tavern with vine-leaves over the lintel,
Six hands at an open door dicing for pieces of silver,
And feet kicking the empty wine-skins.
But there was no information, and so we continued
And arrived at evening, not a moment too soon   30
Finding the place; it was (you may say) satisfactory.

All this was a long time ago, I remember,
And I would do it again, but set down
This set down
This: were we led all that way for   35
Birth or Death? There was a Birth, certainly,
We had evidence and no doubt. I had seen birth and death,
But had thought they were different; this Birth was
Hard and bitter agony for us, like Death, our death.
We returned to our places, these Kingdoms,   40
But no longer at ease here, in the old dispensation,
With an alien people clutching their gods.
I should be glad of another death.

JAMES WELDON JOHNSON

Saint Peter Relates an Incident of the Resurrection Day†

Eternities—now numbering six or seven—
Hung heavy on the hands of all in heaven.
Archangels tall and fair had reached the stage
Where they began to show some signs of age.

The faces of the flaming seraphim   5
Were slightly drawn, their eyes were slightly dim.
The cherubs, too, for now—oh, an infinite while
Had worn but a wistful shade of their dimpling smile.

† From James Weldon Johnson, *Saint Peter Relates an Incident* (New York: Penguin, 1993), 13–22. An American poet and novelist associated with the Harlem Renaissance, Johnson (1871–1938) was also a U.S. diplomat in Latin America, an advocacy journalist, and an early civil rights leader. His political interests are on clear display in this satirical poem about the eschatological resurrection.

The serried singers of the celestial choir
Disclosed a woeful want of pristine fire;   10
When they essayed to strike the glad refrain,
Their attack was weak, their tone revealed voice strain.

Their expression seemed to say, "We must! We must!" though
'Twas more than evident they lacked the gusto;
It could not be elsewise—that fact all can agree on—   15
Chanting the selfsame choral æon after æon.

Thus was it that Saint Peter at the gate[1]
Began a brand new thing in heaven: to relate
Some reminiscences from heavenly history,
Which had till then been more or less a mystery.   20

So now and then, by turning back the pages,
Were whiled away some moments from the ages,
Was gained a respite from the monotony
That can't help settling on eternity.

II

Now, there had been a lapse of ages hoary,
And the angels clamored for another story.
"Tell us a tale, Saint Peter," they entreated;
And gathered close around where he was seated.

Saint Peter stroked his beard,   5
And "Yes," he said
By the twinkle in his eye
And the nodding of his head.

A moment brief he fumbled with his keys—
It seemed to help him call up memories—   10
Straightway there flashed across his mind the one
About the unknown soldier
Who came from Washington.

The hosts stood listening,
Breathlessly awake;   15
And thus Saint Peter spake:

---

1. A tradition ultimately based on Matt 16:19 makes Peter heaven's gatekeeper.

III

'Twas Resurrection morn,
And Gabriel blew a blast upon his horn[2]
That echoed through the arches high and vast
Of Time and Space—a long resounding blast

To wake the dead, dead for a million years;　　　　　　5
A blast to reach and pierce their dust-stopped ears;
To quicken them, wherever they might be,
Deep in the earth or deeper in the sea.

A shudder shook the world, and gaping graves
Gave up their dead. Out from the parted waves　　　　10
Came the prisoners of old ocean.[3] The dead belonging
To every land and clime came thronging.

From the four corners of all the earth they drew,
Their faces radiant and their bodies new.
Creation pulsed and swayed beneath the tread　　　　15
Of all the living, and all the risen dead.

Swift-winged heralds of heaven flew back and forth,
Out of the east, to the south, the west, the north,
Giving out quick commands, and yet benign,
Marshaling the swarming milliards into line.　　　　20

The recording angel in words of thundering might,
At which the timid, doubting souls took fright,
Bade all to await the grand roll-call; to wit,
To see if in the Book their names were writ.[4]

The multitudinous business of the day　　　　　　25
Progressed, but naturally, not without delay.
Meanwhile, within the great American border
There was the issuance of a special order.

IV

The word went forth, spoke by some grand panjandrum,
Perhaps, by some high potentate of Klandom,
That all the trusty patriotic mentors,
And duly qualified Hundred-Percenters[5]

---

2. Cf. 1 Cor 15:52; 1 Thess 4:16.
3. Cf. Rev 20:13.
4. Cf. Rev 20:12, 15.
5. Extreme U.S. nationalists (a term that came into use in the 1920s).

Should forthwith gather together upon the banks   5
Of the Potomac, there to form their ranks,
March to the tomb, by orders to be given,
And escort the unknown soldier up to heaven.[6]

Compliantly they gathered from each region,
The G.A.R., the D.A.R., the Legion,[7]   10
Veterans of wars—Mexican, Spanish, Haitian—
Trustees of the patriotism of the nation;

Key Men, Watchmen, shunning circumlocution,
The Sons of the This and That and of the Revolution;
Not to forget, there gathered every man   15
Of the Confederate Veterans and the Ku-Klux Klan.

The Grand Imperial Marshal gave the sign;
Column on column, the marchers fell in line;
Majestic as an army in review,
They swept up Washington's wide avenue.   20

Then, through the long line ran a sudden flurry,
The marchers in the rear began to hurry;
They feared unless the procession hastened on,
The unknown soldier might be risen and gone.

The fear was groundless; when they arrived, in fact,   25
They found the grave entirely intact.
(Resurrection plans were long, long past completing
Ere there was thought of re-enforced concreting.)

They heard a faint commotion in the tomb,
Like the stirring of a child within the womb;   30
At once they saw the plight, and set about
The job to dig the unknown soldier out.

They worked away, they labored with a will,
They toiled with pick, with crowbar, and with drill
To cleave a breach; nor did the soldier shirk;   35
Within his limits, he helped to push the work.

---

6. That is, the unidentified American soldier whose burial in Arlington National Cemetery, by the Potomac River, commemorates all the "unknowns" who died in World War I; his remains were interred in 1921.
7. The Grand Army of the Republic, an organization of Civil War veterans of the Union Army; the Daughters of the American Revolution, whose members are descendants of revolutionary soldiers; and the American Legion, the largest American veterans organization.

He, underneath the débris, heaved and hove
Up toward the opening which they cleaved and clove;
Through it, at last, his towering form loomed big and bigger—
"Great God Almighty! Look!" they cried, "he is a nigger!"   40

Surprise and consternation and dismay
Swept over the crowd; none knew just what to say
Or what to do. And all fell back aghast.
Silence—but only an instant did it last.

Bedlam: They clamored, they railed, some roared, some bleated;   45
All of them felt that somehow they'd been cheated.
The question rose: What to do with him, then?
The Klan was all for burying him again.

The scheme involved within the Klan's suggestion
Gave rise to a rather nice metaphysical question: 50
Could he be forced again through death's dark portal,
Since now his body and soul were both immortal?

Would he, forsooth, the curious-minded queried,
Even in concrete, re-entombed, stay buried?
In a moment more, midst the pile of broken stone,   55
The unknown soldier stood, and stood alone.

                                    V

The day came to a close.
And heaven—hell too—was filled with them that rose.
I shut the pearly gate and turned the key;
For Time was now merged into Eternity.

I gave one last look over the jasper wall,   5
And afar descried a figure dark and tall:
The unknown soldier, dust-stained and begrimed,
Climbing his way to heaven, and singing as he climbed:
    Deep river, my home is over Jordan,
    Deep river, I want to cross over into camp-ground.[8]   10

Climbing and singing—
    Deep river, my home is over Jordan,
    Deep river, I want to cross over into camp-ground.

---

8. The opening lines of a traditional African American spiritual, "Deep River."

Nearer and louder—
   Deep river, my home is over Jordan, 15
   Deep river, I want to cross over into camp-ground.

At the jasper wall—
   Deep river, my home is over Jordan,
   Deep river,
   Lord, 20
   I want to cross over into camp-ground.

I rushed to the gate and flung it wide,
Singing, he entered with a loose, long stride;
Singing and swinging up the golden street,
The music married to the tramping of his feet. 25

Tall, black soldier-angel marching alone,
Swinging up the golden street, saluting at the great white throne.
Singing, singing, singing, singing clear and strong.
Singing, singing, singing, till heaven took up the song:
   Deep river, my home is over Jordan, 30
   Deep river, I want to cross over into camp-ground.

VI

The tale was done,
The angelic hosts dispersed,
   but not till after
There ran through heaven
Something that quivered 5
   'twixt tears and laughter.

COUNTEE CULLEN†

Simon the Cyrenian Speaks[1]

He never spoke a word to me,
   And yet He called my name;
He never gave a sign to me,
   And yet I knew and came.

† The following selections come from *My Soul's High Song: The Collected Writings of Countee Cullen, Voice of the Harlem Renaissance,* ed. Gerald Lyn Early (New York: Doubleday, 1991), 87, 125–28. Countee Cullen (1903–1946), American poet associated with the Harlem Renaissance.
1. See Mark 15:21 and parallels.

At first I said, "I will not bear
    His cross upon my back;
He only seeks to place it there
    Because my skin is black."[2]   5

But He was dying for a dream,
    And He was very meek,
And in His eyes there shone a gleam   10
    Men journey far to seek.

It was Himself my pity bought;
    I did for Christ alone
What all of Rome could not have wrought   15
    With bruise of lash or stone.

Judas Iscariot[3]

I think when Judas' mother heard
    His first faint cry the night
That he was born, that worship stirred
    Her at the sound and sight.
She thought his was as fair a frame   5
    As flesh and blood had worn;
I think she made this lovely name
    For him—"Star of my morn."[4]

As any mother's son he grew
    From spring to crimson spring;
I think his eyes were black, or blue,   10
    His hair curled like a ring.
His mother's heart-strings were a lute
    Whereon he all day played;
She listened rapt, abandoned, mute,   15
    To every note he made.

I think he knew the growing Christ,
    And played with Mary's son,

2. Simon was from North Africa. (Cyrene is in present-day Libya.)
3. This poem speculates about Judas's motives, participating in a long tradition that originates in the Gospels' contradictory portrayals of him. Was Judas motivated by greed (Matt 26:14–16)? Was he instead (or in addition) possessed by the devil (Luke 22:3–6; John 13:27)? Did he ultimately repent and kill himself out of shame and regret (Matt 27:3–8)? Or did God rather strike the unrepentant traitor dead (Acts 1:18 and note)? The solution at which Cullen tentatively arrives also surfaces, in one form or another, in Nikos Kazantzakis's *The Last Temptation of Christ* (1953) and in the recently discovered ancient gnostic text *The Gospel of Judas*, among other writings.
4. An allusion to Isa 14:12, traditionally understood as a reference to Satan.

And where mere mortal craft sufficed,
   There Judas may have won.   20
Perhaps he little cared or knew,
   So folly-wise is youth,
That He whose hand his hand clung to
   Was flesh-embodied Truth;[5]

Until one day he heard young Christ,   25
   With far-off eyes agleam,
Tell of a mystic, solemn tryst
   Between Him and a dream.
And Judas listened, wonder-eyed,
   Until the Christ was through,   30
Then said, "And I, though good betide,
   Or ill, will go with you."

And so he followed, heard Christ preach,
   Saw how by miracle
The blind man saw, the dumb got speech,   35
   The leper found him well.
And Judas in those holy hours
   Loved Christ, and loved Him much,
And in his heart he sensed dead flowers
   Bloom at the Master's touch.   40

And when Christ felt the death hour creep
   With sullen, drunken lurch,
He said to Peter, "Feed my sheep,
   And build my holy church."[6]
He gave to each the special task   45
   That should be his to do,
But reaching one, I hear him ask,
   "What shall I give to you?"

Then Judas in his hot desire
   Said, "Give me what you will."[7]   50
Christ spoke to him with words of fire,
   "Then, Judas, you must kill[8]
One whom you love, One who loves you
   As only God's son can:

---

5. Cf. John 1:14.
6. Cf. John 21:15–17; Matt 16:16–18.
7. In the Gospels it is Peter who speaks with passion at this point in the narrative (Mark 14:31 and parallels).
8. This exchange imaginatively recasts John 13:26–30.

This is the work for you to do   55
   To save the creature man."

"And men to come will curse your name,
   And hold you up to scorn;
In all the world will be no shame
   Like yours; this is love's thorn.   60
It takes strong will of heart and soul,
   But man is under ban.
Think, Judas, can you play this role
   In heaven's mystic plan?"

So Judas took the sorry part,   65
   Went out and spoke the word,
And gave the kiss that broke his heart,[9]
   But no one knew or heard.
And no one knew what poison ate
   Into his palm that day,   70
Where, bright and damned, the monstrous weight
   Of thirty white coins lay.

It was not death that Judas found
   Upon a kindly tree;
The man was dead long ere he bound   75
   His throat as final fee.[1]
And who can say if on that day
   When gates of pearl swung wide,
Christ did not go His honored way
   With Judas by His side?   80

I think somewhere a table round
   Owns Jesus as its head,
And there the saintly twelve are found
   Who followed where He led.
And Judas sits down with the rest,   85
   And none shrinks from His hand,
For there the worst is as the best,
   And there they understand.

And you may think of Judas, friend,
   As one who broke his word,   90
Whose neck came to a bitter end
   For giving up his Lord.

9. Cf. Mark 14:44–45 and parallels.
1. Cf. Matt 26:14–16; 27:3–5.

But I would rather think of him
   As the little Jewish lad
Who gave young Christ heart, soul, and limb,   95
   And all the love he had.

ELIZABETH BISHOP

Roosters[†]

At four o'clock   1
in the gun-metal blue dark
we hear the first crow of the first cock

just below
the gun-metal blue window
and immediately there is an echo

off in the distance,
then one from the backyard fence,
then one, with horrible insistence,

grates like a wet match
from the broccoli patch,
flares, and all over town begins to catch.

Cries galore   5
come from the water-closet door,
from the dropping-plastered henhouse floor,

where in the blue blur
their rustling wives admire,
the roosters brace their cruel feet and glare

with stupid eyes
while from their beaks there rise
the uncontrolled, traditional cries.

Deep from protruding chests
in green-gold medals dressed,
planned to command and terrorize the rest,

---

† This and the following poem come from Elizabeth Bishop, *The Complete Poems, 1927–1979* (New York: Farrar, Straus and Giroux, 1983), 35–39, 71. Elizabeth Bishop (1911–1979), American poet. (For "Roosters," compare Richard Crashaw, "On St. Peter cutting off Malchus his eare," and Emily Dickinson, "He forgot - and I - remembered," both on the same theme [Appendix, pp. 1286, 1301–02].)

the many wives
who lead hens' lives
of being courted and despised;

deep from raw throats   10
a senseless order floats
all over town. A rooster gloats

over our beds
from rusty iron sheds
and fences made from old bedsteads,

over our churches
where the tin rooster perches,
over our little wooden northern houses,

making sallies
from all the muddy alleys,
marking out maps like Rand McNally's:

glass-headed pins,
oil-golds and copper greens,
anthracite blues, alizarins,

each one an active   15
displacement in perspective;
each screaming, "This is where I live!"

Each screaming
"Get up! Stop dreaming!"
Roosters, what are you projecting?

You, whom the Greeks elected
to shoot at on a post, who struggled
when sacrificed, you whom they labeled

"Very combative . . ."
what right have you to give
commands and tell us how to live,

cry "Here!" and "Here!"
and wake us here where are
unwanted love, conceit and war?

The crown of red   20
set on your little head
is charged with all your fighting blood.

Yes, that excrescence
makes a most virile presence,
plus all that vulgar beauty of iridescence.

Now in mid-air
by twos they fight each other.
Down comes a first flame-feather,

and one is flying,
with raging heroism defying
even the sensation of dying.

And one has fallen,
but still above the town
his torn-out, bloodied feathers drift down;

and what he sung   25
no matter. He is flung
on the gray ash-heap, lies in dung

with his dead wives
with open, bloody eyes,
while those metallic feathers oxidize.

St. Peter's sin[1]
was worse than that of Magdalen
whose sin was of the flesh alone;

of spirit, Peter's,
falling, beneath the flares,
among the "servants and officers."

Old holy sculpture
could set it all together
in one small scene, past and future:

Christ stands amazed,   30
Peter, two fingers raised
to surprised lips, both as if dazed.

But in between
a little cock is seen
carved on a dim column in the travertine,

1. For this section of the poem, see Mark 14:53–54, 66–72, and parallels.

explained by *gallus canit;*
flet Petrus[2] underneath it.
There is inescapable hope, the pivot;

yes, and there Peter's tears
run down our chanticleer's
sides and gem his spurs.

Tear-encrusted thick
as a medieval relic
he waits. Poor Peter, heart-sick,

still cannot guess   35
those cock-a-doodles yet might bless,
his dreadful rooster come to mean forgiveness,

a new weathervane
on basilica and barn,
and that outside the Lateran[3]

there would always be
a bronze cock on a porphyry
pillar so the people and the Pope might see

than even the Prince
of the Apostles long since
had been forgiven, and to convince

all the assembly
that "Deny deny deny"
is not all the roosters cry.

In the morning   40
a low light is floating
in the backyard, and gilding

from underneath
the broccoli, leaf by leaf;
how could the night have come to grief?

gilding the tiny
floating swallow's belly
and lines of pink cloud in the sky,

---

2. The rooster crows; Peter weeps (Latin).
3. The cathedral in Rome where the pope presides.

the day's preamble
like wandering lines in marble.
The cocks are now almost inaudible.

The sun climbs in,
following "to see the end,"[4]
faithful as enemy, or friend.

The Prodigal[5]

The brown enormous odor he lived by
was too close, with its breathing and thick hair,
for him to judge. The floor was rotten; the sty
was plastered halfway up with glass-smooth dung.
Light-lashed, self-righteous, above moving snouts,   5
the pigs' eyes followed him, a cheerful stare—
even to the sow that always ate her young—
till, sickening, he leaned to scratch her head.
But sometimes mornings after drinking bouts
(he hid the pints behind a two-by-four),   10
the sunrise glazed the barnyard mud with red;
the burning puddles seemed to reassure.
And then he thought he almost might endure
his exile yet another year or more.

But evenings the first star came to warn.   15
The farmer whom he worked for came at dark
to shut the cows and horses in the barn
beneath their overhanging clouds of hay,
with pitchforks, faint forked lightnings, catching light,
safe and companionable as in the Ark.   20
The pigs stuck out their little feet and snored.
The lantern—like the sun, going away—
laid on the mud a pacing aureole.
Carrying a bucket along a slimy board,
he felt the bats' uncertain staggering flight,   25
his shuddering insights, beyond his control,
touching him. But it took him a long time
finally to make his mind up to go home.

4. See Matt 26:58.
5. See Luke 15:11–32.

HYMNS AND SPIRITUALS
HYMNS

A hymn is a sacred poem set to music and sung during a religious ceremony. The Psalms are the hymns of the ancient Israelites; their inscriptions often carry musical or liturgical directions, and the texts themselves occasionally refer to congregational worship (e.g., 81:1–3; 118:26–27; 134). The New Testament also mentions the corporate singing of hymns (e.g., Eph 5:19; Col 3:16), and the Epistles seem to contain quotations from hymns sung by the early church (e.g., Phil 2:6–11). Ancient Eastern Christian hymnody is rather conservative, relying on a tonal system for a cappella chant that dates to the Byzantine era and is probably closely related to even more ancient Greek music. Ambrose (340–397) seems to have been central to the early development of Western Christian hymnody. His hymns were incorporated into the important Benedictine Rule for the monastic liturgy in the fifth century and were frequently imitated by other early hymnists. During the Middle Ages the clergy occasionally encouraged the laity to sing during extraliturgical devotions, but vernacular congregational singing during the mass itself was prohibited. The primary impetus for vernacular hymnody therefore had to await the reformer Martin Luther (1483–1546), who translated and paraphrased the Vulgate Psalms and other Latin texts into German verse; these new hymns, set to simple and familiar melodies, were easily incorporated into Protestant liturgies.

The most important hymnists in the English tradition are Isaac Watts and Charles Wesley, both active in the eighteenth century. Watts was the pastor of an Independent church in London and his hymns helped pave the way for the expanded use of music in the worship of English Nonconformist congregations, which before had been largely restricted to the singing of metrical psalms. Charles Wesley was an itinerant minister in the Methodist movement founded by his brother John, but it is as a hymnist that he is most often remembered.

It goes without saying that hymns often draw on biblical texts—probably the Old Testament more than the New. They recast into contemporary idioms the Bible's own hymnody (e.g., Caroline Noel's "At the Name of Jesus" [Phil 2:5–11] and Reginald Heber's "Holy, Holy, Holy! Lord God Almighty" [Rev 4:8–11]), or transform biblical texts into verse (e.g., Nahum Tate's "While Shepherds Watched Their Flocks"). They also meditate on particular moments of the gospel story (e.g., Watts's "Alas! And Did My Savior Bleed") and traditional doctrines drawn from the New Testament (Wesley's "And Can It Be That I Should Gain"). The English tradition of Christian hymnody is particularly rich—Wesley alone wrote words for about 8,000—and the following selection is representative only in that it highlights a variety of interpretive approaches to the New Testament that English hymns typically display.

The hymns that follow are all still sung today and so their texts are fairly fluid. We generally print the earliest versions accessible, which are sometimes not the most familiar.

NAHUM TATE†

While Shepherds Watched Their Flocks by Night¹

While shepherds watch'd their flocks by night,   1
  All seated on the ground,
The angel of the Lord came down,
  And glory shone around.

"Fear not," said he; (for mighty dread   2
  Had seized their troubled mind;)
"Glad tidings of great joy I bring
  To you and all mankind.

"To you in David's town this day   3
  Is born of David's line
The Saviour, who is Christ the Lord;
  And this shall be the sign.

"The Heavenly Babe you there shall find   4
  To human view displayed,
All meanly wrapt in swathing bands,
  And in a manger laid."

Thus spake the Seraph; and forthwith   5
  Appeared a shining throng
Of angels, praising God, and thus
  Addressed their joyful song.

"All glory be to God on high,   6
  And to the earth be peace;
Good will henceforth from Heaven to men
  Begin, and never cease!"

† Nahum Tate (1652–1715), Irish poet and hymnist perhaps most famous as co-editor of a collection of metrical psalms, *A New Version of the Psalms of David* (1696). This hymn originally appeared in its *Supplement* (1700). It is reprinted here from Nahum Tate, *While Shepherds Watched Their Flocks by Night* (Boston: D. Lothrop, 1886).
1. See Luke 2:8–14.

ISAAC WATTS

Alas! And Did My Saviour Bleed†

Alas! and did my Saviour bleed,   1
    And did my Sov'reign die?[1]
Would he devote that sacred head
    For such a worm as I?

[Thy body slain, sweet Jesus, thine,   2
    And bath'd in its own blood,
While all expos'd to wrath divine
    The glorious sufferer stood!]][2]

Was it for crimes that I had done   3
    He groan'd upon the tree?[3]
Amazing pity! grace unknown!
    And love beyond degree!

Well might the sun in darkness hide,   4
    And shut his glories in,
When God the mighty Maker dy'd
    For man the creature's sin.

Thus might I hide my blushing face   5
    While his dear cross appears,
Dissolve my heart in thankfulness,
    And melt my eyes to tears.

But drops of grief can ne'er repay   6
    The debt of love I owe;
Here, Lord, I give myself away,
    Tis all that I can do.

---

† From Isaac Watts, *Hymns and Spiritual Songs in Three Books* (London: W. Strahan, J. and F. Rivington, et al., 1773), 136–37 (though this hymn first appeared in the original edition of Watts's *Hymns and Spiritual Songs,* 3 vols. [1707–09]). Isaac Watts (1674–1748), nonconformist minister, often called the father of English hymnody.
1. Cf. Mark 15:37 and parallels.
2. The brackets indicate that the stanza may be omitted in singing.
3. Cf. Mark 15:34 and parallels.

CHARLES WESLEY[†]

Come, Sinners, to the Gospel Feast[1]

Come, sinners, to the gospel feast,   1
Let every soul be Jesu's guest,
You need not one be left behind,
For God hath bidden all mankind.

Sent by my Lord, on you I call,   2
The invitation is to all,
Come all the world; come, sinner, thou,
All things in Christ are ready now.

Jesus to you His fulness brings,   3
A feast of marrow and fat things:
All, all in Christ is freely given,
Pardon, and holiness, and heaven.

Do not begin to make excuse,   4
Ah! do not you His grace refuse;
Your worldly cares and pleasures leave,
And take what Jesus hath to give.

Your grounds forsake, your oxen quit,   5
Your every earthly thought forget,
Seek not the comforts of this life,
Nor sell your Saviour for a wife.

"Have me excused," why will ye say?   6
Why will ye for damnation pray?
Have you excused—from joy and peace!
Have you excused—from happiness:

Excused from coming to a feast!   7
Excused from being Jesu's guest!
From knowing *now* your sins forgiven,
From tasting *here* the joys of heaven!

Excused, alas! why should you be   8
From health, and life, and liberty,

† Charles Wesley (1707–1788) was a Methodist preacher and prolific English hymnist. The following hymns are reprinted from *The Poetical Works of John and Charles Wesley: Reprinted from the Originals*, ed. George Osborn, 13 vols. (London: Wesleyan-Methodist Conference Office, 1868–72), 4:274–77, 1:105–6. The first hymn originally appeared in Wesley's 1747 collection, *Hymns for those that seek, and those that Have, Redemption in the Blood of Christ*, under the title "The Great Supper." The second appeared in *Hyms and Sacred Poems* (1739), labeled "Free Grace."
1. See Luke 14:15–24; John 6:51–56; etc.

From entering into glorious rest,
From leaning on your Saviour's breast!

Yet must I, Lord, to Thee complain,   9
The world hath made Thy offers vain;
Too busy, or too happy they,
They will not, Lord, Thy call obey.

Go then, my angry Master said,   10
Since these on all My mercies tread,
Invite the rich and great no more,
But preach My gospel to the poor.

Confer not thou with flesh and blood,   11
Go quickly forth, invite the crowd,
Search every lane, and every street,
And bring in all the souls you meet.

Come then, ye souls by sin opprest,   12
Ye restless wanderers after rest,
Ye poor, and maim'd, and halt, and blind,
In Christ a hearty welcome find.

Sinners my gracious Lord receives,   13
Harlots, and publicans, and thieves;
Drunkards, and all ye hellish crew,
I have a message now to you.

Come, and partake the gospel feast,   14
Be saved from sin, in Jesus rest:
O taste the goodness of our God,
And eat His flesh and drink His blood.

'Tis done: my all-redeeming Lord,   15
I have gone forth, and preach'd the word,
The sinners to Thy feast are come,
And yet, O Saviour, there is room.

Go then, my Lord again enjoin'd,   16
And other wandering sinners find;
Go to the hedges and highways,
And offer all My pardoning grace.

The worst unto My supper press,   17
Monsters of daring wickedness,
Tell them My grace for all is free,
They cannot be too bad for Me.

Tell them, their sins are all forgiven, 18
Tell every creature under heaven
I died to save them from all sin,
And force the vagrants to come in.

Ye vagrant souls, on you I call, 19
(O that my voice could reach you all!)
Ye all are freely justified,
Ye all may live, for Christ hath died.

My message as from God receive, 20
Ye all may come to Christ, and live:
O let His love your hearts constrain,
Nor suffer Him to die in vain.

His love is mighty to compel, 21
His conquering love consent to feel;
Yield to His love's resistless power,
And fight against your God no more!

See Him set forth before your eyes, 22
Behold the bleeding Sacrifice!
His offer'd love make haste to' embrace,
And freely now be saved by grace.

Ye who believe His record true 23
Shall sup with Him, and He with you:
Come to the feast; be saved from sin,
For Jesus waits to take you in.

This is the time, no more delay, 24
This is the acceptable day,
Come in, this moment, at His call,
And live for Him who died for all.

And Can It Be, That I Should Gain

And can it be, that I should gain 1
    An interest in the Saviour's blood?
Died He for me?—who caused His pain!
    For me?—who Him to death pursued.
Amazing love! how can it be
That Thou, my God, shouldst die for me?

'Tis mystery all! the' Immortal dies! 2
    Who can explore His strange design?

In vain the first-born seraph tries
　　To sound the depths of Love Divine.
'Tis mercy all! Let earth adore;
Let angel minds inquire no more.

He left His Father's throne above,   3
　　(So free, so infinite His grace!)
Emptied Himself of all but love,
　　And bled for *Adam's* helpless race:[2]
'Tis mercy all, immense and free!
For, O my God! it found out me!

Long my imprison'd spirit lay,   4
　　Fast bound in sin[3] and nature's night:
Thine eye diffused a quickening ray;
　　I woke; the dungeon flamed with light;
My chains fell off, my heart was free,
I rose, went forth, and follow'd Thee.

Still the small inward voice I hear,   5
　　That whispers all my sins forgiven;
Still the atoning blood is near,
　　That quench'd the wrath of hostile Heaven:
I feel the life His wounds impart;
I feel my Saviour in my heart.

No condemnation now I dread,   6
　　Jesus, and all in Him, is mine:
Alive in Him, my Living Head,
　　And clothed in righteousness Divine,
Bold I approach the' eternal throne,
And claim the crown, through Christ, my own.

REGINALD HEBER[†]

Holy, Holy, Holy! Lord God Almighty[1]

Holy, holy, holy, Lord God Almighty!   1
　　Early in the morning our song shall rise to Thee;

2. Cf. Phil 2:5–8.
3. Stanzas 4 and 6 adapt language and imagery from Rom 7:14–8:4.
† Reginald Heber (1783–1826) was an English hymnist and, toward the end of his life, the Anglican Bishop of Calcutta. This hymn is called "Trinity Sunday" in *The Poetical Works of Reginald Heber* (London: John Murray, 1841), 92, from which it is here reprinted. Heber's hymns were published only posthumously, and this one appeared first in *Hymns, Written and Adapted to the Weekly Church Service of the Year* (1827).
1. See Rev 4:6–11.

Holy, holy, holy! merciful and mighty!
    God in three persons, blessed Trinity!

Holy, holy, holy! all the saints adore Thee,   2
    Casting down their golden crowns around the glassy sea;
Cherubim and seraphim falling down before Thee
    Which wert and art and evermore shalt be!

Holy, holy, holy! Though the darkness hide Thee,   3
    Though the eye of sinful man Thy glory may not see,
Only Thou art holy, there is none beside Thee,
    Perfect in power, in love, and purity!

Holy, holy, holy, Lord God Almighty!   4
    All Thy works shall praise Thy name in earth and sky and sea.
Holy, holy, holy! merciful and mighty!
    God in three persons, blessed Trinity!

MATTHEW BRIDGES[†]

Crown Him with Many Crowns[1]

Crown Him with many crowns,   1
    The Lamb upon His throne;
Hark! how the heavenly anthem drowns
    All music but its own!
    Awake, my soul, and sing
    Of Him who died for thee;
And hail Him as thy matchless King,
    Through all eternity.

Crown Him the Virgin's Son!   2
    The God Incarnate born,—
Whose Arm those crimson trophies won
    Which now His Brow adorn!
    Fruit of the Mystic Rose,
    As of that Rose the Stem:

---

† The English hymnist Matthew Bridges (1800–1894) was a convert to Catholicism associated with the Oxford movement and John Henry Newman. "Crown Him with Many Crowns" is known in many versions, especially one with additional verses by Godfrey Thring (1823–1903). This, though, is Bridges's original version, which first appeared in the second edition of his *Hymns of the Heart* (1851). It is reprinted here from *The Poets and the Poetry of the Nineteenth Century*, ed. Alfred H. Miles, vol. 12, *The Sacred Poets of the Nineteenth Century: Edward Hayes Plumptre to Selwyn Image* (London: George Routledge and Sons; New York: E. P. Dutton, 1907), 311.
1. See Rev 19:12; cf. chaps. 4–5, esp. 4:10; 5:6.

The Root, whence Mercy ever flows,—
    The Babe of Bethlehem!

Crown Him the Lord of Love!   3
    Behold His Hands and Side,—
Rich wounds, yet visible above,
    In beauty glorified:
    No angel in the sky
    Can fully bear that sight,
But downward bends his burning eye
    At mysteries so bright!

Crown Him the Lord of Peace!   4
    Whose power a sceptre sways,
From pole to pole,—that wars may cease,
    Absorbed in prayer and praise:
    His reign shall know no end,
    And round His piercèd Feet
Fair flowers of Paradise extend
    Their fragrance ever sweet.

Crown Him the Lord of Years!   5
    The Potentate of Time,—
Creator of the rolling spheres,
    Ineffably sublime!
    Glass'd in a sea of light,
    Where everlasting waves
Reflect His Throne,—the Infinite!
    Who lives,—and loves,—and saves.

Crown Him the Lord of Heaven!   6
    One with the Father known,—
And the blest Spirit, through Him given,
    From yonder triune throne!
    All hail! Redeemer,—hail!
    For Thou hast died for me;
Thy praise shall never, never fail,
    Throughout eternity!

CAROLINE M. NOEL[†]

At the Name of Jesus[1]

At the Name of Jesus   1
   Every knee shall bow.
Every tongue confess Him,
   King of Glory now.
'Tis the Father's pleasure
   We should call Him Lord,
Who from the beginning
   Was the mighty Word.

Mighty and mysterious,   2
   In the highest height,
God from Everlasting,
   Very Light of Light!
In the Father's bosom,
   With the Spirit blest,
Love, in Love Eternal,
   Rest, in perfect rest.

At His voice, Creation   3
   Sprang at once to sight,
All the angel faces,
   All the hosts of light;
Thrones and dominations,
   Stars upon their way,
All the Heavenly orders,
   In their great array.

Humbled for a season,   4
   To receive a Name
From the lips of sinners,
   Amongst whom He came;
Faithfully He bore it,
   Spotless to the last,
Brought it back victorious,
   When from death He passed.

† Caroline Noel (1817–1877), English hymnist. The following hymn is labeled "Ascension Day" in her collection *The Name of Jesus, and Other Poems, for the Sick and Lonely*, new ed. (London: Hatchards, 1876), 65, from which it is here reprinted. It first appeared in the 1870 edition of that volume.
1. See Phil 2:5–11.

Bore it up triumphant,   5
　　With its human light,
Through all ranks of creatures.
　　To the central height;
To the Throne of Godhead,
　　To the Father's breast,
Filled it with the glory
　　Of that perfect rest.

Name Him, brothers, name Him,   6
　　With love as strong as death,
But humbly and with wonder,
　　And with bated breath:
He is God the Saviour,
　　He is Christ the Lord,
Ever to be worshipped,
　　Trusted, and adored.

In your hearts enthrone Him!   7
　　There let Him subdue
All that is not holy,
　　All that is not true.
Crown Him as your Captain,
　　In temptation's hour;
Let His Will enfold you
　　In its light and power.

Brothers, this Lord Jesus   8
　　Shall return again,
With His Father's glory,
　　With His angel train:
For all wreaths of empire
　　Meet upon His brow,
And our hearts confess Him,
　　King of Glory now.

SPIRITUALS

The African American spiritual is one of the most impressive products of the tragic encounter of West African and European cultures resulting from the trans-Atlantic slave trade. Although difficult to discern when only the printed text is consulted, the West African influence on the spiritual's development (as evident, for example, in spirituals' irregular, syncopated rhythms and call-and-response forms) must not be underestimated. Neither can one overlook the prevalence of biblical imagery, which slaves adapted from the Bible and preaching of their European and American captors.

African American slaves were introduced to Christianity by their masters and by Anglican and later, more successful, Evangelical missionaries. Far from simply embracing the Christianity presented to them (which usually emphasized obedience to one's master as a requisite for salvation), African Americans transformed this gospel to make it relevant to their own experiences. Important aspects of the New Testament embraced by African American slaves are evident in the texts of the spirituals that follow, which tend to identify with the powerless and eagerly anticipate God's just eschatological judgment. In addition to expressing faith, spirituals covertly exhorted resistance and were sometimes used as codes for communicating about plans for escape (e.g., "Steal Away to Jesus").

Spirituals are properly works of oral literature. They were composed in the process of performance, and even today performances of the same spiritual are liable to differ radically. No text can legitimately claim to be authoritative, let alone original. Standard collections exist, however. Two of the most important are James Weldon Johnson and J. Rosamond Johnson, eds., *The Books of American Negro Spirituals*, 2 vols. (New York: Viking, 1925–26), and, more exhaustively, Erskine Peters, ed., *Lyrics of the Afro-American Spiritual: A Documentary Collection* (Westport, CT: Greenwood Press, 1993).

Done Found My Lost Sheep[1]

> Done found my lost sheep,
> Done found my lost sheep,
> Done found my lost sheep, Hallelujah!
>
> Done found my lost sheep,
> Done found my lost sheep,
> Done found my lost sheep.
>
> My Lord had a hundred sheep;
> One of them did go astray.
> That just left him ninety-nine.
> Go to the wilderness, seek and find;

1. See Matt 18:10–14; Luke 15:3–7.

If you find him, bring him back,
'Cross your shoulders, 'cross your back.
Tell the neighbors all around:
That lost sheep has done been found!

Done found my lost sheep,
Done found my lost sheep,
Done found my lost sheep.

In that Resurrection Day
Sinner can't find no hiding place.
Go to the mountain, the mountain move;
Run to the hill, the hill run too.[2]
Sinner man traveling on trembling ground;
Poor lost sheep ain't never been found.
Sinner why don't you stop and pray?
Then you'd hear the shepherd say:

Done found my lost sheep,
Done found my lost sheep,
Done found my lost sheep.

Were You There, When They Crucified My Lord?

Were you there, when they crucified my Lord?
Were you there, when they crucified my Lord?
Oh, sometimes, it causes me to tremble, tremble, tremble.
Were you there, when they crucified my Lord?

Were you there, when they nailed him to the tree?
Were you there, when they nailed him to the tree?
Oh, sometimes, it causes me to tremble, tremble, tremble.
Were you there, when they nailed him to the tree?

Were you there, when they pierced him in the side?[3]
Were you there, when they pierced him in the side?
Oh, sometimes, it causes me to tremble, tremble, tremble.
Were you there, when they pierced him in the side?

Were you there, when the sun refused to shine?[4]
Were you there, when the sun refused to shine?
Oh, sometimes, it causes me to tremble, tremble, tremble.
Were you there, when the sun refused to shine?

2. Cf. Rev 6:16.
3. Cf. John 19:34.
4. Cf. Mark 15:33 and parallels.

Were you there, when they laid him in the tomb?
Were you there, when they laid him in the tomb?
Oh, sometimes, it causes me to tremble, tremble, tremble.
Were you there, when they laid him in the tomb?

The Angel Roll the Stone Away

The angel roll the stone away,
The angel roll the stone away.
'Twas on a bright and shiny morn,
When the trumpet begin to sound.[5]
The angel roll the stone away.

(*repeat*)

Sister Mary came a running
At the break of day.
Brought the news from heaven:
The stone done roll away.[6]

I'm-a looking for my savior:
Tell me where he lay.[7]
High up on the mountain,
The stone done roll away.

The soldiers there a-plenty,
standing by the door.
But they could not hinder
The stone done roll away.[8]

Old Pilate and his wise men
Didn't know what to say.
The miracle was on them:
The stone done roll away.

The angel roll the stone away,
The angel roll the stone away.
'Twas on a bright and shiny morn,
When the trumpet begin to sound.
The angel roll the stone away.

(*repeat*)

5. The trumpet signals the general resurrection of the dead (cf. 1 Cor 15:52; 1 Thess 4:16).
6. Cf. John 20:1–2.
7. Cf. John 20:11–15.
8. Cf. Matt 27:62–66; 28:11–15.

I Got a Home in-a That Rock[9]

I got a home in-a that rock, don't you see?
I got a home in-a that rock, don't you see?
Between the earth and sky,
Thought I heard my savior cry:
You got a home in-a that rock, don't you see?

Poor man Lazarus, poor as I, don't you see?
Poor man Lazarus, poor as I, don't you see?
Poor man Lazarus, poor as I;
When he died he found a home on high.
He had a home in-a that rock, don't you see?

Rich man, Dives, he lived so well, don't you see?
Rich man, Dives, he lived so well, don't you see?
Rich man, Dives, he lived so well,
When he died he found a home in Hell.
He had no home in-a that rock, don't you see?

God gave Noah the rainbow sign, don't you see?
God gave Noah the rainbow sign, don't you see?
God gave Noah the rainbow sign:
No more water but fire next time.[1]
Better get a home in-a that rock, don't you see?

Steal Away to Jesus

Steal away, steal away,
Steal away to Jesus!
Steal away, steal away home.
I ain't got long to stay here.

(*repeat*)

My Lord, he calls me,
He calls me by the thunder.
The trumpet sounds within-a my soul,[2]
I ain't got long to stay here.

Steal away, steal away,
Steal away to Jesus!

9. See Luke 16:19–31 and notes.
1. Cf. Gen 9:11–16.
2. An internalization of eschatological imagery (e.g., 1 Cor 15:52; 1 Thess 4:16).

Steal away, steal away home.
I ain't got long to stay here.

Green trees a-bending,
Poor sinner stand a-trembling.
The trumpet sounds within-a my soul,
I ain't got long to stay here.
Oh, Lord, I ain't got long to stay here.

Steal away, steal away,
Steal away to Jesus!
Steal away, steal away home.
I ain't got long to stay here.

EPIC

JUVENCUS

[Christ's Judgment, Crucifixion, and Resurrection]†

570 Because she had seen Peter sad inside, a woman asked him, "Hadn't you, young man, come as a companion of the fellow whom the leaders' derisive judgment condemned?" He denies and tries to bring himself forth from the humble dwelling. But behold, another woman perceiving him stepping out, right at the threshold, betrayed him to the servants with a similar cry. Again he declares that he did not know the man, now swearing. Then many follow her, approaching to question him, and they say that they can recognize from the sound of his voice that all his words rattle in a Galilean dialect. And Peter, swearing everything with solemn words, insists that he does not know him, whoever he may be, denying him. The bird follows Peter's voice with its song, shaking out its cry from the roof's peak, and Christ's prophetic words gather round Simon's sad mind. And when he came out, he wept bitterly.

586 The stars now retreat from the light and the swift sun comes forth, filling the world with trembling rays. And now with a great shout they drag Christ from

---

† Juvencus, *Evangeliorum libri quattuor* 4.570–812, translated by Austin Busch from the edition of Johannes Huemer (Prague: F. Tempsky, 1891). Boldfaced numbers correspond to line numbers in the Latin original.

Our best information about Juvencus comes from Jerome, who tells us that he was an aristocratic priest from Spain who flourished during the emperor Constantine's reign. According to Jerome, in 329 Juvencus published his *Evangeliorum libri quattuor* (*Four Books of the Gospels*), which transformed the gospel story into a Latin narrative poem in dactylic hexameter—the same meter used by Virgil, Lucan, Statius, and other pagan epic poets. Juvencus's poem thereby inaugurates a rich tradition of reimagining the Bible, and the Gospels in particular, as heroic epic. Juvencus is rarely read today and his poem has never been translated into English in its entirety. The following excerpt offers a prose translation of its conclusion, beginning with Peter's betrayal of Christ and ending with Christ's resurrection and an epilogue praising the emperor Constantine. This poem is typical of other epic transformations of the Gospels in that it draws freely from all relevant NT accounts.

the council, bound behind his back, to the bosom of the governor. And the Lord Jesus, standing before the high tribunal, takes from Pilate's words such things as this: "You, as it is said, stand before me king of the Jewish nation?" Christ responds: "From your words I hear this." Hereupon the terrible accusation against the just man emerges, growling, and defiled eloquence presses the holy one. Jesus deigns to respond nothing to these fierce words. Pilate asks why he now keeps quiet. Standing all the more firmly, he preserves an astonishing silence.

599 But as it happened the laws required a pardon on that solemn day, customarily of one condemned to die. A brigand was bound in custody, whose name was well known and whose life the people hostile to Christ were passionate to save. But, terrified in her sleep by fierce visions, Pilate's wife anxiously entreated her husband with commands and prayers to have no part in the just man's punishment. So the judge again questions the leaders' intentions, and he demands that it be made subject to the people's verdict, in accordance with the law, whom they desire to free from the impending punishment. But the leaders were going around canvassing the people, entreating them to demand the brigand for lawful pardon and to deny Christ.

611 After the leaders' words stir up the masses, who ask that the life of the brigand be granted them in place of Christ's, the governor puts it to the people what they want to happen to Jesus. The populace was stirred by evil to form fierce mobs, and again and again they were demanding crucifixion: "Whoever desires the name of king has confessed to being Caesar's enemy and has condemned himself by his own mouth." Finally, overcome by their force and cursing his bloody duty, Pilate cries that he holds his heart free from this blood and before their eyes he washes his hands of the crime, so that the stain might remain on that nation alone. They shout all the more: "Let that blood pursue us, us, and let this curse and guilt overflow onto our descendants." Pilate grants Barabbas to the people, in accordance with the law, and overcome he yields Jesus to the punishment of the cross.

626 But the traitor Judas, as soon as he realized that he, insane, had been the one to give the signal for such crimes after receiving payment for the betrayal, wretchedly condemned his actions and with authentic laments threw the silver into the temple, cursing it. Beginning to assume his punishment with a noose, he seized an ugly death from a fig tree's highest branch. Then the priests, saying that it was forbidden to admit the payment to the temple's entrance because it was polluted by blood—the very payment which they believed it lawful to give when blood was being sold—, signal their unholy pollution with a dreadful deed: they purchased a field with the true name of blood. The true voice of the prophet singing things once hidden disclosed the events' outcome in the succession of the ages: they laid down thirty minas of unclean silver, setting this as the price for the most precious body,[1] which would soon again be changed into a potter's little field.

642 The just man was handed over to the fierce soldiers, servants of villainy. He provided opportunities for ridicule with his afflicted body. They dress him in a purple tunic and a red cape and they cincture his head with bloody thorns, and instead of a scepter a reed attends his right arm. Then, leaning on their knees,

---

1. See Zech 11:12–13.

they hail him king and lord of the Jewish nation, and they bathe his face with spittle, and they entertain themselves by giving heinous blows to his holy head.

650 Once the soldiers had enough of their demented entertainment, they took out his own clothes to put on him and they dragged the holy and just man to the punishment of the cross. But behold, as soon as they departed they seized a certain Simon, of Cyrene by birth, and they commanded him to bear the wood to which, with fierce commands, the insistent, immutable succession of ages was impelling them to affix the lord of light. But after they had arrived at a place outside the city named Golgotha, they gave cups of wine mixed with gall to Christ. But he refuses to let his last taste be from the corrupted drink, so that in this way the ancient sayings may be satisfied,[2] nor does the mocking rage of these men demand all. Now his body was hanging on a tree, affixed to the cross, and a casting of lots awarded one of the soldiers possession of his tunic, which was woven without seam. And they displayed the written title of his accusation, which he deserved, namely "King of the Jewish People and Nation."

667 It happened, in order that there might be shared participation in the punishment, that brigands were with him, on this side and that; but the blind madness of the raging people mocks the affixed Christ: "This is the one who by himself was able to destroy the temple. This is the one who could rebuild it within a three-fold passing of the sun. But now let the Thunderer's venerable progeny descend and let him loose his body and soul from the punishment of the cross." The leaders of the senseless people imitate what they say. The Pharisees and scribes and the frenzied faction mock and shake their heads and their tongues with wild speech so as to bring on themselves the bonds of eternal punishment: "Was he not accustomed to saving others from the fierce bonds of disease? Why is he not strong enough to free himself from punishment? This is the one whom we are to believe is king of our nation? Let him free his body from the wood's strength. Then, in fitting manner, we will be able to believe his holy signs. He trusts in God as his father, so why does that venerable power not want to deliver its own offspring from punishment?" The brigands at his right hand and left reproach him no less, even while they groan, affixed to crosses as the lot for their crimes.

687 Already the light's course had elevated it to the sky's middle point when suddenly it flees from all eyes and puts on dark shadows, and the sun conceals the agitated day in night. But when this turmoil had lasted until the ninth hour, the frantic light returned to its world, and Christ called on the Father with a great voice in the custom of the Hebrew tongue; but the ignorant people suppose he is calling Elijah. Then some man, excited by what was happening, forced him to drink sour juice pressed to his lips from a foul sponge tied to a reed, and the rest of the crowd, raging, made a violent racket with their voice: "Let us look all around lest by chance Elijah comes, sent back from heaven where he rests on his exalted seat, and free the king affixed to this wretched stake." Then a cry sent forth with the Lord's great exertion unites his spirit, once his companion, with the ethereal wind. At the same time the curtains of the holy temple are ripped in two and the fine linens, severed into twin halves, gape open, and the trembling earth is struck by all weight, and

2. See Ps 69:21.

cliffs leap down, broken off from their mass. Then the tombs of ancient men were laid open, the bolts removed from their doors, and just souls returned to their bodies and people were seen wandering widely in every direction within the city walls. Thus do all these things terrify the world, but first to be shaken with fear were the hearts of the soldiers who guarded the bodies consigned to fierce punishment, and they said that he was God's offspring, and confessed Christ.

714 From their places of watch all the mothers who used to attend to Christ's needs observe these great wonders. Now the evening begins to follow the setting sun, when one of the leaders, since he was more just, dares alone to demand the body of Christ for last services. This man, from Arimathea, bore the name of Joseph, and he once offered his ears to Jesus' words. This one, then, asks Pilate, who had lately borne his life to punishment—a crude violence. The governor assented and brilliant linen fabric covers the body, and it is placed in a cave newly carved of stone. A huge rolling mass of rock closes the entrance securely, and from their places of watch the mothers stand guard, observing all.

727 Now day fills the earth with auburn light, which, by ancient law, always commanded rest, but the merciless rage of the leaders keeps no rest. They assemble and in one company overwhelm the ears of the judge: "A most just punishment loosened error's snares. Now it would be good to remember this: that man was accustomed openly to promise the common people—always bandying it about—that with the third return of the sun he would come back in like manner from the shadows of death to the light of life. We request that a division of soldiers guard the new tomb, lest wild boldness to plunder it rise up in the disciples and a fresh delusion disturb the people." Pilate responds to their words: "You may have your soldiers, to guard, as you wish, a body buried in the earth." They assemble and roll gigantic loads of stone, and they safeguard the threshold with a seal and the stone with a band of soldiers.

743 When the stars of night begin to give way to the sun soon to come, then the mothers run together to look at the tomb's enclosure, but all at once a violent motion shakes the entire land and a messenger fallen from the opened heavens descends and rolls the stone from the threshold of the tomb. His visage gleams as lightning's fire, and for clothing his robe glows like the bright sheen of snow. Fright banished all sense from the soldiers and they collapsed together like corpses laid prostrate by violent death. But that one speaks to the mothers like this: "Let no tremulous fear now assail your hearts, for your faithfulness is evident, in that you seek the sacred body which criminal madness affixed to the wood of the cross. Christ has arisen and has received the eternal light of life, along with his body made holy by death's defeat. You may now see that no members lie in the grave where they were interred. Hereafter, return quickly and hasten to tell the disciples that Christ has returned to the shores of light and that he joyfully goes before them into the land of Galilee." At these words and sights an intense stupor pours over the souls of the women, thunderstruck by joy and by wavering fear. Finally, jubilantly celebrating, with a headlong run they go to report these things to the disciples, leaving the tomb behind. But behold, in the middle of their flight, Jesus showed himself clearly and comforted the faithful mothers with a greeting. They rush to meet him and, grasping his knees and his feet, they worship Jesus

who had defeated terrified death. He immediately fortifies their hearts with injunctions such as these: "Let all fear withdraw from your faithful minds and come, quickly bear these commands back to our brothers. If you attend to what you have seen of me, go willingly: quickly run across the land into Galilee."

776 Meanwhile, the hearts of the guards at the tomb were struck with terror. They send some from their number to report to the Jews the wondrousness of the events. But that demented band, already once thoroughly devoted to insane fury, eagerly remunerates the soldiers with large payments, purchasing with silver a false report, namely that the audacious disciples, having violated the threshold of the tomb, furtively plundered it under the cover of darkness and secretly bore the body away.

784 And now, the anxious crowd of his own people ascended the Galilean mountains, assembling at Christ's command. Behold, the venerable offspring of the Thunderer appears to his own. Falling down prostrate, the entire chorus solemnly praises him. But virtue was not poured out in all their hearts equally, for some of them continued to doubt. So Jesus at that time clearly compels the disciples: "My father has made all things in heaven and earth subject to me, and he deigned to send me as a light to you all. No differently have I ordained to send you to all the nations; it is your task to join all nations to me. Go forth and bathe men in the holy name of the father and of his son, washing them with cleansing waves, and at the same time let blow the aspirations of life-giving breezes. And then introduce by teaching our precepts to those who have been washed, in order that they may be able to move onward to eternal life. Nor will our presence ever depart from you, not until the consuming end dissolves the ages."

802 My mind laid hold of this force of faith and of holy fear and so greatly did Christ's grace enlighten me that in our verses the glory of divine law willingly laid hold of the earthly ornaments of language. These words the peace of Christ conferred on me, these the peace of this age too, fostered by Constantine, the known world's kind lord. He is worthy of suitable favor, who alone of kings shudders at the great burden of the holy name placed on him, so that, made more worthy by his just deeds, he may lay hold of eternal life in the divine age through the lord of light Christ, who reigns in that age forever.

ROGER P. H. GREEN

[Juvencus's Inversion of Vergil's *Aeneid*]†

Another example of inversion, again clearly linked to and dependent on the verbal text, is in the depiction of Christ as captive, just before his trial. There is a very close

† From Roger P. H. Green, *Latin Epics of the New Testament: Juvencus, Sedulius, Arator* (Oxford: Oxford University Press, 2006), 63–65. Green offers some paradigmatic observations about the dialogue with pagan epic that Juvencus and other writers of biblical epic orchestrate. Although readers of the present volume will likely be more interested in the relationship of the excerpted epics to the Gospel accounts, the authors' transformations of the NT stories of Jesus into heroic narrative poems involve highly complex fusions of the Gospels and classical literary forms; their informed interpretation thus demands attention to the latter as well as to the former.

resemblance between [Juvencus] 4. 588–9 *Christum post terga revinctum . . . magno clamore trahebant*[1] and Vergil's words on the capture of Sinon, the fake renegade, at A. [*Aeneid*] 2. 57–8 *post terga revinctum . . . magno . . . clamore trahebant.*[2] Moreover, the people at 4. 568 'compete in mocking him', just as they did in Vergil (cf. A. 2. 64 *certantque illudere*). These details of the alluding language serve to reveal, by their surprising exactitude, that Christ is the very opposite of Sinon, and his adversaries are the deceitful ones. He is not, like Sinon, prepared *seu versare dolos seu certae occumbere morti* ('either to ply his tricks or to succumb to certain death', A. 2. 62), but is aware only of the second. At the same time there is a vivid picture of Christ's painful and humiliating isolation among his many enemies. There may even be, in the words *comes additus* (4. 571, shortly preceding), a hint of Ulysses, the trickster who lay behind this ruse, for in A. 6. 528–9 *comes additus una* | *hortator scelerum Aeolides* ('joined with him, his companion Ulysses, inciter of crimes'), this phrase refers to Odysseus, to whom Peter, the *comes additus*, might fleetingly be compared.

At line 4. 714 the words *e speculis matres . . . tuentur* ('the mothers watch from their lookouts') begin an episode about the 'mothers'—Mary Magdalene, Mary the mother of James and Joseph, and the mother of the sons of Zebedee—and others who watch at Christ's grave. Most unusually, the same words, in a slightly different order, end the passage at 726; and the word *matres* is frequent in the whole context. They invite a comparison with A. 11. 877 *e speculis . . . percussae pectora matres* ('from the towers the mothers, beating their breasts . . .') describing women distraught at the danger to themselves and their families and raising a cry to heaven. Mothers, indeed, usually indicated as here by the single stark word *matres*, are frequent in the *Aeneid*: Trojan mothers whose city is sacked in Book 2 (489 and 766), the mothers who are torn 'between love of their present land and the fated kingdoms that are calling them' in Book 5 (654–6), the Latin mothers who answer the call of Amata in Book 7, and the same mothers who witness the downfall of their city in Books 11 and 12. In these passages, as often in the *Aeneid*, 'mothers' have a miserable fate; sometimes they are seen as disruptive. But in Juvencus, though sorrowful—one may note also the *matres* of 1. 265 who actually correspond to 'Rachel weeping for her children' in Matt. 2:18—they are quiet, patient, and soon to be rewarded (4.768). This contrast, highlighted by the simple word *matres* and Juvencus' allusive *e speculis* (the Marys were not exactly ensconced in watchtowers), captures a contrast of values between the male-oriented warfare of the *Aeneid* which subordinates women and makes victims of them and the more universal and internalized virtues that are highlighted, from the outset, in the gospel narratives. Christ is certainly engaged in a conflict, but it is one where the quiet virtues of faith, patience, and suffering are the victorious ones.

After Christ's resurrection (4.793–4) the disciples are commanded to go out into the whole world. The words 'to all races' actually occur in both these lines, and the verbatim repetition is arresting. There is no such closeness at the verbal level to Vergil, but in the *Aeneid* the future emperor Augustus is conspicuous because all races come to him (8. 722 *incedunt victae longo ordine gentes*, 'conquered races

---

1. They dragged Christ, [hands] bound behind his back, with great shouting (Latin).
2. They dragged him, [hands] bound behind his back, with great shouting (Latin).

parade in a long line'); he does not use the word 'all', but this is implied by the choice of remote and exotic races. As a sign of their defeat they present gifts (721). One may see an important reversal or inversion here, for Christ's followers, by contrast, take with them the gifts (*dona*) of salvation, the *munera* of the kingdom of Heaven (cf. 1.419–20, and 3.294–5 . . . *cunctisque dabit sua munera terris*, 'and he will give his gifts to all lands', as a result of his resurrection). The preaching of the gospel goes world-wide, *in cunctas terrae metas* (4.117–18 'to all the ends of the earth'), just as, according to Jupiter's prophecy, the sway of the Romans would. Jupiter had given no limits (*metas*) to the empire, in space or time (*A.* 1. 278–9); but Christian outreach had overshadowed that proud claim, going even beyond the limits of the empire. And after preaching had gone to all nations—as it had by Constantine's time—the end of time would come, as Christ prophesied (4. 120: Matt. 24:14); this recalls the Preface, where true eternity can only be predicated of God, the Christian kerygma, and its faithful messengers, and not of Rome or her poets.

MARCO GIROLAMO VIDA

[The Exorcism of Legion]†

439 "I[1] shudder whenever I recall a certain man who was driven by fierce obsessions and whom I saw at that time when I was gathering my haul of fish on this very shore. In an attack of madness he frothed horribly at the mouth. They say that he was conceived when his parents once lay together in forbidden embrace at a time when sexual union had been interdicted.[2] They had gone to bed when the holy laws of God forbade, when all were solemnizing the dark tragedy of our people. But they did not long enjoy their sacrilege. For all at once, even as they embraced in delight, the unfortunate adulterer breathed his last sinful breath into thin air, and that first short night of unspeakable sacrilege was also his last. And a fever, divinely sent, seized the woman with its burning when the burden of the matured foetus already pressed down upon her; and the same hour would have brought the death of both except that the baby was delivered by cutting it from its mother's womb.

456 "His father's sisters reared the youngster. And he who did not deserve it paid for the evil his parents had done, for his eyes were denied glad light, and he was completely deaf; it was not given him either to hear words or to reply. As soon as he had grown up, then madness also gripped the sick man—a wild violence inflicted by a hellish crew. A hundred furies, a hundred demons dreadfully

† Vida, *Christiad* 4.439–531, from Marco Girolamo Vida, *The Christiad*, ed. and trans. Gertrude C. Drake and Clarence A. Forbes (Carbondale, Il.: Southern Illinois University Press, 1978), 163, 165, 167. Boldfaced numbers correspond to line numbers in the Latin.
    Like Juvencus, Vida (ca. 1485–1566) is not often read today, but his neo-Latin epic on the life of Christ (published in 1535) enjoyed great popularity during the Renaissance. Other than classical poets and the Bible itself, perhaps no work influenced Milton's biblical epics more thoroughly. Virtually every line of the *Christiad* echoes one classical author or another, though only one such allusion is flagged in the notes for the selection that follows, which gives Vida's account of the exorcism of Legion (cf. Matt 8:28–34; Mark 5:1–20; Luke 8:26–39).
1. The speaker here is the apostle John, who in the *Christiad* recounts Jesus' ministry before Pilate.
2. On analogy with Exod 19:15 (cf. Deut 23:10–11; 1 Sam 21:4), Vida plausibly imagines that abstinence was periodically required for ancient Jewish festivals.

vexed and overmastered him; they were a legion driven from the shadows of hell. Producing voices that imitated human speech, they uttered fearful wails and terrifying groans. All men were afraid of him when he raved and shouted gibberish, and they fled in fear to their houses whenever the youth had got free and escaped negligent attendants by wildly bursting his cords and chains.

471 "At times he did not recognize his brothers, nor again his sisters, and he would stay no longer in his father's house, but lived like a wild animal in woods and caverns, wherever there were hollow rocks or tombs worn by time. He was dirty and in need, and, having ripped off his clothes, he was naked.

476 "And so his kin and those who loved him tied his hands behind his back with cord and dragged him forcibly before Christ, hoping he might pity the boy. But the youth kept struggling against them as he tried to break the cords, and frightened everyone by screaming to high heaven. He was like a pugnacious bull, lassoed for sacrifice, that bellows with rage through the city, and flings foam, and beats the air with its curving horns.[3] The attendants prod it here and there, and, crowding in on it, they redouble the lashes, raining blows on its back and forequarters with bludgeons. The people scatter in fear, and, safe behind their gates, they enjoy watching the danger from a distance. Such was the appearance of the young man in his terrible frenzy whom they wearily set before God, asking him to give help, or at least to deliver him from such vexing devils and drive the tormenting demons out of his mind.

492 "Thereupon the Savior raised both his palms to heaven and in formal supplication prayed to the Creator. And now all at once a great and wondrous miracle occurred. Slavering at the mouth, the madman uttered fearful sounds like the howling of wolves and the barking of dogs. A torrential cataract from high cliffs with its crashing floods would not roar so violently if the Pie-di-Lugo[4] should happen to burst its high dam and the whole mass of water should rush down from the heights over the low valleys so that all the district becomes a sea, and the inundated villages round about are afloat, and Rome is deluged and fears for its holy shrines. Again, the uproar is like that in the heavens when the King of angels flashes lightning and shakes the golden zones of the sky with thunder.

505 "Now a sound was heard like the horrible rasping of iron chains when smashed with a tremendous weight, or like the roar of the sea. All the land, all the sky everywhere echoed the din. God attacked the demons with great force and shouted at them when they lingered. And now they trembled within the man and begged for peace: 'True and undoubted Son of God, why do you now thrust us out of the body which was given over to us to torment? At least let us enter this herd now as we leave.' (It so happened that bristly hogs were then grazing near that seashore.) 'Do not plunge us into the fearful abyss. Do not order us to go beneath to the darkness of hell.'

516 "The Savior consented. One could see that the black herd in the distance were immediately forced to scatter helter-skelter every-which-way without rest or peace because of the devils' fierce goading. Wild violence raged within them until they hurled themselves into the deep pools below where every one of them lost its life in the water.

3. For this simile, cf. *Iliad* 20.403–06.
4. A lake in Italy.

522 "But the young man's weary limbs relaxed at once when the restraining cords were finally taken from his arms. With his face pressed to the ground, the sick man lay there a long time grinding his teeth, and continued to moan and pant hard with heaving breast, and forced breath out from his lungs. The Son of God the Father stood near him, and, touching his face with his right hand, he opened his eyes and his ears. And now he saw and spoke, and his heart, so long distraught, was at peace. The outcry of the multitude rejoicing mounted to the golden stars, and they acknowledged him the Son of the highest Father and God."

JOHN MILTON

[Christ's Third Temptation]†

Satan, now   365

Quite at a loss (for all his darts were spent),
Thus to our Saviour with stern brow replied:—
  "Since neither wealth nor honour, arms nor arts,
Kingdom nor empire, pleases thee, nor aught
By me proposed in life contemplative   370
Or active, tended on by glory or fame,
What dost thou in this world? The Wilderness
For thee is fittest place: I found thee there,
And thither will return thee. Yet remember
What I foretell thee; soon thou shalt have cause   375
To wish thou never hadst rejected thus
Nicely or cautiously my offered aid,
Which would have set thee in short time with ease
On David's throne, or throne of all the world,
Now at full age, fulness of time, thy season,   380
When prophecies of thee are best fulfilled.
Now, contrary—if I read aught in heaven,
Or heaven write aught of fate—by what the stars
Voluminous, or single characters
In their conjunction met, give me to spell,   385
Sorrows and labours, opposition, hate,
Attends thee, scorns, reproaches, injuries,
Violence and stripes, and, lastly, cruel death.
A kingdom they portend thee, but what kingdom,
Real or allegoric, I discern not;   390
Nor when: eternal sure—as without end,

---

† John Milton, *Paradise Regained* 4.365–639, from *The Complete Poems of John Milton*, ed. Charles W. Elliot (New York: P. F. Collier and Son Company, 1909), 404–411 (punctuation occasionally altered). For Milton, see note on p. 1289.
   Milton's brief epic on the temptation of Christ (Matt 4:1–11; Luke 4:1–13), the conclusion of which is excerpted here, was published in 1671, a few years after the first edition of *Paradise Lost*. It frequently echoes Greek and Roman poetry, as well as English and Italian Renaissance epics, not to mention the Bible. The notes signal only a handful of the most important allusions.

Without beginning; for no date prefixed
Directs me in the starry rubric[1] set."
     So saying, he took (for still he knew his power
Not yet expired), and to the Wilderness   395
Brought back the Son of God and left him there,
Feigning to disappear. Darkness now rose,
As daylight sunk, and brought in louring Night,
Her shadowy offspring, unsubstantial both,
Privation mere of light and absent day.   400
Our Saviour meek and with untroubled mind
After his aerie jaunt,[2] though hurried sore,
Hungry and cold betook him to his rest,
Wherever, under some concourse of shades
Whose branching arms thick intertwined might shield   405
From dews and damps of night his sheltered head;
But sheltered slept in vain; for at his head
The Tempter watched, and soon with ugly dreams
Disturbed his sleep. And either tropic[3] now
'Gan thunder, and both ends of heaven; the clouds   410
From many a horrid rift abortive poured
Fierce rain with lightning mixed, water with fire
In ruin reconciled; nor slept the winds
Within their stony caves, but rushed abroad
From the four hinges of the world, and fell   415
On the vexed wilderness, whose tallest pines,
Though rooted deep as high, and sturdiest oaks
Bowed their stiff necks, loaden with stormy blasts,
Or torn up sheer. Ill wast thou shrouded then,
O patient Son of God, yet only stood'st   420
Unshaken! Nor yet staid the terror there:
Infernal ghosts and hellish furies round
Environed thee; some howled, some yelled, some shrieked,
Some bent at thee their fiery darts, while thou
Sat'st unappalled in calm and sinless peace.   425
Thus passed the night so foul, till Morning fair
Came forth with pilgrim steps in amice[4] grey,
Who with her radiant finger stilled the roar
Of thunder, chased the clouds, and laid the winds
And griesly spectres, which the Fiend had raised   430
To tempt the Son of God with terrors dire.
And now the sun with more effectual beams
Had cheered the face of earth, and dried the wet

1. An instruction in a book of liturgy, traditionally printed in red (*OED*).
2. An exhausting journey (*OED*).
3. The northern and southern solstitial points.
4. A wrap with gray fur worn by religious orders (*OED*).

From drooping plant, or dropping tree; the birds,
Who all things now behold more fresh and green,   435
After a night of storm so ruinous,
Cleared up their choicest notes in bush and spray[5]
To gratulate the sweet return of morn.
Nor yet, amidst this joy and brightest morn,
Was absent, after all his mischief done,   440
The Prince of Darkness; glad would also seem
Of this fair change, and to our Saviour came;
Yet with no new device (they all were spent),
Rather by this his last affront resolved,
Desperate of better course, to vent his rage   445
And mad despite to be so oft repelled.
Him walking on a sunny hill he found,
Backed on the north and west by a thick wood;
Out of the wood he starts in wonted shape,
And in a careless mood thus to him said:—   450
    "Fair morning yet betides thee, Son of God,
After a dismal night. I heard the wrack,
As earth and sky would mingle; but myself
Was distant; and these flaws, though mortals fear them
As dangerous to the pillared frame of Heaven,[6]   455
Or to the Earth's dark basis underneath,
Are to the main as inconsiderable
And harmless, if not wholesome, as a sneeze
To man's less universe, and soon are gone.
Yet, as being ofttimes noxious where they light   460
On man, beast, plant, wasteful and turbulent,
Like turbulencies in the affairs of men,
Over whose heads they roar, and seem to point,
They oft fore-signify and threaten ill.
This tempest at this desert most was bent;   465
Of men at thee, for only thou here dwell'st.
Did I not tell thee, if thou didst reject
The perfect season offered with my aid
To win thy destined seat, but wilt prolong
All to the push of fate, pursue thy way   470
Of gaining David's throne no man knows when
(For both the when and how is nowhere told),
Thou shalt be what thou art ordained, no doubt;
For Angels have proclaimed it, but concealing
The time and means: each act is rightliest done   475
Not when it must, but when it may be best.

5. Small twigs.
6. Echoing Virgil, *Aeneid* 1.133–34 and Job 26:11.

If thou observe not this, be sure to find
What I foretold thee—many a hard assay
Of dangers, and adversities, and pains,
Ere thou of Israel's sceptre get fast hold;   480
Whereof this ominous night that closed thee round,
So many terrors, voices, prodigies
May warn thee, as a sure foregoing sign."
    So talked he, while the Son of God went on
And staid not, but in brief him answered thus:—   485
    "Me worse than wet thou find'st not; other harm
Those terrors which thou speak'st of did me none.
I never feared they could, though noising loud
And threatening nigh: what they can do as signs
Betokening or ill-boding I contemn   490
As false portents, not sent from God, but thee;
Who, knowing I shall reign past thy preventing,
Obtrud'st thy offered aid, that I, accepting,
At least might seem to hold all power of thee,
Ambitious Spirit! and would'st be thought my God;   495
And storm'st, refused, thinking to terrify
Me to thy will! Desist (thou art discerned
And toil'st in vain), nor me in vain molest."
    To whom the Fiend, now swoln with rage, replied:—
"Then hear, O Son of David, virgin-born!   500
For Son of God to me is yet in doubt.
Of the Messiah I have heard foretold
By all the Prophets; of thy birth, at length
Announced by Gabriel, with the first I knew,
And of the angelic song in Bethlehem field,   505
On thy birth-night, that sung thee Saviour born.
From that time seldom have I ceased to eye
Thy infancy, thy childhood, and thy youth,
Thy manhood last, though yet in private bred;
Till, at the ford of Jordan, whither all   510
Flocked to the Baptist, I among the rest
(Though not to be baptized), by voice from Heaven
Heard thee pronounced the Son of God beloved.
Thenceforth I thought thee worth my nearer view
And narrower scrutiny, that I might learn   515
In what degree or meaning thou art called
The Son of God, which bears no single sense.
The Son of God I also am, or was;
And, if I was, I am; relation stands:
All men are Sons of God,[7] yet thee I thought   520
In some respect far higher so declared.

7. Cf. Job 1:6; Ps 82:6.

Therefore, I watched thy footsteps from that hour,
And followed thee still on to this waste wild,
Where, by all best conjectures, I collect
Thou art to be my fatal enemy.   525
Good reason, then, if I beforehand seek
To understand my adversary, who
And what he is; his wisdom, power, intent;
By parle[8] or composition,[9] truce or league
To win him, or win from him what I can.   530
And opportunity I here have had
To try thee, sift thee, and confess have found thee
Proof against all temptation, as a rock
Of adamant and as a centre, firm
To the utmost of mere man both wise and good,   535
Not more; for honours, riches, kingdoms, glory
Have been before contemned, and may again.
Therefore, to know what more thou art than man,
Worth naming Son of God by voice from Heaven,
Another method I must now begin."   540
    So saying, he caught him up, and, without wing
Of hippogrif,[1] bore through the air sublime,
Over the wilderness and o'er the plain,
Till underneath them fair Jerusalem,
The Holy City, lifted high her towers,   545
And higher yet the glorious Temple reared
Her pile, far off appearing like a mount
Of alablaster, topt with golden spires:
There, on the highest pinnacle, he set
The Son of God, and added thus in scorn:—   550
    "There stand, if thou wilt stand; to stand upright
Will ask thee skill. I to thy Father's house
Have brought thee, and highest placed: highest is best.
Now shew thy progeny;[2] if not to stand,
Cast thyself down, safely, if Son of God;   555
For it is written, 'He will give command
Concerning thee to his Angels; in their hands
They shall uplift thee, lest at any time
Thou chance to dash thy foot against a stone.'"[3]
    To whom thus Jesus: "Also it is written,   560
'Tempt not the Lord thy God.'"[4] He said, and stood;
But Satan, smitten with amazement, fell.

8. Parley.
9. Political reconciliation.
1. A mythological creature, part horse and part griffin.
2. Parentage or ancestry (*OED*).
3. Ps 91:11–12.
4. Deut 6:16.

As when Earth's son, Antæus[5] (to compare
Small things with greatest), in Irassa strove
With Jove's Alcides, and, oft foiled, still rose,   565
Receiving from his mother Earth new strength,
Fresh from his fall, and fiercer grapple joined,
Throttled at length in the air expired and fell;
So, after many a foil, the Tempter proud,
Renewing fresh assaults, amidst his pride   570
Fell whence he stood to see his victor fall.
And, as that Theban monster[6] that proposed
Her riddle, and him who solved it not devoured,
That once found out and solved, for grief and spite
Cast herself headlong from the Ismenian steep,   575
So, strook with dread and anguish, fell the Fiend,
And to his crew that sat consulting brought
Joyless triumphals of his hoped success,
Ruin, and desperation, and dismay,
Who durst so proudly tempt the Son of God.   580
So Satan fell, and straight a fiery globe
Of Angels on full sail of wing flew nigh,
Who on their plumy vans received Him soft
From his uneasy station, and upbore,
As on a floating couch, through the blithe air;   585
Then in a flowery valley set him down
On a green bank, and set before him spread
A table of celestial food, divine
Ambrosial fruits fetched from the Tree of Life,[7]
And from the Fount of Life ambrosial drink   590
That soon refreshed him wearied, and repaired
What hunger, if aught hunger, had impaired,
Or thirst; and, as he fed, Angelic quires
Sung heavenly anthems of his victory
Over temptation and the Tempter proud:—   595
    "True Image of the Father, whether throned
In the bosom of bliss, and light of light
Conceiving, or, remote from Heaven, enshrined
In fleshly tabernacle and human form,[8]
Wandering the wilderness—whatever place,   600
Habit, or state, or motion, still expressing
The Son of God, with Godlike force endued

---

5. The mythical giant defeated by Hercules (Alcides, 565), in Irassa, according to Pindar (*Pythian* 9.106).
6. The Sphinx, who killed those unable to solve her riddle. She destroyed herself when Oedipus answered correctly.
7. Cf. Gen 2:9.
8. Cf. John 1:1–18.

Against the attempter of thy Father's throne
And thief of Paradise!⁹ Him long of old
Thou didst debel,¹ and down from Heaven cast   605
With all his army; now thou hast avenged
Supplanted Adam, and, by vanquishing
Temptation, hast regained lost Paradise
And frustrated the conquest fraudulent.
He never more henceforth will dare set foot   610
In Paradise to tempt; his snares are broke.²
For, though that seat of earthly bliss be failed,³
A fairer Paradise is founded now
For Adam and his chosen sons, whom thou,
A Saviour, art come down to reinstall;   615
Where they shall dwell secure, when time shall be
Of tempter and temptation without fear.
But thou, Infernal Serpent! shalt not long
Rule in the clouds. Like an autumnal star,
Or lightning, thou shalt fall from Heaven, trod down   620
Under his feet.⁴ For proof, ere this thou feel'st
Thy wound (yet not thy last and deadliest wound)⁵
By this repulse received, and hold'st in Hell
No triumph; in all her gates Abaddon⁶ rues
Thy bold attempt. Hereafter learn with awe   625
To dread the Son of God. He, all unarmed,
Shall chase thee with the terror of his voice
From thy demoniac holds, possession foul—
Thee and thy legions; yelling they shall fly
And beg to hide them in a herd of swine,   630
Lest he command them down into the Deep,
Bound, and to torment sent before their time.⁷
Hail, Son of the Most High, heir of both Worlds,
Queller of Satan! On thy glorious work
Now enter, and begin to save Mankind."   635
    Thus they the Son of God, our Saviour meek,
Sung victor, and, from heavenly feast refreshed,
Brought on his way with joy. He, unobserved,
Home to his mother's house private returned.

9. A reference to Satan's supposed role in the primeval transgression (Gen 3), which Milton's *Paradise Lost* famously elaborates.
1. Subdue.
2. Cf. Ps 124:7.
3. Be absent or be wanting (*OED*).
4. Cf. Gen 3:15; Luke 10:18; Rom 16:20.
5. Referring to Satan's eschatological defeat; cf. Rev 20:10.
6. Hell; cf. Rev 9:11 and note.
7. Cf. Matt 8:29–33 and parallels.

Part IV. Case Studies

The Character of Pontius Pilate

A strong ideological impulse—even a propagandistic one—lies behind much ancient Christian writing about Pontius Pilate, the Roman governor who oversaw Jesus' trial and crucifixion. Tertullian calls him a Christian at heart; some go further, making him a Christian martyr (*Paradosis Pilati*). Early Christian transformations of Pilate into a believer, usually complemented by the demonization of Jesus' Jewish opponents, reflect an attempt to reduce tension between this upstart religious sect and the Roman Empire that Pilate represented, which brutally persecuted the church during the early centuries of its existence. By presenting Pilate as a fundamentally just albeit weak man coerced by an evil Jewish high priest into ordering the Lord's execution, ancient Christians suggested that Rome was not inherently hostile to the religion founded in Christ's name. This tendency is not restricted to post–New Testament Christian literature; it is also on display in the Gospels themselves (see Matt 26:1–5, 14–16, 47–68; 27:1–66; 28:11–15; Mark 14:1–2, 10–11, 43–65; 15:1–47; Luke 22:1–6, 47–53, 63–71; 23:1–56; John 11:45–57; 18:1–14, 19–24, 28–40; 19:1–42), which portray Pilate as fraught with ambivalence about the role he is forced to play in Jesus' trial and execution—a historically unlikely portrayal in light of the brutality attributed to him by Philo (see above, pp. 981–83), by Josephus, and by Luke himself outside of his Passion Narrative (13:1). Indeed, Josephus indicates that Pilate left office under a cloud of suspicion after having ordered unjustified executions of Samaritan zealots on a massive scale (*Jewish Antiquities* 18.87–89).

The Pilate tradition ultimately acquired a momentum independent of its original ideological impulse. Later writers present Pilate as a tragic figure, whose inability to exercise justice in his dealings with Jesus calls forth from the audience a combination of pity and scorn. Such versions are represented in this volume, not only in *The Dream of Pilate's Wife*, included below, but also in Emily Dickinson's "One Crucifixion is recorded-only," which tends toward pity (pp. 1303–04), and Richard Crashaw's "To Pontius washing his blood-stained hands" (p. 1287), which tends toward scorn. Perhaps the most compelling literary representation of Pontius Pilate comes from a work that this appendix cannot accommodate: the Master's novel from Mikhail Bulgakov's *The Master and Margarita* (1966–67; chaps. 2, 16, 25–26). Those who find intriguing the diverse portrayals included here would do well to read that wonderful work.

TERTULLIAN

[Pilate: A Christian in Heart] (from *Apology*, chap. 21)[†]

But the Jews were so exasperated by His teaching, by which their rulers and chiefs were convicted of the truth, chiefly because so many turned aside to Him, that at last they brought Him before Pontius Pilate, at that time Roman governor of Syria; and, by the violence of their outcries against Him, extorted a sentence giving Him up to them to be crucified. He Himself had predicted this; which, however, would have signified little had not the prophets of old done it as well. And yet, nailed upon the cross, He exhibited many notable signs by which His death was distinguished from all others. At His own free-will, He with a word dismissed from Him His spirit, anticipating the executioner's work. In the same hour, too, the light of day was withdrawn, when the sun at the very time was in his meridian blaze. Those who were not aware that this had been predicted about Christ no doubt thought it an eclipse. You yourselves have the account of the world-portent still in your archives.[1] Then, when His body was taken down from the cross and placed in a sepulchre, the Jews in their eager watchfulness surrounded it with a large military guard, lest, as He had predicted His resurrection from the dead on the third day, His disciples might remove by stealth His body and deceive even the incredulous. But, lo, on the third day there was a sudden shock of earthquake, and the stone which sealed the sepulchre was rolled away, and the guard fled off in terror: without a single disciple near, the grave was found empty of all but the clothes of the buried One. But nevertheless, the leaders of the Jews, whom it nearly concerned both to spread abroad a lie and keep back a people tributary and submissive to them from the faith, gave it out that the body of Christ had been stolen by His followers. For the Lord, you see, did not go forth into the public gaze, lest the wicked should be delivered from their error and in order that faith also, destined to a great reward, might hold its ground in difficulty. But He spent forty days with some of His disciples down in Galilee, a region of Judea, instructing them in the doctrines they were to teach to others. Thereafter, having given them commission to preach the gospel through the world, He was encompassed with a cloud and taken up to heaven,—a fact more certain far than the assertions of your Proculi concerning Romulus.[2] All these things Pilate did to Christ; and now in fact a Christian in his own convictions, he sent word of Him to the reigning Cæsar, who was at the time Tiberius. Yes, and the Cæsars too would have believed on Christ, if either the Cæsars had not been necessary for the world, or if Christians could have been Cæsars.

[†] From Tertullian, *Apology*, trans. S. Thelwall, in *The Ante-Nicene Fathers*, vol. 3 (1885; reprint, Peabody, MA: Hendrickson, 1994), 35 (occasionally altered). For Tertullian, see note on p. 1090. Tertullian's *Apology* (197 C.E.) is a defense of Christianity ostensibly addressed to Roman officials in North Africa.
1. Perhaps alluding to writings such as the *Letter of Pilate to Claudius* (Appendix, pp. 1360–61); alternatively, Tertullian might simply infer the existence of a record of the eclipse.
2. Proculus publicly reported that the recently deceased Romulus descended from heaven, spoke to him, and ascended again (Livy 1.16). Proculi is the plural of his name.

JOHN CHRYSOSTOM

From Homily on Matthew 27:11–12†

"And Jesus stood before the governor; and the governor asked Him, saying, Art thou the king of the Jews? And Jesus said unto him, Thou sayest. And when He was accused of the chief priests and elders, He answered nothing."

1. Do you see what He is first asked? which thing most of all they [the Jewish leaders] were continually bringing forward in every way? For since they saw Pilate making no account of the matters of the law, they direct their accusation to the state charges. So likewise did they in the case of the apostles, ever bringing forward these things and saying that they were going about proclaiming king one Jesus [Acts 17:7], speaking as of a mere man, and investing them with a suspicion of usurpation.

Whence it is manifest that both the rending the garment and the amazement were a pretense [Matt 26:65]. But all things they got up and plied in order to bring Him to death.

This at any rate Pilate then asked. What then said Christ? "Thou sayest." He confessed that He was a king, but a heavenly king, which elsewhere also He spake more clearly, replying to Pilate, "My kingdom is not of this world" [John 18:36]; that neither they nor this man should have an excuse for accusing Him of such things. And He gives a reason that cannot be gainsaid, saying, "If I were of this world, my servants would fight, that I should not be delivered." For this purpose I say, in order to refute this suspicion, He both paid tribute [Matt 17:24–27] and commanded others to pay it [Matt 22:15–22], and when they would make Him a king, He fled [John 6:15].

Wherefore then did he not bring forward these things, it may be said, at that time, when accused of usurpation? Because having the proofs from His acts, of His power, His meekness, His gentleness, beyond number, they were willfully blind, and dealt unfairly, and the tribunal was corrupt. For these reasons then He replies to nothing, but holds His peace, yet answering briefly (so as not to get the reputation of arrogance from continual silence) when the high priest adjured Him, when the governor asked, but in reply to their accusations, He no longer saith anything; for He was not now likely to persuade them. Even as the prophet declaring this selfsame thing from of old, said, "In His humiliation His judgment was taken away" [LXX Isa 53:8].

At these things the governor marvelled, and indeed it was worthy of admiration to see Him showing such great forbearance and holding His peace, Him

---

† From John Chrysostom, *Homily LXXXVI,* trans. George Prevost, rev. M. B. Riddle, in *The Nicene and Post-Nicene Fathers: First Series,* vol. 10 (1888; reprint, Peabody, MA: Hendrickson, 1994), 511–13 (occasionally altered).
    The brilliant orator John Chrysostom (ca. 354–407 C.E.) was educated in Antioch but served as bishop of the imperial capital Constantinople from 398 until 404, when he was deposed as a result of conflict with other church leaders and the imperial family. His voluminous sermons constitute the earliest extant commentary for much of the New Testament. In the homily excerpted here, Chrysostom attempts to distribute blame for Jesus' unjust execution among the Jewish leaders (with other Jerusalemites) and Pontius Pilate.

that had countless things to say. For neither did they accuse Him from knowing of any evil thing in Him, but from jealousy and envy only. At least when they had set false witness, wherefore, having nothing to say, did they still urge their point? and when they saw Judas was dead and that Pilate had washed his hands of it, why were they not pricked with remorse. For indeed He did many things even at the very time that they might recover themselves, but by none were they amended.

What then saith Pilate? "Hearest thou not how many things these witness against thee?" [Matt 27:13]. He wished that He should defend Himself and be acquitted, wherefore also he said these things; but since He answered nothing, he devises another thing again.

Of what nature was this? It was a custom for them to release one of the condemned, and by this means he attempted to deliver Him. For if you are not willing to release Him as innocent, yet as guilty pardon Him for the feast's sake.

Do you see the order reversed? For the petition in behalf of the condemned it was customary to be with the people, and the granting it with the rulers; but now the contrary has come to pass, and the ruler petitions the people; and not even so do they become gentle, but grow more savage and bloodthirsty, driven to frenzy by the passion of envy. For neither had they whereof they should accuse Him, and this though He was silent, but they were refuted even then by reason of the abundance of His righteous deeds, and being silent He overcame them that say ten thousand things and are maddened.

"And when he was set down on the judgment seat, his wife sent unto him, saying, have thou nothing to do with this just man, for I have suffered many things this day in a dream because of Him" [Matt 27:19]. See what a thing takes place again, sufficient to recall them all. For together with the proof from the things done, the dream too was no small thing. And wherefore does he not see it himself? Either because she was more worthy, or because he, if he had seen it, would not have been equally believed; or would not so much as have told it. Therefore it was ordered that the wife should see it, so that it might be manifest to all. And she does not merely see it, but also suffers many things, that from his feeling towards his wife the man may be made more reluctant to the murder. And the time too contributed not a little, for on the very night she saw it.

But it was not safe, it may be said, for him to let Him go, because they said He made Himself a king. He ought then to have sought for proofs, and a conviction, and for all the things that are infallible signs of an usurpation, as, for instance, whether He levied forces, whether He collected money, whether he forged arms, whether He attempted any other such thing. But he is led away at random, therefore neither doth Christ acquit him of the blame in saying, "He that betrayeth me unto thee hath greater sin" [John 19:11]. So that it was from weakness that he yielded and scourged Him, and delivered Him up.

He then was unmanly and weak; but the chief priests wicked and criminal. For since he had found out a device, namely, the law of the feast requiring him to release a condemned person, what do they contrive in opposition to that? "They persuaded the multitude," it is said, "that they should ask Barabbas" [Matt 27:20].

2. See how much care he taketh for them to relieve them from blame, and how much diligence they employed so as not to leave to themselves so much as a shadow of an excuse. For which was right? to let go the acknowledged criminal, or

Him about whose guilt there was a question? For, if in the case of acknowledged offenders it was fit there should be a liberation, much more in those of whom there was a doubt. For surely this man did not seem to them worse than acknowledged murderers. For on this account, it is not merely said they had a robber; but one noted, that is, who was infamous in wickedness, who had perpetrated countless murders. But nevertheless even him did they prefer to the Saviour of the world, and neither did they reverence the season because it was holy, nor the laws of humanity, nor any other thing of the kind, but envy had once for all blinded them. And besides their own wickedness, they corrupt the people also, that for deceiving them too they might suffer the most extreme punishment.

Since therefore they ask for the other, He saith, "What shall I do then with the Christ" [Matt 27:22], in this way desiring to put them to the blush by giving them the power to choose, that at least out of shame they might ask for Him, and the whole should be of their bountifulness. For though to say, He had not done wrong made them more contentious, yet to require that He should be saved out of humanity carries with it persuasion and entreaty that cannot be gainsaid.

But even then they said, "Crucify Him. But he said, why, what evil hath He done? but they cried out exceedingly; let Him be crucified. But he, when he saw that he profited nothing, washed his hands, saying, I am innocent" [Matt 27:22–24]. Why then did you deliver Him up? Why did you not rescue Him, as the centurion did Paul [Acts 21]? For that man too was aware that he would please the Jews; and a sedition had taken place on his account, and a tumult; nevertheless he stood firm against all. But not so this man, but he was extremely unmanly and weak, and all were corrupt together. For neither did this man stand firm against the multitude, nor the multitude against the Jews,[1] and in in every way their excuse was taken away. For they "cried out exceedingly," that is, cried out the more, "Let Him be crucified." For they desired not only to put Him to death, but also that it should be on a charge of wickedness, and though the judge was contradicting them, they continued to cry out the same thing.

Do you see how many things Christ did in order to recover them? For like as He often times checked Judas, so likewise did He restrain these men too, both throughout all His Gospel and at the very time of His condemnation. For surely when they saw the ruler and the judge washing his hands of it and saying, "I am innocent of this blood," they should have been moved to compunction both by what was said and by what was done, as well when they saw Judas had hanged himself as when they saw Pilate himself entreating them to take another in the place of Him. For when the accuser and traitor condemns himself, and he who gives sentence puts off from himself the guilt, and such a vision appears the very night, and even as condemned he begs Him off, what kind of plea will they have? For if they were not willing that He should be innocent, yet they should not have preferred to him even a robber, one that was acknowledged to be such, and very notorious.

What then did they? When they saw the judge washing his hands and saying, "I am innocent," they cried out "His blood be on us, and on our children" [Matt 27:25]. Then at length when they had given sentence against themselves, he yielded that all should be done.

---

1. *I.e.*, the Jewish rulers [translator's note; cf. John 7:13 and note].

See here too their great madness. For passion and wicked desire are like this. They suffer not men to see anything of what is right. For be it that you curse yourselves; why do you draw down the curse upon your children also?

Nevertheless, the lover of man, though they acted with so much madness, both against themselves and against their children, so far from confirming their sentence upon their children, confirmed it not even on them, but from the one and from the other received those that repented and counts them worthy of good things beyond number. For indeed even Paul was of them, and the thousands that believed in Jerusalem; for, "thou seest it is said, brother, how many thousands of Jews there are which believe" [Acts 21:20]. And if some continued in their sin, to themselves let them impute their punishment.

"Then released he Barabbas unto them, but Jesus, when he had scourged Him, he delivered to be crucified" [Matt 27:26].

And wherefore did he scourge Him. Either as one condemned, or willing to invest the judgment with due form, or to please them. And yet he ought to have resisted them. For indeed even before this he had said, "Take ye Him, and judge Him according to your law" [John 18:31]. And there were many things that might have held back him and those men: the signs and the miracles, and the great patience of Him who was suffering these things, and above all His untold silence. For since both by His defense of Himself and by His prayers, He had shown His humanity, again He shows His exaltedness and the greatness of His nature, both by His silence and by His contemning what is said; by all leading them on to marvel at Himself. But to none of these things did they give way.

THE LETTER OF PILATE TO CLAUDIUS†

Pilate, hearing these words of Annas and Caiaphas, laid them all up in the acts of our Lord and Saviour, in the public records of his prætorium, and wrote a letter to Claudius,[1] king of the city of Rome, saying:

Pontius Pilate to Claudius his king, greeting. It has lately happened, as I myself have also proved, that the Jews, through envy, have punished themselves and their posterity by a cruel condemnation. In short, when their fathers had a promise that their God would send them from heaven his holy one, who should deservedly be called their king, and promised that he would send him by a virgin upon the earth; when, therefore, while I was procurator, he had come into Judæa, and when they saw him enlightening the blind, cleansing the lepers, curing the paralytics, making

---

† From *The Gospel of Nicodemus,* trans. Alexander Walker, in *The Ante-Nicene Fathers,* vol. 8 (1886; reprint, Peabody, MA: Hendrickson, 1994), 454.

Perhaps the earliest of the apocryphal Pilate literature, this forged letter, attached to *The Gospel of Nicodemus* (in one recension), may be related to the epistle mentioned by Tertullian in his *Apology* (see above, p. 1357), in which case it would date to the second century C.E. But this identification is by no means certain, since for apologetic purposes ancient Christians circulated a number of counterfeit correspondences attributed to Pilate and purporting to confirm the Gospel accounts of Christ's death and resurrection. All these writings emphasize the Jews' guilt for Christ's death and portray Pilate as diffident rather than wicked.

1. Tiberius would have been emperor at the time of Jesus' crucifixion.

demons flee from men, even raising the dead, commanding the winds, walking dry-shod upon the waves of the sea, and doing many other signs of miracles; and when all the people of the Jews said that he was the Son of God, the chief priests felt envy against him, and seized him, and delivered him to me; and, telling me one lie after another, they said that he was a sorcerer, and was acting contrary to their law.

And I believed that it was so, and delivered him to be scourged, according to their will. And they crucified him, and set guards over him when buried. And he rose again on the third day, while my soldiers were keeping guard. But so flagrant was the iniquity of the Jews that they gave money to my soldiers, saying, Say that his disciples have stolen his body. But after receiving the money they could not keep secret what had been done; for they bore witness both that he had risen again, that they had seen him,[2] and that they had received money from the Jews.

This accordingly I have done, lest any one should give a different and a false account of it, and lest thou shouldst think that the lies of the Jews are to be believed.

PARADOSIS PILATI[†]

And the writings having come to the city of the Romans, and having been read to the Cæsar, with not a few standing by, all were astounded, because through the wickedness of Pilate the darkness and the earthquake had come over the whole world. And the Cæsar, filled with rage, sent soldiers, and ordered them to bring Pilate a prisoner.

And when he was brought to the city of the Romans, the Cæsar, hearing that Pilate had arrived, sat in the temple of the gods, in the presence of all the senate, and with all the army, and all the multitude of his power; and he ordered Pilate to stand forward.[1] And the Cæsar says to him: Why hast thou, O most impious, dared to do such things, having seen so great miracles in that man? By daring to do an evil deed, thou hast destroyed the whole world.

And Pilate said: O almighty king, I am innocent of these things; but the multitude of the Jews are violent and guilty. And the Cæsar said: And who are they? Pilate says: Herod, Archelaus, Philip, Annas and Caiaphas, and all the multitude of the Jews. The Cæsar says: For what reason didst thou follow out their counsel? And Pilate says: Their nation is rebellious and insubmissive, not submitting themselves to thy power. And the Cæsar said: When they delivered him to thee, thou oughtest to have made him secure, and to have sent him to me, and not to have obeyed them in crucifying such a man, righteous as he was, and one that

---

2. Or, that they had seen that he rose from the dead [translator's note].

† From *The Giving up of Pontius Pilate*, trans. Alexander Walker, in *The Ante-Nicene Fathers*, vol. 8 (1886; reprint, Peabody, MA: Hendrickson, 1994), 464–465.

Although its earliest Greek manuscript dates to the twelfth century, this text was probably composed somewhat earlier, and it may be based on traditions earlier still. Its revisionary transformation of the Roman official is more radical than that in much related literature: it actually presents Pilate as the first Christian martyr, thereby assimilating him to Christ, whose execution he oversaw. The title's *paradosis*, a Latinized Greek word meaning "handing over," is etymologically related to the verb used of Jesus' betrayal in the Gospels (e.g., Matt 26:21). This strange text may have originated in Egypt, where the Coptic Church venerated Pilate as a saint.

1. Or, in the entrance [translator's note].

did such good miracles, as thou hast said in thy report. For from such miracles Jesus was manifestly the Christ, the King of the Jews.

And as the Cæsar was thus speaking, when he named the name of Christ, all the multitude of the gods fell down in a body, and became as dust, where the Cæsar was sitting with the senate. And the people standing beside the Cæsar all began to tremble, on account of the speaking of the word, and the fall of their gods; and being seized with terror, they all went away, each to his own house, wondering at what had happened. And the Cæsar ordered Pilate to be kept in security, in order that he might know the truth about Jesus.

And on the following day, the Cæsar, sitting in the Capitol with all the senate, tried again to question Pilate. And the Cæsar says: Tell the truth, O most impious, because through thy impious action which thou hast perpetrated against Jesus, even here the doing of thy wicked deeds has been shown by the gods having been cast down. Say, then, who is he that has been crucified; because even his name has destroyed all the gods? Pilate said: And indeed the records of him are true; for assuredly I myself was persuaded from his works that he was greater than all the gods whom we worship. And the Cæsar said: For what reason, then, didst thou bring against him such audacity and such doing, if thou wert not ignorant of him, and altogether devising mischief against my kingdom? Pilate said: On account of the wickedness and rebellion of the lawless and ungodly Jews, I did this.

And the Cæsar, being filled with rage, held council with all his senate and his power, and ordered a decree to be written against the Jews as follows:—To Licianus, the governor of the chief places of the East, greeting. The reckless deed which has been done at the present time by the inhabitants of Jerusalem, and the cities of the Jews round about, and their wicked action has come to my knowledge, that they have forced Pilate to crucify a certain god named Jesus, and on account of this great fault of theirs the world has been darkened and dragged to destruction. Do thou then speedily, with a multitude of soldiers, go to them there, and make them prisoners in accordance with this decree. Be obedient and take action against them, and scatter them and make them slaves among all the nations; and having driven them out of the whole of Judæa make them the smallest of nations, so that it may not any longer be seen at all, because they are full of wickedness.[2]

And this decree having come into the region of the East, Licianus, obeying from fear of the decree, seized all the nation of the Jews; and those that were left in Judæa he scattered among the nations, and sold for slaves: so that it was known to the Cæsar that these things had been done by Licianus against the Jews in the region of the East; and it pleased him.

And again the Cæsar set himself to question Pilate; and he orders a captain named Albius to cut off Pilate's head, saying: Just as he laid hands upon the just man named Christ, in like manner also shall he fall, and not find safety.

And Pilate, going away to the place, prayed in silence, saying: Lord, do not destroy me along with the wicked Hebrews, because I would not have laid hands upon Thee, except for the nation of the lawless Jews, because they were exciting rebellion against me. But Thou knowest that I did it in ignorance. Do not then destroy me for this my sin; but remember not evil against me, O Lord, and against Thy servant

2. The text is very corrupt [translator's note].

Procla,[3] who is standing with me in this the hour of my death, whom Thou didst appoint to prophesy that Thou shouldest be nailed to the cross. Do not condemn her also in my sin; but pardon us, and make us to be numbered in the portion of Thy righteous.

And, behold, when Pilate had finished his prayer, there came a voice out of the heaven, saying: All the generations and families of the nations shall count thee blessed, because under thee have been fulfilled all those things said about me by the prophets; and thou thyself shalt be seen as my witness at my second appearing, when I shall judge the twelve tribes of Israel, and those that have not owned my name. And the prefect struck off the head of Pilate; and, behold, an angel of the Lord received it. And his wife Procla, seeing the angel coming and receiving his head, being filled with joy herself also, immediately gave up the ghost, and was buried along with her husband.

THE DREAM OF PILATE'S WIFE[†]

[Scene I, Pilate's judgment hall.]

PILATE: Ye cursed creatures that cruelly are crying,
Restrain you from[1] striving for strength of my strakes.[2]

---

3. Pilate's wife.
† This mystery play composed in Northern Middle English probably dates to the late fourteenth century. It is part of the York cycle, an elaborate collection of dramas recounting biblical history that was performed throughout the city of York on Corpus Christi day. "Mystery" actually refers to a craft guild. Each guild was responsible for producing one play, which involved, among other things, procuring a special wagon for its staging. These wagons were hauled to various stations on the midsummer holiday, enabling multiple performances of each drama over the course of the day.
   The Dream of Pilate's Wife (anonymous, as are all the plays in the cycle) was produced by the Tapiters and Couchers, tapestry makers and upholsterers. Though based on the *Gospel of Nicodemus* (or *Acts of Pilate*), one of the most influential late antique apocryphal writings concerning the Roman governor, *The Dream of Pilate's Wife* is a remarkable work of literature on its own terms. It employs ambiguity and ambivalence not primarily to deflect blame for Jesus' death away from Rome and onto the Jews, but to create a complex and intriguing literary portrayal of the character Pilate. This complexity carries over to its representation of the governor's wife, Procla, initially a partner in carefree erotic banter with her husband but soon haunted by a tormenting dream regarding Jesus' impending doom.
   The text is our reading version based on the early critical edition by Lucy Toulmin Smith (*York Plays: The Plays Performed by the Crafts or Mysteries of York on the Day of Corpus Christi in the 14th, 15th, and 16th Centuries* [Oxford: Clarendon Press, 1885], 270–91), with spelling and punctuation modernized, and archaic vocabulary and diction glossed. Toulmin Smith's edition is fairly conservative: it probably does not emend the text with as much freedom as it ought, in light the York plays' survival, for the most part, in but a single MS, the bulk of which was copied by a scribe of allegedly "average competence" (Richard Beadle, *The York Plays*, p. xxvii). We have therefore introduced into the text of the play a number of emendations Toulmin Smith tentatively proposed in footnotes and we have also adopted a handful suggested by Richard Beadle in *The York Plays: A Critical Edition of the York Corpus Christi Play as Recorded in British Library Additional MS 35290* (Oxford: Oxford University Press, 2009), 255–76. All such emendations are cited in the annotations. For glosses of archaic diction and syntax and for modernization of spelling, we have relied on the *Oxford English Dictionary* and the *Middle English Dictionary*, and have also at times consulted Richard Beadle and Pamela M. King, *York Mystery Plays: A Selection in Modern Spelling* (Oxford: Oxford University Press, 1984), 154–74. As much as feasible, we have maintained the play's rhyme scheme, even at the expense of foregoing an otherwise obvious synonym or standardization of Middle English's archaic and erratic spelling.
1. Adopting Beadle's emendation of the MS, which reads "for."
2. *Strakes*: strokes.

Your plaints in my presence use platly[3] applying,
Or else this brand[4] in your brains soon[5] bursts and breaks.
This brand in his bones breaks   5
What brawl[6] that with brawling me brews.[7]
That wretch may not wry[8] from my wreaks,[9]
Nor his sleights not slyly him slakes.[10]
Let that traitor not trust in my truce.

For sir Caesar was my sire and I soothly[11] his son,   10
That excellent emperor exalted in height,
Who all this wild world with wights had won,
And my mother hight[12] Pila that proud was of plight.[13]
Of Pila that proud and Atus her father he hight:
This Pila was had into Atus.[14]   15
Now, renks,[15] read ye it right?
For thus shortly I have showed you in sight,
How I am proudly proved Pilatus.

Lo! Pilate, I am proved a prince of great pride:
I was put into Pontus[16] the people to press,   20
And sithen[17] Caesar himself, with senators by his side,
Remit me to the realms[18] the renks to redress.
And yet am I granted on ground, as I guess,
To justify and judge all the Jews.
Ah! Love! Here lady! No less.   [*Enter dame Procula.*]   25
Lo! Sirs, my worthy wife, that she is!
So seemly, lo! Certain she shews.[19]

PILATE'S WIFE: Was never judge in this Jewry of so jocund generation,
Nor of so joyful genealogy to gentrice enjoined,
As ye, my duke doughty, deemer[20] of damnation   30
To princes and prelates that your precepts purloined.[21]

---

3. *Platly*: directly, without equivocation.
4. *Brand*: sword (so throughout).
5. *Soon*: adopting Toulmin Smith's suggested emendation of the MS, which reads "schalle."
6. *Brawl*: brawler.
7. *Brews*: injures.
8. *Wry*: turn.
9. *Wreaks*: pain, punishment.
10. *Slakes*: release.
11. *Soothly*: truly (so throughout).
12. *Hight*: is named (so throughout).
13. *Plight*: circumstances (adopting Beadle's emendation of the MS, which reads "pight").
14. The etymology is entirely fabricated.
15. *Renks*: people (so throughout).
16. Suggesting another imaginary etymology.
17. *Sithen*: afterwards.
18. *Remit me to the realms*: sent me to these realms.
19. *Shews*: shows.
20. *Deemer*: judge.
21. *Purlooined*: set aside, i.e., failed to follow (so throughout).

Who that your precepts pertly[22] purloined
With dread in to death shall you drive him.
By my truth, he untruly is throned[23]
That against your behest has honed.[24]   35
All to rags shall ye rent him and rive him.

I am dame precious Procula, of princes the prize,
Wife to sir Pilate, here prince without peer.
All well of all womanhood I am, witty and wise.
Conceive now my countenance so comely and clear: 40
The color of my corpse is full clear
And in riches of robes I am arrayed.
There is no lord in this land, as I lere,[25]
In faith that hath a friendlier fere[26]
Than ye, my lord, myself though I say it.   45

PILATE: Now say it[27] may ye safely, for I will certify the same.
WIFE: Gracious lord, gramercy; your good word is gain.
PILATE: Yet for to comfort my corpse, me must kiss you, my dame!
WIFE: To fulfill your foreward,[28] my fair lord, in faith I am fain.[29]
PILATE: How! How! Fellows! Now in faith I am fain   50
Of these lips, so lovely are lapped—
In bed she[30] is full buxom and bain.[31]
WIFE: Yea, sir, it needeth not to lain,[32]
All ladies we covet then both to be kissed and clapped.[33]

                    [Enter Beadle.]

BEADLE: My liberal lord, O leader of laws,   55
Oh shining show that all shames eschews,
I beseech you, my sovereign, assent to my saws,[34]
As ye are gentle judger and justice of Jews.
WIFE: Do hark! How thou, javel,[35] jangle of Jews!
Why, go bet,[36] whoreson boy, when I bid thee.   60
BEADLE: Madam, I do but that due is.

22. *Pertly*: openly, boldly (so throughout).
23. *Throned*: adopting Beadle's emendation of the MS, which reads "stonyd."
24. *Honed*: been idle.
25. *Lere*: learn (as frequently).
26. *Fere*: spouse or companion.
27. *Say it*: adopting Beadle's emendation of the MS, which reads "say it safe."
28. *Foreward*: pledge, command (so throughout).
29. *Fain*: well-pleased (so throughout).
30. *She*: adopting Beadle's emendation of the MS, which omits the sentence's subject.
31. *Is full buxom and bain*: is entirely yielding and eager (so throughout).
32. *Lain*: be concealed.
33. *Clapped*: clipped, i.e., embraced.
34. *Saws*: speech (so throughout).
35. *Javel*: scoundrel (so throughout).
36. *Go bet*: begone (so throughout).

WIFE: But if[37] thou rest of thy reason,[38] thou rues,
For as a cursed carl[39] hast thou kid[40] thee![41]

PILATE: Do mind you, madam, and your mood be amending,
For me seems it were sitting[42] to see what he says.   65
WIFE: My lord, he told never tale that to me was tending,[43]
But with wrenks[44] and with wiles to wend[45] me my ways.
BEADLE: Iwis[46] of your ways to be wending it longs to our laws.[47]
WIFE: Lo! Lord, this lad with his laws! How think ye it profits well
His preaching to praise?   70
PILATE: Yea, love, he knows
All our custom, I know well.

BEADLE. My seignior, will ye see now the sun in your sight,
For his stately strength he stems[48] in his streams.
Behold over your head how he holds from his height   75
And glides to the ground with his glittering gleams.
To the ground he goes with his beams
And the night is nighing anon.
Ye may doom[49] after no dreams,
But let my lady here with all her light leams[50]   80
Wightly[51] go wend to her wone.[52]

For ye must sit,[53] sir, this same night of life and limb.
It is not lawful for my lady, by the law of this land,
In doom for to dwell from[54] the day wax aught dim.
For she may stagger in the street but she stalwartly stand.   85
****
Let her take her leave while that light is.
PILATE: Now wife, then ye blithely be buskand.[55]

37. *But if*: unless (so throughout).
38. *Rest of thy reason*: leave off your statement, cease talking.
39. *Carl*: man of low birth.
40. *Kid*: revealed.
41. *For as . . . thee*: adapting Beadle's emendation of the MS, which reads "For all is a-cursed carle, hase in, kydde þe."
42. *It were sitting*: it behooves (so throughout).
43. *Tending*: i.e., complimentary.
44. *Wrenks*: tricks.
45. *Wend*: go or cause to go (so throughout).
46. *Iwis*: to be sure, indeed (so throughout).
47. *Of your . . . laws*: i.e., "for you to be going your ways conforms to our law"; but ll. 68–72 are evidently corrupt (the rhyme scheme breaks down, even if laws is changed to "lays") and the meaning is ultimately unclear.
48. *Stems*: checks, dams up.
49. *Doom*: judge (so throughout).
50. *Leams*: radiance.
51. *Wightly*: quickly.
52. *Wone*: abode (so throughout).
53. *Sit*: i.e., in judgment.
54. *From*: from the moment when (as frequently).
55. *Buskand*: busking, i.e., preparing to go or hurrying (so throughout).

WIFE: I am here, sir, hendly[56] at hand.
PILATE: This renk has us rede[57] as right is.   90

WIFE: Your commandment to keep to cair[58] forth I cast me;
My lord, with your leave, no longer I let[59] you.
PILATE: It were a reproof[60] to my person that privily ye passed me,
Or ye went from this wone ere with wine ye had wet you.
Ye shall wend forth with wine when that ye have wet you.   95
Get drink. What does thou? Have done!
Come seemly, beside me, and sit you.
Look! Now it is even here that I ere behet[61] you.
Yea, essay it now sadly[62] and sone.[63]

WIFE: It would glad me, my lord, if ye goodly begin.   100
PILATE: Now I assent to your counsel, so comely and clear.
Now drink, madam. To death all this din!
WIFE: If it like[64] you my own lord, I am not to lere.
This lore[65] I am not to lere.
PILATE: Give[66] eft[67] to your damsel, my dame.   105
WIFE: In thy hand, hold now, and have here.
MAID: Gramercy, my lady so dear.
PILATE: Now fares well, and walk on your way.

****
****
WIFE: Now farewell, ye friendliest, your foemen to fende.[68]
PILATE: Now farewell, ye fairest figure that ever did food feed,   110
And farewell, ye damsel, indeed.
MAID: My lord, I commend me to your royalty.
PILATE: Fair lady, he this shall you lead.
[*To his son.*] Sir, go with this worthy indeed,
And what she bids you do, look that buxom you be.   115

SON: I am proud and pressed to pass on apace,
To go with this gracious, her goodly to guide.
PILATE: Attend to my tale,[69] thou; turn on no trace.

56. *Hendly*: gracefully, courteously (so throughout).
57. *Rede*: advised.
58. *Cair*: go (so throughout).
59. *Let*: hinder.
60. *A reproof*: adopting Beadle's emendation of the MS, which reads "appreue," display.
61. *Behet*: promised.
62. *Sadly*: diligently, seriously (so throughout).
63. *Sone*: soon (so throughout).
64. *Like*: please.
65. *Lore*: instruction (so throughout).
66. *Give*: adopting Beadle's emendation of the MS, which reads "yitt."
67. *Eft*: likewise (so throughout).
68. *Fende*: fend, ward off.
69. *Tale*: i.e., command.

Come tite[70] and tell me if any tidings betide.

SON: If any tidings my lady betide   120
I shall full soon, sir, wit you to say.[71]
This seemly shall I show by her side
Belive,[72] sir. No longer we bide.

PILATE: Now fares well, and walks on your way.

[*Exeunt Procula, son, and maid.*]

Now went is my wife, if[73] it were not her will,   125
And she raiks[74] to her rest as of nothing she rought.[75]
[*To Beadle.*] Time is, I tell thee, thou attend me until,
And busk thee belive, belamy,[76] to bed that I were brought.

****

And look I be richly arrayed.

BEADLE: As your servant I have sadly it sought,   130
And this night, sir, annoy shall ye naught,
I dare lay,[77] from ye lovely be laid.

[*Pilate goes to his couch.*]

PILATE: I command thee to come near, for I will cair to my couch.
Have in thy hands hendly and have me from hyne,[78]
But look that thou teen[79] me not with thy tasting,[80] but tenderly me touch.   135

BEADLE: Ah! Sir, ye weigh well!
                    PILATE: Yea, I have wet me with wine.

****

Yet hield[81] down and lap[82] me even [here],
For I will slyly sleep unto syne.[83]
Look that no man nor no myron[84] of mine
With no noise be nighing me near.   140

BEADLE: Sir, what warlock[85] you wakens with words full wild,
That boy for his brawling were better be unborn.

PILATE: Yea, who chatters, him chastise, be he churl or child,

70. *Tite*: quickly (so throughout).
71. *Wit you to say*: let you know.
72. *Belive*: with speed (so throughout).
73. *If*: i.e., even if.
74. *Raiks*: walks (so throughout).
75. *Of nothing she rought*: she had not a care.
76. *Belamy*: fair friend.
77. *Lay*: i.e., lay wager.
78. *Hyne*: hence.
79. *Teen*: irritate.
80. *Tasting*: touching.
81. *Hield*: incline.
82. *Lap*: wrap or cover (so throughout).
83. *Syne*: later.
84. *Myron*: servant (so throughout).
85. *Warlock*: reprobate (so throughout).

For and[86] he escape scatheless, it were to us a great scorn.
If scatheless he scape, it were a scorn.
What ribald that readily will roar,
I shall meet with that myron tomorn,
And for his lither[87] lewdness him learn to be lorn.[88]
BEADLE: We! So sir, sleep ye, and say no more.   145

[Scene II, Chamber of Procula, Pilate's wife.]

WIFE: Now are we at home; do help if ye may,   150
For I will make me ready and raik to my rest.
MAID: Ye are weary, madam, forewent[89] of your way.
Do boun you[90] to bed, for that hold I best.
SON: Here is a bed arrayed of the best.
WIFE: Do hap[91] me, and fast hence ye hie.   155
MAID: Madam, anon all duly is dressed.
SON: With no stalking nor no strife be ye stressed.
WIFE: Now be ye in peace, both your carping and cry.

[All sleep; enter Satan.]

DEVIL: Out! Out! Harrow! Into bale am I brought; this bargain may I ban.[92]
But if I work some wile, in woe must I won.[93]   160
This gentleman Jesu of cursedness he can.[94]
By any sign that I see, this same is God's son,
And he be slain, our solace will sese.[95]
He will save man's soul from our sound[96]
And reave us the realms that are round.   165
I will on stiffly[97] in this stound[98]
Unto sir Pilate's wife, pertly, and put me in press.

[Whispers to Procula.]

Oh woman! Be wise and ware, and won in thy wit:
There shall a gentleman, Jesu, unjustly be judged
Before thy husband in haste, and with[99] harlots[100] be hit.   170

---

86. *And*: if.
87. *Lither*: base (so throughout).
88. *Lorn*: doomed to destruction.
89. *Forewent*: tired out.
90. *Boun you*: betake yourself (so throughout).
91. *Hap*: cover.
92. *Ban*: curse.
93. *Won*: dwell (so throughout).
94. *Can*: has knowledge.
95. *Sese*: cease.
96. *Sound*: keeping.
97. *On stiffly*: go on with determination.
98. *Stound*: moment.
99. *With*: by (as occasionally).
100. *Harlots*: rogues (so throughout).

And[101] that doughty[102] today to death thus be dighted,[103]
Sir Pilate, for his preaching, and thou
With need shall ye namely[104] be annoyed.
Your strife and your strength shall be stroyed;
Your richesse shall be reft you that is rude,[105]   175
With vengeance, and that dare I avow.

[*Procula awakes, starting.*]

WIFE: Ah! I am dretched[106] with a dream full dreadfully to doubt.
Say, child! Rise up readily and rest for no ro.[107]
Thou must lance[108] to my lord and lowly him lout.[109]
Commend me to his reverence, as right will I do.   180
SON: O! What! Shall I travail thus timely this tide?[110]
Madam, for the dretching of heaven,
Such note is noisesome to neven,[111]
And it nighs unto midnight full even.
WIFE: Go bet, boy; I bid no longer thou bide.   185

And say to my sovereign, this same is sooth that I send him:
All naked this night as I napped,
With teen[112] and with train[113] was I trapped
With a sweven[114] that swiftly me swapped[115]
Of one Jesu, the just man the Jews will undo.   190
She prays attend to that true man—with teen be not trapped—
But as a doomsman duly to be addressing,
And loyally deliver that lede.[116]
SON: Madam, I am dressed to that deed;
But first I will nap in this need,   195
For he has mister[117] of a morn sleep that midnight is missing. [*Sleeps.*]

101. *And*: if.
102. *Doughty*: worthy (so throughout).
103. *Dighted*: appointed (so throughout).
104. *Thou / with need shall ye namely*: you, yourself in particular, will necessarily.
105. *Rude*: common, humble.
106. *Dretched*: afflicted (so throughout).
107. *Ro*: repose.
108. *Lance*: spring quickly, rush.
109. *Lout*: bow to (so throughout).
110. *Shall I . . . tide*: must I exert myself so early now?
111. *Neven*: utter (so throughout).
112. *Teen*: mischief (so throughout).
113. *Train*: treachery.
114. *Sweven*: dream (so throughout).
115. *Swapped*: struck (so throughout).
116. *Lede*: person (so elsewhere).
117. *Mister*: need.

*[Scene III, On the way from the palace of Caiaphas
to Pilate's judgment-hall.]*

ANNAS: Sir Caiaphas, ye ken[118] well this captive we have catched
That oft times in our temple has teached untruly.
Our meinie[119] with might at midnight him matched
And has driven him to his deeming[120] for his deeds unduly.   200
Wherefore I counsel that kindly[121] we cair
Unto sir Pilate, our prince, and pray him
That he for our right will array him,
This faitour[122] for his falsehood to flay him.
For from we say him the sooth I shall sit him full sore.[123]   205

CAIAPHAS: Sir Anna, this sport have ye speedily espied,
As I am pontifical prince of all priests.
We will press to sir Pilate, and present him with pride
With this harlot that has hewed our hearts from our breasts
Through talking of tales untrue. And therefore, sir knights—

                                                    SOLDIERS: Lord![124]   210
CAIAPHAS: Sir knights that are courteous and kind,
We charge you that churl be well chyned.[125]
Do busk you and gradely[126] him bind
And rug[127] him in ropes his race[128] till he rue.

SOLDIER 1: Sir, your saws shall be served shortly and sone.   215
Yea! Do, fellow, by thy faith, let us fasten this faitour full fast.
SOLDIER 2: I am doughty to this deed. Deliver! Have done!
Let us pull on with pride till his power be passed.
SOLDIER 1: Do have fast and hold at his hands.
SOLDIER 2: For this same is he that lightly avaunted[129]
And God's son he gradely him granted.[130]   220
SOLDIER 1: He is hurled from the highness he haunted;
Lo! He stonies[131] for us; he stares where he stands.

---

118. *Ken*: know (so throughout).
119. *Meinie*: retainers.
120. *Deeming*: judgment (so throughout).
121. *Kindly*: as is custom.
122. *Faitour*: infidel or deceiver (so throughout).
123. *Sit him full sore*: cause him great suffering.
124. *And therefore . . . Lord*: this seems to be an interjection in prose, with the poetic line ending at
"untrue."
125. *Chyned*: chained.
126. *Gradely*: promptly (so throughout).
127. *Rug*: pull violently (so throughout).
128. *Race*: course of action.
129. *Avaunted*: boasted.
130. *Him granted*: declared himself.
131. *Stonies*: is stupefied.

SOLDIER 2: Now is the brothel[132] bound for all the boast that he's blown
And the last day he let[133] no lordings[134] might low[135] him.   225
SERVANT: Yea, he weened[136] this world had been wholly his own.
As ye are doughtiest today to his deeming ye draw him,
And then shall we ken how that he can excuse him.[137]
SOLDIER 1: Here, ye gomes,[138] go a-room. Give us gate.
We must step to yon star of estate.   230
SOLDIER 2: We must yaply[139] wend in at this gate,
For he that comes to court, to courtesy must use him.[140]

SOLDIER 1: Do rap[141] on the renks that we may raise with our rolling.[142]
Come forth, sir coward! Why cower ye behind?   [*Knocks at Pilate's hall.*]
BEADLE: [*Within.*] Oh, what javels are ye that japes with gowling?[143]   235
SOLDIER 1: Ah! Good sir, be not wroth, for words are as the wind.
BEADLE: I say, gadlings,[144] go back with your gauds.[145]
SOLDIER 2: Be suffering, I beseech you,
And more of this matter ye meek you.[146]
BEADLE: Why, uncunning knaves, an I cleek you,[147]   240
I shall fell you, by my faith, for all you false frauds.

PILATE [*Within, in bed.*] Say, child—ill cheve you[148]—what churls are so clattering?
BEADLE: My lord, uncunning knaves. They cry and they call.
PILATE: Go boldly, belive, and those brothels be batting,
And put them in prison upon pain that might fall.   245
Yea, speedily speer[149] them if any sport can they spell.[150]
Yea, and look what lordings they be.
BEADLE: My lord that is loveful in lee,[151]
I am buxom and blithe to your blee.[152]
PILATE: And if they talk any tidings come tite and me tell.   250

132. *Brothel*: scoundrel (so throughout).
133. *The last . . . let*: at the end time, he pretends.
134. *Lordings*: lords (so throughout).
135. *Low*: bring him low.
136. *Weened*: believed (so throughout).
137. *Him*: i.e., himself.
138. *Gomes*: men.
139. *Yaply*: nimbly.
140. *Use him*: get used to.
141. *Rap*: rush.
142. *Do rap . . . rolling*: this line is obscure.
143. *Gowling*: howling.
144. *Gadlings*: fellows (so throughout).
145. *Gauds*: pranks.
146. *Ye meek you*: attend to (?).
147. *An I cleek you*: if I lay my hands on you.
148. *Ill cheve you*: let evil fall upon you.
149. *Speer*: inquire of.
150. *Any sport can they spell*: they have anything entertaining to say.
151. *Is loveful in lee*: loves tranquility.
152. *Blee*: visage.

BEADLE: [*To the soldiers.*] Can ye talk any tidings, by your faith, my fellawes?[153]
SOLDIER 1: Yea, sir Caiaphas and Annas are come both together
To sir Pilate of Pontus and prince of our laws,[154]
And they have latched a lorel[155] that is lawless and lither.
BEADLE: [*To Pilate.*] My lord! My lord!
PILATE: How![156]
BEADLE: My lord, unlap you belive where you lie.   255
Sir Caiaphas to your court is carried,
And sir Annas, but a traitor them tarried.
Many wight of that warlock has waried,[157]
They have brought him in a band, his bales to buy.

PILATE: But are these saws certain in sooth that thou says?   260
BEADLE: Yea, lord. The estates[158] yonder stand, for strife are they stunned.
PILATE: Now then am I light as a roe and eath for to raise.[159]
Go bid them come in both, and the boy they have bound.
BEADLE: Sirs, my lord gives leave in for to come.

[*Scene IV; Pilate's judgment hall;*
enter Caiaphas and company.]

CAIAPHAS: Hail, prince that is peerless in price!   265
Ye are leader of laws in this land;
Your help is full hendly at hand.
ANNAS: Hail, strong in your state for to stand!
All this doom must be dressed[160] at your duly device.

PILATE: Who is there? My prelates?   270
CAIAPHAS: Yea, lord.
PILATE: Now be ye welcome, iwis.
CAIAPHAS: Gramecy, my sovereign, but we beseech you all sam,[161]
Because of waking you unwarely[162] be not wroth with this.
For we have brought here a lorel; he looks like a lamb.
PILATE: Come in, you both, and to the bench braid you.[163]
CAIAPHAS: Nay, good sir, lower is leeful for us.   275
PILATE: Ah, sir Caiaphas, be courteous ye bus.[164]

---

153. *Can ye . . . fellawes*: adopting Toulmin Smith's proposed emendation of the MS, where the three clauses appear in a different order. *Fellawes* is fellows.
154. *Laws*: adopting Beadle's emendation of the MS, which reads "law."
155. *Lorel*: blackguard (so throughout).
156. *How* stands independent of the rhyme scheme.
157. *Waried*: cursed.
158. *Estates*: men of high status.
159. *Eath for to raise*: have no objection to rising.
160. *Dressed*: set in order.
161. *Sam*: together.
162. *Unwarely*: without warning.
163. *Braid you*: bring yourselves quickly.
164. *Bus*: behoove, i.e., are in need of (so throughout).

ANNAS: Nay good lord; it may not be thus.

PILATE: Say no more, but come sit you beside me, in sorrow as I said you.

[*Enter Pilate's son.*]

SON: Hail! The seemliest segge[165] under sun sought.

Hail! The dearest duke and doughtiest in deed.   280

PILATE: Now bienvenue,[166] beausire![167] What bodeword hast thou brought?

Has any languor my lady new latched in this hede?[168]

SON: Sir, that comely commends her you to

And says, all naked this night as she napped,

With teen and with tray was she trapped,   285

With a sweven that swiftly her swapped,

Of one Jesu, the just man the Jews will undo.

She beseeches you as her sovereign that simple to save.

Deem him not to death, for dread of vengeance.

PILATE: What! I hope this be he that hither harled[169] ye have.   290

CAIAPHAS: Yea, sir. The same and the self; but this is but a skaunce.[170]

With[171] witchcraft this wile has he wrought.

Some fiend of his sending has he sent

And warned your wife ere he went.

Yow! That shalk[172] should not shamely be shent.[173]   295

This is siker[174] in certain, and sooth should be sought.

ANNAS: Yea, through his phantom and falsehood and fiend's craft

He has wrought many wonder where he walked full wide.

Wherefore my lord it were leeful his life were him raft.[175]

PILATE: Be ye never so breme,[176] ye both bus abide,   300

But if the traitor be taught[177] for untrue.

And therefore sermons[178] you no more.

I will sikerly send himself for,

And see what he says to thee sore.

Beadle, go bring him, for of that renk have I ruth.[179]   305

165. *Segge*: man.
166. *Bienvenue*: welcome (French).
167. *Beausire*: fair sir (French).
168. *Hede*: regard.
169. *Harled*: dragged.
170. *Skaunce*: jest.
171. *With*: adopting Beadle's emendation of the MS, which reads "he with."
172. *Shalk*: man.
173. *Shent*: destroyed.
174. *Siker*: sure (so throughout).
175. *Raft*: reft (from reave).
176. *Breme*: fierce (so throughout).
177. *Taught*: shown.
178. *Sermons*: speak.
179. *Ruth*: compassion (so throughout).

BEADLE: This foreward to fulfill am I fain moved in my heart.
Say, Jesu, the judges and the Jews have me enjoined
To bring thee before them, even bound as thou art.
Yon lordings to lose[180] thee full long have they hoined,[181]
But first shall I worship thee with wit and with will.   310
This reverence I do thee forthy;[182]   [*Bows to Jesus.*]
For wits that were wiser than I,
They worshipped thee full wholly on high
And with solemnity sang Hosanna till.[183]

SOLDIER 1: My Lord that is leader of laws in this land,   315
All beadles to your bidding should be buxom and bain.
And yet this boy here before you full boldly was bowand[184]
To worship this warlock. Me think we work all in vain.
SOLDIER 2: Yea, and in your presence he prayed him of peace:
In kneeling on knees to this knave   320
He besought him his servant to save.
CAIAPHAS: Lo, lord, such error among them they have!
It is great sorrow to see; no segge may it cease.[185]

It is no mensk[186] to your manhood that mickle[187] is of might
To forebear such forfeits[188] that falsely are feigned.   325
Such spites in especial would be eschewed in your sight.
PILATE: Sirs, move you not in this matter, but be mildly demeaned,
For yon courtesy I ken had some cause.
ANNAS: In your sight, sir, the sooth shall I say:
As ye are prince, take heed I you pray.   330
Such a lurdan[189] disloyal dare I lay,
Many lords of our lands might lead from our laws.

PILATE: [*To the Beadle.*] Say, losel,[190] who gave thee leave so for to lout to yon lad
And solace him in my sight so seemly, that I saw?
BEADLE: Ah! Gracious lord, grieve you not, for good case I had.   335
Ye commanded me to cair, as ye ken well and knawe,[191]
To Jerusalem on a journey, with sele;[192]

---

180. *Lose*: ruin, destroy (so throughout).
181. *Hoined*: i.e., honed, waited (adopting Beadle's emendation of the MS, which reads "heyned," an alternative version of the same word that does not seem to fit the rhyme scheme).
182. *Forthy*: unrestrained or therefore (so throughout).
183. *Till*: to (as frequently).
184. *Bowand*: bowing.
185. *It cease*: bring it to an end.
186. *Mensk*: honor (so throughout).
187. *Mickle*: great (so throughout).
188. *Forfeits*: transgressions.
189. *Lurdan*: sluggard, vagabond.
190. *Losel*: rake (so throughout).
191. *Knawe*: know.
192. *Sele*: good fortune.

And then this seemly on an ass was set
And many men mildly him met.
As a god in that ground they him gret,[193]   340
Well psalming[194] him in way with worship leal.[195]

"Hosanna," they sang, "the son of David."
Rich men with their robes they ran to his feet
And poor folk fetched flowers of the frith[196]
And made mirth and melody this man for to meet.   345
PILATE: Now, good sir, by thy faith, what is "Hosanna" to say?
BEADLE: Sir, construe it we may by language of this land as I leve.[197]
It is as much to me for to meve[198]
(Your prelates in this place can it preve[199])
As "our savior and sovereign, thou save us, we pray."   350

PILATE: Lo, seigniors, how seems you the sooth I you said?
CAIAPHAS: Yea, lord, this lad is full lither, by this light.
If his saws were searched and sadly assayed—
Save[200] your reverence—his reason they reckon not with right.
This captive thus cursedly can construe us.   355
BEADLE: Sirs, truly the truth I have told
Of this wight ye have wrapped in wolde.[201]
ANNAS: [Rising.] I say, harlot, thy tongue should thou hold
And not against thy masters to move thus.

PILATE: Do cease of your saying and I shall examine full sore.   360
ANNAS: Sir, deem him to death, or do him away.
PILATE: Sir, have you said?
              ANNAS: Yea, lord.
                          PILATE: Now go sit you with sorrow and care,
For I will lose no lede that is loyal to our lay.[202]
[To Jesus.] But step forth and stand up on height
And busk to my bidding, thou boy,   365
And for the nonce[203] that thou neven us an "oy."
BEADLE: I am here at your hand to hallow a "hoy."
Do move of your master, for I shall mell[204] it with might.

193. Gret: greeted.
194. Psalming: adopting Beadle's interpretation of "semand."
195. Leal: faithful (so throughout).
196. Frith: woods or meadow.
197. Leve: believe (so throughout).
198. Meve: move, i.e., translate.
199. Preve: prove.
200. Save: i.e., God save.
201. Wolde: custody.
202. Lay: adopting Beadle's emendation of the MS, which reads "law"; "lay" is a related word with a similar meaning (so throughout).
203. For the nonce: for the purpose.
204. Mell: sing.

PILATE: Cry "Oyas!"
      BEADLE: "Oyas!"
          PILATE: Yet louder!
             BEADLE: "Oyas!" (aloud).
                PILATE: Yet eft, by thy feithe.[205]

Cry peace in this press,[206] upon pain thereupon;   370
Bid them swage of[207] their sweying[208] both swiftly and swithe,[209]
And stint of[210] their striving and stand still as a stone.
Call Jesu the gentle of Jacob, the Jew.
Come pressed and appear.
To the bar draw thee near,   375
To thy judgment here,
To be deemed for thy[211] deeds undue.

SOLDIER 1: We! Hark how this harlot he hields out of harre.[212]
This lotterel[213] list[214] not my lord to lout.
SOLDIER 2: Say, beggar, why brawlest thou? Go boun thee to the bar.   380
SOLDIER 1: Step on thy standing[215] so stern and so stout.
SOLDIER 2: Step on thy standing so still.
SOLDIER 1: Sir coward, to court must ye cair.
SOLDIER 2: A lesson to learn of our lare.[216]
SOLDIER 1: Flit forth, foul might thou fare.   385
SOLDIER 2: Say, warlock, thou wantest of thy will.

SON: O Jesu ungentle, thy joy is in japes.
Thou cannot be courteous? Thou captive I call thee.
No ruth were it[217] to rug thee and rive thee in ropes.
Why falls thou not flat here—foul fall thee[218]—   390
For fear of my father so free?
Thou wot not his wisdom, iwis.
All thine help in his hand that it is,
How soon he might save thee from this.
Obey him, brothel, I bid thee.   395

PILATE: Now, Jesu, thou art welcome iwis, as I ween.
Be not abashed, but boldly boun thee to the bar.

---

205. Adopting Toulmin Smith's proposed emendation of the MS. *Feithe* is faith.
206. *Press*: crowd.
207. *Swage of*: abate.
208. *Sweying*: sound.
209. *Swithe*: swith, i.e., forcibly.
210. *Stint of*: leave off.
211. *Thy*: adopting Beadle's emendation of the MS, which reads "his."
212. *Out of harre*: out of order.
213. *Lotterel*: scoundrel.
214. *List*: cares (so throughout).
215. *Standing*: i.e., place of standing.
216. *Lare*: i.e., lore (so throughout).
217. *No ruth were it*: i.e., I would not be sorry to.
218. *Foul fall thee*: i.e., may evil befall you.

What seignior will pursue for thee sore, I have seen,
To work on this warlock; his wit is in war.[219]
Come pressed, of a pain,[220] and appear. 400
And sir prelates, your points be proving:
What cause can ye cast of accusing?
This matter ye mark to be moving
And hendly in haste let us hear.

CAIAPHAS: Sir Pilate of Pontus and prince of great price, 405
We trust ye will trow[221] our tales they be true,
To death for to deem him with duly device.
For cursedness yon knave has in case,[222] if ye knew,
In heart would ye hate him in hie.[223]
For if it ne[224] were so 410
We meant not to misdo;
Trust, sir, shall ye thereto,
we had not him taken to thee.

PILATE: Sir, your tales would I trow, but they touch non intent.
What cause can ye find now this freke[225] for to fell? 415
ANNAS: Our Sabbath he saves not, but sadly assent
To work full unwisely, this wot I right well.
****
He works when he will, well I wot,
And therefore in heart we him hate.
It sits you to strength your estate 420
Yon losel to lose for his lay.

PILATE: Ilka[226] lede for to lose for his lay is not leal.
Your laws are leeful, but to your laws longs[227] it
This faitour to feeze[228] well with flaps full fele.[229]
And woe may ye work him by law, for he wrongs it. 425
Therefore take unto you full tite
And like as your laws will you lead,
Ye deem him to death for his deed.
CAIAPHAS: Nay, nay, sir. That doom must us dread.
****

219. *His wit is in war*: his mind is confused.
220. *Of a pain*: on account of a pain (that I will give you).
221. *Trow*: trust.
222. *Case*: heart (unless *cursedness yon knave has in case* means "the evil that knave has prepared").
223. *In hie*: quickly.
224. *Ne*: not (adopting Beadle's emendation of the MS, which lacks this word).
225. *Freke*: man.
226. *Ilka*: every.
227. *Longs*: pertains (so throughout).
228. *Feeze*: flog.
229. *Fele*: many (so throughout).

It longs not to us no lede for to lose.   430
PILATE: What would ye I did then? The devil mote you draw![230]
Full few are his friends, but fele are his foes.
His life for to lose there longs no law,
Nor no cause can I kindly contrive
That why he should lose thus his life.   435
ANNAS: Ah! Good sir, it raiks full rife[231]
In steads[232] where he has stirred mickle strife
Of ledes that are loyal to your life.

CAIAPHAS: Sir, halt men and hurt he healed in haste;
The deaf and the dumb he delivered from doole[233]   440
By witchcraft, I warrant—his wits shall waste—
For the ferlies[234] that he fareth with. Lo how they follow yon fool,
Our folk so thus he frightens in fear.
ANNAS: The dead he raises anon:
This Lazarus that low lay alone,   445
He granted him his gates for to gone[235]
And pertly thus proved he his power.

PILATE: Now good sirs, I say, what would ye?
CAIAPHAS: Sir, to death for to deem[236] him or do him adawe.[237]
PILATE: Yea, for he does well his death for to deem?[238]   450
Go, lake[239] you, sir, lightly. Where learned you such law?
This touches no treason, I tell you.
Ye prelates that proved are for price,
Ye should be both witty and wise
And aledge our law where it lies.   455
Our matters ye move thus amell[240] you.

ANNAS: Misplease not your person, ye prince without peer!
It touches to treason, this tale I shall tell;
Yon briber, full bainly he bad to forebear
The tribute to the emperor. Thus would he compel   460
Our people thus his points to apply.
CAIAPHAS: The people he says he shall save,
And Christ gars he[241] call him, yon knave,

---

230. *The devil . . . draw*: the devil take you!
231. *Raiks full rife*: spreads everywhere.
232. *Steads*: places.
233. *Doole*: dole, hardship.
234. *Ferlies*: wonders.
235. *He grant . . . gone*: he allowed him go his way.
236. *Deem*: adopting Beadle's emendation of the MS, which reads "do."
237. *Do him adawe*: put him out of life.
238. *For he . . . deem*: condemn him to death because he does well?
239. *Lake*: play. The sentence seems to imply that Caiaphas is not being serious.
240. *Amell*: between.
241. *Gars he*: he makes.

And says he will the high kingdom have.
Look whether he deserve to die!   465

PILATE: To die he deserves if he do thus indeed,
But I will see myself what he says.
Speak, Jesu, and spend now thy space for to speed.[242]
These lordings they alledge thee thou list not leve on our lays.
They accuse thee cruelly and keen   470
And therefore, as a chieftain I charge thee:
If thou be Christ that thou tell me,
And God's son thou grudge not to grant ye;
For this is the matter that I mean.

JESUS: Thou sayest so thyself. I am soothly the same,   475
Here woning in world to work all thy will,
My father,[243] is faithful to fell all thy fame.
Without trespass or teen am I taken thee till.
PILATE: Lo, bishops! Why blame ye this boy?
Me seems that it is sooth that he says.   480
Ye move all the malice you may
With your wrenches[244] and wiles to writhe him away,
Unjustly to judge him from joy.

CAIAPHAS: Not so, sir. His[245] saying is full soothly sooth;
It brings our bernes[246] in bale for to bind.   485
ANNAS: Sir, doubtless we deem as due of the death
This fool that ye favor. Great faults can we find
This day for to deem him to die.
PILATE: Say, losel, thou lies, by this light!
Say, thou ribald, thou reckons unright!   490
CAIAPHAS: Advise you, sir, with main[247] and with might,
And wreck not your wrath now forthy.

PILATE: Me likes not this language so largely for to lie.
CAIAPHAS: Ah! Mercy, lord. Meekly, no malice we meant.
PILATE: Now done is it doubtless, bald and be blithe.   495
Talk on that traitor and tell your intent.
Your segge is subtle ye say:
Good sirs, where learned he such lare?
CAIAPHAS: In faith we cannot find where.

242. *Speed*: succeed.
243. *My father*: apparently, both the object of Jesus' address in 1. 476 and the subject of the sentence
in 1. 477.
244. *Wrenches*: devious devices.
245. *His*: i.e., if his.
246. *Bernes*: men.
247. *Main*: force.

PILATE: Yes. His father with some ferlies began fare   500
And has lered[248] this lad of his lay.

ANNAS: Nay, nay, sir. We wist that he was but a wright.[249]
No subtlety he showed that any segge saw.
PILATE: Then mean ye of malice to mar him of might,
Of cursedness convict, no cause can ye know?   505
Me marvels ye malign amiss.
CAIAPHAS: Sir, from Galilee hither and o[250]
The greatest against him gan go,[251]
Yon warlock to waken of woe,[252]
And of this work bears witness, iwis.   510

PILATE: Why, and has he gone in Galilee, yon gadling ungain?[253]
ANNAS: Yea, lord. There was he born, yon brothel, and bred.
PILATE: Now without faging,[254] my friends, in faith I am fain,
For now shall our strife full sternly be stead.[255]
Sir Herod is king there ye ken.   515
His power is proved full pressed
To rid him or reave him of rest;
And therefore, to go with yon guest
Ye mark us out of the manliest men.

CAIAPHAS: As wit and wisdom your will shall be wrought.   520
Here are kemps[256] full keen to the king for to cair.
ANNAS: [To the soldiers.] Now seigniors, I say you, since sooth shall be sought,
But if he shortly be sent it may sit us full sare.[257]
PILATE: Sir knights that are cruel and keen,
That warlock ye·warrok[258] and wraste,[259]   525
And look that he bremely be braste.[260]
And therefore, sir knights, [in haste]
Do take on that traitor you between.

To Herod in haste with that harlot ye hie,
Commend me full meekly unto his most might.   530
Say the doom of this boy, to deem him to die,

248. *Lered*: taught.
249. *Wright*: woodwright.
250. *O*: continually.
251. *The greatest . . . go*: the largest crowds began to go to him.
252. *Yon warlock . . . woe*: to incite that reprobate to evil (so Beadle).
253. *Ungain*: disagreeable or difficult.
254. *Faging*: beguiling with flattery.
255. *Stead*: stayed.
256. *Kemps*: strong warriors.
257. *Sare*: sore.
258. *Warrok*: bind.
259. *Wraste*: wrest.
260. *Braste*: i.e., brast, severely beaten.

Is done upon him duly, to dress or to dight,[261]
or life for to leave at his list.
Say ought I may do him indeed,
His own am I worthily in weed.[262]   535
SOLDIER 1: My lord, we shall spring on a-speed.
Come, hence with this traitor full trist.[263]

PILATE: Beausires, I bid you ye be not too bold,
But attend for our tribute full truly to treat.[264]
SOLDIER 2: My lord, we shall hie this behest for to hold   540
And work it full wisely, in will and in wit.
PILATE: So, sirs, me seems it is sitting.
SOLDIER 1: Mahound, sirs, he mensk you with might.[265]
SOLDIER 2: And save you, sir, seemly in sight.
PILATE: Now in the wild vengeance ye walk with that wight   545
And freshly ye found[266] to be flitting,

E. P. SANDERS

[A Historical Examination of Jesus' Arrest and Trial][†]

Jesus' Arrest

We turn now to our second main question: why did the high priest arrest Jesus? We
have already substantially answered it: most immediately, the cause of Jesus' arrest
was his prophetic demonstration at the Temple. At least some people thought that
he threatened it. If the high priest Caiaphas and his advisers knew that Jesus had
been hailed as 'king' when he entered Jerusalem, they would have already worried
about him. The Temple action sealed his fate. The Markan trial scene seems to
presuppose the high priest's knowledge of both events. Jesus was first accused of
threatening the Temple. The witnesses, however, did not agree. Then Caiaphas
asked Jesus if he were 'the Messiah, the son of the Blessed' (Mark 14.61). In the

261. *To dress or to dight*: to arrange or to ordain.
262. *His own am I worthily in weed*: i.e., I am entirely at his disposal (with "weed" punning on "to
dress" above).
263. *Come, hence . . . trist*: Come, haul here this very sad traitor (adopting Beadle's emendation of
the MS, which reads "Come þens to me þis traitoure full tyte").
264. *Treat*: negotiate.
265. *Mahound, sirs . . . might*: may Mohammed honor you with strength (reflecting a tendency in
the European Middle Ages to view Islam as a relic of pre-Christian paganism).
266. *Found*: hasten.
† From E. P. Sanders, *The Historical Figure of Jesus* (London: Penguin, 1993), 265–74.
    Sanders's historical analysis examines the role played by the high priest Caiaphas in Jesus' arrest
and execution. By situating the events leading to Jesus' crucifixion in the complex political situation
that obtained in Judea at the time, Sanders is able to offer a probable account of the different play-
ers' motivations, including Pilate's. His work thus provides a sober historical foil to the imaginative
portrayals of Pilate and the Jewish leaders presented in this section's other selections.

previous chapter we briefly discussed the different versions of his answer. According to Mark, he answered, 'Yes'; according to Luke, he replied only 'You say that I am'; and, according to Matthew, he said, 'You have said so; *but* [on the other hand] I say that you will see the Son of Man . . .' Whatever Jesus' answer, however, we note that the question implies some knowledge of Jesus' pretensions or (more probably) knowledge of the cries of his followers when he entered the city. Jesus had also been teaching about 'the kingdom' while in Jerusalem, and this would have added to the negative impression. The high priest wanted him dead for the same reason [Herod] Antipas wanted John [the Baptist] dead: he might cause trouble.

We saw above that the high priest was responsible for good order in Judaea in general, and in Jerusalem in particular. Caiaphas served longer than any other high priest during the periods of direct Roman rule, and this is good evidence that he was capable. If the high priest did not preserve order, the Roman prefect would intervene militarily, and the situation might get out of hand. As long as the Temple guards, acting as the high priest's police, carried out arrests, and as long as the high priest was involved in judging cases (though he could not execute anyone), there was relatively little possibility of a direct clash between Jews and Roman troops. To keep his job, he had to remain in control, but any decent high priest—and Caiaphas was pretty decent—also cared about the Jewish populace. The high priest had other obligations to the populace than just the need to prevent clashes with Roman troops. He should also represent their views to the prefect, and he should stand up for Jewish customs and traditions. He was the man in the middle. This second responsibility was important, but it plays no role in our story.

The high priest, together with his counsellors, both formal and informal, often had the task of preventing trouble and stopping trouble-makers. I wish to illustrate this major fact of political life by giving very brief summaries from Josephus[1] of three separate events.

(1) About the year 50 CE, during a clash between Samaritans and Galilean pilgrims passing through Samaria, one of the pilgrims was killed. A crowd came from Galilee, bent on revenge, but 'the best-known' men went to the Roman procurator, Cumanus, to urge him to send troops and punish the murderers, thus putting an end to the matter. He refused to do so. News reached Jerusalem, and many of the people there rushed to Samaria, though 'the magistrates' or 'rulers' tried to restrain them. The magistrates, however, did not give up; clad in sackcloth, and with ashes on their heads (two signs of mourning), they went after the hotheads and tried to persuade them not to do anything rash, since a battle would surely lead Rome to intervene with a heavy hand. This appeal was effective, and the Jewish mob dispersed (though some smaller bands stayed on for pillage). 'The powerful' Samaritans went to Syria to lay their case before the Roman legate, and 'the best-known' Jews, including the high priest, did the same. The legate went to Caesarea and Lydda, in each place ordering executions of some of the guilty parties. He sent others to Rome to be tried by Claudius: two men of the 'highest power', namely, the chief priest Jonathan and the serving high priest Ananias, as well as Ananias' son, other 'best-known' Jews and 'the most distinguished' Samaritans (*War* 2.232–44).

1. Jewish historian (37–ca. 100); his writings include *The Jewish War* and *Antiquities of the Jews* (see Appendix, p. 975).

This event took place during a festival, and it required action in Samaria. It is doubtful, in these circumstances, that the high priest was one of the leading Jews who went to Samaria to stop the mob. But we see, even here, that Rome regarded him as responsible: he went to Syria to see the Roman legate, and he had to go to Rome to be tried. He had nothing to do with the trouble in Samaria, but nevertheless he was responsible for good order. We also see that the high priest was only 'first among equals'. Responsibility to prevent trouble fell, to some degree, on all the leading citizens.

(2) In 62 CE, during a brief period when no Roman procurator was resident in Palestine, the Sadducean high priest Ananus convened 'a council [*synedrion*] of judges' and had James the brother of Jesus and probably others executed. Certain fair-minded, lenient citizens, those most precise about the laws, objected, but the execution took place. Many scholars think that the objectors were Pharisees, and this seems to me likely. In any case the protest was partially successful: Ananus was deposed (*Antiq.* 20.199–203), since he had transgressed the Roman rule that, in an equestrian province, only the highest Roman official could execute.

(3) Jesus' arrest is closer to the third case, which concerns another Jesus, the son of Ananias, about thirty years after the execution of Jesus of Nazareth. At the Feast of Booths (Tabernacles), in a period that was otherwise peaceful, Jesus son of Ananias went to the Temple, where he cried, 'A voice from the east, a voice from the west, a voice from the four winds; a voice against Jerusalem and the sanctuary, a voice against the bridegroom and the bride, a voice against all the people.' This prediction of destruction—that it was such is clear from the reference to the bridegroom and the bride, taken from Jeremiah 7.34—led to his being interrogated and flogged, first by the Jewish authorities, then by the Romans. He answered questions by 'unceasingly reiterat[ing] his dirge over the city' and was finally released as a maniac. He kept up his cries for seven years, especially at the festivals, but otherwise did not address the populace. Finally, a stone from a Roman catapult killed him (*War* 6.300–309).

If we use this case as a guide, we can understand why Jesus of Nazareth was executed rather than merely flogged. Our Jesus' offence was worse than that of Jesus son of Ananias. Jesus of Nazareth had a following, perhaps not very large, but nevertheless a following. He had taught about the kingdom for some time. He had taken physical action in the Temple. He was not a madman. Thus he was potentially dangerous. Conceivably he could have talked his way out of execution had he promised to take his disciples, return to Galilee and keep his mouth shut. He seems not to have tried.

Collectively, the three stories illustrate how Judaea was governed when it was a province of Rome, formally administered by a Roman. * * * The Roman prefect or procurator had to maintain domestic tranquillity and collect tribute. Both tasks he turned over to Jewish aristocrats, especially the priestly aristocrats, headed by the high priest. Rome's choice of the high priest respected Jewish tradition. Judaea had been ruled by high priests for several centuries. When Herod became king he brought this system to an end, and Rome simply reinstated it when Herod's heir in Judaea (Archelaus) proved unable to rule successfully. When Caiaphas ordered Jesus to be arrested, he was carrying out his duties, one of the chief of which was to prevent uprisings.

I shall mention only briefly two other theories of why Jesus was arrested. One is that he was misunderstood. Caiaphas and Pilate thought that he had in mind a kingdom of this world, and that his followers were about to attack the Roman army; they mistakenly executed him as a rebel. This view basically derives from John 18.33–8, a long discussion about what kind of 'king' Jesus claimed to be. It is, however, most unlikely that Caiaphas and Pilate thought that Jesus led an armed force and planned a military takeover. Had they thought this, Caiaphas would have had Jesus' lieutenants arrested too, and his followers would have been executed—as were the followers of other prophets in later years, who made the mistake of marching about in large groups. The solitary execution of the leader shows that they feared that Jesus could rouse the mob, not that he had created a secret army. In other words, they understood Jesus and his followers very well.

The second view has been that Jesus was arrested because of theological differences with the mass of Jews, led by the Pharisees. He believed in love and compassion, ideas that the Pharisees abominated, and he disagreed with petty legalism and ritualism, which they favoured; for these reasons they conspired to have him killed. Scholars who hold this view do not explain the mechanics of how the Pharisees got Jesus arrested, but are content to maintain that Pharisaic opposition played a role. I shall not here repeat my numerous efforts to get Christians to see the Pharisees in a truer light, but only comment that such imagined disagreements explain nothing historically. Jews sometimes killed each other, but not because of these sorts of disagreements. The range of legal dispute between Jesus and others was well within the parameters of normal debate, and there is no reason at all to think that they were in conflict about love, mercy and grace. Conceivably Jesus opposed Pharisaic views about what produce counted as foodstuff and should be tithed (Matt. 23.23), but such criticisms as these were not matters of life and death. Moreover, the Pharisees are almost entirely absent from the last chapters of the gospels, and completely absent from the stories of the arrest and trial. According to the evidence, they had nothing to do with these events. The synoptic descriptions of the high priest and his council agree 100 per cent with Josephus' descriptions of how Jerusalem was governed when it was part of a Roman province. The high priest and the chief priests are the primary actors, and the Pharisees play no role at all.

The theory advanced here—that Caiaphas had Jesus arrested because of his responsibility to put down trouble-makers, especially during festivals—corresponds perfectly with all the evidence. Jesus had alarmed some people by his attack on the Temple and his statement about its destruction, because they feared that he might actually influence God. It is highly probable, however, that Caiaphas was primarily or exclusively concerned with the possibility that Jesus would incite a riot. He sent armed guards to arrest Jesus, he gave him a hearing, and he recommended execution to Pilate, who promptly complied. That is the way the gospels describe the events, and that is the way things really happened, as the numerous stories in Josephus prove.

The Recommendation to Execute

Can we say any more about *why* Caiaphas and his advisers sent Jesus to Pilate to be executed? The trial scenes in the gospels afford the only possible evidence. I have already briefly discussed them, but now we shall look at them more closely. I think that they are accurate enough for general purposes, but there are problems in detail. In this discussion I shall assume that both Matthew and Luke based their accounts of the Jewish trial on Mark. I do not think that we can rely on Mark's description of the trial in a very precise way, as if it were a court-recorder's transcript, but it will form the basis of our examination.

* * *

Mark's view is that Jesus was convicted for claiming titles for himself, and that these claims constituted blasphemy in the eyes of other Jews—or at least one, Caiaphas. In the decades following Jesus' death and resurrection Christians would give Jesus both titles (Messiah and Son of God) and interpret them in ways that some Jews considered blasphemous. 'Son of God' in particular would come to mean that Jesus was not a mere mortal. We saw in [the previous chapter] that on their own these titles have no such meaning. Mark's question, 'Are you the Christ, the Son of the Blessed?' [14:61], supposes that these two titles go together and interpret one another. But that is a Christian achievement. The mere combination is suspicious, and the statement that the two titles, when combined, constitute blasphemy also looks like Christian creativity. Some early Christians wanted to attribute his death to confessing the christology of the church. Christology separated the new movement from its mother, and naturally they wanted their own distinctive views to go back to Jesus. Titles, however, play such a minor part in the synoptic gospels that we must doubt that they were the real issue at the trial.

If, however, we back off from Christianity's preoccupation with titles that supposedly define the person of Jesus and look at Mark's trial scene with fresh eyes, we find that it is perfectly reasonable. If it were a transcript, if these exchanges between Caiaphas and Jesus took place precisely as Mark wrote them, we would still have to conclude that titles were not the real issue. What the passage says is this: Jesus threatened the Temple and gave himself airs. The high priest had him arrested because of his action against the Temple, and that was the charge against him. The testimony was thrown out of court because the witnesses did not say the same things. The high priest, however, *had decided that Jesus had to die*, and so he was not willing to drop the case. He asked Jesus to say something about himself, and then he cried 'blasphemy', rending his garments. The rest of the court went along. That is, as the story reads, the high priest did not want to try Jesus on the basis of claiming titles, but because of the Temple. He fell back on titles, and declared that Jesus' answer was blasphemy—no matter what he said. We do not have to decide whether Jesus answered 'yes' or 'maybe'. The high priest had already made up his mind.

Tearing one's garments was a powerful sign of mourning, and showing the signs of mourning had persuasive power. We saw above that the 'magistrates' or 'rulers' from Jerusalem put ashes on their heads and wore sackcloth (other signs of mourning) when trying to prevent mob violence in Samaria. For the high priest to tear his clothing was the most extreme sign of mourning, since the Bible forbids him to tear his garments, or even to dishevel his hair (Lev. 21.10). Caiaphas' transgression of the law showed horror. Few Jews would have denied him what he wanted, and certainly not his own counsellors. Jesus was sent to Pilate.

I am proposing two ways of reading Mark. One is Mark's own view. During his public ministry Jesus had not claimed titles for himself and had tried to silence others who called him 'Messiah' or 'Son of God'. Therefore the titles, according to Mark's Gospel, do not explain the decision to arrest. Caiaphas had Jesus arrested because he held the mistaken view that Jesus had threatened the Temple. Jesus had not done so, and his trial exonerated him of this charge. The high priest, however, asked a leading question about titles. Jesus accepted the two terms 'Messiah' and 'Son of the Blessed (God)' as applying to himself, and the high priest charged him with blasphemy. The second reading is a critical interpretation of Mark. It arises in part from the observation that Mark attaches to 'Messiah' and 'Son of God' a significance that they did not have prior to the development of the church's christology. Because of this, we may offer a better historical interpretation of Jesus' trial and execution *even if* we accept Mark's narrative, (1) During his teaching and healing ministry, Jesus did not give himself titles; when directly asked he declined to say who he was. (2) Jesus was arrested because he threatened the Temple. (3) When the witnesses failed to agree about Jesus' threat to the Temple, Caiaphas did not have him flogged and then released. He decided, instead, to try again. This shows that he had intended execution from the outset. (4) He then asked Jesus if he was Messiah and Son of God. (5) Jesus said that he was. (6) These titles did not, in and of themselves, constitute blasphemy. (7) The high priest decided to call them blasphemy because he had already decided on execution. (8) Instead of conducting a further inquiry into what the terms meant to Jesus, Caiaphas made an extravagant display of mourning and thereby persuaded his counsellors to join him in condemning the Galilean. An historical construal of Mark's trial scene *as written* is that the titles were an expedient and that the threat to the Temple was the immediate cause of execution.

I wish to distinguish my own view from the previous eight points, which offer a reconstruction of what Mark's account would mean if it gave a verbatim report of a trial. I think that Mark's trial scene is not a transcript and that we must assess the motives of the various actors on more general grounds. When we consider the way in which high priests discharged their civic responsibilities under the Roman prefects and procurators, we should conclude that Caiaphas was carrying out his duties as prescribed: Jesus was dangerous because he might cause a riot, which Roman troops would put down with great loss of life. The author of John attributed to Caiaphas an entirely appropriate statement: 'it is expedient for you that one man should die for the people, and that the whole nation should not perish' (John 11.50). Although it was the Temple scene that decided the issue, other factors were probably contributing causes: Jesus' entry to Jerusalem and his teaching about the kingdom. We do not know how much Caiaphas knew about these other matters, but it would be reasonable to think that, after he learned of Jesus' assault on the pigeon-sellers and money-changers, and before he ordered his arrest, he had sought and attained further information about him. As we shall see immediately below, he probably passed on to Pilate the fact that Jesus thought that he was 'king'. This self-claim is implicit in Jesus' entry into Jerusalem, especially when that symbolic act is combined with Jesus' teaching. While I doubt the Markan combination of 'Messiah', 'Son of God' and 'blasphemy', I do not doubt that Caiaphas and his counsellors knew that Jesus taught about the kingdom and claimed for himself a significant role in it.

I propose, then, that Caiaphas made only one decision: to arrest *and* execute Jesus. If so, he did not act because of theological disagreement, but because of his principal political and moral responsibility: to preserve the peace and to prevent riots and bloodshed. It was Jesus' self-assertion, especially in the Temple, but also in his teaching and in his entry to the city, that motivated the high priest to act.

Pilate's Decision

Why did Pilate order Jesus' execution? Because the high priest recommended it and gave him a telling charge: Jesus thought that he was king of the Jews. Pilate understood that Jesus was a would-be king without an army, and therefore he made no effort to run down and execute Jesus' followers. He probably regarded him as a religious fanatic whose fanaticism had become so extreme that it posed a threat to law and order.

The gospels, especially Matthew and John, want Jesus to have been condemned by the Jewish mob, against Pilate's better judgement. Pilate worried, he was advised by his wife to do nothing, he consulted the crowd, he pleaded on Jesus' behalf; finally, weakling that he was, he could not withstand the clamour of the crowd, and so he had Jesus executed (Matt. 27.11–26; John 18.28–19.16). These elements of the story of Jesus' last hours derive from the desire of the Christians to get along with Rome and to depict Jews as their real opponents. In all probability Pilate received Caiaphas' charge, had Jesus flogged and briefly interrogated, and, when the answers were not completely satisfactory, sent him to the cross with not a second thought. Philo, who was Pilate's contemporary, wrote an appeal to the emperor Gaius (Caligula), which included a description of Pilate. Philo wrote of 'the briberies, the insults, the robberies, the outrages and wanton injuries, the executions without trial constantly repeated, the ceaseless and supremely grievous cruelty' that marked Pilate's rule (*Embassy to Gaius* 302).[2] Moreover, Pilate was eventually dismissed from office because of large-scale and ill-judged executions (*Antiq.* 18.88f.). This evidence agrees precisely with the sequence of events that the gospels narrate: Jesus appeared before Pilate and was executed almost immediately, with no further witnesses and with no trial procedure. The stories of Pilate's reluctance and weakness of will are best explained as Christian propaganda; they are a kind of excuse for Pilate's action which reduces the conflict between the Christian movement and Roman authority.

---

2. See Appendix, pp. 981–83, for a relevant selection from this work.

THE MEANING OF ROMANS 7

Romans 7:7–25 may be the most controversial passage in the New Testament. To begin with, readers from antiquity to the present have struggled to identify its "I." (As many of the exegetes whose works are excerpted below recognize, its equation with Paul's authorial persona cannot be assumed.) Moreover, the relationship this passage describes between sin, the self, and the law is carefully nuanced, to say the least: though the law by definition prohibits sin, sin nonetheless relies on the law in order to bring itself into existence. Its existence in turn brings about a split within the sinning self, entailing this self's paradoxically self-willed actions against its own desires. As if the passage's ambiguity and paradoxes were not challenge enough, a consensus about the proper literary, rhetorical, and social context in which Romans 7 should be situated remains elusive.

The following section aims to tell one coherent story about how this passage has been read throughout history, and about some influential ways in which its interpretive problems have been solved. It perhaps goes without saying that this is not the full story, nor the only story about Romans 7 that could be told. It begins with Origen's careful rhetorical analysis of Paul's argument and then moves via Jerome to Augustine, who in the context of the Pelagian theological controversy takes Paul to be writing about his pre-conversion experience with sin and the law. Augustine thereby articulates an influential reading of the passage that privileges a relatively straightforward autobiographical interpretation over Origen's subtle rhetorical analysis. Augustine's exegesis informed that of Martin Luther, who interpreted Romans 7 in the context of another theological controversy, and the Augustinian-Lutheran interpretive tradition gave rise to a number of brilliant modern readings of the passage, including those of the Swiss theologian Karl Barth and of the German theologian and biblical scholar Rudolf Bultmann, who each deepen and complicate the insights of their predecessors.

In the later twentieth century a "new approach" to Paul emerged, most clearly articulated in E. P. Sanders's *Paul and Palestinian Judaism* (1977) but largely inspired by Kirster Stendahl's important essay "The Apostle Paul and the Introspective Conscience of the West." In order to resist uncritical assimilation of Paul's insights to those of later theologians writing in very different circumstances, the new approach focuses on carefully reconstructing the apostle's own historical context by foregrounding, for instance, the controversies in which he was embroiled, especially those attending the integration of Gentile believers into the originally Jewish early church. Although scholars approaching Paul in this way often recognize as interesting and profound the theological ideas that Augustine, Luther, Barth, Bultmann, and others explore in dialogue with Romans 7, they usually do not consider these interpretations to be viable readings of the text.

In recent years, a number of innovative interpretations of the passage have been proposed, several of which, in addition to reflecting Stendahl and Sanders's enormous influence, reach for inspiration over the heads of Luther and Augustine all the way back to Origen. They capitalize on this very early biblical scholar's astute observations about Paul's conventional employment of rhetorical personae in order to construct interpretations that purportedly locate Paul's argument in its original literary and social contexts. Two such readings are excerpted here: Stanley Stowers's, which focuses on Paul's use of a Greco-Roman literary commonplace that resonated with ancient Jewish stereotypes of Gentile depravity, and J. Albert Harrill's, which investigates Paul's reliance on language associated with slavery in the Roman Empire. This volume's annotations to Romans 7 propose a complementary reading of this passage that emphasizes its employment of the persona of Eve from Genesis 3's story of the primeval transgression.

ORIGEN

[Paul's Laws and Personae]†
(from *Commentary on Romans*, Book 6, Chapter 8)

On Romans 7:7–8

3 Accordingly he says, "What then shall we say? Is the law sin?" Did you think, he says, that I was speaking about the law of Moses [and claiming] that it was sin? "By no means!" The response, "By no means!" should suffice for both clauses: Neither am I speaking about the law of Moses nor am I saying that that law is sin. On the contrary: "I did not know sin except through the law. For I would not have known covetousness had the law not said, 'You shall not covet.'" Understand which law I am speaking about, he says, which, unless it existed, no one would know sin. Is it the law of Moses through which Adam knew his sin and hid himself from the presence of the Lord [Gen 3:8]? Is it the law of Moses through which Cain knew his sin and said, "My sin is greater than that I should be left alive" [Gen 4:13], or through which Pharaoh knew his sin and said, "The Lord is righteous, but I and my people are wicked" [Exod 9:27]? But if all these and innumerable others knew their sin before the law of Moses, it will, doubtless, not be the law of Moses about which the Apostle says, "I did not know sin except through the law," and about which he says, "I would not have known what it is to covet had the law not said, 'You shall not covet'" [Rom 7:7; Exod 20:17]. Rather, it is that law concerning which we have frequently said is in everyone's hearts, "written not with ink, but by the Spirit of the living God" [2 Cor 3:3], and teaches each man what ought to be done and what ought to be avoided. It is the same [law], then, through which a man knows his own sin. For it speaks to us within the conscience and says, "You shall not covet."

---

† From Origen, *Commentary on the Epistle to the Romans, Books 6–10*, trans. Thomas P. Scheck, Fathers of the Church 104 (Washington, DC: Catholic University of America Press, 2002), 30–32, 36–39, 41–42, 44.
   Origen (see headnote on p. 1068) speculates about the identity of the "law" and especially of the "I" in Romans 7:7–25, in the latter case operating under the reasonable assumption that Paul, like many other Greco-Roman writers, frequently and subtly shifts personae as his discourse progresses. Origen's careful rhetorical analysis anticipates and informs much later debate surrounding these interpretive issues.

4 But this law is found in man neither at all times nor from the beginning, when a man is born, but rather he lives without this law for a certain time, while his age does not allow it, just as Paul himself acknowledges when he says, "I was once alive without the law." Therefore, at that time, when we lived without the law, we did not know covetousness. He did not say: I was not having it; but: "I was not knowing it," as if covetousness existed, but it was not known what it was. But when reason arrives and the natural law finds a place within us in the advancement of age, it begins to teach us what is good and to turn us away from evils. Thus, when it says, "You shall not covet," we learn from it what we did not know before: Covetousness is evil.

5 "But sin, receiving an opportunity, worked in me through the commandment all kinds of covetousness." That law of which he says, "For I would not have known covetous desire had the law not said: You shall not covet," is also called the commandment. Thus he says that by an opportunity afforded by this commandment, in which we are forbidden to covet, sin was kindled all the more intensely within us and worked all kinds of covetousness within us. For because the flesh lusts against the Spirit [Gal 5:17], i.e., against the law that says, "You shall not covet," it is likewise opposed to it and engages it in battle in a certain manner, so that not only would it satisfy the covetousness but also it would conquer an enemy.

6 This then is the opportunity that he says comes from the commandment. For these things that are forbidden are somehow longed for more passionately. On this account, though the commandment is holy and just and good—for what prohibits evil must of necessity be good—yet by prohibiting covetousness it instead provokes and kindles it; and through the good it worked death in me. The Apostle is showing by these things, however, that the origin of sin has arisen from covetousness. As long as the law is issuing prohibitions, whether it is Moses' law, which says, "You shall not covet," or even natural law, as I have explained above, whatever is forbidden is desired all the more tenaciously.

(from *Commentary on Romans*, Book 6, Chapter 9)

On Romans 7:14–20, 24–25a

2 If, perhaps, the explanation we were maintaining concerning the different kinds of law appeared to anyone as forced and presumptuous, let him now attend to this section, where not only a diversity of laws is introduced, but a diversity of *personae*.[1] For Paul, who has said elsewhere, "For we do not live according to the flesh nor do we wage war according to the flesh" [2 Cor 10:3], claims in the present passage to be of the flesh. And here he claims to be sold into slavery under sin, whereas elsewhere he had said, "You were bought with a price" [1 Cor 6:20; 7:23], and again, "Christ redeemed us" [Gal 3:13–14]. What is more, in other places he said, "It is no longer I who live but Christ lives in me" [Gal 2:20], and says again, "on account of his Spirit dwelling in us" [Rom 8:11]. But now he says, "Good does

---

1. Roles (e.g., those played by an actor) or characters (Latin).

not dwell in me, that is, in my flesh." Well, if good does not dwell in his flesh, how can he say that our bodies are a temple of God and a temple of the Holy Spirit [1 Cor 3:16; 6:19]? Furthermore, how are all the other things, in which he declares that he is led captive to the law of sin by the law that is in his members and that fights against the law of his mind, congruent with apostolic dignity and especially with Paul, in whom Christ both lives and speaks [Gal 2:20; 2 Cor 13:3]?

3 We should conclude from these things that it is the custom of Holy Scripture to imperceptibly change the *personae* and the subject matter and the reasons that it seems to discuss and the designations. Rather, it uses by all means the same designations at times for some subjects, at other times for others. For example, in the present passage the Apostle says, "For we know that the law is spiritual." Up to this point, what he said, "we know that the law is spiritual," is pronounced with apostolic authority. For one who is of the flesh and sold as a slave under sin does not know that the law is spiritual; on the contrary it is the one who has the Spirit of God in him who knows that the law is spiritual. This statement applies well to the law of Moses. For that law is a spiritual law and a life-giving Spirit for those who understand it spiritually [2 Cor 3:6]. But the one who understands it in a fleshly way recalls it as a law of the letter and a letter that kills [2 Cor 3:6].

4 Yet when he says, "But I am of the flesh, sold into slavery under sin," as if a teacher of the Church, he has now taken upon himself the *persona* of the weak. On this account he has also said elsewhere, "I became weak to the weak to win the weak" [1 Cor 9:22]. Here as well, then, to whoever is weak, i.e., to those who are in the flesh and sold into slavery under sin, Paul becomes fleshly and sold into slavery under sin and he says the same things that are customary for them to say under the pretense of an excuse or accusation. He is therefore talking about himself as if speaking under the *persona* of these others: "But I am of the flesh and sold into slavery under sin," that is to say, living according to the flesh and sold at the price of lust and covetous desire to the authority of sin. "I do not understand my own actions. For I do not do what I want; but I do the very thing I hate." Therefore, when he says, "I do not understand my own actions," he does not so much mean that a person does not understand the thing itself that he is doing, though he may be fleshly, but he is said not to understand the reason for what he is doing.

5 But what he says, "For I do not do what I want; but I do the very thing I hate," shows that even though the one who is saying these things may be of the flesh and sold into slavery under sin, he is nevertheless also attempting to resist the vices to some small extent, obviously by means of the instinct that comes from natural law; but he is conquered by the vices and, against his will, is overwhelmed. This is what frequently occurs, for example, when someone resolves patiently to endure another who is inciting him, but in the end is overcome with wrath and suffers this against his own will. Thus he becomes angry even though he does not want to become angry. The same thing regularly happens with the vice of fear, so that even contrary to one's will a person may be terrified with dread and fright. This also comes to pass quite often in connection with sudden elation or unexpected honor, resulting in one being more arrogant and haughty than one wants.

6 The person who is not yet spiritual but fleshly is therefore conquered by each individual [vice], even contrary to his will. For that will is not yet strong and

robust enough that it may determine for itself that it must struggle even to the point of death for the sake of the truth [cf. Sir 4:28]. Nor is this the kind of will to say, "Yes is yes; no is no" [Matt 5:37], and for that reason it cannot do what it wants, but what it does not want. Nevertheless the part that does not want the evil agrees with the law of God that whatever forbids evil is good. And natural law is brought into a kind of agreement with the law of God so that [the two laws] want the same things and do not want the same things. But if we agree with the law of God according to the will, then the evil that we do is no longer being done by us but by the sin that is in us, that is, the law and will of the flesh, which leads us as captives to the law of sin. Surely here it is the fleshly Paul who says, "It is no longer I that do it, but sin that dwells within me." But elsewhere the spiritual Paul says, "I labored more abundantly than all the others; but not I but the grace of God with me" [1 Cor 15:10]. Therefore, just as he ascribes these labors of his not to himself but to the grace of God, which was working in him, in the same way, as a fleshly man he reckons the works that are not good not to himself but to sin that dwells and works within him. For this reason, then, he says, "It is no longer I that do it, but sin that dwells within me. For good does not dwell within me, that is, in my flesh." For Christ is not yet dwelling within him [cf. Rom 8:10] nor is his body a temple of God [cf. 1 Cor 3:16; 6:19].

* * *

11 Having assumed the *persona* of the weaker person, Paul had taught that struggles occur within a human being. He had shown that a soul may be carried off to sin's jurisdiction, even against the will, through the desires of the flesh by the very practice of sinning. Since this is so, at this point he utters an exclamation, still under the *persona* of the one whom he has described, and says, "Wretched man that I am! Who will set me free from the body of this death?" For he sees himself as wretched, within whom so many laws are fighting with one another, and so many battles are being engaged in. "The flesh fights against the Spirit, and the Spirit against the flesh" [Gal 5:17]; the law in the members fights against the law of the mind. And the captive soul is led away to the law of sin and is put under its yoke, even though the inner man may delight in the law of God. With so many evils of this kind in him, how could a man not say that he is wretched and dwells in a body of death? For a body in which sin dwells is deservedly called a body of death, since sin is the cause of death. This exclamation comes, then, from the *persona* of the one whom the Apostle describes as having received the initial phases of a conversion in that the will for the good is present in him, but he could not yet come to the accomplishment of the good. For he does not manage to perfect the good, because the practice and training in the virtues had not yet grown in him. The answer to what he had said, "Who will set me free from the body of this death?" is given no longer under the *persona* of that person but with apostolic authority: "The grace of God through Jesus Christ our Lord." From this it becomes apparent that the Apostle, because of this, has described all these things and he has set forth these evils that were going on within us in order that he might show clearly and demonstrate to the utmost from how many evils and from how many kinds of death Christ has rescued us [cf 2 Cor 1:10].

(from *Commentary on Romans*, Book 6, Chapter 10)

On Romans 7:25b

2 Someone will possibly say that the Apostle, because up to this point he has spoken not as himself but under the assumed *persona* of another, now, as if indicating a change of *persona*, says, "I myself," so as to show that what is needful to be said pertains to himself, that is, to the Apostle. Yet he says that with the mind he serves the law of God, but with the flesh the law of sin, as if the power of sinning is so great and the tyranny of the flesh is so strong that the Apostle could not escape it. And for this reason he would have said elsewhere, "I punish my body and reduce it to slavery, so that after proclaiming to others I myself should not be rejected" [1 Cor 9:27]. Yet it seems to me that whoever assumes that these things have been spoken under the *persona* of the Apostle smites every soul with hopelessness. For there would then be absolutely no one who does not sin in the flesh [cf. Eccl 7:20]. For that is what it means to serve the law of sin in the flesh. Therefore, it appears more to me that he is still retaining the *persona* that he described above as though it were himself, of a man already converted to better things in the will and purpose, and one who is a slave to the law of God with the mind and soul, but who had thus not yet reached the point of bringing the obedience of the flesh into agreement with the mind.

3 For since he had discussed above the putting to death of the body and had taught that there must be a dying together with Christ [Rom 6:8], in these words he seems now to be pointing out how arduous is this work. He seems to teach that it is not realized immediately in one's actions, as soon as one wills this and purposes to do good. On the contrary, the force of habit is so great and the enticement of the vices is so strong that when the mind is already aiming for virtue and has determined to serve the law of God, nevertheless the desires of the flesh may persuade it to serve sin and submit to its laws.

JEROME

[Free Will and God's Grace]†

5. The better to deceive men they have added to the maxim given above[1] the saving clause "but not without the grace of God"; and this may at the first blush

---

† From Jerome, *Letter* 133, trans. W. H. Fremantle, G. Lewis, and W. G. Martley, in *The Nicene and Post-Nicene Fathers: Second Series*, vol. 6 (1893; reprint, Peabody, MA: Hendrickson, 1994), 275–78. Except as indicated, all notes are the translators'.
    The great biblical scholar and translator of the Latin Vulgate Jerome (ca. 347–420) invokes Romans 7:14–24 alongside a number of other biblical texts in order to refute a controversial doctrine propagated by the Christian ascetic Pelagius and his followers. As the excerpted letter makes clear, Jerome understood Pelagius's teaching to imply that through an exercise of free will independent of God's transforming grace, people could shun sin and sinful desires to commit themselves wholly to virtue.
    1. Viz., "A man may be without sin." See for this and the other statements of Pelagius, Aug. de Gestis Pelagii [Augustine, *On the Deeds of Pelagius*], esp. 2 chap. 5 and 6.

take in some readers. However, when it is carefully sifted and considered, it can deceive nobody. For while they acknowledge the grace of God, they tell us that our acts do not depend upon His help. Rather, they understand by the grace of God free will and the commandments of the Law. They quote Isaiah's words: "God hath given the law to aid men" [LXX Isa 8:20], and say that we ought to thank Him for having created us such that of our own free will we can choose the good and avoid the evil. Nor do they see that in alleging this the devil uses their lips to hiss out an intolerable blasphemy. For if God's grace is limited to this, that He has formed us with wills of our own, and if we are to rest content with free will, not seeking the divine aid lest this should be impaired, we should cease to pray; for we cannot entreat God's mercy to give us daily what is already in our hands, having been given to us once for all. Those who think thus make prayer impossible and boast that free will makes them not merely controllers of themselves but as powerful as God. For they need no external help. Away with fasting, away with every form of self-restraint! For why need I strive to win by toil what has once for all been placed within my reach? The argument that I am using is not mine; it is that put forward by a disciple of Pelagius, or rather one who is the teacher and commander of his whole army.[2] This man, who is the opposite of Paul, for he is a vessel of perdition, roams through thickets—not, as his partisans say, of syllogisms, but of solecisms, and theorizes thus: "If I do nothing without the help of God and if all that I do is His act, I cease to labour and the crown that I shall win will belong not to me but to the grace of God. It is idle for Him to have given me the power of choice if I cannot use it without His constant help. For will that requires external support ceases to be will. God has given me freedom of choice, but what becomes of this if I cannot do as I wish?" Accordingly he propounds the following dilemma: "Either once for all I use the power which is given to me, and so preserve the freedom of my will; or I need the help of another, in which case the freedom of my will is wholly abrogated."

6. Surely the man who says this is no ordinary blasphemer; the poison of his heresy is no common poison. Since our wills are free, they argue, we are no longer dependent upon God; and they forget the Apostle's words: "what hast thou that thou didst not receive? Now if thou didst receive it why dost thou glory as if thou hadst not received it" [1 Cor 4:7]? A nice return, truly, does a man make to God when to assert the freedom of his will he rebels against Him! For our parts we gladly embrace this freedom, but we never forget to thank the Giver; knowing that we are powerless unless He continually preserves in us His own gift. As the Apostle says, "it is not of him that willeth, nor of him that runneth, but of God that sheweth mercy" [Rom 9:16]. To will and to run are mine, but they will cease to be mine unless God brings me His continual aid. For the same apostle says: "it is God which worketh in you both to will and to do" [Phil 2:13]. And in the Gospel the Saviour says: "my Father worketh hitherto and I work" [John 5:17]. He is always a giver, always a bestower. It is not enough for me that he has given me grace once; He must give it me always. I seek that I may obtain, and when I have obtained I seek again. I am covetous of God's bounty; and as He is never slack in giving, so I am never weary in receiving. The more I drink, the more I thirst. For I have read

2. Celestius is meant [a friend and follower of Pelagius].

the song of the psalmist: "O taste and see that the Lord is good" [Ps 34:8]. Every good thing that we have is a tasting of the Lord. When I fancy myself to have finished the book of virtue, I shall then only be at the beginning. For "the fear of the Lord is the beginning of wisdom" [Ps 111:10], and this fear is in its turn cast out by love [1 John 4:18]. Men are only perfect so far as they know themselves to be imperfect. "So likewise ye," Christ says, "when ye shall have done all those things which are commanded you, say, We are unprofitable servants: we have done that which was our duty to do" [Luke 17:10]. If he is unprofitable who has done all, what must we say of him who has failed to do so? This is why the Apostle declares that he has attained in part and apprehended in part, that he is not yet perfect, and that forgetting those things which are behind he reaches forth unto those things which are before [Phil 3:12–13]. Now he who always forgets the past and longs for the future shews that he is not content with the present.

They are for ever objecting to us that we destroy free will. Nay, we reply, it is you who destroy it; for you use it amiss and disown the bounty of its Giver. Which really destroys freedom? the man who thanks God always and traces back his own tiny rill to its source in Him? or the man who says: "come not near to me, for I am holy [LXX Isa 65:5]; I have no need of Thee. Thou hast given me once for all freedom of choice to do as I wish. Why then dost Thou interfere again to prevent me from doing anything unless Thou Thyself first makest Thy gifts effective in me?" To such an one I would say: "your profession of belief in God's grace is insincere. For you explain this of the state in which man has been created and you do not look for God to help him in his actions. To do this, you argue, would be to surrender human freedom. Thus disdaining the aid of God you have to look to men for help."

7. Listen, only listen, to the blasphemer. "Suppose," he avers, "that I want to bend my finger or to move my hand, to sit, to stand, to walk, to run to and fro, to spit or to blow my nose, to perform the offices of nature; must the help of God be always indispensable to me?" Thankless, nay blasphemous wretch, hear the Apostle's declaration: "whether therefore ye eat or drink, or whatsoever ye do, do all to the glory of God" [1 Cor 10:31]. Hear also the words of James: "go to now, ye that say, To-day or to-morrow we will go into such a city and continue there a year, and buy, and sell, and get gain. Whereas ye know not what shall be on the morrow: for what is your life? It is even a vapour that appeareth for a little time, and then vanisheth away. For that ye ought to say, If the Lord will, we shall live, and do this or that. But now ye rejoice in your boastings; all such rejoicing is evil" [Jas 4:13–16]. You fancy that a wrong is inflicted on you and your freedom of choice is destroyed if you are forced to fall back on God as the moving cause of all your actions, if you are made dependent on His Will, and if you have to echo the psalmist's words: "mine eyes are ever toward the Lord: for it is he that shall pluck my feet out of the net" [Ps 25:15]. And so you presume rashly to maintain that each individual is governed by his own choice. But if he is governed by his own choice, what becomes of God's help? If he does not need Christ to rule him, why does Jeremiah write: "the way of man is not in himself" [Jer 10:23], and "the Lord directeth his steps" [Prov 16:9].

You say that the commandments of God are easy, and yet you cannot produce any one who has fulfilled them all. Answer me this: are they easy or are they difficult? If they are easy, then produce some one who has fulfilled them all. Explain also the words of the psalmist: "thou dost cause toil by thy law" [Ps 94:20 (LXX and Vulg.)], and "because of the words of thy lips I have kept hard ways" [LXX Ps 17:4]. And make plain our Lord's sayings in the gospel: "enter ye in at the strait gate" [Matt 7:13]; and "love your enemies"; and "pray for them which persecute you" [Matt 5:44]. If on the other hand the commandments are difficult and if no man has kept them all, how have you presumed to say that they are easy? Do not you see that you contradict yourself? For either they are easy and countless numbers have kept them; or they are difficult and you have been too hasty in calling them easy.

8. It is a common argument with your party to say that God's commandments are either possible or impossible. So far as they are the former you admit that they are rightly laid upon us; but so far as they are the latter you allege that blame attaches not to us who have received them but to God who has imposed them on us. What! has God commanded me to be what He is, to put no difference between myself and my creator, to be greater than the greatest of the angels, to have a power which no angels possess? Sinlessness is made a characteristic of Christ, "who did no sin neither was guile found in his mouth" [1 Pet 2:22]. But if I am sinless as well as He, how is sinlessness any longer His distinguishing mark? for if this distinction exists, your theory becomes fatal to itself.

You assert that a man may be without sin if he will; and then, as though awakening from a deep sleep, you try to deceive the unwary by adding the saving clause "yet not without the grace of God." For if by his own efforts a man can keep himself without sin, what need has he of God's grace? If on the other hand he can do nothing without this, what is the use of saying that he can do what he cannot do? It is argued that a man may be without sin and perfect if he only wills it. What Christian is there who does not wish to be sinless or who would reject perfection if, as you say, it is to be had for the wishing, and if the will is sure to be followed by the power? There is no Christian who does not wish to be sinless; wishing to be so, therefore, they all will be so. Whether you like it or not you will be caught in this dilemma, that you can produce nobody or hardly anybody who is without sin, yet have to admit that everybody may be sinless if he likes. God's commandments, it is argued, are possible to keep. Who denies it? But how this truth is to be understood the chosen vessel thus most clearly explains: "what the law could not do in that it was weak through the flesh, God, sending his own Son in the likeness of sinful flesh and for sin, condemned sin in the flesh" [Rom 8:3]; and again: "by the deeds of the law there shall no flesh be justified" [Rom 3:20]. And to shew that it is not only the law of Moses that is meant or all those precepts which collectively are termed the law, the same Apostle writes:[3] * * *

9. But you will demur to this and say that I follow the teaching of the Manichæans[4] and others who make war against the church's doctrine in the interest of their belief that there are two natures diverse from one another and that there is an evil nature which can in no wise be changed. But it is not against me that you must make this imputation but against the Apostle who knows well that God

3. Here Jerome quotes Rom 7:22–25, 14–20 [editors' note].
4. This is the well known dualism of Manes (Manichæus [Persian religious leader, 216–276 C.E.]), who held that the physical world and the human body are essentially evil.

is one thing and man another, that the flesh is weak and the spirit strong [cf. Matt 26:41]. "The flesh lusteth against the spirit and the spirit against the flesh: and these are contrary the one to the other: so that ye cannot do the things that ye would" [Gal 5:17]. But from me you will never hear that any nature is essentially evil. Let us learn then from him who tells us so in what sense the flesh is weak. Ask him why he has said: "the good that I would, I do not; the evil which I would not, that I do" [Rom 7:19]. What necessity fetters his will? What compulsion commands him to do what he dislikes? And why must he do not what he wishes but what he dislikes and does not wish? He will answer you thus: "nay, but, O man, who art thou that repliest against God? Shall the thing formed say unto him that formed it, Why hast thou made me thus? Hath not the potter power over the clay, of the same lump to make one vessel unto honour and another unto dishonour" [Rom 9:20, 21]? Bring a yet graver charge against God and ask Him why, when Esau and Jacob were still in the womb, He said: "Jacob have I loved, but Esau have I hated" [Mal 1:2, 3; Rom 9:13]. Accuse Him of injustice because, when Achan the son of Carmi stole part of the spoil of Jericho, He butchered so many thousands for the fault of one [Josh 7]. Ask Him why for the sin of the sons of Eli the people were well-nigh annihilated and the ark captured [1 Sam 4]. And why, when David sinned by numbering the people, so many thousands lost their lives [2 Sam 24]. Or lastly make your own the favorite cavil of your associate Porphyry, and ask how God can be described as pitiful and of great mercy when from Adam to Moses and from Moses to the coming of Christ He has suffered all nations to die in ignorance of the Law and of His commandments. For Britain, that province so fertile in despots, the Scottish tribes, and all the barbarians round about as far as the ocean were alike without knowledge of Moses and the prophets. Why should Christ's coming have been delayed to the last times? Why should He not have come before so vast a number had perished? Of this last question the blessed Apostle in writing to the Romans most wisely disposes by admitting that he does not know and that only God does. Do you too, then, condescend to remain ignorant of that into which you inquire. Leave to God His power over what is His own; He does not need you to justify His actions. I am the hapless being against whom you ought to direct your insults, I who am for ever reading the words: "by grace ye are saved" [Eph 2:5], and "blessed is he whose transgression is forgiven, whose sin is covered" [Ps 32:1]. Yet, to lay bare my own weakness, I know that I wish to do many things which I ought to do and yet cannot. For while my spirit is strong and leads me to life my flesh is weak and draws me to death. And I have the warning of the Lord in my ears: "watch and pray that ye enter not into temptation. The spirit indeed is willing, but the flesh is weak" [Matt 26:41].

10. It is in vain that you misrepresent me and try to convince the ignorant that I condemn free will. Let him who condemns it be himself condemned. We have been created endowed with free will; still it is not this which distinguishes us from the brutes. For human free will, as I have said before, depends upon the help of God and needs His aid moment by moment, a thing which you and yours do not choose to admit. Your position is that, if a man once has free will, he no longer needs the help of God. It is true that freedom of the will brings with it freedom of decision. Still man does not act immediately on his free will, but requires God's

aid who Himself needs no aid. You yourself boast that a man's righteousness may
be perfect and equal to God's; yet you confess that you are a sinner. Answer me
this, then; do you or do you not wish to be free from sin? If you do, why on your
principle do you not carry out your desire? And if you do not, do you not prove
yourself a despiser of God's commandments? If you are a despiser, then you are a
sinner. And if you are a sinner, then the scripture says: "unto the wicked God
saith, what hast thou to do to declare my statutes, or that thou shouldest take my
covenant in thy mouth? seeing thou hatest instruction and castest my words behind
thee" [Ps 50:16, 17]. So long as you are unwilling to do what God commands, so
long do you cast His words behind you. And yet like a new apostle you lay down
for the world what to do and what not to do. However, your words and your
thoughts by no means correspond. For when you say that you are a sinner—yet
that a man may be without sin if he will, you wish it to be understood that you
are a saint and free from all sin. It is only out of humility that you call yourself
a sinner; to give you a chance of praising others while you depreciate yourself.

AUGUSTINE

[Paul Speaks of Himself in Romans 7]†

8, 13. "They claim," he says, "that even the apostle Paul or all the apostles had
always been polluted by unbridled passion." Who would dare to say that, even if
one were a unbeliever? But this man surely spreads such lies precisely because
they hold that the apostle did not say with regard to himself, *I know that the good
does not dwell in me, that is, in my flesh. I can will the good, but I find that I cannot
bring it to completion* (Rom 7:18), and other such statements. Rather, they contend that he had assumed the role of some other person who was suffering such
a state of soul.[1] For this reason we must carefully examine and weigh this passage
in his letter so that their error may not be able to find a hiding place in some of
its obscurities.

In this letter the apostle argues at great length, defending grace in his long and
hard struggle against those who boasted in the law, but we will touch on only
a few points relevant to our topic.[2] * * * By these statements and others of this
sort that teacher of the nations shows quite clearly that the law could not take
away sin, but rather increased the sin which grace takes away. For the law is able
to give commands before which weakness gives way, but grace provides help in

† From Augustine, *Answer to the Two Letters of the Pelagians*, book 1, trans. Roland J. Teske, *The
Works of Saint Augustine: A Translation for the 21st Century*, part 1, vol. 24, *Answer to the Pelagians,
II* (Hyde Park, NY: New City Press, 1998), 122–29.
   Augustine (see headnote on pp. 1075–76), like Jerome, invokes Romans 7 to refute the doctrine of
Pelagius and his followers, although Augustine's exegesis is more careful and sustained than his
contemporary's. His interpretation answers in very different ways some of the same questions as
Origen's commentary, which itself influenced Pelagius's thinking.
1. See *The Grace of Christ and Original Sin* I, 39, 43, where Augustine cites Pelagius as holding this
view [translator's note].
2. Augustine here quotes Rom 3:20–24, 27–28; 3:27–28; 4:13–15; 5:20; 7:1–2, 4–6.

bestowing love. But so that no one would blame the law on account of these tes-timonies and maintain that it is evil, the apostle saw what could occur to those who understand incorrectly, and so he posed the same question for himself. *What then shall we say?* he asks. *Is the law sin? Heaven forbid! But I knew sin only through the law* (Rom 7:7). For he had said above, *Knowledge of sin came through the law* (Rom 3:20)—not the removal of sin, but the knowledge of sin!

14. But this is where he begins—and this was the reason that we undertook the examination of this text—to introduce his own person and to speak as if he were talking about himself. In this passage the Pelagians do not want us to understand Paul the apostle himself; rather, they hold that he has depicted himself as some other person, that is, as someone still under the law and not yet set free by grace. Here they should at least grant that *no one is justified by the law* (Gal 3:11), as the same apostle says elsewhere, but that the law suffices only for the knowledge of sin and for the transgression of the law so that, when sin is known and increased, one might seek grace through faith. They are not afraid to take as applicable to the apostle these statements which he could also have made about his past, but they are afraid to apply to him those which follow.[3] * * *

As I said, the apostle could be taken to have mentioned all these things from his past life so that he meant his words, *I was once living without the law* to be under-stood as referring to his first years of infancy before the age of reason. Then his next words, *But with the arrival of the commandment sin came back to life. I, how-ever, died*, would indicate that he was capable of receiving the commandment, but did not carry it out and became a transgressor of the law.

9, 15. Nor should one be disturbed by what he wrote to the Philippians, namely, that in terms of the righteousness which comes from the law he was without reproach [see Phil 3:6]. After all, he could have been a transgressor of the law inte-riorly in his evil desires and still have fulfilled the external works of the law out of fear either of human beings or of God himself, but out of a fear of punishment, not out of a love for and delight in righteousness. It is, after all, one thing to do good out of the desire to do good, and it is something else to be so inclined by the will toward doing evil that one would do evil, if it were possible that one could go unpunished. For in that case one certainly sins in the depths of the will, if one holds back from sin, not because of the will, but because of fear. In his interior acts the apostle knew that he was such a man before receiving the grace of God which is given through Jesus Christ our Lord, and he elsewhere openly admits this.[4] * * * Saul was such a man at that time when, as he says, he was without reproach in terms of the righteousness which comes from the law [see Phil 3:6]. For it was not after this detestable life that he made progress in the law and changed his conduct so that he might be beyond reproach. In the following passage he clearly shows this, where he says that he was changed and freed from these evils only by the grace of the savior. He adds here as well the same idea as he wrote to the Ephesians.[5] * * *

16. His words in this passage of the Letter to the Romans, *In order that sin might be seen as sin, it produced death in me through what was good* (Rom 7:13), fit

3. Augustine here quotes Rom 7:7–13.
4. Augustine here quotes Eph 2:1–5; Titus 3:3.
5. Augustine here quotes Titus 3:4–7.

with the previous text where he said, *But I knew sin only through the law, for I would not have known desire if the law had not said, "You shall not desire"* (Rom 7:7) and with his earlier words, *Knowledge of sin came through the law* (Rom 3:20). For here too he expressed the same idea: *In order that sin might be seen as sin* (Rom 7:13). He did not want us to understand his previous words, *After all, without the law sin lay dead* (Rom 7:8) in any other sense than that sin was hidden, unseen, and completely unknown, as if it were buried in the darkness of ignorance. What do his words, *I was once living without the law* (Rom 7:9a), mean but: "I thought I was living." And what else do the words he added, *But with the arrival of the commandment, sin came back to life* (Rom 7:9b), mean but that sin stood out and was seen? He did not say, "came to life," but *came back to life*. It had, after all, come to life long ago in paradise, when sin was clearly seen to have been committed against the commandment that God had given. But when it is contracted by those who are born, sin lies hidden, as if it were dead, until its prohibition makes us perceive its evil when it resists righteousness, when we are commanded to do one thing and give it our approval, but find delight in something else which has control of us. Then in the conscience of the human being born into this world there somehow comes back to life the sin that had long ago come to life in the conscience of the first human being God made.

10, 17. It is not so easy to show how what follows can be taken as applying to Paul. He says, *For we know that the law is spiritual, but I am carnal* (Rom 7:14). He does not say, "I was," but, *I am*. Was the apostle carnal at the time when he wrote this? Or did he say this with reference to the body? For he was still in the body of this death [see Rom 7:24], since the change which he mentions elsewhere had not yet taken place, *There is sown an animal body, but there arises a spiritual body* (1 Cor 15:44). For he will be a spiritual man in his whole being, that is, in both of the parts of which he is composed, when the body will also be spiritual. It is not, after all, absurd that in that life to come even the flesh will be spiritual, if it is possible that in this life even the spirit is carnal in those whose thoughts are still carnal. Hence, the apostle said, *But I am carnal* (Rom 7:14), because he did not yet have a spiritual body, just as he could have said, "But I am mortal." He would, of course, have been understood to have said this only with reference to his body which was not yet clothed with immortality.

So too, no one should think on account of his next words, *Sold under the power of sin* (Rom 7:14c), that he was not yet redeemed by the blood of Christ. That phrase can also be interpreted in accord with his words, *We too who have the first fruits of the Spirit groan in ourselves as we await the adoption, the redemption of our body* (Rom 8:23). After all, if he says that he was sold under the power of sin in the sense that his body was not as yet redeemed from corruption or that he was formerly sold under the power of sin by the first transgression of the commandment so that he has a corruptible body that weighs down the soul [see Wis 9:15], what prevents one from taking the apostle to be speaking about himself here? For such expressions of his can be taken as also applying to him, even if he intended us to understand in his own person not merely himself, but all who know that they struggle against their carnal inclinations without consenting to them because of their spiritual love.

18. His next words are: *I do not know what I do, for I do not do what I want; rather, I do what I hate* (Rom 7:15). Need we perhaps fear that someone will because of these words suppose that the holy apostle consented to the concupiscence of the flesh to do evil actions? But we must consider what he adds, *But if I do what I do not want, I consent to the law that it is good* (Rom 7:16). He says, after all, that he consents to the law rather than to the concupiscence of the flesh, for the latter he calls sin. He said, then, that his action and conduct do not stem from the will to consent to evil and to do it, but from the impulse of concupiscence. For this reason, then, he says, *I consent to the law that it is good*; I consent, because I do not will what it does not want. Then he says, *But now it is not I who do this, but the sin that dwells in me* (Rom 7:17). What does *But now* mean but: even now under the reign of grace which has set free the delight of the will from consenting to lust? For one cannot interpret, *It is not I who do this*, better than in the sense that he does not consent to hand over his members to sin as weapons of iniquity. For if he desires and consents and acts, how can he not do it, even if he is sorry for doing it and groans deeply over being conquered?

19. Do not the words which follow show with utmost clarity the reason why he says this? *For I know that the good does not dwell in me, that is, in my flesh* (Rom 7:18a). After all, if he did not explain it with the addition, *that is, in my flesh*, his words, *in me*, might be taken in another sense. And for this reason he goes back, repeating and teaching the same point. *I can will the good, but I find that I cannot bring it to completion* (Rom 7:18b). To bring the good to completion means that one does not even have concupiscence, but the good is incomplete when one has concupiscence, even if one does not consent to concupiscence in order to do an evil action. *I do not do the good that I want*, he says, *but I do the evil that I do not want. But if I do what I do not want, it is no longer I who do it, but the sin that dwells in me* (Rom 7:19–20). He repeated this with insistence, as if he were rousing sluggish minds from sleep. He says, *I find, therefore, this law: when I want to do what is good, evil lies at hand for me* (Rom 7:21). The other law, then, is good when one wills to observe it, but evil lies at hand because of concupiscence, though one does not consent to it who says, *It is no longer I who do it.*

20. What comes next explains both points still more clearly. *For I take delight in the law of God in the interior self, but I see another law in my members that resists the law of my mind and holds me captive under the law of sin which is in my members* (Rom 7:22–23). His words, *holds me captive*, can be surprising if there is no consent. Because of these three expressions, namely, the two which we have already discussed, *But I am carnal* (Rom 7:14b) and *Sold under the power of sin* (Rom 7:14c), and this third one, *Holds me captive under the law of sin which is in my members*, the apostle can be thought to describe a person who is still living under the law, not under grace. But just as we explained that he made those first two statements because of the flesh which is still subject to corruption, so we can interpret this statement in the same sense. That is, he meant that it *holds me captive* by the flesh, not by the mind, by its impulse, not by his consent, and thus it *holds me captive*, not because some foreign nature is present in the flesh, but because our own nature is present there. Just as, then, he himself explained his words, *For I know that the good does not dwell in me, that is, in my flesh* (Rom 7:18), so we ought also to interpret this passage, as if he said, *holds me captive*, that is, my flesh, *by the law of sin which is in my members* (Rom 7:23).

21. Then he added the reason why he said all these things: *Wretched man that I am! Who will set me free from the body of this death? The grace of God through Jesus Christ our Lord* (Rom 7:24–25a), and he concluded from this, *Therefore, I serve the law of God with my mind, but the law of sin with my flesh* (Rom 7:25b), the law of sin with my flesh, because I have concupiscence, but the law of God with my mind because I do not consent to the same concupiscence. *Now, then, there is no condemnation for those who are in Christ Jesus* (Rom 8:1). For only one who has consented to the concupiscence of the flesh to do evil is condemned. *For the law of the Spirit of life in Christ Jesus has set you free from the law of sin and death* (Rom 8:2), so that the concupiscence of the flesh does not win for itself your consent. The verses that follow explain the same idea still further, but we need to set a limit.

22. I had once thought that this passage from the apostle described a human being under the law.[6] Later, however, these words, *But now it is not I who do this* (Rom 7:17), made me feel their force. For his later words also belong to this passage, *Now, then, there is no condemnation for those who are in Christ Jesus* (Rom 8:1). Also, I do not see how a human being under the law could say, *I delight in the law of God in the interior self* (Rom 7:22). For we must attribute only to grace that delight in the good by which one also keeps from consenting to evil, not out of fear of punishment, but out of a love of righteousness. That, after all, is what it means to take delight.

11, 23. As for the passage in which he says, *Who will set me free from the body of this death?* (Rom 7:24), who will deny that, when the apostle said this, he was in the body of this death? From that body those who are not believers are not set free, but their same bodies are handed over to eternal torments. To be set free, then, from the body of this death, once the disease of concupiscence of the flesh has been completely healed, is to receive back the body, not for punishment, but for glory. With this passage the following text is quite in agreement, *We too who have the first fruits of the Spirit groan in ourselves as we await the adoption, the redemption of our body* (Rom 8:23). We clearly groan with such a groan when we say, *Wretched man that I am! Who will set me free from the body of this death?* (Rom 7:24).

What else do his words, *I do not know what I do* (Rom 7:15), mean but: I do not will it, I do not approve it, I do not consent to it, I do not do it? Otherwise, it is opposed to his earlier statements: *Knowledge of sin came through the law* (Rom 3:20), and *I knew sin only through the law* (Rom 7:7), and *In order that sin might be seen as sin, it produced death in me through what was good* (Rom 7:13). How, after all, did he know through the law the sin which he does not know? How is sin which is not known seen as sin? He said, *I do not know*, in the sense that I do not do it, since I do it without any consent. In that way the Lord will say to unbelievers, *I do not know you* (Matt 7:23), though surely nothing can lie hidden from him. In the same sense scripture said, *The one who did not know sin* (2 Cor 5:21), that is, the one did not commit sin. He could not, after all, fail to know what he blamed.

6. Earlier Augustine had explicitly stated that Saint Paul was speaking of a human being still under the law. See his *Commentary on Some Statements in the Letter to the Romans* 37, 44, his *Miscellany of Eighty-three Questions*, Question 66, 5, and *Miscellany of Questions in Response to Simplician* I, Questions 1, 1; 4; 9; 11; 12; and 13 [translator's note].

24. Once these points and others of this sort have been carefully considered in
the context of the apostle's writing, we correctly understand that the apostle was
not referring to himself alone in his own person, but also to others who are under
the dispensation of grace, but are not yet in that perfect peace in which death will
be swallowed up in victory [see 1 Cor 15:54]. He speaks of this next, *If Christ is
in you, the body is indeed dead on account of sin, but the spirit is life on account of
righteousness. If, then, the Spirit of him who raised Jesus from the dead dwells in you,
he who raised Christ Jesus from the dead will also bring to life your mortal bodies
through his Spirit dwelling in you* (Rom 8:10–11). When he has, then, given life to
our mortal bodies, not only we will not consent to sin, but we will not even have any
concupiscence of the flesh to which we might consent. In this mortal flesh only he
could be free of this concupiscence that resists the spirit who did not come to dwell
among human beings by means of it. The apostles were human beings and carried
about the body which is being corrupted and weighs down the soul [see Wis 9:15].
But heaven forbid that we should for this reason say, as this fellow falsely claims,
that they "had always been polluted by unbridled passion." We say, rather, that they
were free from consent to evil desires, but because of the concupiscence of the
flesh which they reined in through self-control, they groaned with great humility
and piety, longing not to have concupiscence at all rather than to have to control it.

MARTIN LUTHER

[The Righteous Are at the Same Time Sinners][†]

On Romans 7:7–25

First, this whole passage clearly reveals disapproval and hatred of the flesh and
love for the good and the law. Now such an attitude is not characteristic of a

† From Martin Luther, *Lectures on Romans*, trans. and ed. Wilhelm Pauck, Library of Christian
Classics (Philadelphia: Westminster Press, 1961), 201–5, 207–13. Unless indicated, all notes are
the translator's.

As an Augustinian monk, Martin Luther (1483–1546) suffered from an extremely sensitive conscience: he found it difficult to be convinced that his sins were forgiven and his relationship with
God secure. This painful experience, informed by his thorough biblical scholarship and his disgust
at abuses in the distribution of indulgences (remissions of earthly penances and time in purgatory
assigned for forgiven sins), ultimately led him to develop a theology that undermined the system
of sacraments that the medieval church understood to facilitate Christians' righteous transformation before a forgiving God. Although this German monk desired to reform the church by initiating debate on vital theological issues, his teachings actually precipitated its reorganization in his
homeland and elsewhere, with the emergent Protestant congregations generally characterized by a
more exclusive reliance on the authority of Scripture than the Catholic Church, by a liturgy more
accessible to the laity, and by a set of theological emphases and interpretations of the sacraments
different from the Roman church's (and frequently from Luther's as well).

The first selection comes from a series of lectures that Luther gave on Romans while serving as
chair of biblical studies at the University of Wittenberg. They date to 1515–16, when Luther was
beginning to develop his new understanding of God's righteousness as imputed to believers independently of their intentions or actions. Luther here, like Origen and Augustine before him, wrestles
with the identity of the "I" in Romans 7 and ponders the theological implications of this literary self's
characterization. The second selection, from a series of lectures on Galatians that Luther gave much
later, in 1535, focuses on the role of the law in bringing the believer to righteousness. Although he
is discussing Galatians 3:19, Luther reads that verse in light of Romans 7.

carnal man, for he hates and laughs at the law and follows the inclinations of his flesh.

Yet a spiritual man fights with his flesh and bemoans the fact that he cannot do as he wills. But a carnal man does not fight with it but yields and consents to it. Hence, this well-known judgment of Blessed Augustine: "The will to be righteous is a large part of righteousness."[1]

* * *

The first word, then, which proves that a spiritual man is speaking here is this: **But I am carnal** (Rom. 7:14). Because it is characteristic of a spiritual and wise man that he knows that he is carnal, that he is dissatisfied with himself and hates himself, and that he praises the law of God because it is spiritual. Conversely, it is characteristic of a foolish and carnal man that he thinks he is spiritual or that he is satisfied with himself and that he loves his life here in this world [cf. John 12:25].

* * *

The fourth word. **I consent to the law that it is good.** (Rom. 7:16.) The law wants the good, and he wants the good, and so they agree with one another. A carnal man, however, does not do this, but he always disagrees with the law and he would rather that there were no law (if this were possible). And so he does not want the good but evil. And even though he may do good (as I have said before), he does not really know it, because he acts from the slavish compulsion of fear, always with the strong desire to do the opposite if he can get away with it.

From this we must not think that the apostle wants us to understand his statement that he does the evil he hates and that he does not do the good he wants to do, in a moral and metaphysical sense as if he did no good but only evil; to ordinary human understanding, this may seem to be the meaning of his phrase. But he wants to say that he does not do the good as often and to such an extent and as readily as he would like. For he wants to act from utter single-mindedness, freedom, and cheerfulness, unmolested by the resistance of the flesh, and this he cannot do. It is as with a man who seeks to be chaste: he does not want to be assailed by any excitement but he wants to realize chastity without difficulty. But the flesh does not let him do this; with its inclinations and drives, it makes chastity a most troublesome burden and it stimulates unclean desires however unwilling the spirit may be. He that sets out to watch, to pray, and to help his fellow man will always find that the flesh is rebellious and that it plots and desires something else.

* * *

Now a man who does not know what struggling is and who yields to the flesh and obeys its desires without putting up any resistance, does not say: "What I will not I do," for he does not take delight in the opposite of what he does but in what he does in fact. But "to accomplish" means to realize what one wants to do or desires. So the spirit accomplishes the good it wants to do when it acts without protest according to the law of God. But this cannot be done in this life, for "to accomplish that which is good, I find not."

1. Cf. Augustine, [*Letters*] 127, 5.

The flesh, however, accomplishes what it wants to do in so far as it fulfills its desires with joy and without any struggle and hesitation. This is the way of this life, nay, rather, it is a sign of death; it shows that the world is lost: it is so easy to do evil. Hence, I maintain that this word proves that Paul speaks here not as a carnal man but as a very spiritual man.

The fifth word: **It is no more I that do it, but sin that dwells in me.** (Rom. 7:20.)

So it is not he that sins, because his flesh covets without his consent; indeed, strictly speaking, he himself does not covet, because he does not agree with the coveting of his flesh. And yet he says: "The good that I will, I do not." For one and the same person is spirit and flesh; thus what the flesh does the whole man is said to do. And yet what resists is not the whole man but is rightly called a part of him. Both then are true: it is he that acts and yet it is not he.

It is as with a rider: When his horse does not trot exactly as he wishes, it is he and yet not he that causes it to trot as it does. For the horse is not without him nor he without the horse. But a carnal man does always what sin does, because he always agrees with the law of his members. For in this case, mind and flesh are held together not only by one person but also by one will.

The sixth word: **For I know that there dwells not in me, that is to say, in my flesh, that which is good.** (Rom. 7:18.)

Observe how he attributes the flesh to himself as a part of himself, as if he himself were flesh. This is why he said before: "I am carnal," and so he now confesses himself to be not good but evil because he does evil. Because of the flesh, he is carnal and evil, for the good is not in him and he does evil; because of the spirit, he is spiritual and good, for he does the good. *We must note, therefore, that the words "I will" and "I hate" refer to the spiritual man or to the spirit, but "I do" and "I work" to the carnal man and to the flesh.* Just because one and the same man as a whole consists of flesh and spirit, he attributes to the whole man both of the opposites that come from the opposite parts of him. Thus there comes about a *communio idiomatum:*[2] one and the same man is spiritual and carnal, righteous and sinful, good and evil. Just so the one person of Christ is at the same time both dead and alive, both suffering and blessed, both active and inactive, etc., because of the *communio idiomatum,* even though there belongs to neither of his two natures what is characteristic of the other, for, as everyone knows, they differ absolutely from each other.

But this applies in no way to the carnal man; he is nothing but flesh in his whole person because the Spirit of God did not remain in him. The carnal man can therefore not say: "in me, that is to say, in my flesh," as if he were by his will something else than flesh, but he is identical with his flesh by virtue of his yielding to the desires of the flesh, just as man and wife are figuratively one flesh, yet in the manner of harlots and fornicators.

* * *

2. "Communion of proper qualities" [Latin; traditionally used to describe the conjunction of divinity and humanity in Christ].

The eleventh word: **Wretched man that I am! Who shall deliver me from the body of this death?** (Rom. 7:24.)

This shows even more clearly than the foregoing that a spiritual man is speaking here. For he sighs and grieves and longs to be delivered. Certainly no one will declare himself wretched except one who is a spiritual man. For perfect self-knowledge is perfect humility, and perfect humility is perfect wisdom, and perfect wisdom is perfect spiritualness. Hence, only a perfectly spiritual man can say: "Wretched man that I am!" A carnal man, however, does not long to be delivered and broken up, but he greatly abhors the dissolution of death and is unable to recognize his wretchedness.

So then, when Paul says here: "Who will deliver me from the body of this death?" he says exactly what he says elsewhere: "I desire to be dissolved and to be with Christ" (Phil. 1:23). For this reason, it is astonishing that it could have entered anyone's mind that the apostle speaks these words in the person of the old and carnal man, words which reflect such remarkable perfection, as if it were necessary for the apostle, like a hypocrite, to think and speak only well of himself, i.e., to praise himself and to deny that he is a sinner and thus not to praise grace but to deny its existence.

Indeed, it is a great consolation to us to learn that such a great apostle was involved in the same grievings and afflictions in which we find ourselves when we wish to be obedient to God!

The twelfth word: **Therefore, I myself with the mind serve the law of God, but with the flesh, the law of sin.** (Rom. 7:25.)

This is the most telling passage of all. Notice that one and the same man serves both the law of God and the law of sin, that he is righteous and at the same time he sins. He does not say: "My mind serves the law of God," nor "My flesh serves the law of sin," but he says, "I, this whole man, this person here, stand in this double servitude." He therefore gives thanks that he serves the law of God and he asks for mercy that he serves the law of sin.

Who can say of a carnal man that he serves the law of God? Notice, then, what I stated before: The saints in being righteous are at the same time sinners; they are righteous because they believe in Christ whose righteousness covers them and is imputed to them, but they are sinners because they do not fulfill the law and are not without sinful desires. They are like sick people in the care of a physician: they are really sick, but healthy only in hope and in so far as they begin to be better, or, rather: are being healed, i.e., they will become healthy. Nothing can harm them so much as the presumption that they are in fact healthy, for it will cause a bad relapse.

*   *   *

Without the law sin was dead. (Rom. 7:8.)

Blessed Augustine explains this passage together with the one that follows it with reference to the time of infancy when reason is not yet used. In the second book against Julian,[3] he says: "A little child that does not yet have the use of reason

---

3. Augustine, *Contra Jul.,* II, 4, 8. [Julian, bishop of Eclanum, was an early 5th-century adherent of Pelagianism.]

lives by his own will neither in the good nor in evil. But as he grows older and reason awakens, the commandment comes and sin revives, and, when it begins to fight him as he grows, then there will appear what was latent in the infant; it either conquers and will take domination over him, or it will be conquered, and he will be healed." The law comes to life and sin begins to appear when he begins to recognize the law; then concupiscence, which was latent in infancy, breaks forth and becomes manifest. And when it breaks forth in adolescence, then it brings fully to the fore what lay concealed in infancy. Just so, a young plant does not yet show what kind of fruit it will bear; but when it is in foliage and it bears fruit, one knows what kind of tree it is.

We can find a still profounder meaning in this: There are people who, in their mental attitude, are children, even if they are a hundred years old. They are those who let themselves be bewitched by a messenger of Satan that appears to them in the form of a spiritual good. For this good they long more ardently than an adulterer longs for a woman or a miser for money, and so they forsake the law and the obedience of God, like the Jews, heretics, schismatics, individualists, and nonconformists who have no sin because, as far as they are concerned, the law is not yet given. But if they knew the law against which they sin, they would doubtless recognize their sin at once, because they burn with pious zeal for the law. When, therefore, the law comes to them, sin is awakened in them. Then they long even more ardently for the realization of their special concerns and are even more strongly excited to anger against the law, so that they come to hate it because it prohibits to them what in their own imagination they have chosen to regard as law-conformity. So then when the law says: "You shalt not covet," all coveting is so strictly forbidden that whatever one covets besides God, even if it is coveted for the sake of God, is sin.

This is why many invite their own ruin when they love to practice piety and engage in prayers, studies, readings, devotions, meditations, and other such works as if they alone were good and well pleasing to God, but when they are called upon to render some mean service they get angry and provoked. Fools that they are, they do not know that it is not good works of some kind or number that God requires of them but a quiet and meek and obedient spirit. As it says in Ps. 51:16: *"For if thou hadst wanted it, I would have given sacrifice; with burnt offerings thou wilt not be delighted"* (i.e., thou dost not care for the good works, whatever they may be, that we have chosen to do). What then? *"A sacrifice to God is an afflicted"* (i.e., broken) *"spirit; a contrite"* (i.e., broken) *"and humbled"* (i.e., contrite) *"heart, O God, thou wilt not despise"* (Ps. 51:17), i.e., a heart and spirit which are not hardened by an obstinacy of mind but can be guided and broken in to do thy will. People of such a spirit do not choose their work but they expect to be chosen for it whatever it may be. And all this in order that "he may open our lips and that our mouth shall show forth his praise" (Ps. 51:15). For people who choose on their own initiative what work they shall do cannot refrain from praising themselves. Instead of pleasing God and thereby themselves, they please only themselves even when they want to please God.

We should know that the devil disturbs everyone's mind in order to make void his vocation and in order to seduce and persuade him to something to which he is not called, as if God were stupid and did not know whereto he wanted to call anyone. In this way, the devil is always contending against the wisdom of God and is trying to make God appear foolish in our eyes in order to mislead us to the idolatrous notion that God wills what in fact he does not want. These are certainly the gods of the house of Israel for whom altars have everywhere been set up at all street corners throughout Jerusalem (Jer. 11:13).

It is no more I that do it, but sin that dwells in me. (Rom. 7:17.)

So then, is it not true that the treacherous metaphysics of Aristotle and traditional philosophy have deceived our theologians? For did they not believe to know that sin is done away with in baptism or penance, so that they thought it absurd that the apostle says: **"but sin that dwells in me"**! Thus it was chiefly this word that gave them offense, so that they came to the false and noxious opinion that the apostle was speaking here not in his own name but in the name of a carnal man. And over against his various and very emphatic assertions in many letters, they insist on talking nonsense by saying that he could not possibly have any sin.

This foolish opinion has led to a most harmful deception: people who are baptized or have received absolution think that they are at once without any sin; they become secure in the feeling that they have obtained righteousness and they do nothing because they are not conscious of any sin they should fight against and purge out under groaning and tears and with sorrowful effort.

But we should know that sin is left in the spiritual man for the exercise of grace, for the humiliation of pride, and for the restraint of presumptuousness. For if we do not earnestly endeavor to struggle against sin, we already have it, even though we have ceased to commit any sin for which we could be condemned. For we are not called to a life of ease but to labor against our passions. And they would not be without guilt (for they really are sins and damnable, indeed) unless God in his mercy did not impute them to us. But he does not impute them to those only who, invoking his grace, resolutely attack their faults and fight against them. In the light of this we say that *when a person goes to confession, he must not think that he can put down his burden and live quietly, but he must know that by putting down his burden he becomes a soldier of God and thereby assumes another burden, namely, to fight for God against the devil and his own faults.*

If he does not know this, he will soon relapse. *If therefore, he does not intend to fight henceforth against his sins, why does he pray for absolution and for his enrollment in the ranks of the soldiers of Christ?*

*   *   *

We should note that the apostle does not mean to be understood as saying that the spirit and the flesh are, so to speak, two separate entities. He understands them to be one whole just as a wound and the flesh are one. To be sure, the wound is something by itself and the flesh is something by itself, but because the wound and the flesh are one and because the wound is nothing else than wounded or weakened flesh, we can attribute to the flesh the properties of the wound. In the same way, one and the same man is at the same time spirit and flesh. The flesh is his weakness or wound. In so far as he loves the law of God, he is spirit; but in so far as he covets, he shows the weakness of his spirit and the wound of his sin which must still be healed. As Christ says: "The spirit is willing, but the flesh is weak." (Matt. 26:41.)

And Blessed Augustine says in the second book of *Against Julian:*[4] "When we speak of our faults we generally mean that which from the law of sin resists the law of the mind. When these faults are separated from us, they will not be somewhere else, but as soon as they are healed in us, they will be nowhere. Why do they not perish in baptism? Will you not admit that their guilt perishes but their weakness remains, not a guilt by which they themselves were guilty, but by which they made us guilty in the evil deeds to which they had drawn us? And their weakness does not remain as if they were something alive that has now become weak, but it is our own weakness." This beautiful authoritative work shows in what way concupiscence is that weakness in us which renders us unable to do the good. To be sure, it is guilty in itself, yet we become guilty by it only if we yield to it and commit a sin. This explains the remarkable fact that we are guilty and not guilty. For this weakness and we ourselves are inseparable; hence, it is guilty and we are guilty until it ceases and is healed. Yet we are not guilty as long as we do act in accordance with it, for God in his mercy does not impute the guilt of weakness but the guilt of the will that yields to this weakness.

We can understand this dialectic best in the light of the parable in the Gospel concerning the man who was left half-dead (Luke 10:30 ff.): When the Samaritan poured wine and oil on his wounds, he did not heal him right away but he began to get well. Just so the sick man of whom we are speaking is one and the same man who is weak and in process of being healed. In so far as he is healthy, he desires the good, but in so far as he is weak, he cannot help yielding to his weakness even though he does not want to.

[The Use of the Law][†]

On Galatians 3:19

The other use of the Law is the theological or spiritual one, which serves to increase transgressions. This is the primary purpose of the Law of Moses, that through it sin might grow and be multiplied, especially in the conscience. Paul discusses this magnificently in Rom. 7. Therefore the true function and the chief and proper use of the Law is to reveal to man his sin, blindness, misery, wickedness, ignorance, hate and contempt of God, death, hell, judgment, and the well-deserved wrath of God. Yet this use of the Law is completely unknown to the hypocrites, the sophists in the universities, and to all men who go along in the presumption of the righteousness of the Law or of their own righteousness. To curb and crush this monster and raging beast, that is, the presumption of religion, God is obliged, on Mt. Sinai, to give a new Law with such pomp and with such an awesome spectacle that the entire people is crushed with fear [cf. Exod 19:16; 20:18]. For since the

---

4. Augustine, *Contra Jul.,* II, 5, 12.
† From Martin Luther, *Lectures on Galatians,* 1535, trans. Jaroslav Pelikan, *Luther's Works,* vol. 26 (Saint Louis: Concordia Publishing House, 1961), 309–10, 312–15.

reason becomes haughty with this human presumption of righteousness and imagines that on account of this it is pleasing to God, therefore God has to send some Hercules, namely, the Law, to attack, subdue, and destroy this monster with full force. Therefore the Law is intent only on this beast, not on any other.

Hence this use of the Law is extremely beneficial and very necessary. For if someone is not a murderer, adulterer, or thief, and abstains from external sins, as that Pharisee did (Luke 18:11), he would swear, being possessed by the devil, that he is a righteous man; therefore he develops the presumption of righteousness and relies on his good works. God cannot soften and humble this man or make him acknowledge his misery and damnation any other way than by the Law. Therefore the proper and absolute use of the Law is to terrify with lightning (as on Mt. Sinai), thunder, and the blare of the trumpet, with a thunderbolt to burn and crush that brute which is called the presumption of righteousness. Hence God says through Jeremiah (23:29): "My Word is a hammer which breaks the rock in pieces." For as long as the presumption of righteousness remains in a man, there remain immense pride, self-trust, smugness, hate of God, contempt of grace and mercy, ignorance of the promises and of Christ. The proclamation of free grace and the forgiveness of sins does not enter his heart and understanding, because that huge rock and solid wall, namely, the presumption of righteousness by which the heart itself is surrounded, prevents this from happening.

Therefore this presumption of righteousness is a huge and a horrible monster. To break and crush it, God needs a large and powerful hammer, that is, the Law, which is the hammer of death, the thunder of hell, and the lightning of divine wrath. To what purpose? To attack the presumption of righteousness, which is a rebellious, stubborn, and stiff-necked beast. And so when the Law accuses and terrifies the conscience—"You must do this or that! You have not done so! Then you are condemned to the wrath of God and to eternal death!"—then the Law is being employed in its proper use and for its proper purpose. Then the heart is crushed to the point of despair. This use and function of the Law is felt by terrified and desperate consciences, who yearn for death or want to inflict death on themselves because of the anguish of conscience.

* * *

Therefore it is a matter of no small moment to believe correctly about what the Law is and what its use and function are. Thus it is evident that we do not reject the Law and works, as our opponents falsely accuse us. But we do everything to establish the Law, and we require works. We say that the Law is good and useful, but in its proper use, namely to restrain civic transgressions; and secondly, to reveal spiritual transgressions. Therefore the Law is a light that illumines and shows, not the grace of God or righteousness and life but the wrath of God, sin, death, our damnation in the sight of God, and hell. For just as on Mt. Sinai the lightning, the thunder, the dark cloud, the smoking and burning mountain, and the whole horrendous sight did not make the Children of Israel happy or alive but terrified them, made them almost helpless, and disclosed a presence of God speaking from the cloud that they could not bear for all their sanctity and purity, so when the Law is being used correctly, it does nothing but reveal sin, work wrath, accuse, terrify, and reduce the minds of men to the point of despair. And that is as far as the Law goes.

On the other hand, the Gospel is a light that illumines hearts and makes them alive. It discloses what grace and the mercy of God are; what the forgiveness of sins, blessing, righteousness, life, and eternal salvation are; and how we are to attain to these. When we distinguish the Law from the Gospel this way, we attribute to each its proper use and function. You will not find anything about this distinction between the Law and the Gospel in the books of the monks, the canonists, and the recent and ancient theologians. Augustine taught and expressed it to some extent. Jerome and others like him knew nothing at all about it. In other words, for many centuries there has been a remarkable silence about this in all the schools and churches. This situation has produced a very dangerous condition for consciences; for unless the Gospel is clearly distinguished from the Law, Christian doctrine cannot be kept sound. But when this distinction is recognized, the true meaning of justification is recognized. Then it is easy to distinguish faith from works, and Christ from Moses, as well as from the magistrate and all civil laws. For everything apart from Christ is a ministry of death for the punishment of the wicked. Therefore Paul answers the question this way:

The Law was added because of transgressions [Gal 3:19].

That is, so that transgressions might be increased, recognized, and made more visible. And in fact this is what happens. For when through the Law a man's sin, death, the wrath and judgment of God, and hell are revealed to him, it is impossible for him not to become impatient, murmur, and hate God and His will. He cannot endure the judgment of God and his own death and damnation, and yet he cannot flee. Then he inevitably falls into hate and blasphemy against God. When there was no trouble, he was a big saint; he worshiped and praised God, genuflected, and gave thanks, as that Pharisee did in Luke (18:11). But now that sin and death have been revealed, he would want God not to exist. In this way the Law produces extreme hate toward God. This means that through the Law sin is not only disclosed and recognized, but that through this disclosure sin is increased, inflated, inflamed, and magnified. This is what Paul is saying in Rom. 7:13: "It was sin, working death in me through what is good, in order that sin might be shown to be sin, and through the commandment might become sinful beyond measure." There he discusses this effect of the Law at some length.

To the question, "If the Law does not justify, what is its purpose?" Paul, therefore, replies: "Although the Law does not justify, it is nevertheless extremely useful and necessary. In the first place, it acts as a civic restraint upon those who are unspiritual and uncivilized. In the second place, it produces in a man the knowledge of himself as a sinner, who is therefore subject to death and worthy of eternal wrath." But what is the value of this effect, this humiliation, this wounding and crushing by the hammer? It has this value, that grace can have access to us. Therefore the Law is a minister and a preparation for grace. For God is the God of the humble, the miserable, the afflicted, the oppressed, the desperate, and of those who have been brought down to nothing at all. And it is the nature of God to exalt the humble, to feed the hungry, to enlighten the blind, to comfort the miserable and afflicted, to justify sinners, to give life to the dead, and to save those who are desperate and damned. For He is the almighty Creator, who makes everything out of nothing. In the performance of this, His natural and proper work, He does not allow Himself to be interfered with by that dangerous pest, the presumption of righteousness, which refuses to be sinful, impure, miserable, and damned but wants to be righteous and holy. Therefore God has to make use of that hammer of His, namely, the Law, to break, bruise, crush, and annihilate this beast with its false confidence, wisdom, righteousness, and power, so that it learns that it has been destroyed and damned by its evil. Then, when the conscience has been terrified this way by the Law, there is a place for the doctrine of the Gospel and of grace, which raises it up again and comforts it; it says that Christ did not come into the world to break the bruised reed or to quench the dimly burning wick (Is. 42:3) but to announce the Gospel to the poor, to bind up the brokenhearted, and to proclaim liberty to the captives (Is. 61:1).

KARL BARTH

[The Meaning of Religion in Romans 7]†

[On] vv. 8–11

But sin, taking occasion by the commandment, wrought in me all manner of coveting. In speaking of the process by which Word became Myth it is impossible to avoid mythological language! In its primal form, in the secret of God, sin is the possibility that the union between men and God may be broken. Sin is the possibility of predestination to blessedness OR to damnation. This does not mean, of course, that sin originated in God: but it does mean that He is its final truth. In God men possess—as slaves do—the possibility of rebellion. They can separate themselves from Him who is eternally one. They can lay hold of the shadow which follows the divine glory—but only as its negation—and make it their eternity. Men have the opportunity of making themselves God. The knowledge of this opportunity, and the consequent capacity to make use of it, is sin. When the sluice-gates are opened, the water, by the force of its own inertia, pours through to a lower level. So sin, because its nature is to move downwards and not upwards, because it belongs properly to what is relative, separated, independent, and indirect, bursts into the world of time, breaks into concrete visibility, and stands there in stark contrast with what

---

† From Karl Barth, *The Epistle to the Romans*, trans. Edwyn C. Hoskyns (London: Oxford University Press, 1933), 246–57.
    Karl Barth (1886–1968) is arguably the most influential Christian theologian of the twentieth century. His commentary on Romans, excerpted here from the English translation of the sixth German edition (fundamentally the same as the second edition of 1922, a thorough revision of the 1918 original), eschews, though it does not discount, the historical-critical methodologies that emerged in the Enlightenment's wake and soon came to dominate modern biblical scholarship. It proposes a coherent, creative, and compelling theological interpretation of the epistle in the Lutheran tradition. Indeed, Barth's provocative claims regarding the necessary futility of "religion" may be read as sophisticated developments of Luther's statements about the law in the selections included above. Barth was by no means the first to read Romans 7 in light of the story of the primeval transgression (Gen 2–3), but he is more aggressive than most in drawing out the implications of its allusive and sustained intertextual engagement with that important Old Testament passage.

is unobservable, non-concrete, and eternal. Sin is sin—in so far as the world is manifested as an independent thing over against creation; in so far as the course of the world runs counter to its existence; in so far as men are opposed to God. And yet, it is not immediately obvious that the sluice-gates of the lock which marks the distinction between God and man have been opened. Originally, there was no separation. Men dwelt in the Garden of Eden, in which there were no absolute and relative, no 'Higher' and 'Lower', no 'There' and 'Here': such distinctions marked the Fall. The world was originally one with the Creator, and men were one with God. The natural order then, as such, was holy, because holiness is its characteristic mark. Originally, there was no *coveting*: men were permitted, and indeed commanded, to enjoy all the fruits of the garden. There was, however, one exception. In the midst of the garden stood *the tree of the knowledge of good and evil*. The behaviour of men must not be governed by knowledge of the contrast between the primal state and its contradiction. That is God's secret. Men ought not to be independently what they are in dependence upon God; they ought not, as creatures, to be some second thing by the side of the Creator. Men ought not to know that they are merely—men. God knows this, but in His mercy He has concealed it from them. So long as ignorance prevailed, the Lord walked freely in the garden in the cool of the day, as though in the equality of friendship. Look how Michelangelo has depicted the 'Creation of Eve': in the fullness of her charm and beauty she rises slowly, posing herself in the fatal attitude of—worship. Notice the Creator's warning arm and careworn, saddened eyes, as He replies to Eve's gesture of adoration. She is manifestly behaving as she ought not. Eve—and we must honour her as the first 'religious personality'—was the first to set herself over against God, the first to worship Him; but, inasmuch as SHE worshipped HIM, she was separated from Him in a manner at once terrible and presumptuous. Then the 'well-known serpent' appears upon the scene. He utters words—the archetype of all sermons—about God; he—the first shepherd of the souls of men—first offers advice concerning the commandments of God. Adam's titanic capacity for wisdom already existed before Eve!;—now it is turned into tragic reality. Tragic—because, when men, knowing good and evil, become *like God*, when their direct relation with Him gives birth to independent action, then all direct relationship is broken off. When men stretch out their hands and touch the link which binds them to God, when they touch the tree *in the midst of the garden*, which ought not to be touched, they are by this presumptuous contact separated from Him. They have handled death—that barbed wire loaded with electricity. Stretching out to reach what they are not, men encounter what they are, and they are thereby fenced in and shut out. With open eyes they see that they are separated from God and—naked. Coveting, lusting after, passionately desiring corruptible things, they become themselves corruptible. Why is the question concerning God as the Creator and us as His creation a question which, in spite of its insistent, compelling, desperate urgency, cannot even be formulated—by us? Yet we know no man who has not done as Adam did. We ourselves have touched the tree; we have formulated the question; and in formulating it we have set ourselves in opposition to God. In opposition to God!—this which God withheld from us for our salvation now governs our lives. Immediately we know good AND evil, the commandment of God transforms Paradise into—Paradise Lost. Our present existence is discredited and rendered questionable, already, perhaps, accused and condemned as actually evil, by the demand which names a thing 'good' which—ought to be so and is not. The covetous desire, which causes men to stretch out their hands towards that one tree, renders also more or less forbidden those many desires to enjoy the fruits of all the other trees. For this one lust sets everything which men think and will and do in direct opposition to the relentless and holy and eternal will of God. This is the triumph of sin. Impetuously sin has sought and found its level in the many-sided vitality of men, and their vitality is now named 'lust'. Opposition to God emerges in the critical distinction between seen and unseen, relative and absolute, independence and primal union. And this opposition comes into being through the divine commandment; through the intrusion of the possibility of religion; through the beguilement of the serpent's sermon on the theme of a direct relation between men and God; through the far too great attention paid to it by men, and especially by women, since they are more acutely disturbed than men are by the riddle of direct relationship. So it is that religion becomes the occasion of sin. Religion is the working capital of sin; its fulcrum; the means by which men are removed from direct union with God and thrust into disunion, that is, into the recognition of their—creatureliness.

For apart from the law sin is dead. And I was alive apart from the law once. The words *I was alive* can no more refer to the historical past than can the words *we shall live* (vi. 2, &c.) to some historical future; the reference is to that life which is primal and non-historical, just as the previous reference was to that life which is also final and non-historical. There is no question here of contrasting a particular epoch in the life of a single individual, or of a group, or indeed of all mankind, with some other epoch, past or future. The passages refer to that timeless age to which all men belong. Only in a parable, and, even so, only with the greatest care, can we speak of the 'innocence' of children and of the guilt of those who have passed beyond the 'age of innocence'! Only with great circumspection ought we to speak of 'Child-races' or 'Child-civilizations', &c., or of their 'growing up'. The life defined as past or future must not be depressed into history, because the contrast is concerned with the opposition between eternal life and our present concrete existence. *I was alive* and sin was dead, because I lived *apart from the law: apart from the law* sin is dead, and men are alive. Only when the creature stands over against the Creator may it be defined as sinful. The creation is not questionable, unless it be thought of as mere Nature, independent of God. The recognition of the opposition of the world to God, and of its consequent sinfulness, becomes acute only with the emergence of the titanic possibility of religion. The creature, in its primal, original, unseen history, lives and moves without touching the line of death which marks the separation between God and man; without touching the tree of destiny which stands in the midst of the garden. In this primal life, the union and distinction between the Creator and the creature is not fraught with the tragic significance which comes into being with the emergence of religion. In the fresco of the 'Creation of Adam' Michelangelo depicts God and Adam looking one another straight in the face, their hands stretched out towards one another in a delicious freedom of intercourse. The air is charged with the deep, triumphant, moving peace of the eternal 'Moment' of creation. And yet, the scene is heavy with tragedy; for it portrays the direct relation as not yet lost; it portrays the relation in which religion plays no part. And so it draws attention to the distinction between our present existence and, not only the 'old' Creation, but also the 'new' Creation for which men are now waiting. In this direct relationship mankind lives; not this or that individual man, but mankind as created by God, in His own image, and as He will again create them. Out of this relationship, which never has been, and never will be an event in history, we issue, and towards it we move. Nor can sin destroy this primal union, for it is the act and work of God alone. Marcion[1] described it admirably as the 'Wholly Other' which is our unforgettable home; the reality, the proximity, the glory, which we encounter in the last words of the Gospel—Forgiveness, Resurrection, Redemption, Love, God. These are words in which disturbance and promise are joined together; for they direct us towards the realm where there is no law and no religion (iv. 15). Those concrete and historical events which seem to us (as v. 13) relatively pure and innocent are harmless and fraught with hope and meaning only when we behold reflected in them that life from which we come and to which we move.

But when the commandment came, sin burst into life, and I died. Scattered to the winds is the eternal 'Now' of the Creation. *The commandment came.* It had to come, when men became as God, bearing the burden of the divine secret, knowing good AND evil, election AND damnation, 'Yes' AND 'No'. The time when there was no commandment is beyond our understanding. All we know is that the union between God and man has been changed from divine pre-supposition to human supposition, and that, consequently, every human position has suffered dislocation. On the very brink of human possibility there has, moreover, appeared a final human capacity—the capacity of knowing God to be unknowable and wholly Other; of knowing man to be a creature contrasted with the Creator, and, above all, of offering to the Unknown God gestures of adoration. This possibility of religion sets every other human capacity also under the bright and fatal light of impossibility. Such is human capacity; and we are bound to believe and to make known—for only a weak-chested piety fails to perceive it—that men are compelled to advance along a road which ends in 'Double Predestination'. What then—we are bound to ask the question—are men? *Sin burst into life.* Irrecoverable is the 'Moment' of creation; irretrievable the purity and peace of that existence in which God and men were one and not two. The unity of life has been sundered, and God stands over against men as their counterpart—in power; whereas men stand over against God as His counterpart—in weakness. Men are limited by God, and God is limited by men: both are compromised and rendered questionable. *And I died.* Death is the mark of that passing of eternity into time, which is, of course, not an occurrence in time, but a past happening in primal history. Now everything is concrete and indirect. The whole range of the life we now live is contrasted with our life in God, and consequently stamped with the indelible mark of death. The narrow gate through which our perception widens out from what is finite to what is infinite closes and opens only with critical negation. The recognition that we must die is forced upon us, and such recognition is the point where either we attain wisdom or remain 'fools'—in the most reprehensible sense of the word. In the inexorable 'No' of death, the 'Yes' of God and of life is presented to us: that is to say, it is

---

1. See headnote on p. 1027.

presented to us in the contrast between what we are able to observe and what is beyond our observation; it is presented to us in recognizable time, which is past and future, but never present; in the concrete form of Nature, which is mere 'world'—COSMOS—but never Creation; in visible history, which is only process but never completed occurrence. The only world we can know is the world of time, of things, and of men. The final experience to which we have access in this world is summed up in the words—*and I died*, and this is the pre-supposition of all experience. Now, the religious man is bound to encounter this experience, this pre-supposition of all experience, precisely because he is a religious man: *Then said I, Woe is me! for I am undone:. . . for mine eyes have seen the King, the Lord of hosts* (Isa. vi. 5). There is no escape from this vision or from this undoing.

And the commandment, which was unto life, this I found to be unto death: for sin, taking occasion by the commandment, deceived me, and through it slew me. The supreme possibility to which we can attain within the range of our concrete existence under the dominion of sin consists in our capacity to grasp the line of death, to know both good and evil, and in the consequent emergence of the distinction between God as God and men as men. Now, that this supreme and urgent necessity of our existence should be identical with that capacity by which our direct union with God was destroyed, constitutes the final paradox of the Fall.

When we ask what it is that directs us towards that lost, but recoverable life in God, standing as we do within the world of time and things and men, there is but one possible answer: we are directed by the *commandment*, by our capacity for religion, by a vast critical negation—in fact, by the recognition that *we must die*. Is there any other road where the unseen becomes visible, any other road along which those men have passed who have *seen clearly* and to whom the thought of God has been revealed (i. 20), except the narrow way of the 'wisdom of death'? Since we cannot take up our position beyond the line of death, and since we must take our stand somewhere, have we any alternative but to stand on the line 'across which Adam fell' (Luther)? Daring the best and the highest, our place is on the extremest edge of human possibility, where the 'Jesus of History' stands, where Abraham, Job, and all the prophets and apostles stand; the place where men are most evidently men, where they are most completely removed from direct union with God, and where human existence is most heavily burdened with its own questionableness. There is for us no honourable alternative but to be religious men, repenting in dust and ashes, wrestling in fear and trembling, that we may be blessed; and, since we must take up a position, adopting the attitude of adoration. To all this we are urged by the commandment which directs us unto life. Knowing, then, that we have no alternative, knowing also what that alternative involves, ought we to shrink from advancing to take up our position on the very outermost edge of the precipice, on the very brink of the possibility of religion? We may, however, judge the relentlessness of Calvin, the dialectical audacity of Kierkegaard, Overbeck's sense of awe, Dostoevsky's hunger for eternity, Blumhardt's optimism,[2] too risky

2. John Calvin (1509–1564), French theologian and reformer; Søren Kierkegaard (1813–1855), Danish philosopher; Johann Friedrich Overbeck (1789–1869), German religious painter; Fyodor Dostoevsky (1821–1881), Russian novelist; Johann Christoph Blumhardt (1805–1880), German Lutheran theologian.

and too dangerous for us. We may therefore content ourselves with some lesser, more feeble possibility of religion. We may fall back on some form of rationalism or pietism. Yet these more feeble types of religion are also pregnant with implications pointing towards that outermost edge, and some day they may bring this harsh and dangerous reality to birth. If Adam, easily content with lesser possibilities, should ever forget his proper condition and omit to move to his final possibility, Eve soon reminds him of the possibility of religion, for she is more acutely aware of the loss of direct union with God. And yet—for here is the tragic paradox of religion— should we seriously undertake to turn as pilgrims towards that far-off land which is our home, should we undertake the final concrete human action, we do but display the catastrophe of human impotence in the things of God. What is our action, our taking up of a position, but the supreme betrayal of the true pre-supposition? What is our undertaking of a visible relationship, our scaling of the summit of human possibility, but our completest separation from the true invisible relationship? Seen from God's standpoint, religion is precisely that which we had better leave undone: *And the commandment—this I found to be unto death.* The necessity of the possibility of religion, the necessity of stretching out towards the tree in our midst, the desire to know good and evil, life and death, God and man—this necessity is no more than a manœuvre, undertaken by men within the concrete reality of this world. By it they are defined as evil and passing to corruption; by it they are defined as—men; by it they are thrown into the contrast between relative and absolute, and there imprisoned. At best they are confronted in religion by the 'No' in which the 'Yes' of God is hidden. Death is the meaning of religion; for when we are pressed to the boundary of religion, death pronounces the inner calm of simple and harmless relativity to be at an end. Religion is not at all to be 'in tune with the infinite' or to be at 'peace with oneself'. It has no place for refined sensibility or mature humanity. Let simpleminded Occidentals (!) retain such opinions as long as they are able. But religion is an abyss: it is terror. There demons appear (Ivan Karamazov[3] and Luther!). There the old enemy of man is strangely near. There sin deceives. There the power of the commandment is deadly—*The serpent beguiled me* (Gen. iii. 13). Sin is the place where our destiny becomes a present, concrete possibility, the place where our knowledge of good and evil becomes an urgent, direct knowledge. The deception of sin is the illusion that such direct knowledge is life, whereas in fact it is death. Deceit runs its full course, because men do not perceive that the necessity of independent human action is what should not be in the presence of God. It is successful, because human determination to retain the possibility of independence before God reveals men to be—merely men. The commandment is therefore the lever or *occasion* of sin: clothing time with the garment of eternity, it presents piety as a human achievement, evokes worship which knows not how to be silent before God, and names such worship 'religion'; concealing from the worshipper, not merely how questionable the world is, but how utterly questionable religion is, it compels him to lift up hands in prayer, then lets them drop back wearily, and in this weariness spurs him unto prayer again. And this is, after all, the situation in which men find themselves under the commandment.

3. A character in Dostoevsky's *The Brothers Karamazov* (1879–80).

We have now been able to provide a second answer to our question concerning the meaning of religion. Religion is that human necessity in which the power exercised over men by sin is clearly demonstrated. Once again we are compelled to consider what the freedom of God means when it confronts men imprisoned in the closed circle of humanity.

[On] vv. 12, 13

The law is holy, and the commandment holy, and righteous, and good. What, then, are we to do? This is the urgent question which presses upon the man who has come to himself, who has become religious, and is aware of his rebellion against God and of the terrible weight he has to bear as a man of this world. The answer to the question implies a still greater emphasis upon the question. May God never relieve us of this questioning! May He enclose us with questions on every side! May He defend us from any answer which is not itself a question! May He bar every exit and cut us off from all simplifications! May the cavity at the cart-wheel's centre, which Lao-Tse[4] perceived long ago, be delimited by a ring of questions! In that central void the answer to our questioning is hidden; but since the void is defined by questions, they must never for one moment cease. *The law is holy.* We cannot stand on the definition of religion, or indeed of any human possibility, as though it were merely sin. Religion is the place where every human capacity is enlightened by divine light. Placed outside the region of divinity, religion, nevertheless, represents divinity as its delegate or impress or negative. Moving within the sphere of human activity, religion is without doubt *holy*, because it points from humanity to divinity; it is without doubt *righteous*, because it is correlated with the will of God and parallel to it, being indeed the parable of it; and it is without doubt *good*, for it is that concrete, observable, mediated experience which bears witness to the immediacy which has been lost. Should we remove ourselves consciously or unconsciously from the dangerous ambiguity of religion, either we must take refuge in some other less exalted human possibility—in some possibility that is ethical or logical or aesthetic or even lower; or we must side-step into some ancient or modern variety of religion; and, if we are not fully aware of the ambiguity of all religion, to do so will mean inevitably that the alternative variety which we have selected will be a bad one. There is no human advance beyond the possibility of religion, for religion is the last step in human progress. Standing as it does within humanity but outside divinity, it bears witness to that which is within divinity but outside humanity. Let us therefore—within the possibility of religion, and outside the realm of that charity which does *not covet* (I Cor. xii. 31; xiv. 1; cf. xiii. 4)—*covet earnestly the best gifts.* Let us be convincedly nothing but religious men; let us adore and tarry and hurry with all the energy we possess; let us cultivate, nurse, and stir up religion; and above all, let us reform it; nay more, revolutionize it. This labour in the field of the humanities is well worth the vigour of noble and devoted men.

---

4. *Tao-Teh-King,* ch. xi. 'The thirty spokes of a chariot wheel and the nave to which they are attached would be useless, but for the hollow space in which the axle turns' (G. G. Alexander) [translator's note; Lao-tzu/Laozi (6th c. B.C.E), Chinese philosopher credited with writing the *Tao Te Ching* and with founding Taoism].

But—the more zealously this labour is undertaken, the deeper we penetrate the valley of the shadow of death. It should cause us no surprise that the majority are reluctant to move to the outer edge of the precipice of religion; for there not only does religion itself become ambiguous, but its ambiguity carries with it the questionableness of all human possibility. We ought not to be surprised at the many attempts which have been made to explore the possibility of some compromise between the spiritual lethargy of the man of this world and the holiness and righteousness and goodness of religion and of the law. The question—**Did then that which is good become death unto me?**—corresponds with the earlier question—*Is the law sin?* (vii. 7). These overlapping questions quite naturally entice men to escape from the twilight of religion. We are fully aware of the tension and disturbance and impossibility of our situation as religious men: we have been led far from the flesh-pots of Egypt deep into the desert. Surely, this eccentric and strange occurrence, this pilgrimage of ours, by which we are cast to the ground and dissolved, cannot be—good? Can God deal with us so harshly? How beguiling and attractive, then, are those many simpler alternatives! How enticing to us is some semi-antinomianism, or indeed, complete antinomianism! Shall we not yield to those who attempt to rid men of the terrifying earnestness of religion by inviting them to something less vexatious; by offering them a joyful, less exacting redemption which takes place outside the danger-zone? Here we are presented with something utterly different from that deadly shadow of the law of God, under which the great men of religion have passed their days bearing witness to the salvation which is by grace only. Can we resist the temptation of easing religion of its heavy burden and uncharging it of its dangerous dynamite? Can we not, at least partially, escape from the accursed relativity of every merely human possibility; from the misery of our present indirect relation to God and of our present segregation on this side of the abyss; from the curse which presses so hardly upon the religious man?

God forbid. This is our answer. For, at whatever cost, we must remain at our post and drain the cup to its dregs. Good is not less good because it is not simple or obvious, or because we have no direct access to it. We must submit to the full paradox of our situation. The moment we become aware of ourselves and of our position in the world, through the commandment of God which meets us in the known uncertainty of our present existence we are led onwards to the final possibility of religion. Appealing with tears and longing to the Great Unknown, we stretch out our failing arms towards the 'Yes' which confronts us invisibly in the 'No' by which we are imprisoned. But, nevertheless, we have to learn that we are not justified, not redeemed, not saved, by these appealing cries and tears. Passing, as we are, to corruption, they do but establish and stamp us as—men. I have no alternative but to follow the desire which is above all other desires—the longing for the recovery of the lost immediacy of my life in God. And when I follow it all my desires are thereby turned to sin, and this last desire supremely so. 'Through the law I become aware of how it is betwixt God and me. Therefore I move about anxious with fears and questionings, unnerved by the slightest trembling leaf, terrified by the thunder's noise. Every moment I expect God to come behind me and crash me over the head with a bludgeon. Wherefore, lest I be forced to hold myself a coward and a weakling, I must dare all, surrender all, sacrifice all, that I may attain the One, and be—like God' (Luther). Thither, then, all the vigour of my energy is directed, that

I may attain the eternal 'Moment' of Creation. But, when I have dared, offered, sacrificed everything, I stand with nothing in my hands, mere dust and ashes, separated farther than ever from the One. Do we now at last recognize what sin is, and how impossible it is for us to escape from it? So deeply does it penetrate every human capacity that the attempt to elude it by taking up with religion entangles us more surely in its guilt and plunges us into the destiny of death.—**Sin, that it might be shown to be sin, by working death to me through that which is good.** Death—through that which is good! through what is necessary and unavoidable! through that which honest and upright men are compelled to snatch at, as a drowning man clutches at a straw! through that possibility which, when first discovered, appears as light shining in the darkness of night! through the purest, noblest, and most hopeful element within the sphere of the competence of men. For what are erotics, alcoholics, intellectualists, mammonites, might-is-right-politicians, what are the armies of the Philistines in comparison with one sinner who believes and prays? He it is, not they, who hears and obeys the destructive command 'Halt'. He it is, not they, who dies the death which is the last word uttered over the man of this world. *Surely he hath borne our sickness, and carried our sorrows* (Isa. liii. 4). He is the sinner; yet he is also the guiltless one, for through him there has entered a divine, not a human possibility. In the mercy of God, he announces salvation and life, for *the chastisement of our peace was upon him* (Isa. liii. 5). Do we now perceive what sin is and what is the significance of religion? Do we understand the words— **That through the commandment sin might become incomprehensibly sinful?** Here we have reached the meaning of religion. In the inexorable reality (vii. 7b–11) of this supreme human possibility sin is shown forth as the power which reigns within the closed circle of humanity. Nevertheless, its power is bounded by the freedom of God, of God Himself, and of God alone. But it has no other boundary. This is the meaning of the law: it sharpens our intelligence that we may perceive (vii. 6) the sheer impossibility of our attaining that freedom from the law, that service *in newness of the spirit,* at which we have gazed—outside the frontiers of religion.

RUDOLF BULTMANN

[The Self Split by Sin under the Law][†]

§ 23 Flesh and Sin

The fact that *"flesh,"* and through it also *"sin," can become powers* to which man falls slave finds especially clear expression in the circumstance that Paul can speak

† From Rudolf Bultmann, *Theology of the New Testament*, trans. Kendrick Grobel, vol. 1 (New York: Charles Scribner's Sons, 1951), 244–49. For Bultmann, see headnote on p. 1166
   Bultmann here demythologizes Paul's language about sin and death in order to produce a psychologically penetrating interpretation of Romans 7 as a tragic depiction of the self paradoxically alienated from itself and therefore placed on a trajectory to destruction. His emphasis on the self divided in two deepens and complicates Augustine's insistence on the corrupting influence of the mortal flesh upon the soul and Luther's understanding of the Christian as a peculiar *communio idiomatum,* a conjunction of righteousness and sin.

of both as personal beings as if they were demonic rulers—but in such a way that we do not have the right actually to ascribe to him a mythological concept of "flesh" and "sin." Man is in danger of becoming a "debtor" to the "flesh" (Rom. 8:12) or of opening the door to it, so to say, or of offering it his hand (Gal. 5:13, tr.: "do not [offer] your freedom to the flesh as a base of operations"). Paul can even attribute "desire" to the "flesh" itself (Gal. 5:17: "for the desires of the flesh are against the Spirit"). Or he can speak of the "intent (φρόνημα) of the flesh" (Rom. 8:6f. tr.), or of its "passions" and "desires" (Gal. 5:24) and its "works" (Gal. 5:19) or "deeds" (Rom. 8:13). Moreover, he can personify the world in the same way when he speaks of its "wisdom" and its "knowing" (I Cor. 1:20f.). "Sin" particularly appears in this way as if it were a personal being. It "came into the world" (Rom. 5:12) and "achieved dominion" (Rom. 5:21 Blt.). Man is enslaved to it (Rom. 6:6, 17ff.), sold under it (Rom. 7:14); or man places himself at its disposal (Rom. 6:13) and it pays him wages (Rom. 6:23). Sin is also thought of as if it were a personal being when it is said to have been dead but to have revived (Rom. 7:8f.), or to have used the Torah to rouse desire in man and to have deceived and killed him (Rom. 7:8, 11, 13), or to "dwell" and act in man (Rom. 7:17, 20).

Little as all this constitutes realistic mythology—it is not that, but figurative, rhetorical language—it is, nevertheless, clear that this language stamps *flesh and sin as powers to which man has fallen victim* and against which he is powerless. The personification of these powers expresses the fact that man has lost to them the capacity to be the subject of his own actions. The strongest expression of this is found in Rom. 7:14, "I am carnal (= flesh-ly), sold under sin," and Rom. 7:18, "for I know that nothing good dwells within me, that is, in my flesh." While it may be that "that is" possibly has a limiting meaning here ("so far as I am flesh") and that the true, willing self is thereby dissociating itself from this self that is fallen victim to flesh, it is, nevertheless, significant that "I" and "my flesh" can be equated. Under the viewpoint of "doing," they are identical; but if they can be opposed to each other in regard to "willing," then it is apparent that the subject-self, the true self of a man, is inwardly split. That self which in Rom. 7:17, 20 distinguishes itself from the "sin which dwells within me," is flatly labeled in v. 14 as "carnal" and "sold under sin"—just as the first person is used throughout vv. 14–24 both in regard to willing and to doing. Therefore "I" and "I," self and self, are at war with each other; i.e. to be innerly divided, or not to be at one with one's self, is the essence of human existence under sin.

This inner dividedness means that man himself destroys his true self. In his self-reliant will to be himself, a will that comes to light in "desire" at the encounter with the "commandment," he loses his self, and "sin" becomes the active subject within him (Rom. 7:9). Thereby the self—the "I"—dies; selfhood, of course, belongs to the nature of man, and it is just the "commandment," given "for life," that ought to bring his selfhood to reality. Man fails to achieve it by attempting self-reliantly to realize it in "desire." In this false will toward selfhood man's destination to be a self—his will toward "life"—is pervertedly preserved; that is just the reason why it is possible to describe human existence as the struggle between "self" and "self" within a man. In the fact that man is a self—that he is a being to whom what matters and should matter is his "life," his self—lies the possibility of sin. In the fact that God's commandment is meant to give man "life" lies the possibility of misunderstanding: Man, called to selfhood, tries to live out of his own strength and thus loses his self—his "life"—and rushes into death. This is the domination of sin: All man's doing is directed against his true intention—viz. to achieve life.

§ 24. *Sin and Death*

1. Since all man's pursuit ultimately aims at life, even though in each case it seeks some specific end, it follows that a false, aberrant pursuit walks the way that leads to death.

For Paul, in the train of Old Testament-Jewish tradition, it is axiomatic that sin draws death after it. The "sting" of death is sin, whose power lies in the Torah (I Cor. 15:56); i.e. the transgressing of the Torah, which is occasioned by sin, draws death after it. *Death is the punishment for the sin a man has committed;* sinners are "worthy of death" (Rom. 1:32 KJ), they have "earned" death. So Paul can also say that sin pays her slave his "wage" with death (Rom. 6:16, 23), or that the sinner by his death pays his debt, atones for his sin (Rom. 6:7). In such statements, death, we must recognize, is first thought of as the death which is natural dying, as Rom. 5:12ff. shows, according to which death as the punishment for sin was brought into the world by Adam's sin. Nevertheless, they also presuppose that this death will be confirmed—made final, so to say—by the verdict condemning them to "destruction" which God will pronounce over sinners on the judgment day (Rom. 2:6–11).

2. Still Paul's thoughts on flesh and sin lead beyond this traditional juristic conception of death as punishment. If as we have concluded sin is man's false pursuit of life, and if this consists in leading one's life "after the flesh,"—i.e. living out of the created, the earthly-natural and transitory—*then sin leads with inner necessity into death*: "If you live according to the flesh you will die" (Rom. 8:13). He who derives life out of the transitory must, himself, perish with the perishing of the transitory. "He who sows to his own flesh will from the flesh reap corruption" (Gal. 6:8). "Anxiety for the affairs of the world" clings to "the world," whose σχῆμα ("substance," not just "form") "passes away" (I Cor. 7:31); he who so lives clutches at emptiness, so to say, and all he gets himself is death. "Worldly grief" brings death to him who has it (II Cor. 7:10). Why? Because in it he clings to that which is doomed to death.

Thus, death grows out of flesh-ly life like a fruit—organically, as it were: "While we were living in the flesh, our sinful passions, aroused by the law, were at work in our members to bear fruit for death" (Rom. 7:5). Death is the "end" of the "fruit" of sinful life (Rom. 6:21 KJ). The *soma* [body] of flesh in which sin "dwells" is thereby a "*soma* of death" (Rom. 7:24). When II Cor. 3:6 says: "for the written code kills, but the Spirit gives life," there is no reflection in this context over the question whether the individual under the reign of Law brings death upon himself by transgressing the Law or by his zeal for it. But the sentence is spoken not in regard to Jewish transgressions of the Law, but in polemic against the Jewish esteem for the Torah as an eternal Law diffused with glory. In opposition to this esteem Paul says that the ministry of Moses is a "ministry of death" and its "splendor" or "glory" a fading one. The Torah, therefore, belongs to the sphere of "flesh" in contrast to the "new covenant," which is a "covenant of the Spirit." Hence, serving the Torah leads with inner necessity to death.

The perversion of human striving that pursues life and yet only garners death is described at length in Rom. 7:7–25, a passage in which Paul so depicts the situation of man under the Torah as it has become clear to a backward look from the standpoint of Christian faith. V. 10 says that the commandment was given to man "for life"; and man, whose longing is to have life, completely agrees with this intention (v. 16: "I agree . . .", v. 22: "I delight in . . ."). But the commandment nonetheless leads factually into death; it does so by arousing "desire" in man (vv. 7–11).

It may be that in these verses Paul does not reflect over the question whether "desire" tempts man to transgress the Law or whether it misleads him to a false zeal for fulfilling it. Yet the latter must at least be included; for if 7:7–25 describes the situation of being under the Law in a way that holds true for everyone who is under it, then the attitude (described in Phil. 3:4–6) of being "blameless" "as to righteousness under the Law" must be contained in it. In this case, then, the "desire" aroused by the Law is the "unenlightened zeal for God" of Rom. 10:2 (tr.).

Sin's "deceit" (Rom. 7:11) consists in deluding man to think that if he follows his "desire" he will gain life, whereas he only acquires death. Victimized by this deceit, man does not know what he is doing: "for what I am bringing about I do not know" (v. 15a tr.); i.e. he does not know that by what he is doing he is only reaping death.

These words cannot mean: "I don't know how it happens that my good resolutions always get broken," in the sense of Ovid's line, *video meliora proboque, deteriora sequor* (I see the better and approve; the lower I follow, *Metamorphoses* 7, 21). For nothing is said about good resolutions that come to nothing in actual conduct. What the encounter with the commandment arouses is not good will, but "desire"! Rather, the point of the passage in its context is that what man brings about is an "evil," whereas according to his intention (which is the guiding factor in "desire"), it was to be a "good." Since κατεργάζεσθαι in v. 13 does not mean "do," but "bring about" or "reap," it is natural to take it to mean the same in v. 15 (and then also in v. 17 and v. 20 in spite of 2:9f.) and to supply there the object named in v. 13—"death" (*cf.* also II Cor. 7:10: "worldly grief brings about—κατεργάζεται—death"); then "the good thing" which is the object of the same verb in v. 18 is "life." Then the "doing" (πράσσειν, vv. 16, 19, or ποιεῖν, vv. 19, 20, 21) of evil and good must be correspondingly interpreted as meaning the bringing about of the evil thing (= death) and of the good thing (= life), which might be a conceivable locution in pointed speech. But even if the simple verbs (πράσσειν and ποιεῖν) are understood literally (linguistically the more natural assumption) as the "doing" of evil or of good (in which case κατεργάζεσθαι would also have to be so understood, at least in vv. 17, 18, and 20), the basic meaning still remains the same: In pursuing his "desire" man thinks he is doing something good (i.e. life-bringing) and actually is doing something evil (i.e. life-destroying). In either case, the gruesome contradiction which characterizes human striving is being described: It wants to gain life and only achieves death.

Fundamentally, then, death is already a present reality, for man "sold under sin" (v. 14) has lost himself, is no longer at one with himself. This is clearly expressed in the formulation of vv. 9–11: ". . . but when the commandment came, sin revived and I died . . . for sin . . . deceived me and . . . killed me."

3. The juristic conception of death as the punishment for sin and the conception of death as a fruit organically growing out of sin are not harmonized with each other. Nor does either conception agree with the view set forth in I Cor. 15:45–49 that Adamitic man was created "earthy," and being earthy is flesh and blood (v. 50), and therefore "perishable" (v. 53f.). The disagreement between this view and the two preceding is obscured only by the fact that Paul here avoids the term "fleshly" (σαρκικός) and uses ψυχικός ("animate"—but non-spiritual) instead—which, however, amounts to the same thing (cf. I Cor. 2:14 with 3:1, 3).

KRISTER STENDAHL

The Apostle Paul and the Introspective Conscience of the West[†]

In the history of Western Christianity—and hence, to a large extent, in the history of Western culture—the Apostle Paul has been hailed as a hero of the introspective conscience. Here was the man who grappled with the problem "I do not do the good I want, but the evil I do not want to do is what I do . . ." (Rom. 7:19). His insights as to a solution of this dilemma have recently been more or less identified, for example, with what Jung referred to as the Individuation Process;[1] but this is only a contemporary twist to the traditional Western way of reading the Pauline letters as documents of human consciousness.

Twenty-five years ago Henry J. Cadbury wrote a stimulating study, "The Peril of Modernizing Jesus" (1937). That book and that very title is a good summary of one of the most important insights of biblical studies in the 20th century. It has ramifications far beyond the field of theology and biblical exegesis. It questions the often tacit presupposition that man remains basically the same through the ages. There is little point in affirming or denying such a presupposition in general

---

† A paper delivered at the Annual Meeting of the American Psychological Association, September 3, 1961; published in *Harvard Theological Review* 56 (1963): 199–215. An earlier version appeared in *Svensk exegitisk årsbok* 25 (1960): 62–77.
Stendahl (1921–2008) argues that the Augustinian-Lutheran theological tradition in which Paul—and Romans 7 in particular—has often been interpreted fundamentally misconstrues the apostle's message. Stendahl's important essay helped inaugurate a new era of Pauline studies, challenging scholars to investigate with renewed seriousness the apostle's historical context (especially the social problems associated with the integration of Gentiles into what was originally a Jewish church) and to question a variety of conventional assumptions about Paul's theology (e.g., the centrality of the grace–works dichotomy). Much recent scholarship on Paul owes a direct or indirect debt to Stendahl—including the selections by Stanley Stowers and J. Albert Harrill excerpted below, both of which leap over Luther and Augustine to pursue Origen's insight that Paul in Romans 7 speaks in the voice of another.
1. D. Cox, *Jung and St. Paul: A Study of the Doctrine of Justification by Faith and Its Relation to the Concept of Individuation* (1959) [Stendahl's note; to Carl Jung, individuation (personal integration) was a spiritual as well as a psychological experience].

terms—much would depend on what the foggy word "basically" could mean. But both the historian and the theologian, both the psychologist and the average reader of the Bible, are well advised to assess how this hypothesis of contemporaneity affects their thinking, and their interpretation of ancient writings.

This problem becomes acute when one tries to picture the function and the manifestation of introspection in the life and writings of the Apostle Paul. It is the more acute since it is exactly at this point that Western interpreters have found the common denominator between Paul and the experiences of man, since Paul's statements about "justification by faith" have been hailed as the answer to the problem which faces the ruthlessly honest man in his practice of introspection. Especially in Protestant Christianity—which, however, at this point has its roots in Augustine and in the piety of the Middle Ages—the Pauline awareness of sin has been interpreted in the light of Luther's struggle with his conscience. But it is exactly at that point that we can discern the most drastic difference between Luther and Paul, between the 16th and the 1st century, and, perhaps, between Eastern and Western Christianity.

A fresh look at the Pauline writings themselves shows that Paul was equipped with what in our eyes must be called a rather "robust" conscience. In Phil. 3 Paul speaks most fully about his life before his Christian calling, and there is no indication that he had had any difficulty in fulfilling the Law. On the contrary, he can say that he had been "flawless" as to the righteousness required by the Law (v. 6). His encounter with Jesus Christ—at Damascus, according to Acts 9:1–9— has not changed this fact. It was not to him a restoration of a plagued conscience; when he says that he now forgets what is behind him (Phil. 3:13), he does not think about the shortcomings in his obedience to the Law, but about his glorious achievements as a righteous Jew, achievements which he nevertheless now has learned to consider as "refuse" in the light of his faith in Jesus as the Messiah.

The impossibility of keeping the whole Law is a decisive point in Paul's argumentation in Rom. 2:17–3:20 (cf. 2:1ff.); and also in Gal. 3:10–12 this impossibility is the background for Paul's arguments in favor of a salvation which is open to both Jews and Gentiles in Christ. These and similar Pauline statements have led many interpreters to accuse Paul of misunderstanding or deliberately distorting the Jewish view of Law and Salvation. It is pointed out that for the Jew the Law did not require a static or pedantic perfectionism but supposed a covenant relationship in which there was room for forgiveness and repentance and where God applied the Measure of Grace. Hence Paul should have been wrong in ruling out the Law on the basis that Israel could not achieve the perfect obedience which the Law required. What is forgotten in such a critique of Paul—which is conditioned by the later Western problem of a conscience troubled by the demands of the Law—is that these statements about the impossibility of fulfilling the Law stand side by side with the one just mentioned: "I was blameless as to righteousness—of the Law, that is" (Phil. 3:6). So Paul speaks about his subjective conscience—in full accordance with his Jewish training. But Rom. 2–3 deals with something very different. The actual transgressions in Israel—as a people, not in each and every individual— show that the Jews are not better than the Gentiles, in spite of circumcision and the proud possession of the Law. The "advantage" of the Jews is that they have been entrusted with the Words of God and this advantage cannot be revoked by their disobedience (Rom. 3:1ff.), but for the rest they have no edge on salvation. The Law has not helped. They stand before God as guilty as the Gentiles, and even more so (2:9). All this is said in the light of the new avenue of salvation, which has been opened in Christ, an avenue which is equally open to Jews and Gentiles, since it is not based on the Law, in which the very distinction between the two rests. In such a situation, says Paul, the old covenant, even with its provision for forgiveness and grace, is not a valid alternative any more. The only *metanoia* (repentance/conversion) and the only grace which counts is the one now available in Messiah Jesus. Once this has been seen, it appears that Paul's references to the impossibility of fulfilling the Law is part of a theological and theoretical scriptural argument about the relation between Jews and Gentiles. Judging from Paul's own writings, there is no indication that he had "experienced it in his own conscience" during his time as a Pharisee. It is also striking to note that Paul never urges Jews to find in Christ the answer to the anguish of a plagued conscience.

If that is the case regarding *Paul the Pharisee*, it is, as we shall see, even more important to note that we look in vain for any evidence that *Paul the Christian* has suffered under the burden of conscience concerning personal shortcomings which he would label "sins." The famous formula "simul justus et peccator"—at the same time righteous and sinner—as a description of the status of the Christian may have some foundation in the Pauline writings, but this formula cannot be substantiated as the center of Paul's conscious attitude toward his personal sins. Apparently, Paul did not have the type of introspective conscience which such a formula seems to presuppose. This is probably one of the reasons why "forgiveness" is the term for salvation which is used least of all in the Pauline writings.

It is most helpful to compare these observations concerning Paul with the great hero of what has been called "Pauline Christianity," i.e., with Martin Luther. In him we find the problem of late medieval piety and theology. Luther's inner struggles presuppose the developed system of Penance and Indulgence, and it is significant that his famous 95 theses take their point of departure from the problem of forgiveness of sins as seen within the framework of Penance: "When our Lord and Master Jesus Christ said: 'Repent (*penitentiam agite*) . . . ,' he wanted the whole life of the faithful to be a repentance (or penance)."

When the period of the European mission had come to an end, the theological and practical center of Penance shifted from Baptism, administered once and for all, to the ever repeated Mass, and already this subtle change in the architecture of the Christian life contributed to a more acute introspection. The manuals for self-examination among the Irish monks and missionaries became a treasured legacy in wide circles of Western Christianity. The Black Death may have been significant in the development of the climate of faith and life. Penetrating self-examination reached a hitherto unknown intensity. For those who took this practice seriously— and they were more numerous than many Protestants are accustomed to think— the pressure was great. It is as one of those—and for them—that Luther carries out his mission as a great pioneer. It is in response to *their* question, "How can I find a gracious God?" that Paul's words about a justification in Christ by faith, and without the works of the Law, appears as the liberating and saving answer. Luther's unrelenting honesty, even to the gates of hell (cf. especially his *De servo arbitrio*,

"On the Bondage of the Will"), his refusal to accept the wise and sound consolation from his spiritual directors, these make him into a Christopher Columbus in the world of faith, who finds new and good land on the other side of what was thought to be the abyss.

In these matters Luther was a truly Augustinian monk, since Augustine may well have been one of the first to express the dilemma of the introspective conscience. It has always been a puzzling fact that Paul meant so relatively little for the thinking of the Church during the first 350 years of its history. To be sure, he is honored and quoted but—in the theological perspective of the West—it seems that Paul's great insight into justification by faith was forgotten. It is, however, with Augustine that we find an interpretation of Paul which makes use of what to us is the deeper layer in the thought of the great Apostle. A decisive reason for this state of affairs may well have been that up to the time of Augustine the Church was by and large under the impression that Paul dealt with those issues with which he actually deals: 1) What happens to the Law (the Torah, the actual Law of Moses, not the principle of legalism) when the Messiah has come?—2) What are the ramifications of the Messiah's arrival for the relation between Jews and Gentiles? For Paul had not arrived at his view of the Law by testing and pondering its effect upon his conscience; it was his grappling with the question about the place of the Gentiles in the Church and in the plan of God, with the problem Jews/Gentiles or Jewish Christians/Gentile Christians, which had driven him to that interpretation of the Law which was to become his in a unique way. These observations agree well with the manner in which both Paul himself and the Acts of the Apostles describe his "conversion" as a call to become the Apostle to and of the Gentiles. This was the task for which he—in the manner of the prophets of old—had been earmarked by God from his mother's womb (Gal. 1:15; cf. Acts 9:15). There is not—as we usually think—first a conversion, and then a call to apostleship; there is only the call to the work among the Gentiles. Hence, it is quite natural that at least one of the centers of gravity in Paul's thought should be how to define the place for Gentiles in the Church, according to the plan of God. Rom. 9–11 is not an appendix to chs. 1–8, but the climax of the letter.

This problem was, however, not a live one after the end of the first century, when Christianity for all practical purposes had a non-Jewish constituency. Yet it was not until Augustine that the Pauline thought about the Law and Justification was applied in a consistent and grand style to a more general and timeless human problem. In that connection we remember that Augustine has often been called "the first modern man." While this is an obvious generalization, it may contain a fair amount of truth. His *Confessiones* are the first great document in the history of the introspective conscience. The Augustinian line leads into the Middle Ages and reaches its climax in the penitential struggle of an Augustinian monk, Martin Luther, and in his interpretation of Paul.

Judging at least from a superficial survey of the preaching of the Churches of the East from olden times to the present, it is striking how their homiletical tradition is either one of doxology or meditative mysticism or exhortation—but it does not deal with the plagued conscience in the way in which one came to do so in the Western Churches.

The problem we are trying to isolate could be expressed in hermeneutical terms somewhat like this: The Reformers' interpretation of Paul rests on an analogism when Pauline statements about Faith and Works, Law and Gospel, Jews and Gentiles are read in the framework of late medieval piety. The Law, the Torah, with its specific requirements of circumcision and food restrictions becomes a general principle of "legalism" in religious matters. Where Paul was concerned about the possibility for Gentiles to be included in the messianic community, his statements are now read as answers to the quest for assurance about man's salvation out of a common human predicament.

This shift in the frame of reference affects the interpretation at many points. A good illustration can be seen in what Luther calls the Second Use of the Law, i.e., its function as a Tutor or Schoolmaster unto Christ. The crucial passage for this understanding of the Law is Gal. 3:24, a passage which the King James Version—in unconscious accord with Western tradition—renders: "Wherefore the law was our schoolmaster (R.V. and A.S.V.: tutor) to bring us unto Christ," but which the Revised Standard Version translates more adequately: "So that the law was our custodian until Christ came." In his extensive argument for the possibility of Gentiles becoming Christians without circumcision etc., Paul states that the Law had not come in until 430 years after the promise to Abraham, and that it was meant to have validity only up to the time of the Messiah (Gal. 3:15–22). Hence, its function was to serve as a Custodian for the Jews until that time. Once the Messiah had come, and once the faith in Him—not "faith" as a general religious attitude—was available as the decisive ground for salvation, the Law had done its duty as a custodian for the Jews, or as a waiting room with strong locks (vv. 22f.). Hence, it is clear that Paul's problem is how to explain why there is no reason to impose the Law on the Gentiles, who now, in God's good Messianic time, have become partakers in the fulfillment of the promises to Abraham (v. 29).

In the common interpretation of Western Christianity, the matter looks very different. One could even say that Paul's argument has been reversed into saying the opposite to his original intention. Now the Law is the Tutor *unto* Christ. Nobody can attain a true faith in Christ unless his self-righteousness has been crushed by the Law. The function of the Second Use of the Law is to make man see his desperate need for a Savior. In such an interpretation, we note how Paul's distinction between Jews and Gentiles is gone. "*Our* Tutor/Custodian" is now a statement applied to man in general, not "our" in the sense of "I, Paul, and my fellow Jews." Furthermore, the Law is not any more the Law of Moses which requires circumcision etc., and which has become obsolete when faith in the Messiah is a live option—it is the moral imperative as such, in the form of the will of God. And finally, Paul's argument that the Gentiles must not, and should not come to Christ *via* the Law, i.e., *via* circumcision etc., has turned into a statement according to which all men must come to Christ with consciences properly convicted by the Law and its insatiable requirements for righteousness. So drastic is the reinterpretation once the original framework of "Jews and Gentiles" is lost, and the Western problems of conscience become its unchallenged and self-evident substitute.

Thus, the radical difference between a Paul and a Luther at this one point has considerable ramification for the reading of the actual texts. And the line of Luther appears to be the obvious one. This is true not only among those who find themselves more or less dogmatically bound by the confessions of the Reformation. It is equally true about the average student of "all the great books" in a College course, or the agnostic Westerner in general. It is also true in serious New Testament exegesis. Thus, R. Bultmann—in spite of his great familiarity with the history of religions in early Christian times—finds the nucleus of Pauline thought in the problem of "boasting," i.e., in man's need to be utterly convicted in his conscience.[2] Paul's self-understanding in these matters is the existential, and hence, ever valid center of Pauline theology. Such an interpretation is an even more drastic translation and an even more far-reaching generalization of the original Pauline material than that found in the Reformers. But it is worth noting that it is achieved in the prolongation of the same line. This is more obvious since Bultmann makes, candidly and openly, the statement that his existential hermeneutic rests on the presupposition that man is essentially the same through the ages, and that this continuity in the human self-consciousness is the common denominator between the New Testament and any age of human history. This presupposition is stated with the force of an a priori truth.

What in Bultmann rests on a clearly stated hermeneutic principle plays, however, its subtle and distorting role in historians who do not give account of their presuppositions but work within an unquestioned Western framework. P. Volz, in his comprehensive study of Jewish eschatology,[3] uses man's knowledge of his individual salvation in its relation to a troubled conscience as one of the "trenches" in his reconstruction of the Jewish background to the New Testament. But when it comes to the crucial question and he wants to find a passage which would substantiate that this was a conscious problem in those generations of Judaism, he can find only one example in the whole Rabbinic literature which perhaps could illustrate an attitude of a troubled conscience (b. *Ber.* 28b).

To be sure, no one could ever deny that *harmartia*, "sin," is a crucial word in Paul's terminology, especially in his epistle to the Romans. Rom. 1–3 sets out to show that all—both Jews and Gentiles—have sinned and fallen short of the Glory of God (3:19; cf. v. 23). Rom. 3:21–8:39 demonstrates how and in what sense this tragic fact is changed by the arrival of the Messiah.

It is much harder to gage how Paul subjectively experienced the power of sin in his life and, more specifically, how and in what sense he was conscious of actual sins. One point is clear. The Sin with capital S in Paul's past was that he had persecuted the Church of God. This climax of his dedicated obedience to his Jewish faith (Gal. 1:13; Phil. 3:6) was the shameful deed which made him the least worthy of apostleship (1 Cor. 15:9). This motif, which is elaborated dramatically by the author of the Acts of the Apostles (chs. 9, 22 and 26), is well grounded in Paul's own epistles. Similarly, when 1 Timothy states on Paul's account that "Christ Jesus came into the world to save sinners, of whom I am number one" (1:15), this is not an expression of contrition in the present tense, but refers to how Paul in his ignorance had been a blaspheming and violent persecutor, before God in his mercy and grace had revealed to him his true Messiah and made Paul an Apostle and a prototype of sinners' salvation (1:12–16).

2. See, e.g., Rudolf Bultmann, *Theology of the New Testament*, trans. Kendrick Grobel, vol. 1 (New York: Scribner, 1951), 242–43.
3. Paul Volz, *Die Eschatologie der jüdischen Gemeinde im neutestamentischen Zeitalter* (1934).

Nevertheless, Paul knew that he had made up for this terrible Sin of persecuting the Church, as he says in so many words in 1 Cor. 15:10: ". . . his grace toward me was not in vain; on the contrary, I worked harder than any of them—though it was not I, but the grace of God which is with me."

Thus his call to Apostleship has the same pattern as the more thematic statement that Christ died for us godless ones, while we were yet sinners (Rom. 5:6–11). We note how that statement is only the subsidiary conditional clause in an argument *e majore ad minus*[4]: If now God was so good and powerful that he could justify weak and sinful and rebellious men, how much easier must it not be for him to give in due time the ultimate salvation to those whom he already has justified. Hence, the words about the sinful, the weak and the rebellious have not present-tense meaning, but refer to the past, which is gloriously and gracefully blotted out, as was Paul's enmity to Jesus Christ and his Church.

What then about Paul's consciousness of sins after his conversion? His letters indicate with great clarity that he did not hold to the view that man was free from sin after baptism. His pastoral admonitions show that he had much patience with the sins and weaknesses of Christians. But does he ever intimate that he is aware of any sins of his own which would trouble his conscience? It is actually easier to find statements to the contrary. The tone in Acts 23:1, "Brethren, I have lived before God in all good conscience up to this day" (cf. 24:16), prevails also throughout his letters. Even if we take due note of the fact that the major part of Paul's correspondence contains an apology for his Apostolic ministry—hence it is the antipode to Augustine's *Confessions* from the point of view of form—the conspicuous absence of reference to an actual consciousness of being a sinner is surprising. To be sure, Paul is aware of a struggle with his "body" (1 Cor. 9:27), but we note that the tone is one of confidence, not of a plagued conscience.

In Rom. 9:1 and 2 Cor. 1:12 he witnesses to his good conscience. This tone reaches its highest pitch in 2 Cor. 5:10f.: "For we must all appear before the judgment seat of Christ so that each one may receive the retribution for what he has done while in his body, either good or evil. Aware, therefore, of the fear of the Lord, we try to persuade men, but to God it is clear [what we are]; and I hope that it is clear also to your conscience." Here, with the day of reckoning before his eyes, Paul says that the Lord has approved of him, and he hopes that the Corinthians shall have an equally positive impression of him, and of his success in pleasing the Lord (5:9). This robust conscience is not shaken hut strengthened by his awareness of a final judgment which has not come yet. And when he writes about the tensions between himself and Apollos and other teachers, he states that "I have nothing on my conscience" (1 Cor. 4:4; N.E.B.—literally "I know nothing with me"; the verb is of the same stem as the word for conscience); to be sure, he adds that this does not settle the case, since "the Lord is my judge," but it is clear from the context that Paul is in little doubt about the final verdict. His warning against a premature verdict is not a plea out of humility or fear, but a plea to the Corinthians not to be too rash in a negative evaluation of Paul.

---

4. From the greater to the smaller (Latin).

Thus, we look in vain for a statement in which Paul would speak about himself as an actual sinner. When he speaks about his conscience, he witnesses to his good conscience before men and God. On the other hand, Paul often speaks about his *weakness*, not only ironically as in 2 Cor. 11:21f. In 2 Cor. 12 we find the proudly humble words, "But He said to me: 'My grace is sufficient to you, for the power is fulfilled in weakness.' I will the more gladly boast of my weakness, that the power of Christ may rest upon me. For the sake of Christ, then, I am content with weaknesses, insults, hardships, persecutions, and calamities; for when I am weak, then I am strong" (vv. 9–10). The weakness which Paul here refers to is clearly without any relation to his sin of his conscience. The "thorn in the flesh" (v. 7) was presumably some physical handicap—some have guessed at epilepsy— which interfered with his effectiveness and, what was more important, with his apostolic authority, as we can see from Gal. 4:13; cf. 1 Cor. 11:30. Sickness was seen as a sign of insufficient spiritual endowment. But there is no indication that Paul ever thought of this and other "weaknesses" as sins for which he was responsible. They were caused by the Enemy or the enemies. His weakness became for him an important facet in his identification with the work of Christ, who had been "crucified in weakness" (2 Cor. 13:4; cf. also 4:10 and Col. 1:24).—In the passage from Rom. 5, mentioned above, we find the only use of the word "weak" as a synonym to "sinner," but there these words helped to describe primarily the power of justification as a past act (and the New English Bible consequently renders it by "powerless"). This is the more clear since the third synonym is "enemy" (v. 10), and points to Paul's past when he had been the enemy of Christ.

Yet there is one Pauline text which the reader must have wondered why we have left unconsidered, especially since it is the passage we mentioned in the beginning as the proof text for Paul's deep insights into the human predicament: "I do not do the good I want, but the evil I do not want to do is what I do" (Rom. 7:19). What could witness more directly to a deep and sensitive introspective conscience? While much attention has been given to the question whether Paul here speaks about a pre-Christian or Christian experience of his, or about man in general, little attention has been drawn to the fact that Paul here is involved in an argument about the Law; he is not primarily concerned about man's or his own cloven ego or predicament. The diatribe style of the chapter helps us to see what Paul is doing. In vv. 7–12 he works out an answer to the semi-rhetorical question: "Is the Law sin?" The answer reads: "Thus the Law is holy, just, and good." This leads to the equally rhetorical question: "Is it then this good (Law) which brought death to me?", and the answer is summarized in v. 25b: "So then, I myself serve the Law of God with my mind, but with my flesh I serve the Law of Sin" (i.e., the Law "weakened by sin" [8:3] leads to death, just as a medicine which is good in itself can cause death in a patient whose organism [flesh] cannot take it).

Such an analysis of the formal structure of Rom. 7 shows that Paul is here involved in an interpretation of the Law, a defense for the holiness and goodness of the Law. In vv. 13–25 he carries out this defense by making a distinction between the Law as such and the Sin (and the Flesh) which has to assume the whole responsibility for the fatal outcome. It is most striking that the "I", the *ego*, is not simply identified with Sin and Flesh. The observation that "I do not do the good

I want, but the evil I do not want to do is what I do" does not lead directly over to the exclamation: "Wretched man that I am . . .!", but, on the contrary, to the statement, "Now if I do what I do not want, *then it is not I who do it*, but the sin which dwells in me." The argument is one of acquittal of the ego, not one of utter contrition. Such a line of thought would be impossible if Paul's intention were to describe man's predicament. In Rom. 1–3 the human impasse has been argued, and here every possible excuse has been carefully ruled out. In Rom. 7 the issue is rather to show how in some sense "I gladly agree with the Law of God as far as my inner man is concerned" (v. 22); or, as in v. 25, "I serve the Law of God."

All this makes sense only if the anthropological references in Rom. 7 are seen as means for a very special argument about the holiness and goodness of the Law. The possibility of a distinction between the good Law and the bad Sin is based on the rather trivial observation that every man knows that there is a difference between what he ought to do and what he does. This distinction makes it possible for Paul to blame Sin and Flesh, and to rescue the Law as a good gift of God. "If I now do what I do not want, I agree with the Law [and recognize] that it is good" (v. 16). That is all, but that is what should be proven.

Unfortunately—or fortunately—Paul happened to express this supporting argument so well that what to him and his contemporaries was a common sense observation appeared to later interpreters to be a most penetrating insight into the nature of man and into the nature of sin. This could happen easily once the problem about the nature and intention of God's Law was not any more as relevant a problem in the sense in which Paul grappled with it. The question about the Law became the incidental framework around the golden truth of Pauline anthropology. This is what happens when one approaches Paul with the Western question of an introspective conscience. This Western interpretation reaches its climax when it appears that even, or especially, the will of man is the center of depravation. And yet, in Rom. 7 Paul had said about that will: "The will (to do the good) is there . . ." (v. 18).

What we have called the Western interpretation has left its mark even in the field of textual reconstruction in this chapter in Romans. In Moffatt's translation of the New Testament[5] the climax of the whole argument about the Law (v. 25b, see above) is placed before the words "wretched man that I am . . ." Such a rearrangement—without any basis in the manuscripts—wants to make this exclamation the dramatic climax of the whole chapter, so that it is quite clear to the reader that Paul here gives the answer to the great problem of human existence. But by such arrangements the structure of Paul's argumentation is destroyed. What was a digression is elevated to the main factor. It should not be denied that Paul is deeply aware of the precarious situation of man in this world, where even the holy Law of God does not help—it actually leads to death. Hence his outburst. But there is no indication that this awareness is related to a subjective conscience struggle. If that were the case, he would have spoken of the "body of sin," but he says "body of death" (v. 25; cf. 1 Cor. 15:56). What dominates this

---

5. James Moffatt's *New Testament: A New Translation* (1913) frequently rearranges the NT text on dubious form-critical assumptions.

chapter is a theological concern and the awareness that there is a positive solution available here and now by the Holy Spirit about which he speaks in ch. 8. We should not read a trembling and introspective conscience into a text which is so anxious to put the blame on Sin, and that in such a way that not only the Law but the will and mind of man are declared good and are found to be on the side of God.

We may have wasted too much time in trying to demonstrate a fact well known in human history—and especially in the history of religions: that sayings which originally meant one thing later on were interpreted to mean something else, something which was felt to be more relevant to human conditions of later times.

And yet, if our analysis is on the whole correct, it points to a major question in the history of mankind. We should venture to suggest that the West for centuries has wrongly surmised that the biblical writers were grappling with problems which no doubt are ours, but which never entered their consciousness.

For the historian this is of great significance. It could of course always be argued that these ancients unconsciously were up against the same problems as we are—man being the same through the ages. But the historian is rightly anxious to stress the value of having an adequate picture of what these people actually thought that they were saying. He will always be suspicious of any "modernizing," whether it be for apologetic, doctrinal, or psychological purposes.

The theologian would be quite willing to accept and appreciate the obvious deepening of religious and human insight which has taken place in Western thought, and which reached a theological climax with Luther—and a secular climax with Freud. He could perhaps argue that this Western interpretation and transformation of Pauline thought is a valid and glorious process of theological development. He could even claim that such a development was fostered by elements implicit in the New Testament, and especially in Paul.

The framework of "Sacred History" which we have found to be that of Pauline Theology (cf. our comments on Gal. 3:24 above) opens up a new perspective for systematic theology and practical theology. The Pauline *ephapax* ("once for all", Rom. 6:10) cannot be translated fully and only into something repeated in the life of every individual believer. For Gentiles the Law is *not* the Schoolmaster who leads to Christ; or it is that only by analogy and a secondary one at that. We find ourselves in the new situation where the faith in the Messiah Jesus gives us the right to be called Children of God (1 Jn. 3:1). By way of analogy, one could of course say that in some sense every man has a "legalistic Jew" in his heart. But that *is* an analogy, and should not be smuggled into the texts as their primary or explicit meaning in Paul. If that is done, something happens to the joy and humility of Gentile Christianity.

Thus, the theologian would note that the Pauline original should not be identified with such interpretations. He would try to find ways by which the church—also in the West—could do more justice to other elements of the Pauline original than those catering to the problems raised by introspection. He would be suspicious of a teaching and a preaching which pretended that the only door into the church was that of evermore introspective awareness of sin and guilt. For it appears that the Apostle Paul was a rather good Christian, and yet he seems to have had little such awareness. We note how the bibilical original functions as a critique of inherited presuppositions and an incentive to new thought. Few things are more liberating and creative in modern theology than a clear distinction between the "original" and the "translation" in any age, our own included.

STANLEY K. STOWERS

The Gentile Share in Christ's Life[†]

A Greek Tradition in 7:14–24

[T]here is a solid place to stand in trying to contextualize chapter 7 and treat it in a nonanachronistic way: 7:15 and 19 contain a ubiquitous Greek saying that is central to the Greco-Roman ethic of self-mastery. Some scholars have noted this fact but usually dismiss it because the saying is supposedly trivial while Paul's antimoralistic (that is, Augustinian-Lutheran) "transformation" of it is supposedly profound. In other words, interpreters have judged the historical fact by the ideology of that Christian tradition.

The text remembered as the starting point for this tradition is Euripides' *Medea* 1077–80: "I am being overcome by evils. I know that what I am about to do is evil but passion is stronger than my reasoned reflection and this is the cause of the worst evils for humans." These words of Euripides' Medea became the classic text for the long and varied ancient discussion of *akrasia*, lack of self-mastery. It represents what can be described as the tragic position in literary depictions and philosophical discussion of "the will," or self-mastery in moral psychology. The tragic tradition emphasizes that the good of the human life is vulnerable to luck, conflict of values, and the passions as structures of perception that allow humans to be deeply affected by situations and powers they do not control. Tragedy emphasizes the often evil consequences of these limitations, but it also claims that what is good and beautiful about human life is intrinsically bound to this vulnerability. Just before the text quoted above, Medea, driven by anger and the thought of revenge, determines to follow a terrible plan that includes killing her children. Twice she wavers as she reflects that another course of action would be better (1040–48; 1056–58). Finally, in our text she recognizes how evil her deed will be but says that her desire for revenge is stronger than her reasoned reflections.

The ancients also remembered Phaedra's monologue in Euripides' *Hippolytus* in connection with the failure of self-mastery (377–83):

> I do not think people do evil by nature, for many are good.
> But one must consider that though we know and understand what is good
> We don't act on what we know—some through laziness,
> Others through preferring pleasure more than goodness.

[†] From Stanley K. Stowers, *A Rereading of Romans: Justice, Jews, and Gentiles* (New Haven: Yale University Press, 1994), 260–64, 269–81, 361–63. All notes are Stowers's.

Not only emotions and drives but other habits of character prevent people from doing the good that they know and recognize.

In the Protagoras 352 D, Socrates refers to this view in Euripides as the understanding of the masses: "Most people say that . . . while knowing what is best they do not will to do it although they could do it but instead they do something else. And when I have asked why, they say that those who act this way are acting under pleasure or pain or the power of the things I just mentioned." The other side of the debate was begun by Socrates, who in contrast to the popular view held that akrasia, acting against what one knew was right, was impossible. Plato too, partly under the influence of Socrates and partly for other reasons, opposes the popular view in some of his writing. Plato also opposed the larger tragic perspective. Through ascetic suppression of desire and passion and by valuing the abstract and universal rather than the vulnerable and changeable particular, Plato sought to find a way for humans to become godlike and avoid the limit and vulnerability of human life. Thus in several respects, he sets or anticipates the agenda of the Hellenistic philosophies with which Paul had at least indirect contact. Aristotle, on the other hand, affirmed the tragic and popular view. Book 7 of his *Nicomachean Ethics*, devoted to the discussion of akrasia, distinguishes between lack of self-mastery that is impulsive and lack of self-mastery that is deliberate and fully aware of itself. Later debates focused on whether weakness of will (that is, lack of self-mastery) stemmed from ignorance and false beliefs, the Stoic position, or from inherently rebellious passions, the popular and Platonic position.

The Stoics developed a sophisticated version of the Socratic position that passion and weakness of the will were due to ignorance or false belief. Chrysippus reinterpreted the *Medea* from this perspective: "Medea declared before her infanticide: 'I know what evil I intend to commit, I see it well; but passion is stronger in me than reason.' But this passion is not a sort of foreign power, which wrests dominion from the mind; it is Medea's mind, which in unhealthy agitation chooses the bad. It turns away from itself and from every reasonable reflection. Precisely this conscious turning away from calm reflection and from the mind itself is the essential characteristic of emotion."[1] The early Stoics denied the existence of a distinct, irrational part of the soul, instead arguing for the soul's unity. The passions were disturbed or diseased states of the soul engendered by false beliefs. To be healthy is to have no contrast in the personality between reason and emotion. What most people think of as reason and emotion harmonize in the healthy person.

Chrysippus is said to have studied the *Medea* zealously.[2] Later Stoics showed continued interest in Euripides' tragedy. Paul's nearly exact contemporary Seneca wrote a *Medea* of his own based on Euripides' work. Paul's near contemporary Epictetus has an imaginary interlocutor cite Medea's words to represent the popular view of reason and emotion (*Diss.* [*Dissertations*] 1.28.6–8):

> INTERLOCUTOR: Can't a person believe that something is profitable for him, and yet not choose it?

1. Quoted from [Gerd] Theissen, *Psychological Aspects* [*of Pauline Theology* (Philadelphia: Fortress Press, 1987)], 14–15.
2. *Stoicorum Veterum Fragmenta*, ed. Hans von Arnim, 3 vols. (Leipzig: Teubner, 1903–5), 2.1.

EPICTETUS: He cannot.

ı: What about she [Medea] who said, "Now I understand what evils I intend: But passion overpowers my reasoned reflection?"

E: It is because she regards the very indulgence of her passion and the vengeance against her husband as more profitable than saving her children.

ı: Yes, but she was deceived [cf. Rom 7:11].

E: Show her clearly that she is deceived, and she will not do it; but until you show it, what else has she to follow but that which appears true?

Epictetus elsewhere uses a version of the nearly proverbial saying that we find in Rom 7:15 and 19: "For since he who does wrong [*hamartein*] does not want to, but to be right, it is clear that he is not doing what he wants to do [*ho men thelei ou poiei*]. . . . He, then, who can show to each person that which causes him to do wrong, and can clearly demonstrate to him how he is not doing what he wants, and is doing what he does not want to do [*ho thelei ou poiei kai ho mē thelei poiei*], is strong in argument, and also in both exhortation and moral criticism" (*Diss.* 2.26.1–4). Platonists followed a more popular view in opposing the Stoics and in emphasizing that reason, emotion, and appetite are distinct powers that do battle in the soul. So, for example, Plutarch, with his typical eclecticism, draws heavily on both Plato and Aristotle, quoting Medea's famous words in attacking the Stoics in *On Moral Virtue* (446A). In the following passages, Galen attacks the early Stoics and in the first text specifically Chrysippus's interpretation of Medea's words. According to Galen, the soul consists of distinct powers that can never be completely harmonized. Notice how what one knows or understands about the good or evil of one's actions is an issue in the debate as it also is in Romans 7 (cf. 7:7, 11, 15). Galen writes,

> If Euripides were supporting the teachings of Chrysippus, he would not have said that she understands but just the opposite, that she is ignorant and does not understand what evils she is about to do. But to say, on the one hand, that she knows and, on the other hand, that she is overcome by anger—what else is that but a person introducing two sources for Medea's impulses, one by which we perceive things and come to know them, which is the rational power, and another irrational, whose work is anger? This [anger], then, forced Medea's soul. (*Hippoc. et Plat.* [*On the Doctrines of Hippocrates and Plato*] 4.274.15–22)

> But Medea was not only not persuaded by any reasoning to kill her children but on the contrary, as for reasoning, she says that she understands the evil of the deeds that she is about to commit, but her anger is stronger than her reasoned deliberations; that is, her passion has not been brought into subjection and does not obey and follow reason as if it were a master, but throws off the reins and bolts and disobeys the command, so that it is some other act or passion or power than the rational. For how could any-

thing disobey itself or run away from itself or not follow itself?[3] (*Hippoc. et Plat.* 4.244.2–9)

Finally, the famous Medean saying occurs not only in drama and philosophers' debates, but also in such contexts as letters and public orations.[4] The famous parallel to Paul's words in Ovid *Met.* [*Metamorphoses*] 7.17–21, for example, are the words of Medea dialoguing with herself: "Oh wretched one, drive out these flames that you feel from your maiden breast if you can. If I could, I would be more reasonable. But some strange power holds me back against my will. Desire, impels [or "counsels"] me one way, my mind another. I see what is better and approve it, but I follow the worse. Why do you, a royal maiden, burn for a stranger, and think about marriage in a foreign world?"[5]

These texts illustrate how versions of the saying found in 7:15 and 19 played a central role in the Greek moral tradition. The words of Euripides' *Medea* were widely cited in this connection. In philosophy and literature alike the words were variously interpreted in discussions about the roles of the emotions, deliberation, and knowledge of good and evil in moral psychology. Most aspects of Paul's discussion in 7:7–25 can be paralleled with language from this tradition. No one, however, would deny that Paul's text has its own character. In order to get at Paul's use of the tradition it is first necessary to discuss the style and rhetoric of 7:7–25.

* * *

Toward a Historical Reading with Speech-in-Character

The difficult task of imagining a reading possible for readers in Paul's time must preclude Christian assumptions and readings that make sense only in epochs later than Paul's. The interpreter can neither presuppose the introspective Christian conscience of late antiquity or the middle ages nor assume the much later Christian stereotype of the legalistic Jew who attempts the impossible task of keeping the law. The picture of Paul the Pharisee, who attempted that impossible task, clearly comes from reading the narratives of his conversion in Acts through the lens of later Christian constructions of Judaism and the law.[6] Types and assumptions for reading will have to be those that readers in Paul's time could have made.

The section begins in v. 7 with an abrupt change in voice following a rhetorical question that serves as a transition from Paul's authorial voice, which has previously addressed the readers explicitly described by the letter in 6:1–7:6. This constitutes what the grammarians and rhetoricians described as change of voice (*enallagē* or *metabolē*). These ancient readers would next look for *diaphōnia*, a

3. My translation from the Greek text edited by Phillip DeLacy, *Galen on the Doctrines of Hippocrates and Plato* (Berlin: Akademie Verlag, 1978), 1:274, 244. I have cited Galen's work by book and DeLacy's page and line numbers.
4. Plautus, *Trinummus*, 657–58; Albinus, *Epitome* 243; Aelius Aristides, *Oration* 50; Lucian, *Apology*, 10.
5. I have translated from *P. Ovid Naso Metamorphosen*, 10th ed., ed. Rudolf Ewald (Zurich: Weidmann, 1966).
6. Paula Fredriksen, "Paul and Augustine: Conversion Narratives, Orthodox Traditions, and the Retrospective Self," *Journal of Theological Studies* 37 (1986): 3–34.

difference in characterization from the authorial voice. The speaker in 7:7–25 speaks with great personal pathos of coming under the law at some point, learning about his desire and sin, and being unable to do what he wants to do because of enslavement to sin and flesh. If one asks whether Paul gives his readers any clues elsewhere in the letter that this might be his autobiography, the answer is clearly no. And this picture does not fit what he says about himself in other letters.[7] The passage seems to present a distinctive, coherent ethos with a particular life situation.

* * *

In accord with a form of the technique discussed in the handbooks, Paul's authorial voice does not explicitly introduce the person. In comparison with the preceding context in 6:1–7:6, in which Paul's voice addresses "brothers," the addressee/s of the voice in 7:7–25 is either ambiguous or only Paul. The explicit audience of the letter addressed in its prescript disappears, as it does in 1:18–4:23, which I have elsewhere argued is also dominated by speech-in-character. At one point (7:25–8:2), again fitting prosōpopoiia, dialogue between the speaker in 7:7–25 and Paul occurs. The characterization of 7:7–25 reads like someone personally witnessing to the statement "when we were in the flesh, our sinful passions worked in our bodily parts through the law" (7:5), after the false conclusion and its rejection in 7:7a, "What shall we say? Is the law sin? By no means!" I find the identity of the speaker at 7:7a unclear: perhaps it is Paul, perhaps the person characterized in what follows, perhaps an anonymous objector.

Tragic characters or newly created characterizations of people in emotionally laden tragic situations were favorite subjects of prosōpopoiia.[8] One finds a remarkable intersection of style and content in Romans 7, an intersection of the techniques of prosōpopoiia and motifs and style of the tragic monologue as mediated by the tradition of moral psychology. As we saw in the tradition of Medea's words, such tragic speeches are often in the form of monologues or soliloquies. They usually employ the first person singular. The tragic speeches were models for the teaching of soliloquy in the *progymnasmata* [preparatory exercises] and rhetoric. Ovid, another near contemporary of Paul, not only wrote a *Medea* but also the *Heroides*, which are letters written by means of prosōpopoiia imagining what legendary women might have written. These include letters from Medea to Jason. When Paul wrote Romans, Ovid's works were popular reading in Rome.

One reason the figure of Medea gained such continuing popularity appears in connection with purity of citizenship and ethnicity ("nationality").[9] Medea stood for foreigners who corrupted the purity of the citizen body, and her saying about akrasia connoted the moral degeneracy that mixing with foreigners would supposedly bring. I find great irony in the fact that Paul the Jew resonates these allusions back to Greeks and Romans who apparently now see themselves as gentiles, outsiders to Judaism described as immoral foreigners. The figures of Medea and

---

7. The position of Krister Stendahl is still entirely persuasive ("The Apostle Paul and the Introspective Conscience of the West"; see above, pp. 1426–36).
8. Aphthonius, for instance, suggests the examples of Hecuba and the speech of Achilles to Patrocles. His illustration is Niobe's speech.
9. John K. Davies, "Athenian Citizenship," *Classical Journal* 73 (1977): 111–12.

other passion-bound barbarian women from Greek tragedy became important in imperial Rome. As early as Cicero, the type becomes a prominent oratorical slander (*Pro Caelio* 7.18; *Pro Lege Manilia* 8.21). But the theme rose to a height of public consciousness during the struggle between Antony and Octavian and the early years of the empire. The propagandists for Augustus depicted Antony as a man dominated by passionate foreign women and compared Cleopatra to Medea, Omphale, and Semiramis. Niobe, whom we have already seen recommended as a model for prosōpopoiia, paralleled Medea as a type of the degenerate foreign woman. On the doors of the temple to Apollo in Rome, erected as a votive for the victory at Actium, stood the scene of Niobe slaying her children. This not-so-subtle allusion to the defeat of Antony and Cleopatra used Niobe as the paradigm of God's wrath against barbarian hybris. All of this helps us to fathom how the Medean saying might have played in the public consciousness of Paul's time.

Rom 7:7–25 resembles tragic soliloquy and prosōpopoiia of the person in a tragic situation in several ways. It reveals the conflict of inner thoughts and feelings using the first person singular. The exclamation "wretched man that I am!" (*talaipōros egō anthrōpos*) reads almost as a parody of the tragic outcry. In Seneca's *Medea*, Medea cries "What, wretched woman, have I done?" as she reflects on how her will to do the good has been overpowered by anger. In the *Metamorphoses* (7.18), just before she speaks the famous words about akrasia, Medea calls herself "wretched" (*infelix*). The Vulgate uses the same word to translate *talaipōros* in Rom 7:24. Just before he introduces the example of Medea, Epictetus uses the fictive I: "Who is more wretched than I?" (2.17.18; cf. 26). In 1.4.23–26, Epictetus says that tragedies in which people say "wretched man that I am" are the depiction of people suffering because they admire external things.[1] The cry of despair "oh wretch that I am" is first made prominent in literature by the tragedians and comedians themselves.[2]

Another important feature that Romans 7 shares with the tragic monologue and the soliloquies of prosōpopoiia is the language of external power for moral and psychological states. I have already discussed the importance of "sin as a power" for traditional readings of Romans, and I have argued that one should not take Paul's language as more than rhetorical and metaphorical except in one regard. Now I can be more specific about the tradition of this rhetoric. Such language is not typical of the Hebrew Bible/Old Testament (for example, the Psalms) or earlier Jewish literature but rather of what scholars often call the fragmented personality of Homer and the Greek poets.[3]

Greek polytheism facilitated expression of the common human dilemma of conflicting goods and obligations. Different gods corresponded to different impulses and demands of human life. So, for example, in the *Hippolytus*, Euripides explores the conflicting demands of Aphrodite, goddess of love, and Artemis, goddess of virginity. As her nurse reflects upon Phaedra's dilemma of knowing what she ought to do but yielding to the power of love, she blames Aphrodite (358–59): "The modest

---

1. On the expression *talas egō*, see *Diss.* 1.12.28; 3.13.4.
2. In addition to texts already cited, see Aristophanes, *Thesmophoriazusae* 1039, and Plautus, *Trinummus* 657.
3. A. W. H. Adkins, *From the Many to the One* (Ithaca: Cornell University Press, 1970), 1–126.

forced against their wills to lust after evils! Aphrodite is no god!" Hippolytus's Phaedra speaks of being unable to subdue the goddess by self-mastering mastery (401). The language of outside powers shows itself in the tradition of Medea's saying and the broader discussion of willing and doing. Plutarch quotes from Euripides' lost *Chrysippus:* "Wretched I am, this evil comes to men from God, when one knows the good but does it not."[4] In Hellenistic and Roman times, philosophers and moralists usually rationalized that language. The powers were not really external but internal. Epictetus said, "When a man does something contrary to his opinion under the compulsion of love, while seeing the better thing but lacking the strength to follow, one might think him worthy of being excused, because he is in the power of something violent, and, in a manner of speaking, godlike" (*Diss.* 4.1.147). I find it no surprise, then, that Rom 6–7, with part of its subject matter from Greek moral psychology, uses the language of external power.

Thus in 7 one meets a well-known and highly developed kind of rhetoric that was employed by moralists and philosophers to treat the very issues that Paul discusses.

Gentiles in Chapter 7

Paul uses prosōpopoiia in chapter 7 to characterize not every human or every human who is not a Christian but rather gentiles, especially those who try to live by works of the law. Paul has already introduced and explained the character depicted in the prosōpopoiia of 7 from a historical point of view in chapter 1. Chapter 1 introduces the gentile mind as a motif that reappears at crucial points in the letter's discourse. When the gentile peoples rejected the true God and adopted polytheism, their reasoning became vain and their hearts became senseless and darkened (1:21). The true God, who has been unjustly rejected, now enters the story. He punishes these peoples in a fitting way by handing them over to slavery under a cruel tyrant. They are allowed or caused (which is not clear) to be under the mastery of their appetites and passions. As we saw in chapter 6, Romans treats its audience as having been enslaved to these masters before their baptisms. God handed these gentiles over to the lusts (*epithumiai*) of their hearts so as to practice impurity (*akatharsia*) and dishonor their bodies (1:24). God also handed them over to dishonorable passions (*pathē*), which resulted in perversions of nature and self-deceit (1:26–27). Paul sums it up by saying that God handed these gentiles over to a "base mind" (*nous*). He explains what this means by giving a long catalogue of characteristic vices. Chapter 7 speaks of bondage to both the passions (*ta pathēmata*) and desire (*epithumia*). The law made this bondage to desire known but also increased its hold (7:7–12) on the persona of 7:7–25. This person has been deceived by sin (7:11) and has a mind (*nous*) that is captive to sin and the flesh (7:23, 25). Paul uses the traditional language of external power for these inner forces. But God is the one who has handed the gentile peoples over to the powers, so that even God's law only witnesses to the bondage.

---

4. My translation of Euripides frg. 841 (*Tragicorum Graecorum Fragmenta,* ed. [Augustus] Nauck, [2nd ed. (Leipzig: Teubner, 1889)]). The Plutarch citation is in *Moralia* 33F (cf. 446A).

This view of gentiles enslaved to their appetites and passions appears elsewhere in Paul's letters. In 1 Thess 4:4 he writes, "Each man should know how to possess his own wife in holiness and honor, not in the passion of desire [*en pathē epithumias*] as the gentiles who do not know God."[5] The Thessalonians themselves had just recently turned from idols to the true God (1:10). Paul characterizes the preconversion life of the Corinthians with a mind-boggling list of vices (1 Cor 6:9–11). Nowhere in the letters is there comparable generalizing about Jews. In fact, defining gentiles as captive to their appetites over against Jewish freedom from such captivity constitutes a fundamental feature of self-definition for Paul.

Paul's view of gentiles is, of course, not unique to him but widespread in Jewish sources. The view of gentiles as morally degenerate must be considered a fundamental feature of Jewish self-definition in antiquity. Whether the authors believed what they were saying is a different matter. A few illustrative examples will suffice. The letter of Aristeas contrasts Jewish with gentile sexual practices (152): "For the vast majority of humans pollute themselves by promiscuous intercourse, committing great wickedness, and entire countries and cities pride themselves on such things. For they not only have intercourse with men, but they pollute the mothers who bore them and even their daughters. But we have kept our distance from these sins." Such texts attribute all kinds of abuses of appetites and desires to gentile peoples, but those concerning kinship taboos and relations with the same sex, especially between adults and children, are most prominent. These constitute the great sins against patriliny and patriarchy. An example from the Sibylline Oracles (3.591–99) illustrates the assumption that by such actions the gentiles were transgressing the law of Israel's God to which they were in some unspecified way responsible: "But [the Jews] raise holy hands toward heaven, rising early from their bed and continually purifying their body with water, and they honor Him alone who rules forever, the eternal One, and then their parents; and far more than any other people they remember the purity of the marriage bed. Nor do they hold unholy intercourse with boys, as do the Phoenicians, Egyptians, and Latins and spacious Greece and many other peoples, Persians and Galatians and all Asia, transgressing the holy law of immortal God." Finally, such texts often find the cause of gentile degeneracy in their worship of idols.

This picture of non-Jewish cultures is such a great distortion that it is natural to ask why and how it was maintained. The representation clearly has something to do with Israel's master narrative, which in turn became the mainspring of Jewish social and cultural integrity. Group boundaries of a constantly threatened people may have been a factor, but one must turn to Jewish society's internal organization to understand the role of the representation. The master narrative centers on a certain reading of the books of Moses. The gift of the land to Israel came about because of the perversions of the peoples who occupied it. When Noah curses Canaan, he proclaims that his descendants will be enslaved to the descendants of his brothers because of his sin (Gen 9:24–27). In Gen 15:16 God

---

5. The translation of v. 4 has been a matter of much debate. The word *skeuos* may mean one's own body rather than wife, but I think "wife" more likely. The language of possession actually argues for "wife" given that women were thought of as being property of men. See O. Larry Yarbrough, *"Not Like the Gentiles": Marriage Rules in the Letters of Paul*, Society of Biblical Literature Dissertation Series 80 (Atlanta: Scholars Press, 1985), 7.

promises Abraham that his descendants will inherit the land when the "wickedness of the Amorites is complete." After a list of "abominations," Lev 18:24–25 continues: "Do not pollute yourselves by all of these things, for by all these the peoples I am casting out before you polluted themselves; and the land became polluted, and I paid back their wickedness on account of it, and the land was greatly angered with those who inhabited it." The "peoples of the land" and later "gentiles" more broadly exhibit practices that are opposite to the rules of genealogical purity and inheritance of property and status from father to son. The ascendancy of the hereditary priesthood during the second temple supported by a centralized cult with a powerful written discourse of purity and pollution promoted an almost obsessive consciousness of sexual and kinship rules. Deut 7:1–5 provides the mandate for Israel to erase the other nations from the land and forbids intermarriage and dealings lest "they turn away your sons" from following God. The representation of the lustful gentile who is promiscuous about matters of paternity and ignorant of lawful kinship relations developed from patriarchal and patrilineal ideology and served as a foil to those ideals.

It is not the later Christian focus on Adam and Eve's moment of disobedience in the garden that stands behind chapters 1 and 7 of Romans, but the story of the gentile peoples as a part of Israel's story. In Romans, this view of gentiles has been Hellenized by a retelling of the narrative in terms of the inner mythology of moral psychology. This was not a unique way of conceptualizing the other in the Greco-Roman world. A most fascinating parallel comes to us through Diodorus of Sicily. He draws on the Egyptian historian Hecataeus of Abdera for the following and precedes the passage with a discussion of how even Egyptian kings had to follow the law (*nomos*):

> And in doing what custom required in these matters, they did not become indignant or take offense in their souls, but rather they believed that they lived a most happy life. For they believed that all other men, in irrationally gratifying their natural passions, do many things which bring them injuries and perils, and that often some who know [*eidotas*] that they are about to sin [*hamartein*] nevertheless do base acts when overpowered by love or hate or some other passion, while they, on the other hand, by virtue of their having followed a manner of life which had been chosen before all others [or "judged superior to all others"] by the wisest of men, fell into the fewest faults. (1.71.3)

Here Egyptians prove superior to all the other peoples because they are able to do what they know is right by following their law rather than be overcome by their passions. Hecataeus characterizes the non-Egyptians with the Medean saying, They know what is right but are not able to do it because of their passions. But how is it that the Egyptians are morally superior in such a basic way? Their superiority results from their having a superior politeia, a better social, political, and cultural constitution. Jewish apologists like Philo and Josephus claimed exactly the same for Judaism: Its superior constitution, the divine law, made Jews typically more self-controlled, just, and humane than non-Jews. Jews could better control their passions.

Not only Jews and Egyptians related moral psychology to culture, but also Greeks and Romans. The Greek equivalent of Jew/gentile is Hellene (Greek)/barbarian. The latter classification was made with far wider criteria of taxonomy than just language. The taxonomic indicators for "barbarian" often included much of what we moderns mean by morals and culture. Even Galen, that sophisticated and most educated Greek in the center of the Roman world, has a Greek view of the other. After citing the famous words of Euripides' Medea about akrasia, Galen writes, "Taught by reason, doubtlessly she knows the greatness of the evils she is about to do, but she says that her anger gets the better of her reason, and therefore she is forcibly led by anger to commit the act. . . . Euripides has used Medea as an example of barbarians and uneducated people, in whom anger is stronger than reason; but among Greeks and educated [read Hellenized] people . . . reason prevails over anger" (*Hippoc. et Plat.* 3.189.20–190.1). Elsewhere (*Hippoc. et Plat.* 3.214.10–20) Galen explains that children, wild animals, and barbarians are often slaves of their desires (*epithumiai*).

Rom 1 and 6–7 draw on a Jewish version of a widespread Greco-Roman way of portraying the other. The free adult male of your own people constitutes the norm. As the scale moves away from him, the other becomes less rational and more emotional on the scale of self-mastery. A foreign woman like Medea is doubly dangerous. Jews, Greeks, Romans, and Egyptians all had their own frames of reference, which in Paul's time had been made somewhat ambiguous because of the political dominance of Rome and the cultural dominance of the Greeks. Sexual transgressions and rules of purity and pollution loom large in such conceptions of the other to the extent that the societies are patrilineal or otherwise constructed around lineage and descent. Such societies practice animal or some other form of sacrifice. Since the patrilineal principle of earlier times had been modified and weakened among Greeks, Romans, and Jews, a new order arose that is reflected in the ethic of self-mastery. In Paul's time both codes coexisted and competed. The centrality of the one temple with its hereditary priesthoods, however, reinforced the principles of birth and purity of descent for Jews. The very fact that the Judaism which emerged after the end of the temple so radically moved the focus from ascription by descent to achievement in studying Torah serves as a measure of how important pure blood had been in Paul's time. On the other hand, certain strains of Judaism and Israelite religion that downplayed blood and stressed achievement had always existed.[6] Adaptation to the complexities of the Greco-Roman world made the tension between the two principles even more complex. Thus Paul's talk of gentile immorality, mastery by sexual passions, the theme of works versus adoptive kinship, and his very mission is concerned with working out tensions inherent in Judaism and in similar societies in which purity of birth had been central but achievement had gained a major role.

Ambiguity lay in Paul's own situation. His basic categories for humans are Jew and gentile. He recognizes the dominance of Greek culture in the Roman East by interchanging "gentile" and "Greek." At the same time, however, he views the

---

6. So, for instance, Isa 56:1–8 defines Jewish identity so much by lawkeeping that even foreigners can become Israelites.

world from a Greek perspective. The non-Jewish part of humanity, the gentiles, can be divided into two parts, Greeks and barbarians (Rom 1:13–14). His native language is also Greek. Someone who does not speak Greek is for him a barbarian (1 Cor 14:11). Whatever Paul's Greekness, and the evidence seems to be that it was great, in his self-conception he has assimilated it to his Jewishness.

* * *

All of Paul's rhetoric, including his concern to argue for gentle equality and to argue against gentile judaizing, makes sense if we suppose that Paul's literary audience represents something like those who have traditionally been called godfearers in modern scholarship.[7] From beginning to end, Romans presupposes an audience that consists of gentiles who had or still have a lively interest in Judaism. Such people existed and most likely made up the bulk of the early gentile converts to Christ. Those who know the law in 7:1 were formerly enslaved to their passions and desires while they submitted to the law (7:4–6). Paul supposes that all gentiles are in some sense "under the law" and responsible for teachings that apply to gentiles. The *person* in 7:7–25 whom Paul so carefully constructs by means of prosōpopoiia, however, seems more specific. That person represents those caught between two cultures. Like Medea, he cannot submit to a foreign law because his gentile passions will not allow it. Rom 7:7–25 represents the judaizing gentile's ambiguous status. Neither fully Jew nor fully Greek, he is torn between the passions of an idolator and the law of the one true God.

According to a long, influential line of Western interpretation, Rom 7 and 8 contrast the Jewish and Christian self-understanding. I believe it a great tragedy that generations of Christians have seen Jews through these dark lenses. The currently most influential commentator has written of 7:7–13, "First, it is to be maintained under all circumstances that the apostle is speaking of mankind under the law, or specifically of the pious Jew."[8] In a recent study, Gerd Theissen unfortunately falls into this Western reading.[9] He even makes the chapter autobiographical, a description of Paul's struggle as a Pharisee from the later Christian perspective.[1] In this Western reading, the linchpin is usually pride. The human or the Jewish crime is pride. Jews may be outwardly virtuous and good but their good behavior is at the base evil because it is motivated by pride. Again the ghost of Augustine lives on. But Paul says nothing about pride or anxiety or overachievement. These interpreters have to argue that the concepts are hidden but assumed in the concepts of "sin" and "doing the law."

The ten commandments must have been basic to what gentiles who wanted to identify with Judaism were taught. When Paul caricatures the works of the law that a Jewish teacher taught to gentiles, he cites three commandments from the Decalogue (2:21–22). The gentile *persona* in 7:7 gives the commandment against

---

7. Scott McKnight, *A Light among the Gentiles: Jewish Missionary Activity in the Second Temple Period* (Minneapolis: Fortress Press, 1991), chaps. 6, 7.

8. [Ernst] Käsemann, [*Commentary on*] *Romans* [trans. Geoffrey W. Bromiley (Grand Rapids, MI: Eerdmans, 1980)], 195. Käsemann does recognize that Jews did not understand their own experience in this way.

9. Theissen, *Psychological Aspects.*

1. Ibid., 241–42.

covetousness as an example of what he was taught. This prohibition was given a special significance by Jews who wanted to show the correspondence of Jewish teaching and the Greco-Roman ethic of self-mastery. The LXX's use of *epithumia* to translate the Hebrew allowed Jews like Philo and the author of 4 Maccabees to claim that the Jewish law agreed with Greek moral psychology in its emphasis on the passions as the source of evil impulses. Furthermore, following the appropriate commandments from the Jewish law was an extraordinarily potent therapy for the ravages of rampant desire. Translations introduce an entirely alien idea when they render *epithumēseis* in 7:7 as "you shall not covet," rather than "you shall not desire," hiding the connections with the motif of gentile desire and Paul's Hellenistic conceptualities.

The dilemma of the gentile who tries to base his life on works of the law appears in 7:8–11. Although the law reveals that desire is sin, it can do little to change the fact that *epithumia* forms a fundamental aspect of his character. The gentile ruled by his God-ordained slavery to the desire arising from passions experiences the law against desire as a deceitful, almost teasing condemnation (7:8–11). Instead of controlling excessive desire, the commandment stimulates desire in accordance with God's punishment and adds a knowledge of God's condemnation. Perhaps Paul thought that the gentile was definitively socialized in one way, the Jew in another or that each carried the characteristics of his ancestors. He definitely believed that lifting a few commandments out of the Jewish politeia could only lead the gentile to a knowledge of his bondage to sin and the penalties of God's wrath. Behind Paul's caricature may lie sociological realities. Gentile godfearers may have aspired to live by certain Jewish teachings, but they still lived in gentile society. Could a gentile living in such circumstances really be expected to forge for himself a life truly pleasing to God? The attendant schizophrenia might even make matters worse.

Rather than merely repeat and elaborate the mythological discourse of Hellenistic moral psychology and its ideology, one must understand the social constructions indicated in such discourse. Paul, of course, employs the Hellenistic discourse and not social analysis. Indeed, the discourse often functions to mask these realities. Romans 7 stands forth as a Jewish Christian adaptation of Greco-Roman discourse about the problem of akrasia, in service of an argument against gentiles attempting to gain self-mastery by following the law. Rom 6–8 uses "sin" in a way similar to the concept of *akolasia*, a set disposition to do wrong. Paul adds the assumption that sin is wrongdoing offensive to God and his law. In Hellenistic moral thought, habitual akrasia becomes *akolasia*. Ancient moralists debated as to whether akrasia, weakness of will or lack of self-mastery, was caused by ignorance and false belief or by passions inherent in human nature. In light of modern study, both approaches vastly oversimplify the problem, but the Stoics had the most sophisticated analysis, attributing akrasia to false beliefs and ignorance. Paul in crucial respects sides with the popular and Platonic view against the Stoics. Knowledge alone cannot cure gentile akrasia. Merely knowing the teachings of the law fails to solve the problem. Using the popular view, Romans explains akrasia in terms of desire arising from passions (similar to our emotions and appetites).

Again using the popular and Platonic view, Romans 7 divides the person between a true self identified with the mind or rationality and a lower or false self identified with the body or the flesh. According to Paul, the passions and desire reside in the flesh or the body and its parts (Gal 5:16, 24; Rom 6:12–13, cf. 1:26–27; 7:5, 18, 22; 8:3). The mind rationally apprehends and wills to do the law (7:22), but since it has been corrupted by the turn to idolatry (1:21–22, 28), the desires of the flesh overcome it. Only a mind renewed by infusion with God's Spirit can enable the gentile to resist the flesh and act according to God's law (8:5–8). Thus the law is not the problem but also not the answer (7:9–13, 16; 8:3a). The problem stems from God withholding his divine Spirit from gentiles who are thus not related to him as children (8:12–30) and cannot master the flesh (8:2–11). God effected gentile redemption from the flesh by making his son the pioneer of the movement from life dominated by the flesh to life dominated by the Spirit. Redeemed gentiles do not leave the body for a spiritual existence but are incorporated into Christ's mode of life by infusion with God's (also called Christ's) life principle (spirit/*pneuma*).

* * *

The gentiles need a new mind to replace the mind corrupted by idolatry (1:21, 22, 28). The gentile who is torn between his will to follow the law of God and the life of the flesh cries out in 7:24 asking for a savior. Verse 25 is best read as a parenthetic interjection of the authorial voice within the speech of the imaginary persona. The person's speech continues and concludes in v. 25. Paul then ends his prosōpopoiia by addressing the imaginary gentile in 8:1–2. The apostle tells him that he is freed from condemnation and from the law of sin and death through the Spirit of Jesus Christ, which will effect a renewed mind (8:1–11).

J. ALBERT HARRILL

The Slave Self: Paul and the Discursive "I"†

The Problem

The Apostle Paul considers the inner subjectivity of a slave in Romans 7, one of the most important and controversial passages on the self in the Christian Bible. The traditional reading, which goes back to Augustine, credits Paul with centering his attention on the split internal to the individual and the resulting incapacity of the self to carry out its own will. Augustine first took the passage to depict the introspective conscience of the unregenerate human, and later came to identify Paul's words, assumed to be autobiographical, with his own agonizing struggle against sin, described in the *Confessions*. Interpreting his own conversion retrospectively, in light of the Platonic myth of the soul (its alienation from the good and its return), Augustine created from Romans 7 a normative model of the religious self, which in Western culture has become the archetype for inquiry into the individual, influencing Thomas Aquinas, Martin Luther, John Calvin, and the Protestant

---

† From J. Albert Harrill, *Slaves in the New Testament: Literary, Social, and Moral Dimensions* (Minneapolis: Fortress, 2006), 17–31, 206–12. All notes are Harrill's.

Reformation, as well as Søren Kierkegaard and Sigmund Freud. Biblical scholars advancing this psychologizing model of the self assume that the mythical picture of bondage and helplessness in Romans 7 is direct testimony of Paul's interior, subjective religious life. The claim is that the voice is both personal and realistic.[1]

Viewing Paul's letters from the perspective of Greco-Roman literary conventions, however, sharpens the problem of this psychologizing approach to the ancient Christian self. One of the successes of modern biblical criticism is the discovery that there is little indication that Paul understood himself or the typical convert to be a person who had previously agonized under a subjective sense of incapacitating guilt. In the rare places where Paul speaks about his former life in Judaism, he does so with pride (Gal 1:13–14; Phil 3:4–6).[2] It is therefore unlikely that the first-person singular in Rom 7:7–25 is Paul voicing his inner struggle of his "preconversion" experience, or that it includes the apostle at all. While the particular identification of the *egō* ("I") does not matter to my argument—my point is that the persona is enslaved—I follow current scholarship that identifies Paul's subject as a fictive "I," specifically, the technique of "speech-in-character" (*prosōpopoiia*) familiar from Greco-Roman rhetoric and literature, which I find to be the most convincing explanation of the text.[3] The question that I bring to the text is how an ancient *Roman* audience would have most likely heard Paul's discursive "I," especially in a letter whose opening words assert a slave persona: "Paul, a slave of Jesus Christ" (Rom 1:1).

Speech-in-Character and the Slave Persona

Prosōpopoiia is the introduction of a character whose speech represents not that of the author but that of another person or an invented persona.[4] The technique played a central role in the hypothetical situations posed for declamatory exercises, the preliminary rhetorical drills in formal Roman education, which closely followed Greek teaching methods. The teacher (*grammaticus* or *rhetor*) would ask the student to compose poetry or prose, for the purposes of recitation, by imagining what a certain type of person would say to another in a given situation. The identification of the speaking voice and characters formed particular reading habits attuning the student's ear to standard interpretative conventions of oral speech used in written texts, teaching him or her to ask "Who is speaking?"—a critical skill in an ancient culture where readers faced texts containing dialogues that had

1. For example, Gerd Theissen, *Psychological Aspects of Pauline Theology* (Philadelphia: Fortress Press, 1987), 177–265, in spite of admitting that the *egō* is discursive and a rhetorical device.
2. Wayne A. Meeks, *The First Urban Christians: The Social World of the Apostle Paul* (2d ed.; New Haven: Yale University Press, 2003), 186; the fundamental article is Krister Stendahl, "The Apostle Paul and the Introspective Conscience of the West," in idem, *Paul among Jews and Gentiles and Other Essays* (Philadelphia: Fortress Press, 1976), 78–96 [see above, pp. 1426–36].
3. First proposed in 1929 by Werner Georg Kümmel and reprinted as *Römer 7 und das Bild des Menschen im Neuen Testament: Zwei Studien* (Munich: C. Kaiser, 1974), 1–160. Stanley K. Stowers, "Romans 7.7–25 as a Speech-in-Character (*prosōpopoiia*)," in *Paul in His Hellenistic Context* (ed. Troels Engberg-Pedersen; Edinburgh: T. & T. Clark, 1994), 180–202; idem, [A] *Rereading* [of] *Romans* [: *Justice, Jews, and Gentiles* (New Haven: Yale University Press, 1994)], 264–73 [see above, pp. 1436–48].
4. This paragraph and the next follows the excellent discussion in Stowers, *Rereading Romans*, 16–21 (and idem, "Speech-in-Character," 180–91), with further literature cited there.

no punctuation, no word division, and nothing to indicate change of speakers. Importantly for our study of Romans 7, the exercise figured prominently for training in letter writing.

The technique of speech-in-character is commonplace in Greek and Roman literature. The best evidence comes from Cicero, Quintilian, and the extant handbooks *progymnasmata* (preliminary rhetorical exercises).[5] Aelius Theon of Alexandria, a rhetor of the first century C.E., explains in his handbook that speech-in-character consists of both cases in which one invents through conventional diction the character (*ēthos*) of a known person (*prosōpon*) and cases in which one invents both the *ēthos* and the person. In the latter case, the student conforms the words of the invented persona—the self—to fit the moral habits and inner dispositions of a recognizable stock type, often taken from Greek and Roman drama, such as a husband, soldier, braggart, barbarian, or the slave.[6] While to me the argument that Paul employs this latter case of speech-in-character to invent both the *ēthos* and persona of the "I" in Romans 7 is convincing,[7] what remains unclear in this reading is why a *slave* is chosen for the persona.

Paul writes, "I delight in the law of God in my inmost self (*kata ton esō anthrō-pon*), but I see in my members another law at war with the law of my mind, making me captive to the law of sin that dwells in my members" (Rom 7:22–23). As many commentators have shown, Paul refers to the Greek philosophical concept of an "inner" versus an "outer" human being, an idea of the self that originated from Platonic tradition, going back to the ninth book of the *Republic*. Scholarship emphasizes that although the Platonic tradition identifies the "inner human being" with the *psychē* (soul), *nous* (mind), or *pneuma* (spirit), Paul considers the "inner human being" not to have a higher status than the "outer human being" but thinks that both are two aspects of the same *anthrōpos*, a non-dualistic entity. What commentators overlook in their analysis of "Pauline anthropology" is that Paul does not describe a generic or "typical" *anthrōpos* but one pointedly characterized as enslaved, having specific connotations in the slaveholding culture of Roman imperial society. In the rush to analyze the Platonic "background" of Pauline theology, there has been no serious inquiry into why Paul chooses the persona of the slave as his model of the *anthrōpos* containing both an "outer" and "innermost" self.

At first glance, the slave seems an unlikely model of the *anthrōpos*, if we follow the formal definitions of the slave in Greek philosophy. Aristotle and his epigones claim that the slave does not have the very "inner self" that Paul's speech-in-character requires. Aristotle writes that because the slave is deficient in many

5. Sources: George A. Kennedy, *Progymnasmata: Greek Textbooks of Prose Composition and Rhetoric* (Atlanta: SBL, 2003), 47–49, 115–17, 164–66, 213–17.
6. Aelius Theon, *Progymnasmata* 8 (115–18); Michel Patillon with Giancarlo Bolognesi, eds., *Aelius Théon: Progymnasmata* (Paris: Les Belles Lettres, 1997), 70–71. See also James R. Butts, "The Progymnasmata of Theon: A New Text with Translation and Commentary" (Ph.D. diss., The Claremont Graduate School, 1986), 445–64; Kennedy, *Progymnasmata*, 48 and 214 (slave speech-in-character); and W. Martin Bloomer, "Schooling in Persona: Imagination and Subordination in Roman Education," *Classical Antiquity* 16 (1997): 57–78.
7. For a persuasive reply to objections, see Stanley K. Stowers, "Apostrophe, *Prosōpopoiia* and Paul's Rhetorical Education," in *Early Christianity and Classical Culture: Comparative Studies in Honor of Abraham J. Malherbe* (ed. John T. Fitzgerald, Thomas H. Olbricht, and L. Michael White; Leiden: Brill, 2003), 351–69.

human essentials, such as emotion, virtue, reason, and deliberative powers, the slave is only a partial (outer, bodily) self whose actions are incomplete. Since the slave's actions are incomplete, the slave is and ought to be an "animate tool" (*empsychon organon*) of someone else.[8] After arguing the inherent naturalness (goodness) of slavery, Aristotle raises the subsequent, independent question of whether some slaves are "natural" slaves. His comments on this second topic are, to be sure, scattered and inconsistent, but his overarching theme is clear: the relationship of master and slave in the family is the paradigm that grounds and naturalizes all human relationships of domination. Later Hellenistic and Roman writers, particularly among the Peripatetic school, develop Aristotelian ideas of the natural slave into a coherent theory with detailed elaboration and systemization in technical handbooks on physiognomics, as we shall see in the next chapter. In this theory, the slave's body, by virtue of its very anatomy, is biologically built for servitude. The natural slave is a deficient *anthrōpos*, without the faculty of reason, a human subspecies assimilated to irrational beasts requiring taming and domestication.

Greeks in general defined the slave, like the animal, in terms of its body alone. A common word in Greek for "slave" was simply "body" (*sōma*); other ancient terms included "boy" (Greek *pais*; Latin *puer*), "rogue" (that is, someone who needs a whipping: *mastigia*; *verbero*), "garbage" (*katharma*), and "man-footed creature" (*andrapodon*), the last term derived from a common word for cattle (*tetrapodon*).[9] The somatic vocabulary reflects a cultural habit that tended to define the slave by its (my use of neuter is pointed) outer corporality alone—a mere "body." The semantic and philosophical evidence, therefore, makes Paul's case of a speech-in-character, in which an invented slave persona communicates thoughts from an "innermost self" (and not, as we would expect, the flesh or bodily members), curious. Significantly, the passage in Romans 7 expresses no need to argue that "the slave" has an innermost self. Paul simply presumes that a slave character would naturally have one, and proceeds with the speech. If Paul expected that his encoded Gentile readers (Rom 1:5–6, 13; 15:15–16) would immediately associate the speech-in-character with a recognizable stock type whose special trademark was the innermost self and would thereby catch his wider meaning about baptism, "the slave" seems a poor choice. In classical Greek philosophy, ideology, and even vocabulary the slave has neither a "self" nor an interior experience. The passage does not make sense in the philosophical history-of-ideas context of standard biblical commentary.

Examining Romans 7 in a context wider than Greek philosophy makes Paul's choice of an enslaved *anthrōpos*, to depict the inner and outer aspects of the religious self, more intelligible. Key is attention to different social constructions of the slave in classical culture, focusing on Roman and not Greek (Athenian) ideologies of slavery. The focus on Roman sources serves as a methodological control against exclusive reliance on Aristotle or Plato to interpret the passage and

8. Aristotle, *Politics* 1.1252a–56a; *Nicomachean Ethics* 8.1161b; Eugene Garver, "Aristotle's Natural Slaves: Incomplete *Praxeis* and Incomplete Human Beings," *Journal of the History of Philosophy* 32 (1994): 173–95.
9. Keith Hopkins, "Novel Evidence for Roman Slavery," *Past and Present* 138 (1993): 23; Keith R. Bradley, "Animalizing the Slave: The Truth of Fiction," *Journal of Roman Studies* 90 (2000): 110–11; and Jennifer A. Glancy, *Slavery in Early Christianity* (New York: Oxford University Press, 2002), 3–38.

its ideas of slavery. In contrast to Aristotelian ideas of the slave being only an outer "body" without interior rationality or agency, the main Roman (Stoic) ideology required the ideal slave to possess reason and virtue (*logos* and *aretē*).

Roman law recognized the slave to have inner subjectivity and moral agency. Influential on this principle were Stoic ideas of common humanity, organic cosmology, and fate. A condition of fate and not of nature, slavery in Roman legal categorization belonged to the law of nations (*ius gentium*), by which, contrary to nature (*contra naturam*), one person is subjected to the power (*dominium*) of another. Remarkably, this case is the only one in the entire extant corpus of Roman private law in which the *ius gentium* and the *ius naturale* are in conflict.[1] The legal material reveals also the enormous importance of slaves in commercial and other acquisitions. The centrality of trusted managerial slaves on rural estates, which Roman agricultural writers emphasize, parallels the urban household situation envisioned in the legal texts. Partly because masters employed their slaves as de facto agents, Roman law lacked a concept of agency in the modern sense of a free person representing another—one reason why a slave was often more useful to his master in business transactions than a free client. The importance in the Roman economy and society of trusted slaves who often worked independently and in locations outside the master's hometown rests on an ideology that the master did not need to supervise every decision a slave agent made. The Roman notion of mastery defined the ideal slave not in terms of obedience to individual commands of the master but in terms of having accepted the master's wishes so fully that the slave's innermost self could anticipate the master's wishes and take the initiative. Romans did not want automatons for their slaves.

The Slave as Automaton and the Art of Authority

Roman moral philosophy used the slave automaton and the comedy of its ineffectiveness to teach the art of authority. The *Life of Aesop* (*Vita Aesopi*) offers an illustration. Although the legendary figure of Aesop originates from the early Greek period, the extant biography was written no earlier than the time of the Roman Empire. The *Life of Aesop* is a romance based on themes found in the fables, a repository of slave-savant anecdotes about Aesop and his hapless master, Xanthos, a so-called philosopher. A recurring theme of the biography is Aesop's philosophical game of cat and mouse with his master. Xanthos looks for excuses to beat his slave. Aesop, in turn, evades punishment by his ingenious "misunderstandings" of the orders, repeatedly receiving opportunities to lecture his master on the meaning of self-control and proper household authority. This willful misbehavior frustrates Xanthos (and his wife) so completely that Xanthos finally orders Aesop to act like an automaton, to do nothing more or less than what his commands literally demand. Of course, this move only leads to further situation comedy as Aesop takes his master exactly at his word. Going to the baths, Xanthos

---

1. Justinian, *Institutiones* 1.3.2; *Digesta* 1.5.4.1; W. W. Buckland, *The Roman Law of Slavery: The Conditions of the Slave in Private Law from Augustus to Justinian* (New York: AMS Press, 1969), 1. Translations of the *Digesta* are from *The Digest of Justinian* (4 vols.; ed. Theodor Mommsen with Paul Krueger; trans. Alan Watson; Philadelphia: University of Pennsylvania Press, 1985), altered when not sufficiently literal for my purposes.

instructs Aesop, "to pick up the oil flask." Aesop picks up the flask but not the oil. Xanthos orders the slave home to "cook lentil" for a dinner party. Aesop tosses a single legume into the cooking pot. Xanthos tells Aesop to give his dinner guests "something to drink, right from the bath." Aesop returns with a pitcher full of bathing swill. Succeeding in driving Xanthos nearly mad, Aesop explains that his demonstrations are the same a philosopher would use with students: "You shouldn't have been so precise in laying down the law, and I would have served you properly. But don't feel sorry about it, master. The way you decreed the law to me will be useful to you, for it will teach you not to make mistakes in the classroom. Statements that include or exclude too much are no small mistakes." The moral is that one's subordinate has a self. When they want subordinates to act as automatons—that is, without a self—masters have only themselves to blame for the resulting chaos in the household (and in the classroom). To be properly served, the master needs the slave to have agency and to take some initiative from interior subjectivity. The farcical comedy of the *Life of Aesop* teaches the moral philosophy of proper mastery.

That mastery was *auctoritas*, which routed power through patterns of personalized influence rather than through abstract institutions such as bureaucracy, wage labor, or public office. The Latin term—whose force was something like "influence" or making known one's will based on mutuality—was, as the Greek senator and historian Cassius Dio remarked, quintessentially Roman and untranslatable (Dio, *Roman History* 55.3.5). As I noted in the introduction, *auctoritas* denoted a quality of real power in the individual that colleagues and social lessers granted by willing compliance. * * *

* * *

This personalized view of power recognized subjectivity in the slave. *Auctoritas* was achieved in specific, concrete events in which the slave expressed acceptance of the master's point of view so fully as to anticipate the master's wishes. Rather than merely following individual orders in mechanical fashion, the good slave (*servus frugi*) completed and developed what the master had only suggested or even unconsciously desired—a task that in the practice of Roman slaveholding encouraged the actual slave to develop moral intuition. This social construction imagined the slave with an internal faculty of assent, a function of reason. The ideology reflects the Stoic philosophy of *prohairesis* [volition], which detached an essential self from the outer body ("the flesh") and identified it with an interior moral subject understood to be personal and individualized.[2] The Stoics stressed the importance of the self to such an extent that some scholars are tempted to say that they even discovered the concept.[3]

Personalization of the slave with this kind of subjective self is a central tenet in the Roman discourse of authority. Ancient authors discuss the hard work and

2. Epictetus, *Diatribai* 4.7.32; Seneca, *De Beneficiis* 3.20; *Ad Marciam de consolatione* 24.5; see A. A. Long, "Representation and the Self in Stoicism," in *Companions to Ancient Thought*, vol. 2: *Psychology* (ed. Stephen Everson; Cambridge: Cambridge University Press, 1991), 102–20.
3. Troels Engberg-Pedersen, "Stoic Philosophy and the Concept of the Person," in *The Person and the Human Mind: Issues in Ancient and Modern Philosophy* (ed. Christopher Gill; Oxford: Clarendon, 1990), 122.

constant maintenance that such mastery over a self requires. Epictetus warns his aristocratic students—teenaged masters themselves, and future householders—against allowing their happiness to depend upon the constant obedience of their slaves. "Nothing is got without a price," lectures the Stoic teacher. "And when you call your slave boy, bear in mind that it is possible that he may not heed you, and again, that even if he does heed, he may not do what you want done" (Epictetus, *Encheiridion* 12.2). In actual practice, mastery does not always work. Slaves do not always conform their innermost self to the master's will. Additionally, the moralist Plutarch recounts the "famous case" of a slave resisting mastery to illustrate a lesson about foolish chatter. Ironically, the case involves an orator. Plutarch writes:

> Pupius Piso, the orator, not wishing to be troubled, ordered his slaves to speak only in answer to questions and not a word alone. Subsequently, wishing to pay honour to Clodius when he was a magistrate, Piso gave orders that he be invited to dinner and prepared what was, we may suppose, a sumptuous banquet. When the hour came, the other guests were present, but Clodius was still expected, and Piso repeatedly sent the slave who regularly carried invitations to see if Clodius was approaching. And when evening came and he was finally despaired of, Piso said to his slave, "See here, did you give him the invitation?" "I did," said the slave. "Why hasn't he come then?" "Because he declined." "Then why didn't you tell me at once?" "Because you didn't ask me that." (Plutarch, *Moralia* 551d–e; Helmbold, LCL)

The anecdote resembles the episode discussed above in the *Life of Aesop* and is further evidence that the "automaton slave" is a stock comic type. Plutarch goes on to contrast the back talk of such a "typical Roman slave" with the poetic line an Athenian slave would say to his master, the moral of the story being that people often talk in habituated banter rather than with intelligence.

Cicero provides an additional example. He pleads:

> What law, what decree of the senate, what edict of the magistrates, what pact or agreement or even, if I may speak of the civil law, what will, what judgments or stipulations or formulae of agreement and contract could not be weakened and pulled apart, if we wanted to twist the substance to suit the words and leave unaccounted for the intentions, reasoning, and *auctoritas* of those who wrote the document? By god, everyday household language will make nonsense, if we try to pounce on each other's words; ultimately there would be no household authority (*imperium domesticum*) if we allowed our slaves to obey us in accordance with our words, and not comply with what we understand from the words.[4]

Cicero uses the private discourse of household mastery to illustrate by analogy the public discourse of *auctoritas*. He and the other authors above show the preva-

---

4. Cicero, *Pro Caecina* 51–52 (trans. [Kathleen] McCarthy, *Slaves, [Masters, and Art of Authority in Plautine Comedy* (Princeton, NJ: Princeton University Press, 2000),] 23 n. 36).

lence of *auctoritas* in Roman culture across the board, from education and moral philosophy to law, rhetoric, and religious/political ideology.

This cultural context is critical for the interpretation of Romans 7 because Paul uses the ideology of *auctoritas*, with its model of the slave self, to influence his Roman audience. Establishing this thesis requires locating Roman cultural influence not only on Paul himself but also on early Christians broadly, since Paul's encoded audience, though Gentile, is not "Pauline" in the sense of having the apostle as its founder. Paul had not visited Rome and had not established any of the congregations in that city (see Rom 1:10–15). Comprehensive examination of the Roman imperial context of early Christianity is beyond the scope of my exegetical study, and it hardly needs repeating.

The Parable of the Talents/Pounds

As a prelude to the exegesis of Romans 7, one example of what I find to be the best source outside of the Pauline material must suffice: the parable of the Talents/Pounds. In Matthew's version, a man "going on a journey" summons three slaves and entrusts talents to each "according to his ability" (Matt 25:15). Predictably, and almost as a setup, the slave having the least ability, and so entrusted only with a single talent (his inherent character flaws made explicit in the narrative's introduction), fails to prove his usefulness and worth. While the slave complies with the literal commands, he is "useless" because he has not internalized the master's will that the ideology of *auctoritas* required. Ironically, the paralysis causing the slave to act like an automaton stems from fear of merciless punishment for failure to obey, his master being characterized as a "harsh man" (25:24–25). The slave hides the money in a hole, whereas his more able fellows go out and trade with the talents to make more (25:16–18). The master, in Matthew's reasoning, rightly rewards the entrepreneurship of the good slaves, who receive more responsibility in the household and "enter into the joy of [their] master" (25:21–22), and punishes the bad. "You wicked and lazy slave!" the master yells at the terrified piece of chattel. "You knew, did you not, that I reap where I did not sow, and gather where I did not scatter? Then you ought to have invested my money with the bankers, and on my return I would have received what was my own with interest" (25:26–27). The master then gives the slave the beating of his life: "As for this worthless slave, throw him into the outer darkness, where there will be weeping and gnashing of teeth," the master said, employing domestic torturers used regularly for such purpose (25:30).[5]

The author of Matthew makes explicit his contrast of the "good slave" (who shows loyalty to an absent master) and the "bad slave" (who does not), two stock types in tales of *apsente ero* (when the master's away) familiar from ancient comedy. This contrast echoes what Cicero and Plutarch say above and is a further example story (moral *exemplum*) of the distinctively Roman ideology of

5. Roman masters, weary of the effort, often hired the services of professional torturers; see Moses I. Finley, *Ancient Slavery and Modern Ideology* (enlarged ed.; ed. Brent D. Shaw; Princeton, N.J.: Markus Wiener, 1998), 163; Keith R. Bradley, *Slaves and Masters in the Roman Empire: A Study in Social Control* (1984; repr., New York: Oxford University Press, 1987), 118–23; and Richard Saller, "The Family and Society," in *Epigraphic Evidence: Ancient History from Inscriptions* (ed. John Bodel; London: Routledge, 2001), 111.

auctoritas—personalized power channeled through the master's ethos. The bland moralistic division into good and bad, which the slave parables of the Synoptic Gospels advance, makes the connection to Roman slaveholding ideology (and its stock of comic slave types) even more likely.

*   *   *

Romans 7 and the Slave Self

Paul incorporates Roman slaveholding ideology, the cultivation of the interior motivation of the slave by *auctoritas*, into his discussion of baptism (Rom 6:6–14) and into his speech-in-character (Rom 7:14–25). The opening chapters establish interior motivation as a central theme in Paul's definition of the religious self. First, a set of antitheses (concerning God's impartiality) underscores the point: "visible" (*en tō phanerō*) versus "in secret" (*en tō kryptō*); "on the fleshly surface" (*en sarki*) versus "from the heart" (*kardias*); "literal" (*en grammati*) versus "spiritual" (*en pneumati*) (Rom 2:28–29). Next, Paul reassures his readers that Christ has redeemed them from a curse; by agreeing to go to and die on a cross, Christ displayed trust (*pistis*) in God and his promises, and in so doing generated a proper relationship with God on the model of Abraham's faithfulness to God and the covenant (Rom 3:21–33). The term *pistis* (faith) here carries the sense of faithfulness or trust ("obedience"), not "belief" as in the traditional theological reading.[6] Paul then encourages his readers to think about their participation in the Christ event during the ritual of baptism, knowledge being an explicit warrant for the exhortations: "We know that our old self was crucified with him, so that the body of sin might be destroyed, and we are no longer enslaved to sin (*douleuein hēmas tē hamartia*)" (6:6). Paul asks rhetorically:

> Do you not know that if you present yourselves to anyone as obedient slaves (*doulous eis hypakoēn*), you are slaves of the one whom you obey, either of sin, which leads to death, or of obedience (*hypakoēs*), which leads to (God's) righteousness (*dikaiosynēn*)? But thanks be to God that you, having once been slaves of sin (*douloi tēs hamartias*), have become obedient from the heart (*hypēkousate de ek kardias*) to the standard of the teaching to which you were entrusted, and that you, having been set free from sin (*eleutherōthentes de apo tēs hamartias*), have become slaves of (God's) righteousness (*edoulōthēte tē dikaiosynē*). (6:16–18)

The slave speech-in-character of chapter 7 follows, leading into chapter 8, where Paul expresses apocalyptic knowledge that "creation itself will be set free from its slavery to decay and will obtain freedom" (Rom 8:21). Paul portrays "creation" (8:19) as a person enslaved to the wrong master and suffering under Sin's domination, one of four agents (including the Spirit [8:26], God [8:31–33], and Christ

---

6. The exegetical debate on the "faith of Christ" question has too long a history to repeat here. See Stowers, *Rereading Romans*, 194–226, and literature cited there; see also Jouette M. Bassler, review of *Rereading Romans*, by Stowers, *Journal of Biblical Literature* 115 (1996): 365–68.

[8:34]) personified as friends having all emotions in common. The whole section (Romans 6–8) argues against Gentile adherence to the law, by pairing the law with slavery under Sin.

Redemption from the Persona of Sin

In this context, sin is not something the self does (as in a "crime"), but a personalized demonic power that victimizes the self by residing in the self's fleshly "members" (where sinful passions are located) when the self hears the holy law.[7] The Gentile self remains devoted to God's law but is nonetheless powerless to achieve what it wants, even doing the very opposite of what it avoids (7:18–19). The conflict is not between two different selves, nor two selves at different levels—such as the "rational self" (*nous*) and "irrational self" (*sōma*) in the Platonic tradition—as though one were under the power of Sin and the other not. Both "innermost self" and "members" are two facets of the same self that is "sold under sin" (6:14).

Paul does not, then, simply repeat Platonizing concepts of the self but thinks in terms of a whole *anthrōpos* (both *nous* and *sōma*, but without the flesh [*sarx*]) that will be saved. To be sure, there is an apocalyptic dualism, but not in anthropology. Paul speaks about two different laws—the holy law of God and a demonic law (not just "another law") called the "law of sin," which resides in the outer members of the religious self. The speech-in-character declares allegiance and delight in the first (7:22) and then reports discovery of the second (7:23). The eschatological hope of salvation is not *release of the soul* from the body but *redemption of the self* (the pneumatic *sōma*) from the "law of sin and death" (8:2) for enslavement to God, where it belongs. The problem is not slavery per se, but slavery to the wrong master.

The slavery is also partial and chaotic. The demonic power of Sin possesses external "members" but not the "innermost" part of the religious self, which still delights in the law of God. For this reason, Paul reminds his readers that baptism does not bring a complete end of sinning (in the judicial sense of committing crimes and vice; hence the moral exhortation in Romans 14–15) or manumission from Sin itself (in the participationist sense of a demonic power). The apocalyptic drama imagined has the religious self caught in the eschatological tension of "already and not yet," forced to work against its will like a captured war slave, but already experiencing partial effects of God's redemption because of baptism. Set against an enemy in battle (*antistrateuomenon*) and captured as prisoner of war (*aichmalōtizonta*; cf. 2 Cor 10:3), the self is locked in close-arms combat (Rom 7:23). Paul's imagery of face-to-face fighting corresponds to the visual representation of armed conflict in Greece and Rome that localized all actions to immediate partners or opponents, limited to the reach of the person's limbs and weapons (depicting the individual as part of a comprehensive whole, such as providential Destiny [Fortuna; Tychē]). In Roman depictions, as opposed to Greek, brute physical strength of the enemy loses out to superior technical skill and static loyalty.

---

7. Leander E. Keck, "The Absent Good: The Significance of Rom 7:18a," in *Text und Geschichte: Facetten theologischen Arbeitens aus dem Freundes- und Schülerkreis Dieter Lührmann zum 60. Geburtstag* (ed. Stefan Maser and Egbert Schlarb; Marburg: Elwert, 1999), 68–69.

Paul incorporates the Roman visual representation of close-arms combat into his mental construct of apocalyptic battle. The sustained military imagery typecasts the "I" character as captured but still having a punch, and the loyal hope of ultimate victory, in its self.

Paul's letter evokes the military culture of Rome by use of another cultural symbol—*auctoritas*. The apocalyptic drama personalizes God's power and authority over Sin and other demonic war enemies. Gentile converts are captives of Sin, slaves whom God has now "bought with a price" (see 1 Cor 6:20; 7:23). In Paul's gospel, Christ had demonstrated *pistis* (faithfulness, trust, obedience) to God. Converts must likewise accept God's point of view so fully as to anticipate the divine personal will and to make it effective in the world, even when the Eschaton is not yet present. This theme corresponds to the classical Roman topos of the "faithful slave," who acts and dies on behalf of her or his master (*de fide servorum*).[8] For Paul, baptism is the concrete ritual moment moving the catechumen away from an "I" (the subject of the individual as the normative locus) and toward identification of that subject with Christ. Comparable to the Stoic theory of *oikeiōsis* (appropriation, or taking as one's own), this transference of subjectivity is believed by Paul to be a direct consequence of a transformation in the individual self. The Pauline view of God's mastery recognizes the subjectivity and agency of the converted religious self and sees that true authority consists not in obeying individual commands—as in the automaton who misunderstands, and who obeys only literal instructions of the law—but in total directness toward God.

Paul's overarching combat language echoes themes not only in Jewish apocalyptic eschatology and Roman military culture but also in ancient Mediterranean terms generally that symbolized slavery with the language of "death" and "life." The classic statement comes from Roman law and its discussion on the etymological root of the Latin word for slave: "Slaves (*servi*) are so-called, because generals have a custom of selling their prisoners and thereby preserving (*servare*) rather than killing them: and indeed they are said to be *mancipia*, because they are captives in the hand (*manus*) of their enemies" (*Digesta* 1.5.4.2–3). In Pauline understanding, catechumens present themselves *as if* they were brought from death to life (6:13; note the baptismal cry in 8:15; cf. 7:25), with baptism participating in Christ's death and resurrection. The theme of "being dead to" also confirms for ancient studies the interpretative value of modern definitions of slavery as a "social death."[9] In addition, Paul's theological statements on baptism connect directly to his paraenesis [exhortation] later in the letter, a central plank of which is obedience to Rome's governing authorities (Rom 13:1–7). The paraenesis further confirms Paul's full participation and deep implication in the Augustan imperial ideology of *auctoritas*.[1]

8. E.g., Valerius Maximus 6.8.1–7. To Valerius, such faithfulness was not just an instance of *fides* [faithfulness], but of *benevolentia* [good will] and *pietas* [piety] as well.
9. Orlando Patterson, *Slavery and Social Death: A Comparative Study* (Cambridge, Mass.: Harvard University Press, 1982), 35–76 passim; and J. Albert Harrill, *The Manumission of Slaves in Early Christianity* (Tübingen: Mohr [Siebeck], 1995), 1, 15–17, 32.
1. Paul's advice in Rom 13:1–7 presupposes Christians sharing in the special relationship of Jewish communities to Roman rule. Paul reuses a traditional piece of Jewish paraenesis that was formed in the Greek synagogue, to address *auctoritas* directly: Jewish rights under Roman rule come with mutual

Conclusion

Paul, in the final analysis, does not present a polemical argument against slavery as an ideology or institution in the Roman world. The dramatic persona of "the slave" served Paul as a rhetorical device for thinking about community, social categorization, hierarchy, and one's relation to the divine. The subject of Paul's speech-in-character (Rom 7:14–25) presented for an ancient Roman audience a recognizable stock voice of the slave self. Defining *pietas* [piety] in his gospel, the apostle uses the slave, and especially the trope of the faithful slave (*de fide servorum*), to "think with." Paul offers the slave experience of disassociation by change of owners as a metaphor for the situation of Gentile converts. The metaphor also corresponds to the Stoic philosophy of *prohairesis* (volition) that urged the integrity of the individual self in the face of moral slavery to the passions. Paul could not have been unaware that Gentile converts could not completely forget their former life in paganism. Using stereotypes about slaves familiar from wider "pagan" culture, Paul aims to help his encoded Gentile readers move into a dialogic relation with their old, pre-converted selves. The juxtaposition of two worldviews—the bad enslavement under Sin's domination and the good enslavement under God's *auctoritas*—allows each worldview to throw light on the other. The juxtaposition of one culture over against another is a fundamental feature of self-definition in Paul. Of course, the slave is a common representation of the other, and of a person caught between two cultures.

The specific persona in Romans 7 is a captured war slave who undergoes an agonizing crisis of identity because it is alienated from its rightful owner. Every facet of the *anthrōpos*, both inner and outer, responds. Like all slaves, the persona is answerable to its new master (the demonic power Sin) with its body. The slave cannot control or prevent the violence inflicted on its body; it can only learn to withstand by a known passive strategy of disguised resistance common among all slaves, a "hidden transcript" of slave resistance that the "public transcript" of *auctoritas* created. The persona is compelled to follow the new master, but in its external bodily members alone and only in habitual, mechanical obedience to individual commands (to the law of Sin) like an automaton. The subject of the slave's self takes solace in not letting Sin have *auctoritas* over it. A passive commodity of Sin, the persona delights in a different law (the holy law of God) inwardly. Its innermost self perseveres unwaveringly in total directness toward its true master (God), as a good and faithful slave (and Roman soldier) should, even when the master is not yet present. The enslaved self, though captured, retains its capacity to fight and its inner, subjective agency. Paul thus thinks of "the slave" in terms of *auctoritas*, the quintessentially Roman idea of personalized power.

---

obligations on the part of subordinates; see Wayne A. Meeks, "Corinthian Christians as Artificial Aliens," in *Paul beyond the Judaism/Hellenism Divide* (ed. Troels Engberg-Pedersen; Louisville: Westminster John Knox, 2001), 137; idem, *First Urban Christians*, 208 n. 192, and literature cited there.

APPROACHES TO THE APOCALYPSE

Revelation has always been a controversial New Testament book, and it is not difficult to find Christian readers ancient and modern uncomfortable with its inclusion in the canon. Such important church fathers as Cyril of Jerusalem and Gregory of Nazianzus, for instance, omit it from their early lists of biblical books, and it is partly in this context that the fragment from Dionysius quoted below should be read. Dionysius accepts the book's canonical authority, but at the same time seems intent on qualifying that authority carefully.

Although some readers have found the book's obscurity a major problem, others, virtually from the moment of its composition, have reveled in Revelation's seemingly cryptic prophecies, finding in them encouraging references to their own traumatic historical situations. Indeed, this volume's introduction and annotations to Revelation assume that its author understood his purported vision to address issues of relevance to his own contemporaries, including the increasingly marginalized position of Jesus-believers in the Roman Empire (a position with which later socially and politically dispossessed readers have often identified, as exemplified by the dialogue from Elizabeth Gaskell's *North and South* excerpted below). The details of later prophetic interpretations of Revelation differ widely, depending on the context and concerns of the given interpreter. Excerpts from three such readings are included below: one from the Middle Ages (Nicholas of Lyra), another from the time of the Reformation (the Geneva Bible), and a third from the 1970s (Hal Lindsey). Even a perfunctory reading of these makes it clear that they provide more insight into the anxieties of the interpreters than into the biblical text itself.

Alternative or perhaps complementary approaches to Revelation surface as well in the history of its interpretation, including those that attend carefully to its literary dimensions. These include Dionysius's early discussion of its rhetoric and authorship, Isaac Newton's consideration of its strange symbolism, and Austin Farrer's investigation of its structure. Whatever else it is, Revelation is an imaginative work, at least insofar as it conjures up and calls for thoughtful meditation on provocative and sometimes bizarre images. The imagination may, in fact, be central to Revelation's ultimate purpose. Some readers see the book not so much as a prophetic encryption of future events as a mystical prose poem of praise, a doxological bricolage of Old Testament and pagan religious images. Such readers find themselves awed (and occasionally disturbed) by the vision it finally presents of a world made right by the violent power of God. Many hymnists seem to have read Revelation in such a way, for several of the greatest English hymns are based on passages from this book, including "Holy, Holy, Holy" and "Crown Him with Many Crowns" (both included above; see pp. 1332–34), as well, of course, as the Hallelujah chorus from Handel's *Messiah*.

This section of the appendix samples a variety of interpretive approaches to Revelation in order to give the reader a sense of how this strange biblical book has been read over the ages and of the peculiar problems and possibilities latent in its controversial history of interpretation.

DIONYSIUS OF ALEXANDRIA

[Revelation's Authority and Author]
(from Eusebius, *Church History*, book 7)[†]

25 Afterward he [Dionysius] speaks in this manner of the Apocalypse of John.

"Some before us have set aside and rejected the book altogether, criticising it chapter by chapter, and pronouncing it without sense or argument, and maintaining that the title is fraudulent. For they say that it is not the work of John, nor is it a revelation, because it is covered thickly and densely by a veil of obscurity. And they affirm that none of the apostles, and none of the saints, nor any one in the Church is its author, but that Cerinthus, who founded the sect which was called after him the Cerinthian, desiring reputable authority for his fiction, prefixed the name. For the doctrine which he taught was this: that the kingdom of Christ will be an earthly one. And as he was himself devoted to the pleasures of the body and altogether sensual in his nature, he dreamed that that kingdom would consist in those things which he desired, namely, in the delights of the belly and of sexual passion; that is to say, in eating and drinking and marrying, and in festivals and sacrifices and the slaying of victims, under the guise of which he thought he could indulge his appetites with a better grace.

"But I could not venture to reject the book, as many brethren hold it in high esteem. But I suppose that it is beyond my comprehension, and that there is a certain concealed and more wonderful meaning in every part. For if I do not understand I suspect that a deeper sense lies beneath the words. I do not measure and judge them by my own reason, but leaving the more to faith I regard them as too high for me to grasp. And I do not reject what I cannot comprehend, but rather wonder because I do not understand it."

After this he examines the entire Book of Revelation, and having proved that it is impossible to understand it according to the literal sense, proceeds as follows:

"Having finished all the prophecy, so to speak, the prophet pronounces those blessed who shall observe it, and also himself. For he says, 'Blessed is he that keepeth the words of the prophecy of this book, and I, John, who saw and heard these things' [Rev 22:7–8]. Therefore that he was called John, and that this book is the work of one John, I do not deny. And I agree also that it is the work of a holy and inspired man. But I cannot readily admit that he was the apostle, the son of Zebedee, the brother of James, by whom the Gospel of John and the Catholic Epistle

---

[†] From Eusebius, *Church History*, trans. Arthur Cushman McGiffert, in *The Nicene and Post-Nicene Fathers: Second series*, vol. 1 (1890; reprint, Peabody, MA: Hendrickson, 1994), 309–11.

In this lengthy fragment from his book *On the Promises*, preserved by Eusebius, Dionysius (ca. 200–265 C.E.), bishop of Alexandria, bears witness to Revelation's controversial status in the early church. Although he is not willing to reject its canonical authority, he seems suspicious of the eschatology it espouses, and on the basis of a stylistic analysis he concludes against apostolic authorship. Dionysius rightly infers that Revelation was written by someone other than the author of the Fourth Gospel or 1 John, which he understands John the son of Zebedee to have composed. (Dionysius's statement about the authorship of 2 and 3 John is perhaps ambiguous, but in any case he does not identify their author either with the John of Revelation.)

were written. For I judge from the character of both, and the forms of expression, and the entire execution of the book, that it is not his. For the evangelist nowhere gives his name, or proclaims himself, either in the Gospel or Epistle." Farther on he adds:

"But John never speaks as if referring to himself, or as if referring to another person. But the author of the Apocalypse introduces himself at the very beginning: 'The Revelation of Jesus Christ, which he gave him to show unto his servants quickly; and he sent and signified it by his angel unto his servant John, who bare witness of the word of God and of his testimony, even of all things that he saw' [Rev 1:1–2]. Then he writes also an epistle: 'John to the seven churches which are in Asia, grace be with you, and peace' [Rev 1:4]. But the evangelist did not prefix his name even to the Catholic Epistle; but without introduction he begins with the mystery of the divine revelation itself: 'That which was from the beginning, which we have heard, which we have seen with our eyes' [1 John 1:1]. For because of such a revelation the Lord also blessed Peter, saying, 'Blessed art thou, Simon Bar-Jonah, for flesh and blood hath not revealed it unto thee, but my heavenly Father' [Matt 16:17]. But neither in the reputed second or third epistle of John, though they are very short, does the name John appear; but there is written the anonymous phrase, 'the elder.' But this author did not consider it sufficient to give his name once and to proceed with his work; but he takes it up again: 'I, John, who also am your brother and companion in tribulation, and in the kingdom and in the patience of Jesus Christ, was in the isle that is called Patmos for the Word of God and the testimony of Jesus' [Rev 1:9]. And toward the close he speaks thus: 'Blessed is he that keepeth the words of the prophecy of this book, and I, John, who saw and heard these things' [Rev 22:8].

"But that he who wrote these things was called John must be believed, as he says it; but who he was does not appear. For he did not say, as often in the Gospel, that he was the beloved disciple of the Lord, or the one who lay on his breast [e.g. John 13:23], or the brother of James, or the eyewitness and hearer of the Lord [John 19:35; 21:24]. For he would have spoken of these things if he had wished to show himself plainly. But he says none of them; but speaks of himself as our brother and companion, and a witness of Jesus, and blessed because he had seen and heard the revelations. But I am of the opinion that there were many with the same name as the apostle John who, on account of their love for him, and because they admired and emulated him, and desired to be loved by the Lord as he was, took to themselves the same surname, as many of the children of the faithful are called Paul or Peter. For example, there is also another John, surnamed Mark, mentioned in the Acts of the Apostles, whom Barnabas and Paul took with them [Acts 12:25]; of whom also it is said, 'And they had also John as their attendant' [Acts 13:5]. But that it is he who wrote this, I would not say. For it is not written that he went with them into Asia, but, 'Now when Paul and his company set sail from Paphos, they came to Perga in Pamphylia; and John departing from them returned to Jerusalem' [Acts 13:13]. But I think that he was some other one of those in Asia; as they say that there are two monuments in Ephesus, each bearing the name of John.

"And from the ideas, and from the words and their arrangement, it may be reasonably conjectured that this one is different from that one. For the Gospel and

Epistle agree with each other and begin in the same manner. The one says, 'In the beginning was the Word' [John 1:1]; the other, 'That which was from the beginning' [1 John 1:1]. The one: 'And the Word was made flesh and dwelt among us, and we beheld his glory, the glory as of the only begotten of the Father' [John 1:14]; the other says the same things slightly altered: 'Which we have heard, which we have seen with our eyes; which we have looked upon and our hands have handled of the Word of life,—and the life was manifested' [1 John 1:1–2]. For he introduces these things at the beginning, maintaining them, as is evident from what follows, in opposition to those who said that the Lord had not come in the flesh. Wherefore also he carefully adds, 'And we have seen and bear witness, and declare unto you the eternal life which was with the Father and was manifested unto us. That which we have seen and heard declare we unto you also' [1 John 1:2–3]. He holds to this and does not digress from his subject, but discusses everything under the same heads and names; some of which we will briefly mention. Any one who examines carefully will find the phrases, 'the life,' 'the light,' 'turning from darkness,' frequently occurring in both; also continually, 'truth,' 'grace,' 'joy,' 'the flesh and blood of the Lord,' 'the judgment,' 'the forgiveness of sins,' 'the love of God toward us,' the 'commandment that we love one another,' that we should 'keep all the commandments'; the 'conviction of the world, of the Devil, of Anti-Christ,' the 'promise of the Holy Spirit,' the 'adoption of God,' the 'faith continually required of us,' 'the Father and the Son,' occur everywhere. In fact, it is plainly to be seen that one and the same character marks the Gospel and the Epistle throughout. But the Apocalypse is different from these writings and foreign to them; not touching, nor in the least bordering upon them; almost so to speak, without even a syllable in common with them. Nay more, the Epistle—for I pass by the Gospel—does not mention nor does it contain any intimation of the Apocalypse, nor does the Apocalypse of the Epistle. But Paul, in his epistles, gives some indication of his revelations [2 Cor 12:1–4; Eph 3:3; Col 1:26], though he has not written them out by themselves.

"Moreover, it can also be shown that the diction of the Gospel and Epistle differs from that of the Apocalypse. For they were written not only without error as regards the Greek language, but also with elegance in their expression, in their reasonings, and in their entire structure. They are far indeed from betraying any barbarism or solecism, or any vulgarism whatever. For the writer had, as it seems, both the requisites of discourse, that is, the gift of knowledge and the gift expression,—as the Lord had bestowed them both upon him. I do not deny that the other writer saw a revelation and received knowledge and prophecy. I perceive, however, that his dialect and language are not accurate Greek, but that he uses barbarous idioms, and, in some places, solecisms. It is unnecessary to point these out here, for I would not have any one think that I have said these things in a spirit of ridicule, for I have said what I have only with the purpose of showing clearly the difference between the writings."

NICHOLAS OF LYRA

[On Revelation 13:11–18]†

V. 11. **Then I saw:** having described the persecution of Chosroes[1] and his son, here the same is described under Muhammad and his people. It is divided into three parts. First, this persecution begins; second, it is interrupted by another, at the place: **Then I looked, and there was a white cloud** (14:14); and third, the first part is resumed, at the place: **And the sixth angel** (16:12).

The first section is divided in three parts; because first the situation of the Saracen sect is included; second the persecution of the Christians in the beginning of the following chapter; and third, the punishment of the persecutors, at the place: **I saw another angel.** (14:8)

The first part is again in two parts, because first the situation of the sect is described; and second the veiling of a certain secret judgement, at the place: **This calls for wisdom** (13:18). Concerning the first it should be known that, although the beginning of the sect of Muhammad is spoken of in various ways by various persons, nevertheless, it is more conveniently held that it began around the end of Heraclius's[2] reign discussed in the preceding part.

Muhammad, elevated from poverty to wealth, intended to become the king of the Ishmaelites; for he belonged to this people, who are properly called the children of Hagar. Ishmael was the son of Hagar, the handmaid of Sarah (Gn 16); nevertheless, freed from Sarah, they are inappropriately called Saracens.[3] To obtain his goal, he used the counsel and help of a certain heretical monk, Sergius.[4] By writing a false and carnal law and having colored it with certain authorities from the Old and New Testaments, he was the more easily accepted, not only by Gentiles prone to carnal matters but also by simple Christians and Jews, who lived with the Ishmaelites. He also invented the fiction that this law was revealed by God to the greatest prophet of God.

Therefore, concerning him it is said: **Then I saw another beast,** that is, Muhammad who was leading a licentious life, which is called bestial. For he was lecherous and afire with the ardor of lust for all persons of the eastern region, boasting singlehandedly to have God-given copulating and generative powers greater than forty men, as it is written in Book I, Chapter 5, of the *His-*

---

† From *Nicholas of Lyra's Apocalypse Commentary*, trans. Philip D. W. Krey (Kalamazoo, MI: Medieval Institute Publications, 1997), 151–60.

   This commentary on Revelation, written in 1329 by the important medieval biblical scholar Nicholas of Lyra (1270–1349), betrays anxiety felt by many Europeans at the time about the growing influence of Islam in the Mediterranean world. Nicholas interprets the second beast of Revelation 13:11 as Muhammad and the mark of the beast (13:16) as adherence to the Qur'an.

1. Chosroes II, king of Persia (ca. 590–628).
2. Heraclius, Byzantine emperor (610–641).
3. The etymology is fabricated.
4. Sergius, Patriarch of Constantinople (d. 638), was the most influential exponent of Monothelitism, a christological heresy in which one will and energy was emphasized in Christ. The doctrine of two energies and two wills in Christ was established as orthodox over against monothelitism at the Council of Constantinople in 681 [translator's note].

tory of the Eastern Church, which is otherwise called the book of James of Vitry, who is the author.[5]

Ascending: because through business and through rapine he ascended from poverty to riches, as is said in the same place. **It had two horns like a lamb,** that is, of Christ, whose two horns are called prophecy, insofar as Christ was a wayfarer on earth and the proclaimer of the new law. (Lk declared in 7:16 concerning this, "A great prophet has risen among us.") Muhammad imagined that he was a prophet and a giver of the divine law, as has been said. Therefore, it is said that he had two horns like the horns of a lamb, because they were not truthfully such, but according to human fiction. **And it spoke like a dragon,** namely, cleverly, lyingly, and deceitfully.

V. 12. **It exercises all the authority of the first beast:** some explain this concerning the sin of Chosroes, who was called the beast above. For Muhammad and his followers transferred the authority of the kingdom of the Persians to the Saracens, and thus it is said that he had all the authority of the first beast.

But what follows seems contrary to this exposition: **And it makes the earth . . .** By transferring the authority from the Persians, he did not make them adore their king, but much more to the contrary. On account of which it seems to me, and I submit myself to better judgement, that the first beast was himself Muhammad, who is called a beast by reason of his bestiality, as was said. The first, because he was the first ruler of the Saracens, who were living in a bestial fashion. Moreover, it is the manner of the first ruler in any kingdom to firm up his control and to expand it as much as he is able, which Muhammad did. Therefore it says, **And it exercises all the authority. . . ,** because whatever a first ruler is accustomed to do to firm up and expand his authority, he did the more diligently. **On its behalf,** that is, as it seems expedient to a violent end for him.

And it makes the earth and all it inhabitants worship the first beast, that is, himself, who is called the first beast above, but he does not cause himself to be adored as God, as Chosroes did, but just as the highest prophet of God. **Whose mortal wound had been healed.** In a certain battle Muhammad was seriously wounded but was healed afterwards, as was said in the *History of the Eastern Church*, Chapter 5.

V. 13. **It performs great signs,** nevertheless, false ones. **Even making fire come down from heaven:** this fire is taken metaphorically, just as the other things which are mentioned here. For after Muhammad had a great effect, he began to fall into epileptic fits, and, lest he be despised, he said that he suffered this because of the appearance of the Archangel, Gabriel; a strong man is not able to bear his light, as Daniel said to the angel appearing to him, "My Lord because of the vision such pains have come upon me that I retain no strength" (Dn 10:16). Indeed, angels are called "fire" in Ps 104:4, "You make the winds your messengers, fire and flame your ministers." And because he was deceitful, therefore, it is added: **In the sight of all,** that is, in the erroneous opinion of those believing him. For his disciple said that he

5. Jacques de Vitry, *Historia orientalis*, ed. J Bongars (Douai, 1597), Book I, Ch. 5. James of Vitry (ca. 1160–1240) was an Augustinian Canon Regular known for his preaching and historiography. In 1216 he was consecrated bishop of Acre and also accompanied the army of the Fifth Crusade at Damietta (1218–21) [translator's note].

caused the moon to descend with his voice, which because of its light is associated with fire, and thus according to the opinion of people he made fire descend.

V. 14. **And he deceives:** through him and his disciples. **By the signs** which are erroneously called such. **On behalf of the beast,** that is, of himself; for they knew that the signs were deceitful or otherwise. **On behalf of the beast,** that is, of a bestial people, and easily seduced—the nature that the people of the Ishmaelites living in the desert were. **Telling the inhabitants of the earth:** subjected to him. **Telling them to make an image for the beast:** this is added to designate that the beast is understood as Muhammad himself and not for the people deceived by him. Moreover, his image is called his law in which his nature and life are represented, which he ordered to be kept. And this is what is said: **To make an image,** that is, that his law might be fulfilled.

V. 15. **And it was allowed to give,** that is, permission by God. **Breath to the image of the beast,** that is, the vigor of his law. For the law is called life as long as it flourishes, and death when it is abrogated. **So that the image of the beast could even speak,** that is, demonstrate his judgement, as it is said, "Such a law speaks concerning such a case." For nearly everything here is taken metaphorically. **And cause those who would not worship the beast to be killed.** For he commanded under pain of death that his law be kept in great reverence.

V. 16. **Also it causes all, both small and great,** that is, all persons regardless of condition. **To be marked,** that is, circumcision, as some say. For the Saracens are circumcised just as the Jews. But the following letter seems to disagree, when it says **On the right hand,** for circumcision was not done here. And therefore this mark seems to mean a determinate manner of living according to the law of Muhammad by which the Saracens are distinguished from other peoples. Therefore, it is said **On the right hand,** in relation to the operation. **Or on the forehead,** through open confession.

V. 17. **So that no one can buy or sell,** that is, to take part with the Saracens in their laws. **Who does not have the mark,** that is, the manner of living mentioned above. **That is, the name:** false Saracens, as it were; for just as among Christians there are some who are false, on account of which they are allowed to communicate with true Christians, thus it is also true among the Saracens. **Or the number of its name:** the servants of the Saracens, as it were, of another law, who share with them in human concerns, because they are from the households of the Saracens.

V. 18. **This calls for wisdom:** here, the veiling of a certain secret judgement is included, namely, the number of Muhammad's years. Therefore, it is said: **This calls for wisdom,** that is, a hidden thing, which to grasp properly is wisdom. **Let anyone with understanding,** that is, quick learning and the ability to penetrate secrets. **Calculate the number of the beast,** that is, of Muhammad who is called the beast, as was made clear earlier.

For it is the number, that is, of a year. To what this number definitely refers is clear, and it does not refer to the number of years in his life, because he only flourished for sixty-three years, as *The Speculum of History*[6] reports. Therefore, some have said that it refers to the duration of his law, which ought to last that

---

6. *The Mirror of History* (*Speculum Historiale*), an encyclopedic history of the world by the French Dominican friar Vincent of Beauvais (ca. 1190–1264).

long; however, this does not seem true, because his law was given around the time of Heraclius, as was said above. Heraclius began to rule in the year of our Lord 613, and ruled for thirty years. Moreover, from the end of this to the present time, which is the year of our Lord 1329, more time has passed, as is clear upon reflection, and, moreover, the law of Muhammad still endures.

Therefore, some say that after the death of Muhammad his law was corrected by the wise ones of the Saracens, and from that reform one ought to begin counting the number of years of this law. But this does not seem probable, because this suggestion addresses the law not of Muhammad but of the wise ones. Besides, because these wise ones are said to have been disciples of Muhammad, and that reform was not long after the giving of the law by Muhammad, and from that time already 669 years have passed, the years are very nearly completed. Moreover, the law of Muhammad does not seem near an end but, in the last few years, has grown much stronger. For the Tartars, who are great in number, have accepted that law for a great part of their people, as I have heard asserted by a certain bishop of our order, who lived among the Tartars for many years.

Therefore it seems, but I submit myself to better judgement, that this number of years is to begin from the incarnation of the Lord and to end with the death of Muhammad concerning whom John speaks prophetically. This can be said, because from the year of the Incarnation of the Lord to the end of the reign of Heraclius 643 years passed, as was made evident before. Muhammad lived for sixty-three years, as has been said. Together these numbers make 706 years, from which it is necessary to subtract the years in which he flourished with Heraclius; otherwise they would be counted twice, as is clear by intuition. These years can probably be estimated to be forty, because Muhammad was first poor, and afterwards he grew strong through trade and rapine and fraud before he made himself king and made the law, which he gave at the death of Heraclius. Thus from the life of Muhammad it seems probable that sixty years had passed before the death of Heraclius, which [that is, forty] subtracted from 706 leaves precisely 666 remaining from the incarnation of the Lord to the death of Muhammad—according to this it is possible to explain it according to the letter.

THE GENEVA BIBLE

[Revelation 13:16–17]†

16 ²³ And he made all, both small and great, rich and poore, free and bond, to receiue ²⁴ a ᵇ marke in their right hande or in their foreheads,

---

† From *The Bible: That is, The Holy Scriptures conteined in the Old and New Testament* (London, 1615).
   The most important English translation of the Bible preceding the KJV was originally published in 1560 (though the New Testament appeared on its own in 1557). Unlike KJV, however, the Geneva Bible (so called because it was printed in the Swiss city in which many English Protestant scholars sought refuge during Mary I's reign) included copious and occasionally tendentious interpretive annotations. The expanded notes for Revelation in the edition first published in 1599 were written by Franciscus Junius. As one would expect from a Huguenot scholar writing at the height of the Reformation, they are vehemently anti-Catholic, identifying the mark of the beast as Catholic sacraments and the whore of Babylon as the Roman church.

17 And that no man might [25] buy or sell, saue he that had the [26] marke or the name of the beast or the number of his name.

23 The third place, is a most wicked and most insolent tyranny as was sayd before, vsurped ouer the persons of men in this verse: and ouer their goods and actions, in the next verse. For he is said, both to bring vpon al persons a tyrannous seruitude, that as bondslaues they might serue the beast: and also to exercise ouer all their goods and actions, a pedler like abuse of indulgences and dispensations (as they terme them) amongst their friends, & against others to vse most violent interdictions, and to shoot out cursings, euen in naturall and ciuill, priuate and publike contracts, wherein all good faith ought to haue place. 24 That is, their Chrisme, by which in the Sacrament (as they call it) of Confirmation, they make seruile vnto themselues, the persons and doings of men signing them in their forehead & hands: and as for the signe left by Christ (Of which Chapter 7.3) and the holy Sacrament of Baptisme they make as voyd. For whom Christ hath ioyned vnto himselfe by Baptisme, this beast maketh challenge vnto them by her greasie Chrisme, which hee doubteth not to preferre before Baptisme, both in authoritie and in eificace. *b The marke of the name of the beast.* 25 That is, haue any traffique or entercourse with men, but they onely which haue this anointing and consecration of Clearkely tonsure, as they call it. * * * 26 Here the false Prophets doe require three things, which are set down in the order of their greatnesse, a character, a name, & the number of the name. The meaning is, that man that hath not first their annoynting and clericall tonsure or shauing: secondly holy orders, by receiuing whereof is communicated the name of the beast: or finally hath not attained that high degree of Pontificall knowledge, and of the Law (as they call it) Canonicall, & hath not as it were made vp in account and cast the number of the mysteries thereof: for in these things consisteth the number of that name of the beast. And this is excellently set forth in the next verse.

[Revelation 17:3–6]

3 * * * and I saw a woman sit vpon a [b] scarlet coloured beast, full of names of blasphemie, which had seuen heads, and ten hornes.

4 And [4] the woman was arrayed [5] in purple and scarlet, and gilded with gold, and precious stones, and pearles, [6] and had a cup of gold in her hand full of abomination, and filthinesse of her fornication.

5 [7] And in her forehead *was* a name written, A mystery, [8] that great Babylon that mother of whoredomes, and abominations of the earth.

6 [9] And I saw the woman drunken with the blood of Saints, and with the blood of the Martyrs of IESVS.

b A skarlet colour, that is, with a red and purple garment: & surely it was not without cause that the Romish clergie were so much delighted with this colour. 4 That harlot, the spirituall Babylon, which is Rome. She is described by her attire, profession and deeds. 5 In attire most glorious, triumphant, most rich, & most gorgious.

6 In profession, the nourisher of all, in this verse, and teaching her mysteries vnto all, vers **5.** setting forth all things most magnificently: but indeed most pernicious besotting miserable men with her cup, & bringing vpon them a deadly giddines.

7 Deceiuing with the title of religion, & publike inscription of mystery: which the beast in times past did not beare. 8 An exposition: in which S. John declareth what maner of woman this is. 9 In maner of deeds: She is red with blood, and sheddeth it most licentiously, and therefore is coloured with the blood of the Saints, as on the contrary part, Christ is set forth imbrued with the blood of his enemies, Esa [Isa] 63.1.

HAL LINDSEY

[On Revelation 17:12–14]†

Rome: Phase 2

In phase two of the fourth kingdom, Rome, the kingdom will be in the form of a ten-nation confederacy. "And of the ten horns that were in his head, and of the other which came up, and before whom three fell; even of that horn that had eyes, and a mouth that spake very great things, whose look was more stout than his fellows" (Daniel 7:20 KJV [cf. Rev 17:12–14]).

* * *

United We . . . Must

If the formation of the European Common Market were an isolated development in the line of Biblical prophecy, then it would have no significance for our study. However, combined with the other pieces of the prophetic puzzle which we are attempting to develop for you, it takes on immense importance.

We believe that the Common Market and the trend toward unification of Europe may well be the beginning of the ten-nation confederacy predicted by Daniel and the Book of Revelation.

What particular forces are contributing to the evolvement of this federation that the conquerors of history could not command?

First, there is the threat of Communism. One of the great motivating factors in forming this economic community and NATO was the concern over a common enemy. An article about "Mister Europe at Eighty," quotes Jean Monnet, called

---

† From Hal Lindsay, with C. C. Carlson, *The Late Great Planet Earth* (Grand Rapids, MI: Zondervan, 1970), 92, 94–97, 112–13.

The Late Great Planet Earth (1970) was the best-selling "nonfiction" book of its decade. Its preoccupation with Europe's transformation after World War II—in particular, with the Soviet domination of the East and the emergence of the European Common Market (forerunner of the European Union) in the West—dates the interpretation it proposes to the Cold War era, but the book paved the way for much later Christian apocalyptic speculation. Lindsey's book remains in print today, enjoying continued esteem among many fundamentalist and evangelical Christians.

the father of the Common Market, as saying, "As long as Europe remains divided, it is no match for the Soviet Union. Europe must unite."[1]

The second reason for the formation of the European Common Market was the economic threat of the United States. Europeans realized they could not survive the industrial might of the United States. * * *

The third reason this writer feels Europe will form this ten-nation confederacy is that Europeans sense the basic weakness of the United States in its will to resist Communism. They seem to realize that if Europe were really at stake the U.S. would be dragging its feet in reacting against a Russian invasion. As an American it is difficult to write these words, but Europe does not feel that it can count on us in a real showdown.

A fourth factor is that according to the prophetic outlook the United States will cease being the leader of the West and will probably become in some way a part of the new European sphere of power.

Sheath your weapons, please. We realize that the United States is not mentioned in the Bible. However, it is certain that the leadership of the West must shift to Rome, in its revived form, and if the U.S. is still around at that time, it will not be the power it now is. * * *

A fifth factor in the trend toward the ten nation confederacy is the realization of the great potential of a United Europe.

                               *   *   *

A friend who lives in Germany sent us this translated statement of Dr. Walter Hallstein, who was formerly the president of the European Economic Community. Our correspondent, knowing our interest in Bible prophecy, thought there was significance in Hallstein's words. We'll let you judge.

"Three phases of the European unification are to be noted. First, the customs union, second, the economic union, third, the political union . . . What we have created on the way to uniting Europe is a mighty economic-political union of which nothing may be sacrificed for any reason. Its value exists not only in what it is, but more in what it promises to become . . . At about 1980 we may fully expect the great fusion of all economic, military, and political communities together into the United States of Europe."

Hallstein cited 1980. The timetable may be accelerating. Developments in Europe have changed so rapidly that an American news magazine had a feature headed "Europe's Dreams of Unity Revive."

One sentence in that story leaped from the page: "Should all go according to the most optimistic schedules, the Common Market could someday expand into a ten-nation economic entity whose industrial might would far surpass that of the Soviet Union."[2]

Imagine that. A "ten-nation economic entity."

Is it any wonder that men who have studied prophecy for many years believe that the basic beginning of the unification of Europe has begun?

1. *Look*, November 26, 1968 [Lindsey's note].
2. *Time*, July 4, 1969 [Lindsey's note].

What Else Is New?

At the time that this Roman empire will begin to be revived there will also be a revival of mystery Babylon. If this sound rather spooky bring your head out from under the skeptical cover and examine with us * * * the Biblical basis and the current applications.

Heading the revived Roman Empire will be a man of such magnetism, such power, and such influence, that he will for a time be the greatest dictator the world has ever known. He will be the completely godless, diabolically evil "future fuehrer."

[On Revelation 13:11–18]

The False Prophet

In Revelation 13:11–18 we are introduced to this infamous character. This person, who is called the second beast, is going to be a Jew. Many believe he will be from the tribe of Dan, which is one of the tribes of the original progenitors of the nation of Israel.

The False Prophet (he is called that in Revelation 19:20 and 20:10) will be a master of satanic magic. This future False Prophet is going to be a devilish John the Baptist. He will aid and glorify this Roman Dictator; he will proclaim him the savior of the world and make people worship him as God.

It is logical to ask how the False Prophet will force this worship of the Roman Dictator. He will be given control over the economics of the world system and cause everyone who will not swear allegiance to the Dictator to be put to death or to be in a situation where they cannot buy or sell or hold a job. Everyone will be given a tattoo or mark on either his forehead or forehand, only if he swears allegiance to the Dictator as being God.

Symbolically, this mark will be 666. Six is said to be the number of man in Scripture and a triad or three is the number for God. Consequently, when you triple "six" it is the symbol of man making himself God.

The cleverness of this economic vise is ghastly to contemplate. But no one could ever accuse Satan of not being clever.

O Come Now . . .

Do you believe it will be possible for people to be controlled economically? In our computerized society, where we are all "numbered" from birth to death, it seems completely plausible that some day in the near future the numbers racket will consolidate and we will have just one number for all our business, money, and credit transactions. Leading members of the business community are now planning that all money matters will be handled electronically.

Upstage

We believe that the dramatic elements which are occurring in the world today are setting the stage for this magnetic, diabolical Future Fuehrer to make his entrance. However, we must not indulge in speculation about whether any of the current world figures is the Antichrist. He will not be known until his sudden miraculous recovery from a fatal wound.

There would be no earthly advantage in being alive when the Antichrist rules. We believe that Christians will not be around to watch the debacle brought about by the cruelest dictator of all time.[3]

ISAAC NEWTON

[Biblical Symbolism and Revelation 17:1–6][†]

The nature of the serpent being no more changed by one Decree than that of the bow by the other.[1] Tis agreed that Eve was deceived by the Devil & that the Serpent was only a symbol of the Deceiver{;} [Now to make the sign really punished for the crime of the thing signified is absurd & therefore [the curs of the Serpent must be understood really of the Devil only & be spoken of the serpent] tis not to {be} understood that the serpent] & therefore to make the serpent really metamorphised & condemned to creep on his belly & eat dust because the Devil had offended is to punish one thing for anothers fault & make the signe suffer in a litteral sense for the crime of the thing signified which is absurd & unagreeable to the nature & design of Parables. When the ancient sages would have one thing to be represented by another they feigned a metamorphosis of the one into the other & thence came all the ancient Metamorphoses recited by Ovid & other writers. This was their way of making Parables & Moses in this Parable of the Serpent speaks in the language of the ancient wise men.

---

3. Lindsey believes they will already have been raptured to heaven.

† From Isaac Newton, "Treatise on Revelation," 4v, in Yahuda MS 9, Jewish National and University Library, Jerusalem, as normalized at www.newtonproject.sussex.ac.uk/view/texts/normalized/THEM00216.

　　The copious unpublished manuscripts of Isaac Newton (1643–1727), housed primarily at Cambridge University and the Jewish National and University Library in Jerusalem, became accessible only in 1991, when they were first published on microfilm. The Newton Project now makes many available online. These fascinating texts reveal the scientist and mathematician's deep interest in alchemy, in primitive Christianity and the development of orthodox theology (whose Trinitarianism, it turns out, Newton privately rejected), and in biblical prophecy. They contain something like three million words on theological and biblical themes, including some fascinating textual analysis. The fragment printed here, from a draft "Treatise on Revelation," discusses biblical symbolism. It focuses first on the serpent from Genesis 3 in order to make a programmatic statement about the subject, and then on the whore of Babylon from Revelation 17:1–6, which it persuasively interprets in light of what Newton identifies as the Bible's conventional employment of drunkenness as a figure for "error & confusion."

　　The "Treatise on Revelation," which dates to the mid- to late 1680s, is preserved in Yahuda MS 9, housed in the Jewish National and University Library in Jerusalem. An edited version, as well as a version offering a detailed representation of the original, can be consulted at the Newton Project (www.newtonproject.sussex.ac.uk).

1. A comparison between Gen 3:14–15 and 9:12–17.

As water of life given to the thirsty & wine given to drink in the Eucharist signify the doctrine of truth by which men are nourished to life eternal so the wine of fornication in this Cup [in the golden cup of the Whore of Babylon] must signify the doctrine of idolatry by which as with a Philter she entices her lovers to commit spiritual fornication with her & makes them err & reel to & fro like drunken men & become furious in their inordinate affections & passions towards their spiritual mistress. For drunkenness is the type of error & confusion & therefor the Philter by which she inebriated the nations is afterwards called her sorceries by which she deceived them. They are drunken but not with wine, they stagger but not with strong drink For the Lord hath poured out upon you the spirit of deep, sleep & hath closed your eyes—& the vision of all is become unto you as a book that is sealed—Wherefore, saith the Lord, forasmuch as this people draw near to me with their mouth & with their lips do honour me but have removed their heart far from me & their fear towards me is taught by the precept of men: therefore behold I will proceed to do a marvelous work among this people &c. Isa. 29.9, 11, 13. Which is as much as to say that Moses & the Prophets were to Israel as a book that is sealed up so that they consulted them not but worshipped God as they were taught by the precept of men & by imbibing & swallowing this precept became drunk & staggered & slept like men grown senseless with wine; for which reason God would destroy them. To the same purpose it is that Isaiah in another place saith, The Princes of Noph are deceived, they have also seduced Egypt—the Lord hath mingled a perverse spirit in the midst thereof; & they have caused Egypt to erre in every work thereof as a drunken man staggereth in his vomit. Isa. 19.13, 14. And so where God gives the nations the wine cup of his fury to drink that they may be mad & drunken & spue & fall & rise no more because of the sword which he will send amongst them Ier. 25. the meaning is that he will send amongst them the spirit of delusion giddiness & madness whereby they shall be gathered to battel & therein reel & spue up their & perish. & in the same sense he makes great Babylon drink the wine of his fury in the Apoc. The Golden Cup in the hand of the whore of Bab. is said to be full of abominations & filthiness of her fornication & this filthiness is a little before called the wine of her fornication, that is the doctrine of her idolatry.

ELIZABETH GASKELL

[A Dialogue on Revelation]†

Bessy moved uneasily; then she said:

"I wish father would not speak as he does. He means well, as I telled yo' yesterday, and tell yo' again and again. But yo' see, though I don't believe him a bit by day, yet by night—when I'm in a fever, half-asleep and half-awake—it comes back

† From Elizabeth Gaskell, *North and South*, 2 vols (London: Chapman and Hall, 1855), 1.154–57, 210–14, 230–33.

This series of exchanges from Elizabeth Gaskell's best-known novel between Margaret, a genteel, middle-class newcomer to the fictional northern English industrial town of Milton, and the bed-ridden factory worker Bessy demonstrates how differing attitudes toward Revelation and the apocalyptic-eschatological religion it espouses often map on to distinctions of social status and class.

upon me—oh! so bad! And I think, if this should be th' end of all, and if all I've been born for is just to work my heart and my life away, and to sicken i' this dree place, wi' them mill-noises in my ears for ever, until I could scream out for them to stop, and let me have a little piece o' quiet—and wi' the fluff filling my lungs, until I thirst to death for one long deep breath o' the clear air yo' speak on—and my mother gone, and I never able to tell her again how I loved her, and o' all my troubles—I think if this life is th' end, and that there's no God to wipe away all tears from all eyes[1]—yo' wench, yo'!" said she, sitting up, and clutching violently, almost fiercely, at Margaret's hand, "I could go mad, and kill yo', I could." She fell back completely worn out with her passion. Margaret knelt down by her.

"Bessy—we have a Father in Heaven."

"I know it! I know it," moaned she, turning her head uneasily from side to side. "I'm very wicked. I've spoken very wickedly. Oh! don't be frightened by me and never come again. I would not harm a hair of your head. And," opening her eyes, and looking earnestly at Margaret, "I believe, perhaps, more than yo' do o' what's to come. I read the book o' Revelations until I know it off by heart, and I never doubt when I'm waking, and in my senses, of all the glory I'm to come to."

"Don't let us talk of what fancies come into your head when you are feverish. I would rather hear something about what you used to do when you were well."

"I think I was well when mother died, but I have never been rightly strong sin' somewhere about that time. I began to work in a carding-room soon after, and the fluff got into my lungs, and poisoned me."

"Fluff?" said Margaret, inquiringly.

"Fluff," repeated Bessy. "Little bits, as fly off fro' the cotton, when they're carding it, and fill the air till it looks all fine white dust. They say it winds round the lungs, and tightens them up. Anyhow, there's many a one as works in a carding-room, that falls into a waste, coughing and spitting blood, because they're just poisoned by the fluff."

"But can't it be helped?" asked Margaret.

"I dunno. Some folk have a great wheel at one end o' their carding-rooms to make a draught, and carry off th' dust; but that wheel costs a deal o' money—five or six hundred pound, maybe, and brings in no profit; so it's but a few of th' masters as will put 'em up; and I've heard tell o' men who did'nt like working in places where there was a wheel, because they said as how it made 'em hungry, at after they'd been long used to swallowing fluff, to go without it, and that their wage ought to be raised if they were to work in such places. So between masters and men th' wheels fall through. I know I wish there'd been a wheel in our place, though."

"Did not your father know about it?" asked Margaret.

"Yes! And he were sorry. But our factory were a good one on the whole; and a steady likely set o' people; and father was afeard of letting me go to a strange place, for though yo' would na think it now, many a one then used to call me a gradely lass enough. And I did na like to be reckoned nesh and soft, and Mary's schooling were to be kept up, mother said, and father he were always liking to buy books, and go to lectures o' one kind or another—all which took money—so I just worked on

1. Cf. Rev 21:4.

till I shall ne'er get the whirr out o' my ears, or the fluff out o' my throat i' this world. That's all."

"How old are you?" asked Margaret.

"Nineteen, come July."

"And I too am nineteen." She thought, more sorrowfully than Bessy did, of the contrast between them. She could not speak for a moment or two for the emotion she was trying to keep down.

* * *

Her father went out of doors, evidently to finish his pipe.

Bessy said passionately,

"Now am not I a fool,—am I not, Miss?—there, I knew I ought for to keep father at home, and away fro' the folk that are always ready for to tempt a man, in time o' strike, to go drink,—and there my tongue must needs quarrel with this pipe o' his'n,—and he'll go off, I know he will,—as often as he wants to smoke— and nobody knows where it'll end. I wish I'd letten myself be choked first."

"But does your father drink?" asked Margaret.

"No—not to say drink," replied she, still in the same wild excited tone. "But what win ye have? There are days wi' you, as wi' other folk, I suppose, when yo' get up and go through th' hours, just longing for a bit of a change—a bit of a fillip, as it were. I know I ha' gone and bought a four-pounder out o' another baker's shop to common on such days, just because I sickened at the thought of going on for ever wi' the same sight in my eyes, and the same sound in my ears, and the same taste i' my mouth, and the same thought (or no thought, for that matter) in my head, day after day, for ever. I've longed for to be a man to go spreeing, even if it were only a tramp to some new place in search o' work. And father—all men— have it stronger in 'em than me to get tired o' sameness and work for ever. And what is 'em to do? It's little blame to them if they do go into th' gin-shop for to make their blood flow quicker, and more lively, and see things they never see at no other time—pictures, and looking-glass, and such like. But father never was a drunkard, though maybe, he's got worse for drink, now and then. Only yo' see," and now her voice took a mournful, pleading tone, "at times o' strike there's much to knock a man down, for all they start so hopefully; and where's the comfort to come fro'? He'll get angry and mad—they all do—and then they get tired out wi' being angry and mad, and maybe ha' done things in their passion they'd be glad to forget. Bless yo'r sweet pitiful face! but yo' dunnot know what a strike is yet."

"Come, Bessy," said Margaret, "I won't say you're exaggerating, because I don't know enough about it: but, perhaps, as you're not well, you're only looking on one side, and there is another and a brighter to be looked to."

"It's all well enough for yo' to say so, who have lived in pleasant green places all your life long, and never known want or care, or wickedness either, for that matter."

"Take care," said Margaret, her cheek flushing, and her eye lightening, "how you judge, Bessy. I shall go home to my mother, who is so ill—so ill, Bessy, that there's no outlet but death for her out of the prison of her great suffering; and yet I must speak cheerfully to my father, who has no notion of her real state, and to whom the knowledge must come gradually. The only person—the only one who could sympathise with me and help me—whose presence could comfort my mother more than any other earthly thing—is falsely accused—would run the risk of death if he came to see his dying mother. This I tell you—only you, Bessy. You must not mention it. No other person in Milton—hardly any other person in England knows. Have I not care? Do I not know anxiety, though I go about well-dressed, and have food enough? Oh, Bessy, God is just, and our lots are well portioned out by Him, although none but He knows the bitterness of our souls."

"I ask your pardon," replied Bessy, humbly. "Sometimes, when I've thought o' my life, and the little pleasure I've had in it, I've believed that, maybe, I was one of those doomed to die by the falling of a star from heaven; 'And the name of the star is called Wormwood; and the third part of the waters became wormwood; and men died of the waters, because they were made bitter.'[2] One can bear pain and sorrow better if one thinks it has been prophesied long before for one: somehow, then it seems as if my pain was needed for the fulfilment; otherways it seems all sent for nothing."

"Nay, Bessy—think!" said Margaret. "God does not willingly afflict. Don't dwell so much on the prophecies, but read the clearer parts of the Bible."

"I dare say it would be wiser; but where would I hear such grand words of promise—hear tell o' anything so far different fro' this dreary world, and this town above a', as in Revelations? Many's the time I've repeated the verses in the seventh chapter to myself, just for the sound. It's as good as an organ, and as different from every day, too. No, I cannot give up Revelations. It gives me more comfort than any other book i' the Bible."

"Let me come and read you some of my favourite chapters."

"Ay," said she greedily, "come. Father will maybe hear yo'. He's deaved wi' my talking; he says it's all nought to do with the things o' to-day, and that's his business."

"Where is your sister?"

"Gone fustian-cutting. I were loth to let her go; but somehow we must live; and th' Union can't afford us much."

"Now I must go. You have done me good, Bessy."

"I done you good!"

"Yes. I came here very sad, and rather too apt to think my own cause for grief was the only one in the world. And now I hear how you have had to bear for years, and that makes me stronger."

"Bless yo'! I thought a' the good-doing was on the side of gentlefolk. I shall get proud if I think I can do good to yo'."

"You won't do it if you think about it. But you'll only puzzle yourself if you do, that's one comfort."

"Yo're not like no one I ever seed. I dunno what to make of yo'."

"Nor I of myself. Good-bye!"

Bessy stilled her rocking to gaze after her.

"I wonder if there are many folk like her down South. She's like a breath of country air, somehow. She freshens me up above a bit. Who'd ha' thought that face—as bright and as strong as the angel I dream of—could have known the sorrow she speaks on? I wonder how she'll sin. All on us must sin. I think a deal on her, for sure.

2. Rev 8:11.

But father does the like, I see. And Mary even. It's not often hoo's stirred up to notice much."

*   *   *

"I wish I could see you dressed up," said Bessy. "I reckon, yo're not what folk would ca' pretty; yo've not red and white enough for that. But dun yo' know, I ha' dreamt of yo', long afore ever I seed yo'."

"Nonsense, Bessy!"

"Ay, but I did. Yo'r very face,—looking wi' yo'r clear steadfast eyes out o' th' darkness, wi' yo'r hair blown off from yo'r brow, and going out like rays round yo'r forehead, which was just as smooth and as straight as it is now,[3]—and yo' always came to give me strength, which I seemed to gather out o' yo'r deep comforting eyes,—and yo' were drest in shining raiment—just as yo'r going to be drest. So, yo' see, it was yo'!"

"Nay, Bessy," said Margaret, gently, "it was but a dream."

"And why might na I dream a dream in my affliction as well as others? Did not many a one i' the Bible? Ay, and see visions too! Why, even my father thinks a deal o' dreams! I tell yo' again, I saw yo' as plainly, coming swiftly towards me, wi' yo'r hair blown back wi' the very swiftness o' the motion, just like the way it grows, a little standing off like; and the white shining dress on yo've getten to wear. Let me come and see yo' in it. I want to see yo' and touch yo' as in very deed yo' were in my dream."

"My dear Bessy, it is quite a fancy of yours."

"Fancy or no fancy,—yo've come, as I knew yo' would, when I saw yo'r movement in my dream,—and when yo're here about me, I reckon I feel easier in my mind, and comforted, just as a fire comforts one on a dree day. Yo' said it were on th' twenty-first; please God, I'll come and see yo'."

"Oh Bessy! you may come and welcome; but don't talk so—it really makes me sorry. It does indeed."

"Then I'll keep it to mysel', if I bite my tongue out. Not but what it's true for all that."

Margaret was silent. At last she said,

"Let us talk about it sometimes, if you think it true. But not now. Tell me, has your father turned out?"[4]

"Ay!" said Bessy, heavily—in a manner very different from that she had spoken in but a minute or two before. "He and many another,—all Hamper's men,—and many a one besides. Th' women are as bad as th' men, in their savageness, this time. Food is high,—and they mun have food for their childer, I reckon. Suppose Thorntons sent 'em their dinner out,—th' same money, spent on potatoes and meal, would keep many a crying babby quiet, and hush up its mother's heart for a bit!"

"Don't speak so!" said Margaret. "You'll make me feel wicked and guilty in going to this dinner."

"No!" said Bessy. "Some's pre-elected to sumptuous feasts, and purple and fine linen,—may be yo're one on 'em. Others toil and moil all their lives long—and

3. Cf. Rev 1:13–14; 4:4.
4. I.e., gone on strike.

the very dogs are not pitiful in our days, as they were in the days of Lazarus. But if yo' ask me to cool yo'r tongue wi' th' tip of my finger, I'll come across the great gulf to yo' just for th' thought o' what yo've been to me here."[5]

"Bessy! you're very feverish! I can tell it in the touch of your hand, as well as in what you're saying. It won't be division enough, in that awful day, that some of us have been beggars here, and some of us have been rich,—we shall not be judged by that poor accident, but by our faithful following of Christ."

Margaret got up, and found some water: and soaking her pocket-handkerchief in it, she laid the cool wetness on Bessy's forehead, and began to chafe the stone-cold feet. Bessy shut her eyes, and allowed herself to be soothed. At last she said,

"Yo'd ha' been deaved out o' yo'r five wits, as well as me, if yo'd had one body after another coming in to ask for father, and staying to tell me each one their tale. Some spoke o' deadly hatred, and made my blood run cold wi' the terrible things they said o' th' masters,—but more, being women, kept plaining, plaining (wi' the tears running down their cheeks, and never wiped away, nor heeded), of the price o' meat, and how their childer could na sleep at nights for th' hunger."

"And do they think the strike will mend this?" asked Margaret.

"They say so," replied Bessy. "They do say trade has been good for long, and the masters has made no end o' money; how much father doesn't know, but, in course, th' Union does; and, as is natural, they wanten their share o' th' profits, now that food is getting dear; and th' Union says they'll not be doing their duty if they don't make the masters give 'em their share. But masters has gotten th' upper hand somehow; and I'm feared they'll keep it now and evermore. It's like th' great battle o' Armageddon, the way they keep on, grinning and fighting at each other, till even while they fight, they are picked off into the pit."[6]

AUSTIN FARRER

[The Structure of Revelation]†

The Apocalypse has a great deal of framework; no one can miss that. It bears the promise of formal consistency, of a continuous grand architecture spanning the whole book, into which all the visionary detail is to be fitted. Yet, as we advance, it does not appear to us that the promise is fulfilled. The lines of the schematic architecture elude us, and the work seems in danger of disintegrating into a mere pile of

5. Cf. Luke 16:19–31.
6. Cf. Rev 16:16. For the pit, see, e.g., Rev 9:1–2, 11; 20:1–3.
† From Austin Farrer, *A Rebirth of Images: The Remaking of St. John's Apocalype* (Westminster: Dacre Press, 1949), 36–58. All notes are Farrer's.
   Even if Austin Farrer (1904–1968) had never published any biblical scholarship, his reputation would be secure as a leading twentieth-century philosopher and theologian. Farrer's biblical scholarship was considered eccentric in his own time, for it tended to attribute to New Testament writers an agency analogous if not identical to literary authorship; contemporary scholars usually viewed the Gospels in particular as lightly edited compendia of traditions rather than as creative compositions in their own right. Farrer's writings on the Bible are now regarded somewhat more favorably, especially by critics committed to understanding the literary dimensions of biblical texts.

visions and oracles. Then architectural elements reappear, yet not in such order as plainly to make up the unity of a single edifice. We are left unable to reconcile ourselves either to the hypothesis of formal order or to the hypothesis of its absence. Must we conclude that St John attempted form and broke down in the execution of it? Or must we accept the supposition of a demon-editor who has broken up St John's noble building by his senseless omissions, rearrangements and additions?

Before we capitulate to either of these desperate conclusions let us make one more attempt to construe the formal pattern as it stands. Perhaps a little more flexibility of approach, a little more attention to St John's parallelisms of phrase may yet succeed. Evidently his architecture was not fully successful, in a literary sense, or it would not have proved so baffling to his readers from the second century onwards. He was, perhaps, over-subtle; yet that does not mean that the recovery of his form, if indeed we can recover it, will be unrewarding. There is no absurdity in entertaining hope of the attempt, for we are now possessed of methods and materials for the reconstruction of the Jewish-Christian mind in the first century which the Christian exegete has lacked ever since the second.

In [chapters] I–XI there is a firmly built structure: it is at XII that we lose our way. It seems best, then, to analyse the structure so far as we can already see it, in the hope that a better acquaintance with it here may help us to trace it where we cannot see it yet.

The pattern in I–XI is based on three series of sevens: seven messages, seven unsealings, seven trumpet-blasts. But the form of the seven-term cycle does not simply repeat itself; it becomes elaborated and modified with each repetition, as we shall proceed to show.

The first seven (I–III) is straightforward enough. The seven things are introduced all together in the opening vision. The Son of Man stands among seven candlesticks, which are the seven churches. He holds in his hand seven stars, which are their guardian angels; and to these angels the seven messages are one by one addressed. The serial idea is contained in the very notion of the seven luminaries, for in the universally known Chaldaean system, seven luminaries give their names to the series of seven days, the week:[1] and St John has just told us that his vision falls on the first of the week, the Lord's Day. So the seven messages spell out that favourite apocalyptic period, the symbolical week. The detail of the messages is not, however, prescribed by the special characters of the seven week-days, except for the last, where the sabbath-note is unmistakably heard. Here Christ, significantly named the Amen, the fulfilment and end, stands at the door and knocks, that he may enter and sup with the true believer in a holy sabbath feast.

The introduction to the second seven (IV–VIII, 6) places it carefully in line with the beginning of the first. Again the trumpet-like voice and the spiritual rapture introduce a theophany. In the former vision the Son of Man stood on earth as the apostle of the Ancient of Days, whose features therefore he wore. In the latter, the enthroned Glory himself is seated in heaven, and the Son of Man appears accessory to his throne, a Lamb endued with his Spirit. There is evident climax

---

1. The sun to Sunday, moon to Monday, and so on with the remaining five planets, or planetary gods. We have the names teutonised, except for Saturday, which is Latin = dies Saturni.

here—from the Messiah we proceed to the Glory, from earth we rise to heaven. Again the seven things appear together—the seven seals of the book, and the seven Spirits whereby they are opened. Again the serial treatment of the seven follows—the seven seals are broken one by one, to the accompaniment of visions. And again the seventh is sabbatical in character, introducing a heavenly silence, a sabbath-pause (VIII, 1).

So far the pattern is the same: but when we look at the structure of the six week-day visions (VI–VII) we find much elaboration which had no counterpart in the messages to the Churches. The first four are marked off from the rest and grouped together, by the following features. (a) In addition to the rubric common to the whole series, 'I saw when the Lamb opened the first seal,' or 'the second', or whatever the number may be, they have the additional rubric, 'I heard the first, second, etc. beast say: Come,' a cry to be understood in the sense of the Church's prayer for Advent, 'Maranatha,' 'Come, Lord Jesus' (cf. XXII, 20). (b) This rubric is in each case followed by the appearance of a horse of distinct colour bearing a rider; the further descriptions of the several horsemen are written in careful stylistic parallel to one another. (c) The four visions have their own joint conclusion, when the powers of all four horsemen are epitomised in the fourth: 'and there was given unto them (i.e. to the fourth rider and his companion) authority over the fourth part of the earth, to kill with the sword, the famine and the death, and by the wild beasts of the earth.'

The fifth vision lacks the peculiar features of the first four, and is about twice as long. The Maranatha-prayers of the four cherubim are here paralleled and expanded in the more potent prayers of the martyr-souls run down in blood beneath the altar of their sacrifice, and crying, 'How long?' Their prayer is not, like that of each cherub, immediately followed by a partial vengeance: it receives the assurance of complete vindication soon to follow.

The sixth vision is a pair to the fifth in length, and carries out its idea, for the signs of the Last Day are now manifested to appal the kings and the mighty men of earth. 'The great day of wrath is come: and who is able to stand?' This verse, being the last of the vision, brings us to the most surprising feature of the whole series of unsealings. The sixth unsealing is not directly followed by the seventh, but by a pair of intrusive visions which are not numbered (VII, 1–8, VII, 9–17). We might well begin to think that the series of unsealings is finished and that we are passing into another series altogether, except that we know that the seventh unsealing must yet be fulfilled.

The two intrusive visions do to some extent run on from the sixth unsealing. 'And I saw when the Lamb opened the sixth seal, there was a great earthquake . . . and the stars of the heaven fell to earth as a fig-tree casteth her unripe figs when she is shaken of a great wind.' So the sixth unsealing begins: and the first intrusive vision thus: 'After this I saw four angels standing at the four corners of the earth holding back the four winds of the earth, that no wind should blow on the earth, or the sea, or any tree: and I saw another angel ascend from the sunrising with the seal of the living God.' So the winds of destruction released by the sixth *unsealing* are after all restrained a while for a contrary operation, a *sealing*, to take place. The imposition of the divine seal protects the righteous against the plagues which the breaking of the (seventh) divine seal will let loose upon the wicked. We are given the number of the sealed, and so proceed to the second intrusive vision, there to catch a glimpse of the saints' final bliss, in which their sealing is to have its full effect. The opening phrase is placed in line with that of the sealing vision: 'And after this (vision) I saw four angels . . .'—'And after these (visions) I saw, and lo, a great multitude. . . .'

We have called the vision of the great multitude a glimpse of final bliss. In being this it cannot help being an anticipated conclusion to the whole apocalypse. This fact may afford us a clue to the significance of the two intrusive visions. St John leaves them unnumbered, but the reader is broken in to enumeration by this time, and counts them for himself: they may not be *the* seventh and eighth, but they are *a* seventh and an eighth. Now the Christian, unlike the Jew, sees the climax of the week in the Sunday, not the Sabbath, in the eighth day which is a new first, and not in the seventh. This has already been exemplified in I–V. It is on a first Sunday that the Son of Man appears to St John. The appearance articulates itself into a whole 'week' of messages, formally concluding in the seventh. What follows upon it as an eighth is a new Sunday and a new theophany (IV–V); and this in its turn articulates itself into a 'week', the series of seven unsealings (VI ff.). In the sixth unsealing we reach a climax of action, with the cosmic earthquake. The first intrusive vision follows it up with a sabbatical pause; the work of judgement rests while the saints are sealed. The second intrusive vision adds a spectacle of heavenly glory and final redemption, closely echoing the triumphs and blisses of the Sunday-vision in IV–V, and itself to be understood, surely, as a Sunday-vision.

What St John has done, then, is to permit the week of judgements, which sprang from the breaking of the seals, to run on through a sabbath into a Sunday of final consummation. So he lets us see what the movement of the week is striving after, what its form really signifies. Yet it is not for *this* week to fulfil the movement so perfectly, or reach so absolute a consummation. The two visions after the sixth are therefore left unnumbered, and when the seventh seal is formally broken they are forced back into the position of a cancelled conclusion, and allowed to stand as a mere interlude, an anticipation of the supreme end. Meanwhile the numbered seventh vision introduces a more modest sabbath—the half-hour's silence of incense-offering—and a more modest Sunday—the trumpet-blowing (VIII, 1–6).

We have now to examine the structure of the third seven (VIII, 7–XI, 19). An innovation here, to begin with, is the dropping of the introductory theophany. This is plainly necessary, for the second theophany has already touched the height of theophanic climax. We can proceed from Messiah on earth to the enthroned Glory in heaven, but there is nowhere further to go, no theophany could be an advance on this, unless it should be that of the Last Day; and we have just been made to understand that the Last Day is not yet. Since mounting climax must nevertheless maintain the tension of the Apocalypse until the final consummation relaxes it in everlasting peace, St John finds another stair by which to climb. The theophany of the enthroned Glory took effect in the opening of the book: and this was a process of seven stages, the breaking of the seven seals. Now if one is breaking seven seals to open a scroll, nothing has really been effected until the seventh is broken: for then the scroll is open, and until then it is not. Thus the visions which accompany the six unsealings are by their very position preparatory in character; it is the seventh seal which unseals apocalypse, and the fresh seven in which it proliferates are the proper content of revelation. Now the day arrives, now the sevenfold trump of the archangels is blown.

Just as the simple Maranatha-cries of the four cherubs prepared us for the more expansive treatment of petition in the martyrs' cry from beneath the altar, so the trumpet-like voices which introduce the two theophanies of I and IV prepare us for the vision of the seven trumpet-angels which takes the place of theophany in VIII, 2–6. As the winds were checked until the saints were sealed, so the trumpeters stand by while the prayers of the saints, carried from the altar of slaughter where we heard them at the fifth unsealing, are offered in angelic incense at the golden altar of perfume within the shrine. When the saints' prayers have been thus presented, and cast back in coals of fire on the heads of their persecutors, then the first of the seven trumpet-blasts shatters the quiet of celestial liturgy, and brings down hail and flame upon the wicked earth.

The seven trumpets are presented all together in VIII, 1–6, and then drawn out serially, like the messages and seals: and the last of the serial seven has that sabbatical character which the pattern hitherto has led us to expect. The seventh trumpet is greeted with shouts of heavenly worship, and there follows a heavenly liturgy—the opening of the temple to reveal the ark (XI, 15–19).

All sabbaths, as we know, represent the seventh day of creation-week, when after his six days' work God entered into eternal rest: and it is a simple development of this idea to consider our six working days as representing his six creative labours. In the trumpet-series St John makes this development. The series expresses divine judgements, not divine creations: but he can still draw six judgements into correspondence with six creative works by representing the creatures made in the genesis as used one by one in the judgement to plague the wicked. The works of the six days are these:

1. Elemental light.
2. Firmament.
3. Land, sea and waters, vegetation.
4. Luminaries.
5. Sea beasts.
6. Land beasts.

The first two present difficulties. How can light itself, the light before the sun, which expresses the eternal Word, be made the substance of a plague? And how can the firmament, the very floor of heaven? St John profits by the manifold character of the third day's work, and by dividing it can still obtain a list of six, though he lets go the first two works on the Genesis list. Here is St John's:

1. Land, vegetation.
2. Sea.
3. Waters.
4. Luminaries.
5. Beasts from the abyss (of sea).[2]
6. Beasts from the land.

2. The sea and the infernal abyss are one in Old Testament imagery, and they are equivalents, for St John. XI introduces 'the beast from the abyss' to be understood, presumably, from Daniel VII which says 'sea'. In XIII he appears as a beast rising from the sea; in XVII he comes up out of the abyss. In XXI we learn of new heaven and earth, but no more sea; neither sea nor abyss has any part in the world to come.

The first four, being inanimate, are simply smitten, the land with hail and lightning, the sea and waters with corruption, the luminaries with darkness. The last two play a more active part: demonic monsters swarm first from the abyss, then from the confines of the earth, to vex and slay the enemies of God.

We see, then, that the idea of the week, which had its germ in the two previous series, has its expansion in the series of the trumpets. Two further features of the series of unsealings find their counterpart in the trumpets: the division into a group of four and a group of three; and the intrusive visions between the sixth and the seventh. As to the division of the seven into a four and a three, we have already seen the first four trumpet-plagues grouped together by subject-matter, as simple smitings of four world-elements. They match one another in treatment, and also in brevity. The remaining three are separated from them not only by greater length and expansiveness of style, but also by the insertion of a separate heading: 'I saw and heard an eagle (vulture) flying in mid-heaven,[3] saying with a great voice: Woe, woe, woe to the dwellers upon earth, for the remaining trumpet-blasts of the three angels still to sound' (VIII, 13). This heading is picked up in a heading to the sixth trumpet, 'The first woe is past; behold there come yet two woes hereafter' (IX, 12) and in a similar heading to the seventh: 'The second woe is past: behold the third woe cometh quickly' (XI, 14). And when the third woe comes in Satan's descent to earth, there is a heavenly voice: 'Woe to the earth and to the sea,' closely followed by a vision of Satan's pursuit after the Mother of Messiah, to whom are given 'the two wings of the great eagle, that she may fly into the wilderness' (XII, 12–14). The eagle's voice proclaimed threefold woe to the inhabitants of earth, the eagle's wings prevent the third woe from being misdirected upon an inhabitant of heaven: only the wicked are destroyed by the Satanic invasion.

Now as to the intrusive visions after the sixth trumpet-vision. The sixth trumpet-angel looses 'the four angels bound at the great river Euphrates, prepared for the hour and day and month and year, to slay the third part of mankind', which they proceed to do with the aid of their two myriad myriads of land-demons. The theme of the hour, day, month and year is carried on into the intrusive visions. We have been shown the predestined moment of a third-part judgement; which may well have set us wondering about the moment of the last and total judgement. The next vision brings us the answer: 'Another strong angel descending from heaven arrayed in a cloud and the rainbow over his head, his face as the sun and his feet as pillars of fire' (x, 1) for no other purpose than to swear the oath 'that there shall be delay no more, but in the days of the seventh angel when he shall sound, the secret of God is accomplished'. He carries in his hand a scroll, in which we presume that his essential message is expressed more in detail: there we should find written the history of 'the days of the seventh angel', the series of events leading to the accomplishment of the secret of God, in other words, the substance of the rest of the Apocalypse. St John, like Ezekiel, is told to eat and digest the scroll of revelation.

At the same time he is given a reed (XI, 1). 'Reed' when placed in parallel with 'scroll' obviously means 'pen'; compare the phrase in St John's third epistle,

---

3. The vulture flying in mid-heaven is a proper introduction to a plague by the creatures of the fifth day: for on the fifth day God made not only the monsters of the sea, but also the 'fowl to fly above the earth on the face of the breadth of heaven'.

'Many things . . . I am unwilling to write to thee with ink and reed, but hope shortly to see thee.' 'Take the scroll and scan' was too straightforward for Ezekiel; 'Take the reed and write' is too straightforward for St John. 'Take the scroll and eat' says Ezekiel, and St John after him: 'Take the reed and measure the Temple of God,' says St John, for the reed, *calamus*, is also a measuring-rod. The digesting of the scroll is a metaphorical reading, the measuring of the temple will be a metaphorical writing. St John the inspired prophet by his written prophecy is to effect what the 'measuring' describes: those who heed the word of God become the living sanctuary of God, but those who find their condemnation in the word are left outside the sacred enclosure, to be profaned by invasive heathendom. An oracle which St John hears proceeds to treat of those within, letting go those without. The candles of the sanctuary, it says, are the Lord's two witnesses, prophetic figures like St John himself. His potent reed, 'a reed like a staff,' becomes in their hands the rod of Moses, to 'smite the land with every plague'. They do the works of Moses and Elias; the oracle goes on to tell of their martyrdom and assumption into heaven.

The history of the two witnesses is, indeed, a summary of the reign and fall of Antichrist, of the persecution and final redemption of the saints. These things will be more fully set out in the remaining visions of the Apocalypse. What we have in XI is a foreshortened and premature conclusion, cancelled, and yet permitted to stand by way of interlude; a close parallel, in fact, to the 'intrusive eighth vision' in the series of seals. The sixth trumpet-vision reached a climax of action in the slaughter of a third part of men. Then come the unnumbered visions—first a pause from action, devoted to the 'eating of the scroll', i.e. scriptural meditation: next, in the vision or oracle of the Reed, an action extending through the reign of Antichrist to the brink of Advent. Lastly, the premature conclusion of the trumpet-series offered by X and XI, 1–13 is firmly cancelled when the authentic seventh trumpet sounds (XI, 15).

The very meaning of such a cancellation is, that the week in question (in VI–VIII that of the seals, in VIII-XI that of the trumpets) is not the final week; it aspires, but is not permitted, to be this. So when the seventh trumpet and its sabbath have past, we must expect to find another week stretching out before us towards the ultimate goal. We turn therefore to the sequel (XII, 1 ff.) in the hope of finding a new sevenfold series, bearing some of the marks which the previous sevens have taught us to recognize.

With this clue in our hands we step forward into unmapped country; for with the seventh trumpet the explicit counting of sets of seven breaks off. St John has warned us that it will be so in X. When the Angel of the Oath exerts his lion-like voice, the Seven Thunders speak. With our experience of the seven seals and the seven trumpets, we naturally expect a thunder-apocalypse to follow, seven visions each initiated by a word of thunder. Were not the breakings of the first four seals each accompanied by the cries of a cherub, with a voice like thunder? But St John is told to 'seal' the thunder voices and not write them: there is to be no more delay, no more sevenfold sets of portents are to unroll before the great event begins. In the days of the seventh trumpet-angel when he shall sound, the secret purpose of God is fulfilled. It is this fulfilment, divested of the form of *numbered* series, that we have now to examine. It will be a seven, but not a numbered seven.

Let us pause and consider our situation. Our first inclination may be to complain that St John, after providing us with a clear plan in the three sevens of I–XI, has suddenly let us down. But a little reflection may suggest that he has not really treated us so unkindly. I–XI are roughly the first half of the work, and they consist of the three roughly equal sections which we have analysed, I–III, IV–VII, VIII–XI, 14, the core of each section being a counted seven. In the second half of the book (XI, 15–XXII), and roughly in the middle of it, there occurs a counted seven, the vials (XVI), which, with its exordium and closely attached appendix, occupies roughly a third part of it (XV–XVIII). Thus, all we have to do is to mark off the four counted sevens with their attached material, and the whole book is divided into six equal parts, the four sevens and the two blanks, thus:

> Seven Messages, I–III. (125 lines in my Greek Bible.)
> Seven Seals, IV–VII. (133 lines.)
> Seven Trumpets, VIII–XI, 14. (122 lines.)
> . . . XI, 15–XIV. (144 lines.)
> Seven Vials, XV–XVIII. (159 lines.)
> . . . XIX–XXII. (148 lines.)

St John has not, surely, put too severe a strain on our ingenuity by leaving us to realize for ourselves that the two blanks are sections comparable with the others, and that his whole work falls into six divisions.

It is with the former of the two blanks that we have to do at present. What guidance have we for mapping out its interior structure? We have just above obtained some directions, from what precedes the blank. We have seen that the sense of the 'cancelled conclusion' to the trumpets requires that another seven should directly follow the seventh blast, though it be an uncounted seven. We may derive a similar indication from the other end of the gap. The seven vials are introduced by a sabbath-vision (XV) which is written in the closest possible parallel to the two sabbaths which follow the seventh seal and the seventh trumpet respectively. The conclusion is obvious: XV is the sabbath-vision to the visions in the blank (XI, 15–XIV); in it a sevenfold series ends, just as a sevenfold series (the vials) opens out of it.

But before we proceed to analyse the series in the blank, let us exhibit the parallel between the three sabbath-visions, VIII, 1–6, XI, 15–19, and XV, I–XVI, I. In the last of these, as in the first, the seven angels of the seven coming plagues (the trumpets, the vials) are first introduced, and then left to stand by while a liturgy is performed. When it is finished, the trumpet-angels prepare themselves to blow, and the vial-angels are commanded to pour. In VIII the liturgy is an incense-offering, in XV it is levitical psalmody followed by the opening of the temple and the entry of the Glory-Cloud. The two ceremonies could not, you might say, be more different, and yet they are firmly tied together by the highly significant common use of Ezekiel X. The incense-offering of VIII becomes a scattering of fiery coals over the doomed city of earth by the angelic minister, as we read in Ezekiel. The liturgy of XV is even closer to Ezekiel—it is an entry of the temple by God's Glory, at which a cherub puts liquid fire (the vials of wrath) into angelic hands, to be outpoured upon the world. Now as to the parallel between XV and XI, 15 ff.: XI, 15 ff. is a two-part liturgy, the shouting of heavenly worshippers followed by an opening of the temple of God in heaven, to reveal the Ark of his covenant. The liturgy in xv is equally of two parts, the song of heavenly worshippers, followed by the opening of the 'temple of the tabernacle of the testimony' in heaven, to admit the Glory.

Let it be accepted that the parallel between the three sabbaths needs no more argument. xv, being so careful a match to the two previous sabbath-scenes, is itself the sabbath of the series in the blank: what we have to do is to identify the previous six visions to which it acts as seventh. But what are we to look for? Just six visions, or, as in the seals and trumpets, six visions followed by a set of 'intrusive visions'? Surely there can be no question of 'intrusive visions' here, for the very possibility of intrusive visions depends on the explicit counting of the rest of the series. It is because they are by contrast uncounted that we know them to be intrusive: it is because after them we return to the counting that we know the intrusion to be over. In the section we are examining there are no counted visions, and therefore no intrusion. We have to look for six visions, and no more. And, if we feel inclined to say that the feature of the intrusion, carefully built up and elaborated in VII and X–XI, cannot be allowed to die, a glance at the vials (XVI) may suffice to set us right. Here is a counted series, but the seventh directly follows the sixth. The intrusion-feature has died by this time anyhow. What more likely than that it died in the previous series (XI, 15–XIV), where the absence of counting was of itself enough to kill it?

In dividing the six visions of XII–XIV let us allow ourselves to be guided by the most objective and mechanical of tests. If St John does not mark the introduction of a fresh vision by the numbering of its angel or seal, how does he mark it? By the use of the rubric 'And I saw', for which 'And there was seen' (XII, 1) may be accepted as an equivalent. If we use this simple test, we get the following result:

(i) And a great sign was seen in heaven, a woman . . . and there was seen another sign in heaven, and behold, a dragon . . . (XII i—3).

(ii) And I saw a beast coming up out of the sea (XIII, i).

(iii) And I saw another beast coming up out of the earth (XIII, ii).

(iv) And I saw, and behold, the Lamb standing upon Mount Zion (XIV, 1).

(v) And I saw another angel flying in mid-heaven (XIV, 6).

(vi) And I saw, and behold a white cloud, and on the cloud sitting as a Son of Man (XIV, 14).

(vii) And I saw another sign in heaven great and marvellous, seven angels having seven plagues (xv, 1).

The only informality here is the repetition of the rubric in XII, 3, so that the first vision is made double: it is the vision of the woman, and the vision of the dragon. But it would surely be absurd to cut off the first two verses of XII and call them a separate vision, the vision of the woman: the fortunes of the woman and the dragon are intimately linked throughout the long chapter: it is a single two-headed vision. It is not the only such in St John's book: cf. XXI, 1–2, where we read: 'And I saw a new heaven and a new earth: for the first heaven and the first earth are passed away, and the sea is no more. And the holy city, new Jerusalem, saw I descending out of heaven from God. . . .'

The conclusion derived from the examination of beginnings is confirmed by an examination of endings, for these link into a system of refrains.

(i) And the dragon waxed wroth with the woman; and he went away to make war with the rest of her seed, which keep the commandments of God, and hold the testimony of Jesus; and he stood on the sand of the sea (XII, 17).

(ii) If any man hath an ear, let him hear. If any is for captivity, into captivity he goeth, if any to be killed with the sword, with the sword must he be killed. Here is the patience and faith of the saints (XIII, 9–10).

(iii) Here is wisdom: he that hath understanding, let him count the number of the Beast: for it is number of man. And his number is six hundred and sixty-six (XIII, 18).

(iv) These are they which were not defiled with women, for they are virgins; these are they which follow the Lamb whithersoever he goeth; these were purchased from among men, first fruits to God and the Lamb, and in their mouth was found no lie: they are unblemished (XIV, 4–5).

(v) Here is the patience of the saints, that keep the commandments of God and the faith of Jesus. And I heard a voice from heaven, saying, Write, Blessed are the dead that die in the Lord, and that presently. Yea, saith the Spirit, let them rest from their labours, for their works accompany them (XIV, 12–13).

(vi) And the winepress was trodden without the city, and there came out blood from the winepress even to the bridles of the horses, to the distance of furlongs a thousand and six hundred (XIV, 20).

We observe the theme of the sufferings and merits of the saints (i, ii, iv and v) and the two mysterious figures with sixes in them, which express the apostasy of the wicked and their punishment respectively (iii and vi). The dramatic 'Here is' formula appears in (ii), (iii) and (v).

So much for the beginnings and endings. Let us turn to the substance of the six visions. What we have is this:

> The Woman and the Dragon
> The Beast
> The Second Beast; a false Lamb
> The True Lamb and his followers
> Three flying angels with proclamations
> The Son of Man on clouds, and three angelic harvesters.

The first four form a group, being held together by the theme of Beast-Figures. The first is the vision of (the Woman and) the Dragon, the second is of the Beast, the third of the False Lamb, the fourth of the True. To appreciate the closeness of this sequence one must recall that 'dragon' is the LXX version of 'Leviathan' and 'beast' ($\theta\eta\rho\iota o\nu$) of 'Behemoth': or rather, 'Behemoth' is translated by the completely non-Greek 'plural of majesty' $\theta\eta\rho\iota\alpha$ 'beasts.' So 'Leviathan and Behemoth' will be 'the Dragon and the Beasts'—the two Beasts, says St John. The opposite of the Beast ($\theta\eta\rho\iota o\nu$) is the Lamb ($\check{\alpha}\rho\nu\iota o\nu$), whose appearance therefore brings the procession of animal-figures to a close. The real theme is as continuous as the apparent form—the four visions are concerned with the persecuting tyranny of the instruments of Satan, and the sacrificial loyalty of Christ and the Saints. The last vision of the four both belongs to its predecessors, and is their antithesis; it begins the movement in which divine power reacts against bestial usurpation.

The presence of the Lamb on Mount Zion is to be understood spiritually. It does not represent the Millennium: Zion is that spiritual 'place', neither Jerusalem nor Gerizim, where God through Christ is worshipped in spirit and in truth. The vision does not show the replacing of the throne of the Beast by the visible throne of Christ; it simply reveals the spiritual kingdom of Christ on earth which the Beast's tyranny is powerless to touch, and to which it is destined to succumb. There stand Christ and the saints, signed with the Holy Name, in defiance of the kingdom of the Beast's worshippers, who bear his blasphemous mark. If the primitive Christian wished to image Christ in the act of supplanting the Beast's usurpation, there was only one figure under which he could see him—not the figure of the Lamb, but the figure of the Son of Man on clouds: for this was the figure which Daniel had seen supplanting the Beast from the Sea, in the great vision of his seventh chapter, a vision which evidently supplies the most part of the material to Apocalypse XIII. And so the four beast-visions (XII–XIV, 5) are followed by a pair of visions (XIV, 6 ff.) which culminate in the figure of the Son of Man on clouds, with his attendant reapers and vintagers. That is the sixth vision: the fifth is supplied by forerunners of the Rider on the cloud, angels with warning cries, flying in mid-heaven.

When we were examining the six trumpets, we found there the series of God's creation-works, earth, sea, rivers, luminaries, living things of sky and water, living things of dry land. In the Beast-Visions (as we will now begin to call the whole series in XII–XIV) the theme of the six works reappears, though the first four are taken in reverse order. Why in the world St John should make the reversal, is a question we will reserve for the present: let us rather attend to the facts. The first vision, that of the woman and dragon, is firmly placed among the heavenly luminaries. The woman is a great sign in the sky, clothed with the sun, standing on the moon, and crowned with twelve stars. The dragon is also a celestial sign, and his tail sweeps up a third of the stars and casts them to the earth. When he is himself cast by Michael out of heaven, he must be thought to fall like a star: 'How art thou fallen from heaven, O Lucifer, son of the morning!'

Expelled from the region of the *stars*, he does not abandon his attempts at playing omnipotence: he tries to overcome the woman by shooting after her a *river of water*. Here too he is foiled: the earth swallows the river. His next attempt at mischief is to evoke the Beast out of the *sea*, and this is followed up by the emergence of the False Lamb from the *land*. The futility of his efforts is shown by the True Lamb and his followers, standing on Mount Zion.

So much for the four elements of the world, taken as they are in the reverse of their true order. The first of the flying angels, who initiates the fifth vision, epitomizes the four, calling on men to worship the God who really wields the world, 'the maker of heaven, earth, sea, and the fountains of water.' But this flying angel, while he epitomizes the four previous works, is himself the representation of the fifth work. On the fifth day God made not only living things of the water, but also birds to fly over the breadth of the firmament: and for that reason the plague of the fifth trumpet was introduced by 'an eagle flying in mid-heaven'. The phrase is echoed in the description of our angel, 'flying in mid-heaven', ἐν μεσουρήματι. The eagle cried triple *woe* to the inhabitants of earth from the plagues of the three trumpet-angels yet to sound. Our angel is himself one of three, and proclaims everlasting *gospel* to the dwellers upon earth. That he is the conscious antitype of the flying eagle is evident. He flies like a bird, a form of motion not attributed to an angel anywhere else in the Apocalypse, nor are any other angels even said to be winged, except of course the cherubim of Apocalypse IV.

We might conclude, then, that the angel of this fifth vision is represented bird-wise in allusion to the creation of birds on the fifth day of Genesis; but there is more to it than that. For it was a subject of speculation with the Jews, on which day of creation the angels were made, since scripture says nothing of the matter. There were allowed to be two 'probable answers': either they were made with the firmament of heaven, for it is their country, or else they were made with the birds, for they are included in the description 'winged fowl'. So angels, in so far as birdlike, are actually to be taken as creatures of the fifth day.[4]

From the fifth day we pass to the sixth, from (fishes and) birds to (beasts and) the son of man. As St John's fifth vision takes the second work of its day, so does his sixth. And both consider the work they take in its highest excellence: not any birds, but angels; not any man, but the New Adam, Jesus the Son of Man.

The visionary series of Apocalypse XII–XIV is of peculiar interest, because here St John places the famous symbol of the Son of Man back in that same Genesis-context from which the writer of Daniel had first drawn it; and it is of the highest importance for the understanding of the doctrine of Christ, that we should know his followers to have been still in possession of the clue to the Son of Man riddle, its relation to Genesis 1. Daniel VII is, of course, a spiritual exposition of Genesis 1, 20–28. The seer sees himself in, as it were, the fifth 'day' of the world's history, the day of the monsters which 'come up out of the great sea', always, to the Semitic mind, the symbols of chaotic and godless violence. But he knows that their time is appointed, and the day will come when the Ancient of Days will establish the everlasting dominion of the Son of Man 'over the fishes of the sea and the birds of the heaven and all cattle, over all the earth and all that crawl the earth' (Gen. 1, 28). Of this dominion there can be no end, for the Son of Man is the last work of God. He is not spawned either out of the sea or out of the land, but is especially the creature of heavenly God, made in his image and likeness: so whereas the beasts come up out of the sea, the Son of Man comes with the clouds of heaven. Daniel applies his parable to the history of mankind. There is the age in which the image of Leviathan reigns; the age is coming when the image of Adam will reign, and Adam is the image of God. The image of Adam, for the mere Jew, is to become incarnate in a regenerate Israel, of which Messiah is the representative head. For the Christian, Christ is primarily the image of Adam, and Christians derivatively his members. Allowing for this difference, there is no reason to think that the special title 'Son of

---

4. See [George Foot] Moore, *Judaism [in the First Centuries of the Christian Era: The Age of the Tannaim*, 3 vols. (Cambridge: Harvard UP, 1927–30)], I, 381.

Man' ever meant anything else from the time of Daniel to the time of St John, than what it means to both of them.

A fact which must immediately strike us about the visions in Apocalypse XII–XIV is the new distribution of emphasis. Both the seals and the trumpets run into a climax: their first four visions are preparatory, the weight is in the fifth and sixth. But in the beast-visions the weight is in the first four. The tyranny of the beasts is expansively treated, the triumph of the Son of Man is barely sketched. This curious fact needs to be brought into relation with another, which we have discussed already—the absence from XII–XIV of any 'intrusive visions'. The function of the intrusions after the sixth seal and the sixth trumpet was to carry an 'anticipated conclusion', a foreshadowing of how the whole apocalypse will end; with the result that the series of six seals or six trumpets *plus* the intrusive visions belonging to each could be read each as a complete apocalypse, though with a somewhat shadowy conclusion. Now the same thing can be said of the beast-visions: they provide a complete apocalypse, extending from the Incarnation (Birth of the Man Child) to the Second Advent (Son of Man on Clouds). But the conclusion is a mere shadow, a mere anticipation. The centre of XII–XIV is the Tyranny of Antichrist. The proper place of the Advent is in XIX. There are, as we said, no 'intrusive visions' in XII–XIV, but there is an 'anticipated conclusion' never the less.

We have now crossed the unmapped territory of XII–XIV. With the vials there begins once more a country of fields, lanes and hedgerows. The vials are most carefully modelled on the trumpets. The parallel begins, as we saw, in the sabbaths out of which the two weeks open (VIII, 1–5, XV). It is continued in the detail of the sevenfold series. The four first vials, like the four first trumpets, smite the four elements of the world, and in the same order: earth, sea, waters, luminaries. The fifths also match, though not so simply. The fifth trumpet released the smoke of the pit, whereby the sun and the air were darkened. If this had been the substance of the fifth trumpet-plague, it would have merely duplicated the fourth, in which all the heavenly lights were already darkened by a third part. But in fact the darkening of the air in the fifth trumpet is a mere prelude to a plague of locust-demons. In the fifth vial, no such development takes place: the darkening of the Beast's kingdom is the substance of the plague. To avoid any mere duplication of a precedent darkening of luminaries in the fourth vial, St John completely alters the character of the fourth vision. The sun, touched by the angel's fiery libation, is not darkened, but quickened to an intolerable heat.

In the sixth vision trumpets and vials closely correspond: armies from behind Euphrates are let loose for a predestined day of battle. ('The hour and day and month and year to slay the third of mankind'—'The battle of the great day of God Almighty: behold, I come as a thief'). In the trumpets the soldiers are demons, in the vials they are men.

So much for the six vials. There are, as we have said, no 'intrusive visions' after the sixth. We proceed straight to the seventh, which none the less reflects the character of the seventh trumpet-vision. The seventh trumpet-vision was 'great voices in heaven', declaring that the kingdom had come; and an opening of the temple, to the accompaniment of lightnings, voices, thunders, earthquakes, and great hail. At the seventh vial, a great voice comes out of the temple, saying, 'It is done,' to the accompaniment of lightnings, voices, thunders, earthquakes, and great hail. At the seventh trumpet the accompanying portents are a simple list, but at the seventh vial the two last items are expanded: the earthquake shakes down the cities of earth, cleaving Jerusalem and overthrowing Babylon; the hail falls in stones of a talent's weight, provoking blasphemy from unrepentant man.

This ingenious variation on the theme of the earlier vision is both characteristic of St John, and appropriate to its place. The seventh trumpet is widely separated from the first six, and does not really continue the sequence of judgements: it is rather the liturgy out of which the next sevenfold series opens: it is purely sabbatical in character. It is otherwise with the seventh vial. It is an immediate part of a continuous series, just as the seventh message is, and should conform to its series. And it is widely separated from the next sevenfold action by an interlude: it is not a sabbath-liturgy out of which a new week opens. St John does justice to such sabbatical character as it has by making the great voice 'It is done' the substance of the vision: but he conforms it to the series of active judgements of which it is the conclusion by developing its accompanying portents of earthquake and hail[5] into plagues on their own account. The trumpet plagues, being six, covered four elements of the world and two creations of living things. The vial-plagues are seven, and so the seventh vial requires a seventh sphere of action in which to take effect. It falls on none of the regions of whose creation Genesis makes specific mention, but on the air. On which day was the air created? Let us leave the question to the Rabbis who discuss the occasion of the making of angels.

With the seventh vial the system of numbered visions finally ends, and we step off the map for good. But we have little excuse for getting lost; an interpreter-angel steps forward to be our guide. He is explicitly said to be one of the seven vial-angels, and his business is to shew us in greater detail a mystery all too briefly touched in the seventh vial, the overthrow of Babylon. We may safely, therefore, consider him and the vision he has to shew as an explanatory appendix to the vials: the appendix could scarcely be more emphatically attached than it is. So much for the beginning of it: but where does it end? The interpreter-angel promises a vision of 'the judgement' (i.e. punishment) 'of the great harlot enthroned upon many waters'. But the vision, as it opens, hardly does justice to the description. It is not a shewing of the harlot's punishment, but of her queenly enthronement. True, the *comment* is added that such an enthronement will prove her certain ruin at last. But this comment, even among the comments offered, is not specially prominent: it cannot justify the description of Apocalypse XVII as 'a shewing of the punishment of the great harlot'. The discrepancy between title and contents is no mere clumsiness, however; it is simply another of St John's devices for sustaining climax and preserving continuity. The theme of the harlot's punishment overflows the *Angelus Interpres* vision. Very well, then let supplementary visions do justice to it. Let another angel descend from heaven with the proclamation of Babylon's doom, let voices from the sky exult over the smoke of her burning, let the sinking of a

---

5. The hail has room made for it by the rehandling of the previous plagues. In the trumpets, the first plague smites earth with hail and fire. In the first vial, a plague of boils is substituted, arising out of the infection of the dust of the earth. So the hail is left for the seventh vial, and the fire for the fourth (the sun scorches, instead of being darkened, as we have seen above).

millstone confirm her everlasting annihilation, let the dividing clouds reveal a heavenly host triumphant in the victory of God (Apoc. xvii–xix, 10).

The appendix to the vials trails out to a great length, but then the vial-series itself is very brief, and so the whole vial-section, series *plus* appendix, is still not disproportionate to the other five sections out of which the Apocalypse is made up. We need be in no doubt where it ends. xix, 1–10 builds up into a great scene of heavenly sabbath, an unmistakable companion-piece to the scenes out of which the seals, trumpets, beast-visions and vials each take their spring. And the new series which rises from it is nothing but the Advent itself. When the first seal was broken, and the first cherub cried 'Come', there appeared *a* rider on a white horse. It was not he for whom the cherub prayed, and the saints still cried, 'How long, O Lord?' But here at length is *the* Rider on the White Horse. He initiates the seven-fold series of the last things: there is nothing left for which the saints should pray.

We have now to attempt the formal analysis of this sevenfold series. Let us follow the same procedure as we did with the previous unnumbered series in xii–xiv. First we fix its limits: then we divide it up by the mechanical method of counting 'And I saw's. As to fixing the limits, we already have the beginning, the white-horsed rider of xix, 11. No less evident is the end, for everyone knows that the Apocalypse concludes with a Jerusalem-appendix set in careful balance against the Babylon-appendix to the vials. The comparison is enforced by the introductory phrases of the two appendices. 'And there came one of the seven angels that had the seven bowls, and spake with me, saying: Hither, and I will shew thee the judgement of the great harlot that sitteth upon many waters. . . . And he carried me away by the spirit into a wilderness' (xvii, 1–3). 'And there came one of the angels that had the seven bowls . . . and spake with me, saying: Hither, and I will shew thee the Bride, the Lamb's Wife. And he carried me away by the Spirit to a mountain' (xxi, 9–10). The relation of the two appendices to the previous texts on which they severally hang is the same. The 'judgement of the great harlot' sets forth in detail that fall of Babylon of which there was briefest mention in the last preceding vision (xvi, 19), and the vision of the Bride sets forth at length the establishment of Jerusalem, barely stated in the vision directly preceding (xxi, 2).

We have our end, then (xxi, 8) and we have our beginning (xix, 11). It remains to count the series. Since xxi, 9 ff. is not a sabbath, but an appendix, we ought to suppose that the Last Things, like the Vials, are a complete seven, comprising their own sabbath. Without more ado, let us count the 'I saw's.

(i) And I saw the heaven opened, and behold a white horse (xix, 11).
(ii) And I saw an angel standing in the sun (xix, 17).
(iii) And I saw the Beast and the kings of the earth (xix, 19).
(iv) And I saw an angel descending from heaven (xx, 1).
(v) And I saw thrones, and they sat on them (xx, 4).
(vi) And I saw a great white throne, and him that sat upon it (xx, 11).
(vii) And I saw a new heaven and a new earth . . . and the holy city saw I, New Jerusalem (xxi, 1, 2).

Nothing could be more formally beautiful than this series. There are four visions of the great battle, then two of the kingdom, the many millenial thrones and the one great throne of judgement. Then there is a seventh vision of the final sabbath, in which God will abide with men in a renovated world. The four visions of the battle are perfectly arranged. First there is a vision of the heavenly host, followed by a vision of the angel summoning the kites. Then there is a vision of the earthly host, followed by a vision of the angel haling off the defeated Dragon to his prison. As in the trumpets, beast-visions and vials, these four first visions set forth four elements of the world: here they are taken in vertical order, to express the invasion from above. The firmament opens to let forth the heavenly warriors: on their downward path is an angel standing in the sun to summon the birds who fly below. On earth stand the Beast and his allies: the abyss beneath is opened for Satan, and sealed over his head.

A second battle, the destruction of Gog, is not allowed to appear as a vision on its own account, but is compressed into a narrative appendix to the vision of millennial thrones. In that position, never the less, it makes a certain balance between the visions of the battle (I–IV) and the visions of the kingdom (V–VI). The judgements meted out after the battle become parallel to the judgements meted out after the defeat of Gog, at the Great Assize. In each of the preceding 'weeks' there has been a climax of judgement in the sixth vision. Here in the sixth sixth is the climax of climax, the Last Judgement itself. And so the sabbath which succeeds, and the appendix which, as an eighth, completes the whole, have no longer anything anticipatory about them. This is fulfilment: the throne of God and of the Lamb is set in the heart of the city, and the river of the Holy Ghost pours from beneath their feet to water it with eternal life. The saints look up, and their faces reflect the radiance of the Face of God.

6 And there are diuersities of operations, but it is the same God, which worketh all in all.

7 But the manifestation of the spirit, is giuen to euery man to profit withall.

8 For to one is giuen by the spirit, the word of wisedome, to another the word of knowledge, by the same spirit.

9 To another faith, by the same spirit: to another the gifts of healing, by the same spirit:

10 To another the working of miracles, to another prophecie, to another discerning of spirits, to another *diuers* kindes of tongues, to another the interpretation of tongues.

11 But all these worketh that one and the selfe same spirit, diuiding to euery man seuerally as he will.

12 For as the body is one, and hath many members, and all the membrs of that one body, being many, are one bodie: so also is Christ.

13 For by one spirit are we all baptized into one bodie, whether *wee bee* Jewes or † Gentiles, whether *wee bee* bond or free: and haue beene all made to drinke into one spirit.

†Gr.Greeks.

14 For the body is not one member, but many.

15 If the foot shall say, Because I am not the hand, I am not of the body: is it therefore not of the body?

16 And if the eare shall say, Because I am not the eye, I am not of the body: is it therefore not of the body?

17 If the whole body were an eye, where were the hearing? If the whole were hearing, where were the smelling?

18 But now hath God set the members, euery one of them in the body, as it hath pleased him.

19 And if they were all one member, where were the body?

20 But now are they many members, yet but one body.

21 And the eye cannot say vnto the hand, I haue no need of thee: nor againe, the head to the feete, I haue no neede of you.

22 Nay, much more those members of the bodie, which seeme to bee more feeble, are necessary.

23 And those *members* of the bodie, which wee thinke to bee lesse honourable, vpon these we || bestow more abundant honour, and our vncomely parts

||Or,put on.

haue more abundant comelinesse.

24 For our comely *parts* haue no need: but God hath tempered the bodie together, hauing giuen more abundant honour to that part which lacked:

25 That there should be no||schisme in the body: but that the members should haue the same care one for another.

||Or, diuision.

26 And whether one member suffer, all the members suffer with it: or one member be honoured, all the menbers reioyce with it.

27 Now yee are the body of Christ, and members in particular.

28 And God hath set some in the Church, first Apostles, secondarily Prophets, thirdly Teachers, after that miracles, then gifts of healings, helpes in gouernmёts, ||diuersities of tongues.

||Or,kinds.

29 Are all Apostles? are all Prophets? are all Teachers? are all ||workers of miracles?

||Or, powers.

30 Haue all the gifts of healing? doe all speake with tongues? doe all interpret?

31 But couet earnestly the best gifts: And yet shew I vnto you a more excellent way.

CHAP. XIII.

1 All giftes, 2. 3 how excellent soeuer, are nothing worth without charitie. 4 The praises therof, and 13 prelation before hope & faith.

Though I speake with the tongues of men & of Angels, and haue not charity, I am become as sounding brasse or a tinkling cymbal.

2 And though I haue the gift of prophesie, and vnderstand all mysteries and all knowledge: and though I haue all faith, so that I could remooue mountaines, and haue no charitie, I am nothing.

3 And though I bestowe all my goods to feede the poore, and though I giue my body to bee burned, and haue not charitie, it profiteth me nothing.

4 Charitie suffereth long, and is kinde: charitie enuieth not: charitie || vaunteth not it selfe, is not puffed vp,

||Or,is not rash.

5 Doeth not behaue it selfe vnseemly, seeketh not her owne, is not easily prouoked, thinketh no euill,

6 Reioyceth not in iniquitie, but reioyceth ||in the trueth:

||Or,with the trueth.

7 Beareth all things, beleeueth all things, hopeth all things, endureth all things.

R   3 Cha-

JOHN WYCLIFFE[†]

1 If Y speke with tungis of men and of aungels, and Y haue not charite, Y am maad
2 as bras sownynge, or a cymbal tynkynge. ·And if Y haue prophecie, and knowe
alle mysteries, and al kunnynge, and if Y haue al feith, so that Y meue hillis fro
3 her place, and Y haue not charite, Y am nouȝt. ·And if Y departe alle my goodis in
to the metis of pore men, and yf Y bitake my bodi, so that Y brenne, and if Y haue
4 not charite, it profitith to me no thing. ·Charite is pacient, it is benygne; charite
5 enuyeth not, it doith not wickidli, it is not blowun, ·it is not coueytouse, it sekith
not tho thingis that ben hise owne, it is not stirid to wraththe, it thenkith not
6,7 yuel, ·it ioyeth not on wickidnesse, but it ioieth togidere to treuthe; ·it suffrith
alle thingis, it bileueth alle thingis, it hopith alle thingis, it susteyneth alle thingis.
8 ·Charite fallith neuere doun, whether prophecies schulen be voidid, ethir langa-
9 gis schulen ceesse, ethir science schal be distried. ·For a parti we knowun, and a
10 parti we prophecien; ·but whanne that schal come that is parfit, that thing that
11 is of parti schal be auoidid. ·Whanne Y was a litil child, Y spak as a litil child,
Y vndurstood as a litil child, Y thouȝte as a litil child; but whanne Y was maad a
12 man, Y auoidide tho thingis that weren of a litil child. ·And we seen now bi a
myrour in derknesse, but thanne face to face; now Y knowe of parti, but thanne
13 Y schal knowe, as Y am knowun. ·And now dwellen feith, hope, and charite,
these thre; but the most of these is charite.

WILLIAM TYNDALE[‡]

Though I spake with the tonges of men and angels, and yet had no love, I were
even as soundinge brasse: or as a tynklynge Cymball. And though I coulde
prophesy, and vnderstode all secretes, and all knowledge: yee, yf I had all fayth so
that I coulde move mountayns oute of ther places, and yet had no love, I were

† Two versions of the Bible translated by John Wycliffe (ca. 1324–1384) from the Latin Vulgate survive. This is the later, more idiomatic (i.e., less Latinate) one, from Josiah Forshall and
Frederic Madden's critical edition (4 vols.; Oxford: Oxford University Press, 1850). It seems to
have appeared first in the late 1380s or the 1390s, sometime after Wycliffe's death. It is unclear
to what extent Wycliffe is himself responsible for either version; he certainly had assistance. In
any case, the translations attributed to him are the earliest English versions of the Bible in its
entirety.
‡ From *The New Testament, Translated by William Tyndale, 1534*, ed. N. Hardy Wallis
(Cambridge: Cambridge University Press, 1938).

The scholar and priest William Tyndale (ca. 1494–1536) found no support for his plan to
publish a vernacular New Testament in England, and so the first English translation of the
New Testament from Greek—indeed, the first printed English Bible—was actually published in
Worms (Germany) in 1526. Tyndale's revision, printed in Antwerp eight years later, is included
here. It deeply influenced later English translations, including KJV. Because Tyndale had
aligned himself with the Protestant Reformers once he left England for the continent, he was
arrested by Catholic authorities in Antwerp and executed for heresy.

nothynge. And though I bestowed all my gooddes to fede the poore, and though I gave my body even that I burned, and yet had no love, it profeteth me nothinge.

Love suffreth longe, and is corteous. Love envieth not. Love doth not frowardly, swelleth not dealeth not dishonestly, seketh not her awne, is not provoked to anger, thynketh not evyll, reioyseth not in iniquite: but reioyseth in the trueth, suffreth all thynge, beleveth all thynges, hopeth all thynges, endureth in all thynges. Though that prophesyinge fayle, other tonges shall cease, or knowledge vanysshe awaye, yet love falleth never awaye.

For oure knowledge is vnparfect, and oure prophesyinge is vnperfet. But when that which is parfect is come, then that which is vnparfet shall bedone awaye. When I was a chylde, I spake as a chylde, I vnderstode as a childe, I ymagened as a chylde. But assone as I was a man, I put awaye childesshnes. Now we se in a glasse even in a darke speakynge: but then shall we se face to face. Now I knowe vnparfectly: but then shall I knowe even as I am knowen. Now abideth fayth, hope, and love, even these thre: but the chefe of these is love.

GENEVA BIBLE[†]

1. Thogh I speake with the tongues of men and Angels, and haue not loue, I am *as* sounding brasse, or a tinkling cymbal.

2. And thogh I had the *gift* of prophecie, and knewe all secretes and all knowledge, yea, if I had all faith, so that I colde remoue mountaines and had not loue, I were nothing.

3. And thogh I fede the poore with all my goods, and thogh I giue my bodie, that I be burned, and haue not loue, it profiteth me nothing.

4. Loue suffreth long: it is bountiful: loue enuieth not: loue doeth not boast it self: it is not puffed vp:

5. It disdaineth not: it seketh not her owne things: it is not prouoked to anger: it thinketh not euil:

6. It reioyceth not in iniquitie, but reioyceth in the trueth:

7. It Suffreth all things: it beleueth all things: it hopeth all things: it endureth all things.

8. Loue doeth neuer fall away, thogh that prophecyings be abolished, or the tongues cease, or knowledge vanish away.

9. For we knowe in parte,[1] and we prophecie[2] in parte.

10. But when that which is parfite, is come, then that which is in parte, shalbe abolished.

---

† From *The Geneva Bible: A Facsimile of the 1560 Edition* (Madison: University of Wisconsin Press, 1969). All notes are from the Geneva Bible.

The Geneva Bible was originally published in 1560, though the New Testament appeared on its own in 1557. It was printed in the Swiss city whose name it came to bear because the English Protestant scholars who produced it had fled there during Mary I's reign. Although an excellent translation, it included copious and occasionally tendentious interpretative annotations of a Puritan flavor (not included here), and these came to be seen as somewhat controversial.

1. That is, imperfectly.

2. *Or, teache.*

11. When I was a childe, I spake as a childe, I vnderstode as a childe, I thoght as a childe: but when I became a man, I put away childish things.

12. For now we se through a glasse darkely: but then *shal we se* face to face. Now I knowe in parte: but then shal I knowe euen as I am knowen.[3]

13. And now abideth faith, hope & loue, *euen* these three: but the chiefest of these *is* loue.

RHEIMS NEW TESTAMENT[†]

1. If I speake with the tongues of men, and of Angels, and haue not charitie, I am become as sounding brasse, or a tinkling cymbal. 2. And if I should haue prophecie, and knew al mysteries, and al knowledge, & if I should haue al faith so that I could remoue mountaines, and haue not charitie, I am nothing. 3. And if I should distribute al my goods to be meate for the poore, and if I should deliuer my body so that I burne, and haue not charitie, it doth profit me nothing.

4. Charitie is patient, is benigne: Charitie enuieth not, dealeth not peruersly: is not puffed vp, 5. is not ambitious, seeketh not her owne, is not prouoked to anger, thinketh not euil, 6. reioyceth not vpon iniquitie, but reioyceth with the truth: 7. suffereth al things, beleeueth al things, hopeth al things, beareth al things. 8. Charitie neuer falleth away: whether prophecies shal be made void, or tongues shal cease, or knowledge shal be destroied. 9. For in part we know, & in part we prophecie. 10. But when that shal come that is perfect, that shal be made void that is in part. 11. When I was a litle one, I speake as a litle one, I vnderstood as a litle one, I thought as a litle one. But when I was made a man, I did away the things that belonged to a litle one. 12. We see now by a glasse in a darke sort: but then face to face. Now I know in part: but then I shal know as also I am knowen. 13. And now there remaine, faith, hope, charitie, these three: but the greater of these is charitie.

BISHOPS' BIBLE[‡]

1. Though I speake with the tongues of men, and of angels, and haue not charitie, I am (as) sounding brasse, or (as) a tynckling Cymbale.

---

3. *Or, saught of God.*

† From *The New Testament of Jesus Christ Faithfully translated into English, out of the authentical Latin, diligently conferred with the Greek, & other Editions in divers languages . . . ,* 4th ed. (n.p.: John Cousturier, 1633).

The Rheims New Testament (1582) is a Catholic translation of the Latin Vulgate into English, made primarily by Gregory Martin at the English Catholic College at Rheims (which had been established for British Catholics exiled on the continent after Elizabeth came to the throne). Although it frequently follows earlier English translations, its prose is sometimes bafflingly Latinate. It was therefore revised in the eighteenth century to enhance its intelligibility. The original is included here.

‡ From *The Holie Byble*, rev. ed. (London: R. Jugge, 1572). All notes are from the Bishops' Bible.

2. And though I haue prophecie, and understand al secreces, and al knowl-edge: Yea, if I haue al fayth, so that I can remooue mountaynes, and haue not charitie, I am nothyng.

3. And though I bestowe al my goodes to feede the poore, and though I geue my body that I shoulde be burned, and haue not charitie, it profiteth me nothing.

4. Charitie suffereth long, and is curteous: Charitie enuieth not, charitie doth not frowardly, swelleth not,[1]

5. Dealeth not dishonestly, seeketh not her owne, is not bitter, thinketh not euyl,

6. Reioyceth not in iniquitie, but reioyceth in the trueth:

7. Suffereth al things, beleeueth al things, hopeth al thinges, endureth al thynges.

8. Though that prophesiynges fayle, either tongues ceasse, or knowledge uan-ish away, (yet) charitie falleth neuer away.

9. For our knowledge is unperfect,[2] and our prophesiyng is unperfect:

10. But when that which is perfect is come, then that whiche is unperfect shalbe done away.

11. When I was a childe, I spake as a child. I understoode as a childe, I imag-ined as a childe: but assoone as I was a man, I put away childishnesse.

12. Nowe we see in a glasse, euen in a darke speaking: but then (shal we see) face to face. Nowe I knowe unperfectly: but then shal I knowe, euen as I am knowen.

13. Now abydeth fayth, hope, and charitie, these three, but the cheefe of these is charitie.

KING JAMES VERSION[†]

1 Though I speake with the tongues of men & of Angels, and haue not charity, I am become as sounding brasse or a tinkling cymbal.

The Bishops' Bible, first printed in 1568 with a revised edition in 1572 (included here), was commissioned by Archbishop of Canterbury Matthew Parker, who assigned various portions of the Bible to different bishops for translation and later revised much of their work himself. It was intended to supersede the Geneva Bible, whose popularity was immense but whose Puritan notes and foreign origins made English ecclesiastical authorities suspicious. At the same time, it was to replace the English Bible that the monarchy had previously authorized for public read-ing, the deficient Great Bible, first published in 1539. (That version relied heavily on Tyndale's work; the portions of the Bible Tyndale had not gotten to before his execution were rendered from Latin and German by Miles Cloverdale, who knew no Hebrew.) The bishops were not strong philologists or inspired prose stylists, however, and neither ambition was realized.

1. Or, is not puft up.

2. Or, in part.

† From *The Holy Bible, Conteyning the Old Testament, and the New* (London: Robert Barker, 1611). All notes are from KJV.

KJV (1611), conceived as a revision of the Bishops' Bible and as an answer to the ever popu-lar Geneva, was to rectify the deficiencies of the former and to omit the interpretative annota-tions of the latter, a few of which offended King James himself. About fifty scholars, working in six groups, began the project in 1604. King James commissioned this Bible, but neither he nor any other monarch ever "authorized" it, and it was not commonly referred to as such until the nineteenth century.

2 And though I haue the gift of prophesie, and vnderstand all mysteries and all knowledge: and though I haue all faith, so that I could remooue mountaines, and haue no charitie, I am nothing.

3 And though I bestowe all my goods to feede the poore, and though I giue my body to bee burned, and haue not charitie, it profiteth me nothing.

4 Charitie suffereth long, and is kinde: charite enuieth not: charitie vaunteth not it selfe,[1] is not puffed vp,

5 Doeth not behaue it selfe vnseemly, seeketh not her owne, is not easily prouoked, thinketh no euill,

6 Reioyceth not in iniquitie, but reioyceth in the trueth:[2]

7 Beareth all things, beleeueth all things, hopeth all things, endureth all things.

8 Charitie neuer faileth: but whether there be prophesies, *they* shall faile; whether there bee tongues, *they* shall cease; whether there bee knowledge, *it* shall vanish away.

9 For we know in part, and we prophesie in part.

10 But when that which is perfect is come, then that which is in part, shalbe done away.

11 When I was a childe, I spake as a childe, I vnderstood as a childe, I thought[3] as a childe: but when I became a man, I put away childish things.

12 For now we see through a glasse, darkely:[4] but then face to face: now I know in part, but then shall I know euen as also I am knowen.

13 And now abideth faith, hope, charitie, these three, but the greatest of these is charitie.

REVISED VERSION†

1 If I speak with the tongues of men and of angels, but have not love, I am become
2 sounding brass, or a clanging cymbal. ·And if I have *the gift of* prophecy, and know all mysteries and all knowledge; and if I have all faith, so as to remove mountains, but have not love, I am nothing. ·And if I bestow all my goods to feed
3 *the poor*, and if I give my body to be burned,[1] but have not love, it profiteth me

1. *Or, is not rash.*
2. *Or, with the trueth.*
3. *Or, reasoned.*
4. *Or, in a riddle.*

† From *The New Testament of Our Lord and Saviour Jesus Christ Translated Out of the Greek: Being the Version Set Forth* A.D. *1611 Compared with the Most Ancient Authorities and Revised* A.D. *1881* (Cambridge: Cambridge University Press, 1881). All notes are from the RV.

The 1881 Revised Version of the New Testament was intended primarily to update KJV with reference to modern biblical scholarship, especially textual criticism, for the nineteenth century had seen critical editions of the Greek New Testament far superior to the texts on which KJV was based. The RV was ostensibly a conservative revision, as the preface suggests: its stated intent was "to introduce as few alterations as possible. . . . Our task was revision, not re-translation." Despite its initial popularity, many readers ultimately concluded that the RV had departed from KJV more radically than its own statement of purpose had authorized, and that it unnecessarily ruined KJV's literary qualities—problems its successor resolved.

4 nothing. •Love suffereth long, *and* is kind; love envieth not; love vaunteth not
5 itself, is not puffed up, •doth not behave itself unseemly, seeketh not its own, is
6 not provoked, taketh not account of evil; •rejoiceth not in unrighteousness, but
7 rejoiceth with the truth; •beareth[2] all things, believeth all things, hopeth all
8 things, endureth all things. •Love never faileth: but whether *there be* prophecies,
they shall be done away; whether *there be* tongues, they shall cease; whether
9 *there be* knowledge, it shall be done away. •For we know in part, and we prophesy
10 in part: •but when that which is perfect is come, that which is in part shall be
11 done away. •When I was a child, I spake as a child, I felt as a child, I thought as a
12 child: now that I am become a man, I have put away childish things. •For now we
see in a mirror, darkly[3]; but then face to face: now I know in part; but then shall
13 I know[4] even as also I have been known.[5] •But now abideth faith, hope, love,
these three; and the greatest[6] of these[7] is love.

REVISED STANDARD VERSION†

[1]If I speak in the tongues of men and of angels, but have not love, I am a noisy
gong or a clanging cymbal. [2]And if I have prophetic powers, and understand all
mysteries and all knowledge, and if I have all faith, so as to remove mountains, but
have not love, I am nothing. [3]If I give away all I have, and if I deliver my body to be
burned,[1] but have not love, I gain nothing.

[4]Love is patient and kind; love is not jealous or boastful; [5]it is not arrogant or
rude. Love does not insist on its own way; it is not irritable or resentful; [6]it does not
rejoice at wrong, but rejoices in the right. [7]Love bears all things, believes all things,
hopes all things, endures all things.

[8]Love never ends; as for prophecies, they will pass away; as for tongues, they
will cease; as for knowledge, it will pass away. [9]For our knowledge is imperfect and
our prophecy is imperfect; [10]but when the perfect comes, the imperfect will pass

1. Many ancient authorities read *that I may glory.*
2. Or, *covereth.*
3. Gr. *in a riddle.*
4. Gr. *know fully.*
5. Gr. *known fully.*
6. Gr. *greater.*
7. Or, *but greater than these.*

† From *The New Oxford Annotated Bible,* Revised Standard Version, ed. Herbert G. May
and Bruce M. Metzger (New York: Oxford University Press, 1973). All notes are from the RSV.
The Revised Standard Version of the New Testament (1946; 2nd ed., 1971) is a revision of the
American Standard Version, a translation closely related to the RV, and almost identical in 1 Cor
13. Its preface announces its intent to "stay as close to the Tyndale–King James tradition as it
can in the light of our present knowledge of the Hebrew and Greek texts and their meaning on
the one hand, and our present understanding of English on the other." It negotiated a more
successful compromise than its predecessor between the requirements of modern biblical
scholarship and the great tradition of English Bible translation.
    1. Other ancient authorities read *body that I may glory.*

away. [11]When I was a child, I spoke like a child, I thought like a child, I reasoned like a child; when I became a man, I gave up childish ways. [12]For now we see in a mirror dimly, but then face to face. Now I know in part; then I shall understand fully, even as I have been fully understood. [13]So faith, hope, love abide, these three; but the greatest of these is love.

NEW REVISED STANDARD VERSION[†]

[1]If I speak in the tongues of mortals and of angels, but do not have love, I am a noisy gong or a clanging cymbal. [2]And if I have prophetic powers, and understand all mysteries and all knowledge, and if I have all faith, so as to remove mountains, but do not have love, I am nothing. [3]If I give away all my possessions, and if I hand over my body so that I may boast,[1] but do not have love, I gain nothing.

[4]Love is patient; love is kind; love is not envious or boastful or arrogant [5]or rude. It does not insist on its own way; it is not irritable or resentful; [6]it does not rejoice in wrongdoing, but rejoices in the truth. [7]It bears all things, believes all things, hopes all things, endures all things.

[8]Love never ends. But as for prophecies, they will come to an end; as for tongues, they will cease; as for knowledge, it will come to an end. [9]For we know only in part, and we prophesy only in part; [10]but when the complete comes, the partial will come to an end. [11]When I was a child, I spoke like a child, I thought like a child, I reasoned like a child; when I became an adult, I put an end to childish ways. [12]For now we see in a mirror, dimly,[2] but then we will see face to face. Now I know only in part; then I will know fully, even as I have been fully known. [13]And now faith, hope, and love abide, these three; and the greatest of these is love.

NEW ENGLISH BIBLE[‡]

[1] I may speak in tongues of men or of angels, but if I am without love, I am a
[2] sounding gong or a clanging cymbal. ·I may have the gift of prophecy, and know every hidden truth; I may have faith strong enough to move mountains; but if I

---

† From *The HarperCollins Study Bible: Fully Revised and Updated*, New Revised Standard Version, ed. Harold W. Attridge (San Francisco: HarperCollins, 2006). All notes are from the NRSV.
    The New Revised Standard Version (1989) substantially revises the RSV. It is generally more colloquial, especially in the New Testament, and, as its preface announces, it eliminates "masculine-oriented language . . . as far as this can be done without altering passages that reflect the historical situation of ancient patriarchal culture." The result is a translation that departs much further from the Tyndale–King James tradition than did its immediate predecessor.
    1. Other ancient authorities read *body to be burned*.
    2. Gk *in a riddle*.
    ‡ From *The New English Bible: New Testament* (Oxford: Oxford University Press; Cambridge: Cambridge University Press, 1961). All notes are from the NEB.

3   have no love, I am nothing. ·I may dole out all I possess, or even give my body to
     be burnt,[1] but if I have no love, I am none the better.

4   ·Love is patient; love is kind and envies no one. Love is never boastful, nor
5   conceited, ·nor rude; never selfish, not quick to take offence. Love keeps no score
6,7 of wrongs; ·does not gloat over other men's sins, but delights in the truth. ·There
     is nothing love cannot face; there is no limit to its faith, its hope, and its
     endurance.

8   ·Love will never come to an end. Are there prophets? their work will be over.
     Are there tongues of ecstasy? they will cease. Is there knowledge? it will vanish
9,10 away; ·for our knowledge and our prophecy alike are partial, ·and the partial van-
11   ishes when wholeness comes. ·When I was a child, my speech, my outlook, and
     my thoughts were all childish. When I grew up, I had finished with childish
12   things. ·Now we see only puzzling reflections in a mirror, but then we shall see
     face to face. My knowledge now is partial; then it will be whole, like God's knowl-
13   edge of me. ·In a word, there are three things that last for ever: faith, hope, and
     love; but the greatest of them all is love.

GOOD NEWS BIBLE[†]

[1]I may be able to speak the languages of men and even of angels, but if I have not
love, my speech is no more than a noisy gong or a clanging bell. [2]I may have the
gift of inspired preaching; I may have all knowledge and understand all secrets; I
may have all the faith needed to move mountains—but if I have not love, I am
nothing. [3]I may give away everything I have, and even give up my body to be
burned—but if I have not love, it does me no good.

[4]Love is patient and kind; love is not jealous, or conceited, or proud; [5]love is not
ill-mannered, or selfish, or irritable; love does not keep a record of wrongs; [6]love

---

The New English Bible (NT 1961; OT and Apocrypha 1970) eschews the Tyndale–King James
tradition of English Bible translation. As its preface announces, the NEB is "a completely new
translation . . . rather than a revision" and "the translators [were] free to employ a contemporary
idiom rather than reproduce the traditional 'biblical' English." Perhaps not surprisingly, in light
of its ostensible abandonment of the tradition of English Bible translation, it provoked a hostile
response from T. S. Eliot and other conservative critics. It was revised in 1989 (under the title
Revised English Bible), but the original is included here.

1. Some witnesses read *even seek glory by self-sacrifice.*

† From *Good News for Modern Man: The New Testament in Today's English Version* (New York:
American Bible Society, 1966).

The Good News Bible (NT 1966; OT 1976) aims for simplicity and straightforwardness
throughout: "After ascertaining as accurately as possible the meaning of the original, the translators' next task was to express that meaning in a manner and form easily understood by the
readers. . . . Every effort has been made to use language that is natural, clear, simple, and unambiguous. Consequently there has been no attempt to reproduce in English the parts of speech,
sentence structure, word order, and grammatical devices of the original languages" (preface). Its
stated quest for simplicity results in a somewhat looser translation than most of those sampled in
this section. Although the Good News Bible has been revised repeatedly since its initial publication (most notably in the edition of 1992), the original version is included here.

is not happy with evil, but is happy with the truth. [7]Love never gives up: its faith, hope, and patience never fail.

[8]Love is eternal. There are inspired messages, but they are temporary; there are gifts of speaking, but they will cease; there is knowledge, but it will pass. [9]For our gifts of knowledge and of inspired messages are only partial; [10]but when what is perfect comes, then what is partial disappears.

[11]When I was a child, my speech, feelings, and thinking were all those of a child; now that I am a man, I have no more use for childish ways. [12]What we see now is like the dim image in a mirror; then we shall see face to face. What I know now is only partial; then it will be complete, as complete as God's knowledge of me.

[13]Meanwhile these three remain: faith, hope, and love; and the greatest of these is love.

NEW INTERNATIONAL VERSION[†]

[1]If I speak in the tongues[1] of men or of angels, but do not have love, I am only a resounding gong or a clanging cymbal. [2]If I have the gift of prophecy and can fathom all mysteries and all knowledge, and if I have a faith that can move mountains, but do not have love, I am nothing. [3]If I give all I possess to the poor and give over my body to hardship that I may boast,[2] but do not have love, I gain nothing.

[4]Love is patient, love is kind. It does not envy, it does not boast, it is not proud. [5]It does not dishonor others, it is not self-seeking, it is not easily angered, it keeps no record of wrongs. [6]Love does not delight in evil but rejoices with the truth. [7]It always protects, always trusts, always hopes, always perseveres.

[8]Love never fails. But where there are prophecies, they will cease; where there are tongues, they will be stilled; where there is knowledge, it will pass away. [9]For we know in part and we prophesy in part, [10]but when completeness comes, what is in part disappears. [11]When I was a child, I talked like a child, I thought like a child, I reasoned like a child. When I became a man, I put the ways of childhood behind me. [12]For now we see only a reflection as in a mirror; then we shall see face to face. Now I know in part; then I shall know fully, even as I am fully known.

[13]And now these three remain: faith, hope and love. But the greatest of these is love.

† The New International Version of the Bible (1978; NT in 1973) is an extremely popular translation, especially in evangelical circles. It has been revised numerous times. The latest version (2011) is included here, from www.biblica.com (in partnership with Zondervan, the NIV's current publisher). All notes are from the NIV.

1. Or *languages*.
2. Some manuscripts *body to the flames*.

NEW JERUSALEM BIBLE†

1 Though I command languages both human and angelic—if I speak without love,
2 I am no more than a gong booming or a cymbal clashing. ·And though I have the power of prophecy, to penetrate all mysteries and knowledge, and though I have all the faith necessary to move mountains—if I am without love, I am noth-
3 ing. ·Though I should give away to the poor all that I possess, and even give up my body to be burned[1]—if I am without love, it will do me no good whatever.

4 Love is always patient and kind; love is never jealous; love is not boastful or
5 conceited, ·it is never rude and never seeks its own advantage, it does not take
6 offence or store up grievances. ·Love does not rejoice at wrongdoing, but finds its
7 joy in the truth. ·It is always ready to make allowances, to trust, to hope and to endure whatever comes.

8 Love never comes to an end. But if there are prophecies, they will be done away with; if tongues, they will fall silent; and if knowledge, it will be done away
9,10 with. ·For we know only imperfectly, and we prophesy imperfectly; ·but once per-
11 fection comes, all imperfect things will be done away with. ·When I was a child, I used to talk like a child, and see things as a child does, and think like a child;
12 but now that I have become an adult, I have finished with all childish ways. Now we see only reflections in a mirror, mere riddles, but then we shall be seeing face to face. Now, I can know only imperfectly; but then I shall know just as fully as I am myself known.

13 As it is, these remain: faith, hope and love, the three of them; and the greatest of them is love.

RICHMOND LATTIMORE‡

¶ But now I show you a way that is even better. If I speak with the tongues of men and angels, but have no love, all I am is sounding bronze or a clashing cymbal. And if I have the gift of prophecy and know all mysteries and all understanding, and if I have faith entire so as to move mountains, and have no love, I am nothing.

---

† From *The New Jerusalem Bible* (New York: Doubleday, 1985). All notes are from the NJB. *The Jerusalem Bible* (1966) translates the French *Bible de Jérusalem* (1961), a sophisticated Catholic study Bible produced by scholars associated with the École Biblique in Jerusalem. Its revision in 1973 led to the *New Jerusalem Bible* (1985), excerpted here. Unlike its predecessor, the *New Jerusalem Bible* is translated directly from the original ancient languages, rather than from the French with reference to the originals. It strives for a somewhat literal translation; for instance, it is more careful than perhaps any other English version to ensure that "key terms in the originals . . . (are) rendered throughout . . . by the same English word" (foreword).
1. Var. "I may give all my goods to the poor so that I can boast of it."
‡ From *The New Testament*, trans. Richmond Lattimore (New York: North Point Press, 1996). Toward the end of his career, the American classicist, poet, and translator of ancient Greek literature Richmond Lattimore (1906–1984) turned his talents to the New Testament. His version of Acts and the New Testament Epistles first appeared in 1982.

And if I give all I have in alms, and if I give my body to be burned, and have no love, it does me no good. Love is patient, is kind, love has no jealousy, does not swagger, has no pride, is not immodest, does not look for its own advantage, is not stirred to anger, does not keep count of evil done, is not happy over wrongdoing, shares the happiness of the truth; all-sustaining, all-faithful, all-hopeful, all-enduring. Love never fails. If there are prophecies, they will come to nothing; if there are speeches, they will be stopped; if there is understanding, it will come to nothing. For we understand in part and we prophesy in part; but when completeness comes, what is in part will vanish away. When I was a child, I spoke as a child, and thought as a child, and reasoned as a child; now that I am a man, I am through with childish things. For now we see by a mirror, obscurely; but then face to face. Now I know in part; but then I will know in full, as I myself am fully known. And now there remain faith, hope, love; these three; but the greatest of these is love.

J. B. PHILLIPS[†]

If I were to speak with the combined eloquence of men and angels I should stir men like a fanfare of trumpets or the crashing of cymbals, but unless I had love, I should do nothing more. If I had the gift of foretelling the future and had in my mind not only all human knowledge but the secrets of God, and if, in addition, I had that absolute faith which can move mountains, but had no love, I tell you I should amount to nothing at all. If I were to sell all my possessions to feed the hungry and, for my convictions, allowed my body to be burned, and yet had no love, I should achieve precisely nothing.

This love of which I speak is slow to lose patience—it looks for a way of being constructive. It is not possessive: it is neither anxious to impress nor does it cherish inflated ideas of its own importance.

Love has good manners and does not pursue selfish advantage. It is not touchy. It does not compile statistics of evil or gloat over the wickedness of other people. On the contrary, it is glad with all good men when Truth prevails.

Love knows no limit to its endurance, no end to its trust, no fading of its hope: it can outlast anything. It is, in fact, the one thing that still stands when all else has fallen.

For if there are prophecies they will be fulfilled and done with, if there are "tongues" the need for them will disappear, if there is knowledge it will be swallowed up in truth. For our knowledge is always incomplete and our prophecy is

† From J. B. Phillips, *Letters to Young Churches: A Translation of the New Testament Epistles* (New York: Macmillan, 1954).

The Anglican priest J. B. Phillips (1906–1982) was convinced that the Bible's meaning had been obscured by KJV and the tradition of English Bible translation it represented, not only by archaism but also "by the sheer beauty of language as well as by the familiarity of repetition" ("The Problems of Making a Contemporary Translation," *The Bible Translator* 16 [1965]: 28). He therefore aimed to translate the New Testament into a vivid and contemporary English idiom. Phillips's translation (published in its entirety in 1958) has had many admirers, including C. S. Lewis, who wrote the introduction to its initial installment, *Letters to Young Churches* (1947).

always incomplete, and when the Complete comes, that is the end of the Incomplete.

When I was a little child I talked and felt and thought like a little child. Now that I am a man my childish speech and feeling and thought have no further significance for me.

At present all we see is the baffling reflection of reality; we are like men looking at a landscape in a small mirror. The time will come when we shall see reality whole and face to face! At present all I know is a little fraction of the truth, but the time will come when I shall know it as fully as God now knows me!

In this life we have three great lasting qualities—faith, hope and love. But the greatest of them is love.

JOHN BOIS

[Notes]†

In the Epistle to the Romans

* * *

Cap. 2. 15. μεταξὺ ἀλλήλων] [among themselves, or, meanwhile . . . one another] i.e. as I conjecture, in turn, by turns. ἐναλλάξ [alternately] ἀνὰ μέρος [by turns, in turn] ἐν μέρει [in turn]. *Otherwhiles.* It has been agreed by the chief of my colleagues that τὸ ἀλλήλων [the word, one another] was governed by κατηγορούντων [accusing], which to my mind can in no way be established. At least better than what is not clearly demonstrated: κατηγορούντων, of course αὐτούς [them].

* * *

[Cap. 3.] 9. προεχόμεθα] [are we better] After he had said many things concerning the infidelity and iniquity of the Jews, the Jews might be able to ask, τί οὖν προεχόμεθα; [what then? are we bettered] are we surpassed, are we excelled,

† From John Bois, *Translating for King James: Being a True Copy of the Only Notes Made by a Translator of King James's Bible* . . . , trans. and ed. Ward Allen (Nashville: Vanderbilt University Press, 1969), 37, 39, 45, 47, 49. Allen uses Roman typeface for Bois's Latin and italics for his English. He also includes translations of the Greek in brackets. Included are Bois's notes on 1 Cor 4:9, and Rom 2:15; 3:9; 25–26, which all address issues discussed in the annotations to this volume. Excerpts from his notes on 1 Cor 9–13 are also included.

John Bois (1560–1643) was a member of the company working in Cambridge that drafted the KJV translation of the Apocrypha. He also served on the final committee of review, which revised the drafts that the six groups of translators submitted. The notes he took while revising the translation of Romans through Revelation as a member of that committee survive. They were written in Latin, with a spattering of English and Greek, and their highly technical and deeply learned comments reveal at once the KJV translators' philological sophistication and the meticulous care they took in weighing possible English renderings. Occasional references to interpretations passionately supported by fellow committee member Andrew Downes (A. D. in Bois's notes), but rejected by Bois himself, as well as to other strong disagreements, indicate that the KJV translators did not always work with harmonious collegiality.

plainly by the Greeks. Otherwise in the person of the Jews (for that this must be referred to the Jews is clear from what follows) *What then? Are we safe, and out of danger? are we preferred? are we Gods darlings?*

[Ibid. v. 25. 26.] The Apostle shows, unless I am mistaken, in the justification of the sinner in this way that mercy is tempered with justice, so that neither may be an impediment to the other: there is justice because He has punished our sins; mercy, because in another, not in us. The preposition, διά, means here, as far as it pertains to, *in respect of.* Then there is Ἀντίθεσις [Antithesis] between προγεγονότων [that are past] and ἐν τῷ νῦν καιρῷ [at this time], so that the sense is, that the justice of God stands whole, whether we contemplate sins having been pardoned, or indeed to be pardoned, and which now are pardoned. Scarcely another place is to be found more apt to this point, so that there is exhibited how well the justice of God joins with His mercy: He is δίκαιος [righteous], i.e. at the same time just; and nevertheless δικαιόει [He justifies], i.e. He justifies the sinner, i.e. He is merciful in the highest degree.

* * *

1. Corinthians

* * *

[Cap. 4.] 9. ἐσχάτους ἀπέδειξεν ὡς ἐπιθανατίους [hath set forth . . . last, as it *were* appointed to death] Jos. Scalig. in *Sphaer. Barbar.* of Manilius, p. 417. Those whom the Greeks call ἐφέδρους [a third combatant who sits by to fight the conqueror], the Latins, in the gladiatorial game, call *sequutores* [pursuers]. Old glosses render ἔφεδρον also as *Tertiarium* [the third], because no doubt one having been killed a third was chosen; he follows therefore as a substitute. Likewise the Apostle 1 Cor. 4. 9. Δοκῶ γάρ ὅτι etc. [for I think that], and he does not say τοὺς ἀποστόλους ἐσχάτους [the last apostles], nor indeed does the canon of the Greek tongue permit that; but ἀπέδειξεν ἐσχάτους ἡμᾶς τοὺς Ἀποστόλους [he set forth us last, the Apostles]. He has posted us who are Apostles, so to speak, as certain substitute fighters with beasts. ἔσχατος [last] indeed is here ἔφεδρος. And the context is fitting. However Scaliger in his notes on the Ἀποτελεσματικά of Manilius p. 316. 317. But concerning the parts of animals] [He] understands *bestiarios* not certainly as those who had been doomed to the beasts, whom the Apostle calls ἐπιθανατίους [appointed to death], 1 Cor. 4. but those who having been hired did this, and hired out their service for the mid-day spectacle, or, that I may speak as Manilius, who furnished the carnage for the riotous excess: these on account of their desperate boldness were called παράβολοι [venturesome persons]. Hence the fitting word of the Apostle παραβολεύεσθαι [to risk one's life]: which others translate by [παραβολευσάμενος] [risking his life], Philip. 2. (30.)

* * *

[Cap. 9.] 18. *That I streine not to the utmost my power in the Gospel, or, that I rack not, or, stretch not* etc. καταχρῆσθαι τῇ ἐξουσίᾳ [to abuse the power] is κατεξουσιάζειν [to exercise lordship over], to increase power inflexibly. See 1.

Thess. 2.6. δυνάμενοι ἐν βάρει εἶναι [when we might have been burdensome, when we might have been in authority].

* * *

Cap. 10. 11. Ut ἐντελὴς λόγος sit [that the thought may be complete] read thus, ὡς τύποι ἡμῶν συνέβαινον ἐκείνοις [these things as our examples happened to them]. A. D. [Andrew Downes] sharply and violently ὑπερδιετείνετο [exerted himself beyond measure] for the interpretation of Augustine, that is, that τύποι [the examples] were understood as concerning the types and figures of the people of old: but the scope of the passage does not seem to admit this interpretation.

* * *

Ibid. v. 20. A. D. *and I would not have you partakers with the Devills*, i.e. to be partakers together with those of things having been offered to them.

Ibid. v. 30. *and if I by thanksgiving*] This interpretation, rejected by Beza, A. D. deemed worthy of his advocacy.

* * *

Cap. 12. 17. *and members for the part, or, in particular.* jointly σῶμα [body], separately μέλη [limbs].

Ibid. v. 29. δυνάμεις [powers, authorities] Abstract for the concrete; and, thus perhaps in ἀντιλήψεις [helps], in the preceding verse.

Cap. 13. 5. he does not impute evil. *non* μνησικακεῖ [does not remember past wrongs]. A. D. See Zachar. 7. 10.

Ibid. v. 11. *I understood, I cared as a child, I had a childs mind, I imagined as a child, I was affected as a child.*

PERMISSIONS ACKNOWLEDGMENTS

Anonymous: "The Dream of the Rood" from OLD AND MIDDLE ENGLISH c. 890–c. 1450: AN ANTHOLOGY edited by Elaine Treharne. Copyright © Blackwell Publishing Ltd. Reproduced with permission of Blackwell Publishing Ltd.

Saint Augustine: From ANSWER TO THE PELAGIANS II, translated by Roland J. Teske and edited by John E. Rotelle. Copyright © 1998 Augustinian Heritage Institute. "Sermon on John 6:1–14" from HOMILIES ON THE GOSPEL OF JOHN 1–40, translated by Edmund Hill, edited by Allan D. Fitzgerald. Copyright © 2009 Augustinian Heritage Institute. Reprinted by permission.

Karl Barth: "The Meaning of Religion" from THE EPISTLE TO THE ROMANS by Karl Barth, translated by Edwyn C. Hoskyns (London: Oxford University Press, 1933). Reprinted by permission of Oxford University Press.

Elizabeth Bishop: "Roosters" and "The Prodigal" from THE COMPLETE POEMS 1927–1979 by Elizabeth Bishop. Copyright © 1979, 1983 by Alice Helen Methfessel. Reprinted by permission of Farrar, Straus and Giroux, LLC.

John Bois: Excerpts from TRANSLATING FOR KING JAMES: NOTES MADE BY A TRANSLATOR OF KING JAMES'S BIBLE by John Bois, translated and edited by Ward Allen. Copyright © 1969 by Vanderbilt University Press. Reprinted by permission.

Rudolf Bultmann: Extracts from THEOLOGY OF THE NEW TESTAMENT, Volume 1, translated by Kendrick Grobel, are under copyright in the world outside North America, © SCM Press, 1952, and are reproduced by permission of Hymns Ancient & Modern Ltd. Extracts from THEOLOGY OF THE NEW TESTAMENT, Volume 2, translated by Kendrick Grobel, are under copyright in the world outside North America, © SCM Press, 1955, and are reproduced by permission of Hymns Ancient & Modern Ltd.

Hans Conzelmann: From THE THEOLOGY OF ST. LUKE by Hans Conzelmann, translated by Geoffrey Buswell. Translation copyright © 1961 by Geoffrey Buswell. Copyright © Faber and Faber and Harper & Row, New York 1960. Reprinted by permission of Mohr Siebeck.

Countee Cullen: "Simon the Cyrian Speaks" and "Judas Iscariot" from MY SOUL'S HIGH SONG: THE COLLECTED WRITINGS OF COUNTEE CULLEN, VOICE OF THE HARLEM RENAISSANCE (New York: Doubleday, 1991). Copyrights held by Amistad Research Center, Tulane University, administered by Thompson and Thompson, Brooklyn, NY. Reprinted with permission from the Estate of Ida M. Cullen and the Amistad Research Center.

Emily Dickinson: Poems from THE POEMS OF EMILY DICKINSON: READING EDITION, edited by Ralph W. Franklin. Copyright © 1951, 1955, 1979, 1983 by the President and Fellows of Harvard College. Reprinted by permission of the publishers and the Trustees of Amherst College.

John Donne: Footnotes by Donald R. Dickson, from JOHN DONNE'S POETRY: NORTON CRITICAL EDITION by John Donne, edited by Donald R. Dickson. Copyright © 2007 by W. W. Norton & Company, Inc. Used by permission of W. W. Norton & Company, Inc.

William Dunbar: "Done Is a Battell on the Dragon Blak" from SELECTED POEMS by William Dunbar, edited by Patricia Bawcutt. Copyright © Addison Wesley Longman Ltd., 1996. Reprinted by permission of Pearson Education Ltd.

T. S. Eliot: "The Journey of the Magi" from COLLECTED POEMS 1909–1962 by T. S. Eliot. Copyright 1936 by Harcourt Inc. and renewed 1964 by T. S. Eliot. Reprinted by permission of Houghton Mifflin Harcourt Publishing Company.

Roger P. H. Green: From LATIN EPICS OF THE NEW TESTAMENT by Roger P. H. Green. Copyright © Roger P. H. Green 2006. Reprinted by permission of Oxford University Press.

J. Albert Harrill: Excerpts from "The Slave Self: Paul and the Discursive 'I'" in SLAVES IN THE NEW TESTAMENT by J. Albert Harrill (Minneapolis: Fortress Press, 2006). Reproduced by permission of Augsburg Fortress Publishers.

Richard B. Hays: "Intertextual Echo in Romans" from ECHOES OF SCRIPTURE IN THE LETTERS OF PAUL by Richard B. Hays. Copyright © 1989 by Richard B. Hays. Reprinted by permission of Yale University Press.

James Weldon Johnson: "Saint Peter Relates an Incident of the Resurrection Day" from SAINT PETER RELATES AN INCIDENT by James Weldon Johnson. Copyright © 1917, 1921, 1935 by James Weldon Johnson, copyright renewed © 1963 by Grace Nail Johnson. Used by permission of Viking Penguin, a division of Penguin Group (USA), Inc.

Brigitte Kahl: "No Longer Male: Masculinity Struggles Behind Galatians 3.28" by Brigitte Kahl, from JOURNAL FOR THE STUDY OF THE NEW TESTAMENT 79 (2000). Reprinted by permission of SAGE.

Werner H. Kelber: "The Gospel [of Mark] as Written Parable" from THE ORAL AND WRITTEN GOSPEL by Werner H. Kelber (Minneapolis: Fortress Press, 1997). Reproduced by permission of Augsburg Fortress Publishers.

Frank Kermode: From THE LITERARY GUIDE TO THE BIBLE, edited by Robert Alter and Frank Kermode. Cambridge, MA: The Belknap Press of Harvard University Press. Copyright © 1987 by Robert Alter and Frank Kermode. Reprinted by permission of the publisher and SLL/Sterling Lord Literistic, Inc.

Hal Lindsey: From THE LATE GREAT PLANET EARTH by Hal Lindsey with C. C. Carlson. Copyright © 1970 by Zondervan Publishing House. Reprinted by permission of Zondervan.

Martin Luther: "The Righteous Are at the Same Time Sinners" from LUTHER: LECTURES ON ROMANS, edited and translated by Wilhelm Pauck. Copyright © 1961 by The Westminster Press. Used in North America by permission of Westminster John Knox Press. www.wjkbooks.com. Copyright in the world outside North America by © SCM Press. Reproduced by permission of Hymns Ancient & Modern Ltd. "The Use of the Law" from LUTHER'S WORKS, VOLUME 26, edited by Jaroslav Pelikan. Copyright © 1963, 1991 Concordia Publishing House. Used with permission. www.cph.org.

Dennis R. Macdonald: "Luke's Eutychus and Homer's Elpenor: Acts 20:7–12 and Odyssey 10–12" from JOURNAL OF HIGHER CRITICISM 1 (1994). Reprinted by permission of the author.

SCYTHIANS

GETAE

Olbia

BOSPORAN KINGDOM

Panticapaeum

SARMATIANS

ILLYRIA

Ister

(Danube)

THRACE

BLACK SEA

CAUCASUS

MACEDONIA

Pella

EPIRUS

BITHYNIA

PAPHLA-
GONIA

Ilium

Gordion

Ancyra

PONTUS

Trapezus

COLCHIS

ACHAIA

Athens

Sparta

AEGEAN SEA

ASIA MINOR

ARMENIA

Ephesus

Halicarnassus

Cilician
Gates

Edessa

Arbela

Crete

Tarsus

Thapsacus

Euphrates

MEDIA

Cyprus

Palmyra

Ecbatana

MEDITERRANEAN

SYRIA

Tigris

SEA

Sidon

Damascus

SUSIAN.
(ELAM

LIBYA

Tyre

Babylon

BABYLONIA

Susa

Alexandria

Gaza

Jerusalem

Oracle of
Amon

Pelusium

NABATEANS

Memphis

EGYPT

ARABIA

LIBYAN

Nile

DESERT

RED

Thebes

SEA

Syene

ETHIOPIA
(CUSH)

1512

Territory Conquered by Alexander the Great

	Limits of Alexander's empire, 323 B.C.E.
•	Cities founded by Alexander

MASSAGETAE

ARAL SEA

Jaxartes

CHORASMIA

ASPIAN SEA

• Alexandria Eschata

• Maracanda (Samarkand)

SOGDIANA

HINDU KUSH

Oxus

Alexandria • on Oxus

Bactra •

BACTRIA

HIMALAYAN MOUNTAINS

Cophen

Taxila •

HYRCANIA

Bucephala •• Nicaea

• Hecatompylus

Alexandria Arion (Herat) •

agae

Caspian Gates

PARTHIA

ARIA

ARACHOSIA

Hyphasis (Beas)

• Alexandria Arachosion (Kandahar)

Prophthasia •

INDIA

Indus

Persepolis •

CARMANIA

PERSIS

Alexandria (Golashkerd) •

• Pura

GEDROSIA

Pattala •

Persian Gulf

• Harmozia

ARABIAN SEA

0		200		400 miles
0	300		600 kilometers	

The Roman Empire

ATLANTIC

OCEAN

BRITANNIA

GERMANI

MAGNA

Albis (Elbe)

BELGICA

Augusta
Treverorum

•Lutetia

LUGDUNENSIS

GAUL

Rhine

RAETIA   NORICUM

AQUITANIA

Lugdunum•

ALPS

Aquileia•

PANNONIA

Burdigala•

ALPES

NARBONENSIS

Rubicon

ADRIATIC

ILLYRICU

•Salona

TARRACONENSIS

•Narbo

Caesarea•
Augusta

•Tarraco

CORSICA
& SARDINIA

ITALY

Rome•

SEA

LUSITANIA

Emerita
Augusta•

HISPANIA

Tarentum•

Corduba•
BAETICA

Caralis•

M
E
D
I
T
E
R
R
A
N
E
A
N

Tingis•

Caesarea•

Cirta•   Carthage•

SICILIA

•Syracuse

MAURETANIA

•Leptis Magna

AFRICA

Legend

Boundary of Roman rule and hegemony,
ca. turn of the first millennium C.E.

Boundary of Roman province
or client kingdom

0		200		400 miles
0		300		600 kilometers

SCYTHIA

SARMATIA

Rha (Volga)

CASPIAN SEA

BOSPORAN
KINGDOM

CARPATHIANS

DACIA
(GETAE)

ingidunum

(Danube)

Ister

MOESIA

THRACE

BLACK SEA

CAUCASUS

COLCHIS   IBERIA   ALBANIA

•Sinope

•Trapezus

•Artaxata

ARMENIA

BITHYNIA & PONTUS

Byzantium•

•Ancyra

CAPPADOCIA

PARTHIAN
EMPIRE

1ACEDONIA

Thessalonica•

GALATIA

COMMAGENE

•Edessa

Tigris

Pergamum•

ASIA

AEGEAN

•Ephesus

Tarsus•

CILICIA & SYRIA

•Antioch

Euphrates

ACHAIA•

Corinth•

•Athens

SEA

PAMPHYLIA

•Ctesiphon

LYCIA

CYPRUS

CRETA

SEA

KINGDOM OF
HEROD

Jerusalem•

•Cyrene

Alexandria•

NABATEA

ARABIA

CRETA &
CYRENAICA

Memphis•

EGYPT

Nile

RED

SEA

•Thebes

Po

Ravenna

PANNONIA

Singidunum

DACIAN
KINGDOM

Ister   (Danube)

ILLYRICUM
(DALMATIA)

MOESIA

Salonae

ADRIATIC SEA

Tiber

ITALY   Ortona

Scodra

Hebrus

THRACE

Rome

Ostia

Three Taverns

Forum of
Appius

Beneventum

Puteoli

Paestum   Tarentum

Apollonia

EPIRUS

MACEDONIA   Philippi   Neapolis

Amphipolis   Samothrace

Thessalonica   Apollonia

Beroea

Troas

Assos

Mitylene

Lesbos

AEGEAN SEA

TYRRHENIAN

SEA

Croton

Corcyra

Larisa

Nicopolis

Chios

ACHAIA   Athens

Messana

Rhegium

SICILY

Agrigentum

Syracuse

Corinth   Cenchreae

Sparta

Malta (Melita)

CRETE

Phoenix   Cnossus

Cauda   Lasea

Fair Havens

LESSER
SYRTIS

MEDITERRANEAN

Cyrene

Leptis Magna

GREATER

SYRTIS

AFRICA

CYRENAICA
(LIBYA)

1516

BLACK SEA

Bosphorus

opontis

• esembria

• Sinope

• Amisus

• Trapezus

BITHYNIA & PONTUS

• Heraclea

• Byzantium
Nicomedia •

• Nicaea

PAPHLAGONIA

• Amasia

• Comana

LESSER ARMENIA
(Roman Client Kingdom)

Lake Van

ARMENIA
(Intermittent Roman Client Kingdom)

GALATIA

Sangarius   Ancyra •

• Dorylaeum

Halys

Tavium •

CAPPADOCIA

Tigris

YSIA

ramyttium

ASIA

rgamum •

• Thyatira

• Sardis

nyrna • • Philadelphia

• Pessinus

PHRYGIA

LYDIA

phesus • • Laodicea
• Colossae

Lake Tatta

• Caesarea
Mazaca

• Tyana

COMMAGENE
(Roman Client Kingdom)

• Edessa

PARTHIAN EMPIRE

Euphrates

PISIDIA

• Antioch

LYCAONIA

• Iconium

• Lystra

Derbe •

CILICIA & SYRIA

Tarsus •

• Antioch

imos

Miletus

CABIA

• Cnidus

• Patara

Attalia • • Perga

LYCIA & PAMPHYLIA

• Myra

Seleucia •

os

Rhodes

Cape Salmone

• Salamis

Paphos •

CYPRUS

Sidon •

• Damascus

ARABIAN DESERT

Tyre •

Ptolemais •

SEA

Caesarea •

Joppa •

Jerusalem •

Judea
(satellite province
of Syria)

• Gaza

NABATEANS (Roman Client Kingdom)

• Pelusium

• Petra

Alexandria •

Memphis •

EGYPT

Nile

The Eastern Mediterranean World

0	100	200 miles
0	150	300 kilometers

RED SEA

The Roman Empire's provincial boundaries, ca. mid-first century C.E.

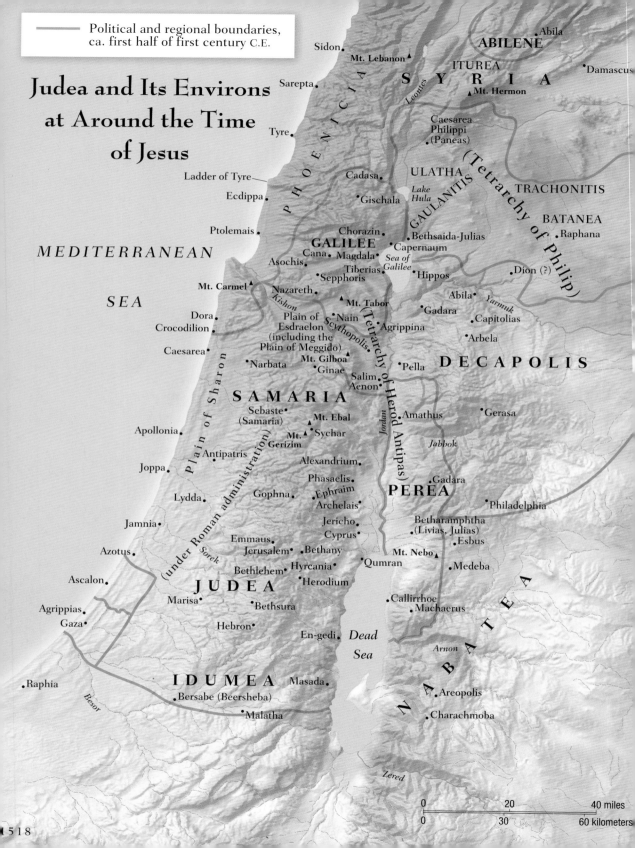

Judea and Its Environs
at Around the Time
of Jesus

MEDITERRANEAN

SEA

Sidon

Mt. Lebanon

Sarepta

PHOENICIA

SYRIA

ABILENE

Abila

ITUREA

Mt. Hermon

Damascus

Leontes

Tyre

Caesarea
Philippi
(Paneas)

Ladder of Tyre

Ecdippa

Cadasa

ULATHA

Lake
Hula

GAULANITIS

(Tetrarchy of Philip)

TRACHONITIS

BATANEA

Ptolemais

Gischala

Chorazin

Bethsaida-Julias

Raphana

GALILEE

Capernaum

Cana

Magdala

Sea of
Galilee

Asochis

Tiberias

Hippos

Dion (?)

Sepphoris

Mt. Carmel

Nazareth

Mt. Tabor

Agrippina

Abila

Yarmuk

Gadara

Capitolias

Dora

Plain of
Esdraelon
(including the
Plain of Meggido)

Nain

Scythopolis

(Tetrarchy of Herod Antipas)

Arbela

Crocodilion

Kishon

Caesarea

Narbata

Mt. Gilboa

Ginae

Salim
Aenon

Pella

DECAPOLIS

SAMARIA

Sebaste
(Samaria)

Mt. Ebal

Sychar

Amathus

Gerasa

Apollonia

Mt.
Gerizim

Plain of Sharon

Antipatris

(under Roman administration)

Joppa

Alexandrium

Jabbok

Jordan

Lydda

Gophna

Phasaelis

Ephraim

Archelais

PEREA

Gadara

Philadelphia

Jamnia

Emmaus

Jerusalem

Jericho

Cyprus

Betharamphtha
(Livias, Julias)

Azotus

Bethany

Sorek

Bethlehem

Hyrcania

Esbus

Qumran

Mt. Nebo

Ascalon

Marisa

Bethsura

Herodium

Callirrhoe

Medeba

Machaerus

Agrippias

Gaza

Hebron

En-gedi

Dead
Sea

Arnon

NABATEA

Raphia

IDUMEA

Masada

Bersabe (Beersheba)

Besor

Malatha

Areopolis

Charachmoba

Zered

0   20   40 miles

0   30   60 kilometers